1997/51st Annual Edition

EDITED BY KEN WARNER

DBI BOOKS
a division of Krause Publications, Inc.

CONTENTS

FEATURES

DEPARTMENTS

CATALOG

ABOUT OUR COVERS

Whoever said the only thing in life that remains constant is change was right on the money. And the pistols on our covers show that things are constantly changing at Heckler & Koch.

Our front cover highlights the newest of the new from this famed German gunmaker, the USP Compact. In fact, we were so anxious to show you this gun that what you see here is actually a prototype; what you eventually see in the dealer's display case may not exactly match the gun shown here.

Details were sketchy at press time, but what we *can* tell you is that the USP Compact will initially be available in 9mm Parabellum and 40 S&W, with the 45 ACP still being talked about. The gun is rated for use with +P ammunition. The overall length is 6.9 inches, width at the slide (the widest part) is 1.14 inches, barrel length 3.5 inches, and the gun weighs 26 ounces. Magazine capacity is ten rounds for civilians and twelve for law enforcement consumption, plus, we're told, the magazines will be metal instead of polymer.

This Compact model is, of course, built off most features of the standard, full-size USP. It uses the modified Browning-type action and has the frame-mounted, easily accessible control lever that's a combination safety and decocking lever. The frame is the same polymer material used for the HK MK23 SOCOM 45 ACP pistol. Nearly indestructible, it's also light in weight.

There are nine different fire modes and control functions available, so like its bigger kin, the USP Compact can be "customized" to a shooter's taste. The control lever can be switched from left to right, and the gun can be changed from one type of firing mode to another—including conventional double action, cocked and locked, and double-action-only. There are nine different fire modes and control functions available.

The two-tone pistol shown on the front cover is HK's USP in 40 S&W with the new stainless steel slide, which is even more durable than the original black-finished version.

Our back cover shows the same stainless steel USP pistol equipped with the HK Quik-Comp muzzlebrake/compensator and a C-More red dot sight riding on an HK USP scope mount.

Specially designed to attach to the universal mounting grooves on the pistol, the Quik-Comp redirects propellant gases through an expansion chamber and directional ports to reduce muzzle climb and tame felt recoil up to 25 percent. It also significantly reduces muzzle flash.

The HK scope mount can be used alone or in combination with the Quik-Comp and supports most pistol scopes and electronic sights, like the very popular and effective C-More unit shown. The mount is made of high-strength alloy and accommodates universal bases with 1-inch rings, and it goes on the gun with no gunsmithing needed. Any of the USP's variants can be turned into a state-of-the-art competitive handgun.

Photos by John Hanusin.

GUN DIGEST STAFF

EDITOR-IN-CHIEF
Ken Warner

SENIOR STAFF EDITORS
Harold A. Murtz
Ray Ordorica

ASSOCIATE EDITOR
Robert S.L. Anderson

PRODUCTION MANAGER
John L. Duoba

EDITORIAL/PRODUCTION ASSOCIATE
Laura M. Mielzynski

EDITORIAL/PRODUCTION ASSISTANTS
Joan Bean
Georgiana Drew
Lisa Norling-Christensen
Karen Rasmussen
Debbie Weinberg

ASSISTANT TO THE EDITOR
Lilo Anderson

CONTRIBUTING EDITORS
Bob Bell
Holt Bodinson
Raymond Caranta
Doc Carlson
John Malloy
Layne Simpson
Larry S. Sterett
Hal Swiggett
Don Zutz

ELECTRONIC PUBLISHING DIRECTOR
Sheldon L. Factor

ELECTRONIC PUBLISHING MANAGER
Nancy J. Mellem

ELECTRONIC PUBLISHING ASSOCIATE
Larry Levine

GRAPHIC DESIGN
John L. Duoba
Bill Limbaugh
Jim Billy

MANAGING EDITOR
Pamela J. Johnson

PUBLISHER
Charles T. Hartigan

Copyright © 1996 by Krause Publications, Inc., 700 E. State St., Iola, WI 54990. All rights reserved. Printed in the United States of America.

No part of this publication may be reproduced, stored in a retrieval system, or transmitted in any form or by any means, electronic, mechanical, photocopying, recording or otherwise, without the prior written permission of the publisher.

The views and opinions contained herein are those of the authors. The editor and publisher disclaim all responsibility for the accuracy or correctness of the authors' views.

Manuscripts, contributions and inquiries, including first class return postage, should be sent to the Gun Digest Editorial Offices, 4092 Commercial Ave., Northbrook, IL 60062. All materials received will receive reasonable care, but we will not be responsible for their safe return. Material accepted is subject to our requirements for editing and revisions. Author payment covers all rights and title to the accepted material, including photos, drawings and other illustrations. Payment is at our current rates.

CAUTION: Technical data presented here, particularly technical data on handloading and on firearms adjustment and alteration, inevitably reflects individual experience with particular equipment and components under specific circumstances the reader cannot duplicate exactly. Such data presentations therefore should be used for guidance only and with caution. Krause Publications, Inc., accepts no responsibility for results obtained using this data.

Arms and Armour Press, London, G.B., exclusive licensees and distributor in Britain and Europe, India and Pakistan. Book Services International, Sandton, Transvaal, exclusive distributor in South Africa and Zimbabwe. Forrester Books N.Z. Limited, Auckland, exclusive distributor in New Zealand.

ISBN 0-87349-181-5

Library of Congress Catalog #44-32588

A Half-Breed COLT

by HOWARD MC CORD

SOMETIMES OLD MEN want most those things that got away in youth. I suppose I wasn't more than six or seven years old when my grandfather let me handle his Colt Peacemaker. He had been the first Anglo child born on the Peñasco, in southern New Mexico in 1881, and he was raised a cowboy. He gave up ranching in 1912 and ended up putting thirty years in with American Smelting and Refining in El Paso. His roots stayed pure cowboy, as was his pistol. He showed me how it worked, and let me see it and handle it whenever I asked, but I never played with it. It was *real*. Eventually I grew up, went away to the Korean War and, while I was there, my grandfather died. Two years later, the Peacemaker was gone. Nobody knew where.

A lot of other pistols and rifles have come my way over the years, but never a Peacemaker. And the prices kept rising. I stayed happy enough with more modern arms, single actions included, and didn't let the thought of my grandfather's pistol ruin my days. I'm a shooter, not a collector, and a man of modest means, so when the Colt clones began to appear I thought seriously of getting one, but never did. Too new, or something. I guess I wanted a sign.

Early in 1994, at a gun show in a small Ohio town, I was walking down the aisle and spotted a Bisley on a table full of shotguns. When I picked it up, what caught my eye first were my own initials engraved on the frame "H.L.M." right under the cylinder. Now I call that a sign. The grips were of some pale wood, hand-carved, with a thumbrest on the left. The barrel was a Colt, $5^{1}/_{2}$ inches, and the cylinder, when I inspected it, had the rampant horse as it should. The frame, however, bore no markings but three discreet small stars—exactly the same as those on the grips. The loading gate had the number #962, which I also found inside the frame under the grips. A serial number, 323012, was stamped on the frame, the trigger guard, and the butt. If it had been a Colt frame, that would have placed its manufacture in 1912, the last year Bisleys were made.

There was still some case coloring, and the piece was in generally tight, excellent condition. The owner admitted that "It's not quite all Colt." And added, "But it's a good shooter."

He had taken it in trade on a deal and was asking a reasonable price for "a half-breed Colt"—one a collector would surely call a fake. But as I said, I'm not a collector, and I figure the odds of finding a pistol with my own initials on it in a configuration I admire—my Ruger Bisleys are among my favorites—were so high that I was clearly destined to own this pistol. It was time to start dickering.

We could have been trading horses for camels, or carpets for spices—it's the oldest and best way of business in the world. We finally reached a deal that made us both happy, secure in our inner selves that we each had put one over on the other. My pleasure was the deeper, I am positive, for he received nothing marked by such a sign, nor such a long fulfillment.

I wondered, of course, who put the gun together with such care and such oddness. Who would put what seemed to be a Colt serial number on a frame clearly not a Colt? Was it the same person who carved the grips with their stars, and then used the same punch to mark the frame with three stars? The fake serial number seemed an intent to deceive. But the stars? And who was the other "H.L.M.?" And those initials, not so properly engraved as just cut in with a scribe. How many hands had left their marks on this revolver? I will never know.

I decided to feed my half-breed ammo appropriate for a piece built in 1912, for who knows what the metallurgy of the receiver was? So I took a box of Remington 45 Colt 250-grain round-noses and a box of Winchester 225-grain Silvertips. The Remington goes about 860 fps, and the Winchester about 960. These were pleasant to shoot in a revolver weighing more than 40 ounces. As a comparison, I took my Ruger Blackhawk in 45 Colt with 4⅝-inch barrel.

Even though the temperature was near zero at the range, and I had to keep my car running and the heater on full blast to thaw out after each string, I had an enjoyable time. I shot at twenty paces from a rolled blanket rest, and this is what I found out about my half-breed: With either load, firing over a rolled blanket, it was good for 3-inch groups, and the Ruger for 2-inchers. The Ruger's fine sights are a tremendous advantage, as my eyes found the half-breed's tiny notch difficult to see.

Both actions are reasonably slick, but the half-breed's trigger pull is a bit smoother. Certainly, its Bisley hammer—a generous half-inch wide, rounded and checkered—is more pleasant to use than the Ruger's quarter-inch hammer with its sharp serrations. It was too cold to be any more precise, and I think both revolvers probably have the same inherent accuracy, but the Ruger's sights gave it a real advantage. Up close and sudden, I would prefer the half-breed's Bisley grip and hammer, which I can work faster than the Ruger. Either one would be a comfort when in need.

A few years ago, I had El Paso Saddlery make up a full floral carved Hardin shoulder holster for my Blackhawk. The half-breed fit it fine. The holster is one of my favorite rigs for mountain rambling. It keeps the pistol up out of the brush, protects it under a jacket if I wear one, and does not interfere with a daypack at all. Each year, I go back to my home country in West Texas and New Mexico and spend a week wandering around a mountain range or two. That April I was returning to the San Mateos, a range about sixty miles by twenty miles, with five peaks over 10,000 feet.

The Apache Kid hid out in the San Mateos from 1886 to 1906, when he was killed, and not much has happened there since. The core of the range is the Apache Kid Wilderness Area, and it is as great a range as I know of. In 1989, I went there to relocate the Apache Kid's grave and did so, as far as I can tell.

This time, I wanted to circle the range on the back roads, driving up those canyons that I can, camping, then walking up the canyons, just poking around. I never know what I'll turn up on these expeditions, and that is one reason I always carry a pistol. I was taking my half-breed back to its natural home—the wild areas of New Mexico—where I feel right at home myself and should be even more comfortable with the gun riding in that shoulder holster. I won't be far from the country my grandfather rode back at the turn of the century, a Peacemaker at his side. I'll never find that one again, but I've got something like it, with mysteries all its own, and marked with my brand.

The writer found his initials on a Colt 45 and took them as a sign—one that appealed to his mystic nature.

Part II

Winter broke late in Ohio, and it was unpleasantly cold still when I left for the Southwest with four pistols in my luggage and a heady desire for sunshine, some heat and wilderness. I walked off the plane in El Paso into sunshine and heat, and wilderness was not far away. In my home country, I navigate more by mountain ranges than I do by towns, as towns don't interest me and mountains do.

Coming in from the northeast, the first good mountains I saw were the Guadalupes, with Texas' highest peak, and scene of several long rambles in the late 1940s, including a memorable winter excursion up the length of McKittrick Canyon, now a national park, carrying a Marlin 39A. The canyon narrows in one spot to only a few feet, and I remember wading in ice-cold water, holding my rifle high. Coming up the steep slopes to the high southern ridge made me wish for a sling, yet I somehow got through the whole trip without putting a ding on the Marlin stock. But I should have carried a pistol.

Driving through my old hometown

of El Paso, I kept one eye on the traffic and the other on the Franklin mountains, checking out some favored hikes of childhood: up along the ridge from Scenic Drive to the radio towers, and the beacons and beyond; then the rugged face of Ranger Peak, and north to the humped shoulders of Mt. Franklin, where Cottonwood Springs—once a part of Albert and Molly Coe's (my great-grandparents) ranch—still flowed. It was the only steady spring on the range.

North of the Franklins, in New Mexico, is the jewel of all the mountain ranges for hundreds of miles, the Organs, where more than a dozen granite spires offer climbers hundreds of possibilities. But I pressed on to the San Mateos, past the Doña Anas, the San Andres, la Sierra de las Uvas (the Grape Mountains), the Caballo, the Fra Cristobal, until just north of the Black Range, to the west, the San Mateos loomed. I knew the southern part of the range fairly well, as that is where the Apache Kid's gravesite is. But the northern part, with the Withington Wilderness Area, would be new to me.

The last time I was in the San Mateos, I had seen two mountain lions stalking a small herd of mule deer. There were bear and coyotes in abundance, and doubtless some bobcat. An access road leads up Mt. Withington to the lookout on top, at 10,115 feet. It's a better ride than most roller coasters and offers a few healthy thrills. Adjacent to Mt. Withington is the wilderness area of the same name, with deep, rough canyons and steep mountainsides.

I found a pull-off on the ridge, parked, slipped on the Wes Hardin rig and the daypack with a water bottle and a few oranges, and decided to explore the canyon below by pushing out the ridge a ways, then angling down. It was April and nearly 80 degrees in the sun, but I found small patches of snow banked on protected northern faces in the forest, and the mix of cool air and hot sun was refreshing.

There was no Forest Service trail here, but I soon came up on a deer trail and began to follow it, believing the best way to get through mountains is to "think like a deer," and a deer trail certainly puts you right in that frame of reference. I had seen no "bear country" signs in the San Mateos, though the warnings were numerous in the Chiricahuas a hundred miles or so from here. But having seen mountain lions in the range, I thought it very likely bear were about as well.

I've run across black bears twice in the woods, each time electrifying the bear about as much as I did myself. The signs always say, "Don't try to run from a bear," and I never have. But both bears I saw sure ran from me. That's the way I hoped all such encounters would end, but one thing about bears is that you can't be too sure they will do what you think they should do. So I was happy to have the semi-Colt along.

The next several days I wandered the San Mateos, went over to the Mogollones at the north edge of the Gila Wilderness, crossed the Big Lou, and then went south to the Chiricahuas, another home range for me for this past quarter-century. There, I ran across a number of mule deer, an exotic long-eared squirrel (dark grey to nearly black, I'll have to look up in a book), heard a few distant turkey gobbles and some fine woodpeckers rapping away. I had no immediate need for my pistol.

Heading back to El Paso, I stopped out in the desert between the Animas range and Columbus, New Mexico, the scene of Pancho Villa's raid in 1916, and spent a happy hour plinking at targets of opportunity out in the big empty. I was refreshed beyond remembering Ohio and the cold, and when I drove into El Paso, I thought one of the first things I wanted to do, after a good Mexican meal, was to drop by El Paso Saddlery and see if Bobby McNellis had something already made up that would fit the half-breed 45.

The first pistol holster I ever bought, a full-flap floral carved masterpiece for my Hi-Standard, I chose in 1946 on the advice of *Tío* Sam Myres himself, at the old Myres Saddlery by the Courthouse. El Paso Saddlery is a descendant of Myres, as more than 2000 Myres patterns are still employed there.

It wasn't long before I was describing my pistol to Bobby and looking at some possible holsters from his small supply of made-up but never collected orders he keeps out back. I picked a nice 1887 model, and Bobby asked me if I had the pistol with me. Sure thing.

I brought it in from the car and handed it to him. He was also a Bisley fancier. He examined it very carefully, removed the cylinder, turned it this way and that, and then he said, "this isn't a fake. This is a *pure* Colt.

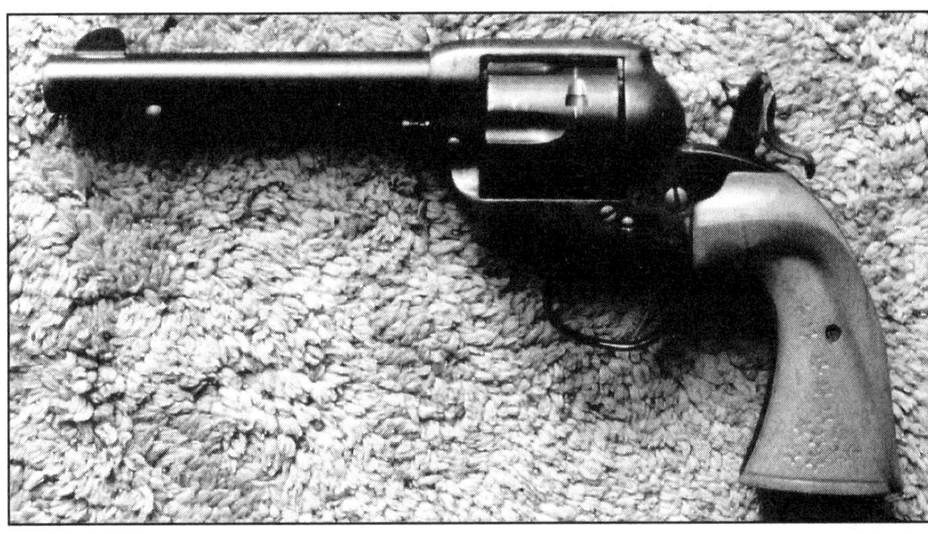

McCord will leave his Colt just as it looked on the gun-show table—the grip and hammer make it easy to shoot.

The Hardin-style shoulder rig has already carried McCord's Colt a many mile—five rounds in the gun, five on the rig.

Look here," and he pointed to a glint of metal under the hammer, and to another glint in a serial number. "This might have been originally nickled. Could be that someone has refinished it. The barrel is not original, but it is an interesting one; that style rollmark was only used briefly after World War II or thereabouts. It's a rare barrel. In fact," he said, "the only thing I see on the pistol that doesn't seem to be Colt is the trigger, and someone has made a fine copy of the original."

He smiled and handed the pistol back, "If I were you, I'd send off for a Colt historical letter and find out where this was originally sent. The serial numbers look quite authentic."

By that time, I was probably wearing the biggest smile I could come up with and felt that for once this crazy world had decided to bless me with a favor. Maybe this old man was going to get something he had pined for half a century and more. I slipped the Colt into its new holster as we talked about the advisability of getting it restored and the nice turn of luck that had occurred. I had also learned once again that, if I knew a bit about guns, there sure were folks out there who knew more than I did. I was glad I had run across such a one as Bobby McNellis.

No more half-breed, but a thoroughbred now. Maybe not all original, but all Colt. That's a metamorphosis denied most other things. I sent for the historical letter and am researching restorers of old Colts. And I carry it in the woods and shoot it when I want to make my memories of the mountains sharper.

Part III

I decided to invest in some research tools, and so I ordered *A Study of the Colt Single Action Army Revolver,* by Ron Graham, John Kopec, and C.K. Moore, a beautiful volume of more than 500 pages filled with more information about the single action than I will ever be able to absorb. But Chapter XI, on the Bisley, taught me a lot; for example, after 1908 the assembly, or bin, number on the loading gate is also found on the right rear frame flat and can be seen when the right stock is removed. On mine, #962 showed in both places. A triangular front left side trigger guard bow stamping was present, though the W on the rear left of trigger guard was missing. Perhaps use had worn it away. The knurling on the hammer was appropriate for the serial range. Another bit of lore this wonderful book includes is that the nickname "hogleg," now applied to all Colt single actions and their clones, was originally used for the distinctive Bisley-style grip. And on page 190 is a photograph of the replacement barrel used by Colt "for a short while" starting in 1955. That is the barrel on my pistol.

Ray Meibaum, who specializes in the sale of Colt single-action revolvers, kindly answered my letter of inquiry about finding an original Bisley trigger with the news that such were not likely to be found. He added, "I personally would not look to change the barrel nor have the gun refinished... The gun is what it is. Shoot it and enjoy it. Don't try to make it into something else."

I thought that was sound advice, and the longer I have my Bisley, admire it and shoot it, the better I like it as it is.

It took a few months, but eventually a letter came from Kathleen J. Hoyt, the Colt Historian, authenticating my pistol. It had been shipped to Belknap Hardware in Louisville, Kentucky, on June 15, 1912. It was blue, with a 4$^3/_4$-inch barrel. The type of stocks was not known. But there I had it: My pistol was a true Bisley with a replacement barrel, and if it was not totally original, it was totally Colt (except maybe the trigger, but I can't tell about that).

I've carried it in five mountain ranges now; and in the Shawnee forest along the Ohio River; in bear country, deer country, easy country and hard country; at my side, under my arm, and stuck in my waistband. I am sure it still shoots better than I can see and will do its job as long as I can do mine. I won't ever go West again without it, and no matter how many pistols I may own between now and then, this one is my favorite. After all, it came marked for me, with my brand. It took a long time to find me, but it's mine. ●

High-power action-mounted scopes such as this on an M77 varmint rifle have taken over from long-tube target styles.

This Leupold 1½-4½x on Pachmayr Swing Mount was Bell's choice to be unbeatable for all-around use.

The Leupold 4x Compact is tops on an M77 Ruger 308—everything in the outfit is medium except its weight.

Scopes are common. Everyone has at least one. Still, there's more to any scope than meets the eye:

The ANATOMY of a SCOPE

by BOB BELL

THERE'S NO DOUBT that a scope is the most popular accessory to a rifle. It's not unusual for guns to be made without metallic sights nowadays, as the manufacturer feels certain the first thing a buyer will do is add a scope. Many rifles are seen in the field without slings—in fact, true slings have almost been replaced by carrying straps—and few shooters these days even know how to install a military-type sling and use it to help them shoot. Fewer know that, properly used, a sling enables a good prone shooter to hold in a half-minute (about ½-inch at 100 yards). That's better than most shooters can hold off a benchrest and sandbags. Nevertheless, slings have almost disappeared, and as a rifle accessory they were the only thing that might rival a scope in popularity.

Scopes are seen everywhere. On rifles, of course, even on such "unscopable" guns as the Model 94 Winchester; on shotguns intended for slug use; on hunting handguns and even those designed for the fastest action pistol shooting. They're even made for bows (although I must admit I've never seen one afield), and I feel certain they'll be made for atlatls if some state makes such things legal for taking deer with thrown spears.

So everyone, almost, uses a scope, or a half-dozen, or more of them. Some guys have a scope on every rifle they own. I mention that because when I was a kid, which admittedly wasn't yesterday, my cousin Dave Bell, who had the first good scope I ever saw, a 2¼x Zeiss Zielklein on an early Model 70 300 H&H, also had a Redfield Jr. base on a Model 30 Remington 30-06 so he could switch the scope whenever he chose to use the slightly less powerful rifle. That was a fairly common procedure back in the '30s and was something gunwriters of those days talked about. Now...well, I won't tell you how many scopes I have at the moment because my wife might read this article, but it's more than anyone can justify.

It's obvious that, under most circumstances, a good scope is superior to the best metallic sight. Maybe not in a driving rain or snow (though it's debatable if anything is much good then), but for most shooting we'd take a scope. The reasons, when you boil them down, are simply magnification and illumination. You have a larger, brighter sight picture (target image) through a properly designed scope than through the best iron sights.

This assumes that the scope being used has adequate field of view for the type of shooting being done, and eye relief sufficient to keep the user from being hit on the eyebrow when the gun recoils. It also assumes there is some method for adjusting the reticle (or image on which the reticle is superimposed), so that the path of the bullet and the aiming point can be made to coincide at some specific range.

It isn't any more necessary to know how a scope works than it is to be a mechanic to know how to drive a car. But the more a person knows about anything, the more generally satisfying it is. So a simple rundown on scopes may be of interest. Only general principles will be covered; the higher mathematics will be left for those who like such things; they know where to find the equations.

Fundamentally, a scope is simple. It's just a metal tube with lenses in certain combinations installed at certain distances, with a movable aiming point (reticle). The reticle can be either actual wires or post(s) normally fastened to a metal ring, or an etched or photo-deposited design on a plano (non-refracting) lens. Metallic deposits on a lens can be used also, particularly in the less complicated designs. Extremely complex and precise designs can be made for photo-depositing as they are made very large to begin with, then "shot" down very small; the proportions remain the same though, and they can be made to subtend any amount of target wanted. Of course, this method requires the installation of another lens, which reduces light transmission somewhat. Each lens in a system, particularly if uncoated, absorbs or scatters or screens a tiny amount of the light which strikes it. Actually, each *surface* of each lens has such an effect.

The reticle can be moved by mechanical adjustments in vertical and lateral directions so the point of aim has the desired relationship to the bullet's path. Nowadays, it's common for each click of adjustment to move the reticle 1/4-MOA, or approximately 1/4-inch at 100 yards. Some target scopes now have 1/8-inch adjustments, and in years gone by it was common for values to be as much as 1 MOA in low-power scopes, or to be non-clicking friction designs which had graduated reference scales. In fact, in the early days of scopes, many had no reference marks on adjustments, and often there was no lateral adjustment at all; such scopes relied on mounts which could be moved, sometimes in both directions, or a key (similar to a skate key) was used to move the scope laterally by actually bending the scope tube left or right. What that did to good lenses inside is best left to the imagination.

To many newer shooters who grew up using 1/4-MOA clicks, a scope with 1-MOA adjustments seems ridiculous. But it's good enough for most big game shooting. Consider: If, when zeroing-in, your group forms a multiple of the 1-inch adjustments from where you want it at 100 yards, you simply adjust so many clicks. If it's 3/4- or 7/8-inch away, one click will put your impact within 1/4-inch. The most you can be off of dead zero is

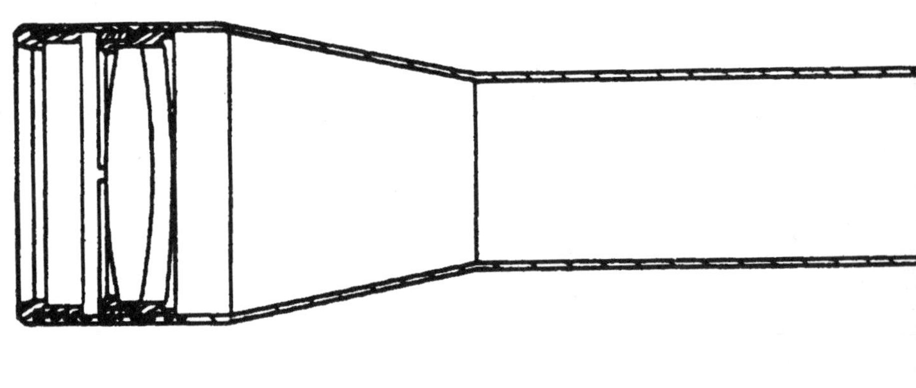

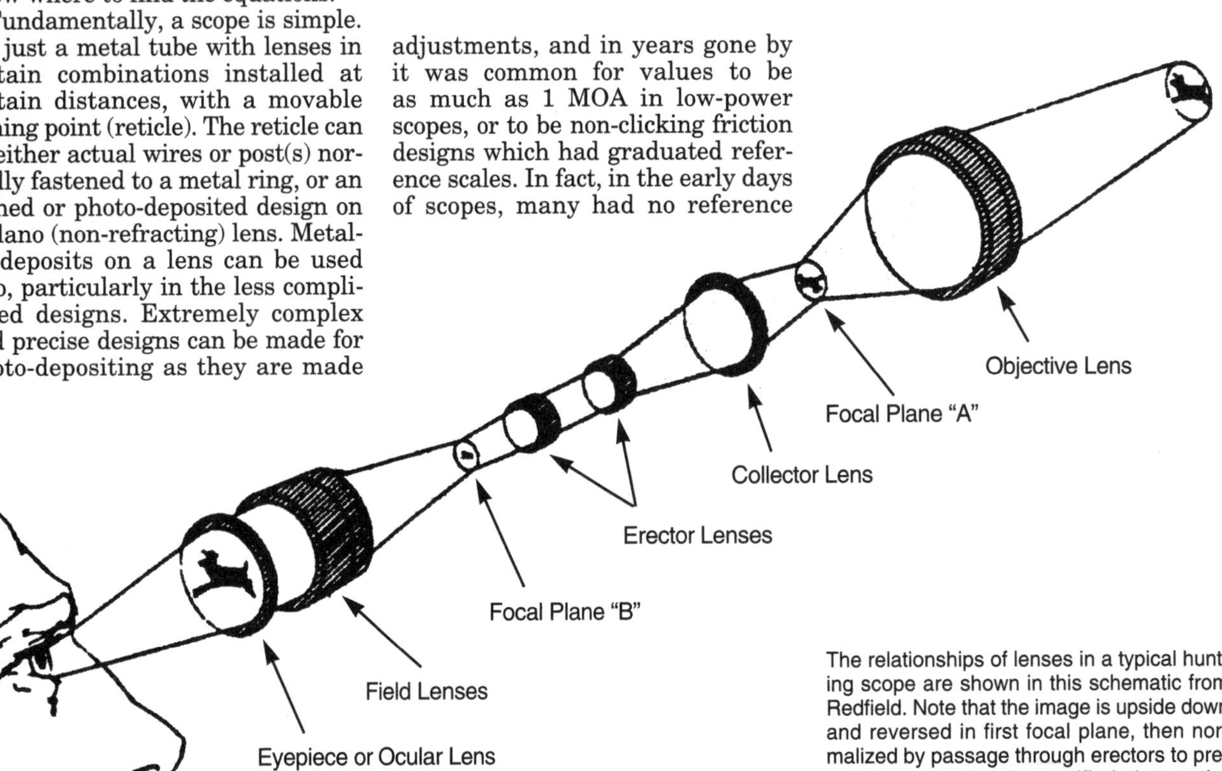

The relationships of lenses in a typical hunting scope are shown in this schematic from Redfield. Note that the image is upside down and reversed in first focal plane, then normalized by passage through erectors to present a conventional magnified view to the eye. (Courtesy Redfield Co.)

$^{1}/_{2}$-inch—and any hunter who thinks that's significant on a deer or elk is more persnickety than anyone I know. Actually, 1-MOA adjustments on low-power scopes would be perfectly suitable nowadays and maybe easier to make, and therefore less expensive. If memory serves correctly, the old Lyman $2^{1}/_{2}$x Alaskan had 1-MOA clicks, and it was a great scope.

The old externally mounted scopes like the Lyman Super TargetSpot had rear mounts which rotated the scope tube around, actually within, the front mount. Each click (which you could both feel and hear if you weren't already partially deaf from firing so many shots with unprotected ears) was made by a tiny metal ball which sat in precisely machined grooves inside the screw-fastened adjustment cap, which also had reference marks so you could easily go to predetermined zeros. This made it easy to use such a scope on several rifles, simply by keeping track of the zeros in a shooting book.

Doc Niklaus likes Bausch & Lomb's 6-24x for small targets at long range on an M700 223.

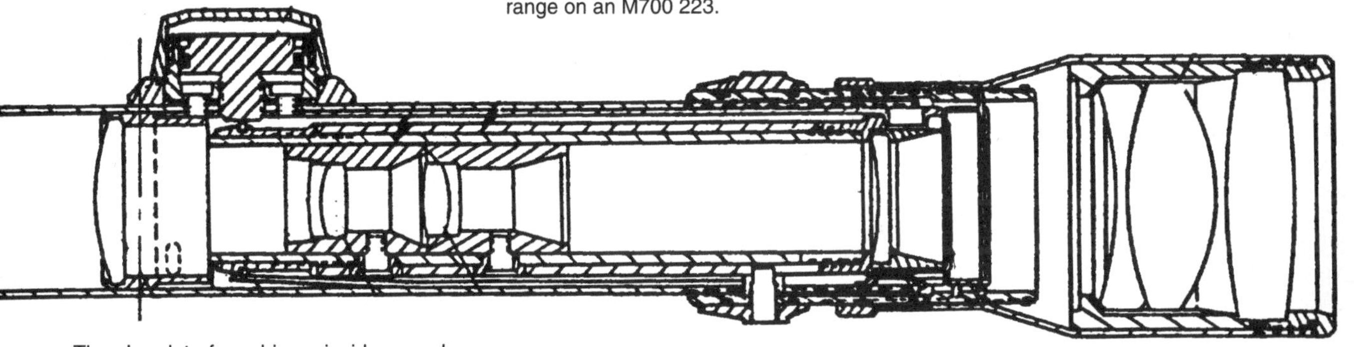

There's a lot of machinery inside a modern riflescope, as this illustration of a Weaver V7 shows.

Maybe the gun wouldn't always be zeroed in when the scope was installed, but it was within a few clicks. It had to be. The external mounts slid over permanently mounted dovetail blocks and were held with a finger-tightened screw in a relief cut, so there was little room for them to get out of whack once zeroed. Any change was usually more due to the way the rifle was held and fired than to mounting problems. These were often called micrometer click mounts, because they were read the same way as a micrometer. Because they actually rotated the scope around the front mount, the distance between front and rear mounts was critical, if each click were to have a $^{1}/_{4}$-inch value for the angle the scope was changing. As I recall, this distance was 7.2 inches. A lesser amount resulted in

This Shepherd Dual Reticle scope provided a two-range zero for Bell's 223 M700, making chucks easy.

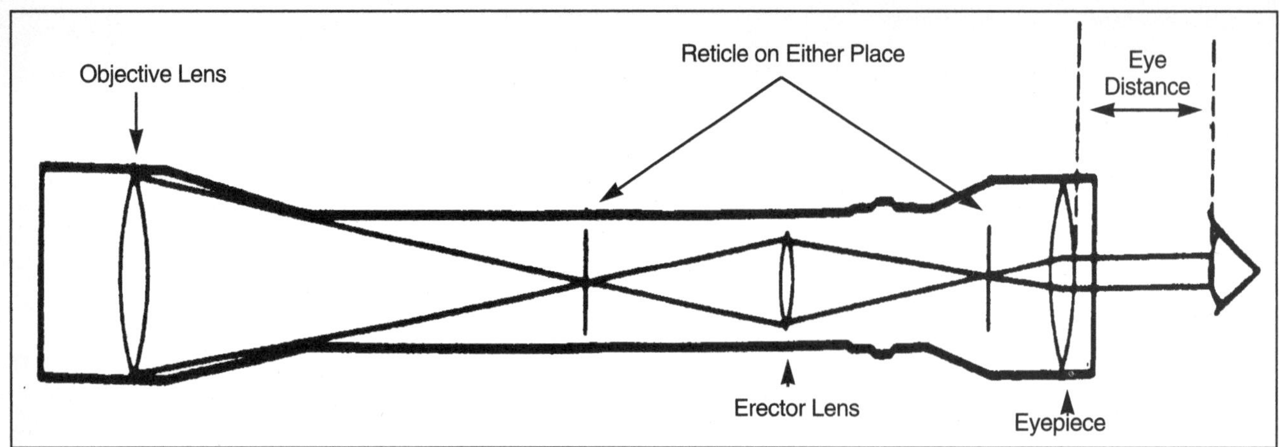

The four basic optical parts of a rifle scope are the objective lens, reticle (crosshairs, dot, etc.), erecting system (to reinvert the image right-side up, and in correct left-to-right position), and the eyepiece. (Courtesy of Bushnell.)

Zeiss' 8x56 was Bob Wise's choice on a Mauser 7mm Magnum for cold weather use on distant whitetails.

a greater angle, so click value was increased, and a greater amount (as when the rear mount was placed on the receiver bridge, say, and the front block remained at its conventional position) gave a lesser value. The shooter could figure click value mathematically, but it was simpler to derive through actual shooting; just fire a group at 100 yards, move twenty clicks, fire another group, and divide the distance between their centers by twenty. Shooting is a lot more fun than figuring.

There are only two places within a scope tube that the reticle can be placed: In the first focal plane, which is where the objective (front) lens (usually a combination of several lenses) brings the image to a focus; or in the second focal plane, which is where an image is formed by the erector lenses. Elsewhere, the reticle would be invisible. If it's placed in the first focal plane, it's no problem in a single-power scope. But in a variable power, because the magnification change is done behind it, it seems to get larger as magnification is increased. Actually, the target gets larger too, in exactly the same proportion, so the reticle subtends no more nor less than at bottom power, but many shooters are annoyed by its conspicuousness at high power. So, years ago, Redfield Scope Co. decided to put the reticle in the second focal plane of their variables. When power was increased in those scopes, the target got bigger, but the reticle didn't; therefore, it seemed to get smaller, because it subtended less of the target. Subtension was in inverse proportion to power; in a 3-9x scope, for instance, a reticle that subtended 3 MOA at 3x subtended (covered) one-third of that, or 1 MOA, at 9x. The target was three times bigger, therefore the reticle covered only one-third as much of it, so it appeared smaller to the shooter.

The idea was great. It allowed medium-power scopes, such as a 3-9x or 4-12x, to be used for varmint shooting at their top magnifications; the small-looking reticles did not cover too much of the target for varmint shooting at top power, yet were conspicuous for big game when used at lower power.

Yet, at first, all was not beer and skittles. A change in scope power requires that machinery inside the scope be moved, which in turn requires that fits are not solid—some clearance is necessary in order for there to be movement. Many makers who quickly latched onto the Redfield design didn't manufacture their scopes to the same precision, and a switch in power often created a change in point of impact. In fact, if a collimator were mounted on the muzzle of the rifle so you could watch the reticle as power was switched, the point of aim often seemed to take a spiral path as you went from bottom to top magnification, or vice versa, ending up in some scopes as much as 6 MOA away from where it started. With such a scope, when power was changed, the harder you held, the more you missed.

It's no wonder that variables had a poor reputation when first marketed en masse. Also, nothing was helped when the materials they were made of had different expansion rates. When the temperature changed, as it's wont to do in hunting season, one material would expand or contract at one rate, another at a different rate, so scopes often bound up—as they sometimes did when the rear mounting ring was tightened enough to minutely compress the scope tube.

But the makers kept finding and correcting the trouble spots, until nowadays a variable from a good manufacturer usually doesn't have enough change in reticle location to be seen against a collimator when going from top to bottom power. There might be some change, but at 1.5x, 2.5x or 3x, it's so small that it can't be seen. And if you can't see it, it doesn't make any difference. When zeroing, I always do so at top magnification. Why not? That usually gives best definition. Then when I crank down to bottom power, the reticle might move a whisper, but what difference does that make on big game in tight cover? Long, precise shooting is done at top power, and that's perfectly zeroed.

free otherwise to be pushed around by the adjustments: Therefore, the erectors pointed at different parts of the forward image when sighted in. The reticle, which was behind the erectors in the second focal plane, was always in the center of the field, no matter how much adjustment was necessary.

With this system, the erectors don't actually utilize the light rays from the full diameter of the objective lens, but when I once asked an optical designer of one of the country's biggest scopemakers about this, he said only about .040-inch of the objective was lost, so that's no big problem.

This Lyman 4x was perfect in thick woods for Darrel Lewis' M88 243—tough conditions, but the scope worked.

At about the same time that Redfield put the reticle in the second focal plane (which had been done much earlier by Weaver and other scopemakers, but for different reasons), they also introduced a method of making the reticle always appear centered in the field of view. For decades, the reticle had been physically moved by the adjustments when the rifle was zeroed. This way, it was not unusual for the aiming point to end up way off-center, which was bothersome. To avoid this, many gunsmiths became adept at shimming or bending the mount to accommodate. But now along comes the erector system, installed in a second, inner, tube which was fastened at one point at the rear end and was

The lenses are thought of, probably correctly, as the most important part of a scope. They provide the optics which are the reason for using a scope. Basically, they're pieces of glass made of several ingredients in proportions accurate, in the best makes, to at least three decimal places; then they're ground to specific shapes to surfaces accurate to hundred-thousandths of an inch. Then they are cleaned, coated and installed immovably in the metal tube, in the proper relationship to each other.

It must be remembered that the basic purpose of a lens is to change the paths of the light rays which strike it. Light is assumed to travel in a straight line through a given medium such as air, and probably does, so far as we can tell, if we ignore such things as Einstein's Theory and distances such as interstellar ones, which have nothing to do with hitting a deer, even if it's 500 yards away.

Lenses are made with differently curved surfaces—convex, concave, etc.—according to what the designer wants them to do. The most common ones in scopes are "positive" or converging lenses. In objective lenses, the most protuberant point, or apex, is located in the absolute center of the surface facing the object being observed. Every other point of that lens is successively lower than the apex, with the outer edge being lowest of all. From the side, the lens surface can be seen to be a curve which, if extended far enough, would be part of a circle. In three dimensions, it is part of a sphere.

When light hits the spherical surface, it passes through the center point in a straight line. However, at all other points (which are infinitely small flats, but nevertheless have surface dimension), its path is angled (refracted) because it hits the inner edge of the spherical surface before it hits the outer edge. It then continues through the lens in a straight line. In other words, the light rays are converged, with the effect that those striking the top wind up at the bottom, those hitting the right side end up on the left. Altogether, they form an image at what is called the focal length of that lens. Because the lens curvature is continuous, even within what may be considered an infinitely small surface or point, the angles of the light rays passing through the lens differ somewhat, so they form their images at minutely different distances behind the lens and the complete image is imperfect—an effect that is called "spherical abberation."

Spherical abberation is noticeable if only one lens is used, but scope makers largely overcome this by using several lenses in such situations, the subsequent lenses correcting most of the faults of the first one. Each lens introduces its own problems, of course, but these are taken into account as far as practicable. The result is an image which isn't perfect, but which, in scopes from the better manufacturers, is probably as good as the human eye (which itself isn't perfect) can resolve.

So we have what is termed the "first image" in the scope. But no

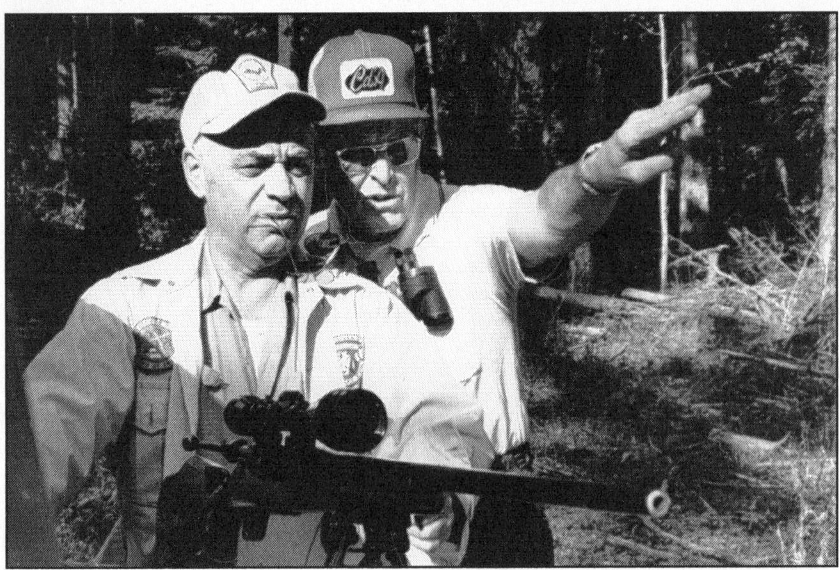

Bud Oakland points out a bunch of Columbian ground squirrels to Bell on an Idaho hunt. The Weatherby 3-9x Supreme on a 224 did well on them.

Tasco's 6-24x on a 40-XB 222 dropped many crows for Dave Wise, providing good optics and accurate adjustments.

matter how good it is, the darn thing is reversed—upside down and left to right. That means little in astronomy—there's no up or down, left or right in the drowned depths of outer space—but it would be disconcerting to look into the rear end of a scope and have a topsy-turvy view.

So a pair of erector lenses is installed behind the first image. They take that upside down, reversed image and reverse it again, which means the "second image," formed at their focal length, is right-side up. The erector lenses can do more than that. Depending upon various things, such as placement, they can add or lessen magnification, or do neither. Magnification normally depends upon the ratio between the objective (front) lens and that of the ocular (rearmost) lens. If the former, for instance, has a focal length four times as long as the latter, and this ratio is not altered by other lenses, the scope is a 4x.

In variable-power scopes, turning the power selector ring ultimately moves the erector lenses in accordion fashion, thus affecting magnification.

The erector lenses, as mentioned, form the second or rear target image, and the reticle can be installed in it. Farther to the rear, nearest the user, is the ocular or eyepiece lens. Actually, this is several lenses functioning as one unit, just as the objective "lens" is actually two or three lenses, and each erector lens is normally a doublet or two lenses. There are usually other lenses in a scope also, a "collector" lens between the objective and the erector lenses, and "field" lenses just forward of the ocular lens. In total, a scope often contains nine or more.

We've mentioned that positive lenses converge light rays. There are also, among a number of other designs, negative lenses, which scatter light rays outward. And there are times that a negative lens is effective. One of these is when increasing magnification, for obviously if the light rays are spread, they get bigger. This was noticed by a camera bug named Wally Siebert, and for some years he made a business of boosting scope power by installing a negative lens near the rear of the optical system, then utilizing the image created before it disintegrated. This also required lengthening the scope tube a bit (about an inch with the Lyman AA 8x he boosted to 16x for me).

This use of a negative lens degrades image quality a trifle at the outer edges, but not enough for the average user to notice. Also, this is the least used portion of the image. A negative lens, incidentally, is also called a Barlow lens, after the English mathematician Peter Barlow, who first noticed its effect some 200 years ago.

I might note that Siebert's work led to many scopemakers' production of the short, action-mounted, high-powered scopes of today. Early on, bench shooters used target-type scopes, but wanted to get the weight of the front end of the scope off the barrel. So Leupold, Lyman, Weaver and many others brought out the numerous models available.

The two focal planes are the only places within a scope tube that images are formed and are therefore visible. So the reticle must go in one of them (or both, sometimes, as in the case of Shepherd's Dual Reticle scope) if it's to be visible to the user. After all, if it's not visible, the scope is of no use to a shooter. However, if the scope is not being used at the exact range for which it is focused, the target image will form just in front of or just behind the reticle's position. Then, if the eye is not consistently aligned, an angle is introduced and the reticle seems to move. That is called parallax. The amount is not enough to be important in a big game scope at woods ranges, but it can be important to a target or varmint shooter. For that reason, scopes of low-medium magnification normally are focused at 100 or 150 yards, in what is called universal focus, while higher-power scopes—say 8x or above—usually have adjustable objective units. These allow precise adaptation for range by screwing or sliding the objective in or out. Occasional scopes adjust for distance by an arrangement which moves the erector lenses fore or aft.

This is most important to target shooters, who spend long periods of time using scopes, as it minimizes eyestrain. Varmint shooters sometimes make range adjustments when they will be spending long sessions of shooting at distances greatly different from their normal range. However, it should be noted that moving the objective unit can change the zero of the rifle. Also, the range marks which the maker puts on the tube rarely match the true distances. It's far better to actually check them from a bench and mark a few distances with sharp pocketknife scratches so you can return to them as necessary.

It also can be mentioned that if the eye is always positioned in exactly the same relationship to the scope, parallax doesn't exist because no angle is introduced. It's when the head is moved sideways or vertically that it's noticeable.

The light rays leave the scope via what is called the exit pupil. This is a beam of light, the size of which is the diameter of the unobstructed objective lens in millimeters divided by the scope's power. For example, if we have a 32mm objective in a 4x scope, the exit pupil will measure 8mm. (Occasionally, the maker installs a baffle to block the rays from the outer edges of the objective lens, because of difficulty in focusing such rays, glare, or whatever. In such cases, the exit pupil is reduced slightly.)

The square of the exit pupil's diameter gives an abstract number called "relative brightness," a term not heard as much nowadays as in years past. It was supposed to indicate which scope gave a brighter image than another. However, to be valid it assumed that all lenses were of equal quality, optical systems were equal, etc. That is rarely the case. Even successive scopes off a production line aren't 100-percent identical.

Also, the only amount of the exit pupil which enters the human eye is that part which doesn't exceed the diameter of the eye's entrance pupil—and that varies from about 2mm to about 7mm, according to ambient light. There's little advantage in having a 10mm exit pupil, with its relative brightness rating of 100, at a time when the eye's entrance pupil is, say, 5mm. A 5mm scope exit pupil, with an RB rating of 25, would supply all the light the eye could use in this instance. Only under extremely dark conditions does the eye's pupil widen to about 7mm (which is why night binoculars are usually made to provide a 7mm exit pupil); most of the time, the entrance pupil does not exceed 5mm, even in early evening.

In an effort to provide a better comparison than relative brightness, European scope makers came up with a method called the twilight factor. I have got a hunch they just looked at the results different scopes gave, then found a formula that fitted—sort of an empirical approach. I may be all wrong about that; maybe it's all super-scientific. Anyway, the twilight factor (TF) is calculated by simply multiplying the objective lens diameter in millimeters by the magnification and taking the square root of the product. For example, a 4x32 has a TF of 11.3 while an 8x56 goes 21+, so it's easy to see why those South Carolina beanfield riflemen prefer the latter for their evening shooting on whitetails.

But 8x seems to be about the limit on power for using the TF formula. Scopes with a 56mm objective are available, but few if any larger ones (after all, you've gotta get the darn things on a gun), and it takes that size to give a 7mm exit pupil with an 8x scope for maximum light transmission in the dark—when the eye's entrance pupil expands to its maximum. Consider: a 20x38mm, such as a target scope, gives a TF of 27+, which would be even more efficient in poor light than an 8x56 if this calculation were always valid, yet anyone who has used the latter type of scope for small varmints under poor light conditions knows it doesn't do the job. Its exit pupil is just too small (1.9mm), and therefore the delivered light is too low.

It seems to me that the twilight factor works only when the scope's exit pupil equals or slightly exceeds the eye's entrance pupil, which means an 8x56 at the moment. A 10x56 with a TF of 23.7 from an exit pupil of 5.6mm might be a trace better, but I can't think of any scope of that size being offered now.

The objective unit has a lot to do with getting maximum light, obviously, but contrary to what many users think, it's not important in creating a scope's field of view. The ocular lens is. The greater its diameter, normally, the greater the field. That is why Redfield's Widefield scopes and Burris's Fullfield, for instance, are larger in ocular lens diameter than regular lenses. Field is also affected by the scope's magnification and its eye relief (distance from the ocular lens to the eye.) When the eye is positioned to get a full field (at its best eye relief distance), a cone of view from the eye's entrance pupil to the outer edge of the ocular lens exists. This cone is actually an angle and it represents the greatest field possible with that scope.

Suppose we are working with a 4x scope and a 24-degree angle. Since the picture we see is magnified by the power, the actual field is the 24-degree angle divided by 4. The 24-degree angle equals about 120 feet at 100 yards, so divided by 4 we get an actual field of about 30 feet. If a larger field is wanted, we can reduce the power to 2.5x, say, and get a 48-foot field. Or we can reduce the eye relief, which would automatically increase the angle, perhaps to 30 degrees. Then a 4x scope would have a 37.5-foot field. Anyway, it's obvious that the ocular unit, not the objective, is important to a scope's field.

The field of view, incidentally, is usually given as the diameter in feet of the maximum circular image that can be seen when using a scope. It's usually expressed in feet per hundred yards. It can also be given as an angle, for it's one-half of the normal number at 50 yards, twice it at 200 yards, etc. In the conventional method, it's a lateral linear dimension, expressing diameter. But since field is concerned with area, and areas of circles are proportionate to the square of their diameters, a 200-yard field is actually four times as big as a 100-yard field with a given scope. This is complicated by scopes that have a wider horizontal view than vertical (such as the Widefields), but you get the idea. (The Widefields, ideally, begin life as circular lenses, then have sections ground off what are eventually their tops and bottoms, resulting in horizontal lenses. The Fullfields are round and give a circular image, but due to their diameter have to be mounted higher.)

Eye relief, perhaps we should mention, is the distance from the apex of the ocular lens to the eye. It is that measurement where a perfect

In past years, straight 4x scopes like this Kollmorgen on Bell's 7x61 S&H Magnum often did it all, from this short-range buck to well over a quarter-mile.

image is formed—where the eye sees a circle of light as large as the lens. In a practical sense, it might be considered the distance from the eyebrow to the rearmost part of the tube, as that's the part that whacks the shooter if he crowds the scope too closely for any reason. It depends on the angle of the light rays coming from the lens perimeter to the eye's entrance pupil. However, the eye's pupil is not a point. It has dimension, at its greatest diameter some 7mm, which is greater than 1/4-inch. Thus some light rays enter at the edge of the pupil, not at its centermost point, which means eye relief is not an absolute measurement, and a part of the field can still be seen when the eye is placed fore or aft a little. The field diminishes, though; in fact, if the scope is held at arm's length, the only thing to be seen is a spot of light—the exit pupil.

Awhile back we mentioned an effect called spherical aberration. This is due to the fact that light passing through the different areas of a convex lens does not form its complete image at exactly the same distance from the lens—because the different parts of the curved surface do not have exactly the same focal lengths. There are other types of aberration. For instance, chromatic. This is because light going through a lens breaks down when its component colors refract differently and therefore comes to focus at slightly different distances. Then there is distortion, which occurs when magnification is not the same throughout the field. If a square appears to have elongated corners, magnification is greater at the outside than center; if it looks barrel-shaped, the reverse is true. And a lens is astigmatic when it cannot sharply focus lines lying at different angles at the same time. Coma can occur when light passes through a lens at an angle and gives an indistinct image, and field curvature exists when an image formed by a lens is formed on a bowl-shaped surface rather than a flat one.

All of these effects and others are largely taken care of by following lenses—their shapes and substances, which alter refracting power. Different kinds of lenses—for instance, those made of crown and flint glass—refract light differently, so each can be used at times to overcome an unwanted effect of the other. These are not simple glasses either. They include, but aren't limited to, zinc; light, medium and dense barium; boro-silicate; and fluor. Each affects light routes in a different way. Fortunately, the shooter doesn't have to worry about such things; the optical engineer already has.

Lenses have been in existence at least as long as our species, *Homo sapiens*, for each human eye contains a lens. When the eye is relaxed, its design, size and shape bring light from an object at optical infinity, about 50 yards, to focus on the retina. Light reflected from a distant object, if not accommodated for, is brought to focus in front of the retina in a condition called myopia or shortsightedness; light which would be focused behind the retina, which is physically impossible, is a result of hyperopia or farsightedness. Automatic alteration of the lens shape, within limitations, brings the transmitted light to focus on the retina. It is interesting that the lens is of the positive shape and therefore the image it transmits is upside down and reversed, but, according to ophthalmologists, the brain somehow accommodates for this and we see things normally. *(Or, perhaps, abnormally, but right-side up.—Editor)*

Manufactured lenses, though, have existed only since about 1266, when the English philosopher Friar Roger Bacon reputedly used a segment of glass sphere to magnify the printing in a book. For seven centuries, lenses didn't significantly change except in quality of materials and precision of manufacture. All of the light which struck the surface of a lens did not pass through it, and it eventually was determined that at least 4 percent was reflected away at each glass-air surface (leaving as well as entering a lens) or was absorbed or scattered by the glass. When you think how many lenses a scope has, the total loss is seen to be great, perhaps 40 percent. Therefore, early scopes had only about 60 percent light transmission. This light loss reduces brilliance of the image, dulls colors, and bounces around inside the scope tube, often causing ghost images. To reduce such reflections, the inside of the tube is often darkened and roughened.

Then in the 1930s, Prof. A. Smakula, an employee of the Carl Zeiss works in Germany, developed a process of anti-reflection lens coating. This was an extremely thin layer of magnesium fluoride (one-fourth the wavelength of light or some .000004- to .000006-inch in thickness). This increased light transmission to about 85 percent. Since then, multi-coating has improved transmission to the mid-90s, percentagewise, at least in some parts of the spectrum. That means there is no place to go, for if transmission can't be improved at least 10 percent, the human eye can't notice. At least that's what some students of the subject say.

There's no doubt that coating improved lenses; in fact, many authorities say it's the most significant advance in the seven centuries lenses have existed.

But scopemakers continue bringing out new and better models. Lenses are improved in perfection (materials and dimensions), installation is better, relationships of parts are improved, more magnifications are made available...

Shooters never had it so good. ●

Rook shooting in Britain in the 1830s: Note that the guy on the extreme right of the left-hand group is using a bullet crossbow.

HOW THE BRITS CULLED THE ROOKS

by JACK BARTLETT

IT MUST BE admitted that the old-time British gamekeeper butchered, with gun, trap and poison, many a rare bird he assumed was thieving his game eggs and chicks. No species was more harried than the family *Corvidae*, the principle members of which, found in the game-rearing counties of Britain, were the rook and the carrion crow.

The carrion was a solitary bird, nesting with his mate in a lone hedgerow tree. From there, his frequent expeditions in search of carrion, game eggs and chicks, as well as many a weakly newborn lamb in season, were launched. His vulture reputation was richly deserved.

The rook, on the other hand, was far more numerous than the carrion and nested in colonies or "rookeries"—collections of dozens of nests built high 'mongst the swaying, dipping, topmost branches of the tall elm trees. Any rook will undoubtedly snap up game bird chicks and eggs, and can do considerable harm to both the farmer and the game rearer; nevertheless, his sins are somewhat balanced by his consumption of wire-worms and grubs.

As the current census of rook-breeding capacity is classified as "abundant," it has been, for many hundreds of years, necessary to institute an annual cull to keep their population within reasonable numbers. During the 19th century, the cull was achieved by shooting the young rooks when they emerged from the parental nests in the latter part of the month of May and perched on the slender twigs of their tree prior to gaining the courage to test their wings in flight. Owners of small coverts boasting a rookery would carefully study the progress of the fledgling birds and, when they judged that sufficient numbers had emerged from the parental home, would invite their friends and neighbors to partake in a "rook shoot."

For the owner of a large estate with abundant rookeries in his coverts, the May rook shoot provided the excuse for a real shindig. His noble pals, together with their ladies, were invited to stay at the mansion and partake of his lavish hospitality before sallying forth to cull the birds. Many of the ladies, who would find the recoil of a 12-bore shotgun unacceptable at a large pheasant covert shoot or on a grouse moor, were able to handle the light rook rifle with expertise. Tho' fashion in the 1880s decreed that ladies' legs were to be veiled from the vulgar masculine gaze, nevertheless we can assume that the gals in my photograph so deftly sighting their light rifles at the quarry 'mongst the high trees had those exquisite limbs positioned correctly in the traditional offhand shooting position.

But let us commence in the earliest days of rook shooting. In the early 18th century, the principal weapon was the flintlock shotgun, until it was usurped by the "bullet crossbow"—an excellent weapon discharging a lead ball from its pouch 'twixt twin bowstrings. Fitted with aperture and bead foresight, it was an exceedingly accurate weapon and was extremely popular until overtaken by muzzle-loading small-bore rook rifles in the 19th century.

In the 1920s, a British working carpenter, one Daniel Higson of Preston in Lancashire, resurrected the ancient bullet crossbow and wrote two fascinating books about the weapon. A current British dealer in field sport literature, David Grayling of Lyvennet, Crosby Ravensworth, Penrith, Cumbria CA1O 3JP, England, has brought out an excellent reprint of both works bound tastefully in one work.

British gunmakers eventually produced excellent muzzle-loading rook rifles in either 80- or 120-bores, using about a quarter of a dram of blackpowder. The other arm, which achieved considerable popularity 'mongst the 20th May rook shooters, was the old air rifle. Unlike the modern spring-operated air gun, these possessed an air reservoir, either in a sharkskin covered metal stock or in a separate copper ball screwed to the weapon in front of the trigger guard. These reservoirs were charged with compressed air via a large hand pump, similar to an automobile tire pump.

An adult bird perched high on the elms.

The operator screwed the end of the pump to the reservoir and then undertook the horrendous task of filling the thing with compressed air. It required some 250 hard strokes of the pump handle to attain a pressure of 400 psi. This pressure was then tapped off by means of a valve, giving the shooter some twenty to thirty shots. Of course, a gentleman estate owner would have his gamekeeper in attendance to undertake the laborious chore of pumping.

These early air rifles were fitted with interchangeable rifled and smoothbore barrels for ball (often up to about .400-inch caliber) and for small charges of shot. With ball, some were quite capable of killing deer or man. Indeed, the old Austrian army possessed a regiment of air gunners, an unsporting action which so incensed their enemy, Napoleon I, that he gave orders that any soldier captured who was armed with an air rifle was to be summarily hung.

With the arrival of the 1860s, the interest in rook shooting increased, and accordingly the British gunmakers put their talents to work designing and building accurate light rifles for rook and rabbit shooting. The 22 rimfire cartridge had not by that date achieved much popular-

Another young gal sights her rook rifle at young birds perched high on the elms ity in England, and these British rook rifles were all chambered for centerfire cartridges, calibers designated 297/230; 297/250; 300; 320; 360; and even 380. However, intrepid rook shooters were to discover that the larger calibers tended to pulverize the game.

The better-class rook rifle was sold cased, together with a full cleaning kit and a full set of reloading tools, complete with bullet mould for casting round balls. We must assume that the large estate owner also delegated the task of reloading and bullet casting to his gamekeeper.

Did one shoot rooks merely for the thrill of seeing them topple from their high perch and the confidence that one was reducing the number of vermin? Most definitely not, for they make a succulent dish. Just after World War I, in the very early 1920s, your reporter was living on a

The late Jack Bartlett, known as "Whiteface" in the U.K. because he hailed from Hereford, has gone on ahead, but he left some writing behind that reflects his love for the countryside he stands in here. This article is one such.

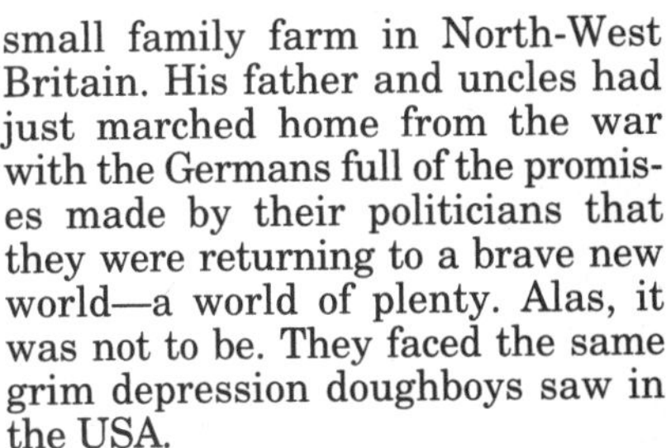

small family farm in North-West Britain. His father and uncles had just marched home from the war with the Germans full of the promises made by their politicians that they were returning to a brave new world—a world of plenty. Alas, it was not to be. They faced the same grim depression doughboys saw in the USA.

My family, existing on a minute farm, had a small covert of some ten acres supporting a rookery. There was, of course, no spare cash to provide a young son with pocket money, so I had to eke out a few coppers by catching rabbits, then selling the carcasses to a local butcher and the skins to a traveling dealer who bought 'em to be converted into "fur felt," which was employed in the manufacture of hats.

The few small amounts of cash money I earned by means of my rabbit enterprise were pushed over the counter of a nearby gun shop for 22 Shorts for my old 1890 Winchester. So when the little rifle (which had started life knocking celluloid ping-pong balls off jets of water at a fairground) was suitably foddered, I'd bag a dozen fledgling rooks and take 'em into the larder. I neatly slit along their breast bones, peeling back skin and feathers, before carefully removing the two chunks of meat on the breasts.

These small chunks of protein were then given to my mother who steeped them in milk overnight before laying them in a pie dish covered with crisp pastry. Tho' 'tis nigh on seventy years since I tasted this succulent dish, the memory still lingers. ●

A charming young lady takes careful aim at a perching rook in the 1880s.

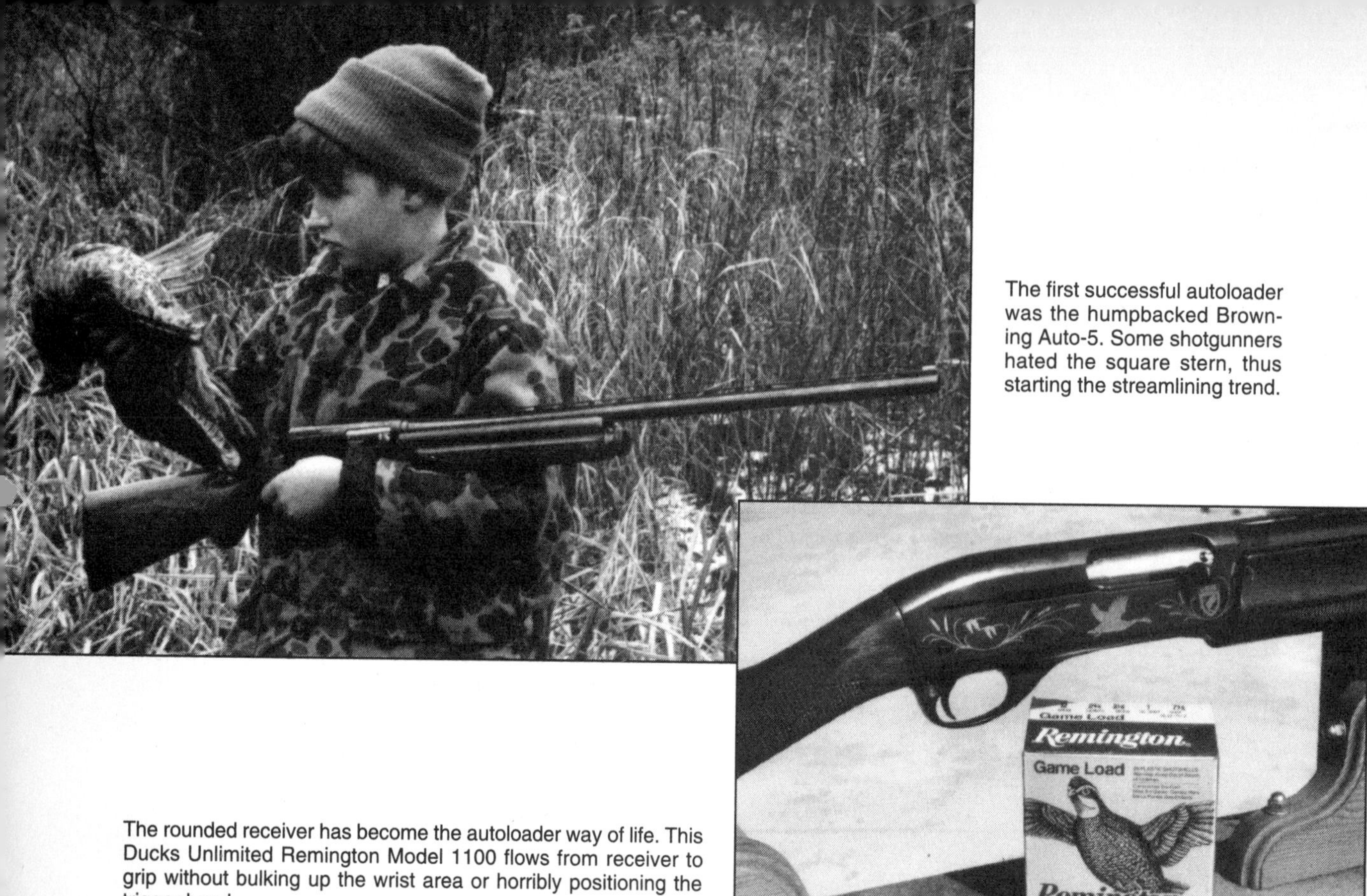

The first successful autoloader was the humpbacked Browning Auto-5. Some shotgunners hated the square stern, thus starting the streamlining trend.

The rounded receiver has become the autoloader way of life. This Ducks Unlimited Remington Model 1100 flows from receiver to grip without bulking up the wrist area or horribly positioning the trigger hand.

SHOTGUN HISTORY: STREAMLINING

by DON ZUTZ

THERE WAS A time when hunters debated the sporting qualities of autoloading shotguns. They were for game hogs, some argued, tragically blessed with a firepower that could massacre flocks and coveys. The hilarious thing about that argument was that, as the debate rolled on, egotistical pumpgunners began to claim that they could get off accurately directed shots as rapidly with their trombone guns as others could with semi-autos! If that were true, why didn't the pumps come in for sharp criticism as well?

And then there were the British who rejected every sort of repeater, only to take a matched pair of doubles with them, along with a loader who kept them fully charged. I have never understood why four shots from two guns were considered more sporting than three shots from one repeater. On the other hand, I've never wanted a king or a queen around, either.

Gradually, however, the autoloading shotgun gained acceptance here. Cooler heads realized that personal ethics were the deciding factor in sportsmanship and conservation, not any gun's mechanical advantages. And the debate fell apart in the 1930s when President Franklin D. Roosevelt signed into law new federal waterfowling regulations, including the three-shell maximum capacity for repeaters. Today, the autoloading shotgun is an integral part of sport shooting, and even the British are using designs like the Beretta Model A303 and Remington Model 1100 for serious Skeet and Sporting Clays tournaments.

But we'll grant one point to those who criticized early autoloaders for their bulky, slab-sided, mechanical lines and dubious cosmetics. Compared to the trim, compact, even racy lines of a classic double, the semi-autos were rather gross. Hardly sleek on the exterior, their metallic nuclei packaged all sorts of springs, latches, dogs, pins and moving parts. On the only successful design of the first half of the 20th century—the Browning long-recoil system—the receiver needed a sharply humpbacked receiver stern to provide an enclosed raceway for the bolt, and this jagged feature didn't go unnoticed by traditionalists who doted on simple elegance.

This is not to say that the Browning Auto-5 was an ineffective shotgun, of course. Many hunters then, as now, swear by the Auto-5's square-sterned receiver as a subconscious reference point; it stood out boldly before the eye, and the frontal ramp and bead stood out as a sharp

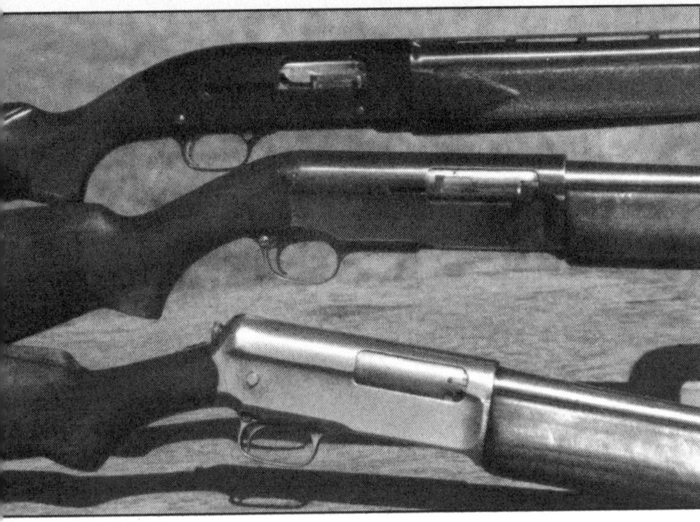

The Winchester autoloaders, ill-fated all: (bottom) the Model 1911 Self-Loader, the Model 40 (middle), and the Model 50. The Model 40 was the first commercial streamlining attempt. Its trigger unit is pulled back and angled upward so the trigger finger can reach it from its elevated location.

To open the Winchester Model 1911 Self-Loader, the hunter had to grab a knurled segment of the barrel and pump it. The original Browning Auto-5's patent covered the operating handle.

contrast for accurate alignment. Not only has much game been bagged with the Auto-5, but the same concept swept many Skeet and some trap tournaments in the period between the World Wars. This was especially so when Remington obtained the manufacturing rights to the Auto-5 and brought it out in Skeet Grade.

When Savage began making autoloaders in 1930, it also used the Browning patents and the humpbacked receiver. An interesting variant was the Model 726 "Upland Sporter," which had only a two-shot magazine capacity. Somewhat later, the Model 726 Savage was updated into a Skeet model with a factory-installed Cutts Compensator and barrel length of 24 inches. Those were the days when Skeet was shot with a low-gun starting position, and any number of shooters thought that the short-barreled piece was *the* answer.

About the only commercial autoloader to counter the Browning Auto-5 was Winchester's Model 1911 "Self-Loader," which perforce went on the market *sans* the important Browning refinements such as the operating handle and friction piece. As a result, the Winchester M1911 became a stock-splitter of the first magnitude. Opening one was hardly a cinch with cold hands, as the hunter had to grab a knurled segment of the barrel and pump it backwards. If I am permitted a bit of sarcasm, it was just a tad more awkward than opening a Holland & Holland self-opening double!

Despite the gun's mechanical shortcomings, however, the Winchester M1911 S-L had good pointing qualities which, in my opinion, outdid those of the Browning Auto-5 design. Its receiver was but moderately humpbacked, semi-rounded, and one's eye tended to flow over it for enhanced target visibility. The Browning Auto-5, on the opposite hand, did much to block out the lower portion of one's viewing area. Indeed, if the Browning mechanisms had been put into the Winchester M1911's frame, it would have been quite the gun! But it wasn't to be. The M1911 S-L sold 82,774 pieces between 1911 and 1925, then folded, while the Remington Model 11 sold about 300,000 from 1911 to 1948, and the Browning Auto-5 is still running after more than 2,000,000 copies have been sold.

During the 1930s, experimenters began to streamline the existing autoloading scatterguns. Some of this demand came from Skeetmen who wanted easier visual access to the target, complaining of the way an Auto-5's wall-like receiver blotted out the field of vision. What they wanted was an autoloader with a

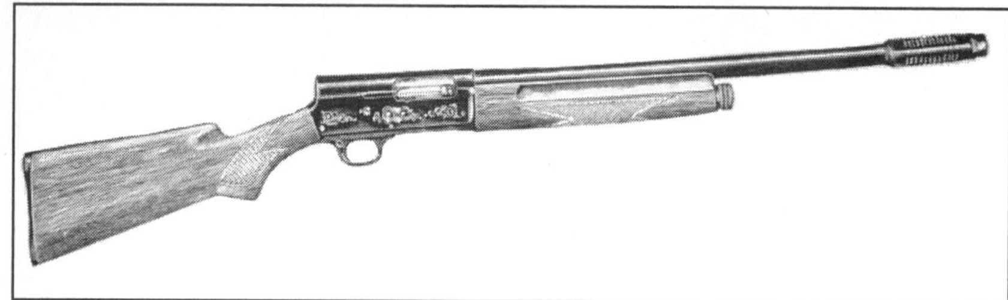

Some early Skeetmen swore by the Cutts-equipped autoloader, humpbacked receiver, *et al.* This is the Savage Model 720-C in Skeet mode.

rounded receiver like the Model 12 Winchester and Model 31 Remington pumps.

Such modifications were no small goals. They meant altering the stock, of course, since the receiver metal couldn't be changed without obstructing the breechbolt's rearward travel.

A couple of eastern outfits took up the challenge. These were Griffin & Howe of New York and Ed Garland of New Jersey. Their approach was to reshape the stock, giving the pistol grip a goosenecky configuration that swept high to fill the space behind the humpback. A nearby photo shows the Griffin & Howe remodeling. But while the goosenecked grip may have salved the feelings of those who were irritated by the abrupt humpback on Browning long-recoil guns, it certainly didn't provide a classic curve!

The fact is that these initial attempts to streamline the Auto-5 upset the effective gripping that John M. Browning had built into the gun. Browning's grips—the first were straight, the next semi-pistol with the famed round knob—were set to position the hands in line for coordinated pointing and swinging. The G&H and Garland goose-neck grips, however, forced the shooter's hand higher at a steep angle; it made him reach farther for the trigger, often contacting it at an angle that necessitated an upward pull rather than a straight-back action. Thus, the modified mode that attempted to streamline the gun turned out to be more cosmetic than effective; people found it uncomfortable, inefficient, and even impossible, all depending upon their hand sizes, of course.

The different grip height, angle, and distance therefore necessitated further modifications to the Auto-5. The trigger unit had to be brought farther back than in the original design. This, too, can be seen in our illustrations. The Garland conversion moved the trigger and guard a pretty good distance back from the receiver, whereas the true

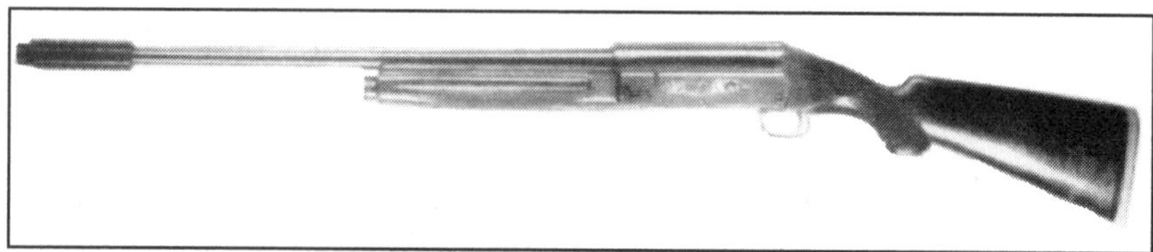

A full-length view of the Griffin & Howe conversion of an Auto-5 taken from *Field & Stream* magazine, 1940. The grip extends upward to fill the rear of the receiver, forcing the shooter's hand upward at an awkward angle.

Val Browning's Double Automatic was that firm's first venture into a rounded receiver; it lasted a long time, but never caught hold.

Browning has repeatedly returned to the semi-humpbacked design, only to meet with public disapproval. This is the Model A-5000. It worked OK, but never hit it big, either.

Browning Auto-5 has its trigger unit and guard ahead of the receiver's back line.

The G&H and Garland conversions were only stopgap projects, of course. Not many were made; those buyers requesting them apparently were Skeet shooters. Having handled Auto-5 guns with goosenecked grips, my conclusion is that it wasn't worth the cost and the effort. But the exercise did set the industry to thinking.

The first commercial attempt to streamline the autoloading shotgun was Winchester's ill-fated Model 40. By the late 1930s, Browning's patents had run out and Winchester was free to use the operating handle and friction assembly. Winchester tacked these onto a gun that had a slightly rounded receiver top. But as on the G&H and Garland conversions, the grip ran high relative to the trigger. Winchester designers rightly positioned the M40's trigger in a rearward location, actually angling it upward slightly. This feature is readily apparent in the nearby photo of the Model 40 vis-a-vis some other Winchester autoloaders. In most respects, the Model 40's grip was comfortable unless one had small hands and short fingers.

The Model 40 felt good and shot well. Bits of history indicate that the motivation behind it may have been the Skeet market. Some beautiful Skeet guns were made with dense burl walnut and factory-attached Cutts Comps. But, alas, a weakness at the juncture of the recoil spring's tubular housing and the rear of the receiver caused many of them to break down, and the gun had little more than a year's life, going out of production in 1941 after roughly 2200 had been made. Examples of this gun can be seen in the Cody Firearms Museum wing of the Buffalo Bill Historical Center in Cody, Wyoming.

In reality, the Model 40's receiver wasn't very streamlined at all. The rear was just slightly radiused. But it proved that the industry's wheels were turning, however slow the rotation.

The closest that the G&H and Garland profilings came to widespread commercial use was on the post-WWII Savage Model 775 series of 1949-1958. These had a gooseneck grip, their triggers also pulled back farther than those of the Browning-licensed Model 720 Savages of an earlier date. A lightweight M755 at 6¾ pounds in 12-gauge made it into the line for 1950 and hung around until about 1965.

None of the Savage Model 775 guns sold all that well. In fact, they were virtually obsolete the instant they hit the dealers' shelves, because in 1949, Remington took a swing at making a streamlined semi-auto shotgun, and it wasn't just a concept copy of the G&H and Garland conversion as was Savage's. Known as the Model 11-48, the new Remington flowed with graceful geometry which, for some conservative hunters of the era, may actually have been ahead of its time. Not only was the 11-48's receiver given a lengthy top curve, but the trigger guard was also streamlined. And although the 11-48 still operated on the Browning long-recoil system, Remington did come up with a friction piece that negated the need to switch rings around for light and heavy loads.

The secret behind the Remington 11-48's geometry was quite simple. To make the breechbolt and barrel extension fit the gun's interior without a high-standing humpback, both of those recoiling parts were sloped to match their environs. *Voila!* The sighting plane on the 11-48 was pretty much akin to that of the Model 31 and Model 870 slide actions. The 11-48 went on to be made in all Skeet gauges, 12 through 410-bore, and to win heavily in all. There is a warm spot in my memory bank for Model 11-48s, like the 20-gauge with which I won my first state championship and my class at the world shoot during the 1960s.

In 1954, Winchester introduced its post-war autoloader, the Model 50. Based on an inertia-block system, it had a somewhat more conservative approach to the rounded receiver and carried a more traditional trigger-guard geometry than did the M11-48. But the M50's receiver was nicely compacted, and it had a sighting plane and overall feel of the Model 12 pumpgun. If ever a gun answered the demands of those Skeeters of the 1930s who wanted an autoloader with the viewing and pointing qualities of the M12, the Model 50 was it. But, alas, those early shooters had left the game or had taken up the over/under, which was then beginning to catch on more widely.

The profiling of the modern American autoloader, then, was hardly an overnight procedure. The time from when Griffin & Howe and Ed Garland began massaging the Browning Auto-5 to the Remington Model 11-48 and Winchester Model 50 covered somewhat more than two decades. World War II obviously slowed the process, but it's a moot question as to whether the Remington Model 11-48 and Winchester Model 50 would have come out much sooner had the Japanese not pounced upon Pearl Harbor. With typical hunters still willing to buy Remington Model 11s, why would Remington have advanced the 11-48 project in the early 1940s, especially with the U.S. economy creeping along and inflated production costs not a major factor?

It was mainly after the war, when production costs and inflated figures began hitting the economy, that gunmakers had to look at new concepts. The Remington Model 11-48 didn't only bring streamlining to the semi-auto shotgun, it brought a whole new way of manufacturing guns. Castings and stampings now became part of the package; machined parts were simply too costly to produce. The Remington 11-48 and 870, for example, were initially called "punch press guns," and shooters were quite critical of them. But in reality, the change in production methods saved American gunmaking. Without stampings and castings, gun prices might have leaped over the moon, as a fully machined sporting gun would have cost more than a typical hunter could have paid. It is only now, with CNC equipment, that machined components are slowly coming back into gunmaking without driving up the price.

But the die has been struck. Modern American shotgunners favor the rounded, streamlined receiver. Browning has tried time and again to popularize the semi-humpbacked models such as the B-80, B-2000, A-500R and A-500G without success. In 1994, Browning gave in and announced a new family of gas-operated autoloaders with rounded receivers—the Gold.

Franchi sticks with the semi-hump, but trails the lot in sales. And despite the super simplicity and dependability of the relatively new Beretta Model A390 ST, the 1994 Beretta International catalog shows target-grade A390 STs with rounded receivers. Once set in motion by the G&H and Garland conversions of the 1930s, the trend to streamline receiver profiles has been the dominant one in autoloading shotguns. ●

THE BROWNING

The gun that changed

by KONRAD F. SCHREIER, JR.

THE U.S. ARMY'S Browning Automatic Rifle, always known as the BAR, was one of the great infantry weapons of its day. It served in World War I, World War II, the Korean War and other conflicts, and some are still in military service.

The U.S. Army adopted the BAR in 1917 and retained it as a standard infantry weapon into the 1960s. From its introduction, this reliable and rugged weapon's accurate and effective fire changed the basic infantry organization and tactics of the U.S. Army and the Marine Corps.

The BAR began as another of the remarkable ideas of the amazing arms inventor John Moses Browning several years before World War I began. He conceived it as an automatic rifle to complement the bolt-action rifles used by infantrymen of the day, but he did not develop it at the time because he realized the U.S. Army of the period would not want it.

Shortly after WWI began, in the fall of 1914, Browning began to develop his "automatic rifle" at the Browning Brothers' experimental gun machine shop in Ogden, Utah. In late 1916, he demonstrated a prototype at the Colt factory in Hartford, Connecticut, and it worked very well. By this time, the U.S. Army was learning to use its existing machineguns in the troubles along the Mexican border, and they were interested in the new Browning's possibilities.

The Army first tested the BAR in February 1917, several months before the United States entered WWI in April 1917. Like so many Browning designs, it showed great promise, and Colt was encouraged to continue with its development, although the Army had neither the organization nor the tactics to use it at the time.

Then in May 1917, the Army adopted the BAR, even though its design had not yet been finished. At the time, no production facility or tooling to manufacture it existed.

Colt could not put the BAR into production quickly because they had massive military orders for their pistols, revolvers and machineguns—all critically needed at the front. The Army negotiated a license with Colt which allowed them to assign production of the BAR to any manufacturer they selected. In September 1917, after several false starts and much confusion, Winchester got a contract manufacture it.

In early 1918, after testing the pre-production Winchester BARs, the Army standardized the weapon as the "Cal. 30 Browning Automatic Rifle, Model of 1918." At the same time, Colt and Marlin-Rockwell were also given BAR production contracts. Winchester began delivering production BARs in June 1918, and Colt and

The first Army unit to use the BAR in combat was the 79th Division in an action on September 13, 1918. While the BAR was an instant comat success, integrating it into the U.S. Army infantry organization was a major project.

Machineguns were regimental weapons in World War I, but the BAR became a company weapon. Originally, a U.S. Army WWI rifle company consisted of four rifle platoons. One of

Teaching a soldier to use and care for a BAR was not difficult. It was fired from the same prone, sitting, kneeling and standing positions as a regular infantry rifle. In addition, the WWI BAR magazine belt provided a special pocket for the butt of the BAR which was used when firing from the hip in the "assault position."

The 18-pound WWI Model 1918 BAR fired from an open bolt, and the forward movement of the bolt caused

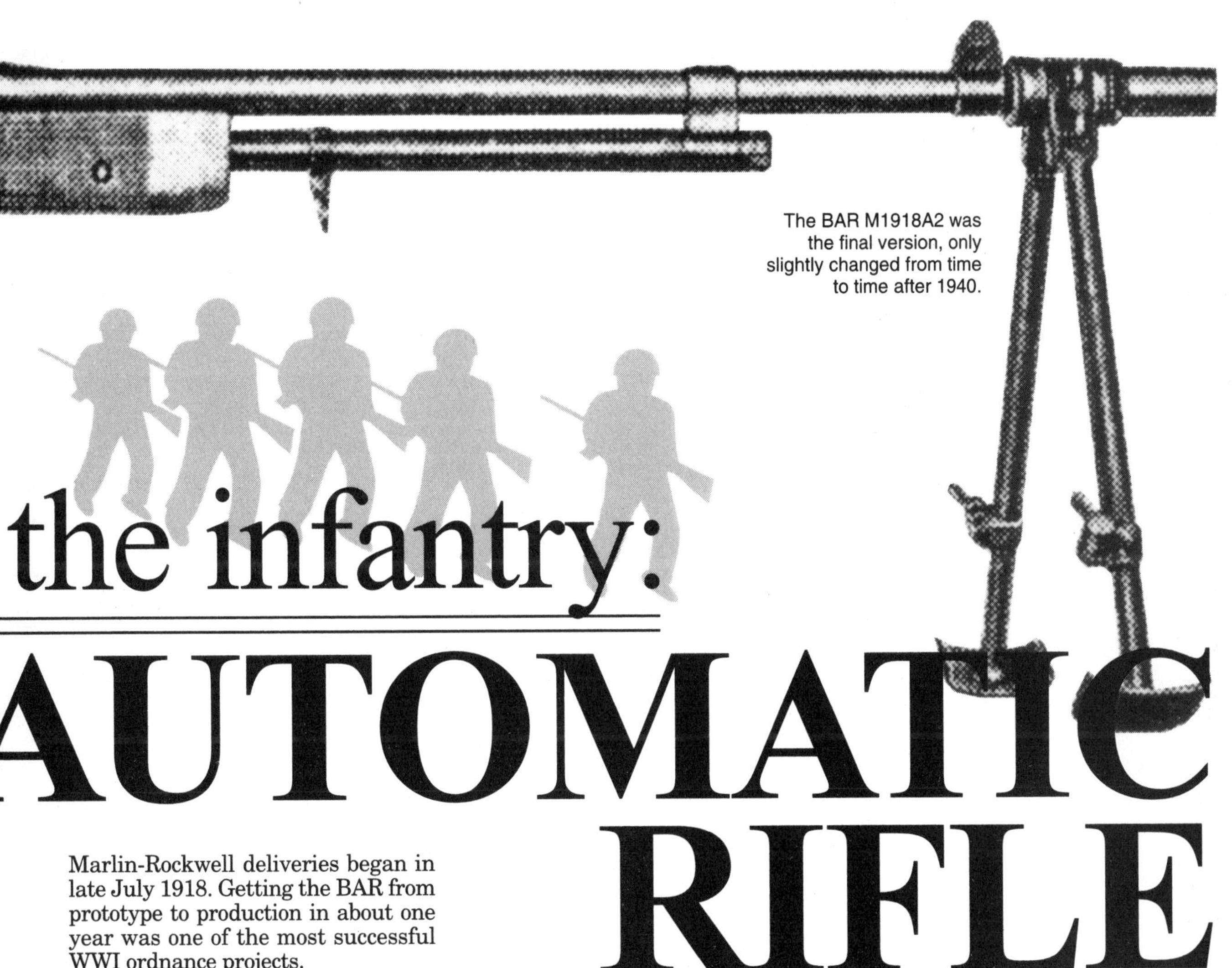

The BAR M1918A2 was the final version, only slightly changed from time to time after 1940.

the infantry: AUTOMATIC RIFLE

Marlin-Rockwell deliveries began in late July 1918. Getting the BAR from prototype to production in about one year was one of the most successful WWI ordnance projects.

The first BARs reached the American Expeditionary Force, the A.E.F., in France in August 1918. They were desperately wanted to replace the marginal French Chauchat machineguns American troops were using in combat at the time. Second Lt. Val A. Browning, the inventor's son, went to France with the first BARs to demonstrate them, and he is supposed to have been the first person to fire one in combat.

these was converted to a BAR platoon of three squads with two BAR sections each. In combat, one BAR squad was assigned to each rifle platoon. At the end of the war, plans were being made to enlarge the BAR platoon so there would be one BAR for each eight-man rifle squad. This organization did not go into use because there weren't enough BARs or BAR men.

some aim disturbance. However, the BAR was a very accurate weapon, particularly when fired from any handy rest. It could be fired in its semi-automatic manner, but it was found to be most effective firing short three- or four-round full-automatic bursts. Longer full-automatic bursts were inaccurate and a waste of ammunition. Short bursts were easily

Inventor John M. Browning (left) and Frank Burton of Winchester with an early production BAR in 1918.

fired by simply pulling and releasing the BAR's trigger quickly. This mode also kept the weapon from overheating.

The BAR saw relatively little combat in World War I, but it proved its worth beyond any doubt, so much so that it was one of the very few weapons kept in production after the end of World War I. Some 102,125 BARs were built during WWI, and about half of them were delivered after the end of the war. At that point, Winchester had built 47,123; Marlin-Rockwell, 39,002; and Colt, 16,000.

The Army's WWI combat success of the BAR caused the British to consider adopting it, and they tested a version in their 303 rifle caliber. The French also considered

The prototype BAR tested in February 1917 differed in many respects, including its open-top receiver. This one still exists in the collection of John M. Browning's arms displayed in Ogden, Utah.

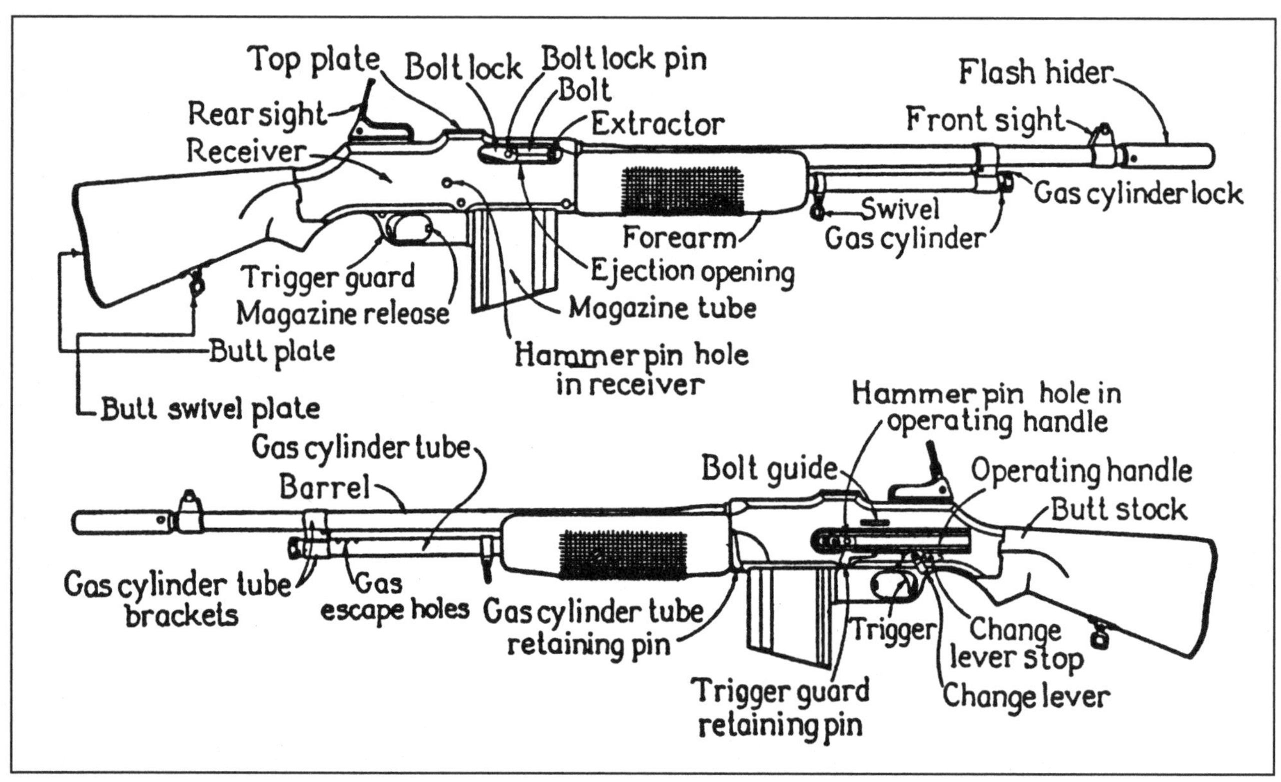

A U.S. Army manual for the Browning Automatic Rifle M1918 with the parts names common to all models of the BAR.

A World War I Doughboy with a BAR and the BAR belt with the "assault fire" butt pocket.

A 1941 BAR man with an M1918A2 BAR, tin hat and leggings.

A 1940 BAR man with the M1918A1 BAR in the "assault fire" position. His belt lacks the "assault fire" pocket.

adopting it in 30-06 caliber. Neither of these projects continued after the end of WWI.

At the end of that war, the BAR manufacturing rights reverted to Colt, and they manufactured BARs in the 1920s and 1930s for export military sales. The calibers included 6.5mm, 7mm and 8mm Mauser. Colt also built a special law enforcement "Monitor" version of the BAR and sold a few of them.

In the 1920s, Browning licensed foreign manufacturers to build the BAR. FN of Belgium built it as their Model 30 and sold them to Belgian, Chilean, Chinese and other armies in limited numbers. After World War II, FN reintroduced their BAR as the improved Model D with a quick-change barrel, something the U.S. Army never considered necessary or desirable. The FN Model D BAR in 30-06 caliber was used by the Belgian army, and the Egyptian army bought a number in 8mm Mauser caliber.

In the center is a BAR man in action in the Pacific in 1944. Note that the BAR's flash hider and bipod have been removed.

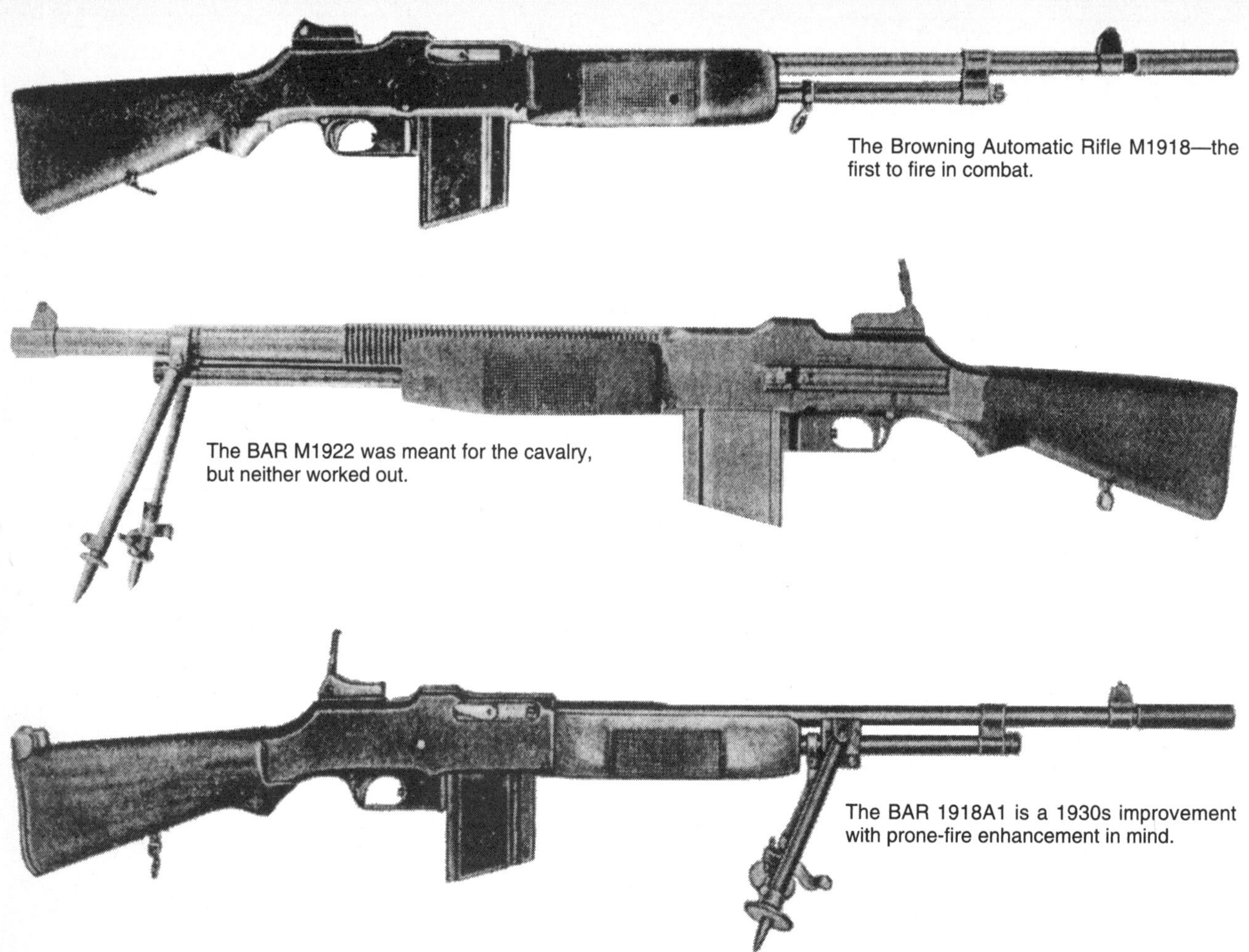

The Browning Automatic Rifle M1918—the first to fire in combat.

The BAR M1922 was meant for the cavalry, but neither worked out.

The BAR 1918A1 is a 1930s improvement with prone-fire enhancement in mind.

The Swedish government also bought a license to build BARs in 1920, and their army adopted it as the M21 in their 6.5mm. In the late 1930s they introduced an improved model with a quick-change barrel as their M37 BAR.

Poland also bought a license to build the BAR in the 1920s, and their army used them in 8mm as the Model 28. The Poles also built an experimental 8mm infantry rifle based on the BAR design, which they never placed in production.

In 1922, the U.S. Army adopted a modified BAR known as the "Cal. 30 Browning Machine Rifle M1922," at the request of the Cavalry Board. It was nothing more than a slightly heavier BAR with a finned barrel, bipod, and buttrest. This model was specifically for use with horse-mounted cavalry, and it became obsolete before World War II. Existing models were converted back to regular BARs.

All through the 1920s and 1930s, our Army worked on finding the best way to integrate the BAR into the infantry organization. By the end of the 1930s, two structures had been developed. One was an infantry platoon with three eight-man rifle squads and a fourth eight-man squad with three BAR teams; that was standard at the end of the 1930s. The second approach involved a new, larger infantry platoon with four twelve-man squads, each with its own BAR team. Extensive troop testing proved the twelve-man squad was tactically superior. It was adopted for Army and Marine Corps infantry in 1941, and it remained standard through WWII and as long after that as the BAR remained in service.

In the 1930s, the Army looked into improving the BAR. It was agreed the most effective fire was delivered prone, so a bipod was added and a hinged buttplate was provided to stabilize the gun in prone firing. This version was adopted in June 1937 as the "Cal. 30 Browning Automatic Rifle M1918A1" and put in production by modifying existing M1918 BARs.

While both the M1918 and M1918A1 BARs were used in combat and for training until about 1942, a better gun, the "Cal. 30 Browning Automatic Rifle M1918A2," was adopted for use in 1940. This was the model used in WWII and thereafter, as long as the BAR remained in military service. Both M1918 and M1918A1 BARs were rebuilt as M1918A2s, and the M1918A2 was the WWII production model.

The M1918A2 BAR had some major changes from the earlier models: It had a bipod attached to its muzzle at its flash hider. A new forend with a metal heat shield was provided. Clip guides were added to the front of the trigger housing to improve magazine loading and survivability. A completely new fire-rate-control buffer mechanism was installed in the buttstock, which allowed the BAR to fire selectively at full-automatic cyclic rates of 350 or 550 rounds per minute. The buttstock was also provided with a hinged fire support buttplate and a detachable butt support.

The M1918A2 BAR was in the hands of troops when WWII began for the U.S. armed forces. All of its modifications proved very successful except the buttstock support, which was no longer used by troops after 1943.

Very few changes were made to the BAR during WWII. An accessory carrying handle, the T4, was adopted in December 1942, but it was seldom issued during the war. It remained available as long as the BAR was standard, but it saw only limited service.

In 1942, a plastic stock for the BAR was developed because of stock-wood shortages and problems with rot encountered in jungle warfare. At the end of WWII, a prong-type flash suppressor, the T35, was developed to replace the old tubular flash hider, but it was not extensively used until later during the Korean War.

The huge expansion of the U.S. armed forces for WWII made it necessary to put the BAR back in production. The project began by using the basic production tooling from Colt, Marlin-Rockwell and Winchester, which had been placed in storage after WWI. Deliveries of new BARs began in 1942, and 208,380 were built: 188,380 by New England Arms Co., a wartime company; and 20,000 by IBM.

The WWII supply of BARs was adequate to allow the Marine Corps to develop a special infantry organization around them for jungle combat. This was a four-squad rifle platoon with three BARs in each squad, or a dozen per platoon. Each squad fought as three "fire teams," each with its own BAR, and it proved very effective in jungle combat. While this organization was used in a number of Marine and Army infantry units during WWII, it was not used much after the end of the war.

Combat conditions, particularly in the jungles of the Pacific theater, caused BAR men to lighten their BARs. They commonly took off the bipod, and sometimes the flash hider, to make the gun handier for jungle or street fighting, but this was never authorized. In open-country warfare, the bipod and flash hider were desirable since they allowed the BAR to deliver accurate and effective fire from the prone position to as far as 1000 yards.

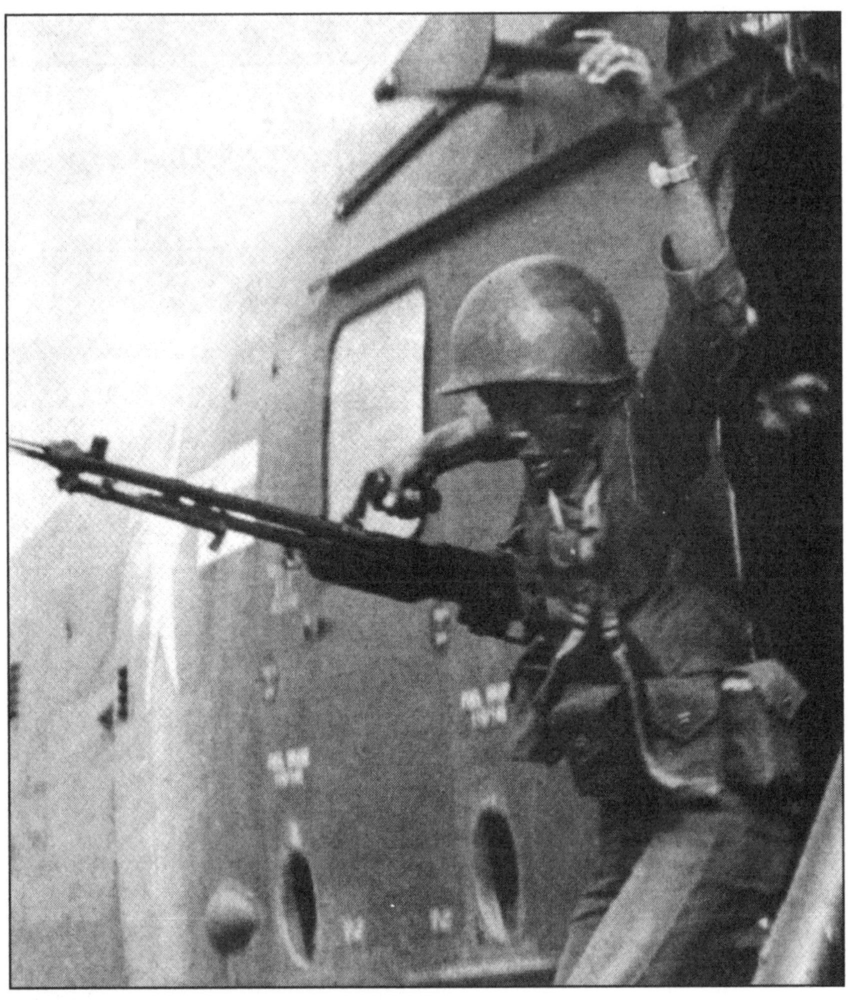

An ARVN BAR man dismounting from a U.S. Army helicopter in Vietnam. His BAR is the last model with the prong-type flash suppressor, a carrying handle, and the improved forend.

From about 1942 until after WWII, the Army experimented with a number of weapons designed to be lighter "squad automatic weapons" than the BAR. A number of these were modifications of the standard M-1 Garand infantry rifle with selective full- or semi-automatic fire, but none of these proved satisfactory. The Winchester Automatic Rifle designed by J.R. Williams of M-1 Carbine fame was more promising when tested in 1945-1946, but the end of the war precluded its adoption.

When the U.S. entered the Korean War in 1950, the Army used its latest and best WWII weapons and tactics, and the BAR was a mainstay of the infantry. Requirements for BARs for our armed forces, as well as those for United Nations allies such as the Republic of Korea, caused the weapon to be put back into production for one last time. The Royal McBee Typewriter Co. manufactured 61,000 guns using tooling which had been saved at the end of World War II.

At the time of the Korean War, the U.S. was preparing to issue new infantry rifles to its armed forces in the new 7.62mm NATO caliber. While it was easy to convert the BAR to the new 7.62mm caliber, the Army did not do it because they considered the gun too heavy for their future squad automatic weapon. At the same time, the Army experimented with a quick-change barrel feature for the BAR to make it more suitable for sustained fire as a light machinegun, but none of this type was ever produced.

The Army adopted the new 7.62mm "Rifle M-14" for its infantry in May 1957. The M-14 fired selectively, and the bipod-equipped, heavy-barrel M-15 version was adopted as the squad automatic weapon (SAW) to replace the BAR. As the M-14 rifles and M-15 SAWs went into service in the late 1950s, the M-1 rifles and BARs they replaced were placed in "war reserve storage," and by the early 1960s, the BAR had been retired from the U.S. armed forces.

However, many BARs had been given to various countries as military assistance, and they again saw service in the Vietnam War. Even today, the BAR is as rugged and reliable a weapon as there is, and they will still be found in service with some foreign armies. ●

There are NO Non-Lethal Bullets

Very few pay attention to the "P" factor

by MARSHALL R. WILLIAMS

MODERN JACKETED hollowpoint pistol bullets first appeared in the late '60s. Since then, a generation of gun writers has made its living drawing fine-line distinctions among an ever-expanding selection of such bullets. Their readers now have an indelible impression that small non-deforming bullets at relatively pedestrian velocities are innocuous. Many believe that a bullet which "merely" penetrates through-and-through without expanding does no damage and has no stopping power. Excepting, of course, the 45 ACP.

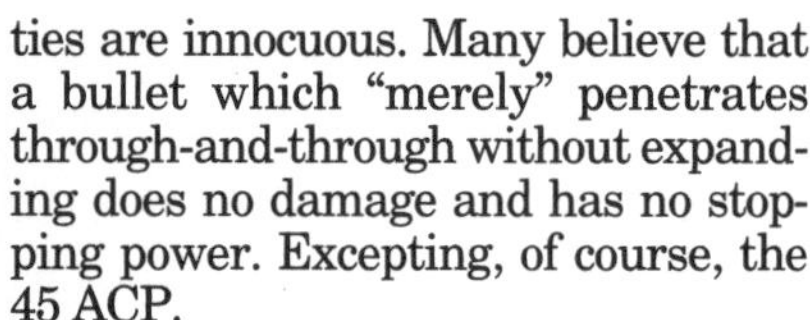

Common sense, that uncommon commodity, tells us that deep through-and-through puncture wounds are serious injuries. In addition, they impede continuing activity and sometimes produce one-shot stops. Thus, "mere" penetration is a significant factor in stopping power and deserves serious attention.

Let me put penetration in perspective. I am 6 feet tall and weigh more than 200 pounds. (Actually, quite a bit more.) Rough measurements of my body indicate that, assuming a reasonably upright posture, a bullet that penetrates 10 inches could reach my spine from virtually any direction. In reaching my spine, it would seriously damage all vital organs along the way. As we shall see, *all* pistol bullets can penetrate 10 inches.

There is a formula that predicts penetration of round-nose bullets in 20-percent ballistic gelatin (and, by implication, flesh) at velocities below 1000 feet per second. That formula demonstrates that all pistol bullets can provide the required penetration. Our nearby table contains predicted penetration in 20-percent gelatin for some common cartridges. Modern tests indicate that penetration in 20-percent gelatin understates penetration in flesh. Therefore, the table is conservative.

Skin is more resistant to penetration than flesh, and the formula takes into account penetrating only a single layer of skin. If a bullet must penetrate more than a single layer, for instance, if it enters and exits an arm and then penetrates into the body, the bullet would have to penetrate three layers of skin and would have much less total penetration.

The table in no way represents a scale of relative stopping power. Instead, it shows that all pistol bullets, even the 22 Short from the shortest barrel, can completely penetrate a large man's body. The following anecdotes illustrate how much stopping power simple penetration can have.

Several years ago, I was in court during a murder case. The evidence established that the deceased was a husky young man, about 5 feet, 8 inches tall and weighing more than 185 pounds. At the time he violently assaulted the defendant, the deceased's blood alcohol content was .33 percent. (A blood alcohol content of .10 percent raises the presumption of drunken driving in most states.) The defendant shot the deceased with a cheap 22 revolver with a 2-inch barrel. The cartridge was a high-velocity 22 Long Rifle with solidpoint bullet.

According to the autopsy, the bullet entered the front of the deceased's chest near the center, damaged a lung, the heart and aorta, and came to rest in his spine. Sworn testi ony of a number of witnesses, all of whom were thoroughly examined and cross-examined, established be-

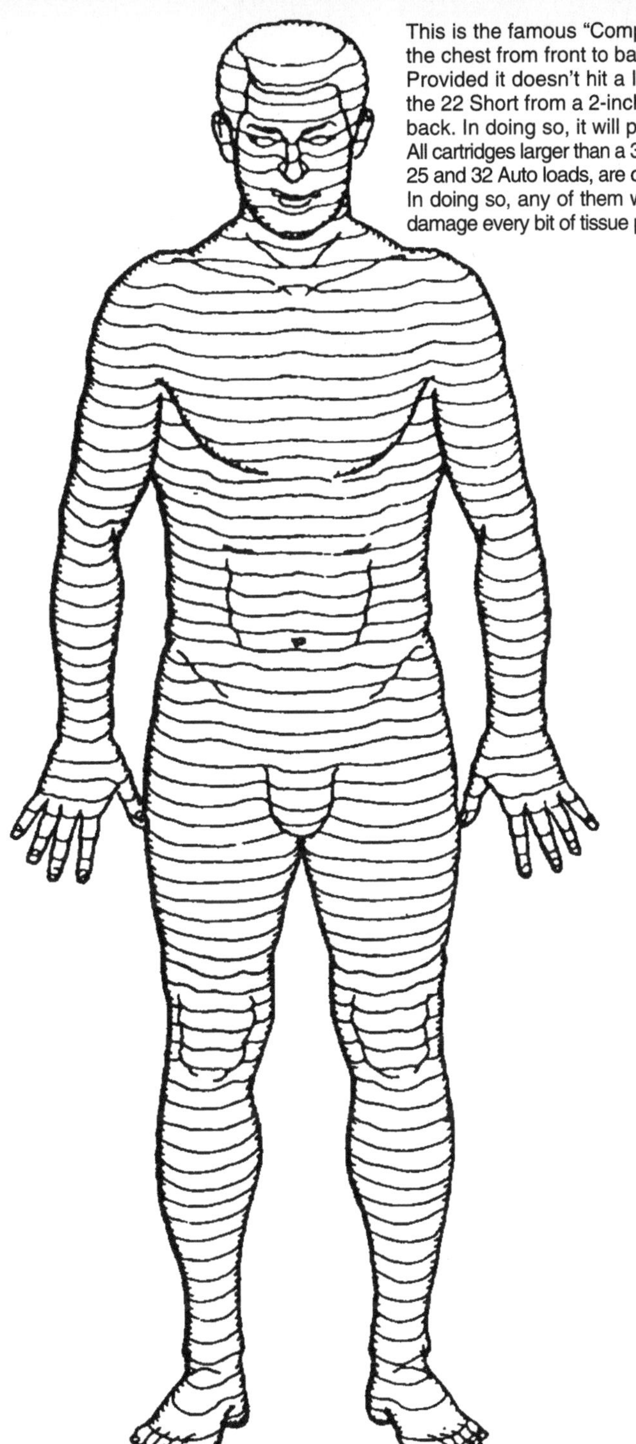

This is the famous "Computer Man." He is about 6 feet tall, about 9 inches thick through the chest from front to back, and about 14 inches through the chest from side to side. Provided it doesn't hit a large bone or other hard obstruction, any pistol bullet, including the 22 Short from a 2-inch barrel, is capable of penetrating through the torso from front to back. In doing so, it will puncture and damage every bit of tissue it penetrates.
All cartridges larger than a 380, plus 22 Long Rifle from a 3-inch or longer barrel, and some hotter 25 and 32 Auto loads, are capable of penetrating completely through the chest from side to side. In doing so, any of them will puncture and damage every bit of tissue penetrated.

Computer Man

For purposes of illustration, I have dusted off the Computer Man from the National Institute of Justice, report 100-83, "Police Handgun Ammunition." That report is now ancient history. It was severely and, in light of later studies, justifiably criticized, being ultimately rejected. Nevertheless, it contains much useful information.

The report was in two volumes. Volume I was slim and contained the Relative Incapacitation Indices (RII) for various loads. Everybody read Volume I. Volume II was thick and contained the empirical information used in Volume I's evaluation. Few people bothered to read it.

Among the most useful information contained in Volume II are plots showing the maximum temporary cavities that different loads produce in 20-percent gelatin. Loads with similar levels of effectiveness as shown by Evan Marshall's study also produce very similar maximum temporary cavities.

In my opinion, the study failed because it attempted to rank potential stopping power based solely on maximum temporary cavities while largely ignoring the effect of mere penetration. The RII rankings, based on maximum temporary cavity, ran from 1.2 for the worst (38 Special) to 67.3 for the best (44 Magnum). If one arbitrarily adds a "fudge factor" of 100 to every score to account for the effect of penetration, the rankings run from 101.2 to 167.3 and give a picture of relative stopping power not dissimilar to more recent studies.

yond doubt that, immediately at the shot, the deceased fell down and never moved again. It was a classic one-shot stop.

By coincidence, within weeks of the above case, I was again in court during a case involving an identical gun and cartridge. In that case, another husky young decedent, under the influence of marijuana and alcohol, was committing a violent assault when the defendant shot him transversely across the chest. No autopsy

PREDICTED PENETRATION IN 20-PERCENT GELATIN

Cartridges	Penetration (ins.)
22 Short (2"); 31-caliber C&B	9.7
22 Short (3"); 22 Short (4"); 25 ACP; 32 S&W; 36-caliber C&B	11.1-11.7
22 LR (2"); 32 S&W Long; 32 ACP; 44-caliber C&B	13.4-13.8
380 ACP; 22 LR (3")	15.3-15.8
22 LR (4"); 38 S&W	17-17.2
38 Special (158-gr.); 38 Special (200-gr.)	19-19.2
45 ACP; 44 Special	20.8-21.3
45 Colt; 38 Special +P	23.8-24

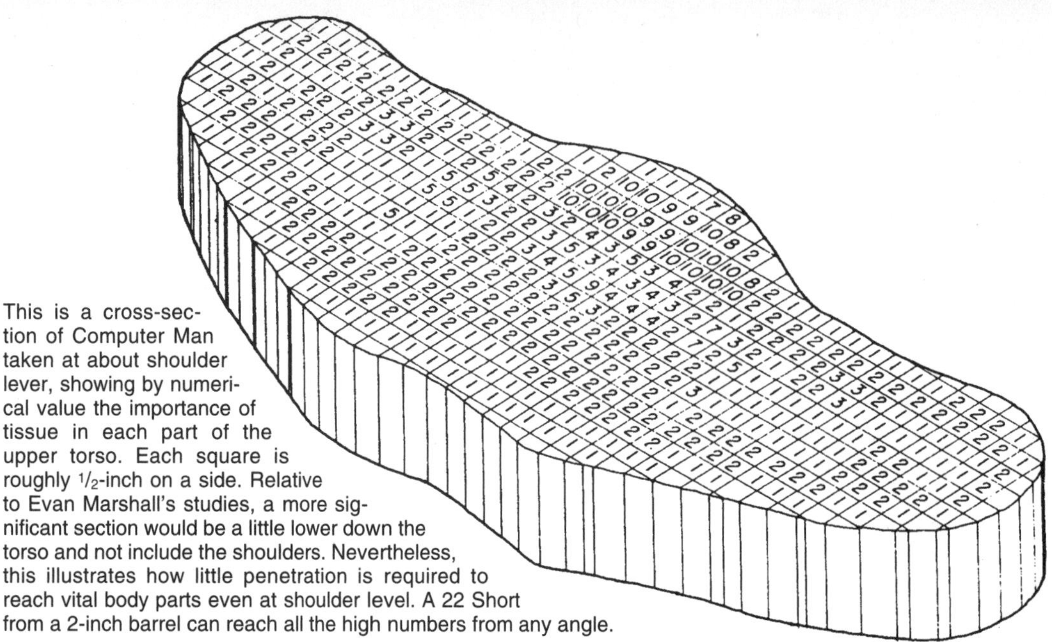

This is a cross-section of Computer Man taken at about shoulder lever, showing by numerical value the importance of tissue in each part of the upper torso. Each square is roughly 1/2-inch on a side. Relative to Evan Marshall's studies, a more significant section would be a little lower down the torso and not include the shoulders. Nevertheless, this illustrates how little penetration is required to reach vital body parts even at shoulder level. A 22 Short from a 2-inch barrel can reach all the high numbers from any angle.

was available in this case. Again, the testimony was overwhelming; at the shot, the deceased immediately fell down and stopped all activity. Another classic.

I could list other similar stories, but these two clearly illustrate the point that small-caliber pistols frequently are very effective stoppers.

Most people who read this will be familiar with Evan Marshall's work. Marshall compiled information from actual shootings in an effort to illustrate cartridge effectiveness in terms of the percentage of one-shot stops by caliber and load. Marshall compiled figures for some cartridges with round-nose bullets at speeds below 1000 fps, among them the 380 Auto, 28 Special, 44 Special, 45 ACP and 45 Colt. With round-nose bullets, these cartridges range from about 50- to about 65-percent effectiveness. When loaded with expanding bullets, these cartridges are more effective.

To date, all of the attention to Marshall's worthy effort emphasizes the differences at the top end of the scale, i.e., the most effective one-shot stoppers for each caliber. That emphasis is entirely appropriate; one needs to know that a 38 Special loaded with a round-nose lead bullet is 55-percent effective, but when loaded with a hollowpoint lead bullet is 65-percent effective. The increase in effectiveness is significant. However, emphasis on the 10-point increase in percentage causes us to overlook the 55 percentage points already there. We should always remember that in Marshall's study no ammunition produces one-shot stops below the rate of 50 percent.

This strongly implies a *threshold* of stopping power which even round-nose, non-expanding pistol bullets have. Since such bullets offer nothing except penetration, this strongly suggests that this threshold represents the stopping effect of *penetration* alone. This is the "P" factor.

None of the foregoing means that small calibers are as effective as large calibers, nor that round-nose, non-expanding bullets are as effective as the expanding or disintegrating types. Clearly they are less effective, but exactly none of them are non-lethal. ●

LOW-POWER BALLISTICS

Cartridge	Bullet (Wgt. grs.)	Barrel (ins.)	Velocity (fps)	Penetration (ins.)	One-Shot Stops (percent)
22 Short†	29	2	853	9.7	
		3	948	11.1	
		4	977	11.5	
22 Long Rifle	40	2	852	13.4	
		3	972	15.8	
		4	1034	17.0	
25 ACP††	50	2	760	11.5	
32 ACP	71	4	905	13.8	
32 S&W	88	3	680	11.7	
32 Long	98	4	705	13.7	
380 ACP	95	4	955	15.3	55
38 S&W	145	4	685	17.2	
38 Spl.	158	4	755	19.2	55*
		2	—	—	51*
		4	895	24.0	
38 Spl.	200	4	635	19.0	
44 Spl.	246	6	755	21.3	65**
45 ACP	230	5	835	20.8	63
45 LC	255	5	860	23.8	64
Blackpowder round balls:					
.319″	50	—	800	10.7	
.375″	81	—	800	13.0	
.451″	138	—	800	15.7	

*In 38 Special, Marshall's figures distinguish between 2-inch and 4-inch barrels, but not between high-speed and standard-velocity loads.

**Marshall's figures for this load are inconsistent. He states eighteen stops for twenty-four attempts, but shows a percentage of 65 percent.

†All 22 rimfire velocities in short barrels are taken from "Expansion Ratio Major Factor in Barrel Length Vs. Velocity," Wm. C. Davis, p. 26, *American Rifleman*, September 1988. All others are from Remington's 1992 catalog.

††The 25 ACP, 32 ACP, 380 ACP and 45 ACP have jacketed bullets; all others have lead bullets. General Hatcher found that jacketed bullets had a lower coefficient of friction than lead bullets and, therefore, more penetration in pine wood. The Lowry article makes no distinction between steel balls and lead shot in gelatin. The implication is that, since the bullet carries a coat of gelatin, the operative coefficient is gelatin against gelatin, not metal against gelatin.

Start Your Collection

What do these firearms have in common? All deliver performance beyond expectations. All are made in the USA. All are made of the finest materials obtainable by modern industry. All are from the world's largest manufacturer of firearms.

ALL ARE RUGER.

For full details see our catalog at your Ruger stocking dealer.

Sturm, Ruger & Company, Inc.
99 Lacey Place
Southport, CT 06490

Instruction manuals for all Ruger firearms are available free upon request. Please specify model.

Arms Makers for Responsible Citizens

No Matter Which Make or Model You Choose,
We Only Make One Kind of Revolver,
The Best
FREEDOM ARMS
PREMIER GRADE
1992
Buckmaster Revolver Champion
I.H.M.S.A. Small Bore Revolver Champion
N.R.A. Big Bore Revolver Champion
1993
Buckmaster Revolver Champion
I.H.M.S.A. Big Bore Revolver Champion
I.H.M.S.A. Small Bore Revolver Champion
N.R.A. Small Bore Revolver Champion
The most acclaimed big game hunting revolver in the world
Hunting and Silhouette models available in:
Model 252: .22 long rifle, .22 Magnum
Model 353: .357 Magnum
.44 Magnum, 454 Casull and 50 A.E.
The World's Finest handguns
FA
FREEDOM ARMS®
Freedom Arms, P.O. Box 1776
Freedom, Wyoming 83120 307-883-2468

Start Your Golden Years Now.

The Gold shotgun is available in 12 and 20 gauge Hunter models and a new 12 gauge Sporting Clays version with front and center beads, tapered rib, barrel porting and a radiused recoil pad with a solid heel insert.

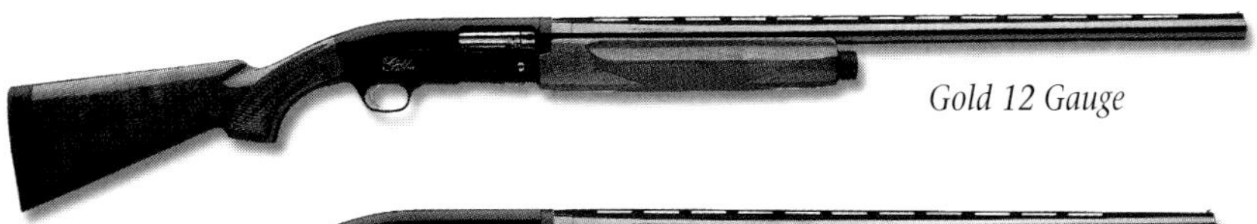

The Browning Gold is designed to last. Better get started using it right away.

Its unique, self-cleaning piston system will provide you years of cleaner, more dependable performance.

You can quickly remove moisture because no tools are required for take-down of the gas or trigger assemblies and there are no small parts to pop out or get lost.

We can't really say whether or not the Gold will be the last gas-operated semi-auto shotgun you ever buy, but we can easily say it will be the best — after all, it's a Browning.

Gold 12 Gauge

Gold 20 Gauge

Visit your Browning dealer for a free 1996 Hunting & Shooting catalog. For $3.00 we'll send you a catalog by priority mail. Call 1-800-333-3504 to order by credit card, or send payment to Browning, Dept. C54, One Browning Place, Morgan, Utah 84050-9326. If you have questions on the Gold or other Browning products please call 1-800-333-3288.

THE BEST THERE IS.

ENCORE *Performance!*

ENCORE™ *Single Shot Excellence*

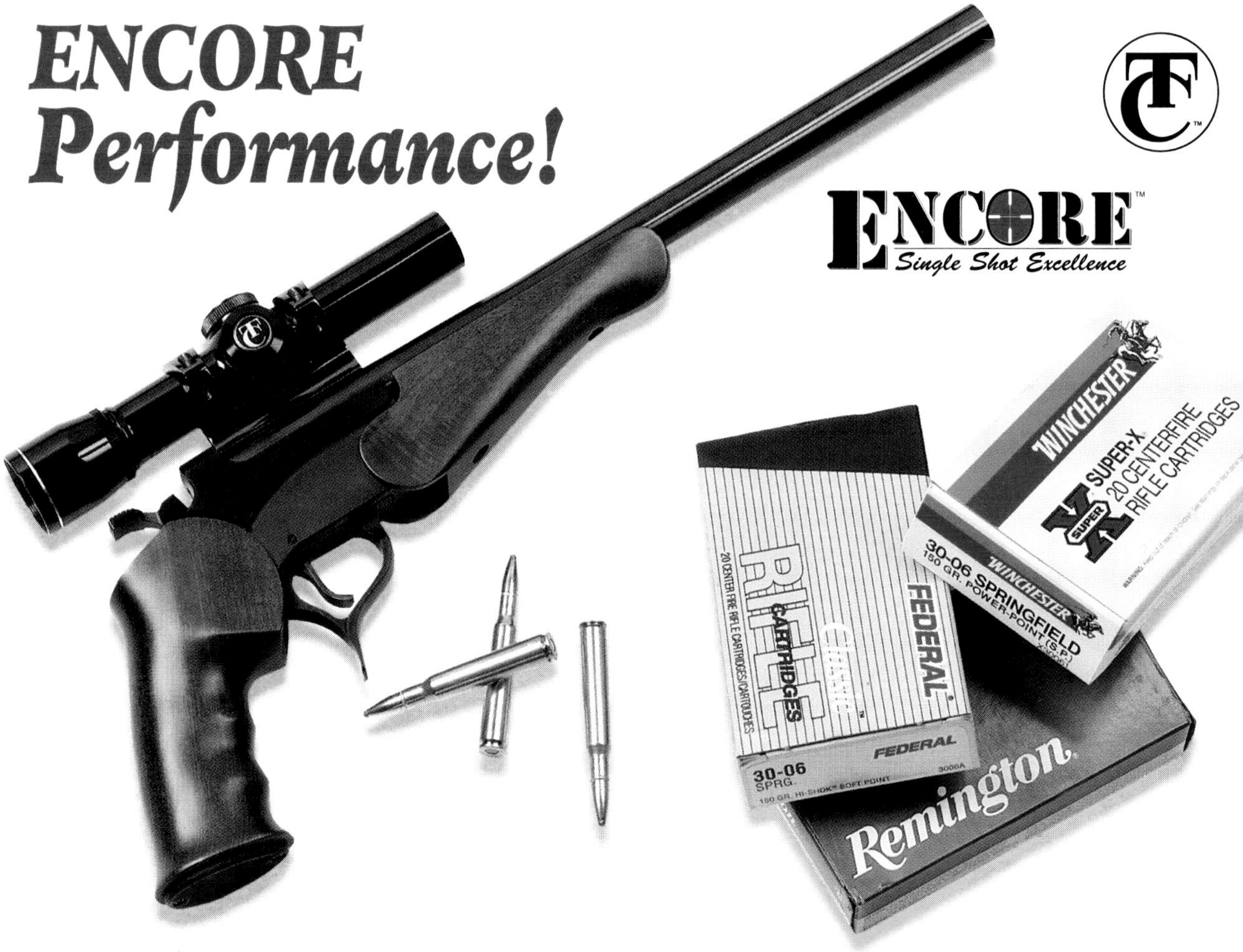

After 29 years of leading the industry in long range handgun hunting and competitive shooting, what could we possibly do for an encore? It's simple, we announce one! Thompson/Center's new Encore™ Pistol.

The Encore™ is destined to be the most versatile big bore handgun in the world, with long range performance and value unequaled by any other pistol on the market.

Like it's predecessor, the world famous Contender®, the Encore is a single shot pistol which "breaks open" by squeezing the trigger guard rearward. Barrels interchange by merely removing the forend and pushing out the pivot pin.

The Encore boasts the same "Minute of Angle" accuracy that the Contender is famous for, but the Encore will be chambered for the "big boys;" those high performance rifle cartridges which have become the mainstay of varmint hunters and big game hunters the world over.

Think of it... 30/06 Springfield, .308 Winchester, 7mm-08 Remington, .223 Remington and 22-250 Remington... all chambered in a hunting handgun that will even out-perform some rifles. Single shot handgun performance has never been so good!

Scheduled for delivery in the Fall of '96, Thompson/Center's new Encore Pistol will certainly set the standard for handgunning excellence in the decades to come.

Now that's an Encore worth waiting for!

by JERRY BURKE

Texas Ranger Lee Trimble at Glenn Springs, Texas, circa 1919, belted into a typical border-style Mexican holster and belt.

(Right) Ranger Lee Trimble and a patrol partner head out in the Texas Big Bend Country—one saddle strapped to hood, another in back.

LEATHER QUICK, LEATHER DEADLY

THE ROCKY GROUND burned my feet through my boots as I stood on the little hill. The air temperature hovered around 106 degrees; the desert floor of the Texas Big Bend Country was even more Hell-like. Just below once stood Glenn Springs, a small community not far from the *Rio Bravo del Norte* (Rio Grande). There once was a simple general store and a few other scattered buildings; the area was so remote the Mexican mail rider used to cross the river to collect postings deposited for his constituents at the old store.

Now, there were just faint outlines where once stood those civilian dwellings and the space temporarily occupied by the U.S. Cavalry. The only sounds were created by a hot desert wind blowing gently through the scattered creosote bushes and ocotillo plants. As I've done infrequently over the last four decades, I wandered around and remembered some of what once happened at this spot where only a desert spring ever caused humanity to establish a tenuous foothold.

In 1916, the very soul of Old Mexico was on fire, and on the night of May 5, "Mexican Revolutionaries"—nothing more than armed cowards looking for defenseless victims—swept across the *Rio Bravo* looking for anything they could destroy that they couldn't steal. Their latest targets were the *gringos*.

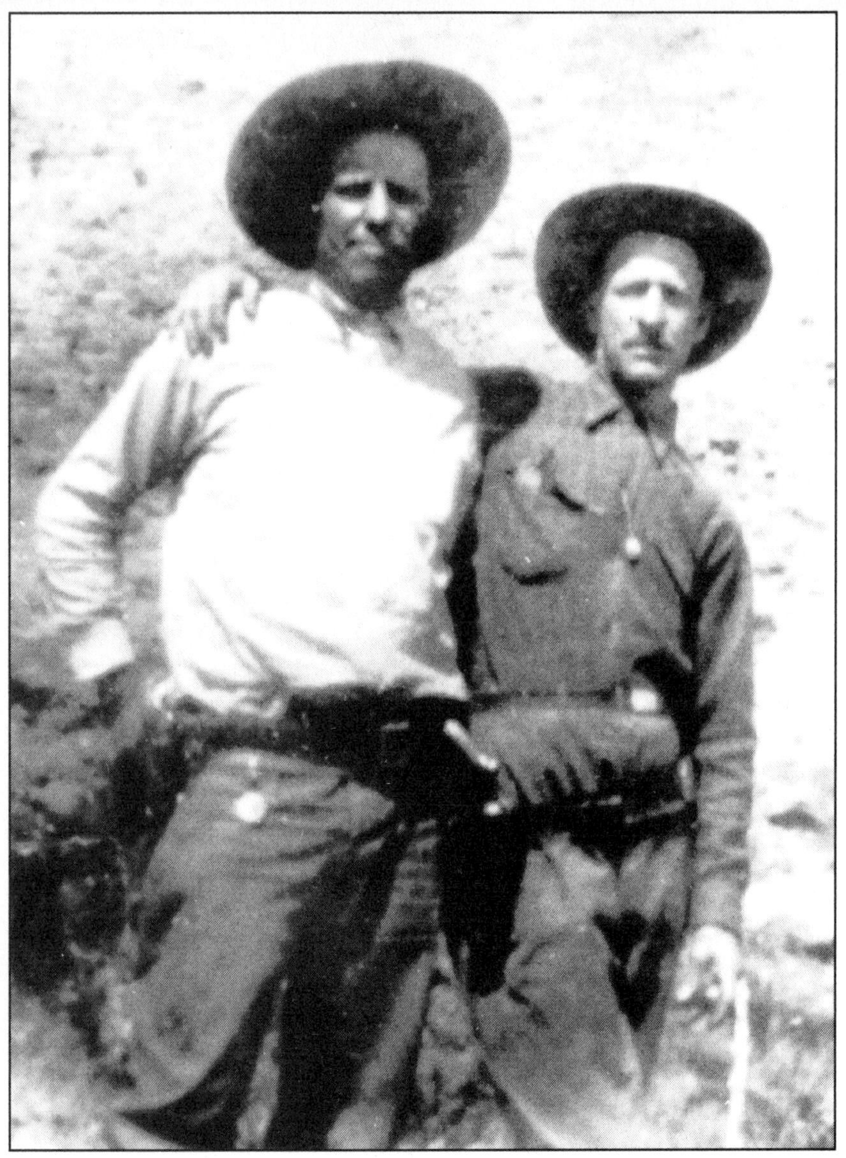

Tom Threepersons (left) with a friend named S.B. wearing Threepersons-style holsters, then revolutionary designs.

went on into Mexico with General Pershing. Thereafter, the humble structure that had been home to the Comptons became Ranger headquarters at Glenn Springs. When the Rangers took it over, small bloody hand prints could still be seen on the floor and walls.

It isn't Mexican bandits that bring me back to this forlorn locale, with terrain features virtually unchanged since the first Comanche warrior took in its vastness. In 1920 here, two professional lawmen, men who would remain great friends for their whole lives, established new design ideas that reconfigured the professional lawman's handgun holster. Those two men were Texas Ranger Lee Trimble and perhaps the last of the old-time gunfighter-lawmen, Tom Threepersons.

In those days, the Mexican loop holster, with its wide back flap folded behind the holster's pouch (the part which actually holds the handgun) including one or more integral leather retaining straps, was still in vogue. It had been since the mid-1870s; both men had worn them.

The reason gun leather was changed in those particular days is usually attributed to the need for increased speed of draw. In reality, speed of draw has always been important to gunmen, including the time when the Mexican loop holster was commonplace. According to Lee Trimble, what sparked their search was the advent of the automobile. Texas Rangers (and other Western lawmen) still operated heavily as horsebackers in the early days of the car, but they

I walked over to where once stood the home of Mr. Compton and his three young children, a girl and two boys. Close by, in 1916, had stood the tents of nine soldiers of the U.S. Army, sent to Glenn Springs as a deterrent against the growing threat of Mexican raiders. The Mexicans came in large numbers that night; nine Rambos couldn't have held them back. Five of the nine were quickly killed; Mr. Compton only had time to grab his daughter, age 11, and flee into the night before the dusky thugs entered his home.

The Compton boy of four years was shot by the marauders and died a horrible death; the older one, a deaf mute, was left unharmed. Texans from the surrounding Big Bend retaliated in kind during the days that followed. Within two weeks, Troop A of the 6th U.S. Cavalry was stationed at Glenn Springs; the rest of the outfit

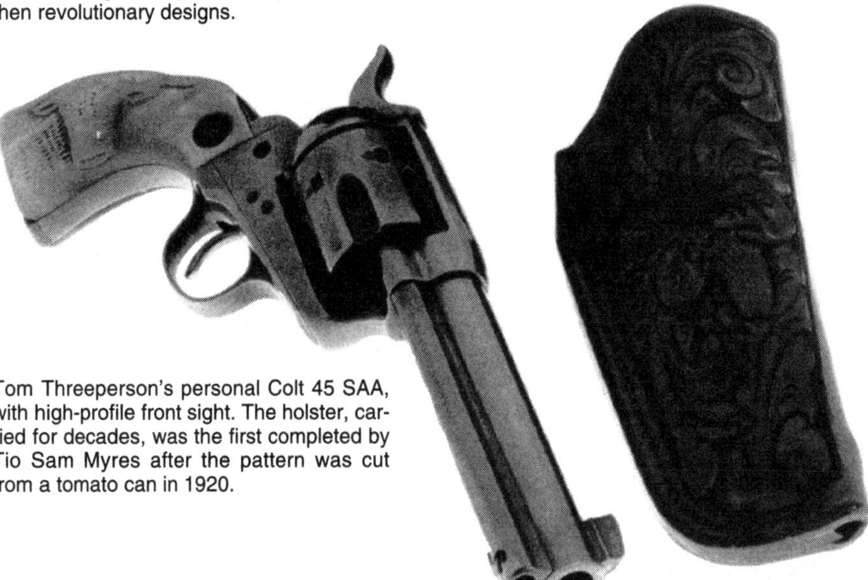

Tom Threeperson's personal Colt 45 SAA, with high-profile front sight. The holster, carried for decades, was the first completed by Tio Sam Myres after the pattern was cut from a tomato can in 1920.

were authorized to use this new-fangled conveyance. When a number of Rangers were ordered out on a scout together, they could use a car to get as far as it would take them. From there, wherever it was, they picked up horses.

If at first the popularization of the automobile seems an odd start for searching for a holster to replace the Mexican loop style, consider this: When a broomtail was the only mode of transportation, a man's need for clearing leather quickly likely came while he was seated in a saddle or while flat-footed on the ground. Buggy rides and train excursions were exceptional activities. If trouble was expected in a barber's chair, the thinking man had gun in hand when the fellow with the red-striped pole covered him with a cloth to keep the hair off his shirt. Same went for a lot of other situations such as at the gaming table, where one or more "stingy guns" were more practical to keep about the person than a full-size Colt beltgun.

But the automobile was something different. Those early seats were pretty much like those on a buggy, but proved more confining... especially from behind a steering wheel. The gunman needed to be able to draw his handgun with ease, sitting behind his desk, seated in a car or perched atop a Western saddle. Extra wide border belts were also common in South and West Texas. These belts, often 4 inches wide, slid easily through the large belt loop area created on the Mexican loop holster and included a single row of loops for rifle cartridges like the 30-40 Krag, as well as double rows for handgun ammunition.

Trimble took the revolutionary holster features he and Threepersons developed to Austin saddler A.W. Brill, who crafted Trimble's own unique version of the concept. El Paso Saddlery Company still makes it.

Picture a number of heavily equipped Texas Rangers all crammed into a touring car resplendent with big-rowelled spurs, border belts and Mexican loop holsters heading out for a long hot ride to the middle of nowhere. They could only hope no gunplay erupted until they could unload, something like clowns in one of those ultra-small circus cars. And so with the advent of the automobile, a new breed of handgun leather was needed. The rest of the world may establish 1890, or even 1900, as the closing of the Old West, but South and West Texas was still plenty wild through most of the 1920s.

Lee Elisha Trimble was born in Globe, Arizona, in September of 1895. As a young man, he migrated to Texas and cowboyed on the Brite Ranch in Presidio County, part of the sprawling Big Bend Country. This was a ranch which, like many others, experienced its share of Mexican terrorism during the often glamorized Revolutionary period of that nation's early 20th century history. While in the ranching business, Trimble had plenty of opportunities to learn what would later serve him well as a Texas Ranger. He learned the ways of cow thieves and smugglers.

Trimble became Texas Ranger Lee Trimble in 1918, joining Captain Jerry Gray's Company B headquartered in the small West Texas border town of Presidio. Captain Gray's Company had been formed to replace one disbanded after some of its members joined the Eighth United States Cavalry on a little payback raid into Old Mexico. Of course, many of the same Rangers served with both companies.

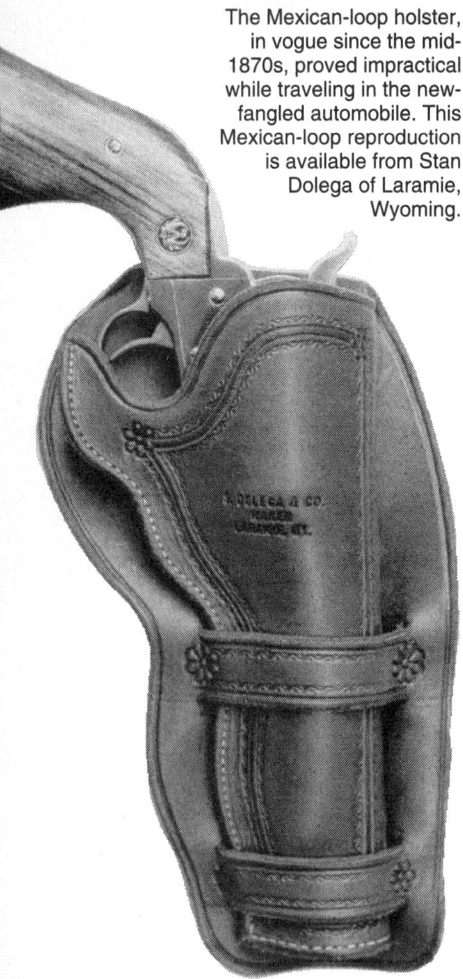

The Mexican-loop holster, in vogue since the mid-1870s, proved impractical while traveling in the new-fangled automobile. This Mexican-loop reproduction is available from Stan Dolega of Laramie, Wyoming.

Ranging across the land he knew best, Lee Trimble served Texans in the tough, violent Big Bend District, and it was there at Glenn Springs that he met Tom Threepersons sometime in 1920.

Tom Threepersons' trip to Glenn Springs was quite different from Trimble's. Threepersons, or as Lee Trimble jokingly called him, "Threepeoples," was a little older than Trimble, having first seen the light of day in 1889, at Vinita, Oklahoma. When Tom was about 10 years old, the Cherokee Threepersons family moved north to Canada to pursue ranching. By the time a second decade had passed, his father was killed by some clumsy Canadian cow thieves. The perpetrators were eventually caught and charged, but on their release, Tom just happened to find a good reason to "smoke" the men who had killed his father.

The Law-Up-North apparently held no grudge against Tom Threepersons, or maybe they just knew a good gunhand when they needed one, but in any case Tom went on to serve with the Northwest Mounted Police. He also plied his talents in another arena; by 1912, he was a celebrated Canadian rodeo champion. Threepersons then returned to the States and did some cowboying on his own, until some of Pancho Villa's Revolutionaries decided to see what might interest them in Columbus, New Mexico, in 1916. Threepersons joined the U.S. Army to help teach some folks south of the border a lesson or two.

Somewhere along the way, Threepersons took a kick to the head from a horse, resulting in a lifelong problem for the big gunfighter. He routinely wore a stiff-brimmed Stetson with high crown to help protect a delicate spot on top of his head covered by a metal plate. By 1920, Threepersons and the Army had parted company, and either on his way from San Antonio to El Paso to join the latter city's police force, or soon thereafter, he found himself at Glenn Springs amongst the Rangers. One way or the other, this is where the two lawmen compared notes and thoughts on a holster more suited to a mechanized and increasingly citified Texas.

Following the Mexican raid in 1916, Glenn Springs continued to be a small rough spot on the ground; life went on, but just barely. Anyone needing supplies, including the Rangers, received same after they'd been hauled a good 90 miles from the nearest town, and law enforcement duties were both difficult and lonely. Time in camp left Rangers little to do.

On more than one of those hot desert evenings, when these horsebackers were enjoying the questionable pleasures of their own cooking, the talk turned to gunleather, and especially how inconvenient their equipment was while perched in an automobile. Some had little interest in the subject, figuring they would continue to make-do with the gun harness and holsters they now had and expected to use for a long time to come. But not Threepersons and Trimble.

Before the mid-1870s, handgun holsters tended to be rather form-fitting, built with no more leather than necessary. They were, however, made of relatively lightweight leather and

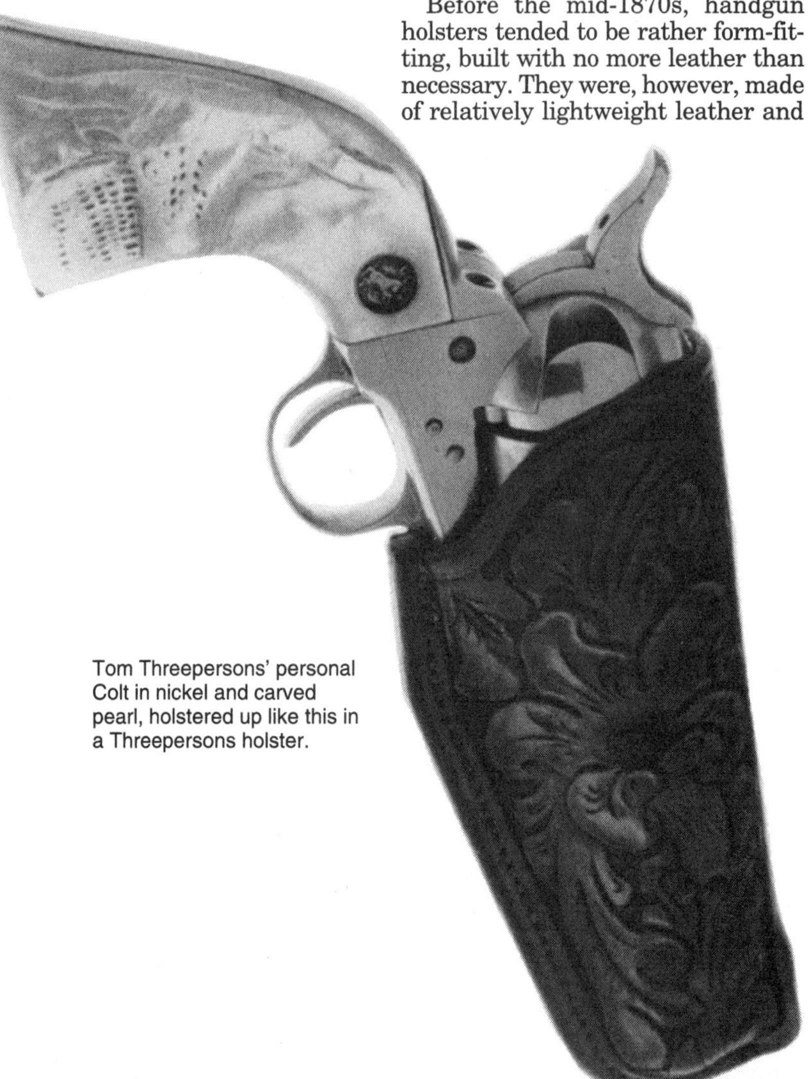

Tom Threepersons' personal Colt in nickel and carved pearl, holstered up like this in a Threepersons holster.

all but swallowed the gun clear up to the grip! The Mexican loop holster which replaced these Slim Jim rigs consisted of a single piece of heavy leather forming both the holster's pouch (the part that holds the gun) and a flap which formed a wide belt loop and provided one or more integral horizontal straps through which the holster pouch passed. The result served the trail hand well, but included entirely too much leather for sure and easy access while riding around in a car. In addition, the large belt loop area on the Mexican loop holster meant it shifted around under almost any circumstance. It was normally crafted to hang perfectly vertical, although the wearer could cant the holster to a variety of angles on the gunbelt.

As these two experienced real-life gunmen compared notes and notions about what a sixgun holster ought to look like and how it needed to perform, Lee Trimble and Tom Threepersons established some basic features to meet their mutual requirements. A holster needed to protect the six-shooter, but its primary purpose was to keep the gun positioned in the same place on the belt and at the same angle so that, when needed, the gun could be put into action speedily and accurately. The hammer needed full exposure; so did the trigger guard. And both men knew from experience that a holster with butt-forward cant would allow them to take advantage of the forward momentum associated with the draw and not require the amount of lift needed when drawing from a vertical holster. The gun needed to ride high on the belt so it wouldn't shift in virtually any position a man might find himself in. And with that, the talk of an evening or two—no doubt over a meal of Mexican strawberries, biscuits and a little venison—the basics for a new breed of six-gun holster were developed, with each man planning to have such a holster constructed by a quality saddler specializing in the making of professional gunleather.

Tom Threepersons strode into the El Paso saddle and harness shop of S.D. "Tio Sam" Myres later that same year (1920). With him was a crude holster pattern, fashioned from a tomato can. There wasn't much to it, but that was the idea—just a minimal holster body with sewn belt loop, just long enough to accept a relatively narrow gunbelt. There seemed little need for wide gunbelts in the new order of things.

The holster was designed to cut under the Colt's trigger guard, completely exposing it for quick access; same for the stylish hammer, which needed manual cocking. Nothing, but *nothing*, was to bar this gunfighter-lawman who sometimes skirted on the edge of the law from getting his weapon into action in a split-second. Finally, the holster needed to be heavily canted butt-forward, perfectly aligning the gun for a quick deadly draw, whether standing or sitting,

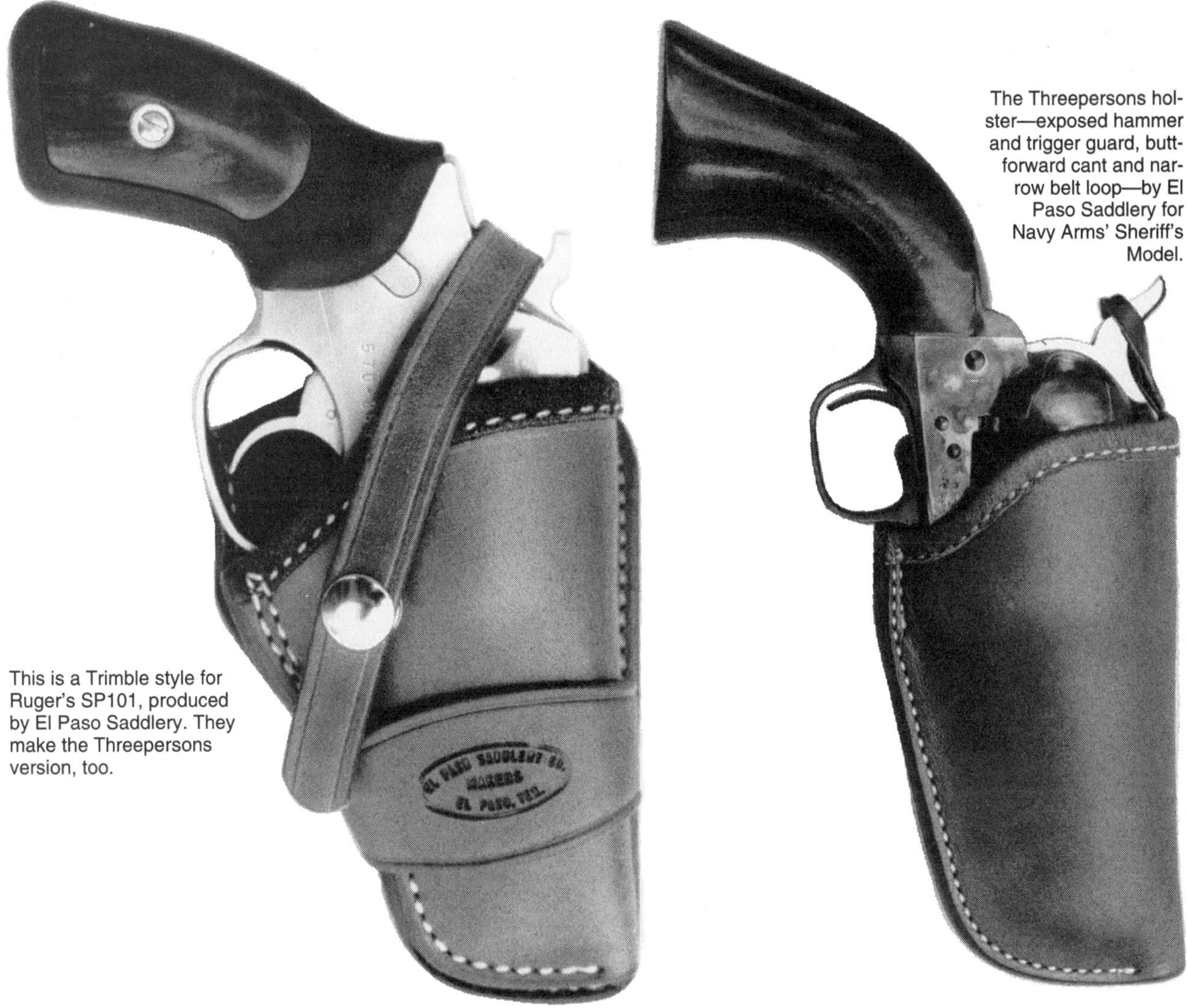

This is a Trimble style for Ruger's SP101, produced by El Paso Saddlery. They make the Threepersons version, too.

The Threepersons holster—exposed hammer and trigger guard, butt-forward cant and narrow belt loop—by El Paso Saddlery for Navy Arms' Sheriff's Model.

even sitting in a car. This angling of the gun butt-forward had the added advantage of reducing the distance the holster dropped below the beltline.

Tio Sam Myres got his nickname from his resemblance to Uncle Sam of U.S. government fame. He had been crafting top-quality leather goods since the 1890s, getting his start in Sweetwater, Texas. By 1920, his El Paso shop had gained a well-deserved reputation for excellence in both custom design and craftsmanship. Many a gunman, on both sides of the law, came to Tio Sam's shop seeking his advice on one gunleather need or another. Included among the shop's clientele were Texas Rangers like Captain John R. Hughes ("The Border Boss") and killer John Wesley Hardin, to name just two.

Threepersons and Myres talked the new holster over and, after the pattern was set—with Myres including a welt between the two pieces of folded leather that formed the seam—that first holster, fully hand-carved, went to Tom Threepersons. The famous "Threepersons" holster was in the S.D. Myres catalog as early as the 1922 edition. Myres was supposed to give Threepersons 25 cents for each Threepersons holster sold by the Myres firm, but no such royalty was ever paid.

Not long after, Lee Trimble also sought the expertise of a leather professional, A.W. Brill, of Austin, Texas. Brill's work was certainly among the finest of the era, reflecting his own design concepts, as well as the popular standards of the day. As Trimble described the basic aspects of the holster he wanted made to his specifications, Brill listened carefully. The request was virtually the same as the one Threepersons had made of Myres—exposed hammer and trigger guard; gun butt canted well forward, holster to carry the gun high on the belt and a belt slot tight enough to hold the gun steady, eliminating any movement of leather at the moment of draw.

Brill became absorbed in the project, but his solution was somewhat different than that of Tio Sam miles away in El Paso. Tradition was important to Texas Ranger Lee Trimble; that's understandable for a law enforcement organization whose exploits had already earned them world-wide fame. Being a little more conservative-minded, A.W. Brill honored the Ranger's request for certain holster features, but Brill followed with a style all his own. First, the Trimble-style holster Brill crafted included a back flap, as had the old Mexican loop style, but it was stylized and slender, just barely extending beyond the outline of the holster's pouch. And, the minimal back flap was sewn to the toe of the holster's body, eliminating possible separation of pouch and flap and changing its position on the belt. A separate strip of leather was wrapped around the holster's body in the cylinder area to add strength and rigidity to the pouch and—another critical point—this secured the pouch to the back flap and created a tight-fitting belt loop in the process.

Trimble's Ranger badge—some Rangers didn't use them.

As with the Threepersons holster, Brill went on to fashion a steady stream of Trimble holsters during his lengthy career in Austin. By the 1930s, many a Texas Ranger took "The Oath" at the state capitol, then simply strolled down Congress Avenue to the gunshop and hardware emporium of J.C. Petmecki to secure an appropriate shootin' iron to go with the new job. From there, they could almost fall into A.W. Brill's shop to place an order for personalized gunleather, often of the Trimble design. As well known as A.W. Brill was for his fine leather products, many a young man made more trips than necessary to check on the status of their ordered goods just on the chance they might glean a smile from Brill's handsome daughter Nellie, known to the world today by her married name, Mrs. John B. Connally.

Tom Threepersons and Lee Trimble remained friends for the rest of their lives, bound by a profession, a rugged lifestyle, a place in time, and their revolutionary handgun holster concept. And they each continued to carry their version of that concept from that point until they hung up their shootin' irons forever. Both were law enforcement professionals, but took very different paths.

After his stint with the El Paso Police Department, Tom Threepersons went on to serve as a federal prohibition agent and a mounted inspector for U.S. Customs, work for a Mexican rancher, and then return to El Paso to serve in both local and county law enforcement capacities. He smiled at an opportunity to get a taste of Hollywood movie magic, but instead returned to ranching for a while. Threepersons, who married the nurse who ministered to him after his head injury, wound up in Silver City, New Mexico, where he spent the rest of his life ranching and offering his services as a hunting guide. Lee Trimble's friend, and a certifiable legendary gunfighter, died in 1969; Silver City, New Mexico, is his final resting place.

Texas Ranger Lee Trimble was promoted to Sergeant of Rangers in 1921 and continued with The Service through 1924. Retaining a Special Ranger Commission, he continued to serve Texas and Texans until his retirement in 1963. In the '40s, Special Texas Ranger Trimble was in charge of ranch security for the Grant family outside Beaumont, Texas. Whatever his assignment, on ranch or war-time shipyard duty, he always carried a holster of the design he first took to the Brill Leather Co. in Austin.

Today, the basic operational features of the Threepersons-Trimble leather are copied worldwide, both as law enforcement tools and for civilian use. If it's the real thing you're after, the trail leads to Bobby McNellis' El Paso Saddlery Company, successor to the original S.D. Myres outfit. The talented craftsmen at El Paso Saddlery, including noted El Paso and Old West historian Bobby McNellis himself, make Threepersons holsters for single- and double-action revolvers and semi-autos alike, using the original patterns. They also offer Lee Trimble's version, faithful to the work of A.W. Brill. And you won't be alone, as Texas Rangers have continued to place orders for both designs for years now. ●

THE FIRST TIME I held Jack Geary's timeworn hunting rifle, I wondered what ranges of the Rocky Mountains the rifle had looked over and what November storms it had weathered. The rifle evoked a different time, when hunters could walk out from town to hunt mule deer in the foothills and timbered shoulders of the mountains.

It is an original-pattern Newton bolt-action rifle chambered for the 256 Newton cartridge. Such Newton rifles are fairly rare now; only about 4350 were made. This one was made in 1916 or 1917. The last of these originals were produced in 1918, when the Newton Arms Company went bankrupt.

From the rifle's condition when I first saw it, the day it was made was the last time anyone gave it any care. The action was gummed up, and the bore looked like a gravel road. The stock had two long splits. At one time, the grip and forearm of the stock had been checkered, but all that remained was a faint outline of the borders. Jack Geary was my godfather; his brother, Bill Geary, had had big plans to refurbish the stock when he was a teenager in the late 1930s. However, about as far as Bill got was to sand the wood surfaces. Perhaps the United States Marines' invitation to tour Pacific Ocean islands, such as Iwo Jima, during World War II occupied too much of Bill's spare time. Of course with no finish, the stock sucked up snow and rain over the decades.

The lines, though, were still pleasing to the eye. The comb was straight, and the slender grip felt good in my hand. The narrow forearm ended in a Schnabel tip. Mr. Newton was not hesitant in removing unnecessary wood, something that cannot be said for many factory rifles, then or now.

The slim stock matched the trim action. The receiver bridge was low. The bolt handle was straight with a small nearly rectangular knob. A gunsmith friend said he had once mounted a scope on a Newton action. On opening the bolt, the small handle had easily cleared the scope.

The seven small locking lugs on the bolt head permitted the action to be made so slim. The wear on the rear of the lugs, however, showed three of them failed to fully engage their recesses in the receiver.

The rifle's front trigger tripped with a light touch when the rear trigger was set. The front blade sight was very thin and was difficult to see in the shallow rear notch. Ahead of the rear sight is a taller leaf sight on the same mount. This sight was for longer ranges and was folded down when not in use.

The last time my godfather had shot the rifle was in the years right after World War II. More than likely, he quit shooting it because he couldn't find ammunition. The last of that was made around 1938 by the Western Cartridge Company. A handful of Western fired cases and one loaded round came with the rifle, and I took apart the loaded round. The 129-grain bullet had a full jacket with an open point. The cylindrical-shaped powder in the case weighed 42.7 grains.

Of course, the minute I picked up the Newton I started formulating plans to shoot it. After swabbing the grime out of the bore, I wondered if it would be a waste of time; it was pitted from the throat to the muzzle. I thought the rifle had been shot so much the bore was worn completely smooth. But a few pages of reading about Newton rifles explained only one side of the lands have an edge to grip a bullet. This is known as parabolic rifling.

The first step toward shooting the Newton was to take it to a gunsmith for a checkup. I interrupted Doug Wells one morning while he was busily crafting a Remington rolling block action into a blackpowder cartridge rifle. Usually these craftsmen of rifles from the last century become cranky when they are interupted, but the Newton was sufficiently old that Wells felt it was worth his time.

SHOOTING A NEWTON

by JOHN HAVILAND

Slim lines and light weight and a hot cartridge make an easy carrier that kicks a bit.

How they did it in the '30s, this time with a '36 Plymouth. The fender was the only place to put the carcasses.

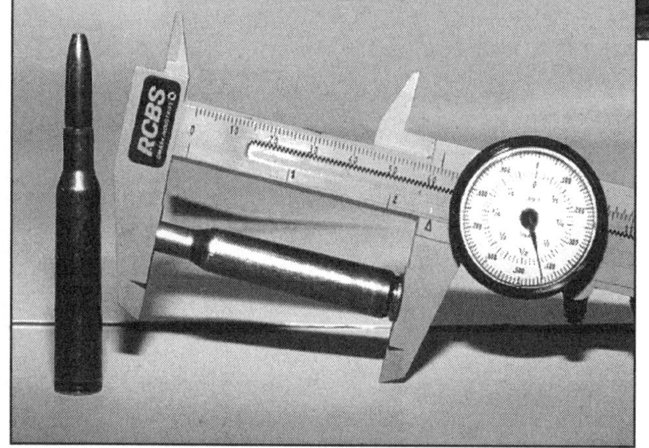

To find the right dimensions, the writer measured a 256 factory cartridge loaded by the Western Cartridge Company—his only one.

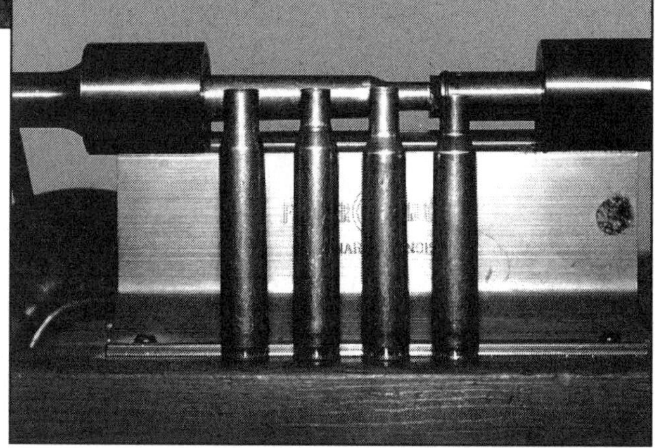

Forming 256 Newton cases from 30-06 cases required several steps and definitely had to include turning the necks.

Everything looked good until he eyed the eroded bore. "Not good," he commented. "It might shoot OK, then again it might not."

To check the chamber headspace, Wells put a piece of masking tape on the face of the factory loaded cartridge. He explained the thickness of a single piece of masking tape measures close to .004-inch. A rifle's headspace is fine if the bolt freely closes on a cartridge with one piece of tape on the face. But with two thicknesses of tape the bolt should only close with some resistance. The Newton closed easily on one thickness of tape, but stopped with two, so the headspace was pronounced to be OK.

Wells handed me the rifle. "It was my pleasure to look over such a unique rifle. That Newton was way ahead of his time," he said. "Keep me posted on how it shoots."

The next step was to find a set of reloading dies. The nice folks at RCBS in Oroville, California, said dies for the 256 Newton were a special-order item, but not that unusual. They said RCBS receives quite a few orders every year for dies for the Newton cartridge.

While waiting, I searched through reloading manuals for loads for the 256 and dimensions of the case. The 256 comes by its name because of the diameter measured between the lands, not the grooves. So the 256 actually shoots a 6.5mm, or .264-inch, bullet.

Cartridges of the World, by Frank Barnes, listed loads for 120-, 130- and 140-grain bullets for the 256 with 4350, 4895 and 4831 powders. Barnes stated the 129-grain factory load had a muzzle velocity of 2760 fps. Volume I of *Handbook for Shooters & Reloaders*, by P.O. Ackley, listed loads for bullets weighing from 87 to 160 grains. Ackley listed the 129-grain factory load at 3100 fps.

I could not find a measurement for the length of the case, so I measured the factory round. It was 2.44 inches long. The length of the fired cases was 2.45 inches. Since the 256 is based on the 30-06 case, I planned to make 256s out of 30-06s. The '06 case measures 2.494-inch, so they would have to be trimmed.

I ran fifty once-fired 30-06 cases through a 270 Winchester sizing die to partially neck down them. The expander rod and plug were removed from the 270 sizing die so the case necks were reduced even farther. I trimmed the cases to 2.44-inch.

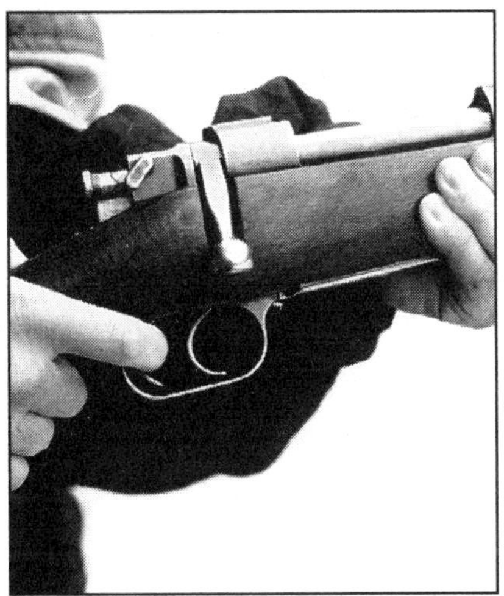

The Newton's rear trigger sets the sear; the front trigger fires the rifle.

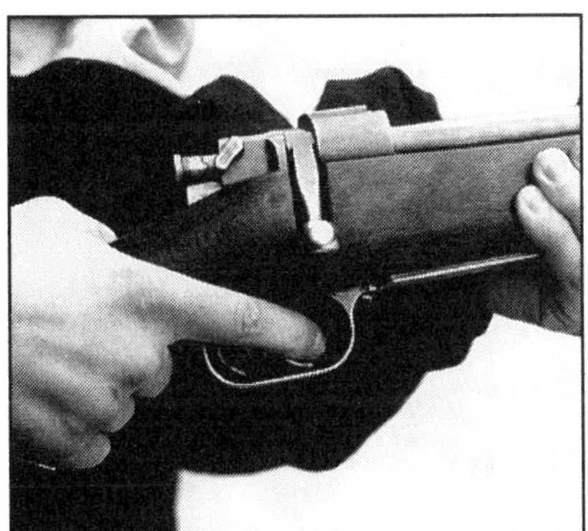

The splits in the rifle's stock also needed attention before shooting. One crack followed the grain of the wood along the top of the forearm for a foot. The other break ran through the middle of the recoil shoulder back through the web and into the grip. I held the splits open with a screwdriver and coated them with Acraglas epoxy, colored to match the stock. The stock remained in a C-clamp overnight. In the morning, the Acraglas was dry and the stock was strong as ever. A light sanding smoothed off the run-over.

The 256 dies arrived two weeks later. I screwed the sizing die into my reloading press, four turns short of touching the raised shellholder, and ran one partially formed 30-06 shell through the die. This reduced the neck down to the proper diameter, but left the shoulder too long. With the same case in place, I started turning in the sizing die a quarter turn, sizing the case, then putting it into the rifle's chamber to see if it fit. When the bolt handle closed without resistance, I tightened the lock ring on the sizing die. The sizing die was set to form cases that fully fit the chamber.

I settled on loads with 120- and 140-grain Speer bullets with H4895, H4350 and H4831 powders. The powder weights were 3 to 9 grains below the ones listed in Ackley's and Barnes' books.

I set the overall length of the loaded cartridges at 3.33 inches, so they'd work through the magazine. Even with the base of a bullet seated nearly at the mouth of a case, the bullet failed to touch the rifling, as is possible in most rifles with sharp-edged rifling.

I ran into a problem with the first shot. The second shot confirmed it. The load with the 140-grain bullet and 43 grains of H4895 flattened the primers and froze the bolt shut so hard I had to pop it open with the palm of my hand.

I scratched my head and stroked my jaw in thought. These loads were supposed to be on the mild side. I tried putting a bullet in the mouth of a fired case. The bullet wouldn't slip into the mouth. The thick case necks had caused the high pressure.

I retreated to my reloading room to start over.

With no measurement of the proper outside neck diameter of the 256 Newton to use as a guide, I sized one of the Western 256 cases. I turned off just enough brass from the outside of the case neck with my neck turner to true the neck. With the neck turner thus set, I neck turned all my formed 30-06 cases.

Back at the range all the loads shot fine. The primers remained nice and round. I have listed the average velocities and standard deviations of loads shot from the Newton's 24-inch barrel over an Oehler Model 33 chronotach, with no adjustment to true muzzle velocity.

These speeds rank right up there with today's popular cartridges, such as the 25-06 Remington and 270 Winchester. Someone once wrote the 256 was Winchester's basis for their 270 cartridge, and I can see why.

The corroded bore, though, spoiled my delight like a large black fly rising to the surface in a bowl of chowder. All the 140-grain bullets keyholed through the target at 25 yards, leaving an oblong tear in the paper and often a smear of lead. They grouped 2 to 3 inches wide.

The 120-grain bullets shot somewhat better—at least they flew straight through the target at 25 yards. The 120s with H4350 grouped 2.3 inches and 1.6 inches with H4831 powder. The best group, at 1.1 inches, came from 46 grains of H4895. At 50 yards, this bunch went into 1.7 inches for three shots. At 100 yards, five shots fell in a 4-inch circle.

So what's next for the Newton? The barrel could be bored out to, say, a 270 Winchester, and at least retain the original barrel markings. Somewhere a gunsmith must be able to rebarrel the rifle for the 256. Or I could leave the rifle alone, hoping next fall's whitetail buck walks past within 100 yards.

But for now, the rifle remains a reminder of when the Rockies were still clean and new. That's plenty. ●

LOADS I TRIED

Bullet Grs./Type	Powder Grs./Type	Velocity fps	Standard Deviation
120 Speer	45/H4895	2999	8
	46/H4985	3034	18
	50/H4350	2878	34
	52/H4831	2740	21
140 Speer	43/H4895	2706	13
	44/H4895	2727	17
	49/H4350	2734	7
	49/H4831	2532	7

A Mauser '98 will make a...

416 RIGBY

The problem in a nutshell is that the original Mauser 1898 action was designed around the 8x57 cartridge (left), and we had to make room for the 416 Rigby while retaining the integrity of the rifle.

THE 416 RIGBY cartridges appear to be nearly as large as the action, yet two of them disappear down into the magazine under my insistent thumb. Holding the top cartridge down, I ease the bolt closed. Then I invert the rifle so the ejection port is facing the floor, and as fast as possible I bang the bolt open and shut twice, then open again. Each cartridge, in turn, is chambered and ejected.

Next, I repeat the entire loading and testing process, but this time I move the bolt on the inverted rifle as slowly as I can move it. The result is the same, the two enormous Rigby cartridges are fed, chambered and ejected perfectly. The rifle does this at any speed and in any position, demonstrating its reliability. Unlikely as it may seem, the action is basically an ordinary large-ring '98 Mauser.

This action was made by FN for Browning, but it is the same basic '98 Mauser that was designed around the 8x57 German military cartridge. This specific rifle began life as a 300 H&H Magnum, complete with an aluminum magazine box long enough for that cartridge or the 375 Holland & Holland Magnum. The Mauser '98 has long been used successfully for those two belted magnum cartridges, but the Rigby round is a bit longer and a whole lot fatter than either of them. At first glance, it seems impossible to get the big Rigbys into the rifle, much less feed them with any de-by RAY ORDORICA

TWO-SHOOTER

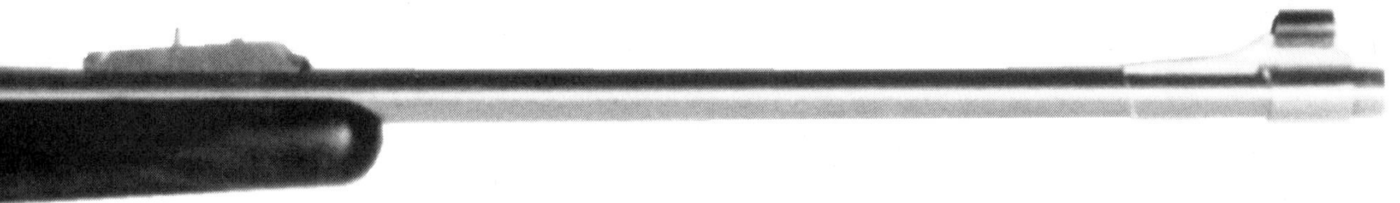

Right- and left-side overall views of Ordorica's completely successful and thoroughly reliable 416 Rigby two-shot on an FN Browning '98 action. The rifle features the author's action modification, stockwork, oil finish and checkering. The barrel is 24 inches long.

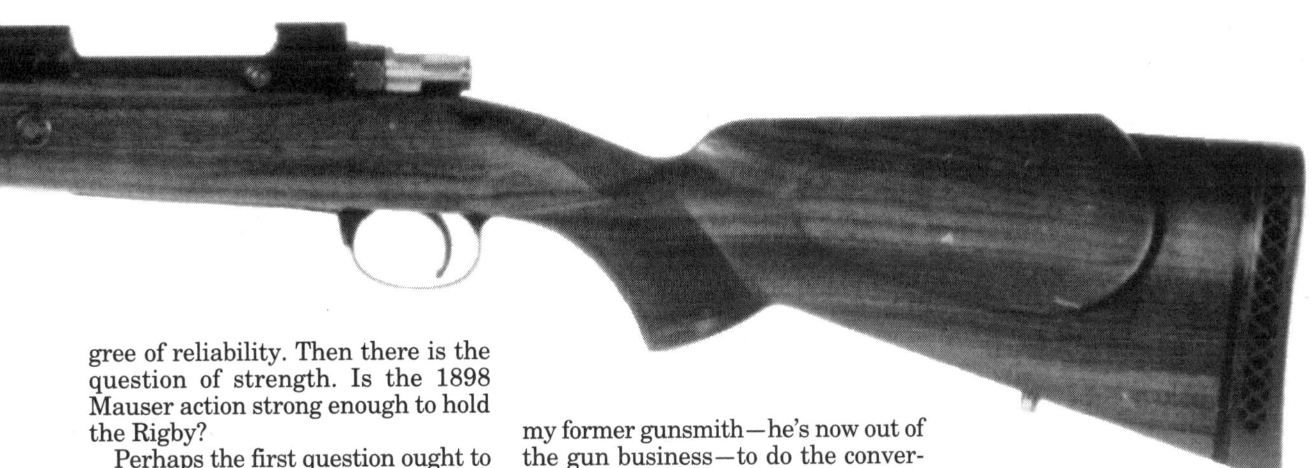

gree of reliability. Then there is the question of strength. Is the 1898 Mauser action strong enough to hold the Rigby?

Perhaps the first question ought to be, "Why would anyone try this conversion in the first place?" One answer is that you end up with a very light, very powerful rifle, albeit one with only two rounds in the magazine. Another answer, and my real reason, is that I had no choice other than to kiss lots of my money goodbye after having waited four years to get anything at all for it.

I had originally wanted a 416 Howell. I thought the Howell, which requires only a standard-length action, would make up into a light rifle that would be perfect for my many wanderings in the Alaskan Bush. I planned to load it with 300- to 350-grain bullets at 2600 fps or so.

I acquired a pre-'64 Featherweight Model 70 action and negotiated with my former gunsmith—he's now out of the gun business—to do the conversion. After a four-year wait and many "deals," I ended up owning an FN Browning that had been rechambered to accept the 378 Weatherby necked to 30-caliber. The 416 Rigby base diameter is the same as the 378 Weatherby's, so it came down to a choice between the Rigby and nothing, because I had grown tired of waiting. I had no need for a 30-caliber rifle.

So now, the gunsmith installed and chambered a barrel in 416 Rigby and got the rifle to shoot. Not feed, *shoot*. He then did exactly nothing to my rifle for more than a year, though he told me he was continually working on it.

I paid for a Shilen match-grade barrel with 1:14-inch twist, and the gunsmith assured me that's what he used. Much later, I discovered I actually have a 1:12-inch twist barrel and a call to Shilen verified that they have never made a 416 barrel with that twist rate.

I assume it is a Douglas barrel, and Douglas makes very good barrels. I had wanted a twist rate that wouldn't over-stabilize shorter 416 bullets. Original Rigbys had 1:16-inch twist, and they work well enough with light, short bullets. My limited accuracy testing to date indicates that with modern homogeneous bullets such as the Barnes X, which are rather long for their weight, the twist of my rifle is not too fast at 1:12 inches.

Getting my rifle out of the gunsmith's shop at the end of this additional year was a good move. One day, a little later, he simply disappeared. And it took me nearly another year of part-time work, doing it myself, to turn the gun into a fully functional, reliable entity.

When I first approached the concept of stuffing the Rigby cartridge into this particular action, I was apprehensive about its strength. I checked my references and found that the bolt diameters of normal-length (1898) and true "magnum" Mausers, around which the original 416 Rigbys were built, are identical (.70-inch). Therefore, there were no problems with the bolt.

The magnum Mauser action is longer than ordinary '98s, and they have more metal behind the lower locking lug. My main concern with this conversion project lay right there. I wondered if there would be sufficient strength in the lower lug of the FN action to support the thrust developed. I knew that the '98 action, when lengthened to accept 375s and 300s, had proven itself more than adequately strong for the job. Therefore, I reasoned, if I kept the thrust on the bolt lugs the same as, or less than, that provided by those two belted magnum cartridges, the rifle would be more than strong enough for the Rigby.

Federal told me they loaded the 416 Rigby to 41,500 CUP nominally, with a maximum of 42,000 CUP acceptable. All those long belted magnums work perfectly in ordinary Mauser actions. These modern magnum cartridges, often handloaded to well over 50,000 CUP, generate acceptable forces on the '98 action, and the Rigby generates less force. And so it proved.

The rifle handles Federal factory-

The action loaded with its maximum capacity of two 416 Rigby cartridges. The magazine box is cut away to permit the lower cartidge more side room. The scope bases are by Warne.

Ordorica's Rigby weighs less than 8 pounds complete with its two cartridges and is built for Alaskan use with 300- and 350-grain bullets at medium velocities, and for lots of carrying. The author feels any outstanding '98 action can be used to get an extremely light 416 Rigby, if one is needed.

loaded cartridges far better than my shoulder does with an 8-pound rifle. There is no need to hot-rod this cartridge in this rifle. My loads with light bullets are very conservative (300-grain Barnes X at 2625 fps; 335-grain Jensen J26 at 2575; and 350-grain Barnes X at 2450 fps) and designed for Alaskan use. In short, the rifle is perfectly safe for my uses, and entirely safe with any current factory loads as well.

First, however, I had to make the cartridges fit the magazine. Right off the bat, I'll say that I didn't alter the width of the action rail lips. They remain at their .60-inch spacing that worked just fine with the 300 H&H cartridge. The main problem was to get the big rounds to stay under those lips, not pop out more easily.

Federal Cartridge Company told me their factory-loaded 416 Rigbys measure 3.75 inches maximum length, 3.63 inches minimum. The standard length of 300 H&H cartridges is given as 3.60 inches, and the unaltered aluminum magazine box of the FN measured 3.68 inches. This meant it would have to be lengthened by approximately .07-inch. I did this by filing the magazine box as thin as I could get it. I achieved an overall inside length of 3.70 inches, which has accepted all the Federal factory loads I've tried in it. I intend to use my own handloads almost exclusively, so I find the magazine length to be fully acceptable.

I had to take a very small amount of metal off the face of the feed ramp, more of a polishing than a grinding action. I don't believe that I removed more than .020-inch from the surface of the ramp, which is not enough to sacrifice the integrity of the bottom lug area. I polished the ramp on both sides under the rails to ensure smooth feeding.

The large diameter of the Rigby

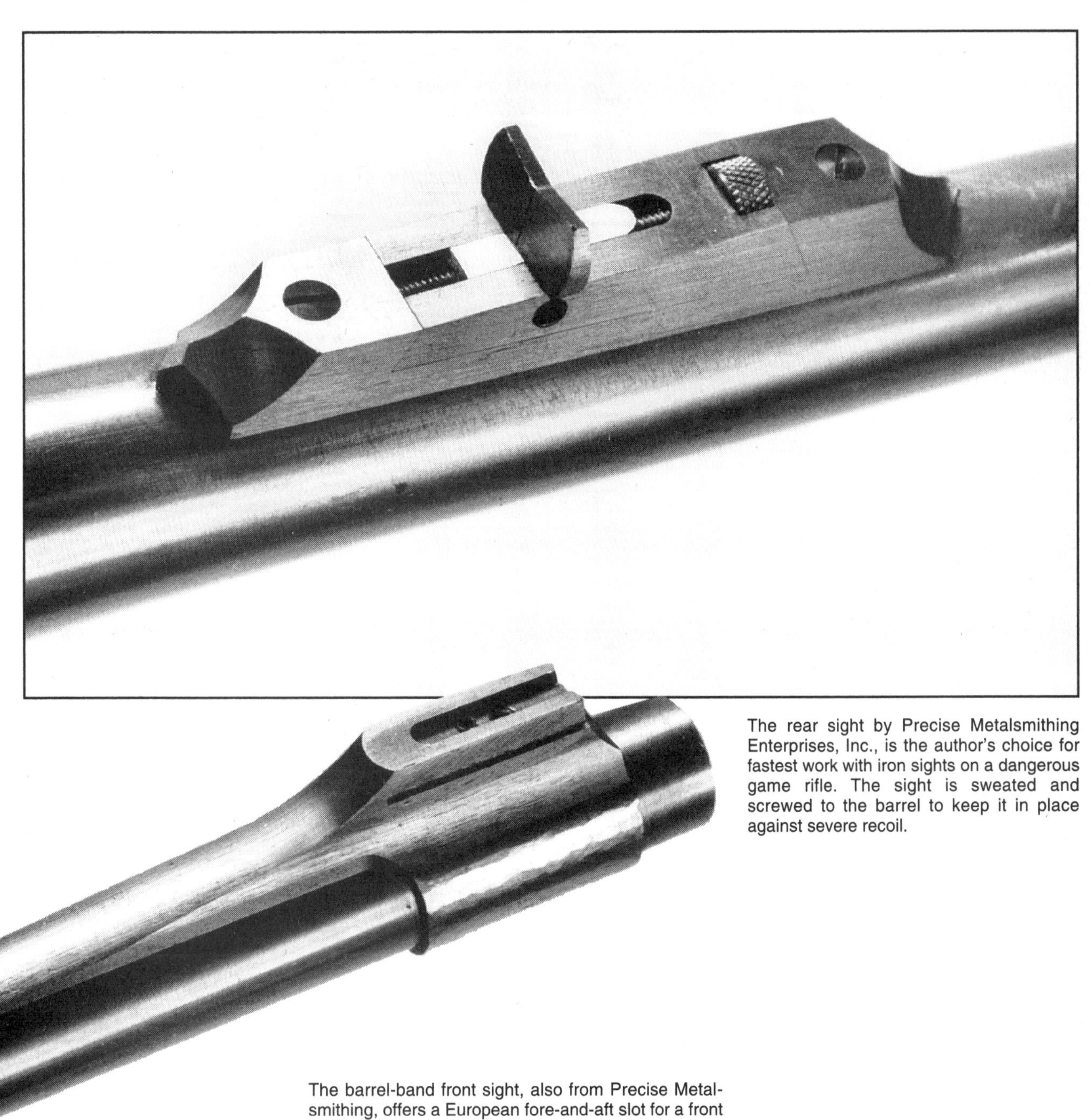

The rear sight by Precise Metalsmithing Enterprises, Inc., is the author's choice for fastest work with iron sights on a dangerous game rifle. The sight is sweated and screwed to the barrel to keep it in place against severe recoil.

The barrel-band front sight, also from Precise Metalsmithing, offers a European fore-and-aft slot for a front bead. The sight also has a quick-detachable hood.

It was necessary to weld a small bead of metal to the nose of the magazine follower (at pencil point) to ensure sufficient pressure from the follower against the cartridge that rides on it. This bead prevents the follower from sagging toward the left.

case requires a wider space within the magazine, and also dictates the action to be wider under the lips of the rails. I went to work, one cartridge at a time. The first cartridge placed into the magazine is held there by the force of the follower, pressing the case against the right action rail. In an unaltered rifle, this spring force tends to push a fat cartridge vertically up and out of the magazine box. The cartridge wants to pop out as soon as it is bumped or jarred, or moved slightly forward by the bolt.

The solution was to find more room under the rail to the right. I went to work with a hand-held grinder and widened the action in that area as much as the magazine would allow, thinned the magazine wall and bent it slightly outward to meet the edge of the widened action.

I also filed the top of the magazine follower to make it conform to the radius of the Rigby cartridge. With the follower pressing hard against the cartridge, and with more room under the right rail, I was able to keep the first (right) cartridge well-restrained and under complete control. I could bang the bolt open hard with a round in the magazine and that first round would stay firmly in place. With the feed ramp smoothed, it would also feed reliably. I was halfway there.

It seemed desirable to open the action's ejection port by grinding the action ring slightly toward the front, as well as the rear bridge toward the rear, just above the right rail. This permits easier loading and also allows ejection of loaded rounds. As the cartridge base strikes the ejector, the bullet swings to the right, clears the ring, and the cartridge is ejected out of the action.

Original Rigbys have a vertical groove ground into the rear center of the front ring to permit easier passage of the bullet nose when loading. Although I did grind a small groove here, it isn't necessary or desirable. On this rifle it accomplishes nothing. One doesn't load this gun by pressing the cartridges straight down...which you can't do anyway with a scope in place, even on original Rigbys. The cartridge must be inserted from the right side.

Now that I had the first cartridge well-controlled, I pressed the second

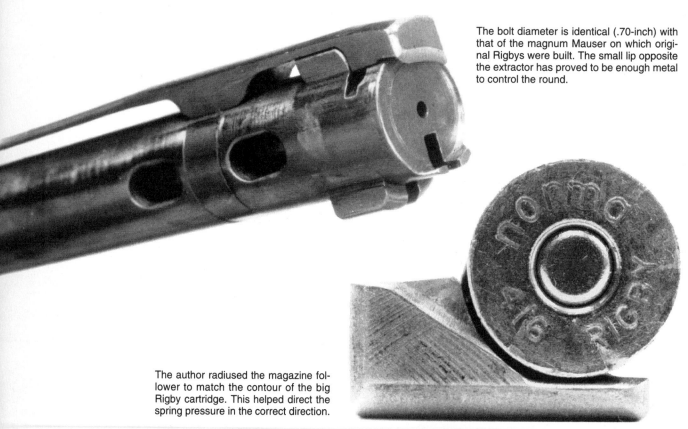

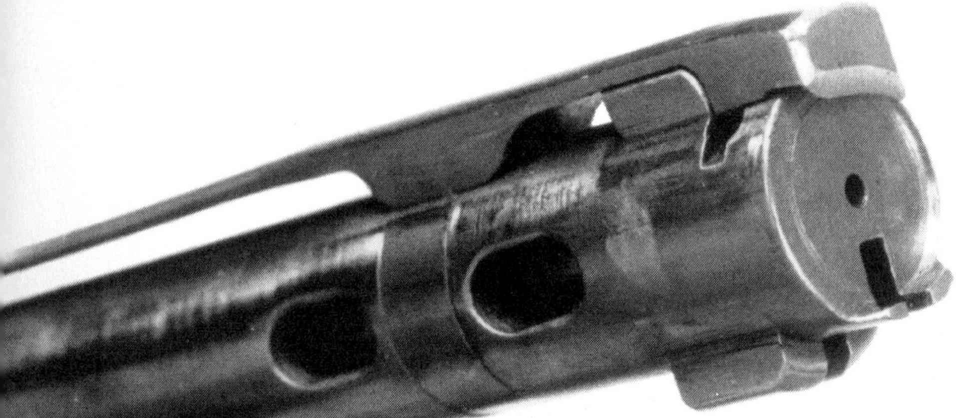

The bolt diameter is identical (.70-inch) with that of the magnum Mauser on which original Rigbys were built. The small lip opposite the extractor has proved to be enough metal to control the round.

The author radiused the magazine follower to match the contour of the big Rigby cartridge. This helped direct the spring pressure in the correct direction.

The magazine box has been filed very thin, and its left wall bent outward. The action, seen from the bottom, has had metal removed below the rails, particularly toward the rear of the action. However, the rails themselves are unaltered.

one down into the magazine on top of the first. Then I went to work under the left rail, widening the action and thinning the left wall of the magazine, then bent it very slightly outward.

After this work, I discovered the magazine follower no longer restrained the first cartridge as it once did. If I had only one round loaded into the magazine it would now pop out. The left front side of the follower now had nothing to press against and sagged to the left.

I cured this by welding a bit of metal onto the left side of the follower, near its front, to keep it pressing against the right cartridge. Now the first (lower) cartridge stayed firmly in place under the right rail.

Once I had room for two rounds, I discovered I couldn't reliably keep both of them in the magazine as I worked the bolt. Any vibration or even just opening the bolt over them could cause one or both to pop out, though the rifle worked perfectly with only one round loaded.

I watched carefully as I pressed the second cartridge down on top of the first and discovered the lower cartridge was being forced to the left, toward the center of the rifle, by the right wall of the magazine box. Thus, the lower round pressed not against the side of the upper one, but against the bottom of it as shown in my diagrams.

I had made as much room as I could under the left rail, and it looked OK. However, that lower cartridge needed to get over to the right more and press the top one tight against the left action rail, thereby restraining it. I could not get the

The action loaded with its maximum capacity of two 416 Rigby cartridges. Note the cutaway portions of the action at front and rear of the ejection port, which permits easier loading and also ejection of loaded cartridges. The trigger and safety are original Browning.

Two Rigby cartridges just fit into the original aluminum FN Browning magazine box with no room to spare. The lower cartridge overhangs the box slightly and is retained by the stock wood. Works perfectly.

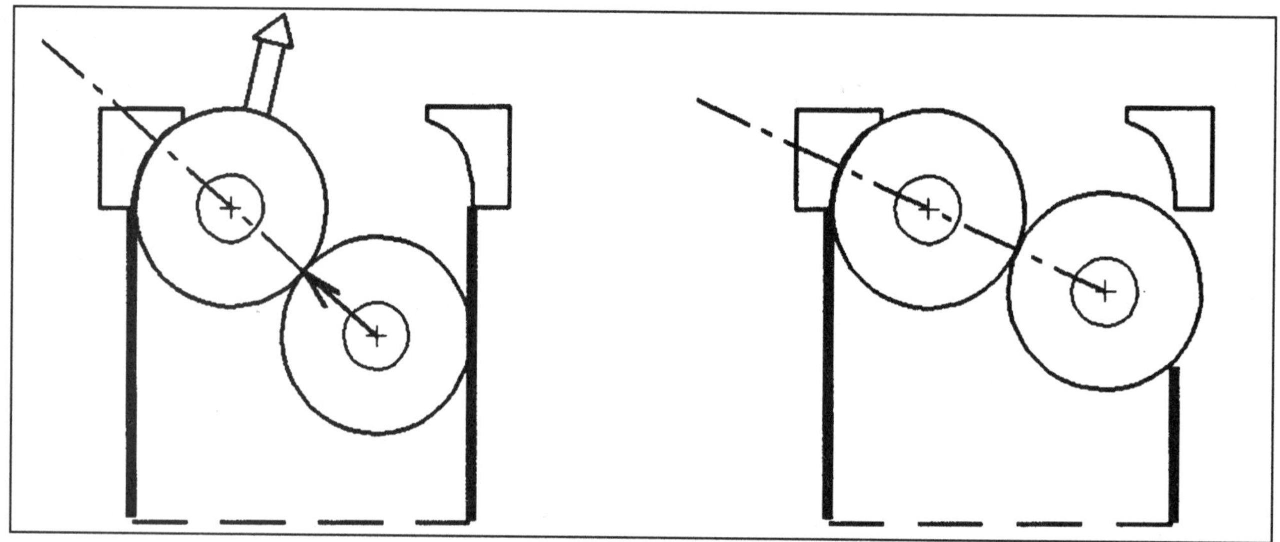

Diagram A (left) illustrates the problem with fitting two 416 Rigby cartridges into a magazine that isn't wide enough for them. The force from the lower cartridge pressing too far down toward the bottom of the upper cartridge causes the upper one to be ejected from the magazine as a result fo the slightest vibration. When the bolt is opened to chamber a round, the jar of the bolt hitting the bolt-stop is enough to cause one or both cartridges to pop out of the box, causing a jam. The spring force retaining the cartridge is represented by the line bisecting the primers. Diagram B shows the author's solution to this problem. By cutting away the right side of the magazine, he created more room for the lower cartridge. Now the line of spring force (between the two primers) becomes more horizontal, keeping both cartridges down under the rails and under complete control.

right side of the magazine box any thinner.

After a very long period of meditation, the solution came: Simply get the magazine box out of the way and let the cartridge rest against the wood of the stock, outside the box. That would effectively give me a wider magazine box. I could chamfer the lower edge of the action rail on the right so the lower cartridge would climb that edge after the first cartridge was fed into the chamber. I cut away the box from where the lower cartridge pressed against it, smoothed the edges, and then tried it. It worked perfectly, much to my satisfaction.

After I did a bit more work, smoothing and fairing the edges of everything, I discovered I had a totally reliable two-shooter in 416 Rigby. It holds the ammunition securely in the magazine and feeds them extremely well from any rifle position and at any speed. I couldn't ask for more, except perhaps for more magazine capacity.

I discovered it is not possible to make the rifle accept a third round without making a new magazine. If I wanted to do that—I don't—I'd try to utilize the stock wood for the walls of the new box.

I don't like to carry a bolt-action rifle with a load in the chamber. I prefer to carry the rifle with its chamber empty and load every round from the magazine at all times. All my bolt-action big game rifles are controlled-feed designs, and I have the habit of loading all of them from the magazine, not dropping one "up the spout." I don't want to change my gun-handling habits just to get a third shot out of the Rigby...though I *can* load three.

Perhaps the biggest advantage of putting together this project is that I ended up with a very light, very powerful rifle. I never feel the recoil when shooting any rifle at game, and I prefer powerful rifles for all my hunting. If I have a choice of two rifles of equal weight for any shooting job, but one is more powerful, I'll usually choose the more powerful rifle (within reason, of course). My FN Rigby 416 weighs just under 8 pounds with iron sights and two rounds, all ready to go. I haven't put a scope on it, but if I do, the total weight will be about $8^{1}/_{2}$ pounds.

A friend has a 425 Express with ballistics similar to the original 416 Rigby that weighs even less than mine, and he had it Mag-na-ported. He says the kick with even very heavy loads is tolerable. I haven't found muzzlebraking to be necessary with this rifle because most of my shooting is with light bullets at moderate velocities, and they don't kick as much as full-power factory 410-grainers at 2400 fps.

When I finally had a fully function-

The feed ramp required only minimal metal removal. The author widened it slightly below the rails and polished the ramp surface. The Rigby cartridges quickly climb the ramp. The author radiused a notch into the right side of the action ring in order to ease loading and permit ejection of loaded rounds. The small vertical notch in the action ring at the rear of scope base is unnecessary.

Author Ray Ordorica put the finishing touches on his 416 Rigby by engraving it in an English-style rose-and-scroll pattern, then rust-bluing it. The scope bases, by Warne, accept a 2.5x Weaver in the latest Warne QD rings.

Africa is the intended hunting ground of most 416 Rigbys. The author (left) took this impala under the guidance of PH Tony Calavrias, Kiboko Safaris, in the Selous Game Reserve in Tanzania. The 416 Rigby is ideal for one-rifle African hunts, well suited for taking plains game at long range or Cape buff up close.

al rifle in my hands, I became considerably more enthusiastic about the project. I shortened the forend 2 inches, reshaped the entire stock, gave it a best-quality oil finish, and checkered it in a 20-line-per-inch pattern. Although the stockwork is done, the metalwork you see in the photos here is quite rough. All of it has now been cleaned up and polished to give smoother feeding and better looks. The trigger needed a bit of work, but now it's perfect. I have engraved the action in a rose-and-scroll pattern, and I'm now rust-bluing the rifle.

I experimented with the new Warne combination aperture sight/scope base, and though it is an excellent sight, and even though I really like aperture rear sights on all-purpose rifles, I decided I didn't want it on this rifle. I installed an adjustable wide-angle express rear sight and a barrel-band, large-bead front sight, both made by Precise Metalsmithing Enterprises.

This project proved that it is possible to stuff the 416 Rigby into an original '98 Mauser action and make it function perfectly with that big cartridge. It ends up lighter than can be built on a magnum-length action. I think the project is viable for any outstanding '98-sized large-ring action, but not for just an ordinary '98 that is of questionable ancestry. No matter how good the action, one must never use heavy handloads in a Rigby built on a '98 action.

I think there are better ways to get a 416 Rigby. Today, you can buy a Ruger 416 Rigby bolt action, and they are great bargains, in my opinion. Ruger also offers their Number One single shot in 416. Dakota offers their Model 76 African rifle in 416 Rigby in either right- or left-hand versions. Original Rigbys also pop up from time to time, though they will never be inexpensive. The 1917 Enfield action is even more suitable to the 416 Rigby than the '98, as is the Korean-made BBK magnum Mauser action, and the Brno ZKK 602.

Paul Roberts, director of John Rigby & Co., told me recently that Rigby did in fact use FN actions to make their 416s shortly after WWII. He said they didn't like doing it, for many of the reasons I've listed. Be that as it may, Mr. Roberts did formally establish the fact that John Rigby & Co. had made this conversion before I did it. Even though my FN doesn't have the original "Rigby's Special 416 Bore for Big Game" engraved on it, I'm happy to be in good company. ●

© 1995 by Charles Fergus. Reprinted from *The Upland Edition* by permission of Lyons & Burford, Publishers, 31 W. 21 St., New York, NY 10010

Fergus and his Hinton 16 in typical central Pennsylvania grouse cover.

This is the book from which we draw this personal view of upland guns. Fergus is just as forthright on the dogs, the ethics, and the birds themselves. He's an amateur in the very best game.

THE GUN

An excerpt from a book by CHARLES FERGUS

GOUGH THOMAS WAS an Englishman and a professional engineer so smitten with shotguns that he once rigged up a device to measure a gun's "moment of inertia," the value that best expresses its liveliness and handling qualities. He fitted a cradle with a spirit level and suspended it from the ceiling on a high-tensile steel wire. He would place a gun in this cradle, slide it forward or backward until it was level, secure it, and then make it pivot from side to side, recording with a stopwatch the time it took to complete a given number of oscillations. The shorter the time, the less energy was required to direct the gun, and the lower its "moment of inertia": The better balanced it was.

Thomas published many technical articles on shotguns from the nineteen sixties to the nineteen eighties; yet his interest was not solely in guns for their own sake. He once wrote, "Guns are fascinating things, but they are only a means to an end": For him, the sport of shooting came first, dogs and dog-work second, the guns themselves third—albeit a necessary third.

One day, Thomas and four companions were on a partridge shoot in the Hampshire Downs. They took lunch sitting against a hay rick and enjoying the bucolic scenery, the spire of Salisbury's famous cathedral on the horizon, pale against a blue September sky. The conversation dwelt on the morning's sport: the skillful shooting, the good dog work, the healthful exercise, the enjoying of these things in the company of friends. "Nobody mentioned the gun until I did," wrote Thomas later. "What about the pleasure of having a good gun in your hands?" he asked. He was met with bland comments and blank stares. Somewhat nettled, he blurted out, "Are you fellows so infernally civilized that you take no pleasure in owning and using a fine, personal weapon?"

I do take such pleasure: I hunt for doves, pheasants, woodcock, and grouse using a pair of side-by-side English game guns, one of them a 12 gauge (or 12 "bore," as Gough Thomas would have put it) and the other a 16. I shoot ducks with a modern American 12-gauge over-and-under.

When I bought my first decent shotgun twenty years ago, I chose without hesitation a side-by-side, an Ithaca SKB in 20 gauge. I may be stretching things a bit when I call it a decent gun. Made for Ithaca by a Japanese company, it was lightweight, looked pretty, and had a straight-hand stock and classic lines. Only later did I discover that it had been cheaply made (the stock split after a few years) and falsely tarted up (a fancy wood "grain" had been stained onto a plain and porous piece of walnut). When I learned more about shotguns, I discovered to my chagrin that the little Ithaca's stock was "cast on" (angled to the left when viewed from above), for a lefthanded shooter. For me, a righthander, this arrangement sent my shots to the left of the target. I needed a stock that was cast *off*, with the stock angling to the right, to align my right, and master, eye with the top rib so the gun would shoot exactly where I was looking. At one point, I had a brace of the SKBs—a 12 along with the 20, both of them inexplicably cast on.

I am lucky (my wife might choose a different adjective) to have a friend and gunning partner whose evolving appreciation of shotguns paralleled my own. I got an inexpensive education watching Carl buy and trade, go through firearms that seemed to both of us, at the time, to be the epitome of bird guns—old Ithacas, a Parker 12 gauge, several Winchester Model 21s, a handsome C-grade Fox 16—only to realize that other shotguns were more effective in the field and finer objects of the gunmakers' art. It was Carl who introduced me to English guns. There is truth to the saying that once you shoot an English gun, there is no going back. Last year, I flew across the Atlantic and bought two of them.

I cannot extol a hunter who buys a fancy gun just to show it off. I cannot dismiss a hunter who uses a beat-up pump, shoots it well and kills cleanly. But I think that the latter misses a certain sweet feeling of dynamism and connection that a good gun can impart.

Many hunters use pump-action or semi-automatic shotguns in the uplands. These repeaters remind me more of military ordnance than of sporting arms. I dislike the clashing sounds they make. They are efficient in a mechanical sense, although, like automatic windows in a car, they are complicated and more prone to misbehave than the simpler double-barrel design. They deliver three shots, certainly, but two are almost always enough.

Nor is a repeater as safe as a double: If I stop to chat with someone in the coverts, I can open my gun's barrels and demonstrate that the piece cannot go off by accident. Years ago, I shot at a woodcock, and heard a *phoosh* and then the pellets raining weakly on the brush; the 'cock flew ahead and landed, and I quickly reloaded and went after it. Then I stopped. I opened my gun, removed the cartridge from the right barrel, and looked down the tube. There, about halfway along, was the plastic wad left by the dud round. Had my gun not been so easy to open—had I been carrying a repeater, which cannot be easily dismantled in the field—I might not have taken the time to check it. I might have flushed the woodcock, pulled the trigger—and lost a barrel, and perhaps my left hand.

The reasons for wanting a double gun go beyond safety. Because of the way its weight centers between the shooter's hands, a well-made double

"...fluent lines, well-finished surfaces, conformable to the hand and pleasant to the sense of touch."

will handle more fluidly than a semi-automatic or a pump, which, with its longer action and extended magazine tube, will have its weight too far forward.

Once the hunter decides to have a double gun, dozens of factors must be considered. Gauge. The gun's weight and balance. The shooter's own size and physical strength. Conditions in the hunting coverts. A preference among game birds: pheasants over grouse, for example. Cost. Barrel length, stock profile and dimensions, type of action, two triggers or one, choking, location of the safety....

Generally the first decision is whether to have an over-and-under or a side-by-side. To me a side-by-side looks sleeker than an over-and-under. I particularly fancy a slim, straight-hand stock (no bulbous pistol grip to interrupt the sweep of the wood from butt to action) and a splinter fore-end; with them, the gun has no excess flesh on its bones.

The combination of a straight stock and a minimalist fore-end places the hands on the same plane as the gun itself, so that the shot passes directly from the hands to the target. A pistol grip combined with a beavertail fore-end also puts the hands on the same plane, but one that is fractionally lower than the plane of the bores. I think I *aim* an over-and-under better (perhaps explaining why I shoot mine fairly well on clay targets, which have a predictable flight), but *direct* a side-by-side more instinctively when shooting at feathered birds.

Gauge is a matter of personal preference. With the exception of distant ducks and pheasants, the birds of the Eastern uplands can be killed cleanly and consistently with an ounce of shot. The 12 gauge, 16 gauge, and 20 gauge all can deliver an ounce. Of the three, the 12 has the best chance of shooting that ounce in an even pattern (with fewer bird-sized gaps in it). The natural load for the 20 is $^7/_8$-ounce; a full ounce of shot, piled high in the 20's skinny cartridge, may throw a patchier pattern compared to the two larger bores. The 28 gauge, which standardly shoots $^3/_4$-ounce, can make a useful grouse and woodcock gun in the hands of one who eschews long shots and regularly centers the target; however, the 28 is too light for pheasants and ducks and only marginally adequate for grouse. Overloaded with an ounce of shot, the 28 may perform poorly.

A handy thing about a 12 gauge is that it can efficiently shoot $1^1/_{16}$-ounce and $1^1/_8$-ounce loads, making it more versatile than the 16 or the 20; and the 12 can also be loaded down to $^7/_8$-ounce. Then there is the matter of recoil. In general, the heavier the powder and shot charges, the more a gun will "kick." The lighter the gun, the less recoil it will absorb and the more it will pass on to the shooter. The trick is to use a gun heavy enough to dampen recoil, yet light enough to be carried comfortably and handled with alacrity.

The typical American 12 gauge weighs seven to eight pounds, usually closer to the second figure. The average American 16 weighs six and a half to seven pounds. The average American 20 weighs a few ounces over six pounds, even up to seven pounds in some models. American guns are sometimes scorned for being excessively heavy, but there is a reason for their heft. In England, the government long ago passed strict laws under which all shotgun barrels must be proven capable of safely firing specific loads: generally, $1^1/_8$ ounces of shot for the 12 bore, 1 ounce for the 16, and $^7/_8$-ounce for the 20, fired from $2^1/_2$-inch cartridges (as opposed to the American standards of $2^3/_4$ and 3 inches) propelled by a gunpowder charge generating a moderate chamber pressure. American manufacturers (and European and Asian makers eyeing the U.S. market) do not have—and never have had—such proof laws to which they can adhere. Instead, they must build firearms capable of withstanding whatever shot and powder charge the most power-hungry shooter crams into them: In 12 gauge, a 2¾-inch shell loaded with 1½ ounces of shot, or even a 3-inch shell with 2¼ ounces, backed by sufficient propellant to send the pellets zipping along at thirteen hundred or so feet per second. Loads of this sort have little or no utility for the upland hunter who nevertheless must tote around a shotgun stout enough to fire them without flying into pieces.

I am of a size that thirty years ago would have been considered "average" and today perhaps is classifiable as "small." (Someone interviewing me for a magazine once characterized me as "slight," which sounded dismissive.) I am five feet, nine inches, and weigh one hundred forty-five pounds. (Make that "lean" or "wiry," please.) My English 12, at six pounds, five ounces, suits me nicely; my English 16, at just six pounds, seems even more appropriate to my frame and approaches the perfect weight for a grouse and woodcock gun. My American over-and-under, a Ruger 12 gauge, weighs seven pounds, twelve ounces. The Ruger balances well and soaks up recoil. Although designed for shooting clay targets, it excels in the duck blind and is usable for jump shooting, although I wouldn't want to haul it through the grouse brush all day.

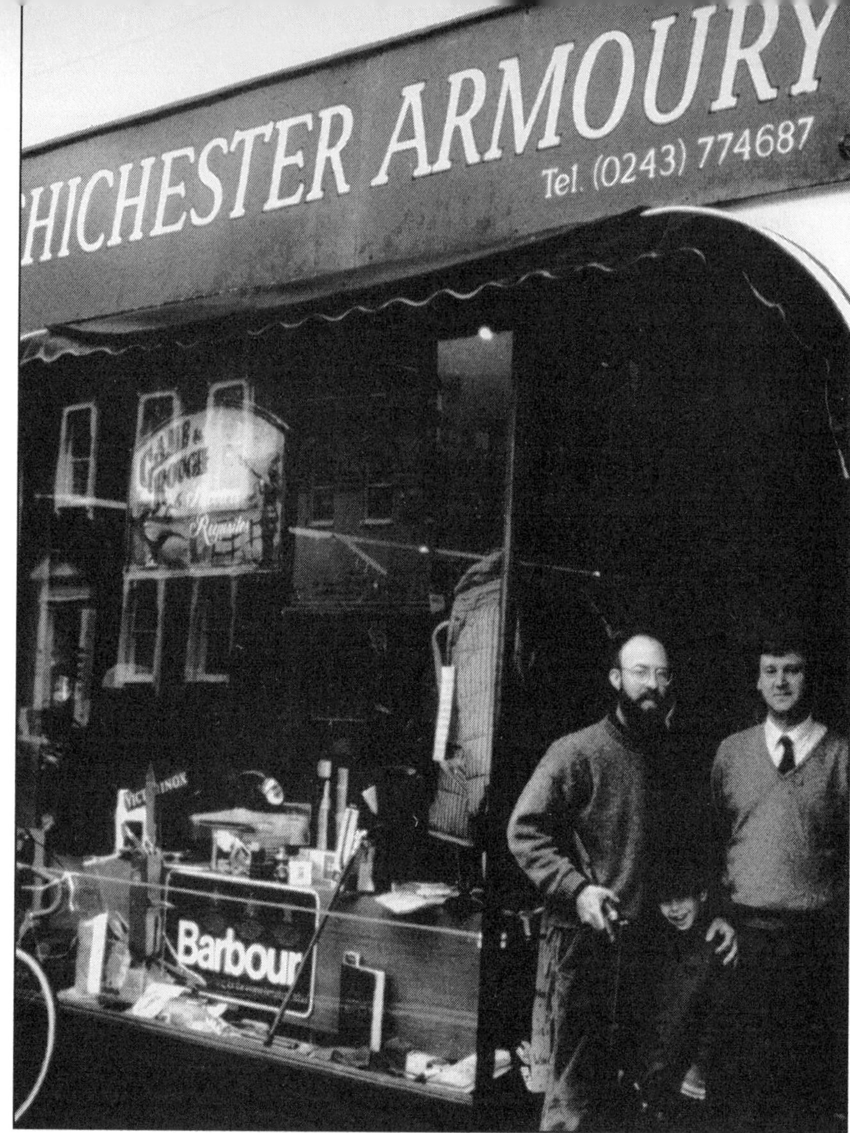

Fergus (bearded), his son William, and John Hancock, proprietor of Chichester Armoury, where Fergus bought the George Hinton 16 bore.

The Ruger's barrels are thirty inches. Those long tubes help me swing through a passing claybird or a duck, but in covert they are slow to get into action. During the last century, barrels of thirty and thirty-two inches were the standard, necessary for the full combustion of blackpowder propellant. When smokeless gunpowder was invented, barrel length could be reduced, since combustion occurred much more rapidly. It took decades to happen, but gun manufacturers finally began making barrels shorter, yielding shotguns that were lighter and livelier.

Today, some observers believe the trend toward short barrels has gone too far. (Don't most trends work that way?) In England, a popular length is twenty-five inches. Here, twenty-six inches is common. Short-barreled guns have their drawbacks, though. They look odd in the hands of large people. In 12 gauge, they have a stubby appearance. More important, short barrels do not show up as obviously in the shooter's vision, making a short-barreled gun more difficult to point accurately than a long-barreled gun. Although easier to get moving, short barrels are harder to keep in motion, to keep swinging with the target, necessary for consistent wingshooting success. And when fired, they are noticeably louder than long barrels, distracting the shooter and damaging his or her hearing. My English 12 bore has twenty-seven-inch barrels, which seems a reasonable compromise for the uplands. Twenty-eight-inch barrels likewise are very fine, especially when mated to light-framed 16- or 20-bore guns.

Certain shotguns, when you pick them up, feel "sweet": They leap to the shoulder and can be pointed swiftly and surely in different directions. As mentioned at the outset of this chapter, Gough Thomas, the English writer and engineer, invented a device for measuring shotgun balance. The best-balanced firearm he tested was a 12-bore side-by-side having twenty-seven-inch barrels and weighing six pounds, three ounces. (He doesn't say, but I suspect it was his own personal gun, made to his specifications by the London firm of Henry Atkin in 1948.) An Italian automatic and a well-known Italian over-and-under each possessed a much higher moment of inertia, showing, Thomas wrote, "how far certain popular guns fall short of the standards of balance, liveliness, and fast-handling that have been attained by the best guns hitherto made in this country." Thomas confirmed that in the best-balanced shotguns the majority of the weight is concentrated between the shooter's hands—neither biased toward the buttstock nor the barrels, but between the appendages that move and direct the gun. Other factors he cited as adding to the overall sensation of good balance were "fluent lines," "well-finished surfaces," and a shape that was "conformable to the hand and pleasant to the sense of touch."

In Thomas's opinion, the fastest-handling guns (light ones having twenty-five-, twenty-six-, or twenty-seven-inch barrels) "show at their best at such sport as partridge driving or rabbit, pigeon, or woodcock shooting in covert," while the slowest-handling guns (heavier ones with thirty-inch barrels) "are least disadvantageous, or, it may be, positively advantageous, for duck flighting and the like."

There are two main types of double-barreled shotgun actions: the boxlock and the sidelock. The sidelock, an older design, is somewhat more exacting and expensive to make. Its operating mechanisms, or locks (as in "lock, stock, and barrel"), attach to the insides of flat metal plates, which in turn are fitted to the sides of the firearm. These side plates, bounded above and below by the stock wood, provide a goodly surface for decorative engraving. The sidelock's trigger pulls are said to be slightly smoother than those of the boxlock. (I can't tell any difference.)

Unlike the boxlock, the sidelock design commonly incorporates "intercepting sears," which prevent the gun from firing should it be jarred, as by being dropped on the ground.

The boxlock is a simpler concept. Invented in Birmingham, England, in 1875 by the gunsmiths William Anson and John Deeley, it requires less-complicated inletting of the stock wood to accept the action. It can be made lighter, having less steel in its mechanism. It is more resistant to water seeping in. These attributes did not prevent, in 1896, the famous English game shot Sir Ralph Payne-Gallwey from pronouncing the boxlock shotgun "a monstrous horrendum, a mere unwieldy log of iron and wood when compared to the perfect article produced in London." To this day in England it is more prestigious to be seen shooting a London-built sidelock (most boxlocks were made in Birmingham), showing that snobbishness is alive and well on the Scepter'd Isle. In the United States, vintage side-by-sides of boxlock design include the Parker, Fox, Ithaca, Lefever, and Winchester Model 21; the current crop of over-and-unders also are boxlocks. The famous L. C. Smith was a sidelock (although it lacked intercepting sears).

Some older American side-by-sides—and almost all British game guns—have two triggers. Double triggers are simpler and less apt to malfunction than single triggers. They offer an instant choice of choke, taking full advantage of the double-barrel design. In the classic side-by-side, the front trigger shoots the right barrel, traditionally having an open choke (cylinder or improved cylinder) to fire a wide swarm of shot at a bird at short range. The left barrel possesses a greater degree of choke (quarter, modified, improved modified, or full), yielding a pattern that is tighter—and therefore more lethal—at longer ranges. The normal sequence is to first shoot the open barrel; then, if the bird is missed, to follow with the choke. But sometimes a bird gets up at a distance—thirty or forty yards, say—so that one wants the tighter barrel for what will be the only shot taken. On a gun with two triggers, it is a simple matter to slide the hand back and pull the rear trigger to instantly fire the tighter choke. A straight-hand stock (as opposed to a pistol grip) facilitates this movement by the trigger hand, either to fire the choke barrel first, or to fire the open and then the choke in the usual sequence.

Today, almost all factory-made shotguns come equipped with single triggers. Usually there is a complicated safety button mounted on the top tang that can be thumbed in one direction to select the open barrel, in the other direction to select the choke. The people in the marketing departments of firearms companies, most of whom obviously have never seen the inside of a thorn-apple thicket or an alder swamp, want us to believe that a selective safety is easy to operate during the heat of a flush. It is not. About the only time a single trigger outperforms double triggers is during frigid weather when a stationary hunter (sitting in a duck blind, for instance) loses feeling in his or her fingers. Both of my English guns have two triggers; I had never shot double triggers before getting them, but reckoned that if I could learn to drive on the left side of the road (over a thousand miles while shopping for guns), I could teach myself to use two trig-

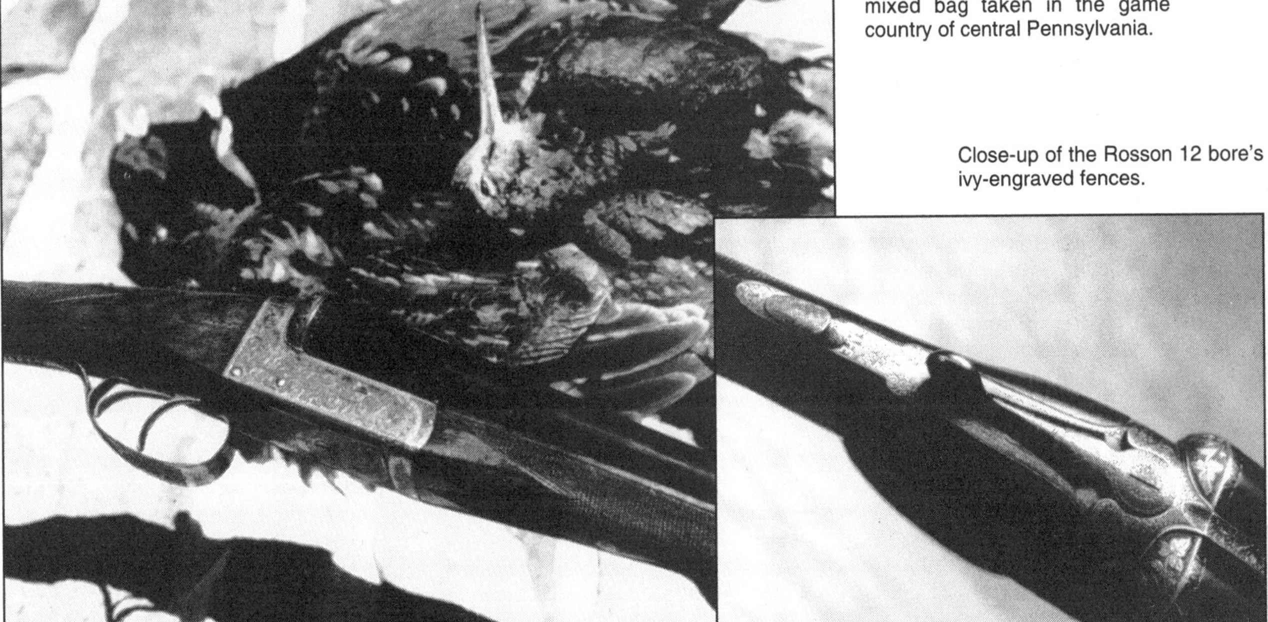

The Rosson gun along with a fine mixed bag taken in the game country of central Pennsylvania.

Close-up of the Rosson 12 bore's ivy-engraved fences.

gers. I could, and did, and it didn't take very long.

After I got shut of my SKBs, I thought long and hard about what kind of gun I wanted. It had to be well-balanced and dynamic, for those snap shots on grouse. It had to carry easily, for the long treks over hill and dale. A gun whose beauty would make me want to get it out and look at it, pick it up and handle it, shoot it often. As I saw it, there were three possible avenues for procuring an excellent upland gun.

The first route—by far the simplest and the most practical—was to buy a modern high quality shotgun. A host of over-and-under boxlocks are manufactured by American, European, and Asian makers. Most are priced at around a thousand dollars (second-hand ones are less) and offer considerable value for the money. They are chambered for cartridges of the standard 2$^{3}/_{4}$- or 3-inch lengths. Many come with interchangeable choke tubes that let the shooter set up the choke combination for the birds and the cover conditions at hand.

Most modern over-and-unders can safely shoot steel shot, currently mandated for hunting ducks. Most of these shotguns are predictably heavy, steering the average shooter toward the 20 rather than the 12 gauge. As far as I can tell, no one makes a 16, which is a shame because the 16 is lighter and trimmer than the 12 and can handle both upland birds and ducks: The 20 is a bit underpowered for shooting waterfowl. I know of no company that makes a good-quality, modestly priced side-by-side, probably because American shooters overwhelmingly prefer over-and-unders.

A normal fellow would have chosen a modern gun. But remember, I had handled Carl's English.

For a while I considered getting an older American side-by-side. These guns hold a treasured place in the hearts of many shooters; they hearken back to what is imagined to be a simpler time, when game was more abundant and a predominantly rural populace held the sport of bird hunting in higher regard than does today's urbanized society. In 12 gauge (the most common gauge then, as now), most of the old Yankee guns are clunky: heavy, thick through the wrist, with pistol grips and wrap-around beavertail fore-ends. I handled many such at gun shows and in shops. Perhaps, I thought, I could be happy with a 16 or a 20.

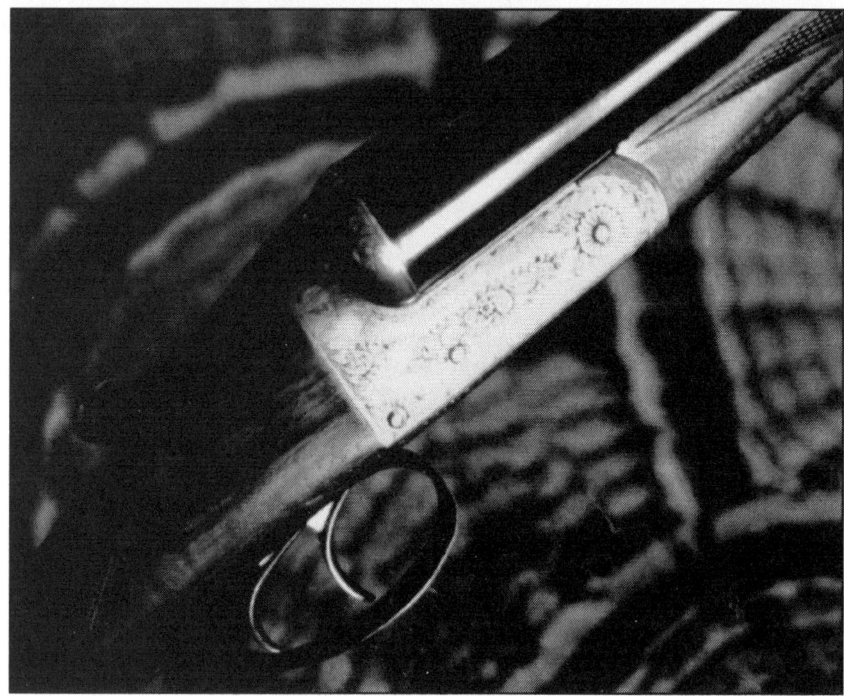

The Hinton has modest good-quality engraving—a "solid Birmingham boxlock" it was characterized by Alfred Gallifent, a Churchill-trained gunsmith.

Mass-produced in factories, most of the vintage American guns did not receive the care and craftsmanship invested in English and European doubles, handwork that resulted in sleek lines, subtle adornment, and good balance. Despite any negative qualities, old American doubles—especially those in original condition—command high prices. Parker shotguns, for example, seem absurdly expensive, as do Winchester Model 21s, especially compared with English guns available at a similar cost.

The higher grades of the American doubles can be downright gaudy. Various models sport checkered side panels, *fleurs de lis* carved into the stock wood, and even gold lightning bolts inlaid in the barrels. The engraving is often copious, although much of it is imprecise, and some of the dogs and birds suggest that Dr. Seuss was manning the engraving tool! To me, the lower grades look better—the V Grade Parker and Fox Sterlingworth, for example, their actions outlined with modest border engraving—and, happily, these simpler guns cost less than the high-grade ones. It would be possible, although not easy, to find an old American double with two triggers and a straight stock. It is also an option to have a gun restocked to modern dimensions.

But really, my case was hopeless. New books had accumulated on my shelves, such as *Gough Thomas's Gun Book* and Geoffrey Boothroyd's *Sidelocks & Boxlocks, the Classic British Shotguns*. Little yellow stick-on markers feathered the back issues of magazines featuring fine guns. I visited toney gun-trading establishments and emerged in a state combining agony and ecstasy. I wrote to English companies for lists. I struck up an over-the-phone friendship with a man who had lived in England and who had bought many shotguns there, for himself and for friends. It was clear that English guns cost considerably less in England than they did here. It was complicated, bringing them over, but it could be done. From my new friend, and from Carl and through my reading, I learned of certain considerations regarding English shotguns: Like the older American doubles, they were not built to handle steel shot. Most English guns have 2$^{1}/_{2}$-inch chambers that will not accept the 2$^{3}/_{4}$-inch shells found in sporting goods shops in the United States. The solution was to buy imported English cartridges (at about twice the cost of American ammunition) or, as I planned to do, reload your own.

I had incurably caught what I sometimes jokingly referred to as "the shotgun bane." Only an English gun would relieve it.

The English game gun is the ultimate evolutionary expression of the side-by-side shotgun. It is as lean as it can be made, and still remain comfortable to shoot. While many English doubles have magnificent stock wood and superb engraving, their beauty does not depend on applied adornment. Scheming after my gun, I realized I could be happy with a twin-triggered, lightweight firearm with little or no metal engraving and plain stock wood: Such a gun still sings out its correctness of form. Gough Thomas had coined a word to describe the best of the English guns, *eumatic*, meaning "the quality in a manually operated device whereby it is totally correlated to the human being who [uses] it."

At that juncture, a fortunate thing happened. Years earlier, I had squirreled away some old sporting art. I learned that the art had value, and sold it. Now I had dollars burning holes in my pockets. Enough dollars, it would seem, for two guns: a plain one and a fancy. The British pound had sunk to one dollar and fifty cents. I pointed out to my wife that the value of English shotguns had steadily risen and would continue to do so. Sidelocks were quite expensive, but boxlocks—so the experts said—remained underpriced. I managed to convince my wife that I was turning one form of investment (the artwork) into another, eminently more usable, form of investment (the guns). And hadn't she always wanted to visit England?

We flew in April. London was rain, traffic, crowds—and places like Holland & Holland and Purdeys, where sleek, gorgeous sidelocks lined the racks, most of them (even the used ones) costing upwards of ten thousand pounds. No doubt about it, boxlocks were the bargains, and I would find them in the countryside.

Spring was just coming on. Outside the city, fruit trees were in blossom, lambs frolicked across kelly-green meadows, and the mustard fields were brilliant yellow coverlets spread on the fertile earth. Our first stop was seventy miles southwest of the metropolis, in the town of Chichester. The proprietor of Chichester Armoury was a sandy-haired, quiet-spoken gent whose John Hancock was... John Hancock. The shop, on West Street not far from the town's imposing Norman cathedral, smelled of gun oil, waxed cotton, and wool. Outside, the rain spattered down, and inside I happily laid my hands on some guns.

I looked at boxlocks and sidelocks, ordinary and dressy, cheap and dear. Finally I picked up the gun that had drawn me to the shop in the first place. (We had also gone to Chichester because it was on the way from London to Cornwall, where my wife, son, and I would be vacationing for two weeks. At the moment, they were enjoying themselves at Chichester Cathedral.)

The gun was a 16-bore boxlock made in the nineteen thirties by George Hinton of Taunton, Somerset. Taunton is a town in the west of England, in Somerset, which is a "shire," similar to our "county" designation. Hinton was one of many "provincial" gunmakers whose businesses were located outside of London. (One source book lists four thousand gunmakers, or firms, that sold shotguns under their own name: In actuality, most boxlocks were made anonymously in shops and factories in Birmingham.) The 16 was not a fancy gun but an honest one—a "bramble divider," as the English call a firearm destined for hard use. It had its share of nicks and scratches, so I wouldn't be afraid to carry it on icy slopes or through the wickedest briars. At six pounds, I could carry it all day and still get onto a grouse flushed in the waning light. The price, twelve hundred fifty pounds, included a leather case and the reblacking of the barrels, trigger guard, and floorplate.

"Done," I said.

Mr. Hancock noted that he had sold the Hinton through his shop five years earlier, the buyer having traded it back in on a rifle. He smiled, hefting the little double. "I don't expect to own it again," he said.

I found my 12 bore in Salisbury, whose cathedral spire had caught Gough Thomas's eye on that September day of partridge shooting. It was market day when we arrived; in the town square, people sold fresh produce, rugs, fabric, shoes, eggs, butchered meat. When I walked into Greenfields, I knew it was my kind of place. Plenty of doubles on the racks—stacked-barrel Browning and Beretta clays guns—but also a fine complement of English side-by-sides. Richard Moore, in green gunmaker's smock, white shirt, and tie, oversaw the gun room. He had a countryman's genial face below a shock of gray-streaked brown hair.

I looked at several guns—Wanless Brothers, a Newnham, a couple of Gallyons, a Martin, a Stensby—all 12 bores, none of them names that I knew, but obviously well-made boxlock game guns, most of them in excellent condition and priced between twelve hundred and three thousand pounds. Forget the names, this is what you look for: good lines, high quality, top condition.

Then I came to the Rosson.

The moment I picked it up, the gun felt at home in my hands. Its light weight resided perfectly about the hinge pin. It came to my shoulder swiftly, stayed there, could be quickly and positively redirected. The stock fit me perfectly. Again and again, I swept the gun to my shoulder, then lowered it and turned it in my hands. English ivy carved impeccably into the fences. A partridge engraved on the floorplate and another on the top lever; fine scrollwork on the action, trigger guard, top and bottom tangs, and fore-end furniture. The metallic blues, reds, greens, and purples of antique case-coloring swirled across the surface of the action. Black lines played through the richly colored French walnut stock.

The Rosson had been made in the nineteen thirties by the now-defunct firm of C. S. Rosson & Company (their address, "Rampant Horse Street, Norwich," was engraved on the top rib). By chance, Mr. Moore had a Rosson catalog from the thirties, which identified the gun as a "Regent" model, their top-of-the-line boxlock. Back then, it cost forty-seven pounds, ten shillings, just five pounds less than their lowest-priced sidelock. (That was at a time when the average English workman made five to ten pounds a month.) Of the Regent, C. S. Rosson & Company stated: "Particular attention is paid to Weight and Balance, and the Gun is a perfect delight to use."

The Rosson was just within my budget. It is a better gun than any old American double I have ever seen. It is a better gun than some English sidelocks costing several thousand pounds more. Indeed, it has proven a perfect delight to use, here in the uplands of Pennsylvania.

I suppose I am odd for going all the way to England to buy my guns. But we had a memorable trip, and I refuse to count the journey's cost into the price of the guns—which admittedly was considerable. My wife thinks I am insane for buying two shotguns whose combined worth is twice that of my pickup truck. Yes, an English game gun is expensive. But the weight is right, the profile classic, and the balance superb. How correct it seems to pursue birds with a firearm as honed and lovely as they. ●

This whitetail buck was taken with the 9x56mm Mannlicher along a creek-bottom thicket. This little carbine is fast and dependable.

The author's Model 1905 Mannlicher carbine in 9x56mm Mannlicher chambering shown in profile. The sling is original. This classic was located in unfired condition in a local gunshop.

ROMANCE OF THE MANNLICHER-SCHOENAUER

by SAM FADALA

MEN AND BOYS are separated by the cost of their toys, and the man who accumulates the most toys in his tenure wins the game of life, or so the story goes. For many years, believing this, I wanted a Mannlicher carbine for the simple joy of ownership. A clipped-out picture of one rested in my wallet when I was a boy. Practicality then outran desire, however, and my first "deer gun" was a 25-35 Model 94 Winchester carbine, bought well used and abused for a double sawbuck. I sold it two years later for fifty bucks, pocketing ten dollars profit.

A Remington rolling block 7x57 came next, then a Model 94 30-30, followed by the rifleman's rifle, a 270 Model 70 Winchester with the admirable 26mm Stith 4x Bear Cub scope. I was set. The romance of the Mannlicher still flickered, now just a tiny flame in a dark corner of my memory.

Years later, I walked into a gun shop in my hometown, and on the used rack was a little carbine that never had been used. It was a Mannlicher-Schoenauer in caliber 9x56mm, purchased, I learned later, in 1921, then doubtless wrapped in cloth like a mummy and placed to rest before it ever fired a shot. Rest it did for a half-century. Its present owner knew its worth, as demonstrated by the lofty price tag, but I learned I had something he wanted, and so a trade ensued. I walked out of the gunshop that day with the old, yet new, Mannlicher tucked under an arm. I remedied the unfired situation next day at the range and bagged a whitetail buck with the little carbine in the fall of the same year.

So what? What's so wonderful about a vintage Mannlicher? Perhaps nothing. That's why I call it a rifle of romance. Many rifles of the same era had more to offer. Plus, if you want to own one today, the modern version is stronger, more accurate, and endowed with a big list of high-intensity cartridges. All the same, my outdated Mannlicher is not for sale.

Aside from some custom-built arms, it's the only rifle I've owned that pays for itself even when it's not in the field or on the shooting range. Handling alone is worth the price of ownership. Perhaps its history has something to do with it. Few rifles were better received by the cognoscenti of the day than the Mannlicher.

Although he also favored a Model 99 Savage for some part of his adventuresome life, American naturalist/explorer Roy Chapman Andrews said his Mannlicher was a "constant companion during more than a quarter of a century," adding that, "To its bullets had fallen game in almost every continent of the world. Two notches on the stock were reminders of how it had saved my life from Chinese Brigands. In Arctic snows or tropic jungles, it never failed."

Walter Winans, well-known shooter of his era, admired the Mannlicher. So did W.D.M. "Karamojo" Bell, the great ivory hunter. "I once had a carbine Mannlicher-Schoenauer 20-inch barrel down to 5½ pounds with a hollowed-out walnut stock that was simply lightning for the brain shot on elephant," reported Bell.

Who was this man Mannlicher? John Moses Browning, known to all who study firearms, deserves each molecule of accorded respect, yet Ritter Ferdinand von Mannlicher has every right to stand alongside Browning. Mannlicher was a gun design genius. But before his many amazing inventions went from his mind to a drawing board to reality, other people prepared Mannlicher's stage for greatness. The "Iron City" of Steyr, Austria, enjoyed a society of rifle and barrel makers, founded in the 1600s. The society fell because Emperor Rudolf hated the Lutheran city of Steyr. A strong Catholic himself, he punished Steyr by employing workers to build military arms, then refusing to pay for the goods.

Steyr survived, and in the 1800s, the city remained a manufacturing center. Leopold Werndl was employed in Steyr making barrels, shoes, steel ramrods, lance points, and other products. He and his wife, Josepha nee Millner, had a son, Josef Werndl, born Febuary 26, 1831. When Josef grew up he had a dream: to invent a machineable firearm action with strong locking lugs.

He did it, and his bolt-action rifle earned a large Austrian army contract, and Steyr became the "arsenal of the world" at the time, because other armies demanded Austrian-made arms.

When Josef Werndl died on April 29, 1889, he left behind a multitude of ideas, including one for a high-class sporting rifle. Eventually, such a rifle was made in Austria. Its designer was Mannlicher, born in Mainz, Germany in 1848. Mannlicher's work continued into the last year of his life in 1904.

Mannlicher was chief engineer for the Austrian Northern Railway for a time, gaining employment later with the Oesterreichische Waffenfabriks-Gessellschaft, which for obvious reasons we'll call the OWG, an armory famous for bolt-action repeating magazine rifles. From 1874 to 1904, Mannlicher invented more designs than John Browning or Paul Mauser, with 150 repeating rifles, some automatics. His was the first production fully automatic military rifle. There was also a straight-pull bolt-action rifle adopted by the Austrian army. Another rifle with front locking lugs at the head of the bolt proved strong enough for smokeless powder. His patents were many.

British Patent No. 2915 was for a bolt-action rifle with a rotary magazine in the buttstock. It enjoyed no commercial success. British Patent No. 632/1888 was granted for another rotary magazine, this one beneath the action of the rifle. It operated with a star wheel, but once again, commercial success was not forthcoming. Mannlicher also gained no fame or dollar reward for the M-1 Garand, yet the M-1 clearly borrowed from the inventor's gas bleed-off system designed in 1895. Nor was he credited for the Canadian Ross rifle, or the Schmidt-Rubin, both straight-pull bolt-action models following the Mannlicher scheme. The principles of Browning's automatic firearms followed closely on Mannlicher's ideas as well, including an accelerator housing, locking action, reciprocating parts associated with the barrel, as well as methods of locking, unlocking, cocking, and the manner of harnessing recoil energy. By 1885, Mannlicher's automatic rifle was perfected, a light machinegun that embodied only five moving parts.

The sun finally shone on the gun inventor in 1900. But not with a military rifle. Mannlicher's sporting rifle appeared in France's *Exposition Universalle* in Paris. Otto Schoenauer (also seen as Schonauer and Schoenhatier) shared his name on the new rifle for perfecting Mannlicher's rotary magazine. Otto was a manager at OWG for many years and was one of six men to work on the rotary magazine. The rifle gained instant approval and evolved into the collectible model we know today. In contrast with many other sporting arms, few

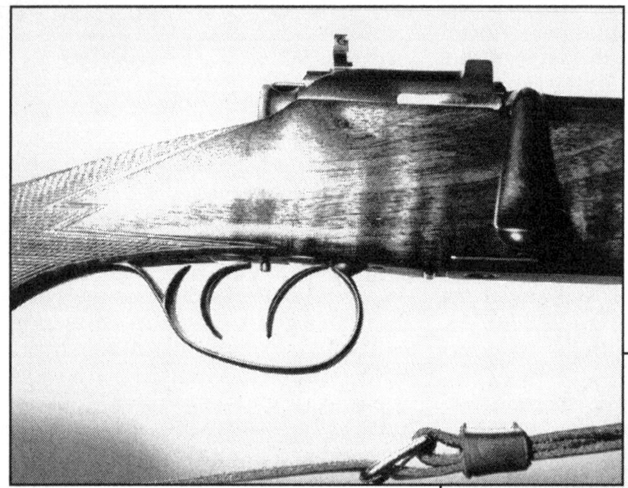

This double-set trigger system with set-screw in between the two triggers suits Fadala, who shoots similar systems in front-stuffers.

Note the shiny knurled piece forward of the butterknife bolt handle. A press on this spring-loaded metal projection clears the magazine.

were manufactured. Records show that, over forty-seven years, the factory turned out only 74,000 original-style Mannlichers, or 3.5 rifles per working day (according to research figures). Why so few? Speedy production of the fine rifle was not possible. Besides, Mannlichers were expensive.

London's W.J. Jeffery Company sold the "Jeffery's New Model No. 8" Mannlicher-Schoenauer Sporting Rifle for £21 in 1912. This model had a removable rotary magazine charged with five rounds from a stripper clip that was discarded after loading. Interchangeable barrels were offered. In the same catalog, Jeffery's finest double-barrel shotgun cost the same. Mannlichers made it to America soon after production began, maintaining sufficient popularity to merit continued sales. The Sequoia Importing Company imported Mannlichers in 1908, contracting with George Knaak, who fit 7mm barrels marked "7.57 1908." Much later, Stoeger's 1932 catalog listed the carbine for $82.50 with 18-inch barrel in 6.5mm (also noted as 6.7mm). The 8mm, 9mm and 9.5mm carbines, all with 20-inch barrels, sold for the same price.

The same catalog carried the Winchester Model 94 30-30 carbine for $36.30 and the Winchester Model 54 for $53.40. In 1939, the Mannlicher carbine sold for $140, while the fine Winchester Model 70 went for $61.25, and the Model 94 carbine for $30.

In the mid-1960s, the Mannlicher carbine retained its original action, albeit with a new stock. It sold for a shade under $200 in 6.5mm, 7mm Mauser, 243 Winchester and other calibers. In the same time slot, the Model 70 retailed at $139.95, and the 94 went for under $85. Obviously, the shooter on a budget went for any of the excellent American bolt-action rifles over the Mannlicher.

Besides, the original-style Mannlicher carbine had its faults, as Elmer Keith pointed out. Four "problems" were bolt design, placement of bolt handle, narrow stock, and high scope mounting. Engineer types shook their heads. It made the fillings in their teeth hurt just to consider the multiple-piece bolt design and a bolt-handle well forward of the trigger(s). Yet, Mannlichers did not blow up, and it took no more than 2½ minutes to get used to operating the bolt, in spite of handle location. The slim stock did a poor job of dispersing recoil, but at the same time it promoted quick handling. Few rifles mount faster to the shoulder than the little Mannlicher, with the shooter's eye instantly locked into a sight picture. Mounted scopes centered, if not prettily, over the bore. Perhaps romance dominates reason, but I've found the Mannlicher, with peep sight, nearly ideal for dropping running bucks in the thicket with one shot per customer.

Theory be hanged, the little Mannlicher was a jewel. The carbine, with its flat bolt handle, slipped in and out of a saddle scabbard slicker than a marble on ice, and it packed into tight corners with nothing sticking out. It loaded into short gun cases for travel and later shot with sufficient accuracy for any type of big game hunting.

Although Mannlicher's original masterpiece escaped the drawing board for the production line in 1900, it is the Model 1903 that caused a stir among hunters. The 6.5mm cartridge had almost as much to do with it as the firearm. Noted as the 6.7x53mm, because Austrians stated caliber by groove diameter rather than bore diameter at the time, the little cartridge performed far beyond its mere 53mm to 54mm length and 26-caliber bullet size. Sectional density was the reason. The 6.5x54, which we call it now, fired a 160-grain bullet that looked like a pencil sticking out of the case.

The 9x56mm round in the Model 1905 was not as well-received as the smaller cartridge that preceded it.

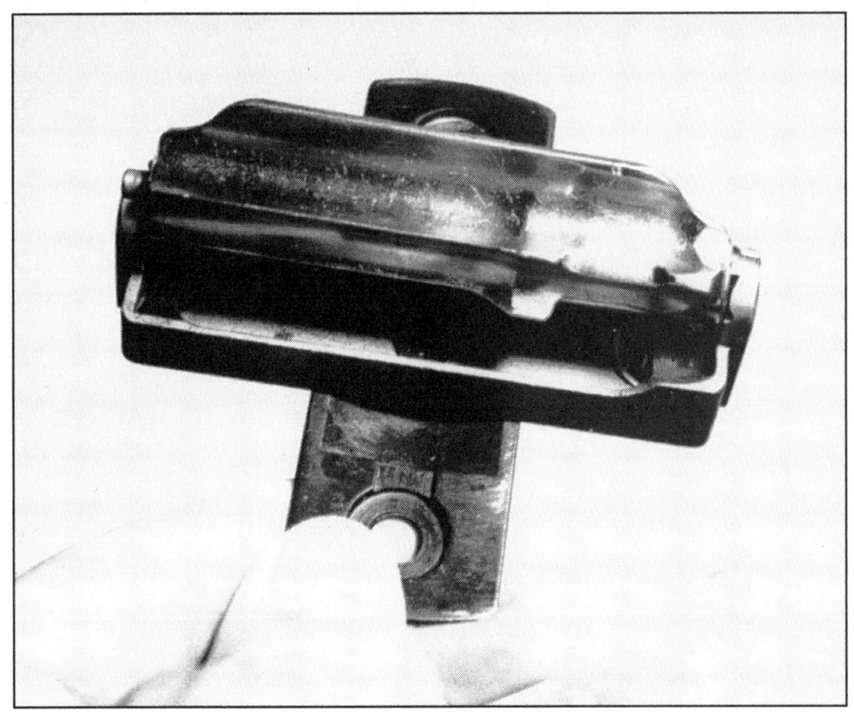

The rotary Schoenauer magazine is quickly and easily removed. It is just as easily and quickly replaced.

The trapdoor in the serrated steel buttplate is spring-loaded. Under the trap are receptacles contoured for two cartridges and a cleaning rod.

The 8x56mm, chambered in the Model 1908, also failed to outstrip the popularity of the 6.5mm. Nor did the 9.5x57mm in the Model 1910 eclipse 6.5x54 sales. Incidentally, the 6.5x53R is essentially the 6.5x54, but with a rim, and the 9.5x57 was also known as the 9.5x56, 9.5x56.7 and 375 Nitro Express Rimless.

Over time, the Mannlicher was chambered for at least thirty different cartridges, but the four named above are of special interest because they are associated with the original Mannlicher carbine. Ballistics from the literature varies with the source, but Keith's listings in *Rifles for Large Game* (1946) showed the 6.5mm with a 160-grain bullet at 2160 fps muzzle velocity and the 9mm with a 280-grain bullet at 2000 fps. The little 6.5mm was a giant-killer, used even on pachyderms.

The 8mm pushed a 200-grain bullet at about 2150 fps, while the 9.5mm drove a 260-grain bullet at around the same velocity. I once studied caliber with regard to ballistic authority by comparing 30-06 cases necked down as small as 6mm and as large as 375. Over 200 yards, the 375 cleaned house for delivered energy. So it is no surprise that the larger calibers on the medium-length Mannlicher case also won the day for sheer authority. All four vintage Mannlicher rounds were buried by better cartridges in time, yet all four were, and still are, surprisingly effective. The 9x56mm became my Mannlicher cartridge of interest for one obvious reason: I owned one. Quickly, I learned that the 9x56mm carbine of 1905 had a problem with consistent bore diameter, or did it?

Some said yes; others no. One "expert" on the subject proclaimed that the problem lay with writers—the first one picking up on false data, the rest of the pack spreading it like a disease. If truly a 9mm bullet, diameter would run .35433-inch, rounded off to .354. I had the bore of my Model 1905 slugged and found that bullets closer to .358-inch were appropriate, which didn't hurt my feelings at all, since America is full of good .358-inch bullets.

It seems that, in spite of claims otherwise, the 9mm did have some variance in bore dimension. Larry Stewart of the Mannlicher Collectors Association (MCA) studied the 9mm problem, concluding that the company intended bullets of .355- to .356-inch diameter. One MCA reader voiced a plea to MCA: "Please, would you help me acquire some bullets to load and fire in my Model 1905 9x56mm...bullets need to be swaged down to .354 or .355." Another 9x56 owner stated, "Regarding the 9x56mm M-S: Mine has a .356 bore." Another wrote, "I have searched and researched, but can't find bullets for my Model 1905 9mm M-S. The bore is .354." Another 9x56mm miked at exactly .3525-inch groove diameter.

Dave Cumberland, of The Old Western Scrounger, solved the 9x56mm bullet problem for Mannlicher Model 1905 fans. Dave offers bullets swaged from .358-inch down to .355-inch for only $5 a box plus the retail price of the bullets. Loading data can be found in older manuals, such as Lyman's No. 42, which shows Hi-Vel powder providing 2200 fps with a 200-grain bullet, 2150 fps for a 220-grain bullet, 2100 fps for a 250-grain bullet, and 2010 fps with a 280-grain bullet in the 9x56mm, noted as the 9mm Mannlicher on page 142. The same manual provides loading data for the 6.5mm Mannlicher, page 122. There's nothing on the 8x56mm or 9.5x57mm in this manual. My 9x56mm likes H335 powder. A 225-grain bullet at 2400 fps MV and a 250-grain bullet at 2200 fps MV are my best loads using H335. My modern loads are powerful, but they do not necessarily outstrip old-time ballistics. For example, Kynoch's factory load for the 9x56mm with a 245-grain bullet showed a muzzle velocity of 2200 fps.

While the four basic Mannlicher cartridges and their interesting ballistics are paramount to understanding the fame and glory of the Mannlicher, it's the firearm itself that caused the stir. Variations were many, including a swept-back bolt similar to the Winchester Model 70. Using my own Model 1905 M-S as an example, here are some statistics that reveal the nature of the carbine. Unloaded, it weighs 7 pounds on the nose. The barrel is 20 inches long, overall length 40.5 inches. The distinctive full-length stock ends with a blued metal nosecap up front and a blued steel rifle-style buttplate. The nosecap is retained in part by a screw located centered and below. The buttplate has a trapdoor held shut by a powerful fingernail-breaking spring. The buttstock has three receptacles—two for cartridges, one for a cleaning rod. Contoured cartridge holders prevent bullet smack-back when the rifle is fired. Some trapdoors are useless for extra ammo because bullets are smashed into the case upon firing the rifle. A bolt release button is located under the receiver sight.

The leather sling fits on non-detachable swivels; the forward loop retained by a crossbolt. The stock is of walnut, with reasonable fiddleback; the house finish appears to be varnish-based. Hand checkering is spare, a couple nice panels at the wrist, with a small wrap-around on the forearm. A gold bead front sight rests in a dovetail notch on a ramp. My gun has a blank where an open rear sight would go. The interesting receiver sight is, according to Keith, a Lyman swinging-arm model, and indeed it is marked "Lyman." It is actually Lyman's No. 36 model, which sold for $10 in the 1930s and was billed as a "no tap or drill needed" sight. The aperture arm can be swung rearward and locked back for open sight use. Otherwise, the spring-loaded arm neatly swings out of the way and back to battery as the bolt is worked. This allows the peep to be centered low. Elevation can be altered in a second with a lever, allowing multiple sight-in ranges.

Most metal parts are blued, including the forend and grip caps. Mannlicher offered single and double triggers interchangeably. Mine has the double-set type. A background in muzzleloaders prepared me for the double-set system. I set the front or "hair" trigger as a matter of common practice, even for brush shooting. The military-like safety is located on the cocking piece. It has a wing that swings full right to lock the bolt and deactivate the front (shooting) trigger. The same condition exists with the safety arm straight up—locked bolt/non-active trigger. In this posture, the peep sight is blocked, and, therefore, a shooter knows instantly that he has left his safety on if he mounts the rifle to take a shot because he can't see his sights.

I carry the Mannlicher with the safety in the upright position when stalking brush or woods, thumb resting on the arm and forefinger on the set (rear) trigger. For jump-shooting, this is fast: the thumb flicks the safety to the left (firing position), while the forefinger simultaneously sets the trigger. The front

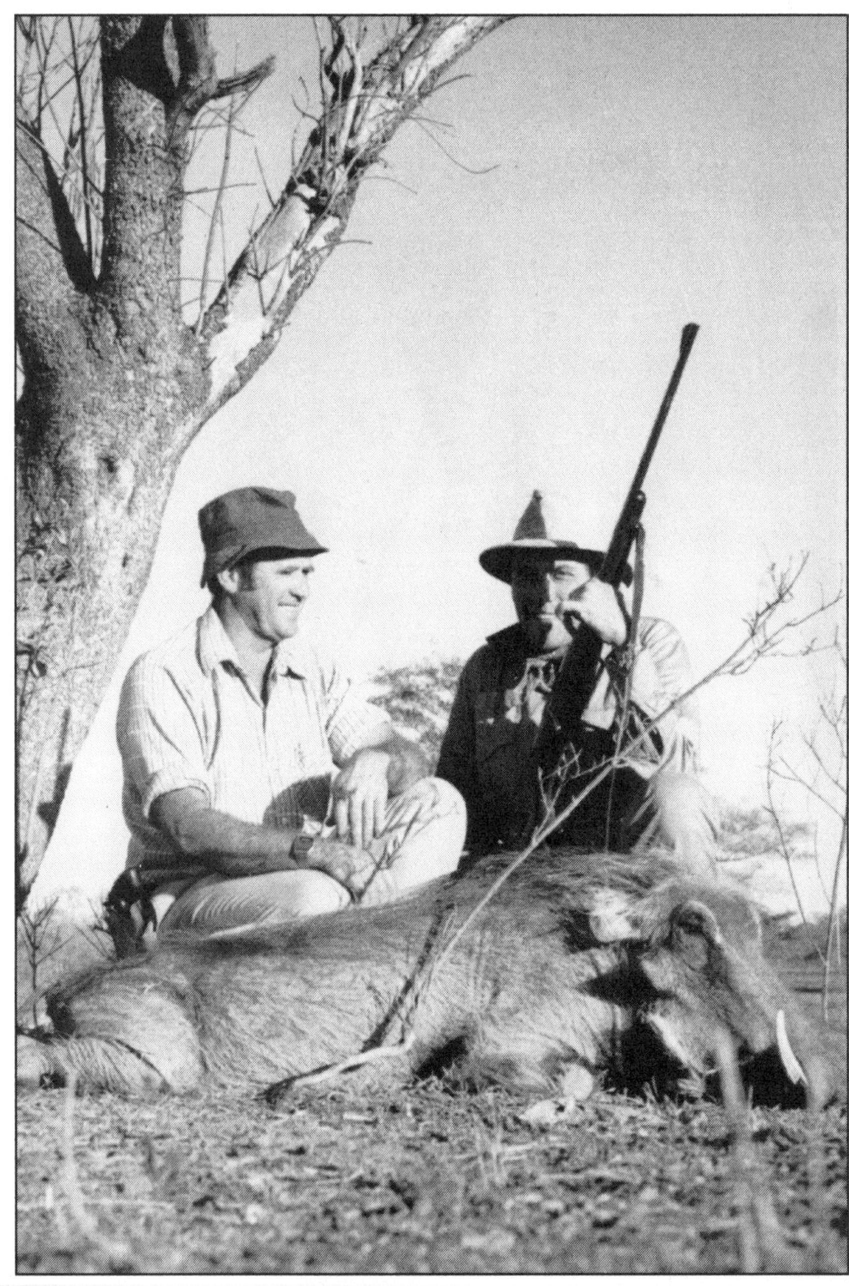

Ivon du Plessis (left) with the author and a warthog taken with Ivon's Mannlicher rifle, caliber 30-06. This was Fadala's first experience with a Mannlicher firearm, not his last.

Gun genius Ferdinand von Mannlicher created hundreds of new guns, but few will outlast the romance of the Mannlicher-Schoenauer carbine.

trigger, unset, on my carbine lets go at 3 pounds. It's actually two-stage, for there is minimal slack to take up before the trigger engages. When set, the front trigger releases cleanly at 1/2-pound. This, of course, is adjustable with a set-screw located between the two triggers. The serrated underside of the butter-knife bolt handle prevents slippage. The Mannlicher bolt works plenty fast enough for follow-up shots. As with most supposed negatives about the Mannlicher, working the bolt is no problem.

The slender stock with pancake cheekpiece promotes fast aim, and a peep is about as easy to get on target as any sight. Jumped deer in the thicket are no problem, and when hit they go down and stay there. The 9mm Mannlicher cartridge is as effective as a 358 Winchester—the way I load mine.

Going on with attributes, there is the famous spool magazine with star rotor. Each cartridge is provided an individual stall, and each round is held firmly in place. The rotary magazine loads easily, is fairly jam-proof, and unloads quickly via an auto-release button. Push the shiny button once and the magazine gives up all its rounds directly into your waiting hand. It's far faster than dropping a floorplate or working rounds from the magazine one at a time. The magazine is removable in one piece for disassembly and cleaning. All it takes is a pointed object to activate a release spring located forward on the floor of the magazine. Spring tension is mild. As with everything else on the little carbine, the magazine cleanly slips in and out with perfect fit.

Those are the major features of the Mannlicher carbine. As noted, there were numerous alternatives. Mannlicher had its own swing-away peep sight, for example, and scope mounts were available. I have not opted for a scope on my carbine, nor will I. Original factory mounts allowed sighting the irons with scope in place, proving how high the mounts truly were. The mounts were touted for their quick on/off design. Some hunters carried the scope in a pocket, relying on the iron sights for all but the long shot. When the long shot was called for, the scope came out of a pocket and was attached to the rifle. I like the easy-carrying carbine as is, no scope. My longest shot to date was around 200 yards on a whitetail buck. I don't plan to shoot farther with the little carbine.

My first experience with a Mannlicher in the field happened in Africa. The rifle, for it was not a carbine, came my way via a loan. Ivon du Plessis asked if I'd like to hunt with his 30-06, and I said sure. I had not taken my own rifles to Africa anyway, so one more model made no difference. The rifle shot beautifully, and I made a couple particularly fortunate shots with it, two on running animals. It was a Mannlicher through and through. Well made. Unique. One of a kind.

Wait for something long enough and the keen edge of expectancy is generally dulled by the grit of reality. Not so with the Mannlicher. Whether in the field, on the range or admired in the den, my little carbine has earned its keep many times over. The original-style Mannlicher may be a rifle of romance, but I can understand why so many serious hunters believed in it. I believe in mine. ●

Roy Chapman Andrews, American naturalist, carried his Savage 99, but he also favored a Mannlicher carbine and said so.

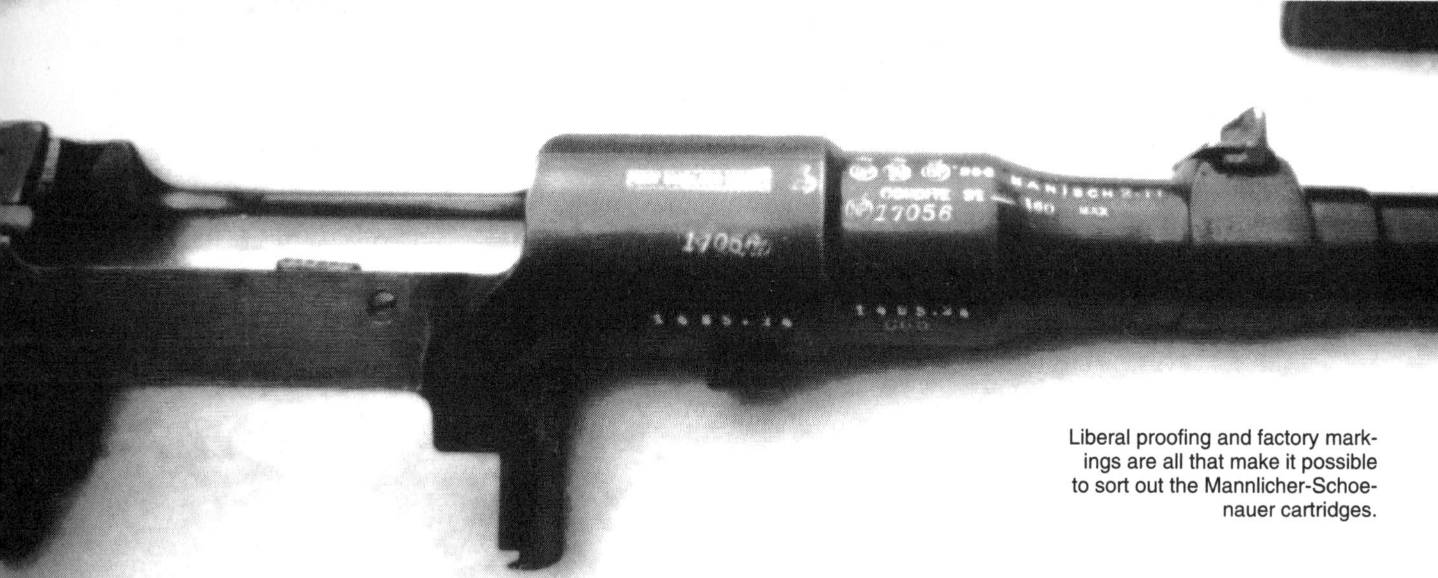

Liberal proofing and factory markings are all that make it possible to sort out the Mannlicher-Schoenauer cartridges.

Cartridges for the MANNLICHER-SCHOENAUER

by DON L. HENRY

COLLECTORS AND shooters have long searched for tidbits of information on Mannlicher rifles. The basic material was tragically "misplaced"—like many other things including entire arms factories—during a ten-year Soviet occupation of Austria which began in 1945. Steyr production records and complete serial number ranges seem irretrievably lost.

Still, that Austrian penchant for detail serves us well in dating individual pieces and directly aids in the tedious reconstruction of production chambering dates. The Austrian proof code is stamped, for instance, on each and every pre-war piece. It may be found either above or beneath the stock wood. The code line suffix is separated from the prefix by a period, dot or hyphen. The first number is the order in which the piece was tested by the proof house. The last digit(s) indicate the year of proofing—in most cases, the year of manufacture. In many cases, there is a middle number from 1 to 12. It indicates the month of proofing. For example: The proof code line 1087 .11 .29 would indicate that the piece was proof number 1087 and was passed in November of 1929. A piece bearing two such code lines would indicate reproofing after repair or refitting of anything from new sights to a new barrel.

Considerable confusion also exists regarding Mannlicher-Schoenauer chamberings. The 8mms are a case in point. There are at least three, possibly four, 8mm chamberings, and they are easily confused. The 8x56 M-S with .323-inch bore is well known. The 8x57 appears to have been chambered in both .318-inch (J) and .323-inch (S) bore rifles. My Winchester 8x57 cartridges manufactured in the '30s carry bullets of .319-inch diameter, as a hedge against uninformed Yankee shooters with .318-inch bore souvenir rifles, and were loaded to about 30-40 Krag power, which may help account for why those who forced them into 8x56 Mannlichers survived with major portions of their anatomy intact. This load, bullet size and low velocity account for the 8mm's reputation for poor accuracy, energy and trajectory. The Western 8x56 M-S load of similar vintage carries a .3215-inch bullet. One should not be surprised that an 8x56 J (.318) bore may have been produced to

CARTRIDGE CHAMBERINGS AVAILABLE IN THE MANNLICHER-SCHOENAUER

Cartridge	Introduction Date	Introduced In M-S	Catalog Listing	Discontinued In M-S	Comments/ Ammo Avail.
22 LR	c.1887	1953	Steyr 1965, Stoeger 1953, 1969	1969	Listed as "Steyr Small Bore Closed Season Model"[1]
243 Win.	1955	1956	—	1972[2]	
244 Rem.	1955	1959	Steyr 1965	U.S. 1961	Stoeger discontinued 1961
257 Robt.	1934	1950	Steyr 1965	U.S. 1961	
257 Wby.	1948	1962	—	1969	
6.5x54 M-S	1900	1900	—	1970[3]	
6.5x55	1894	—	Steyr 1965	—	
6.5x57	—	—	Steyr 1965	—	Ammo. avail. RWS/DWM 1965
6.5x68S	1938	1958	—	1967	Ammo. avail. RWS/DWM 1965
264 Win.	1958	1962	—	1969	
270 Win.	1925	1950	—	1970	Avail. entire post-war prod.
7x57	1892	—	Steyr 1935,1965, not 1929 Stoeger 1934-'39	—	Re-introduced 1952 import.[4]
7x64	1917	—	Steyr 1965 Stoeger 1934-'39	—	Ammo. avail. RWS/DWM 1965[5]
280 Rem.(7x63)	1957	1959	—	1969	
308 Win. (7.62x51)	1952	1953	—	1969	
30-06 U.S. (7.62x63)	1906	1924	Steyr 1929,1935,1965 Stoeger 1929-'39	1970	Avail. to end of production. Stoeger "Alpine" avail. 1970[6]
8x56 M-S (7.92x56)	1908	1908	Steyr 1929,1935 Stoeger 1927-'39	—	Ammo. disc. by Western Ctg. Co. 1938. Avail. RWS/DWM 1965
8x57 (7.92x57)	1903	1908	Steyr 1929,1935,1965[7]	—	
8x60S	1921	—	Steyr 1929,1935,1965 Stoeger 1934-'39	—	Ammo. avail. RWS/DWM 1965[8]
8x68S	1940	1958	—	1967	
338 Win.	1958	1962	—	1969	
358 Win.	1955	1961	—	1969	
9x56 M-S	1905	1905	Steyr 1929,1935 Stoeger 1927-'39		Ammo. disc. by Rem. c.1937, Eley 1963, last ammo. mfg.
9.3x62	1905	—	Steyr 1935 Stoeger 1934-'39	—	Chambering avail. 1952. Ammo from RWS/DWM, Norma in 1965[9]
9.5x57	1910	1910	Stoeger 1927-'39	—	Ammo. avail. from Eley 1963.[10]
9.5x60	—	—	Steyr 1929,1935	—	
400/375 H&H	1904	1910	H&H 1910[11]	—	
10.75x57 M-S	c.1900[12]	—	—	—	
10.75x68	c.1920	—	Steyr 1935 Stoeger 1934-'39	—	Not in 1929 Steyr catalog. Ammo avail. RWS/DWM 1965[13]
458 Win.	1956	1958	—	1969	

[1]The 22 LR caliber Steyr Small Bore Carbine, also known as the "Closed Season Model," while a duplicate of the 6.5 carbine in size and shape, was technically not a Mannlicher-Schoenauer. It was first listed by Stoeger's in 1953. Two three-digit serial-numbered pieces in hand are dated 1953. It was not listed by Stoeger after 1969.

[2]The engraved and carved "Alpine" and "Premier" models were still available from Stoeger's stock through 1972.

[3]Also known as the 6.5x53mm Mannlicher-Schoenauer and the 6.7x53mm (or 54) M-S, depending on whether designated by bore or groove diameter. Known in England as the 256 Mannlicher. Loadings by U.S. manufacturers ceased about 1940.

[4]The date of first Steyr factory chambering in 7x57mm remains a mystery. In 1908 the M-S was independently rebarrelled by George Knaak in 7x57 at the order of Sequoia Importing Company of California and breech marked "7.57, 1908." It was available from Stoeger in the carbine only in 1934. The 7x57 was available in 1952 and listed as late as 1965. The writer has a Model 1910 takedown factory M-S rifle, engraved and with custom dimensions, in 7x57, marked and proofed in November 1929.

[5]Available in this Model 1924 "High-Power" from Stoeger from 1934 through 1939.

[6]Introduced in the U.S. in the Model 1924 rifle by Sequoia in a separate serial number range beginning with number 001.

[7]Some specimens are originally so chambered and factory marked "8x57 Norm." for normal 8x57 cartridge. Herewith confusion may begin as Europeans popularly believed that the .318 (J) bore was inherently more accurate than the .323 (S) bore. The year of introduction of 8x57 chambering in M-S is unknown but would not predate 1908. The "S" or .323-inch chambering was available through end of production.

[8]Available in the Model 1924. This cartridge was popular in Germany to circumvent the Armistice regulation prohibiting the 8x57 cartridge.

[9]Chambered in the Model 1924 rifle, first available from Stoeger in 1934. Available from Steyr in rifle only through 1965.

[10]Also known as the 9.5x56 and 9.5x56.7. The British designation was 375 Nitro Express Rimless and 9.5 Mannlicher-Schoenauer.

[11]A proprietary cartridge designed in 1904 by Holland and offered in their c. 1910 catalog as the 375 H&H Belted Velopex.

[12]Some claim this was a Mannlicher cartridge. The author has not observed a specimen so chambered.

[13]Listed in Stoeger's 1939 catalog as available in the M1924. Not chambered prior to 1929. Available 1934-1939.

The author rests, secure in the knowledge he had done his best for history and in the possession and use of a fine rifle.

accommodate the European preference.

The rechambering of a Mannlicher-Schoenauer required extensive and tedious alteration of both the magazine spool and action rails, or complete replacement of the magazine follower spool, which, while simple in design and unfailingly reliable in function, required extensive machining in manufacture. Some cartridge changes—very few—require less work than others.

It is nearly impossible to state with any precision when various Mannlicher cartridge designs first appeared. His extensive experiments with the 6.5mm (.256 bore, .264 groove) produced the 6.5x53R Roumanian and Dutch rounds designed in 1890 and issued in quantity beginning in 1892. Frank Barnes suggests this is nothing different than a rimmed 6.5x54 M-S design. Still, it would be stretching a point to say that the 6.5 Mannlicher-Schoenauer cartridge was introduced prior to the 1900 rifle for which it was chambered and named, albeit the prototype was well known.

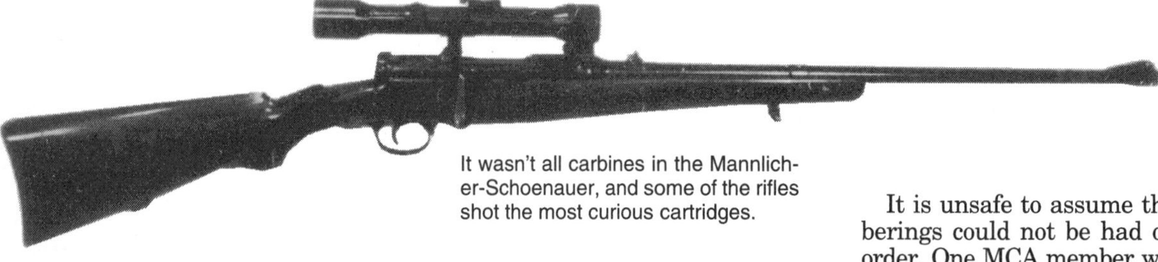

It wasn't all carbines in the Mannlicher-Schoenauer, and some of the rifles shot the most curious cartridges.

The author at a Steyr stand at a show in Europe. Knowledge is where you find it.

It is unsafe to assume that chamberings could not be had on special order. One MCA member who visited the Steyr armory reported "...bins of Mannlicher-Schoenauer cartridge magazines for virtually any caliber that was appropriate length to the action." One should not be surprised to discover a 7.5x55 Swiss chambering, a cartridge for which von Mannlicher designed other rifles and which is chambered in the current Steyr-Mannlicher rifle, although no such Mannlicher-Schoenauers are presently known or were they listed as available.

Using the Steyr proof code, serial numbers supplied by MCA members, the Mannlicher Collectors Association archive, and known model designations, a compilation has been made listing cartridge chamberings available in Mannlicher-Schoenauer rifles and carbines. The year of introduction of seven chamberings has not yet been precisely pinned down. Many were available through "end of production," but production of some obviously ceased before others due to demand or lack thereof. ●

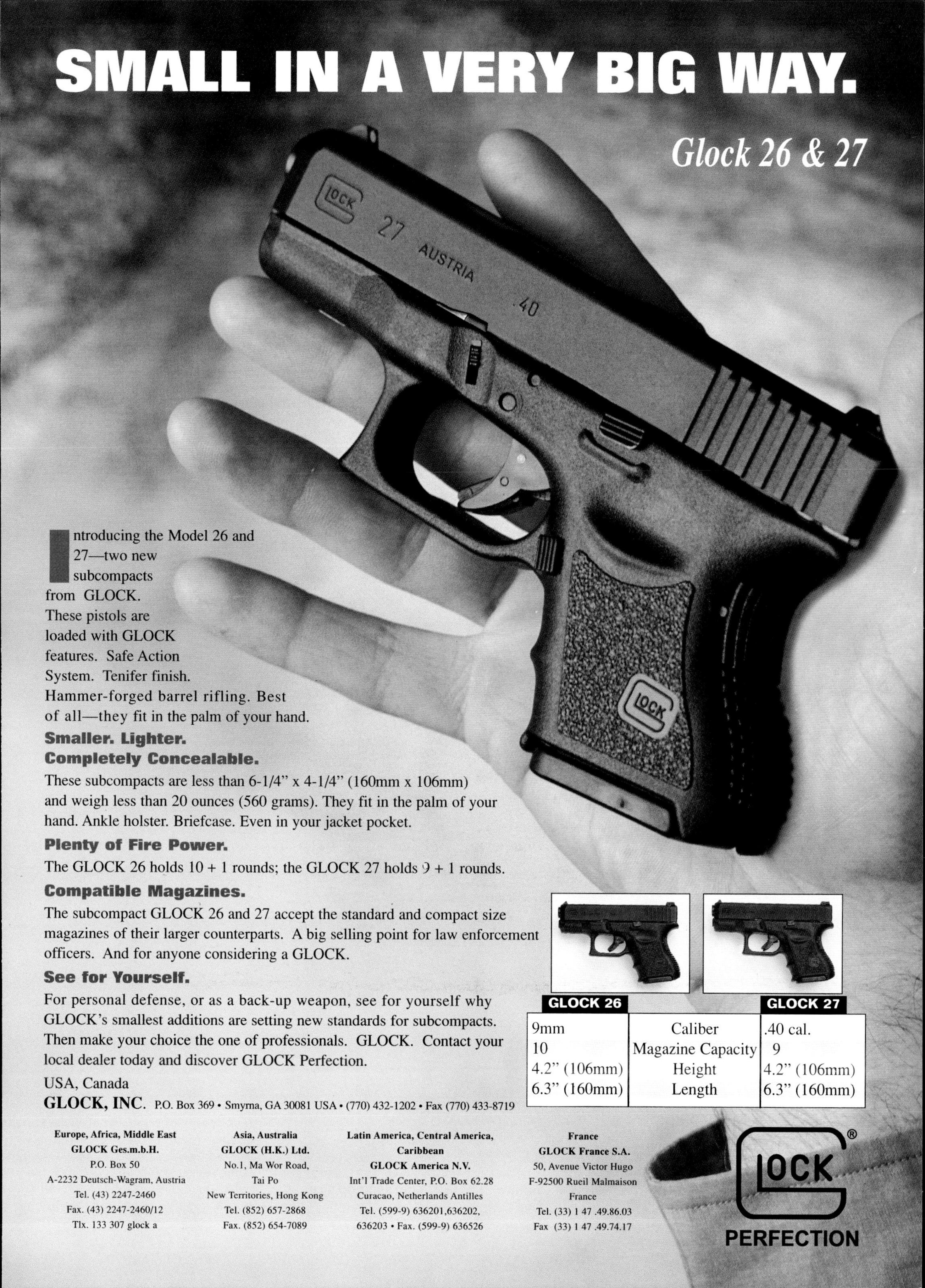

SMALL IN A VERY BIG WAY.

Glock 26 & 27

Introducing the Model 26 and 27—two new subcompacts from GLOCK. These pistols are loaded with GLOCK features. Safe Action System. Tenifer finish. Hammer-forged barrel rifling. Best of all—they fit in the palm of your hand.

Smaller. Lighter.
Completely Concealable.

These subcompacts are less than 6-1/4" x 4-1/4" (160mm x 106mm) and weigh less than 20 ounces (560 grams). They fit in the palm of your hand. Ankle holster. Briefcase. Even in your jacket pocket.

Plenty of Fire Power.

The GLOCK 26 holds 10 + 1 rounds; the GLOCK 27 holds 9 + 1 rounds.

Compatible Magazines.

The subcompact GLOCK 26 and 27 accept the standard and compact size magazines of their larger counterparts. A big selling point for law enforcement officers. And for anyone considering a GLOCK.

See for Yourself.

For personal defense, or as a back-up weapon, see for yourself why GLOCK's smallest additions are setting new standards for subcompacts. Then make your choice the one of professionals. GLOCK. Contact your local dealer today and discover GLOCK Perfection.

GLOCK 26		GLOCK 27
9mm	Caliber	.40 cal.
10	Magazine Capacity	9
4.2" (106mm)	Height	4.2" (106mm)
6.3" (160mm)	Length	6.3" (160mm)

USA, Canada
GLOCK, INC. P.O. Box 369 • Smyrna, GA 30081 USA • (770) 432-1202 • Fax (770) 433-8719

Europe, Africa, Middle East
GLOCK Ges.m.b.H.
P.O. Box 50
A-2232 Deutsch-Wagram, Austria
Tel. (43) 2247-2460
Fax. (43) 2247-2460/12
Tlx. 133 307 glock a

Asia, Australia
GLOCK (H.K.) Ltd.
No.1, Ma Wor Road,
Tai Po
New Territories, Hong Kong
Tel. (852) 657-2868
Fax. (852) 654-7089

Latin America, Central America, Caribbean
GLOCK America N.V.
Int'l Trade Center, P.O. Box 62.28
Curacao, Netherlands Antilles
Tel. (599-9) 636201,636202, 636203 • Fax. (599-9) 636526

France
GLOCK France S.A.
50, Avenue Victor Hugo
F-92500 Rueil Malmaison
France
Tel. (33) 1 47 .49.86.03
Fax (33) 1 47 .49.74.17

Your Best Shot & Your Best Buy...

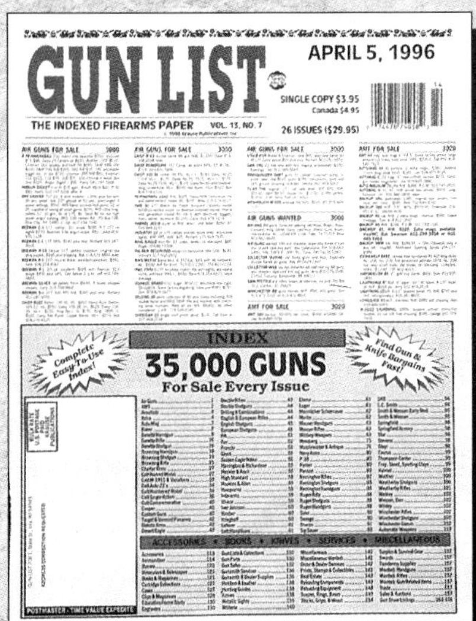

Gun List

The nation's only alphabetized, indexed firearms publication for buyers and sellers of antique and modern guns.

Biweekly • 13 issues (1/2 year) for only **$16.95** (ABAMZN)

6th Edition

Standard Catalog of

Firearms

The latest and most accurate prices available put you in control when buying, selling or trading.

8-1/2x11 • softcover • 1,116 pages • 2,300 b&w photos • **CG06 $29.95**

700 E. State St. Dept DGB1, Iola, WI 54990-0001

Credit Card Calls Toll-free 800-258-0929 Dept. DGB1

Monday-Friday, 7 am. - 8 p.m. Saturday, 8 a.m. - 2 p.m., CST

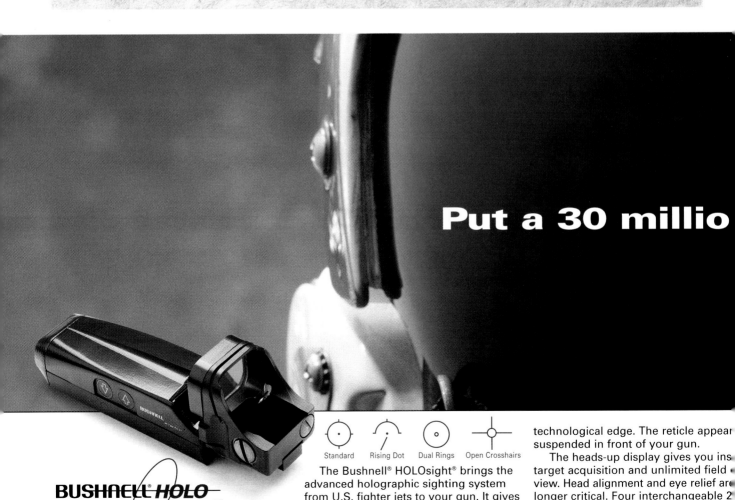

Put a 30 millio

Standard | Rising Dot | Dual Rings | Open Crosshairs

BUSHNELL HOLO sight®

The Bushnell® HOLOsight® brings the advanced holographic sighting system from U.S. fighter jets to your gun. It gives handgunners, slug and wing shooters a technological edge. The reticle appear suspended in front of your gun.

The heads-up display gives you ins target acquisition and unlimited field view. Head alignment and eye relief ar longer critical. Four interchangeable 2 and 3-D reticles give flexibility to char

...Accurate, Invaluable, Yet Affordable

10th Edition – **The Gun Digest Book of**

Modern Gun Values

Current values of all guns from 1900-1995, including more than 1,000 introduced since the last edition.

8-½ x 11 • softcover • 560 pages • 2,500 b&w photos • **MGV10 $21.95**

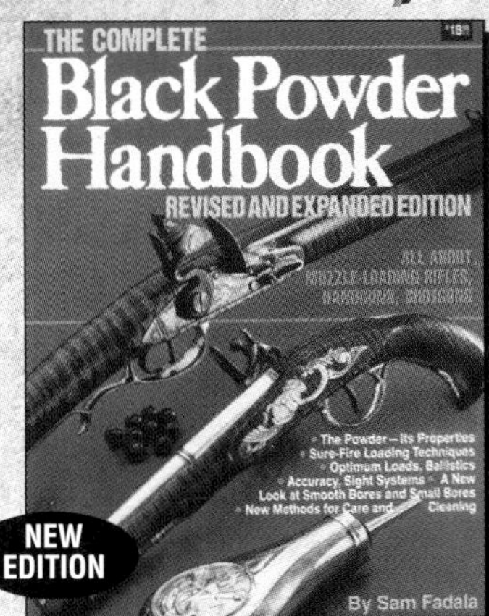

3rd Edition – **The Complete**

Black Powder Handbook

The bible for the black powder shooter, enlarged and rewritten to cover every aspect of the black powder world.

8-1/2 x 11 • softcover • 416 pages • 600 b&w photos • **BPH3 $21.95**

Flayderman's Guide to

Antique American Firearms

and Their Values, 6th Edition

Completely updated. More than 3,600 models and variants, 2,800 individually-priced firearms and much more!

8-1/2 x 11 • softcover • 640 pages •1,600 b&w photos • **FLA6 $29.95**

$3.25 shipping first book, $2.00 each additional
Foreign addresses $10.00 first book, $5.00 each additional
WI residents add 5.5% sales tax; IL residents add 7.75% sales tax.

a division of Krause Publications, Inc.

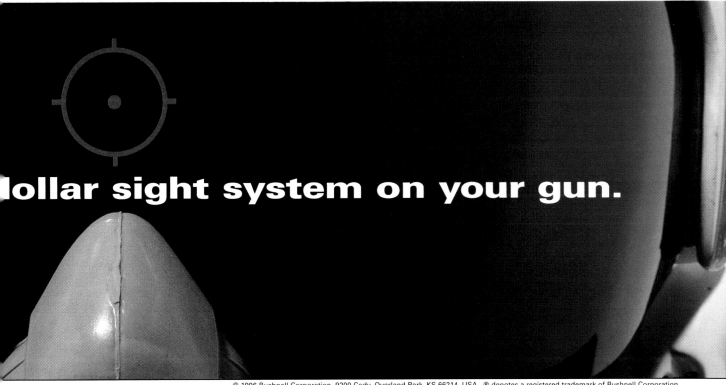

ollar sight system on your gun.

© 1996 Bushnell Corporation. 9200 Cody, Overland Park, KS 66214, USA ® denotes a registered trademark of Bushnell Corporation.

patterns in the field. And it's waterproof and fogproof.

To experience this next generation in gun sight technology, you have to see through it. Call (800) 423-3537 for the dealer nearest you. Bushnell® HOLOsight,® another example of leadership and vision.

BUSHNELL®
HOW THE WORLD LOOKS

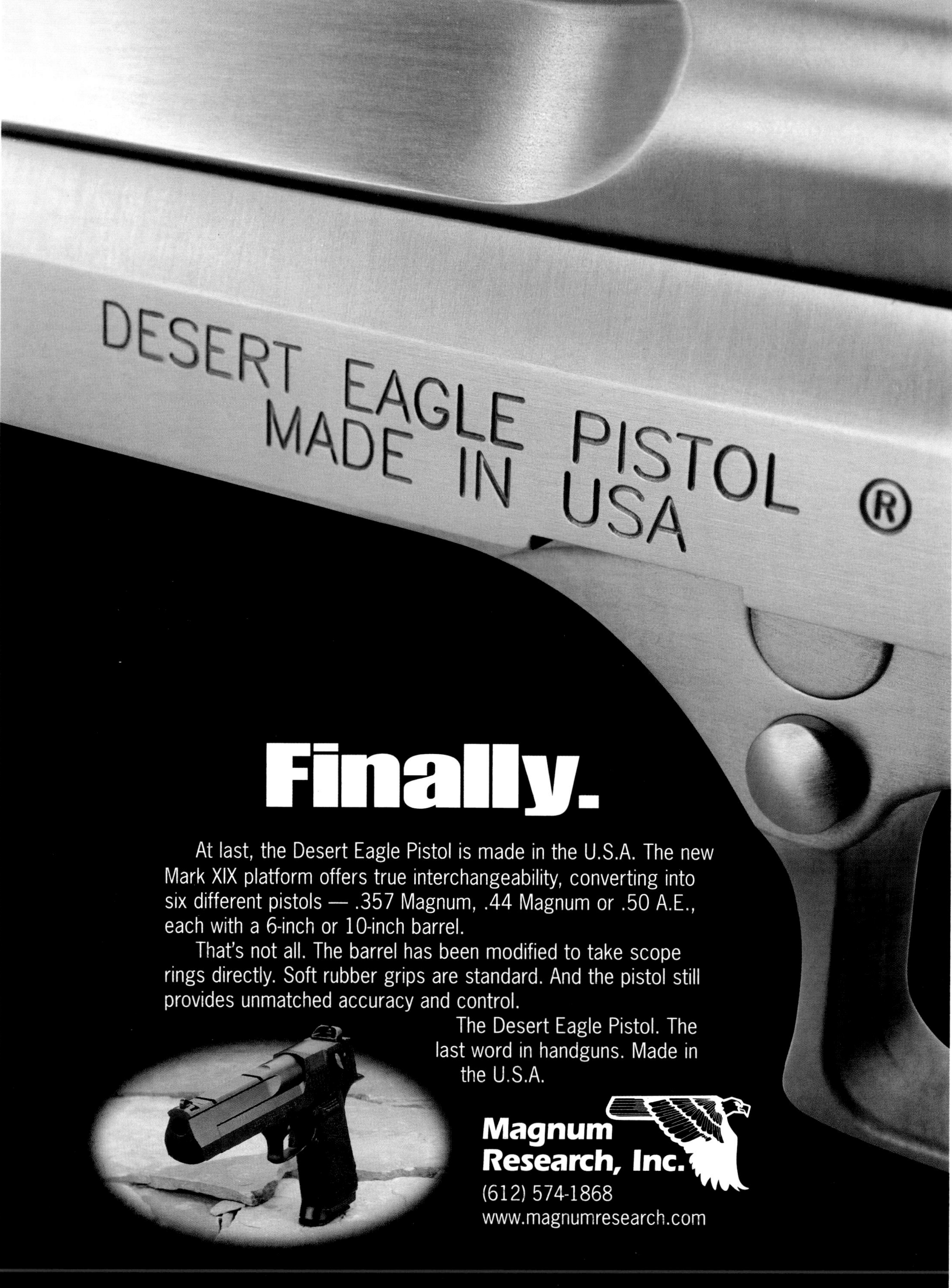
DESERT EAGLE PISTOL ®
MADE IN USA
Finally.
At last, the Desert Eagle Pistol is made in the U.S.A. The new Mark XIX platform offers true interchangeability, converting into six different pistols — .357 Magnum, .44 Magnum or .50 A.E., each with a 6-inch or 10-inch barrel.
That's not all. The barrel has been modified to take scope rings directly. Soft rubber grips are standard. And the pistol still provides unmatched accuracy and control.
The Desert Eagle Pistol. The last word in handguns. Made in the U.S.A.
Magnum Research, Inc.
(612) 574-1868
www.magnumresearch.com

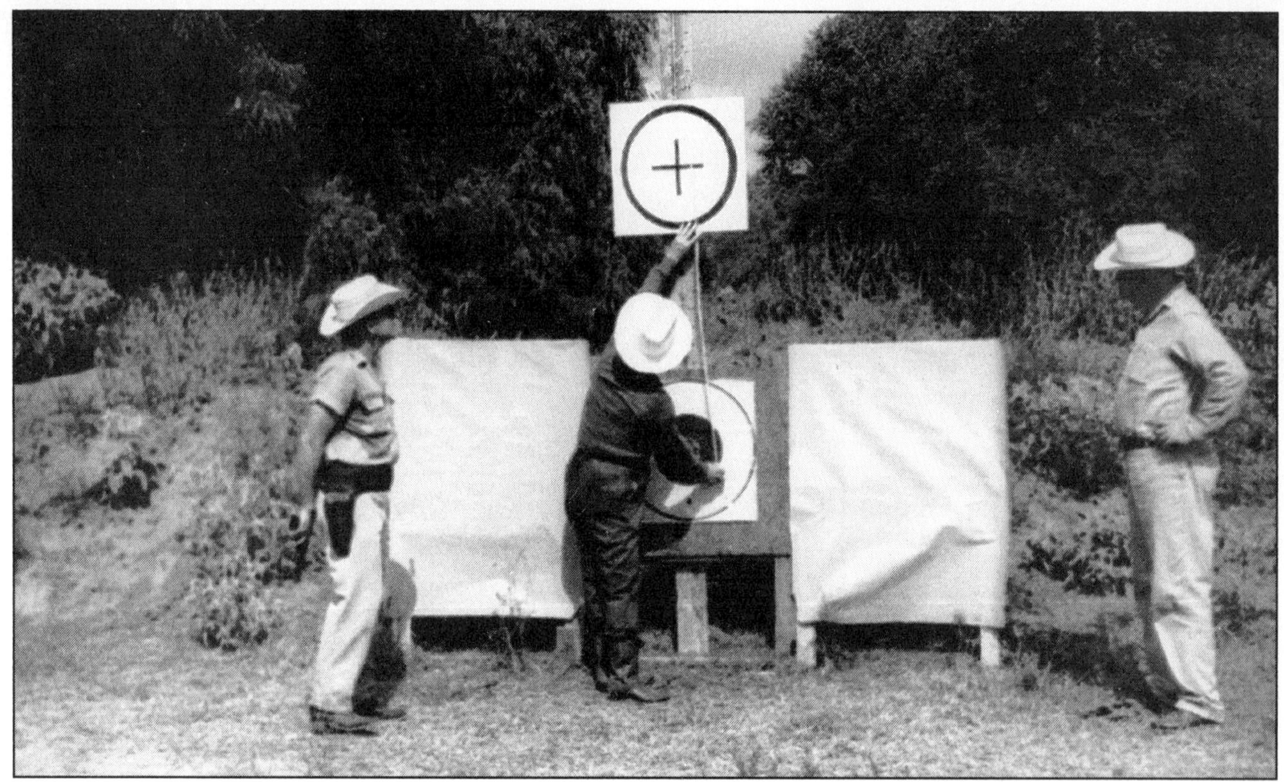

The writer did not get his bullet-drop numbers out of a book, or even a computer. He actually measured them.

GAME FIELD DISTANCES

by Col. CHARLES ASKINS

GAME RANGE YARDAGES are tough to calculate because a feller always wants to make them shorter than they are. There stands a really trophy bull elk, a real old buster with six tines on the one side and seven on the other.

"He's the Bull of the Woods," the guide announced.

"Shall I try him?" the dude whispered, visibly shaking.

He'd been at the La Baca Land & Cattle Co. Rancho for five days, and every day the guide had restrained him. Now they had the biggest wapiti west of the Mississippi virtually in their sights.

"What's the distance, you reckon," the client asked breathlessly.

"Oh, 'bout four-fifty, I figure," the guide speculated. "Better hold over him 'bout a foot-an-a-half."

The brand-new elk hunter got down behind a monster boulder, placed the 30-06 across the support and, after long moments of agonizing, pulled the trigger. The 180-grain spirepoint hit the ground at the feet of the mighty bull. That was all the inducement he wanted; he hightailed it like he had been stung by hornets.

My observation of Western guides when it comes to calculating the gun-to-target yardage is that they are pretty sketchy. Most of them have never stepped off a quarter-mile in all their lives, and looking across the canyon at the mule deer over there is not conducive to any accurate accounting of the actual distance. By the same token, the visiting sportsman travels everywhere he goes by auto so his in-the-field background is even more scanty.

A dozen years ago, an enterprising scope manufacturer announced he had the solution, not only to the poor judgment of the guide, but also the scanty background of the shooter. He had a scope with an adjustable reticle, and all you had to do was to bracket the game between the two stadia wires and a set of figures on the periphery of the scope would tell you the yardage. Of course, this was just ducky. The only small drawbacks were that the old bull wapiti had to be standing broadside, he had to hold that pose until you could fiddle with your adjusting wheel and, maybe even more importantly, the animal had to be of normal dimension. Beyond this, the game couldn't be spooky; he had to hold like a statue while you went through all the mechanics and finally got off the shot. Needless to say, this great scope idea didn't exactly set the woods on fire.

During WWII, I was stuck in Merrie Auld England for a few months awaiting the African invasion, and it fell to my lot to teach mortar gunnery. Now, any idiot can drop an

81mm round down the uptilted tube, but it takes a pretty slick Roger to decide the range. Mortars are high-trajectory weapons, and unless the gunner cranks on the right elevation, his round is just as apt to fall among friendly troops as enemy infantry.

To train the mortar squad to set in the proper range, we taught distance estimation. We did this by carefully chaining off yardages to the crossroads, to the old red barn, to the far clump of trees and to the schoolhouse. After we had measured these targets, we asked the class to write down what they thought the distances might be. The misses would have been ludicrous had it not been so gravely serious. Needless to say, the country boys made the best mortarmen. They had a pretty good idea of the distances simply because they had walked a lot and knew country distances pretty well.

A surprisingly large number of big game hunters honestly believe that the rifle and its cartridge will shoot out to maybe as far as a thousand yards without dropping an inch. I was in a whitetail camp last season, and a feller there told me that his 30-06 would shoot out to 600 yards before the bullet commenced to drop at all: "I get my ammunition from Austria. I wouldn't shoot any of this American stuff, and it goes faster and don't drop hardly at all."

This was interesting news, and I asked to see one of his cartridges. It was Norma, not loaded in Austria, and with the conventional ballistics.

I hunted with an old general officer one time. He was out of the Army Medical Corps, and he said, "I always let my buck get out there about 600 yards before I shoot because I don't want to ruin so much meat."

I never saw him make any of those 600-yard shots, and I have always had some misgivings about his judgment of distance.

Editor's Note

The legendary Col. Charles Askins, who was never called Chuck, has been ill a couple of years now. Thus far, he gets off a pithy, not to say crunchy, note or two each year, but that's about it. We miss this crafty, forthright and outrageous old soldier.

KW

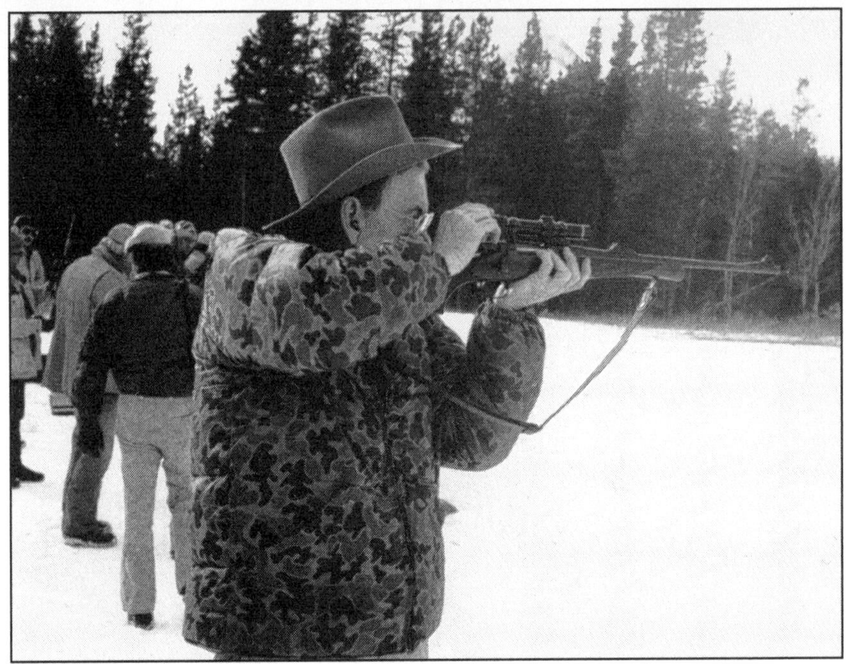

The writer fiddles with his brand-new 7mm-08 Model Seven at a strange range in Alberta. He was properly zeroed, but neither he nor this Editor even saw a deer closer than a mile on that hunt.

Talk to the average camp of sportsmen and you'll have to give each hombre there the third degree with a lot of arm twisting to get him to admit that he ain't much on estimating the muzzle-to-game yardage. On the contrary, the majority will tell you quite confidently that he never has any problems in that regard.

During many autumns, I have journeyed off to Wyoming and there joined up with about twenty-five invitees, all guests of the Tasco Scope Co. These laddy-os are mostly jobbers of the telescope line, and the opportunity to collect a Wyoming pronghorn is a once-in-a-lifetime chance. The misses were frequent, and the wounded animals plentiful.

The little American antelope is visible on a completely bald prairie; there ain't no trees, no shrubbery, nothing to use as a point of reference as to the distance. Viewed through the Tasco scope, he looks pretty goodsized, and the shooter elects to give the game a whirl. The bullet strikes the ground at the little buck's feet, and he fires up the afterburner and goes hence.

If the hunter is honest with himself, he will select a rifle loading that will compensate in great part for his lack of range estimation. There are a half-dozen loadings that out to as far as 300 yards can be depended on to hit the game. Frankly, 300 yards is just one hell of a long way, but I like to limit my chance to only 300 long steps. Even this yardage seems almighty long when you view a piddling little whitetail buck so far away. He may weigh not more than 120 pounds, and the shoulders from top to bottom only measure 16 inches. There are, of course, many much bigger whitetails, but not in my country.

One of the best loads for our most common deer is the 270 Winchester with 140-grain bullet—not 130-grain, mind you, and not the more common 150-grain. Another real performer is the 25-06. This old buster with 120-grain loading will be down only 11 inches at 300 yards. This means you will want to hold right at the top of the shoulders to plop the 120-grain slug into the very middle of his shoulder.

The 6mm is popular with American sportsmen; they fire it in the 243 Winchester and the 6mm Remington, and thousands of whitetails are axed annually with the tiny little cartridges. As for me, I shoot only the best when the 6mm is in contention. I fire the 240 Weatherby Magnum which, with its 100-grain slug, falls only 5.7 inches at our extreme distance.

Another Weatherby offering which is dear to my heart is their 257 Magnum. This hotrock, with the 117-grain bullet sighted in for 100 yards, pitches downward but 6 inches at our max distance of 300 steps. In the 270 Weatherby Magnum, with the 130-grain bullet, the velocity is 3375 fps and the trajectory out to 300 yards permits the ball to strike only 5.5 inches low.

Tasco executive George Rosenfield with a Wyoming pronghorn that didn't get away, deceptive apparent ranges or not.

It is said that more deer have been killed with the ancient 30-30 Winchester than all the other calibers combined. I suspect there is a considerable modicum of truth in this statement, but let me assure you the experienced nimrod who goes afield with the 1894 model is almighty careful not to try any over-in-the-next-county shots. He levels down on his buck at sane yardages. Like 100 short steps. And that is unquestionably the prime reason the 30-30 had accounted for seven trainloads of defunct bucks.

The old 30-30 with its 170-grain bullet falls 31 inches getting out to 300 yards. Another good old-timer is the 7x57mm; it has killed a raft of deer and game around the world as well. With the 140-grain bullet, which is common to this ancient round, it will fall 17 inches at 300 yards. Not bad, but indicative that the 7x57 will be a lot more effective at only 200 steps.

The old '06 with 150-grain bullet will kill whitetail bucks like nuclear reaction, but it is a bit too much gun in my opinion. At our max yardage of 300 steps, the 150-grain falls off only 13 inches, which is quite acceptable. The 308 with the same slug doesn't do quite as well. It pitches downward 16 inches. You wouldn't catch me trying it beyond 200 yards. Or maybe 250.

One happy solution to our problem is to hunt in a country where the game is not only plentiful but anything save wild. I don't know of any spot like that in North America, but that is one solution. I shot one time in Kenya for thirty-five days, and when I returned home I wrote to Jack Boone, who was then the sales manager for Winchester. (My rifles had both been Model 70 shooting irons.) I told Boone the average distance for my kills—I had shot some kind of a beastie every day—was 120 yards, stepped off.

He wrote back and said, "I reckon you are the only honest man who ever reported on his safari shooting. Most of 'em tell me they shoot at not less than 400 yards."

There are a few sensible practices to observe when hunting critters like our whitetail and mule deer, or little pronghorn and the lordly wapiti. Don't try a shot offhand! No one, but no one, can hit a barn off his hindlegs. Find some manner of rest. If you can still assume the sitting position by all means do that; if you are too potbellied, then kneel and, sitting on the left foot, get the shot off that way. If there is any kind of a rest handy, use it—a tree limb, a log, a big boulder or whatever offers. Whatever you find, don't rest the rifle so the naked barrel touches the support.

The truth of the matter is that the run-of-mill big game sportsman ain't much of a marksman. He simply does not get enough practice to have any high degree of skill. This may be because of the press of everyday affairs, or it may be due to the lack of a suitable shooting range, or it may be simply due to his lack of interest. He likes to hunt the wily whitetail in season, but his enthusiasm only bubbles during the active hunting time.

City hunters are god-awful judges of game field yardages because modern living lays a high premium on getting here to there via the ever-present auto. As a solution, the really deeply interested sport ought to join a big bore rifle club. These jazbos fire out to 1000 yards with intermediate ranges like 200, 300, 500, 600 yards, and the city boy who measures his distances in blocks can get a pretty accurate idea of what 300 yards looks like.

It is a popular pastime these modern days to walk. The enthusiast turns out in the early morning and hikes two miles. If he is to gain any real good from the drill, he ought to hit about a 20-minute-to-the-mile gait. This means the morning stint will take up only 40 minutes of his busy day. Also, he should measure his stride. Most of us step 30 inches to the stride. By counting the steps taken, the hiker may look back over his course and get an accurate idea of the distance he has traveled. This is extremely good training for the hunting man. He gets, over a period of time, to judge distance with considerable precision. This is worth a very great deal when he gets into the game fields once again.

These days a bull wapiti will cost well over $3000, a whitetail will go not less than $1000, and a Kodiak brownie will also be more than $5000. If a feller is going to invest his shekels to this extent, he ought to be trained to shoot straight and know his ranges. ●

Big beech logs are often cheaper and easier to get—and beech is tougher than walnut.

An expert tells us about all those military stock woods, which were...

NOT ALWAYS WALNUT

by DAVID A. WEBB

OFTEN, IN ARTICLES concerning military weapons, there is a fair amount of detail with regard to barrel, action, bolt, sight equipment, furniture on the rifle stock (buttplate and sling swivels), bayonet, cleaning rod, and the like. But seldom does one find much of anything written about the wood in the stock.

Occasionally, mention has been made of the fact that American black walnut (*Juglans nigra*) was used to stock, for example, the bolt-action Springfield A303, and the same wood was also used when the Garand M-1 was adopted as the standard foot-soldier's weapon. Also, some not-too-favorable comments have been echoed when the wood stock on the M-1 was changed from walnut to birch (*Betula alleghaniensis*). For the most part, however, the switch in wood species on the M-1 was "down-played" by the military. They even went so far as to stain the lighter colored birch to resemble the dark color of walnut. In some instances, when comparing the physical characteristics of birch and walnut, there are some properties of birch that are superior to those of walnut. Of those, the most important would be "toughness," also often referred to as shock resistance. Birch is tougher than black walnut.

The most commonly used wood *has* been walnut—that includes both the predominant walnut species—black and Old World (*Juglans regia*), which also goes by other common names of Circassian, English, French or Turkish walnut. Essentially, *Juglans regia* has been named according to the region or country in which it grew.

At one time or another, these two walnut species were used to stock the military rifles of most nations in the four continents of North and South America, Europe and Australia. Some of the Asian countries used local wood species for their stocks.

Therein lies one of the major considerations: The availability and supply of a species often determined its use as gunstock material. Of course, of additional concern was the physical characteristics, such as the strength properties of toughness, hardness and shear resistance, along with relative stability concerning movement due to moisture variations. Another primary factor of consideration was a wood's machinability.

And which wood species had the most satisfactory wood properties to make a gunstock? In those early years (i.e., late 19th century), that could be a difficult question to answer. There just were not the types of test procedures and equipment to compare the various wood properties. A wood species was selected as gunstock material based on actual field evaluations—extensive military field tests. To select a military weapon, rigorous field tests were conducted. The wood stock was an integral part of those military arms. The stock was the handle to which the metal was attached. Those field tests showed that walnut was a relatively stable wood and its dark color provided "built-in" camouflage.

Walnut was available and in abundant supply for military stocks, but it wasn't the only wood used. If one looks around, other species will include European beech (*Fagus sylivatica*); birch (*Betula alleghaniensis*); Philippine mahogany or lauan (several species including *Dipterocarpus turbinatus, Pentacme contorta* and *Shorea guiso*); sycamore—both North American and European species (*Platanus occidentalis* and *Platanus acerifolia*); and teak (*Tectona grandis*). Also, believe it or not, I have seen one Austrian Steyr Model 95 and one Swedish Mauser Model 96 manufactured at the Carl Gustaf works stocked with European elm (*Ulmus campestris*). For the most part, these woods were used as solid material; however, there were two exceptions.

With their Model 98k carbines, the Germans introduced the use of laminated wood in military gunstocks.

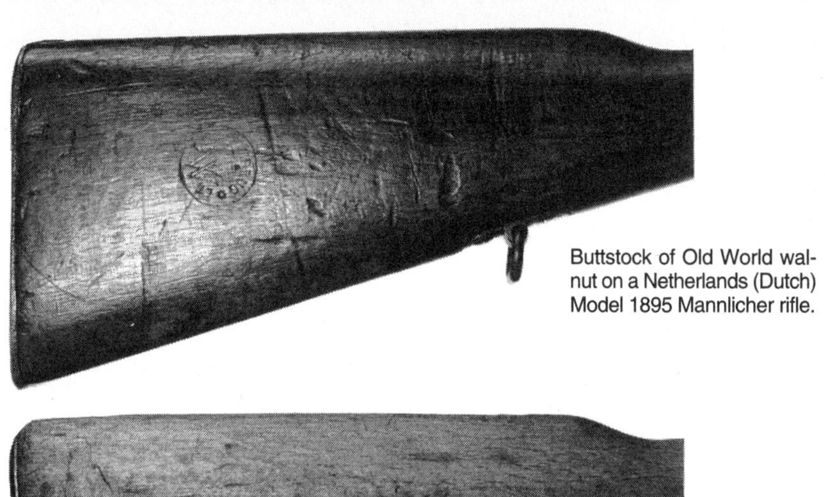

Buttstock of Old World walnut on a Netherlands (Dutch) Model 1895 Mannlicher rifle.

This Berthier buttstock is European sycamore, not your usual stuff.

On top, this is an original black walnut stock on sniper rifle; below, that's a replacement stock of European beech.

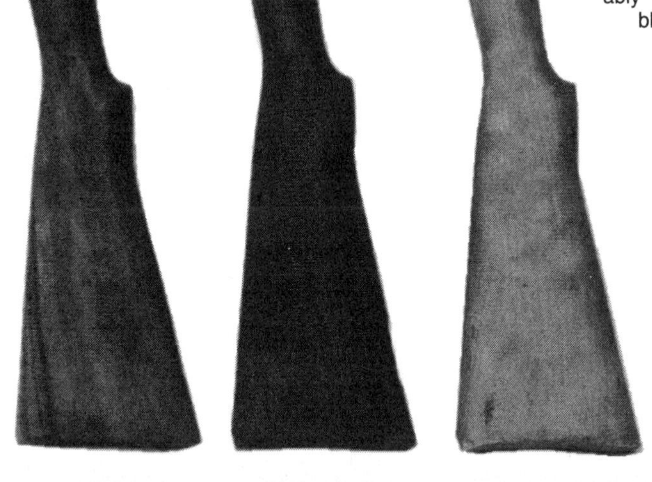

Replacement SMLE and No. 4 buttstocks—used interchangeably—in crabwood, black bean and yellow birch.

The laminated stock was prepared using thin veneers of beech, about 1.5mm thick, glued together under hydraulic pressure with a phenolic-resin adhesive. This construction was stronger, more durable and less liable to warp than solid beech or walnut stocks. The laminated stock was heavier and more difficult to manufacture, but overall it was most efficient for military use.

Another different utilization of wood for military stocks was the

These Berthier Carbines, Model 1892/17, were arsenal reworked in Turkey. At top, it's European sycamore, and on bottom, it's European beech.

Japanese two-piece glued buttstock. Most of the stock was the conventional single piece of wood with a wood handguard forward of the receiver ring; however, the butt portion was two pieces, dovetailed and glued together. This method permitted using relatively narrow boards (from smaller trees) and was initiated with the Arisaka Type 30. Subsequently, stocks for all remaining models of Japanese bolt-action service rifles were made thus.

The Type 30 rifle in my collection and several others I have examined have all been stocked with European beech. The military stock would normally start with a 2x6-inch board. However, by using the dovetail-glue joint technique, it was possible to use a 2x4-inch piece of wood, roughly a 30-percent wood-material savings.

The use of beech was not unusual. Although Old World walnut was generally the preferred stock wood for most European military small arms, European beech was often used interchangeably. The choice depended on availability and cost.

European beech is light brown and was usually given a walnut stain. The practical reason for staining was to darken the wood and reduce light reflection, and to maintain visual uniformity.

The Japanese also used Philippine mahoganies. These woods are also often known as lauan. They are somewhat lighter in weight and not as strong as beech. They are quite similar to our own hemisphere's mahoganies (*Swietenia mahagoni* and *Swietenia macrophylla*). The Philippine varieties are, however, not true mahogany species.

European beech was apparently used quite extensively for gunstock material. Specimens of military weapons stocked with this wood can be found on just about any country's military shoulder arms. Some Brazilian Mauser 98s were stocked with Imbuya (*Phoebe porosa*). The Italian Carcano carbine and rifles were stocked using beech. Often, when the arsenal "reworked" a weapon and it was necessary to replace the stock, the replacement was other than walnut. In my collection, there are two examples of the French Berthier carbine, Model 1892/27, which were reworked at the T.C. Orman Arsenal in Turkey and stocked using both beech and sycamore. The 1948 date stamped on the front of the receiver indicated these carbines were recently reworked by the Turkish for reissue. Bill Rogers of Springfield Sporters, Inc. in Penn Run, Pennsylvania, who recently purchased quite a few of these 8mm Lebel-chambered carbines, was informed the Turkish government reworked the carbines at the T.C. Orman Arsenal for issue to the forestry department for "homeguard" purposes.

The British Lee-Enfield probably has had more different wood species used to stock it than any other military longarm. Ian Skennerton reported in his very excellent book, *The British Service Lee,* that in 1928 the British government initiated a series of tests on alternate supplies of timber for stocking their military weapons.

The alternate wood species and their source locations that were evaluated are listed as follows:

Australia—black bean, Tasmanian myrtle, Tasmanian oak
British Guiana—crabwood
Canada—yellow birch and hard maple
Europe—beech and birch
New Zealand—Southland beech
West Africa—Benin mahogany and iroko.

The woods were tested for their strength properties of hardness, impact bending, compression and tensile strength. Also, other non-strength properties such as moisture retention, pH high acid content which can cause excessive corrosion of the metal hardware, abrasion, and the effect of oil and charing were observed. The results of these tests concluded that an order of preference was developed for stock material for the Lee-Enfield: hard maple, European beech, yellow birch, Tasmanian myrtle and Southland beech.

The Lee-Enfield rifle was also manufactured in Australia. The production was centered at Lithgow, which is west of Sydney in the state of New South Wales. The No. 1 Mark III SMLE was initially stocked in walnut supplied in an unfinished form from England. Shortly thereafter, the Australian wood known as coachwood (*Ceratopetalum apetalum*) was used to stock the Enfield rifles produced in Australia. Skennerton reported that during the 1920s a switch was made to another Australian wood, Queensland maple (*Flindersia brayleyana*).

Coachwood and Queensland maple are lower density woods than walnut, and both are easier to machine and more prone to split. To reduce this tendency, the Aussies put a threaded brass rod in the forearm as a crossbolt.

The nearby table lists more than twenty different woods that were found to have been used to stock military weapons. When the Editor first suggested the subject of different woods and military stocks, I initially thought of a half-dozen or so—birch on the M-1 Garand, European beech on the Lee-Enfield and several others. Most certainly, it was not expected that twenty-four wood species would be uncovered as being used to stock military rifles from various nations. In most instances, Eastern black and Old World walnut were the preferred military stock woods; however, when walnut was in short supply or arsenal "reworking" was to be performed, then locally available woods were substituted for the walnut woods. In general, these woods usually had physical properties somewhat similar to walnut. They were often lighter in color and thus required a dark-colored stain. All twenty-four species worked, however, in the military stock. •

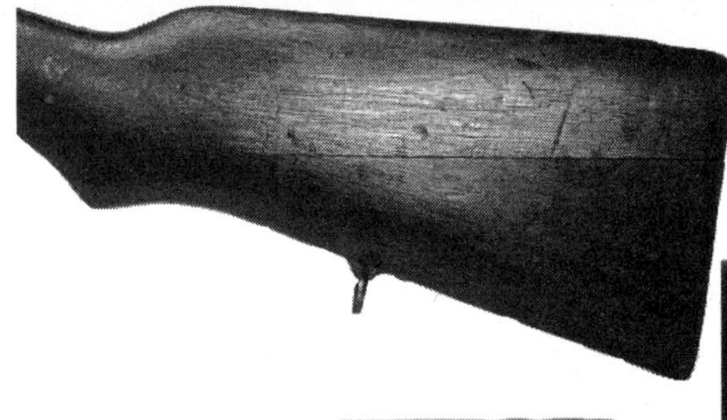

Buttstock showing the dovetail joint of a Siamese Mauser produced at the Japanese Tokyo Arsenal. This one's made of teak.

Typical dovetail-joint on a Japanese Type 99; the wood is lauan (Philippine mahogany).

Laminated stock glued up, using 1.5mm thick veneer layers of European beech. This was standard for the Mauser 98K in World War II.

Military Stock Woods

Common Name	Botanical Name	Density(1) (lbs/cu.ft.)	Shrinkage(2) (%) Volumetric	Color Appearance
Beech, European	*Fagus sylivatica*	42	—	medium reddish brown
Black Bean	*Castanospermum australe*	39	14.0	deep dark brown
Birch, European	*Betula pendula*	42	—	pale light brown
Birch, Yellow	*Betula alleghaniesnsis*	43	13.4	light brown
Borneo Camphorwood	*Dryobalanops spp.*	45	7.0	light to dark reddish brown
Coachwood	*Ceratopetalum*	39	10.2	pinkish brown
Crabwood	*Carapa guianesis*	40	8.3	reddish to dark brown
Elm, European	*Ulmus campestris*	38	—	light to medium brown
Imbuya	*Phoebe porosa*	38	—	golden medium brown
Iroko	*Chlorophora regia*	40	7.5	dark brown
Mahogany, Benin	*Khaya grandifolia*	40	7.5	dark brown
Maple, Hard	*Acer saccharum*	44	11.9	very light brown
Maple, Queensland	*Flindersia brayleyana*	35	9.3	very light pinkish brown
Philippine Mahogany or Lauan	*Dipterocarpus turbinatus, Pentacme contorta, Shorea guiso*	28-45	9.1	pale pink to purple-brown and dark reddish brown
Southland Beech	*Nothofagus menziesii*	39	8.5	light brown
Sycamore, European	*Platanus occidentalis*	35	—	light brown
Sycamore, North American	*Platanus acerifolia*	35	11.4	light brown
Tasmanian Myrtle	*Nothofagus cunninghamii*	44	9.0	reddish brown
Tasmanian Oak	*Eucalyptus obliqua*	38	15.0	light yellowish brown
Teak	*Tectona grandis*	38	4.4	golden brown
Walnut, American Black	*Juglans nigra*	38	10.2	chocolate brown
Walnut, Old World or English	*Juglans regia*	33	9.4	medium brown often with dark brown pigmentation streaks

(1) Based on 12-percent moisture content: data from *Wood Handbook, No. 72*, USDA, Forest Service, Forest Products Laboratory, Madison, WI.

(2) Calculated using data from green to 6-percent moisture content.

by LAYNE SIMPSON

RIFLE REVIEW

THE YEAR 1996 brings us lots of new long guns. There are lever-action rimfire and centerfire rifles from a company that has never offered a lever-action rifle, and a bolt-action rifle from a company best known for its lever actions. Then there's a rather novel bolt-action rifle from a company best known for making screw-in shotgun chokes. And what about a muzzleloader built around the great Remington Model 700 action. Perhaps your cup of tea might be a highly modified custom Remington 700 weighing less than a fistful of feathers. Bush pilots who fly over unforgiving country are sure to take to a custom takedown rifle in 45-70 that stows neatly behind the seat of a Super Cub. Two wildcats are slated for domestication during this year, and a grand old cartridge called the 300 Savage is taking yet another bow. Last, but certainly not smallest or slowest, Roy Weatherby's fastest 30-caliber cartridge, an old wildcat that for many years held the world's record for the smallest ten-shot group fired in 1000-yard competition, is now available in a super-accurate big game rifle. Finding out more about those exciting things requires no more effort than simply moving on to the next paragraph in this report.

A-Square

Now a member of SAAMI, A-Square plans to domesticate a number of semiwildcat cartridges for which its rifles are chambered. Among those scheduled for 1996 are the 7mm STW and 358 STA, cartridges of my design that A-Square has been factory-loading for a couple of years. I have been shooting a couple of Hamilcar-grade rifles in those calibers, and both are extremely accurate.

Briley

In January, I examined a prototype of a bolt-action rifle totally designed and built by Briley Manufacturing. The barreled action was quite conventional in design, but the action rested in an alloy receiver and two-piece stock. I can't say whether or not the rifle will ever go into full production, but I can say its design is quite interesting and rather novel, as centerfire rifles go.

Browning

Called the Lightning BLR, it is a lighter version of Browning's lever-action rifle and is available in calibers ranging from 223 to 7mm Remington Magnum. It has an aluminum alloy receiver, a curved grip and a more hand-filling forend than the standard model.

Also new is a Model 1885 variant in 45-70 called the BPCR which, in case you haven't already figured it out, is short for Black Powder Cartridge Rifle. The oil-finished walnut stock and forend have cut checkering, while the 34-inch barrel has a matte blue finish. The rifle also has a Vernier sight mounted on its tang and a globe-style front sight with spirit level. Other features include case-colored receiver, buttplate and finger lever. While this rifle is obviously aimed directly at long-range blackpowder shooters, I'd really rather don my buckskins and go shoot a bison with it.

The Eclipse is a new A-Bolt variant with thumbhole-style stock of laminated wood. It is available in standard and varmint versions, the latter with a heavy barrel. This rifle and other Browning centerfires are available with a new version of the BOSS system which has no muzzlebrake.

Clark Custom

While the name Jim Clark is most often associated with super-accurate 1911 Colt handguns and Bullseye competition, he also specializes in fine-tuning Ruger Models 77/22 and 10/22. I recently had Clark sprinkle his magic dust on a Model 77/22 in 22 Hornet, and the improvement in accuracy was quite satisfying. While wearing its factory barrel, the rifle had averaged 2.52 inches for two five-shot groups at 100

Look closely and you'll see Simpson's Bausch & Lomb Elite binoculars—as important as the rifle.

Marlin's MR-7 comes with or without open sights and in 270 or 30-60 caliber—very trim.

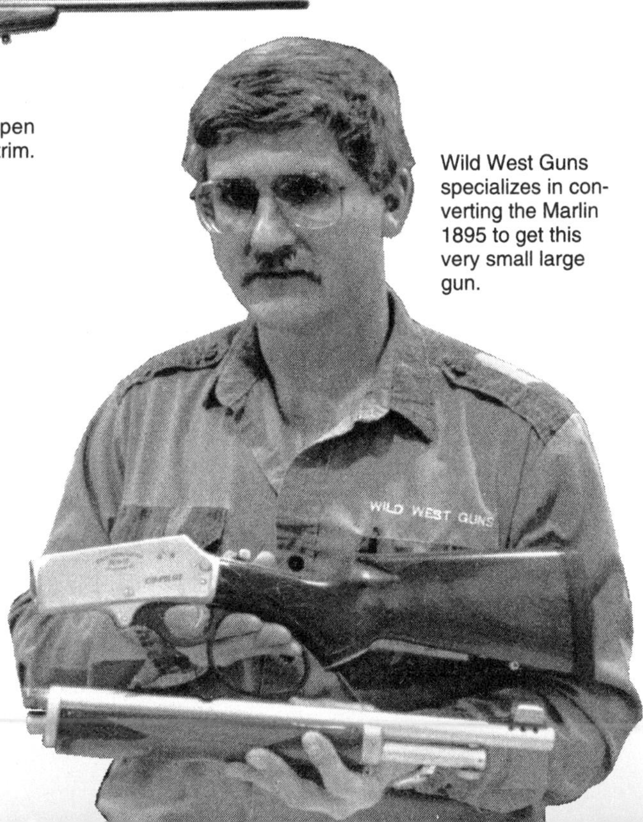

Wild West Guns specializes in converting the Marlin 1895 to get this very small large gun.

yards with each of eleven handloads and four factory loads. The best accuracy I got was 1.78 inches, using the Sierra 50-grain Blitz. The 1:14-inch rifling twist of its barrel allowed the rifle to stabilize heavier (and therefore longer) bullets than is possible with the slower 1:16 twist, which has always been common for barrels in 22 Hornet. After Clark installed a heavy match-grade barrel with 1:16 twist, the rifle chalked up an overall average of 1.20 inches, and six loads averaged less than an inch. The most accurate combination utilized H110 and the Sierra 40-grain hollowpoint.

All in all, I am quite happy with Clark's conversion, but do wish I had specified a 1:14 twist so the new barrel would stabilize longer bullets such as the Nosler 40- and 50-grain Ballistic Tips, the Sierra 50-grain Blitz, the Speer 50-grain TNT and the Hornady 50-grain SX. With their thin jackets and soft lead cores, those bullets will expand just as violently as 40- and 45-grainers made specifically for the 22 Hornet, and they are much easier to find.

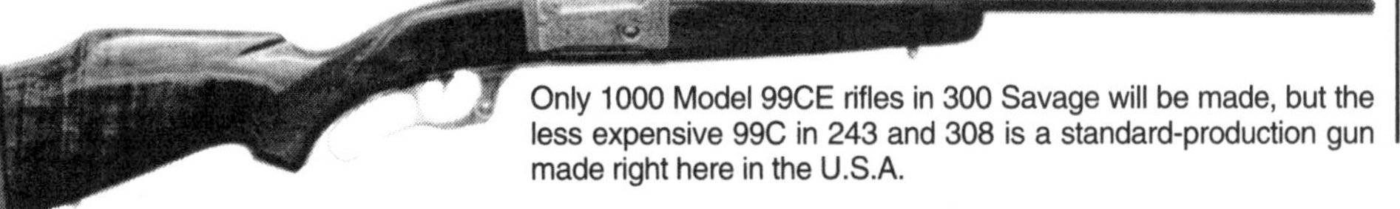

Only 1000 Model 99CE rifles in 300 Savage will be made, but the less expensive 99C in 243 and 308 is a standard-production gun made right here in the U.S.A.

Shorten the barrel on your old Winchester Model 9422 to $16^1/_2$ inches and it will be a lot like USRA's new Model 9422 Trapper.

Ruger's new Model 96 looks like the old 44 autoloader with a lever, but it differs in a number of ways.

H&R 1871

It is said that a portion of the sales from the H&R single shot rifle in 35 Whelen will go to the Rocky Mountain Elk Foundation. The rifle has a 26-inch barrel, a buttstock and forend of laminated wood, and rollmarking on its receiver that identifies it as a limited-production rifle.

Harris Gunworks

Designed for various competitive shooting sports, a new version of the Signature action from Harris Gunworks features a right-hand bolt, but the ejection port is on the left side. For southpaw shooters, a mirror image of that action is available with left-hand bolt and right-side ejection. Standard and belted magnum boltface sizes are available.

Magnum Research, Inc.

The action of the Mountain Eagle is made for MRI by Sako, the Finnish rifle manufacturer, and is quite similar to the action around which that company builds its own rifles. Latest additions to the lineup are a left-hand version in various chamberings from 270 Winchester to 416 Remington Magnum. The Varmint Edition rifle is also new. It comes with a heavy 26-inch stainless steel fluted barrel in calibers 222 and 223 Remington. All variations of the Mountain Eagle have synthetic stocks.

Marlin

Back in the fall of '94, I hunted elk in New Mexico with a prototype rifle built by Marlin. It eventually evolved into the new MR-7, the first bolt-action centerfire rifle built in its entirety by this ultra-conservative old Connecticut company. The MR-7 has a blued steel barreled action, a classic-style walnut stock with cut checkering, and chamberings, for now, in 30-06 and 270 Winchester. Other features include a three-position safety-lever, cocking indicator, and detachable box magazine. Marlin's new bolt action is available with or without open sights made by Williams. The one I shot averaged $1^1/_2$ to 3 inches at 100 yards for five-shot groups with a variety of factory loads.

New variations of existing Marlin rifles for '96 are the Model 1894 Cowboy with its 24-inch tapered octagonal barrel in 45 Colt, the Model 2000L target rifle with a black/grey laminated wood stock, and the Model 880SQ. The latter is an economy-grade, heavy-barrel squirrel rifle with a black synthetic stock.

Precision Sales, Inc.

This long-time importer of Anschutz firearms is now bringing Walther rifles into the U.S. Their lineup includes a variety of competition-grade 22 rimfire and air-powered rifles and pistols.

Remington

The biggest news from Remington for '96 is an in-line muzzleloader built around the famous Model 700 action, in either 50 or 54 calibers. The blued steel gun is called the Model 700ML, and its stainless steel mate is called the Model 700MLS. In October of 1995, I had the opportunity to wring out one of the three rifles then in existence. I also hunted deer with it at as a guest of Hayward Simmons of Cedar Knoll near Allendale, South Carolina. Hayward's operation is top-drawer, and he is one of the most successful whitetail outfitters in the business.

I attached a Leupold 4x scope to the new Remington 50-caliber muzzleloader. I got the best accuracy with the 370-grain Maxi-Ball seated atop 80.0 grains of Pyrodex RS Select. The average muzzle velocity was 1208 fps, and five-shot groups averaged 2.7 inches at 100 yards. Second-best accuracy, of 3.3 inches, was with the Remington 44-caliber 275-grain bullet resting in a T/C sabot and seated atop a T/C Natural Wad. I got a muzzle velocity of 1311 fps with the same charge of Pyrodex. As we have come to expect from any variation of the Model 700, the trigger pull was truly outstanding.

Also new for '96 is a stainless steel version of the extremely accurate Model 700 Sendero. With its medium-heavy 26-inch fluted barrel in 25-06, 7mm Remington Magnum and 300 Winchester Magnum, this one is just the ticket for reaching out to touch a trophy buck. And shooters who simply must have a muzzlebrake can now get one on the Model 700 BDL/SS/DM/B, which is the BDL rifle with a synthetic stock, stainless steel barreled action, detachable magazine and muzzlebrake. Belted magnum chambering options are 7mm Remington, 300 Winchester, 300 Weatherby and 338 Winchester. I shot one in 300 Magnum and found its brake to be most effective—loud, but most effective.

Jim Clark transformed the author's Ruger 77/22 in 22 Hornet into an even better rifle for close- to medium-range varminting.

The receivers of Model 700BDL

bolt action, Model 7600 slide action and Model 7400 autoloader rifles are now covered with some of the most attractive engraving you'll ever see on standard-production guns. Remington officials say it won't increase the prices of those rifles by one cent. The samples I examined were more tastefully executed than some hand engraving I've seen.

Last but certainly not least, during a recent visit to Remington's new research and development center in Elizabethtown, Kentucky, I enjoyed a sneak preview of a new variation of a Model 700 we may see introduced sometime in the near future. On the outside it looked like any other Model 700, but on the inside the rifle had an electronic trigger and ignition system. Remington's version uses plain old brass cartridge cases. I shot the rifle, and one thing was certain—locktime was about as fast as we are likely to get until someone comes up with a telepathic trigger.

Rifles, Inc.

Lex Webernick of Rifles, Inc., specializes in building superlightweight rifles around the Remington Model 700 action. I used one of his rifles on a high-country elk hunt and was most pleased with it. It had a 26-inch barrel in 7mm STW and weighed only 6 pounds with its Leupold 3-9x compact scope. Lex makes rifles that feathery in heft by using a thin barrel and an extremely light synthetic stock made in his shop, and by removing metal from non-stress areas of the action. The rifle I hunted with averaged .80-inch for three shots with one of my favorite elk loads, the Nosler 160-grain Partition seated atop a maximum charge of Hodgdon's old H5010 or Hodgdon's new H50BMG.

Ruger

The big news from Ruger for '96 is their lever-action carbines. They include the Model 96/22 in 22 LR, the Model 96/22M in 22 WMR and the Model 96/44 in 44 Remington Magnum. All have Ruger's extremely successful rotary magazine, a ten-rounder in the 22 LR, a nine-rounder in the 22 WMR, and a four-rounder in the 44-caliber gun. The receivers of the 22s are drilled and tapped for scope mounting. An integral base on the receiver of the 44 accepts Ruger's easy-on, easy-off rings. From a distance, you'd swear one is the 10/22 with a lever and the other is a lever action variation of the handy little 44-caliber autoloading woods gun Ruger once made. The one-piece hardwood stocks have a curved buttplate at the rear and a barrel band up front. Barrel length is 18½ inches for all calibers. Nominal weight is 5¼ pounds for the 96/22, and 6 pounds for the 96/44.

Several years ago, gunsmiths across the country began to discover that the Ruger 10/22 could be transformed into an incredibly accurate shooting machine by simply attaching a top-quality barrel to its aluminum receiver and perhaps tuning its trigger a bit. Not one to let any popular bandwagon travel too far down the road before hopping aboard, Ruger has now introduced a heavy-barrel version of the 10/22. Weighing 7½ pounds, the 10/22 Target also features a laminated wood stock and a lighter trigger than on the standard rifle.

Savage

During 1996, Savage will offer its Centennial Edition of the famous Model 99 lever-action rifle. Only 1000 will be built, with serial numbers running from AS0001 to AS1000. The Model 99CE has a gold-plated trigger, engraved receiver, and fancy American walnut stock with cut checkering. The caliber is that grand old classic, the 300 Savage. Savage is also bringing back a made-in-America Model 99C with a 22-inch barrel in 243 or 308 Winchester.

Several new variants of the Model 110 bolt gun are also new for '96. There's the Model 114CE Classic European, stocked in oil-finished walnut replete with Schnabel forend tip and skip-line checkering. It has a quick-detach magazine and is available in 270, 30-06, 7mm Remington and 300 Winchester.

The Model 111FAK Express has a blued steel barreled action sitting in a synthetic stock. Its features include Savage's popular Adjustable Muzzle Brake and chamberings are the Model 114CE's plus the 338 Winchester Magnum.

Southpaw varmint shooters, beanfield snipers and sendero sitters take note: The extremely accurate Model 112FVSS is now available with a pillar-bedded left-hand action. It wears a synthetic stock, weighs 9 pounds and is available in 223, 22-250, 25-06, 308, 30-06, 7mm Remington and 300 Winchester. Also available in those same calibers, the Model 112BVSS has a pillar-bedded action in a laminated wood stock that was designed for shooting from prone. It weighs 10½ pounds and is also available in a single shot version called the Model 112BVSS-S.

Savage is back in the 22 rimfire business with a line of bolt actions and autoloaders in various configurations. Called the Model 64G, the selfloader has a 20-inch button-rifled barrel, ten-round detachable magazine, rotary safety button and manual bolt hold-open latch. The lightweight alloy receiver is grooved for scope mounting, and the hardwood stock is Monte Carlo in style with checkered wrist and forend. The lineup of bolt actions begins with variations called Mark IG (single shot), Mark IIG (repeater) and Mark IIGXP (gun packaged with 4x scope). The Mark IG and Mark IIG are also available in youth versions replete with 19-inch barrel and short buttstock. Then we have the new Model 93G bolt gun in 22 WMR with its 21-inch barrel and five-round detachable magazine.

Rounding out the line is a series of new target rifles, all with five-round detachable magazines, 21-inch heavy free-floated barrels, and available in right- and left-hand versions. The aperture sight on the receiver of the Target and Biathlon has quarter-minute click adjustments, and the hooded front sight of the latter has a hinged snow cover. The Silhouette has no iron sights, but comes with scope mount already installed.

Sigarms

If you remember the Colt Sauer rifle, you will probably also recall that its bolt traveled to and fro as smoothly as the bolt of a well-oiled 1898 Krag. The Colt Sauer is still available, but today it is called the Sauer 90. It has a Monte Carlo-style stock with cut checkering and high-gloss finish. It is available in various cartridges ranging from 243 Winchester to 375 H&H Magnum. Barrel lengths are 23.6 inches for standard cartridges and 26 inches for belted magnums.

The latest rifle from Sigarms is the switch-barrel Sauer 202 with optional right- or left-hand action. They say its bolt rotation is a bit less (60 versus 65 degrees) than that of the Sauer 90 and its locktime is a bit faster (3 versus 4 milliseconds). Six locking lugs on its bolt engage recesses in the barrel rather than in the receiver ring. Barrels are hammer-forged of Krupp steel and are easily changed with only simple hand tools. One of these rifles with

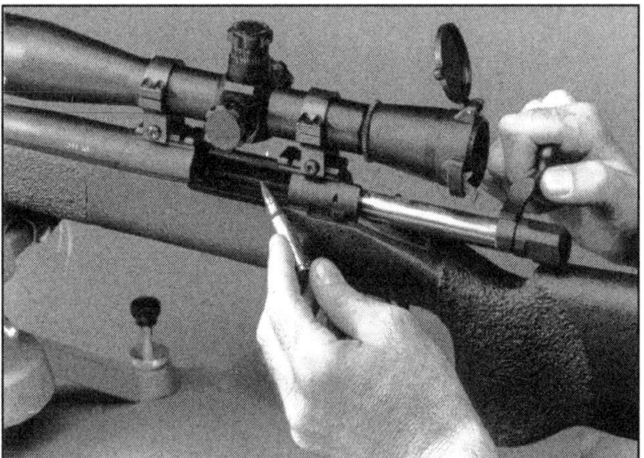

The Harris Gunworks Signature action is available with a right-hand bolt and left-hand load/eject port (shown here) or a mirror image for southpaws.

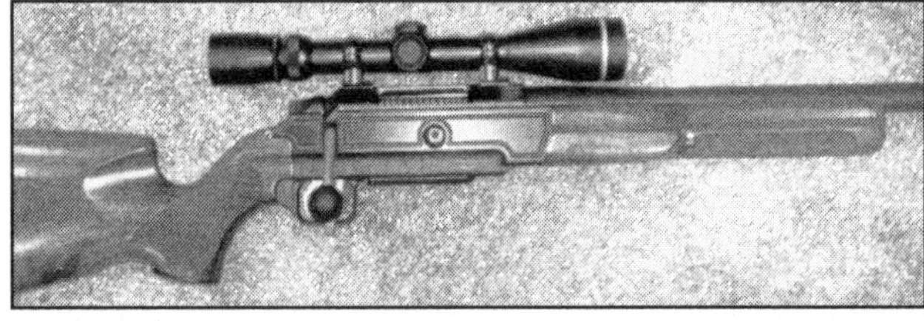

The new Briley rifle has an action of conventional size and shape resting in a precision-machined alloy receiver with two-piece stock.

barrels in 7mm Remington Magnum and 375 H&H Magnum would be both practical and fun. Other caliber options are 243, 270, 308, 30-06 and 300 Winchester Magnum. The Sauer 202 I handled was a bit lighter than the Sauer 90, but the balance was about the same.

USRAC

Plinkers and small game hunters will like what they see from U.S. Repeating Arms for 1996. The Model 9422 Trapper with its 16.5-inch barrel in 22 Long Rifle has an overall length of 33 inches and about half that when taken down for toting in a backpack. Also new is the Model 70 Laredo with its 26-inch barrel in two magnum calibers, 7mm Remington and 300 Winchester. The barreled action rests atop an aluminum bedding block in the synthetic stock.

Weatherby

I hope you will forgive me for taking a tiny bit of credit for Weatherby's domestication of the old 30-378 Magnum wildcat, but I'll have to do so in order to explain how it all came about. On a number of occasions during the past few years, I had urged Ed Weatherby to add this biggest of the Big 30s to his list of chambering options for the Mark V rifle. My persistence began to pay off in 1993 when Ed sent me a Mark V action for rebarreling to 30-378 and asked for a report on its performance. I sent the action to Kenny Jarrett for installation of one of his 26-inch match-grade stainless steel barrels and a Clifton synthetic stock. When the rifle was completed, I was not the least bit surprised by its performance; I mean, after all, it's a Jarrett. The Nosler 180-grain Ballistic Tip and Sierra MatchKing of the same weight seated atop a hefty charge of H5010 averaged just over 3500 fps and consistently punched out three-shot groups at 100 yards measuring less than half an inch. The Nosler 180- and 200-grain Partition bullets (either of which would be fine medicine for use on elk, moose and such) averaged just under .80-inch.

In the 48th edition of GUN DIGEST, I briefly reported on the Jarrett rifle and mentioned that if Weatherby eventually decided to domesticate the 30-378 it would probably be in a new super-accurate version of the Mark V rifle called the Accumark. Then, while on a hunt in Alaska with Ed Weatherby and Brad Ruddell, also of Weatherby, I kept the ball rolling by talking long and hard about what a great long-range big game cartridge the 30-378 is. Finally, in late 1995, I was informed that during 1996 Norma would load the ammo for Weatherby and the chambering would be offered in a new rifle called the Mark V Accumark. For now, this chambering is available only in that rifle, but I expect to see it added to the Custom and Stainless variants of the Mark V in the near future.

The Webernicks of Rifles, Inc., proudly show off their fine custom rifles at the '96 SHOT Show.

I received the first Mark V Accumark built in 30-378 and put it through its paces with three Hodgdon powders, H5010, H870 and the new H50BMG which will eventually replace the old war-surplus H5010. I also burned a bit of Accurate 8700. Two loads averaged less than minute of angle for five-shot groups. I also shot several ten-shot groups at 300 yards, and the Ballistic Tip chalked up the smallest at 2.8 inches. The most accurate elk load for five shots (1.28 inches) was the Nosler 180-grain Partition pushed to 3460 fps by a big charge of H50BMG. Handloaders should note that since the Weatherby chamber is free-bored, it will handle a few grains more powder than rifles with standard-length chamber throats.

Introduction of the Mark V Accumark itself is Weatherby's second big news item for 1996. It has a blued steel action and a match-grade 26-inch medium-heavy stainless steel fluted barrel with a muzzle diameter of .70-inch. The rifle has a synthetic stock with an aluminum bedding block. Weighing about $8^1/_2$ pounds, the Accumark should be just the ticket for hunting in country where the shots are long and the miles are short. I can't imagine a better beanfield rifle for the Southeast, and it's just the ticket for reaching down a long sendero and surprising a big Texas buck. In 30-378 Magnum, it will have no peer among factory-built rifles for sitting on this side of a wide canyon and dropping a big bull elk on that side. Chambering options include all Weatherby Magnums from 257 to 340 as well as the 7mm Remington Magnum and 300 Winchester Magnum.

I can remember when Weatherby offered only one standard-production rifle, the Mark V Deluxe, but that certainly has changed. In addition to the Deluxe and Accumark, there are the Stainless, Euromark, Lazermark, Synthetic, Sporter and Eurosport. Add the three options from the custom shop, Safari Grade Custom, Crown Custom and Weatherby Custom, and you've got eleven choices. I like all the Weatherbys, but will have to admit that the Euromark is my favorite of the standard rifles, with the Sporter in a close second place.

Wild West Guns

I recently examined a Marlin 45-70 Model 1895SS made into a takedown by Wild West Guns. The shop also performs the same trick to the Marlin 444SS in 444-caliber. Called the Alaskan Co-Pilot, it was designed for bush pilots who need lots of power in a compact and relatively light package, one easily stowed behind the seat of a Super Cub or other small plane. Various options include barrel lengths ranging from 16 to 22 inches, muzzle-brake, Pachmayr Decelerator recoil pad, 4-pound trigger pull, custom open sights, blued or chrome finish.

One Great Piece Of Gear

I am asked to field-test many new products each year. Most are used a time or two and then discarded, passed on to someone else, or returned to the manufacturer for various reasons. Every once in a while, an item is so good it stays with me until something better comes along. One case in point is my Bausch & Lomb Elite 8x42mm, a binocular I have used on almost all my hunts during the past eight years simply because nothing better has come along. Truth of the matter is, if something else as good has come along, I have not discovered it.

My B&L Elite has survived the frog-drowning downpours of moose and bear hunts in Alaska; the dust, heat and bouncing safari cars of Africa; and many other places in between. Among the binoculars I've tested (some selling for upwards of three grand), no other has come close to matching the optical quality of the Bausch & Lomb Elite. Even more important, I have looked into its precision-ground lenses for hours and days on end without experiencing the slightest trace if eyestrain. Yep, it's one great piece of gear.

And they say the new Elite is even better. ●

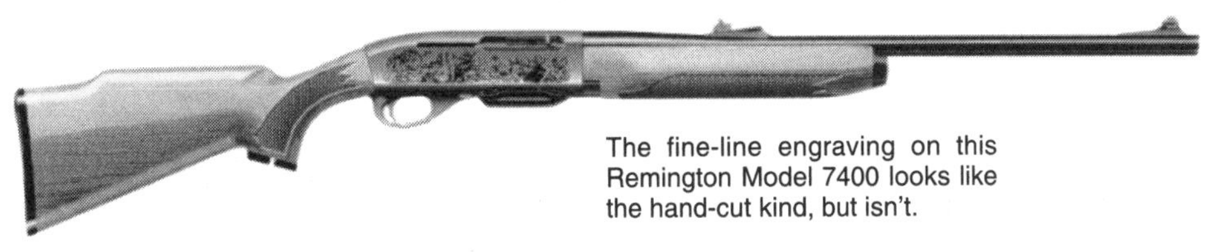
The fine-line engraving on this Remington Model 7400 looks like the hand-cut kind, but isn't.

SHOOTING COMPETITIONS, with live turkeys as bullseyes, were one way 19th-century farmers and homesteaders asserted their proficiency with the rifle, a frontier tool as basic as the axe and the plow. The turkey shoot of days gone by was a social affair, a backwoodsman's holiday and a strong Appalachian tradition since the settlement era of Davy Crockett, Daniel Boone, and their pioneer compatriots. As the bullfight was to Mexico, so was the turkey shoot to Appalachia.

Like Colonial snuff-the-candle and drive-the-nail competitions, turkey shoots let scattered neighbors and mountaineers gather as a community, to be among friends. This Kentucky institution's vitality, color, and appeal hadn't diminished with the turning of the century. The early 20th-century turkey shoot was of tremendous cultural importance, preserving the heritage of fathers and grandfathers. The occasions were always happy ones with a festive gala atmosphere.

Shortly after 1900, most states had banned the use of live birds as targets in sporting contests. Kentucky, in 1910, ignoring the kinder and gentler example legislated by neighboring Ohio, Indiana and West Virginia, was one of the very few states still shooting at living crea-

THE LONG PEWEE

tures. And just an hour's trolley ride eastward of Louisville, past rich truck gardens, cozy villas, and smiling farm houses, lay Pewee Valley. Amongst the bluegrass, in a bottom along the East Fork of Beargrass Creek, was the Swiss range, where the Louisville Rifle and Revolver Club shot.

The Louisville bunch was ardent and active, keenly devoted to preserving and participating in the region's quaint ancestral traditions. So they regularly held turkey shoots and other competitive shooting events. Indeed, they customarily celebrated Thanksgiving, Christmas and New Year's with day-long live turkey shoots.

Their procedure was not complicated. Rules were simple and few. Each

This S&W, the 38 Hand Ejector Target, was preferred by the Long Shooters—they liked a Paine bead with a U-notch adjustable rear sight.

The inaugural turkey shoot of the 1912 season in Pewee Valley. Contestants shot at turkey silhouettes rather than live birds.

by JIM FORAL

SHOOTERS OF VALLEY

shooter provided his own gun and ammunition. Targets were provided by a local entrepreneur known as the gamekeeper, who obtained fowl from area farmers and sold chances to the competitors for ten cents a shot. A nickel bought a ticket for a shot at a duck or a chicken. The targets were tethered. The marksman was compelled to shoot at his assigned turkey in whatever position the bird was in the mood to assume. Any hit on a bird above the knees which drew blood was close enough to claim the poultry. Off to the side of the range waited a boy with a sharp knife. Wounded birds were dispatched swiftly and humanely. The headless bird was brought back to its new owner on the firing point.

Four separate ranges paralleled one another. For the 22 rifle, a range of 300 yards was provided. Turkeys were placed 400 yards from the firing line on the high-power rifle range. All rifles were shot from offhand. A separate range for shotguns was about 100 yards in length. Pistol and revolver shooters fired at birds on a special range at a maximum of 200 yards.

A crowd of bystanders delighted in the activity, applauding good shots and heckling those who were habitually unsuccessful. Enthusiastic and vocal onlookers benefited shooters by calling shots wide or short of the target. And to the rear, the women peeled turnips and potatoes, sliced okra and onions, and fussed over the day's meal. Burgoo bubbled in a big kettle over an open fire. Since flintlock days, this vegetable and beef-rich stew had been traditional fare at Kentucky turkey shoots.

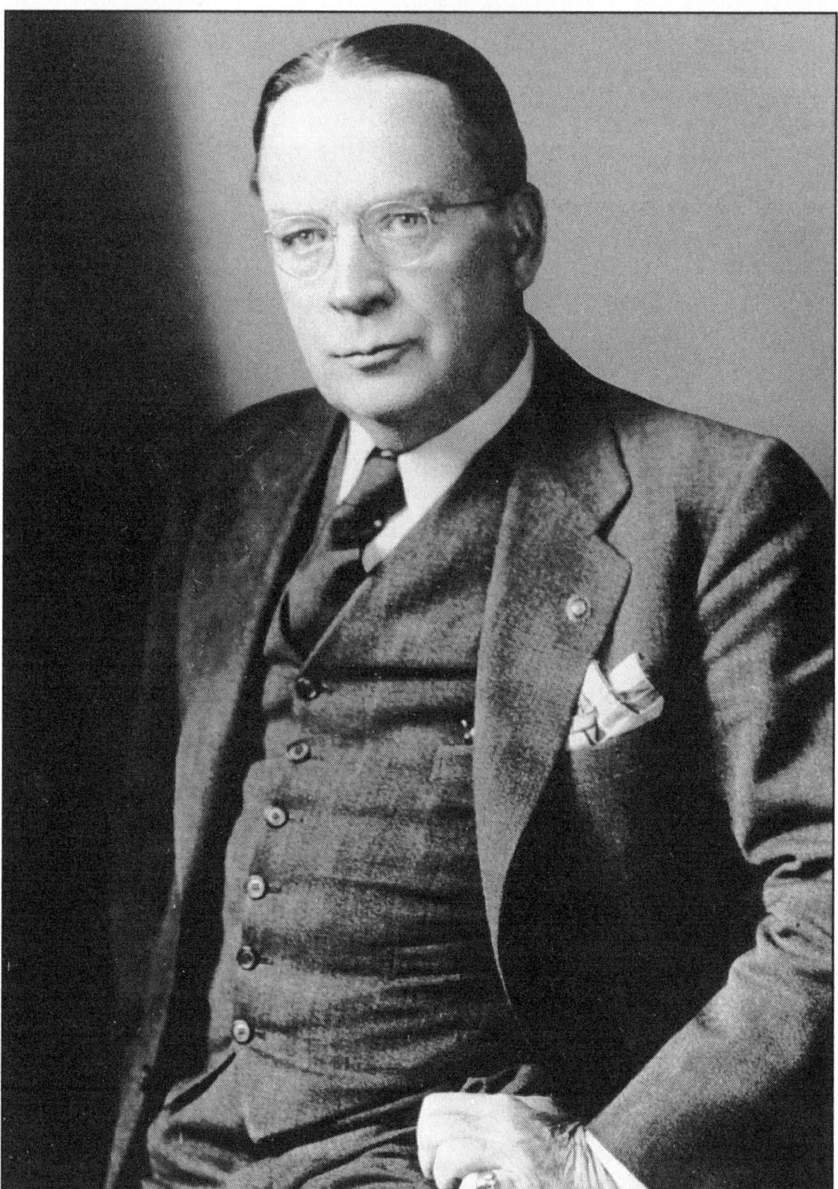

General Drain of the NRA, whose intemperate comments did little to quiet down the Long Shooters.

During the westward movement, the classic Appalachian turkey shoot was modified to suit regional and sometimes ethnic tastes. It remained an interesting diversion when practiced in the Mountain States, or the Southwest, for instance. The turkey shoot, wherever, was basically a sport for the rifleman. However, the most remarkable shooting conducted by the Louisville Rifle and Revolver Club was not over the 400-yard rifle facility, but on the revolver range.

By 1908, some club members more devoted to the handgun than the rifle had been pushing the possibilities of the six-gun beyond a hundred yards. One of the group's converts, William Brent Altsheler, had been introduced to long-range revolver shooting and coached in the arts of range estimation and wind-doping during informal plinking sessions at Pewee Valley during the summer of 1909. Trained under the guidance of the veterans, Altsheler managed to break his first bottle at over 100 yards with his Smith & Wesson 38 Special, fresh from its factory box. An awestruck Altsheler watched the airborne shards scatter and fall. He was entranced. From that moment, shooting at distant targets perched upon the front bead of his new revolver became his passion. There existed sufficient interest among the growing coterie of Long Shooters, as they preferred to be called, to incorporate a pistol match into the regular turkey-shoot program.

Thanksgiving, appropriately enough, was the beginning of the 1910 turkey-shoot season and the occasion of the club's inaugural long-range revolver contest. A small group of chilled shooters amassed on that frosty morning, warming their hands in their pockets as they waited for the gamekeeper to position the feathered targets. At that time, 150 yards from the firing line, a big bronze gobbler went to the stake. With bullets whizzing by, the turkey smugly strutted as contestants groped for the proper elevation.

Photos of William Brent Altsheler are hard to come by. This one was in the April 1913 issue of *Outdoor Life*.

In due time, bullets landing at the bird's feet threw gravel onto his breast. It took Fritz just a cylinderfull of 44s to get the range. Five birds fell to his Smith & Wesson that day. Nat unholstered his pet Smith & Wesson with a special 8-inch barrel that Harry Pope had screwed in. Another serious shooter showed up on line with a peep aperture attached to his spectacles. The gamekeeper quickly megaphoned his disapproval. "Open sights only," he howled in protest to the rule violation. Besides the sight restriction, the only other unwritten rule involved the shooter's position. The Long Shooters further handicapped themselves by adopting the offhand stance customarily taken by gentleman pistol shooters.

Brent Altsheler recorded the predictable misses before finally connecting on a hen. Brent described his revolver as a Model of 1905 Smith & Wesson Hand Ejector, 38 Special, with a 6½-inch barrel. It was equipped with the Paine bead front sight and an adjustable U-notch-rear sight, "just as it came from the factory." This model seemed to be the revolver of choice among the Long Shooters.

The day closed on a cheery note. Participants were pleased and perhaps a little surprised by their performance at 150-yard revolver competition. The affair sparked enough interest that another shoot of the same type was scheduled for Christmas. The only regrets were those expressed by the gamekeeper, Dick Schultze, who complained that for him, it had been an unprofitable experience. At the next event, he assured the cocky Long Shooters, some tables would be turned.

Next month, at the Christmas shoot, the gamekeeper paced off 200 yards and staked the revolver turkey. Brent and associates squinted to find the shifting fowl over the front bead of their pistols.

"It looks like a house fly doing a two-step on the upper deck of the Mauritania," whined Fritz.

"Is that a hummingbird in the perspective?" questioned Nat.

Having registered their kicks, the nonetheless game Long Shooters got out their toothpick screwdrivers and cranked more elevation onto the back sights of their Smith & Wessons. The front beads were blackened with a tallow candle. Getting the 200-yard sight setting proved to be a time- and ammunition-consuming effort. Pat expended a full box of blackpowder 38s and had hit not a feather.

Eventually, Fritz fractured the ice and bored a bird through its middle. In the afternoon, the collective luck of the group turned around. By day's end, most shooters had one or two birds apiece. Fritz boarded the homebound trolley with four birds in hand.

Scores made at the New Year's shoot of 1910 closely matched those recorded on Christmas. While accepting the challenge at 200 yards, the fledgling Long Shooters were killing fewer turkeys, but were gaining experience and enjoying their sport. For the moment, the gamekeeper, now showing a profit, was contented.

During the summer of 1910, the Long Shooters practiced for the upcoming turkey-shoot season by firing at plates at 200 yards. Sight settings were recorded and exchanged. New revolvers were sighted in. Different handloads and various brands of factory ammunition were tested.

The Long Shooters' mastery of the 200-yard turkey during the Thanksgiving and Christmas shoots caused Schultze, the gamekeeper, to devise tactics that would allow him to remain solvent. Further encumbering the already handicapped Long

Shooters, he simply added 25 yards to the Pewee range. The Long Shooters made sight corrections for the extension, commenced perforating turkeys systematically, and the gamekeeper was obliged to step off an additional 25 paces. At 250 yards, the Long Shooters were still sniping Schultze's birds with alarming regularity. When the distance from muzzle to turkey was extended to 275 yards, some of the competitors dropped out. Those who remained merely elevated the rear sight a few turns and proceeded to pick off turkeys with a steady, but much less frequent pace.

"This beats all revolver shooting I have ever witnessed," Schultze wailed. "Move 'em back to 300 yards!" he told the range boy.

At this point, the ranks of the Long Shooters dwindled to four individuals. Only Fred Keller, Henry Mattmiller, a Mr. Hitt, and Brent Altsheler remained on the firing line. After getting accustomed to the 300-yard target, this quartet connected on turkeys at a rather astonishing rate of one hit to every four or five attempts. The coops were emptied. One by one the turkeys were led to the 300-yard stake to meet the same fate as their predecessors, until the supply of turkeys was exhausted. The gamekeeper finished the day with no turkeys, no profit, and no plans to continue furnishing turkeys for the Long Shooters.

The crowd of spectators agreed that the extraordinary 300-yard exhibition was the most striking demonstration of shooting, in any form, that they had ever seen. However, the absence of media coverage of the shoot, coupled with the relative seclusion of communities, especially by today's standards, limited knowledge of the Long Shooters' performance to the locality. Information on the New Year's shoot would have never filtered out of north-central Kentucky had it not been for Brent Altsheler, self-appointed spokesman.

Almost a year after the incident, a brief and inconspicuous article devoted to the subject of the Kentucky turkey shoot, in general, and the 300-yard exercise, in particular, appeared over Altsheler's signature in the December 1910 issue of *Outdoor Life* magazine. Altsheler's incidental description of the 300-yard segment was not included to draw attention to himself or the club, but simply to present an example of an unusual performance at an uncommon sporting event. In Louisville, the account was read, but without much special comment. After all, any resident likely to be reading a sporting magazine already knew about the shoot.

Although Brent's communication was placed where it could easily go unnoticed, it did not escape attention. Accepting on faith a report that a revolver shooter could repeatedly hit turkeys at 300 yards, by design, required an unsuspicious, childlike trust. If Mr. Altsheler was naive enough to suppose his story would be accepted unquestioned, he was mistaken.

"What a shame it is not to tell a true story!" was the editorial reaction of *Arms and The Man*, forerunner of *American Rifleman*. Altsheler's article had drawn the fire of an anonymous staff writer, who wrote a column entirely devoted to denunciation and ridicule of the *Outdoor Life* essay. "Hot-Air Shooting" scorched the pages of the December 15, 1910, issue. The offensive manner of the writer became clearly apparent when he denounced the *Outdoor Life* account as "hot air," "absurd" and "impossible." Mockingly, it was suggested the Long Shooters must have been "honestly mistaken."

The journalist brought the 300-yard turkey marksmanship to a matter of proportion. "How many men of the greatest skill in the use of a revolver are willing to attempt to put one shot in five in a one-inch bullseye at twenty five yards?" he asked.

The fact that he very obviously lacked any knowledge of pistol shooting beyond regulation ranges didn't deter him from advancing his opinion: "But so far as sighting is concerned, the size is not a factor, because the shooter must overhold so much that the target would be out of sight anyway."

Satisfied and confident that he had identified and exposed a villainous fakery, and shielded by his anonymity, he wantonly ridiculed the Peweeites. His sarcastic finale was, "...no other handarm user who ever lived could hold a candle to such experts."

The *Arms and The Man* outburst shocked and enraged Altsheler. His response appeared not in the periodical that had insulted him, but in the February 1911 number of *Outdoor Life*. The managing editor of *Outdoor Life*, J.A. McGuire, had been placed in a unique position. Not only had America's leading military and sporting journal publicly humiliated a group of men and thrust them into the national limelight by way of its columns, but its editor had refused them space to defend themselves. McGuire felt obliged to support individuals and statements published in his magazine and branded as false in another. Editor McGuire may have been motivated to protect his own magazine. Perhaps there was some friction between editors. Reading between the lines, one can perceive a minor rivalry between the periodicals.

In any event, if the Long Shooters would be spitefully attacked on the pages of *Arms and The Man*, they would be just as zealously defended by McGuire. The Long Shooters would have their forum in *Outdoor Life*. Infuriated, Altsheler arrived at the conclusion that his critic was "as unfamiliar as he is obtuse in the discussion of long range shooting with revolvers, the wonder is that he has not inadvertently blown out his own brains; but perhaps the target has proven immune on account of its diminutive size."

H.W. Mattmiller, the president of the Louisville Rifle and Revolver Club and fellow Long Shooter, wrote a letter in support of Altsheler's original article. He politely asked the editor to publish it as a "matter of justice and fair play." Matmiller pledged that Altsheler's December account was true from beginning to end, and that the *Arms and The Man* article contained mistakes made through "inexperience or ill-will, or both." He graciously submitted that the *Arms and The Man* writer was one of the "good many shooters who are unfamiliar with the use and capabilities of the modern revolver."

The importance of the adjustable U-notch rear sight, which Altsheler continually stressed, was lost on the *Arms and The Man* mystery contributor. This sight gave the shooter the same sight picture at both long and conventional six-gun ranges. Common fixed revolver sights at long range do require elevating the front sight over the target. The "Hot Air" artist was either inexperienced or, as Altsheler opined, the details pertaining to the revolver's sight were "carelessly read."

Fred Keller, a well-known figure in Louisville business and shooting

Unidentified Long Shooter at the 200-yard range of the Louisville Rifle and Revolver Club range, January 1910. The crowd was allowed to heckle.

circles, also expressed his opinion in the magazine space provided by *Outdoor Life*: "...the Pewee Valley turkey shoot occurred just as reported, for I was one of the four successful participants he had mentioned," wrote Keller. The statements of the *Arms and The Man* writer's apparent misconception regarding holding the front sight over the target were discussed. Keller was convinced that "he doesn't know what he is talking about." In his eagerness to criticize, the writer had overlooked the excellent Smith & Wesson adjustable rear sight, which had ample adjustment designed into it, even for 300-yard shooting "...we do not hold the bead somewhere over the mark as he seems to believe, for that would be guesswork sure enough. We hold right on it, or just under it...."

The Kentucky bunch demanded the identity of the caustic author of "Hot Air Shooting." Implications that General James A. Drain was the culprit were not well hidden. Not only did General Drain edit the periodical, he was its publisher and owner. Drain, a self-confessed technical expert on ballistic subjects, had recently completed a three-year term as president of the National Rifle Association. Nationally, Drain was a prominent and influential figure, capable of moulding public opinion.

Now under suspicion, Drain responded: "A member of the staff wrote 'Hot Air Shooting.' He added that "the editor is responsible for all it contains." In a supplemental statement, Drain adds: "The article was written...to punish by ridicule what were considered incorrect and exaggerated statements," and that he was "perfectly willing to concede that the author of the article...is honestly mistaken."

In a show of fair-mindedness, and since the affair had drawn a good deal of national attention, Drain demonstrated a willingness to compromise by calling for the "official record:" "If you will send to me a detailed statement of the shots fired upon the occasion mentioned in 'Hot Air Shooting,' the order in which they were fired, the names of the firers, and the number of turkeys actually secured at the 300 yards by this firing by the persons named in this article, you need only sign it, and say that you know—not believe— it to be true to secure it's publication, and to secure the acceptance of what you say is true."

Despite Altsheler's urging, Drain refused to respond through the pages of his publication. Drain's offer, and Altsheler's response, as well as a series of joint communications were published in the March 1911 number of *Outdoor Life*.

Altsheler admitted that he was uninformed that the informal turkey shooting match had ever been standardized and duly apologized for not having maintained an official record. "We shoot for turkeys, and not for records," he wrote.

General Drain was now losing patience: "...this is not what was asked for, nor is it a proper or worthy letter. A perfectly clear way has been offered to you by which you may be set right in the minds of the reading public, if you have been misrepresented."

Drain repeated that only by providing the official record could the story be verified, adding "If it is not true then the original criticism is entirely too mild to fit the case."

Altsheler's response was: "Our statement was sufficiently clear and pointed for the average reader, who is generally fair and intelligent, the exception or exceptions we have met with only proving the rule.

Altsheler offered to produce statements from ten eyewitnesses agreeing in the truth of what they saw, "against the edict of one man who dogmatically asserts without support that the account is untrue, although he was probably one thousand miles away from the occurrence and did not learn of it till nearly a year later...we confess we are powerless in the presence of such omniscience."

A week later, signed statements from the ten, verifying the accuracy of Altsheler's statements, arrived on Editor McGuire's desk.

Certainly, General Drain and his "staff writer" could not have imagined the tremendous consequences resulting from their solitary slur-riddled editorial. The open publication of Drain's correspondence with the slandered Kentuckians built the national exposure even higher. We can safely assume that the 300-yard stunt monopolized the idle talk at gun clubs, behind firing lines, or wherever sportsmen assembled in the spring of 1911.

On one hand there was a handful of obscure Kentuckians, broadcasting that the accomplishment of the seemingly impossible had been achieved, although recognized by them as a mere "unusual occurance." The other hand is occupied by a highly regarded, authoritative personality of national preeminence who declares the claims to be preposterous and not to be swallowed as gospel.

Understandably, some Americans formed opinions of their own. A few took pen in hand and made public their opinions. One notable detractor, who preferred to shroud his identity with the presumptuous pseudonym of "A.L. Iar," succeeded in getting published in the April 1911 issue of *Outdoor Life*: "We all know that the fluid that had made Kentucky famous will make you see things double, but we did not all know until now that it will make you see double the distance. And that sight, Mr. Editor, that wonderful U-sight—is it located on the revolver, in the shooter's eye, or in the bottle?"

Even Editor McGuire considered the piece to be "adverse criticism," but for reasons known only to editors, permitted its publication. Several outraged subscribers voiced their disapproval, effectively summarized by one G.R. Gale. "I, for one, think the Editor of *Outdoor Life* owes it to his readers to uncompromisingly refrain from publishing any contributions from these parties in the future, and when anyone wishes to take a whack at another, do it like a man, and sign your full name and place of residence, not like a footpad, masking under an abbreviated or false name." An irritated Coloradan, Arthur Clark, was provoked to say: "He had better wake up, or rather, sober up, go to a gun store and see a revolver with adjustable sights—and then he will not be so eager to rush into print with his views on revolver shooting and show his ignorance!"

Among the disbelievers was Ned H. Roberts, whose thoughts on the long-shooting matter enlightened the readers of *Outdoor Life*'s, December 1911 issue. "The Editor of *Arms and The Man* knew these facts when he published the article about 'Hot Air Shooting,' and he was so far nearer right than are those who would have us believe that 300-yard turkey hitting with a 38 caliber revolver is a sure thing for a good revolver shot."

Drawing upon his proclaimed thirty years experience with the rifle and various pistols and revolvers, Roberts arrived at the conclusion that "...hitting a turkey at that range with a revolver is simply luck, there is no skill about it. The poorest revolver shot is just as likely to make a hit as the most skillful."

Roberts' message was abundantly clear: "It is not really worth wasting good ammunition on the figure of the turkey at 300 yards with a revolver. Nothing can be learned by it."

Roberts, better known for fathering the 25-caliber rifle cartridge that bears his name than for publicly proclaiming the impossibility of the shooting of others, urged the Long Shooters to demonstrate their talents at Camp Perry: "There are good prizes to win, prizes well worth the effort to capture them, and the shooters will be required to shoot at distances of only 25, 50, or 75 yards to win these prizes. How dead easy that will be compared with hitting a turkey at 300 yards."

Carl Engelhardt, the secretary of the Louisville Rifle and Revolver Club, responded angrily in the same issue. Mr. Roberts' "extraordinary statements" pertaining to luck's hand and the absence of skill involved in the turkey shooting aroused Engelhardt's wrath: "How about this? Does this strike the reader as absurd or reasonable? If this is true (but we all know it is the farthest from the truth possible), then such marksmen as Whelen, Hudson, and others whom we have been calling expert shots are not more certain of getting within the bullseye than the man who knows not the difference between the lever of a gun and a pump handle."

Members of the Louisville Rifle and Revolver Club posed at a turkey shoot in 1909 when they were still shooting live birds—and even a rifle, now and again.

The discussion between the Long Shooters and General Drain continued to vitalize the columns of *Outdoor Life*. The journalistic pot boiled. Drain insisted that the matter be resolved and the Long Shooters be put to the test. In the early summer of 1911, a startling announcement appeared in an *Arms and The Man* editorial. General Drain issued a challenge to the Kentuckians. They were invited to journey to Washington at the General's expense, to shoot on a government rifle range at the General's turkeys, in front of an assembly of the General's spectators. The Long Shooters were enticed with a promise of $500 in prizes if they could collectively repeat their celebrated one hit in "four or five" attempts. If they failed to hit twenty-three turkeys out of 100 shots, however, they were to forfeit $500.

Drain's bet did not silence the Long Shooters: "Is this sport, or fair play, or a burlesque, or both?" was their response in the September, 1911, number of *Outdoor Life*. Editor McGuire's input was, of course, inevitable. He labeled Drain's proposal as "absolutely absurd."

The officers of the Louisville club, perhaps intimidated by General Drain's home-court advantage, suggested a test on Kentucky soil. They countered with a challenge of their own, issued, needless to say, on the pages of the October 1911 issue of *Outdoor Life*. The club would conduct the match, to be held solely for Drain's benefit, on its own ground, in familiar surroundings, and provide the turkeys. Drain was invited to view the range, inspect the revolvers, enjoy a bowl of burgoo, and witness a turkey shooting demonstration, Kentucky style. If the match results averaged one bird out of five, the General paid for the birds. If not, the Long Shooters were stuck with the bill for the turkeys. They tauntingly volunteered: "...and you may take all the side bets offered you."

General Drain published no reply. Apparently, both sides considered the matter to be dropped.

The reading public soon laid aside the question of personality, the authenticity of Altsheler's account, and the confusion over who the genuine authorities were. After all the entertaining squabble, after all the brickbats had been hurled, after all the misspent time and magazine space devoted to the cultivation of mistrust of one's fellow man and the ill will it generated, the crux of the matter remained.

Subscribers were now concentrated on the actual possibilities of the Long Shooters' alleged accomplishments. The question requiring resolution narrowed to substantially a matter of duplication. If the Long Shooters could connect on a turkey, one shot out of "four or five," others could do it, too. A nation lay waiting for the issue's resolving. Some folks sat in judgment, some were skeptical, some condemned either faction. Still others grabbed revolvers and measured off 300 yards.

The Long Shooters 1911-1912, shooting in the summer heat, but still, by the records, nailing right around one out of five turkeys.

One of the first reports of repeating the Long Shooters scores was received from Capt. A.H. Hardy. He was one of the finest revolver shots in the United States and considered the Long Shooters claims to be an impossibility.

"It was perhaps the heated discussion which arose from the publication of this story that got me all the more interested," he wrote. Hardy set up a turkey figure at 300 yards, and after a few sighting shots, proceeded to make three "kills" in fifteen shots. Hardy's shooting was strictly offhand and fortified with the affidavits of nine eye-witnesses.

Hardy's demonstration didn't change malcontented Ned Roberts' contention that such shooting was strictly dependent on luck. Roberts maintained that Hardy made no more hits than someone who "hardly knows the difference between a 38 and 45 caliber revolver." An amateur pistolshooter "holding at the ground ten feet in front of the turkey" stands an equal chance of making a hit as Captain Hardy with a hard hold, Roberts tells us.

Capt. Hardy also put the Hot Air writer's comparison of the 300-yard turkey and a 1-inch target at 25 yards to an actual test. Reports from Hardy, as well as others who tried it, indicated that the inch square was hittable about once in four or five tries.

M.S. Hendricks, a nationally acclaimed gunsmith and barrel maker, admitted in the June 1911 issue of *Outdoor Life* that he'd been an avid competitor in rifle turkey shoots since a schoolboy in the 1850s. After reading the accounts of the Kentucky long-shooting, Hendricks couldn't resist the temptation to try it himself. He painted a picture of a turkey on a piece of cardboard and hunted up a suitable snow-covered pasture beyond the city limits of Aurora, Illinois. After pacing off 200 good long steps, he proceeded to fire twenty shots from his Smith & Wesson 7½-inch 44 Special target revolver at the target. Two of his handloaded bullets hit the turkey, which was better results than Mr. Hendricks had expected for the first trial.

Hendricks offered: "The S&W target revolvers will shoot as good as the average rifle, and it is only a matter of being able to hold on the turkey to get it."

In conclusion, he wrote that he did not take much stock in the unsigned "Hot-Air Shooting" article, but later he was very much surprised to find out that it had been written by the editorial staff. "I thought they were better posted on target revolvers and sights."

Also unstimulated with the *Arms and The Man* editorial was Oregonian Gus Peret. He wrote simply: "I didn't quite agree with what the writer had to say." As the traveling exhibition shooter for the Peter's Cartridge Company, Gus Peret knew something about fancy revolver shooting.

"Those fellows down in Kentucky must be good revolver shots," he said to himself. Still, he had some doubts. To satisfy his own curiosity about the capability of a revolver at long range,

Twenty shots by Arthur Tuttle.

Sergeant Smith's best twenty shots.

Out in Denver, this set of targets showed it could be done.

(Below) An August 1911 *Outdoor Life* published these Ashley Haines targets in support of the Long Shooters' claims.

Cut No. 1.

Cut No. 2.

TURKEY SHOOTING BY ASHLEY A. HAINES. (SEE ARTICLE BY MR. HAINES IN THE JUNE NUMBER.)

Cut No. 1—Six hits on the turkey target at 300 yards out of 25 consecutive shots with .22 S. & W. 8-inch pistol. Cut No. 2—Seven hits on the turkey target at 200 yards out of 25 consecutive shots with .22 Stevens 6-inch off-hand model pistol. Height of both targets, from top of back to tips of toes, 18 in.; length from tip of bill to tip of tail, 32 in.; through body, 12 in.

Gus painted a turkey silhouette on a 5½-foot piece of oilcloth and set it up at 300 measured yards. Shooting Peters factory 38 Special loads in his 1905 S&W target revolver, Peret found the range within four shots. Fifteen shots for record, all of which landed on the oilcloth, resulted in three turkeys. Peret concluded: "In closing I will say that to those that have tried shooting at long range with a revolver, and using the adjustable U-notch sight, it will be a surprise to you how close you can shoot, if you will try it. I know it was for me."

Ashley A. Haines, the Canadian firearms authority from Salmon Arm, British Columbia, was convinced that Mr. Altsheler's first Long Shooting account was unjustly appraised and ridiculed in the *Arms and The Man* article and that its author was more intent on criticizing than investigating the facts. In addition, a printed apology from the editor to the Long Shooters was in order, Haines felt, before the "reading public will afford him a small amount of respect, that, since this little incident occurred, is sadly lacking."

Haines credited the momentary popularity of the long-range pistol shooting to the efforts of the " 'Hot-Air' man and the editor at his heels," for contending and publicizing such marksmanship as being impossible. Uninfluenced by Gen. Drain's opinions, faithful in Mr. Altsheler's report, and completely lacking in revolver-shooting experience beyond fifty yards, Haines proceeded to determine the factual possibilities of the long-range pistol shooting.

Assisted by his youngest brother, Jay, Ashley spent three days "long shooting" with 22 pistols and reported the results in the July 1911 number of *Outdoor Life*. After warming up on some 200-yard targets, the brothers erected a paper target with the likeness of a turkey at the base of a hill 300 yards from the muzzle of their 8-inch Smith & Wesson single shot target pistol, equipped with adjustable sights.

Damp conditions hampered observation of telltale puffs of dirt generated by impacting bullets, which made precise sight adjustment a matter of guesswork. Our Canadian Long Shooters were additionally frustrated by another normally occurring nemesis of long-distance marksmen. Haines reported that it was "...plenty windy, too."

Despite nature's obstacles, Ashley and Jay managed to hit the target regularly enough to make it interesting, the poorest shooting being one hit in ten shots. During a lull in the wind, Ashley connected with six shots in a twenty-five-shot string, while his brother nearly duplicated his performance with five hits. A few days later, with the wind again misbehaving, Ashley fired twenty-five Winchester 22 Shorts, successfully "getting four through his turkeyship." On a windless day shortly thereafter, 200 shots were fired, resulting in 21 hits.

Haines considered his shooting representative of what could be accomplished by someone not familiar with long-range pistol shooting. On the other hand... "It is my opinion that an expert pistol shot, if in practice, could make at least one hit on the turkey target out of five shots at 300 yards under favorable conditions...some might do better."

Incidentally, the Arms and Ammunition section of McGuire's monthly was edited by Ashley Haines. One must wonder if Haines' individual participation was motivated by a memo from *Outdoor Life*'s publishing office.

Meanwhile, a group of America's most preeminent and competitive riflemen observed the distasteful proceedings in the sporting press from the sidelines.

The Denver Rifle Club conducted a 300-yard turkey shoot of their own, for a couple of reasons besides the fellowship these get-togethers provided. Sustaining their assailed Kentucky comrades, with whom they felt a kinship, was a priority. Match results similar to the Louisville club's would finally vindicate the Kentuckians in the critical eyes of a certain Washington, D.C., editor and the rest of America's watchful shooters with little faith. Besides, the suit, necktie, and derby-attired Denver gentlemen were always eager for an excuse to participate in a shooting contest of any sort.

Denver Rifle Club member Arthur Smith described the April 23rd shoot to the readers of the June 1911 issue of *Outdoor Life.* Smith reported that the event was attended by a "fairly good crowd," to include quite a number of the curious and a handful of skeptics.

Also present, we must assume, was one Denver resident with a particular interest in the performances of the competitors, Mr. J.A. McGuire, managing Editor of *Outdoor Life,* coincidentally published in Denver. Whether Mr. McGuire sponsored or influenced the decision to have the match is not recorded. It is known, however, that he personally provided prizes for first and second place.

Competitors and spectators arrived at Golden, site of the club's range, on the 9 a.m. trolley. The rules were simple and perhaps experimental. Any revolver was permitted with no restrictions on ammunition or sights. All shooting was strictly offhand with only one hand allowed to touch the revolver. Each entrant was permitted five sighting shots, and twenty shots were fired for score.

The target, a profile of a 15-pound turkey, was fastened to a stake at 300 measured yards. Twenty-one contestants engaged in the three-hour competition, the last half of which was conducted in a driving wind and rainstorm that "completely spoiled all chances for a record score."

J.H. Parry emerged as the match winner, with three hits, and took home a silver loving cup. Six shooters tied for second place with two hits each. Among them was Denver gunsight manufacturer and nationally celebrated Schuetzen rifleman, D.W. King. Considered one of America's best Schuetzen competitors, A.W. Bitterly was no stranger to the stresses and trials of shooting in inclement weather. Bitterly also recorded two hits. The famed Denver-based barrelmaker, and president of the club, Axel W. Peterson, managed but a single turkey.

Two competitors used Smith & Wesson 44 Russian revolvers. The remainder fired 38 Special S&Ws with adjustable sights. Several shot handloaded shells, but the favorite ammunition was the Peters 165-grain factory load.

Match results, taken as a whole, don't quite measure up to the "one turkey in four or five shots" as broadcast by the pistol shooters of Pewee Valley. In justice to the men who competed under the adverse rainy conditions, and to "leave no doubt in the minds of our readers that the feat of hitting a turkey at 300 yards (with a revolver) is possible, correspondent Smith included some earlier practice scores, fired in the absence of the disruptive elements of wind and rain.

In practice, J.H. Dreher hit two turkeys in five shots twice, as did Axel Peterson and Bitterly. A. Tuttle secured six in twenty. Smith reported that four turkeys succumbed to twenty of his shots. Under favorable weather and visibility conditions, Smith opined, it is entirely possible to duplicate or better the scores of the Kentucky shooters.

Another contest was scheduled for May 14, 1911. In conclusion, Smith wrote: "I am willing to wager...a new record will be established."

The May Denver shoot was plagued by gusty conditions which required some fancy wind doping that competitors were totally unfamiliar with. The previous match winner, J.H. Perry, placed one bullet through the turkey in his first three strings, before he managed to make the necessary windage allowances. Three shots in the final string of five were solid hits. With an aggregate of four hits, Perry retained his crown as the champion Denver Long Shooter. With three hits each, Bitterly and Peterson tied for second place. Some members discussed a change in target form. A military-type of target, with a bullseye and scoring rings, they felt, would serve to "get the possibilities of a revolver at this range down to a more scientific basis than the hit or miss plan as used at the present time."

Sgt. Smith, who again covered the event, expressed the belief that the unjustly persecuted Pewee Valley shooters had been thoroughly vindicated by the Denver Rifle Club and by others "who believe in a square deal." Smith extended a friendly challenge to other clubs and added that he "would particularly like to hear from the Pewee Valley Shooters for a match with them."

After the Denver club got the ball rolling, twenty-four members of the Colorado Springs Revolver Club competed at a 200-yard turkey shoot on May 7, 1911. Shooting in a gale of wind and rain, R.B. Wilson, shooting a 22 Remington pistol, was awarded first prize for four hits in twenty shots. A.H. Hardy, who reported the event in a mid-summer issue of *Outdoor Life*, remarked that "turkey shooting at 200 and 300 yards is fast becoming a popular sport in Colorado."

Brent Altsheler was unconventionally serious about the game he was instrumental in popularizing. By his own admission, he was first a lover of the rifle, but after his first exposure to the long-range revolver, it had cast its spell over him. Long-range pistol shooting, he was convinced, was "the luxury, the dessert, of marksmanship."

As the man responsible for presenting the 300-yard sport to American shooters, Altsheler was the individual singularly qualified to write the book on the subject. The sixty-four page illustrated volume, with an introduction by Ashley Haines, made its appearance in September of 1912. *The Long Shooters and The Origin of 300 Yard Revolver Shooting* was published, to no one's surprise, by our friends at the Outdoor Life Publishing Co. of Denver, Colorado.

Mr. Altsheler was of the firm belief that marksmanship with the revolver is not an inherited trait. Good shooters are not born. They are developed through long periods of practice with the expenditure of a large quantity of ammunition. Altsheler practiced constantly and deliberately at unpaced ranges and under varying field and light conditions, until he acquired an intimate acquaintance with the revolver and its ammunition. He developed an ability to read and dope wind and apply its little-understood effects on a low-velocity pistol bullet at long range. Once the essential 38- or 44-caliber Smith & Wesson revolver with adjustable-U sights and a quantity of the best ammunition had been obtained, the competitor's outfit was complete.

Beyond equipment, Altsheler supposed that seventy-five percent of finding one's self in the winners circle was physical condition. The physical act of shooting, Altsheler's book explains, "...is nerve work, undoubtedly."

He stressed a campaign to maximize efficiency of nervous control through strenuous exercise. It was vital to immerse one's self in a program of physical and mental discipline and training. Outdoor exercise, Altsheler maintained, was essential to acquiring physical poise and balance.

"One must do a great many things to counteract the unnatural tendencies of indoor life," he tells us. His equilibrium was honed by walking along fencetops. Arm and leg extending exercises were conducted daily. He said, "The nerves like a good stretching from toe to fingertips."

Altsheler considered his eyes as his most essential organs. They, too, could benefit from daily outdoor exercise. After bathing his eyes in cold, purified water, he would strengthen them by gazing at distant objects, up to a mile away, until the object came into sharp focus. He then concentrated on closer objects until they, too, became clear and distinct in outline.

Stimulants, such as tobacco, coffee and tea, were shunned. His tonic was exercise and discipline. Altsheler kept a close watch on himself, avoiding stress, overwork, and excesses in food and drink. He modified his daily work practices and sleep habits. Attention was paid to sub-influences such as digestion, will and mental attitude, which played major roles in developing the extremely delicate marksmanship skills involved in long-range revolver shooting.

Like most fads, the 300-yard turkey-shoot craze experienced a widespread, vibrant, but short-lived duration. The possibilities had been proven, the impatient critics were silenced, and the public's awareness of the potential and capability of the revolver had been expanded. The trials of feuding editors and weary Kentuckians lacked the ability to maintain the interest of a readership, and the issue withered. The spotlight on the Long Shooters, along with the fickle public's attention, was redirected to other areas. By late summer of 1912, the drama was in its final scenes.

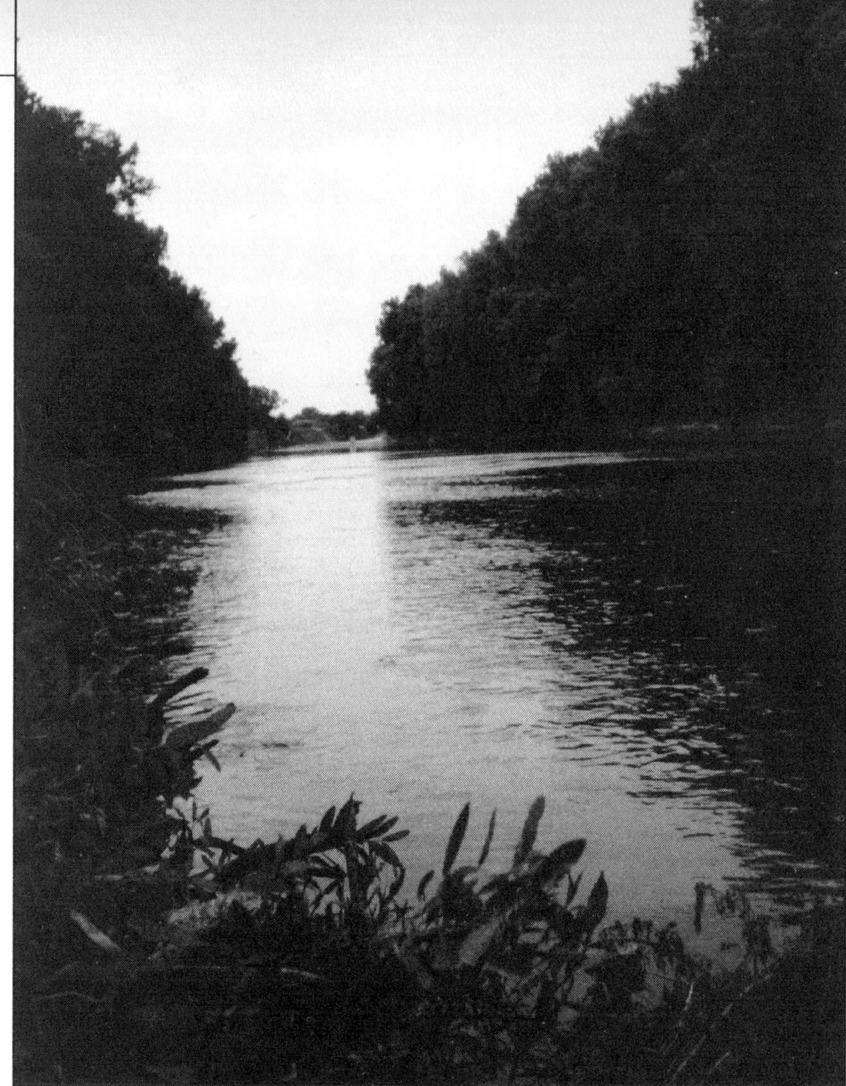

The writer's "official" range in Nebraska gave him the distance needed—and easy zeroing with the help of the splashes.

The Denver Rifle Club held its final turkey shoot of record in November of 1912. A turkey silhouette, 32 inches bill to tail and 9½ inches deep, was the target. Adverse conditions hampered shooters and dampened enthusiasm. Mud, caused by recent storms, made it impossible for contestants to mark the direction of their shots. C.F. MacBeth's score of four hits in twenty shots was enough to win the trophy. Considering the mud and wind, MacBeth's score was considered a remarkable accomplishment by club secretary J.H. Parry, who reported on the event.

The Louisville Rifle and Revolver Club's last publicized revolver turkey match was the fall kick-off shoot of the 1912 season. Participating were seven members of the club, all but one armed with Smith & Wesson 38 Specials. The exception fired a S&W 44 Special. Rather than live birds, competitors shot at turkey silhouettes pasted over the regulation Army "A" target. Although participants were allowed twenty sighting shots, no one required more than fifteen. A telephone connected the pit crew to the firing line. A total of 350 shots were sent downrange, and thirty-six turkeys were scored. With eight turkeys out of fifty shots, Brent Altsheler emerged as the match winner. He was awarded a silver medal with a sedentary gobbler engraved in its center and the inscription "300 yard Revolver Turkey Championship L.R.R.C. 1912." The *Arms and The Man* staff, General Drain, nor the Hot Air specialist had no response that made it into print.

Nebraska Long Shooter Jim Foral and his K-38 and five hits on a turkey under Long Shooter conditions.

William Brent Altsheler, however, did not immediately fade from notoriety in the sporting press. In April of 1913, he organized a self-conducted safari into the wild regions of British East Africa, Uganda and the Belgian Congo. Collecting specimens of white rhino, okapi and bongo for exhibitions at the Chicago Field Museum of Natural History was the journey's objective.

In preparation, Altsheler assembled an African battery which included a sporting Springfield, a 405 and a London-made double elephant rifle. Not as an afterthought, certainly, his 38 Special Smith & Wesson was stuffed into a duffel—"I may need my old turkey revolver for a hyena or jackal and it'll go along, too." Altsheler's serial account of his exciting adventures on the Dark Continent was reported to the readers of *Outdoor Life* in 1914 and 1915.

One shooter's scores arrived too late to be included in the long-range discussion of 1911. This reporter considered that long-range pistol shooting could prove to be an interesting pastime and wondered if the average amateur could hit the turkey at all. In the Summer of 1991, I painted the image of a turkey to the same dimensions used by the Denver Rifle Club on a 4x6-foot sheet of plywood.

If a marksman were allowed to shoot over the water, I reasoned, the strike of the bullets could be clearly observed, and sight adjustments could be made.

For a range, I selected a stretch of Salt Creek near my home in Eastern Nebraska. Due to the Midwestern drought, the water was but a few inches deep. A section of the high-banked creek with a gentle bend behind the target was chosen to prevent ricochets and skipping bullets from landing in cow pastures and other parts of the landscape. The turkey target was a measured 300 yards from my firing position.

The revolver used was the modernized counterpart of the Long Shooter's 38 Special 1905 Smith & Wesson. This 6-inch K-38 has held a hallowed niche in my battery since 1971 when, barely out of my teens, I was obliged to forgo many a meal to produce the $125 required to bring it home.

A few days prior, I'd sighted the gun at a bucket-size clump of mud at about 300 yards on another section of the creek. Hits gradually became frequent enough that I was confident that I could ventilate the 300-yard turkey a time or two. After shooting a dozen sighters off to the side of the plywood to verify windage, I fired sixty-five shots for record, offhand—just one hand supporting the revolver. Forty-six of the handloaded, cast semi-wadcutters missed the turkey, but struck the plywood sheet. Eleven shots missed the target altogether. Eight of the bullets perforated the turkey, including two that landed so close to the bird's knee joint, the hit or miss mark by Kentucky definition, a judgment call was required. I ruled them to be hits. Brent Altsheler, I suspect, would have agreed.

This score may not place me in the same league as the Pewee Valley Long Shooters, but I suppose it could be considered representative of what can be accomplished by someone not practiced at the activity. This long-range revolver shooting is, if nothing else, a distinctly different and interesting sport. Having tried the game, I can appreciate why members of the Louisville Rifle and Revolver Club were captivated by it. All things considered, arcing 38-caliber bullets toward a wooden turkey figure 300 yards upstream was a refreshing way to spend a Saturday.

If American handgunners would be receptive to a new shooting game, perhaps a rejuvenation of 300-yard revolver shooting is it. I would suggest that it be maintained as a sport, easily and inexpensively taken up by beginners and the inexpert. As for the rules, a turkey-shoot revival should be free of optical sights, high-intensity single shot contraptions, and other complicating elements. Keep it restricted to factory revolvers with standard adjustable sights, fired strictly offhand, and make up the rest of the rules as we go along, and thus retain the same simple spirit of the Long Shooters of Pewee Valley. ●

by DON ZUTZ

SHOTGUN REVIEW

THE TERM "GLOBAL economy" is used frequently these days, and the younger generations would have us believe this is something totally new and exciting, a product of their presence. A new college graduate recently told me and a small gathering of my ancient shooting peers that we must learn to live with world marketing or step aside. I guess we weren't impressed, frightened, or chagrined by his erudite pronouncements, because we casually picked up our shotguns and strolled to the Skeet field for a leisurely round, leaving the genius to polish the gold bead in his ear.

Indeed, anyone who knows anything about the history of shotguns fully understands the international nature of trade. For shotguns as economic goods are about as widely distributed as any other products. Americans did not have a domestic firearms industry at the time of the Revolutionary War, and they bought heavily from Belgium and France. The same thing occurred in the War of 1812 and, to varying degrees, during the American Civil War. And even when Sam Colt and Eli Whitney got their acts together, there was still a shortage of firearms in North America.

A variety of importers made a good living because of these conditions, many of them New York merchants who brought in British and European sporting pieces. Among them were Daly, Shoverling & Gales, (New York); E.C. Mecham Arms Co. (St. Louis); Charles J. Godfrey (New York); B. Kittredge & Co. (Cincinnati); Schuyler, Hartley & Graham (New York); and even the Winchester Repeating Arms Co. (New Haven), which imported its doubles from England between 1879-1884. Other minor players could join the list, of course, and one could point out that most, if not all, Damascus barrels used in the U.S. were imported from England or, primarily, Belgium. Indeed, the shops of Birmingham, England; Eibar, Spain; Suhl, Prussia; and the Liege-Herstal region of Belgium did much to supply the North American gun sellers.

And so it is today. Our gun market is still a study in world competition, only more so! The players are many, coming from all points on the compass. Sometimes they still angle in from the Old World, but gunmakers of South America, Asia, and even Asia Minor are now chipping in. Thus, any shotgun review for 1996 must perforce be a global one. Oh, we still salute the flag, stand for the national anthem, and back the U.S. Olympic team. But when it comes to shotguns, we must acknowledge that the great ones aren't all "Made in America."

That's Remington's upgraded Peerless, the Model 396, in Sporting Clays mode. The sideplate has fine acid-etched scroll and game scenes.

American Arms

This importer continues to offer doubles in both vertical and horizontal configurations. The guns of the Silver series of O/Us have excellent handling qualities for bird hunting and sell at a moderate price. The side-by-sides are also affordably priced and have clean lines. Some hefty models in $3\frac{1}{2}$-inch 10- and 12-gauge are handy pieces for the waterfowler and turkey hunter.

Arrieta

One of the best side-by-sides to come out of Spain, the Arrieta is enjoying increased popularity. Most such doubles follow the classic English pattern, and in recent months, they have begun coming to these shores in the novel 2-inch 12-gauge chambering. The importers can point buyers to sources for these 2-inch loads.

AyA

Most British hunters can't afford the fancy prices tagged to their country's handmade doubles, so they seek an alternative. One of their favorites is the AyA No. 1 sidelock, which is again coming to the U.S. There are other less costly AyAs, of course.

The overseas shooting press is carrying notice of a new AyA over/under of a modern design. No mention has been made of its availability over here, but one can keep his eyes peeled. Meanwhile, AyA makes a spittin' image copy of the Merkel O/U called the Model 37 Super.

Browning

When I first reviewed the Browning Gold autoloader a couple years ago, I thought it had excellent field qualities and that its pointability could have serious application in Sporting Clays. Now Browning has made some modifications to the 12-gauge Gold and turned it into a true sporter. It wears an overbored, ported 30-inch barrel and that snazzy radiused buttpad which is equated with Sporting Clays pieces. It has already won one U.S. national championship in the hands of Andy Duffy.

Browning's other shotgun venture is the Model 802 ES Sporting Clays O/U. Although profiled like the popular M325/425 Brownings, the M802 ES has a novel set of screw-in barrel extensions which allows a shooter to increase the barrel length from 28 inches to both 30 inches and 32 inches by the use of Invector Plus extension choke tubes. The appended "ES" of the gun's designation stands for "Extended Swing." To keep the M802 ES manageable, it is given the Superlite barreled action.

Beretta

Whether it's in the U.S. or overseas, Beretta keeps playing games with its basic over/under line. Names keep changing, as do finishes, and this time there may be some additional new features. These are the Gold series. And although we haven't heard much about it here, the overseas press has noticed some barrel weight changes to better balance the stackbarrels, along with a newly shaped grip and a narrower action. The body sports a finish which is said to change shades in different light conditions and can withstand the punishment of tournaments and hunting.

There's also a Silver Pigeon model replacing the former, short-lived 686 Silver Perdiz. It has an electroless nickel finish. The Model 390 Silver Mallard semi-auto has been trimmed by half a pound thanks to a reshaped grip, slimmer forend and lighter forend cap, and will be known as the A390.

As a personal flashback, I must note that the Beretta 686 Essential is still around. I've used one for two seasons, and the more I hunted with it, the more I liked it. Light, pointable and possessed of excellent dynamics, it is a neat entry-level over/under.

hand checkered and given a hand-rubbed oil finish on fancy American walnut. These aren't cheapies, but in today's market they seem worth their price.

Connecticut Shotgun Manufacturing Co.

A couple years ago, these fellows popped onto the scene with a 20-gauge replica of the ol' A.H. Fox double, and they've quietly held onto a niche in the market. Now they've gone several strides further to announce Fox replicas in 16- and 28-gauge as well as 410-bore. These are finely made little doubles and should appeal to fans of the smaller bores. But you'll need deep pockets, as the guns carry big tickets.

Dixie Gun Works

This company is a leader in blackpowder guns and kits, and its Dixie Magnum Percussion Double should interest hunters. Nicely profiled, it is available in 10-, 12-, and 20-gauge with hand checkering, light scroll on the metal works and case-hardened locks.

Harrington & Richardson, 1871

Bull-barreled slug guns are H&R's big thrusts. Their Ultra-Slug Gun was well received in 1995, thanks to the stiff 10-gauge barrel which was made to handle 12-gauge slugs. This year's offering is a super-accurate 20-gauge built on a 12-gauge frame. The 12-gauge barrel leaves lots of metal for stiffness and accuracy around the 20-gauge bore. Some 5/8-inch, three-shot groups have been reported over a 50-yard range. The gun is cataloged as the Model 920, but there's a downsized version, the Model 925, for junior hunters and milady.

Over on the smoothbore side, H&R's companion line, New England Firearms, is bringing back the 32-inch-barreled single shot 10-bore with a green and black camouflage pattern. The same 10-gauge barreled action is also being made into a 22-inch-barreled Turkey Gun, which is drilled and tapped to accommodate the ever-growing trend toward scoped turkey guns.

IGA

From Brazil, IGA shotguns nestle into the lower-priced ranges of today's market. The first such guns were quite basic, but they've been upgraded somewhat in a new O/U called the Condor Supreme. It's a better looking gun than the originals, having a higher grade of Brazilian walnut, checkering fore and aft, a ventilated rib, rolled-on engraving, screw-in chokes, automatic ejectors, and barrels suited for steel shot with 3-inch chambers. It's a step forward by IGA. A 410-bore English-style double is also new at IGA this year, as is a 16-gauge Uplander SxS that should attract some bird hunters.

Laurona

One of the tragedies of U.S. gun sales is the failure of Laurona O/Us to find a home with some importer. These, along with the Lanbers, are some of the best guns built in Spain. The Laurona has a super twin non-selective single trigger setup. The front trigger taps off the lower barrel first, while a second pull fires the upper tube. The rear trigger reverses that firing sequence. A very versatile arrangement, indeed. Hopefully, some Yankee importer will pick up on both the Laurona and Lanber.

Marocchi

For years, Precision Sales International has been bringing Marocchi O/Us from Italy under the Conquista model name. These are nicely made competition guns which are suited for lefties and ladies as well as for right-handed shooters. And now there's a new one, the Classic Doubles Model 92, which is built on a low-profiled action with replaceable trunnions and length-of-pull adjustments. It has 30-inch barrels with 3-inch chambers for hunters who want to use the same gun on Sporting Clays and Skeet. The muzzles are ported, while the screw-in chokes are extra-long units. This is the basic gun, which has been attracting attention in the U.K. under the Classic Doubles moniker, and at $1500 retail, the price will be mighty competitive. There's also a Conquista Sporting Light O/U on the way. It'll scale just 7½ pounds and is for shooters who have difficulty with the more ponderous target guns.

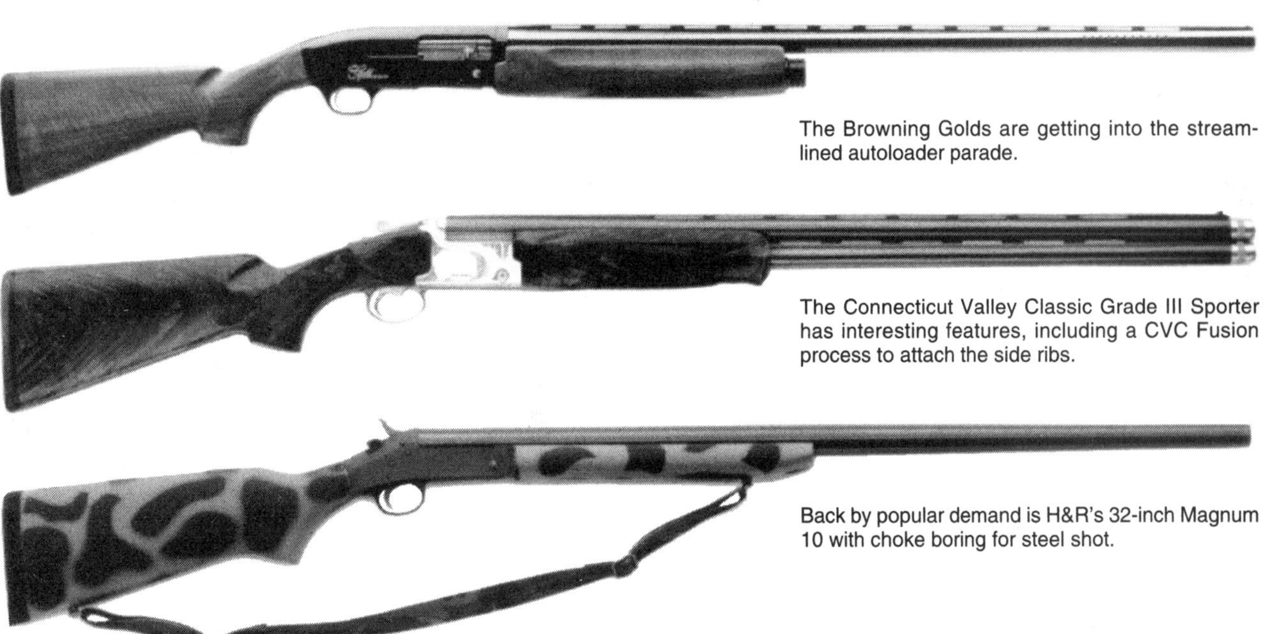

The Browning Golds are getting into the streamlined autoloader parade.

The Connecticut Valley Classic Grade III Sporter has interesting features, including a CVC Fusion process to attach the side ribs.

Back by popular demand is H&R's 32-inch Magnum 10 with choke boring for steel shot.

Connecticut Valley Classic

With ample publicity preceding it, the CVC over/under is breaking out in Sporting, Field, Skeet, Waterfowl and Flyer grades. This gun is built along the lines of the defunct Classic Doubles line, which trailed the earlier Winchester M101. It has nice handling qualities with lively, albeit disciplined, barrels. There's also a straight-gripped bird gun.

The CVC O/Us have their ribs attached by an electron-beam welding process called "CVC Fusion," which is said to achieve added barrel strength at a lighter weight than does lead soldering. The CVCs are

The Model 333 from Turkey via Tristar Sporting Arms, Ltd., is a very affordable O/U with excellent workmanship and materials.

Merkel

From Suhl, the gunmaking capital of Germany, comes a new Sporting Clays gun, the Merkel Model 200 SC. Imported by GSI, Inc., of Alabama, it has the same great pointing qualities as the Merkel field guns. The 30-inch barrels are given Briley chokes, and the woodwork is deluxe stuff. But although it's nice to have a Merkel Sporting Clays gun, it's disappointing to note that the M200 Merkel O/U is being dropped. The Model 201 will now be the lowest grade Merkel stackbarrel available.

Mossberg

Mossberg's 1996 catalog lists two new concepts. One is the Model 695 bolt action, which Mossberg fits into its turkey systems. With a 22-inch barrel and Extra-Full Accu-Choke, it fits a Woodland camouflage synthetics stock. Mossberg's plan is to have it handle like a sporter rifle. One blotch is the protruding magazine well, but turkeys probably won't see it. The gun is drilled and tapped for scopes.

The other Mossberg entry is the so-called Viking line of standard M500, M9200 and M835 repeaters. These have green stock/forend components and sorta blend into the bush without the camo patterns that increase a shotgun's production cost.

Remington

Remington has carried the Peerless forward into a tournament grade gun, the Model 396, which comes in Skeet and Sporting Clays modes. With fancy walnut and chemically etched engraving, it is a truly attractive O/U. Each gun has subtleties common to its specialty. Why no trap grade? I dunno.

Remington has also enhanced the Model 870 Wingmaster and variants of its M11-87 semi-auto by applying fine roll-on engraving in flowing scroll patterns and with lifelike game and dog scenes. The M1100 20-gauge Skeet gun is back, and there's an M1100 28-gauge Sporting Clays gun with screw-in chokes, too. The M870 trap gun also returns, but, alas, all Remington tournament grades are now custom-shop orders at higher prices.

Perhaps the best news for hunters is that the great 12-gauge M1100, arguably the best-pointing repeater ever made, is back in the line as a regular item.

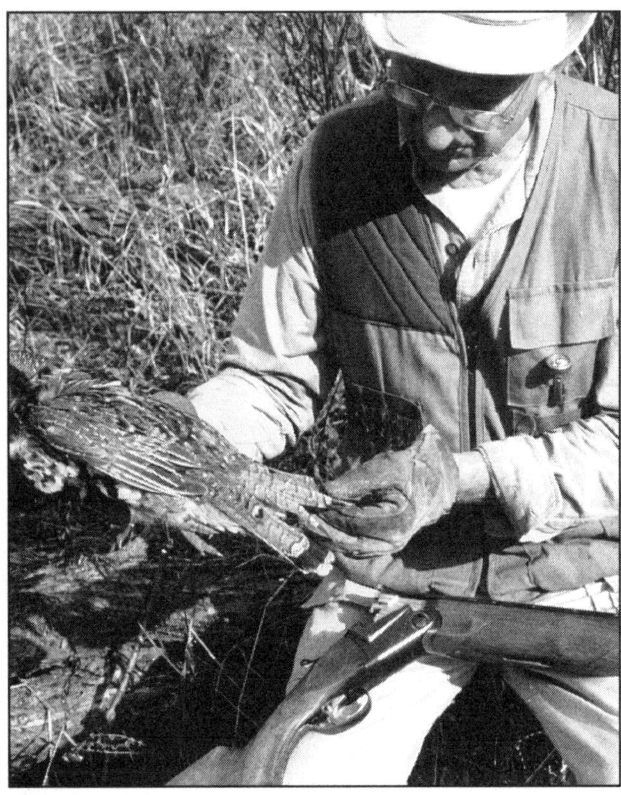

The SKB Model 505 is an affordable, entry-level O/U with field-efficient pointing qualities.

Savage

Savage is using its proven M110 bolt action on a new 12-gauge slug gun, the Model 210 Master Shot. It's designed for optimum accuracy and velocity with sabot slugs. The twist is 1:27 in a 24-inch barrel that's chambered for 3-inch loads. There are no iron sights because anyone opting for this deer gun will surely want a scope. The stock is a nicely profiled synthetic.

SKB

A most titillating announcement is the reappearance of SKB's Model 385 side-by-side. Nobody has ever questioned SKB quality, and these 385s won't be questioned, either. They're neat small gauges, made only in 20 and 28 at this time, with the buyer's choice of pistol-grip or English-style stock. The 385s have silver-nitrided receivers with scroll and game scenes nicely done. The action body is scalloped, and the trigger is a single-selective job. Stocks and forends are shaped from selected American walnut and are given a high-gloss finish. Both gauges come with screw-in choke tubes.

Otherwise, the Model 785 SKB O/Us remain extremely attractive pieces with effective handling qualities, while the M505 is a solid entry-level stackbarrel.

Tristar Sporting Arms, Ltd.

Unknown to most Westerners, Turkey has a solid reputation for gunmaking and as a nation of hunters. Tristar is taking advantage of this by importing Turkish-made doubles that show good quality at affordable prices. The Model 333 O/U is uppermost, but there are side-by-sides as well as a special model designed by Marty Fajen to fit the female shotgunner's special needs.

Turkish Firearms Corp.

This firm also brings Turkish doubles to the U.S., but its line rises to higher prices and more ornate pieces than the Tristar offerings. New this year is a cute 410 side-by-side with super wood and very nice handling qualities. The Turks take pride in their steels, and much of the work is done in a cottage-industry setting as specialists work in their own shops. In general, these guns have good handling qualities.

Watson Bros.

Connoisseurs of fine guns have always related the name of Watson Bros. to ultra-fine smallbore doubles. The name has faded in recent years, but the company's revamped 20-bore deserves mention. Based on the round body concept, the new Watson double has a narrower action strap to utilize more wood, and the forend iron has also been reduced in width for the same reason. The knuckle pin is trimmed by 1/8-inch for a better taper, while the barrels are kept slender. A self-opener, the Watson 20 scales but 6 pounds, while a companion O/U goes a mere 6 1/2 pounds. But here again, you'll need deep pockets, as it's a handmade gem.

Winchester

The Winchester 1400 semi-auto has been dropped with little chance of a resurrection, but the Model 1300 is alive and well. The Ranger version is an economy-priced slide action, but the M1300 Walnut Field is a really solid hunting piece. Winchester likes to say, "No pump is faster." Whatever. The myriad barrels available for any M1300 make it a true all-arounder, and the various camouflage synthetic-stocked models round out the line. ●

THE REBORE STILL WORKS

★ by NORMAN E. JOHNSON ★

THE LONG, TIRING stalk on snowshoes took me to within 260 yards of the suspicious coyote. Having decided about the range, I lay prone, with my rifle resting steady over my shooting pad. I'd made so many shots like this, it almost seemed routine; but after the recoil and the dusting of snow, the coyote was on its way. Missing an ordinarily easy shot prompted a close look at my well-used rifle—including its bore.

That was back in the early '60s and the Model 70 Winchester 243 Varmint rifle I was using had developed extensive bore erosion. It had served me well as one of my first fox and coyote rifles, and noting signs of the gun's imminent failure really bothered me. Becoming attached to a rifle that is losing its usefulness left me with few options, and setting the gun away as a keepsake was not one of them.

Barrel reboring was a preferred alternative to rebarreling, and I soon had a letter off to a company that performed this work. The Atkinson & Marquart Rifle Co. out of Prescott, Arizona, promptly re-

The older Winchester Model 70 rifles rebored to caliber 257 Roberts Improved (Ackley): (top) Target model with Winchester Marksman stock rebored from 220 Swift and Varmint model rebored from 243 Winchester.

sponded to my plea for help. I was encouraged when I was told I could have my rifle rebored to 257 Improved and could opt for a slower rifling pitch which would adapt to my special bullet needs. All I had to do was send the barreled action. They said the rebored barrel could be expected to parallel the accuracy performance of the former caliber. The price was $28.10 for the complete job of reboring, rifling and rechambering.

As my thoughts take me back to my first 257 Improved cartridge and the extended years of shooting made possible through reboring three of my most treasured old rifles, the

The author with a very large red fox and his Model 70 Varmint in 257 Improved. No better rifle is available for Johnson's kind of shooting or he'd have it.

experience has been most pleasant. My enduring enthusiasm had been equally divided between this most capable 257 wildcat cartridge and the attraction of reboring a time-tested old rifle. Now after thirty years, I would like to share these experiences. Regretfully, the Atkinson & Marquart Rifle Co. is no more, nor are 1960s prices, but I will review rifle reboring and show how this could help you realize added shooting pleasure from guns that no longer serve you well.

In October of 1964 I received the first of my two rebored Winchester early Model 70 barreled actions in 257 Roberts Improved from Atkinson & Marquart. I also had an earlier stainless steel varmint barrel rebored from 220 Swift to 270 Winchester in 1965. So it was with a sense of satisfaction that I chose to have my third rifle rebored in early 1967. The measure of a good rifle bore is in its performance, and the first two rebores were producing outstandingly reliable performance.

I had a very well-preserved, older Winchester Model 70 Target with stainless steel barrel in 220 Swift with a badly eroded barrel. I was acquiring considerable experience with the first 257 Improved cartridge, and reboring this one to the same case didn't take much contemplation on my part. The 257 Roberts Improved (Ackley) with its minimum body taper and 40-degree shoulder comes very close to the mythical, all-around cartridge in 25-caliber. It is near case capacity, producing excellent velocity without erratic pressures, and in a pinch, factory ammunition can be fired through the rifle. The Ackley version of the

(Right) Here are the standard 257 Roberts and 257 Roberts Improved (Ackley) with 40-degree shoulder.

(Below) Johnson favors high-power Unertl and Leupold scopes like this M-8 16x Leupold.

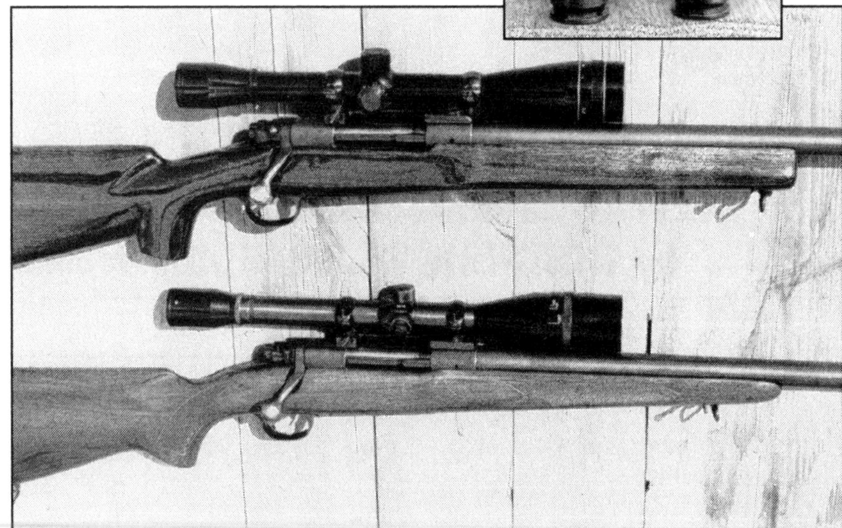

many 257 Improved cartridges will increase velocity over its 257 Roberts cousin by a modest 200 fps. There is no problem attaining 3500 fps velocity with 87-grain bullets in a 26-inch barrel using a few different powders. The Improved case will move a 100-grain bullet at just over 3200 fps and is an ideal cartridge for deer, bear and some other larger game with 100- to 120-grain bullets.

Both rifles had been thoroughly gone over to obviate any inherent accuracy problems that could have originated from sources other than the bore. I left few stones unturned in this area.

My normal procedure with any rifle is to alternately tighten and loosen the receiver screws while carefully feeling for any metal-to-wood movement. Even though the actions of these two guns had been drawn down into the wood for some time, there was noticable action movement as the rear tang screw was moved with the recoil lug screw firm. This is typical of quite a few Model 70 actions where the mid-receiver rail rides unevenly, or higher, on the stock wood here than in the tang area. It must be corrected to avoid group-walking on target.

I proceeded to correct this condition, as I have with many Model 70s, by carefully glass-bedding the action with two-point support, including the recoil lug area and the rear tang. The entire receiver rail is thus left free of wood contact. After that, the front receiver screw is tightened firmly and the rear tang screw receives lesser torque to avoid crushing the somewhat weaker support in this area. The center receiver screw simply goes along for the ride thereafter and is just tightened enough to remain in place, or it will surely spring the rifle's action causing other accuracy problems.

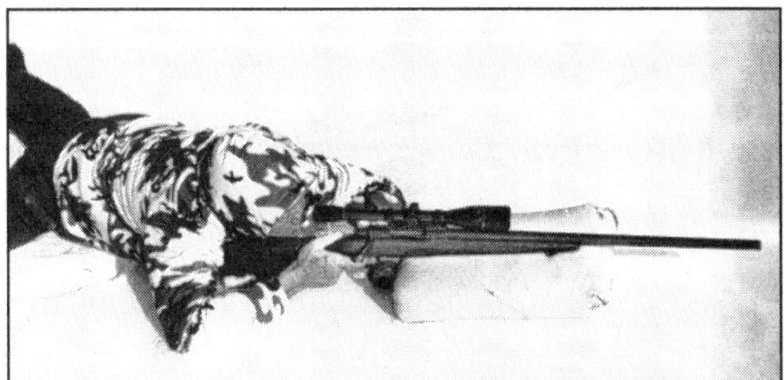

The author's typical long-range shooting position for fox and coyote. The shooting pad has served him well over a variety of conditions, and more than 1000 red fox alone have been taken over the years.

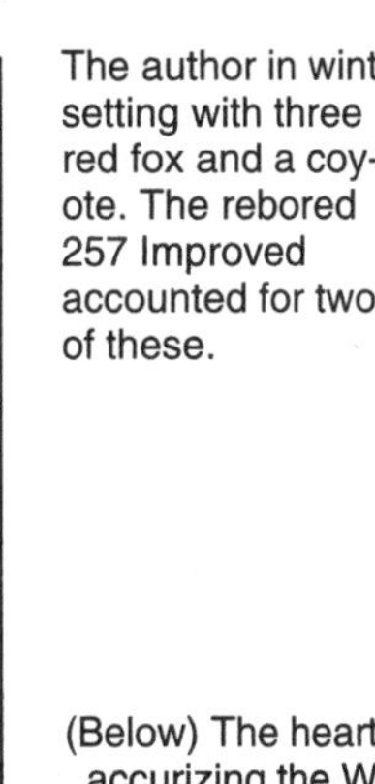

The author in winter setting with three red fox and a coyote. The rebored 257 Improved accounted for two of these.

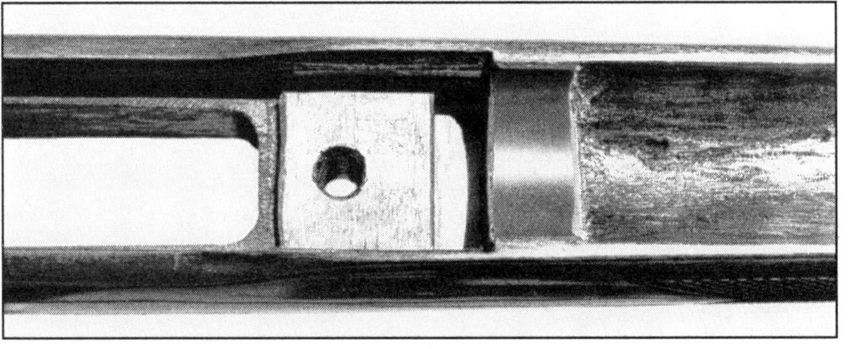

(Below) The heart of accurizing the Winchester Model 70 lies in precise bedding of the area around the recoil lug (and sometimes an inch or so forward) and the rear tang.

Action glass-bedding was just becoming popular at this time, and I had done several rifles with very excellent results. I have since bedded or rebedded more than a hundred rifles using glass-bedding and can strongly recommend this procedure.

Along with action bedding, I have found that barrel free-floating does, in most instances, improve overall accuracy and definitely produces a more dependable point of impact over time as rifles are subjected to precipitant temperature and humidity changes. Therefore, I also free-floated the barrels of these two Model 70s, leaving but an inch or so of barrel bedding surface just forward of the receiver lug.

With a little care and knowledge, the Model 70 trigger can be adjusted to a very crisp 1½ to 2 pounds. This I accomplish by carefully honing all mating surfaces of the trigger and sear, being careful not to round off any edges. As a final polishing effort, I use J.B. Bore Paste, which is an ultra-mild abrasive. I will also substitute the original, overly firm trigger spring with a lighter one and reduce trigger/sear travel and trigger creep as well. Triggers gone over in this way are safe and a pleasure to shoot, and it does enhance accuracy. Should I sell such a rifle, the heavier trigger spring is replaced. If you are inexperienced in this area, seek professional help to avoid possible problems.

The temptation to test a rifle before it is fully ready is often overwhelming. I have sometimes regretted it, but not with these two rifles. My first rebored M70s gave me sufficient indication that fine performance was in store if I would pace myself while preparing the Target model for its debut.

Using the Redfield scope mounting system, I carefully mounted fixed-power scopes on both of these rifles. Today the varmint-weight rifle wears an older 10x Unertl receiver-mounted scope and the Model 70 Target has a Leupold 16x M-8, though each has carried different optics in years past. These are, however, fine long-range

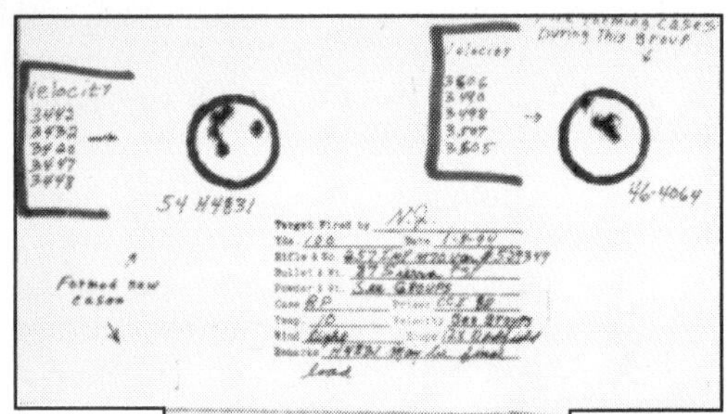

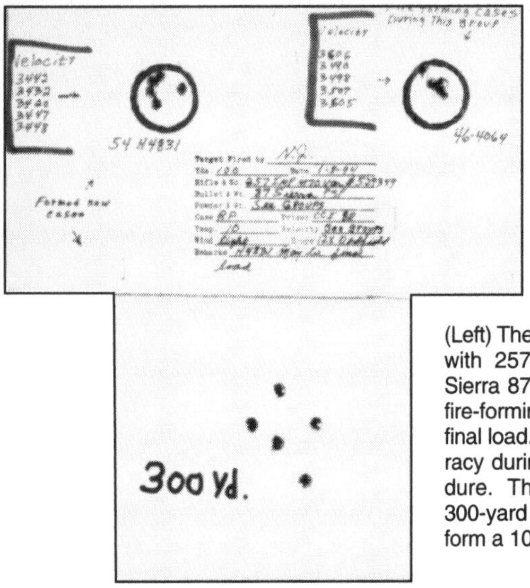

(Left) These 1994 targets were shot with 257 Improved Varmint and Sierra 87-grain bullets (from right): fire-forming of cases and using the final load. Note the incredible accuracy during the fire-forming procedure. The bottom group shows 300-yard accuracy and actual drop form a 100-yard zero.

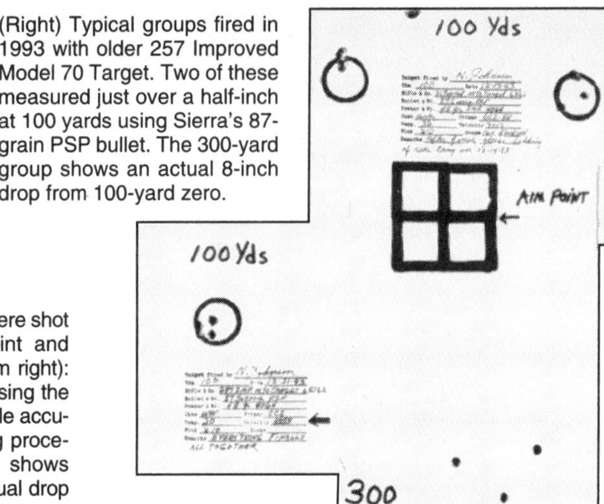

(Right) Typical groups fired in 1993 with older 257 Improved Model 70 Target. Two of these measured just over a half-inch at 100 yards using Sierra's 87-grain PSP bullet. The 300-yard group shows an actual 8-inch drop from 100-yard zero.

varmint scopes and serve equally well while shooting the guns from benchrest.

Working with the two Winchester Model 70s in 257 Roberts Improved (Ackley) has been a most pleasurable experience dating back more than thirty years. I feel I have been part of these rifles and they have been part of me.

Prior to test-shooting any new bore, I frequently lap or polish it. This usually includes all those bores not known to have this work professionally performed on them. While I'll not go into the finer details of this procedure, it continues to serve me well in attaining break-in accuracy as well as in revitalizing bores that often require such a treatment. Following the initial bore conditioning, I selected cases in preparation for fire-forming in each rifle's chamber. I had cut down a set of Weatherby 257 Magnum handloading dies for use in neck-sizing and bullet seating later on. Cases would not, of course, interchange in these two rifles, and limiting case preparation to neck-sizing only has its advantages.

In my attempt to create cases for my first 257 Improved wildcat cartridge—for use in the varmint-weight rifle—I sized down some old 30-06 military match brass. As I look back, this was a mistake, as I had to turn down the thickened necks and anneal them to prevent loss due to neck splitting. Case volume was also somewhat less using these cases, essentially reducing the effectiveness of the Improved case. I would also recommend pre-testing your cases for volume prior to final selection and forming, then use the brand with the greater powder capacity. Cases will vary somewhat

The bench is the other place Johnson finds out if a rifle will shoot. This is the rebored Model 70 Target.

by brand and lot. For example, the empty Winchester primed cases I used weighed 167.3 grains and had a full case capacity of IMR4350 powder of 57½ grains. The Remington cases weighed 172.8 grains and held 55.8 grains of IMR4350 powder. Thus, the expansion ratio (ratio of interior case volume to bore volume) would be of some concern to the handloader.

I lost some cases in the fireforming process. Today, I use and can strongly recommend standard 257 Roberts cases for fire-forming; sizing up the necks of 6mm Remington cases is also an excellent way to get brass for the 257 Improved cartridge. The fire-forming process is uncomplicated and is best done using near-full loads in factory cases. Some of the earlier recommendations suggested forming cases with much reduced loads, which is believed to reduce case splitting loss. In my own experience, such reduced loads actually increased case splitting or separation as they clearly failed to fully form the cases. Using the same load you would use in the standard 257 Roberts will result in a perfectly fire-formed case. Neck-resizing only is used thereafter, and case loss will be virtually nonexistent as you load and use the rifle. The minimal case body taper and the sharp 40-degree shoulder substantially reduce case stretching and neck thickening once cases are formed.

Sometimes I feel I've spent as much time at the bench as most Supreme Court justices and have made as many important decisions while there. Thus, before I approach the shooting bench, I have a pretty good idea of the outcome of a rifle and its load. In both 257 Improved Winchester Model 70 rifles, I had chosen a 1:12-inch rifling pitch over the standard 1:10-inch twist, an option not ordinarily available in factory rifles. My intention here was to improve both velocity and accuracy using a lighter varmint bullet while reducing the bullet energy consumption used to turn or stabilize it on its passage through the bore. Such energy loss can be significantly high, and stabilizing a bullet beyond that which is required to produce best accuracy is not needed or recommended. Further, the 1:12 rifling pitch will stabilize 100-, 117- and 120-grain bullets very well.

During my initial fire-forming process, rifle accuracy—using standard 257 Roberts handloads—was, indeed, encouraging, with most loads producing well under 1 MOA accuracy. I did, however, begin my full-load workup with both rifles prior to fire-forming the whole lot of 100 cases.

Looking back three decades, there never were the bullets or powders available to the handloader as we have today. This was particularly true of the 25-caliber, and that has had a lasting effect to this day on this fine caliber. Sierra, Speer and Hornady produced ideally suited varmint bullets in 87-grain weights when I first started using and testing the Improved cartridge. Today several other bullet manufacturers have followed suit, but the 25 caliber in general does not quite have the fine bullet selection available to other calibers like the 243, 224, et al.

For the Model 70 Target, I had Atkinson & Marquart throat the bore to the Sierra 87-grain PSP bullet (which was delivering outstanding accuracy in my first 257 Improved Model 70). In those days, I used a lot of DuPont's Improved Military Rifle Powder (IMR), mainly because it was excellent and available. Now the array of powders available to handloaders leaves them in awe.

Perhaps because it was there when I needed it—and continues to be available—the Sierra 87-grain pointed softpoint bullet has been a worthy

LOAD & TRAJECTORY COMPARISON

—Bullet— (Wgt.Grs.)	(Type)	Load (Grs./Powder)	Primer	MV (fps)	—Bullet Drop from 100-Yard Zero (26" Barrel)— 100 yds.	200 yds.	250 yds.	300 yds.	350 yds.	375 yds.	400 yds.
257 Roberts Improved (Ackley)											
87	Sierra PSP	48.5/IMR4064	CCI 200	3525	0	1.8	3.8	8	12	16	21
100	Speer PSP-BT	53.0/H4831	Fed. 210	3200	0	2.6	4.8	10	17	21	25
117	Sierra PSP	46.5/IMR4350	CCI 200	2920	0	3	6	12	20	23	27
257 Roberts											
87	Sierra PSP	42.0/IMR4064	CCI 200	3250	0	2.8	5	10.5	16	21	26
117	Speer PSP	40.5/IMR4350	Fed. 210	2780	0	3.8	7	14	20	26	33

REBORING INFORMATION

Rebore Facility	Services Offered/Comments	Basic Reboring Costs	
Ridgetop Sporting Goods **Richard Nickel, Owner**	Complete reboring, rerifling, rechambering and barrel relining, etc. Does stainless barrels. Call for available or special reamers, etc. Uses cut rifling process.	Straight rebore/rerifle with no chamber work up to 308-caliber	$125
		Chamber work over 35-caliber	$135
		Rebore with chambering and headspace	$160
		Over 35-caliber	$170
Redman's Rifling & Reboring **Randall Redman, Owner**	Established 1973. Complete reboring, rifling and rechambering, and barrel relining. Does *not* currently rebore stainless barrels. Call for available or special reamers. Uses cut rifling process. Brochure available.	Rebore and rifle modern barrels starting at	$230
		Rebore and rifle modern barrels including reaming neck and chamber.	$250
		Rechambering work starting at	$40
LaBounty Precision Reboring, Inc. **Clifford F. LaBounty, Owner**	Complete reboring, rerifling, chambering and barrel relining, etc. Does stainless barrels. Call for available or special reamers. Uses cut rifling process. Brochure available.	Rebore and rifle modern barrels	$105
		Barrel larger than 375-caliber	$115
		Complete rebore & conversion including neck and throat	$205
		Rebore and rifling with new chamber	$245

performer in both M70 rifles. For example, with the 87-grain Sierra bullets, the varmint-weight M70 does best with 54 grains of H4831 powder, whereas the Target model performs noticeably better with 48.5 grains of IMR4064 powder with this bullet. Half-minute-of-angle groups are quite common, and long-range trajectory is impressive. As a point of interest, 54 grains of H4831 is a compressed load, whereas the 48.5 IMR4064 load fills the case just below the base of a seated bullet, Neither, however, shows any sign of excessive chamber pressure. In my limited tests using Winchester's Magnum Rifle powder (WMR), accuracy showed promise with bullet weights from 87 to over 100 grains using CCI 250 Magnum primers. Early tests using Hodgdon's new Varget powder in the Target 257 Improved rifle produced excellent accuracy and trajectory. Yet, each rifle is different, and loads should be approached with caution, with particular attention paid to the case capacity of the different brands of formed cases used.

Though I'm not in a posture to cite from first-hand test experience on the present-day performance of rebored barrels, my past experience has proved most favorable. However, my recent extensive communication with three facilities whose mastery includes reboring clearly shows a great deal of knowledge and capability in this field. I'm very encouraged to learn that the state-of-the-art in today's reboring remains on the cutting edge of technology.

As in the past, there is really no mystery in producing a rebored and rifled barrel. In reboring and rifling, a smaller bore is drilled or reamed to a larger caliber. It is generally accepted that there must be about .030-inch difference between the old and new bore for a good cleanup where new riflings can be cut. During the reboring process, the rifling grooves are precisely cut using a special "hook-type" cutting tool. As many as forty or more passes of the tool are often required to cut one of the usual six grooves, shaving as little as .0001-inch of metal at each pass. The average cut rifling groove depth is .0040-inch, as compared to .0025-inch with button rifling. Due to anticipated complications, the button rifling process is not used in the reboring and rifling of modern tapered barrels.

There is a great deal of difference in rifle barrel steels, and this affects the outcome of reboring and rifling. While some facilities may rebore certain barrel steels, others will avoid them. These may include steels such as chrome vanadium, original Sako barrels, some types of stainless steels and others. The properties of some steels make rifling most difficult with unpredictable outcomes. For this reason, reboring is usually performed at the customer's risk where such steels are involved, and some will not attempt to work at all.

One need not look far to see some of the advantages of having a rifle rebored. In my own case, I have continued to enjoy outstanding performance from three treasured rifles brought back through reboring over a period of more than thirty years. There are many claims, backed by proof, that the cut rifling is, indeed, as accurate a method of rifling as is available. Some of these have set world records for accuracy. The degree of precision in making these cut rifled barrels is virtually unlimited.

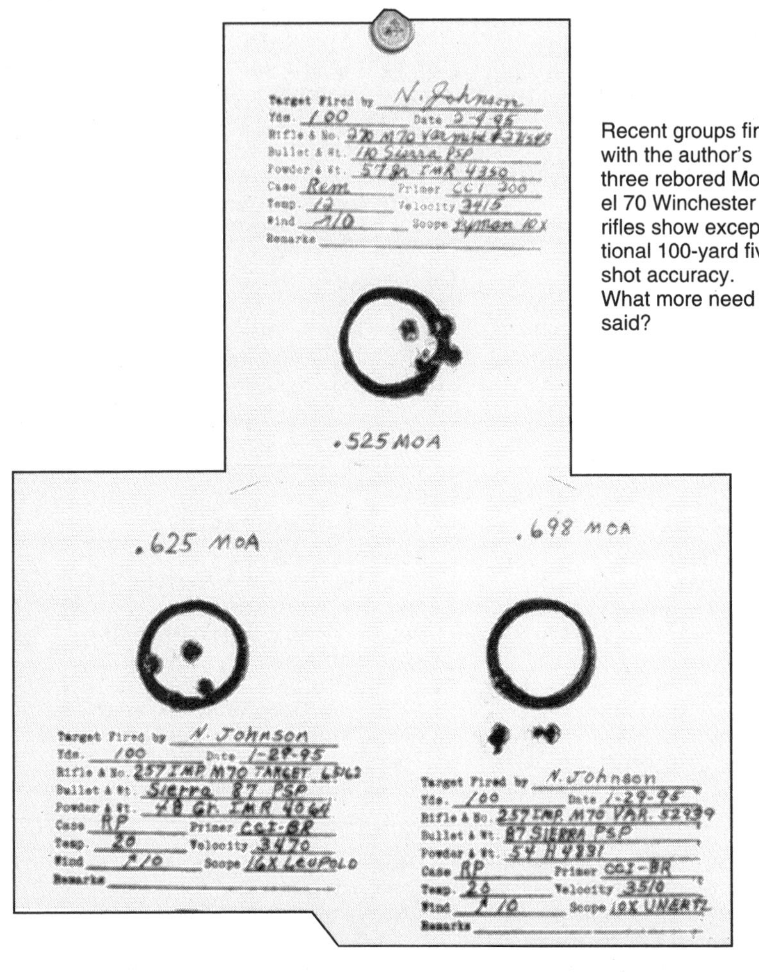

Recent groups fired with the author's three rebored Model 70 Winchester rifles show exceptional 100-yard five-shot accuracy. What more need be said?

Through reboring, the rifle retains its original outward appearance and requires no rebluing or stock inletting. The twist rate of a rebored rifle barrel can also be selected to fit the bullets you plan to use. This can present a great advantage for the knowledgeable rifleman/handloader. Cartridge selection, including those commercially unavailable, is limited only to the chambering reamers available to the reboring facility. The satisfaction in working with some of these cartridges can be very rewarding.

From a cost standpoint, reboring continues to be an economical move, too. In most cases, a rifle can be rebored for less money than the cost of a custom rebarrel job. Of course, prices and services vary, and the consumer must be aware of this. As I reflect back to the 1960s when I had my rifles rebored, the total price for the three guns, including rechambering, was under $75, but I could buy a new Winchester Model 70 for $135 then, and gunpowder sold for about $1.85 a pound.

Now the time has arrived when a few of my faithful old rifles are beginning to show evidence of bore degeneration. Old habits die hard, and I won't hesitate to have them rebored. ●

• ABLE SENTRY • DENY FLIGHT • DESERT STORM • JUST CAUSE • PROVIDE COMFORT • PROVIDE HOPE • PROVIDE PROMISE • RESTORE HOPE • SAFE HAVEN • SHARP GUARD • SUPPORT HOPE • SOUTHERN WATCH •
UPHOLD DEMOCRACY • URGENT FURY • VIGILANT WARRIOR • ABLE SENTRY • DENY FLIGHT • DESERT STORM • JUST CAUSE • PROVIDE COMFORT • PROVIDE HOPE • PROVIDE PROMISE • RESTORE HOPE • SAFE HAVEN • SHARP GUARD • SUPPORT HOPE • SOUTHERN WATCH •
It's good to know your new partner is a combat veteran.
UNITED STATES AIR FORCE
UNITED STATES COAST GUARD 1790
BERETTA U.S.A. CORP. ACKK. MD.—MADE IN USA
BER344070 Z
UNITED STATES ARMY
UNITED STATES NAVY
UNITED STATES MARINE CORPS
If you're serious about personal protection, you need a serious handgun. At the heart of every Beretta large frame pistol is the legendary 92F…10-year veteran of the U.S. Military and choice of thousands of law enforcement agencies in the United States. We've won those honors by beating the competition time after time in things that really matter. Things like reliability and performance. Just as important is the gut-level trust Beretta has won on the world's battlefields.
Select from Beretta 92 (9mm) or 96 (.40 cal.) models. Both offer a choice of two operating systems. Available in Standard and Centurion models, your Beretta dealer can help you pinpoint the model best for you. Remember, it's either a Beretta or something else. For complete information, contact your Beretta dealer or Beretta U.S.A. Corp., 17601 Beretta Drive, Accokeek, Maryland 20607. (301) 283-2191.
Beretta U.S.A.
Model 92/96F. Legendary reliability in 9mm or .40 cal. 10+1 firepower. Double/single action with external safety/decocking lever.
Model 92/96D. Double-action only. Features slick slide system with no external safety lever and bobbed hammer.
Model 92/96F Centurion. New shortened high capacity versions of the 92/96 models (10+1 firepower) with a compact slide and barrel.
Model 92/96D Centurion. Double-action only version of the Centurion. Features slick slide system with no external safety lever and bobbed hammer.
F Models—double/single action with external safety/decocking levers; D Models—double-action-only with no external safety.
When in New York, visit the Beretta Gallery at 718 Madison Avenue. For your copy of the 1996 Beretta Worldwide catalog, call 1-800-528-7453. ($3.00 shipping and handling.)
• UPHOLD DEMOCRACY • URGENT FURY • VIGILANT WARRIOR • ABLE SENTRY • DENY FLIGHT • DESERT STORM • JUST CAUSE • PROVIDE COMFORT • PROVIDE HOPE • PROVIDE PROMISE • RESTORE HOPE •
ABLE SENTRY • DENY FLIGHT • DESERT STORM • JUST CAUSE • PROVIDE COMFORT • PROVIDE HOPE • PROVIDE PROMISE • RESTORE HOPE • SAFE HAVEN • SHARP GUARD • SUPPORT HOPE • SOUTHERN WATCH • UPHOLD DEMOCRACY • URGENT FURY • VIGILANT WARRIOR

The only autoloader that softens the blow

here...

and here.

The Soft Shooting System™ that handles target loads to 3″ Mags without ever changing barrels.

Now, one autoloader can cover every shotgunner's game. When the season changes, you only change chokes, not barrels. Mossberg's exclusive gas compensation system is the key. Its simple, yet rugged, design vents excess pressure while operating the action. The result is a substantial reduction in recoil without any reduction in reliability. You'll also like the reduction in cost compared to other autoloaders.

A. gas from barrel
B. action movement
C. vents excess gas

Camo, Slugs and Combos make the Model 9200 the most versatile autoloader.

Mossy Oak® Treestand, new Realtree® All Purpose Gray and affordable OFM Woodland… turkey hunters and waterfowlers can find a Model 9200 for the cover they hunt. Slug hunters enjoy less recoil and still get all of the accuracy of a scope mounted, fully rifled barrel with the Trophy Slugster™ version. With both a 28" vent rib barrel and a 24" rifled slug barrel, the Model 9200 Combo is Mossberg's best deal.

Even the new, more affordable Viking Grade™ Model 9200 has a Lifetime Limited Warranty.

The new Viking Grade™ Model 9200 delivers soft shooting, gas operated performance in an even more attractively priced model. Outfitted with a rugged, good looking Moss green synthetic stock and a Mil-Spec Parkerized barrel, the Viking Grade Model 9200 is loaded with Mossberg Value.

Just like every other Model 9200, it's backed by Mossberg's Lifetime Limited Warranty.

MOSSBERG®

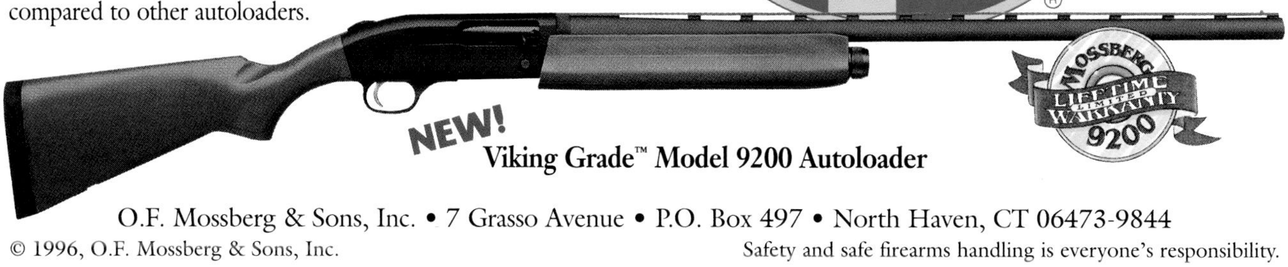

MOSSBERG LIFETIME LIMITED WARRANTY 9200

NEW! Viking Grade™ Model 9200 Autoloader

O.F. Mossberg & Sons, Inc. • 7 Grasso Avenue • P.O. Box 497 • North Haven, CT 06473-9844

© 1996, O.F. Mossberg & Sons, Inc.

Safety and safe firearms handling is everyone's responsibility.

MODELS 908 • 909 • 910 • 410 • 457

THE VALUE SERIES FROM SMITH & WESSON

The new Models 908, 410 and 457 join the Models 909 and 910 as part of the Smith & Wesson Value Series. These no compromise pistols deliver performance in three calibers and two frame sizes. Whether you choose the Model 908, 909 or 910 in the popular 9mm, the Model 410 in the versatile .40 S&W or the compact Model 457 in the old reliable .45 ACP, there is a Smith & Wesson Value Series Pistol that meets your needs.

The new series of utilitarian pistols feature the same attention to detail and precision that has given Smith & Wesson handguns their reputation for quality. All value Series pistols come with three dot sight system to bring the shooter on target quickly. The consistently smooth trigger pull enhances shot to shot accuracy.

The three dot low profile sight system brings the shooter on target quickly, shot after shot.

The combination of the aluminum alloy frames and carbon steel slides create a rugged, lightweight comfortable to carry series of pistols that deliver the performance expected from Smith & Wesson. Bead-blast matte finish and slide mounted manual safety and decocking lever rounds out these high value packages.

With their Traditional Double Action firing system, these pistols can be carried safely yet offer instant access when needed. From the compact Models 908 and 457 to the single stack 909 and the full size Models 910 and 410 these high value pistols don't sacrifice accuracy or compromise performance for price.

Like all Smith & Wesson the value series come with Smith & Wesson's Lifetime Service Policy, just part of the Smith & Wesson ADVANTAGE™ and are backed by a Worldwide Warranty Repair Network. For more information and the location of the Smith & Wesson Stocking Dealer nearest you call 1-800-331-0852, ext 2904.

SPRINGFIELD, MA
QUALITY FIREARMS SINCE 1852

For more information on the Models 909 and 910 and the location of the Smith & Wesson Stocking Dealer nearest you call 1-800-331-0852, extension 2904.

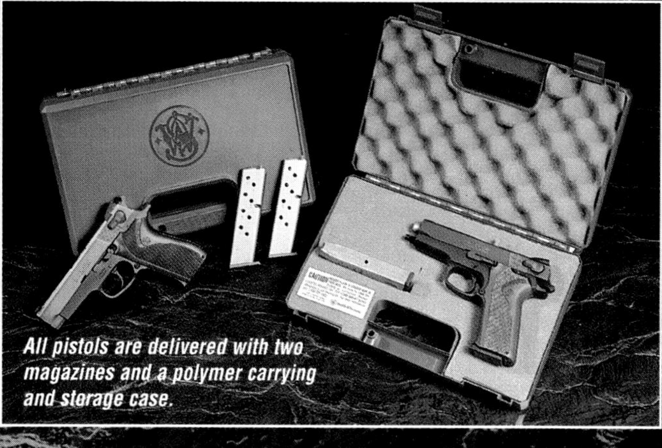

All pistols are delivered with two magazines and a polymer carrying and storage case.

P228 9mm

When the U.S. Army needed a compact sidearm, both for special duty and for concealment, its first choice was the SIG SAUER P228. Similarly, the FBI has chosen the P228 as a compact sidearm for its agents. Despite its small size, this compact pistol packs a *10 round magazine in an easy-pointing, superbly balanced package that's ideal for both law enforcement and personal protection.

SIGARMS

SIGARMS INC.
CORPORATE PARK
EXETER, NH 03833

ENGINEERED RELIABILITY

*13-round magazine available for law enforcement personnel only.

A MAYNARD TALKS

Here I am in 1995, a Long Range Creedmoor Maynard in 44/100 Maynard, ready to shoot another 100 years if I can find an owner who doesn't mind a little recoil.

by MICHAEL PETROV

In its own words, so to speak, an American classic tells how a rifle lasts 132 years.

"MIKE, MY CURRENT caretaker, tells me most gun collectors at one time or another have said 'If only this gun could talk, we would know of the places it has been or who owned it,' so I am going to talk, although from my point of view after 125 years I think of those owners more as my caretakers.

"My first recollection is from about the year 1865, when my action was forged at the Massachusetts Arms Company located at Chicopee Falls, Massachusetts. I was invented by Dr. Edward Maynard, a Washington, D.C., dentist, and I was going to be a 50-caliber percussion saddle-ring carbine and fight in the Civil War. Before I had a chance to serve, the war was over, and I and thousands of others sat at the factory waiting to see what was going to happen to us.

"After the war, many people were resettling out West. With so many surplus percussion carbines on the market, we did not think that the Massachusetts Arms Company would continue to exist, but because our barrels could be changed so easily, and we were now offered in caliber 35 and 40 in sporting rifles and in 55 and 64 in shot barrels, the orders kept coming in. As the workmen returned to the plant, I began to look forward to a trip out West, but instead I just sat on the shelf and watched many friends go.

"In 1873, Dr. Maynard patented a line of centerfire cartridges. All of these had thick rims and Berdan primers. I was taken off the shelf, my

At Shushan, N.Y., in 1911, Ed Leopold, Dr. Baker, A.O. Niedner and Dr. Mann shot woodchucks. Three of them owned me, sooner or later.

saddle ring was removed and the two holes that held it on were filled with screws. Then my percussion nipple was removed and a centerfire firing pin was fitted. My left side was stamped '1873', and back to the shelf I went.

"All the other Maynards were going out with new barrels and stocks and in many different calibers. Many target shooters were using Maynards and writing glowing letters back to the factory about how good the Maynard was. The shooters all liked the fact that you could have several different barrels and only one action.

"A new model rifle was patented in 1882 by Dr. Maynard. The only difference from the Model 1873 was that it was for smaller-diameter, thinner-rimmed cartridges. It could use the same cartridges as the Sharps, Remington, Ballard and others.

"If memory serves me right, it was around the year 1885 the shop foreman announced they had an order for a Model 1802 No. 14 Long Range Creedmoor from E.A. Leopold, of Norristown, Pennsylvania. Leopold was a well-known shooter and author of many articles recommending the Maynard rifle in shooting journals of the time. I will never forget that day, because after sitting around for twenty years I was going to be a Long Range Creedmoor, the most prestigious and expensive rifle of the Maynard line.

"I first went to the action-fitting station where every one of my parts was hand-finished and fitted until I had a crisp trigger pull. Being a Creedmoor rifle, I could only have a single trigger because the rules did not allow a set trigger. At this time, they stamped '1882' on my right side. Next, I was fitted with a 32-inch round barrel in 44-caliber and chambered for the 44-100 Maynard cartridge. I would be shooting a 520-grain paper-patched bullet using 100 grains of blackpowder. A dovetail was cut, a wind-gauge front sight was fitted, and a Maynard rack-and-pinion long-range sight was mounted on my tang.

"I was next fitted with a fancy branch walnut buttstock and forend. The buttstock had a rear sight base back by the buttplate for people who shot lying on their back with their feet toward the target. With the sight back on the heel, you then had a longer sight radius and could make finer sight adjustments.

"After being assembled, I was taken to the range and tested, and I passed with flying colors. I was taken back to the workbench to have my

Jim Foral found this picture of my inventor for Mike. It appeared in the May, 1890, issue of *Forest & Stream.* Nice-looking man, don't you think?

barrel and other parts polished until all the tool marks were removed. I was weighed and came in overweight; the Creedmoor rules said that a rifle had to weigh under 10 pounds. My buttplate was removed and large holes were drilled into the stock to lighten me. Next, my barrel and sights were rust blued and my stock finished.

"Boy, was I handsome!

"I was then sent to shipping where a wooden box was made for me. Included in the box were twenty-five cartridge cases, a cartridge capper and decapper, a charger, a loader, a loading block, a cartridge cleaner, three rods and a brush, two rag holders, a screwdriver, and a hundred patched bullets of 520 grains. I was then shipped Railway Express to Norristown, Pennsylvania, on the Philadelphia and Reading Railway in care of the station agent, who was none other than Edgar A. Leopold.

"Ed took me home and placed me in the gun rack with several other Maynard rifles and two fine old muzzle-loading target rifles, one by Horace Warner and one by Gardner. Ed was a gun crank of the first order, and the next twenty-eight years was the most interesting time in my life. As a station agent, Ed did not make much money, but with a railroad pass we could travel far and wide to visit friends and attend shooting matches. Ed was a member of the rifle clubs of Pottstown, Phoenixville and Norristown. We shot at Walnut Hill, Massachusetts; Stockton, New York; Creedmoor on Long Island; and Sea Girt, New Jersey.

"One of my favorite stories happened at the Sea Girt range. Ed was trying to sight me in at 1000 yards on the day before the match and was having no luck at all. Ed and Harry Pope, the famous barrel maker, walked downrange and found where the bullets had fallen short in the wet sand. Harry then placed a ramrod into the hole and figured out the angle of entry.

"That evening, after careful calculations, Harry told Ed where to set my sight. Ed, however, came up with a different setting.

"The following day, Ed was allowed only two sighting shots, tried his new setting, and missed both times. Ed then moved my sight to the setting suggested by Harry, got on the target with five shots, and won the match.

"Ed was a busy man working for the railroad. When time allowed, he would be out shooting; when not, his time was spent in the gun room writing to his many shooting friends. There was always some experiment he was undertaking. In 1888, Ed made friends with Dr. Franklin W. Mann, who later authored *The Bullet's Flight From Powder To Target.* We made many trips to Dr. Mann's range where he carried out many of the experiments that were suggested by Ed. It was not long before they became close friends, and because I spent much of the time just sitting in the gun room without a lot to do, I counted over 286 letters that Ed wrote to Dr. Mann over a six-year time period.

"Ed wrote for *Shooting and Fishing*, *Western Field*, *Arms and the Man*, and *Outing*. His love was firearms. Many advancements in the field, such as his Banana bullet lubricant and Oleo wads (which were used by many top shooters of the time), were made because of his tireless efforts, yet Mike tells me Ed is unknown to the current shooting fraternity. For a few years, Ed was interested in the art of sailing small vessels and was very proud of the sailing skiff he built to try out some of his theories first hand.

"Ed used me for some of his screen-shooting testing and other experimenting, but as he got older, the recoil bothered him more and more, until one day Ed drilled several holes in the top of my barrel and screwed on a 6-pound bar of lead. Now that I weighed 16 pounds, the recoil was a lot less, and Ed could keep shooting me. We made fewer and fewer trips to

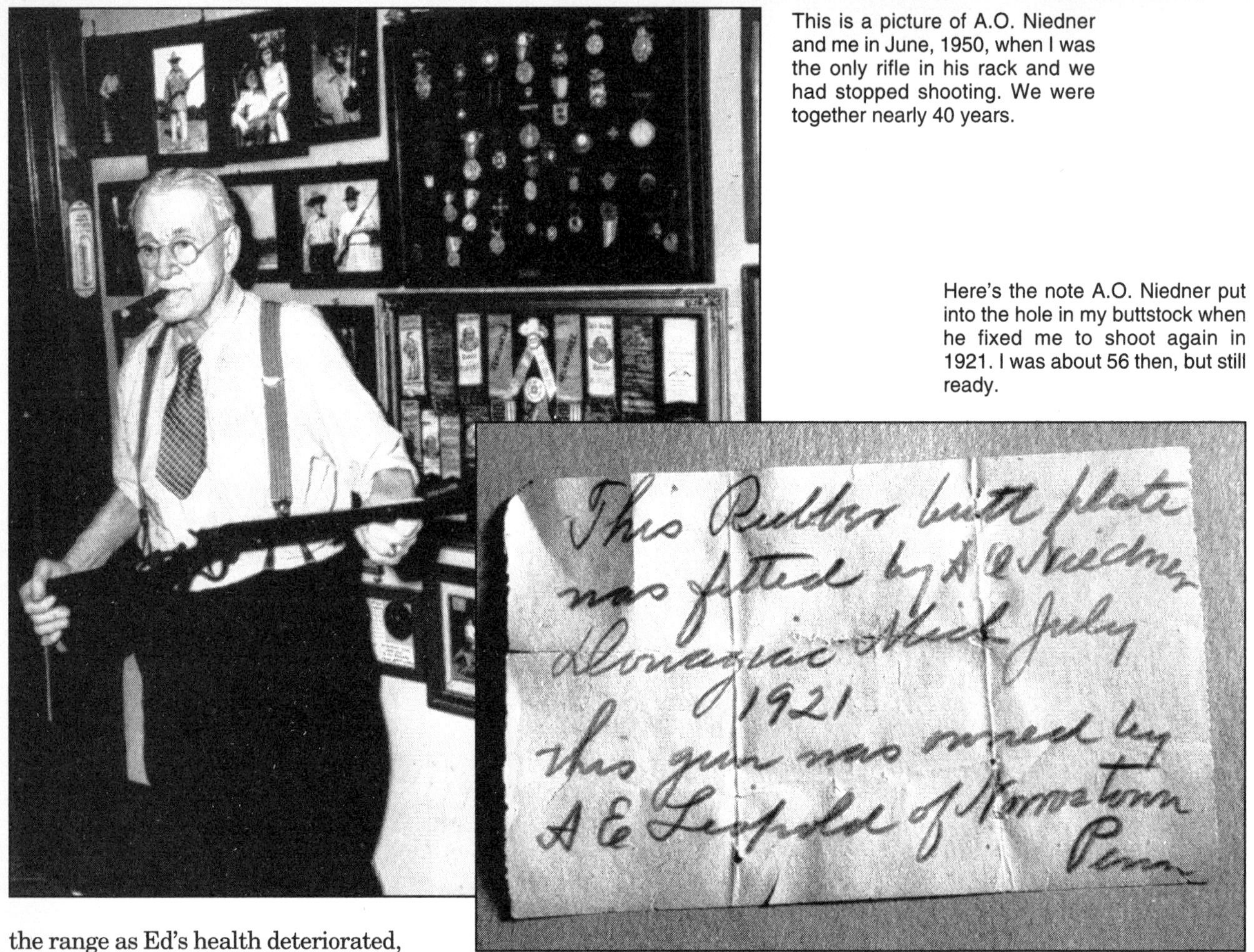

This Rubber butt plate
was fitted by A O Niedner
Dowagiac Mich July
1921
this gun was owned by
A E Leopold of Norristown
Penn

This is a picture of A.O. Niedner and me in June, 1950, when I was the only rifle in his rack and we had stopped shooting. We were together nearly 40 years.

Here's the note A.O. Niedner put into the hole in my buttstock when he fixed me to shoot again in 1921. I was about 56 then, but still ready.

the range as Ed's health deteriorated, until none of us guns were taken to the range any more.

"When Ed died on June 13, 1913, I was sad and scared. What was going to happen to me? I wished Ed were a Viking so his family could place him into his sailing boat, lay me by his side, cover us with wood, raise the sails, set the boat on fire and let us go off into the sunset together.

"Shortly after Ed's death, our friend Dr. Mann came to the house, talked with Ed's wife, and bought me and all the other rifles. We were loaded into Dr. Mann's motor car and driven to our new home in Milford, Massachusetts. Dr. Mann had a very large and wonderful gun room with his easy chair in front of a large fireplace, and books and guns everywhere. I was just getting used to my new home when one day Dr. Mann invited his and Ed's friend Adolph O. Niedner over to the house.

"Niedner was one of the most respected gunsmiths in America and had been a good friend of Ed's. Ed, Dr. Mann, Niedner and Dr. Henry Baker, a well-known shooter from the Boston area, used to go every year together to the Shushan area of New York to shoot woodchucks. Dr. Mann and Niedner talked about Ed's death and how they would both miss him, then Dr. Mann offered Niedner any one of the rifles that had belonged to Ed as a gift and a remembrance of Ed. Niedner didn't hesitate. He walked straight to me and grabbed me up and held me as though we had been together for years. I was so choked up you could not have shot a 22 down my barrel.

"Malden, Massachusetts was my new home. When I called Ed a gun crank, I did not know about the day-to-day activities of Niedner. This man lived and breathed firearms, and every shooter with a new idea brought it to Niedner to see what he could do with it. Me and my kind were no longer in demand. The order of the day was high-speed cartridges in bolt actions shooting metal-jacketed bullets. I remember when Dr. Baker brought his Long Range Creedmoor rifle to Niedner to be converted to a 25 Niedner-Krag varmint rifle. Would this be my fate? Niedner took me out and shot me a few times, but mostly I stayed in his gun rack. After Dr. Mann died in 1916, every time Niedner looked at me he thought of his two best friends. Then he would take me down and clean me even though I did not need it.

"In 1919, Niedner decided to relocate to Milwaukee, Wisconsin, so I was boxed up and shipped across country. When I was unboxed at my new home, I was in Dowagiac, Michigan! What the hell!? I found out later that a customer of Niedner's, W.A. Stolly, offered to put up the land and building for a gunshop if Niedner would move to Dowagiac. A gun cabinet was built on the second floor of our house at 524 Main Street, and I settled into my new home.

"In 1921, Niedner took me to the shop, my first visit to the Niedner Rifle Corporation. There was machinery everywhere and a half dozen busy workmen, but Niedner took me over to his bench.

"The first thing he did was fill in the holes that Ed had put in my barrel to hold that lead. Then he polished my barrel and re-blued it. Niedner bushed my breech face, and a smaller-diameter firing pin was fitted. He removed my hard buttplate and fitted a recoil pad.

"When the fitting of the pad was done, he removed the recoil pad, wrote a note and placed it into the hole that was drilled into my stock to lighten me. The note said 'This rubber buttplate was fitted by A.O. Niedner Dowagiac, Mich., July 1921. This gun was owned by A.E. (sic) Leopold of Norristown, Penn.'

"After the facelift, we would go shooting. Sometimes Niedner would let one of the people at the shop or one of his friends shoot me so they could experience first-hand what the old days were like. As much as Niedner cared for me, I could tell that the recoil was taking its toll and I was shot very little.

"One day Niedner took me out of the cabinet, removed my barrel and took me to the shop where he made and fitted a new barrel in 38-55 smoothbore. He loaded up some shells with small shot and said we were going fishing.

"Fishing? You must be kidding. But no, the next day he was off to his favorite fishing hole with me in tow. We no sooner arrived when he loaded me and shot a dragonfly out of the air. Yes, you heard me right, a dragonfly.

"I had now been around for sixty-five years, but had never seen anything like this. It should have been no surprise to me, really. I remember back in Malden, Niedner had made a 22 single shot shotgun that shot corn meal for a man who was confined to a wheelchair, so the man could shoot flies on his back porch. Niedner was having so much fun, I did not think we would ever go home. After that day, we made many trips after the mighty dragonfly.

"When Niedner's wife died in 1940, he retired from the Niedner Rifle Corporation. He tore out his wife's closet and built a workbench where he spent many days working on new ideas, making powder flasks for friends, making puzzles or some such thing. As Niedner got older and his eyesight began to fail, he started looking for homes for his many guns.

"His fancy Meunier Schuetzen caplock rifle went to a friend in Chicago; his underhammer 40-caliber muzzleloader that he had made with all its tools went to John Amber in Chicago; the Ballard Schuetzen 32-40 and the Niedner Model 1924 rifle went to his friend Bill McQuerry. The 22 Ballard Schuetzen went to his friend Gerald. And on and on they went, until one day they were all gone, even his famous Hamburg rifle which he had given to Rupert, and I sat alone in his gun cabinet.

"On June 25, 1950, Niedner and I were visited by Harry Wandrus, who wrote for *Hobbies*, a magazine for collectors. Niedner told my story and posed for a picture in front of his shooting medals and ribbons holding me.

"The next four years was a period of reflection and quiet times. Niedner's health was such that he hardly left the house. Shortly before he died on December 26, 1954, his friend Bill McQuerry stopped by to say so long. McQuerry had taken a job in Alaska and might not get back this way. Niedner took me down from the gun cabinet and gave me to Bill, saying, 'You know how much this rifle means to me. I would like you to have it.'

"Bill took me out and placed me between two mattresses in the back of his pickup where I was surprised to find myself lying beside Niedner's Model 1924 rifle and his Ballard Schuetzen 32-40, which I had not seen in a couple of years. As Dowagiac fell behind us, I realized that A.O. Niedner and I had been together for forty-one years. So long, my friend.

"I was 89 years old and starting on a 4000-mile trip to my adventure in Alaska. What would I do in Alaska? Maybe the mosquitoes will be as big as dragonflies and we can...*Hey Bill! STOP! Go back! You forgot my 38-55 barrel...Damn!*

"We bumped along forever over that gravel road until we arrived in Kenai, Alaska. Bill McQuerry had taken a job working on the construction of Wildwood Army Base. The job kept him busy most of time, but he did get in lots of hunting and fishing. He would take me out now and then, but never shot me, as he had left my cartridges and loading tools behind.

"I think it was around 1958 that his friend Jim came over to the cabin. Bill took me out and showed me to Jim, then Jim bought me. It happened so fast I could not believe it. As we were heading out the door I remember yelling to Bill: *You have to tell Jim about Ed, about Dr. Mann, about Niedner. I have history! I am important! This is no way to treat a fine old rifle!*

"I do not like to talk about the next twenty-five years. All I can say is that I sat in Jim's closet. We never went shooting, and he never showed me to anyone. Jim did know how to care for a rifle. He kept me clean and oiled, and never a spot of rust appeared on me. Thank you, Jim.

"One day in 1982, Jim took me out of the closet, and I heard that we were going to a gun show, whatever that was. It sounded like fun to me. Jim carried me inside where there were lots of tables covered with guns and there were people everywhere.

"He and I walked up and down the aisles as Jim tried to sell me. Several people looked at me, but no one had ever seen anything like me before, so back out to the truck I went. A little while later, Jim came back with a guy named Dennis who looked me over, said he liked single shot rifles and asked what caliber I was. Jim said, '45-70.'

"*Oh, great!* What a way to end my career. Wonder how far that .458-inch diameter bullet will make it down my .441-inch barrel before something lets loose? Well, Dennis bought me and we headed for Anchorage. I was hoping we were not going to stop somewhere along the way and pick up a box of 45-70s.

"Dennis took me down to his gun room where there were several single shot rifles, all about my age, a nice bunch to be around. None of them were target shooters—all hunting rifles. If I never hear another hunting story, it will be too soon. The next day, Dennis took me out to the shop and made a chamber cast and found out that I was a 44-100, not a 45-70. What a relief that was.

"Dennis did not want to mess around trying to find cartridges for me, so I was sold to a guy named Don. Don lived down on the Kenai Peninsula in a place called Cooper Landing and collected Colt single actions.

"Now, don't get me wrong. I like all guns, but if you have never been locked up with a bunch of single actions, you cannot imagine what it was like. These guys had been everywhere and done everything, and not a one of them was owned by anyone except a Texas Ranger or other famous lawman, famous outlaw, or famous cowboy, according to them.

"Don took my recoil pad off and found the note that Niedner had put in there back in 1921. Shortly after that, Don put me in a case and said that we were going to The Fort. A fort, now that sounds like fun.

"The Fort turned out to be a log-cabin gun shop owned by a man

Mike at The Fort with his new Borchardt Long-Range, the rifle he says he's shooting to protect me from wear-and-tear. Sure.

named Bill Fuller. Inside, it was just like stepping back in time a hundred years. A gun rack held many fine old single shot target rifles. There were side-hammer Sharps, a hammerless Sharps called the Borchardt model, several Ballards and over on the end was a Ballard with a barrel by our old friend H.M. Pope. There were old loading tools hanging from the overhead wooden beams. On the loading bench was a duplex No. 6 Ideal powder measure.

"This was a neat place, and I hoped Bill was going to be my new caretaker. I overheard Don and Bill talking; they were waiting for some guy named Mike to look at me. Well, it wasn't long before Mike came in the shop. My first impression of Mike was *large* and *loud*. He picked me up, looked me all over, looked down my bore, read the note from Niedner, asked Don what he wanted for me and paid the price.

"He set me back in the gun rack, folded up the Niedner note and placed it in his pocket. Hell, he acted no more excited than if he was buying a loaf of bread and putting the shopping list back in his pocket. Mike had brought a Winchester Hi-wall with him, a 32-40 if it matters, and he and Bill spent the rest of the day shooting. When the day was over, Mike's rifle case and shooting box went in back of the car and I sat up front out of my case.

"I could not figure out what was going on. Mike had a smile on his face a doctor would have had trouble removing. He kept looking over at me and every so often just laid his hand on me. About half way to my new home he looked over and said 'I'm going to be shooting you. I have a little range out back where I live, not as fancy as Dr. Mann's, but it will do.'

"*Oh great!* I get to shoot again. *What was that he said?...* something about Dr. Mann's Range...? How does he know about Mann? It did not say anything about Mann on the note.

"When we got to Kasilof, where Mike lived, down to the basement we went, and the first thing I saw were gun books everywhere. Mike put me in his gun rack and I looked at the rifle next to me. I'll be damned if it wasn't Niedner's Model 1924 rifle which I had not seen in over thirty years. Before Mike turned out the light and went upstairs he said 'You two probably have lots to catch up on so I'll leave you alone.'

"This is one strange person.

"Mike got some brass that fit my chamber, and his friend John made me a bullet mould for a 515-grain paper-patch bullet. My load was called a duplex load, 10 grains of 4759 next to the primer, then 85 grains of FFg blackpowder, a cork wad, then the bullet. We got everything together and headed for The Fort.

"Mike touched off that first shot and, boy, did it feel great! Mike was sitting there, though, looking to see if his shoulder was still connected. Hey, big guy! You were the one who put all that powder behind a 515-grain bullet. Welcome to the world of real recoil.

"Back at home, Mike took off the recoil pad Niedner had fitted because it had become hard and was falling apart. He filled the holes that had been used to lighten me with lead shot and put on a new thick recoil pad. There was no 10-pound limit at The Fort.

"For the next few years, we made many trips to The Fort. There was an 18-inch steel plate out at 400 yards and a steel ram at 500, and I worked them over whenever I got the chance. Mike moved to Anchorage and I tagged along. I have been living for several years now in a gun safe and never know what to expect next.

"One day, the door opened and Niedner's underhammer muzzleloader which I have not seen for over thirty-six years came to live with us. Then came Mr. Niedner's 38-72 Pope that I remembered from Malden. A muzzle-loading pistol I had forgotten about and Dr. Baker's Borchardt varmint rifle joined us.

"If Mike keeps going at this rate, some day all of us from Niedner's will be back together. Last year, we had to move over for a new rifle. If I had a nose, it would have been pushed out of shape. Mike came home with a new Sharps Borchardt Long Range Creedmoor. Now when he goes to The Fort, the Borchardt goes.

"My feelings were hurt at first, then Mike explained to me that if he were to do something wrong and I hurt myself, he would feel terrible. He felt that he owed it to Leopold, Mann, and Niedner to look after me.

"So now I am retired, for the present anyway. My bore is mint and I am as strong today as I was in 1885. I also understand that my caretakers will look after me better if they know my story, so that's why I'm telling it now. Someday, Mike, like Niedner, will have to find a new home for me. I know I will be OK and treated with respect if I come to live with you, because now you know who I am." ●

by DOC CARLSON

BLACKPOWDER REVIEW

ACCORDING TO MOST, last year was a downer for the firearms industry. The feeding frenzy of the previous year, caused by the threat of oppressive gun laws, had filled the pipeline and used up the money squirreled away for gun and accessory purchases by shooters. The one area that didn't seem to be affected by all this was blackpowder shooting.

Fueled by special-season hunting in most states, the sale of muzzle-loading guns for hunting remains strong every year. The growing popularity of competitions using blackpowder cartridge firearms, such as Black Powder Cartridge Silhouette, Long Range Black Powder, and Old West Shootists Matches, also kept cartridge firearms of the late 1800s on the front burner. Accessories for both types of guns also enjoyed a pretty good year. This continued interest and growth keeps more new products coming.

Without doubt, the biggest story is **Remington's** entry into the muzzle-loading market. Many of us looked forward to a reproduction of an early Eliphalet Remington, but the folks at Remington felt the market was with hunters who wanted a modern muzzleloader. The result is an in-line rifle built on the Model 700 action.

Other than the solid aluminum ramrod under the barrel, the new rifle looks like a synthetic-stocked 700. The rifle has the same balance and feel as the 700, and the controls—the safety, etc.—are the same. It is available in either blued steel or stainless and in two calibers, 50 and 54.

CVA's Buckmaster provides the very newest technique, apart from its remarkable in-line architecture.

Yes, it's a Remington 700 ML, an in-line that is really like a bolt-action rifle.

In this muzzle-loading version of the 700, the barrel is closed off by a stainless steel breech plug and nipple. The modified bolt, using the same bolt stroke and cocking motion as the standard bolt action, has the firing pin replaced by a cylindrical pin that, on firing, strikes the No. 11 cap on the nipple to fire the rifle. The hammer fall—or in this case, striker fall—is very short, resulting in a very fast lock time of 3 milliseconds. The trigger is the well-proven system found on the 700 for years. The gun is built on the short-action receiver and is drilled and tapped for any standard, short-action scope mount.

The barrel is rifled with eight lands and grooves with a 1:28-inch twist—primarily intended for conical-type bullets, although patched round ball can also be handled. Both the blued and stainless versions of the rifle are finished with a non-glare matte finish. The black synthetic stock is also dull finished. A barrel band has been added to the barrel to support the forward portion of the ramrod.

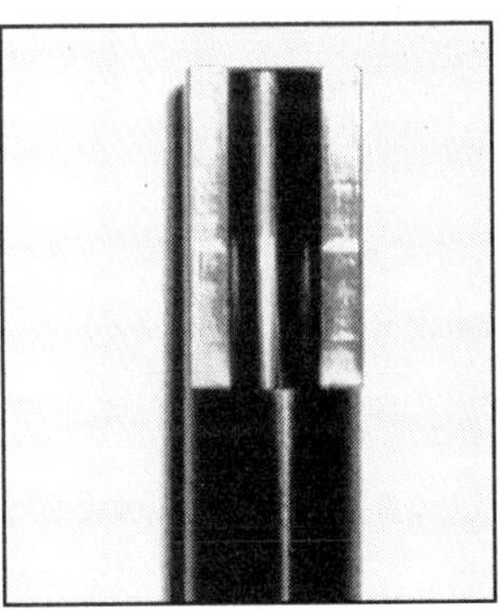

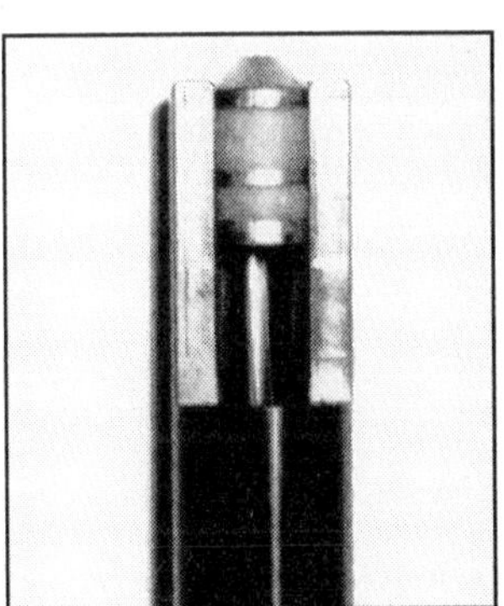

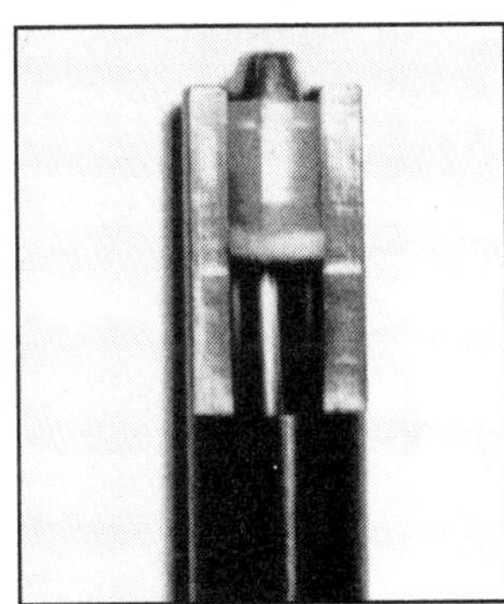

The QLA barrel counterbore system from T/C and how it works for three kinds of bullets.

The guns are supplied with cleaning tube, breech plug and nipple combination wrench, cleaning rod handle and extensions, and a patch jag. Retail prices are $359 for the blue version and $452 for stainless.

Along with the new rifle, Remington is getting into the ammunition and accessory business, too. They are bringing out a line of lead conical solidpoint and hollowpoint bullets in 45, 50, 54 and 58 calibers, ranging in weight from 285 to 535 grains. Plastic-sabotted jacketed Core-Lokt bullets with the patented spiral nose-cut design will also be available in the same four calibers. The sabot is of a stepped-diameter design that should make for easier insertion in the muzzle of the barrel, facilitating faster loading.

Eight calibers of swaged round balls complete the ammunition line, along with the familiar No. 10 and 11 percussion caps. The round balls are made in calibers from 31 to 58, contain 3/4-percent antimony and are copper-plated, a definite departure from other pure lead balls on the market.

Accessories include a starter kit with a short starter, brass powder measure, ball puller, prelubed patches and a belt bag to hold everything. A Cyclone Quick Starter kit is being supplied with three Cyclone shells for quick reloading. There is also a belt bag that is set up to carry the Cyclone Starter kit.

With a broad selection of dry and Wonder Lube patches, cleaning patches, bronze brushes and many other accessories required to run a muzzle-loading

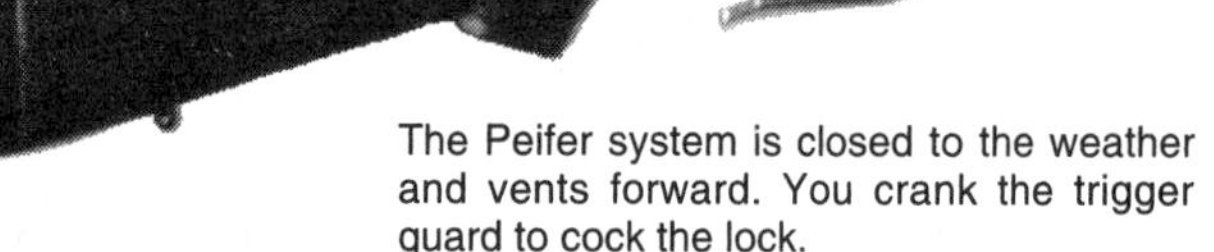

The Peifer system is closed to the weather and vents forward. You crank the trigger guard to cock the lock.

gun in the field, it would appear that Remington is very serious about their entry into the black-powder field.

There is a new company making an in-line rifle with some rather unique features. The rifle, by **Peifer Rifle Co.**, resembles the standard in-line except there is no opening in the top or side of the action for introduction of the primer or cap. The gun utilizes, instead, a primer holder containing a 209 shot-shell primer which is inserted into the bottom of the action in the breech area. When in place, the primer is struck by a firing pin/striker to fire the rifle. The flame of the primer communicates with the powder charge through a small hole in the breech, similar to the touchhole on a flintlock gun. The gasses that escape during firing are vented out through the ramrod channel away from the shooter. This type of system has a couple of advantages. First, there is no opening in the top of the action to admit water during bad weather, and second, the primer holder can be taken out and stored away from the gun, effectively unloading it.

The striker assembly is activated by a 45-pound spring which makes for a very fast lock time. To cock this very heavy spring, the trigger guard is rotated sideways. This uses a great deal of leverage to cock the striker, making a potentially hard task very easy for the shooter.

Another innovation from the Peifer folks is the use of bullets that are swaged and then passed through a die that engraves the rifling of the barrel on the bullet. During loading, the bullet is positioned over the muzzle of the Douglas barrel and rotated until the engraving is felt to "click" into the rifling. The bullet is then seated in the normal manner. This makes for easy loading in a clean barrel and precludes the need for the bullet to upset to fill the rifling. This same system was used in the English Whitworth rifle using a hexagonal bore. The Whitworth had a fine reputation for accuracy.

Connecticut Valley Arms has greatly expanded their line of in-line rifles utilizing different stock materials and styles, combined with either stainless steel or blued barreled actions. This allows the hunter a choice of many different models of, basically, the same gun at very reasonable prices, ranging from around $179 to $300.

The basic rifle has a 1:32-inch twist for use with slugs, combined with the standard and well-known CVA action. Stock materials run the gamut.

The well-known **Thompson/Center Co.** continues to offer their full line of traditional and in-line guns. New this year is what T/C calls their QLA—Quick Load Accurizer— system. The muzzle is counterbored for a distance slightly over two bore diameters. The rifling is thus removed, but the groove diameter of the bore remains to guide the bullet during loading. The advantage of this system is that it is much easier to start the bullet in the bore as it is supported in the correct position for loading. The QLA system acts as a false muzzle, which has been used for well over a hundred years by target shooters. However, this system does not have to be removed prior to shooting, as do false muzzles, or carried separately, making it usable for the average shooter or hunter. There is a good possibility that T/C may make this system available to owners of existing T/C guns as a retrofit option.

Modern Muzzleloading, Inc., the folks who started the in-line movement, have adapted their Knight rifle action to a shotgun. The 12-gauge gun utilizes screw-in chokes and is supplied with an Extra Full choke tube. It was originally set up for turkey hunting, and the Extra Full choke gives a very dense pattern. Other chokes are available, and for added versatility, interchangeable rifle barrels in either 50- or 54-caliber are available. Called the MK-86 Multiple Barrel System, this outfit allows the hunter to have several guns in one at a very reasonable cost. If you add the 22 LR rimfire conversion unit, this is really an all-around, all-season firearm. The gun is available in blue with a black synthetic stock.

Knight is marketing a new bullet by Barnes developed for correct expansion at blackpowder velocities. Called the Hot Bullet, it is a sabotted unit that provides controlled expansion for maximum transfer of energy and good penetration. It is available in 45, 50 and 54 calibers, and gives well over 900 foot pounds of energy at 100 yards, when loaded as recommended.

The line of Knight rifles is available with thumbhole stocks for the first time this year. This stock style seems to be very popular, so I imagine this addition will be well received. Also, the Wolverine Model LK-95 is being sold in a blister-packed "Value Pak" that contains the rifle and everything that one needs to begin shooting except powder and caps. This should be a very popular item with beginners.

An outfit that needs little or no introduction to hunters is **White Shooting Systems**.

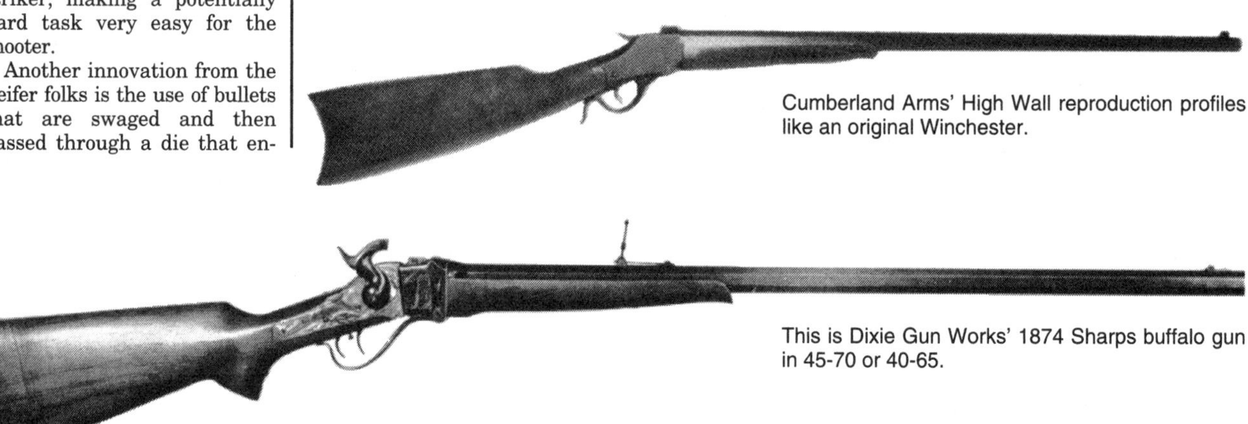

Cumberland Arms' High Wall reproduction profiles like an original Winchester.

This is Dixie Gun Works' 1874 Sharps buffalo gun in 45-70 or 40-65.

They have been in the marketplace with in-line guns for hunters for several years. They are now making the Green River series of guns—a side-hammer, traditional-styled gun reminiscent of the fine English rifles of yesteryear. These will be available as custom-shop rifles for this year and maybe later as production guns, if demand warrants.

The White folks have brought out a new in-line rifle for hunting dangerous game. Called the Grand Alaskan, it weighs in at $7\frac{3}{4}$ pounds in 54-caliber. The 24-inch barrel is heavier than normal and intended for heavy loads. The rifle has a green tundra-design laminated stock and has already proved itself on the largest land animal on earth—the African elephant. They have developed a massive 750-grain bullet to go with it, and backed by 150 to 200 grains of powder, this is a load to be reckoned with—on both ends! If you are looking for a rifle that will take on the biggest and meanest on earth, this is the one.

While on the subject of bullets and projectiles for muzzleloading guns, I talked to the folks who are making bismuth shot as a substitute for lead and steel. It would appear that this shot will be available for reloaders soon. This will make it available for muzzleloader use. Bismuth shot is very close to lead in both weight and hardness, so it should be usable in all those ML shotguns out there that folks don't like to use with steel shot. If bismuth becomes a legal substitute for lead and steel in waterfowl hunting, many of these old guns will get a new lease on life as hunting arms.

Turning to the more traditional type of firearms, **Taylors, Inc.**, is importing a very nice reproduction of the 1842 percussion musket in 69-caliber smoothbore. This was the standard-issue musket between 1842 and the Civil War. Many of these arms were used in the early years of the war by Union troops, and also by Confederate troops as arms were captured from some of the federal arsenals. If you have an interest in U.S. muskets, this one certainly is worth a look. It is an extremely accurate copy of this famous musket and, along with Dixie Gun Works' 1816 flintlock musket and Navy Arms Company's 1777 Charleville, gives the reenactor or military history buff a good selection of early muskets.

The blackpowder cartridge interests are well represented this year. One of the major problems for the growth of this division of the blackpowder sports has been the limited supply of suitable firearms, especially single shot rifles. Certainly, supply is running hard to catch up with demand.

Flintlocks, Inc., is bringing in a nice group of single shot cartridge guns. They have several Pedersoli-made reproductions, including the Remington rolling block in standard and target styles; the Sharps 1874 in carbine-length round barrel and 28-inch octagon-barreled sporting version, with either straight-grip or pistol-grip shotgun buttstock; and the venerable 1873 Trapdoor Springfield carbine in both standard and Officers Model. All of the above are available in 45-70 only, at present.

Dixie Gun Works is now importing an 1874 Sharps with a 30-inch tapered octagon barrel, twisted 1:18 inches for 45-70 and 1:16 inches in 40-65. The gun is available with either a pistol-grip shotgun-type or a straight military-type buttstock. These guns are intended to be used for the Black Powder Cartridge Silhouette (BPCS) game and, from early accuracy tests, seem to be well suited for that. Dixie is also marketing a couple of newly designed bullet moulds for use in these and other rifles in the BPCS program, in both 45 and 40 calibers.

And now there's a video on classic blackpowder shooting and its cartridges from Dixie Gun Works.

If you are thinking about getting into BPCS competition, it might be worth your time to get a copy of the new video that Dixie has just brought out. The price is $24.95 plus $4.75 shipping. It's worth looking at before you jump into this fun game.

Browning Arms has also discovered the BPCS market and is offering a redesigned version of their Model 1885 single shot rifle. The 1885, a coil-spring version of the Winchester High Wall originally designed by John Moses Browning, is being offered with a color case-hardened receiver with a top tang added for mounting a Vernier tang sight. The gun is supplied with a 30-inch tapered octagon barrel in either 45-70 or 40-65 calibers. It comes with a Soule-type Vernier tang sight coupled with a globe front using eight inserts and an integral spirit level.

The gun is intended to be useable right out of the box for BPCS shooting. The prototype was at the last two BPCS nationals at Raton, New Mexico, and showed that it will be a definite competitor on the firing lines around the country.

Lyman Corp., the folks who have been making bullet moulds and sights for blackpowder guns for more than 100 years, have a couple new spitzer-type bullet moulds for the 45-70 and the 40-65, the two most popular calibers in both the BPCS and the Long Range Black Powder Matches.

An outfit called **Cumberland Mountain Arms** is tooling up to make a reproduction of the tried-and-true Winchester High Wall action for use with blackpowder cartridges. It will be available as a completed action, as a machined kit or as a kit of raw castings with the receiver square hole broached. They will also have a completed rifle, walnut stock blanks, sights, and other accessories for these rifles. The action will also be available for use as a muzzleloader. It's worth a look if you have any interest in blackpowder cartridge shooting or want a muzzleloader with a High Wall action.

This was only a very light onceover of the many guns and accessories available to the shooter who likes blackpowder firearms, be they muzzleloader or cartridge. If you look over the catalog section of this book, you'll see that the shooter of this type firearm has a wider selection available to him than ever before, probably including the blackpowder era. The vast array of guns, both front-loading and cartridge, in pistols, rifles and shotguns, military and civilian, is truly a joy to see. The sport is in fine shape and set to grow way beyond what most of us, in the game a long time, ever imagined. ●

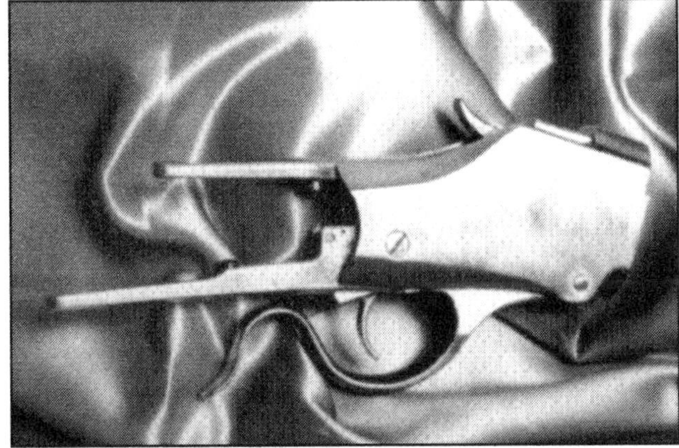

The Cumberland action will also be available for those who want to build their own.

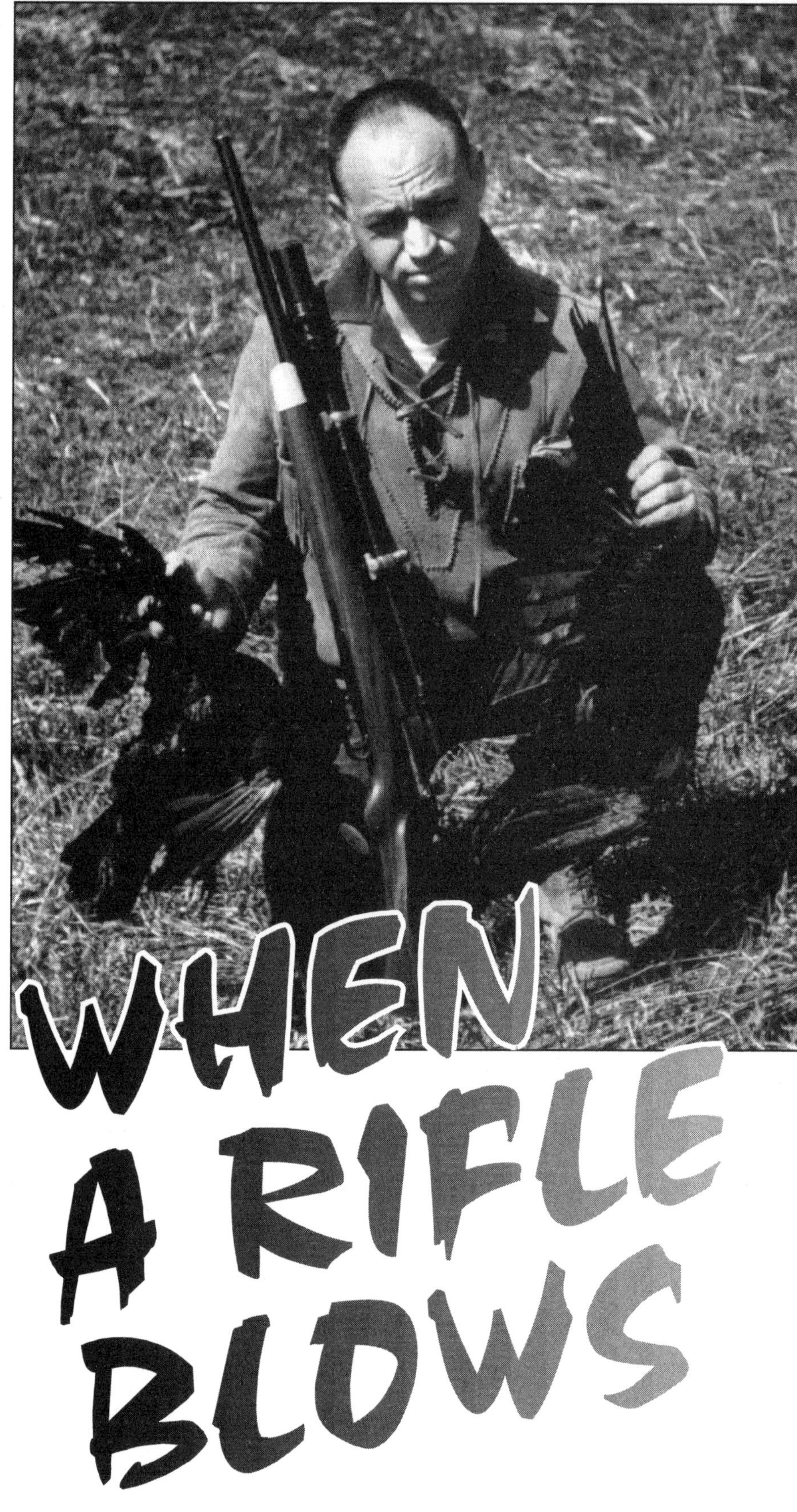

Bell with his replacement 22-250—an '03 with the old Unertl scope on top.

WHEN A RIFLE BLOWS

by BOB BELL

I GUESS I'M a conservative when it comes to loads. At least some people accuse me of that. There's a reason, and it goes back a long ways, to 1950 or so.

It was before I got married, and I was still living with my parents in a ranch-style house my father and I had just built a few miles outside of town on a small farm. Across the highway was a steep wooded hill, and one day I saw several crows land in a thick oak on top of it, maybe 135 yards away. Mostly they disappeared in the foliage, but one was visible, tipping and swelling as he cawed mightily.

"Might as well pop him," I told myself, and went over to the built-in gun cabinet in one corner of the room and got my 22-250.

My Bausch & Lomb shooting glasses were handy on a shelf, but I didn't bother putting them on. After all, I was going to fire only one shot. I wound the window open and sat down on the floor so I could rest the back of my left hand on the window sill. The crow was still there, oblivious to everything. I fed a handload into the chamber, closed the bolt and found the crow in the big 12x Unertl target scope. It was an easy shot, and he exploded nicely.

My parents were home, but they paid no attention to the shot. I was shooting all the time around there so the blast was normal, even if I didn't usually shoot from an open window. The crow was dead, but he didn't fall far; he hung up in the thick oak, feathers flared out all over.

"Might as well knock him out of there," I muttered and reloaded.

That's when it happened. It felt like I'd been hit in the face with a board. Man, I really popped a primer, I thought. I just sat there on the floor, my eyes scrunched shut. Then my hands moved across the gun and I felt broken pieces and I was suddenly afraid to open my eyes. I'd had three years in the Army, with combat duty in five Northern European countries during World War II, and knew that seriously wounded soldiers sometimes didn't feel their injuries for a little bit.

My parents came running into the bedroom. They'd paid no attention to the first shot, but the second one hadn't sounded right. I forced my eyes open. I could see. For a little bit, I wasn't sure that I'd be able to.

"What happened!" Mom yelled. "Are you all right?"

I don't know what I said, or if I said anything. After a moment I gestured at the gun. It was a wreck.

My face burned. It felt as if I had a new sunburn. I went into the bathroom and looked in a mirror. My eyes and the upper part of my face were reddish. But at least I could see.

Dad phoned a doctor who had been our neighbor in Danville, the next town down the river. He was the head ophthalmologist at Geisinger Memorial Hospital, and moments later we were driving there. It was a Sunday, so not normally a working day for the doctor, but he said he'd be waiting for us.

I spent the next hour or so on a table of some sort—I don't think it was a bed, but I don't really remember—while the doctor examined my eyes with all sorts of optical equipment. He then cocained them—a local anesthesia, so I wasn't asleep—and then used a sort of wire pick to remove a number of tiny pieces of brass, mostly from my left eyeball. The scope had apparently protected my right eye momentarily when the head of the cartridge case evaporated.

I can tell you right now, looking at a steel pick coming toward your eye, seeing it come too close to be in focus, then feeling it tug at particles of brass embedded in your eyeball is not an enjoyable way to spend an afternoon, no matter who is doing the tugging. I've been grateful ever since for Dr. Jacob's skill, but I have to say that anyone with a lick of sense would rather not experience it.

Later, while lying at home for some days with my eyes bandaged up, I remembered those Ray-Bans in the gun cabinet that I hadn't bothered putting on 'cause I was only going to fire one shot. Fact is, I spent considerable time thinking about them.

When things normalized a bit, I examined the rifle. It had been a pretty case-hardened M98 action I'd made a swap for. I wanted it because it was a 98 and because it was better looking than most. An acquaintance had brought it back from Germany when the war ended, a commercial 9x57 with a ribbed barrel, double-set triggers, and a nice sporter stock. The receiver ring had been dovetailed to accept a claw mount base.

As it turned out, I didn't like the triggers. The front (firing) one was too far forward for my short trigger finger, so I replaced the German design with a Mashburn trigger, which worked very well. And I filed a piece of steel to fit the notch left when the mount base was removed. Then a heavy Pfeiffer barrel was installed, chambered for the popular wildcat (in those days) 22-250 cartridge. "Bump" Lynn, a patternmaker who occasionally made stocks, bedded it airtight in a dense piece of walnut, and a 12x Unertl 1½-inch target scope was mounted.

It proved to be quite a gun. Groups were normally under an inch at 100 yards, and in those days we fired ten-shotters. When not being shot from the bench, it accounted for countless chucks and crows, and even an occasional housecat that strayed too far from home. In those days, such critters were viewed with a jaundiced eye. Maybe we were wrong.

Then came the last of maybe 1200 or 1500 shots with that rifle.

Investigation showed that one piece of the receiver ring went through the birch-paneled door some feet to my right. Another piece went through a window pane in the opposite side of the room, to my left and somewhat behind. When the receiver ring blew apart, the barrel fell out. The bolt opened and started to come back—in the direction of my head, of course; however, somewhere in the process, the action bent lengthwise, both vertically and horizontally, and the bolt cramped in place after traveling about an inch. The magazine well bulged significantly, splintering the stock, and the Unertl scope was U-shaped, as if someone had taken it by the small end and wrapped it around a pole. What was left of the headless case was in the chamber of the now-unsupported barrel. All in all, it wasn't the truly impressive varmint rifle that it had been earlier.

From the rifle, I salvaged the Mashburn trigger. I sent the scope back to John Unertl to see if anything could be done with it. I didn't expect anything, but some weeks later got a package in the mail. It was my scope and it looked like new. There was a handwritten note from Ol' John. "That was a helluva way to treat a good scope," he said.

I knew that already.

Eventually, I collected the pieces and took them down to Phil Sharpe, the author of *Complete Guide to Handloading* and other things, who lived on a farm between Fairfield, Pennsylvania, and Emmitsburg, Maryland. We had been friends for years. He examined the pieces and wrote me a 2½-page, single-spaced letter on his conclusions, and later used the remains of the rifle to try to convince other handloaders to be careful.

Boiled down, his letter said that the action was one of many Mausers made during the period between the two World Wars and sold to gunsmiths throughout the world. It had no stamping to indicate who manufactured it, something I should have noticed but didn't. Apparently it had been case-hardened by the gunsmith who built the original 9x57, and he had little or no means of controlling the depth of hardness on an action like the M98 which has many different thicknesses. Therefore, it had been burned in places, and a crack had formed on the inside of the receiver ring about in line with the top edge of the right rail. The crack was about one-third the depth of the receiver, much older and duller in appearance than the remainder of the break, where it finally let go. The surprising part is that it held together as long as it did. Actually, it was never safe. The next-to-last shot had killed the crow, so I know there was nothing in the bore.

A few months later, I had another 22-250, built on a good '03 Springfield action, with the same Unertl on it. I was a bit hesitant before firing the first group, but eventually touched off five rounds. They went into a whisper less than ¾-inch at 100 yards, so I felt I was holding OK. That was all that could be expected in those days.

If I learned anything from the experience, it was to always start building a new rifle with a good action. That's the heart of it and everything depends on it. There's nothing wrong with a solid 98; probably more research went into its design than into any action before or since. But over 100 million 98s were reportedly built at various times and places around the world, and some have been horribly mistreated over the years. If you start with one—or for that matter any other—have it fully examined and tested by a good gunsmith. Be sure it's ready to go with high-pressure loads.

And then—be conservative. •

by JOHN MALLOY

HANDGUNS TODAY:

AUTOLOADERS

A NUMBER OF factors are influencing new developments in autoloading pistols. Certainly, the effect of the purported Crime Bill of September 1994, with its ten-round limit on magazine capacity, is a major one. A full-size, large-capacity pistol loses some of its advantage without a large capacity magazine. Newly-introduced 9mm pistols are generally smaller. Many provide a legal limit of ten rounds in a more compact package.

Because the 9mm no longer has the advantage of large magazine capacity, more attention is being given to larger calibers. The 45 ACP, especially, is being looked at with greater favor. Seven or more rounds of 45 no longer seem such a disadvantage when compared to only ten rounds of 9mm. A number of new 45s have been introduced, most of them based on the 1911 Colt/Browning design.

Another factor is the encouraging passage of right-to-carry legislation in more and more states. A growing number of people able to be legally armed has created a demand for pistols that ordinary people, who are not in law enforcement and who are perhaps not dyed-in-the-wool firearms enthusiasts, can buy and use. Lower-priced models, more compact designs, and uncomplicated user-friendly models are being offered to this market.

Increased interest in pistol shooting for personal protection has brought about a greater interest in pistol competition, and thus more competition pistols are being offered. Low maintenance is a factor with many people—stainless steel, polymer frames and corrosion-resistant finishes are becoming more common.

Add in a little nostalgia, some concern over product-liability litigation, and lots of new high-tech manufacturing procedures. Put all this together and there are plenty of special ideas and plenty of niches in the world of autoloading pistols.

Let's take a look at what the companies are doing:

A. A. Arms

A.A. Arms of Monroe, North Carolina, includes a new semi-automatic pistol in their line. The new AP 9 Mini/5 has a tubular receiver with the magazine forward of the trigger guard. It is offered in black or nickel finish, with either a 3- or 5-inch barrel. A ten-round magazine is standard, but a five-shot is also available.

AMT

AMT has added the 357 SIG to its Back Up line. AMT's Back Up series has gained acceptance since their introduction a few years ago. The guns are double action only (DAO) and were first introduced in the blowback 380, followed by the locked-breech 45, 40, 9mm and 38 Super versions.

The pistols are compact and, as the name implies, are designed for a backup function. No frills, such as sights, are provided; a groove on the top of the slide allows alignment. The trigger pull is long and heavy. The weight is rather light, 18-23 ounces, but recoil—even in the big calibers—is controllable.

American Arms

This Missouri company has introduced the Aussie. The pistol

Once called the Baby Browning, the PSA-25 pistol is now available to American shooters from Precision Small Arms.

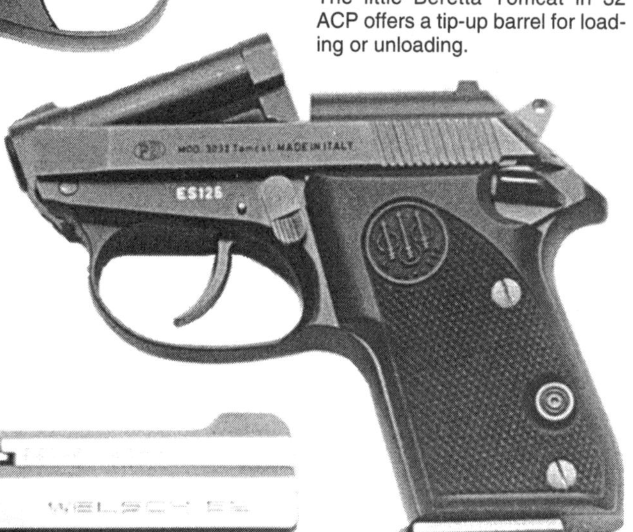

The little Beretta Tomcat in 32 ACP offers a tip-up barrel for loading or unloading.

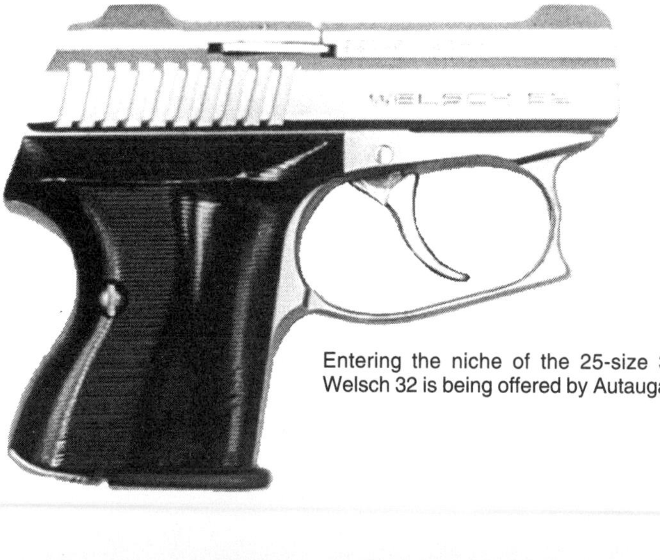

Entering the niche of the 25-size 32, the Welsch 32 is being offered by Autauga Arms.

was, as you may have guessed, designed in Australia. Looking a bit like the result of a mating between a Beretta and a Glock, the Aussie has a polymer frame with an open-top steel slide.

It has a Glock-type action, but unlike the Glock has a positive safety on the rear of the trigger. This safety is not automatic. The shooter rotates it back, where it prevents the trigger from moving rearward. The safety can be rotated forward, from either side, to allow the pistol to be fired.

The Aussie is made in 9mm and 40 S&W, and a compact version is in the works.

Autauga Arms

This Prattville, Alabama, firm has introduced the Welsch 32, a vest-pocket-size pistol chambered for 32 ACP. Autauga's vice-president, Dan Hanson, explained that the tiny Seecamp 32, introduced some years back, had been well-received, but was essentially impossible to obtain. The time seemed appropriate for another 32 pistol to enter that niche. The Welsch 32 is a seven-shot (six shots in the magazine, plus one more in the chamber) DAO with no manual safety.

It is designed for Winchester Silvertip ammunition. This load has proven effective and has made the 32 ACP a viable option in cases where only a tiny pistol will do. The Welsch is getting pretty close to being tiny; at 4.3 inches long and 3.2 inches high, it can almost hide under a 3x5 note card. The pistol, named for its designer, Manford Welsch, is made of stainless steel and weighs 11 ounces.

Beretta

Beretta's big news is a little gun. Also eyeing the niche of a 25-size 32, the company has introduced the 32 ACP Tomcat. It is the approximate size and weight of their little Bobcat 25- and 22-caliber pistols.

Like those earlier pistols, the Tomcat has a tip-up barrel for loading and unloading the chamber without working the slide. This feature has some appeal for those without great strength in their hands and as an added measure of safety.

The action of the new pistol is what has come to be called conventional double action. That is, double action for the first shot, single action thereafter.

It is designed for Winchester Silvertip loads and was introduced with a promotional offer giving a discount on the purchase of two boxes of 32 ACP Silvertips. The Tomcat 32 has 7+1 capacity, is 5 inches long and weighs 15 ounces. Plans are to offer it also in a 22 Long Rifle version.

Brolin

Brolin Arms of Pomona, California, now offers three lines of 45-caliber pistols in both 5- and 4-inch barrels. Models range from near-traditional "Government"-style guns to compensated match competition pistols. All are based on the 1911 design with the modifications favored by many of today's shooters, such as larger sights, lowered ejection port, and skeletonized hammer and trigger. Custom-shop work and parts are also offered.

Browning

Browning has introduced two 9mm pistols from Fabrique Nationale in Belgium. The FN BDA is a conventional double action, with a decocking lever; the FN BDAO is double action only. The pistols have the feel and general appearance of the original Browning Hi-Power.

Lots of people shoot Bullseye pistol matches, and Browning now has the 22-caliber Buck Mark Bullseye pistol to appeal to them. The new target pistol has precision sights and a 7¼-inch fluted barrel.

Desert Eagle pistols are now being made in the U.S., with 6- and 10-inch barrels available.

(Above) The Walther P99 didn't make its debut at the 1996 SHOT Show, but its picture was there. It may be imported by Interarms.

(Right) A.A. Arms' AP 9—here in a 3-inch-barrel, black-finish version—is also offered in 5-inch and nickel versions.

(Below) AMT now has five calibers of locked-breech Back Up pistols in their line. No frills, yet.

Ultima Technologies offers the "recoilless" Piranha in 9mm; other calibers are planned later.

Colt

The basic 1911-design 45 has been a mainstay of the Colt line since...well, 1911. New versions have appeared from time to time to make sure every niche is being filled. The no-frills 1991A1, introduced a few years ago, is now available in a matte-finish stainless steel.

A new Combat Target Model is also now offered; it has target sights, lightened trigger and hammer, and other currently favored features. It comes in a black matte finish—what many shooters want anyway—that allows more competitive pricing.

Daewoo

The new DH 45 MK II is the first 45 ACP pistol to feature the Daewoo "Tri-Action." The pistol can be fired either double action or single action for the first shot. Then, from the cocked single-action position, the pistol can be made safe by simply pushing the hammer forward. Pressing the trigger will again raise the hammer, with a lighter pull than the conventional double action. Daewoo pistols are imported by Kimber and are distributed by Nationwide Sports Distributors.

Erma

For Bullseye shooters, Erma of Germany offers the ESP 85A Competition pistol, available in the U.S. through Precision Sales International. The pistol can be had in 22 LR or 32 S&W Long, or as a conversion outfit in both calibers. New options for 1996 included a simple removable dry-fire device and an accessory base that permits the use of optical or electronic sights. The new base was designed for Erma by Jacksonville, Florida, gunsmith Steven K. Moore, of 10-Ring Service.

European American Armory

EAA is now importing the Astra A-100 in a new stainless-steel version, the A-100 Inox. A new polymer-frame Tanfoglio pistol in the Witness series is a possibility at presstime, but we couldn't get details.

Fort Worth Firearms

This Texas-based company produced 22-caliber target pistols of the High Standard design for another firm. Now it is making pistols under the Fort Worth name.

There is the original High Standard-style pistol, and there are three new models in an improved line. The improved pistols feature twin extractors, beveled magazine well and push-button magazine release. The new release still allows operation of the original release at the forward bottom of the grip. However, the location of the new release is at the upper forward portion of the right grip, and it is designed to be operated by the right index finger. This placement serves as a safety feature when a magazine is removed while the chamber is still loaded; it gets the trigger finger away from the trigger. Vent-rib models of the improved series also have the rear of the slide flared to allow more purchase for retraction.

Glock

Commemorating the 10th anniversary of their operations in the U.S., Glock, Inc., introduced the Model 26 (in 9mm) and the Model 27 (in 40 S&W) in 1996. Both are shortened versions of full-size models—shortened front-to-back and top-to-bottom, pistols just big enough to hold a ten-round magazine. The 9mm is a 10+1 pistol, and the 40 holds 9+1. Either model will accept appropriate older, high-capacity magazines.

The new guns are over 4 inches tall, about the same as a Walther PPK, and run just over 6 inches long. They are not quite, but almost, hidden under a 4x6 index card. The low sights, newly designed, are fully adjustable for windage and elevation.

And what is that strange-looking dimple and hump at the top of the grip? Why, it is a target thumbrest, placed there along with the adjustable sights and grooved trigger so the pis-

Ruger's compact P95, a new 9mm pistol, has a polymer frame and Ruger looks.

S&W's value-line 45-caliber pistol is the new Model 457—very purposeful.

The first SIG/Sauer pistol made in the USA, the compact P239 is available in 9mm.

tols can be imported under the GCA '68 point system.

Grizzly

The big Grizzly pistol—the one that looks like a 1911 that has taken up bodybuilding—can now be had in 50 Action Express (50 AE). A new conversion kit in that caliber has just been offered by LAR Manufacturing of West Jordan, Utah.

Heckler & Koch

Heckler & Koch has introduced the Mark 23 and the stainless USP, both in 45 ACP. The new guns move toward more conventional pistol design, reflecting American influence about the location of controls and how things should work. There's a tilting barrel-locking system with polymer frame and steel slide. HK has made polymer frames since the 1960s, so they probably know what they are doing.

The Mark 23 is a civilian version of the HK Special Operations pistol, the one adopted by the U.S. Special Operations Command. First deliveries of the military pistols were scheduled for mid-1996. The Mark 23, with its 5.9-inch barrel (threaded at the muzzle as is that of the military version), is almost 10 inches long and 6 inches high. It differs from the government-contract pistol in markings and its ten-round magazine. A limited number will be available to civilian customers.

The newest version of the USP 45 (Universal Self-Loading Pistol) is in stainless steel.

The USP is a commercial version of the SOCOM design with some control changes, no threaded muzzle and a somewhat smoother appearance. It is offered in conventional double action, DAO, safety, decocker, left-hand, right-hand—nine variants in all. Those variants are also available in 9mm and 40 S&W.

Heritage

Heritage Manufacturing, Inc., of Opa Locka, Florida, introduced the Stealth, a slim, compact 9mm pistol, at the 1996 SHOT Show. It weighs about 20 ounces and is just 4 inches high and 6 inches long.

The little 9mm is a delayed blowback, with the delay provided by a gas piston arrangement. The frame is polymer, with the other parts of 17-4 stainless steel, an alloy which has self-lubricating properties. Magazine capacity is ten rounds. A 40 S&W version is scheduled.

High Standard

High Standard is back in business making pistols and has completed the move of its manufacturing facilities from Hartford, Connecticut, to Houston, Texas.

Production of the newly made High Standard target pistols began in 1994, and a number of the original models are currently in the line. New items introduced at the 1996 SHOT Show were the Olympic Rapid Fire Pistol and the Supermatic Citation MS.

The Rapid Fire pistol is in 22 Short, with a 4-inch barrel, muzzle brake and compensator to reduce recoil for the Olympic Rapid Fire course. The special International grips require a handprint of the shooter for fitting; the pistol is almost worn, not just held.

The "MS" of the other new offering stands for Metallic Silhouette, and the pistol comes with a 10-inch barrel, hooded front and adjustable rear sights.

Hi-Point

Hi-Point Firearms is now the single name used for the line of inexpensive blowback centerfire pistols known previously as Stallard, Haskell, Iberia and Hi-Point. Makes it easier for dealers and customers to keep track of things, and it certainly simplifies my files on all those guns. Hi-Point pistols are marketed through MKS Supply of Dayton, Ohio.

Ithaca

Ithaca has licensed a 50th Anniversary 45 based on the 1911A1 design. Ithaca was one of the major manufacturers of 1911A1 pistols during WWII. The new pistol is not, however, a re-creation of the wartime pistol. The plan was to produce one that took into account the modifications that have become popular during the past fifty years.

The new Ithaca has better sights, altered hammer, trigger and grip safety, and other mod-

A new electroless nickel finish is now available on the Kahr 9mm pistol.

Heritage Manufacturing has introduced the 9mm Stealth, in stainless steel and polymer frame, a gas-delayed blowback action.

(Below) Glock's Caroline Sizer beautifully demonstrates the compact size of the new Glock 26.

The no-frills S&W Model 908 is another value-line pistol, but in 9mm.

ern features. To prove that nostalgia isn't dead, though, it is offered with early-type diamond-pattern checkered grips. A production run of only 2500 pistols is planned. The Ithaca is made in America and is offered by All America Sales of Memphis, Tennessee. That firm also now handles the BUL M-5, a high-capacity steel and polymer pistol based on the 1911 design. The BUL was introduced in 1995.

J.O. Arms

J.O. Arms, of Houston, Texas, imports pistols from Israel. The 9mm Kareen, based on the Browning Hi-Power, has been around for some time. More recent is the Golan, a 9mm or 40 S&W pistol styled after the SIG-Sauer design. The latest offering—it arrived just two days before the January SHOT Show—is the GAL. It is a 45-caliber pistol based on the tried-and-true 1911 design, with modern add-ons.

KBI

KBI, Inc., of Harrisburg, Pennsylvania, has announced that they will be importing a 1911-type pistol made by Armscor of the Philippines. The new 45 has an extended slide release, beavertail tang, three-dot sights, a lightened hammer and other features. Plans were to begin shipments by mid-1996. A wide-grip prototype for a large-capacity magazine was also shown at the SHOT Show and may be produced at a later date.

Kahr

Kahr Arms was in the forefront of the compact 9mm trend, having displayed prototypes early in 1994. Production models were shipped early in 1995. The little American-made K9 pistols are all steel, with a tilting-barrel locked-breech system. The guns measure about $4^{1}/_{2}$ by 6 inches and weigh 25 ounces.

A new variation, introduced in 1996, has a glare-free electroless nickel finish. The finish material has a Teflon-like component that provides dry lubricating qualities.

Kel-Tec

The compact, lightweight Kel-Tec P-11 9mm pistol made its debut at the 1995 SHOT Show. For 1996, variations with corrosion-resistant finishes were introduced. The pistols can now be had with a stainless slide and a grey polymer frame, or with a parkerized slide and a green frame. All the Kel-Tec pistols are about $5^{1}/_{2}$ by 4 inches and weigh 14 ounces. They hold 10+1 rounds and are made in America.

Kimber

First displayed at the January 1996 SHOT Show, the Kimber Classic 45 is a 45 ACP pistol of the 1911 design. McCormick match-grade parts and eight-round magazines are standard.

Llama

Just a short time ago, the 1911-style Llama pistols were redesigned to suit American tastes. For 1996, a new compact 45 was added to the line. The MiniMax 45—Minimum size and Maximum firepower—has a $3^{1}/_{2}$-inch barrel and is about 7 inches long and 5 inches high. Magazine capacity is six rounds, only one shot less

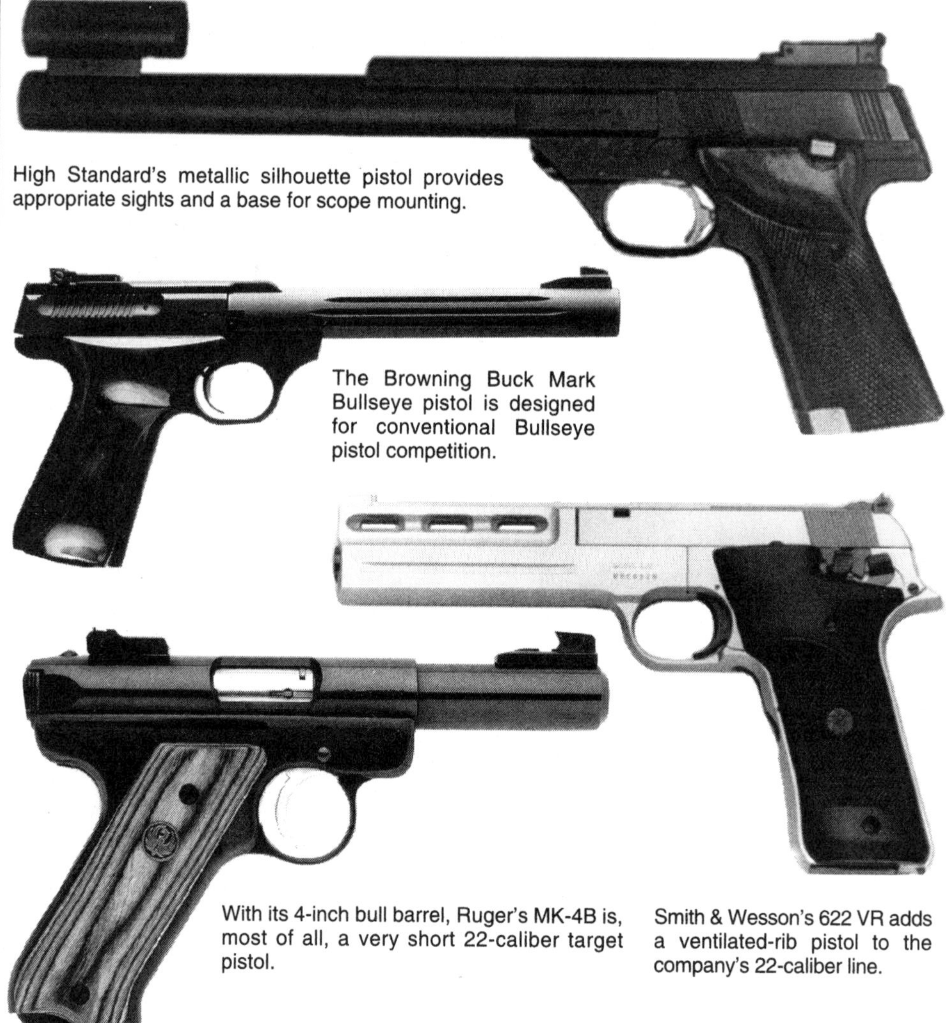

High Standard's metallic silhouette pistol provides appropriate sights and a base for scope mounting.

The Browning Buck Mark Bullseye pistol is designed for conventional Bullseye pistol competition.

With its 4-inch bull barrel, Ruger's MK-4B is, most of all, a very short 22-caliber target pistol.

Smith & Wesson's 622 VR adds a ventilated-rib pistol to the company's 22-caliber line.

than a full-size 1911. The new Llamas are imported from Spain by Import Sports, Inc., of New Jersey.

Four grades are offered. The Custom is matte black, with plastic grips; the Custom Stainless has a satin-finish stainless steel slide and frame; the Custom Royal has a polished blue finish with diamond-pattern walnut grips; and the Gold Match is a Custom Royal with Bo-Mar target sights.

All models have beavertail grip safeties, skeletonized triggers and hammers, and other refinements. All are 5-inch-barrel "Government" size. The Kimber 45 pistols are made in America.

Magnum Research

The Desert Eagle pistol, formerly made in Israel, is now being made in the U.S.A.—in Saco, Maine, to be exact. The magnum-caliber Desert Eagles are now all built on the 50 Action Express (50 AE) platform. This means frames and slides are now identical for 357-, 44- and 50-caliber pistols. Thus, 44 and 50 conversions consist simply of substituting barrels and magazines. For the 357, a bolt is also needed. Pistols and conversion kits are available with 6- and 10-inch barrels.

Mitchell Arms

Mitchell 45-caliber 1911-style pistols have been shipped since May 1995, but the 1996 SHOT Show was the first public display of production models. At the same time, the Jeff Cooper Signature model, built to Cooper's specifications and bearing his signature, was introduced. No variations of this particular model will be offered.

A wide-body version of the 45 line was scheduled for introduction in mid-1996. The basic 1911 design has also been enlarged by Mitchell to handle the 44 Magnum chambering for 1996. Scheduled for early 1996 availability, the big 44 was designed as a hunting pistol and is offered with an adjustable rear sight.

Mitchell has changed the

names of the company's line of 22 target pistols to avoid confusion with similar High Standard models. The line now consists of the Sportster, Baron, Monarch, Medallion, Sovereign and Medalist.

Mossberg

Mossberg started out making pistols in 1919, and in the late 1970s they advertised a 45-caliber autoloader that was never actually put into production. Now it looks as if Mossberg may be back in the pistol business. At the January 1996 SHOT Show, Mossberg quietly added a display of Israeli-made IMI semiautomatic pistols to its other displays. Company representatives said the deal was in the process of being finalized at the time. With an eye to law enforcement sales in particular, they felt the IMI products would supplement their line of shotguns.

Precision Small Arms

The tiny 25-caliber pistol known as the Baby Browning is still in production. In a sort of role reversal, an American company has been making the pistols for export by Browning, to Europe and Asia.

That company, Precision Small Arms, of Beverly Hills California, is now making the pistol available for North American customers. As the PSA-25, it is available in traditional black, satin chrome and engraved finishes.

President Bennett Brachman says that with MagSafe ammunition, the 25 ACP has reasonable stopping power, and the small size of the PSA-25 allows it to go along when more powerful pistols would have to be left behind. Small it is. At about 4 by 3 inches, it is completely hidden beneath a 3 by 5 note card. Thickness is about $^{7}/_{8}$-inch, and the weight is $9^{1}/_{2}$ ounces. A $7^{1}/_{2}$-ounce lightweight version is in the works.

Ruger

The P95 is a compact 9mm with a polymer frame. Ruger's entry into the centerfire polymer world did not come without extensive testing. The final design fired over 20,000 rounds of +P+ ammunition without harm to the pistol or loss of accuracy, Ruger says. The P95 comes in two styles—DAO and conventional double action with a decocker. For either version, length is about 7 inches and weight is 27 ounces. Magazine capacity is ten rounds, but the pistols will accept any Ruger P-series magazine.

The MK-4B is a new version of the company's traditional 22 autoloader. It has adjustable sights and a 4-inch bull barrel—a very short target pistol. Ruger's Robert Stutler says the pistol will fill a need for a compact, accurate outdoor pistol.

All Ruger autoloaders now come with a lockable case, a lock and an extra magazine.

Sigarms

The P239 is the first SIG/Sauer pistol made completely in the U.S. The design was a joint effort between U.S. and Swiss engineers. In 9mm only at this time, the compact pistol is about $6^{1}/_{2}$ by 5 inches. The slide is blackened stainless steel, and the frame is darkened aluminum alloy. Weight is about 25 ounces, and the magazine holds eight rounds. A 357 SIG version, and possible other calibers, are in the works for the future.

Smith & Wesson

Four new S&W pistols were introduced at the 1996 SHOT Show. The Model 622 VR (Ventilated Rib) is essentially a cosmetic addition to the company's line of 22-caliber semi-automatic pistols. The light 23-ounce gun is a full-size pistol with a 6-inch barrel. Its new vent rib probably doesn't really do much, but it makes for an eye-catching pistol.

The remaining three new offerings are additions to S&W's value-line pistols, utility guns with few frills. They all have matte-finish black steel slides and black alloy frames, and are conventional double action:

The Model 908 is in 9mm, with a 3.5-inch barrel and overall length (OAL) of 6.9 inches, and weighs 26 ounces.

The Model 410 is a 40 S&W, with a 4-inch barrel, OAL of 7.5 inches, weighing 29 ounces.

The Model 457 is in 45 ACP caliber. It has a 3.75-inch barrel, is 7.25 inches overall, and weighs 29 ounces.

High Standard offers a new Olympic Rapid Fire pistol in 22 Short. Grips are sized to the shooter's hand, and the pistol is worn as much as held.

The Stoeger Luger now is available with a dark finish on its stainless steel parts, for a more traditional look.

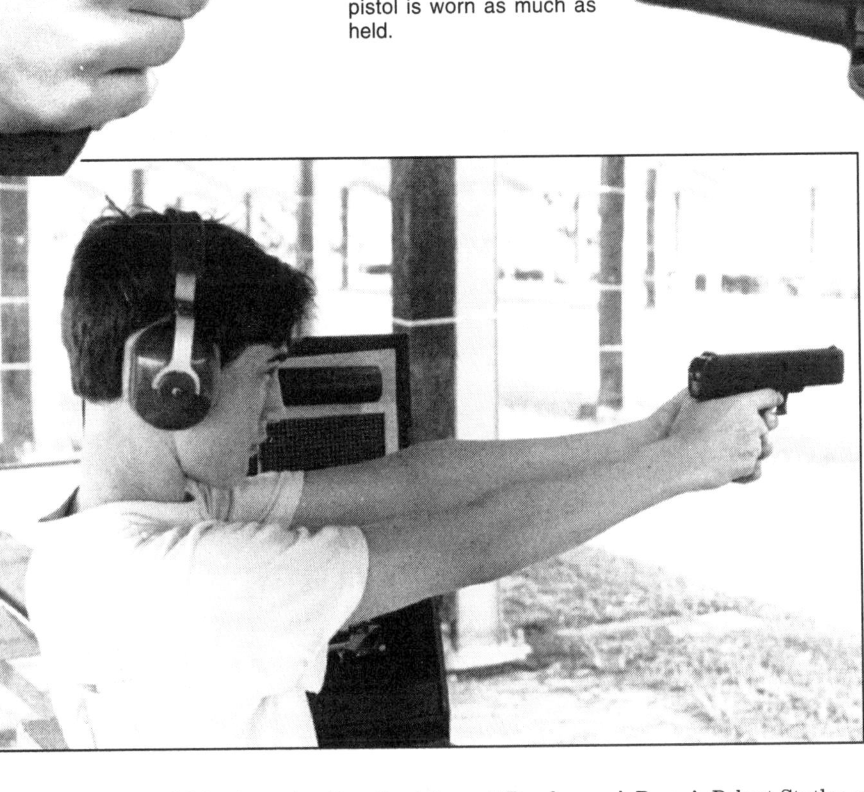

A young Patrick Malloy shot a 9mm Stallard pistol in times past. Now, Stallard, Haskell and Iberia pistols are all marketed under the Hi-Point tradename.

Stoeger

Stoeger introduced a line of High Standard-type 22 pistols, designated the PRO-95 line. A number of models are offered.

The American-made Stoeger 9mm Luger pistol (Stoeger retains the "Luger" tradename and can legitimately call the pistol by that name) was introduced in 1995 in stainless steel. Nice it was, but some wanted a more traditional look. Now, the Luger is available, still stainless steel, but with a matte black finish to make it look more like the originals. Both P08 (short) and Navy (long) models are now offered.

Ultima Technologies

This company has introduced a 9mm pistol named the Piranha. The unusual gun has a certain nostalgic look to it. The grip angle and rear receiver say "Luger," while the magazine forward of the trigger guard suggests "Mauser." In construction, though, everything is new.

To disassemble the gun, a barrel shroud is removed at the front of the receiver. The split receiver, which is hinged at the rear, can then be opened, clamshell fashion. All internal parts are held in place, but the barrel can simply be lifted out. This allows rapid barrel changes, and the gun can quickly be switched to other calibers of the same cartridge base size.

Inventor Walter Perrine describes the action as a hesitation lock, and because of the geometry of the parts, recoil effect is minimized without a compensator. Full production was expected by mid-1996. The Piranha was introduced in 9mm, but prototypes of other calibers, including 44 AutoMag and 50 AE, are under development.

Ultramatic

An Austrian firm has introduced a pistol that at first glance looks a bit like a 1911, but really isn't anything like it at all. The Ultramatic LV pistol has a fixed barrel and "fixed slide." What moves is an internal bolt, retarded after firing by two locking studs, in a fashion somewhat similar to that of the MG-42, the German machinegun of WWII. Ultramatic calls this a "torus segment locking system."

This is a big pistol, about 10 inches long and 6 inches high with a 6-inch barrel. It has conventional double action and a staggered-column magazine. A manual safety combined with a decocker conforms to IPSC rules.

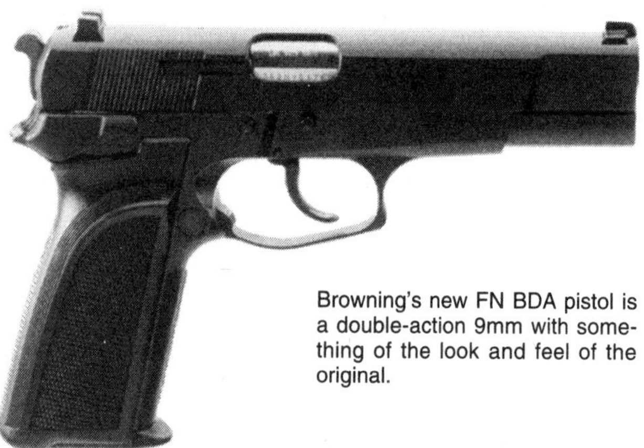

Browning's new FN BDA pistol is a double-action 9mm with something of the look and feel of the original.

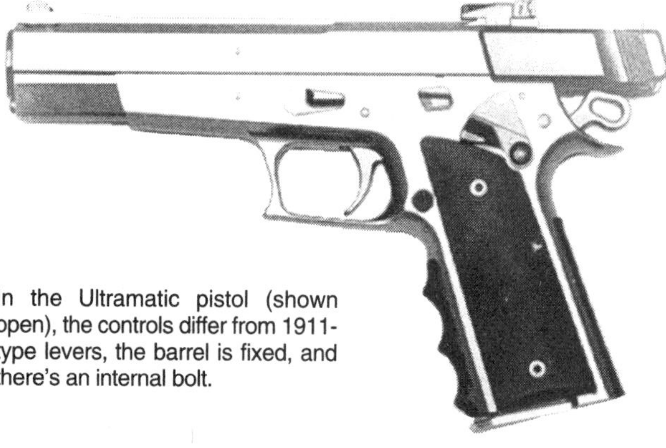

In the Ultramatic pistol (shown open), the controls differ from 1911-type levers, the barrel is fixed, and there's an internal bolt.

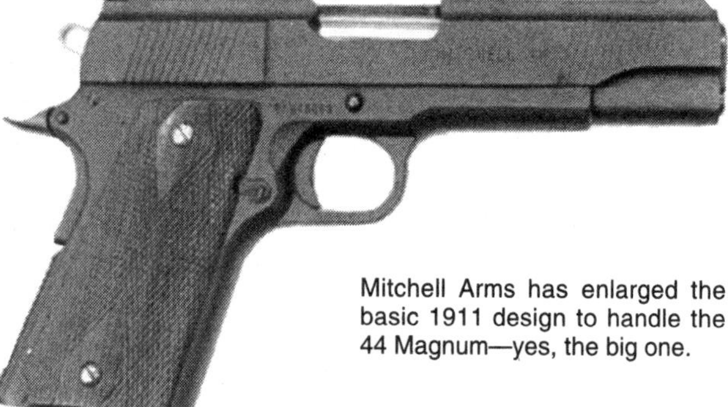

Mitchell Arms has enlarged the basic 1911 design to handle the 44 Magnum—yes, the big one.

The Kimber Gold Match 45 is the company's top-of-the-line pistol.

Here's the Jeff Cooper Signature model from Mitchell Arms. A 45? Of course.

KBI now sells the Armscor 45, a 1911-style pistol made in the Philippines.

Imported from Israel, the GAL is a 45 based on the 1911 design, newly trimmed up.

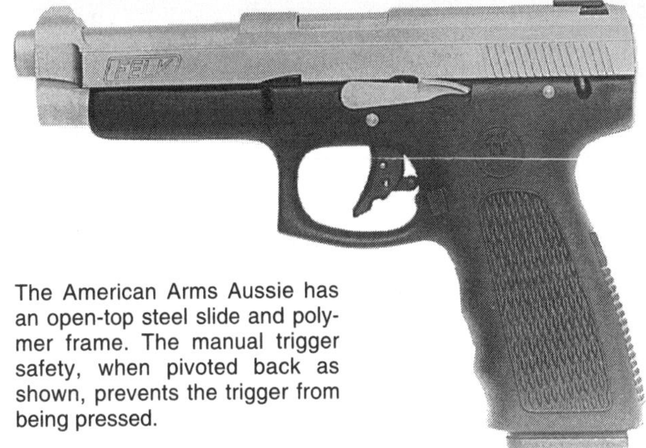

The American Arms Aussie has an open-top steel slide and polymer frame. The manual trigger safety, when pivoted back as shown, prevents the trigger from being pressed.

HK's USP is a stainless steel and polymer commercial version of the basic design of the Special Operations pistol.

The big Heckler & Koch Special Operations pistol is also in limited production as the Mark 23, a civilianized version which still has the threaded muzzle, but only a ten-shot magazine.

Ithaca has licensed a 50th Anniversary Model 45, only updated with the modifications currently in favor.

Daewoo has added a 45 ACP pistol, the DH 45 MK II, to its line and installs the exclusive Daewoo "Tri-Action" in it.

The pistol is offered as a 9mm now, but others in 40, 45, 10mm and 50 AE are in the works. Pistols have reportedly been in production since late 1995. The company plans to incorporate in the United States and open an office in Atlanta, Georgia.

Walther

A picture of the Walther P99 was displayed at the 1996 SHOT Show, but not the pistol itself. The new 9mm compact pistol is a real departure for Walther—striker-fired, and with a polymer frame, yet. If it is imported, Interarms will handle it.

Western Munitions

A family-operated company from Beulah, North Dakota, Western Munitions introduced their 9mm Patriot pistol at the 1996 SHOT Show. This pistol has a grip angle similar to that of the Luger. It is made of polycarbonate and steel components, a blowback design with a fixed $4^{1}/_{2}$-inch barrel. It has adjustable sights and a DAO action.

Postscript

Along with new autoloading pistols, a plethora of sights and accessories is being offered.

Items that might appeal to those with an interest in old autoloading pistols are the reloadable brass cartridge cases made by Bertram Bullet Company of Australia. Bertram produces cases in rifle and handgun calibers to keep some of the old-timers going. Currently offered for autoloading handguns are 30 Mauser, 7.5 French MAS, 9mm Basic (which can be trimmed to 9mm Mauser, 9mm Steyr, 9mm Largo and others) and 8mm Nambu. Bertram brass is available in the U.S. through Huntington's and The Old Western Scrounger. ●

THE 28-GAUGE IS, for me, the elite among shotgun gauges. Maintained for generations by a clique of Skeet shooters and a coterie of bird hunters, it survived comfortably in its special niche while the 14, the 24, and the 32 gauges and the 9mm shotshell virtually disappeared from the memory of living man. The 28 has held its tiny own while the sporting 10-gauge disappeared from everywhere but a few goose blinds, while the once-popular 16-bore lapsed into ignominy, and while the 10-gauge started a comeback. In its small way, the 28-gauge actually prospered, even became somewhat fashionable recently among a few yuppie shooters.

Doubtless, the main factor in the 28's life is its status as one of the four gauges chosen for Skeet competitions by the originators of the game. That is quite the opposite of why the 16-gauge faltered.

When I was a regular Skeet shooter, the 28-gauge event usually drew the fewest competitors of any. Many competitors used their .410-bore guns with the 3-inch shell loaded with 3/4-ounce of shot. Nevertheless, the winners usually used 28s. Skeet shooting provided a small but dependable market for what otherwise would be a marginal sales item.

SHOOTING THE 28

by MARSHALL R. WILLIAMS

With such incentives, the manufacturers produced some of their best models as 28s. Among the nice doubles available early on were Parkers, Ithacas, Iver Johnsons, and a rare few Winchester Model 21s. They were available in special Skeet models and in all of the higher grades. Strangely, L.C. Smith apparently made only one 28-gauge gun, although they probably made more Skeet guns than any other manufacturer of doubles. (As a matter of information, some specialty shops made 28-gauge barrels for L.C. Smiths, rather like the multi-gauge sets popular for Skeet.)

Winchester, High Standard, and Remington all eventually produced pumps in 28-gauge. Remington offered their fine and reliable Model 11-48 in 28, and I have seen at least one 28-gauge "F Grade" with gold inlays, their very best gun. Remington's Model 1100 would dominate Skeet in 28, as well as in all the other gauges.

Among the various English makers, Greener appears to have delighted in making beautiful little guns, as did Webley and Scott. If you had the bucks and the patience, all of the London best gunmakers would make 28s. I have even seen a photograph of a 28-gauge "Paradox gun" called a Fauneta by its manufacturer.

In point of fact, small shot charges are much more effective than many shooters realize. Without going into the math involved, a 3/4-ounce shot charge will be as effective at 35 yards as a 1-ounce charge will be at 40 yards.

Over the years, I have shot a variety of game with a number of 28-gauges. Off the top of my head, I remember the following: blue quail, bobwhite quail, whitewing doves, mourning doves, pigeons, woodcock, ruffed grouse, jackrabbits, cottontails, pigmy cottontails, squirrels, crows, one large hawk, one small owl, and a number of rattlesnakes, including one that was 7 feet long and must have weighed 20 pounds. Among the guns I have used in taking that game were a Winchester Model 12, with 28-inch Full choke barrel; a very attractive Italian double imported by Atlas and choked Improved Cylinder and Modified; a Remington Model 11-48 Skeet gun; and a Remington Model 870 Skeet gun. Thus, I feel qualified to make a few observations and comments on the 28 for hunting.

My first was the Winchester Model 12 with the only 28-inch Full choke barrel I ever saw on a 28-gauge gun. It was an old one, marked for the 2 5/8-inch shell. I bought it from a secondhand store for $20 because the stock was broken, it was rusty, and the owner didn't know where to get shells for it. The Herter's mail-order sporting-goods business was in full swing at the time, and I sent the gun to them. They restocked it in bird's-eye maple, reblued it, and put a full-length ventilated rib on it, all for about $100. When I got it back, it looked like the best prize ever from a Crackerjack box, weighed 7 pounds, and was the best shooting shotgun I ever owned. It fit me like a glove and shot good near and far. I once broke 25/25 at Skeet with it and stepped over to the trap range and broke 24/25 with it. That is what I mean when I say it shot good, near and far.

During this same period, both Federal and Winchester-Western offered a "magnum" shell loaded with an ounce of shot. The recoil from this load could be fairly stiff in a light gun. The velocity of this load was lower than other 28-gauge loads, on the order of 1150 fps. In my relatively heavy Model 12, the recoil was tame enough. I really liked this load for crow shooting. Crow calling was a popular off-season sport among my friends, and I did my share. This load seemed as good as any I ever used on crows, and I killed them

If you shoot a 28, an old plaid shirt is OK for Skeet.

as far and as cleanly as I did with any bigger gun.

The old Model 12 was a splendid gun, but its value increased all out of reason, and I grew reluctant to carry it. Groceries must be bought, house payments must be made, and doctor's bills have to be taken care of, so I eventually sold it. I hope its present owner gets as much enjoyment out of it as I did. Should you ever see it, some Herter's employee wrote my name inside the forearm in pencil.

Shooting in my home state of Virginia has always been at much closer ranges than one sees in South Texas. Consequently, less choke is needed. I have done virtually all my bird shooting with Skeet-choked guns, primarily a Remington Model 11-48 and Model 870. However, I did use an Improved Cylinder/Modified double, a really delightful little gun, imported by Atlas Arms. It had a straight grip with 25½-inch barrels and, typical of older guns, was choked a little tight for shells with plastic wads.

I shot a number of bobwhite quail and a few woodcocks with the Skeet-choked guns using both #8s and #9s. Both were effective to 30 yards, and I rarely get a shot any further away. Because the ranges are generally short, I find small shot very effective.

I firmly believe there is little magic in the bore diameter from which a shot charge is launched. An ounce of shot from a 28 is as effective as an ounce of shot from a 12-bore of comparable choke, but no more so. Such differences as they exist are important in the minds of those who practice shooting as theology and concern themselves with the number of angels who can dance on a bead sight.

My experience, then, is that the 28-gauge is a very satisfactory shotgun for game shooting where the ranges are moderate, such as forested and brushy areas. In the more open spaces found in much of our West and Southwest, the 28 needs some choke and the heavier loads. I really doubt many shooters can be consistently effective beyond the range of the 28, regardless of gauge.

I have never seen a reference to a 3-inch 28-gauge shell. Such a shell could be made to hold 1⅛ ounces of shot, but recoil would be uncomfortable in most 28-gauge guns and internal ballistics would be a problem. I covered the 1-ounce loads above. They were loaded in 2¾-inch shells, as were the ⅞-ounce loads.

I do not find the limited number of shot sizes to be a problem. True, I don't shoot geese or ducks, but if I did, I would not use a 28. For hunting, the 28 is essentially a short-range bird and game gun. At the shorter ranges, the smaller shot sizes have velocity, energy and penetration comparable to the larger sizes at longer ranges. Blue quail are considered tougher than bobwhites, and I have killed large numbers of blue quail with #9s.

I usually reload with #8s for hunting the uplands. I would use #7½s for rabbits, or perhaps #6s. I consider #8½s ideal for quail, and #9s for doves. I have found that the denser patterns of the smaller shot are more effective in the smaller gauges.

Reloading the 28-gauge differs little from reloading the larger gauges. My general observation is that reloading the 28 is like reloading all the others: Follow the manufacturer's instructions and expect success; don't follow them and expect trouble.

I have taken one flyer in the adventurous realm of load development for the 28-gauge. There is no longer a slug load available, and I set out to remedy this. One of my friends is an ardent muzzle-loading enthusiast with a 54-caliber rifle. He kindly gave me a few .535-inch diameter round balls which I used to produce a few "punkin' ball" loads. I used 17 grains of Unique, enough card and fiber wads to get the correct wad column, put the ball on top, and ran it through my MEC 600 Jr. crimper. This pushed the crimp section of the shell inside the case and secured the ball. It looks ugly but works. Five shots from my Model 870 Skeet gun averaged 1505 fps, for an energy of 1130 foot pounds, and resulted in a 5-inch group at 25 yards. The level of accuracy is uninspiring, but would be adequate for deer hunting at close range. No doubt a little refining could improve accuracy. The performance equals that of my friends's muzzle-loading rifle, a size which the mountain men considered adequate for buffalo and grizzly b'ar. Thus, I have a 6-pound buffalo gun.

Traditional wisdom regarding "punkin' ball" loads tells us that the ball should be smaller than the choke section it must pass through. A simple test is to roll the ball into the choke of the barrel and check for daylight around it. A better way is to measure with a dial caliper or micrometer. Balls should be at least .010-inch smaller than choke diameter.

In comparing the 28 to the larger gauges, it is largely a matter of using equivalent loads and getting equivalent performance. The 20, 16 and 12 bores are superior to the 28 to the extent they can handle heavier shot charges. I have used ¾-ounce loads in the 20, and ⅞-ounce and 1-ounce loads in all three. Frankly, I could discern no differences between any of them and the 28 when using similar shot charges.

The 28 suffers in comparison to the larger gauges in several minor respects. Shells are not nearly as widely distributed as shells for the other gauges, only a single weight of shot charge is available and shells cost more than the larger gauges. Additionally, there are no cheap promotional loads in 28-gauge at the discount stores. Of course, if elitism came cheap, everybody would do it. ●

Loads for the 28 are no longer $2.39 a box, but here's about as much variety as ever.

28-GAUGE BALLISTICS

Shot Charges	Comparative Range*
⅝-ounce	31.6 yards (79%)
¾-ounce	34.6 yards (86.6%)
⅞-ounce	37.4 yards (93.5%)
1-ounce	40.0 yards (100%)

*The comparison is based on arbitrarily setting the effective range of the 1-ounce charge at 40 yards. Obviously, effective range depends on a number of variables, particularly shot size, intended quarry and choke. The actual percentage of range is shown in parenthesis.

by HAL SWIGGETT

HANDGUNS TODAY:

SIXGUNS AND OTHERS

MAYBE THAT SHOULD read: Ten-shooters or less. Multi-stacked autoloaders started it; now revolvers have joined the many-shots crowd. Can't help but wonder what happened to that ever-so-important aimed first shot?

We are up to ten chambers in a revolver cylinder, and we also have them with nine, eight and seven holes. Cartridge case dimensions, for the moment, are the only limiting factor.

Smith & Wesson makes the ten-shot, Harrington & Richardson 1871/New England Firearms has *always* had a nine-shot, but now Taurus has joined that bandwagon, and they also have two eight-shooters. Let's start in that order and pray no one gets left out. Watch out for the surprise from Thompson/Center once we get to them in alphabetical order. And, yes, a lot of old Iver Johnson 22s were seven-shooters, but not now.

Smith & Wesson

The Model 17 22 Long Rifle revolver now offers a ten-round cylinder capacity, a 6-inch full lug barrel, Hogue rubber grips, Patridge front and adjustable black rear blade sights, and it's drilled and tapped for scope mounting. On the other end, the Model 625 Mountain Gun is offered in 45 Colt. It has a 4-inch tapered barrel, pinned black ramp front and micrometer-click-adjustable black rear blade, Hogue round-butt rubber Monogrip, stainless steel construction, and is also drilled and tapped for scope mounting (on a 4-inch barrel?).

The Model 686 Magnum Plus holds seven 357 Magnum rounds, making it the smallest seven-shooter 357 offered. It has a micrometer click-adjustable black blade rear sight on the $2^1/_2$-inch version and a white-outline rear blade on the 4- and 6-inch models. S&W's sixty-year-old five-shot, 2-inch Chief Special has grown up. Now it's offered with $2^1/_8$-inch barrel and is chambered in 357 Magnum. Of stainless steel, it weighs 20 ounces, is $6^5/_{16}$ inches overall and gives you a choice of single or double action. The Model 640 Centennial with concealed hammer is still double-action-only, but in 357 Magnum, $2^1/_2$-inch barrel. You really need their catalog.

Taurus

Their Model 94 22 Long Rifle is a nine-shot, with 4-inch barrel in blue or stainless. There is also a 3-inch version in stainless. Chambered for 22 Winchester Rimfire Magnum, Taurus' Model 921 has a heavy barrel with full-length underlug. The cylinder holds eight cartridges. The gun is in stainless or blue in 3-inch, blue only in 4-inch.

The Model 607 is a new large-frame 357 Magnum, vent-ribbed and Taurus-compensated, with your choice of 4- or 6-inch barrel. The one on display at the SHOT Show was blue and had seven chambers in its cylinder.

H&R 1871

An H&R might have been the first modern revolver with more than the usual six chambers. The very popular H&R Model 999 was first offered in 1950, nearly half a century back. There was an earlier Model 6, a 22 seven-shot only, issued in 1906.

Their newest listing, this time around, is the "Trapper." This one rang my bell. I was a trapper a lot of years and still buy a Texas trapper's license every year—though I haven't set a trap for more than twenty years.

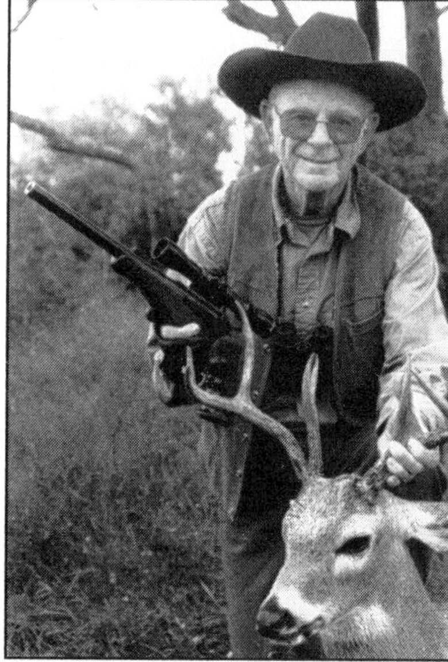

The first-ever whitetail buck with T/C's new Encore pistol, bagged by Swiggett, who else?

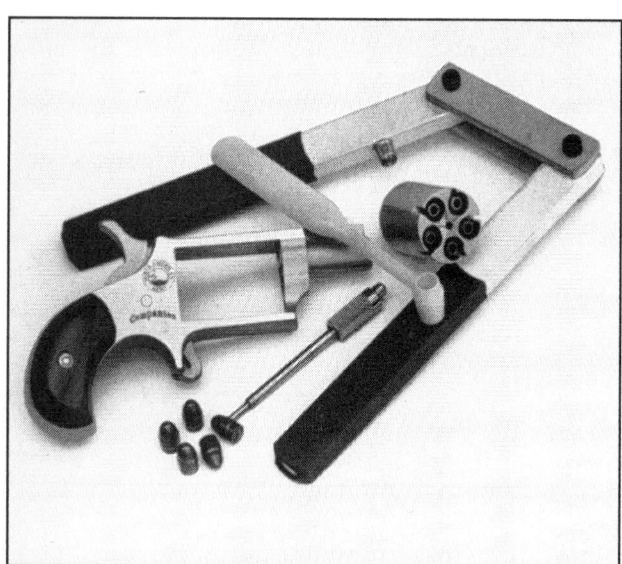

NAA's Companion is a 5-ounce cap-and-ball revolver, delivered with loading tool, powder measure and bullets.

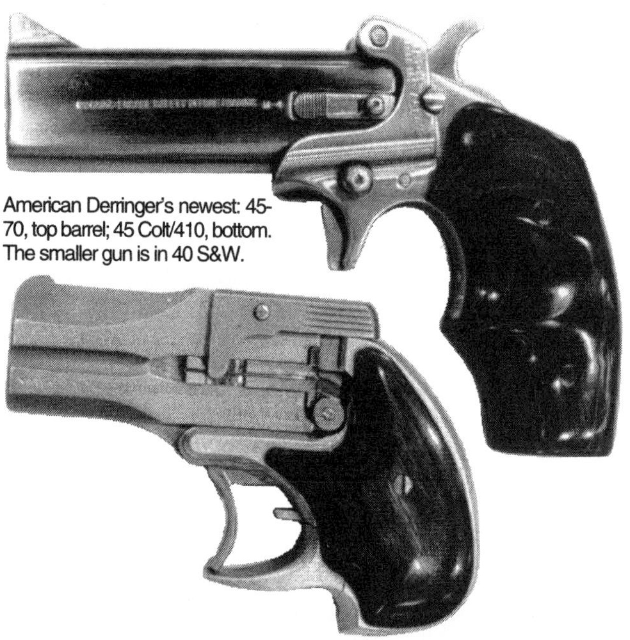

American Derringer's newest: 45-70, top barrel; 45 Colt/410, bottom. The smaller gun is in 40 S&W.

Rifle, shotgun, even handgun hunting is easy compared to making an animal step on that tiny 1 3/4-inch pan.

This Trapper is H&R's regulation Model 929 Sidekick, but with a gray laminated grip. Its heavy 4-inch barrel, fixed sights, and weight of 30 ounces make it an easy-to-handle revolver. H&R donates a portion of each sale to the National Trapper's Association. This *is* a limited issue.

Erma Werke and H&R 1871 have joined forces. Their combined effort is called the AMTEC 2000, and it is a five-shot 38 Special revolver with 2- or 3-inch barrel. Finishes are high-polish blue, electroless matte nickel or stainless. This new tiny—7 1/8 inches overall with 2-inch barrel—shortie weighs 24 ounces. Could be this one will fit well with concealed-carry laws.

American Derringer

Elizabeth Saunders, wife of the late Robert Saunders, tells me they have a couple of new models: The DA 38 Double Action is billed as the "World's Smallest & Lightest 40 S&W" and is also chambered for 357 Magnum, 38 Special and 9mm Luger.

Their other addition is a 45-70 in the M-4 Alaskan Survival Model. Its top barrel is 45-70, and the lower is either 45 Colt or 3-inch 410. The barrel length is 4.1 inches, overall length 6 inches, and weight is 16 1/2 ounces.

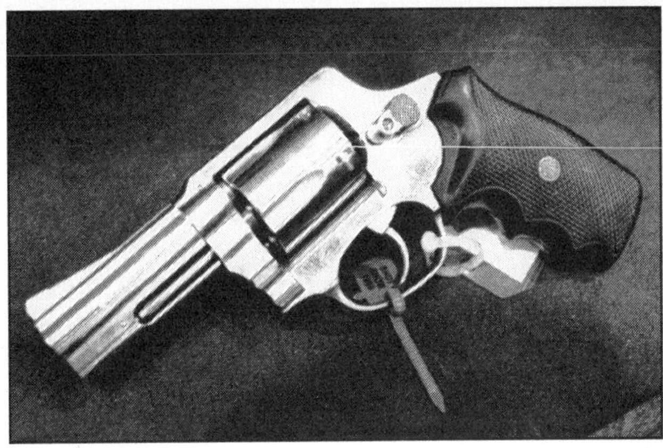

This 3-inch 44 Special Rossi with shrouded hammer is double-action-only.

Back as an Airweight, S&W's Model 642—38 Special, 15.8 ounces, five-shot, 6 5/16 inches in length.

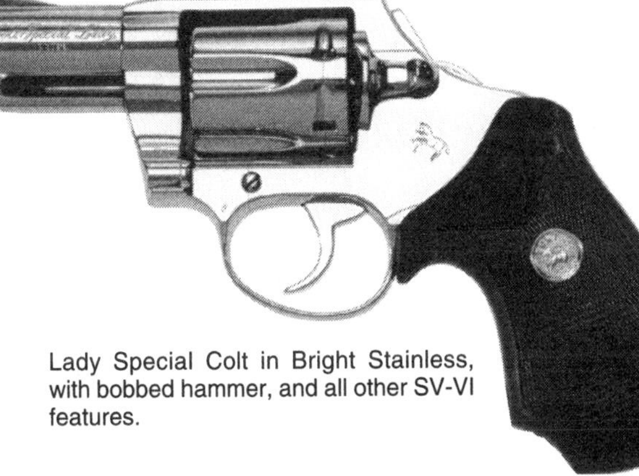

Lady Special Colt in Bright Stainless, with bobbed hammer, and all other SV-VI features.

American Frontier Firearms

This company's open-top single actions—1871-72 Open-Top, Remington New Model (1863-1875), Richards Metallic Cartridge Conversion (based on the 1860 percussion), Richards and Mason Metallic Cartridge Conversion (based on the 1851 Navy Percussion), and several pocket models—are authentic stuff in all but caliber.

Each revolver looks and feels like those old originals, but is designed and built to handle regulation 38 Special or 44 Special ammunition. Finishes are blue or silver. You will have to see them to believe.

A.M.T. (Arcadia Machine & Tool)

How did this one get in *Sixguns and Others*? Widely known as a manufacturer of fine autoloaders, Harry Sanford has added a new ingredient—bolt-action receivers for handguns. His new receivers are built specifically for pistols and are available to all custom gun manufacturers. It is, and nearly always has been, illegal to alter any rifle action to pistol use. Through A.M.T., fine bolt actions are available, legally built for such use.

Cimarron

Widely known for their excellent reproductions of golden oldies revolvers, Cimarron's newest is the Schofield Wells Fargo 5-inch 44 Russian and Special, in nickel finish. This gun is also

Erma Werke and H&R 1871 team up to offer this 38 Special, five-shot, 2- or 3-inch barrel.

Taurus' 431 Carry Pak—2 1/2 inch, five-shot, 44 Special with patented Hydra-port.

available in 45 S&W, known as the 45 Short Colt. You really do need, if you're at all interested in excellent reproductions of fine old revolvers, the beautifully and expensively printed color catalog.

Colt

New this time around is the SF-VI, a double-action six-shot built on a 400 stainless steel small frame that, to use their words, "makes it notably effective as a personal protection and woman's firearm."

The internal mechanism combines the Anaconda safety connector, Detective Special leaf spring and hand, a frame-mounted firing pin, and a new bolt design. Barrel length is 2 or 4 inches. The 4-inch version is offered with choice of Bright Stainless or their new Black Stainless. The Special Lady has all the above features, Bright Stainless, 2-inch only, and with a bobbed hammer.

Initially, last year, Colt's Realtree Anaconda was offered with 2.5-7x scope, mounts, rings and a soft camo gun pouch. Now the big double action comes by itself: 8-inch barrel, Realtree camo pattern, thermoplastic combat-style Hogue Monogrip, free-floating ejector rod and full-length housing, enhanced balance, and integral ventilated rib.

Competitor

Al Straitiff and his cannon-breech single shot are alive and well. New for this year is the 414 E.T.Gates cartridge. Designed by Elgin Gates for silhouette shooting, he called it, I believe, the 414 Super Magnum IHMSA. It is simply a lengthier case—.314-inch longer, unless my measurement is amiss—so a heavy bullet can be launched downrange 300 or so fps faster than regulation 41s.

Both cases and dies are available from Robert Gates at The Silhouette. He has on hand an abundance of brass plus those necessary dies.

Long talked about, and finally on hand, is the 5mm centerfire. Competitor offers barrels so chambered, plus brass, bullets and dies. It's a reloadable version of the old 5mm rimfire.

Crosman's Python Look-Alike

Colt's 6-inch-barreled Python weighs in at 44.5 ounces on my postal scale. Crosman's 357, with the same length barrel, weighs 31 ounces. Both of them are six-shooters.

Why compare these two? Easy. Almost every day, right here in my office, I get in a few practice shots with my Crosman pellet revolver. My target is a Sheridan Products bullet trap mounted on a closet door, 16 feet from the muzzle as I sit here at my typewriter.

This is mighty good practice. Its trigger pull is 3¼ pounds, or 52 ounces. This is better, in fact, than a lot of cartridge revolvers as delivered from manufacturers. Accuracy, with fresh CO_2 cylinders, is more than sufficient to let any shooter know where the fault lay with a wayward pellet.

D-Max Sidewinder 45/410

It's 3¾ pounds of stainless steel, which includes a 3-inch cylinder that, by itself, weighs a fraction over a pound. Barrel length is 6½ inches; overall length is 13¾ inches. Barrel diameter is .806-inch, from frame to muzzle. This is not, obviously, a quick-draw six-shooter.

Shotshells out of a rifled barrel? You bet! The gun arrives with two choke tubes and a hex wrench for installation/removal. One is labeled "scatter choke," and it measures .480-inch inside diameter. The other tube is not labeled, and it measures .438-inch.

Unlike conventional single actions, the Sidewinder has only two hammer positions—cocked to fire and all the way down. A transfer bar rises to cover the firing pin as the trigger is pulled. With the hammer down, that firing pin cannot be reached by the hammer, providing a degree of safety.

How does it shoot?

First, make certain this dual-purpose sixgun's choke tube is removed before firing bullets. My tests were made with Black Hills' 255-grain 45 Colt lead bullet load, a semi-wadcutter, and CCI's 255-grain pointed bullet. At 25 yards, groups were about the same as I shoot with open sights regularly, meaning with seventy-four-year-old cataract-implanted eyes and glasses. A cottontail's head, at that distance, would be in serious trouble.

Having more than limited experience with a well-known single shot 45/410 pistol, I learned, two years back while shooting grouse, that heavier shot does better than light, so my tests were with 3-inch #6s and #4s. I'm not one to be bothered with details—maybe that's a flaw, but it's the end result that whets my interest—my targets were quail-size styrofoam hot drink cups. At 15 yards, what I considered max for this barrel length/shot charge, both shot sizes would have dropped birds. I used the unmarked tighter choke tube, not the "scatter choke."

(Left) Rossi's stainless steel 22 WMR is an eight-shooter, Kit Gun-styled.

(Right) H&R's Trapper—a 4-inch nine-shot 22 LR. A portion of each sale goes to the National Trapper's Association.

S&W's Long Rifle Model 17—ten-shot cylinder, full lug, serious looks.

My decision about the Sidewinder: It does everything its manufacturer claims, maybe to the point he is a bit modest.

European American Armory

This company, like so many, has become obsessed with self-shuckers, and they list only two revolvers. I've preached it for years, and it's still true: nothing beats an aimed first shot...unless the intent is to give the antagonist pneumonia from wind blowing around him as bullets fly by.

E.A.A. offers the Big Bore Bounty Hunter with 4½- or 7½-inch barrels and chambered for 357 Magnum/38 Special, 44 Remington Magnum or 45 Colt. They also list their double-action Windicator. This one is in 22 LR, 22 WRM, 38 Special or 357 Mag-

This is a ten-shot S&W 22 LR cylinder—some serious drilling.

Taurus gets up a 357 eight-shooter; this one's their Model 607.

S&W's Model 686 Magnum Plus goes seven 357 rounds without feeding.

Taurus' eight-shot 22 WMR cylinder has a lot of holes in it.

num. Barrel lengths are 2 or 4 inches in centerfire and 4 or 6 inches, rimfire.

Freedom Arms

Wyoming-based Freedom Arms' newest is a 3-inch 454 Casull called the "Packer." It has a fixed sight and an octagon barrel, and I feel certain, it will definitely be a handful when spitting out that heavy 45-caliber bullet. It could well be the perfect backup for those hunting dangerous game—easy to carry and immediately handy.

My pair of 454s have been in southern Africa several times and served well. One has a 9½-inch barrel with muzzlebrake and is scoped. The other is a 4¾-incher and rides on my hip (my hunting handguns are *always* in my hands). It has proven itself more than a few times to be a top-rate troubleshooter. Maybe *finisher* is a better description. This new Packer might be even handier.

Now there is a Freedom Arms Collectors Association. For information, write to them in Miami.

Medusa

Medusa's Model 47 double-action revolver is billed as "Like no other gun in the world." How come? It is specially designed to fire and extract, without the use of half-moon clips, fourteen different cartridges of "38 caliber." The list includes the 9mm Winchester Magnum, and all 380, 38, 38 Special, 9mm, and 357 Magnum cartridges. It does this through the use of a single six-shot cylinder. Available barrel lengths are 2½, 3, 4, 5 or 6 inches. Finish is matte blue. It has gripper-style rubber grips and a

In 22 Long Rifle, Taurus gets yet another hole—a nine-shooter.

American Frontier Firearms offers two versions of the 1871-72 open-top blackpowder revolver. They're chambered for modern 38 or 44 Special cartridges.

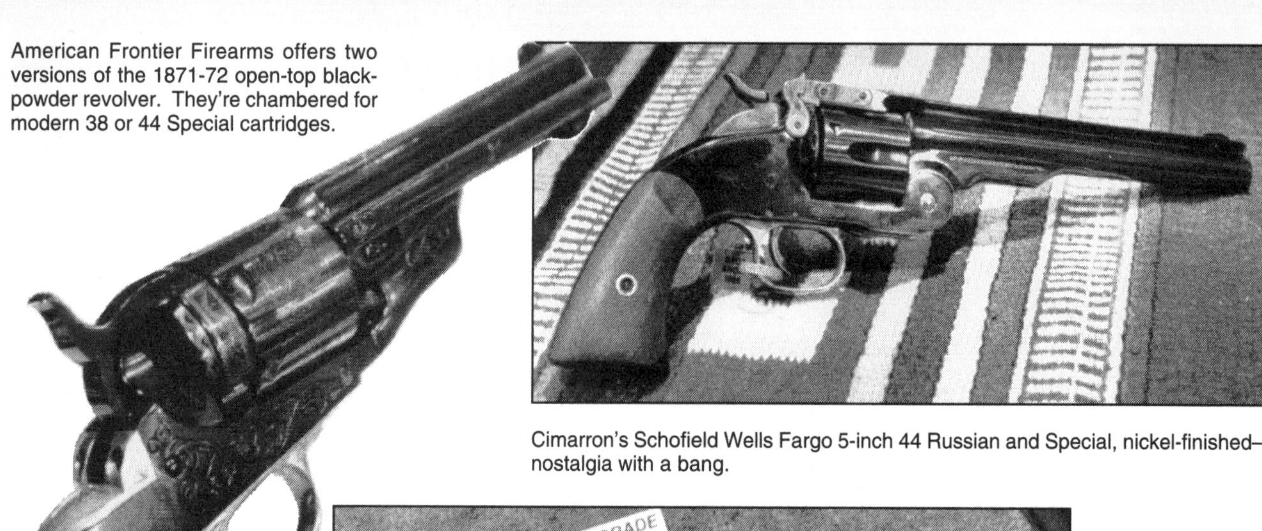

Cimarron's Schofield Wells Fargo 5-inch 44 Russian and Special, nickel-finished—nostalgia with a bang.

Freedom Arms' 3-inch 454 Casull Packer—octagonal barrel and fixed sights.

changeable front sight. The Medusa's frame is cast from 8620 steel, heat-treated to 28 Rockwell "C" hardness. Cylinders are of 4330 modified vanadium steel, heat-treated to 36 Rockwell.

This company also manufactures cylinders for Ruger Blackhawk and S&W 686 revolvers to accept twenty-five cartridges, 9mm through 357 Magnum. Also listed is a replacement cylinder for Ruger Blackhawk 45 Colt-chambered single actions that will accept 45 ACP and 45 Colt. Another of their listings is a five-shot 45 Colt/45 Winchester Magnum cylinder for Ruger Blackhawks.

This company can also take your 44 Remington Magnum New Model Ruger and turn it into a five-shot 50 Action Express. Barrel lengths offered are $4^{5}/_{8}$ to 8 inches. Phillips & Rodgers is the name of the company building these innovative revolvers, and they are in Conroe, Texas.

North American Arms

Now there are five different single actions offered by this Utah-based manufacturer. First

Screw-in chokes for the D-Max. Tubes MUST be removed before firing bullets.

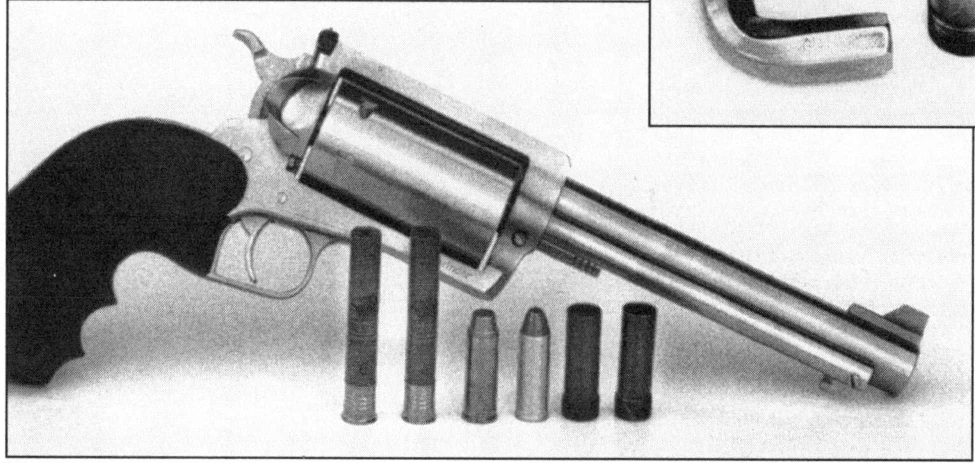

D-Max's 45 Colt/410 was tested with 3-inch #6 and #4 shot along with CCI's Blazer and Black Hills' 255-grain lead bullet loads. It worked.

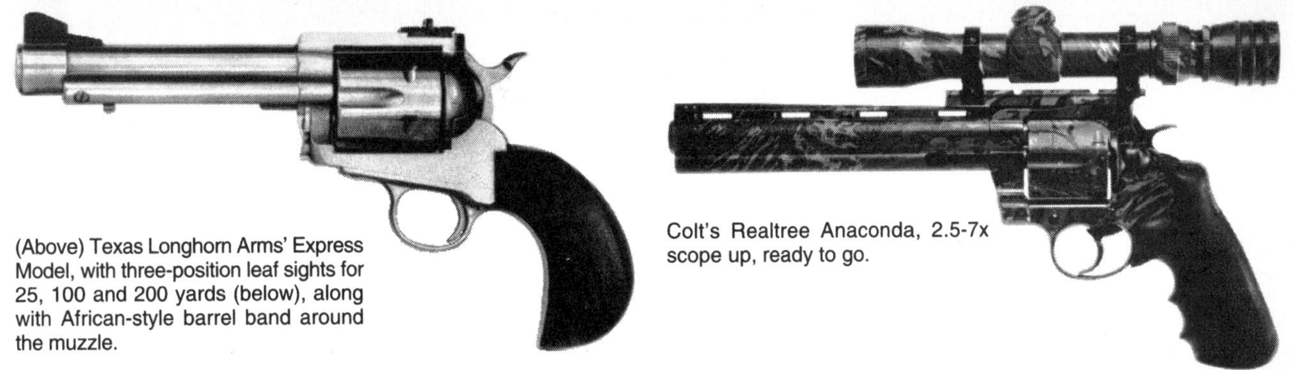

(Above) Texas Longhorn Arms' Express Model, with three-position leaf sights for 25, 100 and 200 yards (below), along with African-style barrel band around the muzzle.

Colt's Realtree Anaconda, 2.5-7x scope up, ready to go.

Thompson/Center's newest, the Encore, a heavier/beefier version of the Contender. Works fine.

were the little $1\frac{1}{8}$- and $1\frac{5}{8}$-inch-barreled five-shooters in 22 Short, 22 Long Rifle and 22 Winchester Magnum Rimfire. Then came their Mini-Master, a 4-inch heavy barrel with dual cylinders in 22 Long Rifle and 22 WMR, with an adjustable rear sight. Shortly after the Mini-Master's introduction came their Black Widow—a 2-inch version of the Mini-Master. Dual cylinders were available here, too, along with the adjustable rear sight.

Number five was a cap-and-baller called the Companion. Weighing 5 ounces on my postal scale, the Companion is delivered with a dipper (2.5 grains of FFFFG or Pyrodex in the Long Rifle, 4 grains in the Magnum version). That charge is set off with the ever-popular #11 percussion caps. Bullet weight is 30 grains. A seating tool is supplied with the Companion along with complete instructions on loading, bullet seating and percussion cap installation. This is a "fun" five-shooter if ever I've seen one.

Rossi

Imported by Interarms, Rossi revolvers are alive and well, and several new models are offered to back up that statement: A nine-shot 22 Long Rifle; eight-shot 22 WMR; seven-shot 357 Magnum; the Lady Rossi, a five-shot 38 Special; and a 3-inch-barreled, double-action-only, shrouded-hammer 44 Special. This last is also offered with an exposed hammer and in double/single action. Both 44s wear 3-inch barrels. Again, you really need their catalog.

Ruger

Nothing new from Ruger this time around, so far as this section is concerned. However, concerning my mention in last year's GUN DIGEST of a need for original grips to fit an early Bearcat, a reader, K.A. Wiseman, referred me to Lett Custom Grips, the manufacturer of those original Bearcat grips. They are still in business. Thank you, K.A.

Texas Longhorn Arms

Bill Grover, he of right-hand-single-action fame, has done it again. His newest innovation is a three-leaf folding rear sight on his Express Model revolver.

Grover used his new Express Model on the Y.O. Ranch during Safari Club International's annual Handgun Meat Hunt for the Needy. He took a whitetail buck at 158 yards (agreed on by several witnesses). His ammunition was Cor-Bon's 300-grain Swift-bullet load, sighted dead-on at 25 yards. Using the new sight's 100-yard blade, he held up a wee bit of front sight and held for the shoulder. The point of impact for his one-shot kill was on that shoulder.

Thompson/Center

The T/C Encore is a beefed-up—meaning stronger and a bit heavier—frame, with all new inner workings including the trigger and guard, chambered in 308 Winchester and 30-06 Springfield (1:10 twist), 7mm-08 (1:9), and 22-250 (1:12). Barrel lengths offered are $10\frac{5}{8}$ and 15 inches. Overall length is 15 or $19\frac{1}{2}$ inches. Approximate weight is 4 pounds with the $10\frac{5}{8}$-inch barrel. The Encore's rear sight is fully adjustable, and the new gun has a ramp-style front sight.

T/C's easy-to-change barrel-switching system remains intact. Their patented automatic hammer block with bolt interlock ensures this pistol will not fire until it is completely locked. Grips and forends are of American black walnut.

This writer shot the Encore before it had a name. The serial number was Z.2, and it was chambered in 308 Winchester.

How did it shoot? My first five-shot group measured 1.234 inches. Muzzle velocity for the five averaged 2554 fps.

T/C has, at least in my opinion, another winner. In fact, my name for the prototype used deer hunting was "Champion." As with most of my suggestions/ideas, it didn't fly.

Wrist Injuries

As this is written, two handgunners of note, both of them widely known and read, are wearing casts on their right wrists. The damage came from excessive shooting with h-e-a-v-y loads.

My grandfather, Louis H. Spray (1870-1951), on July 22, 1927, started me shooting "real" guns. That day was my sixth birthday. He gave me the most valuable advice anyone ever gave any handgunner. "God gave you two hands, use them both. God gave you two eyes, keep both open." Then he added, "Push lightly forward with the gun-holding hand, pull lightly back with the other." Some call it the Weaver method. I prefer to call it the Louis H. Spray method.

It still works, call it "Weaver" or "Spray." Using both hands on heavy-recoiling handguns will go a long way toward lack of injury to one's wrists. Think on it. ●

TENITE and the early SYNTHETICS In the LONG ARMS INDUSTRY

by LARRY S. STERETT

BUTTPLATES FOR LONG guns have been manufactured of wood, iron, steel, aluminum, brass, silver, pewter, ivory, leather, rubber and various synthetics starting with bakelite, possibly even other materials. The butts on some shotguns, usually English doubles of high quality, have been checkered and left without a plate or pad. Except for reproduction blackpowder arms, iron or brass buttplates aren't used on modern small arms, nor is leather, except for some leather-covered pads on expensive shotguns. Thus, the majority of buttplates are of some synthetic material, just as they have been for the past eighty-plus years.

With the exception of leather, and possibly rubber, trigger guards have been made from the same materials as buttplates. Up to and following World War II, most of the trigger guards on rimfire rifles in the lower price ranges were of stamped steel. Even recently, some of the more economical centerfire rifles also used stamped steel trigger guards, such as on the excellent Remington Model 788 of a few years past, and the earlier Models 721 and 722. The trigger guards on the most expensive rifles and shotguns have sometimes been horn and ivory, but steel is the most common material used.

Then synthetic guards began appearing, particularly on rimfire rifles, some shotguns, and a few centerfire rifles. The ventilated rib and synthetic trigger guard were the only really poor features of the Remington Model 600 rifle, and the rib on the XP-100 wasn't a real beauty.

Pistol grip caps were made of synthetic materials, as well as iron, steel, wood, aluminum, pewter, silver, gold and ivory, to mention the more common materials. Forearm tips were also made of similar materials, with brass and iron being used on muzzleloading arms, blued steel on such rifles as the lever-action Winchesters, horn and ivory on some of the more expensive rifles and shotguns, and exotic woods on the more expensive arms. Then plastic forearm tips began to appear prior to World War II. Ivory-colored or black to resemble real ivory or ebony, such tips were more common on replacement stocks such as those available from E.C. Bishop, Reinhart Fajen, and the late great Herter's, Inc. It is still possible to purchase a new stock, complete with plastic forend tip, grip cap, and buttplate for a sporterized Mauser, Springfield, Enfield and others.

Remington introduced their line of Nylon rifles featuring the entire stock assembly of a form of thermo-setting nylon. Consisting of tubular and detachable box magazine autoloaders, a lever action, and three bolt-action models—single shot, tubular and detachable box magazine repeaters—the rifles really gained a following, or at least the autoloaders did, with the other versions fading quickly.

ArmaLite, the successor to Fairchild Engine, the parent of the original AR-15 design which followed the AR-10 and others, made lavish use of synthetics in manufacturing small arms. Witness the AR-7, the survival rifle with the synthetic buttstock assembly into which the metal parts of the rifle could be stored. Or the wonderful AR-17 autoloading shotgun which had many unique features, including a synthetic buttstock and forend, detachable choke tubes, and a golden glow; hence the "Golden Gun" label.

Without getting into the current use of synthetics to produce handgun receivers and stocks, such as on the Remington XP-100 221 Fireball pistol, the list of synthetic parts on sporting arms could go on and on. Sight bases, sights, magazines, cartridge guides, safety slides and levers, pistol grips, magazine plugs and followers, all have been and are being made from synthetic materials for use on sporting arms.

Many of these parts have evolved over the past few decades, and all have seemed an innovative use of plastic, and they may well have been. Especially noteworthy are the Nylon 66, ArmaLite AR-7 and AR-17 stocks. But these were not the first synthetic stocks for sporting arms, not by nearly thirty years. That credit has to go to the Stevens Arms Co. division of Savage Arms.

The time? Over fifty years ago, in the mid-1930s. Tennessee Eastman Corp. of Kingsport, Tennessee, a subsidiary of Eastman Kodak, developed a new synthetic thermo-plastic called Tenite. Tests showed the new synthetic to be extremely hard and durable, easily colored and moulded, polishable, and weatherproof. It was advertised as not swelling, shrinking, warping, checking, cracking or splitting, sales talk which later proved to be a bit much. Table telephone hous-

The Beauty of your TENITE GUNSTOCK lasts longer!
A TENITE GUNSTOCK is as hard and tough as good to look at. It resists marring and scratching, when, for example, it is dragged through thickets. But if it sustains a scratch, its original beauty can be restored simply by polishing with a fine abrasive. You can keep it looking new . . . indefinitely.
TENITE is not affected by extremes of weather. It won't swell, split, warp or crack. It is ideally suited to gunstock requirements.
STEVENS No. 530-M
Double Barrel Shotgun
with stock and fore-end of TENITE
12, 16, 20 Gauge and .410 Bore
Note handsome, paneled stock with fluted comb and richly checkered, capped full pistol grip. Also, checkering on fore-end. Other refinements: two white bead Ivoroid sights, polished, case-hardened frame. A stand-out in shotgun value!
ELABORATE CHECKERING AT NO EXTRA COST
STEVENS No. 530-M
$22.95
SEND FOR FREE CATALOG
STEVENS
J. STEVENS ARMS COMPANY
Division of Savage Arms Corporation
Dept. A-44, Chicopee Falls, Mass.
Please send free catalog.
Name
Address

(Right) This advertisement from the late 1940s is one of the few noted in which Tennessee Eastman promoted the use of Tenite for gunstocks.

for greater durability
ask for the gun with the
TENITE STOCK
Noble model 33 slide action .22 caliber rifle—with Tenite stock, fore-end, and slide handle, Noble Manufacturing Co., Inc., Haydenville, Mass.
Savage model 311 double-barrel 16 gauge shotgun—with Tenite stock and fore-end, Savage Arms Corporation, Chicopee Falls, Mass.
● Tough Tenite stocks and fore-ends are noted for their ability to take hard blows without splitting or cracking.
They offer other important advantages too: dimensional stability under varying temperature and moisture conditions—custom-built features and detail – smooth, eye-appealing finish – rich, molded-in colors.
Ask your dealer to show you the range of gun models now equipped with Tenite stocks and fore-ends.
TENITE
an Eastman plastic

(Above) Cellulose acetate was first produced in 1856-1869. In 1929, moulding compounds became available, and in 1938, cellulose acetate-butyrate was introduced by Tennessee Eastman Corporation as Tenite II. Tenite I had been introduced in 1933. This new acetate-butyrate plastic had superior moisture resistance, higher impact strength, and improved dimensional stability. This advertisement for the Stevens 530-M shotgun is from the 1940s.

(Above) The Stevens Model 94 was available in 12-, 16-, 20-ga. and 410-bore in Tenite. The buttstocks were hollow, or partially hollow, and weighed less than similar walnut stocks, so Tenite-stocked firearms recoil a bit more, particularly in 12-gauge. With light loads, this 20-gauge Model 94 is a joy to carry and shoot, its Tenite stock still new-looking after nearly fifty years.

RESISTS SCRATCHING
WEATHERPROOF
Why THIS MODERN GUNSTOCK MATERIAL GIVES YOU BETTER SERVICE
TENITE by STEVENS
Tenite is extremely hard, strong, durable. It is richly colored and polished to a handsome luster. It needs no applied surface coating and has none. You can carry a gun with Tenite stock through the worst tangle of alders or briars without risking disfiguring scratches. You can keep it looking like new indefinitely.
You can take it out in the rain, sun, snow or frost, and it will not swell, shrink, warp, check, crack or split. Tenite is weatherproof.
The TENITE Gunstock
is an exclusive Stevens development . . . another in the long list of improvements pioneered by Stevens. Available on the following models:
No. 530-M Double Barrel Shotgun
No. 22-410 Over and Under .22 rifle and .410 shotgun
No. 240 Over and Under .410 shotgun
SEND FOR FREE CATALOG
and current price list
J. STEVENS ARMS COMPANY
Division of Savage Arms Corporation
Dept. C-50, Chicopee Falls, Mass.

By the time this 1940s advertisement appeared, Stevens was using Tenite on the Model 530-M side-by side, the Model 22-410 over/under and the Model 240 over/under.

ings were being manufactured from it as early as 1936.

The new material was cellulose acetate-butyrate. It could be moulded merely by the application of heat (around 250-350 degrees F.) and pressure (about 2000 psi), and it set by cooling, unlike phenol and urea plastics, which are set by curing under heat. Tenite undergoes no chemical change in moulding and is one of the few plastics adapted to both compression and injection moulding. It takes an exceptionally smooth finish and has no odor or taste. Because it is a low conductor of heat, it is pleasant to touch, making it particularly adapted to the moulding of articles which may come in contact with the skin. It supports combustion with difficulty, burning like hard rubber; the Underwriters' Laboratories rated its hazards "to be small and in storage somewhat less than would be presented by common newsprint paper in the same form and quantity." Exposure to temperatures of 160 degrees F., or higher, will cause softening, but ordinary temperatures had no affect.

Tenite I—or cellulose acetate-propionate—while tough and extremely shock resistant, was less soluble in fewer chemical solutions than the later Tenite II, making the finished products more expensive to produce. Raw Tenite I was apparently cheaper to produce than Tenite II. Tenite II was found to have less than half the water absorption of the Tenite I, if completely immersed in water for a long period of time, making it ideal for use outdoors.

Thus, by 1939, more than seventy different moulded Tenite parts were being used on automobiles, in addition to such items as vanity cases, reel and spool ends, buttons, desk accessories, film cores, pencils and fountain pens, to mention only a few.

Engineers at the J. Stevens Arms Co. examined this new synthetic and used it to develop a new line of weatherproof gunstocks. According to Mr. Roe Clark, a gentleman and Savage/Stevens scholar *par excellence*, first mention of Tenite stocks was in the 1940 Stevens catalog, with the last mention being around 1950. The first mention this writer has found was an advertisement dated August 15, 1939, for the Stevens Model 530-M, stocked in Tenite and available in 12-, 16- and 20-gauge for $21.50.

During World War II, Savage/Stevens was busy manufacturing Enfield No. 4 Mk 1 rifles and Thompson submachine guns. Sporting rifles and shotguns, including those models with Tenite stocks, were put on the shelf. Reintroduction of Tenite-stocked arms was in 1946. The bolt-action Model 124 shotgun was stocked with wood, starting in 1951, but it wasn't until 1954 that the Tenite buttstock on the Model 820 was replaced with wood.

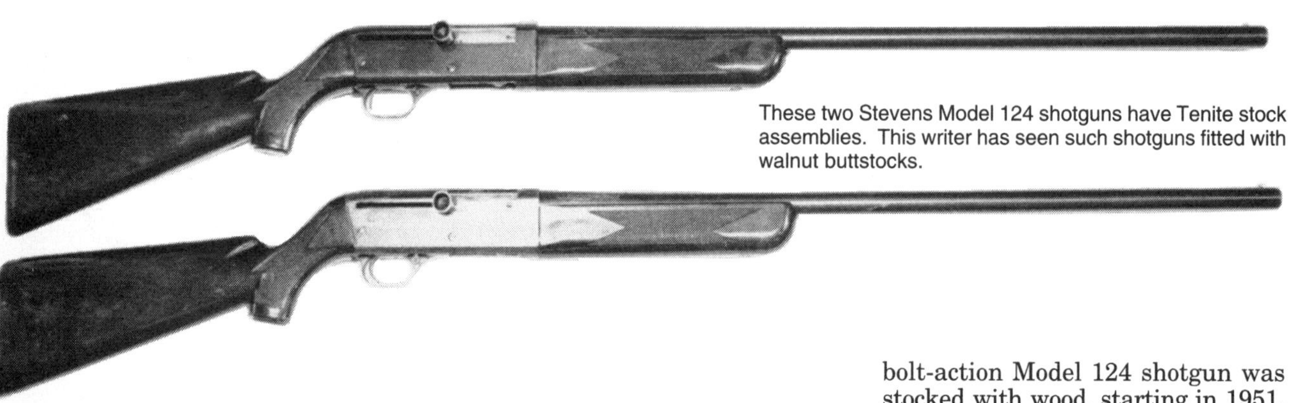

These two Stevens Model 124 shotguns have Tenite stock assemblies. This writer has seen such shotguns fitted with walnut buttstocks.

The total number of Stevens models featuring Tenite stocks was around eight, not counting the possible variations and models produced for firms such as Montgomery Ward under the Western Field label, and the like. Included are the Model 22-410 combination gun, or the Model 24, as it became known; the Model 87 autoloading rimfire rifle; the Model 311 side-by-side shotgun; the Model 530-M side-by-side shotgun; the Model 94 single-barrel shotgun; the Model 124 bolt-action shotgun; the Model 240 over/under shotgun; and the Model 820 pump-action shotgun.

According to "Savage-Stevens-Fox Component Parts Catalog No. 51," issued November 1, 1951, Tenite stocks were still available for the following models: Stevens-Springfield 87/76 series, Model 24, Model 240, Model 820, Model 124, Model 311T and Model 94T. However, some stocks would fit more than one model—the

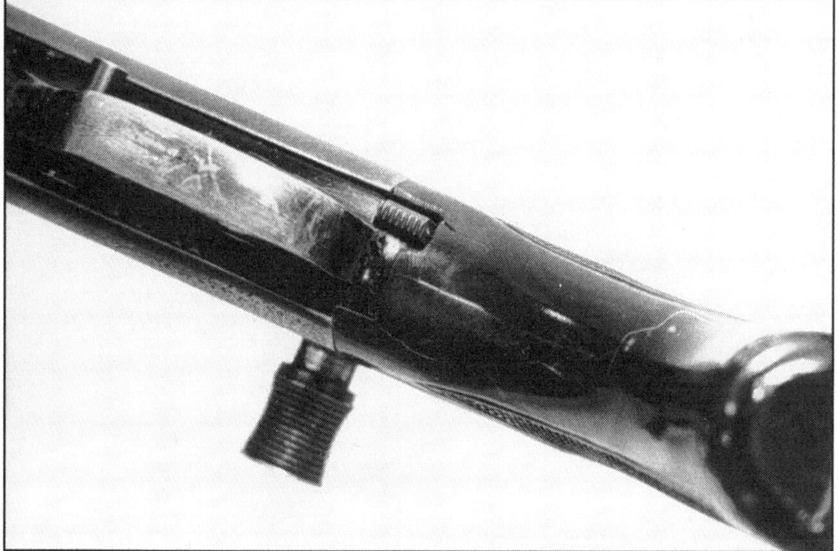

Tenite has a tensile strength of 4300-5000 psi and a compressive strength of 12,000-16,000 psi, and could withstand an impact of 5.2 ft. lbs. per square inch under the Charpy test. It excelled in toughness and resilience, and it was not brittle, but it was not unbreakable. Extended firing in some shotguns, such as this 12-gauge Model 124, did tend to produce cracks in the tang area, as can be seen here. This was more apt to occur during severe cold weather.

same stock could be used for the 94, 24 and 240 models, while the Model 820 used the same stock as the Model 124, and the 530 and 311 models were interchangeable.

After Savage/Stevens phased out the Tenite stocks, there were still barrels of them left. Many were sold to Numrich Arms as surplus parts, but what happened to the balance is not known. They may still exist somewhere, but were probably scrapped when the firm moved from Chicopee Falls to Westfield, Massachusetts.

Former Savage official Gene Noble Davidson left the firm in the late '40s to form his own outfit, Noble Manufacturing Co., of Haydenville, Massachusetts. One of the first products was the Nobel 33 slide-action 22 rimfire rifle, available with a choice of Tenite or walnut stock and slide handle. Interestingly, if you take a stock for the Stevens 87 autoloading rifle and cut it off a few inches forward of the trigger guard, it's almost a perfect fit as a buttstock for the Nobel 33. It would have been an excellent way to use surplus Tenite stocks.

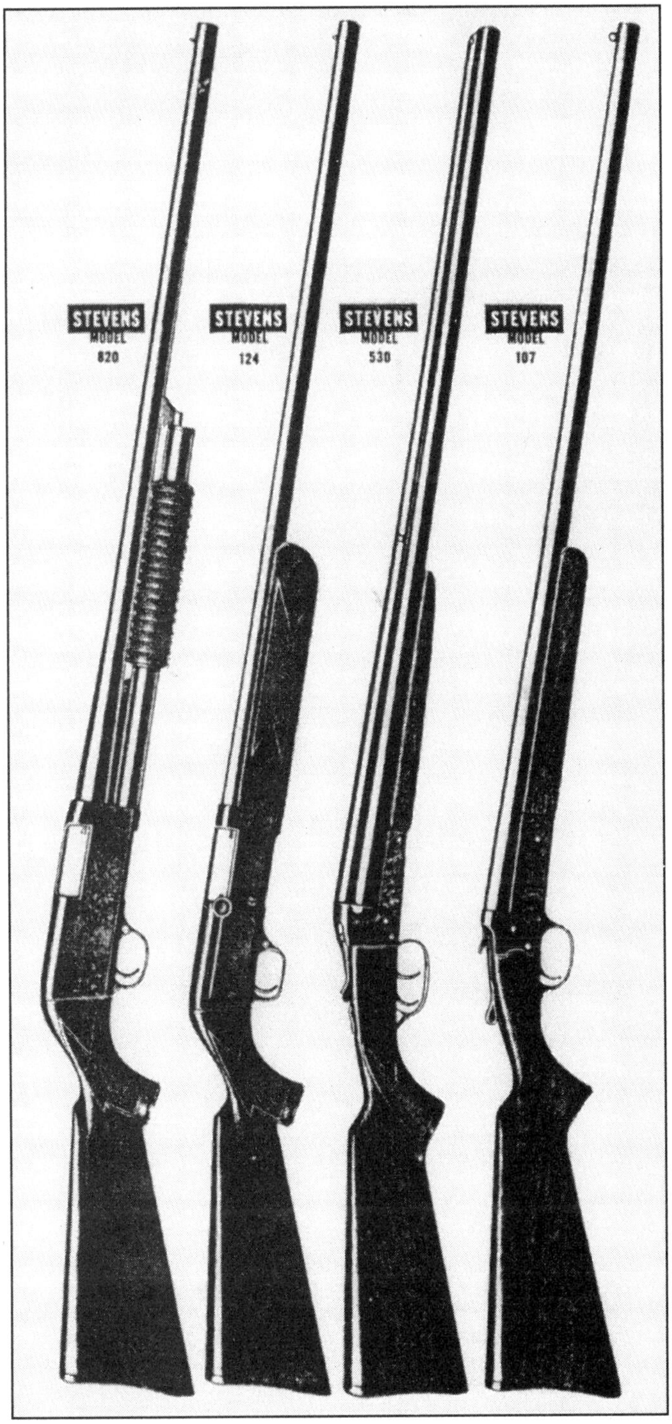

STEVENS MODEL 820

STEVENS MODEL 124

STEVENS MODEL 530

STEVENS MODEL 107

These four shotguns in the later 1940s advertisement were available with Tenite stocks. The Model 820 and the Model 124 purportedly could use the same buttstock assembly, and the Model 94 single barrel could use the same assembly as the Models 240 and 24-410.

It was thought that maybe Daisy Manufacturing Co. had used Tenite for some of their airgun stocks in the early 1950s, but it doesn't seem cost-efficient to do so on an airgun. Tenite was never exactly low priced. Although a new Tenite stock for the 87T cost only $4.27 in 1947, it would not make sense to put Tenite on a $2.95 airgun. It would, however, on a $30 rifle or shotgun.

Another gun reportedly made mainly of Tenite was the Johnson Indoor Target Gun. Designed by Melvin M. Johnson of Johnson rifle and machinegun fame, the Indoor Target Gun featured a Tenite stock assembly with both front and rear pistol grips, *a la* Thompson SMG. It shot steel ball bearings, had an adjustable rear sight, and was said to be reasonably accurate at short ranges.

Not exactly sporting arms, but definitely related to their use, are duck decoys, and in 1950, Herter's, Inc., was offering triple-guaranteed duck decoys of Tenite for $18.75 per dozen, shipped express collect. Available in a choice of mallard, black mallard, bluebill, redhill or canvasback, the decoys weighed 1 pound each, dull painted and keel equipped. By 1952, the decoys were $15 per dozen, or in a larger-than-life version for $23.75 per dozen, plus shipping.

There was another firm, Majestic Molding Co., that also produced duck decoys of Tenite. Available in mallard, black duck or pintail versions, they were more expensive than the Herter's models, costing $40 per dozen, f.o.b. Advertised as waterproof and shockproof, with built-in ballast, they were supposed to duplicate the natural duck plumage.

Tenite was not used just for stocks and duck decoys, it was also used for the scales and stocks on knives and handguns. Examples advertised in the late '40s and early '50s include the Franzite models by Sports, Inc., of Chicago, and Hyscore stocks by Midwest Gun & Mfg. Co. of the same city. One of the most interesting was "Duel Duty" by the Gary, Indiana, Niles Corp. Designed by a policeman for use on the S&W Police revolver and moulded with a knurled, slip-resistant surface, the grip had a trapdoor on the bottom which held six 38 Special cartridges in individual cavities.

Today, there are many custom knifemakers, and the name Randall still is one of the best. Starting in the early '50s, Bo Randall introduced Tenite scales on designs No. 14 and 15, and later 16. Other materials could probably have been ordered, as the knives were custom-made to a basic design, but Tenite was Randall's material of choice. Today, many other synthetic materials are available to knifemakers, and Tenite is not so frequently seen.

Tenite was not the first synthetic material of what we refer to as plastics. It was the first to be used so extensively in major sporting arms' components. A rifle or shotgun without a stock assembly is incomplete, and while Tenite didn't quite prove to be the ideal replacement for wood, it was an interesting change...even today. ●

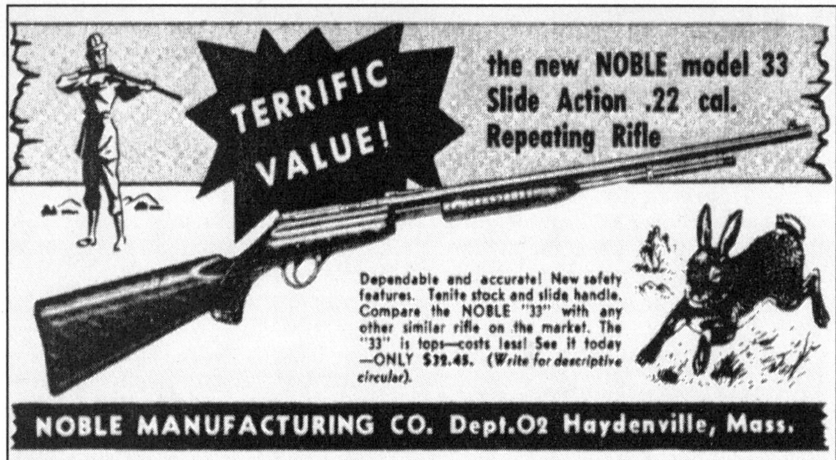

This advertisement for the Noble 33 slide-action rimfire rifle stresses its Tenite stock and slide handle.

Tenite is pleasant to touch, takes an exceptionally smooth finish, does not conduct heat well, does not absorb moisture as does wood, and can be moulded to precision tolerances. This made it ideal for use on a sporting arm, such as this Johnson Indoor Target Gun.

MOLDED TENITE
SENSATIONAL VALUE!
Bishop stocks now fitted with molded tenite foreend cap, pistol grip cap and butt plate, with length of pull cut to customer's requirements; no advance in price. Same high quality Ozark growth American Walnut, noted for fine texture and color. For all standard actions. Standard inletting; semi-finished. Price $5.00. Send postage for 4 pounds.
Mannlicher Type Bishop stocks also available, now, for 22" barrels, with tenite butt plate and grip cap—$7.50. Send postage for 5 pounds. New Catalog on request.
E. C. BISHOP & SON
Warsaw, Missouri

Forearm tips, grip caps and buttplates of Tenite have been and are used by many stock producing firms, but this four-decades-old Bishop advertisement is one of the few actually stressing such use.

FINEST MOLDED PLASTIC DECOYS

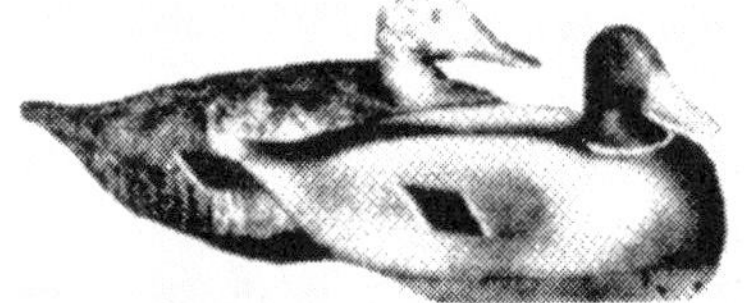

FULL SIZE!
LIGHT WEIGHT!
COLORFUL!

WATERPROOF—May be left out all season
RUGGED—Molded of tough shock-proof Tenite
COLOR—Plastic Duplicates natural duck
BALLAST—Built-in ballast makes them self-righting
Any Shot Damage Easily Repaired
Mallard, Black Duck and Pintail
$4.00 each, $40.00 per dozen—f.o.b. Elvria
SEND FOR FREE LITERATURE!
MAJESTIC MOLDING CO. - Elyria, Ohio

Since Tenite II could be completely immersed in water for 24 hours and absorb only 1.4 to 1.7 percent, it was ideal for gunstocks and duck decoys. It also had excellent color retention. Its cost was about one-third that of nylon, selling for 50 cents per pound in 1945 when purchased in 5000-pound lots of a plain color. Tenite I sold for 60 cents per pound in April, 1944, with the Tenite II used for gunstocks selling for 70 cents per pound when introduced on December 1, 1938.

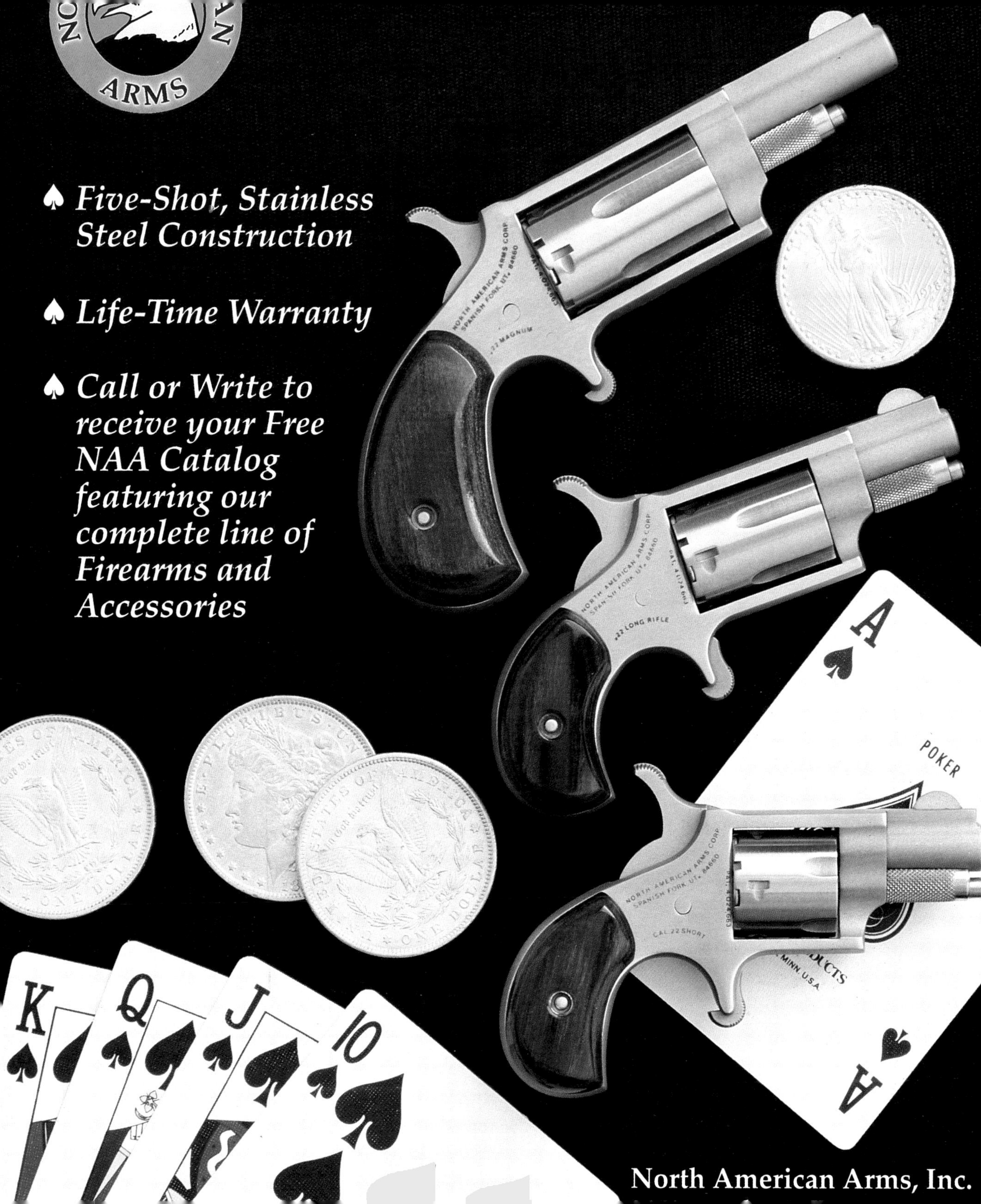
ARMS
♠ Five-Shot, Stainless Steel Construction
♠ Life-Time Warranty
♠ Call or Write to receive your Free NAA Catalog featuring our complete line of Firearms and Accessories
POKER
North American Arms, Inc.

SIMMONS ANNOUNCES THE MOST SIGNIFICANT ADVANCE IN RIFLESCOPE TECHNOLOGY SINCE VARIABLE POWER.

The new AETEC™ Scope with Aspherical Lens System. HOT!

The aspherical lens system was first used in very expensive binoculars and cameras. It was not used in riflescopes because it couldn't take the pounding that scopes demanded. *Not any more!*

Simmons has made a breakthrough in riflescope technology. They have created a new aspherical lens system, just for riflescopes. It now performs beautifully in their new, 44mm scope, the AETEC.

It creates the widest field of view in the industry, with a completely flat image. There is no distortion of the image at the edges of your view, *and* the edges are as bright as the center.

Plus, it has a 5 inch eye relief (almost double the length of conventional wide angle systems). Easier to see. Easier to mount.

Every single lens in the AETEC system is multi-coated. You just can't get any brighter than that, or should we say "hotter."

Simmons Outdoor Corp., 201 Plantation Oak Drive, Thomasville, GA 31792

MODEL 70

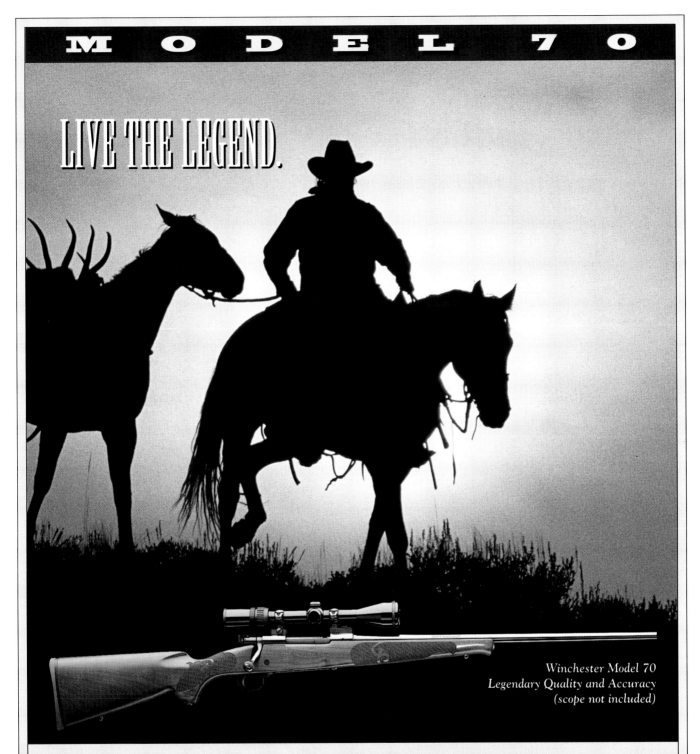

LIVE THE LEGEND.

Winchester Model 70
Legendary Quality and Accuracy
(scope not included)

Accept no imitation. When you go hunting, go with the original: a Winchester Model 70® Classic. Its design is considered so reliable, its feel so natural, and its appearance so perfect that it's known the world-over as *"The Rifleman's Rifle."* Its Pre-'64 style bolt with claw extractor, three position safety, blade type ejector, field-strippable firing pin and accurate hammer-forged rifling (on blued models), all contribute to a feeling of confidence no other bolt action can match. And with the optional BOSS® system, you can now tune your rifle's accuracy to match the loads you want to shoot. So get a Model 70 and get ready for adventure. (Warning: The "BOSS" includes a recoil reducing muzzle brake which provides substantial increased noise/muzzle blast. Always wear hearing protection to prevent hearing loss or damage.) For more information write for our free catalog: U. S. Repeating Arms Co., Dept. R12, 275 Winchester Avenue, Morgan, Utah 84050-9333.

Winchester and Model 70 are registered trademarks of the Olin Corporation.

We don't make the best pistols in the world *only* for the U.S. Special Operations Forces.

The HK Special Operations Handgun
and the HK USP...
the same design team,
the same technology,
the same rigorous testing,
and the same power—.45 ACP.

Heckler & Koch, the leader in high technology firearms for defense and law enforcement, has developed the two most advanced .45 ACP pistols in the world today.

To put an HK pistol in your hand, see your authorized dealer. For the location nearest you, call 703-450-1900.

HK USP .45 ACP (also available in 9mm and .40 caliber). The HK USP parallels the MK23 Special Operations Handgun in every significant facet of its development. The USP is shown with the HK UTL (Universal Tactical Light) attached.

HK MK23, MOD 0 .45 ACP Special Operations Handgun with its detachable sound suppressor and a Laser Aiming Module. The HK MK23 was developed especially for the U.S. Special Operations Command. A civilian version of the Special Operations Handgun, the HK Mark 23, will be available in limited numbers.

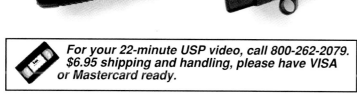

For your 22-minute USP video, call 800-262-2079. $6.95 shipping and handling, please have VISA or Mastercard ready.

HECKLER & KOCH, INC.
21480 Pacific Boulevard
Sterling, Virginia 20166 U.S.A.

by BOB BELL

SCOPES AND MOUNTS

QUITE A FEW items deserve mention this year, and space is rather limited, so we'll get right into it: **Bushnell** has a couple of high-tech units that should be available by the time you read this, the HOLOsight and the Lytespeed 400 rangefinder. The latter isn't a scope, but it's so useful to any long-range hunter that it has to be mentioned.

The HOLOsight at 1x can be installed on a Weaver-type base on a rifle, shotgun or handgun. A hologram of a reticle is recorded on a display window. When illuminated by laser light, a holographic image becomes visible in the window, superimposed over the target. Critical eye alignment is not necessary. You simply look through the window, place the reticle image on the target, and shoot. Field is unlimited, as is eye relief. Reticle brightness is battery-powered and adjustable. Several reticle designs are available and can be quickly changed in the field without losing zero. If the HOLOsight reminds you of the target-acquisition system jetfighter pilots see from their cockpits, you're on the right track.

The Lytespeed 400 Laser Rangefinder measures distances between 16 and 400 yards to ±1 yard if the target is low-reflective—and gives the same accuracy to about 1000 yards if it's high-reflective. This 4x, 18-ounce battery-powered unit sorta resembles a binocular. You simply look into it, place a small square reticle on the target and push a button. Instantly, the range in yards or meters is displayed. Sophisticated circuitry and a high-speed clock calculate distance by measuring the time it takes for the laser pulse to travel from the Lytespeed to the target and back. Advantages for the sheep, pronghorn or woodchuck hunter are obvious. Even a golfer would find it handy.

Bausch & Lomb has a new 4-16x Elite with an adjustable 50mm objective. Bushnell has four new Sportviews, a 6-18x40 AO, 3-9x40 with Bullet Drop Compensator, and 4x models for 22s and blackpowder guns.

In case you haven't heard, Worldwide Sports and Recreation, Inc., has purchased the B&L Sports Optics Division, and Bushnell Corp. is now a subsidiary of Worldwide, which will continue to market B&L, Bushnell, and Jason products. The new corporate name is Bushnell.

Autauga Arms is rather new on the scope scene, but is offering a number of large **Hakko**-built variables. Currently, 5-20x, 3-10x, 3-12x and a straight 16x are offered, all with one-piece 30mm aluminum tubes and 56mm objectives. Several of the models have battery-powered zoom switches to change magnification while looking into the scope. We've examined a 3-12x that was fine optically, but heavy—over 2 pounds. This one is more suitable to beanfield watching than brush hunting.

Burris has figured a way to keep the size of a lighted dot reticle small and has introduced it in three variables this year, 3-9x scopes in the Signature and Fullfield series, and a 6-24x Signature. Called the Electro-Dot, it subtends about 1 MOA at 3x and 1/8-MOA at 24x. It's integrated with their Plex reticle.

Other Burris scopes are offered with additional finishes, features, etc. Pos-Align rings are now available for Ruger's integral base system. These use pivoting inserts within the steel outer rings, allowing stress-free scope alignment. This is a fine idea, for when rings don't align perfectly, they can put tremendous stress on a tube as the rings are snugged down, easily bending the scope, which obviously is not good for the lenses, seals, or whatever.

Pentax has updated three of their excellent scopes into Lightseeker II with Perm-Align models—a 3-9x, 4-16x and 6-24x, the latter with 1/8-MOA clicks. All are available with several finishes. The Perm-Align system allows the shooter to lock in the windage and elevation settings with solid metal-to-metal contact, eliminating the possibility of reticle movement from recoil or vibration. A new entry, the 1.75-6x Lightseeker, is intended to cover most of the big game hunter's needs, especially the guy who goes after dangerous game. Field at bottom power is large—71 feet; the objective is slightly enlarged for plenty of light; eye relief is long, about 4

This was a 91-yard shot—not 90, not 92—because the Lytespeed rangefinder said so.

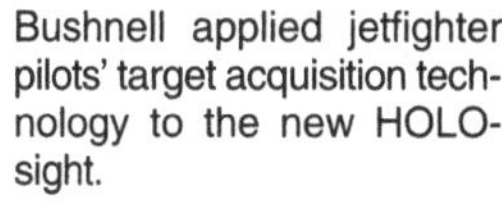

Bushnell applied jetfighter pilots' target acquisition technology to the new HOLOsight.

(Below) This 4x28 Simmons is made specifically for 22 Magnums. It's the Mag Mini.

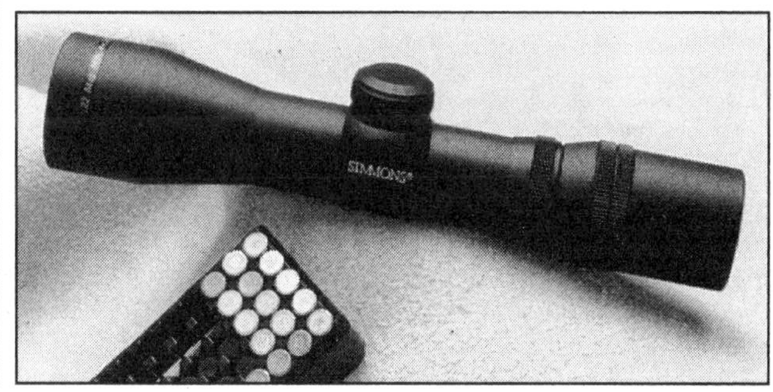

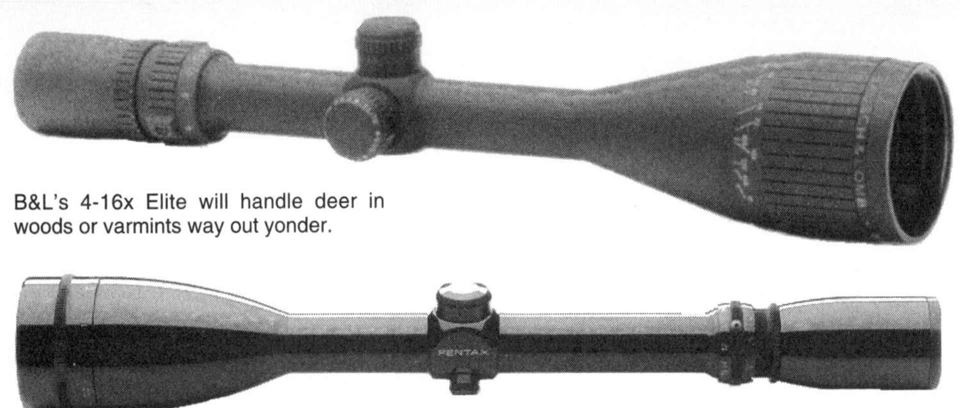

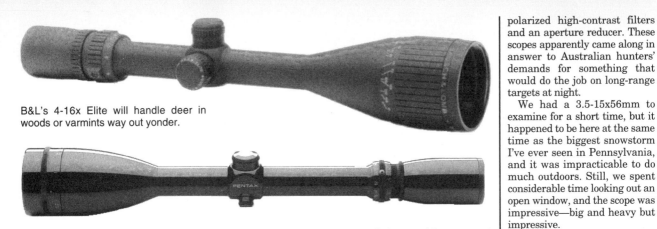

B&L's 4-16x Elite will handle deer in woods or varmints way out yonder.

Pentax's 4-16x Lighseeker II AO uses the Perm-Align metal-to-metal system to elimintate reticle movement.

inches; and adjustments are 1/2-MOA, which makes sense for this power scope.

Millett has long been known for their many strong mounts and other gun-related items, and this year they offer more of these then ever. Now they've added several REDOT electronic 1x scopes (1 inch or 30mm, Compact or Wide View) for use on rifles, shotguns or handguns. Dots subtend 3, 5, or 10 MOA, and are red, of course.

Hensoldt is a name we haven't seen in decades. Their scopes were rated among the world's best back in the '30s. Now a division of the Zeiss Group in Germany, they are offering two models in the U.S.: the ZF500 and AF800. Both are 10x with 42mm objectives, and both have bullet-drop compensators, cammed for the 308 cartridge. All are available from GSI, Inc.

Leupold somehow found room in its extensive line to add two scopes this year, a big one and a little one. First is a Vari-X II 6-18x40/AO, the most powerful scope Leupold offers in this line. New erector assembly lens technology allows making this model just a bit over 12 inches long and 14 ounces in weight, and image quality is typical of Leupold's high-level performance. The other model is the 2.5x32mm Scout with 9 to 17 inches of eye relief. Obviously, it's intended to be mounted ahead of the action on lever or bolt guns, or perhaps on handguns, though it seems a bit long for handguns. Also new are the QRW detachable mounts, which utilize the Weaver-style cross-slot bases, and Torx screws for installing all Leupold mounts. These are said to be improvements on hex heads, allowing more torque without stripping.

Nikon has added a couple of binoculars and a spotting scope to their line of optics, but no scopes. None is really necessary, as the current Monarch UCC (Ultra ClearCoat) models cover the field, ranging from a 4x40mm to a 6.5-20x44mm AO for riflemen, plus a 2x20 EER for handgun use. We've used several of these, including the big variable on Dakota prairie dogs, and results were great.

(Above) This new version of the Weaver 3-9x has a 50mm objective unit for lots of light.

This is Schmidt & Bender's 3-12x50 Police/Marksman model and a special reticle design for it.

Nightforce currently supplies eight big scopes, mostly high-powers with 56mm objectives and 1/8-minute adjustments. A very sophisticated rangefinder reticle is offered—also simple crosshairs, and there are three other styles. Reticles are etched on glass and vacuum-coated; most are illuminated. There are a number of accessories, such as polarized high-contrast filters and an aperture reducer. These scopes apparently came along in answer to Australian hunters' demands for something that would do the job on long-range targets at night.

We had a 3.5-15x56mm to examine for a short time, but it happened to be here at the same time as the biggest snowstorm I've ever seen in Pennsylvania, and it was impracticable to do much outdoors. Still, we spent considerable time looking out an open window, and the scope was impressive—big and heavy but impressive.

Barrelmaker Dan Lilja is quoted as saying he's seen 50-caliber bullet holes at 1000 yards with a 5.5-22x56 Nightforce. I've never had a chance to try that, but it gives you some idea of the quality of these scopes.

Schmidt & Bender recently made the P/M (Police/Marksman) line available. It consists of six scopes, 6x42 and 10x42 fixed powers as well as four variables from 1.5-6x to 3-12x50. Intended primarily, but not exclusively, for SWAT and tactical teams, they come with two elevation-adjustment rings that can be interchanged. The first has 1/4-MOA clicks, while the other is calibrated for the 168-grain 308 load, so you can just dial it to the range you want.

Simmons offers scopes for any need that I can think of—for crossbows and airguns as

A 1/8-MOA dot is available in Swarovski's new 6-25x50 Professional Hunter—a big scope and a pretty big ticket.

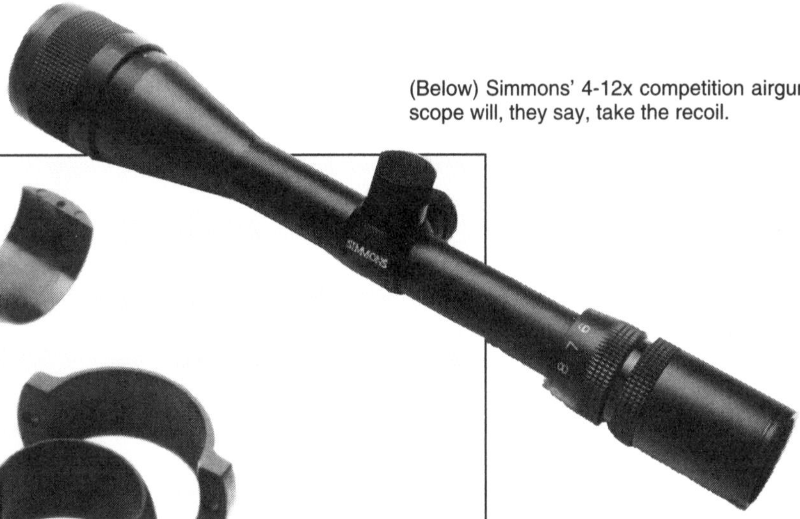

(Below) Simmons' 4-12x competition airgun scope will, they say, take the recoil.

(Left) Burris' Pos-Align mounts allow the scope to be mounted in perfect alignment to the bore so optics can be centered.

(Left) A Bullet Drop Compensator can be had on all Z models from Zeiss.

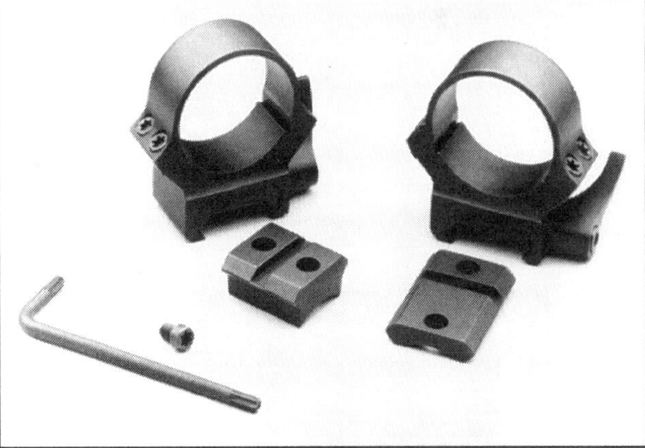

(Above) QRW lever-tightening rings from Leupold utilize the long-familiar Weaver-style cross-slot bases.

well as long guns and handguns—and more models than I feel like counting, topped by the aspherical lens Aetec, discussed here last year. Another Aetec now is a 3.8-12x44. It has a wide-angle eyepiece—which gives a large field completely flat to the edges—edges as bright as the optical center, and longer-than-normal eye relief. These advantages accrue from the aspherical lens. Also new this year are the high-tech V-Tac, a 3-9x40 with 1/8-MOA adjustments and a reticle designed for range estimating; a 4.5-14x AO Whitetail Classic; a 6.5-20x44 AO; ProHunters of 3.5-10x50 and 4-12x50; a 4x28 Mini specifically for 22 Rimfire Magnums; and a 4-12x40 for airgun competition. Don't chuckle condescendingly; you might be surprised at the accuracy some airguns deliver, and their strange recoil batters those scopes not built for it. *(Simmons was recently purchased by Blount, Inc.—Editor)*

Weaver scopes have been available for over a half-century now, and it's interesting that the K2.5, K4 and K6, which were introduced just after WWII, are with us still. It's impossible to explain the impact these models had on hunters when announced. Built on 1-inch diameter tubes which have become standard over the years, their large lenses offered a brilliance which was hard to believe even when you were using one. They transmitted much more light than earlier Weavers, which had been built on .75-inch tubes.

Weavers have been made in many larger sizes since—the V9 3-9x50 being one example—but I still have a soft spot for those first Ks. I still have an early K2.5 and won't part with it.

Swarovski has added a 6-24x50mm to its Professional Hunter series and a 3-10x42mm to its Nova-A line. The "A" is for "American" and indicates these scopes are made on 1-inch tubes to fit our common mounts. They have the reticle installed in the second focal plane—so it seems to decrease in thickness when the power is boosted, as most Americans prefer—and are made of light alloy instead of steel. Several reticles are available, and the lenses are laser-aligned. A 1/8-MOA dot can be had in the 6-24x, which has 1/6-minute external adjustments in waterproof turrets, with a coil-spring suspension system to ensure reticle dependability. This scope has a 30mm main tube, as do many Professional Hunters, with most Novas being 26mm. A choice of seven reticles is available in most models.

Kahles, a Swarovski company for some time now, makes a number of scopes, including the ZF95 in either 6x42 or 10x42. Built on a 1-inch steel tube, it can be had with simple crosshairs, several kinds of plex, a rangefinder, or Mil-Dot reticle. Bullet-drop compensators are also available for various 308 and 223 loads.

Tasco has added three riflescopes and two ProPoints to an already extensive line of optical equipment. Included are the 1.5-6x42, 3-9x42 and 3-12x52 in the Titan series, all of which have 30/30 reticles and black-matte finish. The ProPoints are red-dot models for Action handgunners. Both are 1x, the PDP3CMP having a 30mm objective and 10-MOA dot, the PDP5 a 40mm and 4-, 8-, or 12-minute dot (interchangeable). Ring sets for a dovetail-style base are supplied, as are other accessories.

B-Square's extensive lines of mounts are made to fit most anything anyone wants to shoot, including military rifles such as the British SMLE, 1917 Enfield, M-1, '98 Mauser, and '03 Springfield, without the necessity of alterations. Their Interlock system is simple and strong, with a dovetail base slotted for easy ring positioning to adjust eye relief.

Redfield already offers so many fine lines—eight or ten—that it has to be hard to find a need that they haven't covered. But this year they've squeezed in a 2 1/2x20 for those blackpowder shooters allowed to use a scope. Seems an appropriate power for a muzzle-loading gun. They also have two models for law enforcement use, a 3-12x56 AO and a 3-9x50, both with target knobs.

New this year are Leupold's Torx head screws, which allow more torque without stripping.

(Above) Kahles' ZF-95 scopes are made in 6x42 and 10x42. They have Ballistic Cams for 308 use.

(Above) Swift's 658 is one of the top models of their inexpensive line; it has a Quadraplex reticle

(Below) Extended Eye Relief Fullfields are offered in 1x or 1-4x by Burris.

The 3-9x is built on a 1-inch tube, the larger one on 30mm, with 1/4-MOA clicks in both. A special, but not extremely complicated, rangefinding reticle is standard in these models.

Dave Talley's beautifully machined TnT rings are made for three scope diameters, 7/8-, 1-inch and 30mm. They snug onto the bases with allen screws if you want a solid setup or levers for a quick-detachable arrangement. An efficient peep sight that fits the rear mount base can be carried in a TnT pistol-grip cap in case the scope should become damaged. Dave also makes bases for a number of popular bolt guns that will accept Ruger rings, and his regular rings have .500-inch wide dovetails to fit quarter ribs.

Swift started importing optical units of various kinds from Germany and France in 1926, and after WWII began working with the Japanese optical industry on the development of a Swift line. For many years, they've supplied scopes from 4x to 6-18x for rifles, others for handguns, and a 1x shotgun model. They have a straight 4x and a 3-7x with mounts to fit dovetail-grooved 22s, which is nice to know when so many scopemakers seem to have forgotten about the small rimfires.

Sightron, which has relocated from South Florida to Wake Forest, North Carolina, has added three S11 variables—1.5-6x, 4-16x AO and a 6-24x AO. All

B-Square's mount keeps the scope low and solid on this Model 870 Remington with no drilling, no tapping.

have 42mm objectives and Exac-Track technology for reticle stability; all are built on one-piece 1-inch aluminum tubes with matte finishes. Sightron scopes all have 4-inch eye relief, which is longer than most, and if mounted to take advantage of this, it provides a positive full-time safety factor for those shooters who tend to crawl the stock..

Aimtech mount systems provide a simple and strong way to get a scope on many revolvers, autoloading pistols, and numerous rifles and shotguns—even muzzleloaders and compound bows. They are one-piece units that utilize screw holes in the grip and frame to position a scope on top, centered. The base accepts most brands of standard scope rings and all electronic sights. One rifle base provides a low see-through mount.

Conetrol is now making DapTar bases for the Ruger mounting system. They attach to M77s with mounting cuts to accept Ruger rings. Each base segment has two locknuts positioned in flush contact with Ruger's quarter-moon cuts. These slide up into the bottom of the segment. When the screws in the top of each segment are tightened, the base is pulled down and locked securely to the action. No drilling or tapping is needed. Hidden recoil shoulders incorporated in the bases engage the radiused concavities in the top of the Ruger mounting rails to complete the integrity of the connection. After the bases are installed, Conetrol rings are attached in the conventional way. And don't forget—Conetrol gives "the NRA percent."

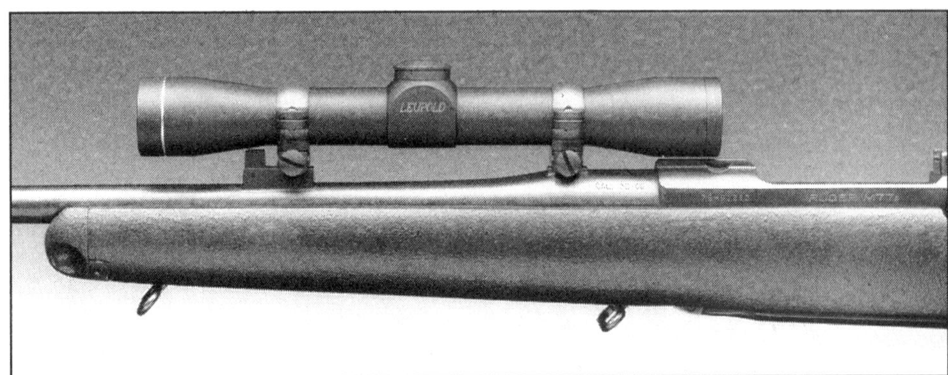

(Above) Leupold's 2.5x Scout can be mounted ahead of the action, comes in matte or silver finish, and has a duplex reticle.

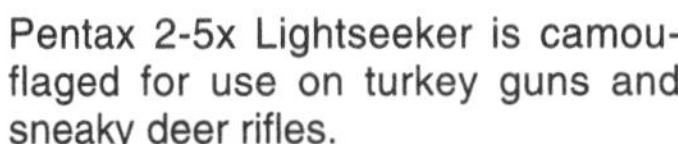

Pentax 2-5x Lightseeker is camouflaged for use on turkey guns and sneaky deer rifles.

Docter Optic of Wetzlar-Jena is offering a whole line of high-grade scopes. All have that Germanic look, especially the VZF 1-4x24, but there's nothing wrong with that, especially when you're gazing into the rear end of one and thus taking advantage of that German optical quality. Other powers are available: 4x32, 6x42, 8x56 and 2.5-10x48, each having a choice of a dozen reticles (CH, post, dot, and variations of the plex style—long available in Germany). They can be supplied either with an integral mounting rail or to fit mounting rings.

Steiner is now offering three Hunting Z scopes. Manufactured in the U.S. in a joint venture with Leupold, and using German-made CAT/AC optics for exceptional light transmission, these scopes are made in 1.5-5x20, 2.5-8x36 and 3.5-10x50. Either a heavy duplex or European #4 reticle can be had; the latter is essentially a duplex without the 12-o'clock post. Tubes are one-piece aluminum with black matte finish. From Pioneer Research.

Center Lock is making an unusual, probably unique, set of scope rings in 1 inch and 30mm. A series of six small stainless steel ball bearings around a stud projecting from the bottom of the rings locks into a recess in a circular base to give precise alignment and replacement. The scope can be removed with an allen wrench. Early production bases are made for the '98 Mauser, Model 70 Winchester and Model 700 Remington

Zeiss has introduced a Diavari 1.25-4x24 to their Z-Series, for big game hunting at normal range. It has a field of well over 100 feet at lowest power, which is wide enough for use against dangerous game at close range. It's built on a 30mm tube and is 11.5 inches long, which makes it easy to get the proper eye relief on even a magnum-length action, something that isn't always true of compact models. The Z scopes are now made with a stainless finish to go with stainless guns, and the Diavari Z 3-12x56 can be had with a battery-powered illuminated reticle. Also available on all Z models is a bullet-drop compensator, which can be retrofitted to the earlier ZA-Series. ●

Beretta's 626: A classic collectible-to-be

by NIKITAS KYPRIDEMOS

(Above) Bird's-eye view of the 626 action reveals the rounded fences and sculpted top strap—and good looks.

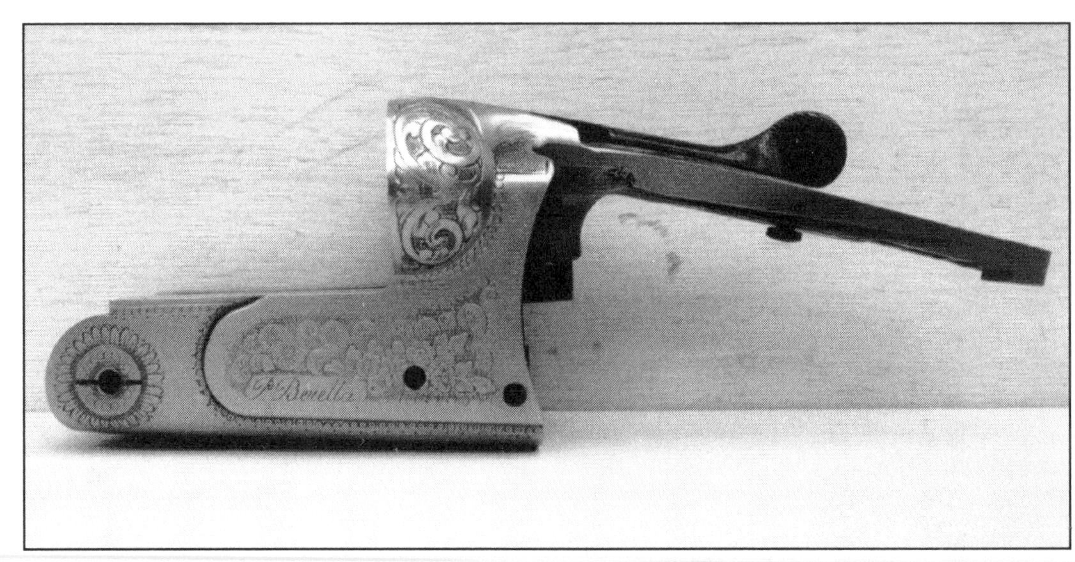

The cocking lug axle goes right through the hinge pin, the tumbler axle is drilled low in the action to minimize stresses, and at the rear is the hole for the sear axle.

THE MOMENT THE word "collectible" is mentioned with regard to shotguns, images of London sidelocks and their clones spring to mind. We forget why these guns are so valued and so desirable today. A pre-war London gun was in its time a modern product, the best that could be produced with the technology of the time. The same holds true for great factory-made guns, the Winchester Model 12, the Browning Auto-5 and many others.

So while sorting the guns made today that will be valued in the future, we must overcome the Holland & Holland sidelock-copy syndrome. It is more worthwhile to seek the best combination of today's technology and design work. Modern copies of the great guns of the 1920s are well-made; some are definitely great guns. They do not, however, represent today's best available design philosophy or technological capability.

Then there is the cost factor. A future collectible, as a product of its time, must be affordable today. After all, it is made so it will sell to today's buyers at prices and conditions that reflect current market trends. The Holland copies are made to sell to informed admirers of yesterday, and they carry price tags and delivery times to match those tastes. No offense is meant to the buyers of the Holland types, but the facts are undeniable.

One shotgun, almost in a class of its own in terms of design and technological refinement, will most probably be a collectible in the future. It's the Beretta 626 side-by-side. There are sound reasons for this view.

To appreciate, one must analyze. In gun terms, this means taking the gun apart, and from the beginning of the dismantling procedure, the advances in the 626 are plainly visible. The stock is attached to the action with a through bolt, which means it comes off easily and quickly without the need for specialized tools or knowledge. With the stock removed, the action is visible and can be inspected, cleaned and lubricated in place.

Dismantling any further is easy. Only a drift punch and screwdrivers are needed to take the gun apart. There is no need for spring compressors or specially fitted turnscrews as in traditional guns. With the gun apart, it is possible to examine each piece, and we will.

The action body or receiver is made of modern steel, hardened throughout. The only file-soft part on the 626 is the trigger guard; the rest is impervious to even the best Swiss file, although it is not recommended here that you carry out this kind of test on your gun.

The action type is not the classic English Anson & Deeley boxlock, but a Beretta design which borrows some features from other guns and offers its own unique refinements. Gone are V-springs and long cocking levers with their inefficient friction and vulnerability. The 626 has sturdy coil mainsprings on equally sturdy guides with ball points where they contact the tumblers. In addition to the guides, the springs are housed in cylindrical recesses at the underside of the action. As an experiment, I installed a broken coil spring in a Beretta 626. It worked flawlessly trapped as it was between the internal guide and the cylindrical recess. The mainsprings act on the underside of the tumblers during the firing sequence.

Cocking is via two 5mm pushrods working in cylindrical recesses under the action flats. These cocking rods work back and forth, not around a pivot as in the Anson & Deeley. This means that during cocking they are compressed rather than put under tension as in the old lever cockers. Steel is strongest in compression, so the advantage is obvious. Each cocking rod has its own return coil spring.

The tumblers are chunky, 6mm through at their thickest section, and relieved in part of their surface to minimize friction. The relieving is not a necessary operation: That it is done shows the sound design thinking. The sear bent is on the rear upper part of the tumbler, not underneath as in the Anson & Deeley. This allows the sear greater mechanical advantage during the trigger-pulling phase. It also means that if the gun falls, resulting in a blow to the back of the action, the inertia forces developed reinforce the sear engagement. However, should the sear engagement fail, there is a secondary safety sear to catch the tumbler and prevent discharge.

The firing pin is one-piece with the tumbler, an arrangement which is stronger than the separate disc-set firing pin. The advantage of the latter is theoretical, as everyone who has ever tried to undo a disc pounded into its threads by hundreds of shots will know. The shape of the tumbler minimizes the risk of breakage. The front surfaces most stressed during firing are curved, and the lower part is con-

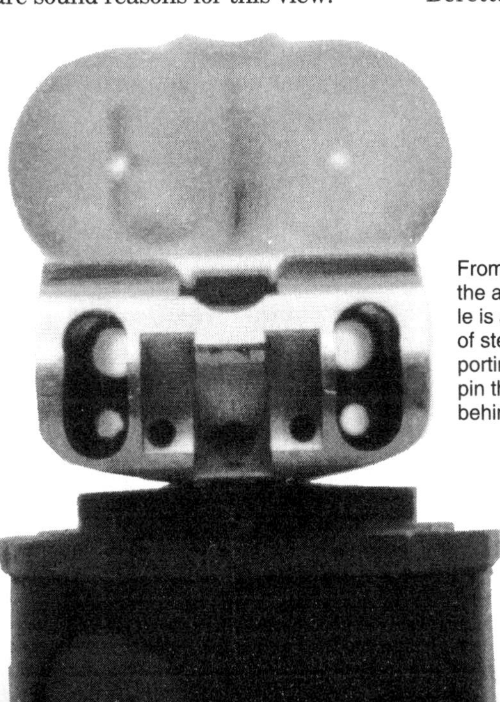

From the front, the action knuckle is a solid mass of steel fully supporting the hinge pin that lies behind it.

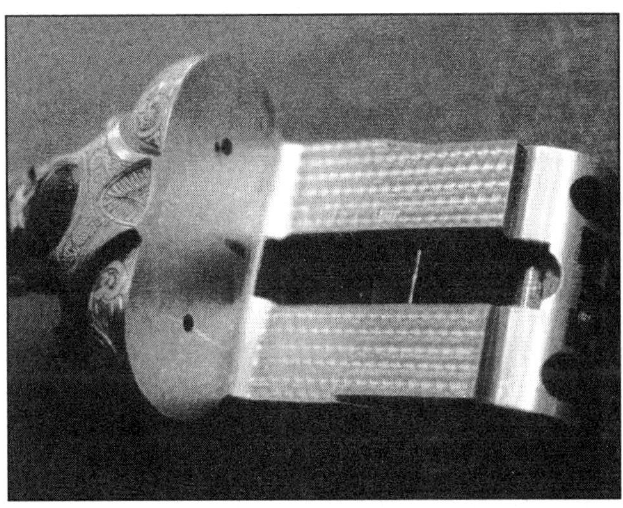

Here are fully radiused edges for the lump recesses and the fully supported hinge pin. Radiusing at the corner of the flats and breech face is generous.

vex and chamfered, all to make the tumbler better able to deal with the stress of thousands of cycles of cocking and firing.

The tumbler axle is set low, in the lower third of the receiver's depth, which is the part of the receiver that is put in compression during firing. The area just under the standing breech, the most stressed part of a double gun, is free of axle holes and the square section cuts found in the old Anson & Deeley action. The effort to minimize the effect of stress is evident in the width of the action at the out of engagement with the tumbler. This motion is the reverse of that which would occur if the gun were dropped on its back.

The trigger blades and triggers are one-piece, made of steel and polished. The front trigger in the double-trigger model is articulated as standard. It is interesting to note here that the replacement of the articulated front trigger on an English gun costs more than a good used 626 in England. Single-trigger versions employ the tried and tested inertia mechanism, and have the selector situated in the

The Beretta presents some refinements in the radiusing where the lumps meet the action flats, as well as the shape and size of the lumps. Also, the ejector hole is smaller by 1mm than the standard 6.5mm found in most doubles, leaving more metal around the chambers. The barrels are made of the same steel used in the Beretta over/unders of the 6 series and are internally chromed. They will accept steel shot. The internal and external finish is good with a minimum of ripples.

The use of coil springs extends to

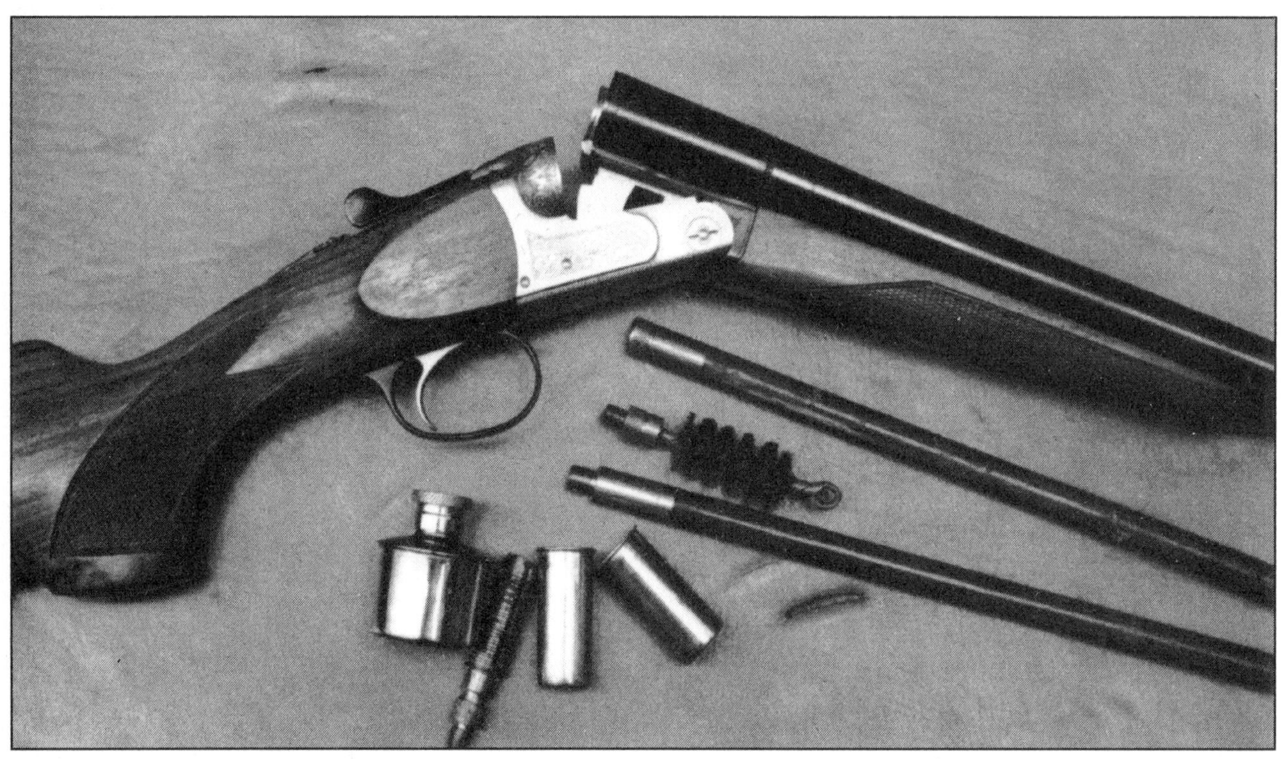

The overall appearance is still that of a classic double, despite the modern internal design and the use of better machined tougher steel.

foot of the standing breech and the radiusing both here and at the internal edges of the barrel flats. Most double guns have a sharp ridge here on the barrel flats.

The sears hinge on an axle set low and well to the rear of the action. There is one wire spring for both sears. This wire spring needs careful handling when disassembling and assembling the 626; it is the only part of the gun that can be easily broken. The sears themselves are chunky, and their surfaces formed for maximum strength. The sear tails, where they engage with the triggers, are rounded to minimize friction with the trigger blade. The trigger blade presses the sear tail downward during firing and thus levers the sear up and

safety button, like the Beretta over/under. The manual safety is a trigger-blocking device.

The locking system is the classic underbolt. The underbolt in the action mates with twin bites in the lumps under the barrels. The underbolt has its own coil spring housed in the rear of the action. The barrels hinge on a massive 11mm cross pin, fixed in the action with a grub screw. The action knuckle supports the cross pin throughout its width.

The barrels are constructed on the monoblock system and are joined by friction and a low melting-point solder, as are the ribs. The advantages of the monoblock over the other systems of double-barrel construction are strength and repairability.

ejectors in the 626. Again, the coil springs work with internal guides, and the ejector system is two-piece—ejector kicker and ejector sear. The use of coil springs, in addition to greater reliability, offers the advantage of easy cocking. It is possible to fire and reset the 626 ejectors using a ball point pen and simple finger pressure. To the user, this means easy closing of the fired gun. To the gun, it means less friction and less wear on the parts that do the recocking—on the ejector legs and the breech face.

The ejectors are actuated through long rods linked to the tumblers and housed in long 2mm holes drilled in the action body. When the tumbler is tripped, the end of the rod protrudes from the knuckle and catches the ejector sear as the gun is opened, thus pushing it out of its bent and freeing the ejector kicker. Notable in its simplicity and strength is the primary extraction. A simple recess in the knuckle mates with the extractor leg and effects extraction.

The 626 is the last in a long line of boxlock side-by-side models made by Beretta. In the post-war era, the company brought out its series 400 which went through improvements to reach the 626. The changes were aesthetic and functional. The 626 has ball fences instead of the Webley-type straight fence. Gone is the Greener-type crossbolt. Internally, the lock parts of the 626 offer refinements such as the secondary safety notches and improved sear geometry. The action body has leaner lines and superior surface finish. The improvements are part of an evolutionary process which shows an active design approach and attention to the things that matter. It is the reverse of the usual progression which focuses mostly on production shortcuts. The 626 is definitely superior to every model that preceded it.

All internal parts are hardened throughout; they are not simply case-hardened. The surface finish is superior, although not to the level of the mirror finish seen on the SO range of Beretta's other hand-built guns. All parts, tumblers, sears, cocking rods and triggers are well shaped without polishing faults or evidence of slips and shoddy workmanship. The surfaces are dark, the result of the hardening process, except for the triggers which have been mirror-polished.

The fitting is excellent, and 626 parts are replaceable without any need for prior interfitting or fitting in the action body. This is a great asset for most shooters today as very few of us have access to gunsmiths able to hand-fit broken V springs or tumblers. The ability to disassemble a quality double without special tools, then drop in the replacement part and reassemble the gun, and be certain that it will work, is a self-evident asset. This alone puts the 626 in a special category as one of the few side-by-sides easily repaired. The probability that such repairs will be needed is very small, but knowing it is possible is an asset.

As it is, the 626 is a quality firearm. Asked how much it would cost to have similar gun built in England, an English gunmaker gave a figure four times the price of the 626 new, assuming that a factory were tooled up to the task. However, one test for the quality of a factory-built gun is how good a foundation it is for further improvement. Refinement is only worthwhile on a solid foundation. The 626 is such a foundation. With a little effort and a comparatively small investment, it can be brought up to what the shotgun lovers call "best quality standard."

For the double gun man who wants to have mirror-polished internal parts, the 626 offers a suitable foundation on which to lavish hours of hand-polishing. Bearing in mind the warning to keep away from the sear noses and sear bents, the enthusiastic owner can devote time and effort to polishing the internal parts to a mirror finish. Given the hardness of the parts, it will not be easy; on the other hand, the polishing can proceed without the fear that it will endanger surface hardness.

Little can be done for the shape of the action body. Aesthetics are a subjective factor anyway. The 626 offers acceptable machine engraving and a harmonious blend of curved surfaces, round fences and rounded edges. It should please the majority of double gun lovers. For external upgrading, one must look to the woodwork, which comes in a matte finish. This finish can easily be upgraded with linseed oil to enhance the feel and look of the stock.

For some, the black finish on the

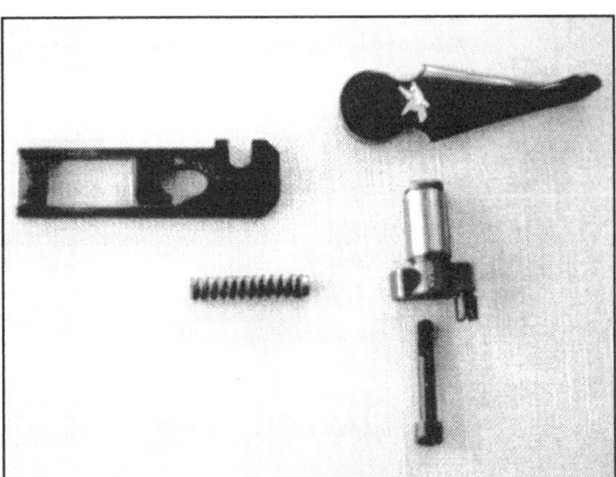

Lock-up is via the classic flat underbolt actuated by the top lever. Note the finish on the spindle, the simple coil spring and retaining screw.

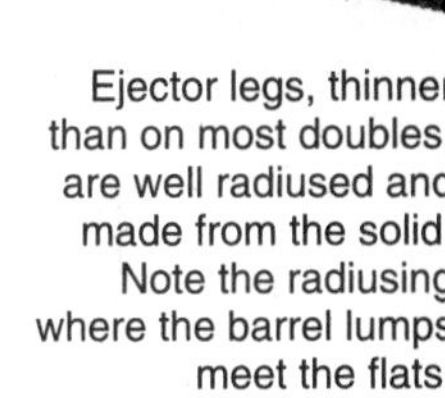

Ejector legs, thinner than on most doubles, are well radiused and made from the solid. Note the radiusing where the barrel lumps meet the flats.

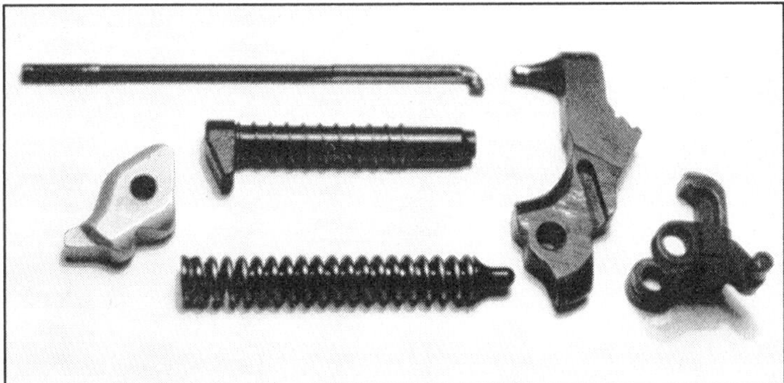

Lock parts: the cocking dog, the cocking rod with its coil spring, the tumbler, the sear (note the twin anchoring holes for the sear axle), the mainspring with its guide. The long rod at the top is the auto ejector actuating rod.

trigger guard, forend iron and top lever will look out of place with the satin action. They can easily be brushed to match the action.

The most radical aesthetic upgrade on a double is restocking with a high-grade piece of walnut. On the 626, with its central stock bolt and round mating surfaces where stock meets metal, restocking is easier than most double guns with their complicated stock pins through the grip. The inherent quality of the 626 makes such a move feasible and worthwhile.

Balancing a double is tricky business. It is not simply a matter of adding or subtracting weight. Each and every part, barrels, forend and receiver with the stock attached are balanced, then the whole gun is checked to make it balance with that in-between-the-hands feel. The 626 is a gun made to withstand all available $2^{3}/_{4}$-inch shells, including baby magnums. This requirement imposes barrels that are thicker, therefore more front-heavy, than $2^{1}/_{2}$-inch classic guns. It *can* be done, and the 626 can balance like the best of them.

For the more finicky, it is possible to go to great lengths and resort to unchroming the barrels, regulating them to pattern, maybe making them ribless to enhance front end lightness. Everything is possible given time and money. Some time ago, Gun Digest published an article about the conversion of a 626 into a double rifle, proving the action's inherent strength and its worth as a customizing foundation.

Barrel flats show Gardone Val Trompia proof house marks and stamps indicating the barrels are choked by the Beretta method.

Yes, you can see the joint where the barrels are fitted into the monoblock. You can also see the concave English-style rib.

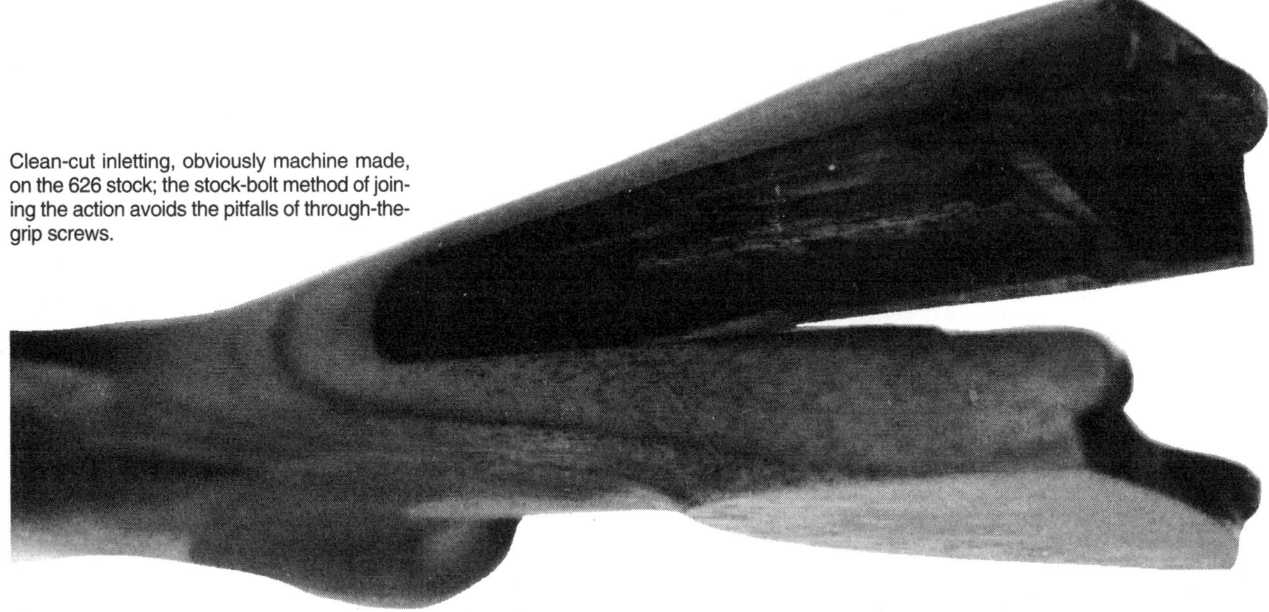

Clean-cut inletting, obviously machine made, on the 626 stock; the stock-bolt method of joining the action avoids the pitfalls of through-the-grip screws.

Beretta lately dropped the 626 from its catalogs. Word has it that the gun will be offered only with false sideplates in the EL and EELL grades. False sideplates detract both aesthetically and functionally, but that is mostly a personal thing. The fact of the matter is that a 626 is expensive to make, and it never provided a market for spares. They just do not break easily.

Still, there are new guns in stock and used 626s appear frequently. It is an even bet that the market will dry up soon, as more and more people realize the inherent quality and the elegant possibilities of this gun. For those that have the foresight and the cash, it can mean a good usable investment. In case you are wondering, I did not buy one when they were plentiful and affordable. One might hope the evolutionary process would continue and Beretta will come out with a side-by-side to improve on the 626, but that seems unlikely in this age of the over/under. ●

The robust solid one-piece Beretta (right) looks strong compared to the hollowed-out original Westley Richards boxlock design. The overall lines are not that far apart. And the 626 is factory-made.

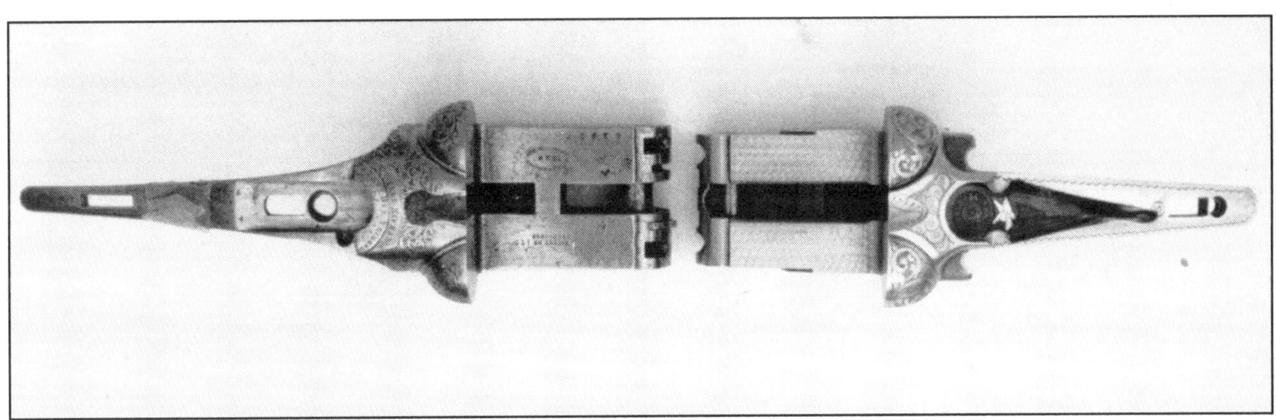

The Westley Richards (left) owns somewhat more flowing lines, but it's mild steel, not modern hardened steel.

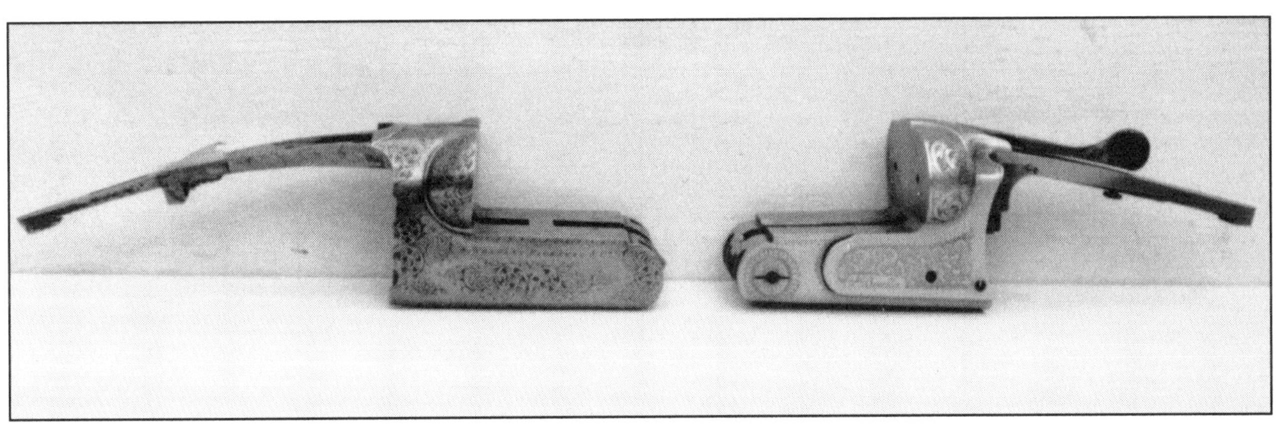

The 1910 Westley Richards detachable boxlock action (left) shows the handwork. The Beretta 626 shows, for instance, a straight top strap compared to the graceful curve of the Westley Richards. But they're not *that* different.

by RAYMOND CARANTA

THE GUNS OF EUROPE

PRE-WWII POCKET PISTOLS

WHEN THE BROWNING pistol chambered in 7.65mm (32 ACP, in the United States, from 1903) arrived in 1900, it created quite a stir. When one million such guns were sold in twelve years, the day of the European commercial revolver was over, at least for a while—some have always been made in Great Britain, Spain, Italy, and even France.

Early on, people relied mostly on penetration in fir boards and computation of kinetic energy to determine the efficiency of a gun. They didn't give serious consideration to the way the energy was spent. At this, the 7.65mm Browning looked good. With a nominal muzzle velocity of 950 fps and a full-jacketed bullet weighing 70 grains, the kinetic energy was 145 foot pounds, and the bullet penetrated five 7/8-inch dry pine boards, comparing favorably to the French 8mm Model 1892 service revolver data—120-grain bullet moving at 720 fps—3 1/2 boards.

It is flat, but the seven-shot Browning M1900 pistol was too long (6.35 inches) and heavy (21.4 ounces) for a genuine pocket pistol. As a matter of fact, there is a considerable variation between the pocket pistol definitions of the various writers and manufacturers. For some, it is sufficient that a gun can enter a pocket—even a large pocket—to be considered such, while for others it must be capable of being conveniently carried in the pocket as long as desirable. According to the definition stated in my book. *Le Pistolet de Poche,* a genuine pocket pistol should not exceed *1 pound loaded and 5.3 inches of length;* for the maximum of ease, this weight should be reduced *by one half* and the length *by 25 percent.* Finally, the thickness should not exceed 1 inch, and the height 3.5 inches.

The stringent thickness requirement practically precludes the conventional revolver for actual pocket use because of the cylinder bulge (even the old Smith & Wesson 32 New Departure was 1.12 inches thick). Most revolvers, even small ones, are carried in holsters.

The Belgian Fabrique Nationale, distinguished manufacturers of the Browning pistols in Europe, certainly believed this, since they introduced, in 1906, another Browning design chambered in a new caliber, the 6.35mm (called the 25 ACP in the United States after 1909). The 7.65mm Browning 1900 required a screwdriver for disassembly, but the Model 1906 could be easily field-stripped without tools.

Called the "Triple Sureté," it features, in addition to the conventional thumb safety— a grip safety, then erroneously considered as an adequate answer to the revolver's double action—and, later, a magazine safety to prevent firing when the magazine is removed. It was the "triple safety" model. At 4.45 inches in length, 3 inches high, and just .94-in. thick, the 6.35mm Browning weighed 13.4 ounces, empty. It was the first modern pocket semi-automatic pistol.

A gun on this patent was made in large quantities in the United States by Colt after 1909, so the capabilities were well known in North America. In Europe, the Browning 1906 was instantly successful—100,000 were sold in five years—as was the larger Model 1900. Many competitors, in Great Britain and Germany but mostly in Belgium and Spain, were ready this time to board the bandwagon. Within a few years, a crop of new semi-automatic pistols were developed in the same caliber. No article could cover all these models and variations seriously. In English, the remarkably well-documented book by J. Howard Mathews, *Firearms Identification,* does that; in French, my own does.

Among the vest-pocket Browning competitors of the pre-1914 era, one deserves a particular mention. It is the Bayard pocket pistol as made by the Anciens Etablissement Pieper in Liege. Patented by Clarus in 1905, the Bayard was first produced in 32 ACP in 1909; then in 380 ACP in 1911 and, finally, in 25 ACP in 1912. The 1914-18 War, unfortunately, stopped its distribution. Production was not resumed thereafter.

The Bayard was very accurate with its fixed barrel. A sample in 32 ACP I have fired holds the black well—7.75-inch diameter—at 25 meters with the original sight setting when shot offhand. The gun was also very reliable and sturdy; it could be field-stripped without any tools. Its most highly recommended feature was its compactness for the calibers chambered. The Bayard was just 5 inches long and 1 inch thick. It weighed 1 pound, empty, in 380. The trigger pull was set at a very clean 5.5 pounds. The recoil was a little stiff in 32 ACP (recoil velocity of 10 feet per second) and on

Pocket guns once popular in France (from top): 32 Smith & Wesson New Departure, the Triple Sureté Browning 1906, the Bayard pocket pistol, a "Le Bossu" hammerless revolver in 32 ACP, and the Le Francais semi-automatic pistol.

the verge of being heavy in 380 (12 fps), but very mild in 25 ACP (5.1 fps).

With the exception of the very rare German Mann and Walther models and the French Mikros pistols chambered in 32 ACP, no other genuine pocket pistol has been chambered in these calibers since then. *(There have been some developments in the U.S.A.— Editor.)* The only European pistols coming close to our requirements in calibers over 25 are the Star DKI chambered in 32 ACP and the DKL in 380 ACP with light alloy receivers (total length 5.7 inches; weight 15 ounces). These guns are not now available in the United States because of the Firearms Act of 1968. Let us say only that they are very accurate and reliable.

The 25 ACP is the centerpiece for all pocket pistols made in Europe from 1906 to 1969, as well as for many of those manufactured during the last twelve years. Why has this tiny and expensive ammunition been so popular for such a long period of time?

First, it represents a good compromise as far as practical accuracy and ease of operation are concerned.

It is also generally thought that, among the design parameters, the recoil velocity is a significant one, and that 8 fps is a good value for an *average* combat shooter, and 10 fps a maximum for *fast and accurate shooting*. The recoil velocity is the bullet momentum divided by the gun weight, so it is obvious that for a 1-pound pistol and an 8 fps recoil velocity, the bullet energy should not exceed 129 foot pounds, or about that of the 32 ACP. If gun weight is reduced by 50 percent, as is desirable, further reduction in power is needed to avoid difficult recoil.

The only modern ammunition falling within this range are the 25 ACP and the 22 Long Rifle. Except for new Winchester Silvertip loadings and for a Fiocchi round-nose lead bullet designed for target shooting, all 25 ACP bullets are round-nose full-jacketed types weighing 49 grains.

The actual muzzle velocity ranges from 623 to 738 fps when fired from a 2-inch barrel, and 705 fps can be considered as an average for European ammunition. Higher velocities often quoted are obtained from test barrels having no connection with reality. The fastest 25 ACP loading I have tested to date is the Hirtenberger at 738 fps, average value for ten rounds, and the most accurate and reliable are from Geco, FN and Fiocchi. About 2.4-inch diameter ten-round groupings can be obtained *from a bench* at 25 meters. Some American cartridges have case diameters at the maximum of the tolerance and may require sanding or resizing, particularly in the "Baby Browning."

The muzzle energy ranges from 50 to 60 foot pounds, and penetration from 2 to 3 boards; with 3.35-inch barrels, these values may be exceeded by half a board. The cavity in clay may vary from the ridiculous value of .08-liter when the bullet goes straight after impact to .21-liter—greater than that of the 32 ACP when it tumbles. In this connection, it can be stated that this effect is well-known by experimenters, and according to my experience, the Austrian Hirtenberger, the Belgian FN, the French Gevelot and the German Geco tumble from three to four times out of five when hitting solid wet 55-pound clay blocks from 10 feet away.

The 25 ACP is a centerfire round with a grooved rimmed case. It is well sealed and can be stored for more than ten years, and thanks to its jacketed bullet, it feeds well in pistols in good condition. It has served European pocket pistol purposes well.

Among the other early competitors to the Browning were the various Star models with fixed barrels, the Pieper models of 1909 called "Petits basculants" and "Petits démontants" with removable and hinged barrels, and the Mauser 1910, which was at the maximum of our requirements with a length of 5.3 inches and an empty weight of just under 1 pound, but comfortable to shoot, reliable and accurate.

In the 1914 issue of a famous French catalog, the Le Francais pistol, designed at Saint-Etienne and patented in 1913, was disclosed to the public. Thanks to the originality of the design and to a long and strong advertising campaign, this small gun became quite famous in spite of its drawbacks.

In the 25 ACP caliber, there are two types of Le Francais: the Pocket Model with a 2.36-inch barrel, made from 1914 to 1966, and the Policeman Model with a 3.34-inch protruding barrel and striker shroud, made from 1922 to 1968. The magazine attachment was changed from the early unsafe "tilting" type to the conventional rear latch design in 1935, and the shape of the grip was improved. A tube for carrying the eighth round was also added to the Policeman's magazine floorplate the same year.

The author shooting the small Walther Model 9 at 25 meters (27 yards)—his regular practice for years.

The Walther Model 8 pistol was the most accurate pocket pistol of its time, but barely holds its own today.

The author's favorite target set. He needs no bag to carry his pet Walther TPH, Zeiss 8x20 monocular, ear plugs and a box of 22 Long Rifle ammunition.

A plain model and three styles of engraving were available for each type of Le Francais up to World War II. A very rare "Modèle Extra-léger" with fluted short barrel, lightened slide and light alloy receiver was even marketed the year before the Hitler War as the Number 812. It was said to weigh only 8.57 ounces, but production was not resumed after the war. For the minor variations of these models and their illustrations, the reader may refer to the excellent book of my friend Jean Huon or to the applicable catalogs of the "Manufacture francaise d'Armes et Cycles de Saint-Etienne," which are now prized collector's items.

The sample Le Francais used for our tests is a variation of the Pocket Model with the short barrel and the lower tube for the spare round normally fitted only to the "Policeman." The gun is 4.58 inches long, 3.3 inches high without the lower tube and .94-inch thick. The empty weight is 12.5 ounces.

To load the gun, remove the magazine; the barrel automatically swings up. Then, fill up the magazine with seven rounds, place the eighth round (the spare one) in the firing chamber and press the barrel down to lock it. Since people who did not want to have a round permanently chambered also hated to carry it loose in the pocket, and with this gun you cannot operate the slide for chambering a round, the manufacturer provided the floorplate tube for that purpose. The eighth round was chambered manually after opening the barrel using a sidelock lever.

With a round in the chamber, the Le Francais can be fired *double action only* eight times consecutively. "Never cocked, always ready," said the advertising. This sounded nice as far as safety was concerned, but that gun unfortunately combined the defects of the revolver—hard pull every time—with those of the automatic pistol—possibility of jamming and fragility of magazines.

Moreover, it had no extractor in case of misfire, ejected empty cases are often very hot, the barrel lock spring was complicated and fragile, and, on guns made before 1935, the magazine could be easily lost. Also, the rear of the slide was cut square and kept getting caught in the pocket. The worst defect was the hard double-action pull, which was 10 pounds on pre-World War II guns and up to a terrific 14 pounds on those made after the war.

As the 25 ACP is not a powerful round, its only justification for defense is shooting accuracy. Here the Le Francais was behind the pack, due to its long and hard double-action pull, so difficult to control. Furthermore, our test sample (in mint condition, with the original box and wrapper) was shooting 2.75 inches too low at 17 feet (i.e., 14 inches at 25 meters or 27 yards) and would have required a higher rear sight. However, if we extrapolate our 17-foot target to 25 meters with the proper correction, all bullets would have hit the black of the I.S.U. target; that is, our Le Francais grouped well.

After World War I, when target shooting with 25 ACP pistols became a popular sport in France, the manufacturers designed a special target version of the Le Francais with a longer grip, 6-inch barrel, adjustable rear sight and a special striker arrangement. Single-action shots were possible by manually cocking the striker. However, this gun, called "Le Francais Champion," was not a pocket pistol.

Among the German competitors was Carl Walther, who designed his Model 1 in 1908, a small pistol chambered in 25 ACP. This gun looks quite prehistoric, but sold enough to convince its manufacturer to proceed, and the Walther factory poured out, during the Great War, quite a large quantity of blowback pistols numbered from Model 1 to Model 7. All these guns were ugly but amazingly accurate with their fixed barrels and good trigger pulls.

After Germany lost the war, Fritz Walther, successor to his father, was allowed to make, in 1920 under the authority of the League of Nations, a new pistol chambered in 25 ACP of the same class as the earlier Mauser Model 1910. This gun, the Model 8, also had a fixed barrel but a much sleeker appearance. In fact, it is the forerunner of the later Model PP, too big to be commented on in this article. The Walther Model 8 is 5.23 inches long, 3.7 inches high and .86-inch thick. Its empty weight is 13.2 ounces, and the barrel is 2.83 inches long. Magazine capacity is eight rounds.

The Model 8 was immediately appreciated by the European 25 ACP target shooters. According to my old shooting partner, Dr. Cantegrit, who died in 1978, the Walther Model 8 was considered as the most accurate in its class. Therefore, I decided to test a mint specimen belonging to a collector. First, I found the trigger pull very long, but not creepy; it was soft (in a sort of "ideal Luger" style) up to the moment when it suddenly became quite hard. Of course, the trigger finger position is short, but the gun is comfortable in the hand, and the recoil is mild.

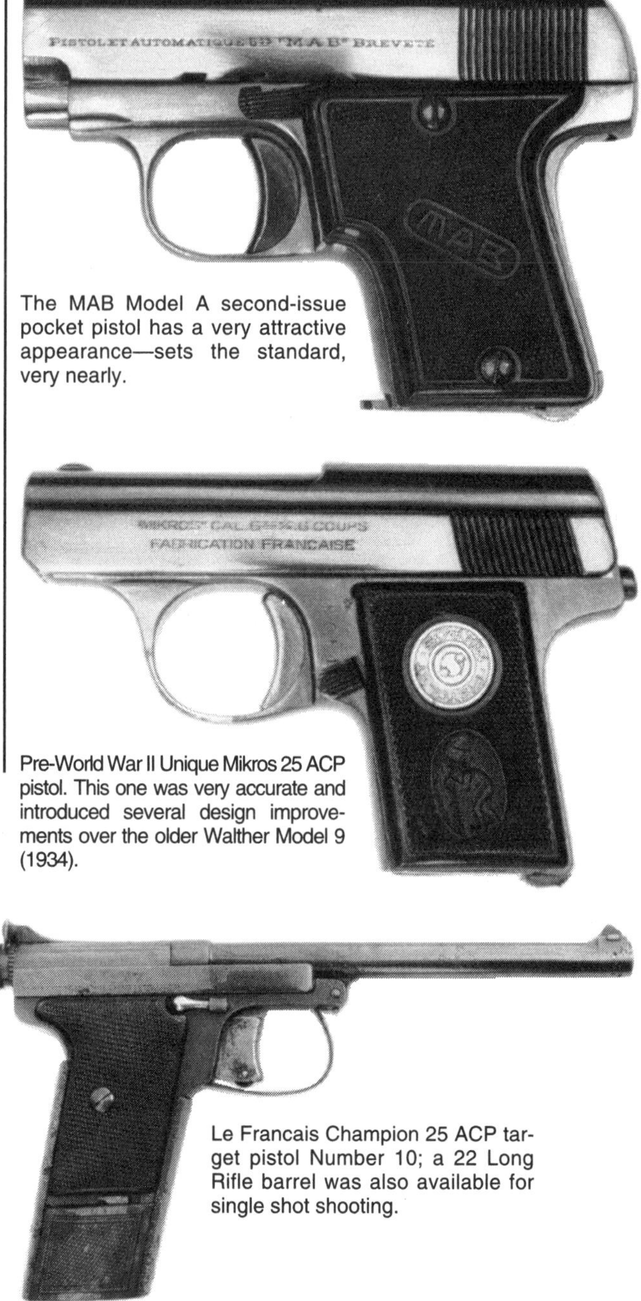

The MAB Model A second-issue pocket pistol has a very attractive appearance—sets the standard, very nearly.

Pre-World War II Unique Mikros 25 ACP pistol. This one was very accurate and introduced several design improvements over the older Walther Model 9 (1934).

Le Francais Champion 25 ACP target pistol Number 10; a 22 Long Rifle barrel was also available for single shot shooting.

This is the 25 ACP Le Francais "Modele de Poche" with the police-model spare-cartridge floorplate.

At 17 feet, the gun shot 2 inches low, but produced a decent grouping. At 25 meters, I aimed at one target to hit another as we did not want to adjust the sights and damage a specimen in such a perfect condition. The score would have been excellent with a modern TPH or Astra 7000. Probably, the champions of the Twenties improved the trigger pulls and modified the rear sight as applicable. Even now, beyond its outstanding workmanship, the Walther Model 8 is a good, accurate and reliable gun which would require only small honing and a higher rear sight.

The Model 9, much smaller, was marketed in 1921 and made, like the Model 8, up to the end of World War II. It also features a fixed barrel, but is striker-fired where the Model 8 has a hammer. The Model 9 is 3.9 inches long, 2.75 inches high and .82-inch thick. The barrel length is exactly 2 inches. The empty weight is 9.5 ounces, and the magazine capacity is six rounds.

The sights of both Walther pistols are the same: a small U machined in the slide and a thin rounded blade. With its beautiful blue and perfect workmanship, the Walther Model 9 looks like a black jewel. It is also said to be very accurate.

This is probably true, but for me this pistol has a bad defect: the slide pinches the hand when recoiling, and if I want to preserve my skin, I must hold it too gingerly to get pinpoint accuracy. At 17 feet, my sample shot 1.5 inches low, but the grouping would not be contained in the black of the I.S.U. target. The trigger pull is set at 6 pounds; it is progressive, without any creep. For somebody not fearing to be pinched, the Walther Model 9 would require only a higher rear sight to shoot straight. Reliability seems perfect with the German Geco ammunition.

The Unique Model II was the top-quality 25 ACP model of the line, styled in the Browning/Colt tradition.

The extremely compact Walther Model 9 was a model of design and displays some of the best workmanship the author has ever seen on a production semi-automatic pistol.

MAB, a French company, was founded in 1921 in Bayonne for making, first, a gun very similar to the Spanish variations of the Browning 1906, featuring a thumb safety acting on the trigger and no grip safety. This first model was soon followed, in 1925, by a more sophisticated second-issue Model A (the one illustrated); then followed by, in 1932, a rare Model B featuring a grip safety and a fixed barrel; and finally by a more common Model E with a nine-round magazine, looking somewhat like a scaled-down version of the MAB 32 ACP pistols. The MAB Model A, second issue, was made for about forty years and was widely exported.

It is very similar to the Browning 1906, from which it differs principally by the trigger mechanism involving a different thumb safety and by more modern lines and stockplates. It is 4.5 inches long, 3.15 inches high and .86-inch thick. The barrel is 2 inches long. The magazine has a six-round capacity, and the empty weight is 13.2 ounces.

The sights are a very small U and an even smaller blade machined in a long groove above the slide. The trigger pull is usually set at about 5.5 pounds. Normally, these guns are quite reliable and shoot low, but the trigger mechanism is the weak point of the design.

Unique was founded at Hendaye, on the Spanish border, in 1923, by Mr. Uria, the father of the current owners. They produced, up to World War II, an amazing number of Basque-style blowback pistols, mostly in 25 ACP and 32 ACP, under several trade names, sold directly or through jobbers.

The most popular Unique pistol was the Model 10 which has the same weight and dimensions as the MAB Model A second issue. However, the Unique Model 10 is disassembled like the World War I Spanish Ruby pistols and has no grip safety. It has, however, beside the conventional thumb safety acting on the trigger, a magazine safety. Also, an ugly 3.3-inch long protruding barrel was available as an option. This barrel gives a higher muzzle velocity and may be used for fitting a silencer.

The Model 10 was made up until 1956 and is very common. It is usually made of excellent materials and produces groupings quite as good as those of my modern Astra 7000. However, it has no sights, except the long groove machined in the top of the slide, and when used off the shelf, it normally shoots about 3 inches low at 17 feet.

If you want to use this otherwise fine gun properly, you need to fit it with conventional sights, which is a very easy task. The trigger pull is also improved by removing the magazine safety. For instance, I have fitted to my personal sample, which belonged to my father, a night sight of my invention which gives excellent results at 17 feet, which is 5 meters, in the dark. At that range, I practice night shooting on the I.S.U. 10-meter air pistol target which has a .47-inch 10-ring and a 2.36-inch black.

Before World War II, Unique produced five different 25 ACP pistols under their own trademark numbered Models 10, 11, 12, 13 and 14, using the same general construction, plus a Mikros pistol separately dealt with. The Model 11, which displays the best workmanship and most sophistication, is quite a collector's item. It has the same dimensions as the Model 10, but weighs only 12.5 ounces and has both grip safety and cocking indicator. The trigger pull is usually excellent and needs no improvement for target shooting. Also, as the slide contour is lower, the balance is improved. Some specimens have a thumb safety acting on the trigger, while that of others acts on the sear. The Model 11 has no sights, and my sample shoots 2.75 inches too low at 17 feet.

When fitted with good Patridge sights, the Unique Model 11 makes a pleasant pocket target pistol, as the recoil is very mild and the grip is quite decent. The real target model of the Unique line of 25 ACP pistols before World War II was the Mikros with a fixed barrel and a six-round magazine capacity, obviously inspired by the handsome Walther Model 9.

The Mikros is 4.2 inches long, 2.83 inches high and .86-inch thick, weighing only 10.6 ounces, empty. The barrel is 2 inches long, and workmanship is very good. The trigger pull of my sample, which shoots 1.90 inches high at 17 feet, is set at 5.7 pounds. The slide does not pinch the hand, and curiously, the gun ejects *to the left*. The trigger pull is very long, but displays no creep. The rear sight is a small U machined in the slide, while the front sight is a thin rounded blade on the barrel. If it were not for the magnificent bluing, I would have changed the front sight to a higher undercut square one for shooting straight at 25 meters.

Besides these pre-WWII pistols that I have tested along the same schedule, there are many others worthy of interest, such as the Mauser 1910, the British Webleys, the Spanish Stars and the Belgian Piepers. I have shot

(Above and below) The author's Unique Model 10 is fitted with the sight he has devised for night shooting at 17 feet. The sight offers two radium-painted half-circles which are matched to form a complete circle in the dark.

all of them at one time or another and know most can produce good groups. As I have testfired all the modern European pocket pistols as well, for my book, and regularly use them for target shooting at 25 meters—my pet guns are a Walther TPH, an Astra 7000 chambered in 22 Long Rifle, and a Bernardelli 68 chambered in 25 ACP—a comparison between the old and the new can be easily drawn.

The Walther pistols Models 8 and 9 unquestionably display the best workmanship and finish, and many pre-World War II pistols such as the Le Francais, MAB Model A and Unique Model 11 show a better appearance than their modern counterparts as far as polishing and bluing are concerned, and their letoffs are not creepy. All seem reasonably reliable when shot with good-quality European ammunition.

On the other side, the Walther Model 9 pinches the hand (which is the case for no modern design, including the "Baby" Browning marketed in 1931, which is, however, marginal on this aspect), and none of them shoots to the sights at 25 meters, while most modern pistols tested need no correction for use at that range.

In this connection, I regularly score between 240 and 250 out of 300 with all my modern pocket guns on the I.S.U. target at 25 meters, which would require quite a significant tuning for most of their pre-war ancestors. Also, while many modern pocket pistols have somewhat creepy trigger pulls, they seem to be fitted with better barrels and are better finished *as far as the essentials are concerned,* even if they may show some tool marks.

For instance, the modern Walther TPH is unquestionably superior to the pre-war Model 8 in all respects. Also, the chambering of the Astra 7000 and Walther TPH in 22 Long Rifle has considerably improved the overall efficiency of these guns, which have more man-sized grips and do not rely anymore on a hypothetical bullet tumbling to obtain a minimum of efficiency.

As a matter of fact, any high-velocity 22 Long Rifle round produces a .24- liter capacity when fired from the 2.3-inch barrel of an Astra 7000 at wet clay, thanks to expansion, which is unquestionably larger than most tumbling 25 ACP jacketed bullet performance. The Remington Yellow Jacket is a true giant in its class with an *actual* 997 fps average velocity and a cavity within the .4 to .5-liter range, not to speak of penetration of 1mm of steel at 10 feet. Finally, the 22 rimfire rounds are less expensive than the 25 ACP and are available everywhere. The last advantages remaining to the latter are in compactness, better sealing and ease of feeding in self-loading mechanisms. ●

Three 25 ACP rounds in the dark, under the rain, at 17 feet (5m).

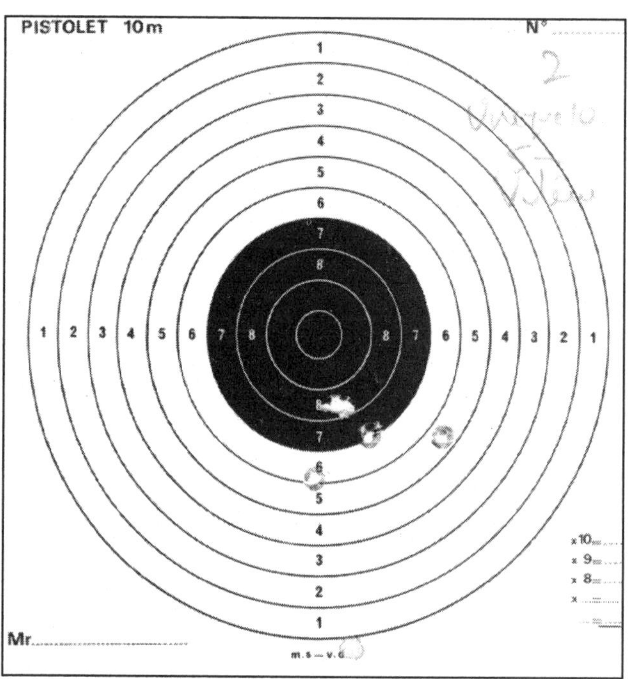

A rapid fire five-round string at 17 feet, in the dark, with the Unique Model 10 and night sight.

CUSTOM GUNS

◀ DON ROBINSON
Restored Westley-Richards 577/450 Martini sporter—new wood, rust blue, all standard touches.

▲ RICHARD BINGER
Providence Tool Peabody in 45-70, 34-inch barrel, done for Stott's Creek Armory—fully sighted.

▶ STEVEN DODD HUGHES
Sharps M77 Long-Range Rifle—45x2.4-inch. Madole metal, Ron Long barrel, Gold engraved.

▲ JOHN M. BOLTIN
Turkish walnut in a long and lean sporting rifle—Tomalin engraving, five-facet bolt knob. (Carter photo).

◀ DAVE COSTA
Roy Johnson owns this classic Mauser GEHA 16-gauge with Claro walnut and 22 l.p.i. checkering.

◀ MAURICE OTTMAR
Terry Wallace-engraved Hagn action in 220 Swift sports Leupold scope in Conetrol rings.

◀ DENNIS ERHARDT
This 9.3x64mm VZ-24 action is square-bridged for Warne rings and has a Precise Metalsmithing dropped magazine.

◀▶ DARWIN HENSLEY
This is a *pair* of 243s built on original Model 98 Kurz actions with Sooter metalwork—square-bridged and quarter-rib sights.

▶ DAVE COSTA
GEHA 16-gauge now has 22-inch barrel, Weaver K1.5 scope, Timney trigger, Grisel safety—shoots slugs well.

▶ MAURICE OTTMAR
That's French walnut, a Half-Moon barrel, and all work is by Ottmar.

▶ DENNIS ERHARDT
Stocked in California English, this rifle has a Half-Moon barrel and idealized Africa rifle lines.

▼ R.H. "DICK" DEVEREAUX
For his retirement rifle, the last one in a string, Devereaux did a 284 on a lightened Sako action, hand-laid a Kevlar stock, and finished it up at 5 pounds and a single ounce. It shoots four-shot groups under .5-inch. Devereaux is trying to buy it back.

▲ STEPHEN E. NELSON
This M2 Springfield is done up as a rimfire understudy big game rifle—recontoured some places, restocked in English walnut. (Hughes photo)

▲ STEVEN DODD HUGHES
A 1930s Fox 20-gauge completely updated—metalwork, stock, checkering by Hughes, engraved by Eric Gold—is now a 5½-pound bird gun.

▲ KENT BOWERLY
Matching English walnut stock blanks make a pair—280 Remington and 338 Winchester Magnum—of deluxe sporters (at top) with engraving by Sherwood, metal by Noreen. The 338 has quarter-rib sights. Then Bowerly made a 223 with Noreen action to the same dimensions for the same customer.

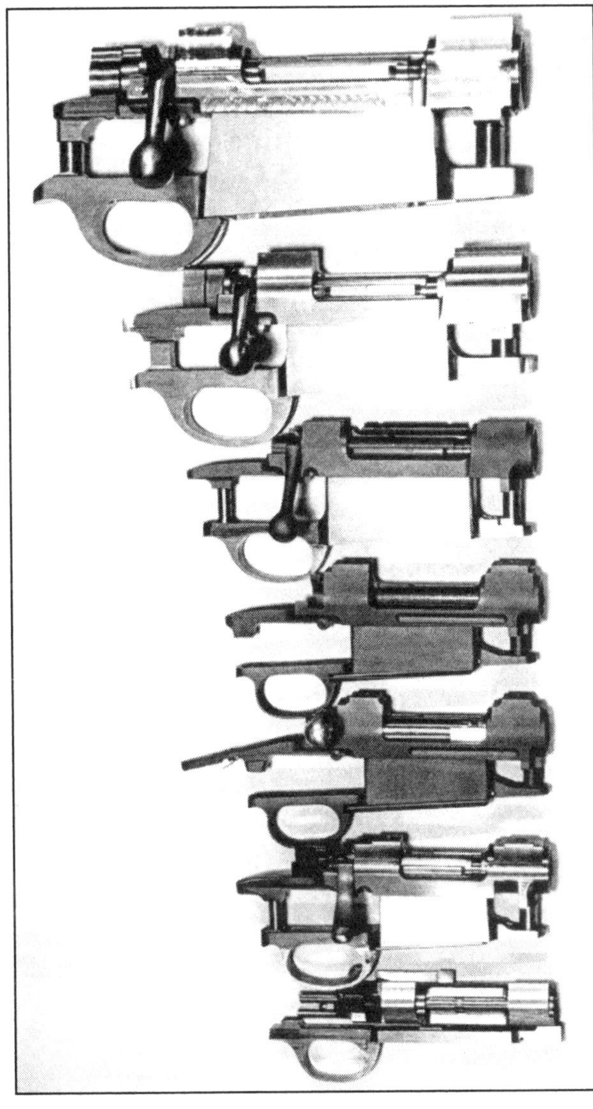

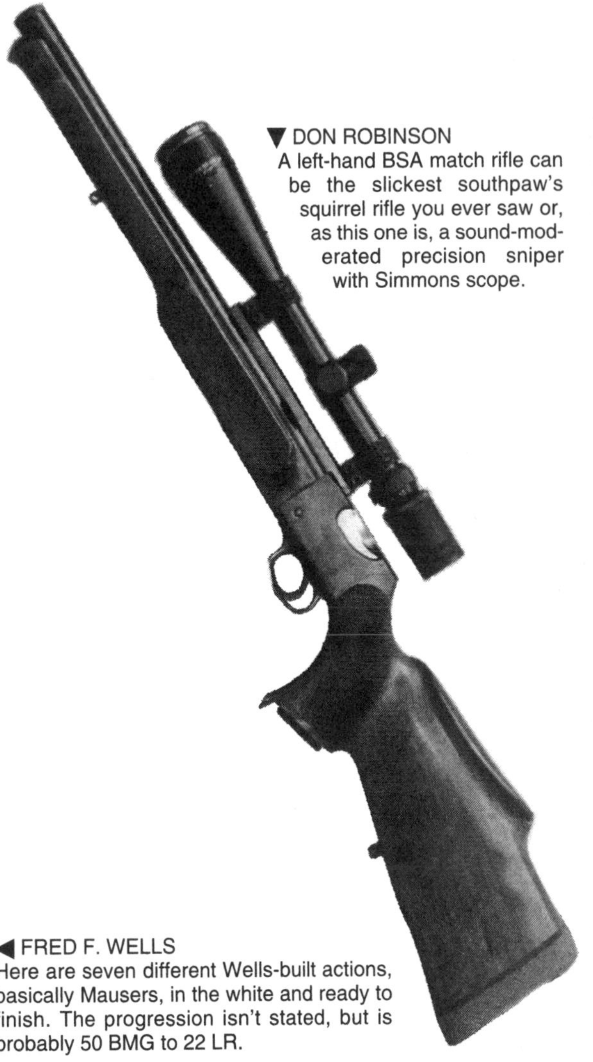

▼ DON ROBINSON
A left-hand BSA match rifle can be the slickest southpaw's squirrel rifle you ever saw or, as this one is, a sound-moderated precision sniper with Simmons scope.

◀ FRED F. WELLS
Here are seven different Wells-built actions, basically Mausers, in the white and ready to finish. The progression isn't stated, but is probably 50 BMG to 22 LR.

One Good Gun

by PAT DEPASQUALE

Sometimes It Takes Three Chipmunks

ABOUT ELEVEN YEARS ago, I was selling guns at Lew Horton's retail store in Framingham, Massachusetts. My leisure time in the winter was spent at the outdoor range or shooting indoor gallery targets at the Hopedale Rifle and Pistol Club. As spring unfolded that year, my six-year-old daughter, Katie, said she wanted to spend more time with her Old Man, so I looked over the available firearms to see what a skinny little kid might use to learn to shoot.

Obviously, a 22 rifle was the ticket, but mine were all too big, uniformly too long and too heavy. I kicked this puzzle around for a few weeks until my glance fell across the Chipmunk rifle hanging on the wall of the store. There was the answer as plain as day, so I had only to justify the expense of the acquisition. That took less time than you might think, and the little single shot was on the way home that day.

It had nice figure in the wood, weighed well under 3 pounds, and was so short that no adult could see the sights while holding the piece to their shoulder. Perfect.

Well, almost perfect. I took it to Hopedale range to test its accuracy. The first problem was how to hold the gun because a grown-up just can't get his head down to see through the simple factory peep sight. I wound up shooting with the plastic buttplate on my cheekbone, which felt strange but worked fine. From the 50-foot line, I fired groups with the rifle balanced on my cheek, and for comparison, then I shot groups using the same ammunition out of my High Standard Citation, a terrifically accurate target pistol, using two hands resting on the bench. The Chipmunk shot tighter, went off every time, and the fired cases looked good. It was time to take Katie to the range.

I set her up with muff-type hearing protectors; she wore glasses anyway, so no other eye protection was needed. Chipmunks are chambered for 22 Long Rifle shells, but I wanted the least possible recoil and noise to interfere with her learning sight picture, breath control, and trigger squeeze. CB caps were the ammunition of choice in the CCI CB Long flavor. I had always found them to have a very practical level of accuracy, though certainly not the best. Group size was easily manipu-

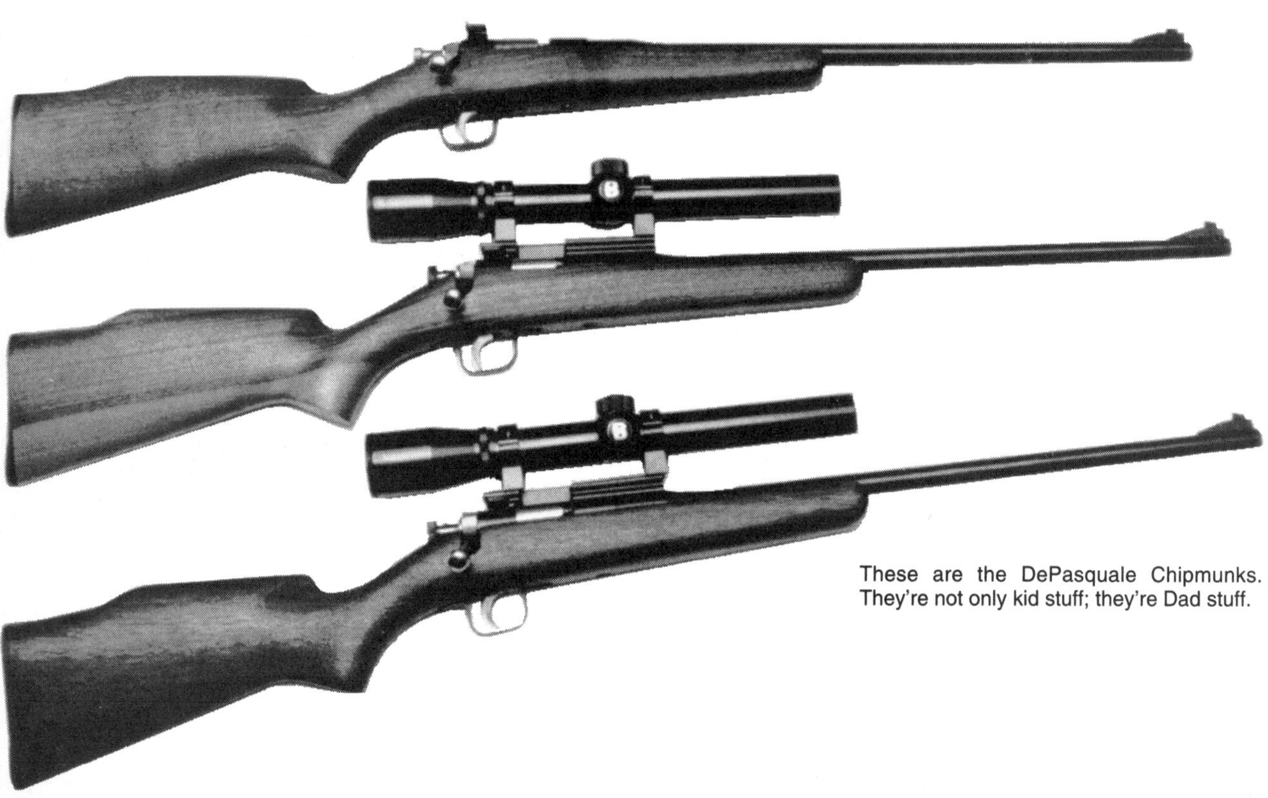

These are the DePasquale Chipmunks. They're not only kid stuff; they're Dad stuff.

The deal includes a special Chipmunk case, which makes great kid sense.

lated by moving the target closer to the gun, so any inherent lack of accuracy in the rifle/ammo combination was compensated for, and Katie's confidence was maintained by seeing the bullet holes fall close together.

The second problem was more subtle. It took a little while to realize that the kiddo was struggling with the 6-pound trigger. I had thought it was pretty good, but didn't consider that an easy pull for an adult might be a very hard pull for a child. The Chipmunk has a lot of nice features, but an adjustable trigger isn't one of them. A customer at the store had recently completed gunsmithing school and suggested that he could install a simple system that would allow substantial lightening of the trigger. I had him do it, and the difference was immediate and positive. Kate's trigger control improved tremendously, and so then did her accuracy. She could even shoot longer without fatigue, which had been noticeable before.

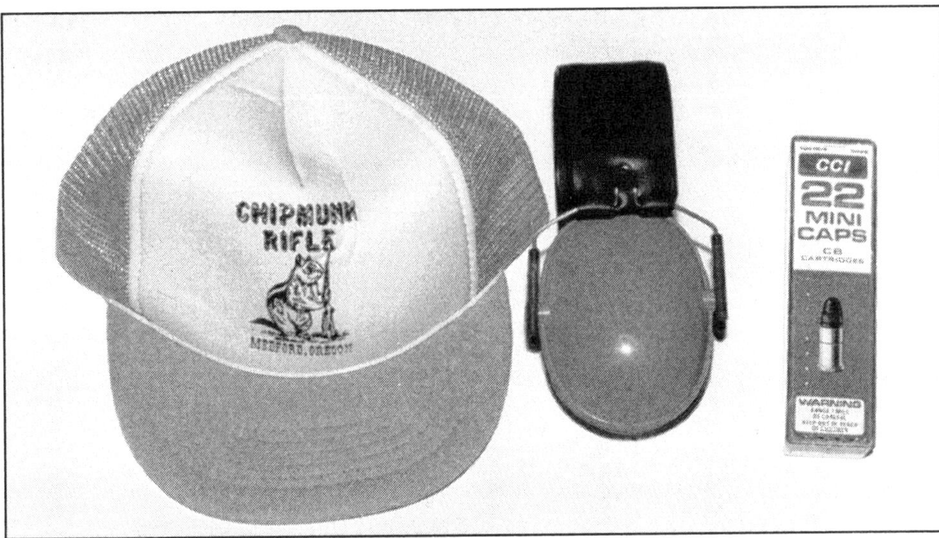

The kiddos' shooting equipment: hearing protectors, Chipmunk hat and CB caps—the long ones.

The third problem came up after a couple of years of shooting. The Chipmunk stays small, but kids do not. The short stock, such a good fit for three or four years, became too short. Firing from the cheek was alright for casual function testing, but not as a useful long-term technique. Taking a chance (a very small one), I ordered a Chipmunk scope base and a Bushnell 4x 1-inch 22 scope. The plan was to mount the base and rings, then cobble up a stock extension. It turned out that the eye relief was fine if the glass was mounted far forward in the rings, which also picked up the sight high enough that you didn't have to kink your neck to see through it. *Voilà*—a simple elegant solution that did not require my simple but inelegant carpentry skills.

So we had the ultimate little-kid shooting setup: a pair of orange hearing protectors, glasses, a box of CB caps, and one of the only two customized Chipmunk rifles in the world. Naturally, the whole set-up was duplicated for my other offspring, Amy. The two of them were given Chipmunk hats and Chipmunk rifle cases, padded blue ones just the right size for their guns, including scopes.

And why *three* Chipmunks, you ask? Ah, you have caught me. Time and familiarity have caused a great admiration for these tiny rifles. They are accurate, reliable, and they don't weigh anything to speak of. I got one for myself. The trigger is unaltered and I still use the gun from the cheek. It is sighted in with high-speed Long Rifle stuff and goes along on hikes during small game season in New Hampshire. The factory sights are fine for my purpose. In fact, you could say that about the whole gun, or all three. ●

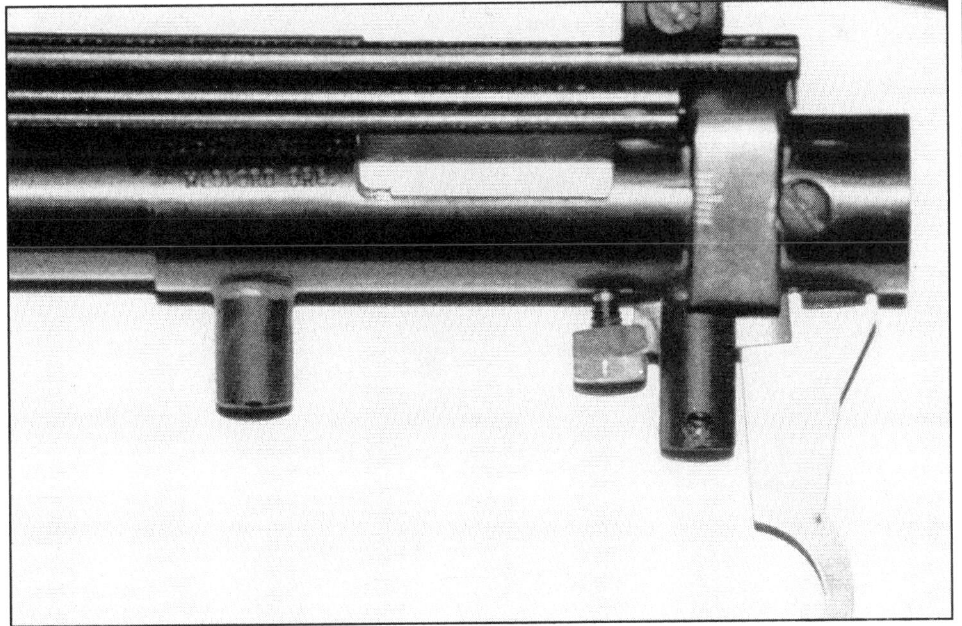

For adjustable trigger arrangements, a nut was attached to the trigger, and the screw and lock nut added to provide both adjustability and stability.

by KENNETH BOLIN

Many Good Rifles And One Good Scope

I HUNTED FOR about eleven years before I realized people who used riflescopes might be on to something. I had begun to frequent a small gunsmith shop in a rather secluded area of Northeast Texas about 35 miles from my home. The gunsmith was a genius with guns, both repairing them and making them from scratch. A custom riflemaker, he was known in Oklahoma, in Arkansas and to the well-heeled members of the Dallas Gun Club.

I couldn't afford a custom gun, but I had him do jobs like bluing 22 rimfires, adjusting triggers, refinishing old shotguns, and buying reloading equipment. A scope had been on my deer rifle for about a year when the gunsmith encouraged me to change it for a better one.

He sold only Leupolds and put them on his customer's high-priced rifles. I believed him when he said there was none better. In fact, for the next twenty-five years, I believed everything he said about guns, scopes or ammunition. This was 1965, and I never knew him to be wrong.

He said, "Put your hand in front of the lens, you can see the crosswires in the dark. And the centerwire is thin so you can aim at small targets at long range."

This was, of course, my introduction to the duplex recticule. I didn't have to think long. I had just bought a Leupold 4x M8 scope.

There have been numerous advances in the development of the riflescope in the last thirty years. Since 1965, we have seen things like compact scopes, mini-scopes, low-light scopes, battery-powered dots, multi-coated lenses, micro-track adjustments, all-steel scopes, all-aluminum scopes, even graphite scopes. They have silver finishes, matte finishes, and glossy finishes; some are camouflaged. There are range-finding devices, many sizes and types of variable-power scopes, and internal advances I'm sure I neither know about nor understand. For all that, my thirty-year-old scope does everything an up-to-date one will do.

I bought another Leupold 4x in 1978 for another rifle, and with these 4xs, I have tallied something like twenty-three whitetails, four mule deer, one elk, one pronghorn, two black bear, nine coyotes and a bobcat. I've used scopes other than the 4xs at times, but not very much.

My first Leupold 4x was fitted to a pre-'64 M70 Winchester 30-06. It was only 1965, and we didn't understand the "pre-'64" business. So in five years, I traded it, but not the scope, for an FN Mauser 7mm Magnum as I was going on an elk hunt. The 30-06 took a 275-pound mule deer at 325 yards; the 7mm Magnum killed an elk at 336 steps. No problem—I didn't need higher power.

Later on, with the scope on another Model 70 it did fine when a whitetail trotted by at 25 yards. Four power was not too much on that one. Four power is enough scope for any big game animal at reasonable ranges. Well, I was stupid enough to trade off that Model 70 too, but smart enough to keep the scope. A couple of rifles later, about 1975, that Leupold landed on a Ruger M77, a 270, and there it has found a home.

One of the good things about the Leupold 4x is the length of the scope between the objective bell and adjustment housing,

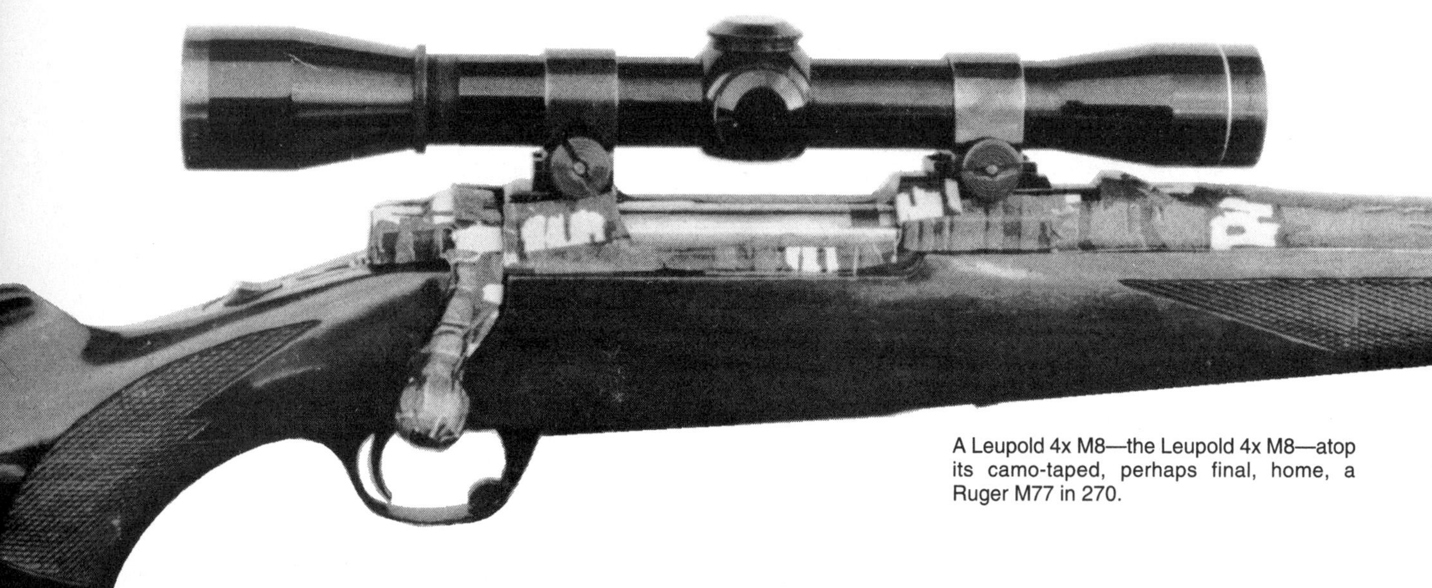

A Leupold 4x M8—the Leupold 4x M8—atop its camo-taped, perhaps final, home, a Ruger M77 in 270.

Bolin's good scope is basically a Texas whitetail killer, and it's worked on dozens of them.

And every once in a while, some other critter, like this largish coyote, proves 4x is power enough.

and thence to the eyepiece. The adjustments are directly in the center. I never had any trouble mounting that scope on any rifle. This is certainly not so with some of the shorter variables on long-action rifles. I have the Leupold mounted as low as possible on the Ruger 77 with old Weaver mounts and rings. There is nothing wrong with Weaver rings as long as you tighten them down good, and I mean *tight*.

The popular thing today is to use a big scope with high power and a large objective bell. They gather light, it is said, and many animals are taken at dawn and dusk. That is true, and I've taken my share at those times. However, you don't need a big objective bell on a 4x scope. Most experts say to multiply the power times the exit pupil of the eye, which is about 7mm in the dark, and you should have the objective size you need. Like 4x7=28mm for a 4x scope. So, the objective on my 4x Leupold is a bit more than that, although small by today's standards. I've taken five whitetails in the fading dusk, and I was a bit apprehensive while walking over to them, afraid I had not actually seen horns after all. They always had 'em, I'm happy to say. It's probably not wise to take such late afternoon shots, even with big scopes.

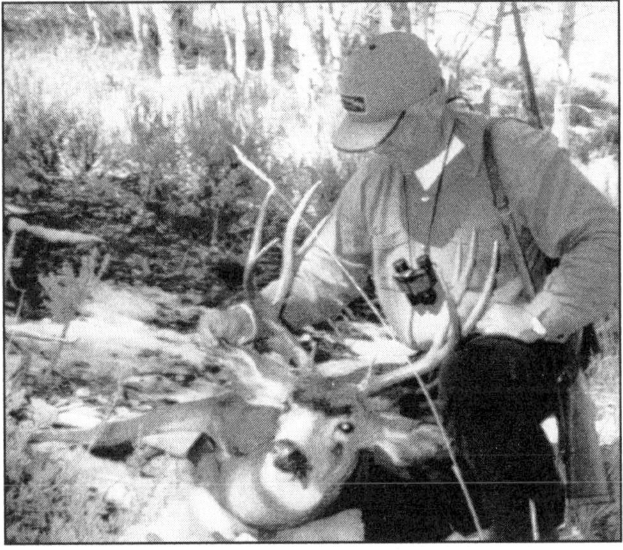

Sufficient practice in Texas obviously worked in the mountains on mule deer—this is a nice buck.

I believe the adjustments on that old scope were calibrated for an inch per mark on the dial at 100 yards. I never tested that for accuracy because you just turn them however much you need until you are zeroed and leave the scope be until resighting or mounting it on some other gun. One thing I like about adjustments on the Leupold is the amount of latitude and longitude you have. It's 100 inches at 100 yards, whereas with some variables it's only 28 inches.

This is important when the mounting holes in your rifle have been drilled and tapped a bit off center. And don't think some of them are not off, even straight from the factory. I've seen some out of whack so much that a variable could not be sighted in—that is, with the Weaver mounts of the non-adjustable type I prefer. And, too, a scope that is aligned with the barrel is clearer because, no matter that the crosswires look centered, a scope is clearest at the center. The less movement made from side to side with the adjustments, the better. It's a personal thing, but I like friction adjustments better than clicks. I just trust them more.

I've hunted in the rain, the cold, and the snow with the Leupold 4x. No leaks. Leupold prides itself on making waterproof optics and has from its beginning, I suppose.

I could say more, but enough. I know I can think of nothing critical about the scope. It has been and is yet a very good sight. Most of the rifles it sat atop have been sold or traded off, but I plan to keep the scope. My big game hunting is mostly whitetails in the woods these days, and shots are about 20 to 100 yards. What scope would serve me better? I've thought about a $1^1/_2$-5x variable, but I've found you don't have time to turn rings in the whitetail woods. I'm going to stick with my one good 4x scope. ●

One Good Gun

by ROB LUCAS

A Second-Choice M29

THE FRUGAL SCOT'S advice, "Get what you want the first time, laddie, or you'll pay twice," is good for guns. Buy the Colt, in other words, if that's what you want, and don't settle for the clone.

I have bought and sold some clones, so to speak, including a semi-auto 22 target gun, a belt gun, a home-defense gun, and a couple of big-bore revolvers. So, I've paid twice for my first choice several times. My wife, whose family name is Burns, understands when I say "I must have had a fit of cheap."

On the other hand, second choice doesn't always mean second best. Sometimes the gun firmly in hand is good enough to make you forget the elusive one in your dreams, and my very good Smith & Wesson Model 29 is a gun like that.

Introduced in 1955, the Model 29 was the only double-action 44 Magnum on the market for almost a quarter century. Between 1955 and 1960, about 20,000 N-frame Model 29s were made, compared to an average single-year figure of 30,000 K frames. In the 1960s and early '70s, the legend of caliber 44 Magnum grew, and the N-frame Model 29—extolled for its quality and accuracy by writers named Keith, Skelton, Askins, Lachuk, and Cooper—came off the S&W assembly line in less conservative quantities, but there were still more buyers than guns. For me, Jeff Cooper's experience with the Model 29 had the most impact.

Cooper was—and still is—the pointman of the Practical Pistol movement, where the Colt semi-automatic pistol is regarded as king. His 1974 book, *Cooper On Handguns,* wasn't exactly the same old stuff. Cooper's cogent argument against wheelguns startled a law enforcement community that mostly

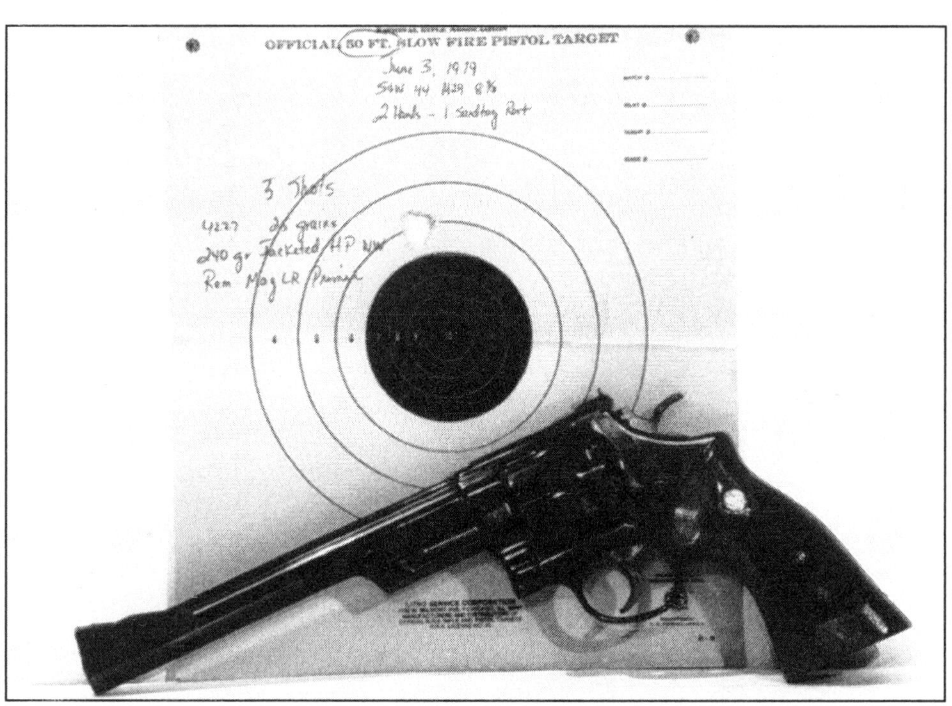

A revolver that does a lot of this for almost two decades can be forgiven a long barrel.

Lucas and the 8 3/8-inch Model 29, both posing; after thousands of rounds, the gun looks good.

The Lucas $8^{3}/_{8}$-inch 44 is a 29-2, which gives it a counterbored cylinder and stuff.

This was all it took for thousands of happy 44-caliber rounds.

The Ray Baker underarm rig keeps the big Model 29 about as unobtrusive as a $3^{1}/_{2}$-pound object can be.

issued 38 Special Colts and Smith to its people. Today, you almost never see a cop wearing a revolver.

Cooper found the revolver bulky, slow to reload, and hard to shoot well, but the very practical Col. Cooper owned and revered at least one revolver, the S&W Model 29 44 Magnum, calling it the "Great One." Cooper added but two caveats: 1) Shoot magnum ammunition in this finely tuned revolver only sparingly; and 2) be prepared to pay double the new gun price for a good used Model 29 if one could be found for sale at all.

That's because, you'll remember, another champion of the Model 29 emerged in 1971. Surly, fictitious street detective Harry Callahan really screwed things up. In the movies, Dirty Harry chased San Francisco punks and thugs carrying a 3-pound $6^{1}/_{2}$-inch S&W 44 Magnum in preference to the usual plain-clothes 38 snubby. Callahan's 44 Magnum was, as he liked to remind the uninitiated, "the world's most powerful handgun," and for the rest of the 1970s we all had to have one like Harry's.

It was in 1975 that I decided to buy a Model 29, more Cooper's influence than Clint's, but by then it was "take a number." The $6^{1}/_{2}$-inch gun had become virtually unobtainable; the 4-inch, which was Elmer Keith's choice in a portable 44 Magnum, was rare; the gargantuan $8^{3}/_{8}$-inch target 29 was merely hard to find.

Around the 4th of July 1976, I found one new $6^{1}/_{2}$-inch Model 29 priced at $699, never mind the 1977 GUN DIGEST price of $235. The following summer, another appeared in a local gunshop, and the call went to the guy at the top of the list. Despite a first-refusal price of $800, that gun sold before it was ever displayed.

Well, you see in the photographs I got my second choice, an $8^{3}/_{8}$-inch Model 29. In December of 1978, my wife bought it new in a felt-lined mahogany box for about what it's worth today, just under $500, and she stuck it under the Christmas tree. She definitely did not cheap out; it was the only Model 29 she could find; and so she said I could sell it or trade it without hurting her feelings. That's exactly what I planned to do—at first.

I shot that handcannon the day after it was officially mine with full-house Winchester 240-grain jacketed magnums and 246-grain Winchester Lubaloy 44 Specials. Those old Winchester 44 Magnums were hot...they belched flame and torqued that long barrel to a 45-degree angle every time the hammer fell. Straight from the box, the factory sights threw magnum jacketed slugs 3 inches high and left, but a cylinderful would stay on a 50-cent piece. With comparatively recoilless 44 Specials, I had to hold on the bottom of the paper to hit the top of the black, but those light loads shot almost as tight as the magnums.

The gun was accurate, but it was barrel-heavy—not clumsy but not graceful either. Sure, the single-action pull was perfect, as you'd expect in a deluxe-grade S&W, and the DA pull was slick, too, but who besides Dirty Harry fired a 44 Magnum double-action anyway, let alone one with an $8^{3}/_{8}$-inch barrel? The factory target grips looked good, felt great, but in full 44 Magnum recoil they were, as Cooper described, too fat at the bottom and too slender up top. This hard-kicking 29 was tough to hang onto, but I thought 2 extra inches of barrel might have something to do with that. The sight picture, a red-ramped black blade about two miles ahead of a white-outlined notch, was pretty clean... once you found it.

These shortcomings I could live with because I planned to dump this gun the day the first $6^{1}/_{2}$-incher became available. My name was still on a few waiting lists, and meantime, the $8^{3}/_{8}$ became a proving ground for Jeff Cooper's Prescription for Long Life in a Magnum Revolver: Shoot a bunch of light loads and relatively few gun-pounding magnums.

Cooper wrote, "Note what you feel in your hand," correlating that palm-bashing sensation to the physical blow absorbed by the gun mechanism. He recommended keeping a close count of rounds fired and saving full-house magnum ammo for "seri-

The 44 Magnum and 44 Special 250-grain Keith loads at left, the 250-grain Mastercast at right, loaded straight out of the bag.

ous work," limiting these to about 10 percent of the total. He thought 90 percent of all 44 Magnum shooting should be single-action target work and controlled double-action practice with light or medium loads. That way, an expensive, hard-to-find handgun like the Model 29 wouldn't shoot loose in a lifetime.

I started reloading the 44s with a set of Lee 44 Special hand dies and a Lee aluminum mould that dropped 240-grain round-nose slugs from wheelweights. I had the idea I should learn double-action shooting and speed reloading. My round-nose slugs fed smoothly through Safariland speed loaders, and 5 grains of Bullseye and the 240 cast Lee in 44 Special cases made an accurate, indoor load that barely lifted that long barrel.

Avoiding trial-and-error 44 Magnum shooting, I began with Elmer Keith's famous load—22.0/Hercules 2400 with 240-grain JSPs—and found it OK, but another storied 44 Magnum load—25.0/IMR4227—was deadly accurate in my gun. With this heavy load, new Pachmayr rubber grips nested in a sandbag and both hands clamped on Weaver-style, the long barrel and I shot great groups.

How great? In 1979 I fired my best-ever group with any handgun, five handloads of 25.0 4227/Win 240 JSP that went into 1/2-inch at 50 feet. If I hadn't saved that target and had a witness, I wouldn't even mention it. The load clocks 1530 fps in the 8 3/8-inch gun, meaning it's not only twice as fast as most factory 44 Specials, it's also twice as accurate.

In 1980 I graduated from the Lee hand dies to an RCBS single-stage Jr. press and RCBS 44 Magnum dies. With this setup, I shot a 50-pound box of wheelweights, almost 1400 rounds, through the gun in two years, load-testing the way the famous gun writers did for their revolvers, using just a single chamber.

With Bullseye, WW 630 and greasy old Unique, I fired hundreds of five-shot groups single-loading one chamber. The plan was to duplicate 44 Special velocity in 44 Magnum cases and develop *the* accurate practice cartridge for *my next* Model 29, but the long-barreled gun would not cooperate. Some groups were good, a few were great, but the experiment was a failure: five rounds of a good load fired from a single chamber didn't always group as tight as five rounds of the same load fired from five chambers, and that wasn't supposed to happen. It seemed like the gun outshot the best ammunition I could make for it.

Reloading notes show that in 1983, after 2200 cast round-nose bullets had gone down my barrel, I gave up on "intrinsic" accuracy, double-action speed shooting, and round-nose bullets. With an all-around 44 Magnum load in mind for *my next* Model 29, I switched from the Lee bullet to an RCBS Keith-style SWC, and from quick-burning Bullseye to slower Blue Dot. I upgraded my reloading operation again with a Ponsness-Warren Metal-Matic pistol press. Most Blue Dot/Keith 245-grain SWC recipes shot well in the gun, but I finally found one that clocked a respectable 950 fps and shot "lights out."

So, by the end of 1986, I had the 44 field covered, an accurate all-purpose +P 44 Special load for everyday use and a super-accurate Magnum load for special occasions. Both these loads were for that dream revolver, the 6 1/2-inch Model 29. In seven years, having melted a 50-pound box and most of a 5-gallon can of wheelweights into bullets, the number of rounds fired through my 8 3/8-inch gun stood just shy of 4000. Of that total, less than 250 were factory or handload-equivalent 44 Magnums.

The Cooper formula worked: My revolver was in fine shape, clean, tight, accurate, and still valuable in a trade. Although not as urgently as ten years earlier, I still wanted that 6 1/2-inch Model 29, and by 1986, those pistols were out there. Smith & Wesson had made some design changes in their famous 44, though.

The 8 3/8-inch was not perfect. Like when one round grain of WW 630 ball powder under the extractor rendered the gun unshootable. And twenty or thirty quick double-action shots invariably meant cylinder sluggishness cocking the hammer. A tight flashgap, though it held down side-spitting, was the problem and a royal pain. For awhile, I lived with it; then I took a closer look and found a sharp edge of metal between 11 and 1 o'clock on the barrel in constant contact with the cylinder, hot or cold.

You know what's coming: I got turned around on the long gun and kept it. It outlasted me. I pulled off the Pachmayrs and went back to the original Goncalo Alves factory wood. Deciding to shoot just 44 Magnum cases in my gun, I bought another pistol so I could shoot the accumulated 44 Special cases.

My S&W Model 29, now eighteen years old, is stamped 29-2 on the crane, indicating a model with Design Change 1 from 1960, a left-hand-threaded extractor rod, and Design Change 2 from 1961, a new cylinder stop which eliminated a hole in the front of the trigger guard. The designation 29-2 also means my gun has a couple nice features missing from post-1982 Model 29s—a barrel crosspin through the topstrap and a counterbored cylinder to support 44 Magnum cartridge rims. S&W found that 44 Magnum case rims didn't need support in their guns, and counterboring was a redundancy, as was pinning barrels to keep them from unscrewing. I think the slightly longer counterbored cylinder and the very thin band of light passing between it and the standing breech makes the old 29-2 one sleek, handsome revolver.

These days, the 8 3/8-inch gun stays sighted-in at 25 yards for my utility-target load, 14.0/ Blue Dot/250 lead SWC. I don't shoot it as much as I used to, but I have upward of 500 handloads in the cabinet, and when they're gone the 44 will have passed its next milestone, 9000 rounds fired. On targets at 75 feet, it still shoots golfball-size groups every time out. I still cast Keith 245-grain SWCs from the RCBS mould, but I also like Mastercast .429-inch alloy slugs that come in 500-count plastic bags. I just load 'em and shoot 'em.

Except when I'm packing back into game country or packing around my old 22 Bearcat in snake country, I use the 44 and utility load for everything, plinking at tin cans and targets, single-action bowling pins, the occasional furry critter, and even teaching the six-gun to a newcomer. A 250-grain lead semi-wadcutter at 950 fps from a 51-ounce pistol doesn't kick a lot, but it does slam bowling pins off the table. Of late, I've gotten into coyote-calling with this gun in hand; I shot at just one near-sighted coyote 35 yards away, and he went over about like a bowling pin.

In the movies, Harry Callahan hauled around his 6 1/2-inch Model 29 in a shoulder holster, but it wasn't until 1981 that I saw Roy Baker's shoulder rig for long-barreled revolvers, and in 1984 I bought one. It's not a fast holster, but it comfortably handles my long-barreled 44 whether I'm snowshoe stalking or coyote sitting.

Mostly, I don't shoot this 44 in the ways that take advantage of its special cartridge and barrel length, like for big game hunting or silhouette shooting. My good 8 3/8-inch is an everyday gun, a little bigger and a little heavier than the average plinker, but that's a lot of what I like about it. The rest is its accuracy. I've fired it nearly 9000 times, but I haven't shot it loose and don't expect to in my lifetime. And I expect to own this second choice of mine as long as I breathe. ●

by BOB ARGANBRIGHT

A Special Colt SAA

TO MY EYES, the Colt Single Action Army (SAA) revolver has a grace and beauty equalled by no other handgun. And while a new-in-the-box Second Generation SAA will make my pulse race, it is older pre-WWII First Generation Colts that have been personalized by their early users that fascinate me the most. I envied the late Skeeter Skelton for the custom SAAs he had, built from salvaged First Generation models that had been worn to the point of having no collector value. I treasure those issues of *Shooting Times* magazine featuring Skeeter's articles about his custom Colt SAAs.

I had considered purchasing one of the Italian Colt clones to personalize, but it just wouldn't be the same. And then, the chance of a lifetime, a blackpowder model Colt SAA frame was offered to me on a trade. The deal was made, and I had the beginning of my special Colt.

Wanting a revolver for fun shooting and not wanting to strain the old frame, which was manufactured in 1891, I chose a Second Generation 5½-inch barrel and cylinder in 357 Magnum, intending to use mild 38 Special ammunition. At the time, 357 barrels and cylinders were plentiful, as collectors weren't interested in the caliber, and many Colts had been converted to 44 or 45. Today, the popularity of Cowboy Action Shooting has caused the supply of 357 SAA parts to dry up.

After cleaning up the frame by careful filing and hand polishing, I had friend and SAA specialist Ray Meibaum install the barrel and fit the cylinder bushing. My parts box yielded a usable hammer and the other necessary action parts, and I ordered a trigger guard and ejector assembly from Peacemaker Specialists. A friend supplied the perfect backstrap for my pet project. Inscribed on it is "TO ANDY ANDERSON FROM ARVO OJALA FEB. 1957." These men were two of the giants of the Hollywood holster industry of the 1950s and '60s.

(Left) The author's new/old Colt has character. One can see the cut trigger guard, beveled cylinder, and subtle reshaping of hammer spur. The playing cards were shot offhand at 10 feet.

(Right) The Colt is at home in this vintage flower-carved George Lawrence "Threepersons" hip holster.

While the details are beyond the scope of this article, I did an action job on my emerging SAA, ending up with one that is light and smooth as glass. Next I could start on modifying the six-shooter, which is what really intrigues me. For SAAs, the Colt with hammer spur modified, trigger tied back or removed, front sight filed off, and trigger guard chopped tops my list.

Such an easy-pointing Colt is ideal for fast point-shooting, but I will also use mine for a fast run at five Bianchi plates or bowling pins, so the front sight stayed, as did the trigger, as I do not have time to perfect the slip-shooting technique. So that left just the trigger guard and hammer to be modified.

An hour with several files and emery paper, and I had reshaped the hammer spur, deepening the hollow in front of the spur, increasing its angle for sure speed cocking, and removing the checkering to save my thumb. Then, a few more minutes with a hacksaw, files and emery paper, and I had removed the front of the guard. While Colt's FitzGerald popularized this modification some fifty to sixty years ago on his New Service "Fitz Specials," I have seen numerous photos of First Generation SAAs modified in this way.

A trip to a gun show provided a pair of stag grips. I thinned these down to the proper feel, resulting in an exceptional pair of stag ivory grips with only traces of the original stag texture. For finishing touches, I beveled the end of the ejector housing and the cylinder to save wear and tear on my holsters, and capped the right-side grip screw hole with an ivory plug.

Finally, a local engraver set up at the next gun show cut my initials into the trigger guard flat. All that was left was selecting a proper holster and seeing how my custom Colt shot.

You may know from my articles in previous GUN DIGESTS that I collect holsters. This special Colt needed a special holster. I wanted comfort, light weight, speed and relative security. A search through my holster chest yielded a George Lawrence "Threepersons"-style holster marked "C SA 5½," for Colt Single Action 5½-inch barrel. The Threepersons was originated by S.D. Myres of El Paso, Texas, for El Paso gunfighter Tom Threepersons, and this beautiful, full, hand flower carved version by one of the legends of the holster industry will be the perfect complement for my special Colt. All that was left was a shooting session—the "proof of the pudding."

The original V-notch rear sight, combined with my over-fifty eyesight, makes precise aiming difficult. So I tried something in line with the fun gun theory. Legendary Texas gunslinger John Wesley Hardin, when living in El Paso in the 1890s, is known to have shot for group at playing cards, and then autographed them.

Once I had shot my Colt to find where it hit, compared to point of aim, I broke out the playing cards. Shooting offhand, with 38 Special full wadcutters, at a distance of 10 feet, all shots touching each other was the norm. I finished up my session by shooting at the spots on a card. Most shots cut some part of the spot. Finally, backing up to 30 feet, I put four or five shots on a playing card. Good enough for this Saturday matinee gunslinger. ●

Editor's Note

There are two things (maybe more) to note about Arganbright's creation: Such alterations were not uncommon; they were done by actual users; Arganbright is himself a notable gunhandler, a tested national champion quick-drawer and, so, well-versed in the safety aspects of gun handling.

K.W.

One Good Gun

by LEE ARTEN

The Surprising Bronco

MY BRONCO 410 was the first gun I bought without a lot of plotting and planning. I'd seen it in the magazine ads and decided I was going to get one, someday. That time, someday didn't take as long as it had before, or has since.

I was out of high school and had saved a few bucks from driving cabs and washing dishes, so when I walked into Ace Hardware in Calumet, Michigan, and saw the Bronco, all it took was a trip to the bank. I graduated in 1969, so it must have been 1971. I paid (prepare to sing "Those Were The Days, My Friend") $19 for the brand-new single shot shotgun.

I had bought one new gun before, a Glenfield Model 70 semi-auto 22 with vague M-1 Carbine styling and a seven-shot box magazine. I picked it up for around $30 while I was in high school, after months of shoveling snow and saving up. I'd owned my grandfather's old single-barrel 12-gauge since 1966. My great-uncle let me talk him out of it when I started hunting deer. By the time I ran across the Bronco, I had a much more effective shotgun, a 16-gauge Winchester Model 12 that I'd gotten as a graduation present. Still, the Bronco just appealed to me. I had to have it.

I've always had a fondness for odd and little guns. The Bronco was both, but I found out at the gravel pit that it fit pretty well. I was then, and am now, one of the world's worst shotgunners, but I managed to break more clays in the air, and rolling on the ground, than I was used to. My scattergunning deficiencies stem mostly from a lack of practice. I seem to pick up a little when I am trying out a new smoothbore. I'm in a real slump now—it's been a couple of years since I bought one.

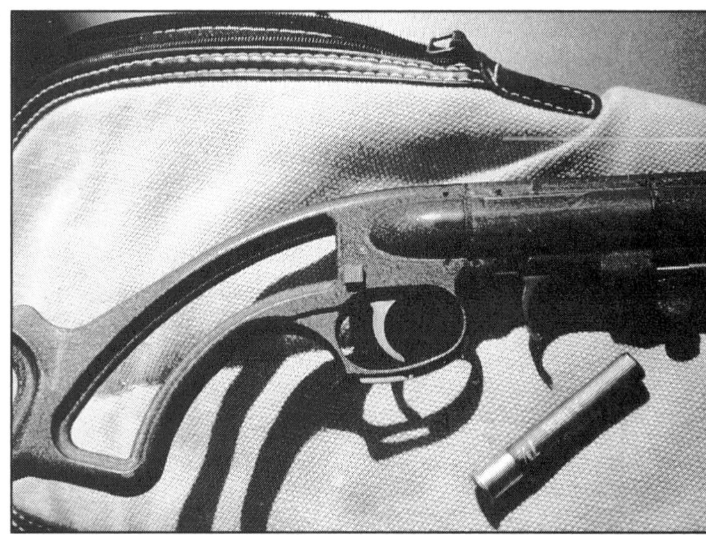

The author finds the spartan simplicity of the Bronco very sensible and usable.

The "new" factor was in operation with the Bronco. I had to pick it up twenty times a day and admire the clever arrangement of the lock, the neat lines of the brown metal stock, and the blue of the barrel. Every time I did, I checked to be sure it wasn't loaded, closed the action on the empty chamber, and threw it to my shoulder. Usually, I found my face in the right place on the skeletonized stock and my eye looking right down the barrel. The little gun might look strange compared to my Winchester, or any other "standard" shotgun, but it did not feel strange, it felt good.

Somebody may have told me the little 410 wasn't a thing of beauty, but if they did, I don't remember it. What I remember is walking bush roads early in grouse season and meeting bear hunters. They also had a season going and would grind up in big muddy pickups, with a strike dog fidgeting on the hood. Nearly all of them stopped me to ask, many in out-of-state accents, "What kind of gun is that?" I'd tell them. Then they'd want to see it, so I'd open the action, drop the shell into my hand and hand the Bronco over. When they gave it back, they'd almost always say "Who'd you say made it?" and "That'd make a great little gun to carry in the truck." I probably sold a few Broncos for Firearms International (FI) talking to those bear hunters.

It's a small fellow who really needs the Bronco's size.

(Above) It takes a big man, however, to understand a really neat little gun.

Small fingers find the Bronco's unequivocal handling requirements easy to meet.

Other people were intrigued with the gun, too. One of my brother's friends borrowed it several times. He brought it back once with what looked like white scratches on its brown stock and receiver. I was unhappy, until the scratches wore off and the crackle finish reappeared.

At the gravel pit, everyone wanted to try it. I usually used the 3-inch "magnum" 410 shells for hunting. With $2\frac{1}{2}$-inch Remington shells, the Bronco was mild enough for almost everyone to shoot. Over the years, several kids fired their first shots from a shotgun with the Bronco. My son, Isaac, is the latest one. He has fired several shotguns by now, but needs more practice. One of the first things we are going to do, before his first small game season, is shoot up all the shells we have for the Bronco. He may start hunting with something else, but the little 410 will be a big part of our preparations. My daughter and my younger son will probably shoot the Bronco first, too.

My wife, Kathleen, carried the Bronco when she used to go grouse hunting with me. I thought the two of them fit together so well that, in a fit of romantic weakness, I gave her the gun. Luckily, she has never been mad enough to sell it, or to divorce me and leave with it. Kathleen is small; other guns I had available then were too heavy and too long in the stock for her. She easily handled the Bronco.

Other novice hunters handled it well, too. I think the Bronco is actually a bit safer for a young hunter than the standard single barrel with an outside hammer. I have known beginners who had trouble opening, closing, cocking and uncocking a single shot with an outside hammer. The Bronco's side-swinging action locks securely on two steel pins. It unlocks easily with a hook or trigger-like cocking lever, and has no hammer to slip out from under a novice's thumb. The safety is a serrated block of steel above the trigger guard. Push it to the left and it is off, push it back to the right and it's on; there is no fumbling like there can be with an external hammer. (The cocking lever could lead to confusion between it and the trigger, but I haven't seen it happen much after the first five minutes of instruction.) There is a manual extractor worked by an extractor slide on the left side of the chamber. Beginners sometimes have to look for it. Once they discover it, it works fine.

Despite all this, there are a couple of drawbacks to the Bronco. One is that it is a single shot. As a bad shotgun shot, I have often had the need for a second, third or, if it was there and legal, fourth shot. Even with all the time spent handling the Bronco, I never learned to reload it quickly enough for a second shot on game. The other drawback is the gauge. While the 410 worked well on clay birds, it didn't hold up when the birds wore feathers.

There were a lot of days during bird seasons years ago when I wanted to carry the Bronco more than any other shotgun. There were also days when, I'm convinced, I'd have hit and killed birds with the 16-gauge that I missed clean with the 410. I didn't think the 410 was the problem at the time, but as I shifted from the Bronco to the larger Winchester, my bag slowly increased.

I still liked the Bronco and shot it when I was practicing or plinking. I also liked the Bronco 22, a single shot rifle similar to the 410, but finished in black. The one time I saw one I was so broke I couldn't have afforded the ammo, much less the gun. I thought the Bronco 22/410 was the best idea of all. I had my hands on one once, but it was going for $80, I was in college, and if I had the money, which is unlikely, I couldn't afford to spend it.

I was disappointed to see all Broncos go out of production by the late 1970s. I was interested when the Bauer company brought the over/under back as the Bauer Rabbit a year or two later. It got away from me, too, and disappeared soon afterward. Maybe I should have paid the $80 for the only 22/410 I saw—I've been waiting a long time to find a used one cheaper.

The Broncos were sold by FI, Garcia and Bauer. Either not many were sold or everyone who bought one likes it as much as I like mine. Either hypothesis could be true, but I lean toward the second one. It would explain, better than simple scarcity, why I have yet to see a used Bronco or Rabbit for sale. I've been looking for years, and I'm going to keep looking. While I look, I'll also be shooting the good gun I did manage to get, my (or my wife's) Bronco 410. ●

One Good Gun

by KENNETH BOLIN

My Browning Auto 22 Squirrel Gun

I WAS BITTEN by the gun bug at a very early age. And now, after more than forty years, I'm still severely infected. Consequently, many guns have come and gone from my possession during that time. One that came but didn't go is a beautiful little 22 rimfire, the Browning Auto 22.

Designed by John M. Browning and first produced by Fabrique Nationale in 1914, the rifle has always enjoyed immense popularity. In the United States, Remington Arms Co. exercised a license to produce essentially the same rifle from 1922 until 1950. It was known as the Model 24 at first and later redesigned as the Model 241.

In 1956, the gun was modernized and marketed by Browning. FN-made, the new model was first reviewed by the *American Rifleman* magazine in the September 1956 issue.

Mine came to me in 1960. I was a young, impoverished school teacher living in West Texas. I saw it in the window of a hardware store in Abilene and knew I had to have it. The price was $69.50, no mean sum for a young family man. I traded in the only other gun I owned at the time.

My Browning Auto 22 has spent more time in my hands than any gun I have owned. Mostly it has hunted squirrels. Also a few rabbits, paper targets, tin cans, frogs, snakes, pine cones, and anything that makes a 22 target.

Two foxes and four coyotes have fallen to it, taken incidentally to squirrel hunting. Credit fast-functioning repeating shots for a couple of those. But if you say the word "squirrel" as you walk past the gun case, I swear, you can see that Browning jump a little. It's ready to go.

With a Redfield 4x rimfire scope, the one once called the "Westerner," the gun weighs $5\frac{1}{2}$ pounds. You can grasp the rifle with scope all the way around at the receiver and it's especially delightful to carry.

I used the four-position rear sight set at 25 yards for about fifteen years. My eyes were good then, and I wasn't missing many squirrels. Later, I noticed that it was sometimes taking more than one shot per squirrel. So, I got the aforementioned scope, attached it to the grooved receiver, then realized I had a tack-driver.

It was an injustice to the squirrels. I am a record keeper. I have records on my squirrel shooting for the past forty years. The Browning has shot *at* 294 squirrels; 238 of them went in the bag. That's more than 80 percent. I am not currently holding that average, but I remember one year when it was forty-six for fifty-two.

After firing thousands of rounds of ammo, the little gun's accuracy fell off. Inspection revealed that the barrel-receiver connection had become slightly loose, and it doesn't take much play here to affect accuracy. The Browning is a takedown gun, and no tools are needed. Just push the thumb-latch in the front of the receiver, pull back on the cocking mechanism, and simultaneously turn the barrel right while holding the buttstock firmly. The barrel will disconnect and the trigger housing and firing mechanism will slip from the receiver. This takedown procedure also makes for easy cleaning. The barrel and the receiver mate with interrupted threads. An adjusting ring surrounds the barrel. Tightening the connection of barrel and receiver is easy by turning this adjustment ring ever so slightly.

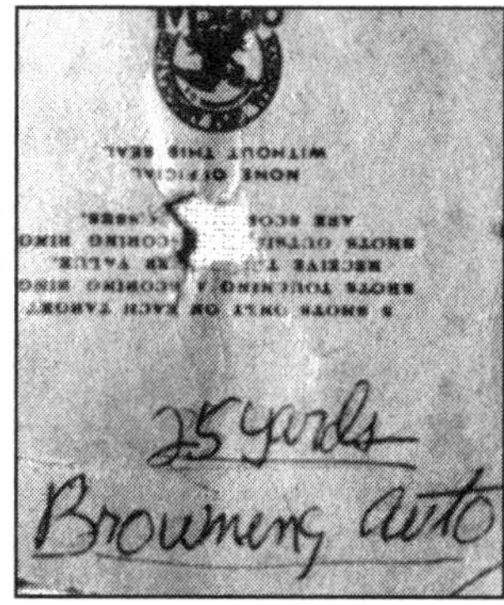

(Above) Bolin's 22 still punches 25-yard one-holers.

(Right) Bolin and Browning in the much-preferred habitat—the squirrel woods.

The reason my gun shoots so well, I am convinced, is the fact that I tightened that adjustment ring too tight. I had to force the barrel-receiver back together, slightly cracking the stock ahead of the grip. I glued it and it's hardly noticeable. Take my advice and *don't* do that. But, is it tight! And does it shoot! A longtime gunsmith friend of mine, who once accurized old Remington M241s, says he's never seen a gun of this type shoot like mine does. I'll sit at his bench and plop round after round into $\frac{1}{2}$-inch or less at 25 yards.

My Browning has a friendly, easy trigger which is conducive to good shooting. It has a slight bit of creep, but is soft and easy to control.

I've owned a lot of 22 rimfires in my time. I've owned super-accurate bolt actions, pumps, target rifles, but how can you beat this one? It has a French walnut stock, fine checkering, engraved receiver, and excellent bluing that's wearing well after thiry-five years of honest use. It's small enough for a youngster, yet big enough for an adult to hold on to, accurate as almost any 22, and capable of making head shots on squirrels to 50 yards or more. I once made seven head shots in one morning with that gun. No telling how many times I could see only a squirrel's eye with about $\frac{1}{4}$-inch of head above that eye as it lay flattened on the back side of a limb, but it was enough to shoot at.

There are good guns and there are *really* good guns. I vote my Browning Auto 22 for the latter. It is easy to carry, easy to hit with, and enjoyable to look at. Mine will never be for sale—not in this lifetime. ●

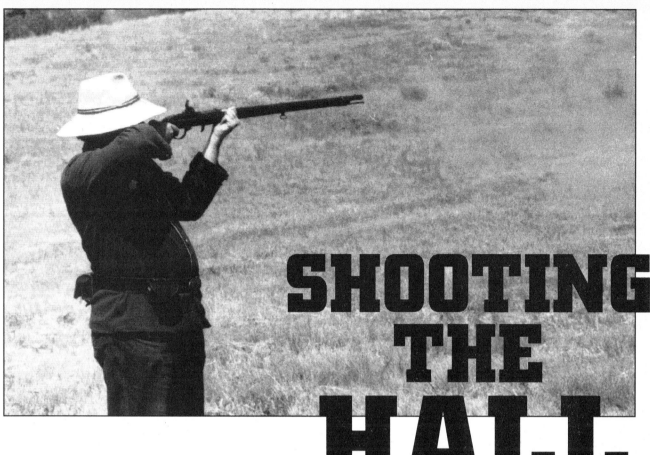

SHOOTING THE HALL BREECHLOADER

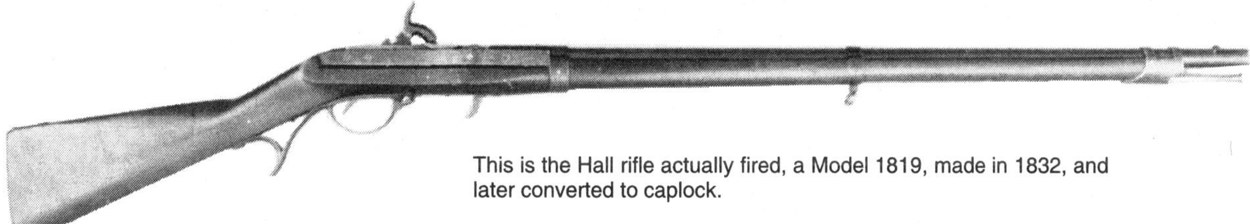

This is the Hall rifle actually fired, a Model 1819, made in 1832, and later converted to caplock.

by DENNIS BRUNS

THE BASIC DESIGN for the Hall breechloader was patented by New Englander John Hancock Hall in 1811. The Hall was not the first breech-loading mechanism to be tried, but it was the first to be adopted by a military service, manufactured, issued and used in quantity. It is probably also the only breechloader which, having been produced and used in quantity, was replaced after several years of successful service by a muzzleloader.

The Hall breechloader was still just a little bit ahead of its time. In fact, years later during the Civil War, the Confederate government had a number of Hall rifles converted to muzzleloaders.

John Hall spent most of his life trying to produce his invention. From 1812 to 1817, he manufactured Hall breechloaders in his own shop. Unfortunately, his breech-loading mechanism was difficult to build with the limited equipment then available to a small shop.

This initial venture was a failure which left Hall so deeply in debt that he spent the next twenty years paying off his losses. The experience convinced Hall that successful production of his breech-loading mechanism depended on developing machinery and techniques of mass production to reduce the cost per rifle to a level comparable to competing muzzleloaders.

The most likely source of support for his efforts was the United States government. In 1817, Hall succeeded in interesting the U.S. Army in his breech-loading rifle, and in that year

Hall rifle with action open. Note the gas escape gap below the iron receiver bands.

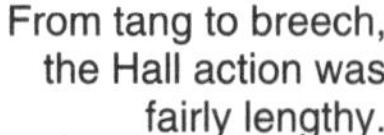

From tang to breech, the Hall action was fairly lengthy.

he delivered 100 of them for testing. Results of the testing were favorable, and in 1819 Hall was given a contract for 1000 additional rifles. These were to be produced in the government arsenal at Harper's Ferry under Hall's supervision. The Hall was to be identified as the U.S. Rifle, Model 1819.

John Hall concentrated on the development of machinery and manufacturing techniques needed to mass-produce his breechloader with interchangeable parts. In many respects, Hall functioned much like a modern defense contractor, doing research and development for the military using government facilities. He was employed as much for his work in developing the techniques and machinery of mass production as for the breech-loading arms he produced.

The first Hall rifles were completed at Harper's Ferry in 1823, and by 1841, some 19,682 rifles and 2020 carbines had been produced. These guns were all made with flintlock ignition, but many were later converted to percussion during the 1840s. In 1841 and 1842, an additional 3190 rifles and 1001 carbines were produced with percussion ignition. Arms manufacturer Simeon North made an additional 30,364 Hall rifles and carbines under government contract between 1830 and 1852.

The Hall breech-loading mechanism was a reasonably good design in 1811, but it had several flaws. The worst was that it allowed gas to escape upon firing.

Hall guns were made with a one-piece wood stock. The main part of the action consists of two iron bands screwed to each side of the back of the barrel in front and bolted together, and to the stock at the back. The breechblock (or chamber) is held in place by two lugs (Hall called them chocks) set into the bands on each side just back of the barrel, which are engaged by projections on each side of the front of the breechblock. These chocks are removable and control the size of the gap between chamber and barrel. The chamber does not make a tight seal against the barrel, and considerable gas escapes upon firing. The stock is protected from the escaping powder gas by a $^1/_{16}$-inch thick iron plate inletted into the stock under the gap. In addition, a space is left between the stock and the iron receiver bands to allow escaping powder gas to vent without putting pressure on the stock.

In service, the Hall breechloaders appear to have been accepted favorably at first, but then general opinion went against them. It was a more complicated mechanism than most people of the 1820s and 1840s were used to. Most problems were caused by careless handling, storage and maintenance. The Hall also seems to have developed a reputation for blowing apart.

In spite of Hall's efforts at standardization, there were slight variations between chambers. They were not numbered or otherwise identified with the rifle and could, therefore, be mixed up in cleaning. When a breechblock was put back into a rifle other than the one it was fitted to, problems developed. In some cases, the action would stick closed after firing. Worse yet were those which were too loose and allowed excessive amounts of powder gas to escape on firing. We still have the same basic problem today. You do not casually swap bolts between different rifles without eventually having something go wrong. We know that now (more or less), but back in the early 1800s when breechloaders with interchangeable parts were a new development, they often didn't.

It also appears that under the stress of repeated firing, the chocks could compress or the bands holding them stretch, gradually increasing headspace. Whatever the cause, I have seen Hall rifles and carbines with gaps between chamber and barrel in excess of 1/8-inch. When the gap becomes too large, there is great danger of blowing the stock apart upon firing due to the high pressure of escaping gas.

Hall was aware of this problem and designed his action to allow for it. This was the purpose of the removable chocks. In the book of instructions for use of his rifle, published in 1816, Hall advised that the chocks could be renewed at pleasure, whenever the joint may grow too open. Thus the Hall action was designed so that with proper and careful maintenance, headspace could be kept to a safe minimum.

I once walked into a blackpowder shoot just as a Hall rifle blew apart. The rifle had excessive gap between barrel and chamber, and a previous owner had blown apart the stock. This person evidently glued the stock back together with epoxy then sold the rifle. In the process of gluing the stock, the ventilation slits between the iron straps and the stock were filled with epoxy. When the new owner fired the rifle, the pressure of powder gas, unable to escape easily through the slits, blew the stock apart again. The rifle was repaired by a local gunsmith who did a much better job, this time keeping the slits open. I was also able to suggest ways of closing up the excess headspace. The owner later fired the rifle without difficulty, but he never really trusted it. He kept remembering it blowing apart in his hands and eventually quit firing it.

In much the same way, the reputation of the Hall breechloader for blowing up probably contributed to its loss of popularity. Soldiers might understandably be nervous about a rifle they had been told could literally blow apart in their hands. This problem could have been eliminated by redesigning the action so that it used a metal receiver, but in his later years, John Hall seems to have been strongly opposed to any changes in his design. In the end, the Hall breechloaders were replaced by muzzleloaders. Simeon North patented a Hall-type carbine with a metal receiver in 1847, but by that time the Hall design had fallen from favor with the military and few were built. The Burnside carbine, patented in 1856, is essentially a much improved Hall action with an iron receiver.

From 1817, when the first 100 Hall rifles were issued for trial on the Western frontier, Hall's breechloaders saw almost fifty years of service. They saw action in Florida during the Seminole Indian war and were carried on the Western plains in the 1830s and 1840s. By the time of the Mexican War, the Hall had been replaced by newer muzzleloaders. However, due to a shortage of the new arms, some soldiers were equipped with Hall rifles and carbines.

The Hall was last used during the Civil War. Available accounts indicate that, in both of these wars, the volunteers equipped with the breechloaders were glad to have them and preferred them to muzzleloaders. Apparently, when someone was shooting back at you, the higher rate of fire of the breechloader was more important than any problems of gas leakage.

One of the best accounts involving the use of the Hall rifle in action during the Mexican War is contained in the memoirs of Samuel E. Chamberlain. He was a private in the First Regiment of U.S. Dragoons, fighting in the battle of Buena Vista and in a number of skirmishes with Mexican guerrillas.

The First Dragoons at that time were armed with Hall carbines. Standard practice then for the cavalry appears to have been to use sabers as the primary weapon when charging the enemy and to use the carbines as secondary weapons for skirmishing or for holding a position.

Sam Chamberlain never made any particular mention of the advantages or disadvantages of the Hall carbines. He seemed to have been more impressed with, and made better use of, a Colt revolver which he was issued shortly after the battle of Buena Vista. On two occasions, while closely chased on horseback by Mexican guerrillas, Sam was able to reload his Hall carbine and use it to hold back his pursuers; a feat which would have been more difficult with a muzzleloader.

On another occasion, Sam was part of a small patrol that had to fort up behind their dead horses and fight a much larger group of Mexican guerrillas. They augmented their Hall carbines with captured Mexican muzzle-loading carbines and ammunition, so that with four or five guns per man, they were able to keep up a heavy volume of fire. Even the breech-loading Halls couldn't be loaded and fired fast enough on this occasion.

In describing the battle of Buena Vista, Sam mentioned the use of a "Hall's long range rifle" to shoot down a Mexican officer who was examining the American lines from about four hundred yards away. Presumably this was either the standard Hall rifle (which would have been long ranged compared to the smoothbore carbine) or possibly a Hall rifle fitted with some sort of elevating rear sight. This was a good shot, and if the rifle was fitted with the standard sights regulated for 100 yards, it was a very good example of holding high to hit a distant target.

When Sam separated from the Dragoons (he was listed as a deserter), he took with him this, or a similar, Hall rifle. He joined a band of scalp hunters headed by John Glanton. Again the Hall rifle and Colt revolver appeared to have served him well. Sam described shooting an Apache scout at 400 yards, and with his group he fought through the surrounding war party. Sam was one of twenty-four men who made it. Another fourteen of his party were killed, and four of the survivors were seriously wounded. At a time when muzzleloaders were the standard armament, the combination of a Colt revolver and a Hall breechloader appear to have given Sam a significant advantage.

The Hall breechloaders do not seem to have been popular with civilians. As a new military arm manufactured at a government arsenal, the Hall would not have been readily available to civilians. By the late 1830s, when Hall breechloaders might have become available for civilian purchase, its bad reputation appears to have been established. The gun was carried West by civilians but, apparently, was not very highly regarded. I have seen several references dating from the late 1840s through the early 1860s which refer somewhat disparagingly to "old army breechloaders."

The Hall rifle I have shot is a standard Model 1819 rifle as made in 1832. It has been converted to percussion. The rifle weighs about 10½ pounds, has a 23¾-inch barrel, and is 52½ inches long overall. The barrel has sixteen lands and grooves of approximately equal width. Land diameter is .516-inch with no detectable variation. Groove diameter is .538-inch near the muzzle and .540-inch at the breech. There is a slight choke about 4 inches below the muzzle, and the grooves are slightly deeper for the last 8 inches at the breech. Most of the .002-inch enlargement of groove diameter occurs in the last 8 inches at the breech. The barrel is reamed to .540-inch for the last 1.3 inches at the muzzle, apparently to aid in loading from the muzzle.

The rate of twist is surprisingly slow at 1:130 inches. This is one feature of the Hall breechloaders that has always puzzled me. Unlike a muzzleloader, where the presence of rifling makes loading more difficult and a slow twist is easier to load than a fast twist, there was no penalty for the presence of rifling in the Hall breechloader. Why then, were the carbines made as smoothbores and the rifles with a rate of twist so slow as to be nearly straight?

The breechblock has a two-diameter chamber. With the rust cleaned out, the chamber measures .542-inch at the mouth. The chamber is 2.4 inches deep and is reduced in diameter about halfway down to provide a shoulder which prevents the ball from being seated too deep. The chamber holds 85 grains of FFg powder when filled to the point where a ball can just be seated. The top front of the breechblock is stamped J.H. HALL, H. FERRY, U.S., 1832 in four lines. This is the only identification on the rifle.

This particular Hall rifle started with a gap between chamber and barrel of about .016-inch, I removed the chocks, and by striking about sixty careful, moderate blows along the back edge of each with a hammer, I was able to peen metal out on the back edges of the chocks and reduce the gap to .004-inch. I also checked to make sure that the flanges on the breechblock bore equally on both chocks. Hall intended that headspace be controlled by using the chocks in some such manner as indicated in his instructions.

The metal at the front of the chocks should not be disturbed as this could change the slight curvature there. The front of the chamber moves up and down in an arc and the back sides of the flanges and the front of the chocks are curved slightly to allow for this arc. A gap of .003- to .005-inch between the chamber and barrel seems necessary as the buildup of powder fouling will cause fouling. Trigger pull is adjustable by a small screw running through the bottom of the sear which controls depth of sear engagement with the full-cock notch. I set the pull of the Hall I shot to about 2½ pounds.

Loading the Hall is simple. Pull the catch to the rear and push up, tilting the front of the chamber up for loading. Then pour in the powder charge, press a ball in on top, push the chamber back down, cap and fire.

The stock is somewhat clumsy to look at, but it holds well for offhand shooting. The long projection in back of the trigger guard acts much like the finger lever of a scheutzen rifle and helps position the hand. The front sight is offset to the left side of the barrel and angles out to the left, then up. In addition, it is low, rather wide, and rounded on top. I had difficulty in identifying the top center of the sight for precision shooting. The rear sight is also low and offset to the

With left hand out ahead of the rear band, the author sets for the shot.

the breechblock to stick to the barrel if the gap is less. Where a Hall has extreme headspace, new chocks can be made and fitted to close up the gap.

When closed, the catch allows the front of the chamber to shift up and down about .05-inch. There is about the same amount of vertical play at the back of the chamber where it is held in by a loosely fitted screw running through the iron straps. There is also noticeable lateral play between chamber and action. This appears to be intentional, to allow for gas escape and the buildup of powder

left to clear the flintlock pan and frizzen (now removed).

The rifle is sighted to hit point of aim at 100 yards. I found it difficult to hit anything beyond 150 yards with these low sights. I think that if I were living back then and had this rifle, I would cut 4 to 8 inches off the barrel and fit a high, dovetailed blade front sight and some sort of elevating rear sight. This would have made a much handier rifle with more versatile sights than the military issue.

When shooting the Hall, I always hold it with my left hand forward of the lower barrel band. This keeps my hand and wrist away from gas escape vents and chamber latch where hot powder gases are escaping. In the unlikely event the stock blows apart, the splitting of the wood will be stopped by the lower barrel band, thus protecting my hand.

The original load for the Hall rifle is reported to have been 100 grains of powder with a .525-inch round ball.

Since my rifle will only hold about 85 grains of powder in the chamber, I presume 10-15 grains of the original powder charge were used for priming the flintlock. In my first shooting sessions, I used a .525-inch diameter round ball as recommended by several sources. I fired a few shots with 75-80 grains of FFg powder, but then dropped to 55 grains of FFg to reduce the possibility of wear or damage to the old rifle. Accuracy was something less than wonderous—groups of 4 to 6 inches at 50 yards and a foot at 100 yards when fired with a clean barrel.

I took the rifle out to a local blackpowder shoot which consisted of a series of informal primitive matches. Using the .525-inch ball, it wasn't capable of the precision needed to compete with a well-handled muzzleloader. I did notice that the gun seemed to shoot more accurately when I fired without wiping the barrel. Shooting this way, I managed finally to win one elimination match by hitting an 8-inch gong at about 75 yards offhand. In reality, it was less a case of my winning the match than of the other shooters losing it, as the Hall scattered its shots all over the target rather than consistently centering them.

When a round-ball rifle shoots better with the barrel fouled, this is often an indication that the ball is too small. After this first match, I slugged the barrel and discovered it might more correctly be called a 54-caliber than a 52 as usually described. I tried it with a .535-inch round ball, which improved accuracy. I cleaned a spotty coating of rust out of the mouth of the chamber and found I could use a .542-inch ball, provided I wiped out the mouth of the chamber every shot and used a short starter to drive the ball in. This produced the best accuracy yet—groups of 2 to 3 inches at 50 yards and 6 to 8 inches at 100 yards. Accuracy with the .542-inch ball dropped off if I didn't clean the barrel every shot. Since this size ball was hard to load anyway, I finally settled on the .535-inch ball for most shooting. For events where greater accuracy was needed, I used the larger ball and wiped out the barrel and chamber after every shot.

He gets two clouds of smoke, one forward of the rifle from the muzzle and the second above the rifle from leakage at the breech.

There are two other means of controlling fouling buildup in a Hall rifle. Basically, it can be treated like a one-chamber revolver. Grease can be put on top of the ball after it's loaded into the chamber or a grease wad can be loaded between powder and ball. Either method takes about as long as wiping out the barrel, but might be more useful for hunting.

I then took the Hall to another blackpowder shoot. The first event was a three-man rapid-fire team event, and I was partnered with a couple of beginners. We were supposed to cut three 1- by 2-inch stakes driven into the ground about 40 yards in front of us. I remember feeling a bit guilty, thinking about the tremendous advantage I had over the other competitors with their muzzle-loading replica Hawkens. At the same time, they couldn't complain that my breech-loading rifle wasn't authentic because the Hall rifle actually predated the Hawken.

As it turned out, I had nothing to feel guilty about. I found I could fire four to six carefully aimed shots a minute, about twice the rate of fire I get with a Minie rifle, and about four times as fast as the competing shooters with their muzzle-loading patched round-ball rifles. Unfortunately, what I gained in rate of fire I more than lost in accuracy. Any shot that misses the target might as well not have been fired, and I was missing those little stakes most of the time.

After the first couple of minutes, I was having trouble even seeing the stakes through the blur of heat rising from the barrel. I could still have hit a man-sized target easily at 50 yards and most of the time at 100 yards, but with the barrel hot and badly fouled, the Hall just couldn't group on those little 2-inch wide stakes. I didn't even make a good start at cutting them.

Finally, I tried wiping the barrel out, but made the mistake of doing it with the breechblock closed and got the cleaning jag stuck in the gap between chamber and barrel. I had to unscrew the rod from the stuck cleaning jag, remove the chamber from the rifle, and then screw the rod back onto the jag to pull it out—and none of this helped.

Later in the match, we had to shoot a playing card in half edgewise at 15 yards. I nicked the card but didn't cut it on my first shot. As I remember, the winner of this event cut three straight with his replica Hawken.

The final event was an elimination on metal gongs starting at 25 yards and ending up at 100 yards. By then, the wind was blowing 20 to 30 miles per hour. I won that event on the fifth shot, holding on the upwind side of an 8-inch gong at 100 yards. The ball drifted downwind and just hit the other edge of the gong. My final opponent failed to hold enough into the wind and just missed on the downwind side. If he had estimated the wind drift a little better, he would probably eventually have won the match as his replica Hawken seemed to be holding a closer group than my Hall rifle.

The Hall has one other minor, but possibly useful advantage. You can remove the breechblock/chamber and use it as a pocket pistol. This is something you can't do with a muzzle-loading rifle. Getting a Hawken rifle inconspicuously into your coat pocket takes some doing. Samuel Chamberlain mentions using the chamber of his Hall carbine as a pistol in his memoirs. Naturally I had to try it.

Being cautious, I started with a 10-grain powder charge and worked up. I found it most convenient to hold the chamber between thumb and forefinger with my last three fingers on the trigger. The chamber became unpleasant to fire with more than 30 grains of powder. Firing with a full powder charge would probably cause injury to the hand unless heavy gloves were worn. Even then, I doubt most people could manage to hold on.

Accuracy was best with a 20-grain powder charge which allowed the ball to seat deeply enough that the front of the chamber served as a barrel. Even then, accuracy was poor. I would rate the chamber as effective out to 15 feet when fired as a pistol. Beyond that distance, any hits would be accidental.

I did try the chamber as a pistol in one of the blackpowder matches I attended. I can honestly state that I shot as well with it as three-quarters of the people in the match did with their muzzle-loading pistols or revolvers. That is, I missed and so did they. On the other hand, I didn't have to haul an extra gun around and clean it afterward to blow the match. I just had to take the chamber out of my rifle.

Taken overall, I found the Hall rifle to be a sound and serviceable, if somewhat complicated rifle. It was slightly less accurate than a good muzzle-loading rifle, but it shot well enough by the military standards of the time. The Hall breechloaders were probably capable of twice the rate of fire of smooth bore muskets with much better accuracy, and two to four times the rate of fire of muzzle-loading round-ball rifles with only slightly inferior accuracy. The Hall breechloader does require more careful cleaning and maintenance.

Because breech-loading rifles eventually replaced the old muzzleloaders, there is a tendency to assume that any breech-loading rifle is automatically more accurate than any muzzleloader. We seem to have forgotten that the early breechloaders were favored primarily for their rate of fire. Good accuracy was desirable but strictly secondary. When compared to the muzzleloading rifles of their day, the early breechloaders were more like a submachine gun as compared to the bolt-action sporting rifles of today. They were also heavier, more complicated, and more likely to get out of order.

(Above) Fired thus, the Hall breechblock will deliver the 54-caliber ball accurately enough well beyond knife range.

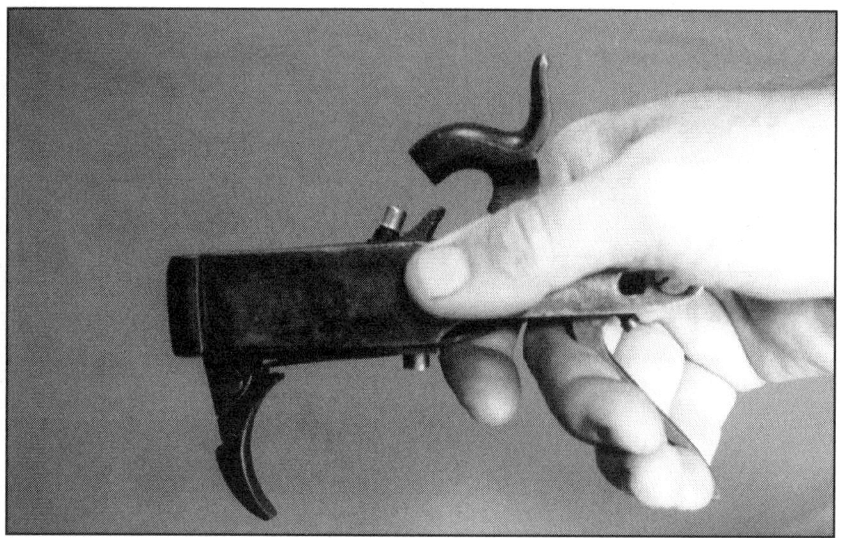

(Below) If you're going to shoot the Hall breechlock as a pistol, you hold it like this and shoot light charges.

The Hall rifle was also slightly more expensive than comparable muzzleloaders of its day. In 1829, the North-Hall rifle was contracted at a price of $17.50 each. At the same time, Simeon North was building the Model 1817 Common rifles at $14 each. A good serviceable civilian muzzle-loading rifle could be bought for as little as $8 or $9. The more expensive civilian rifles sold for up to $35. If this seems cheap, remember that an ounce of gold was worth about $16 at that time. Therefore, the North-Hall rifles actually cost about 1.1 ounces of gold or $400-$450 in modern currency. ●

References

Chamberlain, Samuel E. *My Confessions.* New York: Harper & Brothers, 1956.

Huntington, R.T. *Halls Breechloaders.* York, PA.: George Shumway, Publisher, 1972.

ART OF THE ENGRAVER

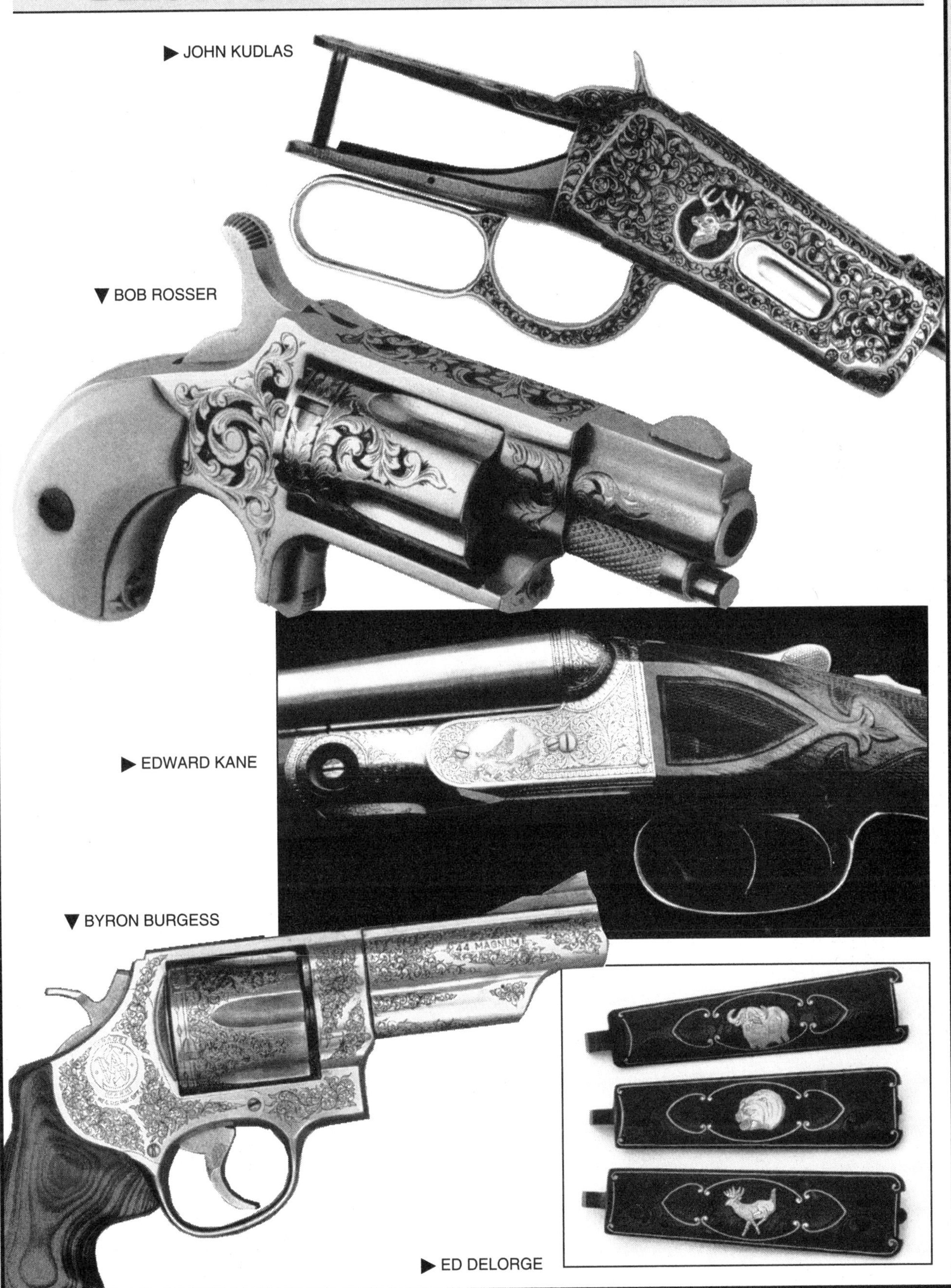

▶ JOHN KUDLAS

▼ BOB ROSSER

▶ EDWARD KANE

▼ BYRON BURGESS

▶ ED DELORGE

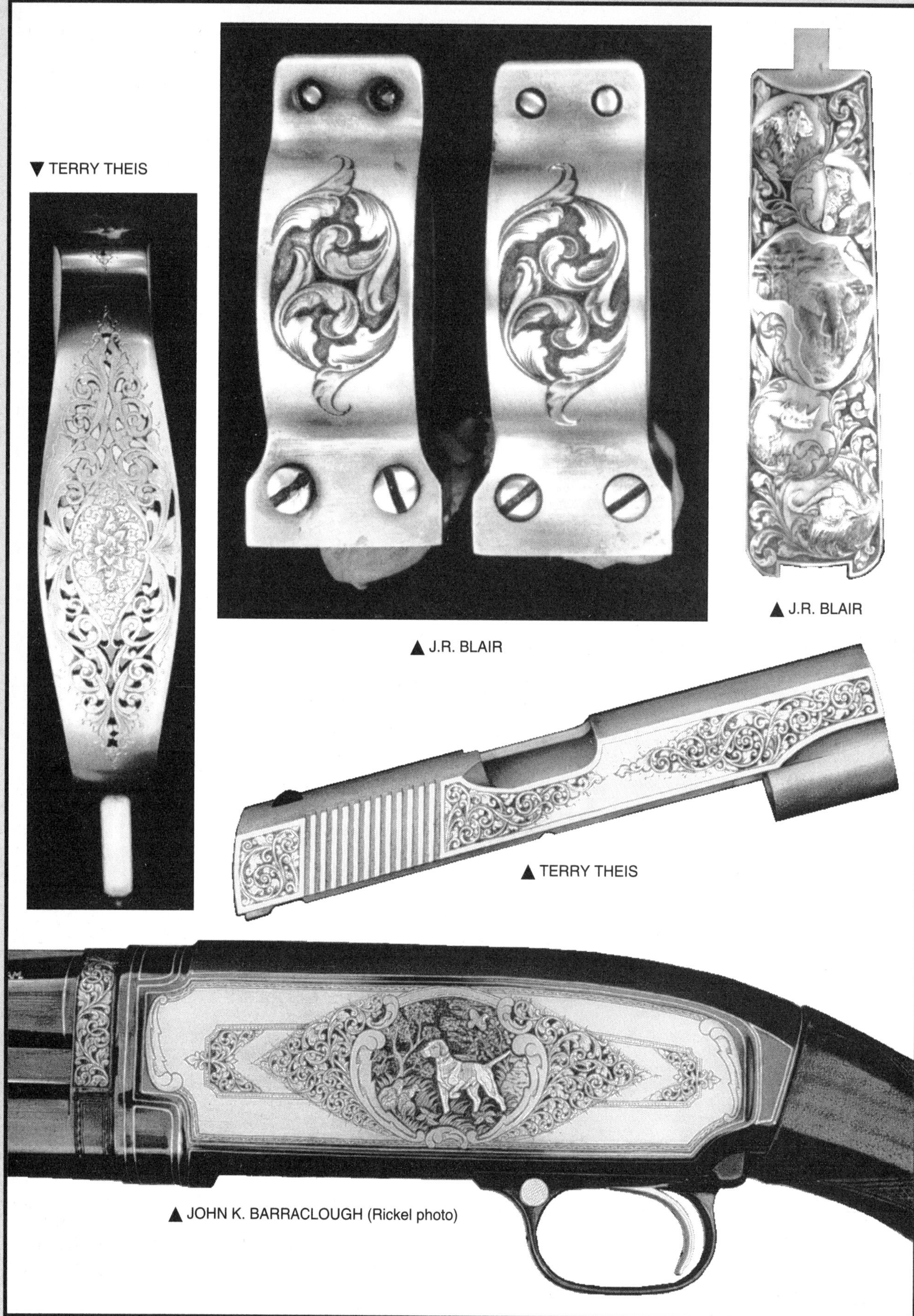

▼ TERRY THEIS

▲ J.R. BLAIR

▲ J.R. BLAIR

▲ TERRY THEIS

▲ JOHN K. BARRACLOUGH (Rickel photo)

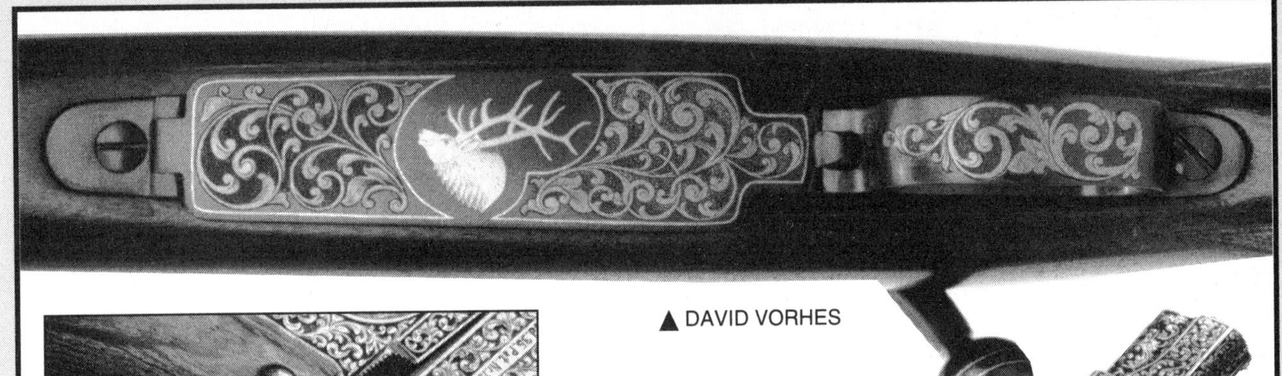

▲ DAVID VORHES

◀▼ BOB ROSSER

▼ SCOTT PILKINGTON

▶ GERALD DESQUESNES

▼ EDWARD KANE

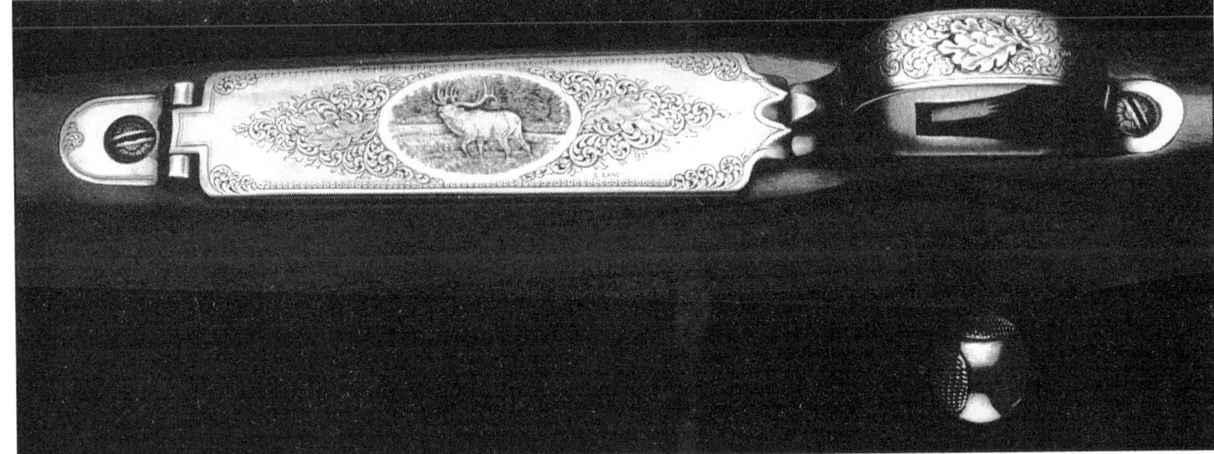

by LARRY S. STERETT

HANDLOADING UPDATE

HANDLOADERS ARE always looking for new equipment and accessories that will allow them to load more accurate cartridges faster, thus providing more time for shooting, and every year the manufacturers attempt to oblige. There is more comprehensive loading data available now than ever, and more components, and even more equipment. Here we are with the following, covering some of what is new:

A-Square, the ammunition and big-bore rifle firm, has a new handloading manual available. Titled *Any Shot You Want*, the new manual covers eighty-seven different rifle cartridges from the 22 Hornet up, and includes data on such oddballs as the 400 Pondoro, 416 Gerlach, 577 Tyrannosaur and 600 Nitro Express. A chapter is devoted to each cartridge, and a great deal of material, besides loading data, is provided.

Alliant Techsystems now manufactures what used to be Hercules Smokeless Powder, and their new *Reloader's Guide* is available. Loading data included in the *Guide* covers shotshells from the 10-gauge to the 410-bore, rifle cartridges from the 17 Remington to the 458 Winchester Magnum, and handgun cartridges from the 25 ACP to the 45 Winchester Magnum.

Shotgunners doing a lot of handloading for hunting purposes with any kind of shot should consider **Ballistic Products, Inc.** This Minnesota firm not only has popular-brand handloading equipment, ammunition and components, but more shotshell loading data than anyone. Currently, BPI has nearly two dozen different manuals for just about all gauges, none costing over $7 (plus shipping), and some fourteen different "special load information brochures" costing just under half a buck. The subjects range from loading specific brand hulls such as the Activ, Victory or AA, to wads, loading steel shot, slugs, roll crimping, turkey loads, and even hot- and cold-weather hunting loads.

BPI has all sorts of accessories to make handloading of shotshells easier. A couple of the handier ones are the Hull Skiver and the Hull Shape-Up tools. The former is intended to make new plastic shells easier to fold or roll crimp, while the latter is used to shape the case mouth of previously fired hulls for easier wad insertion. Years ago, Herter's offered a heated tool that would perfectly shape the mouths of wax-treated paper shotshells, but the heat was a bit much for plastic.

Barnes Bullets has a new computer software program—"Barnes Ballistics 2." This Windows-based program will run on any PC 486 with 8 Mb of RAM. One enters the specifics for a particular gun and load, and the data appears, along with a trajectory table and a graph of the table. An on-line help directory is available. The user can calculate trajectory, velocity, wind deflection and striking velocity for any load desired, and can determine what effect altitude, temperature, barrel length, humidity and other factors have on bullet flight.

Shooters turning out handloads in bulk using cast bullets might find the products from **Ben's Machines** handy. Ben's currently has two lubers including an air-powered model; an automatic feeder; a heater for a lubricator/sizer; an air-powered brass resizer that will handle 380, 9mm, 10mm or 45 ACP brass at a rate of more than 2000 cases per hour; and two case sorters. The machines are designed for use with handgun brass only, and they could be great timesavers for police departments and gun clubs.

At the 1996 SHOT Show, there were nearly a dozen different rifles being shown chambered for the 50 BMG cartridge. These included single shot bolt-action models, five-shot bolt-action repeaters, and ten-shot autoloaders. There was even a new model chambered for a wildcat consisting of a 20mm case necked down to handle 50 BMG bullets. These rifles are, for the most part, used in 1000-yard matches. Since not every sporting-goods store or gunshop carries 50 BMG cartridges, handloading is a must. Components are becoming more readily available, and loading data is also available from several sources. That leaves only the equipment—presses and dies.

RCBS produces dies for the 50 BMG cartridge with either $1\frac{1}{2}$- or $1\frac{3}{8}$-inch thread diameter, and the dies will fit the RCBS Big Max, Ammomaster, A-2 and Rock Crusher presses; the Hollywood; and three Corbin presses (CHP-1, CSP-2 and CSP-2H). Hornady has also introduced a two-die set to handle the 50 BMG cartridge, plus a file-type trim die and a neck-sizing die.

Corbin can also produce dies to swage 50 BMG bullets, such as the 50 BMG ULD (Ultra Low Drag) design. Currently, the firm manufactures a wide range of swaging dies and presses for swaging and handloading. The CSP-2H and CHP-1 presses are capable of loading up to 4-bore,

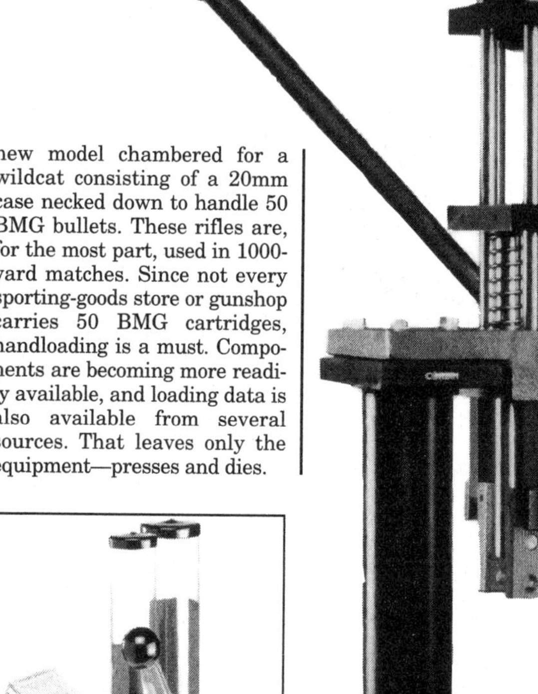

The Corbin CSP-2 MegaMite press can do the 50 BMG, operated from either side.

Hornady's new Apex 3.1 progressive shotshell reloader, in 12 and 20 gauges, offers a unique shellplate.

Lyman Products' LE-500 electronic scale has a capacity of 65 grains, working accuracy to ±0.1-grain.

and will easily swage 12-gauge slugs.

Dillon Precision Products—the Blue Press people—now offer a new progressive five-station shotshell reloader. At one station, the wad is seated, followed by the shot at the same station, but further along on the stroke. Die heads are interchangeable, and the first presses are in 12-gauge, with the 410 and 20-gauge following in that order. Having many of the features of the Dillon presses for reloading metallic cartridges, the new Blue Press should become a popular item. Its price will be in the $500 range.

Other new Dillon products include two- and three-die sets for rifle cartridges ranging from the 223 to the 30-06, with some neck-sizing and taper-crimp dies available. Another item handloaders can use is a pistol case gauge. Dillon has ten new stainless steel gauges for cartridges ranging from the 380 ACP to the 45 Colt. Manufactured to SAAMI specs, the gages are accurate to ±0.001-inch and allow checking of all critical dimensions, including maximum cartridge length and base diameter.

The **Hodgdon Powder Company** celebrated its 50th anniversary in 1996 with a new *Basic Reloaders Manual*, containing up-to-date data on the most popular handgun, shotgun and rifles calibers, including the Big Fifty cartridge. For additional information, the *26th Data Manual* is still available.

It was the Apex 3.0, but now there's a new Apex 3.1 progressive shotshell reloader from **Hornady Manufacturing**. Available in 12 and 20 gauges, the 3.1 features a unique shellplate which requires no shell retainer ring. Instead, the shellplate opens and closes automatically, securing each shotshell throughout the cycle, but still permitting removal or replacement without binding. The shellplate is spring-loaded and opens automatically at the deprime station to allow inserting a shell, and again after the finish crimp station to release the loaded round. Other 3.1 features include auto advance, auto primer feed with shell detect, auto powder and shot drop with shell detects, two-stage crimp, and swing-out hopper castings.

Mountain State's Tru-Charger is an adjustable measure for loading blackpowder cartridges—just three major parts.

The ProJector progressive press for loading metallics is now available as a +P Package with automatic powder drop, deluxe powder measure and shellplate (no dies). The +P Package comes with any one of seven different shellplates, and dies can be purchased separately for more than 170 different calibers. The 00-7 Loader is now packed with an automatic primer feed, but dies and shellholder must be purchased separately. Hornady also has a couple of new two-die sets available, one for the 7mm STW cartridge and one for the 50 BMG cartridge, plus a trim die and a neck-size die for the latter.

Lyman Products has several new things for handloaders, including a couple of new electronic reloading scales, the LE-300 and the LE-500. These two scales have weight capacities of 330 and 650 grains, and are accurate to .1-grain. Powered by four AAA cells, they feature auto-touch calibration and come complete with a calibration weight and a storage/carrying case. Also new from Lyman are moulds for a 20-gauge sabot slug and a 40-caliber 385-grain pointed bullet, in addition to the actual bullets and slugs. The 4th edition of the Lyman *Shotshell Reloading Handbook* is now out, and it covers the subject thoroughly with chapters on components, shotshell ballistics, and how to reload. There's plenty of data on handloading shotshells from the 10-gauge to the 410-bore with lead or steel shot.

The **Magma Engineering Co.** is known for its bullet casting equipment, including the Bullet Master and Master Caster, but it also manufactures a Lube Master and accessories for the Star Lubrisizer. Now there is also a new Case Master Case Sizer which will resize over 5000 cases per hour, making it ideal for clubs or shooters who go through lots of ammunition. The sizer comes with one die of choice—380 ACP, 9mm, 10mm, 9x21mm, 40 S&W or 45 ACP—but extra dies can be ordered, and other calibers may be available later.

Handloaders or clubs considering getting into the the business in a big way might want to consider **Mast Technology, Inc.** This firm, founded by Jim Bell—the founder and CEO of Brass Extrusion Labs, Ltd., prior to its purchase by PMC—not only produces brass cases for some rifle manufacturers, but also produces some ammunition. Mast has machinery available for producing ammunition in sizes from 22-caliber to 20mm. The machines range from "as is" to fully reconditioned and tooled, individual pieces or full production lines. Mast has also qualified as a supplier of specialized ammunition to the U.S. government.

Shotshell handloaders owning **MEC** equipment should stop by their local dealers and pick up one of the new MEC Powder Bushing Charts. The latest edition lists what various MEC bushings will throw of currently available Accurate, Alliant, Hodgdon, IMR, VihtaVuori and Winchester powders. Information is provided on charge bars and what bushings will fit. There's even a chilled-shot conversion table.

Midway, one of the Midwest's largest sources of handloading supplies, has several items carrying their own name, including a heavy shop apron made of cotton duck, reloaders' labels, empty shotshell and bullet boxes, and hardwood loading trays in a dozen sizes that will hold fifty cases from 25 ACP to 460 Weatherby Magnum. Midway also has a *Shooter's Notebook* that has space for recording plenty of handloading data.

Mountain State Muzzleloading Supplies celebrated its silver anniversary in 1996 with the introduction of several new items, including an adjustable powder measure intended for use by handloaders of blackpowder cartridges. This new measure, the Tru-

The RCBS priming strip loader permits handloaders to load loose primers into the system.

The RCBS APS bench-type tool—handle angle is adjustable.

The RCBS APS press-type priming system mounted and ready to prime—there's a special priming punch.

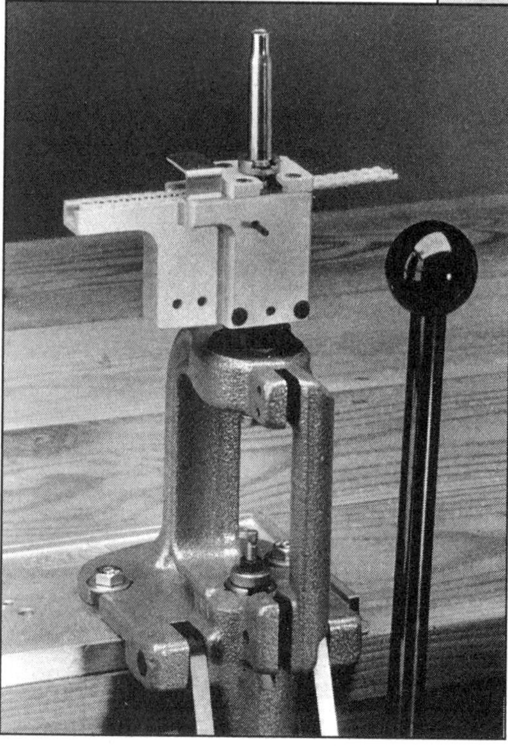

Charger, can be mounted on the reloading bench for loading cartridges or used for measuring charges for muzzleloaders. It is constructed of non-sparking brass and consists of three major parts, a main body with cut-off valve, an adjustable sliding gauge with cut-off value, and a powder hopper. The Tru-Charger allows accurate duplication of loads.

Handloaders always need boxes in which to carry and to store ammunition, particularly if they purchase once-fired cases in bulk or happen to find some empties at the range. **MTM Products** produces plastic boxes that will hold from five to a hundred rounds of handgun, rifle or shotgun ammunition. The capacity depends on the caliber or gauge, but if there has been a demand for a particular case, MTM probably manufactures a box to hold it. Although handloaders do not need them, MTM also manufactures boxes to hold 22 rimfire cartridges, a decided improvement over paper boxes for carrying in pockets. Both hinged-lid and slip-top boxes are available, and for handloaders of African-size cartridges there is a ten-round Ammo-Wallet that will hold anything from 378 Weatherby Magnum cartridges to the big Nitro Expresses.

MTM also has load labels to assist in keeping track of what load is in what box, a primer flipper, powder funnels, die storage boxes, and loading traps. The newest item is a *Handloaders Log*, with 150 pages in a vinyl-covered loose-leaf three-ring binder. It provides space for handgun, rifle and shotshell loading data; pet loads; and firearms inventory.

Nostalgia Enterprises produces specialized handloading equipment for dedicated shooters. The Concentricity, Wall Thickness and Runout Gauge will help produce the best ammunition it is possible to assemble. The Standard Gauge will handle cartridge cases from 22 to 45-70, and with an optional chord anvil also the 17 calibers. A longer 50 Gauge will handle the Standard cases, plus the 50 BMG case. Bullets can also be checked for concentricity with the use of removable guides.

NECO produces a Cartridge Case Holder that will rigidly and precisely hold an empty 50 BMG case for trimming to overall length on a drill press. Handloaders who use hard plastic wads beneath plain-base cast bullets will find the NECO Wad Insertion Tool handy. Available in most common calibers, the tool allows the P-wads to be seated squarely, uniformly and to a controlled seating depth.

The firm having the most interesting new handloading product has to be **RCBS**. Developed jointly by RCBS and CCI, sister companies within Blount Sporting Equipment Division, the APS Priming System is the culmination of a two-year project. The system consists of an APS bench- or press-mounted priming tool, a strip loader and empty color-coded priming strips. (Pre-loaded CCI primer strips will sell for the same price as conventionally packaged primers.) Each strip holds twenty-five primers, and strips can be hooked together for continuous feeding. The bench-mounted tool is a free-standing unit with its own handle, while the press-mounted tool fits into conventional presses. Both units accept regular shellholders. In use, an unprimed case is slipped into the shellholder and the handle is operated to prime the case. An indexing system automatically advances the strips one primer at a time, and seating depth is fully adjustable on the bench tool. The angle of the operating handle is also adjustable. On the reloading press unit, the shellholder in the press ram is replaced by a special assembly that permits adjustment for primer seating depth.

RCBS also has a new cutter head for its case trimmers. The new cutter functions as a regular case trimmer, but also simultaneously chamfers the inside of the case mouth and deburrs the outside. Currently available to trim 22- and 30-caliber cases, it replaces the stan-

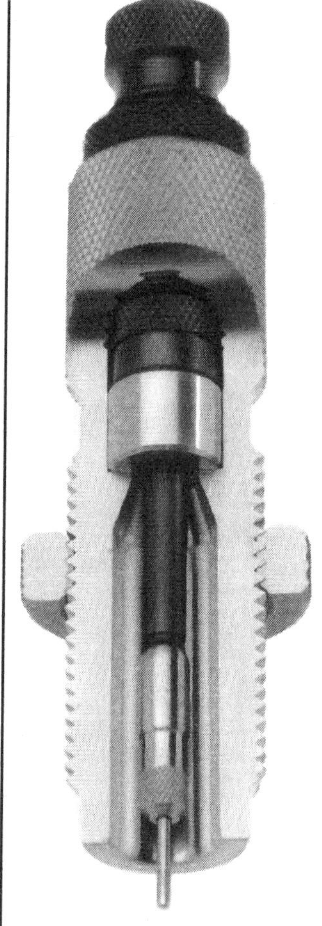

Redding's standard bushing-style neck-sizing die, available in .001-inch increments.

dard cutter by simply unscrewing the original cutter head and installing the new Three-Way version. Hopefully, other calibers will be available later.

Redding Reloading Equipment, which also owns Saeco Bullet Casting products, has been a big name among silhouette and benchrest shooters the past decade or more. For 1996, their 50th year, they managed to make improvements on what was already excellent by introducing two new neck-sizing dies and a bullet-seating die. The new bushing-style neck-sizing dies, both standard and Benchrest Competition, allow the case neck to be resized as little as .001-inch. The dies are available in forty-two calibers, without the bushings, which are available in .001 size increments throughout the range of .235 to .340, or approximately calibers 22 thru 30. The main difference between the two types of dies is the micrometer adjustment available on the Benchrest Competition models.

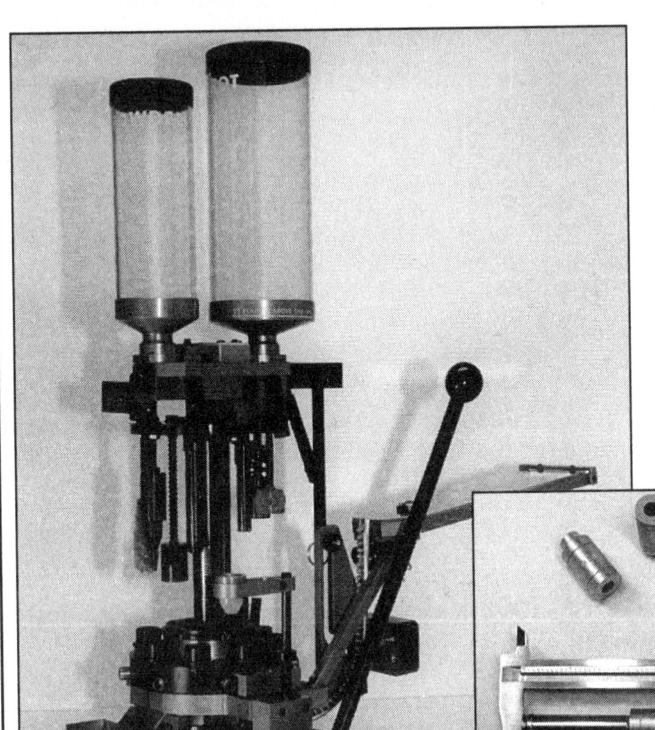

The Spolar Power Load Golden Premier progressive shotshell loading press can be operated from either side, or changed to hydraulic operation. Comes in all Skeet gauges.

Stoney Point Products' cartridge headspace gauge uses five bushings, a B-2000 body and calipers to measure headspace to the datum line on the case shoulder.

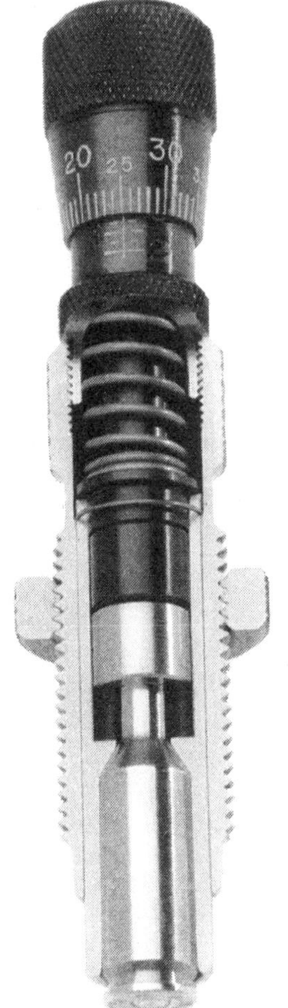

Redding's Benchrest Competition bushing-style neck-sizing die has micrometer adjustments.

In the Saeco line, Redding has four new moulds for blackpowder shooters. Two are in 40-caliber, two in 45-caliber, all with five lubricating grooves. Mould 640 produces a 370-grain bullet, while mould 740 produces a 410-grain bullet; both will size to .408/.410-inch. For the 45s, mould 645 will cast a 480-grain bullet, and mould 745 will cast a 525-grain bullet, either sizing to .458/.460. Other changes include cutting all blackpowder moulds from oversize or magnum-size blocks—the single Magnum is cut from normal double-cavity blocks, while double-cavity Magnum moulds are cut from triple cavity-blocks.

The third edition of **Reloading Specialties, Inc.**'s, *Steel Shotshell Reloading Handbook* is out. New data is included for use in loading 20-, 12- and 10-gauge shells with steel shot, and while only the magnum-length 20-and 10-gauge shells are covered, the 12-gauge loads are included for the three common lengths—2¾, 3, and 3½ inches.

1996 was a big year for celebrating anniversaries, at least in the handloading/reloading business. Or maybe 1946, and the startup of new businesses following World War II was the real biggie. Regardless, **The Bulletsmiths (Sierra)** got started in 1946, and for 1996 they produced the 4th edition of the *Sierra Rifle and Handgun Reloading Manual*. This latest edition been completely rewritten to make it one of the most complete manuals available anywhere.

Spolar Power Load Inc. has introduced a new Golden Premier shotshell reloading press that is top-of-the-line. A complete gauge change, if desired, can be accomplished in less than ten minutes, and the leverage mechanism is ball-bearing enhanced. The handle can be placed either left or right, and the machine is hydraulic-ready. Features include an electronic setting system for shot, powder and primer, and simultaneous wad and shot drop. It has a 25-pound shot capacity; shot and powder hoppers are threaded for stability. Two final crimps are provided, and shells can be removed at any time from any position. The press is available in 12, 20 and 28 gauges, plus 410-bore. A counter is included, along with full instructions.

Incorrect headspace can create problems, which is why shoving the shoulder back too far on a case when resizing is a no-no. **Stoney Point Products** has helped solve the problem with their introduction of a Cartridge Headspace Gauge. Measuring from the case head to the datum line on the case shoulder, the new Headspace Gauge allows the handloader to measure headspace of cases before and after firing, with or without bullets seated. It will handle most bottleneck cases from the 17 Remington to the belted 375 H&H Magnum. Five bushings, with a B-2000 Body to fit onto the blade of a caliper, are all that are needed. Handloaders already owning a Stoney Point Comparator will have the B-2000 Body and will need only to purchase the five bushings.

VihtaVuori Oy released their second hardbound reloading manual last year, but there is a new 6th edition of the softbound *Reloading Guide* available at dealers handling this fine line of powders. This *Guide* has data on handgun, shotgun and rifle cartridges, and includes more than two dozen loads for the 50 BMG cartridge. Rifle cartridge data ranges from the 17 Remington to the 50 BMG, with many loads for the excellent 6.5x55 Swedish, and a few for some less-often-seen calibers, such as the 7x33 Sako, 8.2x53R Finnish, 338 Lapua Magnum, and 9.3x53R Finnish. Handgun data covers cartridges from the 25 ACP to the 454 Casull, but shotshells are limited to 12, 20 and 28 gauges. ●

HERE'S WHAT HAPPENED

THIRTY OR FORTY years ago, or perhaps a few more or less, and for a long time before that, the 16-gauge shotgun was the *beau ideal* in the United States. Never as popular as the 12, it was far more popular than everything else lumped together and had an excellent following among all types of shotgunners. Waterfowlers, upland hunters, deer hunters, anyone who used a shotgun was likely to use a 16.

Just thirty years ago, the 16 was still the second most popular gauge, but the 20 had made strong inroads into its popularity. Sales figures for new shotshells about 1965 showed the 16-gauge at about 21 percent, the 20 about 19 percent. A 1965 gun catalog showed nearly every make and model of gun available in 16-gauge. The 20-gauges were mostly new models or new offerings in old models.

A 1975 gun catalog showed a number of models had been discontinued in 16-gauge. By 1985 no major manufacturer offered its top-of-the-line repeaters in 16. There were just a couple of single-barrel guns and the Stevens double.

What caused the decline? I recently looked through a 1920s mail-order catalog. It showed only two loads offered in the 12-gauge, a 1-ounce load and $1\frac{1}{8}$-ounce load. The 16-gauge offering was a 1-ounce load. The only 20 was a $\frac{7}{8}$-ounce load. Well, one might say, as they all did, that the 16 had as much power as the 12—in the 1-ounce load they were identical.

By the late 1950s or the early 1960s, however, gun writers no longer praised the 16. They discovered the 20 and praised it. No one, at least no one who knew anything about guns and was honest, said anything bad about the 16; they simply said nothing at all about it.

The reason, of course, was the improvement in the loads for the 12s and 20s. "Magnumization" set in. The 12 got it two ways—there was a 3-inch $1\frac{3}{8}$-ounce 12 load, and this was increased to $1\frac{7}{8}$ ounces, thereby nearly killing off the 10-gauge. A new $1\frac{1}{2}$-ounce load came out in the standard $2\frac{3}{4}$-inch 12-gauge shell. Similarly, the standard 20 was now loaded with $1\frac{1}{8}$ ounces (the 1-ounce load had been around for some time) and a new 3-inch shell was loaded first with $1\frac{3}{16}$ ounces of shot, later increased to a full $1\frac{1}{4}$ ounces.

The 16 got little of the same treatment. The standard shell was offered with $1\frac{1}{4}$ ounces of shot and was called a *magnum*, but most people simply considered it an express load. No 3-inch load was forthcoming.

Gun writers as a group, it must be said, thrive on hyperbole, and there wasn't any hyperbole left in the 16-gauge. It could hardly be said to equal the 12 anymore, and even worse was the other new truth: the *20* was the *equal* of the 12-gauge express load. The 20 had stolen the 16's thunder. All the power of the 12-gauge express load in a 6-pound 20! The writers didn't mention recoil, which is some hyperbole they missed. From then on, the 16 wasn't maligned—it was never maligned—but it was ignored, and that is anathema.

There is little magic in any particular size of shotgun shell. It is a package for holding powder and shot. Its power is dependent on its capacity. The more it holds, the more powerful it is. It is that simple.

The 16-gauge has a 10-percent greater volume than the 3-inch 20. Therefore it will hold that much more powder and shot. And, a 16 could be loaded with $1\frac{3}{8}$ ounces of shot. Had a 3-inch 16 been developed, it could hold $1\frac{1}{2}$ ounces of shot. Those loads might have made it more competitive. A friend of mine used to load $1\frac{3}{8}$ ounces of shot in his 16 for a heavy duck and goose load, and thought it very effective.

The 16's slug load is a good bit more powerful than the 20's was. They both go about the same speed, so their kinetic energy and momentum are proportional to their weights. The standard 16 weighs $\frac{7}{8}$-ounce to the $\frac{5}{8}$-ounce of the 20. And it remains slightly more powerful than the new heavyweight 20, which weighs $\frac{4}{5}$-ounce.

A curious real advantage is enjoyed by the 20 in buckshot. The standard 20-gauge buckshot load is twenty #3 buck, which weighs 1.126 ounces. The standard 16-gauge buckshot load is twelve #1 buckshot, which weighs 1.11 ounces. The 3-inch 20-gauge buckshot load of eighteen #2 buck weighs 1.24 ounces. I call this curious for two reasons—I have never seen it observed in print, and among my acquaintances who use buckshot, the 16 is considered more effective.

The 16 lost ground again when gunmakers dropped double-barrel guns and redesigned all their repeaters around just the 12-gauge frame.

Modern practice has mostly been to design a single frame size and fit it with different-size barrels and such small parts as are necessary for proper function with different-size shells, keeping as many parts as possible in a common size. Different gauge guns of a given model thus all weigh about the same.

When Skeet shooting was invented about 1930, it was formalized according to gauge. The gauges chosen were 410-bore, 28-gauge, 20, and "all-bore." Skeet's inventors didn't see any difference in the power of the 16 and the 12 and lumped them together.

And one of the first national championships was won with a 16-gauge double. The maximum load allowed in "all bore" is $1\frac{1}{8}$ ounces of shot, the 12-gauge load. The standard 16 load for clays was only 1 ounce. There is no practical difference in effectiveness. However, there was some slight advantage to the heavier load, and as a result practically nobody now shoots Skeet seriously with a 16. Still, old 16 users may ruefully mark the near-universal use of 1-ounce loads in competition these days.

I have seen trap guns in 16-gauge. They were never as popular for trap as they were for Skeet. In trap, shots are taken at longer ranges, around 35 yards, and the advantage of the extra $^1/_8$-ounce of shot is less theoretical. Other things being equal, in

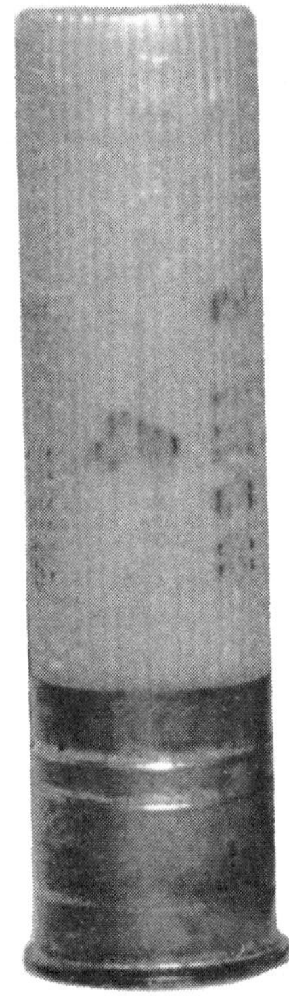

The 3-inch 20 (left) isn't the only thing, but it was the biggest thing, and for no ballistic reason.

TO THE 16-GAUGE

by MARSHALL R. WILLIAMS

fact, it gives a 6 percent increase in range. That's about 2 yards, which might be significant.

You could, of course, shoot the heavier loads in the 16, and Federal Cartridge Co., an innovative firm, offered a $1^1/_8$-ounce target load in the late '60s or early '70s, but it did not catch on. A 16-gauge shooting the heavier load kicks harder, a complication a good shooter can do without.

And then the over/under shotgun became fashionable. The only such gun to enjoy much popularity in 16-gauge was the Marlin Model 90, which was discontinued in 1959. Browning never made a 16-gauge over/under to my knowledge. Neither did Beretta, so far as I know. The fine German makers such as Simpson and Merkel made them, but they were never imported into the United States in quantity.

There you have it. The 16 disappeared in just thirty years without any real faults. And it had some real virtues. Above all, it works fine in the real shooting world.

I generally shoot Skeet with the $^7/_8$-ounce load in the 16. It's a great target breaker and has no noticeable recoil. I usually hunt with a 1-ounce load in either the 12 or 16. Most of my hunting is for quail, rabbit, grouse, dove and woodcock, so I rarely shoot a heavier load.

I like the 16-gauge and, strange as it may seem, so does every other shooter of my acquaintance. Some will go so far as to attribute special powers to it. Notwithstanding, few of them shoot a 16 or want to acquire one. So I really don't foresee any brighter future for the shell. A lot of first-class guns remain in use. And the factories will turn out shells for them for a long time yet. At this writing, it appears only one factory now loads the $1^1/_4$-ounce load; and only one continues to supply 16-gauge wads, and it has dropped one of its two types. Trap and Skeet shooters are rediscovering that the 1-ounce load is effective for their games, but the 12- and 20-gauge guns they already own handle that. They are unlikely to clamor for 16-gauge replacements.

The 16 remains nearly as versatile and light as the 20, even the 3-inch 20. It remains nearly as powerful as the standard-length 12. A shooter can do all the shotgunning that can be done using a 16-gauge gun. The same was probably true of the long-forgotten 14-gauge guns. •

TAKING THE SHOT

...when the game is up close

by FRANCIS E. SELL

THERE IS NO substitute for complete utilization of the limited time for an off-hand shot in heavy cover when deer is the quarry. The chance for an accurate snapshot comes and goes within a matter of seconds. If these seconds are properly used, the shot is accurate and unhurried.

This snapshooting technique starts with the hunter's feet, on through to the actual shot. In short, if the feet are not in place, the shot is inaccurate and hurried.

Once, watching an overgrown reforesting with the late Al Lyman, we saw another hunter following a deer trail along a draw below us. His hunting direction for the time of day was correct, as he was still moving toward the security cover at the tag end of the morning feeding period. His trail technique, however, was something else again.

A fairly large windfall tree lay across the trail he followed, and when he came to it he stepped over, or more correctly scrambled over, right foot first—no pause at the windfall to give the cover a careful examination, no thought at all.

From the way he carried his rifle, he unquestionably shot from the right shoulder, and in getting over the windfall, he placed himself completely out of shooting position. Al Lyman's remark was to the point: "That fellow is no great threat to the deer."

Actually, if that deer hunter got a shot then, he would be completely out of position for it. If a deer got up while he was getting over the log, he would have had to get his left foot over, then take another step before he would be in any position to shoot, unless the deer came out of the cover well to his left.

Consider the rifle routine in heavy cover, where an experienced deer hunter is in command of the situation from first to last. If such a rifleman had crossed that windfall, there would have been a pause before he took this step. The entire cover within the short range of the expected shot would have been examined in detail, especially the shadow areas. He would have stepped across the windfall with his left foot first, assuming he shot from the right shoulder. If a deer got up while he made the crossing, he would have been in a position for the shot. After he had crossed the windfall, he would have only to slide his left foot forward a bit to be in proper position for taking a shot.

One thing that is well to put out of mind is any five-shot, 1-inch group at 100-150 yards. What is needed in snapshooting, short range in heavy cover, is the ability to put one shot in a 4-inch circle, off-hand, at 40-50 yards. The target presented is usually moving, but sometimes, with careful still hunting, there is an opportunity to take the shot at standing or slow moving deer.

Certainly off-hand snapshooting places a limit on effective ranges in taking running deer. I place this at not more than 90-100 yards. Usually, though, the range will be much shorter. The actual target presented by the game for a clean kill is the heart and lung area, about 12 inches long by 10 inches high, and if the game is viewed broadside, it is indicated by the shoulder area, well down.

In getting on a running deer target, there is always the thought of proper lead. Most deer, while capable of much faster speed, move out if put up

A cleanly killed buck is the deer hunter's goal; making the right shot is the way to reach it.

in heavy cover at about 18 or so miles an hour—a figure I have established by putting up a lot of deer and timing their getaways with a stopwatch.

Beyond the actual speed, there is also the matter of apparent speed. Most deer put up by a hunter move away from him at an angle that makes the apparent speed much slower than the actual speed. The angle of the shot is fully compensated by the size of the target in the vital area of the game.

Swinging with the target is quite often impossible in heavy cover. Trees interfere. Brush and fern conceal the deer to the extent that there is only a glimpse of the target in the small clear openings. The hunter must make his play for one of these openings, getting on the deer, making the shot at the vital area. The rifle must come up already aligned, and the shot taken as the sights come on target. There is no other way to take such a shot effectively.

I recall one such hunting instance while prowling an overgrown logging slash. The cover was a thick waste of low-growing trees, vine maple and black huckle bushes. When I jumped this deer from its bed, I could mark its going along the trail by the violent movement of the brush.

Forward along the trail there was a huge fir windfall, and I knew the deer would clear this in its flight. So it was at this point I made my play, the range about forty yards. When the deer cleared the windfalls, it came into my sights beautifully. I could see it was a legal buck, four points to a side, and I took the shot.

It was a comparatively easy shot, as the deer was going away from me at an angle, and the size of the vital area target compensated for lead requirements.

The rifle pointing, the aiming, the total blend of the snapshot was just about as easy as if the target had been stationary. The bullet entered just behind the left shoulder, pushed through the heart and lung area, and emerged in front of the right shoulder.

It was a shot any competent snapshot could have made, and one I have made many times; not at deer jumping over a windfall, but when they presented the shot in a small opening clear of intervening brush.

Once I had a young and inexperienced hunter with me, trying to teach him the intricacy of getting a telling shot on deer in heavy cover. I put out a forked horn to him and it crossed a small and comparatively open draw, affording the young hunter an easy killing shot. The range was about thirty-five yards. He emptied his 30-06 Model 70 Winchester without so much as disturbing a hair on the target.

Afterward, when I was more or less holding a review of the episode, questioning him about his shooting, I asked him about his gunning plan. At what point did he feel the target was most stable for the shot? He looked at me as though I had lost some of my marbles.

"Stable for the shot! That deer was jumping around like a chicken with its head cut off. I bet any stability it had was about four hundred yards down the trail, long after I had stopped shooting. You trying to tell me there was a best time and place for the shot?"

"Certainly," I replied. "A lot of that erratic jumping around was in your attitude. You thought, he's getting away. Shoot fast or you'll lose him. That deer wasn't greatly alarmed. Looking at the tracks will tell you that. He probably went out at about ten miles an hour, trotting mostly, jumping over a bit of down stuff."

"There were two points when jumping where he was most stable for the shot: at the top of the leap when the upward movement is spent and downward movement hasn't started—an instant to be sure, but sufficient for a snapshot at such short range. The other point where the target is most stable is at the time it touches the ground.

When he was trotting, you only had to put your sights on the vital chest and shoulder area for a clean kill. The size of the target was sufficient in all cases to compensate for the required lead.

Later, I suggested that this young rifleman-hunter leave his gun at my cabin and go out and jump a few deer and just look—nothing more. Just observe in detail. The jumping of deer in heavy cover is a comparatively easy undertaking.

He went out. He came back late in the evening filled with a lot of enthusiasm, some of which he will lose later. He now saw how easy a shot is, even though the target was moving. Most of all he realized how much time there is for a telling shot, if it is all properly used.

Beyond this, he came to realize that some shots are rejected because there is no sure opportunity for a clean kill, only wounding, and perhaps losing the quarry, so it will go off and suffer and die. Unless a rifleman has the ability to bring off a clean kill, he is under a solemn obligation not to take the shot. And that, incidentally, is the difference between the experienced hunter and the casual, once-a-year woods prowler. More to the point, don't expect the quarry to comply with a preconception of the

Sell increased the time he had to make any shot by rebuilding his rifles so they pointed for him.

hunter about the best place for getting the shot. That is brought about by the game.

I once posted a hunter on a sure-shot stand, where the opportunity for the kill would come and go in a matter of seconds. But, as I said, it was a sure-shot setup.

I put deer through, a beautiful big buck I saw briefly as he came out of his security bedding. He took the proper trail directly over the stand, but there was no shot. When I came through the cover, directly on the trail of the buck I put out, there was no hunter on the stand!

After the posting and I had left to make the still-hunting drive, this once-a-year hunter found a more open spot nearby which would afford a beautiful chance for a shot, and here he took up his watch, losing a dead-sure chance at a wonderful trophy. He did learn one element of hunting—it's the game instead of the hunter who picks the spot for the shot.

Of all the many backwoods hunters with whom I have shared deer hunting in the wilderness, the truly great have an innate ability to reject a shot and can wait out the moment knowing a better, sure-kill opportunity was in the making. This I have especially noted among the many Indian friends of my early-day hunting.

Some of these came to their deer hunting with their lever-action Winchesters and Marlins with all the ammunition they had in the magazines of the rifles. Once, I recall hunting with a Siwash who had only three 38-55 cartridges for his rifle. He didn't have enough money for a full box that cost 75¢. Besides, he explained, he only wanted one deer. He used one of those cartridges to snip off the head of a blue grouse, which we had for our evening meal.

He got his deer and returned home with one cartridge. While I was trail-watching with him, he rejected four shots because they didn't afford chances for a clean kill. Being a comparatively young hunter at the time, I know I would have taken some of those shots, but always he placed a restraining hand on my half-raised rifle. It was a deer hunting lesson I will never forget. In hunting deer in heavy cover—still-hunting, trail-watching, feeding area watching—never gamble on a shot where there is a chance for a wounding hit.

A hunter in heavy cover can never take anything for granted. How he steps over a windfall, like the one in front, can make or break the shot, maybe the hunt.

There are compensations for deer hunting restraint. Quite often, waiting out the situation produces a much better chance for a clean, humane kill later. I recall the last deer season when I took my buck. I waited out the shot for the better part of a quarter-hour, while this buck browsed through some heavy cover. It was late evening, with the shooting light rapidly passing. Eventually, he stepped into a small opening and I took the shot, a clean kill, the bullet ranging through the neck just below his ears.

On another occasion, trail-watching, there was a large buck feeding in low-growing, heavy cover that gave no chance for a shot. Occasionally, I got a flash of ivory-tipped antlers, a glimpse of his head as he raised it to test the downdraft of wind. I picked up a small limb and broke it, and up came his head, but with no chance for a shot. He stood motionless for several moments, then resumed his browsing. I waited a bit, then I broke another limb. He went through the same routine of standing perfectly still for a few moments, listening. Then, again, he resumed feeding.

I waited a short time, then broke another limb. This time he began moving out. He was cautiously taking a few steps, then listening, testing the wind with that sensitive black nose. I had him dead to rights in just a little bit.

I have killed more than my share of deer. And out of this welter of hunting experience, I have decided opinions about shooting. My view is essentially this. It is more important to match the rifle to the hunter than it is to match it to the game. In short, some hunters are better served with a bolt action because it has a steadying influence on their shooting. This is especially true of a nervous type. Other hunters will find a lever action just enough work to be steady for a second, more accurate shot. Very few deer hunters have the disposition or ability to handle an autoloader. They tend to depend on volume of fire instead of making each individual shot take the emphasis.

I live in the wilderness. I see deer almost daily in going about my reforestings. Yet the thrill is always there, the challenge is always there! I think that if there is time enough for two hasty shots, there is plenty of time for one accurate killing shot, and that, when the season rolls around and I am on the prowl again, rifle in hand, I put the thought into practice! •

Editor's Note

The late Francis E. Sell made his mark on hunting practice with thinking like this. He's still missed. By the way, I handled his guns; they did what he says.

KW

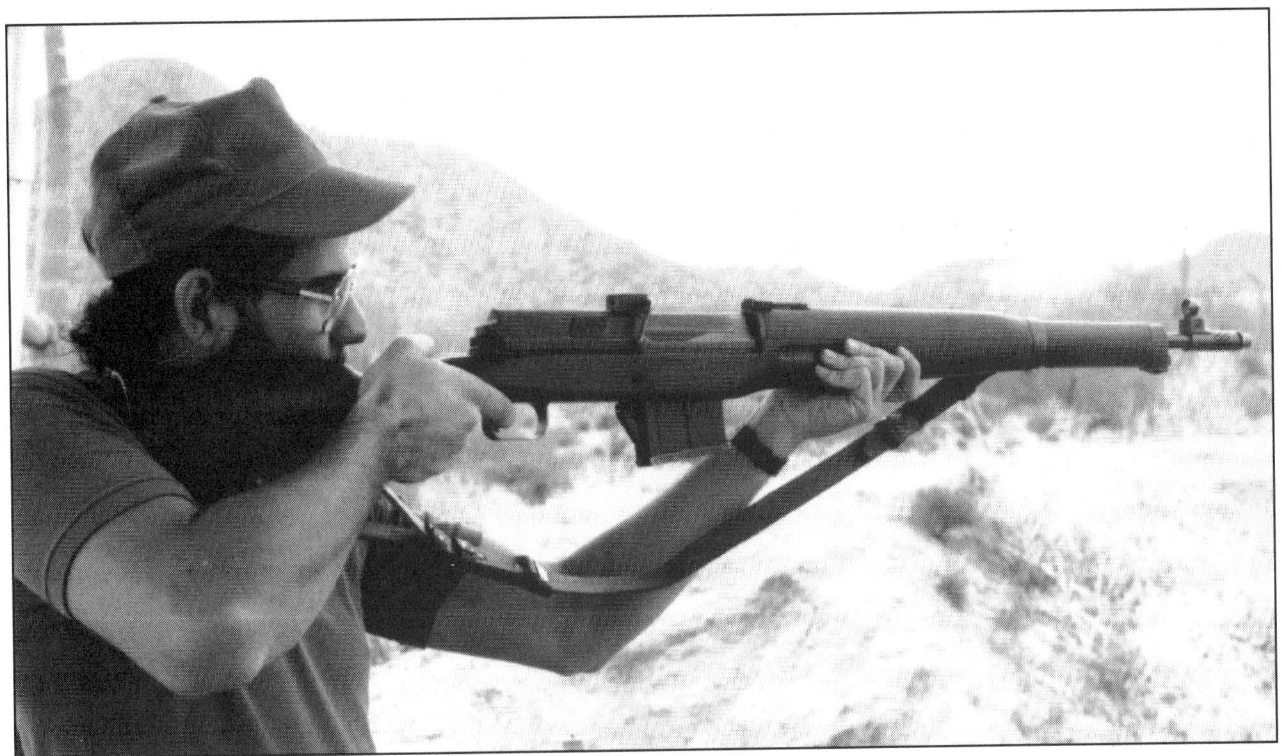

In a desert war, many Egyptian soldiers must have wished for something else...ANYTHING ELSE...than a Hakim autoloading rifle.

Seven Selected TURKEYS of the 20th CENTURY... and why they were.

by
JIM THOMPSON

BY AND LARGE, firearms are pretty good products. Once in a while, a mediocre one sneaks out. Sometimes, it's a minor player and that's no big deal, because it's only a few guns. Sometimes, though, it's a major production item for which customers—some of them national governments—laid down their money in the mistaken impression that their new weapons were world-beaters. There are individual lemons all the time, but they can be easily isolated and handled.

The subjects of this article are military or self-defense guns manufactured in quantity at great expense to someone, but which failed miserably in their intended duties. Some still have virtues, like the Ross rifle which is very accurate. So is the M-14. But others are so weird, unsafe or unreliable, any virtues they might have had are lost in a tangle of complicated malfunctions. Thus, their failures represent the loss of dollars and, potentially, lives.

If a hunting or target gun fails at its assigned task, someone may get angry, but no one gets dead. Not so with the turkey.

It's sometimes fortunate when a gun is so plagued early on that even the illusion of reliability can't be maintained. The Bren Ten, which got into production several years late, had so many complex feed problems, many of them completely insoluble, that no one who had reliable data on or had tested a production gun was foolish enough to bet his life on the pistol. Had the French Chauchat or the Ross been properly "torture tested" early on, thousands more Allied soldiers would have lived to old age. Unless, of course, as they say at the track, "the fix was in."

"The fix" implies corruption. But that's only part of it. Petty grudges,

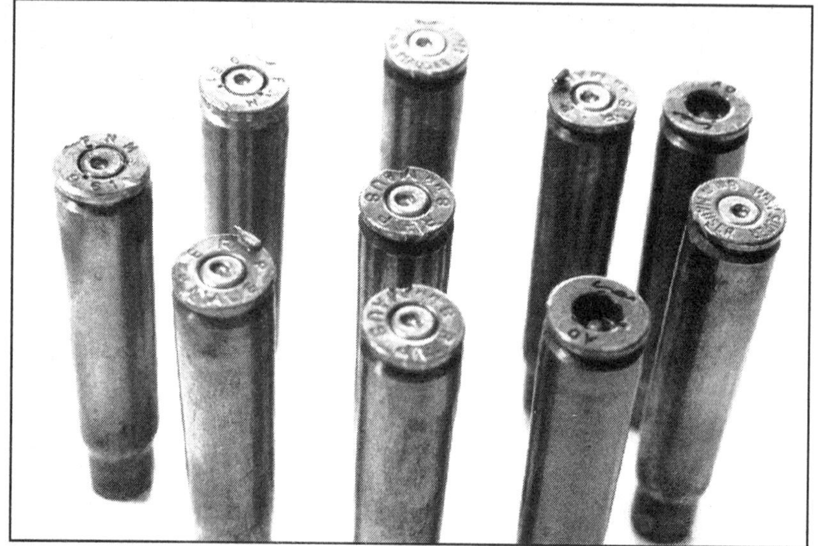

The Hakim tears up brass with an unpolished extractor. Even after extractor rework, Egyptian rounds popped primers fairly frequently.

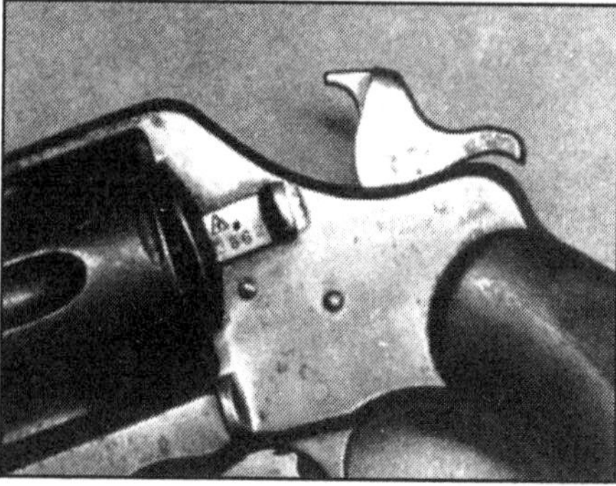

That hammer-and-nail firing pin arrangement was not even nearly the worst feature of these old Colts.

The turn-of-the-century Colt and S&W military models led directly to the current generation of high-quality medium- and large-format revolvers so popular on the American market.

rampant chauvinism, and just plain stupidity and stubbornness probably play as big a part as under-the-table money.

Having some experience in the manufacturing end of this business, I know there are some sharks out there, people who put no real emphasis on production itself, so you get the specifications chronically unmet, returns not honored, every delivery late, ending up one day with phones disconnected, letters returned, offices empty, the former "president" of the company unavailable, but still driving his Rolls Royce.

And there are salesmen who will say or do anything to make the right sale. Vested interests inside military organizations often serve exactly the same purpose, sometimes with money on the line, more often rank and power. It has always amused me when the military establishments of the world point accusing fingers at civilians in government for this or that, but remain strangely mute themselves when equipment failures in their pet projects become obvious.

A recently retired GI said something to me not long ago that still burns in my memory. He'd served with NATO troops in Europe most of his career and was fully familiar with current weaponry worldwide. "Y'know," he mused, looking through my MG-42 manual, "I kinda figger the only damned reason the Army didn't adopt this gun was 'cause it didn't cost enough!"

He had no beef with M-60. He just felt it wasn't as good or as flexible as the German or Italian versions of the World War II classic.

Some of the turkeys were merely out of place—anachronisms—or underpowered. One thing they all were was oversold. Which is why they failed.

It's worth adding that enthusiastic gun writers sometimes contribute to the hype. Testing handmade prototypes is one bugaboo we all have to avoid. A lot of writers were enthusiastic about Ruger's 308-caliber XG-1 and wrote much joyous copy based on their contacts with the prototypes. Ruger, however, to their eternal credit, found the rifle could not be mass-produced at an acceptable combination of quality and price, and canceled the rifle.

I've tested one such prototype in my life and found some serious glitches, which I reported back to the manufacturer. Much to my surprise, most of them were corrected on the production pistols. But I've seen plenty of excessive enthusiasm in the firearms press. This is nothing new.

Remember that totalitarian countries produce very few really lousy weapons. The Soviets' first Tokarev M-38 rifles were rather fragile, but the Russians knew this and restricted the rifle to use by snipers and specialists where firepower and accuracy were what counted. The Nazis spent a lot of money and effort on blind-alley prototypes, but none of them were issued in quantity.

In a totalitarian state, the price for some errors is death, so designers are disinclined to press the issue for undeveloped or unreliable designs. Also, totalitarian states have plenty of chances to test their weapons in combat, often against their own citizens, who are always milling around and handy for target practice. In fact, many first-rate weapons issued in Latin America bear mismatched bolts or other critical parts because various dictators found it handy at times to have certain parts removed to assure that they were not one of the citizen targets of military *insurrecto* plinkers. In the world's democracies, mistakes are more easily forgotten, especially in the warm glow of victory.

The M-73 (7.62mm) and M-85 (caliber 50) short-breech machineguns—which cost many millions to develop and are now breaking into pieces in U.S. service and/or being replaced by much older, cheaper and more reliable designs—may one day be included in an article like this. Certainly, you have the right to ask about how your tax dollars are spent, just as the government has a right—they seem to believe an obligation—to ignore your query, but until I have more data I'll put such an entry on hold.

The British Sten gun certainly had a lot of glitches, especially the famous jam by one of Reinhard Heydrich's assassins just a few feet in front of his car. Fortunately, the startled driver killed the engine, and assassin number two lobbed a highly reliable #2 Mills bomb into the Mercedes. Heydrich still had time to empty his Luger and chase his tormentors. He died from an abdominal infection.

All of which is interesting mainly to those who like to dwell on the reliability of this or that magic formula of "killing power." If a very potent hand grenade can't kill someone reliably, perhaps all this talk about cartridges is irrelevant.

Still, the Sten was legitimately famous for its jams, mainly due to bad magazines from subcontractors who in peacetime made toys or kitchen appliances or, yes, tin cans. Crude, cheap (cost was less than £2 by 1943) and disgusting looking in general, by the end of World War II, the gun was a very reliable weapon. It was also issued in quantities where the failure of one gun meant only that someone a few feet away would continue the effort, while the soldier in question grabbed another Sten. By '45, this was a rare occurrence. The Sten was, in fact, copied in several countries, in versions sometimes more posh than the original, sometimes even cruder.

Friends and associates have suggested firearms they felt were bad enough to be "Turkeys of the Twentieth Century." Many were guns I'm not fond of, but of which I have heard some good rumors. Mostly they were individual lemons or failed variants of otherwise satisfactory weapons. A few were just worn-out classics or greats mangled by enthusiastic, but inept hands. And a lot of people buy the wrong gun for the wrong reasons.

A few almost made the list.

Colt's first-generation military-style semi-automatics (1905-1908) were certainly awkward, had lousy sights, and were stripped with difficulty. But they were very accurate, quite reliable, and really not much more than production prototypes.

The Reising submachine gun was mentioned frequently. Yet, I've fired several and never had any difficulty. Rumors persist that the Reising guns that failed at Guadalcanal were jumbled around or damaged en route in 1942. Many of the same guns were sold or given to police departments after the war and have been sold as registered weapons since, and I haven't been able to find a really disappointed owner. So the jams and other malfunctions seem to have been some kind of fluke...very real, but a fluke.

The double-action 380/38 Enfield and Webley breaktop revolvers of World War II wouldn't hit much and were unlikely to stop much if they did. But they saw little use that demanded much precision and seemed to have been emptied into what few human targets popped up. And they worked. Just barely, but they worked.

There have been far more spectacular failures, real turkeys, as you will note:

Colt Military 38s

There's really nothing inherently wrong with the design of the military revolvers and civilian versions Colt built from 1889 to about 1911. Sure, they were fairly crude, first-generation swing-out types, with pretty lousy double-action yanks and those malevolent nail firing pins. The cylinders rotated counterclockwise, which tended to push the cylinder out of the frame. Most specimens now seem to have badly beat up lockwork, even if they haven't seen much use, so they were perhaps a little more fragile than their successors.

While the Colts are named here, the Smith & Wesson Hand Ejector Models of 1899 and 1902 were chambered for the same cartridge, and thus the same specific weaknesses apply. The Colt New Navy M1889 and New Army M1892 are the original variants, though Models of 1894, 1895, 1896, 1901 and 1903 are also 38 Long Colts and basically the same revolver. Civilian variants were produced during and after military runs, based on the same frame and in the same caliber.

These pistols appear to have been introduced in a general sweep toward modernism. The old M1873 pistols seem to have been viewed as too powerful. Unfortunately, the 38 Long Colt was about as bad a cartridge as could have been devised. Among today's ballistics buffs, there's the velocity school, the large frontal area/knockdown power group, the big bullet school, and the bullet design troops, and combinations thereof. None of them would have been satisfied with a 148-grain round-nose traveling, most authorities think, well below the stated factory velocity of 765 fps. Horse-mounted U.S. troops armed only with pistols suffered greatly during the campaigns in the Phillipines from 1898-1900. In fact, it was this cartridge which led directly to the U.S. refusal to even consider the similarly sized 9mm cartridge already gaining popularity in the rest of the world by the turn of the century. A great deal was made about the itty-bitty bullet being incapable of stopping hopping mad Moro tribesmen, but the truth is, that same itty-bitty bullet moving about 300-350 fps faster or in a little more effective configuration, or both, would probably have saved a lot of lives, at least among our troops.

The next two revolvers—the last major handgun issues for seventy years in a bore size other than 45—were the Colt M1905 USMC Double Action and Army Special M1908, both in the 38 Special caliber, still not quite what the military was looking for. On the M1908, the cylinder rotation finally went clockwise, and the weak lockwork of the earlier models was improved. The frame on the latter was also enlarged. In the future, military revolvers would be modified or off-the-shelf civilian items, seldom procured in much quantity. The M1909 New Service was an enlarged reversion to the old 45 Colt cartridge.

In combat, the service Colts in 38-caliber proved to be underpowered. They gave birth, however, to a whole generation of solid, reliable revolvers from both Colt and S&W.

Ross Rifle

If you opt to shoot a Ross, carefully check the condition of the locking lugs and *make sure* you tear down the bolt with the manual right in front of you. Failure to do either could get you killed. These were the Ross' two great weaknesses, and they were significant enough that the rifle was withdrawn from general issue to Canadian forces at the height of World War I, in 1916, to be replaced by the British SMLE.

In addition to primary extraction weaknesses, the Ross bolt-stop bore against the rearmost lug set and tended to tear up and/or jam the bolt, especially when the abrasive and often wet filth of WWI battlefields was added to the mix. Misassembly of the bolt can also cause the striker assembly to act as a projectile.

As this is written, I have just inspected a Ross in a sporting goods store with its bolt assembled incorrectly and with three cracked screw lugs. An accident waiting to happen. I have informed the store's owner that the gun should really be disas-

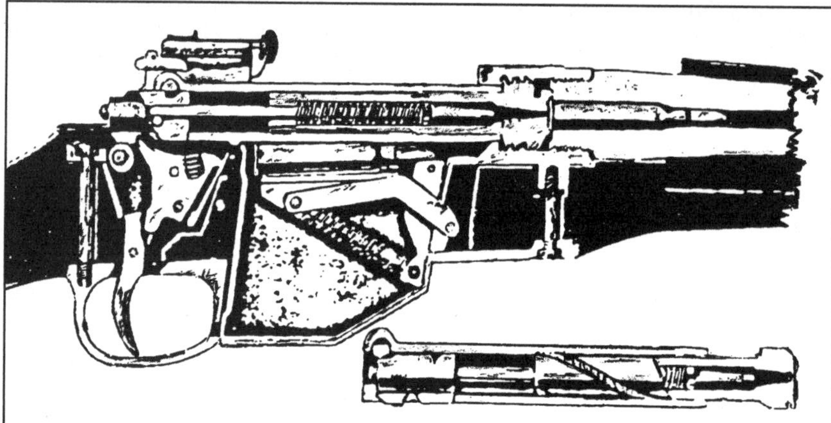

This is a road map to combat difficulties. Beautiful they were, the Rosses, but too complex, too fitted.

sembled for parts, the receiver and bolt body discarded.

That said, my only experience with a Ross as a shooter was a splendidly positive experience. The rifle's owner, a Canadian emigré and very old when I met him back in the '60s, was a hard-nosed WWI veteran with failing eyesight, a scoped Ross Mark 3 (S) T rifle with a huge Zeiss Jena scope of 1930s vintage, and a very large box of Canadian match ammunition already then approaching thirty years old. The ammo, he said, was "superb"...

In his odd French-Scottish-laced accent, he explained: "They load special for me to shoot targets. I keep in refridge. My wife, she think I'm crayzee, no?"

Old, perhaps eccentric, but crazy... definitely not. I wondered why this rifle sported a long, very narrow-angle 16x Zeiss scope when all my references said Canadian sniper rifles used Warner-Swasey scopes. It was mounted very strangely, with many rings and a lot of external micrometer knobs and gee-gaws. I didn't want to touch anything, so I asked the owner, who seemed very eager to have me shoot his rifle, what I should do. "Use the crosshair at 200 yards."

I paced off the range, planted targets, marched back and read the manual with special emphasis on bolt assembly. Every thing was OK. I loaded singly, operated the slick, well-lubricated bolt, kept reminding myself that chances of imminent death were really quite nominal, rehearsed my breathing technique and, after running out of reasons to delay, squeezed off a shot.

Relieved to be alive and seemingly not wounded, I slicked the straight-pull bolt back again and snugged it forward, trying to realign my eye to jibe with the strange scope's ultra-critical eye relief. There was a hole in the "x." I fired several more magazines full before I heard, "Now we clean." And so we did. The rifle put twenty shots in about 4 inches, and with my jittery nerves, I'm by no means sure I was milking the rifle's full potential. Its owner assured me that most Ross rifles could shoot like that and that sloppy cleaning was partly responsible for its failures.

"What," I asked, "did you do for the Canadian army?"

"I train the sniper."

One authority says there were at least eighty-five models and variants of the Ross, consolidated for purposes of simple coverup to eleven service models. Almost 420,000 were built, but the British, who extensively tested the rifle, noted in their 1910 report on the Ross Mark 2**: "It seems clear that this rifle is designed as a target rifle, pure and simple, without regard to the requirements of active service or of the training of large bodies of men of average attainment."

Well made of excellent materials, rifled to tolerances which are still challenging to today's match barrel manufacturers, the Ross was indeed a precision instrument in an environment where crude hammers were more appropriate. It could be fired very fast if well lubricated and clean, but British troops, in joint operations with Canadian personnel in 1916 and before, described Canadian troops kicking, pounding, and hammering on their rifles' bolt handles in vain attempts to operate them. Authorities had warned of the rifle's potential for failure since its adoption in 1902, but not only were the reports denied and their authors suppressed, each new "fix" was claimed to have solved the problems which the ordnance authorities had not too long before denied.

Sometimes, accurate rifles are adopted in spite of everything else that can go wrong. The Ross is one.

Bren Ten

The Bren gun of the British army was and is a wonderful light machinegun based on the Czech ZB26/30, manufactured mostly at the great British armory at Enfield Lock. It got its name from the home of the ZB, Brno (BR), and the home of British ordnance, Enfield (EN). Apparently the Bren Ten derives its name from those features loosely copied from the Brno-built CZ-75 pistol and the "EN" in the number of its centimetric bore. Any similarities begin and end with those four letters.

The problems all came from the Ross bolt system. The "interrupted threads" on this on are about to fail completely.

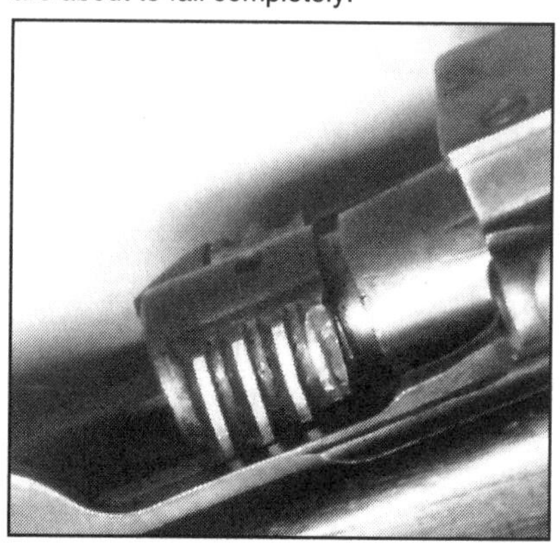

Misassembly of the Ross' bolt could result in a terminal departure of the same from the receiver as it attempted to be a semi-automatic, without staying in the breech.

I tried three times to test a Bren Ten. Three times, the pistols failed to feed with sufficient reliability to obtain any sensible data. One of the pistols, with less than 100 rounds through it, already showed visible cracking on its slide rails. That said, the 10mm round developed by Norma in Sweden for the Bren Ten is superb, accurate and powerful, and firing it in Colt Government models we converted from 38 Super was a real joy. Recoil is profound, but accuracy exceeds anything I've ever fired from a handgun of normal proportions.

The Bren Ten's problems began with the conception and then immediate collection of money on a pistol whose design was never really complete, and whose deliveries, when finally made several years late, caused profound disappointment. Many parts on guns I examined ran excessively hard, as high as 65 on the Rockwell "C" scale, in places where fractures can be problems and showed much evidence of emergency "crash" fitting; magazines, when furnished, couldn't be made to function properly with production guns. The tolerances and clearances from the magazine feed rails to the outside of the ejection port are just too narrow and tight, yet are essential to retain the gun's physical proportions and balance.

The Bren Ten has some virtues. It shoots straight (when it shoots); it inherited some of the ergonomic qualities of the CZ-75, so that shooter fatigue is minimized; the sights are good; and the double-action trigger pull approaches the quality of some of the better and later "super-nines."

Sold with much of the Barnum-like enthusiasm of a traveling medicine show for several years, pre-sold like British custom rifles, relentlessly advertised in the firearms media with handmade prototypes handed to gun writers like candied bon-bons, the banner carriers of the Bren Ten seemed to promise perfection. The production items proved incapable even of mediocrity.

It's generally a lot easier to scale down a design than scale up one. The excellent 223-caliber Spanish Ameli CETME MG-82, which some consider the finest machinegun in its chambering, was directly derived from the venerable German MG-42. Ruger's Mini-14 flows directly from the M-1 and M-14, fine semi-automatic designs. Even the "puffed up" incarnations can work, with a little careful analysis. A whole family of heavy-caliber aircraft machineguns of a very high order of reliability were "enlarged" from Browning and Maxim designs. But with a pistol, going up in size changes proportions and weights to a far more critical degree. In particular, to inherit all the design features and reliability of the CZ-75 in 10mm and 45 would have entailed a far larger pistol than could be readily marketed.

One of my correspondents owns a Bren Ten which was delivered as and still is the world's neatest and perhaps only semi-automatic single shot pistol. Rather than ejecting the nasty, old spent brass cartridge outside the gun, the extractor neatly places it back inside the magazine, thus saving owners from potential damage suits by those who might stumble on same.

There is virtually no leeway in the ejector or extractor fit and interrelationship, and the case must leave the chamber at exactly the right horizontal attitude. Nose down, the case can re-enter the magazine. Nose up, the ejector doesn't hit the case properly, usually causing messy stovepipe jams.

The main negative effect of the Bren Ten's failure is the chill which reverberated through the market. Consumers were disinclined to welcome new designs for a time, and even excellent pistols had tough rows to hoe with consumers.

Chauchat Gun

My first experience with the Chauchat was also my last. Even that distant memory has a heavily negative connotation for three reasons: (1) In order to shoot the weapon, its owner insisted that I cooperate in cleaning out forty-five to fifty years of grease and grit accumulation from the minty, seemingly unfired weapon; (2) I had to buy, retail, 250 rounds of what must have been Remington's last few batches of 8mm Lebel ammo; and (3) on the same day, I fired a

An accident that really never happened, the Bren Ten simply did not, could not, work as designed.

The 10mm Norma automatic cartridge (center), shown with 9mm and 38 Special, was a real winner.

group of other World War I classics, all of them were tough, durable, reliable and singularly, deadly efficient. Like many French weapons, this old "Sho-Sho" was painted dark green. We tore it down to small parts and inspected everything. The machine work looked good. As it turned out, both the design and the fundamental metallurgy weren't so hot.

Firing in short bursts of three to six rounds at 100 yards, each squeeze would produce a hit or two on the 14-inch square target, the rest striking well above the target holder. This was the case firing prone and hanging weights on the bipod. Also somewhat disconcerting was the tendency for the gun, despite its slow rate of fire, to tap out an additional round or two after I'd let up on the trigger. After firing a few more vintage classics, we cleaned everything and only then noticed: (1) the receiver tube had a 1½-inch longitudinal crack; and (2) between sloppy machining/fit and excessive length, the firing pin and sear were both in a malfunctioning condition. The Chauchat's owner had the crack re-welded, green paint retouched, and deactivated the gun by welding the chamber shut, changing its registration status.

My experience with the Chauchat is actually comparatively positive. As if the weapon's other glitches and constant malfunctions weren't enough, the U.S. M1918 version in 30-06 and many of the original French Model 1915 guns were far more dangerous, and magazine explosions were quite common among those which could be made to shoot for a while.

The long-recoil system, with its inherently high vibrations and violence, is partly to blame for the Chauchat's inadequacies. This system requires that the barrel and breech recoil together for a length greater than the cartridge, the breeching unit then separating to complete the extraction-to-rechambering process. In all likelihood, the gun would have worked had the subcontractors adhered to the specifications, especially as to welding and metallurgy.

Evidence suggests that U.S. General of Ordnance Crozier despised the designer of the Lewis gun, Colonel Isaac Newton Lewis of the Coastal Artillery, who had been told repeatedly to mind his cannon. The Lewis was coldly rejected by the U.S. Ordnance Board, despite the fact that it outperformed anything close to its weight. Lewis then sold the design on a royalty basis to the Belgians, British, and Savage.

Crozier vowed that no Lewis gun would ever serve with American troops. It's never been firmly established that it was by his personal order that Lewis guns were replaced by Chauchats before our soldiers went into combat, but it was done. Many of them probably still litter roadside subsoil in France, for American troops were quick to appreciate that a machinegun which will not shoot is merely an inert fire-drawing device. That's if the Chauchat itself didn't kill or injure its operator during a magazine explosion. Better units, especially those of the U.S. Marines, suddenly acquired all sorts of non-issue automatic weapons; Army troops lugging this French abomination quickly learned to carry a Lebel or Berthier (8mm Lebel) or U.S. Springfield so that *when*—not if—their Chauchat failed, they could at least defend themselves and make some use of themselves and their generous supply of ammunition.

The Chauchat's use in the French army involved using the gun in great quantity whenever possible, and even then the French seem to have experienced a lot of unit-wide failures. The placing of this weapon with American troops seems to owe much to tunnel vision on the part of the U.S. Ordnance Board, a deep personal grudge, and unwillingness to inspect weapons before acceptance. Wherever the weapon was used—it was actually sold to the Belgians and Greeks after the war—its cheap construction of ordinary plumbing and tool materials and poor overall quality and fit caused it to fail. Many soldiers died because of this. There is no record of a procurement official, contractor, or major ordnance figure anywhere having been even questioned about his decisions in regard to the Chauchat.

The Chauchat's problem wasn't just cheapness. Even a brilliantly executed Chauchat of very high quality materials would still experience a lot of jams, partly owing to the magazine design, partly because of the odd ejector—and the gun would still be inaccurate. This is a lousy design. If you own a registered Chauchat, I strongly suggest you either deactivate it and make it into a planter, or hang it someplace where you'll never even think of shooting it.

Hakim

The Hakim rifle is the Egyptian son of a pedigreed Swedish sire, accurate and powerful, if a trifle heavy. Chambered for the potent 7.92x57mm (8mm Mauser) cartridge, and using the straightforward Eklund-Ljungmann gas system in which the gas flows directly to the bolt, this beefy rifle can shoot minute-of-angle groups with high-quality ammo. So why is the Hakim in this article? It served in Egypt, which means deserts, so it seldom had the good fortune to be serviced by technically sophisticated soldiers, or to be fed first-rate ammo.

Because of tight tolerances in the bolt components, the Hakim is far more prone to stoppages from grains of sand jamming its operation than any other semi-automatic rifle I've ever tested. I discovered this in a fairly mild sandstorm in Arizona. Had it been actually dropped in the sand, I'm not sure I'd have even been able to detail strip and clean the rifle. On the other hand, you could once have bought this gun for less than $200 almost anywhere. They've *all* been imported to the U.S.

Among its other eccentricities, the Hakim requires exact positioning of its magazine group, to the extent that the screws must be in *precisely* the correct position for the hammer mechanism and magazine feed to function properly. To emphasize the point, hardened wire loops and stakes register and assure that position, making the rifle difficult to detail disassemble. Also, stripping the bolt assembly can be hazardous to one's health because of the powerful spring.

The manufacturing glitches of this Egyptian-built Swedish design involve the extractor, which is often too sharp and a bit too hard. It tends to chop slots in harder brass, making extraction, therefore ejection, impossible.

The excessively tight tolerances elsewhere amount to design deficiencies, for the rifle should have been redesigned for the Egyptians. The extractor is easily removed and polished, and only a bit of "melting" is usually necessary to assure reliable function. However, the Egyptian ammo is made from very brittle brass and may continue to ding rather badly. I got mediocre performance from all U.S. 8mm ammo, but Norma and other European commercial stuff shot superbly.

The adjustable gas system works off a valve near the center of the barrel and will require considerable adjustment with dirty ammo. With the underloaded American rounds,

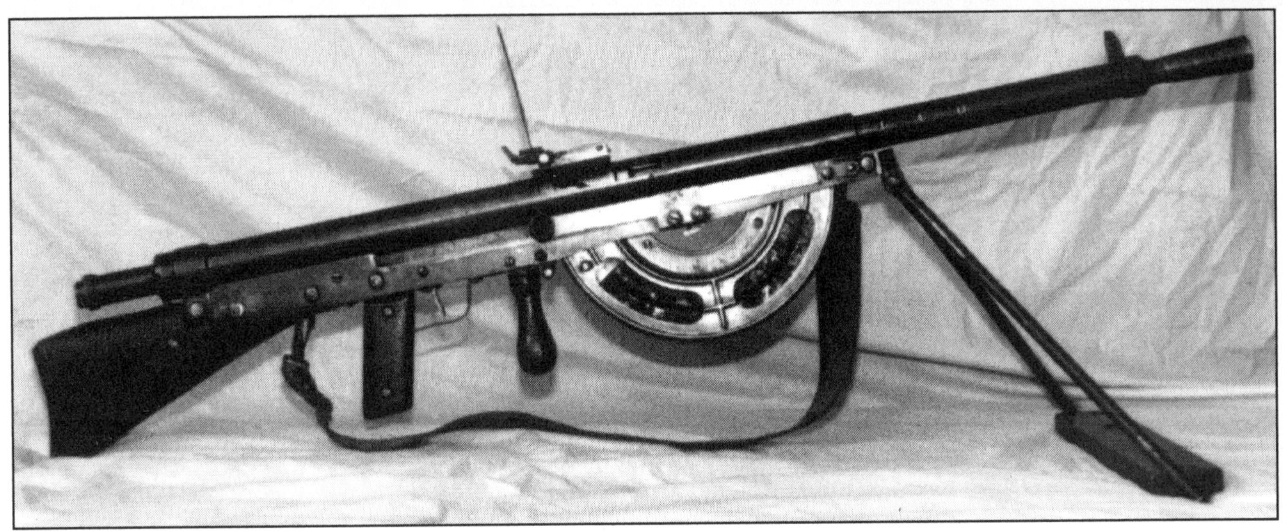

The Chauchat looks like a concoction of leftover gas pipe and plumbing parts. Its single virtue was its low cost.

you'll be shooting with the gas valve nearly wide open. Normal loads give reliable function near the center position. The compensator works superbly.

Had it stayed closer to the Arctic Circle, the Hakim would never have made this list. But in Egypt, it must have been a real loser. Adopted in the late '40s when King Farouk was in power, the sales presentations for firearm and factory setup must have been very interesting. Its only known front line use was in the 1956 Suez War, when it was heavily supplemented by the SAFN 49.

It is nice to know that, even in a refined, reserved socialist state like Sweden, there were, at least in the late '40s, a few salesmen good enough to have warmed the heart of P.T. Barnum. And they even managed to get rid of a rather splendid factory and set of machine tools for which they had no further use.

M-14

I was ten or eleven years old when I first saw an M-14 at my local National Guard Armory, with an exhibition of other new and historic weapons. I hadn't done much high-powered rifle shooting then, but I read a lot of weapons' history. And I hankered to own the M-1, which the M-14 had just replaced officially (it was 1957 or '58) if not in fact. The M-14 was still called T-44, with the "M-14" in parentheses. I turned to my brother and said, "Why did they make it so light in front *and* try to make the M-1 into a machinegun?"

Someone smiled indulgently and remarked, "I'm sure they know a lot of things we don't."

I shut up, but I was never quite comfortable with "them" knowing laws of physics undiscovered by the rest of the world.

The U.S. M-14 was, in essence, a product-improved M-1, born of a very long gestation period beginning almost as soon as the first M-1s were issued. Gripes about the M-1's weight, eight-round en bloc clip, and complex tear-down procedure led to a whole series of modified rifles with larger magazine capacity, lightened receivers, simplified operating rod setups, etc. The T-20E2 led to the T-44, which was tested against the T-48 (FAL), a Belgian design actually constructed in test quantities in the U.S. by H&R (500 made) and High Standard (13 produced). The FAL seems to have won all the field comparisons. It would've cost about the same in large quantities, probably less over the long run because it was a fully developed design.

As the leaders of NATO, the United States had developed the 308/7.62x51mm cartridge from the 300 Savage family. And by suggestion and the occasional twisting of arms, they persuaded experimenters in Britain to abandon the revolutionary EM2 rifle and its 7mm cartridge and influenced designers of the CETME and FAL in Spain and Belgium to forget the intermediate 7.92 Kurz cartridge as "terribly underpowered."

CETME became the Spanish standard and was developed into the Heckler & Koch G3/HK91 rifle, and FAL became the standard rifle of much of the non-communist world. Both, because they were originally prototyped in that form, proved to be readily adaptable to a later generation of "intermediate" cartridges and have been directly downscaled to 223. Their fully automatic forms, with heavier barrels and beefed up parts, work reasonably well, though they are by no means considered good substitutes for general-purpose or heavy machineguns.

Meantime, in Italy, with much less expense and hoopla, Beretta, who had been making M-1s since the early 1950s, produced the BM-59, a rifle very similar to the M-14 in purpose and function, whose receiver was closer to the original M-1. It was adopted by the Italians in 1962, five years after M-14, but after only four years' development time and very little expense.

The M-14 proved to be a dead end. The M-15, the initial 14-pound automatic rifle variant, was dropped almost immediately because, even with the added weight, it was a very mediocre automatic weapon. The M-14 was supposed to replace every weapon in the military inventory, from the M-3 submachine gun—some authorities say the pistol, too—and M-1 Carbine, up to and including the BAR and the odds and ends of Browning M1919A6 and other light machineguns developed since 1940. It proved to be an adequate replacement only for the M-1 and the carbine, which is why it was the undisputed U.S. service rifle only from 1957 to 1964-5, when the M-16 began to replace it.

Having said all that, it should be noted that I am an M-14 fan of the first order. For precision, semi-automatic fire, there's nothing better. The gun's failure is that it is one of the world's *worst* fully automatic weapons. During the early stages of the Vietnam war, the *American Rifleman* (February 1965) put it succinctly, implying what was about to happen: "...it has been the general opinion that M-14 control in full-automatic fire is not sufficient. The operational significance of this matter never has been settled."

It has now. Perhaps a reduced NATO load, especially for full-automatic fire, coupled with modifications similar to those which allow the Spanish CETME to function with reduced or standard loads, would've prevented the problem; it would also have complicated the engineering, implying a variable gas system and/or springs. But it might have allowed the rifle to stay in service in situations like Vietnam, where bullet-hosing devices were handy. Instead, those weapons are gathering dust or being demilitarized with welding torches, and our military depends on a 22 which many feel has neither adequate range nor punch for theaters like the Middle East, where visibility is excellent and long-range shooting can often decide battles.

The M-14 cost $68.75, complete, through most of its procurement life. M-1s averaged around $100, some twenty years earlier. The rifle was simplified, meeting most of the complaints of the World War II infantry soldier. With a five-round magazine, the M-14 by Armscorp or M-1A by Springfield Armory (Illinois) is light enough for field carry on a genuine hunt. The M-14's early production problems—too tight stocks, cracked receivers, defective extractors and ejectors—proved to be teething problems a little more severe than, but similar to, those experienced with M-1 back in the '30s. The real problem was a center of gravity too high and too far to the rear for automatic fire.

The rifle was adopted because it was familiar to soldiers trained on the M-1, contractors who were set up to produce the M-1, and to critics, because it "looked like a rifle," whereas the FAL was "upside down." Production totaled about 1,380,000 guns, of which only a few thousand seem to be in issue now. Production of military M-14s ceased in 1964.

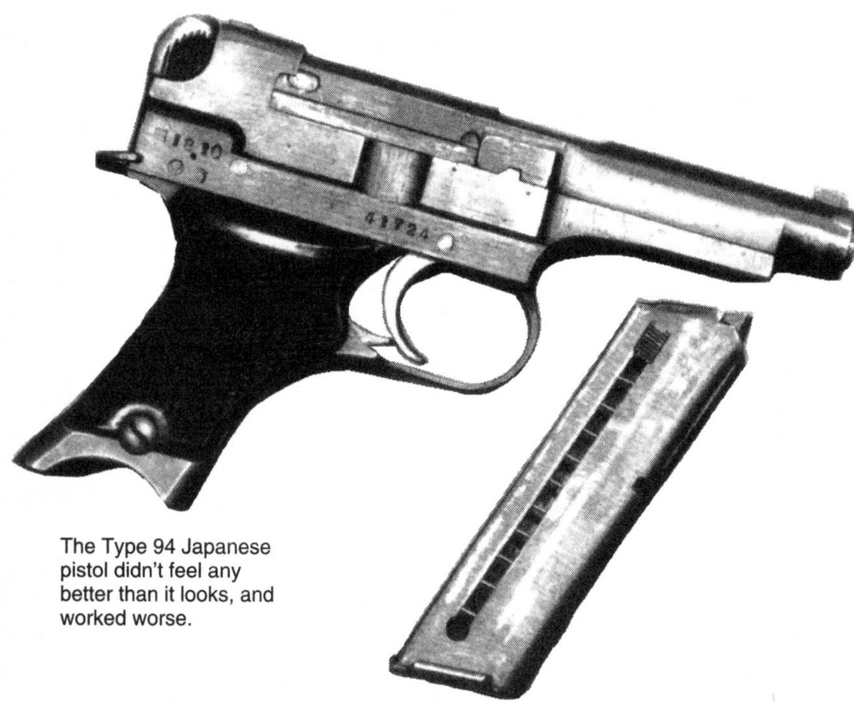

The Type 94 Japanese pistol didn't feel any better than it looks, and worked worse.

If the M-14's only failing was in full-automatic fire, how bad was it? Back in the early '60s, I watched a group of veteran Marines at a military range answer just that question. The M-14 was compared to a BAR, M-1, and an FN commercial FAL/HB. All three weapons, including the M-1, fired semi-automatically, landed several times more hits at 100-, 200- and 500-yard ranges than the M-14 fired full auto. The longer the M-14's bursts, the more profound the differences. The BAR, of course, excelled, but the full-auto FN was not far behind.

To the military, the M-14 was an expensive failure. We *might* have been better served by modified M-1s with nothing more sophisticated than a jazzed-up, twenty-round magazine added. Like a lot of American hardware, and even more ideas, the unique character of the Vietnam war rendered the rifle obsolete.

Japanese Type 94

Japanese issue handguns before 1945 were a strange lot. Even the beautifully made Nambus were held to a standard of mediocrity by their fairly accurate but grossly underpowered cartridge. The mass-produced Type 14 was a modified production version of the Nambu system, whose reliability varied according to its quality of construction. The Type 94, though, was a genuine freak. The gun was probably more reliable than it looked, but it happens to be just about the ugliest handgun ever designed.

The failings of the Type 94 are well known. A sharp blow on the exposed sear bar on the pistol's left side can cause force a discharge, even if the pistol is on safe. And, especially with worn internals, the pistol could also fire unlocked and open at the breech. Feed was reasonably good, until quality completely disappeared about 1944, and the magazine design, though skimpy at six shots, was exceptionally sturdy.

About 3000 pistols were sold commercially to somebody, somewhere (no one seems to know to whom) before the military began purchasing them in 1937. One Japanese authority said the gun was preferred by motorized troops because it would fit the pistol ports on Japanese armored vehicles. The gun is uncomfortable and awkward, even for shooters with tiny hands. Trigger pull on most specimens is rough, raspy and stiff. About 72,000 appear to have been made.

One authority says the Type 94 was "designed to eliminate most of the bad features of Type 14." If so, someone spent a lot of time concocting new bad features. Added to which, most of the guns are sloppy shooters.

The genuine unmistakable turkey, it is clear, may be a gun that won't shoot at all, or one that shoots unreliably and/or inaccurately, or one that requires a specific, but unavailable environment, generally a nice clean one.

Turkeys are born everywhere, everywhere they can be designed and approved and produced without being tested more or less publicly by anyone who knows. Sound familiar? ●

by EDWARD R. CREWS

The Guns of Jamestown

CAPTAIN JOHN SMITH knew when he heard the first screams that Indians had ambushed his two men at their camp along Virginia's Chickahominy River. Smith and a native guide had left the site fifteen minutes earlier to reconnoiter. Now, with his men dead or captured, Smith had to rely on himself. No rescuers were close, and the ambushers surely soon would search for him.

A veteran of hard-fought campaigns in the Low Countries and Eastern Europe, Smith acted swiftly, knowing that delay in battle meant death. The English explorer grabbed his guide, tore a garter from his own clothing and with it bound the man's arm to his. Smith now had a shield and a hostage. Within seconds, two Indians appeared from the forest. They immediately began shooting arrows. One grazed Smith's right thigh. He returned fire with his pistol, apparently a French snaphaunce, an early type of muzzle-loading flintlock.

From other skirmishes, the Indians knew about the destructive power of European firearms, and Smith's attackers retreated into the woods as the captain reloaded. It was obvious that the Indians would return shortly, so Smith fled into the nearby Chickahominy Swamp, dragging his human shield along.

Only about eight months earlier, in April 1607, Smith and more than a hundred other adventurers had arrived in Virginia following a four-month voyage from England in three tiny sailing ships. The expedition was underwritten by the Virginia Company, a commercial enterprise with a royal charter to colonize North America.

The men established a settlement at Jamestown on the James River, determined to make their fortunes

The matchlock was imperfect for the American frontier. Its burning match was a signal in the forest. (Jamestown-Yorktown Foundation photo)

and to create an English toehold in the New World. Few realized then that they had come to a place of intense danger. Disease, starvation and internal discord would plague the colony. So would the natives who alternately treated the newcomers with kindness and ferocity, offering food one moment and hails of arrows the next.

An English prisoner could find himself an honored guest or a victim of torture as did George Cassen, member of another section of the Smith-led Chickahominy River trip. According to contemporary accounts, Cassen was "sacrificed as they (the Indians) thought, to the Divell, being stripped naked, and bound to two stakes, with his backe against a great fire: then did they rippe him and burne his bowels, and dried his flesh to the bones, which they kept above ground in a byeroome."

The Indians somehow hoped that a policy of sporadic warfare, terrorism and friendly persuasion would convince the colonists to leave. However, given the schizophrenic quality of their relationship with the natives, the English settlers naturally came to rely heavily on experienced military leaders, like Smith, as well as on the technological edge provided by their guns, instead of leaving.

"Jamestown might have succeeded without firearms," said Thomas E. Davidson, senior curator for the Jamestown-Yorktown Foundation, which maintains a museum and living history park in Virginia. "But these weapons gave the English a big advantage in dealing with the wilderness. Firearms certainly made the process easier, not only as weapons but also as tools."

As the Smith story demonstrates, firearms were constant companions to early settlers and often made the difference between life and death. Smith, by the way, eventually was captured in the swamp, taken to Chief Powhatan, sentenced to be executed and allegedly saved by the Indian leader's daughter, Pocahontas. For the student of American folklore, the story remains one of the nation's most enduring legends, one constantly reinvented and retold—most recently, successfully and inaccurately, by Disney studios.

The early Jamestown defenses include cannon for the walls, matchlock muskets for the citizen soldiers, and armor to preserve those scarce soldiers, in close combat. (Jamestown-Yorktown Foundation photo)

This 1612 print of John Smith's map of Virginia is on exhibit in the Jamestown Settlement. Smith's map, the result of exploration he undertook during his $2\frac{1}{2}$ years in Virginia—1607 to 1609—was the first accurate representation of the Chesapeake Bay and its environs. North is the right.

The guns of Jamestown, however, were not brought to Virginia primarily to defend the colonists against North American natives. They mainly were part of English preparations to protect the settlement from Spaniards. When the settlers left England in 1606, their nation's chief rival was Spain, which already had thriving colonies in Central and South America.

The two countries had been locked in conflict for years. This fight was rooted in a struggle for dominance of Europe's economy and politics. It also had a strong religious dimension. Spain's ruler, Philip II, was a staunch Roman Catholic and enemy of Protestantism, which held sway in England.

Furious at English support for Protestant rebels in other countries, Philip pledged to destroy the English heretics. He dispatched a great armed fleet, the Armada, to crush the island kingdom. However, bad luck, foul weather and daring English sea captains wrecked this endeavor in 1588, breaking Spain's control of the seas. That opening allowed English colonists to travel to the New World and English privateers, like Francis Drake and John Hawkins, to plunder Spanish treasure ships and outposts.

The men who came to Jamestown believed that they would suffer similar retaliatory raids. They never did, but operating on that assumption, one of their first projects was to build a triangular fort. This structure was patterned on English fortifications in Ireland. It had a high wooden palisade, watch towers and cannon emplacements at each corner.

Besides relying on sturdy walls and cannon, the colonists also would defend themselves with longarms. The initial mainstay of Jamestown's early defenses was the matchlock musket.

"For the first 15 or so years of the Jamestown colony, the matchlock was the basic arm. It hung on for a long time because it was cheap, comparatively easy to mass produce, robust and anyone could fix it," Davidson said. "The gun's dimensions varied, as did its styles and grades. It might weigh about 12 pounds, maybe more. In Europe, it was fired from a rest. It was smoothbore and not particularly accurate at long ranges. At 100 yards, firing and hitting anything was largely a random matter. It was popular with European armies for many years."

The weapon took its name from its ignition system, a burning cord that had been soaked in saltpeter. Firing the gun was a fairly simple process. The gunner merely pushed up on the trigger. This caused the match, held in place by an arm called a serpentine, to fall into a pan of powder. This burned through a hole in the barrel and ignited the main charge, which fired the bullet.

Like all muzzleloaders, the matchlock required a soldier to load blackpowder and a projectile separately. The powder was carried in wooden cylinders, each containing a measured amount suitable for one shot. Cylinders were worn on a bandolier. Bullets were carried in a pouch. A rammer was used to seat the bullet atop the powder after it was poured down the barrel. A wad of paper came last to hold the load in place.

The matchlock's biggest drawback was the burning cord, which was lit at both ends. During loading, the musketeer removed it from the serpentine. He then folded it in half

Simon van de Passe created this picture of John Smith for Smith's *Description of New England,* 1616. The engraving is about 8x10 inches. (Virginia Historical Society photo)

and gripped it underneath the weapon with his left hand, the same hand he used to hold the gun while loading. One can imagine the delicate balancing act required to keep the burning cord and powder separated. Add an attacking enemy and the reloading picture becomes really interesting.

Used on the steady ramparts at Jamestown fort, the matchlock offered a powerful form of protection and intimidation. Once the Englishmen moved outside the walled town, however, the gun had serious defects. It was heavy, big and bulky, and therefore could not be brought into action quickly. The match had to be lit and kept burning. Wary Indians and skittish deer probably could smell it smoldering. Wet weather made firing difficult if not impossible, and a night assault could not be hidden.

Accidents were always possible. Smith, the cool-headed warrior, was hurt when a lit match ignited a powder bag he was carrying. His injuries forced his evacuation to England.

Given the matchlock's drawbacks, it's easy to understand why some colonists from Jamestown's earliest days preferred longarms using the snaphaunce ignition system, which was an early form of flintlock. It relied on a piece of flint, placed in a movable arm, striking a piece of steel to create sparks. Those sparks ignited powder in a pan and that ultimately set off the main charge. The snaphaunce was far more complicated mechanically than the matchlock. It also eliminated the burning match and therefore was a much more portable, practical weapon for the frontier.

Snaphaunce longarms, like the matchlock, came in a variety of sizes, weights and calibers. According to Davidson, a snaphaunce might weigh between 10 and 15 pounds. Caliber might be anything from 45 to more than 60. By about 1625, the snaphaunce largely had replaced the matchlock in Virginia. The real value of the snaphaunce, though, can be measured not by English enthusiasm for it but by native interest in it.

"Indians adapted quickly to the gun's presence in Virginia," said Davidson. "They clearly wanted guns, and colonial leaders constantly were attempting to stop them from getting guns."

Native fascination for English weaponry was demonstrated when Smith was captured. One of the first things his captors asked the captain to do was show them how to fire his pistol. Smith, fearful that native knowledge of guns would harm the colony, was vague about the process and broke the gun's arm that held the flint. Indians especially were eager to get snaphaunces, and archaeological digs have found snaphaunce parts at native American sites.

In fact, the power of firearms was recognized quickly by the Indians, who continually tried to trade for them or capture them if possible. One historian has theorized that during a critical period in 1608 when Jamestown faced starvation, Powhatan assisted the colonists largely to win their friendship and the use of their weapons to extend his empire. If so, his hopes went unfulfilled.

Besides longarms, some colonists, like Smith on the Chickahominy, carried pistols. Smith's apparently had a snaphaunce ignition system. And some men carried wheellocks, a more mechanically sophisticated weapon that had been available in Europe early in the 1500s.

Firearms were not the only weapons Jamestown settlers used. The men soon found that sometimes in Virginia's thick forests close-range weapons were more effective than guns. In the quick, merciless, close-in nature of Indian warfare, the settlers only had time to fire one round and then were forced to draw swords and fight hand-to-hand. The colonists carried swords, pikes and halberds. Halberds typically were not used for fighting and remained in the garrison when military expeditions went into the wilderness. Another edged weapon found in the Virginia colony was the bill. This polearm was immensely popular in England. Archaeologists have found evidence of these at Jamestown, and apparently 950 of them were shipped to Jamestown in 1623. Swords, we are told, were carried by all men regardless of rank. Archaeologists have found several different types of swords from the period, including broadswords and rapiers.

Smith reportedly used a falchion, a single-edged cutting sword. And a story about his using it in a fight with Paspehegh Indians illustrates, again, his calmness in battle and the skills needed to survive in Virginia. According to one version of the story, Smith and twenty armed men were patrolling near Jamestown, looking for a Dutchman who was aiding the Indians. The English band was headed into an ambush of forty bowmen led by Wowinchopunck, the Paspeheghs' king.

The natives became rattled when they realized that Smith was leading the unit and they fled. Smith sent his men after them and headed back to Jamestown alone. The Indian chief had remained behind, saw Smith and moved from behind his cover, drawing his bow. Smith rushed him and the two wrestled furiously. They eventually fell into the nearby river where Smith choked the king into submission, then dragged his assailant from the water, drew his sword and prepared to behead him. Then Smith's usual coolness asserted itself—a live king as hostage was worth a lot more than a dead one. The Englishman spared his valuable prisoner.

For anybody interested in early American edged weapons, Smith's choice of a falchion tells much about his character. This sword's blade curved somewhat like a Turkish scimitar, a weapon Smith knew about from his European campaigning. Northern European soldiers used the falchion extensively in the 14th and 15th centuries. By 1607, it was not as popular. But Smith chose it, perhaps, as one historian has suggested, to draw attention to himself and to his previous military experience.

Like guns, the Indians recognized that English swords, pikes and hatchets were superior to their wooden clubs and swords. The natives naturally traded for these items if they could and tried to capture them when they couldn't.

Interestingly enough (and oddly enough for anybody familiar with Virginia's muggy summers and overgrown woods), Jamestown's earliest soldiers were liberally supplied with armor. A foot soldier could find himself wearing a breast plate, back plate, helmet, gorget and tassets, which were thigh protectors. Some men wore chain mail. Musketeers wore quilted cloth tunics called jacks or heavy leather coats called buff coats.

Some historians question how much the men wore the armor, but apparently the equipment saw some use. Regulations developed about 1610 directed all Jamestown's men to wear their armor while guarding the settlement. This was to familiarize them with it before they went campaigning.

George Percy, a colony official, wrote that the men typically wore helmets and jacks during Smith's time. A tougher military policy toward the Indians was adopted by colonial leaders about 1610. After that date, Percy reported that heavier plate armor was worn in the field. He also wrote that "nott beinge acquainted nor acustomed to encownter w(i)th men in Armour, (the Indians had) mutche wondered thereatt especyally that they did nott see any of our men fall as they had done in other conflictts."

One surviving report also describes a raid led by Sir Thomas Dale against the Indians after plate armor and mail shirts were issued to the English. In this fight, English records show that about a hundred colonists wearing armor attacked the Nansemond tribe. Dale was wearing a helmet, which saved his life when its brim was struck by an arrow. Percy relates that even with this armor the shot was a close call. If the arrow had gone a bit lower, it might have "shott him in the braynes and indangered his lyfe."

All of this equipment, of course, was designed for use on European battlefields, not Virginia's woodlands. Western combat in the late 16th and early 17th centuries centered on massing infantry in tight groups and then closing and firing on the enemy.

"The European battlefield of the period also saw the employment of artillery and cavalry, something that didn't happen in America," said historian Davidson. "Battles were set-piece affairs with one side firing until the other broke. Then, the cavalry rode in and cut up the retreating force."

The model for this fighting came from Holland where the Dutch fought for independence from Spain. Military professionals took an intense interest in the conflict and adopted techniques and innovations developed there. Historians believe that early Virginia settlers may have brought Dutch military manuals, like Jacob DeGheyn's "The Exercise of Arms," to the New World and used them to train the militia.

Unfortunately for the colonists, little of this knowledge could be applied in Virginia. For starters, European tactics relied on having large masses of men. The first group of colonists numbered only slightly more than a hundred. They had scant ammunition, limited maneuvering room, no mounted troops, few cannon and no way to haul them.

Besides, the Indians were not going to bunch up and throw themselves on a fort in a pitched battle. Indian warfare by 1607 had evolved to match their technology and the terrain. That combat was based on ambushes with warriors using trees and brush for cover and concealment. Sometimes the Indians used formations—half-moons and squares—and sometimes extra warriors were hired or drafted for larger battles. Wounding and disabling the enemy was more important than killing him. Warriors took scalps as trophies and would cut off, dry and wear an enemy's hand as a symbol of courage.

Relations between colonists and Indians were shaky from the start. Neither party appeared particularly interested in peaceful coexistence. The English were determined to stay; the Indians were determined they should leave.

When the Englishmen first landed on Virginia's soil near Cape Henry on April 26, 1607, they were attacked by the natives. This hostility continued, and once before the fort was completed, the Paspeheghs attacked the exposed and inexperienced settlers. The fight lasted about an hour and only ended when musket fire and ship cannons were used effectively. Once the fort was completed, natives ambushed working parties outside it and occasionally fired arrows over the walls and into the compound.

The colonists were blockaded inside their fort through much of

Some of the guns of Jamestown are still there in the museum on the Jamestown site. A colonist's gear included matchlock, pikes, swords and armor. (Jamestown-Yorktown Foundation photo)

In 1608, John Smith listed 25 "peeces of ordinances" (cannon) mounted in the fort at Jamestown. This is a reproduction of an early 17th-century English saker. The gun and carriage weigh about 3000 pounds. The saker fired a 6-pound ball. (Jamestown-Yorktown Foundation photo)

1607 and well into 1608. Scared, disorganized and burdened with ineffective leadership, they could not find a means to get outside to farm, hunt or fish without risking attack.

This dismal period ended in autumn, 1608, when Smith became president of the settlement. He embarked upon an aggressive military policy designed to give the English a secure environment to get food and to cow the Indians into leaving them alone. The veteran officer quickly rebuilt the fort, which had burned, into a pentagon, and constructed and manned nearby blockhouses.

He then began turning the men into soldiers. They drilled every Saturday on a piece of open ground near the fort, called Smithfield. They quickly gained basic fighting skills, and Smith wasted no time in launching offensive actions against the natives.

The one-time mercenary readily and successfully abandoned European tactics and borrowed Indian ones. Under Smith, the English adopted the ambush and raid as the centerpiece of campaigns. The policy kept the Indians off-guard and even allowed Smith to recover some stolen items.

This promising policy (at least from the colonial viewpoint) did not continue. Smith was injured badly in 1609 in the accident mentioned earlier. With his departure, the colonists returned to the ineffective ways, and the Indians immediately returned to their tough and aggressive behavior.

The Virginia Company realized Smith's methods worked. The company eventually adopted a much harder line with the Indians and ultimately sent three tough-minded, experienced soldiers to lead the colony: Sir Thomas West, Sir Thomas Gates and Sir Thomas Dale. These men reintroduced drill, guards and Smith's "good defense is a good offense" policy.

As early as August in 1610, Jamestown's leaders sent Captain George Percy to raid a major Paspehegh village near the settlement. Percy took seventy men in two boats up river, off-loaded and then marched three miles to the village. The men approached quietly behind a captive guide named Percy, a color bearer and a drummer. The Englishmen struck when a pistol shot signalled the beginning of the attack. Fifteen Indians were killed; others fled or were captured. Houses were burned; corn in the field was destroyed. Percy sent a party further inland to destroy another village. The English had embraced fully their foe's ideas of warfare.

The fighting between Indians and Englishmen would continue in a sporadic way until 1614 when Pocahontas married English planter John Rolfe. An eight-year period of peace followed.

In 1622, a massive Indian uprising disrupted life in the colony and forced the settlers to develop a better organized militia whose membership was composed of all free white males under the leadership of wealthy planters. This force played a dominant role in Virginia's military history for the remainder of the 17th century.

The Indians in Eastern Virginia mounted one last major offensive against the settlers in 1644, but they were decisively defeated and found themselves totally controlled by the English. Although their numbers dwindled and they offered no real threat to England's Virginia colony, the Powhatan people endured. Their descendants live in Virginia today.

The guns of Jamestown were a key factor in the colony's survival. Without these weapons, English success in the New World probably would have been much more difficult and taken much longer. European firearms gave the colonists a vital technological edge during the settlement's uneasy early days.

In addition, the Jamestown experience nurtured many of the weapons-related traditions that survive in the United States almost 390 years after John Smith made his stand in the Chickahominy Swamp, including notions about hunting and self-sufficiency. Perhaps, though, the most important legacy of Jamestown was the idea that an armed American could play a major role in defending his family, his property and his community. ●

by J.I. GALAN

Realism in AIR POWER

The superb Gamo R-77 is an eight-shot 177 pellet snubby powered by CO_2.

This Webley representative proudly displays the Beeman Bearcub carbine, a potent barrel-cocker despite its overall length of just 37.8 inches.

LONG-TIME OBSERVERS now find it difficult, if not impossible, to keep up with all the new airguns, pellets and accessories. I am hard-pressed to gather all the pertinent information, let alone test each and every new model coming down the pike, and I'm working at it.

There *are* lots of new airguns coming along these days. At the 1996 SHOT Show, I counted seventeen new air pistols and probably eight new air rifles. This was hardly surprising, given the huge growth of the airgun market and the stiff competition among them for a decent share of that market.

Air pistols are showing a decidedly intriguing upsurge in variety after years of lagging behind air rifles. The trend toward air pistols that look like regular firearms has become more pronounced, something that I personally welcome because I've always been a staunch advocate of air pistols in the firearms training role. Many of the new models are, in fact, nearly exact copies of a variety of popular powder-burning handguns, which makes them useful trainers.

Let's begin, then, with the new air pistols.

Air Pistols

A newcomer with its headquarters in Moscow, Russia, **Anics Firm, Inc.,** is producing and marketing six superb CO_2-powered BB handguns, four of which are incredibly faithful look-alikes of popular autoloaders, while the other two are thirty-shot revolvers. The samples I saw were pleasantly heavy, solidly made and extremely well finished. They boast muzzle velocities of up to 460 fps with one standard 12-gram CO_2 cartridge. The semi-auto replicas have fifteen-shot magazines that fit in the grip, just like the real McCoys. Although at the time of this writing I have not had the opportunity to test these Russian BB guns, they certainly look impressive, and their retail prices are supposed to be close to those of American-made CO_2 plinking pistols.

Arms United Corp. from the Midwest is currently importing the Gamo line of airguns from

The GP-1 is a high-tech pre-charged pneumatic rifle of extremely compact dimensions that packs plenty of oomph.

Spain, including Gamo's latest handgun model, the R-77 revolver. This eight-shot DA/SA 177-caliber pellet wheelgun is powered by a 12-gram CO_2 cartridge and generates a muzzle velocity of about 350 fps, fired single or double action. The Gamo R-77, incidentally, has the distinction of being the smallest pellet revolver made so far. I have been shooting a sample for about five months and can tell you that it is fun to shoot.

By the time you read this, **Crosman Corporation/Benjamin Sheridan**'s new air pistol offerings, the Black Fang and Black Venom, will be on dealers' shelves. Intended for the budget-priced plinking-pistol market, these two similar-looking spring-piston models are faithful copies of the Colt 22 Target autoloader. Although both pistols have seventeen-shot BB magazines, the Black Venom model can also shoot 177-caliber pellets or darts as a single shot and can muster 250 fps, while the BB-only Black Fang reaches 220 fps.

Daisy's most recent models consist of a pair of CO_2-powered repeating pistols. Following in

The Daisy Power Line 2003 is the first handgun to employ Daisy's revolutionary thirty-five-shot helical pellet magazine.

(Above) For fast-paced plinking fun, the Daisy 454 semi-auto BB pistol is hard to beat. Its slide goes back and forth, like a cartridge autoloader.

The Russian BB pistols are coming! These hefty semi-auto CO_2 BB pistols from Anics Firm even house the magazine in the grip.

their now well-established tradition of top quality at easily affordable prices, their new Power Line Models 454 and 2003 are top examples of state-of-the-art CO_2 technology. The Power Line 454 is a semi-auto with reciprocating slide and can empty its twenty-round BB magazine real quick, at about 420 fps. The Power Line 2003 is a thiry-five-shot 177-caliber pellet semi-auto using the same helical magazine developed for Daisy's highly popular Models 2001 and 2002 repeating rifles. With a rifled steel barrel—as opposed to smooth brass for the 454—and an MV of 400 fps, this semi-auto is a real handful. These are not replicas, but have the generic styling of the full-size combat autoloaders so much in vogue today.

Although not brand-new, the potent BSA 240 Magnum air pistol from **Precision Sales International, Inc. (BSA)** is finally becoming widely available in the United States. It's a spring-piston pistol in 177- or 22-caliber that utilizes a top-cocking action. Another salient point of this very well made air pistol is that despite its compactness (9 inches overall), it can produce around 510 fps in 177 and 420 fps or so in 22. In addition, this punchy British model also has the generic looks of a deadly serious "wondernine" for those, like myself, who fancy such looks in an air pistol.

Unfortunately, **Rutten Airguns** of Belgium does not have an established importer here in the U.S. at this time. A real pity, because Rutten airguns certainly exhibit a high level of workmanship, and are reliable and accurate. Rutten's latest offering is a spring-piston pistol resembling rather closely the famous Webley Hurricane.

Hammerli's world-class Model 480 and 480K match air pistols are currently available in the U.S. from Sigarms. The pistols, quite similar on the outside, have different grip material; walnut for the 480 and synthetic for the 480K. Typically, these Olympic-grade 10-meter pistols will put a sizeable hole in your wallet, but, as they say, you only go around once...

In 1996, **Walther** gave us all a real surprise with the CP88 pistol, a CO_2-powered 177-caliber pellet semi-auto replica of the Walther P88 combat autoloader. The CP88 uses an eight-shot rotary magazine fairly similar to that of the Crosman 1008 pistol, and is also powered by one standard 12-gram CO_2 cartridge housed in the grip.

Crosman's new Black Venom pistol can shoot BBs as a repeater, or pellets and darts in single shot mode.

The Crosman Black Fang is a seventeen-shot BB plinker patterned after the Colt 22 Target autoloader.

Even Walther is jumping into the replica game with the CP88, a CO_2-powered pellet semi-auto copy of the pricey Walther P88 "wondernine." Shown is the long barrel "competition" version.

Another new model from Walther is the LP200. This 10-meter world-class competition air pistol can give up to 500 shots from one canister of compressed air, something that dedicated match shooters appreciate. Like all such pistols, the Walther LP200 carries a pretty stiff price tag.

Air Rifles

Air Rifle Trade Suppliers of Britain recently announced their new GP-1 (Gun Power 1) pre-charged pneumatic rifle. Actually designed here in the Colonies by a Texan, the GP-1 looks like something out of a sci-fi thriller with its stubby profile, folding bipod and all-black finish. Intended mainly for serious field applications, the GP-1 is a compact powerhouse with a bolt-action pellet-loading system and an air bottle that doubles as the buttstock. The pre-production prototype I saw at the 1996 SHOT Show appeared extremely well made and was a real attention-grabber.

Arms United Corp. is importing the new Gamo Hunter 880, a barrel-cocking airsporter in the magnum class with its sizzling 1000-plus fps muzzle velocity in 177-caliber. This potent rifle should retail for around $179.

Beeman Precision Airguns

did not introduce a new air pistol, but unveiled several new sporting-class adult air rifles. In the pre-charged pneumatic (PCP) group, Beeman's MAKO FT (Field Target) is a beautifully made, potent 177-caliber rifle. Imported from England, it comes with a deluxe walnut thumbhole stock. In the spring-piston barrel-cocking group, the Beeman Bearcub is destined to become a hot item, given its carbine length of just 37.8 inches overall and punchy 915 fps muzzle velocity in 177. If you prefer a full-size barrel-cocker, the new Beeman R9 is made by the famous Weihrauch firm in Germany and is available in 177- and 20-caliber, giving muzzle velocities of

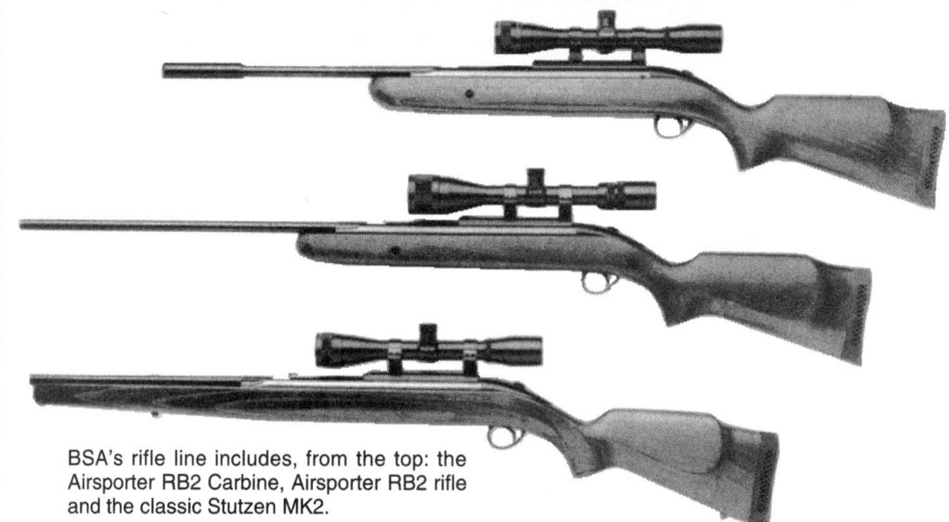

BSA's rifle line includes, from the top: the Airsporter RB2 Carbine, Airsporter RB2 rifle and the classic Stutzen MK2.

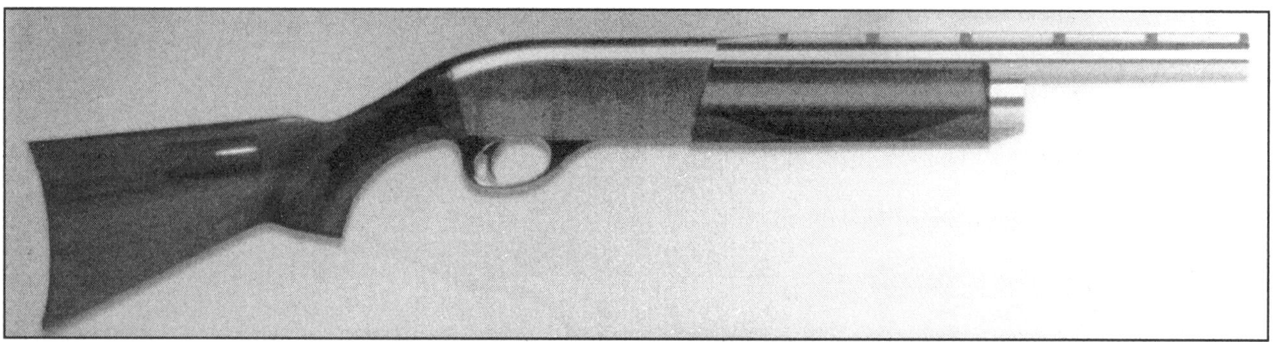

Crosman's new Black Lightning is a single-pump pneumatic BB repeater with an MV of 350 fps.

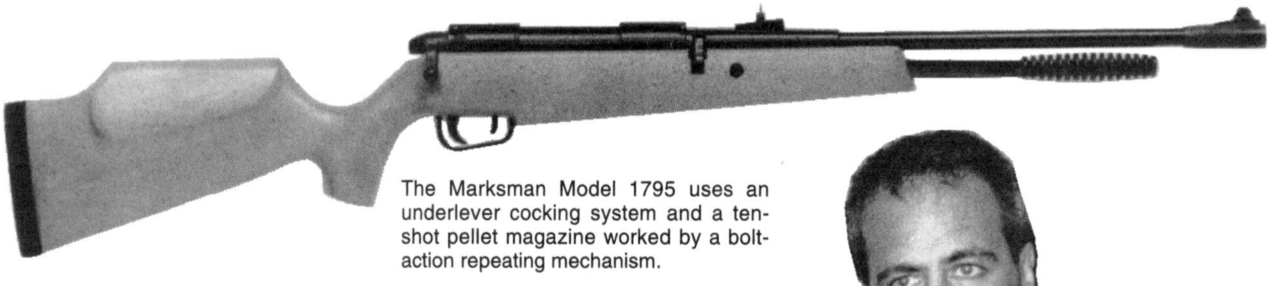

The Marksman Model 1795 uses an underlever cocking system and a ten-shot pellet magazine worked by a bolt-action repeating mechanism.

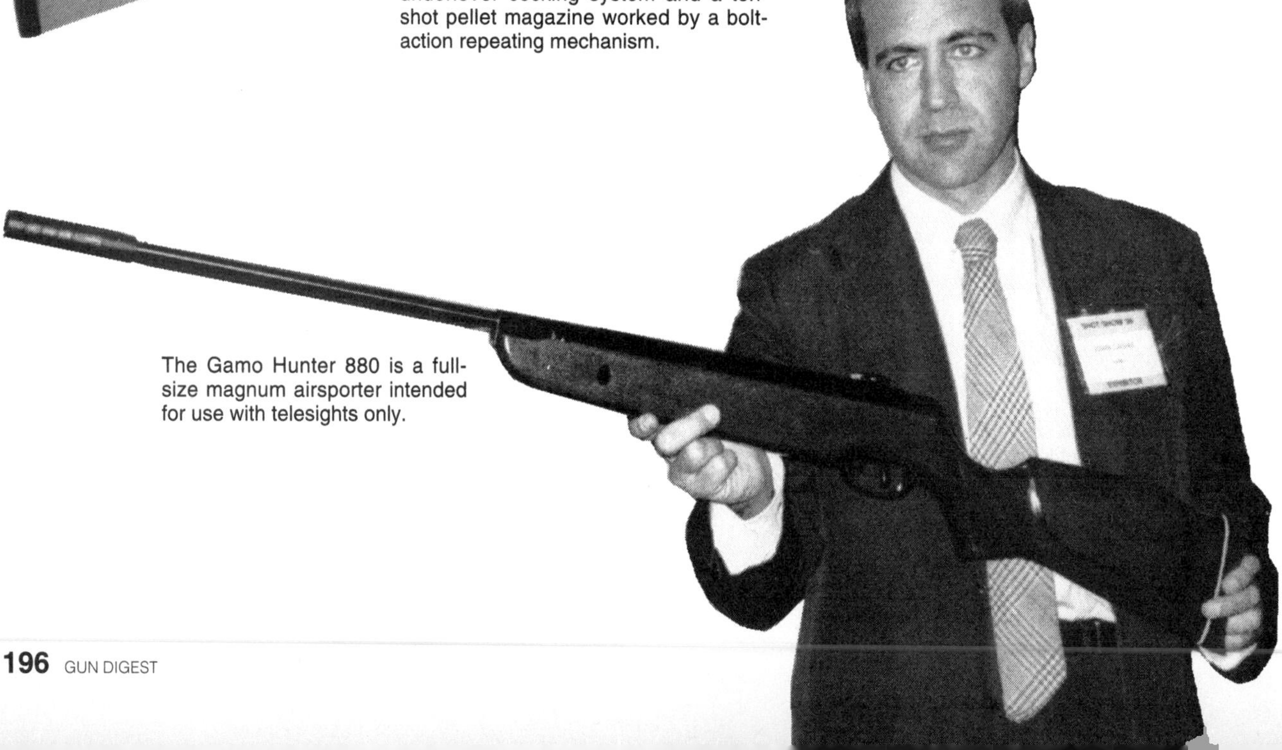

The Gamo Hunter 880 is a full-size magnum airsporter intended for use with telesights only.

The superb BSA Gold Star (top) is a ten-shot repeater. The Super Star MK2 (middle) and Super Star MK2 Carbine are also magnum class air rifles. All three are available in 177, 22 and 25 calibers.

The RWS Model 48SC is a magnum sporter in an elegant, yet practical package.

Dynamit Nobel-RWS also introduced the Model 46 this year, another magnum spring-piston sporter.

Beeman now has the Aim Brace shoulder stock from Webley, shown here converting the Webley Nemesis air pistol into a handy mini-carbine.

1000 and 800 fps, respectively. Beeman's new R1-AW adds a truly modern look to one of this company's all-time top sellers. It combines a nickel-plated barrel and action with a black composite stock. This magnum airsporter is available in 20-caliber, producing a respectable 900 fps at the muzzle.

The only *really* new long gun in **Crosman Corp.**'s lineup this year is called the Black Lightning. Styled after the Remington 11-87 scattergun, this new model is a single-pump pneumatic BB repeater that can spit out those BBs at an MV of 350 fps. Featuring a twenty-round BB magazine, plus a reservoir with capacity for 300 BBs, the Black Lightning will become a favorite as soon as it reaches store shelves.

Crosman Models 788 and 781—beginner-oriented pneumatic smoothbores—have been given facelifts and are now marketed as the Black Fire and Black Serpent. The two fun guns are black throughout.

There are two new magnum airsporters from **Dynamit Nobel-RWS, Inc.**, this year: The RWS Model 48SC is an intriguing rendition of the powerful RWS 48 with a black epoxy-coated thumbhole stock and folding bipod. The second rifle is made by Diana in Germany; the RWS Model 46 should become a true classic in the world of adult air rifles, mainly due to its underlever cocking action and elegant lines.

Marksman's new Model 1795 air rifle offers an underlever-cocking spring-piston power plant and a bolt-action loading system using a ten-shot magazine for 177-caliber pellets. Each time the bolt is worked, the rotary magazine automatically indexes one pellet up to the breech. Muzzle velocity hovers around 500 fps, and there's a stylish synthetic stock, elevation-adjustable open sights and a grooved receiver.

Precision Sales International, Inc. offers the splendid BSA line of adult air rifles—eight models, in all—including the new Super Star MK2 Carbine, the Airsporter RB2 Carbine and the light but powerful Super Sport America. The latter is a barrel cocker, while the first two are underlever cockers. The Super Sport America also has a textured matte black stock and, like most of the air rifles in the BSA line, a choice of 177-, 22- or 25-caliber. The quarter-bore, in particular, is a real whacker for small game hunting. Personally, I am delighted to see BSA air rifles become available once again here in America; the hiatus has lasted fifteen years. ●

The New CZ-75B

TESTFIRE

COMBINING THE lines, feel, pointing qualities, caliber and high magazine capacity of the Browning Hi-Power with the locking cam and internal slide rails of the SIG P210, the Czech CZ-75 emerged in 1975, one of the earliest of the double-action "wondernines." That appearance was coupled with political reality—firearms made in Communist countries were embargoed by the United States, so the CZ-75 simply was not available to U.S. citizens.

With the genuine Ceskoslovenska Zbrojovka (CZ) product unavailable, the prized design was cloned in Italy by Fratelli Tanfoglio and introduced in the U.S. under such model designations as TZ-75, TA-90 and P9. Now, the "real thing," is finally arriving in the U.S. in a variety of models imported and distributed by Magnum Research.

What's impressive about the 1996 models is the continual advancement and refinement of the basic design. A year or so ago, Magnum Research was importing two very distinct models—the CZ-75 and the CZ-85. The CZ-75 had a traditional spur hammer, and the CZ-85 hammer was rounded. The trigger guard of the CZ-75 was rounded in the traditional style; the CZ-85 was squared-off and checkered. And there were other differences. The CZ-85 fea-

The CZ-75B is thoughtfully designed, fully enhanced and naturally pointing.

The newest version of the oldest "Super-Nine," the CZ-75B has lost none of the original appeal.

The field-stripped CZ-75B reveals its basic simplicity—not much to go wrong here.

(Below) To create the infamous ten-round bureaucrat's magazine, CZ either inserts a plastic plug or heavily crimps the original fifteen-round magazine.

tured an ambidextrous safety and a slide release—the CZ-75 did not. The top of the CZ-85 slide was grooved to break up reflected light—that on the CZ-75 was not.

What CZ has accomplished in the last year is the gradual integration of the finer features of the CZ-85 into the basic CZ-75 that now sports a rounded hammer spur, squared-off and checkered trigger guard, three-dot sights, non-reflective grooved slide and firing-pin safety block at a price that is still "basic" in the realm of wondernines. The new CZ-75B is as enhanced a full-size 9mmP as one could wish for, lacking only a decocking lever—a modern amenity this writer feels is another gimmick to clutter up an otherwise sleek semi-automatic. A secure firing-pin safety block—indicated by the "B" in CZ-75B—is another recent upgrade. At the end of the trigger squeeze, the trigger bar lug acts on a plunger lever to unlock the firing pin.

Missing today, of course, is CZ's full-capacity magazine holding fifteen rounds. The new ten-rounder is furnished by the factory with either a plastic plug in its base or with two deep detents that pinch the original fifteen-round magazine down to the ten-round level. Excellent fifteen-round magazines are still available from parts purveyors like Tom Forrest—a little pricey, but available.

The finish on the CZ-75B is a black, non-reflective polymer that is often seen on military firearms of the former Eastern Bloc. It is a very tough finish that resists corrosion and holster wear.

The 35-ounce CZ-75B is a pleasure to shoot in 9mmP caliber. The CZ can safely be carried in the cocked-and-locked mode, secured by an excellent frame-mounted safety, or fired double action from the hammer-down position. Due to a well-designed system, the double-action squeeze is smooth, fairly light and uninterrupted, although shooters with very small hands may find the forward starting position of the trigger in the double action a little difficult to fully master. The single-action let-off is nicely crisp.

On the range, the CZ-75B was tested with 400 rounds of various factory loads and favorite 9mmP handloads. Fired from a sandbag rest at 25 yards, the new CZ-75B performed as follows: the 115-grain Federal Gold Dot averaged 1268 fps and 2 inches; the 124-grain Gold Dot averaged 1212 fps and 2 inches; the 147-grain Gold Dot registered 941 fps and 2 inches. If this pistol is beginning to sound like a 2-inch grouper, you're right. The only load that consistently delivered smaller groups was a handload featuring 8.0 grains of Blue Dot and a Winchester 115-grain hollowpoint, with Winchester cases and primers. That load averaged 1306 fps and 1½ inches. All loads were well centered and approximately 2 inches high. In 400 rounds, the CZ failed to cycle twice, only with lighter handloads of PB. The CZ has a reputation; given its all-steel construction, I expect that reputation is warranted.

In summary, the Czech CZ-75B is a thoughtfully designed, well-made, accurate and attractively priced 9mmP. It's a natural pointer and can now be purchased in a variety of styles, finishes and models, including a compact, semicompact and adjustable-sighted combat model from Magnum Research. Having been in production for two decades, the CZ-75 just gets better and better.

Holt Bodinson

Mitchell's M9109 Riot Gun

TESTFIRE

Nice spreads at 20 yards with both #4 Buck and #00 Buck—standard loads.

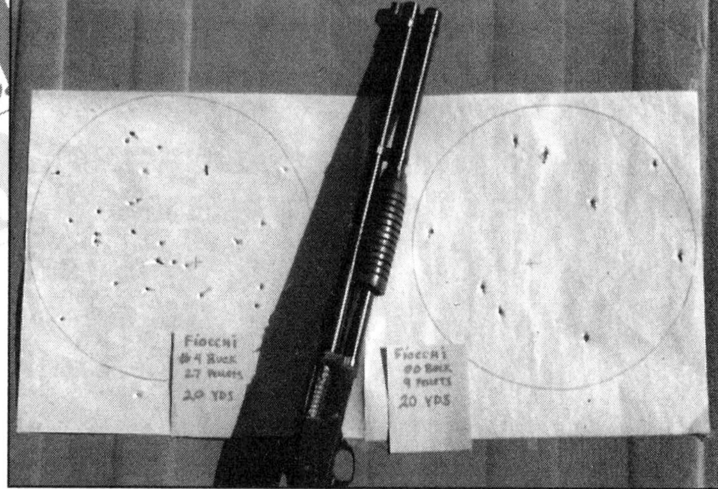

THIS IS A solid blued-steel, mahogany-stocked, well-built shotgun. It will load seven in the tubular magazine plus one in the chamber, a total of eight. Many police departments had very similar guns as standard issue for years. This is a dedicated police-use smoothbore.

The barrel is .890-inch outside diameter at the muzzle, while the bore is .745-inch, and appears well polished. All metal work is nicely blued; sights are a hooded bead front and an adjustable open sliding leaf rear dovetailed into the barrel in some versions.

Deserving comment is the shellcarrier. I've had a pump gun malfunction and release a cartridge from the magazine while the gun was in battery, thereby jamming the gun completely. One must find something to slip between the magazine loading port and shell carrier so as to force the jammed cartridge back into the magazine tube, thereby clearing the jam. The Model 9109 shellcarrier (or lifter, if you prefer) offers a large open center section through which one may easily push a jammed shell back into its proper place in the magazine tube.

(Above) There have not been many mahogany-stocked riot guns, but here's one.

The mahogany stock is smoothly finished. There is a pistol grip cap of a contrasting wood and a black plastic buttplate. The slide handle is slim, cylindrical and grooved for a very positive non-slip feel.

Felt recoil of the gun, while noticeable when firing slugs and buckshot, wasn't objectionable. I was pleasantly surprised at the rather good groups fired with full-size Rottweil Brenneke slugs. Five of the Brennekes went into $1^1/_2$ inches, centered at 50 yards from a standing post rest with the forearm resting on a sandbag atop the post. I also tried a few 675-caliber round-ball handloads, and one of those five-shot groups went into $2^1/_2$ inches at 50 yards.

The crisp trigger was a help, to be sure, and I'd guess the

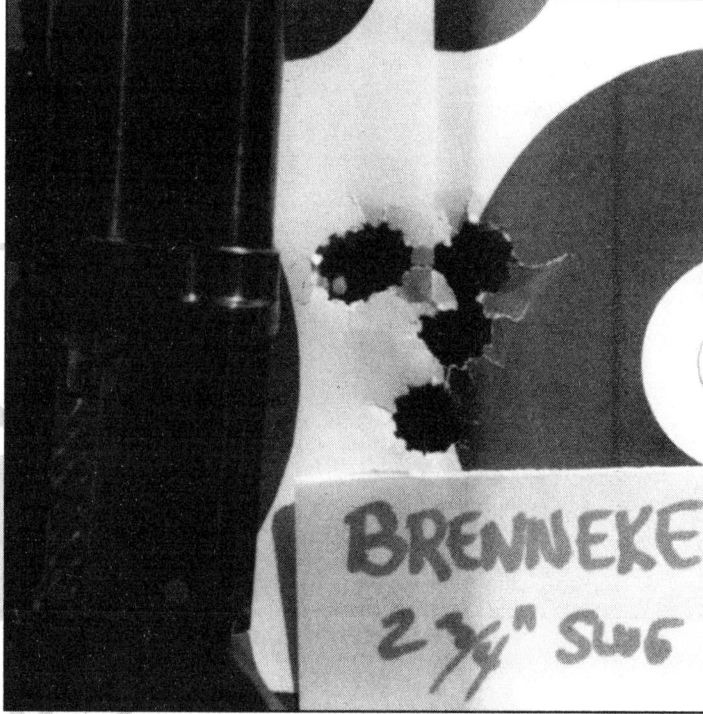

A tight Brenneke group at 50 yards.

The see-through carrier is an advantage.

rigidly mounted barrel did its share also. At any rate, I feel the accuracy potential of this gun is quite good indeed. I fired #00 and #4 buckshot at 20 yards and, not surprisingly, patterns opened up. Still, all but one #4 buck was within a 15-inch circle, and *all* the #00 Buck was. So at close range, this gun is most impressive.

The $2\frac{3}{4}$-inch chambering is in no way a handicap. Standard cartridges in new "tactical" loads are now gaining in popularity. They represent a good and sensible balance of power, controllability and recovery. If you feel the need for more shot, the short magnums will serve you well.

In firing this Mitchell shotgun, I encountered no problems of any kind. The gun was positive in loading, feeding, firing and ejection. It was impressive in terms of the firepower it delivered on target, and it could be easily reloaded in the middle of a shooting string, if need be. Mitchell offers eight different 12-gauge pumps. I've only tried the 9109, but I certainly liked this all-steel shotgun, finding it well suited for its purpose and well worth the price.

M.T. Lumley

Beretta's Cougar

Beretta Cougar, Model 8040D, clean-lined, uncluttered—this one is in 40 S&W.

Here the Cougar is field-stripped. The barrel-rotation block is at right center.

This arrow on the barrel rotation block points toward the muzzle.

FIRST OF ALL, it doesn't look like a Beretta. Over the years, we have all gotten used to the familiar open-top slide, exposing the barrel, that has been a feature of most Beretta pistols since the first Tullio Marengoni design of 1915.

Well, there's a good reason for the new full-slide configuration. The Beretta Cougar has a turning-barrel locking system, and for this to work you need a slide that covers the barrel.

The turn-barrel system is not new. Back around 1905, Searle did it for Savage, and in Austria, Roth did it for Steyr. In modern times, MAB of France used this system well in their PA-15 pistol.

This locking system has some notable advantages. It allows a level, non-tilting barrel, and it takes up less space than most other types. In the Cougar, Beretta has used the "less space" feature to make the new pistol in one size—compact.

There is another notable difference in the design of the new Beretta: the shape of the grip frame. It is similar to the grip of the Browning HP and the Czech 75, with a deep incurve at upper rear and a straight line at lower rear. It feels just right in the hand.

At the time of this writing, the only version of the Cougar available for testing was a Model 8040D. The designation translates to 40 S&W chambering and a double-action-only trigger system. This one has no manual safety and no hammer spur. The hammer is contoured

The barrel-rotation system is locked here, the top lug tilted to the right.

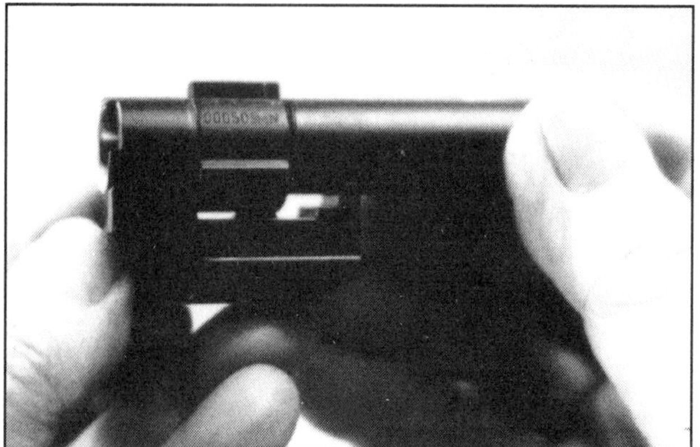

Here it is unlocked, the barrel to the rear, and the lug now at the top.

to match the rear curve of the slide.

There are two other basic versions. Model F has selective double/single action and the same safety system as the Model 92F. The Model G has a decock-only system, with the lever returning to horizontal after you have used it to drop the hammer.

The Cougar is designated Model 8000 in 9x19mm, 9x21mm, and 41 Action Express. At present, we civilians will have ten-round magazines in all versions. For police, and elsewhere in the world, it will be fifteen rounds for the 9mm, and eleven for the 40 S&W.

All of the controls on the Cougar are in the familiar locations, easy to reach and operate without changing the hand position. The magazine release is reversible for left-handed shooters. The trigger is nicely shaped and has no serrations.

At the range, I tried the pistol with seven different loads, all hollowpoints. Two of these were special items—the Cor-Bon Plus-P and the Federal Hydra-Shok. The Beretta fired everything without a single malfunction. I was not surprised.

The DAO trigger pull is quite smooth, with no increase of tension (stacking) at the end of the trigger arc. There is, though, if you pull very slowly, a little pause you can feel just before the hammer is released. This allowed some random plinking, and I found the pistol to be quite accurate.

The sight picture is square post and square notch, with ample margins for quick eye pick-up. The front sight has a white dot, and the rear notch is flanked by white dots. Both sights are dovetail-mounted.

The slide is deeply recessed behind the ejection port to ensure that the ejected case has a clear path out. The front of the trigger guard is curved and cross-grooved, for those who put a finger there while using that weird version of the two-hand hold.

The Cougar is going to be well-liked by law enforcement people, especially in the D version. I think I'd prefer the Model 8000F, in 9x19mm. The new pistol is sleek, compact and totally reliable. It may not look like one, but it is, after all, a Beretta.

J.B. Wood

Norinco's Nine

In a surplus issue holster, the Norinco 213 makes a nice belt gun package.

THIS CHINESE variant of the Russian 7.62x25mm Tokarev pistol is chambered for the 9x19mm (Luger) cartridge. It reminds me of the slim pocket pistols of Colt and Browning in years gone by, but there are a few things to spoil this vision. There's the too-tall rear sight, the reverse-tapering grip, the spur hammer, and the reversed safety—mostly all cosmetic.

All of these pistols I've seen have initially been quite stiff, so much so that break-in is necessary. Manually cycling the action for a hundred (or more) times should do it. You'll find the springs extremely strong, both the slide return and hammer spring.

The Model 213 incorporates the Browning/Colt pivoting linked barrel with locked breech and separate barrel bushing and slide stop. The push-button magazine release, while a bit small, is in proportion to the size of the pistol. A notable departure is the drop-in sear mechanism, a novel unit enabling quick cleaning and inspection.

The safety is too small to facilitate easy operation, but that is tolerable. The reversal of positions is not. *Forward* is the safe position, *back* is fire. I don't trust a lifetime of conditioning.

And it's flat enough to be comfy inside the pants in a Brauer holster—conceals well, too.

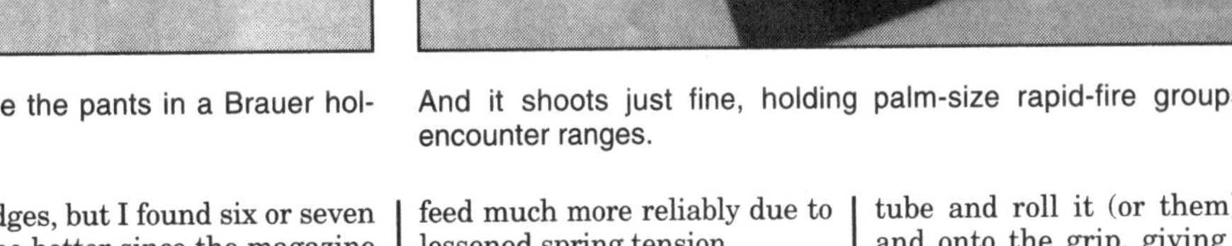

And it shoots just fine, holding palm-size rapid-fire groups at encounter ranges.

I would carry this pistol with an empty chamber. The hammer may be left cocked to get easy manipulation of the slide to chamber a round. The magazines are rated for eight cartridges, but I found six or seven to be better since the magazine springs are extremely robust. It *may* be possible to remove a few coils to cure this. This could make them easier to load and feed much more reliably due to lessened spring tension.

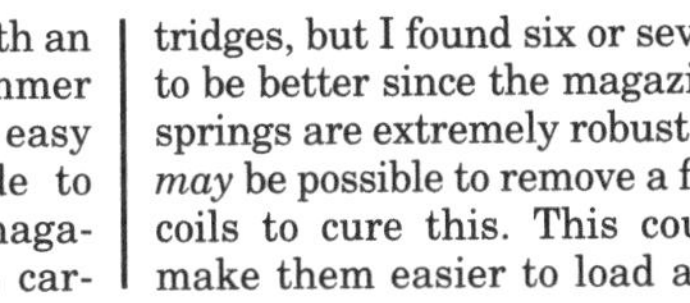

The slightly reverse-tapered grip, while visually unpleasing, had little effect in use, at least for me. It seemed neutral in feel, but if it's a problem for you, an inexpensive fix is to slice a band or bands of bicycle inner-tube and roll it (or them) up and onto the grip, giving it a tacky feel.

This 9mm is an easy pistol to handle, especially for those with small hands. The trigger broke at about 6 pounds after some noticeable takeup. Its sights offer a good sight picture.

At 25 yards, I used a six-o'clock hold while firing offhand and felt the groups, though high, were quite respectable given the fact this piece wasn't intended to be used on paper targets. Recoil was mild, and cycling was quick.

As to ammunition, I found it best to stay with ball because this pistol is designed for ball. The factory brochure with the pistol states service life is 2000 rounds. With proper maintenance and care, I have no reason to believe that this figure wouldn't be exceeded.

For the 9mm Luger in a Browning/Colt design, this pistol seems about ideal in size. Even with its flaws, there are several good points. Price is certainly the biggest of them, and the all-steel construction is another. Mine had an extra magazine, too.

M.T. Lumley

The battle-tested Tokarev in the more convenient 9mm Luger is a sound budget-minded gun today.

Ruger's Workhorse: The 45 P90DC

TESTFIRE

(Above) Shooting groups, which include shots fired DA-mode, takes concentration.

The P90DC is quite manageable, even in full benchrest recoil—gun is back in battery here.

HANDGUNNERS trained and experienced with the single-action M1911A1 service pistol resist accepting the new generation of double-action semi-automatic pistols. Some veteran handgunners feel a DA 45 is "an ingenious solution to a non-existent problem." Were this simplistic dismissal only true, millions of dollars could have been saved defending manufacturers in product liability lawsuits. It is, however, fact that a hammer-down, double-action semi-auto pistol is safer to carry loaded than a cocked-and-locked, single-action semi-automatic. Despite the old Colt warhorse's reputation as a manstopper, the safety record of the M1911, human error or not, is far from perfect.

Bringing the 45 auto into the 21st century required careful scrutiny of the weaknesses in previous pistol designs. Appropriately, William B. Ruger would be the one to do it. Ruger has a special talent for combining the best features of proven designs and blending them harmoniously into a simple combination which: 1) works; and 2) is practical to manufacture.

The ability to learn from earlier mistakes is demonstrated in product improvements made between the P85, Ruger's first centerfire double-action self-loader in 9mm, and the 45 ACP decocker-only (no safety-lever) P90DC. The heavy trigger pull of early P85s made first-round hits under stress a sometime thing. This problem has been fixed, and the P90DC has one of the best trigger pulls of any DA autoloader I have handled, including those costing several times more. When the P85 was first envisioned, market forces clearly directed Ruger toward 9mm as the caliber of choice. The U.S. Army was testing 9mm pistols, and the whole law enforcement community was on the verge of adopting semi-automatic pistols because the "perceived nature of the threat" had changed. Ruger needed a 9mm semi-automatic handgun to maintain market share, to complete the product line, and to be competitive in foreign markets.

When I demonstrated the Ruger pistol at trade shows and the armorer's school group when it was first introduced, the initial reaction of experienced handgunners was, "Gee, this would sure be nice if it were a 45!" I was always polite and stifled my skeptical reaction. After all, in 1986 we all knew the 45 was dead, wasn't it? Bill Ruger himself would hint at a future 45, but nobody in the field took him seriously.

That was because the then-new P85 was having growing pains, and none of us involved with its development could see beyond our immediate concerns of simply getting the thing into production. Ruger must have sensed that America's love affair with "the nine" would eventually cool. And, in fact, it was only a matter of time before the pendulum of demand swung back to something more proven and familiar. Now, military Special Operations forces (Army Green Berets, Navy SEALs, and Air Force Commandos) have, in fact, specified 45 ACP as the caliber of choice for their new "offensive pistol" (supergun) developed by H&K.

There is still a need for a 9mm pistol for foreign sales and for customers who require light recoil or simply prefer the large magazine capacity. While the demand for 9mm pistols has peaked, these pistols, because of their worldwide use, will continue to be strong sellers. So Ruger has chosen to produce pistols in both calibers.

When I was first exposed to

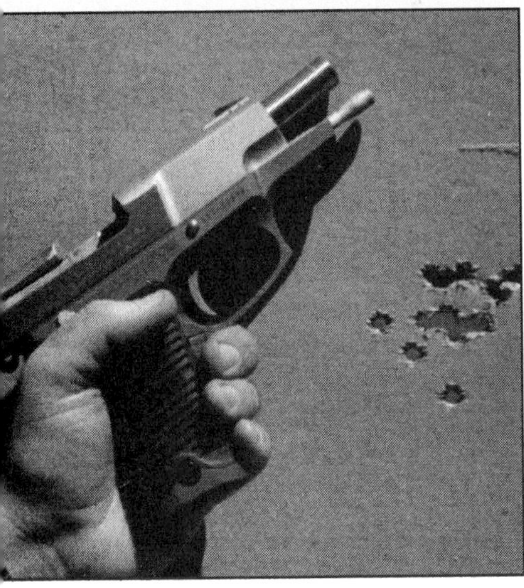

Ten shots, mind you, from this handful of gun in 45 ACP look like this.

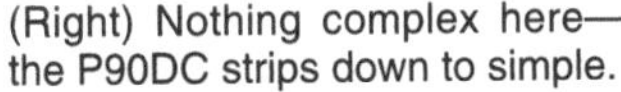

(Right) Nothing complex here—the P90DC strips down to simple.

It's a nice little outfit, this Ruger, in a nice big caliber—the one they're going back to rapidly.

the P85 at Ruger's Newport, New Hampshire, factory, the Bostomatic computerized machinery and tooling was being tested in pilot-run trials prior to packing off the whole caboodle to Prescott, Arizona, where the P85 would be manufactured. As with any newly manufactured item, the initial production wasn't perfect. To ensure the P85 had enough striker energy to fire hard foreign primers, the gun had heavy springs and trigger pulls. Reliable functioning under adverse conditions required some of the sloppiness of fit like the M1911 we all know and love, but this precluded the pistol being a tight grouper. The design intent seemed to be for a safe and reliable pistol that "worked all the time" and was "accurate enough," like an issued Model 1911.

On those early P85s, the trigger pulls were awful, the safeties were awkward, and accuracy was mediocre. When I left the company in 1986, I wouldn't have traded my Browning Hi-Power for a whole trainload of P85s. I could not look past the problems I had dealt with to realize the potential of the pistol once they were fixed. I was expecting an ideal world where everything was perfect on the first try.

Before marketing a 45, Ruger waited a few years, as usual, to work out the bugs in his new design and test the market. The finished product shows what folks in the government procurement business call "design maturity," which in plain words says people at Prescott have done their homework well. In both handling and shooting, the new P90DC is a much-improved pistol from the early pilot-run P85s with which I was familiar from 1985-86.

The first thing I noticed was that the trigger pull is much improved in both single and double action. It isn't the same gun I worked on in 1985. The curvature of the trigger has been changed to eliminate the stacking tendency of earlier models, so shooters with short fingers can completely follow through in DA, which was difficult before. The 4½-pound single-action let-off feels lighter than it is. While not as crisp as your proverbial glass rod, it feels better than most DA semiautomatics on the market and is excellent for a duty pistol.

Law enforcement agencies like decocking DA semi-automatics because they are revolver-like in operation. The P90DC's double-action pull certainly feels revolver-like and doesn't require a white-knuckle death grip. These are good, safe, serviceable trigger pulls for the price-conscious practical pistol or self-defense user.

The *Too Fat Polka,* a popular song of some years ago, would be considered grossly insensitive today. Sample line: "I don't want her, you can have her, she's too fat for me." This lyric sums up my reaction to many of the wide-gripped, staggered-magazine autoloaders now in vogue. The P90DC, with its trim seven-shot-in-line magazine well, escapes that category. Geometry and leverage indicate more strength or bigger hands are necessary to handle the big-gripped behemoths. The slim P90DC has a comfortable, controllable grip, manageable in recoil.

Another important, but often overlooked, ergonomic factor is the plastic foot at the base of the P90DC magazine. Most semiautomatic rifle or handgun malfunctions are initiated because the user fails to seat the magazine fully. The plastic foot is simple, but very important, in that it permits the P90DC magazine to be fully seated in normal insertion without interference from the lanyard loop, unlike the Beretta M92S and many other pistols.

The simplicity of the Ruger pistol is noteworthy. It contains about the same number of parts as an M1911 pistol and is easily field-stripped without tools. The magazine catch has been changed from early P85s to resemble that of the M1911, and it can be reversed if desired for left-handed users.

Ruger makes the P90DC barrel from a one-piece stainless steel investment casting. This differs from earlier P85 pistols in which a cast breech monobloc and separate barrel were welded into an assembly and finish-machined together.

The P90DC's decocking lever is a great improvement. It is easily operated either by the thumb of the firing hand, or the supporting hand. The recommended safe carrying mode for most civilian users for any semi-automatic pistol is with the slide closed and the hammer down on an empty chamber. For P90DC duty carry, when *immediate* use of the pistol may be required, the top round can be chambered, and the decocking lever used to lower the hammer. This blocks the firing pin positively so that the pistol is safe if ures to eject. This is not a criticism of the P90DC, because it is a service-type pistol, rather than one intended for target work.

Ruger does not recommend use of reloaded ammunition, and the owner's manual contains warnings against its use. Shooters will find that long-nose semi-wadcutter bullets like the H&G No. 130 will feed ammunition did not do quite as well, about like as-issued M1911-type pistols firing the same ammunition. I got five consecutive ten-shot groups averaging 4.16 inches, with the smallest group 3.6 inches and the largest 5.2 inches.

It was easy to obtain solid first-round hits in the torso of a military "E" silhouette, snap-

My brief encounter with the Ruger P90DC has demonstrated the value of patience and constant reevaluation in gun manufacture. Browning's 45 semi-automatic required about fifteen years of revisions and design changes from 1905 into the 1920s before it assumed the form with which we are now familiar. The P90DC appears to

A Decocker Primer

No "Official" definition of decockers likely exists—if one did, exceptions doubtless abound to "prove the rule." Generally, a decocker is a double-action autoloading pistol on which the hammer can be uncocked safely *without* manipulating its trigger. Extant models often have a decocking lever and no safety-lever. The absence of a safety-lever does not pose additional risk with firearms designed to arrest forward firing pin motion until the trigger is fully rearward, i.e., employ a passive firing pin block.

Decocking double-action semi-automatic pistols eases the training transition from revolvers to autos, because they are "revolver-like" in operation. They can be carried with the hammer down and the chamber loaded, and fired immediately without having to deliberately disengage a safety. This is not a new concept. The Walther PP, PPK and P-38 pistols were developed in the 1930s and have been successful in military and police service for many years. Newer designs have simply improved the ergonomics of hammer-dropping safeties and made them more convenient, and practical.

Why? Although autoloading rifles *must* be cocked to carry a live round in their chambers, no one seems to get particularly excited when the SWAT team shows up with their M-16s cocked and locked. A visible cocked hammer on a handgun, however, panics some hearts and minds. While aficionados argue with conviction that their M1911-style autos in "Condition One" carry, i.e., cocked and locked, are as safe as the day is long, it ain't necessarily so:

- Although improbable, the uncocked inertial firing pins of Browning-designed autos can, and sometimes (rarely) do, fire a chambered round inadvertently when dropped, regardless whether they are cocked or uncocked, with safety on or off.
- While in the hands of a conscientious, competent shooter (say, for example, Bill Blankenship), who remains in complete control of his pistol, cocked and locked is pretty safe. But in the hands of the average bear, in unexpected and unpredictable operational situations, wipe-off of the safety-lever from Safe to Fire (by brush, struggle, fall, impeded draw, etc.) can render the pistol capable of firing with only the light single-action trigger pull.

Thus, conventional wisdom suggests an uncocked pistol is less prone to an unintentional discharge than a cocked one. Safety incentives therefore encouraged production of a decocking pistol.

Operational rather than safety considerations, however, gave decockers their greatest recent encouragement. The German (then *West* German) government upgraded police pistols in the 1970s (from 32 ACP to 9mm Parabellum) to counter the terrorist threat. The specification for the new pistols contained a functional requirement, poetically beautiful for its crystalline clarity, profound meaning, and sensible intent:

> The firearm must be safely carried with a round in the chamber and capable of immediate action without manipulating external levers.

In other words, the requirement demanded the safety and readiness of a modern revolver (think about it) in an autoloading pistol. Does the cocked-and-locked Colt Model 1911 make it under this specification? No, because even IPSC pistoleros must manipulate the safety-lever before they blast away.

Fruits of this German procurement include the Walther P5, the SIG-Sauer P6, and the Heckler & Koch P7. Each of these pistols is a decocker, with the H&K entry uniquely uncocking itself automatically when left unattended. (These pistol models have all spawned their own expanded nuclear families of additional model types, such as the Walther P5K/P88, the SIG P220/225-229, and the H&K P7M8/M13/K3.

America is a litigious society. This understatement means anyone and everyone—individual, company, government agency, fraternal group, Sunday school class, whatever—is vulnerable to lawsuits by anyone for anything. Police departments are especially lucrative targets in the current defendant-rights-sensitivity climate, and so they dread inadvertent discharges and their attendant liability.

One hopes concerned departments redouble their training, revise their doctrine, and increase range time and training ammunition budgets to minimize inadvertent shootings. They have attempted to eliminate single-action (light trigger pull) first shots by equipment choice—New York and Los Angeles PDs disabled the single-action features of their service revolvers, in the time before autoloaders were issued. Administrators want their officers to carry uncocked sidearms on duty in the hope unintentional shootings will be minimized.

Modern decockers offer bureaucratic peace of mind without unduly compromising the operational readiness of the cops on the street. Lest we forget, however, training and doctrine are much more important than firearm type. No pistol yet invented can compensate for inadequate training and bad judgment.

James P. Cowgill

---

dropped, yet it may be fired immediately.

My sample Ruger P90DC fired over 300 rounds with full-power service ammunition, both jacketed hollowpoints and round-nose FMJ loads, and there were no malfunctions. Fifty rounds of factory 185-grain mid-range wadcutter loads were tried, and there were four fail- more reliably than short-nose designs.

Accuracy of the P90DC was quite good out-of-the-box. Five consecutive ten-shot groups fired hand-held from a sandbag rest at 25 yards with match-grade hardball ammunition averaged 2.54 inches, with the smallest group 2.1 inches and the largest 3.1 inches. Surplus military ball shooting the first round double-action from a chamber-loaded, hammer-down mode. Rapid follow-up shots in "double-taps" came naturally and could be directed accurately and with rapidity. The rugged fixed sights are drift-adjustable for windage and offer a three-dot sight picture for improved visibility in subdued light.

have assumed all the attributes of a fully developed design in only a third of that time. Its future track record remains to be determined, but if somebody would offer me a trainload of P90DCs for my Browning Hi-Power, I'd be willing to reconsider my earlier smart-mouthed position.

C.E. Harris

The beginning of a very long story.

The almost-mythical Czech CZ-75 spawned copies and near copies, which makes it the first Super-Nine.

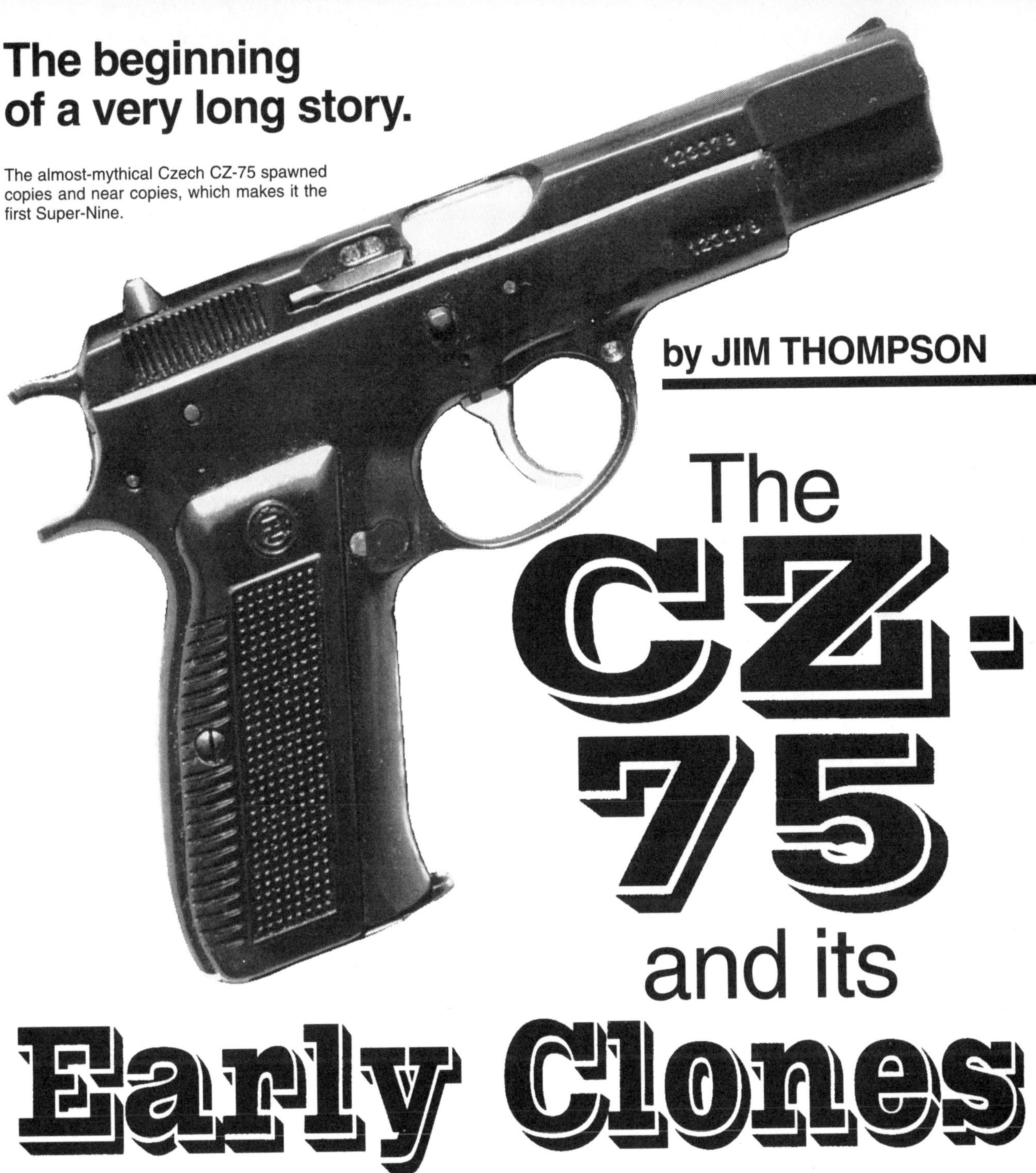

by JIM THOMPSON

The CZ-75 and its Early Clones

FIREARMS STORIES ARE generally pretty straightforward—test an item, report on the results. Not so the '70s *Wunderkind*, the 9mm that turned so many heads eastward, the CZ-75. The Iron Curtain and the trade barriers which protected us from it or it from us have almost disappeared; factories marketing copies and clones have arisen, prospered, and also disappeared; and while the form and function of the original pistol have become supremely well-known in the United States, this only happened because the duplicates got very good, and because reporters and analysts simply refused to give up. It usually takes about a half-century for a firearms tale to become so tangled and ebullient; but the CZ-75 is not yet twenty years old, boasts almost as many progeny as a hyperhormonal rabbit, and still isn't common here, but it's getting that way. (See "Testfire," p. 198)

If the history of the CZ-75 and its brethren seems odd and tangled, so are its roots in the Czech arms industry. For seventy years or so, Brno-marked arms produced at *Ceska Zbrojovka* at Strakonica have been universally recognized as high-quality bargains. Many of their designs have been adopted by well-established arms industries elsewhere. The British Bren began life in Czechoslovakia; likewise the British Besa. Germany, the Soviet Union, most of Eastern Europe and much of Latin America as recently as the 1950s used Czech Mausers and Czech cannon. The tendency continued whether the Czech factory was in capitalist or communist hands, Czech or German, Soviet or Czech reformist control. From time to time, authorities in Europe and elsewhere have complained it was very difficult to sell their nationally produced firearms output when a better-made Czech product was available, despite tariffs and barriers, for about half the price. In France and Germany, from the '30s until quite recently, Czech shotguns and hunting rifles accounted for a very high percentage of products available and sold. Even now, the CZ-75 is sold in Europe quite cheaply.

This preamble is necessary because there are still some in the U.S. who describe the CZ-75 as what it is not. It has elements derived from evolved components of more ancient and/or far inferior handguns, but the slide/frame interface and most of the rest of the pistol's functional details come from the Petter-Neuhausen patents of the late 1930s. The trigger combines beefed-up Radom geometry with a much more sophisticated base hinge spun off a Walther original. If anything in the CZ-75 seems ordinary in the 1990s, the observer should page through a GUN DIGEST from the early 1970s looking for an all-steel, double-action fifteen-shot handgun. For the CZ-75 was and remains the original "Super-Nine," and European pistolsmiths who've been working with the gun for more than fifteen years still believe it's the one with the most potential for truly precise shooting in the real or simulated combat arenas.

All of which is amazing, after all this time and after the fact that nearly every firearms firm in the world with the capacity to do so has produced and sold at least one gun either inspired by or is a direct copy of the Czech original. This kind of market impact is precisely what was intended by the gun's designers; for the CZ-75 was conceived, designed and sold with virtually no domestic civilian or military market. The guns have seen military use worldwide, but virtually always as an individual's private purchase. And they sell to this day in that most personal and competitive market.

In 1988, the TZ-75 from Tanfoglio in hard chrome had a lot of advantages.

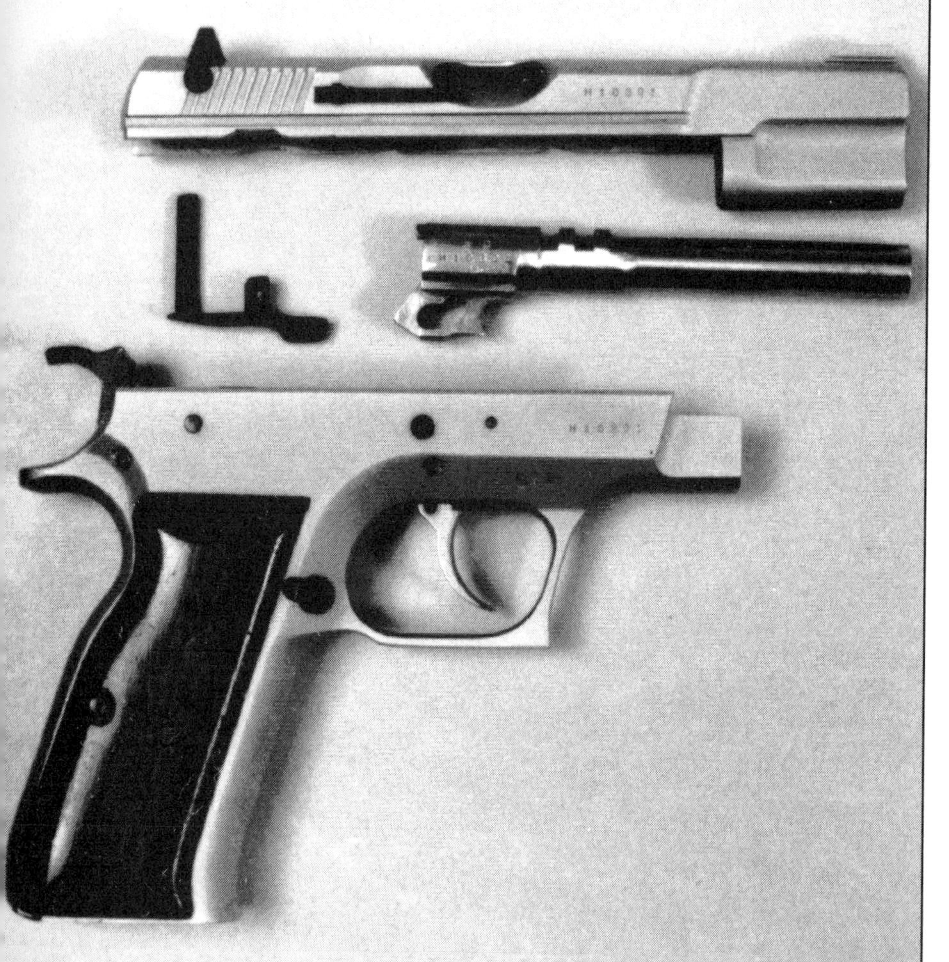

(Left) The CZ-75 and/or TZ-75 are stripped according to the time-honored Browning method, *a la* Hi-Power.

I said the real market history of the pistol was tangled and confused. It is, in fact, so tangled that, by the time this sees ink, much will have changed. This is only the story of the earliest days of CZ-75, and its early clones and stepchildren.

I had to wait only ten days to get my first CZ-75 from P.I.M.C. back in 1986, but I was terribly impatient anyway because I had been waiting, in real terms, eleven long years. Tariffs, import restrictions on "Communist Bloc" products, a crazy quilt of erratic importers and undelivered product, and lots of promises had preceded my order and kept the pistol from me. Enticing ads for the gun in *Deutsches Waffen Journal* and the Swiss *Waffen Digest*—for less than half the wholesale price I paid, mind you—had held my attention. At one point, I had even made elaborate arrangements with a German firm to acquire a Peter F. Stahl-modified custom gun, a deal which fell apart, congealed again, fell apart again, and finally, became real in early 1991, when I took delivery of the gun and owned it for two days, total. A fellow shooter decided he couldn't live without it and, like many who wind up with CZ-75s, gobbled it up with a few too many dollars before I even got a chance to properly photograph it. By then, of course, I had too much time and money in the pistol, and no matter what it did for me, it couldn't possibly have satisfied me.

The same was essentially true of that first 1986 baked-enamel gun. By the time it actually showed up, praise and promises had me anticipating some sort of model of perfection which would do more or less everything, including assist me in leaping tall buildings in a single bound. I'd heard the double-action pull was smooth, slick, and truly useful; and it was, at what my weights told me was about 14 pounds, through it felt lighter. Butter smooth and predictable, I eventually slicked it a bit more with careful stone and fitting work, once the gun was broken in. I had heard the CZ-75 was beautifully made. This was mostly true, though the barrel fit was very average. To say, however, I hate paint finishes on handguns is something of an understatement; phosphated underneath, the baked-on look is my least favorite finish, ranking somewhere *after* rust. The magazines were crudely scratched with the pistol's serial number. Sights were decent, but nothing special.

That pistol was one of a batch imported by and marked "Bauska." The finish is sometimes referred to as "military gloss"...and if I'd had a surefire way to cleanly strip it off without damaging anything, I'd have been down to the phosphate more or less instantly. It's too hard, therefore brittle, and chips badly. The single-action trigger broke neatly at 4½ pounds, preceded by the gentle "takeup"—calling it "creep" suggests more tension than there really is—so common on today's semi-autos. Despite excellent overall conformance to the gun's specifications, the long wait and the opportunity to handle so many slick and graceful 9mm guns since the mid-'70s had me in a mindset to be at least slightly dissatisfied no matter what.

I sat down with the instructions and test target to do some studying. Part of the reason European guns function so well is their detailed testing and proofing. One of the tougher requirements in the Czech factory is the final approval, which requires a signature and the test target, also requiring a signature. Comrade Bobcik did mine. What I, for a long time, thought was six rounds on paper was in fact ten. Very disturbing, however, was the fact that there were two very tight groups—one dead-center and tiny, another 2½ inches away, tight, at about 1 o'clock—and a single bullet hole, fully 5¼ inches from center at 4 o'clock, completely out of the black on the 25-meter test target. Two groups and a flyer. Ah, well, I thought, probably strange ammo or bad shooting. At the time, I hadn't even a single inkle that the pistol would replicate that pattern as long as the original barrel remained in place. Later fiddling with a Tanfoglio barrel partially exorcised the demon, but fitting a tight match barrel eventually did the job. But it was aggravating.

Detailed study of the gun's innards and bore with high magnification equipment showed a lot of very atypical attention to detail and some unusual processes used in the gun's fabrication, part of which I'm still pondering. The bore was exceptionally bright, its finish approximating a #8 R.M.S. finish. The slide and frame appear to be extremely high-quality investment casting, though the exporter, Merkuria, claims all parts are forged. Some of the internal machining of the slide and especially the frame left no "tracks" even under very high magnification, and so the amount of machine-induced stress in the metal's crystalline structure proved to be very low. Some extremely gentle process or treatment is used on these parts, which may be worked hot or cold, or manipulated electronically or robotically; none of the machinists I talked to could really provide much insight, though the one who said, half jokingly, "maybe it's a laser" may have been closer than he knew.

I did some measuring and checking on the barrel, and at least in this gun, it's configured more like an American tube than a typical European unit. Six grooves, right twist, roughly one turn in 10 inches (probably four per meter). But the hood and muzzle fit were well-executed, clean, loose. This is done on many semi-automatics today because manufacturers know that nothing irritates consumers more than unreliable equipment, and nothing causes more fouling/dirt malfunctions than excessively tight fit on a semi-auto. But I keep my guns well-lubricated with MDS/graphite greases and cleaner than my plates or silverware, I do not shoot in pigpens, and I demand accuracy, even at the cost of some reliability. The barrel leade cut ahead of the smooth chamber appeared to have a sharper step than I am accustomed to seeing in European semi-automatics, and I suspected this could cause problems with some fatter-nosed hollowpoints.

Determined to leave the gun in a factory-stock condition for initial testing, I still went ahead with some steps I execute with all semi-automatics. My good friend and pistolsmith John Student taught me to check everything, prevent "unexplained" problems as I work, gently polishing and closely studying parts. I merely detail polished the mainspring, recoil spring, firing pin and firing pin spring with gentle touches of 600-grit emery cloth and, afterward, pumice and oil and a silicone cloth. One removes virtually no functioning metal in these processes. I then packed the mainspring and firing pin with heavy grease and reassembled. Contrary to advice from some smiths, modern MDS greases remain viable at very low temperatures and do not migrate all over your pistol, holster and clothing, as oil does; and the lubricity of modern greases is superb, preventing corrosion in areas one cannot reach without tearing the gun apart.

The general takedown procedure is simple, and the trigger assembly is much easier to deal with than the Hi-Power or Model 1911 because it's semi-modular. There is no magazine disconnector/safety. There is nothing in this pistol of fragile design, and there are *no* sheet metal stirrups in the trigger mechanism.

The safety and slide stop on the CZ-75 and most of the current generation of clones are located on the same plane at the pistol's left. The newer CZ-85 is ambidextrous, and I've seen a European 30-caliber (7.65mm) pistol equipped with smooth, handsome wood grips and gracefully extended controls. Who knows what the future might hold?

In several thousand rounds of firing, no "regular" jams of any sort have been encountered with the CZ-75. With the original barrel, some failures to fully chamber were encountered with jacketed hollowpoints conflicting slightly with the leade.

Also digested by the CZ-75 were vast quantities of surplus ammunition. And herein lies a wonderful tale. Most European ammo for 9mm is at or slightly above the old SAAMI 9mm specification, and virtually all American ammo well below the so-called "redline." NATO specifications for the cartridge are very hot by U.S. civilian standards, normal to soft by European specifications, so I hoard Geco, Norma, Lapua and Fiocchi 9mm loads. When I could still afford Lugers, I was pleased to take a superb Artillery Model for minimal money from an owner who, though advised properly, refused to shoot either European ammo or "warmish" handloads, and who was therefore convinced his gun just didn't work. Didn't work? I put 5000 rounds through it without a single malfunction. The CZ-75, especially with the Geco and Fiocchi loads, was more than accurate enough to save anyone's life; the groups thus made were essentially miniatures of Comrade Bobcik's work.

Later, with the match barrel fitted, the flyers totally disappeared. And the pistol, across a padded rest or from a Ransom rest, began to perform brilliantly. Groups of just 1 inch at 25 yards were about maximum, and with carefully controlled handloads, Geco, Fiocchi, Norma, and Federal Match, groups became ragged bullet holes. The key to this is simple, and it was about what I had expected thousands of rounds earlier: slide/frame interface on my specimen—and on all the Czech 75s I've examined—is near perfect. Only "service" barrel fit retards performance.

The "Bobcik Syndrome" was solved by the installation of $160 worth of barrel. But I'd rather it hadn't been necessary. Proof that it would be was early on, for installing the Tanfoglio-produced barrel from my TZ-75 alleviated the flyers. And the Stahl-prepared match pistol shot about the same from day one.

Looking back, I was displeased with the CZ-75 early on mainly because, in the 1980s, I had handled and tested the big-magazine Astras and Stars, Steyrs and Llamas, Bernardellis, Berettas, the Walther P-88, every one of which either aped the Czech gun or was inspired by it. And, of course, I paid over twice what the CZ sells for in Europe.

It has proven durable and, at long last, accurate. The CZ-75 contains not a single part or system not adapted from another firearm, but it's not really a copy of anything.

Known in the '50s and '60s for a set of competent but rather boring pocket semi-automatics, Fratelli Tanfoglio then made new inroads in manufacturing firearms clones and have found the horses to market their output. From F.I.E. and ExCam's early efforts to current output from a half-dozen firms, virtually all the CZ-75 clones use Tanfoglio-produced parts and are often Tanfoglio-produced and finished guns.

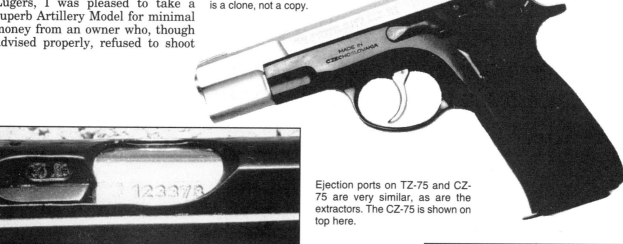

This mixture of parts—the TZ-75's slide and CZ-75's frame—fired and worked rather well. The TZ-75 is a clone, not a copy.

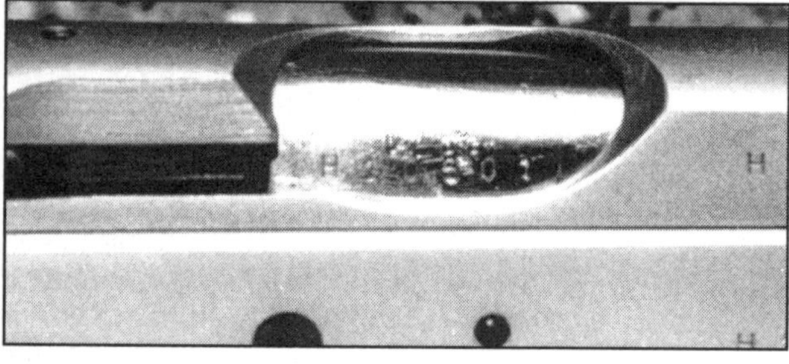

Ejection ports on TZ-75 and CZ-75 are very similar, as are the extractors. The CZ-75 is shown on top here.

The CZ-75 can be carried "cocked and locked," and lacks a modern pin/hammer drop safety.

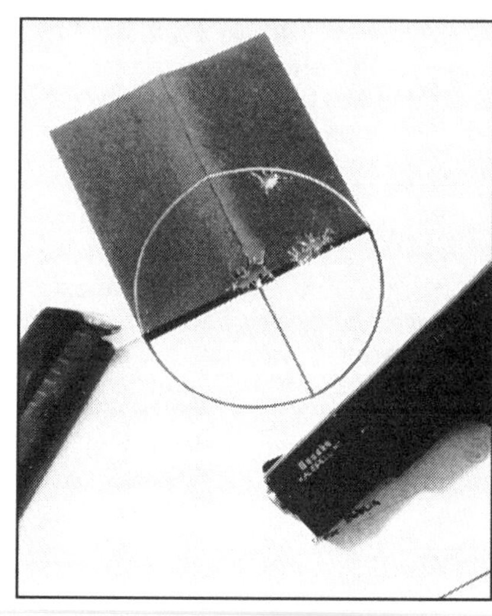

Here is the Bobcik Syndrome—two groups and a flier—out of the box.

I've done most of my testing of CZ-75 clones with guns from the defunct F.I.E. line. European American Armory of Florida marketed many of the same models under the Witness name, and their literature showed guns in 9mm, 41 AE, 40 S&W and 45. Springfield's P9 came in many versions; it, too, had Tanfoglio parts, though in an American-finished and assembled configuration. The Action Arms AT-84 and AT-88 employ Tanfoglio parts, but were Swiss-assembled and finished. It's all part of the CZ-75 story.

Variations on a selling theme included both bigger and smaller TZ-75s.

Why clone guns? Historically, there have always been several reasons. Often, the original is too expensive. Sometimes—especially so in the CZ-75's case—the original is hard to get for political/competitive reasons. Sometimes, desirable options aren't available on the original. Tanfoglio got into this market smart and early. Some of those early blued guns were misfitted and displayed odd metallurgical anomalies which led to early failures. The hard-chromed pistols, however, quickly established an excellent reputation, for the hard, flexible "crust" of their finish concealed mediocre materials. By late '86, the guns were vastly improved, and by '88, the high-mounted firing pin safety had been replaced by a unit similar to the Czech original, target and compensated versions were on the market and, as nearly as anyone could tell, the F.I.E. TZ series and ExCam's TA pistols were prospering and proliferating.

All the Tanfoglio guns sport better sights than the Czech originals. Prices were much lower. Finish options and combinations could teach anybody a lesson. The Millett-style sights on the match gun are, simply put, wonderful. And the internal manufacturing techniques are as sophisticated as the Czech guns. The externals are at least as well done. Slide/frame interface is not quite as good, but is easily adjusted in a press.

In shooting all the variants, including a couple of custom guns, some interesting information developed. A TA90C purchased after ExCam ceased to exist shot better than any of the other stock pistols, including the big match gun. It was largely a case of better-than-average frame/slide fit and a barrel that happened to be very tight. Another gun of the same model wouldn't shoot close to that particular example. Most stock guns delivered 3- to 3½-inch groups with most factory loads at 25 yards, but the little TA90C, carefully rested and shot with Federal Match or careful handloads, cut group size in half. All the Czech-built and Czech-inspired pistols handle and balance well, owing to the dished out tang area of the backstrap, but the Tanfoglios run a little deeper and feel a bit better. Among all the Italian and Czech pistols—and for that matter, later with the AT-84—there were no malfunctions at all.

I preferred the high-set firing pin safety, mostly because I'm accustomed to the Walther P-38, but I seem to be the only person on the planet who does. That may account for the fact that all the recent pistols have returned to the original's frame-mounted conventional safety.

Double action on most guns evinced a 17- to 20-pound pull, which

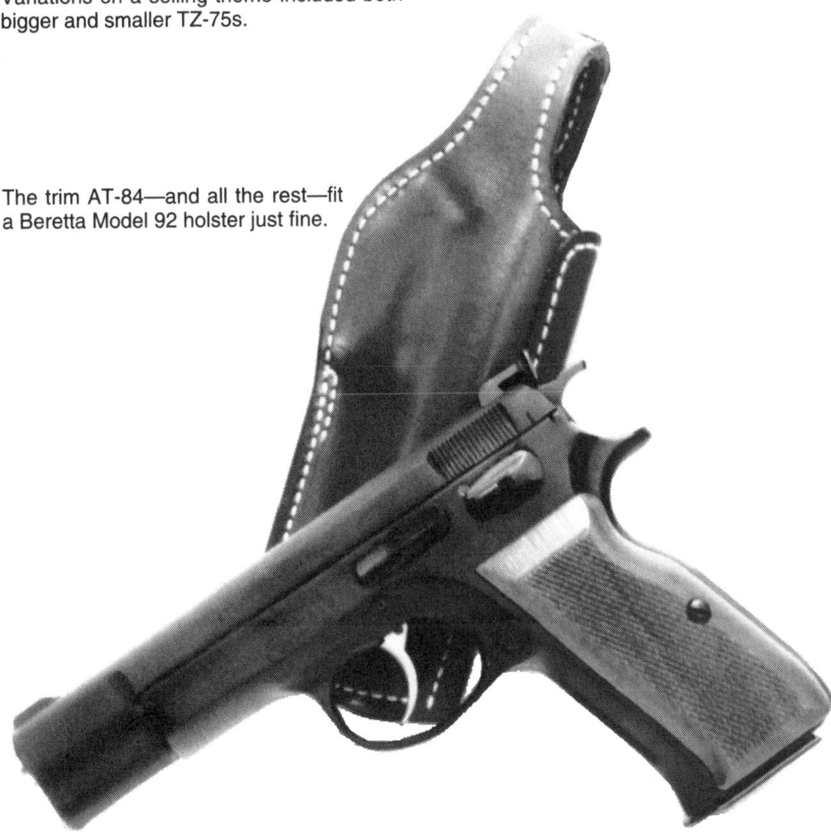

The trim AT-84—and all the rest—fit a Beretta Model 92 holster just fine.

I was able to modify gradually to a smooth 9 to 12 pounds on two specimens which particularly irritated me. I am finally beginning to use the double action properly, by the way, and now that I'm accustomed to the varying pulls, the "grip readjustment" which is supposed to cause round one and two to land in different places just doesn't happen. The recurved combat trigger guard is one of those which can actually be used without drawing blood, unlike many that are beautifully covered with razor-sharp checkering. Single action on all guns was very like the CZ-75.

Almost all Tanfoglio guns use a recoil guide rod similar to those used by custom pistolsmiths, projecting through a hole in the slide. Whether these actually do much of anything is moot, but they generally make operations smooth and are easy to strip. Unfortunately, it is not easy to replace grips on any of the guns in this whole family from standard items.

All the Tanfoglio-produced and finished guns have netted me good performance at very reasonable prices. And the eight years of continuous improvement is indeed an impressive record.

Tanfoglio is, of course, neither the beginning nor the end of the CZ-75 story. Even the Chinese are producing a CZ-75 clone, Norinco's China Sports NZ-75. John Slough Armorers in England produce a pistol called the SpitFire which appears from photos to be a clone or near clone. But the best CZ-75 clone I've handled and tested so far came from Action Arms, the late, lamented AT-84.

Just the words "made in Switzerland" can pole-vault the price of almost anything into the low stratosphere. SIG knows this, which is why their recent service pistols are actually built by Sauer in Germany. But the Swiss also have high internal industrial standards, and they fancy their machine-tool quality.

Swiss firearms have been rather strange for a long time. The Schmidt-Rubin straight-pull rifles, even the recent StG-57, are oddly configured and unusually built, but incredibly accurate. The SIG-Neuhausen P-210s specifications don't outdazzle any 9mms of the '30s or '40s, let alone the '90s, but none will outshoot it. Their guns seem to be designed for a system where cleaning weapons is almost an obsession and where everyone is essentially a well-informed technocrat. My pistol sold for a little more than the CZ-75. It was money well spent.

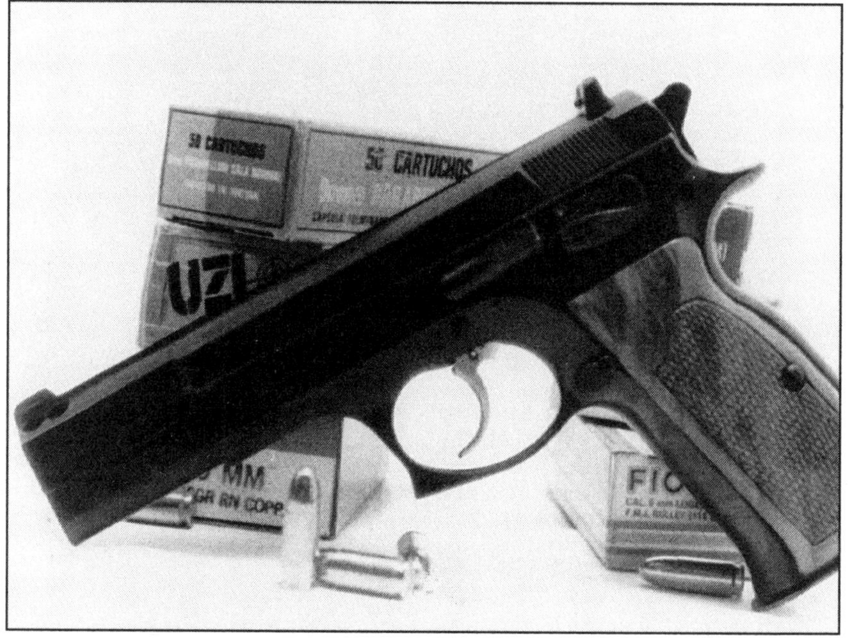

The TZ-75 Special Match had a six-inch barrel, four-port compensator and a long slide.

General fit, finish and machine work were exceptional. I began to get the feeling that AT-84 was a seriously excellent pistol, or that mine was a specially prepared ringer, so I ran up to Mandall's in Scottsdale, Arizona, the only store I know that stocks several of most anything, and was able to confirm by measurement and eyeball that they're all beautifully made. I tested for roundness, uniformity of fit, left-right symmetry, and parallelism of major surfaces on slide and frame and their relationship to each other. Everything was close to perfect. In fact, I did not adjust the trigger or polish the springs on this gun, as I am inclined to do on others; that work was pretty much already done. It was so well-fitted I began to wonder if it might malfunction without dirt or heat.

I needn't have worried. There were no malfunctions of any kind in 2500 rounds. After my most recent teardown, even my 20x viewing glass could find no galling or abrasion in the slide/frame interface. Barrel fit was the tightest of all these pistols, which may account for the tiny downrange groups. The first ammo shot was RIO-CBC and cheap Egyptian surplus, and both gave tiny groups shooting very casually. So the theory of good fit equalling good accuracy is borne out.

My nephew greatly admired this pistol, and he wound up with it. Otherwise, I'd probably never have found out that all these pistols fit easily into leather for the Government Model and/or Beretta 92, for Bob immediately ordered an expensive Lawrence (G&G) shoulder holster, and what arrived, from the imprinted codes, was a very nice rig set up for the 92F. And it worked and fit well, though as I advised my nephew only phoney-baloney movie detectives actually ever really use shoulder holsters, *especially* under their clothes. However, after only a few months' instruction, he figured out how to get it on, after which he, too, used only the companion belt holster, also from Lawrence.

For a while, and almost by default, Springfield Armory was in a position to ship more CZ-75 clones and variants than anyone else. However, the General Agreement on Tariffs and Trade allows the government to lift politically motivated trade barriers and/or to extend to any nation the MFN (most favored nation) status which largely eliminates tariffs and duties on products from the country specified. Which is another way of saying that the CZ-75 in its original Czech form is here and so is the CZ-85.

There are so many CZ-75 guns and clones that J.M. Ramos has written a genealogy of the pistols called *The CZ-75 Family*, from Paladin Press. That book may require lengthy addenda tomorrow...or next week...*surely* by next month! The story is a long way from over for the world's first and arguably most sensible Super-Nine. ●

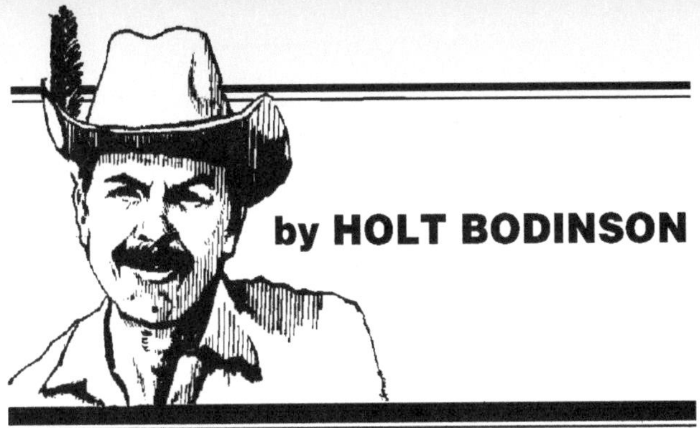

by HOLT BODINSON

AMMUNITION, BALLISTICS AND COMPONENTS

AMMUNITION VARIETY and component performance continue to accelerate this year. Factory ammunition is increasing in velocity while maintaining safe pressures, thanks to improved powder chemistry. Old firms like Speer introduce a complete new line of premium rifle ammunition. And entrepreneurs like John Lazzeroni develop four new hyper-velocity big game cartridges to enliven the ballistics race. Premium hunting and benchrest bullets offered by an assemblage of smaller makers provide everything one could desire in accuracy and performance on game. For the shooter and handloader, this will be a great year with the cupboard full of new items to try.

Action Bullets

Action Bullets is a prime source for hard-cast handgun bullets in calibers 380 Auto (95 grains) to 45 Colt (250 grains) in lots of 500 at very reasonable prices coupled with free freight. A nice touch to the whole line is the variety of sizing offered. For example, their 32-caliber 110-grain bullet is offered in .312-inch diameter for the 32-20 and .314 diameter for the H&R 32 Magnum. Also offered by the firm is an excellent selection of casting alloys ranging in hardness from 5 to 22 Brinell, including their DB alloy that closely duplicates the old and very popular Lyman #2 blend.

Accurate Arms

Accurate Arms' first reloading manual is proving very popular with handloaders. It contains among other things up-to-date data for Scheutzen, obsolete blackpowder and modern target cartridges. A reloading data flyer is now available for the recently reintroduced XMP-5744 powder, and AA's useful "Technical Booklet" has recently been completely updated. This year Accurate Arms is releasing a new powder, XMR-4064—a short-cut grain, single-base rifle powder manufactured in the Czech Republic. XMR-4064 meters well and is providing excellent shot-to-shot and lot-to-lot consistency. To differentiate their ball powders from their extruded powders, AA has now adopted the "XMR" label as a prefix for their entire series of extruded offerings.

AFSCO Ammunition

When I need obsolete or hard-to-get ammunition, one of the first places I turn to is AFSCO, which is run by Tony Sailer of C-H. If you need some 5.6x61 Vom Hofe, 6mm Navy, 8x56 M-S, 50-110, or even 9mm shot, AFSCO has it.

Alliant Powder

Formerly Hercules Powder, Alliant's new pistol powder, they say, has already been used commercially to load over one billion 9mm Luger rounds. Appropriately named "Power Pistol," the new propellant features small granules that meter well and have a slow burn rate. Outstanding in the 9mm Luger giving 1280 fps with the 115-grain bullet, Power Pistol is also recommended for use in the 9x18 Makarov, 357 Magnum, 38 Super Auto +P, 38 Special +P, 380 Auto, 40 S&W, 44 Magnum, 45 ACP and 45 ACP +P. Also new this year is a very clean-burning shotgun powder labeled "American Select," a single-base powder that parallels Green Dot's pressures and velocities but eliminates Green Dot's dirty residues. And introduced across the whole Alliant powder line is new packaging that features plastic, screw top containers replacing the cardboard pop-top units of yore. "Good riddance," says I.

Alpha LaFranck Enterprises

As a high-quality custom bullet maker, Jerry Franck specializes in 458-, 416-, 452-, 430-, and 357-caliber jacketed and cold-swaged lead bullets in an alone, Franck currently supplies over 97 jacketed bullet and 100 swaged lead bullet combinations. I have used his 350-grain heavy-jacketed 4S spitzers with a ballistic coefficient of .310 in a 458 Winchester Magnum (registering 2510 fps over my Chrony) as an elk load in heavy timbered cover. Sighted in at 200 yards, this combination is 2$^3/_4$ inches high at 100 yards and only 11$^3/_4$ inches low at 300 yds. That load is flat, accurate, deadly and puts the "magnum" back in *magnum*. Franck's bullets are carefully packaged, and he offers trial packs of various mixes of bullets at reasonable prices.

Armfield Custom Bullets

Armfield makes a full line of pure copper-jacketed, bonded-core premium-quality hunting

Speer's Nitrex line of centerfire includes five-round packets in the grand tradition.

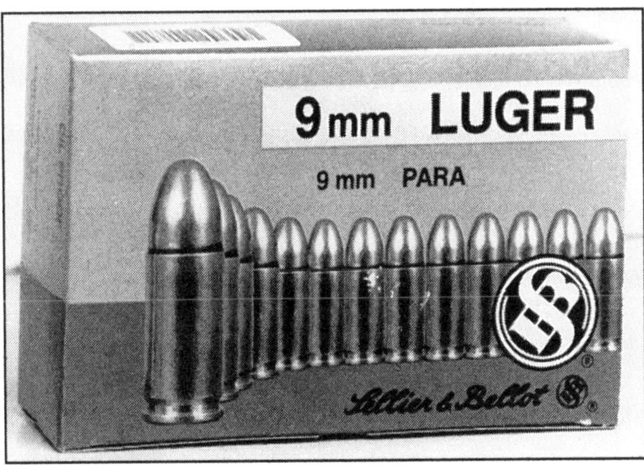

Sellier & Bellot's good stuff—not new, not widely marketed, but here and very handsomely boxed.

amazing variety of weights and point designs. The most intriguing designs are his 458-caliber jacketed spitzer rifle bullets available in 2S, 3S and 4S ogives, five jacket thicknesses, and in weights from 325 to 550 grains. Indeed, in 458-caliber bullets in 243, 257, 264, 277, 284, 308 and 338 calibers under the label "Plainsbond." In addition, this maker offers a parallel line of non-ricocheting, gilding-jacketed bullets that contain a pre-fragmented core designed for varmint shooting and pest control.

A-Square

Called the 300 Petersen but never released under that name, A-Square's beltless super-thirty will finally make its debut this year as the 300 Pegasus. This is a large 3.75-inch case that is designed to boost a 180-grain bullet to a muzzle velocity of 3500 feet per second. Similar in design is another new cartridge offering, the 338 Excalibur that launches a 250-grain bullet at 3250 fps and a 200-grain bullet at 3600 fps. A-Square will load the 338-06 wildcat as a standard offering this year and will release its first reloading manual entitled, "Any Shot You Want."

Ballistic Products Inc.

Ballistic Products, Inc. (BPI), continues to be a shotshell loader's Mecca. BPI has been selected by the Bismuth Cartridge Company to be the exclusive distributor of bismuth shot. In concert with this development, BPI has developed specialty wads, buffer compounds, and loading data for bismuth loads. Also new this year is a drop shipment program from Estate Cartridge, new spreader loads from Polywad, a variety of new wads, and a 1³/₈-ounce slug named the G/BP "Thunderbolt" designed specifically for the 12-gauge 3-inch and 3¹/₂-inch hulls.

Ballard Built Custom Bullets

Dennis Ballard is another custom bullet maker who specializes in the larger caliber rifle and pistol bullets. He currently offers a variety of jacketed designs and point forms for 475 and 510 calibers in weights from 300 to 600 grains. Ballard also offers copper tubing jackets and lead wire.

Barnes

Continuing to expand and refine their X-Bullet line, Barnes has introduced two 224-caliber X-Bullets—a 45-grain boattail and a 53-grain flat base. The bullets were developed for use on deer- and antelope-size game as well as small game, and exhibit classic X-Bullet expansion over a wide variety of velocities. Due to the acquisition of a high-tech tool and die operation, Barnes tolerances and quality control throughout their bullet line is top flight. To make their excellent computer ballistics program even more user friendly, Barnes is now offering its program in a Windows format that includes additional new ways of combining, displaying and printing the generated data.

Once it was Hercules, now it is Alliant, but the new Power Pistol has experience.

Beartooth Bullets

Beartooth is a custom bullet caster of rifle and handgun bullets that emphasizes quality over quantity. They feature LBT bullet designs heat-treated to a BHN of 21+ and rigid inspection procedures. Like the better casters, Beartooth offers custom sizing to properly fit individual bores and handgun cylinder throat dimensions. They have also just released a well-written technical guide to lead bullet use and management, and can supply fire-lapping supplies as well.

Berger Bullets

The Berger benchrest-quality bullet line continues to expand with the addition this year of a 17-caliber 37-grain boattail and two "Length Tolerant Bullets"—a 224-caliber 73-grain LTB and a 30-caliber 155-grain LTB. The Length Tolerant Bullet (LTB) label refers to the unique ogive form that delivers fine accuracy at various seating depths as opposed to Berger's very low drag competition bullets that are seating-depth critical.

Bertram Bullets

A manufacturer of obsolete and specialty caliber rifle brass ranging from the 25-21 Stevens to the 11.2x72 Schuler, Bruce Bertram is introducing yet another basic case this year—the 43 Beaumont—as well as formed cases for the 50-90 Government and the 45-75 Winchester. Through his efforts, Bertram has extended the shooting life of many fine,old guns, and if you need an oddball caliber, like, let's say, a 350 Rigby, or a 25-21 Stevens, or a 40-82 Winchester, check Bertram's current catalog for brass. You will be amazed at the sheer variety of cases he is making available.

Brenneke of America

Offering a full selection of Brenneke slugs in all gauges, Brenneke has introduced a new 1³/₄-ounce slug designed especially for the rifled shotgun barrel. Loaded in the 3-inch 12-gauge case, the new slug carries the name "Super Magnum" and sails forth at 1476 fps.

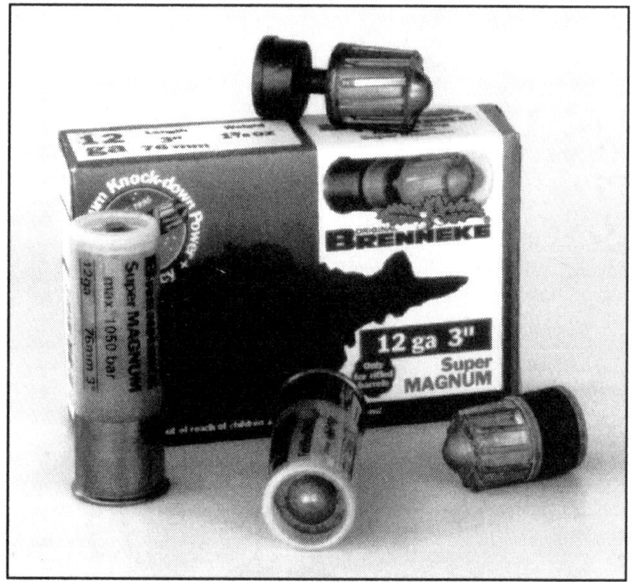

More big boys—Brenneke has a new 12-gauge 3-inch Super Magnum slug load.

James Calhoon

James Calhoon has gained a well-deserved reputation as a supplier of high-quality 224-caliber varmint bullets featuring rebated boattails, deep hollowpoints and an anti-fouling coating at very reasonable bulk prices. This year he has added a full line of 17-caliber bullets in 19-, 22-, 25- and 28-grain weights with all the unique features of his original 224-caliber line.

Cor-Bon

Noted for their high-velocity handgun ammunition featuring bonded-core hollowpoint bullets, Cor-Bon has completed its move to Sturgis, South Dakota, and this year is offering a number of new loads, including a line of rifle ammunition with Barnes' X-Bullets. The new handgun loads are a 90-grain 9mm +P at 1475 fps; two 356 TSW and two 357 SIG loads featuring a 115-grain JHP at 1520 fps and a 124 BHP at 1450 fps; and a 45 ACP +P with a 165-grain JHP at 1250 fps.

Estate Cartridges

Offering a full line of custom loaded, custom headstamped, custom labeled, and custom boxed shotgun shells featuring your or your company's name and logo, Estate Cartridge is unique in the ammunition field and has developed an enviable reputation for quality products.

Eldorado

Home of the PMC cartridge and component line, Eldorado is once again offering reloaders a full selection of PMC brass and bullets, including the successful Starfire handgun bullet. New this year in PMC's loaded ammunition lineup are a 250-grain loading for the venerable 45 Long Colt, and 40-grain soft-point and hollowpoint loads for the 22 Winchester Magnum. PMC is entering the shotshell business, too. This year they'll offer a low-base, 2³/₄-inch Quail & Dove load for 12 and 20 gauges. Finally, at the request of hunters, the cartridge boxes containing PMC's factory-loaded X-Bullet rifle ammunition will now carry a complete ballistics table on the side panel of the box.

Federal

Federal is introducing sixty new or improved ammunition

products this year. At the top of the list are their new Premium High Energy rifle loads that feature Trophy Bonded Bear Claw or Nosler Partition bullets at velocities up to 200 fps faster than former factory loads. Available in 308 Winchester, 30-06, 300 Winchester Magnum and 338 Winchester Magnum loads, the new high-velocity ammunition provides ballistics like a 308 Winchester load with a 165-grain Trophy Bonded Bear Claw at 2870 fps.

One of the more intriguing new offerings is a 22 Winchester Rimfire Magnum load featuring a 30-grain jacketed hollowpoint by Sierra at 2200 fps. With the EPA breathing hot and heavy down the necks of indoor shooting-range operators to eliminate airborne lead, Federal is introducing BallistiClean in calibers 380 Auto, 9mm Luger, 38 Special, 40 S&W and 45 ACP. The heart of BallistiClean is a Toxic-Metal-Free primer and a zinc-core bullet with a copper-alloy jacket.

To improve steel shot shotgun performance, Federal is introducing high-velocity (1425- 1450 fps) loads in 10- and 12-gauge with a new decomposable wad they indicate can provide 90-percent patterns at 40 yards. The shells are headstamped "STEEL" to assure the most skeptical of game wardens.

Following on their successful development of the Olympic-winning Gold Medal Ultra Match 22 rimfire ammunition, Federal is introducing a sub-sonic-velocity version of the same load. Finally, the company continues to expand its Premium ammunition line with new loads for the 220 Swift, 25-06, 257 Weatherby, 270 Winchester, 7mm-08 Remington, 7mm Remington Magnum, 300 Winchestyer Magnum, 300 Weatherby, 35 Whelen, 375 H&H, 416 Remington, 356 TSW, and 357 SIG.

Fiocchi USA

Always a good source for oddball ammunition like the 5.57 Velo Dog or the 7.62 Nagant, Fiocchi's primary focus is quality shotgun ammunition. This year they are introducing six new 12-gauge loads, including an upland steel load featuring #4, #6, and #7 size shot at 1400 fps; a $1^{1}/_{8}$-ounce spreader load; a pheasant load featuring $1^{3}/_{8}$ ounces of nickel-plated shot at 1250 fps; and a 1-ounce slug at 1560 fps.

Fusilier Precision Casting

This is a custom bullet casting outfit that offers a new twist. Their extensive line of rifle and pistol caliber bullets are selectively annealed—tempered to produce a super hard base and shank, and a very soft nose to facilitate expansion. Their complete line is gas-checked and lubricated with a Teflon-impregnated compound.

Gonic Bullet Works

Looking for a bonded-core bullet for your favorite lever-action rifle or Ruger 44 Magnum semi-auto? Gonic specializes in 357-, 44-, 45- and 30-caliber bonded-core bullets with various point styles, including a plastic point for slick feeding in semi-autos and lever guns. This bullet line is equally suitable for revolvers and pistols.

Green Bay Bullets

Years ago and for a pittance, Lyman would send sample batches of 100 cast bullets from any of their mould designs thus permitting the prospective buyer to try a particular bullet of interest before investing in a mould. Opening up Green Bay's well-illustrated catalog of cast bullet offerings is almost like looking at a Lyman mould catalog. Here are some very classic designs from 22-caliber rifle bullets to .760-inch musket balls—some designs I've been wanting to try for years. All bullets are hand cast so that Green Bay can also offer its customers special sizing and custom hardness upon request.

Hawk Precision Bullets

Using dead-soft copper jackets and pure lead cores, Hawk is producing a premium hunting bullet capable of 2- to 3-diameters expansion and 80- to 95-percent weight retention. Offered in a staggering variety of calibers from 6.5mm through 577, Hawk bullets are held to a tolerance of $^{1}/_{2}$-grain and provided in various bullet jacket thicknesses and point profiles to match bullet performance to cartridge velocity. I've tried Hawks in a 33 Winchester, and they performed very well on deer—accurate, too, in my old Model 1886 takedown.

Hornady

Hornady is introducing its own version of a polymer-tipped 224-caliber varmint bullet labeled the V-Max. Available in 40-, 50-, and 55-grain weights, V-Maxes will be offered as components or in loaded ammunition under the Varmint Express designation in calibers 222, 223, 22-250 and 220 Swift. Continuing to expand the Light Magnum ammunition line, Hornady is adding new loadings for the 6.5x55mm, 270 Winchester, 308 Winchester, 300 Winchester Magnum and 338 Winchester Magnum. The Vector illuminated-trajectory handgun ammunition line is being expanded to include 115- and 124-grain loads for the 9mm Luger and a 180-grain loading for the 40 S&W. Factory ammunition for the 357 SIG featuring 124- and 147-grain loads will be offered, and a new 180-grain 30-caliber match bullet will be released this year.

HT Bullets

Individually turned from solid copper with a reverse-tangent radius nose and a grooved shank, an HT Bullet looks much like a flying Coke bottle crossed with a Titan missile. These radically designed hunting bullets have a tremendous sectional density and ballistic coefficient, and typically retain 90- to 100-percent bullet weight (if they are recovered, but usually they exit on game). Annealed to match the bullet to cartridge velocity and the size of the game, HTs are offered in 224 through 475 calibers.

Huntington

Huntington is a great source for hard-to-find loading components and ammunition. While perusing their latest catalog, I found such goodies as 310 Cadet lead bullets and 470 N.E. cases by Norma; .287-inch 140-grain jacketed bullets for the 280 Ross; 5.6x61 Vom Hofe cases by Wal-

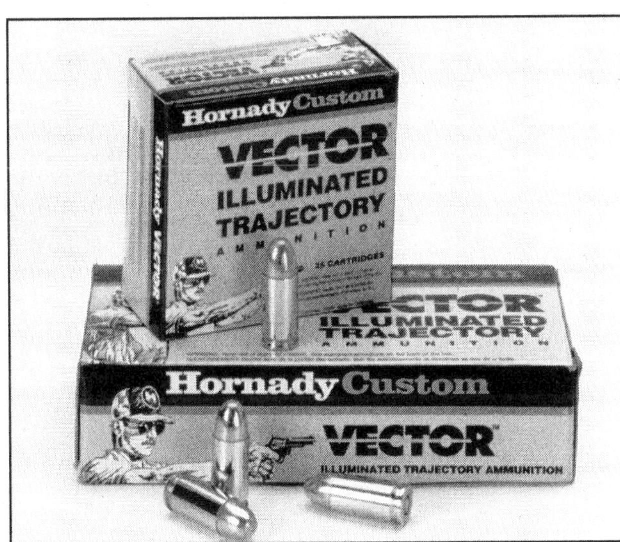

When something that looks like a tracer is needed, Hornady has Vector.

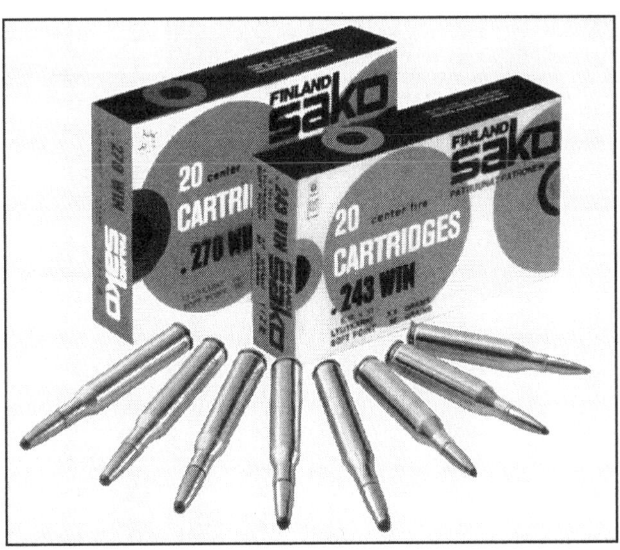

Not much changed, not even the boxes, but Sako is still with us.

ter Gehmann; Woodleigh bullets and Bertram cases; and a hundred other components that just can't be found at your local gun shop.

IMR Powder Company

IMR has released a thoroughly updated and expanded edition of its "Handloader's Guide" featuring new data for the 7.62x39mm, 9mm Luger, 10mm Auto, 40 S&W, and the increasingly popular 24-gram and 1-ounce loadings for the 12-gauge. Emphasizing uniformity and compatibility with other published reloading data, IMR now lists chamber pressures for all shotgun target loads in psi.

Kynoch Ltd.

An agreement has been made between Eley Ltd. and Kynamco Ltd. to reintroduce the entire Kynoch big game ammunition line. Standard double rifle calibers such as the 500, 470, 465, 500/450, 375 Flanged, and 333 Jeffrey Flanged will be loaded as close as possible to original ballistics to maintain the regulation of the fine doubles. New calibers to be offered are the 700 H&H and the 450 Rigby Magnum Rimless. The revived ammunition line will feature solid and softpoint bullets from Woodleigh.

Lapua

Keng's Firearms Speciality, Inc., is the exclusive U.S. importer of the excellent Lapua ammunition and components line. Keng's now has the first English edition of the *Lapua Reloading Manual* that covers standard rifle and handgun cartridges as well as some obscure Finish cartridges like the 8.2x53R—an 8mm hunting cartridge that was widely popular after WWII in converted Mosin-Nagants (as the manual reads, "eh, 'confiscated merchandise' after the Russo-Finnish war."). The colorful and entertaining descriptive text is worth the price of the manual. For example in discussing the 30-30 Winchester, the Finnish editor writes: "Lately, there have been some discordant notes that there would be more efficient tools available for the deer than an almost 100 years old cartridge. But what the heck. There are many millions of 30-30 Winchester rifles and shooters around. It is a hopeless task convincing them that the cartridge is marginal for deer, that it should not be tried for anything bigger than deer, that it should be confined to 100 meter shooting distance, that there are better, more modern choices available. So just skip the above!" The editor's wit is as refreshing as his wisdom.

Lazzeroni Arms Company

John Lazzeroni has created a complete family of rimless hyper-velocity rifle cartridges in 257, 7mm, 308, and 338 calibers, named respectively the 6.53 Scramjet, 7.21 Firehawk, 7.82 Warbird and the 8.59 Titan. The proprietary cases, which are drawn by Jim Bell of MAST Technology, share an overall length of 2.790 inches, a 30-degree shoulder and a .300-inch neck. And they perform. From 26-inch barrels, the Scramjet reaches 3700+ fps with a 100-grain bullet; the Firehawk, 3600 fps with a 140-grain projectile; the Warbird, 3400 fps with a 180-grain bullet; and the Titan, 3225 fps with a 225-grain bullet. The first run of factory ammunition is loaded exclusively with Nosler Partition bullets. The development and standardization of the Lazzeroni cartridges stands as one of the most exciting ballistic developments of the year. Lazzeroni has available the loaded cartridges, brass, RCBS dies, and custom rifles.

Your 7x30 Waters can be happy again—the 120-grain flatpoint 7mm Nosler is back.

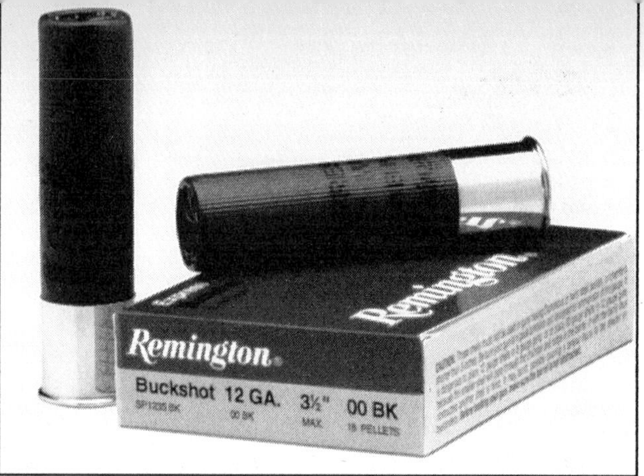

Play with the big boys—eighteen #00 pellets—in a new Remington $3^1/_2$-inch load.

Lyman

Considered the bible for shotgun shell reloaders, the 4th edition of Lyman's *Shotshell Reloading Handbook* has been released, featuring updated and new data for many of the newest components including Remington RTL, Activ and Fiocchi cases; Winchester, Hodgdon, Accurate Arms, Scot, and VihtaVuori powders; the Federal 209A primer; and additional special sections on steel shot, buckshot and slugs. The *Handbook* numbering 372 pages also contains valuable new technical articles on Sporting Clays loads.

Mast Technology

Providing a variety of brass cartridge cases for major ammunition companies, governments and proprietary manufacturers, MAST Technology under the leadership of Jim Bell, Jr., will be offering its own line of fine rifle cases this year. First off the machines will be the 404 Jeffrey and the 416 Rigby.

Montana Precision Swaging

While supplying a variety of cast rifle and handgun bullets, this company stands out as a source of swaged paper patch bullets in 38, 40, 43, 44, 45, and 50 calibers, either straight-sided or tapered.

Norma

The complete Norma line of ammunition and components is imported and distributed in the U.S. by the Paul Company. New this year is 6mm Norma BR brass and loaded match ammunition; a 6.5mm 130-grain VLD match bullet with a BC of .583; basic forming brass in 30-06, H&H, 45- and 50-caliber $3^1/_4$-inch sizes; and a revolutionary new Diamond Line of target bullets and cartridges (6.5x55mm and 6mm Norma BR) that feature a fine coating of molybdenum disulfide and carnauba wax. Norma's tests of the new coating, developed and licensed by NECO of California, show a decrease in pressure and barrel fouling, improved accuracy, better bullet ballistic characteristics, and longer barrel life. The 6mm Norma BR cartridge, which is the Remington case with a smaller flash hole, loaded with a coated 107-grain Sierra VLD match bullet at 2820 fps, has been cleaning up at the European 300-meter matches. Norma will also be releasing a new pistol powder this year with a burning rate midway between R-1 and R-123.

Northern Precision

Noted for producing unique 416-caliber bullets suitable for everything from squirrel to elephant, Northern Precision has expanded its line of jacketed and "base guard" swaged lead bullets to the 358, 429, and 458 calibers. Available in an endless variety of weights, bonded-core or not, with a poly tip or "sabr-star" hollowpoint, the new offerings are designed for both handgun and rifle cartridges.

Nosler

Ever expanding their line of fine projectiles, Nosler is adding a 55-grain 6mm Ballistic Tip varmint bullet; a 45-grain Hornet Solid Base bullet; a 120-grain 7mm Solid Base flatpoint for the 7-30 Waters; and a 38-caliber 115-grain hollowpoint IPSC handgun bullet for a major power load for the 38 Super. Nosler Ballistic Tips will be packaged in boxes of fifty this year.

Old Western Scrounger

One of the most valuable sources for hard-to-get ammunition and components, Old Western Scrounger is expanding its line of custom-loaded obsolete-caliber ammunition. New this year are the 351 Winchester Self-Loader, 33 Winchester and 9mm Winchester Magnum, as well as blackpowder loadings for the 8mm Kropatschek, 45-75 Winchester, and 577-450 Martini Henry. Their annual catalog continues to be highly informative, entertaining and filled with excellent reference material. The Scrounger will be a prime source for the new Kynoch line.

Paragon

Always a source for great buys in military ammunition, Paragon's latest offerings include such exotic numbers as plastic-core 7.62x39mm, 6.5x55mm light bullet gallery ammo, and 223 subsonic and frangible light bullet training rounds.

Polywad

Manufacturer and distributor of the popular and effective Spred-R insert wad that turns tight chokes into open chokes, Polywad will now offer factory-loaded Spred-R shotgun ammunition featuring a transparent case, high antimony shot and, of course, a Spred-R wad.

Precision Custom Bullets

Here is a 50-caliber Browning Machine Gun specialty house that offers target-quality 50 BMG match bullets in a selection of weights, ogives, drag and point forms. Bullets that show less than the highest target specs are sold as hunting or varmint bullets. Precision also offers 50 BMG brass, primers and military-quality plinking bullets.

Remington

Remington is introducing a 12-gauge Premier STS Target load line in trap, Skeet and Sporting Clays specifications that features an exceptional-quality, tapered-mouth plastic case with high-crimp memory loaded with high antimony-grade shot. For the 3½-inch 12-gauge users, there is a new #00 buckshot load containing eighteen pellets. Two popular big game calibers have been added to the Safari Grade ammunition line—a 300 Weatherby load featuring a 200-grain Swift A-Frame bullet at 2925 fps and a 458 Winchester Magnum load with a 450-grain A-Frame bullet at 2150 fps. A new 140-grain Core-Lokt bullet will be offered in the 7x57, 7x64, 7mm-08 Remington, 280 Remington, and 7mm Remington Magnum, while the 338 Winchester Magnum will be loaded with 225-grain and 250-grain Core-Lokt bullets. In the handgun line, Remington will offer a 185-grain (+P) Golden Saber load in the 45 ACP at 1140 fps as well as a new 230-grain JHP load in the old warhorse. The increasingly popular 357 SIG will be offered with a 125-grain JHP at 1350 fps. New Leadless target loads will include the 9mm Luger, 357 Magnum, 38 Special and 380 Auto. Finally expanding their economy UMC line, Remington is adding metal-case bullet loads for the 303 British, 30-06, 32 ACP, 357 SIG and 10mm.

Seller & Bellot U.S.A.

Here is a popular European line soon more available in the States. Sellier & Bellot is an excellent source of the metric cartridges and this year is introducing 12-gauge nickel-plated buckshot loads of #00 through #4 buck; a 131-grain softpoint load for the 6.5x55; and standard loads for the 40 S&W and 45 ACP.

Shilen

A benchrest barrel, trigger and bullet maker, Shilen has introduced a completely new 65-grain 6mm benchrest bullet. What sets the new bullet apart from the company's earlier 224-caliber bullet is the uniform jacket being produced by Shilen in their own shop. Called the MicroJacket, Shilen is now able to completely control the quality of their bullets as a result of producing a jacket with an average runout of only .0001- to .0002-inch. It is not uncommon for commercial-quality benchrest jackets to have thickness variations up to .0008-inch, so Shilen has truly upped the precision ante in benchrest circles. The new benchrest bullet is flat-based and has a 7S ogive. The production lots are dated so that lot integrity is maintained upon sale.

Sierra

For their 50th anniversary, Sierra is celebrating by releasing a 50th anniversary bullet board featuring 158 bullets and a new, updated 50th anniversary edition of their excellent two-volume reloading manual. New bullets this year consist of a 30-caliber 175 HPBT Matchking suitable for 1000-yard competition in the M-1, M-1A and M-14; a 125-grain 311-caliber Pro-Hunter bullet suitable for deer in the 7.62x39mm cartridge and for varmints in the 303 British, 7.7 Arisaka and 7.65 Mauser; a 174-grain 311-caliber HPBT Matchking for shooters who are competing with classic calibers like the 303 British; and a lightweight 135-grain 40/10mm-caliber JHP bullet designed for plinking, small game, USPSA competition and defensive applications. Sierra's rifle and handgun handloading videos continue to be the finest ever produced and are as useful for the most experienced as they are for the novice.

Speer

The big news from Speer is that they are aggressively entering the premium rifle ammunition market. Under the label NITREX (nitro-express), the new line initially features Speer's premium Grand Slam bullets loaded in nickel-plated cases for the 243 and 270 Winchester, 7mm Remington Magnum, 308 Winchester, 30-06, 300 and 338 Winchester Magnum, and 375 H&H. A NITREX load for the

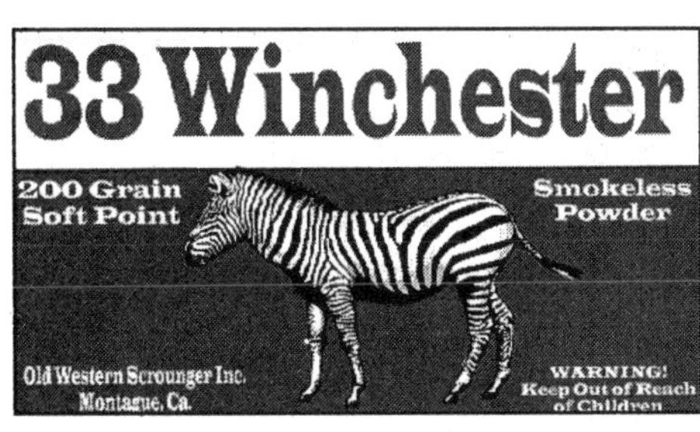

Glorious packaging for wonderful old cartridges for veterans that can shoot once more—from Old Western Scrounger, naturally.

venerable 30-30 Winchester sports a totally new 150-grain bonded-core bullet.

As interesting as the new loads is their packaging. Each twenty-round box contains four shirt pocket-sized five-round packs reminiscent of the early Kynoch packaging. The pocket-sized packs are handy in the field, and, undoubtedly, dealers will be willing to sell the five-round packs separately.

New offerings from Speer in their highly effective Gold Dot handgun ammunition line include a 35-grain 25 Auto load at 900 fps; a 60-grain 32 Auto load at 960 fps; and a 125-grain 357 SIG load at 1350 fps. Another new SIG load consisting of a 125-grain Totally Metal Jacketed bullet at 1350 fps is included in the Lawman series.

New component bullets consist of the Gold Dot bullets for the 25 Auto, 32 Auto and 357 SIG, plus a 165-grain 40-caliber bullet for the 40 S&W. New Totally Metal Jacketed component bullets are available for the 357 SIG, with a 165-grain bullet for the 40-calibers.

Finally, some news on the primer front. CCI rifle and pistol primers will be offered preloaded in color-coded APS strips for the new RCBS Automatic Priming System. And CCI has developed a 209SC Sporting Clays shotgun primer matched carefully to the burning characteristics of Hodgdon's Clays powders.

Sperry Sporting Specialties

Sperry has found a unique niche in the reloading market. As a service, it provides handloaders with two-, six-, twelve- or twenty-five-packs of virtually every component rifle and pistol bullet made, thus eliminating the problem most of us have with numerous partially-used boxes of component bullets that just didn't work out. This is a great way to experiment with a variety of bullets before putting your cash on the line for full boxes of a hundred or more.

Stoeger

Stoeger has added the full line of high-quality Sako centerfire rifle and pistol ammunition to its offerings, including factory-loaded 22 PPC and 6mm PPC cartridges.

Szczepanski Bullet Swaging

Ron Szczepanski makes one thing and one thing well—swaged straight-sided paper-patched bullets. He currently offers 40- and 45-caliber paper-patched bullets in a variety of diameters, weights and ogives.

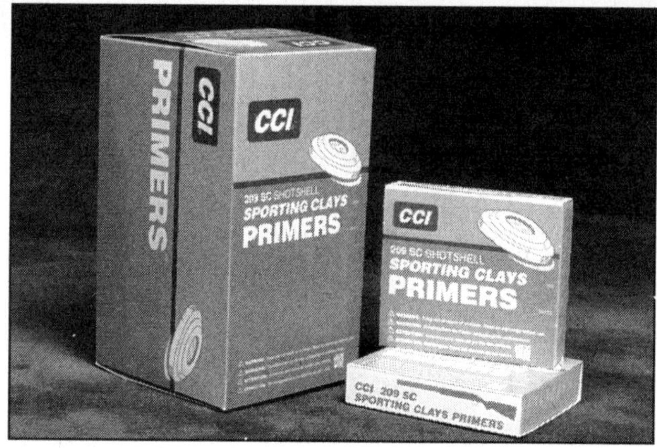

The 209 SC is a primer for Sporting Clays loads. Wow, is that game going or what?

Triton Cartridge

Triton has developed a new line of Quik-Shok Premium Plus handgun ammunition featuring a unique Hyper-Stressed bullet designed by Tom Burczynski, the designer of the Hydra-Shok and Starfire bullets. According to Triton, during penetration, the Hyper-Stressed bullet expands rapidly and then splits into three sections that continue to penetrate in three directions producing multiple wound channels and maximum energy transfer to the target.

VihtaVuori Oy

This diverse Finnish powder line is imported into the United States by Kaltron Pettibone. The big news this year is the release of the high-energy N500 series of powder and accompanying loading data in the company's 6th edition *Reloading Guide*. The Finnish powdersmiths have taken single-base powders, impregnated them with nitroglycerine and then added special coatings to achieve a progressive burn while reducing barrel wear. The result is higher velocities at standard pressures. The release of these powders to handloaders opens up a whole new world for experimentation. The second edition of VihtaVuori's *Reloading Manual* is available this year. Written by the same witty scribe who produces the Lapua manual, the VihtaVuori book contains the best explanation and graphic presentation of internal and external ballistics concepts ever produced for the layman.

Weatherby

They once said they would never do it, but they have. Weatherby will be offering rifles and factory ammunition for the 30-378, boosting a 180-grain bullet to a stratospheric velocity of 3500 fps. Weatherby will also be offering Barnes X-Bullets in all Weatherby magnum calibers.

New, cleaner, more efficient—AA Plus is better than Super Target, they say.

Widener's

This mail-order supply house is the best source of Israel Military Industries (IMI) cases and bullets like 62-grain match bullets and SS-109 bullets for the 223 Remington, and 647-grain match bullets for the 50 BMG. Occasionally available is match brass for the 308 Winchester and 45 ACP. Quality at very reasonable bulk-rate prices.

Winchester

The handloading component pipeline continues to improve at Winchester with the release of the 270-grain 375-caliber Fail Safe bullet and Silvertip hollow-point handgun bullets for the 380 Auto, 38 Special and 45 ACP. The Supreme Fail Safe rifle ammunition line is being expanded to include a 180-grain loading for the 300 H&H, a 165-grain load for the 300 Winchester Magnum, and a 270-grain load for the 375 H&H. Similarly, the Supreme SXT handgun ammunition line now includes a 130-grain loading for the 38 Special +P and a 165-grain load for the 40 S&W.

Meeting the challenge to deliver leadless practice ammunition to the marketplace with bullet weights and velocities that are equivalent to service ammunition, Winchester is adding a 158-grain 38 Special +P, a 165-grain 40 S&W and a 147-grain 9mm Luger load to its Super-X Super Unleaded series.

In the shotgun line, Winchester is releasing a new component powder labeled AA Plus that is more clean-burning and efficient than the Super Target powder that has been a sterling performer in the 2$^{3}/_{4}$-inch, 3-dram equivalent loads, permitting the handloader to duplicate factory AA ballistics and patterns. New, too, this year are 10- and 12-gauge 3$^{1}/_{2}$-inch magnum turkey loads, as well a 20-gauge 3-inch turkey loading featuring #5 and #6 shot, and a $^{7}/_{8}$-ounce Double A wad for the 12-gauge.

Zonic Bullets

Zonic offers a wide variety of cast handgun bullets. Particularly interesting is their line of heavyweight hunting bullets based on LBT designs, including a 170-grain 357 bullet; 250-, 275- and 300-grain 44 bullets; and a 300-grain 45 bullet. Reasonably priced, too. ●

AVERAGE CENTERFIRE RIFLE CARTRIDGE BALLISTICS AND PRICES

	Caliber	Bullet weight grains	-VELOCITY (fps)- Muzzle	100 yds.	200 yds.	300 yds.	400. yds.	-ENERGY (ft. lbs.)- Muzzle	100 yds.	200 yds.	300 yds.	400 yds.	-TRAJ. (in.)- 100 yds.	200 yds.	300 yds.	400 yds.	Approx. Price per box
17	17 Remington	25	4040	3284	2644	2086	1606	906	599	388	242	143	+2.0	+1.7	-4.0	-17.0	$17
	221 Fireball	50	2800	2137	1580	1180	988	870	507	277	155	109	0.0	-7.0	-28.0	NA	$14
22	22 Hornet	45	2690	2042	1502	1128	948	723	417	225	127	90	0.0	-7.7	-31.0	NA	$27**
	218 Bee	46	2760	2102	1550	1155	961	788	451	245	136	94	0.0	-7.2	-29.0	NA	$46**
	222 Remington	40	3600	3117	2673	2269	1911	1151	863	634	457	324	+1.07	0.0	-6.13	-18.9	NA
	222 Remington	50	3140	2602	2123	1700	1350	1094	752	500	321	202	+2.0	-0.4	-11.0	-33.0	$11
	222 Remington	55	3020	2562	2147	1773	1451	1114	801	563	384	257	+2.0	-0.4	-11.0	-33.0	$12
	22 PPC	52	3400	2930	2510	2130	NA	1335	990	730	525	NA	+2.0	1.4	-5.0	NA	NA
	223 Remington	40	3650	3010	2450	1950	1530	1185	805	535	340	265	+2.0	+1.0	-6.0	-22.0	$14
	223 Remington	52/53	3330	2882	2477	2106	1770	1305	978	722	522	369	+2.0	+0.6	-6.5	-21.5	$14
	223 Remington	55	3240	2748	2305	1906	1556	1282	922	649	444	296	+2.0	-0.2	-9.0	-27.0	$12
	223 Remington	60	3100	2712	2355	2026	1726	1280	979	739	547	397	+2.0	+0.2	-8.0	-24.7	$16
	223 Remington	64	3020	2621	2256	1920	1619	1296	977	723	524	373	+2.0	-0.2	-9.3	-23.0	$14
	223 Remington	69	3000	2720	2460	2210	1980	1380	1135	925	750	600	+2.0	+0.8	-5.8	-17.5	$15
	222 Rem. Mag.	55	3240	2748	2305	1906	1556	1282	922	649	444	296	+2.0	-0.2	-9.0	-27.0	$14
	225 Winchester	55	3570	3066	2616	2208	1838	1556	1148	836	595	412	+2.0	+1.0	-5.0	-20.0	$19
	224 Wea. Mag.	55	3650	3192	2780	2403	2057	1627	1244	943	705	516	+2.0	+1.2	-4.0	-17.0	$32
	22-250 Rem.	40	4000	3320	2720	2200	1740	1420	980	660	430	265	+2.0	+1.8	-3.0	-16.0	$14
	22-250 Rem.	52/55	3680	3137	2656	2222	1832	1654	1201	861	603	410	+2.0	+1.3	-4.0	-17.0	$13
	22-250 Rem.	60	3600	3195	2826	2485	2169	1727	1360	1064	823	627	+2.0	+2.0	-2.4	-12.3	$19
	220 Swift	40	4200	3678	3190	2739	2329	1566	1201	904	666	482	+0.51	0.0	-4	-12.9	NA
	220 Swift	50	3780	3158	2617	2135	1710	1586	1107	760	506	325	+2.0	+1.4	-4.4	-17.9	$20
	220 Swift	55	3650	3194	2772	2384	2035	1627	1246	939	694	506	+2.0	+2.0	-2.6	-13.4	$19
	220 Swift	60	3600	3199	2824	2475	2156	1727	1364	1063	816	619	+2.0	+1.6	-4.1	-13.1	$19
	22 Savage H.P	71	2790	2340	1930	1570	1280	1225	860	585	390	190	+2.0	-1.0	-10.4	-35.7	NA
	6mm BR Rem.	100	2550	2310	2083	1870	1671	1444	1185	963	776	620	+2.5	-0.6	-11.8	NA	$22
nm	6mm Norma BR	107	2822	2667	2517	2372	2229	1893	1690	1506	1337	1181	+1.73	0.0	-7.24	-20.6	NA
	6mm PPC	70	3140	2750	2400	2070	NA	1535	1175	895	665	NA	+2.0	+1.4	-5.0	NA	NA
24)	243 Winchester	60	3600	3110	2660	2260	1890	1725	1285	945	680	475	+2.0	+1.8	-3.3	-15.5	$17
	243 Winchester	75/80	3350	2955	2593	2259	1951	1993	1551	1194	906	676	+2.0	+0.9	-5.0	-19.0	$16
	243 Winchester	85	3320	3070	2830	2600	2380	2080	1770	1510	1280	1070	+2.0	+1.2	-4.0	-14.0	$18
	243 Winchester*	100	2960	2697	2449	2215	1993	1945	1615	1332	1089	882	+2.5	+1.2	-6.0	-20.0	$16
	243 Winchester	105	2920	2689	2470	2261	2062	1988	1686	1422	1192	992	+2.5	+1.6	-5.0	-18.4	$21
	243 Light Mag.	100	3100	2839	2592	2358	2138	2133	1790	1491	1235	1014	+1.5	0.0	-6.8	-19.8	NA
	6mm Remington	80	3470	3064	2694	2352	2036	2139	1667	1289	982	736	+2.0	+1.1	-5.0	-17.0	$16
	6mm Remington*	100	3100	2829	2573	2332	2104	2133	1777	1470	1207	983	+2.5	+1.6	-5.0	-17.0	$16
	6mm Remington	105	3060	2822	2596	2381	2177	2105	1788	1512	1270	1059	+2.5	+1.1	-3.3	-15.0	$21
	240 Wea. Mag.	87	3500	3202	2924	2663	2416	2366	1980	1651	1370	1127	+2.0	+2.0	-2.0	-12.0	$32
	240 Wea. Mag.*	100	3395	3106	2835	2581	2339	2559	2142	1785	1478	1215	+2.5	+2.8	-2.0	-11.0	$43
25	25-20 Win.	86	1460	1194	1030	931	858	407	272	203	165	141	0.0	-23.5	NA	NA	$32**
	25-35 Win.	117	2230	1866	1545	1282	1097	1292	904	620	427	313	+2.5	-4.2	-26.0	NA	$24
	250 Savage	100	2820	2504	2210	1936	1684	1765	1392	1084	832	630	+2.5	+0.4	-9.0	-28.0	$17
	257 Roberts	100	2980	2661	2363	2085	1827	1972	1572	1240	965	741	+2.5	-0.8	-5.2	-21.6	$20
	257 Roberts+P	117	2780	2411	2071	1761	1488	2009	1511	1115	806	576	+2.5	-0.2	-10.2	-32.6	$18
	257 Roberts+P*	120	2780	2560	2360	2160	1970	2060	1750	1480	1240	1030	+2.5	+1.2	-6.4	-23.6	$22
	257 Roberts	122	2600	2331	2078	1842	1625	1831	1472	1169	919	715	+2.5	0.0	-10.6	-31.4	$21
	257 Light Mag.	117	2940	2694	2460	2240	2031	2245	1885	1572	1303	1071	+1.7	0.0	-7.6	-21.8	NA
	25-06 Rem.	87	3440	2995	2591	2222	1884	2286	1733	1297	954	686	+2.0	+1.1	-2.5	-14.4	$17
	25-06 Rem.	90	3440	3043	2680	2344	2034	2364	1850	1435	1098	827	+2.0	+1.8	-3.3	-15.6	$17
	25-06 Rem.	100	3230	2893	2580	2287	2014	2316	1858	1478	1161	901	+2.0	+0.8	-5.7	-18.9	$17
	25-06 Rem.	117	2990	2770	2570	2370	2190	2320	2000	1715	1465	1246	+2.5	+1.0	-7.9	-26.6	$19
	25-06 Rem.*	120	2990	2730	2484	2252	2032	2382	1985	1644	1351	1100	+2.5	+1.2	-5.3	-19.6	$17
	25-06 Rem.	122	2930	2706	2492	2289	2095	2325	1983	1683	1419	1189	+2.5	+1.8	-4.5	-17.5	$23
	257 Wea. Mag.	87	3825	3456	3118	2805	2513	2826	2308	1870	1520	1220	+2.0	+2.7	-0.3	-7.6	$32
	257 Wea. Mag.	100	3555	3237	2941	2665	2404	2806	2326	1920	1576	1283	+2.5	+3.2	0.0	-8.0	$32
	257 Scramjet	100	3745	3450	3173	2912	2666	3114	2643	2235	1883	1578	+2.1	+2.77	0.0	-6.93	NA
	6.5x50mm Jap.	139	2360	2160	1970	1790	1620	1720	1440	1195	985	810	+2.5	-1.0	-13.5	NA	NA
6.5	6.5x50mm Jap.	156	2070	1830	1610	1430	1260	1475	1155	900	695	550	+2.5	-4.0	-23.8	NA	NA
	6.5x52mm Car.	139	2580	2360	2160	1970	1790	2045	1725	1440	1195	985	+2.5	0.0	-9.9	-29.0	NA
	6.5x52mm Car.	156	2430	2170	1930	1700	1500	2045	1630	1285	1005	780	+2.5	-1.0	-13.9	NA	NA
	6.5x55mm Light Mag.	129	2770	2561	2361	2171	1994	2197	1878	1597	1350	1136	+1.98	0.0	-8.25	-23.2	NA
	6.5x55mm Swe.	140	2550	NA	NA	NA	NA	2020	NA	NA	NA	NA	NA	NA	NA	NA	$18
	6.5x55mm Swe.*	139/140	2850	2640	2440	2250	2070	2525	2170	1855	1575	1330	+2.5	+1.6	-5.4	-18.9	$18
	6.5x55mm Swe.	156	2650	2370	2110	1870	1650	2425	1950	1550	1215	945	+2.5	0.0	-10.3	-30.6	NA
	6.5 Rem. Mag.	120	3210	2905	2621	2353	2102	2745	2248	1830	1475	1177	+2.5	+1.7	-4.1	-16.3	Disc.
	264 Win. Mag.	140	3030	2782	2548	2326	2114	2854	2406	2018	1682	1389	+2.5	+1.4	-5.1	-18.0	$24
	270 Winchester	100	3430	3021	2649	2305	1988	2612	2027	1557	1179	877	+2.0	+1.0	-4.9	-17.5	$17
27	270 Winchester	130	3060	2776	2510	2259	2022	2702	2225	1818	1472	1180	+2.5	+1.4	-5.3	-18.2	$17
	270 Winchester	135	3000	2780	2570	2369	2178	2697	2315	1979	1682	1421	+2.5	+1.4	-6.0	-17.6	$23
	270 Winchester*	140	2940	2700	2480	2260	2060	2685	2270	1905	1590	1315	+2.5	+1.8	-4.6	-17.9	$20
	270 Win. Light Mag.	140	3100	2894	2697	2508	2327	2987	2604	2261	1955	1684	+1.37	0.0	-6.32	-18.3	NA
	270 Winchester*	150	2850	2585	2336	2100	1879	2705	2226	1817	1468	1175	+2.5	+1.2	-6.5	-22.0	$17

CAUTION: PRICES SHOWN ARE SUPPLIED BY THE MANUFACTURER OR IMPORTER. CHECK YOUR LOCAL GUNSHOP.

Caliber	Bullet weight grains	-VELOCITY (fps)- Muzzle	100 yds.	200 yds.	300 yds.	400. yds.	-ENERGY (ft. lbs.)- Muzzle	100 yds.	200 yds.	300 yds.	400 yds.	-TRAJ. (in.)- 100 yds.	200 yds.	300 yds.	400 yds.	Approx. Price per box
27 (cont.)																
270 Wea. Mag.	100	3760	3380	3033	2712	2412	3139	2537	2042	1633	1292	+2.0	+2.4	-1.2	-10.1	$32
270 Wea. Mag.	130	3375	3119	2878	2649	2432	3287	2808	2390	2026	1707	+2.5	+2.9	-0.9	-9.9	$32
270 Wea. Mag.*	150	3245	3036	2837	2647	2465	3507	3070	2681	2334	2023	+2.5	+2.6	-1.8	-11.4	$47
7mm																
7mm BR	140	2215	2012	1821	1643	1481	1525	1259	1031	839	681	+2.0	-3.7	-20.0	NA	$23
7mm Mauser*	139/140	2660	2435	2221	2018	1827	2199	1843	1533	1266	1037	+2.5	0.0	-9.6	-27.7	$17
7mm Mauser	145	2690	2442	2206	1985	1777	2334	1920	1568	1268	1017	+2.5	+0.1	-9.6	-28.3	$18
7mm Mauser	154	2690	2490	2300	2120	1940	2475	2120	1810	1530	1285	+2.5	+0.8	-7.5	-23.5	$17
7mm Mauser	175	2440	2137	1857	1603	1382	2313	1774	1340	998	742	+2.5	-1.7	-16.1	NA	$17
7mm Light Mag.	139	2830	2620	2450	2250	2070	2475	2135	1835	1565	1330	+1.8	0.0	-7.6	-22.1	NA
7x30 Waters	120	2700	2300	1930	1600	1330	1940	1405	990	685	470	+2.5	-0.2	-12.3	NA	$18
7mm-08 Rem.	120	3000	2725	2467	2223	1992	2398	1979	1621	1316	1058	+2.0	0.0	-7.6	-22.3	$18
7mm-08 Rem.*	140	2860	2625	2402	2189	1988	2542	2142	1793	1490	1228	+2.5	+0.8	-6.9	-21.9	$18
7mm-08 Rem.	154	2715	2510	2315	2128	1950	2520	2155	1832	1548	1300	+2.5	+1.0	-7.0	-22.7	$23
7mm-08 Light Mag.	139	3000	2790	2590	2399	2216	2777	2403	2071	1776	1515	+1.5	0.0	-6.7	-19.4	NA
7x64mm Bren.	140	Not Yet Announced														$17
7x64mm Bren.	154	2820	2610	2420	2230	2050	2720	2335	1995	1695	1430	+2.5	+1.4	-5.7	-19.9	NA
7x64mm Bren.*	160	2850	2669	2495	2327	2166	2885	2530	2211	1924	1667	+2.5	+1.6	-4.8	-17.8	$24
7x64mm Bren.	175	Not yet announced														$17
284 Winchester	150	2860	2595	2344	2108	1886	2724	2243	1830	1480	1185	+2.5	+0.8	-7.3	-23.2	$24
280 Remington	120	3150	2866	2599	2348	2110	2643	2188	1800	1468	1186	+2.0	+0.6	-6.0	-17.9	$17
280 Remington	140	3000	2758	2528	2309	2102	2797	2363	1986	1657	1373	+2.5	+1.4	-5.2	-18.3	$17
280 Remington*	150	2890	2624	2373	2135	1912	2781	2293	1875	1518	1217	+2.5	+0.8	-7.1	-22.6	$17
280 Remington	160	2840	2637	2442	2556	2078	2866	2471	2120	1809	1535	+2.5	+0.8	-6.7	-21.0	$20
280 Remington	165	2820	2510	2220	1950	1701	2913	2308	1805	1393	1060	+2.5	+0.4	-8.8	-26.5	$17
7x61mm S&H Sup.	154	3060	2720	2400	2100	1820	3200	2520	1965	1505	1135	+2.5	+1.8	-5.0	-19.8	NA
7mm Dakota	160	3200	3001	2811	2630	2455	3637	3200	2808	2456	2140	+2.1	+1.9	-2.8	-12.5	NA
7mm Rem. Mag.*	139/140	3150	2930	2710	2510	2320	3085	2660	2290	1960	1670	+2.5	+2.4	-2.4	-12.7	$21
7mm Rem. Mag.	150/154	3110	2830	2085	2320	2085	3221	2667	2196	1792	1448	+2.5	+1.6	-4.6	-16.5	$21
7mm Rem. Mag.*	160/162	2950	2730	2520	2320	2120	3090	2650	2250	1910	1600	+2.5	+1.8	-4.4	-17.8	$34
7mm Rem. Mag.	165	2900	2699	2507	2324	2147	3081	2669	2303	1978	1689	+2.5	+1.2	-5.9	-19.0	$28
7mm Rem. Mag.	175	2860	2645	2440	2244	2057	3178	2718	2313	1956	1644	+2.5	+1.0	-6.5	-20.7	$21
7mm Wea. Mag.	140	3225	2970	2729	2501	2283	3233	2741	2315	1943	1621	+2.5	+2.0	-3.2	-14.0	$35
7mm Wea. Mag.	154	3260	3023	2799	2586	2382	3539	3044	2609	2227	1890	+2.5	+2.8	-1.5	-10.8	$32
7mm Wea. Mag.*	160	3200	3004	2816	2637	2464	3637	3205	2817	2469	2156	+2.5	+2.7	-1.5	-10.6	$47
7mm Wea. Mag.	165	2950	2747	2553	2367	2189	3188	2765	2388	2053	1756	+2.5	+1.8	-4.2	-16.4	$43
7mm Wea. Mag.	175	2910	2693	2486	2288	2098	3293	2818	2401	2033	1711	+2.5	+1.2	-5.9	-19.4	$35
7mm STW	140	3450	3254	3067	2888	2715	3700	3291	2924	2592	2292	+2.42	+3.04	0.0	-7.27	NA
7mm STW	160	3250	3087	2930	2778	2631	3752	3385	3049	2741	2460	+2.78	+3.42	0.0	-7.97	NA
7mm Firehawk	140	3625	3373	3135	2909	2695	4084	3536	3054	2631	2258	+2.2	+2.87	0.0	-7.03	NA
30																
30 Carbine	110	1990	1567	1236	1035	923	977	600	373	262	208	0.0	-13.5	NA	NA	$28**
303 Savage	190	1890	1612	1327	1183	1055	1507	1096	794	591	469	+2.5	-7.6	NA	NA	$24
30 Remington	170	2120	1822	1555	1328	1153	1696	1253	913	666	502	+2.5	-4.7	-26.3	NA	$20
30-30 Win.	55	3400	2693	2085	1570	1187	1412	886	521	301	172	+2.0	0.0	-10.2	-35.0	$18
30-30 Win.	125	2570	2090	1660	1320	1080	1830	1210	770	480	320	+2.0	-2.6	-19.9	NA	$13
30-30 Win.	150	2390	1973	1605	1303	1095	1902	1296	858	565	399	+2.5	-3.2	-22.5	NA	$13
30-30 Win.	160	2300	1997	1719	1473	1268	1879	1416	1050	771	571	+2.5	-2.9	-20.2	NA	$18
30-30 Win.*	170	2200	1895	1619	1381	1191	1827	1355	989	720	535	+2.5	-5.8	-23.6	NA	$13
300 Savage	150	2630	2354	2094	1853	1631	2303	1845	1462	1143	886	+2.5	-0.4	-10.1	-30.7	$17
300 Savage	180	2350	2137	1935	1754	1570	2207	1825	1496	1217	985	+2.5	-1.6	-15.2	NA	$17
30-40 Krag	180	2430	2213	2007	1813	1632	2360	1957	1610	1314	1064	+2.5	-1.4	-13.8	NA	$18
7.65x53mm Arg.	180	2590	2390	2200	2010	1830	2685	2280	1925	1615	1345	+2.5	0.0	-27.6	NA	NA
307 Winchester	150	2760	2321	1924	1575	1289	2530	1795	1233	826	554	+2.5	-1.5	-13.6	NA	Disc.
307 Winchester	180	2510	2179	1874	1599	1362	2519	1898	1404	1022	742	+2.5	-1.6	-15.6	NA	$20
7.5x55 Swiss	180	2650	2450	2250	2060	1880	2805	2390	2020	1700	1415	+2.5	+0.6	-8.1	-24.9	NA
308 Winchester	55	3770	3215	2726	2286	1888	1735	1262	907	638	435	+2.0	+1.4	-3.8	-15.8	$22
308 Winchester	150	2820	2533	2263	2009	1774	2648	2137	1705	1344	1048	+2.5	+0.4	-8.5	-26.1	$17
308 Winchester	165	2700	2440	2194	1963	1748	2670	2180	1763	1411	1199	+2.5	0.0	-9.7	-28.5	$20
308 Winchester	168	2680	2493	2314	2143	1979	2678	2318	1998	1713	1460	+2.5	0.0	-8.9	-25.3	$18
308 Winchester	178	2620	2415	2220	2034	1857	2713	2306	1948	1635	1363	+2.5	0.0	-9.6	-27.6	$23
308 Winchester*	180	2620	2393	2178	1974	1782	2743	2288	1896	1557	1269	+2.5	-0.2	-10.2	-28.5	$17
308 Light Mag.*	150	2980	2703	2442	2195	1964	2959	2433	1986	1606	1285	+1.6	0.0	-7.5	-22.2	NA
308 Light Mag.	165	2870	2658	2456	2263	2078	3019	2589	2211	1877	1583	+1.7	0.0	-7.5	-21.8	NA
308 High Energy	165	2870	2600	2350	2120	1890	3020	2485	2030	1640	1310	+1.8	0.0	-8.2	-24.0	NA
308 Light Mag.	168	2870	2658	2456	2263	2078	3019	2589	2211	1877	1583	+1.7	0.0	-7.5	-21.8	NA
308 High Energy	180	2740	2550	2370	2200	2030	3000	2600	2245	1925	1645	+1.9	0.0	-8.2	-23.5	NA
30-06 Spfd.	55	4080	3485	2965	2502	2083	2033	1483	1074	764	530	+2.0	+1.9	-2.1	-11.7	$22
30-06 Spfd.	125	3140	2780	2447	2138	1853	2736	2145	1662	1279	953	+2.0	+1.0	-6.2	-21.0	$17
30-06 Spfd.	150	2910	2617	2342	2083	1853	2820	2281	1827	1445	1135	+2.5	+0.8	-7.2	-23.4	$17
30-06 Spfd.	152	2910	2654	2413	2184	1968	2858	2378	1965	1610	1307	+2.5	+1.0	-6.6	-21.3	$23
30-06 Spfd.*	165	2800	2534	2283	2047	1825	2872	2352	1909	1534	1220	+2.5	+0.4	-8.4	-25.5	$17
30-06 Spfd.	168	2710	2522	2346	2169	2003	2739	2372	2045	1754	1497	+2.5	+0.4	-8.0	-23.5	$18
30-06 Spfd.	178	2720	2511	2311	2121	1939	2924	2491	2111	1777	1486	+2.5	+0.4	-8.2	-24.6	$23
30-06 Spfd.*	180	2700	2469	2250	2042	1846	2913	2436	2023	1666	1362	+2.5	0.0	-9.3	-27.0	$17
30-06 Spfd.	220	2410	2130	1870	1632	1422	2837	2216	1708	1301	988	+2.5	-1.7	-16.0	NA	$17

CAUTION: PRICES SHOWN ARE SUPPLIED BY THE MANUFACTURER OR IMPORTER. CHECK YOUR LOCAL GUNSHOP.

AVERAGE CENTERFIRE RIFLE CARTRIDGE BALLISTICS AND PRICES (cont.)

Caliber	Bullet weight grains	-VELOCITY (fps)- Muzzle	100 yds.	200 yds.	300 yds.	400. yds.	-ENERGY (ft. lbs.)- Muzzle	100 yds.	200 yds.	300 yds.	400 yds.	-TRAJ. (in.)- 100 yds.	200 yds.	300 yds.	400 yds.	Approx. Price per box
30-06 Light Mag.	150	3100	2815	2548	2295	2058	3200	2639	2161	1755	1410	+1.4	0.0	-6.8	-20.3	NA
30-06 Light Mag.	180	2880	2676	2480	2293	2114	3316	2862	2459	2102	1786	+1.7	0.0	-7.3	-21.3	NA
30-06 High Energy	180	2880	2690	2500	2320	2150	3315	2880	2495	2150	1845	+1.7	0.0	-7.2	-21.0	NA
308 Norma Mag.	180	3020	2820	2630	2440	2270	3645	3175	2755	2385	2050	+2.5	+2.0	-3.5	-14.8	NA
300 Dakota	200	3000	2824	2656	2493	2336	3996	3542	3131	2760	2423	+2.2	+1.5	-4.0	-15.2	NA
300 H&H Magnum*	180	2880	2640	2412	2196	1990	3315	2785	2325	1927	1583	+2.5	+0.8	-6.8	-21.7	$24
300 H&H Magnum	220	2550	2267	2002	1757	NA	3167	2510	1958	1508	NA	+2.5	-0.4	-12.0	NA	NA
300 Peterson	180	3500	3319	3145	2978	2817	4896	4401	3953	3544	3172	+2.3	+2.9	0.0	-6.8	NA
300 Win. Mag.	150	3290	2951	2636	2342	2068	3605	2900	2314	1827	1424	+2.5	+1.9	-3.8	-15.8	$22
300 Win. Mag.	165	3100	2877	2665	2462	2269	3522	3033	2603	2221	1897	+2.5	+2.4	-3.0	-16.9	$24
300 Win. Mag.	178	2980	2769	2568	2375	2191	3509	3030	2606	2230	1897	+2.5	+1.4	-5.0	-17.6	$29
300 Win. Mag.*	180	2960	2745	2540	2344	2157	3501	3011	2578	2196	1859	+2.5	+1.2	-5.5	-18.5	$22
300 W.M. High Energy	180	3100	2830	2580	2340	2110	3840	3205	2660	2190	1790	+1.4	0.0	-6.6	-19.7	NA
300 W.M. Light Mag.	180	3100	2879	2668	2467	2275	3840	3313	2845	2431	2068	+1.39	0.0	-6.45	-18.7	NA
300 Win. Mag.	190	2885	2691	2506	2327	2156	3511	3055	2648	2285	1961	+2.5	+1.2	-5.7	-19.0	$26
300 W.M. High Energy	200	2930	2740	2550	2370	2200	3810	3325	2885	2495	2145	+1.6	0.0	-6.9	-20.1	NA
300 Win. Mag.*	200	2825	2595	2376	2167	1970	3545	2991	2508	2086	1742	+2.5	+1.6	-4.7	-17.2	$36
300 Win. Mag.	220	2680	2448	2228	2020	1823	3508	2927	2424	1993	1623	+2.5	0.0	-9.5	-27.5	$23
300 Wea. Mag.	110	3900	3441	3038	2652	2305	3714	2891	2239	1717	1297	+2.0	+2.6	-0.6	-8.7	$32
300 Wea. Mag.	150	3600	3307	3033	2776	2533	4316	3642	3064	2566	2137	+2.5	+3.2	0.0	-8.1	$32
300 Wea. Mag.	165	3450	3210	3000	2792	2593	4360	3796	3297	2855	2464	+2.5	+3.2	0.0	-7.8	NA
300 Wea. Mag.	178	3120	2902	2695	2497	2308	3847	3329	2870	2464	2104	+2.5	-1.7	-3.6	-14.7	$43
300 Wea. Mag.*	180	3120	2866	2667	2400	2184	3890	3284	2758	2301	1905	+2.5	+1.7	-3.8	-15.0	$35
300 Wea. Mag.	190	3030	2830	2638	2455	2279	3873	3378	2936	2542	2190	+2.5	+1.6	-4.3	-16.0	$38
300 Wea. Mag.	220	2850	2541	2283	1984	1736	3967	3155	2480	1922	1471	+2.5	+0.4	-8.5	-26.4	$35
300 Warbird	180	3400	3180	2971	2772	2582	4620	4042	3528	3071	2664	+2.59	+3.25	0.0	-7.95	NA
300 Pegasus	180	3500	3319	3145	2978	2817	4896	4401	3953	3544	3172	+2.28	+2.89	0.0	-6.79	NA
32-20 Win.	100	1210	1021	913	834	769	325	231	185	154	131	0.0	-32.3	NA	NA	$23**
303 British	150	2685	2441	2210	1992	1787	2401	1984	1627	1321	1064	+2.5	+0.6	-8.4	-26.2	$18
303 British	180	2460	2124	1817	1542	1311	2418	1803	1319	950	687	+2.5	-1.8	-16.8	NA	$18
303 Light Mag.	150	2830	2570	2325	2094	1884	2667	2199	1800	1461	1185	+2.0	0.0	-8.4	-24.6	NA
7.62x39mm Rus.	123/125	2300	2030	1780	1550	1350	1445	1125	860	655	500	+2.5	-2.0	-17.5	NA	$13
7.62x54mm Rus.	146	2950	2730	2520	2320	NA	2820	2415	2055	1740	NA	+2.5	+2.0	-4.4	-17.7	NA
7.62x54mm Rus.	180	2580	2370	2180	2000	1820	2650	2250	1900	1590	1100	+2.5	0.0	-9.8	-28.5	NA
7.7x58mm Jap.	180	2500	2300	2100	1920	1750	2490	2105	1770	1475	1225	+2.5	0.0	-10.4	-30.2	NA
8x57mm JS Mau.	165	2850	2520	2210	1930	1670	2965	2330	1795	1360	1015	+2.5	+1.0	-7.7	NA	NA
32 Win. Special	170	2250	1921	1626	1372	1175	1911	1393	998	710	521	+2.5	-3.5	-22.9	NA	$14
8mm Mauser	170	2360	1969	1622	1333	1123	2102	1464	993	671	476	+2.5	-3.1	-22.2	NA	$18
8mm Rem. Mag.	185	3080	2761	2464	2186	1927	3896	3131	2494	1963	1525	+2.5	+1.4	-5.5	-19.7	$30
8mm Rem. Mag.	220	2830	2581	2346	2123	1913	3912	3254	2688	2201	1787	+2.5	+0.6	-7.6	-23.5	Disc.
338-06	200	2750	2553	2364	2184	2011	3358	2894	2482	2118	1796	+1.9	0.0	-8.22	-23.6	NA
330 Dakota	250	2900	2719	2545	2378	2217	4668	4103	3595	3138	2727	+2.3	+1.3	-5.0	-17.5	NA
338 Lapua	250	2963	2795	2640	2493	NA	4842	4341	3881	3458	NA	+1.9	0.0	-7.9	NA	NA
338 Win. Mag.	200	2960	2658	2375	2110	1862	3890	3137	2505	1977	1539	+2.5	+1.0	-6.7	-22.3	$27
338 Win. Mag.*	210	2830	2590	2370	2150	1940	3735	3130	2610	2155	1760	+2.5	+1.4	-6.0	-20.9	$33
338 Win. Mag.*	225	2785	2517	2266	2029	1808	3871	3165	2565	2057	1633	+2.5	+0.4	-8.5	-25.9	$27
338 W.M. Heavy Mag.	225	2920	2678	2449	2232	2027	4259	3583	2996	2489	2053	+1.75	0.0	-7.65	-22.0	NA
338 W.M. High Energy	225	2940	2690	2450	2230	2010	4320	3610	3000	2475	2025	+1.7	0.0	-7.5	-22.0	NA
338 Win. Mag.	230	2780	2573	2375	2186	2005	3948	3382	2881	2441	2054	+2.5	+1.2	-6.3	-21.0	$40
338 Win. Mag.*	250	2660	2456	2261	2075	1898	3927	3348	2837	2389	1999	+2.5	+0.2	-9.0	-26.2	$27
338 W.M. High Energy	250	2800	2610	2420	2250	2080	4350	3775	3260	2805	2395	+1.8	0.0	-7.8	-22.5	NA
340 Wea. Mag.*	210	3250	2991	2746	2515	2295	4924	4170	3516	2948	2455	+2.5	_1.9	-1.8	-11.8	$56
340 Wea. Mag.*	250	3000	2806	2621	2443	2272	4995	4371	3812	3311	2864	+2.5	+2.0	-3.5	-14.8	$56
338 A-Square	250	3120	2799	2500	2220	1958	5403	4348	3469	2736	2128	+2.5	+2.7	-1.5	-10.5	NA
338 Titan	225	3230	3010	2800	2600	2409	5211	4524	3916	3377	2898	+3.07	+3.80	0.0	-8.95	NA
338 Excalibur	200	3600	3361	3134	2920	2715	5755	5015	4363	3785	3274	+2.23	+2.87	0.0	-6.99	NA
338 Excalibur	250	3250	2922	2618	2333	2066	5863	4740	3804	3021	2370	+1.3	0.0	-6.35	-19.2	NA
348 Winchester	200	2520	2215	1931	1672	1443	2820	2178	1656	1241	925	+2.5	-1.4	-14.7	NA	$42
357 Magnum	158	1830	1427	1138	980	883	1175	715	454	337	274	0.0	-16.2	-33.1	NA	$25**
35 Remington	150	2300	1874	1506	1218	1039	1762	1169	755	494	359	+2.5	-4.1	-26.3	NA	$16
35 Remington	200	2080	1698	1376	1140	1001	1921	1280	841	577	445	+2.5	-6.3	-17.1	-33.6	$16
356 Winchester	200	2460	2114	1797	1517	1284	2688	1985	1434	1022	732	+2.5	-1.8	-17.1	NA	$31
356 Winchester	250	2160	1911	1682	1476	1299	2591	2028	1571	1210	937	+2.5	-3.7	-22.2	NA	$31
358 Winchester	200	2490	2171	1876	1619	1379	2753	2093	1563	1151	844	+2.5	-1.6	-15.6	NA	$31
358 STA	275	2850	2562	2292	2039	NA	4958	4009	3208	2539	NA	+1.9	0.0	-8.6	NA	NA
350 Rem. Mag.	200	2710	2410	2130	1870	1631	3261	2579	2014	1553	1181	+2.5	-0.2	-10.0	-30.1	$33
35 Whelen	200	2675	2378	2100	1842	1606	3177	2510	1958	1506	1145	+2.5	-0.2	-10.3	-31.1	$20
35 Whelen	225	2500	2300	2110	1930	1770	3120	2650	2235	1870	1560	+2.6	0.0	-10.2	-29.9	NA
35 Whelen	250	2400	2197	2005	1823	1652	3197	2680	2230	1844	1515	+2.5	-1.2	-13.7	NA	$20
358 Norma Mag.	250	2800	2510	2230	1970	1730	4350	3480	2750	2145	1655	+2.5	+1.0	-7.6	-25.2	NA
358 STA	275	2850	2562	2292	2039	1764	4959	4009	3208	2539	1899	+1.9	0.0	-8.58	-26.1	NA
9.3x57mm Mau.	286	2070	1810	1590	1390	1110	2710	2090	1600	1220	955	+2.5	-2.6	-22.5	NA	NA
9.3 x 62mm Mau.	286	2360	2089	1844	1623	NA	3538	2771	2157	1670	1260	+2.5	-1.6	-21.0	NA	NA
9.3 x 64mm	286	2700	2505	2318	2139	1968	4629	3984	3411	2906	2460	+2.5	+2.7	-4.5	-19.2	NA

CAUTION: PRICES SHOWN ARE SUPPLIED BY THE MANUFACTURER OR IMPORTER. CHECK YOUR LOCAL GUNSHOP.

	Caliber	Bullet weight grains	-VELOCITY (fps)- Muzzle	100 yds.	200 yds.	300 yds.	400. yds.	-ENERGY (ft. lbs.)- Muzzle	100 yds.	200 yds.	300 yds.	400 yds.	-TRAJ. (in.)- 100 yds.	200 yds.	300 yds.	400 yds.	Approx. Price per box
	9.3 x 74Rmm	286	2360	2089	1844	1623	NA	3538	2771	2157	1670	NA	+2.5	-2.0	-11.0	NA	NA
375	38-55 Win.	255	1320	1190	1091	1018	963	987	802	674	587	525	0.0	-23.4	NA	NA	$25
	375 Winchester	200	2200	1841	1526	1268	1089	2150	1506	1034	714	527	+2.5	-4.0	-26.2	NA	$27
	375 Winchester	250	1900	1647	1424	1239	1103	2005	1506	1126	852	676	+2.5	-6.9	-33.3	NA	$27
	375 Dakota	300	2600	2316	2051	1804	1579	4502	3573	2800	2167	1661	+2.4	0.0	-11.0	-32.7	NA
	375 N.E. 2½"	270	2000	1740	1507	1310	NA	2398	1815	1362	1026	NA	+2.5	-6.0	-30.0	NA	NA
	375 Flanged	300	2450	2150	1886	1640	NA	3998	3102	2369	1790	NA	+2.5	-2.4	-17.0	NA	NA
	375 H&H Magnum	250	2670	2450	2240	2040	1850	3955	3335	2790	2315	1905	+2.5	-0.4	-10.2	-28.4	NA
	375 H&H Magnum	270	2690	2420	2166	1928	1707	4337	3510	2812	2228	1747	+2.5	0.0	-10.0	-29.4	$28
	375 H&H Magnum*	300	2530	2245	1979	1733	1512	4263	3357	2608	2001	1523	+2.5	-1.0	-10.5	-33.6	$28
	375 Wea. Mag.	300	2700	2420	2157	1911	1685	4856	3901	3100	2432	1891	+2.5	-0.4	-10.7	-	NA
	378 Wea. Mag.	270	3180	2976	2781	2594	2415	6062	5308	4635	4034	3495	+2.5	+2.6	-1.8	-11.3	$71
	378 Wea. Mag.	300	2929	2576	2252	1952	1680	5698	4419	3379	2538	1881	+2.5	+1.2	-7.0	-24.5	$77
	375 A-Square	300	2920	2626	2351	2093	1850	5679	4594	3681	2917	2281	+2.5	+1.4	-6.0	-21.0	NA
	38-40 Win.	180	1160	999	901	827	764	538	399	324	273	233	0.0	-33.9	NA	NA	$42**
40	450/400-3"	400	2150	1932	1730	1545	1379	4105	3316	2659	2119	1689	+2.5	-4.0	-9.5	-30.3	NA
41	416 Dakota	400	2450	2294	2143	1998	1859	5330	4671	4077	3544	3068	+2.5	-0.2	-10.5	-29.4	NA
	416 Taylor	400	2350	2117	1896	1693	NA	4905	3980	3194	2547	NA	+2.5	-1.2	_15.0	NA	NA
	416 Hoffman	400	2380	2145	1923	1718	1529	5031	4087	3285	2620	2077	+2.5	-1.0	-14.1	NA	NA
	416 Rigby	350	2600	2449	2303	2162	2026	5253	4661	4122	3632	3189	+2.5	-1.8	-10.2	-26.0	NA
	416 Rigby	400	2370	2210	2050	1900	NA	4990	4315	3720	3185	NA	+2.5	-0.7	-12.1	NA	NA
	416 Rigby	410	2370	2110	1870	1640	NA	5115	4050	3165	2455	NA	+2.5	-2.4	-17.3	NA	$110
	416 Rem. Mag.*	350	2520	2270	2034	1814	1611	4935	4004	3216	2557	2017	+2.5	-0.8	-12.6	-35.0	$82
	416 Rem. Mag.*	400	2400	2175	1962	1763	1579	5115	4201	3419	2760	2214	+2.5	-1.5	-14.6	NA	$80
	416 Wea. Mag.*	400	2700	2397	2115	1852	1613	6474	5104	3971	3047	2310	+2.5	0.0	-10.1	-30.4	$96
	404 Jeffrey	400	2150	1924	1716	1525	NA	4105	3289	2614	2064	NA	+2.5	-4.0	-22.1	NA	NA
	425 Express	400	2400	2160	1934	1725	NA	5115	4145	3322	2641	NA	+2.5	-1.0	-14.0	NA	NA
425	44-40 Win.	200	1190	1006	900	822	756	629	449	360	300	254	0.0	-33.3	NA	NA	$36**
	44 Rem. Mag.	210	1920	1477	1155	982	880	1719	1017	622	450	361	0.0	-17.6	NA	NA	$14
44	44 Rem. Mag.	240	1760	1380	1114	970	878	1650	1015	661	501	411	0.0	-17.6	NA	NA	$13
	444 Marlin	240	2350	1815	1377	1087	941	2942	1753	1001	630	472	+2.5	-15.1	-31.0	NA	$22
	444 Marlin	265	2120	1733	1405	1160	1012	2644	1768	1162	791	603	+2.5	-6.0	-32.2	NA	Disc.
	45-70 Govt.	300	1810	1497	1244	1073	969	2182	1492	1031	767	625	0.0	-14.8	NA	NA	$21
45	45-70 Govt.	405	1330	1168	1055	977	918	1590	1227	1001	858	758	0.0	-24.6	NA	NA	$21
	458 Win. Magnum	350	2470	1990	1570	1250	1060	4740	3065	1915	1205	870	+2.5	-2.5	-21.6	NA	$43
	458 Win. Magnum	400	2380	2170	1960	1770	NA	5030	4165	3415	2785	NA	+2.5	-0.4	-13.4	NA	$73
	458 Win. Magnum	465	2220	1999	1791	1601	NA	5088	4127	3312	2646	NA	+2.5	-2.0	-17.7	NA	NA
	458 Win. Magnum	500	2040	1823	1623	1442	1237	4620	3689	2924	2308	1839	+2.5	-3.5	-22.0	NA	$61
	458 Win. Magnum	510	2040	1770	1527	1319	1157	4712	3547	2640	1970	1516	+2.5	-4.1	-25.0	NA	$41
	450 Dakota	500	2450	2235	2030	1838	1658	6663	5544	4576	3748	3051	+2.5	-0.6	-12.0	-33.8	NA
	450 N.E.-3¼"	465	2190	1970	1765	1577	NA	4952	4009	3216	2567	NA	+2.5	-3.0	-20.0	NA	NA
	450 N.E.-3¼"	500	2150	1920	1708	1514	NA	5132	4093	3238	2544	NA	+2.5	-4.0	-22.9	NA	NA
	450 No. 2	465	2190	1970	1765	1577	NA	4952	4009	3216	2567	NA	+2.5	-3.0	-20.0	NA	NA
	450 No. 2	500	2150	1920	1708	1514	NA	5132	4093	3238	2544	NA	+2.5	-4.0	-22.9	NA	NA
	458 Lott	465	2380	2150	1932	1730	NA	5848	4773	3855	3091	NA	+2.5	-1.0	-14.0	NA	NA
	458 Lott	500	2300	2062	1838	1633	NA	5873	4719	3748	2960	NA	+2.5	-1.6	-16.4	NA	NA
	450 Ackley Mag	465	2400	2169	1950	1747	NA	5947	4857	3927	3150	NA	+2.5	-1.0	-13.7	NA	NA
	450 Ackley Mag.	500	2320	2081	1855	1649	NA	5975	4085	3820	3018	NA	+2.5	-1.2	-15.0	NA	NA
	460 Short A-Sq.	500	2420	2175	1943	1729	NA	6501	5250	4193	3319	NA	+2.5	-0.8	-12.8	-	NA
	460 Wea. Mag.	500	2700	2404	2128	1869	1635	8092	6416	5026	3878	2969	+2.5	+0.6	-8.9	-28.0	$72
	500/465 N.E.	480	2150	1917	1703	1507	NA	4926	3917	3089	2419	NA	+2.5	-4.0	-22.2	-	NA
475	470 Rigby	500	2150	1940	1740	1560	NA	5130	4170	3360	2695	NA	+2.5	-2.8	-19.4	NA	NA
	470 Nitro Ex.	480	2190	1954	1735	1536	NA	5111	4070	3210	2515	NA	+2.5	-3.5	-20.8	NA	NA
	470 Nitro Ex.	500	2150	1890	1650	1440	1270	5130	3965	3040	2310	1790	+2.5	-4.3	-24.0	NA	$177
	475 No. 2	500	2200	1955	1728	1522	NA	5375	4243	3316	2573	NA	+2.5	-3.2	-20.9	NA	NA
	505 Gibbs	525	2300	2063	1840	1637	NA	6166	4922	3948	3122	NA	+2.5	-3.0	-18.0	NA	NA
50	500 N.E.-3"	570	2150	1928	1722	1533	NA	5850	4703	3752	2975	NA	+2.5	-3.7	-22.0	NA	NA
58	500 N.E.-3"	600	2150	1927	1721	1531	NA	6158	4947	3944	3124	NA	+2.5	-4.0	-22.0	NA	NA
	495 A-Square	570	2350	2117	1896	1693	NA	5850	4703	3752	2975	NA	+2.5	-1.0	-14.5	NA	NA
	495 A-Square	600	2280	2050	1833	1635	NA	6925	5598	4478	3562	NA	+2.5	-2.0	-17.0	NA	NA
	500 A-Square	600	2380	2144	1922	1766	NA	7546	6126	4920	3922	NA	+2.5	-3.0	-17.0	NA	NA
	500 A-Square	707	2250	2040	1841	1567	NA	7947	6530	5318	4311	NA	+2.5	-2.0	-17.0	NA	NA
	500 BMG PMC	660	3080	2854	2639	2444	2248	13688		500 yd. zero			+3.1	+3.90	+4.7	+2.8	NA
	577 Nitro Ex.	750	2050	1793	1562	1360	NA	6990	5356	4065	3079	NA	+2.5	-5.0	-26.0	NA	NA
	577 Tyrannosaur	750	2400	2141	1898	1675	NA	9591	7633	5996	4671	NA	+3.0	0.0	-12.9	NA	NA
6-700	600 N.E.	900	1950	1680	1452	NA	NA	7596	5634	4212	NA	NA	+5.6	0.0	NA	NA	NA
	700 N.E.	1200	1900	1676	1472	NA	NA	9618	7480	5774	NA	NA	+5.7	0.0	NA	NA	NA

Notes: NA in vel. or eng. column = This data not available from manufacturer. NA in trajectory column = Bullet has fallen more than 3 feet below line of sight and further hold-over is not practical. Wea. Mag. = Weatherby Magnum. Spfd. = Springfield. A-Sq. = A-Square. N.E.= Nitro Express. Many manufacturer's do not supply suggested retail prices. Others did not get their pricing to us before press time. All pricing can vary dependent on the exact brand and style of ammo selected and/or the retail outlet from which you make your purchase. Pricing has been rounded to the nearest dollar and represent our best estimate of average pricing. An * after the bullet weight means these loads are available with Nosler Partition or Swift A-Frame bullets. Listed pricing may or may not reflect this bullet type. ** = these are packed 50 to box, all others are 20 to box.

CAUTION: PRICES SHOWN ARE SUPPLIED BY THE MANUFACTURER OR IMPORTER. CHECK YOUR LOCAL GUNSHOP.

CENTERFIRE HANDGUN CARTRIDGES—BALLISTICS AND PRICES

Caliber	Bullet Wgt. Grs.	Velocity (fps) MV	Velocity (fps) 50 yds.	Velocity (fps) 100 yds.	Energy (ft. lbs.) ME	Energy (ft. lbs.) 50 yds.	Energy (ft. lbs.) 100 yds.	Mid-Range Traj. (in.) 50 yds.	Mid-Range Traj. (in.) 100 yds.	Bbl. Lgth. (in.)	Est. Price /box
221 Rem. Fireball	50	2650	2380	2130	780	630	505	0.2	0.8	10.5"	$15
25 Automatic	35	900	813	742	63	51	43	NA	NA	2"	$18
25 Automatic	45	815	730	655	65	55	40	1.8	7.7	2"	$21
25 Automatic	50	760	705	660	65	55	50	2.0	8.7	2"	$17
7.5mm Swiss	107	1010	NA	NA	240	NA	NA	NA	NA	NA	NEW
7.62mm Tokarev	87	1390	NA	NA	365	NA	NA	0.6	NA	4.5"	NA
7.62mm Nagant	97	1080	NA	NA	350	NA	NA	NA	NA	NA	NEW
7.63mm Mauser	88	1440	NA	NA	405	NA	NA	NA	NA	NA	NEW
30 Luger	93†	1220	1110	1040	305	255	225	0.9	3.5	4.5"	$34
30 Carbine	110	1790	1600	1430	785	625	500	0.4	1.7	10"	$28
32 S&W	88	680	645	610	90	80	75	2.5	10.5	3"	$17
32 S&W Long	98	705	670	635	115	100	90	2.3	10.5	4"	$17
32 Short Colt	80	745	665	590	100	80	60	2.2	9.9	4"	$19
32 H&R Magnum	85	1100	1020	930	230	195	165	1.0	4.3	4.5"	$21
32 H&R Magnum	95	1030	940	900	225	190	170	1.1	4.7	4.5"	$19
32 Automatic	60	970	895	835	125	105	95	1.3	5.4	4"	$22
32 Automatic	71	905	855	810	130	115	95	1.4	5.8	4"	$19
8mm Lebel Pistol	111	850	NA	NA	180	NA	NA	NA	NA	NA	NEW
8mm Steyr	113	1080	NA	NA	290	NA	NA	NA	NA	NA	NEW
8mm Gasser	126	850	NA	NA	200	NA	NA	NA	NA	NA	NEW
380 Automatic	60	1130	960	NA	170	120	NA	1.0	NA	NA	NA
380 Automatic	85/88	990	920	870	190	165	145	1.2	5.1	4"	$20
380 Automatic	90	1000	890	800	200	160	130	1.2	5.5	3.75"	$10
380 Automatic	95/100	955	865	785	190	160	130	1.4	5.9	4"	$20
38 Super Auto +P	115	1300	1145	1040	430	335	275	0.7	3.3	5"	$26
38 Super Auto +P	125/130	1215	1100	1015	425	350	300	0.8	3.6	5"	$26
38 Super Auto +P	147	1100	1050	1000	395	355	325	0.9	4.0	5"	NA
9x18mm Makarov	95	1000	NA	NA	NA	NA	NA	NA	NA	NA	NEW
9x18mm Ultra	100	1050	NA	NA	240	NA	NA	NA	NA	NA	NEW
9x23mm Largo	124	1190	1055	966	390	306	257	0.7	3.7	4"	NA
9mm Steyr	115	1180	NA	NA	350	NA	NA	NA	NA	NA	NEW
9mm Luger	88	1500	1190	1010	440	275	200	0.6	3.1	4"	$24
9mm Luger	90	1360	1112	978	370	247	191	NA	NA	4"	$26
9mm Luger	95	1300	1140	1010	350	275	215	0.8	3.4	4"	NA
9mm Luger	100	1180	1080	NA	305	255	NA	0.9	NA	4"	NA
9mm Luger	115	1155	1045	970	340	280	240	0.9	3.9	4"	$21
9mm Luger	123/125	1110	1030	970	340	290	260	1.0	4.0	4"	$23
9mm Luger	140	935	890	850	270	245	225	1.3	5.5	4"	$23
9mm Luger	147	990	940	900	320	290	265	1.1	4.9	4"	$26
9mm Luger +P	90	1475	NA	NA	437	NA	NA	NA	NA	NA	NA
9mm Luger +P	115	1250	1113	1019	399	316	265	0.8	3.5	4"	$27
9mm Federal	115	1280	1130	1040	420	330	280	0.7	3.3	4"V	$24
9mm Luger Vector	115	1155	1047	971	341	280	241	NA	NA	4"	NA
9mm Luger +P	124	1180	1089	1021	384	327	287	0.8	3.8	4"	NA
38 S&W	146	685	650	620	150	135	125	2.4	10.0	4"	$19
38 Short Colt	125	730	685	645	150	130	115	2.2	9.4	6"	$19
38 Special	100	950	900	NA	200	180	NA	1.3	NA	4"V	NA
38 Special	110	945	895	850	220	195	175	1.3	5.4	4"V	$23
38 Special	130	775	745	710	175	160	120	1.9	7.9	4"V	$22
38 (Multi-Ball)	140	830	730	505	215	130	80	2.0	10.6	4"V	$10**
38 Special	148	710	635	565	165	130	105	2.4	10.6	4"V	$17
38 Special	158	755	725	690	200	185	170	2.0	8.3	4"V	$18
38 Special +P	95	1175	1045	960	290	230	195	0.9	3.9	4"V	$23
38 Special +P	110	995	925	870	240	210	185	1.2	5.1	4"V	$23
38 Special +P	125	975	929	885	264	238	218	1	5.2	4"	NA
38 Special +P	125	945	900	860	250	225	205	1.3	5.4	4"V	$23
38 Special +P	129	945	910	870	255	235	215	1.3	5.3	4"V	$11
38 Special +P	130	925	887	852	247	227	210	1.3	5.50	4"V	NA
38 Special +P	147/150(c)	884	NA	NA	264	NA	NA	NA	NA	4"V	$27
38 Special +P	158	890	855	825	280	255	240	1.4	6.0	4"V	$20
357 SIG	115	1520	NA	NA	593	NA	NA	NA	NA	NA	NA
357 SIG	124	1450	NA	NA	578	NA	NA	NA	NA	NA	NA
357 SIG	125	1350	1190	1080	510	395	325	0.7	3.1	4"	NA
357 SIG	150	1130	1030	970	420	355	310	0.9	4.0	NA	NA
356 TSW	115	1520	NA	NA	593	NA	NA	NA	NA	NA	NA
356 TSW	124	1450	NA	NA	578	NA	NA	NA	NA	NA	NA
356 TSW	135	1280	1120	1010	490	375	310	0.8	3.50	NA	NA
356 TSW	147	1220	1120	1040	485	410	355	0.8	3.5	5"	NA
357 Magnum	110	1295	1095	975	410	290	230	0.8	3.5	4"V	$25
357 (Med. Vel.)	125	1220	1075	985	415	315	270	0.8	3.7	4"V	$25
357 Magnum	125	1450	1240	1090	585	425	330	0.6	2.8	4"V	$25
357 (Multi-Ball)	140	1155	830	665	420	215	135	1.2	6.4	4"V	$11**
357 Magnum	140	1360	1195	1075	575	445	360	0.7	3.0	4"V	$25
357 Magnum	145	1290	1155	1060	535	430	360	0.8	3.5	4"V	$26
357 Magnum	150/158	1235	1105	1015	535	430	360	0.8	3.5	4"V	$25
357 Magnum	165	1290	1189	1108	610	518	450	0.7	3.1	8 3/8"	NA
357 Magnum	180	1145	1055	985	525	445	390	0.9	3.9	4"V	$25
357 Rem. Maximum	158	1825	1590	1380	1170	885	670	0.4	1.7	10.5"	$14**
40 S&W	135	1140	1070	NA	390	345	NA	0.9	NA	4"	NA
40 S&W	155	1140	1026	958	447	362	309	0.9	4.1	4"	$14***
40 S&W	165	1150	NA	NA	485	NA	NA	NA	NA	4"	$18***
40 S&W	180	985	936	893	388	350	319	1.4	5.0	4"	$14***
40 S&W	180	1015	960	914	412	368	334	1.3	4.5	4"	NA
10mm Automatic	155	1125	1046	986	436	377	335	0.9	3.9	5"	$26
10mm Automatic	170	1340	1165	1145	680	510	415	0.7	3.2	5"	$31
10mm Automatic	175	1290	1140	1035	650	505	420	0.7	3.3	5.5"	$11**
10mm Auto.(FBI)	180	950	905	865	361	327	299	1.5	5.4	4"	$16**
10mm Automatic	180	1030	970	920	425	375	340	1.1	4.7	5"	$16**
10mm Auto H.V.	180†	1240	1124	1037	618	504	430	0.8	3.4	5"	$27
10mm Automatic	200	1160	1070	1010	495	510	430	0.9	3.8	5"	$14**
10.4mm Italian	177	950	NA	NA	360	NA	NA	NA	NA	NA	NEW
41 Action Exp.	180	1000	947	903	400	359	326	0.5	4.2	5"	$13**
41 Rem. Magnum	170	1420	1165	1015	760	515	390	0.7	3.2	4"V	$33
41 Rem. Magnum	175	1250	1120	1030	605	490	410	0.8	3.4	4"V	$14**
41 (Med. Vel.)	210	965	900	840	435	375	330	1.3	5.4	4"V	$30
41 Rem. Magnum	210	1300	1160	1060	790	630	535	0.7	3.2	4"V	$33
44 S&W Russian	247	780	NA	NA	335	NA	NA	NA	NA	NA	NA
44 S&W Special	180	980	NA	NA	383	NA	NA	NA	NA	6.5"	NA
44 S&W Special	180	1000	935	882	400	350	311	NA	NA	7.5"V	NA
44 S&W Special	200†	875	825	780	340	302	270	1.2	6.0	6"	$13**
44 S&W Special	200	1035	940	865	475	390	335	1.1	4.9	6.5"	$13**
44 S&W Special	240/246	755	725	695	310	285	265	2.0	8.3	6.5"	$26
44 Rem. Magnum	180	1610	1365	1175	1035	745	550	0.5	2.3	4"V	$18***
44 Rem. Magnum	200	1400	1192	1053	870	630	492	0.6	NA	6.5"	$20
44 Rem. Magnum	210	1495	1310	1165	1040	805	635	0.6	2.5	6.5"	$18***
44 (Med. Vel.)	240	1000	945	900	535	475	435	1.1	4.8	6.5"	$17
44 R.M.(Jacketed)	240	1180	1080	1010	740	625	545	0.9	3.7	4"V	$18***
44 R.M. (Lead)	240	1350	1185	1070	970	750	610	0.7	3.1	4"V	$29
44 Rem. Magnum	250	1180	1100	1040	775	670	600	0.8	3.6	6.5"V	$21
44 Rem. Magnum	275	1235	1142	1070	931	797	699	0.8	3.3	6.5"	NA
44 Rem. Magnum	300	1200	1100	1026	959	806	702	NA	NA	7.5"	$17
450 Short Colt	226	830	NA	NA	350	NA	NA	NA	NA	NA	NEW
45 Automatic	165	1030	930	NA	385	315	NA	1.2	NA	5"	NA
45 Automatic	185	1000	940	890	410	360	325	1.1	4.9	5"	$28
45 Auto. (Match)	185	770	705	650	245	204	175	2.0	8.7	5"	$28
45 Auto. (Match)	200	940	890	840	392	352	312	2.0	8.6	5"	$20
45 Automatic	200	975	917	860	421	372	328	1.4	5.0	5"	$18
45 Automatic	230	830	800	675	355	325	300	1.6	6.8	5"	$27
45 Automatic	230	880	846	816	396	366	340	1.5	6.1	5"	NA
45 Automatic +P	165	1250	NA	NA	573	NA	NA	NA	NA	NA	NA
45 Automatic +P	185	1140	1040	970	535	445	385	0.9	4.0	5"	$31
45 Automatic +P	200	1055	982	925	494	428	380	NA	NA	5"	NA
45 Win. Magnum	230	1400	1230	1105	1000	775	635	0.6	2.8	5"	$14**
45 Win. Magnum	260	1250	1137	1053	902	746	640	0.8	3.3	5"	$16**
455 Webley MKII	262	850	NA	NA	420	NA	NA	NA	NA	NA	NA
45 Colt	200	1000	938	889	444	391	351	1.3	4.8	5.5"	$21
45 Colt	225	960	890	830	460	395	345	1.3	5.5	5.5"	$22
45 Colt	250/255	860	820	780	410	375	340	1.6	6.6	5.5"	$27
50 Action Exp.	325	1400	1209	1075	1414	1055	835	0.2	2.3	6"	$24**

Notes: Blanks are available in 32 S&W, 38 S&W, and 38 Special. V after barrel length indicates test barrel was vented to produce ballistics similar to a revolver with a normal barrel-to-cylinder gap. Ammo prices are per 50 rounds except when marked with an ** which signifies a 20 round box; *** signifies a 25-round box. Not all loads are available from all ammo manufacturers. Listed loads are those made by Remington, Winchester, Federal, and others. DISC. is a discontinued load. Prices are rounded to nearest whole dollar and will vary with brand and retail outlet. †= new bullet weight this year; "c" indicates a change in data.

RIMFIRE AMMUNITION—BALLISTICS AND PRICES

Cartridge type	Bullet Wt. Grs.	Velocity (fps) 22 1/2" Barrel Muzzle	Velocity (fps) 22 1/2" Barrel 50 Yds.	Velocity (fps) 22 1/2" Barrel 100 Yds.	Energy (ft. lbs.) 22 1/2" Barrel Muzzle	Energy (ft. lbs.) 22 1/2" Barrel 50 Yds.	Energy (ft. lbs.) 22 1/2" Barrel 100 Yds.	Velocity (fps) 6" Barrel Muzzle	Velocity (fps) 6" Barrel 50 Yds.	Energy (ft. lbs) 6" Barrel Muzzle	Energy (ft. lbs) 6" Barrel 50 Yds.	Approx. Price Per Box 50 Rds.	Approx. Price Per Box 100 Rds.
22 Short Blank						Not applicable						$4	NA
22 CB Short	30	725	667	610	34	29	24	706	—	32	—	$2	NA
22 Short Match	29	830	752	695	44	36	31	786	—	39	—	—	NA
22 Short Std. Vel.	29	1045	—	810	70	—	42	865	—	48	—	Discontinued	
22 Short High Vel.	29	1095	—	903	77	—	53	—	—	—	—	$2	NA
22 Short H.V. H.P.	27	1120	—	904	75	—	49	—	—	—	—	—	NA
22 CB Long	30	725	667	610	34	29	24	706	—	32	—	$2	NA
22 Long Std. Vel.	29	1180	1038	946	90	69	58	1031	—	68	—	—	—
22 Long High Vel.	29	1240	—	962	99	—	60	—	—	—	—	$2	NA
22 L.R. Sub Sonic	38/40	1070	970	890	100	80	70	940	—	—	—	$2	NA
22 L.R. Std. Vel.	40	1138	1047	975	116	97	84	1027	925	93	76	$2	NA
22 L.R. High Vel.	40	1255	1110	1017	140	109	92	1060	—	100	—	$2	NA
22 L.R. H.V. Sil.	42	1220	—	1003	139	—	94	1025	—	98	—	$2	NA
22 L.R. H.V. H.P.	36/38	1280	1126	1010	131	101	82	1089	—	95	—	$2	NA
22 L.R. Shot	#11 or #12	1047	—	—	—	—	—	950	—	—	—	$5	NA
22 L.R. Hyper Vel	36	1410	1187	1056	159	113	89	—	—	—	—	$2	NA
22 L.R. Hyper H.P	32/33/34	1500	1240	1075	165	110	85	—	—	—	—	$2	NA
22 WRF	45	1320	—	1055	175	—	111	—	—	—	—	NA	$5
22 Win. Mag.	30	2200	1750	1373	322	203	127	1610	—	—	—	—	NA
22 Win. Mag.	40	1910	1490	1326	324	197	156	1428	—	181	—	$6	NA
22 Win. Mag.	50	1650	—	1280	300	180	—	—	—	—	—	NA	NA
22 Win. Mag. Shot	#11	1126	—	—	—	—	—	—	—	—	—	NA	NA

Note: The actual ballistics obtained with your firearm can vary considerably from the advertised ballistics. Also ballistics can vary from lot to lot with the same brand and type load. Prices can vary with manufacturer and retail outlet. NA in the price column indicates this size packaging currently unavailable.

SHOTSHELL LOADS AND PRICES

Dram Equivalent	Shot Ozs.	Load Style	Shot Sizes	Brands	Avg.Nom. Price /box	Velocity (fps)
10 Gauge 3½" Magnum						
4½	2¼	premium	BB, 2, 4, 5, 6	Win., Fed., Rem.	$33	1205
4¼	2	high velocity	BB, 2, 4	Rem.	$22	1210
4½	2¼	duplex	4x6	Rem.	$14*	1205
Max	18 pellets	premium	00 buck	Fed., Win.	$7**	1100
4¼	1¾	steel	TT, T, BBB, BB, 1, 2, 3	Win., Rem.	$27	1260
Mag	1⅝	steel	T, BBB	Win.	$27	1285
4⅝	1⅝	steel	F, T, BBB	Fed.	$26	1350
Max	1⅜	Steel	BBB, BB	Fed.	NA	1425
Max	1¾	slug, rifled	slug	Fed.	NA	1280
12 Gauge 3½" Magnum						
Max	2¼	premium	4, 5, 6	Fed., Rem., Win.	$13*	1150
Max	18 pellets	premium	00 buck	Fed., Win., Rem.	$7**	1100
4⅛	19/16	steel	TT, F, T, BBB, BB, 1, 2	Rem., Win., Fed.	$22	1335
Max	1⅜	steel	BBB, BB	Fed.	NA	1450
12 Gauge 3" Magnum						
4	2	premium	BB, 2, 4, 5, 6	Win., Fed., Rem.	$9*	1175
4	2	duplex	4x6	Rem.	$10	1175
4	1⅞	premium	BB, 2, 4, 6	Win., Fed., Rem.	$19	1210
4	1⅞	duplex	4x6	Rem., Fio.	$9*	1210
Max	1¾	turkey	4, 5, 6	Fio.	NA	1150
4½	1¾	duplex	2x4, 4x6	Fio.	NA	1150
4	1⅝	premium	2, 4, 5, 6	Win., Fed., Rem.	$18	1290
4	24 pellets	buffered	1 buck	Win., Fed., Rem.	$5**	1040
4	15 pellets	buffered	00 buck	Win., Fed., Rem.	$6**	1210
4	10 pellets	buffered	000 buck	Win., Fed., Rem.	$6**	1225
4	41 pellets	buffered	4 buck	Win., Fed., Rem.	$6**	1210
Max	1⅜	slug	slug	Bren.	NA	1476
Max	1¼	slug, rifled	slug	Fed.	NA	1600
Max	13/16	saboted slug	copper slug	Rem.	NA	1500
Max	1	slug, rifled	slug, magnum	Win., Rem.	$5**	1760
Max	1	saboted slug	slug	Win., Fed.	$10**	1550
3⅝	1⅜	steel	TT, F, T, BBB, BB, 1, 2, 3, 4	Win., Fed., Rem.	$19	1275
Max	1⅛	steel	BBB, BB	Fed.	NA	1450
4	1¼	steel	TT, F, T, BBB, BB, 1, 2, 3, 4, 6	Win., Fed., Rem.	$18	1375
12 gauge 2¾"						
Max	1⅝	magnum	4, 5, 6	Win., Fed.	$8*	1250
Max	1⅜	turkey	4, 5, 6	Fio.	NA	1250
Max	1⅜	duplex	2x4, 4x6	Fio.	NA	1200
3¾	1½	magnum	BB, 2, 4, 5, 6	Win., Fed., Rem.	$16	1260
3¾	1½	duplex	BBx4, 2x4, 2x6, 4x6	Rem., Fio.	$9*	1260
3¾	1¼	high velocity	BB, 2, 4, 5, 6, 7½, 8, 9	Win., Fed., Rem., Fio.	$13	1330
3½	1¼	mid velocity	7, 8, 9	Win.	Disc.	1275
3¼	1¼	standard velocity	6, 7½, 8, 9	Win., Fed., Rem., Fio.	$11	1220
3¼	1⅛	standard velocity	4, 6, 7½, 8, 9	Win., Fed., Rem., Fio.	$9	1255
3¼	1	standard velocity	6, 7½, 8	Rem., Fed., Fio.	$6	1290
3¼	1¼	target	7½, 8, 9	Win., Fed., Rem.	$10	1220
3	1⅛	spreader	7½, 8, 8½, 9	Fio.	NA	1200
3	1⅛	duplex target	7½x8	Rem.	NA	1200
3	1⅛	target	7½, 8, 9, 7½x8	Win., Fed., Rem., Fio.	$7	1200
3	1⅛	duplex clays	7½x8½	Rem.	NA	1200
2¾	1⅛	target	7½, 8, 8½, 9, 7½x8	Win., Fed., Rem., Fio.	$7	1145
2¾	1⅛	duplex target	7½x8	Rem.	NA	1145
2¾	1⅛	low recoil	7½, 8	Rem.	NA	1145
2¼	1⅛	target	7½, 8, 8½, 9	Rem., Fed.	$7	1080
Max	1	spreader	7½, 8, 8½, 9	Fio.	NA	1300
3¼	28grams(1oz)	target	7½, 8, 9	Win., Fed., Rem., Fio.	$8	1290
3	1	target	7½, 8, 8½, 9	Win., Fio.	NA	1235
2¾	1	target	7½, 8, 8½, 9	Fed., Rem., Fio.	NA	1180
3¼	24grams	target	7½, 8, 9	Fed., Win., Fio.	NA	1325
3	⅞	light	8	Fio.	NA	1200
3¾	8 pellets	buffered	000 buck	Win., Fed., Rem.	$4**	1325
4	12 pellets	premium	00 buck	Win., Fed., Rem.	$5**	1290
3¾	9 pellets	buffered	00 buck	Win., Fed., Rem., Fio.	$19	1325
3¾	12 pellets	buffered	0 buck	Win., Fed., Rem.	$4**	1275
4	20 pellets	buffered	1 buck	Win., Fed., Rem.	$4**	1075
3¾	16 pellets	buffered	1 buck	Win., Fed., Rem.	$4**	1250
4	34 pellets	premium	4 buck	Fed., Rem.	$5**	1250
3¾	27 pellets	buffered	4 buck	Win., Fed., Rem., Fio.	$4**	1325
Max	1	saboted slug	slug	Win., Fed., Rem.	$10**	1450
Max	1¼	slug, rifled	slug	Fed.	NA	1520
Max	1	slug, rifled	slug, magnum	Rem., Fio.	$5**	1680
Max	1	slug, rifled	slug	Win., Fed., Rem.	$4**	1610
3	1⅛	steel target	6½, 7	Rem.	NA	1200
2¾	1⅛	steel target	7, 8	Rem.	NA	1145
3	1#	steel	7	Win.	$11	1235
3½	1¼	steel	T, BBB, BB, 1, 2, 3, 4, 5, 6	Win., Fed., Rem.	$18	1275
3¾	1⅛	steel	BB, 1, 2, 3, 4, 5, 6	Win., Fed., Rem., Fio.	$16	1365
3¾	1	steel	2, 3, 4, 5, 6, 7	Win., Fed., Rem., Fio.	$13	1390
Max	⅞	steel	7	Fio.	NA	1440
16 Gauge 2¾"						
3¼	1¼	magnum	2, 4, 6	Fed., Rem.	$16	1260
3¼	1⅛	high velocity	4, 6, 7½	Win., Fed., Rem., Fio.	$12	1295
2¾	1⅛	standard velocity	6, 7½, 8	Fed., Rem., Fio.	$9	1185
2½	1	dove	6, 7½, 8, 9	Fio.	NA	1165
2¾	1		6, 7½, 8	Fio.	NA	1200
Max	15/16	steel	2, 4	Fed., Rem.	NA	1300
Max	⅞	steel	2, 4	Win.	$16	1300
3	12 pellets	buffered	1 buck	Win., Fed., Rem.	$4**	1225
Max	⅘	slug, rifled	slug	Win., Fed., Rem.	$4**	1570
20 Gauge 3" Magnum						
3	1¼	premium	2, 4, 5, 6, 7½	Win., Fed., Rem.	$15	1185
3	1¼	turkey	4, 6	Fio.	NA	1200
Max	18 pellets	buck shot	2 buck	Fed.	NA	1200
Max	24 pellets	buffered	3 buck	Win.	$5**	1150
2¾	20 pellets	buck	3 buck	Rem.	$4**	1200
3¼	1	steel	1, 2, 3, 4, 5, 6	Win., Fed., Rem.	$15	1330
Mag.	⅝	saboted slug	275 gr.	Fed.	NA	1450
20 Gauge 2¾"						
2¾	1⅛	magnum	4, 6, 7½	Win., Fed., Rem.	$14	1175
2¾	1	high velocity	4, 5, 6, 7½, 8, 9	Win., Fed., Rem., Fio.	$12	1220
2½	1	standard velocity	6, 7½, 8	Win., Rem., Fed., Fio.	$6	1165
2½	⅞	clays	8	Rem.	NA	1200
2½	⅞	promotional	6, 7½, 8	Win., Rem., Fio.	$6	1210
2½	1#	target	8, 9	Win., Rem.	$8	1165
2½	⅞	target	8, 9	Win., Fed., Rem.	$8	1200
Max	20 pellets	buffered	3 buck	Win., Fed.	$4	1200
Max	⅝	slug, saboted	slug	Win.	$9**	1400
2¾	⅝	slug, rifled	slug	Rem.	$4**	1580
Max	¾	saboted slug	copper slug	Rem.	NA	1450
Max	¾	slug, rifled	slug	Win., Fed., Rem., Fio.	$4**	1570
Max	¾	steel	2, 3, 4, 6	Win., Fed., Rem.	$14	1425
28 Gauge 2¾"						
2	1	high velocity	6, 7½, 8	Win.	$12	1125
2¼	¾	high velocity	6, 7½, 8, 9	Win., Fed., Rem., Fio.	$11	1295
2	¾	target	8, 9	Win., Fed., Rem.	$9	1200
410 Bore 3"						
Max	11/16	high velocity	4, 5, 6, 7½, 8, 9	Win., Fed., Rem., Fio.	$10	1135
410 Bore 2½"						
Max	½	high velocity	4, 6, 7½	Win., Fed., Rem.	$9	1245
Max	⅕	slug, rifled	slug	Win., Fed., Rem.	$4**	1815
1½	½	target	8, 8½, 9	Win., Fed., Rem., Fio.	$8	1200

NOTES: * = 10 rounds per box. ** = 5 rounds per box. Pricing variations and number of rounds per box can occur with type and brand of ammunition. Listed pricing is the average nominal cost for load style and box quantity shown. Not every brand is available in all shot size variations. Some manufacturers do not provide suggested list prices. All prices rounded to nearest whole dollar. The price you pay will vary dependent upon outlet of purchase. # = new load spec this year; "C" indicates a change in data.

THE 1997 GUN DIGEST SHOOTER'S MARKETPLACE

GUNSMITHING TOOLS AND MACHINERY

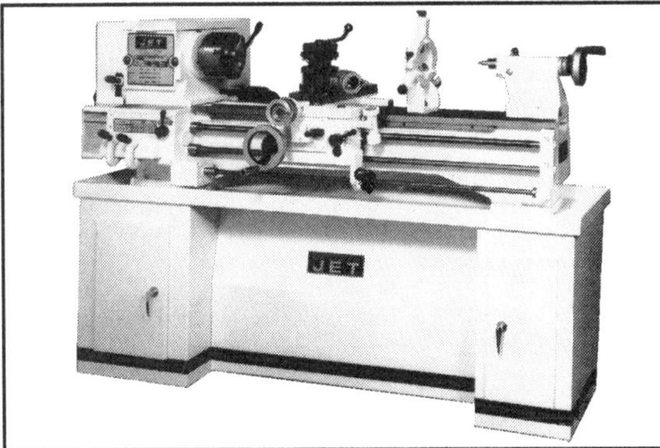

Blue Ridge offers a wide selection of top name-brand machinery and tools for the gunsmith and hobbyist. From lathes, milling machines, drill presses, mill/drills to measuring tools, metals, books and videos, Blue Ridge can provide all the tools you need to build that custom rifle or rechamber an old favorite. Some of the well-known industry standards featured in their catalog are: Baldor, Clausing, Dykem, Foredom, Kasenit, Lagun, Mitutoyo, Morse, Myford and Sherline. All new for 1997 is the Jet BD-1336N lathe (shown with optional stand) which comes with a full one-year warranty on all parts and labor. Though the list price is $3,175.00, Blue Ridge is offering a special price on this and other Jet equipment if you mention *Shooter's Marketplace*. Call Blue Ridge's toll-free number to receive their special offer and a free catalog.

BLUE RIDGE MACHINERY & TOOLS, INC.

NEW BARREL PORTING SYSTEM

Almost 30 years ago, Mag-Na-Port International, Inc. introduced the firearms industry to the advantages of barrel porting using EDM or Electrical Discharge Machining. Today, the company continues as an innovator and leader in barrel porting systems for all types of firearms. Their newest porting option, called the Miss Mag-Na-Port Custom package, is especially useful for magnum revolvers with barrels 3″ or larger. "Dual Trapezoidal" ports on each side of the barrel reduce felt recoil and muzzle flip. The package also includes custom services such as the installation of the C-More front sight blade, a velvet hone finish, jeweled and polished hammer and trigger, fine-tuned action and custom pin-striping. Write or call for a free catalog.

MAG-NA-PORT INTERNATIONAL, INC.

See manufacturers' addresses on page 250.

QUALITY GUN SAFES

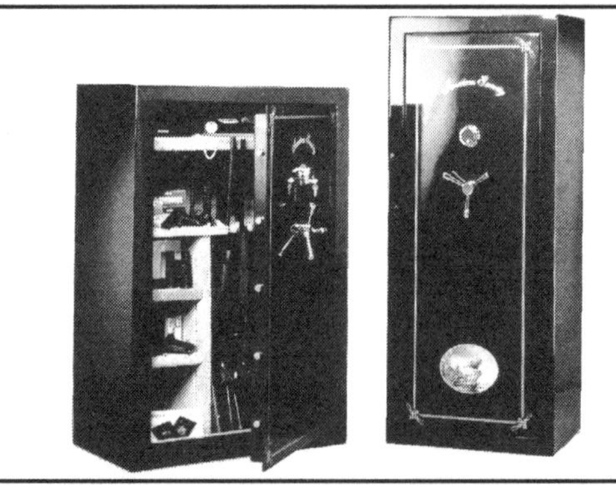

Manufacturers of firearms safes for the security industry for 50 years, American Security Products Company offers the firearms enthusiast a complete line of pistol and gun safes, vault doors and gun cabinets for secure storage of firearms. All AMSEC safes have passed the U.L. burglary testing procedures for drill, punch and pry attacks. Standard features include recessed doors, independent relocking devices, Sargent and Greenleaf keylocking dials, an ABR™ automatic bolt retraction system and twelve massive 1″ diameter tri-bolt design locking bolts that lock both horizontally and vertically behind the door jambs. Certified fireliners are also available. Interior design options offer storage capacity from eight to sixty firearms. For more information, a free brochure or the location of their nearest warehouse contact AMSEC.

AMERICAN SECURITY PRODUCTS COMPANY (AMSEC)

RIFLE ACCESSORIES

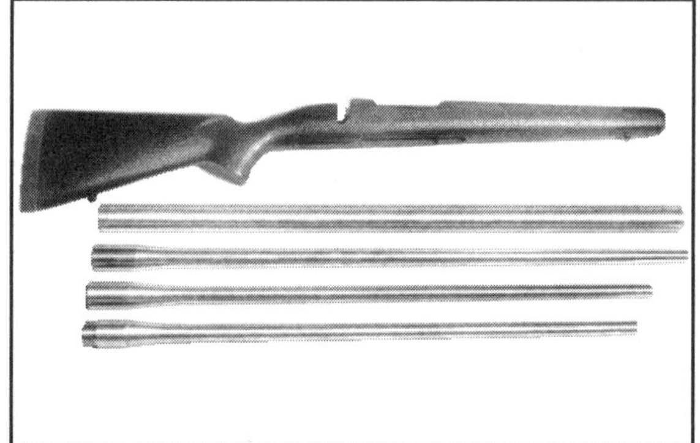

B. Perazone-Gunsmith offers a full range of rifle accessories and services for sporterizing Mauser 93 through 98 rifles from pre-threaded and chambered barrels to synthetic stocks, adjustable triggers, low-swing safeties and scope mounts. Barrels and accessories are also available for the Ruger 10/22 and 77/22 rifles from heavy barrels and synthetic stocks to scope mounts. Perazone also offers: Wilson Arms air-gauged, lead-lapped, match-grade barrels; Dayton Traister triggers and safeties; Butler Creek and Bell & Carlson stocks; Volquartsen Ruger 10/22 accessories; PM Enterprises scope mounts, safeties and speed locks; and Power Custom titanium parts for Ruger 10/22 rifles. Also, special sale items and closeouts. Their catalog is free with order or send $3.00. Dealer inquiries welcome; send a copy of your F.F.L.

BRIAN PERAZONE—GUNSMITH

NEW PORTABLE KNIFE SHARPENER

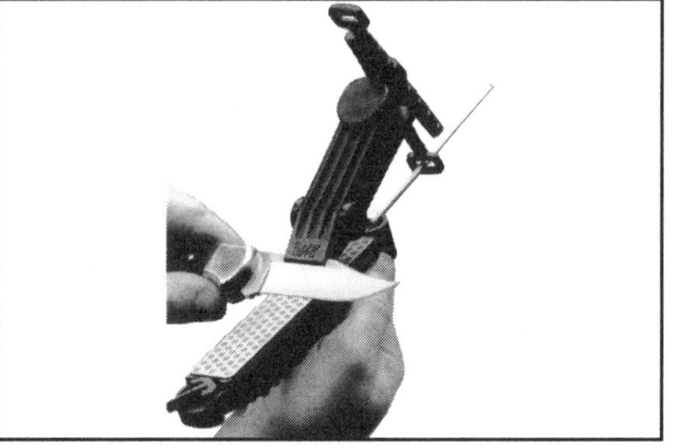

Diamond Machining Technology's new Diamond Aligner™ knife sharpening system maintains a consistent bevel for restoring the sharpness of any knife blade. Highly portable, the new Diamond Aligner is available with two or four Diamond Whetstones™. Each 4″ Whetstone displays DMT's unique polka-dot pattern surface which prevents loading and speeds sharpening. The Whetstones can be used dry or with just a few drops of water for lubrication and, unlike conventional knife sharpening abrasives, they will never hollow or groove. A cam-lock handle enables quick changes between grits and allows stones to be used separately. The strong glass-reinforced polycarbonate clamp holds knives securely. All Aligner components come in a convenient roll-up fabric pouch for portability to the field.

DIAMOND MACHINING TECHNOLOGY, INC.

RANGE-FINDING SCOPE

Shepherd Scope offers a German-design Speed Focus eyepiece that provides razor sharp images with a twist of the rear ring.

The eyepiece remains rock solid throughout focusing and zooming.

Also available is an adjustable objective lens housing which will accept Shepherd Scope's sunshade. The scopes have a scratch-resistant 340 hard matte finish.

All scopes have Shepherd's patented dual reticle system that provides one-shot zeroing, instant range finding, bullet drop and constant visual verification of the original zero.

Call, write or fax Shepherd Scope direct for a free brochure.

SHEPHERD SCOPE LTD.

See manufacturers' addresses on page 250.

BARREL ACCURIZING SERVICE

BlackStar Barrel Accurizing significantly enhances the performance of custom and factory rifle and pistol barrels. In addition to 30-55 percent accuracy improvements, it also reduces barrel fouling by nearly 90 percent, and boosts velocities by up to 10 percent. The program includes a detailed cleaning of your barrel followed by a borescope and bore gauge inspection. If the barrel meets their inspection criteria, it is cryogenically stress-relieved at -300° Fahrenheit in BlackStar's own state-of-the-art CryoStar™ processor which stabilizes the barrel steel, making it less likely to warp as it heats up during sustained fire. The final step is a precise electrochemical micro-polishing of the bore. Mention *Shooter's Marketplace* and receive 10 percent off the retail price of BlackStar Barrel Accurizing. Limit one discount per customer. Visa and MasterCard accepted.

BLACKSTAR ACCURIZING

NEW BORESCOPES

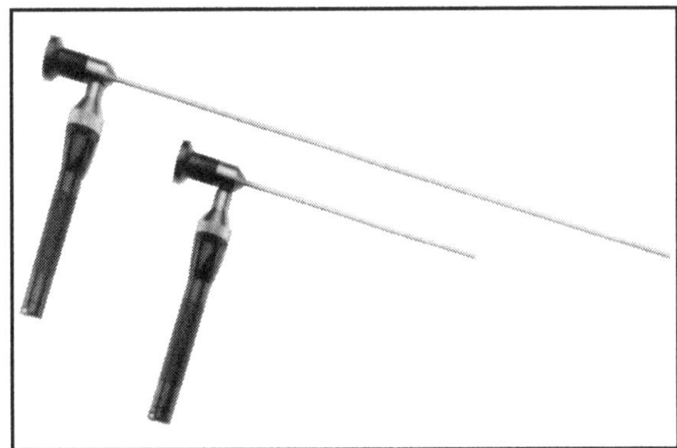

BlackStar Accurizing offers a line of high-quality, affordable borescopes for the serious shooter and gunsmith. Powered by a modified Mini-Mag™ flashlight, the Hawkeye borescope is one of the most compact and convenient to use scopes on the market. Crafted in the U.S. from state-of-the-art fiber optics and durable stainless steel, they allow detailed 360° inspection of your rifle bore and throat as well as chamber, lockwork, magazine well and other critical areas. The scopes come in three lengths—7″, 12″ or 17″—and are complete with detailed instructions and tips for use. Optional accessories are available on special order. BlackStar is offering $20.00 off the retail price of a Hawkeye 17″ borescope if you mention *Shooter's Marketplace*. Limit one per customer. Visa and MasterCard accepted.

BLACKSTAR ACCURIZING

CERAMIC BORE TREATMENT

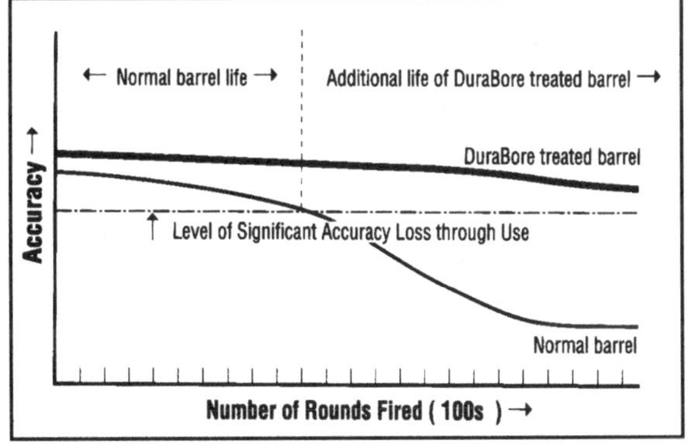

The DuraBore™ process from BlackStar Accurizing is a unique barrel hardening technology with the proven capability of extending barrel life without destroying accuracy. By transforming the top .005-.007″ of the bore surface of new or unfired barrels into a high-performance ceramic, barrel bore hardness is boosted to 75-80 Rc without changing the Rockwell hardness of the core material. DuraBore hardens the inner bore surface against erosion and heat damage. Used in benchrest, high-power and other competitive rifle as well as military-type weapons, DuraBore improves the performance and life of your barrel. Mention *Shooter's Marketplace* and receive 15 percent off the retail price of your first DuraBore treatment. Limit one discount per customer. Visa and MasterCard accepted. Dealer program requires FFL and applicable tax certificate.

BLACKSTAR ACCURIZING

CUSTOM RIFLE BARRELS

BlackStar produces precision cut-rifled barrels that are cryogenically stress-relieved, electro-polished and taper-bored for enhanced accuracy and performance. Used by hunters and varmint shooters, these 416R stainless AccuMax barrels are also top performers for benchrest, high-power BR-50 and IBS 1,000-yard competitors as well as for the U.S. military and various police organizations in sniper applications. AccuMax barrels can cut fouling by 80 to 90 percent. They come fluted or non-fluted and in any size, contour, and twist rate from 172- to 585-caliber with larger calibers up to 20mm available by special order. Dealer program requires FFL and applicable tax certificate. Mention *Shooter's Marketplace* and you'll receive 15 percent off the retail price of barrel fluting. Limit one per customer. Visa and MasterCard accepted.

BLACKSTAR ACCURIZING

See manufacturers' addresses on page 250.

GUNSMITH'S MAINTENANCE CENTER

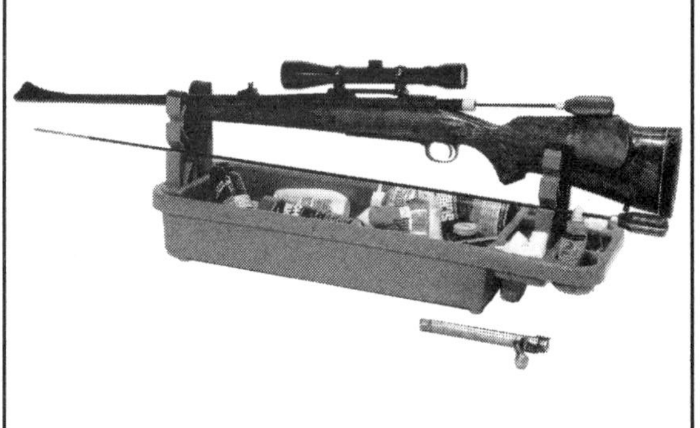

The new RMC-5 portable maintenance center from MTM Case-Gard makes working on rifles and shotguns a hassle-free project. On the workbench, at the range or on a hunting trip, the handy RMC-5 is ideal for mounting scopes, swivels, bedding actions or for routine cleaning. To help eliminate spills, compartments are provided to hold bore cleaners, rust preventatives, and other solvents. The large open middle section is designed to store all the needed tools and cleaning supplies. The RMC-5's removable forks have moulded-on rubber padding to protect against scratches and abrasion while holding the rifle or shotgun securely in place. Each fork has two height adjustments, allowing firearms to be held in three positions, level upright, slanted or upsidedown. For more information, write or call MTM Case-Gard.

MTM MOLDED PRODUCTS CO., INC.

TRIGGER GUARD ASSEMBLY

Williams Manufacturing of Oregon, a maker of high-quality firearm parts and accessories, introduces their full bottom metal trigger guard assembly for Remington Model 700 BDL short and long-action rifles. Fully CNC-machined from 1215 alloy steel solid drop-hammer forgings and solid bar stock, each assembly is professionally polished and blued to match Remington factory finish. Close attention to edges and screw holes ensures crisp and clean edges. William's time-proven floorplate release design allows easy assembly to existing factory stocks. Slightly inletting and shortening the magazine box also adapts this unit to Remington's Models 700 ADL, 721 and 722 rifles. Suggested retail price is $48.00; dealer inquiries welcome. Mention *Shooter's Marketplace* and you'll receive a 10% discount on your first order.

WILLIAMS MANUFACTURING OF OREGON, INC.

SHOOTERS' NEWSPAPER

SHOTGUNS • RIFLES • HANDGUNS • ACCESSORIES • MODERN & ANTIQUE

Shotgun News

THE WORLD'S LARGEST GUN SALES PUBLICATION — VOLUME 50, ISSUE 14, 1996

Announcing 50th Anniversary Sweepstakes

Established 1946 — Published Three Times Each Month

SEE SUPER CLASSIFIED INDEX ON PAGE 5

Established in 1946, *The Shotgun News* is the original and still one of the largest firearms sales publications available today. At less that $.62 per issue (36 issues for $22.00) *The Shotgun News* is a low-price leader with a volume readership. Three times each month, more than 140,000 firearms enthusiasts read, enjoy and profit from this newspaper. Thousands of alphabetically indexed classified ads and hundreds of display ads help readers locate money-saving prices on pistols, revolvers, rifles, shotguns, edged weapons, militaria, antique and collectible firearms, ammunition, optics and many other accessories and services.

Celebrating their 50th year of service in 1996 to firearms enthusiasts nationwide, it is, as the cover says, "the trading post for anything that shoots."

THE SHOTGUN NEWS

CUSTOM PRESENTATION CASES

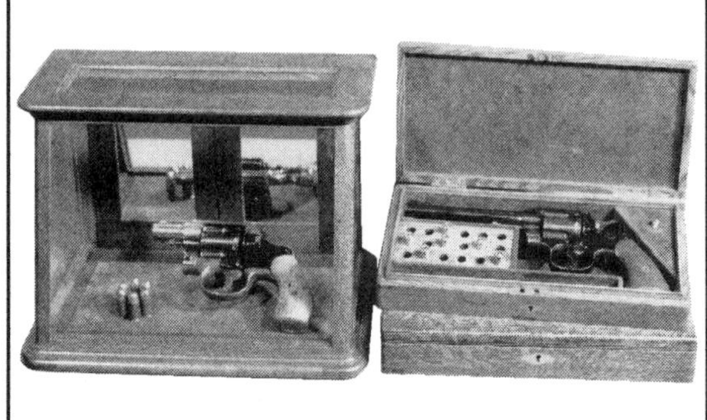

Continuing in the formal woodworking traditions of the past, Bison Studios offers fine old-style pistol presentation cases and an array of 19th century-style showcases for collectors, dealers and merchants. Handmade in traditional American or English patterns from oak, mahogany, rosewood or walnut, the pistol cases come with full velvet-lined partitions for handgun and accessories. Inlays and detailing can be in brass, silver, ivory or ebony. Small, medium and large display cases for counter top, wall mounting or free-standing floor display are available in walnut, mahogany, lacewood or oak with curved glass, flat glass or both and may be ordered as single units or in sets. All woodwork features finely fitted joints and a hand-rubbed finish over polished wood. For more information contact Bison Studios.

BISON STUDIOS, PHILIP POBURKA, CASE MAKER

See manufacturers' addresses on page 250.

NEW BIPOD MODELS

B-SQUARE bipods are offered in several models. The Rigid Bipod provides strong support and is available with swivel stud "Sporter" or barrel clamp "Service" attachment. The Tilt Bipod offers rigid support and cants from side to side for fine tuning aim. Tilt Bipods are also available with swivel stud or barrel clamp attachment. The Roto-Tilt provides that same support and side-to-side canting, but also swivels in a 30-degree angle, enabling shooters to follow perfectly aimed shots. It is available with swivel stud or barrel clamp attachment. All B-SQUARE bipods are available in blue or stainless finish and feature an Unlimited Leg Extension System with 7″ leg extenders, sold separately. The bipods range in price from $39.95 to $159.95. To order, call B-SQUARE's toll-free order line.

B-SQUARE COMPANY, INC.

NEW INTERLOCK RINGS AND MOUNTS

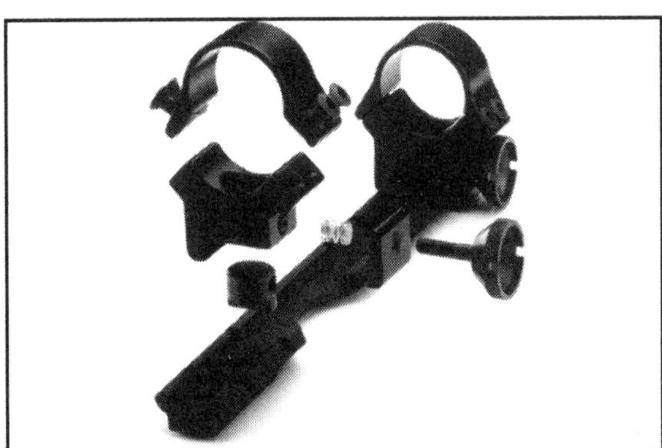

B-SQUARE's new Interlock Rings and Bases create a strong, shock-proof mounting system. The wrap-around design of the ring caps provides twice the clamping power area of conventional rings. The four extra-heavy 8x40 hex screws secure the cap to the ring saddle and the sculpted and contoured one-piece base is likewise secured with 8x40 hex head screws. The strength of this system is achieved with an over-size cross-bolt threaded completely through a solid steel barrel-shaped recoil key that extends fully into the base cross-slot, creating a solid recoil barrier to keep stress off the dovetails. The knurled cross-bolt knobs tighten and loosen easily. Retail price of the Interlock Ring ranges from $34.95 to $64.95; the bases from $14.95 to $19.95. See your local dealer or call B-SQUARE's toll-free order line.

B-SQUARE COMPANY, INC.

NEW AIRGUN RINGS AND BASES

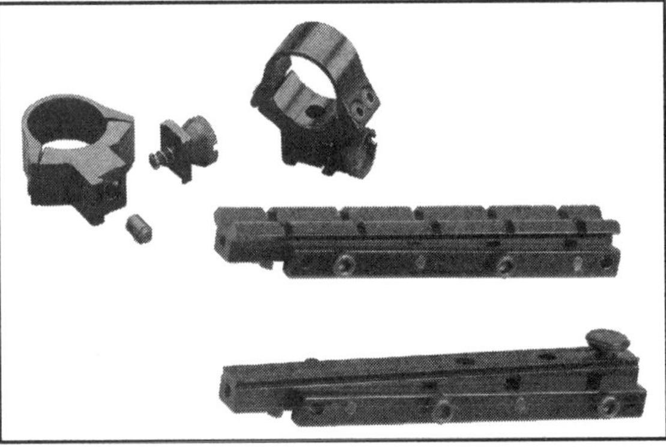

B-SQUARE introduces a major advancement in airgun scope mounting systems. Their 11mm dovetail rings use the new Interlock design which features steel recoil stops to fit RWS/Beeman/FWB/Weihrach/BSA plus other airgun receivers. The rings are available for 1″, 30mm and 26mm scope tubes.

B-SQUARE offers an 11mm to 11mm base as well as an 11mm to standard dovetail (Weaver-style)—both providing elevation adjustment and extended base length.

The airgun Interlock rings retail starting at $34.95; the bases retail for $39.95. See your local dealer or call B-SQUARE's toll-free order line. A catalog featuring the complete line of their products is available upon request.

B-SQUARE COMPANY, INC.

FREE SCREWDRIVER KIT OFFER

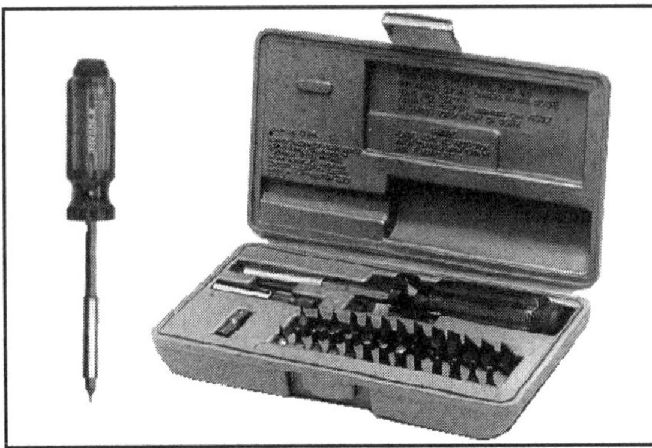

B-SQUARE will include one of their new 31-piece Gunsmith Screwdriver Kits with an order of any one of the following B-SQUARE products: Interlock Ring and Base combination; handgun, rifle or shotgun mount; bi-pod; or laser sight. The screwdriver kit, featuring hardened, gunsmith ground bits and ergonomically designed handle, is a $32.95 value and includes the popular-sized Torx, Hex, Phillips, and slot-head bits.

The free gunsmith screwdriver kit can be ordered in the U.S. by calling B-SQUARE's toll-free line or by mail. For international orders write or fax B-SQUARE. You must mention *Shooter's Marketplace* to take advantage of this free offer.

B-SQUARE COMPANY, INC.

See manufacturers' addresses on page 250.

PRECISION RIFLE

AMTEC 2000, Inc. now imports the Erma SR-100 precision rifle to the U.S. A military-specification firearm, the SR-100 bolt-action rifle provides uncompromising accuracy. Features include a detachable magazine, quick detachable barrel and fully-adjustable tactical stock. The two-part receiver is of forged alloy, its lower section acting as a massive bedding block. The bolt lugs lock into the barrel, not the receiver, assuring lock-up strength and precise headspace. The trigger assembly is fully-adjustable for take-up, weight and length of pull, pre-load and overtravel. Available in 308 Win., 300 Win. Mag. and 338 Lapua Mag., this rifle incorporates a number of new patentable technologies. Production is extremely limited and intended primarily for the military and law enforcement. For additional information write or call AMTEC.

AMTEC 2000, INC.

SELF-ADHESIVE RECOIL PAD

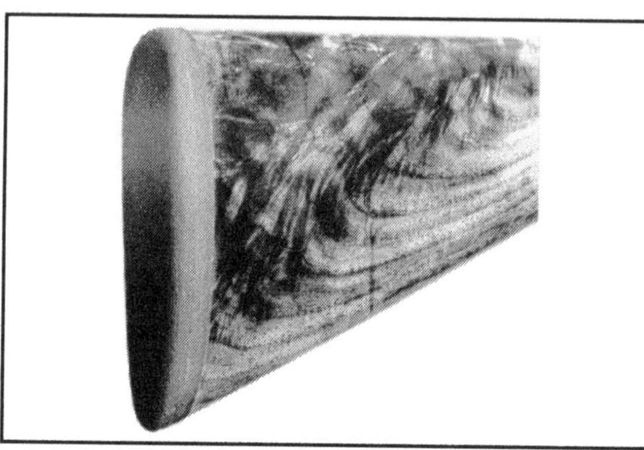

Add-A-Pad, for rifles or shotguns, can be installed in minutes by simply pressing a pad on the end of the butt, trimming it with a sharp knife and then sanding it to the exact shape of the stock.

Add-A-Pad is made from a shock-absorbent blended neoprene with a specially formulated adhesive backing.

The package includes two 1/4″ and one 1/2″ pads, allowing the use of any one pad or a combination of pads to build a recoil pad up to 1″ thick. The result is an economical pad which looks professionally installed.

Add-A-Pad costs $10.95 and comes with complete installation instructions. Call or write Palsa Outdoor Products for more information.

PALSA OUTDOOR PRODUCTS

NEW AMERICAN DA REVOLVERS

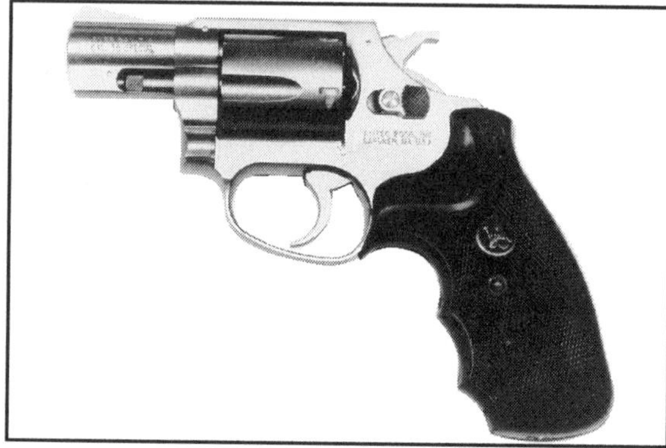

AMTEC 2000, Inc. is a joint venture that merges the engineering skills of Erma Werke of Germany and the manufacturing know-how of H&R 1891, Inc. Together they have created the new H&R American Double Action Revolvers. Sophisticated CAD system designers in the U.S. teamed with skilled Erma Werke engineers in Germany to bring high-level precision to each component of this new revolver series. Chambered for the 38 Special cartridge, American Double-Action revolvers are constructed of high tensile alloy or stainless steel in 2″ and 3″ barrel configurations. The high tensile alloy model is also available in a high-polish blue or electroless matte nickel finish. All models feature a transfer bar safety system, standard fixed sights, Pachmayr® finger-groove grips and 5-shot capacity. Contact AMTEC 2000, Inc. for more information.

AMTEC 2000, INC.

RIFLE AND PISTOL MAGAZINES

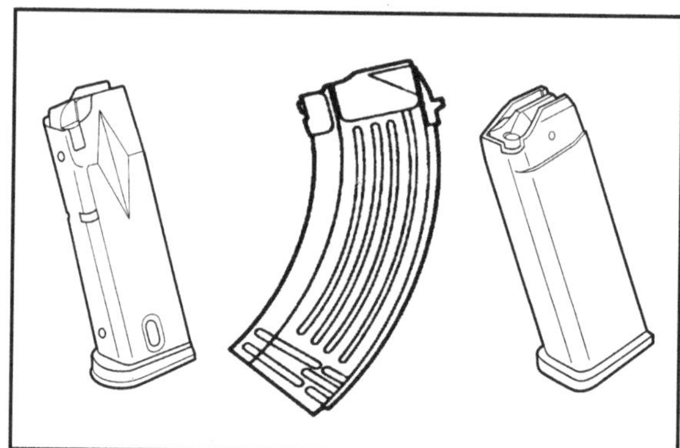

Forrest Inc. offers shooters one of the largest selections of standard and extended high-capacity magazines in the United States. Whether you're looking for a few spare magazines for that obsolete 22 rifle or pistol, or wish to replace a reduced-capacity ten-shot magazine with the higher-capacity pre-ban original, all are available from this California firm. They offer competitive pricing especially for dealers wanting to buy in quantity.

Forrest Inc. also stocks parts and accessories for the Colt 1911 45 Auto pistol, the SKS and MAK-90 rifles as well as many U.S. military rifles. One of their specialty parts is firing pins for obsolete weapons.

Call or write Forrest Inc. for more information and a free brochure. Be sure and mention *Shooter's Marketplace.*

FORREST INC.

See manufacturers' addresses on page 250.

CUSTOM 1911 PISTOLS AND PARTS

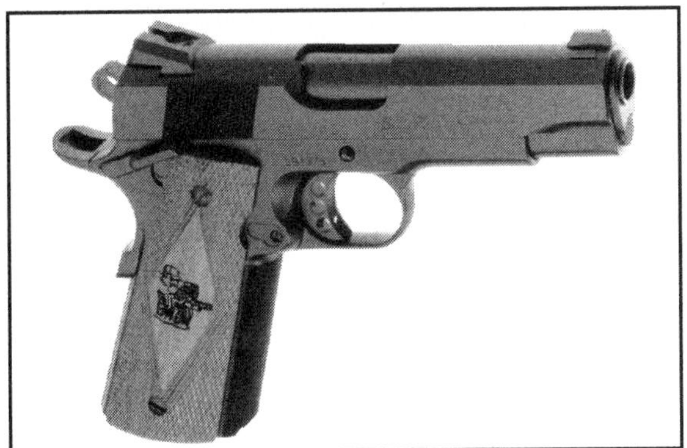

Les Baer manufactures top-quality 1911-style custom pistols and offers a complete line of precision-machined custom 1911 parts and accessories.

More than 20 high-performance pistol models are available for defense, law enforcement and competition use. Each pistol is custom-built and hand-fitted on Baer's American-made, National Match forged frames, slides and barrels by Baer custom gunsmiths. Match-grade accuracy is guaranteed. Baer also offers standard and reduced "Commanche" sizes, stainless steel and aluminum models, some high-capacity 1911s and their new precision 22. Their exclusive forged steel, stainless steel and aluminum frames and slides in standard and reduced sizes, and Baer National Match barrels are also available as separate components.

LES BAER CUSTOM, INC.

CHECKERING TOOLS

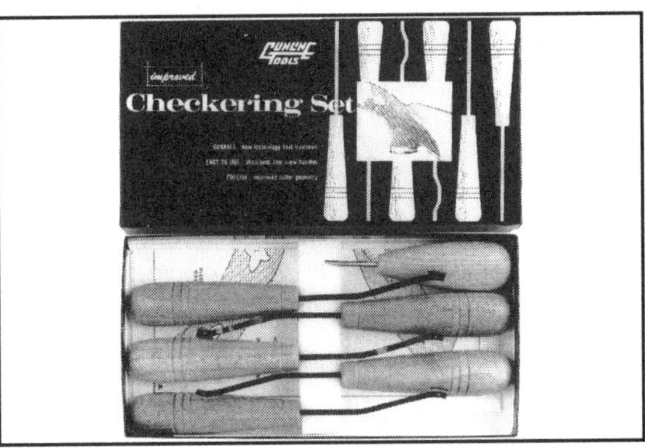

Gunline Checkering Tools are precisely made and come with illustrated instructions and easy-to-follow sample checkering patterns.

Easy to use, the cutting qualities and simple design of the checkering tools are useful for hobbyists and professional gunstockers.

Gunline offers a full line of medium and fine replaceable cutters from 16 to 32 lines per inch. They are available in 60° to 90°, in short or long sizes. Three types of handles are available, one with an offset rear-view feature.

Tool set prices start at $37.75. The Camp Perry Set of six tools lists for $57.50. Add $4.00 for shipping. Mention *Shooter's Marketplace* and receive a free brochure.

GUNLINE TOOLS

FOLDING BIPODS

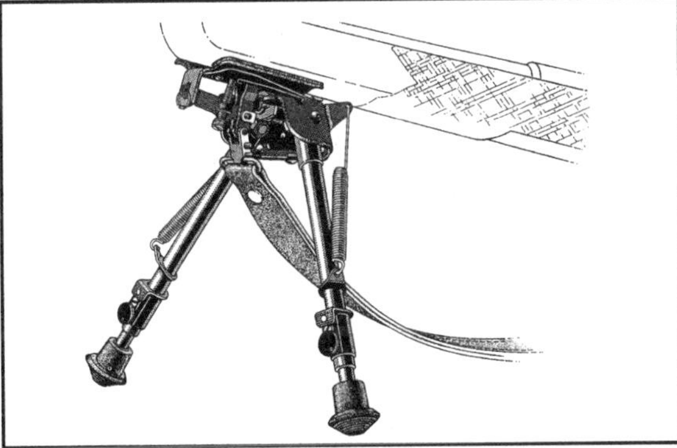

Harris Bipods clamp securely to most stud-equipped bolt-action rifles and are quick-detachable. With adapters, they will fit some other guns. On all models except the Model LM, folding legs have completely adjustable spring-return extensions. The sling swivel attaches to the clamp. This time-proven design is manufactured with heat-treated steel and hard alloys and has a black anodized finish.

Series S Bipods rotate 45° for instant leveling on uneven ground. Hinged base has tension adjustment and buffer springs to eliminate tremor or looseness in crotch area of bipod. They are otherwise similar to non-rotating Series 1A2.

Eleven models are available from Harris Engineering; literature is free.

HARRIS ENGINEERING, INC.

BARREL BEDDING TOOLS

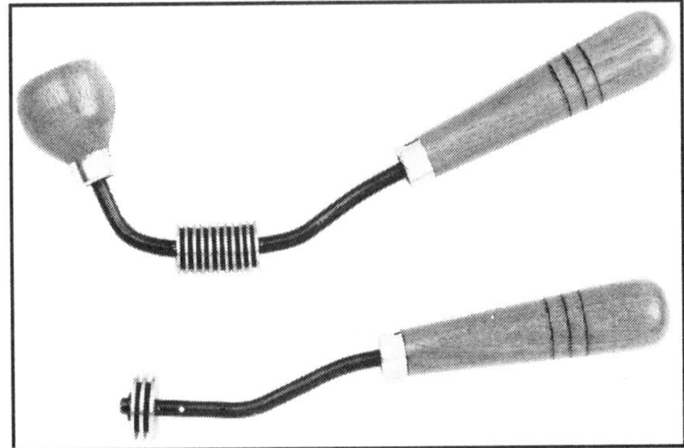

Gunline Barrel Bedding Tools are essential for accurate bedding of rifle to stock, especially when free-floating barrels. With BBT the job is made easy; heavy and light cuts result in a smooth and accurate finish without sanding. The BBT full-size tool has forward and rear handles for full control of cushioned cutters. The single-handled BJ, Barrel Bedder Jr., is suitable for lighter duty. The GS, Groove Shave, is similar to the BJ, but with fewer and larger cutting discs.

The BBT comes in seven sizes from 1/2″ to 1″ diameter for $18.95 and $20.50 respectively; the BJ Tool Set comes with 1/2″, 3/8″ and 3/4″ cutter discs (6 each) for $28.50; the GS Set has 7/8″, 1″ and 11/8″ sizes (3 each) for $22.95. Add $4.00 for shipping. Receive a free brochure for mentioning *Shooter's Marketplace.*

GUNLINE TOOLS

See manufacturers' addresses on page 250.

NEW SHOTSHELL HANDBOOK

The 4th Edition of Lyman's respected *Shotshell Handbook* is one of the most comprehensive shotshell manuals available on the market and is one of the first to offer a complete reloading data section for steel shot.

Covering all gauges from 410-bore to 10-gauge, including the new 12-gauge 3½″, the *Shotshell Handbook* includes data for all the newest components—Remington RTL, Activ and Fiocchi cases; Winchester, Hodgdon, Accurate and Vihtavuori powders; and Federal 209A primers.

In addition to data sections on shotgun slugs, steel shot target and hunting loads, the handbook also features articles written by well known shotgunners.

The suggested retail price for the handbook is $24.95.

LYMAN PRODUCTS CORPORATION

NEW SHOTGUN SLING SYSTEM

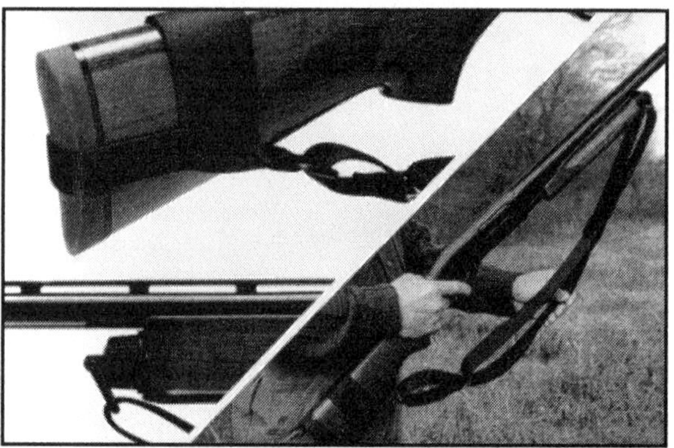

The Total Shotgun Sling from The Outdoor Connection is a complete, fully assembled sling system for 12-gauge Remington shotguns, Models 870, 1100 and 11-87.

The system includes a unique magazine tube cap, called the Total Cap, a reliable buttstock attaching device and the 1¼″-wide Super Sling-2. The Total Cap is designed to fit all models of 12-gauge Remington shotguns and is installed by simply removing and replacing the original tube cap by hand; no tools are required.

The Total Sling System can be installed or removed in less than 1-minute and requires no drilling, screws, tools or alterations to the shotgun. It is a safe, secure, easily manageable system for the serious hunter and shooter.

THE OUTDOOR CONNECTION, INC.

METAL PREPARATION VIDEO

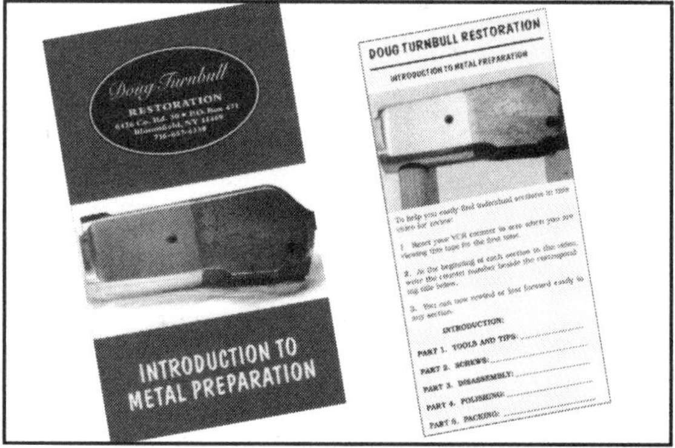

Doug Turnbull Restoration's new video *Introduction to Metal Preparation* provides the hobby gunsmith as well as semi-professional with all the step-by-step instruction necessary to prepare the metal surfaces and parts of firearms for finish work. The video and accompanying handbook clearly outline each step, from the tools needed for the job to disassembly tips and polishing techniques used by the professionals. This instructional tape also illustrates the various finishes applied by manufacturers to their original parts, providing a complete set of guidelines to follow so you can do a professional job and save money. This 37-minute video has a suggested retail price of $19.95 plus $3.00 shipping and handling. Write or call Doug Turnbull Restoration or use his internet address for more information.

DOUG TURNBULL RESTORATION, INC.

SIZING AND FORMING LUBE

Imperial Sizing Wax from E-Z-Way Systems was developed in the early 1970s to allow simple, easy and effective reloading and reforming.

A blend of two waxes and two oils, a thin film of high-lubricity Imperial applied to the outside of a rifle case with your fingertips will ensure smooth loading tool operation with no stuck or dented cases. The lube can be removed simply with a paper towel.

Because it is used sparingly, it is very economical—one tin will size several thousand cases. It is available in 1- and 2-ounce tins with suggested retail prices of $3.75 and $6.00, respectively.

See your local dealer or write directly to E-Z-Way Systems for more information.

E-Z-WAY SYSTEMS

See manufacturers' addresses on page 250.

NEW 65MM SPOTTING SCOPE

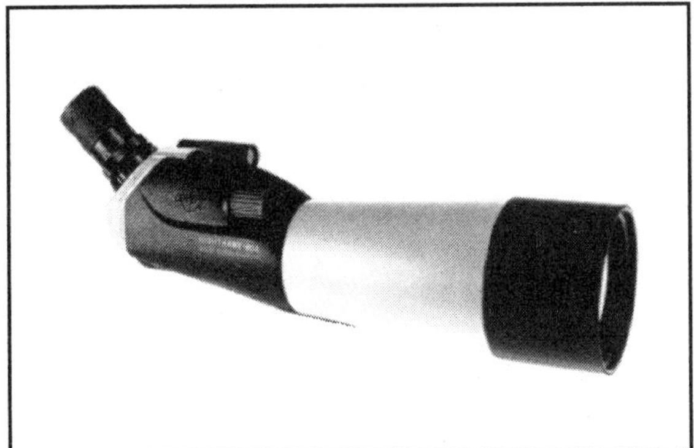

The Model 850U Nighthawk 65mm spotting scope is among the world's most compact, lightweight scopes. Manufactured of modern materials, including polycarbon, aluminum, zamex and rubber, it offers the same optics as the 80mm but a different objective lens. Features include a focal length of 386mm, a retractable hood to protect the objective lens, a rubber-armored main body housing and a 1.8x optical finder. Interchangeable eyepieces (15x, 20x, 25x, 40x, 60x), a zoom lens from 16-48x, an ingenious carrying case that can be left on the scope while viewing and telephotographic equipment are available as accessories. All optics are multi-coated and eyepieces have a bayonet-type mounting for quick lens attachment. Also offered as a straight viewing scope (Model 850). Both come attractively gift-boxed.

SWIFT INSTRUMENTS, INC.

NEW 80MM SPOTTING SCOPE

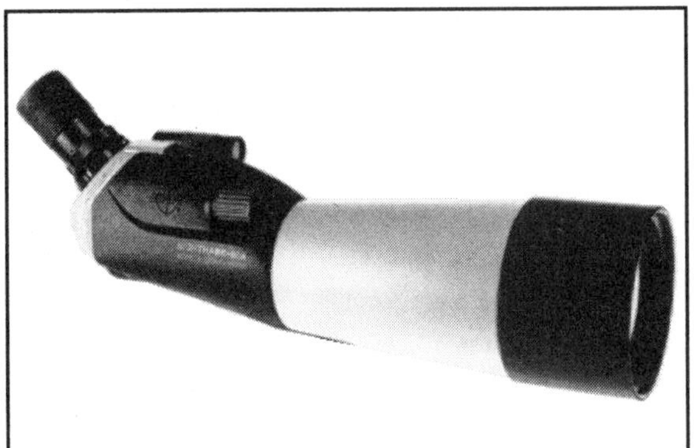

The Model 849U Nighthawk from Swift Instruments is geared for the hunter and nature photographer. Measuring 350mm in length without the eyepiece, this compact, lightweight spotting scope is virtually free from chromatic aberration or distortion and offers excellent depth of field and resolving power. The rubber-armored main body housing features a 1.8x optical finder and a retractable hood to protect the objective lens from direct exposure to sunlight and dew. Accessories include interchangeable eyepieces, 19x, 25x, 31x, 50x, 75x; a zoom eyepiece, 20-60x; a soft carrying case; and telephotographic equipment. All optics are multi-coated and eyepieces feature a bayonet-type mounting for quick lens attachment. Also available as a straight viewing scope (Model 849). Both come attractively gift-boxed.

SWIFT INSTRUMENTS, INC.

NEW BINOCULARS

Swift Instrument's Model 719 Jaguar 8x23 binocular is an ideal all-weather companion for the hiker, hunter or bird watcher. It is light, weighing only 11.4 ounces, and waterproof, sporting a rubber armored exterior that can withstand immersion for five minutes in three feet of water. It features the ability to focus on objects as close as nine feet and has a wide interpupillary adjustment from 57 to 74mm. The patented pop-up eyecups provide comfortable and protected viewing. Also available from Swift is the more powerful 720 Bobcat, a 10x23 binocular. Immersible for five minutes in depths of one meter, it possesses the same fine features of the 8x Jaguar. Both binoculars come attractively gift boxed complete with case and broad woven neck strap.

SWIFT INSTRUMENTS, INC.

NEW RIFLESCOPE

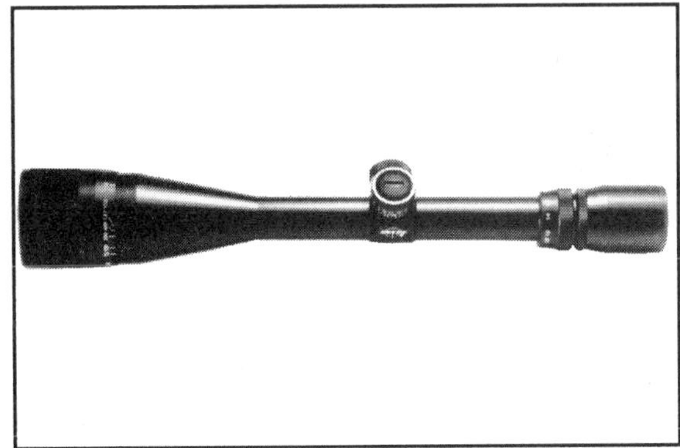

The Model 669M from Swift Instruments is a wide angle, multi-coated riflescope designed especially for varmint hunters and silhouette shooters. With a maximum effective objective lens diameter of 44mm and a power range from 6 to 18, this riflescope is extremely effective in poor light conditions.

The 669M features a hard-anodized matte finish, fully multi-coated optics, parallax adjustable objective lens and comes equipped with a fine self-centering crosshair reticle plus sunshade. This tough riflescope is fog-, water- and shock-proof and comes attractively gift-boxed.

For more information on the this and other available products, write or call Swift Instruments.

SWIFT INSTRUMENTS, INC.

See manufacturers' addresses on page 250.

MODULAR SHOOTING REST SYSTEM

Keng's Firearms Specialty's Versa-Pod® is a revolutionary system of interchangeable shooting rests and mounting adapters. The system consists of two prone-position bipods (Models 1 & 2), a sitting position bipod (Model 3) and a shooting stick/monopod (Solo™). A wide selection of mounting adaptors ensures compatibility with most popular long guns. Featuring sturdy one-piece telescopic legs with convenient push-button adjustments, the Versa-Pod offers true one-hand operation. The multi-pivot head of the bipod allows a wide range of movement for shots that require tilting, panning or canting of the rifle. The telescopic Solo Shooting Stick, available in late 1996, features a unique trigger release for quick, one-hand height adjustment.

KENG'S FIREARMS SPECIALTY, INC.

LEAD REMOVAL SYSTEM FOR HANDGUNS

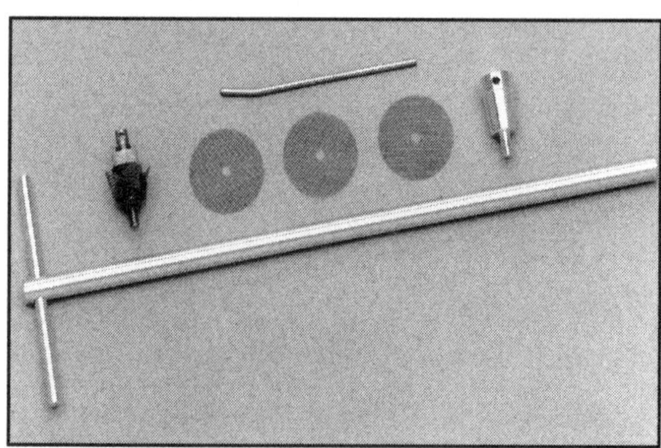

Shooting large numbers of unjacketed lead bullets causes lead to accumulate in the forcing cones of revolvers and in the barrels of both revolvers and semiautomatic pistols. This buildup can noticeably affect accuracy and in extreme situations lead to malfunctions. The Lewis Lead Remover, marketed since 1954 by L.E.M. Gun Specialties, Inc., is designed specifically to remove these deposits without the use of chemicals. The Lewis Lead remover is available in kit form, complete with brass cloth patches, two accessory tips and a 9½" handle for 38/357/9mm, 41, 44 and 45 calibers at a retail price of $13.75 plus $2.00 shipping, or as individual components to be purchased separately. If you mention *Shooter's Marketplace* an extra package of brass patches will be included. Call or write for a free brochure.

L.E.M. GUN SPECIALTIES, INC.

AMMUNITION AND COMPONENTS

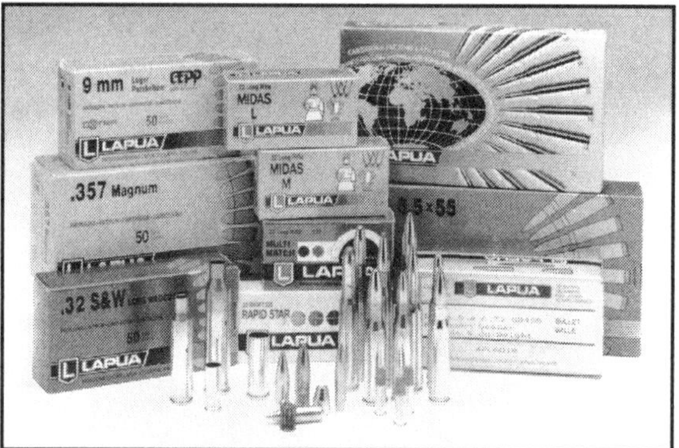

Lapua of Finland has been producing top-quality ammunition and components for discriminating sportsmen and competitive shooters since 1923. Manufactured to exacting industry standards in one of the most modern facilities in the world, Lapua ammunition is recognized by top national teams in international shooting competition and elite military/police agencies for its consistency and dependability. Keng's Firearms Specialty, Inc. is Lapua's exclusive U.S. importer and is making available to U.S. shooters the complete line of Lapua centerfire rifle and pistol and 22 rimfire ammunition, along with the wide selection of brass and bullet reloading components. For more information, call or write Keng's Firearms Specialty, Inc.

KENG'S FIREARMS SPECIALTY, INC.

TACTICAL RESPONSE SHOTGUNS

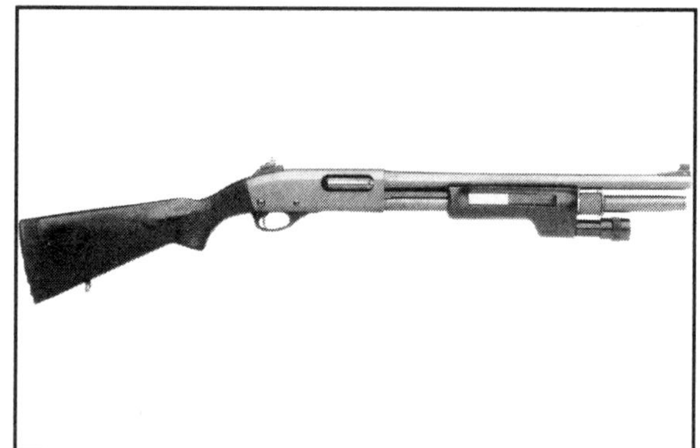

Chosen by special response teams worldwide, Scattergun Technologies' Tactical Response shotguns offer utility, reliability and accuracy. There are seventeen different models to choose from, each designed for a specific purpose. Standard features include Trak-Lock Ghost Ring sight system, an extended magazine, a high-performance spring and follower, a jumbo head safety, a synthetic stock and fore grip, a tactical light, a Side Saddle II shell carrier, a three-way tactical sling, various barrel lengths and choke configurations. For Remington 870, 1100 or 1187 owners a retro-fitting service to one of their stock models is also available. For the more ambitious, the entire line of replacement parts and accessories is available for customer installation. To receive their 49-page 1996 catalog, send $3.00 to SGT.

SCATTERGUN TECHNOLOGIES INC.

See manufacturers' addresses on page 250.

COMPACT PISTOLS

Phoenix Arms® introduces two affordable compact semi-automatics in their HP Series line of personal protection pistols. The HP-22-LR is chambered for 22 Long Rifle and the HP-25-ACP for the 25 ACP cartridge. Weighing less than 20 ounces, they offer features associated with larger caliber semi-automatics such as adjustable rear sights, quick-release takedown, manual hold-open, magazine interlocks, firing pin block safety and 10-shot magazines in a package that measures only 4.1 inches in length and 5.5 inches in depth. Both can be converted into range-ready target pistols with Phoenix Arms' 2-in1 Extended Target Barrel and Magazine Conversion Kit™. Available in satin blue and polished nickel, the HP-22-LR and HP-25-ACP retail for under $100.00 and are backed by Phoenix Arms' no-nonsense lifetime warranty.

PHOENIX ARMS

ACCESSORY/SERVICE BROCHURE

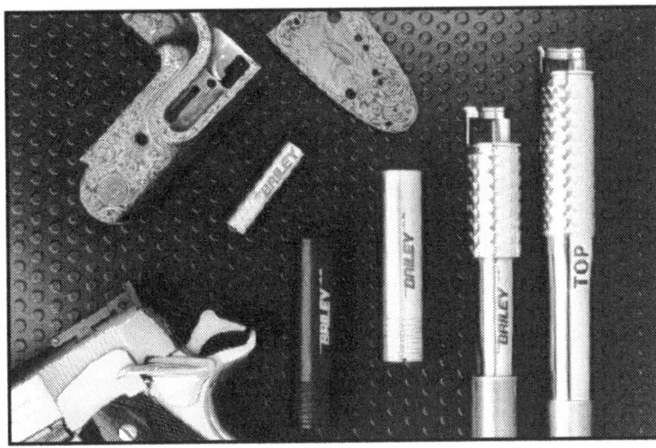

This Houston-based firm is well-known for providing precision products to the avid shotgunner. The Briley tradition of attention to detail and complete customer satisfaction keeps the hunter and competition shooter happy.

Their brochure describes Briley's line of shotgun and now pistol and revolver services. Briley has added a new division for the discerning handgun enthusiast.

Everything from screw-in chokes to competition Skeet tubes to pistol and revolver customizing and accessories is available. Briley offers an extensive line of products and services for the shotgunner and handgunner.

Write or call toll-free for a free brochure.

BRILEY MFG., INC.

GUN REPAIR SCHOOL

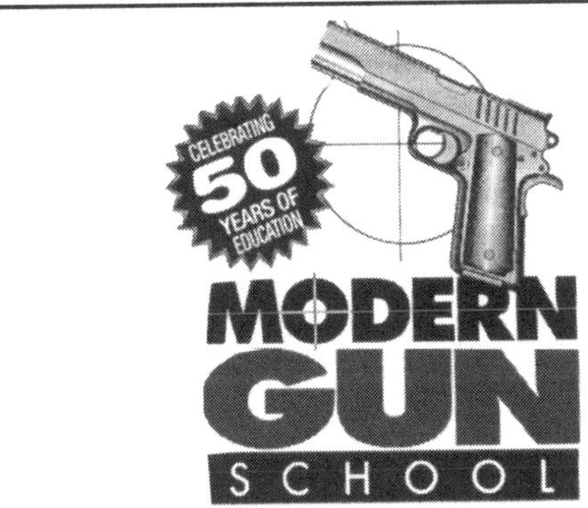

Gun repair techniques can be learned at home in six months or less through Modern Gun School's home-study program. Since 1946 this nationally-accredited school has taught firearm repair to over 50,000 students who have learned basic and advanced gunsmithing at their own pace. Whether your desire is to make gunsmithing techniques your vocation or avocation, Modern Gun's program teaches gunsmithing skills and repairs step-by-step and even provides the tools needed for the projects. Current industry catalogs and firearms publications also accompany their curriculum. Topics and techniques covered include shotguns, handguns, scopes, chokes, wholesale buying, accurizing, sporterizing, and bluing as well as professional ballistics. To receive a no-obligation information packet write or call Modern Gun School's toll-free number.

MODERN GUN SCHOOL

DROP-IN CONVERSION TUBES

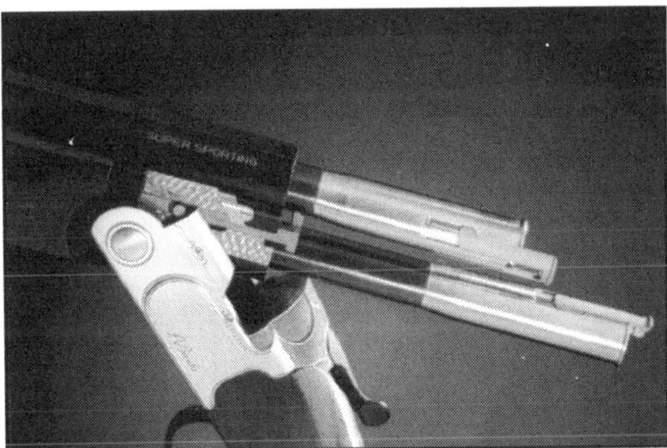

The Companion from Briley Mfg. is a 28-gauge drop-in tube insert set designed to fit all 12-gauge double-barrel shotguns.

Each tube set comes in a vinyl slip cover containing full instructions, two Briley screw-in chokes, a wrench, and a power knock-out tool for insertion and removal. No additional tools and no alterations to the shotgun are necessary. You simply insert the tubes and shoot.

Additional screw-in chokes for the tube set are available and include: Cylinder, Skeet, Improved Cylinder, Light Modified, Modified, Improved Modified, Light Full, Full and Extra Full. Briley also manufactures .410-bore and 20-gauge inserts on a fitted basis. See your local dealer or call Briley toll-free for more information. Mention *Shooter's Marketplace.*

BRILEY MFG., INC.

See manufacturers' addresses on page 250.

ADJUSTABLE BORE SAVER ROD GUIDES

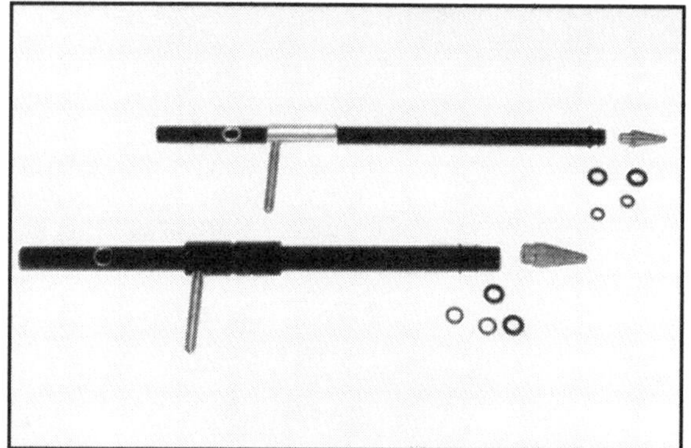

The Dewey Bore Saver cleaning rod guide replaces the bolt in your action while cleaning. The cleaning rod enters the bore straight, without harming the chamber or throat. Made from anodized aluminum in six bore sizes, the aluminum rod guide collar with threaded brass adjustment pin allows for quick adjustment to any bolt length. Chamber-sealing O-rings prohibit solvents from entering the action, trigger and magazine areas.

The guide can be used with all cleaning rods; all models fit .695- to .700-inch bolt diameter rifles. All guides allow brush clearance through tube I.D. and come with solvent port, spare O-rings and O-ring assembly tool. Weatherby and Sako models available. Write or fax J. Dewey Mfg. Co., Inc. for more information.

J. DEWEY MFG. CO., INC.

RIFLE REST

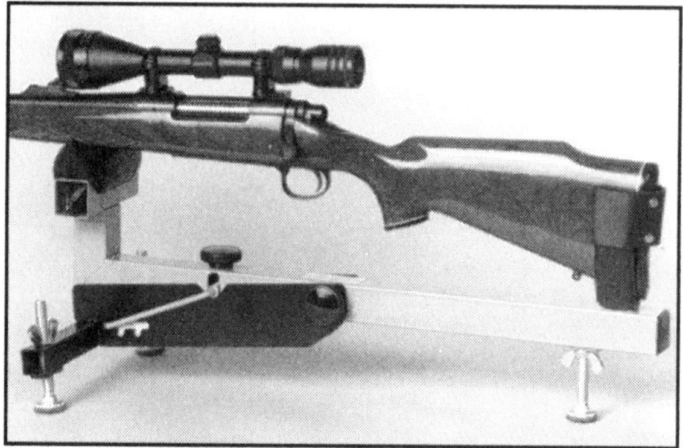

The Bench Master rifle rest from Desert Mountain Mfg. offers precision line-up and recoil reduction for load testing, varmint shooting or just sighting-in.

It features three coarse positions totaling $5^1/_2''$ with $1^1/_2''$ fine adjustment in each position, plus leveling and shoulder height adjustments for maximum control and comfort.

Because of its unique design, the Bench Master can easily double as a rifle vise for scope mounting, bore sighting, cleaning and more.

The Bench Master comes with a Lifetime Warranty and a list price of $119.95.

Contact your local dealer, or call or write Desert Mountain Mfg. for additional information or a free brochure.

DESERT MOUNTAIN MFG.

NYLON COATED GUN CLEANING RODS

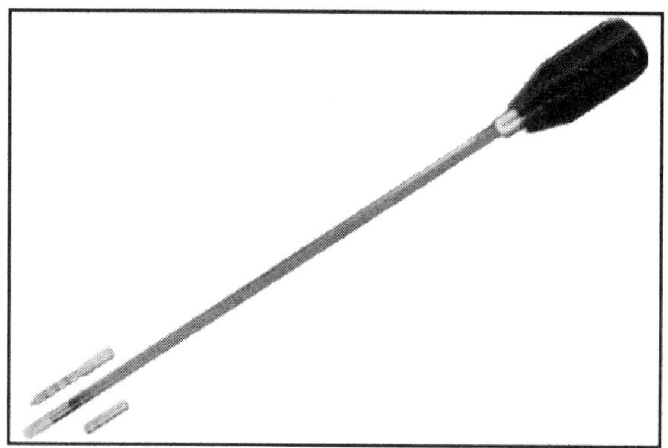

J. Dewey cleaning rods have been used by the U.S. Olympic shooting team and the benchrest community for over 20 years. These one-piece, spring-tempered, steel-base rods will not gall delicate rifling or damage the muzzle area of front-cleaned firearms. The nylon coating eliminates the problem of abrasives adhering to the rod during the cleaning operation. Each rod comes with a hard non-breakable plastic handle supported by ball-bearings, top and bottom, for ease of cleaning.

The brass cleaning jags are designed to pierce the center of the cleaning patch or wrap around the knurled end to keep the patch centered in the bore.

Coated rods are available from 17-caliber to shotgun bore size in several lengths to meet the needs of any shooter. Write for more information.

J. DEWEY MFG. CO., INC.

COLD-SWAGED MUZZLE-LOADING BULLETS

Buffalo Bullet Company has been supplying the black-powder shooter with innovative projectile designs since 1981. They offer the enthusiast a complete line of muzzle-loading balls, bullets, sabots and Ball-ets, their new patented rifle projectile which is half bullet, half ball.

All Buffalo Bullet Company projectiles are cold-swaged in precision dies under tons of pressure. Tight manufacturing tolerances help elminate air pockets, parting lines and other deformities commonly found in cast projectiles. Each bullet comes pre-lubricated with a non-petroleum lube which extends shelf-life of the projectile and provides less bullet-to-barrel friction for a higher muzzle-loading velocity.

Write, call or fax Buffalo Bullet Company for more information and a free catalog.

BUFFALO BULLET COMPANY

See manufacturers' addresses on page 250.

NEW YOUTH SLUG GUN

Harrington & Richardson's® new 20-gauge SB1-925 Ultra™ Youth Slug Hunter mates a heavy target-style barrel and scope capability with stock dimensions appropriate for shooters of smaller stature who require moderate recoil. The Ultra delivers rifle-like 100-yard groups utilizing 20-gauge sabot-style slugs. Built on a 20-gauge action, the SB1-925 uses a 12-gauge barrel blank underbored to 20-gauge with a 1 in 35″ twist and shortened to 22″. This gives it the extra heavy barrel profile while keeping the balance point to the rear. Features include a factory-mounted Weaver-style scope base, walnut-stained American hardwood Monte Carlo stock and forend, ventilated recoil pad, sling swivels, black nylon sling, a matte black receiver and low-luster blued barrel to help minimize reflection. See your local dealer or write H&R direct.

HARRINGTON & RICHARDSON

NEW 22 REVOLVER

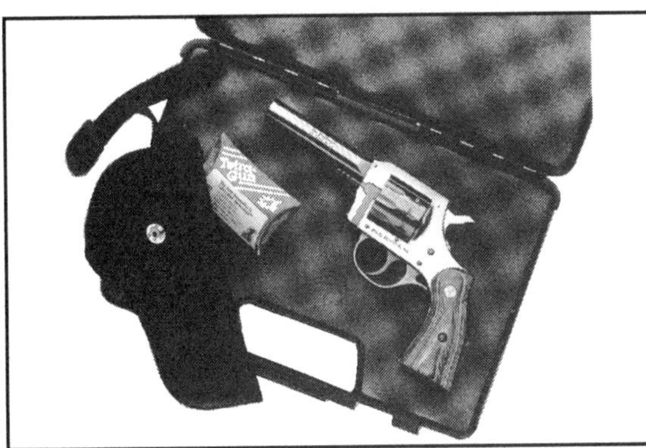

The new Model 929 Sidekick® 22-caliber revolver from Harrington & Richardson® is designed specifically for the beginning shooter. It comes as a complete package with lockable plastic storage case, Uncle Mikes® ballistic nylon holster and trial size package of Tetra® Gun oil and grease. The Sidekick features a steel square-butt frame with cinnamon hardwood laminate grips, swing-out nine-shot cylinder to handle 22 Short, 22 Long and 22 Long Rifle interchangeably, a transfer bar safety system and fixed sights—a blade front and a notch rear milled into the topstrap. The entire revolver is highly polished and hot blued, a color and finish reminiscent of pre-war handguns. For more information on this 100% American-made revolver, see your local Harrington & Richardson dealer, or contact H&R direct.

HARRINGTON & RICHARDSON

NEW 357 MAGNUM SURVIVAL RIFLE

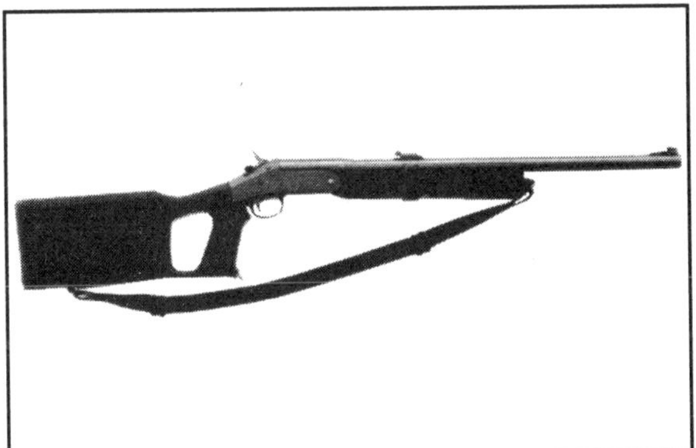

Another new offering in New England Firearms' Survivor® product line is the 357 Magnum Survivor Rifle. Featuring NEF's single shot break-action design with patented transfer bar safety, the Survivor sports a 22″ barrel with adjustable rifle sights to handle either the 357 Magnum or 38 Special cartridge. The receiver comes drilled and tapped for optional NEF scope base. The thumbhole stock and beavertail forend are constructed of high-impact synthetic and feature integral storage compartments. Also standard are integral sling swivels and a black nylon sling. Available in either a low visibility matte blue or a highly weather resistant electroless matte nickel, this rifle is ideal for camp, home or informal target practice. For more information see your local dealer or write New England Firearms.

NEW ENGLAND FIREARMS

NEW 223 REMINGTON SURVIVAL RIFLE

The new Survivor® Rifle from New England Firearms chambered in 223 Rem. features their single shot break-action design with transfer bar safety and fully-rifled 22″ barrel. Durable and easy to use, this survival/utility rifle provides excellent protection on the trail and is equally at home on a boat, in the cab of a tractor or on a light aircraft. It's also a highly effective varmint rifle.

The thumbhole stock and beavertail forend are made of high-impact synthetic, and both feature integral tool-free access storage compartments for survival supplies and additional ammunition. A factory installed scope base as well as three-point integral sling swivels and a black nylon sling come as standard equipment. Available in either matte blue or electroless matte nickel for extra durability.

NEW ENGLAND FIREARMS

See manufacturers' addresses on page 250.

NEW CHOKE MEASURING TOOL

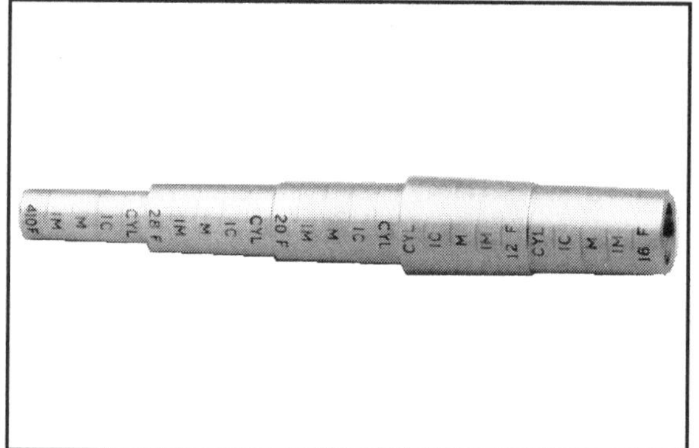

Galazan of New Britain Connecticut has just introduced an innovative new tool to measure the choke in 12-, 16-, 20-, 28-gauge and .410-bore shotguns. This compact $5\frac{1}{2}$", $3\frac{1}{2}$-ounce one-piece gauge accurately measures choke for each of the five most popular gauges. It features precision brass construction with bore choking clearly indicated for each of the five gauges. The newly designed choke gauge is easy to read and is calibrated to standard constriction designations of Cylinder (CYL), Improved Cylinder (IC), Modified (M), Improved Modified (IM) and Full (F). Manufactured in the United States, the 12/410 Choke Gauge is available from Galazan for $27.00. If you place an order and mention *Shooter's Marketplace*, you'll also receive the new *Galazan Quality Gun Products Catalog #2*.

GALAZAN

RIFLE/SHOTGUN SIGHT-IN VISE

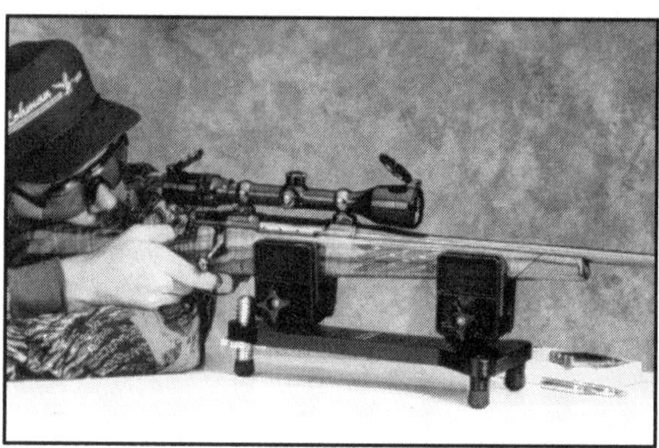

Ideal for any caliber firearm, the Sight-Vise SSV-2 from Lohman Game Call Company is a precision instrument that makes accurate rifle sighting and shotgun patterning easy. The Sight-Vise features adjustable dual clamps to hold the gun stock firmly, regardless of size or shape, and padded jaws to prevent stock marring. An adjustable rear post and wide stable base combine to reduce recoil and provide a solid rest for accurate, precise shotgun patterning or rifle sighting. For extra support and stability, lead shot can be added to the compartment in the base. The American-made SSV-2 also serves to secure guns for scope mounting, cleaning or repair work.

Contact Lohman for more information.

LOHMAN GAME CALL COMPANY

10/22 TARGET HAMMER

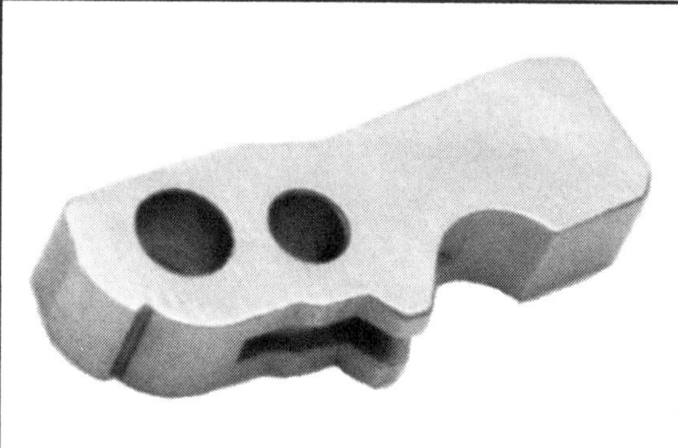

This new target hammer with replacement hammer spring from Volquartsen Custom is designed to give the stock Ruger 10/22 a superb "trigger job" by simply installing it in place of the factory hammer. No stoning or fitting is required to the sear or springs.

This hammer may appear similar to the production hammer, but is geometrically advanced in the sear engagement area. The hammers are heat-treated to achieve 60-61 Rc, then sapphire-honed for ultra smooth RMS. Trigger pull is reduced to $1\frac{1}{3}$ pounds to $1\frac{3}{4}$ pounds, depending on the gun.

The target hammer sells for $33.00 plus $4.00 shipping and handling, satisfaction guaranteed. To receive a catalog, send $4.00; mention *Shooter's Marketplace* and that catalog is yours for just $3.00.

VOLQUARTSEN CUSTOM LTD.

GUNSMITHING PROGRAM

The Pennsylvania Gunsmith School was founded in 1949 as a private vocational technical school specializing in gunsmithing. Their 2500-hour career-oriented program of study covers all major areas of rifle, shotgun, pistol and revolver function and design. Courses include bluing, stockmaking, rebarreling, sight mounting, machine work, reloading, ballistics, repairing and custom alterations. The type of work performed by the student during his course work is of the type typically performed by professional gunsmiths and is closely monitored and supervised by the PGS faculty. Pennsylvania Gunsmith School is accredited by the Accrediting Commission of Career Schools and Colleges of Technology. Financial assistance is available to those who qualify. Call or write PGS for more information.

PENNSYLVANIA GUNSMITH SCHOOL

See manufacturers' addresses on page 250.

AMBIDEXTROUS HANDGUN LASER

The BA-1 laser sight's ergonomic design allows it to perform flawlessly with the movements of the handgunner. Upgraded, sophisticated and easy to install, the BA-1 has been computer-designed to fit each handgun without any modification, while still remaining field-strippable. The ambidextrous bottom toggle switch allows turning the unit on and off while leaving a finger on the trigger. An optional slip-on Hogue grip with a pressure-sensitive switch is also available. The BA-1 is a true 5mW output and available with daytime laser diode. Laser Devices also offers leather duty holsters at a special price when laser and holster are purchased together. For an instruction video and/or catalog, contact Laser Devices and mention *Shooter's Marketplace*.

LASER DEVICES, INC.

PERSONAL DEFENSE AMMUNITION

Glaser Safety Slug's state-of-the-art, professional-grade personal defense ammunition is offered in two bullet styles: Blue uses a #12 compressed shot core for maximum ricochet protection; and Silver uses a #6 compressed shot core for maximum penetration.

The Glaser Safety Slug manufacturing process results in outstanding accuracy with documented groups of less than 1″ at 100 yards. This is one reason Glaser has been a top choice of professional and private law enforcement agencies worldwide for more than sixteen years.

Currently available in every caliber from 25 ACP through 30-06, plus 40 S&W, 10mm, 223 and 7.62x39.

Write Glaser Safety Slug for a free brochure.

GLASER SAFETY SLUG, INC.

NEW LASER SIGHT SYSTEM

Laser Devices, Inc. has recently introduced its new Universal Laser System, the ULS-2001 laser sight and tactical light combination. The system features a quick-detachable laser housing and universal mount to fit most popular semi-automatic pistols. The quick-detachable tactical light provides four hours of continuous battery life and has a bright 84-lumen Xenon bulb. It can be removed from the laser housing without affecting sight alignment or functioning of the pistol. The laser sight has easy-to-access external windage and elevation adjustments and is activated through either a toggle switch, optional Hogue grip and/or optional patented tactical thumb switch. The ULS-2001 system is also available with their Super Power Point™, an option that offers laser visibility up to 45 yards in sunlight conditions. Call or write for more information.

LASER DEVICES, INC.

STOCK KIT AND BIPOD

Glaser's MG-42 Stock Kit transforms your Ruger 10/22™ into a 2/3-scale semi-auto replica of the WWII MG-42 machine gun. The lightweight MG-42 stock fully encloses the 10/22 receiver and barrel to give the appearance and feel of the original machine gun. Ventilation slots in the barrel shroud provide barrel cooling just like the original, and front and rear sights come with adjustments for both windage and elevation. Fully assembled, the replica weighs no more than the original 10/22, maintains excellent balance and has the feel and appearance of a totally new gun. For authenticity, a Featherweight Bipod can be added to enhance prone and bench shooting accuracy. No alterations to the 10/22 are required and the old stock can be replaced in minutes. For a free brochure, contact Glaser Safety Slug.

GLASER SAFETY SLUG, INC.

See manufacturers' addresses on page 250.

PRECISION RIFLE REST

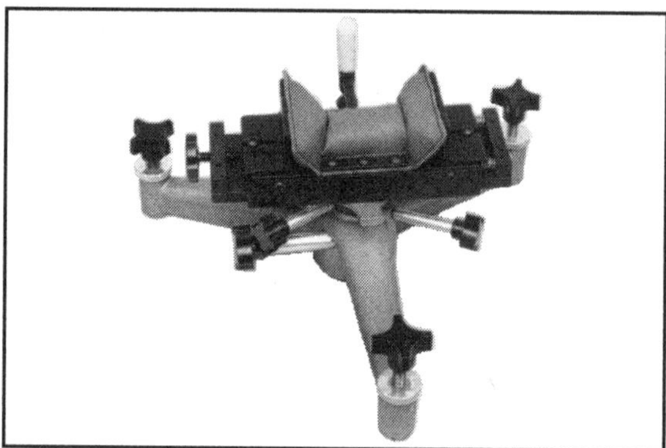

Bald Eagle Precision Machine Co. offers a rifle rest perfect for the serious benchrester or the dedicated varminter.

The rest is constructed of aircraft-quality aluminum and weighs 7 pounds, 12 ounces. It's finished with three coats of Imron Clear. Height adjustments are made with a rack and pinion and a mariner wheel. A fourth leg allows lateral movement on the bench.

Bald Eagle offers approximately 56 rest models to choose from, including windage adjustments, right or left hand, cast aluminum or cast iron. The Standard Rest with rifle stop and bag is pictured above.

Prices: $99.95 to $260.00. For more information or a free brochure, contact Bald Eagle.

BALD EAGLE PRECISION MACHINE CO.

RIMFIRE CARTRIDGE GAGE

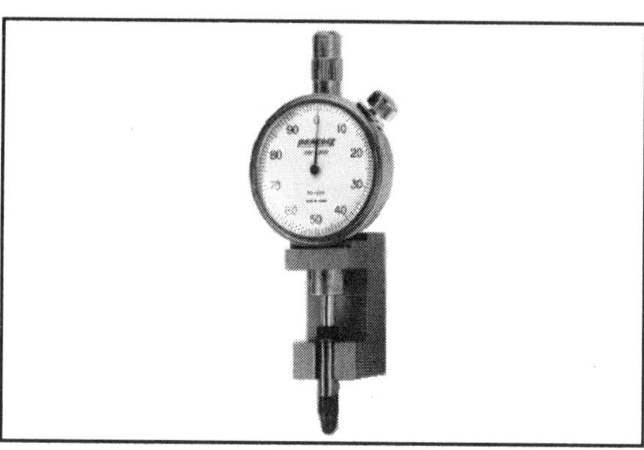

The Rimfire Cartridge Gage from Bald Eagle Precision Machine Co. can improve overall group size by up to 25% by sorting rimfire ammo into uniform rim-thickness lots.

The more consistent the rim thickness, the more consistent the ignition of the primer and powder charge, and the firing pin travel remains uniform from shot-to-shot.

The Cartridge Gage is a snap to use—grab a box or two of rimfire ammo and start sorting. It is ideal for BR-50 benchrest competitors and serious small game hunters.

Normally $80.00, mention *Shooter's Marketplace* and it's only $74.95. Write Bald Eagle for a free brochure.

BALD EAGLE PRECISION MACHINE CO.

FREE CHRONOGRAPH CATALOG

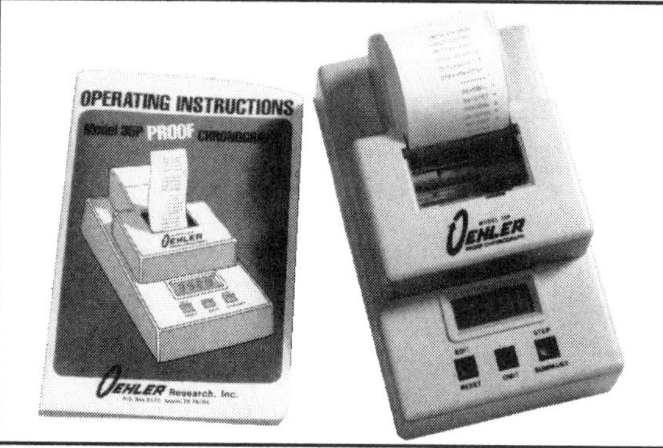

Oehler Research, Inc. offers shooters and reloaders their encyclopedic catalog of ballistic test equipment free of charge. This 40-page catalog describes and illustrates Oehler's family of ballistic testing equipment, from reliable chronographs for handloaders to their personal ballistics laboratory, a computer-based system that calculates and integrates chamber pressure, muzzle and downrange velocity and acoustic target measurements. Used by industry and military laboratories, Oehler's ballistic laboratory is invaluable for serious load development and costs little more than a good factory rifle with scope. For the serious handloader and hunter, Oehler offers their Ballistic Explorer exterior ballistics software. Available for both DOS and Windows, the programs have established a reputation for both ease of use and technical accuracy.

OEHLER RESEARCH, INC.

HIGH SECURITY PISTOL SAFE

NESCI Enterprises offers the handgunner a high-security safe for the storage of handguns, cash or small valuables. Constructed from A-36 steel tubing and entirely tig-welded, the Cash & Pistol Stash safe will resist most types of cutting or prying and has a fire-resistant factor of approximately one-half hour. Locking is accomplished with a high-security tubular lock. Available in three compact sizes, 4″x4″x8″, 4″x6″x8″ or 4″x6″x10″, the unit can be bolted to the inside of a drawer, on a closet shelf, under furniture or other concealed locations. Two 3/8″ bolt holes in the bottom of the safe and fasteners supplied with each unit allow secure installation. An optional mounting plate is available. For delivery and price information, call or write NESCI Enterprises.

NESCI ENTERPRISES, INC.

See manufacturers' addresses on page 250.

NEW ULTRA LASER SIGHTS

Quarton USA is now offering the Beamshot™ 1000S and 1000U laser sights. The 650nm 1000 Super is five times brighter than standard Beamshot Lasersights; the 635nm 1000 Ultra is ten times brighter for long-range visibility range of 800 yards. Both laser sights are powered by a single 3-volt lithium battery, providing up to 20 hours of continuous usage.

Made of aircraft-grade 6061 aluminum, both lasersights have a window lens, are available in black or silver, have windage and elevation adjustments and come with mounts for rifle, pistol, revolver, shotgun or crossbow. The 1000S and 1000U are easily holstered and come with a 1-year warranty. Longer cable switches are available. Call, write or fax Quarton USA for a free copy of their brochure.

QUARTON USA, LTD. CO.

NEW BORE SIGHTING KIT

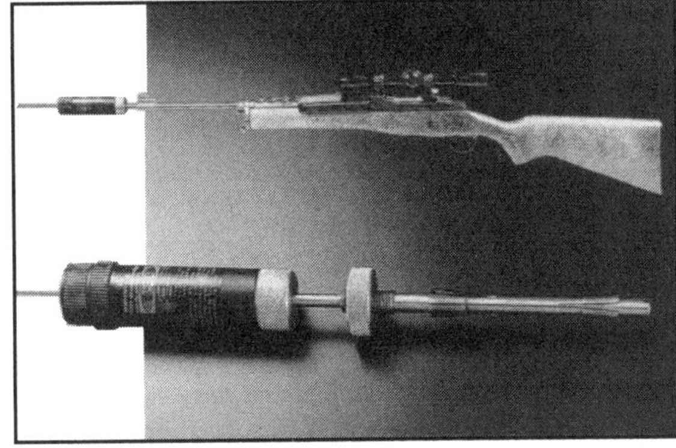

A new high-tech Laser Bore Sighting Kit is now available from Quarton USA, manufacturers of the Beamshot™ line of lasersights.

The kit consists of three parts, available either in kit form or sold separately. The three parts are the Arbor #1, for .22″ through .264″ diameter bullets; the Arbor #2, for .264″ through .308″ diameter bullets; and the bore sight laser.

This Laser Bore Sighting Kit provides an easy, inexpensive way to bore sight a rifle before taking it to the range. Sighting-in before you get to the range saves both time and ammunition.

For more information about any of their products or for a free copy of their brochure, contact Quarton USA and mention *Shooter's Marketplace*.

QUARTON USA, LTD. CO.

NEW LONG-RANGE LASER SIGHT

The Beamshot™ 1000 from Quarton USA is a long-range laser sight precision-engineered for acute accuracy and performance plus rugged durability. Constructed of aircraft-grade 6061 aluminum, the Beamshot's pin-point laser sight is activated by an adjustable pressure switch mounted on the handgrip. With a single 3-volt lithium battery providing up to 20 hours of continuous use, the super lightweight 1000 has 670nm wave length, windage and elevation adjustments and range to 300 yards. It is easily holstered, is available in black or silver and comes with a 1-year warranty. The Beamshot 1000 comes standard with one mount. Easily interchangeable, extra mounts may be purchased to fit most any pistol, revolver, rifle, shotgun, crossbow or compound bow. Call, write or fax Quarton USA for a free copy of their brochure.

QUARTON USA, LTD. CO.

NEW MINIATURE LASERSIGHT

Quarton USA introduces the newest member of its Beamshot™ lasersight family. The Beamshot 3000S represents a high-quality lasersight in a more convenient, miniature model. The ultra lightweight 3000S adds only 2 ounces of total weight to any large or small gun and is powered with three SR44 silver oxide watch batteries to allow for a minimum of four hours of continuous usage. Constructed from aircraft-grade aluminum, the 3000S is adjustable for windage and elevation and has a range to 500 yards. Complete with black finish and window lens, the 3000S fits existing Beamshot mounts and is easily holstered. This Beamshot lasersight comes with a 1-year limited warranty. Contact Quarton USA for a free copy of their brochure.

QUARTON USA, LTD. CO.

See manufacturers' addresses on page 250.

SAFARI SLING

Boonie Packer's Safari Sling attaches easily to both 1″ and 1¼″ swivels interchangeably and allows rifles and shotguns to be carried upright in front of or at the side of the body. The patented design allows hunters to quickly bring their guns up and aim because there is nothing to undo or release.

The sling, which has been adopted by the U.S. military, stays securely on the shoulder and allows hunters' hands to be free, which reduces fatigue and permits them to perform other tasks, such as use binoculars. The sling also works well with backpacks.

The 2″-wide carrying strap is available in Black, Woodland Camo, Realtree™ Camo and Blaze Orange. Write or call for free literature.

BOONIE PACKER PRODUCTS

TARGET SCOPES

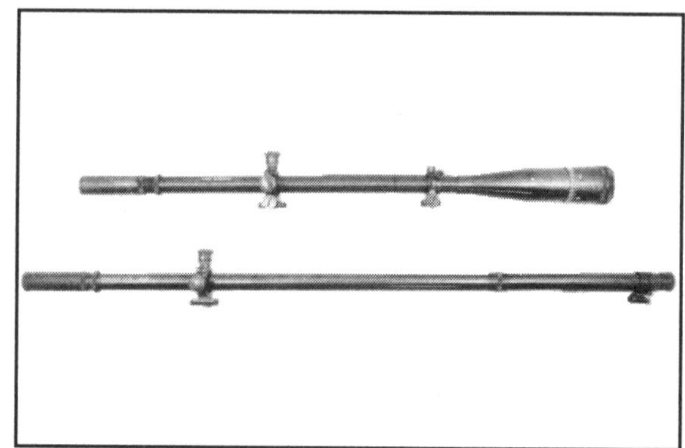

Parsons Optical offers two high-grade target scopes—the Lyman Super Targetspot and the Parsons Long Scope. Manufactured completely in the U.S., both scopes are all blued steel and use the finest of coated optics.

The Super Targetspot is made using original Lyman blueprints and in all the original powers. It comes with steel mounts, lens caps, rubber eye cup and three-point suspension rear mount with ¼-micrometer click adjustments. The Long Scope, designed by Gil Parsons, uses turn-of-the-century specifications, but with modern improvements. Available in 6x only and in lengths beginning at 28″, it comes with blued steel mounts and four-point suspension rear mount with micrometer click adjustments. Accessories for both scopes are available. Parsons also operates a full-service repair shop.

PARSONS OPTICAL MFG. CO.

VENTILATED SHOTGUN RIBS

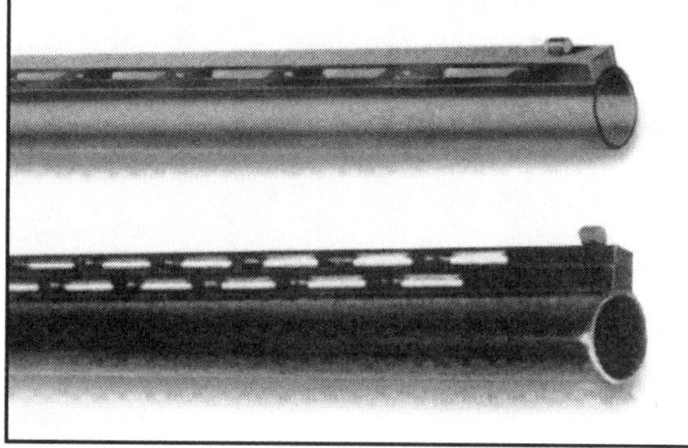

Adding Marble Arms' Poly-Choke® anodized, ventilated rib to your over/under, pump, semi-automatic or single shot shotgun will help you get on target more quickly and easily. The rib weighs less than two ounces, is factory installed with no drilling or tapping of the barrel and comes with mid and front sights in a choice of colors. The cost is a mere $79.75 installed, plus shipping. The High Rise International rib with or without taper can be installed on a plain barrel for $190.00 or a top rib installed on an existing rib for $95.00, plus shipping. There is a three-to-four day turn-around on all installations. For a free catalog and information on Poly-Choke adjustable chokes, rifle and shotgun sights and many other firearm accessories, write, fax or call Marble Arms.

MARBLE ARMS

NEW SCOPE MOUNT

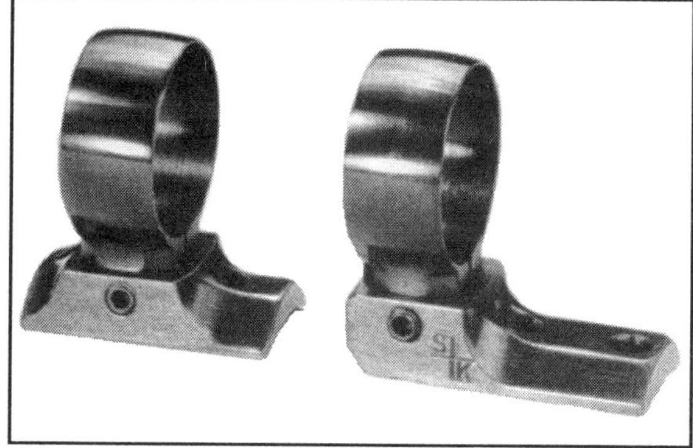

S&K Manufacturing Co. offers their new scope mount with SKulptured Base and Smooth Kontoured Rings for most factory drilled and tapped rifles.

Available in stainless steel, matte or polished blued finish, the mounts feature front and rear base windage adjustments and ring interchangeability. In addition there are no projections, bulges, lobes or joints and no ring halves to join together with fragile caps.

Made from steel, the base weighs approximately 1 ounce, the rings ½-ounce each. They are not interchangeable with any other brands.

S&K carries a complete inventory for all popular rifles. The mounts come with a lifetime guarantee. For a current catalog, send $1.00 to S&K Manufacturing Co.

S&K MANUFACTURING CO.

See manufacturers' addresses on page 250.

NEW BIG-BORE SUB-COMPACT SEMI-AUTO

European American Armory offers the Spanish-made Astra A-75, a sub-compact semi-automatic pistol with big-bore firepower. Available in 9mm, 40 S&W, 45 ACP, it features dimensions and weight of a sub-compact—3½″ barrel; 6½″ (9mm, 40 S&W) or 6¾″ (45 ACP) overall length; 1¼″ width; and weight of 23½-oz. for the Featherweight model to 34¼-oz. for the 45 ACP. Its size, weight and caliber choices make it an ideal back-up, carry or home-defense pistol. Other features include double/single action firing, decocker carry system, three dot sights, internal firing pin block, checkered frame and trigger guard, and optional caliber conversion kits. Available in matte blue, satin nickel or stainless steel finish. Comes with a limited lifetime warranty and has a suggested retail price starting at under $350.00.

EUROPEAN AMERICAN ARMORY CORP.

BIG BORE REVOLVER

The Bounty Hunter from European American Armory Corp. is a Western-style single-action revolver that has the look and feel of the original single actions that won the West. Featuring solid steel German construction, it combines the traditional three frame screws, hammer loading position, fixed sights and cylinder bushing reminiscent of the originals with modern safety features, including a transfer bar firing system and recessed chambers. The Bounty Hunter is offered in a choice of four calibers—357 Mag./38 Special, 44 Mag., 45 Long Colt—and two barrel lengths, 4½″ or 7½″. The finish options include either an overall deep polished blue, or color case-hardened receiver with blued cylinder and barrel. The Bounty Hunter comes with a limited lifetime warranty and has a suggested retail price of under $300.00.

EUROPEAN AMERICAN ARMORY CORP.

RELIABLE AND DURABLE SEMI-AUTO

The Witness semi-automatic pistol imported by European Armory Corp. is world renown for its quality and durability. Featuring precision-machined forged steel frames, cut-rifled barrels and cold-drawn barstock slides, the Witness is available in four calibers, 9mm, 40 S&W, 38 Super and 45 ACP; two frame sizes, standard or competition; and two frame styles, full-size or sub-compact. Magazine capacity for the full-size models range from 10+1 in 40 S&W and 45 ACP to a limited supply of high-capacity 15+1 and 19+1 magazines for the 9mm and 38 Super, respectively. The sub-compact models carry 10+1 in 9mm, 9+1 in 40 S&W and 8+1 in 45 ACP. Witness models come in either blue or Wonder finish, a stainless steel-like finish, and carry E.A.A.'s limited lifetime warranty. The suggested retail price starts at a reasonable $350.00.

EUROPEAN AMERICAN ARMORY CORP.

TOUGH DA SERVICE REVOLVER

The Windicator from European American Armory is made in Germany by the HWM Company. This tough double-action revolver is available in 357 Magnum or 38 Special with six-shot capacity. Weighing in at 30 ounces, it features 2″ or 4″ barrels, an internal firing pin block safety, all steel firing train, modular trigger assembly, floating firing pin, long coil mainspring, heavy-duty crane, grooved target trigger and knurled cylinder release latch and hammer spur. The sights are adjustable low-profile for non-snag carry and come as standard equipment on some models. The thumbrest finger-grooved rubber grips give the Windicator a sure and hefty feel. Covered by E.A.A.'s Limited Lifetime Warranty, the Windicator comes reasonably priced at a starting suggested retail of $185.00.

EUROPEAN AMERICAN ARMORY CORP.

See manufacturers' addresses on page 250.

SHOOTING GLASSES

The Randolph Ranger shooting glass is one of the finest eye protection systems available for the shooting sports. With frames built of rugged monel 400 steel, the Ranger features 2.5mm polycarbonate lenses which are designed to withstand a 12-gauge shotgun blast from 12 meters. Choose any three of the ten lens colors offered: clear, yellow, canary, orange, sunset, vermilion, purple, brown, bronze, or gray. Ranger shooting glasses are available in two finishes—23k gold-plate or matte black and come packed in a hard-shell belt clip case. The Ranger can be purchased with the three-lens system or as Rx frame only for prescription wearers. For more information, write, call or fax Randolph Engineering, or see your local gun dealer or sporting goods store.

RANDOLPH ENGINEERING, INC.

AVIATOR GLASSES

The Aviators are genuine U.S. military-issue sunglasses (mil-spec 25948) made only by Randolph Engineering. The glasses combine safety, comfort, and visual acuity and are built to exacting military standards. Randolph Aviators offer maximum glare-checking UV-absorbing ophthalmic crown glass. These lenses are crystal clear and offer the highest level of UV protection available. Crafted in the U.S.A., Aviator frames come with a lifetime warranty against frame/joint separation. Aviators come in several frame colors, temples and lens combinations.

For more information, call or write Randolph Engineering. Be sure and mention *Shooter's Marketplace.*

RANDOLPH ENGINEERING, INC.

GUN PARTS CATALOG

The Gun Parts Corp. is one of the world's largest suppliers of gun parts, and this year introduces its newly updated 20th Edition Catalog—a standard reference for gunsmiths, shooters, collectors and for military organizations worldwide.

Its 750-plus pages contain complete listings and prices for more than 500 million gun parts currently in stock.

Machinegun, military, U.S., foreign, commercial and antique gun parts are included, as well as hundreds of schematic drawings.

To order, U.S. customers send $7.95; foreign surface mail orders $13.00; airmail delivery $25.00.

THE GUN PARTS CORP.

MULTI-CALIBER ADAPTERS

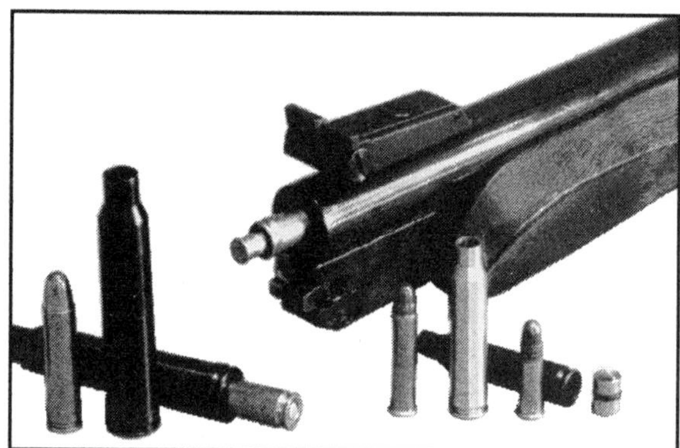

MCA Sports offers adapters and conversion devices for all types of firearms, including inserts for break-open shotguns and chamber adapters for rifles and pistols.

These inserts/adapters add versatility to any firearm. Big-bore shooters can practice on urban indoor ranges or take small game using the same rifle they used for big game hunting. For survival purposes, these adapters are unequaled, allowing a single rifle or pistol to fire a variety of ammunition. Wildcat and odd calibers are their specialty.

Write for prices; hundreds of combinations available. Offered in blue or stainless steel. Send self-addressed, stamped envelope (52¢ postage) to MCA Sports for information.

MCA SPORTS

See manufacturers' addresses on page 250.

NEW 30MM RIFLESCOPE

Swarovski's 6-24x50 30mm riflescope is designed for long-range competition, hunting and varmint shooting. Its precise 1/6" click adjustments and large internal optics yield optimum accuracy and twilight performance. The light, one-piece alloy tube has a 50m to infinity parallax adjustment ring and an exclusive, reticle suspension system with four coil springs for extreme accuracy with any rifle caliber. The reticle is positioned in the second image plane and thus retains the same size at all power settings. The 6-24x50 scope is nitrogen filled and sealed to be waterproof and submersible with the target turret caps removed and comes with a warranty to back it up. For a free catalog and the name of their nearest dealer call Swarovski Optik toll-free.

SWAROVSKI OPTIK NORTH AMERICA LTD.

HAMMER SHROUDS FOR HANDGUNS

W. Waller & Son, Inc. offers hammer shrouds for Smith & Wesson J-frame and Colt D-frame revolvers. Available in blue or stainless steel finish, the hammer shrouds are precision, aluminum investment castings finished to Waller's exacting specifications and standards. The S&W J-frame shrouds will fit the Chief's Special Models 36, 37 and 60 plus the LadySmith revolvers. The Colt D-frame version fits the Detective Special, Agent, Cobra and other Colts, from the earliest models with exposed ejector rods to their newest stainless models.

Retail price is $49.95 plus $4.00 for UPS-insured ground shipping in the contiguous U.S. For more information, call or write W. Waller & Sons or visit their Web site on the Internet.

W. WALLER & SON INC.

CLAY TARGET TRAPS

Trius Traps offers shotgunners low-cost, easy-cocking mechanical clay target traps. Lay-on loading of singles, doubles and piggy-back doubles makes it possible to launch four birds in the air at one time. For the casual shooter, Trius offers four models: the Birdshooter, a quality trap at an affordable price; the Model 92 with high angle clip and can-thrower; the TrapMaster with sit-down comfort and pivoting action; and the New Trius 1-Step. The innovative 1-Step offers cocking and target release in one easy, effortless motion. Set the arm and place the targets on the arm without tension. Stepping on the trap's pedal puts tension on the arm and launches targets in one continuous motion. To receive a free catalog for more information on these models plus their Sporting Clays line of traps, contact Trius.

TRIUS TRAPS, INC.

MARINER'S BAG

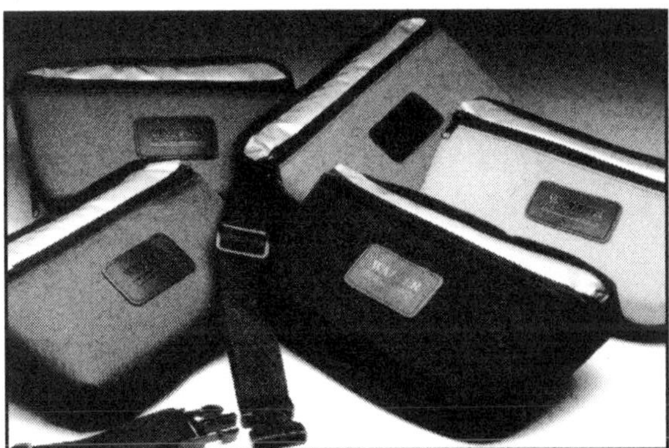

Created to meet the needs of law enforcement agents assigned to maritime duties, the floatable Mariner™ bag protects and reduces the risk of losing your valuables should they go overboard. It can support the weight of a full-size handgun, spare magazine, knife, pocket flashlight, handcuffs, keys, badge and ID, and the reflective silver band sewn across the top of the bag increases the chance of recovery in low light. Made of water repellent materials, the Mariner features two separate padded, zippered compartments for securing valuables without shifting. The mil-spec adjustable web belt and parachute-style quick release buckle secures the bag around the waist. Available in black, dark gray, arctic blue, safety yellow and international orange, the Mariner retails for $58.00 plus $6.00 UPS-insured ground shipping in the contiguous U.S.

W. WALLER & SON, INC.

See manufacturers' addresses on page 250.

22 RIMFIRE ACCURACY GAUGE

The 22 Rimfire Accuracy Gauge from Neil Jones Custom Products measures the thickness of the cartridge rim and enables ammunition to be sorted for consistent headspacing. The use of this gauge helps eliminate flyers, which results in smaller groups.

The rimfire gauge has been used for 15 years by thousands of satisfied customers. It is 100% safe, with nothing to wear out or break. It is easily modified for use with 22 Rimfire Magnum ammunition.

Shooter's Marketplace readers can send for a free catalog of prices and information on this and other Neil Jones accuracy products for shooters and handloaders.

NEIL JONES CUSTOM PRODUCTS

NEW CHRONOGRAPHS

Shooting Chrony announces their new Master Line of chronographs for shooters, reloaders and bowhunters. Master Chronys are available either as an up-grade option for owners of their F-2, Alpha-, Beta-, Delta- or Gamma-Chrony or come as complete units. Featuring a new 1/2″ LCD readout remote control unit with 16″ cord, the Master Chrony allows shooters to bring shot velocities and statistics directly to the shooting bench. To up-grade your Shooting Chrony chronograph to the Master version, send your unit to their U.S. address along with $30.00 plus $5.00 shipping and handling. Complete Master Chrony units start at a retail price of $109.95. For more information and a free brochure, call, fax or write Shooting Chrony.

SHOOTING CHRONY INC.

TELESCOPING BIPODS

Stoney Point's new shooting rests set up quickly, providing hunters with a steady, accurate shot on any type of terrain. The tempered-aluminum, tri-section legs telecope from 15″ to 38″ (Ultra-Light model—$42.50) or from 25″ to 67″ (Extra-Height model—$55.50) and lock in place with a half-turn twist to provide the height needed for shooting over vegetation and ground contours. Their compact, lightweight design assures quick set-up for sitting, kneeling or squatting shots, or stand-up shots if using the Extra-Height model. A multi-function rest top permits instant leg angle adjustments and allows the firearm to pivot in the cushion-foam "V"-shaped cradle for rapid sight alignment and the tracking of moving game. An optional belt clip attaches the rests to belt or sling for field carry. From your local dealer or Stoney Point.

STONEY POINT PRODUCTS, INC.

QUALITY GUNSTOCK BLANKS

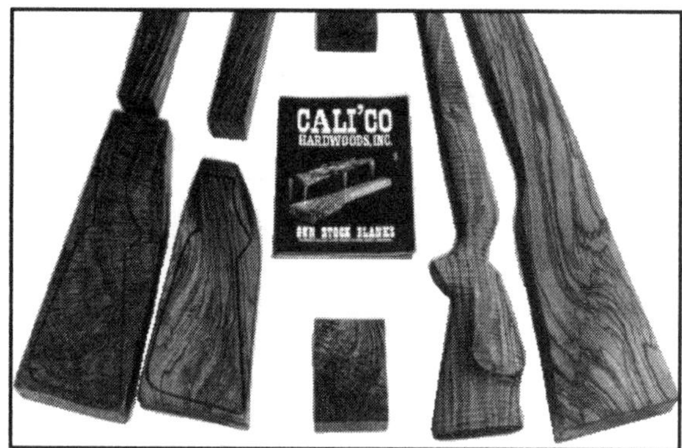

Cali'co Hardwoods has been cutting superior-quality shotgun and rifle blanks for more than 31 years. Cali'co supplies blanks to many of the major manufacturers—Browning, Weatherby, Ruger, Holland & Holland, to name a few—as well as custom gunsmiths the world over.

Profiled rifle blanks are available, ready for inletting and sanding. Cali'co sells superior California hardwoods in Claro walnut, French walnut, Bastogne, maple and myrtle.

Cali'co offers good, serviceable blanks and some of the finest exhibition blanks available. Satisfaction guaranteed.

Color catalog, retail and dealer price list (FFL required) free upon request.

CALI'CO HARDWOODS, INC.

See manufacturers' addresses on page 250.

RUGER 10/22® TARGET BARREL

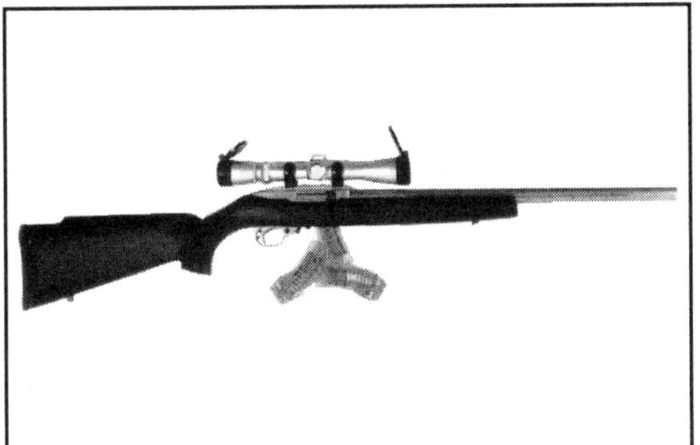

Butler Creek is offering their new Ruger 10/22® target barrels and matching stocks either as individual accessories or as a combination package.

The 20″ barrels include a Bentz/Match chamber to ensure top accuracy and have proven MOA groups of 1/2″ at 50 yards. Available in blued and stainless steel, fluted and non-fluted, all barrels are .920″ in diameter.

The 10/22 target stock offers true drop-in fit and includes a fuller forearm, semi-Monte Carlo comb for scope mounting, palm swells, raised checkering and swivel studs. Suggested retail for the target barrel is $119.00 to $219.00; target barrel stock, $94.00; the combination package of stock and barrel, $196.00 to $304.00. Call or write for more information.

BUTLER CREEK CORPORATION

NEW RIFLE SLING

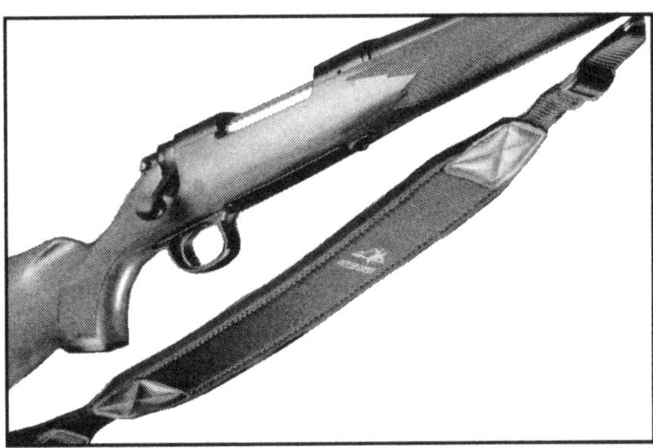

Butler Creek introduces their new Highlander™ Rifle Sling for North American hunters.

The newly patented design combines comfort with style offering an internal controlled-stretch sling design with two layers of neoprene padding, finished seams and sewn edging. A top-quality black leather panel has been added at each end for additonal strength and support.

Butler Creek's Highlander comes with a Lifetime Warranty and is available at a suggested retail price of $29.95.

For more information, call or write Butler Creek Corporation.

Be sure and mention *Shooter's Marketplace*.

BUTLER CREEK CORPORATION

QUALITY VARIABLE RIFLESCOPES

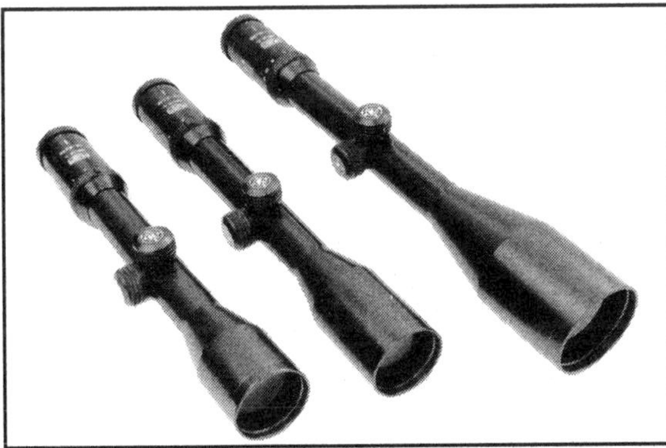

For over 100 years, Kahles of Vienna, Austria has provided premium-quality variable-power riflescopes at the lowest possible price for hunters and sportsmen worldwide. Three 30mm models are available to American shooters, the 1.5x42, 2.2-9x42 and 3-12x56. These scopes are rugged, extremely accurate, dependable and as bright or brighter than other traditional European riflescopes. Each features an etched glass reticle for zero impact shift when changing magnifications; parallax free shooting with factory preset at 109 yards; anti-reflection transmax coating; hammered aluminum main tubes; full four-time magnification factor with fast, focus adjustment ring; and fogproof and waterproof body. Call Swarovski Optik toll-free for a catalog and the name of their nearest dealer.

SWAROVSKI OPTIK NORTH AMERICA LTD.

GATLING GUN BUILDER'S PACKAGE

Complete plans for the 22-caliber Long Rifle Gatling are now available and have been fully adapted to incorporate obtainable materials and makeable parts. No castings are required.

The to-scale blueprints are fully dimensioned and toleranced. A 40-page instruction booklet lists materials and explains each part and how it is made.

The package includes drawings and instructions for making rifled barrels, wooden spoked wheels and all internal parts. The finished piece has 10 rifled barrels and is 3 feet long by 2 feet high.

Plans for the gun and carriage are $58.56; priority postage within the U.S. included. Overseas air add $14.00. Materials kits also available. Major credit cards, check or money order accepted. Include a self-addressed card.

R.G.-G., INC.

See manufacturers' addresses on page 250.

NEW RELOADING MANUAL

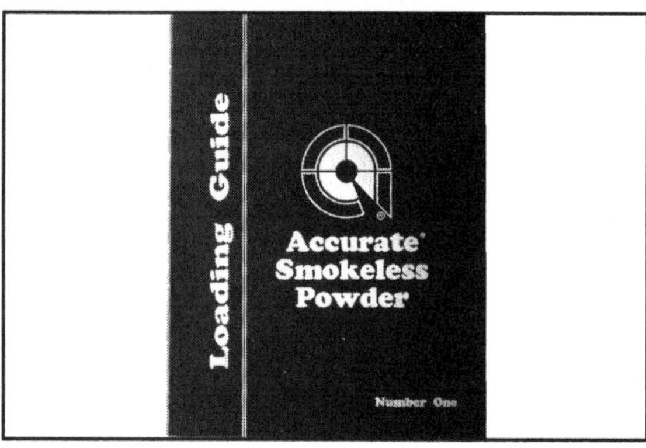

Accurate Arms' *Accurate Smokeless Powder Loading Guide, Number One* is the first reloading manual to receive an Award of Merit from *American Firearms Industry*. Packed with all the information a serious handloader needs, this 345-page guide provides load data for popular pistol and rifle cartridges from the 25 ACP to the 50 Browning and most everything in between with special attention given to obsolete and blackpowder cartridges. Articles contributed by well-recognized shooting sports writers cover the important facets of the art of reloading. The *Accurate Smokeless Powder Loading Guide, Number One* is available at most gun shops or from your local reloading supplies dealer. For the dealer nearest you or to order Accurate Arms' reloading guide by phone, call their toll-free Customer Service Line.

ACCURATE ARMS COMPANY, INC.

CASE GAUGE

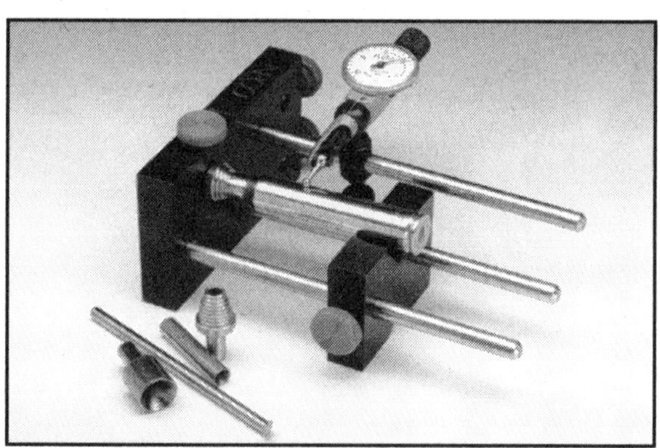

The NECO Concentricity, Wall Thickness and Runout Gauge™ identifies and measures the imperfections in brass cartridge cases, case head squareness, bullets and loaded ammunition. It verifies possible accuracy problems caused by imperfections in rifle chambers, sizing and bullet seating dies and/or reloading techniques. Handmade to precision tolerances from solid stainless steel and hard-anodized aluminum, it is equipped with a Gem Model 222 all-angle dial indicator, two removable guides for bullet tips, two step cones for empty cases, a chord anvil for case wall thickness measurements and an instruction manual. Standard model handles 22 to 45-70 cartridge cases (17-caliber and 50 BMG models also available) and retails for $137.15 plus shipping.

NECO/NOSTALGIA ENTERPRISES COMPANY

RIFLE, PISTOL AND SHOTSHELL POWDERS

Accurate Arms offers a full line of pistol, rifle and shotshell propellants for handloaders. Whether reloading for hunting, competition or just practice, Accurate Arms propellants have been formulated to meet your needs. Their disc, flake, ball and extruded powders offer burning speeds for all popular cartridges as well as some of the more esoteric. Four burning speed formulations are available for shotshell and pistol reloaders plus twelve more geared specifically to the rifle-class cartridge. For the rifle cartridge reloader, two types of propellants are available—ball propellants, including the popular Accurate 2230, and the newly updated X-truded™ line, featuring Accurate's versatile XMP-5744 powder. For more information, to place an order or for a free copy of their reloading booklet, call their toll-free Customer Service Line or write them direct.

ACCURATE ARMS COMPANY, INC.

FULLY-ADJUSTABLE PISTOL SIGHTS

Last year Miniature Machine Corp. (MMC) introduced their new line of low-profile, snag-free, fully-adjustable pistol sights designed for Glocks, Colt 1911s and H&K USPs. Machined from 4140 steel and heat-treated to 40 Rc for rugged durability, these sights provide a target-quality sight picture. The sights feature MMC's patented eccentric cam elevation mechanism with twenty-two positive detent positions. The sturdy ears are machined integral to the base to protect the target-quality blade. This year, MMC added three new models for S&W semi-automatic pistols, including the Sigma. Premium finishes of high-density Teflon from Rocky Mountain Arms and 400 stainless steel are now available for most models. They have also introduced a Banded Tactical Shotgun Front Sight with Tritium to complement their Ghost Ring Rear Sight.

MINIATURE MACHINE CORP.

See manufacturers' addresses on page 250.

NEW HIGH VISIBILITY TARGETS

Birchwood Casey introduces their new Shoot·N·C™ high-visibility, self-adhesive target system. Featuring a fluorescent background with flat black coating, the targets allow bullet holes to be seen instantly. As the bullet strikes the target, the black coating gives way to the fluorescent background, leaving a bright halo effect around each bullet hole. Shoot·N·C targets allow shooters to make immediate sight corrections, even during rapid fire. They are excellent for indoor and outdoor range use in both bright and low light conditions. Shoot·N·C targets are available in six sizes: 3″, 5½″ and 8″ round bull's-eyes for rifles; or 4″, 7″ and 9″ oval silhouettes for handguns. For more information see your local dealer or call Birchwood Casey's toll-free number and receive a free catalog and sample target sheet.

BIRCHWOOD CASEY

PRECISION RELOADING DIES

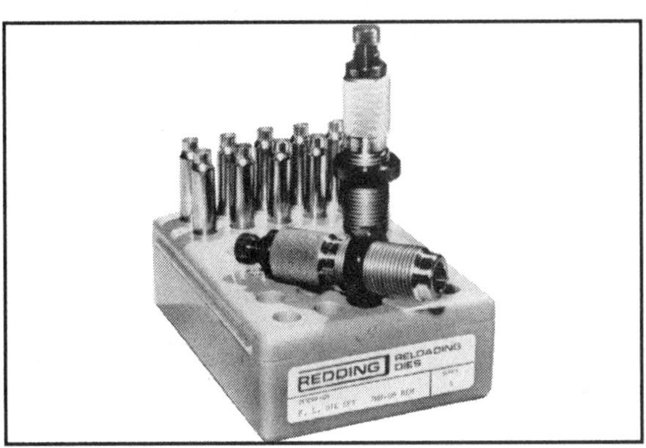

REDDING has built a reputation equal to the quality of the reloading gear they produce, and they continue to expand their line of reloading dies.

Their newest introduction is a line of bushing-style neck sizing dies with interchangeable sizing bushings in .001″ increments from 17 through 30-caliber.

The latest catalog from REDDING lists dies for over 400 different calibers and a whole host of special-purpose dies. There are competition seating and neck-sizing dies, special purpose crimping dies, trim dies, custom-made dies and a section on case-forming that lists everything you need to form one caliber from another.

Write, call or fax REDDING to receive their latest catalog.

REDDING RELOADING EQUIPMENT

PREMIUM BIG GAME SCOPE

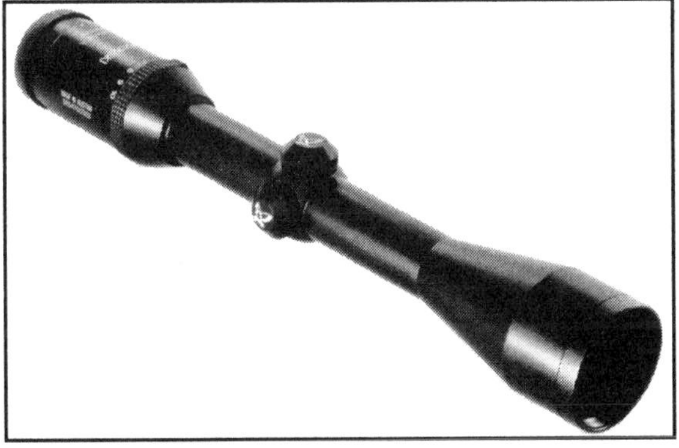

This American-style 3-10x42mm rifle scope from Swarovski Optik is engineered for bean field, black timber and Eastern brush and hill hunting. The 42mm objective lens and Swarotop™ multi-coatings on all lens surfaces transmit more light in the early morning or late afternoon than most other scopes sporting a 50mm objective lens.

Light in weight, fully shock-proof and waterproof, even when submerged, Swarovski Optik's 3-10x42mm riflescope is known for its precision and accuracy. It is truly a riflescope for all game and all seasons and comes complete with a warranty to back it up.

For a free catalog and the name of their nearest dealer, call Swarovski Optik's toll-free number. Be sure and mention *Shooter's Marketplace.*

SWAROVSKI OPTIK NORTH AMERICA LTD.

COMPETITION POWDER MEASURES

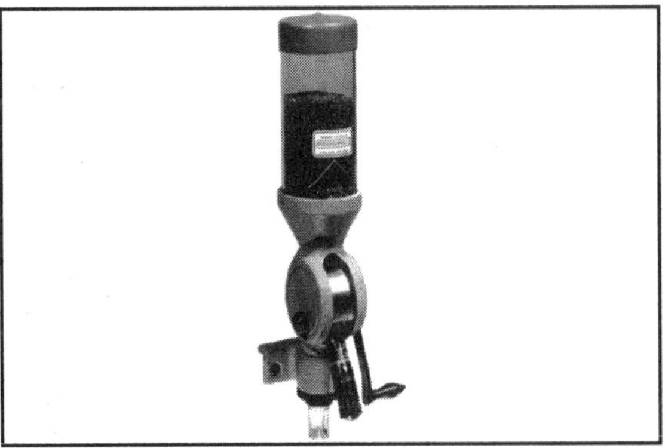

REDDING powder measures have earned a dedicated following among benchrest shooters. Featuring close tolerance, hand-fitted drums and super-accurate micrometer adjustments, REDDING measures are designed for reloaders who strive for top accuracy from their handloads.

Their newest BR-30 Competition Model has a reduced diameter, cup-shaped metering cavity that minimizes irregular powder settling and enhances charge-to-charge uniformity. Designed specifically for benchrest competition, the BR-30 is also popular among silhouette shooters and varmint hunters. Its charging range is limited to approxmately 10 to 50 grains with optimum uniformity at about 30 grains. Write, call or fax REDDING for their latest catalog.

REDDING RELOADING EQUIPMENT

See manufacturers' addresses on page 250.

ADJUSTABLE DISC APERTURE

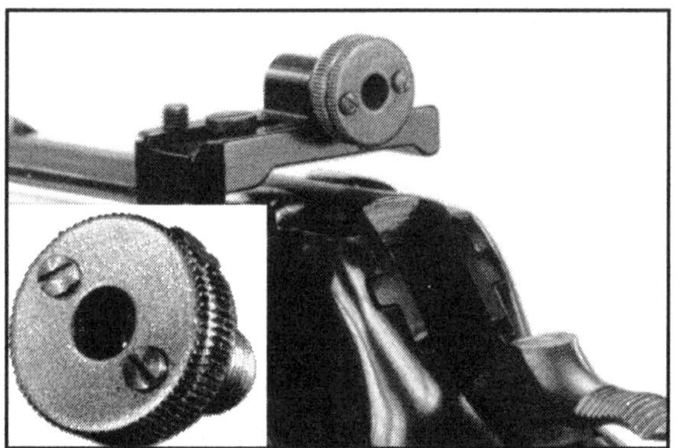

Hunters in the field are constantly faced with continually changing light conditions. A receiver sight with a fixed aperture is adequate for only one light condition.

The Merit Hunting Disc aperture is instantly adjustable from .025- to .155-inch in diameter, allowing a clear sight picture to be maintained under changing light conditions.

The aperture leaves are supported to withstand recoil from heavy calibers, and the shank is tapered to provide solid lockup of the disc to your receiver sight.

Contact Merit Corp. for a free copy of their brochure describing this and other sighting aids for shooters.

MERIT CORPORATION

SHOOTING GLASSES APERTURE

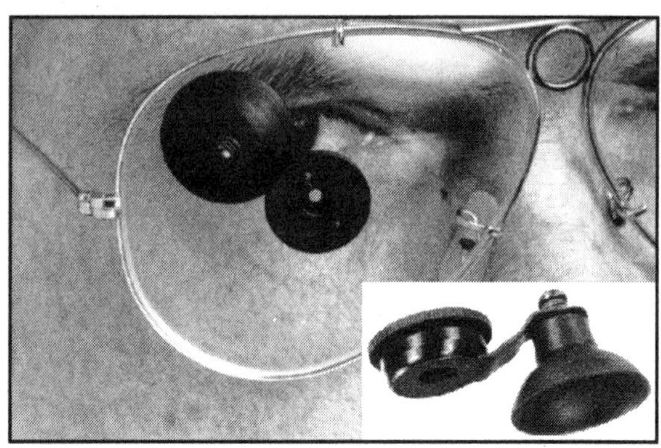

Pistol shooters are able to see their sights and target clearly with the Merit Optical Attachment and its instantly adjustable diameter aperture.

An aperture (pinhole) increases the eyes' depth of field (range of focus) dramatically.

The Merit Optical Attachment is instantly adjustable from .022- to .156-inch in diameter to accommodate different light conditions. Thus the sights and target remain in clear focus.

Additionally, using an aperture improves a shooter's concentration by helping maintain a consistent head position. This device works equally well with bifocals, trifocals and plain-lensed shooting glasses.

Contact Merit Corporation for a free brochure.

MERIT CORPORATION

SHOOTER'S MARKETPLACE MANUFACTURERS' ADDRESSES

ACCURATE ® *(Pg. 248)*
Attn: Dept. GDM97
5891 Hwy. 230 West
McEwen, TN 37101
Phone: 800-416-3006; Fax: 615-729-4211

AMERICAN SECURITY PRODUCTS COMPANY (AMSEC) *(Pg. 226)*
Attn: Dept. SM'97
11925 Pacific Ave.
Fontana, CA 92337
Phone: 800-421-6142, Ext.31; Fax: 909-681-9056

AMTEC 2000, INC. *(Pg. 230)*
Attn: Dept. SM'97
84 Industrial Rowe
Gardner, MA 01440
Phone: 508-632-9608

LES BAER CUSTOM, INC. *(Pg. 231)*
Attn: Dept. SM'97
29601 34th Ave.
Hillsdale, IL 61257
Phone: 309-658-2716; Fax: 309-658-2610

BALD EAGLE PRECISION MACHINE *(Pg. 240)*
Attn: Dept. SM'97
101-K Allison St.
Lock Haven, PA 17745
Phone: 717-748-6772; Fax: 717-748-4443

BIRCHWOOD CASEY *(Pg. 249)*
Attn: Dept. SM'97
7900 Fuller Road
Eden Prairie, MN 55344
Phone: 800-328-6156
Fax: 612-937-7979

BISON STUDIOS, PHILIP POBRUKA, CASE MAKER *(Pg. 228)*
Attn: Dept. SM'97
1409 South Commerce St.
Las Vegas, NV 89102
Phone: 702-388-2891

BLACKSTAR ACCURIZING *(Pg. 227)*
Attn: Dept. SM'97
11501 Brittmoore Park Drive
Houston, TX 77041
Phone: 713-849-9999
Fax: 713-849-5445

BLUE RIDGE MACHINERY & TOOLS, INC. *(Pg. 225)*
Attn: Dept. SM'97
P.O. Box 536
Hurricane, WV 25526
Phone: 800-872-6500 or 304-562-3538
Fax: 304-562-5311

BONNIE PACKER PRODUCTS *(Pg. 242)*
Attn: Dept. SM'97
P.O. Box 12204
Salem, OR 97309
Phone: 800-477-3244
Fax: 503-581-3191

BRILEY MFG., INC. *(Pg. 235)*
Attn: Dept. SM'97
1230 Lumpkin
Houston, TX 77043
Phone: 800-331-5718
Fax: 713-932-1043

B-SQUARE COMPANY, INC. *(Pg. 229)*
Attn: Dept. SM'97
P.O. Box 11281
Fort Worth, TX 76110
Phone: 800-433-2909 or 817-923-0964
Fax: 817-926-7012

BUFFALO BULLET CO., INC. *(Pg. 236)*
Attn: Dept. SM'97
12637 Los Nietos Road, Unit "A"
Santa Fe Springs, CA 90670
Phone: 310-944-0322
Fax: 310-944-5054

BUTLER CREEK CORPORATION *(Pg. 247)*
Attn: Dept. SM'97
290 Arden Drive
Belgrade, MT 59714
Phone: 800-423-8327 or 406-388-1356
Fax: 406-388-7204

CALI'CO HARDWOODS, INC. *(Pg. 246)*
Attn: Dept. SM'97
3580 Westwind Blvd.
Santa Rosa, CA 95403
Phone: 707-546-4045
Fax: 707-546-4027

DESERT MOUNTAIN MFG. *(Pg. 236)*
Attn: Dept. SM'97
P.O. Box 2767
Columbia Falls, MT 59912
Phone: 800-477-0762 or 406-892-7772
Fax: 406-892-7772

J. DEWEY MFG. CO., INC. *(Pg. 236)*
Attn: Dept. SM'97
P.O. Box 2014
Southbury, CT 06488
Phone: 203-264-3064
Fax: 203-262-6907

DIAMOND MACHINING TECHNOLOGY, INC.(DMT) *(Pg. 226)*
Attn: Dept. SM'97
85 Hayes Memorial Drive
Marlborough, MA 01752-1892
Phone: 508-481-5944; Fax: 508-485-3924

EUROPEAN AMERIAN ARMORY CORP. (E.A.A. Corp.) *(Pg. 243)*
Attn: Dept. SM'97
P.O. Box 1299
Sharpes, FL 32959
Phone: 407-639-4842; Fax: 407-639-7006

E-Z-WAY SYSTEMS *(Pg. 232)*
Attn: Dept. SM'97
P.O. Box 4310
Newark, OH 43058-4310
Phone: 614-345-6645 or 800-848-2072
Fax: 614-345-6600

FORREST INC. *(Pg. 230)*
Attn: Dept. SM'97
P.O. Box 326
Lakeside, CA 92040
Phone: 619-561-5800
Fax: 619-561-0227

GALAZAN *(Pg. 238)*
Attn: Dept. SM'97
P.O. Box 1692
New Britain, CT 06051-1692
Phone: 203-225-6581
Fax: 203-832-8707

GLASER SAFETY SLUG, INC. *(Pg. 239)*
Attn: Dept. SM'97
P.O. Box 8223
Foster City, CA 94404-8223
Phone: 800-221-3489
Fax: 415-345-8217

GUNLINE TOOLS *(Pg. 231)*
Attn: Dept. SM'97
2950 Saturn St., Ste. "O"
Brea, CA 92621
Phone: 714-993-5100; Fax: 714-572-4128

THE GUN PARTS CORP. *(Pg. 244)*
Attn: Dept SM'97
226 Williams Lane
West Hurley, NY 12491
Phone: 914-679-2417; Fax: 914-679-5849

HARRINGTON & RICHARDSON® *(Pg. 237)*
Attn: Dept. SM'97
60 Industrial Rowe
Gardner, MA 01440
Phone: 508-632-9393; Fax: 508-632-2300

HARRIS ENGINEERING, INC. *(Pg. 231)*
Attn: Dept. SM'97
Rt. 1
Barlow, KY 42024

NEIL JONES CUSTOM PRODUCTS *(Pg. 246)*
Attn: Dept. SM'97
17217 Brookhouser Road
Saegerstown, PA 16433
Phone: 814-763-2769; Fax: 814-763-4228

KENG'S FIREARMS SPECIALTY, INC. *(Pg. 234)*
Attn: Dept. SM'97
P.O. Box 44405
Atlanta, GA 30336
Phone: 404-691-7611; Fax: 404-505-8445

LASER DEVICES, INC. *(Pg. 239)*
Attn: Dept. SM'97
2 Harris Court, A-4
Monterey, CA 93940
Phone: 800-235-2162; Fax: 408-373-0903

L.E.M. GUN SPECIALTIES, INC. *(Pg. 234)*
Attn: Dept. SM'97
P.O. Box 2855
Peachtree City, GA 30269-2024
Phone: 770-487-0556

LOHMAN GAME CALL COMPANY *(Pg. 238)*
Attn: Dept. SM'97
4500 Doniphan Drive
Neosho, MO 64850
Phone: 417-451-4438; Fax: 417-451-2576

LYMAN PRODUCTS CORPORATION *(Pg. 232)*
Attn: Dept. 119
475 Smith Street
Middletown, CT 06457
Phone: 800-225-9626; Fax: 860-632-1699

MAG-NA-PORT INTERNATIONAL, INC. *(Pg. 225)*
Attn: Dept. SM'97
41302 Executive Drive
Harrison Twp. MI 48045-1306
Phone: 810-469-6727; Fax: 810-469-0425

MARBLE ARMS *(Pg. 242)*
Attn: Dept. SM'97
P.O. Box 111
Gladstone, MI 49837
Phone: 906-428-3710; Fax: 906-428-3711

MCA SPORTS *(Pg. 244)*
Attn: Dept. SM'97
P.O. Box 8868
Palm Springs, CA 92263
Phone/Fax: 619-770-2005

MERIT CORPORATION *(Pg. 250)*
Attn: Dept. SM'97
P.O. Box 9044
Schenectady, NY 12309
Phone: 518-346-1420

MINIATURE MACHINE CORP. *(Pg. 248)*
Attn: Dept. SM'97
2513 East Loop 820 North
Fort Worth, TX 76118
Phone: 800-998-SITE or 817-595-0404
Fax: 817-595-3074

MODERN GUN SCHOOL *(Pg. 235)*
Attn: Dept. SM'97
500 N. Kimball Ave., Suite 105
Southlake, TX 76092
Phone: 800-774-5112

MTM MOLDED PRODUCTS CO., INC. *(Pg. 228)*
Attn: Dept. SM'97
3370 Obco Ct.
Dayton, OH 45414
Phone: 513-890-7461

NECO/NOSTALGIA ENTERPRISES COMPANY *(Pg. 248)*
Attn: Dept. SM'97
P.O. Box 427
Lafayette, CA 94549
Phone: 510-450-0420
Fax: 510-450-0421

NESCI ENTERPRISES, INC. *(Pg. 240)*
Attn: Dept. SM'97
P.O. Box 119
East Hampton, CT 06424
Phone: 860-267-2588
Fax: 860-267-2589

NEW ENGLAND FIREARMS *(Pg. 237)*
Attn: Dept. SM'97
60 Industrial Rowe
Gardner, MA 01440
Phone: 508-632-9393
Fax: 508-632-2300

OEHLER RESEARCH, INC. *(Pg. 240)*
Attn: Dept. SM'97
P.O. Box 9135
Austin, TX 78766
Phone: 512-327-6900 or 800-531-5125
Fax: 512-327-6903

THE OUTDOOR CONNECTION, INC. *(Pg. 232)*
Attn: Dept. SM'97
P.O. Box 7751, 201 Cotton Drive
Waco, TX 76714-7751
Phone: 800-533-6076 or 817-772-5575
Fax: 817-776-3553

PALSA OUTDOOR PRODUCTS *(Pg. 230)*
Attn: Dept. SM'97
P.O. Box 81336
Lincoln, NE 68501-1336
Phone: 800-456-9281
Fax: 402-488-2321

PARSONS OPTICAL MFG. CO. *(Pg. 242)*
Attn: Dept. SM'97
P.O. Box 192
Ross, OH 45061
Phone: 513-867-0820; Fax: 513-867-8380

PENNSYLVANIA GUNSMITH SCHOOL *(Pg. 238)*
Attn: Dept. SM'97
812 Ohio River Blvd. (Avalon)
Pittsburgh, PA 15202
Phone/Fax: 412-766-1812

BRIAN PERAZONE-GUNSMITH *(Pg. 226)*
Attn: Dept. SM'97
P.O. Box 275GD, Cold Spring Road
Roxbury, NY 12474
Phone: 607-326-4088; Fax: 607-326-3140

PHOENIX ARMS *(Pg. 235)*
Attn: Dept. SM'97
1420 S. Archibald Ave.
Ontario, CA 91761
Phone: 909-947-4843; Fax: 909-947-6798

QUARTON USA, LTD. CO. *(Pg. 241)*
Attn: Dept. SM'97
7042 Alamo Downs Pkwy., Suite 370
San Antonio, TX 78238-4518
Phone: 800-520-8435 or 210-520-8430
Fax: 210-520-8433

RANDOLPH ENGINEERING, INC. *(Pg. 244)*
Attn: Dept. SM'97
26 Thomas Patten Drive
Randolph, MA 02368
Phone: 800-541-1405 or 617-961-6070
Fax: 617-986-0337

REDDING RELOADING EQUIPMENT *(Pg. 249)*
Attn: Dept. SM'97
1097 Starr Road
Cortland, NY 13045
Phone: 607-753-3331
Fax: 607-756-8445

R.G.-G., INC. *(Pg. 247)*
Attn: Dept. SM'97
P.O. Box 1261
Conifer, CO 80433-1261

S&K MANUFACTURING CO. *(Pg. 242)*
Attn: Dept. SM'97
P.O. Box 247
Pittsfield, PA 16340
Phone/Fax: 814-563-7808

SCATTERGUN TECHNOLOGIES INC. *(Pg. 234)*
Attn: Dept. SM'97
620 8th Ave., South
Nashville, TN 37203
Phone: 615-254-1441
Fax: 615-254-1449
Internet: http://www.scattergun.com

SHEPHERD SCOPE LTD. *(Pg. 226)*
Attn: Dept. SM'97
P.O. Box 189
Waterloo, NE 68069
Phone: 402-779-2424
Fax: 402-779-4010

SHOOTING CHRONY, INC. *(Pg. 246)*
Attn: Dept. SM'97
3269 Niagara Falls Blvd.
N. Tonawanda, NY 14120
Phone: 905-276-6292
Fax: 905-276-6295

THE SHOTGUN NEWS *(Pg. 228)*
Attn: Dept. SM'97
P.O. Box 669
Hastings, NE 68902
Phone: 402-463-4589
Fax: 402-463-3893

STONEY POINT PRODUCTS, INC. *(Pg. 246)*
Attn: Dept. SM'97
P.O. Box 234
New Ulm, MN 56073-0234
Phone: 507-354-3360
Fax: 507-354-7236

SWAROVSKI OPTIK NORTH AMERICA LTD. *(Pg. 245, 247, 249)*
Attn: Dept. SM'97
One Wholesale Way
Cranston, RI 02920
Phone: 800-426-3089; Fax: 401-946-2587

SWIFT INSTRUMENTS, INC. *(Pg. 233)*
Attn: Dept. SM'97
952 Dorchester Avenue
Boston, MA 02125
Phone: 800-446-1116; Fax: 617-436-3232

TRIUS TRAPS, INC. *(Pg. 245)*
Attn: Dept. SM'97
P.O. Box 25
Cleves, OH 45002
Phone: 513-941-5682
Fax: 513-941-7970

DOUG TURNBULL RESTORATION *(Pg. 232)*
Attn: Dept. SM'97
P.O. Box 471
Bloomfield, NY 14469
Phone: 716-657-6338
Internet: http://gunshop.com/dougt.htm

VOLQUARTSEN CUSTOM LTD. *(Pg. 238)*
Attn: Dept. SM'97
P.O. Box 271
Carroll, IA 51401
Phone: 712-792-4238
Fax: 712-792-2542
E-mail: vcl@netins.net

W. WALLER & SON, INC. *(Pg. 245)*
Attn: Dept. SM'97
59 Stoney Brook Road
Grantham, NH 03753
Phone: 603-863-4177
Internet: http://www.shooters.com

WILLIAMS MFG. OF OREGON, INC. *(Pg. 228)*
Attn: Dept. SM'97
110 East "B" Street
Drain, OR 97435
Phone: 800-357-3006 or 541-836-7461
Fax: 541-836-7245

1997 GUN DIGEST

Complete Compact

CATALOG

GUNDEX®

C

D

E

F

G

H

I

J

K

L

M

GUNDEX

N

O

P

Q

R

S

T

U

V

W

Z

Includes models suitable for several forms of competition and other sporting purposes.

AA ARMS AP9 PISTOL
Caliber: 9mm Para., 10-shot magazine.
Barrel: 5″.
Weight: 3.5 lbs. **Length:** 12″ overall.
Stocks: Checkered black synthetic.
Sights: Post front adjustable for elevation, rear adjustable for windage
Features: Ventilated barrel shroud; blue or electroless nickel finish. Made in U.S. by AA Arms.
Price: Blue **$299.00**
Price: Nickel **$312.00**
Price: AP9 Target (11″ barrel) **$399.00**

ACCU-TEK MODEL AT-9SS AUTO PISTOL
Caliber: 9mm Para., 8-shot magazine.
Barrel: 3.2″.
Weight: 28 oz. **Length:** 6.25″ overall.
Stocks: Black checkered nylon.
Sights: Blade front, rear adjustable for windage; three-dot system.
Features: Stainless steel construction. Double action only. Firing pin block with no external safeties. Lifetime warranty. Introduced 1992. Made in U.S. by Accu-Tek.
Price: Satin stainless **$317.00**

Accu-Tek AT-45SS Auto Pistol
Same as the Model AT-9SS except chambered for 45 ACP, 6-shot magazine. Introduced 1995. Made in U.S. by Accu-Tek.
Price: Stainless steel **$327.00**

ACCU-TEK MODEL AT-380SS AUTO PISTOL
Caliber: 380 ACP, 5-shot magazine.
Barrel: 2.75″.
Weight: 20 oz. **Length:** 5.6″ overall.
Stocks: Grooved black composition.
Sights: Blade front, rear adjustable for windage.
Features: Stainless steel frame and slide. External hammer; manual thumb safety; firing pin block, trigger disconnect. Lifetime warranty. Introduced 1991. Made in U.S. by Accu-Tek.
Price: Satin stainless **$191.00**
Price: Black finish over steel (AT-380B) **$196.00**

Accu-Tek Model AT-32SS Auto Pistol
Same as the AT-380SS except chambered for 32 ACP. Introduced 1991.
Price: Satin stainless **$185.00**
Price: Black finish over steel (AT-32B) **$190.00**

ACCU-TEK MODEL HC-380SS AUTO PISTOL
Caliber: 380 ACP, 10-shot magazine.
Barrel: 2.75″.
Weight: 28 oz. **Length:** 6″ overall.
Stocks: Checkered black composition.
Sights: Blade front, rear adjustable for windage.
Features: External hammer; manual thumb safety with firing pin and trigger disconnect; bottom magazine release. Stainless finish. Introduced 1993. Made in U.S. by Accu-Tek.
Price: Satin stainless **$243.00**
Price: Black finish over stainless **$248.00**

AMERICAN ARMS AUSSIE PISTOL
Caliber: 9mm Para., 40 S&W, 10-shot magazine.
Barrel: 4¾″.
Weight: 23 oz. **Length:** 7⅞″ overall.
Stocks: Integral; checkered polymer.
Sights: Blade front, rear adjustable for windage.
Features: Double action only. Polymer frame. Has five safeties—firing pin block; positive trigger safety; magazine safety; slide lock safety; loaded chamber indicator. Introduced 1996. From American Arms, Inc.
Price: **$425.00**

AA Arms AP9 Mini, AP9 Mini/5 Pistol
Similar to AP9 except scaled-down dimensions with 3″ or 5″ barrel.
Price: 3″ barrel, blue **$239.00**
Price: 3″ barrel, electroless nickel **$259.00**
Price: Mini/5, 5″ barrel, blue **$259.00**
Price: Mini/5, 5″ barrel, electroless nickel **$279.00**

Acc-Tek AT-9SS

Accu-Tek AT-40SS Auto Pistol
Same as the Model AT-9 except chambered for 40 S&W, 7-shot magazine. Introduced 1992.
Price: Stainless **$317.00**

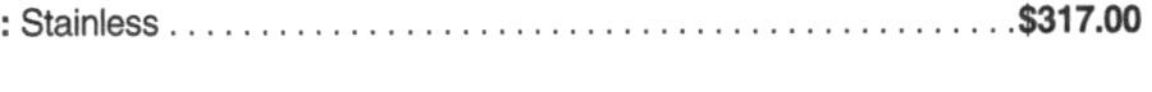

Acc-Tek AT 380SS

Accu-Tek HC-380SS

American Arms Escort

AMERICAN ARMS ESCORT AUTO PISTOL
Caliber: 380 ACP, 7-shot magazine.
Barrel: $3\frac{3}{8}$″.
Weight: 19 oz. **Length:** $6\frac{1}{8}$″ overall.
Stocks: Soft polymer.
Sights: Blade front, rear adjustable for windage.
Features: Double-action-only trigger; stainless steel construction; chamber loaded indicator. Introduced 1995. From American Arms, Inc.
Price: $349.00

AMERICAN ARMS MODEL PK22 DA AUTO PISTOL
Caliber: 22 LR, 8-shot magazine.
Barrel: 3.3″.
Weight: 22 oz. **Length:** 6.3″ overall.
Stocks: Checkered plastic.
Sights: Fixed.
Features: Double action. Polished blue finish. Slide-mounted safety. Made in the U.S. by American Arms, Inc.
Price: $199.00

AMERICAN ARMS MODEL P-98 AUTO PISTOL
Caliber: 22 LR, 8-shot magazine.
Barrel: 5″.
Weight: 25 oz. **Length:** $8\frac{1}{8}$″ overall.
Stocks: Grooved black polymer.
Sights: Blade front, rear adjustable for windage.
Features: Double action with hammer-block safety, magazine disconnect safety. Alloy frame. Has external appearance of the Walther P-38 pistol. Introduced 1989. Made in U.S. by American Arms, Inc.
Price: $209.00

ARMSCOR M-1911-A1P AUTOLOADING PISTOL
Caliber: 45 ACP, 7- or 10-shot magazine.
Barrel: 5″.
Weight: 38 oz. **Length:** $8\frac{3}{4}$″ overall.
Stocks: Checkered.
Sights: Blade front, rear drift adjustable for windage; three-dot system.
Features: Skeletonized combat hammer and trigger; beavertail grip safety; extended slide release; oversize thumb safety; Parkerized finish. Introduced 1996. Imported from the Philippines by K.B.I., Inc.
Price: $399.99

AMT AUTOMAG II AUTO PISTOL
Caliber: 22 WMR, 9-shot magazine (7-shot with $3\frac{3}{8}$″ barrel).
Barrel: $3\frac{3}{8}$″, $4\frac{1}{2}$″, 6″.
Weight: About 23 oz. **Length:** $9\frac{3}{8}$″ overall.
Stocks: Grooved carbon fiber.
Sights: Blade front, adjustable rear.
Features: Made of stainless steel. Gas-assisted action. Exposed hammer. Slide flats have brushed finish, rest is sandblast. Squared trigger guard. Introduced 1986. From AMT.
Price: $405.95

AMT AUTOMAG III PISTOL
Caliber: 30 Carbine, 8-shot magazine.
Barrel: $6\frac{3}{8}$″.
Weight: 43 oz. **Length:** $10\frac{1}{2}$″ overall.
Stocks: Carbon fiber.
Sights: Blade front, adjustable rear.
Features: Stainless steel construction. Hammer-drop safety. Slide flats have brushed finish, rest is sandblasted. Introduced 1989. From AMT.
Price: $469.79

AMT AUTOMAG IV PISTOL
Caliber: 45 Winchester Magnum, 6-shot magazine.
Barrel: 6.5″.
Weight: 46 oz. **Length:** 10.5″ overall.
Stocks: Carbon fiber.
Sights: Blade front, adjustable rear.
Features: Made of stainless steel with brushed finish. Introduced 1990. Made in U.S. by AMT.
Price: $699.99

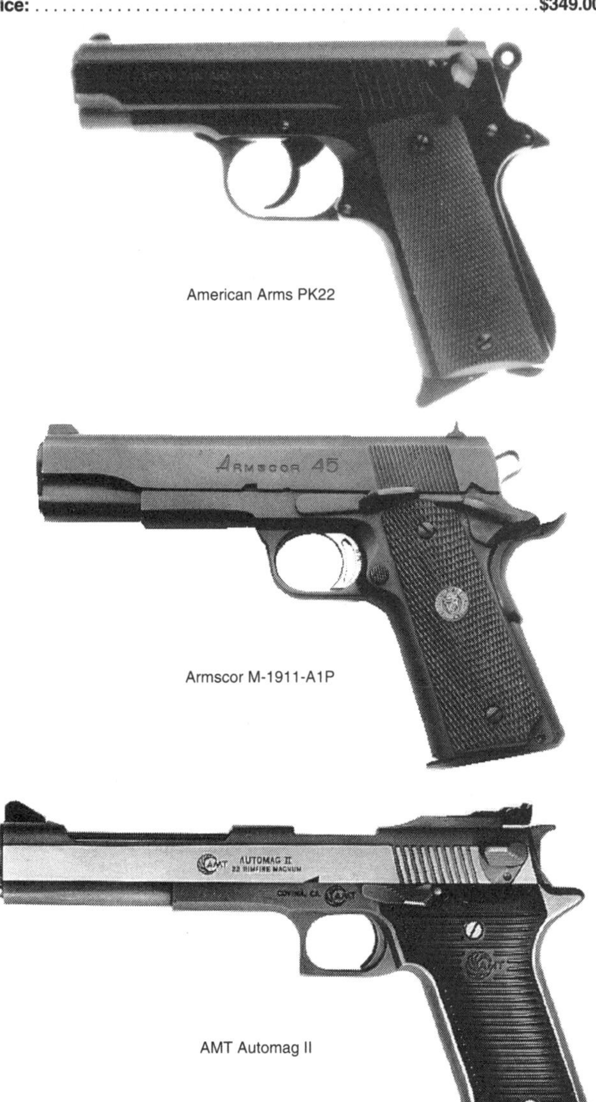

American Arms PK22

Armscor M-1911-A1P

AMT Automag II

AMT 45 ACP HARDBALLER
Caliber: 45 ACP.
Barrel: 5″.
Weight: 39 oz. **Length:** $8\frac{1}{2}$″ overall.
Stocks: Wrap-around rubber.
Sights: Adjustable.
Features: Extended combat safety, serrated matte slide rib, loaded chamber indicator, long grip safety, beveled magazine well, adjustable target trigger. All stainless steel. From AMT.
Price: $549.95
Price: Government model (as above except no rib, fixed sights) $489.99

AMT 45 ACP HARDBALLER LONG SLIDE
Caliber: 45 ACP.
Barrel: 7″. **Length:** $10\frac{1}{2}$″ overall.
Stocks: Wrap-around rubber.
Sights: Fully adjustable rear sight.
Features: Slide and barrel are 2″ longer than the standard 45, giving less recoil, added velocity, longer sight radius. Has extended combat safety, serrated matte rib, loaded chamber indicator, wide adjustable trigger. From AMT.
Price: $595.99

CAUTION: PRICES SHOWN ARE SUPPLIED BY THE MANUFACTURER OR IMPORTER. CHECK YOUR LOCAL GUN SHOP.

AMT BACK UP II AUTO PISTOL
Caliber: 380 ACP, 5-shot magazine.
Barrel: 2 1/2″.
Weight: 18 oz. **Length:** 5″ overall.
Stocks: Carbon fiber.
Sights: Fixed, open, recessed.
Features: Concealed hammer, blowback operation; manual and grip safeties. All stainless steel construction. Smallest domestically-produced pistol in 380. From AMT.
Price: **$309.99**

AMT 45 ACP Backup

AMT Back Up Double Action Only Pistol
Similar to the standard Back Up except has double-action-only mechanism, enlarged trigger guard, slide is rounded ar rear. Has 5-shot magazine. Introduced 1992. From AMT.
Price: **$329.99**
Price: 9mm Para., 38 Super, 40 S&W, 45 ACP **$449.99**

ARGENTINE HI-POWER 9MM AUTO PISTOL
Caliber: 9mm Para., 10-shot magazine.
Barrel: 4 21/32″.
Weight: 32 oz. **Length:** 7 3/4″ overall.
Stocks: Checkered walnut.
Sights: Blade front, adjustable rear.
Features: Produced in Argentina under F.N. Browning license. Introduced 1990. Imported by Century International Arms, Inc.
Price: About **$299.95**

Argentine Hi-Power

Argentine Hi-Power Detective Model
Similar to the standard model except has 3.8″ barrel, 6.9″ overall length and weighs 33 oz. Grips are finger-groove, checkered soft rubber. Matte black finish. Introduced 1994. Imported by Century International Arms, Inc.
Price: About **$310.00**

ASTRA A-70 AUTO PISTOL
Caliber: 9mm Para., 8-shot; 40 S&W, 7-shot magazine.
Barrel: 3.5″.
Weight: 29.3 oz. **Length:** 6.5″ overall.
Stocks: Checkered black plastic.
Sights: Blade front, rear adjustable for windage.
Features: All steel frame and slide. Checkered grip straps and trigger guard. Nickel or blue finish. Introduced 1992. Imported from Spain by European American Armory.
Price: Blue, 9mm Para. **$360.00**
Price: Blue, 40 S&W **$360.00**
Price: Nickel, 9mm Para. **$385.00**
Price: Nickel, 40 S&W **$385.00**
Price: Stainless steel, 9mm **$450.00**
Price: Stainless steel, 40 S&W **$450.00**

Astra A-75

Astra A-75 Decocker Auto Pistol
Same as the A-70 except has decocker system, double or single action, different trigger, contoured pebble-grain grips. Introduced 1993. Imported from Spain by European American Armory.
Price: Blue, 9mm or 40 S&W **$415.00**
Price: Nickel, 9mm or 40 S&W **$440.00**
Price: Blue, 45 ACP **$445.00**
Price: Nickel, 45 ACP **$460.00**
Price: Stainless steel, 9mm, 40 S&W **$495.00**
Price: Featherweight (23.5 oz.), 9mm, blue **$440.00**

Consult our Directory pages for the location of firms mentioned.

Astra A-100

ASTRA A-100 AUTO PISTOL
Caliber: 9mm Para., 10-shot; 40 S&W, 10-shot; 45 ACP, 9-shot magazine.
Barrel: 3.9″.
Weight: 29 oz. **Length:** 7.1″ overall.
Stocks: Checkered black plastic.
Sights: Blade front, interchangeable rear blades for elevation, screw adjustable for windage.
Features: Double action. Decocking lever permits lowering hammer onto locked firing pin. Automatic firing pin block. Side button magazine release. Introduced 1993. Imported from Spain by European American Armory.
Price: Blue, 9mm, 40 S&W, 45 ACP **$450.00**
Price: As above, nickel **$475.00**

AUTO-ORDNANCE 1911A1 AUTOMATIC PISTOL

Caliber: 9mm Para., 38 Super, 9-shot; 10mm, 45 ACP, 7-shot magazine.
Barrel: 5″.
Weight: 39 oz. **Length:** 8½″ overall.
Stocks: Checkered plastic with medallion.
Sights: Blade front, rear adjustable for windage.
Features: Same specs as 1911A1 military guns—parts interchangeable. Frame and slide blued; each radius has non-glare finish. Made in U.S. by Auto-Ordnance Corp.
Price: 45 ACP, blue **$397.50**
Price: 45 ACP, Parkerized **$389.95**
Price: 45 ACP, satin nickel **$425.95**
Price: 9mm, 38 Super **$435.00**
Price: 10mm (has three-dot combat sights, rubber wrap-around grips) .. **$435.00**
Price: 45 ACP General Model (Commander style) **$465.00**
Price: Duo Tone (nickel frame, blue slide, three-dot sight system, textured black wrap-around grips) **$435.00**

Auto-Ordnance 1911A1 Competition Model

Similar to the standard Model 1911A1 except has barrel compensator. Commander hammer, flat mainspring housing, three-dot sight system, low-profile magazine funnel, Hi-Ride beavertail grip safety, full-length recoil spring guide system, black-textured rubber, wrap-around grips, and extended slide stop, safety and magazine catch. In 45 or 38 Super. Introduced 1994. Made in U.S. by Auto-Ordnance Corp.
Price: **$635.00**

Baby Eagle FS

BAER 1911 CONCEPT I AUTO PISTOL

Caliber: 45 ACP, 7-shot magazine.
Barrel: 5″.
Weight: 37 oz. **Length:** 8.5″ overall.
Stocks: Checkered rosewood.
Sights: Baer dovetail front, Bo-Mar deluxe low-mount rear with hidden leaf.
Features: Baer forged steel frame, slide and barrel with Baer stainless bushing; slide fitted to frame; double serrated slide; Baer beavertail grip safety, checkered slide stop, tuned extractor, extended ejector, deluxe hammer and sear, match disconnector; lowered and flared ejection port; fitted recoil link; polished feed ramp, throated barrel; Baer fitted speed trigger, flat serrated mainspring housing. Blue finish. Made in U.S. by Les Baer Custom, Inc.
Price: **$1,428.00**
Price: Concept II (with Baer adjustable rear sight) **$1,428.00**

Baer Premier II

Baer 1911 Prowler III Auto Pistol

Same as the Premier II except also has tapered cone stub weight and reverse recoil plug. Made in U.S. by Les Baer Custom, Inc.
Price: Standard size, blued **$1,795.00**

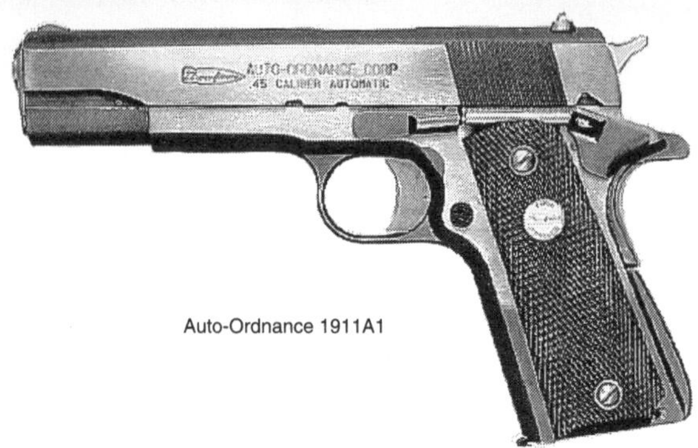

Auto-Ordnance 1911A1

Auto-Ordnance ZG-51 Pit Bull Auto

Same as the 1911A1 except has 3½″ barrel, weighs 36 oz. and has an over-all length of 7¼″. Available in 45 ACP only; 7-shot magazine. Introduced 1989.
Price: **$455.00**

BABY EAGLE AUTO PISTOL

Caliber: 9mm Para., 40 S&W, 41 A.E.
Barrel: 4.37″.
Weight: 35 oz. **Length:** 8.14″ overall.
Stocks: High-impact black polymer.
Sights: Combat.
Features: Double-action mechanism; polygonal rifling; ambidextrous safety. Model 9mm F has frame-mounted safety on left side of pistol; Model 9mm FS has frame-mounted safety and 3.62″ barrel. Introduced 1992. Imported by Magnum Research.
Price: 40 S&W, 41 A.E., 9mm (9mm F, 9mm FS), black finish **$569.00**
Price: Conversion kit, 9mm Para. to 41 A.E. **$239.00**
Price: 9mm FS, chrome finish **$659.00**
Price: 9mm FSS, matte black finish, frame-mounted safety, short grip, short barrel **$569.00**
Price: As above, chrome finish **$659.00**

Baer 1911 Concept III Auto Pistol

Same as the Concept I except has forged stainless frame with blued steel slide, Bo-Mar rear sight, 30 lpi checkering on front strap. Made in U.S. by Les Baer Custom, Inc.
Price: **$1,500.00**
Price: Concept IV (with Baer adjustable rear sight) **$1,499.00**
Price: Concept V (all stainless, Bo-Mar sight, checkered front strap) .. **$1,598.00**
Price: Concept VI (stainless, Baer adjustable sight, checkered front strap) **$1,598.00**

Baer 1911 Concept VII Auto Pistol

Same as the Concept I except reduced Commanche size with 4.25″ barrel, weighs 27.5 oz., 7.75″ overall. Blue finish, checkered front strap. Made in U.S. by Les Baer Custom, Inc.
Price: **$1,480.00**
Price: Concept VIII (stainless frame and slide, Baer adjustable rear sight) **$1,598.00**

Baer 1911 Concept IX Auto Pistol

Same as the Commanche Concept VII except has Baer lightweight forged aluminum frame, blued steel slide, Baer adjustable rear sight. Chambered for 45 ACP, 7-shot magazine. Made in U.S. by Les Baer Custom, Inc.
Price: **$1,598.00**
Price: Concept X (as above with stainless slide) **$1,598.00**

BAER 1911 PREMIER II AUTO PISTOL

Caliber: 45 ACP, 7- or 10-shot magazine.
Barrel: 5″.
Weight: 37 oz. **Length:** 8.5″ overall.
Stocks: Checkered rosewood, double diamond pattern.
Sights: Baer dovetailed front, low-mount Bo-Mar rear with hidden leaf.
Features: Baer NM forged steel frame and barrel with stainless bushing; slide fitted to frame; double serrated slide; lowered, flared ejection port; tuned, polished extractor; Baer extended ejector, checkered slide stop, aluminum speed trigger with 4-lb. pull, deluxe Commander hammer and sear, beavertail grip safety with pad, beveled magazine well, extended ambidextrous safety; flat mainspring housing; polished feed ramp and throated barrel; 30 lpi checkered front strap. Made in U.S. by Les Baer Custom, Inc.
Price: Blued **$1,428.00**
Price: Stainless **$1,559.00**
Price: 6″ model, blued **$1,690.00**

CAUTION: PRICES SHOWN ARE SUPPLIED BY THE MANUFACTURER OR IMPORTER. CHECK YOUR LOCAL GUN SHOP.

Baer Custom Carry

BAER LIGHTWEIGHT 22

Caliber: 22 LR.
Barrel: 5″.
Weight: 25 oz. **Length:** 8.5″ overall.
Stocks: Checkered walnut.
Sights: Blade front.
Features: Aluminum frame and slide. Baer beavertail grip safety with pad, checkered slide stop, deluxe hammer and sear, match disconnector, flat serrated mainspring housing, Baer fitted speed trigger, tuned extractor. Has total reliability tuning package, action job. Baer Ultra Coat finish. Introduced 1996. Made in U.S. by Les Baer Custom, Inc.
Price: Government model size, fixed sights **$1,428.00**
Price: Government model, Bo-Mar sights **$1,498.00**
Price: Commanche size, fixed sights **$1,428.00**

BAIKAL IJ-70 DA AUTO PISTOL

Caliber: 9x18mm Makarov, 8-shot magazine.
Barrel: 4″.
Weight: 25 oz. **Length:** 6.25″ overall.
Stocks: Checkered composition.
Sights: Blade front, rear adjustable for windage and elevation.
Features: Double action; all-steel construction; frame-mounted safety with decocker. Comes with two magazines, cleaning rod, universal tool. Introduced 1994. Imported from Russia by Century International Arms, K.B.I., Inc.
Price: 9x18mm, blue **$199.00**
Price: IJ-70HC, 9x18, 10-shot magazine, from K.B.I. **$239.00**
Price: As above, 380 ACP (K.B.I.) **$249.00**

BERETTA MODEL 80 CHEETAH SERIES DA PISTOLS

Caliber: 380 ACP, 10-shot magazine (M84); 8-shot (M85); 22 LR, 7-shot (M87), 22 LR, 8-shot (M89).
Barrel: 3.82″.
Weight: About 23 oz. (M84/85); 20.8 oz. (M87). **Length:** 6.8″ overall.
Stocks: Glossy black plastic (wood optional at extra cost).
Sights: Fixed front, drift-adjustable rear.
Features: Double action, quick takedown, convenient magazine release. Introduced 1977. Imported from Italy by Beretta U.S.A.
Price: Model 84 Cheetah, plastic grips **$529.00**
Price: Model 84 Cheetah, wood grips **$557.00**
Price: Model 84 Cheetah, wood grips, nickel finish **$600.00**
Price: Model 85 Cheetah, plastic grips, 8-shot **$499.00**
Price: Model 85 Cheetah, wood grips, 8-shot **$530.00**
Price: Model 85 Cheetah, wood grips, nickel, 8-shot **$599.00**
Price: Model 87 Cheetah wood, 22 LR, 7-shot **$493.00**

Beretta Model 86 Cheetah

Similar to the 380-caliber Model 85 except has tip-up barrel for first-round loading. Barrel length is 4.33″, overall length of 7.33″. Has 8-shot magazine, walnut grips. Introduced 1989.
Price: **$514.00**

BERETTA MODEL 92FS PISTOL

Caliber: 9mm Para., 10-shot magazine.
Barrel: 4.9″.
Weight: 34 oz. **Length:** 8.5″ overall.
Stocks: Checkered black plastic; wood optional at extra cost.
Sights: Blade front, rear adjustable for windage. Tritium night sights available.
Features: Double action. Extractor acts as chamber loaded indicator, squared trigger guard, grooved front- and backstraps, inertia firing pin. Matte finish. Introduced 1977. Made in U.S. and imported from Italy by Beretta U.S.A.
Price: With plastic grips **$626.00**
Price: With wood grips **$647.00**
Price: Tritium night sights, add **$90.00**

BAER 1911 CUSTOM CARRY AUTO PISTOL

Caliber: 45 ACP, 7- or 10-shot magazine.
Barrel: 5″.
Weight: 37 oz. **Length:** 8.5″ overall.
Stocks: Checkered walnut.
Sights: Baer improved ramp-style dovetailed front, Novak low-mount rear.
Features: Baer forged NM frame, slide and barrel with stainless bushing; fitted slide to frame; double serrated slide (full-size only); Baer speed trigger with 4-lb. pull; Baer deluxe hammer and sear, tactical-style extended ambidextrous safety, beveled magazine well; polished feed ramp and throated barrel; tuned extractor; Baer extended ejector, checkered slide stop; lowered and flared ejection port, full-length recoil guide rod; recoil buff. Made in U.S. by Les Baer Custom, Inc.
Price: Standard size, blued **$1,490.00**
Price: Standard size, stainless **$1,580.00**
Price: Commanche size, blued **$1,490.00**
Price: Commanche size, stainless **$1,580.00**
Price: Commanche size, aluminum frame, blued slide **$1,530.00**
Price: Commanche size, aluminum frame, stainless slide **$1,590.00**

BAER 1911 S.R.P. PISTOL

Caliber: 45 ACP.
Barrel: 5″.
Weight: 37 oz. **Length:** 8.5″ overall.
Stocks: Checkered walnut.
Sights: Trijicon night sights.
Features: Similar to the F.B.I. contract gun except uses Baer forged steel frame. Has Baer match barrel with supported chamber, Wolff springs, complete tactical action job. All parts Mag-na-fluxed; deburred for tactical carry. Has Baer Ultra Coat finish. Tuned for reliability. Contact Baer for complete details. Introduced 1996. Made in U.S. by Les Baer Custom, Inc.
Price: Government or Commanche length **$2,495.00**

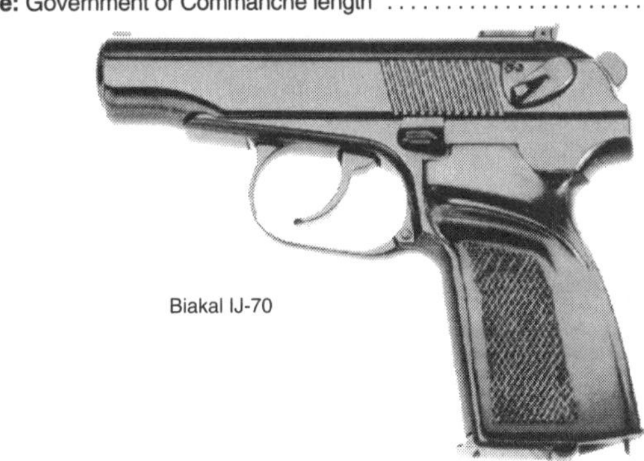
Biakal IJ-70

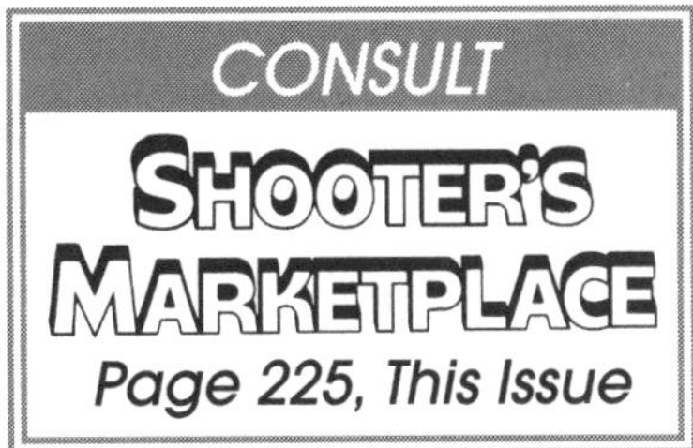
CONSULT
SHOOTER'S
MARKETPLACE
Page 225, This Issue

Beretta Model 92FS

Beretta Model 92F Stainless Pistol

Same as the Model 92FS except has stainless steel barrel and slide, and frame of aluminum-zirconium alloy. Has three-dot sight system. Introduced 1992.
Price: **$757.00**
Price: For tritium sights, add **$90.00**

Beretta Models 92FS/96 Centurion Pistols

Identical to the Model 92FS and 96F except uses shorter slide and barrel (4.3″). Tritium or three-dot sight systems. Plastic or wood grips. Available in 9mm or 40 S&W. Also available in D Models (double-action-only). Introduced 1992.

Price: Model 92FS Centurion, three-dot sights, plastic grips $626.00
Price: Model 92FS Centurion, wood grips $647.00
Price: Model 96 Centurion, three-dot sights, plastic grips $643.00
Price: Model 92D Centurion $586.00
Price: Model 96D Centurion $607.00
Price: For tritium sights, add $90.00

Beretta 96D

Beretta Model 96 Auto Pistol

Same as the Model 92F except chambered for 40 S&W. Ambidextrous safety mechanism with passive firing pin catch, slide safety/decocking lever, trigger bar disconnect. Has 10-shot magazine. Available with tritium or three-dot sights. Introduced 1992.

Price: Model 96, plastic grips $643.00
Price: Model 96D, double-action-only, three-dot sights $607.00
Price: For tritium sights, add $90.00

Beretta Model 92D Pistol

Same as the Model 92FS except double-action-only and has bobbed hammer, no external safety. Introduced 1992.

Price: With plastic grips, three-dot sights $586.00
Price: As above with tritium sights $676.00

Beretta 950 Jetfire

BERETTA MODEL 950 JETFIRE AUTO PISTOL

Caliber: 25 ACP, 8-shot.
Barrel: 2.4″.
Weight: 9.9 oz. **Length:** 4.7″ overall.
Stocks: Checkered black plastic or walnut.
Sights: Fixed.
Features: Single action, thumb safety; tip-up barrel for direct loading/unloading, cleaning. From Beretta U.S.A.

Price: Jetfire plastic, blue $187.00
Price: Jetfire plastic, nickel $221.00
Price: Jetfire wood, engraved $267.00
Price: Jetfire plastic, matte blue $159.00

Beretta Model 21 Bobcat Pistol

Similar to the Model 950 BS. Chambered for 22 LR or 25 ACP. Both double action. Has 2.4″ barrel, 4.9″ overall length; 7-round magazine on 22 cal.; 8 rounds in 25 ACP, 9.9 oz., available in nickel, matte, engraved or blue finish. Plastic or walnut grips. Introduced in 1985.

Price: Bobcat, 22-cal. $244.00
Price: Bobcat, nickel, 22-cal. $254.00
Price: Bobcat, 25-cal. $244.00
Price: Bobcat, nickel, 25-cal. $254.00
Price: Bobcat wood, engraved, 22 or 25 ....$294.00
Price: Bobcat plastic matte, 22 or 25 ....$194.00

Beretta M8000/8040 Cougar

BERETTA MODEL 8000/8040 COUGAR PISTOL

Caliber: 9mm Para., 10-shot, 40 S&W, 10-shot magazine.
Barrel: 3.6″.
Weight: 33.5 oz. **Length:** 7″ overall.
Stocks: Checkered plastic.
Sights: Blade front, rear drift adjustable for windage.
Features: Slide-mounted safety; rotating barrel; exposed hammer. Matte black Bruniton finish. Announced 1994. Imported from Italy by Beretta U.S.A.

Price: $699.00
Price: D models $663.00

BERNARDELLI PO18 DA AUTO PISTOL

Caliber: 9mm Para., 10-shot magazine.
Barrel: 4.8″.
Weight: 34.2 oz. **Length:** 8.23″ overall.
Stocks: Checkered plastic; walnut optional.
Sights: Blade front, rear adjustable for windage and elevation; low profile, three-dot system.
Features: Manual thumb half-cock, magazine and auto-locking firing pin safeties. Thumb safety decocks hammer. Reversible magazine release. Imported from Italy by Mitchell Arms.

Price: Blue $505.00
Price: Chrome $568.00

Bernardelli PO18 Compact DA Auto Pistol

Similar to the PO18 except has 4″ barrel, 7.44″ overall length, 10-shot magazine. Weighs 31.7 oz. Imported from Italy by Mitchell Arms.

Price: Blue $552.00
Price: Chrome $600.00

BERETTA MODEL 3032 TOMCAT PISTOL

Caliber: 32 ACP, 7-shot magazine.
Barrel: 2.45″.
Weight: 15 oz. **Length:** 5″ overall.
Stocks: Checkered black plastic.
Sights: Blade front, drift-adjustable rear.
Features: Double action with exposed hammer; tip-up barrel for direct loading/unloading; thumb safety; polished or matte blue finish. Imported from Italy by Beretta U.S.A. Introduced 1996.

Price: Polished blue $299.00
Price: Matte blue $240.00

Bernadelli PO18

CAUTION: PRICES SHOWN ARE SUPPLIED BY THE MANUFACTURER OR IMPORTER. CHECK YOUR LOCAL GUNSHOP.

BERNARDELLI MODEL USA AUTO PISTOL
Caliber: 22 LR, 10-shot, 380 ACP, 7-shot magazine.
Barrel: 3.5″.
Weight: 26.5 oz. **Length:** 6.5″ overall.
Stocks: Checkered plastic with thumbrest.
Sights: Ramp front, white outline rear adjustable for windage and elevation.
Features: Hammer-block slide safety; loaded chamber indicator; dual recoil buffer springs; serrated trigger; inertia-type firing pin. Imported from Italy by Mitchell Arms.
Price: Blue, either caliber **$387.00**
Price: Chrome, either caliber **$412.00**
Price: Model AMR (6″ barrel, target sights) **$440.00**

Bernadelli USA

BERNARDELLI P. ONE DA AUTO PISTOL
Caliber: 9mm Para., 16-shot, 40 S&W, 10-shot magazine.
Barrel: 4.8″.
Weight: 34 oz. **Length:** 8.35″ overall.
Stocks: Checkered black plastic.
Sights: Blade front, rear adjustable for windage and elevation; three dot system.
Features: Forged steel frame and slide; full-length slide rails; reversible magazine release; thumb safety/decocker; squared trigger guard. Introduced 1994. Imported from Italy by Mitchell Arms.
Price: 9mm Para., blue/black **$530.00**
Price: 9mm Para., chrome **$580.00**
Price: 40 S&W, blue/black **$530.00**
Price: 40 S&W, chrome **$580.00**

Bernardelli P. One Practical VB Pistol
Similar to the P. One except chambered for 9x21mm, two- or four-port compensator, straight trigger, micro-adjustable rear sight. Introduced 1994. Imported from Italy by Mitchell Arms.
Price: Blue/black, two-port compensator **$1,425.00**
Price: As above, four-port compensator **$1,475.00**
Price: Chrome, two-port compensator **$1,498.00**
Price: As above, four-port compensator **$1,540.00**
Price: Customized VB, four-plus-two-port compensator **$2,150.00**
Price: As above, chrome **$2,200.00**

BERSA THUNDER 9 AUTO PISTOL
Caliber: 9mm Para., 10-shot magazine.
Barrel: 4″.
Weight: 30 oz. **Length:** 7 3/8″ overall.
Stocks: Checkered black polymer.
Sights: Blade front, rear adjustable for windage and elevation; three-dot system.
Features: Double action. Ambidextrous safety, decocking levers and slide release; internal automatic firing pin safety; reversible extended magazine release; adjustable trigger stop; alloy frame. Link-free locked breech design. Matte blue finish. Introduced 1993. Imported from Argentina by Eagle Imports, Inc.
Price: Matte finish **$474.95**
Price: Satin nickel **$524.95**
Price Duo-Tone finish **$491.95**

Bersa Thunder 9

BERSA THUNDER 22 AUTO PISTOL
Caliber: 22 LR, 10-shot magazine.
Barrel: 3.5″.
Weight: 24.2 oz. **Length:** 6.6″ overall.
Stocks: Black polymer.
Sights: Blade front, notch rear adjustable for windage; three-dot system.
Features: Double action; firing pin and magazine safeties. Available in blue or nickel. Introduced 1995. Distributed by Eagle Imports, Inc.
Price: Blue **$249.95**
Price: Nickel **$266.95**

BERSA SERIES 95 AUTO PISTOL
Caliber: 380 ACP, 7-shot magazine.
Barrel: 3.5″.
Weight: 22 oz. **Length:** 6.6″ overall.
Stocks: Wrap-around textured rubber.
Sights: Blade front, rear adjustable for windage; three-dot system.
Features: Double action; firing pin and magazine safeties; combat-style trigger guard. Matte blue or satin nickel. Introduced 1992. Distributed by Eagle Imports, Inc.
Price: Matte blue **$224.95**
Price: Satin nickel **$241.95**

BERSA THUNDER 380 AUTO PISTOLS
Caliber: 380 ACP, 7-shot (Thunder 380), 10-shot magazine (Thunder 380 Plus).
Barrel: 3.5″.
Weight: 25.75 oz. **Length:** 6.6″ overall.
Stocks: Black rubber.
Sights: Blade front, notch rear adjustable for windage; three-dot system.
Features: Double action; firing pin and magazine safeties. Available in blue or nickel. Introduced 1995. Distributed by Eagle Imports, Inc.
Price: Thunder 380, 7-shot, deep blue finish **$249.95**
Price: As above, satin nickel **$266.95**
Price: Thunder 380 Plus, 10-shot, matte blue **$316.95**
Price: As above, satin nickel **$349.95**

Brolin Legend L45

BROLIN LEGEND L45 STANDARD PISTOL
Caliber: 45 ACP, 7-shot magazine.
Barrel: 5″.
Weight: 36 oz. **Length:** 8.5″ overall.
Stocks: Checkered walnut.
Sights: Orange ramp front, white outline rear.
Features: Throated match barrel; polished feed ramp; lowered and flared ejection port; beveled magazine well; flat top slide; flat mainspring housing; lightened aluminum match trigger; slotted Commander hammer; modified high-relief grip safety; matte blue finish. Introduced 1996. Made in U.S. by Brolin Arms.
Price: **$449.00**

Brolin Legend L45C Compact Pistol
Similar to the L45 Standard pistol except has 4″ barrel with conical lock up; overall length 7.5″; weighs 32 oz. Matte blue finish. Introduced 1996. Made in U.S. by Brolin Arms.
Price: **$459.00**

BROLIN PATRIOT P45 STANDARD CARRY COMP
Caliber: 45 ACP, 7-shot magazine.
Barrel: 4″.
Weight: 37 oz. **Length:** 8.5″ overall.
Stocks: Checkered wood.
Sights: Orange ramp front, white outline rear.
Features: Dual-port compensator is integral with the throated match barrel; conical lock-up system; polished feed ramp; lowered and flared ejection port; beveled magazine well; flat-top slide; four-legged sear spring; serrated flat mainspring housing; high relief cut front strap; adjustable aluminum match trigger; beavertail grip safety; slotted Commander hammer. Introduced 1996. Made in U.S. by Brolin Arms.
Price: Blue or two-tone $649.00

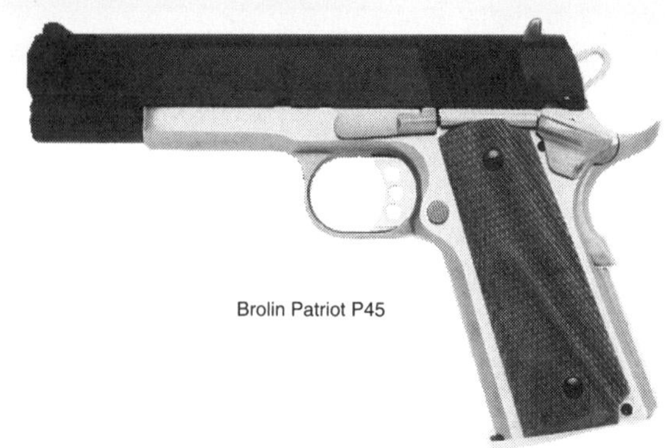
Brolin Patriot P45

Brolin P45C Compact Carry Comp
Similar to the P45 Standard Carry Comp except has 3.25″ barrel with integral milled compensator; overall length 7.5″; weighs 33 oz. Introduced 1996. Made in U.S. by Brolin Arms.
Price: Blue or two-tone $679.00

BROWNING HI-POWER 9mm AUTOMATIC PISTOL
Caliber: 9mm Para., 40 S&W, 10-shot magazine.
Barrel: $4\frac{21}{32}$″.
Weight: 32 oz. **Length:** $7\frac{3}{4}$″ overall.
Stocks: Walnut, hand checkered, or black Polyamide.
Sights: $\frac{1}{8}$″ blade front; rear screw-adjustable for windage and elevation. Also available with fixed rear (drift-adjustable for windage).
Features: External hammer with half-cock and thumb safeties. A blow on the hammer cannot discharge a cartridge; cannot be fired with magazine removed. Fixed rear sight model available. Ambidextrous safety available only with matte finish, moulded grips. Imported from Belgium by Browning.
Price: Fixed sight model, walnut grips $584.75
Price: 9mm with rear sight adj. for w. and e., walnut grips $635.95
Price: Mark III, standard matte black finish, fixed sight, moulded grips, ambidextrous safety $550.75
Price: Silver chrome, adjustable sight, Pachmayr grips $650.95

Browning FN BDA

Browning BDA 380

Browning 40 S&W Hi-Power Mark III Pistol
Similar to the standard Hi-Power except chambered for 40 S&W, 10-shot magazine, weighs 35 oz., and has $4\frac{3}{4}$″ barrel. Comes with matte blue finish, low profile front sight blade, drift-adjustable rear sight, ambidextrous safety, moulded polyamide grips with thumb rest. Introduced 1993. Imported from Belgium by Browning.
Price: Mark III $550.95

Browning Capitan Hi-Power Pistol
Similar to the standard Hi-Power except has adjustable tangent rear sight authentic to the early-production model. Also has Commander-style hammer. Checkered walnut grips, polished blue finish. Reintroduced 1993. Imported from Belgium by Browning.
Price: 9mm only $692.95

Browning Hi-Power HP-Practical Pistol
Similar to the standard Hi-Power except has silver-chromed frame with blued slide, wrap-around Pachmayr rubber grips, round-style serrated hammer and removable front sight, fixed rear (drift-adjustable for windage). Available in 9mm Para. or 40 S&W. Introduced 1991.
Price: $629.75
Price: With fully adjustable rear sight $681.95

BROWNING BDM DA AUTO PISTOL
Caliber: 9mm Para., 10-shot magazine.
Barrel: 4.73″.
Weight: 31 oz. **Length:** 7.85″ overall.
Stocks: Moulded black composition; checkered, with thumbrest on both sides.
Sights: Low profile removable blade front, rear screw adjustable for windage.
Features: Mode selector allows switching from DA pistol to "revolver" mode via a switch on the slide. Decocking lever/safety on the frame. Two redundant, passive, internal safety systems. All steel frame; matte black finish. Introduced 1991. Made in the U.S. From Browning.
Price: $612.95

BROWNING FN BDA/BDAO PISTOLS
Caliber: 9mm Para., 10-shot magazine.
Barrel: $4\frac{5}{8}$″.
Weight: 31 oz. **Length:** $7\frac{7}{8}$″ overall.
Stocks: Checkered, contoured composition.
Sights: Low profile three-dot system; blade front, rear adjustable for windage.
Features: All-steel slide and frame; tilt-barrel design; reversible magazine release; grooved front strap; matted blue finish; ambidextrous decocking lever on BDA. Available as DA or DAO. Introduced 1996. Imported from Belgium by Browning.
Price: Double action or double-action-only $612.95

BROWNING BDA-380 DA AUTO PISTOL
Caliber: 380 ACP, 10-shot magazine.
Barrel: $3\frac{13}{16}$″.
Weight: 23 oz. **Length:** $6\frac{3}{4}$″ overall.
Stocks: Smooth walnut with inset Browning medallion.
Sights: Blade front, rear drift-adjustable for windage.
Features: Combination safety and decocking lever will automatically lower a cocked hammer to half-cock and can be operated by right- or left-hand shooters. Inertia firing pin. Introduced 1978. Imported from Italy by Browning.
Price: Blue $563.95
Price: Nickel $606.95

CAUTION: PRICES SHOWN ARE SUPPLIED BY THE MANUFACTURER OR IMPORTER. CHECK YOUR LOCAL GUNSHOP.

Browning Micro Buck Mark Standard

Browning Buck Mark Varmint

BRYCO MODEL 48 AUTO PISTOLS
Caliber: 22 LR, 32 ACP, 380 ACP, 6-shot magazine.
Barrel: 4″.
Weight: 19 oz. **Length:** 6.7″ overall.
Stocks: Polished resin-impregnated wood.
Sights: Fixed.
Features: Safety locks sear and slide. Choice of satin nickel, bright chrome or black Teflon finishes. Announced 1988. From Jennings Firearms.
Price: 22 LR, 32 ACP, about **$139.00**
Price: 380 ACP, about **$139.00**

BRYCO MODEL 59 AUTO PISTOL
Caliber: 9mm Para., 10-shot magazine.
Barrel: 4″.
Weight: 33 oz. **Length:** 6.5″ overall.
Stocks: Black composition.
Sights: Blade front, fixed rear.
Features: Striker-fired action; manual thumb safety; polished blue finish. Comes with two magazines. Introduced 1994. From Jennings Firearms.
Price: About **$169.00**
Price: Model 58 (5.5″ overall length, 30 oz.) **$169.00**

CENTURY FEG P9R PISTOL
Caliber: 9mm Para., 10-shot magazine.
Barrel: 4.6″.
Weight: 35 oz. **Length:** 8″ overall.
Stocks: Checkered walnut.
Sights: Blade front, rear drift adjustable for windage.
Features: Double action with hammer-drop safety. Polished blue finish. Comes with spare magazine. Imported from Hungary by Century International Arms.
Price: About **$263.00**
Price: Chrome finish, about **$375.00**

Century FEG P9RK Auto Pistol
Similar to the P9R except has 4.12″ barrel, 7.5″ overall length and weighs 33.6 oz. Checkered walnut grips, fixed sights, 10-shot magazine. Introduced 1994. Imported from Hungary by Century International Arms, Inc.
Price: About **$290.00**

COLT 22 AUTOMATIC PISTOL
Caliber: 22 LR, 10-shot magazine.
Barrel: 4.5″.
Weight: 33 oz. **Length:** 8.62″ overall.
Stocks: Textured black polymer.
Sights: Blade front, rear drift adjustable for windage.
Features: Stainless steel construction; ventilated barrel rib; single action mechanism; cocked striker indicator; push-button safety. Introduced 1994. Made in U.S. by Colt's Mfg. Co.
Price: **$248.00**

BROWNING BUCK MARK 22 PISTOL
Caliber: 22 LR, 10-shot magazine.
Barrel: 5½″.
Weight: 32 oz. **Length:** 9½″ overall.
Stocks: Black moulded composite with skip-line checkering.
Sights: Ramp front, Browning Pro Target rear adjustable for windage and elevation.
Features: All steel, matte blue finish or nickel, gold-colored trigger. Buck Mark Plus has laminated wood grips. Made in U.S. Introduced 1985. From Browning.
Price: Buck Mark, blue **$256.95**
Price: Buck Mark, nickel finish with contoured rubber stocks **$301.95**
Price: Buck Mark Plus **$313.95**

Browning Micro Buck Mark
Same as the standard Buck Mark and Buck Mark Plus except has 4″ barrel. Available in blue or nickel. Has 16-click Pro Target rear sight. Introduced 1992.
Price: Blue **$256.95**
Price: Nickel **$301.95**
Price: Micro Buck Mark Plus **$313.95**

Browning Buck Mark Varmint
Same as the Buck Mark except has 9⅞″ heavy barrel with .900″ diameter and full-length scope base (no open sights); walnut grips with optional forend, or finger-groove walnut. Overall length is 14″, weighs 48 oz. Introduced 1987.
Price: **$390.95**

BRYCO MODEL 38 AUTO PISTOLS
Caliber: 22 LR, 32 ACP, 380 ACP, 6-shot magazine.
Barrel: 2.8″.
Weight: 15 oz. **Length:** 5.3″ overall.
Stocks: Polished resin-impregnated wood.
Sights: Fixed.
Features: Safety locks sear and slide. Choice of satin nickel, bright chrome or black Teflon finishes. Introduced 1988. From Jennings Firearms.
Price: 22 LR, 32 ACP, about **$109.95**
Price: 380 ACP, about **$129.95**

Calico M-110

CALICO M-110 AUTO PISTOL
Caliber: 22 LR. 100-shot magazine.
Barrel: 6″.
Weight: 3.7 lbs. (loaded). **Length:** 17.9″ overall.
Stocks: Moulded composition.
Sights: Adjustable post front, notch rear.
Features: Aluminum alloy frame; flash suppressor; pistol grip compartment; ambidextrous safety. Uses same helical-feed magazine as M-100 Carbine. Introduced 1986. Made in U.S. From Calico.
Price: **$359.00**

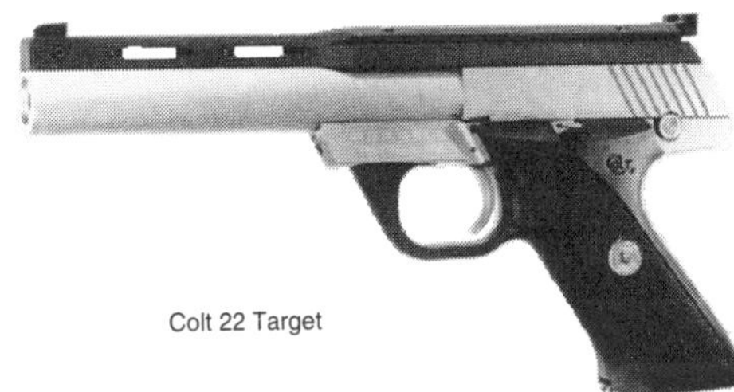
Colt 22 Target

Colt 22 Target Pistol
Similar to the Colt 22 pistol except has 6″ bull barrel, full-length sighting rib with lightening cuts and mounting rail for optical sights; fully adjustable rear sight; removable sights; two-point factory adjusted trigger travel. Stainless steel frame. Introduced 1995. Made in U.S. by Colt's Mfg. Co.
Price: **$377.00**

COLT COMBAT COMMANDER AUTO PISTOL
Caliber: 38 Super, 9-shot; 45 ACP, 8-shot.
Barrel: 4¼″.
Weight: 36 oz. **Length:** 7¾″ overall.
Stocks: Checkered rubber composite.
Sights: Fixed, glare-proofed blade front, square notch rear; three-dot system.
Features: Long trigger; arched housing; grip and thumb safeties.
Price: 45, blue **$735.00**
Price: 45, stainless **$789.00**
Price: 38 Super, stainless **$789.00**

Colt Lightweight Commander MK IV/Series 80
Same as Commander except high strength aluminum alloy frame, checkered rubber composite stocks, weighs 27½ oz. 45 ACP only.
Price: Blue **$735.00**

COLT DOUBLE EAGLE MKII/SERIES 90 DA PISTOL
Caliber: 45 ACP, 8-shot magazine.
Barrel: 4½″, 5″.
Weight: 39 oz. **Length:** 8½″ overall.
Stocks: Black checkered Xenoy thermoplastic.
Sights: Blade front, rear adjustable for windage. High profile three-dot system. Colt Accro adjustable sight optional.
Features: Made of stainless steel with matte finish. Checkered and curved extended trigger guard, wide steel trigger; decocking lever on left side; traditional magazine release; grooved frontstrap; beveled magazine well; extended grip guard; rounded, serrated combat-style hammer. Announced 1989.
Price: **$727.00**
Price: Combat Comm., 45, 4½″ bbl. **$727.00**

Colt Double Eagle Officer's ACP
Similar to the regular Double Eagle except 45 ACP only, 3½″ barrel, weighs 35 oz., 7¼″ overall length. Has 5¼″ sight radius. Introduced 1991.
Price: **$727.00**

COLT GOVERNMENT MODEL MK IV/SERIES 80
Caliber: 38 Super, 9-shot; 45 ACP, 8-shot magazine.
Barrel: 5″.
Weight: 38 oz. **Length:** 8½″ overall.
Stocks: Black composite.
Sights: Ramp front, fixed square notch rear; three-dot system.
Features: Grip and thumb safeties and internal firing pin safety, long trigger.
Price: 45 ACP, blue **$735.00**
Price: 45 ACP, stainless **$789.00**
Price: 45 ACP, bright stainless **$863.00**
Price: 38 Super, blue **$735.00**
Price: 38 Super, stainless **$789.00**
Price: 38 Super, bright stainless **$863.00**

Colt 10mm Delta Elite
Similar to the Government Model except chambered for 10mm auto cartridge. Has three-dot high profile front and rear combat sights, checkered rubber composite stocks, internal firing pin safety, and new recoil spring/buffer system. Introduced 1987.
Price: Blue **$807.00**
Price: Stainless **$860.00**

Colt Combat Elite MK IV/Series 80
Similar to the Government Model except has stainless frame with ordnance steel slide and internal parts. High profile front, rear sights with three-dot system, extended grip safety, beveled magazine well, checkered rubber composite stocks. Introduced 1986.
Price: 45 ACP, STS/B **$895.00**
Price: 38 Super, STS/B **$895.00**

COLT MODEL 1991 A1 AUTO PISTOL
Caliber: 45 ACP, 7-shot magazine.
Barrel: 5″.
Weight: 38 oz. **Length:** 8.5″ overall.
Stocks: Checkered black composition.
Sights: Ramped blade front, fixed square notch rear, high profile.
Features: Parkerized finish. Continuation of serial number range used on original G.I. 1911 A1 guns. Comes with one magazine and moulded carrying case. Introduced 1991.
Price: **$538.00**
Price: Stainless **$590.00**

Colt Model 1991 A1 Compact Auto Pistol
Similar to the Model 1991 A1 except has 3½″ barrel. Overall length is 7″, and gun is ⅜″ shorter in height. Comes with one 6-shot magazine, moulded case. Introduced 1993.
Price: **$538.00**

Colt Double Eagle Combat

Colt Government Model

Consult our Directory pages for the location of firms mentioned.

Colt 1991 A1 Compact

COLT GOVERNMENT MODEL 380
Caliber: 380 ACP, 7-shot magazine.
Barrel: 3¼″.
Weight: 21¾ oz. **Length:** 6″ overall.
Stocks: Checkered composition.
Sights: Ramp front, square notch rear, fixed.
Features: Scaled-down version of the 1911 A1 Colt G.M. Has thumb and internal firing pin safeties. Introduced 1983.
Price: Blue **$462.00**
Price: Stainless **$493.00**
Price: Pocketlite 380, blue **$462.00**

Colt Model 1991 A1 Commander Auto Pistol
Similar to the Model 1991 A1 except has 4¼″ barrel. Parkerized finish. 7-shot magazine. Comes in moulded case. Introduced 1993.
Price: **$538.00**

CAUTION: PRICES SHOWN ARE SUPPLIED BY THE MANUFACTURER OR IMPORTER. CHECK YOUR LOCAL GUNSHOP.

Colt Mustang 380, Mustang Pocketlite

Similar to the standard 380 Government Model. Mustang has steel frame (18.5 oz.), Pocketlite has aluminum alloy (12.5 oz.). Both are 1/2" shorter than 380 G.M., have 2 3/4" barrel. Introduced 1987.

Price: Mustang 380, blue $462.00
Price: As above, stainless $493.00
Price: Mustang Pocketlite, blue $462.00
Price: Mustang Pocketlite STS/N $493.00

Colt Mustang Plus II

Similar to the 380 Government Model except has the shorter barrel and slide of the Mustang. Introduced 1988.

Price: Blue $462.00
Price: Stainless $493.00

Colt Mustang 380

COLT OFFICER'S ACP MK IV/SERIES 80

Caliber: 45 ACP, 6-shot magazine.
Barrel: 3 1/2".
Weight: 34 oz. (steel frame); 24 oz. (alloy frame). **Length:** 7 1/4" overall.
Stocks: Checkered rubber composite.
Sights: Ramp blade front with white dot, square notch rear with two white dots.
Features: Trigger safety lock (thumb safety), grip safety, firing pin safety; long trigger; flat mainspring housing. Also available with lightweight alloy frame and in stainless steel. Introduced 1985.

Price: Blue $735.00
Price: L.W., blue finish $789.00
Price: Stainless $735.00
Price: Bright stainless $863.00

COLT COMBAT TARGET MODEL

Caliber: 45 ACP, 7-shot magazine.
Barrel: 5".
Weight: 39 oz. **Length:** 8 1/2" overall.
Stocks: Black composition.
Sights: Patridge-style front, Colt Accro adjustable rear.
Features: Steel target trigger with cut-out; flat-top slide; flared and lowered ejection port; beveled magazine well. Introduced 1996. Made in U.S. by Colt's Mfg. Co.

Price: Matte blue $768.00
Price: Matte stainless $820.00

COONAN 357 MAGNUM PISTOL

Caliber: 357 Mag., 7-shot magazine.
Barrel: 5".
Weight: 42 oz. **Length:** 8.3" overall.
Stocks: Smooth walnut.
Sights: Interchangeable ramp front, rear adjustable for windage.
Features: Stainless steel construction. Unique barrel hood improves accuracy and reliability. Linkless barrel. Many parts interchange with Colt autos. Has grip, hammer, half-cock safeties, extended slide latch. Made in U.S. by Coonan Arms, Inc.

Price: 5" barrel $720.00
Price: 6" barrel $755.00
Price: With 6" compensated barrel $999.00
Price: Classic model (Teflon black two-tone finish, 8-shot magazine, fully adjustable rear sight, integral compensated barrel) $1,400.00

Coonan 357 Magnum

Coonan Compact Cadet 357 Magnum Pistol

Similar to the 357 Magnum full-size gun except has 3.9" barrel, shorter frame, 6-shot magazine. Weight is 39 oz., overall length 7.8". Linkless bull barrel, full-length recoil spring guide rod, extended slide latch. Introduced 1993. Made in U.S. by Coonan Arms, Inc.

Price: $841.00

CZ 75 9MM

CZ 75 AUTO PISTOL

Caliber: 9mm Para., 40 S&W, 10-shot magazine.
Barrel: 4.7".
Weight: 34.3 oz. **Length:** 8.1" overall.
Stocks: High impact checkered plastic.
Sights: Square post front, rear adjustable for windage; three-dot system.
Features: Single action/double action design; choice of black polymer, matte or high-polish blue finishes. All-steel frame. Imported from the Czech Republic by Magnum Research.

Price: Black polymer finish $539.00
Price: Nickel $569.00

CZ 75 Compact Auto Pistol

Similar to the CZ 75 except has 10-shot magazine, 3.9" barrel and weighs 32 oz. Has removable front sight, non-glare ribbed slide top. Trigger guard is squared and serrated; combat hammer. Introduced 1993. Imported from the Czech Republic by Magnum Research.

Price: Black polymer finish $539.00

CZ 75 Semi-Compact Auto Pistol

Uses the shorter slide and barrel of the CZ 75 Compact with the full-size frame of the standard CZ 75. Has 10-shot magazine; 9mm Para. only. Introduced 1994. Imported from the Czech Republic by Magnum Research.

Price: Black polymer finish $519.00
Price: Matte blue finish $539.00
Price: High-polish blue finish $559.00

CZ 85 Auto Pistol

Same gun as the CZ 75 except has ambidextrous slide release and safety-levers; non-glare, ribbed slide top; squared, serrated trigger guard; trigger stop to prevent overtravel. Introduced 1986. Imported from the Czech Republic by Magnum Research.

Price: Black polymer finish $549.00

CZ 85 Combat Auto Pistol

Same as the CZ 85 except has walnut grips, round combat hammer, fully adjustable rear sight, extended magazine release. Trigger parts coated with friction-free beryllium copper. Introduced 1992. Imported from the Czech Republic by Magnum Research.

Price: Black polymer finish $649.00

CZ 83 DOUBLE-ACTION PISTOL

Caliber: 32, 380 ACP, 10-shot magazine.
Barrel: 3.8″.
Weight: 26.2 oz. **Length:** 6.8″ overall.
Stocks: High impact checkered plastic.
Sights: Removable square post front, rear adjustable for windage; three-dot system.
Features: Single action/double action; ambidextrous magazine release and safety. Blue finish; non-glare ribbed slide top. Imported from the Czech Republic by Magnum Research.
Price: **$409.00**

CZ 83 380

CZ 100 AUTO PISTOL

Caliber: 9mm Para., 40 S&W, 10-shot magazine.
Barrel: 3.7″.
Weight: 24 oz. **Length:** 6.9″ overall.
Stocks: Grooved polymer.
Sights: Blade front with dot, white outline rear drift adjustable for windage.
Features: Double action only with firing pin block; polymer frame, steel slide; has laser sight mount. Introduced 1996. Imported from the Czech Republic by Magnum Research.
Price: **$489.00**

DAEWOO DP51 FASTFIRE AUTO PISTOL

Caliber: 9mm Para., 40 S&W, 10-shot magazine.
Barrel: 4.1″.
Weight: 28.2 oz. **Length:** 7.5″ overall.
Stocks: Checkered composition.
Sights: 1/8″ blade front, square notch rear drift adjustable for windage. Three dot system.
Features: Patented Fastfire mechanism. Ambidextrous manual safety and magazine catch, automatic firing pin block. Alloy frame, squared trigger guard. Matte black finish. Introduced 1991. Imported from South Korea by Kimber of America, distributed by Kimber and Nationwide Sports Dist.
Price: DP51 .... **$400.00**
Price: DH40 (40 S&W) **$450.00**

Daewoo DP51 Fastfire

Daewoo DP51C, DP51S Auto Pistols

Same as the DP51 except DP51C has 3.6″ barrel, 1/4″ shorter grip frame, flat mainspring housing, and is 2 oz. lighter. Model DP51S has 3.6″ barrel, same grip as standard DP51, weighs 27 oz. Introduced 1995. Imported from South Korea by Kimber of America, Inc., distributed by Kimber and Nationwide Sports Dist.
Price: DP51C **$445.00**
Price: DP51S **$420.00**

DAEWOO DP52, DH380 AUTO PISTOLS

Caliber: 22 LR, 10-shot magazine.
Barrel: 3.8″.
Weight: 23 oz. **Length:** 6.7″ overall.
Stocks: Checkered black composition with thumbrest.
Sights: 1/8″ blade front, rear drift adjustable for windage; three-dot system.
Features: All-steel construction with polished blue finish. Dual safety system with hammer block. Introduced 1994. Imported from South Korea by Kimber of America, distributed by Kimber and Nationwide Sports Distributors.
Price: **$380.00**
Price: DH380 (as above except 380 ACP, 7-shot magazine) **$410.00**

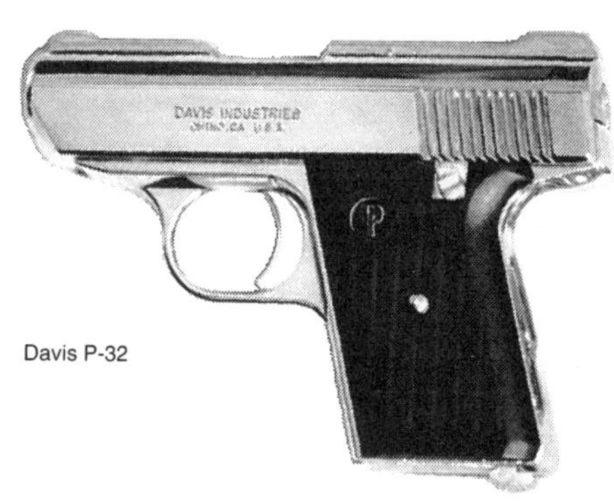
Davis P-32

DAVIS P-32 AUTO PISTOL

Caliber: 32 ACP, 6-shot magazine.
Barrel: 2.8″.
Weight: 22 oz. **Length:** 5.4″ overall.
Stocks: Laminated wood.
Sights: Fixed.
Features: Choice of black Teflon or chrome finish. Announced 1986. Made in U.S. by Davis Industries.
Price: **$87.50**

E.A.A. EUROPEAN MODEL AUTO PISTOLS

Caliber: 32 ACP or 380 ACP, 7-shot magazine.
Barrel: 3.88″.
Weight: 26 oz. **Length:** 7 3/8″ overall.
Stocks: European hardwood.
Sights: Fixed blade front, rear drift-adjustable for windage.
Features: Chrome or blue finish; magazine, thumb and firing pin safeties; external hammer; safety-lever takedown. Imported from Italy by European American Armory.
Price: Blue **$160.00**
Price: Chrome **$175.00**
Price: Ladies Model **$225.00**

DAVIS P-380 AUTO PISTOL

Caliber: 32 ACP, 6-shot, 380 ACP, 5-shot magazine.
Barrel: 2.8″.
Weight: 22 oz. **Length:** 5.4″ overall.
Stocks: Black composition.
Sights: Fixed.
Features: Choice of chrome or black Teflon finish. Introduced 1991. Made in U.S. by Davis Industries.
Price: **$98.00**

ERMA KGP68 AUTO PISTOL

Caliber: 32 ACP, 6-shot, 380 ACP, 5-shot.
Barrel: 4″.
Weight: 22 1/2 oz. **Length:** 7 3/8″ overall.
Stocks: Checkered plastic.
Sights: Fixed.
Features: Toggle action similar to original "Luger" pistol. Action stays open after last shot. Has magazine and sear disconnect safety systems. Imported from Germany by Mandall Shooting Supplies.
Price: **$499.95**

CAUTION: PRICES SHOWN ARE SUPPLIED BY THE MANUFACTURER OR IMPORTER. CHECK YOUR LOCAL GUNSHOP.

Desert Eagle Magnum

DESERT EAGLE MAGNUM PISTOL

Caliber: 357 Mag., 9-shot; 44 Mag., 8-shot; 50 Magnum, 7-shot.
Barrel: 6″, 10″, interchangeable.
Weight: 357 Mag.—62 oz.; 41 Mag., 44 Mag.—69 oz.; 50 Mag.—72 oz.
Length: 10¼″ overall (6″ bbl.).
Stocks: Hogue rubber.
Sights: Blade on ramp front, combat-style rear. Adjustable available.
Features: Rotating three-lug bolt; ambidextrous safety; combat-style trigger guard; adjustable trigger optional. Military epoxy finish. Satin, bright nickel, hard chrome, polished and blued finishes available. Made in U.S. From Magnum Research, Inc.
Price: 357, 6″ bbl., standard pistol **$979.00**
Price: 44 Mag., 6″, standard pistol **$999.00**
Price: 50 Magnum, 6″ bbl., standard pistol **$1,049.00**

Desert Industries War Eagle

DESERT INDUSTRIES WAR EAGLE PISTOL

Caliber: 380 ACP, 8- or 10-shot; 9mm Para., 14-shot; 10mm, 10-shot; 40 S&W, 10-shot; 45 ACP, 10-shot.
Barrel: 4″.
Weight: 35.5 oz. **Length:** 7.5″ overall.
Stocks: Rosewood.
Sights: Fixed.
Features: Double action; matte finish stainless steel; slide mounted ambidextrous safety. Announced 1986. From Desert Industries, Inc.
Price: **$795.00**
Price: 380 ACP **$725.00**

DESERT INDUSTRIES DOUBLE DEUCE, TWO BIT SPECIAL PISTOLS

Caliber: 22 LR, 6-shot; 25 ACP, 5-shot.
Barrel: 2½″.
Weight: 15 oz. **Length:** 5½″ overall.
Stocks: Rosewood.
Sights: Special order.
Features: Double action; stainless steel construction with matte finish; ambidextrous slide-mounted safety. From Desert Industries, Inc.
Price: 22 .... **$399.95**
Price: 25 (Two-Bit Special) **$399.95**

E.A.A. WITNESS DA AUTO PISTOL

Caliber: 9mm Para., 10-shot magazine; 38 Super, 40 S&W, 10-shot magazine; 45 ACP, 10-shot magazine.
Barrel: 4.50″.
Weight: 35.33 oz. **Length:** 8.10″ overall.
Stocks: Checkered rubber.
Sights: Undercut blade front, open rear adjustable for windage.
Features: Double-action trigger system; round trigger guard; frame-mounted safety. Introduced 1991. Imported from Italy by European American Armory.
Price: 9mm, blue **$399.00**
Price: 9mm, satin chrome **$425.00**
Price: 9mm Compact, blue, 10-shot **$399.00**
Price: As above, chrome **$425.00**
Price: 40 S&W, blue **$425.00**
Price: As above, chrome **$450.00**
Price: 40 S&W Compact, 8-shot, blue **$425.00**
Price: As above, chrome **$450.00**
Price: 45 ACP, blue **$525.00**
Price: As above, chrome **$550.00**
Price: 45 ACP Compact, 8-shot, blue **$525.00**
Price: As above, chrome **$550.00**
Price: 9mm/40 S&W Combo, blue, compact or full size **$595.00**
Price: 9mm or 40 S&W Carry Comp, blue **$550.00**

E.A.A. Witness

CONSULT
SHOOTER'S
MARKETPLACE
Page 225, This Issue

FEG B9R AUTO PISTOL

Caliber: 380 ACP, 10-shot magazine.
Barrel: 4″.
Weight: 25 oz. **Length:** 7″ overall.
Stocks: Hand-checkered walnut.
Sights: Blade front, drift-adjustable rear.
Features: Hammer-drop safety; grooved backstrap; squared trigger guard. Comes with spare magazine. Introduced 1993. Imported from Hungary by Century International Arms.
Price: About **$312.00**

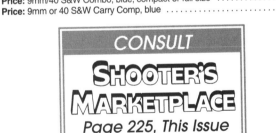

FEG B9R

FEG FP9 AUTO PISTOL
Caliber: 9mm Para., 10-shot magazine.
Barrel: 5″.
Weight: 35 oz. **Length:** 7.8″ overall.
Stocks: Checkered walnut.
Sights: Blade front, windage-adjustable rear.
Features: Full-length ventilated rib. Polished blue finish. Comes with extra magazine. Introduced 1993. Imported from Hungary by Century International Arms.
Price: About **$269.00**

FEG GKK-45

FEG GKK-45C DA AUTO PISTOL
Caliber: 45 ACP, 8-shot magazine.
Barrel: 4 1/8″.
Weight: 36 oz. **Length:** 7 3/4″ overall.
Stocks: Hand-checkered walnut.
Sights: Blade front, rear adjustable for windage; three-dot system.
Features: Combat-type trigger guard. Polished blue finish. Comes with two magazines, cleaning rod. Introduced 1995. Imported from Hungary by K.B.I., Inc.
Price: Blue **$399.00**
Price: GKK-40C (40 S&W, 9-shot magazine) **$399.00**

FEG PJK-9HP

FEG PJK-9HP AUTO PISTOL
Caliber: 9mm Para., 10-shot magazine.
Barrel: 4.75″.
Weight: 32 oz. **Length:** 8″ overall.
Stocks: Hand-checkered walnut.
Sights: Blade front, rear adjustable for windage; three dot system.
Features: Single action; polished blue or hard chrome finish; rounded combat-style serrated hammer. Comes with two magazines and cleaning rod. Imported from Hungary by K.B.I., Inc.
Price: Blue **$349.00**
Price: Hard chrome **$429.00**

Consult our Directory pages for the location of firms mentioned.

FEG P9R AUTO PISTOL
Caliber: 9mm Para., 10-shot magazine.
Barrel: 4.6″.
Weight: 35 oz. **Length:** 7.9″ overall.
Stocks: Checkered walnut.
Sights: Blade front, rear adjustable for windage.
Features: Double-action mechanism; slide-mounted safety. All-Steel construction with polished blue finish. Comes with extra magazine. Introduced 1993. Imported from Hungary by Century International Arms.
Price: About **$262.00**

FEG SMC-380 AUTO PISTOL
Caliber: 380 ACP, 6-shot magazine.
Barrel: 3.5″.
Weight: 18.5 oz. **Length:** 6.1″ overall.
Stocks: Checkered composition with thumbrest.
Sights: Blade front, rear adjustable for windage.
Features: Patterned after the PPK pistol. Alloy frame, steel slide; double action. Blue finish. Comes with two magazines, cleaning rod. Imported from Hungary by K.B.I., Inc.
Price: **$279.00**

Glock 19

FEG SMC-22 DA AUTO PISTOL
Caliber: 22 LR, 8-shot magazine.
Barrel: 3.5″.
Weight: 18.5 oz. **Length:** 6.12″ overall.
Stocks: Checkered composition with thumbrest.
Sights: Blade front, rear adjustable for windage.
Features: Patterned after the PPK pistol. Alloy frame, steel slide; blue finish. Comes with two magazines, cleaning rod. Introduced 1994. Imported from Hungary by K.B.I., Inc.
Price: **$279.00**

FEG SMC-918 Auto Pistol
Same as the SMC-380 except chambered for 9x18 Makarov. Alloy frame, steel slide, blue finish. Comes with two magazines, cleaning rod. Introduced 1995. Imported from Hungary by K.B.I., Inc.
Price: **$279.00**

GAL COMPACT AUTO PISTOL
Caliber: 45 ACP, 8-shot magazine.
Barrel: 4.25″.
Weight: 36 oz. **Length:** 7.75″ overall.
Stocks: Rubberized wrap-around.
Sights: Low profile, fixed, three-dot system.
Features: Forged steel frame and slide; competition trigger, hammer, slide stop magazine release, beavertail grip safety; front and rear slide grooves; two-tone finish. Introduced 1996. Imported from Israel by J.O. Arms, Inc.
Price: **$525.00**

GLOCK 17 AUTO PISTOL
Caliber: 9mm Para., 10-shot magazine.
Barrel: 4.49″.
Weight: 21.9 oz. (without magazine). **Length:** 7.28″ overall.
Stocks: Black polymer.
Sights: Dot on front blade, white outline rear adjustable for windage.
Features: Polymer frame, steel slide; double-action trigger with "Safe Action" system; mechanical firing pin safety, drop safety; simple takedown without tools; locked breech, recoil operated action. Adopted by Austrian armed forces 1983. NATO approved 1984. Imported from Austria by Glock, Inc.
Price: With extra magazine, magazine loader, cleaning kit **$606.00**
Price: Model 17L (6″ barrel) **$790.00**

Glock 19 Auto Pistol
Similar to the Glock 17 except has a 4″ barrel, giving an overall length of 6.85″ and weight of 20.99 oz. Magazine capacity is 10 rounds. Fixed or adjustable rear sight. Introduced 1988.
Price: **$606.00**

 CAUTION: PRICES SHOWN ARE SUPPLIED BY THE MANUFACTURER OR IMPORTER. CHECK YOUR LOCAL GUNSHOP.

Glock 21

Glock 20 10mm Auto Pistol
Similar to the Glock Model 17 except chambered for 10mm Automatic cartridge. Barrel length is 4.60″, overall length is 7.59″, and weight is 26.3 oz. (without magazine). Magazine capacity is 10 rounds. Fixed or adjustable rear sight. Comes with an extra magazine, magazine loader, cleaning rod and brush. Introduced 1990. Imported from Austria by Glock, Inc.
Price: **$658.00**

Glock 21 Auto Pistol
Similar to the Glock 17 except chambered for 45 ACP, 10-shot magazine. Overall length is 7.59″, weight is 25.2 oz. (without magazine). Fixed or adjustable rear sight. Introduced 1991.
Price: **$658.00**

Glock 22 Auto Pistol
Similar to the Glock 17 except chambered for 40 S&W, 10-shot magazine. Overall length is 7.28″, weight is 22.3 oz. (without magazine). Fixed or adjustable rear sight. Introduced 1990.
Price: **$606.00**

Glock 23 Auto Pistol
Similar to the Glock 19 except chambered for 40 S&W, 10-shot magazine. Overall length is 6.85″, weight is 20.6 oz. (without magazine). Fixed or adjustable rear sight. Introduced 1990.
Price: **$606.00**

GLOCK 26, 27 AUTO PISTOLS
Caliber: 9mm Para. (M26), 10-shot magazine; 40 S&W (M27), 9-shot magazine.
Barrel: 3.47″.
Weight: 21.75 oz. **Length:** 6.3″ overall.
Stocks: Integral. Stippled polymer.
Sights: Dot on front blade, fixed or fully adjustable white outline rear.
Features: Subcompact size. Polymer frame, steel slide; double-action trigger with "Safe Action" system, three safeties. Matte black Tenifer finish. Hammer-forged barrel. Imported from Austria by Glock, Inc. Introduced 1996.
Price: Fixed sight **$606.00**
Price: Adjustable sight **$634.00**

Glock 27 40 S&W

GOLAN AUTO PISTOL
Caliber: 9mm Para., 40 S&W, 10-shot magazine.
Barrel: 3.9″.
Weight: 34 oz. **Length:** 7″ overall.
Stocks: Textured composition.
Sights: Fixed.
Features: Fully ambidextrous double/single action; forged steel slide, alloy frame; matte blue finish. Introduced 1994. Imported from Israel by J.O. Arms, Inc.
Price: **$684.50**

HECKLER & KOCH MARK 23 SPECIAL OPERATIONS PISTOL
Caliber: 45 ACP, 10-shot magazine.
Barrel: 5.87″.
Weight: 43 oz. **Length:** 9.65″ overall.
Stocks: Integral with frame; black polymer.
Sights: Blade front, rear drift adjustable for windage; three-dot.
Features: Polymer frame; double action; exposed hammer; short recoil, modified Browning action. Civilian version of the SOCOM pistol. Introduced 1996. Imported from Germany by Heckler & Koch, Inc.
Price: **$1,995.00**

Heckler & Koch Mark 23

HECKLER & KOCH USP AUTO PISTOL
Caliber: 9mm Para., 10-shot magazine, 40 S&W, 10-shot magazine.
Barrel: 4.25″.
Weight: 28 oz. (USP40). **Length:** 6.9″ overall.
Stocks: Non-slip stippled black polymer.
Sights: Blade front, rear adjustable for windage.
Features: New HK design with polymer frame, modified Browning action with recoil reduction system, single control lever. Special "hostile environment" finish on all metal parts. Available in SA/DA, DAO, left- and right-hand versions. Introduced 1993. Imported from Germany by Heckler & Koch, Inc.
Price: Right-hand **$636.00**
Price: Left-hand **$656.00**
Price: Stainless steel, right-hand **$681.00**
Price: Stainless steel, left-hand **$701.00**

Heckler & Koch USP 45 Auto Pistol
Similar to the 9mm and 40 S&W USP except chambered for 45 ACP, 10-shot magazine. Has 4.13″ barrel, overall length of 7.87″ and weighs 30.4 oz. Has adjustable three-dot sight system. Available in SA/DA, DAO, left- and right-hand versions. Introduced 1995. Imported from Germany by Heckler & Koch, Inc.
Price: Right-hand **$696.00**
Price: Left-hand **$716.00**
Price: Stainless steel right-hand **$696.00**
Price: Stainless steel left-hand **$716.00**

Heckler & Koch USP 45

HECKLER & KOCH P7M8 AUTO PISTOL
Caliber: 9mm Para., 8-shot magazine.
Barrel: 4.13″.
Weight: 29 oz. **Length:** 6.73″ overall.
Stocks: Stippled black plastic.
Sights: Blade front, adjustable rear; three dot system.
Features: Unique "squeeze cocker" in frontstrap cocks the action. Gas-retarded action. Squared combat-type trigger guard. Blue finish. Compact size. Imported from Germany by Heckler & Koch, Inc.
Price: P7M8, blued **$1,187.00**

HERITAGE STEALTH AUTO PISTOL
Caliber: 9mm Para., 40 S&W, 10-shot magazine.
Barrel: 3.9″.
Weight: 20.2 oz. **Length:** 6.3″ overall.
Stocks: Black polymer; integral.
Sights: Blade front, rear drift adjustable for windage.
Features: Gas retarded blowback action; polymer frame, 17-4 stainless slide; frame mounted ambidextrous trigger safety, magazine safety. Introduced 1996. Made in U.S. by Heritage Mfg., Inc.
Price: **$299.95**

HI-POINT FIREARMS 40 S&W AUTO
Caliber: 40 S&W, 8-shot magazine.
Barrel: 4.5″.
Weight: 39 oz. **Length:** 7.72″ overall.
Stocks: Checkered acetal resin.
Sights: Fixed; low profile.
Features: Internal drop-safe mechansim; all aluminum frame. Introduced 1991. From MKS Supply, Inc.
Price: Matte black **$148.95**

HI-POINT FIREARMS 45 CALIBER PISTOL
Caliber: 45 ACP, 7-shot magazine.
Barrel: 4.5″.
Weight: 39 oz. **Length:** 7.95″ overall.
Stocks: Checkered acetal resin.
Sights: Fixed; low profile.
Features: Internal drop-safe mechanism; all aluminum frame. Introduced 1991. From MKS Supply, Inc.
Price: Matte black **$148.95**

HI-POINT FIREARMS MODEL 9MM COMPACT PISTOL
Caliber: 380 ACP, 9mm Para., 8-shot magazine.
Barrel: 3.5″.
Weight: 29 oz. **Length:** 6.7″ overall.
Stocks: Textured acetal plastic.
Sights: Combat-style fixed three-dot system; low profile.
Features: Single-action design; frame-mounted magazine release. Scratch-resistant matte finish. Introduced 1993. From MKS Supply, Inc.
Price: **$124.95**
Price: With polymer frame (29 oz.), non-slip grips **$132.95**
Price: 380 ACP **$89.95**

Intratec Cat 9

INTRATEC CAT 9 AUTO PISTOL
Caliber: 380 ACP, 9mm Para., 7-shot magazine.
Barrel: 3″.
Weight: 21 oz. **Length:** 5.5″ overall.
Stocks: Textured black polymer.
Sights: Fixed channel.
Features: Black polymer frame. Introduced 1993. Made in U.S. by Intratec.
Price: About **$235.00**

Heritage Stealth

Hi-Point 40 S&W

HI-POINT FIREARMS 9MM AUTO PISTOL
Caliber: 9mm Para., 9-shot magazine.
Barrel: 4.5″.
Weight: 39 oz. **Length:** 7.72″ overall.
Stocks: Textured acetal plastic.
Sights: Fixed, low profile.
Features: Single-action design. Scratch-resistant, non-glare blue finish. Introduced 1990. From MKS Supply, Inc.
Price: Matte black **$139.95**

HUNGARIAN T-58 AUTO PISTOL
Caliber: 7.62mm and 9mm Para., 8-shot magazine.
Barrel: 4.5″.
Weight: 31 oz. **Length:** 7.68″ overall.
Stocks: Grooved composition.
Sights: Blade front, rear adjustable for windage.
Features: Comes with both barrels and magazines. Thumb safety locks hammer. Blue finish. Imported by Century International Arms.
Price: About **$187.00**

INTRATEC CAT 45
Caliber: 40 S&W, 45 ACP; 6-shot magazine.
Barrel: 3.25″.
Weight: 19 oz. **Length:** 6.35″ overall.
Stocks: Moulded composition.
Sights: Fixed, channel.
Features: Black polymer frame. Introduced 1996. Made in U.S. by Intratec.
Price: **$255.00**

INTRATEC PROTEC-22, 25 AUTO PISTOLS
Caliber: 22 LR, 10-shot; 25 ACP, 8-shot magazine.
Barrel: 2½″.
Weight: 14 oz. **Length:** 5″ overall.
Stocks: Wraparound composition in gray, black or driftwood color.
Sights: Fixed.
Features: Double-action only trigger mechanism. Choice of black, satin or TEC-KOTE finish. Announced 1991. Made in U.S. by Intratec.
Price: 22 or 25, black finish **$112.00**
Price: 22 or 25, satin or TEC-KOTE finish **$117.00**

INTRATEC SPORT 22 AUTO PISTOL
Caliber: 22 LR, 10-shot magazine.
Barrel: 4″.
Weight: 28 oz. **Length:** 11$^{3}/_{16}$″ overall.
Stocks: Moulded composition.
Sights: Protected post front, adjustable for windage, rear adjustable elevation.
Features: Ambidextrous cocking knobs and safety. Matte black finish. Accepts any 10/22-type magazine. Introduced 1988. Made in U.S. by Intratec.
Price: **$130.00**

CAUTION: PRICES SHOWN ARE SUPPLIED BY THE MANUFACTURER OR IMPORTER. CHECK YOUR LOCAL GUNSHOP.

Jennings J-25

JENNINGS J-22, J-25 AUTO PISTOLS

Caliber: 22 LR, 25 ACP, 6-shot magazine.
Barrel: 2½".
Weight: 13 oz. (J-22). **Length:** 4 15/16" overall (J-22).
Stocks: Walnut on chrome or nickel models; grooved black Cycolac or resin-impregnated wood on Teflon model.
Sights: Fixed.
Features: Choice of bright chrome, satin nickel or black Teflon finish. Introduced 1981. From Jennings Firearms.
Price: J-22, about **$79.95**
Price: J-25, about **$79.95**

KAHR K9 DA AUTO PISTOL

Caliber: 9mm Para., 7-shot magazine.
Barrel: 3.5".
Weight: 25 oz. **Length:** 6" overall.
Stocks: Wrap-around textured soft polymer.
Sights: Blade front, rear drift adjustable for windage; bar-dot combat style.
Features: Trigger-cocking double-action mechanism with passive firing pin block. Made of 4140 ordnance steel with matte black finish. Introduced 1994. Made in U.S. by Kahr Arms.
Price: **$595.00**
Price: Matte black, night sights **$692.00**
Price: Matte nickel finish **$678.00**
Price: Nickel, night sights **$775.00**

Kahr K9

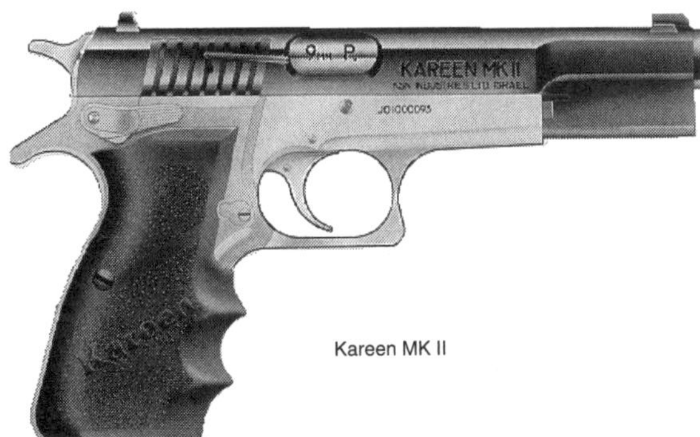
Kareen MK II

KAREEN MK II AUTO PISTOL

Caliber: 9mm Para., 10-shot magazine.
Barrel: 4.75".
Weight: 34 oz. **Length:** 7.85" overall.
Stocks: Textured composition.
Sights: Blade front, rear adjustable for windage.
Features: Single-action mechanism; ambidextrous external hammer safety; magazine safety; combat trigger guard. Two-tone finish. Introduced 1985. Imported from Israel by J.O. Arms & Ammunition.
Price: **$425.00**
Price: Kareem Mk II Compact 9mm (3.75" barrel, 30 oz., 6.75" overall length) **$495.00**

KEL-TEC P-11 AUTO PISTOL

Caliber: 9mm Para., 10-shot magazine.
Barrel: 3.1".
Weight: 14 oz. **Length:** 5.6" overall.
Stocks: Checkered black polymer.
Sights: Blade front, rear adjustable for windage.
Features: Ordnance steel slide, aluminum frame. Double-action-only trigger mechanism. Introduced 1995. Made in U.S. by Kel-Tec CNC Industries, Inc.
Price: Blue **$309.00**
Price: Stainless **$407.00**
Price: Parkerized **$350.00**

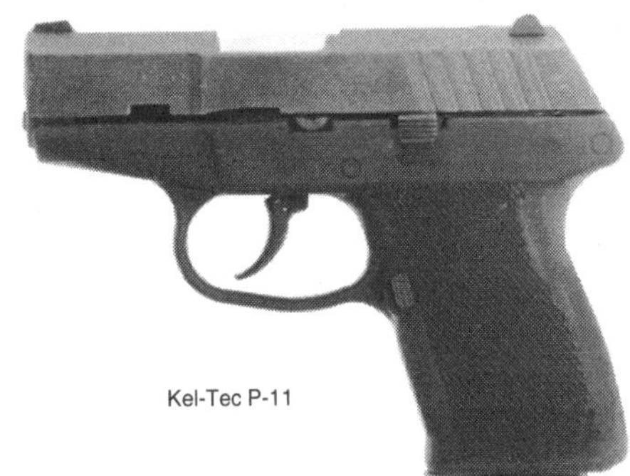
Kel-Tec P-11

Kimber Classic 45 Custom

KIMBER CLASSIC 45 CUSTOM AUTO PISTOL

Caliber: 45 ACP, 8-shot magazine.
Barrel: 5".
Weight: 38 oz. **Length:** 8.5" overall.
Stocks: Black synthetic.
Sights: McCormick dovetailed front, low combat rear.
Features: Uses Chip McCormick Corp. forged frame and slide, match-grade barrel, extended combat thumb safety, high beavertail grip safety, skeletonized lightweight composite trigger, skeletonized Commander-type hammer, elongated Commander ejector, and 8-shot magazine. Bead-blasted black oxide finish; flat mainspring housing; lowered and flared ejection port; serrated front and rear of slide; relief cut under trigger guard; Wolff spring set; beveled magazine well. Introduced 1995. Made in U.S. by Kimber of America, Inc.
Price: Custom **$575.00**
Price: Custom Stainless **$650.00**

Kimber Classic 45 Gold Match Auto Pistol

Same as the Custom Royal except also has Bo-Mar BMCS low-mount adjustable rear sight, fancy walnut grips, tighter tolerances. Comes with one 10-shot and one 8-shot magazine and factory proof target. Introduced 1995. Made in U.S. by Kimber of America, Inc.
Price: **$925.00**

Kimber Classic 45 Custom Royal Auto Pistol

Same as the Custom model except has checkered diamond-pattern walnut grips, long guide rod, polished blue finish, and comes with two 8-shot magazines. Introduced 1995. Made in U.S. by Kimber of America, Inc.
Price: **$715.00**

L.A.R. GRIZZLY WIN MAG MK I PISTOL

Caliber: 357 Mag., 357/45, 10mm, 44 Mag., 45 Win. Mag., 45 ACP, 7-shot magazine.
Barrel: 5.4″, 6.5″.
Weight: 51 oz. **Length:** $10\frac{1}{2}$″ overall.
Stocks: Checkered rubber, non-slip combat-type.
Sights: Ramped blade front, fully adjustable rear.
Features: Uses basic Browning/Colt 1911A1 design; interchangeable calibers; beveled magazine well; combat-type flat, checkered rubber mainspring housing; lowered and back-chamfered ejection port; polished feed ramp; throated barrel; solid barrel bushings. Available in satin hard chrome, matte blue, Parkerized finishes. Introduced 1983. From L.A.R. Mfg., Inc.
Price: 45 Win. Mag. **$1,000.00**
Price: 357 Mag. **$1,014.00**
Price: Conversion units (357 Mag.) **$248.00**
Price: As above, 45 ACP, 10mm, 45 Win. Mag., 357/45 Win. Mag. **$233.00**

L.A.R. Grizzly 50 Mark V Pistol

Similar to the Grizzly Win Mag Mark I except chambered for 50 Action Express with 6-shot magazine. Weight, empty, is 56 oz., overall length $10\frac{5}{8}$″. Choice of 5.4″ or 6.5″ barrel. Has same features as Mark I, IV pistols. Introduced 1993. From L.A.R. Mfg., Inc.
Price: **$1,152.00**

LASERAIM ARMS SERIES I AUTO PISTOL

Caliber: 10mm Auto, 8-shot, 45 ACP, 7-shot magazine.
Barrel: 6″, with compensator.
Weight: 46 oz. **Length:** 9.75″ overall.
Stocks: Pebble-grained black composite.
Sights: Blade front, fully adjustable rear.
Features: Single action; barrel compensator; stainless steel construction; ambidextrous safety-levers; extended slide release; matte black Teflon finish; integral mount for laser sight. Introduced 1993. Made in U.S. by Laseraim Technologies, Inc.
Price: Standard, fixed sight **$552.95**
Price: Standard, Compact ($4\frac{3}{8}$″ barrel), fixed sight **$552.95**
Price: Adjustable sight **$579.95**
Price: Standard, fixed sight, Auto Illusion red dot sight system **$649.95**
Price: Standard, fixed sight, Laseraim Laser with Hotdot **$694.95**

LLAMA MAX-I AUTO PISTOLS

Caliber: 9mm Para., 9-shot, 45 ACP, 7-shot.
Barrel: $4\frac{1}{4}$″ (Compact); $5\frac{1}{8}$″ (Government).
Weight: 34 oz. (Compact); 36 oz. (Government). **Length:** $7\frac{3}{8}$″ overall (Compact).
Stocks: Black rubber.
Sights: Blade front, rear adjustable for windage; three-dot system.
Features: Single-action trigger; skeletonized combat-style hammer; steel frame; extended manual and grip safeties. Introduced 1995. Imported from Spain by Import Sports, Inc.
Price: 9mm, 9-shot, Government model **$349.95**
Price: As above, Compact model **$349.95**
Price: 45 ACP, 7-shot, Government model **$349.95**
Price: As above, Duo-Tone finish **$366.95**
Price: As above, Compact model **$382.95**

LLAMA IX-C LARGE FRAME AUTO PISTOL

Caliber: 45 ACP, 10-shot.
Barrel: $5\frac{1}{8}$″.
Weight: 41 oz. **Length:** $8\frac{1}{2}$″ overall.
Stocks: Black rubber.
Sights: Blade front, rear adjustable for windage; three-dot system.
Features: Grip and manual safeties, ventilated rib. Imported from Spain by Import Sports, Inc.
Price: Matte finish **$399.95**

LLAMA IX-D COMPACT FRAME AUTO PISTOL

Caliber: 45 ACP, 10-shot.
Barrel: $4\frac{1}{4}$″.
Weight: 39 oz.
Stocks: Black rubber.
Sights: Blade front, rear adjustable for windage; three-dot system.
Features: Scaled-down version of the Large Frame gun. Locked breech mechanism; manual and grip safeties. Introduced 1995. Imported from Spain by Import Sports, Inc.
Price: Matte finish **$399.95**

L.A.R. Girzzly MK I

L.A.R. Grizzly 44 Mag MK IV

Similar to the Win Mag Mk I except chambered for 44 Magnum, has beavertail grip safety. Matte blue finish only. Has 5.4″ or 6.5″ barrel. Introduced 1991. From L.A.R. Mfg., Inc.
Price: **$1,014.00**

Laseraim Arms Series III Auto Pistol

Similar to the Series II except has 5″ barrel only, with dual-port compensator; weighs 43 oz.; overall length is $7\frac{5}{8}$″. Choice of fixed or adjustable rear sight. Introduced 1994. Made in U.S. by Laseraim Technologies, Inc.
Price: Fixed sight **$533.95**
Price: Adjustable sight **$559.95**
Price: Fixed sight Dream Team Laseraim laser sight **$629.95**

Laseraim Arms Series II Auto Pistol

Similar to the Series I except without compensator, has matte stainless finish. Standard Series II has 5″ barrel, weighs 43 oz., Compact has $3\frac{3}{8}$″ barrel, weighs 37 oz. Blade front sight, rear adjustable for windage or fixed. Introduced 1993. Made in U.S. by Laseraim Technologies, Inc.
Price: Standard or Compact ($3\frac{3}{8}$″ barrel), fixed sight **$399.95**
Price: Adjustable sight, 5″ only **$429.95**
Price: Standard, fixed sight, Auto Illusion red dot sight **$499.95**
Price: Standard, fixed sight, Laseraim Laser **$499.95**

Llama Max-I

Llama Large Frame

CAUTION: PRICES SHOWN ARE SUPPLIED BY THE MANUFACTURER OR IMPORTER. CHECK YOUR LOCAL GUNSHOP.

LLAMA III-A SMALL FRAME AUTO PISTOL
Caliber: 380 ACP.
Barrel: 3 11/16″.
Weight: 23 oz. **Length:** 6 1/2″ overall.
Stocks: Checkered polymer, thumbrest.
Sights: Fixed front, adjustable notch rear.
Features: Ventilated rib, manual and grip safeties. Imported from Spain by Import Sports, Inc.
Price: Blue **$248.95**
Price: Satin Chrome **$291.95**

Llama Max-1 Compensator

LLAMA MAX-I COMPENSATOR
Caliber: 45 ACP, 7-, 10-shot magazine.
Barrel: 4 7/8″ (without compensator, 6 1/3″ with).
Weight: 42 oz. (7-shot). **Length:** 9 7/8″ overall.
Stocks: Checkered rubber.
Sights: Dovetail blade front, fully adjustable rear.
Features: Extended beavertail grip safety, skeletonized combat hammer, extended slide release. Introduced 1996. Imported from Spain by Import Sports, Inc.
Price: 7-shot **$491.95**
Price: 10-shot **$516.95**

LORCIN L-22 AUTO PISTOL
Caliber: 22 LR, 9-shot magazine.
Barrel: 2.5″.
Weight: 16 oz. **Length:** 5.25″ overall.
Stocks: Black combat, or pink or pearl.
Sights: Fixed three-dot system.
Features: Available in chrome or black Teflon finish. Introduced 1989. From Lorcin Engineering.
Price: About **$89.00**

LORCIN L9MM AUTO PISTOL
Caliber: 9mm Para., 10-shot magazine.
Barrel: 4.5″.
Weight: 31 oz. **Length:** 7.5″ overall.
Stocks: Grooved black composition.
Sights: Fixed; three-dot system.
Features: Matte black finish; hooked trigger guard; grip safety. Introduced 1994. Made in U.S. by Lorcin Engineering.
Price: **$159.00**

LORCIN L-25, LT-25 AUTO PISTOLS
Caliber: 25 ACP, 7-shot magazine.
Barrel: 2.4″.
Weight: 14.5 oz. **Length:** 4.8″ overall.
Stocks: Smooth composition.
Sights: Fixed.
Features: Available in choice of finishes: chrome, black Teflon or camouflage. Introduced 1989. From Lorcin Engineering.
Price: L-25 .... **$69.00**
Price: LT-25 .... **$79.00**

LORCIN L-32, L-380 AUTO PISTOLS
Caliber: 32 ACP, 380 ACP, 7-shot magazine.
Barrel: 3.5″.
Weight: 27 oz. **Length:** 6.6″ overall.
Stocks: Grooved composition.
Sights: Fixed.
Features: Black Teflon or chrome finish with black grips. Introduced 1992. From Lorcin Engineering.
Price: L-32 32 ACP **$89.00**
Price: L-380 380 ACP **$100.00**

MITCHELL ARMS ALPHA AUTO PISTOL
Caliber: 45 ACP, 8- and 10-shot magazine.
Barrel: 5″.
Weight: 41 oz. **Length:** 8.5″ overall.
Stocks: Smooth polymer.
Sights: Interchangeable blade front, fully adjustable rear or drift adjustable rear.
Features: Interchangeable trigger modules permit double-action-only, single-action-only or SA/DA fire. Accepts any single-column, 8-shot 1911-style magazine. Frame-mounted decocker/safety; extended ambidextrous safety; extended slide latch; serrated combat hammer; beveled magazine well; heavy bull barrel (no bushing design); extended slide underlug; full-length recoil spring guide system. Introduced 1995. Made in U.S. From Mitchell Arms, Inc.
Price: Blue, fixed sight **$695.00**
Price: Blue, adjustable sight **$725.00**
Price: Stainless, fixed sight **$725.00**
Price: Stainless, adjustable sight **$749.00**

LLAMA MINIMAX SERIES
Caliber: 9mm Para., 40 S&W, 45 ACP, 6-shot magazine.
Barrel: 3 1/2″.
Weight: 35 oz. **Length:** 7 1/3″ overall.
Stocks: Checkered rubber.
Sights: Three-dot combat.
Features: Single action, skeletonized combat-style hammer, extended slide release, cone-style barrel, flared ejection port. Introduced 1996. Imported from Spain by Import Sports, Inc.
Price: Blue **$366.95**
Price: Duo-Tone finish (45 only) **$382.95**
Price: Satin chrome **$408.95**
Price: Stainless steel finish **$432.95**

Lorcin L9MM

Lorcin L-25

Mitchell Arms Alpha

MITCHELL GOLD SERIES AMBIDEXTROUS AUTO
Caliber: 9mm Para., 40 S&W.
Barrel: 4.4″.
Weight: 33 oz. **Length:** NA.
Stocks: Checkered wood.
Sights: Dovetail blade front, drift-adjustable rear; three-dot system.
Features: Ambidextrous controls, including magazine release; chrome lined barrel; forged steel slide, aluminum frame. Announced 1996. Made in U.S. by Mitchell Arms.
Price: Black pearl **$650.00**
Price: Diamond **$725.00**
Price: Gold **$795.00**

Mitchell 45 Gold Tactical Model
Similar to the Standard model except fixed or adjustable sight; adjustable trigger; ambidextrous safety; extended slide stop; checkered walnut grips; skeleton hammer. Announced 1996. Made in U.S. by Mitchell Arms.
Price: With fixed sight **$750.00**
Price: With adjustable sight **$775.00**

Mitchell 45 Gold Wide Body Standard
Similar to the 45 Gold Standard except comes with 10-shot magazine; rear slide serrations only; satin-finished slide; walnut composite grips. Announced 1994. Made in U.S. by Mitchell Arms.
Price: **$775.00**

MITCHELL 45 GOLD STANDARD MODEL
Caliber: 45 ACP, 8-shot magazine.
Barrel: 5″.
Weight: 32 oz. **Length:** 8.75″ overall.
Stocks: Wrap-around rubber.
Sights: Blade front, fixed rear.
Features: Stainless steel with bright/satin finish; front and rear slide serrations; flat grooved mainspring housing; full-length mainspring guide rod; Commander hammer; beavertail grip safety. Announced 1994. Made in U.S. by Mitchell Arms.
Price: **$675.00**

MITCHELL ARMS SPORTSTER AUTO PISTOL
Caliber: 22 LR, 10-shot magazine.
Barrel: 4.5″, 6.75″.
Weight: 39 oz. (4.5″ barrel). **Length:** 9″ overall (4.5″ barrel).
Stocks: Checkered black plastic.
Sights: Blade front, rear adjustable for windage.
Features: Military grip; standard trigger; push-button barrel takedown. Stainless steel or blue. Introduced 1992. From Mitchell Arms, Inc.
Price: **$325.00**

Consult our Directory pages for the location of firms mentioned.

MITCHELL 44 MAGNUM AUTO PISTOL
Caliber: 44 Mag., 6-shot magazine.
Barrel: 5.5″.
Weight: 46 oz. **Length:** NA.
Stocks: Checkered walnut.
Sights: Dovetail blade front, fully adjustable rear.
Features: Front and rear slide serrations; skeleton hammer. Announced 1996. Made in U.S. by Mitchell Arms.
Price: **$1,190.00**

Mountain Eagle Target

Mitchell 45 Gold Tactical

Mitchell 45 Gold Wide Body Tactical
Similar to the 45 Gold Standard except 10-shot magazine; adjustable sight; ambidextrous safety; checkered mainspring housing; adjustable trigger; extended slide release; match barrel; skeleton Commander hammer; polished slide; black composite grips. Announced 1994. Made in U.S. by Mitchell Arms.
Price: **$895.00**

MITCHELL JEFF COOPER SIGNATURE AUTO
Caliber: 45 ACP, 8-shot magazine.
Barrel: 5″ heavy match, no bushing.
Weight: 32 oz. **Length:** NA.
Stocks: Thin checkered composite.
Sights: Ramped front, fixed rear.
Features: Cooper's signature roll-marked on slide; slenderized frame; completely dehorned; short adjustable trigger; grooved arched mainspring housing; extended safety; military slide serrations; military guide rod; burn hammer. Announced 1996. Made in U.S. by Mitchell Arms.
Price: Satin black finish **$795.00**

Mitchell Jeff Cooper Commemorative Model
Similar to the Signature model except has polished frame; engraved signature; polished and gold-plated trigger; checkered walnut grips with medallion; gold-filled lettering. Limited edition gun comes with red and Marine gold lanyard with gold trim, certificate of authenticity, special case. Announced 1996. Made in U.S. by Mitchell Arms.
Price: **$1,895.00**

Mitchell Sportster

MOUNTAIN EAGLE AUTO PISTOL
Caliber: 22 LR, 10-shot magazine.
Barrel: 4.5″, 6.5″, 8″.
Weight: 21 oz., 23 oz. **Length:** 10.6″ overall (with 6.5″ barrel).
Stocks: One-piece impact-resistant polymer in "conventional contour"; checkered panels.
Sights: Serrated ramp front with interchangeable blades, rear adjustable for windage and elevation; interchangeable blades.
Features: Injection moulded grip frame, alloy receiver; hybrid composite barrel replicates shape of the Desert Eagle pistol. Flat, smooth trigger. Introduced 1992. From Magnum Research.
Price: Mountain Eagle Compact **$199.00**
Price: Mountain Eagle Standard **$239.00**
Price: Mountain Eagle Target Edition (8″ barrel) **$279.00**

NORTH AMERICAN MUNITIONS MODEL 1996
Caliber: 9mm Para., 9-shot magazine.
Barrel: 4.5″.
Weight: 40 oz. **Length:** 8.38″ overall.
Stocks: Black polycarbonate.
Sights: Blade front, adjustable rear; three-dot system.
Features: Gas-delayed blowback system; no external safeties; fixed 10-groove barrel. Introduced 1996. Made in U.S. From Intercontinental Munitions Distributors, Ltd.
Price: **$275.00**

CAUTION: PRICES SHOWN ARE SUPPLIED BY THE MANUFACTURER OR IMPORTER. CHECK YOUR LOCAL GUNSHOP.

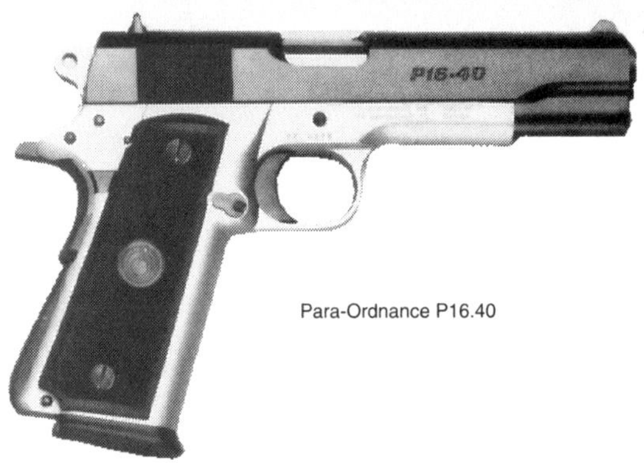
Para-Ordnance P16.40

PHOENIX ARMS MODEL RAVEN AUTO PISTOL
Caliber: 25 ACP, 6-shot magazine.
Barrel: $2\frac{7}{16}$″.
Weight: 15 oz. **Length:** $4\frac{3}{4}$″ overall.
Stocks: Ivory-colored or black slotted plastic.
Sights: Ramped front, fixed rear.
Features: Available in blue, nickel or chrome finish. Made in U.S. Available from Phoenix Arms.
Price: **$79.00**

PHOENIX ARMS HP22, HP25 AUTO PISTOLS
Caliber: 22 LR, 10-shot (HP22), 25 ACP, 10-shot (HP25).
Barrel: 3″.
Weight: 20 oz. **Length:** $5\frac{1}{2}$″ overall.
Stocks: Checkered composition.
Sights: Blade front, adjustable rear.
Features: Single action, exposed hammer; manual hold-open; button magazine release. Available in satin nickel, polished blue finish. Introduced 1993. Made in U.S. by Phoenix Arms.
Price: **$99.00**

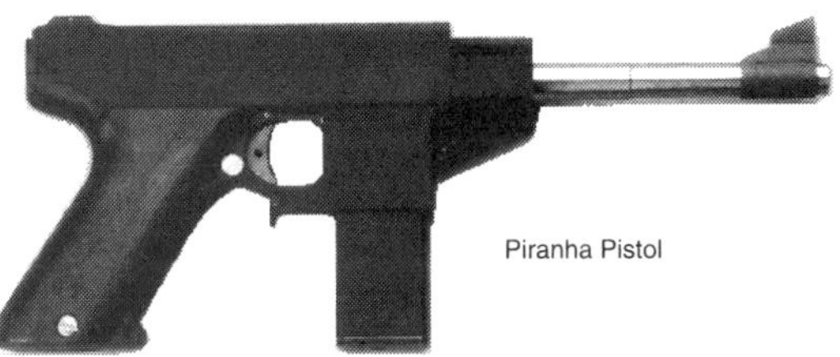
Piranha Pistol

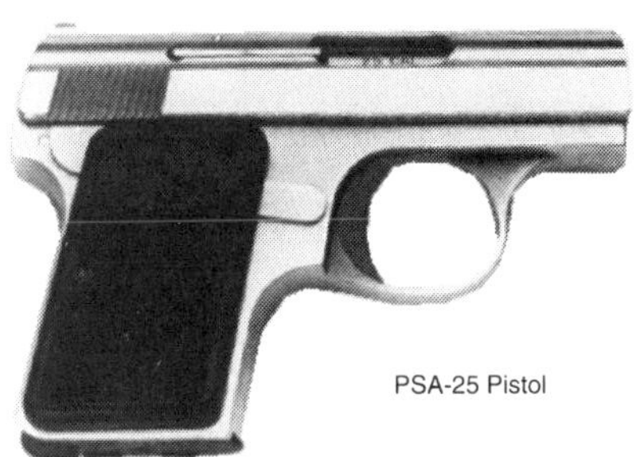
PSA-25 Pistol

ROCKY MOUNTAIN ARMS PATRIOT PISTOL
Caliber: 223, 10-shot magazine.
Barrel: 7″, with muzzle brake.
Weight: 5 lbs. **Length:** 20.5″ overall.
Stocks: Black composition.
Sights: None furnished.
Features: Milled upper receiver with enhanced Weaver base; milled lower receiver from billet plate; machined aluminum National Match handguard. Finished in DuPont Teflon-S matte black or NATO green. Comes with black nylon case, one magazine. Introduced 1993. From Rocky Mountain Arms, Inc.
Price: With A-2 handle top ....**$2,500.00** to **$2,800.00**
Price: Flat top model ....**$3,000.00** to **$3,500.00**

PARA-ORDNANCE P-SERIES AUTO PISTOLS
Caliber: 40 S&W, 45 ACP, 10-shot magazine.
Barrel: 5″.
Weight: 28 oz. (alloy frame). **Length:** 8.5″ overall.
Stocks: Textured composition.
Sights: Blade front, rear adjustable for windage. High visibility three-dot system.
Features: Available with alloy, steel or stainless steel frame with black finish (silver or stainless gun). Steel and stainless steel frame guns weighs 38 oz. (P14.45), 35 oz. (P13.45), 33 oz. (P12.45). Grooved match trigger, rounded combat-style hammer. Beveled magazine well. Manual thumb, grip and firing pin lock safeties. Solid barrel bushing. Contact maker for full details. Introduced 1990. Made in Canada by Para-Ordnance.
Price: P14.45ER (steel frame) **$750.00**
Price: P14.45RR (alloy frame) **$705.00**
Price: P12.45RR ($3\frac{1}{2}$″ bbl., 24 oz., alloy) **$705.00**
Price: P13.45RR ($4\frac{1}{4}$″ barrel, 28 oz., alloy) **$705.00**
Price: P12.45ER (steel frame) **$750.00**
Price: P16.40ER (steel frame) **$750.00**

Phoenix Arms HP22

PIRANHA AUTOLOADING PISTOL
Caliber: 9mm Para., 9mm Largo, 30 Luger, 10-shot magazine.
Barrel: 4″, 6″, 8″, 10″, 16″.
Weight: About 2.7 lbs. **Length:** 9″ overall with 4″ barrel.
Stocks: Smooth walnut.
Sights: Blade front, rear adjustable for windage.
Features: Nearly recoilless action; stainless steel construction; fires from closed bolt; change caliber by changing barrel. Introduced 1996. Made in U.S. by Recoillers Technologies, Inc.
Price: **$600.00**

CONSULT
SHOOTER'S
MARKETPLACE
Page 225, This Issue

PSA-25 AUTO PISTOL
Caliber: 25 ACP, 6-shot magazine.
Barrel: $2\frac{1}{8}$″.
Weight: 9.5 oz. **Length:** $4\frac{1}{8}$″ overall.
Stocks: Checkered black plastic.
Sights: Fixed.
Features: All steel construction with polished finish. Introduced 1984. Made in the U.S. by PSP.
Price: Black oxide **$249.00**
Price: Brushed satin chrome **$301.00**
Price: Featherweight **$375.00**

RUGER P89 AUTOMATIC PISTOL
Caliber: 9mm Para., 10-shot magazine.
Barrel: 4.50″.
Weight: 32 oz. **Length:** 7.84″ overall.
Stocks: Grooved black Xenoy composition.
Sights: Square post front, square notch rear adjustable for windage, both with white dot inserts.
Features: Double action with ambidextrous slide-mounted safety-levers. Slide is 4140 chrome-moly steel or 400-series stainless steel, frame is a lightweight aluminum alloy. Ambidextrous magazine release. Blue or stainless steel. Introduced 1986; stainless introduced 1990.
Price: P89, blue, with extra magazine and magazine loading tool, plastic case **$410.00**
Price: KP89, stainless, with extra magazine and magazine loading tool, plastic case **$452.00**

Ruger P89D Decocker Automatic Pistol

Similar to the standard P89 except has ambidextrous decocking levers in place of the regular slide-mounted safety. The decocking levers move the firing pin inside the slide where the hammer can not reach it, while simultaneously blocking the firing pin from forward movement—allows shooter to decock a cocked pistol without manipulating the trigger. Conventional thumb decocking procedures are therefore unnecessary. Blue or stainless steel. Introduced 1990.

Price: P89D, blue with extra magazine and loader, plastic case **$410.00**
Price: KP89D, stainless, with extra magazine, plastic case **$452.00**

Ruger P89 Double-Action-Only Automatic Pistol

Same as the KP89 except operates only in the double-action mode. Has a spurless hammer, gripping grooves on each side of the rear of the slide; no external safety or decocking lever. An internal safety prevents forward movement of the firing pin unless the trigger is pulled. Available in 9mm Para., stainless steel only. Introduced 1991.

Price: With lockable case, extra magazine, magazine loading tool **$452.00**

RUGER P90 SAFETY MODEL AUTOMATIC PISTOL

Caliber: 45 ACP, 7-shot magazine.
Barrel: 4.50″.
Weight: 33.5 oz. **Length:** 7.87″ overall.
Stocks: Grooved black Xenoy composition.
Sights: Square post front, square notch rear adjustable for windage, both with white dot inserts.
Features: Double action with ambidextrous slide-mounted safety-levers which move the firing pin inside the slide where the hammer can not reach it, while simultaneously blocking the firing pin from forward movement. Stainless steel only. Introduced 1991.
Price: KP90 with plastic case, extra magazine, loader **$488.65**

RUGER P93 COMPACT AUTOMATIC PISTOL

Caliber: 9mm Para., 10-shot magazine.
Barrel: 3.9″.
Weight: 31 oz. **Length:** 7.3″ overall.
Stocks: Grooved black Xenoy composition.
Sights: Square post front, square notch rear adjustable for windage.
Features: Front of slide is crowned with a convex curve; slide has seven finger grooves; trigger guard bow is higher for a better grip; 400-series stainless slide, lightweight alloy frame. Decocker-only or DAO-only. Introduced 1993. Made in U.S. by Sturm, Ruger & Co.
Price: **$520.00**

Ruger KP94 Automatic Pistol

Sized midway between the full-size P-Series and the compact P93. Has 4.25″ barrel, 7.5″ overall length and weighs about 33 oz. KP94 is manual safety model; KP94DAO is double-action-only (both 9mm Para., 10-shot magazine); KP94D is decocker-only in 40 S&W with 10-shot magazine. Slide gripping grooves roll over top of slide. KP94 has ambidextrous safety-levers; KP94DAO has no external safety, full-cock hammer position or decocking lever; KP94D has ambidextrous decocking levers. Matte finish stainless slide, barrel, alloy frame. Introduced 1994. Made in U.S. by Sturm, Ruger & Co.

Price: KP94 (9mm), KP944 (40) **$520.00**
Price: KP94DAO (9mm), KP944DAO (40) **$520.00**
Price: KP94D (9mm), KP9440 (40 S&W) **$520.00**

Ruger P94L Automatic Pistol

Same as the KP94 except mounts a laser sight in a housing cast integrally with the frame. Allen-head screws control windage and elevation adjustments. Announced 1994. Made in U.S. by Sturm, Ruger & Co.

Price: For law enforcement only .... **NA**

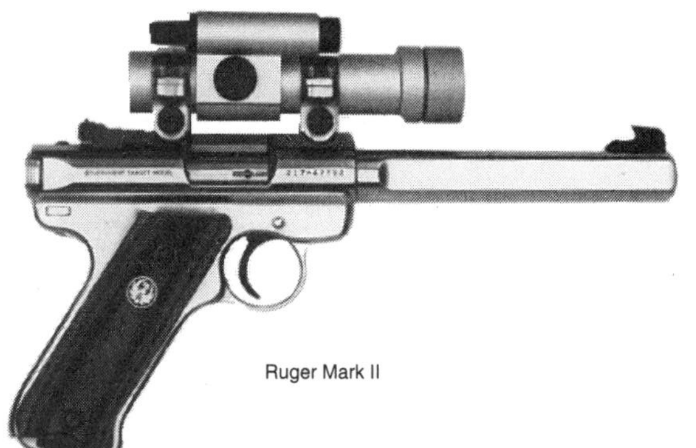

Ruger Mark II

Ruger KP89D

Ruger P90 Decocker Automatic Pistol

Similar to the P90 except has a manual decocking system. The ambidextrous decocking levers move the firing pin inside the slide where the hammer can not reach it, while simultaneously blocking the firing pin from forward movement—allows shooter to decock a cocked pistol without manipulating the trigger. Available only in stainless steel. Overall length 7.87″, weighs 34 oz. Introduced 1991.

Price: P90D with lockable case, extra magazine, and magazine loading tool **$488.65**

Ruger P93 DAO

RUGER P95 AUTOMATIC PISTOL

Caliber: 9mm Para., 10-shot magazine.
Barrel: 3.9″.
Weight: 27 oz. **Length:** 7.3″ overall.
Stocks: Grooved; integral with frame.
Sights: Blade front, rear drift adjustable for windage; three-dot system.
Features: Moulded grip frame, stainless steel or chrome-moly slide. Suitable for +P+ ammunition. Decocker or DAO. Introduced 1996. Made in U.S. by Sturm, Ruger & Co. Comes with lockable plastic case, spare magazine, loading tool.
Price: P95 DAO double-action-only **$343.00**
Price: P95D decocker only **$351.00**

RUGER MARK II STANDARD AUTO PISTOL

Caliber: 22 LR, 10-shot magazine.
Barrel: 4 3/4″ or 6″.
Weight: 25 oz. (4 3/4″ bbl.). **Length:** 8 5/16″ (4 3/4″ bbl.).
Stocks: Checkered plastic.
Sights: Fixed, wide blade front, square notch rear adjustable for windage.
Features: Updated design of the original Standard Auto. Has new bolt hold-open latch. 10-shot magazine, magazine catch, safety, trigger and new receiver contours. Introduced 1982.
Price: Blued (MK 4, MK 6) **$252.00**
Price: In stainless steel (KMK 4, KMK 6) **$330.25**

Ruger 22/45 Mark II Pistol

Similar to the other 22 Mark II autos except has grip frame of Zytel that matchs the angle and magazine latch of the Model 1911 45 ACP pistol. Available in 4 3/4″ standard and 5 1/2″ bull barrel. Introduced 1992.

Price: KP4 (4 3/4″ barrel) **$280.00**
Price: KP512 (5 1/2″ bull barrel) **$330.00**
Price: P512 (5 1/2″ bull barrel, all blue) **$237.50**

CAUTION: PRICES SHOWN ARE SUPPLIED BY THE MANUFACTURER OR IMPORTER. CHECK YOUR LOCAL GUNSHOP.

Ruger MK-4B Compact

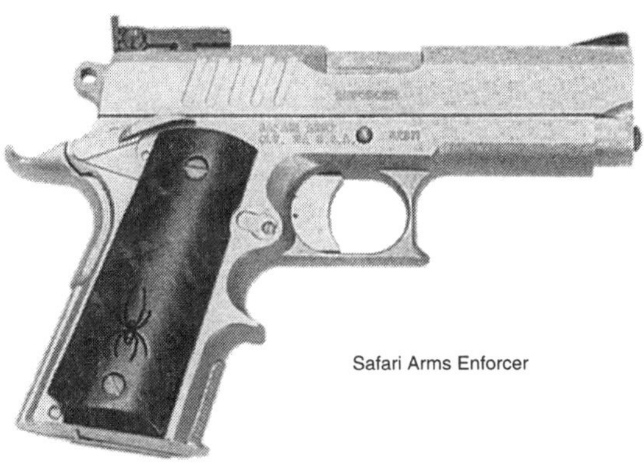
Safari Arms Enforcer

SCHUETZEN PISTOL WORKS BIG DEUCE PISTOL
Caliber: 45 ACP, 7-shot magazine.
Barrel: 6″, 416 stainless steel.
Weight: 40.3 oz. **Length:** 9.5″ overall.
Stocks: Smooth walnut.
Sights: Ramped blade front, LPA adjustable rear.
Features: Beavertail grip safety; extended thumb safety and slide release; Commander-style hammer. Throated, polished and tuned. Parkerized matte black slide with satin stainless steel frame. Introduced 1995. Made in U.S. by Safari Arms, Inc.
Price: $849.00

SCHUETZEN PISTOL WORKS GRIFFON PISTOL
Caliber: 45 ACP, 10-shot magazine.
Barrel: 5″, 416 stainless steel.
Weight: 40.5 oz. **Length:** 8.5″ overall.
Stocks: Smooth walnut.
Sights: Ramped blade front, LPA adjustable rear.
Features: 10+1 1911 enhanced 45. Beavertail grip safety; long aluminum trigger; full-length recoil spring guide; Commander-style hammer. Throated, polished and tuned. Grip size comparable to standard 1911. Satin stainless steel finish. Introduced 1996. Made in U.S. by Olympic Arms, Inc.
Price: $910.00

SCHUETZEN PISTOL WORKS RELIABLE PISTOL
Caliber: 45 ACP, 7-shot magazine.
Barrel: 5″, 416 stainless steel.
Weight: 39 oz. **Length:** 8.5″ overall.
Stocks: Checkered walnut.
Sights: Ramped blade front, LPA adjustable rear.
Features: Beavertail grip safety; long aluminum trigger; full-length recoil spring guide; Commander-style hammer. Throated, polished and tuned. Satin stainless steel finish. Introduced 1996. Made in U.S. by Safari Arms, Inc.
Price: $815.00

SCHUETZEN PISTOL WORKS RENEGADE
Caliber: 45 ACP, 7-shot magazine.
Barrel: 5″, 416 stainless steel.
Weight: 39 oz. **Length:** 8.5″ overall.
Stocks: Checkered walnut.
Sights: Ramped blade, LPA adjustable rear.
Features: True left-hand pistol. Beavertail grip safety; long aluminum trigger; full-length recoil spring guide; Commander-style hammer; satin stainless finish. Throated, polished and tuned. Introduced 1996. Made in U.S. by Safari Arms, Inc.
Price: $1,075.00

Ruger MK-4B Compact Pistol
Similar to the Mark II Standard pistol except has 4″ bull barrel, Patridge-type front sight, fully adjustable rear, and smooth laminated hardwood thumbrest stocks. Weighs 38 oz., overall length of 8 3/16″. Comes with extra magazine, plastic case, lock. Introduced 1996. Made in U.S. by Sturm, Ruger & Co.
Price: $336.50

SAFARI ARMS COHORT PISTOL
Caliber: 45 ACP, 7-shot magazine.
Barrel: 3.8″, 416 stainless.
Weight: 37 oz. **Length:** 8.5″ overall.
Stocks: Smooth walnut with laser-etched black widow logo.
Sights: Ramped blade front, LPA adjustable rear.
Features: Combines the Enforcer model, slide and MatchMaster frame. Beavertail grip safety; extended thumb safety and slide release; Commander-style hammer. Throated, polished and tuned. Satin stainless finish. Introduced 1996. Made in U.S. by Safari Arms, Inc.
Price: $780.00

SAFARI ARMS ENFORCER PISTOL
Caliber: 45 ACP, 6-shot magazine.
Barrel: 3.8″, stainless.
Weight: 36 oz. **Length:** 7.3″ overall.
Stocks: Smooth walnut with etched black widow spider logo.
Sights: Ramped blade front, LPA adjustable rear.
Features: Extended safety, extended slide release; Commander-style hammer; beavertail grip safety; throated, polished, tuned. Parkerized matte black or satin stainless steel finishes. Made in U.S. by Safari Arms.
Price: $740.00

Schuetzen Pistol Works Enforcer Carrycomp II Pistol
Similar to the Enforcer except has Wil Schueman-designed hybrid compensator system. Introduced 1993. Made in U.S. by Safari Arms, Inc.
Price: 3.8″ barrel $1,150.00
Price: 5″ barrel $1,300.00

SAFARI ARMS GI SAFARI PISTOL
Caliber: 45 ACP, 7-shot magazine.
Barrel: 5″, 416 stainless.
Weight: 39.9 oz. **Length:** 8.5″ overall.
Stocks: Checkered walnut.
Sights: G.I.-style blade front, drift-adjustable rear.
Features: Beavertail grip safety; extended thumb safety and slide release; Commander-style hammer. Parkerized finish. Reintroduced 1996.
Price: .... $585.00.

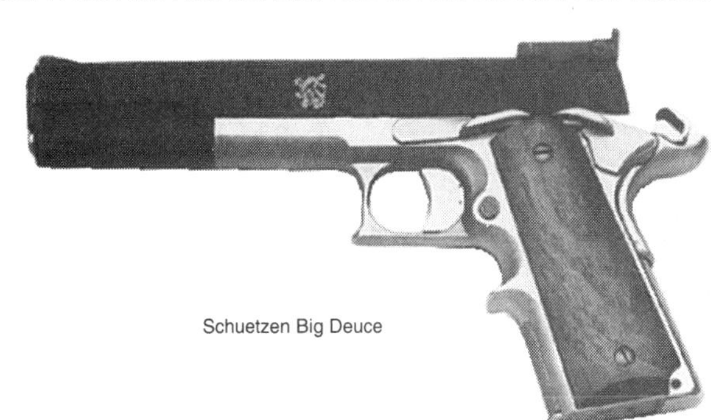
Schuetzen Big Deuce

Schuetzen Pistol Works Reliable 4-Star Pistol
Similar to the Reliable except has 4.5″ barrel, 7.5″ overall length, and weighs 35.7 oz. Introduced 1996. Made in U.S. by Safari Arms, Inc.
Price: $875.00

SEECAMP LWS 32 STAINLESS DA AUTO
Caliber: 32 ACP Win. Silvertip, 6-shot magazine.
Barrel: 2″, integral with frame.
Weight: 10.5 oz. **Length:** 4 1/8″ overall.
Stocks: Glass-filled nylon.
Sights: Smooth, no-snag, contoured slide and barrel top.
Features: Aircraft quality 17-4 PH stainless steel. Inertia-operated firing pin. Hammer fired double-action-only. Hammer automatically follows slide down to safety rest position after each shot—no manual safety needed. Magazine safety disconnector. Polished stainless. Introduced 1985. From L.W. Seecamp.
Price: $375.00

SIG SAUER P220 "AMERICAN" AUTO PISTOL

Caliber: 38 Super, 45 ACP, (9-shot in 38 Super, 7 in 45).
Barrel: $4^{3}/_{8}$″.
Weight: $28^{1}/_{4}$ oz. (9mm). **Length:** $7^{3}/_{4}$″ overall.
Stocks: Checkered black plastic.
Sights: Blade front, drift adjustable rear for windage.
Features: Double action. Decocking lever permits lowering hammer onto locked firing pin. Squared combat-type trigger guard. Slide stays open after last shot. Imported from Germany by SIGARMS, Inc.
Price: "American," blue (side-button magazine release, 45 ACP only) . . . **$805.00**
Price: 45 ACP, blue, Siglite night sights . . . **$905.00**
Price: K-Kote finish . . . **$850.00**
Price: K-Kote, Siglite night sights . . . **$950.00**

SIG SAUER P225 DA AUTO PISTOL

Caliber: 9mm Para., 8-shot magazine.
Barrel: 3.8″.
Weight: 26 oz. **Length:** $7^{3}/_{32}$″ overall.
Stocks: Checkered black plastic.
Sights: Blade front, rear adjustable for windage. Optional Siglite night sights.
Features: Double action. Decocking lever permits lowering hammer onto locked firing pin. Square combat-type trigger guard. Shortened, lightened version of P220. Imported from Germany by SIGARMS, Inc.
Price: Blue, SA/DA or DAO . . . **$780.00**
Price: With Siglite night sights, blue, SA/DA or DAO . . . **$880.00**
Price: K-Kote finish . . . **$850.00**
Price: K-Kote with Siglite night sights . . . **$950.00**

SIG Sauer P228 DA Auto Pistol

Similar to the P226 except has 3.86″ barrel, with 7.08″ overall length and 3.35″ height. Chambered for 9mm Para. only, 10-shot magazine. Weight is 29.1 oz. with empty magazine. Introduced 1989. Imported from Germany by SIGARMS, Inc.
Price: Blue . . . **$825.00**
Price: Blue, with Siglite night sights . . . **$925.00**
Price: Blue, double-action-only . . . **$825.00**
Price: Blue, double-action-only, Siglite night sights . . . **$975.00**
Price: K-Kote finish . . . **$875.00**
Price: K-Kote, Siglite night sights . . . **$975.00**
Price: K-Kote, double-action-only . . . **$875.00**
Price: K-Kote, double-action-only, Siglite night sights . . . **$975.00**

SIG SAUER P230 DA AUTO PISTOL

Caliber: 32 ACP, 8-shot; 380 ACP, 7-shot.
Barrel: $3^{3}/_{4}$″.
Weight: 16 oz. **Length:** $6^{1}/_{2}$″ overall.
Stocks: Checkered black plastic.
Sights: Blade front, rear adjustable for windage.
Features: Double action/single action or DAO. Same basic action design as P220. Blowback operation, stationary barrel. Introduced 1977. Imported from Germany by SIGARMS, Inc.
Price: Blue . . . **$510.00**
Price: In stainless steel (P230 SL) . . . **$595.00**
Price: With stainless steel slide, blue frame . . . **$545.00**

SIG P210-6 AUTO PISTOL

Caliber: 9mm Para., 8-shot magazine.
Barrel: $4^{3}/_{4}$″.
Weight: 32 oz. **Length:** $8^{1}/_{2}$″ overall.
Stocks: Checkered walnut.
Sights: Blade front, notch rear drift adjustable for windage.
Features: Mechanically locked, short-recoil operation; single action only; target trigger with adjustable stop; magazine safety; all-steel construction with matte blue finish. Optional 22 LR conversion kit consists of barrel, slide, recoil spring and magazine. Imported from Switzerland by SIGARMS, Inc.
Price: . . . **$2,300.00**
Price: With 22LR conversion kit . . . **$2,900.00**

SMITH & WESSON MODEL 422, 622 AUTO

Caliber: 22 LR, 10-shot magazine.
Barrel: $4^{1}/_{2}$″, 6″.
Weight: 22 oz. ($4^{1}/_{2}$″ bbl.). **Length:** $7^{1}/_{2}$″ overall ($4^{1}/_{2}$″ bbl.).
Stocks: Checkered simulated woodgrain polymer.
Sights: Field—serrated ramp front, fixed rear; Target—serrated ramp front, adjustable rear.
Features: Aluminum frame, steel slide, brushed stainless steel or blue finish; internal hammer. Introduced 1987. Model 2206 introduced 1990.
Price: Blue, $4^{1}/_{2}$″, 6″, fixed sight . . . **$235.00**
Price: As above, adjustable sight . . . **$290.00**
Price: Stainless (Model 622), $4^{1}/_{2}$″, 6″, fixed sight . . . **$284.00**
Price: As above, adjustable sight . . . **$337.00**

SIG Sauer P228

SIG Sauer P226 DA Auto Pistol

Similar to the P220 pistol except has 4.4″ barrel, and weighs $26^{1}/_{2}$ oz. 357 SIG or 9mm. Imported from Germany by SIGARMS, Inc.
Price: Blue . . . **$825.00**
Price: With Siglite night sights . . . **$925.00**
Price: Blue, double-action-only . . . **$825.00**
Price: Blue, double-action-only, Siglite night sights . . . **$925.00**
Price: K-Kote finish . . . **$875.00**
Price: K-Kote, Siglite night sights . . . **$975.00**
Price: K-Kote, double-action-only . . . **$875.00**
Price: K-Kote, double-action-only, Siglite night sights . . . **$975.00**

SIG Sauer P229 DA Auto Pistol

Similar to the P228 except chambered for 9mm Para., 40 S&W, 357 SIG. Has 3.86″ barrel, 7.08″ overall length and 3.35″ height. Weight is 30.5 oz. Introduced 1991. Frame made in Germany, stainless steel slide assembly made in U.S.; pistol assembled in U.S. From SIGARMS, Inc.
Price: Blue . . . **$875.00**
Price: With nickel slide . . . **$900.00**
Price: Blue, double-action-only . . . **$875.00**
Price: With Siglite night sights . . . **$975.00**

SIG Sauer P230

SIG P-210-2 AUTO PISTOL

Caliber: 7.65mm or 9mm Para., 8-shot magazine.
Barrel: $4^{3}/_{4}$″.
Weight: $31^{3}/_{4}$ oz. (9mm). **Length:** $8^{1}/_{2}$″ overall.
Stocks: Checkered black composition.
Sights: Blade front, rear adjustable for windage.
Features: Lanyard loop; matte finish. Conversion unit for 22 LR available. Imported from Switzerland by Mandall Shooting Supplies.
Price: P-210-2 Service Pistol . . . **$3,500.00**

Smith & Wesson Model 422

CAUTION: PRICES SHOWN ARE SUPPLIED BY THE MANUFACTURER OR IMPORTER. CHECK YOUR LOCAL GUNSHOP.

Smith & Wesson Model 622 VR Auto

Similar to the Model 622 except 6″ barrel only with ventilated rib, glass-beaded serrated sight line with revised ramped front sight; matte black trigger, barrel and extractor; revised trigger guard. Introduced 1996. Made in U.S. by Smith & Wesson.

Price: **$310.00**

Smith & Wesson Model 2213, 2214 Sportsman Auto

Similar to the Model 422 except has 3″ barrel, 8-shot magazine; dovetail Patridge front sight with white dot, fixed rear with two white dots; matte blue finish, black composition grips with checkered panels. Overall length 6$^{1}/_{8}$″, weight 18 oz. Introduced 1990.

Price: **$269.00**
Price: Model 2213 (stainless steel) **$314.00**

Smith & Wesson Model 2206 Target Auto

Same as the Model 2206 except 6″ barrel only; Millett Series 100 fully adjustable sight system; Patridge front sight; smooth contoured Herrett walnut target grips with thumbrest; serrated trigger with adjustable stop. Frame is bead-blasted along sighting plane, drilled and tapped for optics mount. Introduced 1994. Made in U.S. by Smith & Wesson.

Price: **$433.00**

SMITH & WESSON MODEL 410 DA AUTO PISTOL

Caliber: 40 S&W, 10-shot magazine.
Barrel: 4″.
Weight: 28.5 oz. **Length:** 7.5 oz.
Stocks: One-piece Xenoy, wrap-around with straight backstrap.
Sights: Post front, fixed rear; three-dot system.
Features: Aluminum alloy frame; blued carbon steel slide; traditional double action with left-side slide-mountd decocking lever. Introduced 1996. Made in U.S. by Smith & Wesson.
Price: **$490.00**

SMITH & WESSON MODEL 457 DA AUTO PISTOL

Caliber: 45 ACP, 7-shot magazine.
Barrel: 3$^{3}/_{4}$″.
Weight: 29 oz. **Length:** 7$^{1}/_{4}$″ overall.
Stocks: One-piece Xenoy, wrap-around with straight backstrap.
Sights: Post front, fixed rear, three-dot system.
Features: Aluminum alloy frame, matte blue carbon steel slide; bobbed hammer; smooth trigger. Introduced 1996. Made in U.S. by Smith & Wesson.
Price: **$490.00**

SMITH & WESSON MODEL 909, 910 DA AUTO PISTOLS

Caliber: 9mm Para., 10-shot magazine.
Barrel: 4″.
Weight: 28 oz. **Length:** 7$^{3}/_{8}$″ overall.
Stocks: One-piece Xenoy, wrap-around with straight backstrap.
Sights: Post front with white dot, fixed two-dot rear.
Features: Alloy frame, blue carbon steel slide. Slide-mounted decocking lever. Introduced 1995.
Price: Model 910 . . . .**$443.00**
Price: Model 909 (9-shot magazine, curved backstrap, 27 oz.) **$443.00**

SMITH & WESSON MODEL 3913 DOUBLE ACTION

Caliber: 9mm Para., 8-shot magazine.
Barrel: 3$^{1}/_{2}$″.
Weight: 26 oz. **Length:** 6$^{13}/_{16}$″ overall.
Stocks: One-piece Delrin wrap-around, textured surface.
Sights: Post front with white dot, Novak LoMount Carry with two dots, adjustable for windage.
Features: Aluminum alloy frame, stainless slide (M3913) or blue steel slide (M3914). Bobbed hammer with no half-cock notch; smooth .304″ trigger with rounded edges. Straight backstrap. Extra magazine included. Introduced 1989.
Price: **$622.00**

Smith & Wesson Model 3913 LadySmith Auto

Similar to the standard Model 3913 except has frame that is upswept at the front, rounded trigger guard. Comes in frosted stainless steel with matching gray grips. Grips are ergonomically correct for a woman's hand. Novak LoMount Carry rear sight adjustable for windage, smooth edges for snag resistance. Extra magazine included. Introduced 1990.

Price: **$640.00**

Smith & Wesson Model 3953DA Pistol

Same as the Model 3913 except double-action-only. Model 3953 has stainless slide with alloy frame. Overall length 7″; weighs 25.5 oz. Extra magazine included. Introduced 1990.

Price: **$622.00**

Smith & Wesson Model 622 VR

Smith & Wesson Model 2206 Auto

Similar to the Model 422/622 except made entirely of stainless steel with non-reflective finish. Weight is 39 oz. Introduced 1990.

Price: With adjustable sight **$385.00**

Smith & Wesson Model 457

SMITH & WESSON MODEL 908 AUTO PISTOL

Caliber: 9mm Para., 8-shot magazine.
Barrel: 3$^{1}/_{2}$″.
Weight: 26 oz. **Length:** 6$^{13}/_{16}$″.
Stocks: One-piece Xenoy, wrap-around with straight backstrap.
Sights: Post front, fixed rear, three-dot system.
Features: Aluminum alloy frame, matte blue carbon steel slide; bobbed hammer; smooth trigger. Introduced 1996. Made in U.S. by Smith & Wesson.
Price: **$443.00**

Smith & Wesson Model 910

Smith & Wesson 3913 LadySmith

SMITH & WESSON MODEL 4006 DA AUTO
Caliber: 40 S&W, 10-shot magazine.
Barrel: 4″.
Weight: 38.5 oz. **Length:** 7⅞″ overall.
Stocks: Xenoy wrap-around with checkered panels.
Sights: Replaceable post front with white dot, Novak LoMount Carry fixed rear with two white dots, or micro. click adjustable rear with two white dots.
Features: Stainless steel construction with non-reflective finish. Straight backstrap. Extra magazine included. Introduced 1990.
Price: With adjustable sights **$775.00**
Price: With fixed sight **$745.00**
Price: With fixed night sights **$855.00**

SMITH & WESSON MODEL 4013, 4053 AUTOS
Caliber: 40 S&W, 8-shot magazine.
Barrel: 3½″.
Weight: 26 oz. **Length:** 7″ overall.
Stocks: One-piece Xenoy wrap-around with straight backstrap.
Sights: Post front with white dot, fixed Novak LoMount Carry rear with two white dots.
Features: Model 4013 is traditional double action; Model 4053 is double-action-only; stainless slide on alloy frame. Introduced 1991.
Price: Model 4013 . . . . **$722.00**
Price: Model 4053 . . . . **$722.00**

SMITH & WESSON MODEL 4500 SERIES AUTOS
Caliber: 45 ACP, 7-shot (M4516), 8-shot magazine for M4506, 4566/4586.
Barrel: 3¾″ (M4516), 5″ (M4506).
Weight: 41 oz. (4506). **Length:** 7⅛″ overall (4516).
Stocks: Xenoy one-piece wrap-around, arched or straight backstrap on M4506, straight only on M4516.
Sights: Post front with white dot, adjustable or fixed Novak LoMount Carry on M4506.
Features: M4506 has serrated hammer spur. Extra magazine included. Contact Smith & Wesson for complete data. Introduced 1989.
Price: Model 4506, fixed sight **$774.00**
Price: Model 4506, adjustable sight **$806.00**
Price: Model 4516, fixed sight **$774.00**
Price: Model 4566 (stainless, 4¼″, traditional DA, ambidextrous safety, fixed sight) **$774.00**
Price: Model 4586 (stainless, 4¼″, DA only) **$774.00**

SMITH & WESSON MODEL 5900 SERIES AUTO PISTOLS
Caliber: 9mm Para., 10-shot magazine.
Barrel: 4″.
Weight: 28½ to 37½ oz. (fixed sight); 38 oz. (adjustable sight). **Length:** 7½″ overall.
Stocks: Xenoy wrap-around with curved backstrap.
Sights: Post front with white dot, fixed or fully adjustable with two white dots.
Features: All stainless, stainless and alloy or carbon steel and alloy construction. Smooth .304″ trigger, .260″ serrated hammer. Extra magazine included. Introduced 1989.
Price: Model 5903 (stainless, alloy frame, traditional DA, fixed sight, ambidextrous safety) **$690.00**
Price: Model 5904 (blue, alloy frame, traditional DA, adjustable sight, ambidextrous safety) **$642.00**
Price: Model 5906 (stainless, traditional DA, adjustable sight, ambidextrous safety) **$742.00**
Price: As above, fixed sight **$707.00**
Price: With fixed night sights **$817.00**
Price: Model 5946 (as above, stainless frame and slide) **$707.00**

Smith & Wesson Model 6904/6906 Double-Action Autos
Similar to the Models 5904/5906 except with 3½″ barrel, 10-shot magazine, fixed rear sight, .260″ bobbed hammer. Extra magazine included. Introduced 1989.
Price: Model 6904, blue **$614.00**
Price: Model 6906, stainless **$677.00**
Price: Model 6906 with fixed night sights **$788.00**
Price: Model 6946 (stainless, DA only, fixed sights) **$677.00**

SMITH & WESSON SIGMA SW380 AUTO
Caliber: 380 ACP, 6-shot magazine.
Barrel: 3″.
Weight: 14 oz. **Length:** 5.8″ overall.
Stocks: Integral.
Sights: Fixed groove in the slide.
Features: Polymer frame; double-action-only trigger mechanism; grooved/serrated front and rear straps; two passive safeties. Introduced 1995. Made in U.S. by Smith & Wesson.
Price: **$308.00**

Smith & Wesson Model 4046 DA Pistol
Similar to the Model 4006 except is double-action-only. Has a semi-bobbed hammer, smooth trigger, 4″ barrel; Novak LoMount Carry rear sight, post front with white dot. Overall length is 7½″, weighs 28 oz. Extra magazine included. Introduced 1991.
Price: **$745.00**
Price: With fixed night sights **$855.00**

Smith & Wesson Model 4053

Smith & Wesson Model 4506

Smith & Wesson Sigma

SMITH & WESSON SIGMA SERIES PISTOLS
Caliber: 9mm Para., 40 S&W, 10-shot magazine.
Barrel: 4.5″.
Weight: 26 oz. **Length:** 7.4″ overall.
Stocks: Integral.
Sights: White dot front, fixed rear; three-dot system. Tritium night sights available.
Features: Ergonomic polymer frame; low barrel centerline; internal striker firing system; corrosion-resistant slide; Teflon-filled, electroless-nickel coated magazine. Introduced 1994. Made in U.S. by Smith & Wesson.
Price: Model SW9F (9mm Para.) **$593.00**
Price: Model SW40F (40 S&W) **$593.00**
Price: Model Compact, SW9C, SW 40C (4″ bbl., 24.4 oz.) **$593.00**
Price: With fixed tritium night sights **$697.00**

CAUTION: PRICES SHOWN ARE SUPPLIED BY THE MANUFACTURER OR IMPORTER. CHECK YOUR LOCAL GUNSHOP.

SPHINX AT-380 AUTO PISTOL
Caliber: 380 ACP, 10-shot magazine.
Barrel: 3.27″.
Weight: 25 oz. **Length:** 6.03″ overall.
Stocks: Checkered plastic.
Sights: Fixed.
Features: Double-action-only mechanism, Chamber loaded indicator; ambidextrous magazine release and slide latch. Introduced 1993. Imported from Switzerland by Sphinx USA, Inc.
Price: Two-tone **$493.95**
Price: Black finish **$513.95**
Price: Nickel/Palladium finish **$564.95**

SPHINX AT-2000S DOUBLE-ACTION PISTOL
Caliber: 9mm Para., 9x21mm, 40 S&W, 10-shot magazine.
Barrel: 4.53″.
Weight: 36.3 oz. **Length:** 8.03″ overall.
Stocks: Checkered neoprene.
Sights: Fixed, three-dot system.
Features: Double-action mechanism changeable to double-action-only. Stainless frame, blued slide. Ambidextrous safety, magazine release, slide latch. Introduced 1993. Imported from Switzerland by Sphinx USA, Inc.
Price: 9mm, two-tone **$1,090.00**
Price: 40 S&W, two-tone **$1,120.00**

Sphinx AT-2000P, AT-2000PS Auto Pistols
Same as the AT-2000S except AT-2000P has shortened frame, 3.74″ barrel, 7.25″ overall length, and weighs 34 oz. Model AT-2000PS has full-size frame. Both have stainless frame with blued slide. Introduced 1993. Imported from Switzerland by Sphinx USA, Inc.
Price: 9mm, two-tone **$940.00**
Price: 40 S&W, two-tone **$980.00**

Sphinx AT-2000H Auto Pistol
Similar to the AT-2000P except has shorter slide with 3.54″ barrel, shorter frame, 10-shot magazine, with 7″ overall length. Weight is 32.2 oz. Stainless frame with blued slide. Introduced 1993. Imported from Switzerland by Sphinx USA, Inc.
Price: 9mm, two-tone **$940.00**
Price: 40 S&W, two-tone **$980.00**

Springfield Standard

Consult our Directory pages for the location of firms mentioned.

Springfield, Inc. 1911A1 High Capacity Pistol
Similar to the Standard 1911A1 except available in 45 ACP and 9mm with 10-shot magazine (45 ACP). Has Commander-style hammer, walnut grips, ambidextrous thumb safety, beveled magazine well, plastic carrying case. Introduced 1993. From Springfield, Inc.
Price: 45 ACP **$622.00**
Price: 9mm **$638.00**
Price: 45 ACP Factory Comp **$964.00**
Price: 45 ACP Comp Lightweight, matte finish **$840.00**
Price: 45 ACP Compact, blued **$609.00**
Price: As above, stainless steel **$648.00**

Sphinx AT-380M

Sphinx AT-2000P

SPRINGFIELD, INC. 1911A1 AUTO PISTOL
Caliber: 9mm Para., 9-shot; 38 Super, 9-shot; 45 ACP, 8-shot.
Barrel: 5″.
Weight: 35.6 oz. **Length:** $8\frac{5}{8}$″ overall.
Stocks: Checkered plastic or walnut.
Sights: Fixed three-dot system.
Features: Beveled magazine well; lowered and flared ejection port. All forged parts, including frame, barrel, slide. All new production. Introduced 1990. From Springfield, Inc.
Price: Basic, 45 ACP, Parkerized **$476.00**
Price: Standard, 45 ACP, blued **$527.00**
Price: Basic, 45 ACP, stainless **$572.00**
Price: Lightweight (28.6 oz., matte finish) **$527.00**
Price: Standard, 9mm, 38 Super, blued **$557.00**
Price: Standard, 9mm, stainless steel **$587.00**

Springfield, Inc. 1911A1 Custom Carry Gun
Similar to the standard 1911A1 except has fixed three-dot low profile sights, Videki speed trigger, match barrel and bushing; extended thumb safety, beavertail grip safety; beveled, polished magazine well, polished feed ramp and throated barrel; match Commander hammer and sear, tuned extractor; lowered and flared ejection port; recoil buffer system, full-length spring guide rod; walnut grips. Comes with two magazines with slam pads, plastic carrying case. Available in all popular calibers. Introduced 1992. From Springfield, Inc.
Price: **$1,388.00**

Springfield, Inc. 1911A1 Factory Comp
Similar to the standard 1911A1 except comes with bushing-type dual-port compensator, adjustable rear sight, extended thumb safety, Videki speed trigger, and beveled magazine well. Checkered walnut grips standard. Available in 38 Super or 45 ACP, blue only. Introduced 1992.
Price: 38 Super **$947.00**
Price: 45 ACP **$984.00**

Springfield, Inc. N.R.A. PPC Pistol
Specifically designed to comply with NRA rules for PPC competition. Has custom slide-to-frame fit; polished feed ramp; throated barrel; total internal honing; tuned extractor; recoil buffer system; fully checkered walnut grips; two fitted magazines; factory test target; custom carrying case. Introduced 1995. From Springfield, Inc.
Price: **$1,632.00**

Springfield Champion

Springfield, Inc. 1911A1 Defender Pistol

Similar to the 1911A1 Champion except has tapered cone dual-port compensator system, rubberized grips. Has reverse recoil plug, full-length recoil spring guide, serrated frontstrap, extended thumb safety, skeletonized hammer with modified grip safety to match and a Videki speed trigger. Bi-Tone finish. Introduced 1991.

Price: 45 ACP $993.00

STAR FIRESTAR AUTO PISTOL

Caliber: 9mm Para., 7-shot; 40 S&W, 6-shot.
Barrel: 3.39″.
Weight: 30.35 oz. **Length:** 6.5″ overall.
Stocks: Checkered rubber.
Sights: Blade front, fully adjustable rear; three-dot system.
Features: Low-profile, combat-style sights; ambidextrous safety. Available in blue or weather-resistant Starvel finish. Introduced 1990. Imported from Spain by Interarms.

Price: Blue, 9mm $450.00
Price: Starvel finish 9mm $450.00
Price: Blue, 40 S&W $465.00
Price: Starvel finish, 40 S&W $465.00

Star Firestar M45 Auto Pistol

Similar to the standard Firestar except chambered for 45 ACP with 6-shot magazine. Has 3.6″ barrel, weighs 35 oz., 6.85″ overall length. Reverse-taper Acculine barrel. Introduced 1992. Imported from Spain by Interarms.

Price: Blue $490.00
Price: Starvel finish $490.00

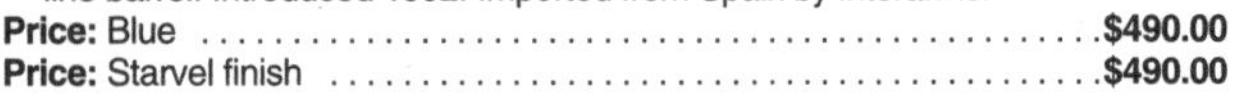

Star Firestar Plus

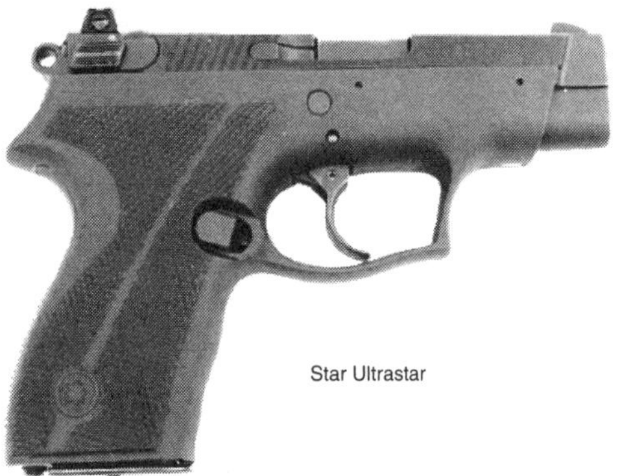

Star Ultrastar

Springfield, Inc. 1911A1 Champion Pistol

Similar to the standard 1911A1 except slide is 4.025″. Has low-profile three-dot sight system. Comes with skeletonized hammer and walnut stocks. Available in 45 ACP only; blue or stainless. Introduced 1989.

Price: Blue $543.00
Price: Stainless $582.00
Price: Mil-Spec $476.00
Price: Champion Comp (single-port compensator) $871.00

Springfield, Inc. 1911A1 Compact Pistol

Similar to the Champion model except has a shortened frame height, 7.75″ overall length. Magazine capacity is 7 shots. Has shortened hammer, checkered walnut grips. Available in 45 ACP only. Introduced 1989.

Price: Blued $543.00
Price: Stainless $582.00
Price: Compact Lightweight $543.00
Price: Mil-Spec $476.00

Springfield, Inc. V10 Ultra Compact Pistol

Similar to the 1911A1 Compact except has shorter slide, 3.5″ barrel, recoil reducing compensator built into the barrel and slide. Beavertail grip safety, beveled magazine well, "hi-viz" combat sights, Videcki speed trigger, flared ejection port, stainless steel frame, blued slide, match grade barrel, walnut grips. Introduced 1996. From Springfield, Inc.

Price: V10 45 ACP $659.00
Price: Ultra Compact (no compensator), 45 ACP $569.00

Star Firestar

Star Firestar Plus Auto Pistol

Same as the standard Firestar except has 10-shot magazine. Introduced 1994. Imported from Spain by Interarms.

Price: Blue, 9mm $460.00
Price: Starvel, 9mm $485.00

STAR ULTRASTAR DOUBLE-ACTION PISTOL

Caliber: 9mm Para., 9-shot magazine; 40 S&W, 8-shot.
Barrel: 3.57″.
Weight: 26 oz. **Length:** 7″ overall.
Stocks: Checkered black polymer.
Sights: Blade front, rear adjustable for windage; three-dot system.
Features: Polymer frame with inside steel slide rails; ambidextrous two-position safety (Safe and Decock). Introduced 1994. Imported from Spain by Interarms.

Price: $490.00

Stoeger American Eagle Luger

STOEGER AMERICAN EAGLE LUGER

Caliber: 9mm Para., 7-shot magazine.
Barrel: 4″, 6″.
Weight: 32 oz. **Length:** 9.6″ overall.
Stocks: Checkered walnut.
Sights: Blade front, fixed rear.
Features: Recreation of the American Eagle Luger pistol in stainless steel. Chamber loaded indicator. Introduced 1994. From Stoeger Industries.

Price: $695.00
Price: Navy Model, 6″ barrel $695.00

CAUTION: PRICES SHOWN ARE SUPPLIED BY THE MANUFACTURER OR IMPORTER. CHECK YOUR LOCAL GUNSHOP.

SUNDANCE MODEL A-25 AUTO PISTOL
Caliber: 25 ACP, 7-shot magazine.
Barrel: 2.5″.
Weight: 16 oz. **Length:** 4 7/8″ overall.
Stocks: Grooved black ABS or simulated smooth pearl; optional pink.
Sights: Fixed.
Features: Manual rotary safety; button magazine release. Bright chrome or black Teflon finish. Introduced 1989. Made in U.S. by Sundance Industries, Inc.
Price: $79.95

Sundance Laser 25

SUNDANCE BOA AUTO PISTOL
Caliber: 25 ACP, 7-shot magazine.
Barrel: 2 1/2″.
Weight: 16 oz. **Length:** 4 7/8″.
Stocks: Grooved ABS or smooth simulated pearl; optional pink.
Sights: Fixed.
Features: Patented grip safety, manual rotary safety; button magazine release; lifetime warranty. Bright chrome or black Teflon finish. Introduced 1991. Made in the U.S. by Sundance Industries, Inc.
Price: $95.00

SUNDANCE LASER 25 PISTOL
Caliber: 25 ACP, 7-shot magazine.
Barrel: 2 1/2″.
Weight: 18 oz. **Length:** 4 7/8″ overall.
Stocks: Grooved black ABS.
Sights: Class IIIa laser, 670 NM, 5mW, and fixed open.
Features: Factory installed and sighted laser sight activated by squeezing the grip safety; manual rotary safety; button magazine release. Bright chrome or black finish. Introduced 1995. Made in U.S. by Sundance Industries, Inc.
Price: With laser $219.00
Price: Lady Laser (as above except different name, bright chrome only) .$219.00

TAURUS MODEL PT 22/PT 25 AUTO PISTOLS
Caliber: 22 LR, 9-shot (PT 22); 25 ACP, 8-shot (PT 25).
Barrel: 2.75″.
Weight: 12.3 oz. **Length:** 5.25″ overall.
Stocks: Smooth Brazilian hardwood.
Sights: Blade front, fixed rear.
Features: Double action. Tip-up barrel for loading, cleaning. Blue or stainless. Introduced 1992. Made in U.S. by Taurus International.
Price: 22 LR or 25 ACP $187.00
Price: Nickel $195.00

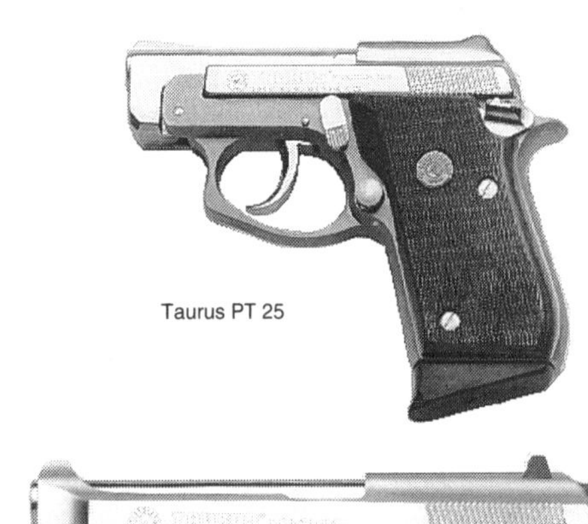
Taurus PT 25

TAURUS MODEL PT58 AUTO PISTOL
Caliber: 380 ACP, 10-shot magazine.
Barrel: 4.01″.
Weight: 30 oz. **Length:** 7.2″ overall.
Stocks: Brazilian hardwood.
Sights: Integral blade on slide front, notch rear adjustable for windage. Three-dot system.
Features: Double action with exposed hammer; inertia firing pin. Introduced 1988. Imported by Taurus International.
Price: Blue $429.00
Price: Stainless steel $470.00

Taurus PT 92

TAURUS MODEL PT 92AF AUTO PISTOL
Caliber: 9mm Para., 10-shot magazine.
Barrel: 4.92″.
Weight: 34 oz. **Length:** 8.54″ overall.
Stocks: Brazilian hardwood.
Sights: Fixed notch rear. Three-dot sight system.
Features: Double action, exposed hammer, chamber loaded indicator, ambidextrous safety, inertia firing pin. Imported by Taurus International.
Price: Blue $479.00
Price: Blue, Deluxe Shooter's Pak (extra magazine, case) $477.00
Price: Stainless steel $493.00
Price: Stainless, Deluxe Shooter's Pak (extra magazine, case) $522.00

Taurus PT 99AF Auto Pistol
Similar to the PT-92 except has fully adjustable rear sight, smooth Brazilian walnut stocks and is available in stainless steel or polished blue. Introduced 1983.
Price: Blue $471.00
Price: Blue, Deluxe Shooter's Pak (extra magazine, case) $500.00
Price: Stainless steel $518.00
Price: Stainless, Deluxe Shooter's Pak (extra magazine, case) $546.00

Taurus PT 101

Taurus PT 92AFC Compact Pistol
Similar to the PT-92 except has 4.25″ barrel, 10-shot magazine, weighs 31 oz. and is 7.5″ overall. Available in stainless steel or blue. Introduced 1991. Imported by Taurus International.
Price: Blue $449.00
Price: Stainless steel $493.00

Taurus PT 101 Auto Pistol
Same as the PT 100 except has micro-click rear sight adjustable for windage and elevation, three-dot combat-style. Introduced 1991.
Price: Blue $491.00
Price: Blue, Deluxe Shooter's Pak (extra magazine, case) $519.00
Price: Stainless $537.00
Price: Stainless, Deluxe Shooter's Pak (extra magazine, case) $565.00

TAURUS PT 100 AUTO PISTOL
Caliber: 40 S&W, 10-shot magazine.
Barrel: 5″.
Weight: 34 oz.
Stocks: Smooth Brazilian hardwood.
Sights: Fixed front, drift-adjustable rear. Three-dot combat.
Features: Double action, exposed hammer. Ambidextrous hammer-drop safety; inertia firing pin; chamber loaded indicator. Introduced 1991. Imported by Taurus International.
Price: Blue $469.00
Price: Blue, Deluxe Shooter's Pak (extra magazine, case) $497.00
Price: Stainless $514.00
Price: Stainless, Deluxe Shooter's Pak (extra magazine, case) $542.00

TAURUS MODEL PT-908 AUTO PISTOL
Caliber: 9mm Para., 8-shot magazine.
Barrel: 3.8″.
Weight: 30 oz. **Length:** 7.05″ overall.
Stocks: Santoprene II.
Sights: Drift-adjustable front and rear; three-dot combat.
Features: Double action, exposed hammer; manual ambidextrous hammer-drop; inertia firing pin; chamber loaded indicator. Introduced 1993. Imported by Taurus International.
Price: Blue **$435.00**
Price: Stainless steel **$473.00**
Price: Blue, Deluxe Shooter's Pak **$459.00**
Price: Stainless, Deluxe Shooter's Pak **$496.00**

Taurus PT-940 Auto Pistol
Same as the PT-908 except chambered for 40 siW, 9-shot magazine. Introduced 1996. Imported by Taurus International.
Price: Blue **$453.00**
Price: Stainless **$497.00**
Price: Blue, Deluxe Shooter's Pak **$476.00**
Price: Stainless, Deluxe Shooter's Pack **$520.00**

TAURUS PT-945 AUTO PISTOL
Caliber: 45 ACP, 8-shot magazine.
Barrel: 4.25″.
Weight: 29.5 oz. **Length:** 7.48″ overall.
Stocks: Santoprene II.
Sights: Drift-adjustable front and rear; three-dot system.
Features: Double-action mechanism. Has manual ambidextrous hammer drop safety, intercept notch, firing pin block, chamber loaded indicator, last-shot hold-open. Introduced 1995. Imported by Taurus International.
Price: Blue **$453.00**
Price: Stainless **$497.00**
Price: Blue, Deluxe Shooter's Pak **$476.00**
Price: Stainless, Deluxe Shooter's Pak **$520.00**

WALTHER P-5 AUTO PISTOL
Caliber: 9mm.
Barrel: 3.6″
Weight: 28 oz. **Length:** 7″ overall.
Stocks: Checkered polymer.
Sights: Blade front, adjustable rear.
Features: Uses the basic Walther P-38 double-action mechanism. Polished blue finish. Imported from Germany by Interarms.
Price: **$900.00**

WALTHER PP AUTO PISTOL
Caliber: 32 ACP, 380 ACP, 7-shot magazine.
Barrel: 3.86″.
Weight: $23\frac{1}{2}$ oz. **Length:** 6.7″ overall.
Stocks: Checkered plastic.
Sights: Fixed, white markings.
Features: Double action; manual safety blocks firing pin and drops hammer; chamber loaded indicator on 32 and 380; extra finger rest magazine provided. Imported from Germany by Interarms.
Price: 32 .... **$999.00**
Price: 380 .... **$999.00**
Price: Engraved models .... **On Request**

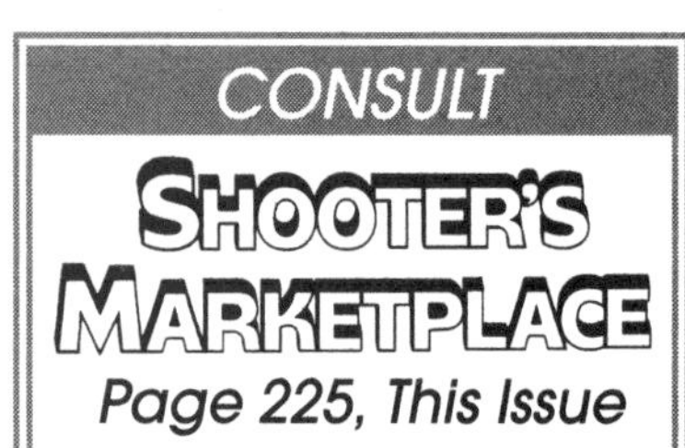
CONSULT
SHOOTER'S
MARKETPLACE
Page 225, This Issue

WALTHER MODEL TPH AUTO PISTOL
Caliber: 22 LR, 25 ACP, 6-shot magazine.
Barrel: $2\frac{1}{4}$″.
Weight: 14 oz. **Length:** $5\frac{3}{8}$″ overall.
Stocks: Checkered black composition.
Sights: Blade front, rear drift-adjustable for windage.
Features: Made of stainless steel. Scaled-down version of the Walther PP/PPK series. Made in U.S. Introduced 1987. From Interarms.
Price: Blue or stainless steel, 22 or 25 .... **$440.00**

Taurus PT 945

Walther P-5 Compact

Walther P-5 Compact
Similar to the P-5 except has 3.2″ barrel, weighs 26 oz., and has magazine release on left side of grip. Imported from Germany by Interarms.
Price: **$900.00**

Walther PPK/S American

Walther PPK American Auto Pistol
Similar to Walther PPK/S except weighs 21 oz., has 6-shot capacity. Made in the U.S. Introduced 1986.
Price: Stainless, 380 ACP only **$540.00**
Price: Blue, 380 ACP only **$540.00**

Walther TPH

Walther PPK/S American Auto Pistol
Similar to Walther PP except made entirely in the United States. Has 3.27″ barrel with 6.1″ length overall. Introduced 1980.
Price: 380 ACP only, blue **$540.00**
Price: As above, stainless **$540.00**

CAUTION: PRICES SHOWN ARE SUPPLIED BY THE MANUFACTURER OR IMPORTER. CHECK YOUR LOCAL GUNSHOP.

WALTHER P88 COMPACT PISTOL

Caliber: 9mm Para., 10-shot magazine.
Barrel: 3.93″.
Weight: 28 oz. **Length:** NA.
Stocks: Checkered black polymer.
Sights: Blade front, drift adjustable rear.
Features: Double action with ambidextrous decocking lever and magazine release; alloy frame; loaded chamber indicator; matte blue finish. Imported from Germany by Interarms.
Price: $900.00

Walther P88 Compact

WILDEY AUTOMATIC PISTOL

Caliber: 10mm Wildey Mag., 11mm Wildey Mag., 30 Wildey Mag., 357 Peterbuilt, 45 Win. Mag., 475 Wildey Mag., 7-shot magazine.
Barrel: 5″, 6″, 7″, 8″, 10″, 12″, 14″ (45 Win. Mag.); 8″, 10″, 12″, 14″ (all other cals.). Interchangeable.
Weight: 64 oz. (5″ barrel). **Length:** 11″ overall (7″ barrel).
Stocks: Hardwood.
Sights: Ramp front (interchangeable blades optional), fully adjustable rear. Scope base available.
Features: Gas-operated action. Made of stainless steel. Has three-lug rotary bolt. Double or single action. Polished and matte finish. Made in U.S. by Wildey, Inc.
Price: .... $1,175.00 to $1,495.00

WILKINSON "LINDA" AUTO PISTOL

Caliber: 9mm Para.
Barrel: 8 5/16″.
Weight: 4 lbs., 13 oz. **Length:** 12 1/4″ overall.
Stocks: Checkered black plastic pistol grip, walnut forend.
Sights: Protected blade front, aperture rear.
Features: Fires from closed bolt. Semi-auto only. Straight blowback action. Cross-bolt safety. Removable barrel. From Wilkinson Arms.
Price: $533.33

WILKINSON "SHERRY" AUTO PISTOL

Caliber: 22 LR, 8-shot magazine.
Barrel: 2 1/8″.
Weight: 9 1/4 oz. **Length:** 4 3/8″ overall.
Stocks: Checkered black plastic.
Sights: Fixed, groove.
Features: Cross-bolt safety locks the sear into the hammer. Available in all blue finish or blue slide and trigger with gold frame. Introduced 1985.
Price: $195.00

Wilkinson Sherry

HANDGUNS—COMPETITION HANDGUNS

Includes models suitable for several forms of competition and other sporting purposes.

AUTO-ORDNANCE 1911A1 COMPETITION MODEL

Caliber: 45 ACP.
Barrel: 5″.
Weight: 42 oz. **Length:** 10″ overall.
Stocks: Black textured rubber wrap-around.
Sights: Blade front, rear adjustable for windage; three-dot system.
Features: Machined compensator, combat Commander hammer; flat mainspring housing; low profile magazine funnel; metal form magazine bumper; high-ride beavertail grip safety; full-length recoil spring guide system; extended slide stop, safety and magazine catch; Videcki adjustable speed trigger; extended combat ejector. Introduced 1994. Made in U.S. by Auto-Ordnance Corp.
Price: $635.50

Auto-Ordnance Competition Model

Baer 1911 Ultimate Master

Baer 1911 Ultimate Master "Steel Special" Pistol

Similar to the Ultimate Master except chambered for 38 Super with supported chamber (other calibers available), lighter slide, bushing-type compensator; two-piece guide rod. Designed for maximum 150 power factor. Comes without sights—scope and mount only. Hard chrome finish. Made in U.S. by Les Baer Custom, Inc.
Price: $2,670.00

BAER 1911 ULTIMATE MASTER COMBAT PISTOL

Caliber: 45 ACP (others available), 10-shot magazine.
Barrel: 5″; Baer NM.
Weight: 37 oz. **Length:** 8.5″ overall.
Stocks: Checkered rosewood.
Sights: Baer dovetail front, low-mount Bo-Mar rear with hidden leaf.
Features: Full-house competition gun. Baer forged NM blued steel frame and double serrated slide; Baer triple port, tapered cone compensator; fitted slide to frame; lowered, flared ejection port; Baer reverse recoil plug; full-length guide rod; recoil buff; beveled magazine well; Baer Commander hammer, sear; Baer extended ambidextrous safety, extended ejector, checkered slide stop, beaver-tail grip safety with pad, extended magazine release button; Baer speed trigger. Made in U.S. by Les Baer Custom, Inc.
Price: Compensated, open sights $1,996.00
Price: Uncompensated "Limited" Model $1,843.00
Price: Compensated, with Baer optics mount $2,360.00

Baer 1911 Bullseye Wadcutter

BAER 1911 NATIONAL MATCH HARDBALL PISTOL

Caliber: 45 ACP, 7-shot magazine.
Barrel: 5″.
Weight: 37 oz. **Length:** 8.5″ overall.
Stocks: Checkered walnut.
Sights: Baer dovetail front with undercut post, low-mount Bo-Mar rear with hidden leaf.
Features: Baer NM forged steel frame, double serrated slide and barrel with stainless bushing; slide fitted to frame; Baer match trigger with 4-lb. pull; polished feed ramp, throated barrel; checkered front strap, arched mainspring housing; Baer beveled magazine well; lowered, flared ejection port; tuned extractor; Baer extended ejector, checkered slide stop; recoil buff. Made in U.S. by Les Baer Custom, Inc.
Price: **$1,180.00**

Baer 1911 Target Master Pistol

Similar to the National Match Hardball except available in 45 ACP and other calibers, has Baer post-style dovetail front sight, flat serrated mainspring housing, standard trigger. Made in U.S. by Les Baer Custom, Inc.
Price: **$1,263.00**
Price: With 6″ barrel **$1,540.00**

Baer 1911 Bullseye Wadcutter Pistol

Similar to the National Match Hardball except designed for wadcutter loads only. Has polished feed ramp and barrel throat; Bo-Mar rib on slide; full-length recoil rod; Baer speed trigger with 3½-lb. pull; Baer deluxe hammer and sear; Baer beavertail grip safety with pad; flat mainspring housing checkered 20 lpi. Blue finish; checkered walnut grips. Made in U.S. by Les Baer Custom, Inc.
Price: **$1,347.00**
Price: With 6″ barrel **$1,597.00**

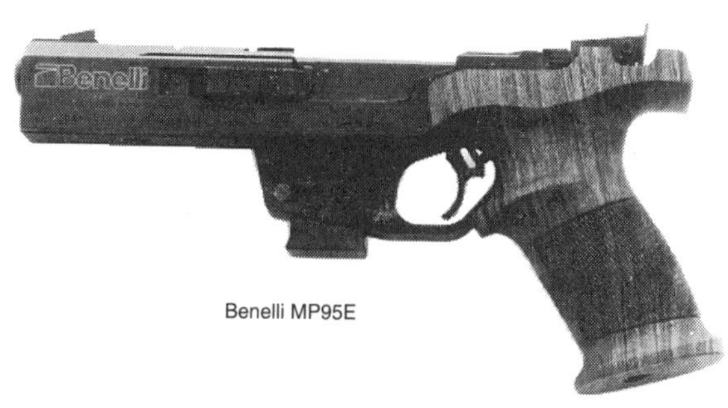

Benelli MP95E

BENELLI MP95E MATCH PISTOL

Caliber: 22 LR, 9-shot magazine, or 32 S&W WC, 5-shot magazine.
Barrel: 4.33″.
Weight: 38.8 oz. **Length:** 11.81″ overall.
Stocks: Checkered walnut match type; anatomically shaped.
Sights: Match type. Blade front, click-adjustable rear for windage and elevation.
Features: Removable, trigger assembly. Special internal weight box on sub-frame below barrel. Cut for scope rails. Introduced 1993. Imported from Italy by European American Armory.
Price: Blue **$550.00**
Price: Chrome **$599.00**
Price: MP90S (competition version of MP95E), 22 LR **$1,295.00**
Price: As above, 32 S&W **$1,495.00**

Beretta Model 89

BERNARDELLI MODEL 69 TARGET PISTOL

Caliber: 22 LR, 10-shot magazine.
Barrel: 5.9″.
Weight: 38 oz. **Length:** 9″ overall.
Stocks: Wrap-around, hand-checkered walnut with thumbrest.
Sights: Fully adjustable and interchangeable target type.
Features: Conforms to U.I.T. regulations. Has 7.1″ sight radius, .27″ wide grooved trigger. Manual thumb safety and magazine safety. Introduced 1987. Imported from Italy by Mitchell Arms.
Price: **$612.00**

BERETTA MODEL 89 GOLD STANDARD PISTOL

Caliber: 22 LR, 8-shot magazine.
Barrel: 6″
Weight: 41 oz. **Length:** 9.5″ overall.
Stocks: Target-type walnut with thumbrest.
Sights: Interchangeable blade front, fully adjustable rear.
Features: Single action target pistol. Matte black, Bruniton finish. Imported from Italy by Beretta U.S.A.
Price: **$736.00**

BF SINGLE SHOT PISTOL

Caliber: 22 LR, 357 Mag., 44 Mag., 7-30 Waters, 30-30 Win., 375 Win., 45-70; custom chamberings from 17 Rem. through 45-cal.
Barrel: 10″, 10.75″, 12″, 15+″.
Weight: 52 oz. **Length:** NA.
Stocks: Custom Herrett finger-groove grip and forend.
Sights: Undercut Patridge front, ½-MOA match-quality fully adjustable RPM Iron Sight rear; barrel or receiver mounting. Drilled and tapped for scope mounting.
Features: Rigid barrel/receiver; falling block action with short lock time; automatic ejection; air-gauged match barrels by Wilson or Douglas; matte black oxide finish standard, electroless nickel optional. Barrel has 11-degree recessed target crown. Introduced 1988. Made in U.S. by E.A. Brown Mfg.
Price: 10″, no sights **$499.95**
Price: 10″, RPM sights **$564.95**
Price: 10.75″, no sights **$529.95**
Price: 10.75″, RPM sights **$594.95**
Price: 12″, no sights **$562.95**
Price: 12″, RPM sights **$643.75**
Price: 15″, no sights **$592.95**
Price: 15″, RPM sights **$675.00**
Price: 10.75″ Ultimate Silhouette (heavy barrel, special forend, RPM rear sight with hooded front, gold-plated trigger) **$687.95**

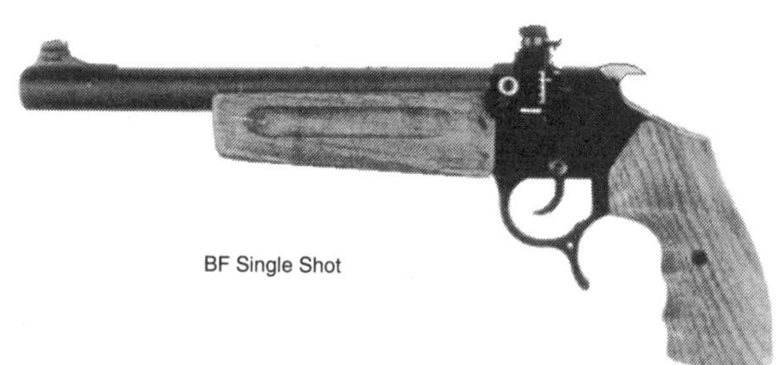
BF Single Shot

CAUTION: PRICES SHOWN ARE SUPPLIED BY THE MANUFACTURER OR IMPORTER. CHECK YOUR LOCAL GUNSHOP.

Browning Buck Mark Bullseye

Browning Buck Mark Bullseye
Similar to the Buck Mark Silhouette except has 7 1/4" heavy barrel with three flutes per side; trigger is adjustable from 2 1/2 to 5 lbs.; specially designed rosewood target or three-finger-groove stocks with competition-style heel rest, or with contoured rubber grip. Overall length is 11 5/16", weighs 36 oz. Introduced 1996. Made in U.S. From Browning.
Price: With rubber stocks **$376.95**
Price: With rosewood stocks **$484.95**

Browning Buck Mark Target 5.5
Same as the Buck Mark Silhouette except has a 5 1/2" barrel with .900" diameter. Has hooded sights mounted on a scope base that accepts an optical or reflex sight. Rear sight is a Browning fully adjustable Pro Target, front sight is an adjustable post that customizes to different widths, and can be adjusted for height. Contoured walnut grips with thumbrest, or finger-groove walnut. Matte blue finish. Overall length is 9 5/8", weighs 35 1/2 oz. Has 10-shot magazine. Introduced 1990. From Browning.
Price: **$411.95**
Price: Target 5.5 Gold (as above with gold anodized frame and top rib) .**$462.95**
Price: Target 5.5 Nickel (as above with nickel frame and top rib) **$462.95**

BROLIN PRO-STOCK COMPETITION PISTOL
Caliber: 45 ACP, 8-shot magazine.
Barrel: 5".
Weight: 37 oz. **Length:** 8.5" overall.
Stocks: Checkered with Brolin logo.
Sights: Ramp front, fully adjustable rear.
Features: Throated heavy match barrel; full-length recoil spring guide; polished feed ramp; lowered and flared ejection port; beveled magazine well; flat-top slide; serrated flat mainspring housing; high relief front strap cut; four-legged sear spring; adjustable match trigger; slotted Commander hammer; beavertail grip safety; ambidextrous thumb safety; front slide serrations. Introduced 1996. Made in U.S. by Brolin Arms.
Price: Blue **$779.00**
Price: Blue/stainless two-tone **$799.00**

COLT GOLD CUP NATIONAL MATCH MK IV/SERIES 80
Caliber: 45 ACP, 8-shot magazine.
Barrel: 5", with new design bushing.
Weight: 39 oz. **Length:** 8 1/2".
Stocks: Checkered rubber composite with silver-plated medallion.
Sights: Patridge-style front, Colt-Elliason rear adjustable for windage and elevation, sight radius 6 3/4".
Features: Arched or flat housing; wide, grooved trigger with adjustable stop; ribbed-top slide, hand fitted, with improved ejection port.
Price: Blue **$937.00**
Price: Stainless **$1,003.00**
Price: Bright stainless **$1,073.00**
Price: Delta Gold Cup (10mm, stainless) **$1,027.00**

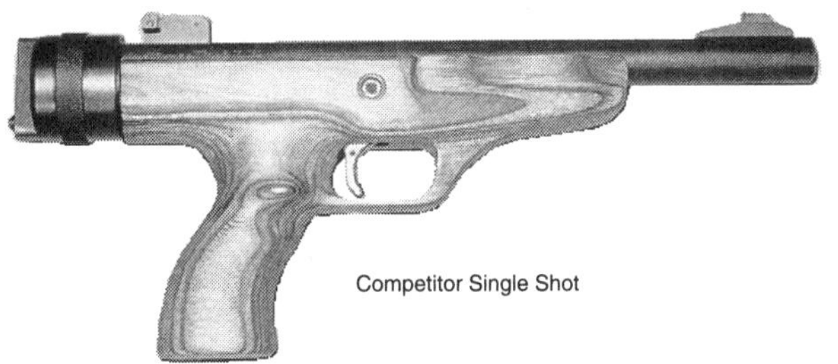
Competitor Single Shot

BROWNING BUCK MARK SILHOUETTE
Caliber: 22 LR, 10-shot magazine.
Barrel: 9 7/8".
Weight: 53 oz. **Length:** 14" overall.
Stocks: Smooth walnut stocks and forend, or finger-groove walnut.
Sights: Post-type hooded front adjustable for blade width and height; Pro Target rear fully adjustable for windage and elevation.
Features: Heavy barrel with .900" diameter; 12 1/2" sight radius. Special sighting plane forms scope base. Introduced 1987. Made in U.S. From Browning.
Price: **$434.95**

Browning Buck Mark Unlimited Match
Same as the Buck Mark Silhouette except has 14" heavy barrel. Conforms to IHMSA 15" maximum sight radius rule. *Introduced 1991.
Price: **$535.95**

Browning Buck Mark Target 5.5

Browning Buck Mark Field 5.5
Same as the Target 5.5 except has hoodless ramp-style front sight and low profile rear sight. Matte blue finish, contoured or finger-groove walnut stocks. Introduced 1991.
Price: **$411.95**

Brolin Pro-Comp Competition Pistol
Similar to the Pro-Stock model except has integral milled DPC Comp on the heavy match barrel; barrel length 4", overall length 8.5"; weighs 37 oz.; 8-shot magazine. Introduced 1996. Made in U.S. by Brolin Arms.
Price: Blue **$909.00**
Price: Blue/stainless two-tone **$929.00**

Colt Gold Cup National Match

COMPETITOR SINGLE SHOT PISTOL
Caliber: 22 LR through 50 Action Express, including belted magnums.
Barrel: 14" standard; 10.5" silhouette; 16" optional.
Weight: About 59 oz. (14" bbl.). **Length:** 15.12" overall.
Stocks: Ambidextrous; synthetic (standard) or laminated or natural wood.
Sights: Ramp front, adjustable rear.
Features: Rotary canon-type action cocks on opening; cammed ejector; interchangeable barrels, ejectors. Adjustable single stage trigger, sliding thumb safety and trigger safety. Matte blue finish. Introduced 1988. From Competitor Corp., Inc.
Price: 14", standard calibers, synthetic grip **$399.95**
Price: Extra barrels, from **$149.95**

E.A.A. WITNESS GOLD TEAM AUTO
Caliber: 9mm Para., 9x21, 38 Super, 40 S&W, 45 ACP.
Barrel: 5.1″.
Weight: 41.6 oz. **Length:** 9.6″ overall.
Stocks: Checkered walnut, competition style.
Sights: Square post front, fully adjustable rear.
Features: Triple-chamber cone compensator; competition SA trigger; extended safety and magazine release; competition hammer; beveled magazine well; beavertail grip. Hand-fitted major components. Hard chrome finish. Match-grade barrel. From E.A.A. Custom Shop. Introduced 1992. From European American Armory.
Price: **$2,195.00**

E.A.A. Witness Gold Team

E.A.A. Witness Silver Team Auto
Similar to the Witness Gold Team except has double-chamber compensator, oval magazine release, black rubber grips, double-dip blue finish. Comes with Super Sight and drilled and tapped for scope mount. Built for the intermediate competition shooter. Introduced 1992. From European American Armory Custom Shop.
Price: 9mm Para., 9x21, 38 Super, 40 S&W, 45 ACP **$975.00**

ERMA ER MATCH REVOLVER
Caliber: 32 S&W Long, 6-shot.
Barrel: 6″.
Weight: 47.3 oz. **Length:** 11.2″ overall.
Stocks: Stippled walnut, adjustable match-type.
Sights: Blade front, micrometer rear adjustable for windage and elevation.
Features: Polished blue finish. Introduced 1989. Imported from Germany by Precision Sales International.
Price: 32 S&W Long **$1,248.00**

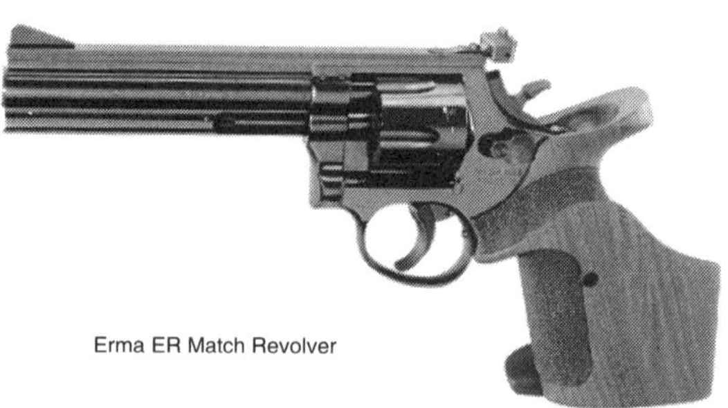
Erma ER Match Revolver

ERMA ESP 85A MATCH PISTOL
Caliber: 22 LR, 6-shot; 32 S&W, 6-shot magazine.
Barrel: 6″.
Weight: 39 oz. **Length:** 10″ overall.
Stocks: Match-type of stippled walnut; adjustable.
Sights: Interchangeable blade front, micrometer adjustable rear with interchangeable leaf.
Features: Five-way adjustable trigger; exposed hammer and separate firing pin block allow unlimited dry firing practice. Blue or matte chrome; right- or left-hand. Introduced 1989. Imported from Germany by Precision Sales International.
Price: 22 LR **$1,695.00**
Price: 22 LR, left-hand **$1,735.00**
Price: 22 LR, matte chrome **$1,890.00**
Price: 32 S&W **$1,790.00**
Price: 32 S&W, left-hand **$1,830.00**
Price: 32 S&W, matte chrome **$2,095.00**
Price: 32 S&W, matte chrome, left-hand **$2,135.00**

Consult our Directory pages for the location of firms mentioned.

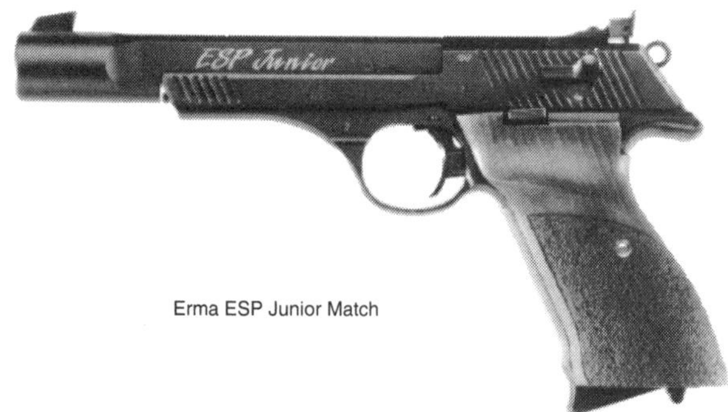

Erma ESP Junior Match

Erma ESP Junior Match Pistol
Similar to the ESP 85A Match except chambered only for 22 LR, blue finish only. Stippled non-adjustable walnut match grips (adjustable grips optional). Introduced 1995. Imported from Germany by Precision Sales International.
Price: **$1,295.00**

FAS 607 MATCH PISTOL
Caliber: 22 LR, 5-shot.
Barrel: 5.6″.
Weight: 37 oz. **Length:** 11″ overall.
Stocks: Walnut wrap-around; sizes small, medium, large or adjustable.
Sights: Match. Blade front, open notch rear fully adjustable for windage and elevation. Sight radius is 8.66″.
Features: Line of sight is only 11/32″ above centerline of bore; magazine is inserted from top; adjustable and removable trigger mechanism; single lever takedown. Full 5-year warranty. Imported from Italy by Nygord Precision Products.
Price: **$1,175.00**
Price: Model 603 (32 S&W) **$1,175.00**

FAS 601 Match Pistol
Similar to Model 607 except has different match stocks with adjustable palm shelf, 22 Short only for rapid fire shooting; weighs 40 oz., 5.6″ bbl.; has gas ports through top of barrel and slide to reduce recoil; slightly different trigger and sear mechanisms. Imported from Italy by Nygord Precision Products.
Price: **$1,250.00**

FAS 607 Match

FREEDOM ARMS CASULL MODEL 252 SILHOUETTE
Caliber: 22 LR, 5-shot cylinder.
Barrel: 9.95″.
Weight: 63 oz. **Length:** NA
Stocks: Black micarta, western style.
Sights: 1/8″ Patridge front, Iron Sight Gun Works silhouette rear, click adjustable for windage and elevation.
Features: Stainless steel. Built on the 454 Casull frame. Two-point firing pin, lightened hammer for fast lock time. Trigger pull is 3 to 5 lbs. with pre-set overtravel screw. Introduced 1991. From Freedom Arms.
Price: Silhouette Class **$1,509.00**
Price: Extra fitted 22 WMR cylinder **$253.00**

CAUTION: PRICES SHOWN ARE SUPPLIED BY THE MANUFACTURER OR IMPORTER. CHECK YOUR LOCAL GUNSHOP.

Freedom Arms Casull Model 252 Varmint

Similar to the Silhouette Class revolver except has 7.5″ barrel, weighs 59 oz., has black and green laminated hardwood grips, and comes with brass bead front sight, express shallow V rear sight with windage and elevation adjustments. Introduced 1991. From Freedom Arms.

Price: Varmint Class **$1,454.00**
Price: Extra fitted 22 WMR cylinder **$253.00**

Freedom Arms Casull 252 Varmint

GAUCHER GP SILHOUETTE PISTOL

Caliber: 22 LR, single shot.
Barrel: 10″.
Weight: 42.3 oz. **Length:** 15.5″ overall.
Stocks: Stained hardwood.
Sights: Hooded post on ramp front, open rear adjustable for windage and elevation.
Features: Matte chrome barrel, blued bolt and sights. Other barrel lengths available on special order. Introduced 1991. Imported by Mandall Shooting Supplies.
Price: **$425.00**

CONSULT
SHOOTER'S
MARKETPLACE
Page 225, This Issue

GLOCK 17L COMPETITION AUTO

Caliber: 9mm Para., 10-shot magazine.
Barrel: 6.02″.
Weight: 23.3 oz. **Length:** 8.85″ overall.
Stocks: Black polymer.
Sights: Blade front with white dot, fixed or adjustable rear.
Features: Polymer frame, steel slide; double-action trigger with "Safe Action" system; mechanical firing pin safety, drop safety; simple takedown without tools; locked breech, recoil operated action. Introduced 1989. Imported from Austria by Glock, Inc.
Price: **$790.00**

Glock 24 Competition

GLOCK 24 COMPETITION MODEL PISTOL

Caliber: 40 S&W, 10-shot magazine.
Barrel: 6.02″.
Weight: 29.5 oz. **Length:** 8.85″ overall.
Stocks: Black polymer.
Sights: Blade front with dot, white outline rear adjustable for windage.
Features: Long-slide competition model available as compensated or non-compensated gun. Factory-installed competition trigger; drop-free magazine. Introduced 1994. Imported from Austria by Glock, Inc.
Price: **$790.00**

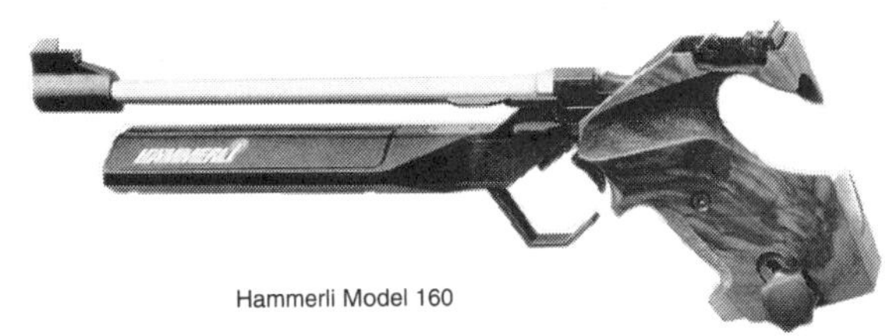
Hammerli Model 160

HAMMERLI MODEL 160/162 FREE PISTOLS

Caliber: 22 LR, single shot.
Barrel: 11.30″.
Weight: 46.94 oz. **Length:** 17.52″ overall.
Stocks: Walnut; full match style with adjustable palm shelf. Stippled surfaces.
Sights: Changeable blade front, open, fully adjustable match rear.
Features: Model 160 has mechanical set trigger; Model 162 has electronic trigger; both fully adjustable with provisions for dry firing. Introduced 1993. Imported from Switzerland by Sigarms, Inc.
Price: Model 160, about **$2,085.00**
Price: Model 162, about **$2,295.00**

HAMMERLI MODEL 208s PISTOL

Caliber: 22 LR, 8-shot magazine.
Barrel: 5.9″.
Weight: 37.5 oz. **Length:** 10″ overall.
Stocks: Walnut, target-type with thumbrest.
Sights: Blade front, open fully adjustable rear.
Features: Adjustable trigger, including length; interchangeable rear sight elements. Imported from Switzerland by Sigarms, Inc.
Price: About **$1,925.00**

HAMMERLI MODEL 280 TARGET PISTOL

Caliber: 22 LR, 6-shot; 32 S&W Long WC, 5-shot.
Barrel: 4.5″.
Weight: 39.1 oz. (32). **Length:** 11.8″ overall.
Stocks: Walnut match-type with stippling, adjustable palm shelf.
Sights: Match sights, micrometer adjustable; interchangeable elements.
Features: Has carbon-reinforced synthetic frame and bolt/barrel housing. Trigger is adjustable for pull weight, take-up weight, let-off, and length, and is interchangeable. Interchangeable metal or carbon fiber counterweights. Sight radius of 8.8″. Comes with barrel weights, spare magazine, loading tool, cleaning rods. Introduced 1990. Imported from Sigarms, Inc.
Price: 22-cal., about **$1,565.00**
Price: 32-cal., about **$1,765.00**

HARRIS GUNWORKS SIGNATURE JR. LONG RANGE PISTOL

Caliber: Any suitable caliber.
Barrel: To customer specs.
Weight: 5 lbs.
Stock: Gunworks fiberglass.
Sights: None furnished; comes with scope rings.
Features: Right- or left-hand benchrest action of titanium or stainless steel; single shot or repeater. Comes with bipod. Introduced 1992. Made in U.S. by Harris Gunworks, Inc.
Price: **$2,400.00**

Hammerli Model 280

HIGH STANDARD OLYMPIC MILITARY
Caliber: 22 Short, 5-shot magazine.
Barrel: 5.5″ bull.
Weight: 44 oz. **Length:** 9.50″ overall.
Stocks: Checkered hardwood with thumbrest.
Sights: Undercut ramp front, micro-click rear adjustable for windage and elevation.
Features: Removable barrel stabilizer; high strength aluminum slide, carbon steel frame; adjustable trigger and sear. Overall blue finish. Reintroduced 1994. Made in U.S. by High Standard Mfg. Co., Inc.
Price: **$536.00**

High Standard Olympic Rapid Fire

HIGH STANDARD OLYMPIC RAPID FIRE
Caliber: 22 Short, 5-shot magazine.
Barrel: 4″.
Weight: 46 oz. **Length:** 11.5″ overall.
Stocks: International-style stippled hardwood.
Sights: Undercut ramp front, fully adjustable rear.
Features: Integral muzzle brake and forward mounted compensator; trigger adjustable for weight of pull, travel; gold-plated trigger, slide stop, safety, magazine release; stippled front and backstraps; push-button barrel takedown. Introduced 1996. Made in U.S. by High Standard Mfg. Co.
Price: **$1,995.00**

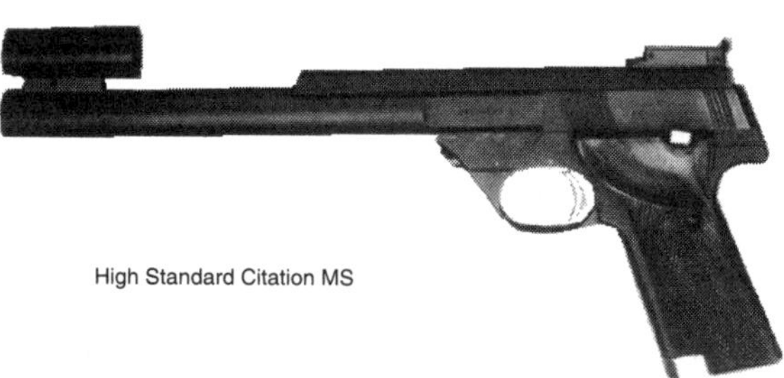
High Standard Citation MS

HIGH STANDARD SUPERMATIC TOURNAMENT PISTOL
Caliber: 22 LR, 10-shot magazine.
Barrel: 5.5″; push-button takedown.
Weight: 43 oz. **Length:** 8.5″ overall.
Stocks: Black rubber; ambidextrous.
Sights: Undercut ramp front, micro-click rear adjustable for windage and elevation.
Features: Slide-mounted rear sight. Blue finish. Reintroduced 1994. From High Standard Mfg. Co., Inc.
Price: **$399.00**

HIGH STANDARD SUPERMATIC TROPHY PISTOL
Caliber: 22 LR, 10-shot magazine.
Barrel: 5.5″ or 7.25″; push-button takedown; drilled and tapped for scope mount.
Weight: 44 oz. **Length:** 9.5″ overall.
Stocks: Checkered hardwood with thumbrest.
Sights: Undercut ramp front, micro-click rear adjustable for windage and elevation.
Features: Gold-plated trigger, slide lock, safety-lever and magazine release; stippled front grip and backstrap; adjustable trigger and sear. Barrel weights optional. A 22 Short version is available. Reintroduced 1994. From High Standard Mfg. Co., Inc.
Price: **$516.00**

HIGH STANDARD 10X MODEL TARGET PISTOL
Caliber: 22 LR, 10-shot magazine.
Barrel: 5.5″; push-button takedown.
Weight: 44 oz. **Length:** 9.5″ overall.
Stocks: Checkered black epoxied walnut; ambidextrous.
Sights: Undercut ramp front, micro-click rear adjustable for windage and elevation.
Features: Hand built with select parts. Adjustable trigger and sear; Parkerized finish; stippled front grip and backstrap. Barrel weights optional. Comes with test target, extended warranty. Reintroduced 1994. From High Standard Mfg. Co., Inc.
Price: .... **$869.00** to **$1,095.00**

MITCHELL ARMS MONARCH PISTOL
Caliber: 22 LR, 10-shot magazine.
Barrel: 5.5″ bull, 7.25″ fluted.
Weight: 44.5 oz. **Length:** 9.75″ overall (5.5″ barrel).
Stocks: Checkered walnut with thumbrest.
Sights: Undercut ramp front, click-adjsutable frame-mounted rear.
Features: Grip duplicates feel of military 45; positive action magazine latch; front and rear straps stippled. Trigger adjustable for pull, over-travel; gold-filled roll marks, gold-plated trigger, safety, magazine release; push-button barrel takedown. Introduced 1992. From Mitchell Arms, Inc.
Price: Stainless steel or blue **$489.00**

Mitchell Arms Monarch II Pistol
Same as the Monarch except has nickel-plated trigger, safety and magazine release, and has silver-filled roll marks. Available in satin finish stainless steel or blue. Introduced 1992. From Mitchell Arms, Inc.
Price: **$498.00**

High Standard Supermatic Citation Pistol
Same as the Supermatic Trophy except has nickel-plated trigger, slide lock, safety lever, magazine release, and has slightly heavier trigger pull. Has stippled front-grip and backstrap, checkered hardwood thumbrest grips, adjustable trigger and sear. Matte blue finish. 5.5″ barrel only. Conversion unit for 22 Short available. Reintroduced 1994. From High Standard Mfg. Co., Inc.
Price: **$446.00**
Price: With scope mount, rings, no sights **$416.00**

High Standard Supermatic Citation MS
Same as the Supermatic Citation except has 10″ barrel and RPM sights. Introduced 1996. Made in U.S. by High Standard Mfg. Co., Inc.
Price: **$695.00**

HIGH STANDARD VICTOR TARGET PISTOL
Caliber: 22 LR, 10-shot magazine.
Barrel: 4.5″ or 5.5″; push-button takedown.
Weight: 46 oz. **Length:** 9.5″ overall.
Stocks: Checkered hardwood with thumbrest.
Sights: Undercut ramp front, micro-click rear adjustable for windage and elevation. Also available with scope mount, rings, no sights.
Features: Full-length aluminum vent rib (steel optional).Gold-plated trigger, slide lock, safety-lever and magazine release; stippled front grip and backstrap; adjustable trigger and sear. Comes with barrel weight. Blue or Parkerized finish. Reintroduced 1994. From High Standard Mfg. Co., Inc.
Price: **$532.00**
Price: Victor 10X **$1,195.00**
Price: With scope mount, rings, no sights **$479.00**

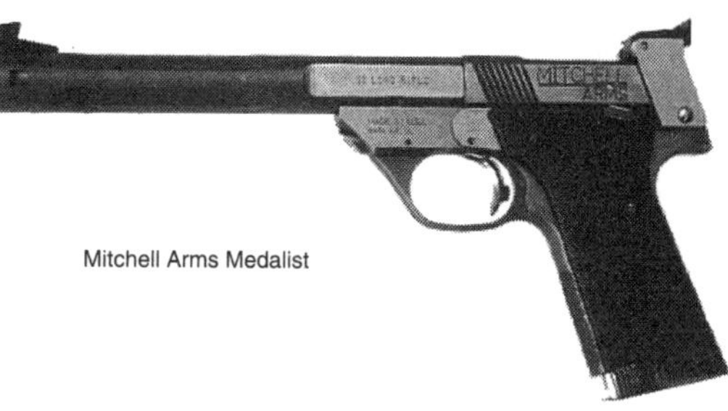
Mitchell Arms Medalist

MITCHELL ARMS MEDALIST AUTO PISTOL
Caliber: 22 Short, 22 LR, 10-shot magazine.
Barrel: 6.75″ round tapered, with stabilizer.
Weight: 40 oz. **Length:** 11.25″ overall.
Stocks: Checkered walnut with thumbrest.
Sights: Undercut ramp front, frame-mounted click adjustable square notch rear.
Features: Integral stabilizer with two removable weights. Trigger adjustable for pull and over-travel; blue finish or stainless or combo; stippled front and backstraps; push-button barrel takedown. Announced 1992. From Mitchell Arms.
Price: **$599.00**

CAUTION: PRICES SHOWN ARE SUPPLIED BY THE MANUFACTURER OR IMPORTER. CHECK YOUR LOCAL GUNSHOP.

MITCHELL ARMS BARON PISTOL
Caliber: 22 LR, 10-shot magazine.
Barrel: 5.5″ bull.
Weight: 45 oz. **Length:** 10.25″ overall.
Stocks: Checkered walnut.
Sights: Ramp front, slide-mounted square notch rear adjustable for windage and elevation.
Features: Military grip. Slide lock; smooth grip straps; push-button takedown; drilled and tapped for barrel weights. Introduced 1992. From Mitchell Arms, Inc.
Price: Stainless steel, blue or combo **$395.00**

MITCHELL ARMS SOVEREIGN AUTO PISTOL
Caliber: 22 LR, 10-shot magazine.
Barrel: 4.5″ vent rib, 5.5″ vent, dovetail or Weaver ribs.
Weight: 44 oz. **Length:** 9.75″ overall.
Stocks: Military-type checkered walnut with thumbrest.
Sights: Blade front, fully adjustable rear mounted on rib.
Features: Push-button takedown for barrel interchangeability. Bright stainless steel combo or royal blue finish. Introduced 1994. Made in U.S. From Mitchell Arms.
Price: Vent rib, 4.5″ barrel **$595.00**
Price: Dovetail rib, 5.5″ barrel **$595.00**
Price: Weaver rib, 5.5″ barrel **$675.00**

Mitchell Arms 45 Gold IPSC Limited Model
Similar to the Bullseye model except has hard-chromed frame; ghost-ring or adjustable sight; match trigger tuning; ambidextrous safety; fitted barrel and slide; extended magazine release; hex-head grip screws. Announced 1996. Made in U.S. by Mitchell Arms.
Price: **$1,195.00**

MORINI MODEL 84E FREE PISTOL
Caliber: 22 LR, single shot.
Barrel: 11.4″.
Weight: 43.7 oz. **Length:** 19.4″ overall.
Stocks: Adjustable match type with stippled surfaces.
Sights: Interchangeable blade front, match-type fully adjustable rear.
Features: Fully adjustable electronic trigger. Introduced 1995. Imported from Switzerland by Nygord Precision Products.
Price: **$1,495.00**

PARDINI K50 FREE PISTOL
Caliber: 22 LR, single shot.
Barrel: 9.8″.
Weight: 34.6 oz. **Length:** 18.7″ overall.
Stocks: Wrap-around walnut; adjustable match type.
Sights: Interchangeable post front, fully adjustable match open rear.
Features: Removable, adjustable match trigger. Barrel weights mount above the barrel. Introduced 1995. Imported from Italy by Nygord Precision Products.
Price: **$995.00**

Ruger Government Target

Ruger Mark II Government Target Model
Same gun as the Mark II Target Model except has 6⅞″ barrel, higher sights and is roll marked "Government Target Model" on the right side of the receiver below the rear sight. Identical in all aspects to the military model used for training U.S. armed forces except for markings. Comes with factory test target. Introduced 1987.
Price: Blued (MK-678G) **$356.50**
Price: Stainless (KMK-678G) **$427.25**

Mitchell Arms Sovereign

MITCHELL ARMS 45 BULLSEYE MODEL
Caliber: 45 ACP, 8-shot magazine.
Barrel: 5″, match.
Weight: 32 oz. **Length:** 8.75″ overall.
Stocks: Checkered walnut.
Sights: Blade front, adjustable rear.
Features: Stainless steel construction; adjustable trigger; flat checkered mainspring housing; extended slide stop; front and rear slide serrations; checkered front strap; full-length guide rod; wadcutter recoil spring. Announced 1996. Made in U.S. by Mitchell Arms.
Price: **$950.00**

PARDINI GP RAPID FIRE MATCH PISTOL
Caliber: 22 Short, 5-shot magazine.
Barrel: 4.6″.
Weight: 43.3 oz. **Length:** 11.6″ overall.
Stocks: Wrap-around stippled walnut.
Sights: Interchangeable post front, fully adjustable match rear.
Features: Model GP Schuman has extended rear sight for longer sight radius. Introduced 1995. Imported from Italy by Nygord Precision Products.
Price: Model GP **$995.00**
Price: Model GP Schuman **$1,395.00**

PARDINI MODEL SP, HP TARGET PISTOLS
Caliber: 22 LR, 32 S&W, 5-shot magazine.
Barrel: 4.7″.
Weight: 38.9 oz. **Length:** 11.6″ overall.
Stocks: Adjustable; stippled walnut; match type.
Sights: Interchangeable blade front, interchangeable, fully adjustable rear.
Features: Fully adjustable match trigger. Introduced 1995. Imported from Italy by Nygord Precision Products.
Price: Model SP (22 LR) **$950.00**
Price: Model HP (32 S&W) **$1,095.00**

RUGER MARK II TARGET MODEL AUTO PISTOL
Caliber: 22 LR, 10-shot magazine.
Barrel: 6⅞″.
Weight: 42 oz. **Length:** 11⅛″ overall.
Stocks: Checkered hard plastic.
Sights: .125″ blade front, micro-click rear, adjustable for windage and elevation. Sight radius 9⅜″.
Features: Introduced 1982.
Price: Blued (MK-678) **$310.50**
Price: Stainless (KMK-678) **$389.00**

Ruger Mark II Bull Barrel
Same gun as the Target Model except has 5½″ or 10″ heavy barrel (10″ meets all IHMSA regulations). Weight with 5½″ barrel is 42 oz., with 10″ barrel, 51 oz.
Price: Blued (MK-512) **$310.50**
Price: Blued (MK-10) **$294.50**
Price: Stainless (KMK-10) **$373.00**
Price: Stainless (KMK-512) **$389.00**

Ruger Stainless Government Competition Model 22 Pistol
Similar to the Mark II Government Target Model stainless pistol except has 6⅞″ slab-sided barrel; the receiver top is drilled and tapped for a Ruger scope base adaptor of blued, chrome moly steel; comes with Ruger 1″ stainless scope rings with integral bases for mounting a variety of optical sights; has checkered laminated grip panels with right-hand thumbrest. Has blued open sights with 9¼″ radius. Overall length is 11⅛″, weight 45 oz. Introduced 1991.
Price: KMK-678GC **$441.00**

SMITH & WESSON MODEL 41 TARGET
Caliber: 22 LR, 10-shot clip.
Barrel: 5½", 7".
Weight: 44 oz. (5½" barrel). **Length:** 9" overall (5½" barrel).
Stocks: Checkered walnut with modified thumbrest, usable with either hand.
Sights: ⅛" Patridge on ramp base; micro-click rear adjustable for windage and elevation.
Features: ⅜" wide, grooved trigger; adjustable trigger stop.
Price: S&W Bright Blue, either barrel **$753.00**

Smith & Wesson Model 41

SPHINX AT-2000C, CS COMPETITOR PISTOL
Caliber: 9mm Para., 9x21mm, 40 S&W, 10-shot.
Barrel: 5.31".
Weight: 40.56 oz. **Length:** 9.84" overall.
Stocks: Checkered neoprene.
Sights: Fully adjustable Bo-Mar or Tasco Pro-Point dot sight in Sphinx mount.
Features: Extended magazine release. Competition slide with dual-port compensated barrel. Two-tone finish only. Introduced 1993. Imported from Switzerland by Sphinx U.S.A., Inc.
Price: With Bo-Mar sights **$1,902.00**
Price: With Tasco Pro-Point and mount (AT-2000CS) **$2,189.00**

Sphinx AT-2000c Competitor

Sphinx AT-2000GM Grand Master Pistol
Similar to the AT-2000C except has single-action-only trigger mechanism, squared trigger guard, extended beavertail grip, safety and magazine release; notched competition slide for easier cocking. Two-tone finish only. Has dual-port compensated barrel. Available with fully adjustable Bo-Mar sights or Tasco Pro-Point and Sphinx mount. Introduced 1993. Imported from Switzerland by Sphinx U.S.A., Inc.
Price: With Bo-Mar sights (AT-2000GMS) **$2,894.00**
Price: With Tasco Pro-Point and mount (AT-2000GM) **$2,972.00**

SAFARI ARMS MATCHMASTER PISTOL
Caliber: 45 ACP, 7-shot magazine.
Barrel: 5", 6"; stainless steel.
Weight: 38 oz. **Length:** 8.5" overall.
Stocks: Smooth walnut with etched scorpion logo.
Sights: Ramped blade front, LPA adjustable rear.
Features: Beavertail grip safety, extended safety, extended slide release, Commander-style hammer; throated, polished, tuned. Finishes: Parkerized matte black, or satin stainless steel. Made in U.S. by Safari, Inc.
Price: 5" barrel **$715.00**
Price: 6" barrel **$844.00**

Springfield 1911A1 Trophy Match

Springfield, Inc. Basic Competition Pistol
Has low-mounted Bo-Mar adjustable rear sight, undercut blade front; match throated barrel and bushing; polished feed ramp; lowered and flared ejection port; fitted Videki speed trigger with tuned 3.5-lb. pull; fitted slide to frame; recoil buffer system; checkered walnut grips; serrated, arched mainspring housing. Comes with two magazines with slam pads, plastic carrying case. Introduced 1992. From Springfield, Inc.
Price: 45 ACP, blue, 5" only **$1,439.00**

Springfield, Inc. Expert Pistol
Similar to the Competition Pistol except has triple-chamber tapered cone compensator on match barrel with dovetailed front sight; lowered and flared ejection port; fully tuned for reliability; fitted slide to frame; extended ambidextrous thumb safety, extended magazine release button; beavertail grip safety; Pachmayr wrap-around grips. Comes with two magazines, plastic carrying case. Introduced 1992. From Springfield, Inc.
Price: 45 ACP, Duotone finish **$1,915.00**
Price: Expert Ltd. **$1,804.00**

Safari Arms Matchmaster Carrycomp I
Similar to the Matchmaster except has Wil Schueman-designed hybrid compensator system. Introduced 1993. Made in U.S. by Safari Arms, Inc.
Price: 3.8" barrel **$1,150.00**
Price: 5" barrel **$1,300.00**

SPRINGFIELD, INC. 1911A1 BULLSEYE WADCUTTER PISTOL
Caliber: 45 ACP.
Barrel: 5".
Weight: 45 oz. **Length:** 8.59" overall (5" barrel).
Stocks: Checkered walnut.
Sights: Bo-Mar rib with undercut blade front, fully adjustable rear.
Features: Built for wadcutter loads only. Has full-length recoil spring guide rod, fitted Videki speed trigger with 3.5-lb. pull; match Commander hammer and sear; beavertail grip safety; lowered and flared ejection port; tuned extractor; fitted slide to frame; recoil buffer system; beveled and polished magazine well; checkered front strap and steel mainspring housing (flat housing standard); polished and throated National Match barrel and bushing. Comes with two magazines with slam pads, plastic carrying case, test target. Introduced 1992. From Springfield, Inc.
Price: **$1,665.00**

Springfield, Inc. 1911A1 Trophy Match Pistol
Similar to the 1911A1 except factory accurized, Videki speed trigger, skeletonized hammer; has 4- to 5½-lb. trigger pull, click adjustable rear sight, match-grade barrel and bushing. Comes with checkered walnut grips. Introduced 1994. From Springfield, Inc.
Price: Blue **$954.00**
Price: Stainless steel **$985.00**

Springfield, Inc. Competition Pistol
Similar to the 1911A1 Basic Competition Wadcutter Pistol except has brazed, serrated improved ramp front sight; Videki speed trigger with 3½-lb. pull; extended ambidextrous thumb safety; match Commander hammer and sear; serrated rear slide; Pachmayr flat mainspring housing; extended magazine release; beavertail grip safety; full-length recoil spring guide; Pachmayr wrap-around grips. Comes with two magazines with slam pads, plastic carrying case. Introduced 1992. From Springfield, Inc.
Price: 45 ACP, blue **$1,598.00**

Springfield, Inc. Distinguished Pistol
Has all the features of the 1911A1 Expert except is full-house pistol with deluxe Bo-Mar low-mounted adjustable rear sight; full-length recoil spring guide rod and recoil spring retainer; checkered frontstrap; S&A magazine well; walnut grips. Hard chrome finish. Comes with two magazines with slam pads, plastic carrying case. From Springfield, Inc.
Price: 45 ACP **$2,717.00**
Price: Distinguished Limited **$2,606.00**

CAUTION: PRICES SHOWN ARE SUPPLIED BY THE MANUFACTURER OR IMPORTER. CHECK YOUR LOCAL GUNSHOP.

Springfield, Inc. 1911A1 N.M. Hardball Pistol
Has Bo-Mar adjustable rear sight with undercut front blade; fitted match Videki trigger with 4-lb. pull; fitted slide to frame; throated National Match barrel and bushing, polished feed ramp; recoil buffer system; tuned extractor; Herrett walnut grips. Comes with two magazines, plastic carrying case, test target. Introduced 1992. From Springfield, Inc.
Price: 45 ACP, blue $1,485.00

STOEGER PRO SERIES 95 VENT RIB
Caliber: 22 LR, 10-shot magazine.
Barrel: 5½″.
Weight: 48 oz. **Length:** 9⅝″ overall.
Stocks: Pachmayr wrap-around checkered rubber.
Sights: Blade front, fully adjustable micro-click rear mounted on rib.
Features: Stainless steel construction; full-length ventilated rib; gold-plated trigger, slide lock, safety-lever and magazine release; adjustable trigger; interchangeable barrels. Introduced 1996. From Stoeger Ind.
Price: $565.00

Stoeger Pro Series 95 Bull Barrel
Similar to the Vent Rib model except has 5½″ bull barrel, rear sight mounted on slide bridge. Introduced 1996. From Stoeger Ind.
Price: $460.00

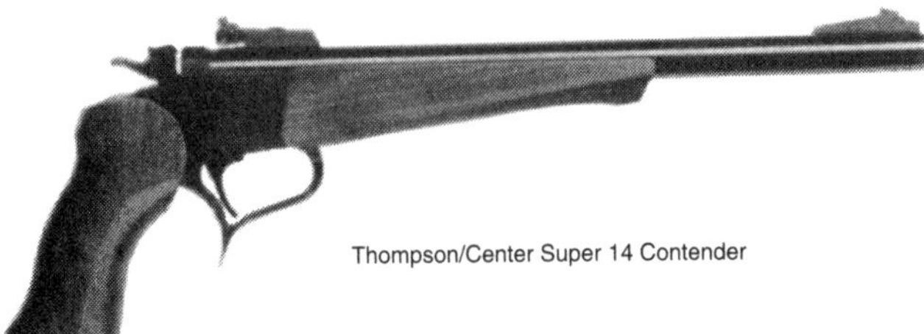

Thompson/Center Super 14 Contender

Thompson/Center Super 16 Contender
Same as the T/C Super 14 Contender except has 16¼″ barrel. Rear sight can be mounted at mid-barrel position (10¾″ radius) or moved to the rear (using scope mount position) for 14¾″ radius. Overall length is 20¼″. Comes with T/C Competitor Grip of walnut and rubber. Available in 22 LR, 22 WMR, 223 Rem., 7-30 Waters, 30-30 Win., 35 Rem., 44 Mag., 45-70 Gov't. Also available with 16″ vent rib barrel with internal choke, caliber 45 Colt/410 shotshell.
Price: Blue $478.90
Price: Stainless steel $509.90
Price: 45-70 Gov't., blue $484.10
Price: As above, stainless steel $530.50
Price: Super 16 Vent Rib, blued $509.90
Price: As above, stainless steel $540.80
Price: Extra 16″ barrel, blued $229.20
Price: As above, stainless steel $244.50
Price: Extra 45-70 barrel, blued $234.30
Price: As above, stainless steel $265.50
Price: Extra Super 16 vent rib barrel, blue $260.10
Price: As above, stainless steel $265.50

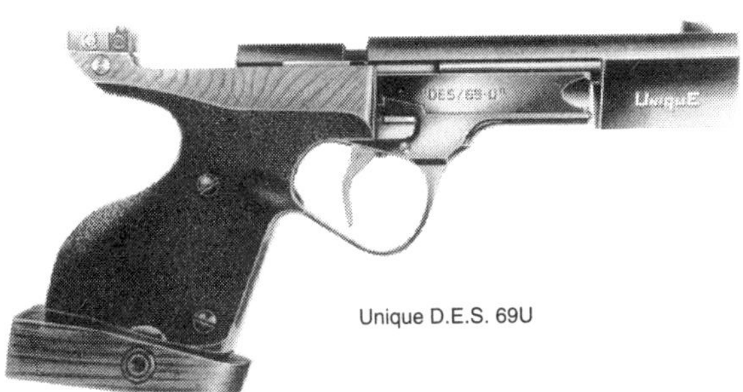

Unique D.E.S. 69U

UNIQUE D.E.S. 69U TARGET PISTOL
Caliber: 22 LR, 5-shot magazine.
Barrel: 5.91″.
Weight: 35.3 oz. **Length:** 10.5″ overall.
Stocks: French walnut target-style with thumbrest and adjustable shelf; hand-checkered panels.
Sights: Ramp front, micro. adjustable rear mounted on frame; 8.66″ sight radius.
Features: Meets U.I.T. standards. Comes with 260-gram barrel weight; 100, 150, 350-gram weights available. Fully adjustable match trigger; dry-firing safety device. Imported from France by Nygord Precision Products.
Price: Right-hand, about $1,250.00
Price: Left-hand, about $1,290.00

Stoeger Pro Series 95 Fluted

Stoeger Pro Series 95 Fluted Barrel
Similar to the Vent Rib model except has 7½″ heavy fluted barrel, rear sight mounted on slide bridge. Overall length 11¼″, weighs 50 oz. Introduced 1996. From Stoeger Ind.
Price: $490.00

THOMPSON/CENTER SUPER 14 CONTENDER
Caliber: 22 LR, 222 Rem., 223 Rem., 7mm TCU, 7-30 Waters, 30-30 Win., 35 Rem., 357 Rem. Maximum, 44 Mag., 10mm Auto, 445 Super Mag., single shot.
Barrel: 14″.
Weight: 45 oz. **Length:** 17¼″ overall.
Stocks: T/C "Competitor Grip" (walnut and rubber).
Sights: Fully adjustable target-type.
Features: Break-open action with auto safety. Interchangeable barrels for both rimfire and centerfire calibers. Introduced 1978.
Price: Blued $473.80
Price: Stainless steel $504.70
Price: Extra barrels, blued $244.00
Price: Extra barrels, stainless steel $239.50

UNIQUE D.E.S. 32U TARGET PISTOL
Caliber: 32 S&W Long wadcutter.
Barrel: 5.9″.
Weight: 40.2 oz.
Stocks: Anatomically shaped, adjustable stippled French walnut.
Sights: Blade front, micrometer click rear.
Features: Trigger adjustable for weight and position; dry firing mechanism; slide stop catch. Optional sleeve weights. Introduced 1990. Imported from France by Nygord Precision Products.
Price: Right-hand, about $1,350.00
Price: Left-hand, about $1,380.00

WALTHER GSP MATCH PISTOL
Caliber: 22 LR, 32 S&W Long (GSP-C), 5-shot magazine.
Barrel: 4.22″.
Weight: 44.8 oz. (22 LR), 49.4 oz. (32). **Length:** 11.8″ overall.
Stocks: Walnut.
Sights: Post front, match rear adjustable for windage and elevation.
Features: Available with either 2.2-lb. (1000 gm) or 3-lb. (1360 gm) trigger. Spare magazine, barrel weight, tools supplied. Imported from Germany by Nygord Precision Products.
Price: GSP, with case $1,495.00
Price: GSP-C, with case $1,595.00

WICHITA SILHOUETTE PISTOL
Caliber: 308 Win. F.L., 7mm IHMSA, 7mm-308.
Barrel: 14 15/16″.
Weight: 4½ lbs. **Length:** 21⅜″ overall.
Stock: American walnut with oil finish. Glass bedded.
Sights: Wichita Multi-Range sight system.
Features: Comes with left-hand action with right-hand grip. Round receiver and barrel. Fluted bolt, flat bolt handle. Wichita adjustable trigger. Introduced 1979. From Wichita Arms.
Price: Center grip stock $1,417.50
Price: As above except with Rear Position Stock and target-type Lightpull trigger $1,417.50

WICHITA CLASSIC SILHOUETTE PISTOL
Caliber: All standard calibers with maximum overall length of 2.800″.
Barrel: 11¼″.
Weight: 3 lbs., 15 oz.
Stocks: AAA American walnut with oil finish, checkered grip.
Sights: Hooded post front, open adjustable rear.
Features: Three locking lug bolt, three gas ports; completely adjustable Wichita trigger. Introduced 1981. From Wichita Arms.
Price: $3,450.00

CAUTION: PRICES SHOWN ARE SUPPLIED BY THE MANUFACTURER OR IMPORTER. CHECK YOUR LOCAL GUNSHOP.

Includes models suitable for hunting and competitive courses for fire, both police and international.

ARMSCOR M-200DC REVOLVER
Caliber: 38 Spec., 6-shot cylinder.
Barrel: 2½″, 4″.
Weight: 22 oz. (2½″ barrel). **Length:** 7⅜″ overall (2½″ barrel).
Stocks: Checkered rubber.
Sights: Blade front, fixed notch rear.
Features: All-steel construction; floating firing pin, transfer bar ignition; shrouded ejector rod; blue finish. Reintroduced 1996. Imported from the Philippines by K.B.I., Inc.
Price: **$199.99**

Armscor M-200DC

COLT ANACONDA REVOLVER
Caliber: 44 Rem. Magnum, 45 Colt, 6-shot.
Barrel: 4″, 6″, 8″.
Weight: 53 oz. (6″ barrel). **Length:** 11⅝″ overall.
Stocks: TP combat style with finger grooves.
Sights: Red insert front, adjustable white outline rear.
Features: Stainless steel; full-length ejector rod housing; ventilated barrel rib; offset bolt notches in cylinder; wide spur hammer. Introduced 1990.
Price: **$612.00**
Price: 45 Colt, 6″, 8″ barrel only **$612.00**
Price: With complete Realtree camouflage coverage **$740.00**
Price: As above with scope and mount **$999.00**

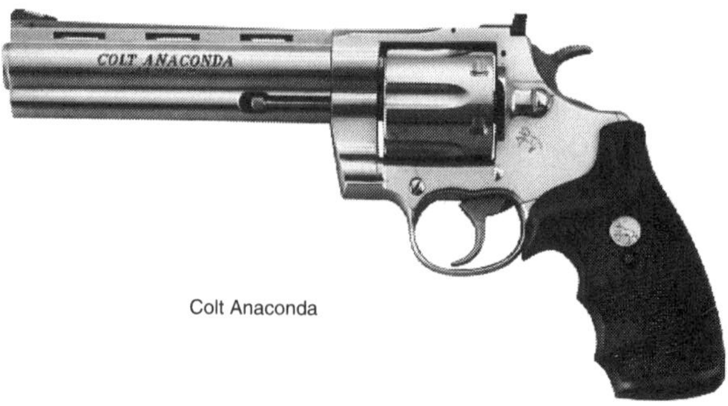
Colt Anaconda

COLT 38 SF-VI REVOLVER
Caliber: 38 Special, 6-shot.
Barrel: 2″.
Weight: 21 oz. **Length:** 7″ overall.
Stocks: Checkered black composition.
Sights: Ramp front, fixed rear.
Features: Has new lockwork. Made of stainless steel. Introduced 1995. From Colt's Mfg. Co.
Price: **$408.00**

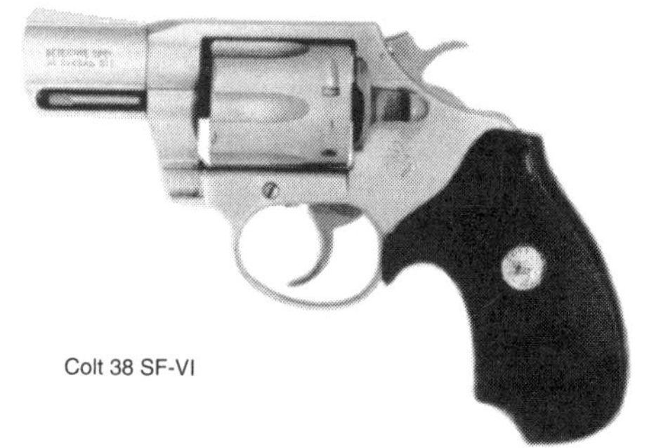
Colt 38 SF-VI

COLT KING COBRA REVOLVER
Caliber: 357 Magnum, 6-shot.
Barrel: 4″, 6″.
Weight: 42 oz. (4″ bbl.). **Length:** 9″ overall (4″ bbl.).
Stocks: TP combat style.
Sights: Red insert ramp front, adjustable white outline rear.
Features: Full-length contoured ejector rod housing, barrel rib. Introduced 1986.
Price: Stainless **$455.00**

COLT PYTHON REVOLVER
Caliber: 357 Magnum (handles all 38 Spec.), 6-shot.
Barrel: 4″, 6″ or 8″, with ventilated rib.
Weight: 38 oz. (4″ bbl.). **Length:** 9¼″ (4″ bbl.).
Stocks: Hogue Monogrip (4″), TP combat style (6″, 8″).
Sights: ⅛″ ramp front, adjustable notch rear.
Features: Ventilated rib; grooved, crisp trigger; swing-out cylinder; target hammer.
Price: Royal blue, 4″, 6″, 8″ **$815.00**
Price: Stainless, 4″, 6″, 8″ **$904.00**
Price: Bright stainless, 4″, 6″, 8″ **$935.00**

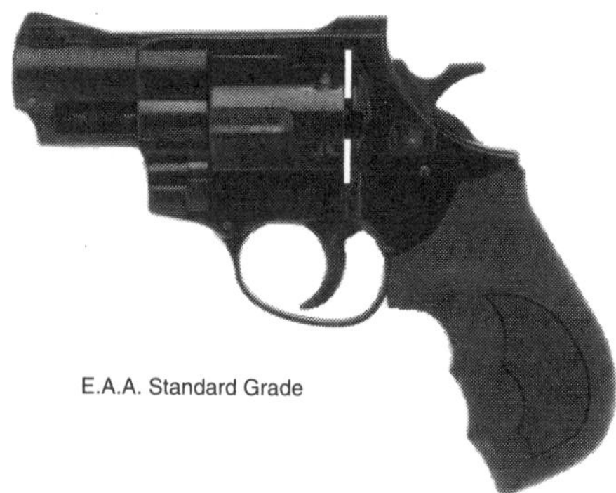
E.A.A. Standard Grade

E.A.A. STANDARD GRADE REVOLVERS
Caliber: 22 LR, 22 LR/22 WMR, 8-shot; 38 Spec., 6-shot; 357 magnum, 6-shot.
Barrel: 4″, 6″ (22 rimfire); 2″, 4″ (38 Spec.).
Weight: 38 oz. (22 rimfire, 4″). **Length:** 8.8″ overall (4″ bbl.).
Stocks: Rubber with finger grooves.
Sights: Blade front, fixed or adjustable on rimfires; fixed only on 32, 38.
Features: Swing-out cylinder; hammer block safety; blue finish. Introduced 1991. Imported from Germany by European American Armory.
Price: 38 Special 2″ **$180.00**
Price: 38 Special, 4″ **$199.00**
Price: 357 Magnum **$199.00**
Price: 22 LR, 6″ **$199.00**
Price: 22 LR/22 WMR combo, 4″ **$200.00**
Price: As above, 6″ **$200.00**

ERMA ER-777 SPORTING REVOLVER
Caliber: 357 Mag., 6-shot.
Barrel: 5½″.
Weight: 43.3 oz. **Length:** 9½″ overall (4″ barrel).
Stocks: Stippled walnut service-type.
Sights: Interchangeable blade front, micro-adjustable rear for windage and elevation.
Features: Polished blue finish. Adjustable trigger. Imported from Germany by Precision Sales Int'l. Introduced 1988.
Price: **$1,019.00**

CAUTION: PRICES SHOWN ARE SUPPLIED BY THE MANUFACTURER OR IMPORTER. CHECK YOUR LOCAL GUNSHOP.

HARRINGTON & RICHARDSON 939 PREMIER REVOLVER
Caliber: 22 LR, 9-shot cylinder.
Barrel: 6″ heavy.
Weight: 36 oz. **Length:** NA.
Stocks: Walnut-finished hardwood.
Sights: Blade front, fully adjustable rear.
Features: Swing-out cylinder with plunger-type ejection; solid barrel rib; high-polish blue finish; double-action mechanism; Western-style grip. Introduced 1995. Made in U.S. by H&R 1871, Inc.
Price: **$189.95**

Harrington & Richardson 939

HARRINGTON & RICHARDSON SPORTSMAN 999 REVOLVER
Caliber: 22 Short, Long, Long Rifle, 9-shot.
Barrel: 4″, 6″.
Weight: 30 oz. (4″ barrel). **Length:** 8.5″ overall.
Stocks: Walnut-finished hardwood.
Sights: Blade front adjustable for elevation, rear adjustable for windage.
Features: Top-break loading; polished blue finish; automatic shell ejection. Reintroduced 1992. From H&R 1871, Inc.
Price: **$279.95**

Harrington & Richardson Sportsman 999

HARRINGTON & RICHARDSON 949 WESTERN REVOLVER
Caliber: 22 LR, 9-shot cylinder.
Barrel: 5½″, 7½″.
Weight: 36 oz. **Length:** NA.
Stocks: Walnut-stained hardwood.
Sights: Blade front, adjustable rear.
Features: Color case-hardened frame and backstrap, traditional loading gate and ejector rod. Introduced 1994. Made in U.S. by H&R 1871, Inc.
Price: About **$189.95**

HARRINGTON & RICHARDSON AMERICAN REVOLVERS
Caliber: 38 Spec., 5-shot.
Barrel: 2″, 3″.
Weight: 24 oz. **Length:** 7⅛″ overall.
Stocks: Pachmayr rubber.
Sights: Ramp front, fixed notch rear.
Features: Available in blue or nickel. Introduced 1996. Made in U.S. by Amtec 2000.
Price: .... **NA**

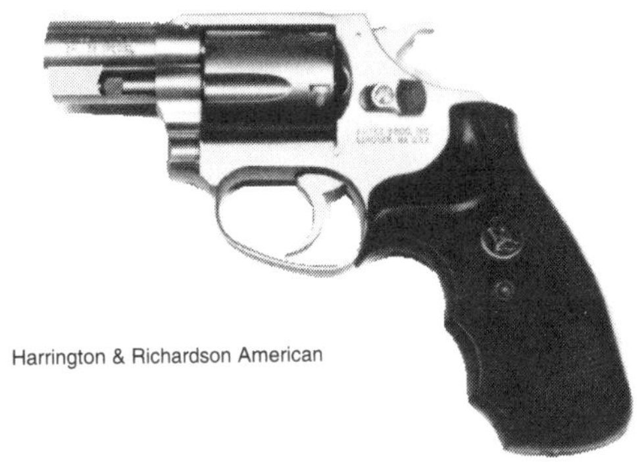
Harrington & Richardson American

HARRINGTON & RICHARDSON 929 SIDEKICK
Caliber: 22 LR, 9-shot cylinder.
Barrel: 4″ heavy.
Weight: 30 oz. **Length:** NA.
Stocks: Cinnamon-color laminated wood.
Sights: Blade front, notch rear.
Features: Double action; swing-out cylinder, traditional loading gate; blued frame and barrel. Comes with lockable storage case, Uncle Mike's Sidekick holster. Introduced 1996. Made in U.S. by H&R 1871, Inc.
Price: **$159.95**
Price: NTA Trapper Edition, special rollmark, gray laminate grips **$174.95**

Manurhin MR73 Sport Revolver

Heritage Sentry

MANURHIN MR 73 SPORT REVOLVER
Caliber: 357 Magnum, 6-shot cylinder.
Barrel: 6″.
Weight: 37 oz. **Length:** 11.1″ overall.
Stocks: Checkered walnut.
Sights: Blade front, fully adjustable rear.
Features: Double action with adjustable trigger. High-polish blue finish, straw-colored hammer and trigger. Comes with extra sight. Introduced 1984. Imported from France by Century International Arms.
Price: About **$1,500.00**

HERITAGE SENTRY DOUBLE-ACTION REVOLVERS
Caliber: 38 Spec., 6-shot.
Barrel: 2″.
Weight: 23 oz. **Length:** 6¼″ overall (2″ barrel).
Stocks: Checkered plastic.
Sights: Ramp front, fixed rear.
Features: Pull-pin-type ejection; serrated hammer and trigger. Polished blue or nickel finish. Introduced 1993. Made in U.S. by Heritage Mfg., Inc.
Price: .... **$129.95** to **$139.95**

MANURHIN MR 73 REVOLVER
Caliber: 32 S&W, 38 Spec., 357 Mag.
Barrel: 3″, 4″, 5¼″, 5¾″, 6″.
Weight: 38 oz. (6″ barrel). **Length:** 11″ overall (6″ barrel).
Stocks: Checkered hardwood.
Sights: Blade front, fully adjustable rear.
Features: Polished bright blue finish; hammer-forged barrel. Imported from France by Sphinx U.S.A., Inc.
Price: Police model, 3″ or 4″ barrel **$1,885.00**
Price: Sport model, 5¼″ or 6″ barrel, undercut blade front sight **$1,885.00**
Price: 38 Spec. Match, 5¾″ barrel, single action only **$1,975.00**
Price: 32 S&W Match, 6″ barrel, single action only **$1,975.00**

Manurhin MR 96

MANURHIN MR 88 REVOLVER
Caliber: 357 Magnum, 6-shot.
Barrel: 4″, 5¼″, 6″.
Weight: 33.5 oz. **Length:** 8.1″ overall.
Stocks: Checkered wood.
Sights: Blade front, fully adjustable rear.
Features: Stainless steel construction; hammer-forged barrel. Imported from France by Sphinx U.S.A., Inc.
Price: **$877.95**

Consult our Directory pages for the location of firms mentioned.

NEW ENGLAND FIREARMS LADY ULTRA REVOLVER
Caliber: 32 H&R Mag., 5-shot.
Barrel: 3″.
Weight: 31 oz. **Length:** 7.25″ overall.
Stocks: Walnut-finished hardwood with NEF medallion.
Sights: Blade front, fully adjustable rear.
Features: Swing-out cylinder; polished blue finish. Comes with lockable storage case. Introduced 1992. From New England Firearms.
Price: **$174.95**

NEW ENGLAND FIREARMS ULTRA REVOLVER
Caliber: 22 LR, 9-shot; 22 WMR, 6-shot.
Barrel: 4″, 6″.
Weight: 36 oz. **Length:** 10⅝″ overall (6″ barrel).
Stocks: Walnut-finished hardwood with NEF medallion.
Sights: Blade front, fully adjustable rear.
Features: Blue finish. Bull-style barrel with recessed muzzle, high "Lustre" blue/black finish. Introduced 1989. From New England Firearms.
Price: **$174.95**
Price: Ultra Mag 22 WMR **$174.95**

NEW ENGLAND FIREARMS STANDARD REVOLVERS
Caliber: 22 LR, 9-shot; 32 H&R Mag., 5-shot.
Barrel: 2½″, 4″.
Weight: 26 oz. (22 LR, 2½″). **Length:** 8½″ overall (4″ bbl.).
Stocks: Walnut-finished American hardwood with NEF medallion.
Sights: Fixed.
Features: Choice of blue or nickel finish. Introduced 1988. From New England Firearms.
Price: 22 LR, 32 H&R Mag., blue **$134.95**
Price: 22 LR, 2½″, 4″, nickel, 32 H&R Mag. 2½″ nickel **$144.95**

ROSSI LADY ROSSI REVOLVER
Caliber: 38 Spec., 5-shot.
Barrel: 2″, 3″.
Weight: 21 oz. **Length:** 6.5″ overall (2″ barrel).
Stocks: Smooth rosewood.
Sights: Fixed.
Features: High-polish stainless steel with "Lady Rossi" engraved on frame. Comes with velvet carry bag. Introduced 1995. Imported from Brazil by Interarms.
Price: **$285.00**

ROSSI MODEL 68 REVOLVER
Caliber: 38 Spec.
Barrel: 2″, 3″.
Weight: 22 oz.
Stocks: Checkered wood and rubber.
Sights: Ramp front, low profile adjustable rear.
Features: All-steel frame, thumb latch operated swing-out cylinder. Introduced 1978. Imported from Brazil by Interarms.
Price: 38, blue, 3″, wood or rubber grips **$225.00**
Price: M68/2 (2″ barrel), wood or rubber grips **$225.00**
Price: 3″, nickel **$225.00**

MANURHIN MR 96 REVOLVER
Caliber: 357 Magnum, 6-shot.
Barrel: 3″, 4″, 5¼″, 6″.
Weight: 38.4 oz. **Length:** 8.8″ overall.
Stocks: Checkered rubber.
Sights: Blade front, fully adjustable rear.
Features: Polished blue finish; removable sideplate holds action parts; separate barrel and shroud. Introduced 1996. Imported from France by Sphinx U.S.A., Inc.
Price: **$857.95**

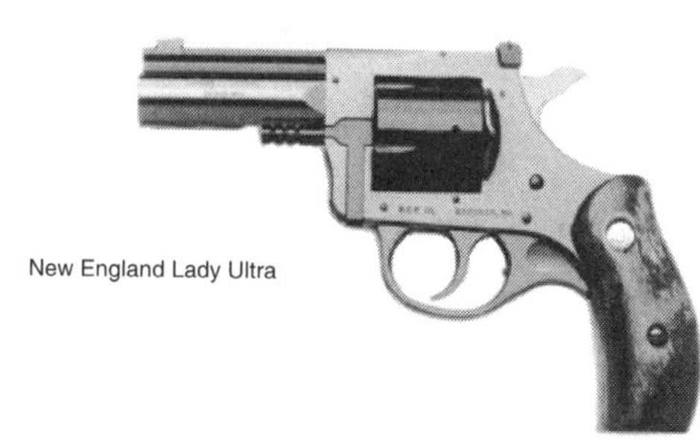
New England Lady Ultra

Rossi Lady Rossi

Rossi Model 518

ROSSI MODEL 88 STAINLESS REVOLVER
Caliber: 38 Spec., 5-shot.
Barrel: 2″, 3″.
Weight: 22 oz. **Length:** 7.5″ overall.
Stocks: Checkered wood, service-style, and rubber.
Sights: Ramp front, square notch rear drift adjustable for windage.
Features: All metal parts except springs are of 440 stainless steel; matte finish; small frame for concealability. Introduced 1983. Imported from Brazil by Interarms.
Price: 3″ barrel, wood or rubber grips **$255.00**
Price: 2″ barrel, wood or rubber grips **$255.00**

ROSSI MODEL 515, 518 REVOLVERS
Caliber: 22 LR (Model 518), 22 WMR (Model 515), 6-shot.
Barrel: 4″.
Weight: 30 oz. **Length:** 9″ overall.
Stocks: Checkered wood and finger-groove wrap-around rubber.
Sights: Blade front with red insert, rear adjustable for windage and elevation.
Features: Small frame; stainless steel construction; solid integral barrel rib. Introduced 1994. Imported from Brazil by Interarms.
Price: Model 518, 22 LR **$255.00**
Price: Model 515, 22 WMR **$270.00**

CAUTION: PRICES SHOWN ARE SUPPLIED BY THE MANUFACTURER OR IMPORTER. CHECK YOUR LOCAL GUNSHOP.

ROSSI MODEL 720 REVOLVER
Caliber: 44 Spec., 5-shot.
Barrel: 3″.
Weight: 27.5 oz. **Length:** 8″ overall.
Stocks: Checkered rubber, combat style.
Sights: Red insert front on ramp, fully adjustable rear.
Features: All stainless steel construction; solid barrel rib; full ejector rod shroud. Introduced 1992. Imported from Brazil by Interarms.
Price: **$290.00**
Price: Model 720C, spurless hammer, DA only **$290.00**

ROSSI MODEL 851 REVOLVER
Caliber: 38 Spec., 6-shot.
Barrel: 3″ or 4″.
Weight: 27.5 oz. (3″ bbl.). **Length:** 8″ overall (3″ bbl.).
Stocks: Checkered Brazilian hardwood.
Sights: Blade front with red insert, rear adjustable for windage.
Features: Medium-size frame; stainless steel construction; ventilated barrel rib. Introduced 1991. Imported from Brazil by Interarms.
Price: **$255.00**

ROSSI MODEL 877 REVOLVER
Caliber: 357 Mag., 6-shot cylinder.
Barrel: 2″.
Weight: 26 oz. **Length:** NA.
Stocks: Stippled synthetic.
Sights: Blade front, fixed groove rear.
Features: Stainless steel construction; fully enclosed ejector rod. Introduced 1996. Imported from Brazil by Interarms.
Price: **$290.00**

ROSSI MODEL 971 REVOLVER
Caliber: 357 Mag., 6-shot.
Barrel: $2^{1}/_{2}$″, 4″, 6″, heavy.
Weight: 36 oz. **Length:** 9″ overall.
Stocks: Checkered Brazilian hardwood. Stainless models have checkered, contoured rubber.
Sights: Blade front, fully adjustable rear.
Features: Full-length ejector rod shroud; matted sight rib; target-type trigger, wide checkered hammer spur. Introduced 1988. Imported from Brazil by Interarms.
Price: 4″, stainless **$290.00**
Price: 6″, stainless **$290.00**
Price: 4″, blue **$255.00**
Price: $2^{1}/_{2}$″, stainless **$290.00**

CONSULT
SHOOTER'S
MARKETPLACE
Page 225, This Issue

RUGER GP-100 REVOLVERS
Caliber: 38 Spec., 357 Mag., 6-shot.
Barrel: 3″, 3″ heavy, 4″, 4″ heavy, 6″, 6″ heavy.
Weight: 3″ barrel—35 oz., 3″ heavy barrel—36 oz., 4″ barrel—37 oz., 4″ heavy barrel—38 oz.
Sights: Fixed; adjustable on 4″ heavy, 6″, 6″ heavy barrels.
Stocks: Ruger Santoprene Cushioned Grip with Goncalo Alves inserts.
Features: Uses action and frame incorporating improvements and features of both the Security-Six and Redhawk revolvers. Full length and short ejector shroud. Satin blue and stainless steel. Available in high-gloss stainless steel finish. Introduced 1988.
Price: GP-141 (357, 4″ heavy, adj. sights, blue) **$440.00**
Price: GP-160 (357, 6″, adj. sights, blue) **$440.00**
Price: GP-161 (357, 6″ heavy, adj. sights, blue) **$440.00**
Price: GPF-331 (357, 3″ heavy), GPF-831 (38 Spec.) **$423.00**
Price: GPF-340 (357, 4″), GPF-840 (38 Spec.) **$423.00**
Price: GPF-341 (357, 4″ heavy), GPF-841 (38 Spec.) **$423.00**
Price: KGP-141 (357, 4″ heavy, adj. sights, stainless) **$474.00**
Price: KGP-160 (357, 6″, adj. sights, stainless) **$474.00**
Price: KGP-161 (357, 6″ heavy, adj. sights, stainless) **$474.00**
Price: KGPF-330 (357, 3″, stainless), KGPF-830 (38 Spec.) **$457.00**
Price: KGPF-331 (357, 3″ heavy, stainless), KGPF-831 (38 Spec.) **$457.00**
Price: KGPF-340 (357, 4″, stainless), KGPF-840 (38 Spec.) **$457.00**
Price: KGPF-341 (357, 4″ heavy, stainless), KGPF-841 (38 Spec.) **$457.00**

Rossi Model 877

Rossi Model 971 VRC

Rossi Model 971 VRC Revolver
Similar to the Model 971 except has Rossi's 8-port Vented Rib Compensator; checkered finger-groove rubber grips; stainless steel construction. Available with 2.5″, 4″, 6″ barrel; weighs 30 oz. with $2^{5}/_{8}$″ barrel. Introduced 1996. Imported from Brazil by Interarms.
Price: **$340.00**

Rossi Model 971 Comp Gun
Same as the Model 971 stainless except has $3^{1}/_{4}$″ barrel with integral compensator. Overall length is 9″, weighs 32 oz. Has red insert front sight, fully adjustable rear. Checkered, contoured rubber grips. Introduced 1993. Imported from Brazil by Interarms.
Price: **$290.00**

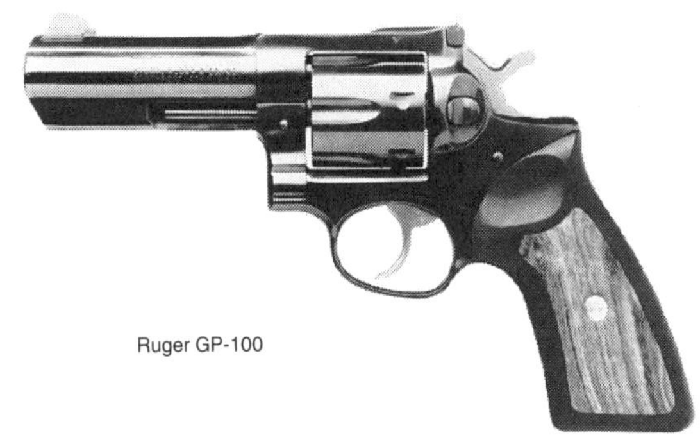
Ruger GP-100

RUGER SP101 REVOLVERS
Caliber: 22 LR, 32 H&R Mag., 6-shot, 9mm Para., 38 Spec. +P, 357 Mag., 5-shot.
Barrel: $2^{1}/_{4}$″, $3^{1}/_{16}$″, 4″.
Weight: $2^{1}/_{4}$″—25 oz.; $3^{1}/_{16}$″—27 oz.
Sights: Adjustable on 22, 32, fixed on others.
Stocks: Ruger Santoprene Cushioned Grip with Xenoy inserts.
Features: Incorporates improvements and features found in the GP-100 revolvers into a compact, small frame, double-action revolver. Full-length ejector shroud. Stainless steel only. Available with high-polish finish. Introduced 1988.
Price: KSP-821 ($2^{1}/_{2}$″, 38 Spec.) **$443.00**
Price: KSP-831 ($3^{1}/_{16}$″, 38 Spec.) **$443.00**
Price: KSP-221 ($2^{1}/_{4}$″, 22 LR) **$443.00**
Price: KSP-240 (4″, 22 LR) **$443.00**
Price: KSP-241 (4″ heavy bbl., 22 LR) **$443.00**
Price: KSP-3231 ($3^{1}/_{16}$″, 32 H&R) **$443.00**
Price: KSP-921 ($2^{1}/_{4}$″, 9mm Para.) **$443.00**
Price: KSP-931 ($3^{1}/_{16}$″, 9mm Para.) **$443.00**
Price: KSP-321 ($2^{1}/_{4}$″, 357 Mag.) **$443.00**
Price: KSP-331 ($3^{1}/_{16}$″, 357 Mag.) **$443.00**

Ruger SP101 DAO

Ruger SP101 Double-Action-Only Revolver
Similar to the standard SP101 except is double-action-only with no single-action sear notch. Has spurless hammer for snag-free handling, floating firing pin and Ruger's patented transfer bar safety system. Available with $2^{1}/_{4}$″ barrel in 38 Special +P and 357 Magnum only. Weighs $25^{1}/_{2}$ oz., overall length 7.06″. Natural brushed satin or high-polish stainless steel. Introduced 1993.
Price: KSP821L (38 Spec.), KSP321XL (357 Mag.) **$443.00**

RUGER REDHAWK
Caliber: 44 Rem. Mag., 6-shot.
Barrel: $5^{1}/_{2}$″, $7^{1}/_{2}$″.
Weight: About 54 oz. ($7^{1}/_{2}$″ bbl.). **Length:** 13″ overall ($7^{1}/_{2}$″ barrel).
Stocks: Square butt Goncalo Alves.
Sights: Interchangeable Patridge-type front, rear adjustable for windage and elevation.
Features: Stainless steel, brushed satin finish, or blued ordnance steel. Has a $9^{1}/_{2}$″ sight radius. Introduced 1979.
Price: Blued, 44 Mag., $5^{1}/_{2}$″, $7^{1}/_{2}$″ **$490.00**
Price: Blued, 44 Mag., $7^{1}/_{2}$″, with scope mount, rings **$527.00**
Price: Stainless, 44 Mag., $5^{1}/_{2}$″, $7^{1}/_{2}$″ **$547.00**
Price: Stainless, 44 Mag., $7^{1}/_{2}$″, with scope mount, rings **$589.00**

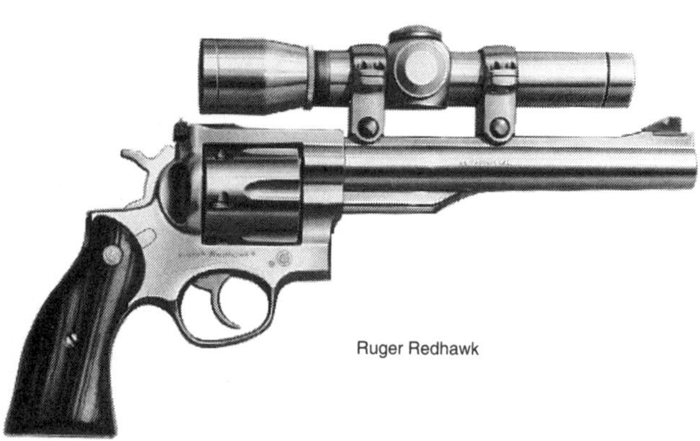
Ruger Redhawk

Ruger Super Redhawk Revolver
Similar to the standard Redhawk except has a heavy extended frame with the Ruger Integral Scope Mounting System on the wide topstrap. The wide hammer spur has been lowered for better scope clearance. Incorporates the mechanical design features and improvements of the GP-100. Choice of $7^{1}/_{2}$″ or $9^{1}/_{2}$″ barrel, both with ramp front sight base with Redhawk-style Interchangeable Insert sight blades, adjustable rear sight. Comes with Ruger "Cushioned Grip" panels of Santoprene with Goncalo Alves wood panels. Satin or high-polished stainless steel. Introduced 1987.
Price: KSRH-7 ($7^{1}/_{2}$″), KSRH-9 ($9^{1}/_{2}$″) **$589.00**

SMITH & WESSON MODEL 10 M&P REVOLVER
Caliber: 38 Spec., 6-shot.
Barrel: 2″, 4″.
Weight: 30 oz. **Length:** $9^{5}/_{16}$″ overall.
Stocks: Uncle Mike's Combat soft rubber; square butt. Wood optional.
Sights: Fixed, ramp front, square notch rear.
Price: Blue **$383.00**

Smith & Wesson Model 65LS

Smith & Wesson Model 10 38 M&P Heavy Barrel
Same as regular M&P except has heavy 4″ ribbed barrel with square butt grips. Weighs $33^{1}/_{2}$ oz.
Price: Blue **$390.00**

SMITH & WESSON MODEL 13 H.B. M&P
Caliber: 357 Mag. and 38 Spec., 6-shot.
Barrel: 3″ or 4″.
Weight: 34 oz. **Length:** $9^{5}/_{16}$″ overall (4″ bbl.).
Stocks: Uncle Mike's Combat soft rubber; wood optional.
Sights: $^{1}/_{8}$″ serrated ramp front, fixed square notch rear.
Features: Heavy barrel, K-frame, square butt (4″), round butt (3″).
Price: Blue **$394.00**
Price: Model 65, as above in stainless steel **$427.00**

Smith & Wesson Model 65 Revolver
Smiliar to the Model 13 except made of stainless steel. Has Uncle Mike's Combat grips, smooth combat trigger, fixed notch rear sight. Made in U.S. by Smith & Wesson.
Price: 3″ or 4″ **$427.00**

Consult our Directory pages for the location of firms mentioned.

SMITH & WESSON MODEL 14 FULL LUG REVOLVER
Caliber: 38 Spec., 6-shot.
Barrel: 6″, full lug.
Weight: 47 oz. **Length:** $11^{1}/_{8}$″ overall.
Stocks: Hogue soft rubber; wood optional.
Sights: Pinned Patridge front, adjustable micrometer click rear.
Features: Has .500″ target hammer, .312″ smooth combat trigger. Polished blue finish. Reintroduced 1991. Limited production.
Price: **$465.00**

Smith & Wesson Model 14

SMITH & WESSON MODEL 15 COMBAT MASTERPIECE
Caliber: 38 Spec., 6-shot.
Barrel: 4″.
Weight: 32 oz. **Length:** $9^{5}/_{16}$″ (4″ bbl.).
Stocks: Uncle Mike's Combat soft rubber; wood optional.
Sights: Front, Baughman Quick Draw on ramp, micro-click rear adjustable for windage and elevation.
Price: Blued **$419.00**

CAUTION: PRICES SHOWN ARE SUPPLIED BY THE MANUFACTURER OR IMPORTER. CHECK YOUR LOCAL GUNSHOP.

Smith & Wesson Model 17

SMITH & WESSON MODEL 17 K-22 MASTERPIECE
Caliber: 22 LR, 10-shot cylinder.
Barrel: 6″.
Weight: 42 oz. **Length:** 11 1/8″ overall.
Stocks: Hogue rubber.
Sights: Pinned Patridge front, fully adjustable rear.
Features: Polished blue finish; smooth combat trigger; semi-target hammer. The 10-slot version of this model introduced 1996.
Price: $490.00

Smith & Wesson Model 19

SMITH & WESSON MODEL 19 COMBAT MAGNUM
Caliber: 357 Mag. and 38 Spec., 6-shot.
Barrel: 2 1/2″, 4″, 6″.
Weight: 36 oz. **Length:** 9 9/16″ (4″ bbl.).
Stocks: Uncle Mike's Combat soft rubber; wood optional.
Sights: Serrated ramp front 2 1/2″ or 4″ bbl., red ramp on 4″, 6″ bbl., micro-click rear adjustable for windage and elevation.
Price: S&W Bright Blue, adj. sights . . . . $416.00 to $430.00

SMITH & WESSON MODEL 29, 629 REVOLVERS
Caliber: 44 Magnum, 6-shot.
Barrel: 6″, 8 3/8″ (Model 29); 4″, 6″, 8 3/8″ (Model 629).
Weight: 47 oz. (6″ bbl.). **Length:** 11 3/8″ overall (6″ bbl.).
Stocks: Soft rubber; wood optional.
Sights: 1/8″ red ramp front, micro-click rear, adjustable for windage and elevation.
Price: S&W Bright Blue, 6″ $554.00
Price: S&W Bright Blue, 8 3/8″ $566.00
Price: Model 629 (stainless steel), 4″ $587.00
Price: Model 629, 6″ $592.00
Price: Model 629, 8 3/8″ barrel $606.00

Smith & Wesson Model 629 PowerPort

Smith & Wesson Model 629 Classic Revolver
Similar to the standard Model 629 except has full-lug 5″, 6 1/2″ or 8 3/8″ barrel; chamfered front of cylinder; interchangable red ramp front sight with adjustable white outline rear; Hogue grips with S&W monogram; the frame is drilled and tapped for scope mounting. Factory accurizing and endurance packages. Overall length with 5″ barrel is 10 1/2″; weighs 51 oz. Introduced 1990.
Price: Model 629 Classic (stainless), 5″, 6 1/2″ $629.00
Price: As above, 8 3/8″ $650.00

Smith & Wesson Model 629 Classic DX Revolver
Similar to the Model 629 Classic except offered only with 6 1/2″ or 8 3/8″ full-lug barrel; comes with five front sights: 50-yard red ramp; 50-yard black Patridge; 100-yard black Patridge with gold bead; 50-yard black ramp; and 50-yard black Patridge with white dot. Comes with Hogue combat-style round butt grip. Introduced 1991.
Price: Model 629 Classic DX, 6 1/2″ $811.00
Price: As above, 8 3/8″ $838.00

Smith & Wesson Model 37

Smith & Wesson Model 629 Classic PowerPort Revolver
Similar to the Model 629 Classic with 6 1/2″ full-lug barrel except has PowerPort compensator. Introduced 1996. Made in U.S. by Smith & Wesson.
Price: 6 1/2″ barrel only $629.00

SMITH & WESSON MODEL 36, 37 CHIEFS SPECIAL & AIRWEIGHT
Caliber: 38 Spec., 5-shot.
Barrel: 2″.
Weight: 19 1/2 oz. (2″ bbl.); 13 1/2 oz. (Airweight). **Length:** 6 1/2″ (2″ bbl. and round butt).
Stocks: Round butt soft rubber; wood optional.
Sights: Fixed, serrated ramp front, square notch rear.
Price: Blue, standard Model 36 . . . . $377.00
Price: Blue, Airweight Model 37, 2″ only $412.00

Smith & Wesson Model 60LS

Smith & Wesson Model 637 Airweight Revolver
Similar to the Model 37 Airweight except has stainless steel barrel, cylinder and yoke; Uncle Mike's Boot Grip. Introduced 1996. Made in U.S. by Smith & Wesson.
Price: $428.00

Smith & Wesson Model 60 Chiefs Special Stainless
Same as Model 36 except 357 Magnum or 38 Special (only). All stainless construction, 2″ bbl. and round butt only.
Price: Stainless steel $431.00

Smith & Wesson Model 36LS, 60LS LadySmith
Similar to the standard Model 36. Available with 2″ barrel. Comes with smooth, contoured rosewood grips with the S&W monogram. Has a speedloader cutout. Comes in a fitted carry/storage case. Introduced 1989.
Price: Model 36LS $408.00
Price: Model 60LS (as above except in stainless) $461.00

Smith & Wesson Model 649

Smith & Wesson Model 63

SMITH & WESSON MODEL 65LS LADYSMITH
Caliber: 357 Magnum, 6-shot.
Barrel: 3″.
Weight: 31 oz. **Length:** 7.94″ overall.
Stocks: Rosewood, round butt.
Sights: Serrated ramp front, fixed notch rear.
Features: Stainless steel with frosted finish. Smooth combat trigger, service hammer, shrouded ejector rod. Comes with soft case. Introduced 1992.
Price: $461.00

SMITH & WESSON MODEL 66 STAINLESS COMBAT MAGNUM
Caliber: 357 Mag. and 38 Spec., 6-shot.
Barrel: 2½″, 4″, 6″.
Weight: 36 oz. (4″ barrel). **Length:** 9⁹⁄₁₆″ overall.
Stocks: Soft rubber; wood optional.
Sights: Red ramp front, micro-click rear adjustable for windage and elevation.
Features: Satin finish stainless steel.
Price: 2½″ $466.00
Price: 4″, 6″ $471.00

SMITH & WESSON MODEL 67 COMBAT MASTERPIECE
Caliber: 38 Special, 6-shot.
Barrel: 4″.
Weight: 32 oz. **Length:** 9⁵⁄₁₆″ overall.
Stocks: Soft rubber; wood optional.
Sights: Red ramp front, micro-click rear adjustable for windage and elevation.
Features: Stainless steel with satin finish. Smooth combat trigger, semi-target hammer. Introduced 1994.
Price: $467.00

SMITH & WESSON MODEL 586, 686 DISTINGUISHED COMBAT MAGNUMS
Caliber: 357 Magnum.
Barrel: 4″, 6″, full shroud.
Weight: 46 oz. (6″), 41 oz. (4″).
Stocks: Soft rubber; wood optional.
Sights: Baughman red ramp front, four-position click-adjustable front, S&W micrometer click rear. Drilled and tapped for scope mount.
Features: Uses L-frame, but takes all K-frame grips. Full-length ejector rod shroud. Smooth combat-type trigger, semi-target type hammer. Trigger stop on 6″ models. Also available in stainless as Model 686. Introduced 1981.
Price: Model 586, blue, 4″, from $461.00
Price: Model 586, blue, 6″ $466.00
Price: Model 686, 6″, ported barrel $528.00
Price: Model 686, 8⅜″ $515.00
Price: Model 686, 2½″ $481.00

Smith & Wesson Model 686 Magnum Plus Revolver
Similar to the Model 686 except has 7-shot cylinder, 2½″, 4″ or 6″ barrel. Weighs 34½ oz., overall length 7½″ (2½″ barrel). Hogue rubber grips. Introduced 1996. Made in U.S. by Smith & Wesson.
Price: 2½″ barrel $498.00
Price: 4″ barrel $506.00
Price: 6″ barrel $514.00

Smith & Wesson Model 60 3″ Full-Lug Revolver
Similar to the Model 60 Chief's Special except has 3″ full-lug barrel, adjustable micrometer click black blade rear sight; rubber Uncle Mike's Custom Grade Boot Grip. Overall length 7½″; weighs 24½ oz. Introduced 1991.
Price: $458.00

SMITH & WESSON MODEL 38 BODYGUARD
Caliber: 38 Spec., 5-shot.
Barrel: 2″.
Weight: 14½ oz. **Length:** 6⁵⁄₁₆″ overall.
Stocks: Soft rubber; wood optional.
Sights: Fixed serrated ramp front, square notch rear.
Features: Alloy frame; internal hammer.
Price: Blue $444.00
Price: Nickel $460.00

Smith & Wesson Model 49, 649 Bodyguard Revolvers
Same as Model 38 except steel construction, weighs 20½ oz.
Price: Blued, Model 49 .... $409.00
Price: Stainless, Model 649 .... $469.00

SMITH & WESSON MODEL 63 KIT GUN
Caliber: 22 LR, 6-shot.
Barrel: 2″, 4″.
Weight: 24 oz. (4″ bbl.). **Length:** 8⅜″ (4″ bbl. and round butt).
Stocks: Round butt soft rubber; wood optional.
Sights: Red ramp front, micro-click rear adjustable for windage and elevation.
Features: Stainless steel construction.
Price: 2″ $458.00
Price: 4″ $462.00

SMITH & WESSON MODEL 64 STAINLESS M&P
Caliber: 38 Spec., 6-shot.
Barrel: 2″, 3″, 4″.
Weight: 34 oz. **Length:** 9⁵⁄₁₆″ overall.
Stocks: Soft rubber; wood optional.
Sights: Fixed, ⅛″ serrated ramp front, square notch rear.
Features: Satin finished stainless steel, square butt.
Price: 2″ $415.00
Price: 3″, 4″ $423.00

SMITH & WESSON MODEL 617 FULL LUG REVOLVER
Caliber: 22 LR, 6-shot.
Barrel: 4″, 6″, 8⅜″.
Weight: 42 oz. (4″ barrel). **Length:** NA.
Stocks: Soft rubber; wood optional.
Sights: Patridge front, adjustable rear. Drilled and tapped for scope mount.
Features: Stainless steel with satin finish; 4″ has .312″ smooth trigger, .375″ semi-target hammer; 6″ has either .312″ combat or .400″ serrated trigger, .375″ semi-target or .500″ target hammer; 8⅜″ with .400″ serrated trigger, .500″ target hammer. Introduced 1990.
Price: 4″ $460.00
Price: 6″, target hammer, combat trigger $490.00
Price: 8⅜″ $501.00

Smith & Wesson Model 625

SMITH & WESSON MODEL 625 REVOLVER
Caliber: 45 ACP, 6-shot.
Barrel: 5″.
Weight: 46 oz. **Length:** 11.375″ overall.
Stocks: Soft rubber; wood optional.
Sights: Patridge front on ramp, S&W micrometer click rear adjustable for windage and elevation.
Features: Stainless steel construction with .400″ semi-target hammer, .312″ smooth combat trigger; full lug barrel. Introduced 1989.
Price: $597.00

CAUTION: PRICES SHOWN ARE SUPPLIED BY THE MANUFACTURER OR IMPORTER. CHECK YOUR LOCAL GUNSHOP.

Smith & Wesson Model 442

Smith & Wesson Model 642

SMITH & WESSON MODEL 640 CENTENNIAL
Caliber: 357 Mag., 38 Spec., 5-shot.
Barrel: 2 1/8".
Weight: 25 oz. **Length:** 6 3/4" overall.
Stocks: Uncle Mike's Boot Grip.
Sights: Serrated ramp front, fixed notch rear.
Features: Stainless steel version of the original Model 40 but without the grip safety. Fully concealed hammer, snag-proof smooth edges. Introduced 1995 in 357 Magnum.
Price: $469.00
Price: Model 940 (9mm Para.) $474.00

Smith & Wesson Model 442 Centennial Airweight
Similar to the Model 640 Centennial except has alloy frame giving weight of 15.8 oz. Chambered for 38 Special, 2" carbon steel barrel; carbon steel cylinder; concealed hammer; Uncle Mike's Custom Grade Santoprene grips. Fixed square notch rear sight, serrated ramp front. Introduced 1993.
Price: Blue $427.00

Smith & Wesson Model 642 Airweight Revolver
Similar to the Model 442 Centennial Airweight except has stainless steel barrel, cylinder and yoke with matte finish; Uncle Mike's Boot Grip; weights 15.8 oz. Introduced 1996. Made in U.S. by Smith & Wesson.
Price: $442.00

Smith & Wesson Model 642LS LadySmith Revolver
Same as the Model 642 except has smooth combat wood grips, and comes with case; frosted matte finish. Introduced 1996. Made in U.S. by Smith & Wesson.
Price: $471.00

SMITH & WESSON MODEL 651 REVOLVER
Caliber: 22 WMR, 6-shot cylinder.
Barrel: 4".
Weight: 24 1/2 oz. **Length:** 8 11/16" overall.
Stocks: Soft rubber; wood optional.
Sights: Red ramp front, adjustable micrometer click rear.
Features: Stainless steel construction with semi-target hammer, smooth combat trigger. Reintroduced 1991. Limited production.
Price: $460.00

SMITH & WESSON MODEL 657 REVOLVER
Caliber: 41 Mag., 6-shot.
Barrel: 6".
Weight: 48 oz. **Length:** 11 3/8" overall.
Stocks: Soft rubber; wood optional.
Sights: Pinned 1/8" red ramp front, micro-click rear adjustable for windage and elevation.
Features: Stainless steel construction.
Price: $528.00

TAURUS MODEL 66 REVOLVER
Caliber: 357 Mag., 6-shot.
Barrel: 2.5", 4", 6".
Weight: 35 oz.(4" barrel).
Stocks: Soft black rubber.
Sights: Serrated ramp front, micro-click rear adjustable for windage and elevation. Red ramp front with white outline rear on stainlees models only.
Features: Wide target-type hammer spur, floating firing pin, heavy barrel with shrouded ejector rod. Introduced 1978. Imported by Taurus International.
Price: Blue, 2.5", 4", 6" $318.00
Price: Stainless, 2.5", 4", 6" $392.00

Taurus Model 65 Revolver
Same as the Model 66 except has fixed rear sight and ramp front. Available with 2.5" or 4" barrel only, round butt grip. Imported by Taurus International.
Price: Blue, 2.5", 4" $290.00
Price: Stainless, 2.5", 4" $357.00

TAURUS MODEL 80 STANDARD REVOLVER
Caliber: 38 Spec., 6-shot.
Barrel: 3" or 4".
Weight: 30 oz. (4" bbl.). **Length:** 9 1/4" overall (4" bbl.).
Stocks: Soft black rubber.
Sights: Serrated ramp front, square notch rear.
Features: Imported by Taurus International.
Price: Blue $252.00
Price: Stainless $299.00

Smith & Wesson Model 651

TAURUS MODEL 44 REVOLVER
Caliber: 44 Mag., 6-shot.
Barrel: 4", 6 1/2", 8 3/8".
Weight: 44 3/4 oz. (4" barrel). **Length:** NA.
Stocks: Soft black rubber.
Sights: Serrated ramp front, micro-click rear adjustable for windage and elevation.
Features: Heavy solid rib on 4", vent rib on 6 1/2", 8 3/8". Compensated barrel. Blued model has color case-hardened hammer and trigger. Introduced 1994. Imported by Taurus International.
Price: Blue, 4" $425.00
Price: Blue, 6 1/2", 8 3/8" $443.00
Price: Stainless, 4" $484.00
Price: Stainless, 6 1/2", 8 3/8" $504.00

Taurus Model 66

TAURUS MODEL 82 HEAVY BARREL REVOLVER
Caliber: 38 Spec., 6-shot.
Barrel: 3″ or 4″, heavy.
Weight: 34 oz. (4″ bbl.). **Length:** 9 1/4″ overall (4″ bbl.).
Stocks: Soft black rubber.
Sights: Serrated ramp front, square notch rear.
Features: Imported by Taurus International.
Price: Blue **$252.00**
Price: Stainless **$295.00**

Taurus Model 82

TAURUS MODEL 83 REVOLVER
Caliber: 38 Spec., 6-shot.
Barrel: 4″ only, heavy.
Weight: 34 oz.
Stocks: Soft black rubber.
Sights: Ramp front, micro-click rear adjustable for windage and elevation.
Features: Blue or nickel finish. Introduced 1977. Imported by Taurus International.
Price: Blue **$265.00**
Price: Stainless **$309.00**

Taurus Model 85CH Revolver
Same as the Model 85 except has 2″ barrel only and concealed hammer. Soft rubber boot grip. Introduced 1991. Imported by Taurus International.
Price: Blue **$239.00**
Price: Stainless **$287.00**

TAURUS MODEL 94 REVOLVER
Caliber: 22 LR, 9-shot cylinder.
Barrel: 3″, 4″, 5″.
Weight: 25 oz.
Stocks: Soft black rubber.
Sights: Serrated ramp front, click-adjustable rear for windage and elevation.
Features: Floating firing pin, color case-hardened hammer and trigger. Introduced 1989. Imported by Taurus International.
Price: Blue **$293.00**
Price: Stainless **$339.00**

Consult our Directory pages for the location of firms mentioned.

TAURUS MODEL 85 REVOLVER
Caliber: 38 Spec., 5-shot.
Barrel: 2″, 3″.
Weight: 21 oz.
Stocks: Black rubber, boot grip.
Sights: Ramp front, square notch rear.
Features: Blue finish or stainless steel. Introduced 1980. Imported by Taurus International.
Price: Blue, 2″, 3″ **$239.00**
Price: Stainless steel **$287.00**

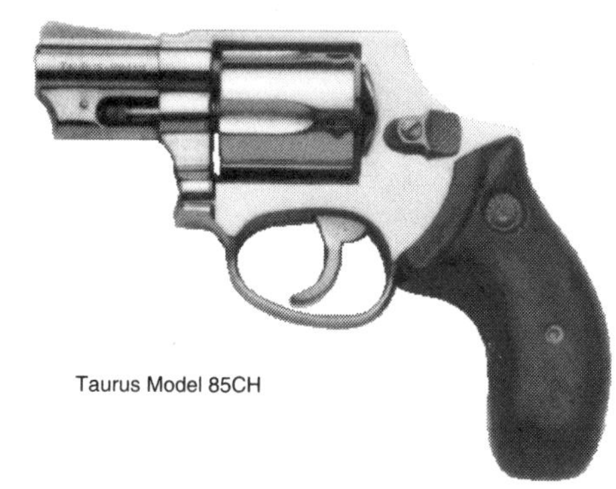
Taurus Model 85CH

TAURUS MODEL 96 REVOLVER
Caliber: 22 LR, 6-shot.
Barrel: 6″.
Weight: 34 oz. **Length:** NA.
Stocks: Soft black rubber.
Sights: Patridge-type front, micrometer click rear adjustable for windage and elevation.
Features: Heavy solid barrel rib; target hammer; adjustable target trigger. Blue only. Imported by Taurus International.
Price: **$358.00**

TAURUS MODEL 441/431 REVOLVERS
Caliber: 44 Spec., 5-shot.
Barrel: 3″, 4″, 6″.
Weight: 40.4 oz. (6″ barrel). **Length:** NA.
Stocks: Soft black rubber.
Sights: Serrated ramp front, micrometer click rear adjustable for windage and elevation.
Features: Heavy barrel with solid rib and full-length ejector shroud. Introduced 1992. Imported by Taurus International.
Price: Model 441, Blue, 3″, 4″, 6″ **$298.00**
Price: Model 441, Stainless, 3″, 4″, 6″ **$374.00**
Price: Model 431 (fixed sights), blue, 2″, 3″, 4″ **$256.00**
Price: Model 431 (fixed sights), stainless, 2″, 3″, 4″ **$350.00**

TAURUS MODEL 605 REVOLVER
Caliber: 357 Mag., 5-shot.
Barrel: 2 1/4″, 3″.
Weight: 24.5 oz. **Length:** NA.
Stocks: Finger-groove Santoprene I.
Sights: Serrated ramp front, fixed notch rear.
Features: Heavy, solid rib barrel; floating firing pin. Blue or stainless. Introduced 1995. Imported by Taurus International.
Price: Blue **$262.00**
Price: Stainless **$312.00**
Price: Model 605CH (concealed hammer) 2 1/4″, blue **$262.00**
Price: Model 605CH, stainless, 2 1/4″ **$312.00**

Taurus Model 607

TAURUS MODEL 607 REVOLVER
Caliber: 357 Mag., 7-shot.
Barrel: 4″, 6 1/2″.
Weight: 44 oz. **Length:** NA.
Stocks: Santoprene I with finger grooves.
Sights: Serrated ramp front, fully adjustable rear.
Features: Ventilated rib with built-in compensator on 6 1/2″ barrel. Available in blue or stainless. Introduced 1995. Imported by Taurus international.
Price: Blue, 4″ **$425.00**
Price: Blue, 6 1/2″ **$443.00**
Price: Stainless, 4″ **$484.00**
Price: Stainless, 6 1/2″ **$504.00**

Taurus Model 608 Revolver
Same as the Model 607 except has 8-shot cylinder. Introduced 1996. Imported by Taurus International.
Price: Blue, 4″ **$425.00**
Price: Blue, 6 1/2″ **$443.00**
Price: Stainless, 4″ **$484.00**
Price: Stainless, 6 1/2″ **$504.00**

CAUTION: PRICES SHOWN ARE SUPPLIED BY THE MANUFACTURER OR IMPORTER. CHECK YOUR LOCAL GUNSHOP.

TAURUS MODEL 669 REVOLVER
Caliber: 357 Mag., 6-shot.
Barrel: 4″, 6″.
Weight: 37 oz., (4″ bbl.).
Stocks: Black rubber.
Sights: Serrated ramp front, micro-click rear adjustable for windage and elevation.
Features: Wide target-type hammer, floating firing pin, full-length barrel shroud. Introduced 1988. Imported by Taurus International.
Price: Blue, 4″, 6″ **$327.00**
Price: Blue, 4″, 6″ compensated **$346.00**
Price: Stainless, 4″, 6″ **$401.00**
Price: Stainless, 4″, 6″ compensated **$421.00**

Taurus Model 669

TAURUS MODEL 941 REVOLVER
Caliber: 22 WMR, 8-shot.
Barrel: 3″, 4″.
Weight: 27.5 oz. (4″ barrel). **Length:** NA.
Stocks: Soft black rubber.
Sights: Serrated ramp front, rear adjustable for windage and elevation.
Features: Solid rib heavy barrel with full-length ejector rod shroud. Blue or stainless steel. Introduced 1992. Imported by Taurus International.
Price: Blue **$315.00**
Price: Stainless **$366.00**

Taurus Model 689 Revolver
Same as the Model 669 except has full-length ventilated barrel rib. Available in blue or stainless steel. Introduced 1990. From Taurus International.
Price: Blue, 4″ or 6″ **$341.00**
Price: Stainless, 4″ or 6″ **$415.00**

HANDGUNS—SINGLE-ACTION REVOLVERS

Both classic six-shooters and modern adaptations for hunting and sport.

AMERICAN ARMS REGULATOR SINGLE-ACTIONS
Caliber: 357 Mag. 44-40, 45 Colt.
Barrel: 4$^{3}/_{4}$″, 5$^{1}/_{2}$″, 7$^{1}/_{2}$″.
Weight: 32 oz. (4$^{3}/_{4}$″ barrel). **Length:** 8$^{1}/_{6}$″ overall (4$^{3}/_{4}$″ barrel).
Stocks: Smooth walnut.
Sights: Blade front, groove rear.
Features: Blued barrel and cylinder, brass trigger guard and backstrap. Introduced 1992. Imported from Italy by American Arms, Inc.
Price: Regulator, single cylinder **$349.00**
Price: Regulator, dual cylinder (44-40/44 Spec. or 45 Colt/45 ACP) **$399.00**
Price: Regulator DLX (all steel) **$395.00**

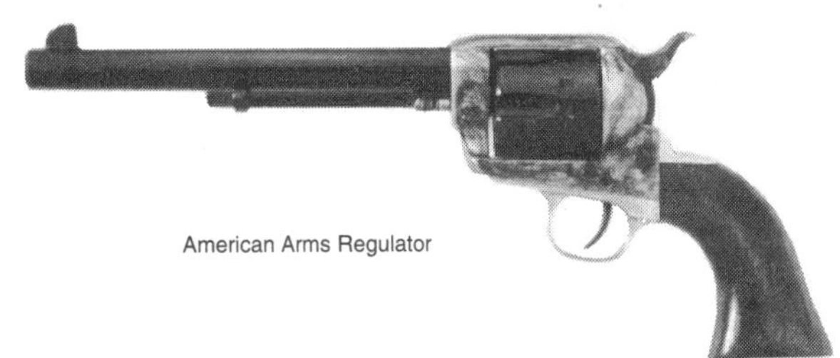
American Arms Regulator

American Frontier 1871-1872 Open-Top

AMERICAN FRONTIER POCKET RICHARDS & MASON NAVY
Caliber: 32, 5-shot cylinder.
Barrel: 4$^{3}/_{4}$″, 5$^{1}/_{2}$″.
Weight: NA. **Length:** NA.
Stocks: Varnished walnut.
Sights: Blade front, fixed rear.
Features: Shoots metallic-cartridge ammunition. Non-rebated cylinder; high-polish blue, silver-plated brass backstrap and trigger guard; ejector assembly; color case-hardened hammer and trigger. Introduced 1996. Imported from Italy by American Frontier Firearms Co.
Price: From **$495.00**

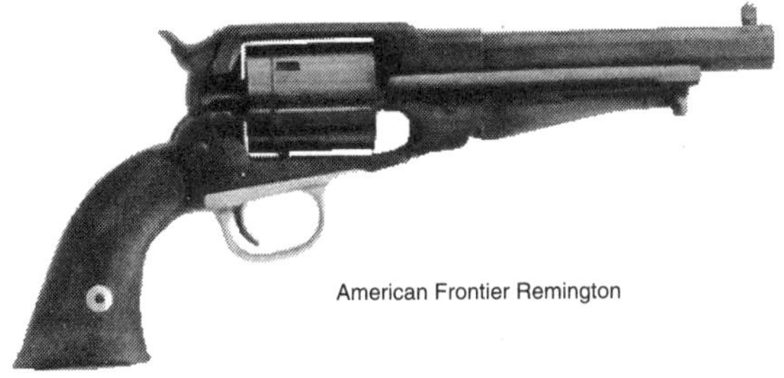
American Frontier Remington

AMERICAN FRONTIER 1871-1872 OPEN-TOP REVOLVERS
Caliber: 38, 44.
Barrel: 4$^{3}/_{4}$″, 5$^{1}/_{2}$″, 7$^{1}/_{2}$″, 8″ round.
Weight: NA. **Length:** NA.
Stocks: Varnished walnut.
Sights: Blade front, fixed rear.
Features: Reproduction of the early cartridge conversions from percussion. Made for metallic cartridges. High polish blued steel, silver-plated brass backstrap and trigger guard, color case-hardened hammer; straight non-rebated cylinder with naval engagement engraving; stamped with original patent dates. Does not have conversion breechplate. Introduced 1996. Imported from Italy by American Frontier Firearms Co.
Price: **$795.00**
Price: Tiffany model with Tiffany grips, silver and gold finish with engraving **$995.00**

AMERICAN FRONTIER 1871-1872 POCKET MODEL REVOLVER
Caliber: 32, 5-shot cylinder.
Barrel: 4$^{3}/_{4}$″, 5$^{1}/_{2}$″ round.
Weight: NA. **Length:** NA.
Stocks: Varnished walnut or Tiffany.
Sights: Blade front, fixed rear.
Features: Based on the 1862 Police percussion revolver converted to metallic cartridge. High polish blue finish with silver-plated brass backstrap and trigger guard, color case-hardened hammer. Introduced 1996. Imported from Italy by American Frontier Firearms Co.
Price: From **$495.00**

AMERICAN FRONTIER REMINGTON NEW MODEL REVOLVER
Caliber: 38, 44.
Barrel: 5$^{1}/_{2}$″, 7$^{1}/_{2}$″
Weight: NA. **Length:** NA.
Stocks: Varnished walnut.
Sights: Blade front, fixed rear.
Features: Replica of the factory conversions by Remington between 1863 and 1875. High polish blue or silver finish with color case-hardened hammer; with or without ejector rod and loading gate. Introduced 1996. Imported from Italy by American Frontier Firearms Co.
Price: **$695.00**

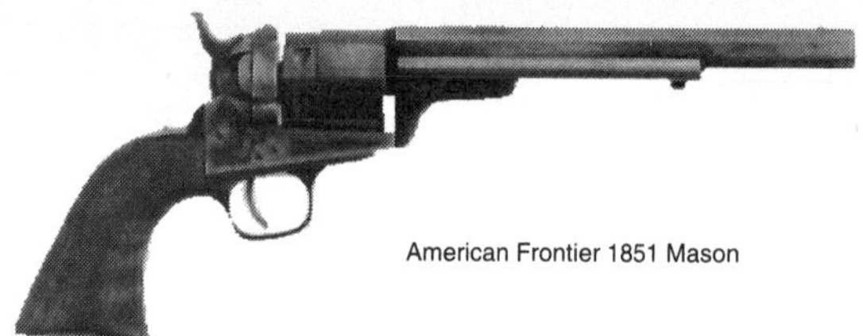

American Frontier 1851 Mason

American Frontier 1851 Navy Richards & Mason Conversion

Similar to the 1851 Navy Conversion except has Mason ejector assembly. Introduced 1996. Imported from Italy by American Frontier Firearms Co.

Price: **$695.00**

CENTURY GUN DIST. MODEL 100 SINGLE-ACTION

Caliber: 30-30, 375 Win., 444 Marlin, 45-70, 50-70.
Barrel: $6^{1}/_{2}$" (standard), 8", 10", 12".
Weight: 6 lbs. (loaded). **Length:** 15" overall (8" bbl.).
Stocks: Smooth walnut.
Sights: Ramp front, Millett adjustable square notch rear.
Features: Highly polished high tensile strength manganese bronze frame, blue cylinder and barrel; coil spring trigger mechanism. Calibers other than 45-70 start at $2,000.00. Contact maker for full price information. Introduced 1975. Made in U.S. From Century Gun Dist., Inc.
Price: $6^{1}/_{2}$" barrel, 45-70 .... **$1,250.00**

CIMARRON 1873 FRONTIER SIX SHOOTER

Caliber: 38 WCF, 357 Mag., 44 WCF, 44 Spec., 45 Colt.
Barrel: $4^{3}/_{4}$", $5^{1}/_{2}$", $7^{1}/_{2}$".
Weight: 39 oz. **Length:** 10" overall (4" barrel).
Stocks: Walnut.
Sights: Blade front, fixed or adjustable rear.
Features: Uses "old model" blackpowder frame with "Bullseye" ejector or New Model frame. Imported by Cimarron Arms.
Price: $4^{3}/_{4}$" barrel **$439.95**
Price: $5^{1}/_{2}$" barrel **$439.95**
Price: $7^{1}/_{2}$" barrel **$439.95**

CIMARRON U.S. CAVALRY MODEL SINGLE-ACTION

Caliber: 45 Colt
Barrel: $7^{1}/_{2}$".
Weight: 42 oz. **Length:** $13^{1}/_{2}$" overall.
Stocks: Walnut.
Sights: Fixed.
Features: Has "A.P. Casey" markings; "U.S." plus patent dates on frame, serial number on backstrap, trigger guard, frame and cylinder, "APC" cartouche on left grip; color case-hardened frame and hammer, rest charcoal blue. Exact copy of the original. Imported by Cimarron Arms.
Price: **$469.00**

Cimarron Rough Rider Artillery Model Single-Action

Similar to the U.S. Cavalry model except has $5^{1}/_{2}$" barrel, weighs 39 oz., and is $11^{1}/_{2}$" overall. U.S. markings and cartouche, case-hardened frame and hammer; 45 Colt only.

Price: **$469.00**

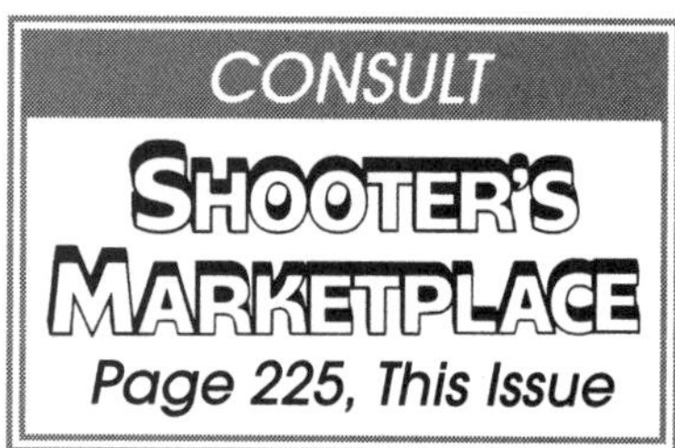
CONSULT
SHOOTER'S
MARKETPLACE
Page 225, This Issue

COLT SINGLE ACTION-ARMY REVOLVER

Caliber: 44-40, 45 Colt, 6-shot.
Barrel: $4^{3}/_{4}$", $5^{1}/_{2}$", $7^{1}/_{2}$".
Weight: 40 oz. ($4^{3}/_{4}$" barrel). **Length:** $10^{1}/_{4}$" overall ($4^{3}/_{4}$" barrel).
Stocks: Black Eagle composite.
Sights: Blade front, notch rear.
Features: Available in full nickel finish with nickel grip medallions, or Royal Blue with color case-hardened frame, gold grip medallions. Reintroduced 1992.
Price: **$1,213.00**

AMERICAN FRONTIER RICHARDS 1860 ARMY

Caliber: 38, 44.
Barrel: $4^{3}/_{4}$", $5^{1}/_{2}$", $7^{1}/_{2}$", round.
Weight: NA. **Length:** NA.
Stocks: Varnished walnut, Army size.
Sights: Blade front, fixed rear.
Features: Shoots metallic cartridge ammunition. Rebated cylinder; available with or without ejector assembly; high-polish blue including backstrap; silver-plated trigger guard; color case-hardened hammer and trigger. Introduced 1996. Imported from Italy by American Frontier Firearms Co.
Price: **$695.00**

AMERICAN FRONTIER 1851 NAVY CONVERSION

Caliber: 38, 44.
Barrel: $4^{3}/_{4}$", $5^{1}/_{2}$", $7^{1}/_{2}$", octagon.
Weight: NA. **Length:** NA.
Stocks: Varnished walnut, Navy size.
Sights: Blade front, fixed rear.
Features: Shoots metallic cartridge ammunition. Non-rebated cylinder; blued steel backstrap and trigger guard; color case-hardened hammer, trigger, ramrod, plunger; no ejector rod assembly. Introduced 1996. Imported from Italy by American Frontier Firearms Co.
Price: **$695.00**

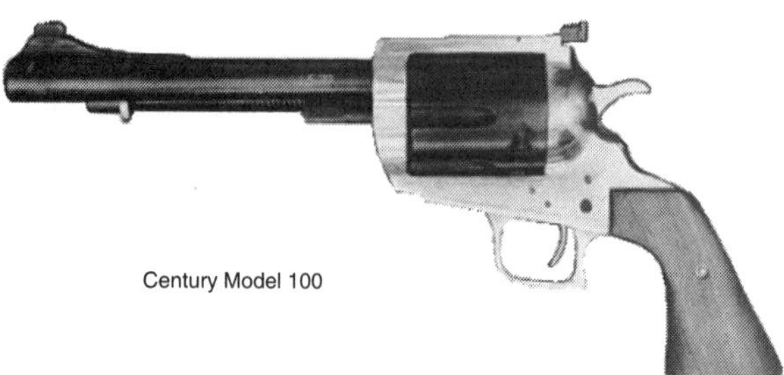

Century Model 100

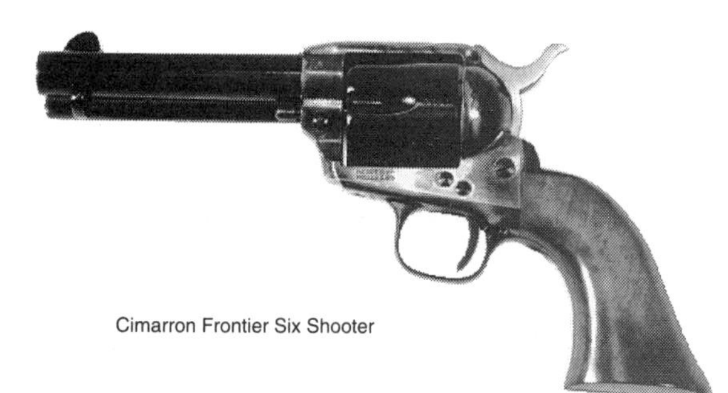

Cimarron Frontier Six Shooter

CIMARRON NEW THUNDERER REVOLVER

Caliber: 357 Mag., 44 WCF, 44 Spec., 45 Colt, 6-shot.
Barrel: $3^{1}/_{2}$", $4^{3}/_{4}$", with ejector.
Weight: 38 oz. ($3^{1}/_{2}$" barrel). **Length:** NA.
Stocks: Hand-checkered walnut.
Sights: Blade front, notch rear.
Features: Thunderer grip; color case-hardened frame with balance blued, or nickel finish. Introduced 1993. Imported by Cimarron Arms.
Price: Color case-hardened **$439.95**
Price: Nickeled **$559.95**

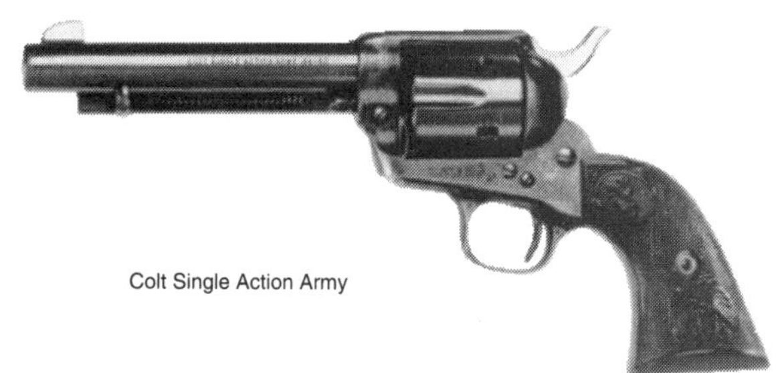

Colt Single Action Army

CAUTION: PRICES SHOWN ARE SUPPLIED BY THE MANUFACTURER OR IMPORTER. CHECK YOUR LOCAL GUNSHOP.

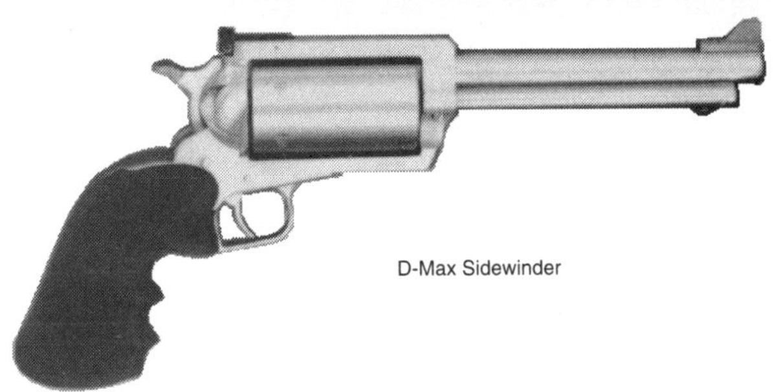
D-Max Sidewinder

D-MAX SIDEWINDER REVOLVER
Caliber: 45 Colt/410 shotshell, 6-shot.
Barrel: 6.5″, 7.5″.
Weight: 57 oz. (6.5″). **Length:** 14.1″ (6.5″ barrel).
Stocks: Hogue black rubber with finger grooves.
Sights: Blade on ramp front, fully adjustable rear.
Features: Stainless steel construction. Has removable choke for firing shotshells. Grooved, wide-spur hammer; transfer bar ignition; satin stainless finish. Introduced 1992. Made in U.S. by D-Max, Inc.
Price: **$750.00**

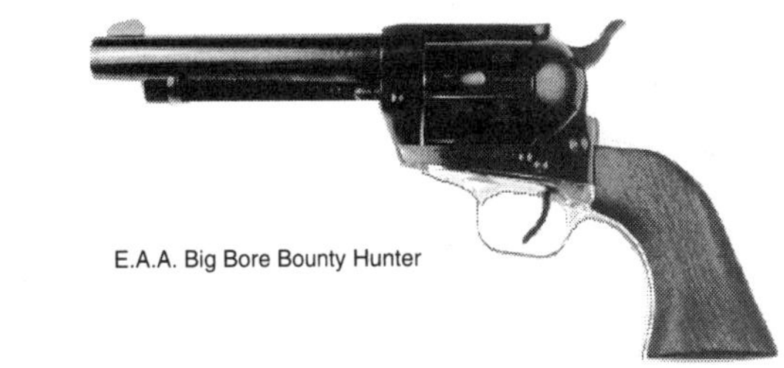
E.A.A. Big Bore Bounty Hunter

E.A.A. BIG BORE BOUNTY HUNTER SA REVOLVERS
Caliber: 357 Mag., 44 Mag., 45 Colt, 6-shot.
Barrel: 4$^1/_2$″, 7$^1/_2$″.
Weight: 2.5 lbs. **Length:** 11″ overall (4$^5/_8$″ barrel).
Stocks: Smooth walnut.
Sights: Blade front, grooved topstrap rear.
Features: Transfer bar safety; three position hammer; hammer forged barrel. Introduced 1992. Imported by European American Armory.
Price: Blue **$299.00**
Price: Color case-hardened frame **$310.00**

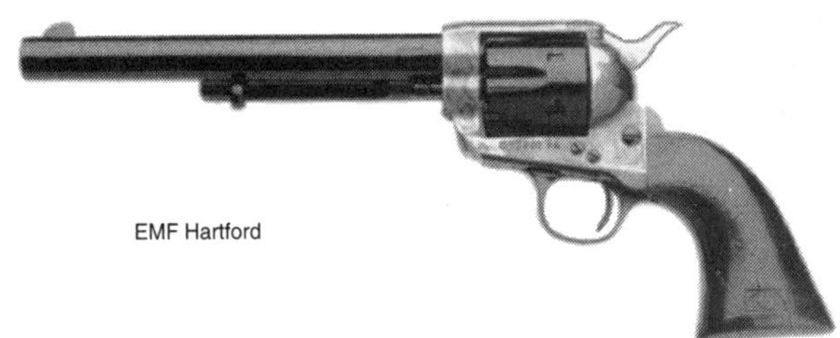
EMF Hartford

EMF HARTFORD SINGLE-ACTION REVOLVERS
Caliber: 22 LR, 357 Mag., 32-20, 38-40, 44-40, 44 Spec., 45 Colt.
Barrel: 4$^3/_4$″, 5$^1/_2$″, 7$^1/_2$″.
Weight: 45 oz. **Length:** 13″ overall (7$^1/_2$″ barrel).
Stocks: Smooth walnut.
Sights: Blade front, fixed rear.
Features: Identical to the original Colts with inspector cartouche on left grip, original patent dates and U.S. markings. All major parts serial numbered using original Colt-style lettering, numbering. Bullseye ejector head and color case-hardening on frame and hammer. Introduced 1990. From E.M.F.
Price: **$600.00**
Price: Cavalry or Artillery **$655.00**
Price: Nickel plated **$725.00**
Price: Engraved, nickel plated **$840.00**
Price: Pinkerton (bird's-head grip), 45 Colt, 4″ barrel **$680.00**

EMF DAKOTA 1875 OUTLAW REVOLVER
Caliber: 357 Mag., 44-40, 45 Colt.
Barrel: 7$^1/_2$″.
Weight: 46 oz. **Length:** 13$^1/_2$″ overall.
Stocks: Smooth walnut.
Sights: Blade front, fixed groove rear.
Features: Authentic copy of 1875 Remington with firing pin in hammer; color case-hardened frame, blue cylinder, barrel, steel backstrap and brass trigger guard. Also available in nickel, factory engraved. Imported by E.M.F.
Price: All calibers **$465.00**
Price: Nickel **$550.00**
Price: Engraved **$600.00**
Price: Engraved Nickel **$710.00**

Freedom Arms Premier

Freedom Arms Model 353 Revolver
Similar to the Premier 454 Casull except chambered for 357 Magnum with 5-shot cylinder; 4$^3/_4$″, 6″, 7$^1/_2$″ or 9″ barrel. Weighs 59 oz. with 7$^1/_2$″ barrel. Field grade model has adjustable sights, matte finish, Pachmayr grips, 7$^1/_2$″ or 10″ barrel; Silhouette has 9″ barrel, Patridge front sight, Iron Sight Gun Works Silhouette adjustable rear, Pachmayr grips, trigger over-travel adjustment screw. All stainless steel. Introduced 1992.
Price: Field Grade **$1,253.00**
Price: Premier Grade (brushed finish, impregnated hardwood grips, Premier Grade sights) **$1,627.00**
Price: Silhouette (9″, 357 Mag., 10″, 44 Mag.) **$1,347.00**

EMF 1894 Target Bisley Revolver
Similar to the Hartford single-action revolver except has special grip frame and trigger guard, wide spur hammer; available in 45 Colt only, 5$^1/_2$″ or 7$^1/_2$″ barrel. Introduced 1995. Imported by E.M.F.
Price: Blue **$680.00**
Price: Nickel **$805.00**

EMF Dakota 1890 Police Revolver
Similar to the 1875 Outlaw except has 5$^1/_2$″ barrel, weighs 40 oz., with 12$^1/_2$″ overall length. Has lanyard ring in butt. No web under barrel. Calibers 357, 44-40, 45 Colt. Imported by E.M.F.
Price: All calibers **$470.00**
Price: Nickel **$560.00**
Price: Engraved **$620.00**
Price: Engraved nickel **$725.00**

EMF Dakota New Model Single-Action Revolvers
Similar to the standard Dakota except has color case-hardened forged steel frame, black nickel backstrap and trigger guard. Calibers 357 Mag., 44-40, 45 Colt only.
Price: **$460.00**
Price: Nickel **$585.00**

FREEDOM ARMS PREMIER SINGLE-ACTION REVOLVER
Caliber: 44 Mag., 454 Casull with 45 Colt, 45 ACP, 45 Win. Mag. optional cylinders, 5-shot.
Barrel: 4$^3/_4$″, 6″, 7$^1/_2$″, 10″.
Weight: 50 oz. **Length:** 14″ overall (7$^1/_2$″ bbl.).
Stocks: Impregnated hardwood.
Sights: Blade front, notch or adjustable rear.
Features: All stainless steel construction; sliding bar safety system. Lifetime warranty. Made in U.S. by Freedom Arms, Inc.
Price: Field Grade (matte finish, Pachmayr grips), adjustable sights, 4$^3/_4$″, 6″, 7$^1/_2$″, 10″ **$1,301.00**
Price: Field Grade, fixed sights, 4$^3/_4$″, 6″, 7$^1/_2$″, 10″ **$1,207.00**
Price: Field Grade, 44 Rem. Mag., adjustable sights, all lengths **$1,253.00**
Price: Premier Grade 454 (brush finish, impregnated hardwood grips) adjustable sights, 4$^3/_4$″, 6″, 7$^1/_2$″, 10″ **$1,677.00**
Price: Premier Grade, fixed sights, all barrel lengths **$1,568.00**
Price: Premier Grade, 44 Rem. Mag., adjustable sights, all lengths . . . **$1,627.00**
Price: Fitted 45 ACP, 45 Colt or 45 Win. Mag cylinder, add **$253.00**

Freedom Arms Model 555 Revolver
Same as the 454 Casull except chambered for the 50 A.E. (Action Express) cartridge. Offered in Premier and Field Grades with adjustable sights, 4$^3/_4$″, 6″, 7$^1/_2$″ or 10″ barrel. Introduced 1994. Made in U.S. by Freedom Arms, Inc.
Price: Premier Grade **$1,677.00**
Price: Field Grade **$1,301.00**

HERITAGE ROUGH RIDER REVOLVER
Caliber: 22 LR, 22 LR/22 WMR combo, 6-shot.
Barrel: 2¾", 3½", 4¾", 6½", 9".
Weight: 31 to 38 oz. **Length:** NA
Stocks: Exotic hardwood.
Sights: Blade front, fixed rear.
Features: Hammer block safety. High polish blue or nickel finish. Introduced 1993. Made in U.S. by Heritage Mfg., Inc.
Price: .....$109.95 to $169.95
Price: 2¾", 3½", 4¾" birdshead grip .....$129.95 to $149.95

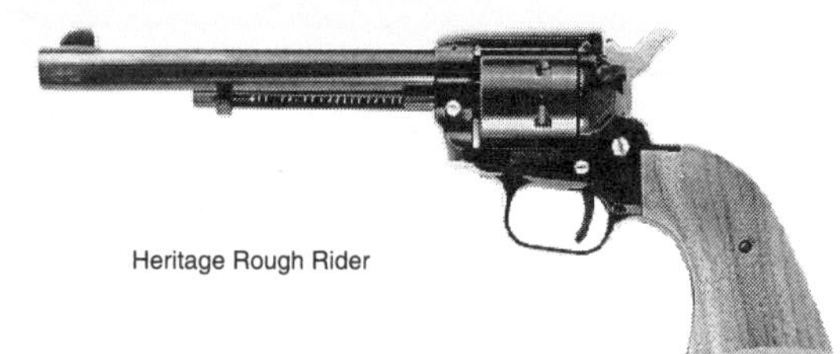
Heritage Rough Rider

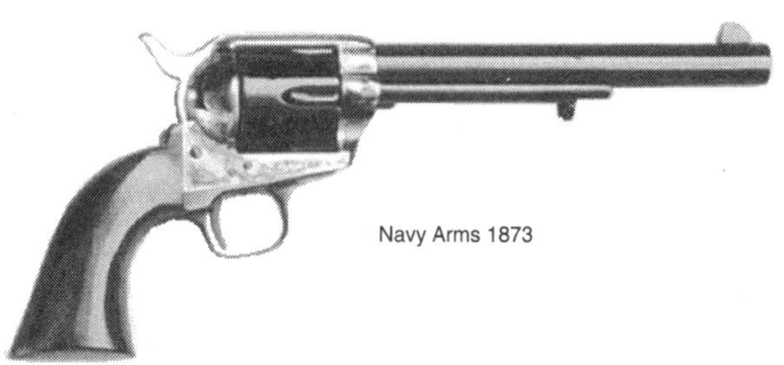
Navy Arms 1873

NAVY ARMS 1873 SINGLE-ACTION REVOLVER
Caliber: 44-40, 45 Colt, 6-shot cylinder.
Barrel: 3", 4¾", 5½", 7½".
Weight: 36 oz. **Length:** 10¾" overall (5½" barrel).
Stocks: Smooth walnut.
Sights: Blade front, groove in topstrap rear.
Features: Blue with color case-hardened frame, or nickel. Introduced 1991. Imported by Navy Arms.
Price: Blue **$390.00**
Price: Nickel **$455.00**
Price: 1873 U.S. Cavalry Model (7½", 45 Colt, arsenal markings) **$480.00**
Price: 1895 U.S. Artillery Model (as above, 5½" barrel) **$480.00**

Consult our Directory pages for the location of firms mentioned.

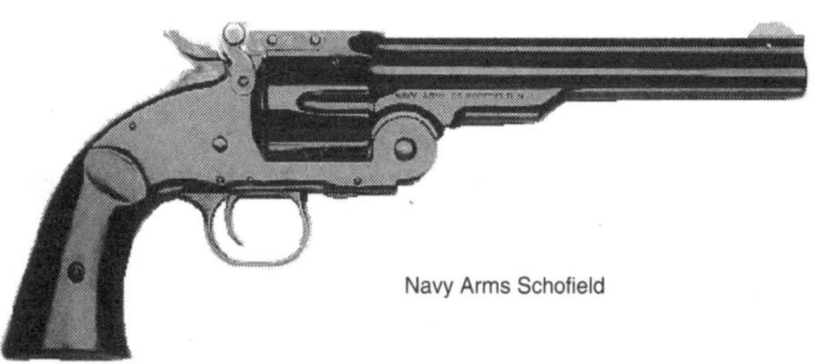
Navy Arms Schofield

NAVY ARMS 1875 SCHOFIELD REVOLVER
Caliber: 44-40, 44 S&W Spec., 45 Colt, 6-shot cylinder.
Barrel: 5", 7".
Weight: 39 oz. **Length:** 10¾" overall (5" barrel).
Stocks: Smooth walnut.
Sights: Blade front, notch rear.
Features: Replica of Smith & Wesson Model 3 Schofield. Single-action, top-break with automatic ejection. Polished blue finish. Introduced 1994. Imported by Navy Arms.
Price: Wells Fargo (5" barrel, Wells Fargo markings) **$795.00**
Price: U.S. Cavalry model (7" barrel, military markings **$795.00**

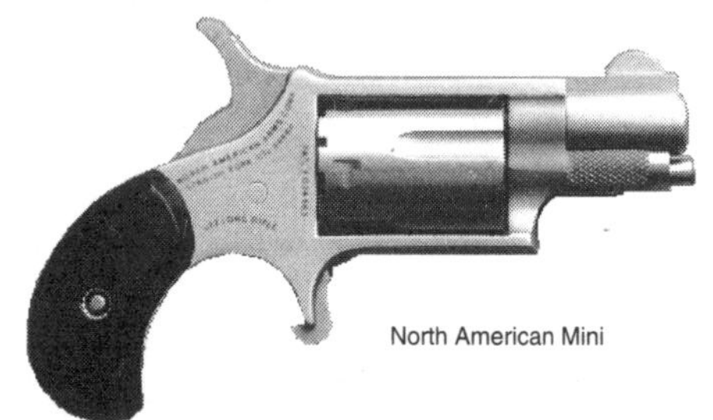
North American Mini

NORTH AMERICAN MINI-REVOLVERS
Caliber: 22 Short, 22 LR, 22 WMR, 5-shot.
Barrel: 1⅛", 1⅝".
Weight: 4 to 6.6 oz. **Length:** 3⅝" to 6⅛" overall.
Stocks: Laminated wood.
Sights: Blade front, notch fixed rear.
Features: All stainless steel construction. Polished satin and matte finish. Engraved models available. From North American Arms.
Price: 22 Short, 22 LR, 1⅛" bbl. **$157.00**
Price: 22 LR, 1⅝" bbl. **$157.00**
Price: 22 WMR, 1⅝" bbl. **$178.00**
Price: 22 WMR, 1⅛" or 1⅝" bbl. with extra 22 LR cylinder **$210.00**

NORTH AMERICAN MINI-MASTER
Caliber: 22 LR, 22 WMR, 5-shot cylinder.
Barrel: 4".
Weight: 10.7 oz. **Length:** 7.75" overall.
Stocks: Checkered hard black rubber.
Sights: Blade front, white outline rear adjustable for elevation, or fixed.
Features: Heavy vent barrel; full-size grips. Non-fluted cylinder. Introduced 1989.
Price: Adjustable sight, 22 WMR or 22 LR **$279.00**
Price: As above with extra WMR/LR cylinder **$317.00**
Price: Fixed sight, 22 WMR or 22 LR **$264.00**
Price: As above with extra WMR/LR cylinder **$302.00**

North American Black Widow Revolver
Similar to the Mini-Master except has 2" heavy vent barrel. Built on the 22 WMR frame. Non-fluted cylinder, black rubber grips. Available with either Millett Low Profile fixed sights or Millett sight adjustable for elevation only. Overall length 5⅞", weighs 8.8 oz. From North American Arms.
Price: Adjustable sight, 22 LR or 22 WMR **$249.00**
Price: As above with extra WMR/LR cylinder **$285.00**
Price: Fixed sight, 22 LR or 22 WMR **$235.00**
Price: As above with extra WMR/LR cylinder **$270.00**

Ruger Blackhawk

RUGER BLACKHAWK REVOLVER
Caliber: 30 Carbine, 357 Mag./38 Spec., 41 Mag., 45 Colt, 6-shot.
Barrel: 4⅝" or 6½", either caliber; 7½" (30 Carbine, 45 Colt only).
Weight: 42 oz. (6½" bbl.). **Length:** 12¼" overall (6½" bbl.).
Stocks: American walnut.
Sights: ⅛" ramp front, micro-click rear adjustable for windage and elevation.
Features: Ruger transfer bar safety system, independent firing pin, hardened chrome-moly steel frame, music wire springs throughout.
Price: Blue, 30 Carbine (7½" bbl.), BN31 .....**$360.00**
Price: Blue, 357 Mag. (4⅝", 6½"), BN34, BN36 .....**$360.00**
Price: Blue, 357/9mm Convertible (4⅝", 6½"), BN34X, BN36X **$360.00**
Price: Blue, 41 Mag., 45 Colt (4⅝", 6½"), BN41, BN42, BN45 .....**$360.00**
Price: Stainless, 357 Mag. (4⅝", 6½"), KBN34, KBN36 .....**$443.00**
Price: High-gloss stainless, 357 Mag. (4⅝", 6½"), GKBN34, GKBN36 .....**$443.00**
Price: High-gloss stainless, 45 Colt (4⅝", 7½"), GKBN44, GKBN45 .....**$443.00**

CAUTION: PRICES SHOWN ARE SUPPLIED BY THE MANUFACTURER OR IMPORTER. CHECK YOUR LOCAL GUNSHOP.

Ruger New Super Bearcat

RUGER SUPER SINGLE-SIX CONVERTIBLE
Caliber: 22 LR, 6-shot; 22 WMR in extra cylinder.
Barrel: 4 5/8", 5 1/2", 6 1/2", or 9 1/2" (6-groove).
Weight: 34 1/2 oz. (6 1/2" bbl.). **Length:** 11 13/16" overall (6 1/2" bbl.).
Stocks: Smooth American walnut.
Sights: Improved Patridge front on ramp, fully adjustable rear protected by integral frame ribs; or fixed sight.
Features: Ruger transfer bar safety system, gate-controlled loading, hardened chrome-moly steel frame, wide trigger, music wire springs throughout, independent firing pin.
Price: 4 5/8", 5 1/2", 6 1/2", 9 1/2" barrel, blue, fixed or adjustable sight (5 1/2", 6 1/2") **$313.00**
Price: 5 1/2", 6 1/2" bbl. only, high-gloss stainless steel, fixed or adjustable sight **$353.00**

Ruger SSM Single-Six Revolver
Similar to the Super Single-Six revolver except chambered for 32 H&R Magnum (also handles 32 S&W and 32 S&W Long). Weighs about 34 oz. with 6 1/2" barrel. Barrel lengths: 4 5/8", 5 1/2", 6 1/2", 9 1/2". Introduced 1985.
Price: **$313.00**

Ruger Bisley Small Frame Revolver
Similar to the Single-Six except frame is styled after the classic Bisley "flat-top." Most mechanical parts are unchanged. Hammer is lower and smoothly curved with a deeply checkered spur. Trigger is strongly curved with a wide smooth surface. Longer grip frame designed with a hand-filling shape, and the trigger guard is a large oval. Adjustable dovetail rear sight; front sight base accepts interchangeable square blades of various heights and styles. Has an unfluted cylinder and roll engraving. Weighs about 41 oz. Chambered for 22 LR and 32 H&R Mag., 6 1/2" barrel only. Introduced 1985.
Price: **$360.00**

Ruger Bisley Single-Action Revolver
Similar to standard Blackhawk except the hammer is lower with a smoothly curved, deeply checkered wide spur. The trigger is strongly curved with a wide smooth surface. Longer grip frame has a hand-filling shape. Adjustable rear sight, ramp-style front. Has an unfluted cylinder and roll engraving, adjustable sights. Chambered for 357, 41, 44 Mags. and 45 Colt; 7 1/2" barrel; overall length of 13". Introduced 1985.
Price: **$430.00**

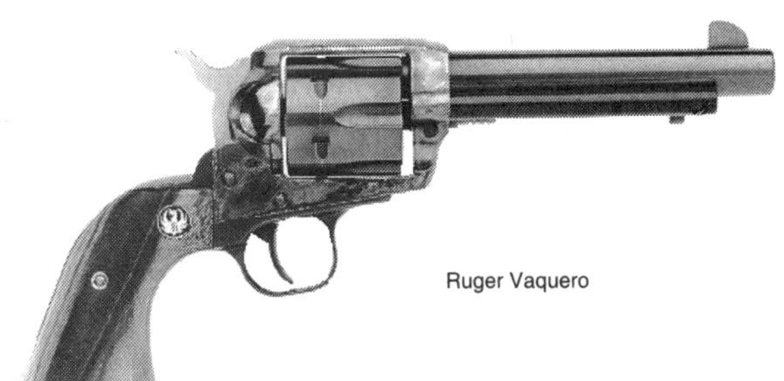
Ruger Vaquero

TEXAS LONGHORN ARMS RIGHT-HAND SINGLE-ACTION
Caliber: All centerfire pistol calibers.
Barrel: 4 3/4".
Weight: 40 oz. **Length:** 10 1/4" overall.
Stocks: One-piece fancy walnut.
Sights: Blade front, grooved topstrap rear.
Features: Loading gate and ejector housing on left side of gun. Cylinder rotates to the left. All steel construction; color case-hardened frame; high polish blue; music wire coil springs. Lifetime guarantee to original owner. Introduced 1984. From Texas Longhorn Arms.
Price: South Texas Army Limited Edition—handmade, only 1,000 to be produced; "One of One Thousand" engraved on barrel **$1,595.00**

RUGER SUPER BLACKHAWK
Caliber: 44 Mag., 6-shot. Also fires 44 Spec.
Barrel: 4 5/8", 5 1/2", 7 1/2", 10 1/2".
Weight: 48 oz. (7 1/2" bbl.), 51 oz. (10 1/2" bbl.). **Length:** 13 3/8" overall (7 1/2" bbl.).
Stocks: American walnut.
Sights: 1/8" ramp front, micro-click rear adjustable for windage and elevation.
Features: Ruger transfer bar safety system, non-fluted cylinder, steel grip and cylinder frame, square back trigger guard, wide serrated trigger and wide spur hammer.
Price: Blue (S45N, S47N, S411N) **$413.00**
Price: Stainless (KS45N, KS47N, KS411N) **$450.00**
Price: High-gloss stainless (4 5/8", 5 1/2", 7 1/2"), GKS458N, GKS45N, GKS47N **$450.00**

RUGER NEW SUPER BEARCAT SINGLE-ACTION
Caliber: 22 LR, 6-shot.
Barrel: 4".
Weight: 23 oz. **Length:** 8 7/8" overall.
Stocks: Smooth rosewood with Ruger medallion.
Sights: Blade front, fixed notch rear.
Features: Reintroduction of the Ruger Super Bearcat with slightly lengthened frame, Ruger patented transfer bar safety system. Available in blue only. Introduced 1993. From Sturm, Ruger & Co.
Price: SBC4, blue **$298.00**

Ruger Bisley Single-Action

RUGER VAQUERO SINGLE-ACTION REVOLVER
Caliber: 44-40, 44 Mag., 45 Colt, 6-shot.
Barrel: 4 5/8", 5 1/2", 7 1/2".
Weight: 41 oz. **Length:** 13 3/8" overall (7 1/2" barrel).
Stocks: Smooth rosewood with Ruger medallion.
Sights: Blade front, fixed notch rear.
Features: Uses Ruger's patented transfer bar safety system and loading gate interlock with classic styling. Blued model has color case-hardened finish on the frame, the rest polished and blued. Stainless model has high-gloss polish. Introduced 1993. From Sturm, Ruger & Co.
Price: BNV44 (4 5/8"), BNV445 (5 1/2"), BNV45 (7 1/2"), blue **$434.00**
Price: KBNV44 (4 5/8"), KBNV455 (5 1/2"), KBNV45 (7 1/2"), stainless **$434.00**

Texas Longhorn Grover's No. Five

TEXAS LONGHORN ARMS GROVER'S IMPROVED NO. FIVE
Caliber: 44 Mag., 6-shot.
Barrel: 5 1/2".
Weight: 44 oz. **Length:** 11 1/2" overall.
Stocks: Smooth walnut.
Sights: Square blade front on ramp, fully adjustable rear.
Features: Music wire coil spring action with double locking bolt; polished blue finish. Handmade in limited 1,200-gun production. Grip contour, straps, over-sized base pin, lever latch and lockwork identical copies of Elmer Keith design. Lifetime warranty to original owner. Introduced 1988.
Price: **$1,195.00**

Texas Longhorn Arms Sesquicentennial Model Revolver
Similar to the South Texas Army Model except has 3/4-coverage Nimschke-style engraving, antique golden nickel plate finish, one-piece elephant ivory grips. Comes with handmade solid walnut presentation case, factory letter to owner. Limited edition of 150 units. Introduced 1986.
Price: **$2,500.00**

Texas Longhorn Arms Texas Border Special
Similar to the South Texas Army Limited Edition except has 4″ barrel, bird's-head style grip. Same special features. Introduced 1984.
Price: **$1,595.00**

Texas Longhorn Arms West Texas Flat Top Target
Similar to the South Texas Army Limited Edition except choice of barrel length from 7$^{1}/_{2}$″ through 15″; flat-top style frame; $^{1}/_{8}$″ contoured ramp front sight, old model steel micro-click rear adjustable for windage and elevation. Same special features. Introduced 1984.
Price: **$1,595.00**

Texas Longhorn Arms Cased Set
Set contains one each of the Texas Longhorn Right-Hand Single-Actions, all in the same caliber, same serial numbers (100, 200, 300, 400, 500, 600, 700, 800, 900). Ten sets to be made (#1000 donated to NRA museum). Comes in hand-tooled leather case. All other specs same as Limited Edition guns. Introduced 1984.
Price: **$5,750.00**
Price: With $^{3}/_{4}$-coverage "C-style" engraving **$7,650.00**

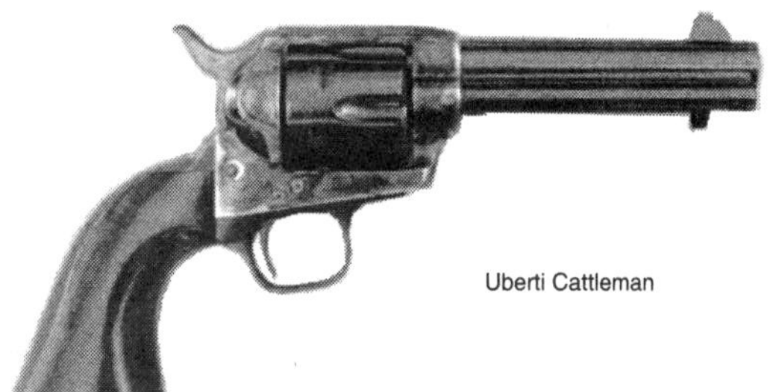
Uberti Cattleman

Uberti 1873 Buckhorn Single-Action
A slightly larger version of the Cattleman revolver. Available in 44 Magnum or 44 Magnum/44-40 convertible, otherwise has same specs.
Price: Steel backstrap, trigger guard, fixed sights **$410.00**
Price: Convertible (two cylinders) **$475.00**

UBERTI 1875 SA ARMY OUTLAW REVOLVER
Caliber: 357 Mag., 44-40, 45 Colt, 45 Colt/45 ACP convertible, 6-shot.
Barrel: 5$^{1}/_{2}$″, 7$^{1}/_{2}$″.
Weight: 44 oz. **Length:** 13$^{3}/_{4}$″ overall.
Stocks: Smooth walnut.
Sights: Blade front, notch rear.
Features: Replica of the 1875 Remington S.A. Army revolver. Brass trigger guard, color case-hardened frame, rest blued. Imported by Uberti U.S.A.
Price: **$435.00**
Price: 45 Colt/45 ACP convertible **$475.00**

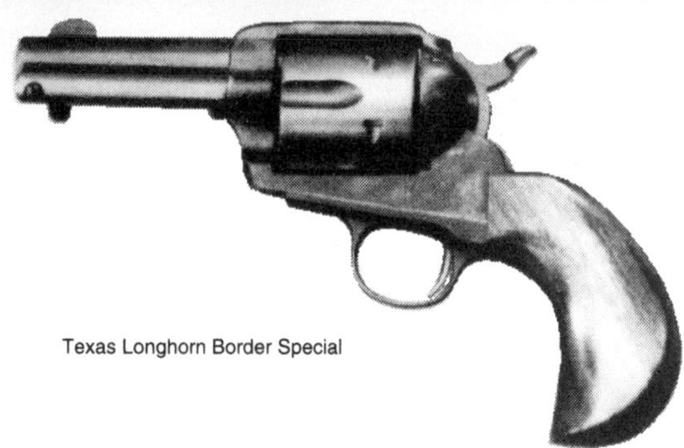
Texas Longhorn Border Special

UBERTI 1873 CATTLEMAN SINGLE-ACTIONS
Caliber: 22 LR/22 WMR, 38 Spec., 357 Mag., 44 Spec., 44-40, 45 Colt/45 ACP, 6-shot.
Barrel: 4$^{3}/_{4}$″, 5$^{1}/_{2}$″, 7$^{1}/_{2}$″; 44-40, 45 Colt also with 3″, 3$^{1}/_{2}$″, 4″.
Weight: 38 oz. (5$^{1}/_{2}$″ bbl.). **Length:** 10$^{3}/_{4}$″ overall (5$^{1}/_{2}$″ bbl.).
Stocks: One-piece smooth walnut.
Sights: Blade front, groove rear; fully adjustable rear available.
Features: Steel or brass backstrap, trigger guard; color case-hardened frame, blued barrel, cylinder. Imported from Italy by Uberti U.S.A.
Price: Steel backstrap, trigger guard, fixed sights **$435.00**
Price: Brass backstrap, trigger guard, fixed sights **$365.00**
Price: Bisley model **$435.00**

Uberti 1875 Army

UBERTI 1890 ARMY OUTLAW REVOLVER
Caliber: 357 Mag., 44-40, 45 Colt, 45 Colt/45 ACP convertible, 6-shot.
Barrel: 5$^{1}/_{2}$″, 7$^{1}/_{2}$″.
Weight: 37 oz. **Length:** 12$^{1}/_{2}$″ overall.
Stocks: American walnut.
Sights: Blade front, groove rear.
Features: Replica of the 1890 Remington single-action. Brass trigger guard, rest is blued. Imported by Uberti U.S.A.
Price: **$435.00**
Price: 45 Colt/45 ACP convertible **$475.00**

HANDGUNS—MISCELLANEOUS

Specially adapted single-shot and multi-barrel arms.

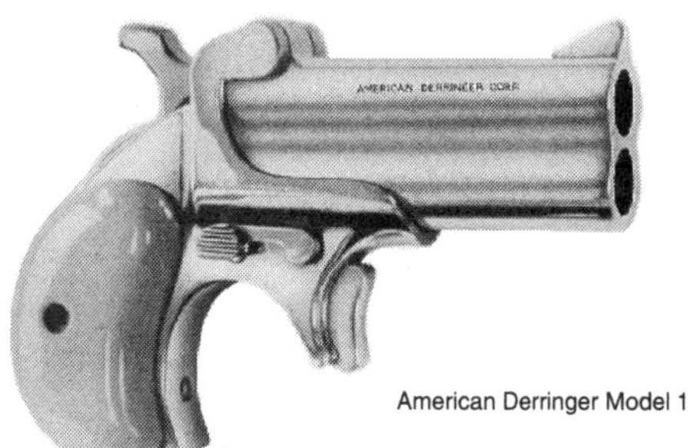

American Derringer Model 1

AMERICAN DERRINGER MODEL 1
Caliber: 22 LR, 22 WMR, 30 Carbine, 30 Luger, 30-30 Win., 32 H&R Mag., 32-20, 380 ACP, 38 Super, 38 Spec., 38 Spec. shotshell, 38 Spec. +P, 9mm Para., 357 Mag., 357 Mag./45/410, 357 Maximum, 10mm, 40 S&W, 41 Mag., 38-40, 44-40 Win., 44 Spec., 44 Mag., 45 Colt, 45 Win. Mag., 45 ACP, 45 Colt/410, 45-70 single shot.
Barrel: 3″.
Weight: 15$^{1}/_{2}$ oz. (38 Spec.). **Length:** 4.82″ overall.
Stocks: Rosewood, Zebra wood.
Sights: Blade front.
Features: Made of stainless steel with high-polish or satin finish. Two-shot capacity. Manual hammer block safety. Introduced 1980. Available in almost any pistol caliber. Contact the factory for complete list of available calibers and prices. From American Derringer Corp.
Price: 22 LR **$245.00**
Price: 38 Spec. **$245.00**
Price: 357 Maximum **$265.00**
Price: 357 Mag. **$257.00**
Price: 9mm, 380, ... **$245.00**
Price: 40 S&W **$257.00**
Price: 44 Spec., ... **$320.00**
Price: 44-40 Win., 45 Colt **$320.00**
Price: 30-30, 41, 44 Mags., 45 Win. Mag. .... **$375.00** to **$385.00**
Price: 45-70, single shot **$312.00**
Price: 45 Colt, 410, 2$^{1}/_{2}$″ **$320.00**
Price: 45 ACP, 10mm Auto **$257.00**

CAUTION: PRICES SHOWN ARE SUPPLIED BY THE MANUFACTURER OR IMPORTER. CHECK YOUR LOCAL GUNSHOP.

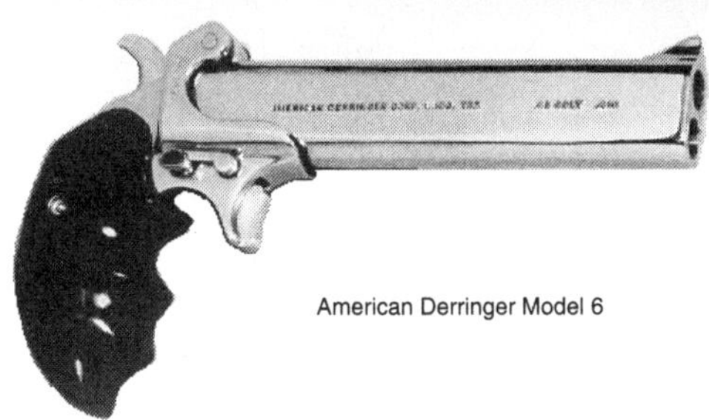
American Derringer Model 6

American Derringer Model 7 Ultra Lightweight
Similar to Model 1 except made of high strength aircraft aluminum. Weighs 7½ oz., 4.82″ o.a.l., rosewood stocks. Available in 22 LR, 22 WMR, 32 H&R Mag., 380 ACP, 38 Spec., 44 Spec. Introduced 1986.
Price: 22 LR, WMR **$240.00**
Price: 38 Spec. **$240.00**
Price: 380 ACP **$240.00**
Price: 32 H&R Mag. **$240.00**
Price: 44 Spec. **$500.00**

American Derringer Lady Derringer
Same as the Model 1 except has tuned action, is fitted with scrimshawed synthetic ivory grips; chambered for 32 H&R Mag. and 38 Spec.; 357 Mag., 45 Colt. Deluxe Grade is highly polished; Deluxe Engraved is engraved in a pattern similar to that used on 1880s derringers. All come in a French fitted jewelry box. Introduced 1991.
Price: 32 H&R Mag. **$280.00**
Price: 357 Mag. **$300.00**
Price: 38 Spec. **$200.00**
Price: 45 Colt **$345.00**

ANSCHUTZ EXEMPLAR BOLT-ACTION PISTOL
Caliber: 22 LR, 5-shot; 22 Hornet, 5-shot.
Barrel: 10″.
Weight: 3½ lbs. **Length:** 17″ overall.
Stock: European walnut with stippled grip and forend.
Sights: Hooded front on ramp, open notch rear adjustable for windage and elevation.
Features: Uses Match 64 action with left-hand bolt; Anschutz #5091 two-stage trigger set at 9.85 oz. Receiver grooved for scope mounting; open sights easily removed. The 22 Hornet version uses Match 54 action with left-hand bolt, Anschutz #5099 two-stage trigger set at 19.6 oz. Introduced 1987. Imported from Germany by AcuSport Corp.
Price: 22 LR **$580.75**
Price: 22 LR, left-hand **$473.14**
Price: 22 Hornet (no sights, 10″ bbl.) **$1,009.89**

DAVIS DERRINGERS
Caliber: 22 LR, 5-shot; 22 Hornet, 5-shot.
Barrel: 2.4″.
Weight: 9.5 oz. **Length:** 4″ overall.
Stocks: Laminated wood.
Sights: Blade front, fixed notch rear.
Features: Choice of black Teflon or chrome finish; spur trigger. Introduced 1986. Made in U.S. by Davis Industries.
Price: **$75.00**

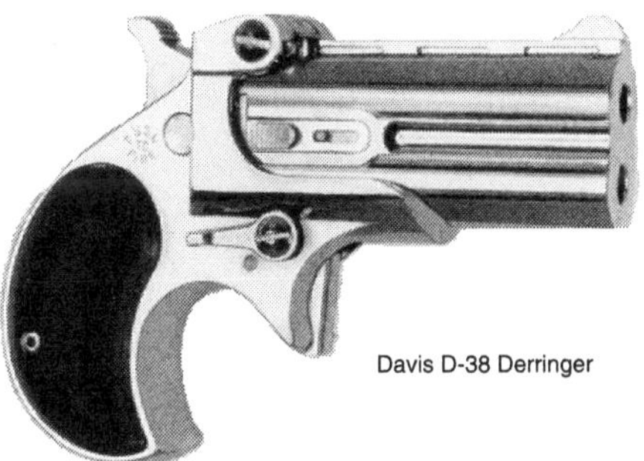
Davis D-38 Derringer

American Derringer Model 4
Similar to the Model 1 except has 4.1″ barrel, overall length of 6″, and weighs 16½ oz.; chambered for 357 Mag., 357 Maximum, 45-70, 3″ 410-bore shotshells or 45 Colt or 44 Mag. Made of stainless steel. Manual hammer block safety. Introduced 1985.
Price: 3″ 410/45 Colt **$352.00**
Price: 3″ 410/45 Colt or 45-70 (Alaskan Survival model) **$388.00**
Price: 44 Mag. with oversize grips **$422.00**
Price: Alaskan Survival model (45-70 upper, 410 or 45 Colt lower) **$388.00**

American Derringer Model 6
Similar to the Model 1 except has 6″ barrel chambered for 3″ 410 shotshells or 22 WMR, 357 Mag., 45 ACP, 45 Colt; rosewood stocks; 8.2″ o.a.l. and weighs 21 oz. Shoots either round for each barrel. Manual hammer block safety. Introduced 1986.
Price: 22 WMR **$300.00**
Price: 357 Mag. **$300.00**
Price: 45 Colt/410 .... **$363.00**
Price: 45 ACP **$345.00**

American Derringer Model 10 Lightweight
Similar to the Model 1 except frame is of aluminum, giving weight of 10 oz. Stainless barrels. Available in 38 Spec., 45 Colt or 45 ACP only. Matte gray finish. Introduced 1989.
Price: 45 Colt **$320.00**
Price: 45 ACP **$257.00**
Price: 38 Spec. **$240.00**

American Derringer Texas Commemorative
A Model 1 Derringer with solid brass frame, stainless steel barrel and rosewood grips. Available in 38 Spec., 44-40 Win., or 45 Colt. Introduced 1987.
Price: 38 Spec. **$280.00**
Price: 44-40 or 45 Colt **$345.00**

AMERICAN DERRINGER DA 38 MODEL
Caliber: 22 LR, 9mm Para., 38 Spec., 357 Mag., 40 S&W.
Barrel: 3″.
Weight: 14.5 oz. **Length:** 4.8″ overall.
Stocks: Rosewood, walnut or other hardwoods.
Sights: Fixed.
Features: Double-action only; two-shots. Manual safety. Made of satin-finished stainless steel and aluminum. Introduced 1989. From American Derringer Corp.
Price: 22 LR, 38 Spec. **$300.00**
Price: 9mm Para. **$325.00**
Price: 357 Mag., 40 S&W **$350.00**

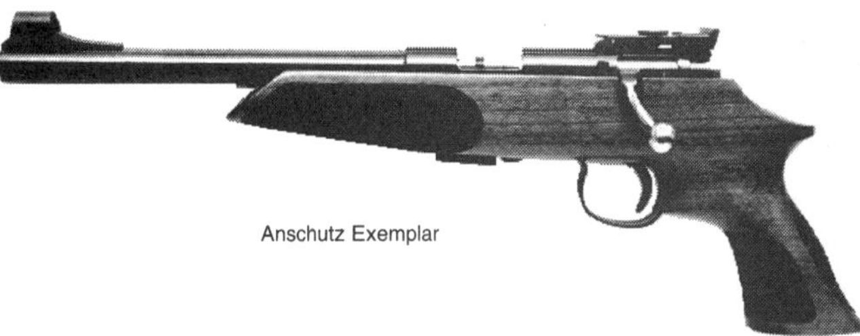
Anschutz Exemplar

DAVIS LONG-BORE DERRINGERS
Caliber: 22 WMR, 32 H&R Mag., 38 Spec., 9mm Para.
Barrel: 3.5″.
Weight: 16 oz. **Length:** 5.4″ overall.
Stocks: Textured black synthetic.
Sights: Fixed.
Features: Chrome or black teflon finish. Larger than Davis D-Series models. Introduced 1995. Made in U.S. by Davis Industries.
Price: **$104.00**
Price: Big-Bore models (same calibers, ¾″ shorter barrels) **$98.00**

DAVIS D-SERIES DERRINGERS
Caliber: 22 WMR, 32 H&R, 38 Spec..
Barrel: 2.75″.
Weight: 11.5 oz. **Length:** 4.65″ overall.
Stocks: Textured black synthetic.
Sights: Blade front, fixed notch rear.
Features: Alloy frame, steel-lined barrels, steel breech block. Plunger-type safety with integral hammer block. Chrome or black Teflon finish. Introduced 1992. Made in U.S. by Davis Industries.
Price: **$98.00**

HJS LONE STAR DERRINGER
Caliber: 380 ACP.
Barrel: 2″.
Weight: 6 oz. **Length:** 3 15/16″ overall.
Stocks: Brown plastic.
Sights: Groove.
Features: Stainless steel construction. Beryllium copper firing pin. Button-rifled barrel. Introduced 1993. Made in U.S. by HJS Arms, Inc.
Price: $185.00

HJS FRONTIER FOUR DERRINGER
Caliber: 22 LR.
Barrel: 2″.
Weight: 5 1/2 oz. **Length:** 3 15/16″ overall.
Stocks: Brown plastic.
Sights: None.
Features: Four barrels fire with rotating firing pin. Stainless steel construction. Introduced 1993. Made in U.S. by HJS Arms, Inc.
Price: $165.00

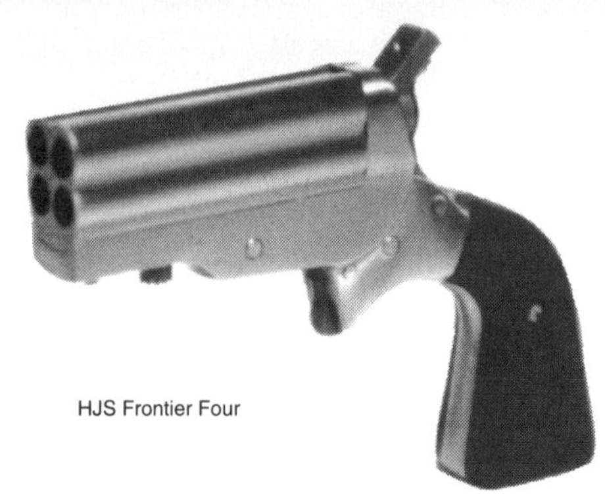
HJS Frontier Four

HJS Antigua Derringer
Same as the Frontier Four except blued barrel, brass frame, brass pivot pins. Brown plastic grips. Introduced 1994. Made in U.S. by HJS Arms, Inc.
Price: $180.00

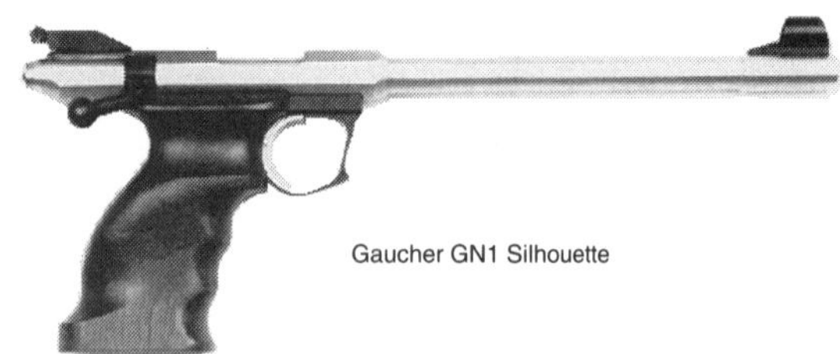
Gaucher GN1 Silhouette

GAUCHER GN1 SILHOUETTE PISTOL
Caliber: 22 LR, single shot.
Barrel: 10″.
Weight: 2.4 lbs. **Length:** 15.5″ overall.
Stocks: European hardwood.
Sights: Blade front, open adjustable rear.
Features: Bolt action, adjustable trigger. Introduced 1990. Imported from France by Mandall Shooting Supplies.
Price: About $525.00
Price: Model GP Silhouette $425.00

MAGNUM RESEARCH LONE EAGLE SINGLE SHOT PISTOL
Caliber: 22 Hornet, 223, 22-250, 243, 7mm BR, 7mm-08, 30-30, 7.62x39, 308, 30-06, 357 Max., 35 Rem., 358 Win., 44 Mag., 444 Marlin.
Barrel: 14″, interchangable.
Weight: 4lbs., 3 oz. to 4 lbs., 7 oz. **Length:** 15″ overall.
Stocks: Ambidextrous.
Sights: None furnished; drilled and tapped for scope mounting and open sights. Open sights optional.
Features: Cannon-type rotating breech with spring-activated ejector. Ordnance steel with matte blue finish. Cross-bolt safety. External cocking lever on left side of gun. Introduced 1991. Available from Magnum Research, Inc.
Price: Complete pistol $408.00
Price: Barreled action only $289.00
Price: Scope base $14.00
Price: Adjustable open sights $35.00

LORCIN OVER/UNDER DERRINGER
Caliber: 38 Spec./357 Mag., 45 ACP.
Barrel: 3.5″.
Weight: NA. **Length:** 6.5″ overall.
Stocks: Black composition.
Sights: Blade front, fixed rear.
Features: Stainless steel construction. Rebounding hammer. Introduced 1996. Made in U.S. by Lorcin Engineering.
Price: $129.00

Consult our Directory pages for the location of firms mentioned.

Magnum Research Lone Eagle

MANDALL/CABANAS PISTOL
Caliber: 177, pellet or round ball; single shot.
Barrel: 9″.
Weight: 51 oz. **Length:** 19″ overall.
Stock: Smooth wood with thumbrest.
Sights: Blade front on ramp, open adjustable rear.
Features: Fires round ball or pellets with 22 blank cartridge. Automatic safety; muzzlebrake. Imported from Mexico by Mandall Shooting Supplies.
Price: $139.95

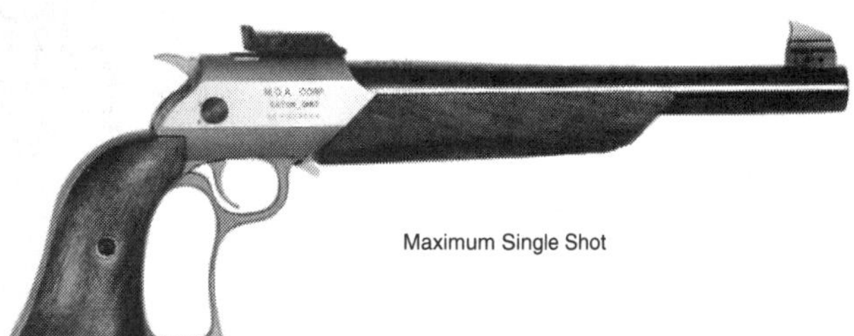
Maximum Single Shot

MAXIMUM SINGLE SHOT PISTOL
Caliber: 22 LR, 22 Hornet, 22 BR, 22 PPC, 223 Rem., 22-250, 6mm BR, 6mm PPC, 243, 250 Savage, 6.5mm-35M, 270 MAX, 270 Win., 7mm TCU, 7mm BR, 7mm-35, 7mm INT-R, 7mm-08, 7mm Rocket, 7mm Super Mag., 30 Herrett, 30 Carbine, 30-30, 308 Win., 30x39, 32-20, 350 Rem. Mag., 357 Mag., 357 Maximum, 358 Win., 44 Mag., 454 Casull.
Barrel: 8 3/4″, 10 1/2″, 14″.
Weight: 61 oz. (10 1/2″ bbl.); 78 oz. (14″ bbl.). **Length:** 15″, 18 1/2″ overall (with 10 1/2″ and 14″ bbl., respectively).
Stocks: Smooth walnut stocks and forend. Also available with 17° finger groove grip.
Sights: Ramp front, fully adjustable open rear.
Features: Falling block action; drilled and tapped for M.O.A. scope mounts; integral grip frame/receiver; adjustable trigger; Douglas barrel (interchangeable). Introduced 1983. Made in U.S. by M.O.A. Corp.
Price: Stainless receiver, blue barrel $653.00
Price: Stainless receiver, stainless barrel $711.00
Price: Extra blued barrel $164.00
Price: Extra stainless barrel $222.00
Price: Scope mount $52.00

CAUTION: PRICES SHOWN ARE SUPPLIED BY THE MANUFACTURER OR IMPORTER. CHECK YOUR LOCAL GUNSHOP.

MITCHELL ARMS GUARDIAN ANGEL PISTOL
Caliber: 22 LR, 22 WMR, 2-shot.
Barrel: 1 3/4″.
Weight: 7 1/2 oz. **Length:** 4 3/4″ overall.
Stocks: Checkered black synthetic.
Sights: Fixed channel.
Features: Uses a pre-loaded, drop-in 2-shot removable breechblock; double-action-only. Available in nickel, black nickel, satin steel, gold finishes. Deluxe comes in jewel box with angel charm. Introduced 1996. Made in U.S. by Mitchell Arms.
Price: .... **$142.95** to **$199.95**

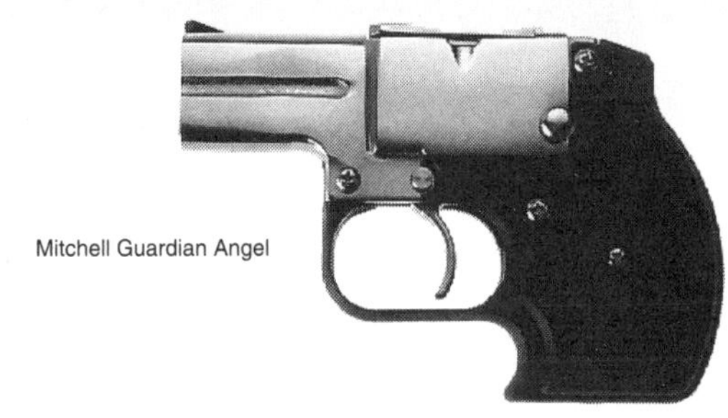
Mitchell Guardian Angel

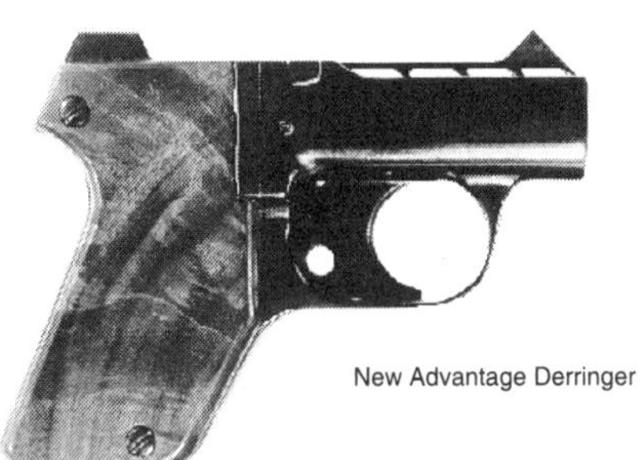
New Advantage Derringer

NEW ADVANTAGE ARMS DERRINGER
Caliber: 22 LR, 22 WMR, 4-shot.
Barrel: 2 1/2″.
Weight: 15 oz. **Length:** 4 1/2″ overall.
Stocks: Smooth walnut.
Sights: Fixed.
Features: Double-action mechanism, four barrels, revolving hammer with four firing pins. Rebounding hammer. Blue or stainless. Reintroduced 1989. From New Advantage Arms Corp.
Price: 22 LR, 22 WMR, blue, about **$249.99**
Price: As above, stainless, about **$249.99**

RPM XL SINGLE SHOT PISTOL
Caliber: 22 LR through 45-70.
Barrel: 8″, 10 3/4″, 12″, 14″.
Weight: About 60 oz. **Length:** NA.
Stocks: Smooth Goncalo Alves with thumb and heel rests.
Sights: Hooded front with interchangeable post, or Patridge; ISGW rear adjustable for windage and elevation.
Features: Barrel drilled and tapped for scope mount. Visible cocking indicator. Spring-loaded barrel lock, positive hammer-block safety. Trigger adjustable for weight of pull and over-travel. Contact maker for complete price list. Made in U.S. by RPM.
Price: Hunter model (stainless frame, 5/16″ underlug, latch lever and positive extractor) **$1,195.00**
Price: Silhouette model (chrome-moly frame, blue or hard chrome finish) **$857.50**
Price: Extra barrel, 8″ through 10 3/4″ **$287.50**
Price: Muzzle brake **$100.00**

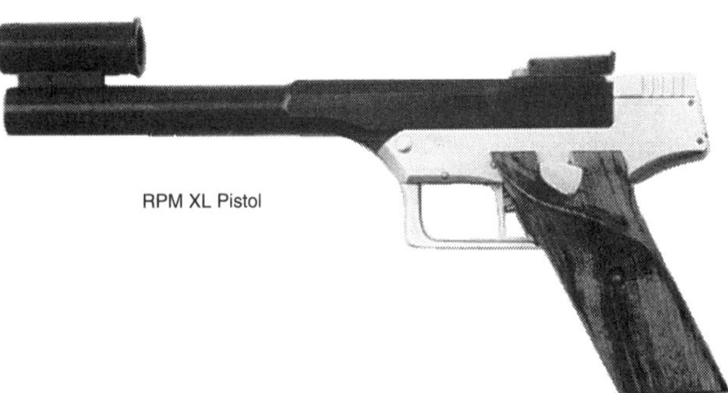
RPM XL Pistol

SUNDANCE POINT BLANK O/U DERRINGER
Caliber: 22 LR, 2-shot.
Barrel: 3″.
Weight: 8 oz. **Length:** 4.6″ overall.
Stocks: Grooved composition.
Sights: Blade front, fixed notch rear.
Features: Double-action trigger, push-bar safety, automatic chamber selection. Fully enclosed hammer. Matte black finish. Introduced 1994. Made in U.S. by Sundance Industries.
Price: **$99.00**

Sundance Point Blank

Texas Armory Defender

TEXAS ARMORY DEFENDER DERRINGER
Caliber: 9mm Para., 357 Mag., 44 Mag., 45 ACP, 45 Colt/410.
Barrel: 3″.
Weight: 21 oz. **Length:** 5″ overall.
Stocks: Smooth wood.
Sights: Blade front, fixed rear.
Features: Interchangeable barrels; retracting firing pins; rebounding hammer; cross-bolt safety; removable trigger guard; automatic extractor. Blasted finish stainless steel. Introduced 1993. Made in U.S. by Texas Armory.
Price: **$310.00**
Price: Extra barrel **$100.00**

TEXAS LONGHORN "THE JEZEBEL" PISTOL
Caliber: 22 Short, Long, Long Rifle, single shot.
Barrel: 6″.
Weight: 15 oz. **Length:** 8″ overall.
Stocks: One-piece fancy walnut grip (right- or left-hand), walnut forend.
Sights: Bead front, fixed rear.
Features: Handmade gun. Top-break action; all stainless steel; automatic hammer block safety; music wire coil springs. Barrel is half-round, half-octagon. Announced 1986. From Texas Longhorn Arms.
Price: About **$250.00**

THE JUDGE SINGLE SHOT PISTOL
Caliber: 22 Hornet, 22 K-Hornet, 218 Bee, 7-30 Waters, 30-30.
Barrel: 10″ or 16.2″.
Weight: NA. **Length:** NA.
Stocks: Walnut.
Sights: Bead on ramp front, open adjustable rear.
Features: Break-open design; made of 17-4 stainless steel. Also available as a kit. Introduced 1995. Made in U.S. by Cumberland Mountain Arms.
Price: .... **NA**

Thompson/Center Encore

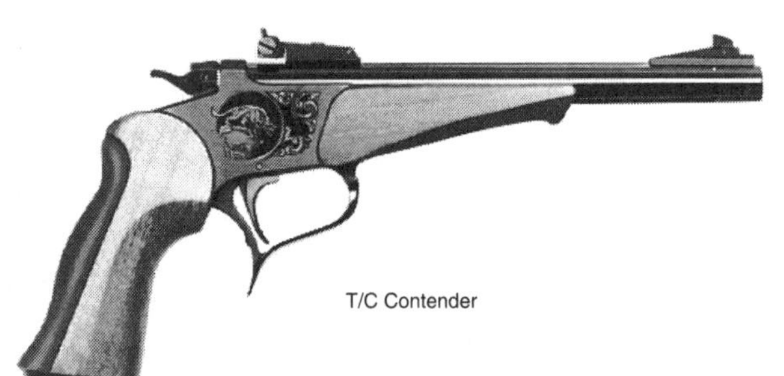
T/C Contender

Thompson/Center Contender Hunter Package

Package contains the Contender pistol in 223, 7-30 Waters, 30-30, 375 Win., 357 Rem. Maximum, 35 Rem., 44 Mag. or 45-70 with 14″ barrel with T/C's Muzzle Tamer, a 2.5x Recoil Proof Long Eye Relief scope with lighted reticle, q.d. sling swivels with a nylon carrying sling. Comes with a suede leather case with foam padding and fleece lining. Introduced 1990. From Thompson/Center Arms.

Price: Blued **$798.00**
Price: Stainless **$829.00**

Thompson/Center Stainless Super 14, Super 16 Contender

Same as the standard Super 14 and Super 16 except they are made of stainless steel with blued sights. Both models have black Rynite forend and finger-groove, ambidextrous grip with a built-in rubber recoil cushion that has a sealed-in air pocket. Receiver has a different cougar etching. Available in 22 LR, 22 LR Match, 22 Hornet, 223 Rem., 30-30 Win., 35 Rem. (Super 14), 45-70 (Super 16 only), 45 Colt/410. Introduced 1993.

Price: 14″ bull barrel **$504.70**
Price: 16¼″ bull barrel **$509.90**
Price: 45 Colt/410, 14″ **$535.60**
Price: 45 Colt/410, 16″ **$530.50**

UBERTI ROLLING BLOCK TARGET PISTOL

Caliber: 22 LR, 22 WMR, 22 Hornet, 357 Mag., 45 Colt, single shot.
Barrel: 9⅞″, half-round, half-octagon.
Weight: 44 oz. **Length:** 14″ overall.
Stocks: Walnut grip and forend.
Sights: Blade front, fully adjustable rear.
Features: Replica of the 1871 rolling block target pistol. Brass trigger guard, color case-hardened frame, blue barrel. Imported by Uberti U.S.A.
Price: **$410.00**

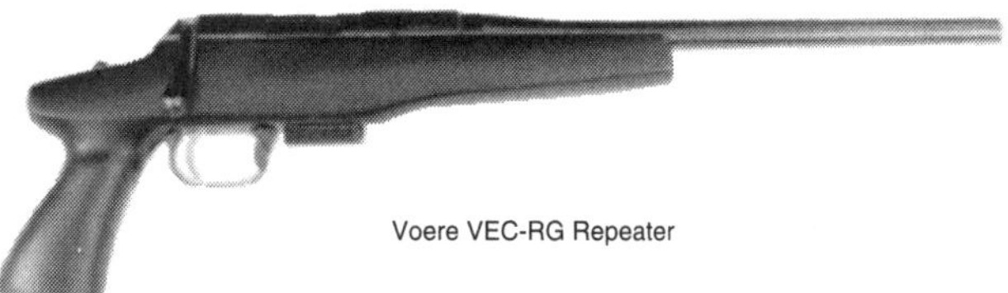
Voere VEC-RG Repeater

Voere VEC-RG Repeater pistol

Similar to the VEC-95CG except has rear grip stock and detachable 5-shot magazine. Available with 12″ or 14″ barrel. Introduced 1995. Imported from Austria by JagerSport, Ltd.

Price: **$1,495.00**

THOMPSON/CENTER ENCORE PISTOL

Caliber: 22-250, 223, 7mm-08, 308, 30-06, single shot.
Barrel: 10″, 15″, tapered round.
Weight: NA **Length:** 19″ overall with 10″ barrel.
Stocks: American walnut with finger grooves, walnut forend.
Sights: Blade on ramp front, adjustable rear, or none.
Features: Interchangeable barrels; action opens by squeezing the trigger guard; drilled and tapped for scope mounting; blue finish. Announced 1996. Made in U.S. by Thompson/Center Arms.
Price: About **$500.00**

THOMPSON/CENTER CONTENDER

Caliber: 7mm TCU, 30-30 Win., 22 LR, 22 WMR, 22 Hornet, 223 Rem., 270 Ren, 7-30 Waters, 32-20 Win., 357 Mag., 357 Rem. Max., 44 Mag., 10mm Auto, 445 Super Mag., 45/410, single shot.
Barrel: 10″, tapered octagon, bull barrel and vent. rib.
Weight: 43 oz. (10″ bbl.). **Length:** 13¼″ (10″ bbl.).
Stocks: T/C "Competitor Grip." Right or left hand.
Sights: Under-cut blade ramp front, rear adjustable for windage and elevation.
Features: Break-open action with automatic safety. Single-action only. Interchangeable bbls., both caliber (rim & centerfire), and length. Drilled and tapped for scope. Engraved frame. See T/C catalog for exact barrel/caliber availability.
Price: Blued (rimfire cals.) **$463.50**
Price: Blued (centerfire cals.) **$463.50**
Price: Extra bbls. (standard octagon) **$213.70**
Price: 45/410, internal choke bbl. **$218.90**

Thompson/Center Stainless Contender

Same as the standard Contender except made of stainless steel with blued sights, black Rynite forend and ambidextrous finger-groove grip with a built-in rubber recoil cushion that has a sealed-in air pocket. Receiver has a different cougar etching. Available with 10″ bull barrel in 22 LR, 22 LR Match, 22 Hornet, 223 Rem., 30-30 Win., 357 Mag., 44 Mag., 45 Colt/410. Introduced 1993.

Price: **$494.40**
Price: 45 Colt/410 . . . . **$499.60**
Price: With 22 LR match chamber **$504.70**

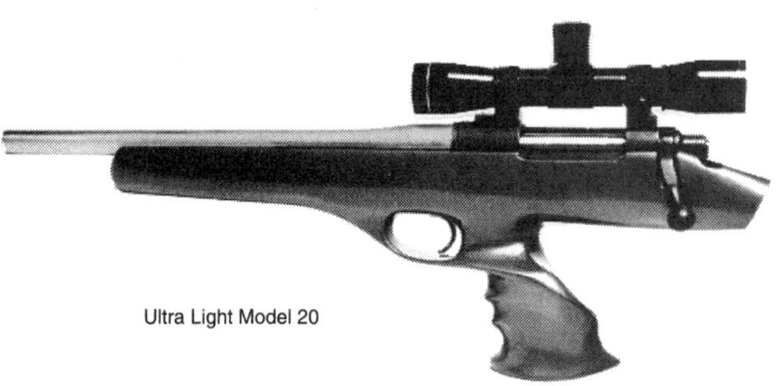
Ultra Light Model 20

ULTRA LIGHT ARMS MODEL 20 REB HUNTER'S PISTOL

Caliber: 22-250 thru 308 Win. standard. Most silhouette calibers and others on request. 5-shot magazine.
Barrel: 14″, Douglas No. 3.
Weight: 4 lbs.
Stock: Composite Kevlar, graphite reinforced. Du Pont Imron paint in green, brown, black and camo.
Sights: None furnished. Scope mount included.
Features: Timney adjustable trigger; two-position, three-function safety; benchrest quality action; matte or bright stock and metal finish; right- or left-hand action. Shipped in hard case. Introduced 1987. From Ultra Light Arms.
Price: **$1,600.00**

VOERE VEC-95CG SINGLE SHOT PISTOL

Caliber: 5.56mm, 6mm UCC caseless, single shot.
Barrel: 12″, 14″.
Weight: 3 lbs. **Length:** NA.
Stock: Black synthetic; center grip.
Sights: None furnished.
Features: Fires caseless ammunition via electronic ignition; two batteries in the grip last about 500 shots. Bolt action has two forward locking lugs. Tang safety. Drilled and tapped for scope mounting. Introduced 1995. Imported from Austria by JagerSport, Ltd.
Price: **$1,495.00**

CAUTION: PRICES SHOWN ARE SUPPLIED BY THE MANUFACTURER OR IMPORTER. CHECK YOUR LOCAL GUNSHOP.

CENTERFIRE RIFLES—AUTOLOADERS

Both classic arms and recent designs in American-style repeaters for sport and field shooting.

AA ARMS AR9 SEMIAUTOMATIC RIFLE
Caliber: 9mm Para., 10-shot magazine.
Barrel: 16″.
Weight: 6 lbs. **Length:** 31″ overall.
Stock: Folding metal skeleton.
Sights: Post front adjustable for elevation, open rear for windage.
Features: Ventilated barrel shroud. Blue or electroless nickel finish. Made in U.S. by AA Arms, Inc.
Price: Blue **$695.00**

ARMALITE AR-10A4 RIFLE
Caliber: 308 Win., 10-slot magazine.
Barrel: 20″ HBAR, 1:12″ twist.
Weight: 9.75 lbs. **Length:** 41.5″ overall.
Stock: Black composition.
Sights: Optional. Has Weaver-type rail.
Features: One-piece international-style flattop receiver; three-slot Picatinny rail gas system. Optional NM two-stage trigger; detachable carry handle with NM sight; detachable front sight assembly; scope mount; stainless barrel. Introduced 1995. Made in U.S. by ArmaLite, Inc.
Price: **$1,325.00**

ArmaLite M15A2 Heavy Barrel

ARMALITE M15A2 POST BAN HEAVY BARREL RIFLE
Caliber: 223, 10-shot magazine.
Barrel: 20″ heavy, 1:9″ twist.
Weight: 9.75 lbs. **Length:** 39.5″ overall.
Stock: Black composition.
Sights: Elevation-adjustable front, E-2-style NM rear with $1/2$-MOA adjustments.
Features: Upper and lower receivers have push-type pivot pin; hard-coat anodized; A2-style forward assist; M-16A2-type raised fence around magazine release button; recoil check brake. Introduced 1995. Made in U.S. by ArmaLite, Inc.
Price: **$895.00**

CONSULT
SHOOTER'S MARKETPLACE
Page 225, This Issue

ArmaLite M15A4 Post Ban M4A1C Carbine
Similar to the M15A2 Heavy Barrel rifle except has 16″ heavy barrel with 1:9″ twist; one-piece international-style flattop receiver with Picatinny (Weaver-type) rail including case deflector; detachable carry handle assembly; NM sights. Introduced 1995. Made in U.S. by ArmaLite, Inc.
Price: **$935.00**

ARMALITE M15A2 POST BAN GOLDEN EAGLE RIFLE
Caliber: 223, 10-shot magazine.
Barrel: 20″, heavy premium stainless, 1:8″ twist, 1.2″ diameter.
Weight: 10.75 lbs. **Length:** 38.25″ overall.
Stock: Black composition.
Sights: NM .050″ front, NM rear with $1/4$ MOA wandage, $1/2$ MOA elevation.
Features: DCM approved; ArmaLite NM two-stage trigger; A2-style forward assist; hard-coat anodized receivers. Introduced 1995. Made in U.S. by ArmaLite, Inc.
Price: **$1,200.00**

ArmaLite M4C Carbine

ArmaLite M15A2 Post Ban M4C Carbine
Similar to the M15A2 Heavy Barrel rifle except has 16″ heavy barrel with 1:9″ twist. Weighs 8.25 lbs., overall length 35.4″. Introduced 1996. Made in U.S. by ArmaLite, Inc.
Price: **$870.00**

Thompson M1

Auto-Ordnance Thompson M1
Similar to the Model 27 A-1 except is in the M-1 configuration with side cocking knob, horizontal forend, smooth unfinned barrel, sling swivels on butt and forend. Matte black finish. Introduced 1985.
Price: **$772.50**

AUTO-ORDNANCE 27 A-1 THOMPSON
Caliber: 45 ACP, 30-shot magazine.
Barrel: 16″.
Weight: $11\frac{1}{2}$ lbs. **Length:** About 42″ overall (Deluxe).
Stock: Walnut stock and vertical forend.
Sights: Blade front, open rear adjustable for windage.
Features: Recreation of Thompson Model 1927. Semi-auto only. Deluxe model has finned barrel, adjustable rear sight and compensator; Standard model has plain barrel and military sight. From Auto-Ordnance Corp.
Price: Deluxe **$795.00**
Price: 1927A1C Lightweight model **$767.00**

Barrett Model 82A-1

BARRETT MODEL 82A-1 SEMI-AUTOMATIC RIFLE
Caliber: 50 BMG, 10-shot detachable box magazine.
Barrel: 29″.
Weight: 28.5 lbs. **Length:** 57″ overall.
Stock: Composition with Sorbothane recoil pad.
Sights: Scope optional.
Features: Semi-automatic, recoil operated with recoiling barrel. Three-lug locking bolt; muzzlebrake. Self-leveling bipod. Fires same 50-cal. ammunition as the M2HB machinegun. Introduced 1985. From Barrett Firearms.
Price: From **$6,800.00**

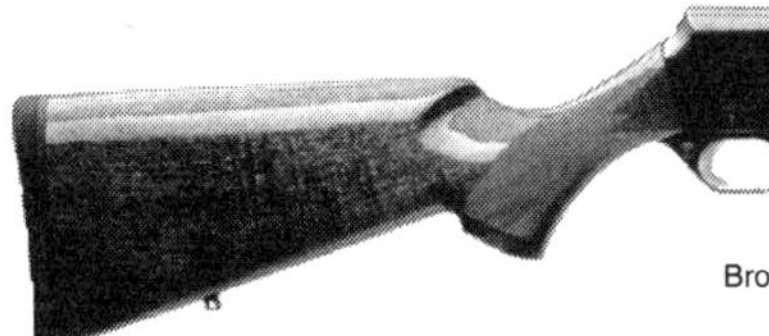

Browning Mark II Safari

BROWNING BAR MARK II SAFARI SEMI-AUTO RIFLE
Caliber: 243, 270, 30-06, 308.
Barrel: 22″ round tapered.
Weight: 7$^{3}/_{8}$ lbs. **Length:** 43″ overall.
Stock: French walnut pistol grip stock and forend, hand checkered.
Sights: Gold bead on hooded ramp front, click adjustable rear, or no sights.
Features: Has new bolt release lever; removable trigger assembly with larger trigger guard; redesigned gas and buffer systems. Detachable 4-round box magazine. Scroll-engraved receiver is tapped for scope mounting. BOSS barrel vibration modulator and muzzlebrake system available only on models without sights. Mark II Safari introduced 1993. Imported from Belgium by Browning.
Price: Safari, with sights **$729.95**
Price: Safari, no sights **$713.95**
Price: Safari, no sights, BOSS **$811.95**

Browning BAR Mark II Safari Magnum Rifle
Same as the standard caliber model, except weighs 8$^{3}/_{8}$ lbs., 45″ overall, 24″ bbl., 3-round mag. Cals. 7mm Mag., 300 Win. Mag., 338 Win. Mag. BOSS barrel vibration modulator and muzzlebrake system available only on models without sights. Introduced 1993.
Price: Safari, with sights **$781.95**
Price: Safari, no sights **$765.95**
Price: Safari, no sights, BOSS **$863.95**

BUSHMASTER SHORTY XM-15 E2S CARBINE
Caliber: 223, 30-shot magazine.
Barrel: 16″, heavy; 1:9″ twist.
Weight: 7.3 lbs. **Length:** 34.5″ overall.
Stock: Fixed black composition.
Sights: Adjustable post front, adjustable aperture rear.
Features: Patterned after Colt M-16A2. Chrome-lined barrel with manganese phosphate finish. "Shorty" handguards. Has E-2 lower receiver with push-pin. Made in U.S. by Bushmaster Firearms Inc./Quality Parts Co.
Price: **$730.00**
Price: XM-15 E-2S Dissipator ("Dissipator" full-length handguard) **$740.00**

BUSHMASTER M17S BULLPUP RIFLE
Caliber: 223, 10-shot magazine.
Barrel: 21.5″, heavy; 1:9″ twist.
Weight: 8.2 lbs. **Length:** 30″ overall.
Stock: Fiberglass-filled nylon.
Sights: Has 25-meter open emergency sights; designed for optics mounted to rail on carrying handle for Weaver-type rings.
Features: Gas-operated, short-stroke piston system; ambidextrous magazine release. Introduced 1993. Made in U.S. by Bushmaster Firearms, Inc./Quality Parts Co.
Price: **$575.00**

Calico Liberty 50

CALICO LIBERTY 50, 100 CARBINES
Caliber: 9mm Para.
Barrel: 16.1″.
Weight: 7 lbs. **Length:** 34.5″ overall.
Stock: Glass-filled, impact resistant polymer,
Sights: Adjustable front post, fixed notch and aperture flip rear.
Features: Helical feed magazine; ambidextrous, rotating sear/striker block safety; static cocking handle; retarded blowback action; aluminum alloy receiver. Introduced 1995. Made in U.S. by Calico.
Price: Liberty 50 . . . . **$503.00**
Price: Liberty 100 . . . . **$517.00**

Century FAL Sporter

CENTURY INTERNATIONAL FAL SPORTER RIFLE
Caliber: 308 Win.
Barrel: 20.75″.
Weight: 9 lbs., 13 oz. **Length:** 41.125″ overall.
Stock: Bell & Carlson thumbhole sporter.
Sights: Protected post front, adjustable aperture rear.
Features: Matte blue finish; rubber butt pad. From Century International Arms.
Price: About **$625.00**

CENTURY INTERNATIONAL M-14 SEMI-AUTO RIFLE
Caliber: 308 Win., 10-shot magazine.
Barrel: 22″.
Weight: 8.25 lbs. **Length:** 40.8″ overall.
Stock: Walnut with rubber recoil pad.
Sights: Protected blade front, fully adjustable aperture rear.
Features: Gas-operated; forged receiver; Parkerized finish. Imported from China by Century International Arms.
Price: About **$468.95**

CENTURY TIGER DRAGUNOV RIFLE
Caliber: 7.62x54R, 5-shot magazine.
Barrel: 20.8″.
Weight: 8.5 lbs. **Length:** 42.9″ overall.
Stock: Thumbhole design of laminated European hardwood, black composition forend.
Sights: Blade front, open rear adjustable for elevation; comes with 4x rangefinding scope with sunshade, lighted reticle.
Features: Shortened version of Russian SVD sniper rifle. New manufacture. Blued metal. Quick-detachable scope mount. Comes with sling, cleaning kit, gas regulator tool, case. Imported from Russia by Century International Arms.
Price: About **$1,350.00**

Colt Match Target Lightweight

COLT MATCH TARGET LIGHTWEIGHT RIFLE
Caliber: 9mm Para., 223 Rem., 7.62x39mm, 5-shot magazine.
Barrel: 16″.
Weight: 6.7 lbs. (223); 7.1 lbs. (9mm Para.). **Length:** 34.5″ overall.
Stock: Composition stock, grip, forend.
Sights: Post front, rear adjustable for windage and elevation.
Features: 5-round detachable box magazine, flash suppressor, sling swivels. Forward bolt assist included. Introduced 1991.
Price: **$987.00**
Price: 7.62x39mm **$987.00**

Daewoo DR200

DAEWOO DR200 DR300 AUTOLOADING RIFLES
Caliber: 223 Rem., 7.62x39mm, 6-shot magazine.
Barrel: 18.3″.
Weight: 9 lbs. **Length:** 39.2″ overall.
Stock: Synthetic thumbhole style with rubber buttpad.
Sights: Post front in ring, aperture rear adjustable for windage and elevation.
Features: Forged aluminum receiver; bolt, bolt carrier, firing pin, piston and recoil spring contained in one assembly. Rotating bolt locking. Uses all AR-15 magazines. Introduced 1995. Imported from Korea by Kimber of America, Inc.
Price: DR200, 223 Rem. **$535.00**
Price: DR300, 7.62x39mm **$750.00**

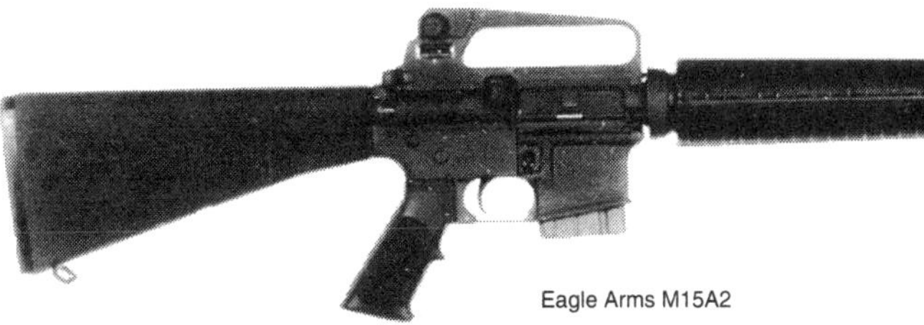
Eagle Arms M15A2

Eagle Arms M4C Carbine
Collapsible carbine-type buttstock, 16″ heavy carbine barrel. Has M15A2-style upper receiver; full front sight housing; M177-type flash supressor. Weighs about 7 lbs., 3 oz. Introduced 1989. Made in U.S. by Eagle Arms, Inc.
Price: **$1,100.00**
Price: M4A1C (as above except one-piece international-style upper receiver for scope mounting) **$1,100.00**

EAGLE ARMS M15A2 POST-BAN HEAVY BARREL RIFLE
Caliber: 223 Rem., 10-shot magazine.
Barrel: 20″, premium, heavy; 1:9″ twist.
Weight: 8 lbs., 2 oz. **Length:** 38 3/8″ overall.
Stock: Black composition; weighted.
Sights: Elevation-adjustable front, E-2-style NM rear with 1/2-MOA adjustments, NM aperture.
Features: Upper and lower receivers have push-type pivot pin for easy takedown. Receivers hard coat anodized. A2-style forward assist mechanism. Integral raised M-16A2-type fence around magazine release button. Introduced 1995. Made in U.S. by Eagle Arms, Inc.
Price: **$895.00**

Hi-Point 9mm Carbine

HI-POINT 9mm CARBINE
Caliber: 9mm Para., 10-shot magazine.
Barrel: 16 1/2″.
Weight: NA. **Length:** 31 1/2″ overall.
Stock: Black polymer.
Sights: Protected post front, aperture rear. Integral scope mount.
Features: Grip-mounted magazine release. Parkerized or chrome finish. Sling swivels. Introduced 1996. Made in U.S. by MKS Supply, Inc.
Price: **$169.00**

IBUS M17S Bullpup

IBUS M17S 223 BULLPUP RIFLE

Caliber: 223, 10-shot magazine.
Barrel: 21.5″.
Weight: 8.2 lbs. **Length:** 30″ overall.
Stock: Zytel glass-filled nylon.
Sights: None furnished. Comes with scope mount for Weaver-type rings.
Features: Gas-operated, short-stroke piston system. Ambidextrous magazine release. Introduced 1993. Made in U.S. by Bushmaster Firearms Inc./Quality Parts Co.
Price: **$975.00**

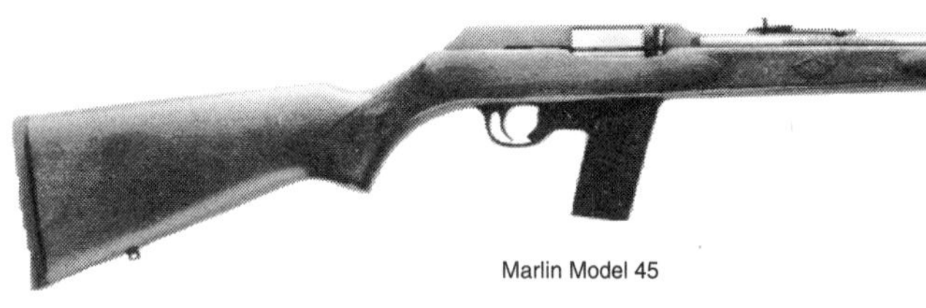
Marlin Model 45

Marlin Model 45 Carbine

Similar to the Model 9 except chambered for 45 ACP, 7-shot magazine. Introduced 1986.
Price: **$424.40**

MARLIN MODEL 9 CAMP CARBINE

Caliber: 9mm Para., 12-shot magazine.
Barrel: 16½″, Micro-Groove® rifling.
Weight: 6¾ lbs. **Length:** 35½″ overall.
Stock: Press-checkered walnut-finished Maine birch; rubber buttpad; Mar-Shield™ finish; swivel studs.
Sights: Ramp front with orange post, cutaway Wide-Scan™ hood, adjustable open rear.
Features: Manual bolt hold-open; Garand-type safety, magazine safety; loaded chamber indicator; receiver drilled, tapped for scope mounting. Introduced 1985.
Price: **$424.40**

Mitchell Arms LW9

MITCHELL ARMS LW9 SEMI-AUTO CARBINE

Caliber: 9mm Para., 10-shot magazine.
Barrel: 17″.
Weight: 5 lbs. **Length:** 35″ overall.
Stock: Black foam or fixed skeleton.
Sights: Protected post front, adjustable aperture rear.
Features: Blue finish; removable stock and barrel. Introduced 1996. Made in U.S. by Mitchell Arms.
Price: Skeleton stock **$499.95**
Price: Black foam stock **$534.95**

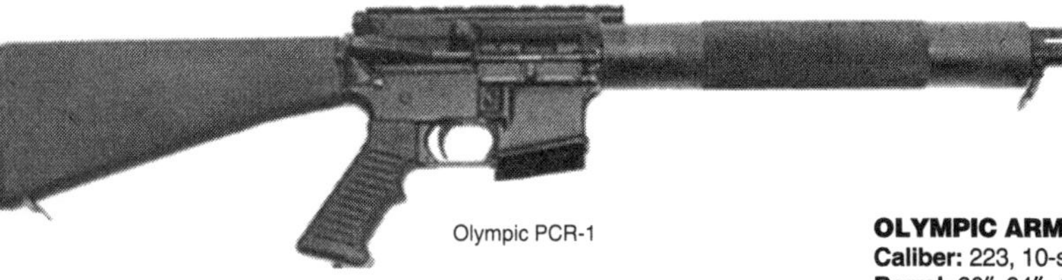
Olympic PCR-1

Olympic Arms PCR-2, PCR-3 Rifles

Similar to the PCR-1 except has 16″ barrel, weighs 8 lbs., 2 oz.; has post front sight, fully adjustable aperture rear. Model PCR-3 has flattop upper receiver, cut-down front sight base. Introduced 1994. Made in U.S. by Olympic Arms, Inc.
Price: **$1,025.00**

OLYMPIC ARMS PCR-1 RIFLE

Caliber: 223, 10-shot magazine.
Barrel: 20″, 24″; 416 stainless steel.
Weight: 10 lbs., 3 oz. **Length:** 38.25″ overall with 20″ barrel.
Stock: A2 stowaway grip and trapdoor butt.
Sights: None supplied; flattop upper receiver, cut-down front sight base.
Features: Based on the AR-15 rifle. Broach-cut, free-floating barrel with 1:8.5″ or 1:10″ twist. No bayonet lug. Crowned barrel; fluting available. Introduced 1994. Made in U.S. by Olympic Arms, Inc.
Price: **$1,100.00**

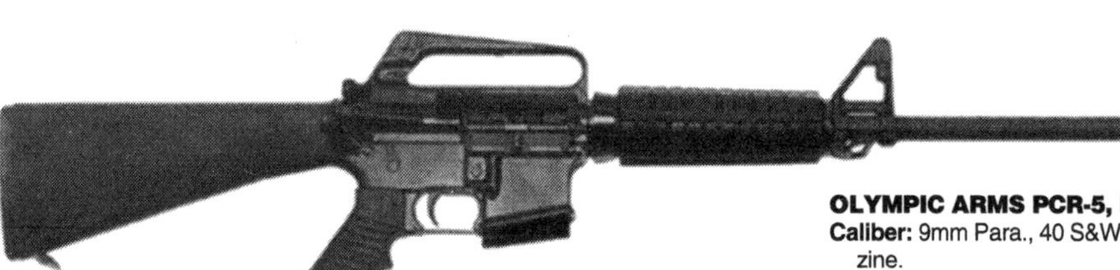
Olympic PCR-5

OLYMPIC ARMS PCR-4 RIFLE

Caliber: 223, 10-shot magazine.
Barrel: 20″.
Weight: 8 lbs., 5 oz. **Length:** 38.25″ overall.
Stock: A2 stowaway grip, trapdoor buttstock.
Sights: Post front, A1 rear adjustable for windage.
Features: Based on the AR-15 rifle. Barrel is button rifled with 1:9″ twist. No bayonet lug. Introduced 1994. Made in U.S. by Olympic Arms, Inc.
Price: **$810.00**

OLYMPIC ARMS PCR-5, PCR-6 RIFLES

Caliber: 9mm Para., 40 S&W, 45 ACP, 223, 7.62x39mm (PCR-6), 10-shot magazine.
Barrel: 16″.
Weight: 7 lbs. **Length:** 34.75″ overall.
Stock: A2 stowaway grip, trapdoor buttstock.
Sights: Post front, A1 rear adjustable for windage.
Features: Based on the CAR-15. No bayonet lug. Button-cut rifling. Introduced 1994. Made in U.S. by Olympic Arms, Inc.
Price: 9mm Para., 40 S&W, 45 ACP **$820.00**
Price: 223 Rem. **$775.00**
Price: 7.62x39mm (PCR-6) **$835.00**

 CAUTION: PRICES SHOWN ARE SUPPLIED BY THE MANUFACTURER OR IMPORTER. CHECK YOUR LOCAL GUN SHOP.

Remington Model 7400

REMINGTON MODEL 7400 AUTO RIFLE
Caliber: 243 Win., 270 Win., 280 Rem., 308 Win., 30-06, 4-shot magazine.
Barrel: 22″ round tapered.
Weight: 7$^{1}/_{2}$ lbs. **Length:** 42″ overall.
Stock: Walnut, deluxe cut checkered pistol grip and forend. Satin or high-gloss finish.
Sights: Gold bead front sight on ramp; step rear sight with windage adjustable.
Features: Redesigned and improved version of the Model 742. Positive cross-bolt safety. Receiver tapped for scope mount. Comes with green Remington hard case. Introduced 1981.
Price: About **$573.00**
Price: Carbine (18$^{1}/_{2}$″ bbl., 30-06 only) **$573.00**

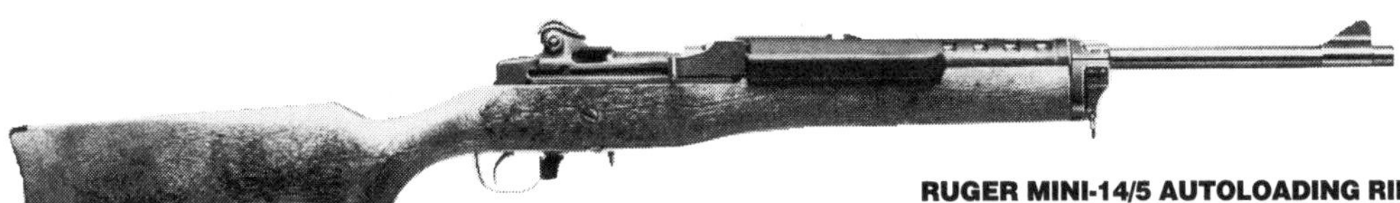

Ruger Mini-14/5

RUGER MINI-14/5 AUTOLOADING RIFLE
Caliber: 223 Rem., 5-shot detachable box magazine.
Barrel: 18$^{1}/_{2}$″. Rifling twist 1:9″.
Weight: 6.4 lbs. **Length:** 37$^{1}/_{4}$″ overall.
Stock: American hardwood, steel reinforced.
Sights: Ramp front, fully adjustable rear.
Features: Fixed piston gas-operated, positive primary extraction. New buffer system, redesigned ejector system. Ruger S100RH scope rings included. 20-, 30-shot magazine available to police departments and government agencies only.
Price: Mini-14/5R, Ranch Rifle, blued, scope rings **$556.00**
Price: K-Mini-14/5R, Ranch Rifle, stainless, scope rings **$609.00**
Price: Mini-14/5, blued, no scope rings **$516.00**
Price: K-Mini-14/5, stainless, no scope rings **$569.00**

Ruger Mini Thirty Rifle
Similar to the Mini-14 Ranch Rifle except modified to chamber the 7.62x39 Russian service round. Weight is about 7 lbs., 3 oz. Has 6-groove barrel with 1:10″ twist, Ruger Integral Scope Mount bases and folding peep rear sight. Detachable 5-shot staggered box magazine. Blued finish. Introduced 1987.
Price: Blue **$556.00**
Price: Stainless **$609.00**

Springfield M1A

SPRINGFIELD, INC. M1A RIFLE
Caliber: 7.62mm NATO (308), 5-, 10- or 20-shot box magazine.
Barrel: 25$^{1}/_{16}$″ with flash suppressor, 22″ without suppressor.
Weight: 8$^{3}/_{4}$ lbs. **Length:** 44$^{1}/_{4}$″ overall.
Stock: American walnut with walnut-colored heat-resistant fiberglass handguard. Matching walnut handguard available. Also available with fiberglass stock.
Sights: Military, square blade front, full click-adjustable aperture rear.
Features: Commercial equivalent of the U.S. M-14 service rifle with no provision for automatic firing. From Springfield, Inc.
Price: Standard M1A rifle, about **$1,329.00**
Price: National Match, about **$1,670.00**
Price: Super Match (heavy premium barrel), about **$1,980.00**
Price: M1A-A1 Bush Rifle, walnut stock, about **$1,359.00**

SA-85M SEMI-AUTO RIFLE
Caliber: 7.62x39mm, 6-shot magazine.
Barrel: 16.3″.
Weight: 7.6 lbs. **Length:** 34.7″ overall.
Stock: European hardwood; thumbhole design.
Sights: Post front, Ipen adjustable rear.
Features: BATF-approved version of the Kalashnikov rifle. Gas operated. Black phosphate finish. Comes with one magazine, cleaning rod, cleaning/tool kit. Introduced 1995. Imported from Hungary by K.B.I., Inc.
Price: **$399.00**

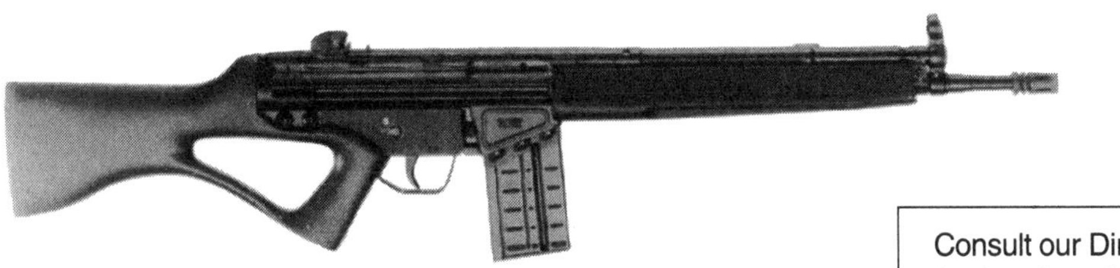

Springfield SAR-8

Consult our Directory pages for the location of firms mentioned.

SPRINGFIELD, INC. SAR-8 SPORTER RIFLE
Caliber: 308 Win., 20-shot magazine.
Barrel: 18″.
Weight: 8.7 lbs. **Length:** 40.3″ overall.
Stock: Black composition, thumbhole buttstock.
Sights: Protected post front, rotary-style adjustable rear.
Features: Delayed roller-lock action; fluted chamber; matte black finish. Reintroduced 1995. From Springfield, Inc.
Price: **$1,175.00**

SPRINGFIELD, INC. SAR-4800 RIFLE
Caliber: 5.56, 7.62 NATO (308 Win.), 20-shot magazine.
Barrel: 21″.
Weight: 9.5 lbs. **Length:** 43.3″ overall.
Stock: Fiberglass forend, composite thunbhole butt.
Sights: Protected post front, adjustable peep rear.
Features: New production. Reintroduced 1995. From Springfield, Inc.
Price: **$1,199.00**

Stoner Sr-25 Sporter

STONER SR-25 SPORTER RIFLE
Caliber: 7.62 NATO, 10-shot steel magazine, 5-shot optional.
Barrel: 20″.
Weight: 8.75 lbs. **Length:** 40″ overall.
Stock: Black synthetic AR-15A2 design, AR-15A2-type synthetic round forend.
Sights: AR-15A2-style front adjustable for elevation, detachable rear is adjustable for windage.
Features: AR-15 trigger; AR-15-style seven-lug rotating bolt. Upper and lower receivers made of lightweight aircraft aluminum alloy. Quick-detachable carrying handle/rear sight assembly. Two-stage target trigger, shell deflector, bore guide, scope rings optional. Introduced 1993. Made in U.S. by Knight's Mfg. Co.
Price: $2,995.00

Stoner SR-25 Carbine
Similar to the SR-25 Sporter except has 16″ light/hunting contour barrel, weighs 7.75 lbs., 36″ overall. No sights furnished; has integral Weaver-style rail. Scope rings, iron sights optional. Introduced 1995. Made in U.S. by Knight's Mfg. Co.
Price: $2,995.00

WILKINSON TERRY CARBINE
Caliber: 9mm Para., 31-shot magazine.
Barrel: 16 3/16″.
Weight: 6 lbs., 3 oz. **Length:** 30″ overall.
Stock: Maple stock and forend.
Sights: Protected post front, aperture rear.
Features: Semi-automatic blowback action fires from a closed breech. Bolt-type safety and magazine catch. Ejection port has automatic trap door. Receiver equipped with dovetail for scope mounting. Made in U.S. From Wilkinson Arms.
Price: $636.29

CENTERFIRE RIFLES—LEVER & SLIDE

Both classic arms and recent designs in American-style repeaters for sport and field shooting.

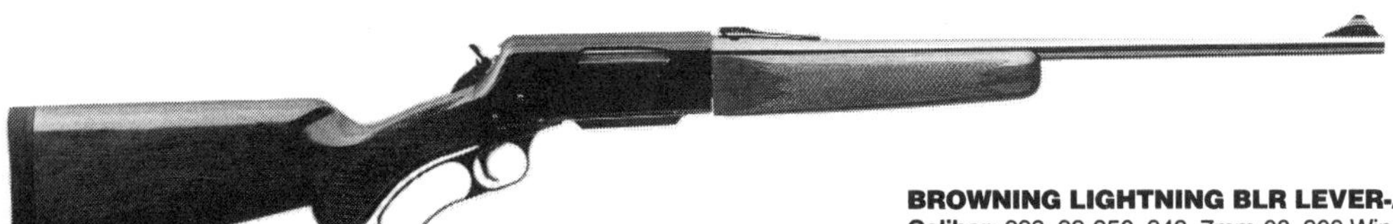
Browning Lightning BLR

Browning Lightning BLR Long Action
Similar to the standard Lightning BLR except has long action to accept 30-06, 270 and 7mm Rem. Mag. Barrel lengths are 22″ for 30-06 and 270, 24″ for 7mm Rem. Mag. Has six-lug rotary bolt; bolt and receiver are full-length fluted. Fold-down hammer at half-cock. Weighs about 7 lbs., overall length 42 7/8″ (22″ barrel). Introduced 1996.
Price: $608.95

CABELA'S CATTLEMAN'S CARBINE
Caliber: 44-40, 6-shot.
Barrel: 18″.
Weight: 4 lbs. **Length:** 34″ overall.
Stock: European walnut.
Sights: Blade front, notch rear.
Features: Revolving carbine. Color case-hardened frame, rest blued. Introduced 1994. Imported by Cabela's.
Price: $299.95

CABELA'S 1858 HENRY REPLICA
Caliber: 44-40, 13-shot magazine.
Barrel: 24 1/4″.
Weight: 9.5 lbs. **Length:** 43″ overall.
Stock: European walnut.
Sights: Bead front, open adjustable rear.
Features: Brass receiver and buttplate. Uses original Henry loading system. Faithful to the original rifle. Introduced 1994. Imported by Mitchell Arms, Inc.
Price: $649.95

CIMARRON 1860 HENRY REPLICA
Caliber: 44 WCF, 13-shot magazine.
Barrel: 24 1/4″ (rifle), 22″ (carbine).
Weight: 9 1/2 lbs. **Length:** 43″ overall (rifle).
Stock: European walnut.
Sights: Bead front, open adjustable rear.
Features: Brass receiver and buttplate. Uses original Henry loading system. Faithful to the original rifle. Introduced 1991. Imported by Cimarron Arms.
Price: $899.95

BROWNING LIGHTNING BLR LEVER-ACTION RIFLE
Caliber: 223, 22-250, 243, 7mm-08, 308 Win., 4-shot detachable magazine.
Barrel: 20″ round tapered.
Weight: 6 lbs., 8 oz. **Length:** 39 1/2″ overall.
Stock: Walnut. Checkered grip and forend, high-gloss finish.
Sights: Gold bead on ramp front; low profile square notch adjustable rear.
Features: Wide, grooved trigger; half-cock hammer safety; fold-down hammer. Receiver tapped for scope mount. Recoil pad installed. Introduced 1996. Imported from Japan by Browning.
Price: $576.95

CABELA'S 1866 WINCHESTER REPLICA
Caliber: 44-40, 13-shot.
Barrel: 24 1/4″.
Weight: 9 lbs. **Length:** 43″ overall.
Stock: European walnut.
Sights: Bead front, open adjustable rear.
Features: Solid brass receiver, buttplate, forend cap. Octagonal barrel. Faithful to the original Winchester `66 rifle. Introduced 1994. Imported by Cabela's.
Price: $499.95

Consult our Directory pages for the location of firms mentioned.

CABELA'S 1873 WINCHESTER REPLICA
Caliber: 44-40, 45 Colt, 13-shot.
Barrel: 24 1/4″, 30″.
Weight: 8.5 lbs. **Length:** 43 1/4″ overall.
Stock: European walnut.
Sights: Bead front, open adjustable rear; globe front, tang rear.
Features: Color case-hardened steel receiver. Faithful to the original Model 1873 rifle. Introduced 1994. Imported by Cabela's.
Price: With tang sight, globe front $639.95
Price: Sporting model, 30″ barrel, 44-40, 45 Colt $599.95
Price: With half-round/half-octagon barrel, half magazine $639.95

CAUTION: PRICES SHOWN ARE SUPPLIED BY THE MANUFACTURER OR IMPORTER. CHECK YOUR LOCAL GUN SHOP.

CIMARRON 1866 WINCHESTER REPLICAS
Caliber: 22 LR, 22 WMR, 38 Spec., 44 WCF.
Barrel: 24¼″ (rifle), 19″ (carbine).
Weight: 9 lbs. **Length:** 43″ overall (rifle).
Stock: European walnut.
Sights: Bead front, open adjustable rear.
Features: Solid brass receiver, buttplate, forend cap. Octagonal barrel. Faithful to the original Winchester '66 rifle. Introduced 1991. Imported by Cimarron Arms.
Price: Rifle **$689.95**
Price: Carbine **$679.95**

CIMARRON 1873 SHORT RIFLE
Caliber: 22 LR, 22 WMR, 357 Mag., 44-40, 45 Colt.
Barrel: 20″ tapered octagon.
Weight: 7.5 lbs. **Length:** 39″ overall.
Stock: Walnut.
Sights: Bead front, adjustable semi-buckhorn rear.
Features: Has half "button" magazine. Original-type markings, including caliber, on barrel and elevator and "Kings" patent. From Cimarron Arms.
Price: **$899.95**

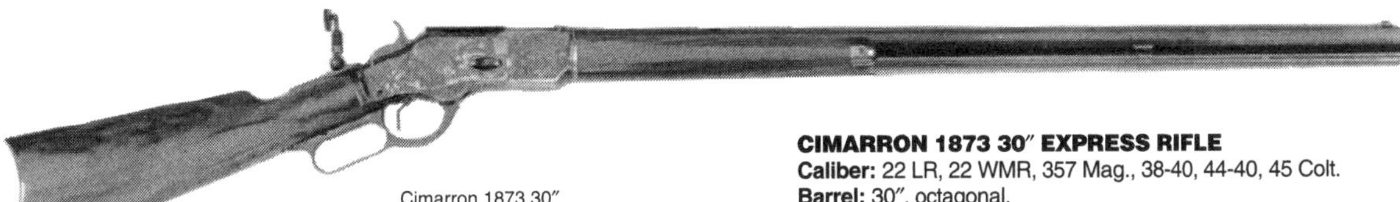

Cimarron 1873 30″

Cimarron 1873 Sporting Rifle
Similar to the 1873 Express except has 24″ barrel with half-magazine.
Price: **$899.95**
Price: 1873 Saddle Ring Carbine, 19″ barrel **$899.95**

CIMARRON 1873 30″ EXPRESS RIFLE
Caliber: 22 LR, 22 WMR, 357 Mag., 38-40, 44-40, 45 Colt.
Barrel: 30″, octagonal.
Weight: 8½ lbs. **Length:** 48″ overall.
Stock: Walnut.
Sights: Blade front, semi-buckhorn ramp rear. Tang sight optional.
Features: Color case-hardened frame; choice of modern blue-black or charcoal blue for other parts. Barrel marked "Kings Improvement." From Cimarron Arms.
Price: **$949.95**

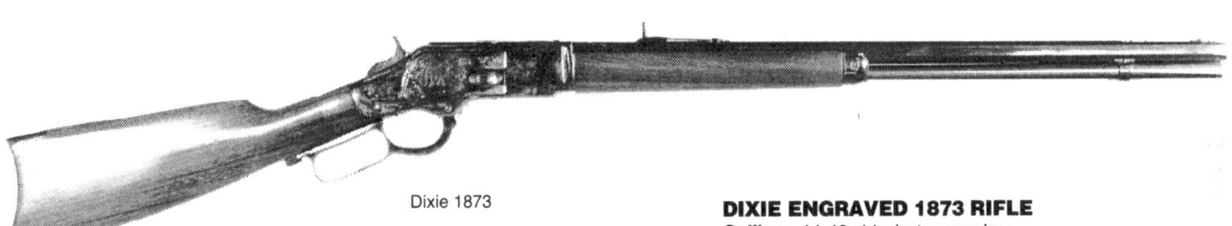

Dixie 1873

E.M.F. 1860 HENRY RIFLE
Caliber: 44-40 or 44 rimfire.
Barrel: 24.25″.
Weight: About 9 lbs. **Length:** About 43.75″ overall.
Stock: Oil-stained American walnut.
Sights: Blade front, rear adjustable for elevation.
Features: Reproduction of the original Henry rifle with brass frame and buttplate, rest blued. From E.M.F.
Price: Standard **$1,100.00**

E.M.F. MODEL 73 LEVER-ACTION RIFLE
Caliber: 357 Mag., 44-40, 45 Colt.
Barrel: 24″.
Weight: 8 lbs. **Length:** 43¼″ overall.
Stock: European walnut.
Sights: Bead front, rear adjustable for windage and elevation.
Features: Color case-hardened frame (blue on carbine). Imported by E.M.F.
Price: Rifle **$1,050.00**
Price: Carbine, 19″ barrel **$1,020.00**

DIXIE ENGRAVED 1873 RIFLE
Caliber: 44-40, 11-shot magazine.
Barrel: 20″, round.
Weight: 7¾ lbs. **Length:** 39″ overall.
Stock: Walnut.
Sights: Blade front, adjustable rear.
Features: Engraved and case-hardened frame. Duplicate of Winchester 1873. Made in Italy. From Dixie Gun Works.
Price: **$1,250.00**
Price: Plain, blued carbine **$895.00**

E.M.F. 1866 YELLOWBOY LEVER ACTIONS
Caliber: 38 Spec., 44-40.
Barrel: 19″ (carbine), 24″ (rifle).
Weight: 9 lbs. **Length:** 43″ overall (rifle).
Stock: European walnut.
Sights: Bead front, open adjustable rear.
Features: Solid brass frame, blued barrel, lever, hammer, buttplate. Imported from Italy by E.M.F.
Price: Rifle **$848.00**
Price: Carbine **$825.00**

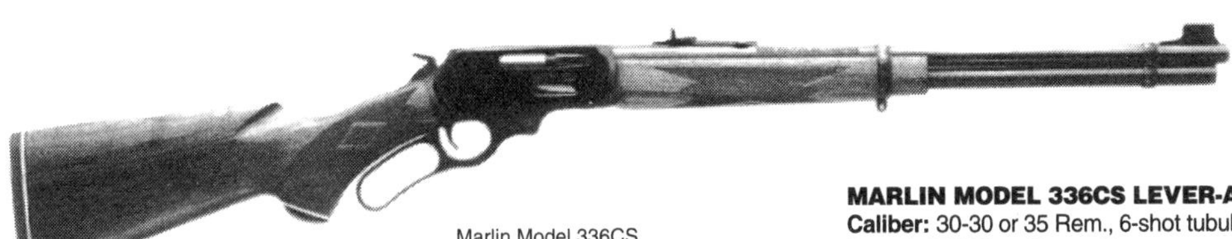

Marlin Model 336CS

Marlin Model 30AS Lever-Action Carbine
Same as the Marlin 336CS except has press-checkered, walnut-finished Maine birch pistol grip stock, 30-30 only, 6-shot. Hammer-block safety. Adjustable rear sight, brass bead front.
Price: **$377.60**

MARLIN MODEL 336CS LEVER-ACTION CARBINE
Caliber: 30-30 or 35 Rem., 6-shot tubular magazine.
Barrel: 20″ Micro-Groove®.
Weight: 7 lbs. **Length:** 38½″ overall.
Stock: Checkered American black walnut, capped pistol grip with white line spacers. Mar-Shield® finish; rubber buttpad; swivel studs.
Sights: Ramp front with Wide-Scan™ hood, semi-buckhorn folding rear adjustable for windage and elevation.
Features: Hammer-block safety. Receiver tapped for scope mount, offset hammer spur; top of receiver sand blasted to prevent glare.
Price: **$443.50**

MARLIN MODEL 444SS LEVER-ACTION SPORTER
Caliber: 444 Marlin, 5-shot tubular magazine.
Barrel: 22″ Micro-Groove®.
Weight: 7½ lbs. **Length:** 40½″ overall.
Stock: Checkered American black walnut, capped pistol grip with white line spacers, rubber rifle buttpad. Mar-Shield® finish; swivel studs.
Sights: Hooded ramp front, folding semi-buckhorn rear adjustable for windage and elevation.
Features: Hammer-block safety. Receiver tapped for scope mount; offset hammer spur.
Price: **$522.60**

Marlin 1894 Cowboy

MARLIN MODEL 1894S LEVER-ACTION CARBINE
Caliber: 44 Spec./44 Mag., 10-shot tubular magazine.
Barrel: 20″ Micro-Groove®.
Weight: 6 lbs. **Length:** 37½″ overall.
Stock: Checkered American black walnut, straight grip and forend. Mar-Shield® finish. Rubber rifle buttpad; swivel studs.
Sights: Wide-Scan™ hooded ramp front, semi-buckhorn folding rear adjustable for windage and elevation.
Features: Hammer-block safety. Receiver tapped for scope mount, offset hammer spur, solid top receiver sand blasted to prevent glare.
Price: $459.35

MARLIN MODEL 1894 COWBOY
Caliber: 45 Colt, 10-shot magazine.
Barrel: 24″ tapered octagon, deep cut rifling.
Weight: 7½ lbs. **Length:** 41½″ overall.
Stock: Straight grip American black walnut with cut checkering, hard rubber buttplate, Mar-Shield® finish.
Sights: Marble carbine front, adjustable Marble semi-buckhorn rear.
Features: Squared finger lever; straight grip stock; blued steel forend tip. Designed for Cowboy Shooting events. Introduced 1996. Made in U.S. by Marlin.
Price: $668.00

MARLIN MODEL 1895SS LEVER-ACTION RIFLE
Caliber: 45-70, 4-shot tubular magazine.
Barrel: 22″ round.
Weight: 7½ lbs. **Length:** 40½″ overall.
Stock: Checkered American black walnut, full pistol grip. Mar-Shield® finish; rubber buttpad; quick detachable swivel studs.
Sights: Bead front with Wide-Scan™ hood, semi-buckhorn folding rear adjustable for windage and elevation.
Features: Hammer-block safety. Solid receiver tapped for scope mounts or receiver sights; offset hammer spur.
Price: $522.60

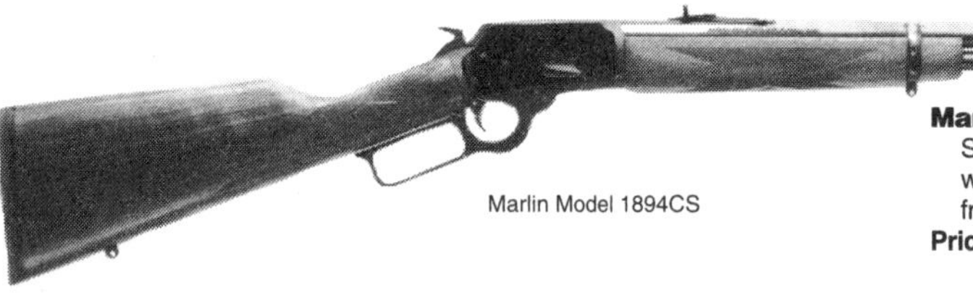
Marlin Model 1894CS

Marlin Model 1894CS Carbine
Similar to the standard Model 1894S except chambered for 38 Spec./357 Mag. with full-length 9-shot magazine, 18½″ barrel, hammer-block safety, brass bead front sight. Introduced 1983.
Price: $459.35

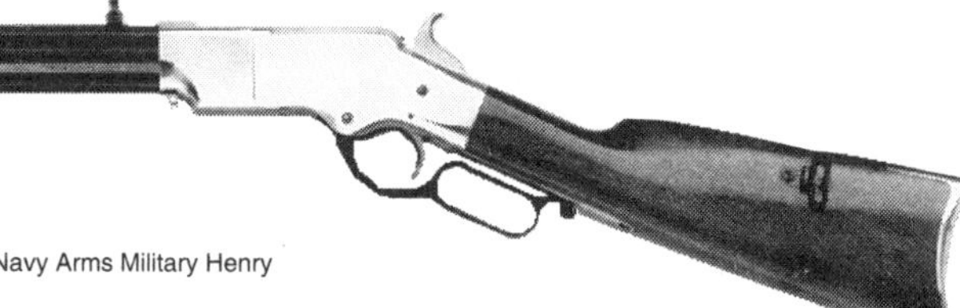
Navy Arms Military Henry

NAVY ARMS MILITARY HENRY RIFLE
Caliber: 44-40, 12-shot magazine.
Barrel: 24¼″.
Weight: 9 lbs., 4 oz.
Stock: European walnut.
Sights: Blade front, adjustable ladder-type rear.
Features: Brass frame, buttplate, rest blued. Recreation of the model used by cavalry units in the Civil War. Has full-length magazine tube, sling swivels; no forend. Imported from Italy by Navy Arms.
Price: $895.00

Navy Arms Henry Trapper
Similar to the Military Henry Rifle except has 16½″ barrel, weighs 7½ lbs. Brass frame and buttplate, rest blued. Introduced 1991. Imported from Italy by Navy Arms.
Price: $875.00

Navy Arms Henry Carbine
Similar to the Military Henry rifle except has 22″ barrel, weighs 8 lbs., 12 oz., is 41″ overall; no sling swivels. Caliber 44-40. Introduced 1992. Imported from Italy by Navy Arms.
Price: $875.00

Navy Arms Iron Frame Henry
Similar to the Military Henry Rifle except receiver is blued or color case-hardened steel. Imported by Navy Arms.
Price: $945.00

NAVY ARMS 1866 YELLOWBOY RIFLE
Caliber: 44-40, 12-shot magazine.
Barrel: 24″, full octagon.
Weight: 8½ lbs. **Length:** 42½″ overall.
Stock: European walnut.
Sights: Blade front, adjustable ladder-type rear.
Features: Brass frame, forend tip, buttplate, blued barrel, lever, hammer. Introduced 1991. Imported from Italy by Navy Arms.
Price: $680.00
Price: Carbine, 19″ barrel $670.00

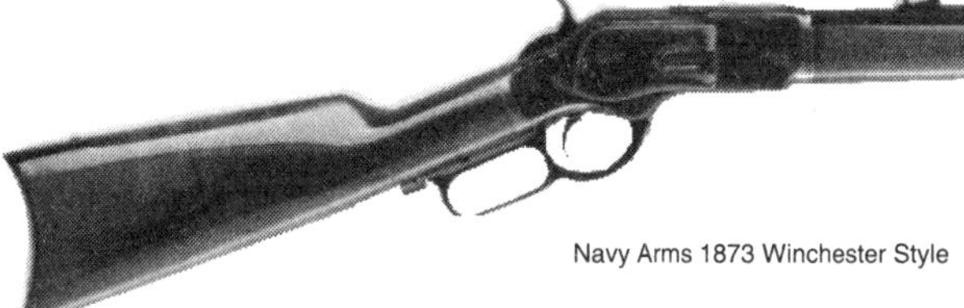
Navy Arms 1873 Winchester Style

Navy Arms 1873 Sporting Rifle
Similar to the 1873 Winchester-Style rifle except has checkered pistol grip stock, 30″ octagonal barrel (24″ available). Introduced 1992. Imported by Navy Arms.
Price: 30″ barrel $960.00
Price: 24″ barrel $930.00

NAVY ARMS 1873 WINCHESTER-STYLE RIFLE
Caliber: 44-40, 45 Colt, 12-shot magazine.
Barrel: 24″.
Weight: 8¼ lbs. **Length:** 43″ overall.
Stock: European walnut.
Sights: Blade front, buckhorn rear.
Features: Color case-hardened frame, rest blued. Full-octagon barrel. Imported by Navy Arms.
Price: $820.00
Price: Carbine, 19″ barrel $800.00

CAUTION: PRICES SHOWN ARE SUPPLIED BY THE MANUFACTURER OR IMPORTER. CHECK YOUR LOCAL GUN SHOP.

Remington 7600 Rifle

REMINGTON 7600 SLIDE ACTION
Caliber: 243, 270, 280, 30-06, 308.
Barrel: 22″ round tapered.
Weight: $7^1/_2$ lbs. **Length:** 42″ overall.
Stock: Cut-checkered walnut pistol grip and forend, Monte Carlo with full cheekpiece. Satin or high-gloss finish.
Sights: Gold bead front sight on matted ramp, open step adjustable sporting rear.
Features: Redesigned and improved version of the Model 760. Detachable 4-shot clip. Cross-bolt safety. Receiver tapped for scope mount. Also available in high grade versions. Comes with green Remington hard case. Introduced 1981.
Price: About **$540.00**
Price: Carbine ($18^1/_2$″ bbl., 30-06 only) **$540.00**

Rossi Model 92

ROSSI MODEL 92 SADDLE-RING CARBINE
Caliber: 38 Spec./357 Mag., 44 Spec./44-40, 44 Mag., 45 Colt, 10-shot magazine.
Barrel: 20″.
Weight: $5^3/_4$ lbs. **Length:** 37″ overall.
Stock: Walnut.
Sights: Blade front, buckhorn rear.
Features: Recreation of the famous lever-action carbine. Handles 38 and 357 interchangeably. Introduced 1978. Imported by Interarms.
Price: **$360.00**
Price: 44 Spec./44 Mag. (Model 65) **$360.00**

Rossi Model 92 Short Carbine
Similar to the standard M92 except has 16″ barrel, overall length of 33″, in 38 Spec./357 Mag. only. Introduced 1986.
Price: **$360.00**

Ruger Model 96/44

RUGER MODEL 96/44 LEVER-ACTION RIFLE
Caliber: 44 Mag., 4-shot rotary magazine.
Barrel: $18^1/_2$″.
Weight: $5^7/_8$ lbs. **Length:** $37^5/_{16}$″ overall.
Stock: American hardwood.
Sights: Gold bead front, folding leaf rear.
Features: Manual cross-bolt safety, visible cocking indicator; short-throw lever action; integral scope mount; blued finish. Introduced 1996. Made In U.S. by Sturm, Ruger & Co.
Price: **$365.00**

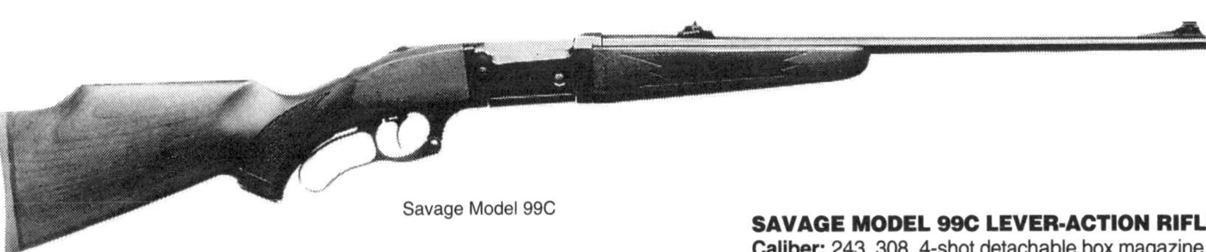

Savage Model 99C

SAVAGE MODEL 99C LEVER-ACTION RIFLE
Caliber: 243, 308, 4-shot detachable box magazine.
Barrel: 22″.
Weight: $7^3/_4$ lbs. **Length:** $45^1/_2$″ overall.
Stock: American walnut; Monte Carlo comb; cut-checkered grip and forend.
Sights: Bead on blade front, open fully adjsutable rear. Drilled and tapped for scope mounts.
Features: Polished blue finish; solid red buttpad; swivel studs. From Savage Arms. Reintroduced 1996.
Price: **$650.00**

Savage Model 99CE Centennial Edition
Similar to the Model 99C except chambered only for 300 Savage; serially numbered AS0001 through AS1000; gold-plated trigger and tang safety; fully engraved receiver with gold-plated figures; wrap-around forend checkering; nickel-plated swivel studs. Production of 1000 rifles. From Savage Arms. Introduced 1996.
Price: **$1,660.00**

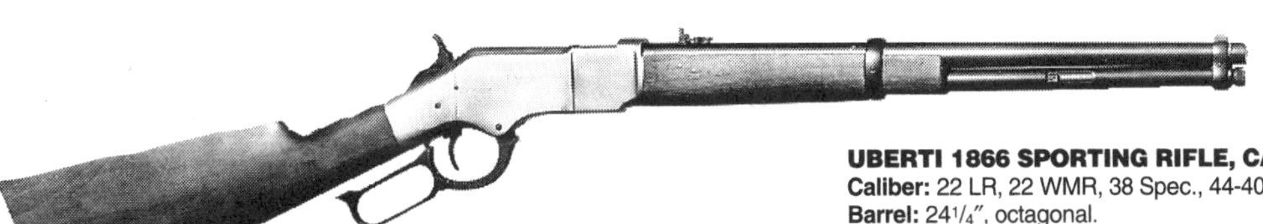

Uberti 1866 Sporting

UBERTI 1866 SPORTING RIFLE, CARBINE
Caliber: 22 LR, 22 WMR, 38 Spec., 44-40, 45 Colt.
Barrel: $24^1/_4$″, octagonal.
Weight: 8.1 lbs. **Length:** $43^1/_4$″ overall.
Stock: Walnut.
Sights: Blade front adjustable for windage, rear adjustable for elevation.
Features: Frame, buttplate, forend cap of polished brass, balance charcoal blued. Imported by Uberti USA Inc.
Price: **$840.00**
Price: Yellowboy Carbine (19″ round bbl.) **$760.00**

UBERTI 1873 SPORTING RIFLE, CARBINE
Caliber: 22 LR, 22 WMR, 38 Spec., 357 Mag., 44-40, 45 Colt.
Barrel: $24\frac{1}{4}$" half-octagon, $24\frac{1}{4}$", 30", octagonal.
Weight: 8.1 lbs. **Length:** $43\frac{1}{4}$" overall.
Stock: Walnut.
Sights: Blade front adjustable for windage, open rear adjustable for elevation.
Features: Color case-hardened frame, blued barrel, hammer, lever, buttplate, brass elevator. Also available with pistol grip stock ($100.00 extra). Imported from Italy by Uberti USA Inc.
Price: **$970.00**
Price: 1873 Carbine (19" round barrel) **$920.00**

UBERTI HENRY RIFLE
Caliber: 44-40, 45 Colt.
Barrel: $18\frac{1}{2}$", $22\frac{1}{4}$", $24\frac{1}{4}$", half-octagon.
Weight: 9.2 lbs. **Length:** $43\frac{3}{4}$" overall.
Stock: American walnut.
Sights: Blade front, rear adjustable for elevation.
Features: Frame, elevator, magazine follower, buttplate are brass, balance blue (also available in polished steel). Imported by Uberti USA Inc.
Price: **$940.00**
Price: Henry Carbine ($22\frac{1}{4}$" bbl.) **$950.00**
Price: Henry Trapper (16", 18" bbl.) **$950.00**

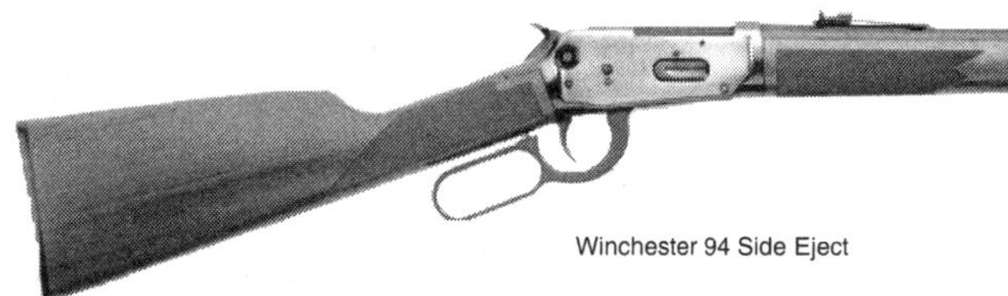
Winchester 94 Side Eject

WINCHESTER MODEL 94 SIDE EJECT LEVER-ACTION RIFLE
Caliber: 30-30 Win., 6-shot tubular magazine.
Barrel: 20".
Weight: $6\frac{1}{2}$ lbs. **Length:** $37\frac{3}{4}$" overall.
Stock: Straight grip walnut stock and forend.
Sights: Hooded blade front, semi-buckhorn rear. Drilled and tapped for scope mount. Post front sight on Trapper model.
Features: Solid frame, forged steel receiver; side ejection, exposed rebounding hammer with automatic trigger-activated transfer bar. Specially inscribed with "1894-1994" on the receiver. Introduced 1984.
Price: Checkered walnut **$393.00**
Price: No checkering, walnut **$363.00**
Price: With WinTuff laminated hardwood stock, 30-30 only **$404.00**

Winchester Model 94 Ranger Side Eject Lever-Action Rifle
Same as Model 94 Side Eject except has 5-shot magazine, American hardwood stock and forend, post front sight. Specially inscribed with "1894-1994" on the receiver. Introduced 1985.
Price: **$320.00**
Price: With 4x32 Bushnell scope, mounts **$376.00**

Winchester Model 94 Wrangler Side Eject
Same as the Model 94 except has 16" barrel and large loop lever for large and/or gloved hands. Has 9-shot capacity (5-shot for 30-30), stainless steel claw extractor. Available in 30-30, 44 Magnum/44 Special. Specially inscribed with "1894-1994" on the receiver. Reintroduced 1992.
Price: 30-30 .... **$384.00**
Price: 44 Magnum/44 Special **$404.00**

Winchester Model 94 Trapper Side Eject
Same as the Model 94 except has 16" barrel, 5-shot magazine in 30-30, 9-shot in 357 Mag., 44 Magnum/44 Special, 45 Colt. Has stainless steel claw extractor, saddle ring, hammer spur extension, walnut wood. Specially inscribed with "1894-1994" on the receiver.
Price: 30-30 .... **$363.00**
Price: 357 Mag., 44 Mag./44 Spec., 45 Colt **$384.00**

Winchester 94 Legacy

Winchester Model 94 Legacy
Similar to the Model 94 Side Eject except has half pistol grip walnut stock, checkered grip and forend. Chambered only for 30-30. Introduced 1995. Made in U.S. by U.S. Repeating Arms Co., Inc.
Price: **$393.00**

WINCHESTER MODEL 94 BIG BORE SIDE EJECT
Caliber: 307 Win., 356 Win., 6-shot magazine.
Barrel: 20".
Weight: 7 lbs. **Length:** $38\frac{5}{8}$" overall.
Stock: American walnut. Satin finish.
Sights: Hooded ramp front, semi-buckhorn rear adjustable for windage and elevation.
Features: All external metal parts have Winchester's deep blue finish. Rifling twist 1:12". Rubber recoil pad fitted to buttstock. Specially inscribed with "1894-1994" on the receiver. Introduced 1983. From U.S. Repeating Arms Co., Inc.
Price: **$404.00**

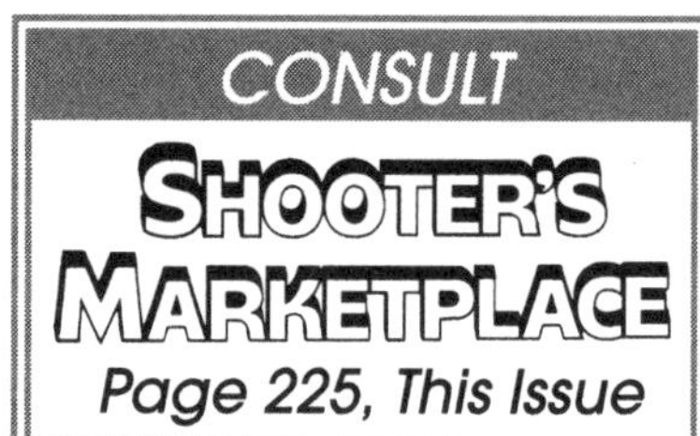
CONSULT
SHOOTER'S
MARKETPLACE
Page 225, This Issue

Winchester Model 1895

WINCHESTER MODEL 1895 LEVER-ACTION RIFLE
Caliber: 30-06, 4-shot magazine.
Barrel: 24", round.
Weight: 8 lbs. **Length:** 42" overall.
Stock: American walnut.
Sights: Gold bead front, buckhorn rear adjustable for elevation.
Features: Recreation of the original Model 1895. Polished blue finish with Nimschke-style scroll engraving on receiver. Scalloped receiver, two-piece cocking lever, schnabel forend, straight-grip stock. Introduced 1995. Only 4000 rifles made. From U.S. Repeating Arms Co., Inc.
Price: Grade I **$853.00**

Winchester Model 1895 High Grade Rifle
Same as the Grade I except has silvered receiver with extensive engraving: right side shows two scenes portraying large big horn sheep; left side has bull elk and cow elk. Gold borders accent the scenes. Magazine and cocking lever also engraved. Has classic Winchester H-style checkering pattern on fancy grade American walnut. Only 4000 rifles made. Introduced 1995. From U.S. Repeating Arms Co., Inc.
Price: **$1,360.00**

CAUTION: PRICES SHOWN ARE SUPPLIED BY THE MANUFACTURER OR IMPORTER. CHECK YOUR LOCAL GUN SHOP.

Includes models for a wide variety of sporting and competitive purposes and uses.

AMT BOLT-ACTION RIFLE
Caliber: Single shot—22 Hornet, 222, 223, 22-250, 243 Win., 243 A, 22 PPC, 6mm PPC, 6.5x08, 7mm-08, 308; repeater—223, 22-250, 243 Win., 243 A, 6mm PPC, 25-06, 6.5x08, 270, 7mm-08, 308, 30-06, 7mm Rem. Mag; 300 Win. Mag., 338 Win. Mag., 375 H&H, 416 Rem; 458 Win. Mag., 416 Rigby, 7.62x39, 7x57.
Barrel: Up to 28″, #3 contour.
Weight: About 8 1/2 lbs.
Stock: Classic composite on Standard grade; McMillan or H-S Precision on Deluxe.
Sights: None furnished; drilled and tapped for scope mounting.
Features: Single shot uses cone breach action with post-64-type extractor, pre-64-type three-position safety; repeater has Mauser-type extractor and magazine, pre-64 three-position safety; plunger-type ejector; short, medium, long action, right- or left-handed. Introduced 1996. Made in U.S. by AMT. Deluxe has Mauser controlled feed action with plunger ejector, claw-type extractor; Standard uses push-feed post-64 Winchester-type action.
Price: Single shot **$2,399.99**
Price: Repeater Standard **$1,109.99**
Price: Repeater Deluxe **$1,595.99**

AAO MODEL 2000 50-CALIBER RIFLE
Caliber: 50 BMG, 5-shot magazine.
Barrel: 30″; 1:15″ twist; muzzlebrake.
Weight: 24 lbs. **Length:** NA.
Stock: Cast alloy with gray anodized finish, Kick-Ease recoil pad.
Sights: None furnished. Drilled and tapped for scope base.
Features: Controlled feeding via rotating enclosed claw extractor; 90-degree bolt rotation; cone bolt face and barrel; trigger-mounted safety blocks sear; fully adjustable, detachable tripod. Introduced 1994. From American Arms & Ordnance.
Price: **$4,000.00**

Anschutz 1700D Custom

ANSCHUTZ 1700D CUSTOM RIFLE
Caliber: 22 Hornet, 5-shot clip; 222 Rem., 3-shot clip.
Barrel: 24″.
Weight: 7 1/2 lbs. **Length:** 43″ overall.
Stock: Select European walnut.
Sights: Hooded ramp front, folding leaf rear; drilled and tapped for scope mounting.
Features: Adjustable single stage trigger. Stock has roll-over Monte Carlo cheekpiece, slim forend with Schnabel tip, Wundhammer palm swell on grip, rosewood grip cap with white diamond insert. Skip-line checkering on grip and forend. Introduced 1988. Imported from Germany by AcuSport.
Price: **$1,297.56**

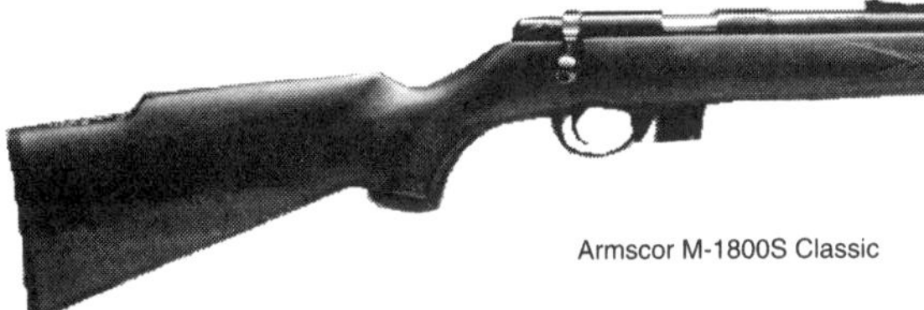
Armscor M-1800S Classic

Armscor M-1800SC Super Classic Rifle
Similar to the M-1800S except has oil-finished American walnut stock with 18 lpi hand checkering; black hardwood grip cap and forend tip; highly polished barreled action; jewelled bolt; recoil pad; swivel studs. Imported from the Philippines by K.B.I., Inc.
Price: **$430.00**

ARMSCOR M-1800S CLASSIC BOLT-ACTION RIFLE
Caliber: 22 Hornet, 5-shot magazine.
Barrel: 22.6″.
Weight: 6.6 lbs. **Length:** 41.25″ overall.
Stock: Walnut-finished hardwood with Monte Carlo comb and checkpiece.
Sights: Ramped blade front, fully adjustable open rear.
Features: Receiver dovetailed for tip-off scope mount. Introduced 1996. Imported from the Philippines by K.B.I., Inc.
Price: **$340.00**

Consult our Directory pages for the location of firms mentioned.

ARNOLD ARMS ALASKAN BUSH RIFLE
Caliber: 223 to 338 Magnum.
Barrel: 22″ to 26″.
Weight: NA. **Length:** NA.
Stock: Synthetic; black, woodland or arctic camouflage.
Sights: Optional; drilled and tapped for scope mounting.
Features: Uses the Apollo action with controlled round feed or push feed; chrome-moly steel or stainless; one-piece bolt, handle, knob; cone head bolt and breech; three-position safety; fully adjustable trigger. Introduced 1996. Made in U.S. by Arnold Arms Co.
Price: Chrome-moly steel **$2,995.00**
Price: Stainless steel **$3,145.00**

Arnold Arms Alaskan Trophy Rifle
Similar to the Alaskan Bush rifle except chambered for 300 Magnums to 458 Win. Mag.; 24″ to 26″ barrel; Fibergrain or black synthetic stock, or AA English walnut; comes with barrel band on 375 H&H and larger; scope mount; iron sights. Introduced 1996. Made in U.S. by Arnold Arms Co.
Price: Chrome-moly steel **$3,525.00**
Price: Stainless steel **$3,990.00**
Price: Chrome-moly steel, walnut stock **$5,140.00**
Price: Stainless steel, walnut stock **$5,299.00**

Arnold Arms High Country Mountain Rifle
Simliar to the Alaskan Bush rifle except chambered for 257 to 338 Magnum; choice of AA English walnut or synthetic stock; scope mount only. Introduced 1996. Made in U.S. by Arnold Arms Co.
Price: Chrome-moly steel, synthetic stock **$2,995.00**
Price: Stainless steel, synthetic stock **$3,170.00**
Price: Chrome-moly steel, walnut stock **$4,489.00**
Price: Stainless steel, walnut stock **$4,839.00**

Arnold Arms Grand Alaskan Rifle
Similar to the Alaskan Bush rifle except has AAA fancy select or exhibition-grade English walnut; barrel band swivel; comes with iron sights and scope mount; 24″ to 26″ barrel; 300 Magnum to 458 Win. Mag. Introduced 1996. Made in U.S. by Arnold Arms Co.
Price: Chrome-moly steel, from **$6,550.00**
Price: Stainless steel, from **$6,710.00**

ARNOLD ARMS SAFARI RIFLE
Caliber: 243 to 458 Win. Mag.
Barrel: 22″ to 26″.
Weight: NA. **Length:** NA.
Stock: Grade A and AA Fancy English walnut.
Sights: Optional; drilled and tapped for scope mounting.
Features: Uses the Apollo action with controlled or push round feed; one-piece bolt, handle, knob; cone head bolt and breech; three-position safety; fully adjustable trigger; chrome-moly steel in matte blue, polished, or bead blasted stainless. Introduced 1996. Made in U.S. by Arnold Arms Co.
Price: Grade A walnut, chrome-moly **$4,435.00**
Price: Grade A walnut, stainless steel **$4,695.00**
Price: Grade AA walnut, chrome-moly steel **$4,690.00**
Price: Grade AA walnut, stainless steel **$4,840.00**

Arnold Arms Grand African Rifle
Similar to the Safari rifle except has Exhibition Grade stock; polished blue chrome-moly steel or bead-blasted or teflon-coated stainless; barrel band; scope mount, express sights; calibers 338 Magnum to 458 Win. Mag.; 24″ to 26″ barrel. Introduced 1996. Made in U.S. by Arnold Arms Co.
Price: Chrome-moly steel **$7,630.00**
Price: Stainless steel **$7,780.00**

Arnold Arms African Trophy Rifle
Similar to the Safari rifle except has AAA Extra Fancy English walnut stock with wrap-around checkering; matte blue chrome-moly or polished or bead blasted stainless steel; scope mount standard or optional Express sights. Introduced 1996. Made in U.S. by Arnold Arms Co.
Price: Blued chrome-moly steel **$6,098.00**
Price: Stainless steel **$6,255.00**

Arnold Arms Serengeti Synthetic Rifle
Similar to the Safari except has Fibergrain synthetic stock in classic or Monte Carlo style; traditional checkering pattern or stipple finish; polished or matte blue or bead-blast stainless finish; chambered for 243 to 300 Magnum. Introduced 1996. Made in U.S. by Arnold Arms Co.
Price: Chrome-moly steel **$2,995.00**
Price: Stainless steel **$3,170.00**

Arnold Arms African Synthetic Rifle
Similar to the Safari except has Fibergrain synthetic stock with or without cheekpiece and traditional checkering pattern, or stipple finish; standard iron sights or Express folding leaf optional; chambered for 338 Magnum to 458 Win. Mag.; 24″ to 26″ barrel. Introduced 1996. Made in U.S. by Arnold Arms Co.
Price: Chrome-moly steel **$2,995.00**
Price: Stainless steel **$3,170.00**

A-SQUARE CAESAR BOLT-ACTION RIFLE
Caliber: 7mm Rem. Mag., 7mm STW, 30-06, 300 Win. Mag., 300 H&H, 300 Wea. Mag., 8mm Rem. Mag., 338 Win. Mag., 340 Wea. Mag., 338 A-Square, 9.3x62, 9.3x64, 375 Wea. Mag., 375 H&H, 375 JRS, 375 A-Square, 416 Hoffman, 416 Rem. Mag., 416 Taylor, 404 Jeffery, 425 Express, 458 Win. Mag., 458 Lott, 450 Ackley, 460 Short A-Square, 470 Capstick, 495 A-Square.
Barrel: 20″ to 26″ (no-cost customer option).
Weight: 8$^1/_2$ to 11 lbs.
Stock: Claro walnut with hand-rubbed oil finish; classic style with A-Square Coil-Chek® features for reduced recoil; flush detachable swivels. Customer choice of length of pull.
Sights: Choice of three-leaf express, forward or normal-mount scope, or combination (at extra cost).
Features: Matte non-reflective blue, double cross-bolts, steel and fiberglass reinforcement of wood from tang to forend tip; three-position positive safety; three-way adjustable trigger; expanded magazine capacity. Right- or left-hand. Introduced 1984. Made in U.S. by A-Square Co., Inc.
Price: Walnut stock **$2,995.00**
Price: Synthetic stock **$3,345.00**

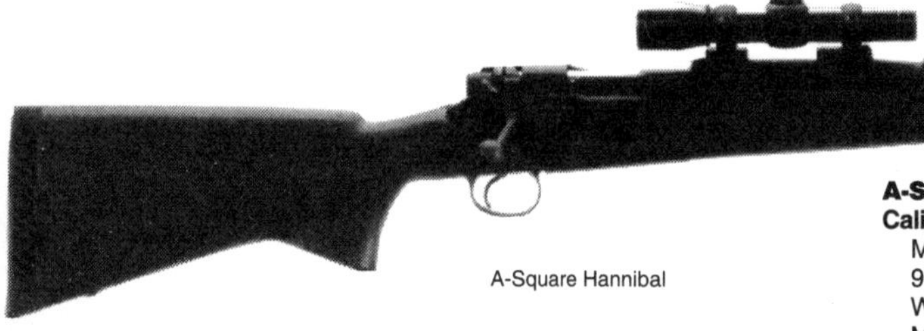
A-Square Hannibal

A-Square Hamilcar Bolt-Action Rifle
Similar to the A-Square Hannibal rifle except chambered for 25-06, 6.5x55, 270 Win., 7x57, 280 Rem., 30-06, 338-06, 9.3x62, 257 Wea. Mag., 264 Win. Mag., 270 Wea. Mag., 7mm Rem. Mag., 7mm Wea. Mag., 7mm STW, 300 Win. Mag., 300 Wea. Mag. Weighs 8-8$^1/_2$ lbs. Introduced 1994. From A-Square Co., Inc.
Price: **$2,995.00**

A-SQUARE HANNIBAL BOLT-ACTION RIFLE
Caliber: 7mm Rem. Mag., 7mm STW, 30-06, 300 Win. Mag., 300 H&H, 300 Wea. Mag., 8mm Rem. Mag., 338 Win. Mag., 340 Wea. Mag., 338 A-Square Mag., 9.3x62, 9.3x64, 375 H&H, 375 Wea. Mag., 375 JRS, 375 A-Square Mag., 378 Wea. Mag., 416 Taylor, 416 Rem. Mag., 416 Hoffman, 416 Rigby, 416 Wea. Mag., 404 Jeffery, 425 Express, 458 Win. Mag., 458 Lott, 450 Ackley, 460 Short A-Square Mag., 460 Wea. Mag., 470 Capstick, 495 A-Square Mag., 500 A-Square Mag.
Barrel: 20″ to 26″ (no-cost customer option).
Weight: 9 to 11$^3/_4$ lbs.
Stock: Claro walnut with hand-rubbed oil finish; classic style with A-Square Coil-Chek® features for reduced recoil; flush detachable swivels. Customer choice of length of pull. Available with synthetic stock.
Sights: Choice of three-leaf express, forward or normal-mount scope, or combination (at extra cost).
Features: Matte non-reflective blue, double cross-bolts, steel and fiberglass reinforcement of wood from tang to forend tip; Mauser-style claw extractor; expanded magazine capacity; two-position safety; three-way target trigger. Right-hand only. Introduced 1983. Made in U.S. by A-Square Co., Inc.
Price: Walnut stock **$2,995.00**
Price: Synthetic stock **$3,345.00**

Barrett Model 95

BARRETT MODEL 95 BOLT-ACTION RIFLE
Caliber: 50 BMG, 5-shot magazine.
Barrel: 29″.
Weight: 22 lbs. **Length:** 45″ overall.
Stock: Sorbothane recoil pad.
Sights: Scope optional.
Features: Updated version of the Model 90. Bolt-action, bullpup design. Disassembles without tools; extendable bipod legs; match-grade barrel; high efficiency muzzlebrake. Introduced 1995. From Barrett Firearms Mfg., Inc.
Price: From **$4,700.00**

CAUTION: PRICES SHOWN ARE SUPPLIED BY THE MANUFACTURER OR IMPORTER. CHECK YOUR LOCAL GUN SHOP.

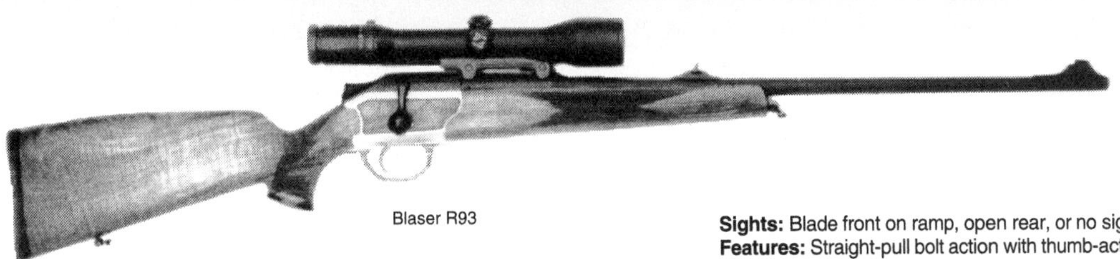
Blaser R93

BLASER R93 BOLT-ACTION RIFLE

Caliber: 222, 243, 6.5x55, 270, 7x57, 308, 30-06, 7mm Rem. Mag., 300 Win. Mag., 300 Wea. Mag., 338 Win. Mag., 375 H&H, 416 Rem. Mag., 3-shot magazine.
Barrel: 22″ (standard calibers), 24″ (magnum calibers).
Weight: 6.5 to 7.5 lbs. **Length:** 40″ overall (22″ barrel).
Stock: Two-piece European walnut.
Sights: Blade front on ramp, open rear, or no sights.
Features: Straight-pull bolt action with thumb-activated safety slide/cocking mechanism. Interchangeable barrels and bolt heads. Introduced 1994. Imported from Germany by Autumn Sales, Inc.
Price: Standard **$2,800.00**
Price: Deluxe (better wood, engraving) **$3,100.00**
Price: Super Deluxe (best wood, gold animal inlays) **$3,500.00**
Price: Safari, standard grade, 375 H&H, 416 Rem. Mag. **$3,300.00**
Price: Safari Deluxe **$3,600.00**
Price: Safari Super Deluxe **$4,000.00**

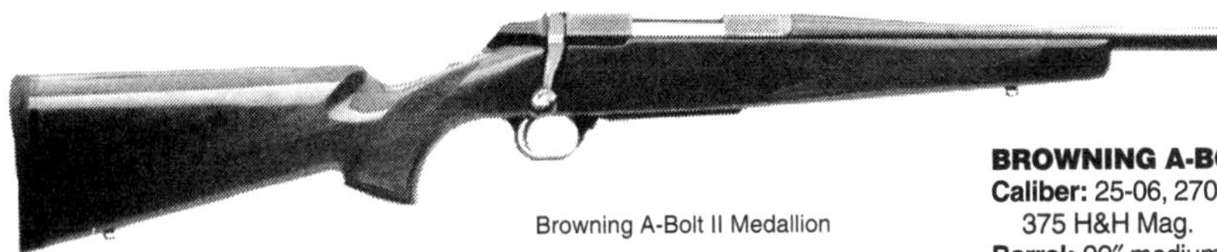
Browning A-Bolt II Medallion

Browning A-Bolt II Left Hand

Same as the Medallion model A-Bolt except has left-hand action and is available only in 270, 30-06, 7mm Rem. Mag., 375 H&H. BOSS barrel vibration modulator and muzzlebrake system not available in 375 H&H. Introduced 1987.
Price: **$734.95**
Price: With BOSS **$832.95**
Price: 375 H&H, with sights **$846.95**

Browning A-Bolt II Gold Medallion

Similar to the standard A-Bolt except has select walnut stock with brass spacers between rubber recoil pad and between the rosewood grip cap and forend tip; gold-filled barrel inscription; palm-swell pistol grip, Monte Carlo comb, 22 lpi checkering with double borders; engraved receiver flats. In 270, 30-06, 7mm Rem. Mag. only. Introduced 1988.
Price: **$949.95**
Price: For BOSS, add **$98.00**

Browning A-Bolt II Composite Stalker

Similar to the A-Bolt II Hunter except has black graphite-fiberglass stock with textured finish. Matte blue finish on all exposed metal surfaces. Available in 223, 22-250, 243, 7mm-08, 308, 30-06, 270, 280, 25-06, 7mm Rem. Mag., 300 Win. Mag., 338 Win. Mag. BOSS barrel vibration modulator and muzzlebrake system offered in all calibers. Introduced 1994.
Price: No sights **$624.95**
Price: No sights, BOSS **$722.95**

Browning A-Bolt II Stainless Stalker

Similar to the Hunter model A-Bolt except receiver and barrel are made of stainless steel; the rest of the exposed metal surfaces are finished with a durable matte silver-gray. Graphite-fiberglass composite textured stock. No sights are furnished. Available in 223, 22-250, 243, 308, 7mm-08, 270, 30-06, 7mm Rem. Mag., 375 H&H. Introduced 1987.
Price: **$786.95**
Price: With BOSS **$884.95**
Price: Left-hand, no sights **$811.95**
Price: With BOSS **$909.95**
Price: 375 H&H, with sights **$895.95**
Price: 375 H&H, left-hand, with sights **$923.95**

BROWNING A-BOLT II RIFLE

Caliber: 25-06, 270, 30-06, 280, 7mm Rem. Mag., 300 Win. Mag., 338 Win. Mag., 375 H&H Mag.
Barrel: 22″ medium sporter weight with recessed muzzle; 26″ on mag. cals.
Weight: 6½ to 7½ lbs. **Length:** 44¾″ overall (magnum and standard); 41¾″ (short action).
Stock: Classic style American walnut; recoil pad standard on magnum calibers.
Features: Short-throw (60°) fluted bolt, three locking lugs, plunger-type ejector; adjustable trigger is grooved and gold-plated. Hinged floorplate, detachable box magazine (4 rounds std. cals., 3 for magnums). Slide tang safety. Medallion has glossy stock finish, rosewood grip and forend caps, high polish blue. BOSS barrel vibration modulator and muzzlebrake system not available in 375 H&H. Introduced 1985. Imported from Japan by Browning.
Price: Medallion, no sights **$706.95**
Price: Hunter, no sights **$605.95**
Price: Hunter, with sights **$681.95**
Price: Medallion, 375 H&H Mag., with sights **$818.95**
Price: For BOSS add **$98.00**

Browning A-Bolt II Short Action

Similar to the standard A-Bolt except has short action for 223, 22-250, 243, 257 Roberts, 7mm-08, 284 Win., 308 chamberings. Available in Hunter or Medallion grades. Weighs 6½ lbs. Other specs essentially the same. BOSS barrel vibration modulator and muzzlebrake system optional. Introduced 1985.
Price: Medallion, no sights **$706.95**
Price: Hunter, no sights **$605.95**
Price: Hunter, with sights **$681.95**
Price: Composite, no sights **$624.95**
Price: For BOSS, add **$98.00**

Browning A-Bolt II Micro Medallion

Similar to the standard A-Bolt except is a scaled-down version. Comes with 20″ barrel, shortened length of pull (13 5/16″); three-shot magazine capacity; weighs 6 lbs., 1 oz. Available in 22 Hornet, 243, 308, 7mm-08, 257 Roberts, 223, 22-250. BOSS feature not available for this model. Introduced 1988.
Price: No sights **$706.95**

Browning A-Bolt II Varmint Rifle

Same as the A-Bolt II Hunter except has heavy varmint/target barrel, laminated wood stock with special dimensions, flat forend and palm swell grip. Chambered only for 223, 22-250, 308. Comes with BOSS barrel vibration modulator and muzzlebrake system. Introduced 1994.
Price: With BOSS, gloss or matte finish **$939.95**

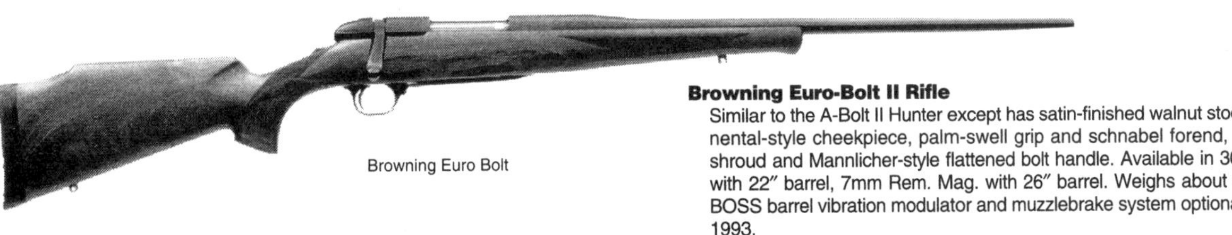
Browning Euro Bolt

Browning Euro-Bolt II Rifle

Similar to the A-Bolt II Hunter except has satin-finished walnut stock with Continental-style cheekpiece, palm-swell grip and schnabel forend, rounded bolt shroud and Mannlicher-style flattened bolt handle. Available in 30-06 and 270 with 22″ barrel, 7mm Rem. Mag. with 26″ barrel. Weighs about 6 lbs., 11 oz. BOSS barrel vibration modulator and muzzlebrake system optional. Introduced 1993.
Price: **$823.95**
Price: For BOSS, add **$98.00**

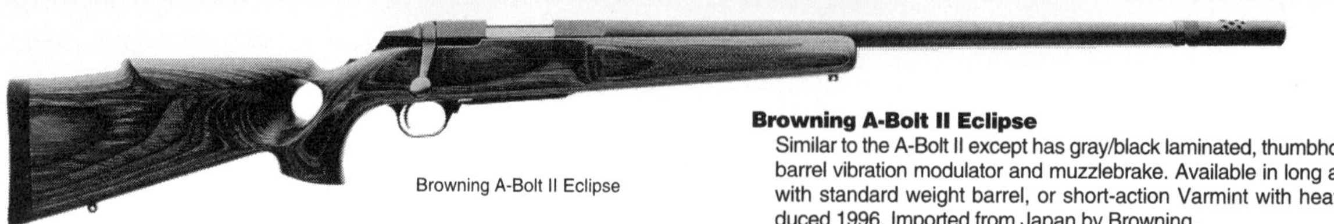
Browning A-Bolt II Eclipse

Browning A-Bolt II Eclipse

Similar to the A-Bolt II except has gray/black laminated, thumbhole stock, BOSS barrel vibration modulator and muzzlebrake. Available in long and short action with standard weight barrel, or short-action Varmint with heavy barrel. Introduced 1996. Imported from Japan by Browning.

Price: Standard barrel $1,024.95
Price: Varmint $1,054.95

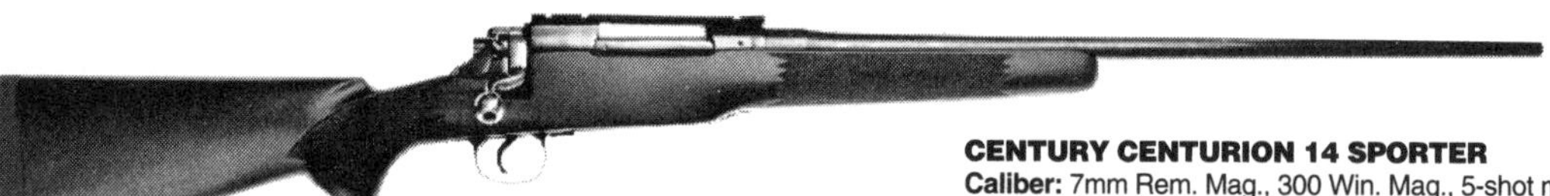
Century Centurion 14

CENTURY CENTURION 14 SPORTER

Caliber: 7mm Rem. Mag., 300 Win. Mag., 5-shot magazine.
Barrel: 24″.
Weight: NA. **Length:** 43.3″ overall.
Stock: Walnut-finished European hardwood. Checkered pistol grip and forend. Monte Carlo comb.
Sights: None furnished.
Features: Uses modified Pattern 14 Enfield action. Drilled and tapped; scope base mounted. Blue finish. From Century International Arms.
Price: About $275.00

CENTURY DELUXE CUSTOM SPORTER

Caliber: 243, 270, 308, 30-06.
Barrel: 24″.
Weight: NA. **Length:** 44″ overall.
Stock: Black synthetic.
Sights: None furnished. Scope base installed.
Features: Mauser 98 action; bent bolt handle for scope use; low-swing safety; matte black finish; blind magazine. Introduced 1992. From Century International Arms.
Price: About $288.00

CENTURY ENFIELD SPORTER #4

Caliber: 303 British, 10-shot magazine.
Barrel: 25.2″.
Weight: 8 lbs., 5 oz. **Length:** 44.5″ overall.
Stock: Beechwood with checkered pistol grip and forend, Monte Carlo comb.
Sights: Blade front, adjustable aperture rear.
Features: Uses Lee-Enfield action; blue finish. Trigger pinned to receiver. Introduced 1987. From Century International Arms.
Price: About $156.00

Century Custom Sporting Rifle

CENTURY SWEDISH SPORTER #38

Caliber: 6.5x55 Swede, 5-shot magazine.
Barrel: 24″.
Weight: NA. **Length:** 44.1″ overall.
Stock: Walnut-finished European hardwood with checkered pistol grip and forend; Monte Carlo comb.
Sights: Blade front, adjustable rear.
Features: Uses M38 Swedish Mauser action; comes with Holden Ironsighter see-through scope mount. Introduced 1987. From Century International Arms.
Price: About $237.50

CENTURY CUSTOM SPORTING RIFLE

Caliber: 308, 7.62x39mm.
Barrel: 22″.
Weight: 6.7 lbs. **Length:** 43.75″.
Stock: Walnut-finished hardwood.
Sights: None furnished; comes with two-piece Weaver-type base.
Features: Uses small ring Model 98 action; low-swing safety; blue finish. Introduced 1994. From Century International Arms.
Price: About $275.00

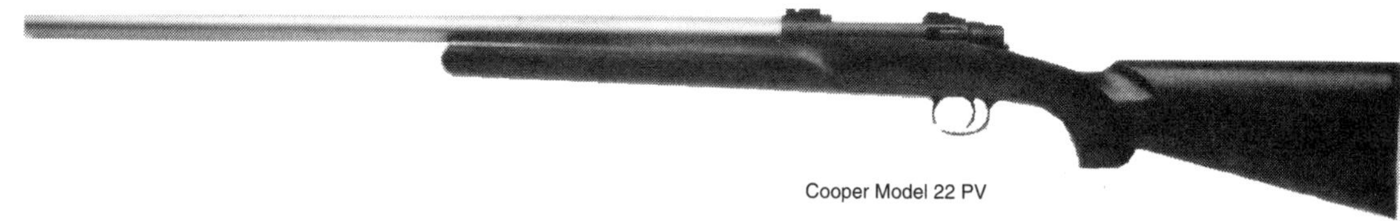
Cooper Model 22 PV

COOPER ARMS MODEL 22 PRO VARMINT EXTREME

Caliber: 22-250, 220 Swift, 243, 25-06, 6mm PPC, 308, single shot.
Barrel: 26″; stainless steel match grade, straight taper; free-floated.
Weight: NA. **Length:** NA.
Stock: AAA Claro walnut, oil finish, 22 lpi wrap-around borderless ribbon checkering, beaded cheekpiece, steel grip cap, flared varminter forend, Pachmayr pad.
Sights: None furnished; drilled and tapped for scope mounting.
Features: Uses a three front locking lug system. Available with sterling silver inlaid medallion, skeleton grip cap, and French walnut. Introduced 1995. Made in U.S. by Cooper Arms.
Price: $1,785.00
Price: Benchrest model with Jewell trigger $2,140.00
Price: Black Jack model (McMillan synthetic stock) $1,575.00

COOPER ARMS MODEL 21 VARMINT EXTREME RIFLE

Caliber: 17 Rem., 17 Mach IV, 221 Fireball, 222, 222 Rem. Mag., 223, 22 PPC, single shot.
Barrel: 23.75″; stainless steel, with competition step crown; free-floated.
Weight: NA. **Length:** NA.
Stock: AAA Claro walnut with flared oval forend, ambidextrous palm swell, 22 lpi checkering, oil finish, Pachmayr buttpad.
Sights: None furnished; drilled and tapped for scope mounting.
Features: Action has three mid-bolt locking lugs; adjustable trigger; glass bedded; swivel studs. Introduced 1994. Made in U.S. by Cooper Arms.
Price: $1,675.00
Price: Benchrest with Jewell trigger $2,140.00
Price: Classic model $1,675.00
Price: Custom Classic $1,960.00

CAUTION: PRICES SHOWN ARE SUPPLIED BY THE MANUFACTURER OR IMPORTER. CHECK YOUR LOCAL GUN SHOP.

COOPER ARMS MODEL 40 CENTERFIRE SPORTER
Caliber: 22 Hornet, 22 K-Hornet, 5-shot magazine.
Barrel: 23″.
Weight: 7 lbs. **Length:** 42 1/2″ overall.
Stock: AAA Claro walnut with 22 lpi borderless wrap-around ribbon checkering, oil finish, steel grip cap, Pachmayr pad.
Sights: None furnished.
Features: Action has three mid-bolt locking lugs, 45-degree bolt rotation; fully adjustable trigger; swivel studs. Pachmayr butt pad. Introduced 1994. Made in U.S. by Cooper Arms.
Price: Classic **$1,825.00**
Price: Custom Classic (AAA Claro walnut, Monte Carlo beaded cheekpiece, oil finish) **$2,025.00**

CZ 550 BOLT-ACTION RIFLE
Caliber: 243, 308 (4-shot detachable magazine), 308, 270, 30-06, 7mm Rem. Mag., 300 Win. Mag. (5-shot internal magazine).
Barrel: 23.6″.
Weight: 7.2 lbs. **Length:** 44.7″ overall.
Stock: Walnut with high comb; checkered grip and forend.
Sights: None furnished; drilled and tapped for Remington 700-style bases.
Features: Polished blue finish. Introduced 1995. Imported from the Czech Republic by Magnum Research.
Price: .... **$649.00** to **$679.00**
Price: Full Stock **$849.00**

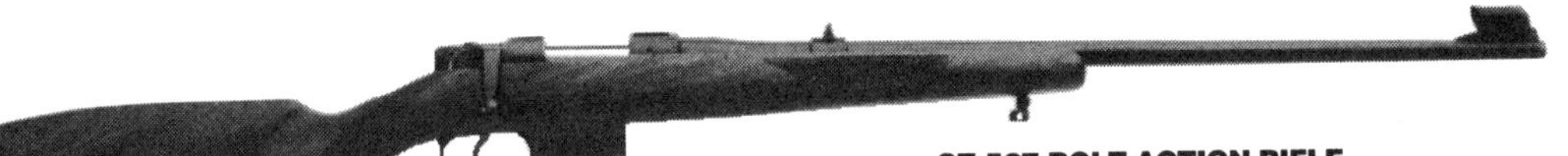

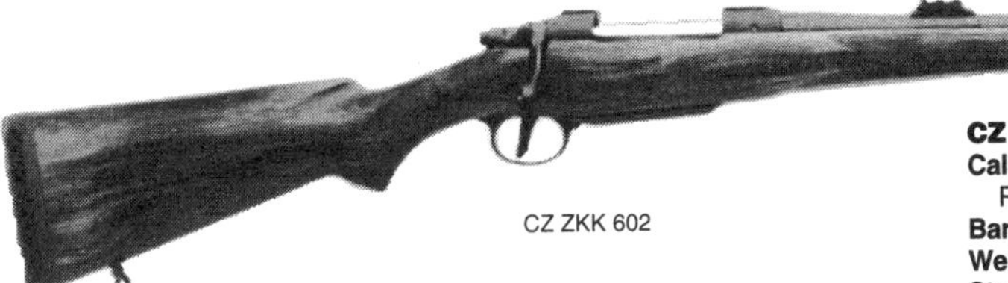
CZ 527

CZ 527 BOLT-ACTION RIFLE
Caliber: 22 Hornet, 222 Rem., 223 Rem., detachable 5-shot magazine.
Barrel: 23 1/2″; standard or heavy barrel.
Weight: 6 lbs., 1 oz. **Length:** 42 1/2″ overall.
Stock: European walnut with Monte Carlo.
Sights: Hooded front, open adjustable rear.
Features: Improved mini-Mauser action with non-rotating claw extractor; grooved receiver. Imported from the Czech Republic by Magnum Research.
Price: Standard **$629.00**

CZ ZKK 602

CZ ZKK 602 BOLT-ACTION RIFLES
Caliber: 7x57, 30-06, 270 (M600); 243, 308 (M601); 375 H&H, 416 Rigby, 416 Rem., 458 Win. Mag. (M602), 5-shot magazine.
Barrel: 25″.
Weight: 7 lbs., 3 oz. to 9 lbs., 9 oz. **Length:** 43″ overall.
Stock: Classic-style checkered walnut.
Sights: Hooded ramp front, open folding leaf adjustable rear.
Features: Improved Mauser action with controlled feed, claw extractor; safety blocks trigger and locks bolt; sling swivels. Imported from the Czech Republic by Magnum Research.
Price: **$799.00**

Dakota 76 Classic

Dakota 76 Short Action Rifles
A scaled-down version of the standard Model 76. Standard chamberings are 22-250, 243, 6mm Rem., 250-3000, 7mm-08, 308, others on special order. Short Classic Grade has 21″ barrel; Alpine Grade is lighter (6 1/2 lbs.), has a blind magazine and slimmer stock. Introduced 1989.
Price: Short Classic **$2,300.00**

DAKOTA 76 CLASSIC BOLT-ACTION RIFLE
Caliber: 257 Roberts, 270, 280, 30-06, 7mm Rem. Mag., 338 Win. Mag., 300 Win. Mag., 375 H&H, 458 Win. Mag.
Barrel: 23″.
Weight: 7 1/2 lbs. **Length:** 43 1/2″ overall.
Stock: Medium fancy grade walnut in classic style. Checkered pistol grip and forend; solid buttpad.
Sights: None furnished; drilled and tapped for scope mounts.
Features: Has many features of the original Model 70 Winchester. One-piece rail trigger guard assembly; steel grip cap. Model 70-style trigger. Many options available. Left-hand rifle available at same price. Introduced 1988. From Dakota Arms, Inc.
Price: **$2,500.00**

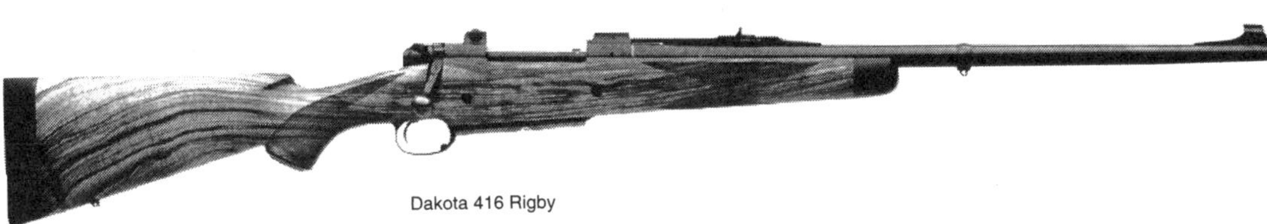
Dakota 416 Rigby

Dakota 416 Rigby African
Similar to the 76 Safari except chambered for 404 Jeffery, 416 Rigby, 416 Dakota, 450 Dakota, 4-round magazine, select wood, two stock cross-bolts. Has 24″ barrel, weight of 9-10 lbs. Ramp front sight, standing leaf rear. Introduced 1989.
Price: **$3,750.00**

Dakota 76 Varmint Rifle
Similar to the Dakota 76 except is a single shot with heavy barrel contour and special stock dimensions for varmint shooting. Chambered for 17 Rem., 22 BR, 222 Rem., 22-250, 220 Swift, 223, 6mm BR, 6mm PPC. Introduced 1994. Made in U.S. by Dakota Arms, Inc.
Price: **$2,300.00**

DAKOTA 76 SAFARI BOLT-ACTION RIFLE
Caliber: 270 Win., 7x57, 280, 30-06, 7mm Dakota, 7mm Rem. Mag., 300 Dakota, 300 Win. Mag., 330 Dakota, 338 Win. Mag., 375 Dakota, 458 Win. Mag., 300 H&H, 375 H&H, 416 Rem.
Barrel: 23″.
Weight: 8 1/2 lbs. **Length:** 43 1/2″ overall.
Stock: XXX fancy walnut with ebony forend tip; point-pattern with wrap-around forend checkering.
Sights: Ramp front, standing leaf rear.
Features: Has many features of the original Model 70 Winchester. Barrel band front swivel, inletted rear. Cheekpiece with shadow line. Steel grip cap. Introduced 1988. From Dakota Arms, Inc.
Price: Wood stock **$3,300.00**

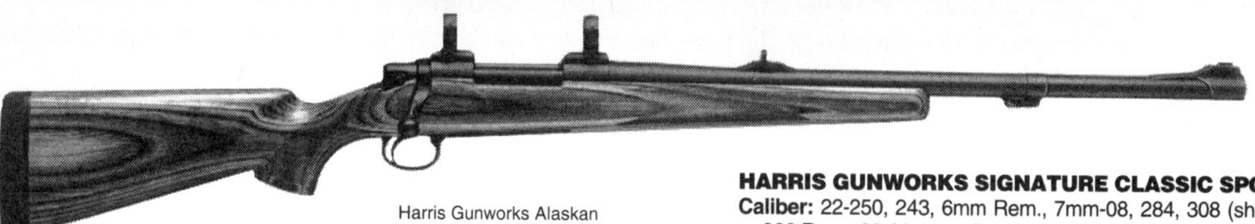
Harris Gunworks Alaskan

AUGUSTE FRANCOTTE BOLT-ACTION RIFLES
Caliber: 243, 270, 7x64, 30-06, 308, 300 Win. Mag., 338, 7mm Rem. Mag., 375 H&H, 458 Win. Mag.; others on request.
Barrel: 23½" to 26½".
Weight: 8 to 10 lbs.
Stock: Fancy European walnut. To customer specs.
Sights: To customer specs.
Features: Basically a custom gun, Francotte offers many options. Imported from Belgium by Armes de Chasse.
Price: From about (no engraving) .... **$10,600.00** to **$14,800.00**

Harris Gunworks Signature Super Varminter
Similar to the Classic Sporter except has heavy contoured barrel, adjustable trigger, field bipod and special hand-bedded fiberglass stock. Chambered for 223, 22-250, 220 Swift, 243, 6mm Rem., 25-06, 7mm-08, 7mm BR, 308, 350 Rem. Mag. Comes with 1" rings and bases. Introduced 1989.
Price: **$2,600.00**

HARRIS GUNWORKS SIGNATURE CLASSIC SPORTER
Caliber: 22-250, 243, 6mm Rem., 7mm-08, 284, 308 (short action); 25-06, 270, 280 Rem., 30-06, 7mm Rem. Mag., 300 Win. Mag., 300 Wea. (long action); 338 Win. Mag., 340 Wea., 375 H&H (magnum action).
Barrel: 22", 24", 26".
Weight: 7 lbs. (short action).
Stock: Fiberglass in green, beige, brown or black. Recoil pad and 1" swivels installed. Length of pull up to 14¼".
Sights: None furnished. Comes with 1" rings and bases.
Features: Uses right- or left-hand action with matte black finish. Trigger pull set at 3 lbs. Four-round magazine for standard calibers; three for magnums. Aluminum floorplate. Wood stock optional. Introduced 1987. From Harris Gunworks, Inc.
Price: **$2,600.00**

Harris Gunworks Signature Alaskan
Similar to the Classic Sporter except has match-grade barrel with single leaf rear sight, barrel band front, 1" detachable rings and mounts, steel floorplate, electroless nickel finish. Has wood Monte Carlo stock with cheekpiece, palm-swell grip, solid buttpad. Chambered for 270, 280 Rem., 30-06, 7mm Rem. Mag., 300 Win. Mag., 300 Wea., 358 Win., 340 Wea., 375 H&H. Introduced 1989.
Price: **$3,300.00**

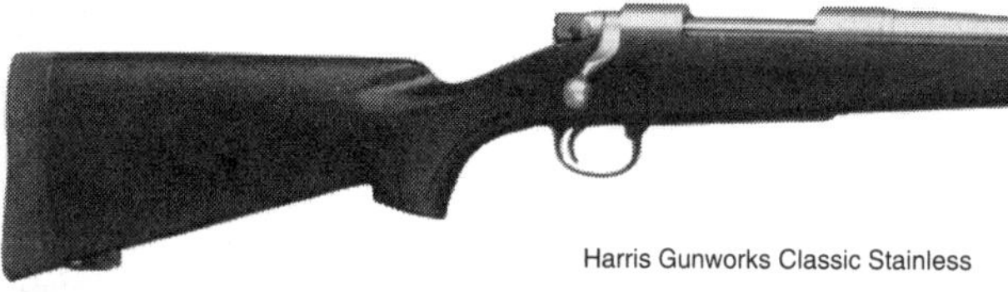
Harris Gunworks Classic Stainless

Harris Gunworks Signature Titanium Mountain Rifle
Similar to the Classic Sporter except action made of titanium alloy, barrel of chrome-moly steel. Stock is of graphite reinforced fiberglass. Weight is 5½ lbs. Chambered for 270, 280 Rem., 30-06, 7mm Rem. Mag., 300 Win. Mag. Fiberglass stock optional. Introduced 1989.
Price: **$3,200.00**

HARRIS GUNWORKS TALON SAFARI RIFLE
Caliber: 300 Win. Mag., 300 Wea. Mag., 300 Phoenix, 338 Win. Mag., 30/378, 338 Lapua, 300 H&H, 340 Wea. Mag., 375 H&H, 404 Jeffery, 416 Rem. Mag., 458 Win. Mag. (Safari Magnum); 378 Wea. Mag., 416 Rigby, 416 Wea. Mag., 460 Wea. Mag. (Safari Super Magnum).
Barrel: 24".
Weight: About 9-10 lbs. **Length:** 43" overall.
Stock: Gunworks fiberglass Safari.
Sights: Barrel band front ramp, multi-leaf express rear.
Features: Uses Harris Gunworks Safari action. Has quick detachable 1" scope mounts, positive locking steel floorplate, barrel band sling swivel. Match-grade barrel. Matte black finish standard. Introduced 1989. From Harris Gunworks, Inc.
Price: Talon Safari Magnum **$3,500.00**
Price: Talon Safari Super Magnum **$3,600.00**

Harris Gunworks Classic Stainless Sporter
Similar to the Classic Sporter except barrel and action made of stainless steel. Same calibers, in addition to 416 Rem. Mag. Comes with fiberglass stock, right- or left-hand action in natural stainless, glass bead or black chrome sulfide finishes. Introduced 1990. From Harris Gunworks, Inc.
Price: **$2,600.00**

Consult our Directory pages for the location of firms mentioned.

HARRIS GUNWORKS TALON SPORTER RIFLE
Caliber: 22-250, 243, 6mm Rem., 6mm BR, 7mm BR, 7mm-08, 25-06, 270, 280 Rem., 284, 308, 30-06, 350 Rem. Mag. (Long Action); 7mm Rem. Mag., 7mm STW, 300 Win. Mag., 300 Wea. Mag., 300 H&H, 338 Win. Mag., 340 Wea. Mag., 375 H&H, 416 Rem. Mag.
Barrel: 24" (standard).
Weight: About 7½ lbs. **Length:** NA.
Stock: Choice of walnut or fiberglass.
Sights: None furnished; comes with rings and bases. Open sights optional.
Features: Uses pre-'64 Model 70-type action with cone breech, controlled feed, claw extractor and three-position safety. Barrel and action are of stainless steel; chrome-moly optional. Introduced 1991. From Harris Gunworks, Inc.
Price: **$2,600.00**

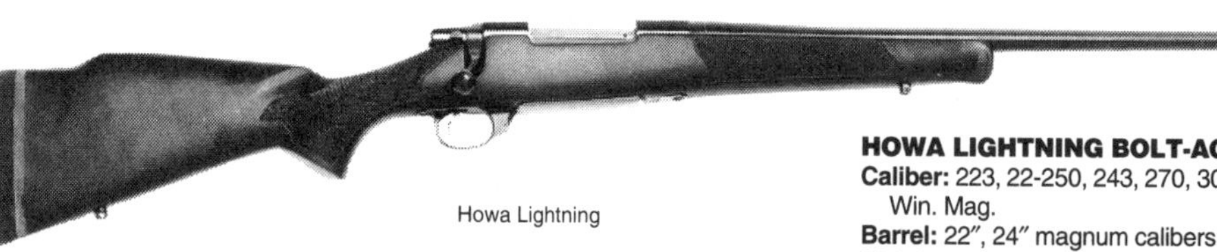
Howa Lightning

HOWA LIGHTNING BOLT-ACTION RIFLE
Caliber: 223, 22-250, 243, 270, 308, 30-06, 7mm Rem. Mag., 300 Win. Mag., 338 Win. Mag.
Barrel: 22", 24" magnum calibers.
Weight: 7½ lbs. **Length:** 42" overall (22" barrel).
Stock: Black Bell & Carlson Carbelite composite with Monte Carlo comb; checkered grip and forend.
Sights: None furnished. Drilled and tapped for scope mounting.
Features: Sliding thumb safety; hinged floorplate; polished blue/black finish. Introduced 1993. From Interarms.
Price: Standard calibers **$425.00**
Price: Magnum calibers **$425.00**

CAUTION: PRICES SHOWN ARE SUPPLIED BY THE MANUFACTURER OR IMPORTER. CHECK YOUR LOCAL GUNSHOP.

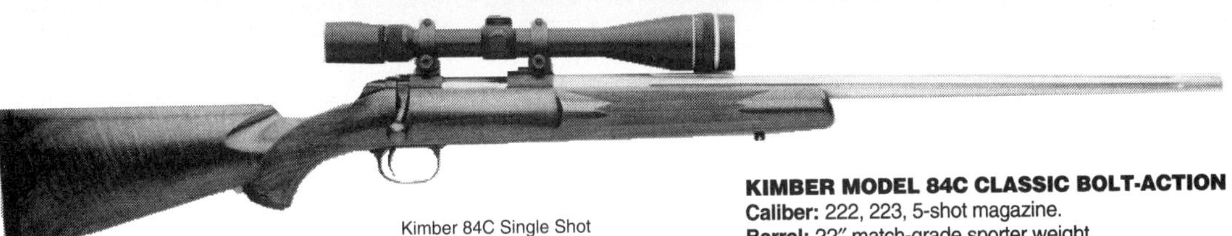

Kimber 84C Single Shot

KIMBER MODEL 84C CLASSIC BOLT-ACTION RIFLE

Caliber: 222, 223, 5-shot magazine.
Barrel: 22″ match-grade sporter weight.
Weight: $6\frac{3}{4}$ lbs. **Length:** $40\frac{1}{2}$″ overall.
Stock: Select A Claro walnut.
Sights: None furnished; drilled and tapped for Warne, Leupold or Millett scope mounts.
Features: Controlled round feed with Mauser-style extractor; pillar-bedded action; free-floating barrel; fully adjustable trigger; steel floorplate and trigger guard. Reintroduced 1996. Made in U.S. by Kimber of America, Inc.
Price: $1,145.00

Kimber Model 84C Single Shot Varmint

Similar to the Model 84C except is a single shot chambered only for 17 Rem. and 223 Rem.; 25″ fluted match-grade stainless barrel with target crown; and has varmint-profile stock with wide forend. Introduced 1996. Made in U.S. by Kimber of America, Inc.
Price: $999.00

Kimber Model 84C SuperAmerica

Similar to the Model 84C Classic except has AAA Claro walnut stock with beaded checkpiece, ebony forend tip, wrap-around 22 lpi checkering, and black rubber butt pad. Chambered for 17 Rem., 222 Rem., 223 Rem. Reintroduced 1996. Made in U.S. by Kimber of America, Inc.
Price: $1,595.00

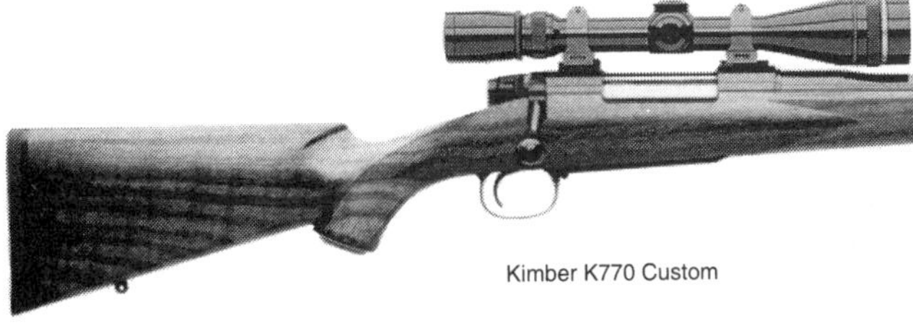

Kimber K770 Custom

KIMBER MODEL K770 CUSTOM RIFLE

Caliber: 270 Win., 30-06.
Barrel: 24″ match grade, sporter weight.
Weight: About $7\frac{1}{2}$ lbs. **Length:** 43″ overall.
Stock: Classic-style select Claro walnut, hand-cut panel checkering, solid rubber recoil pad, blued steel grip cap.
Sights: None furnished; drilled and tapped for Warne, Leupold or Millett scope mounts.
Features: Bolt locks into barrel breach; 60° bolt throw; pillar bedding; free-gloated barrel; hinged floorplate. Introduced 1996. Made in U.S. by Kimber of America, Inc.
Price: $745.00

Kimber Model K770 SuperAmerica Bolt-Action Rifle

Similar to the K770 Custom except has AAA Fancy Claro walnut stock with beaded checkpiece, ebony forend tip, and wrap-around hand-cut 22 lpi checkering. Introduced 1996.
Price: $1,260.00

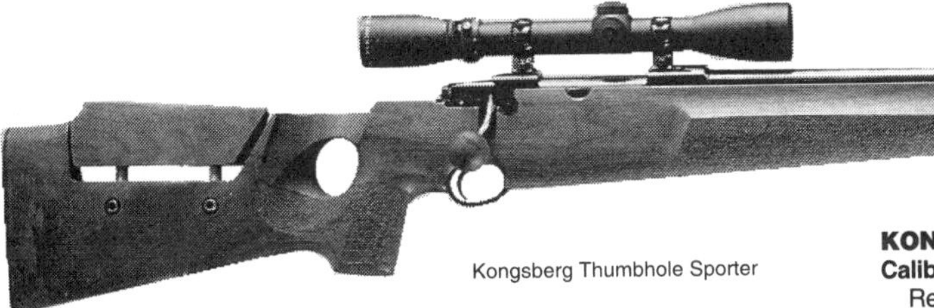

Kongsberg Thumbhole Sporter

KONGSBERG THUMBHOLE SPORTER RIFLE

Caliber: 22-250, 308 Win., 4-shot magazine.
Barrel: 23″ heavy barrel (.750″ muzzle).
Weight: About $8\frac{1}{2}$ lbs. **Length:** NA.
Stock: Oil-finished American walnut with stippled thumbhole grip, wide stippled forend, cheekpiece fully adjustable for height.
Sights: None furnished. Receiver dovetailed for scope mounting, and is drilled and tapped.
Features: Large bolt knob; rotary magazine; adjustable trigger; three-position safety; 60° bolt throw; claw extractor. Introduced 1993. Imported from Norway by Kongsberg America L.L.C.
Price: Right-hand $1,580.00
Price: Left-hand $1,718.00

KONGSBERG CLASSIC RIFLE

Caliber: 22-250, 243, 6.5x55, 270 Win., 30-06, 308 Win., 4-shot magazine; 7mm Rem. Mag., 300 Win. Mag., 338 Win. Mag., 3-shot magazine.
Barrel: 23″ in standard calibers, 26″ for magnums.
Weight: About $7\frac{1}{2}$ lbs. **Length:** 44″ overall (23″ barrel).
Stock: Oil-finished European walnut with straight fluted comb; 18 lpi checkering; rubber buttpad.
Sights: Hooded blade front, open adjustable rear. Receiver dovetailed for Weaver-type scope mount, and drilled and tapped.
Features: Rotary magazine; adjustable trigger; three-position safety; 60° bolt throw; claw extractor. Introduced 1993. Imported from Norway by Kingsberg America L.L.C.
Price: Right-hand, standard calibers $995.00
Price: Right-hand, magnum calibers $1,109.00
Price: Left-hand, standard calibers $1,133.00
Price: Left-hand, magnum calibers $1,245.00

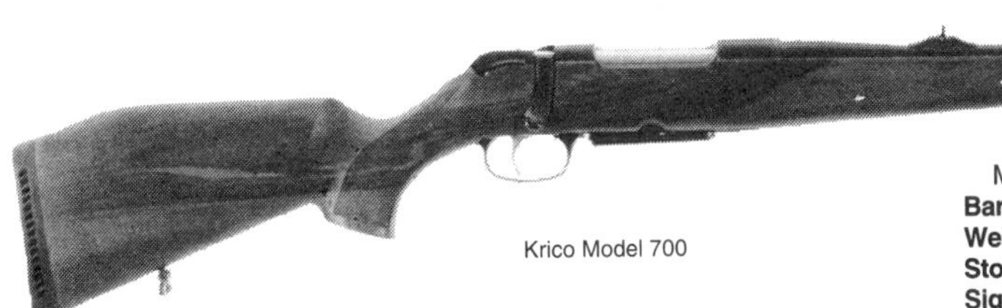

Krico Model 700

KRICO MODEL 700 BOLT-ACTION RIFLES

Caliber: 17 Rem., 222, 222 Rem. Mag., 223, 5.6x50 Mag., 243, 308, 5.6x57 RWS, 22-250, 6.5x55, 6.5x57, 7x57, 270, 7x64, 30-06, 9.3x62, 6.5x68, 7mm Rem. Mag., 300 Win. Mag., 8x68S, 7.5 Swiss, 9.3x64, 6x62 Freres.
Barrel: 23.6″ (std. cals.); 25.5″ (mag. cals.).
Weight: 7 lbs. **Length:** 43.3″ overall (23.6″ bbl.).
Stock: European walnut, Bavarian cheekpiece.
Sights: Blade on ramp front, open adjustable rear.
Features: Removable box magazine; sliding safety. Drilled and tapped for scope mounting. Imported from Germany by Mandall Shooting Supplies.
Price: Model 700 ....$995.00
Price: Model 700 Deluxe S $1,495.00
Price: Model 700 Deluxe $1,025.00
Price: Model 700 Stutzen (full stock) $1,249.00

L.A.R. Grizzly 50

L.A.R. GRIZZLY 50 BIG BOAR RIFLE
Caliber: 50 BMG, single shot.
Barrel: 36″.
Weight: 28.4 lbs. **Length:** 45.5″ overall.
Stock: Integral. Ventilated rubber recoil pad.
Sights: None furnished; scope mount.
Features: Bolt-action bullpup design; thumb safety. All-steel construction. Introduced 1994. Made in U.S. by L.A.R. Mfg., Inc.
Price: $2,570.00

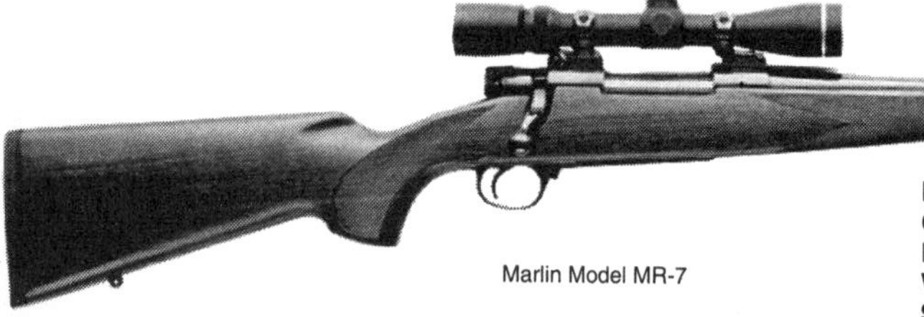
Marlin Model MR-7

MARLIN MODEL MR-7 BOLT-ACTION RIFLE
Caliber: 270, 30-06, 4-shot detachable box magazine.
Barrel: 22″; six-groove rifling.
Weight: 7½ lbs. **Length:** 43″ overall.
Stock: American black walnut with cut-checkered grip and forend, rubber buttpad, Mar-Shield® finish.
Sights: Bead on ramp front, adjustable rear, or no sights.
Features: Three-position safety; shrouded striker; red cocking indicator; adjustable 3-6 lb. trigger; quick-detachable swivel studs. Introduced 1996. Made in U.S. by Marlin.
Price: $610.90

MAUSER MODEL 96 BOLT-ACTION RIFLE
Caliber: 270, 30-06, 5-shot magazine.
Barrel: 22″.
Weight: About 6.25 lbs. **Length:** 42″ overall.
Stock: European walnut with checkered grip and forend.
Sights: None furnished; drilled and tapped for Remington 700 scope mounts.
Features: "Slide-bolt" straight-pull action with 16 locking lugs; tang mounted three-position safety; quick detachable sling swivels. Introduced 1996. Imported from Germany by GSI, Inc.
Price: .... $NA

REMINGTON 700 ADL BOLT-ACTION RIFLE
Caliber: 243, 270, 308, 30-06 and 7mm Rem. Mag.
Barrel: 22″ or 24″ round tapered.
Weight: 7 lbs. **Length:** 41½″ to 43½″ overall.
Stock: Walnut. Satin-finished pistol grip stock with fine-line cut checkering, Monte Carlo.
Sights: Gold bead ramp front; removable, step-adjustable rear with windage screw.
Features: Side safety, receiver tapped for scope mounts.
Price: About $472.00
Price: 7mm Rem. Mag., about $499.00

Remington 700 ADL Synthetic

Remington 700 ADL Synthetic
Similar to the 700 ADL except has a fiberglass-reinforced synthetic stock with straight comb, raised cheekpiece, positive checkering, and black rubber buttpad. Metal has matte finish. Available in 243, 270, 308, 30-06 with 22″ barrel, 7mm Rem. Mag. with 24″ barrel. Introduced 1996.
Price: $412.00
Price: 7mm Rem. Mag. $439.00

Remington 700 BDL Bolt-Action Rifle
Same as the 700 ADL except chambered for 222, 223 (short action, 24″ barrel), 22-250, 25-06, 6mm Rem. (short action, 22″ barrel), 243, 270, 7mm-08, 280, 300 Savage, 30-06, 308; skip-line checkering; black forend tip and grip cap with white line spacers. Matted receiver top, quick-release floorplate. Hooded ramp front sight; q.d. swivels.
Price: About $576.00
Also available in 17 Rem., 7mm Rem. Mag., 300 Win. Mag. (long action, 24″ barrel), 338 Win. Mag., 35 Whelen (long action, 22″ barrel). Overall length 44½″, weight about 7½ lbs.
Price: About $603.00
Price: Custom Grade, about $2,507.00

Remington 700 VLS Varmint Laminated Stock
Similar to the 700 BDL except has 26″ heavy barrel without sights, brown laminated stock with forend tip, grip cap, rubber buttpad. Available in 222 Rem., 223 Rem., 22-250, 243, 308. Polished blue finish. Introduced 1995.
Price: $609.00

Remington 700 VS SF Rifle
Similar to the Model 700 Varmint Synthetic except has satin-finish stainless barreled action with 26″ fluted barrel, spherical concave muzzle crown. Chambered for 223, 220 Swift, 22-250, 308. Introduced 1994.
Price: $826.00

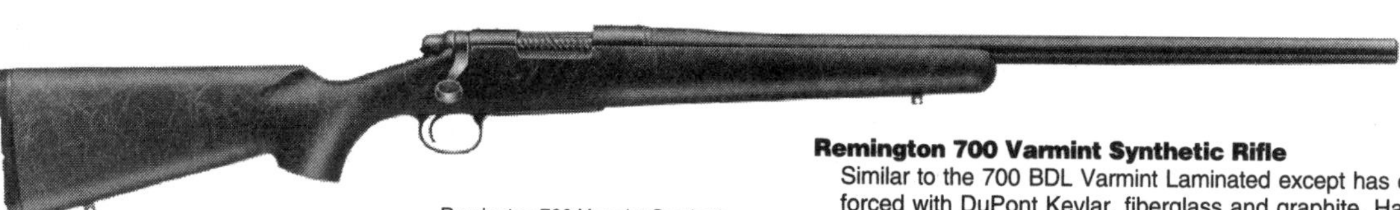
Remington 700 Varmint Synthetic

Remington 700 Varmint Synthetic Rifle
Similar to the 700 BDL Varmint Laminated except has composite stock reinforced with DuPont Kevlar, fiberglass and graphite. Has aluminum bedding block that runs the full length of the receiver. Free-floating 26″ barrel. Metal has black matte finish; stock has textured black and gray finish and swivel studs. Available in 220 Swift, 223, 22-250, 308. Introduced 1992.
Price: $686.00

CAUTION: PRICES SHOWN ARE SUPPLIED BY THE MANUFACTURER OR IMPORTER. CHECK YOUR LOCAL GUNSHOP.

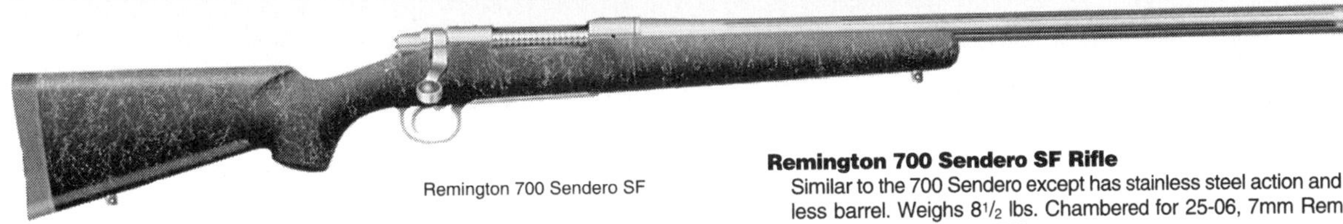

Remington 700 Sendero SF

Remington 700 Sendero Rifle

Similar to the Model 700 Varmint Synthetic except has long action for magnum calibers. Has 26″ heavy varmint barrel with spherical concave crown. Chambered for 25-06, 270, 7mm Rem. Mag., 300 Win. Mag. Introduced 1994.

Price: 25-06, 270 .... $686.00
Price: 7mm Rem. Mag., 300 Win. Mag. $713.00

Remington 700 Custom KS Mountain Rifle

Similar to the 700 BDL except custom finished with Kevlar reinforced resin synthetic stock. Available in both left- and right-hand versions. Chambered for 270 Win., 280 Rem., 30-06, 7mm Rem. Mag., 300 Win. Mag., 300 Wea. Mag., 35 Whelen, 338 Win. Mag., 8mm Rem. Mag., 375 H&H, all with 24″ barrel only. Weighs 6 lbs., 6 oz. Introduced 1986.

Price: Right-hand $1,089.00
Price: Left-hand $1,156.00
Price: Stainless $1,241.00

Remington 700 BDL SS DM Rifle

Same as the 700 BDL SS except has detachable box magazine. Barrel, receiver and bolt made of #416 stainless steel; black synthetic stock. Available in 243, 25-06, 270, 280, 7mm-08, 308, 30-06, 7mm Rem. Mag., 300 Win. Mag., 300 Wea. Mag., 338 Win. Mag. Introduced 1995.

Price: Standard calibers $676.00
Price: Magnum calibers $702.00

Remington 700 Sendero SF Rifle

Similar to the 700 Sendero except has stainless steel action and 26″ fluted stainless barrel. Weighs $8^{1}/_{2}$ lbs. Chambered for 25-06, 7mm Rem. Mag. and 300 Win. Mag. Introduced 1996.

Price: 25-06 .... $826.00
Price: 7mm Rem. Mag., 300 Win. Mag $853.00

Remington 700 BDL SS Rifle

Similar to the 700 BDL rifle except has hinged floorplate, 24″ standard weight barrel in all calibers; magnum calibers have magnum-contour barrel. No sights supplied, but comes drilled and tapped. Has corrosion-resistant follower and fire control, stainless BDL-style barreled action with fine matte finish. Synthetic stock has straight comb and cheekpiece, textured finish, positive checkering, plated swivel studs. Calibers—270, 30-06; magnums—7mm Rem. Mag., 300 Win. Mag. Weighs $6^{3}/_{4}$-7 lbs. Introduced 1993.

Price: Standard calibers, about $623.00
Price: Magnum calibers, about $649.00

Remington 700 BDL Left Hand

Same as 700 BDL except mirror-image left-hand action, stock. Available in 270, 30-06 only.

Price: About $603.00
Price: 7mm Rem. Mag. $629.00

Remington 700 BDL SS DM-B

Remington 700 Safari

Similar to the 700 BDL except custom finished and tuned. In 8mm Rem. Mag., 375 H&H, 416 Rem. Mag. or 458 Win. Mag. calibers only with heavy barrel. Hand checkered, oil-finished stock in classic or Monte Carlo style with recoil pad installed. Delivery time is about 5 months.

Price: About $1,093.00
Price: Classic stock, left-hand $1,160.00
Price: Safari Custom KS (Kevlar stock), right-hand $1,258.00
Price: As above, left-hand $1,326.00

Remington 700 BDL SS DM-B

Same as the 700 BDL SS DM except has muzzlebrake. Available only in 7mm Rem. Mag., 300 Win. Mag., 300 Wea. Mag., 338 Win. Mag. Introduced 1996.

Price: $762.00

Remington 700 APR African Plains Rifle

Similar to the Model 700 BDL except has magnum receiver and specially contoured 26″ Custom Shop barrel with satin finish, laminated wood stock with raised cheekpiece, satin finish, black buttpad, 20 lpi cut checkering. Chambered for 7mm Rem. Mag., 300 Win. Mag., 300 Wea. Mag., 338 Win. Mag., 375 H&H. Introduced 1994.

Price: $1,466.00

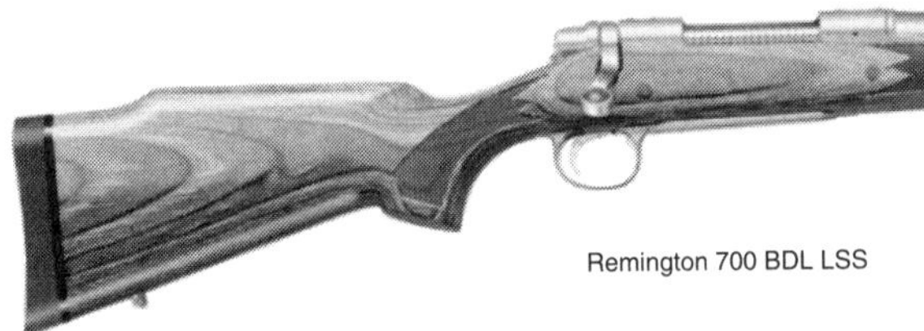

Remington 700 BDL LSS

Remington 700 BDL DM Rifle

Same as the 700 BDL except has detachable box magazine (4-shot, standard calibers, 3-shot for magnums). Has glossy stock finish, open sights, recoil pad, sling swivels. Right-hand action calibers: 6mm, 243, 25-06, 270, 280, 7mm-08, 30-06, 308, 7mm Rem. Mag., 300 Win. Mag., 338 Win. Mag.; left-hand calibers: 270, 30-06, 7mm Rem. Mag., 300 Win. Mag. Introduced 1995.

Price: Right-hand, standard calibers $628.00
Price: Left-hand, standard calibers $656.00
Price: Right-hand, magnum calibers $656.00
Price: Left-hand, magnum calibers $682.00

Remington 700 AWR Alaskan Wilderness Rifle

Similar to the Model 700 BDL except has stainless barreled action with satin blue finish; special 24″ Custom Shop barrel profile; matte gray stock of fiberglass and graphite, reinforced with DuPont Kevlar, straight comb with raised cheekpiece, magnum-grade black rubber recoil pad. Chambered for 7mm Rem. Mag., 300 Win. Mag., 300 Wea. Mag., 338 Win. Mag., 375 H&H. Introduced 1994.

Price: $1,318.00

Remington 700 LSS Rifle

Similar to the 700 BDL except has stainless steel barreled action, gray laminated wood stock with Monte Carlo comb and cheekpiece. No sights furnished. Available in 7mm Rem. Mag. and 300 Win. Mag. Introduced 1996.

Price: $676.00

REMINGTON 700 CLASSIC RIFLE

Caliber: 375 H&H Mag.
Barrel: 24″.
Weight: About $7^{3}/_{4}$ lbs. **Length:** $44^{1}/_{2}$″ overall.
Stock: American walnut, 20 lpi checkering on pistol grip and forend. Classic styling. Satin finish.
Sights: None furnished. Receiver drilled and tapped for scope mounting.
Features: A "classic" version of the M700 ADL with straight comb stock. Fitted with rubber recoil pad. Sling swivel studs installed. Hinged floorplate. Limited production in 1996 only.
Price: About $623.00

Remington 700 MTN DM Rifle

Similar to the 700 BDL except weighs $6^{3}/_{4}$ lbs., has a 22″ tapered barrel. Redesigned pistol grip, straight comb, contoured cheekpiece, hand-rubbed oil stock finish, deep cut checkering, hinged floorplate and magazine follower, two-position thumb safety. Chambered for 243, 270 Win., 7mm-08, 25-06, 280 Rem., 30-06, 4-shot detachable box magazine. Overall length is $42^{1}/_{2}$″. Introduced 1995.

Price: About $629.00

Remington Model Seven

REMINGTON MODEL SEVEN BOLT-ACTION RIFLE

Caliber: 223 Rem. (5-shot); 243, 7mm-08, 308 (4-shot).
Barrel: 18½″.
Weight: 6¼ lbs. **Length:** 37½″ overall.
Stock: Walnut, with modified schnabel forend. Cut checkering.
Sights: Ramp front, adjustable open rear.
Features: Short-action design; silent side safety; free-floated barrel except for single pressure point at forend tip. Introduced 1983.
Price: About $569.00

Remington Model Seven Youth Rifle

Similar to the Model Seven except has hardwood stock with 12³⁄₁₆″ length of pull and chambered for 243, 7mm-08. Introduced 1993.
Price: About $465.00

Remington Model Seven Custom MS Rifle

Similar to the Model Seven except has full-length Mannlicher-style stock of laminated wood with straight comb, solid black recoil pad, black steel forend tip, cut checkering, gloss finish. Barrel length 20″, weighs 6¾ lbs. Available in 222 Rem., 223, 22-250, 243, 6mm Rem., 7mm-08 Rem., 308, 350 Rem. Mag. Calibers 250 Savage, 257 Roberts, 35 Rem. available on special order. Polished blue finish. Introduced 1993. From Remington Custom Shop.
Price: About $1,093.00

Remington Model Seven Custom KS

Similar to the standard Model Seven except has custom finished stock of lightweight Kevlar aramid fiber and chambered for 223 Rem., 7mm-08, 308, 35 Rem. and 350 Rem. Mag. Barrel length is 20″, weighs 5¾ lbs. Comes with iron sights and is drilled and tapped for scope mounting. Special order through Remington Custom Shop. Introduced 1987.
Price: $1,089.00

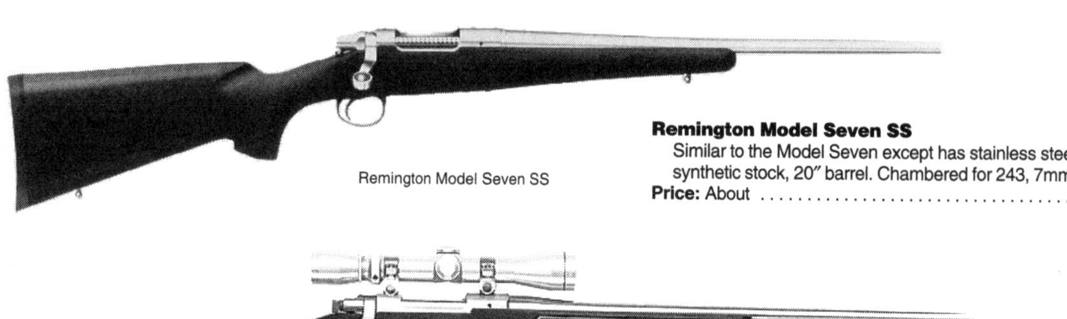

Remington Model Seven SS

Remington Model Seven SS

Similar to the Model Seven except has stainless steel barreled action and black synthetic stock, 20″ barrel. Chambered for 243, 7mm-08, 308. Introduced 1994.
Price: About $623.00

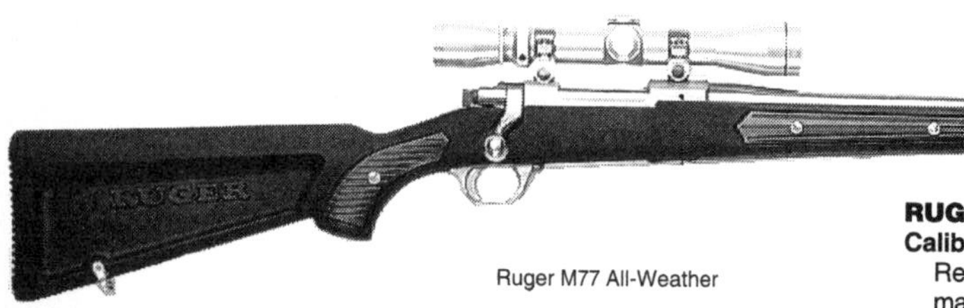

Ruger M77 All-Weather

RUGER M77 MARK II RIFLE

Caliber: 223, 243, 6mm Rem., 257 Roberts, 25-06, 6.5x55 Swedish, 270, 280 Rem., 308, 30-06, 7mm Rem. Mag., 300 Win. Mag., 338 Win. Mag., 4-shot magazine.
Barrel: 20″, 22″; 24″ (magnums).
Weight: About 7 lbs. **Length:** 39¾″ overall.
Stock: Hand-checkered American walnut; swivel studs, rubber butt pad.
Sights: None furnished. Receiver has Ruger integral scope mount base, comes with Ruger 1″ rings. Some models have iron sights.
Features: Short action with new trigger and three-position safety. New trigger guard with redesigned floorplate latch. Left-hand model available. Introduced 1989.
Price: M77RMKII (no sights) $574.00
Price: M77RSMKII (open sights) $635.00
Price: M77LRMKII (left-hand, 270, 30-06, 7mm Rem. Mag., 300 Win. Mag.) $574.00

Ruger M77 Mark II All-Weather Stainless Rifle

Similar to the wood-stock M77 Mark II except all metal parts are of stainless steel, and has an injection-moulded, glass-fiber-reinforced Du Pont Zytel stock. Chambered for 223, 243, 270, 308, 30-06, 7mm Rem. Mag., 300 Win. Mag., 338 Win. Mag. Has the fixed-blade-type ejector, three-position safety, and new trigger guard with patented floorplate latch. Comes with integral Scope Base Receiver and 1″ Ruger scope rings, built-in sling swivel loops. Introduced 1990.
Price: KM77RPMKII $574.00
Price: KM77RSPMKII, open sights $635.00

Ruger M77RL Ultra Light

Similar to the standard M77 except weighs only 6 lbs., chambered for 223, 243, 308, 270, 30-06, 257; barrel tapped for target scope blocks; has 20″ Ultra Light barrel. Overall length 40″. Ruger's steel 1″ scope rings supplied. Introduced 1983.
Price: M77RLMKII $610.00

Ruger M77RSI International Carbine

Same as the standard Model 77 except has 18½″ barrel, full-length International-style stock, with steel forend cap, loop-type steel sling swivels. Integral-base receiver, open sights, Ruger 1″ steel rings. Improved front sight. Available in 243, 270, 308, 30-06. Weighs 7 lbs. Length overall is 38⅜″.
Price: M77RSIMKII $642.00

Ruger M77VT Target

RUGER M77VT TARGET RIFLE

Caliber: 22 PPC, 22-250, 220 Swift, 223, 243, 6mm PPC, 25-06, 308.
Barrel: 26″ heavy stainless steel with target gray finish.
Weight: Approx. 9.25 lbs. **Length:** Approx. 44″ overall.
Stock: Laminated American hardwood with beavertail forend, steel swivel studs; no checkering or grip cap.
Sights: Integral scope mount bases in receiver.
Features: Ruger diagonal bedding system. Ruger steel 1″ scope rings supplied. Fully adjustable trigger. Steel floorplate and trigger guard. New version introduced 1992.
Price: KM77VTMKII $684.00

RUGER M77 MARK II MAGNUM RIFLE

Caliber: 375 H&H, 4-shot magazine; 416 Rigby, 3-shot magazine.
Barrel: 26″, with integral steel rib; hammer forged.
Weight: 9.25 lbs. (375); 10.25 lbs. (416, 458). **Length:** 40.5″ overall.
Stock: Circassian walnut with hand-cut checkering, swivel studs, steel grip cap, rubber butt pad.
Sights: Ramp front, two leaf express on serrated integral steel rib. Rib also serves as base for front scope ring.
Features: Uses an enlarged Mark II action with three-position safety, stainless bolt, steel trigger guard and hinged steel floorplate. Controlled feed. Introduced 1989.
Price: M77RSMMKII $1,550.00

CAUTION: PRICES SHOWN ARE SUPPLIED BY THE MANUFACTURER OR IMPORTER. CHECK YOUR LOCAL GUNSHOP.

RUGER 77/22 HORNET BOLT-ACTION RIFLE

Caliber: 22 Hornet, 6-shot rotary magazine.
Barrel: 20″.
Weight: About 6 lbs. **Length:** 39¾″ overall.
Stock: Checkered American walnut, black rubber buttpad.
Sights: Brass bead front, open adjustable rear; also available without sights.
Features: Same basic features as the rimfire model except has slightly lengthened receiver. Uses Ruger rotary magazine. Three-position safety. Comes with 1″ Ruger scope rings. Introduced 1994.
Price: 77/22RH (rings only) $489.00
Price: 77/22RSH (with sights) $499.00
Price: K77/22VHZ Varmint, laminated stock, no sights $535.00

Ruger 77/22 Hornet

CONSULT
SHOOTER'S
MARKETPLACE
Page 225, This Issue

RUGER M77 MARK II EXPRESS RIFLE

Caliber: 270, 30-06, 7mm Rem. Mag., 300 Win. Mag., 4-shot magazine.
Barrel: 22″, with integral steel rib; barrel-mounted front swivel stud; hammer forged.
Weight: 7.5 lbs. **Length:** 42.125″ overall.
Stock: Hand-checkered medium quality French walnut with steel grip cap, black rubber butt pad, swivel studs.
Sights: Ramp front, V-notch two-leaf express rear adjustable for windage mounted on rib.
Features: Mark II action with three-position safety, stainless steel bolt, steel trigger guard, hinged steel floorplate. Introduced 1991.
Price: M77RSEXMKII $1,550.00

Sako Long-Range Rifle

Sako Long-Range Hunting Rifle

Similar to the long action Hunter model except has 26″ fluted barrel and is chambered for 25-06, 270 Win., 7mm Rem. Mag., 300 Win. Mag. Introduced 1996. Imported from Finland by Stoeger.
Price: 25-06 .... $1,275.00
Price: 7mm Rem. Mag., 300 Win. Mag $1,290.00

Sako Mannlicher-Style Carbine

Same as the Hunter except has full "Mannlicher" style stock, 18½″ barrel, weighs 7½ lbs., chambered for 243, 25-06, 270, 308 and 30-06, 7mm Rem. Mag., 300 Win. Mag., 338 Win. Mag., 375 H&H. Introduced 1977. From Stoeger.
Price: 243, 308 .... $1,275.00
Price: 270, 30-06 .... $1,310.00
Price: 338 Win. Mag. $1,335.00
Price: 375 H&H $1,350.00

Sako Super Deluxe Sporter

Similar to Hunter except has select European walnut with high-gloss finish and deep-cut oak leaf carving. Metal has super high polish, deep blue finish. Special order only.
Price: $3,100.00

Sako Classic Bolt Action

Similar to the Hunter except has classic-style stock with straight comb. Has 21¾″ barrel, weighs 6 lbs. Matte finish wood. Introduced 1993. Imported from Finland by Stoeger.
Price: 243 .... $1,050.00
Price: 270, 30-06 .... $1,085.00
Price: 7mm Rem. Mag. $1,100.00

SAKO HUNTER RIFLE

Caliber: 17 Rem., 222, 223 (short action); 22-250, 243, 7mm-08, 308 (medium action); 25-06, 270, 270 Wea. Mag., 7mm Wea. Mag., 30-06, 7mm Rem. Mag., 300 Win. Mag., 338 Win. Mag., 340 Wea. Mag., 375 H&H Mag., 300 Wea. Mag., 416 Rem. Mag. (long action).
Barrel: 22″ to 24″ depending on caliber.
Weight: 5¾ lbs. (short); 6¼ lbs. (med.); 7¼ lbs. (long).
Stock: Hand-checkered European walnut.
Sights: None furnished.
Features: Adjustable trigger, hinged floorplate. Imported from Finland by Stoeger.
Price: 17 Rem., 222, 223 .... $1,050.00
Price: 22-250, 243, 308, 7mm-08 .... $1,050.00
Price: Long action cals. (except magnums) $1,085.00
Price: Magnum cals. $1,100.00
Price: 375 H&H, 416 Rem. Mag., from $1,120.00
Price: 300 Wea. $1,120.00

Sako Varmint Heavy Barrel

Same as Hunter except has heavy varmint barrel, beavertail forend; available in 17 Rem., 222, 223 (short action), 22 PPC, 6mm PPC (single shot), 22-250, 243, 308, 7mm-08 (medium action). Weight from 8¼ to 8½ lbs., 5-shot magazine capacity.
Price: 17 Rem., 222, 223 (short action) $1,240.00
Price: 22-250, 243, 308 (medium action) $1,240.00
Price: 22 PPC, 6mm PPC (single shot) $1,475.00

Sako Hunter Left-Hand Rifle

Same gun as the Sako Hunter except has left-hand action, stock with dull finish. Available in medium, long and magnum actions. Introduced 1987.
Price: Standard calibers, 22-250 to 7mm-08 .... $1,135.00
Price: Magnum calibers $1,180.00
Price: 375 H&H, 416 Rem. Mag. $1,200.00
Price: Long action, 25-06, 270, 280, 30-06 .... $1,165.00

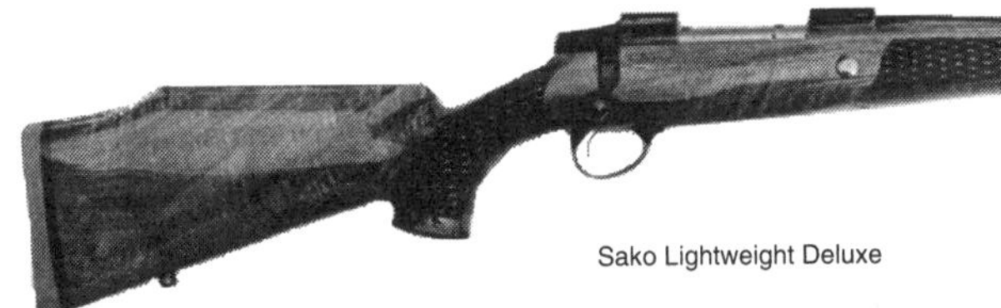
Sako Lightweight Deluxe

Sako Lightweight Deluxe

Same action as Hunter except has select wood, rosewood pistol grip cap and forend tip. Fine checkering on top surfaces of integral dovetail bases, bolt sleeve, bolt handle root and bolt knob. Vent. recoil pad, skip-line checkering, mirror finish bluing.
Price: 17 Rem., 222, 223, 22-250, 243, 308, 7mm-08 .... $1,475.00
Price: 25-06, 270, 280 Rem., 30-06 .... $1,510.00
Price: 7mm Rem. Mag., 300 Win. Mag., 338 Win. Mag. $1,525.00
Price: 300 Wea., 375 H&H, 416 Rem. Mag. $1,545.00

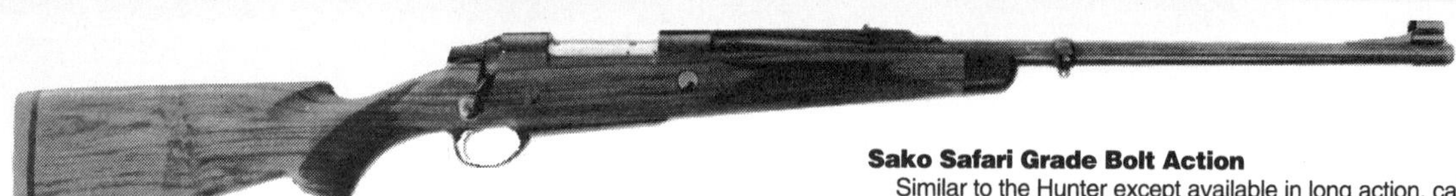
Sako Safari Grade

Sako Fiberclass Sporter
Similar to the Hunter except has a black fiberglass stock in the classic style, with wrinkle finish, rubber buttpad. Barrel length is 23″, weight 7 lbs., 2 oz. Introduced 1985.
Price: 25-06, 270, 280 Rem., 30-06 .... **$1,385.00**
Price: 7mm Rem. Mag., 300 Win. Mag., 338 Win. Mag. **$1,405.00**
Price: 375 H&H, 416 Rem. Mag. **$1,425.00**

Sako Safari Grade Bolt Action
Similar to the Hunter except available in long action, calibers 338 Win. Mag. or 375 H&H Mag. or 416 Rem. Mag. only. Stocked in French walnut, checkered 20 lpi, solid rubber buttpad; grip cap and forend tip; quarter-rib "express" rear sight, hooded ramp front. Front sling swivel band-mounted on barrel.
Price: **$2,765.00**

Sako TRG-S

SAKO TRG-S BOLT-ACTION RIFLE
Caliber: 243, 7mm-08, 270, 6.5x55, 30-06, 7mm Rem. Mag., 300 Win. Mag., 338 Win. Mag., 270 Wea. Mag., 7mm Wea. Mag., 340 Wea. Mag., 375 H&H, 416 Rem. Mag., 5-shot magazine (4-shot for 375 H&H).
Barrel: 22″, 24″ (magnum calibers).
Weight: 7.75 lbs. **Length:** 45.5″ overall.
Stock: Reinforced polyurethane with Monte Carlo comb.
Sights: None furnished.
Features: Resistance-free bolt with 60-degree lift. Recoil pad adjustable for length. Free-floating barrel, detachable magazine, fully adjustable trigger. Matte blue metal. Introduced 1993. Imported from Finland by Stoeger.
Price: 243, 7mm-08, 270, 30-06 .... **$790.00**
Price: Magnum calibers **$830.00**

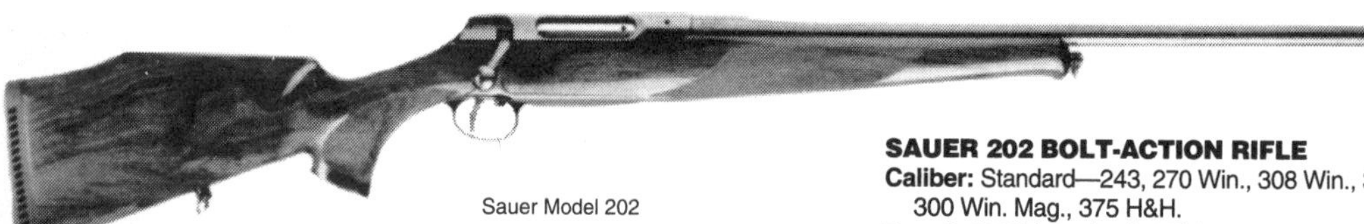
Sauer Model 202

SAUER 90 BOLT-ACTION RIFLE
Caliber: 243, 25-06, 270 Win., 308 Win., 30-06, 7mm Rem. Mag., 300 Win. Mag., 300 Wea. Mag., 375 H&H.
Barrel: 23.6″ (standard calibers); 26″ (magnums).
Weight: About 7.5 lbs. **Length:** 42.5″ overall (23.6″ barrel).
Stock: Select American Claro walnut with high-gloss epoxy finish, rosewood grip and forend caps; 22 lpi checkering.
Sights: None furnished; drilled and tapped for scope mounting.
Features: Three cam-actuated locking lugs on center of bolt; internal extractor; 65° bolt throw; detachable box magazine; tang safety; loaded chamber indicator; cocking indicator; adjustable trigger. Introduced 1986. Imported from Germany by SIGARMS, Inc.
Price: Standard or magnum **$1,300.00**

SAUER 202 BOLT-ACTION RIFLE
Caliber: Standard—243, 270 Win., 308 Win., 30-06; magnum—7mm Rem. Mag., 300 Win. Mag., 375 H&H.
Barrel: 23.6″ (standard), 26″ (magnum).
Weight: 7.7 lbs. (standard) **Length:** 44.3″ overall (23.6″ barrel).
Stock: Select American Claro walnut with high-gloss epoxy finish, rosewood grip and forend caps; 22 lpi checkering.
Sights: None furnished; drilled and tapped for scope mounting.
Features: Short 60° bolt throw; detachable box magazine; six-lug bolt; quick-change barrel; tapered bore; adjustable two-stage trigger; firing pin cocking indicator. Introduced 1994. Imported from Germany by SIGARMS, Inc.
Price: Standard or magnum **$900.00**

Consult our Directory pages for the location of firms mentioned.

SAVAGE MODEL 110FP TACTICAL RIFLE
Caliber: 223, 25-06, 308, 30-06, 300 Win. Mag., 7mm Rem. Mag., 4-shot magazine.
Barrel: 24″, heavy; recessed target muzzle.
Weight: 8½ lbs. **Length:** 45.5″ overall.
Stock: Black graphite/fiberglass composition; positive checkering.
Sights: None furnished. Receiver drilled and tapped for scope mounting.
Features: Pillar-bedded stock. Black matte finish on all metal parts. Double swivel studs on the forend for sling and/or bipod mount. Right or left-hand. Introduced 1990. From Savage Arms, Inc.
Price: **$429.00**

SAVAGE MODEL 110CY LADIES/YOUTH RIFLE
Caliber: 223, 243, 270, 300 Sav., 308, 5-shot magazine.
Barrel: 22″.
Weight: About 6.5 lbs. **Length:** 42.5″ overall.
Stock: Walnut-stained hardwood with high comb, cut checkering.
Sights: Ramp front, fully adjustable rear.
Features: Length of pull is 12.5″, with red rubber buttpad. Drilled and tapped for scope mounting. Uses standard Model 110 barreled action. Introduced 1991. Made in U.S. by Savage Arms, Inc.
Price: **$358.00**

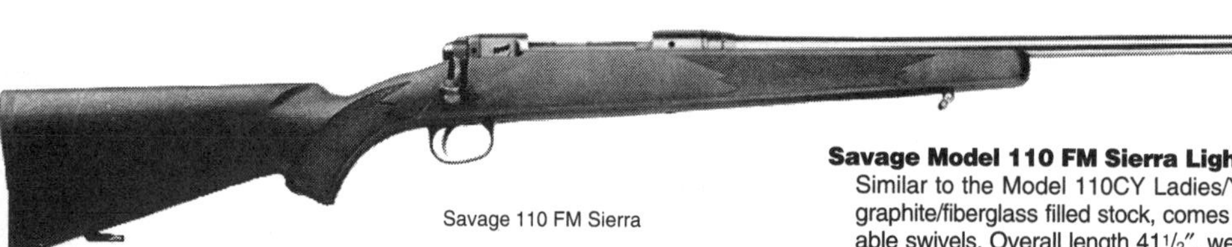
Savage 110 FM Sierra

Savage Model 110 FM Sierra Light Weight Rifle
Similar to the Model 110CY Ladies/Youth rifle except has 20″ barrel, black graphite/fiberglass filled stock, comes with black nylon sling and quick detachable swivels. Overall length 41½″, weighs 6¼ lbs. Available in 243, 270, 308, 30-06. No sights furnished; drilled and tapped for scope mounting. Made in U.S. by Savage Arms, Inc. Introduced 1996.
Price: **$410.00**

 CAUTION: PRICES SHOWN ARE SUPPLIED BY THE MANUFACTURER OR IMPORTER. CHECK YOUR LOCAL GUNSHOP.

Savage Model 111FXP3, 111FCXP3 Package Guns

Similar to the Model 110 Series Package Guns except with lightweight, black graphite/fiberglass composite stock with non-glare finish, positive checkering. Same calibers as Model 110 rifles, plus 338 Win. Mag. Model 111FXP3 has fixed top-loading magazine; Model 111FCXP3 has detachable box. Both come with mounted 3-9x32 scope, quick-detachable swivels, sling. Introduced 1994. Made in U.S. by Savage Arms, Inc.

Price: Model 111FXP3, right- or left-hand **$447.00**
Price: Model 111FCXP3, right- or left-hand **$489.00**

SAVAGE MODEL 110GXP3, 110GCXP3 PACKAGE GUNS

Caliber: 223, 22-250, 243, 250 Savage, 25-06, 270, 300 Sav., 30-06, 308, 7mm Rem. Mag., 7mm-08, 300 Win. Mag. (Model 110GXP3); 270, 30-06, 7mm Rem. Mag., 300 Win. Mag. (Model 110GCXP3).
Barrel: 22″ (standard calibers), 24″ (magnum calibers).
Weight: 7.25-7.5 lbs. **Length:** 43.5″ overall (22″ barrel).
Stock: Monte Carlo-style hardwood with walnut finish, rubber buttpad, swivel studs.
Sights: None furnished.
Features: Model 110GXP3 has fixed, top-loading magazine, Model 110GCXP3 has detachable box magazine. Rifles come with a factory-mounted and bore-sighted 3-9x32 scope, rings and bases, quick-detachable swivels, sling. Left-hand models available in all calibers. Introduced 1991 (GXP3); 1994 (GCXP3). Made in U.S. by Savage Arms, Inc.
Price: Model 110GXP3, right- or left-hand **$418.00**
Price: Model 110GCXP3, right- or left-hand **$482.00**

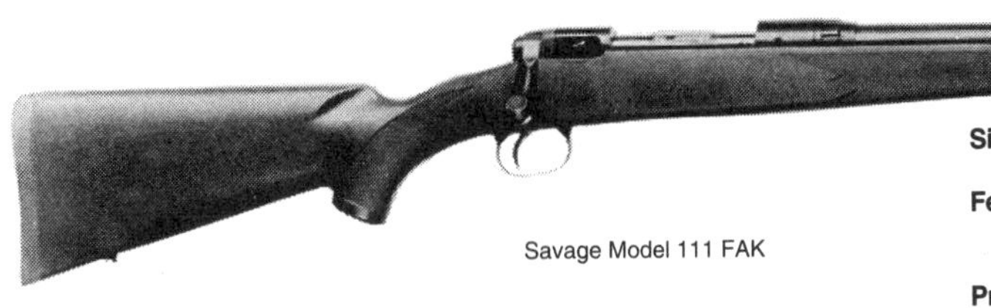

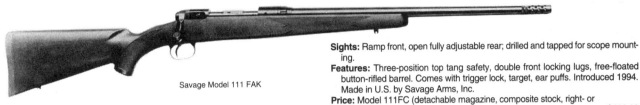

Savage Model 111 FAK

SAVAGE MODEL 111 CLASSIC HUNTER RIFLES

Caliber: 223, 22-250, 243, 250 Sav., 25-06, 270, 300 Sav., 30-06, 308, 7mm Rem. Mag., 7mm-08, 300 Win. Mag., 338 Win. Mag. (Models 111G, GL, GNS, F, FL, FNS); 270, 30-06, 7mm Rem. Mag., 300 Win. Mag. (Models 111GC, GLC, FAK, FC, FLC).
Barrel: 22″, 24″ (magnum calibers).
Weight: 6.3 to 7 lbs. **Length:** 43.5″ overall (22″ barrel).
Stock: Walnut-finished hardwood (M111G, GC); graphite/fiberglass filled composite.
Sights: Ramp front, open fully adjustable rear; drilled and tapped for scope mounting.
Features: Three-position top tang safety, double front locking lugs, free-floated button-rifled barrel. Comes with trigger lock, target, ear puffs. Introduced 1994. Made in U.S. by Savage Arms, Inc.
Price: Model 111FC (detachable magazine, composite stock, right- or left-hand) **$418.00**
Price: Model 111F (top-loading magazine, composite stock, right- or left-hand) **$376.00**
Price: Model 111FNS (as above, no sights, right-hand only) **$372.00**
Price: Model 111G (wood stock, top-loading magazine, right- or left-hand) **$358.00**
Price: Model 111GC (as above, detachable magazine) **$407.00**
Price: Model 111GNS (wood stock, top-loading magzine, no sights, right-hand only) **$353.00**
Price: Model 111FAK Express (blued, composite stock, top loading magazine, Adjustable Muzzle Brake) **$450.00**

SAVAGE MODEL 112 VARMINT RIFLES

Caliber: 22-250, 223, 5-shot magazine.
Barrel: 26″ heavy.
Weight: 8.8 lbs. **Length:** 47.5″ overall.
Stock: Black graphite/fiberglass filled composite with positive checkering.
Sights: None furnished; drilled and tapped for scope mounting.
Features: Pillar-bedded stock. Blued barrel with recessed target-style muzzle. Double front swivel studs for attaching bipod. Introduced 1991. Made in U.S. by Savage Arms, Inc.
Price: Model 112FV **$400.00**
Price: Model 112FVSS (cals. 223, 22-250, 25-06, 7mm Rem. Mag., 300 Win. Mag., stainless barrel, bolt handle, trigger guard) **$510.00**
Price: Model 112FVSS-S (as above, single shot) **$500.00**
Price: Model 112BVSS (heavy-prone laminated stock with high comb, Wundhammer swell, fluted stainless barrel, bolt handle, trigger guard) **$535.00**
Price: Model 112BVSS-S (as above, single shot) **$535.00**

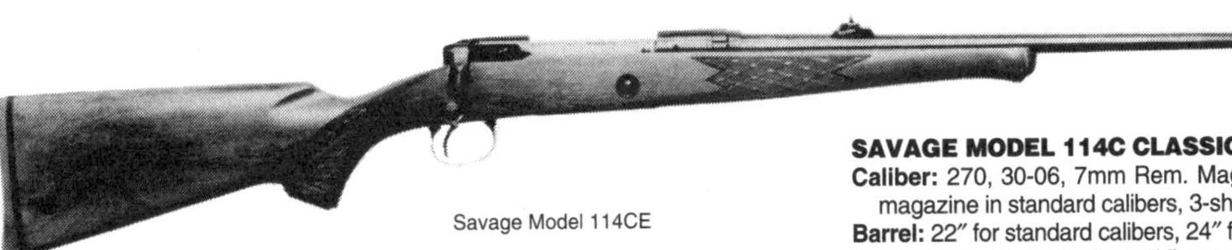

Savage Model 114CE

Savage Model 114CE Classic European

Similar to the Model 114C except the oil-finished walnut stock has a schnabel forend tip, cheekpiece and skip-line checkering; bead on blade front sight, fully adjustable open rear; solid red buttpad. Chambered for 270, 30-06, 7mm Rem. Mag., 300 Win. Mag. Introduced 1996. Made in U.S. by Savage Arms, Inc.

Price: **$600.00**

SAVAGE MODEL 114C CLASSIC RIFLE

Caliber: 270, 30-06, 7mm Rem. Mag., 300 Win. Mag.; 4-shot detachable box magazine in standard calibers, 3-shot for magnums.
Barrel: 22″ for standard calibers, 24″ for magnums.
Weight: $7^{1}/_{8}$ lbs. **Length:** $45^{1}/_{2}$″ overall.
Stock: Oil-finished American walnut; checkered grip and forend.
Sights: None furnished; drilled and tapped for scope mounting.
Features: High polish blue on barrel, receiver and bolt handle; Savage logo laser-etched on bolt body; push-button magazine release. Made in U.S. by Savage Arms, Inc. Introduced 1996.
Price: **$525.00**

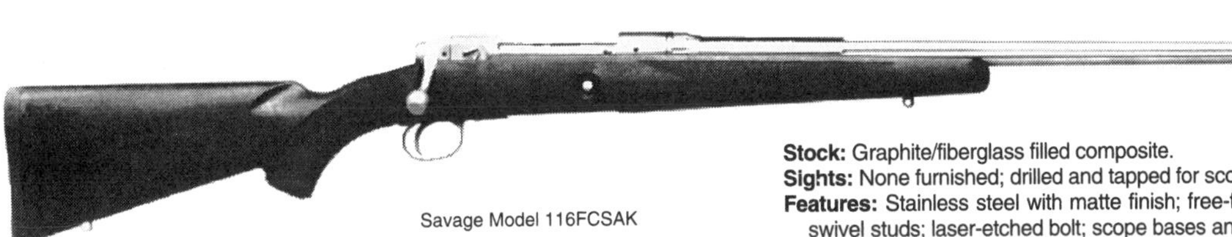

Savage Model 116FCSAK

SAVAGE MODEL 116 WEATHER WARRIORS

Caliber: 223, 243, 270, 30-06, 7mm Rem. Mag., 300 Win. Mag., 338 Win. Mag. (Model 116FSS); 270, 30-06, 7mm Rem. Mag., 300 Win. Mag. (Models 116FCSAK, 116FCS); 270, 30-06, 7mm Rem. Mag., 300 Win. Mag., 338 Win. Mag. (Models 116FSAK, 116FSK).
Barrel: 22″, 24″ for 7mm Rem. Mag., 300 Win. Mag., 338 Win. Mag. (M116FSS only).
Weight: 6.25 to 6.5 lbs. **Length:** 43.5″ overall (22″ barrel).
Stock: Graphite/fiberglass filled composite.
Sights: None furnished; drilled and tapped for scope mounting.
Features: Stainless steel with matte finish; free-floated barrel; quick-detachable swivel studs; laser-etched bolt; scope bases and rings. Left-hand models available in all models, calibers at same price. Models 116FCS, 116FSS introduced 1991; Model 116FSK introduced 1993; Model 116FCSAK, 116FSAK introduced 1994. Made in U.S. by Savage Arms, Inc.
Price: Model 116FSS (top-loading magazine) **$491.00**
Price: Model 116FCS (detachable box magazine) **$554.00**
Price: Model 116FCSAK (as above with Savage Adjustable Muzzle Brake system) **$644.00**
Price: Model 116FSAK (top-loading magazine, Savage Adjustable Muzzle Brake system) **$581.00**
Price: Model 116FSK Kodiak (as above with 22″ Shock-Suppressor barrel) **$554.00**

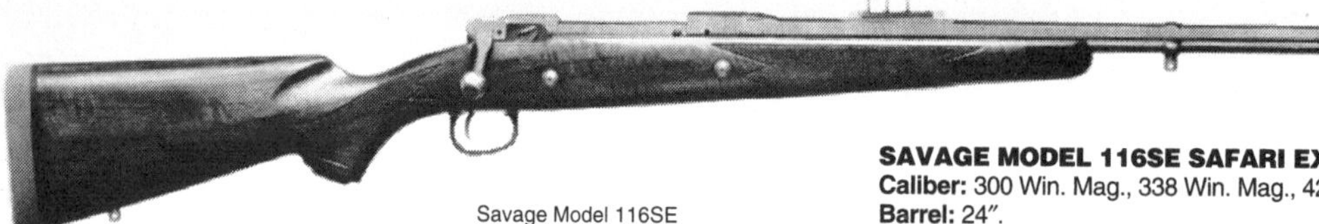
Savage Model 116SE

Savage Model 116US Ultra Stainless Rifle
Similar to the Model 116SE except chambered for 270, 30-06, 7mm Rem. Mag., 300 Win. Mag.; stock has high-gloss finish; no open sights. Stainless steel barreled action with satin finish. Introduced 1995. Made in U.S. by Savage Arms, Inc.
Price: **$700.00**

SAVAGE MODEL 116SE SAFARI EXPRESS RIFLE
Caliber: 300 Win. Mag., 338 Win. Mag., 425 Express, 458 Win. Mag.
Barrel: 24″.
Weight: 8.5 lbs. **Length:** 45.5″ overall.
Stock: Classic-style select walnut with ebony forend tip, deluxe cut checkering. Two cross bolts; internally vented recoil pad.
Sights: Bead on ramp front, three-leaf express rear.
Features: Controlled-round feed design; adjustable muzzlebrake; one-piece barrel band stud. Satin-finished stainless steel barreled action. Introduced 1994. Made in U.S. by Savage Arms, Inc.
Price: **$900.00**

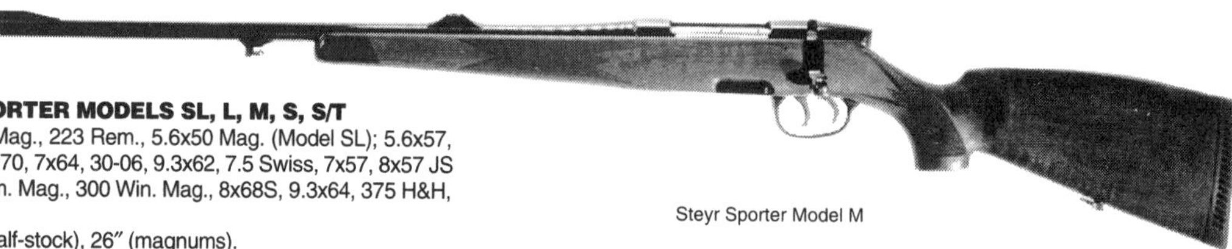
Steyr Sporter Model M

STEYR-MANNLICHER SPORTER MODELS SL, L, M, S, S/T
Caliber: 222 Rem., 222 Rem. Mag., 223 Rem., 5.6x50 Mag. (Model SL); 5.6x57, 243, 308 (Model L); 6.5x57, 270, 7x64, 30-06, 9.3x62, 7.5 Swiss, 7x57, 8x57 JS (Model M); 6.5x68, 7mm Rem. Mag., 300 Win. Mag., 8x68S, 9.3x64, 375 H&H, 458 Win. Mag. (Model S).
Barrel: 20″ (full-stock), 23.6″ (half-stock), 26″ (magnums).
Weight: 6.8 to 7.5 lbs. **Length:** 39″ (full-stock), 43″ (half-stock).
Stock: Hand-checkered European walnut. Full Mannlicher or standard half-stock with Monte Carlo comb and rubber recoil pad.
Sights: Ramp front, open adjustable rear.
Features: Choice of single- or double-set triggers. Detachable 5-shot rotary magazine. Drilled and tapped for scope mounting. Model M actions available in left-hand models; S (magnum) actions available in half-stock only. Imported by GSI, Inc.
Price: Models SL, L, M, half-stock **$2,023.00**
Price: As above, full-stock, 20″ barrel **$2,179.00**
Price: Models SL, L Varmint, 26″ heavy barrel **$2,179.00**
Price: Model M left-hand, half-stock (270, 30-06, 7x64) **$2,179.00**
Price: As above, full-stock (270, 7x57, 7x64, 30-06) **$2,335.00**
Price: Model S Magnum **$2,179.00**
Price: Model S/T, 26″ heavy barrel (375 H&H, 9.3x64, 458 Win. Mag.) **$2,335.00**

Steyr-Mannlicher MIII Professional Rifle
Similar to the Sporter series except has black ABS Cycolac half-stock, 23.6″ barrel, no sights. Available in 270, 30-06, 7x64, single trigger or optional double-set. Weighs about 7 lbs., 5 oz. Introduced 1994. Imported by GSI, Inc.
Price: **$995.00**
Price: With stipple-checkered walnut stock **$1,125.00**

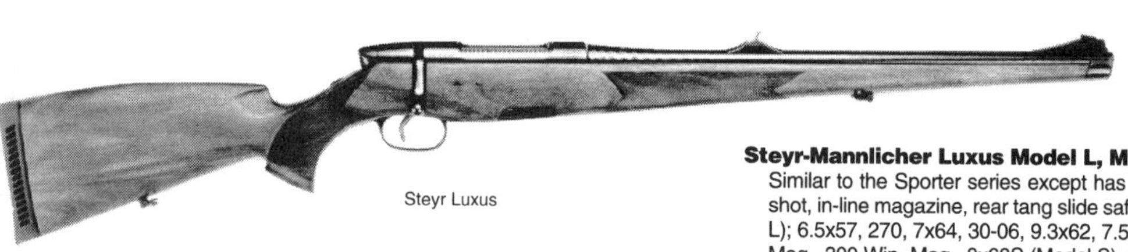
Steyr Luxus

Steyr-Mannlicher Luxus Model L, M, S
Similar to the Sporter series except has single set trigger, detachable steel 3-shot, in-line magazine, rear tang slide safety. Calibers: 5.6x57, 243, 308 (Model L); 6.5x57, 270, 7x64, 30-06, 9.3x62, 7.5 Swiss (Model M); 6.5x68, 7mm Rem. Mag., 300 Win. Mag., 8x68S (Model S). S (magnum) calibers available in half-stock only. Imported by GSI, Inc.
Price: Model L, M, half-stock **$2,648.00**
Price: As above, full-stock **$2,804.00**
Price: Model S (magnum) **$2,804.00**

Tikka Whitetail Hunter

Tikka Whitetail Hunter Synthetic Rifle
Similar to the Whitetail Hunter except has black synthetic stock; calibers 223, 308, 25-06, 270 Win., 30-06, 7mm Rem. Mag., 300 Win. Mag., 338 Win. Mag. Introduced 1996. Imported from Finland by Stoeger.
Price: Standard calibers **$559.00**
Price: Magnum calibers **$589.00**

Tikka Continental Varmint Rifle
Similar to the standard Tikka rifle except has 26″ heavy barrel, extra-wide forend. Chambered for 22-250, 223, 308. Reintroduced 1996. Made in Finland by Sako. Imported by Stoeger.
Price: **$644.00**

TIKKA WHITETAIL HUNTER BOLT-ACTION RIFLE
Caliber: 22-250, 223, 243, 25-06, 270, 308, 30-06, 7mm Rem. Mag., 300 Win. Mag., 338 Win. Mag.
Barrel: 22½″ (std. cals.), 24½″ (magnum cals.).
Weight: 7⅛ lbs. **Length:** 43″ overall (std. cals.).
Stock: European walnut with Monte Carlo comb, rubber buttpad, checkered grip and forend.
Sights: None furnished.
Features: Detachable four-shot magazine (standard calibers), three-shot in magnums. Receiver dovetailed for scope mounting. Reintroduced 1996. Imported from Finland by Stoeger Industries.
Price: Standard calibers **$559.00**
Price: Magnum calibers **$589.00**

Tikka Continental Long Range Hunting Rifle
Similar to the Whitetail Hunter except has 26″ heavy barrel. Available in 25-06, 270 Win., 7mm Rem. Mag., 300 Win. Mag. Introduced 1996. Imported from Finland by Stoeger.
Price: 25-06, 270 Win. **$644.00**
Price: 7 Rem. Mag., 300 Win. Mag. **$674.00**

CAUTION: PRICES SHOWN ARE SUPPLIED BY THE MANUFACTURER OR IMPORTER. CHECK YOUR LOCAL GUNSHOP.

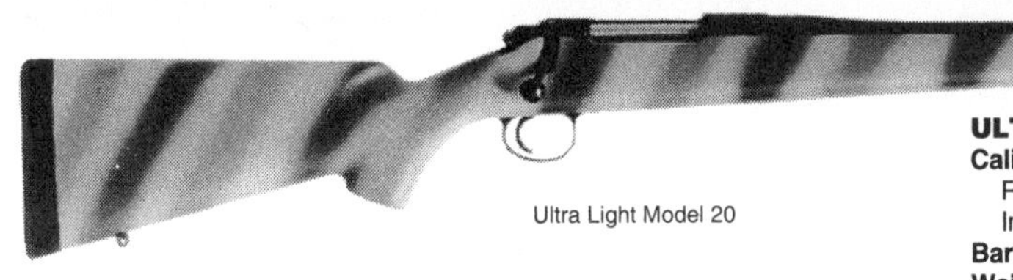

Ultra Light Model 20

ULTRA LIGHT ARMS MODEL 20 RIFLE

Caliber: 17 Rem., 22 Hornet, 222 Rem., 223 Rem. (Model 20S); 22-250, 6mm Rem., 243, 257 Roberts, 7x57, 7x57 Ackley, 7mm-08, 284 Win., 308 Savage. Improved and other calibers on request.

Barrel: 22″ Douglas Premium No. 1 contour.

Weight: 4½ lbs. **Length:** 41½″ overall.

Stock: Composite Kevlar, graphite reinforced. DuPont imron paint colors—green, black, brown and camo options. Choice of length of pull.

Sights: None furnished. Scope mount included.

Features: Timney adjustable trigger; two-position three-function safety. Benchrest quality action. Matte or bright stock and metal finish. 3″ magazine length. Shipped in a hard case. From Ultra Light Arms, Inc.

Price: Right-hand **$2,400.00**

Price: Model 20 Left Hand (left-hand action and stock) **$2,500.00**

Price: Model 24 (25-06, 270, 280 Rem., 30-06, 3⅜″ magazine length) **$2,500.00**

Price: Model 24 Left Hand (left-hand action and stock) **$2,600.00**

Ultra Light Arms Model 28, Model 40 Rifles

Similar to the Model 20 except in 264, 7mm Rem. Mag., 300 Win. Mag., 338 Win. Mag. (Model 28), 300 Wea. Mag., 416 Rigby (Model 40). Both use 24″ Douglas Premium No. 2 contour barrel. Weighs 5½ lbs., 45″ overall length. KDF or ULA recoil arrestor built in. Any custom feature available on any ULA product can be incorporated.

Price: Right-hand, Model 28 or 40 .... **$2,900.00**

Price: Left-hand, Model 28 or 40 .... **$3,000.00**

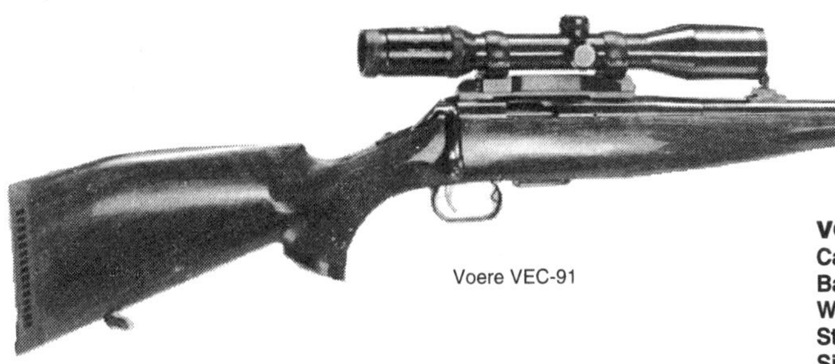

Voere VEC-91

VOERE VEC-91 LIGHTNING BOLT-ACTION RIFLE

Caliber: 5.56 UCC (223-cal.), 6mm UCC caseless, 5-shot magazine.

Barrel: 20″.

Weight: 6 lbs. **Length:** 39″ overall.

Stock: European walnut with cheekpiece, checkered grip and schnabel forend.

Sights: Blade on ramp front, open adjustable rear.

Features: Fires caseless ammunition via electric ignition; two batteries housed in the pistol grip last for about 5000 shots. Trigger is adjustable from 5 oz. to 7 lbs. Bolt action has twin forward locking lugs. Top tang safety. Drilled and tapped for scope mounting. Ammunition available from importer. Introduced 1991. Imported from Austria by JagerSport, Ltd.

Price: About **$1,995.00**

Voere VEC-91BR Caseless Rifle

Similar to the VEC-91 except has heavy 20″ barrel, synthetic benchrest stock, and is a single shot. Drilled and tapped for scope mounting. Introduced 1995. Imported from Austria by JagerSport, Ltd.

Price: **$1,995.00**

Voere VEC-91HB Varmint Special Caseless Rifle

Similar to the VEC-91 except has 22″ heavy sporter barrel, black synthetic or laminated wood stock. Drilled and tapped for scope mounts. Introduced 1995. Imported from Austria by JagerSport, Ltd.

Price: **$1,695.00**

Voere VEC-91SS Caseless Rifle

Similar to the VEC-91 except has synthetic stock with straight comb, matte-finished metal. Drilled and tapped for scope mounting. No open sights furnished. Introduced 1995. Imported from Austria by JagerSport, Ltd.

Price: 5.56mm UCC or 6mm UCC **$1,495.00**

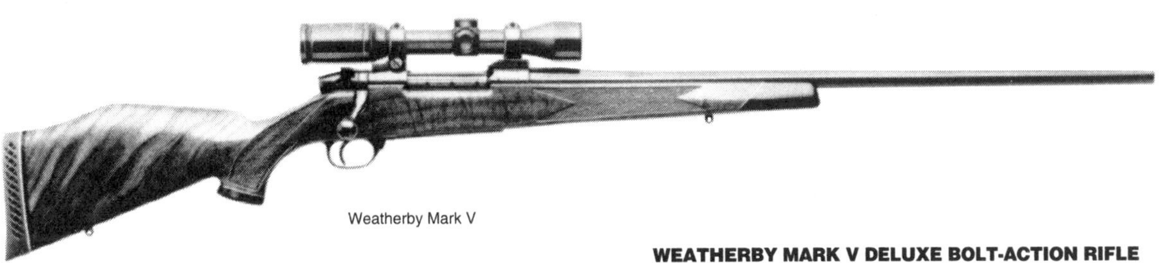

Weatherby Mark V

WEATHERBY MARK V DELUXE BOLT-ACTION RIFLE

Caliber: All Weatherby cals., plus 22-250, 30-06, 460 Wea. Mag.

Barrel: 24″ or 26″ round tapered.

Weight: 6½-10½ lbs. **Length:** 43¼″-46½″ overall.

Stock: Walnut, Monte Carlo with cheekpiece, high luster finish, checkered pistol grip and forend, recoil pad.

Sights: Optional (extra).

Features: Cocking indicator, adjustable trigger, hinged floorplate, thumb safety, quick detachable sling swivels.

Price: 240, 257, 270, 7mm Wea. Mag., 26″ **$1,399.00**

Price: 300 Wea. Mag., left-hand available, 340 Wea. Mag., right-hand, 26″ **$1,399.00**

Price: 378 Wea. Mag., 26″ **$1,475.00**

Price: 416 Wea. Mag., 26″ **$1,534.00**

Price: 460 Wea. Mag., 26″ **$1,892.00**

Consult our Directory pages for the location of firms mentioned.

Weatherby Mark V Sporter Rifle

Same as the Mark V Deluxe without the embellishments. Metal has low-luster blue, stock is Claro walnut with high-gloss epoxy finish, Monte Carlo comb, recoil pad. Introduced 1993.

Price: 257 270, 7mm, 300, 340 Wea. Mags., 26″ **$899.00**

Price: 375 H&H, 24″ **$899.00**

Price: 7mm Rem. Mag., 300 Win. Mag., 338 Win. Mag., 24″, ... **$899.00**

Weatherby Mark V Eurosport Rifle

Similar to the Mark V except has raised-comb Monte Carlo stock with hand-rubbed satin oil finish, low-luster blue metal. No grip cap or forend tip. Right-hand only. Introduced 1995. Made in U.S. From Weatherby.

Price: 257, 270, 7mm, 300, 340 Wea. Mags., 26″ barrel **$899.00**

Price: 7mm Rem. Mag., 300, 338 Win. Mags., 24″ barrel **$899.00**

Price: 375 H&H, 24″ barrel **$899.00**

Weatherby Mark V Stainless Rifle

Similar to the Mark V except made of 400-series stainless steel. Has lightweight injection-moulded synthetic stock with raised Monte Carlo comb, checkered grip and forend, custom floorplate release. Right-hand only. Introduced 1995. Made in U.S. From Weatherby.

Price: 257, 270, 7mm, 300, 340 Wea. Mags. **$999.00**

Price: 7mm Rem. Mag., 300, 338 Win. Mags., 24″ barrel **$999.00**

Price: 375 H&H, 24″ barrel **$999.00**

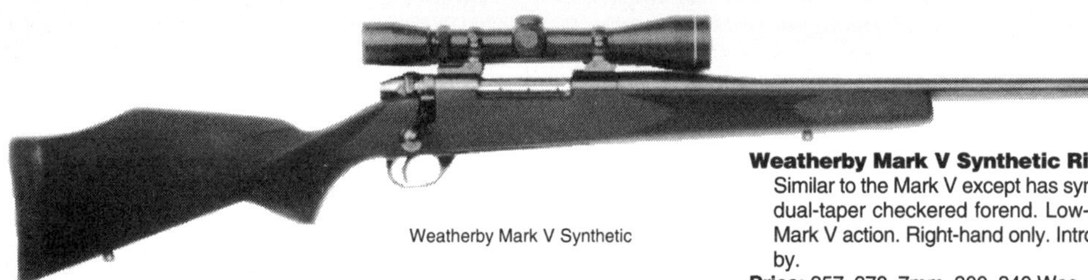

Weatherby Mark V Synthetic

Weatherby Mark V Synthetic Rifle

Similar to the Mark V except has synthetic stock with raised Monte Carlo comb, dual-taper checkered forend. Low-luster blued metal. Weighs $7^{1}/_{2}$ lbs. Uses Mark V action. Right-hand only. Introduced 1995. Made in U.S. From Weatherby.

Price: 257, 270, 7mm, 300, 340 Wea. Mags., 26″ barrel **$749.00**
Price: 7mm Rem. Mag., 300, 338 Win. Mags., 24″ barrel **$749.00**
Price: 375 H&H, 24″ barrel **$749.00**

Weatherby Euromark Rifle

Similar to the Mark V except has raised-comb Monte Carlo stock with hand-rubbed oil finish, fine-line hand-cut checkering, ebony grip and forend tips. All metal has low-luster blue. Right-hand only. Uses Mark V action. Introduced 1995. Made in U.S. From Weatherby.

Price: 257, 270, 7mm Wea. Mags., 26″ barrel **$1,449.00**
Price: 300, 340 Wea. Mags, 26″ barrel **$1,449.00**
Price: 416 Wea. Mag., 26″ barrel **$1,449.00**

Weatherby Lazermark V Rifle

Same as standard Mark V except stock has extensive laser carving under cheekpiece on butt, pistol grip and forend. Introduced 1981.

Price: 240, 257, 270, 7mm Wea. Mag., 300, 340, right-hand, 26″ **$1,499.00**
Price: 378 Wea. Mag., 26″ **$1,594.00**
Price: 416 Wea. Mag., 26″ **$1,644.00**
Price: 460 Wea. Mag., 26″ **$2,037.00**

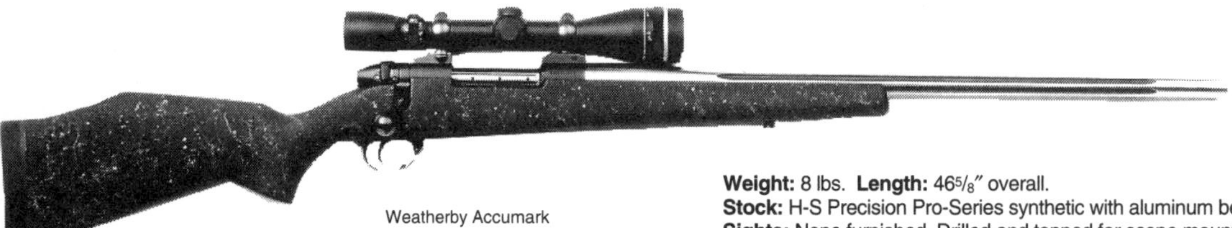

Weatherby Accumark

WEATHERBY ACCUMARK RIFLE

Caliber: 257, 270, 7mm, 300, 340 Wea. Mags., 7mm Rem. Mag., 300 Win. Mag.
Barrel: 26″.
Weight: 8 lbs. **Length:** $46^{5}/_{8}$″ overall.
Stock: H-S Precision Pro-Series synthetic with aluminum bedding plate.
Sights: None furnished. Drilled and tapped for scope mounting.
Features: Uses Mark V action with heavy-contour stainless barrel with flutes, muzzle diameter of .705″. Action coated with black oxide. Introduced 1996. Made in U.S. From Weatherby.
Price: **$1,199.00**

WICHITA CLASSIC RIFLE

Caliber: 17-222, 17-222 Mag., 222 Rem., 222 Rem. Mag., 223 Rem., 6x47; other calibers on special order.
Barrel: $21^{1}/_{8}$″.
Weight: 8 lbs. **Length:** 41″ overall.
Stock: AAA Fancy American walnut. Hand-rubbed and checkered (20 lpi). Hand-inletted, glass bedded, steel grip cap. Pachmayr rubber recoil pad.
Sights: None. Drilled and tapped for scope mounting.
Features: Available as single shot only. Octagonal barrel and Wichita action, right- or left-hand. Checkered bolt handle. Bolt is hand-fitted, lapped and jeweled. Adjustable trigger is set at 2 lbs. Side thumb safety. Firing pin fall is $^{3}/_{16}$″. Non-glare blue finish. From Wichita Arms.
Price: Single shot **$3,495.00**

WICHITA VARMINT RIFLE

Caliber: 222 Rem., 222 Rem. Mag., 223 Rem., 22 PPC, 6mm PPC, 22-250, 243, 6mm Rem., 308 Win.; other calibers on special order.
Barrel: $20^{1}/_{8}$″.
Weight: 9 lbs. **Length:** $40^{1}/_{8}$″ overall.
Stock: AAA Fancy American walnut. Hand-rubbed finish, hand checkered, 20 lpi pattern. Hand-inletted, glass bedded, steel grip cap. Pachmayr rubber recoil pad.
Sights: None. Drilled and tapped for scope mounts.
Features: Right- or left-hand Wichita action with three locking lugs. Available as a single shot only. Checkered bolt handle. Bolt is hand fitted, lapped and jeweled. Side thumb safety. Firing pin fall is $^{3}/_{16}$″. Non-glare blue finish. From Wichita Arms.
Price: Single shot **$2,695.00**

Winchester Model 70 Classic

WINCHESTER MODEL 70 CLASSIC SPORTER

Caliber: 25-06, 270 Win., 270 Wea., 30-06, 264 Win. Mag., 7mm Rem. Mag., 300 Win. Mag., 300 Wea. Mag., 338 Win. Mag., 3-shot magazine; 5-shot for 25-06, 270 Win., 30-06.
Barrel: 24″, 26″ for magnums.
Weight: $7^{3}/_{4}$ lbs. **Length:** $44^{3}/_{4}$″ overall.
Stock: American walnut with cut checkering and satin finish. Classic style with straight comb.
Sights: Optional hooded ramp front, adjustable folding leaf rear. Drilled and tapped for scope mounting.
Features: Uses pre-64-type action with controlled round feeding. Three-position safety, stainless steel magazine follower; rubber buttpad; epoxy bedded receiver recoil lug. BOSS barrel vibration modulator and muzzlebrake system optional. From U.S. Repeating Arms Co.
Price: With sights **$651.00**
Price: Without sights **$613.00**
Price: With BOSS (25-06, 264 Win. Mag., 270 Win., 270 Wea. Mag., 30-06, 7mm Rem. Mag., 300 Win. Mag., 300 Wea. Mag., 338 Win. Mag.) . . . **$728.00**

Winchester Model 70 Classic SM

Same as the Model 70 Sporter except has pre-64 controlled feed action, black composite, graphite-impregnated stock and matte-finished metal. Available in 270, 30-06, 7mm Rem. Mag., 300 Win. Mag., 338 Win. Mag., 375 H&H. Weighs about 7.8 lbs. BOSS barrel vibration modulator and muzzlebrake system optional. Introduced 1994.

Price: **$620.00**
Price: 375 H&H, with sights **$672.00**
Price: With BOSS (270, 30-06, 7mm Rem. Mag., 300 Win. Mag., 338 Win. Mag.) **$735.00**

Winchester Model 70 Classic Stainless Rifle

Same as the Model 70 Classic Sporter except has stainless steel barrel and pre-64-style action with controlled round feeding and matte gray finish, black composite stock impregnated with fiberglass and graphite, contoured rubber recoil pad. Available in 22-250, 243, 308, 270, 30-06, 7mm Rem. Mag., 300 Win. Mag., 300 Wea. Mag., 338 Win. Mag., 375 H&H Mag. (24″ barrel), 3- or 5-shot magazine. Weighs 6.75 lbs. BOSS barrel vibration modulator and muzzlebrake system optional. Introduced 1994.

Price: Without sights **$672.00**
Price: 375 H&H Mag., with sights **$724.00**
Price: With BOSS **$788.00**

CAUTION: PRICES SHOWN ARE SUPPLIED BY THE MANUFACTURER OR IMPORTER. CHECK YOUR LOCAL GUNSHOP.

Winchester Model 70 Synthetic Heavy Varmint Rifle
Similar to the Model 70 Classic Sporter except has fiberglass/graphite stock, 26″ heavy stainless steel barrel, blued receiver. Weighs about 10¾ lbs. Available in 220 Swift, 223, 22-250, 243, 308. Uses full-length Pillar Plus Accu Block bedding system. Introduced 1993.
Price: **$746.00**

WINCHESTER MODEL 70 CLASSIC SUPER EXPRESS MAGNUM
Caliber: 375 H&H Mag., 416 Rem. Mag., 458 Win. Mag., 3-shot magazine.
Barrel: 24″ (375, 416), 22″ (458).
Weight: 8¼ to 8½ lbs.
Stock: American walnut with Monte Carlo cheekpiece. Wrap-around checkering and finish.
Sights: Hooded ramp front, open rear.
Features: Controlled round feeding. Two steel cross bolts in stock for added strength. Front sling swivel stud mounted on barrel. Contoured rubber buttpad. From U.S. Repeating Arms Co.
Price: **$865.00**

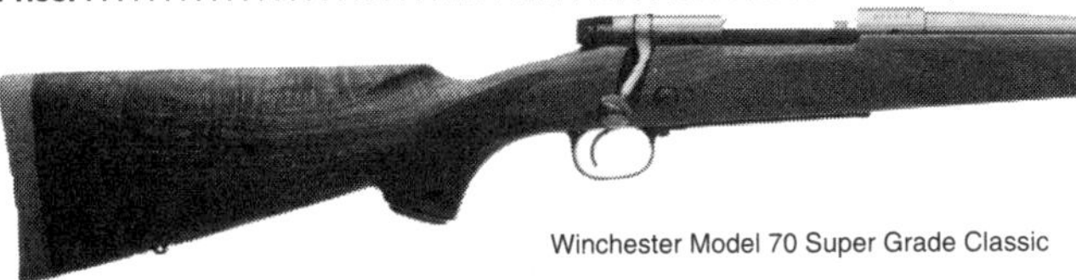
Winchester Model 70 Super Grade Classic

WINCHESTER RANGER RIFLE
Caliber: 223, 243, 270, 30-06.
Barrel: 22″.
Weight: 7¾ lbs. **Length:** 42″ overall.
Stock: Stained hardwood.
Sights: Hooded blade front, adjustable open rear.
Features: Three-position safety; push feed bolt with recessed-style bolt face; polished blue finish; drilled and tapped for scope mounting. Introduced 1985. From U.S. Repeating Arms Co.
Price: **$482.00**
Price: Ranger Ladies/Youth, 243, 308 only, scaled-down stock **$482.00**

Winchester Model 70 Classic Featherweight
Same as the Model 70 Classic except has claw controlled-round feeding system; action is bedded in a standard-grade walnut stock. Available in 22-250, 243, 308, 7mm-08, 270 Win., 280 Rem., 30-06. Drilled and tapped for scope mounts. Weighs 7.25 lbs. Introduced 1992.
Price: **$620.00**
Price: With BOSS **$735.00**

Winchester Model 70 Classic Featherweight All-Terrain
Similar to the Model 70 Classic Featherweight except has black, fiberglass/graphite stock in same style as the Classic Featherweight, barreled action made of stainless steel. Calibers 270 Win., 30-06, 7mm Rem. Mag., 300 Win. Mag. Introduced 1996.
Price: **$672.00**
Price: With BOSS **$788.00**

WINCHESTER MODEL 70 CLASSIC SUPER GRADE
Caliber: 270, 30-06, 5-shot magazine; 7mm Rem. Mag., 300 Win. Mag., 338 Win. Mag., 3-shot magazine.
Barrel: 24″, 26″ for magnums.
Weight: About 7¾ lbs. to 8 lbs. **Length:** 44½″ overall (24″ bbl.)
Stock: Walnut with straight comb, sculptured cheekpiece, wrap-around cut checkering, tapered forend, solid rubber buttpad.
Sights: None furnished; comes with scope bases and rings.
Features: Controlled round feeding with stainless steel claw extractor, bolt guide rail, three-position safety; all steel bottom metal, hinged floorplate, stainless magazine follower. BOSS barrel vibration modulator and muzzlebrake system optional. Introduced 1994. From U.S. Repeating Arms Co.
Price: **$840.00**
Price: With BOSS system **$956.00**

Winchester Model 70 Laredo

WINCHESTER MODEL 70 CLASSIC LAREDO
Caliber: 7mm Rem. Mag., 300 Win. Mag., 3-shot magazine.
Barrel: 26″ heavy; 1:10″ (300), 1:9.5″ (7mm).
Weight: 9½ lbs. **Length:** 46¾″ overall.
Stock: H-S Precision gray, synthetic with "Pillar Plus Accu-Block" bedding system, wide beavertail forend.
Sights: None furnished; drilled and topped for scope mounting.
Features: Pre-64-style, controlled round action with claw extractor, receiver-mounted blade ejector; matte blue finish. Introduced 1996. Made in U.S. by U.S. Repeating Arms Co.
Price: **$764.00**
Price: With BOSS **$879.00**

CENTERFIRE RIFLES—SINGLE SHOT

Classic and modern designs for sporting and competitive use.

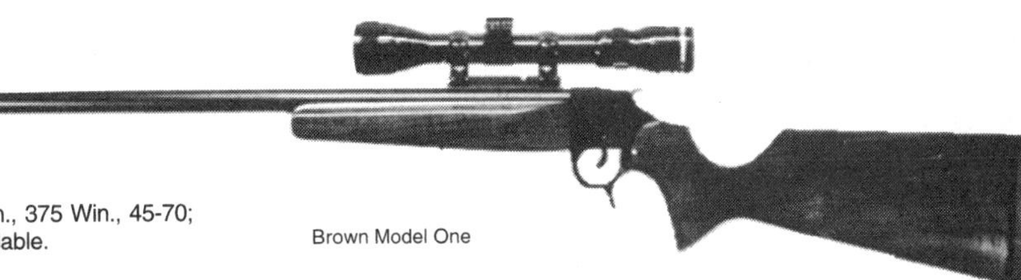
Brown Model One

BROWN MODEL ONE SINGLE SHOT RIFLE
Caliber: 22 LR, 357 Mag., 44 Mag., 7-30 Waters, 30-30 Win., 375 Win., 45-70; custom chamberings from 17 Rem. through 45-caliber available.
Barrel: 22″ or custom, bull or tapered.
Weight: 6 lbs. **Length:** NA.
Stock: Smooth walnut; custom takedown design by Woodsmith. Palm swell for right- or left-hand; rubber butt pad.
Sights: Optional. Drilled and tapped for scope mounting.
Features: Rigid barrel/receiver; falling block action with short lock time, automatic case ejection; air-gauged barrels by Wilson and Douglas. Muzzle has 11-degree target crown. Matte black oxide finish standard, polished and electroless nickel optional. Introduced 1988. Made in U.S. by E.A. Brown Mfg.
Price: **$750.00**

ARMSPORT 1866 SHARPS RIFLE, CARBINE
Caliber: 45-70.
Barrel: 28″, round or octagonal.
Weight: 8.10 lbs. **Length:** 46″ overall.
Stock: Walnut.
Sights: Blade front, folding adjustable rear. Tang sight set optionally available.
Features: Replica of the 1866 Sharps. Color case-hardened frame, rest blued. Imported by Armsport.
Price: **$860.00**
Price: With octagonal barrel **$880.00**
Price: Carbine, 22″ round barrel **$830.00**

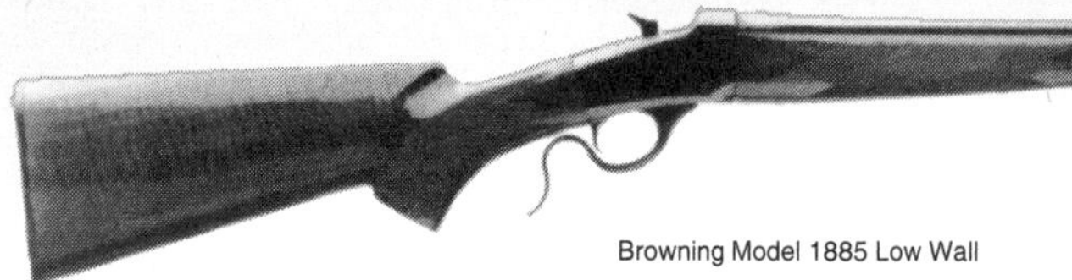
Browning Model 1885 Low Wall

BROWNING MODEL 1885 HIGH WALL SINGLE SHOT RIFLE
Caliber: 22-250, 30-06, 270, 7mm Rem. Mag., 45-70.
Barrel: 28″.
Weight: About 8½ lbs. **Length:** 43½″ overall.
Stock: Walnut with straight grip, schnabel forend.
Sights: None furnished; drilled and tapped for scope mounting.
Features: Replica of J.M. Browning's high-wall falling block rifle. Octagon barrel with recessed muzzle. Imported from Japan by Browning. Introduced 1985.
Price: **$939.95**

Browning Model 1885 BPCR Rifle
Similar to the 1885 High Wall rifle except the ejector system and shell deflector have been removed; chambered only for 40-65 and 45-70; color case-hardened full-tang receiver, lever, buttplate and grip cap; matte blue 30″ part octagon, part round barrel. The Vernier tang sight has indexed elevation, is screw adjustable windage, and has three peep diameters. The hooded front sight has a built-in spirit level and comes with sight interchangeable inserts. Adjustable trigger. Overall length 46⅛″, weighs about 11 lbs. Introduced 1996. Imported from Japan by Browning.
Price: **$1,664.95**

Browning Model 1885 Low Wall Rifle
Similar to the Model 1885 High Wall except has trimmer receiver, thinner 24″ octagonal barrel. Forend is mounted to the receiver. Adjustable trigger. Walnut pistol grip stock, trim schnabel forend with high-gloss finish. Available in 22 Hornet, 223 Rem., 243 Win. Overall length 39½″, weighs 6 lbs., 4 oz. Rifling twist rates: 1:16″ (22 Hornet); 1:12″ (223); 1:10″ (243). Polished blue finish. Introduced 1995. Imported from Japan by Browning.
Price: **$939.95**

CABELA'S SHARPS SPORTING RIFLE
Caliber: 45-70.
Barrel: 32″, tapered octagon.
Weight: 9 lbs. **Length:** 47¼″ overall.
Stock: Checkered walnut.
Sights: Blade front, open adjustable rear.
Features: Color case-hardened receiver and hammer, rest blued. Introduced 1995. Imported by Cabela's.
Price: **$749.95**

CUMBERLAND MOUNTAIN PLATEAU RIFLE
Caliber: 40-65, 45-70.
Barrel: Up to 32″; round.
Weight: About 10½ lbs. (32″ barrel). **Length:** 48″ overall (32″ barrel).
Stock: American walnut.
Sights: Marble's bead front, Marble's open rear.
Features: Falling block action with underlever. Blued barrel and receiver. Stock has lacquer finish, crescent buttplate. Introduced 1995. Made in U.S. by Cumberland Mountain Arms, Inc.
Price: **$1,085.00**

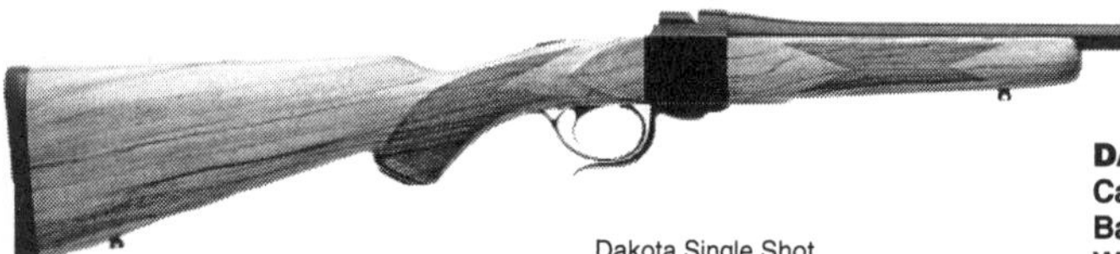
Dakota Single Shot

DAKOTA SINGLE SHOT RIFLE
Caliber: Most rimmed and rimless commercial calibers.
Barrel: 23″.
Weight: 6 lbs. **Length:** 39½″ overall.
Stock: Medium fancy grade walnut in classic style. Checkered grip and forend.
Sights: None furnished. Drilled and tapped for scope mounting.
Features: Falling block action with under-lever. Top tang safety. Removable trigger plate for conversion to single set trigger. Introduced 1990. Made in U.S. by Dakota Arms.
Price: **$2,500.00**
Price: Barreled action **$1,850.00**
Price: Action only **$1,500.00**

DESERT INDUSTRIES G-90 SINGLE SHOT RIFLE
Caliber: 22-250, 220 Swift, 223, 6mm, 243, 25-06, 257 Roberts, 270 Win., 270 Wea. Mag., 280, 7x57, 7mm Rem. Mag., 30-06, 300 Win. Mag., 300 Wea. Mag., 338 Win. Mag., 375 H&H, 45-70, 458 Win. Mag.
Barrel: 20″, 22″, 24″, 26″; light, medium, heavy.
Weight: About 7.5 lbs.
Stock: Walnut.
Sights: None furnished. Drilled and tapped for scope mounting.
Features: Cylindrical falling block action. All steel construction. Blue finish. Announced 1990. From Desert Industries, Inc.
Price: **$795.00**

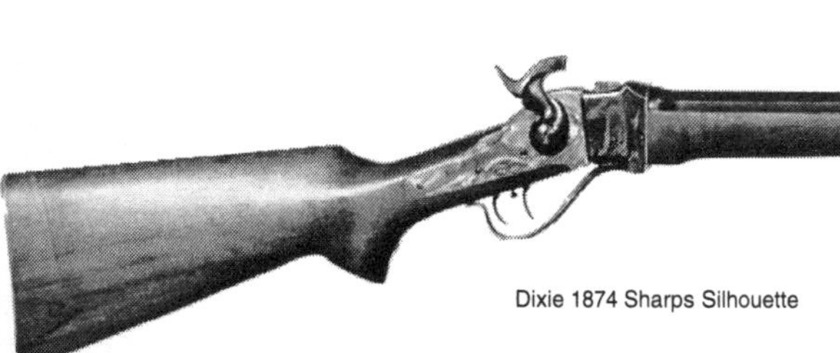
Dixie 1874 Sharps Silhouette

DIXIE 1874 SHARPS BLACKPOWDER SILHOUETTE RIFLE
Caliber: 45-70.
Barrel: 30″; tapered octagon; blued; 1:18″ twist.
Weight: 10 lbs., 3 oz. **Length:** 47½″ overall.
Stock: Oiled walnut.
Sights: Blade front, ladder-type hunting rear.
Features: Replica of the Sharps #1 Sporter. Shotgun-style butt with checkered metal buttplate; color case-hardened receiver, hammer, lever and buttplate. Tang is drilled and tapped for tang sight. Double-set triggers. Meets standards for NRA blackpowder cartridge matches. Introduced 1995. Imported from Italy by Dixie Gun Works.
Price: **$895.00**

Dixie 1874 Sharps Lightweight Hunter/Target Rifle
Same as the Dixie 1874 Sharps Blackpowder Silhouette model except has a straight-grip buttstock with military-style buttplate. Based on the 1874 military model. Introduced 1995. Imported from Italy by Dixie Gun Works.
Price: **$895.00**

E.M.F. SHARPS RIFLE
Caliber: 45-70.
Barrel: 28″, octagon.
Weight: 10¾ lbs. **Length:** NA.
Stock: Oiled walnut.
Sights: Blade front, flip-up open rear.
Features: Replica of the 1874 Sharps Sporting rifle. Color case-hardened lock; double-set trigger; blue finish. Imported by E.M.F.
Price: **$950.00**
Price: With browned finish **$1,000.00**
Price: Carbine (round 22″ barrel, barrel band) **$860.00**

 CAUTION: PRICES SHOWN ARE SUPPLIED BY THE MANUFACTURER OR IMPORTER. CHECK YOUR LOCAL GUNSHOP.

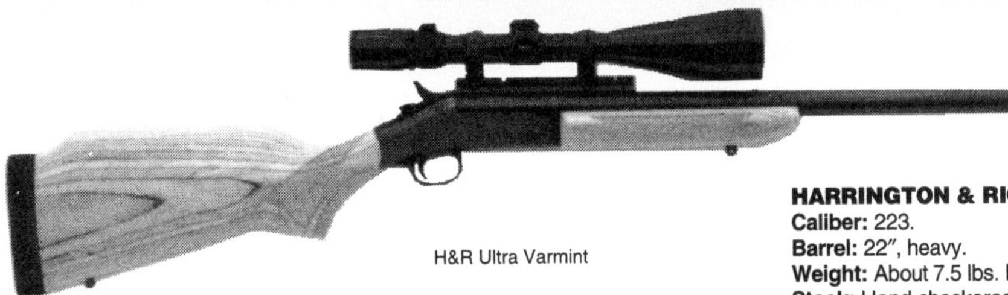

H&R Ultra Varmint

Harrington & Richardson Ultra Hunter Rifle

Similar to the Ultra Varmint rifle except chambered for 25-06 with 26″ barrel, or 308 Win. and 357 Rem. Mag. with 22″ barrel. Stock and forend are of cinnamon-colored laminate; hand-checkered grip and forend. Introduced 1995. Made in U.S. by H&R 1871, Inc.

Price: $249.95

Price: Rocky Mountain Elk Foundation Commemorative (35 Whelen 26″ barrel) $269.95

MODEL 1885 HIGH WALL RIFLE

Caliber: 30-40 Krag, 32-40, 38-55, 40-65 WCF, 45-70.
Barrel: 26″ (30-40), 28″ all others. Douglas Premium #3 tapered octagon.
Weight: NA. **Length:** NA.
Stock: Premium American black walnut.
Sights: Marble's standard ivory bead front, #66 long blade top rear with reversible notch and elevator.
Features: Recreation of early octagon top, thick-wall High Wall with Coil spring action. Tang drilled, tapped for High Wall tang sight. Receiver, lever, hammer and breechblock color case-hardened. Introduced 1991. Available from Montana Armory, Inc.
Price: $1,095.00

HARRINGTON & RICHARDSON ULTRA VARMINT RIFLE

Caliber: 223.
Barrel: 22″, heavy.
Weight: About 7.5 lbs. **Length:** NA.
Stock: Hand-checkered laminated birch with Monte Carlo comb.
Sights: None furnished. Drilled and tapped for scope mounting.
Features: Break-open action with side-lever release, positive ejection. Comes with scope mount. Blued receiver and barrel. Swivel studs. Introduced 1993. From H&R 1871, Inc.
Price: $249.95

HARRIS GUNWORKS ANTIETAM SHARPS RIFLE

Caliber: 40-65, 45-75.
Barrel: 30″, 32″, octagon or round, hand-lapped stainless or chromemoly.
Weight: 11.25 lbs. **Length:** 47″ overall.
Stock: Choice of straight grip, pistol grip or Creedmoor with schnabel forend; pewter tip optional. Standard wood is A Fancy; higher grades available.
Sights: Montana Vintage Arms #111 Low Profile Spirit Level front, #108 mid-range tang rear with windage adjustments.
Features: Recreation of the 1874 Sharps sidehammer. Action is color case-hardened, barrel satin black. Chrome-moly barrel optionally blued. Optional sights include #112 Spirit Level Globe front with windage, #107 Long Range rear with windage. Introduced 1994. Made in U.S. by Harris Gunworks.
Price: $2,000.00

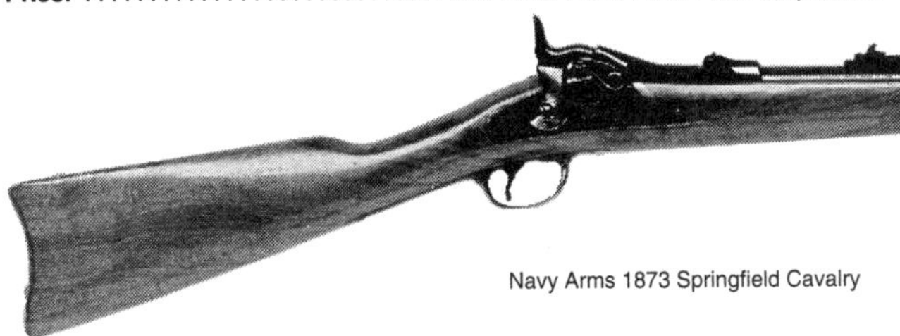

Navy Arms 1873 Springfield Cavalry

NAVY ARMS 1874 SHARPS CAVALRY CARBINE

Caliber: 45-70.
Barrel: 22″.
Weight: 7lbs., 12 oz. **Length:** 39″ overall.
Stock: Walnut.
Sights: Blade front, military ladder-type rear.
Features: Replica of the 1874 Sharps miltary carbine. Color case-hardened receiver and furniture. Imported by Navy Arms.
Price: $935.00

NAVY ARMS 1873 SPRINGFIELD CAVALRY CARBINE

Caliber: 45-70.
Barrel: 22″.
Weight: 7 lbs. **Length:** 40 1/2″ overall.
Stock: Walnut.
Sights: Blade front, military ladder rear.
Features: Blued lockplate and barrel; color case-hardened breechblock; saddle ring with bar. Replica of 7th Cavalry gun. Imported by Navy Arms.
Price: .... NA

Navy Arms 1874 Sharps Sniper Rifle

Similar to the Navy Arms Sharps Carbine except has 30″ barrel, double-set triggers; weighs 8 lbs., 8 oz., overall length 46 3/4″. Introduced 1984. Imported by Navy Arms.

Price: $1,115.00
Price: 1874 Sharps Infantry Rifle (three-band) $1,060.00

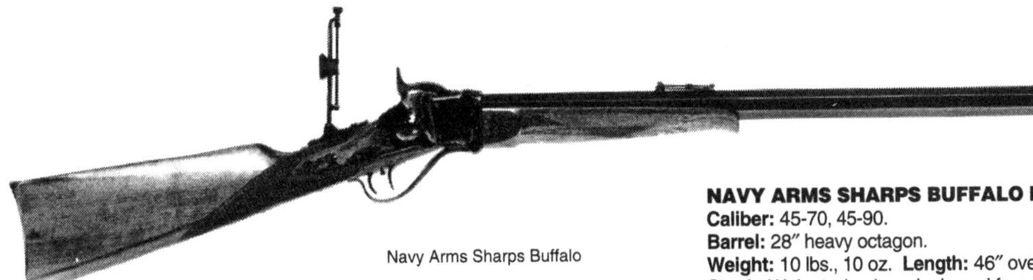

Navy Arms Sharps Buffalo

Navy Arms Sharps Plains Rifle

Similar to the Sharps Buffalo rifle except has 32″ medium-weight barrel, weighs 9 lbs., 8 oz., and is 49″ overall. Imported by Navy Arms.

Price: $1,050.00

Navy Arms #2 Creedmoor Rifle

Similar to the Navy Arms Buffalo Rifle except has 30″ tapered octagon barrel, checkered full-pistol grip stock, blade front sight, open adjustable rear sight and Creedmoor tang sight. Imported by Navy Arms.

Price: $875.00

NAVY ARMS SHARPS BUFFALO RIFLE

Caliber: 45-70, 45-90.
Barrel: 28″ heavy octagon.
Weight: 10 lbs., 10 oz. **Length:** 46″ overall.
Stock: Walnut; checkered grip and forend.
Sights: Blade front, ladder rear; tang sight optional.
Features: Color case-hardened receiver, blued barrel; double-set triggers. Imported by Navy Arms.
Price: $1,080.00

NAVY ARMS ROLLING BLOCK BUFFALO RIFLE

Caliber: 45-70.
Barrel: 26″, 30″.
Stocks: Walnut.
Sights: Blade front, adjustable rear.
Features: Reproduction of classic rolling block action. Available with full-octagon or half-octagon-half-round barrel. Color case-hardened action. From Navy Arms.
Price: $650.00

New England Firearms Survivor

NEW ENGLAND FIREARMS SURVIVOR RIFLE
Caliber: 223, 357 Mag., single shot.
Barrel: 22″.
Weight: 6 lbs. **Length:** 36″ overall.
Stock: Black polymer, thumbhole design.
Sights: Blade front, fully adjustable open rear.
Features: Receiver drilled and tapped for scope mounting. Stock and forend have storage compartments for ammo, etc.; comes with integral swivels and black nylon sling. Introduced 1996. Made in U.S. by New England Firearms.
Price: Blue **$219.95**
Price: Electroless nickel **$234.95**

NEW ENGLAND FIREARMS HANDI-RIFLE
Caliber: 22 Hornet, 223, 243, 30-30, 270, 280 Rem., 30-06, 44 Mag., 45-70.
Barrel: 22″, 26″ for 280 Rem..
Weight: 7 lbs.
Stock: Walnut-finished hardwood; black rubber recoil pad.
Sights: Ramp front, folding rear (22 Hornet, 30-30, 45-70). Drilled and tapped for scope mount; 223, 243, 270, 280, 30-06 have no open sights, come with scope mounts.
Features: Break-open action with side-lever release. The 223, 243, 270 and 30-06 have recoil pad and Monte Carlo stock for shooting with scope. Swivel studs on all models. Blue finish. Introduced 1989. From New England Firearms.
Price: **$214.95**

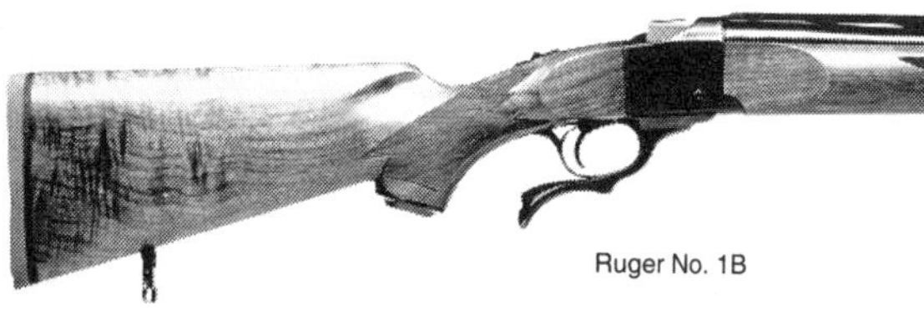
Ruger No. 1B

Ruger No. 1A Light Sporter
Similar to the No. 1B Standard Rifle except has lightweight 22″ barrel, Alexander Henry-style forend, adjustable folding leaf rear sight on quarter-rib, dovetailed ramp front with gold bead. Calibers 243, 30-06, 270 and 7x57. Weighs about 7¼ lbs.
Price: No. 1A **$665.00**
Price: Barreled action **$450.00**

Ruger No. 1S Medium Sporter
Similar to the No. 1B Standard Rifle except has Alexander Henry-style forend, adjustable folding leaf rear sight on quarter-rib, ramp front sight base and dovetail-type gold bead front sight. Calibers 218 Bee, 7mm Rem. Mag., 338 Win. Mag., 300 Win. Mag. with 26″ barrel, 45-70 with 22″ barrel. Weighs about 7½ lbs. In 45-70.
Price: No. 1S **$665.00**
Price: Barreled action **$440.00**

RUGER NO. 1B SINGLE SHOT
Caliber: 218 Bee, 22 Hornet, 220 Swift, 22-250, 223, 243, 6mm Rem., 25-06, 257 Roberts, 270, 280, 30-06, 7mm Rem. Mag., 300 Win. Mag., 338 Win. Mag., 270 Wea., 300 Wea.
Barrel: 26″ round tapered with quarter-rib; with Ruger 1″ rings.
Weight: 8 lbs. **Length:** 43⅜″ overall.
Stock: Walnut, two-piece, checkered p.g. and semi-beavertail forend.
Sights: None, 1″ scope rings supplied for integral mounts.
Features: Under-lever, hammerless falling block design has auto ejector, top tang safety.
Price: **$665.00**
Price: Barreled action **$450.00**

Ruger No. 1H Tropical Rifle
Similar to the No. 1B Standard Rifle except has Alexander Henry forend, adjustable folding leaf rear sight on quarter-rib, ramp front with dovetail gold bead, 24″ heavy barrel. Calibers 375 H&H, 404 Jeffery, 416 Rem. Mag. (weighs about 8¼ lbs.), 416 Rigby, and 458 Win. Mag. (weighs about 9 lbs.).
Price: No. 1H **$665.00**
Price: Barreled action **$440.00**

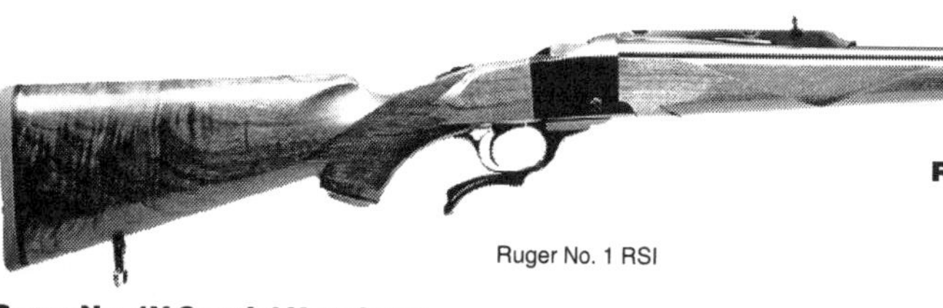
Ruger No. 1 RSI

Ruger No. 1V Special Varminter
Similar to the No. 1B Standard Rifle except has 24″ heavy barrel. Semi-beavertail forend, barrel tapped for target scope block, with 1″ Ruger scope rings. Calibers 22 PPC, 22-250, 220 Swift, 223, 6mm PPC, 25-06. Weight about 9 lbs.
Price: No. 1V **$665.00**
Price: Barreled action **$440.00**

Ruger No. 1 RSI International
Similar to the No. 1B Standard Rifle except has lightweight 20″ barrel, full-length International-style forend with loop sling swivel, adjustable folding leaf rear sight on quarter-rib, ramp front with gold bead. Calibers 243, 30-06, 270 and 7x57. Weight is about 7¼ lbs.
Price: No. 1 RSI **$668.00**
Price: Barreled action **$450.00**

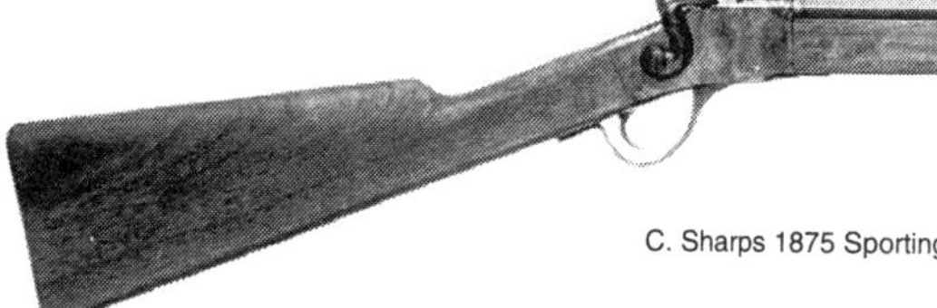
C. Sharps 1875 Sporting

C. SHARPS ARMS NEW MODEL 1875 RIFLE
Caliber: 22LR, 32-40 & 38-55 Ballard, 38-56 WCF, 40-65 WCF, 40-90 3¼″, 40-90 2⅝″, 40-70 2¹/₁₀″, 40-70 2¼″, 40-70 2½″, 40-50 1¹¹/₁₆″, 40-50 1⅞″, 45-90, 45-70, 45-100, 45-110, 45-120. Also available on special order only in 50-70, 50-90, 50-140.
Barrel: 24″, 26″, 30″ (standard), 32″, 34″ optional.
Weight: 8-12 lbs.
Stocks: Walnut, straight grip, shotgun butt with checkered steel buttplate.
Sights: Silver blade front, Rocky Mountain buckhorn rear.
Features: Recreation of the 1875 Sharps rifle. Production guns will have case colored receiver. Available in Custom Sporting and Target versions upon request. Announced 1986. From C. Sharps Arms Co. and Montana Armory, Inc.
Price: 1875 Carbine (24″ tapered round bbl.) **$725.00**
Price: 1875 Saddle Rifle (26″ tapered oct. bbl.) **$825.00**
Price: 1875 Sporting Rifle (30″ tapered oct. bbl.) **$850.00**
Price: 1875 Business Rifle (28″ tapered round bbl.) **$775.00**

CAUTION: PRICES SHOWN ARE SUPPLIED BY THE MANUFACTURER OR IMPORTER. CHECK YOUR LOCAL GUNSHOP.

C. Sharps Arms 1875 Classic Sharps

Similar to the New Model 1875 Sporting Rifle except has 26″, 28″ or 30″ full octagon barrel, crescent buttplate with toe plate, Hartford-style forend with cast German silver nose cap. Blade front sight, Rocky Mountain buckhorn rear. Weighs 10 lbs. Introduced 1987. From C. Sharps Arms Co. and Montana Armory, Inc.

Price: **$1,075.00**

C. Sharps Arms New Model 1875 Target & Long Range

Similar to the New Model 1875 except available in all listed calibers except 22 LR; 34″ tapered octagon barrel; globe with post front sight, Long Range Vernier tang sight with windage adjustments. Pistol grip stock with cheek rest; checkered steel buttplate. Introduced 1991. From C. Sharps Arms Co. and Montana Armory, Inc.

Price: **$1,165.00**

SHARPS 1874 OLD RELIABLE

Caliber: 45-70.
Barrel: 28″, octagonal.
Weight: 9¼ lbs. **Length:** 46″ overall.
Stock: Checkered walnut.
Sights: Blade front, adjustable rear.
Features: Double set triggers on rifle. Color case-hardened receiver and buttplate, blued barrel. Imported from Italy by E.M.F.
Price: Rifle or carbine **$950.00**
Price: Military rifle, carbine **$860.00**
Price: Sporting rifle **$860.00**

Shiloh Sharps 1874 Montana Roughrider

Similar to the No. 1 Sporting Rifle except available with half-octagon or full-octagon barrel in 24″, 26″, 28″, 30″, 34″ lengths; standard supreme or semi-fancy wood, shotgun, pistol grip or military-style butt. Weight about 8½ lbs. Calibers 30-40, 30-30, 40-50x1 11/16″ BN, 40-70x2 1/10″ BN, 45-70x2 1/10″ ST. Globe front and tang sight optional.

Price: Standard supreme **$904.00**
Price: Semi-fancy **$988.00**

C. SHARPS ARMS NEW MODEL 1874 OLD RELIABLE

Caliber: 40-50, 40-70, 40-90, 45-70, 45-90, 45-100, 45-110, 45-120, 50-70, 50-90, 50-140.
Barrel: 26″, 28″, 30″ tapered octagon.
Weight: About 10 lbs. **Length:** NA.
Stock: American black walnut; shotgun butt with checkered steel buttplate; straight grip, heavy forend with schnabel tip.
Sights: Blade front, buckhorn rear. Drilled and tapped for tang sight.
Features: Recreation of the Model 1874 Old Reliable Sharps Sporting Rifle. Double set triggers. Reintroduced 1991. Made in U.S. by C. Sharps Arms. Available from Montana Armory, Inc.
Price: **$995.00**

SHILOH SHARPS 1874 LONG RANGE EXPRESS

Caliber: 40-50 BN, 40-70 BN, 40-90 BN, 45-70 ST, 45-90 ST, 45-110 ST, 50-70 ST, 50-90 ST, 50-110 ST, 32-40, 38-55, 40-70 ST, 40-90 ST.
Barrel: 34″ tapered octagon.
Weight: 10½ lbs. **Length:** 51″ overall.
Stock: Oil-finished semi-fancy walnut with pistol grip, shotgun-style butt, traditional cheek rest, schnabel forend.
Sights: Globe front, sporting tang rear.
Features: Recreation of the Model 1874 Sharps rifle. Double set triggers. Made in U.S. by Shiloh Rifle Mfg. Co.
Price: **$1,134.00**
Price: Sporting Rifle No. 1 (similar to above except with 30″ bbl., blade front, buckhorn rear sight) **$1,108.00**
Price: Sporting Rifle No. 3 (similar to No. 1 except straight-grip stock, standard wood) **$1,004.00**
Price: 1874 Hartford model **$1,174.00**

Shiloh Sharps 1874 Business Rifle

Similar to No. 3 Rifle except has 28″ heavy round barrel, military-style buttstock and steel buttplate. Weight about 9½ lbs. Calibers 40-50 BN, 40-70 BN, 40-90 BN, 45-70 ST, 45-90 ST, 50-70 ST, 50-100 ST, 32-40, 38-55, 40-70 ST, 40-90 ST.

Price: **$1,010.00**
Price: 1874 Saddle Rifle (similar to Carbine except has 26″ octagon barrel, semi-fancy shotgun butt) **$1,062.00**

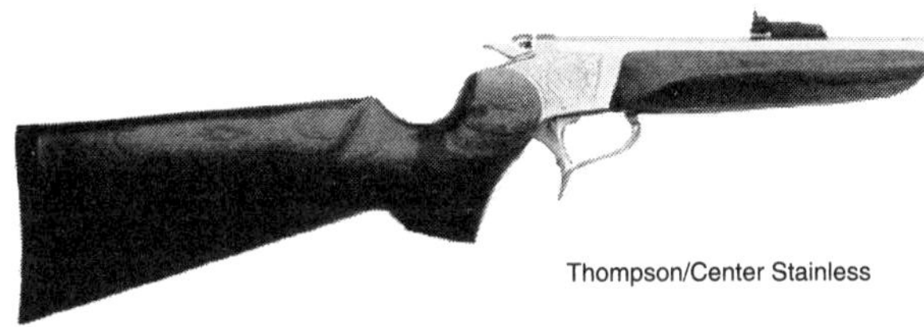

Thompson/Center Stainless

Thompson/Center Stainless Contender Carbine

Same as the blued Contender Carbine except made of stainless steel with blued sights. Available with walnut or Rynite stock and forend. Chambered for 22 LR, 22 Hornet, 223 Rem., 7-30 Waters, 30-30 Win., 410-bore. Youth model has walnut buttstock with 12″ pull length. Introduced 1993.

Price: Rynite stock, forend **$509.90**

CONSULT
SHOOTER'S
MARKETPLACE
Page 225, This Issue

THOMPSON/CENTER CONTENDER CARBINE

Caliber: 22 LR, 22 Hornet, 223 Rem., 7mm T.C.U., 7x30 Waters, 30-30 Win., 357 Rem. Maximum, 35 Rem., 44 Mag., 410, single shot.
Barrel: 21″.
Weight: 5 lbs., 2 oz. **Length:** 35″ overall.
Stock: Checkered American walnut with rubber buttpad. Also with Rynite stock and forend.
Sights: Blade front, open adjustable rear.
Features: Uses the T/C Contender action. Eleven interchangeable barrels available, all with sights, drilled and tapped for scope mounting. Introduced 1985. Offered as a complete Carbine only.
Price: Rifle calibers **$515.00**
Price: Extra barrels, rifle calibers, each **$234.30**
Price: 410 shotgun **$535.60**
Price: Extra 410 barrel **$260.10**

Thompson/Center Contender Carbine Youth Model

Same as the standard Contender Carbine except has 16¼″ barrel, shorter buttstock with 12″ length of pull. Comes with fully adjustable open sights. Overall length is 29″, weight about 4 lbs., 9 oz. Available in 22 LR, 22 WMR, 223 Rem., 7x30 Waters, 30-30, 35 Rem., 44 Mag. Also available with 16¼″, rifled vent. rib barrel chambered for 45/410.

Price: **$479.00**
Price: Extra barrels **$234.30**
Price: Extra 45/410 barrel **$260.10**
Price: Extra 45-70 barrel **$234.30**

UBERTI ROLLING BLOCK BABY CARBINE

Caliber: 22 LR, 22 WMR, 22 Hornet, 357 Mag., single shot.
Barrel: 22″.
Weight: 4.8 lbs. **Length:** 35½″ overall.
Stock: Walnut stock and forend.
Sights: Blade front, fully adjustable open rear.
Features: Resembles Remington New Model No. 4 carbine. Brass trigger guard and buttplate; color case-hardened frame, blued barrel. Imported by Uberti USA Inc.
Price: **$490.00**

WESSON & HARRINGTON BUFFALO CLASSIC RIFLE

Caliber: 45-70.
Barrel: 32″ heavy.
Weight: 9 lbs. **Length:** 52″ overall.
Stock: American black walnut.
Sights: None furnished; drilled and tapped for peep sight; barrel dovetailed for front sight.
Features: Color case-hardened Handi-Rifle action with exposed hammer; color case-hardened crescent buttplate; 19th century checkering pattern. Introduced 1995. Made in U.S. by H&R 1871, Inc.
Price: About **$349.95**

DRILLINGS, COMBINATION GUNS, DOUBLE RIFLES

Designs for sporting and utility purposes worldwide.

Beretta 455EELL Express

BERETTA EXPRESS SSO O/U DOUBLE RIFLES

Caliber: 375 H&H, 458 Win. Mag., 9.3x74R.
Barrel: 25.5″.
Weight: 11 lbs.
Stock: European walnut with hand-checkered grip and forend.
Sights: Blade front on ramp, open V-notch rear.
Features: Sidelock action with color case-hardened receiver (gold inlays on SSO6 Gold). Ejectors, double triggers, recoil pad. Introduced 1990. Imported from Italy by Beretta U.S.A.
Price: SSO6 .... **$21,000.00**
Price: SSO6 Gold **$23,500.00**

AUGUSTE FRANCOTTE BOXLOCK DOUBLE RIFLE

Caliber: 243, 270, 30-06, 7x64, 7x65R, 8x57JRS, 9.3x74R, 375 H&H, 470 N.E.; other calibers on request.
Barrel: 23.5″ to 26″.
Weight: NA. **Length:** NA.
Stock: Deluxe European walnut to customer specs; pistol grip or straight grip with Francotte cheekpiece; checkered butt; oil finish.
Sights: Bead front on long ramp, quarter-rib with fixed V rear.
Features: Side-by-side barrels; Anson & Deeley boxlock action with double triggers (front hinged), manual safety, floating firing pins and gas vent safety screws. Splinter or beavertail forend. English scroll engraving; coin finish or color case-hardening. Many options available. Made to customer specs. Imported from Belgium by Armes de Chasse.
Price: From about (no engraving) **$16,500.00**

AUGUSTE FRANCOTTE SIDELOCK DOUBLE RIFLES

Caliber: 243, 7x64, 7x65R, 8x57JRS, 270, 30-06, 9.3x74R, 375 H&H, 470 N.E.; others on request.
Barrel: 23$^1/_2$″ to 26″.
Weight: 7.61 lbs. (medium calibers), 11.1 lbs. (mag. calibers).
Stock: Fancy European walnut; dimensions to customer specs. Straight or pistol grip style. Checkered butt, oil finish.
Sights: Bead on ramp front, leaf rear on quarter-rib; to customer specs.
Features: Custom made to customer's specs. Special extractor for rimless cartridges; back-action sidelocks; double trigger with hinged front trigger. Automatic or free safety. Wide range of options available. Imported from Belgium by Armes de Chasse.
Price: From about (no engraving) .... **$30,000.00** to **$36,000**

Consult our Directory pages for the location of firms mentioned.

MERKEL OVER/UNDER COMBINATION GUNS

Caliber/Gauge: 12, 16, 20 (2$^3/_4$″ chamber) over 22 Hornet, 5.6x50R, 5.6x52R, 222 Rem., 243 Win., 6.5x55, 6.5x57R, 7x57R, 7x65R, 308 Win., 30-06, 8x57JRS, 9.3x74R, 375 H&H.
Barrel: 25.6″.
Weight: About 7.6 lbs. **Length:** NA.
Stock: Oil-finished walnut; pistol grip, cheekpiece.
Sights: Bead front, fixed rear.
Features: Kersten double cross-bolt lock; scroll-engraved, color case-hardened receiver; Blitz action; double triggers. Imported from Germany by GSI.
Price: Model 210E **$6,195.00**
Price: Model 211E (silver-grayed receivcer, fine hunting scene engraving) **$6,995.00**
Price: Model 213E (sidelock action, English-style, large scroll Arabesque engraving) **$13,595.00**
Price: Model 313E (as above, medium-scroll engraving) **$20,695.00**

BERETTA MODEL 455 SxS EXPRESS RIFLE

Caliber: 375 H&H, 458 Win. Mag., 470 NE, 500 NE 3″, 416 Rigby.
Barrel: 23$^1/_2$″ or 25$^1/_2$″.
Weight: 11 lbs.
Stock: European walnut with hand-checkered grip and forend.
Sights: Blade front, folding leaf V-notch rear.
Features: Sidelock action with easily removable sideplates; color case-hardened finish (455), custom big game or floral motif engraving (455EELL). Double triggers, recoil pad. Introduced 1990. Imported from Italy by Beretta U.S.A.
Price: Model 455 .... **$36,000.00**
Price: Model 455EELL **$47,000.00**

AUGUSTE FRANCOTTE BOXLOCK MOUNTAIN RIFLE

Caliber: 5.6x57R, 5.6x65R, 6.5x57R, 7x57R, 7x65R.
Barrel: 24.5″.
Weight: NA. **Length:** NA.
Stock: Deluxe walnut to customer specifications.
Sights: Ramp front, quarter-rib fixed rear.
Features: Anson & Deeley boxlock action; many options available. Made to customer specifications. Imported from Belgium by Armes de Chasse.
Price: From about (no engraving) **$15,000.00**

AUGUSTE FRANCOTTE SIDELOCK MOUNTAIN RIFLE

Caliber: Rimmed calibers from 5mm to 9mm.
Barrel: 23″ to 26″; chopper lump.
Weight: NA. **Length:** NA.
Stock: Deluxe walnut to customer specifications.
Sights: Ramp front, quarter-rib fixed rear.
Features: True Holland & Holland system; many options available. Made to customer specifications. Imported from Belgium by Armes de Chasse.
Price: From about (no engraving) **$28,000.00**

MERKEL MODEL 160 SIDE-BY-SIDE DOUBLE RIFLE

Caliber: 22 Hornet, 5.6x50R Mag., 5.6x52R, 222 Rem., 243 Win., 6.5x55, 6.5x57R, 7x57R, 7x65R, 308, 30-06, 8x57JRS, 9.3x74R, 375 H&H.
Barrel: 25.6″.
Weight: About 7.7 lbs, depending upon caliber. **Length:** NA.
Stock: Oil-finished walnut with pistol grip, cheekpiece.
Sights: Blade front on ramp, fixed rear.
Features: Sidelock action. Double barrel locking lug with Greener cross-bolt; fine engraved hunting scenes on sideplates; Holland & Holland ejectors; double triggers. Imported from Germany by GSI.
Price: From **$10,995.00**

Merkel Boxlock Double Rifles

Similar to the Model 160 double rifle except with Anson & Deely boxlock action with cocking indicators, double triggers, engraved color case-hardened receiver. Introduced 1995. Imported from Germany by GSI.
Price: Model 140-1 .... **$4,995.00**
Price: Model 140-1.1 (engraved silver-gray receiver) **$5,595.00**
Price: Model 150-1 (false sideplates, silver-gray receiver, Arabesque engraving) **$5,995.00**
Price: Model 150-1.1 (as above with English Arabesque engraving) **$6,995.00**

MERKEL OVER/UNDER DOUBLE RIFLES

Caliber: 22 Hornet, 5.6x50R Mag., 5.6x52R, 222 Rem., 243 Win., 6.5x55, 6.5x57R, 7x57R, 7x65R, 308, 30-06, 8x57JRS, 9.3x74R.
Barrel: 25.6″.
Weight: About 7.7 lbs, depending upon caliber. **Length:** NA.
Stock: Oil-finished walnut with pistol grip, cheekpiece.
Sights: Blade front, fixed rear.
Features: Kersten double cross-bolt lock; scroll-engraved, case-hardened receiver; Blitz action with double triggers. Imported from Germany by GSI.
Price: Model 221 E (silver-grayed receiver finish, hunting scene engraving) **$9,995.00**
Price: Model 223E (sidelock action, English-style large-scroll Arabesque engraving) **$16,295.00**
Price: Model 323E (as above with medium-scroll engraving) **$24,595.00**

CAUTION: PRICES SHOWN ARE SUPPLIED BY THE MANUFACTURER OR IMPORTER. CHECK YOUR LOCAL GUNSHOP.

MERKEL DRILLINGS

Caliber/Gauge: 12, 20, 3″ chambers, 16, $2\frac{3}{4}$″ chambers; 22 Hornet, 5.6x50R Mag., 5.6x52R, 222 Rem., 243 Win., 6.5x55, 6.5x57R, 7x57R, 7x65R, 308, 30-06, 8x57JRS, 9.3x74R, 375 H&H.
Barrel: 25.6″.
Weight: 7.9 to 8.4 lbs. depending upon caliber. **Length:** NA.
Stock: Oil-finished walnut with pistol grip; cheekpiece on 12- , 16-gauge.
Sights: Blade front, fixed rear.
Features: Double barrel locking lug with Greener cross-bolt; scroll-engraved, case-hardened receiver; automatic trigger safety; Blitz action; double triggers. Imported from Germany by GSI.
Price: Model 90S (selective sear safety) **$5,995.00**
Price: Model 90K (manually cocked rifle system) **$6,495.00**
Price: Model 95S (selective sear safety) **$7,195.00**
Price: Model 95K (manually cocked rifle system) **$7,695.00**

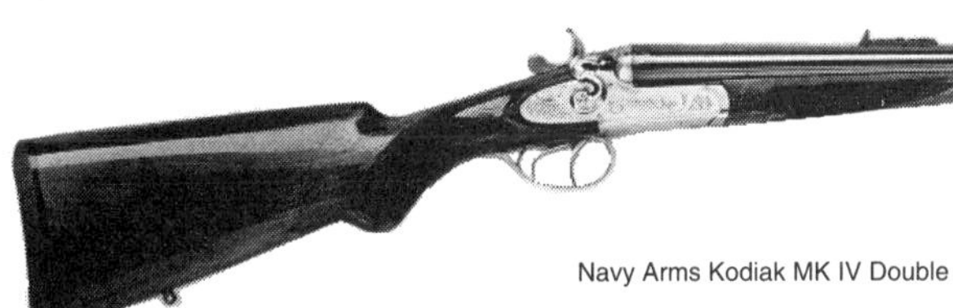

Navy Arms Kodiak MK IV Double

NAVY ARMS KODIAK MK IV DOUBLE RIFLE

Caliber: 45-70.
Barrel: 24″.
Weight: 10 lbs., 3 oz. **Length:** $39\frac{3}{4}$″ overall.
Stock: Checkered European walnut.
Sights: Bead front, folding leaf express rear.
Features: Blued, semi-regulated barrels; color case-hardened receiver and hammers; double triggers. Replica of Colt double rifle 1879-1885. Introduced 1996. Imported by Navy Arms.
Price: **$3,125.00**
Price: Engraved satin-finished receiver, browned barrels **$4,000.00**

SABATTI OVER/UNDER COMBINATION GUN

Caliber/Gauge: 12, 3″ over 223 Rem.
Barrel: 25″ (Imp. Mod.).
Weight: 8 lbs.
Stock: Checkered European walnut.
Sights: Bead on ramp front, fixed rear.
Features: Double triggers; blued, engraved receiver; automatic safety. Introduced 1996. Imported from Italy by K.B.I., Inc.
Price: **$879.00**

Savage 24F Predator

SAVAGE 24F PREDATOR O/U COMBINATION GUN

Caliber/Gauge: 22 Hornet, 223, 30-30 over 12 (24F-12) or 22 LR, 22 Hornet, 223, 30-30 over 20-ga. (24F-20); 3″ chambers.
Action: Takedown, low rebounding visible hammer. Single trigger, barrel selector spur on hammer.
Barrel: 24″ separated barrels; 12-ga. has Full, Mod., Imp. Cyl. choke tubes, 20-ga. has fixed Mod. choke.
Weight: 8 lbs. **Length:** $40\frac{1}{2}$″ overall.
Stock: Black Rynite composition.
Sights: Ramp front, rear open adjustable for elevation. Grooved for tip-off scope mount.
Features: Removable butt cap for storage and accessories. Introduced 1989.
Price: 24F-12 . . . . **$400.00**
Price: 24F-20 . . . . **$400.00**

SAUER DRILLING

Caliber/Gauge: 12, $2\frac{3}{4}$″ chambers/243, 6.5x57R, 7x57R, 7x65R, 30-06, 9.3x74R; 16, $2\frac{3}{4}$″ chambers/6.5x57R, 7x57R, 7x65R, 30-06.
Barrel: 25″.
Weight: 7.5 lbs. **Length:** 46″ overall.
Stock: Fancy French walnut with checkered grip and forend, hog-back comb, sculptured cheekpiece, hand-rubbed oil finish.
Sights: Bead front, automatic pop-up rifle rear.
Features: Greener boxlock cross-bolt action with double underlugs, Greener side safety; separate rifle cartridge extractor. Side-by-side shotgun barrels over rifle barrel. Nitride-coated, hand-engraved receiver available with English Arabesque or relief game animal scene engraving. Lux has profuse relief-engraved game scenes, extra-fancy stump wood. Imported from Germany by SIGARMS, Inc.
Price: Standard **$4,600.00**
Price: Lux **$6,100.00**

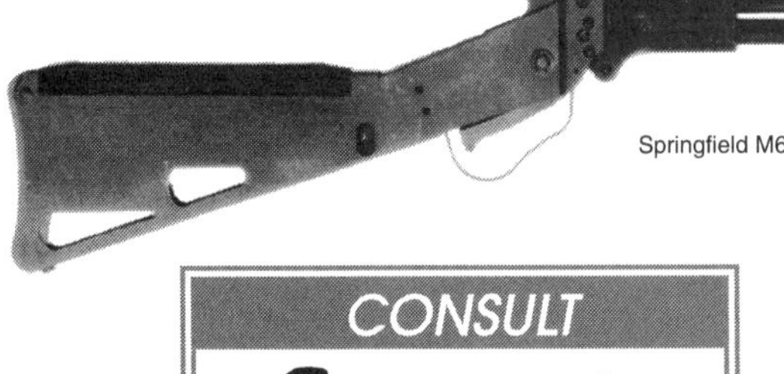

Springfield M6 Scout

SPRINGFIELD, INC. M6 SCOUT RIFLE/SHOTGUN

Caliber/Gauge: 22 LR or 22 Hornet over 410-bore.
Barrel: 18.25″.
Weight: 4 lbs. **Length:** 32″ overall.
Stock: Folding detachable with storage for 15 22 LR, four 410 shells.
Sights: Blade front, military aperture for 22; V-notch for 410.
Features: All-metal construction. Designed for quick disassembly and minimum maintenance. Folds for compact storage. Introduced 1982; reintroduced 1996. Imported from the Czech Republic by Springfield, Inc.
Price: Parkerized **$160.00**
Price: Stainless steel **$190.00**

CONSULT
SHOOTER'S MARKETPLACE
Page 225, This Issue

TIKKA MODEL 512S DOUBLE RIFLE

Caliber: 300, 30-06, 9.3x74R.
Barrel: 24″.
Weight: $8\frac{5}{8}$ lbs.
Stock: American walnut with Monte Carlo style.
Sights: Ramp front, adjustable open rear.
Features: Barrel selector mounted in trigger. Cocking indicators in tang. Recoil pad. Valmet scope mounts available. Introduced 1980. Imported from Italy by Stoeger.
Price: With ejectors **$1,800.00**

TIKKA MODEL 512S COMBINATION GUN

Caliber/Gauge: 12 over 222, 308, 30-06.
Barrel: 24″ (Imp. Mod.).
Weight: $7\frac{5}{8}$ lbs.
Stock: American walnut, with recoil pad. Monte Carlo style. Standard measurements 14″x$1\frac{3}{5}$″x2″x$2\frac{3}{5}$″.
Sights: Blade front, flip-up-type open rear.
Features: Barrel selector on trigger. Hand-checkered stock and forend. Barrels are screw-adjustable to change bullet point of impact. Barrels are interchangeable. Introduced 1980. Imported from Italy by Stoeger.
Price: **$1,400.00**
Price: Extra barrels, from **$775.00**

Designs for hunting, utility and sporting purposes, including training for competition.

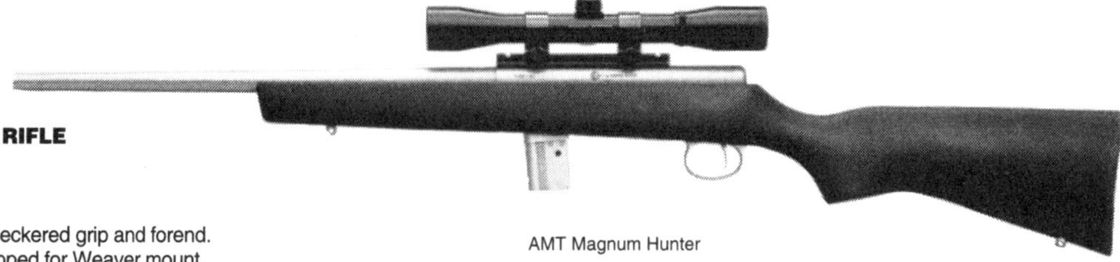

AMT Magnum Hunter

AMT MAGNUM HUNTER AUTO RIFLE
Caliber: 22 WMR, 10-shot magazine.
Barrel: 20″.
Weight: 6 lbs. **Length:** 40½″ overall.
Stock: Black fiberglass-filled nylon; checkered grip and forend.
Sights: None furnished; drilled and tapped for Weaver mount.
Features: Stainless steel construction. Free-floating target-weight barrel. Introduced 1995. Made in U.S. by AMT.
Price: $549.99

Armscor M-20P Standard Rifle
Similar to the M-20C except has 20.75″ barrel, walnut-finished hardwood stock with Monte Carlo comb. Introduced 1990. Imported from the Philippines by K.B.I., Inc.
Price: $119.00

ARMSCOR MODEL AK22 AUTO RIFLE
Caliber: 22 LR, 10-shot magazine.
Barrel: 18.5″.
Weight: 7.5 lbs. **Length:** 38″ overall.
Stock: Plain mahogany.
Sights: Adjustable post front, leaf rear adjustable for elevation.
Features: Resembles the AK-47. Matte black finish. Introduced 1987. Imported from the Philippines by K.B.I., Inc.
Price: About $189.00

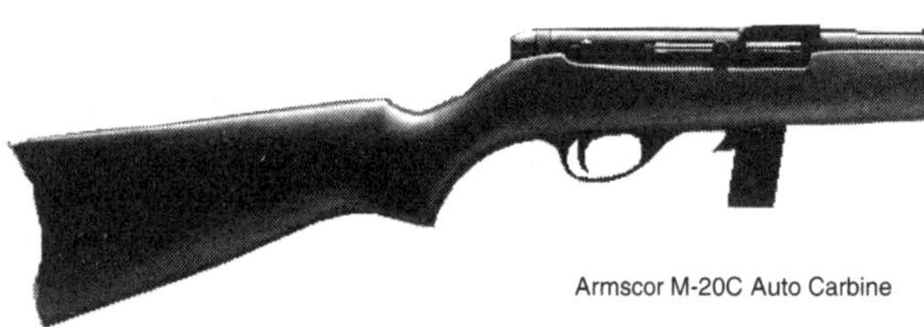

Armscor M-20C Auto Carbine

Armscor M-2000S Classic Auto Rifle
Similar to the M-20C except has 20.75″ barrel; hand-checkered stock has Monte Carlo comb and cheekpiece; fully adjustable rear sight. Introduced 1990. Imported from the Philippines by K.B.I., Inc.
Price: $320.00

Armscor M-2000SC Super Classic Rifle
Similar to the M-2000S except has oil-finished American walnut stock with 18 lpi hand checkering; black hardwood grip cap and forend tip; highly polished barreled action; jewelled bolt; recoil pad; swivel studs. Imported from the Philippines by K.B.I., Inc.
Price: $320.00

ARMSCOR M-20C AUTO CARBINE
Caliber: 22 LR, 10-shot magazine.
Barrel: 18.25″.
Weight: 6.5 lbs. **Length:** 38″ overall.
Stock: Walnut-finished mahogany.
Sights: Hooded front, rear adjustable for elevation.
Features: Receiver grooved for scope mounting. Blued finish. Introduced 1990. Imported from the Philippines by Ruko Products.
Price: $139.99

ARMSCOR M-1600 AUTO RIFLE
Caliber: 22 LR, 10-shot magazine.
Barrel: 18.25″.
Weight: 6.2 lbs. **Length:** 38.5″ overall.
Stock: Black finished mahogany.
Sights: Post front, aperture rear.
Features: Resembles Colt AR-15. Matte black finish. Introduced 1987. Imported from the Philippines by K.B.I., Inc.
Price: About $175.00

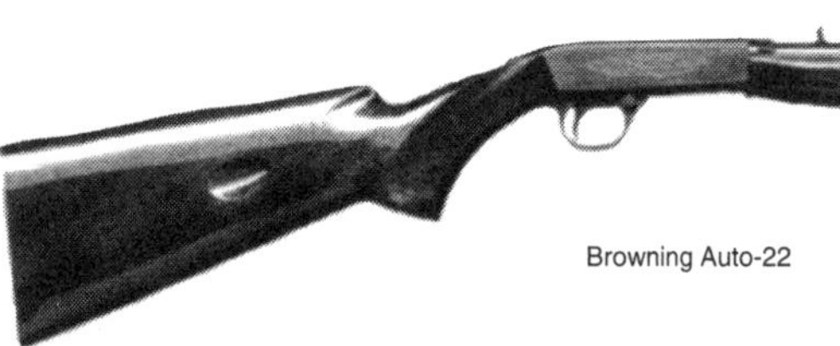

Browning Auto-22

Browning Auto-22 Grade VI
Same as the Grade I Auto-22 except available with either grayed or blued receiver with extensive engraving with gold-plated animals: right side pictures a fox and squirrel in a woodland scene; left side shows a beagle chasing a rabbit. On top is a portrait of the beagle. Stock and forend are of high-grade walnut with a double-bordered cut checkering design. Introduced 1987.
Price: Grade VI, blue or gray receiver $819.00

ERMA EM1 CARBINE
Caliber: 22 LR, 10-shot magazine.
Barrel: 18″.
Weight: 5.6 lbs. **Length:** 35.5″ overall.
Stock: Polished beech or oiled walnut.
Sights: Blade front, fully adjustable aperture rear.
Features: Blowback action. Receiver grooved for scope mounting. Imported from Germany by Mandall Shooting Supplies.
Price: $499.95

BROWNING AUTO-22 RIFLE
Caliber: 22 LR, 11-shot.
Barrel: 19¼″.
Weight: 4¾ lbs. **Length:** 37″ overall.
Stock: Checkered select walnut with pistol grip and semi-beavertail forend.
Sights: Gold bead front, folding leaf rear.
Features: Engraved receiver with polished blue finish; cross-bolt safety; tubular magazine in buttstock; easy takedown for carrying or storage. Imported from Japan by Browning.
Price: Grade I $398.95

BRNO ZKM 611/621 AUTO RIFLE
Caliber: 22 WMR, 6-shot magazine.
Barrel: 20″.
Weight: 6 lbs., 2 oz. **Length:** 37″ overall.
Stock: Walnut; checkered grip and forend.
Sights: Blade front, open rear.
Features: Removable box magazine; polished blue finish; grooved receiver for scope mounting; sling swivels; thumbscrew takedown. Introduced 1995. Imported from the Czech Republic by Magnum Research.
Price: Model 611 .... $569.00
Price: Model 621 (beech stock) $499.00

CAUTION: PRICES SHOWN ARE SUPPLIED BY THE MANUFACTURER OR IMPORTER. CHECK YOUR LOCAL GUN SHOP.

E.A.A./SABATTI MODEL 1822 AUTO RIFLE
Caliber: 22 LR, 10-shot magazine.
Barrel: 18½" round tapered; bull barrel on Heavy and Thumbhole Heavy models.
Weight: 5¼ lbs. (Sporter). **Length:** 37" overall.
Stock: Stained hardwood; Thumbhole model has one-piece stock.
Sights: Bead front, folding leaf rear adjustable for elevation on Sporter model. Heavy and Thumbhole models only dovetailed for scope mount.
Features: Cross-bolt safety. Blue finish. Lifetime warranty. Introduced 1993. Imported from Italy by European American Armory.
Price: Sporter **$190.00**
Price: Heavy **$205.00**
Price: Thumbhole Heavy **$350.00**

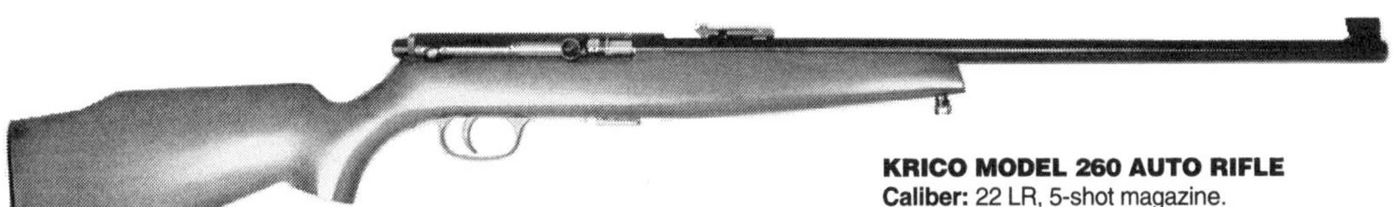
Krico Model 260

KRICO MODEL 260 AUTO RIFLE
Caliber: 22 LR, 5-shot magazine.
Barrel: 19.6".
Weight: 6.6 lbs. **Length:** 38.9" overall.
Stock: Beech.
Sights: Blade on ramp front, open adjustable rear.
Features: Receiver grooved for scope mounting. Sliding safety. Imported from Germany by Mandall Shooting Supplies.
Price: **$700.00**

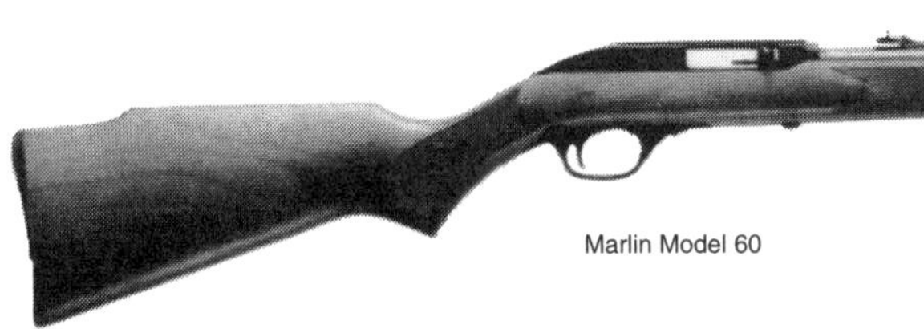
Marlin Model 60

MARLIN MODEL 60 SELF-LOADING RIFLE
Caliber: 22 LR, 14-shot tubular magazine.
Barrel: 22" round tapered.
Weight: About 5½ lbs. **Length:** 40½" overall.
Stock: Press-checkered, walnut-finished Maine birch with Monte Carlo, full pistol grip; Mar-Shieldr finish.
Sights: Ramp front, open adjustable rear.
Features: Matted receiver is grooved for scope mount. Manual bolt hold-open; automatic last-shot bolt hold-open.
Price: **$158.40**

Marlin Model 60SS Self-Loading Rifle
Same as the Model 60 except breech bolt, barrel and outer magazine tube are made of stainless steel; most other parts are either nickel-plated or coated to match the stainless finish. Monte Carlo stock is of black/gray Maine birch laminate, and has nickel-plated swivel studs, rubber butt pad. Introduced 1993.
Price: **$244.20**

MARLIN 70PSS STAINLESS RIFLE
Caliber: 22 LR, 7-shot magazine.
Barrel: 16¼" stainless steel, Micro-Groove® rifling.
Weight: 3¼ lbs. **Length:** 35¼" overall.
Stock: Black fiberglass-filled synthetic with abbreviated forend, nickel-plated swivel studs, moulded-in checkering.
Sights: Romp front with orange post, cutaway Wide Scan® hood; adjustable open rear. Receiver grooved for scope mounting.
Features: Takedown barrel; cross-bolt safety; manual bolt hold-open; last shot bolt hold-open; comes with padded carrying case. Introduced 1986. Made in U.S. by Marlin.
Price: **$255.25**

Marlin Model 922

MARLIN MODEL 922 MAGNUM SELF-LOADING RIFLE
Caliber: 22 WMR, 7-shot magazine.
Barrel: 20.5".
Weight: 6.5 lbs. **Length:** 39.75" overall.
Stock: Checkered American black walnut with Monte Carlo comb, swivel studs, rubber buttpad.
Sights: Ramp front with bead and removable Wide-Scan® hood, adjustable folding semi-buckhorn rear.
Features: Action based on the centerfire Model 9 Carbine. Receiver drilled and tapped for scope mounting. Automatic last-shot bolt hold open; magazine safety. Introduced 1993.
Price: **$410.75**

MARLIN MODEL 995SS SELF-LOADING RIFLE
Caliber: 22 LR, 7-shot clip magazine.
Barrel: 18" Micro-Groove®; stainless steel.
Weight: 5 lbs. **Length:** 37" overall.
Stock: Black fiberglass-filled synthetic with nickel-plated swivel studs, moulded-in checkering.
Sights: Ramp front with orange post and cut-away Wide-Scan® hood; screw-adjustable open rear.
Features: Stainless steel breechbolt and barrel. Receiver grooved for scope mount; bolt hold-open device; cross-bolt safety. Introduced 1979.
Price: **$237.60**

Mitchell Arms LW-22

MITCHELL ARMS LW22 SEMI-AUTO CARBINE
Caliber: 22 LR, 10-shot magazine.
Barrel: 17".
Weight: 3.25 lbs. **Length:** 35" overall.
Stock: Black foam or fixed skeleton.
Sights: Protected post front, adjustable aperture rear.
Features: Blue finish; removable stock and barrel. Introduced 1996. Made in U.S. by Mitchell Arms.
Price: Skeleton stock **$274.95**
Price: Black foam stock **$304.95**

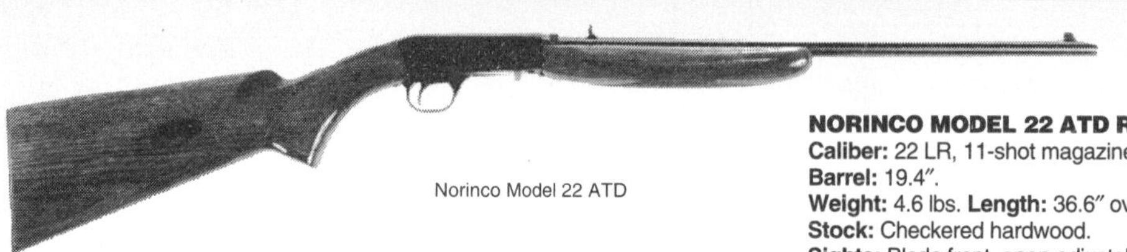
Norinco Model 22 ATD

NORINCO MODEL 22 ATD RIFLE
Caliber: 22 LR, 11-shot magazine.
Barrel: 19.4″.
Weight: 4.6 lbs. **Length:** 36.6″ overall.
Stock: Checkered hardwood.
Sights: Blade front, open adjustable rear.
Features: Browning-design takedown action for storage, transport. Cross-bolt safety. Tube magazine loads through buttplate. Blue finish with engraved receiver. Introduced 1987. Imported from China by Interarms.
Price: **$150.00**

Remington 522 Viper

REMINGTON MODEL 522 VIPER AUTOLOADING RIFLE
Caliber: 22 LR, 10-shot magazine.
Barrel: 20″.
Weight: 4 5/8 lbs. **Length:** 40″ overall.
Stock: Black synthetic with positive checkering, beavertail forend.
Sights: Bead on ramp front, fully adjustable open rear. Integral grooved rail for scope mounting.
Features: Synthetic stock and receiver with overall matte black finish. Has magazine safety, cocking indicator; manual and last-shot hold-open; trigger mechanism has primary and secondary sears; integral ejection port shield. Introduced 1993.
Price: **$165.00**

REMINGTON 552 BDL SPEEDMASTER RIFLE
Caliber: 22 S (20), L (17) or LR (15) tubular mag.
Barrel: 21″ round tapered.
Weight: About 5 3/4 lbs. **Length:** 40″ overall.
Stock: Walnut. Checkered grip and forend.
Sights: Bead front, step open rear adjustable for windage and elevation.
Features: Positive cross-bolt safety, receiver grooved for tip-off mount.
Price: About **$340.00**

Ruger 10/22T Target

RUGER 10/22 AUTOLOADING CARBINE
Caliber: 22 LR, 10-shot rotary magazine.
Barrel: 18 1/2″ round tapered.
Weight: 5 lbs. **Length:** 37 1/4″ overall.
Stock: American hardwood with pistol grip and bbl. band.
Sights: Brass bead front, folding leaf rear adjustable for elevation.
Features: Detachable rotary magazine fits flush into stock, cross-bolt safety, receiver tapped and grooved for scope blocks or tip-off mount. Scope base adaptor furnished with each rifle.
Price: Model 10/22 RB (blue) **$213.00**
Price: Model K10/22RB (bright finish stainless barrel) **$255.00**

Ruger 10/22T Target Rifle
Similar to the 10/22 except has 20″ heavy, hammer-forged barrel with tight chamber dimensions, improved trigger pull, laminated hardwood stock dimensioned for optical sights. No iron sights supplied. Introduced 1996. Made in U.S. by Sturm, Ruger & Co.
Price: **$392.50**

Ruger 10/22 International

Ruger 10/22 International Carbine
Similar to the Ruger 10/22 Carbine except has full-length International stock of American hardwood, checkered grip and forend; comes with rubber buttpad, sling swivels. Reintroduced 1994.
Price: Blue (10/22RBI) **$262.00**
Price: Stainless (K10/22RBI) **$282.00**

Ruger 10/22 Deluxe Sporter
Same as 10/22 Carbine except walnut stock with hand checkered pistol grip and forend; straight buttplate, no barrel band, has sling swivels.
Price: Model 10/22 DSP **$274.00**

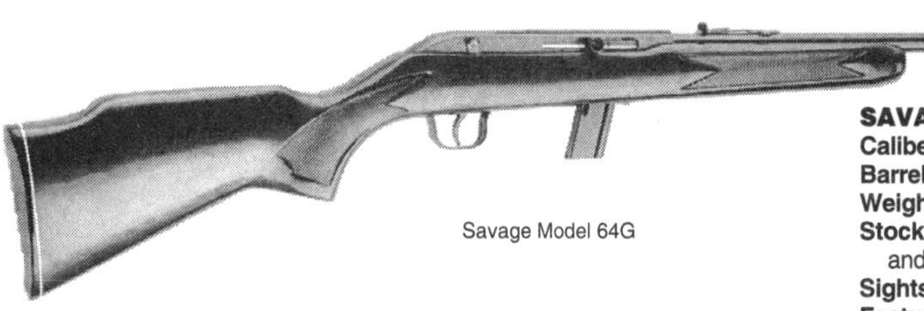
Savage Model 64G

SAVAGE MODEL 64G AUTO RIFLE
Caliber: 22 LR, 10-shot magazine.
Barrel: 20″.
Weight: 5 1/2 lbs. **Length:** 40″ overall.
Stock: Walnut-finished hardwood with Monte Carlo-type comb, checkered grip and forend.
Sights: Bead front, open adjustable rear. Receiver grooved for scope mounting.
Features: Thumb-operated rotating safety. Blue finish. Side ejection, bolt hold-open device. Introduced 1990. Made in Canada, from Savage Arms.
Price: **$123.00**
Price: Model 64GXP Package Gun includes 4x15 scope and mounts **$129.00**

CAUTION: PRICES SHOWN ARE SUPPLIED BY THE MANUFACTURER OR IMPORTER. CHECK YOUR LOCAL GUN SHOP.

Classic and modern models for sport and utility, including training.

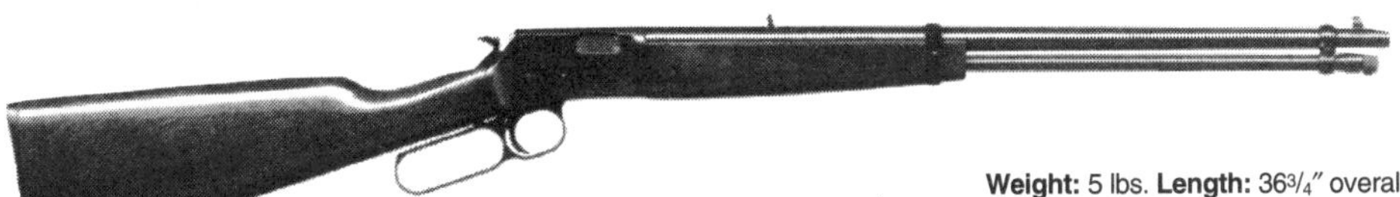

Browning BL-22

BROWNING BL-22 LEVER-ACTION RIFLE

Caliber: 22 S (22), L (17) or LR (15), tubular magazine.
Barrel: 20″ round tapered.
Weight: 5 lbs. **Length:** 36 3/4″ overall.
Stock: Walnut, two-piece straight grip Western style.
Sights: Bead post front, folding-leaf rear.
Features: Short throw lever, half-cock safety, receiver grooved for tip-off scope mounts. Imported from Japan by Browning.
Price: Grade I $345.95
Price: Grade II (engraved receiver, checkered grip and forend) $395.95

Marlin Model 39AS

MARLIN MODEL 39AS GOLDEN LEVER-ACTION RIFLE

Caliber: 22 S (26), L (21), LR (19), tubular magazine.
Barrel: 24″ Micro-Groove®.
Weight: 6 1/2 lbs. **Length:** 40″ overall.
Stock: Checkered American black walnut with white line spacers at pistol grip cap and buttplate; Mar-Shield® finish. Swivel studs; rubber buttpad.
Sights: Bead ramp front with detachable Wide-Scan™ hood, folding rear semi-buckhorn adjustable for windage and elevation.
Features: Hammer-block safety; rebounding hammer. Takedown action, receiver tapped for scope mount (supplied), offset hammer spur; gold-plated steel trigger.
Price: $444.80

REMINGTON 572 BDL FIELDMASTER PUMP RIFLE

Caliber: 22 S (20), L (17) or LR (14), tubular magazine.
Barrel: 21″ round tapered.
Weight: 5 1/2 lbs. **Length:** 42″ overall.
Stock: Walnut with checkered pistol grip and slide handle.
Sights: Blade ramp front; sliding ramp rear adjustable for windage and elevation.
Features: Cross-bolt safety; removing inner magazine tube converts rifle to single shot; receiver grooved for tip-off scope mount.
Price: About $353.00

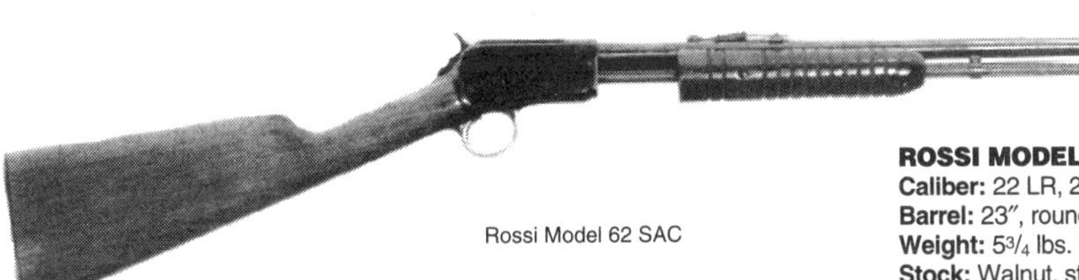

Rossi Model 62 SAC

ROSSI MODEL 62 SA PUMP RIFLE

Caliber: 22 LR, 22 WMR.
Barrel: 23″, round or octagonal.
Weight: 5 3/4 lbs. **Length:** 39 1/4″ overall.
Stock: Walnut, straight grip, grooved forend.
Sights: Fixed front, adjustable rear.
Features: Capacity 20 Short, 16 Long or 14 Long Rifle. Quick takedown. Imported from Brazil by Interarms.
Price: Blue $240.00
Price: Nickel $250.00
Price: Blue, with octagonal barrel $250.00
Price: 22 WMR, as Model 59 .... $280.00

Rossi Model 62 SAC Carbine

Same as standard model except 22 LR, has 16 1/4″ barrel. Magazine holds slightly fewer cartridges.
Price: Blue $240.00
Price: Nickel $250.00

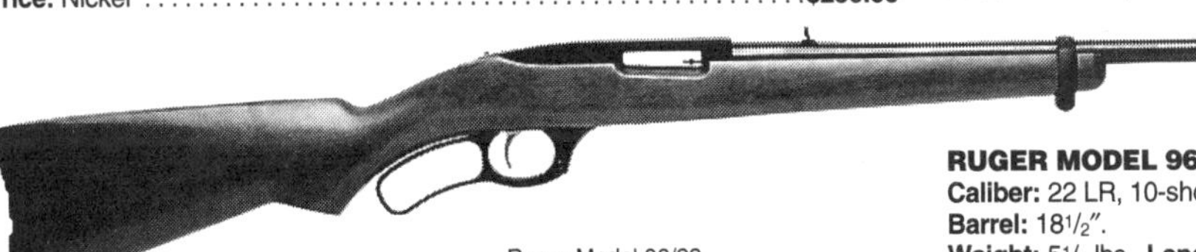

Ruger Model 96/22

RUGER MODEL 96/22 LEVER-ACTION RIFLE

Caliber: 22 LR, 10-shot rotary, magazine; 22 WMR, 9-shot rotary magazine.
Barrel: 18 1/2″.
Weight: 5 1/4 lbs. **Length:** 37 1/4″ overall.
Stock: American hardwood.
Sights: Gold bead front, folding leaf rear.
Features: Cross-bolt safety, visible cocking indicator; short-throw lever action. Screw-on dovetail scope base. Introduced 1996. Made in U.S. by Sturm, Ruger & Co.
Price: 96/22 (22 LR) $327.50
Price: 96/22M (22 WMR) $345.00

Winchester 9422 High Grade

WINCHESTER MODEL 9422 LEVER-ACTION RIFLE

Caliber: 22 S (21), L (17), LR (15), tubular magazine.
Barrel: 20 1/2″.
Weight: 6 1/4 lbs. **Length:** 37 1/8″ overall.
Stock: American walnut, two-piece, straight grip (no pistol grip).
Sights: Hooded ramp front, adjustable semi-buckhorn rear.
Features: Side ejection, receiver grooved for scope mounting, takedown action. From U.S. Repeating Arms Co.
Price: Walnut $407.00
Price: With WinTuff laminated stock $407.00

Winchester Model 9422 Trapper

Winchester Model 9422 High Grade Rifle
Same as the standard Model 9422 except has high grade walnut with gloss finish, blued and engraved receiver with a coonhound on the right side, a racoon profile on the left, both framed with detailed Nimschke-style scrollwork. Chambered only for 22 LR. Introduced 1995. From U.S. Repeating Arms Co., Inc.
Price: $489.00

Winchester Model 9422 Trapper
Similar to the Model 9422 with walnut stock except has 16$^{1}/_{2}$″ barrel, overall length of 33$^{1}/_{8}$″, weighs 5$^{1}/_{2}$ lbs. Magazine holds 15 Shorts, 12 Longs, 11 Long Rifles. Introduced 1996.
Price: $407.00

Winchester Model 9422 Magnum Lever-Action Rifle
Same as the 9422 except chambered for 22 WMR cartridge, has 11-round mag. capacity.
Price: Walnut $424.00
Price: With WinCam green stock $424.00
Price: With WinTuff brown laminated stock $424.00

RIMFIRE RIFLES—BOLT ACTIONS & SINGLE SHOTS

Includes models for a variety of sports, utility and competitive shooting.

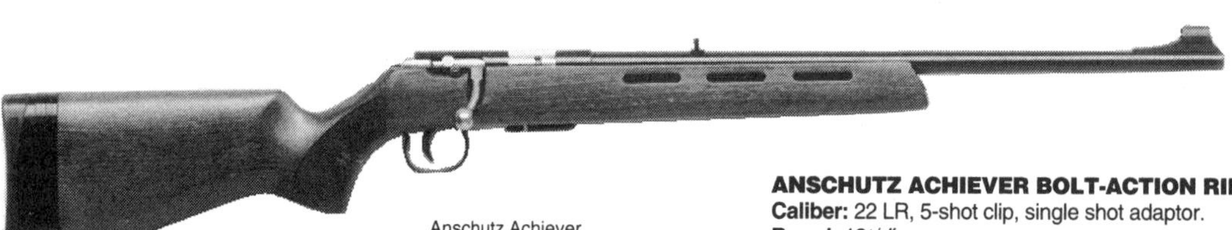
Anschutz Achiever

ANSCHUTZ 1710D CUSTOM RIFLE
Caliber: 22 LR, 5-shot clip.
Barrel: 24$^{1}/_{4}$″.
Weight: 7$^{3}/_{8}$ lbs. **Length:** 42$^{1}/_{2}$″ overall.
Stock: Select European walnut.
Sights: Hooded ramp front, folding leaf rear; drilled and tapped for scope mounting.
Features: Match 54 action with adjustable single-stage trigger; roll-over Monte Carlo cheekpiece, slim forend with schnabel tip, Wundhammer palm swell on pistol grip, rosewood grip cap with white diamond insert; skip-line checkering on grip and forend. Introduced 1988. Imported from Germany by AcuSport Corp.
Price: $1,161.64

ANSCHUTZ ACHIEVER BOLT-ACTION RIFLE
Caliber: 22 LR, 5-shot clip, single shot adaptor.
Barrel: 19$^{1}/_{2}$″.
Weight: 5 lbs. **Length:** 35$^{1}/_{2}$″ to 36$^{2}/_{3}$″ overall.
Stock: Walnut-finished hardwood with adjustable buttplate, vented forend, stippled pistol grip. Length of pull adjustable from 11$^{7}/_{8}$″ to 13″.
Sights: Hooded front, open rear adjustable for windage and elevation.
Features: Uses Mark 2000-type action with adjustable two-stage trigger. Receiver grooved for scope mounting. Designed for training in junior rifle clubs and for starting young shooters. Introduced 1987. Imported from Germany by AcuSport Corp.
Price: $372.60

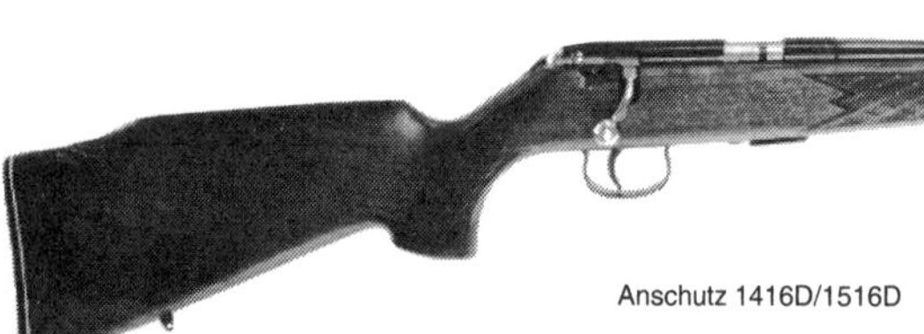
Anschutz 1416D/1516D

Anschutz 1416D/1516D Deluxe Rifles
Similar to the Classic models except have European walnut stocks with roll-over Monte Carlo cheekpiece, slim forend with schnabel tip, fine cut checkering on grip and forend. Introduced 1988. Imported from Germany by AcuSport Corp.
Price: 1416D (22 LR) $673.11
Price: 1516D (22 WMR) $693.78

ANSCHUTZ 1416D/1516D CLASSIC RIFLES
Caliber: 22 LR (1416D), 5-shot clip; 22 WMR (1516D), 4-shot clip.
Barrel: 22$^{1}/_{2}$″.
Weight: 6 lbs. **Length:** 41″ overall.
Stock: European walnut; classic style with straight comb, checkered pistol grip and forend.
Sights: Hooded ramp front, folding leaf rear.
Features: Uses Match 64 action. Adjustable single stage trigger. Receiver grooved for scope mounting. Imported from Germany by AcuSport Corp.
Price: 1416D, 22 LR $604.72
Price: 1516D, 22 WMR $633.58
Price: 1416D Classic left-hand $633.58

Armscor M-14P

Armscor M-14P Standard Rifle
Similar to the M-1400S except has short walnut-finished hardwood stock for small shooters. Introduced 1987. Imported from the Philippines by K.B.I., Inc.
Price: $119.00
Price: M-14Y Youth (17.5″ barrel) $119.00

ARMSCOR M-1400S CLASSIC BOLT-ACTION RIFLE
Caliber: 22 LR, 10-shot magazine.
Barrel: 22$^{5}/_{8}$″.
Weight: 6.7 lbs. **Length:** 41.25″ overall.
Stock: Walnut-finished mahogany.
Sights: Bead front, rear adjustable for elevation.
Features: Receiver grooved for scope mounting. Blued finish. Introduced 1987. Imported from the Philippines by K.B.I., Inc.
Price: $190.00

CAUTION: PRICES SHOWN ARE SUPPLIED BY THE MANUFACTURER OR IMPORTER. CHECK YOUR LOCAL GUNSHOP.

Armscor M-1400SC Super Classic Rifle

Similar to the M-1400S except has oil-finished American walnut stock with 18 lpi hand checkering; black hardwood grip cap and forend tip; highly polished barreled action; jewelled bolt; recoil pad; swivel studs. Imported from the Philippines by K.B.I., Inc.

Price: **$340.00**

Armscor M-12Y Youth Rifle

Similar to the M-1400S except has 17.5″ barrel, and is a single shot. Weight is 4.1 lbs., overall length 34.4″. Imported from the Philippines by K.B.I., Inc.

Price: **$99.00**

CABANAS LASER RIFLE

Caliber: 177.
Barrel: 19″.
Weight: 6 lbs., 12 oz. **Length:** 42″ overall.
Stock: Target-type thumbhole.
Sights: Blade front, open fully adjustable rear.
Features: Fires round ball or pellets with 22 blank cartridge. Imported from Mexico by Mandall Shooting Supplies.
Price: **$159.95**

Cabanas Espronceda IV Bolt-Action Rifle

Similar to the Leyre model except has full sporter stock, 18¾″ barrel, 40″ overall length, weighs 5½ lbs.

Price: **$134.95**

Consult our Directory pages for the location of firms mentioned.

CHIPMUNK SINGLE SHOT RIFLE

Caliber: 22, S, L, LR, single shot.
Barrel: 16⅛″.
Weight: About 2½ lbs. **Length:** 30″ overall.
Stocks: American walnut, or camouflage.
Sights: Post on ramp front, peep rear adjustable for windage and elevation.
Features: Drilled and tapped for scope mounting using special Chipmunk base ($9.95). Made in U.S. Introduced 1982. From Oregon Arms.
Price: Standard **$174.95**
Price: Deluxe (better wood, checkering) **$225.00**

Armscor M-1500SC Super Classic Rifle

Similar to the M-1500S except has oil-finished American walnut stock with 18 lpi hand checkering; black hardwood grip cap and forend tip; highly polished barreled action; jewelled bolt; recoil pad; swivel studs. Imported from the Philippines by K.B.I., Inc.

Price: **$350.00**

Armscor M-1500S Classic Rifle

Similar to the Model 1400S except chambered for 22 WMR. Has 22.6″ barrel, double lug bolt, checkered stock, weighs 6.5 lbs. Introduced 1987.

Price: About **$210.00**

CABANAS MASTER BOLT-ACTION RIFLE

Caliber: 177, round ball or pellet; single shot.
Barrel: 19½″.
Weight: 8 lbs. **Length:** 45½″ overall.
Stocks: Walnut target-type with Monte Carlo.
Sights: Blade front, fully adjustable rear.
Features: Fires round ball or pellet with 22-cal. blank cartridge. Bolt action. Imported from Mexico by Mandall Shooting Supplies. Introduced 1984.
Price: **$189.95**
Price: Varmint model (has 21½″ barrel, 4½ lbs., 41″ overall length, varmint-type stock) **$119.95**

Cabanas Leyre Bolt-Action Rifle

Similar to Master model except 44″ overall, has sport/target stock.

Price: **$149.95**
Price: Model R83 (17″ barrel, hardwood stock, 40″ o.a.l.) **$79.95**
Price: Mini 82 Youth (16½″ barrel, 33″ overall length, 3½ lbs.) **$69.95**
Price: Pony Youth (16″ barrel, 34″ overall length, 3.2 lbs.) **$69.95**

COOPER ARMS MODEL 36 CLASSIC SPORTER RIFLE

Caliber: 22 LR, 5-shot magazine.
Barrel: 22¾″.
Weight: 7 lbs. **Length:** 42½″ overall.
Stock: AAA Claro walnut with 22 lpi checkering, oil finish.
Sights: None furnished.
Features: Action has three mid-bolt locking lugs, 45-degree bolt rotation; fully adjustable single stage match trigger; swivel studs. Pachmayr butt pad. Introduced 1991. Made in U.S. by Cooper Arms.
Price: **$1,675.00**
Price: Custom Classic (AAA Claro walnut, Monte Carlo beaded cheekpiece, oil finish) **$1,960.00**
Price: Model 36 Featherweight (black synthetic stock, 6.5 lbs.) **$1,740.00**
Price: Model 36 Montana Trailblazer (lighter weight, sporter barrel profile) **$1,475.00**

CZ ZKM-452 Deluxe

CZ ZKM-452 DELUXE BOLT-ACTION RIFLE

Caliber: 22 LR, 22 WMR, detachable 6- or 10-shot magazine.
Barrel: 23.6″.
Weight: 6.9 lbs. **Length:** 43.5″ overall.
Stock: Checkered walnut.
Sights: Hooded bead front, open rear adjustable for windage and elevation.
Features: Dual claw extractors, safety locks firing pin. Blue finish; grooved receiver; oiled stock; sling swivels. Introduced 1992. Imported from the Czech Republic by Magnum Research.
Price: 22 LR, 10-shot, standard **$299.00**
Price: 22 LR, 10-shot, Lux, ... **$329.00**
Price: 22 WMR, 6-shot, standard **$379.00**
Price: 22 WMR, 6-shot, Lux **$399.00**

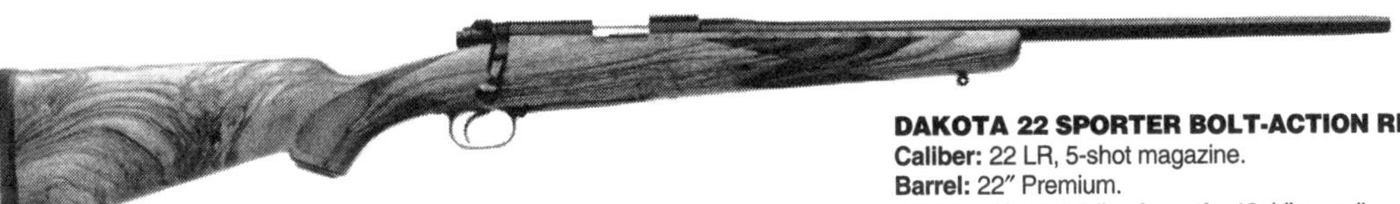

Dakota 22 Sporter

DAKOTA 22 SPORTER BOLT-ACTION RIFLE

Caliber: 22 LR, 5-shot magazine.
Barrel: 22″ Premium.
Weight: About 6.5 lbs. **Length:** 42½″ overall.
Stock: Claro or English walnut in classic design; 13.6″ length of pull. Point panel hand checkering. Swivel studs. Black buttpad.
Sights: None furnished.
Features: Combines features of Winchester 52 and Dakota 76 rifles. Full-sized receiver; rear locking lug and bolt machined from bar stock. Trigger and striker-blocking safety; Model 70-style trigger. Introduced 1992. From Dakota Arms, Inc.
Price: **$1,500.00**

Kimber Model 82C Classic

KIMBER MODEL 82C CLASSIC BOLT-ACTION RIFLE
Caliber: 22 LR, 4-shot magazine (10-shot available).
Barrel: 22″, premium air-gauged, free-floated.
Weight: 6.5 lbs. **Length:** 40.5″ overall.
Stock: Classic style of Claro walnut; 13.5″ length of pull; hand-checkered; red rubber buttpad; polished steel grip cap.
Sights: None furnished; drilled and tapped for Warne, Leupold or Millett scope mounts (optionally available from factory).
Features: Action uses aluminum pillar bedding for consistent accuracy; single-set trigger with 2.5-lb. pull is fully adjustable. Reintroduced 1994. Made in U.S. by Kimber of America, Inc.
Price: **$785.00**

Kimber Model 82C Custom Match Bolt-Action Rifle
Same as the Model 82C Classic except has high grade stock of AA French walnut with black ebony forend tip, full coverage 22 lpi borderless checkering, steel Neidner (uncheckered) buttplate, and satin rust blue finish. Reintroduced 1995. Made in U.S. by Kimber of America, Inc.
Price: **$2,075.00**

Kimber Model 82C Varmint Synthetic Bolt-Action Rifle
Similar to the Model 82C Classic except has a synthetic stock with a slightly larger forend to accommodate the medium/heavy barrel profile. Has fluted, 20″ stainless steel match-grade barrel. Weighs about 7½ lbs. Matte blue action. Introduced 1996. Made in U.S. by Kimber of America, Inc.
Price: **$885.00**

Kimber Model 82C SuperAmerica Bolt-Action Rifle
Similar to the Model 82C Classic except has AAA fancy grade Claro walnut with beaded cheekpiece, ebony forend tip; hand-checkered 22 lpi patterns with wrap-around coverage; black rubber buttpad. Reintroduced 1994. Made in U.S. by Kimber of America, Inc.
Price: **$1,326.00**

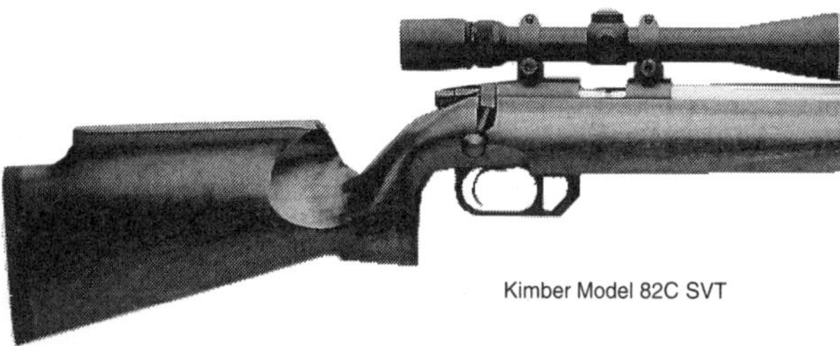
Kimber Model 82C SVT

Kimber Model 82C Stainless Classic Bolt-Action Rifle
Similar to the Model 82C except has a match-grade stainless steel barrel and matte-finished receiver. Introduced 1996. Made in U.S. by Kimber of America, Inc.
Price: **$899.00**

Kimber Model 82C SVT Bolt-Action Rifle
Simliar to the Model 82C except has an offhand high comb target-style stock; 18″ fluted, stainless steel, target weight, match-grade barrel; single shot action; A Claro walnut; weighs 7½ lbs. Designed for off-hand plinking, varmint shooting and competition. Introduced 1996. Made in U.S. by Kimber of America, Inc.
Price: **$785.00**

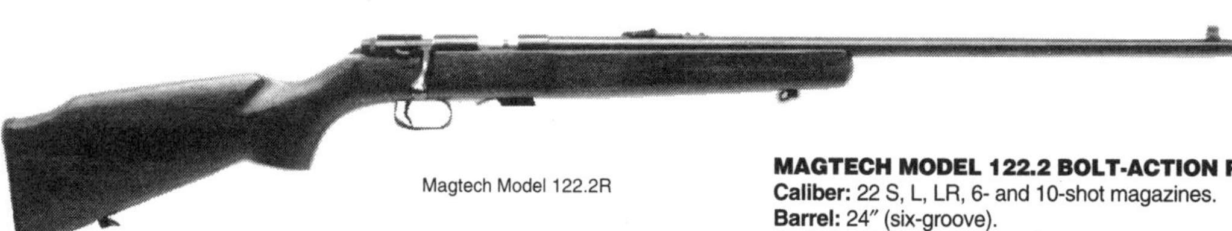
Magtech Model 122.2R

KRICO MODEL 300 BOLT-ACTION RIFLE
Caliber: 22 LR, 22 WMR, 22 Hornet.
Barrel: 19.6″ (22 RF), 23.6″ (Hornet).
Weight: 6.3 lbs. **Length:** 38.5″ overall (22 RF).
Stock: Walnut-stained beech.
Sights: Blade on ramp front, open adjustable rear.
Features: Double triggers, sliding safety. Checkered grip and forend. Imported from Germany by Mandall Shooting Supplies.
Price: Model 300 Standard **$700.00**
Price: Model 300 Deluxe **$795.00**
Price: Model 300 Stutzen (walnut full-length stock) **$825.00**
Price: Model 300 SA (walnut Monte Carlo stock) **$750.00**

MAGTECH MODEL 122.2 BOLT-ACTION RIFLE
Caliber: 22 S, L, LR, 6- and 10-shot magazines.
Barrel: 24″ (six-groove).
Weight: 6.5 lbs. **Length:** 43″ overall.
Stock: Brazilian hardwood.
Sights: Blade front, open rear adjustable for windage and elevation.
Features: Sliding safety; double extractors; receiver grooved for scope mount. Introduced 1994. Imported from Brazil by Magtech Recreational Products, Inc.
Price: Model 122.2S (no sights) **$139.95**
Price: Model 122.2R (open sights) **$149.95**
Price: Model 122.2T (ramp front, micro-type open rear) **$169.95**

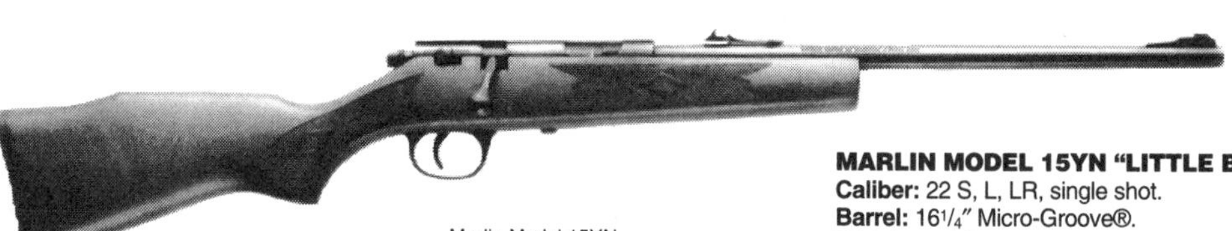
Marlin Model 15YN

MARLIN MODEL 15YN "LITTLE BUCKAROO"
Caliber: 22 S, L, LR, single shot.
Barrel: 16¼″ Micro-Groove®.
Weight: 4¼ lbs. **Length:** 33¼″ overall.
Stock: One-piece walnut-finished, press-checkered Maine birch with Monte Carlo; Mar-Shield® finish.
Sights: Ramp front, adjustable open rear.
Features: Beginner's rifle with thumb safety, easy-load feed throat, red cocking indicator. Receiver grooved for scope mounting. Introduced 1989.
Price: **$171.80**

CAUTION: PRICES SHOWN ARE SUPPLIED BY THE MANUFACTURER OR IMPORTER. CHECK YOUR LOCAL GUNSHOP.

Marlin Model 880

Marlin Model 880SS Stainless Steel Bolt-Action Rifle
Same as the Model 880 except barrel, receiver, front breech bolt, striker knob, trigger stud, cartridge lifter stud and outer magazine tube are made of stainless steel. Most other parts are nickel-plated to match the stainless finish. Has black fiberglass-filled AKZO synthetic stock with moulded-in checkering, stainless steel swivel studs. Introduced 1994. Made in U.S. by Marlin Firearms Co.
Price: $256.65

MARLIN MODEL 880 BOLT-ACTION RIFLE
Caliber: 22 LR; 7-shot clip magazine.
Barrel: 22″ Micro-Groove®.
Weight: 5½ lbs. **Length:** 41″.
Stock: Checkered Monte Carlo American black walnut with checkered pistol grip and forend. Rubber buttpad, swivel studs. Mar-Shield® finish.
Sights: Wide-Scan™ ramp front, folding semi-buckhorn rear adjustable for windage and elevation.
Features: Receiver grooved for scope mount. Introduced 1989.
Price: $240.25

Marlin Model 880SQ

Marlin Model 25N Bolt-Action Repeater
Similar to Marlin 880, except walnut-finished pistol grip stock, adjustable open rear sight, ramp front.
Price: $173.30

Marlin Model 25MN Bolt-Action Rifle
Similar to the Model 25N except chambered for 22 WMR. Has 7-shot clip magazine, 22″ Micro-Groove® barrel, checkered walnut-finished Maine birch stock. Introduced 1989.
Price: $198.20

Marlin Model 882SS Bolt-Action Rifle
Same as the Marlin Model 882 except has stainless steel front breech bolt, barrel, receiver and bolt knob. All other parts are either stainless steel or nickel-plated. Has black Monte Carlo stock of fiberglass-filled polycarbonate with moulded-in checkering, nickel-plated swivel studs. Introduced 1995. Made in U.S. by Marlin Firearms Co.
Price: $282.65

Marlin Model 883 Bolt-Action Rifle
Same as Marlin 882 except tubular magazine holds 12 rounds of 22 WMR ammunition.
Price: $274.60

Marlin Model 883SS Bolt-Action Rifle
Same as the Model 883 except front breech bolt, striker knob, trigger stud, cartridge lifter stud and outer magazine tube are of stainless steel; other parts are nickel-plated. Has two-tone brown laminated Monte Carlo stock with swivel studs, rubber butt pad. Introduced 1993.
Price: $292.35

Marlin Model 880SQ Squirrel Rifle
Similar to the Model 880 except uses the heavy target barrel of Marlin's Model 2000L target rifle. Black synthetic stock with moulded-in checkering; double bedding screws; matte blue finish. Comes without sights, but has plugged dovetail for a rear sight, filled screw holes for front; receiver grooved for scope mount. Weighs 7 lbs. Introduced 1996. Made in U.S. by Marlin.
Price: $263.85

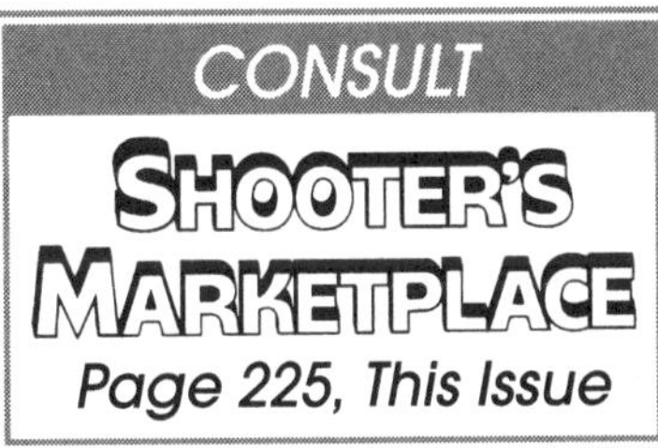
CONSULT
SHOOTER'S
MARKETPLACE
Page 225, This Issue

Marlin Model 881 Bolt-Action Rifle
Same as the Marlin 880 except tubular magazine, holds 17 Long Rifle cartridges. Weighs 6 lbs.
Price: $250.25

Marlin Model 882 Bolt-Action Rifle
Same as the Marlin 880 except 22 WMR cal. only with 7-shot clip magazine; weight about 6 lbs. Comes with swivel studs.
Price: $264.90
Price: Model 882L (laminated hardwood stock) $280.85

Norinco JW-27

NORINCO JW-15 BOLT-ACTION RIFLE
Caliber: 22 LR, 5-shot detachable magazine.
Barrel: 24″.
Weight: 5 lbs., 12 oz. **Length:** 41¾″ overall.
Stock: Walnut-stained hardwood.
Sights: Hooded blade front, open rear drift adjustable for windage.
Features: Polished blue finish; sling swivels; wing-type safety. Introduced 1991. Imported by Interarms.
Price: About $109.00

NORINCO JW-27 BOLT-ACTION RIFLE
Caliber: 22 LR, 5-shot magazine.
Barrel: 22.75″.
Weight: 5 lbs., 14 oz. **Length:** 41.75″ overall.
Stock: Walnut-finished hardwood with checkered grip and forend.
Sights: Dovetailed bead on blade front, fully adjustable rear.
Features: Receiver grooved for scope mounting. Blued finish. Introduced 1992. Imported from China by Century International Arms.
Price: About $106.95

REMINGTON 40-XR RIMFIRE CUSTOM SPORTER
Caliber: 22 LR.
Barrel: 24″.
Weight: 10 lbs. **Length:** 42½″ overall.
Stock: Full-sized walnut, checkered pistol grip and forend.
Sights: None furnished; drilled and tapped for scope mounting.
Features: Custom Shop gun. Duplicates Model 700 centerfire rifle.
Price: Grade I $2,507.00

Remington 541-T

REMINGTON 541-T
Caliber: 22 S, L, LR, 5-shot clip.
Barrel: 24″.
Weight: $5^7/_8$ lbs. **Length:** $42^1/_2$″ overall.
Stock: Walnut, cut-checkered pistol grip and forend. Satin finish.
Sights: None. Drilled and tapped for scope mounts.
Features: Clip repeater. Thumb safety. Reintroduced 1986.
Price: About **$455.00**

Remington 541-T HB Bolt-Action Rifle
Similar to the 541-T except has a heavy target-type barrel without sights. Receiver is drilled and tapped for scope mounting. American walnut stock with straight comb, satin finish, cut checkering, black checkered buttplate, black grip cap and forend tip. Weight is about $6^1/_2$ lbs. Introduced 1993.
Price: **$481.00**

Ruger K77/22RSP

RUGER 77/22 RIMFIRE BOLT-ACTION RIFLE
Caliber: 22 LR, 10-shot rotary magazine; 22 WMR, 9-shot rotary magazine.
Barrel: 20″.
Weight: About $5^3/_4$ lbs. **Length:** $39^3/_4$″ overall.
Stock: Checkered American walnut or injection-moulded fiberglass-reinforced DuPont Zytel with Xenoy inserts in forend and grip, stainless sling swivels.
Sights: Brass bead front, adjustable folding leaf rear or plain barrel with 1″ Ruger rings.
Features: Mauser-type action uses Ruger's 10-shot rotary magazine. Three-position safety, simplified bolt stop, patented bolt locking system. Uses the dual-screw barrel attachment system of the 10/22 rifle. Integral scope mounting system with 1″ Ruger rings. Blued model introduced in 1983. Stainless steel model and blued model with the synthetic stock introduced in 1989.
Price: 77/22R (no sights, rings, walnut stock) **$473.00**
Price: 77/22RS (open sights, rings, walnut stock) **$481.00**
Price: K77/22RP (stainless, no sights, rings, synthetic stock) **$473.00**
Price: K77/22RSP (stainless, open sights, rings, synthetic stock) **$481.00**
Price: 77/22RM (22 WMR, blue, walnut stock) **$473.00**
Price: K77/22RSMP (22 WMR, stainless, open sights, rings, synthetic stock) **$481.00**
Price: K77/22RMP (22 WMR, stainless, synthetic stock) **$473.00**
Price: 77/22RSM (22 WMR, blue, open sights, rings, walnut stock) **$481.00**

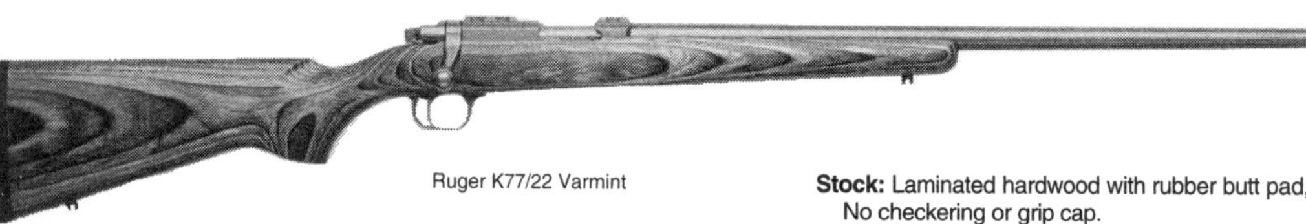
Ruger K77/22 Varmint

RUGER K77/22 VARMINT RIFLE
Caliber: 22 LR, 10-shot, 22 WMR, 9-shot detachable rotary magazine.
Barrel: 24″, heavy.
Weight: 7.25 lbs. **Length:** 43.25″ overall.
Stock: Laminated hardwood with rubber butt pad, quick-detachable swivel studs. No checkering or grip cap.
Sights: None furnished. Comes with Ruger 1″ scope rings.
Features: Made of stainless steel with target gray finish. Three-position safety, dual extractors. Stock has wide, flat forend. Introduced 1993.
Price: K77/22VBZ, 22 LR **$499.00**
Price: K77/22VMB, 22 WMR **$499.00**

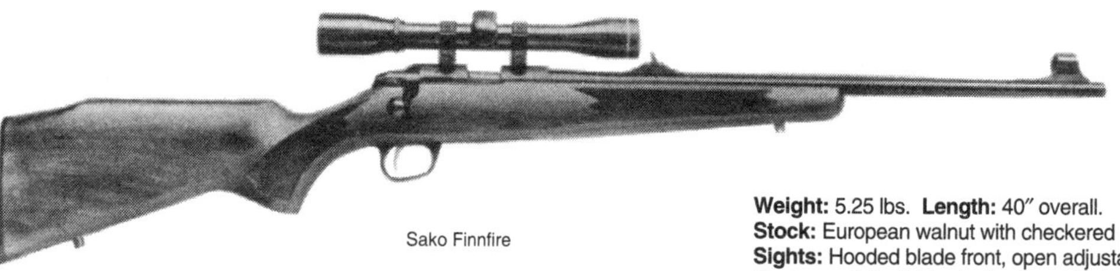
Sako Finnfire

SAKO FINNFIRE BOLT-ACTION RIFLE
Caliber: 22 LR, 5-shot magazine.
Barrel: 22″.
Weight: 5.25 lbs. **Length:** 40″ overall.
Stock: European walnut with checkered grip and forend.
Sights: Hooded blade front, open adjustable rear.
Features: Adjustable single-stage trigger; has 50-degree bolt lift. Introduced 1994. Imported from Finland by Stoeger Industries.
Price: **$732.00**
Price: With heavy barrel **$815.00**

Savage Mark II-GPX

SAVAGE MARK II-G BOLT-ACTION RIFLE
Caliber: 22 LR, 10-shot magazine.
Barrel: $20^1/_2$″.
Weight: $5^1/_2$ lbs. **Length:** $39^1/_2$″ overall.
Stock: Walnut-finished hardwood with Monte Carlo-type comb, checkered grip and forend.
Sights: Bead front, open adjustable rear. Receiver grooved for scope mounting.
Features: Thumb-operated rotating safety. Blue finish. Introduced 1990. Made in Canada, from Savage Arms.
Price: **$126.00**
Price: Mark II-GY (youth), 19″ barrel, 37″ overall, 5 lbs. **$126.00**
Price: Mark II-GL, left-hand **$126.00**
Price: Mark II-Y (youth) left-hand **$126.00**
Price: Mark II-GXP includes 4x15 scope and mount **$131.00**
Price: Mark II-GXP Package Gun (comes with 4x15 scope) **$131.00**

CAUTION: PRICES SHOWN ARE SUPPLIED BY THE MANUFACTURER OR IMPORTER. CHECK YOUR LOCAL GUNSHOP.

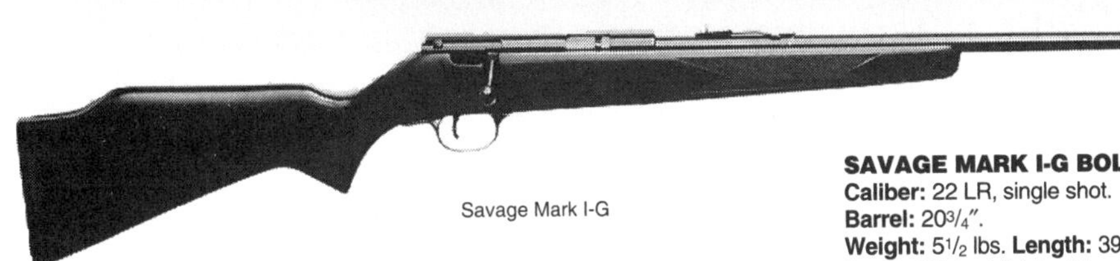

Savage Mark I-G

SAVAGE MODEL 93G MAGNUM BOLT-ACTION RIFLE
Caliber: 22 WMR, 5-shot magazine.
Barrel: $20\frac{3}{4}$".
Weight: $5\frac{3}{4}$ lbs. **Length:** $39\frac{1}{2}$" overall.
Stock: Walnut-finished hardwood with Monte Carlo-type comb, checkered grip and forend.
Sights: Bead front, adjustable open rear. Receiver grooved for scope mount.
Features: Thumb-operated rotary safety. Blue finish. Introduced 1994. Made in Canada, from Savage Arms.
Price: About **$145.00**

SAVAGE MARK I-G BOLT-ACTION RIFLE
Caliber: 22 LR, single shot.
Barrel: $20\frac{3}{4}$".
Weight: $5\frac{1}{2}$ lbs. **Length:** $39\frac{1}{2}$" overall.
Stock: Walnut-finished hardwood with Monte Carlo-type comb, checkered grip and forend.
Sights: Bead front, open adjustable rear. Receiver grooved for scope mounting.
Features: Thumb-operated rotating safety. Blue finish. Rifled or smooth bore. Introduced 1990. Made in Canada, from Savage Arms.
Price: Mark I, rifled or smooth bore **$119.00**
Price: Mark I-GY (Youth), 19" barrel, 37" overall, 5 lbs. **$119.00**

Ultra Light Arms Model 20

ULTRA LIGHT ARMS MODEL 20 RF BOLT-ACTION RIFLE
Caliber: 22 LR, single shot or 5-shot repeater.
Barrel: 22" Douglas Premium, #1 contour.
Weight: 5 lbs., 3 oz. **Length:** $41\frac{1}{2}$" overall.
Stock: Composite Kevlar, graphite reinforced. DuPont Imron paint; $13\frac{1}{2}$" length of pull.
Sights: None furnished. Drilled and tapped for scope mounting.
Features: Available as either single shot or repeater with 5-shot removable magazine. Comes with scope mounts. Introduced 1993. Made in U.S. by Ultra Light Arms, Inc.
Price: **$800.00**

COMPETITION RIFLES—CENTERFIRE & RIMFIRE

Includes models for classic American and ISU target competition and other sporting and competitive shooting.

Anschutz BR-50

ANSCHUTZ ACHIEVER ST SUPER TARGET RIFLE
Caliber: 22 LR, single shot.
Barrel: 22", .75" diameter.
Weight: About 6.5 lbs. **Length:** 38.75" to 39.75" overall.
Stock: Walnut-finished European hardwood with hand-stippled panels on grip and forend; 13.5" accessory rail on forend.
Sights: Optional. Receiver grooved for scope mounting.
Features: Designed for the advanced junior shooter with adjustable length of pull from 13.25" to 14.25" via removable butt spacers. Two-stage #5066 adjustable trigger factory set at 2.6 lbs. Introduced 1994. Imported from Germany by Accuracy International, Champion's Choice, Champion Shooter's Supply, Gunsmithing, Inc.
Price: **$329.95**
Price: Sight Set A **$142.75**

ANSCHUTZ 64-MSR, 64-MS LEFT SILHOUETTE RIFLE
Caliber: 22 LR, 5-shot magazine.
Barrel: $21\frac{1}{2}$", medium heavy; $\frac{7}{8}$" diameter.
Weight: 8 lbs. **Length:** 39.5" overall.
Stock: Walnut-finished hardwood, silhouette-type.
Sights: None furnished. Receiver drilled and tapped for scope mounting.
Features: Uses Match 64 action. Designed for metallic silhouette competition. Stock has stippled checkering, contoured thumb groove with Wundhammer swell. Two-stage #5091 trigger. Slide safety locks sear and bolt. Introduced 1980. Imported from Germany by AcuSport Corp., Accuracy International, Champion's Choice, Champion Shooter's Supply, Gunsmithing, Inc.
Price: 64-MS **$783.70**
Price: 64-MS Left .... **NA**

ANSCHUTZ BR-50 BENCHREST RIFLE
Caliber: 22 LR, single shot.
Barrel: 19.75" (without 11-oz. muzzle weight).
Weight: About 11 lbs. **Length:** 37.75" to 42.5" overall.
Stock: Benchrest style of European hardwood with stippled grip. Cheekpiece vertically adjustable to 1". Stock length adjustable via spacers and buttplate. Finished with glossy blue-black paint.
Sights: None furnished. Receiver grooved for mounts, barrel drilled and tapped for target mounts.
Features: Uses the Anschutz 2013 target action, #5018 two-stage adjustable target trigger factory set at 3.9 oz. Introduced 1994. Imported from Germany by Accuracy International, Champion's Choice, Champion Shooter's Supply, Gunsmithing, Inc.
Price: **$2,304.00**

ANSCHUTZ 1827B BIATHLON RIFLE
Caliber: 22 LR, 5-shot magazine.
Barrel: $21\frac{1}{2}$".
Weight: $8\frac{1}{2}$ lbs. with sights. **Length:** $42\frac{1}{2}$" overall.
Stock: European walnut with cheekpiece, stippled pistol grip and forend.
Sights: Optional globe front specially designed for Biathlon shooting, micrometer rear with hinged snow cap.
Features: Uses Super Match 54 action and nine-way adjustable trigger; adjustable wooden buttplate, Biathlon butthook, adjustable hand-stop rail. Introduced 1982. Imported from Germany by Accuracy International, Champion's Choice, Champion Shooter's Supply, Gunsmithing, Inc.
Price: Right-hand **$1,537.80**
Price: With laminated stock **$1,593.60**
Price: #6827 Sight Set **$264.10**

Anschutz 1827BT Fortner Biathlon Rifle
Similar to the Anschutz 1827B Biathlon rifle except uses Anschutz/Fortner system straight-pull bolt action. Introduced 1982. Imported from Germany by Accuracy International, Champion's Choice, Champion Shooter's Supply, Gunsmithing, Inc.
Price: Right-hand **$2,312.90**
Price: Right-hand, laminated stock **$2,344.60**
Price: Left-hand **$2,542.80**
Price: #6827 Sight Set **$264.10**

ANSCHUTZ 1808D-RT SUPER RUNNING TARGET RIFLE
Caliber: 22 LR, single shot.
Barrel: 32½".
Weight: 9.4 lbs. **Length:** 50.5" overall.
Stock: European walnut. Heavy beavertail forend; adjustable cheekpiece and buttplate. Stippled grip and forend.
Sights: None furnished. Grooved for scope mounting.
Features: Designed for Running Target competition. Nine-way adjustable single-stage trigger, slide safety. Introduced 1991. Imported from Germany by Accuracy International, Champion's Choice, Champion Shooter's Supply, Gunsmithing, Inc.
Price: Right-hand **$1,430.40**

ANSCHUTZ 1911 PRONE MATCH RIFLE
Caliber: 22 LR, single shot.
Barrel: 27¼".
Weight: 11 lbs. **Length:** 46" overall.
Stock: Walnut-finished European hardwood; American prone style with Monte Carlo, cast-off cheekpiece, checkered pistol grip, beavertail forend with swivel rail and adjustable swivel, adjustable rubber buttplate.
Sights: None furnished. Receiver grooved for Anschutz sights (extra). Scope blocks.
Features: Two-stage #5018 trigger adjustable from 2.1 to 8.6 oz. Extremely fast lock time. Imported from Germany by Accuracy International, Champion's Choice, Champion Shooter's Supply, Gunsmithing, Inc.
Price: Right-hand, no sights **$1,673.50**

Anschutz 1907 ISU Standard Match Rifle
Same action as Model 1913 but with 7/8" diameter 26" barrel. Length is 44.5" overall, weighs 10 lbs. Choice of stock configurations. Vented forend. Designed for prone and position shooting ISU requirements; suitable for NRA matches. Imported from Germany by AcuSport Corp., Accuracy International, Champion's Choice, Champion Shooter's Supply, Gunsmithing, Inc.
Price: Right-hand, no sights, European hardwood stock **$1,445.70**
Price: With laminated hardwood stock **$1,532.10**
Price: Right-hand, no sights, walnut stock **$1,500.80**
Price: M1907-L (true left-hand action and stock) **$1,516.90**

ANSCHUTZ 1903 MATCH RIFLE
Caliber: 22 LR, single shot.
Barrel: 25", .75" diameter.
Weight: 8.6 lbs. **Length:** 43.75" overall.
Stock: Walnut-finished hardwood with adjustable cheekpiece; stippled grip and forend.
Sights: None furnished.
Features: Uses Anschutz Match 64 action and #5098 two-stage trigger. A medium weight rifle for intermediate and advanced Junior Match competition. Introduced 1987. Imported from Germany by AcuSport Corp., Accuracy International, Champion's Choice, Champion Shooter's Supply, Gunsmithing, Inc.
Price: Right-hand **$829.60**
Price: Left-hand **$869.90**

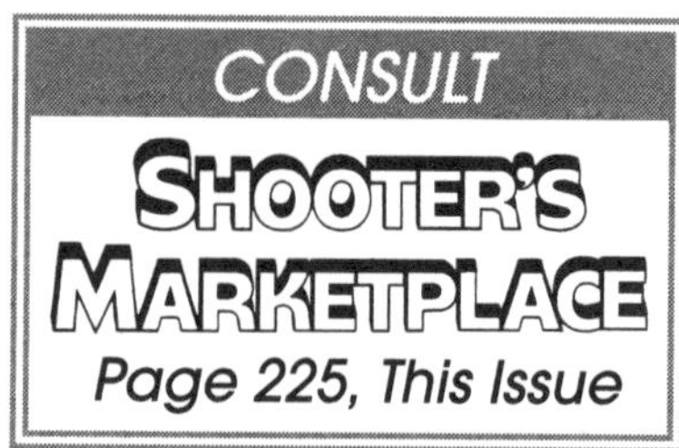
CONSULT
SHOOTER'S
MARKETPLACE
Page 225, This Issue

Anschutz 1913 Super Match Rifle
Same as the Model 1911 except European walnut International-type stock with adjustable cheekpiece, adjustable aluminum hook buttplate, adjustable hand stop, weighs 15.5 lbs., 46" overall. Imported from Germany by AcuSport Corp., Accuracy International, Champion's Choice, Champion Shooter's Supply, Gunsmithing, Inc.
Price: Right-hand, no sights **$2,432.30**
Price: M1913 left-hand **$2,560.90**

Anschutz 1910 Super Match Rifle
Similar to the Super Match 1913 rifle except has a stock of European hardwood with tapered forend and deep receiver area. Hand and palm rests not included. Uses Match 54 action. Adjustable hook buttplate and cheekpiece. Sights not included. Introduced 1982. Imported from Germany by Accuracy International, Champion's Choice, Champion Shooter's Supply, Gunsmithing, Inc.
Price: Right-hand **$2,300.00**

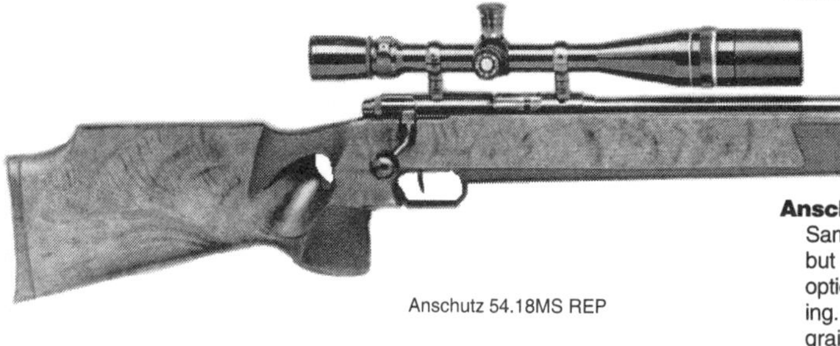
Anschutz 54.18MS REP

Anschutz 54.18MS REP Deluxe Silhouette Rifle
Same basic action and trigger specifications as the Anschutz 1913 Super Match but with removable 5-shot clip magazine, 22" barrel extendable to 30" using optional extension and weight set. Receiver drilled and tapped for scope mounting. Silhouette stock with thumbhole grip is of fiberglass with walnut wood Fibergrain finish. Introduced 1990. Imported from Germany by Accuracy International, Champion's Choice, Champion Shooter's Supply, Gunsmithing, Inc.
Price: 54.18MS REP Deluxe **$1,237.80**
Price: 54.18MS E single shot **$1,154.70**
Price: 54.18MS Standard with fiberglass stock .... **$NA**

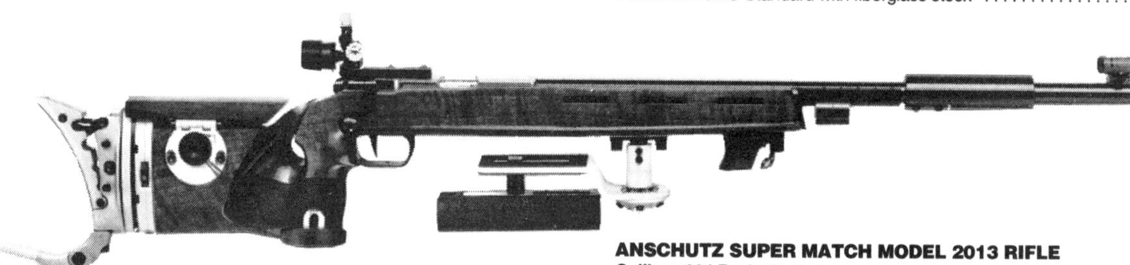
Anschutz 2013

Anschutz Super Match Model 2007 ISU Standard Rifle
Similar to the Model 2013 except has ISU Standard design. European walnut or blonde hardwood stock. Sights optional. Introduced 1992. Imported from Germany by Accuracy International, Champion's Choice, Champion Shooter's Supply, Gunsmithing, Inc.
Price: Right-hand, beech stock **$1,975.00**
Price: Left-hand, beech stock **$2,102.00**
Price: Right-hand, walnut stock **$2,003.80**

ANSCHUTZ SUPER MATCH MODEL 2013 RIFLE
Caliber: 22 LR, single shot.
Barrel: 19.75" (26" with tube installed).
Weight: 15.5 lbs. **Length:** 43" to 45.5" overall.
Stock: European walnut; target adjustable.
Sights: Optional. Uses #7020/20 sight set.
Features: Improved Super Match 54 action, #5018 trigger give fastest consistent lock time for a production target rifle. Barrel is micro-honed; trigger has nine points of adjustment, two stages. Slide safety. Comes with test target. Introduced 1992. Imported from Germany by Accuracy International, Champion's Choice, Champion Shooter's Supply, Gunsmithing, Inc.
Price: Right-hand **$2,769.70**
Price: Left-hand **$2,899.20**

 CAUTION: PRICES SHOWN ARE SUPPLIED BY THE MANUFACTURER OR IMPORTER. CHECK YOUR LOCAL GUNSHOP.

ArmaLite AR-10(T) Target

ARMALITE AR-10(T) TARGET MODEL
Caliber: 308, 10-shot magazine.
Barrel: 24″ target weight with 1:10″ twist.
Weight: 11 lbs. **Length:** 43.5″ overall.
Stock: Black composition butt, fiberglass tubular forend.
Sights: Optional. Has one-piece international-style flattop receiver with Picatinny (Weaver-type) rail for scope mounting.
Features: Forged upper receiver with case deflector; receivers are hard-coat anodized. Optional detachable carry handle with NM sight; detachable front sight assembly; 30mm or 1″ scope mount; stainless barrel. Introduced 1995. Made in U.S. by ArmaLite, Inc.
Price: $1,995.00

Bushmaster XM-15-E2S

BUSHMASTER XM-15 E2S V-MATCH RIFLE
Caliber: 223, 10-shot magazine.
Barrel: 20″, 24″, 26″; 1:9″ twist; heavy.
Weight: 8.2 lbs. **Length:** 38.25″ overall (20″ barrel).
Stock: Black composition.
Sights: None furnished; comes with scope mount base installed.
Features: E2 lower receiver with push-pin-style takedown. Barrel is .950″ outside diameter with counter-bored crown; upper receiver has brass deflector; free-floating steel handguard. Made in U.S. by Bushmaster Firearms Co./Quality Parts Co.
Price: 20″ barrel $795.00
Price: 24″ barrel $805.00
Price: 26″ barrel $815.00

BUSHMASTER XM-15-E2S TARGET MODEL RIFLE
Caliber: 223, 10-shot magazine.
Barrel: 20″, 24″, 26″; 1:9″ twist; heavy.
Weight: 8.1 lbs. **Length:** 38.25″ overall (20″ barrel).
Stock: Black composition.
Sights: Adjustable post front, adjustable aperture rear.
Features: Patterned after Colt M-16A2. Chrome-lined barrel with manganese phosphate exterior. Has E-2 lower receiver with push-pin. Made in U.S. by Bushmaster Firearms Co./Quality Parts Co.
Price: 20″ match heavy barrel $740.00
Price: 24″ match heavy barrel $750.00
Price: 26″ match heavy barrel $760.00

Colt Match Target HBAR

COLT MATCH TARGET MODEL RIFLE
Caliber: 223 Rem., 5-shot magazine.
Barrel: 20″.
Weight: 7.5 lbs. **Length:** 39″ overall.
Stock: Composition stock, grip, forend.
Sights: Post front, aperture rear adjustable for windage and elevation.
Features: Five-round detachable box magazine, standard-weight barrel, sling swivels. Has forward bolt assist. Military matte black finish. Model introduced 1991.
Price: $1,019.00

Colt Match Target HBAR Rifle
Similar to the Target Model except has heavy barrel, 800-meter rear sight adjustable for windage and elevation. Introduced 1991.
Price: $1,067.00

Colt Match Target Competition HBAR II Rifle
Similar to the Match Target Competition HBAR except has 16.1″ barrel, weighs 7.1 lbs., overall length 34.5″; 1:9″ twist barrel. Introduced 1995.
Price: $1,044.00

Colt Match Target Competition HBAR Rifle
Similar to the Sporter Target except has flat-top receiver with integral Weaver-type base for scope mounting. Counter-bored muzzle, 1:9″ rifling twist. Introduced 1991.
Price: Model R6700 ....$1,073.00

Cooper Model 36 BR-50

COOPER ARMS MODEL 36 BR-50
Caliber: 22 LR, single shot.
Barrel: 22″, .860″ straight.
Weight: 6.8 lbs. **Length:** 40.5″ overall.
Stock: McMillan Benchrest.
Sights: None furnished.
Features: Action has three mid-bolt locking lugs; fully adjustable match grade trigger; stainless barrel. Introduced 1994. Made in U.S. by Cooper Arms.
Price: $1,850.00

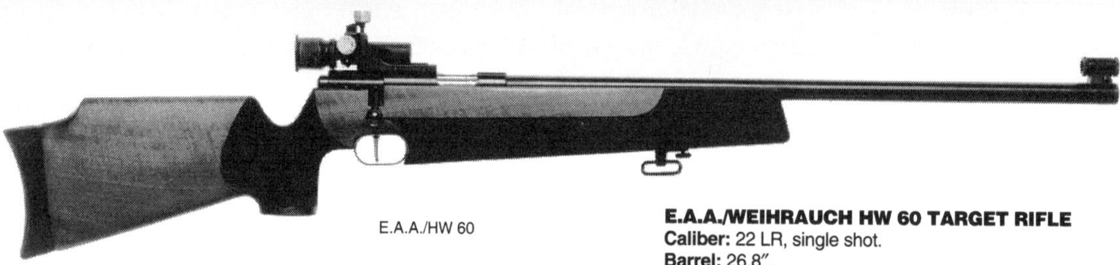
E.A.A./HW 60

E.A.A./HW 660 MATCH RIFLE

Caliber: 22 LR.
Barrel: 26″.
Weight: 10.7 lbs. **Length:** 45.3″ overall.
Stock: Match-type walnut with adjustable cheekpiece and buttplate.
Sights: Globe front, match aperture rear.
Features: Adjustable match trigger; stippled pistol grip and forend; forend accessory rail. Introduced 1991. Imported from Germany by European American Armory.
Price: About $874.95

E.A.A./WEIHRAUCH HW 60 TARGET RIFLE

Caliber: 22 LR, single shot.
Barrel: 26.8″.
Weight: 10.8 lbs. **Length:** 45.7″ overall.
Stock: Walnut with adjustable buttplate. Stippled pistol grip and forend. Rail with adjustable swivel.
Sights: Hooded ramp front, match-type aperture rear.
Features: Adjustable match trigger with push-button safety. Left-hand version also available. Introduced 1991. Imported from Germany by European American Armory.
Price: Right-hand $695.00
Price: Left-hand $875.00

Erma SR-100 Precision

EAGLE ARMS M15A2 GOLDEN EAGLE RIFLE

Caliber: 223 Rem.
Barrel: 20″ extra-heavy NM; 1:8″ twist.
Weight: 9 lbs., 10 oz. **Length:** 39 5/8″ overall.
Stock: Black composition; weighted.
Sights: Elevation-adjustable NM extra-fine front with set screw, E2-style NM rear with 1/2-min. adjustments for windage and elevation; NM aperture.
Features: Upper and lower receivers have push-type pivot pin for easy takedown. Receivers hard coat anodized. Fence-type magazine release. Introduced 1989. Made in U.S. by Eagle Arms, Inc.
Price: $1,300.00

HARRIS GUNWORKS NATIONAL MATCH RIFLE

Caliber: 7mm-08, 308, 5-shot magazine.
Barrel: 24″, stainless steel.
Weight: About 11 lbs. (std. bbl.). **Length:** 43″ overall.
Stock: Fiberglass with adjustable buttplate.
Sights: Barrel band and Tompkins front; no rear sight furnished.
Features: Gunworks repeating action with clip slot, Canjar trigger. Match-grade barrel. Available in right-hand only. Fiberglass stock, sight installation, special machining and triggers optional. Introduced 1989. From Harris Gunworks, Inc.
Price: $2,600.00

ERMA SR-100 PRECISION RIFLE

Caliber: 308 Win. (10-shot), 300 Win. Mag. (8-shot), 338 Lapua Mag. (5-shot); detachable box magazine.
Barrel: 25.5″ (308), 29.5″ (300, 338).
Weight: 14.1 lbs. **Length:** 49.6″ overall (25.5″ barrel).
Stock: Thumbhole style of laminated wood with adjustable recoil pad and comb; aluminum forend rail for bipod or sling swivel.
Sights: None furnished.
Features: Interchangeable barrels; three-lug bolt locks into barrel; 60° bolt rotation; forged aluminum alloy receiver; fully adjustable match trigger; integral muzzlebrake. Inroduced 1996. Imported from Germany by Amtec 2000, Inc.
Price: About $8,000.00

FINNISH LION STANDARD TARGET RIFLE

Caliber: 22 LR, single shot.
Barrel: 27 5/8″.
Weight: 10 1/2 lbs. **Length:** 44 9/16″ overall.
Stock: French walnut, target style.
Sights: Globe front, International micrometer rear.
Features: Optional accessories: palm rest, hook buttplate, forend stop and swivel assembly, buttplate extension, five front sight aperture inserts, three rear sight apertures, Allen wrench. Adjustable trigger. Imported from Finland by Mandall Shooting Supplies.
Price: Without sights $695.00
Price: Sight set $195.00

Harris Gunworks M-86

HARRIS GUNWORKS M-86 SNIPER RIFLE

Caliber: 308, 30-06, 4-shot magazine; 300 Win. Mag., 3-shot magazine.
Barrel: 24″, Gunworks match-grade in heavy contour.
Weight: 11 1/4 lbs. (308), 11 1/2 lbs. (30-06, 300). **Length:** 43 1/2″ overall.
Stock: Specially designed McHale fiberglass stock with textured grip and forend, recoil pad.
Sights: None furnished.
Features: Uses Gunworks repeating action. Comes with bipod. Matte black finish. Sling swivels. Introduced 1989. From Harris Gunworks, Inc.
Price: $2,700.00
Price: Takedown model $2,900.00

HARRIS GUNWORKS COMBO M-87 SERIES 50-CALIBER RIFLES

Caliber: 50 BMG, single shot.
Barrel: 29, with muzzlebrake.
Weight: About 21 1/2 lbs. **Length:** 53″ overall.
Stock: Gunworks fiberglass.
Sights: None furnished.
Features: Right-handed Gunworks stainless steel receiver, chrome-moly barrel with 1:15″ twist. Introduced 1987. From Harris Gunworks, Inc.
Price: $3,735.00
Price: M87R 5-shot repeater $4,150.00
Price: M-87 (5-shot repeater) "Combo" $4,035.00
Price: M-92 Bullpup (shortened M-87 single shot with bullpup stock) .. $4,000.00
Price: M-93SN (10-shot repeater with folding stock, detachable magazine) $4,300.00

CAUTION: PRICES SHOWN ARE SUPPLIED BY THE MANUFACTURER OR IMPORTER. CHECK YOUR LOCAL GUNSHOP.

Harris Gunworks Long Range

HARRIS GUNWORKS M-89 SNIPER RIFLE

Caliber: 308 Win., 5-shot magazine.
Barrel: 28″ (with suppressor).
Weight: 15 lbs., 4 oz.
Stock: Fiberglass; adjustable for length; recoil pad.
Sights: None furnished. Drilled and tapped for scope mounting.
Features: Uses Gunworks repeating action. Comes with bipod. Introduced 1990. From Harris Gunworks, Inc.
Price: Standard (non-suppressed) **$2,700.00**

HARRIS GUNWORKS LONG RANGE RIFLE

Caliber: 300 Win. Mag., 7mm Rem. Mag., 300 Phoenix, 338 Lapua, single shot.
Barrel: 26″, stainless steel, match-grade.
Weight: 14 lbs. **Length:** 46½″ overall.
Stock: Fiberglass with adjustable buttplate and cheekpiece. Adjustable for length of pull, drop, cant and cast-off.
Sights: Barrel band and Tompkins front; no rear sight furnished.
Features: Uses Gunworks solid bottom single shot action and Canjar trigger. Barrel twist 1:12″. Introduced 1989. From Harris Gunworks, Inc.
Price: **$2,600.00**

Heckler & Koch PSG-1

HECKLER & KOCH PSG-1 MARKSMAN RIFLE

Caliber: 308, 5- and 20-shot magazines.
Barrel: 25.6″, heavy.
Weight: 17.8 lbs. **Length:** 47.5″ overall.
Stock: Matte black high impact plastic, adjustable for length, pivoting butt cap, vertically-adjustable cheekpiece; target-type pistol grip with adjustable palm shelf.
Sights: Hendsoldt 6x42 scope.
Features: Uses HK-91 action with low-noise bolt closing device, special Marksman trigger group; special forend with T-way rail for sling swivel or tripod. Gun comes in special foam-fitted metal transport case with tripod, two 20-shot and two 5-shot magazines, tripod. Imported from Germany by Heckler & Koch, Inc. Introduced 1986.
Price: **$10,497.00**

KRICO MODEL 600 SNIPER RIFLE

Caliber: 222, 223, 22-250, 243, 308, 4-shot magazine.
Barrel: 23.6″.
Weight: 9.2 lbs. **Length:** 45.2″ overall.
Stock: European walnut with adjustable rubber buttplate.
Sights: None supplied; drilled and tapped for scope mounting.
Features: Match barrel with flash hider; large bolt knob; wide trigger shoe. Parkerized finish. Imported from Germany by Mandall Shooting Supplies.
Price: **$2,645.00**

KRICO MODEL 400 MATCH RIFLE

Caliber: 22 LR, 22 Hornet, 5-shot magazine.
Barrel: 23.2″ (22 LR), 23.6″ (22 Hornet).
Weight: 8.8 lbs. **Length:** 42.1″ overall (22 RF).
Stock: European walnut, match type.
Sights: None furnished; receiver grooved for scope mounting.
Features: Heavy match barrel. Double-set or match trigger. Imported from Germany by Mandall Shooting Supplies.
Price: **$950.00**

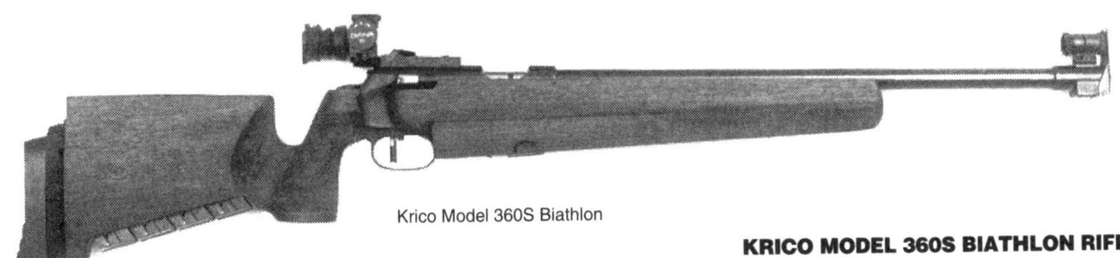

Krico Model 360S Biathlon

KRICO MODEL 500 KRICOTRONIC MATCH RIFLE

Caliber: 22 LR, single shot.
Barrel: 23.6″.
Weight: 9.4 lbs. **Length:** 42.1″ overall.
Stock: European walnut, match type with adjustable butt.
Sights: Globe front, match micrometer aperture rear.
Features: Electronic ignition system for fastest possible lock time. Completely adjustable trigger. Barrel has tapered bore. Imported from Germany by Mandall Shooting Supplies.
Price: **$3,950.00**

KRICO MODEL 600 MATCH RIFLE

Caliber: 222, 223, 22-250, 243, 308, 5.6x50 Mag., 4-shot magazine.
Barrel: 23.6″.
Weight: 8.8 lbs. **Length:** 43.3″ overall.
Stock: Match stock of European walnut with cheekpiece.
Sights: None furnished; drilled and tapped for scope mounting.
Features: Match stock with vents in forend for cooling, rubber recoil pad, sling swivels. Imported from Germany by Mandall Shooting Supplies.
Price: **$1,250.00**

KRICO MODEL 360S BIATHLON RIFLE

Caliber: 22 LR, 5-shot magazine.
Barrel: 21.25″.
Weight: 9.26 lbs. **Length:** 40.55″ overall.
Stock: Walnut with high comb, adjustable buttplate.
Sights: Globe front, fully adjustable Diana 82 match peep rear.
Features: Straight-pull action with 17.6-oz. match trigger. Comes with five magazines (four stored in stock recess), muzzle/sight snow cap. Introduced 1991. Imported from Germany by Mandall Shooting Supplies.
Price: **$1,695.00**

KRICO MODEL 360 S2 BIATHLON RIFLE

Caliber: 22 LR, 5-shot magazine.
Barrel: 21.25″.
Weight: 9 lbs., 15 oz. **Length:** 40.55″ overall.
Stock: Biathlon design of black epoxy-finished walnut with pistol grip.
Sights: Globe front, fully adjustable Diana 82 match peep rear.
Features: Pistol grip-activated action. Comes with five magazines (four stored in stock recess), muzzle/sight snow cap. Introduced 1991. Imported from Germany by Mandall Shooting Supplies.
Price: **$1,595.00**

CAUTION: PRICES SHOWN ARE SUPPLIED BY THE MANUFACTURER OR IMPORTER. CHECK YOUR LOCAL GUNSHOP.

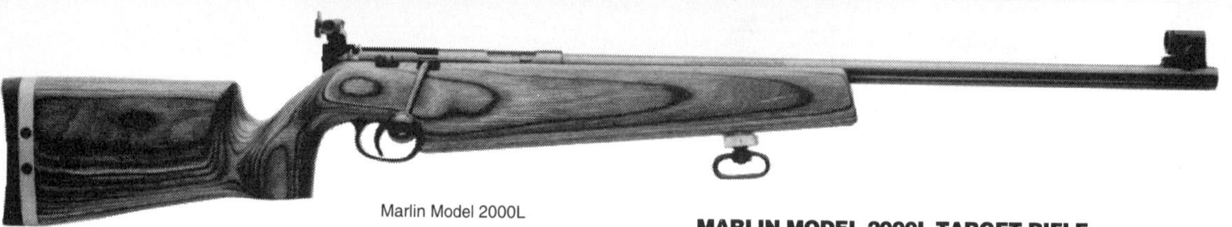
Marlin Model 2000L

OLYMPIC ARMS PCR-SERVICEMATCH RIFLE
Caliber: 223, 10-shot magazine.
Barrel: 20″, broach-cut 416 stainless steel.
Weight: About 10 lbs. **Length:** 39.5″ overall.
Stock: A2 stowaway grip and trapdoor buttstock.
Sights: Post front, E2-NM fully adjsutable operture rear.
Features: Based on the AR-15. Conforms to all DCM standards. Free-floating 1:8.5″ or 1:10″ barrel; crowned barrel; no bayonet lug. Introduced 1996. Made in U.S. by Olympic Arms, Inc.
Price: **$1,135.00**

MARLIN MODEL 2000L TARGET RIFLE
Caliber: 22 LR, single shot.
Barrel: 22″ heavy, Micro-Groove® rifling, match chamber, recessed muzzle.
Weight: 8 lbs. **Length:** 41″ overall.
Stock: Laminated black/gray with ambidextrous pistol grip.
Sights: Hooded front with ten aperture inserts, fully adjustable target rear peep.
Features: Buttplate adjustable for length of pull, height and angle. Aluminum forend rail with stop and quick-detachable swivel. Two-stage target trigger; red cocking indicator. Five-shot adaptor kit available. Introduced 1991. From Marlin.
Price: **$602.30**

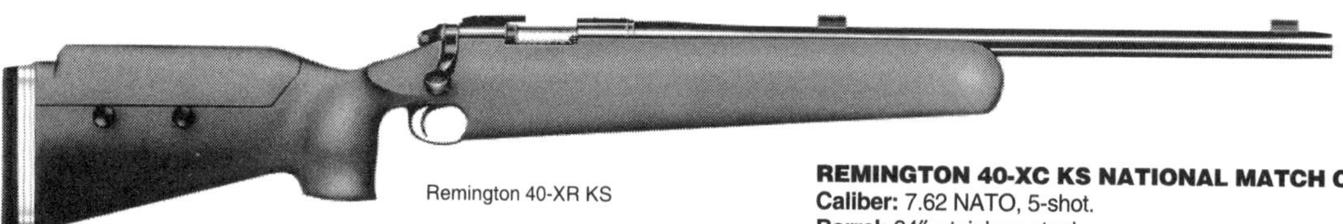
Remington 40-XB

REMINGTON 40-XBBR KS
Caliber: 22 BR Rem., 222 Rem., 222 Rem. Mag., 223, 6mmx47, 6mm BR Rem., 7.62 NATO (308 Win.).
Barrel: 20″ (light varmint class), 24″ (heavy varmint class).
Weight: 7¼ lbs. (light varmint class); 12 lbs. (heavy varmint class).
Length: 38″ (20″ bbl.), 42″ (24″ bbl.).
Stock: Kevlar.
Sights: None. Supplied with scope blocks.
Features: Unblued stainless steel barrel, trigger adjustable from 1½ lbs. to 3½ lbs. Special 2-oz. trigger at extra cost. Scope and mounts extra.
Price: With Kevlar stock **$1,484.00**
Price: Extra for 2-oz. trigger, about **$168.00**

REMINGTON 40-XB RANGEMASTER TARGET CENTERFIRE
Caliber: 222 Rem., 222 Rem. Mag., 223, 220 Swift, 22-250, 6mm Rem., 243, 25-06, 7mm BR Rem., 7mm Rem. Mag., 30-338 (30-7mm Rem. Mag.), 300 Win. Mag., 7.62 NATO (308 Win.), 30-06, single shot.
Barrel: 27¼″.
Weight: 11¼ lbs. **Length:** 47″ overall.
Stock: American walnut or Kevlar with high comb and beavertail forend stop. Rubber non-slip buttplate.
Sights: None. Scope blocks installed.
Features: Adjustable trigger. Stainless barrel and action. Receiver drilled and tapped for sights.
Price: Standard single shot, stainless steel barrel, about **$1,333.00**
Price: Repeater model **$1,433.00**
Price: Model 40-XB KS **$1,504.00**
Price: Repeater model (KS) **$1,604.00**
Price: Extra for 2-oz. trigger **$168.00**

Remington 40-XR KS

REMINGTON 40-XR KS RIMFIRE POSITION RIFLE
Caliber: 22 LR, single shot.
Barrel: 24″, heavy target.
Weight: 10 lbs. **Length:** 43″ overall.
Stock: Kevlar. Position-style with front swivel block on forend guide rail.
Sights: Drilled and tapped. Furnished with scope blocks.
Features: Meets all ISU specifications. Deep forend, buttplate vertically adjustable, wide adjustable trigger.
Price: About **$1,428.00**

REMINGTON 40-XC KS NATIONAL MATCH COURSE RIFLE
Caliber: 7.62 NATO, 5-shot.
Barrel: 24″, stainless steel.
Weight: 11 lbs. without sights. **Length:** 43½″ overall.
Stock: Kevlar, position-style, with palm swell, handstop.
Sights: None furnished.
Features: Designed to meet the needs of competitive shooters firing the national match courses. Position-style stock, top loading clip slot magazine, anti-bind bolt and receiver, stainless steel barrel and action. Meets all ISU Army Rifle specifications. Adjustable buttplate, adjustable trigger.
Price: About **$1,484.00**

Sako TRG-21

SAKO TRG-21 BOLT-ACTION RIFLE
Caliber: 308 Win., 10-shot magazine.
Barrel: 25.75″.
Weight: 10.5 lbs. **Length:** 46.5″ overall.
Stock: Reinforced polyurethane with fully adjustable cheekpiece and buttplate.
Sights: None furnished. Optional quick-detachable, one-piece scope mount base, 1″ or 30mm rings.
Features: Resistance-free bolt, free-floating heavy stainless barrel, 60-degree bolt lift. Two-stage trigger is adjustable for length, pull, horizontal or vertical pitch. Introduced 1993. Imported from Finland by Stoeger.
Price: **$4,265.00**

CAUTION: PRICES SHOWN ARE SUPPLIED BY THE MANUFACTURER OR IMPORTER. CHECK YOUR LOCAL GUNSHOP.

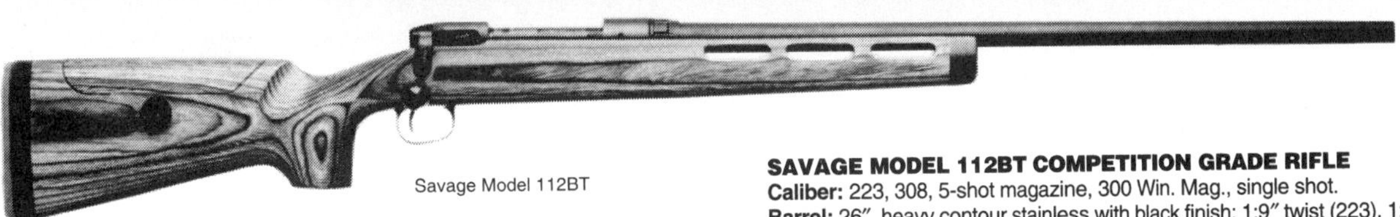

Savage Model 112BT

SAUER 202 TR TARGET RIFLE

Caliber: 6.5x55mm, 308 Win., 5-shot magazine.
Barrel: 26″ or 28.5″, heavy match target.
Weight: 12.1 lbs. **Length:** 44.5″ overall.
Stock: One-piece true target type of laminated beechwood/epoxy; adjustable buttplate and cheekpiece.
Sights: Globe front, Sauer-Busk 200-600m diopter rear. Drilled and tapped for scope mounting.
Features: Interchangeable free-floating, hammer-forged barrel; two-stage adjustable trigger; vertical slide safety; 3 millisecond lock time; rail for swivel, bipod; right- or left-hand; Converts to 22 rimfire. Introduced 1994. Imported from Germany by SIGARMS, Inc.
Price: **$1,900.00**
Price: Spare Match-Target barrel **$425.00**

SAVAGE MODEL 112BT COMPETITION GRADE RIFLE

Caliber: 223, 308, 5-shot magazine, 300 Win. Mag., single shot.
Barrel: 26″, heavy contour stainless with black finish; 1:9″ twist (223), 1:10″ (308).
Weight: 10.8 lbs. **Length:** 47.5″ overall.
Stock: Laminated wood with straight comb, adjustable cheek rest, Wundhammer palm swell, ventilated forend. Recoil pad is adjustable for length of pull.
Sights: None furnished; drilled and tapped for scope mounting and aperture target-style sights. Recessed target-style muzzle has .812″ diameter section for universal target sight base.
Features: Pillar-bedded stock, matte black alloy receiver. Bolt has black titanium nitride coating, large handle ball. Has alloy accessory rail on forend. Comes with safety gun lock, target and ear puffs. Introduced 1994. Made in U.S. by Savage Arms, Inc.
Price: **$1,000.00**
Price: 300 Win. Mag. (single shot 112BT-S) **$1,000.00**

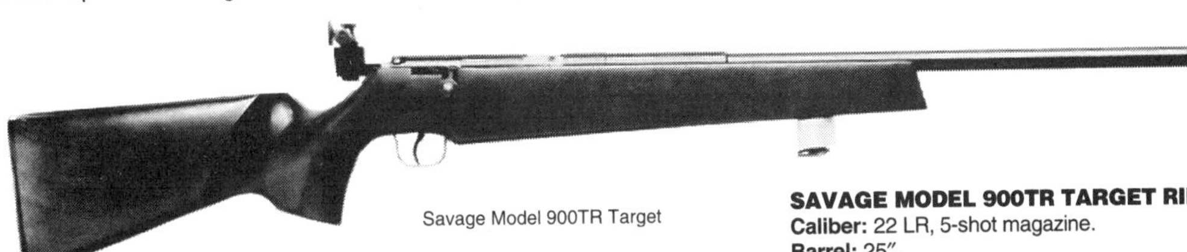

Savage Model 900TR Target

SAVAGE MODEL 900B BIATHALON

Caliber: 22 LR, 5-shot magazine.
Barrel: 21″.
Weight: 8 1/4 lbs. **Length:** 39 5/8″ overall.
Stock: Natural finish hardwood with clip holder, carrying and shooting rails, butt hook, hand stop.
Sights: Target front with inserts, peep rear with 1/4-minute click adjustments.
Features: Biathlon-style rifle with snow cap muzzle protector. Comes with five magazines. Introduced 1991. Made in Canada, from Savage Arms.
Price: About **$498.00**

SAVAGE MODEL 900TR TARGET RIFLE

Caliber: 22 LR, 5-shot magazine.
Barrel: 25″.
Weight: 8 lbs. **Length:** 43 5/8″ overall.
Stock: Target-type, walnut-finished hardwood.
Sights: Target front with inserts, peep rear with 1/4-minute click adjustments.
Features: Comes with shooting rail and hand stop. Introduced 1991. Made in Canada, from Savage Arms.
Price: **$415.00**

Savage Model 900S Silhouette Rifle

Similar to the Model 900B except has high-comb target-type stock of walnut-finished hardwood, one 5-shot magazine. Comes without sights, but receiver is drilled and tapped for scope base. Weighs about 8 lbs. Introduced 1992. Made in Canada, from Savage Arms.
Price: **$346.00**

Springfield M1A/M-21

Springfield, Inc. M1A/M-21 Tactical Model Rifle

Similar to the M1A Super Match except has special sniper stock with adjustable cheekpiece and rubber recoil pad. Weighs 11.2 lbs. From Springfield, Inc.
Price: **$2,204.00**

SPRINGFIELD, INC. M1A SUPER MATCH

Caliber: 308 Win.
Barrel: 22″, heavy Douglas Premium or National Match.
Weight: About 10 lbs. **Length:** 44.31″ overall.
Stock: Heavy walnut competition stock with longer pistol grip, contoured area behind the rear sight, thicker butt and forend, glass bedded.
Sights: National Match front and rear.
Features: Has figure-eight-style operating rod guide. Introduced 1987. From Springfield, Inc.
Price: About **$2,050.00**

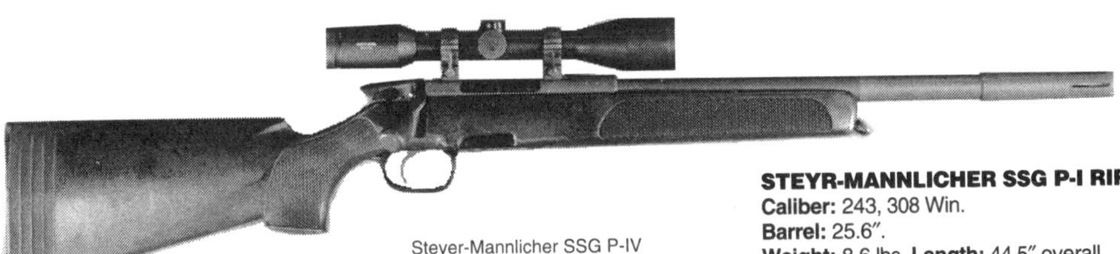

Steyer-Mannlicher SSG P-IV

Steyr-Mannlicher SSG P-IV Rifle

Similar to the SSG P-I except has 16.75″ heavy barrel with flash hider. Available in 308 only. ABS Cycolac synthetic stock in green or black. Introduced 1992. Imported from Austria by GSI, Inc.
Price: **$2,660.00**

STEYR-MANNLICHER SSG P-I RIFLE

Caliber: 243, 308 Win.
Barrel: 25.6″.
Weight: 8.6 lbs. **Length:** 44.5″ overall.
Stock: ABS Cycolac synthetic half-stock. Removable spacers in butt adjusts length of pull from 12 3/4″ to 14″.
Sights: Hooded blade front, folding leaf rear.
Features: Parkerized finish. Choice of interchangeable single- or double-set triggers. Detachable 5-shot rotary magazine (10-shot optional). Receiver grooved for Steyr and Bock Quick Detach mounts. Imported from Austria by GSI, Inc.
Price: Synthetic half-stock **$1,995.00**
Price: SSG-PII (as above except has large bolt knob, heavy bbl., no sights, forend rail). **$1,995.00**

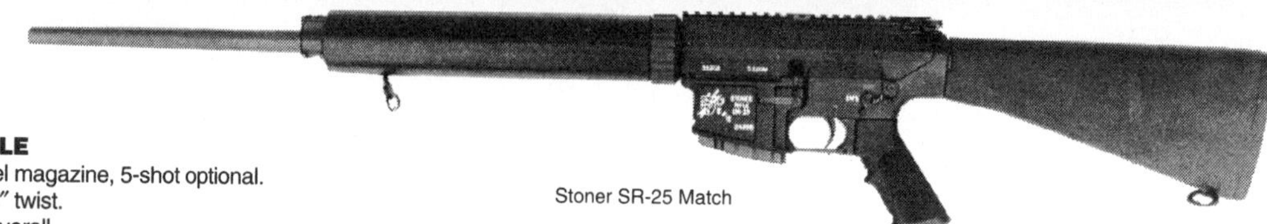
Stoner SR-25 Match

STONER SR-25 MATCH RIFLE
Caliber: 7.62 NATO, 10-shot steel magazine, 5-shot optional.
Barrel: 24″ heavy match; 1:11.25″ twist.
Weight: 10.75 lbs. **Length:** 44″ overall.
Stock: Black synthetic AR-15A2 design. Full floating forend of Mil-spec synthetic attaches to upper receiver at a single point.
Sights: None furnished. Has integral Weaver-style rail. Rings and iron sights optional.
Features: Improved AR-15 trigger; AR-15-style seven-lug rotating bolt. Gas block rail mounts detachable front sight. Introduced 1993. Made in U.S. by Knight's Mfg. Co.
Price: $2,995.00
Price: SR-25 Lightweight Match (20″ medium match target contour barrel, 9.5 lbs., 40″ overall) $2,995.00

STEYR-MANNLICHER MATCH SPG-UIT RIFLE
Caliber: 308 Win.
Barrel: 25.5″.
Weight: 10 lbs. **Length:** 44″ overall.
Stock: Laminated and ventilated. Special UIT Match design.
Sights: Steyr globe front, Steyr peep rear.
Features: Double-pull trigger adjustable for let-off point, slack, weight of first-stage pull, release force and length; buttplate adjustable for height and length. Meets UIT specifications. Introduced 1992. Imported from Austria by GSI, Inc.
Price: $3,995.00
Price: SPG-CISM $4,295.00
Price: SPG-T $3,695.00

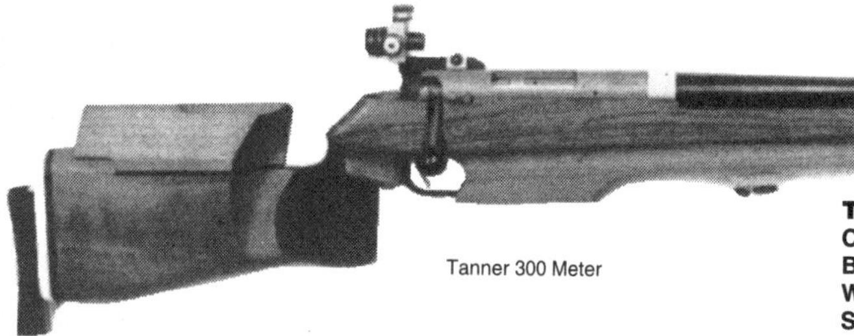
Tanner 300 Meter

TANNER STANDARD UIT RIFLE
Caliber: 308, 7.5mm Swiss, 10-shot.
Barrel: 25.9″.
Weight: 10.5 lbs. **Length:** 40.6″ overall.
Stock: Match style of seasoned nutwood with accessory rail; coarsely stippled pistol grip; high cheekpiece; vented forend.
Sights: Globe front with interchangeable inserts, Tanner micrometer-diopter rear with adjustable aperture.
Features: Two locking lug revolving bolt encloses case head. Trigger adjustable from 1/2 to 6 1/2 lbs.; match trigger optional. Comes with 300-meter test target. Imported from Switzerland by Mandall Shooting Supplies. Introduced 1984.
Price: About $4,700.00

TANNER 300 METER FREE RIFLE
Caliber: 308 Win., 7.5 Swiss, single shot.
Barrel: 27.58″.
Weight: 15 lbs. **Length:** 45.3″ overall.
Stock: Seasoned walnut, thumbhole style, with accessory rail, palm rest, adjustable hook butt.
Sights: Globe front with interchangeable inserts, Tanner-design micrometer-diopter rear with adjustable aperture.
Features: Three-lug revolving-lock bolt design; adjustable set trigger; short firing pin travel; supplied with 300-meter test target. Imported from Switzerland by Mandall Shooting Supplies. Introduced 1984.
Price: About $4,900.00

TANNER 50 METER FREE RIFLE
Caliber: 22 LR, single shot.
Barrel: 27.7″.
Weight: 13.9 lbs. **Length:** 44.4″ overall.
Stock: Seasoned walnut with palm rest, accessory rail, adjustable hook buttplate.
Sights: Globe front with interchangeable inserts, Tanner micrometer-diopter rear with adjustable aperture.
Features: Bolt action with externally adjustable set trigger. Supplied with 50-meter test target. Imported from Switzerland by Mandall Shooting Supplies. Introduced 1984.
Price: About $3,900.00

SHOTGUNS—AUTOLOADERS

Includes a wide variety of sporting guns and guns suitable for various competitions.

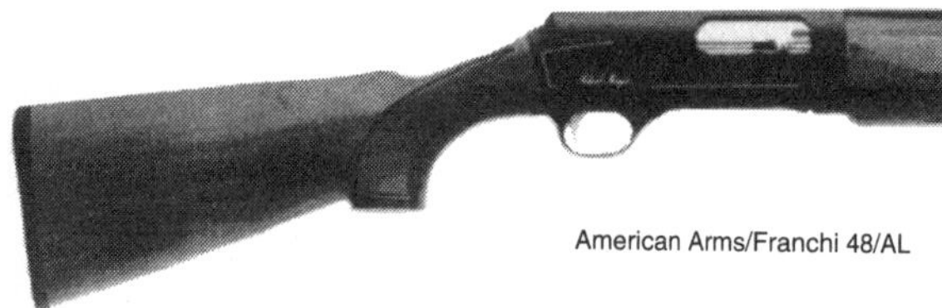
American Arms/Franchi 48/AL

AMERICAN ARMS/FRANCHI BLACK MAGIC 48/AL
Gauge: 12, 20 or 28, 2 3/4″ chamber.
Barrel: 24″, 26″, 28″ (Franchoke Imp. Cyl., Mod., Full choke tubes), 28 ga. has fixed Imp. Cyl. Vent. rib.
Weight: 5.2 lbs. (20-gauge). **Length:** NA
Stock: 14 1/4″x1 5/8″x2 1/2″. Walnut with checkered grip and forend.
Features: Recoil-operated action. Chrome-lined bore; cross-bolt safety. Imported from Italy by American Arms, Inc.
Price: 12, 20 ....$649.00
Price: 28 ga. $725.00

BENELLI BLACK EAGLE COMPETITION AUTO SHOTGUN
Gauge: 12, 3″ chamber.
Barrel: 26″, 28″ (Full, Mod., Imp. Cyl., Imp. Mod., Skeet choke tubes). Mid-bead sight.
Weight: 7.1 to 7.6 lbs. **Length:** 49 5/8″ overall (26″ barrel).
Stock: European walnut with high-gloss finish. Special competition stock comes with drop adjustment kit.
Features: Uses the Montefeltro rotating bolt inertia recoil operating system with a two-piece steel/aluminum etched receiver (bright on lower, blue upper). Drop adjustment kit allows the stock to be custom fitted without modifying the stock. Black lower receiver finish, blued upper. Introduced 1989. Imported from Italy by Heckler & Koch, Inc.
Price: $1,205.00

CAUTION: PRICES SHOWN ARE SUPPLIED BY THE MANUFACTURER OR IMPORTER. CHECK YOUR LOCAL GUNSHOP.

Benelli Super Black Eagle

Benelli Super Black Eagle Slug Gun

Similar to the Benelli Super Black Eagle except has 24″ E.R. Shaw Custom rifled barrel with 3″ chamber, and comes with scope mount base. Uses the Montefeltro inertia recoil bolt system. Matte-finish receiver. Weight is 7.5 lbs., overall length 45.5″. Wood or polymer stocks available. Introduced 1992. Imported from Italy by Heckler & Koch, Inc.

Price: $1,220.00
Price: With polymer stock $1,220.00

BENELLI M1 SUPER 90 FIELD AUTO SHOTGUN

Gauge: 12, 3″ chamber.
Barrel: 21″, 24″, 26″, 28″ (choke tubes).
Weight: 7 lbs., 4 oz.
Stock: High impact polymer; wood on 26″, 28″.
Sights: Metal bead front.
Features: Sporting version of the military & police gun. Uses the rotating Montefeltro bolt system. Ventilated rib; blue finish. Comes with set of five choke tubes. Imported from Italy by Heckler & Koch, Inc.
Price: $884.00
Price: Wood stock version $900.00

BENELLI SUPER BLACK EAGLE SHOTGUN

Gauge: 12, 3$^{1}/_{2}$″ chamber.
Barrel: 24″, 26″, 28″ (Imp. Cyl., Mod., Imp. Mod., Full choke tubes).
Weight: 7 lbs., 5 oz. **Length:** 49$^{5}/_{8}$″ overall (28″ barrel).
Stock: European walnut with satin finish, or polymer. Adjustable for drop.
Sights: Bead front.
Features: Uses Montfeltro inertia recoil bolt system. Fires all 12-gauge shells from 2$^{3}/_{4}$″ to 3$^{1}/_{2}$″ magnums. Introduced 1991. Imported from Italy by Heckler & Koch, Inc.
Price: With 28″ barrel $1,192.00
Price: With 24″, 26″ barrel, polymer stock $1,170.00

Benelli Executive Series Shotguns

Similar to the Black Eagle except has grayed steel lower receiver, hand-engraved and gold inlaid (Type III), and has highest grade of walnut stock with drop adjustment kit. Barrel lengths of 21″, 24″, 26″, 28″; 3″ chamber. **Special order only.** Introduced 1995. Imported from Italy by Heckler & Koch, Inc.

Price: Type I (about two-thirds engraving coverage) $4,550.00
Price: Type II (full coverage engraving) $5,200.00
Price: Type III (full coverage, gold inlays) $6,032.00

Benelli Montefeltro Super 90 20-Gauge Shotgun

Similar to the 12-gauge Montefeltro Super 90 except chambered for 3″ 20-gauge, 24″ or 26″ barrel (choke tubes), weighs 5 lbs., 12 oz. Has drop-adjustable walnut stock with gloss finish, blued receiver. Overall length 47.5″. Introduced 1993. Imported from Italy by Heckler & Koch, Inc.

Price: $905.00
Price: Limited Edition (26″ barrel, special nickel-plated and engraved receiver inlaid with gold) $2,080.00

Benelli Montefeltro Super 90 Shotgun

BENELLI M1 SPORTING SPECIAL AUTO SHOTGUN

Gauge: 12, 3″ chamber.
Barrel: 18.5″ (Imp. Cyl. Mod., Full choke tubes).
Weight: 6 lbs., 8 oz. **Length:** 39.75″ overall.
Stock: Sporting-style polymer with drop adjustment.
Sights: Ghost ring.
Features: Uses Montefeltro inertia recoil bolt system. Matte-finish receiver. Introduced 1993. Imported from Italy by Heckler & Koch, Inc.
Price: $905.00

Beretta A-303 Upland Model

Similar to the field A-303 except has straight English-style stock, 26″ vent. rib barrel with Mobilchoke choke tubes, 3″ chamber. Introduced 1989.

Price: $772.00

Benelli Montefeltro Super 90 Shotgun

Similar to the M1 Super 90 except has checkered walnut stock with high-gloss finish. Uses the Montefeltro rotating bolt system with a simple inertia recoil design. Full, Imp. Mod, Mod., Imp. Cyl. choke tubes. Weighs 7-7$^{1}/_{2}$ lbs. Finish is matte black. Introduced 1987.

Price: 21″, 24″, 26″, 28″ $905.00
Price: Left-hand, 26″, 28″ $925.00
Price: 20-ga., Montefeltro Super 90, 24″ 26″, 5$^{3}/_{4}$ lbs. $905.00

BERETTA A-303 AUTO SHOTGUN

Gauge: 20, 2$^{3}/_{4}$″ or 3″ chamber.
Barrel: 24″, 26″, 28″ Mobilchoke choke tubes.
Weight: About 6$^{1}/_{2}$ lbs.
Stock: American walnut; hand-checkered grip and forend.
Features: Gas-operated action, alloy receiver, magazine cut-off, push-button safety. Mobilchoke models come with three interchangeable flush-mounted screw-in choke tubes. Imported from Italy by Beretta U.S.A. Introduced 1983.
Price: Mobilchoke, 20-ga. $772.00
Price: A-303 Youth Gun, 20-ga., 2$^{3}/_{4}$″ chamber, 24″ barrel $772.00
Price: A-303 Sporting Clays with Mobilchoke, 20 gauge $822.00

Beretta 390 Silver Mallard

BERETTA 390 SILVER MALLARD AUTO SHOTGUN

Gauge: 12, 3″ chamber.
Barrel: 24″, 26″, 28″, 30″, Mobilchoke choke tubes.
Weight: 7.6 lbs.
Stock: Select walnut or matte black synthetic. Adjustable drop and cast.
Features: Gas-operated action with self-compensating valve allows shooting all loads without adjustment. Alloy receiver, reversible safety; chrome-plated bore; floating vent. rib. Matte-finish models for turkey/waterfowl and Deluxe with gold, engraving also available. Slug model available. Introduced 1992. Imported from Italy by Beretta U.S.A.
Price: Walnut or synthetic $822.00
Price: Waterfowl/Turkey (matte finish) $822.00
Price: Gold Mallard $987.00
Price: Slug model $822.00

Beretta 390 Sport Trap/Skeet/Sporting Shotguns

Similar to the 390 Silver Mallard except has lower-contour, rounded receiver. Available with ported barrel. Trap has 30″, 32″ barrel (Full, Imp. Mod., Mod. choke tubes); Skeet has 26″, 28″ barrel (fixed Skeet); Sporting has 28″, 30″ (Full, Mod., Imp. Cyl., Skeet tubes). Introduced 1995. Imported from Italy by Beretta U.S.A.

Price: 390 Sport Trap $865.00
Price: As above, fixed Full choke $851.00
Price: 390 Sport Skeet $849.00
Price: 390 Sport Sporting $865.00
Price: Ported barrel, above models, add about $100.00

Beretta 390 Super Trap, Super Skeet Shotguns

Similar to the 390 Field except have adjustable-comb stocks that allow height adjustments via interchangeable comb inserts. Rounded recoil pad system allows adjustments for length of pull. Wide ventilated rib with orange front sight. Factory ported barrels in 28″ (fixed Skeet), 30″, 32″ Trap (Mobilchoke tubes). Weighs 8.3 lbs. In 12-gauge only, with 3″ chamber. Introduced 1993. Imported from Italy by Beretta U.S.A.

Price: 390 Super Trap $1,258.00
Price: 390 Super Skeet $1,199.00

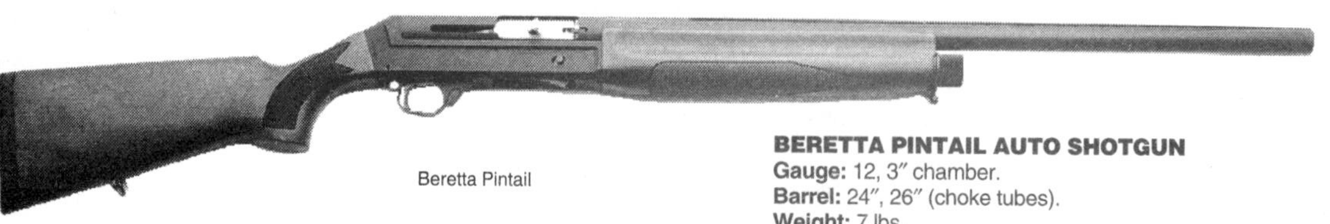

Beretta Pintail

BERETTA PINTAIL AUTO SHOTGUN

Gauge: 12, 3″ chamber.
Barrel: 24″, 26″ (choke tubes).
Weight: 7 lbs.
Stock: Checkered walnut.
Features: Montefeltro-type short recoil action. Matte finish on wood and metal. Comes with sling swivels. Introduced 1993. Imported from Italy by Beretta U.S.A.
Price: $743.00

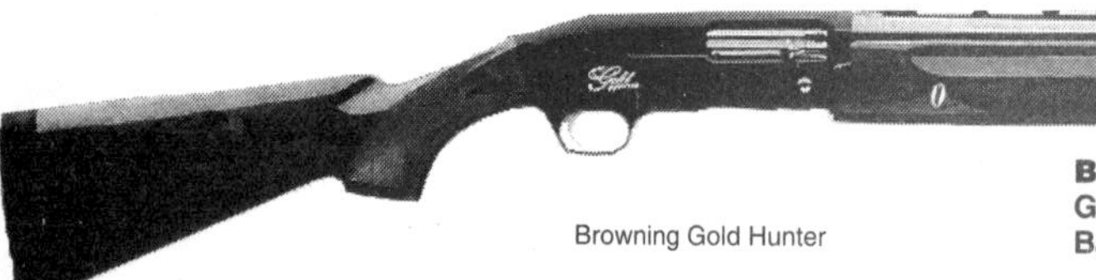

Browning Gold Hunter

BROWNING GOLD HUNTER AUTO SHOTGUN

Gauge: 12, 20, 3″ chamber.
Barrel: 12-ga.—26″, 28″, 30″, Invector Plus choke tubes; 20-ga.—26″, 30″, Invector choke tubes.
Weight: 7 lbs., 9 oz. (12-ga.), 6 lbs., 12 oz. (20-ga.) **Length:** 46¼″ overall (20-ga., 26″ barrel).
Stock: 14″x1½″x2⅓″; select walnut with gloss finish; palm swell grip.
Features: Self-regulating, self-cleaning gas system shoots all loads; lightweight receiver with special non-glare deep black finish; large reversible safety button; large rounded trigger guard, gold trigger. The 20-gauge has slightly smaller dimensions; 12-gauge have back-bored barrels, Invector Plus tube system. Introduced 1994. Imported by Browning.
Price: 12- or 20-gauge $734.95
Price: Extra barrels $272.95

Browning Gold Sporting Clays Auto

Similar to the Gold Hunter except 12-gauge only with 28″ or 30″ barrel; front and center beads on tapered ventilated rib; ported and back-bored Invector Plus barrel; 2¾″ chamber; satin-finished stock with solid, radiused recoil pad with hard heel insert; non-glare black alloy receiver has "Sporting Clays" inscribed in gold. Introduced 1996. Imported from Japan by Browning.

Price: $759.95

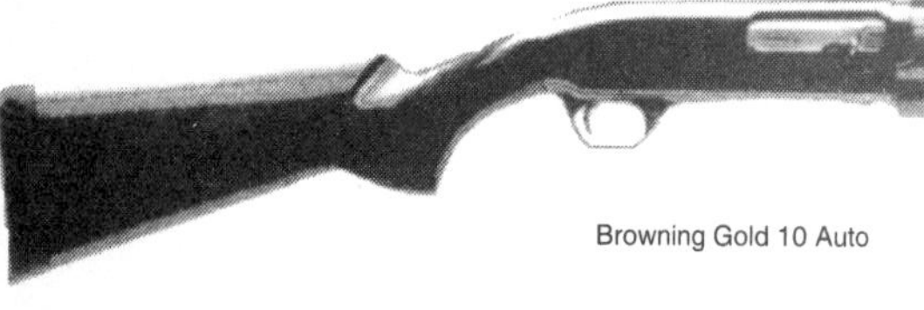

Browning Gold 10 Auto

BROWNING GOLD 10 AUTO SHOTGUN

Gauge: 10, 3½″ chamber, 5-shot magazine.
Barrel: 26″, 28″, 30″ (Imp. Cyl., Mod., Full standard Invector).
Weight: 10 lbs, 7 oz. (28″ barrel).
Stock: 14⅜″x1½″x2⅜″. Select walnut with gloss finish, cut checkering, recoil pad.
Features: Short-stroke, gas-operated action, cross-bolt safety. Forged steel receiver with polished blue finish. Introduced 1993. Imported by Browning.
Price: $1,007.95
Price: Extra barrel $261.95

Browning Gold 10 Stalker Auto Shotgun

Same as the standard Gold 10 except has non-glare metal finish and black graphite-fiberglass composite stock with dull finish and checkering. Introduced 1993. Imported by Browning.

Price: $1,007.95
Price: Extra barrel $261.95

Browning Auto-5 Stalker

BROWNING AUTO-5 LIGHT 12 AND 20

Gauge: 12, 20, 5-shot; 3-shot plug furnished; 2¾″ or 3″ chamber.
Action: Recoil operated autoloader; takedown.
Barrel: 26″, 28″, 30″ Invector (choke tube) barrel; also available with Light 20-ga. 28″ (Mod.) or 26″ (Imp. Cyl.) barrel.
Weight: 12-, 16-ga. 7¼ lbs.; 20-ga. 6⅜ lbs.
Stock: French walnut, hand checkered half-pistol grip and forend. 14¼″x1⅝″x2½″.
Features: Receiver hand engraved with scroll designs and border. Double extractors, extra bbls. Interchangeable without factory fitting; mag. cut-off; cross-bolt safety. All models except Buck Special and game guns have back-bored barrels with Invector Plus choke tubes. Imported from Japan by Browning.
Price: Light 12, 20, vent. rib., Invector Plus $839.95
Price: Extra Invector barrel $307.95
Price: Light 12 Buck Special $828.95
Price: 12, 12 magnum barrel $307.95
Price: Light 12, Hunting, Invector Plus $839.95
Price: Buck Special barrel $269.95

Browning Auto-5 Stalker

Similar to the Auto-5 Light and Magnum models except has matte blue metal finish and black graphite-fiberglass stock and forend. Stock is scratch and impact resistant and has checkered panels. Light Stalker has 2¾″ chamber, 26″ or 28″ vent. rib barrel with Invector choke tubes, weighs 8 lbs., 1 oz. (26″). Magnum Stalker has 3″ chamber, 28″ or 30″ back-bored vent. rib barrel with Invector choke tubes, weighs 8 lbs., 11 oz. (28″). Introduced 1992.

Price: Light Stalker $839.95
Price: Magnum Stalker $865.95

CAUTION: PRICES SHOWN ARE SUPPLIED BY THE MANUFACTURER OR IMPORTER. CHECK YOUR LOCAL GUN SHOP.

Browning Auto-5 Magnum 12

Same as standard Auto-5 except chambered for 3″ magnum shells (also handles $2\frac{3}{4}$″ magnum and $2\frac{3}{4}$″ HV loads). 28″ Mod., Full; 30″ and 32″ (Full) bbls. Back-bored barrel comes with Invector choke tubes. 14″x$1\frac{5}{8}$″x$2\frac{1}{2}$″ stock. Recoil pad. Weighs $8\frac{3}{4}$ lbs.

Price: With back-bored barrel, Invector Plus $865.95
Price: Extra Invector Plus barrel $307.95

Browning Auto-5 Magnum 20

Same as Magnum 12 except 20-gauge, 26″ or 28″ barrel with Invector Plus choke tubes with back-bored barrels. With ventilated rib, weighs $7\frac{1}{2}$ lbs.

Price: Invector Plus $865.95
Price: Extra Invector barrel $307.95

CHURCHILL TURKEY AUTOMATIC SHOTGUN

Gauge: 12, 3″ chamber, 5-shot magazine.
Barrel: 25″ (Mod., Full, Extra Full choke tubes).
Weight: 7 lbs. **Length:** NA.
Stock: Walnut with satin finish, hand checkering.
Features: Gas-operated action, magazine cut-off, non-glare metal finish. Gold-colored trigger. Introduced 1990. Imported by Ellett Bros.
Price: $569.95

Consult our Directory pages for the location of firms mentioned.

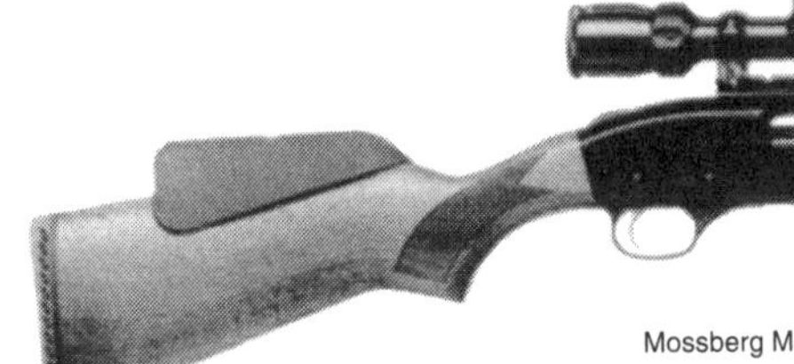

Mossberg Model 9200

MOSSBERG MODEL 9200 CROWN GRADE AUTO SHOTGUN

Gauge: 12, 3″ chamber.
Barrel: 24″ (rifled bore), 24″, 28″ (Accu-Choke tubes); vent. rib.
Weight: About 7.5 lbs. **Length:** 48″ overall (28″ bbl.).
Stock: Walnut with high-gloss finish, cut checkering.
Features: Shoots all $2\frac{3}{4}$″ or 3″ loads without adjustment. Alloy receiver, ambidextrous top safety. Introduced 1992.
Price: 28″, vent. rib $478.00
Price: Turkey, 24″ vent. rib $478.00
Price: Trophy, 24″ with scope base, rifled bore, Dual-Comb stock $500.00
Price: 24″, rifle sights, rifled bore $478.00

Mossberg Model 9200 Persuader

Similar to the Model 9200 Crown Grade except has black synthetic stock and forend, $18\frac{1}{2}$″ plain barrel with fixed Cyl. choke, swivel studs. Weighs 7 lbs. Made in U.S. by Mossberg. Introduced 1996.

Price: $390.00

Mossberg Model 9200 Viking

Similar to the Model 9200 Crown Grade except has black matte metal finish, moss-green synthetic stock and forend; 28″ Accu-Choke vent. rib barrel with Mod. tube. Made in U.S. by Mossberg. Introduced 1996.

Price: $404.00

Mossberg Model 9200 USST Autoloading Shotgun

Same as the Model 9200 Crown Grade except has "United States Shooting Team" custom engraved receiver. Comes with 26″ vent. rib barrel with Accu-Choke tubes (including Skeet), cut-checkered walnut-finish stock and forend. Introduced 1993.

Price: $478.00

Mossberg 9200 Camo

Mossberg Model 9200 Bantam

Same as the Model 9200 Crown Grade except has 1″ shorter stock, 22″ vent. rib barrel with three Accu-Choke tubes. Made in U.S. by Mossberg. Introduced 1996.

Price: $478.00

Mossberg Model 9200 Camo Shotgun

Same as the Model 9200 Crown Grade except completely covered with Mossy Oak Tree Stand, Realtree AP gray or OFM camouflage finish. Available with 24″ barrel with Accu-Choke tubes. Has synthetic stock and forend. Introduced 1993.

Price: Turkey, 24″ vent. rib, Mossy Oak or Realtree finish $562.00
Price: 28″ vent. rib, Accu-Chokes, OFM camo finish $463.00

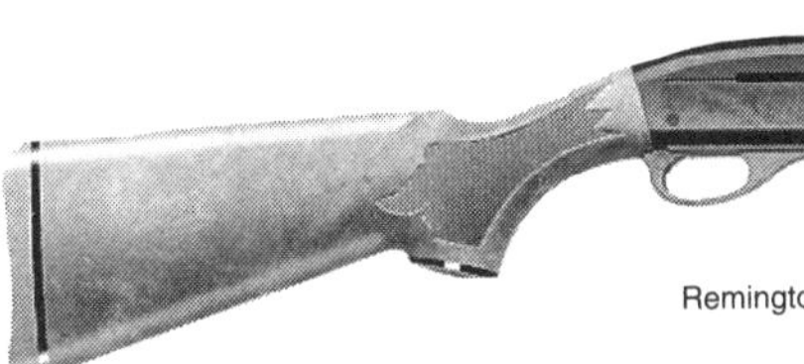

Remington 11-87 Sporting Clays

REMINGTON 11-87 PREMIER SHOTGUN

Gauge: 12, 3″ chamber.
Barrel: 26″, 28″, 30″ Rem Choke tubes. Light Contour barrel.
Weight: About $8\frac{1}{4}$ lbs. **Length:** 46″ overall (26″ bbl.).
Stock: Walnut with satin or high-gloss finish; cut checkering; solid brown buttpad; no white spacers.
Sights: Bradley-type white-faced front, metal bead middle.
Features: Pressure compensating gas system allows shooting $2\frac{3}{4}$″ or 3″ loads interchangeably with no adjustments. Stainless magazine tube; redesigned feed latch, barrel support ring on operating bars; pinned forend. Introduced 1987.
Price: $670.00
Price: Left-hand $720.00
Price: Premier Cantilever Deer Barrel, sling, swivels, Monte Carlo stock $725.00

REMINGTON 11-87 SPORTING CLAYS

Gauge: 12, $2\frac{3}{4}$″ chamber
Barrel: 26″, 28″, vent. rib, Rem Choke (Skeet, Imp. Cyl., Mod., Full); Light Contour barrel. Medium height rib.
Weight: 7.5 lbs. **Length:** 46.5″ overall (26″ barrel).
Stock: $14\frac{3}{16}$″x$1\frac{1}{2}$″x$2\frac{1}{4}$″. Walnut, with cut checkering; sporting clays butt pad.
Features: Top of receiver, barrel and rib have matte finish; shortened magazine tube and forend; lengthened forcing cone; ivory bead front sight; competition trigger. Special no-wrench choke tubes marked on the outside. Comes in two-barrel fitted hard case. Introduced 1992.
Price: $732.00

Remington 11-87 Premier Trap

Similar to 11-87 Premier except trap dimension stock with straight or Monte Carlo combs; select walnut with satin finish and Tournament-grade cut checkering; 30″ barrel with Rem Chokes (Trap Full, Trap Extra Full, Trap Super Full). Gas system set for $2\frac{3}{4}$″ shells only. Introduced 1987.

Price: With Monte Carlo stock $725.00

Remington 11-87 Premier Skeet

Similar to 11-87 Premier except Skeet dimension stock with cut checkering, satin finish, two-piece buttplate; 26″ barrel with Skeet or Rem Chokes (Skeet, Imp. Skeet). Gas system set for $2\frac{3}{4}$″ shells only. Introduced 1987.

Price: $718.00

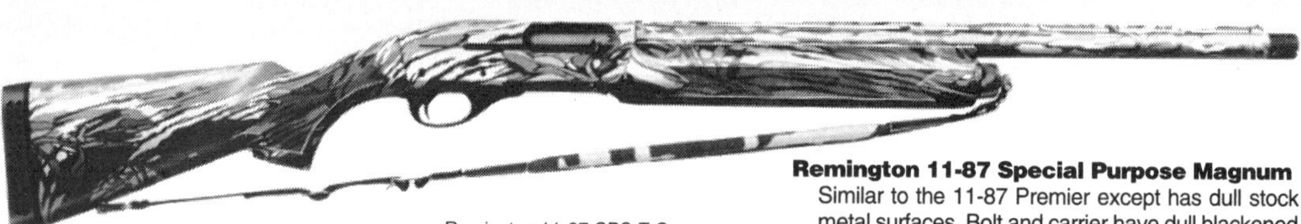
Remington 11-87 SPS-T Camo

Remington 11-87 SPS-T Camo Auto Shotgun
Similar to the 11-87 Special Purpose Magnum except with synthetic stock, 21″ vent. rib barrel with Super-Full Turkey (.665″ diameter with knurled extension) and Imp. Cyl. Rem Choke tubes. Completely covered with Mossy Oak Green Leaf camouflage. Bolt body, trigger guard and recoil pad are non-reflective black. Introduced 1993.
Price: $744.00

Remington 11-87 Special Purpose Synthetic Camo
Similar to the 11-87 Special Purpose Magnum except has synthetic stock and all metal (except bolt and trigger guard) and stock covered with Mossy Oak Bottomland camo finish. In 12-gauge only, 26″, Rem Choke. Comes with camo sling, swivels. Introduced 1992.
Price: $730.00

Remington 11-87 Special Purpose Magnum
Similar to the 11-87 Premier except has dull stock finish, Parkerized exposed metal surfaces. Bolt and carrier have dull blackened coloring. Comes with 26″ or 28″ barrel with Rem Chokes, padded Cordura nylon sling and quick detachable swivels. Introduced 1987.
Price: $644.00
Price: With synthetic stock and forend (SPS) $644.00
Price: Magnum-Turkey with synthetic stock (SPS-T) $657.00

Remington 11-87 SPS-Deer Shotgun
Similar to the 11-87 Special Purpose Camo except has fully-rifled 21″ barrel with rifle sights, black non-reflective, synthetic stock and forend, black carrying sling. Introduced 1993.
Price: $665.00

Remington 11-87 SPS Cantilever Shotgun
Similar to the 11-87 SPS except has fully rifled barrel; synthetic stock with Monte Carlo comb; cantilever scope mount deer barrel. Comes with sling and swivels. Introduced 1994.
Price: $725.00

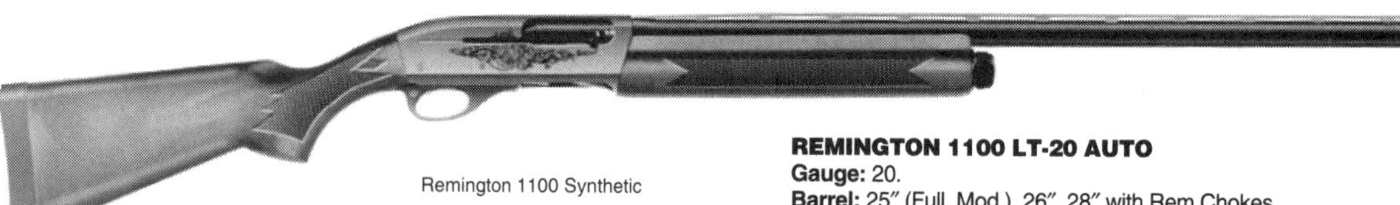
Remington 1100 Synthetic

Remington 1100 Synthetic
Simliar to the 1100 LT magnum except in 12- or 20-gauage, and has black synthetic stock; vent. rib 28″ barrel on 12-gauge, 26″ on 20, both with Mod. Rem Choke tube. Weighs about $7\frac{1}{2}$ lbs. Introduced 1996.
Price: $492.00

Remington 1100 20-Gauge Deer Gun
Same as 1100 except 20-ga. only, 21″ barrel (Imp. Cyl.), rifle sights adjustable for windage and elevation; recoil pad with white spacer. Weighs $7\frac{1}{4}$ lbs.
Price: About $584.00

REMINGTON 1100 LT-20 AUTO
Gauge: 20.
Barrel: 25″ (Full, Mod.), 26″, 28″ with Rem Chokes.
Weight: $7\frac{1}{2}$ lbs.
Stock: 14″x$1\frac{1}{2}$″x$2\frac{1}{2}$″. American walnut, checkered pistol grip and forend.
Features: Quickly interchangeable barrels. Matted receiver top with scroll work on both sides of receiver. Cross-bolt safety.
Price: With Rem Chokes, 20-ga. about $625.00
Price: Youth Gun LT-20 (21″ Rem Choke) $625.00
Price: 20-ga., 3″ magnum $625.00
Price: Skeet, 26″, cut checkering, Rem. Choke $710.00

Remington 1100 Special Field
Similar to Standard Model 1100 except 12- and 20-ga. only, comes with 23″ Rem Choke barrel. LT-20 version $6\frac{1}{2}$ lbs.; has straight-grip stock, shorter forend, both with cut checkering. Comes with vent. rib only; matte finish receiver without engraving. Introduced 1983.
Price: 12- and 20-ga., 23″ Rem Choke, about $625.00

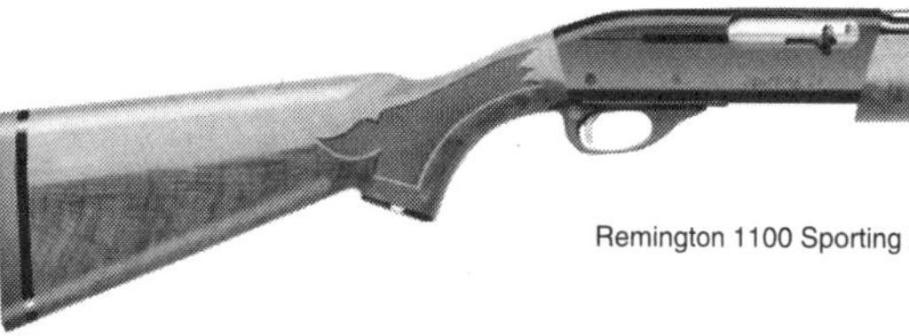
Remington 1100 Sporting 28

Remington 1100 Sporting 28
Similar to the 1100 LT-20 except in 28-gauge with 25″ barrel; comes with Skeet, Imp. Cyl., Light Mod., Mod. Rem Choke tubes. Fancy walnut with gloss finish, Sporting rubber buttpad. Made in U.S. by Remington. Introduced 1996.
Price: $725.00

REMINGTON 11-96 EURO LIGHTWEIGHT AUTO SHOTGUN
Gauge: 12, 3″ chamber.
Barrel: 26″, 28″, Rem Chokes.
Weight: $6\frac{7}{8}$ lbs. (26″ barrel). **Length:** 46″ overall (26″ barrel).
Stock: Semi-fancy Claro walnut with cut checkering; solid rubber butt pad.
Features: Pressure-compensating gas system allows shooting $2\frac{3}{4}$″ or 3″ loads interchangeably with no adjustments. Lightweight steel receiver with scroll-engraved panels; stainless steel magazine tube; 6mm ventilated rib on light contour barrel. Introduced 1996. Made in U.S. by Remington.
Price: $849.00

Remington SP-10 Magnum-Camo

Remington SP-10 Magnum-Camo Auto Shotgun
Similar to the SP-10 Magnum except buttstock, forend, receiver, barrel and magazine cap are covered with Mossy Oak Bottomland camo finish; bolt body and trigger guard have matte black finish. Comes with Extra-Full Turkey Rem Choke tube, 23″ vent. rib barrel with mid-rib bead and Bradley-style front sight, swivel studs and quick-detachable swivels, and a non-slip Cordura carrying sling in the same camo pattern. Introduced 1993.
Price: $1,121.00

REMINGTON SP-10 MAGNUM AUTO SHOTGUN
Gauge: 10, $3\frac{1}{2}$″ chamber, 3-shot magazine.
Barrel: 26″, 30″ (Full and Mod. Rem Chokes).
Weight: 11 to $11\frac{1}{4}$ lbs. **Length:** $47\frac{1}{2}$″ overall (26″ barrel).
Stock: Walnut with satin finish. Checkered grip and forend.
Sights: Metal bead front.
Features: Stainless steel gas system with moving cylinder; $\frac{3}{8}$″ ventilated rib. Receiver and barrel have matte finish. Brown recoil pad. Comes with padded Cordura nylon sling. Introduced 1989.
Price: $1,033.00

CAUTION: PRICES SHOWN ARE SUPPLIED BY THE MANUFACTURER OR IMPORTER. CHECK YOUR LOCAL GUN SHOP.

SHOTGUNS—SLIDE ACTIONS

Includes a wide variety of sporting guns and guns suitable for competitive shooting.

Armscor M-30 Field

ARMSCOR M-30 FIELD PUMP SHOTGUN

Gauge: 12, 3″ chamber.
Barrel: 28″ fixed Mod., or with Mod. and Full choke tubes.
Weight: 7.6 lbs.
Stock: Walnut-finished hardwood.
Features: Double action slide bars; blued steel receiver; damascened bolt. Introduced 1996. Imported from the Philippines by K.B.I., Inc.
Price: With fixed choke **$209.00**
Price: With choke tubes **$259.00**

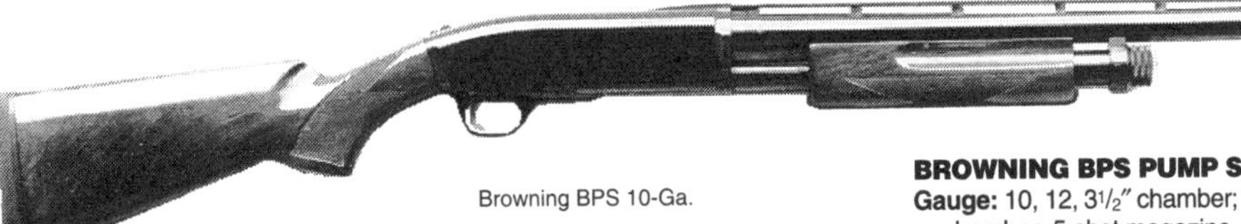

Browning BPS 10-Ga.

BROWNING BPS PUMP SHOTGUN

Gauge: 10, 12, 3½″ chamber; 12 or 20, 3″ chamber (2¾″ in target guns), 28, 2¾″ chamber, 5-shot magazine.
Barrel: 10-ga.—24″ Buck Special, 28″, 30″, 32″ Invector; 12-, 20- ga.—22″, 24″, 26″, 28″, 30″, 32″ (Imp. Cyl., Mod. or Full). Also available with Invector choke tubes, 12- or 20-ga.; Upland Special has 22″ barrel with Invector tubes. BPS 3″ and 3½″ have back-bored barrel.
Weight: 7 lbs., 8 oz. (28″ barrel). **Length:** 48¾″ overall (28″ barrel).
Stock: 14¼″x1½″x2½″. Select walnut, semi-beavertail forend, full pistol grip stock.
Features: All 12-gauge 3″ guns except Buck Special and game guns have back-bored barrels with Invector Plus choke tubes. Bottom feeding and ejection, receiver top safety, high post vent. rib. Double action bars eliminate binding. Vent. rib barrels only. All 12- and 20-gauge guns with 3″ chamber available with fully engraved receiver flats at no extra cost. Each gauge has its own unique game scene. Introduced 1977. Imported from Japan by Browning.
Price: 10-ga., Hunting, Invector **$671.95**
Price: 12-ga., 3½″ Mag., Hunting, Invector Plus **$671.95**
Price: 12-, 20-ga., Hunting, Invector Plus **$534.95**
Price: 12-, 20-ga., Upland Special, Invector Plus **$534.95**
Price: 10-ga. Buck Special **$676.95**
Price: 12-ga. Buck Special **$519.95**
Price: 28-ga., Hunting, Invector **$534.95**

Browning BPS Pigeon Grade Pump Shotgun
Same as the standard BPS except has select high grade walnut stock and forend, and gold-trimmed receiver. Available in 12-gauge only with 26″ or 28″ vent. rib barrels. Introduced 1992.
Price: **$713.95**
Price: 10-gauge Waterfowl Model **$860.95**

CONSULT
SHOOTER'S MARKETPLACE
Page 225, This Issue

Browning BPS Game Gun Turkey Special
Similar to the standard BPS except has satin-finished walnut stock and dull-finished barrel and receiver. Receiver is drilled and tapped for scope mounting. Rifle-style stock dimensions and swivel studs. Has Extra-Full Turkey choke tube. Introduced 1992.
Price: **$571.95**

Browning BPS Pump Shotgun Ladies and Youth Model
Same as BPS Upland Special except 20-ga. only, 22″ Invector barrel, stock has pistol grip with recoil pad. Length of pull is 13¼″. Introduced 1986.
Price: **$534.95**

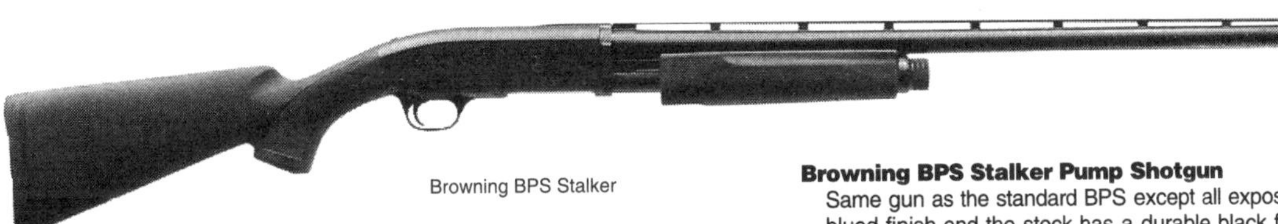

Browning BPS Stalker

Browning BPS Stalker Pump Shotgun
Same gun as the standard BPS except all exposed metal parts have a matte blued finish and the stock has a durable black finish with a black recoil pad. Available in 10-ga. (3½″) and 12-ga. with 3″ or 3½″ chamber, 22″, 28″, 30″ barrel with Invector choke system. Introduced 1987.
Price: 12-ga., 3″ chamber, Invector Plus **$534.95**
Price: 10-, 12-ga., 3½″ chamber **$671.95**

Browning BPS Game Gun Deer Special
Similar to the standard BPS except has newly designed receiver/magazine tube/barrel mounting system to eliminate play, heavy 20.5″ barrel with rifle-type sights with adjustable rear, solid receiver scope mount, "rifle" stock dimensions for scope or open sights, sling swivel studs. Gloss or matte finished wood with checkering, polished blue metal. Introduced 1992.
Price: **$603.95**

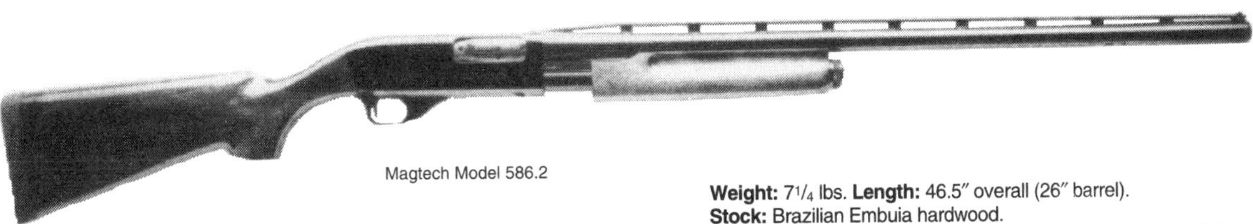

Magtech Model 586.2

MAGTECH MODEL 586.2-VR PUMP SHOTGUN

Gauge: 12, 3″ chamber.
Barrel: 26″, 28″, choke tubes.
Weight: 7¼ lbs. **Length:** 46.5″ overall (26″ barrel).
Stock: Brazilian Embuia hardwood.
Features: Double action slide bars. Ventilated rib with bead front sight. Polished blue finish. Introduced 1995. Imported from Brazil by Magtech Recreational Products.
Price: About **$255.00**

CAUTION: PRICES SHOWN ARE SUPPLIED BY THE MANUFACTURER OR IMPORTER. CHECK YOUR LOCAL GUNSHOP.

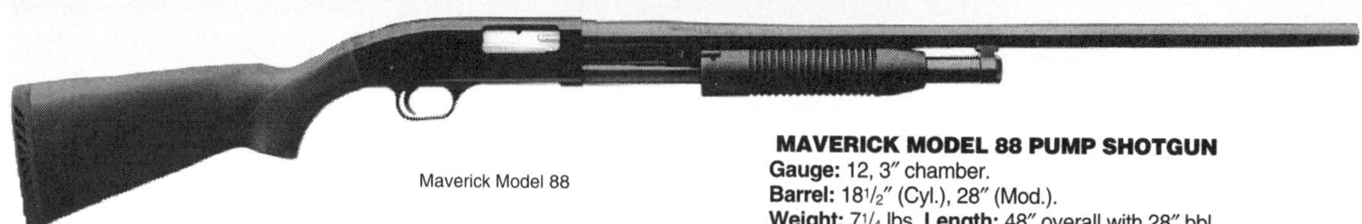

Maverick Model 88

MAVERICK MODEL 88 PUMP SHOTGUN

Gauge: 12, 3″ chamber.
Barrel: 18½″ (Cyl.), 28″ (Mod.).
Weight: 7¼ lbs. **Length:** 48″ overall with 28″ bbl.
Stock: Black synthetic with ribbed synthetic forend.
Sights: Bead front.
Features: Alloy receiver with blue finish; dual slide bars; cross-bolt safety in trigger guard; interchangeable barrels. Rubber recoil pad. Mossberg Cablelock included. Introduced 1989. From Maverick Arms, Inc.
Price: Model 88, synthetic stock, 28″ Mod. $221.00
Price: Model 88, synthetic stock, 28″ ACCU-TUBE, Mod. $235.00
Price: Model 88, synthetic stock, 24″ with rifle sights $235.00

Mossberg Model 500 Sporting

MOSSBERG MODEL 500 SPORTING PUMP

Gauge: 12, 20, 410, 3″ chamber.
Barrel: 18½″ to 28″ with fixed or Accu-Choke, plain or vent. rib.
Weight: 6¼ lbs. (410), 7¼ lbs. (12). **Length:** 48″ overall (28″ barrel).
Stock: 14″x1½″x2½″. Walnut-stained hardwood. Cut-checkered grip and forend.
Sights: White bead front, brass mid-bead.
Features: Ambidextrous thumb safety, twin extractors, disconnecting safety, dual action bars. Quiet Carry forend. Mossberg Cablelock included. From Mossberg.
Price: From about $281.00
Price: Sporting Combos (field barrel and Slugster barrel), from $312.00

Mossberg Model 500 Camo Pump

Same as the Model 500 Sporting Pump except 12-gauge only and entire gun is covered with special camouflage finish. Receiver drilled and tapped for scope mounting. Comes with quick detachable swivel studs, swivels, camouflage sling, Mossberg Cablelock.
Price: From about $296.00
Price: Camo Combo (as above with extra Slugster barrel), from about . .$379.00

Mossberg Turkey Model 500 Pump

Same as the Model 500 Sporting Pump except has overall OFM camo finish, Ghost-Ring sights, Accu-Choke barrel with Imp. Cyl., Mod., Full, Extra-Full lead shot choke tubes, 24″ barrel, swivel studs, camo sling. Introduced 1992.
Price: $384.00

Mossberg Model 500 Muzzleloader Combo

Same as the Model 500 Sporting Pump except comes with 24″ rifled bore, rifle-sighted Slugster barrel and 24″ fully rifled 50-caliber muzzleloading barrel and ramrod. Uses #209 standard primer. Introduced 1992.
Price: $385.00

MOSSBERG MODEL 500 TROPHY SLUGSTER

Gauge: 12, 3″ chamber.
Barrel: 24″, rifled bore. Integral scope mount.
Weight: 7¼ lbs. **Length:** 44″ overall.
Stock: 14″ pull, 1⅜″ drop at heel. Walnut; Dual Comb design for proper eye positioning with or without scoped barrels. Recoil pad and swivel studs.
Features: Ambidextrous thumb safety, twin extractors, dual slide bars. Comes with scope mount. Mossberg Cablelock included. Introduced 1988.
Price: Rifled bore, with scope mount $354.00
Price: Cyl. bore, rifle sights $288.00
Price: Rifled bore, rifle sights $326.00
Price: With Marinecoat finish $415.00

Mossberg Model 500 Bantam Pump

Same as the Model 500 Sporting Pump except 20-gauge only, 22″ vent. rib Accu-Choke barrel with Mod. choke tube; has 1″ shorter stock, reduced length from pistol grip to trigger, reduced forend reach. Introduced 1992.
Price: $281.00

Mossberg Model 500 Viking

Similar to the Model 500 Sporting except in 12-gauge with 24″ rifled bore, rifle sights or 28″ vent. rib with Mod. Accu-Choke tube, or 20-gauge 26″ vent. rib with Mod. Accu-Choke tube; moss-green synthetic stock and forend, matte metal finish. Made in U.S. by Mossberg. Introduced 1996.
Price: $266.00
Price: With rifled barrel $312.00

Mossberg American Field Model 835 Pump Shotgun

Same as the Model 835 Crown Grade except has walnut-stained hardwood stock and comes only with Modified choke tube, 28″ barrel. Introduced 1992.
Price: $313.00

Mossberg Model 835 Viking

Similar to the Model 835 Crown Grade except has moss-green synthetic stock and forend, matte metal finish, 28″ vent. rib Accu-Mag. barrel with Mod. tube. Made in U.S. by Mossberg. Introduced 1996.
Price: $301.00

Mossberg Model 835 Crown Grade

MOSSBERG MODEL 835 CROWN GRADE ULTI-MAG PUMP

Gauge: 12, 3½″ chamber.
Barrel: 24″ rifled bore, 24″, 28″, Accu-Mag with four choke tubes for steel or lead shot.
Weight: 7¾ lbs. **Length:** 48½″ overall.
Stock: 14″x1½″x2½″. Dual Comb. Cut-checkered walnut or camo synthetic; both have recoil pad.
Sights: White bead front, brass mid-bead.
Features: Shoots 2¾″, 3″ or 3½″ shells. Backbored barrel to reduce recoil, improve patterns. Ambidextrous thumb safety, twin extractors, dual slide bars. Mossberg Cablelock included. Introduced 1988.
Price: 28″ vent. rib, Dual-Comb stock $412.00
Price: As above, standard stock $404.00
Price: 24″ Trophy Slugster, rifled bore, scope base, Dual-Comb stock . .$369.00
Price: Combo, 24″ rifled bore, rifle sights, 28″ vent. rib, Accu-Mag choke tubes, Dual-Comb stock $384.00
Price: Combo, 24″ Trophy Slugster rifled bore, 28″ vent. rib, Accu-Mag Mod. tube, Dual-Comb stock $407.00
Price: Realtree or Mossy Oak Camo Turkey, 24″ vent. rib, Accu-Mag Extra-Full tube, synthetic stock $493.00
Price: Realtree Camo, 28″ vent. rib, Accu-Mag tubes, synthetic stock . . .$493.00
Price: Realtree Camo Combo, 24″ rifled bore, rifle sights, 24″ vent. rib Accu-Mag choke tubes, synthetic stock, hard case $601.00
Price: OFM Camo, 28″ vent. rib, Accu-Mag tubes, synthetic stock $441.00
Price: OFM Camo Combo, 24″ rifled bore, rifle sights, 28″ vent. rib, Accu-Mag tubes, synthetic stock $515.00

CAUTION: PRICES SHOWN ARE SUPPLIED BY THE MANUFACTURER OR IMPORTER. CHECK YOUR LOCAL GUNSHOP.

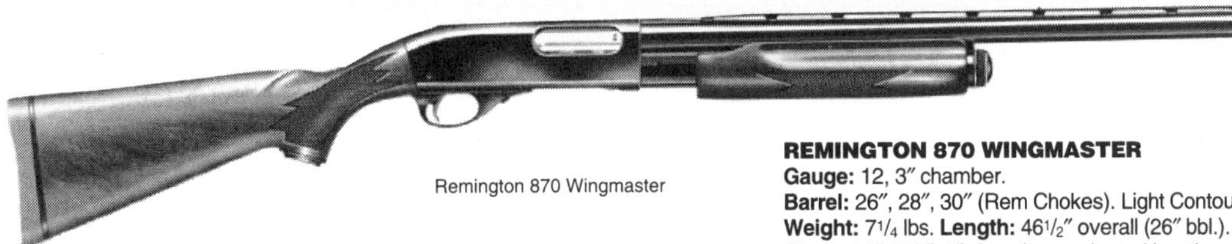
Remington 870 Wingmaster

REMINGTON 870 WINGMASTER
Gauge: 12, 3″ chamber.
Barrel: 26″, 28″, 30″ (Rem Chokes). Light Contour barrel.
Weight: 7¼ lbs. **Length:** 46½″ overall (26″ bbl.).
Stock: 14″x2½″x1″. American walnut with satin or high-gloss finish, cut-checkered pistol grip and forend. Rubber buttpad.
Sights: Ivory bead front, metal mid-bead.
Features: Double action bars; cross-bolt safety; blue finish. Available in right- or left-hand style. Introduced 1986.
Price: $505.00
Price: LW-20 20-ga., vent. rib, 26″, 28″ (Rem Choke) $492.00
Price: Fully rifled Cantilever, 20″ $585.00

Remington 870 Marine Magnum
Similar to the 870 Wingmaster except all metal is plated with electroless nickel and has black synthetic stock and forend. Has 18″ plain barrel (Cyl.), bead front sight, 7-shot magazine. Introduced 1992.
Price: $500.00

Remington 870 TC Trap Gun
Similar to the 870 Wingmaster except has tournament-grade, satin-finished American walnut stock with straight or Monte Carlo comb, over-bored 30″ vent. rib barrel with 2¾″ chamber, over-bore-matched Rem Choke tubes. Made in U.S. by Remington. Reintroduced 1996.
Price: $632.00
Price: With Monte Carlo stock $647.00

Remington 870 SPS Cantilever Shotgun
Similar to the 870 SPS-Deer except has rifled barrel; synthetic stock with Monte Carlo comb; cantilever scope mount deer barrel. Comes with sling and swivels. Introduced 1994.
Price: With fully rifled barrel $483.00

Remington 870 SPS-Deer Shotgun
Has fully-rifled 20″ barrel with rifle sights, black non-reflective, synthetic stock and forend, black carrying sling. Introduced 1993.
Price: $423.00

Remington 870 SPS-T Camo Pump Shotgun
Similar to the 870 Special Purpose Magnum except with synthetic stock, 21″ vent. rib barrel with Super-Full Turkey (.665″ diameter with knurled extension) and Imp. Cyl. Rem Choke tubes. Completely covered with Mossy Oak Green Leaf camouflage. Bolt body, trigger guard and recoil pad are non-reflective black. Introduced 1993.
Price: $497.00

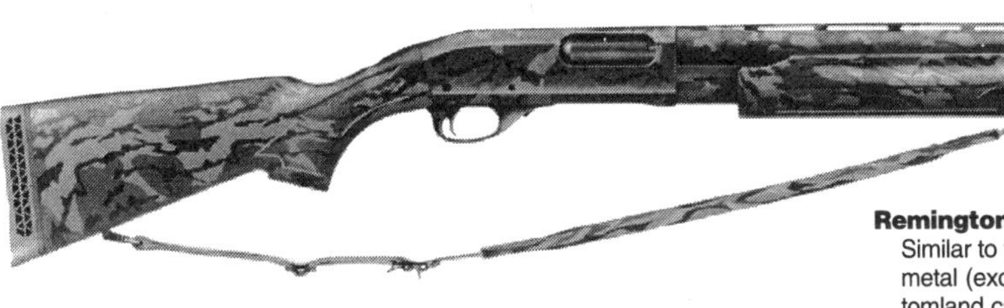
Remington 870 SPS Camo

Remington 870 SPS-T Special Purpose Magnum
Similar to the Model 870 except chambered only for 12-ga., 3″ shells, 26″ or 28″ Rem Choke barrel. All exposed metal surfaces are finished in dull, non-reflective black. Black synthetic stock and forend. Comes with padded Cordura 2″ wide sling, quick-detachable swivels. Chrome-lined bores. Dark recoil pad. Introduced 1985.
Price: $412.00

Remington 870 High Grades
Same as 870 except better walnut, hand checkering. Engraved receiver and barrel. Vent. rib. Stock dimensions to order.
Price: 870D, about $2,610.00
Price: 870F, about $5,377.00
Price: 870F with gold inlay, about $8,062.00

Remington 870 Express Rifle-Sighted Deer Gun
Same as the Model 870 Express except comes with 20″ barrel with fixed Imp. Cyl. choke, open iron sights, Monte Carlo stock. Introduced 1991.
Price: $287.00
Price: With fully rifled barrel $325.00

Remington Model 870 Express Youth Gun
Same as the Model 870 Express except comes with 12½″ length of pull, 21″ barrel with Mod. Rem Choke tube. Hardwood stock with low-luster finish. Introduced 1991.
Price: 20-ga. Express Youth (1″ shorter stock) $292.00
Price: 20-ga. Express Youth Deer (rifle sights, fully rifled barrel) $325.00

Remington 870 Special Purpose Synthetic Camo
Similar to the 870 Special Purpose Magnum except has synthetic stock and all metal (except bolt and trigger guard) and stock covered with Mossy Oak Bottomland camo finish, In 12-gauge only, 26″ vent. rib, Rem Choke. Comes with camo sling, swivels. Introduced 1992.
Price: $483.00

Remington 870 Express
Similar to the 870 Wingmaster except has a walnut-toned hardwood stock with solid, black recoil pad and pressed checkering on grip and forend. Outside metal surfaces have a black oxide finish. Comes with 26″ or 28″ vent. rib barrel with a Mod. Rem Choke tube. Introduced 1987.
Price: 12 or 20 .... $292.00
Price: Express Combo (with extra 20″ Deer barrel), 12 or 20 .... $395.00
Price: Express 20-ga., 28″ with Mod. Rem Choke tubes $292.00

Remington 870 Express Turkey
Same as the Model 870 Express except comes with 3″ chamber, 21″ vent. rib turkey barrel and Extra-Full Rem Choke Turkey tube; 12-ga. only. Introduced 1991.
Price: $305.00

Remington 870 Express Synthetic
Similar to the 870 Express with 26″, 28″ barrel except has synthetic stock and forend. Introduced 1994.
Price: $299.00

Remington 870 Express Small Gauge
Similar to the 870 Express except is scaled down for 28-gauge and 410-bore. Has 25″ vent. rib barrel with fixed Mod. choke; solid black rubber buttpad. Reintroduced 1996.
Price: $307.00

Remington 870 Express HD

Remington 870 Express HD
Similar to the 870 Express except in 12-gauge only, 18″ (Cyl.) barrel with bead front sight, synthetic stock and forend with non-reflective black finish and positive checkering. Introduced 1995.
Price: $292.00

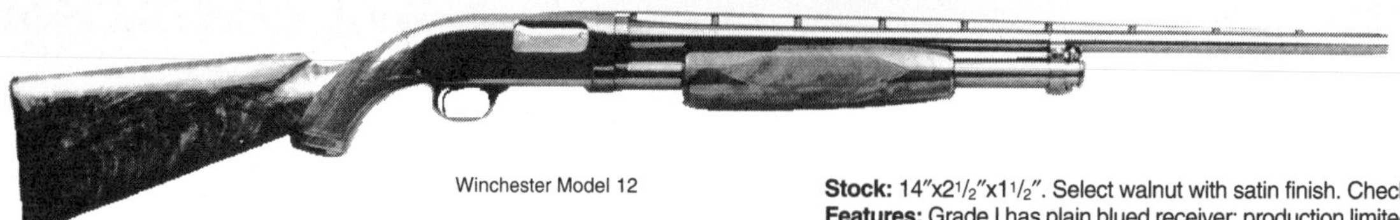

Winchester Model 12

WINCHESTER MODEL 12 PUMP SHOTGUN

Gauge: 20, 2$^3/_4$″ chamber, 5-shot magazine.
Barrel: 26″ (Imp. Cyl.). Vent. rib.
Weight: 7 lbs. **Length:** 45″ overall.
Stock: 14″x2$^1/_2$″x1$^1/_2$″. Select walnut with satin finish. Checkered grip and forend.
Features: Grade I has plain blued receiver; production limited to 4000 guns. Grade IV receiver has engraved game scenes and gold highlights identical to traditional Grade IV, and is limited to 1000 guns. Introduced 1993. From U.S. Repeating Arms Co., Inc.
Price: Grade I **$879.00**
Price: Grade IV **$1,431.00**

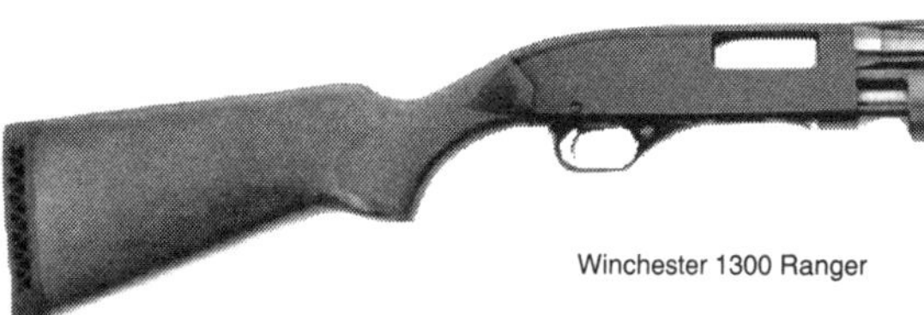

Winchester 1300 Ranger

Winchester Model 1300 Ranger Pump Gun Combo & Deer Gun

Similar to the standard Ranger except comes with two barrels: 22″ (Cyl.) deer barrel with rifle-type sights and an interchangeable 28″ vent. rib Winchoke barrel with Full, Mod. and Imp. Cyl. choke tubes. Drilled and tapped; comes with rings and bases. Available in 12- and 20-gauge 3″ only, with recoil pad. Introduced 1983.
Price: Deer Combo with two barrels **$379.00**
Price: 12-ga., 22″ rifled barrel **$343.00**
Price: 12-ga., 22″ (Imp. Cyl., rifled sabot tubes) **$404.00**
Price: Combo 12-ga. with 18″ (Cyl.) and 28″ (Mod. tube) **$393.00**
Price: Rifled Deer Combo (22″ rifled and 28″ vent. rib barrels,12 or 20-ga.) **$404.00**

Winchester Model 1300 Black Shadow Field Gun

Similar to the Model 1300 Walnut except has black composite stock and forend, matte black finish. Have vent. rib 26″ or 28″ barrel, 3″ chamber, comes with Mod. Winchoke tube. Introduced 1995. From U.S. Repeating Arms Co., Inc.
Price: **$296.00**

WINCHESTER MODEL 1300 RANGER PUMP GUN

Gauge: 12, 20, 3″ chamber, 5-shot magazine.
Barrel: 26″, 28″ vent. rib with Full, Mod., Imp. Cyl. Winchoke tubes.
Weight: 7 to 7$^1/_4$ lbs. **Length:** 48$^5/_8$″ to 50$^5/_8$″ overall.
Stock: Walnut-finished hardwood with ribbed forend.
Sights: Metal bead front.
Features: Cross-bolt safety, black rubber recoil pad, twin action slide bars, front-locking rotating bolt. From U.S. Repeating Arms Co., Inc.
Price: Vent. rib barrel, Winchoke **$309.00**

WINCHESTER MODEL 1300 WALNUT PUMP

Gauge: 12, 20, 3″ chamber, 5-shot capacity.
Barrel: 26″, 28″, vent. rib, with Full, Mod., Imp. Cyl. Winchoke tubes.
Weight: 6$^3/_8$ lbs. **Length:** 42$^5/_8$″ overall.
Stock: American walnut, with deep cut checkering on pistol grip, traditional ribbed forend; high luster finish.
Sights: Metal bead front.
Features: Twin action slide bars; front-locking rotary bolt; roll-engraved receiver; blued, highly polished metal; cross-bolt safety with red indicator. Introduced 1984. From U.S. Repeating Arms Co., Inc.
Price: **$340.00**
Price: Model 1300 Ladies/Youth, 20-ga., 22″ vent. rib **$309.00**

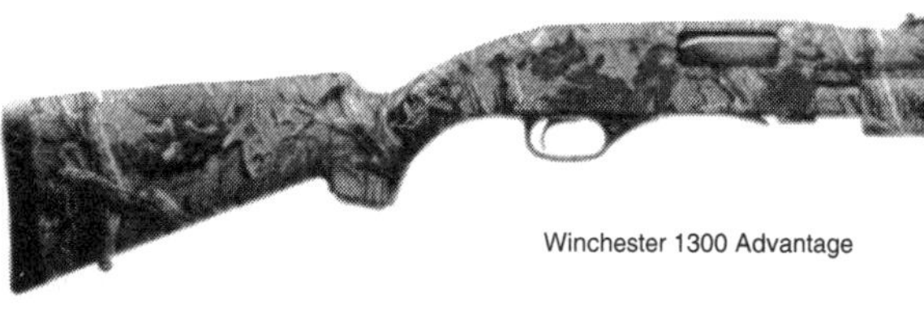

Winchester 1300 Advantage

Winchester Model 1300 Advantage Camo Deer Gun

Similar to the Model 1300 Black Shadow Deer Gun except has full coverage Advantage camouflage. Has 22″ rifled or smoothbore barrel, padded camouflage sling, swivels and swivel posts, rifle sights. Receiver drilled and tapped for scope mounting. Introduced 1995. From U.S. Repeating Arms Co., Inc.
Price: Rifled bore **$432.00**
Price: Smoothbore **$410.00**

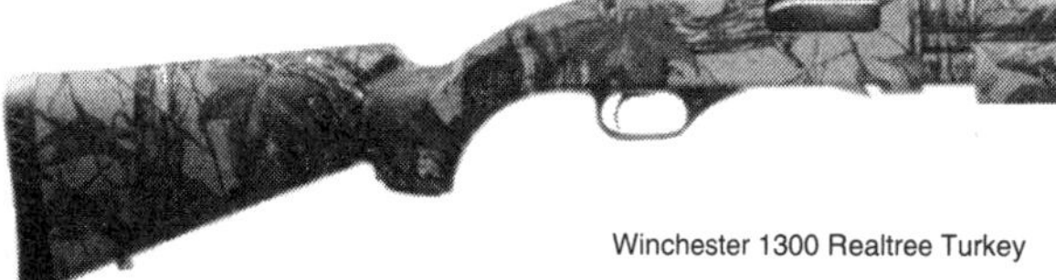

Winchester 1300 Realtree Turkey

Winchester Model 1300 Realtree® Turkey Gun

Similar to the standard Model 1300 except has synthetic Realtree® camo stock and forend, matte finished barrel and receiver, 22″ barrel with Extra Full, Full and Mod. Winchoke tubes. Drilled and tapped for scope mounting. Comes with padded, adjustable sling. In 12-gauge only, 3″ chamber; weighs about 7 lbs. Introduced 1994. From U.S. Repeating Arms Co., Inc.
Price: **$370.00**
Price: With full coverage All-Purpose Realtree® camo **$432.00**

Winchester Model 1300 Black Shadow Turkey Gun

Similar to the Model 1300 Realtree® Turkey except synthetic stock and forend are matte black, and all metal surfaces finished matte black. Drilled and tapped for scope mounting. In 12-gauge only, 3″ chamber, 22″ vent. rib barrel; comes with one Full Winchoke tube. Introduced 1994. From U.S. Repeating Arms Co., Inc.
Price: **$296.00**

Winchester Model 1300 Black Shadow Deer Gun

Similar to the Model 1300 Black Shadow Turkey Gun except has ramp-type front sight, fully adjustable rear, drilled and tapped for scope mounting. Black composite stock and forend, matte black metal. Smoothbore 22″ barrel with one Imp. Cyl. Winchoke tube; 12-gauge only, 3″ chamber. Weighs 7$^1/_4$ lbs. Introduced 1994. From U.S. Repeating Arms Co., Inc.
Price: **$296.00**

CAUTION: PRICES SHOWN ARE SUPPLIED BY THE MANUFACTURER OR IMPORTER. CHECK YOUR LOCAL GUNSHOP.

SHOTGUNS—OVER/UNDERS

Includes a variety of game guns and guns for competitive shooting.

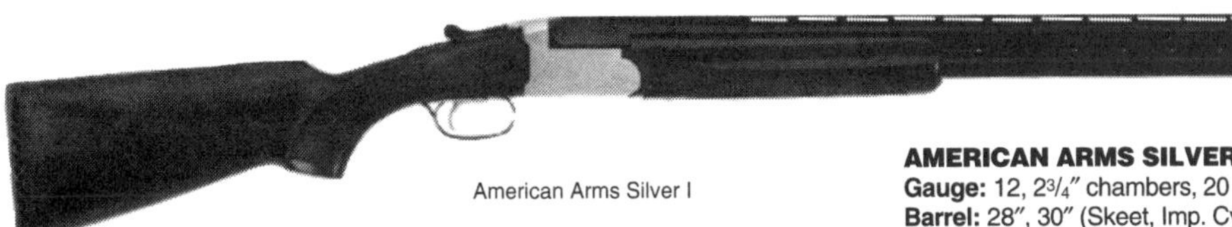

American Arms Silver I

AMERICAN ARMS SILVER I O/U

Gauge: 12, 20, 28, 410, 3″ chamber (28 has 2¾″).
Barrel: 26″ (Imp. Cyl. & Mod., all gauges), 28″ (Mod. & Full, 12, 20).
Weight: About 6¾ lbs.
Stock: 14⅛″x1⅜″x2⅜″. Checkered walnut.
Sights: Metal bead front.
Features: Boxlock action with scroll engraving, silver finish. Single selective trigger, extractors. Chrome-lined barrels. Manual safety. Rubber recoil pad. Introduced 1987. Imported from Italy by American Arms, Inc.
Price: 12- or 20-gauge $599.00
Price: 28 or 410 . . . . $625.00

American Arms Silver Upland Lite

Similar to the Silver I except weighs 6 lbs., 4 oz. (12-gauge), 5 lbs., 12 oz. (20-gauge). Single selective trigger, automatic selective ejectors. Franchoke tubes, vent. rib, engraved frame with antique silver finish. Introduced 1994. Imported by American Arms, Inc.
Price: 12- , 20-ga., 3″ chambers, 26″ $899.00

AMERICAN ARMS SILVER SPORTING O/U

Gauge: 12, 2¾″ chambers, 20 3″ chambers.
Barrel: 28″, 30″ (Skeet, Imp. Cyl., Mod., Full choke tubes).
Weight: 7⅜ lbs. **Length:** 45½″ overall.
Stock: 14⅜″x1½″x2⅜″. Figured walnut, cut checkering; Sporting Clays quick-mount buttpad.
Sights: Target bead front.
Features: Boxlock action with single selective mechanical trigger, automatic selective ejectors; special broadway channeled rib; vented barrel rib; chrome bores. Chrome-nickel finish on frame, with engraving. Introduced 1990. Imported from Italy by American Arms, Inc.
Price: $899.00

American Arms Silver II Shotgun

Similar to the Silver I except 26″ barrel (Imp. Cyl., Mod., Full choke tubes, 12- and 20-ga.), 28″ (Imp. Cyl., Mod., Full choke tubes, 12-ga. only), 26″ (Imp. Cyl. & Mod. fixed chokes, 28 and 410), automatic selective ejectors. Weight is about 6 lbs., 15 oz. (12-ga., 26″).
Price: $699.00
Price: 28, 410 . . . . $725.00

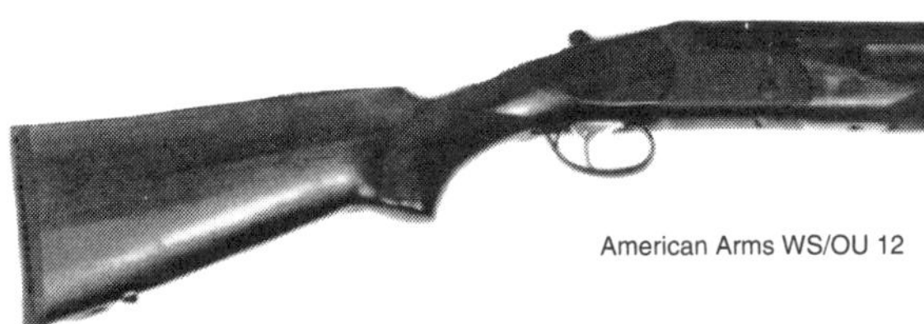

American Arms WS/OU 12

American Arms WT/OU 10 Shotgun

Similar to the WS/OU 12 except chambered for 10-gauge 3½″ shell, 26″ (Full & Full, choke tubes) barrel. Single selective trigger, extractors. Non-reflective finish on wood and metal. Imported by American Arms, Inc.
Price: $950.00

AMERICAN ARMS WS/OU 12, TS/OU 12 SHOTGUNS

Gauge: 12, 3½″ chambers.
Barrel: WS/OU—28″ (Imp. Cyl., Mod., Full choke tubes); TS/OU—24″ (Imp. Cyl., Mod., Full choke tubes).
Weight: 6 lbs., 15 oz. **Length:** 46″ overall.
Stock: 14⅛″x1⅛″x2⅜″. European walnut with cut checkering, black vented recoil pad, matte finish.
Features: Boxlock action with single selective trigger, automatic selective ejectors; chrome bores. Matte metal finish. Imported by American Arms, Inc.
Price: $725.00

ARMSPORT 2700 SERIES O/U

Gauge: 12, 20.
Barrel: 26″ (Imp. Cyl. & Mod.); 28″ (Mod. & Full); vent. rib.
Weight: 8 lbs.
Stock: European walnut, hand-checkered pistol grip and forend.
Features: Single selective trigger, automatic ejectors, engraved receiver. Imported by Armsport. Contact Armsport for complete list of models.
Price: M2733/2735 (Boss-type action, 12, 20, extractors) $790.00
Price: M2741 (as above with ejectors) $825.00
Price: M2730/2731 (as above with single trigger, screw-in chokes) $975.00
Price: M2742 Sporting Clays (12-ga., 28″, choke tubes) $930.00
Price: M2744 Sporting Clays (20-ga., 26″, choke tubes) $930.00
Price: M2750 Sporting Clays (12-ga., 28″, choke tubes, sideplates) . . . $1,050.00
Price: M2751 Sporting Clays (20-ga., 26″, choke tubes, sideplates) . . . $1,050.00

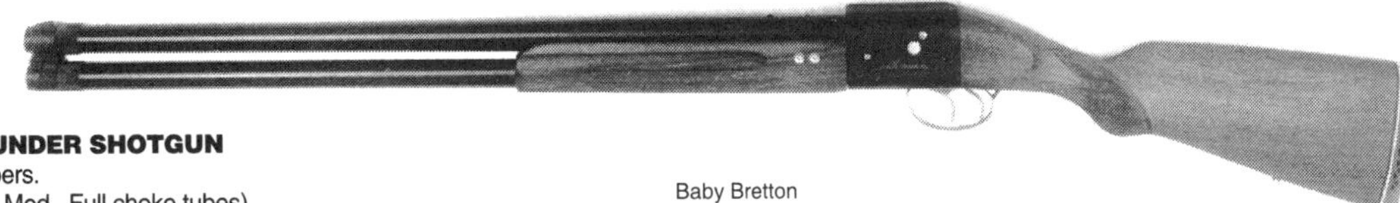

Baby Bretton

BABY BRETTON OVER/UNDER SHOTGUN

Gauge: 12 or 20, 2¾″ chambers.
Barrel: 27½″ (Cyl., Imp. Cyl., Mod., Full choke tubes).
Weight: About 5 lbs.
Stock: Walnut, checkered pistol grip and forend, oil finish.
Features: Receiver slides open on two guide rods, is locked by a large thumb lever on the right side. Extractors only. Light alloy barrels. Imported from France by Mandall Shooting Supplies.
Price: Sprint Standard $895.00
Price: Sprint Deluxe $975.00
Price: Model Fairplay $1,025.00

BAIKAL IJ-27 OVER/UNDER SHOTGUN

Gauge: 12, 2¾″ chambers.
Barrel: 28″ (Mod. & Full).
Weight: 7 lbs.
Stock: Checkered walnut.
Features: Double triggers; extractors; blued receiver with engraving. Reintroduced 1994. Imported from Russia by K.B.I., Inc.
Price: $299.00
Price: IJ-27 EIC (single trigger, automatic ejectors) $339.00

BAIKAL IJ-27M OVER-UNDER SHOTGUN

Gauge: 12, 2¾″ chambers.
Barrel: 28.5″ (Mod. & Full).
Weight: 7.5 lbs. **Length:** 44.5″ overall.
Stock: European hardwood.
Features: Engraved boxlock action with double triggers, extractors; chrome-lined barrels; sling swivels. Imported from Russia by Century International Arms.
Price: About $340.00
Price: IJ-27EM (selective automatic ejectors), about $365.00

BAIKAL TOZ-34P OVER/UNDER SHOTGUN
Gauge: 12, 2¾″ chambers.
Barrel: 28″ (Full & Imp. Cyl.).
Weight: 7.5 lbs. **Length:** 44″ overall.
Stock: European walnut.
Features: Engraved, blued receiver; cocking indicator; double triggers. Ventilated rib, ventilated rubber buttpad. Imported from Russia by Century International Arms.
Price: About **$405.00**
Price: With ejectors, about **$475.00**

BERETTA MODEL ULTRALIGHT ONYX O/U
Gauge: 12, 2¾″ chambers.
Barrel: 26″, 28″, Mobilchoke choke tubes.
Weight: About 5 lbs., 13 oz.
Stock: Select American walnut with checkered grip and forend.
Features: Low-profile aluminum alloy receiver with titanium breech face insert. Silvered receiver with game scene engraving. Single selective trigger; automatic safety. Introduced 1992. Imported from Italy by Beretta U.S.A.
Price: **$1,716.00**

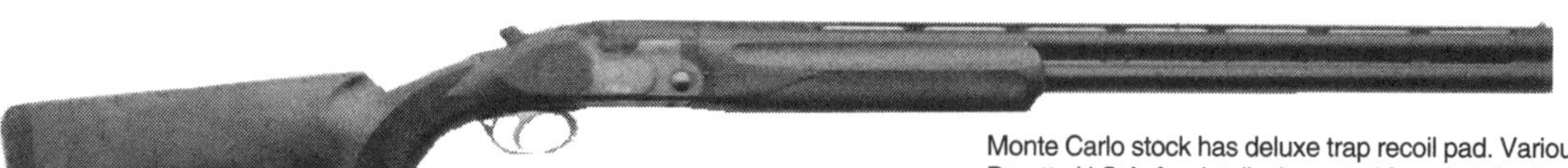

Beretta 682 Gold Skeet

BERETTA SERIES 682 GOLD SKEET, TRAP OVER/UNDERS
Gauge: 12, 2¾″ chambers.
Barrel: Skeet—26″ and 28″; trap—30″ and 32″, Imp. Mod. & Full and Mobilchoke; trap mono shotguns—32″ and 34″ Mobilchoke; trap top single guns—32″ and 34″ Full and Mobilchoke; trap combo sets—from 30″ O/U, to 32″ O/U, 34″ top single.
Stock: Close-grained walnut, hand checkered.
Sights: White Bradley bead front sight and center bead.
Features: Receiver has Greystone gunmetal gray finish with gold accents. Trap Monte Carlo stock has deluxe trap recoil pad. Various grades available; contact Beretta U.S.A. for details. Imported from Italy by Beretta U.S.A.
Price: 682 Gold Skeet **$2,731.00**
Price: 682 Gold Trap **$2,789.00**
Price: 682 Gold Trap Top Combo . . . . . . **$3,689.00** to **$3,832.00**
Price: 682 Gold Super Trap Top Combo **$4,190.00**
Price: 686 Silver Perdiz Skeet (28″) **$1,499.00**
Price: 687 EELL Diamond Pigeon Trap **$4,991.00**
Price: 687 EELL Diamond Pigeon Skeet (4-bbl. set) **$8,899.00**
Price: 687 EELL Diamond Pigeon Trap Top Mono . . . . . . **$5,241.00** to **$5,291.00**
Price: 682 Super Skeet (adjustable comb and butt pads, bbl. porting) . **$3,006.00**
Price: 682 Super Trap (adjustable comb and butt pad, barrel porting) . . . . . . **$2,907.00** to **$3,983.00**
Price: ASE Gold Skeet **$8,737.00**
Price: ASE Gold Trap **$8,815.00**
Price: ASE Gold Trap Top Combo **$10,287.00**

BERETTA MODEL 686 ESSENTIAL O/U
Gauge: 12, 3″ chambers.
Barrel: 26″, 28″, Mobilchoke tubes (Imp. Cyl., Mod., Full).
Weight: 6.7 lbs. **Length:** 45.7″ overall (28″ barrels).
Stock: 14.5″x2.2″x1.4″. American walnut; radiused black buttplate.
Features: Matte finish on receiver and barrels; hard-chrome bores; low-profile receiver with dual conical locking lugs; single selective trigger, ejectors. Introduced 1994. Imported from Italy by Beretta U.S.A.
Price: **$1,186.00**

BERETTA ONYX SPORTING O/U SHOTGUN
Gauge: 12, 3″ chambers.
Barrel: 28″, 30″ (Mobilchoke tubes).
Weight: 7.7 lbs.
Stock: Checkered American walnut.
Features: Intended for the beginning sporting clays shooter. Has wide, vented 12.5mm target rib, radiused recoil pad. Matte black finish on receiver and barrels. Introduced 1993. Imported from Italy by Beretta U.S.A.
Price: **$1,499.00**
Price: 686 Silver Pigeon Sporting (as above except coin silver receiver with scroll engraving; 12- or 20-ga.) **$1,573.00**

Beretta 682 Gold Sporting

BERETTA SPORTING CLAYS SHOTGUNS
Gauge: 12 and 20, 2¾″ chambers.
Barrel: 28″, 30″, 32″ Mobilchoke.
Stock: Close-grained walnut.
Features: Equipped with Beretta Mobilchoke flush-mounted screw-in choke tube system. Dual-purpose O/U for hunting and Sporting Clays.12- or 20-gauge, 28″, 30″ Mobilchoke tubes (four, Skeet, Imp. Cyl., Mod., Full). Wide 12.5mm top rib with 2.5mm center groove; 686 Onyx models have matte black receiver, 686 Silver Pigeon has silver receiver with scroll engraving; 687 Silver Pigeon Sporting has silver receiver, highly figured walnut; 687 EL Pigeon Sporting has game scene engraving with gold inlaid animals on full sideplate. Introduced 1994. Imported from Italy by Beretta U.S.A.
Price: 682 Gold Sporting, 28″, 30″, 32″ (with case) **$2,789.00**
Price: 682 Gold Sporting, 28″, 30″, ported, adj. l.o.p. **$2,999.00**
Price: 682 Onyx Sporting **$1,499.00**
Price: 682 Continental Course Sporting, 2¾″ chambers, 28″ **$2,431.00**
Price: 686 Silver Pigeon Sporting **$1,573.00**
Price: 687L Silver Pigeon Sporting **$2,354.00**
Price: 687 Silver Pigeon Sporting (20 gauge) **$2,354.00**
Price: 687 Diamond Pigeon EELL Sporter (hand engraved sideplates, deluxe wood) **$5,098.00**
Price: 687 Silver Pigeon Sporting Combo, 28″ and 30″ **$3,518.00**
Price: ASE Gold Sporting Clay **$8,815.00**

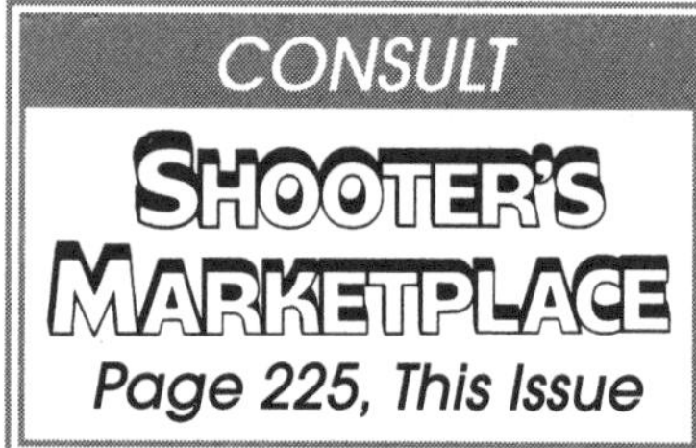
CONSULT
SHOOTER'S
MARKETPLACE
Page 225, This Issue

BERETTA MODEL SO5, SO6, SO9 SHOTGUNS
Gauge: 12, 2¾″ chambers.
Barrel: To customer specs.
Stock: To customer specs.
Features: SO5—Trap, Skeet and Sporting Clays models SO5; SO6—SO6 and SO6 EELL are field models. SO6 has a case-hardened or silver receiver with contour hand engraving. SO6 EELL has hand-engraved receiver in a fine floral or "fine English" pattern or game scene, with bas-relief chisel work and gold inlays. SO6 and SO6 EELL are available with sidelocks removable by hand. Imported from Italy by Beretta U.S.A.
Price: SO5 Trap, Skeet, Sporting **$13,000.00**
Price: SO6 Trap, Skeet, Sporting **$17,500.00**
Price: SO6 EELL Field, custom specs **$28,000.00**
Price: SO9 (12, 20, 28, 410, 26″, 28″, 30″, any choke) **$31,000.00**

Beretta 687EL Gold Pigeon Sporting O/U
Similar to the 687 Silver Pigeon Sporting except has sideplates with gold inlay game scene, vent. side and top ribs, bright orange front sight. Stock and forend are of high grade walnut with fine-line checkering. Available in 12-gauge only with 28″ or 30″ barrels and Mobilchoke tubes. Weight is 6 lbs., 13 oz. Introduced 1993. Imported from Italy by Beretta U.S.A.
Price: **$3,320.00**

CAUTION: PRICES SHOWN ARE SUPPLIED BY THE MANUFACTURER OR IMPORTER. CHECK YOUR LOCAL GUNSHOP.

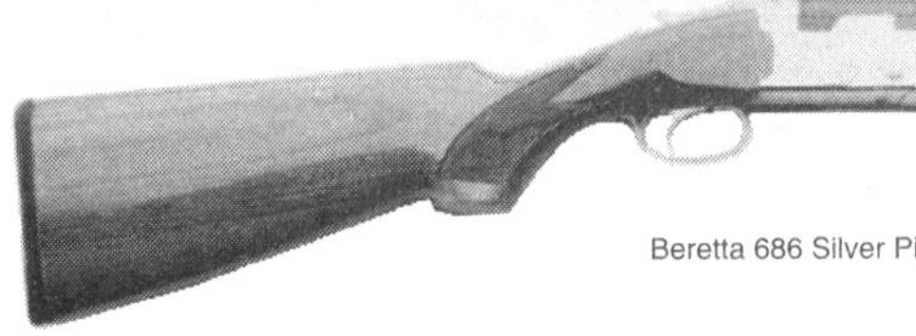

Beretta 686 Silver Pigeon Field

BERETTA OVER/UNDER FIELD SHOTGUNS

Gauge: 12, 20, 28, and 410 bore, 2³/₄", 3" and 3¹/₂" chambers.
Barrel: 26" and 28" (Mobilchoke tubes).
Stock: Close-grained walnut.
Features: Highly-figured, American walnut stocks and forends, and a unique, weather-resistant finish on barrels. The 686 Onyx bears a gold P. Beretta signature on each side of the receiver. Silver designates standard 686, 687 models with silver receivers; 686 Silver Pigeon has enhanced engraving pattern, schnabel forend; Gold indicates higher grade 686EL, 687EL models with full sideplates; Diamond is for 687EELL models with highest grade wood, engraving. Case provided with Gold and Diamond grades. Silver Gold, Diamond grades introduced 1994. Imported from Italy by Beretta U.S.A.

Price: 686 Onyx **$1,473.00**
Price: 686 Silver Pigeon two-bbl. set **$2,259.00**
Price: 686 Silver Pigeon **$1,544.00**
Price: 686EL Gold Perdiz (engraved sideplates, hard case) **$1,999.00**
Price: 687L Silver Pigeon **$2,031.00**
Price: 687EL Gold Pigeon (gold inlays, sideplates) **$3,446.00**
Price: 687EL Gold Pigeon, 410, 26", 28-ga., 28" **$3,599.00**
Price: 687EELL Diamond Pigeon (engraved sideplates) **$4,999.00**
Price: 687EELL Diamond Pigeon, 28-ga., 26" **$4,999.00**
Price: 687EELL Diamond Pigeon Combo, 20- and 28-ga., 26" **$5,577.00**

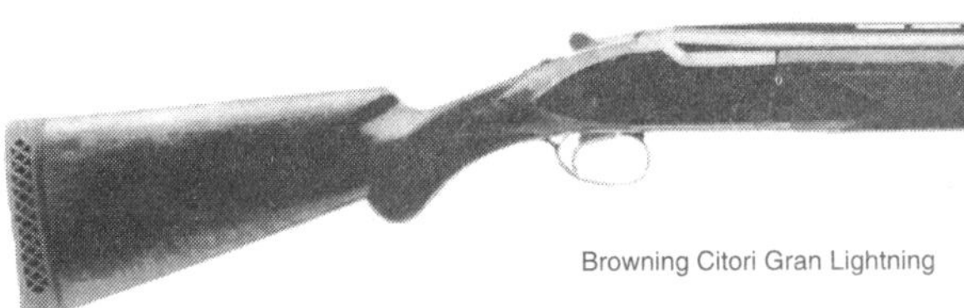

Browning Citori Gran Lightning

BROWNING CITORI O/U SHOTGUN

Gauge: 12, 20, 28 and 410.
Barrel: 26", 28" in 28 and 410. Offered with Invector choke tubes. All 12- and 20-gauge models have back-bored barrels and Invector Plus choke system.
Weight: 6 lbs., 8 oz. (26" 410) to 7 lbs., 13 oz. (30" 12-ga.).
Length: 43" overall (26" bbl.).
Stock: Dense walnut, hand checkered, full pistol grip, beavertail forend. Field-type recoil pad on 12-ga. field guns and trap and Skeet models.
Sights: Medium raised beads, German nickel silver.
Features: Barrel selector integral with safety, automatic ejectors, three-piece takedown. Imported from Japan by Browning. Contact Browning for complete list of models and prices.

Price: Grade I, Hunting, Invector, 12 and 20 .... **$1,134.00**
Price: Grade I, Lightning, 28 and 410, Invector **$1,418.00**
Price: Grade III, Lightning, 28 and 410, Invector **$2,242.00**
Price: Grade VI, 28 and 410 Lightning, Invector **$3,145.00**
Price: Grade I, Lightning, Invector Plus, 12, 20 .... **$1,376.00**
Price: Grade I, Hunting, 28", 30" only, 3¹/₂", Invector Plus **$1,418.00**
Price: Grade III, Lightning, Invector, 12, 20 .... **$2,000.00**
Price: Grade VI, Lightning, Invector, 12, 20 .... **$2,919.00**
Price: Gran Lightning, 26", 28", Invector, 12 ,20 .... **$1,869.00**
Price: Gran Lightning, 28, 410 .... **$1,969.00**

Browning Citori Special Trap Models

Similar to standard Citori except 12 gauge only; 30", 32" ported or non-ported (Invector Plus); Monte Carlo cheek piece (14³/₈"x1³/₈"x1³/₈"x2"); fitted with trap-style recoil pad; high post target rib, ventilated side ribs.

Price: Grade I, Invector Plus, ported bbls. **$1,580.00**
Price: Grade III, Invector Plus Ported **$2,179.00**
Price: Golden Clays **$3,239.00**
Price: Adjustable comb stock, add **$210.00**

Browning Superlight Citori Over/Under

Similar to the standard Citori except available in 12, 20 with 24", 26" or 28" Invector barrels, 28 or 410 with 26" barrels choked Imp. Cyl. & Mod. or 28" choked Mod. & Full. Has straight grip stock, Schnabel forend tip. Superlight 12 weighs 6 lbs., 9 oz. (26" barrels); Superlight 20, 5 lbs., 12 oz. (26" barrels). Introduced 1982.

Price: Grade I only, 28 or 410, Invector **$1,439.00**
Price: Grade III, Invector, 12 or 20 .... **$2,000.00**
Price: Grade III, 28 or 410, Invector **$2,242.00**
Price: Grade VI, Invector, 12 or 20 .... **$2,919.00**
Price: Grade VI, 28 or 410, Invector **$3,145.00**
Price: Grade I Invector, 12 or 20 .... **$1,386.00**
Price: Grade I Invector, Upland Special (24" bbls.), 12 or 20 .... **$1,386.00**

Browning Lightning Sporting Clays

Similar to the Citori Lightning with rounded pistol grip and classic forend. Has high post tapered rib or lower hunting-style rib with 30" back-bored Invector Plus barrels, ported or non-ported, 3" chambers. Gloss stock finish, radiused recoil pad. Has "Lightning Sporting Clays Edition" engraved and gold filled on receiver. Introduced 1989.

Price: Low-rib, ported **$1,490.00**
Price: High-rib, ported **$1,565.00**
Price: Golden Clays, low rib, ported **$3,203.00**
Price: Golden Clays, high rib, ported **$3,092.00**
Price: Adjustable comb stock, all models, add **$210.00**

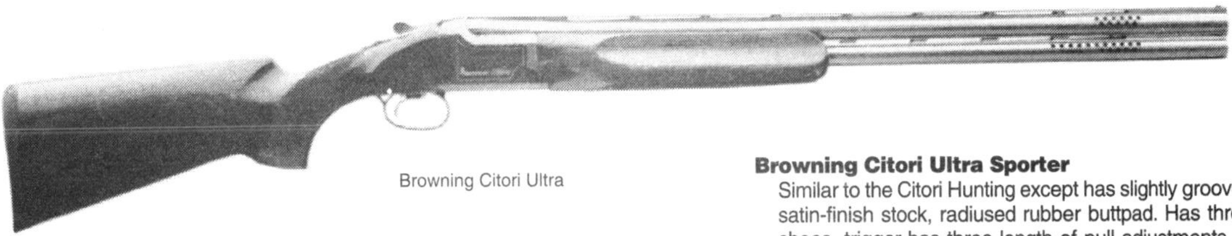

Browning Citori Ultra

Browning Micro Citori Lightning

Similar to the standard Citori 20-ga. Lightning except scaled down for smaller shooter. Comes with 24" Invector Plus back-bored barrels, 13³/₄" length of pull. Weighs about 6 lbs., 3 oz. Introduced 1991.

Price: Grade I **$1,428.00**

Browning Special Sporting Clays

Similar to the Citori Ultra Sporter except has full pistol grip stock with palm swell, gloss finish, 28", 30" or 32" barrels with back-bored Invector Plus chokes (ported or non-ported); high post tapered rib. Also available as 28" and 30" two-barrel set. Introduced 1989.

Price: With ported barrels **$1,565.00**
Price: As above, adjustable comb **$1,775.00**
Price: Golden Clays **$3,203.00**
Price: With adjustable comb stock **$3,413.00**

Browning Citori Ultra Sporter

Similar to the Citori Hunting except has slightly grooved, semi-beavertail forend, satin-finish stock, radiused rubber buttpad. Has three interchangeable trigger shoes, trigger has three length of pull adjustments. Ventilated rib tapers from 13mm to 10mm, 28" or 30" barrels (ported or non-ported) with Invector Plus choke tubes. Ventilated side ribs. Introduced 1989.

Price: With ported barrels, gray or blue receiver **$1,722.00**
Price: Golden Clays **$3,203.00**

Browning Citori O/U Special Skeet

Similar to standard Citori except 26", 28" barrels, ventilated side ribs, Invector choke tubes; stock dimensions of 14³/₈"x1¹/₂"x2", fitted with Skeet-style recoil pad; conventional target rib and high post target rib.

Price: Grade I Invector, 12-, 20-ga., Invector Plus (high post rib) **$1,586.00**
Price: Grade I, 28 and 410 (high post rib) **$1,549.00**
Price: Grade III, 28, 410 (high post rib) **$2,184.00**
Price: Golden Clays **$3,239.00**
Price: Grade III, 12-ga. Invector Plus **$2,179.00**
Price: Adjustable comb stock, add **$210.00**

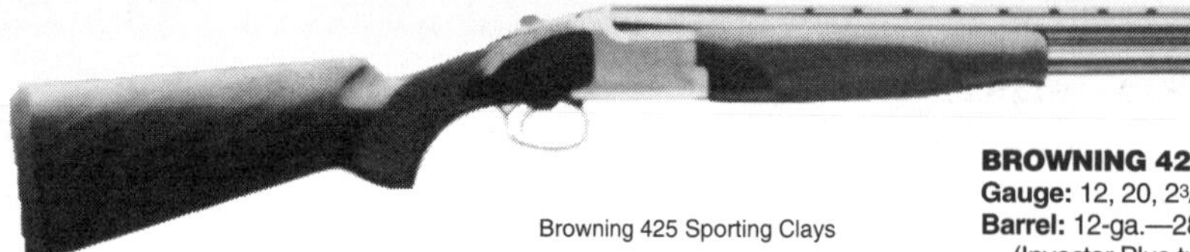
Browning 425 Sporting Clays

BROWNING 425 SPORTING CLAYS

Gauge: 12, 20, 2¾″ chambers.
Barrel: 12-ga.—28″, 30″, 32″ (Invector Plus tubes), back-bored; 20-ga.—28″, 30″ (Invector Plus tubes).
Weight: 7 lbs., 13 oz. (12-ga., 28″).
Stock: 14 13/16″ (±1/8″)x1 7/16″x2 3/16″ (12-ga.). Select walnut with gloss finish, cut checkering, schnabel forend.
Features: Grayed receiver with engraving, blued barrels. Barrels are ported on 12-gauge guns. Has low 10mm wide vent rib. Comes with three interchangeable trigger shoes to adjust length of pull. Introduced in U.S. 1993. Imported by Browning.
Price: Grade I, 12-, 20-ga., Invector Plus **$1,775.00**
Price: Golden Clays, 12-, 20-ga., Invector Plus **$3,305.00**
Price: Adjustable comb stock, add **$210.00**

Browning 425 WSSF Shotgun

Similar to the 425 Sporting Clays except in 12-gauge only, has stock dimensions specifically tailored to women shooters (14¼″x1½″x1½″); top lever and takedown lever are easier to operate. Stock and forend have teal-colored finish with WSSF logo. Introduced 1995. Imported by Browning.
Price: **$1,775.00**

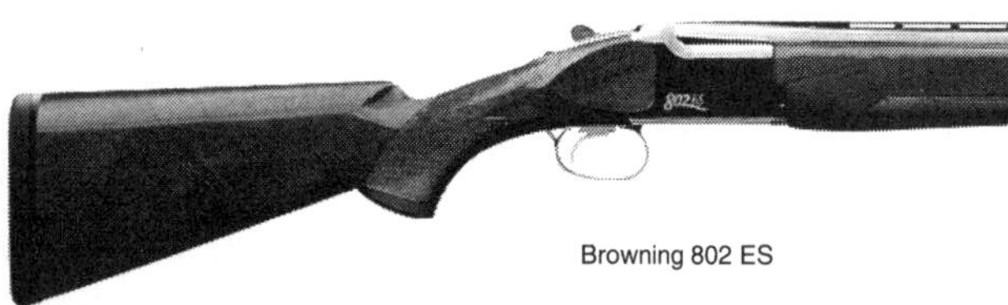
Browning 802 ES

BROWNING LIGHT SPORTING 802 ES O/U

Gauge: 12, 2¾″ chambers.
Barrel: 28″, back-bored Invector Plus. Comes with flush-mounted Imp. Cyl. and Skeet; 2″ extended Imp. Cyl. and Mod.; and 4″ extended Imp. Cyl. and Mod. tubes.
Weight: 7 lbs., 5 oz. **Length:** 45″ overall.
Stock: 14⅜″±1/8″x1 9/16″x1¾. Select walnut with radiused solid recoil pad, schnabel-type forend.
Features: Trigger adjustable for length of pull; narrow 6.2mm ventilated rib; ventilated barrel side rib; blued receiver. Introduced 1996. Imported from Japan from Browning.
Price: **$1,880.00**

CENTURY CENTURION OVER/UNDER SHOTGUN

Gauge: 12, 2¾″ chambers.
Barrel: 28″ (Mod. & Full).
Weight: 7.3 lbs. **Length:** 44.5″ overall.
Stock: European walnut.
Features: Double triggers; extractors. Polished blue finish. Introduced 1993. Imported by Century International Arms.
Price: About **$380.00**

Churchill Windsor Sporting Clays Over/Under

Similar to the Windsor IV except 12-gauge only, with 28″ or 30″ barrels (choke tubes); barrels are ported, back-bored and have lengthened forcing cones; tapered ventilated rib, ventilated side rib; Sporting-style forend with finger grooves; select walnut stock with palm swell grip. Introduced 1995. Imported by Ellett Bros.
Price: **$1,125.00**

CHURCHILL WINDSOR IV OVER/UNDER SHOTGUN

Gauge: 12, 20, 3″ chambers.
Barrel: 12 ga.—26″, 28″; 20 ga.—26″; choke tubes.
Weight: About 7.5 lbs.
Stock: Walnut; rubber recoil pad.
Features: Automatic ejectors, single selective trigger; ventilated top and side ribs; silvered receiver. Introduced 1995. Imported by Ellett Bros.
Price: **$932.00**

Consult our Directory pages for the location of firms mentioned.

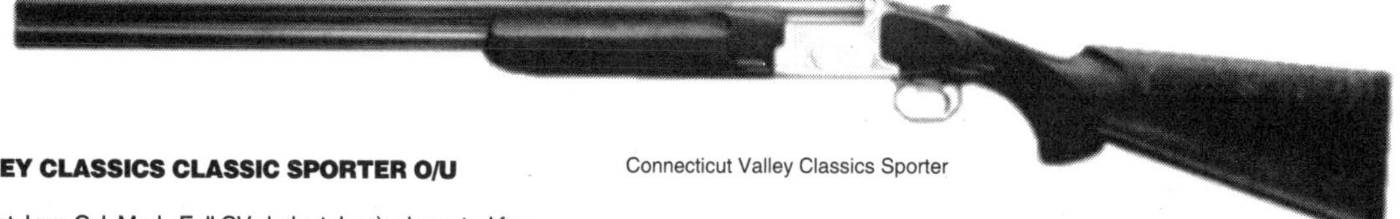
Connecticut Valley Classics Sporter

CONNECTICUT VALLEY CLASSICS CLASSIC SPORTER O/U

Gauge: 12, 3″ chambers.
Barrel: 28″, 30″, 32″ (Skeet, Imp. Cyl. Mod., Full CV choke tubes); elongated forcing cones.
Weight: 7¾ lbs. **Length:** 44⅞″ overall (28″ barrels).
Stock: 14½″x1½″x2⅛″. AA grade semi-fancy American black walnut with 20 lpi hand-checkered grip and forend; hand rubbed oil finish.
Features: Receiver duplicates Classic Doubles M101 specifications. Stainless receiver with fine engraving. Bores and chambers suitable for steel shot. Optionally available are CV Plus (2⅜″ tubes) choke tubes. Introduced 1993. Made in U.S. by Connecticut Valley Classics.
Price: Grade I **$3,195.00**
Price: Grade II, AAA fancy walnut, 22 lpi checkering, enhanced engraving **$3,795.00**
Price: Grade III, AAA select fancy walnut, 22 lpi Fleur de lis checkering, enhanced engraving, bird scenes, gold inlay, gold-plated trigger **$4,195.00**
Price: Women's Classic Sporter, 28″ only, shorter stock, different stock dimensions **$3,195.00**

Connecticut Valley Classics Classic Skeet

Similar to the Classic Sporter except has 29″ barrel with 9mm Skeet rib. AA American black or Claro walnut, 20 lpi checkering. Introduced 1995. Made in U.S. by Century International Arms.
Price: **$3,195.00**

Connecticut Valley Classics Classic Field O/U

Similar to the Classic Sporter except 27½″ barrels with standard choke tubes, slightly different stock shape and dimensions for hunting. Over-bored barrels with lengthened forcing cones. Introduced 1995. Made in U.S. by Century International Arms.
Price: Grade I **$3,195.00**
Price: Grade II (see Sporter prices) **$3,595.00**
Price: Grade III **$4,195.00**

Connecticut Valley Classics Classic Flyer

Similar to the Classic Sporter except has AAA American black or Claro walnut, Premier Grade 22 lpi checkering, choice of standard or schnabel forend, special engraving pattern, gold inlay, gold-plated trigger, 11mm tapered top rib. Introduced 1995. Made in U.S. by Century International Arms.
Price: **$3,995.00**

Connecticut Valley Classics Classic Field Waterfowler

Similar to the Classic Sporter except with 30″ barrel only, blued, non-reflective overall finish. Interchangeable CV choke tube system includes Skeet, Imp. Cyl., Mod. Full tubes. Introduced 1995. Made in U.S. by Connecticut Valley Classics.
Price: **$2,995.00**

CAUTION: PRICES SHOWN ARE SUPPLIED BY THE MANUFACTURER OR IMPORTER. CHECK YOUR LOCAL GUNSHOP.

CHARLES DALY FIELD GRADE O/U
Gauge: 12 or 20, 3″ chambers.
Barrel: 12- and 20- ga.—26″ (Imp. Cyl. & Mod.), 12-ga.—28″ (Mod. & Full).
Weight: 6 lbs., 15 oz. (12-ga.); 6 lbs., 10 oz. (20-ga.). **Length:** 43 1/2″ overall (26″).
Stock: 14 1/8″x1 3/8″x2 3/8″. Walnut with cut-checkered grip and forend. Black, vent. rubber recoil pad. Semi-gloss finish.
Features: Boxlock action with manual safety; extractors; single selective trigger. Color case-hardened receiver with engraving. Introduced 1989. Imported from Europe by Outdoor Sports Headquarters.
Price: **$545.00**
Price: Sporting Clays model (12-ga., 30″, choke tubes) **$895.00**

Charles Daly Deluxe Over/Under
Similar to the Field Grade except available in 12 and 20 gauge, has automatic selective ejectors, antique silver finish on frame, and has choke tubes for Imp. Cyl., Mod. and Full. Introduced 1989.
Price: **$770.00**

HATFIELD UPLANDER OVER/UNDER SHOTGUN
Gauge: 20, 28, 3″ chambers.
Barrel: 26″ (Imp. Cyl. & Mod.).
Weight: 5 lbs., 4 oz.
Stock: Straight English grip of special select XXX fancy walnut; hand-checkered grip and forend; hand-rubbed oil finish.
Features: Boxlock action with single selective trigger; half-coverage hand engraving; French gray finish. Comes with English-style oxblood leather luggage case with billiard felt interior. Special engraving, stock dimensions, metal finish available. Introduced 1994. From Hatfield Gun Co.
Price: Grade I **$3,749.00**

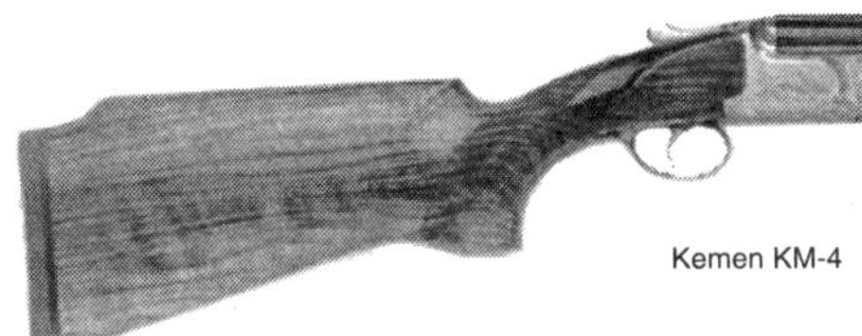
Kemen KM-4

KEMEN OVER/UNDER SHOTGUNS
Gauge: 12, 2 3/4″ or 3″ chambers.
Barrel: 27 5/8″ (Hunting, Pigeon, Sporting Clays, Skeet), 30″, 32″ (Sporting Clays, Trap).
Weight: 7.25 to 8.5 lbs.
Stock: Dimensions to customer specs. High grade walnut.
Features: Drop-out trigger assembly; ventilated flat or step top rib, ventilated, solid or no side ribs. Low-profile receiver with black finish on Standard model, antique silver on sideplate models and all engraved, gold inlaid models. Barrels, forend, trigger parts interchangeable with Perazzi. Comes with hard case, accessory tools, spares. Introduced 1989. Imported from Spain by U.S.A. Sporting Clays.
Price: KM-4 Standard **$6,179.00**
Price: KM-4 Luxe-A (engraved scroll), Luxe-B (game scenes) **$10,644.00**
Price: KM-4 Super Luxe (engraved game scene) **$12,064.00**
Price: KM-4 Extra Luxe-A (scroll engraved sideplates) **$13,960.00**
Price: KM-4 Extra Luxe-B (game scene sideplates) **$16,030.00**
Price: KM-4 Extra Gold (inlays, game scene) **$19,607.00**

HHF MODEL 101 B 12 ST TRAP O/U
Gauge: 12, 3″ chambers.
Barrel: 30″, fixed chokes or choke tubes; 16mm rib.
Weight: About 8 lbs.
Stock: Circassian walnut to trap dimensions; Monte Carlo comb, palm swell grip, recoil pad.
Features: Single selective trigger; manual safety; automatic ejectors or extractors. Many custom features available. Silvered frame with 50 percent envgraving coverage. Introduced 1995. Imported from Turkey by Turkish Firearms Corp.
Price: With extractors **$1,050.00**
Price: With ejectors **$1,680.00**
Price: Model 101 B 12 AT-DT (trap combo, 32″ barrels) **$2,295.00**

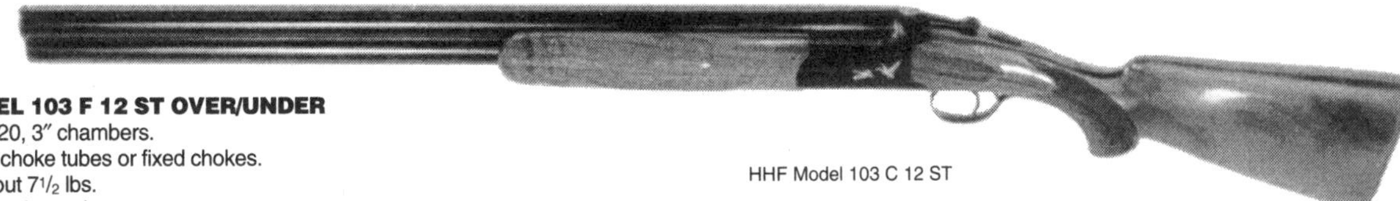
HHF Model 103 C 12 ST

HHF MODEL 103 F 12 ST OVER/UNDER
Gauge: 12, 20, 3″ chambers.
Barrel: 28″, choke tubes or fixed chokes.
Weight: About 7 1/2 lbs.
Stock: Circassian walnut.
Features: Boxlock action with dummy sideplates. Single selective trigger; manual safety; extractors. Can be ordered with many custom options. Has 100 percent engraving coverage, inlaid animals on blackened sideplates. Introduced 1995. Imported from Turkey by Turkish Firearms Corp.
Price: With extractors **$1,120.00**
Price: With automatic ejectors **$1,750.00**
Price: Model 103 C 12 ST (black receiver, 50 percent engraving coverage, extractors) **$1,050.00**
Price: As above, ejectors **$1,680.00**
Price: Model 103 D 12 ST (standard boxlock with 80 percent engraving coverage, extractors) **$1,050.00**
Price: As above, ejectors **$1,680.00**
Price: Model 103 B 12 ST (double triggers, extractors, 80 percent engraving coverage, fixed chokes) **$995.00**
Price: As above, 28, 410 .... **$1,550.00**
Price: With choke tubes, extractors (12, 20) **$1,050.00**

HHF MODEL 104 A 12 ST OVER/UNDER
Gauge: 12, 3″ chambers.
Barrel: 28″, fixed chokes or choke tubes.
Weight: About 7 1/2 lbs.
Stock: Circassian walnut, field dimensions.
Features: Boxlock action with manual safety, extractors, double triggers. Silvered, engraved receiver. Has 15 percent engraving coverage. Introduced 1995. Imported from Turkey by Turkish Firearms Corp.
Price: Fixed chokes, extractors **$925.00**
Price: As above, 28, 410 .... **$1,295.00**
Price: Choke tubes, ejectors (12, 20) **$925.00**

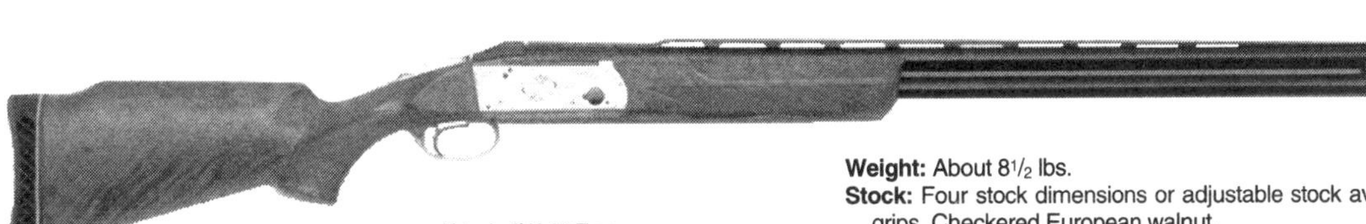
Krieghoff K-80 Trap

KRIEGHOFF K-80 O/U TRAP SHOTGUN
Gauge: 12, 2 3/4″ chambers.
Barrel: 30″, 32″ (Imp. Mod. & Full or choke tubes).
Weight: About 8 1/2 lbs.
Stock: Four stock dimensions or adjustable stock available; all have palm-swell grips. Checkered European walnut.
Features: Satin nickel receiver. Selective mechanical trigger, adjustable for position. Ventilated step rib. Introduced 1980. Imported from Germany by Krieghoff International, Inc.
Price: K-80 O/U (30″, 32″, Imp. Mod. & Full), from **$7,100.00**
Price: K-80 Unsingle (32″, 34″, Full), Standard, from **$7,650.00**
Price: K-80 Combo (two-barrel set), Standard, from **$9,970.00**

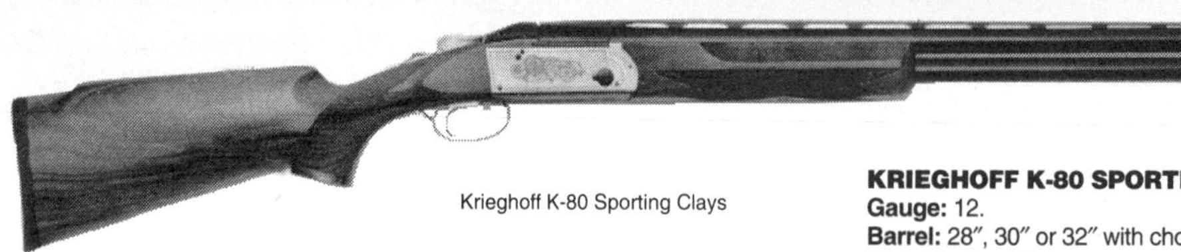
Krieghoff K-80 Sporting Clays

KRIEGHOFF K-80 SKEET SHOTGUN
Gauge: 12, 2¾″ chambers.
Barrel: 28″ (Skeet & Skeet, optional Tula or choke tubes).
Weight: About 7¾ lbs.
Stock: American Skeet or straight Skeet stocks, with palm-swell grips. Walnut.
Features: Satin gray receiver finish. Selective mechanical trigger adjustable for position. Choice of ventilated 8mm parallel flat rib or ventilated 8-12mm tapered flat rib. Introduced 1980. Imported from Germany by Krieghoff International, Inc.
Price: Standard, Skeet chokes **$6,650.00**
Price: As above, Tula chokes **$7,450.00**
Price: Lightweight model (weighs 7 lbs.), Standard **$6,650.00**
Price: Two-Barrel Set (tube concept), 12-ga., Standard **$11,305.00**
Price: Skeet Special (28″, tapered flat rib, Skeet & Skeet choke tubes) **$7,300.00**

Krieghoff K-80 Four-Barrel Skeet Set
Similar to the Standard Skeet except comes with barrels for 12, 20, 28, 410. Comes with fitted aluminum case.
Price: Standard grade **$15,950.00**

LAURONA SILHOUETTE 300 SPORTING CLAYS
Gauge: 12, 2¾″ or 3″ chambers.
Barrel: 28″, 29″ (Multichoke tubes, flush-type or knurled).
Weight: 7 lbs., 12 oz.
Stock: 14⅜″x1⅜″x2½″. European walnut with full pistol grip, beavertail forend. Rubber buttpad.
Features: Selective single trigger, automatic selective ejectors. Introduced 1988. Imported from Spain by Galaxy Imports.
Price: **$1,250.00**
Price: Silhouette Ultra-Magnum, 3½″ chambers **$1,265.00**

Laurona Silhouette 300 Trap
Same gun as the Silhouette 300 Sporting Clays except has 29″ barrels, trap stock dimensions of 14⅜″x1 7/16″x1⅝″, weighs 7 lbs., 15 oz. Available with flush or knurled Multichokes.
Price: **$1,310.00**

KRIEGHOFF K-80 SPORTING CLAYS O/U
Gauge: 12.
Barrel: 28″, 30″ or 32″ with choke tubes.
Weight: About 8 lbs.
Stock: #3 Sporting stock designed for gun-down shooting.
Features: Choice of standard or lightweight receiver with satin nickel finish and classic scroll engraving. Selective mechanical trigger adjustable for position. Choice of tapered flat or 8mm parallel flat barrel rib. Free-floating barrels. Aluminum case. Imported from Germany by Krieghoff International, Inc.
Price: Standard grade with five choke tubes **$7,850.00**

Krieghoff K-80/RT Shotguns
Same as the standard K-80 shotguns except has a removable internally selective trigger mechanism. Can be considered an option on all K-80 guns of any configuration. Introduced 1990.
Price: RT (removable trigger) option on K-80 guns, add **$1,000.00**
Price: Extra pull trigger mechanisms **$1,275.00**

Krieghoff K-80 International Skeet
Similar to the Standard Skeet except has ½″ ventilated Broadway-style rib, special Tula chokes with gas release holes at muzzle. International Skeet stock. Comes in fitted aluminum case.
Price: Standard grade **$7,450.00**

LAURONA SUPER MODEL OVER/UNDERS
Gauge: 12, 20, 2¾″ or 3″ chambers.
Barrel: 26″, 28″ (Multichoke), 29″ (Multichokes and Full).
Weight: About 7 lbs.
Stock: European walnut. Dimensions may vary according to model. Full pistol grip.
Features: Boxlock action, silvered with engraving. Automatic selective ejectors; choke tubes available on most models; single selective or twin single triggers; black chrome barrels. Has 5-year warranty, including metal finish. Imported from Spain by Galaxy Imports.
Price: Model 83 MG, 12- or 20-ga. **$1,215.00**
Price: Model 84S Super Trap (fixed chokes) **$1,340.00**
Price: Model 85 Super Game, 12- or 20-ga. **$1,215.00**
Price: Model 85 MS Super Trap (Full/Multichoke) **$1,390.00**
Price: Model 85 MS Super Pigeon **$1,370.00**
Price: Model 85 S Super Skeet, 12-ga. **$1,300.00**

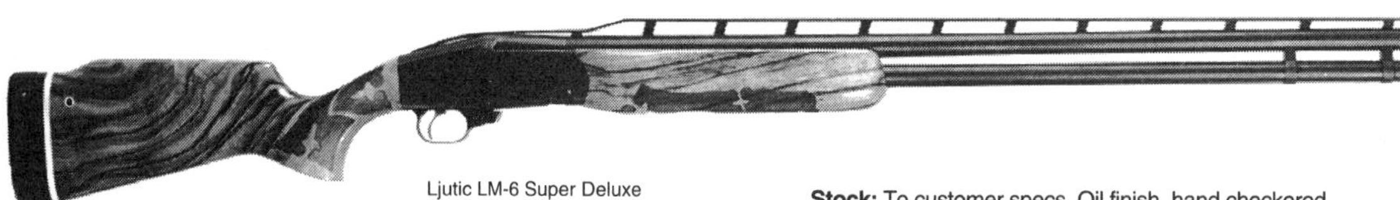
Ljutic LM-6 Super Deluxe

LJUTIC LM-6 SUPER DELUXE O/U SHOTGUN
Gauge: 12.
Barrel: 28″ to 34″, choked to customer specs for live birds, trap, International Trap.
Weight: To customer specs.
Stock: To customer specs. Oil finish, hand checkered.
Features: Custom-made gun. Hollow-milled rib, pull or release trigger, pushbutton opener in front of trigger guard. From Ljutic Industries.
Price: Super Deluxe LM-6 O/U **$19,995.00**
Price: Over/under Combo (interchangeable single barrel, two trigger guards, one for single trigger, one for doubles) **$26,995.00**
Price: Extra over/under barrel sets, 29″-32″ **$5,995.00**

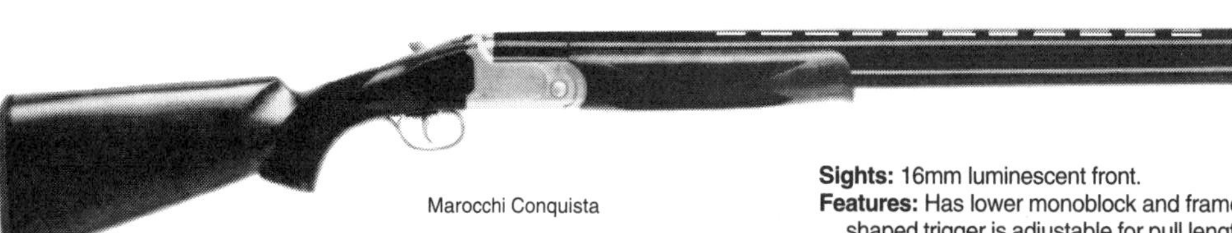
Marocchi Conquista

MAROCCHI CONQUISTA SPORTING CLAYS O/U SHOTGUNS
Gauge: 12, 2¾″ chambers.
Barrel: 28″, 30″, 32″ (Contrechoke tubes); 10mm concave vent. rib.
Weight: About 8 lbs.
Stock: 14½″-14⅞″x2 3/16″x1 7/16″; American walnut with checkered grip and forend; Sporting Clays butt pad.
Sights: 16mm luminescent front.
Features: Has lower monoblock and frame profile. Fast lock time. Ergonomically-shaped trigger is adjustable for pull length and weight. Automatic selective ejectors. Coin-finished receiver, blued barrels. Comes with five choke tubes, hard case, stock wrench. Also available as true left-hand model—opening lever operates from left to right; stock has left-hand cast. Introduced 1994. Imported from Italy by Precision Sales International.
Price: Grade I, right-hand **$1,895.00**
Price: Grade I, left-hand **$1,945.00**
Price: Grade II, right-hand **$2,285.00**
Price: Grade II, left-hand **$2,335.00**
Price: Grade III, right-hand, from **$3,250.00**
Price: Grade III, left-hand, from **$3,350.00**

CAUTION: PRICES SHOWN ARE SUPPLIED BY THE MANUFACTURER OR IMPORTER. CHECK YOUR LOCAL GUNSHOP.

Marocchi Lady Sport O/U Shotgun

Ergonomically designed specifically for women shooters. Similar to the Conquista Sporting Clays model except has 28″ or 30″ barrels with five Contrechoke tubes, stock dimensions of $13\frac{7}{8}$″-$14\frac{1}{4}$″x$1\frac{11}{32}$″x$2\frac{9}{32}$″; weighs about $7\frac{1}{2}$ lbs. Also available as left-hand model—opening lever operates from left to right; stock has left-hand cast. Also available with colored graphics finish on frame and opening lever. Introduced 1995. Imported from Italy by Precision Sales International.

Price: Grade I, right-hand **$1,945.00**
Price: Grade II, right-hand **$2,335.00**
Price: Grade III, right-hand, from **$3,350.00**
Price: Left-hand, add (all grades) **$50.00**
Price: Colored graphics frame (Grade I only), add **$50.00**

Marocchi Conquista Trap Over/Under Shotgun

Similar to the Conquista Sporting Clays model except has 30″ or 32″ barrels choked Full & Full, stock dimensions of $14\frac{1}{2}$″-$14\frac{7}{8}$″x$1\frac{11}{16}$″x$1\frac{9}{32}$″; weighs about $8\frac{1}{4}$ lbs. Introduced 1994. Imported from Italy by Precision Sales International.

Price: Grade I, right-hand **$1,895.00**
Price: Grade II, right-hand **$2,285.00**
Price: Grade III, right-hand, from **$3,250.00**

Marocchi Conquista Skeet Over/Under Shotgun

Similar to the Conquista Sporting Clays except has 28″ (Skeet & Skeet) barrels, stock dimensions of $14\frac{3}{8}$″-$14\frac{3}{4}$″x$2\frac{3}{16}$″x$1\frac{1}{2}$″. Weighs about $7\frac{3}{4}$ lbs. Introduced 1994. Imported from Italy by Precision Sales International.

Price: Grade I, right-hand **$1,895.00**
Price: Grade II, right-hand **$2,285.00**
Price: Grade III, right-hand, from **$3,250.00**

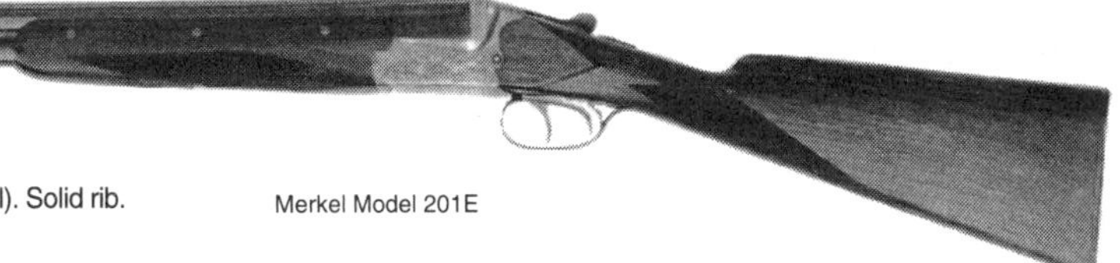

Merkel Model 201E

MERKEL MODEL 200E O/U SHOTGUN

Gauge: 12, 3″ chambers, 16, $2\frac{3}{4}$″ chambers, 20, 3″ chambers.
Barrel: 12-, 16-ga.—28″; 20-ga.—$26\frac{3}{4}$″ (Imp. Cyl. & Mod., Mod. & Full). Solid rib.
Weight: About 7 lbs. (12-ga.).
Stock: Oil-finished walnut; straight English or pistol grip.
Features: Scroll engraved, color case-hardened receiver. Single selective or double triggers; ejectors. Imported from Germany by GSI.

Price: Model 200E **$3,395.00**
Price: Model 201E (as above except silver-grayed receiver with engraved hunting scenes, also 28-ga.) **$4,895.00**
Price: Model 202E (as above except has false sideplates, fine hunting scenes with Arabesque engraving) **$8,895.00**

Merkel Model 200E Skeet, Trap Over/Unders

Similar to the Model 200E except in 12-gauge only with $2\frac{3}{4}$″ chambers, tapered ventilated rib, competition stock with full pistol grip, half-coverage Arabesque engraving on silver-grayed receiver. Single selective trigger only. Model 200ES has $26\frac{3}{4}$″ (Skeet & Skeet) barrels; Model 200ET has 30″ (Full & Full) barrels. Imported from Germany by GSI.

Price: Model 200ET **$4,895.00**
Price: Model 201ES (full-coverage engraving) **$7,495.00**
Price: Model 201ET (full-coverage engraving) **$7,495.00**
Price: Model 203ES (sidelock action, Skeet) **$12,950.00**
Price: Model 203ET (sidelock action, Trap) **$12,950.00**

Merkel Model 200 SC Sporting Clays O/U

Similar to the Model 200E except has 30″ barrels with lengthened forcing cones, five Briley choke tubes. Kersten double cross-bolt lock, color case-hardened receiver, Blitz action; single selective trigger adjustable for length of pull. Select grade stock with competition recoil pad; tapered vent. rib. Comes with fitted luggage case. Introduced 1995. Imported from Germany by GSI.

Price: **$7,495.00**
Price: With fixed Imp. Cyl. and light mod. chokes **$6,995.00**

Merkel Model 203E, 303E Over/Under Shotguns

Similar to the Model 200E except with Holland & Holland-style sidelocks, both quick-detachable: Model 203E with cranked screw, 303E with integral retracting hook. Model 203E has coil spring ejectors; 303E H&H ejectors. Both have silver-grayed receiver with English-style Arabesque engraving—large scrolls on 203E, medium on 303E. Imported from Germany by GSI.

Price: Model 203E **$10,695.00**
Price: Model 303E **$19,950.00**

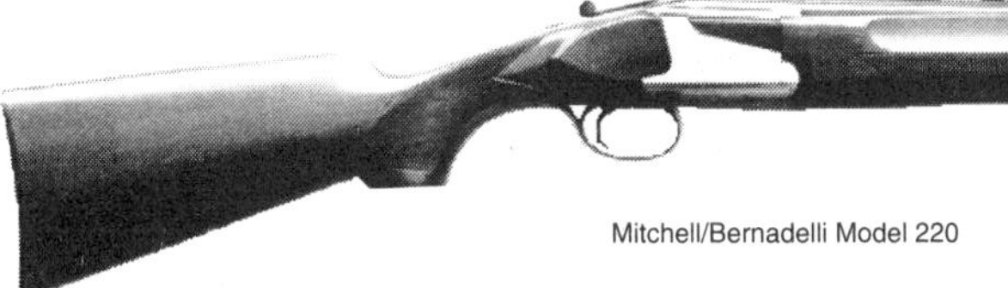

Mitchell/Bernadelli Model 220

Mitchell/Bernardelli Model 115 Over/Under Shotgun

Similar to the Model 192 except designed for competition shooting with thicker barrel walls, specially designed stock with anatomical grip. Leather-faced recoil pad and schnabel forend on Sporting Clays and Skeet guns. Concave top rib, ventilated middle rib. Imported from Italy by Mitchell Arms.

Price: Model 115 S (inclined-plane locking, ejectors, selective or non-selective trigger, Multichoke standard on Sporting Clays) **$2,895.00**
Price: Model 115 S Trap/Skeet **$2,799.00**

MITCHELL/BERNARDELLI MODEL 192 MS-MC O/U SHOTGUN

Gauge: 12, $2\frac{3}{4}$″ chambers.
Barrel: $25\frac{1}{2}$″ (Imp. Cyl. & Imp. Mod., Cyl. & Mod.), $26\frac{3}{4}$″ (Imp. Cyl. & Imp. Mod., Mod. & Full), 28″ (Mod. & Full), $29\frac{1}{2}$″ (Imp. Mod. & Full); or with Multichoke tubes.
Weight: About 7 lbs.
Stock: 14″x$1\frac{3}{8}$″x$2\frac{3}{8}$″. Hand-checkered European walnut. English or pistol grip style.
Features: Boxlock action; single selective trigger. Silvered, engraved action. Imported from Italy by Mitchell Arms.

Price: With Multichokes **$1,340.00**
Price: Model 192 Waterfowler ($3\frac{1}{2}$″ chambers, three Multichoke tubes) **$1,460.00**
Price: Model 192 MS (Sporting Clays, non-selective or selective trigger) **$2,140.00**
Price: Model 220 MS (similar to M192 except 20-ga., different frame) **$1,490.00**
Price: Model 220 (20-ga., 3″ chambers) **$1,420.00**

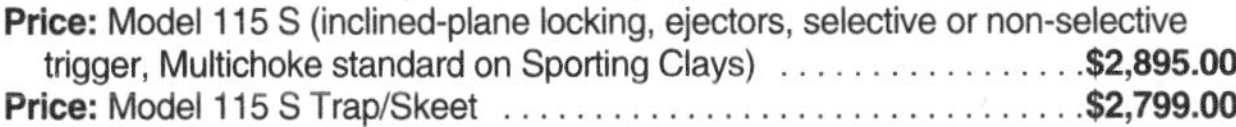

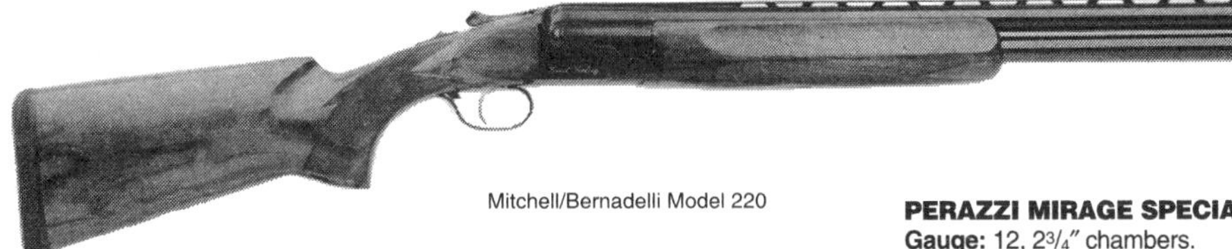

Mitchell/Bernadelli Model 220

Perazzi Mirage Special Four-Gauge Skeet

Similar to the Mirage Sporting model except has Skeet dimensions, interchangeable, adjustable four-position trigger assembly. Comes with four barrel sets in 12, 20, 28, 410, flat $\frac{5}{16}$″x$\frac{5}{16}$″ rib.

Price: From **$19,385.00**

PERAZZI MIRAGE SPECIAL SPORTING O/U

Gauge: 12, $2\frac{3}{4}$″ chambers.
Barrel: $28\frac{3}{8}$″ (Imp. Mod. & Extra Full), $29\frac{1}{2}$″ (choke tubes).
Weight: 7 lbs., 12 oz.
Stock: Special specifications.
Features: Has single selective trigger; flat $\frac{7}{16}$″x$\frac{5}{16}$″ vent. rib. Many options available. Imported from Italy by Perazzi U.S.A., Inc.

Price: **$9,160.00**

CAUTION: PRICES SHOWN ARE SUPPLIED BY THE MANUFACTURER OR IMPORTER. CHECK YOUR LOCAL GUNSHOP.

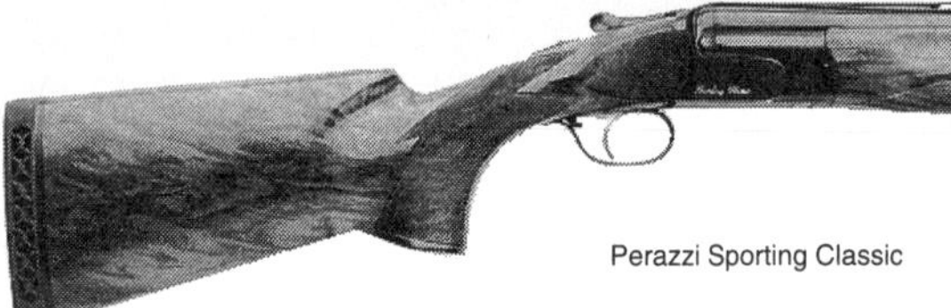
Perazzi Sporting Classic

PERAZZI MX8/MX8 SPECIAL TRAP, SKEET
Gauge: 12, 2¾″ chambers.
Barrel: Trap—29½″ (Imp. Mod. & Extra Full), 31½″ (Full & Extra Full). Choke tubes optional. Skeet—27⅝″ (Skeet & Skeet).
Weight: About 8½ lbs. (Trap); 7 lbs., 15 oz. (Skeet).
Stock: Interchangeable and custom made to customer specs.
Features: Has detachable and interchangeable trigger group with flat V springs. Flat 7/16″ ventilated rib. Many options available. Imported from Italy by Perazzi U.S.A., Inc.
Price: From **$8,090.00**
Price: MX8 Special (adj. four-position trigger), from **$8,570.00**
Price: MX8 Special Single (32″ or 34″ single barrel, step rib), from **$8,300.00**
Price: MX8 Special Combo (o/u and single barrel sets), from **$11,280.00**

PERAZZI MX10 OVER/UNDER SHOTGUN
Gauge: 12, 2¾″ chambers.
Barrel: 29.5″, 31.5″ (fixed chokes).
Weight: NA.
Stock: Walnut; cheekpiece adjustable for elevation and cast.
Features: Comes with six pattern adjustment rib inserts. Vent. side rib. Externally selective trigger. Available in single barrel, combo, over/under trap, Skeet, pigeon and sporting models. Introduced 1993. Imported from Italy by Perazzi U.S.A., Inc.
Price: From **$10,300.00**

PERAZZI MX28, MX410 GAME O/U SHOTGUNS
Gauge: 28, 2¾″ chambers, 410, 3″ chambers.
Barrel: 26″ (Imp. Cyl. & Full).
Weight: NA.
Stock: To customer specifications.
Features: Made on scaled-down frames proportioned to the gauge. Introduced 1993. Imported from Italy by Perazzi U.S.A., Inc.
Price: From **$16,170.00**

Perazzi Sporting Classic O/U
Same as the Mirage Special Sporting except is deluxe version with select wood and engraving, Available with flush mount choke tubes, 29.5″ barrels. Introduced 1993.
Price: From **$10,200.00**

Perazzi Mirage Special Skeet Over/Under
Similar to the MX8 Skeet except has adjustable four-position trigger, Skeet stock dimensions.
Price: From **$8,570.00**

Perazzi MX8/20 Over/Under Shotgun
Similar to the MX8 except has smaller frame and has a removable trigger mechanism. Available in trap, Skeet, sporting or game models with fixed chokes or choke tubes. Stock is made to customer specifications. Introduced 1993.
Price: From **$8,090.00**

PERAZZI MX12 HUNTING OVER/UNDER
Gauge: 12, 2¾″ chambers.
Barrel: 26″, 27⅝″, 28⅜″, 29½″ (Mod. & Full); choke tubes available in 27⅝″, 29½″ only (MX12C).
Weight: 7 lbs., 4 oz.
Stock: To customer specs; Interchangeable.
Features: Single selective trigger; coil springs used in action; schnabel forend tip. Imported from Italy by Perazzi U.S.A., Inc.
Price: From **$8,090.00**
Price: MX12C (with choke tubes), from **$8,680.00**

Perazzi MX20 Hunting Over/Under
Similar to the MX12 except 20-ga. frame size. Available in 20, 28, 410 with 2¾″ or 3″ chambers. 26″ standard, and choked Mod. & Full. Weight is 6 lbs., 6 oz.
Price: From **$8,090.00**
Price: MX20C (as above, 20-ga. only, choke tubes), from **$8,680.00**

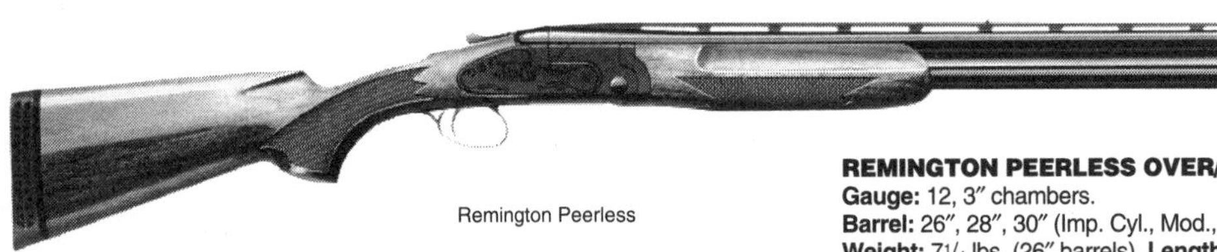
Remington Peerless

PIOTTI BOSS OVER/UNDER SHOTGUN
Gauge: 12, 20.
Barrel: 26″ to 32″, chokes as specified.
Weight: 6.5 to 8 lbs.
Stock: Dimensions to customer specs. Best quality figured walnut.
Features: Essentially a custom-made gun with many options. Introduced 1993. Imported from Italy by Wm. Larkin Moore.
Price: From **$36,600.00**

REMINGTON PEERLESS OVER/UNDER SHOTGUN
Gauge: 12, 3″ chambers.
Barrel: 26″, 28″, 30″ (Imp. Cyl., Mod., Full Rem Chokes).
Weight: 7¼ lbs. (26″ barrels). **Length:** 43″ overall (26″ barrels).
Stock: 14 3/16″x1½″x2¼″. American walnut with Imron gloss finish, cut-checkered grip and forend. Black, ventilated recoil pad.
Features: Boxlock action with removable sideplates. Gold-plated, single selective trigger, automatic safety, automatic ejectors. Fast lock time. Mid-rib bead, Bradley-type front. Polished blue finish with light scrollwork on sideplates, Remington logo on bottom of receiver. Introduced 1993.
Price: **$1,225.00**

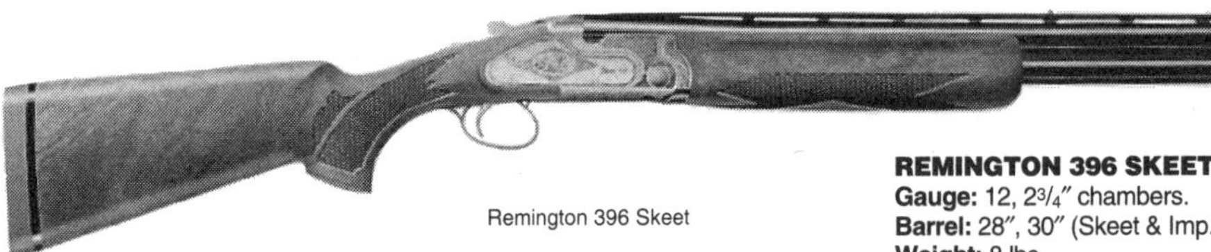
Remington 396 Skeet

Remington 396 Sporting O/U
Similar to the 396 Skeet except the 28″, 30″ barrels are factory ported, and come with Skeet, Imp. Skeet, Imp. Cyl. and Mod. Rem Choke tubes. Made in U.S. by Remington. Introduced 1996.
Price: **$2,659.00**

REMINGTON 396 SKEET O/U
Gauge: 12, 2¾″ chambers.
Barrel: 28″, 30″ (Skeet & Imp. Skeet Rem. Choke tubes).
Weight: 8 lbs.
Stock: 14 3/16″x1½″x2¼″. Fancy, figured American walnut. Target-style forend, larger-radius comb, grip palm swell.
Features: Boxlock action with removable sideplates. Barrels have lengthened forcing cones; 10mm non-stepped, parallel rib; engraved receiver, sideplates, trigger guard, top lever, forend iron are finished with gray nitride. Made in U.S. by Remington. Introduced 1996.
Price: **$2,526.00**

CAUTION: PRICES SHOWN ARE SUPPLIED BY THE MANUFACTURER OR IMPORTER. CHECK YOUR LOCAL GUNSHOP.

RIZZINI AURUM OVER/UNDER SHOTGUN

Gauge: 12, 16, 20, 28, 410.
Barrel: 26", 27 1/2", Mod. & Full, Imp. Cyl. & Imp. Mod. choke tubes.
Weight: About 6.6 lbs.
Stock: 14"x1 1/2"x2 1/8".
Features: Boxlock action; single selective trigger; ejectors; profuse engraving on silvered receiver. Comes with fitted case. Introduced 1996. Imported from Italy by Wm. Larkin Moore & Co.
Price: From $1,875.00

Rizzini Artemis Over/Under Shotgun

Same as the Aurum model except has dummy sideplates with extensive game scene engraving. Fancy European walnut stock. Comes with fitted case. Introduced 1996. Imported from Italy by Wm. Larkin Moore & Co.
Price: From $2,120.00

RIZZINI S782 EMEL OVER/UNDER SHOTGUN

Gauge: 12, 2 3/4" chambers.
Barrel: 26", 27.5" (Imp. Cyl. & Imp. Mod.).
Weight: About 6.75 lbs.
Stock: 14"x1 1/2"x2 1/8". Extra fancy select walnut.
Features: Boxlock action with dummy sideplates; extensive engraving with gold inlaid game birds; silvered receiver; automatic ejectors; single selective trigger. Comes with Nizzoli leather case. Introduced 1996. Imported from Italy by Wm. Larkin Moore & Co.
Price: From $10,300.00

RIZZINI S790 SPORTING EL OVER/UNDER

Gauge: 12, 2 3/4" chambers.
Barrel: 28", 29.5", Imp. Mod., Mod., Full choke tubes.
Weight: 8.1 lbs.
Stock: 14"x1 1/2"x2". Extra-fancy select walnut.
Features: Boxlock action; automatic ejectors; single selective trigger; 10mm top rib. Comes with case. Introduced 1996. Imported from Italy by Wm. Larkin Moore & Co.
Price: $3,060.00

RIZZINI S790 EMEL OVER/UNDER SHOTGUN

Gauge: 20, 28, 410.
Barrel: 26", 27.5" (Imp. Cyl. & Imp. Mod.).
Weight: About 6 lbs.
Stock: 14"x1 1/2"x2 1/8". Extra-fancy select walnut.
Features: Boxlock action with profuse engraving; automatic ejectors; single selective trigger; silvered receiver. Comes with Nizzoli leather case. Introduced 1996. Imported from Italy by Wm. Larkin Moore & Co.
Price: From $8,750.00

Rizzini S792 EMEL Over/Under Shotgun

Similar to the S790 EMEL except has dummy sideplates with extensive engraving coverage. Comes with Nizzoli leather case. Introduced 1996. Imported from Italy by Wm. Larkin Moore & Co.
Price: From $8,750.00

ROTTWEIL PARAGON OVER/UNDER

Gauge: 12, 2 3/4" chambers.
Barrel: 28", 30", five choke tubes.
Weight: 7 lbs.
Stock: 14 1/2"x1 1/2"x2 1/2"; European walnut.
Features: Boxlock action. Detachable trigger assembly; ejectors can be deactivated; convertible top lever for right- or left-hand use; trigger adjustable for position. Imported from Germany by Dynamit Nobel-RWS, Inc.
Price: $5,995.00

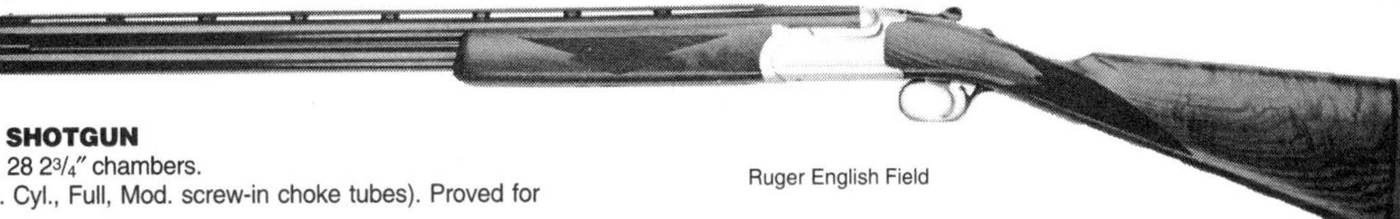

Ruger English Field

RUGER RED LABEL O/U SHOTGUN

Gauge: 12, 20, 3" chambers; 28 2 3/4" chambers.
Barrel: 26", 28" (Skeet, Imp. Cyl., Full, Mod. screw-in choke tubes). Proved for steel shot.
Weight: About 7 lbs. (20-ga.); 7 1/2 lbs. (12-ga.). **Length:** 43" overall (26" barrels).
Stock: 14"x1 1/2"x2 1/2". Straight grain American walnut. Checkered pistol grip and forend, rubber butt pad.
Features: Choice of blue or stainless receiver. Single selective mechanical trigger, selective automatic ejectors; serrated free-floating vent. rib. Comes with two Skeet, one Imp. Cyl., one Mod., one Full choke tube and wrench. Made in U.S. by Sturm, Ruger & Co.
Price: Red Label with pistol grip stock $1,215.00
Price: English Field with straight-grip stock $1,215.00

Ruger Sporting Clays O/U Shotgun

Similar to the Red Label except 30" back-bored barrels, stainless steel choke tubes. Weighs 7.75 lbs., overall length 47". Stock dimensions of 14 1/8"x1 1/2"x2 1/2". Free-floating serrated vent. rib with brass front and mid-rib beads. No barrel side spacers. Comes with two Skeet, one Imp. Cyl., one Mod. choke tubes. Full and Extra-Full available at extra cost. 12 ga. introduced 1992, 20 ga. introduced 1994.
Price: 12 or 20 .... $1,349.00

Ruger Woodside

RUGER WOODSIDE OVER/UNDER SHOTGUN

Gauge: 12, 3" chambers.
Barrel: 26", 28" (Full, Mod., Imp. Cyl. and two Skeet tubes), 30" (Mod., Imp. Cyl. and two Skeet tubes).
Weight: 7 1/2 to 8 lbs.
Stock: 14 1/8"x1 1/2"x2 1/2". Select Circassian walnut; pistol grip or straight English grip.
Features: Has a newly patented Ruger cocking mechanism for easier, smoother opening. Buttstock extends forward into action as two side panels. Single selective mechanical trigger, selective automatic ejectors; serrated free-floating rib; back-bored barrels with stainless steel choke tubes. Blued barrels, stainless steel receiver. Engraved action available. Introduced 1995. Made in U.S. by Sturm, Ruger & Co.
Price: $1,675.00
Price: Woodside Sporting Clays (30" barrels) $1,675.00

SABATTI SPORTING CLAYS OVER/UNDER SHOTGUN

Gauge: 12, 3" chambers.
Barrel: 28", five ICT choke tubes.
Weight: 7.3 lbs.
Stock: Checkered European walnut; solid rubber butt pad.
Features: Blued, engraved receiver; single selective trigger; automatic ejectors; automatic safety. Introduced 1996. Imported from italy by K.B.I., Inc.
Price: $809.00

Sabatti Trap O/U Shotgun

Similar to the Sporting Clays model except has 30" Imp. Mod. & Full barrels, trap stock dimensions; weighs 8 lbs.; 2 3/4" chambers. Introduced 1996. Imported from Italy by K.B.I., Inc.
Price: $819.00

Consult our Directory pages for the location of firms mentioned.

Sabatti Skeet O/U Shotgun

Simliar to the Sporting Clays model except 2 3/4" chambers, 26" Skeet 1 & Skeet 2 barrels; weighs 7 lbs. Introduced 1996. Imported from Italy by K.B.I., Inc.
Price: $799.00

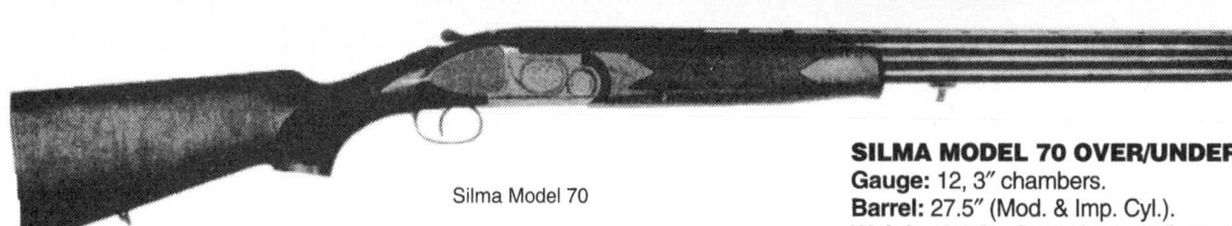

Silma Model 70

SILMA MODEL 70 OVER/UNDER SHOTGUN
Gauge: 12, 3″ chambers.
Barrel: 27.5″ (Mod. & Imp. Cyl.).
Weight: 6.8 lbs. **Length:** 44.75″ overall.
Stock: European walnut.
Features: Engraved, blued boxlock action with single trigger; sling swivels. Introduced 1995. Imported from Italy by Century International Arms.
Price: About **$540.00**

SKB Model 585

SKB MODEL 585 OVER/UNDER SHOTGUN
Gauge: 12 or 20, 3″; 28, $2^{3}/_{4}$″; 410, 3″.
Barrel: 12-ga.—26″, 28″, 30″, 32″, 34″ (Inter-Choke tube); 20-ga.—26″, 28″ (Inter-Choke tube); 28—26″, 28″ (Inter-Choke tube); 410—26″, 28″ (Imp. Cyl. & Mod., Mod. & Full). Ventilated side ribs.
Weight: 6.6 to 8.5 lbs. **Length:** 43″ to $51^{3}/_{8}$″ overall.
Stock: $14^{1}/_{8}$″x$1^{1}/_{2}$″x$2^{3}/_{16}$″. Hand checkered walnut with high-gloss finish. Target stocks available in standard and Monte Carlo.
Sights: Metal bead front (field), target style on Skeet, trap, Sporting Clays.
Features: Boxlock action; silver nitride finish with Field or Target pattern engraving; manual safety, automatic ejectors, single selective trigger. All 12-gauge barrels are back-bored, have lengthened forcing cones and longer choke tube system. Sporting Clays models in 12-gauge with 28″ or 30″ barrels available with optional $^{3}/_{8}$″ step-up target-style rib, matte finish, nickel center bead, white front bead. Introduced 1992. Imported from Japan by G.U., Inc.
Price: Field **$1,179.00**
Price: Two-barrel Field Set, 12 & 20 . . . . . **$1,929.00**
Price: Two-barrel Field Set, 20 & 28 or 28 & 410) **$1,989.00**
Price: Trap, Skeet **$1,279.00**
Price: Two-barrel trap combo **$1,929.00**
Price: Sporting Clays model . . . . . **$1,329.00** to **$1,379.00**
Price: Skeet Set (20, 28, 410) **$2,999.00**

SKB Model 585 Waterfowler Shotgun
Similar to the Model 585 Field except 12-gauge only, 28″ or 30″ barrels with Imp. Cyl., Skeet 1, Mod. Inter-Choke tubes. Bead-blasted receiver with silver nitride finish; bead-blasted, blued barrels. Oil-finished stock and forend. Introduced 1995. Imported from Japan by G.U., Inc.
Price: **$1,329.00**

SKB Model 585 Youth Model Shotgun
Similar to the Field Model 585 except has $13^{1}/_{2}$″ length of pull. Available in 12-gauge with 26″ or 28″, or 20-gauge with 26″ barrels. The 12-gauge has .755″ bores, lengthened forcing cones and competition series choke tubes. Introduced 1994. Imported from Japan by G.U., Inc.
Price: **$1,179.00**

SKB MODEL 785 OVER/UNDER SHOTGUN
Gauge: 12, 20, 3″; 28, $2^{3}/_{4}$″; 410, 3″.
Barrel: 26″, 28″, 30″, 32″ (Inter-Choke tubes).
Weight: 6 lbs., 10 oz. to 8 lbs.
Stock: $14^{1}/_{8}$″x$1^{1}/_{2}$″x$2^{3}/_{16}$″ (Field). Hand-checkered American black walnut with high-gloss finish; semi-beavertail forend. Target stocks available in standard or Monte Carlo styles.
Sights: Metal bead front (Field), target style on Skeet, trap, Sporting Clays models.
Features: Boxlock action with Greener-style cross bolt; single selective chrome-plated trigger, chrome-plated selective ejectors; manual safety. Chrome-plated, over-size, back-bored barrels with lengthened forcing cones. Introduced 1995. Imported from Japan by G.U. Inc.
Price: Field, 12 or 20 . . . . . **$1,899.00**
Price: Field, 28 or 410 . . . . . **$1,949.00**
Price: Field set, 12 and 20 . . . . . **$2,749.00**
Price: Field set, 20 and 28 or 28 and 410 . . . . . **$2,819.00**
Price: Sporting Clays, 12 or 20 . . . . . **$2,029.00**
Price: Sporting Clays, 28 . . . . . **$2,079.00**
Price: Sporting Clays set, 12 and 20 . . . . . **$2,889.00**
Price: Skeet, 12 or 20 . . . . . **$1,949.00**
Price: Skeet, 28 or 410 . . . . . **$1,999.00**
Price: Skeet, three-barrel set, 20, 28, 410 . . . . . **$3,929.00**
Price: Trap, standard or Monte Carlo **$1,949.00**
Price: Trap combo, standard or Monte Carlo **$2,719.00**

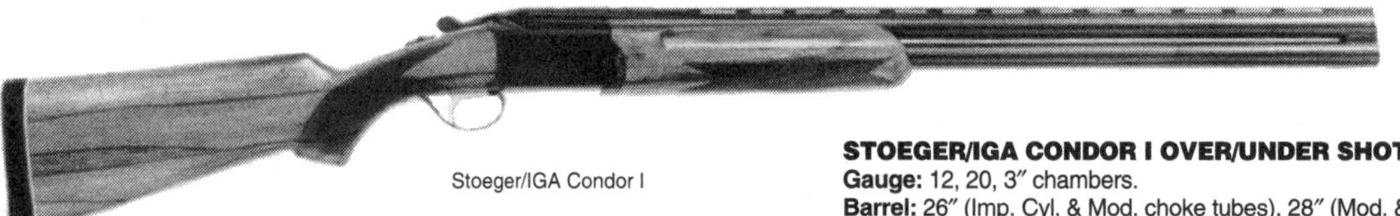

Stoeger/IGA Condor I

STOEGER/IGA CONDOR I OVER/UNDER SHOTGUN
Gauge: 12, 20, 3″ chambers.
Barrel: 26″ (Imp. Cyl. & Mod. choke tubes), 28″ (Mod. & Full choke tubes).
Weight: $6^{3}/_{4}$ to 7 lbs.
Stock: $14^{1}/_{2}$″x$1^{1}/_{2}$″x$2^{1}/_{2}$″. Oil-finished hardwood with checkered pistol grip and forend.
Features: Manual safety, single trigger, extractors only, ventilated top rib. Introduced 1983. Imported from Brazil by Stoeger Industries.
Price: With choke tubes **$500.00**
Price: Condor II (sames as Condor I except has double triggers, moulded buttplate) **$415.00**
Price: Condor Supreme (same as Condor I with single trigger, choke tubes, but with auto. ejectors), 12- or 20-ga., 26″, 28″ **$599.00**

CONSULT
SHOOTER'S
MARKETPLACE
Page 225, This Issue

TIKKA MODEL 512S FIELD GRADE OVER/UNDER
Gauge: 12, 20, 3″ chambers.
Barrel: 26″, 28″, with stainless steel screw-in chokes (Imp. Cyl, Mod., Imp. Mod., Full); 20-ga., 28″ only.
Weight: About $7^{1}/_{4}$ lbs.
Stock: American walnut. Standard dimensions—$13^{9}/_{10}$″x$1^{1}/_{2}$″x$2^{2}/_{5}$″. Checkered pistol grip and forend.
Features: Free interchangeability of barrels, stocks and forends into double rifle model, combination gun, etc. Barrel selector in trigger; auto. top tang safety; barrel cocking indicators. Introduced 1980. Imported from Italy by Stoeger.
Price: Model 512S (ejectors), Field Grade **$1,290.00**
Price: Model 512S Sporting Clays, 12-ga., 28″, choke tubes **$1,325.00**

CAUTION: PRICES SHOWN ARE SUPPLIED BY THE MANUFACTURER OR IMPORTER. CHECK YOUR LOCAL GUNSHOP.

Tristar Model 333

Tristar Model 333SC Over/Under

Same as the Model 333 except has 11mm rib with target sight beads, elongated forcing cones, porter barrels, stainless extended Sporting choke tubes (Skeet, Imp. Cyl., Imp. Cyl., Mod.), Sporting Clays recoil pad. Introduced 1996. Imported from Turkey by Tristar Sporting Arms, Ltd.

Price: **$899.95**

TRISTAR MODEL 333 OVER/UNDER

Gauge: 12, 20, 3″ chambers.

Barrel: 12 ga.—26″, 28″, 30″; 20 ga.—26″, 28″; five choke tubes.

Weight: $7\frac{1}{2}$-$7\frac{3}{4}$ lbs. **Length:** 45″ overall.

Stock: Hand-checkered fancy grade Turkish walnut; full pistol grip, semi-beavertail forend; black recoil pad.

Features: Boxlock action with slivered, hand-engraved receiver; automatic selective ejectors, mechanical single selective trigger; stainless steel firing pins; auto safety; hard chrome bores. Introduced 1995. Imported from Turkey by Tristar Sporting Arms, Ltd.

Price: **$799.95**

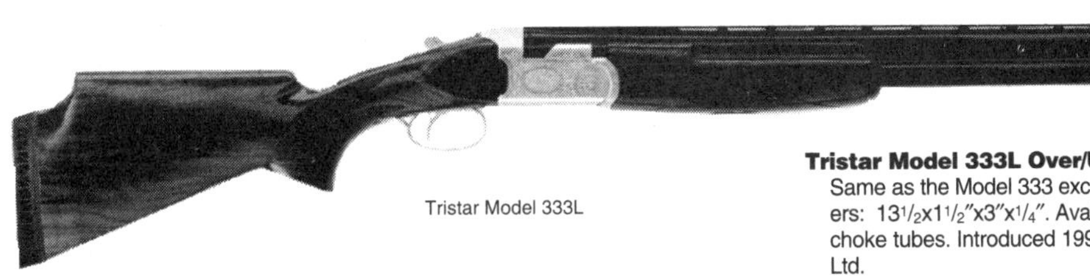

Tristar Model 333L

Tristar Model 333SCL Over/Under

Same as the Model 333SC except has special stock dimensions for female shooters: $13\frac{1}{2}$x$1\frac{1}{2}$″x3″x$\frac{1}{4}$″. Introduced 1996. Imported from Turkey by Tristar Sporting Arms, Ltd.

Price: **$899.95**

Tristar Model 300 Over/Under

Similar to the Model 333 except has standard grade walnut, extractors, etched frame, double triggers, manual safety, plastic buttplate. Available in 12-ga. only with 26″ (Imp. Cyl. & Mod.) or 28″ (Mod. & Full) barrels. Introduced 1996. Imported from Turkey by Tristar Sporting Arms, Ltd.

Price: **$429.95**

Tristar Model 333L Over/Under

Same as the Model 333 except has special stock dimensions for female shooters: $13\frac{1}{2}$x$1\frac{1}{2}$″x3″x$\frac{1}{4}$″. Available in 12-ga. with 26″, 28″ or 20 ga. 26″, with five choke tubes. Introduced 1996. Imported from Turkey by Tristar Sporting Arms, Ltd.

Price: **$799.95**

Tristar Model 330 Over/Under

Similar to the Model 333 except has standard grade walnut, etched engraving, fixed chokes, extractors only. Introduced 1996. Imported from Turkey by Tristar Sporting Arms, Ltd.

Price: **$549.00**

Price: Model 330D (as above except with three choke tubes, ejectors) . . **$689.00**

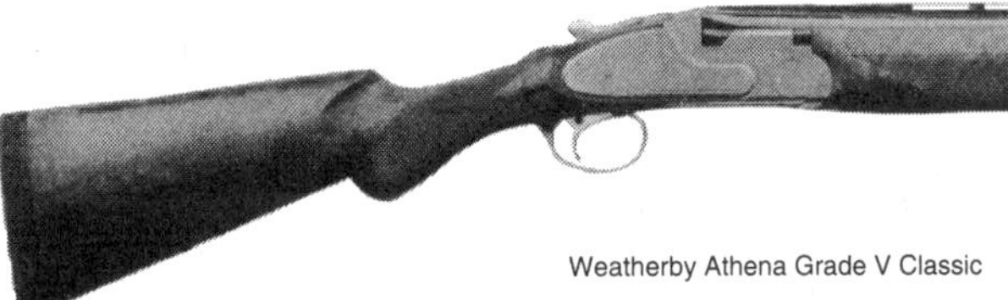

Weatherby Athena Grade V Classic

Weatherby Athena Grade V Classic Field O/U

Similar to the Athena Grade IV except has rounded pistol grip, slender forend, oil-finished Claro walnut stock with fine-line checkering, Old English recoil pad. Sideplate receiver has rose and scroll engraving. Available in 12-gauge, 26″, 28″, 30″, 20-gauge, 26″, 28″, all with 3″ chambers. Introduced 1993.

Price: **$2,527.00**

WEATHERBY ORION O/U SHOTGUNS

Gauge: 12, 20, 3″ chambers.

Barrel: 12-gauge—26″, 28″, 30″; 20-gauge— 26″, 30″; IMC Multi-Choke tubes.

Weight: $6\frac{1}{2}$ to 9 lbs.

Stock: American walnut, checkered grip and forend. Rubber recoil pad. Dimensions for Field and Skeet models, $14\frac{1}{4}$″x$1\frac{1}{2}$″x$2\frac{1}{2}$″.

Features: Selective automatic ejectors, single selective mechanical trigger. Top tang safety, Greener cross bolt. Orion I has plain blued receiver, no engraving; Orion III has silver-gray receiver with engraving. Imported from Japan by Weatherby.

Price: Orion I, Field, 12, IMC, 26″, 28″, 30″ **$1,289.00**

Price: Orion I, Field, 20, IMC, 26″, 28″ **$1,289.00**

Price: Orion III, Field, 12, IMC, 26″, 28″, 30″ **$1,626.00**

Price: Orion III, Field, 20, IMC, 26″, 28″ **$1,626.00**

Weatherby Orion II Classic Sporting Clays O/U

Similar to the Orion II Sporting Clays except has rounded pistol grip, slender forend, high-gloss wood finish. Silver-gray nitride receiver has scroll engraving with clay pigeon monogram in gold-plate overlay. Stepped Broadway-style competition vent. rib, vent. side rib. Available in 12-gauge, 28″, 30″ with choke tubes. Introduced 1993.

Price: **$1,460.00**

WEATHERBY ATHENA GRADE IV O/U SHOTGUNS

Gauge: 12, 20, 3″ chambers.

Action: Boxlock (simulated sidelock) top lever break-open. Selective auto ejectors, single selective trigger (selector inside trigger guard).

Barrel: 26″, 28″, IMC Multi-Choke tubes.

Weight: 12-ga., $7\frac{3}{8}$ lbs.; 20-ga. $6\frac{7}{8}$ lbs.

Stock: American walnut, checkered pistol grip and forend ($14\frac{1}{4}$″x$1\frac{1}{2}$″x$2\frac{1}{2}$″).

Features: Mechanically operated trigger. Top tang safety, Greener cross bolt, fully engraved receiver, recoil pad installed. IMC models furnished with three interchangeable flush-fitting choke tubes. Imported from Japan by Weatherby. Introduced 1982.

Price: 12-ga., IMC, 26″, 28″ **$2,200.00**

Price: 20-ga., IMC, 26″, 28″ **$2,200.00**

Weatherby Orion II, III Classic Field O/Us

Similar to the Orion II, Orion III except with rounded pistol grip, slender forend, high gloss Claro walnut stock with fine-line checkering, Old English recoil pad. Sideplate receiver has rose and scroll engraving. Available in 12-gauge, 26″, 28″, 30″ (IMC tubes), 20-gauge, 26″, 28″ (IMC tubes), 28-gauge, 26″ (IMC tubes), 3″ chambers. Introduced 1993.

Price: Orion II Classic Field **$1,363.00**

Price: Orion III Classic Field (12 and 20 only) **$1,626.00**

Weatherby Orion II Sporting Clays O/U

Similar to the Orion II Field except in 12-gauge only with $2\frac{3}{4}$″ chambers, 28″, 30″ barrels with Imp. Cyl., Mod., Full chokes. High-gloss stock finish. Stock dimensions are $14\frac{1}{4}$″x$1\frac{1}{2}$″x$2\frac{1}{4}$″; weighs 7.5 to 8 lbs. Matte finish, competition center vent. rib, mid-barrel and enlarged front beads. Rounded recoil pad. Receiver finished in silver nitride with acid-etched, gold-plate clay pigeon monogram. Barrels have lengthened forcing cones. Introduced 1992.

Price: **$1,460.00**

SHOTGUNS—SIDE BY SIDES

Variety of models for utility and sporting use, including some competitive shooting.

American Arms Brittany

AMERICAN ARMS BRITTANY SHOTGUN

Gauge: 12, 20, 3″ chambers.
Barrel: 12-ga.—27″; 20-ga.—25″ (Imp. Cyl., Mod., Full choke tubes).
Weight: 6 lbs., 7 oz. (20-ga.).
Stock: $14\frac{1}{8}$″x$1\frac{3}{8}$″x$2\frac{3}{8}$″. Hand-checkered walnut with oil finish, straight English-style with semi-beavertail forend.
Features: Boxlock action with case-color finish, engraving; single selective trigger, automatic selective ejectors; rubber recoil pad. Introduced 1989. Imported from Spain by American Arms, Inc.
Price: **$849.00**

American Arms Gentry

AMERICAN ARMS GENTRY DOUBLE SHOTGUN

Gauge: 12, 20, 410, 3″ chambers; 28 ga. $2\frac{3}{4}$″ chambers.
Barrel: 26″ (Imp. Cyl. & Mod., all gauges), 28″ (Mod., & Full, 12 and 20 gauges).
Weight: $6\frac{1}{4}$ to $6\frac{3}{4}$ lbs.
Stock: $14\frac{1}{8}$″x$1\frac{3}{8}$″x$2\frac{3}{8}$″. Hand-checkered walnut with semi-gloss finish.
Sights: Metal bead front.
Features: Boxlock action with English-style scroll engraving, color case-hardened finish. Double triggers, extractors. Independent floating firing pins. safety. Five-year warranty. Introduced 1987. Imported from Spain by American Arms, Inc.
Price: 12 or 20 . . . . **$725.00**
Price: 28 or 410 . . . . **$757.00**

AMERICAN ARMS TS/SS 12 DOUBLE

Gauge: 12, $3\frac{1}{2}$″ chambers.
Barrel: 26″, choke tubes; solid raised rib.
Weight: 7 lbs., 6 oz.
Stock: Walnut; cut-checked grip and forend.
Features: Non-reflective metal and wood finishes; boxlock action; single trigger; extractors. Imported by American Arms, Inc.
Price: **$750.00**

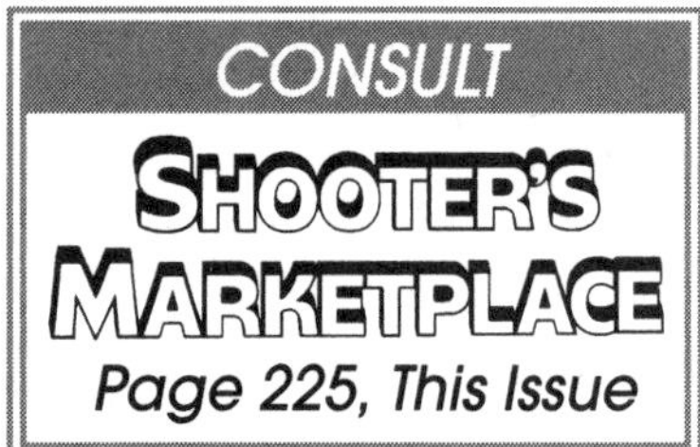
CONSULT
SHOOTER'S
MARKETPLACE
Page 225, This Issue

ARMSPORT 1050 SERIES DOUBLE SHOTGUNS

Gauge: 12, 20, 410, 28, 3″ chambers.
Barrel: 12-ga.—28″ (Mod. & Full); 20-ga.—26″ (Imp. & Mod.); 410—26″ (Full & Full); 28-ga.—26″ (Mod. & Full).
Weight: About $6\frac{3}{4}$ lbs.
Stock: European walnut.
Features: Chrome-lined barrels. Boxlock action with engraving. Imported from Italy by Armsport.
Price: 12, 20 . . . . **$785.00**
Price: 28, 410 . . . . **$860.00**

ARRIETA SIDELOCK DOUBLE SHOTGUNS

Gauge: 12, 16, 20, 28, 410.
Barrel: Length and chokes to customer specs.
Weight: To customer specs.
Stock: $14\frac{1}{2}$″x$1\frac{1}{2}$″x$2\frac{1}{2}$ (standard dimensions), or to customer specs. Straight English with checkered butt (standard), or pistol grip. Select European walnut with oil finish.
Features: Essentially a custom gun with myriad options. Holland & Holland-pattern hand-detachable sidelocks, selective automatic ejectors, double triggers (hinged front) standard. Some have self-opening action. Finish and engraving to customer specs. Imported from Spain by Wingshooting Adventures.
Price: Model 557, auto ejectors, from **$2,750.00**
Price: Model 570, auto ejectors, from **$3,380.00**
Price: Model 578, auto ejectors, from **$3,740.00**
Price: Model 600 Imperial, self-opening, from **$4,990.00**
Price: Model 601 Imperial Tiro, self-opening, from **$5,750.00**
Price: Model 801, from **$7,950.00**
Price: Model 802, from **$7,950.00**
Price: Model 803, from **$5,850.00**
Price: Model 871, auto ejectors, from **$4,290.00**
Price: Model 872, self-opening, from **$9,790.00**
Price: Model 873, self-opening, from **$6,850.00**
Price: Model 874, self-opening, from **$7,950.00**
Price: Model 875, self-opening, from **$12,950.00**

AYA Model XXV Boxlock

AYA BOXLOCK SHOTGUNS

Gauge: 12, 16, 20, 28, 410.
Barrel: 26″, 27″, 28″, depending upon gauge.
Weight: 5 to 7 lbs.
Stock: European walnut.
Features: Anson & Deeley system with double locking lugs; chopper lump barrels; bushed firing pins; automatic safety and ejectors; articulated front trigger. Imported by Armes de Chasse.
Price: Model 931, self-opening, from **$14,500.00**
Price: Model XXV, 12 or 20 . . . . **$3,000.00**
Price: Model 4 Deluxe, 12, 16, 20, 28, 410 . . . . **$3,000.00**
Price: Model 4, 12, 16, 20, 28, 410 . . . . **$1,700.00**

ARIZAGA MODEL 31 DOUBLE SHOTGUN

Gauge: 12, 16, 20, 28, 410.
Barrel: 26″, 28″ (standard chokes).
Weight: 6 lbs., 9 oz. **Length:** 45″ overall.
Stock: Straight English style or pistol grip.
Features: Boxlock action with double triggers; blued, engraved receiver. Imported by Mandall Shooting Supplies.
Price: **$550.00**

CAUTION: PRICES SHOWN ARE SUPPLIED BY THE MANUFACTURER OR IMPORTER. CHECK YOUR LOCAL GUNSHOP.

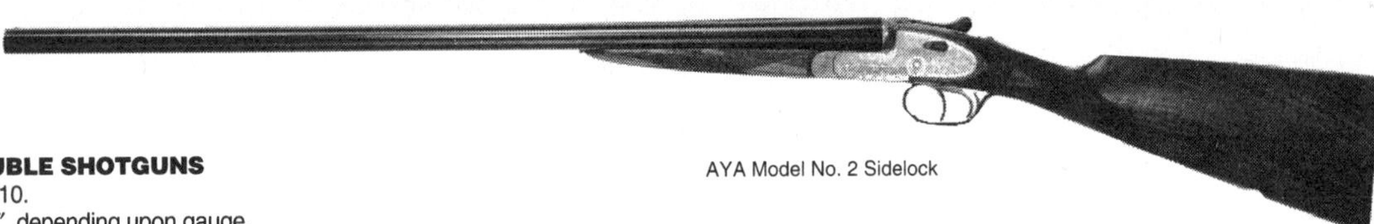

AYA Model No. 2 Sidelock

AYA SIDELOCK DOUBLE SHOTGUNS
Gauge: 12, 16, 20, 28, 410.
Barrel: 26", 27", 28", 29", depending upon gauge.
Weight: NA.
Stock: Figured European walnut; cut checkering; oil finish.
Features: Sidelock actions with double triggers (articulated front), automatic safety, automatic ejectors, cocking indicators, bushed firing pins, replaceable hinge pins, chopper lump barrels. Many options available. Imported by Armes de Chasse.
Price: Model 1, 12 or 20, exhibition-quality wood **$6,600.00**
Price: Model 2, 12, 16, 20, 28, 410 .... **$3,200.00**
Price: Model 53, 12, 16, 20 .... **$5,000.00**
Price: Model 56, 12 only **$8,000.00**
Price: Model XXV, 12 or 20, Churchill-type rib **$4,000.00**

BAIKAL IJ-43M DOUBLE SHOTGUN
Gauge: 12, 2¾" chambers.
Barrel: 28.5" (Mod. & Full).
Weight: NA. **Length:** 44.5" overall.
Stock: European hardwood.
Features: Blued boxlock action with double triggers, extractors, automatic safety; sling swivels. Chrome-lined bores. Imported from Russia by Century International Arms.
Price: About **$255.00**
Price: IJ-43EM (automatic ejectors), about **$270.00**

AUGUSTE FRANCOTTE BOXLOCK SHOTGUN
Gauge: 12, 16, 20, 28 and 410-bore, 2¾" or 3" chambers.
Barrel: 26" to 29", chokes to customer specs.
Weight: NA. **Length:** NA.
Stock: Deluxe European walnut to customer specs. Straight or pistol grip; checkered butt; oil finish; splinter or beavertail forend.
Sights: Bead front.
Features: Anson & Deeley boxlock action with double locks, double triggers (front hinged), manual or automatic safety, Holland & Holland ejectors. English scroll engraving, coin finish or color case-hardening. Custom made to customer's specs. Many options available. Imported from Belgium by Armes de Chasse.
Price: From about (no engraving) **$16,500.00**

BAIKAL IJ-43 DOUBLE SHOTGUN
Gauge: 12, 2¾" chambers.
Barrel: 20" (Cyl. & Cyl.), 28" (Mod. & Full).
Weight: About 6.75 lbs.
Stock: Checkered walnut.
Features: Double triggers; extractors; blued, engraved receiver. Reintroduced 1994. Imported from Russia by K.B.I., Inc.
Price: **$249.00**

BERETTA MODEL 452 SIDELOCK SHOTGUN
Gauge: 12, 2¾" or 3" chambers.
Barrel: 26", 28", 30", choked to customer specs.
Weight: 6 lbs., 13 oz.
Stock: Dimensions to customer specs. Highly figured walnut; Model 452 EELL has walnut briar.
Features: Full sidelock action with English-type double bolting; automatic selective ejectors, manual safety; double triggers, single or single non-selective trigger on request. Essentially custom made to specifications. Model 452 is coin finished without engraving; 452 EELL is fully engraved. Imported from Italy by Beretta U.S.A.
Price: 452 .... **$22,500.00**
Price: 452 EELL **$31,000.00**

AUGUSTE FRANCOTTE SIDELOCK SHOTGUN
Gauge: 12, 16, 20, 28 and 410-bore, 2¾" or 3" chambers.
Barrel: 26" to 29", chokes to customer specs.
Weight: NA. **Length:** NA.
Stock: Deluxe European walnut to customer specs. Straight or pistol grip; checkered butt; oil finish; splinter or beavertail forend.
Sights: Bead front.
Features: True Holland & Holland sidelock action with double locks, double triggers (front hinged), manual or automatic safety, Holland & Holland ejectors. English scroll engraving, coin finish or color case-hardening. Many options available. Imported from Belgium by Armes de Chasse.
Price: From about (no engraving) .... **$20,000.00** to **$25,000.00**

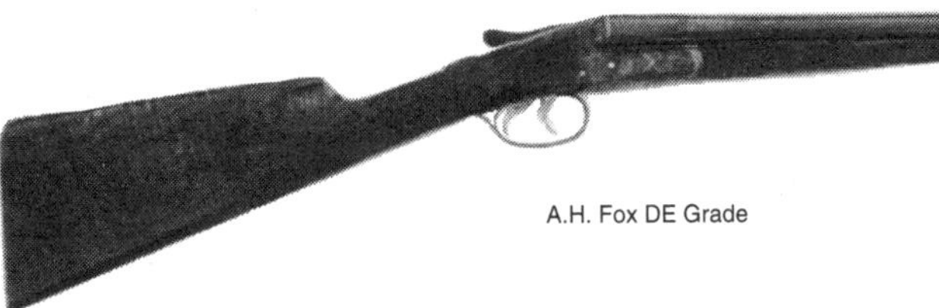

A.H. Fox DE Grade

A.H. FOX SIDE-BY-SIDE SHOTGUNS
Gauge: 16, 20, 28, 410.
Barrel: Length and chokes to customer specifications. Rust-blued Chromox or Krupp steel.
Weight: 5½ to 6¾ lbs.
Stock: Dimensions to customer specifications. Hand-checkered Turkish Circassian walnut with hand-rubbed oil finish. Straight, semi- or full pistol grip; splinter, schnabel or beavertail forend; traditional pad, hard rubber buttplate or skeleton butt.
Features: Boxlock action with automatic ejectors; double or Fox single selective trigger. Scalloped, rebated and color case-hardened receiver; hand finished and hand-engraved. Grades differ in engraving, inlays, grade of wood, amount of hand finishing. Introduced 1993. Made in U.S. by Connecticut Shotgun Mfg.
Price: CE Grade **$7,200.00**
Price: XE Grade **$8,500.00**
Price: DE Grade **$12,500.00**
Price: FE Grade **$17,500.00**
Price: Exhibition Grade **$25,000.000**
Price: 28/410 CE Grade **$8,200.00**
Price: 28/410 XE Grade **$9,700.00**
Price: 28/410 DE Grade **$13,800.00**
Price: 28/410 FE Grade **$14,700.00**
Price: 28/410 Exhibition Grade **$25,000.00**

Garbi Model 100

Garbi Model 103A, B Side-by-Side
Similar to the Garbi Model 100 except has Purdey-type fine scroll and rosette engraving. Better overall quality than the Model 101. Model 103B has nickel-chrome steel barrels, H&H-type easy opening mechanism; other mechanical details remain the same. Imported from Spain by Wm. Larkin Moore.
Price: Model 103A, from **$7,100.00**
Price: Model 103B, from **$9,800.00**

GARBI MODEL 100 DOUBLE
Gauge: 12, 16, 20, 28.
Barrel: 26", 28", choked to customer specs.
Weight: 5½ to 7½ lbs.
Stock: 14½"x2¼"x1½". European walnut. Straight grip, checkered butt, classic forend.
Features: Sidelock action, automatic ejectors, double triggers standard. Color case-hardened action, coin finish optional. Single trigger; beavertail forend, etc. optional. Five other models are available. Imported from Spain by Wm. Larkin Moore.
Price: From **$4,500.00**

Garbi Model 101 Side-by-Side

Similar to the Garbi Model 100 except is hand engraved with scroll engraving, select walnut stock. Better overall quality than the Model 100. Imported from Spain by Wm. Larkin Moore.

Price: From $5,800.00

HATFIELD UPLANDER SHOTGUN

Gauge: 20, 3″ chambers.
Barrel: 26″ (Imp. Cyl. & Mod.).
Weight: $5\frac{3}{4}$ lbs.
Stock: Straight English style, special select XXX fancy maple. Hand-rubbed oil finish. Splinter forend.
Features: Double locking under-lug boxlock action; color case-hardened frame; single non-selective trigger. Grades differ in engraving, finish, gold work. Introduced 1988. From Hatfield.
Price: Grade I $2,249.00
Price: Grade II $2,995.00

CRUCELEGUI HERMANOS MODEL 150 DOUBLE

Gauge: 12, 16 or 20, $2\frac{3}{4}$″ chambers.
Action: Greener triple cross bolt.
Barrel: 20″, 26″, 28″, 30″, 32″ (Cyl. & Cyl., Full & Full, Mod. & Full, Mod. & Imp. Cyl., Imp. Cyl. & Full, Mod. & Mod.).
Weight: 5 to $7\frac{1}{4}$ lbs.
Stock: Hand-checkered walnut, beavertail forend.
Features: Double triggers; color case-hardened receiver; sling swivels; chrome-lined bores. Imported from Spain by Mandall Shooting Supplies.
Price: $450.00

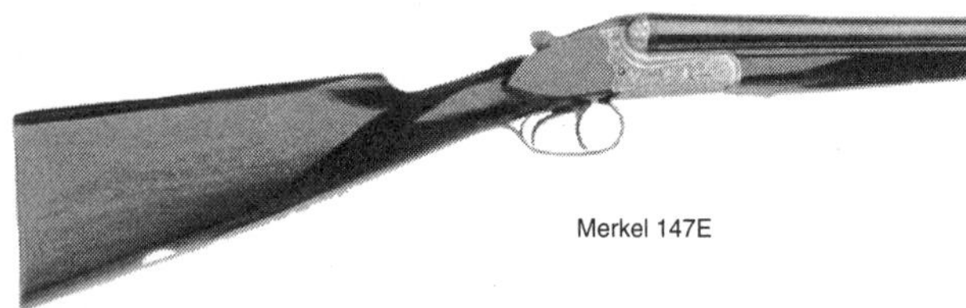

Merkel 147E

Merkel Model 47S, 147S Side-by-Sides

Similar to the Model 122 except with Holland & Holland-style sidelock action with cocking indicators, ejectors. Silver-grayed receiver and sideplates have Arabesque engraving, engraved border and screws (Model 47S), or fine hunting scene engraving (Model 147S). Imported from Germany by GSI.

Price: Model 47S $4,495.00
Price: Model 147S $5,595.00
Price: Model 247S (English-style engraving, large scrolls) $6,895.00
Price: Model 347S (English-style engraving, medium scrolls) $7,895.00
Price: Model 447S (English-style engraving, small scrolls) $8,995.00

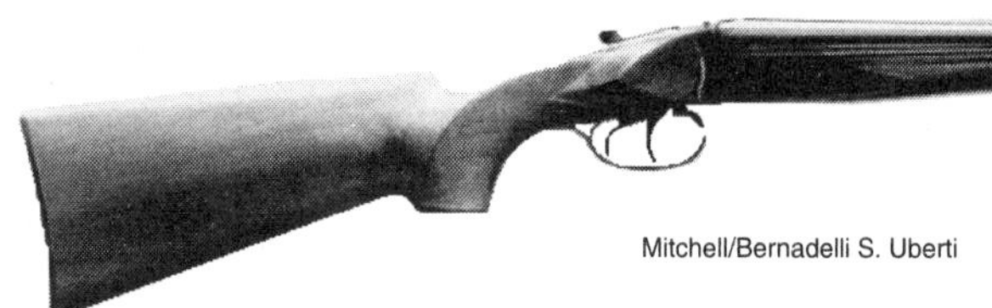

Mitchell/Bernadelli S. Uberti

Mitchell/Bernardelli Series Roma Shotguns

Similar to the Series S. Uberto models except with dummy sideplates to simulate sidelock action. In 12-, 16-, 20-, 28-gauge, $25\frac{1}{2}$″, $26\frac{3}{4}$″, 28″, 29″ barrels. Straight English or pistol grip stock. Chrome-lined barrels, boxlock action, double triggers, ejectors, automatic safety. Checkered butt. Special choke combinations, barrel lengths available. Imported from Italy by Mitchell Arms.

Price: Roma 3, extractors, about $1,470.00
Price: Roma 4, about $1,800.00
Price: Roma 6, about $1,970.00
Price: Roma 7M, ejectors, about $2,750.00
Price: Roma 8M, ejectors, about $3,250.00
Price: Roma 9M, ejectors, about $3,850.00
Price: Las Palomas, 12, 20, about $3,350.00

Garbi Model 200 Side-by-Side

Similar to the Garbi Model 100 except has heavy-duty locks, magnum proofed. Very fine Continental-style floral and scroll engraving, well figured walnut stock. Other mechanical features remain the same. Imported from Spain by Wm. Larkin Moore.

Price: $9,375.00

Hatfield Uplander

HHF MODEL 200 A 12 ST SIDE-BY-SIDE

Gauge: 12, 3″ chambers.
Barrel: 28″, fixed chokes or choke tubes.
Weight: About $7\frac{1}{2}$ lbs.
Stock: Circassian walnut, field dimensions.
Features: Boxlock action with single selective trigger, extractors, manual safety. Silvered receiver with 15 percent engraving coverage. Many options available. Introduced 1995. Imported from Turkey by Turkish Firearms Corp.
Price: Fixed chokes, extractors $1,050.00
Price: As above, 28, 410 .... $1,495.00
Price: Choke tubes, extractors $1,050.00
Price: Model 202 A 12 ST (double triggers, 30 percent engraving coverage $1,025.00
Price: As above, 28, 410 .... $1,495.00
Price: With extractors, choke tubes, 12, 20 .... $1,025.00

MERKEL MODEL 8, 47E SIDE-BY-SIDE SHOTGUNS

Gauge: 12, 3″ chambers, 16, $2\frac{3}{4}$″ chambers, 20, 3″ chambers.
Barrel: 12-, 16-ga.—28″; 20-ga.—$26\frac{3}{4}$″ (Imp. Cyl. & Mod., Mod. & Full).
Weight: About $6\frac{3}{4}$ lbs. (12-ga.).
Stock: Oil-finished walnut; straight English or pistol grip.
Features: Anson & Deeley-type boxlock action with single selective or double triggers, automatic safety, cocking indicators. Color case-hardened receiver with standard Arabesque engraving. Imported from Germany by GSI.
Price: Model 8 (extractors only) $1,395.00
Price: Model 47E (H&H ejectors) $1,795.00
Price: Model 147 (extractors, silver-grayed receiver with hunting scenes) $1,895.00
Price: Model 147E (as above with ejectors) $2,295.00
Price: Model 122 (as above with false sideplates, fine engraving) $3,795.00

MITCHELL/BERNARDELLI SERIES S. UBERTO DOUBLES

Gauge: 12, 20, 28, $2\frac{3}{4}$″ or 3″ chambers.
Barrel: $25\frac{5}{8}$″, $26\frac{3}{4}$″, 28″, $29\frac{1}{2}$″ (Mod. & Full).
Weight: 6 to $6\frac{1}{2}$ lbs.
Stock: $14\frac{3}{16}$″x$2\frac{3}{8}$″x$1\frac{9}{16}$″ standard dimensions. Select walnut with hand checkering.
Features: Anson & Deeley boxlock action with Purdey locks, choice of extractors or ejectors. Custom options available. Imported from Italy by Mitchell Arms.
Price: With ejectors $1,555.00
Price: With extractors $1,435.00
Price: F.S. model, ejectors $1,750.00

MITCHELL/BERNARDELLI HEMINGWAY LIGHTWEIGHT DOUBLES

Gauge: 12, 20, $2\frac{3}{4}$″ or 3″, 16, $2\frac{3}{4}$″ chambers.
Barrel: $23\frac{1}{2}$″ to 28″ (Cyl. & Imp. Cyl. to Mod. & Full).
Weight: $6\frac{1}{4}$ lbs.
Stock: Straight English grip of checkered European walnut.
Features: Silvered and engraved boxlock action. Folding front trigger on double-trigger models. Ejectors. Imported from Italy by Mitchell Arms.
Price: 12 or 20 .... $1,750.00
Price: With single trigger $1,800.00
Price: Deluxe, double trigger $1,900.00
Price: As above, single trigger $2,000.00

CAUTION: PRICES SHOWN ARE SUPPLIED BY THE MANUFACTURER OR IMPORTER. CHECK YOUR LOCAL GUNSHOP.

PARKER REPRODUCTIONS SIDE-BY-SIDE SHOTGUN
Gauge: 12, 16/20 combo, 20, 28, 2¾″ and 3″ chambers.
Barrel: 26″ (Skeet 1 & 2, Imp. Cyl. & Mod.), 28″ (Mod. & Full, 2¾″ and 3″, 12, 20, 28; Skeet 1 & 2, Imp. Cyl. & Mod., Mod. & Full 16-ga. only).
Weight: 6¾ lbs. (12-ga.)
Stock: Checkered (26 lpi) AAA fancy California English or Claro walnut, skeleton steel and checkered butt. Straight or pistol grip, splinter or beavertail forend.
Features: Exact reproduction of the original Parker—parts interchange. Double or single selective trigger, selective ejectors, hard-chromed bores, designed for steel shot. One, two or three (16-20, 20) barrel sets available. Hand-engraved snap caps included. Introduced 1984. Made by Winchester. Imported from Japan by Parker Division, Reagent Chemical.
Price: D Grade, one-barrel set **$3,370.00**
Price: Two-barrel set, same gauge **$4,200.00**
Price: Two-barrel set, 16/20 .... **$4,870.00**
Price: Three-barrel set, 16/20/20 .... **$5,630.00**
Price: A-1 Special two-barrel set **$11,200.00**
Price: A-1 Special three-barrel set **$13,200.00**

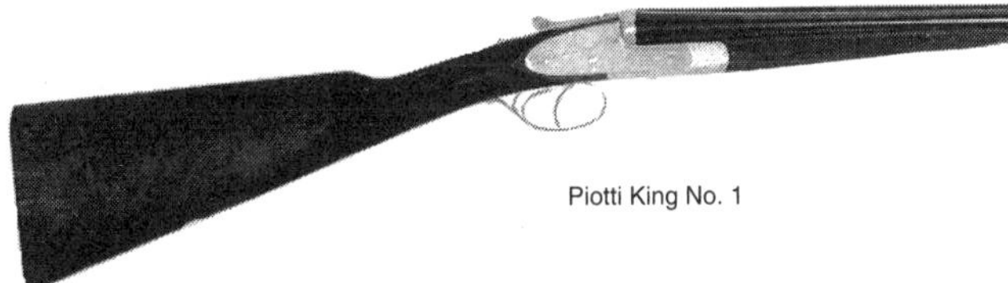
Piotti King No. 1

Piotti Lunik Side-by-Side
Similar to the Piotti King No. 1 except better overall quality. Has Renaissance-style large scroll engraving in relief, gold crown in top lever, gold name and gold crest in forend. Best quality Holland & Holland-pattern sidelock ejector double with chopper lump (demi-bloc) barrels. Other mechanical specifications remain the same. Imported from Italy by Wm. Larkin Moore.
Price: From **$22,200.00**

Piotti King Extra Side-by-Side
Similar to the Piotti King No. 1 except highest quality wood and metal work. Choice of either bulino game scene engraving or game scene engraving with gold inlays. Engraved and signed by a master engraver. Exhibition grade wood. Other mechanical specifications remain the same. Imported from Italy by Wm. Larkin Moore.
Price: From **$26,500.00**

RIZZINI SIDELOCK SIDE-BY-SIDE
Gauge: 12, 16, 20, 28, 410.
Barrel: 25″ to 30″ (12-, 16-, 20-ga.), 25″ to 28″ (28, 410). To customer specs. Chokes as specified.
Weight: 6½ lbs. to 8 lbs. (12-ga. to customer specs).
Stock: Dimensions to customer specs. Finely figured walnut; straight grip with checkered butt with classic splinter forend and hand-rubbed oil finish standard. Pistol grip, beavertail forend, satin luster finish optional.
Features: Holland & Holland pattern sidelock action, auto ejectors. Double triggers with front trigger hinged optional; non-selective single trigger standard. Coin finish standard. Top rib level, file cut standard; concave optional. Imported from Italy by Wm. Larkin Moore.
Price: 12-, 20-ga., from **$43,700.00**
Price: 28, 410 bore, from **$48,700.00**

PIOTTI KING NO. 1 SIDE-BY-SIDE
Gauge: 12, 16, 20, 28, 410.
Barrel: 25″ to 30″ (12-ga.), 25″ to 28″ (16, 20, 28, 410). To customer specs. Chokes as specified.
Weight: 6½ lbs. to 8 lbs. (12-ga. to customer specs.).
Stock: Dimensions to customer specs. Finely figured walnut; straight grip with checkered butt with classic splinter forend and hand-rubbed oil finish standard. Pistol grip, beavertail forend, satin luster finish optional.
Features: Holland & Holland pattern sidelock action, automatic ejectors. Double trigger with front trigger hinged standard; non-selective single trigger optional. Coin finish standard; color case-hardened optional. Top rib; level, file-cut standard; concave, ventilated optional. Very fine, full coverage scroll engraving with small floral bouquets, gold crown in top lever, name in gold, and gold crest in forend. Imported from Italy by Wm. Larkin Moore.
Price: From **$20,600.00**

PIOTTI PIUMA SIDE-BY-SIDE
Gauge: 12, 16, 20, 28, 410.
Barrel: 25″ to 30″ (12-ga.), 25″ to 28″ (16, 20, 28, 410).
Weight: 5½ to 6¼ lbs. (20-ga.).
Stock: Dimensions to customer specs. Straight grip stock with walnut checkered butt, classic splinter forend, hand-rubbed oil finish are standard; pistol grip, beavertail forend, satin luster finish optional.
Features: Anson & Deeley boxlock ejector double with chopper lump barrels. Level, file-cut rib, light scroll and rosette engraving, scalloped frame. Double triggers with hinged front standard, single non-selective optional. Coin finish standard, color case-hardened optional. Imported from Italy by Wm. Larkin Moore.
Price: From **$11,800.00**

Consult our Directory pages for the location of firms mentioned.

SKB Model 385

SKB MODEL 385 SIDE-BY-SIDE
Gauge: 20, 3″ chambers; 28, 23/4″ chambers.
Barrel: 26″ (Imp. Cyl., Mod., Skeet choke tubes).
Weight: 6¾ lbs. **Length:** 42½″ overall.
Stock: 14⅛″x1½″x2½″ American walnut with straight or pistol grip stock, semi-beavertail forend.
Features: Boxlock action. Silver nitrided receiver with engraving; solid barrel rib; single selective trigger, selective automatic ejectors, automatic safety. Introduced 1996. Imported from Japan by G.U. Inc.
Price: **$1,695.00**

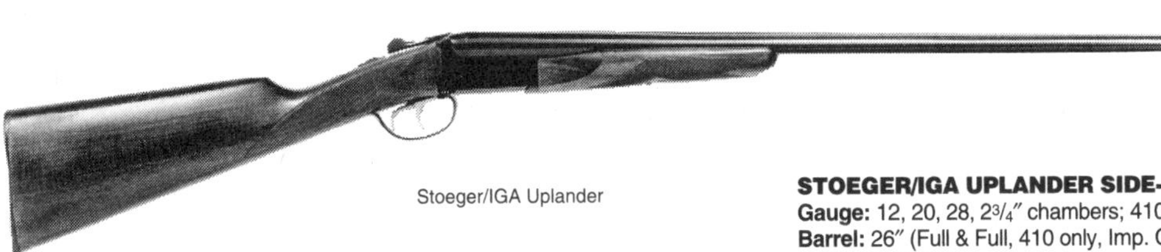
Stoeger/IGA Uplander

Stoeger/IGA English Stock Side-by-Side
Similar to the Uplander except in 410-bore only with 24″ barrels (Mod. & Mod.), straight English stock and beavertail forend. Has automatic safety, extractors, double triggers. Intro 1996. Imported from Brazil by Stoeger.
Price: **$398.00**

STOEGER/IGA UPLANDER SIDE-BY-SIDE SHOTGUN
Gauge: 12, 20, 28, 2¾″ chambers; 410, 3″ chambers.
Barrel: 26″ (Full & Full, 410 only, Imp. Cyl. & Mod.), 28″ (Mod. & Full).
Weight: 6¾ to 7 lbs.
Stock: 14½″x1½″x2½″. Oil-finished hardwood. Checkered pistol grip and forend.
Features: Automatic safety, extractors only, solid matted barrel rib. Double triggers only. Introduced 1983. Imported from Brazil by Stoeger Industries.
Price: **$398.00**
Price: With choke tubes **$442.00**
Price: Coach Gun, 12, 20, 410, 20″ bbls. **$382.00**
Price: Coach Gun, nickel finish, black stock **$424.00**
Price: Coach Gun, engraved stock **$412.00**

Stoeger/IGA Youth Side-by-Side
Similar to the Uplander except in 410-bore with 24″ barrels (Mod. & Full), 13″ length of pull, ventilated recoil pad. Has double triggers, extractors, auto safety. Intro 1996. Imported from Brazil by Stoeger.
Price: $408.00

Stoeger/IGA Ladies Side-by-Side
Similar to the Uplander except in 20-ga. only with 24″ barrels (Imp. Cyl. & Mod. choke tubes), 13″ length of pull, ventilated rubber recoil pad. Has extractors, double triggers, automatic safety. Introduced 1996. Imported from Brazil by Stoeger.
Price: $450.00

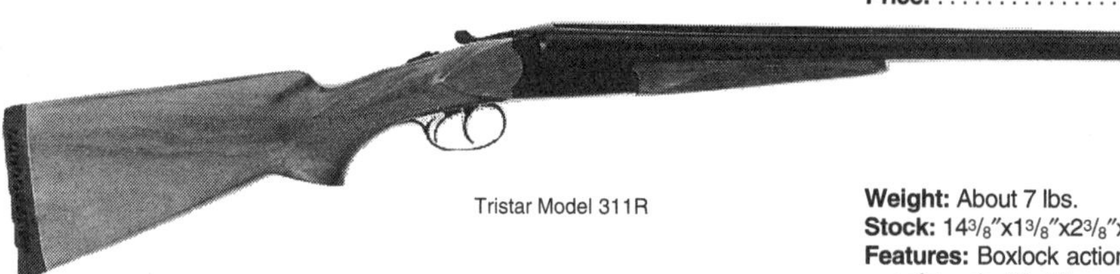
Tristar Model 311R

TRISTAR MODEL 311 DOUBLE
Gauge: 12, 20, 3″ chambers.
Barrel: 26″, 28″, five choke tubes.
Weight: About 7 lbs.
Stock: 14 3/8″x1 3/8″x2 3/8″x3/8″; hand-checkered Turkish walnut; recoil pad.
Features: Boxlock action; underlug and Greener bolt lockup; extractors, manual safety, double triggers. Black chrome finish. Introduced 1996. Imported from Turkey by Tristar Sporting Arms, Ltd.
Price: $599.00
Price: Model 311R (20″ Cyl. & Cyl. barrels) $429.00

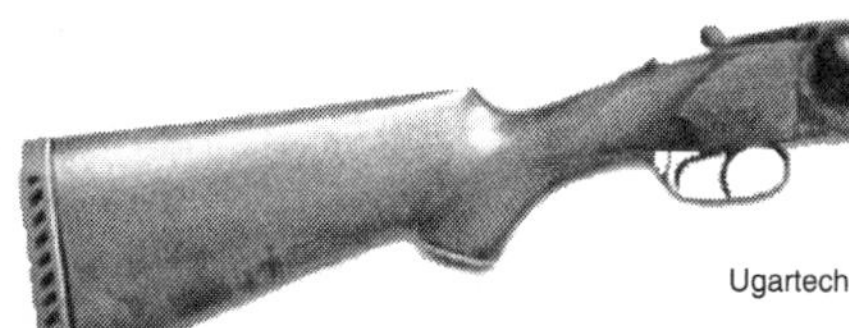
Ugartechea 10-Gauge Magnum

UGARTECHEA 10-GAUGE MAGNUM SHOTGUN
Gauge: 10, 3 1/2″ chambers.
Action: Boxlock.
Barrel: 32″ (Full).
Weight: 11 lbs.
Stock: 14 1/2″x1 1/2″x2 5/8″. European walnut, checkered at pistol grip and forend.
Features: Double triggers; color case-hardened action, rest blued. Front and center metal beads on matted rib; ventilated rubber recoil pad. Forend release has positive Purdey-type mechanism. Imported from Spain by Mandall Shooting Supplies.
Price: $699.50

SHOTGUNS—BOLT ACTIONS & SINGLE SHOTS

Variety of designs for utility and sporting purposes, as well as for competitive shooting.

BAIKAL IJ-18 SINGLE BARREL SHOTGUN
Gauge: 12, 3″ chamber.
Barrel: 28.5″.
Weight: 6 lbs. **Length:** 44.5″ overall.
Stock: European hardwood.
Features: Chrome-lined bore; extractor; cocking indicator; cross-bolt safety. Imported from Russia by Century International Arms.
Price: About $95.00
Price: IJ-18EM (automatic ejector), about $108.00

BAIKAL IJ-18M SHOTGUN
Gauge: 12, 16, 2 3/4″, 20, 410, 3″ chamber.
Barrel: 12, 20-ga.—26″ (Imp. Cyl.), 410 (Full); 12, 20-ga.—28″ (Full, Mod.).
Weight: 5.5 to 6 lbs.
Stock: Stained hardwood.
Features: External hammer with cocking indicator; trigger block safety; engraved, blued receiver. Reintroduced 1994. Imported from Russia by K.B.I., Inc.
Price: $69.00

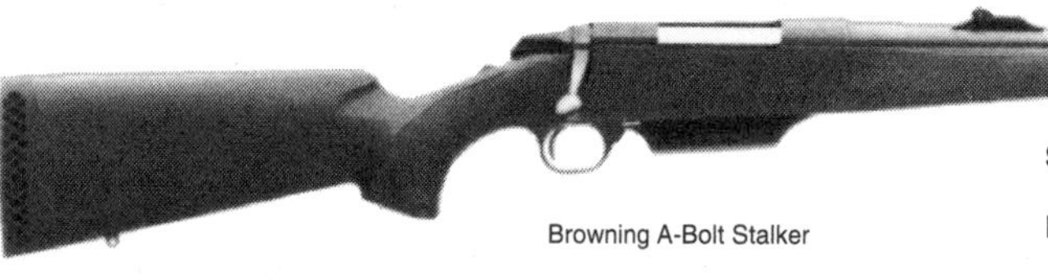
Browning A-Bolt Stalker

BROWNING A-BOLT SHOTGUN
Gauge: 12, 3″ chamber, 2-shot detachable magazine.
Barrel: 22″ (fully rifled), 23″ (5″ Invector choke tubes).
Weight: 7 lbs., 2 oz. **Length:** 44 3/4″ overall.
Stock: 14″x5/8″x1/2″. Walnut with satin finish on Hunter; Stalker has black graphite fiberglass composite. Swivel studs.
Sights: Blade front with red insert, open adjustable rear or none. Drilled and tapped for scope mounting.
Features: Uses same bolt system as A-Bolt rifle with 60° bolt throw; front-locking bolt with claw extractor; hinged floorplate. Matte finish on barrel and receiver. Introduced 1995. Imported by Browning.
Price: Hunter, rifled choke tube, open sights $828.95
Price: As above, no sights $804.95
Price: Hunter, rifled barrel, open sights $881.95
Price: As above, no sights $856.95
Price: Stalker, rifled, choke tube, open sights $744.95
Price: As above, no sights $719.95
Price: Stalker, rifled barrel, no sights $772.95

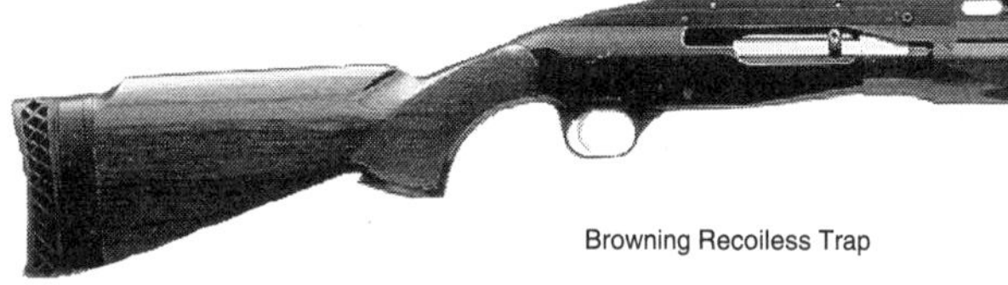
Browning Recoiless Trap

BROWNING RECOILLESS TRAP SHOTGUN
Gauge: 12, 2 3/4″ chamber.
Barrel: Back-bored 30″ (Invector Plus tubes).
Weight: 9 lbs., 1 oz. **Length:** 51 5/8″ overall.
Stock: 14″-14 3/4″x1 3/8″-1 3/4″x1 1/8″-1 3/4″. Select walnut with high gloss finish, cut checkering.
Features: Eliminates up to 72 percent of recoil. Mass of the inner mechansim (barrel, receiver and inner bolt) is driven forward when trigger is pulled, cancelling most recoil. Forend is used to cock action when the action is forward. Ventilated rib adjusts to move point of impact; drop at comb and length of pull adjustable. Introduced 1993. Imported by Browning.
Price: $1,995.00

Browning Micro Recoilless Trap Shotgun
Same as the standard Recoilless Trap except has 27″ barrel, weighs 8 lbs., 10 oz., and stock length of pull adjustable from 13″ to 13 3/4″, Overall length 47 5/8″. Introduced 1993. Imported by Browning.
Price: $1,995.00

CAUTION: PRICES SHOWN ARE SUPPLIED BY THE MANUFACTURER OR IMPORTER. CHECK YOUR LOCAL GUNSHOP.

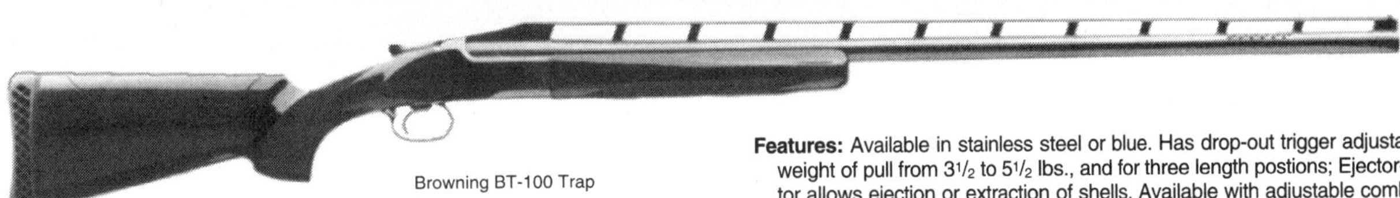
Browning BT-100 Trap

BROWNING BT-100 TRAP SHOTGUN

Gauge: 12, 2$^{3}/_{4}$″ chamber.
Barrel: 32″, 34″ (Invector Plus); back-bored; also with fixed Full choke.
Weight: 8 lbs., 9 oz. **Length:** 48$^{1}/_{2}$″ overall (32″ barrel).
Stock: 14$^{3}/_{8}$″x1$^{9}/_{16}$″x1$^{7}/_{16}$x2″ (Monte Carlo); 14$^{3}/_{8}$″x1$^{3}/_{4}$″x1$^{1}/_{4}$″x2$^{1}/_{8}$″ (thumbhole). Walnut with high gloss finish; cut checkering. Wedge-shaped forend with finger groove.
Features: Available in stainless steel or blue. Has drop-out trigger adjustable for weight of pull from 3$^{1}/_{2}$ to 5$^{1}/_{2}$ lbs., and for three length postions; Ejector-Selector allows ejection or extraction of shells. Available with adjustable comb stock and thumbhole style. Introduced 1995. Imported from Japan by Browning.
Price: Grade I, blue, Monte Carlo, Invector Plus **$1,995.00**
Price: As above, fixed Full choke **$1,948.00**
Price: Stainless steel, Monte Carlo, Invector Plus **$2,415.00**
Price: As above, fixed Full choke **$2,368.00**
Price: Thumbhole stock, blue, Invector Plus **$2,270.00**
Price: Thumbhole stock, stainless, Invector Plus **$2,690.00**
Price: Adjustable comb stock, add **$210.00**
Price: Replacement trigger assembly **$525.00**

H&R SB2-980 Ultra Slug

HARRINGTON & RICHARDSON SB2-980 ULTRA SLUG

Gauge: 12, 20, 3″ chamber.
Barrel: 22″ (20 ga. Youth) 24″, fully rifled.
Weight: 9 lbs. **Length:** NA.
Stock: Walnut-stained hardwood.
Sights: None furnished; comes with scope mount.
Features: Uses the H&R 10-gauge action with heavy-wall barrel. Monte Carlo stock has sling swivels; comes with black nylon sling. Introduced 1995. Made in U.S. by H&R 1871, Inc.
Price: **$209.95**

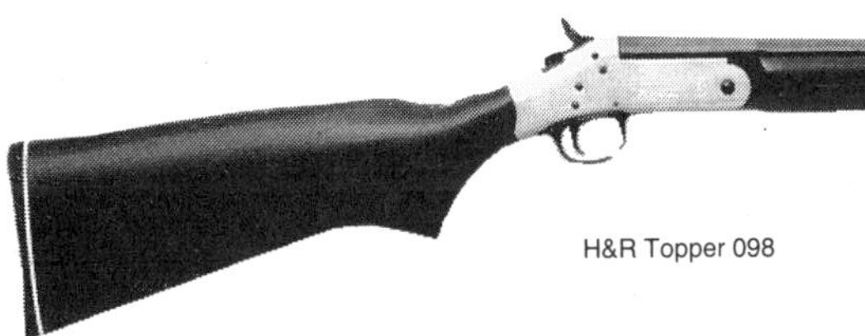
H&R Topper 098

HARRINGTON & RICHARDSON TOPPER MODEL 098

Gauge: 12, 16, 20, 28 (2$^{3}/_{4}$″), 410, 3″ chamber.
Barrel: 12 ga.—28″ (Mod., Full); 16 ga.— 28″ (Mod.); 20 ga.—26″ (Mod.); 28 ga.—26″ (Mod.); 410 bore—26″ (Full).
Weight: 5-6 lbs.
Stock: Black-finish hardwood with full pistol grip; semi-beavertail forend.
Sights: Gold bead front.
Features: Break-open action with side-lever release, automatic ejector. Satin nickel frame, blued barrel. Reintroduced 1992. From H&R 1871, Inc.
Price: **$114.95**
Price: Topper Junior 098 (as above except 22″ barrel, 20-ga. (Mod.), 410-bore (Full), 12$^{1}/_{2}$″ length of pull) **$119.95**

Consult our Directory pages for the location of firms mentioned.

Harrington & Richardson Topper Junior Classic Shotgun

Similar to the Topper Junior 098 except available in 20-gauge (3″, Mod.), 410-bore (Full) with 3″ chamber; 28-gauge, 2$^{3}/_{4}$″ chamber (Mod.); all have 22″ barrel. Stock is American black walnut with cut-checkered pistol grip and forend. Ventilated rubber recoil pad with white line spacers. Blued barrel, blued frame. Introduced 1992. From H&R 1871, Inc.
Price: **$144.95**

Harrington & Richardson Topper Deluxe Model 098

Similar to the standard Topper 098 except 12-gauge only with 3$^{1}/_{2}$″ chamber, 28″ barrel with choke tube (comes with Mod. tube, others optional). Satin nickel frame, blued barrel, black-finished wood. Introduced 1992. From H&R 1871, Inc.
Price: **$134.95**

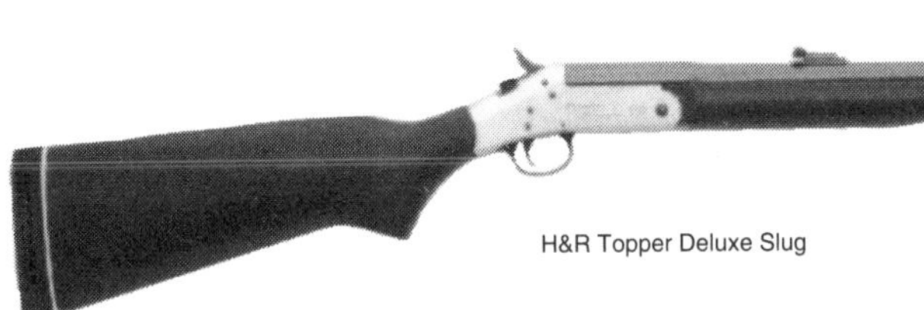
H&R Topper Deluxe Slug

Harrington & Richardson Topper Deluxe Rifled Slug Gun

Similar to the 12-gauge Topper Model 098 except has fully rifled and ported barrel, ramp front sight and fully adjustable rear. Barrel twist is 1:35″. Nickel-plated frame, blued barrel, black-finished stock and forend. Introduced 1995. Made in U.S. by H&R 1871, Inc.
Price: **$169.95**

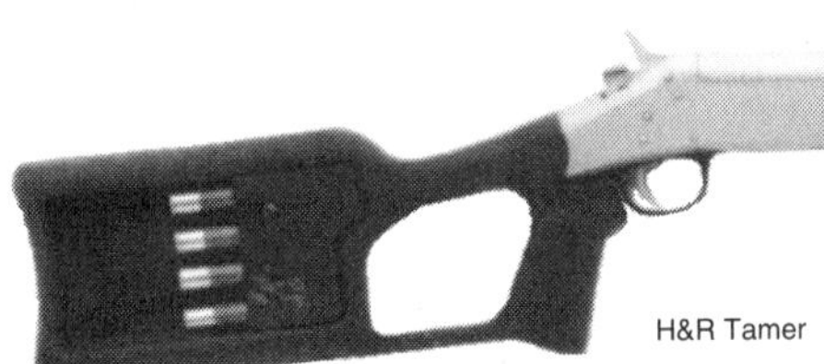
H&R Tamer

HARRINGTON & RICHARDSON TAMER SHOTGUN

Gauge: 410, 3″ chamber.
Barrel: 19$^{1}/_{2}$″ (Full).
Weight: 5-6 lbs. **Length:** 33″ overall.
Stock: Thumbhole grip of high density black polymer.
Features: Uses H&R Topper action with matte electroless nickel finish. Stock holds four spare shotshells. Introduced 1994. From H&R 1871, Inc.
Price: **$124.95**

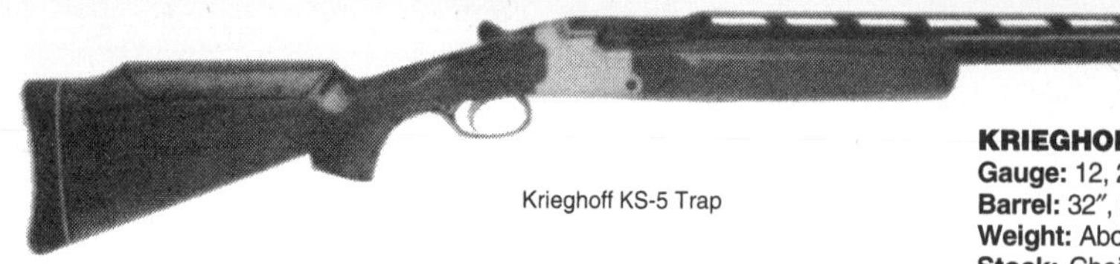
Krieghoff KS-5 Trap

KRIEGHOFF KS-5 TRAP GUN
Gauge: 12, $2^3/_4$″ chamber.
Barrel: 32″, 34″; Full choke or choke tubes.
Weight: About $8^1/_2$ lbs.
Stock: Choice of high Monte Carlo ($1^1/_2$″), low Monte Carlo ($1^3/_8$″) or factory adjustable stock. European walnut.
Features: Ventilated tapered step rib. Adjustable trigger or optional release trigger. Satin gray electroless nickel receiver. Comes with fitted aluminum case. Introduced 1988. Imported from Germany by Krieghoff International, Inc.
Price: Fixed choke, cased $3,575.00
Price: With choke tubes $3,975.00

Krieghoff KS-5 Special
Same as the KS-5 except the barrel has a fully adjustable rib and adjustable stock. Rib allows shooter to adjust point of impact from 50%/50% to nearly 90%/10%. Introduced 1990.
Price: $4,480.00

KRIEGHOFF K-80 SINGLE BARREL TRAP GUN
Gauge: 12, $2^3/_4$″ chamber.
Barrel: 32″ or 34″ Unsingle; 34″ Top Single. Fixed Full or choke tubes.
Weight: About $8^3/_4$ lbs.
Stock: Four stock dimensions or adjustable stock available. All hand-checkered European walnut.
Features: Satin nickel finish with K-80 logo. Selective mechanical trigger adjustable for finger position. Tapered step vent. rib. Adjustable point of impact on Unsingle.
Price: Standard grade full Unsingle $7,595.00
Price: Standard grade full Top Single combo (special order), from $9,595.00
Price: RT (removable trigger) option, add $1,000.00

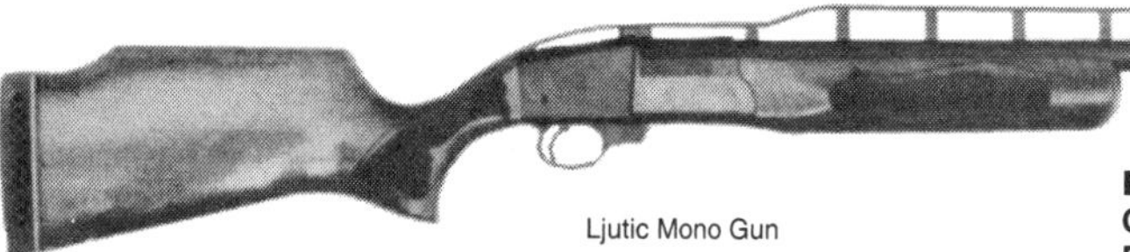
Ljutic Mono Gun

LJUTIC MONO GUN SINGLE BARREL
Gauge: 12 only.
Barrel: 34″, choked to customer specs; hollow-milled rib, $35^1/_2$″ sight plane.
Weight: Approx. 9 lbs.
Stock: To customer specs. Oil finish, hand checkered.
Features: Totally custom made. Pull or release trigger; removable trigger guard contains trigger and hammer mechanism; Ljutic pushbutton opener on front of trigger guard. From Ljutic Industries.
Price: With standard, medium or Olympic rib, custom 32″-34″ bbls. ... $4,795.00
Price: As above with screw-in choke barrel $5,000.00

Ljutic LTX Super Deluxe Mono Gun
Super Deluxe version of the standard Mono Gun with high quality wood, extra-fancy checkering pattern in 24 lpi, double recessed choking. Available in two weights: $8^1/_4$ lbs. or $8^3/_4$ lbs. Extra light 33″ barrel; medium-height rib. Introduced 1984. From Ljutic Industries.
Price: $5,895.00
Price: With three screw-in choke tubes $6,095.00

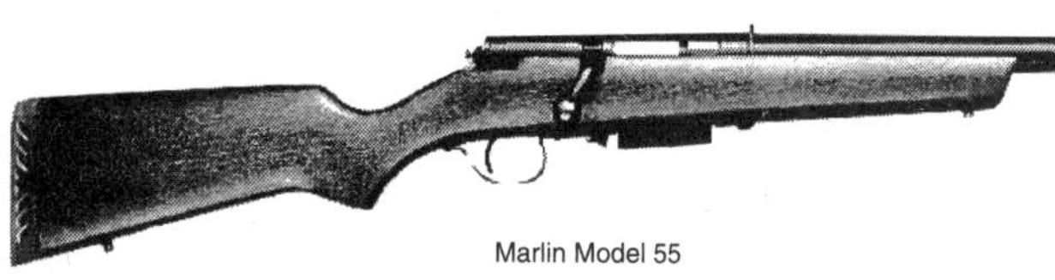
Marlin Model 55

MARLIN MODEL 55 GOOSE GUN BOLT ACTION
Gauge: 12 only, $2^3/_4$″ or 3″ chamber.
Action: Bolt action, thumb safety, detachable two-shot clip. Red cocking indicator.
Barrel: 36″ (Full).
Weight: 8 lbs. **Length:** $56^3/_4$″ overall.
Stock: Walnut-finished hardwood, pistol grip, ventilated recoil pad. Swivel studs, MarShield® finish.
Features: Brass bead front sight, U-groove rear sight.
Price: $307.55

Marlin 512 Slugmaster

MARLIN MODEL 512 SLUGMASTER SHOTGUN
Gauge: 12, 3″ chamber; 2-shot detachable box magazine.
Barrel: 21″, rifled (1:28″ twist).
Weight: 8 lbs. **Length:** $44^3/_4$″ overall.
Stock: Walnut-finished, press-checkered Maine birch with Mar-Shield® finish, ventilated recoil pad.
Sights: Ramp front with brass bead and removable Wide-Scan™ hood, adjustable folding semi-buckhorn rear. Drilled and tapped for scope mounting.
Features: Uses Model 55 action with thumb safety. Designed for shooting sabot-ed slugs. Comes with special Weaver scope mount. Introduced 1994. Made in U.S. by Marlin Firearms Co.
Price: $353.35

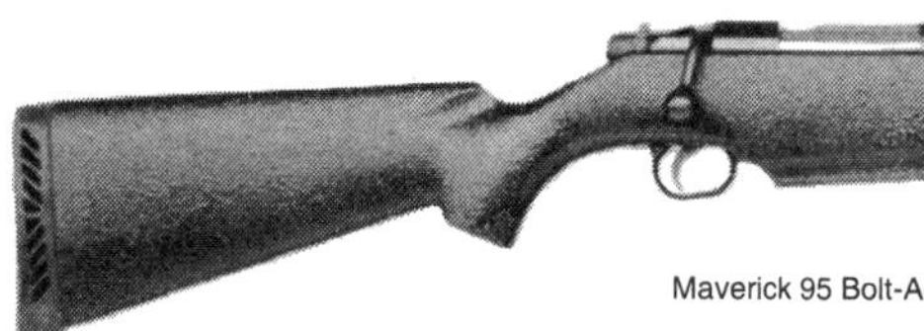
Maverick 95 Bolt-Action

MAVERICK MODEL 95 BOLT-ACTION SHOTGUN
Gauge: 12, 3″ chamber, 2-shot magazine.
Barrel: 25″ (Mod.).
Weight: 6.5 lbs.
Stock: Textured black synthetic.
Sights: Bead front.
Features: Full-length stock with integral magazine; ambidextrous rotating safety; twin extractors; rubber recoil pad. Blue finish. Introduced 1995. From Maverick Arms.
Price: $184.00

CAUTION: PRICES SHOWN ARE SUPPLIED BY THE MANUFACTURER OR IMPORTER. CHECK YOUR LOCAL GUNSHOP.

Mossberg Model 695 Slugster

Mossberg Model 695 Turkey
Same as the Model 695 Slugster except has smoothbore 22″ barrel with Extra-Full Turkey Accu-Choke tube, full OFM camouflage finish, fixed U-notch rear sight, bead front. Made in U.S. by Mossberg. Introduced 1996.
Price: $276.00

MOSSBERG MODEL 695 SLUGSTER
Gauge: 12, 3″ chamber.
Barrel: 22″; fully rifled, ported.
Weight: $7\frac{1}{2}$ lbs.
Stock: Black synthetic, with swivel studs and rubber recoil pad.
Sights: Blade front, folding rifle-style leaf rear. Comes with Weaver-style scope bases.
Features: Matte metal finish; rotating thumb safety; detachable 2-shot magazine. Mossberg Cablelock. Made in U.S. by Mossberg. Introduced 1996.
Price: $293.00

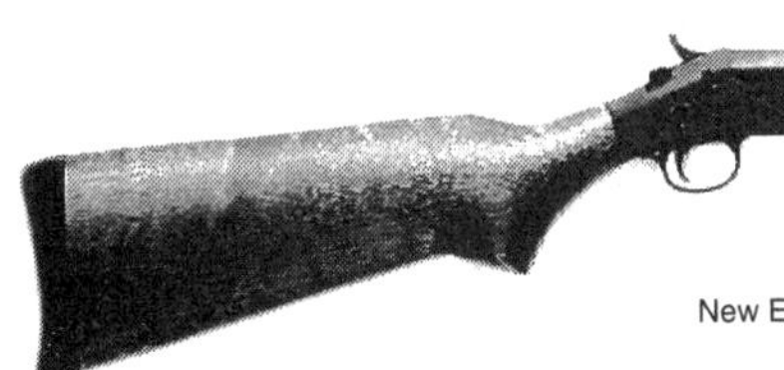

New England Turkey and Goose

NEW ENGLAND FIREARMS STANDARD PARDNER
Gauge: 12, 20, 410, 3″ chamber; 16, 28, $2\frac{3}{4}$″ chamber.
Barrel: 12-ga.—28″ (Full, Mod.), 32″ (Full); 16-ga.—28″ (Full), 32″ (Full); 20-ga.—26″ (Full, Mod.); 28-ga.—26″ (Mod.); 410-bore—26″ (Full).
Weight: 5-6 lbs. **Length:** 43″ overall (28″ barrel).
Stock: Walnut-finished hardwood with full pistol grip.
Sights: Bead front.
Features: Transfer bar ignition; break-open action with side-lever release. Introduced 1987. From New England Firearms.
Price: $99.95
Price: Youth model (20- , 28-ga., 410, 22″ barrel, recoil pad) $109.95
Price: 12-ga., 32″ (Full) $104.95

NEW ENGLAND FIREARMS SURVIVOR
Gauge: 12, 20, 410/45 Colt, 3″ chamber.
Barrel: 22″ (Mod.); 20″ (410/45 Colt, rifled barrel, choke tube).
Weight: 6 lbs. **Length:** 36″ overall.
Stock: Black polymer with thumbhole/pistol grip, sling swivels; beavertail forend.
Sights: Bead front.
Features: Buttplate removes to expose storage for extra ammunition; forend also holds extra ammunition. Black or nickel finish. Introduced 1993. From New England Firearms.
Price: Black $129.95
Price: Nickel $145.95
Price: 410/45 Colt, black $145.95
Price: 410/45 Colt, nickel $164.95

NEW ENGLAND FIREARMS TURKEY AND GOOSE GUN
Gauge: 10, $3\frac{1}{2}$″ chamber.
Barrel: 28″ (Full), 32″ (Mod.).
Weight: 9.5 lbs. **Length:** 44″ overall.
Stock: American hardwood with walnut, or matte camo finish; ventilated rubber recoil pad.
Sights: Bead front.
Features: Break-open action with side-lever release; ejector. Matte finish on metal. Introduced 1992. From New England Firearms.
Price: Walnut-finish wood $149.95
Price: Camo finish, sling and swivels $159.95
Price: Camo finish, 32″, sling and swivels $179.95
Price: Black matte finish, 24″, Turkey Full choke tube, sling and swivels . $184.95

NEW ENGLAND FIREARMS TRACKER SLUG GUN
Gauge: 12, 20, 3″ chamber.
Barrel: 24″ (Cyl.).
Weight: 6 lbs. **Length:** 40″ overall.
Stock: Walnut-finished hardwood with full pistol grip, recoil pad.
Sights: Blade front, fully adjustable rifle-type rear.
Features: Break-open action with side-lever release; blued barrel, color case-hardened frame. Introduced 1992. From New England Firearms.
Price: Tracker $129.95
Price: Tracker II (as above except fully rifled bore) $139.95

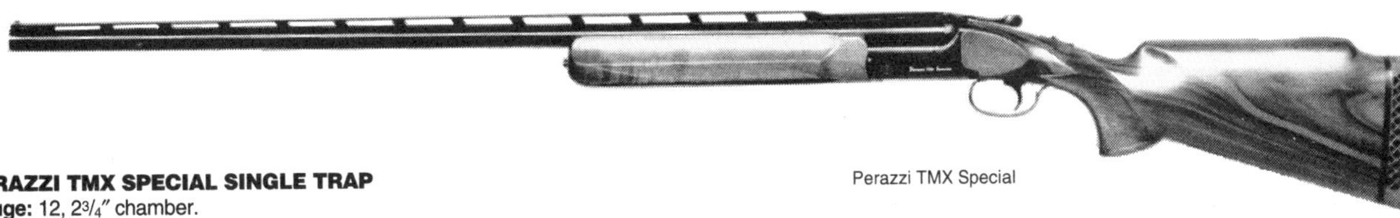

Perazzi TMX Special

PERAZZI TMX SPECIAL SINGLE TRAP
Gauge: 12, $2\frac{3}{4}$″ chamber.
Barrel: 32″ or 34″ (Extra Full).
Weight: 8 lbs., 6 oz.
Stock: To customer specs; interchangeable.
Features: Special high rib; adjustable four-position trigger. Also available with choke tubes. Imported from Italy by Perazzi U.S.A., Inc.
Price: From $6,590.00

SAVAGE MODEL 210F MASTER SHOT SLUG GUN
Gauge: 12, 3″ chamber; 2-shot magazine.
Barrel: 24″ 1:35″ rifling twist.
Weight: $7\frac{1}{2}$ lbs. **Length:**43.5 ″ overall.
Stock: Glass-filled polymer with positive checkering.
Features: Based on the Savage Model 110 action; 60° bolt lift; controlled round feed; comes with scope mount. Introduced 1996. Made in U.S. by Savage Arms.
Price: .... NA

REMINGTON 90-T SUPER SINGLE SHOTGUN
Gauge: 12, $2\frac{3}{4}$″ chamber.
Barrel: 30″, 32″, 34″, fixed choke or Rem Choke tubes; ported or non-ported. Medium-high tapered, ventilated rib; white Bradley-type front bead, stainless center bead.
Weight: About $8\frac{3}{4}$ lbs.
Stock: $14\frac{3}{8}$″x$1\frac{3}{8}$″ (or $1\frac{1}{2}$″ or $1\frac{1}{4}$″)x$1\frac{1}{2}$″. Choice of drops at comb, pull length available plus or minus 1″. Figured American walnut with low-luster finish, checkered 18 lpi; black vented rubber recoil pad. Cavity in forend and buttstock for added weight.
Features: Barrel is over-bored with elongated forcing cones. Removable sideplates can be ordered with engraving; drop-out trigger assembly. Metal has non-glare matte finish. Available with extra barrels in different lengths, chokes, extra trigger assemblies and sideplates, porting, stocks. Introduced 1990. From Remington.
Price: Depending on options $3,199.00
Price: With high post adjustable rib $3,992.00

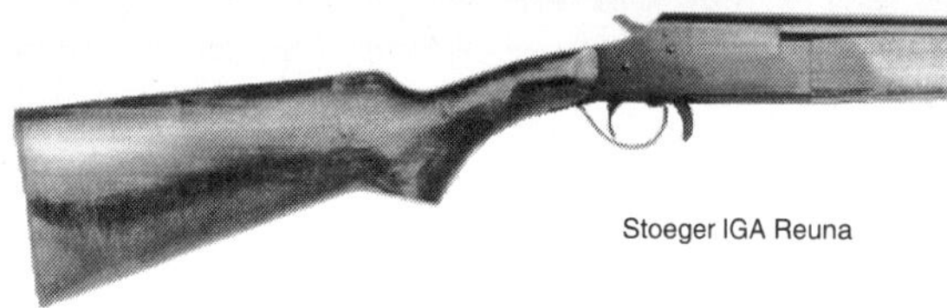

Stoeger IGA Reuna

SNAKE CHARMER II SHOTGUN
Gauge: 410, 3″ chamber.
Barrel: 18¼″.
Weight: About 3½ lbs. **Length:** 28⅝″ overall.
Stock: ABS grade impact resistant plastic.
Features: Thumbhole-type stock holds four extra rounds. Stainless steel barrel and frame. Reintroduced 1989. From Sporting Arms Mfg., Inc.
Price: **$149.00**
Price: New Generation Snake Charmer (as above except with black carbon steel bbl.) **$139.00**

STOEGER/IGA REUNA SINGLE BARREL SHOTGUN
Gauge: 12, 2¾″ chamber; 20, 410, 3″ chamber.
Barrel: 12-ga.—26″ (Imp. Cyl.), 28″ (Full); 20-ga.—26″ (Full); 410 bore—26″ (Full).
Weight: 5¼ lbs.
Stock: 14″x1½″x2½″. Brazilian hardwood.
Sights: Metal bead front.
Features: Exposed hammer with half-cock safety; extractor; blue finish. Introduced 1987. Imported from Brazil by Stoeger Industries.
Price: **$120.00**
Price: 12-, 20-ga., Full choke tube **$142.00**
Price: Youth model (20-ga., 410, 22″ Full) **$132.00**

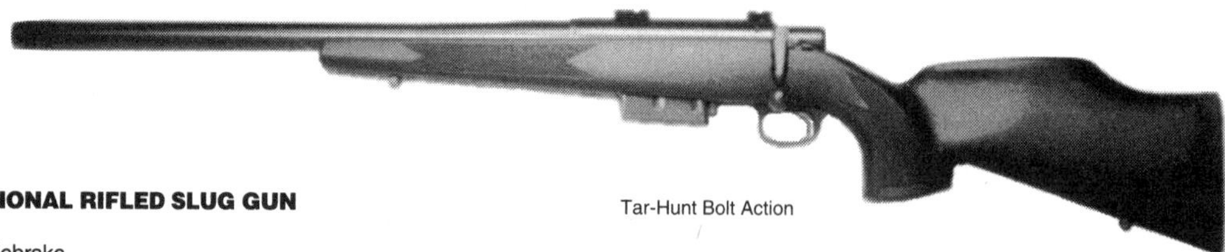

Tar-Hunt Bolt Action

TAR-HUNT RSG-12 PROFESSIONAL RIFLED SLUG GUN
Gauge: 12, 20, 2¾″ chamber.
Barrel: 21½″; fully rifled, with muzzlebrake.
Weight: 7¾ lbs. **Length:** 41½″ overall.
Stock: Matte black McMillan fiberglass with Pachmayr Decelerator pad.
Sights: None furnished; comes with Weaver-style bases and Burris Zee steel rings.
Features: Uses new rifle-style action with two locking lugs; two-position safety; single-stage, adjustable rifle trigger; muzzlebrake. Many options available. Right- and left-hand models at same prices. Introduced 1991. Made in U.S. by Tar-Hunt Custom Rifles, Inc.
Price: Professional model , right- or left hand **$1,395.00**
Price: Turkey model (smoothbore, black McMillan fiberglass stock, Remington Rem-Choke thread system), right- or left-hand **$1,439.00**
Price: Matchless model (400-grit gloss metal finish, McMillan Fibergrain or camouflage stock), right- or left-hand **$1,783.50**
Price: Peerless model NP-3 nickel/teflon metal finish, McMillan Fibergrain fiberglass stock), right- or left-hand **$1,973.25**

SHOTGUNS—MILITARY & POLICE

Designs for utility, suitable for and adaptable to competitions and other sporting purposes.

Armscor M-30R8 Security

ARMSCOR M-30 SECURITY SHOTGUNS
Gauge: 12, 3″ chamber.
Barrel: 18.5″, 20″ (Cyl.).
Weight: About 7 lbs.
Stock: Walnut-finished hardwood.
Sights: Metal bead front.
Features: Dual action slide bars; damascened bolt; blued steel receiver. Imported from the Philippines by K.B.I., Inc.
Price: M-30R6 (5-shot) **$199.00**
Price: M-30R8 (7-shot) **$210.00**

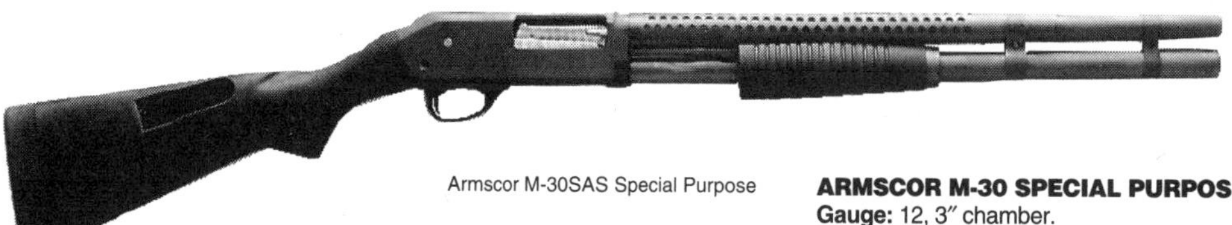

Armscor M-30SAS Special Purpose

ARMSCOR M-30 SPECIAL PURPOSE SHOTGUNS
Gauge: 12, 3″ chamber.
Barrel: 20″ (Cyl.).
Weight: 7.5 lbs.
Stock: Walnut-finished hardwood, or synthetic speedfeed.
Sights: Rifle sights on M-30DG, metal bead front on M-305AS.
Features: M-30DB has 7-shot magazine, polished blue receiver; M-305AS based on Special Air Services gun with 7-shot magazine, ventilated barrel shroud, Parkerized finish. Introduced 1996. Imported from the Philippines by K.B.I., Inc.
Price: M-30DG **$249.00**
Price: M-30SAS **$279.00**

Consult our Directory pages for the location of firms mentioned.

CAUTION: PRICES SHOWN ARE SUPPLIED BY THE MANUFACTURER OR IMPORTER. CHECK YOUR LOCAL GUNSHOP.

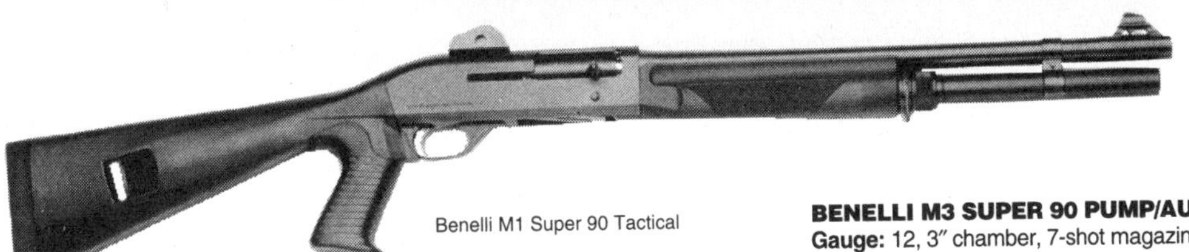

Benelli M1 Super 90 Tactical

Benelli M1 Super 90 Tactical Shotgun

Similar to the M1 Super 90 except has 18.5″ barrel with Imp. Cyl., Mod., Full choke tubes, rifle sights of Ghost Ring system (tritium night sights optional), 5-shot magazine. In 12-gauge (3″ chamber) only, matte-finish receiver. Overall length 39.75″. Introduced 1993. Imported from Italy by Heckler & Koch, Inc.

Price: With rifle sights, standard stock **$860.00**
Price: As above, pistol grip stock **$895.00**
Price: With Ghost Rifle sights, standard stock **$902.00**
Price: As above, pistol grip stock **$936.00**

Benelli M1 Super 90 Defense Shotgun

Similar to the M1 Super 90 except has 18.5″ barrel, rifle sights or Ghost Ring system (tritium night sights optional), 3-shot magazine with 2-shot extension. In 12-gauge (3″ chamber) only, matte finish receiver. Overall length 39¾″. Introduced 1993. Imported from Italy by Heckler & Koch, Inc.

Price: With rifle sights, pistol grip stock **$851.00**
Price: With Ghost Ring sights, pistol grip stock **$892.00**

BENELLI M3 SUPER 90 PUMP/AUTO SHOTGUN

Gauge: 12, 3″ chamber, 7-shot magazine.
Barrel: 19¾″ (Cyl.).
Weight: 7 lbs., 8 oz. **Length:** 41″ overall.
Stock: High-impact polymer with sling loop in side of butt; rubberized pistol grip on stock.
Sights: Post front, buckhorn rear adjustable for windage. Ghost ring system available.
Features: Combination pump/auto action. Alloy receiver with inertia recoil rotating locking lug bolt; matte finish; automatic shell release lever. Introduced 1989. Imported by Heckler & Koch, Inc.
Price: With standard stock **$1,016.00**
Price: With Ghost Ring sight system, standard stock **$1,086.00**

Benelli M1 Super 90

Similar to the M3 Super 90 except is semi-automatic only, has overall length of 39¾″ and weighs 6.5 lbs. Introduced 1986.

Price: Slug Gun with standard stock **$819.00**
Price: With pistol grip stock (Defense) **$851.00**
Price: With ghost ring sight system (standard stock) **$860.00**
Price: With ghost ring sight system, pistol grip stock (Defense) **$892.00**

Beretta Model 1201FP3

BERETTA MODEL 1201FP3 AUTO SHOTGUN

Gauge: 12, 3″ chamber.
Barrel: 20″ (Cyl.).
Weight: 6.3 lbs. **Length:** NA
Stock: Special strengthened technopolymer, matte black finish.
Stock: Fixed rifle type.
Features: Has 6-shot magazine. Introduced 1988. Imported from Italy by Beretta U.S.A.
Price: **$715.00**

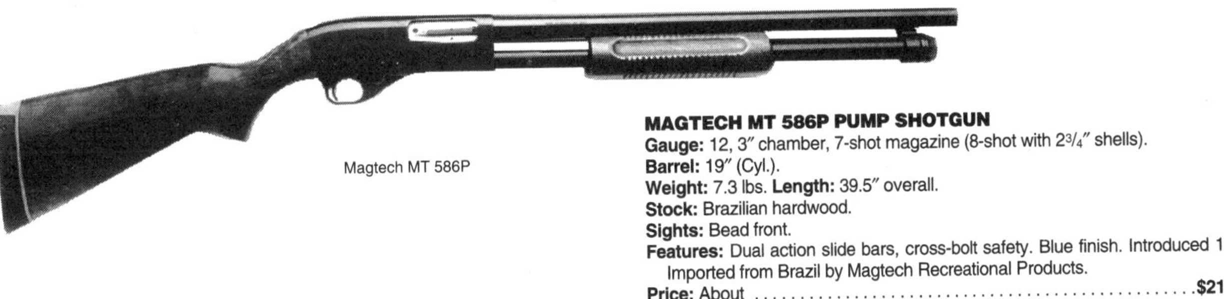

Magtech MT 586P

MAGTECH MT 586P PUMP SHOTGUN

Gauge: 12, 3″ chamber, 7-shot magazine (8-shot with 2¾″ shells).
Barrel: 19″ (Cyl.).
Weight: 7.3 lbs. **Length:** 39.5″ overall.
Stock: Brazilian hardwood.
Sights: Bead front.
Features: Dual action slide bars, cross-bolt safety. Blue finish. Introduced 1991. Imported from Brazil by Magtech Recreational Products.
Price: About **$219.00**

Mossberg Model 500

Mossberg Model HS410 Shotgun

Similar to the Model 500 Security pump except chambered for 20 gauge or 410 with 3″ chamber; has pistol grip forend, thick recoil pad, muzzlebrake and has special spreader choke on the 18.5″ barrel. Overall length is 37.5″, weight is 6.25 lbs. Blue finish; synthetic field stock. Mossberg Cablelock and video included. Introduced 1990.

Price: HS 410 .... **$293.00**

MOSSBERG MODEL 500 PERSUADER SECURITY SHOTGUNS

Gauge: 12, 20, 410, 3″ chamber.
Barrel: 18½″, 20″ (Cyl.).
Weight: 7 lbs.
Stock: Walnut-finished hardwood or synthetic field.
Sights: Metal bead front.
Features: Available in 6- or 8-shot models. Top-mounted safety, double action slide bars, swivel studs, rubber recoil pad. Blue, Parkerized, Marinecote finishes. Mossberg Cablelock included. From Mossberg.
Price: 12- or 20-ga., 18½″, blue, wood or synthetic stock, 6-shot **$281.00**
Price: As above, Parkerized finish, synthetic stock, 6-shot **$315.00**
Price: Cruiser, 12- or 20-ga., 18½″, blue, pistol grip, heat shield **$272.00**
Price: As above, 410-bore **$279.00**
Price: 12-ga., 8-shot, blue, wood or synthetic stock **$281.00**
Price: As above with rifle sights **$304.00**
Price: 6- or 8-shot with Accu-Choke barrel **$281.00**

Mossberg Model 500 Mariner

Mossberg Model 590 Ghost-Ring

Mossberg Model 500, 590 Mariner Pump

Similar to the Model 500 or 590 Security except all metal parts finished with Marinecote metal finish to resist rust and corrosion. Synthetic field stock; pistol grip kit included. Mossberg Cablelock included.

Price: 6-shot, 18½″ barrel $403.00
Price: As above with Ghost-Ring sights $459.00
Price: 9-shot, 20″ barrel $415.00
Price: As above with Ghost-Ring sights $471.00

Mossberg Model 500, 590 Ghost-Ring Shotguns

Similar to the Model 500 Security except has adjustable blade front, adjustable Ghost-Ring rear sight with protective "ears." Model 500 has 18.5″ (Cyl.) barrel, 6-shot capacity; Model 590 has 20″ (Cyl.) barrel, 9-shot capacity. Both have synthetic field stock. Mossberg Cablelock included. Introduced 1990. From Mossberg.

Price: Model 500, blue $331.00
Price: As above, Parkerized $384.00
Price: Model 590, blue $379.00
Price: As above, Parkerized $432.00
Price: Parkerized, Speedfeed stock $465.00
Price: Parkerized, synthetic stock, Accu-Choke barrel $454.00

MOSSBERG MODEL 590 SHOTGUN

Gauge: 12, 3″ chamber.
Barrel: 20″ (Cyl.).
Weight: 7¼ lbs.
Stock: Synthetic field or Speedfeed.
Sights: Metal bead front.
Features: Top-mounted safety, double slide action bars. Comes with heat shield, bayonet lug, swivel studs, rubber recoil pad. Blue, Parkerized or Marinecote finish. Mossberg Cablelock included. From Mossberg.

Price: Blue, synthetic stock $329.00
Price: Parkerized, synthetic stock $379.00
Price: Blue, Speedfeed stock $362.00
Price: Parkerized, Speedfeed stock $412.00

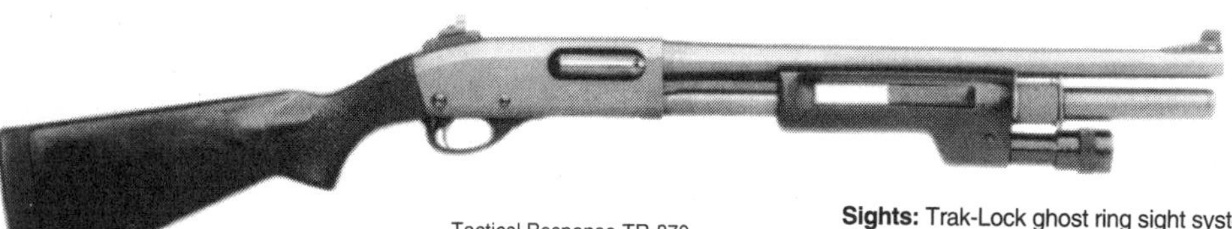

Tactical Response TR-870

TACTICAL RESPONSE TR-870 STANDARD MODEL SHOTGUN

Gauge: 12, 3″ chamber, 7-shot magazine.
Barrel: 18″ (Cyl.).
Weight: 9 lbs. **Length:** 38″ overall.
Stock: Fiberglass-filled polypropolene with non-snag recoil absorbing butt pad. Nylon tactical forend houses flashlight.
Sights: Trak-Lock ghost ring sight system. Front sight has tritium insert.
Features: Highly modified Remington 870P with Parkerized finish. Comes with nylon three-way adjustable sling, high visibility non-binding follower, high performance magazine spring, Jumbo Head safety, and Side Saddle extended 6-shot shell carrier on left side of receiver. Introduced 1991. From Scattergun Technologies, Inc.

Price: Standard model $815.00
Price: FBI model $770.00
Price: Patrol model $595.00
Price: Border Patrol model $605.00
Price: Military model $690.00
Price: K-9 model (Rem. 11-87 action) $860.00
Price: Urban Sniper, Rem. 11-87 action $1,290.00
Price: Louis Awerbuck model $705.00
Price: Practical Turkey model $725.00

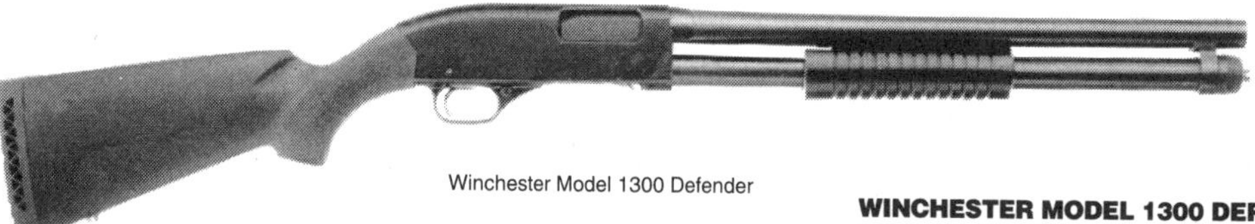

Winchester Model 1300 Defender

WINCHESTER MODEL 1300 DEFENDER PUMP GUN

Gauge: 12, 20, 3″ chamber, 5- or 8-shot capacity.
Barrel: 18″ (Cyl.).
Weight: 6¾ lbs. **Length:** 38⅝″ overall.
Stock: Walnut-finished hardwood stock and ribbed forend, or synthetic; or pistol grip.
Sights: Metal bead front.
Features: Cross-bolt safety, front-locking rotary bolt, twin action slide bars. Black rubber buttpad. From U.S. Repeating Arms Co.

Price: 8-shot, wood or synthetic stock $290.00
Price: 5-shot, wood stock $290.00
Price: Defender Field Combo with pistol grip $393.00

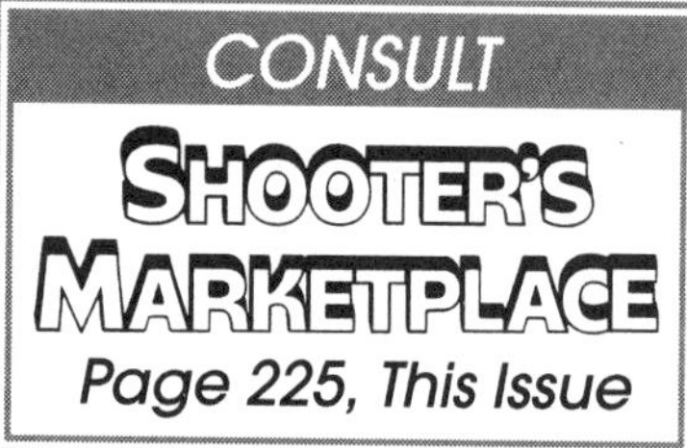
CONSULT
SHOOTER'S
MARKETPLACE
Page 225, This Issue

Winchester 8-Shot Pistol Grip Pump Security Shotguns

Same as regular Defender Pump but with pistol grip and forend of high-impact resistant ABS plastic with non-glare black finish. Introduced 1984.

Price: Pistol Grip Defender $290.00

Winchester Model 1300 Stainless Marine Pump Gun

Same as the Defender except has bright chrome finish, stainless steel barrel, rifle-type sights only. Phosphate coated receiver for corrosion resistance. Pistol grip optional.

Price: $460.00

CAUTION: PRICES SHOWN ARE SUPPLIED BY THE MANUFACTURER OR IMPORTER. CHECK YOUR LOCAL GUNSHOP.

CVA Hawken

CVA HAWKEN PISTOL
Caliber: 50.
Barrel: 9 3/4"; 15/16" flats.
Weight: 50 oz. **Length:** 16 1/2" overall.
Stock: Select hardwood.
Sights: Beaded blade front, fully adjustable open rear.
Features: Color case-hardened lock, polished brass wedge plate, nose cap, ramrod thimble, trigger guard, grip cap. Imported by CVA.
Price: $149.95
Price: Kit $119.95
Price: With laminated stock $159.95

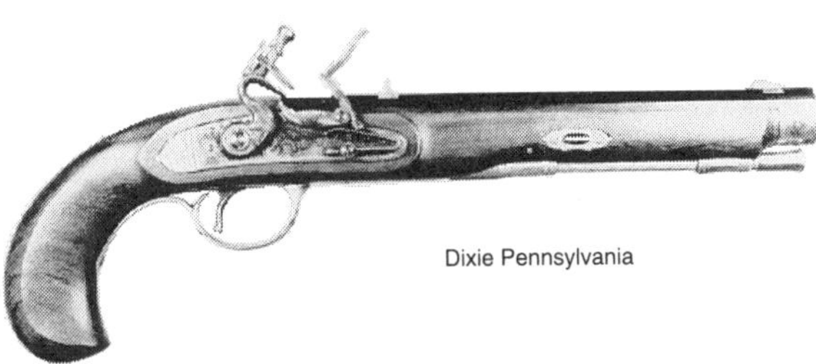
Dixie Pennsylvania

DIXIE PENNSYLVANIA PISTOL
Caliber: 44 (.430" round ball).
Barrel: 10" (7/8" octagon).
Weight: 2 1/2 lbs.
Stock: Walnut-stained hardwood.
Sights: Blade front, open rear drift-adjustable for windage; brass.
Features: Available in flint only. Brass trigger guard, thimbles, nosecap, wedgeplates; high-luster blue barrel. Imported from Italy by Dixie Gun Works.
Price: Finished $159.95
Price: Kit $119.95

Dixie Screw Barrel

DIXIE SCREW BARREL PISTOL
Caliber: .445".
Barrel: 2 1/2".
Weight: 8 oz. **Length:** 6 1/2" overall.
Stock: Walnut.
Features: Trigger folds down when hammer is cocked. Close copy of the originals once made in Belgium. Uses No. 11 percussion caps. From Dixie Gun Works.
Price: $99.95
Price: Kit $79.95

FRENCH-STYLE DUELING PISTOL
Caliber: 44.
Barrel: 10".
Weight: 35 oz. **Length:** 15 3/4" overall.
Stock: Carved walnut.
Sights: Fixed.
Features: Comes with velvet-lined case and accessories. Imported by Mandall Shooting Supplies.
Price: $295.00

Dixie Harper's Ferry

HARPER'S FERRY 1806 PISTOL
Caliber: 58 (.570" round ball).
Barrel: 10".
Weight: 40 oz. **Length:** 16" overall.
Stock: Walnut.
Sights: Fixed.
Features: Case-hardened lock, brass-mounted browned barrel. Replica of the first U.S. Gov't.-made flintlock pistol. Imported by Navy Arms, Dixie Gun Works.
Price: .... $275.00 to $405.00
Price: Kit (Dixie) $199.95
Price: Cased set (Navy Arms) $335.00

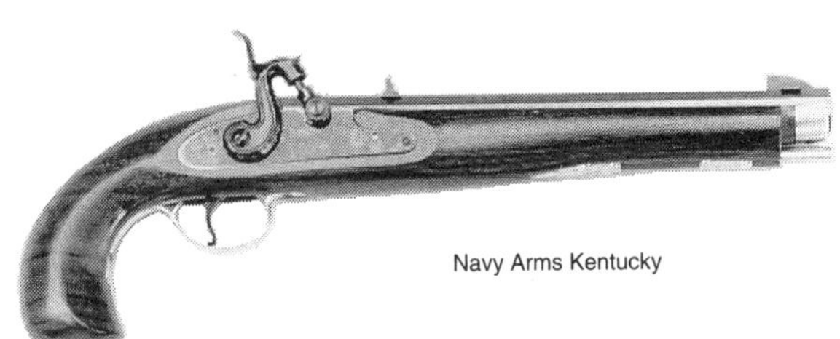
Navy Arms Kentucky

KENTUCKY FLINTLOCK PISTOL
Caliber: 44, 45.
Barrel: 10 1/8".
Weight: 32 oz. **Length:** 15 1/2" overall.
Stock: Walnut.
Sights: Fixed.
Features: Specifications, including caliber, weight and length may vary with importer. Case-hardened lock, blued barrel; available also as brass barrel flint Model 1821. Imported by Navy Arms (44 only), The Armoury.
Price: .... $145.00 to $225.00
Price: In kit form, from .... $90.00 to $112.00
Price: Single cased set (Navy Arms) $350.00
Price: Double cased set (Navy Arms) $580.00

Kentucky Percussion Pistol
Similar to flint version but percussion lock. Imported by The Armoury, Navy Arms, CVA (50-cal.).
Price: .... $129.95 to $250.00
Price: Steel barrel (Armoury) $179.00
Price: Single cased set (Navy Arms) $335.00
Price: Double cased set (Navy Arms) $550.00

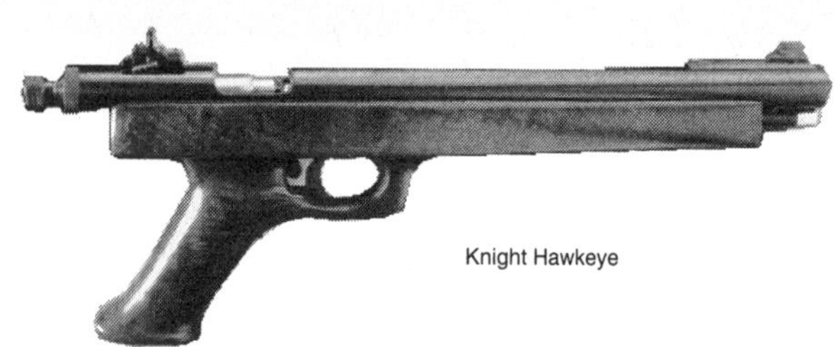
Knight Hawkeye

KNIGHT HAWKEYE PISTOL
Caliber: 50.
Barrel: 12″, 1:20″ twist.
Weight: 3¼ lbs. **Length:** 20″ overall.
Stock: Black composite, autumn brown or shadow black laminate.
Sights: Bead front on ramp, open fully adjustable rear.
Features: In-line ignitiion design; patented double safety system; removable breech plug; fully adjustable trigger; receiver drilled and tapped for scope mounting. Made in U.S. by Modern Muzzle Loading, Inc.
Price: Blued **$359.95**
Price: Stainless **$429.95**

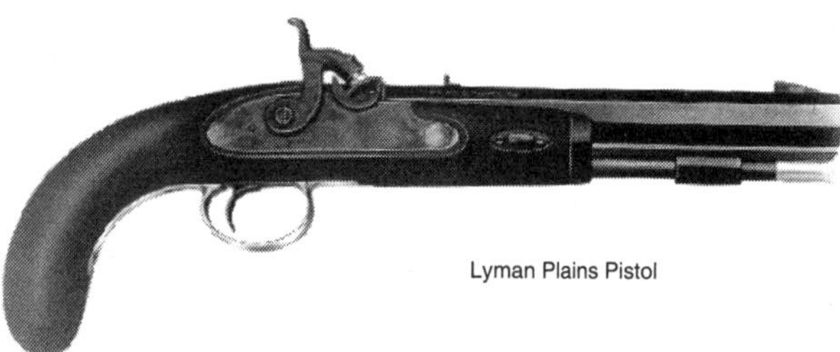
Lyman Plains Pistol

LE PAGE PERCUSSION DUELING PISTOL
Caliber: 44.
Barrel: 10″, rifled.
Weight: 40 oz. **Length:** 16″ overall.
Stock: Walnut, fluted butt.
Sights: Blade front, notch rear.
Features: Double-set triggers. Blued barrel; trigger guard and buttcap are polished silver. Imported by Dixie Gun Works.
Price: **$425.00**

LYMAN PLAINS PISTOL
Caliber: 50 or 54.
Barrel: 8″, 1:30″ twist, both calibers.
Weight: 50 oz. **Length:** 15″ overall.
Stock: Walnut half-stock.
Sights: Blade front, square notch rear adjustable for windage.
Features: Polished brass trigger guard and ramrod tip, color case-hardened coil spring lock, spring-loaded trigger, stainless steel nipple, blackened iron furniture. Hooked patent breech, detachable belt hook. Introduced 1981. From Lyman Products.
Price: Finished **$224.95**
Price: Kit **$179.95**

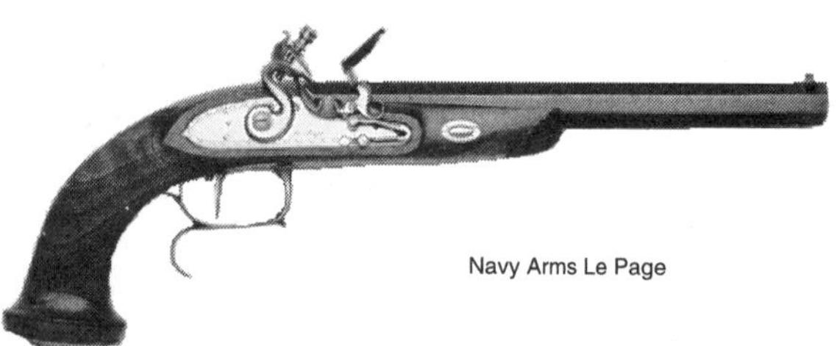
Navy Arms Le Page

NAVY ARMS LE PAGE DUELING PISTOL
Caliber: 44.
Barrel: 9″, octagon, rifled.
Weight: 34 oz. **Length:** 15″ overall.
Stock: European walnut.
Sights: Adjustable rear.
Features: Single-set trigger. Polished metal finish. From Navy Arms.
Price: Percussion **$500.00**
Price: Single cased set, percussion **$775.00**
Price: Double cased set, percussion **$1,300.00**
Price: Flintlock, rifled **$625.00**
Price: Flintlock, smoothbore (45-cal.) **$625.00**
Price: Flintlock, single cased set **$900.00**
Price: Flintlock, double cased set **$1,575.00**

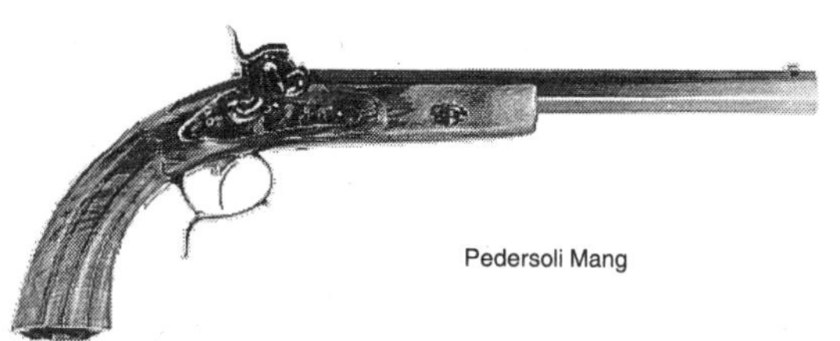
Pedersoli Mang

PEDERSOLI MANG TARGET PISTOL
Caliber: 38.
Barrel: 10.5″, octagonal; 1:15″ twist,
Weight: 2.5 lbs. **Length:** 17.25″ overall.
Stock: Walnut with fluted grip.
Sights: Blade front, open rear adjustable for windage.
Features: Browned barrel, polished breech plug, rest color case-hardened. Imported from Italy by Dixie Gun Works.
Price: **$749.00**

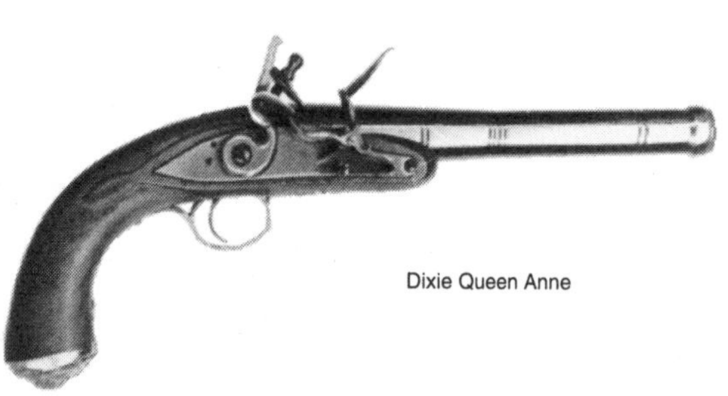
Dixie Queen Anne

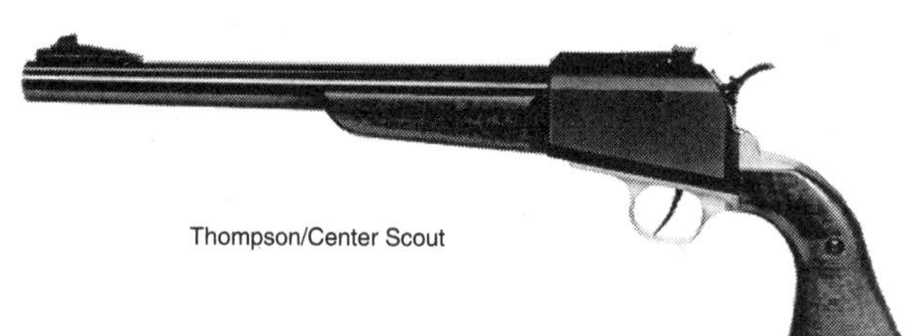
Thompson/Center Scout

THOMPSON/CENTER SCOUT PISTOL
Caliber: 45, 50 and 54.
Barrel: 12″, interchangeable.
Weight: 4 lbs., 6 oz. **Length:** NA.
Stocks: American black walnut stocks and forend.
Sights: Blade on ramp front, fully adjustable Patridge rear.
Features: Patented in-line ignition system with special vented breech plug. Patented trigger mechanism consists of only two moving parts. Interchangeable barrels. Wide grooved hammer. Brass trigger guard assembly. Introduced 1990. From Thompson/Center.
Price: 45-, 50- or 54-cal. **$350.00**

QUEEN ANNE FLINTLOCK PISTOL
Caliber: 50 (.490″ round ball).
Barrel: 7½″, smoothbore.
Stock: Walnut.
Sights: None.
Features: Browned steel barrel, fluted brass trigger guard, brass mask on butt. Lockplate left in the white. Made by Pedersoli in Italy. Introduced 1983. Imported by Dixie Gun Works.
Price: **$189.95**
Price: Kit **$138.50**

CAUTION: PRICES SHOWN ARE SUPPLIED BY THE MANUFACTURER OR IMPORTER. CHECK YOUR LOCAL GUN SHOP.

TRADITIONS BUCKHUNTER PRO IN-LINE PISTOL
Caliber: 50, 54.
Barrel: 10″ round.
Weight: 48 oz. **Length:** 14″ overall.
Stock: Smooth walnut or black epoxy coated grip and forend.
Sights: Beaded blade front, folding adjustable rear.
Features: Thumb safety; removable stainless steel breech plug; adjustable trigger, barrel drilled and tapped for scope mounting. From Traditions.
Price: With walnut grip **$230.00**
Price: Nickel with black grip **$247.00**

Traditions Buckhunter

TRADITIONS BUCKSKINNER PISTOL
Caliber: 50.
Barrel: 10″ octagonal, 7/8″ flats, 1:20″ twist.
Weight: 40 oz. **Length:** 15″ overall.
Stocks: Stained beech or laminated wood.
Sights: Blade front, fixed rear.
Features: Percussion ignition. Blackened furniture. Imported by Traditions.
Price: Beech stocks **$165.00**
Price: Laminated stocks **$180.00**

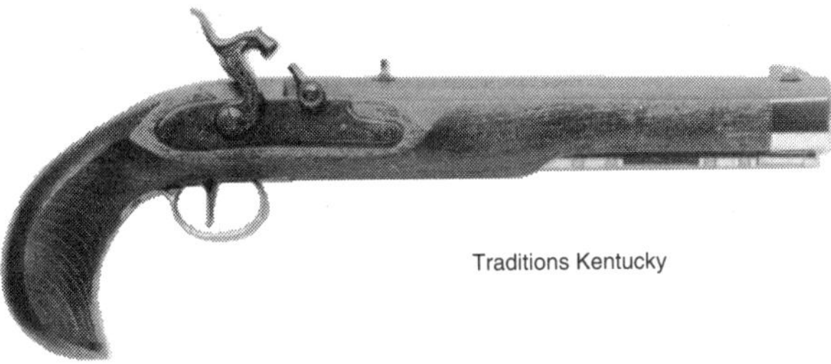
Traditions Kentucky

Traditions Pioneer

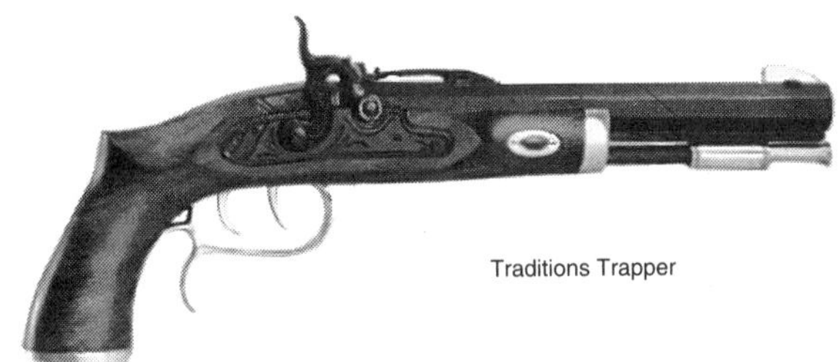
Traditions Trapper

TRADITIONS KENTUCKY PISTOL
Caliber: 50.
Barrel: 10″; octagon with 7/8″ flats; 1:20″ twist.
Weight: 40 oz. **Length:** 15″ overall.
Stock: Stained beech.
Sights: Blade front, fixed rear.
Features: Birds-head grip; brass thimbles; color case-hardened lock. Percussion only. Introduced 1995. From Traditions.
Price: Finished **$142.00**
Price: Kit **$115.00**

TRADITIONS PIONEER PISTOL
Caliber: 45.
Barrel: 9 5/8″, 13/16″ flats, 1:16″ twist.
Weight: 31 oz. **Length:** 15″ overall.
Stock: Beech.
Sights: Blade front, fixed rear.
Features: V-type mainspring. Single trigger. German silver furniture, blackened hardware. From Traditions.
Price: **$157.00**
Price: Kit **$126.00**

TRADITIONS TRAPPER PISTOL
Caliber: 50.
Barrel: 9 3/4″, 7/8″ flats, 1:20″ twist.
Weight: 2 3/4 lbs. **Length:** 16″ overall.
Stock: Beech.
Sights: Blade front, adjustable rear.
Features: Double-set triggers; brass buttcap, trigger guard, wedge plate, forend tip, thimble. From Traditions.
Price: Percission **$190.00**
Price: Flintlock **$207.00**
Price: Kit **$148.00**

TRADITIONS WILLIAM PARKER PISTOL
Caliber: 50.
Barrel: 10 3/8″, 15/16″ flats; polished steel.
Weight: 37 oz. **Length:** 17 1/2″ overall.
Stock: Walnut with checkered grip.
Sights: Brass blade front, fixed rear.
Features: Replica dueling pistol with 1:20″ twist, hooked breech. Brass wedge plate, trigger guard, cap guard; separate ramrod. Double-set triggers. Polished steel barrel, lock. Imported by Traditions.
Price: **$282.00**

BLACKPOWDER REVOLVERS

ARMY 1860 PERCUSSION REVOLVER
Caliber: 44, 6-shot.
Barrel: 8″.
Weight: 40 oz. **Length:** 13 5/8″ overall.
Stocks: Walnut.
Sights: Fixed.
Features: Engraved Navy scene on cylinder; brass trigger guard; case-hardened frame, loading lever and hammer. Some importers supply pistol cut for detachable shoulder stock, have accessory stock available. Imported by American Arms, Cabela's (1860 Lawman), E.M.F., Navy Arms, The Armoury, Cimarron, Dixie Gun Works (half-fluted cylinder, not roll engraved), Euroarms of America (brass or steel model), Armsport, Traditions (brass or steel), Uberti U.S.A. Inc.
Price: About . . . . **$92.95** to **$300.00**
Price: Hartford model, steel frame, German silver trim, cartouches (E.M.F.) **$215.00**
Price: Single cased set (Navy Arms) **$300.00**

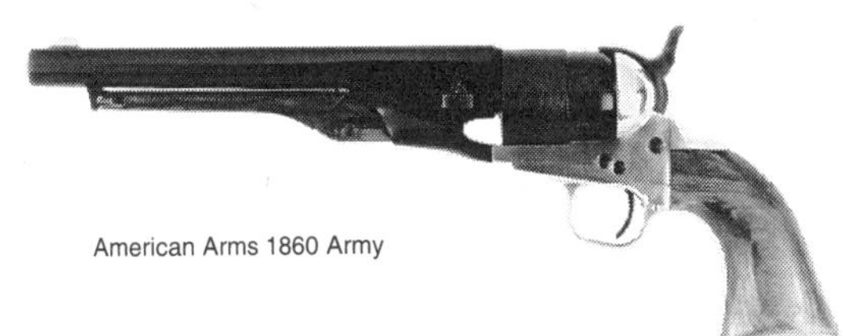
American Arms 1860 Army

Price: Double cased set (Navy Arms) **$490.00**
Price: 1861 Navy: Same as Army except 36-cal., 7 1/2″ bbl., weighs 41 oz., cut for shoulder stock; round cylinder (fluted available), from CVA (brass frame, 44-cal.) . . . . **$99.95** to **$249.00**
Price: Steel frame kit (E.M.F., Euroarms) . . . . **$125.00** to **$216.25**
Price: Colt Army Police, fluted cyl., 5 1/2″, 36-cal. (Cabela's) **$124.95**

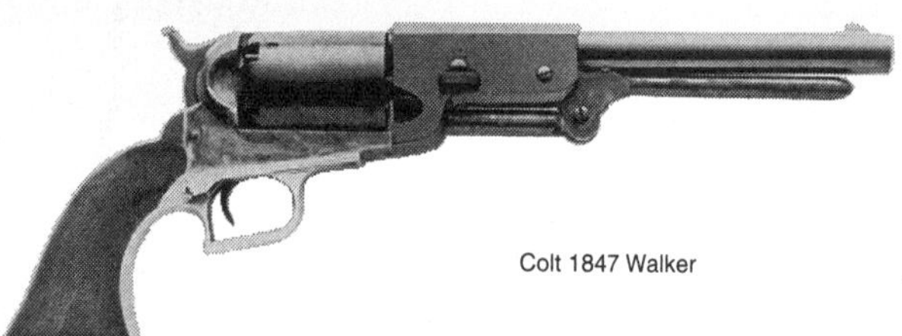
Colt 1847 Walker

COLT 1847 WALKER PERCUSSION REVOLVER
Caliber: 44.
Barrel: 9″, 7 groove, right-hand twist.
Weight: 73 oz.
Stocks: One-piece walnut.
Sights: German silver front sight, hammer notch rear.
Features: Made in U.S. Faithful reproduction of the original gun, including markings. Color case-hardened frame, hammer, loading lever and plunger. Blue steel backstrap, brass square-back trigger guard. Blue barrel, cylinder, trigger and wedge. From Colt Blackpowder Arms Co.
Price: $442.50

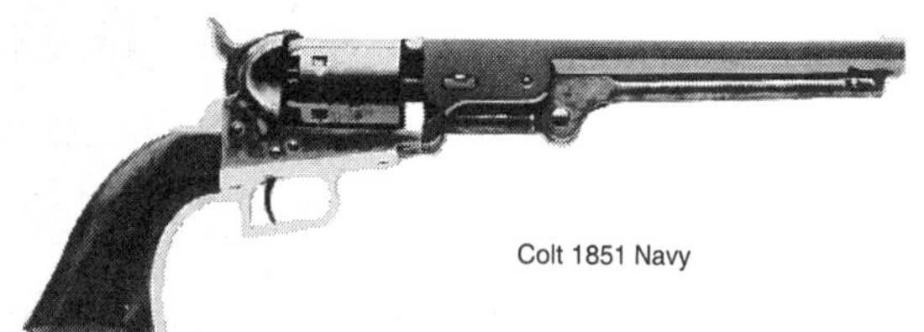
Colt 1851 Navy

COLT 1851 NAVY PERCUSSION REVOLVER
Caliber: 36.
Barrel: 7$^1/_2$″, octagonal, 7 groove left-hand twist.
Weight: 40$^1/_2$ oz.
Stocks: One-piece oiled American walnut.
Sights: Brass pin front, hammer notch rear.
Features: Faithful reproduction of the original gun. Color case-hardened frame, loading lever, plunger, hammer and latch. Blue cylinder, trigger, barrel, screws, wedge. Silver-plated brass backstrap and square-back trigger guard. From Colt Blackpowder Arms Co.
Price: $427.50

Uberti 1861 Navy Percussion Revolver
Similar to 1851 Navy except has round 7$^1/_2$″ barrel, rounded trigger guard, German silver blade front sight, "creeping" loading lever. Available with fluted or round cylinder. Imported by Uberti USA Inc.
Price: Steel backstrap, trigger guard, cut for stock $300.00

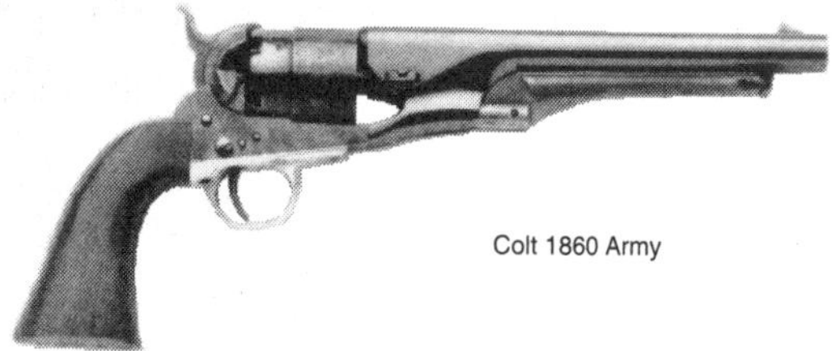
Colt 1860 Army

COLT 1861 NAVY PERCUSSION REVOLVER
Caliber: 36.
Barrel: 7$^1/_2$″.
Weight: 42 oz. **Length:** 13$^1/_8$″ overall.
Stocks: One-piece walnut.
Sights: Blade front, hammer notch rear.
Features: Color case-hardened frame, loading lever, plunger; blued barrel, backstrap, trigger guard; roll-engraved cylinder and barrel. From Colt Blackpowder Arms Co.
Price: $465.00

ARMY 1851 PERCUSSION REVOLVER
Caliber: 44, 6-shot.
Barrel: 7$^1/_2$″.
Weight: 45 oz. **Length:** 13″ overall.
Stocks: Walnut finish.
Sights: Fixed.
Features: 44-caliber version of the 1851 Navy. Imported by The Armoury, Armsport.
Price: $129.00

BABY DRAGOON 1848, 1849 POCKET, WELLS FARGO
Caliber: 31.
Barrel: 3″, 4″, 5″, 6″; seven-groove, RH twist.
Weight: About 21 oz.
Stocks: Varnished walnut.
Sights: Brass pin front, hammer notch rear.
Features: No loading lever on Baby Dragoon or Wells Fargo models. Unfluted cylinder with stagecoach holdup scene; cupped cylinder pin; no grease grooves; one safety pin on cylinder and slot in hammer face; straight (flat) mainspring. From Armsport, Dixie Gun Works, Uberti USA Inc., Cabela's.
Price: 6″ barrel, with loading lever (Dixie Gun Works) $254.95
Price: 4″ (Cabela's, Uberti USA Inc.) $169.95

CABELA'S PATERSON REVOLVER
Caliber: 36, 5-shot cylinder.
Barrel: 7$^1/_2$″.
Weight: 24 oz. **Length:** 11$^1/_2$″ overall.
Stocks: One-piece walnut.
Sights: Fixed.
Features: Recreation of the 1836 gun. Color case-hardened frame, steel backstrap; roll-engraved cylinder scene. Imported by Cabela's.
Price: $229.95

COLT 1849 POCKET DRAGOON REVOLVER
Caliber: 31.
Barrel: 4″.
Weight: 24 oz. **Length:** 9$^1/_2$″ overall.
Stocks: One-piece walnut.
Sights: Fixed. Brass pin front, hammer notch rear.
Features: Color case-hardened frame. No loading lever. Unfluted cylinder with engraved scene. Exact reproduction of original. From Colt Blackpowder Arms Co.
Price: $390.00

Stone Mountain Arms Sheriff's Model
Similar to the Uberti 1861 Navy except has 5$^1/_2$″ barrel, brass or steel frame, semi-fluted cylinder. In 44-caliber only.
Price: Steel frame, finished $179.95
Price: Brass frame (Armsport) $155.00
Price: Steel frame (Armsport) $193.00

Consult our Directory pages for the location of firms mentioned.

COLT 1860 ARMY PERCUSSION REVOLVER
Caliber: 44.
Barrel: 8″, 7 groove, left-hand twist.
Weight: 42 oz.
Stocks: One-piece walnut.
Sights: German silver front sight, hammer notch rear.
Features: Steel backstrap cut for shoulder stock; brass trigger guard. Cylinder has Navy scene. Color case-hardened frame, hammer, loading lever. Reproduction of original gun with all original markings. From Colt Blackpowder Arms Co.
Price: $427.50

Colt 1860 "Cavalry Model" Percussion Revolver
Similar to the 1860 Army except has fluted cylinder. Color case-hardened frame, hammer, loading lever and plunger; blued barrel, backstrap and cylinder, brass trigger guard. Has four-screw frame cut for optional shoulder stock. From Colt Blackpowder Arms Co.
Price: $465.00

CAUTION: PRICES SHOWN ARE SUPPLIED BY THE MANUFACTURER OR IMPORTER. CHECK YOUR LOCAL GUN SHOP.

Griswold & Gunnison

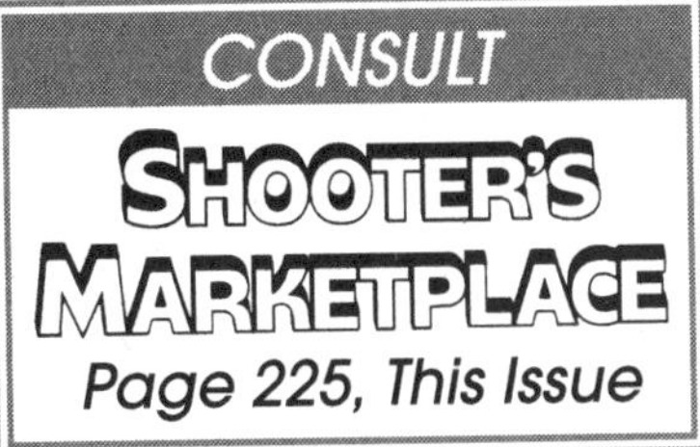
CONSULT
SHOOTER'S
MARKETPLACE
Page 225, This Issue

GRISWOLD & GUNNISON PERCUSSION REVOLVER

Caliber: 36 or 44, 6-shot.
Barrel: 7 1/2".
Weight: 44 oz. (36-cal.). **Length:** 13" overall.
Stocks: Walnut.
Sights: Fixed.
Features: Replica of famous Confederate pistol. Brass frame, backstrap and trigger guard; case-hardened loading lever; rebated cylinder (44-cal. only). Rounded Dragoon-type barrel. Imported by Navy Arms as Reb Model 1860.
Price: **$115.00**
Price: Kit **$90.00**
Price: Single cased set **$235.00**
Price: Double cased set **$365.00**

LE MAT REVOLVER

Caliber: 44/65.
Barrel: 6 3/4" (revolver); 4 7/8" (single shot).
Weight: 3 lbs., 7 oz.
Stocks: Hand-checkered walnut.
Sights: Post front, hammer notch rear.
Features: Exact reproduction with all-steel construction; 44-cal. 9-shot cylinder, 65-cal. single barrel; color case-hardened hammer with selector; spur trigger guard; ring at butt; lever-type barrel release. From Navy Arms.
Price: Cavalry model (lanyard ring, spur trigger guard) **$595.00**
Price: Army model (round trigger guard, pin-type barrel release) **$595.00**
Price: Naval-style (thumb selector on hammer) **$595.00**
Price: Engraved 18th Georgia cased set **$795.00**
Price: Engraved Beauregard cased set **$1,000.00**

CVA 1851 Navy

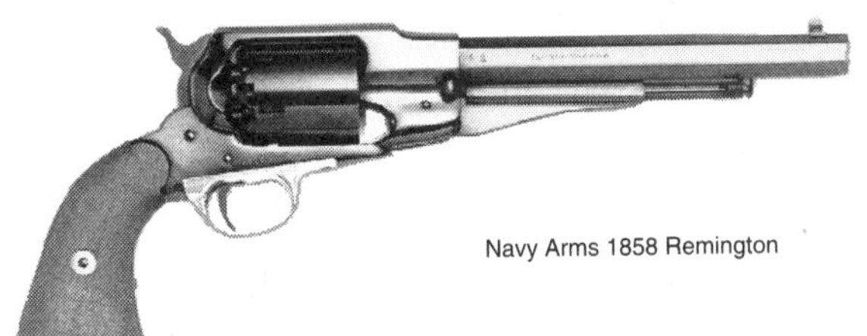
Navy Arms 1858 Remington

COLT THIRD MODEL DRAGOON

Caliber: 44.
Barrel: 7 1/2".
Weight: 66 oz. **Length:** 13 3/4" overall.
Stocks: One-piece walnut.
Sights: Blade front, hammer notch rear.
Features: Color case-hardened frame, hammer, lever and plunger; round trigger guard; flat mainspring; hammer roller; rectangular bolt cuts. From Colt Blackpowder Arms Co.
Price: Three-screw frame with brass grip straps **$487.50**
Price: Four-screw frame with blued steel grip straps, shoulder stock cuts, dovetailed folding leaf rear sight **$502.50**

COLT 1862 POCKET POLICE "TRAPPER MODEL" REVOLVER

Caliber: 36.
Barrel: 3 1/2".
Weight: 20 oz. **Length:** 8 1/2" overall.
Stocks: One-piece walnut.
Sights: Blade front, hammer notch rear.
Features: Has separate 4 5/8" brass ramrod. Color case-hardened frame and hammer; silver-plated backstrap and trigger guard; blued semi-fluted cylinder, blued barrel. From Colt Blackpowder Arms Co.
Price: **$442.50**

DIXIE WYATT EARP REVOLVER

Caliber: 44.
Barrel: 12" octagon.
Weight: 46 oz. **Length:** 18" overall.
Stocks: Two-piece walnut.
Sights: Fixed.
Features: Highly polished brass frame, backstrap and trigger guard; blued barrel and cylinder; case-hardened hammer, trigger and loading lever. Navy-size shoulder stock ($45) will fit with minor fitting. From Dixie Gun Works.
Price: **$130.00**

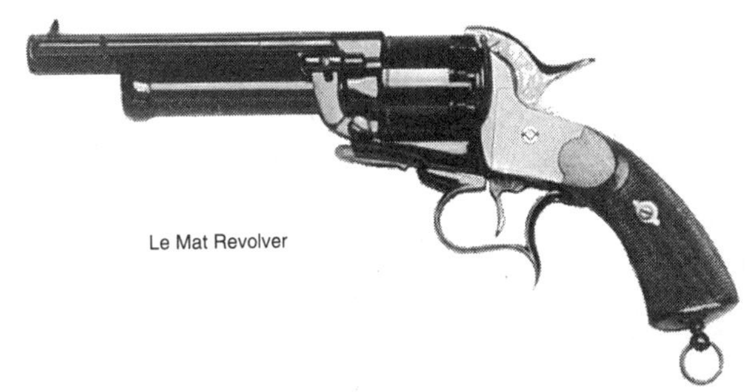
Le Mat Revolver

NAVY MODEL 1851 PERCUSSION REVOLVER

Caliber: 36, 44, 6-shot.
Barrel: 7 1/2".
Weight: 44 oz. **Length:** 13" overall.
Stocks: Walnut finish.
Sights: Post front, hammer notch rear.
Features: Brass backstrap and trigger guard; some have 1st Model squareback trigger guard, engraved cylinder with navy battle scene; case-hardened frame, hammer, loading lever. Imported by American Arms, The Armoury, Cabela's, Navy Arms, E.M.F., Dixie Gun Works, Euroarms of America, Armsport, CVA (36-cal. only), Traditions (44 only), Uberti USA Inc., Stone Mountain Arms.
Price: Brass frame . . . . . **$99.95** to **$280.00**
Price: Steel frame . . . . . **$130.00** to **$285.00**
Price: Kit form . . . . . **$110.00** to **$123.95**
Price: Engraved model (Dixie Gun Works) **$139.95**
Price: Single cased set, steel frame (Navy Arms) **$280.00**
Price: Double cased set, steel frame (Navy Arms) **$455.00**
Price: Confederate Navy (Cabela's) **$69.95**
Price: Hartford model, steel frame, German silver trim, cartouche (E.M.F.) **$190.00**

NAVY ARMS DELUXE 1858 REMINGTON-STYLE REVOLVER

Caliber: 44.
Barrel: 8".
Weight: 2 lbs., 13 oz.
Stocks: Smooth walnut.
Sights: Dovetailed blade front.
Features: First exact reproduction—correct in size and weight to the original, with progressive rifling; highly polished with blue finish, silver-plated trigger guard. From Navy Arms.
Price: Deluxe model **$415.00**

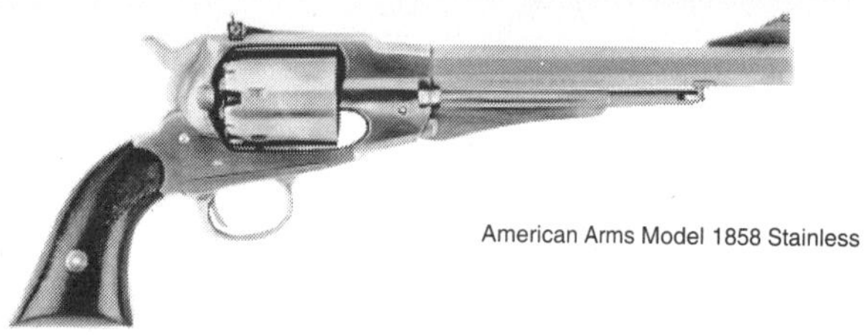
American Arms Model 1858 Stainless

NEW MODEL 1858 ARMY PERCUSSION REVOLVER

Caliber: 36 or 44, 6-shot.
Barrel: 6 1/2" or 8".
Weight: 38 oz. **Length:** 13 1/2" overall.
Stocks: Walnut.
Sights: Blade front, groove-in-frame rear.
Features: Replica of Remington Model 1858. Also available from some importers as Army Model Belt Revolver in 36-cal., a shortened and lightened version of the 44. Target Model (Uberti USA Inc., Navy Arms) has fully adjustable target rear sight, target front, 36 or 44. Imported by American Arms, Cabela's, Cimarron, CVA (as 1858 Army, steel or brass frame, 44 only), Dixie Gun Works, Navy Arms, The Armoury, E.M.F., Euroarms of America (engraved, stainless and plain), Armsport, Traditions (44 only), Uberti USA Inc. Stone Mountain Arms.
Price: Steel frame, about . . . . **$99.95** to **$280.00**
Price: Steel frame kit (Euroarms, Navy Arms) . . . . **$115.95** to **$242.00**
Price: Single cased set (Navy Arms) **$290.00**
Price: Double cased set (Navy Arms) **$480.00**
Price: Stainless steel Model 1858 (American Arms, Euroarms, Uberti USA Inc., Cabela's, Navy Arms, Armsport, Traditions) . . . . **$169.95** to **$380.00**
Price: Target Model, adjustable rear sight (Cabela's, Euroarms, Uberti USA Inc., Navy Arms, Stone Mountain Arms) . . . . **$95.95** to **$399.00**
Price: Brass frame (CVA, Cabela's, Traditions, Navy Arms) . . . **$79.95** to **$212.95**
Price: As above, kit (Dixie Gun Works, Navy Arms) . . . . **$145.00** to **$188.95**
Price: Buffalo model, 44-cal. (Cabela's) **$129.95**
Price: Hartford model, steel frame, German silver trim, cartouche (E.M.F.) **$215.00**

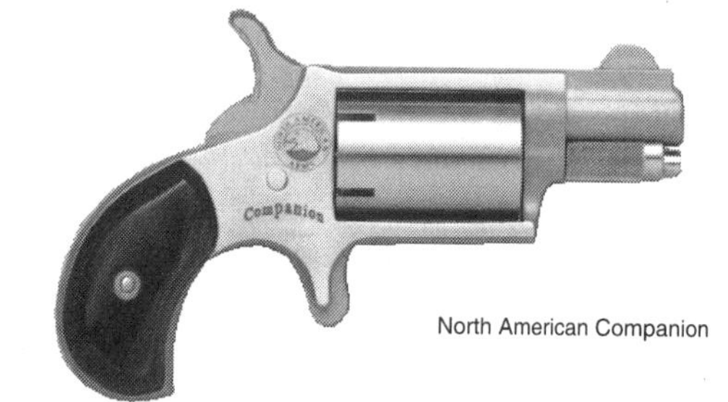

North American Companion

NORTH AMERICAN COMPANION PERCUSSION REVOLVER

Caliber: 22.
Barrel: 1 1/8".
Weight: 5.1 oz. **Length:** 4 5/10" overall.
Stocks: Laminated wood.
Sights: Blade front, notch fixed rear.
Features: All stainelss steel construction. Uses standard #11 percussion caps. Comes with bullets, powder measure, bullet seater, leather clip holster, gun rag. Long Rifle or Magnum frame size. Introduced 1996. Made in U.S. by North American Arms.
Price: Long Rifle frame **$160.00**

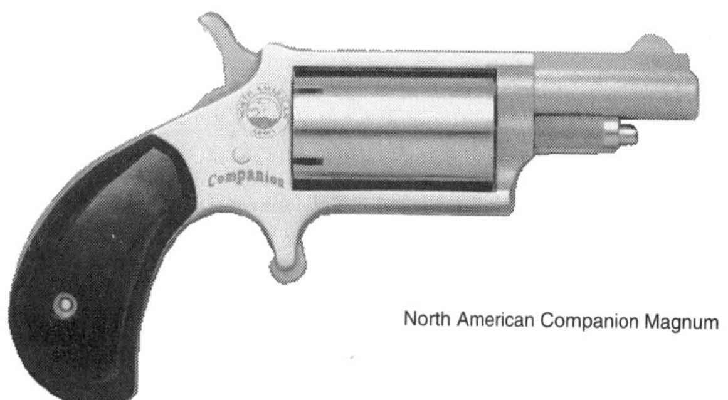

North American Companion Magnum

North American Magnum Companion Percussion Revolver

Similar to the Companion except has larger frame. Weighs 7.2 oz., has 1 5/8" barrel, measures 5 7/16" overall. Comes with bullets, powder measure, bullet seater, leather clip holster, gun rug. Introduced 1996. Made in U.S. by North American Arms.
Price: **$180.00**

POCKET POLICE 1862 PERCUSSION REVOLVER

Caliber: 36, 5-shot.
Barrel: 4 1/2", 5 1/2", 6 1/2", 7 1/2".
Weight: 26 oz. **Length:** 12" overall (6 1/2" bbl.).
Stocks: Walnut.
Sights: Fixed.
Features: Round tapered barrel; half-fluted and rebated cylinder; case-hardened frame, loading lever and hammer; silver or brass trigger guard and backstrap. Imported by CVA (7 1/2" only), Navy Arms (5 1/2" only), Uberti USA Inc. (5 1/2", 6 1/2" only).
Price: About . . . . **$139.95** to **$310.00**
Price: Single cased set with accessories (Navy Arms) **$365.00**
Price: Hartford model, steel frame, German silver trim, cartouche (E.M.F.) **$215.00**

Uberti 1862 Pocket

Consult our Directory pages for the location of firms mentioned.

ROGERS & SPENCER PERCUSSION REVOLVER

Caliber: 44.
Barrel: 7 1/2".
Weight: 47 oz. **Length:** 13 3/4" overall.
Stocks: Walnut.
Sights: Cone front, integral groove in frame for rear.
Features: Accurate reproduction of a Civil War design. Solid frame; extra large nipple cut-out on rear of cylinder; loading lever and cylinder easily removed for cleaning. From Euroarms of America (standard blue, engraved, burnished, target models), Navy Arms, Stone Mountain Arms.
Price: . . . . **$160.00** to **$289.00**
Price: Nickel-plated **$215.00**
Price: Engraved (Euroarms) **$287.00**
Price: Kit version . . . . **$245.00** to **$252.00**
Price: Target version (Euroarms, Navy Arms) . . . . **$239.00** to **$270.00**
Price: Burnished London Gray (Euroarms, Navy Arms) . . . . . **$245.00** to **$270.00**

Euroarms Rogers & Spencer

CAUTION: PRICES SHOWN ARE SUPPLIED BY THE MANUFACTURER OR IMPORTER. CHECK YOUR LOCAL GUNSHOP.

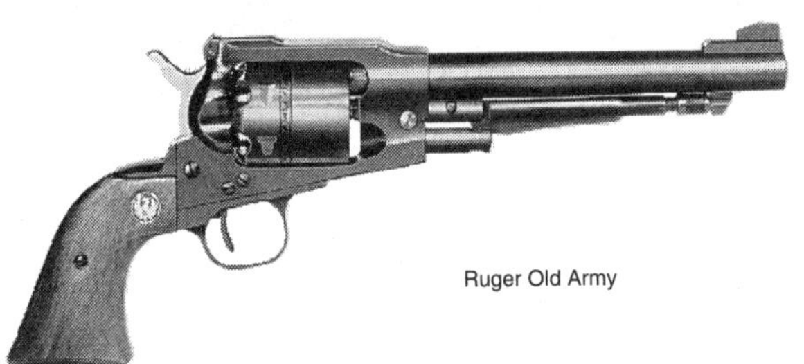
Ruger Old Army

RUGER OLD ARMY PERCUSSION REVOLVER

Caliber: 45, 6-shot. Uses .457″ dia. lead bullets.
Barrel: 7 1/2″ (6-groove, 16″ twist).
Weight: 46 oz. **Length:** 13 3/4″ overall.
Stocks: Smooth walnut.
Sights: Ramp front, rear adjustable for windage and elevation; or fixed (groove).
Features: Stainless steel; standard size nipples, chrome-moly steel cylinder and frame, same lockwork as in original Super Blackhawk. Also available in stainless steel. Made in USA. From Sturm, Ruger & Co.
Price: Stainless steel (Model KBP-7) **$465.00**
Price: Blued steel (Model BP-7) **$413.00**
Price: Stainless steel, fixed sight (KBP-7F) **$465.00**
Price: Blued steel, fixed sight (BP-7F) **$413.00**

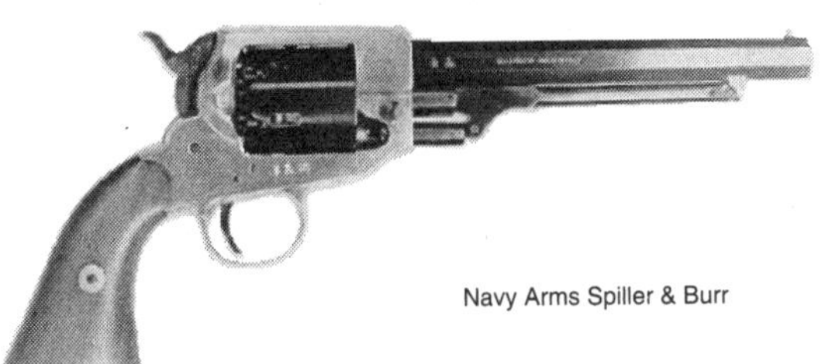
Navy Arms Spiller & Burr

SHERIFF MODEL 1851 PERCUSSION REVOLVER

Caliber: 36, 44, 6-shot.
Barrel: 5″.
Weight: 40 oz. **Length:** 10 1/2″ overall.
Stocks: Walnut.
Sights: Fixed.
Features: Brass backstrap and trigger guard; engraved navy scene; case-hardened frame, hammer, loading lever. Imported by E.M.F., Stone Mountain Arms (5 1/2″ barrel).
Price: Steel frame (E.M.F.) **$172.00**
Price: Brass frame (E.M.F.) **$140.00**
Price: Steel frame (Stone Mountain Arms) **$159.95**

SPILLER & BURR REVOLVER

Caliber: 36 (.375″ round ball).
Barrel: 7″, octagon.
Weight: 2 1/2 lbs. **Length:** 12 1/2″ overall.
Stocks: Two-piece walnut.
Sights: Fixed.
Features: Reproduction of the C.S.A. revolver. Brass frame and trigger guard. Also available as a kit. From Cabela's, Dixie Gun Works, Navy Arms.
Price: .... **$89.95** to **$199.00**
Price: Kit form **$129.95**
Price: Single cased set (Navy Arms) **$270.00**
Price: Double cased set (Navy Arms) **$430.00**

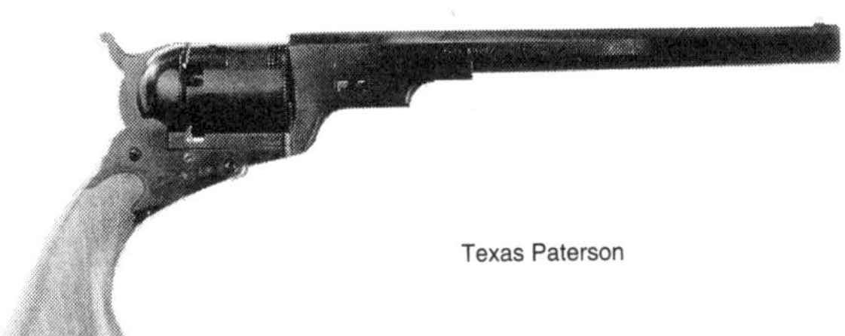
Texas Paterson

TEXAS PATERSON 1836 REVOLVER

Caliber: 36 (.375″ round ball).
Barrel: 7 1/2″.
Weight: 42 oz.
Stocks: One-piece walnut.
Sights: Fixed.
Features: Copy of Sam Colt's first commercially-made revolving pistol. Has no loading lever but comes with loading tool. From Dixie Gun Works, Navy Arms, Uberti USA Inc.
Price: About .... **$325.00** to **$395.00**
Price: With loading lever (Uberti USA Inc.) **$450.00**
Price: Engraved (Navy Arms) **$465.00**

UBERTI 1862 POCKET NAVY PERCUSSION REVOLVER

Caliber: 36, 5-shot.
Barrel: 5 1/2″, 6 1/2″, octagonal, 7-groove, LH twist.
Weight: 27 oz. (5 1/2″ barrel). **Length:** 10 1/2″ overall (5 1/2″ bbl.).
Stocks: One-piece varnished walnut.
Sights: Brass pin front, hammer notch rear.
Features: Rebated cylinder, hinged loading lever, brass or silver-plated backstrap and trigger guard, color-cased frame, hammer, loading lever, plunger and latch, rest blued. Has original-type markings. From Uberti USA Inc.
Price: With brass backstrap, trigger guard **$310.00**

UBERTI 1st MODEL DRAGOON

Caliber: 44.
Barrel: 7 1/2″, part round, part octagon.
Weight: 64 oz.
Stocks: One-piece walnut.
Sights: German silver blade front, hammer notch rear.
Features: First model has oval bolt cuts in cylinder, square-back flared trigger guard, V-type mainspring, short trigger. Ranger and Indian scene roll-engraved on cylinder. Color case-hardened frame, loading lever, plunger and hammer; blue barrel, cylinder, trigger and wedge. Available with old-time charcoal blue or standard blue-black finish. Polished brass backstrap and trigger guard. From Uberti USA Inc.
Price: **$325.00**

Uberti 2nd Model Dragoon Revolver

Similar to the 1st Model except distinguished by rectangular bolt cuts in the cylinder.
Price: **$325.00**

Uberti 3rd Model Dragoon Revolver

Similar to the 2nd Model except for oval trigger guard, long trigger, modifications to the loading lever and latch. Imported by Uberti USA Inc.
Price: Military model (frame cut for shoulder stock, steel backstrap) **$330.00**
Price: Civilian (brass backstrap, trigger guard) **$325.00**

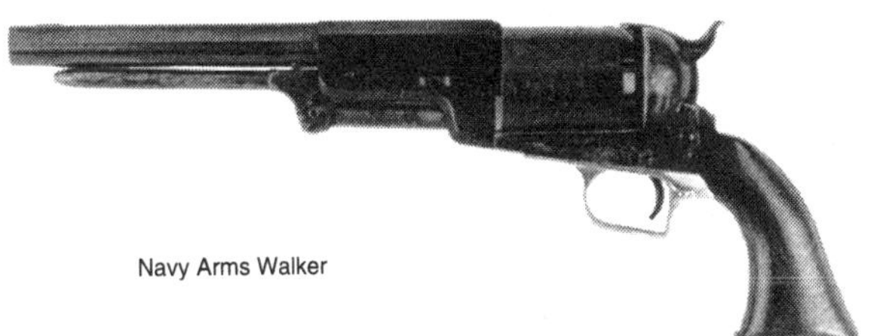
Navy Arms Walker

WALKER 1847 PERCUSSION REVOLVER

Caliber: 44, 6-shot.
Barrel: 9″.
Weight: 84 oz. **Length:** 15 1/2″ overall.
Stocks: Walnut.
Sights: Fixed.
Features: Case-hardened frame, loading lever and hammer; iron backstrap; brass trigger guard; engraved cylinder. Imported by Cabela's, CVA, Navy Arms, Dixie Gun Works, Uberti USA Inc., E.M.F., Cimarron, Traditions.
Price: About .... **$225.00** to **$360.00**
Price: Single cased set (Navy Arms) **$405.00**
Price: Deluxe Walker with French fitted case (Navy Arms) **$505.00**
Price: Hartford model, steel frame, German silver trim, cartouche (E.M.F.) **$295.00**

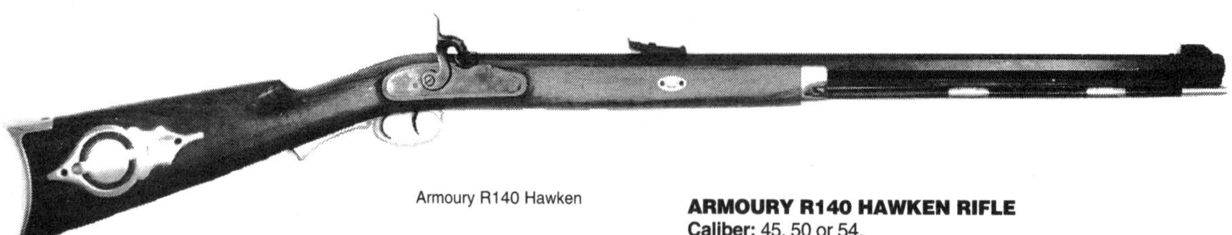
Armoury R140 Hawken

ARMSPORT 1863 SHARPS RIFLE, CARBINE
Caliber: 45, 54.
Barrel: 28″, round.
Weight: 8.4 lbs. **Length:** 46″ overall.
Stock: Walnut.
Sights: Blade front, folding adjustable rear. Tang sight set optionally available.
Features: Replica of the 1863 Sharps. Color case-hardened frame, rest blued. Imported by Armsport.
Price: **$740.00**
Price: Carbine, 54 caliber, 22″ barrel **$640.00**

CABELA'S BLUE RIDGE RIFLE
Caliber: 32, 36, 45, 50, 54.
Barrel: 39″, octagonal.
Weight: About 7 3/4 lbs. **Length:** 55″ overall.
Stock: American black walnut.
Sights: Blade front, rear drift adjustable for windage.
Features: Color case-hardened lockplate and cock/hammer, brass trigger guard and buttplate, double set, double-phased triggers. From Cabela's.
Price: Percussion **$299.95**
Price: Flintlock **$319.95**
Price: Percussion carbine (28″ barrel) **$259.95**

CABELA'S RED RIVER RIFLE
Caliber: 45, 50, 54, 58.
Barrel: NA.
Weight: About 7 lbs. **Length:** 45″ overall.
Stock: Walnut-stained hardwood.
Sights: Blade front, adjustable buckhorn rear.
Features: Brass trigger guard, forend cap, thimbles; color case-hardened lock and hammer; rubber recoil pad. Introduced 1995. Imported by Cabela's.
Price: **$119.95**

CABELA'S SHARPS SPORTING RIFLE
Caliber: 45, 54.
Barrel: 31″, octagonal.
Weight: About 10 lbs. **Length:** 49″ overall.
Stock: American walnut with checkered grip and forend.
Sights: Blade front, ladder-type adjustable rear.
Features: Color case-hardened lock and buttplate. Adjustable double set, double-phased triggers. From Cabela's.
Price: **$649.00**

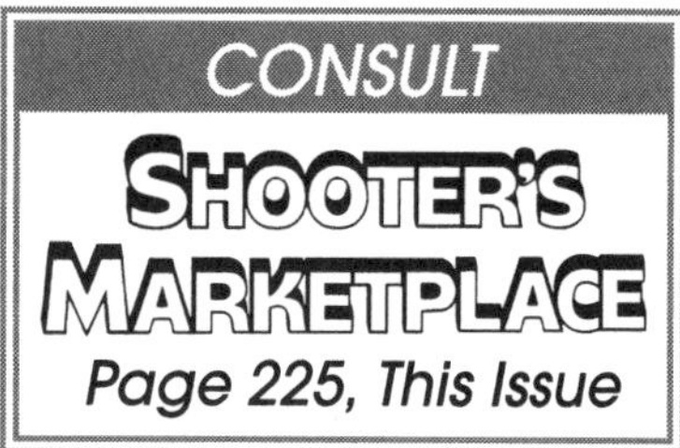
CONSULT
SHOOTER'S
MARKETPLACE
Page 225, This Issue

ARMOURY R140 HAWKEN RIFLE
Caliber: 45, 50 or 54.
Barrel: 29″.
Weight: 8 3/4 to 9 lbs. **Length:** 45 3/4″ overall.
Stock: Walnut, with cheekpiece.
Sights: Dovetail front, fully adjustable rear.
Features: Octagon barrel, removable breech plug; double set triggers; blued barrel, brass stock fittings, color case-hardened percussion lock. From Armsport, The Armoury.
Price: .... **$225.00** to **$245.00**

BOSTONIAN PERCUSSION RIFLE
Caliber: 45.
Barrel: 30″, octagonal
Weight: 7 1/4 lbs. **Length:** 46″ overall.
Stock: Walnut.
Sights: Blade front, fixed notch rear.
Features: Color case-hardened lock, brass trigger guard, buttplate, patchbox. Imported from Italy by E.M.F.
Price: **$285.00**

CABELA'S ROLLING BLOCK MUZZLELOADER
Caliber: 50, 54.
Barrel: 26 1/2″ octagonal; 1:32″ (50), 1:48″ (54) twist.
Weight: About 9 1/4 lbs. **Length:** 43 1/2″ overall.
Stock: American walnut, rubber butt pad.
Sights: Blade front, adjustable buckhorn rear.
Features: Uses in-line ignition system, Brass trigger guard, color case-hardened hammer, block and buttplate; black-finished, engraved receiver; easily removable screw-in breech plug; black ramrod and thimble. From Cabela's.
Price: **$289.95**

Cabela's Rolling Block Muzzleloader Carbine
Similar to the rifle version except has 22 1/4″ barrel, weighs 8 1/4 lbs. Has bead on ramp front sight, modern fully adjustable rear. From Cabela's.
Price: **$269.95**

CABELA'S TRADITIONAL HAWKEN
Caliber: 45, 50, 54, 58.
Barrel: 29″.
Weight: About 9 lbs.
Stock: Walnut.
Sights: Blade front, open adjustable rear.
Features: Flintlock or percussion. Adjustable double-set triggers. Polished brass furniture, color case-hardened lock. Imported by Cabela's.
Price: Percussion, right-hand **$159.95**
Price: Percussion, left-hand **$169.95**
Price: Flintlock, right-hand **$184.95**

Cabela's Sporterized Hawken Hunter Rifle
Similar to the Traditional Hawken's except has more modern stock style with rubber recoil pad, blued furniture, sling swivels. Percussion only, in 45-, 50-, 54- or 58-caliber.
Price: Carbine or rifle, right-hand **$179.95**
Price: Carbine or rifle, left-hand **$189.95**

COLT MODEL 1861 MUSKET
Caliber: 58.
Barrel: 40″.
Weight: 9 lbs., 3 oz. **Length:** 56″ overall.
Stock: Oil-finished walnut.
Sights: Blade front, adjustable folding leaf rear.
Features: Made to original specifications and has authentic Civil War Colt markings. Bright-finished metal, blued nipple and rear sight. Bayonet and accessories available. From Colt Blackpowder Arms Co.
Price: **$615.00**

CAUTION: PRICES SHOWN ARE SUPPLIED BY THE MANUFACTURER OR IMPORTER. CHECK YOUR LOCAL GUNSHOP.

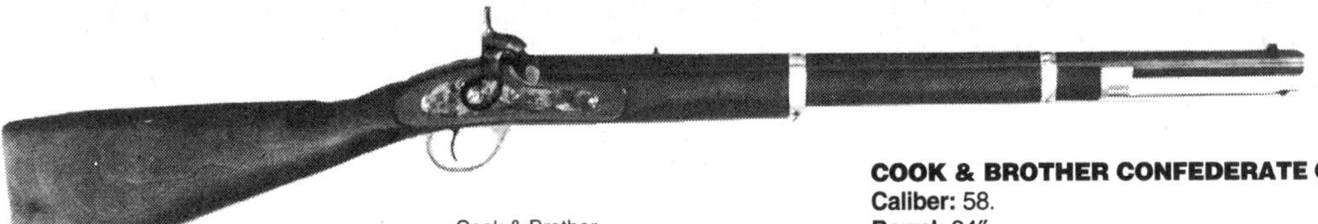
Cook & Brother

COOK & BROTHER CONFEDERATE CARBINE
Caliber: 58.
Barrel: 24″.
Weight: 7½ lbs. **Length:** 40½″ overall.
Stock: Select walnut.
Features: Recreation of the 1861 New Orleans-made artillery carbine. Color case-hardened lock, browned barrel. Buttplate, trigger guard, barrel bands, sling swivels and nose cap of polished brass. From Euroarms of America.
Price: **$449.00**
Price: Cook & Brother rifle (33″ barrel) **$480.00**

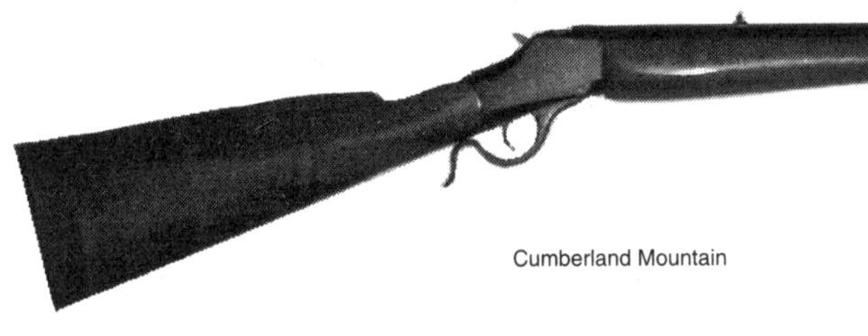
Cumberland Mountain

CUMBERLAND MOUNTAIN BLACKPOWDER RIFLE
Caliber: 50.
Barrel: 26″, round.
Weight: 9½ lbs. **Length:** 43″ overall.
Stock: American walnut.
Sights: Bead front, open rear adjustable for windage.
Features: Falling block action fires with shotshell primer. Blued receiver and barrel. Introduced 1993. Made in U.S. by Cumberland Mountain Arms, Inc.
Price: **$931.50**

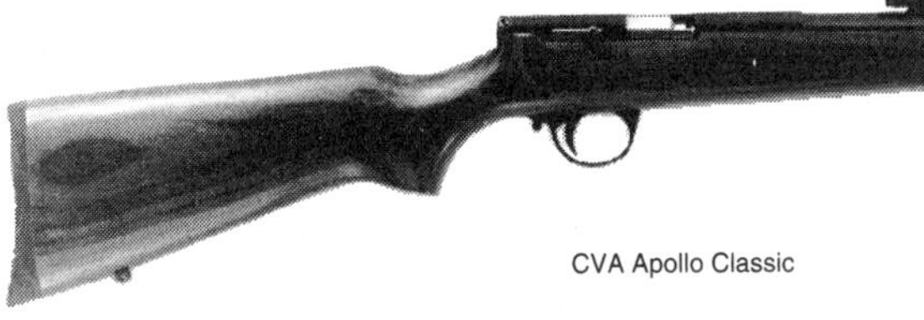
CVA Apollo Classic

CVA APOLLO SHADOW, CLASSIC RIFLES
Caliber: 50, 54.
Barrel: 24″; round with octagon integral receiver; 1:32″ twist.
Weight: 7-7½ lbs. **Length:** 42″ overall.
Stock: Synthetic Dura-Grip (Shadow); brown laminate with swivel studs (Classic); pistol grip, solid rubber buttpad.
Sights: Blade on ramp front, fully adjustable rear; drilled and tapped for scope mounting.
Features: In-line ignition, modern-style trigger with automatic safety; oversize trigger guard; synthetic ramrod. From CVA.
Price: Shadow **$229.95**
Price: Classic **$259.95**

CVA Buckmaster Rifle
Similar to the Apollo Comet except has Dura-Grip synthetic stock with Advantage camouflage pattern, and blued barrel and action. Introduced 1996. From CVA.
Price: **$239.00**

CVA Apollo Comet Rifle
Similar to the Apollo Shadow except stainless steel barrel and action, synthetic stock with matte black finish. Available in 50-caliber only. Introduced 1995. From CVA.
Price: **$279.95**

CVA Staghorn

CVA Staghorn Rifle
Similar to the Apollo Comet except has blued barrel and action, and is available in 50, 54 caliber. Drilled and tapped receiver for scope mount or aperture sight. Introduced 1996.
Price: **$179.00**

CVA BOBCAT RIFLE
Caliber: 50 and 54.
Barrel: 26″; 1:48″ twist.
Weight: 6½ lbs. **Length:** 40″ overall.
Stock: Dura-Grip synthetic.
Sights: Blade front, open rear.
Features: Oversize trigger guard; wood ramrod; matte black finish. Introduced 1995. From CVA.
Price: **$99.95**

CVA Bobcat Hunter
Similar to the Bobcat except has black synthetic stock with checkered wrist and forend, drilled and tapped for scope mounting, engraved, blued lockplate and offset hammer, and has sporter adjustable rear sight. Available in 50- and 54-caliber. Introduced 1995. From CVA.
Price: **$149.95**

CVA Apollo Dominator
Similar to the Apollo Shadow except has a Bell & Carlson synthetic thumbhole stock, stainless steel barrel and action, Williams micro adjustable rear sight, bead on blade front. Drilled and tapped for scope mounting. Introduced 1996. From CVA.
Price: **$329.95**

CVA Apollo Brown Bear
Similar to the CVA Classic except has select grade hardwood stock with oil finish, raised comb and cheekpiece; bead front sight, Williams Hunter rear; blued barrel, receiver; drilled and tapped for scope mounting. Introduced 1996. From CVA.
Price: **$229.95**

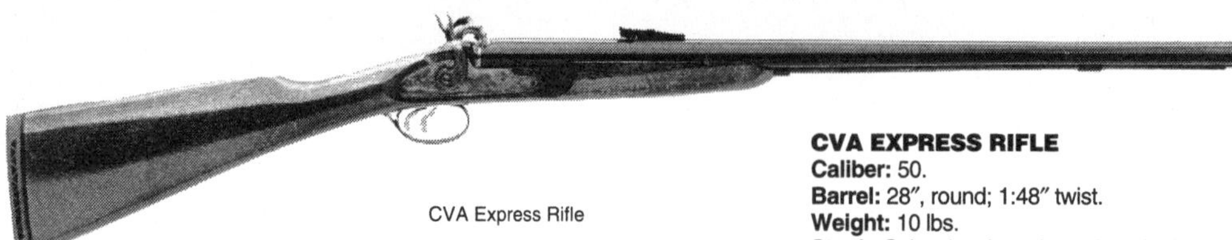

CVA Express Rifle

CVA EXPRESS RIFLE
Caliber: 50.
Barrel: 28″, round; 1:48″ twist.
Weight: 10 lbs.
Stock: Select hardwood; ventilated rubber recoil pad.
Sights: Bead and blade front, adjustable rear.
Features: Double rifle with twin percussion locks and triggers, adjustable barrels. Button breech. Introduced 1989. From CVA.
Price: Finished **$429.95**

CVA FRONTIER HUNTER CARBINE
Caliber: 50, 54.
Barrel: 24″; 15/16″ flats; 1:32″ twist.
Weight: 6¾ lbs. **Length:** 40″ overall.
Stock: Laminated hardwood.
Sights: Bead front, Patridge-style click-adjustable rear.
Features: Offset hammer; black-chromed furniture; solid buttpad; barrel drilled and tapped for scope mounting. From CVA.
Price: **$219.95**

CVA St. Louis Hawken

CVA HAWKEN RIFLE
Caliber: 50, 54.
Barrel: 28″, octagon; 15/16″ across flats; 1:48″ twist.
Weight: 8 lbs. **Length:** 44″ overall.
Stock: Select hardwood.
Sights: Beaded blade front, fully adjustable open rear.
Features: Fully adjustable double-set triggers; synthetic ramrod (kits have wood); brass patch box, wedge plates, nosecap, thimbles, trigger guard and buttplate; blued barrel; color case-hardened, engraved lockplate. V-type mainspring. Button breech. Introduced 1981. From CVA.
Price: St. Louis Hawken, finished (50-, 54-cal.) **$209.95**
Price: As above, combo kit (50-, 54-cal. bbls.) **$229.95**
Price: Left-hand, percussion **$234.95**
Price: Flintlock, 50-cal. only **$234.95**
Price: Flintlock, left-hand **$249.95**
Price: Percussion kit (50-cal., blued, wood ramrod) **$169.95**
Price: St. Louis Hawken Classic (laminated stock) **$249.95**

CVA KENTUCKY RIFLE
Caliber: 50.
Barrel: 33½″, rifled, octagon; 7/8″ flats.
Weight: 7½ lbs. **Length:** 48″ overall.
Stock: Select hardwood.
Sights: Brass Kentucky blade-type front, fixed open rear.
Features: Available in percussion only. Color case-hardened lockplate. Stainless steel nipple included. From CVA.
Price: Percussion **$279.95**
Price: Percussion kit **$189.95**

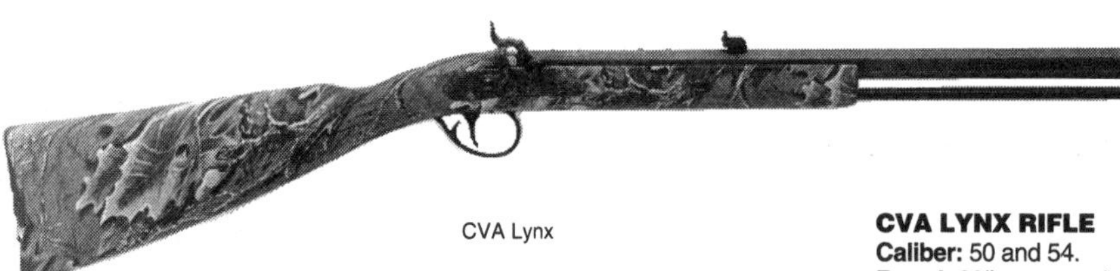

CVA Lynx

CVA LYNX RIFLE
Caliber: 50 and 54.
Barrel: 26″, octagonal; 15/16″ flats; 1:48″ twist.
Weight: About 6½ lbs. **Length:** 40″ overall.
Stock: Dura-Grip synthetic.
Sights: Beaded blade front, rear adjustable for windage.
Features: Oversize trigger guard; color case-hardened lock, blued barrel, Realtree All Purpose® camo stock. Drilled and tapped for scope mounting. Synthetic ramrod. Introduced 1995. From CVA.
Price: **$179.95**

CVA PLAINSHUNTER RIFLE
Caliber: 50.
Barrel: 26″, octagonal; 15/16″ flats; 1:48″ twist.
Weight: About 6½ lbs. **Length:** 40″ overall.
Stock: Select hardwood.
Sights: Brass blade front, semi-buckhorn rear.
Features: Brass nosecap, thimbles, wedge plates; wood ramrod. Introduced 1995. From CVA.
Price: **$174.95**

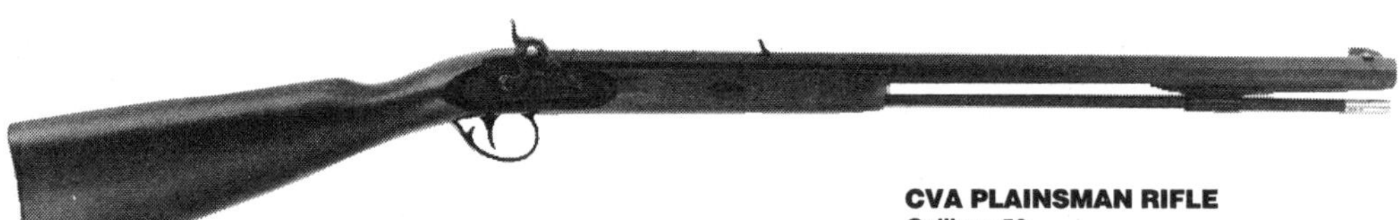

CVA Plainsman

CVA PLAINSMAN RIFLE
Caliber: 50.
Barrel: 26″, octagonal; 15/16″ flats; 1:48″ twist.
Weight: 6½ lbs. **Length:** 40″ overall.
Stock: Stained hardwood.
Sights: Brass blade front, fixed rear.
Features: Oversize trigger guard; color case-hardened lock; wood ramrod; matte finish. Introduced 1995. From CVA.
Price: **$159.95**

CAUTION: PRICES SHOWN ARE SUPPLIED BY THE MANUFACTURER OR IMPORTER. CHECK YOUR LOCAL GUNSHOP.

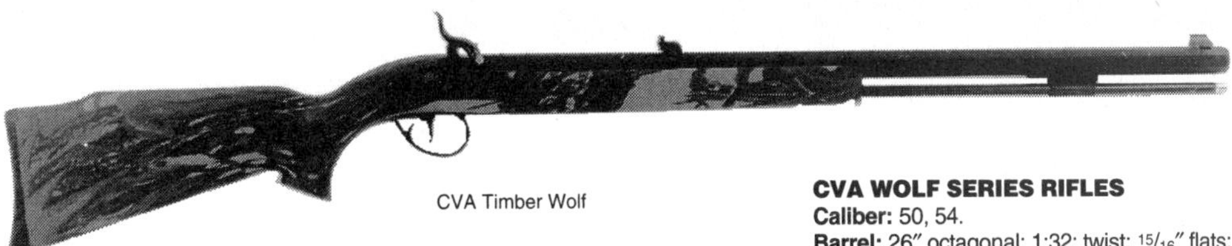

CVA Timber Wolf

CVA VARMINT RIFLE

Caliber: 32.
Barrel: 24″ octagonal; $^{7}/_{8}$″ flats; 1:48″ rifling.
Weight: $6^{3}/_{4}$ lbs. **Length:** 40″ overall.
Stock: Select hardwood.
Sights: Blade front, Patridge-style click adjustable rear.
Features: Brass trigger guard, nose cap, wedge plate, thimble and buttplate. Drilled and tapped for scope mounting. Color case-hardened lock. Single trigger. Aluminum ramrod. Imported by CVA.
Price: $219.95

CVA WOLF SERIES RIFLES

Caliber: 50, 54.
Barrel: 26″ octagonal; 1:32: twist; $^{15}/_{16}$″ flats; blue finish.
Weight: $6^{1}/_{2}$ lbs. **Length:** 40″ overall.
Stock: Tuff-Lite polymer—gray finish, solid buttplate (Grey Wolf); Realtree All Purpose® camo finish, solid buttplate (Timber Wolf); checkered grip.
Sights: Blade front on ramp, fully adjustable open rear; drilled and tapped for scope mounting.
Features: Oversize trigger guard; synthetic ramrod; offset hammer. From CVA.
Price: Grey Wolf $199.95
Price: Timber Wolf (50-cal. only) $229.95

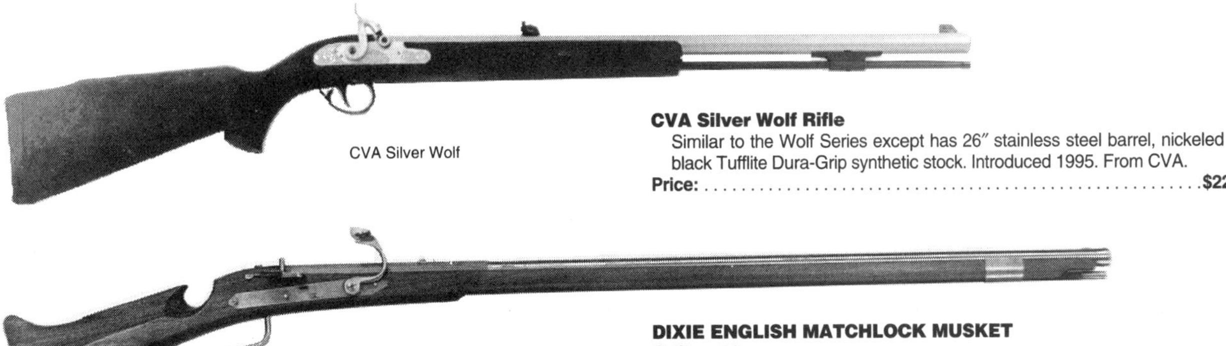

CVA Silver Wolf

CVA Silver Wolf Rifle

Similar to the Wolf Series except has 26″ stainless steel barrel, nickeled lock, black Tufflite Dura-Grip synthetic stock. Introduced 1995. From CVA.
Price: $229.95

Dixie English Matchlock

DIXIE ENGLISH MATCHLOCK MUSKET

Caliber: 72.
Barrel: 44″.
Weight: 8 lbs. **Length:** 57.75″ overall.
Stock: Walnut with satin oil finish.
Sights: Blade front, open rear adjustable for windage.
Features: Replica of circa 1600-1680 English matchlock. Getz barrel with 11″ octagonal area at rear, rest is round with cannon-type muzzle. All steel finished in the white. Imported by Dixie Gun Works.
Price: $895.00

DIXIE DELUX CUB RIFLE

Caliber: 40.
Barrel: 28″.
Weight: $6^{1}/_{2}$ lbs.
Stock: Walnut.
Sights: Fixed.
Features: Short rifle for small game and beginning shooters. Brass patchbox and furniture. Flint or percussion. From Dixie Gun Works.
Price: Finished $335.00
Price: Kit $259.00
Price: Deerslayer (50-caliber) $350.00

Dixie 1859 Sharps

DIXIE SHARPS NEW MODEL 1859 MILITARY RIFLE

Caliber: 54.
Barrel: 30″, 6-groove; 1:48″ twist.
Weight: 9 lbs. **Length:** $45^{1}/_{2}$″ overall.
Stock: Oiled walnut.
Sights: Blade front, ladder-style rear.
Features: Blued barrel, color case-hardened barrel bands, receiver, hammer, nose cap, lever, patchbox cover and buttplate. Introduced 1995. Imported from Italy by Dixie Gun Works.
Price: $895.00

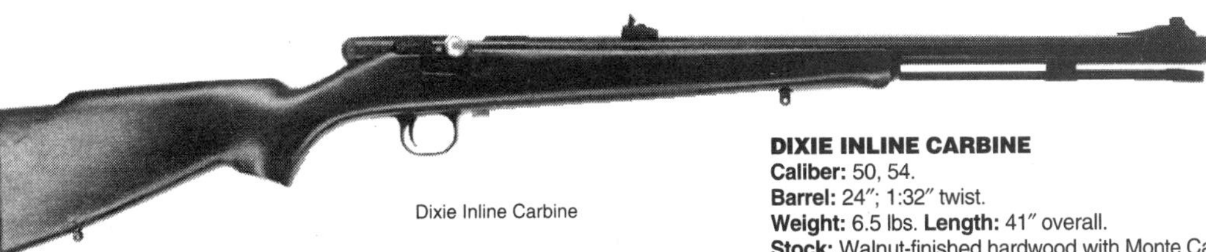

Dixie Inline Carbine

DIXIE INLINE CARBINE

Caliber: 50, 54.
Barrel: 24″; 1:32″ twist.
Weight: 6.5 lbs. **Length:** 41″ overall.
Stock: Walnut-finished hardwood with Monte Carlo comb.
Sights: Ramp front with red insert, open fully adjustable rear.
Features: Sliding "bolt" fully encloses cap and nipple. Fully adjustable trigger, automatic safety. Aluminum ramrod. Imported from Italy by Dixie Gun Works.
Price: $349.95

DIXIE TENNESSEE MOUNTAIN RIFLE
Caliber: 32 or 50.
Barrel: $41^1/_2$″, 6-groove rifling, brown finish. **Length:** 56″ overall.
Stock: Walnut, oil finish; Kentucky-style.
Sights: Silver blade front, open buckhorn rear.
Features: Recreation of the original mountain rifles. Early Schultz lock, interchangeable flint or percussion with vent plug or drum and nipple. Tumbler has fly. Double-set triggers. All metal parts browned. From Dixie Gun Works.
Price: Flint or percussion, finished rifle, 50-cal. **$575.00**
Price: Kit, 50-cal. **$495.00**
Price: Left-hand model, flint or percussion **$575.00**
Price: Left-hand kit, flint or perc., 50-cal. **$495.00**
Price: Squirrel Rifle (as above except in 32-cal. with $^{13}/_{16}$″ barrel flats), flint or percussion **$575.00**
Price: Kit, 32-cal., flint or percussion **$495.00**

DIXIE 1863 SPRINGFIELD MUSKET
Caliber: 58 (.570″ patched ball or .575″ Minie).
Barrel: 50″, rifled.
Stocks: Walnut stained.
Sights: Blade front, adjustable ladder-type rear.
Features: Bright-finish lock, barrel, furniture. Reproduction of the last of the regulation muzzleloaders. Imported from Japan by Dixie Gun Works.
Price: Finished **$595.00**
Price: Kit **$525.00**

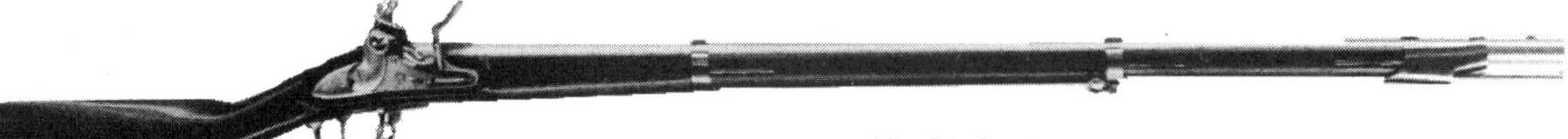

Dixie Model 1816

DIXIE U.S. MODEL 1861 SPRINGFIELD
Caliber: 58.
Barrel: 40″.
Weight: About 8 lbs. **Length:** $55^{13}/_{16}$″ overall.
Stock: Oil-finished walnut.
Sights: Blade front, step adjustable rear.
Features: Exact recreation of original rifle. Sling swivels attached to trigger guard bow and middle barrel band. Lockplate marked "1861" with eagle motif and "U.S. Springfield" in front of hammer; "U.S." stamped on top of buttplate. From Dixie Gun Works.
Price: **$595.00**
Price: From Stone Mountain Arms **$599.00**
Price: Kit **$525.00**

DIXIE U.S. MODEL 1816 FLINTLOCK MUSKET
Caliber: 69.
Barrel: 42″, smoothbore.
Weight: 9.75 lbs. **Length:** 56.5″ overall.
Stock: Walnut with oil finish.
Sights: Blade front.
Features: All metal finished "National Armory Bright"; three barrel bands with springs; steel ramrod with button-shaped head. Imported by Dixie Gun Works.
Price: **$725.00**

Consult our Directory pages for the location of firms mentioned.

E.M.F. 1863 SHARPS MILITARY CARBINE
Caliber: 54.
Barrel: 22″, round.
Weight: 8 lbs. **Length:** 39″ overall.
Stock: Oiled walnut.
Sights: Blade front, military ladder-type rear.
Features: Color case-hardened lock, rest blued. Imported by E.M.F.
Price: **$860.00**

Euroarms Volunteer

EUROARMS VOLUNTEER TARGET RIFLE
Caliber: .451.
Barrel: 33″ (two-band), 36″ (three-band).
Weight: 11 lbs. (two-band). **Length:** 48.75″ overall (two-band).
Stock: European walnut with checkered wrist and forend.
Sights: Hooded bead front, adjustable rear with interchangeable leaves.
Features: Alexander Henry-type rifling with 1:20″ twist. Color case-hardened hammer and lockplate, brass trigger guard and nose cap, rest blued. Imported by Euroarms of America.
Price: Two-band **$720.00**
Price: Three-band **$773.00**

EUROARMS BUFFALO CARBINE
Caliber: 58.
Barrel: 26″, round.
Weight: $7^3/_4$ lbs. **Length:** 42″ overall.
Stock: Walnut.
Sights: Blade front, open adjustable rear.
Features: Shoots .575″ round ball. Color case-hardened lock, blue hammer, barrel, trigger; brass furniture. Brass patchbox. Imported by Euroarms of America.
Price: **$440.00**

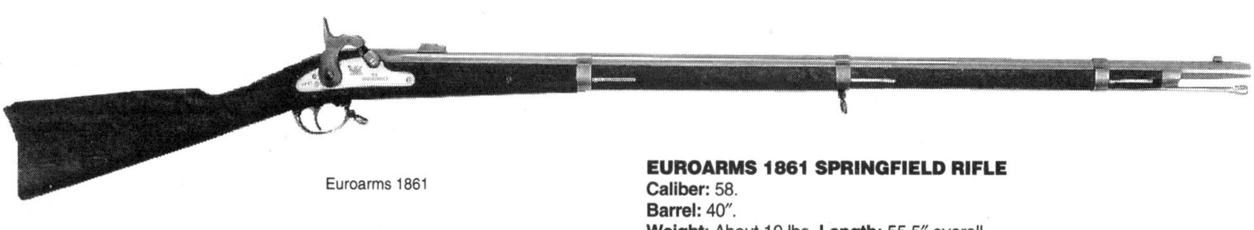

Euroarms 1861

EUROARMS 1861 SPRINGFIELD RIFLE
Caliber: 58.
Barrel: 40″.
Weight: About 10 lbs. **Length:** 55.5″ overall.
Stock: European walnut.
Sights: Blade front, three-leaf military rear.
Features: Reproduction of the original three-band rifle. Lockplate marked "1861" with eagle and "U.S. Springfield." Metal left in the white. Imported by Euroarms of America.
Price: **$564.00**

CAUTION: PRICES SHOWN ARE SUPPLIED BY THE MANUFACTURER OR IMPORTER. CHECK YOUR LOCAL GUNSHOP.

Gonic GA-87

Gonic GA-93 Magnum M/L Rifle

Similar to the GA-87 except has open bolt mechanism, single safety, 22″ barrel and comes only in 50-caliber. Stock is black wrinkle-finish wood or gray or brown, standard or thumbhole laminate. **Partial listing shown.** Introduced 1993. From Gonic Arms, Inc.

Price: Black stock, blue, no sights **$483.30**
Price: As above, stainless **$562.25**
Price: Laminated stock, blue, no sights **$554.25**
Price: As above, stainless **$650.65**
Price: Black stock, blue, open sights **$500.57**
Price: As above, stainless **$603.04**
Price: Laminated stock, blue, open sights **$595.24**
Price: As above, stainless **$691.44**

GONIC GA-87 M/L RIFLE

Caliber: 45, 50
Barrel: 26″.
Weight: 6 to 6$^1/_2$ lbs. **Length:** 43″ overall (Carbine).
Stock: American walnut with checkered grip and forend, or laminated stock.
Sights: Optional bead front, open or peep rear adjustable for windage and elevation; drilled and tapped for scope bases (included).
Features: Closed-breech action with straight-line ignition. Modern trigger mechanism with ambidextrous safety. Satin blue finish on metal, satin stock finish. Introduced 1989. From Gonic Arms, Inc.
Price: Standard rifle, no sights **$800.41**
Price: As above, with sights, from **$869.93**
Price: Walnut stock, peep sight **$800.41**

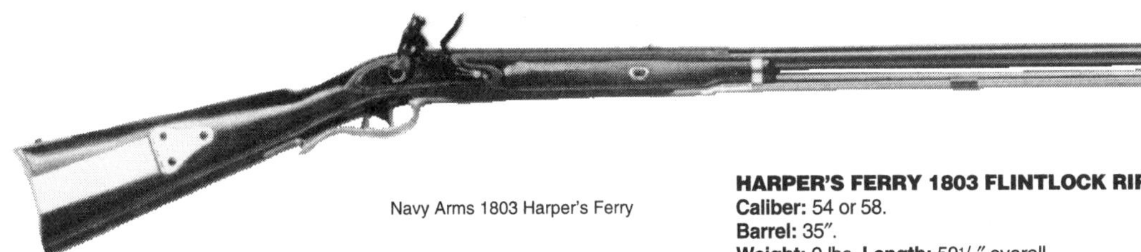

Navy Arms 1803 Harper's Ferry

HATFIELD MOUNTAIN RIFLE

Caliber: 50, 54.
Barrel: 32″.
Weight: 8 lbs. **Length:** 49″ overall.
Stock: Select American fancy maple. Half-stock with nose cap.
Sights: Silver blade front on brass base, fixed buckhorn rear.
Features: Traditional leaf spring and fly lock with extra-wide tumbler of 4140 steel. Slow rust brown metal finish. Double-set triggers. From Hatfield Gun Co.
Price: **$950.00**

HARPER'S FERRY 1803 FLINTLOCK RIFLE

Caliber: 54 or 58.
Barrel: 35″.
Weight: 9 lbs. **Length:** 59$^1/_2$″ overall.
Stock: Walnut with cheekpiece.
Sights: Brass blade front, fixed steel rear.
Features: Brass trigger guard, sideplate, buttplate; steel patch box. Imported by Euroarms of America, Navy Arms (54-cal. only), Cabela's, Stone Mountain Arms.
Price: .... **$495.95** to **$729.00**
Price: 54-cal. (Navy Arms) **$615.00**

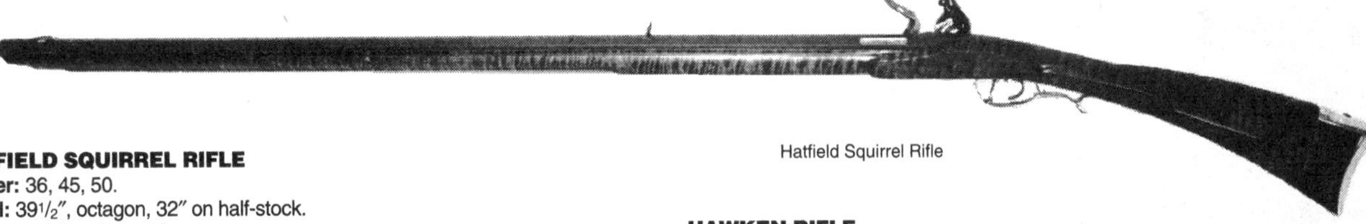

Hatfield Squirrel Rifle

HATFIELD SQUIRREL RIFLE

Caliber: 36, 45, 50.
Barrel: 39$^1/_2$″, octagon, 32″ on half-stock.
Weight: 7$^1/_2$ lbs. (32-cal.).
Stock: American fancy maple.
Sights: Silver blade front, buckhorn rear.
Features: Recreation of the traditional squirrel rifle. Available in flint or percussion with brass trigger guard and buttplate. From Hatfield Rifle Works. Introduced 1983.
Price: Full stock, percussion, Grade II **$819.00**
Price: As above, flintlock **$819.00**
Price: As above, Grade III, flint or percussion **$969.00**

HAWKEN RIFLE

Caliber: 45, 50, 54 or 58.
Barrel: 28″, blued, 6-groove rifling.
Weight: 8$^3/_4$ lbs. **Length:** 44″ overall.
Stock: Walnut with cheekpiece.
Sights: Blade front, fully adjustable rear.
Features: Coil mainspring, double-set triggers, polished brass furniture. From Armsport, Navy Arms, E.M.F.
Price: .... **$220.00** to **$345.00**

Ithaca-Navy Hawken

ITHACA-NAVY HAWKEN RIFLE

Caliber: 50.
Barrel: 32″ octagonal, 1″ dia.
Weight: About 9 lbs.
Stocks: Walnut.
Sights: Blade front, rear adjustable for windage.
Features: Hooked breech, 1$^7/_8$″ throw percussion lock. Attached twin thimbles and under-rib. German silver barrel key inlays, Hawken-style toe and buttplates, lock bolt inlays, barrel wedges, entry thimble, trigger guard, ramrod and cleaning jag, nipple and nipple wrench. Introduced 1977. From Navy Arms.
Price: Complete, percussion **$400.00**

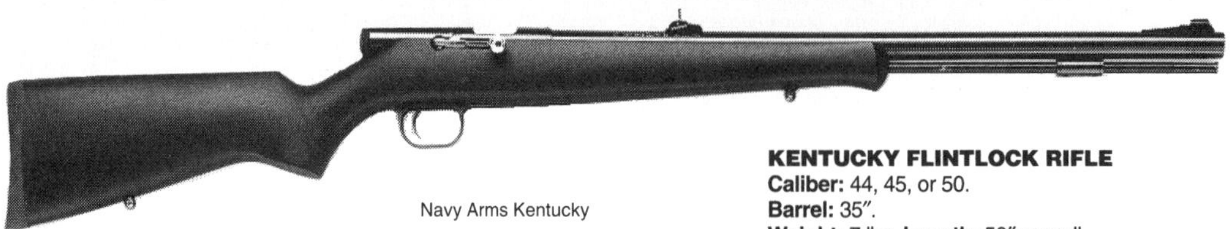

Navy Arms Kentucky

KENTUCKY FLINTLOCK RIFLE
Caliber: 44, 45, or 50.
Barrel: 35″.
Weight: 7 lbs. **Length:** 50″ overall.
Stock: Walnut stained, brass fittings.
Sights: Fixed.
Features: Available in carbine model also, 28″ bbl. Some variations in detail, finish. Kits also available from some importers. Imported by Navy Arms, The Armoury.
Price: About . . . . **$217.95** to **$345.00**
Price: Flintlock, 45 or 50-cal. (Navy Arms) **$410.00**

KENTUCKIAN RIFLE & CARBINE
Caliber: 44.
Barrel: 35″ (Rifle), 27 1/2″ (Carbine).
Weight: 7 lbs. (Rifle), 5 1/2 lbs. (Carbine). **Length:** 51″ overall (Rifle), 43″ (Carbine).
Stock: Walnut stain.
Sights: Brass blade front, steel V-ramp rear.
Features: Octagon barrel, case-hardened and engraved lockplates. Brass furniture. Imported by Dixie Gun Works.
Price: Rifle or carbine, flint, about **$269.95**
Price: As above, percussion, about **$259.95**

Kentucky Percussion Rifle
Similar to flintlock except percussion lock. Finish and features vary with importer. Imported by Navy Arms, The Armoury, CVA.
Price: About **$259.95**
Price: 45- or 50-cal. (Navy Arms) **$400.00**
Price: Kit, 50-cal. (CVA) **$189.95**

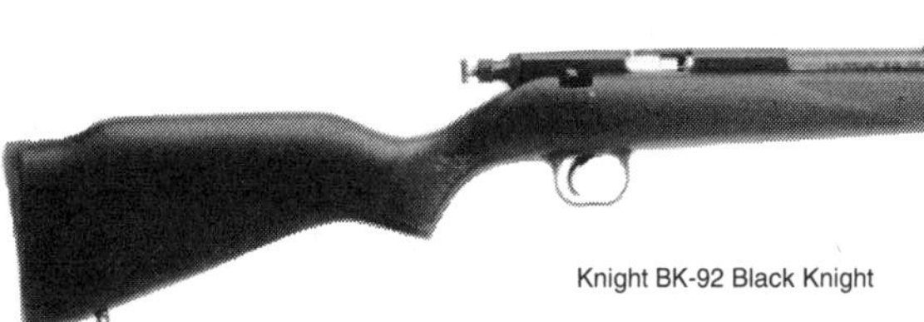

Knight BK-92 Black Knight

KNIGHT BK-92 BLACK KNIGHT RIFLE
Caliber: 50, 54.
Barrel: 24″, blued.
Weight: 6 1/2 lbs.
Stock: Black composition.
Sights: Blade front on ramp, open adjustable rear.
Features: Patented double safety system; removable breech plug for cleaning; adjustable Accu-Lite trigger; Green Mountain barrel; receiver drilled and tapped for scope bases. Made in U.S. by Modern Muzzleloading, Inc.
Price: With composition stock **$399.95**

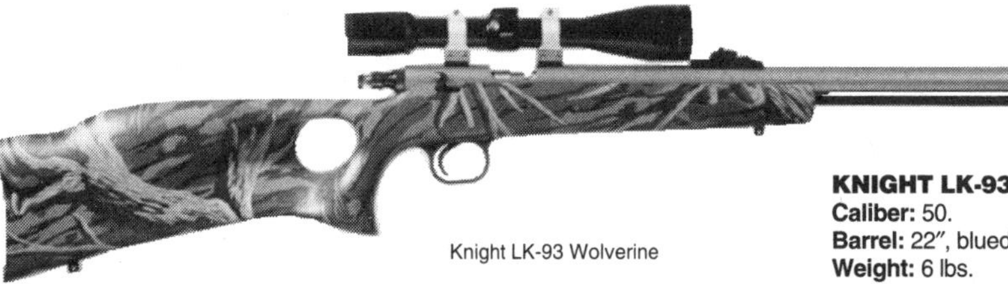

Knight LK-93 Wolverine

KNIGHT LK-93 WOLVERINE RIFLE
Caliber: 50.
Barrel: 22″, blued.
Weight: 6 lbs.
Stock: Black Fiber-Lite synthetic.
Sights: Blade front on ramp, open adjustable rear.
Features: Patented double safety system; removable breech plug; Sure-Fire in-line percussion ignition system. Made in U.S. by Modern Muzzleloading, Inc.
Price: **$319.95**
Price: LK-93 Stainless **$399.95**
Price: LK-93 Thumbhole **$409.95**

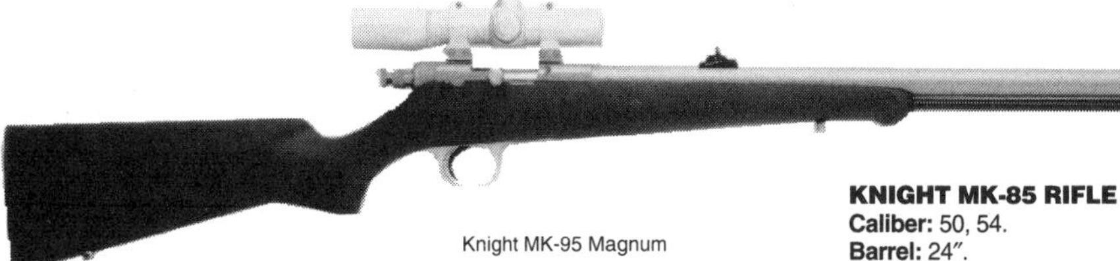

Knight MK-95 Magnum

KNIGHT MK-85 RIFLE
Caliber: 50, 54.
Barrel: 24″.
Weight: 6 3/4 lbs.
Stock: Walnut, laminated or composition.
Sights: Hooded blade front on ramp, open adjustable rear.
Features: Patented double safety; Sure-Fire in-line percussion ignition; Timney Featherweight adjustable trigger; aluminum ramrod; receiver drilled and tapped for scope bases. Made in U.S. by Modern Muzzleloading, Inc.
Price: Hunter, walnut stock **$539.95**
Price: Stalker, laminated or composition stock **$679.95**
Price: Predator (stainless steel), laminated or composition stock **$759.95**
Price: Knight Hawk, blued, composition thumbhole stock **$779.95**
Price: As above, stainless steel **$869.95**

KNIGHT MK-95 MAGNUM ELITE RIFLE
Caliber: 50, 54.
Barrel: 24″, stainless.
Weight: 6 3/4 lbs.
Stock: Composition; black or Realtree All-Purpose camouflage.
Sights: Hooded blade front on ramp, open adjustable rear.
Features: Enclosed Posi-Fire ignition system uses large rifle primers; Timney Featherweight adjustable trigger; Green Mountain barrel; receiver drilled and tapped for scope bases. Made in U.S. by Modern Muzzleloading, Inc.
Price: Black composition stock **$839.95**

CAUTION: PRICES SHOWN ARE SUPPLIED BY THE MANUFACTURER OR IMPORTER. CHECK YOUR LOCAL GUNSHOP.

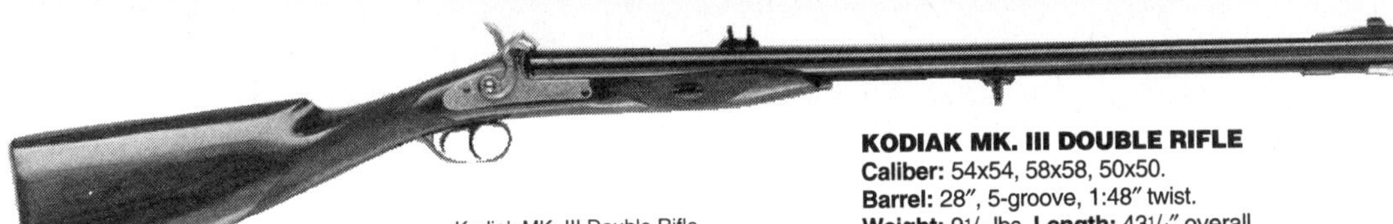
Kodiak MK. III Double Rifle

KODIAK MK. III DOUBLE RIFLE
Caliber: 54x54, 58x58, 50x50.
Barrel: 28″, 5-groove, 1:48″ twist.
Weight: 9½ lbs. **Length:** 43¼″ overall.
Stock: Czechoslovakian walnut, hand-checkered.
Sights: Adjustable bead front, adjustable open rear.
Features: Hooked breech allows interchangeability of barrels. Comes with sling, swivels, bullet mould and bullet starter. Engraved lockplates, top tang and trigger guard. Locks and top tang polished, rest browned. Introduced 1976. Imported from Italy by Navy Arms.
Price: 50-, 54-, 58-cal. SxS **$775.00**

LONDON ARMORY 3-BAND 1853 ENFIELD
Caliber: 58 (.577″ Minie, .575″ round ball, .580″ maxi ball).
Barrel: 39″.
Weight: 9½ lbs. **Length:** 54″ overall.
Stock: European walnut.
Sights: Inverted "V" front, traditional Enfield folding ladder rear.
Features: Recreation of the famed London Armory Company Pattern 1853 Enfield Musket. One-piece walnut stock, brass buttplate, trigger guard and nose cap. Lockplate marked "London Armoury Co." and with a British crown. Blued Baddeley barrel bands. From Dixie Gun Works, Euroarms of America, Navy Arms.
Price: About .... **$350.00** to **$484.00**
Price: Assembled kit (Dixie, Euroarms of America) .... **$425.00** to **$431.00**

LONDON ARMORY 2-BAND 1858 ENFIELD
Caliber: .577″ Minie, .575″ round ball.
Barrel: 33″.
Weight: 10 lbs. **Length:** 49″ overall.
Stock: Walnut.
Sights: Folding leaf rear adjustable for elevation.
Features: Blued barrel, color case-hardened lock and hammer, polished brass buttplate, trigger guard, nosecap. From Navy Arms, Euroarms of America, Dixie Gun Works.
Price: .... **$385.00** to **$531.00**

London Armory 1861

LONDON ARMORY 1861 ENFIELD MUSKETOON
Caliber: 58, Minie ball.
Barrel: 24″, round.
Weight: 7-7½ lbs. **Length:** 40½″ overall.
Stock: Walnut, with sling swivels.
Sights: Blade front, graduated military-leaf rear.
Features: Brass trigger guard, nose cap, buttplate; blued barrel, bands, lockplate, swivels. Imported by Euroarms of America, Navy Arms.
Price: .... **$300.00** to **$427.00**
Price: Kit .... **$365.00** to **$373.00**

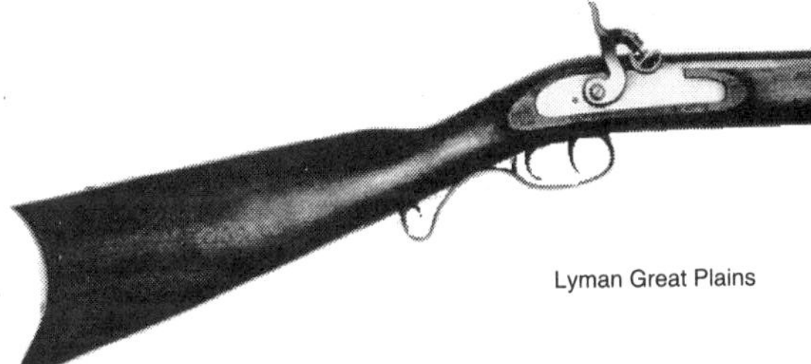
Lyman Great Plains

LYMAN GREAT PLAINS RIFLE
Caliber: 50- or 54-cal.
Barrel: 32″, 1:66″ twist.
Weight: 9 lbs.
Stock: Walnut.
Sights: Steel blade front, buckhorn rear adjustable for windage and elevation and fixed notch primitive sight included.
Features: Blued steel furniture. Stainless steel nipple. Coil spring lock, Hawken-style trigger guard and double-set triggers. Round thimbles recessed and sweated into rib. Steel wedge plates and toe plate. Introduced 1979. From Lyman.
Price: Percussion **$416.95**
Price: Flintlock **$445.95**
Price: Percussion kit **$329.95**
Price: Flintlock kit **$359.95**
Price: Left-hand percussion **$416.95**
Price: Left-hand flintlock **$445.95**

Lyman Deerstalker Custom Carbine
Similar to the Deerstalker rifle except in 50-caliber only with 21″ stepped octagon barrel; 1:24″ twist for optimum performance with conical projectiles. Comes with Lyman 37MA front sight, Lyman 16A folding rear. Weighs 6¾ lbs., measures 38½″ overall. Percussion or flintlock. Comes with Delrin ramrod, modern sling and swivels. Introduced 1991.
Price: Percussion **$309.95**
Price: Percussion, left-hand **$309.95**

LYMAN COUGAR IN-LINE RIFLE
Caliber: 50 or 54.
Barrel: 22″; 1:24″ twist.
Weight: NA. **Length:** NA.
Stock: Smooth walnut; swivel studs.
Sights: Bead on ramp front, folding adjustable rear. Drilled and tapped for Lyman 57WTR receiver sight and Weaver scope bases.
Features: Blued barrel and receiver. Has bolt safety notch and trigger safety. Rubber recoil pad. Delrin ramrod. Introduced 1996. From Lyman.
Price: **$299.95**

LYMAN TRADE RIFLE
Caliber: 50, 54.
Barrel: 28″ octagon, 1:48″ twist.
Weight: 8¾ lbs. **Length:** 45″ overall.
Stock: European walnut.
Sights: Blade front, open rear adjustable for windage or optional fixed sights.
Features: Fast twist rifling for conical bullets. Polished brass furniture with blue steel parts, stainless steel nipple. Hook breech, single trigger, coil spring percussion lock. Steel barrel rib and ramrod ferrules. Introduced 1980. From Lyman.
Price: Percussion **$299.95**
Price: Flintlock **$319.95**

LYMAN DEERSTALKER RIFLE
Caliber: 50, 54.
Barrel: 24″, octagonal; 1:48″ rifling.
Weight: 7½ lbs.
Stock: Walnut with black rubber buttpad.
Sights: Lyman #37MA beaded front, fully adjustable fold-down Lyman #16A rear.
Features: Stock has less drop for quick sighting. All metal parts are blackened, with color case-hardened lock; single trigger. Comes with sling and swivels. Available in flint or percussion. Introduced 1990. From Lyman.
Price: 50- or 54-cal., percussion **$299.95**
Price: 50- or 54-cal., flintlock **$319.95**
Price: 50- or 54-cal., percussion, left-hand **$299.95**
Price: 50-cal., flintlock, left-hand **$319.95**

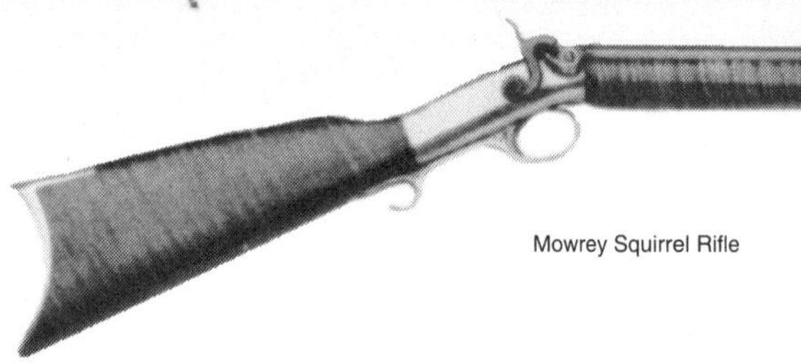

Mowrey Squirrel Rifle

MOWREY SQUIRREL RIFLE
Caliber: 32, 36 or 45.
Barrel: 28″; 13/1″ flats; 1:66″ twist.
Weight: About 7.5 lbs. **Length:** 43″ overall.
Stock: Curly maple; crescent buttplate.
Sights: German silver blade front, semi-buckhorn rear.
Features: Brass or steel boxlock action; cut-rifled barrel. Steel rifles have browned finish, brass have browned barrel. Adjustable sear and trigger pull. Made in U.S. by Mowrey Gun Works.
Price: Brass or steel **$350.00**
Price: Kit **$300.00**

Mowrey Silhouette Rifle
Similar to the Squirrel Rifle except in 40-caliber with 32″ barrel. Available in brass or steel frame.
Price: Brass frame **$350.00**
Price: Steel frame **$350.00**
Price: Kit, brass or steel **$300.00**

Mowrey 1 N 30 Conical Rifle
Similar to the Squirrel Rifle except in steel frame only, 45-, 50- or 54-caliber. Has special 1:24″ twist barrel for conical- and sabot-style bullets. The 50- and 54-caliber barrels have 1″ flats.
Price: **$350.00**
Price: Kit **$300.00**

Mowrey Plains Rifle
Similar to the Squirrel Rifle except in 50- or 54-caliber with 32″ barrel. Available in brass or steel frame.
Price: Brass frame **$350.00**
Price: Steel frame **$350.00**
Price: Rocky Mountain Hunter (as above except 28″ bbl.), brass **$350.00**
Price: As above, steel frame **$350.00**
Price: All above in kit form **$300.00**

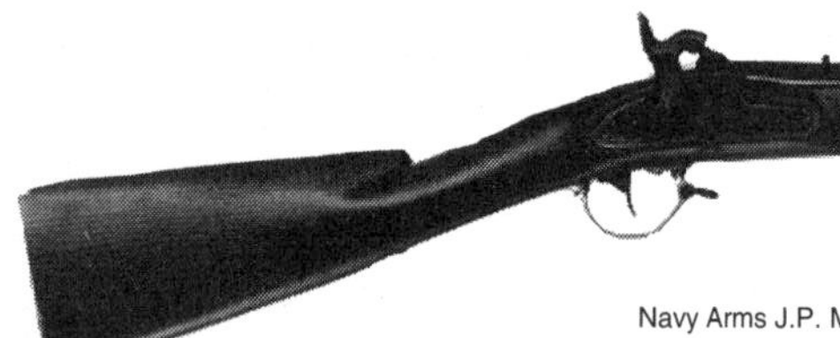

Navy Arms J.P. Murray

J.P. MURRAY 1862-1864 CAVALRY CARBINE
Caliber: 58 (.577″ Minie).
Barrel: 23″.
Weight: 7 lbs., 9 oz. **Length:** 39″ overall.
Stock: Walnut.
Sights: Blade front, rear drift adjustable for windage.
Features: Browned barrel, color case-hardened lock, blued swivel and band springs, polished brass buttplate, trigger guard, barrel bands. From Navy Arms, Euroarms of America.
Price: .... **$405.00** to **$440.00**

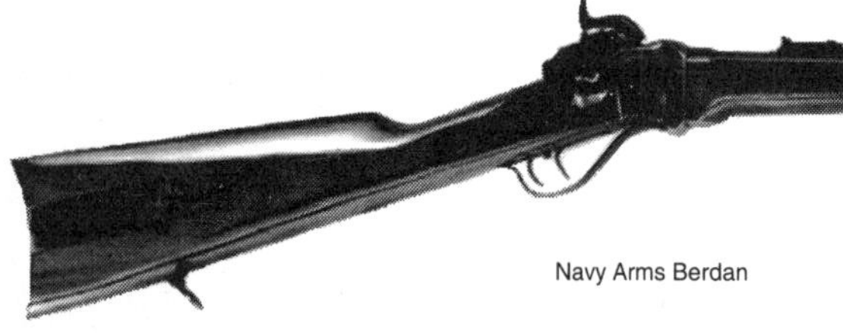

Navy Arms Berdan

NAVY ARMS BERDAN 1859 SHARPS RIFLE
Caliber: 54.
Barrel: 30″.
Weight: 8 lbs., 8 oz. **Length:** 46¾″ overall.
Stock: Walnut.
Sights: Blade front, folding military ladder-type rear.
Features: Replica of the Union sniper rifle used by Berdan's 1st and 2nd Sharpshooter regiments. Color case-hardened receiver, patch box, furniture. Double-set triggers. Imported by Navy Arms.
Price: **$1,095.00**
Price: 1859 Sharps Infantry Rifle (three-band) **$1,030.00**

NAVY ARMS HAWKEN HUNTER RIFLE/CARBINE
Caliber: 50, 54, 58.
Barrel: 22½″ or 28″; 1:48″ twist.
Weight: 6 lbs., 12 oz. **Length:** 39″ overall.
Stock: Walnut with cheekpiece.
Sights: Blade front, fully adjustable rear.
Features: Double-set triggers; all metal has matte black finish; rubber recoil pad; detachable sling swivels. Imported by Navy Arms.
Price: Rifle or Carbine **$240.00**

Navy Arms Country Boy

NAVY ARMS COUNTRY BOY IN-LINE RIFLE
Caliber: 50.
Barrel: 24″.
Weight: 8 lbs. **Length:** 41″ overall.
Stock: Black composition.
Sights: Bead front, fully adjustable open rear.
Features: Chrome-lined barrel; receiver drilled and tapped for scope mount; buttstock has trap containing takedown tool for nipple and breech plug removal. Introduced 1996. From Navy Arms.
Price: **$175.00**

CAUTION: PRICES SHOWN ARE SUPPLIED BY THE MANUFACTURER OR IMPORTER. CHECK YOUR LOCAL GUNSHOP.

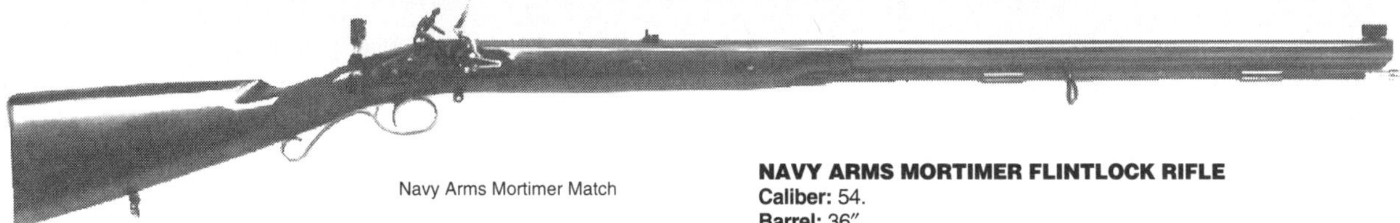
Navy Arms Mortimer Match

NAVY ARMS MORTIMER FLINTLOCK RIFLE

Caliber: 54.
Barrel: 36″.
Weight: 9 lbs. **Length:** 52¼″ overall.
Stock: Checkered walnut.
Sights: Bead front, rear adjustable for windage.
Features: Waterproof pan, roller frizzen; sling swivels; browned barrel; external safety. Introduced 1991. Imported by Navy Arms.
Price: **$780.00**
Price: Mortimer Match Rifle (hooded globe front sight, fully adjustable target aperture rear, color case-hardened lock) **$900.00**

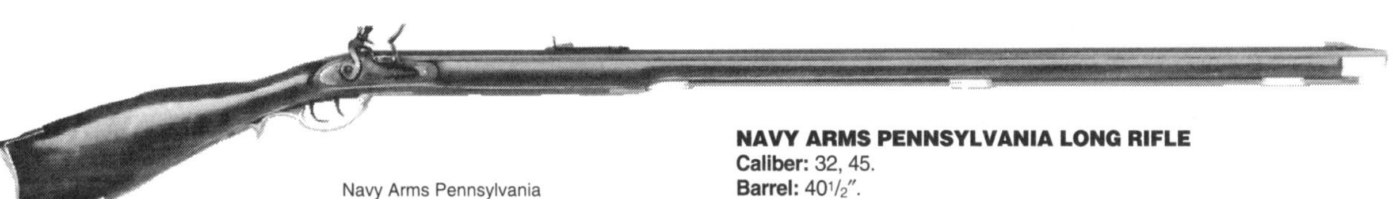
Navy Arms Pennsylvania

NAVY ARMS PENNSYLVANIA LONG RIFLE

Caliber: 32, 45.
Barrel: 40½″.
Weight: 7½ lbs. **Length:** 56½″ overall.
Stock: Walnut.
Sights: Blade front, fully adjustable rear.
Features: Browned barrel, brass furniture, polished lock with double-set triggers. Imported by Navy Arms.
Price: Percussion **$460.00**
Price: Flintlock **$475.00**

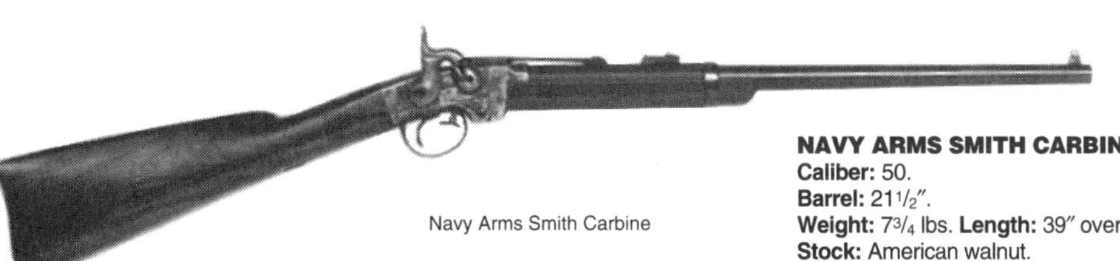
Navy Arms Smith Carbine

NAVY ARMS SMITH CARBINE

Caliber: 50.
Barrel: 21½″.
Weight: 7¾ lbs. **Length:** 39″ overall.
Stock: American walnut.
Sights: Brass blade front, folding ladder-type rear.
Features: Replica of the breech-loading Civil War carbine. Color case-hardened receiver, rest blued. Cavalry model has saddle ring and bar, Artillery model has sling swivels. Imported by Navy Arms.
Price: Cavalry model **$600.00**
Price: Artillery model **$600.00**

Navy Arms Whitworth

NAVY ARMS VOLUNTEER RIFLE

Caliber: .451″.
Barrel: 32″.
Weight: 9½ lbs. **Length:** 49″ overall.
Stock: Walnut, checkered wrist and forend.
Sights: Globe front, adjustable ladder-type rear.
Features: Recreation of the type of gun issued to volunteer regiments during the 1860s. Rigby-pattern rifling, patent breech, detented lock. Stock is glass bedded for accuracy. Imported by Navy Arms.
Price: **$775.00**

NAVY ARMS 1859 SHARPS CAVALRY CARBINE

Caliber: 54.
Barrel: 22″.
Weight: 7¾ lbs. **Length:** 39″ overall.
Stock: Walnut.
Sights: Blade front, military ladder-type rear.
Features: Color case-hardened action, blued barrel. Has saddle ring. Introduced 1991. Imported from Navy Arms.
Price: **$885.00**

NAVY ARMS WHITWORTH MILITARY TARGET RIFLE

Caliber: 45.
Barrel: 36″.
Weight: 9¼ lbs. **Length:** 52½″ overall.
Stock: Walnut. Checkered at wrist and forend.
Sights: Hooded post front, open step-adjustable rear.
Features: Faithful reproduction of the Whitworth rifle, only bored for 45-cal. Trigger has a detented lock, capable of being adjusted very finely without risk of the sear nose catching on the half-cock bent and damaging both parts. Introduced 1978. Imported by Navy Arms.
Price: **$835.00**

NAVY ARMS 1777 CHARLEVILLE MUSKET

Caliber: 69.
Barrel: 44⅝″.
Weight: 10 lbs., 4 oz. **Length:** 59¾″ overall.
Stock: Walnut.
Sights: Brass blade front.
Features: Exact copy of the musket used in the French Revolution. All steel is polished, in the white. Brass flashpan. Introduced 1991. Imported by Navy Arms.
Price: **$810.00**
Price: 1816 M.T. Wickham Musket **$810.00**

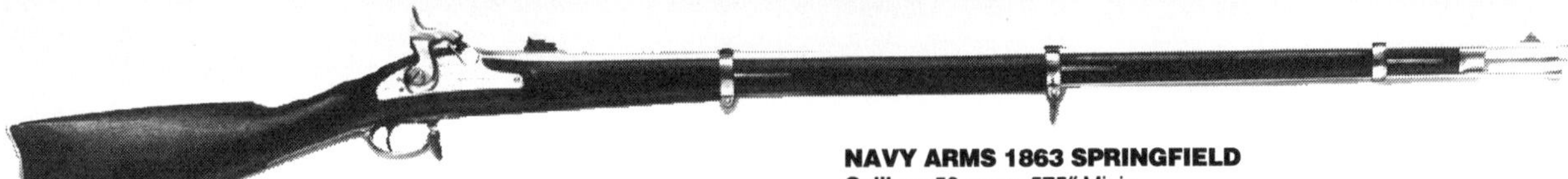
Navy Arms 1863

NAVY ARMS 1863 SPRINGFIELD
Caliber: 58, uses .575″ Minie.
Barrel: 40″, rifled.
Weight: 9 1/2 lbs. **Length:** 56″ overall.
Stock: Walnut.
Sights: Open rear adjustable for elevation.
Features: Full-size three-band musket. Polished bright metal, including lock. From Navy Arms.
Price: Finished rifle $550.00

NAVY ARMS 1861 SPRINGFIELD RIFLE
Caliber: 58.
Barrel: 40″
Weight: 10 lbs., 4 oz. **Length:** 56″ overall.
Stock: Walnut.
Sights: Blade front, military leaf rear.
Features: Steel barrel, lock and all furniture have polished bright finish. Has 1855-style hammer. Imported by Navy Arms.
Price: $550.00

NAVY ARMS 1863 C.S. RICHMOND RIFLE
Caliber: 58.
Barrel: 40″.
Weight: 10 lbs. **Length:** NA.
Stock: Walnut.
Sights: Blade front, adjustable rear.
Features: Copy of the three-band rifle musket made at Richmond Armory for the Confederacy. All steel polished bright. Imported by Navy Arms.
Price: $550.00

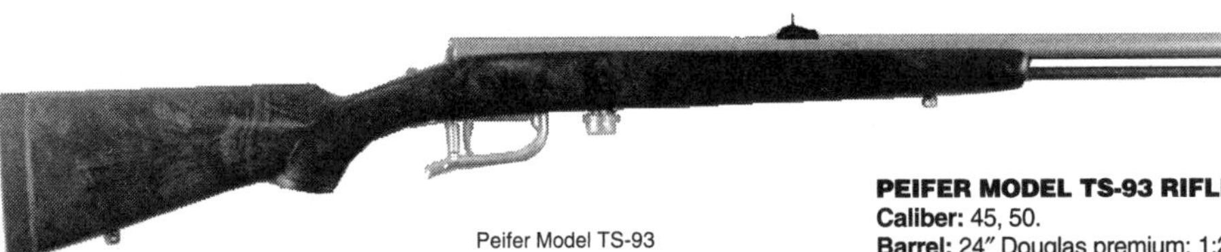
Peifer Model TS-93

PEIFER MODEL TS-93 RIFLE
Caliber: 45, 50.
Barrel: 24″ Douglas premium; 1:20″ twist in 45, 1:28″ in 50.
Weight: 7 lbs. **Length:** 43 1/4″ overall.
Stock: Bell & Carlson solid composite, with recoil pad, swivel studs.
Sights: Williams bead front on ramp, fully adjustable open rear. Drilled and tapped for Weaver scope mounts with dovetail for rear peep.
Features: In-line ignition uses #209 shotshell primer; extremely fast lock time; fully enclosed breech; adjustable trigger; automatic safety; removal primer holder. Blue or stainless. Made in U.S. by Peifer Rifle Co. Introduced 1996.
Price: Blue, black stock $663.00
Price: Blue, wood or camouflage composite stock, or stainless with black composite stock $728.75
Price: Stainless, wood or camouflage composite stock $795.00

PENNSYLVANIA FULL-STOCK RIFLE
Caliber: 45 or 50.
Barrel: 32″ rifled, 15/16″ dia.
Weight: 8 1/2 lbs.
Stock: Walnut.
Sights: Fixed.
Features: Available in flint or percussion. Blued lock and barrel, brass furniture. Offered complete or in kit form. From The Armoury.
Price: Flint $250.00
Price: Percussion $225.00

Prairie River Bullpup

PRAIRIE RIVER ARMS PRA BULLPUP RIFLE
Caliber: 50, 54.
Barrel: 28″; 1:28″ twist.
Weight: 7 1/2 lbs. **Length:** 31 1/2″ overall.
Stock: Hardwood or black all-weather.
Sights: Blade front, open adjustable rear.
Features: Bullpup design thumbhole stock. Patented internal percussion ignition system. Left-hand model available. Dovetailed for scope mount. Introduced 1995. Made in U.S. by Prairie River Arms.
Price: 4140 alloy barrel, hardwood stock $375.00
Price: As above, black stock $390.00
Price: Stainless barrel, hardwood stock $425.00
Price: As above, black stock $440.00

Prairie River Classic

PRAIRIE RIVER ARMS PRA CLASSIC RIFLE
Caliber: 50, 54.
Barrel: 26″; 1:28″ twist.
Weight: 7 1/2 lbs. **Length:** 40 1/2″ overall.
Stock: Hardwood or black all-weather.
Sights: Blade front, open adjustable rear.
Features: Patented internal percussion ignition system. Drilled and tapped for scope mount. Introduced 1995. Made in U.S. by Prairie River Arms, Ltd.
Price: 4140 alloy barrel, hardwood stock $375.00
Price: As above, stainless barrel $425.00
Price: 4140 alloy barrel, black all-weather stock $390.00
Price: As above, stainless barrel $440.00

CAUTION: PRICES SHOWN ARE SUPPLIED BY THE MANUFACTURER OR IMPORTER. CHECK YOUR LOCAL GUNSHOP.

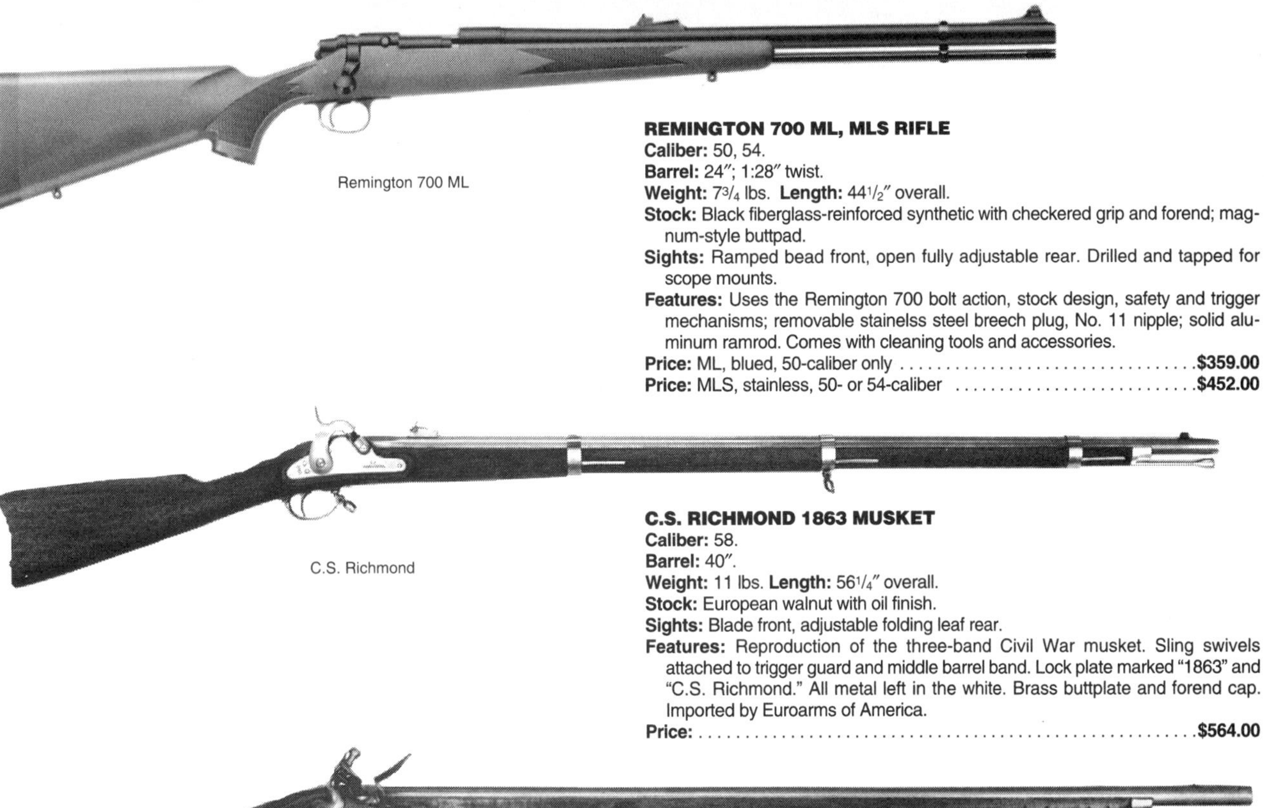

Remington 700 ML

C.S. Richmond

Navy Arms Brown Bess

REMINGTON 700 ML, MLS RIFLE
Caliber: 50, 54.
Barrel: 24″; 1:28″ twist.
Weight: 7¾ lbs. **Length:** 44½″ overall.
Stock: Black fiberglass-reinforced synthetic with checkered grip and forend; magnum-style buttpad.
Sights: Ramped bead front, open fully adjustable rear. Drilled and tapped for scope mounts.
Features: Uses the Remington 700 bolt action, stock design, safety and trigger mechanisms; removable stainelss steel breech plug, No. 11 nipple; solid aluminum ramrod. Comes with cleaning tools and accessories.
Price: ML, blued, 50-caliber only **$359.00**
Price: MLS, stainless, 50- or 54-caliber **$452.00**

C.S. RICHMOND 1863 MUSKET
Caliber: 58.
Barrel: 40″.
Weight: 11 lbs. **Length:** 56¼″ overall.
Stock: European walnut with oil finish.
Sights: Blade front, adjustable folding leaf rear.
Features: Reproduction of the three-band Civil War musket. Sling swivels attached to trigger guard and middle barrel band. Lock plate marked "1863" and "C.S. Richmond." All metal left in the white. Brass buttplate and forend cap. Imported by Euroarms of America.
Price: **$564.00**

STONE MOUNTAIN 1853 ENFIELD MUSKET
Caliber: 58.
Barrel: 39″.
Weight: About 9 lbs. **Length:** 54″ overall.
Stock: Walnut.
Sights: Inverted V front, rear step adjustable for elevation.
Features: Three-band musket. Barrel, tang, breech plug are blued, color case-hardened lock, brass nose cap, trigger guard and buttplate. From Stone Mountain Arms.
Price: **$550.00**

THOMPSON/CENTER BIG BOAR RIFLE
Caliber: 58.
Barrel: 26″ octagon; 1:48″ twist.
Weight: 7¾ lbs. **Length:** 42½″ overall.
Stock: American black walnut; rubber buttpad; swivels.
Sights: Bead front, fullt adjustable open rear.
Features: Percussion lock; single trigger with wide bow trigger guard. Comes with soft leather sling. Introduced 1991. From Thompson/Center.
Price: **$355.00**

SECOND MODEL BROWN BESS MUSKET
Caliber: 75, uses .735″ round ball.
Barrel: 42″, smoothbore.
Weight: 9½ lbs. **Length:** 59″ overall.
Stock: Walnut (Navy); walnut-stained hardwood (Dixie).
Sights: Fixed.
Features: Polished barrel and lock with brass trigger guard and buttplate. Bayonet and scabbard available. From Navy Arms, Dixie Gun Works, Cabela's.
Price: Finished . . . . **$475.00** to **$850.00**
Price: Kit (Dixie Gun Works, Navy Arms) . . . . **$510.00** to **$625.00**
Price: Carbine (Navy Arms) **$750.00**

STONE MOUNTAIN SILVER EAGLE RIFLE
Caliber: 50.
Barrel: 26″, octagonal; 15/16″ flats; 1:48″ twist.
Weight: About 6½ lbs. **Length:** 40″ overall.
Stock: Dura-Grip synthetic; checkered grip and forend.
Sights: Blade front, fixed rear.
Features: Weatherguard nickel finish on metal; oversize trigger guard. Introduced 1995. From Stone Mountain Arms.
Price: **$139.95**
Price: Silver Eagle Hunter (adjustable sight, drilled and tapped for scope mount, swivel studs, synthetic ramrod) **$159.95**

Thompson/Center Fire Hawk

THOMPSON/CENTER FIRE HAWK RIFLE
Caliber: 32, 50, 54, 58.
Barrel: 24″; 1:38″ twist.
Weight: 7 lbs. **Length:** 41¾″ overall.
Stock: American black walnut or black Rynite; Rynite thumbhole style; all with cheekpiece and swivel studs.
Sights: Ramp front with bead, adjustable leaf-style rear.
Features: In-line ignition with sliding thumb safety; free-floated barrel; exposed nipple; adjustable trigger. Available in blue or stainless. Comes with Weaver-style scope mount bases. Introduced 1995. Made in U.S. by Thompson/Center Arms.
Price: Blue, walnut stock, 32, 50, 54, 58 . . . . **$365.00**
Price: Stainless, walnut stock, 50, 54 . . . . **$405.00**
Price: Stainless, Rynite stock, 50, 54 . . . . **$395.00**
Price: Blue, thumbhole stock, 50, 54 . . . . **$385.00**
Price: Stainless, thumbhole stock, 50, 54 . . . . **$425.00**
Price: Bantam model with 13¼″ pull, 21″ barrel **$365.00**
Price: Blue, Advantage camo stock, 50, 54 . . . . **$395.00**

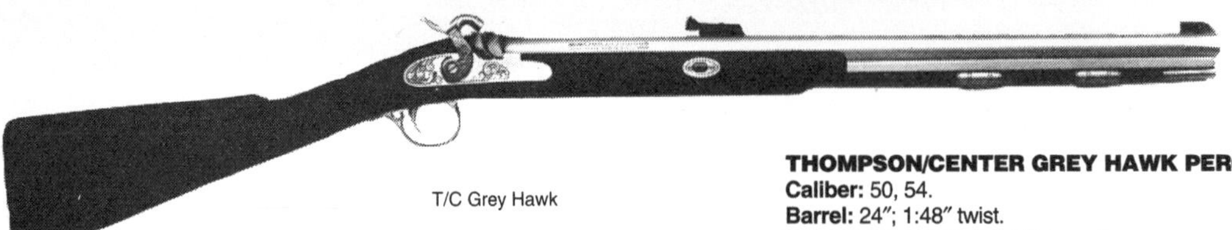

T/C Grey Hawk

THOMPSON/CENTER GREY HAWK PERCUSSION RIFLE
Caliber: 50, 54.
Barrel: 24″; 1:48″ twist.
Weight: 7 lbs. **Length:** 41″ overall.
Stock: Black Rynite with rubber recoil pad.
Sights: Bead front, fully adjustable open hunting rear.
Features: Stainless steel barrel, lock, hammer, trigger guard, thimbles; blued sights. Percussion only. Introduced 1993. From Thompson/Center Arms.
Price: $330.00

T/C Hawken

Thompson/Center Hawken Silver Elite Rifle
Similar to the 50-caliber Hawken except all metal is satin-finished stainless steel. Has semi-fancy American walnut stock without patchbox. Percussion only. Introduced 1996. Made in U.S. by Thompson/Center Arms.
Price: $495.00

THOMPSON/CENTER PENNSYLVANIA HUNTER RIFLE
Caliber: 50.
Barrel: 31″, half-octagon, half-round.
Weight: About 7½ lbs. **Length:** 48″ overall.
Stock: Black walnut.
Sights: Open, adjustable.
Features: Rifled 1:66″ for round ball shooting. Available in flintlock or percussion. From Thompson/Center.
Price: Flintlock $375.00

Thompson/Center Pennsylvania Hunter Carbine
Similar to the Pennsylvania Hunter except has 21″ barrel, weighs 6.5 lbs., and has an overall length of 38″. Designed for shooting patched round balls. Available in percussion or flintlock styles. Introduced 1992. From Thompson/Center.
Price: Percussion $340.00
Price: Flintlock $355.00

Thompson/Center Renegade Hunter
Similar to standard Renegade except has single trigger in a large-bow shotgun-style trigger guard, no brass trim. Available in 50- or 54-caliber. Color case-hardened lock, rest blued. Introduced 1987. From Thompson/Center.
Price: $335.00

Thompson/Center Scout Rifle
Similar to the Scout Carbine except has 24″ part octagon, part round barrel (round only on Rynite-stocked model), solid brass forend cap on walnut-stocked gun. Barrel twist is 1:38″. Available in 50- and 54-caliber. Introduced 1995. Made in U.S. by Thompson/Center Arms.
Price: With walnut stock $435.00
Price: With Rynite stock $360.00

THOMPSON/CENTER HAWKEN RIFLE
Caliber: 45, 50 or 54.
Barrel: 28″ octagon, hooked breech.
Stock: American walnut.
Sights: Blade front, rear adjustable for windage and elevation.
Features: Solid brass furniture, double-set triggers, button rifled barrel, coil-type mainspring. From Thompson/Center.
Price: Percussion model (45-, 50- or 54-cal.) $455.00
Price: Flintlock model (50-cal.) $425.00
Price: Percussion kit $315.00
Price: Flintlock kit $335.00

THOMPSON/CENTER NEW ENGLANDER RIFLE
Caliber: 50, 54.
Barrel: 28″, round.
Weight: 7 lbs., 15 oz.
Stock: American walnut or Rynite.
Sights: Open, adjustable.
Features: Color case-hardened percussion lock with engraving, rest blued. Also accepts 12-ga. shotgun barrel. Introduced 1987. From Thompson/Center.
Price: Right-hand model $310.00
Price: As above, Rynite stock $295.00
Price: Left-hand model $330.00
Price: Accessory 12-ga. barrel, right-hand $170.00

Thompson/Center Pennsylvania Match Rifle
Similar to the Pennsylvania Hunter except has a tang peep sight, globe front with Seven interchangeable inserts. Introduced 1996. Made in U.S. by Thompson/Center Arms.
Price: $400.00

THOMPSON/CENTER RENEGADE RIFLE
Caliber: 50 and 54.
Barrel: 26″, 1″ across the flats.
Weight: 8 lbs.
Stock: American walnut.
Sights: Open hunting (Patridge) style, fully adjustable for windage and elevation.
Features: Coil spring lock, double-set triggers, blued steel trim. From Thompson/Center.
Price: Percussion model $360.00
Price: Flintlock model, 50-cal. only $370.00
Price: Percussion kit $275.00
Price: Left-hand percussion, 50- or 54-cal. $370.00

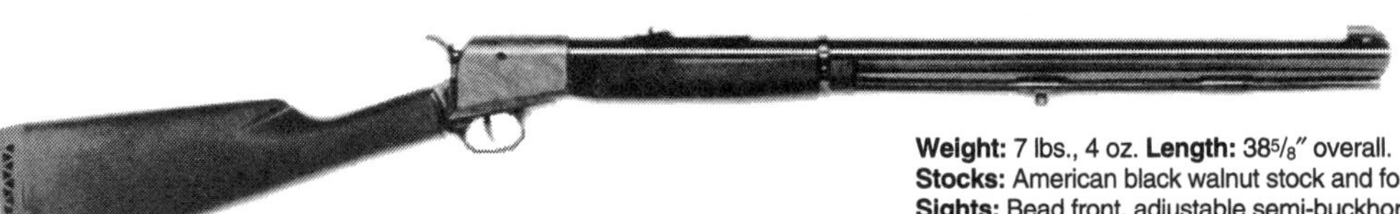

T/C Scout Rifle

THOMPSON/CENTER SCOUT CARBINE
Caliber: 50 and 54.
Barrel: 21″, interchangeable, 1:38″ twist.
Weight: 7 lbs., 4 oz. **Length:** 38⅝″ overall.
Stocks: American black walnut stock and forend.
Sights: Bead front, adjustable semi-buckhorn rear.
Features: Patented in-line ignition system with special vented breech plug. Patented trigger mechanism consists of only two moving parts. Interchangeable barrels. Wide grooved hammer. Brass trigger guard assembly, brass barrel band and buttplate. Ramrod has blued hardware. Comes with quick detachable swivels and suede leather carrying sling. Drilled and tapped for standard scope mounts. Introduced 1990. From Thompson/Center.
Price: 50- or 54-cal. $425.00
Price: With black Rynite stock $350.00

CAUTION: PRICES SHOWN ARE SUPPLIED BY THE MANUFACTURER OR IMPORTER. CHECK YOUR LOCAL GUNSHOP.

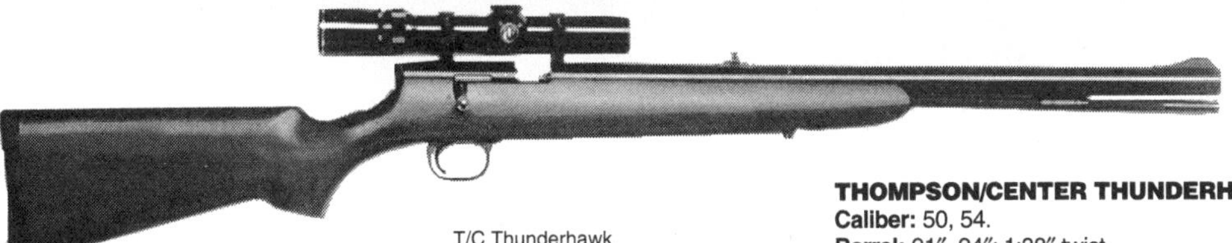
T/C Thunderhawk

THOMPSON/CENTER THUNDERHAWK CARBINE
Caliber: 50, 54.
Barrel: 21″, 24″; 1:38″ twist.
Weight: 6.75 lbs. **Length:** 38.75″ overall.
Stock: American walnut or black Rynite with rubber recoil pad.
Sights: Bead on ramp front, adjustable leaf rear.
Features: Uses modern in-line ignition system, adjustable trigger. Knurled striker handle indicators for Safe and Fire. Black wood ramrod, Drilled and tapped for T/C scope mounts. Introduced 1993. From Thompson/Center Arms.
Price: Blue with walnut stock **$315.00**
Price: Stainless steel with Rynite stock **$345.00**
Price: Blue with Rynite stock **$305.00**

Thompson/Center ThunderHawk Shadow
Similar to the ThunderHawk except 24″ barrel only, blued barrel and receiver, composite stock, polycarbonate adjustable rear sight. Available in 50- or 54-caliber. Introduced 1996. Made in U.S. by Thompson/Center Arms.
Price: **$275.00**

Traditions In-Line Buckhunter

TRADITIONS IN-LINE BUCKHUNTER SERIES RIFLES
Caliber: 50, 54.
Barrel: 24″, round; 1:32″ (50), 1:48″ (54) twist.
Weight: 7 lbs., 6 oz. to 8 lbs. **Length:** 41″ overall.
Stock: Beech, epoxy coated beech, laminated or fiberglass thumbhole; rubber recoil pad.
Sights: Beaded blade front, click adjustable rear. Drilled and tapped for scope mounting.
Features: Removable breech plug; PVC ramrod; sling swivels. Fifteen models available with blackened furniture, blued, C-nickel barrels, thumbhole stock. Introduced 1995. From Traditions.
Price: . . . . **$222.00** to **$345.00**

Traditions Buckhunter In-Line Scout
Similar to the Buckhunter except has 22″ C-Nickel barrel, 50-caliber only; 1:32″ twist; black epoxied beech stock with 13″ pull length. Introduced 1996. Imported by Traditions.
Price: **$239.00**

Traditions Buckhunter Pro In-Line

TRADITIONS BUCKHUNTER PRO IN-LINE RIFLES
Caliber: 50 (1:32″ twist), 54 (1:48″ twist).
Barrel: 24″ tapered round.
Weight: 7½ lbs. **Length:** 42″ overall.
Stock: Beech, composite or laminated; thumbhole available in black Mossy Oak Treestand or Realtree® Advantage camouflage.
Sights: Beaded blade front, fully adjustable open rear. Drilled and tapped for scope mounting.
Features: In-line percussion ignition system; adjustable trigger; manual thumb safety; removable stainless steel breech plug. Seventeen models available. Introduced 1996. From Traditions.
Price: . . . . **$222.00** to **$406.00**

TRADITIONS BUCKSKINNER CARBINE
Caliber: 50.
Barrel: 21″, 15/16″ flats, half octagon, half round; 1:20″ or 1:66″ twist.
Weight: 6 lbs. **Length:** 37″ overall.
Stock: Beech or black laminated.
Sights: Beaded blade front, hunting-style open rear click adjustable for windage and elevation.
Features: Uses V-type mainspring, single trigger. Non-glare hardware. From Traditions.
Price: Flintlock **$264.00**
Price: Flintlock, laminated stock **$336.00**
Price: Percussion, 50 . . . . **$236.00**
Price: Percussion, laminated stock, 50 . . . . **$305.00**
Price: Percussion, left-hand **$255.00**

Consult our Directory pages for the location of firms mentioned.

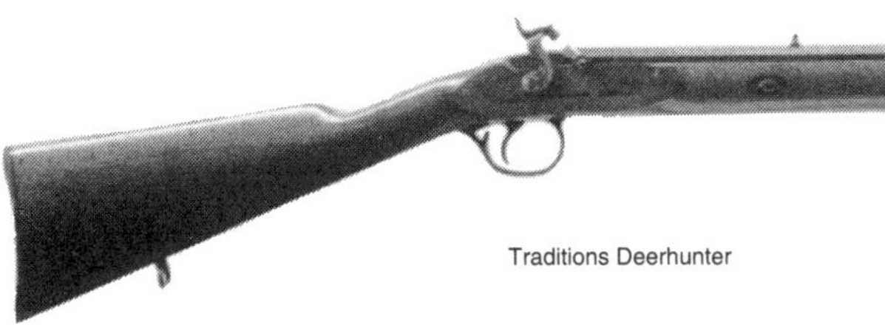
Traditions Deerhunter

TRADITIONS DEERHUNTER RIFLE SERIES
Caliber: 32, 50 or 54.
Barrel: 24″, octagonal, 15/16″ flats; 1:48″ or 1:66″ twist.
Weight: 6 lbs. **Length:** 40″ overall.
Stock: Stained beech with rubber buttpad, sling swivels.
Sights: Blade front, fixed rear.
Features: Flint or percussion with color case-hardened lock. Hooked breech, oversized trigger guard, blackened furniture, PVC ramrod. All-Weather has epoxied beech stock and C-Nickel barrel. Drilled and tapped for scope mounting. Imported by Traditions, Inc.
Price: Percussion, 50 or 54, 1:48″ twist **$189.00**
Price: Flintlock, 50-caliber only, 1:66″ twist **$198.00**
Price: Percussion kit, 50 or 54 . . . . **$153.00**
Price: Flintlock, All-Weather, 50-cal. **$166.00**
Price: Percussion, All-Weather, 50 or 54 . . . . **$198.00**
Price: Small Game, 32-cal., percussion **$189.00**

Traditions Deerhunter Scout Rifle
Similar to the Deerhunter except in 32-caliber percussion only with 22″ octagon barrel; 1:48″ twist; weighs 5 lbs., 10 oz.; 36½″ overall length; beech stock; drilled and tapped for scope mounting; hooked breech; PVC ramrod. Introduced 1996. Imported by Traditions.
Price: **$172.00**

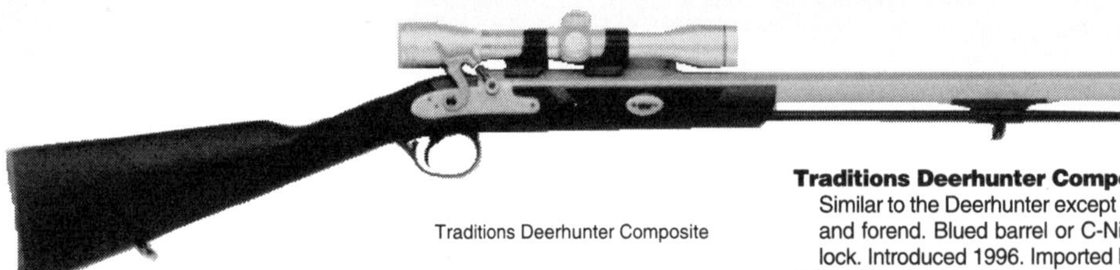

Traditions Deerhunter Composite

TRADITIONS HAWKEN WOODSMAN RIFLE

Caliber: 50 and 54.
Barrel: 28″; 15/16″ flats.
Weight: 7 lbs., 11 oz. **Length:** 44 1/2″ overall.
Stock: Walnut-stained hardwood.
Sights: Beaded blade front, hunting-style open rear adjustable for windage and elevation.
Features: Percussion only. Brass patchbox and furniture. Double triggers. From Traditions.
Price: 50 or 54 .... **$247.00**
Price: 50-cal., left-hand **$264.00**

Traditions Deerhunter Composite Rifle

Similar to the Deerhunter except has black composite stock with checkered grip and forend. Blued barrel or C-Nickel finish, 50, 54 percussion, 50-caliber flintlock. Introduced 1996. Imported by Traditions.
Price: Blued, percussion **$172.00**
Price: C-Nickel barrel, 50-cal. percussion and flintlock, 54-cal. percussion **$189.00**

TRADITIONS KENTUCKY RIFLE

Caliber: 50.
Barrel: 33 1/2″; 7/8″ flats; 1:66″ twist.
Weight: 7 lbs. **Length:** 49″ overall.
Stock: Beech; inletted toe plate.
Sights: Blade front, fixed rear.
Features: Full-length, two-piece stock; brass furniture; color case-hardened lock. Introduced 1995. From Traditions.
Price: Finished **$247.00**
Price: Kit **$198.00**

Traditions Tennessee

TRADITIONS PENNSYLVANIA RIFLE

Caliber: 50.
Barrel: 40 1/4″, 7/8″ flats; 1:66″ twist, octagon.
Weight: 9 lbs. **Length:** 57 1/2″ overall.
Stock: Walnut.
Sights: Blade front, adjustable rear.
Features: Brass patchbox and ornamentation. Double-set triggers. From Traditions.
Price: Flintlock **$506.00**
Price: Percussion **$496.00**

TRADITIONS TENNESSEE RIFLE

Caliber: 50.
Barrel: 24″, octagon with 15/16″ flats; 1:32″ twist.
Weight: 6 lbs. **Length:** 40 1/2″ overall.
Stock: Stained beech.
Sights: Blade front, fixed rear.
Features: One-piece stock has inletted brass furniture, cheekpiece; double-set trigger; V-type mainspring. Flint or percussion. Introduced 1995. From Traditions.
Price: Percussion **$297.00**
Price: Flintlock **$313.00**

TRADITIONS PIONEER RIFLE

Caliber: 50, 54.
Barrel: 28″, 15/16″ flats.
Weight: 7 lbs. **Length:** 44″ overall.
Stock: Beech with pistol grip, recoil pad.
Sights: German silver blade front, buckhorn rear with elevation ramp.
Features: V-type mainspring, adjustable single trigger; blackened furniture; color case-hardened lock; large trigger guard. From Traditions.
Price: Percussion only, rifle **$214.00**

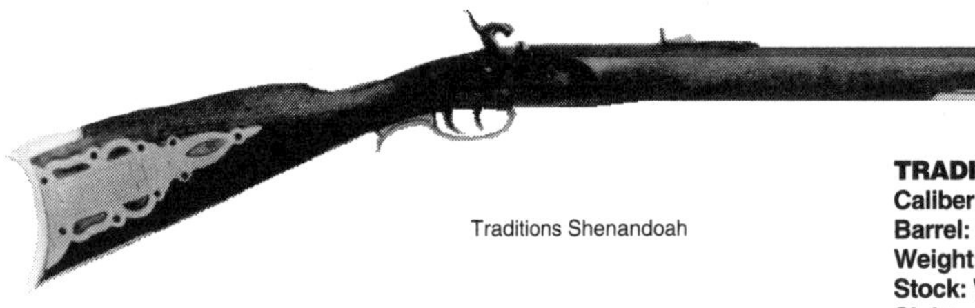

Traditions Shenandoah

TRADITIONS SHENANDOAH RIFLE

Caliber: 50.
Barrel: 33 1/2″ octagon, 1:66″ twist.
Weight: 7 lbs., 3 oz. **Length:** 49 1/2″ overall.
Stock: Walnut.
Sights: Blade front, buckhorn rear.
Features: V-type mainspring; double-set trigger; solid brass buttplate, patchbox, nose cap, thimbles, rigger guard. Introduced 1996. From Traditions.
Price: Flintlock **$366.00**
Price: Percussion **$348.00**

Traditions Model 1853

TRADITIONS 1853 THREE-BAND ENFIELD

Caliber: 58.
Barrel: 39″; 1:48″ twist.
Weight: 10 lbs. **Length:** 55″ overall.
Stock: Walnut.
Sights: Military front, adjustable ladder-type rear.
Features: Color case-hardened lock; brass buttplate, trigger guard, nose cap. Has V-type mainspring; steel ramrod; sling swivels. Introduced 1995. From Traditions.
Price: **$595.00**

CAUTION: PRICES SHOWN ARE SUPPLIED BY THE MANUFACTURER OR IMPORTER. CHECK YOUR LOCAL GUNSHOP.

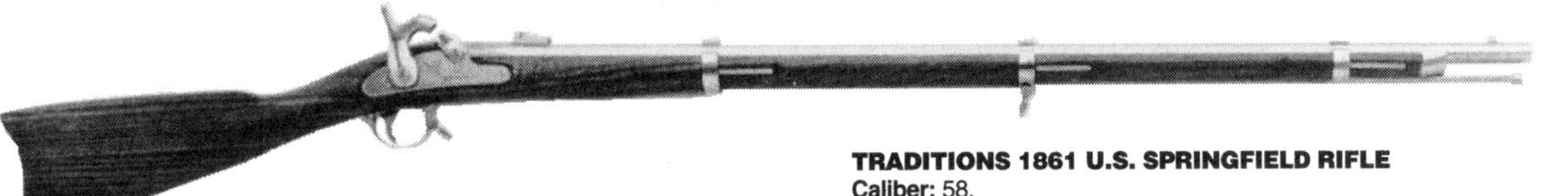

Traditions Model 1861

TRADITIONS 1861 U.S. SPRINGFIELD RIFLE
Caliber: 58.
Barrel: 40″; 1:66″ twist.
Weight: 10 lbs. **Length:** 56″ overall.
Stock: Walnut.
Sights: Military front, adjustable ladder-type rear.
Features: Full-length stock with white steel barrel, buttplate, ramrod, trigger guard, barrel bands, swivels, lockplate. Introduced 1995. From Traditions.
Price: **$645.00**

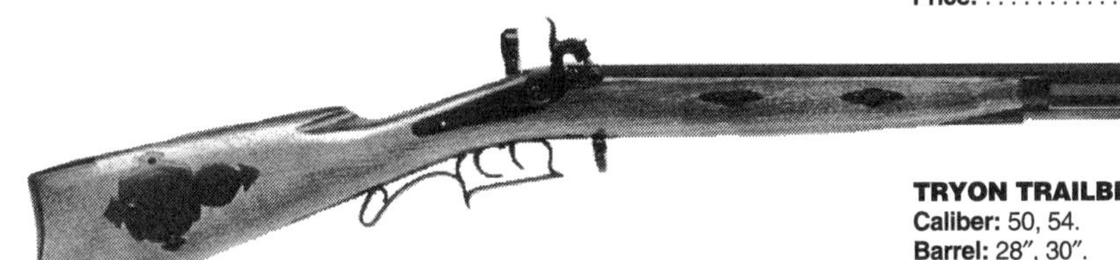

Navy Arms Tryon Creedmoor

Navy Arms Tryon Creedmoor Target Model
Similar to the standard Tryon rifle except 45-caliber only, 33″ octagon barrel, globe front sight with inserts, fully adjustable match rear. Has double-set triggers, sling swivels. Imported by Navy Arms.
Price: **$780.00**

UFA TETON RIFLE
Caliber: 45, 50, 12-bore (rifled, 72-cal.), 12-gauge.
Barrel: 26″.
Weight: 8 lbs. **Length:** 42″ overall.
Stock: Black or brown laminated wood; 1″ recoil pad.
Sights: Marble's bead front, Marble's fully adjustable rear.
Features: Removable, interchangeable barrel; removable one-piece breech plug/nipple, hammer/trigger assembly; hammer blowback block; glass-bedded stock and forend. Introduced 1994. Made in U.S. by UFA, Inc.
Price: Stainless or blued **$834.00**
Price: With premium walnut or maple **$984.00**
Price: Extra barrels **$165.00**

TRYON TRAILBLAZER RIFLE
Caliber: 50, 54.
Barrel: 28″, 30″.
Weight: 9 lbs. **Length:** 48″ overall.
Stock: European walnut with cheekpiece.
Sights: Blade front, semi-buckhorn rear.
Features: Reproduction of a rifle made by George Tryon about 1820. Double-set triggers, back action lock, hooked breech with long tang. From Armsport.
Price: About **$825.00**

UFA Grand Teton Rifle
Similar to the Teton model except has 30″ tapered octagon barrel in 45- or 50-caliber only. Available in blue or stainless steel with brushed or matte finish, brown or black laminated wood stock and forend. Weighs 9 lbs., overall length 46″. Introduced 1994. Made in U.S. by UFA, Inc.
Price: **$995.00**
Price: With premium walnut or maple **$1,145.00**

UFA Teton Blackstone Rifle
Similar to the Teton model except in 50-caliber only, 26″ barrel with shallow groove 1:26″ rifling. Available only in stainless steel with matte finish. Has hardwood stock with black epoxy coating, 1″ recoil pad. Weighs 7$^{1}/_{2}$ lbs., overall length 42″. Introduced 1994. Made in U.S. by UFA, Inc.
Price: **$534.00**

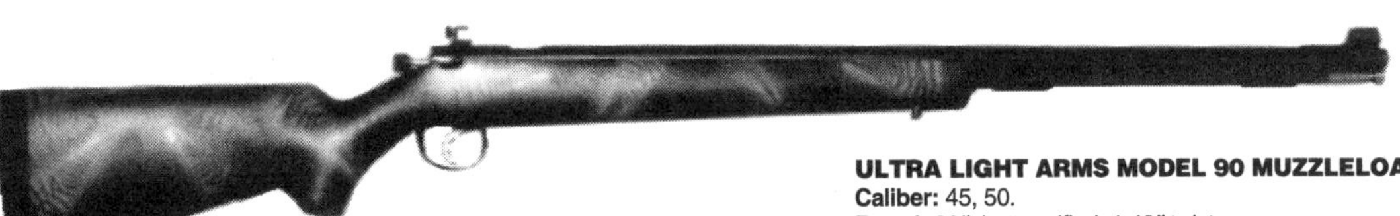

Ultra Light Model 90

ULTRA LIGHT ARMS MODEL 90 MUZZLELOADER
Caliber: 45, 50.
Barrel: 28″, button rifled; 1:48″ twist.
Weight: 6 lbs.
Stock: Kevlar/graphite, colors optional.
Sights: Hooded blade front on ramp, Williams aperture rear adjustable for windage and elevation.
Features: In-line ignition system with top loading port. Timney trigger; integral side safety. Comes with recoil pad, sling swivels and hard case. Introduced 1990. Made in U.S. by Ultra Light Arms.
Price: **$950.00**

White Shooting Systems Super 91

White Shooting Systems Super Safari Rifle
Same as the stainless Super 91 except has Mannlicher-style stock of black composite. Introduced 1993. From White Shooting Systems, Inc.
Price: **$799.00**

WHITE SHOOTING SYSTEMS SUPER 91 BLACKPOWDER RIFLE
Caliber: 41, 45 or 50.
Barrel: 26″.
Weight: 7$^{1}/_{2}$ lbs. **Length:** 43.5″ overall.
Stock: Black laminate or black composite; recoil pad, swivel studs.
Sights: Bead front on ramp, fully adjustable open rear.
Features: Insta-Fire straight-line ignition system; all stainless steel construction; side-swing safety; fully adjustable trigger; full barrel under-rib with two ramrod thimbles. Introduced 1991. Made in U.S. by White Shooting Systems, Inc.
Price: Blue, hardwood stock, 50-cal. **$599.00**
Price: Stainless **$659.00**
Price: Stainless, laminate stock **$699.95**

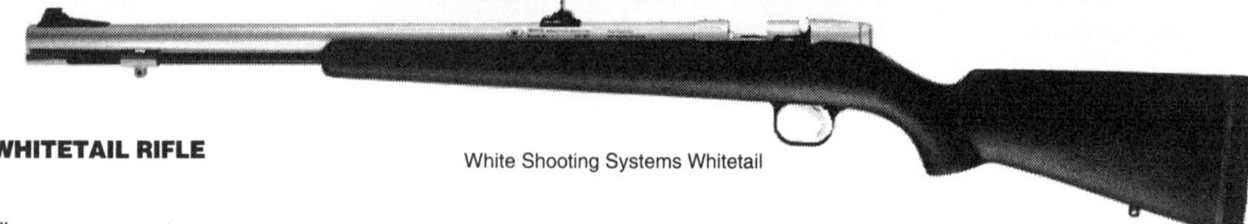
White Shooting Systems Whitetail

WHITE SHOOTING SYSTEMS WHITETAIL RIFLE
Caliber: 41, 45 or 50.
Barrel: 22″.
Weight: 6.5 lbs. **Length:** 39.5″ overall.
Stock: Black composite; classic style; recoil pad, swivel studs.
Sights: Bead front on ramp, fully adjustable open rear.
Features: Insta-Fire straight-line ignition; action and trigger safeties; adjustable trigger; stainless steel. Introduced 1992. Made in U.S. by White Shooting Systems, Inc.
Price: Blue, wood stock, bull bbl., 50-cal. **$399.00**
Price: Stainless, composite stock **$499.00**
Price: Stainless, laminate stock **$549.00**

Consult our Directory pages for the location of firms mentioned.

White Shooting Systems Bison Blackpowder Rifle
Similar to the blued Whitetail model except in 54-caliber (1:28″ twist) with 22″ ball barrel. Uses Insta-Fire in-line percussion system, double safety. Adjustable sight, black-finished hardwood stock, matte blue metal finish, Delron ramrod, swivel studs. Drilled and tapped for scope mounting. Weighs 7¼ lbs. Introduced 1993. From White Shooting Systems, Inc.
Price: **$399.95**

White Shooting Systems White Lightning Rifle
Similar to the Whitetail stainless rifle except uses smaller action with cocking lever and secondary safety on right side, primary safety on the left. Available only in 50-caliber with 22″ barrel. Weighs 6.4 lbs., 40″ overall. Has black hardwood stock. Introduced 1995. From White Shooting Systems, Inc.
Price: **$299.95**

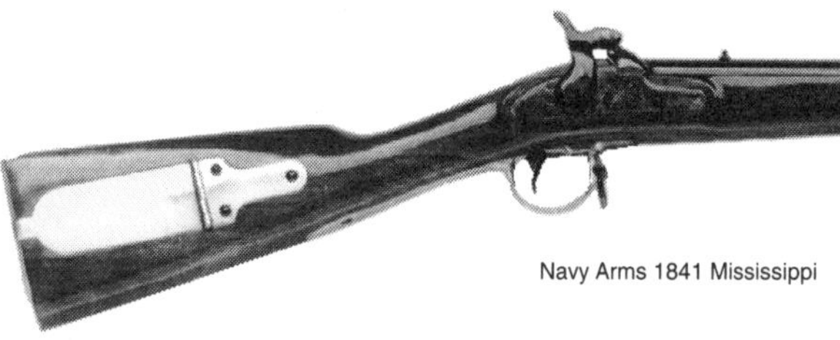
Navy Arms 1841 Mississippi

Mississippi 1841 Percussion Rifle
Similar to Zouave rifle but patterned after U.S. Model 1841. Imported by Dixie Gun Works, Euroarms of America, Navy Arms, Stone Mountain Arms.
Price: .... **$430.00** to **$487.00**

ZOUAVE PERCUSSION RIFLE
Caliber: 58, 59.
Barrel: 32½″.
Weight: 9½ lbs. **Length:** 48½″ overall.
Stock: Walnut finish, brass patchbox and buttplate.
Sights: Fixed front, rear adjustable for elevation.
Features: Color case-hardened lockplate, blued barrel. From Navy Arms, Dixie Gun Works, Euroarms of America (M1863), E.M.F., Cabela's.
Price: About .... **$325.00** to **$465.00**
Price: Kit (Euroarms 58-cal. only) **$331.00**

BLACKPOWDER SHOTGUNS

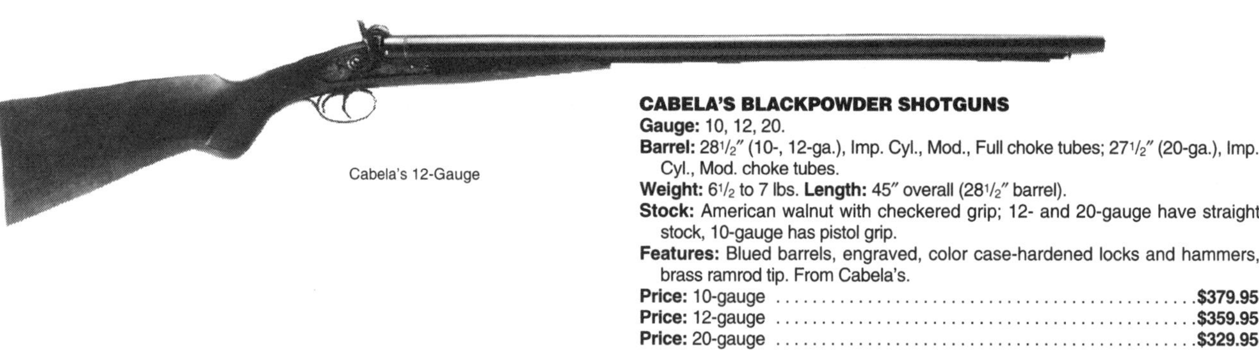
Cabela's 12-Gauge

CABELA'S BLACKPOWDER SHOTGUNS
Gauge: 10, 12, 20.
Barrel: 28½″ (10-, 12-ga.), Imp. Cyl., Mod., Full choke tubes; 27½″ (20-ga.), Imp. Cyl., Mod. choke tubes.
Weight: 6½ to 7 lbs. **Length:** 45″ overall (28½″ barrel).
Stock: American walnut with checkered grip; 12- and 20-gauge have straight stock, 10-gauge has pistol grip.
Features: Blued barrels, engraved, color case-hardened locks and hammers, brass ramrod tip. From Cabela's.
Price: 10-gauge **$379.95**
Price: 12-gauge **$359.95**
Price: 20-gauge **$329.95**

CVA Classic Turkey

CVA CLASSIC TURKEY DOUBLE SHOTGUN
Gauge: 12.
Barrel: 28″.
B>Weight: 9 lbs. **Length:** 45″ overall.
Stock: European walnut; classic English style with checkered straight grip, wrap-around forend with bottom screw attachment.
Sights: Bead front.
Features: Hinged double triggers; color case-hardened and engraved lockplates, trigger guard and tang. Polymer-coated fiberglass ramrod. Rubber recoil pad. Not suitable for steel shot. Introduced 1990. Imported by CVA.
Price: **$429.95**

CAUTION: PRICES SHOWN ARE SUPPLIED BY THE MANUFACTURER OR IMPORTER. CHECK YOUR LOCAL GUNSHOP.

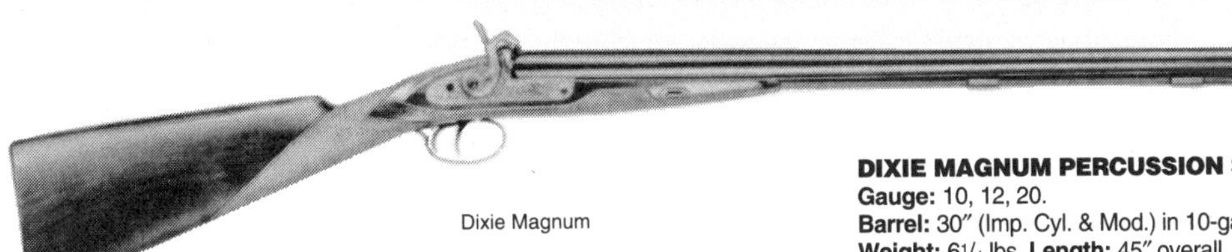
Dixie Magnum

DIXIE MAGNUM PERCUSSION SHOTGUN

Gauge: 10, 12, 20.
Barrel: 30″ (Imp. Cyl. & Mod.) in 10-gauge; 28″ in 12-gauge.
Weight: $6^1/_4$ lbs. **Length:** 45″ overall.
Stock: Hand-checkered walnut, 14″ pull.
Features: Double triggers; light hand engraving; case-hardened locks in 12-gauge, polished steel in 10-gauge; sling swivels. From Dixie Gun Works.
Price: Upland $449.00
Price: 12-ga. kit $375.00
Price: 20-ga. $495.00
Price: 10-ga. $495.00
Price: 10-ga. kit $375.00

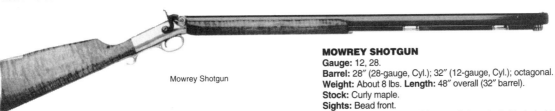

CVA TRAPPER PERCUSSION

Gauge: 12.
Barrel: 28″.
Weight: 6 lbs. **Length:** 46″ overall.
Stock: English-style checkered straight grip of walnut-finished hardwood.
Sights: Brass bead front.
Features: Single blued barrel; color case-hardened lockplate and hammer; screw adjustable sear engagements, V-type mainspring; brass wedge plates; color case-hardened and engraved trigger guard and tang. From CVA.
Price: Finished $239.95

Mowrey Shotgun

MOWREY SHOTGUN

Gauge: 12, 28.
Barrel: 28″ (28-gauge, Cyl.); 32″ (12-gauge, Cyl.); octagonal.
Weight: About 8 lbs. **Length:** 48″ overall (32″ barrel).
Stock: Curly maple.
Sights: Bead front.
Features: Brass or steel frame; shotgun butt. Made in U.S. by Mowrey Gun Works.
Price: Finished $350.00
Price: Kit $300.00

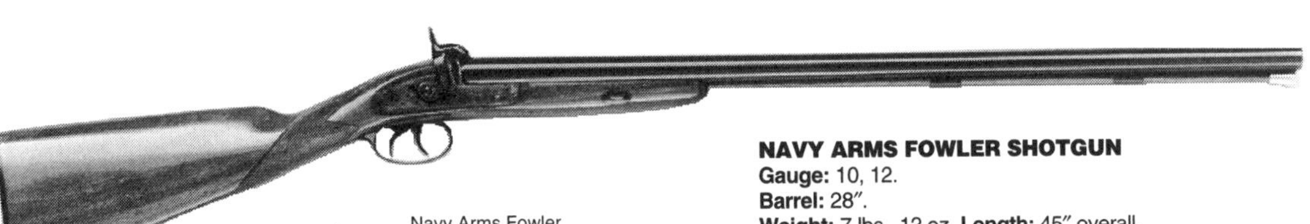
Navy Arms Fowler

NAVY ARMS FOWLER SHOTGUN

Gauge: 10, 12.
Barrel: 28″.
Weight: 7 lbs., 12 oz. **Length:** 45″ overall.
Stock: Walnut-stained hardwood.
Features: Color case-hardened lockplates and hammers; checkered stock. Imported by Navy Arms.
Price: $340.00

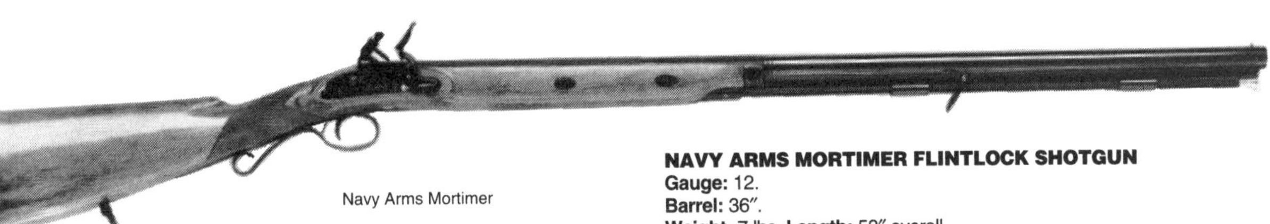
Navy Arms Mortimer

NAVY ARMS MORTIMER FLINTLOCK SHOTGUN

Gauge: 12.
Barrel: 36″.
Weight: 7 lbs. **Length:** 53″ overall.
Stock: Walnut, with cheekpiece.
Features: Waterproof pan, roller frizzen, external safety. Color case-hardened lock, rest blued. Imported by Navy Arms.
Price: $735.00

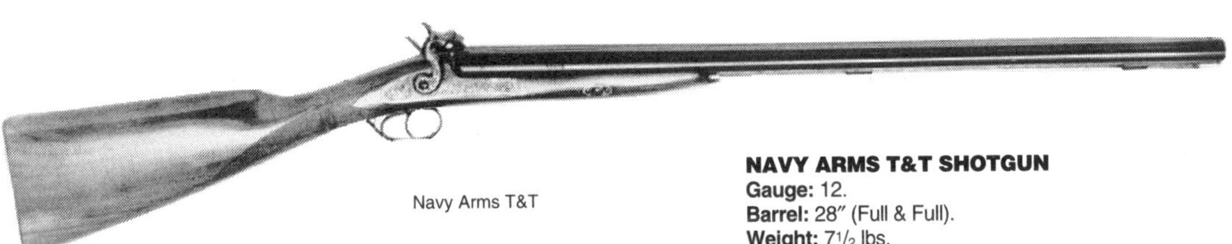
Navy Arms T&T

NAVY ARMS STEEL SHOT MAGNUM SHOTGUN

Gauge: 10.
Barrel: 28″ (Cyl. & Cyl.).
Weight: 7 lbs., 9 oz. **Length:** $45^1/_2$″ overall.
Stock: Walnut, with cheekpiece.
Features: Designed specifically for steel shot. Engraved, polished locks; sling swivels; blued barrels. Imported by Navy Arms.
Price: $560.00

NAVY ARMS T&T SHOTGUN

Gauge: 12.
Barrel: 28″ (Full & Full).
Weight: $7^1/_2$ lbs.
Stock: Walnut.
Sights: Bead front.
Features: Color case-hardened locks, double triggers, blued steel furniture. From Navy Arms.
Price: $540.00

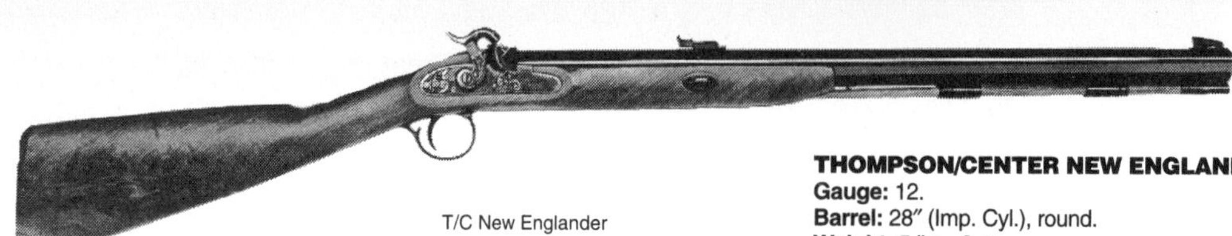
T/C New Englander

THOMPSON/CENTER NEW ENGLANDER SHOTGUN
Gauge: 12.
Barrel: 28″ (Imp. Cyl.), round.
Weight: 5 lbs., 2 oz.
Stock: Select American black walnut with straight grip.
Features: Percussion lock is color case-hardened, rest blued. Also accepts 26″ round 50- and 54-cal. rifle barrel. Introduced 1986. From Thompson/Center.
Price: Right-hand **$330.00**

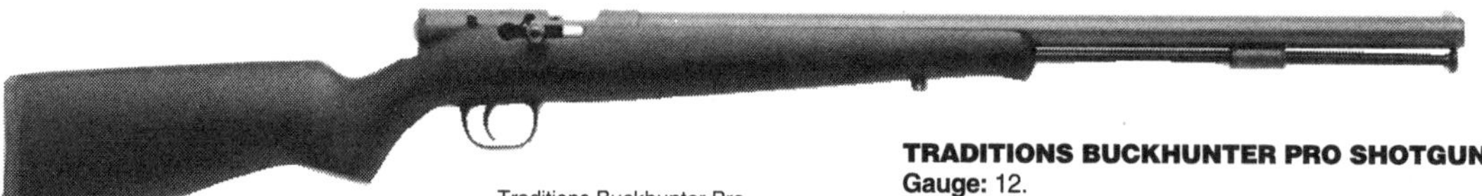
Traditions Buckhunter Pro

TRADITIONS BUCKHUNTER PRO SHOTGUN
Gauge: 12.
Barrel: 24″; choke tube.
Weight: 6 lbs., 4oz. **Length:** 43″ overall.
Stock: Composite matte black, Mossy Oak Treestand or Advantage camouflage.
Features: In-line action with removable stainless steel breech plug; thumb safety; adjustable trigger; rubber buttpad. Introduced 1996. From Traditions.
Price: With black stock **$313.00**
Price: With camouflage stock **$366.00**

White Shooting Systems White Thunder

WHITE SHOOTING SYSTEMS WHITE THUNDER SHOTGUN
Gauge: 12.
Barrel: 26″ (Imp. Cyl., Mod., Full choke tubes); ventilated rib.
Weight: About 5 3/4 lbs.
Stock: Black hardwood.
Features: InstaFire in-line ignition; double safeties; match-grade trigger; Delron ramrod. Introduced 1995. From White Shooting Systems, Inc.
Price: **$459.95**

White Shooting Systems "Tominator" Shotgun
Similar to the White Thunder except has Imp. Cyl., Mod., Full and Super Full Turkey choke tubes; black laminate stock. Introduced 1995. From White Shooting Systems, Inc.
Price: **$549.95**

AIRGUNS—HANDGUNS

AIRROW MODEL A6 AIR PISTOL
Caliber: #2512 10.75″ arrow.
Barrel: 10.75″.
Weight: 1.75 lbs. **Length:** 16.5″ overall.
Power: CO_2 or compressed air.
Stocks: Checkered composition.
Sights: Bead front, fully adjustable Williams rear.
Features: Velocity to 375 fps. Pneumatic air trigger. Floating barrel. All aircraft aluminum and stainless steel construction; Mil-spec materials and finishes. Announced 1993. From Swivel Machine Works, Inc.
Price: About **$597.00**

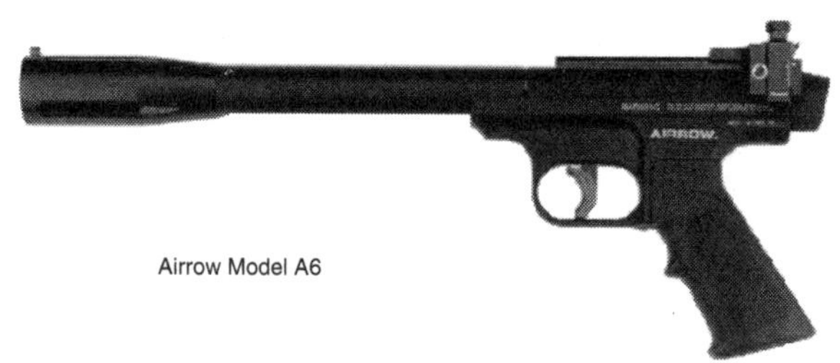

Airrow Model A6

Anics A-101 Magnum

ANICS A-101 AIR PISTOL
Caliber: 177, 4.5mm, BB; 15-shot magazine.
Barrel: 4.5″ steel smoothbore.
Weight: 35 oz. **Length:** 7″ overall.
Power: CO_2
Stocks: Checkered plastic.
Sights: Blade front, fixed rear.
Features: Velocity to 460 fps. Semi-automatic action; double action only; cross-bolt safety; black and silver finish. Comes with two 15-shot magazines. Introduced 1996. Imported by Anics, Inc.
Price: With case, about **$65.00**

Anics A-101 Magnum Air Pistol
Similar to the A-101 except has 6″ barrel with compensator, gives about 490 fps. Introduced 1996. Imported by Anics, Inc.
Price: With case, about **$72.00**

CAUTION: PRICES SHOWN ARE SUPPLIED BY THE MANUFACTURER OR IMPORTER. CHECK YOUR LOCAL GUNSHOP.

ANICS A-201 AIR REVOLVER
Caliber: 177, 4.5mm, BB; 36-shot cylinder.
Barrel: 4″, 6″ steel smoothbore.
Weight: 36 oz. **Length:** 9.75″ overall.
Power: CO_2
Stocks: Checkered plastic.
Sights: Blade front, fully adjustable rear.
Features: Velocity about 425 fps. Fixed barrel; single/double action; rotating cylinder; manual cross-bolt safety; blue and silver finish. Introduced 1996. Imported by Anics, Inc.
Price: **$75.00**

BEEMAN P1 MAGNUM AIR PISTOL
Caliber: 177, 5mm, single shot.
Barrel: 8.4″.
Weight: 2.5 lbs. **Length:** 11″ overall.
Power: Top lever cocking; spring-piston.
Stocks: Checkered walnut.
Sights: Blade front, square notch rear with click micrometer adjustments for windage and elevation. Grooved for scope mounting.
Features: Dual power for 177 and 20-cal.: low setting gives 350-400 fps; high setting 500-600 fps. Rearward expanding mainspring simulates firearm recoil. All Colt 45 auto grips fit gun. Dry-firing feature for practice. Optional wooden shoulder stock. Introduced 1985. Imported by Beeman.
Price: 177, 5mm **$405.00**

Beeman/Feinwekbau 102

BEEMAN/FEINWERKBAU 102 PISTOL
Caliber: 177, single shot.
Barrel: 10.1″, 12-groove rifling.
Weight: 2.5 lbs. **Length:** 16.5″ overall.
Power: Single-stroke pneumatic, underlever cocking.
Stocks: Stippled walnut with adjustable palm shelf.
Sights: Blade front, open rear adjustable for windage and elevation. Notch size adjustable for width. Interchangeable front blades.
Features: Velocity 460 fps. Fully adjustable trigger. Cocking effort 12 lbs. Introduced 1988. Imported by Beeman.
Price: Right-hand **$1,530.00**
Price: Left-hand **$1,580.00**

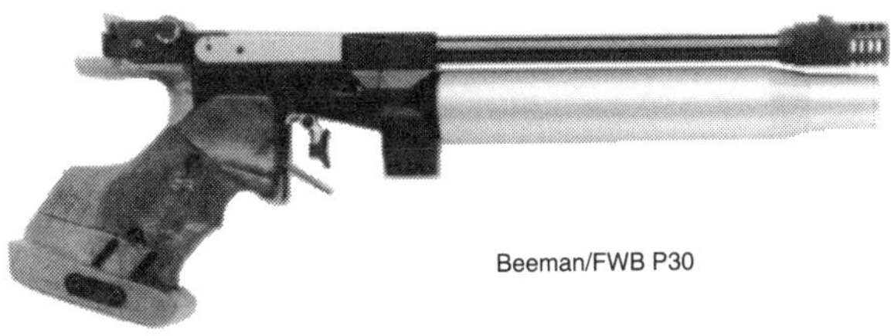
Beeman/FWB P30

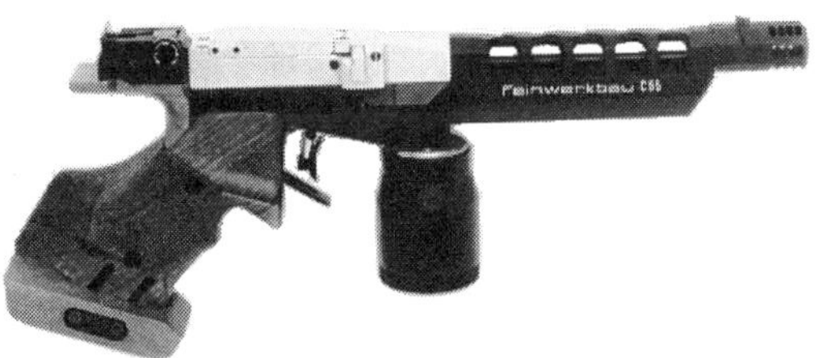
Feinwerkbau C55
Beeman/FWB C55

Beeman P1

Beeman P2 Match Air Pistol
Similar to the Beeman P1 Magnum except shoots only 177 pellets; completely recoilless single-stroke pnuematic action. Weighs 2.2 lbs. Choice of thumbrest match grips or standard style. Introduced 1990.
Price: 177, 5mm, standard grip **$435.00**
Price: 177, match grip **$465.00**

BEEMAN/FEINWERKBAU 65 MKII AIR PISTOL
Caliber: 177, single shot.
Barrel: 6.1″, removable bbl. wgt. available.
Weight: 42 oz. **Length:** 13.3″ overall.
Power: Spring, sidelever cocking.
Stocks: Walnut, stippled thumbrest; adjustable or fixed.
Sights: Front, interchangeable post element system, open rear, click adjustable for windage and elevation and for sighting notch width. Scope mount available.
Features: New shorter barrel for better balance and control. Cocking effort 9 lbs. Two-stage trigger, four adjustments. Quiet firing, 525 fps. Programs instantly for recoil or recoilless operation. Permanently lubricated. Steel piston ring. Imported by Beeman.
Price: Right-hand **$1,170.00**
Price: Left-hand **$1,220.00**

BEEMAN/FWB P30 MATCH AIR PISTOL
Caliber: 177, single shot.
Barrel: 10$\frac{5}{16}$″, with muzzlebrake.
Weight: 2.4 lbs. **Length:** 16.5″ overall.
Power: Pre-charged pneumatic.
Stocks: Stippled walnut; adjustable match type.
Sights: Undercut blade front, fully adjustable match rear.
Features: Velocity to 525 fps; up to 200 shots per CO_2 cartridge. Fully adjustable trigger; built-in muzzlebrake. Introduced 1995. Imported from Germany by Beeman.
Price: Right-hand **$1,530.00**
Price: Left-hand **$1,580.00**

CONSULT
SHOOTER'S
MARKETPLACE
Page 225, This Issue

BEEMAN/FWB C55 CO_2 RAPID FIRE PISTOL
Caliber: 177, single shot or 5-shot magazine.
Barrel: 7.3″.
Weight: 2.5 lbs. **Length:** 15″ overall.
Power: Special CO_2 cylinder.
Stocks: Anatomical, adjustable.
Sights: Interchangeable front, fully adjustable open micro-click rear with adjustable notch size.
Features: Velocity 510 fps. Has 11.75″ sight radius. Built-in muzzlebrake. Introduced 1993. Imported by Beeman Precision Airguns.
Price: Right-hand **$1,705.00**
Price: Left-hand **$1,755.00**

BEEMAN HW70A AIR PISTOL
Caliber: 177, single shot.
Barrel: 6¼", rifled.
Weight: 38 oz. **Length:** 12¾" overall.
Power: Spring, barrel cocking.
Stocks: Plastic, with thumbrest.
Sights: Hooded post front, square notch rear adjustable for windage and elevation. Comes with scope base.
Features: Adjustable trigger, 24-lb. cocking effort, 410 fps MV; automatic barrel safety. Imported by Beeman.
Price: $215.00
Price: HW70S, black grip, silver finish $240.00

Beeman HW70A

BEEMAN/WEBLEY NEMESIS AIR PISTOL
Caliber: 177, single shot.
Barrel: 7".
Weight: 2.2 lbs. **Length:** 9.8" overall.
Power: Single-stroke pneumatic.
Stocks: Checkered black composition.
Sights: Blade on ramp front, fully adjustable rear. Integral scope rail.
Features: Velocity to 400 fps. Adjustable two-stage trigger, manual safety. Recoilless action. Introduced 1995. Imported from England by Beeman.
Price: $190.00

Beeman/Webley Nemesis

BEEMAN/WEBLEY TEMPEST AIR PISTOL
Caliber: 177, 22, single shot.
Barrel: 6⅞".
Weight: 32 oz. **Length:** 8.9" overall.
Power: Spring-piston, break barrel.
Stocks: Checkered black plastic with thumbrest.
Sights: Blade front, adjustable rear.
Features: Velocity to 500 fps (177), 400 fps (22). Aluminum frame; black epoxy finish; manual safety. Imported from England by Beeman.
Price: $200.00

Beeman/Webley Hurricane Air Pistol
Similar to the Tempest except has extended frame in the rear for a click-adjustable rear sight; hooded front sight; comes with scope mount. Imported from England by Beeman.
Price: $225.00

Beeman/Webley Tempest

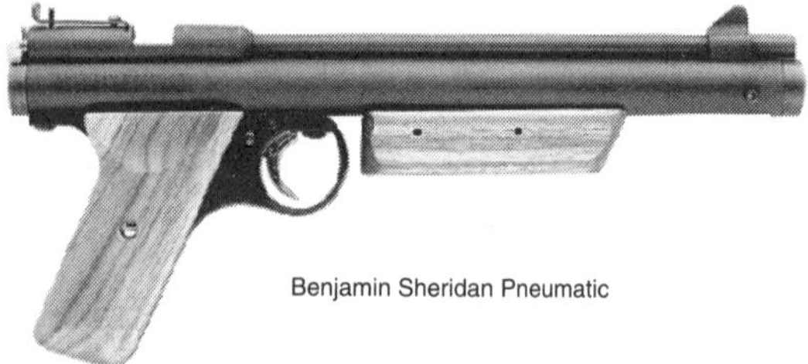
Benjamin Sheridan Pneumatic

Benjamin Sheridan CO_2

BRNO Tau-7 Match

BENJAMIN SHERIDAN PNEUMATIC PELLET PISTOLS
Caliber: 177, 20, 22, single shot.
Barrel: 9⅜", rifled brass.
Weight: 38 oz. **Length:** 13⅛" overall.
Power: Underlever pnuematic, hand pumped.
Stocks: Walnut stocks and pump handle.
Sights: High ramp front, fully adjustable notch rear.
Features: Velocity to 525 fps (variable). Bolt action with cross-bolt safety. Choice of black or nickel finish. Made in U.S. by Benjamin Sheridan Co.
Price: Black finish, HB17 (177), HB20 (20), HB22 (22), about $106.00
Price: Nickel finish, H17 (177), H20 (20), H22 (22), about $112.75

BENJAMIN SHERIDAN CO_2 PELLET PISTOLS
Caliber: 177, 20, 22, single shot.
Barrel: 6⅜", rifled brass.
Weight: 29 oz. **Length:** 9.8" overall.
Power: 12-gram CO_2 cylinder.
Stocks: Walnut.
Sights: High ramp front, fully adjustable notch rear.
Features: Velocity to 500 fps. Turn-bolt action with cross-bolt safety. Gives about 40 shots per CO_2 cylinder. Black or nickel finish. Made in U.S. by Benjamin Sheridan Co.
Price: Black finish, EB17 (177), EB20 (20), EB22 (22), about $97.25
Price: Nickel finish, E17 (177), E20 (20), E22 (22), about $110.50

BRNO TAU-7 CO_2 MATCH PISTOL
Caliber: 177.
Barrel: 10.24".
Weight: 37 oz. **Length:** 15.75" overall.
Power: 12.5-gram CO_2 cartridge.
Stocks: Stippled hardwood with adjustable palm rest.
Sights: Blade front, open fully adjustable rear.
Features: Comes with extra seals and counterweight. Blue finish. Imported by Century International Arms, Great Lakes Airguns.
Price: About $326.50

CAUTION: PRICES SHOWN ARE SUPPLIED BY THE MANUFACTURER OR IMPORTER. CHECK YOUR LOCAL GUN SHOP.

BSA 240 MAGNUM AIR PISTOL
Caliber: 177, 22
Barrel: 5 1/2", rifled.
Weight: 28 oz. **Length:** 8 1/2" overall.
Power: Spring-air.
Stocks: Oil-finish hardwood.
Sights: Post front, fully adjustable rear.
Features: Velocity about 390 fps (177). Automatic safety; adjustable trigger; matte finish. Introduced 1996. Imported frmo England by Great Lakes Airguns.
Price: **$224.75**

COPPERHEAD BLACK VENOM PISTOL
Caliber: 177 pellets, BB, 17-shot magazine.
Barrel: 4.75" smoothbore.
Weight: 16 oz. **Length:** 10.8" overall.
Power: Spring.
Stocks: Checkered.
Sights: Blade front, adjustable rear.
Features: Velocity to 260 fps (BBs), 250 fps (pellets). Spring-fed magazine; cross-bolt safety. Introduced 1996. Made in U.S. by Crosman Corp.
Price: About **$16.00**

COPPERHEAD BLACK FANG PISTOL
Caliber: 177 BB, 17-shot magazine.
Barrel: 4.75" smoothbore.
Weight: 10 oz. **Length:** 10.8" overall.
Power: Spring.
Stocks: Checkered.
Sights: Blade front, fixed notch rear.
Features: Velocity to 240 fps. Spring-fed magazine; cross-bolt safety. Introduced 1996. Made in U.S. by Crosman Corp.
Price: About **$14.00**

Crosman Auto Air II

Crosman Model 1008

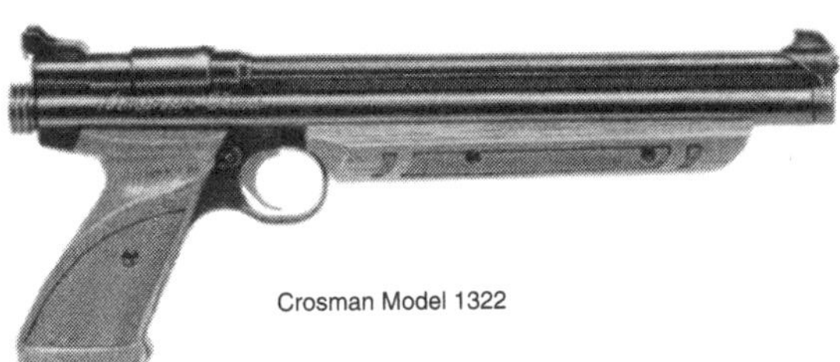
Crosman Model 1322

BSA 240 Magnum

CROSMAN AUTO AIR II PISTOL
Caliber: BB, 17-shot magazine, 177 pellet, single shot.
Barrel: 8 5/8" steel, smoothbore.
Weight: 13 oz. **Length:** 10 3/4" overall.
Power: CO_2 Powerlet.
Stocks: Grooved plastic.
Sights: Blade front, adjustable rear; highlighted system.
Features: Velocity to 480 fps (BBs), 430 fps (pellets). Semi-automatic action with BBs, single shot with pellets. Silvered finish. Introduced 1991. From Crosman.
Price: About **$29.00**

CROSMAN MODEL 357 AIR PISTOL
Caliber: 177, 6- and 10-shot pellet clips.
Barrel: 4" (Model 357-4), 6" (Model 357-6), rifled steel; 8" (Model 357-8), rifled brass.
Weight: 32 oz. (6"). **Length:** 11 3/8" overall (357-6).
Power: CO_2 Powerlet.
Stocks: Checkered wood-grain plastic.
Sights: Ramp front, fully adjustable rear.
Features: Average 430 fps (Model 357-6). Break-open barrel for easy loading. Single or double action. Vent. rib barrel. Wide, smooth trigger. Two cylinders come with each gun. Model 357-8 has matte gray finish, black grips. From Crosman.
Price: 4" or 6", about **$46.50**
Price: 8", about **$53.25**
Price: Model 1357 (same gun as above, except shoots BBs, has 6-shot clip), about **$46.50**

CROSMAN MODEL 1008 REPEAT AIR
Caliber: 177, 8-shot pellet clip
Barrel: 4.25", rifled steel.
Weight: 17 oz. **Length:** 8.625" overall.
Power: CO_2 Powerlet.
Stocks: Checkered plastic.
Sights: Post front, adjustable rear.
Features: Velocity about 430 fps. Break-open barrel for easy loading; single or double semi-automatic action; two 8-shot clips included. Optional carrying case available. Introduced 1992. From Crosman.
Price: About **$45.00**
Price: With case, about **$55.00**
Price: Model 1008SB (silver and black finish), about **$47.00**

CROSMAN MODEL 1322, 1377 AIR PISTOLS
Caliber: 177 (M1377), 22 (M1322), single shot.
Barrel: 8", rifled steel.
Weight: 39 oz. **Length:** 13 5/8".
Power: Hand pumped.
Sights: Blade front, rear adjustable for windage and elevation.
Features: Moulded plastic grip, hand size pump forearm. Cross-bolt safety. Model 1377 also shoots BBs. From Crosman.
Price: About **$53.00**

DAISY MODEL 288 AIR PISTOL
Caliber: 177 pellets, 24-shot.
Barrel: Smoothbore steel.
Weight: .8 lb. **Length:** 12.1" overall.
Power: Single stroke spring-air.
Stocks: Moulded resin with checkering and thumbrest.
Sights: Blade and ramp front, open fixed rear.
Features: Velocity to 215 fps. Cross-bolt trigger block safety. Black finish. From Daisy Mfg. Co.
Price: About **$26.00**

DAISY MODEL 91 MATCH PISTOL
Caliber: 177, single shot.
Barrel: 10.25″, rifled steel.
Weight: 2.5 lbs. **Length:** 16.5″ overall.
Power: CO_2, 12-gram cylinder.
Stocks: Stippled hardwood; anatomically shaped and adjustable.
Sights: Blade and ramp front, changeable-width rear notch with full micrometer adjustments.
Features: Velocity to 476 fps. Gives 55 shots per cylinder. Fully adjustable trigger. Imported by Daisy Mfg. Co.
Price: About **$670.00**

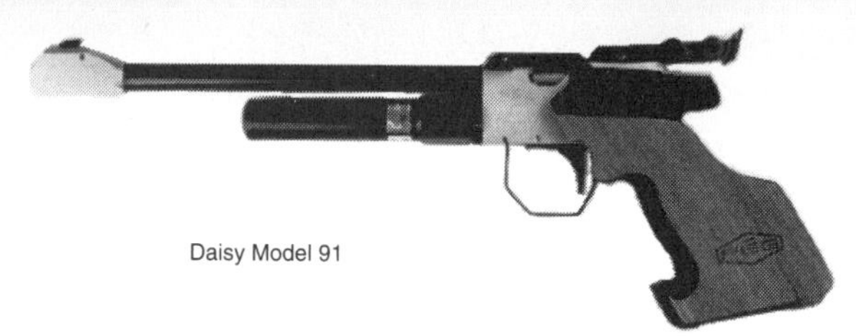
Daisy Model 91

Daisy Model 500

DAISY MODEL 500 RAVEN AIR PISTOL
Caliber: 177 pellets, single shot.
Barrel: Rifled steel.
Weight: 36 oz. **Length:** 8.5″ overall.
Power: CO_2.
Stocks: Moulded plastic with checkering.
Sights: Blade front, fixed rear.
Features: Velocity up to 500 fps. Hammer-block safety. Resembles semi-auto centerfire pistol. Barrel tips up for loading. Introduced 1993. From Daisy Mfg. Co.
Price: About **$65.00**

DAISY/POWER LINE 44 REVOLVER
Caliber: 177 pellets, 6-shot.
Barrel: 6″, rifled steel; interchangeable 4″ and 8″.
Weight: 2.7 lbs.
Power: CO_2.
Stocks: Moulded plastic with checkering.
Sights: Blade on ramp front, fully adjustable notch rear.
Features: Velocity up to 400 fps. Replica of 44 Magnum revolver. Has swingout cylinder and interchangeable barrels. Introduced 1987. From Daisy Mfg. Co.
Price: **$70.00**

Daisy/Power Line 45

DAISY/POWER LINE 45 AIR PISTOL
Caliber: 177, 13-shot clip.
Barrel: 5″, rifled steel.
Weight: 1.25 lbs. **Length:** 8.5″ overall.
Power: CO_2.
Stocks: Checkered plastic.
Sights: Fixed.
Features: Velocity 400 fps. Semi-automatic repeater with double-action trigger. Manually operated lever-type trigger block safety; magazine safety. Introduced 1990. From Daisy Mfg. Co.
Price: About **$80.00**
Price: Model 645 (nickel-chrome plated), about **$85.00**

Daisy/Power Line 93

DAISY/POWER LINE 93 PISTOL
Caliber: 177, BB, 15-shot clip.
Barrel: 5″, steel.
Weight: 17 oz. **Length:** NA.
Power: CO_2.
Stocks: Checkered plastic.
Sights: Fixed.
Features: Velocity to 400 fps. Semi-automatic repeater. Manual lever-type trigger-block safety. Introduced 1991. From Daisy Mfg. Co.
Price: About **$80.00**
Price: Model 693 (nickel-chrome plated), about **$85.00**

Daisy/Power Line 400

DAISY/POWER LINE 400 BB PISTOL
Caliber: BB, 20-shot magazine.
Barrel: Smoothbore steel.
Weight: 1.4 lbs. **Length:** 10.7″ overall.
Power: 12-gram CO_2.
Stocks: Moulded black checkered plastic.
Sights: Blade front, fixed open rear.
Features: Velocity to 420 fps. Blowback slide cycles automatically on firing. Rotary trigger block safety. Introduced 1994. From Daisy Mfg. Co.
Price: About **$83.00**

DAISY/POWER LINE MATCH 777 PELLET PISTOL
Caliber: 177, single shot.
Barrel: 9.61″ rifled steel by Lothar Walther.
Weight: 32 oz. **Length:** 13$^1/_2$″ overall.
Power: Sidelever, single-pump pneumatic.
Stocks: Smooth hardwood, fully contoured with palm and thumbrest.
Sights: Blade and ramp front, match-grade open rear with adjustable width notch, micro. click adjustments.
Features: Adjustable trigger; manual cross-bolt safety. MV of 385 fps. Comes with cleaning kit, adjustment tool and pellets. From Daisy Mfg. Co.
Price: About **$335.00**

CAUTION: PRICES SHOWN ARE SUPPLIED BY THE MANUFACTURER OR IMPORTER. CHECK YOUR LOCAL GUN SHOP.

DAISY/POWER LINE 717 PELLET PISTOL
Caliber: 177, single shot.
Barrel: 9.61″.
Weight: 2.8 lbs. **Length:** 13½″ overall.
Stocks: Moulded wood-grain plastic, with thumbrest.
Sights: Blade and ramp front, micro-adjustable notch rear.
Features: Single pump pneumatic pistol. Rifled steel barrel. Cross-bolt trigger block. Muzzle velocity 385 fps. From Daisy Mfg. Co. Introduced 1979.
Price: About **$80.00**

Daisy/Power Line 747 Pistol
Similar to the 717 pistol except has a 12-groove rifled steel barrel by Lothar Walther, and adjustable trigger pull weight. Velocity of 360 fps. Manual cross-bolt safety.
Price: About **$160.00**

Daisy/Power Line 717

Daisy/Power Line 1140

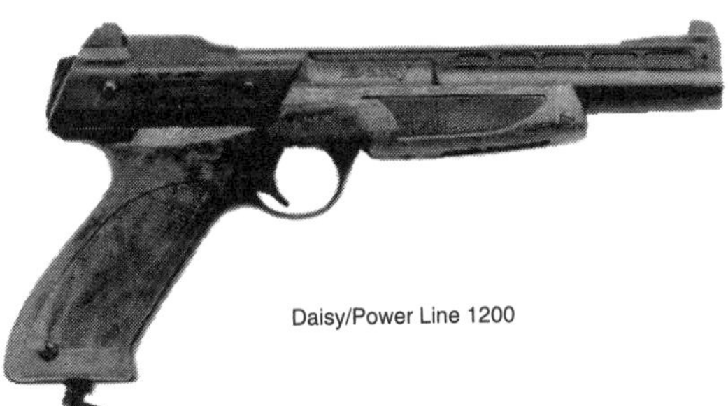
Daisy/Power Line 1200

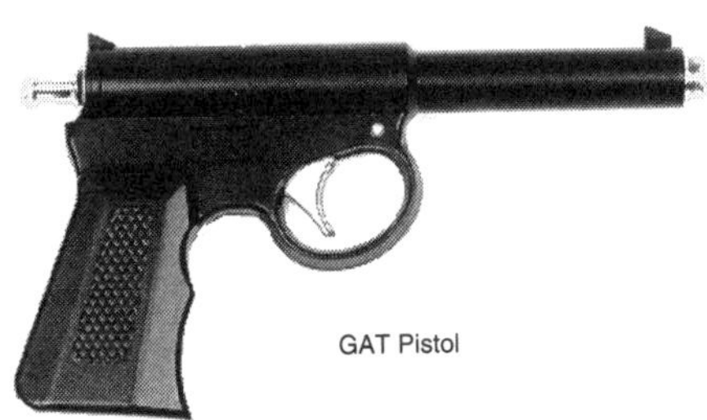
GAT Pistol

DAISY/POWER LINE 1140 PELLET PISTOL
Caliber: 177, single shot.
Barrel: Rifled steel.
Weight: 1.3 lbs. **Length:** 11.7″ overall.
Power: Single-stroke barrel cocking.
Stocks: Checkered resin.
Sights: Hooded post front, open adjustable rear.
Features: Velocity to 325 fps. Made of black lightweight engineering resin. Introduced 1995. From Daisy.
Price: About **$45.50**

DAISY/POWER LINE CO_2 1200 PISTOL
Caliber: BB, 177.
Barrel: 10½″, smooth.
Weight: 1.6 lbs. **Length:** 11.1″ overall.
Power: Daisy CO_2 cylinder.
Stocks: Contoured, checkered moulded wood-grain plastic.
Sights: Blade ramp front, fully adjustable square notch rear.
Features: 60-shot BB reservoir, gravity feed. Cross-bolt safety. Velocity of 420-450 fps for more than 100 shots. From Daisy Mfg. Co.
Price: About **$37.50**

DAISY/POWER LINE 1700 AIR PISTOL
Caliber: 177 BB, 60-shot magazine.
Barrel: Smoothbore steel.
Weight: 1.4 lbs. **Length:** 11.2″ overall.
Power: CO_2.
Stocks: Moulded checkered plastic.
Sights: Blade front, adjustable rear.
Features: Velocity to 420 fps. Cross-bolt trigger block safety; matte finish. Has ⅜″ dovetail mount for scope or point sight. Introduced 1994. From Daisy Mfg. Co.
Price: About **$40.00**

"GAT" AIR PISTOL
Caliber: 177, single shot.
Barrel: 7½″ cocked, 9½″ extended.
Weight: 22 oz.
Power: Spring-piston.
Stocks: Cast checkered metal.
Sights: Fixed.
Features: Shoots pellets, corks or darts. Matte black finish. Imported from England by Stone Enterprises, Inc.
Price: **$21.95**

HAMMERLI 480 MATCH AIR PISTOL
Caliber: 177, single shot.
Barrel: 9.8″.
Weight: 37 oz. **Length:** 16.5″ overall.
Power: Air or CO_2.
Stocks: Walnut with 7-degree rake adjustment. Stippled grip area.
Sights: Undercut blade front, fully adjustable open match rear.
Features: Under-barrel cannister charges with air or CO_2 for power supply; gives 320 shots per filling. Trigger adjustable for position. Introduced 1994. Imported from Switzerland by Hammerli Pistols U.S.A.
Price: **$1,325.00**

Hammerli 480k Match Air Pistol
Similar to the 480 except has a short, detachable aluminum air cylinder for use only with compressed air; can be filled while on the gun or off; special adjustable barrel weights. Muzzle velocity of 470 fps, gives about 180 shots. Has stippled black composition grip with adjustable palm shelf and rake angle. Comes with air pressure gauge. Introduced 1996. Imported from Switzerland by SIGARMS, Inc.
Price: **$1,155.00**

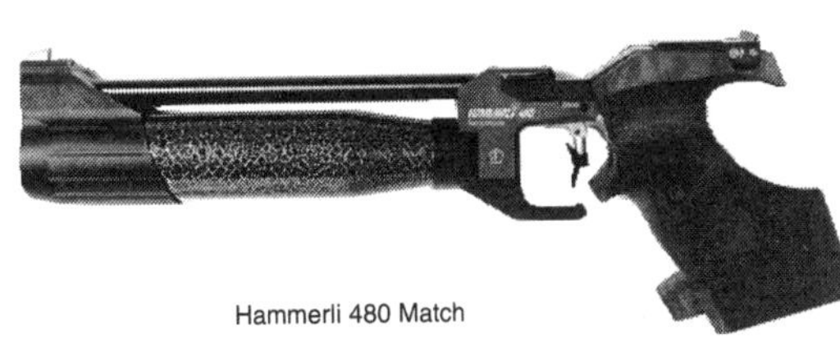
Hammerli 480 Match

MARKSMAN 1010 REPEATER PISTOL
Caliber: 177, 18-shot repeater.
Barrel: 2½″, smoothbore.
Weight: 24 oz. **Length:** 8¼″ overall.
Power: Spring.
Features: Velocity to 200 fps. Thumb safety. Black finish. Uses BBs, darts or pellets. Repeats with BBs only. From Marksman Products.
Price: Matte black finish **$25.50**
Price: Model 1010X (as above except nickel-plated) **$33.50**

MARKSMAN 1015 SPECIAL EDITION AIR PISTOL
Caliber: 177, 24-shot repeater.
Barrel: 3.8″, rifled.
Weight: 22 oz. **Length:** 10.3″ overall.
Power: Spring-air.
Stocks: Checkered brown composition.
Sights: Fixed.
Features: Velocity about 230 fps. Skeletonized trigger, extended barrel with "ported compensator." Shoots BBs, pellets, darts or bolts. From Marksman Products.
Price: $31.75

Marksman 1015

MORINI 162E MATCH AIR PISTOL
Caliber: 177, single shot.
Barrel: 9.4″.
Weight: 32 oz. **Length:** 16.1″ overall.
Power: Pre-charged CO_2.
Stocks: Adjustable match type.
Sights: Interchangeable blade front, fully adjustable match-type rear.
Features: Power mechanism shuts down when pressure drops to a pre-set level. Adjustable electronic trigger. Introduced 1995. Imported from Switzerland by Nygord Precision Products.
Price: $950.00

PARDINI K58 MATCH AIR PISTOL
Caliber: 177, single shot.
Barrel: 9.0″.
Weight: 37.7 oz. **Length:** 15.5″ overall.
Power: Pre-charged compressed air; single-stroke cocking.
Stocks: Adjustable match type; stippled walnut.
Sights: Interchangeable post front, fully adjustable match rear.
Features: Fully adjustable trigger. Introduced 1995. Imported from Italy by Nygord Precision Products.
Price: $650.00
Price: K60 model (CO_2) $650.00

Record Champion Repeater

RECORD CHAMPION REPEATER PISTOL
Caliber: 177, 12-shot magazine.
Barrel: 7.6″, rifled.
Weight: 2.8″, rifled. **Length:** 10.2″ overall.
Power: Spring-air.
Stocks: Oil-finished walnut.
Sights: Post front, fully adjustable rear.
Features: Velocity about 420 fps. Magazine loads through bottom of the grip. Full-length dovetail for scope mounting. Manual safety. Introduced 1996. Imported from Germany by Great Lakes Airguns.
Price: $161.50

Record Jumbo

RECORD JUMBO DELUXE AIR PISTOL
Caliber: 177, single shot.
Barrel: 6″, rifled.
Weight: 1.9 lbs. **Length:** 7.25″ overall.
Power: Spring-air, lateral cocking lever.
Stocks: Smooth walnut.
Sights: Blade front, fully adjustable open rear.
Features: Velocity to 322 fps. Thumb safety. Grip magazine compartment for extra pellet storage. Introduced 1983. Imported from Germany by Great Lakes Airguns.
Price: $121.34

Consult our Directory pages for the location of firms mentioned.

RWS/Diana Model 6M

RWS/Diana Model 5G

RWS/DIANA MODEL 5G AIR PISTOL
Caliber: 177, single shot.
Barrel: 7″.
Weight: $2^3/_4$ lbs. **Length:** 15″ overall.
Power: Spring-air, barrel cocking.
Stocks: Plastic, thumbrest design.
Sights: Tunnel front, micro-click open rear.
Features: Velocity of 450 fps. Adjustable two-stage trigger with automatic safety. Imported from Germany by Dynamit Nobel-RWS, Inc.
Price: $260.00

RWS/DIANA MODEL 6M MATCH AIR PISTOL
Caliber: 177, single shot.
Barrel: 7″.
Weight: 3 lbs. **Length:** 15″ overall.
Power: Spring-air, barrel cocking.
Stocks: Walnut-finished hardwood with thumbrest.
Sights: Adjustable front, micro. click open rear.
Features: Velocity of 410 fps. Recoilless double piston system, movable barrel shroud to protect from sight during cocking. Imported from Germany by Dynamit Nobel-RWS, Inc.
Price: Right-hand $585.00
Price: Left-hand $640.00

CAUTION: PRICES SHOWN ARE SUPPLIED BY THE MANUFACTURER OR IMPORTER. CHECK YOUR LOCAL GUNSHOP.

RWS/Diana Model 6G

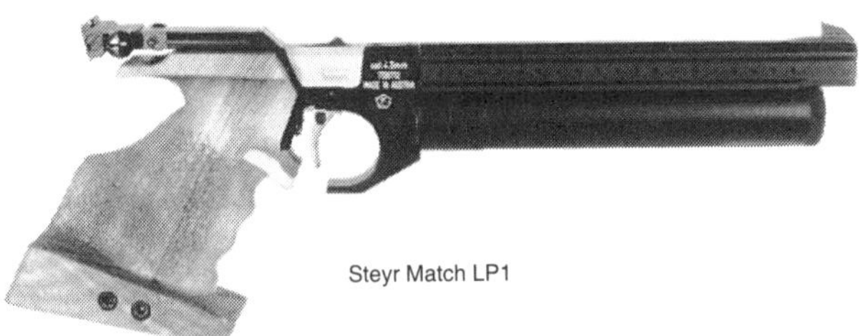
Steyr Match LP1

RWS/Diana Model 6G Air Pistols

Similar to the Model 6M except does not have the movable barrel shroud. Has click micrometer rear sight, two-stage adjustable trigger, interchangeable tunnel front sight. Available in right- or left-hand models.

Price: Right-hand **$450.00**
Price: Left-hand **$490.00**

STEYR CO_2 MATCH LP1 PISTOL

Caliber: 177, single shot.
Barrel: 9″.
Weight: 38.7 oz. **Length:** 15.3″ overall.
Power: Pre-compressed CO_2 cylinders.
Stocks: Fully adjustable Morini match with palm shelf; stippled walnut.
Sights: Interchangeable blade in 4mm, 4.5mm or 5mm widths, fully adjustable open rear with interchangeable 3.5mm or 4mm leaves.
Features: Velocity about 500 fps. Adjustable trigger, adjustable sight radius from 12.4″ to 13.2″. Imported from Austria by Nygord Precision Products.
Price: About **$1,095.00**
Price: LP1C (compensated) **$1,150.00**

STEYR LP5 MATCH PISTOL

Caliber: 177, 5-shot magazine.
Barrel: NA.
Weight: 40.2 oz. **Length:** 13.39″ overall.
Power: Pre-compressed CO_2 cylinders.
Stocks: Adjustable Morini match with palm shelf; stippled walnut.
Sights: Movable 2.5mm blade front; 2-3mm interchangeable in .2mm increments; fully adjustable open match rear.
Features: Velocity about 500 fps. Fully adjustable trigger; has dry-fire feature. Barrel and grip weights available. Introduced 1993. Imported from Austria by Nygord Precision Products.
Price: About **$1,250.00**

WALTHER CPM-1 CO_2 MATCH PISTOL

Caliber: 177, single shot.
Barrel: 8.66″.
Weight: NA. **Length:** 15.1″ overall.
Power: CO_2.
Stocks: Orthopaedic target type.
Sights: Undercut blade front, open match rear fully adjustable for windage and elevation.
Features: Adjustable velocity; matte finish. Introduced 1995. Imported from Germany by Nygord Precision Products.
Price: **$950.00**

STEYR LP 5C MATCH AIR PISTOL

Caliber: 177, 5-shot magazine.
Barrel: NA.
Weight: 40.7 oz. **Length:** 15.2″ overall.
Power: Pre-charged air cylinder.
Stocks: Adjustable match type.
Sights: Interchangeable blade front, fully adjustable match rear.
Features: Adjustable sight radius; fully adjustable trigger. Has barrel compensator. Introduced 1995. Imported from Austria by Nygord Precision Products.
Price: **$1,325.00**

AIRGUNS—LONG GUNS

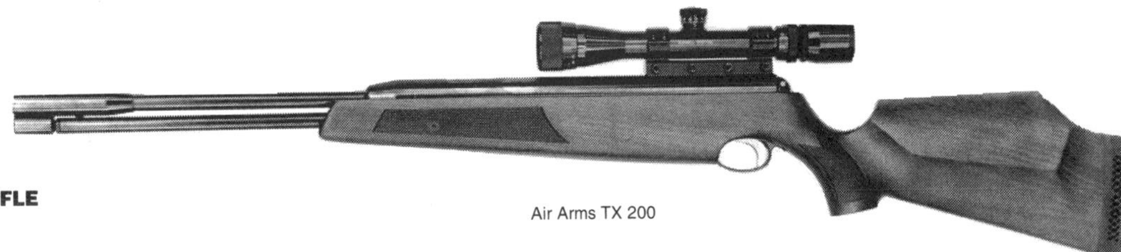
Air Arms TX 200

AIR ARMS TX 200 AIR RIFLE

Caliber: 177; single shot.
Barrel: 15.7″.
Weight: 9.3 lbs. **Length:** 41.5″ overall.
Power: Spring-air; underlever cocking.
Stock: Oil-finished hardwood; checkered grip and forend; rubber buttpad.
Sights: None furnished.
Features: Velocity about 900 fps. Automatic safety; adjustable two-stage trigger. Imported from England by Great Lakes Airguns.
Price: **$489.81**

Airrow A-8S1P

AIRROW MODEL A-8S1P STEALTH AIR GUN

Caliber: #2512 16″ arrow.
Barrel: 16″.
Weight: 4.4 lbs. **Length:** 30.1″ overall.
Power: CO_2 or compressed air; variable power.
Stock: Telescoping CAR-15-type.
Sights: Scope rings only.
Features: Velocity to 650 fps with 260-grain arrow. Pneumatic air trigger. All aircraft aluminum and stainless steel construction. Mil-spec materials and finishes. Waterproof case. Introduced 1991. From Swivel Machine Works, Inc.
Price: About **$1,699.00**

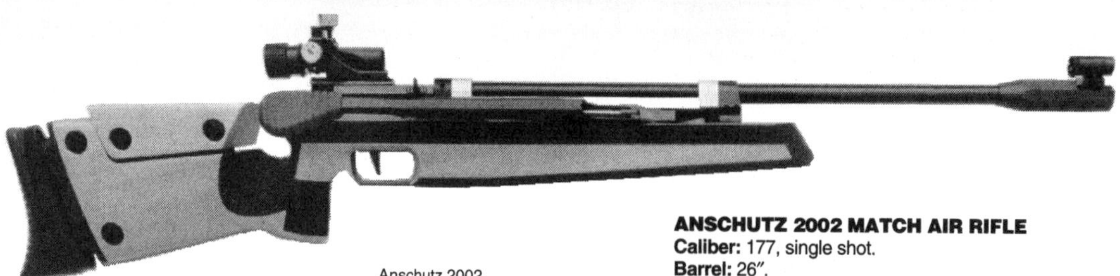

Anschutz 2002

ANSCHUTZ 2002 MATCH AIR RIFLE

Caliber: 177, single shot.
Barrel: 26″.
Weight: 10½ lbs. **Length:** 44.5″ overall.
Stock: European walnut, blonde hardwood or colored laminated hardwood; stippled grip and forend.
Sights: Optional sight set #6834.
Features: Muzzle velocity 575 fps. Balance, weight match the 1907 ISU smallbore rifle. Uses #5021 match trigger. Recoil and vibration free. Fully adjustable cheekpiece and buttplate; accessory rail under forend. Introduced 1988. Imported from Germany by Gunsmithing, Inc., Champion's Choice, Champion Shooter's Supply, Accuracy International.
Price: Right-hand, blonde hardwood stock **$1,212.20**
Price: Left-hand, blonde hardwood stock **$1,272.80**
Price: Right-hand, walnut stock **$1,261.40**
Price: Right-hand, color laminated stock **$1,291.60**
Price: Left-hand, color laminated stock **$1,355.30**
Price: Model 2002D-RT Running Target, right-hand, no sights **$1,419.20**
Price: #6834 Sight Set **$245.90**

AIRROW MODEL A-8SRB STEALTH AIR GUN

Caliber: 177, 22, 25, 38, 9-shot.
Barrel: 19.7″; rifled.
Weight: 6 lbs. **Length:** 34″ overall.
Power: CO_2 or compressed air; variable power.
Stock: Telescoping CAR-15-type.
Sights: Scope rings only.
Features: Velocity 1100 fps in all calibers. Pneumatic air trigger. All aircraft aluminum and stainless steel construction. Mil-spec materials and finishes. Introduced 1992. From Swivel Machine Works, Inc.
Price: About **$2,299.00**

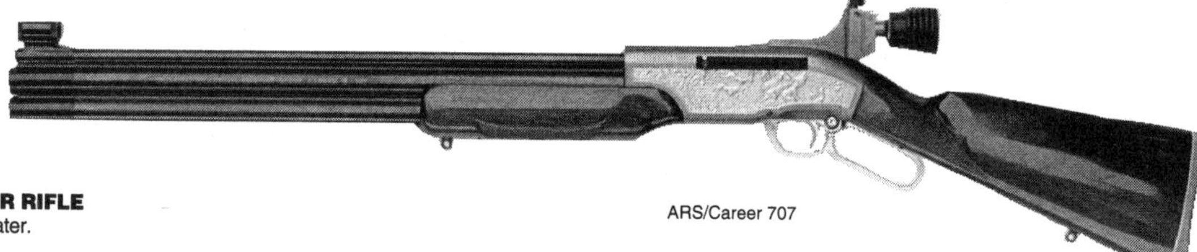

ARS/Career 707

ARS/CAREER 707 AIR RIFLE

Caliber: 22, 6-shot repeater.
Barrel: 23″.
Weight: 7.75 lbs. **Length:** 40.5″ overall.
Power: Pre-compressed air; variable power.
Stock: Indonesian walnut with checkered grip, gloss finish.
Sights: Hooded post front with interchangeable inserts, fully adjustable diopter rear.
Features: Velocity to 1000 fps. Lever-action with straight feed magazine; pressure gauge in lower front air reservoir; scope mounting rail included. Introduced 1996. Imported from the Philippines by Air Rifle Specialists.
Price: **$580.00**

ARS/FARCO FP SURVIVAL AIR RIFLE

Caliber: 22, 25, single shot.
Barrel: 22¾″.
Weight: 5¾ lbs. **Length:** 42¾″ overall.
Power: Multi-pump foot pump.
Stock: Philippine hardwood.
Sights: Blade front, fixed rear.
Features: Velocity to 850 fps (22 or 25). Receiver grooved for scope mounting. Imported from the Philippines by Air Rifle Specialists.
Price: **$295.00**

ARS/FARCO CO_2 AIR SHOTGUN

Caliber: 51 (28-gauge).
Barrel: 30″.
Weight: 7 lbs. **Length:** 48½″ overall.
Power: 10-oz. refillable CO_2 tank.
Stock: Hardwood.
Sights: Blade front, fixed rear.
Features: Gives over 100 ft. lbs. energy for taking small game. Imported from the Philippines by Air Rifle Specialists.
Price: **$460.00**

ARS/Farco CO_2 Stainless Steel Air Rifle

Similar to the ARS/Farco CO_2 shotgun except in 22- or 25-caliber with 21½″ barrel; weighs 6¾ lbs., 42½″ overall; Philippine hardwood stock with stippled grip and forend; blade front sight, adjustable rear, grooved for scope mount. Uses 10-oz. refillable CO_2 cylinder. Made of stainless steel. Imported from the Philippines by Air Rifle Specialists.
Price: Including CO_2 cylinder **$460.00**

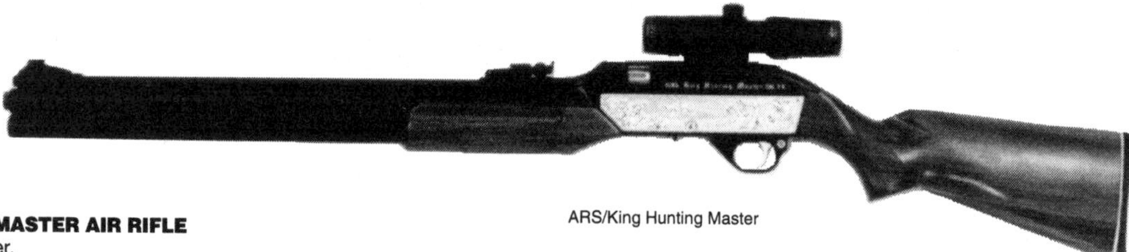

ARS/King Hunting Master

ARS/KING HUNTING MASTER AIR RIFLE

Caliber: 22, 5-shot repeater.
Barrel: 22¾″.
Weight: 7¾ lbs. **Length:** 42″ overall.
Power: Pre-compressed air from 3000 psi diving tank.
Stock: Indonesian walnut with checkered grip and forend; rubber buttpad.
Sights: Blade front, fully adjustable open rear. Receiver grooved for scope mounting.
Features: Velocity over 1000 fps with 32-grain pellet. High and low power switch for hunting or target velocities. Side lever cocks action and inserts pellet. Rotary magazine. Imported from Korea by Air Rifle Specialists.
Price: **$580.00**
Price: Hunting Master 900 (9mm, limited production) **$1,000.00**

ARS HUNTING MASTER AR6 AIR RIFLE

Caliber: 22, 6-shot repeater.
Barrel: 25½″.
Weight: 7 lbs. **Length:** 41¼″ overall.
Power: Pre-compressed air from 3000 psi diving tank.
Stock: Indonesian walnut with checkered grip; rubber buttpad.
Sights: Blade front, adjustable peep rear.
Features: Velocity over 1000 fps with 32-grain pellet. Receiver grooved for scope mounting. Has 6-shot rotary magazine. Imported by Air Rifle Specialists.
Price: **$580.00**

CAUTION: PRICES SHOWN ARE SUPPLIED BY THE MANUFACTURER OR IMPORTER. CHECK YOUR LOCAL GUNSHOP.

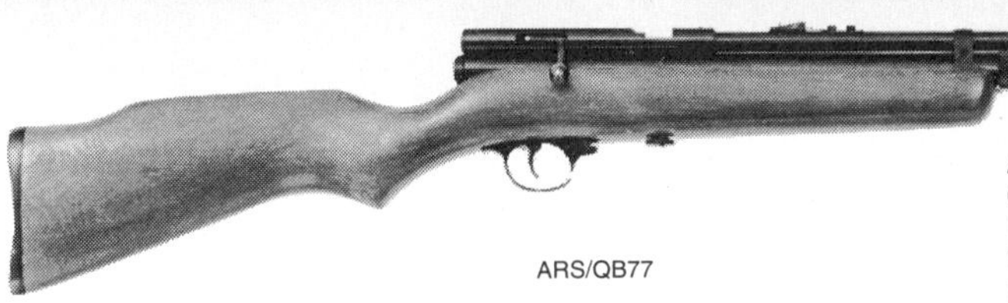
ARS/QB77

ARS/Magnum 6 Air Rifle
Similar to the King Hunting Master except is 6-shot repeater with 23 3/4″ barrel, weighs 8 1/4 lbs. Stock is walnut-stained hardwood with checkered grip and forend; rubber buttpad. Velocity of 1000+ fps with 32-grain pellet. Imported from Korea by Air Rifle Specialists.
Price: $500.00

BEEMAN CROW MAGNUM AIR RIFLE
Caliber: 20, 22, 25, single shot.
Barrel: 16″; 10-groove rifling.
Weight: 8.5 lbs. **Length:**46″ overall.
Power: Gas-spring; adjustable power to 32 foot pounds muzzle energy. Barrel-cocking.
Stock: Classic-style hardwood; hand checkered.
Sights: For scope use only; built-in base and 1″ rings included.
Features: Adjustable two-stage trigger. Automatic safety. Also available in 22-caliber on special order. Introduced 1992. Imported by Beeman.
Price: $1,220.00

ARS/QB77 DELUXE AIR RIFLE
Caliber: 177, 22, single shot.
Barrel: 21 1/2″.
Weight: 5 1/2 lbs. **Length:** 40″ overall.
Power: Two 12-oz. CO_2 cylinders.
Stock: Walnut-stained hardwood.
Sights: Blade front, adjustable rear.
Features: Velocity to 625 fps (22), 725 fps (177). Receiver grooved for scope mounting. Comes with bulk-fill valve. Imported by Air Rifle Specialists.
Price: $195.00

BEEMAN/FEINWERKBAU 300-S MINI-MATCH
Caliber: 177, single shot.
Barrel: 17 1/8″.
Weight: 8.8 lbs. **Length:** 40″ overall.
Power: Spring-piston, single stroke sidelever cocking.
Stock: Walnut. Stippled grip, adjustable buttplate. Scaled-down for youthful or slightly built shooters.
Sights: Globe front with interchangeable inserts, micro. adjustable rear. Front and rear sights move as a single unit.
Features: Recoilless, vibration free. Grooved for scope mounts. Steel piston ring. Cocking effort about 9 1/2 lbs. Barrel sleeve optional. Left-hand model available. Introduced 1978. Imported by Beeman.
Price: Right-hand $1,270.00
Price: Left-hand $1,370.00

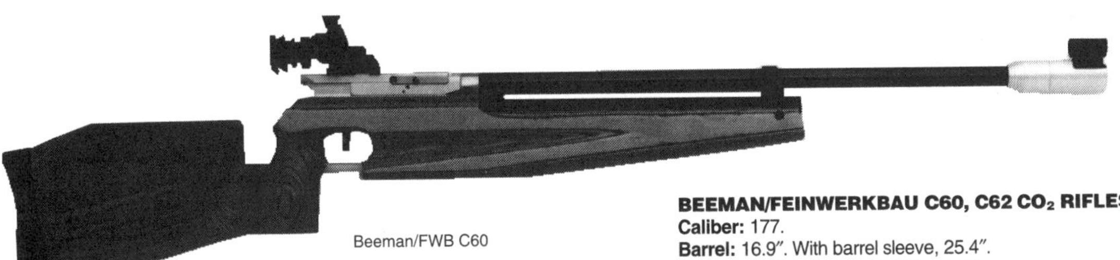
Beeman/FWB C60

BEEMAN BEARCUB AIR RIFLE
Caliber: 177, single shot.
Barrel: 13″.
Weight: 7.2 lbs. **Length:** 37.8″ overall.
Power: Spring-piston, barrel cocking.
Stock: Stained hardwood.
Sights: Hooded post front, open fully adjustable rear.
Features: Velocity to 915 fps. Polished blue finish; receiver dovetailed for scope mounting. Imported from England by Beeman Precision Airguns.
Price: $310.00

BEEMAN/FEINWERKBAU C60, C62 CO_2 RIFLES
Caliber: 177.
Barrel: 16.9″. With barrel sleeve, 25.4″.
Weight: 10 lbs. **Length:** 42.6″ overall.
Stock: Laminated hardwood and hard rubber.
Sights: Tunnel front with interchangeable inserts, quick release micro. click match aperture rear.
Features: Similar features, performance as Beeman/FWB 601. Virtually no cocking effort. Right- or left-hand. Running target version available. Introduced 1987. Imported from Germany by Beeman.
Price: Right-hand, C62 .... $1,750.00
Price: Left-hand, C62 .... $1,900.00
Price: Running Target, right-hand, C60 .... $1,675.00
Price: Running Target, left-hand, C60 .... $1,825.00
Price: Mini C60, right-hand, C60 .... $1,675.00

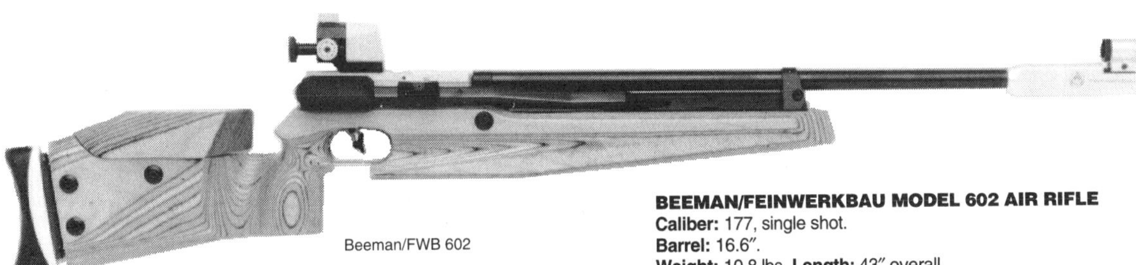
Beeman/FWB 602

BEEMAN/FEINWERKBAU 300-S SERIES MATCH RIFLE
Caliber: 177, single shot.
Barrel: 19.9″, fixed solid with receiver.
Weight: Approx. 10 lbs. with optional bbl. sleeve. **Length:** 42.8″ overall.
Power: Spring-piston, single stroke sidelever.
Stock: Match model—walnut, deep forend, adjustable buttplate.
Sights: Globe front with interchangeable inserts. Click micro. adjustable match aperture rear. Front and rear sights move as a single unit.
Features: Recoilless, vibration free. Five-way adjustable match trigger. Grooved for scope mounts. Permanent lubrication, steel piston ring. Cocking effort 9 lbs. Optional 10-oz. barrel sleeve. Available from Beeman.
Price: Right-hand $1,270.00
Price: Left-hand $1,370.00

BEEMAN/FEINWERKBAU MODEL 602 AIR RIFLE
Caliber: 177, single shot.
Barrel: 16.6″.
Weight: 10.8 lbs. **Length:** 43″ overall.
Power: Single stroke pneumatic.
Stock: Special laminated hardwoods and hard rubber for stability.
Sights: Tunnel front with interchangeable inserts, click micrometer match apperture rear.
Features: Recoilless action; double supported barrel; special, short rifled area frees pellet from barrel faster so shooter's motion has minimum effect on accuracy. Fully adjustable match trigger. Trigger and sights blocked when loading latch is open. Imported by Beeman.
Price: Right-hand $1,875.00
Price: Left-hand $2,035.00

Beeman/Feinwerkbau 601 Running Target
Similar to the standard Model 601. Has 16.9″ barrel (33.7″ with barrel sleeve); special match trigger, short loading gate which allows scope mounting. No sights—built for scope use only. Introduced 1987.
Price: Right-hand $1,750.00

Beeman/HW 97

BEEMAN/HW 97 AIR RIFLE
Caliber: 177, 20, single shot.
Barrel: 17.75″.
Weight: 9.2 lbs. **Length:** 44.1″ overall.
Power: Spring-piston, underlever cocking.
Stock: Walnut-stained beech; rubber buttpad.
Sights: None. Receiver grooved for scope mounting.
Features: Velocity 830 fps (177). Fixed barrel with fully opening, direct loading breech. Adjustable trigger. Introduced 1994. Imported by Beeman Precision Airguns.
Price: Right-hand only $535.00

BEEMAN KODIAK AIR RIFLE
Caliber: 25, single shot.
Barrel: 17.6″.
Weight: 9 lbs. **Length:** 45.6″ overall.
Power: Spring-piston, barrel cocking.
Stock: Stained hardwood.
Sights: Blade front, open fully adjustable rear.
Features: Velocity to 820 fps. Up to 30 foot pounds muzzle energy. Introduced 1993. Imported by Beeman.
Price: $595.00

Beeman Mako

BEEMAN MAKO AIR RIFLE
Caliber: 177, single shot.
Barrel: 20″, with compensator.
Weight: 7.3 lbs. **Length:** 38.5″ overall.
Power: Pre-charged pneumatic.
Stock: Stained beech; Monte Carlo cheekpiece; checkered grip.
Sights: None furnished.
Features: Velocity to 930 fps. Gives over 50 shots per charge. Manual safety; brass trigger blade; vented rubber butt pad. Requires scuba tank for air. Introduced 1994. Imported from England by Beeman.
Price: $875.00
Price: Mako FT (thumbhole stock) $1,250.00

BEEMAN R1 CARBINE
Caliber: 177, 20, 22, 25, single shot.
Barrel: 16.1″.
Weight: 8.6 lbs. **Length:** 41.7″ overall.
Power: Spring-piston, barrel cocking.
Stock: Stained beech; Monte Carlo comb and checkpiece; cut checkered pistol grip; rubber buttpad.
Sights: Tunnel front with interchangeable inserts, open adjustable rear; receiver grooved for scope mounting.
Features: Velocity up to 1000 fps (177). Non-drying nylon piston and breech seals. Adjustable metal trigger. Machined steel receiver end cap and safety. Right- or left-hand stock. Imported by Beeman.
Price: 177, 20, 22, 25, right-hand $525.00
Price: As above, left-hand $575.00
Price: R1-AW (synthetic stock, nickel plating) $650.00

BEEMAN R1 AIR RIFLE
Caliber: 177, 20 or 22, single shot.
Barrel: 19.6″, 12-groove rifling.
Weight: 8.5 lbs. **Length:** 45.2″ overall.
Power: Spring-piston, barrel cocking.
Stock: Walnut-stained beech; cut-checkered pistol grip; Monte Carlo comb and cheekpiece; rubber buttpad.
Sights: Tunnel front with interchangeable inserts, open rear click-adjustable for windage and elevation. Grooved for scope mounting.
Features: Velocity of 940-1000 fps (177), 860 fps (20), 800 fps (22). Non-drying nylon piston and breech seals. Adjustable metal trigger. Milled steel safety. Right- or left-hand stock. Available with adjustable cheekpiece and buttplate at extra cost. Custom and Super Laser versions available. Imported by Beeman.
Price: Right-hand, 177, 20, 22 .... $525.00
Price: Left-hand, 177, 20, 22 .... $575.00

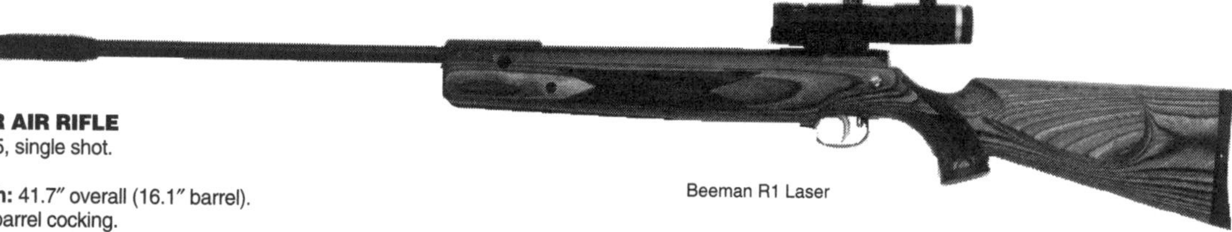
Beeman R1 Laser

BEEMAN R1 LASER AIR RIFLE
Caliber: 177, 20, 22, 25, single shot.
Barrel: 16.1″ or 19.6″.
Weight: 8.4 lbs. **Length:** 41.7″ overall (16.1″ barrel).
Power: Spring-piston, barrel cocking.
Stock: Laminated wood with Monte Carlo comb and cheekpiece; checkered pistol grip and forend; rubber buttpad.
Sights: Tunnel front with interchangeable inserts, open adjustable rear.
Features: Velocity up to 1150 fps (177). Special powerplant components. Built from the Beeman R1 rifle by Beeman.
Price: 177, 20, 22, 25 .... $995.00

BEEMAN R6 AIR RIFLE
Caliber: 177, single shot.
Barrel: NA.
Weight: 7.1 lbs. **Length:** 41.8″ overall.
Power: Spring-piston, barrel cocking.
Stock: Stained hardwood.
Sights: Tunnel post front, open fully adjustable rear.
Features: Velocity to 815 fps. Two-stage Rekord adjustable trigger; receiver dovetailed for scope mounting; automatic safety. Introduced 1996. Imported from Germany by Beeman Precision Airguns.
Price: $325.00

BEEMAN R8 AIR RIFLE
Caliber: 177, single shot.
Barrel: 18.3″.
Weight: 7.2 lbs. **Length:** 43.1″ overall.
Power: Spring-piston, barrel cocking.
Stock: Walnut with Monte Carlo cheekpiece; checkered pistol grip.
Sights: Globe front, fully adjustable rear; interchangeable inserts.
Features: Velocity of 735 fps. Similar to the R1. Nylon piston and breech seals. Adjustable match-grade, two-stage, grooved metal trigger. Milled steel safety. Rubber buttpad. Imported by Beeman.
Price: $380.00

Beeman R7 Air Rifle
Similar to the R8 model except has lighter ambidextrous stock, match-grade trigger block; velocity of 680-700 fps; barrel length 17″; weighs 5.8 lbs. Milled steel safety. Imported by Beeman.
Price: 177 .... $325.00

CAUTION: PRICES SHOWN ARE SUPPLIED BY THE MANUFACTURER OR IMPORTER. CHECK YOUR LOCAL GUNSHOP.

BEEMAN R9 AIR RIFLE
Caliber: 177, 20, single shot.
Barrel: NA.
Weight: 7.3 lbs. **Length:** 43″ overall.
Power: Spring-piston, barrel cocking.
Stock: Stained hardwood.
Sights: Tunnel post front, fully adjustable open rear.
Features: Velocity to 1000 fps (177), 800 fps (20). Adjustable Rekord trigger; automatic safety; receiver dovetailed for scope mounting. Introduced 1996. Imported from Germany by Beeman Precision Airguns.
Price: $335.00

BEEMAN SUPER 12 AIR RIFLE
Caliber: 22, 25, 12-shot magazine.
Barrel: 19″, 12-groove rifling.
Weight: 7.8 lbs. **Length:** 41.7″ overall.
Power: Pre-charged pneumatic; external air reservoir.
Stock: European walnut.
Sights: None furnished; drilled and tapped for scope mounting; scope mount included.
Features: Velocity to 850 fps (25-caliber). Adjustable power setting gives 30-70 shots per 400 cc air bottle. Requires scuba tank for air. Introduced 1995. Imported by Beeman.
Price: $1,675.00

Beeman R11

BEEMAN R11 AIR RIFLE
Caliber: 177, single shot.
Barrel: 19.6″.
Weight: 8.8 lbs. **Length:** 47″ overall.
Power: Spring-piston, barrel cocking.
Stock: Walnut-stained beech; adjustable buttplate and cheekpiece.
Sights: None furnished. Has dovetail for scope mounting.
Features: Velocity 910-940 fps. All-steel barrel sleeve. Imported by Beeman.
Price: $530.00

BEEMAN S1 MAGNUM AIR RIFLE
Caliber: 177, single shot.
Barrel: 19″.
Weight: 7.1 lbs. **Length:** 45.5″ overall.
Power: Spring-piston, barrel cocking.
Stock: Stained beech with Monte Carlo cheekpiece; checkered grip.
Sights: Hooded post front, fully adjustable micrometer click rear.
Features: Velocity to 900 fps. Automatic safety; receiver grooved for scope mounting; two-stage adjustable trigger; curved rubber buttpad. Introduced 1995. Imported by Beeman.
Price: $210.00

BEEMAN RX-1 GAS-SPRING MAGNUM AIR RIFLE
Caliber: 177, 20, 22, 25, single shot.
Barrel: 19.6″, 12-groove rifling.
Weight: 8.8 lbs.
Power: Gas-spring piston air; single stroke barrel cocking.
Stock: Walnut-finished hardwood, hand checkered, with cheekpiece. Adjustable cheekpiece and buttplate.
Sights: Tunnel front, click-adjustable rear.
Features: Velocity adjustable to about 1200 fps. Uses special sealed chamber of air as a mainspring. Gas-spring cannot take a set. Introduced 1990. Imported by Beeman.
Price: 177, 20, 22 or 25 regular, right-hand $575.00
Price: 177, 20, 22, 25, left-hand $675.00

BENJAMIN SHERIDAN CO_2 AIR RIFLES
Caliber: 177, 20 or 22, single shot.
Barrel: 19³/₈″, rifled brass.
Weight: 5 lbs. **Length:** 36¹/₂″ overall.
Power: 12-gram CO_2 cylinder.
Stock: American walnut with buttplate.
Sights: High ramp front, fully adjustable notch rear.
Features: Velocity to 680 fps (177). Bolt action with ambidextrous push-pull safety. Gives about 40 shots per cylinder. Black or nickel finish. Introduced 1991. Made in the U.S. by Benjamin Sheridan Co.
Price: Black finish, Model G397 (177), Model G392 (22), about $115.25
Price: Black finish, Model FB9 (20), about $124.50

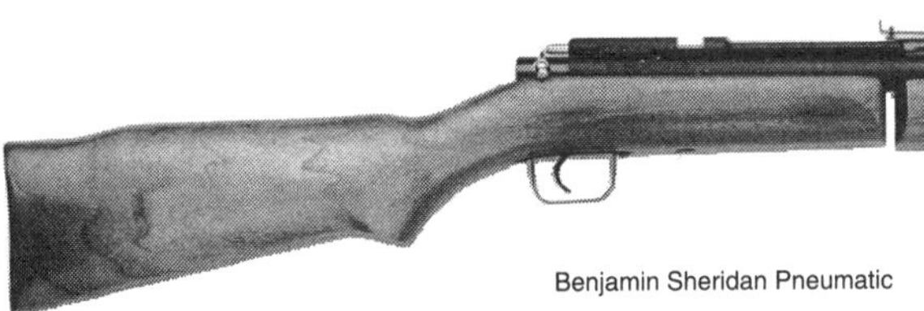
Benjamin Sheridan Pneumatic

Benjamin Sheridan 397C Pneumatic Carbine
Similar to the standard Model 397 except has 16³/₄″ barrel, weighs 4 lbs., 3 oz. Velocity about 650 fps. Introduced 1995. Made in U.S. by Benjamin Sheridan Co.
Price: About $122.50

BENJAMIN SHERIDAN PNEUMATIC (PUMP-UP) AIR RIFLES
Caliber: 177 or 22, single shot.
Barrel: 19³/₈″, rifled brass.
Weight: 5¹/₂ lbs. **Length:** 36¹/₄″ overall.
Power: Underlever pneumatic, hand pumped.
Stock: American walnut stock and forend.
Sights: High ramp front, fully adjustable notch rear.
Features: Variable velocity to 800 fps. Bolt action with ambidextrous push-pull safety. Black or nickel finish. Introduced 1991. Made in the U.S. by Benjamin Sheridan Co.
Price: Black finish, Model 397 (177), Model 392 (22), about $126.50
Price: Nickel finish, Model S397 (177), Model S392 (22), about $135.25

BRNO TAU-200

BRNO TAU-200 AIR RIFLE
Caliber: 177, single shot
Barrel: 19″, rifled.
Weight: 8 lbs. **Length:** 42″ overall.
Power: 6-oz. CO_2 cartridge.
Stock: Wood match style with adjustable comb and buttplate.
Sights: Globe front with interchangeable inserts, fully adjustable open rear.
Features: Adjustable trigger. Comes with sling, extra seals, CO_2 cartridges, large CO_2 bottle, counterweight. Introduced 1993. Imported by Century International Arms, Great Lakes Airguns..
Price: About $423.25
Price: Junior Match (synthetic stock, 7 lbs.) $259.95

Consult our Directory pages for the location of firms mentioned.

BSA Supersport MK II

BSA SUPERSPORT MKII AIR RIFLE
Caliber: 177, single shot.
Barrel: 18″.
Weight: 6.5 lbs. **Length:** 41″ overall.
Power: Spring-air, barrel cocking.
Stock: Walnut-stained beech; rubber recoil pad.
Sights: Bead or blade front, fully adjsutable open rear.
Features: Velocity to 935 fps. Adjustable trigger; manual safety; receiver grooved for scope mounting. Imported from England by Great Lakes Airguns.
Price: $225.81
Price: Carbine, 14″ barrel, 37″ overall $252.97

COPPERHEAD BLACK FIRE RIFLE
Caliber: 177 BB only.
Barrel: 14″ smoothbore steel.
Weight: 2 lbs., 7 oz. **Length:** 31½″ overall.
Power: Pneumatic, hand pumped.
Stock: Textured plastic.
Sights: Blade front, open adjustable rear.
Features: Velocity to 437 fps. Introduced 1996. Made in U.S. by Crosman Corp.
Price: About $25.00

COPPERHEAD BLACK LIGHTNING RIFLE
Caliber: 177 BB, 15-shot magazine.
Barrel: 14″ smoothbore.
Weight: 2 lbs. **Length:** 32″ overall.
Power: Single-stroke pneumatic.
Stock: Textured plastic.
Sights: Bead front.
Features: Velocity to 350 fps. Cross-bolt safety. Introduced 1996. Made in U.S. by Crosman Corp.
Price: About $22.00

COPPERHEAD BLACK SERPENT RIFLE
Caliber: 177 pellets, 5-shot, on BB, 195-shot magazine.
Barrel: 19½″ smoothbore steel.
Weight: 2 lbs., 14 oz. **Length:** 35⅞″ overall.
Power: Pneumatic, single pump.
Stock: Textured plastic.
Sights: Blade front, open adjustable rear.
Features: Velocity to 405 fps. Introduced 1996. Made in U.S. by Crosman Corp.
Price: About $34.00

CROSMAN MODEL 66 POWERMASTER
Caliber: 177 (single shot pellet) or BB, 200-shot reservoir.
Barrel: 20″, rifled steel.
Weight: 3 lbs. **Length:** 38½″ overall.
Power: Pneumatic; hand pumped.
Stock: Wood-grained ABS plastic; checkered pistol grip and forend.
Sights: Ramp front, fully adjustable open rear.
Features: Velocity about 645 fps. Bolt action, cross-bolt safety. Introduced 1983. From Crosman.
Price: About $44.00
Price: Model 66RT (as above with Realtree® camo finish), about $50.00
Price: Model 664X (as above, with 4x scope) $55.00
Price: Model 664SB (as above with silver and black finish), about $57.00

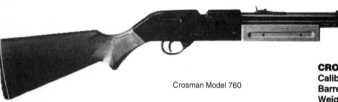

Crosman Model 760

CROSMAN MODEL 782 BLACK DIAMOND AIR RIFLE
Caliber: 177 pellets (5-shot clip) or BB (195-shot reservoir).
Barrel: 18″, rifled steel.
Weight: 3 lbs.
Power: CO_2 Powerlet.
Stock: Wood-grained ABS plastic; checkered grip and forend.
Sights: Blade front, open adjustable rear.
Features: Velocity up to 595 fps (pellets), 650 fps (BB). Black finish with white diamonds. Introduced 1990. From Crosman.
Price: About $42.75

CROSMAN MODEL 1389 BACKPACKER RIFLE
Caliber: 177, single shot.
Barrel: 14″, rifled steel.
Weight: 3 lbs. 3 oz. **Length:** 31″ overall.
Power: Hand pumped, pneumatic.
Stock: Composition, skeletal type.
Sights: Blade front, rear adjustable for windage and elevation.
Features: Velocity to 560 fps. Detachable stock. Receiver grooved for scope mounting. Metal parts blued. From Crosman.
Price: About $54.75

CROSMAN MODEL 760 PUMPMASTER
Caliber: 177 pellets (single shot) or BB (200-shot reservoir).
Barrel: 19½″, rifled steel.
Weight: 2 lbs., 12 oz. **Length:** 33.5″ overall.
Power: Pneumatic, hand pumped.
Stock: Walnut-finished ABS plastic stock and forend
Features: Velocity to 590 fps (BBs, 10 pumps). Short stroke, power determined by number of strokes. Post front sight and adjustable rear sight. Cross-bolt safety. Introduced 1966. From Crosman.
Price: About $32.00
Price: Model 760SB (silver and black finish), about $45.25

CROSMAN MODEL 795 SPRING MASTER RIFLE
Caliber: 177, single shot.
Barrel: Rifled steel.
Weight: 4 lbs., 8 oz. **Length:** 42″ overall.
Power: Spring-piston.
Stock: Black synthetic.
Sights: Hooded front, fully adjustable rear.
Features: Velocity about 550 fps. Introduced 1995. From Crosman.
Price: About $65.00

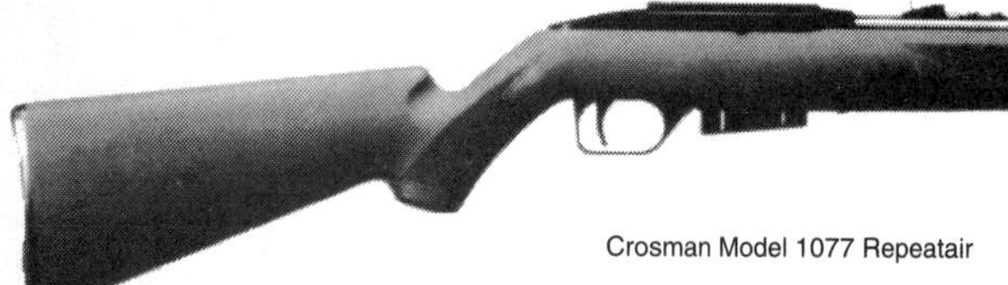

Crosman Model 1077 Repeatair

CROSMAN MODEL 1077 REPEATAIR RIFLE
Caliber: 177 pellets, 12-shot clip
Barrel: 20.3″, rifled steel.
Weight: 3 lbs., 11 oz. **Length:** 38.8″ overall.
Power: CO_2 Powerlet.
Stock: Textured synthetic.
Sights: Blade front, fully adjustable rear.
Features: Velocity 590 fps. Removable 12-shot clip. True semi-automatic action. Introduced 1993. From Crosman.
Price: About $62.75
Price: 1077SB Silver Series (black stock, silver bbl.) $65.00

CAUTION: PRICES SHOWN ARE SUPPLIED BY THE MANUFACTURER OR IMPORTER. CHECK YOUR LOCAL GUNSHOP.

CROSMAN MODEL 2100 CLASSIC AIR RIFLE

Caliber: 177 pellets (single shot), or BB (200-shot BB reservoir).
Barrel: 21″, rifled.
Weight: 4 lbs., 13 oz. **Length:** 39¾″ overall.
Power: Pump-up, pneumatic.
Stock: Wood-grained checkered ABS plastic.
Features: Three pumps give about 450 fps, 10 pumps about 755 fps (BBs). Cross-bolt safety; concealed reservoir holds over 200 BBs. From Crosman.
Price: About **$58.50**
Price: Model 2100SB (silver and black finish), about **$60.25**

CROSMAN MODEL 2200 MAGNUM AIR RIFLE

Caliber: 22, single shot.
Barrel: 19″, rifled steel.
Weight: 4 lbs., 12 oz. **Length:** 39″ overall.
Stock: Full-size, wood-grained ABS plastic with checkered grip and forend.
Sights: Ramp front, open step-adjustable rear.
Features: Variable pump power—three pumps give 395 fps, six pumps 530 fps, 10 pumps 595 fps (average). Full-size adult air rifle. Has white line spacers at pistol grip and buttplate. Introduced 1978. From Crosman.
Price: About **$58.50**

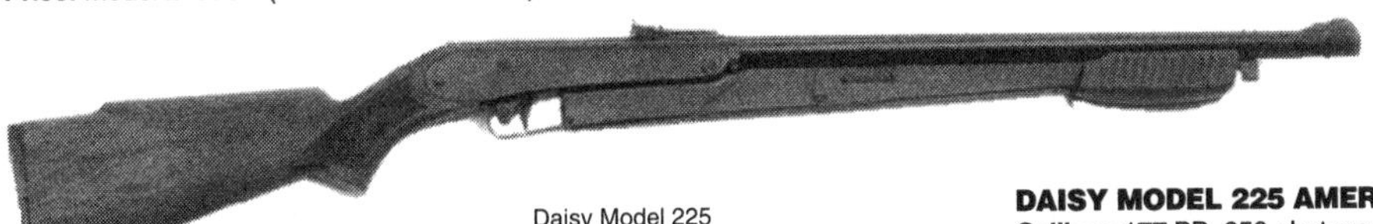

Daisy Model 225

DAISY/YOUTH LINE RIFLES

Model:	95	111	105
Caliber:	BB	BB	BB
Barrel:	18″	18″	13½″
Length:	35.2″	34.3″	29.8″
Power:	Spring	Spring	Spring
Capacity:	700	650	400
Price: About	**$45.00**	**$35.00**	**$29.00**

Features: Model 95 stock and forend are wood; 105 and 111 have plastic stocks. From Daisy Mfg. Co.

DAISY/POWER LINE 753 TARGET RIFLE

Caliber: 177, single shot.
Barrel: 20.9″, Lothar Walther.
Weight: 6.4 lbs. **Length:** 39.75″ overall.
Power: Recoilless pneumatic, single pump.
Stock: Walnut with adjustable cheekpiece and buttplate.
Sights: Globe front with interchangeable inserts, diopter rear with micro. click adjustments.
Features: Includes front sight reticle assortment, web shooting sling. From Daisy Mfg. Co.
Price: About **$412.00**

DAISY MODEL 225 AMERICAN LEGEND

Caliber: 177 BB, 650-shot magazine.
Barrel: Smoothbore steel.
Weight: 2.8 lbs. **Length:** 37.2″ overall.
Power: Single-pump spring air.
Stock: Moulded woodgrain plastic.
Sights: Blade and ramp front, adjustable open rear,
Features: Velocity to 330 fps. Grooved pump handle; Monte Carlo-style stock with cheekpiece and checkered grip. Cross-bolt trigger block safety. Introduced 1994. From Daisy Mfg. Co.
Price: About **$50.00**

DAISY MODEL 1894 BB RIFLE

Caliber: BB, 40-shot magazine.
Barrel: 17.5″. Round shroud.
Weight: 2.2 lbs. **Length:** 39.5″ overall.
Power: Spring-air.
Stock: Moulded woodgrain plastic.
Sights: Blade on ramp front, adjustable open rear.
Features: Velocity 300 fps. Side loading port; sliding sear-block safety; die-cast receiver. Made in U.S. From Daisy Mfg. Co.
Price: **$42.00**

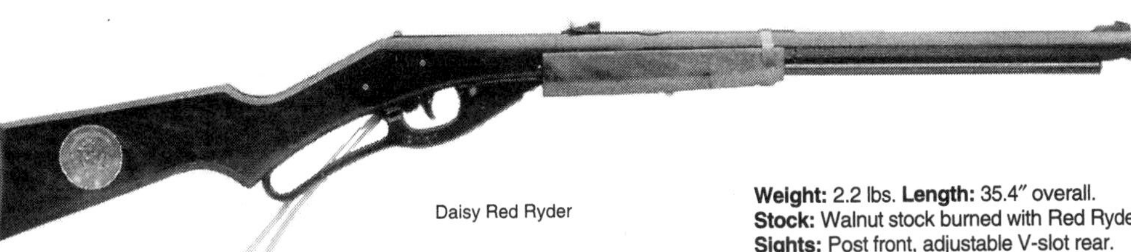

Daisy Red Ryder

DAISY 1938 RED RYDER CLASSIC

Caliber: BB, 650-shot repeating action.
Barrel: Smoothbore steel with shroud.
Weight: 2.2 lbs. **Length:** 35.4″ overall.
Stock: Walnut stock burned with Red Ryder lariat signature.
Sights: Post front, adjustable V-slot rear.
Features: Walnut forend. Saddle ring with leather thong. Lever cocking. Gravity feed. Controlled velocity. One of Daisy's most popular guns. From Daisy Mfg. Co.
Price: About **$45.00**

DAISY/POWER LINE 853

Caliber: 177 pellets.
Barrel: 20.9″; 12-groove rifling, high-grade solid steel by Lothar Walther™, precision crowned; bore size for precision match pellets.
Weight: 5.08 lbs. **Length:** 38.9″ overall.
Power: Single-pump pneumatic.
Stock: Full-length, select American hardwood, stained and finished; black buttplate with white spacers.
Sights: Globe front with four aperture inserts; precision micrometer adjustable rear peep sight mounted on a standard ⅜″ dovetail receiver mount.
Features: Single shot. From Daisy Mfg. Co.
Price: About **$245.00**

Daisy Model 840

DAISY/POWER LINE 856 PUMP-UP AIRGUN

Caliber: 177 pellets (single shot) or BB (100-shot reservoir).
Barrel: Rifled steel with shroud.
Weight: 2.7 lbs. **Length:** 37.4″ overall.
Power: Pneumatic pump-up.
Stock: Moulded wood-grain with Monte Carlo cheekpiece.
Sights: Ramp and blade front, open rear adjustable for elevation.
Features: Velocity from 315 fps (two pumps) to 650 fps (10 pumps). Shoots BBs or pellets. Heavy die-cast metal receiver. Cross-bolt trigger-block safety. Introduced 1984. From Daisy Mfg. Co.
Price: About **$45.00**

DAISY MODEL 840

Caliber: 177 pellet single shot; or BB 350-shot.
Barrel: 19″, smoothbore, steel.
Weight: 2.7 lbs. **Length:** 36.8″ overall.
Power: Pneumatic, single pump.
Stock: Moulded wood-grain stock and forend.
Sights: Ramp front, open, adjustable rear.
Features: Muzzle velocity 335 fps (BB), 300 fps (pellet). Steel buttplate; straight pull bolt action; cross-bolt safety. Forend forms pump lever. Introduced 1978. From Daisy Mfg. Co.
Price: About **$40.00**

DAISY/POWER LINE 880 PUMP-UP AIRGUN
Caliber: 177 pellets, BB.
Barrel: Rifled steel with shroud.
Weight: 4.5 lbs. **Length:** 37¾″ overall.
Power: Pneumatic pump-up.
Stock: Wood-grain moulded plastic with Monte Carlo cheekpiece.
Sights: Ramp front, open rear adjustable for elevation.
Features: Crafted by Daisy. Variable power (velocity and range) increase with pump strokes. 10 strokes for maximum power. 100-shot BB magazine. Cross-bolt trigger safety. Positive cocking valve. From Daisy Mfg. Co.
Price: About **$60.00**

DAISY/POWER LINE 922
Caliber: 22, 5-shot clip.
Barrel: Rifled steel with shroud.
Weight: 4.5 lbs. **Length:** 37¾″ overall.
Stock: Moulded wood-grained plastic with checkered pistol grip and forend, Monte Carlo cheekpiece.
Sights: Ramp front, fully adjustable open rear.
Features: Muzzle velocity from 270 fps (two pumps) to 530 fps (10 pumps). Straight-pull bolt action. Separate buttplate and grip cap with white spacers. Introduced 1978. From Daisy Mfg. Co.
Price: About **$85.00**
Price: Models 970/920 (same as Model 922 except with hardwood stock and forend), about **$120.00**

DAISY MODEL 990 DUAL-POWER AIR RIFLE
Caliber: 177 pellets (single shot) or BB (100-shot magazine).
Barrel: Rifled steel.
Weight: 4.1 lbs. **Length:** 37.4″ overall.
Power: Pneumatic pump-up and 12-gram CO_2.
Stock: Moulded woodgrain.
Sights: Ramp and blade front, adjustable open rear.
Features: Velocity to 650 fps (BB), 630 fps (pellet). Choice of pump or CO_2 power. Shoots BBs or pellets. Heavy die-cast receiver dovetailed for scope mount. Cross-bolt trigger block safety. Introduced 1993. From Daisy Mfg. Co.
Price: About **$70.00**

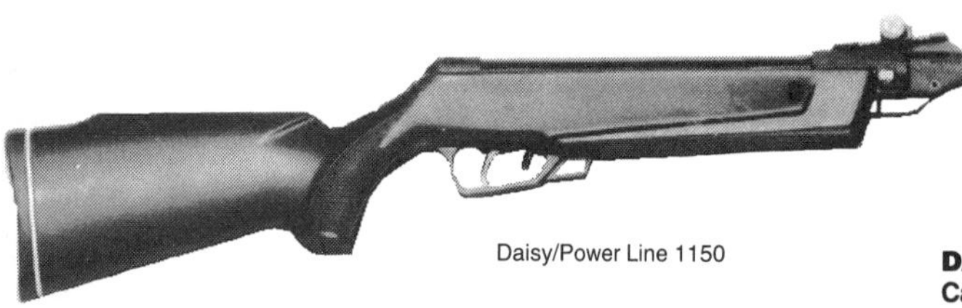
Daisy/Power Line 1150

DAISY/POWER LINE 1150 PELLET RIFLE
Caliber: 177, single shot.
Barrel: Rifled steel.
Weight: NA. **Length:** 37″ overall.
Power: Spring-air, barrel cocking.
Stock: Black moulded plastic.
Sights: Blade on ramp front, micrometer adjustable open rear.
Features: Velocity to 600 fps. Introduced 1995. From Daisy Mfg. Co.
Price: About **$90.00**

DAISY/POWER LINE 1170 PELLET RIFLE
Caliber: 177, single shot.
Barrel: Rifled steel.
Weight: 5.5 lbs. **Length:** 42.5″ overall.
Power: Spring-air, barrel cocking.
Stock: Hardwood.
Sights: Hooded post front, micrometer adjustable open rear.
Features: Velocity to 800 fps. Monte Carlo comb. Introduced 1995. From Daisy Mfg. Co.
Price: About **$162.00**

Daisy/Power Line 2001

DAISY/POWER LINE 2001 AIR RIFLE
Caliber: 177 pellets, 35-shot helical magazine.
Barrel: Rifled steel.
Weight: 3.1 lbs. **Length:** 37.4″ overall.
Power: CO_2.
Stock: Moulded woodgrain with Monte Carlo comb.
Sights: Ramp and blade front, fully adjustable open rear.
Features: Velocity to 625 fps. Bolt-action repeater with cross-bolt trigger block safety; checkered grip and forend; white buttplate spacer. Introduced 1994. From Daisy Mfg. Co.
Price: About **$75.00**

Consult our Directory pages for the location of firms mentioned.

DAISY/POWER LINE EAGLE 7856 PUMP-UP AIRGUN
Caliber: 177 (pellets), BB, 100-shot BB magazine.
Barrel: Rifled steel with shroud.
Weight: 2¾ lbs. **Length:** 37.4″ overall.
Power: Pneumatic pump-up.
Stock: Moulded wood-grain plastic.
Sights: Ramp and blade front, open rear adjustable for elevation.
Features: Velocity from 315 fps (two pumps) to 650 fps (10 pumps). Finger grooved forend. Cross-bolt trigger-block safety. Introduced 1985. From Daisy Mfg. Co.
Price: With 4x scope, about **$60.00**

DAISY/POWER LINE 2002 PELLET RIFLE
Caliber: 177, 35-shot magazine.
Barrel: Rifled steel.
Weight: 3.6 lbs. **Length:** 37.5″ overall.
Power: 12-gram CO_2.
Stock: Moulded polymer.
Sights: Ramped blade front, open fully adjustable rear.
Features: Velocity to 630 fps. Continuous feed helical design Mag Clip. Cross-bolt trigger block safety. Introduced 1995. From Daisy Mfg. Co.
Price: About **$82.50**

FAMAS SEMI-AUTO AIR RIFLE
Caliber: 177, 10-shot magazine.
Barrel: 19.2″.
Weight: About 8 lbs. **Length:** 29.8″ overall.
Power: 12-gram CO_2.
Stock: Synthetic bullpup design.
Sights: Adjustable front, aperture rear.
Features: Velocity of 425 fps. Duplicates size, weight and feel of the centerfire MAS French military rifle in caliber 223. Introduced 1988. Imported from France by Century International Arms.
Price: About **$275.00**

"GAT" AIR RIFLE
Caliber: 177, single shot.
Barrel: 17¼″ cocked, 23¼″ extended.
Weight: 3 lbs.
Power: Spring-piston.
Stock: Composition.
Sights: Fixed.
Features: Velocity about 450 fps. Shoots pellets, darts, corks. Imported from England by Stone Enterprises, Inc.
Price: **$34.95**

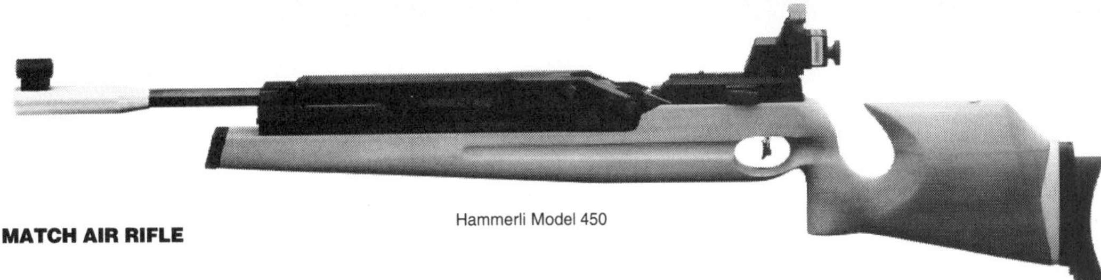
Hammerli Model 450

HAMMERLI MODEL 450 MATCH AIR RIFLE
Caliber: 177, single shot.
Barrel: 19.5″.
Weight: 9.8 lbs. **Length:** 43.3″ overall.
Power: Pneumatic.
Stock: Match style with stippled grip, rubber buttpad. Beach or walnut.
Sights: Match tunnel front, Hammerli diopter rear.
Features: Velocity about 560 fps. Removable sights; forend sling rail; adjustable trigger; adjustable comb. Introduced 1994. Imported from Switzerland by SIGARMS, Inc.
Price: Beech stock **$1,355.00**
Price: Walnut stock **$1,395.00**

MARKSMAN 28 INTERNATIONAL AIR RIFLE
Caliber: 177, single shot.
Barrel: 17″.
Weight: 5¾ lbs.
Power: Spring-air, barrel cocking.
Stock: Hardwood.
Sights: Hooded front, adjustable rear.
Features: Velocity of 580-620 fps. Introduced 1989. Imported from Germany by Marksman Products.
Price: **$220.00**

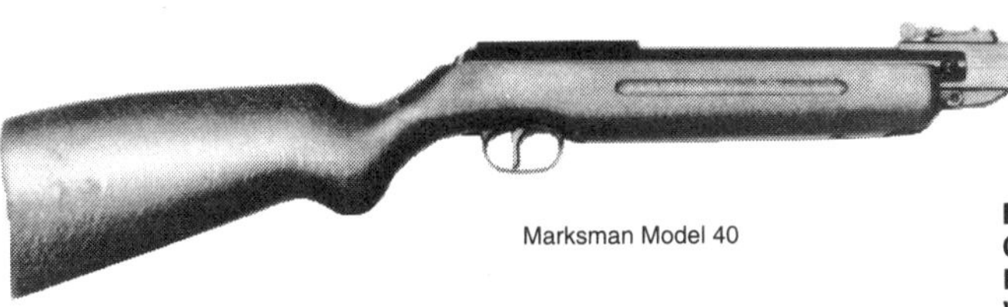
Marksman Model 40

MARKSMAN 40 INTERNATIONAL AIR RIFLE
Caliber: 177, single shot.
Barrel: 18⅜″.
Weight: 7⅓ lbs.
Power: Spring-air, barrel cocking.
Stock: Hardwood.
Sights: Hooded front, adjustable rear.
Features: Velocity of 700-720 fps. Introduced 1989. Imported from Germany by Marksman Products.
Price: **$245.00**

MARKSMAN MODEL 60 AIR RIFLE
Caliber: 177, single shot.
Barrel: 18.5″, rifled.
Weight: 8.9 lbs. **Length:** 44.75″ overall.
Power: Spring-piston, underlever cocking.
Stock: Walnut-stained beech with Monte Carlo comb, hand-checkered pistol grip, rubber butt pad.
Sights: Blade front, open, micro. adjustable rear.
Features: Velocity of 810-840 fps. Automatic button safety on rear of receiver. Receiver grooved for scope mounting. Fully adjustable Rekord trigger. Introduced 1990. Imported from Germany by Marksman Products.
Price: **$485.00**
Price: Model 61 Carbine **$485.00**

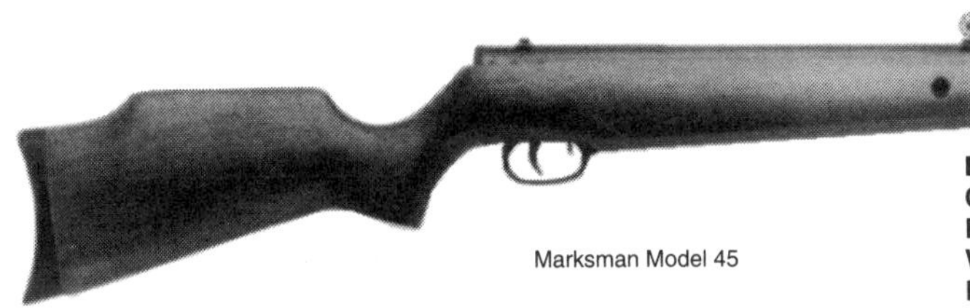
Marksman Model 45

MARKSMAN 70T AIR RIFLE
Caliber: 177, single shot.
Barrel: 19.75″.
Weight: 8 lbs. **Length:** 45.5″ overall.
Power: Spring-air, barrel cocking.
Stock: Stained hardwood with Monte Carlo cheekpiece, rubber buttpad, cut checkered pistol grip.
Sights: Hooded front, open fully adjustable rear.
Features: Velocity of 910-940 fps; adjustable Rekord trigger. Introduced 1988. Imported from Germany by Marksman Products.
Price: 177 .... **$350.00**

MARKSMAN MODEL 45 AIR RIFLE
Caliber: 177, single shot.
Barrel: 19.1″.
Weight: 7.3 lbs. **Length:** 46.75″ overall.
Power: Spring-air, barrel cocking.
Stock: Stained hardwood with Monte Carlo cheekpiece, butt pad.
Sights: Hooded front, fully adjustable micrometer rear.
Features: Velocity 900-930 fps. Adjustable trigger; automatic safety. Introduced 1993. Imported from Spain by Marksman Products.
Price: **$189.00**

Marksman 55 Air Rifle
Similar to the Model 70T except has uncheckered hardwood stock, no cheekpiece, plastic buttplate. Adjustable Rekord trigger. Overall length is 45.25″, weight is 7½ lbs. Available in 177-caliber only.
Price: **$295.00**

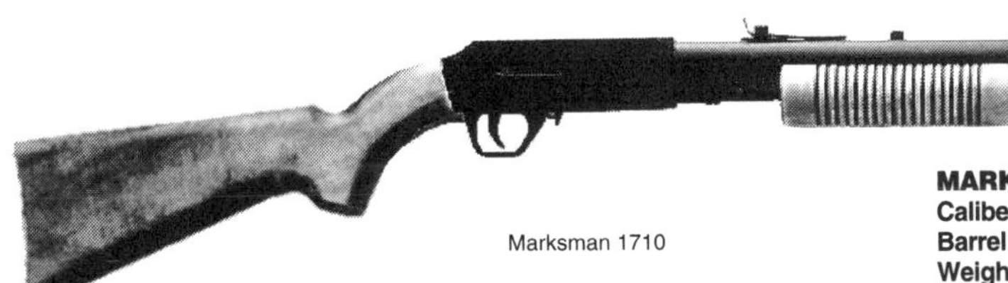
Marksman 1710

MARKSMAN 1710 PLAINSMAN AIR RIFLE
Caliber: BB, 20-shot repeater.
Barrel: Smoothbore steel with shroud.
Weight: 2.25 lbs. **Length:** 34″ overall.
Power: Spring-air.
Stock: Stained hardwood.
Sights: Blade on ramp front, adjustable V-slot rear.
Features: Velocity about 275 fps. Positive feed; automatic safety. Introduced 1994. Made in U.S. From Marksman Products.
Price: **$36.00**

MARKSMAN 1740 AIR RIFLE
Caliber: 177 or 18-shot BB repeater.
Barrel: 15½″, smoothbore.
Weight: 5 lbs., 1 oz. **Length:** 36½″ overall.
Power: Spring, barrel cocking.
Stock: Moulded high-impact ABS plastic.
Sights: Ramp front, open rear adjustable for elevation.
Features: Velocity about 450 fps. Automatic safety; fixed front, adjustable rear sight; positive feed BB magazine; shoots 177-cal. BBs, pellets and darts. From Marksman Products.
Price: **$50.00**
Price: Model 1780 (deluxe sights, rifled barrel, shoots only pellets) **$66.00**

MARKSMAN 1792 COMPETITION TRAINER AIR RIFLE
Caliber: 177, single shot.
Barrel: 15″, rifled.
Weight: 4.7 lbs.
Power: Spring-air, barrel cocking.
Stock: Synthetic.
Sights: Hooded front, match-style diopter rear.
Features: Velocity about 450 fps. Automatic safety. Introduced 1993. More economical version of the 1790 Biathlon Trainer. Made in U.S. From Marksman Products.
Price: **$60.00**

MARKSMAN 1750 BB BIATHLON REPEATER RIFLE
Caliber: BB, 18-shot magazine.
Barrel: 15″, smoothbore.
Weight: 4.7 lbs.
Power: Spring-piston, barrel cocking.
Stock: Moulded composition.
Sights: Tunnel front, open adjustable rear.
Features: Velocity of 450 fps. Automatic safety. Positive Feed System loads a BB each time gun is cocked. Introduced 1990. From Marksman Products.
Price: **$57.00**

Marksman 1790

MARKSMAN 1790 BIATHLON TRAINER
Caliber: 177, single shot.
Barrel: 15″, rifled.
Weight: 4.7 lbs.
Power: Spring-air, barrel cocking.
Stock: Synthetic.
Sights: Hooded front, match-style diopter rear.
Features: Velocity of 450 fps. Endorsed by the U.S. Shooting Team. Introduced 1989. From Marksman Products.
Price: **$69.00**

RWS Model 75S T01

RWS MODEL CA 100 AIR RIFLE
Caliber: 177, single shot.
Barrel: 22″.
Weight: 11.4 lbs. **Length:** 44″ overall.
Power: Compressed air; interchangeable cylinders.
Stock: Laminated hardwood with adjustable cheekpiece and buttplate.
Sights: Optional.
Features: Gives 250 shots per full charge. Double-sided power regulator. Introduced 1995. Imported from England by Dynamit Nobel-RWS, Inc.
Price: **$2,100.00**

RWS MODEL 75S T01 MATCH
Caliber: 177, single shot.
Barrel: 19″.
Weight: 11 lbs. **Length:** 43.7″ overall.
Power: Dual spring piston.
Stock: Oil-finished beech with stippled grip; adjustable cheekpiece, buttplate.
Sights: Globe front, fully adjustable match peep rear.
Features: Velocity of 580 fps. Fully adjustable trigger; recoilless action. Introduced 1990. Imported from Germany by Dynamit Nobel-RWS.
Price: **$1,650.00**

RWS/Diana Model 34 Air Rifle
Similar to the Model 24 except has 19″ barrel, weighs 7.5 lbs. Gives velocity of 1000 fps (177), 800 fps (22). Adjustable trigger, synthetic seals. Comes with scope rail.
Price: 177 or 22 . . . . **$285.00**
Price: Model 34N (nickel-plated metal, black epoxy-coated wood stock) . **$330.00**
Price: Model 34BC (matte black metal, black stock, 4x32 scope, mounts) **$485.00**

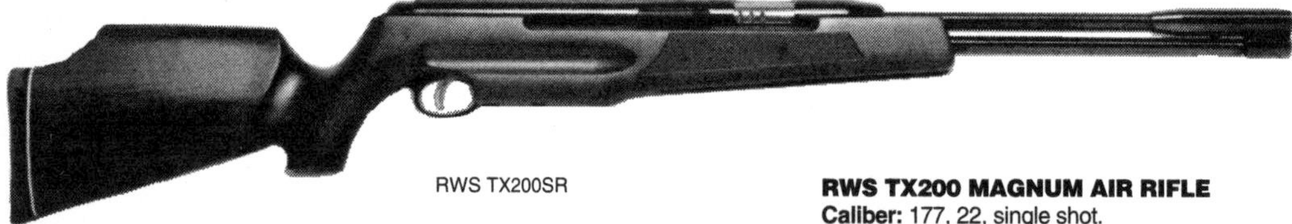
RWS TX200SR

RWS/DIANA MODEL 24 AIR RIFLE
Caliber: 177, 22, single shot.
Barrel: 17″, rifled.
Weight: 6 lbs. **Length:** 42″ overall.
Power: Spring-air, barrel cocking.
Stock: Beech.
Sights: Hooded front, adjustable rear.
Features: Velocity of 700 fps (177). Easy cocking effort; blue finish. Imported from Germany by Dynamit Nobel-RWS, Inc.
Price: **$205.00**
Price: Model 24C **$205.00**

RWS TX200 MAGNUM AIR RIFLE
Caliber: 177, 22, single shot.
Barrel: 14¾″; 12-groove Walther with choke.
Weight: 8½ lbs. **Length:** 42″ overall.
Power: Spring-air, underlever cocking.
Stock: Beech or walnut (177 only) with Monte Carlo cheekpiece; checkered grip and forend; rubber recoil pad.
Sights: None furnished; scope rail.
Features: Adjustable two-stage match trigger; automatic safety; floating piston. Made by Air Arms. Introduced 1995. Imported from England by Dynamit Nobel-RWS, Inc.
Price: **$560.00**
Price: TX200SR (recoilless version of above, slightly different stock), from **$660.00**

CAUTION: PRICES SHOWN ARE SUPPLIED BY THE MANUFACTURER OR IMPORTER. CHECK YOUR LOCAL GUNSHOP.

RWS/DIANA MODEL 45 AIR RIFLE
Caliber: 177, single shot.
Weight: 8 lbs. **Length:** 45″ overall.
Power: Spring-air, barrel cocking.
Stock: Walnut-finished hardwood with rubber recoil pad.
Sights: Globe front with interchangeable inserts, micro. click open rear with four-way blade.
Features: Velocity of 820 fps. Dovetail base for either micrometer peep sight or scope mounting. Automatic safety. Imported from Germany by Dynamit Nobel-RWS, Inc.
Price: **$330.00**

Consult our Directory pages for the location of firms mentioned.

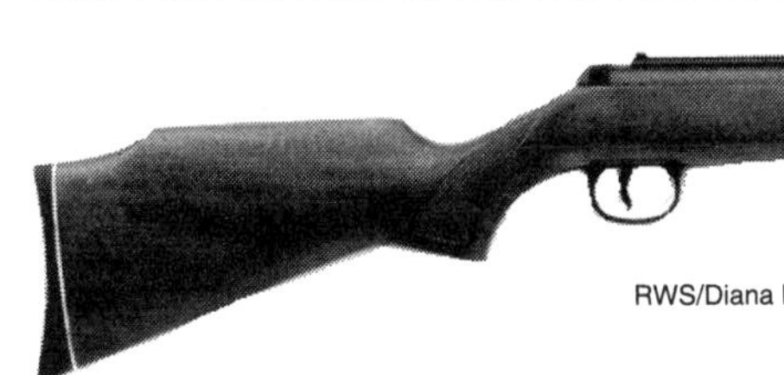

RWS/Diana Model 36

RWS/DIANA MODEL 36 AIR RIFLE
Caliber: 177, 22, single shot.
Barrel: 19″, rifled.
Weight: 8 lbs. **Length:** 45″ overall.
Power: Spring-air, barrel cocking.
Stock: Beech.
Sights: Hooded front (interchangeable inserts available), adjustable rear.
Features: Velocity of 1000 fps (177-cal.). Comes with scope mount; two-stage adjustable trigger. Imported from Germany by Dynamit Nobel-RWS, Inc.
Price: **$415.00**
Price: Model 36 Carbine (same as Model 36 except has 15″ barrel) **$415.00**

RWS/Diana Model 52 Deluxe

RWS/DIANA MODEL 52 AIR RIFLE
Caliber: 177, 22, single shot.
Barrel: 17″, rifled.
Weight: 8½ lbs. **Length:** 43″ overall.
Power: Spring-air, sidelever cocking.
Stock: Beech, with Monte Carlo, cheekpiece, checkered grip and forend.
Sights: Ramp front, adjustable rear.
Features: Velocity of 1100 fps (177). Blue finish. Solid rubber buttpad. Imported from Germany by Dynamit Nobel-RWS, Inc.
Price: **$535.00**
Price: Model 52 Deluxe (select walnut stock, rosewood grip and forend caps, palm swell grip) **$775.00**
Price: Model 48B (as above except matte black metal, black stock) **$535.00**
Price: Model 48 (same as Model 52 except no Monte Carlo, cheekpiece or checkering) **$530.00**

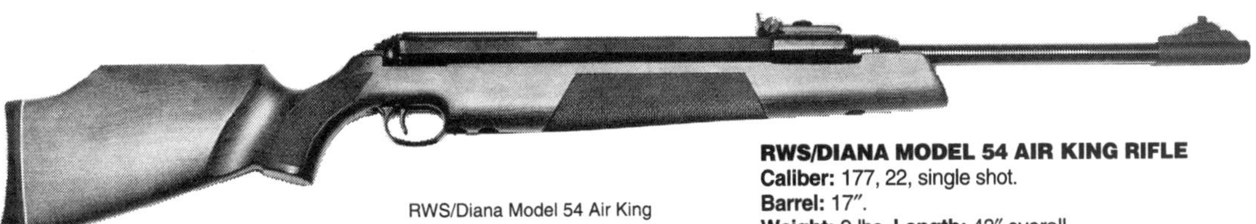

RWS/Diana Model 54 Air King

RWS/DIANA MODEL 54 AIR KING RIFLE
Caliber: 177, 22, single shot.
Barrel: 17″.
Weight: 9 lbs. **Length:** 43″ overall.
Power: Spring-air, sidelever cocking.
Stock: Walnut with Monte Carlo cheekpiece, checkered grip and forend.
Sights: Ramp front, fully adjustable rear.
Features: Velocity to 1000 fps (177), 900 fps (22). Totally recoilless system; floating action absorbs recoil. Imported from Germany by Dynamit Nobel-RWS, Inc.
Price: **$750.00**

RWS/Diana Model 100

RWS/DIANA MODEL 100 MATCH AIR RIFLE
Caliber: 177, single shot.
Barrel: 19″.
Weight: 11 lbs. **Length:** 43″ overall.
Power: Spring-air, sidelever cocking.
Stock: Walnut.
Sights: Tunnel front, fully adjustable match rear.
Features: Velocity of 580 fps. Single-stroke cocking; cheekpiece adjustable for height and length; recoilless operation. Cocking lever secured against rebound. Introduced 1990. Imported from Germany by Dynamit Nobel-RWS, Inc.
Price: Right-hand only **$1,650.00**

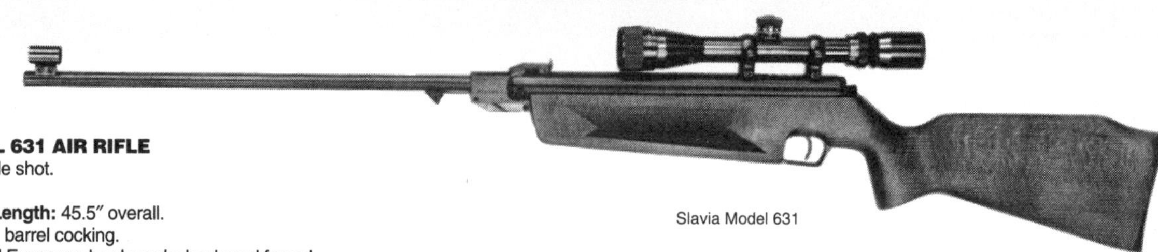
Slavia Model 631

SLAVIA MODEL 631 AIR RIFLE
Caliber: 177, single shot.
Barrel: 21″.
Weight: 6.8 lbs. **Length:** 45.5″ overall.
Power: Spring-air; barrel cocking.
Stock: Oil-finished European hardwood; checkered forend.
Sights: Hooded post front, fully adjustable open rear.
Features: Velocity to 630 fps. Adjustable two-stage trigger; receiver grooved for scope mounting; automatic safety. Introduced 1996. Imported from the Czech Republic by Great Lakes Airguns.
Price: **$112.50**

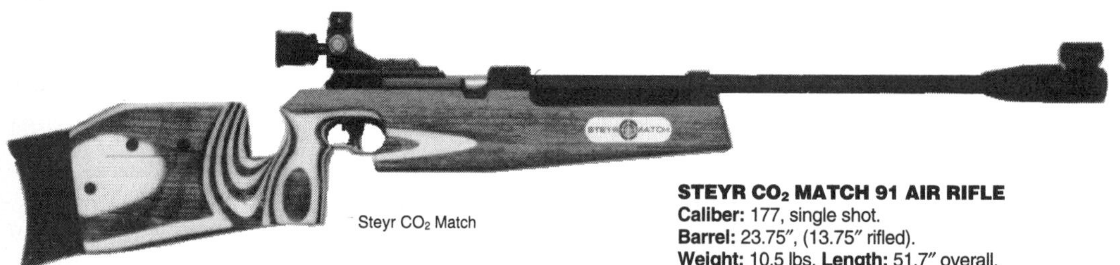
STEYR MATCH
Steyr CO_2 Match

STEYR CO_2 MATCH 91 AIR RIFLE
Caliber: 177, single shot.
Barrel: 23.75″, (13.75″ rifled).
Weight: 10.5 lbs. **Length:** 51.7″ overall.
Power: CO_2.
Stock: Match. Laminated wood. Adjustable buttplate and cheekpiece.
Sights: None furnished; comes with scope mount.
Features: Velocity 577 fps. CO_2 cylinders are refillable; about 320 shots per cylinder. Designed for 10-meter shooting. Introduced 1990. Imported from Austria by Nygord Precision Products.
Price: About **$1,350.00**
Price: Left-hand, about **$1,400.00**
Price: Running Target Rifle, right-hand, about **$1,450.00**
Price: As above, left-hand, about **$1,425.00**

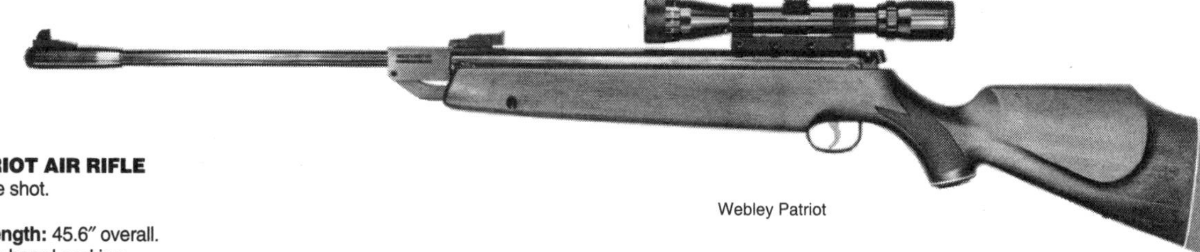
Webley Patriot

WEBLEY PATRIOT AIR RIFLE
Caliber: 22, single shot.
Barrel: 17.5″.
Weight: 9 lbs. **Length:** 45.6″ overall.
Power: Spring-air; barrel cocking.
Stock: Walnut-stained beech; checkered grip; rubber buttpad.
Sights: Post front, fully adjustable open rear.
Features: Velocity to 932 fps. Automatic safety; receiver grooved for scope mounting. Imported from England by Great Lakes Airguns.
Price: **$497.72**

Whiscombe JW70 FB

WHISCOMBE JW SERIES AIR RIFLES
Caliber: 177, 20, 22, 25, single shot.
Barrel: 17″, Lothar Walther.
Weight: 9 lbs., 8 oz. **Length:** 39″ overall.
Power: Dual spring-piston, multi-stroke; underlever cocking.
Stock: Walnut with adjustable buttplate.
Sights: None furnished; grooved scope rail.
Features: Velocity 660-890 fps (22-caliber, fixed barrel) depending upon model. Interchangeable barrels; automatic safety; muzzle weight; semi-floating action; twin opposed pistons with counter-wound springs; adjustable trigger. Introduced 1995. Imported from England by Pelaire Products.
Price: JW50, fixed barrel only **$1,440.00**
Price: JW60, fixed barrel only **$1,495.00**
Price: JW70, fixed barrel only **$1,550.00**
Price: JW75, fixed barrel only **$1,575.00**
Price: JW75 High Power, fixed barrel avail. **$1,595.00**

CONSULT
SHOOTER'S
MARKETPLACE
Page 225, This Issue

CAUTION: PRICES SHOWN ARE SUPPLIED BY THE MANUFACTURER OR IMPORTER. CHECK YOUR LOCAL GUNSHOP.

WARRANTY SERVICE CENTER DIRECTORY

A

A&M Sales, 23 W. North Ave., Northlake, IL 60264/708-562-8190
A-Square Co., Inc., One Industrial Park, Bedford, KY 40006-9667/502-255-7456; FAX: 502-255-7657
Accu-Tek, 4525 Carter Ct., Chino, CA 91710/909-627-2404; FAX: 909-627-7817
Accuracy Gun Shop, 1240 Hunt Ave., Columbus, GA 31907/706-561-6386
Accuracy Gun Shop, Inc., 5903 Boulder Highway, Las Vegas, NV 89122/702-458-3330
Ace Custom 45's, 1880½ Upper Turtle Creek Rd., Kerrville, TX 78028/210-257-4290; FAX: 210-257-5724
Adventure A.G.R., 2991 St. Jude, Waterford, MI 48329/810-673-3090
Ahlman's Custom Gun Shop, Inc., 9525 West 230th St., Morristown, MN 55052/507-685-4244
Aimpoint, Inc., 580 Herndon Parkway, Suite 500, Herndon, VA 22070/703-471-6828; FAX: 703-689-0575
Aimtech Mount Systems, P.O. Box 223, 101 Inwood Acres, Thomasville, GA 31799/912-226-4313; FAX: 912-227-0222
Air Arms, Hailsham Industrial Park, Diplocks Way, Hailsham, E. Sussex, BN27 3JF ENGLAND/011-0323-845853 (U.S. importers—Air Werks International; World Class Airguns)
Air Gun Shop, The, 2312 Elizabeth St., Billings, MT 59102/406-656-2983
Air Guns Unlimited, 15866 Main St., La Puente, CA 91744/818-333-4991
Air Rifle Specialists, 311 East Water St., Elmira, NY 14901/607-734-7340; FAX: 607-733-3261
Air Venture, 9752 E. Flower St., Bellflower, CA 90706/310-867-6355
Air Werks International, 403 W. 24th St., Norfolk, VA 23517-1204/800-247-9375
Airgun Repair Centre, 3227 Garden Meadows, Lawrenceburg, IN 47025/812-637-1463; FAX: 812-637-1463
Airguns International, 3451 G Airway Dr, Santa Rosa, CA 95403/707-578-7900; FAX: 707-578-0951
Airrow (See Swivel Machine Works, Inc.)
Alessandri and Son, Lou, 24 French St., Rehoboth, MA 02769/508-252-3436, 800-248-5652; FAX: 508-252-3436
Alexander, Gunsmith, W.R., 1406 Capitol Circle N.E. #D, Tallahassee, FL 32308/904-656-6176
All Game Sport Center, 6076 Guinea Pike, Milford, OH 45150/513-575-0134
Allison & Carey Gun Works, 17311 S.E. Stark, Portland, OR 97233/503-256-5166
Alpine Arms Corp., 6716 Fort Hamilton Pkwy., Brooklyn, NY 11219/718-833-2228
American Arms & Ordnance, Inc., P.O. Box 2691, 1303 S. College Ave., Bryan, TX 77805/409-822-4983
American Arms, Inc., 715 Armour Rd., N. Kansas City, MO 64116/816-474-3161; FAX: 816-474-1225
American Derringer Corp., 127 N. Lacy Dr., Waco, TX 76705/800-642-7817, 817-799-9111; FAX: 817-799-7935
Ammo Load, Inc., 1560 E. Edinger, Suite G, Santa Ana, CA 92705/714-558-8858; FAX: 714-569-0319
AMT, 6226 Santos Diaz St., Irwindale, CA 91702/818-334-6629; FAX: 818-969-5247
Anderson Manufacturing Co., Inc., P.O. Box 2640, 2741 N. Crosby Rd., Oak Harbor, WA 98277/360-675-7300; FAX: 360-675-3939
Anderson, Inc., Andy, 2125 NW Expressway, Oklahoma City, OK 73112/405-842-3305
Anschutz GmbH, Postfach 1128, D-89001 Ulm, Donau, GERMANY (U.S. importer—PSI, Inc.)
Answer Products Co., 1519 Westbury Drive, Davison, MI 48423/810-653-2911
Argonaut Gun Shop, 607 McHenry Ave., Modesto, CA 95350/209-522-5876
Arizaga (See U.S. importer—Mandall Shooting Supplies, Inc.)
Armadillo Air Gun Repair, 5892 Hampshire Rd., Corpus Christi, TX 78408/512-289-5458
Armas Azor, J.A. (See U.S. importer—Armes de Chasse)
Armes de Chasse, P.O. Box 827, Chadds Ford, PA 19317/610-388-1146; FAX: 610-388-1147
Armi Sport (See U.S. importers—Cape Outfitters; Taylor's & Co., Inc.)
Armoury, Inc., The, Rt. 202, Box 2340, New Preston, CT 06777/203-868-0001
Armscorp USA, Inc., 4424 John Ave., Baltimore, MD 21227/410-247-6200; FAX: 410-247-6205
Armsport, Inc., 3950 NW 49th St., Miami, FL 33142/305-635-7850; FAX: 305-633-2877
Armurier De L'Outaouais, 28 Rue Bourque, Hull, Quebec, CANADA J8Y 1X1/819-777-9824
Arrieta, S.L., Morkaiko, 5, Elgoibar, E-20870, SPAIN/(43) 74 31 50; FAX: (43) 74 31 54 (U.S. importers—Hi-Grade Imports; Jansma, Jack J.; New England Arms Co.; The Orvis Co., Inc.; Quality Arms, Inc.)
Astra Sport, S.A., Apartado 3, 48300 Guernica, Espagne, SPAIN/34-4-6250100; FAX: 34-4-6255186 (U.S. importer—E.A.A. Corp.)
ATIS Armi S.A.S., via Gussalli 24, Zona Industriale-Loc. Fornaci, 25020 Brescia, ITALY
Atlantic Guns, Inc., 944 Bonifant St., Silver Spring, MD 20910/301-585-4448/301-279-7983
Atlas Gun Repair, 4908 E. Judge Perez Dr., Violet, LA 70092/504-277-4229
Auto Electric & Parts, Inc., 24 W. Baltimore Ave., Media, PA 19063/215-565-2432
Auto-Ordnance Corp., Williams Lane, West Hurley, NY 12491/914-679-4190; FAX: 914-679-2698
Autumn Sales, Inc. (Blaser), 1320 Lake St., Fort Worth, TX 76103/817-335-1634; FAX: 817-338-0119
AWC Systems Technology, P.O. Box 41938, Phoenix, AZ 85080-1938/602-780-1050
AYA (See U.S. importer—Armes de Chasse)

B

B&B Supply Co., 4501 Minnehaha Ave., Minneapolis, MN 55406/612-724-5230
B&T, Inc., 1777 Central Ave., Albany, NY 12205/518-869-7934
B&W Gunsmithing, 505 Main Ave. N.W., Cullman, AL 35055/205-737-9595
B-Square Company, Inc., P.O. Box 11281, 2708 St. Louis Ave., Ft. Worth, TX 76110/817-923-0964, 800-433-2909; FAX: 817-926-7012
Bachelder Custom Arms, 1229 Michigan N.E., Grand Rapids, MI 49503/616-459-3636
Badger Gun & Ammo, Inc., 2339 S. 43rd St., West, Milwaukee, WI 53219/414-383-0855
Badger's Shooters Supply, Inc., 202 N. Harding, Owen, WI 54460/715-229-2101; FAX: 715-229-2332
Baer Custom, Inc., Les, 29601 34th Ave., Hillsdale, IL 61257/309-658-2716; FAX: 309-658-2610
Baikal (See U.S. importers—Air Werks International; K.B.I., Inc.)
Bain & Davis, Inc., 307 E. Valley Blvd., San Gabriel, CA 91776-3522/818-573-4241, 213-283-7449
Baity's Custom Gunworks, 2623 Boone Trail, N. Wilkesboro, NC 28659/919-667-8785
Baltimore Gunsmiths, 218 South Broadway, Baltimore, MD 21231/410-276-6908
Barrett Firearms Manufacturer, Inc., P.O. Box 1077, Murfreesboro, TN 37133/615-896-2938; FAX: 615-896-7313
Bausch & Lomb Sports Optics Div., 9200 Cody, Overland Park, KS 66214/913-752-3400, 800-423-3537; FAX: 913-752-3550
Bausch & Lomb, Inc., 42 East Ave., Rochester, NY 14603/913-752-3433, 800-828-5423; FAX: 913-752-3489
Beard's Sport Shop, 811 Broadway, Cape Girardeau, MO 63701/314-334-2266
Beauchamp & Son, Inc., 160 Rossiter Rd., Richmond, MA 01254/413-698-3822; FAX: 413-698-3866
Bedlan's Sporting Goods, Inc., 1318 E. Street, P.O. Box 244, Fairbury, NE 68352/402-729-6112
Beeman Precision Airguns, 5454 Argosy Dr., Huntington Beach, CA 92649/714-890-4800; FAX: 714-890-4808
Bell's Legendary Country Wear, 22 Circle Dr., Bellmore, NY 11710/516-679-1158
Belleplain Supply, Inc., Box 346, Handsmill Rd., Belleplain, NJ 08270/609-861-2345
Bellrose & Son, L.E., 21 Forge Pond Rd., Granby, MA 01033-0184/413-467-3637
Ben's Gun Shop, 1151 S. Cedar Ridge, Duncanville, TX 75137/214-780-1807
Benelli Armi, S.p.A., Via della Stazione, 61029 Urbino, ITALY/39-722-328633; FAX: 39-722-327427 (U.S. importers—E.A.A. Corp.; Heckler & Koch, Inc.; Sile Distributors)
Benjamin (See page 503)
Benson Gun Shop, 35 Middle Country Rd., Coram L.I., NY 11727/516-736-0065
Benton & Brown Firearms, Inc., 311 W. First, P.O. Box 326, Delhi, LA 71232-0326/318-878-2499; FAX: 817-284-9300
Beretta Firearms, Pietro, 25063 Gardone V.T., ITALY (U.S. importer—Beretta U.S.A. Corp.)
Beretta U.S.A. Corp., 17601 Beretta Drive, Accokeek, MD 20607/301-283-2191; FAX: 301-283-0435
Beretta, Dr. Franco, via Rossa, 4, Concesio (BC), Italy I-25062/030-2751955; FAX: 030-218-0414 (U.S. importer—Nevada Cartridge Co.
Bernardelli Vincenzo S.p.A., 125 Via Matteotti, P.O. Box 74, Gardone V.T., Brescia ITALY, 25063/39-30-8912851-2-3; FAX: 39-30-8910249 (U.S. importer—Armsport, Inc.)
Bertuzzi (See U.S. importers—Cape Outfitters; Moore & Co., Wm. Larkin; New England Arms Co.)
Bickford's Gun Repair, 426 N. Main St., Joplin, MO 64801/417-781-6440
Billings Gunsmiths, Inc., 1940 Grand Ave., Billings, MT 59102/406-652-3104
Blaser Jagdwaffen GmbH, D-88316 Isny Im Allgau, GERMANY (U.S. importer—Autumn Sales, Inc.)
Blount, Inc., Sporting Equipment Div., 2299 Snake River Ave., P.O. Box 856, Lewiston, ID 83501/800-627-3640, 208-746-2351; FAX: 208-746-2915
Blue Ridge Outdoor Sports, Inc., 2314 Spartansburg Hwy., E. Flat Rock, NC 28726/704-697-3006
Bob's Crosman Repair, 2510 E. Henry Ave., Cudahy, WI 53110/414-769-8256
Bob's Gun & Tackle Shop, (Blaustein & Reich, Inc.), 746 Granby St., Norfolk, VA 23510/804-627-8311/804-622-9786
Boggus Gun Shop, 1402 W. Hopkins St., San Marcos, TX 78666/512-392-3513
Bohemia Arms Co., 17101 Los Modelos, Fountain Valley, CA 92708/619-442-7005; FAX: 619-442-7005
Bolsa Gunsmithing, 7404 Bolsa Ave., Westminster, CA 92683/714-894-9100
Boracci, E. John, Village Sport Center, 38-10 Merrick Rd., Seaford L.I., NY 11783/516-785-7110
Borden's Accuracy, RD 1, Box 250BC, Springville, PA 18844/717-965-2505; FAX: 717-965-2328
Borgheresi, Enrique, 106 E. Tallalah, P.O. Box 8063, Greenville, SC 29604/803-271-2664
Bosis (See U.S. importer—New England Arms Co.)
Boudreaux, Gunsmith, Preston, 412 W. School St., Lake Charles, LA 70605/318-478-0640
Bradys Sportsmans Surplus, P.O. Box 4166, Missoula, MT 59806/406-721-5500; FAX: 406-721-5581
Braverman Corp., R.J., 88 Parade Rd., Meridith, NH 03293/800-736-4867
Brenneke KG, Wilhelm, Ilmenauweg 2, 30851 Langenhagen, GERMANY/0511/97262-0; FAX: 0511/97262-62 (U.S. importer—Dynamit Nobel-RWS, Inc.)
Brenner Sport Shop, Charlie, 344 St. George Ave., Rahway, NJ 07065/908-382-4066
Bretton, 19, rue Victor Grignard, F-42026 St.-Etienne (Cedex 1) FRANCE/77-93-54-69; FAX: 77-93-57-98 (U.S. importer—Mandall Shooting Supplies, Inc.)
Bridge Sportsmen's Center, 1319 Spring St., Paso Robles, CA 93446/805-238-4407
BRNO (See U.S. importers—Bohemia Arms Co.)
Broadway Arms, 4116 E. Broadway, N. Little Rock, AR 72117/501-945-9348
Brock's Gunsmithing, Inc., North 2104 Division St., Spokane, WA 99207/509-328-9788
Brolin Arms, 2755 Thompson Creek Rd., Pomona, CA 91767/909-392-2345; FAX: 909-392-2354
Brown Co., E. Arthur, 3404 Pawnee Dr., Alexandria, MN 56308/612-762-8847
Brown, Don, Gunsmith, 1085 Tunnel Rd., Ashville, NC 28805/704-298-4867
Browning (See page 503)
Browning Arms Co. (Parts & Service), 3005 Arnold Tenbrook Rd., Arnold, MO 63010-9406/314-287-6800; FAX: 314-287-9751
Bryan & Associates, 201 S. Gosset, Anderson, SC 29623/803-261-6810
Bryco Arms (See U.S. distributor—Jennings Firearms, Inc.)
BSA Guns Ltd., Armoury Rd. Small Heath, Birmingham, ENGLAND B11 2PX/011-021-772-8543; FAX: 011-021-773-0845 (U.S. importer—John Groenewold)
Buffalo Arms, 123 S. Third, Suite 6, Sandpoint, ID 83864/208-263-6953; FAX: 208-265-2096
Buffalo Gun Center, Inc., 3385 Harlem Rd., Buffalo, NY 14225/716-835-1546
Bullseye Gun Works, 7949 E. Frontage Rd.. Overland Park, KS 66204/913-648-4867
Burby, Inc. Guns & Gunsmithing, Rt. 7 South RR #3, Box 345, Middlebury, VT 05753/802-388-7365
Burgins Gun Shop, RD #1 Box 66, Mericksville Rd., Sidney Center, NY 13839/607-829-8668
Burris Co., Inc., P.O. Box 1747, 331 E. 8th St., Greeley, CO 80631/303-356-1670; FAX: 303-356-8702
Burton Hardware, 200 N. Huntington, Sulphur, LA 70663/318-527-8651
Bushmaster Firearms (See Quality Parts Co./Bushmaster Firearms)
Bushnell (See Bausch & Lomb)

C

C-H Tool & Die Corp. (See 4-D Custom Die Co.)
Cabanas (See U.S. importer—Mandall Shooting Supplies, Inc.)
Cabela's, 812 13th Ave., Sidney, NE 69160/308-254-6644; FAX: 308-254-6669
Cal's Customs, 110 E. Hawthorne, Fallbrook, CA 92028/619-728-5230
Calico Light Weapon Systems, 405 E. 19th St., Bakersfield, CA 93305/805-323-1327; FAX: 805-323-7844
Camdex, Inc., 2330 Alger, Troy, MI 48083/810-528-2300; FAX: 810-528-0989
Cape Outfitters, 599 County Rd. 206, Cape Girardeau, MO 63701/314-335-4103; FAX: 314-335-1555
Capitol Sports & Western Wear, 1092 Helena Ave., Helena, MT 59601/406-443-2978

Carl's Gun Shop, 100 N. Main, El Dorado Springs, MO 64744/417-876-4168
Carpenter's Gun Works, RD 1 Box 43D, Newton Rd., Proctorsville, VT 05153/802-226-7690
Carroll's Gun Shop, Inc., 1610 N. Alabama Rd., Wharton, TX 77488/409-532-3175
Carter's Country, 8925 Katy Freeway, Houston, TX 77024/713-461-1844
Casey's Gun Shop, 59 Des E Rables, P.O. Box 100, Rogersville, New Brunswick E0A 2T0 CANADA/506-775-6822
Catfish Guns, 900 Jeffco-Executive Park, Imperial, MO 63052/314-464-1217
CBC, Avenida Humberto de Campos, 3220, 09400-000 Ribeirao Pires-SP-BRAZIL/55-11-742-7500; FAX: 55-11-459-7385 (U.S. importer—MAGTECH Recreational Products, Inc.)
Central Ohio Police Supply, c/o Wammes Guns, 225 South Main St., Bellefontaine, OH 43311
Century Gun Dist., Inc., 1467 Jason Rd., Greenfield, IN 46140/317-462-4524
Century International Arms, Inc., P.O. Box 714, St. Albans, VT 05478-0714/802-527-1252; FAX: 802-527-0470
Cervera, Albert J., Rt. 1 Box 808, Hanover, VA 23069/804-994-5783
CHAA, Ltd., P.O. Box 565, Howell, MI 48844/800-677-8737; FAX: 313-894-6930
Chapuis Armes, 21 La Gravoux, BP15, 42380 St. Bonnet-le-Chateau, FRANCE/(33)77.50.06.96 (U.S. importer—Chapuis USA)
Chapuis USA, 416 Business Park, Bedford, KY 40006
CHARCO, 26 Beaver St., Ansonia, CT 06401/203-735-4686; 203-735-6569
Charlie's Sporting Goods, Inc., 7401-H Menaul Blvd. N.E., Albuquerque, NM 87110/505-884-4545
Charlton Co., Ltd., M.D., Box 153, Brentwood Bay, B.C., CANADA V0S 1A0/604-652-5266
Charter Arms (See CHARCO)
Cherry Corners, Inc., 11136 Congress Rd., P.O. Box 38, Lodi, OH 44254/216-948-1238
Chet Paulson Outfitters, 1901 South 72nd St., Suite A-14, Tacoma, WA 98408/206-475-8831
Christopher Firearms Co., E., Inc., Route 128 & Ferry St., Miamitown, OH 45041/513-353-1321
Chuck's Gun Shop, P.O. Box 597, Waldo, FL 32694/904-468-2264
Chung, Gunsmith, Mel, 8 Ing Rd., P.O. Box 1008, Kaunakakai, HI 96748/808-553-5888
Churchill (See U.S. importer—Ellett Bros.)
Cimarron Arms, P.O. Box 906, Fredericksburg, TX 78624-0906/210-997-9090; FAX: 210-997-0802
Clark's Custom Guns, Inc., P.O. Box 530, 11462 Keatchie Rd., Keithville, LA 71047/318-925-0836; FAX: 318-925-9425
Colabaugh Gunsmith, Inc., Craig, R.D. 4, Box 4168 Gumm St., Stroudsburg, PA 18360/717-992-4499
Coleman, Inc., Ron, 1600 North I-35 #106, Carrollton, TX 75006/214-245-3030
Coliseum Gun Traders, Ltd., 1180 Hempstead Turnpike, Uniondale, NY 11553/516-481-3593
Colonial Repair, P.O. Box 372, Hyde Park, MA 02136-9998/617-469-4951
Colt Blackpowder Arms Co., 5 Centre Market Place, New York, NY 10013/212-925-2159; FAX: 212-966-4986
Colt's Mfg. Co., Inc., P.O. Box 1868, Hartford, CT 06144-1868/800-962-COLT, 203-236-6311; FAX: 203-244-1449
Competitor Corp., Inc., P.O. Box 244, 293 Townsend Rd., West Groton, MA 01472/508-448-3521; FAX: 508-448-6691
Connecticut Shotgun Mfg. Co., P.O. Box 1692, 35 Woodland St., New Britain, CT 06051-1692/203-225-6581; FAX: 203-832-8707
Connecticut Valley Arms Co. (See CVA)
Connecticut Valley Classics, P.O. Box 2068, 12 Taylor Lane, Westport, CT 06880/203-435-4600; FAX: 203-256-1180
Coonan Arms, 1465 Selby Ave., St. Paul, MN 55104/612-641-1263; FAX: 612-641-1173
Cooper Arms, P.O. Box 114, Stevensville, MT 59870/406-777-5534; FAX: 406-777-5228
Corbin, Inc., 600 Industrial Circle, P.O. Box 2659, White City, OR 97503/503-826-5211; FAX: 503-826-8669
Cosmi Americo & Figlio s.n.c., Via Flaminia 307, Ancona, ITALY I-60020/071-888208; FAX: 071-887008 (U.S. importer—New England Arms Co.)
Creekside Gun Shop, Inc., East Main St., Holcomb, NY 14469/716-657-6131; FAX: 716-657-7900
Crosman (See page 503)
Crosman Airguns, Rts. 5 and 20, E. Bloomfield, NY 14443/716-657-6161; FAX: 716-657-5405
Crucelegui Hermanos (See U.S. importer—Mandall Shooting Supplies, Inc.)
Cumberland Arms, Rt. I, Box 1150 Shafer Rd., Blantons Chapel, Manchester, TN 37355/800-797-8414
Cumberland Knife & Gun Works, 5661 Bragg Blvd., Fayetteville, NC 28303/919-867-0009
Custom Firearms Shop, The, 1133 Indiana Ave., Sheboygan, WI 53081/414-457-3320
Custom Gun Service, 1104 Upas Ave., McAllen, TX 78501/210-686-4670
Custom Gun Shop, 12505 97th St., Edmonton, Alberta, CANADA T5G 1Z8/403-477-3737
Custom Gun Works, 4952 Johnston St., Lafayette, LA 70503/318-984-0721
CVA, 5988 Peachtree Corners East, Norcross, GA 30071/800-251-9412; FAX: 404-242-8546
Cylinder & Slide, Inc., William R. Laughridge, 245 E. 4th St., Fremont, NE 68025/402-721-4277; FAX: 402-721-0263
CZ (See U.S. importer—Magnum Research, Inc.)

D

D&D Sporting Goods, 108 E. Main, Tishomingo, OK 73460/405-371-3571
D&J Bullet Co., 426 Ferry St., Russel, KY 41169/606-836-2663
D&J Coleman Service, 4811 Guadalupe Ave., Hobbs, NM 88240/505-392-5318
D&L Gunsmithing/Guns & Ammo, 3615 Summer Ave., Memphis, TN 38122/901-327-4384
D&L Shooting Supplies, 2663 W. Shore Rd., Warwick, RI 02886/401-738-1889
D-Max, Inc., RR1, Box 473, Bagley, MN 56621/218-785-2278
Daenzer, Charles E., 142 Jefferson Ave., Otisville, MI 48463/810-631-2415
Daewoo Precision Industries Ltd., 34-3 Yeoeuido-Dong, Yeongdeungoo-GU, 15th, Fl./Seoul, KOREA (U.S. importer—Nationwide Sports Distributors)
Daisy Mfg. Co., P.O. Box 220, Rogers, AR 72757/501-636-1200; FAX: 501-636-1601
Dakota (See U.S. importer—EMF Co., Inc.)
Dakota Arms, Inc., HC 55, Box 326, Sturgis, SD 57785/605-347-4686; FAX: 605-347-4459
Dale's Guns & Archery Center, 3915 Eighteenth Ave., S.W. Rte. 8, Rochester, MN 55902/507-289-8308
Damiano's Field & Stream, 172 N. Highland Ave., Ossining, NY 10562/914-941-6005
Danny's Gun Repair, Inc., 811 East Market St., Louisville, KY 40206/502-583-7100
Darnall's Gun Works, RR #3, Box 274, Bloomington, IL 61704/309-379-4331
Daryl's Gun Shop, Inc., R.R. #2 Highway 30 West, Box 145, State Center, IA 50247/515-483-2656
Dave's Airgun Service, 1525 E. LaVieve Ln., Tempe, AZ 85284/602-491-8304
Davidson's of Canada, 584 Neal Dr., Box 479, Peterborough, Ontario, CANADA K9J 6Z6/705-742-5405; 800-461-7663
Davis Industries, 15150 Sierra Bonita Ln., Chino, CA 91710/909-597-4726; FAX: 909-393-9771
Dayton Traister, 4778 N. Monkey Hill Rd., P.O. Box 593, Oak Harbor, WA 98277/206-679-4657; FAX:206-675-1114
Delhi Small Arms, 22B Argyle Ave., Delhi, Ontario, CANADA N4B 1J3/519-582-0522
Delisle Thompson Sporting Goods, Ltd., 1814A Loren Ave., Saskatoon, Saskatchewan, CANADA S7H 1Y4/306-653-2171
Denver Instrument Co., 6542 Fig St., Arvada, CO 80004/800-321-1135, 303-431-7255; FAX: 303-423-4831
Desert Industries, Inc., P.O. Box 93443, Las Vegas, NV 89193-3443/702-597-1066; FAX: 702-871-9452
Diana (See U.S. importer—Dynamit Nobel-RWS, Inc.)
Dillon Precision Products, Inc., 8009 East Dillon's Way, Scottsdale, AZ 85260/602-948-8009, 800-762-3845; FAX: 602-998-2786
Dixie Gun Works, Inc., Hwy. 51 South, Union City, TN 38261/901-885-0561, order 800-238-6785; FAX: 901-885-0440
Dollar Drugs, Inc., 15A West 3rd, Lee's Summit, MO 64063/816-524-7600
Don & Tim's Gun Shop, 3724 Northwest Loop 410 and Fredricksburg, San Antonio, TX 78229/512-736-0263
Don's Sport Shop, Inc., 7803 E. McDowell Rd., Scottsdale, AZ 85257/602-945-4051
Dorn's Outdoor Center, 4388 Mercer University Drive, Macon, GA 31206/912-471-0304
Douglas Sporting Goods, 138 Brick Street, Princeton, WV 24740/304-425-8144
Down Under Gunsmiths, 318 Driveway, Fairbanks, AK 99701/907-456-8500
Dubbs, Gunsmith, Dale R., 32616 U.S. Hwy. 90, Seminole, AL 36574/205-946-3245
Duncan Gun Shop, Inc., 414 Second St., North Wilksboro, NC 28659/919-838-4851
Duncan's Gunworks, Inc., 1619 Grand Ave., San Marcos, CA 92069/619-727-0515
Dynamit Nobel-RWS, Inc., 81 Ruckman Rd., Closter, NJ 07624/201-767-7971; FAX: 201-767-1589

E

E&L Mfg., Inc., 4177 Riddle by Pass Rd., Riddle, OR 97469/503-874-2137; FAX: 503-874-3107
E.A.A. Corp., P.O. Box 1299, Sharpes, FL 32959/407-639-4842, 800-536-4442; FAX: 407-639-7006
Eagle Arms, Inc., 128 E. 23rd Ave., Coal Valley, IL 61240/309-799-5619, 800-336-0184; FAX: 309-799-5150
Ed's Gun & Tackle Shop, Inc., Suite 90, 2727 Canton Rd. (Hwy. 5), Marietta, GA 30066/404-425-8461
Elbe Arms Co., Inc., 610 East 27th St., Cheyenne, WY 82001/307-634-5731
Ellett Bros., P.O. Box 128, 267 Columbia Ave., Columbia, SC 29036/803-345-3751, 800-845-3711; FAX: 803-345-1820
Emerging Technologies, Inc., 721 Main St., Little Rock, AR 72201/501-375-2227; FAX: 501-372-1445
EMF Co., Inc., 1900 E. Warner Ave. Suite 1-D, Santa Ana, CA 92705/714-261-6611; FAX: 714-756-0133
Enstad & Douglas, 211 Hedges, Oregon City, OR 97045/503-655-3751
Epps, Ellwood, RR 3, Hwy. 11 North, Orillia, Ontario CANADA L3V 6H3/705-689-5333
Erma Werke GmbH, Johan Ziegler St., 13/15/FeldiglSt., D-8060 Dachau, GERMANY (U.S. importers—Mandall Shooting Supplies, Inc.; PSI, Inc.)
Ernie's Gun Shop, Ltd., 1031 Marion St., Winnipeg, Manitoba, CANADA R2J 0L1/204-233-1928
Essex Arms, P.O. Box 345, Island Pond, VT 05846/802-723-4313
Euroarms of America, Inc., 208 E. Piccadilly St., Winchester, VA 22601/703-662-1863; FAX: 703-662-4464
Europtik Ltd., P.O. Box 319, Dunmore, PA 18512/717-347-6049; FAX: 717-969-4330
Eversull, Ken, #1 Tracemont, Boyce, LA 71409/318-793-8728
Ewell Cross Gun Shop, Inc., 8240 Interstate 30W, Ft. Worth, TX 76108/817-246-4622
Eyster Heritage Gunsmiths, Inc., Ken, 6441 Bishop Rd., Centerburg, OH 43011/614-625-6131

F

F&D Guns, 5140 Westwood Drive, St. Charles, MO 63304/314-441-5897
Fabarm S.p.A., Via Averolda 31, 25039 Travagliato, Brescia, ITALY/030-6863629; FAX: 030-6863684 (U.S. importer—Ithaca Acquisition Corp.)
Famas (See U.S. importer—Century International Arms, Inc.)
FAS, Via E. Fermi, 8, 20019 Settimo Milanese, Milano, ITALY/02-3285846; FAX: 02-33500196 (U.S. importer—Nygord Precision Products)
Fausti Cav. Stefano & Figlie snc, Via Martiri Dell Indipendenza, 70, Marcheno, ITALY 25060 (U.S. importer—American Arms, Inc.)
Feather Industries, Inc., 37600 Liberty Dr., Trinidad, CO 81082/719-846-2699; FAX: 719-846-2644
Federal Engineering Corp., 1090 Bryn Mawr, Bensenville, IL 60106/708-860-1938; FAX: 708-860-2085
Federal Firearms Co., Inc., 5035 Thom's Run Rd., Oakdale, PA 15071/412-221-0300
FEG, Budapest, Soroksariut 158, H-1095 HUNGARY (U.S. importers—Century International Arms, Inc.; K.B.I., Inc.)
Feinwerkbau Westinger & Altenburger GmbH (See FWB)
Felton, James, Custom Gunsmith, 1033 Elizabeth St., Eugene, OR 97402/503-689-1687
FERLIB, Via Costa 46, 25063 Gardone V.T. (Brescia) ITALY/30 89 12 586; FAX: 30 89 12 586 (U.S. importers—Wm. Larkin Moore & Co.; New England Arms Co., Pachmayr Co.)
Fiocchi Munizioni s.p.a. (See U.S. importer—Fiocchi of America)
Fiocchi of America, Inc., 5030 Fremont Rd., Ozark, MO 65721/417-725-4118, 800-721-2666; FAX: 417-725-1039
Firearms Co. Ltd./Alpine (See U.S. importer—Mandall Shooting Supplies, Inc.)
Firearms Repair & Refinish Shoppe, 639 Hoods Mill Rd., Woodbine, MD 21797/410-795-5859
Firearms Service Center, 2140 Old Shepherdsville Rd., Louisville, KY 40218/502-458-1148
Fix Gunshop, Inc., Michael D., 334 Mt. Penn Rd., Reading, PA 19607/215-775-2067
FN Herstal, Voie de Liege 33, Herstal 4040, BELGIUM/(32)41.40.82.83; FAX: (32)41.40.86.79
Foothills Shooting Center, 7860 W. Jewell Ave., Lakewood, CO 80226/303-985-4417
Forgett Jr., Valmore J., 689 Bergen Blvd., Ridgefield, NJ 07657/201-945-2500; FAX: 201-945-6859
Forster Products, 82 E. Lanark Ave., Lanark, IL 61046/815-493-6360; FAX: 815-493-2371
Four Seasons, 76 R Winn St., Woburn, MA 01801/617-932-3133/3255
4-D Custom Die Co., 711 N. Sandusky St., P.O. Box 889, Mt. Vernon, OH 43050-0889/614-397-7214; FAX: 614-397-6600
Fox & Company, 2211 Dutch Valley Rd., Knoxville, TN 37918/615-687-7411
Franchi S.p.A., Luigi, Via del Serpente, 12, 25020 Fornaci, ITALY (U.S. importer—American Arms, Inc.)
Francotte & Cie S.A., Auguste, rue du Trois Juin 109, 4400 Herstal-Liege, BELGIUM/41-48.13.18; FAX: 41-48.11.79 (U.S. importer—Armes de Chasse)
Franklin Sports, Inc., 3941 Atlanta Hwy., Bogart, GA 30622/706-543-7803
Freedom Arms, Inc., P.O. Box 1776, Freedom, WY 83120/307-883-2468, 800-833-4432 (orders only); FAX: 307-883-2005
Freer's Gun Shop, Building B-1, 8928 Spring Branch Dr., Houston, TX 77080/713-467-3016
Fremont Tool Works, 1214 Prairie, Ford, KS 67842/316-369-2327
Friedman's Army Surplus, 2617 Nolenville Rd., Nashville, TN 37211/615-244-1653
Frontiersman's Sports, 6925 Wayzata Blvd., Minneapolis, MN 55426/612-544-3775
FWB, Neckarstrasse 43, 78727 Oberndorf a. N., GERMANY/07423-814-0; FAX: 07423-814-89 (U.S. importer—Beeman Precision Airguns, Inc.)

G

G.H. Outdoor Sports, 520 W. "B" St., McCook, NE 69001/308-345-1250
G.I. Loan Shop, 1004 W. Second St., Grand Island, NE 68801/308-382-9573
G.U. Inc., 4325 S. 120th St., Omaha, NE 68137/402-330-4492; FAX: 402-330-8029
Galaxy Imports Ltd., Inc., P.O. Box 3361, Victoria, TX 77903/512-573-4867; FAX: 512-576-9622
Galazan, Div. of Connecticut Shotgun Mfg. Co., P.O. Box 622, 35 Woodland St., New Britain, CT

06051-0622/203-225-6581; FAX: 203-832-8707
Gamba, USA, P.O. Box 60452, Colorado Springs, CO 80960/719-578-1145; FAX: 719-444-0731
Gamba-Societa Armi Bresciane Srl., Renato, Via Artigiani, 93, 25063 Gardone Val Trompia (BS), ITALY/30-8911640, 30-8911648 (U.S. importers—Cape Outfitters; Giacomo Sporting, Inc.; New England Arms Co.)
Gamo (See U.S. importers—Daisy Mfg. Co.; Dynamit Nobel-RWS, Inc.)
Gander Mountain, Inc., P.O. Box 128, Hwy. W, Wilmot, WI 53192/414-862-2331
Gander Mt. Inc., 1307 Miller Trunk Highway, Duluth, MN 55811/218-726-1100
Garbi, Armas Urki, 12-14, 20.600 Eibar (Guipuzcoa) SPAIN/43-11 38 73 (U.S. importer—Moore & Co., Wm. Larkin)
Garfield Gunsmithing, 237 Wessington Ave., Garfield, NJ 07026/201-478-0171
Garrett Gunsmiths, Inc., Peter, 838 Monmouth St., Newport, KY 41071-1821/606-261-1855
Gart Brothers Sporting Goods, 1000 Broadway, Denver, CO 80203/303-861-1122
Gary's Gun Shop, 905 W. 41st St., Sioux Falls, SD 57104/605-332-6119
Gene's Gunsmithing, Box 34 GRP 326 R.R. 3, Selkirk, Manitoba, CANADA R1A 2A8/204-757-4413
Genecco Gun Works, K., 10512 Lower Sacramento Rd., Stockton, CA 95210/209-951-0706
Gentry Custom Gunmaker, David, 314 N. Hoffman, Belgrade, MT 59714/406-388-4867
GFR Corp., P.O. Box 430, Andover, NH 03216/603-735-5300
Giacomo Sporting, Inc., Delta Plaza, Rt. 26N, Rome, NY 13440
Gibbs Rifle Co., Inc., Cannon Hill Industrial Park, Rt. 2, Box 214 Hoffman, Rd./Martinsburg, WV 25401/304-274-0458; FAX: 304-274-0078
Gilbert Equipment Co., Inc., 960 Downtowner Rd., Mobile, AL 36609/205-344-3322
Girard, Florent, Gunsmith, 598 Verreault, Chicoutimi, Quebec, CANADA G7H 2B8/418-696-3329
Glades Gunworks, 4360 Corporate Square, Naples, FL 33942/813-643-2922
Glenn's Reel & Rod Repair, 2210 E. 9th St., Des Moines, IA 50316/515-262-2990
Glock GmbH, P.O. Box 50, A-2232 Deutsch Wagram, AUSTRIA (U.S. importer—Glock, Inc.)
Glock, Inc., 6000 Highlands Parkway, Smyrna, GA 30082/404-432-1202: FAX: 404-433-8719
Gonic Arms, Inc., 134 Flagg Rd., Gonic, NH 03839/603-332-8456, 603-332-8457
Gonzalez Guns, Ramon B., P.O. Box 370, Monticello, NY 12701/914-794-4515
Gordon's Wigwam, 501 S. St. Francis, Wichita, KS 67202/316-264-5891
Gorenflo Gunsmithing, 1821 State St., Erie, PA 16501/814-452-4855
Great Lakes Airguns, 6175 S. Park Ave., Hamburg, NY 14075/716-648-6666; FAX: 716-648-5279
Green Acres Sporting Goods, Inc., 8774 Normandy Blvd., Jacksonville, FL 32221/904-786-5166
Greene's Gun Shop, 4778 Monkey Hill Rd., Oak Harbor, WA 98277/206-675-3421
Greenwood Precision, P.O. Box 468, Nixa, MO 65714-0468/417-725-2330
Grenada Gun Works, 942 Lakeview Drive, Grenada, MS 38901/601-226-9272
Grice Gun Shop, Inc., 216 Reed St., P.O. 1028, Clearfield, PA 16830/814-765-9273
Griffiths & Sons, E.J., 1014 N. McCullough St., Lima OH 45801/419-228-2141
Groenwold, John, P.O. Box 830, Mundelein, IL 60060-0830/708-566-2365
Grulla Armes, Apartado 453, Avda Otaloa, 12, Eiber, SPAIN (U.S. importer—American Arms, Inc.)
Grundman's, Inc., 75 Wildwood Ave., Rio Dell, CA 95562/707-764-5744
GSI, Inc., 108 Morrow Ave., P.O. Box 129, Trussville, AL 35173/205-655-8299; FAX: 205-655-7078
Gun & Tackle Store, The, 6041 Forrest Ln., Dallas, TX 75230/214-239-8181
Gun Ace Gunsmithing, 3975 West I-40 North, Hurricane, UT 84737/801-635-5212
Gun Center, The, 5831 Buckeystown Pike, Frederick, MD 21701/301-694-6887
Gun City USA, Inc., 573 Murfreesboro Rd., Nashville, TN 37210/615-256-6127
Gun City, 212 W. Main Ave., Bismarck, ND 58501/701-223-2304
Gun Corral, Inc., 2827 East College Ave., Decatur, GA 30030/404-299-0288
Gun Doc, Inc., 5405 N.W. 82nd Ave., Miami, FL 33166/305-477-2777
Gun Exchange, Inc., 5317 W. 65th St., Little Rock, AR 72209/501-562-4668
Gun Hospital, The, 45 Vineyard Ave., E. Providence, RI 02914/401-438-3495
Gun Rack, Inc., The, 213 Richland Ave., Aiken, SC 29801/803-648-7100
Gun Room, The, 201 Clark St., Chapin, SC 29036/803-345-2199
Gun Shop, The, 5550 S. 900 East, Salt Lake City, UT 84117/801-263-3633
Gun World, 392 Fifth Street, Elko, NV 89801/702-738-2666
Gunshop, Inc., The, 44633 N. Sierra Hwy., Lancaster CA 93534/805-942-8377
Gunsite Training Center, P.O. Box 700, Paulden, AZ 86334/602-636-4565; FAX: 602-636-1236
Gunsmith Co., The, 3435 S. State St., Salt Lake City, UT 84115/801-467-8244; FAX: 801-467-8256
Gunsmith, Inc., The, 1410 Sunset Blvd., West Columbia, SC 29169/803-791-0250
Gunsmithing Ltd., 57 Unquowa Rd., Fairfield, CT 06430/203-254-0436
Gunsmithing Specialties Co., 110 North Washington St., Papillion, NE 68046/402-339-1222

H

H&B Service, Inc., 7150 S. Platte Canyon Road, Littleton, CO 80123/970-979-5447
H&R 1871, Inc., 60 Industrial Rowe, Gardner, MA 01440/508-632-9393; FAX: 508-632-2300
H-S Precision, Inc., 1301 Turbine Dr., Rapid City, SD 57701/605-341-3006; FAX: 605-342-8964
Hämmerli Ltd., Seonerstrasse 37, CH-5600 Lenzburg, SWITZERLAND/064-50 11 44; FAX: 064-51 38 27 (U.S. importer—Hammerli USA)
Hagstrom, E.G., 2008 Janis Dr., Memphis, TN 38116/901-398-5333
Hal's Gun Supply, 320 Second Avenue SE, Cullman, AL 35055/205-734-7546
Hammerli USA, 19296 Oak Grove Circle, Groveland, CA 95321/209-962-5311; FAX: 209-962-5931
Hampel's, Inc., 710 Randolph, Traverse City, MI 49684/616-946-5485
Harris-McMillan Gunworks, 302 W. Melinda Lane, Phoenix, AZ 85027/602-582-9627; FAX: 602-582-5178
Harry's Army & Navy Store, 691 NJSH Rt. 130, Yardville, NJ 08691/609-585-5450
Hart & Son, Inc., Robert W., 401 Montgomery St., Nescopeck, PA 18635/717-752-3655, 800-368-3656; FAX: 717-752-1088
Hart's Gun Supply, Ed, U.S. Route 415, Bath, NY 14810/607-776-4228
Hatfield Gun Co., Inc., 224 N. 4th St., St. Joseph, MO 64501/816-279-8688; FAX: 816-279-2716
Hawken Shop, The (See Dayton Traister)
Heckler & Koch GmbH, Postfach 1329, D-7238 Oberndorf, Neckar, GERMANY (U.S. importer—Heckler & Koch, Inc.)
Heckler & Koch, Inc., 21480 Pacific Blvd., Sterling, VA 20166-8903/703-450-1900; FAX: 703-450-8160
Heckman Arms Company, 1736 Skyline Dr., Richmond Heights, OH 44143/216-289-9182
Helwan (See U.S. importer—Interarms)
Hemlock Gun Shop, Box 149, Rt. 590 & Crane Rd., Lakeville, PA 18438/717-226-9410
Henry's Airguns, 1204 W. Locust, Belvidere, IL 61008/815-547-5091
Herold's Gun Shoppe, 1498 E. Main Street, Box 350, Waynesboro, PA 17268/717-762-4010
Heym GmbH & Co. KG, Friedrich Wilh, Coburger Str.8, D-97702 Muennerstadt, GERMANY
Hi-Grade Imports, 8655 Monterey Rd., Gilroy, CA 95021/408-842-9301; FAX: 408-842-2374
Hi-Point Firearms, 5990 Philadelphia Dr., Dayton, OH 45415/513-275-4991; FAX: 513-275-4991
High Standard Mfg. Co., Inc., 264 Whitney St., Hartford, CT 06105-2270/203-586-8220; FAX: 203-231-0411
Hill Top Gunsmithing, Rt. 3, Box 85, Canton, NY 13617/315-386-4875
Hill's Hardware & Sporting Goods, 1234 S. Second St., Union City, TN 38261/901-885-1510
Hill's, Inc., 1720 Capital Blvd., Raleigh, NC 27604/919-833-4884
HJS Arms, Inc., P.O. Box 3711, Brownsville, TX 78523-3711/800-453-2767, 210-542-2767
Hobbs Bicycle & Gun Sales, 406 E. Broadway, Hobbs, NM 88240/505-393-9815
Hodson & Son Pell Gun Repair, 4500 S. 100 E., Anderson, IN 46013/317-643-2055
Hoffman's Gun Center, Inc., 2208 Berlin Turnpike, Newington, CT 06111/203-666-8827
Hollywood Engineering, 10642 Arminta St., Sun Valley, CA 91352/818-842-8376
Holston Ent., Inc., P.O. Box 493, Piney Flats, TN 37686
Horchler's Gun Shop, 100 Ratlum Rd. RFD, Collinsville, CT 06022/203-379-1977
Hornady Mfg. Co., P.O. Box 1848, Grand Island, NE 68802/800-338-3220, 308-382-1390; FAX: 308-382-5761
Houma Gun Works, 1520 Grand Caillou Rd., Houma, LA 70363/504-872-2782
Howa Machinery, Ltd., Sukaguchi, Shinkawa-cho, Nishikasugai-gun, Aichi 452, JAPAN (U.S. importer—Interarms)
Huntington Die Specialties, 601 Oro Dam Blvd., Oroville, CA 95965/916-534-1210; FAX: 916-534-1212
Hutch's, 50 E. Main St., Lehi, UT 84043/801-768-3461
Hutchinson's Gun Repair, 507 Clifton St., Pineville, LA 71360/318-640-4315

I

IAI, 6226 Santos Diaz St., Irwindale, CA 91702/818-334-1200
IGA (See U.S. importer—Stoeger Industries)
Imbert & Smithers, Inc., 1144 El Camino Real, San Carlos, CA 94070/415-593-4207
IMI, P.O. Box 1044, Ramat Hasharon 47100, ISRAEL/972-3-5485222 (U.S. importer—Magnum Research, Inc.)
Interarms, 10 Prince St., Alexandria, VA 22314/703-548-1400; FAX: 703-549-7826
Intermountain Arms & Tackle, Inc., 105 E. Idaho St., Meridian, ID 83642/208-888-4911; FAX: 208-888-4381
Intermountain Arms & Tackle, Inc., 1375 E. Fairfield Ave., Meridian, ID 83642/208-888-4911; FAX: 208-888-4381
Intratec, 12405 SW 130th St., Miami, FL 33186/305-232-1821; FAX: 305-253-7207
Island Pond Gunshop, P.O. Box 428 Cross St., Island Pond, VT 05846/802-723-4546
Ithaca Aquisition Corp., Ithaca Gun, 891 Route 34B, King Ferry, NY 13081/315-364-7171; FAX: 315-364-5134

J

J&G Gunsmithing, 625 Vernon St., Roseville, CA 95678/916-782-7075
J&T Services, 12$^1/_2$ Woodlawn Ave., Bradford, PA 16701/814-368-3034
J.O. Arms Inc., 5709 Hartsdale, Houston, TX 77036/713-789-0745; FAX: 713-789-7513
Jack First, 1201 Turbine Drive, Rapid City, SD 57701/605-343-9544
Jack's Lock & Gun Shop, 32 4th St., Fond Du Lac, WI 54935/414-922-4420
Jackalope Gun Shop, 1048 S. 5th St., Douglas, WY 82633/307-358-3441
Jackson, Inc., Bill, 9501 U.S. 19 N., Pinellas Park, FL 34666/813-576-4169
Jacobsen's Gun Center, 612 Broadway St., Story City, IA 50248/515-733-2995
Jaeger, Inc., Paul/Dunn's, P.O. Box 449, 1 Madison Ave., Grand Junction, TN 38039/901-764-6909; FAX: 901-764-6503
JagerSport, Ltd., One Wholesale Way, Cranston, RI 02920/800-962-4867, 401-944-9682; FAX: 401-946-2587
Jansma, Jack J., 4320 Kalamazoo Ave., Grand Rapids, MI 49508/616-455-7810; FAX: 616-455-5212
Jay's Sports, Inc., North 88 West 15263 Main St., Menomonee Falls, WI 53051/414-251-0550
Jennings Firearms, Inc., 17692 Cowan, Irvine, CA 92714/714-252-7621; FAX: 714-252-7626
Jensen's Custom Ammunition, 5146 E. Pima, Tucson, AZ 85712/602-325-3346; FAX: 602-322-5704
Jerry's Gun Shop, P.O. Box 88, 100 Main St., Glenarm, IL 62536/217-483-4606
Jim's Gun & Service Center, 514 Tenth Ave. S.E., Aberdeen, SD 57401/605-225-9111
Jim's Trading Post, #10 Southwest Plaza, Pine Bluff, AR 71603/501-534-8591
Joe's Gun Shop, 4430 14th St., Dorr, MI 49323/616-877-4615
Joe's Gun Shop, 5215 W. Edgemont Ave., Phoenix, AZ 85035/602-233-0694
John Q's Quality Gunsmithing, 5165 Auburn Blvd., Sacramento, CA 95841/916-344-7669
Johnson Service, Inc., W., 3654 N. Adrian Rd., Adrian, MI 49221/517-265-2545
Jones, J.D. (See SSK Industries)
Jordan Gun Shop, 28 Magnolia Dr., Tifton, GA 31794/912-382-4251
JSL (Hereford) Ltd., 35 Church St., Hereford HR1 2LR ENGLAND/0432-355416; FAX: 0432-355242 (U.S. importer—Specialty Shooters Supply, Inc.)

K

K&M Industries, Inc., Box 66, 510 S. Main, Troy, ID 83871/208-835-2281; FAX: 208-835-5211
K.B.I., Inc., P.O. Box 5440, Harrisburg, PA 17110-0440/717-540-8518; FAX: 717-540-8567
Kahles U.S.A., P.O. Box 81071, Warwick, RI 02888/800-752-4537: FAX: 401-946-2587
Kahnke Gunworks, 206 West 11th St., Redwood Falls, MN 56283/507-637-2901
Kahr Arms, P.O. Box 220, 630 Route 303, Blauvelt, NY 10913/914-353-5996; FAX: 914-353-7833
Karrer's Gunatorium, 5323 N. Argonne Rd., Spokane, WA 99212/509-924-3030
Kassnar (See U.S. importer—K.B.I., Inc.)
Keidel's Gunsmithing Service, 927 Jefferson Ave., Washington, PA 15301/412-222-6379
Kel-Tec CNC Industries, Inc., P.O. Box 3427, Cocoa, FL 32924/407-631-0068; FAX: 407-631-1169
Kelbly, Inc., 7222 Dalton Fox Lake Rd., North Lawrence, OH 44666/216-683-4674; FAX: 216-683-7349
Keller's Co., Inc., 511 Spielman Hwy., Rt. 4, Burlington, CT 06013/203-583-2220
Keng's Firearms Specialty, Inc., 875 Wharton Dr. SW, Atlanta, GA 30336/404-691-7611; FAX: 404-505-8445
Kesselring Gun Shop, 400 Hwy. 99 North, Burlington, WA 98233/206-724-3113; FAX: 206-724-7003
Kesselring Gun Shop, 400 Pacific Hwy. 99 North, Burlington, WA 98233/206-724-3113; FAX: 206-724-7003
Kick's Sport Center, 300 Goodge St., Claxton, GA 30417/912-739-1734
Kielon, Gunsmith, Dave, 57 Kittleberger Park, Webster, NY 14580/716-872-2256
Kimber of America, Inc., 9039 SE Jannsen Rd., Clackamas, OR 97015/503-656-1704, 800-880-2418; FAX: 503-656-5357
Kimel Industries, 3800 Old Monroe Rd., P.O. Box 335, Matthews, NC 28105/800-438-9288; FAX: 704-821-6339
King's Gun Shop, Inc., 32301 Walter's Hwy., Franklin, VA 23851/804-562-4725
Kingyon, Paul L., 607 N. 5th St., Burlington, IA 52601/319-752-4465
Kirkpatrick, Gunsmith, Larry, 707 79th St., Lubbock, TX 79404/806-745-5308
Knight's Mfg. Co., 7750 9th St. SW, Vero Beach, FL 32968/407-562-5697; FAX: 407-569-2955
Kopp, Prof. Gunsmith, Terry K., 1301 Franklin, Lexington, MO 64067/816-259-2636
Korth, Robert-Bosch-Str. 4, P.O. Box 1320, 23909 Ratzeburg, GERMANY/0451-4991497; FAX: 0451-4993230 (U.S. importers—Interarms; Mandall Shooting Supplies, Inc.)
Kotila Gun Shop, 726 County Rd. 3SW, Cokato, MN 55321/612-286-5636
Kowa Optimed, Inc., 20001 S. Vermont Ave., Torrance, CA 90502/310-327-1913; FAX: 310-327-4177

Krebs Gunsmithing, 7417 N. Milwaukee Ave., Niles, IL 60714/708-647-6994
Krico/Kriegeskorte GmbH, A., Nurnbergerstrasse 6, D-90602 Pyrbaum GERMANY/0911-796092; FAX: 0911-796074 (U.S. importer—Mandall Shooting Supplies, Inc.)
Krieghoff Gun Co., H., Boschstrasse 22, D-89079 Ulm, GERMANY/731-401820; FAX: 731-4018270 (U.S. importer—Krieghoff International, Inc.)
Krieghoff International, Inc., 7528 Easton Rd., Ottsville, PA 18942/610-847-5173; FAX: 610-847-8691
KSN Industries, Ltd. (See U.S. importer—J.O. Arms Inc.)

L

L&S Technologies, Inc. (See Aimtech Mount Systems)
L'Armurier Alain Bouchard, Inc., 420 Route 143, Ulverton, Quebec CANADA J0B 2J0/819-826-6611
L.A.R. Mfg., Inc., 4133 W. Farm Rd., West Jordan, UT 84088/801-280-3505; FAX: 801-280-1972
Labs Air Gun Shop, 2307 N. 62nd St., Omaha, NE 68104/402-553-0990
LaFrance Specialties, P.O. Box 178211, San Diego, CA 92177-8211/619-293-3373
Laib's Gunsmithing, North Hwy. 23, R.R. 1, Spicer, MN 56288/612-796-2686
Lakefield Arms Ltd., 248 Water St., P.O. Box 129, Lakefield, Ont. K0L 2H0, CANADA/705-652-6735, 705-652-8000; FAX: 705-652-8431
Lapua Ltd., P.O. Box 5, Lapua, FINLAND SF-62101/64-310111; FAX: 64-4388951 (U.S. importers—Champion's Choice; Keng's Firearms Specialty, Inc.
Laser Devices, Inc., 2 Harris Ct. A-4, Monterey, CA 93940/408-373-0701; FAX: 408-373-0903
Laseraim, Inc. (See Emerging Technologies, Inc.)
Laurona Armas Eiber, S.A.L., Avenida de Otaola 25, P.O. Box 260, 20600 Eibar, SPAIN/34-43-700600; FAX: 34-43-700616 (U.S. importers—Continental Imports & Distribution; Galaxy Imports Ltd., Inc.)
Lawson's Custom Firearms, Inc., Art, 313 S. Magnolia Ave., Ocala, FL 32671/904-629-7793
Lebeau-Courally, Rue St. Gilles, 386, 4000 Liege, BELGIUM/041 52 48 43; FAX: 041 52 20 08 (U.S. importer—New England Arms Co.
Lee Precision, Inc., 4275 Hwy. U, Hartford, WI 53027/414-673-3075
LeFever & Sons, Inc., Frank, 6234 Stokes-Lee Center Rd., Lee Center, NY 13363/315-337-6722
Leica USA, Inc., 156 Ludlow Ave., Northvale, NJ 07647/201-767-7500; FAX: 201-767-8666
Leo's Custom Stocks, 1767 Washington Ave., Library, PA 15129/412-835-4126
Les Gun & Pawn Shop, 1423 New Boston Rd., Texarkana, TX 75501/903-793-2201
Leupold & Stevens, Inc., P.O. Box 688, Beaverton, OR 97075/503-646-9171; FAX: 503-526-1455
Levan's Sporting Goods, 433 N. Ninth St., Lebanon, PA 17042/717-273-3148
Lew's Mountaineer Gunsmithing, Route 2, Box 330A, Charleston, WV 25314/304-344-3745
Lewis Arms, 1575 Hooksett Rd., Hooksett, NH 03106/603-485-7334
Llama Gabilondo Y Cia, Apartado 290, E-01080, Victoria, SPAIN (U.S. importer—SGS Importers International, Inc.)
Lock Stock & Barrel, 115 SW H St., Grants Pass, OR 97526/503-474-0775
Loftin & Taylor, 2619 N. Main St., Jacksonville, FL 32206/904-353-9634
Log Cabin Sport Shop, 8010 Lafayette Rd., Lodi, OH 44254/216-948-1082
Lolo Sporting Goods, 1026 Main St., Lewiston, ID 83501/208-743-1031
Lone Star Guns, Inc., 2452 Avenue K, Plano, TX 75074/214-424-4501; 800-874-7923
Long Beach Uniform Co., Inc., 2789 Long Beach Blvd., Long Beach, CA 90806/310-424-0220
Longacres, Inc., 358 Chestnut St., Abilene, TN 79602/915-672-9521
Longs Gunsmithing Ltd., W.R., P.O. Box 876, 2 Coverdale St., Cobourg, Ontario CANADA K9A 4H1/416-372-5955
Lorcin Engineering Co., Inc., 10427 San Sevaine Way, Ste. A, Mira Loma, CA 91752/909-360-1406; FAX: 909-360-0623
Lounsbury Sporting Goods, Bob, 104 North St., Middletown, NY 10940/914-343-1808
Lusignant, Armurier, A. Richard, 15820 St. Michel, St. Hyacinthe, Quebec, CANADA, J2T 3R7/514-773-7997
Lutter, Robert E., 3547 Auer Dr., Ft. Wayne, IN 46835/219-485-8319
Lyman Products Corp., Rt. 147, Middlefield, CT 06455/203-349-3421, 800-22-LYMAN; FAX: 203-349-3586

M

M.O.A. Corp., 2451 Old Camden Pike, Eaton, OH 45320/513-456-3669
Mac-1 Distributors, 13974 Van Ness Ave., Gardena, CA 90249/310-327-3582
Magasin Latulippe, Inc., 637 West St. Vallier, P.O. Box 395, Quebec City, Quebec, CANADA G1K 6W8/418-529-0024; FAX: 418-529-6381
Magma Engineering Co., P.O. Box 161, 20955 E. Ocotillo Rd., Queen Creek, AZ 85242/602-987-9008; FAX: 602-987-0148
Magnum Gun Service, 357 Welsh Track Rd., Newark, DE 19702/302-454-0141
Magnum Research, Inc., 7110 University Ave. NE, Minneapolis, MN 55432/612-574-1868; FAX: 612-574-0109
MAGTECH Recreational Products, Inc., 4737 College Park, Ste. 101, San Antonio, TX 78249/210-493-4427; FAX: 210-493-9534
Mandall Shooting Supplies, Inc., 3616 N. Scottsdale Rd., Scottsdale, AZ 85252/602-945-2553; FAX: 602-949-0734
Marksman Products, 5482 Argosy Dr., Huntington Beach, CA 92649/714-898-7535, 800-822-8005; FAX: 714-372-3041
Marlin Firearms Co., 100 Kenna Dr., New Haven, CT 06473/203-239-5621; FAX: 203-234-7991
Marocchi F.lli S.p.A., Via Galileo Galilei, I-25068 Zanano di Sarezzo, ITALY (U.S. importers—PSI, Inc.; Sile Distributors)
Martin Gun Shop, Henry, 206 Kay Lane, Shreveport, LA 71115/318-797-1119
Martin's Gun Shop, 3600 Laurel Ave., Natchez, MS 39120/601-442-0784
Mashburn Arms Co., Inc., 1218 North Pennsylvania Ave., Oklahoma City, OK 73107/405-236-5151
Mason, Guns & Ammo Co., Tom, 68 Lake Avenue, Danbury, CT 06810/203-778-6421
Master Gunsmiths, Inc., 12621 Tyconderoga, Houston, TX 77044/713-459-1631
Matt's 10X Gunsmithing, Inc., 5906 Castle Rd., Duluth, MN 55803/218-721-4210
Mauser Werke Oberndorf Waffensysteme GmbH, Postfach 1349, 78722 Oberndorf/N. GERMANY (U.S. importer—Gibbs Rifle Co., Inc.)
Maverick Arms, Inc., 7 Grasso Ave., P.O. Box 497, North Haven, CT 06473/203-230-5300; FAX: 203-230-5420
May & Company, Inc., P.O. Box 1111, 838 W. Capitol St., Jackson, MS 39203/601-354-5781
McBride's Guns, Inc., 2915 San Gabriel, Austin, TX 78705/512-472-3532
McBros Rifle Co., P.O. Box 86549, Phoenix, AZ 85080/602-780-2115; FAX: 602-581-3825
McCann's Machine & Gun Shop, P.O. Box 641, Spanaway, WA 98387/206-537-6919; FAX: 206-537-6993
McClelland Gun Shop, 1533 Centerville Rd., Dallas, TX 75228-2597/214-321-0231
McDaniel Co., Inc., B., 8880 Pontiac Tr., P.O. Box 119, South Lyon, MI 48178/313-437-8989
McGuns, W.H., N. 22nd Ave. at Osborn St., Humboldt, TN 38343/901-784-5742
McMillan Rifle Barrels, P.O. Box 3427, Bryan, TX 77805/409-690-3456; FAX: 409-690-0156
MCS, Inc., 34 Delmar Dr., Brookfield, CT 06804/203-775-1013; FAX: 203-775-9462
MEC, Inc., 715 South St., Mayville, WI 53050/414-387-4500; FAX: 414-387-5802
MEC-Gar S.R.L., Via Madonnina 64, Gardone V.T., Brescia, ITALY 25063/39-30-8912687; FAX: 39-30-8910065 (U.S. importer—MEC-Gar U.S.A., Inc.)
MEC-Gar U.S.A., Inc., Box 112, 500B Monroe Turnpike, Monroe, CT 06468/203-635-8662; FAX: 203-635-8662
Merkel Freres, Strasse 7 October, 10, Suhl, GERMANY (U.S. importer—GSI, Inc.)
Metro Rod & Reel, 236 S.E. Grand Ave., Portland, OR 97214/503-232-3193
Meydag, Peter, 12114 East 16th, Tulsa, OK 74128/918-437-1928
Miclean, Bill, 499 Theta Ct., San Jose, CA 95123/408-224-1445
Midwestern Shooters Supply, Inc., 150 Main St., Lomira, WI 53048/414-269-4995
Mike's Crosman Service, 5995 Renwood Dr., Winston-Salem, NC 27106/910-922-1031
Mill Creek Sport Center, 8180 Main St., Dexter, MI 48104/313-426-3445
Miller Arms, Inc., P.O. Box 260 Purl St., St. Onge, SD 57779/605-642-5160; FAX: 605-642-5160
Miller's Sport Shop, 2 Summit View Dr., Mountaintop, PA 18707/717-474-6931
Millers Gun Shop, 915 23rd St., Gulfport, MS 39501/601-684-1765
Milliken's Gun Shop, Rt. 2, Box 167, Elm Grove, WV 26003/304-242-0827
Mines Gun Shack, Rt. 4 Box 4623, Tullahoma, TN 37388/615-455-1414
Mirador Optical Corp., P.O. Box 11614, Marina Del Rey, CA 90295-7614/310-821-5587; FAX: 310-305-0386
Miroku, B.C./Daly, Charles (See U.S. importer—Bell's Legendary Country Wear; U.S. distributor—Outdoor Sports Headquarters, Inc.)
Mitchell Arms, Inc., 3400-I W. MacArthur Blvd., Santa Ana, CA 92704/714-957-5711; FAX: 714-957-5732
MKS Supply, Inc., 174 S. Mulberry St., Mansfield, OH 44902/419-522-8330; FAX: 513-522-8330
Mo's Competitor Supplies (See MCS, Inc.)
Moates Sport Shop, Bob, 10418 Hull St. Rd., Midlothian, VA 23112/804-276-2293
Modern Guncraft, 148 N. Branford Rd., Wallingford, CT 06492/203-265-1015
Modern MuzzleLoading, Inc., 234 Airport Rd., P.O. Box 130, Centerville, IA 52544/515-856-2626; FAX: 515-856-2628
Moneymaker Guncraft Corp., 1420 Military Ave., Omaha, NE 68131/402-556-0226
Montana Armory, Inc., 100 Centennial Dr., Big Timber, MT 59011/406-932-4353
Montana Gun Works, 3017 10th Ave. S., Great Falls, MT 59405/406-761-4346
Moore & Co., Wm. Larkin, 31360 Via Colinas, Suite 109, Westlake Village, CA 91361/818-889-1986
Moreau, Gunsmith, Pete, 1807 S. Erie, Bay City, MI 48706/517-893-7106
Morini (See U.S. importers—Mandall Shooting Shpplies, Inc.; Nygord Precision Products)
Morrison Gun Shop, Middle Rd., Bradford, ME 04410/207-327-1116
Mossberg (See page 503)
Mowrey Gun Works, P.O. Box 246, Waldron, IN 46182/317-525-6181; FAX: 317-525-6181
Mueschke Manufacturing Co., 1003 Columbia St., Houston, TX 77008/713-869-7073
Mulvey's Marine & Sport Shop, 994 E. Broadway, Monticello, NY 12701/914-794-2000

N

N.A. Guns, Inc., 10220 Florida Blvd., Baton Rouge, LA 70815/504-272-3620
Nagel Gun Shop, Inc., 6201 San Pedro Ave., San Antonio, TX 78216/210-342-5420; 210-342-9893
Nationwide Sports Distributors, Inc., 70 James Way, Southampton, PA 18966/215-322-2050, 800-355-3006; FAX: 702-358-2093
Navy Arms Co., 689 Bergen Blvd., Ridgefield, NJ 07657/201-945-2500; FAX: 201-945-6859
NCP Products, Inc., 721 Maryland Ave. SW, Canton, OH 44710
Nelson's Engine Shop, 620 State St., Cedar Falls, IA 50613/319-266-4497
Nesika Bay Precision, 22239 Big Valley Rd., Poulsbo, WA 98370/206-697-3830
Nevada Air Guns, 3297 "J" Las Vegas Blvd. N., Las Vegas, NV 89115/702-643-8532
Nevada Cartridge Co., 44 Montgomery St., Suite 500, San Francisco, CA 94104/415-925-9394; FAX: 415-925-9396
New Advantage Arms Corp., 2843 N. Alvernon Way, Tucson, AZ 85712/602-881-7444; FAX: 602-323-0949
New England Arms Co., Box 278, Lawrence Lane, Kittery Point, ME 03905/207-439-0593; FAX: 207-439-6726
New England Firearms, 60 Industrial Rowe, Gardner, MA 01440/508-632-9393; FAX: 508-632-2300
Newby, Stewart, Gunsmith, Main & Cross Streets, Newburgh, Ontario CANADA K0K 2S0/613-378-6613
Nicholson's Gunsmithing, 35 Hull St., Shelton, CT 06484/203-924-5635
Nikon, Inc., 1300 Walt Whitman Rd., Melville, NY 11747/516-547-8623; FAX: 516-547-0309
Noreen, Peter H., 5075 Buena Vista Dr., Belgrade, MT 59714/406-586-7383
Norinco, 7A, Yun Tan N Beijing, CHINA (U.S. importers—Century International Arms, Inc.; Interarms)
Norma Precision AB (See U.S. importers—Dynamit Nobel-RWS Inc.; Paul Co. Inc., The)
Norman Custom Gunstocks, Jim, 14281 Cane Rd., Valley Center, CA 92082/619-749-6252
Norrell Arms, John, 2608 Grist Mill Rd., Little Rock, AR 72207/501-225-7864
North American Arms, Inc., 2150 South 950 East, Provo, UT 84606-6285/800-821-5783, 801-374-9990; FAX: 801-374-9998
Northern Precision Airguns, 1161 Grove St., Tawas City, MI 48763/517-362-6949
Northern Virginia Gun Works, Inc., 7518-K Fullerton Road, Springfield, VA 22153/703-644-6504
Northland Sport Center, 1 Mile W. on U.S. Rt. 2, Bagley, MN 56621/218-694-2464
Northwest Arms Service, 720 S. Second St., Atwood, KS 67730/913-626-3700
Nu-Line Guns, Inc., 1053 Caulks Hill Rd., Harvester, MO 63304/314-441-4500; FAX: 314-447-5018
Nusbaum Enterprises, Inc., 1364 Ridgewood Dr., Mobile, AL 36608/205-344-1079
Nygord Precision Products, P.O. Box 8394, La Crescenta, CA 91224/818-352-3027; FAX: 818-352-3378

O

Old Dominion Engravers, 100 Progress Drive, Lynchburg, VA 24502/804-237-4450
Old Western Scrounger, Inc., 12924 Hwy. A-l2, Montague, CA 96064/916-459-5445; FAX: 916-459-3944
Olympic Arms, 620-626 Old Pacific Hwy. SE, Olympic, WA 98503/360-456-3471; FAX: 360-491-3447
On Target Gunshop, Inc., 6984 West Main St., Kalamazoo, MI 49009/616-375-4570
Oregon Arms, Inc., 790 Stevens St., Medford, OR 97504-6746/503-560-4040
Orvis Co., The, Rt. 7, Manchester, VT 05254/802-362-3622 ext. 283; FAX: 802-362-3525
Oshman's Sporting Goods, Inc., 975 Gessner, Houston, TX 77024/713-467-1155
Ott's Gun Service, Rt. 2, Box 169A, Atmore, AL 36502/205-862-2588
Outdoor America Store, 1925 N. MacArthur Blvd., Oklahoma City, OK 73127/405-789-0051
Outdoorsman Sporting Goods Co., The, 1707 Radner Ct., Geneva, IL 60134/708-232-9518
Outdoorsman, The, Village West Shopping Center, Fargo, ND 58103/701-282-0131
Outpost, The, 2451 E. Maple Rapids Rd., Eureka, MI 48833/517-224-9562
Ozark Shooters, Inc., P.O. Box 6518, Branson, MO 65616/417-587-3093

P

Pace Marketing, Inc., P.O. Box 2039, Stuart, FL 34995/407-223-2189; FAX: 407-286-9547
Pachmayr, Ltd., 1875 S. Mountain Ave., Monrovia, CA 91016/818-357-7771, 800-423-9704; FAX: 818-358-7251
Pacific International Service Co., Mountain Way, P.O. Box 3, Janesville, CA 96114/916-253-2218

Paducah Shooters Supply, Inc., 3919 Cairo St., Paducah, KY 42001/502-443-3758
Para-Ordnance Mfg., Inc., 3411 McNicoll Ave., Unit 14, Scarborough, Ont. M1V 2V6, CANADA/416-297-7855; FAX: 416-297-1289 (U.S. importer—Para-Ordnance, Inc.)
Para-Ordnance, Inc., 1919 NE 45th St., Ft. Lauderdale, FL 33308
Pardini Armi Srl, Via Italica 154, 55043 Lido Di Camaiore Lu, ITALY/584-90121; FAX: 584-90122 (U.S. importers—MCS, Inc.; Nygord Precision Products)
Pasadena Gun Center, 206 E. Shaw, Pasadena, TX 77506/713-472-0417; FAX: 713-472-1322
Paul Co., The, 27385 Pressonville Rd., Wellsville, KS 66092/913-883-4444; FAX: 913-883-2525
Pedersoli Davide & C., Via Artigiani 57, Gardone V.T., Brescia, ITALY 25063/030-8912402; FAX: 030-8911019 (U.S. importers—Beauchamp & Son, Inc.; Cabela's; Cape Outfitters; Dixie Gun Works; EMF Co., Inc.; Navy Arms Co.; Taylor's & Co., Inc.)
Pederson Co., C.R., 2717 S. Pere Marquette, Ludington, MI 49431/616-843-2061
Pekin Gun & Sporting Goods, 1304 Derby St., Pekin, IL 61554/309-347-6060
Pentax Corp., 35 Inverness Dr. E., Englewood, CO 80112/303-799-8000; FAX: 303-790-1131
Perazzi m.a.p. S.P.A., Via Fontanelle 1/3, 1-25080 Botticino Mattina, ITALY (U.S. importer—Perazzi USA, Inc.)
Perazzi USA, Inc., 1207 S. Shamrock Ave., Monrovia, CA 91016/818-303-0068; FAX: 818-303-2081
Peregrine Sporting Arms, Inc., 14155 Brighton Rd., Brighton, CO 80601/303-654-0850
Perry's Gunshop, P.O. Box 10, 21 E. Third St., Wendell, NC 27591/919-365-4200
Pete's Gun Shop, 31 Columbia St., Adams, MA 01220/413-743-0780
Peters Stahl GmbH, Stettiner Strasse 42, D-33106 Paderborn, GERMANY/05251-750025; FAX: 05251-75611 (U.S. importers—Harris-McMillan Gunworks; Olympic Arms)
Phillips, D.J., Gunsmith, Rt. 1, N31-W22087 Shady Ln., Pewaukee, WI 53072/414-691-2165
Phoenix Armoury, Inc., 248 Miami Ave., Norristown, PA 19403/215-539-0733
Phoenix Arms, 1420 S. Archibald Ave., Ontario, CA 91761/909-947-4843; FAX: 909-947-6798
PHOXX Shooters Supply, 5807 Watt Ave., N. Highlands, CA 95660/800-280-8668
Pietta (See U.S. importers—Navy Arms Co.; Taylor's & Co., Inc.)
Pintos Gun Shop, 827 N. Central #102, Kent, WA 98032/206-859-6333
Pioneer Arms Co., 355 Lawrence Rd., Broomall, PA 19008/215-356-5203
Piotti (See U.S. importer—Moore & Co., Wm. Larkin)
Plaza Gunworks, Inc., 983 Gasden Highway, Birmingham, AL 35235/205-836-6206
Ponsness/Warren, P.O. Box 8, Rathdrum, ID 83858/208-687-2231; FAX: 208-687-2233
Poor Borch's, Inc., 1204 E. College Dr., Marshall, MN 56258/507-532-4880
Potter Gunsmithing, 13960 Boxhorn Dr., Muskego, WI 53150/414-425-4830
Powell & Son (Gunmakers) Ltd., William, 35-37 Carrs Lane, Birmingham B4 7SX ENGLAND/21-643-0689; FAX: 21-631-3504 (U.S. importer—The William Powell Agency)
Powell Agency, William, The, 22 Circle Dr., Bellmore, NY 11710/516-679-1158
Prairie River Arms, 1220 N. Sixth St., Princeton, IL 61356/815-875-1616; FAX: 815-875-1402
Precision Airgun Sales, Inc., 5139 Warrensville Center Rd., Maple Hts., OH 44137-1906/216-587-5005
Precision Arms & Gunsmithing Ltd., Hwy. 27 & King Road Box 809, Nobleton, Ontario, CANADA L0G 1N0/416-859-0965
Precision Gun Works, 4717 State Rd. 44, Oshkosh, WI 54904/414-233-2274
Precision Gunsmithing, 2723 W. 6th St., Amarillo, TX 79106/806-376-7223
Precision Pellet, 1016 Erwin Dr., Joppa, MD 21085/410-679-8179
Precision Reloading, Inc., P.O. Box 122, Stafford Springs, CT 06076/203-684-7979; FAX: 203-684-6788
Precision Sales International, Inc., P.O. Box 1776, Westfield, MA 01086/413-562-5055; FAX: 413-562-5056
Precision Small Arms, 155 Carlton Rd., Charlottesville, VA 22902/804-293-6124; FAX: 804-295-0780
Precision Sport Optics, 15571 Producer Lane, Unit G, Huntington Beach, CA 92649/714-891-1309; FAX: 714-892-6920
Preuss Gun Shop, 4545 E. Shepherd, Clovis, CA 93612/209-299-6248
Professional Armaments, Inc., 3695 South Redwood Rd., West Valley City, UT 84119/801-975-7422

Q

Quad City Gun Repair, 220 N. Second St., Eldridge, IA 52748/319-285-4153
Quality Arms, Inc., Box 19477, Dept. GD, Houston, TX 77224/713-870-8377; FAX: 713-870-8524
Quality Firearms of Idaho, Inc., 114 13th Ave. S., Nampa, ID 83651/208-466-1631
Quality Parts Co./Bushmaster Firearms, 999 Roosevelt Trail, Bldg. 3, Windham, ME 04062/800-998-7928, 207-892-2005; FAX: 207-892-8068

R

R&R Shooters Supply, W6553 North Rd., Mauston, WI 53948/608-847-4562
R.D.P. Tool Co., Inc., 49162 McCoy Ave., East Liverpool, OH 43920/216-385-5129
R.L. "Skeet" Hill Gun Shop, 209 1/2 Raymond Street, P.O. Box 457, Verona, MS 38879/601-566-8353
Rajo Corporation, 2106 W. Franklin St., Evansville, IN 47712/812-422-6945
Ralph's Gun Shop, 200 Fourth St., South, Niverville, Manitoba, CANADA R0A 1E0/204-338-4581
Ram-Line, Inc., 545 Thirty-One Rd., Grand Junction, CO 81504/303-434-4500; FAX: 303-434-4004
Randy's Gun Repair, P.O. Box 106, 231 Hierlihy High, Tabustinac, N.B. CANADA E0C 2A0/506-779-4768
Ranging, Inc., Routes 5 & 20, East Bloomfield, NY 14443/716-657-6161; FAX: 716-657-5405
Rapids Gun Shop, 7811 Buffalo Ave., Niagara Falls, NY 14304/716-283-7873
Ravell Ltd., 289 Diputacion St., 08009, Barcelona SPAIN
Ray's Gunsmith Shop, 3199 Elm Ave., Grand Junction, CO 81504/970-434-6162
Ray's Liquor and Sporting Goods, 1956 Solano St., Box 677, Corning, CA 96021/916-824-5625
Ray's Rod & Reel Service, 414 Pattie St., Wichita, KS 67211/316-267-9462
Ray's Sport Shop, Inc., 559 Route 22, North Plainfield, NJ 07060/908-561-4400
Ray's Sporting Goods, 730 Singleton Blvd., Dallas, TX 75212/214-747-7916
RCBS, Div. of Blount, Inc., 605 Oro Dam Blvd., Oroville, CA 95965/800-533-5000, 916-533-5191; FAX: 916-533-1647
Red's Gunsmithing, P.O. Box 1251, Chickaloon, AK 99674/907-745-4500
Redding Reloading Equipment, 1089 Starr Rd., Cortland, NY 13045/607-753-3331; FAX: 607-756-8445
Redfield, Inc., 5800 E. Jewell Ave., Denver, CO 80227/303-757-6411; FAX: 303-756-2338
Reliable Gun & Tackle, Ltd., 3227 Fraser St., Vancouver, British Columbia CANADA V5V 4B8/604-874-4710
Reloading Center, 515 W. Main St., Burley, ID 83318/208-678-5053
Remington (See page 503)
Reynold's Gun Shop, Inc., 3502A S. Broadway, Tyler, TX 75702/903-592-1531
Reynolds Gun Shop, 314 N. Western Ave., Peoria, IL 61606/309-674-5790
Richland Gun Shop, 207 Park St., Box 645, Richland, PA 17087/717-866-4246
Richmond Gun Shop, 517 E. Main St., Richmond, VA 23219/804-644-7207
Rigby & Co., John, 66 Great Suffolk St., London SE1 OBU, ENGLAND
River Bend Sport Shop, 230 Grand Seasons Dr., Waupaca, WI 54981/715-258-3583
Rizzini, Battista, Via 2 Giugno, 7/7Bis-25060 Marcheno (Brescia), ITALY (U.S. importers—Alessandri & Son, Lou; New England Arms Co.)
Rizzini, F.LLI (See U.S. importers—Moore & Co. Wm. Larkin; New England Arms Co.)
Robinson's Sporting Goods, Ltd., 1307 Broad St., Victoria, British Columbia CANADA V8W 2A8/604-385-3429
Rocking S Gun Shop, 316 VC Ranches, Hwy. 287, P.O. Box 1469, Ennis, MT 59729/406-682-5229
Rocky Mountain Arms, Inc., 600 S. Sunset, Unit C, Longmont, CO 80501/303-768-8522; FAX: 303-678-8766
Ron's Gun Repair, 1212 Benson Road, Sioux Falls, SD 57104/605-338-7398
Rossi S.A., Amadeo, Rua: Amadeo Rossi, 143, Sao Leopoldo, RS, BRAZIL 93030-220/051-592-5566 (U.S. importer—Interarms)
Ruko Products, Inc., 2245 Kenmore Ave., No. 102, Buffalo, NY 14207/716-874-2707; FAX: 905-826-1353
Rusk Gun Shop, Inc., 6904 Watts Rd., Madison, WI 53719/608-274-8740
Russell's Sporting Goods, 8228 Macleod Trail SE, Calgary, Alberta, CANADA T2M 2B8/403-276-9222
Rutko Corp. d/b/a Stonewall Range, 100 Ken-Mar Dr., Broadview Heights, OH 44147/216-526-0029
RWS (See U.S. importer—Dynamit Nobel-RWS, Inc.)

S

S.E.M. Gun Works, 3204 White Horse Rd., Greenville, SC 29611/803-295-2948
S.K. Guns, Inc., 302 25th St. South, Suite A, Fargo, ND 58103/701-293-4867; FAX: 701-232-0001
Sabatti S.R.L., via Alessandro Volta 90, 25063 Gardone V.T., Brescia, ITALY/030-8912207-831312; FAX: 030-8912059 (U.S. importer—E.A.A. Corp.)
Safari Arms/SWG (See Olympic Arms)
Sako Ltd., P.O. Box 149, SF-11101, Riihimaki, FINLAND (U.S. importer—Stoeger Industries)
Sams Gunsmithing, David, 225 Front St., Lititz, PA 17543/717-626-0021
San Marco (See U.S. importers—Cape Outfitters; EMF Co., Inc.)
Sanders Custom Gun Service, 2358 Tyler Ln., Louisville, KY 40205/502-454-3338
Sanders Custom Gun Shop, P.O. Box 5967, 2031 Bloomingdale Ave., Augusta, GA 30906/706-798-5220
Sanders Gun Shop, 3001 Fifth St., P.O. Box 4181, Meridian, MS 39301/601-485-5301
Saskatoon Gunsmith Shoppe, Ltd., 2310 Avenue C North, Saskatoon, Saskachewan, CANADA S7L 5X5/306-244-2023
Sauer (See U.S. importer—Paul Co., The)
Savage Arms, Inc., 100 Springdale Rd., Westfield, MA 01085/413-568-7001; FAX: 413-562-7764
Saville Iron Co. (See Greenwood Precision)
Scalzo's Sporting Goods, 1520 Farm to Market Road, Endwell, NY 13760/607-746-7586
Scattergun Technologies, Inc., 518 3rd Ave. S., Nashville, TN 37202/615-254-1441; FAX: 615-254-1449
Scharch Mfg., Inc., 10325 Co. Rd. 120, Unit C, Salida, CO 81201/719-539-7242; FAX: 719-539-3021
Schmidt & Bender, Inc., Brook Rd., P.O. Box 134, Meriden, NH 03770/603-469-3565, 800-468-3450; FAX: 603-469-3471
Schultheis Sporting Goods, 8 Main St., Arkport, NY 14807/607-295-7485
Sea Gull Marina, 1400 Lake, Two Rivers, WI 54241/414-794-7533
Seecamp Co., Inc., L.W., P.O. Box 255, New Haven, CT 06502/203-877-3429
Selin Gunsmith, Ltd., Del, 2803 23rd Street, Vernon, British Columbia, CANADA V1T 4Z5/604-545-6413
SGS Importers International, Inc., 1750 Brielle Ave., Unit B1, Wanamassa, NJ 07712/908-493-0302; FAX: 908-493-0301
Shaler Eagle, 102 Arrow Wood, Jonesbrough, TN 37659/615-753-7620
Shamburg's Wholesale Spt. Gds., 403 Frisco Ave., Clinton, OK 73601/405-323-0209
Shapel's Gun Shop, 1708 N. Liberty, Boise, ID 83704/208-375-6159
Sharp (See U.S. importer—Great Lakes Airguns)
Sharps Arms Co., Inc., C. (See Montana Armory, Inc.)
Shepherd Scope Ltd., Box 189, Waterloo, NE 68069/402-779-2424; FAX: 402-779-4010
Sheridan USA, Inc., Austin, P.O. Box 577, 36 Haddam Quarter Rd., Durham, CT 06422/203-349-1772; FAX: 203-349-1771
Shiloh Rifle Mfg., 201 Centennial Dr., Big Timber, MT 59011/406-932-4454; FAX: 406-932-5627
Shockley, Harold, 2204 E. Farmington Road, Hanna City, IL 61536/309-565-4524
Shooters Supply, 1120 Tieton Dr., Yakima, WA 98902/509-482-1181; FAX: 509-575-0315
Shooting Gallery, The, 249 Seneca, Weirton, WV 26062/304-723-3298
Siegle's Gunshop, Inc., 508 W. MacArthur Blvd., Oakland, CA 94609/415-655-8789
Sievert's Guns 4107 W. Northern, Pueblo, CO 81005/719-564-0035
SIG, CH-8212 Neuhausen, SWITZERLAND (U.S. importer—Mandall Shooting Supplies, Inc.)
SIG-Sauer (See U.S. importer—Sigarms, Inc.)
Sigarms, Inc., Corporate Park, Exeter, NH 03833/603-772-2302; FAX: 603-772-9082
Sile Distributors, Inc., 7 Centre Market Pl., New York, NY 10013/212-925-4111; FAX: 212-925-3149
Sillman, Hal, Associated Services, 1514 NE 205 Terrace, Miami, FL 33179/305-651-4450
Simmons Enterprises, Ernie, 709 East Elizabethtown Rd., Manheim, PA 17545/717-664-4040
Simmons Gun Repair, 700 S. Rodgers Rd., Olathe, KS 66062/913-782-3131
Simmons Outdoor Corp., 2120 Killearney Way, Tallahassee, FL 32308-3402/904-878-5100; FAX: 904-878-0300
Sipes Gun Shop, 7415 Asher Ave., Little Rock, AR 72204/501-565-8480
SKB Arms Co., C.P.O. Box 1401, Tokyo, JAPAN (U.S. importer—G.U., Inc.)
Skeet's Gun Shop, Rt. 3, Box 235, Tahlequah, OK 74464/918-456-4749
Skip's Gunshop, 3 Pleasant St., Bristol, NH 03222/603-744-3100
Smith & Smith Gun Shop, Inc., 2589 Oscar Johnson Drive, North Charleston, SC 29405/803-744-2024
Smith & Wesson (See page 503)
Smith's Lawn & Marine Svc., 9100 Main St., Clarence, NY 14031/716-633-7868
Societa Armi Bresciane Srl. (See U.S. importer—Gamba, USA)
Sodak Sport & Bait, 850 South Hwy 281, Aberdeen, SD 57401/605-225-2737
Solvay Home & Outdoor Center, 102 First St., Solvay, NY 13209/315-468-6285
Southland Gun Works, Inc., 1134 Hartsville Rd., Darlington, SC 29532/803-393-6291
Southwest Airguns, 3311 Ryan St., Lake Charles, LA 70601/318-474-6038
Southwest Shooters Supply, Inc., 1940 Linwood Blvd., Oklahoma City, OK 73106/405-235-4476; FAX: 405-235-7022
Specialty Shooters Supply, Inc., 3325 Griffin Rd., Suite 9mm, Fort Lauderdale, FL 33317
Speer Products, Div. of Blount, Inc., P.O. Box 856, Lewiston, ID 83501/208-746-2351; FAX: 208-746-2915
Sporting Arms Mfg., Inc., 801 Hall Ave., Littlefield, TX 79339/806-385-5665; FAX: 806-385-3394
Sports Mart, The, 828 Ford St., Ogdensburg, NY 13669/315-393-2865
Sports Shop, The, 8055 Airline Highway, Baton Rouge, LA 70815/504-927-2600
Sports World, Inc., 5800 S. Lewis Ave., Suite 154, Tulsa, OK 74105/918-742-4027
Sports World, Route 52, Liberty, NY 12754/914-292-3077
Sportsman's Center, U.S. Hwy. 130, Box 731, Bordentown, NJ 08505/609-298-5300
Sportsman's Depot, 644 Miami St., Urban, OH 43078/513-653-4429
Sportsman's Haven, 14695 E. Pike Rd., Cambridge, OH 43725/614-432-7243
Sportsman's Paradise Gunsmith, 640 Main St., Pineville, LA 71360/318-443-6041

Sportsman's Shop, 101 W. Main St., New Holland, PA 17557/717-354-4311
Sportsmen's Exchange & Western Gun Traders, Inc., 560 South C St., Oxnard, CA 93030/805-483-1917
Sportsmen's Repair Ctr., Inc., 106 S. High St., Box 134, Columbus Groves, OH 45830/419-659-5818
Spradlin's, 113 Arthur St., Pueblo, CO 81004/719-543-9462
Springfield, Inc., 420 W. Main St., Geneseo, IL 61254/309-944-5631; FAX: 309-944-3676
SSK Industries, 721 Woodvue Lane, Wintersville, OH 43952/614-264-0176; FAX: 614-264-2257
Stalwart Corporation, P.O. Box 357, Pocatello, ID 83204/208-232-7899; FAX: 208-232-0815
Stan's Gun Repair, RR #2 Box 48, Westbrook, MN 56183-9521/507-274-5649
Star Bonifacio Echeverria S.A., Torrekva 3, Eibar, SPAIN 20600/43-107340; FAX: 43-101524 (U.S. importer—Interarms)
Star Machine Works, 418 10th Ave., San Diego, CA 92101/619-232-3216
Starnes, Ken, 32900 SW Laurelview Rd., Hillsboro, OR 97123/503-628-0705
Steyr Mannlicher AG, Mannlicherstrasse 1, P.O.B. 1000, A-4400 Steyr, AUSTRIA/0043-7252-896-0; FAX: 0043-7252-68621 (U.S. importer—GSI, Inc.)
Stocker's Shop, 5199 Mahoning Ave., Warren, OH 44483/216-847-9579
Stoeger (See page 503)
Stoeger Industries, 5 Mansard Ct., Wayne, NJ 07470/201-872-9500, 800-631-0722; FAX: 201-872-0722
Sundance Industries, Inc., 25163 W. Avenue Stanford, Valencia, CA 91355/805-257-4807
Surplus Center, 515 S.E. Spruce Street, Roseburg, OR 97470/503-672-4312
Survival Arms, Inc., 4500 Pine Cone Place, Cocoa, FL 32922/407-633-4880; FAX: 407-633-4975
Swarovski Optik North America Ltd., One Wholesale Way, Cranston, RI 02920/401-942-3380, 800-426-3089; FAX: 401-946-2587
Swift Instruments, Inc., 952 Dorchester Ave., Boston, MA 02125/617-436-2960; FAX: 617-436-3232
Swivel Machine Works, Inc., 167 Cherry St., Suite 286, Milford, CT 06460/203-926-1840; FAX: 203-874-9212

T

T.J.'s Firing Line Gunsmith, 692-A Peoria Street, Aurora, CO 80011/303-363-1911
Tanfoglio S.r.l., Fratelli, via Valtrompia 39, 41, 25068 Gardone V.T., Brescia, ITALY/30-8910361; FAX: 30-8910183 (U.S. importer—E.A.A. Corp.)
Tank's Rifle Shop, P.O. Box 474, Fremont, NE 68025/402-727-1317; FAX: 402-721-2573
Tanner (See U.S. importer—Mandall Shooting Supplies, Inc.)
Tapco, Inc., 3615 Kennesaw N. Ind. Pkwy, Kennesaw, GA 30144/800554-1445; FAX: 404-425-1510
Tar-Hunt Custom Rifles, Inc., RR3, P.O. Box 572, Bloomsburg, PA 17815-9351/717-784-6368; FAX: 717-784-6368
Tasco Sales, Inc., 7600 NW 26th St., Miami, FL 33156/305-591-3670; FAX: 305-592-5895
Taurus Firearms, Inc., 16175 NW 49th Ave., Miami, FL 33014/305-624-1115; FAX: 305-623-7506
Taurus International Firearms (See U.S. importer—Taurus Firearms, Inc.)
Taylor & Vadney, Inc., 303 Central Ave., Albany, NY 12206/518-472-9183
Taylor's & Co., Inc., 304 Lenoir Dr., Winchester, VA 22603/703-722-2017; FAX: 703-722-2018
Taylor's Sporting Goods, Gene, 445 W. Gunnison Ave., Grand Junction, CO 81505/303-242-8165
Ted's Gun & Reel Repair, 311 Natchitoches St. Box 1635, W. Monroe, LA 71291/318-323-0661
Ten Ring Service, 2227 West Lou Dr., Jacksonville, FL 32216/904-724-7419
Texas Armory, P.O. Box 154906, Waco, TX 76715/817-867-6972
Texas Longhorn Arms, Inc., 5959 W. Loop South, Suite 424, Bellaire, TX 77401/713-341-0775; FAX: 713-660-0493
Theoben Engineering, Stephenson Road, St. Ives, Huntingdon, Cambs., PE17 4WJ ENGLAND/011-0480-461718
Thompson's Gunshop, Inc., 10254 84th St., Alto, MI 49302/616-891-0440
Thompson/Center (See page 503)
300 Gunsmith Service Inc., at Cherry Creek Park Shooting Center, 12500 E. Bellview Ave., Englewood, CO 80111/303-690-3300
Thunder Mountain Arms, P.O. Box 593, Oak Harbor, WA 98277/206-679-4657; FAX: 206-675-1114
Tikka (See U.S. importer—Stoeger Industries)
Time Precision, Inc., 640 Federal Rd., Brookfield, CT 06804/203-775-8343
TOZ (See Nygord Precision Products)
Traders, The, 885 E. 14th St., San Leandro, CA 94577/510-569-0555
Trading Post, The, 412 Erie St. S., Massillon, OH 44646/216-833-7761
Traditions, Inc., P.O. Box 235, Deep River, CT 06417/203-526-9555; FAX: 203-526-4564
Trester, Inc., Verne, 3604 West 16th St., Indianapolis, IN 46222/317-638-6921
Trijicon, Inc., 49385 Shafer Ave., P.O. Box 6029, Wixom, MI 48393-6029/810-960-7700; FAX: 810-960-7725

U

U.S. General Technologies, Inc., 145 Mitchell Ave., South San Francisco, CA 94080/415-634-8440; FAX: 415-634-8452
Uberti USA, Inc., 362 Limerock Rd., P.O. Box 509, Lakeville, CT 06039/203-435-8068; FAX: 203-435-8146
Uberti, Aldo, Casella Postale 43, I-25063 Gardone V.T., ITALY (U.S. importers—American Arms, Inc.; Cape Outfitters; Cimarron Arms; Dixie Gun Works; EMF Co., Inc.; Forgett Jr., Valmore J.; Navy Arms Co; Taylor's & Co., Inc.; Uberti USA, Inc.)
Ugartechea S.A., Ignacio, Chonta 26, Eibar, SPAIN 20600/43-121257; FAX: 43-121669 (U.S. importer—Mandall Shooting Supplies, Inc.)
Ultimate Accuracy, 121 John Shelton Rd., Jacksonville, AR 72076/501-985-2530
Ultra Light Arms, Inc., P.O. Box 1270, 214 Price St., Granville, WV 26505/304-599-5687; FAX: 304-599-5687
Ultralux (See U.S. importer—Keng's Firearms Specialty, Inc.)
Unertl Optical Co., Inc., John, 308 Clay Ave., P.O. Box 818, Mars, PA 16046-0818/412-625-3810
Unique Sporting Goods, 1538 Columbia St., Lorreto, PA 15940/814-674-8889
Unique/M.A.P.F., 10, Les Allees, 64700 Hendaye, FRANCE 64700/33-59 20 71 93 (U.S. importer—Nygord Precision Products)
Upper Missouri Trading Co., 304 Harold St., Crofton, NE 68730/402-388-4844
Upton's Gun Shop, 810 Croghan St., Fremont, OH 43420/419-332-1326

V

Valley Gun Shop, 7719 Harford Rd., Baltimore, MD 21234/410-668-2171
Valley Gunsmithing, John A. Foster, 619 Second St., Webster City, IA 50595/515-832-5102
Valor Corp., 5555 NW 36th Ave., Miami, FL 33142/305-633-0127; FAX: 305-634-4536
Van's Gunsmith Service, Rt. 69A, Parish, NY 13131/315-625-7251
VanBurnes Gun Shop, 2706 Sylvania Ave., Toledo, OH 43613/419-475-9526
Voere-KGH m.b.H., P.O. Box 416, A-6333 Kufstein, Tirol, AUSTRIA/0043-5372-62547; FAX: 0043-5372-65752 (U.S. importers—JagerSport, Ltd.)
Volquartsen Custom Ltd., RR 1, Box 33A, P.O. Box 271, Carroll, IA 51401/712-792-4238; FAX: 712-792-2542

W

Walker Arms Co., Inc., 499 County Rd. 820, Selma, AL 36701/334-872-6231
Wallace & Cockrell Gunsmiths, Inc., 8240 I-30 West, Fort Worth, TX 76108/817-246-4622
Wallace Gatlin Gun Repair, 140 Gatlin Rd., Oxford, AL 36203/205-831-6993
Walther GmbH, Carl, B.P. 4325, D-89033 Ulm, GERMANY (U.S. importer—Interarms)
Warren's Sports Hdqts., 240 W. Main St., Washington, NC 27889/919-946-0960
Way It Was Sporting, The, 620 Chestnut Street, Moorestown, NJ 08057/609-231-0111
Weapon Works, The, 7017 N. 19th Ave., Phoenix, AZ 85021/602-995-3010
Weatherby (See page 503)
Weaver Scope Repair Service, 1121 Larry Mahan Dr., Suite B, El Paso, TX 79925/915-593-1005
Webley and Scott Ltd., Frankley Industrial Park, Tay Rd., Rubery, Rednal, Birmingham B45 0PA, ENGLAND/011-021-453-1864; FAX: 021-457-7846 (U.S. importer—Beeman Precision Airguns, Inc.)
Weihrauch KG, Hermann, Industriestrasse 11, 8744 Mellrichstadt, GERMANY/09776-497-498 (U.S. importers—Beeman Precision Airguns; E.A.A. Corp.)
Welsh, Bud, 80 New Road, E. Amherst, NY 14051/716-688-6344
Wessel Gun Service, 4000 E. 9-Mile Rd., Warren, MI 48091/313-756-2660
Wessinger Custom Guns & Engraving, 268 Limestone Rd., Chapin, SC 29036/803-345-5677
Wesson Firearms Co., Inc., Maple Tree Industrial Center, Rt. 20, Wilbraham, Rd./Palmer, MA 01069
West Gate Gunsports, Inc., 10116 175th Street, Edmonton, Alberta, CANADA T5S 1A1/403-489-9633
West Luther Gun Repair, R.R. #1, Conn, Ontario, CANADA N0G 1N0/519-848-6260
Westley Richards & Co., 40 Grange Rd., Birmingham, ENGLAND B29 6AR/010-214722953 (U.S. importer—Cape Outfitters)
Wheeler Gun Shop, C., 1908 George Washington Way Bldg. F, Richland, WA 99352/509-946-4634
White Dog Gunsmithing, 62 Central Ave., Ilion, NY 13357/315-894-6211
White Shooting Systems, Inc., 25 E. Hwy. 40, Box 330-12, Roosevelt, UT 84066/801-722-3085; FAX: 801-722-3054
Wholesale Sports, 12505 97 St., Edmonton, Alberta, CANADA T5G 1Z8/403-426-4417; 403-477-3737
Wichita Arms, Inc., 923 E. Gilbert, P.O. Box 11371, Wichita, KS 67211/316-265-0661; FAX: 316-265-0760
Wichita Guncraft, Inc., 4607 Barnett Rd., Wichita Falls, TX 76310/817-692-5622
Wild West Guns, Inc., 7521 Old Seward Highway #A, Anchorage, Alaska 99518/907-344-4500; FAX: 907-344-4005
Wildey, Inc., P.O. Box 475, Brookfield, CT 06804/203-355-9000; FAX: 203-354-7759
Wilkinson Arms, 26884 Pearl Rd., Parma, ID 83660/208-722-6771; FAX: 208-722-5197
Will's Gun Shop, 5603 N. Hubbard Lake Rd., Spruce, MI 48762/517-727-2500
Willborn Outdoors & Feed, 505 Main Avenue N.W., Cullman, AL 35055/205-737-9595
William's Gun Shop, Ben, 1151 S. Cedar Ridge, Duncanville, TX 75137/214-780-1807
Williams Gun Sight & Outfitters, 7389 Lapeer Rd., Rt. #1, Davison, MI 48423/313-653-2131, 800-530-9028; FAX: 313-658-2140
Williams Gunsmithing, 4985 Cole Rd., Saginaw, MI 48601/517-777-1240
Williamson Precision Gunsmithing, 117 W. Pipeline, Hurst, TX 76053/817-285-0064; FAX: 817-285-0064
Winchester (See page 503)
Windsor Gun Shop, 8410 Southeastern Ave., Indianapolis, IN 46239/317-862-2512
Wiseman and Co., Bill, P.O. Box 3427, Bryan, TX 77805/409-690-3456; FAX: 409-690-0156
Wisner's Gun Shop, Inc., 287 NW Chehalis Ave., Chehalis, WA 98532/206-748-8942; FAX: 206-748-7011
Wolf Custom Gunsmithing, Gregory, c/o Albright's Gun Shop, 36 E. Dover St., Easton, MD 21601/410-820-8811
Wolfer Brothers, Inc., 1701 Durham, Houston, TX 77007/713-869-7640
Woodman's Sporting Goods, 223 Main Street, Norway, ME 04268/207-743-6602
World Class Airguns, 2736 Morningstar Dr., Indianapolis, IN 46229/317-897-5548
Wortner Gun Works, Ltd., 433 Queen St., Chatham, Ont., CANADA N7M 5K5/519-352-0924
Wright's Hardwood Gunstock Blanks, 8540 SE Kane Rd., Gresham, OR 97080/503-666-1705
Wyoming Armory, Inc., Box 28, Farson, WY 82932/307-273-5556

Y

Ye Olde Blk Powder Shop, 994 W. Midland Rd., Auburn, MI 48611/517-662-2271; FAX: 512-662-2666

Z

Zabala Hermanos S.A., P.O. Box 97, Eibar, SPAIN 20600/43-768085, 43-768076; FAX: 43-768201 (U.S. importer—American Arms, Inc.)
Zanes Gun Rack, 4167 N. High St., Columbus, OH 43214/614-263-0369
Zanoletti, Pietro, Via Monte Gugielpo, 4, I-25063 Gardone V.T., ITALY (U.S. importer—Mandall Shooting Supplies, Inc.)
Zeiss Optical, Carl, 1015 Commerce St., Petersburg, VA 23803/804-861-0033; FAX: 804-733-4024

Warranty Service Centers

■BE=Benjamin BR=Browning ■CR=Crosman ■MO=Mossberg ■RE=Remington ■ST=Stoeger ■SW=Smith & Wesson ■TC=Thompson/Center ■WN=Winchester ■WE=Weatherby

SERVICE CENTER	CITY	BE	BR	CR	MO	RE	ST	SW	TC	WN	WE
ALABAMA											
B&W Gunsmithing	Cullman					●					
Dubbs, Gunsmith, Dale R.	Seminole					●					
Hal's Gun Supply	Cullman		●								
Nusbaum Enterprises, Inc.	Mobile				●	●					
Ott's Gun Service	Atmore		●			●					
Plaza Gunworks, Inc.	Birmingham					●		●			
Walker Arms Co., Inc.	Selma		●		●	●	●	●	●	●	●
Wallace Gatlin Gun	Oxford					●					
Willborn Outdoors & Feed	Cullman									●	
ALASKA											
Down Under Gunsmiths	Fairbanks										●
Red's Gunsmithing	Chickaloon		●		●	●		●			
Wild West Guns, Inc.	Anchorage								●		
ARIZONA											
Dave's Airgun Service	Tempe	●		●							
Don's Sport Shop, Inc.	Scottsdale		●			●				●	
Jensen's Custom Ammunition	Tucson		●		●	●		●	●	●	
Joe's Gun Shop	Phoenix			●							
Weapon Works, The	Phoenix					●					
ARKANSAS											
Broadway Arms	North Little Rock					●				●	
Gun Exchange, Inc.	Little Rock					●		●			
Jim's Trading Post	Pine Bluff		●								
Sipes Gun Shop	Little Rock		●		●	●			●		
CALIFORNIA											
Air Guns Unlimited	La Puente			●							
Air Venture Air Guns	Bellflower	●		●							
Airguns International	Santa Rosa	●		●							
Argonaut Gun Shop	Modesto					●					
Bain & Davis	San Gabriel				●	●				●	
Beeman Precision Arms, Inc.	Santa Rosa			●							
Bolsa Gunsmithing	Westminster		●		●	●	●			●	
Bridge Sportsman's Ctr.	Paso Robles					●					
Cal's Customs	Fallbrook			●		●					
Duncan's Gunworks	San Marcos										●
Grundman's	Rio Dell					●					
Gunshop, Inc., The	Lancaster		●		●	●				●	
Huntington Sportsman's Store	Oroville		●			●				●	●
Imbert & Smithers, Inc.	San Carlos		●			●				●	
J&G Gunsmithing	Roseville					●					
John Q's Quality Gunsmithing	Sacramento		●								
Long Beach Uniform Co., Inc.	Long Beach							●			
Mac-1	Gardena	●		●							
Miclean, Bill	San Jose	●		●							
Pacific International Service Co.	Janesville		●	●	●	●	●	●	●		
PHOXX Shooters Supply	N. Highlands	●		●							
Preuss Gun Shop	Clovis	●		●							
Ray's Liquor and Sporting Goods	Corning		●								
Siegle's Gunshop, Inc.	Oakland		●								
Sportsman's Exchange, Inc.	Oxnard		●			●					
Traders, The	San Leandro			●							
COLORADO											
Foothills Shooting Ctr.	Lakewood					●					
Gart Brothers Sporting Goods	Denver		●		●	●				●	
H&B Service, Inc.	Littleton	●		●							
Ray's Gunsmith Shop	Grand Junction	●		●							
Sievert's Guns	Pueblo								●		
Spradlin's	Pueblo					●					
Taylor's Sporting Goods, Gene	Grand Junction					●					
300 Gunsmith Service (Wichita Guncraft)	Englewood					●			●	●	●
T.J.'s Firing Line Gunsmith	Aurora					●		●			
CONNECTICUT											
Gunsmithing Limited	Fairfield		●			●				●	
Hoffman's Gun Center, Inc.	Newington					●					
Horchler's Gun Shop	Collinsville			●							
Keller's Co., Inc.	Burlington					●					
Mason, Gun & Ammo Co., Tom	Danbury							●			
Modern Guncraft	Wallingford	●		●							
Nicholson's Gunsmithing	Shelton				●	●					
DELAWARE											
Magnum Gun Service	Newark					●					

See page 445 for Service Center addresses.

Warranty Service Centers (cont.)

■BE=Benjamin ■BR=Browning ■CR=Crosman ■MO=Mossberg ■RE=Remington ■ST=Stoeger ■SW=Smith & Wesson ■TC=Thompson/Center ■WN=Winchester ■WE=Weatherby

SERVICE CENTER	CITY	BE	BR	CR	MO	RE	ST	SW	TC	WN	WE
FLORIDA											
Air Gun Rifle Repair	Sebring			●							
Alexander, Gunsmith, W.R.	Tallahassee					●					
Glades Gunworks	Naples					●		●			
Green Acres Sporting Goods, Inc.	Jacksonville		●	●	●	●		●		●	
Gun Doc, Inc.	Miami					●					
Jackson, Inc., Bill	Pinellas Park			●							
Lawsons Custom Firearms, Inc., Art	Ocala				●	●				●	
Loftin & Taylor	Jacksonville					●					
Sillman, Hal, Associated Services	Miami	●		●							
Ten Ring Service	Jacksonville								●		
GEORGIA											
Accuracy Gun Shop	Columbus		●			●				●	
Dorn's Outdoor Center	Macon		●		●	●				●	
Ed's Gun & Tackle Shop, Inc.	Marietta	●	●	●							
Franklin Sports, Inc.	Bogart		●			●		●			
Gun Corral, Inc.	Decatur					●				●	
Jordan Gun & Pawn Shop	Tifton		●								
Kick's Sport Center	Claxton					●					
Sanders Custom Gun Shop	Augusta					●				●	
HAWAII											
Chung, Gunsmith, Mel	Kaunakakai		●		●	●		●		●	
IDAHO											
Intermountain Arms & Tackle, Inc.	Meridian		●			●			●	●	●
Lolo Sporting Goods	Lewiston					●				●	
Quality Firearms	Nampa		●		●					●	
Reloading Center	Burley					●					
Shapel's Gun Shop	Boise					●					
ILLINOIS											
A&M Sales	North Lake	●		●							
Darnall's Gun Works	Bloomington				●	●				●	
Groenwald, John	Mundelein	●		●							
Henry's Airguns	Belvidere			●							
Jerry's Gunshop	Glenarm									●	
Krebs Gunsmithing	Niles					●					
Outdoorsman Sporting Goods Co.	Geneva	●		●							
Pekin Gun & Sporting Goods	Pekin			●							
Reynolds Gun Shop	Peoria		●								
Shockley, Harold	Hanna City		●								
INDIANA											
Airgun Centre, Ltd.	Lawrenceburg			●							
Hodson & Son Pell Gun Repair	Anderson			●							
Lutter, Robert E.	Ft. Wayne			●							
Rajo Corporation	Evansville			●							
Trester, Inc.	Indianapolis					●					
Windsor Gun Shop	Indianapolis			●	●						
IOWA											
Daryl's Gun Shop, Inc.	State Center					●					
Glenn's Reel & Rod Repair	Des Moines			●							
Jacobson's Gun Center	Story City										●
Nelson's Engine Shop	Cedar Falls			●							
Quad City Gun Repair	Eldridge				●	●					
Valley Gunsmithing, John A. Foster	Webster City				●	●				●	
KANSAS											
Bullseye Gun Works	Overland Park					●					
Gordon's Wigwam	Wichita		●	●							
Northwest Arms Service	Atwood					●					
Ray's Rod & Reel Service	Wichita			●							
Simmons Gun Repair	Olathe				●	●				●	
KENTUCKY											
D&J Bullet Co.	Russel							●			
Danny's Gun Repair, Inc.	Louisville					●				●	
Firearms Service Center	Louisville					●					
Garrett Gunsmiths, Inc.	Newport					●					
Paducah Shooters Supply, Inc.	Paducah				●	●					
LOUISIANA											
Atlas Gun Repair	Violet		●			●					
Boudreaux, Gunsmith	Lake Charles					●					
Burton Hardware	Sulphur					●					
Clark's Custom Guns, Inc.	Keithville							●			
Custom Gun Works	Lafayette					●					
Eversull, Ken	Boyce		●								
Houma Gun Works	Houma		●								
Hutchinson's Gun Repair	Pineville				●	●					
Martin Gun Shop	Shreveport					●					
N.A. Guns, Inc.	Baton Rouge					●					
Southwest Airguns	Lake Charles	●		●							
Sports Shop, The	Baton Rouge		●								
Sportsman's Paradise Gunsmith	Pineville					●				●	
Ted's Gun & Reel Repair	W. Monroe					●					
MAINE											
Brunswick Gun Shop	Brunswick				●	●		●		●	●
Morrison Gun Shop	Bradford									●	
Woodman's Sporting Goods	Norway					●					

See page 445 for Service Center addresses.

Warranty Service Centers (cont.)

■BE=Benjamin ■BR=Browning ■CR=Crosman ■MO=Mossberg ■RE=Remington ■ST=Stoeger ■SW=Smith & Wesson ■TC=Thompson/Center ■WN=Winchester ■WE=Weatherby

SERVICE CENTER	CITY	BE	BR	CR	MO	RE	ST	SW	TC	WN	WE
MARYLAND											
Atlantic Guns, Inc.	Silver Spring		●		●	●		●		●	
Baltimore Gunsmiths	Baltimore				●						
Firearms Repair & Refinish Shoppe	Woodbine										●
Gun Center, The	Frederick			●							
Precision Pellet	Joppa	●		●							
Valley Gun Shop	Baltimore		●		●	●				●	
Wolf Custom Gunsmithing, Gregory, c/o Albright's Gun Shop	Easton		●			●					
MASSACHUSETTS											
Bellrose & Son, L.E.	Granby			●							
Four Seasons	Woburn				●						
Pete's Gun Shop	Adams				●						
MICHIGAN											
Adventure A.G.R.	Waterford			●							
Bachelder Custom Arms	Grand Rapids				●	●	●	●		●	●
Daenzer, Charles E.	Otisville	●		●							
Hampel's, Inc.	Traverse City					●					
Joe's Gun Shop	Dorr			●							
Johnson Service, Inc., W.	Adrian					●					
McDaniel Co., Inc., B.	South Lyon					●					
Mill Creek Sport Center	Dexter					●					
Moreau, Gunsmith, Pete	Bay City	●		●							
Northern Precision Airguns	Tawas City			●							
On Target Gunshop, Inc.	Kalamazoo		●		●	●					
Outpost, The	Eureka			●							
Pederson Co., C.R.	Ludington					●					
Thompson's Gunshop, Inc.	Alto			●							
Wessel Gun Service	Warren		●								
Williams Gun Sight & Outfitters	Davison		●		●	●				●	
Williams Gunsmithing	Saginaw					●					
Will's Gun Shop	Spruce			●							●
Ye Olde Blk Powder Shop	Auburn								●		
MINNESOTA											
Ahlman's Custom Gun Shop, Inc.	Morristown		●		●	●	●	●		●	●
B&B Supply Co.	Minneapolis	●		●							
Dale's Gunshop	Rochester					●					
Gander Mt., Inc.	Duluth				●						
Frontiersman's Sports	Minneapolis		●			●					
Kotila Gun Shop	Cokato					●					
Laib's Gunsmithing	Spicer					●					
Matt's 10X Gunsmithing, Inc.	Duluth					●					
Northland Sport Center	Bagley					●					

SERVICE CENTER	CITY	BE	BR	CR	MO	RE	ST	SW	TC	WN	WE
Poor Borch's, Inc.	Marshall					●					
Stan's Gun Repair	Westbrook					●					
MISSISSIPPI											
Grenada Gun Works	Grenada					●					
Martins Gun Shop	Natchez					●					
May & Company, Inc.	Jackson			●							
Millers Gun Shop	Gulfport								●		
Saffle Repair Service	Jackson			●							
R.L. "Skeet" Hill Gun Shop	Verona		●								
MISSOURI											
Beard's Sport Shop	Cape Girardeau					●					
Bickford's Gun Repair	Joplin				●	●				●	●
Carl's Gun Shop	El Dorado Springs					●					
Catfish Guns	Imperial					●		●			
Dollar Drugs, Inc.	Lee's Summit	●		●							
F&D Guns	St. Charles										●
Kopp, Prof. Gunsmith, Terry K.	Lexington		●			●		●			
Nu-Line Guns, Inc.	Harvester		●		●	●		●		●	●
Ozark Shooters, Inc.	Branson					●					
MONTANA											
Air Gun Shop, The	Billings			●							
Billings Gunsmiths	Billings					●				●	
Brady's Sportsmans Surplus	Missoula			●					●		
Capitol Sports & Western Wear	Helena				●	●				●	●
Montana Gun Works	Great Falls							●			
Rocking S Gunshop	Ennis					●					
NEBRASKA											
Bedlan's Sporting Goods, Inc.	Fairbury		●								
Cylinder & Slide, Inc.	Fremont							●			
G.H. Outdoor Sports	McCook				●	●					●
G.I. Loan Shop	Grand Island					●				●	
Gunsmithing Specialties, Co.	Papillion		●			●					
Labs Air Gun Shop	Omaha	●		●							
Moneymaker Gun Craft, Inc.	Omaha									●	
Upper Missouri Trading Co., Inc.	Crofton				●	●			●		●
NEVADA											
Accuracy Gun Shop, Inc.	Las Vegas				●	●				●	
Gun World	Elko					●					
Nevada Air Guns	Las Vegas	●		●							
NEW HAMPSHIRE											
Lewis Arms	Hooksett		●		●	●				●	●
Skip's Gunshop	Bristol					●					

See page 445 for Service Center addresses.

Warranty Service Centers (cont.)

■BE=Benjamin ■BR=Browning ■CR=Crosman ■MO=Mossberg ■RE=Remington ■ST=Stoeger ■SW=Smith & Wesson ■TC=Thompson/Center ■WN=Winchester ■WE=Weatherby

SERVICE CENTER	CITY	BE	BR	CR	MO	RE	ST	SW	TC	WN	WE
NEW JERSEY											
Belleplain Supply, Inc.	Belleplain		●								
Brenner Sport Shop, Charlie	Rahway	●		●							
Garfield Gunsmithing	Garfield		●		●	●				●	
Harry's Army & Navy Store	Robbinsville		●	●							
Ray's Sport Shop, Inc.	North Plainfield		●		●	●		●		●	
Sportsman's Center	Bordentown					●					
The Way It Was Sporting	Moorestown		●		●	●					
NEW MEXICO											
Charlie's Sporting Goods, Inc.	Albuquerque			●		●		●		●	
D&J Coleman Service	Hobbs			●							
Hobbs Bicycle & Gun Sales	Hobbs					●					
NEW YORK											
Alpine Arms Corp.	Brooklyn							●			
B&T, Inc.	Albany				●						
Benson Gun Shop	Coram L.I.	●		●							
Boracci, E. John, Village Sport Ctr.	Seaford L.I.	●		●							
Buffalo Gun Center, Inc.	Buffalo					●					
Burgins Gun Shop	Sidney Center				●	●					
Coliseum Gun Traders, Ltd.	Uniondale				●						
Creekside Gun Shop	Holcomb		●			●		●		●	
Damiano's Field & Stream	Ossining			●							
Hart's Gun Supply, Ed	Bath				●	●					
Hill Top Gunsmithing	Canton					●					
Kielon, Gunsmith, Dave	Webster			●							
LeFever & Sons, Inc., Frank	Lee Center									●	
Lounsbury Sporting Goods, Bob	Middletown			●							
Mulvey's Marine & Sport Shop	Monticello			●							
Rapids Gun Shop	Niagara Falls			●							
Scalzo's Sporting Goods	Endwell			●							
Schultheis Sporting Goods	Arkport					●					
Smith's Lawn & Marine Svc.	Clarence			●							
Solvay Home & Outdoor Center	Solvay					●		●			●
Sports Mart, The	Ogdensburg			●							
Sports World	Liberty	●		●							
Taylor & Vadney, Inc.	Albany			●							
Van's Gunsmith Service	Parish					●					
White Dog Gunsmithing	Ilion					●					
NORTH CAROLINA											
Baity's Custom Gunworks	North Wilksboro				●	●		●		●	
Blue Ridge Outdoor Sports, Inc.	E. Flat Rock		●			●					
Brown, Don, Gunsmith	Ashville			●							
Cumberland Knife & Gun Works	Fayetteville									●	
Duncan Gun Shop, Inc.	North Wilksboro								●		
Hill's, Inc.	Raleigh		●			●					
Mike's Crosman Service	Winston-Salem	●		●							
Perry's Gunshop	Wendell					●					
Warren's Sports Hdqts.	Washington					●					
NORTH DAKOTA											
Gun City, Inc.	Bismarck		●								
Outdoorsman, The	Fargo		●			●					●
S.K. Guns, Inc.	Fargo									●	
OHIO											
All Game Sport Center	Milford			●							
Central Ohio Police Supply, c/o Wammes Guns	Bellefontaine								●		
Cherry Corners, Inc.	Lodi					●				●	
Eyster Heritage Gunsmiths, Ken	Centerburg		●								
Griffiths & Sons, E.J.	Lima				●						
Heckman Arms Company	Richmond Heights									●	
Log Cabin Sport Shop	Lodi								●		
Precision Airgun Sales	Maple Heights	●		●							
Rutko Corp. (Stonewall Range)	Broadview Heights							●			
Sportsman's Depot	Urban			●							
Sportsman's Haven	Cambridge		●		●	●		●	●		●
Sportsmen's Repair Ctr., Inc.	Columbus Groves			●							
Stocker's Shop	Warren			●							
Trading Post, The	Massillon	●		●							
Upton's Gun Shop	Fremont			●							
VanBurne's Gun Shop	Toledo			●							
Zanes Gun Rack	Columbus			●							
OKLAHOMA											
Anderson, Andy	Oklahoma City		●								
D&D Sporting Goods	Tishomingo					●					
Mashburn Arms Co., Inc.	Oklahoma City		●			●					
Meydag, Peter	Tulsa			●							
Outdoor America Store	Oklahoma City					●					
Shamburg's Wholesale Spt. Gds.	Clinton	●		●							
Skeet's Gun Shop	Tahlequah					●					
Southwest Shooters Supply, Inc.	Oklahoma City		●							●	
Sports World, Inc.	Tulsa		●		●	●		●		●	
OREGON											
Allison & Carey Gun Works	Portland		●		●	●				●	
Enstad & Douglas	Oregon City					●			●		
Felton, James	Eugene					●					

See page 445 for Service Center addresses.

Warranty Service Centers (cont.)

■BE=Benjamin ■BR=Browning ■CR=Crosman ■MO=Mossberg ■RE=Remington ■ST=Stoeger ■SW=Smith & Wesson ■TC=Thompson/Center ■WN=Winchester ■WE=Weatherby

SERVICE CENTER	CITY	BE	BR	CR	MO	RE	ST	SW	TC	WN	WE
Lock Stock & Barrel	Grants Pass									●	
Metro Rod & Reel	Portland	●		●							
Starnes, Gunmaker, Ken	Hillsboro					●					
Surplus Center	Roseburg				●	●					
PENNSYLVANIA											
Auto Electric & Parts, Inc.	Media			●							
Colabaugh Gunsmith, Inc., Craig	Stroudsburg					●					
Federal Firearms Co., Inc.	Oakdale					●					
Fix Gunshop, Inc., Michael D.	Reading					●					
Gorenflo Gunsmithing	Erie					●					
Grice Gun Shop, Inc.	Clearfield					●				●	
Hart & Son, Robert W.	Nescopeck							●			
Hemlock Gun Shop	Lakeville			●							
Herold's Gun Shoppe	Waynesboro		●			●					
J&T Services	Bradford			●							
Keidel's Gunsmithing Service	Washington				●	●					
Leo's Custom Stocks	Library		●			●				●	
Levan's Sporting Goods	Lebanon	●		●		●					
Miller's Sport Shop	Mountaintop			●							
Phoenix Armoury, Inc.	Norristown				●						
Richland Gun Shop	Richland					●					
Sams Gunsmithing, David	Lititz					●					
Sportsman's Shop	New Holland		●		●	●					
Unique Sporting Goods	Lorreto			●							
RHODE ISLAND											
D&L Shooting Supplies	Warwick					●				●	
Gun Hospital, The	E. Providence			●							
SOUTH CAROLINA											
Borgheresi, Enrique	Greenville									●	
Bryan & Associates	Anderson			●							
Gun Rack, Inc., The	Aiken					●					
Gun Room, The	Chapin				●			●			
Gunsmith, Inc., The	West Columbia				●	●					
S.E.M. Gun Works	Greenville	●		●							
Smith & Smith Gun Shop, Inc.	North Charleston		●								
Southland Gun Works, Inc.	Darlington					●				●	
SOUTH DAKOTA											
Gary's Gun Shop	Sioux Falls					●					
Jack First	Rapid City				●					●	
Jim's Gun & Service Center	Aberdeen									●	
Ron's Gun Repair	Sioux Falls		●		●	●				●	
Sodak Sport & Bait	Aberdeen		●		●	●				I	
TENNESSEE											
D&L Gunsmithing/Guns & Ammo	Memphis		●		●	●		●		●	
Fox & Company	Knoxville					●					
Friedman's Army Surplus	Nashville			●							
Gun City USA, Inc.	Nashville		●		●	●		●	●	●	
Hagstrom, E.G.	Memphis			●							
Hill's Hardware & Sporting Goods	Union City					●					
McGuns, W.H.	Humboldt		●			●					●
Mines Gun Shack	Tullahoma					●					
Shaler Eagle	Jonesbrough			●							
TEXAS											
Armadillo Air Gun Repair	Corpus Christi	●		●							
Ben's Gun Shop	Duncanville	●		●		●					
Boggus Gun Shop	San Marcos					●					
Carroll's Gun Shop, Inc.	Wharton		●			●					
Carter's Country	Houston					●					
Coleman, Inc., Ron	Carrollton		●			●					
Custom Gun Service	McAllen									●	
Don & Tim's Gun Shop	San Antonio					●					
Ewell Cross Gun Shop, Inc.	Ft. Worth		●								
Freer's Gun Shop	Houston		●			●				●	
Gun & Tackle Store, The	Dallas					●					
Kirkpatrick, Gunsmith, Larry	Lubbock					●					
Les Gun & Pawn Shop	Texarkana									●	
Lone Star Guns, Inc.	Plano				●	●		●			●
Longacre's, Inc.	Abilene					●					
Master Gunsmiths, Inc.	Houston		●			●					
McBride's Guns, Inc.	Austin		●		●	●		●		●	
McClelland Gun Shop	Dallas		●			●	●			●	
Mueschke Manufacturing Co.	Houston							●			
Nagel Gun Shop, Inc.	San Antonio		●			●				●	
Oshman's Sporting Goods, Inc.	Houston	●	●	●		●				I	
Pasadena Gun Center	Pasadena				●	●	●		●		
Precision Gunsmithing	Amarillo					●					
Ray's Sporting Goods	Dallas					●					●
Reynold's Gun Shop, Inc.	Tyler					●					
Wallace & Cockrell, Gunsmiths, Inc.	Fort Worth					●				●	
Wichita Guncraft, Inc.	Wichita Falls								●		
Williamson Precision	Hurst					●					●
Wolfer Brothers, Inc.	Houston			●							
UTAH											
Gun Ace Gunsmithing	Hurricane					●					
Gun Shop, The	Salt Lake City		●								

See page 445 for Service Center addresses.

Warranty Service Centers (cont.)

■BE=Benjamin ■BR=Browning ■CR=Crosman ■MO=Mossberg ■RE=Remington ■ST=Stoeger ■SW=Smith & Wesson ■TC=Thompson/Center ■WN=Winchester ■WE=Weatherby

SERVICE CENTER	CITY	BE	BR	CR	MO	RE	ST	SW	TC	WN	WE
Gunsmith Co., The	Salt Lake City				●	●			●		
Hutch's	Lehi			●							
Professional Armaments, Inc.	West Valley City			●	●	●		●			
VERMONT											
Burby, Inc. Guns & Gunsmithing	Middlebury					●					
Carpenter's Gun Works	Proctorsville								●		
Island Pond Gunshop	Island Pond					●				●	
VIRGINIA											
Bob's Gun & Tackle Shop, (Blaustein & Reich, Inc.)	Norfolk		●		●	●		●		●	
Cervera, Albert J.	Hanover			●							
King's Gun Shop, Inc.	Franklin		●			●					
Moates Sport Shop, Bob	Midlothian		●								
Northern Virginia Gun Works, Inc.	Springfield				●	●					
Old Domimion Engraver, Inc.	Lynchburg									●	
Richmond Gun Shop	Richmond					●					
WASHINGTON											
Brock's Gunsmithing, Inc.	Spokane					●				●	
Chet Paulson Outfitters	Tacoma		●			●				●	
Greene's Gun Shop	Oak Harbor					●					
Karrer's Gunatorium	Spokane					●					
Kesselring Gun Shop	Burlington		●			●					
Pintos Gun Shop	Kent	●		●							
Shooters Supply	Yakima								●		
Wisner's Gun Shop, Inc.	Chehalis		●		●	●		●	●	●	●
Wheeler Gun Shop, C.	Richland				●	●					
WEST VIRGINIA											
Douglas Sporting Goods	Princeton							●			
Lew's Mountaineer Gunsmithing	Charleston				●	●					
Milliken's Gun Shop	Elm Grove									●	
Shooting Gallery, The	Weirton	●		●							
WISCONSIN											
Badger Gun & Ammo, Inc.	Milwaukee					●					
Badger's Shooters Supply, Inc.	Owen					●					
Bob's Crosman Repair	Cudahy			●							
Custom Firearms Shop, The	Sheboygan		●								
Gander Mountain, Inc.	Wilmot		●		●	●		●		●	●
Jack's Lock & Gun Shop	Fond Du Lac			●							
Jay's Sports, Inc.	Menomonee Falls		●							●	
Midwestern Shooters Supply, Inc.	Lomira		●			●					
Phillips, D.J., Gunsmith	Pewaukee					●					

SERVICE CENTER	CITY	BE	BR	CR	MO	RE	ST	SW	TC	WN	WE
Potter Gunsmithing	Muskego					●					
Precision Gun Works	Oshkosh					●					
River Bend Sport Shop	Waupaca				●	●					
R&R Shooters Supply	Mauston	●		●							
Rusk Gun Shop, Inc.	Madison		●			●				●	●
Sea Gull Marina	Two Rivers			●							
WYOMING											
Elbe Arms Co., Inc.	Cheyenne					●					
Jackalope Gun Shop	Douglas					●					
CANADA											
Armurier De L'Outaouais	Hull, PQ				●	●		●		●	
Casey's Gun Shop	Rogersville, NB		●			●				●	
Charlton Co., Ltd., M.D.	Brentwood Bay, BC							●			
Custom Gun Shop	Edmonton, AB		●		●	●					
Davidson's of Canada	Peterborough, ON				●	●				●	
Delhi Small Arms	Delhi, ON									●	
Delisle Thompson Sport Goods	Saskatoon, SK					●					
Epps, Ellwood	Orillia, ON					●				●	
Ernie's Gun Shop, Ltd.	Winnipeg, MB					●			●		
Gene's Gunsmithing	Selkirk, MB				●	●			●	●	
Girard, Florent, Gunsmith	Chicoutimi, PQ					●					
L'Armurier Alain Bouchard, Inc.	Ulverton, PQ		●			●				●	●
Longs Gunsmithing Ltd., W.R.	Coburg, ON		●		●	●				●	
Lusignant Armurier, A. Richard	St. Hyacinthe, PQ					●					
Magasin Latulippe, Inc.	Quebec City, PQ		●			●					●
Newby, Stewart, Gunsmith	New Burgh, ON					●					
Precision Arms & Gunsmithing Ltd.	Nobleton, ON					●					
Ralph's Gun Shop	Niverville, MB					●					
Randy's Gun Repair	Tabustinac, NB				●	●					
Reliable Gun & Tackle, Ltd.	Vancouver, BC					●				●	
Robinson's Sporting Goods, Ltd.	Victoria, BC									●	
Russell's Sporting Goods	Calgery, AB									●	
Saskatoon Gunsmith Shoppe, Ltd.	Saskatoon, SK				●	●				●	
Selin Gunsmith, Ltd., Del	Vernon, BC				●	●					
West Gate Gunsports, Inc.	Edmonton, AB					●					●
West Luther Gun Repair	Conn, ON					●					
Wholesale Sports	Edmonton, AB									●	
Wortner Gun Works, Ltd.	Chatham, ON				●	●		●		●	

See page 445 for Service Center addresses.

METALLIC SIGHTS

Sporting Leaf and Open Sights

ERA EXPRESS SIGHTS A wide variety of open sights and bases for custom installation. Partial listing shown. From New England Custom Gun Service.

Price: One-leaf express **$66.00**
Price: Two-leaf express **$71.50**
Price: Three-leaf express **$77.00**
Price: Bases for above **$27.50**
Price: Standing rear sight, straight **$13.25**
Price: Base for above **$16.50**

ERA PROFESSIONAL EXPRESS SIGHTS Standing or folding leaf sights are securely locked to the base with the ERA Magnum Clamp, but can be loosened for sighting in. Base can be attached with two socket-head cap screws or soldered. Finished and blued. Barrel diameters from .600″ to .930″.

Price: Standing leaf **$54.00**
Price: One-leaf express **$96.00**
Price: Two-leaf express **$101.00**
Price: Three-leaf express **$109.00**

ERA MASTERPIECE REAR SIGHT Adjustable for windage and elevation, and adjusted and locked with a small screwdriver. Comes with 8-36 socket-head cap screw and wrench. Barrel diameters from .600″ to .930″.

Price: **$75.00**

LYMAN No. 16 Middle sight for barrel dovetail slot mounting. Folds flat when scope or peep sight is used. Sight notch plate adjustable for elevation. White triangle for quick aiming. 3 heights: A—.400″ to .500″, B—.345″ to .445″, C—.500″ to .600″.

Price: **$14.40**

MARBLE FALSE BASE #76, #77, #78 New screw-on base for most rifles replaces factory base. 3/8″ dovetail slot permits installation of any folding rear sight. Can be had in sweat-on models also.

Price: **$7.95**

MARBLE FOLDING LEAF Flat-top or semi-buckhorn style. Folds down when scope or peep sights are used. Reversible plate gives choice of "U" or "V" notch. Adjustable for elevation.

Price: **$14.60**
Price: Also available with both windage and elevation adjustment **$16.70**

MARBLE SPORTING REAR With white enamel diamond, gives choice of two "U" and two "V" notches or different sizes. Adjustment in height by means of double step elevator and sliding notch piece. For all rifles; screw or dovetail installation.

Price: . . . . . **$14.60-$16.70**

MARBLE #20 UNIVERSAL New screw or sweat-on base. Both have .100″ elevation adjustment. In five base sizes. Three styles of U-notch, square notch, peep. Adjustable for windage and elevation.

Price: Screw-on **$23.00**
Price: Sweat-on **$21.00**

MILLETT SPORTING & BLACKPOWDER RIFLE Open click adjustable rear fits 3/8″ dovetail cut in barrel. Choice of white outline, target black or open express V rear blades. Also available is a replacement screw-on sight with express V, .562″ hole centers. Dovetail fronts in white or blaze orange in seven heights (.157″-.540″).

Price: Dovetail or screw-on rear **$55.60**
Price: Front sight **$12.34**

MILLETT SCOPE-SITE Open, adjustable or fixed rear sights dovetail into a base integral with the top scope-mounting ring. Blaze orange front ramp sight is integral with the front ring half. Rear sights have white outline aperture. Provides fast, short-radius, Patridge-type open sights on the top of the scope. Can be used with all Millett rings, Weaver-style bases, Ruger 77 (also fits Redhawk), Ruger Ranch Rifle, No. 1, No. 3, Rem. 870, 1100; Burris, Leupold and Redfield bases.

Price: Scope-Site top only, windage only **$31.15**
Price: As above, fully adjustable **$66.10**
Price: Scope-Site Hi-Turret, fully adjustable, low, medium, high **$66.10**

WICHITA MULTI RANGE SIGHT SYSTEM Designed for silhouette shooting. System allows you to adjust the rear sight to four repeatable range settings, once it is pre-set. Sight clicks to any of the settings by turning a serrated wheel. Front sight is adjustable for weather and light conditions with one adjustment. Specify gun when ordering.

Price: Rear sight **$104.47**
Price: Front sight **$78.59**

WILLIAMS DOVETAIL OPEN SIGHT (WDOS) Open rear sight with windage and elevation adjustment. Furnished with "U" notch or choice of blades. Slips into dovetail and locks with gib lock. Heights from .281″ to .531″.

Price: With blade **$15.86**
Price: Less Blade **$9.92**

WILLIAMS GUIDE OPEN SIGHT (WGOS) Open rear sight with windage and elevation adjustment. Bases to fit most military and commercial barrels. Choice of square "U" or "V" notch blade, 3/16″, 1/4″, 5/16″, or 3/8″ high.

Price: Less blade **$15.86**
Price: Extra blades, each **$6.18**

WILLIAMS WGOS OCTAGON Open rear sight for 1″ octagon barrels. Installs with two 6-48 screws and uses same hole spacing as most T/C muzzleloading rifles. Four heights, choice of square, U, V, B blade.

Price: **$21.16**

WILLIAMS WSKS, WAK47 Replaces original military-type rear sight. Adjustable for windage and elevation. No drilling or tapping. Peep aperture or open. For SKS carbines, AK-47.

Price: Aperture **$23.95**
Price: Open **$21.95**

WILLIAMS WM-96 Fits Mauser 96-type military rifles, replaces original rear sight with open blade or aperture. Fully adjustable for windage and elevation. No drilling; tapping.

Price: Aperture **$23.95**
Price: Open **$21.95**

Micrometer Receiver Sights

BEEMAN/FEINWERKBAU 5454 MATCH APERTURE SIGHT Small size, new-design sight uses constant-pressure flat springs to eliminate point of impact shifts.

Price: **$299.00**

BEEMAN SPORT APERTURE SIGHT Positive click micrometer adjustments. Standard units with flush surface screwdriver adjustments. Deluxe version has target knobs. For air rifles with grooved receivers.

Price: Standard **$36.50**
Price: Deluxe **$47.00**

EAW RECEIVER SIGHT A fully adjustable aperture sight that locks securely into the EAW quick-detachable scope mount rear base. Imported by New England Custom Gun Service.

Price: **$95.00**

LYMAN NO. 2 TANG SIGHT Designed for the Winchester Model 94. Has high index marks on aperture post; comes with both .093″ quick sighting aperture, .040″ large disk aperture, and replacement mounting screws.

Price: **$77.50**
Price: For Marlin lever actions **$82.50**

LYMAN No. 57 1/4-minute clicks. Stayset knobs. Quick release slide, adjustable zero scales. Made for almost all modern rifles.

Price: **$69.50**
Price: No. 57SME, 57SMET (for White Systems Model 91 and Whitetail rifles) **$69.50**

LYMAN No. 66 Fits close to the rear of flat-sided receivers, furnished with Stayset knobs. Quick release slide, 1/4-min. adjustments. For most lever or slide action or flat-sided automatic rifles.

Price: **$69.50**
Price: No. 66MK (for all current versions of the Knight MK-85 in-line rifle with flat-sided receiver) **$69.50**
Price: No. 66 SKS fits Russian and Chinese SKS rifles; large and small apertures **$69.50**

LYMAN No. 66U Light weight, designed for most modern shotguns with a flat-sided, round-top receiver. 1/4-minute clicks. Requires drilling, tapping. Not for Browning A-5, Rem. M11.

Price: **$69.50**

LYMAN 90MJT RECEIVER SIGHT Mounts on standard Lyman and Williams FP bases. Has 1/4-minute audible micrometer click adjustments, target knobs with direction indicators. Adjustable zero scales, quick release slide. Large 7/8″ diameter aperture disk.

Price: **$82.50**

MILLETT PEEP RIFLE SIGHTS Fully adjustable, heat-treated nickel steel peep aperture receiver sight for the AR-15A-1 and Mini-14. Has fine windage and elevation adjustments; replaces original.

Price: Rear sight, Mini-14 . . . . . **$49.00**
Price: Front sight, Mini-14 . . . . . **$18.75**
Price: Rear sight, AR-15A-1 . . . . . **$51.45**
Price: Serrated ramp front sight, AR-15A-1 . . . . . **$12.25**

WILLIAMS FP Internal click adjustments. Positive locks. For virtually all rifles, T/C Contender, Heckler & Koch HK-91, Ruger Mini-14, plus Win., Rem. and Ithaca shotguns.

Price: From **$58.77**
Price: With Target Knobs **$69.81**
Price: With Square Notched Blade **$61.80**
Price: With Target Knobs & Square Notched Blade **$72.99**
Price: FP-GR (for dovetail-grooved receivers, 22s and air guns) **$58.77**
Price: FP-94BBSE (for Win. 94 Big Bore A.E.; uses top rear scope mount holes) **$58.77**

WILLIAMS TARGET FP Similar to the FP series but developed for most bolt-action rimfire rifles. Target FP High adjustable from 1.250″ to 1.750″ above centerline of bore; Target FP Low adjustable from .750″ to 1.250″. Attaching bases for Rem. 540X, 541-S, 580, 581, 582 (#540); Rem. 510, 511, 512, 513-T, 521-T (#510); Win. 75 (#75); Savage/Anschutz 64 and Mark 12 (#64). Some rifles

require drilling, tapping.
Price: High or Low $77.15
Price: Base only $12.98
Price: FP-T/C Scout rifle, from $58.77
Price: FP-94BBSE (for Win. 94 Big Bore A.E.; uses top rear scope mount holes) $58.77

WILLIAMS 5-D SIGHT Low cost sight for shotguns, 22s and the more popular big game rifles. Adjustment for windage and elevation. Fits most guns without drilling and tapping. Also for British SMLE, Winchester M94 Side Eject.
Price: From $30.85
Price: With Shotgun Aperture $30.85

WILLIAMS GUIDE (WGRS) Receiver sight for 30 M1 Carbine, M1903A3 Springfield, Savage 24s, Savage-Anschutz and Weatherby XXII. Utilizes military dovetail; no drilling. Double-dovetail windage adjustment, sliding dovetail adjustment for elevation.
Price: $30.85
Price: WGRS-CVA (for rifles with octagon barrels, receivers) $30.85

FRONT SIGHTS

ERA FRONT SIGHTS European-type front sights inserted from the front. Various heights available. From New England Custom Gun Service.
Price: 1/16″ silver bead $11.50
Price: 3/32″ silver bead $16.00
Price: Sourdough bead $14.50
Price: Tritium night sight $44.00
Price: Folding night sight with ivory bead $39.50

LYMAN HUNTING SIGHTS Made with gold or white beads 1/16″ to 3/32″ wide and in varying heights for most military and commercial rifles. Dovetail bases.
Price: $10.50

MARBLE STANDARD Ivory, red, or gold bead. For all American-made rifles, 1/16″ wide bead with semi-flat face which does not reflect light. Specify type of rifle when ordering.
Price: $8.75

MARBLE CONTOURED Has 3/8″ dovetail base, .090″ deep, is 5/8″ long. Uses standard 1/16″ or 3/32″ bead, ivory, red, or gold. Specify rifle type.
Price: $10.15

WILLIAMS RISER BLOCKS For adding .250″ height to front sights when using a receiver sight. Two widths available: .250″ for Williams Streamlined Ramp or .340″ on all standard ramps having this base width. Uses standard 3/8″ dovetail.
Price: $5.46

Globe Target Front Sights

LYMAN 20 MJT TARGET FRONT Has 7/8″ diameter, one-piece steel globe with 3/8″ dovetail base. Height is .700″ from bottom of dovetail to center of aperture; height on 20 LJT is .750″. Comes with seven Anschutz-size steel inserts—two posts and five apertures .126″ through .177″.
Price: 20 MJT or 20 LJT $36.00

LYMAN No. 17A TARGET Includes seven interchangeable inserts: four apertures, one transparent amber and two posts .50″ and .100″ in width.
Price: $29.95
Price: Insert set $10.50

LYMAN No. 93 MATCH Has 7/8″ diameter, fits any rifle with a standard dovetail mounting block. Comes with seven target inserts and accepts most Anschutz accessories. Hooked locking bolt and nut allows quick removal, installation. Base available in .860″ (European) and .562″ (American) hole spacing.
Price: $49.50

WILLIAMS TARGET GLOBE FRONT Adapts to many rifles. Mounts to the base with a knurled locking screw. Height is .545″ from center, not including base. Comes with inserts.
Price: $30.85
Price: Dovetail base (low) .220″ $17.00
Price: Dovetail base (high) .465″ $17.00
Price: Screw-on base, .300″ height, .300″ radius $15.45
Price: Screw-on base, .450″ height, .350″ radius $15.45
Price: Screw-on base, .215″ height, .400″ radius $15.45

Ramp Sights

ERA MASTERPIECE Banded ramps; 21 sizes; hand-detachable beads and hood; beads inserted from the front. Various heights available. From New England Custom Gun Service.
Price: Banded ramp $54.00
Price: Hood $10.50
Price: 1/16″ silver bead $11.50
Price: 3/32″ silver bead $16.00
Price: Sourdough bead $14.50
Price: Tritium night sight $44.00
Price: Folding night sight with ivory bead $39.50

LYMAN SCREW-ON RAMP Used with 8-40 screws but may also be brazed on. Heights from .10″ to .350″. Ramp without sight.
Price: $16.50

MARBLE FRONT RAMPS Available in either screw-on or sweat-on style, five heights: 3/16″, 5/16″, 3/8″, 7/16″, 9/16″. Standard 3/8″ dovetail slot.
Price: $16.80
Price: Hoods for above ramps $3.70

WILLIAMS SHORTY RAMP Companion to "Streamlined" ramp, about 1/2″ shorter. Screw-on or sweat-on. It is furnished in 1/8″, 3/16″, 9/32″, and 3/8″ heights without hood only. Also for shotguns.
Price: $13.74
Price: With dovetail lock $16.39

WILLIAMS STREAMLINED RAMP Available in screw-on or sweat-on models. Furninshed in 9/16″, 7/16″, 3/8″, 5/16″, 3/16″ heights.
Price: $16.50
Price: Sight hood $3.80

WILLIAMS STREAMLINED FRONT SIGHTS Narrow (.250″ width) for Williams Streamlined ramps and others with 1/4″ top width; medium (.340″ width) for all standard factory ramps. Available with white, gold or flourescent beads, 1/16″ or 3/32″.
Price: ....$8.75 to $9.07

Handgun Sights

BO-MAR DELUXE BMCS Gives 3/8″ windage and elevation adjustment at 50 yards on Colt Gov't 45; sight radius under 7″. For GM and Commander models only. Uses existing dovetail slot. Has shield-type rear blade.
Price: $65.95
Price: BMCS-2 (for GM and 9mm) $65.95
Price: Flat bottom $65.95
Price: BMGC (for Colt Gold Cup), angled serrated blade, rear $65.95
Price: BMGC front sight $12.00
Price: BMCZ-75 (for CZ-75, TZ-75, P-9 and most clones. Works with factory front **$65.95**

BO-MAR FRONT SIGHTS Dovetail style for S&W 4506, 4516, 1076; undercut style (.250″, .280″, 5/16″ high); Fast Draw style (.210″, .250″, .230″ high).
Price $12.00

BO-MAR BMU XP-100/T/C CONTENDER No gunsmithing required; has .080″ notch.
Price: $77.00

BO-MAR BMML For muzzleloaders; has .062″ notch, flat bottom.
Price: $65.95
Price: With 3/8″ dovetail $65.95

BO-MAR RUGER "P" ADJUSTABLE SIGHT Replaces factory front and rear sights.
Price: Rear sight $65.95
Price: Front sight $12.00

BO-MAR BMR Fully adjustable rear sight for Ruger MKI, MKII Bull barrel autos.
Price: Rear $65.95
Price: Undercut front sight $12.00

BO-MAR BMSW SMITH & WESSON SIGHTS Replace the S&W Novak-style fixed sights. A .385″ high front sight and minor machining required. For models 4506, 4516, 1076; all 9mms with 53/4″ and 63/16″ radius.
Price: $65.95
Price: .385″ front sight $12.00
Price: BM-645 rear sight (for S&W 645, 745), uses factory front $65.95
Price: BMSW-52 rear sight (for Model 52), fits factory dovetail, uses factory front . **$65.95**

BO-MAR LOW PROFILE RIB & ACCURACY TUNER Streamlined rib with front and rear sights; 71/8″ sight radius. Brings sight line closer to the bore than standard or extended sight and ramp. Weight 5 oz. Made for Colt Gov't 45, Super 38, and Gold Cup 45 and 38.
Price: $123.00

BO-MAR COMBAT RIB For S&W Model 19 revolver with 4″ barrel. Sight radius 53/4″, weight 51/2 oz.
Price: $110.00

BO-MAR HUNTER REAR SIGHT Replacement rear sight in two models—S&W K and L frames use 23/4″ Bo-Mar base with 7/16″ overhang, has two screw holes; S&W N frame has 3″ base, three screw holes. A .200″ taller front blade is required.
Price: $79.00

BO-MAR WINGED RIB For S&W 4″ and 6″ length barrels—K-38, M10, HB 14 and 19. Weight for the 6″ model is about 71/4 oz.
Price: $123.00

BO-MAR COVER-UP RIB Adjustable rear sight, winged front guards. Fits right over revolver's original front sight. For S&W 4″ M-10HB, M-13, M-58, M-64 & 65, Ruger 4″ models SDA-34, SDA-84, SS-34, SS-84, GF-34, GF-84.
Price: $117.00

C-MORE SIGHTS Replacement front sight blades offered in two types and five styles. Made of Du Pont Acetal, they come in a set of five high-contrast colors: blue, green, pink, red and yellow. Easy to install. Patridge style for Colt Python (all barrels), Ruger Super Blackhawk (71/2″), Ruger Blackhawk (45/8″); ramp style for Python (all barrels), Blackhawk (45/8″), Super Blackhawk (71/2″ and 101/2″). From C-More Systems.
Price: Per set $19.95

JP GHOST RING Replacement bead front, ghost ring rear for Glock and M1911 pistols. From JP Enterprises.
Price: $79.95
Price: Bo-Mar replacement leaf with JP dovetail front bead $99.95

MMC COMBAT FIXED REAR SIGHT (Colt 1911-Type Pistols) This veteran MMC sight is well known to those who prefer a true combat sight for "carry" guns. Steel construction for long service. Choose from a wide variety of front sights.
Price: Combat Fixed Rear, plain $19.35
Price: As above, white outline $24.80
Price: Combat Front Sight for above, six styles, from $6.15

MMC STANDARD ADJUSTABLE REAR SIGHT Available for Colt 1911 type, Ruger Standard Auto, and now for S&W 469, and 659 pistols. No front sight change is necessary, as this sight will work with the original factory front sight.
Price: Standard Adjustable Rear Sight, plain leaf $48.40
Price: Standard Adjustable Rear Sight, white outline $53.85

MMC MINI-SIGHT Miniature size for carrying, fully adjustable, for maximum accuracy with your pocket auto. MMC's Mini-Sight will work with the factory front sight. No machining is necessary; easy installation. Available for Walther PP, PPK, and PPK/S pistols. Will also fit fixed sight Browning Hi-Power (P-35).
Price: Mini-Sight, plain **$60.00**
Price: Mini-Sight, white bar **$60.00**

MEPROLIGHT TRITIUM NIGHT SIGHTS Replacement sight assemblies for use in low-light conditions. Available for rifles, shotguns, handguns and bows. **TRU-DOT** models carry a 12-year warranty on the useable illumination, while non-TRU-DOT have a 5-year warranty. Contact Hesco, Inc. for complete details.
Price: Shotgun bead sight **$22.95**
Price: AR-15/M-16 front sight only **$34.95**
Price: AR-15/M-16 sight sets, Rem. rifle sights **$89.95**
Price: TRU-DOT fixed sight sets **$94.95**
Price: TRU-DOT adjustable sight sets, pistols **$139.95**
Price: TRU-DOT adjustable sights for Python, King Cobra, Taurus 669, Ruger GP-100 .... **$124.95**
Price: H&K MP5, SR9 front sight only **$49.95**
Price: H&K MP5, SR9 sight sets **$94.95**

MILLETT DOVETAIL FRONT All-steel replacement front sights with highly visible white or orange bar, serrated ramp, or 3-dot. For Browning, SIG Sauer and S&W autos.
Price: **$16.00**

MILLETT SERIES 100 REAR SIGHTS All-steel highly visible, click adjustable. Blades in white outline, target black, silhouette, 3-dot, and tritium bars. Fit most popular revolvers and autos.
Price: .... **$49.30** to **$55.60**

MILLETT ULTRA SIGHT Fully adjustable rear works with factory front. Steel and carbon fiber. Easy to install. For most automatics. White outline, target black or 3-dot.
Price: **$49.95**

MILLETT BAR-DOT-BAR TRITIUM NIGHT SIGHTS Replacement front and rear combos fit most automatics. Horizontal tritium bars on rear, dot front sight.
Price: **$145.00**

MILLETT 3-DOT SYSTEM SIGHTS The 3-Dot System sights use a single white dot on the front blade and two dots flanking the rear notch. Fronts available in Dual-Crimp and Wide Stake-On styles, as well as special applications. Adjustable rear sight available for most popular auto pistols and revolvers.
Price: Front, from **$16.00**
Price: Adjustable rear .... **$55.60** to **$56.80**

MILLETT REVOLVER FRONT SIGHTS All-steel replacement front sights with either white or orange bar. Easy to install. For Ruger GP-100, Redhawk, Security-Six, Police-Six, Speed-Six, Colt Trooper, Diamondback, King Cobra, Peacemaker, Python, Dan Wesson 22 and 15-2.
Price: .... **$13.60** to **$16.00**

MILLETT DUAL-CRIMP FRONT SIGHT Replacement front sight for automatic pistols. Dual-Crimp uses an all-steel two-point hollow rivet system. Available in eight heights and four styles. Has a skirted base that covers the front sight pad. Easily installed with the Millett Installation Tool Set. Available in Blaze Orange Bar, White Bar, Serrated Ramp, Plain Post.
Price: **$16.00**

MILLETT STAKE-ON FRONT SIGHT Replacement front sight for automatic pistols. Stake-On sights have skirted base that covers the front sight pad. Easily installed with the Millet Installation Tool Set. Available in seven heights and four styles—Blaze Orange Bar, White Bar, Serrated Ramp, Plain Post.
Price: **$16.00**

OMEGA OUTLINE SIGHT BLADES Replacement rear sight blades for Colt and Ruger single action guns and the Interarms Virginian Dragoon. Standard Outline available in gold or white notch outline on blue metal. From Omega Sales, Inc.
Price: **$8.95**

OMEGA MAVERICK SIGHT BLADES Replacement "peep-sight" blades for Colt, Ruger SAs, Virginian Dragoon. Three models available—No. 1, Plain; No. 2, Single Bar; No. 3, Double Bar Rangefinder. From Omega Sales, Inc.
Price: Each **$6.95**

P-T TRITIUM NIGHT SIGHTS Self-luminous tritium sights for most popular handguns, Colt AR-15, H&K rifles and shotguns. Replacement handgun sight sets available in 3-Dot style (green/green, green/yellow, green/orange) with bold outlines around inserts; Bar-Dot available in green/green with or without white outline rear sight. Functional life exceeds 15 years. From Innovative Weaponry, Inc.
Price: Handgun sight sets **$99.95**
Price: Rifle sight sets **$99.95**
Price: Rifle, front only **$49.95**
Price: Shotgun, front only **$49.95**

TRIJICON NIGHT SIGHTS Three-dot night sight system uses tritium inserts in the front and rear sights. Tritium "lamps" are mounted in silicone rubber inside a metal cylinder. A polished crystal sapphire provides protection and clarity. Inlaid white outlines provide 3-dot aiming in daylight also. Available for most popular handguns with fixed or adjustable sights. From Trijicon, Inc.
Price: .... **$19.95 to $175.00**

THOMPSON/CENTER SILHOUETTE SIGHTS Replacement front and rear sights for the T/C Contender. Front sight has three interchangeable blades. Rear sight has three notch widths. Rear sight can be used with existing soldered front sights.
Price: Front sight **$35.80**
Price: Rear sight **$92.40**

WICHITA SERIES 70/80 SIGHT Provides click windage and elevation adjustments with precise repeatability of settings. Sight blade is grooved and angled back at the top to reduce glare. Available in Low Mount Combat or Low Mount Target styles for Colt 45s and their copies, S&W 645, Hi-Power, CZ 75 and others.
Price: Rear sight, target or combat **$75.02**
Price: Front sight, Patridge or ramp **$12.60**

WICHITA GRAND MASTER DELUXE RIBS Ventilated rib has wings machined into it for better sight acquisition and is relieved for Mag-Na-Porting. Milled to accept Weaver see-thru-style rings. Made of stainless or blued steel; front and rear sights blued. Has Wichita Multi-Range rear sight system, adjustable front sight. Made for revolvers with 6″ barrel.
Price: Model 301S, 301B (adj. sight K frames with custom bbl. of 1″ to 1.032″ dia. L and N frame with 1.062″ to 1.100″ dia. bbl.) **$180.60**
Price: Model 303S, 303B (adj. sight K, L, N frames with factory barrel) .. **$180.60**

Shotgun Sights

ACCURA-SITE For shooting shotgun slugs. Three models to fit most shotguns—"A" for vent. rib barrels, "B" for solid ribs, "C" for plain barrels. Rear sight has windage and elevation provisions. Easily removed and replaced. Includes front and rear sights. From All's, The Jim Tembeils Co.
Price: .... **$27.95** to **$34.95**

FIRE FLY EM-109 SL SHOTGUN SIGHT Made of aircraft-grade aluminum, this 1/4-oz. "channel" sight has a thick, sturdy hollowed post between the side rails to give a Patridge sight picture. All shooting is done with both eyes open, allowing the shooter to concentrate on the target, not the sights. The hole in the sight post gives reduced-light shooting capability and allows for fast, precise aiming. For sport or combat shooting. Model EM-109 fits all vent. rib and double barrel shotguns and muzzleloaders with octagon barrel. Model MOC-110 fits all plain barrel shotguns without screw-in chokes. From JAS, Inc.
Price: **$35.00**

LYMAN Three sights of over-sized ivory beads. No. 10 Front (press fit) for double barrel or ribbed single barrel guns...**$5.20**; No. 10D Front (screw fit) for non-ribbed single barrel guns (comes with wrench)...**$6.60**; No. 11 Middle (press fit) for double and ribbed single barrel guns...**$5.70**.

MMC M&P COMBAT SHOTGUN SIGHT SET A durable, protected ghost ring aperture, combat sight made of steel. Fully adjustable for windage and elevation.
Price: M&P Sight Set (front and rear) **$73.45**
Price: As above, installed **$83.95**

MARBLE SHOTGUN BEAD SIGHTS No. 214—Ivory front bead, 11/64″, tapered shank...**$4.40**; No. 223—Ivory rear bead, .080″, tapered shank...**$4.40**; No. 217—Ivory front bead, 11/64″, threaded shank...**$4.75**; No. 223-T—Ivory rear bead, .080″, threaded shank...**$5.95**. Reamers, taps and wrenches available from Marble Arms.

MILLETT SHURSHOT SHOTGUN SIGHT A sight system for shotguns with ventilated rib. Rear sight attaches to the rib, front sight replaces the front bead. Front has an orange face, rear has two orange bars. For 870, 1100 or other models.
Price: Rear **$13.15**
Price: Adjustable rear **$22.00**
Price: Front **$12.95**

POLY-CHOKE Replacement front shotgun sights in four styles—Xpert, Poly Bead, Xpert Mid Rib sights, and Bev-L-Block. Xpert Front available in 3x56, 6x48 thread, 3/32″ or 5/32″ shank length, gold, ivory...**$4.70**; or Sun Spot orange bead...**$5.95**; Poly Bead is standard replacement 1/8″ bead, 6x48...**$2.95**; Xpert Mid Rib in tapered carrier (ivory only) **$5.95**, or 3x56 threaded shank (gold only)...**$2.95**; Hi and Lo Blok sights with 6x48 thread, gold or ivory...**$5.25**. From Marble Arms.

SLUG SIGHTS Made of non-marring black nylon, front and rear sights stretch over and lock onto the barrel. Sights are low profile with blaze orange front blade. Adjustable for windage and elevation. For plain-barrel (non-ribbed) guns in 12-, 16- and 20-gauge, and for shotguns with 5/16″ and 3/8″ ventilated ribs. From Innovision Ent.
Price: **$11.95**

WILLIAMS GUIDE BEAD SIGHT Fits all shotguns, 1/8″ ivory, red or gold bead. Screws into existing sight hole. Various thread sizes and shank lengths.
Price: **$4.77**

WILLIAMS SLUGGER SIGHTS Removable aluminum sights attach to the shotgun rib. High profile front, fully adjustable rear. Fits 1/4″, 5/16″ or 3/8″ (special) ribs.
Price: **$34.95**

Sight Attachments

MERIT IRIS SHUTTER DISC Eleven clicks give 12 different apertures. No. 3 Disc and Master, primarily target types, 0.22″ to .125″; No. 4, 1/2″ dia. hunting type, .025″ to .155″. Available for all popular sights. The Master Deluxe, with flexible rubber light shield, is particularly adapted to extension, scope height, and tang sights. All Merit Deluxe models have internal click springs; are hand fitted to minimum tolerance.
Price: Master Deluxe **$66.00**
Price: No. 3 Disc **$55.00**
Price: No. 4 Hunting Disc **$45.00**

MERIT LENS DISC Similar to Merit Iris Shutter (Model 3 or Master) but incorporates provision for mounting prescription lens integrally. Lens may be obtained locally from your optician. Sight disc is 7/16″ wide (Model 3), or 3/4″ wide (Master). Model 3 Target.
Price: **$68.00**
Price: Master Deluxe **$78.00**

MERIT OPTICAL ATTACHMENT For revolver and pistol shooters, instantly attached by rubber suction cup to regular or shooting glasses. Any aperture .020″ to .156″.
Price: Deluxe (swings aside) **$63.00**

WILLIAMS APERTURES Standard thread, fits most sights. Regular series 3/8″ to 1/2″ O.D., .050″ to .125″ hole. "Twilight" series has white reflector ring.
Price: Regular series **$4.97**
Price: Twilight series **$6.74**
Price: Wide open 5/16″ aperture for shotguns fits 5-D or Foolproof sights (specify model) **$8.77**

CHOKES & BRAKES

Briley Screw-In Chokes

Installation of these choke tubes requires that all traces of the original choking be removed, the barrel threaded internally with square threads and then the tubes are custom fitted to the specific barrel diameter. The tubes are thin and, therefore, made of stainless steel. Cost of installation for single-barrel guns (pumps, autos), lead shot, 12-gauge, **$129.00**, 20-gauge **$139.00**; steel shot **$159.00** and **$169.00**, all with three chokes; un-single target guns run **$190.00**; over/unders and side-by-sides, lead shot, 12-gauge, **$349.00**, 20-gauge **$369.00**; steel shot **$449.00** and **$469.00**, all with five chokes. For 10-gauge auto or pump with two steel shot chokes, **$149.00**; over/unders, side-by-sides with three steel shot chokes, **$329.00**. For 16-gauge auto or pump, three lead shot chokes, **$239.00**; over/unders, side-by-sides with five lead shot chokes, **$429.00**. The 28 and 410-bore run **$159.00** for autos and pumps with three lead shot chokes, **$429.00** for over/unders and side-by-sides with five lead shot chokes.

Cutts Compensator

The Cutts Compensator is one of the oldest variable choke devices available. Manufactured by Lyman Gunsight Corporation, it is available with a steel body. A series of vents allows gas to escape upward and downward. For the 12-ga. Comp body, six fixed-choke tubes are available: the Spreader—popular with Skeet shooters; Improved Cylinder; Modified; Full; Superfull, and Magnum Full. Full, Modified and Spreader tubes are available for 12 or 20, and an Adjustable Tube, giving Full through Improved Cylinder chokes, is offered in 12 and 20 gauges. Cutts Compensator, complete with wrench, adaptor and any single tube **$81.45**; with adjustable tube **$105.50**. All single choke tubes **$22.95** each; adjustable tube **$47.00**. No factory installation available.

Dayson Automatic Brake System

This system fits most single barrel shotguns threaded for choke tubes, and cuts away 30 grooves on the exterior of a standard one-piece wad as it exits the muzzle. This slows the wad, allowing shot and wad to separate faster, reducing shot distortion and tightening patterns. The A.B.S. Choke Tube is claimed to reduce recoil by about 25 percent, and with the Muzzle Brake up to 60 percent. Ventilated Choke Tubes available from .685" to .725", in .005" increments. Model I Ventilated Choke Tube for use with A.B.S. Muzzle Brake, **$49.95**; for use without Muzzle Brake, **$52.95**; A.B.S. Muzzle Brake, from **$69.95**. Contact Dayson Arms for more data.

Gentry Quiet Muzzle Brake

Developed by gunmaker David Gentry, the "Quiet Muzzle Brake" is said to reduce recoil by up to 85 percent with no loss of accuracy or velocity. There is no increase in noise level because the noise and gases are directed away from the shooter. The barrel is threaded for installation and the unit is blued to match the barrel finish. Price, installed, is **$150.00**. Add **$15.00** for stainless steel, **$45.00** for knurled cap to protect threads. Shipping extra.

Intermountain Arms Recoil Brake

The Custom Compact Recoil Brake is said to reduce felt recoil by 50 percent in most calibers. Machined with an expansion chamber to maximize efficiency. There are 42 ports to direct gases away from the shooter. Individually machined, polished and blued to match each barrel. Adds 1¾" to the barrel. Blued or stainless steel, **$169.00**. From Intermountain Arms.

JP Muzzle Brake

Designed for single shot handguns, AR-15, Ruger Mini-14, Ruger Mini Thirty and other sporting rifles, the JP Muzzle Brake redirects high pressure gases against a large frontal surface which applies forward thrust to the gun. All gases are directed up, rearward and to the sides. Priced at **$79.95** (AR-15 or sporting rifles), **$89.95** (bull barrel and SKS, AK models), **$89.95** (Ruger Minis), Dual Chamber model **$79.95.** From JP Enterprises, Inc.

KDF Slim Line Muzzle Brake

This threaded muzzlebrake has 30 pressure ports that direct combustion gases in all directions to reduce felt recoil up to a claimed 80 percent without affecting accuracy or ballistics. It is said to reduce felt recoil of a 30-06 to that of a 243. Price, installed, is **$179.00**. From KDF, Inc.

Mag-Na-Port

Electrical Discharge Machining works on any firearm except those having non-conductive shrouded barrels. EDM is a metal erosion technique using carbon electrodes that control the area to be processed. The Mag-Na-Port venting process utilizes small trapezoidal openings to direct powder gases upward and outward to reduce recoil. No effect is had on bluing or nickeling outside the Mag-Na-Port area so no refinishing is needed. Rifle-style porting on single shot or large caliber handguns with barrels 7½" or longer is **$95.00**; Dual Trapezoidal porting on most handguns with minimum barrel length of 3", **$95.00**; standard revolver porting, **$65.00**; porting through the slide and barrel for semi-autos, **$90.00**; traditional rifle porting, **$115.00**. Prices do not include shipping, handling and insurance. From Mag-Na-Port International.

Mag-Na-Brake

A screw-on brake under 2" long with progressive integrated exhaust chambers to neutralize expanding gases. Gases dissipate with an opposite twist to prevent the brake from unscrewing, and with a 5-degree forward angle to minimize sound pressure level. Available in blue, satin blue, bright or satin stainless. Standard and Light Contour installation cost **$159.00** for bolt-action rifles, many single action and single shot handguns. A knurled thread protector costs **$30.00**. Also available in Varmint style with exhaust chambers covering 220 degrees for prone-position shooters. From Mag-Na-Port International.

Poly-Choke

Marble Arms Corp., manufacturer of the Poly-Choke adjustable shotgun choke, now offers two models in 12-, 16-, 20-, and 28-gauge—the Ventilated and Standard style chokes. Each provides nine choke settings including Xtra-Full and Slug. The Ventilated model reduces 20 percent of a shotgun's recoil, the company claims, and is priced at **$95.00**. The Standard Model is **$88.00**. Postage not included. Contact Marble Arms for more data.

Reed-Choke

Reed-Choke is a system of interchangeable choke tubes that can be installed in any single or double-barreled shotgun, including over/unders. The existing chokes are bored out, the muzzles over-bored and threaded for the tubes. A choice of three Reed-Choke tubes are supplied—Skeet, Imp. Cyl., Mod., Imp. Mod., or Full. Flush fitting, no notches exposed. Designed for thin-walled barrels. Made from 174 stainless steel. Cost of the installation is **$179.95** for single-barrel guns, **$229.95** for doubles. Extra tubes cost **$40.00** each. Postage and handling charges are **$8.50**. From Clinton River Gun Service.

Pro-port

A compound ellipsoid muzzle venting process similar to Mag-Na-Porting, only exclusively applied to shotguns. Like Mag-Na-Porting, this system reduces felt recoil, muzzle jump, and shooter fatigue. Very helpful for trap doubles shooters. Pro-Port is a patented process and installation is available in both the U.S. and Canada. Cost for the Pro-Port process is **$110.00** for over/unders (both barrels); **$80.00** for only the top or bottom barrel; and **$69.00** for single-barrel shotguns. Optional pigeon porting costs **$25.00** extra per barrel. Prices do not include shipping and handling. From Pro-port Ltd.

SSK Arrestor Brake

This is a true muzzlebrake with an expansion chamber. It takes up about 1" of barrel and reduces velocity accordingly. Some Arrestors are added to a barrel, increasing its length. Said to reduce the felt recoil of a 458 to that approaching a 30-06. Can be set up to give zero muzzle rise in any caliber, and can be added to most guns. For handgun or rifle. Prices start at **$95.00**. Contact SSK Industries for full data.

Walker Choke Tubes

This interchangeable choke tube system uses an adaptor fitted to the barrel without swaging. Therefore, it can be fitted to any single-barreled gun. The choke tubes use the conical-parallel system as used on all factory-choked barrels. These tubes can be used in Winchester, Mossberg, Smith & Wesson, Weatherby, or similar barrels made for the standard screw-in choke system. Available for 10-, 12-, 16- and 20-gauge. Factory installation (single barrel) with standard Walker choke tube is **$95.00**, **$190.00** for double barrels with two choke tubes. A full range of constriction is available. Contact Walker Arms for more data.

Walker Full Thread Choke Tubes

An interchangeable choke tube system using fully threaded inserts. No swaging, adaptor or change in barrel exterior dimensions. Available in 12- or 20-gauge. Factory installation cost: **$95.00** with one tube; extra tubes **$20.00** each. Contact Walker Arms Co. for more data.

SCOPES & MOUNTS

Maker and Model	Magn.	Field at 100 Yds. (feet)	Eye Relief (in.)	Length (in.)	Tube Dia. (in.)	W&E Adjust-ments	Weight (ozs.)	Price	Other Data
AAL OPTICS									
Micro-Dot Scopes[1]									
1.5-4.5x20 Rifle	1.5-4.5	80-26	3	9.8	1	Int.	10.5	**$287.00**	[1]Brightness-adjustable fiber optic red dot reticle. Waterproof, nitrogen-filled one-piece tube tube. Tinted see-through lens covers and battery included. [2]Parallax adjustable. [3]Ultra Dot sights include rings, battery, polarized filter, and 5-year warranty. All models available in black or satin finish. [4]Illuminated red dot has eleven brightness settings. Shock-proof aluminum tube. [5]Fiber optic red dot has five brightness settings. Shock-proof polymer tube. From AAL Optics.
2-7x32	2-7	54-18	3	11.0	1	Int.	12.1	**299.00**	
3-9x40	3-9	40-14	3	12.2	1	Int.	13.3	**319.00**	
4x-12x56[2]	4-12	30-10	3	14.3	1	Int.	18.3	**409.00**	
Ultra-Dot Sights[3]									
Ultra-Dot 25[4]	1	—	—	5.1	1	Int.	3.9	**139.00**	
Ultra-Dot 30[4]	1	—	—	5.1	30mm	Int.	4.0	**149.00**	
Ultra Dot Patriot[5]	1	—	—	5.1	1	Int.	2.9	**119.00**	
ADCO									[1]Multi-Color Dot system changes from red to green. [2]For airguns, paintball, rimfires. Uses common lithium wafer battery. [3]Comes with standard dovetail mount. [4]⅜" dovetail mount; poly body; adj. intensity diode. [5]Adj. dot size—5, 10, 15 MOA.
MiRAGE Ranger 1"	0	—	—	5.2	1	Int.	3.9	**159.00**	
MiRAGE Ranger 30mm	0	—	—	5.5	30mm	Int.	5.0	**179.00**	
MiRAGE Sportsman[1]	0	—	—	5.2	1	Int.	4.5	**249.00**	
MiRAGE Competitor[1]	0	—	—	5.5	30mm	Int.	5.5	**269.00**	
MiRAGE Trident[5]	0	—	—	6.0	30mm	Int.	6.5	**499.00**	
IMP Sight[2]	0	—	—	4.5	—	Int.	1.3	**19.95**	
Square Shooter[3]	0	—	—	5.0	—	Int.	5	**129.00**	
MiRAGE Eclipse[1]	0	—	—	5.5	30mm	Int.	5.5	**249.00**	
MiRAGE Champ Red Dot	0	—	—	4.5	—	Int.	2	**39.95**	
AIMPOINT									Illuminates red dot in field of view. Noparallax (dot does not need to be centered). Unlimited field of view and eye relief. On/off, adj. intensity. Dot covers 3" @ 100 yds. Mounts avail. for all sights and scopes. [1]Comes with 30mm rings, battery, lens cloth. [2]Requires 1" rings. Black or stainless finish. 3x scope attachment (for rifles only), **$129.95**. [3]Projects red dot of visible laser light onto target. Black finish (LSR-2B) or stainless (LSR-2S); or comes with rings and accessories. Optional toggle switch, **$34.95**. Lithium battery life up to 15 hours. [4]Black finish (AP 5000-B) or stainless (AP 5000-S); avail. with regular 3-min. or 10-min. Mag Dot as B2 or S2. [5]For Beretta, Browning, Colt Gov't., Desert Eagle, Glock, Ruger, SIG-Sauer, S&W. [6]For Colt, S&W. From Aimpoint U.S.A.
Comp	0	—	—	4.6	30mm	Int.	4.3	**308.00**	
Series 5000[4]	0	—	—	5.75	30mm	Int.	5.8	**277.00**	
Series 3000 Universal[2]	0	—	—	5.5	1	Int.	5.5	**232.00**	
Series 5000/2x[1]	2	—	—	7	30mm	Int.	9	**367.00**	
Laserdot[3]	—	—	—	3.5	1	Int.	4.0	**319.95**	
Autolaser[5]	—	—	—	3.75	1	Int.	4.3	**351.00**	
Revolver Laser[6]	—	—	—	3.5	1	Int.	3.6	**339.00**	
ARMSON O.E.G.									Shows red dot aiming point. No batteries needed. Standard model fits 1" ring mounts (not incl.). Other models available for many popular shotguns, para-military rifles and carbines. [1]Daylight Only Sight with ⅜" dovetail mount for 22s. Does not contain tritium. From Trijicon, Inc.
Standard	0	—	—	5⅛	1	Int.	4.3	**175.00**	
22 DOS[1]	0	—	—	3¾	—	Int.	3.0	**104.00**	
22 Day/Night	0	—	—	3¾	—	Int.	3.0	**146.00**	
M16/AR-15	0	—	—	5⅛	—	Int.	5.5	**209.00**	
Colt Pistol	0	—	—	3¾	—	Int.	3.0	**209.00**	
BAUSCH & LOMB									
Elite 4000									[1]Adj. objective, sunshade. [2]Also in matte and silver finish, **$632.00.** [3]Also in matte finish, **$589.00.** [4]Also in matte finish, **$370.95**; silver finish, **$370.95.** [5]Also in matte finish, **$361.95.** [6]50mm objective; matte finish, **$453.95.** [7]Also in matte finish, **$430.95.** [8]Also in silver finish, **$321.95.** [9]Also in silver finish, **$432.95 Partial listing shown. Contact Bausch & Lomb Sports Optics Div. for details.**
40-6244A[1]	6-24	18-4.5	3	16.9	1	Int.	20.2	**702.00**	
40-2104G[2]	2.5-10	41.5-10.8	3	13.5	1	Int.	16	**606.00**	
40-1636G[3]	1.5-6	61.8-16.1	3	12.8	1	Int.	15.4	**565.00**	
40-1040	10	10.5	3.6	13.8	1	Int.	22.1	**1,745.00**	
Elite 3000									
30-4124A[1]	4-12	26.9-9	3	13.2	1	Int.	15.0	**421.95**	
30-3940G[4]	3-9	33.8-11.5	3	12.6	1	Int.	13.0	**348.95**	
30-2732G[5]	2-7	44.6-12.7	3	11.6	1	Int.	12.0	**342.95**	
30-3950G[6]	3-9	31.5-10.5	3	15.7	1	Int.	19	**434.95**	
30-1545M[7]	1.5-4.5	63-20	3.3	12.5	1	Int.	13	**434.95**	
30-3955E	3-9	31.5-10.5	3	15.6	30mm	Int.	22	**633.95**	
Elite 3000 Handgun									
30-2028G[8]	2	23	9-26	8.4	1	Int.	6.9	**301.95**	
30-2632G[9]	2-6	10-4	20	9.0	1	Int.	10.0	**413.95**	
BEEMAN									All scopes have 5-point reticle, all glass, fully coated lenses. [1]Includes mount. [2]Also as 66RL with lighted color reticle, **$355.00.** [3]Also as SS-2L 3x with color 4pt. reticle. Imported by Beeman
Blue Ribbon SS-3[1]	1.5-4	42-25	3	5.8	⅞	Int.	8.5	**300.00**	
Blue Ribbon 66R[2]	2-7	62-16	3	11.4	1	Int.	14.9	**315.00**	
Blue Ribbon SS-2[1,3]	4	25	3.5	7.0	1.4	Int.	13.7	**305.00**	
Blue Ribbon 25 Pistol	2	19	10-24	9.1	1	Int.	7.4	**155.00**	
B-SQUARE									[1]Blue finish; stainless, **$209.95**. T-slot mount; cord or integral switch. [2]Blue finish; stainless, **$259.95**. T-slot mount; cord or integral switch. Uses common A76 batteries. [3]High intensity 635 beam, **$349.95** (blue), **$359.95** (stainless). Dimensions 1.1"x1.1"x.6". From B-Square.
BSL-1[1]	—	—	—	2.75	.75	Int.	2.25	**199.95**	
Mini-Laser[2,3]	—	—	—	1.1	—	Int.	2.9	**239.95**	
BURRIS									
Fullfield									All scopes avail. in Plex reticle. Steel-on-steel click adjustments. [1]Dot reticle on some models. [2]Post crosshair reticle extra. [3]Matte satin finish. [4]Available with parallax adjustment (standard on 10x, 12x, 4-12x, 6-12x, 6-18x, 6x HBR and 3-12x Signature). [5]Silver matte finish extra. [6]Target knobs extra, standard on silhouette models, LER and XER with P.A., 6x HBR. [7]Sunshade avail. [8]Avail. with Fine Plex reticle. [9]Available with Heavy Plex reticle. [10]Available with Posi-Lock. [11]Available with Peep Plex reticle. [12]Also avail. for rimfires, airguns.
1x LER[3]	1	51	4.5-20	8.8	1	Int.	7.9	**278.00**	
1½x[9]	1.6	62	3.5-3.75	10¼	1	Int.	9.0	**268.00**	
2½x[9]	2.5	55	3.5-3.75	10¼	1	Int.	9.0	**282.00**	
4x[1,2,3]	3.75	36	3.5-3.75	11¼	1	Int.	11.5	**285.00**	
6x[1,3]	5.8	23	3.5-3.75	13	1	Int.	12.0	**312.00**	
12x[1,4,6,7,8]	11.8	10.5	3.5-3.75	15	1	Int.	15	**392.00**	
1-4x XER[3]	1.0-3.8	53-15	4.25-30	8.8	1	Int.	10.3	**342.00**	
1¾-5x[1,2,9,10]	1.7-4.6	66-25	3.5-3.75	10⅞	1	Int.	13	**340.00**	

Maker and Model	Magn.	Field at 100 Yds. (feet)	Eye Relief (in.)	Length (in.)	Tube Dia. (in.)	W&E Adjust-ments	Weight (ozs.)	Price	Other Data
Burris (cont.)									
2-7x[1,2,3]	2.5-6.8	47-18	3.5-3.75	12	1	Int.	14	**364.00**	
3-9x[1,2,3,10]	3.3-8.7	38-15	3.5-3.75	12⅝	1	Int.	15	**339.00**	
3.5-10x50mm[3,5,10]	3.7-9.7	29.5-11	3.5-3.75	14	1	Int.	19	**450.00**	
4-12x[1,4,8,11]	4.4-11.8	27-10	3.5-3.75	15	1	Int.	18	**458.00**	
6-18x[1,3,4,6,7,8]	6.5-17.6	16-7	3.5-3.75	15.8	1	Int.	18.5	**479.00**	
Compact Scopes									
4x[4,5]	3.6	24	3¾-5	8¼	1	Int.	7.8	**239.00**	
6x[1,4]	5.5	17	3¾-5	9	1	Int.	8.2	**254.00**	
6x HBR[1,5,8]	6.0	13	4.5	11¼	1	Int.	13.0	**329.00**	
2-7x	2.5-6.9	32-14	3¾-5	12	1	Int.	10.5	**327.00**	
3-9x[5]	3.6-8.8	25-11	3¾-5	12⅝	1	Int.	11.5	**335.00**	
4-12x[1,4,6]	4.5-11.6	19-8	3¾-4	15	1	Int.	15	**442.00**	
Signature Series									LER=Long Eye Relief; IER=Intermediate Eye Relief; XER=Extra Eye Relief. Partial listing shown, contact maker for complete data. From Burris.
1.5-6x[2,3,5,9,10]	1.7-5.8	70-20	3.5-4.0	10.8	1	Int.	13.0	**429.00**	
4x[3]	4.0	30	3.5-4.0	12⅛	1	Int.	14	**349.00**	
6x[3]	6.0	20	3.5-4.0	12⅛	1	Int.	14	**358.00**	
2-8x[3,5,11]	2.1-7.7	53-17	3.5-4.0	11.75	1	Int.	14	**498.00**	
3-9x[3,5,10]	3.3-8.8	36-14	3.5-4.0	12⅞	1	Int.	15.5	**509.00**	
2½-10x[3,5,10]	2.7-9.5	37-10.5	3.5-4.0	14	1	Int.	19.0	**552.00**	
3-12x[3,10]	3.3-11.7	34-9	3.5-4.0	14¼	1	Int.	21	**612.00**	
4-16x[1,3,5,6,8,10]	4.3-15.7	33-9	3.5-4.0	15.4	1	Int.	23.7	**624.00**	
6-24x[1,3,5,6,8,10]	6.6-23.8	17-6	3.5-4.0	16.0	1	Int.	22.7	**664.00**	
8-32x[8,10,12]	8.6-31.4	13-3.8	3.5-4.0	17	1	Int.	24	**727.00**	
Handgun									
1½-4x LER[1,5,10]	1.6-3.	16-11	11-25	10¼	1	Int.	11	**365.00**	
2-7x LER[3,4,5,10]	2-6.5	21-7	7-27	9.5	1	Int.	12.6	**358.00**	
3-9x LER[4,5,10]	3.4-8.4	12-5	22-14	11	1	Int.	14	**402.00**	
1x LER[1]	1.1	27	10-24	8¾	1	Int.	6.8	**228.00**	
2x LER[4,5,6]	1.7	21	10-24	8¾	1	Int.	6.8	**235.00**	
3x LER[4,6]	2.7	17	10-20	8⅞	1	Int.	6.8	**252.00**	
4x LER[1,4,5,6,10]	3.7	11	10-22	9⅝	1	Int.	9.0	**262.00**	
7x IER[1,4,5,6]	6.5	6.5	10-16	11¼	1	Int.	10	**329.00**	
10x IER[1,4,6]	9.5	4	8-12	13½	1	Int.	14	**388.00**	
Scout Scope									
1½x XER[3,9]	1.5	22	7-18	9	1	Int.	7.3	**238.00**	
2¾x XER[3,9]	2.7	15	7-14	9⅜	1	Int.	7.5	**235.00**	
BUSHNELL									
Trophy									
73-0130[1]	1	61	—	5.25	30mm	Int.	5.5	**282.95**	[1]45mm objective. [2]Wide angle; silver or matte finish, **$297.95.** [3]Also silver finish, **$205.95**. [4]Also silver finish, **$267.95**. [5]56mm objective. [6]Selective red L.E.D. dot for low light hunting. [7]Also silver finish, **$65.95**. [8]Adj. obj. [9]Variable intensity; interchangeable extra reticles (Dual Rings, Open Cross Hairs, Rising Dot) **$128.95**; fits Weaver-style base.
73-2545[1]	2.5-10	39-10	3	13.75	1	Int.	14	**310.95**	
73-1500[2]	1.75-5	68-23	3.5	10.8	1	Int.	12.3	**258.95**	
73-4124[2]	4-12	32-11	3	12.5	1	Int.	16.1	**288.95**	
73-3940	3-9	42-14	3	11.7	1	Int.	13.2	**186.95**	
73-6184	6-18	17.3-6	3	14.8	1	Int.	17.9	**338.95**	
HOLOsight[9]	1	—	—	6	—	Int.	8.7	**599.95**	
Trophy Handgun									
73-0232[3]	2	20	9-26	8.7	1	Int.	7.7	**190.95**	
73-2632[4]	2-6	21-7	9-26	9.1	1	Int.	9.6	**252.95**	
Banner Standard									
71-2520	2.5	44	3.6	10	1	Int.	7.5	**84.95**	
71-3956[5]	3-9	37-12	3.5	13.7	1	Int.	17.3	**288.95**	
Lite-Site									
71-3940[6]	3-9	36-13	3.1	12.8	1	Int.	15.5	**368.95**	
Sportview									
79-0004	4	31	4	11.7	1	Int.	11.2	**92.95**	
79-0039	3-9	38-13	3.5	10.75	1	Int.	11.2	**109.95**	
79-0412[8]	4-12	27-9	3.2	13.1	1	Int.	14.6	**132.95**	
79-0640	6	20.5	3	12.25	1	Int.	10.4	**91.95**	
79-1393[7]	3-9	35-12	3.5	11.75	1	Int.	10	**66.95**	
79-1545	1.5-4.5	69-24	3	10.7	1	Int.	8.6	**88.95**	
79-3145	3.5-10	36-13	3	12.75	1	Int.	13.9	**145.95**	
79-1403	4	29	4	11.75	1	Int.	9.2	**53.95**	
79-6184	6-18	19.1-6.8	3	14.5	1	Int.	15.9	**159.95**	
79-3938	3-9	42-14	3	12.7	1	Int.	12.5	**105.95**	
79-3720	3-7	23-11	2.6	11.3	.75	Int.	5.7	**40.95**	
Turkey & Brush									
73-1420	1.75-4	73-30	3.5	10.8	32mm	Int.	10.9	**263.95**	
CHARLES DALY									
4x32	4	28	3.25	11.75	1	Int.	9.5	**70.00**	Waterproof, fog-proof. [1]Shotgun scope. From Outdoor Sports Headquarters.
4x32[1]	4	16	6	8.8	1	Int.	9.2	**90.00**	
4x40 WA	4	36	3.25	13	1	Int.	11.5	**98.00**	
2-7x32 WA	2-7	56-17	3	11.5	1	Int.	12	**125.00**	
3-9x40	3-9	35-14	3	12.5	1	Int.	11.25	**110.00**	
3-9x40 WA	3-9	36-13	3	12.75	1	Int.	12.5	**125.00**	
4-12x40 WA	4-12	30-11	3	13.75	1	Int.	14.5	**133.00**	

CAUTION: PRICES SHOWN ARE SUPPLIED BY THE MANUFACTURER OR IMPORTER. CHECK YOUR LOCAL GUNSHOP.

Maker and Model	Magn.	Field at 100 Yds. (feet)	Eye Relief (in.)	Length (in.)	Tube Dia. (in.)	W&E Adjust-ments	Weight (ozs.)	Price	Other Data
DOCTER OPTIC									Matte black and matte silver finish available. All lenses multi-coated. Illuminated reticle avail., choice of reticles. Rail mount, aspherical lenses avail. [1]Aspherical lens model, **$1,375.00**. Imported from Germany by Docter Optic Technologies, Inc.
Fixed Power									
4x32	4	31	3	10.7	26mm	Int.	10.0	**898.00**	
6x42	6	20	3	12.8	26mm	Int.	12.7	**1,004.00**	
8x56[1]	8	15	3	14.7	26mm	Int.	15.6	**1,240.00**	
Variables									
1-4x24	1-4	79.7-31.3	3	10.8	30mm	Int.	13	**1,300.00**	
1.2-5x32	1.2-5	65-25	3	11.6	30mm	Int.	15.4	**1,345.00**	
1.5-6x42	1.5-6	41.3-20.6	3	12.7	30mm	Int.	16.8	**1,378.00**	
2.5-10x48	2.5-10	36.6-12.4	3	13.7	30mm	Int.	18.6	**1,378.00**	
2-12x56	3-12	44.2-13.8	3	14.8	30mm	Int.	20.3	**1,425.00**	
FROM JENA									[1]Military scope with adjustable parallax. Fixed powers have 26mm tubes, variables have 30mm tubes. Some models avail. with steel tubes. All lenses multi-coated. Dust and water tight. From Jena, Europtik, Ltd.
4x36	4	39	3.5	11.6	26mm	Int.	14	**695.00**	
6x36	6	21	3.5	12	26mm	Int.	14	**795.00**	
6x42	6	21	3.5	13	26mm	Int.	15	**860.00**	
8x56	8	18	3.5	14.4	26mm	Int.	20	**890.00**	
1.5-6x42	1.5-6	61.7-23	3.5	12.6	30mm	Int.	17	**975.00**	
2-8x42	2-8	52-17	3.5	13.3	30mm	Int.	17	**1,050.00**	
2.5-10x56	2.5-10	40-13.6	3.5	15	30mm	Int.	21	**1,195.00**	
3-12x56	3-12	NA	NA	NA	30mm	Int.	NA	**1,195.00**	
4-16x56	4-16	NA	NA	NA	30mm	Int.	NA	**1,225.00**	
3-9x40	3-9	NA	NA	NA	1	Int.	NA	**1,120.00**	
2.5-10x46	2.5-10	NA	NA	NA	30mm	Int.	NA	**1,150.00**	
4-16x56[1]	4-16	NA	NA	NA	30mm	Int.	NA	**1,695.00**	
INTERAIMS									Intended for handguns. Comes with rings. Dot size less than 1½" @ 100 yds. Waterproof. Battery life 50-10,000 hours. Black or nickel finish. 2x booster, 1" or 30mm, **$139.00** Imported by Stoeger.
One V	0	—	—	4.5	1	Int.	4	**159.95**	
One V 30	0	—	—	4.5	30mm	Int.	4	**176.95**	
KAHLES									[1]Steel tube. [2]Ballistic cam system with military rangefinder. Waterproof, fogproof, nitrogen filled. Choice of reticles. Imported from Austria by Swarovski Optic NA.
K1.5-6x42-L	1.5-6	61-21	—	12.5	30mm	Int.	15.8	**721.12**	
K2.2-9x42-L	2.2-9	39.5-15	—	13.3	30mm	Int.	15.5	**887.78**	
K3-12x56-L	3-12	30-11	—	15.2	30mm	Int.	18	**943.33**	
KZF84-6[1,2]	6	23	—	12.5	1	Int.	17.6	**1,245.00**	
KZF84-10[1,2]	10	13	—	13.25	1	Int.	18	**1,245.00**	
KILHAM									Unlimited eye relief; internal click adjustments; crosshair reticle. Fits Thompson/Center rail mounts, for S&W K, N, Ruger Blackhawk, Super, Super Single-Six, Contender.
Hutson Handgunner II	1.7	8	—	5½	⅞	Int.	5.1	**119.95**	
Hutson Handgunner	3	8	10-12	6	⅞	Int.	5.3	**119.95**	
LASERAIM									[1]Red dot/laser combo; 300-yd. range; LA3XHD Hotdot has 500-yd. range **$249.00**; 4 MOA dot size, laser gives 2" dot size at 100 yds. [2]30mm obj. lens; 4 MOA dot at 100 yds.; fits Weaver base. [3]300-yd. range; 2" dot at 100 yds.; rechargeable Nicad battery. [4]1.5-mile range; 1" dot at 100 yds.; 20+ hrs. batt. life. [5]1.5-mile range; 1" dot at 100 yds.; rechargeable Nicad battery (comes with in-field charger); [6]Black or satin finish. With mount, **$169.00**. [7]Laser projects 2" dot at 100 yds.; with rotary switch; with Hotdot **$237.00**; with Hotdot, touch switch **$357.00**. [8]For Glock 17-27; G1 Hotdot **$299.00**; price installed. [10]Fits std. Weaver base, no rings required; 6-MOA dot; seven brightness settings. All have w&e adj.; black or satin silver finish. From Laseraim Technologies, Inc.
LA3X Dualdot[1]	—	—	—	6	—	Int.	12	**199.00**	
LA5[3]	—	—	—	2	.75	Int.	1.2	**236.00**	
LA10 Hotdot[4]	—	—	—	3.87	.75	Int.	NA	**396.00**	
LA11 Hotdot[5]	—	—	—	2.75	.75	Int.	NA	**292.00**	
LA14	—	—	—	NA	NA	Int.	NA	**314.00**	
LA16 Hotdot Mighty Sight[6]	—	—	—	1.5	NA	Int.	1.5	**169.00**	
Red Dot Sights									
LA93 Illusion III[2]	—	—	—	6.0	—	Int.	5.0	**139.00**	
LA9750 Grand Illusion[10]	—	—	—	5.5	50mm	Int.	7.0	**199.00**	
Lasers									
MA3 Mini Aimer[7]	—	—	—	1.5	⅝	Int.	1.0	**155.00**	
G1 Laser[8]	—	—	—	1.5	—	Int.	2.0	**289.00**	
LASER DEVICES									Projects high intensity beam of laser light onto target as an aiming point. Adj. for w. & e. [1]Diode laser system. From Laser Devices, Inc.
He Ne FA-6	—	—	—	6.2	—	Int.	11	**229.50**	
He Ne FA-9	—	—	—	12	—	Int.	16	**299.00**	
He Ne FA-9P	—	—	—	9	—	Int.	14	**299.00**	
FA-4[1]	—	—	—	4.5	—	Int.	3.5	**299.00**	
LEUPOLD									Constantly centered reticles, choice of Duplex, tapered CPC, Leupold Dot, Crosshair and Dot. CPC and Dot reticles extra. [1]2x and 4x scopes have from 12"-24" of eye relief and are suitable for handguns, top ejection arms and muzzleloaders. [2]3x9 Compact, 6x Compact, 12x, 3x9, 3.5x10 and 6.5x20 come with adjustable objective. [3]Target scopes have 1-min. divisions with ¼-min. clicks, and adjustable objectives. 50-ft. Focus Adaptor available for indoor target ranges, **$53.60**. Sunshade available for all adjustable objective scopes, **$21.40-39.30**. [4]Also available in matte finish for about **$15.00** extra. [5]Silver finish about **$15.00** extra. [6]Matte finish. [7]Battery life 60 min.; dot size .625" @ 25 yds. Black matte finish Partial listing shown. **Contact Leupold for complete details.**
Vari-X III 3.5x10 STD Tactical	3.5-10	29.5-10.7	3.6-4.6	12.5	1	Int.	13.5	**716.10**	
M8-2X EER[1]	1.7	21.2	12-24	7.9	1	Int.	6.0	**271.40**	
M8-2X EER Silver[1]	1.7	21.2	12-24	7.9	1	Int.	6.0	**292.90**	
M8-4X EER[1]	3.7	9	12-24	8.4	1	Int.	7.0	**367.90**	
M8-4X EER Silver[1]	3.7	9	12-24	8.4	1	Int.	7.0	**367.90**	
Vari-X 2.5-8 EER	2.5-8.0	13-4.3	11.7-12	9.7	1	Int.	10.9	**530.40**	
M8-4X Compact	3.6	25.5	4.5	9.2	1	Int.	7.5	**335.70**	
Vari-X 2-7x Compact	2.5-6.6	41.7-16.5	5-3.7	9.9	1	Int.	8.5	**421.40**	
Vari-X 3-9x Compact	3.2-8.6	34-13.5	4.0-3.0	11-11.3	1	Int.	11.0	**435.70**	
Vari-X 6-18x40	6.7-17.1	14.5-6.6	4.7-3.7	13.4	1	Int.	14.0	**821.40**	
M8-4X[4]	4.0	24	4.0	10.7	1	Int.	9.3	**335.70**	
M8-6X[6]	5.9	17.7	4.3	11.4	1	Int.	10.0	**358.90**	
M8-6x 42mm	6.0	17	4.5	12	1	Int.	11.3	**444.60**	
M8-12x A.O. Varmint	11.6	9.1	4.2	13.0	1	Int.	13.5	**498.20**	
BR-24X[3]	24.0	4.7	3.2	13.8	1	Int.	15.3	**896.40**	
BR-36X[3]	36.0	3.2	3.4	14.1	1	Int.	15.6	**937.50**	
Vari-X 3-9x Compact EFR A.O.	3.8-8.6	34.0-13.5	4.0-3.0	11.0	1	Int.	11	**491.10**	
Vari-X-II 1x4	1.6-4.2	70.5-28.5	4.3-3.8	9.2	1	Int.	9.0	**360.70**	
Vari-X-II 2x7[4]	2.5-6.6	42.5-17.8	4.9-3.8	11.0	1	Int.	10.5	**391.10**	
Vari-X-II 3x9[1,4,5]	3.3-8.6	32.3-14.0	4.1-3.7	12.3	1	Int.	13.5	**394.60**	
Vari-X-II 3-9x50mm[4]	3.3-8.6	32.3-14	4.7-3.7	12	1	Int.	13.6	**501.80**	
Vari-X-II 4-12 A.O. Matte	4.4-11.6	22.8-11.0	5.0-3.3	12.3	1	Int.	13.5	**542.90**	
M8-2.5x32 IER Scout	2.3	22	9-17	10.0	1	Int.	7.5	**353.60**	
Vari-X-III 1.5x5	1.5-4.5	66.0-23.0	5.3-3.7	9.4	1	Int.	9.5	**551.80**	

CAUTION: PRICES SHOWN ARE SUPPLIED BY THE MANUFACTURER OR IMPORTER. CHECK YOUR LOCAL GUNSHOP.

Maker and Model	Magn.	Field at 100 Yds. (feet)	Eye Relief (in.)	Length (in.)	Tube Dia. (in.)	W&E Adjust-ments	Weight (ozs.)	Price	Other Data
Leupold (cont.)									
Vari-X-III 1.75-6x 32	1.9-5.6	47-18	4.8-3.7	9.8	1	Int.	11	**575.40**	
Vari-X-III 2.5x8[4]	2.6-7.8	37.0-13.5	4.7-3.7	11.3	1	Int.	11.5	**594.60**	
Vari-X-III 3.5-10x50 A.O.	3.3-9.7	29.5-10.7	4.6-3.6	12.4	1	Int.	13.0	**769.60**	
Vari-X-III 3.5-10x50[2,4]	3.3-9.7	29.5-10.7	4.6-3.6	12.4	1	Int.	14.4	**714.30**	
Vari-X-III 4.5-14	4.7-13.7	20.8-7.4	5.0-3.7	12.4	1	Int.	14.5	**691.10**	
Vari-X-III 4.5-14x50	4.7-13.7	20.8-7.4	5.0-3.7	12.4	1	Int.	14.5	**828.60**	
Vari-X-III 6.5-20 A.O. Varmint	6.5-19.2	14.2-5.5	5.3-3.6	14.2	1	Int.	17.5	**839.30**	
Vari-X-III 6.5-20x Target EFR A.O.	6.5-19.2	—	5.3-3.6	14.2	1	Int.	16.5	**812.50**	
Mark 4 M3-6x	6	17.7	4.5	13.1	30mm	Int.	21	**1,612.50**	
Mark 4 M1-10x[6]	10	11.1	3.6	13⅛	1	Int.	21	**1,612.50**	
Mark 4 M1-16x[6]	16	6.6	4.1	12⅞	1	Int.	22	**1,612.50**	
Mark 4 M3-10x[6]	10	11.1	3.6	13⅛	1	Int.	21	**1,612.50**	
Vari-X-III 6.5x20[2]	6.5-19.2	14.2-5.5	5.3-3.6	14.2	1	Int.	16.0	**719.60**	
Rimfire									
Vari-X-II 2-7x RF Special	3.6	25.5	4.5	9.2	1	Int.	7.5	**421.40**	
Shotgun									
M8 4x	3.7	9.0	12-24	8.4	1	Int.	6.0	**357.10**	
Vari-X-II 1x4	1.6-4.2	70.5-28.5	4.3-3.8	9.2	1	Int.	9.0	**382.10**	
Vari-X-II 2x7	2.5-6.6	42.5-17.8	4.9-3.8	11.0	1	Int.	9.0	**412.50**	
Laser									
LaserLight[7]	—	—	—	1.18	NA	Int.	.5	**292.90**	
LYMAN									
Super TargetSpot[1]	10,12,15,20, 25,30	5.5	2	24.3	.75	Int.	27.5	**685.00**	Made under license from Lyman to Lyman's orig. specs. Blue steel. Three-point suspension rear mount with ¼-min. click adj. Data listed are for 20x model. [1]Price approximate. Made in U.S. by Parsons Optical Mfg. Co.
McMILLAN									
Vision Master 2.5-10x	2.5-10	14.2-4.4	4.3-3.3	13.3	30mm	Int.	17.0	**1,250.00**	42mm obj. lens; ¼-MOA clicks; nitrogen filled, fogproof, waterproof; etched duplex-type reticle. [1]Tactical Scope with external adj. knobs, military reticle; 60+ min. adj.
Vision Master Model I[1]	2.5-10	14.2-4.4	4.3-3.3	13.3	30mm	Int.	17.0	**1,250.00**	
MILLETT									
Red Dot 1 Inch	1	36.65	—	NA	1	Int.	NA	**189.95**	Full coated lenses; parallax-free; three lenses; 30mm has 10-min. dot, 1-Inch has 3-min. dot. Black or silver finish. From Millett Sights.
Red Dot 30mm	1	58	—	NA	30mm	Int.	NA	**289.95**	
MIRADOR									
RXW 4x40[1]	4	37	3.8	12.4	1	Int.	12	**179.95**	[1]Wide Angle scope. Multi-coated objective lens. Nitrogen filled; waterproof; shockproof. From Mirador Optical Corp.
RXW 1.5-5x20[1]	1.5-5	46-17.4	4.3	11.1	1	Int.	10	**188.95**	
RXW 3-9x40	3-9	43-14.5	3.1	12.9	1	Int.	13.4	**251.95**	
NIKON									
4x40[2]	4	26.7	3.5	11.7	1	Int.	11.7	**284.00**	Super multi-coated lenses and blackening of all internal metal parts for maximum light gathering capability; positive ¼-MOA; fogproof; waterproof; shockproof; luster and matte finish. [1]Also available in matte silver finish. [2]Available in silver matte finish. From Nikon, Inc.
1.5-4.5x20	1.5-4.5	67.8-22.5	3.7-3.2	10.1	1	Int.	9.5	**358.00**	
1.5-4.5x24 EER	1.5-4.4	13.7-5.8	24-18	8.9	1	Int.	9.3	**352.00**	
2-7x32	2-7	46.7-13.7	3.9-3.3	11.3	1	Int.	11.3	**367.00**	
3-9x40[1]	3-9	33.8-11.3	3.6-3.2	12.5	1	Int.	12.5	**371.00**	
3.5-10x50	3.5-10	25.5-8.9	3.9-3.8	13.7	1	Int.	15.5	**489.00**	
4-12x40 A.O.	4-12	25.7-8.6	3.6-3.2	14	1	Int.	16.6	**476.00**	
4-12x50 A.O.	4-12	25.4-8.5	3.6-3.5	14.0	1	Int.	18.3	**578.00**	
6.5-20x44	6.5-19.4	16.2-5.4	3.5-3.1	14.8	1	Int.	19.6	**591.00**	
2x20 EER	2	22	26.4	8.1	1	Int.	6.3	**213.00**	
PARSONS									
Parsons Long Scope	6	10	2	28-34+	¾	Ext.	13	**475.00-525.00**	Adjustable for parallax, focus. Micrometer rear mount with ¼-min. click adjustments. Price is approximate. Made in U.S. by Parsons Optical Mfg. Co.
PENTAX									
Lightseeker 2-8x[1]	2-8	53-17	3-3.5	11.7	1	Int.	14.0	**530.00**	[1]Glossy finish; matte finish, **$530.00**; satin chrome, **$550.00**. [2]Glossy finish; matte finish, **$560.00**; satin chrome, **$580.00**. [3]Glossy finish; matte finish, **$580.00**; satin chrome, **$600.00**. [4]Glossy-XL finish; matte-XL finish, **$720.00**; satin chrome-XL, **$740.00**. [5]Glossy finish; matte finish, **$770.00.** [6]Glossy finish, Fine Plex; matte finish, Fine Plex, **$810.00**; dot reticle, add **$10.00**. [7]Glossy finish; matte finish, **$504.00**; satin chrome, **$524.00**. [8]Glossy finish; matte finish, **$420.00;** satin chrome **$440.00**. [9]Lightseeker II **$624.00** glossy, **$648.00** matte. [10]Lightseeker II **$804.00** glossy, **$828.00** matte. [11]Glossy finish; matte finish, **$360.00**. [12]Glossy finish; matte finish, **$440.00**. [13]Glossy finish; matte finish, **$310.00**; Mossy Oak, **$330.00**. [14]Glossy finish; satin chrome, **$260.00**. [15]Glossy finish; satin chrome, **$380.00**. [16]Glossy finish; satin chrome, **$390.00**. [17]Lightseeker II **$836.00** glossy, **$844.00** satin chrome. Imported by Pentax Corp.
Lightseeker 3-9x[2,9]	3-9	36-14	3-3.5	12.7	1	Int.	15.0	**560.00**	
Lightseeker 1.75-6x[7]	1.75-6	71-20	3.5-4	10.75	1	Int.	13.0	**484.00**	
Lightseeker 3.5-10x[3]	3.5-10	29.5-11	3-3.25	14.0	1	Int.	19.5	**588.00**	
Lightseeker 3-11x[4]	3-11	38.5-13	3-3.25	13.3	1	Int.	19	**700.00**	
Lightseeker 4-16x AO[5,10]	4-16	3-3.5	33-9	15.4	1	Int.	23.7	**760.00**	
Lightseeker 6-24 AO[6,17]	6-24	18-5.5	3-3.25	16	1	Int.	22.7	**800.00**	
3-9x[8]	3-9	38-14.7	3-3.25	13.0	1	Int.	15.0	**400.00**	
Shotgun									
Lightseeker Zero-X SG Plus[11]	0	51	4.5-15	8.9	1	Int.	7.9	**340.00**	
Lightseeker Zero-X/V SG Plus[12]	0-4	53.8-15	3.5-7	8.9	1	Int.	10.3	**420.00**	
Lightseeker 2.5x SG Plus[13]	2.5	55	3-3.5	10.0	1	Int.	9.0	**346.00**	
Pistol									
2x[14]	2	21	10-24	8.8	1	Int.	6.8	**230.00**	
1.5-4x[15]	1.5-4	16-11	11-25, 11-18	10.0	1	Int.	11.0	**350.00**	
2.5-7x[16]	2.5-7	12-7.5	11-28, 9-14	12.0	1	Int.	12.5	**370.00**	
RWS									
300	4	36	3.5	11¾	1	Int.	13.2	**170.00**	Air gun scopes. All have Dyna-Plex reticle. Model 800 is for air pistols. [1]M450, 3-9x40mm, **$200.00**. Imported from Japan by Dynamit Nobel-RWS.
400[1]	2-7	55-16	3.5	11¾	1	Int.	13.2	**190.00**	
450	3-9	43-14	3.5	12	1	Int.	14.3	**215.00**	
500	4	36	3.5	12¼	1	Int.	13.9	**225.00**	
550	2-7	55-16	3.5	12¾	1	Int.	14.3	**235.00**	
600	3-9	43-14	3.5	13	1	Int.	16.5	**260.00**	

CAUTION: PRICES SHOWN ARE SUPPLIED BY THE MANUFACTURER OR IMPORTER. CHECK YOUR LOCAL GUNSHOP.

Maker and Model	Magn.	Field at 100 Yds. (feet)	Eye Relief (in.)	Length (in.)	Tube Dia. (in.)	W&E Adjust-ments	Weight (ozs.)	Price	Other Data
REDFIELD									
Ultimate Illuminator 3-9x	3.4-9.1	27-9	3-3.5	15.1	30mm	Int.	20.5	705.95	*Accutrac feature avail. on these scopes at extra cost. Traditionals have round lenses. 4-Plex reticle is standard. [1]Magnum proof. Specially designed for magnum and auto pistols. Uses Double Dovetail mounts. Also in nickel-plated finish, 2x, **$239.95**, 4x, **$239.95**, 2½-7x, **$322.95**, 2½-7x matte black, **$322.95**. [2]With matte finish **$619.95**. [3]Also available with matte finish at extra cost. [4]All Golden Five Star scopes come with Butler Creek flip-up lens covers. [5]56mm adj. objective; European #4 or 4-Plex reticle; comes with 30mm steel rings with Rotary Dovetail System. ¼-min. click adj. Also in matte finish, **$805.95**. [6]Also available nickel-plated **$363.95**. [7]With target knob, **$439.95**; black matte finish, **$493.95**; black matte with target knob, **$446.95**. [8]Black matte finish, **$400.95**. [9]Also avail. in black matte, **$246.95**. [10]Also avail. in black matte, **$462.95**; black matte with target knobs, **$480.95**; with Accu-Trac, black matte,**$512.95**. [11]Fine crosshair, black finish; **$681.95** dot reticle or black or fine crosshair and matte finish; **$737.95** with dot, matte; Quick-Zero target knobs, ⅛-MOA reticle, adj. obj. [12]Comes with rings, see-through lens covers, variable intensity, four dial-in sight patterns. Selected models shown. **Contact Redfield for full data.**
Ultimate Illuminator 3-12x[5]	2.9-11.7	27-10.5	3-3½	15.4	30mm	Int.	23	805.95	
Widefield Illuminator 2-7x	2.0-6.8	56-17	3-3.5	11.7	1	Int.	13.5	539.95	
Widefield Illuminator 3-9x*[2]	2.9-8.7	38-13	3½	12¾	1	Int.	17	609.95	
Widefield Illuminator 3-10x	3-10.1	29-10.5	3-3.5	14.75	1	Int.	18.0	681.95	
Tracker 4x[3]	3.9	28.9	3½	11.02	1	Int.	9.8	187.95	
Tracker 6x[3]	6.2	18	3.5	12.4	1	Int.	11.1	217.95	
Tracker 8x	8.1	13.5	3.5	12.4	1	Int.	11.1	226.95	
Tracker 2-7x[3]	2.3-6.9	36.6-12.2	3½	12.20	1	Int.	11.6	239.95	
Tracker 3-9x[3]	3.0-9.0	34.4-11.3	3½	14.96	1	Int.	13.4	269.95	
Traditional 4x ¾"	4	24½	3½	9⅜	¾	Int.	—	229.95	
Traditional 2½x	2½	43	3½	10¼	1	Int.	8½	161.95	
Golden Five Star 4x[4]	4	28.5	3.75	11.3	1	Int.	9.75	259.95	
Golden Five Star 6x[4]	6	18	3.75	12.2	1	Int.	11.5	282.95	
Golden Five Star 2-7x[4]	2.4-7.4	42-14	3-3.75	11.25	1	Int.	12	333.95	
Golden Five Star 3-9x[4,6]	3.0-9.1	34-11	3-3.75	12.50	1	Int.	13	409.95	
Golden Five Star 3-9x 50mm[4]	3.0-9.1	36.0-11.5	3-3.5	12.8	1	Int.	16	440.95	
Golden Five Star 4-12x A.O.*[4,10]	3.9-11.4	27-9	3-3.75	13.8	1	Int.	16	505.95	
Golden Five Star 6-18x A.O.*[4,7]	6.1-18.1	18.6	3-3.75	14.3	1	Int.	18	483.95	
6-24x Varmint[11]	5.9-23.8	15-5.5	3-3.5	15.75	1	Int.	26	664.95	
I.E.R. 1-4x Shotgun	1.3-3.8	48-16	6	10.2	1	Int.	12	373.95	
Compact Scopes									
Golden Five Star Compact 2-7x	2.4-7.1	40-16	3-3.5	9.75	1	Int.	9.8	329.95	
Golden Five Star Compact 3-9x	3.3-9.1	32-11.25	3-3.5	10.7	1	Int.	10.5	346.95	
Golden Five Star Compact 4-12x	4.1-12.4	22.4-8.3	3-3.5	12	1	Int.	13	439.95	
Hunter									
3-9x	3-9	34.4-11.3	3.5	12.4	1	Int.	12.6	NA	
Handgun Scopes									
Golden Five Star 2x	2	24	9.5-20	7.88	1	Int.	6	223.95	
Golden Five Star 4x	4	75	13-19	8.63	1	Int.	6.1	223.95	
Golden Five Star 2½-7x	2½-7	11-3.75	11-26	9.4	1	Int.	9.3	303.95	
Widefield Low Profile Compact									
Widefield 4xLP Compact	3.7	33	3.5	9.35	1	Int.	10	303.95	
Widefield 3-9x LP Compact	3.3-9	37.0-13.7	3-3.5	10.20	1	Int.	13	387.95	
ESD[12]	—	14.9	—	5.25	30mm	Int.	6.0	NA	
Low Profile Scopes									
Widefield 2¾xLP	2¾	55½	3½	10½	1	Int.	8	283.95	
Widefield 4xLP	3.6	37½	3½	11½	1	Int.	10	317.95	
Widefield 6xLP	5.5	23	3½	12¾	1	Int.	11	340.95	
Widefield 1¾x-5xLP[8]	1¾-5	70-27	3½	10¾	1	Int.	11½	389.95	
Widefield 2x-7xLP*	2-7	49-19	3½	11¾	1	Int.	13	400.95	
Widefield 3x-9xLP*	3-9	39-15	3½	12½	1	Int.	14	445.95	
SCHMIDT & BENDER									
Fixed									
4x36	4	30	3.25	11	1	Int.	14	725.00	All scopes have 30-yr. warranty, click adjustments, centered reticles, rotation indicators. [1]Glass reticle; steel or aluminum. Available in aluminum with mounting rail. [2]Aluminum only. [3]Aluminum tube. Choice of two bullet drop compensators, choice of two sunshades, two rangefinding reticles. From Schmidt & Bender, Inc.
6x42	6	21	3.25	13	1	Int.	17	795.00	
8x56	8	16.5	3.25	14	1	Int.	22	915.00	
10x42	10	10.5	3.25	13	1	Int.	18	910.00	
Variables									
1.25-4x20[1]	1.25-4	96-16	3.25	10	30mm	Int.	15.5	980.00	
1.5-6x42[1]	1.5-6	60-19.5	3.25	12	30mm	Int.	19.7	1,073.00	
2.5-10x56[1]	2.5-10	37.5-12	3.25	14	30mm	Int.	24.6	1,298.00	
3-12x42[2]	3-12	34.5-11.5	3.25	13.5	30mm	Int.	19.0	1,222.00	
3-12x50[1]	3-12	33.3-12.6	3.25	13.5	30mm	Int.	22.9	1,262.00	
Police/Marksman									
Fixed									
6x42[3]	6	21	3.25	13.0	30mm	Int.	17.0	980.00	
10x42[3]	10	10.5	3.25	13.0	30mm	Int.	18	1,055.00	
Variables									
3-12x42[3]	3-12	34.5-11.5	3.25	13.5	30mm	Int.	NA	1,510.00	
3-12x50[3]	3-12	33.3-12.6	3.25	13.5	30mm	Int.	NA	1,550.00	
1.5-6x42[3]	1.5-6	60-19.5	3.25	12.0	30mm	Int.	NA	1,350.00	
SHEPHERD									
3940-E	3-9	43.5-15	3.3	13	1	Int.	17	1,039.40	[1]Also avail. as 310-P, 310-PE, **$524.25**. [2]Also avail. as 310-P1, 310-P2, 310-P3, 310-Pla, 310-PE1, 310-P22, 310-P22 Mag., 310-PE, **$524.95**. All have patented Dual Reticle system with rangefinder bullet drop compensation; multi-coated lenses, waterprooof, shockproof, nitrogen filled, matte finish. From Shepherd Scope, Ltd.
310-2[1,2]	3-10	35.3-11.6	3-3.75	12.8	1	Int.	18	524.25	

CAUTION: PRICES SHOWN ARE SUPPLIED BY THE MANUFACTURER OR IMPORTER. CHECK YOUR LOCAL GUNSHOP.

Maker and Model	Magn.	Field at 100 Yds. (feet)	Eye Relief (in.)	Length (in.)	Tube Dia. (in.)	W&E Adjust-ments	Weight (ozs.)	Price	Other Data
SIGHTRON									
Electronic Red Dot									
S33-3[1,2]	1	58	—	5.15	33mm	Int.	5.43	**279.99**	[1]Black finish; also stainless. [2]3 MOA dot; also with 5 or 10 MOA dot. [3]Variable 3, 5, 10 MOA dot; black finish; also stainless. [4]Satin black; also stainless. Electronic Red Dot scopes come with ring mounts, front and rear extension tubes, polarizing filter, battery, haze filter caps, wrench. Rifle, pistol, shotgun scopes have aluminum tubes, Exac Trak adjustments. Lifetime warranty. From Sightron, Inc.
S33-30[3]	1	58	—	5.74	33mm	Int.	6.27	**369.99**	
Riflescopes									
Variables									
SII 1.56x42	1.5-6	51-16	3.8-4.0	11.8	1	Int.	15.35	**377.99**	
SII 39x42[4]	3-9	34-12	3.6-4.2	12.34	1	Int.	13.22	**358.99**	
Fixed									
SII 4x42	4	31	4.0	12.48	1	Int.	12.34	**289.99**	
SII 6x42[4]	6	20	4.0	12.48	1	Int.	12.34	**289.99**	
SII 8x42[4]	8	16	4.0	12.48	1	Int.	12.34	**289.99**	
Target									
SII 24x44	24	4	4.33	13.26	1	Int.	15.87	**406.99**	
SII 416x42	4-16	27-7	3.5-3.6	13.74	1	Int.	16.0	**426.99**	
SII 624-42	6-24	16-5	3.7-3.8	14.7	1	Int.	18.7	**449.99**	
Compact									
SII 4x32	4	25	4.5	9.72	1	Int.	9.34	**247.99**	
Shotgun									
SII 2.5x20SG	2.5	41	4.3	10.23	1	Int.	8.46	**232.99**	
Pistol									
SII 1x28P[1]	1	30	9.0-24.0	9.44	1	Int.	8.46	**197.99**	
SII 2x28P[1]	2	16-10	9.0-24.0	9.56	1	Int.	8.28	**196.99**	
SIMMONS									
AETEC									
2100[8]	2.8-10	44-14	5	11.9	1	Int.	15.5	**349.95**	[1]Matte; also polished finish. [2]Silver; also black matte or polished. [3]Black matte finish. [4]Granite finish; black polish **$216.95**; silver $218.95; also with 50mm obj., black granite **$336.95**. [5]Camouflage. [6]Black polish. [7]With ring mounts. [8]Black polished; also black or silver matte. [9]Lighted reticle, Black Granite finish. [10]50mm obj.; black matte. [11]Black or silver matte. [12]75-yd. parallax; black or silver matte. [13]TV view. [14]Adj. obj. [15]V-TAC reticle in 1st focal plane; 4" sunshade; flat black. [16]Adj. objective; 4" sunshade; black matte. [17]Black Granite finish; 50-yd. parallax; ProDiamond reticle. [18]Octagon body; rings included; black matter or silver finish. [19]Black matte finish; also available in silver. **Only selected models shown.** Contact Simmons Outdoor Corp. for complete details.
2104[16]	3.8-12	33-11	4	13.5	1	Int.	20.0	**364.95**	
V-TAC									
3006[15]	3-9	33-11	4.1-3.0	12⅜	1	Int.	25.25	**699.95**	
44 Mag									
M-1044[11]	3-10	36.2-10.5	3.4-3.3	13.1	1	Int.	16.3	**259.95**	
M-1045	4-12	27-9	3	12.6	1	Int.	19.5	**279.95**	
M-1047	6.5-20	14-.5	2.6-3.4	12.8	1	Int.	19.5	**289.95**	
Prohunter									
7700[1]	2-7	58-17	3.25	11.6	1	Int.	12.4	**169.95**	
7710[2]	3-9	40-15	3	12.6	1	Int.	13.4	**179.95**	
7716	4-12	29.6-10.0	3	13.6	1	Int.	20	**199.95**	
7720	6-18	38-13	2.5	12.5	1	Int.	13.5	**224.95**	
7740[3]	6	34.1	3	12.6	1	Int.	9.5	**144.95**	
Prohunter Handgun									
7732[19]	2	21.5	10.5-26.4	7.8	1	Int.	5.75	**179.95**	
7738[19]	4	7	10.5-26.4	8.5	1	Int.	7.25	**189.95**	
7744[19]	2.5-7	11-4	15.7-19.7	9.3	1	Int.	9.0	**229.95**	
Whitetail Classic									
WTC9[9]	3	11.5	11-20	9.0	1	Int.	9.2	**329.95**	
WTC11	1.5-5	80-23.5	3.4-3.2	12.6	1	Int.	11.8	**184.95**	
WTC12	2.5-8	46.5-14.5	3.2-3	12.6	1	Int.	12.8	**199.95**	
WTC13	3.5-10	35-12	3.2-3	12.4	1	Int.	12.8	**219.95**	
WTC16	4	36.8	4	9.9	1	Int.	12	**149.95**	
WTC17	4-12	26-7.9	3	12.8	1	Int.	19.5	**329.95**	
Pro50									
8830[10]	2.5-10	30.5-11	3.2	12.75	1	Int.	13.0	**169.95**	
8800[10]	4-12	27-9	3.5	13.2	1	Int.	18.25	**179.95**	
8810[10]	6-18	17-5.8	3.6	13.2	1	Int.	18.25	**199.95**	
Master Red Dot									
51004[11]	1	40	—	5.25	30mm	Int.	4.8	**269.95**	
Deerfield									
21006	4	28	4	12.0	1	Int.	9.1	**74.95**	
21029	3-9	32-11	3.4	12.6	1	Int.	12.3	**104.95**	
21031	4-12	28-11	3-2.8	13.9	1	Int.	14.6	**139.95**	
Gold Medal Silhouette									
23002	6-20	17.4-5.4	3	14.5	1	Int.	18.3	**529.95**	
Gold Medal Handgun									
22002[6]	2.5-7	9.7-4.0	8.9-19.4	9.25	1	Int.	9.0	**329.95**	
22004[6]	2	3.9	8.6-19.5	7.3	1	Int.	7.4	**229.95**	
22006[6]	4	8.9	9.8-18.7	9	1	Int.	8.8	**269.95**	
Shotgun									
21005	2.5	29	4.6	7.1	1	Int.	7.2	**99.95**	
7789D	2	27	6	8.8	1	Int.	8.1	**129.95**	
7788	1	60	3.8	9.4	1	Int.	10.2	**129.95**	
7790D	4	16	5.5	8.8	1	Int.	9.2	**139.95**	
7791D	1.5-5	75-23	3.4	9.3	1	Int.	9.7	**139.95**	
WTC89D[17]	2	31	5.5	8.8	1	Int.	8.75	**159.95**	
Rimfire									
1022[7]	4	36	3.5	11.5	1	Int.	10	**74.95**	
Blackpowder									
BP0420M[18]	4	19.5	4	7.5	1	Int.	8.3	**139.95**	
BP2520M[12]	2.5	24	6	7.4	1	Int.	7.3	**109.95**	
BP420M[12]	4	19.5	4	7.5	1	Int.	8.3	**109.95**	
BP2732M[12]	2-7	57.7-16.6	3	11.6	1	Int.	12.4	**129.95**	

CAUTION: PRICES SHOWN ARE SUPPLIED BY THE MANUFACTURER OR IMPORTER. CHECK YOUR LOCAL GUNSHOP.

Maker and Model	Magn.	Field at 100 Yds. (feet)	Eye Relief (in.)	Length (in.)	Tube Dia. (in.)	W&E Adjust-ments	Weight (ozs.)	Price	Other Data
Simmons (cont.)									
Fireview									
215071[13]	4	34	3.3	12.8	1	Int.	9	**89.95**	
215131[13]	3-9	40-13	3.5-2.6	12.8	1	Int.	11.7	**99.95**	
Competition Air Gun									
21612[14]	4-12	25-9	3.1-2.9	13.1	1	Int.	15.8	**179.95**	
21618[14]	6-18	18-7	2.9-2.7	13.8	1	Int.	18.2	**189.95**	
STEINER									
Penetrator									
6x42	6	20.4	3.1	14.8	26mm	Int.	14	**1,099.00**	Waterproof, fogproof, nitrogen filled, accordion-type eye cup. [1]Heavy-duplex or European #4 reticle. Aluminum tubes; matte black finish. From Pioneer Research.
8x56	8	15	3.1	14.8	26mm	Int.	17	**1,299.00**	
Hunting Z									
1.5-5x20[1]	1.5-5	32-12	4.3	9.6	30mm	Int.	11.7	**1,499.00**	
2.5-8x36[1]	2.5-8	40-15	4	11.6	30mm	Int.	13.4	**1,799.00**	
3.5-10x50[1]	3.5-10	77-25	4	12.4	30mm	Int.	16.9	**1,899.00**	
SWAROVSKI HABICHT									
PH Series									
1.25-4x24[1]	1.25-4	86-27	4.5	10.6	30mm	Int.	15.9	**987.78**	All models offered in either steel or lightweight alloy tubes. Weights shown are for lightweight versions. Choice of nine constantly centered reticles. Eyepiece recoil mechanism and rubber ring shield to protect face. American-style plex reticle available in 2.2-9x42 and 3-12x56 traditional European scopes. [1]Alloy weighs 12.3 oz. [2]Alloy weighs 15.9 oz. [3]Alloy weighs 14.8 oz. [4]Alloy weighs 18.3 oz. [5]Alloy weighs 16.6 oz. Imported by Swarovski Optik North America Ltd.
1.5-6x42[2]	1.5-6	65.4-21	3.75	13	30mm	Int.	20.5	**1,100.00**	
2.5-10x42[3]	2.5-10	39.6-12.3	3.75	13.2	30mm	Int.	19.4	**1,276.67**	
2.5-10x56[4]	2.5-10	39.6-12.3	3.75	14.7	30mm	Int.	24.3	**1,376.67**	
3-12x50[5]	3-12	33-10.5	3.75	14.3	30mm	Int.	22.0	**1,698.89**	
6x42	6	23	3.25	12.6	1	Int.	17.9	**921.11**	
8x50	8	17	3.25	14.4	30mm	Int.	19.9	**954.44**	
8x56	8	17	3¼	14.4	30mm	Int.	23	**998.89**	
AL Series									
4x32A	4	30	3.2	11.5	1	Int.	10.8	**554.44**	
6x36A	6	21	3.2	11.9	1	Int.	11.5	**610.00**	
1.5-4.5x20A	1.5-4.5	75-25.8	3.5	9.53	1	Int.	10.6	**656.56**	
3-9x36	3-9	39-13.5	3.3	11.9	1	Int.	13	**698.89**	
SWIFT									
600 4x15	4	16.2	2.4	11	¾	Int.	4.7	**24.00**	All Swift scopes, with the exception of the 4x15, have Quadraplex reticles and are fogproof and waterproof. The 4x15 has crosshair reticle and is non-waterproof. [1]Available in black or silver finish—same price. [2]Comes with ring mounts, wrench, lens caps, extension tubes, filter, battery. From Swift Instruments.
601 3-7x20	3-7	25-12	3-2.9	11	1	Int.	5.6	**53.00**	
649 4-12x50	4-12	30-10	3-2.8	13.2	1	Int.	14.6	**216.00**	
650 4x32	4	29	3.5	12	1	Int.	9	**80.00**	
653 4x40WA[1]	4	35.5	3.75	12.25	1	Int.	12	**98.00**	
654 3-9x32	3-9	35.75-12.75	3	12.75	1	Int.	13.75	**95.00**	
656 3-9x40WA[1]	3-9	42.5-13.5	2.75	12.75	1	Int.	14	**103.00**	
657 6x40	6	18	3.75	13	1	Int.	10	**99.50**	
660 4x20	4	25	4	11.8	1	Int.	9	**80.00**	
664 4-12x40[1]	4-12	27-9	3-2.8	13.3	1	Int.	14.8	**143.00**	
665 1.5-4.5x21	1.5-4.5	69-24.5	3.5-3	10.9	1	Int.	9.6	**98.00**	
666 Shotgun 1x20	1	113	3.2	7.5	1	Int.	9.6	**102.00**	
667 Fire-Fly[2]	1	—	—	5.3	30mm	Int.	5	**215.00**	
668M 4x32	4	25	4	10	1	Int.	8.9	**95.00**	
Pistol Scopes									
661 4x32	4	90	10-22	9.2	1	Int.	9.5	**115.00**	
662 2.5x32	2.5	14.3	9-22	8.9	1	Int.	9.3	**110.00**	
663 2x20[1]	2	18.3	9-21	7.2	1	Int.	8.4	**115.00**	
TASCO									
Titan									[1]Water, fog & shockproof; fully coated optics; ¼-min. click stops; haze filter caps; 30-day/limited lifetime warranty. [2]30/30 range finding reticle. [3]World Class Wide Angle; Supercon multi-coated optics; Opti-Centered® 30/30 range finding reticle; lifetime warranty. [4]⅓ greater zoom range. [5]Trajectory compensating scopes, Opti-Centered® stadia reticle. [6]Anodized finish. [7]True one-power scope. [8]Coated optics; crosshair reticle; ring mounts included to fit most 22, 10mm receivers. [9]Fits Remington 870, 1100, 11-87. [10]Electronic dot reticle with rheostat; coated optics; adj. for windage and elevation; waterproof, shockproof, fogproof; Lithium battery; 3x power booster avail.; matte black or matte aluminum finish; dot or T-3 reticle. [11]TV view. [12]Also matte aluminum finish. [13]Also with crosshair reticle. [14]Also 30/30 reticle. [15]Dot size 1.5" at 100 yds.; waterproof. [16]Also in stainless finish. [17]Black matte or stainless finish. [18]Also with stainless finish. [19]Also in matte black. [20]Available with 5-min. or 10-min. dot. [21]Available with 10, 15, 20-min. dot. [22]20mm; also 32mm. [23]20mm; black matte; also stainless steel; also 32mm. **Contact Tasco for details on complete line.**
T1.56x42N	1.5-6	59-20	3.5	12	30mm	Int.	16.4	**680.00**	
T39x42N	3-9	37-13	3.5	12.5	30mm	Int.	16.8	**645.00**	
T312x52N	3-12	27-10	4.5	14	30mm	Int.	20.7	**764.00**	
Big Horn									
BH2.510x50	2.5-10	44-11	4	13.5	1	Int.	16	**611.00**	
BH4.518x50	4.5-18	30-7.3	4	13.5	1	Int.	16	**679.00**	
World Class									
WA4x40	4	36	3	13	1	Int.	11.5	**135.00**	
WA6x40	6	23	3	12.75	1	Int.	11.5	**144.00**	
WA13.5x20[1,3,10]	1-3.5	115-31	3.5	9.75	1	Int.	10.2	**161.00**	
WA1.75-5x20[1,3]	1.75-5	72-24	3	10⅝	1	Int.	10.0	**152.00**	
WA2.58x40[18]	2.5-8	44-14	3	11.75	1	Int.	14.25	**178.00**	
WA27x32[1,3,9]	2-7	56-17	3.25	11.5	1	Int.	12	**161.00**	
WA39x40[1,3,6,11,18]	3-9	43.5-15	3	12.75	1	Int.	13.0	**199.00**	
World Class Airgun									
AG4x40WA	4	36	3	13	1	Int.	14	**374.00**	
AG39x50WA	3-9	41-14	3	15	1	Int.	17.5	**509.00**	
World Class Electronic									
ERD39x40WA	3-9	41-14	3	12.75	1	Int.	16	**323.00**	
World Class Mag IV-44									
WC2510x44[6,19]	2.5-10	41-11	3.5	12.5	1	Int.	14.4	**305.00**	
World Class TS									
TS24x44[19]	24	4.5	3	14	1	Int.	17.9	**407.00**	
TS36x44[19]	36	3	3	14	1	Int.	17.9	**441.00**	
TS832x44[19]	8-24	11-3.5	3	14	1	Int.	19.5	**492.00**	
TS624x44[19]	6-24	15-4.5	3	14	1	Int.	18.5	**475.00**	

CAUTION: PRICES SHOWN ARE SUPPLIED BY THE MANUFACTURER OR IMPORTER. CHECK YOUR LOCAL GUNSHOP.

Maker and Model	Magn.	Field at 100 Yds. (feet)	Eye Relief (in.)	Length (in.)	Tube Dia. (in.)	W&E Adjust-ments	Weight (ozs.)	Price	Other Data
Tasco (cont.)									
World Class TR									
TR39x40WA	3-9	41-14	3	13.0	1	Int.	12.5	**305.00**	
World Class Pistol									
PWC2x22[12]	2	25	11-20	8.75	1	Int.	7.3	**288.00**	
PWC4x28[12]	4	8	12-19	9.45	1	Int.	7.9	**340.00**	
P1.254x28[12]	1.25-4	23-9	15-23	9.25	1	Int.	8.2	**339.00**	
Mag IV									
W312x40[1,2,4]	3-12	35-9	3	12.25	1	Int.	12	**152.00**	
W416x40[1,2,4,16,17]	4-16	26-7	3	14.25	1	Int.	15.6	**203.00**	
W624x40	6-24	17-4	3	15.25	1	Int.	16.8	**255.00**	
Golden Antler									
GA4x32TV	4	32	3	13	1	Int.	12.7	**79.00**	
GA4x40TV	4	32	3	12	1	Int.	12.5	**85.00**	
GA39x32TV[11]	3-9	39-13	3	—	1	Int.	12.2	**102.00**	
GA39x40TV	3-9	39-13	3	12.5	1	Int.	13	**135.00**	
GA39x40WA	3-9	41-15	3	12.75	1	Int.	13	**152.00**	
Silver Antler									
SA2.5x32	2.5	42	3¼	11	1	Int.	10	**99.00**	
SA4x40	4	32	3	12	1	Int.	12.5	**85.00**	
SA39x32	3-9	39-13	3	13.25	1	Int.	12.2	**101.00**	
SA39x40[12]	3-9	41-15	3	12.75	1	Int.	13	**152.00**	
SA39x40	3-9	39-13	3	12.5	1	Int.	13	**135.00**	
SA4x32[12]	4	32	3	13	1	Int.	12.7	**79.00**	
Pronghorn									
PH2.5x32	2.5	42	3.25	11	1	Int.	10	**76.00**	
PH4x32	4	32	3	12	1	Int.	12.5	**61.00**	
PH4x40	4	36	3	13	1	Int.	11.5	**83.00**	
PH6x40	6	20	3	12.5	1	Int.	11.5	**90.00**	
PH39x32	3-9	39-13	3	12	1	Int.	11	**83.00**	
PH39x40	3-9	39-13	3	13	1	Int.	12.1	**110.00**	
High Country									
HC416x40	4-16	26-7	3.25	14.25	1	Int.	15.6	**254.00**	
HC624x10	6-24	17-4	3	15.25	1	Int.	16.8	**280.00**	
HC39x40	3-9	41-15	3	12.75	1	Int.	13.0	**195.00**	
HC3.510x40	3.5-10	30-10.5	3	11.75	1	Int.	14.25	**220.00**	
Rubber Armored									
RC39x40A	3-9	35-12	3.25	12.5	1	Int.	14.3	**255.00**	
TR Scopes									
TR39x40WA	3-9	41-14	3	13	1	Int.	12.5	**305.00**	
TR416x40	4-16	26-7	3	14.25	1	Int.	16.8	**373.00**	
TR624x40	6-24	17-4	3	15.5	1	Int.	17.5	**407.00**	
Bantam									
S1.5-45x20[22]	1.5-4.5	69.5-23	4	10.25	1	Int.	10	**NA**	
S2.5x20[23]	2.5	22	6	7.5	1	Int.	7.5	**NA**	
Airgun									
AG4x20	4	20	2.5	10.75	.75	Int.	5	**40.00**	
AG4x40WA	4	36	3	13.0	1	Int.	14	**373.00**	
AG4x32N	4	30	3	—	1	Int.	12.25	**144.00**	
AG27x32	2-7	48-17	3	12.25	1	Int.	14	**178.00**	
AG37x20	3-7	24-11	3	11.5	1	Int.	6.5	**73.00**	
AG39x50WA	3-9	41-14	3	15	1	Int.	17.5	**475.00**	
Rimfire									
RF4x15[8]	4	22.5	2.5	11	.75	Int.	4	**17.00**	
RF4x32[19]	4	31	3	12.25	1	Int.	12.6	**86.00**	
RF37x20	3-7	24-11	2.5	11.5	.75	Int.	5.7	**45.00**	
P1.5x15	1.5	22.5	9.5-20.75	8.75	.75	Int.	3.25	**37.00**	
Propoint									
PDP2[10,12,20]	1	40	—	5	30mm	Int.	5	**254.00**	
PDP3[10,12,20]	1	52	—	5	30mm	Int.	5	**367.00**	
PDP4[17,21]	1	82	—	—	45mm	Int.	6.1	**458.00**	
PB1[13]	3	35	3	5.5	30mm	Int.	6.0	**183.00**	
PB3	2	30	—	1.25	30mm	Int.	2.6	**214.00**	
PDP3CMP	1	68	—	4.75	33mm	Int.	—	**390.00**	
PDP5	1	82	—	5.5	45mm	Int.	9.1	**340.00**	
World Class Plus									
WCP4x44	4	32	3¼	12.75	1	Int.	13.5	**271.00**	
WCP3.510x50[19]	3.5-10	30-10.5	3¾	13	1	Int.	17.1	**407.00**	
WCP6x44	6	21	3.25	12.75	1	Int.	13.6	**288.00**	
WCP39x44[1,17]	3-9	39-14	3.5	12.75	1	Int.	15.8	**305.00**	
LaserPoint LP2[15]	—	—	—	2	⅝	Int.	.75	**374.00**	
THOMPSON/CENTER RECOIL PROOF SCOPES									
Pistol Scopes									
8356[1]	2	22.1	10.5-26.4	7⅘	1	Int.	6.4	**264.00**	
8312[2]	2.5	15	9-21	7⅖	1	Int.	6.6	**227.00**	
8315[3]	2.5-7	15-5	8-21, 8-11	9¼	1	Int.	9.2	**324.00**	
8352[4]	4	22.1	10.5-26.4	7⅘	1	Int.	6.4	**300.00**	
8320[5]	2.5	15	9-21	7⅖	1	Int.	8.2	**342.00**	
8326[6]	2.5-7	15-5	8-21, 8-11	9¼	1	Int.	10.5	**389.00**	
8650[7]	1	40	—	5¼	30mm	Int.	4.8	**265.00**	

[1]Black finish; silver, **$269.00**. [2]Rail mount. [3]Black finish; silver, **$357.00**. [4]Black; silver, **$305.00**. [5]Lighted reticle, black, rail mount; std. mount, **$314.00**; silver, std., **$329**. [6]Lighted reticle, black. [7]Red dot scope. [8]lighted reticle. [9]Adj. obj. [10]Adj. obj. [11]Matte black; silver finish **$165.00**. From Thompson/Center.

CAUTION: PRICES SHOWN ARE SUPPLIED BY THE MANUFACTURER OR IMPORTER. CHECK YOUR LOCAL GUNSHOP.

Maker and Model	Magn.	Field at 100 Yds. (feet)	Eye Relief (in.)	Length (in.)	Tube Dia. (in.)	W&E Adjust-ments	Weight (ozs.)	Price	Other Data
Thompson/Center (cont.)									
Muzzleloader Scopes									
8626[8]	3-9	33-11	3	10¾	1	Int.	10.1	**411.00**	
8658	1	60	3.8	9⅛	1	Int.	10.2	**128.00**	
8656[11]	1.5-5	53-16	3	11½	1	Int.	12.5	**160.00**	
8664[9]	6-18	18.8-6.2	3	14⅓	1	Int.	13.5	**210.00**	
8666[10]	4-12	26.7-9	3	12⅘	1	Int.	19.5	**263.00**	
TRIJICON									[1]Also 24mm. [2]Also 20mm, **$495.00** to **$595.00**. [3]Advanced Combat Optical Gunsight for AR-15, M-16, with integral mount. From Trijicon, Inc.
Reflex	1	—	—	4.25	1.35	Int.	—	**299.00**	
1x16[1]	1	43.8	4.4	4.6	—	Int.	—	**467.00**	
1.5x16[1]	1.5	43.8	2.4	4.1	—	Int.	—	**495.00-595.00**	
2x16[2]	2	43.8	1.6	3.7	—	Int.	—	**485.00-585.00**	
2.5x20	2.5	43.8	1.4	4.2	—	Int.	—	**519.00-619.00**	
2.25x24	2.25	28.9	2	5.1	—	Int.	—	**519.00-619.00**	
3x24	3	28.9	1.4	4.8	—	Int.	—	**519.00-619.00**	
Variables									
2.5-10x42	2.5-10	7.4-2.3	4.3-3.3	13.4	—	Int.	—	**1,276.00**	
3-12x56	3-12	6.6-1.9	3.9-3.3	14.4	—	Int.	—	**1,396.00**	
8-24x56	8-24	—	—	—	—	Int.	—	**1,700.00**	
ACOG 3.5x35	3.5	29	2.4	8.0	—	Int.	14.0	**1,295.00**	
ACOG 4x32[3]	4	37	1.5	5.8	—	Int.	9.7	**1,195.00**	
UNERTL									[1]Dural ¼-MOA click mounts. Hard coated lenses. Non-rotating objective lens focusing. [2]¼-MOA click mounts. [3]With target mounts. [4]With calibrated head. [5]Same as 1" Target but without objective lens focusing. [6]With new Posa mounts. [7]Range focus unit near rear of tube. Price is with Posa or standard mounts. Magnum clamp. From Unertl.
1" Target	6,8,10	16-10	2	21½	¾	Ext.	21	**307.00**	
1¼" Target[1]	8,10,12,14	12-16	2	25	¾	Ext.	21	**399.00**	
1½" Target	10,12,14, 16,18,20	11.5-3.2	2¼	25½	¾	Ext.	31	**416.00**	
2" Target[2]	10,12,14, 16,18,24, 30,32,36	8	2¼	26¼	1	Ext.	44	**549.00**	
Varmint, 1¼"[3]	6,8,10,12	1-7	2½	19½	⅞	Ext.	26	**395.00**	
Ultra Varmint, 2"[4]	8,10,12,15	12.6-7	2½	24	1	Ext.	34	**538.00**	
Small Game[5]	3,4,6	25-17	2¼	18	¾	Ext.	16	**243.00**	
Programmer 200[7]	10,12,14, 16,18,20, 24,30,36	11.3-4	—	26½	1	Ext.	45	**688.00**	
BV-20[8]	20	8	4.4	17⅞	1	Ext.	21¼	**508.00**	
Tube Sight	—	—	—	17	—	Ext.	—	**226.00**	
U.S. OPTICS									Prices shown are estimates; scopes built as ordered, to order; choice of reticles; choice of front or rear focal plane; extra-heavy MIL-SPEC construction; extra-long turrets; individual w&e rebound springs; up to 88mm dia. objectives; up to 50mm tubes; all lenses multi-coated. Made in U.S. by U. S. Optics.
SN-1/TAR Fixed Power System									
9.6x	10	11.3	3.8	14.5	30mm	Int.	24	**1,100.00**	
16.2x	15	8.6	4.3	16.5	30mm	Int.	27	**1,200.00**	
22.4x	20	5.8	3.8	18.0	30mm	Int.	29	**1,300.00**	
26x	24	5.0	3.4	18.0	30mm	Int.	31	**1,400.00**	
31x	30	4.6	3.5	18.0	30mm	Int.	32	**1,500.00**	
37x	36	4.0	3.6	18.0	30mm	Int.	32	**1,600.00**	
42x	40	3.6	3.7	18.0	30mm	Int.	32	**1,700.00**	
48x	50	3.0	3.8	18.0	30mm	Int.	32	**1,800.00**	
Variables									
SN-2	4-22	26.8-5.8	5.4-3.8	18.0	30mm	Int.	24	**1,256.00**	
SN-3	1.6-8	—	4.4-4.8	18.4	30mm	Int.	36	**1,010.00**	
SN-4	1-4	116-31.2	4.6-4.9	18.0	30mm	Int.	35	**680.00**	
Fixed Power									
SN-6	4,6,8,10	—	4.2-4.8	9.2	30mm	Int.	18	**655.00**	
SN-8	4, 10, 20, 40	32	3.3	7.5	30mm	Int.	11.1	**620.00**	
WEAVER									Micro-Trac adjustment system with ¼-minute clicks on all T-Series. All have Dual-X reticle. One-piece aluminum tube, satin finish, nitrogen filled, multi-coated lenses, waterproof. [1]Also available in matte finish: V3, **$208.29**; K4, **$171.91**; V9, **$226.86**; V10, **$241.15**; V10 stainless, **$238.42**. [2]Available with Dual-X, fine crosshair or ¼-min. dot reticles. [3]4 MOA red dot; also with 12 MOA dot; comes with Weaver q.d. rings. [4]Variable 4, 8, 12 MOA red dot; comes with Weaver q.d. rings; matte finish **$382.34**. [5]4 MOA, 12 MOA, variable 4, 8, 12 MOA **$364.86**; matte finish **$383.11**. [6]Stainless finish, **$226.42**. [7]Stainless finish, **$232.04**. [8]Stainless finish, **$287.58**. [9]Gloss; matte **$285.04**; stainless **$292.36**. [10]Stainless or matte finish. [11]Matte finish **$312.58**. [12]Matte or stainless finish **$321.54**. From Weaver.
K2.5	2.5	35	3.7	9.5	1	Int.	7.3	**150.93**	
K4[1]	3.7	26.5	3.3	11.3	1	Int.	10	**171.15**	
K6	5.7	18.5	3.3	11.4	1	Int.	10	**185.43**	
V3[1]	1.1-2.8	88-32	3.9-3.7	9.2	1	Int.	8.5	**192.29**	
V9[1]	2.8-8.7	33-11	3.5-3.4	12.1	1	Int.	11.1	**213.16**	
V9x50[11]	3-9	29.4-9.9	3.6-3.0	13.1	1	Int.	14.5	**310.63**	
V10[1]	2.2-9.6	38.5-9.5	3.4-3.3	12.2	1	Int.	11.2	**231.15**	
V10x50[12]	2.3-9.7	40.2-9.2	2.9-2.8	13.75	1	Int.	15.2	**310.69**	
V16[2]	3.8-15.5	26.8-6.8	3.1	13.9	1	Int.	16.5	**401.15**	
KT15	14.6	7.5	3.2	12.9	1	Int.	14.7	**364.00**	
T-10 Varminter	10	9.3	3.0	15.1	1	Int.	16.7	**824.02**	
T-16	16	6.5	3.0	15.1	1	Int.	16.7	**830.49**	
T-24	24	4.4	3.0	15.1	1	Int.	16.7	**837.00**	
T-36	36	3.0	3.0	15.1	1	Int.	16.7	**843.47**	
Rimfire									
R4[10]	3.9	29	3.7	9.7	1	Int.	8.8	**136.07**	
RV7[10]	2.5-7	37-13	3.3	10.75	1	Int.	10.7	**158.73**	
Qwik-Point									
QP30[3]	1	12.6	—	5.39	30mm	Int.	5.3	**235.81**	
QP33[4]	1	14.4	—	5.74	33mm	Int.	6.3	**383.11**	

Maker and Model	Magn.	Field at 100 Yds. (feet)	Eye Relief (in.)	Length (in.)	Tube Dia. (in.)	W&E Adjust-ments	Weight (ozs.)	Price	Other Data
Weaver (cont.)									
QP45[5]	1	21.8	—	4.8	45mm	Int.	8.46	**296.19**	
Handgun									
2x28[6]	2	21	4-29	8.5	1	Int.	6.7	**214.52**	
VH8 2.5-8x28[9]	2.5-8	8.5-3.7	12-16	9.3	1	Int.	8.3	**280.58**	
4x28[7]	4	18	11.5-18	8.5	1	Int.	6.7	**226.42**	
1.5-4x20[8]	1.5-4	13.5-5.8	12-24, 10.5-17	8.6	1	Int.	8.1	**275.68**	
ZEISS									All scopes have ¼-minute click-stop adjustments. Choice of Z-Plex or fine crosshair reticles. Rubber armored objective bell, rubber eyepiece ring. Lenses have T-Star coating for highest light transmission. Z-Series scopes offered in non-rail tubes with duplex reticles only; 1" and 30mm. [1]Black matte finish. [2]Also in stainless matte finish. [3]Also with illuminated reticle, **$1,738.00**. Bullet Drop Compensator avail. for all Z-Series scopes. Imported from Germany by Carl Zeiss Optical, Inc.
Diatal Z 6x42	6	22.9	3.2	12.7	1.02 (26mm)	Int.	13.4	**917.00**	
Diatal Z 8x56	8	18	3.2	13.8	1.02 (26mm)	Int.	17.6	**1,092.00**	
Diavari 1.25-4x24	1.25-4	105-33	3.2	11.46	30mm	Int.	17.3	**1,041.00**	
Diavari Z 2.5x10x48[1,2]	2.5-10	33-11.7	3.2	14.5	30mm	Int.	24	**1,407.00**	
Diavari C 3-9x36	3-9	36-13	3.5	11.2	1	Int.	15.2	**783.00**	
Diavari Z 1.5-6x42[1,2]	1.5-6	65.5-22.9	3.2	12.4	1.18 (30mm)	Int.	18.5	**1,190.00**	
Diavari Z 3-12x56[1,2,3]	3-12	27.6-9.9	3.2	15.3	1.18 (30mm)	Int.	25.8	**1,515.00**	

Hunting scopes in general are furnished with a choice of reticle—crosshairs, post with crosshairs, tapered or blunt post, or dot crosshairs, etc. The great majority of target and varmint scopes have medium or fine crosshairs but post or dot reticles may be ordered. W—Windage E—Elevation MOA—Minute of angle or 1" (approx.) at 100 yards, etc.

Laseraim G1/G1 HOT.

Bushnell HOLOsight.

Laseraim LA93 Illusion III.

Weaver V9x50 3-9x.

ADCO MiRAGE Ranger 1" Red Dot.

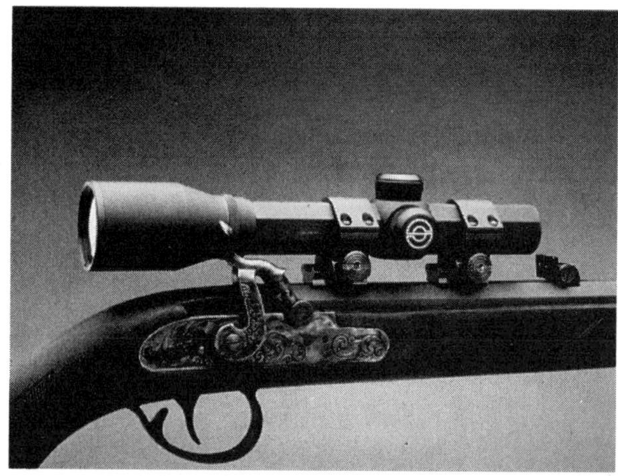

Simmons 4x20 Black Powder scope.

CAUTION: PRICES SHOWN ARE SUPPLIED BY THE MANUFACTURER OR IMPORTER. CHECK YOUR LOCAL GUNSHOP.

SCOPE MOUNTS

Maker, Model, Type	Adjust.	Scopes	Price
AIMPOINT	No	1"	**$49.95-89.95**
Laser Mounts[1]	No	1", 30mm	**51.95**

Mounts/rings for all Aimpoint sights and 1" scopes. For many popular revolvers, auto pistols, shotguns, military-style rifles/carbines, sporting rifles. Most require no gunsmithing. [1]Mounts Aimpoint Laser-dot below barrel; many popular handguns, military-style rifles. Contact Aimpoint.

Maker, Model, Type	Adjust.	Scopes	Price
AIMTECH			
Handguns			
AMT Auto Mag II, III	No	1"	**56.99-64.95**
Auto Mag IV	No	1"	**64.95**
Astra revolvers	No	1"	**63.25**
Beretta/Taurus auto	No	1"	**63.25**
Browning Buck Mark/Challenger II	No	1"	**56.99**
Browning Hi-Power	No	1"	**63.25**
Glock 17, 17L, 19, 22, 23	No	1"	**63.25**
Govt. 45 Auto	No	1"	**63.25**
Rossi revolvers	No	1"	**63.25**
Ruger Mk I, Mk II	No	1"	**49.95**
S&W K,L,N frame	No	1"	**63.25**
S&W Model 41 Target	No	1"	**63.25**
S&W Model 52 Target	No	1"	**63.25**
S&W 45, 9mm autos	No	1"	**56.99**
S&W 422/622/2206	No	1"	**56.99**
Taurus revolvers	No	1"	**63.25**
TZ/CZ/P9 9mm	No	1"	**63.25**
Rifles			
AR-15	No	1"	**21.95**
Browning A-Bolt	No	1"	**21.95**
Knight MK85	No	1"	**21.95**
Remington 700	No	1"	**21.95**
Ruger 10/22	No	1"	**21.95**
Savage 110G	No	1"	**21.95**
Winchester 70	No	1"	**21.95**
Winchester 94	No	1"	**21.95**
Shotguns			
Benelli Super 90	No	1"	**40.95**
Ithaca 37	No	1"	**40.95**
Mossberg 500	No	1"	**40.95**
Mossberg 835 Ultimag	No	1"	**40.95**
Mossberg 5500	No	1"	**40.95**
Remington 870/1100	No	1"	**40.95**
Winchester 1300/1400	No	1"	**40.95**

Mount scopes, lasers, electronic sights using Weaver-style base. All mounts allow use of iron sights; no gunsmithing. Available in satin black or satin stainless finish. **Partial listing shown.** Contact maker for full details. From L&S Technologies, Inc.

Maker, Model, Type	Adjust.	Scopes	Price
A.R.M.S.			
M16A1/A2/AR-15	No	Weaver-type rail	**59.95**
Multibase	No	Weaver-type rail	**59.95**
M21/14 Mount	No	—	**159.00**
#19 Weaver/STANAG Throw Lever Rail	No	Weaver-type rail	**140.00**
STANAG Rings	No	30mm	**75.00**
Ring Inserts	No	1", 30mm	**29.00**
#38 Std. Swan Sleeve[1]	No	—	**150.00**

[1]Avail in three lengths. From A.R.M.S., Inc.

Maker, Model, Type	Adjust.	Scopes	Price
ARMSON			
AR-15[1]	No	1"	**45.00**
Mini-14[2]	No	1"	**66.00**
H&K[3]	No	1"	**82.00**

[1]Fastens with one nut. [2]Models 181, 182, 183, 184, etc. [3]Claw mount. From Trijicon, Inc.

Maker, Model, Type	Adjust.	Scopes	Price
ARMSPORT			
100 Series[1]	No	1" rings. Low, med., high	**10.75**
104 22-cal.	No	1"	**10.75**
201 See-Thru	No	1"	**13.00**
1-Piece Base[2]	No	—	**5.50**
2-Piece Base[2]	No	—	**2.75**

[1]Weaver-type rings. [2]Weaver-type base; most poular rifles. Made in U.S. From Armsport.

Maker, Model, Type	Adjust.	Scopes	Price
B-SQUARE			
Pistols			
Beretta/Taurus 92/99[6]	—	1"	**69.95**
Browning Buck Mark[6]	No	1"	**49.95**
Colt 45 Auto	E only	1"	**69.95**
Colt Python/MkIV, 4",6",8"[1,6]	E	1"	**59.95**
Dan Wesson Clamp-On[2,6]	E	1"	**59.95**
Ruger 22 Auto Mono-Mount[3]	No	1"	**59.95**
Ruger Single-Six[4]	No	1"	**59.95**
Ruger Blackhawk, Super B'hwk[8]	W&E	1"	**59.95**
Ruger GP-100[9]	No	1"	**59.95**
Ruger Redhawk[8]	W&E	1"	**59.95**
S&W 422/2206[9]	No	1"	**59.95**
Taurus 66[9]	No	1"	**59.95**
S&W K, L, N frame[2,6]	No	1"	**59.95**
T/C Contender (Dovetail Base)	W&E	1"	**39.95**
Rifles			
Charter AR-7	No	1"	**29.95**
Mini-14 (dovetail/NATO Stanag)[5,6]	W&E	1"	**59.95**
M-94 Side Mount	W&E	1"	**49.95**
RWS, Beeman/FWB, Anschutz, Diana, Walther Air Rifles	E only	—	**39.95**
SMLE Side Mount with rings	W&E	1"	**69.95**
Military			
AK-47/AKS/SKS-56[10]	No	1"	**59.95**
AK-47, SKS-56[11]	No	1"	**59.95**
M1-A[7]	W&E	1"	**99.95**
AR-15/16[7]	W&E	1"	**59.95**
FN-LAR/FAL[6,7]	E only	1"	**99.95**
HK-91/93/94[6,7]	E only	1"	**99.95**
Shotguns[6]			
Ithaca 37[6]	No	1"	**49.95**
Mossberg 500, 712, 5500[6]	No	1"	**49.95**
Rem. 870/1100 (12 & 20 ga.)[6]	No	1"	**49.95**
Rem. 870, 1100 (and L.H.)[6]	No	1"	**49.95**
BSL Laser Mounts			
Scope Tube Clamp[12,13,16]	No	—	**39.95**
45 Auto[12,13,16]	No	—	**39.95**
SIG P226[12,13,16]	No	—	**39.95**
Beretta 92F/Taurus PT99[12,13,16]	No	—	**39.95**
Colt King Cobra, Python, MkV[12,13,16]	No	—	**39.95**
S&W L Frame[13,16]	No	—	**39.95**
Browning HP[12,13,16]	No	—	**39.95**
Glock	No	—	**39.95**
Star Firestar[12,13,16]	No	—	**39.95**
Rossi small frame revolver[12,13,16]	No	—	**39.95**
Taurus 85 revolver[12,13,16]	No	—	**39.95**
Interlock Rings			
Standard Dovetail[17]	No	1", 30mm	**34.95**
Vertical Split[18]	No	1", 30mm	**12.95**
High/View Thru[19]	No	1"	**15.95**
Tip-Off 3/8" Dovetail[20]	No	1", 30mm	**29.95**
Interlock Bases			
One-Piece[21]	No	Standard dovetail rings	**9.95-10.95**

[1]Clamp-on, blue finish; stainless finish **$59.95**. [2]Blue finish; stainless finish **$59.95**. [3]Clamp-on, blue; stainless finish **$59.95.** [4]Dovetail; stainless finish **$59.95**. [5]No gunsmithing, no sight removal; blue; stainless finish **$79.95.** [6]Weaver-style rings. Rings not included with Weaver-type bases; stainless finish add $10. [7]NATO Stanag dovetail model, **$99.50**. [8]Blue; stainless **$69.95.** [9]Blue; stainless **$69.95**. [10]Handguard mounts. [11]Receiver mounts. [12]Stainless finish add $10. [13]Under-barrel mount, no gunsmithing. [14]Ejector rod mount. [15]Guide rod mount. [16]Used with B-Square BSL-1 Laser Sight only. [17] With recoil key. Blue, black matte; stainless finish, **$39.95**. [18]Blue; stainless finish, **$14.95**; 30mm, blue **$16.95**, stainless **$18.95**. [19]Blue; stainless finish, **$18.95**. [20]Blue; stainless finish, **$34.95**; 30mm, blue, **$39.95**, stainless **$44.95**. [21]Most popular sporting rifles. Mounts for many shotguns, airguns, military and law enforcement guns also available. **Partial listing of mounts shown here. Contact B-Square for more data.**

B-Square makes mounts for the following military rifles: AK47/AKS, Egyptian Hakim, French MAS 1936, M91 Argentine Mauser, Model 98 Brazilian and German Mausers, Model 93, Spanish Mauser (long and short), Model 1916 Mauser, Model 38 and 96 Swedish Mausers, Model 91 Russian (round and octagon receivers), Chinese SKS 56, SMLE No. 1, Mk. III, 1903 Springfield, U.S. 30-cal. Carbine, and others.

Those following replace gun's rear sight: AK47/AKS, P14/1917 Enfield, FN49, M1 Garand, M1-A/M14 (no sight removal), SMLE No. 1, Mk III/No. 4 & 5, Mk. 1, 1903/1903-A3 Springfield, Beretta AR 70 (no sight removal).

Maker, Model, Type	Adjust.	Scopes	Price
BEEMAN			
Two-Piece, Med.	No	1"	**31.50**
Deluxe Two-Piece, High	No	1"	**33.00**
Deluxe Two-Piece	No	30mm	**41.00**
Deluxe One-Piece	No	1"	**50.00**
Dampamount	No	1"	**110.00**

All grooved receivers and scope bases on all known air rifles and 22-cal. rimfire rifles (1/2" to 5/8"—6mm to 15mm).

Maker, Model, Type	Adjust.	Scopes	Price
BOCK			
Swing ALK[1]	W&E	1", 26mm, 30mm	**349.00**
Safari KEMEL[2]	W&E	1", 26mm, 30mm	**149.00**
Claw KEMKA[3]	W&E	1", 26mm, 30mm	**224.00**

Maker, Model, Type	Adjust.	Scopes	Price
Bock (cont.)			
ProHunter Fixed[4]	No	1", 26mm, 30mm	**95.00**

[1]Q.D.; pivots right for removal. For Steyr-Mannlicher, Win. 70, Rem. 700, Mauser 98, Dakota, Sako, Sauer 80, 90. Magnum has extra-wide rings, same price. [2]Heavy-duty claw-type; reversible for front or rear removal. For Steyr-Mannlicher rifles. [3]True claw mount for bolt-action rifles. Also in extended model. For Steyr-Mannlicher, Win. 70, Rem. 700. Also avail. as Gunsmith Bases—bases not drilled or contoured—same price. [4]Extra-wide rings. Imported from Germany by GSI, Inc.

Maker, Model, Type	Adjust.	Scopes	Price
BURRIS			
Supreme (SU) One Piece (T)[1]	W only	1" split rings, 3 heights	**1 piece base— 27.00-34.00**
Trumount (TU) Two Piece (T)	W only	1" split rings, 3 heights	**2 piece base— 25.00-39.00**
Trumount (TU) Two Piece Ext.	W only	1" split rings	**31.00**
Browning 22-cal. Auto Mount[2]	No	1" split rings	**21.00**
1" 22-cal. Ring Mounts[3]	No	1" split rings	**1" rings— 23.00-46.00**
L.E.R. (LU) Mount Bases[4]	W only	1" split rings	**25.00-66.00**
L.E.R. No Drill-No Tap Bases[4,7,8]	W only	1" split rings	**46.00-52.00**
Extension Rings[5]	No	1" scopes	**44.00-52.00**
Ruger Ring Mount[6,9]	W only	1" split rings	**52.00-74.00**
Std. 1" Rings[9]	—	Low, medium, high heights	**35.00-48.00**
Zee Rings[9]	—	Fit Weaver bases; medium and high heights	**33.00-46.00**

[1]Most popular rifles. Universal rings, mounts fit Burris, Universal, Redfield, Leupold and Browning bases. Comparable prices. [2]Browning Standard 22 Auto rifle. [3]Grooved receivers. [4]Universal dovetail; accept Burris, Universal, Redfield, Leupold rings. For Dan Wesson, S&W, Virginian, Ruger Blackhawk, Win. 94. [5]Medium standard front, extension rear, per pair. Low standard front, extension rear, per pair. [6]Compact scopes, scopes with 2" bell, for M77R. [7]Selected rings and bases available with matte Safari or silver finish. [8]For S&W K,L,N frames, Colt Python, Dan Wesson with 6" or longer barrels. [9]Also in 30mm.

Maker, Model, Type	Adjust.	Scopes	Price
CAPE OUTFITTERS			
Quick Detachable	No	1" split rings, lever quick detachable	**99.95**

Double rifles; Rem. 700-721, Colt Sauer, Sauer 200, Kimber, Win. 61-63-07-100-70, Browning High Power, 22, BLR, BAR, BBR, A-Bolt; Wea. Mark V, Vanguard; Modern Muzzle Loading, Knight, Thompson/Center, CVA rifles, Dixie rifles. All steel; returns to zero. From Cape Outfitters.

Maker, Model, Type	Adjust.	Scopes	Price
CLEAR VIEW			
Universal Rings, Mod. 101[1]	No	1" split rings	**21.95**
Standard Model[2]	No	1" split rings	**21.95**
Broad View[3]	No	1"	**21.95**
22 Model[4]	No	¾", ⅞", 1"	**13.95**
SM-94 Winchester[5]	No	1" split rings	**23.95**
94 EJ[6]	No	1" split rings	**21.95**

[1]Most rifles by using Weaver-type base; allows use of iron sights. [2]Most popular rifles; allows use of iron sights. [3]Most popular rifles; low profile, wide field of view. [4]22 rifles with grooved receiver. [5]Side mount. [6]For Win. A.E. From Clear View Mfg.

Maker, Model, Type	Adjust.	Scopes	Price
CONETROL			
Huntur[1]	W only	1", 26mm, 26.5mm solid or split rings, 3 heights	**59.88**
Gunnur[2]	W only	1", 26mm, 26.5mm solid or split rings, 3 heights	**79.92**
Custum[3]	W only	1", 26mm, 26.5mm solid or split rings, 3 heights	**99.96**
One Piece Side Mount Base[4]	W only	1", 26mm, 26.5mm solid or split rings, 3 heights	—
DapTar Bases[5]	W only	1", 26mm, 26.5mm solid or split rings, 3 heights	—
Pistol Bases, 2 or 3-ring[6]	W only	1" scopes	—
Fluted Bases[7]	W only	Standard Conetrol rings	**99.96**
30mm Rings[8]	W only	30mm	**59.88-79.92**

[1]All popular rifles, including metric-drilled foreign guns. Price shown for base, two rings. Matte finish. [2]Gunnur grade has mirror-finished rings, satin-finish base. Price shown for base, two rings. [3]Custum grade has mirror-finished rings and mirror-finished, streamlined base. Price shown for base, two rings. [4]Win. 94, Krag, older split-bridge Mannlicher-Schoenauer, Mini-14, etc. Prices same as above. [5]For all popular guns with integral mounting provision, including Sako, BSA, Ithacagun, Ruger, Tikka, H&K, BRNO—**$29.94-$49.98**—and many others. Also for grooved-receiver rimfires and air rifles. Prices same as above. [6]For XP-100, T/C Contender, Colt SAA, Ruger Blackhawk, S&W. [7]Sculptured two-piece bases as found on fine custom rifles. Price shown is for base alone. Also available unfinished—**$79.92**, or finished but unblued—**$89.91**. [8]30mm rings made in projectionless style, medium height only. Three-ring mount available for T/C Contender and other pistols in Conetrol's three grades. Any Conetrol mount available in stainless or Teflon for double regular cost of grade.

Maker, Model, Type	Adjust.	Scopes	Price
EAW			
Quick-Loc Mount	W&E	1",26mm	**253.00**
	W&E	30mm	**291.00**
Magnum Fixed Mount	W&E	1", 26mm	**198.00**
	W&E	30mm	**215.00**

Fit most popular rifles. Avail. in 4 heights, 4 extensions. Reliable return to zero. Stress-free mounting. Imported by New England Custom Gun Svc.

Maker, Model, Type	Adjust.	Scopes	Price
GENTRY			
Feather-Light Rings	No	1", 30mm	**75.00**

One-piece of stainless or chrome moly; matte blue or gray. From David Gentry.

Maker, Model, Type	Adjust.	Scopes	Price
GRIFFIN & HOWE			
Standard Double Lever (S)	No	1" or 26mm split rings.	**405.00**

All popular models (Garand **$255**). All rings **$105.** Top ejection rings available. Price installed for side mount.

Maker, Model, Type	Adjust.	Scopes	Price
G. G. & G.			
Swan G-3[1]	No	Weaver-type rail	**225.00**
FN FAL[2]	No	Weaver-type rail	**149.00**
Remington 700, Win. 70	No	Weaver base	**85.00**
Sniper Grade Rings	No	1", 30mm	**125.00**
M-14 Mount	No	1", 30mm	**175.00**
M-16 Carry Handle Mount	No	—	**80.00**

[1]Universal top claw lock. [2]Paratrooper model, **$169.00.** From Guns, Gear & Gadgets.

Maker, Model, Type	Adjust.	Scopes	Price
IRONSIGHTER			
Wide Ironsighter™	No	1" split rings	**35.98**
Ironsighter Center Fire[1]	No	1" split rings	**32.95**
Ironsighter S-94	No	1" split rings	**39.95**
Ironsighter AR-15/M-16[8]	No	1", 30mm	**$103.95**
Ironsighter 22-Cal.Rimfire			
Model #570[9]	No	1" split rings	**32.95**
Model #573[9]	No	30mm split rings	**32.95**
Model #722	No	1" split rings	**17.75**
Model #727	No	⅞" split rings	**17.75**
Series #700[5]	No	1" split rings	**32.95**
Ruger Base Mounts[6]	No	1" split rings	**83.95**
Ironsighter Handguns[4]	No	1" split rings	**38.95**
Blackpowder Mount[7]	No	1"	**32.95-76.95**

[1]Most popular rifles, including Ruger Mini-14, H&R M700, and muzzleloaders. Rings have oval holes to permit use of iron sights. [2]For 1" dia. scopes. [3]For ⅞" dia. scopes. [4]For 1" dia. extended eye relief scopes. [5]702—Browning A-Bolt; 709—Marlin 39A. [6]732—Ruger 77/22 R&RS, No. 1, Ranch Rifle; 778 fits Ruger 77R, RS. Both 733, 778 fit Ruger integral bases. [7]Fits most popular blackpowder rifles; one model for Holden Ironsighter mounts, one for Weaver rings. [8]Model 716 with 1" #540 rings; Model 717 with 30mm #530 rings. [9]Fits mount rail on Rem. 522 Viper. Adj. rear sight is integral. Some models in stainless finish. From Ironsighter Co.

Maker, Model, Type	Adjust.	Scopes	Price
K MOUNT By KENPATABLE			
Shotgun Mount	No	1", laser or red dot device	**49.95**
SKS[1]	No	1"	**39.95**

Wrap-around design; no gunsmithing required. Models for Browning BPS, A-5 12-ga., Sweet 16, 20, Rem. 870/1100 (LTW and L.H.), S&W 916, Mossberg 500, Ithaca 37 & 51 12-ga., S&W 1000/3000, Win. 1400. [1] Requires simple modification to gun. From KenPatable Ent.

Maker, Model, Type	Adjust.	Scopes	Price
KRIS MOUNTS			
Side-Saddle[1]	No	1", 26mm split rings	**12.98**
Two Piece (T)[2]	No	1", 26mm split rings	**8.98**
One Piece (T)[3]	No	1", 26mm split rings	**12.98**

[1]One-piece mount for Win. 94. [2]Most popular rifles and Ruger. [3]Blackhawk revolver. Mounts have oval hole to permit use of iron sights.

Maker, Model, Type	Adjust.	Scopes	Price
KWIK-SITE			
KS-See-Thru[1]	No	1"	**31.95**
KS-22 See-Thru[2]	No	1"	**23.95**
KS-W94[3]	No	1"	**39.95**
Bench Rest	No	1"	**31.95**
KS-WEV	No	1"	**31.95**
KS-WEV-HIGH	No	1"	**37.95**
KS-T22 1"[4]	No	1"	**23.95**
KS-FL Flashlite[5]	No	Mini or C cell flashlight	**49.95**
KS-T88[6]	No	1"	**11.95**
KS-T89	No	30mm	**14.95**
KSN 22 See-Thru	No	1", ⅞"	**20.95**
KSN-T22	No	1", ⅞"	**20.95**
KSN-M16 See-Thru	No	1"	**99.95**
KS-202[1]	No	1"	**31.95**
KS-203	No	30mm	**43.95**
KSBP[7]	No	Intergral	**76.95**
KSSM[8]	No	1"	**31.95**

CAUTION: PRICES SHOW ARE SUPPLIED BY THE MANUFACTURER OR IMPORTER. CHECK YOUR LOCAL GUNSHOP.

Maker, Model, Type	Adjust.	Scopes	Price
Kwik-Site (cont.)			
KSB Base Set	—	—	**5.95**
Combo Bases & Rings	No	1"	**31.95**
Bases interchangeable with Weaver bases. [1]Most rifles. Allows use of iron sights. [2]22-cal. rifles with grooved receivers. Allows use of iron sights. [3]Model 94, 94 Big Bore. No drilling or tapping. Also in adjustable model **$49.95**. [4]Non-see-through model for grooved receivers. [5]Allows Mag Lite or C or D, Mini Mag Lites to be mounted atop See-Thru mounts. [6]Fits any Redfield, Tasco, Weaver or universal-style Kwik-Site dovetail base. [7]Blackpowder mount with integral rings and sights. [8]Shotgun side mount. Bright blue, black matte or satin finish. Standard, high heights.			
LASER AIM	No	Laser Aim	**19.00-69.00**
Mounts Laser Aim above or below barrel. Avail. for most popular handguns, rifles, shotguns, including militaries. From Laseraim Technologies, Inc.			
LEUPOLD			
STD Bases[1]	W only	One- or two-piece bases	**23.80**
STD Rings[2]	—	1" super low, low, medium, high	**31.40**
STD Handgun mounts[3]	No	—	**57.00**
Dual Dovetail Bases[1,4]	No	—	**23.80**
Dual Dovetail Rings[9]	—	1", super low, low	**31.40**
Ring Mounts[5,6,7]	No	⅞", 1"	**79.80**
22 Rimfire[9]	No	⅞", 1"	**58.20**
Gunmaker Base[8]	W only	1"	**16.50**
Quick Release Rings	—	1", low, med., high	**31.90-68.90**
Quick Release Bases[10]	No	1", one- or two-piece	**69.30**
[1]Rev. front and rear combinations; matte finish **$22.90**. [2]Avail. polished, matte or silver (low, med. only) finish. [3]Base and two rings; Casull, Ruger, S&W, T/C; add $5.00 for silver finish. [4]Rem. 700, Win. 70-type actions. [5]For Ruger No. 1, 77, 77/22; interchangeable with Ruger units. [6]For dovetailed rimfire rifles. [7]Sako; high, medium, low. [8]Must be drilled, tapped for each action. [9]Most dovetail-receiver 22s. [10]BSA Monarch, Rem. 40X, 700, 721, 725, Ruger M77, S&W 1500, Weatherby Mark V, Vanguard, Win M70.			
MARLIN			
One Piece QD (T)	No	1" split rings	**10.10**
Most Marlin lever actions.			
MILLETT			
Black Onyx Smooth	—	1", low, medium, high	**31.15**
Chaparral Engraved	—	engraved	**46.15**
One-Piece Bases[6]	Yes	1"	**23.95**
Universal Two-Piece Bases			
700 Series	W only	Two-piece bases	**25.15**
FN Series	W only	Two-piece bases	**25.15**
70 Series[1]	W only	1", two-piece bases	**25.15**
Angle-Loc Rings[2]	W only	1", low, medium, high	**32.20-47.20**
Ruger 77 Rings[3]	—	1"	**47.20**
Shotgun Rings[4]	—	1"	**28.29**
Handgun Bases, Rings[5]	—	1"	**34.60-69.15**
30mm Rings[7]	—	30mm	**37.75-42.95**
Extension Rings[8]	—	1"	**35.65**
See-Thru Mounts[9]	No	1"	**27.95-32.95**
Shotgun Mounts[10]	No	1"	**49.95**
Rem. 40X, 700, 722, 725, Ruger 77 (round top), Weatherby, FN Mauser, FN Brownings, Colt 57, Interarms Mark X, Parker-Hale, Sako (round receiver), many others. [1]Fits Win. M70, 70XTR, 670, Browning BBR, BAR, BLR, A-Bolt, Rem. 7400/7600, Four, Six, Marlin 336, Win. 94 A.E., Sav. 110. [2]To fit Weaver-type bases. [3]Engraved. Smooth **$34.60**. [4]For Rem. 870, 1100; smooth. [5]Two and three-ring sets for Colt Python, Trooper, Diamondback, Peacekeeper, Dan Wesson, Ruger Redhawk, Super Redhawk. [6]Turn-in bases and Weaver-style for most popular rifles and T/C Contender, XP-100 pistols. [7]Both Weaver and turn-in styles; three heights. [8]Med. or high; ext. front—std. rear, ext. rear—std. front, ext. front—ext. rear; **$40.90** for double extension. [9]Many popular rifles, Knight MK-85, T/C Hawken, Renegade, Mossberg 500 Slugster, 835 Slug. [10]For Rem. 870/1100, Win. 1200, 1300/1400, 1500, Mossberg 500. Some models available in nickel at extra cost. From Millett Sights.			
OAKSHORE			
Handguns			
Browning Buck Mark	No	1"	**29.00**
Colt Cobra, Diamondback, Python, 1911	No	1"	**38.00-52.00**
Ruger 22 Auto, GP100	No	1"	**33.00-49.00**
S&W N Frame	No	1"	**45.00-60.00**
S&W 422	No	1"	**35.00-38.00**
Rifles			
Colt AR-15	No	1"	**26.00-34.00**
H&K 91, 93, 94, MP-5, G-3	No	1"	**56.00**
Galil	No	1"	**75.00**

Maker, Model, Type	Adjust.	Scopes	Price
Marlin 336 & 1800 Series	No	1"	**21.00**
Win. 94	No	1"	**39.00**
Shotguns			
Mossberg 500	No	1"	**40.00**
Rem. 870, 1100	No	1"	**33.00-52.00**
Rings	—	1", med., high	**5.20-9.80**
See Through offered in some models. Black or silver finish; 1" rings also avail. for ⅜" grooved receivers (See Through). From Oakshore Electronic Sights, Inc.			
PEM'S			
22T Mount[1]	No	1"	**17.95**
The Mount[2]	Yes	1"	**29.50**
[1]Fit all ⅜" dovetail on rimfire rifles. [2]Base and ring set; for over 100 popular rifles; low, medium rings. From Pem's.			
RAM-LINE			
Mini-14 Mount	Yes	1"	**24.97**
No drilling or tapping. Use std. dovetail rings. Has built-in shell deflector. Made of solid black polymer. From Ram-Line, Inc.			
REDFIELD			
American Rings[6]	No	1", low, med., high	**16.95**
American Bases[6]	No	—	**2.65-10.55**
American Widefield See-Thru[7]	No	1"	**16.95**
JR-SR (T)[1]	W only	¾", 1", 26mm, 30mm	**JR—26.95-52.95** **SR—20.95-22.95**
Ring (T)[2]	No	¾" and 1"	**30.95-45.95**
Three-Ring Pistol System SMP[3]	No	1" split rings (three)	**56.95-62.95**
Widefield See-Thru Mounts	No	1"	**16.95**
Ruger Rings[4]	No	1", med., high	**36.95**
Ruger 30mm[5]	No	1"	**47.95**
Midline Ext. Rings	No	1"	**24.95**
[1]Low, med. & high, split rings. Reversible extension front rings for 1". 2-piece bases for Sako. Colt Sauer bases **$39.95**. Med. Top Access JR rings nickel-plated, **$28.95**. SR two-piece ABN mount nickel-plated, **$22.95**; [2]Split rings for grooved 22s; 30mm, black matte **$42.95**.. [3]Used with MP scopes for: S&W K, L or N frame, XP-100, T/C Contender, Ruger receivers. [4]For Ruger Model 77 rifles, medium and high; medium only for M77/22. [5]For Model 77. Also in matte finish, **$45.95**. [6]Aluminum 22 groove mount **$14.95**; base and medium rings **$18.95**. [7]Fits American or Weaver-style base.			
S&K			
Insta-Mount (T) bases and rings[1]	W only	Use S&K rings only	**47.00-117.00**
Conventional rings and bases[2]	W only	1" split rings	**From 65.00**
Skulptured Bases, Rings[2]	W only	1", 26mm, 30mm	**From 65.00**
Smooth Kontoured Rings[3]	Yes	1", 26mm, 30mm	**90.00-120.00**
[1]1903, A3, M1 Carbine, Lee Enfield #1, Mk. III, #4, #5, M1917, M98 Mauser, AR-15, AR-180, M-14, M-1, Ger. K-43, Mini-14, M1-A, Krag, AKM, Win. 94, SKS Type 56, Daewoo, H&K. [2]Most popular rifles already drilled and tapped. [3]No projections; weigh ½-oz. each; matte or gloss finish. Horizontally and vertically split rings, matte or high gloss.			
SSK INDUSTRIES			
T'SOB	No	1"	**65.00-145.00**
Quick Detachable	No	1"	**From 160.00**
Custom installation using from two to four rings (included). For T/C Contender, most 22 auto pistols, Ruger and other S.A. revolvers, Ruger, Dan Wesson, S&W, Colt DA revolvers. Black or white finish. Uses Kimber rings in two- or three-ring sets. In blue or SSK Khrome. For T/C Contender or most popular revolvers. Standard, non-detachable model also available, from **$65.00**.			
SAKO			
QD Dovetail	W only	1" only	**70.00-155.00**
Sako, or any rifle using Sako action, 3 heights available. Stoeger, importer.			
SPRINGFIELD, INC.			
M1A Third Generation	No	1" or 30mm	**123.00**
M1A Standard	No	1" or 30mm	**77.00**
SAR-4800 Mount	No	—	**96.00**
M6 Scount Mount	No	—	**29.00**
Weaver-style bases. From Springfield, Inc.			
TASCO			
World Class			
Universal "W" Ringmount[1]	No	1", 30mm	**25.50-30.00**
Ruger[2]	No	1", 30mm	**31.00-73.00**
22, Air Rifle[3]	No	1", 30mm	**18.00-82.00**
Ringsets[4]	No	1", 26mm, 30mm	**39.00-66.00**
Handgun Revolver	No	1"	**33.50-58.00**
Handgun Competition	No	1"	**103.00**

CAUTION: PRICES SHOWN ARE SUPPLIED BY THE MANUFACTURER OR IMPORTER. CHECK YOU LOCAL GUNSHOP.

Maker, Model, Type	Adjust.	Scopes	Price
Traditional Ringsets	No	1"	33.00-66.00
Tasco (cont.)			
See-Thru	No	1"	**19.00**
Bases[5]	Yes	—	**24.00-61.00**

[1]Steel; low, high only; also high-profile see-through; fit Tasco, Weaver, other universal bases; black gloss or satin chrome. [2]Low, high only; for Redhawk and Super, No.1, Mini-14 & Thirty, 77, 77/22; blue or stainless. [3]Low, med., high; 3/8" grooved receivers; black or satin chrome. [4]Low, med., high; black gloss, matte satin chrome; also Traditional Ringsets **$31.00** (1"), **$42.00** (26mm), **$53.00** (30mm). [5]For popular rifles and shotguns; one-piece, two-piece, Q.D., long and short action, extension. Handgun bases have w&e adj. From Tasco.

THOMPSON/CENTER			
Contender 9741[1]	No	2½, 4 RP	**20.00**
Duo-Ring Mount[2]	No	1"	**65.00**
Weaver-Style Bases[3]	No	—	**13.00**
Weaver-Style Rings[4]	No	1"	**29.00-41.00**
Weaver-Style See-Through Rings[5]	No	1"	**29.00**
Quick Release System[6]	No	1"	**Rings 56.00** **Base 30.00**

[1]T/C rail mount scopes; all Contenders except vent. rib. [2]Attaches directly to T/C Contender bbl., no drilling/tapping; also for T/C M/L rifles, needs base adapter; blue or stainless; for M/L guns, **$59.80**. [3]For T/C ThunderHawk, FireHawk rifles; blue; silver, **$37.00.** [4]Medium and high; blue or silver finish. [5]For T/C FireHawk, ThunderHawk; blue; silver, **$25.00**. [6]For Contender pistol, Carbine, Scout, all M/L long guns. From Thompson/Center.

UNERTL			
¼ Click[1]	Yes	¾", 1" target scopes	**Per set 165.00**

[1]Unertl target or varmint scopes. Posa or standard mounts, less bases. From Unertl

WARNE			
Deluxe Series (all steel non-Q.D. rings)			
Standard	No	1", 4 heights 30mm, 2 heights	**95.50** **107.50**
Sako	No	1", 4 heights 30mm, 3 heights	**95.50** **107.50**
Deluxe Series Rings fit Premier Series Bases			
Premier Series (all-steel Q.D. rings)			
Adjustable Double Levers	No	1", 4 heights 26mm, 2 heights 30mm, 3 heights	**105.50** **117.50** **117.50**
Thumb Knob	No	1", 4 heights 26mm, 2 heights 30mm, 3 heights	**95.50** **107.50** **107.50**
Brno 19mm	No	1", 3 heights 30mm, 2 heights	**105.50** **117.50**
Brno 16mm		1" 2 heights	**105.50**
Ruger	No	1", 4 heights 30mm, 3 heights	**105.50** **117.50**
Ruger M77	No	1", 3 heights 30mm, 2 heights	**105.50** **117.50**
Sako Medium & Long Action	No	1", 4 heights 30mm, 3 heights	**105.50** **117.50**
Sako Short Action	No	1", 3 heights	**105.50**
All-Steel One-Piece Base, ea.			**32.00**
All-Steel Two-Piece Base, ea.			**12.50**
Maxima Series (fits all Weaver-style bases)			
Permanently Attached[1]	No	1", 3 heights 30mm, 3 heights	**31.40** **35.40**
Adjustable Double Lever[2]	No	1", 3 heights 30mm, 3 heights	**65.50** **69.50**
Thumb Knob	No	1", 3 heights 30mm, 3 heights	**55.50** **59.50**
All-Steel Two-Piece Base, ea.			**12.50**

Vertically split rings with dovetail clamp, precise return to zero. Fit most popular rifles, handguns. Regular blue, matte blue, silver finish. [1]All-steel, non-q.d. rings. [2]All-steel, q.d. rings. From Warne Mfg. Co.

WEAVER			
Detachable Mounts			
Top Mount[1]	No	7/8", 1"	**25.00-38.00**
Side Mount[2]	No	1", 1" Long	**29.00-35.00**
Pivot Mount[3]	No	1"	**39.00**
Tip-Off Mount[4]	No	7/8", 1"	**21.00-27.00**
See-Thru Mount			
Traditional[5]	No	1"	**16.00-23.00**

Maker, Model, Type	Adjust.	Scopes	Price
Tip-Off[4]	No	1", 7/8"	**14.00-16.00**
Pro View[5]	No	1"	**14.00-16.00**
Mount Base System[6]			
Blue Finish	No	1"	**75.00**
Stainless Finish	No	1"	**105.00**
Shotgun Converta-Mount System[7]	No	1"	**75.00**
Rifle Mount System[8]	No	1"	**33.00**

[1]Nearly all modern rifles. Low, med., high. 1" extension **$25.00**. 1" low, med., high stainless steel **$38.00**. [2]Nearly all modern rifles, shotguns. [3]Most modern big bore rifles; std., high. [4]22s with 3/8" grooved receivers. [5]Most modern big bore rifles. Some in stainless finish, **$20.00-21.00**. [6]No drilling, tapping. For Colt Python, Trooper, 357, Officer's Model, Ruger Blackhawk & Super, Mini-14, Security-Six, 22 auto pistols, Single-Six 22, Redhawk, Blackhawk SRM 357, S&W current K, L with adj. sights. [7]For Rem. 870, 1100, 11-87, Browning A-5, BPS, Ithaca 37, 87, Beretta A303, Beretta A-390, Winchester 1200-1500, Mossberg 500. [8]For some popular sporting rifles. From Weaver.

WEIGAND			
1911 PDP4[1]	No	40mm, PDP4	**69.95**
1911 General Purpose[2]	No	—	**59.95**
Ruger Mark II[3]	No	—	**49.95**
3rd Generation[4]	No	—	**99.95**
Pro Ringless[5]	No	30mm	**99.95**
Stabilizer I Ringless[6,7]	No	30mm	**99.95**
Revolver Mount[8]	No	—	**35.50**
Ruger 10/22[9]	No	—	**39.95**

[1]For Tasco PDP4 and similar 40mm sights. [2]Weaver rail; takes any standard rings. [3]No drilling, tapping. [4]For M1911; grooved top for Weaver-style rings; requires drilling, tapping. [5]Two-piece design; for M1911, P9/EA-9, CZ-75 copies; integral rings; silver alum. finish. [6]Three-piece design; fits M1911, P9/EA-9, TZ, CZ-75 copies; silver alum. finish. [7]Stabilizer II —more forward position; for M1911, McCormick frames. [8]Frame mount. [9]Barrel mount. From Weigand Combat Handguns, Inc.

WIDEVIEW			
Premium 94 Angle Eject	No	1"	**24.00**
Premium See-Thru	No	1"	**22.00**
22 Premium See-Thru	No	¾", 1"	**16.00**
Universal Ring Angle Cut	No	1"	**24.00**
Universal Ring Straight Cut	No	1"	**22.00**
Solid Mounts			
Lo Ring Solid[1]	No	1"	**16.00**
Hi Ring Solid[1]	No	1"	**16.00**
SR Rings	—	1", 30mm	**18.64**
22 Grooved Receiver	No	1"	**16.00**
94 Side Mount	No	1"	**26.00**
Blackpowder Mounts[2]	No	1"	**22.00-44.00**

[1]For Weaver-type bases. Models for many popular rifles. Low ring, high ring and grooved receiver types. [2]No drilling, tapping; for T/C Renegade, Hawken, CVA, Knight Traditions guns. From Wideview Scope Mount Corp.

WILLIAMS			
Sidemount with HCO Rings[1]	No	1", split or extension rings.	**74.21**
Sidemount, offset rings[2]	No	Same	**61.08**
Sight-Thru Mounts[3]	No	1", 7/8" sleeves	**18.95**
Streamline Mounts	No	1" (bases form rings).	**25.70**
Guideline Handgun[4]	No	1" split rings.	**61.75**

[1]Most rifles, Br. S.M.L.E. (round rec.) **$14.41** extra. [2]Most rifles including Win. 94 Big Bore. [3]Many modern rifles, including CVA Apollo, others with 1" octagon barrels. [4]No drilling, tapping required; heat treated alloy. For Ruger MkII Bull Barrel (**$61.75**); Streamline Top Mount for T/C Contender (**$41.15**), Scout Rifle, (**$24.00**), High Top Mount with sub-base (**$51.45**). From Williams Gunsight Co.

YORK			
M-1 Garand	Yes	1"	**39.95**

Centers scope over the action. No drilling, tapping or gunsmithing. Uses standard dovetail rings. From York M-1 Conversions.

NOTES

(S)—Side Mount (T)—Top Mount; 22mm=.866"; 25.4mm=1.024"; 26.5mm=1.045"; 30mm=1.81"

CAUTION: PRICES SHOW ARE SUPPLIED BY THE MANUFACTURER OR IMPORTER. CHECK YOUR LOCAL GUNSHOP.

SPOTTING SCOPES

BAUSCH & LOMB PREMIER HDR 60mm objective, 15-45x zoom. Straight or 45° eyepiece. Field at 1000 yds. 125 ft. (15x), 68 ft. (45x). Length 13.0"; weight 38 oz. Interchangeable bayonet-style eyepieces.
Price: Straight or angled, 15-45x **$554.95**
Price: Angled, 15-45x **$599.95**
Price: 22x wide angle eyepiece **$81.95**
Price: 30x long eye relief eyepiece **$128.95**

BAUSCH & LOMB DISCOVERER 15x to 60x zoom, 60mm objective. Constant focus throughout range. Field at 1000 yds. 38 ft (60x), 150 ft. (15x). Comes with lens caps. Length 17½"; weight 48.5 oz.
Price: **$367.95**

BAUSCH & LOMB ELITE 15x to 45x zoom, 60mm objective. Field at 1000 yds., 119-62 ft. Length is 12.2"; weight, 26.5 oz. Waterproof, armored. Tripod mount. Comes with black case.
Price: **$719.95**

BAUSCH & LOMB 77MM ELITE 20x, 30x or 20-60x zoom, 77mm objective. Field of view at 1000 yds. 175 ft. (20x), 78 ft. (30x), 108-62 ft. (zoom). Weight 51 oz. (20x, 30x), 54 oz. (zoom); length 16.8". Interchangeable bayonet-style eyepieces. Built-in peep sight.
Price: With EDPrime Glass **$1,132.95**
Price: 20-60x zoom eyepiece **$314.95**
Price: 20x wide angle eyepiece **$199.95**
Price: 30x eyepiece **$207.95**

BURRIS 20x SPOTTER 20x, 50mm objective. Straight type. Field at 100 yds. 15 ft. Length 10"; weight 21 oz. Rubber armor coating, multi-coated lenses, 22mm eye relief. Recessed focus adjustment. Nitrogen filled. Retractable sunshade.
Price: 20x 50mm **$565.00**
Price: 24x 60mm **$583.00**
Price: 30x 60mm **$609.00**

BUSHNELL COMPACT TROPHY 50mm objective, 20-50x zoom. Field at 1000 yds. 84 ft. (20x), 48 ft. (50x). Length 11"; weight 16.5 oz. Black rubber armored, waterproof.
Price: **$306.95**

BUSHNELL BANNER SENTRY 18-36x zoom, 50mm objective. Field at 1000 yds. 115-78 ft. Length 14.5", weight 27 oz. Black rubber armored. Built-in peep sight. Comes with tripod.
Price: **$190.95**
Price: With 45° field eyepiece, includes tripod **$211.95**

BUSHNELL SENTRY WATERPROOF 18-36X zoom, 50mm objective. Field at 1000 yds. 115 ft. (18x), 38 ft. (36x). Overall length 14.7", weighs 31 oz. Black rubber armored. Built-in peep sight.
Price: With tripod **$233.95**

BUSHNELL SPACEMASTER 15x-45x zoom. Rubber armored, prismatic. 60mm objective. Field at 1000 yds. 125-65 ft. Minimum focus 20 ft. Length with caps 11.6"; weight 38.4 oz.
Price: With tripod and carrying case. **$526.95**
Price: Interchangeable eyepieces 20x, 25x, 60x, each **$59.95**
Price: 22x Wide Angle **$94.95**
Price: 15-45x zoom eyepiece **$171.95**

BUSHNELL STALKER 10x to 30x zoom, 50mm objective. Field at 1000 yds. 142 ft. (10x) to 86 ft. (30x). Length 10.5"; weight 16 oz. Camo armored. Comes with tripod.
Price: **$416.95**

KOWA TSN SERIES° Offset 45° or straight body. 77mm objective, 20x WA, 25x, 25x LER, 30x WA, 40x, 60x, 77x and 20-60x zoom. Field at 1000 yds. 179 ft. (20xWA), 52 ft. (60x). Available with flourite lens.
Price: TSN-1 (without eyepiece) 45° offset scope **$696.00**
Price: TSN-2 (without eyepiece) Straight scope **$660.00**
Price: 20x W.A. (wide angle) eyepiece **$230.00**
Price: 25x eyepiece **$143.00**
Price: 25x LER (long eye relief) eyepiece **$214.00**
Price: 30x W.A. (wide angle) eyepiece **$266.00**
Price: 40x eyepiece **$159.00**
Price: 60x W.A. (wide angle) eyepiece **$230.00**
Price: 77x eyepiece **$235.00**
Price: 20-60x zoom eyepiece **$302.00**

KOWA TS-610 SERIES Offset 45° or straight body. 60mm objective, 20x WA, 25x, 25x LER, 27x WA, 40x and 20-60x zoom. Field at 1000 yds. 162 ft. (20x WA), 51 ft. (60x). Available with ED lens.
Price: TS-611 (without eyepiece) 45° offset scope **$510.00**
Price: TS-612 (without eyepiece) Straight scope **$462.00**
Price: 20x W.A. (wide angle) eyepiece **$111.00**
Price: 25x eyepiece **$95.00**
Price: 25x LER (long eye relief) eyepiece **$214.00**
Price: 27x W.A. (wide angle) eyepiece **$166.00**
Price: 40x eyepiece **$98.00**
Price: 20-60x zoom eyepiece **$207.00**

KOWA TS-9 SERIES Offset 45°, straight or rubber armored (straight only). 50mm objective, 15x, 20x and 11-33x zoom. Field at 1000 yds. 188 ft. (15x), 99 ft. (33x).
Price: TS-9B (without eyepiece) 45° offset scope **$223.00**
Price: TS-9C (without eyepiece) straight scope **$176.00**
Price: TS-9R (without eyepiece) straight rubber armored scope/black ... **$197.00**
Price: 15x eyepiece **$38.00**
Price: 20x eyepiece **$36.00**
Price: 11-33x zoom eyepiece **$122.00**

LEUPOLD 12-40x60 VARIABLE 60mm objective, 12-40x. Field at 100 yds. 17.5-5.3 ft.; eye relief 1.2" (20x). Overall length 11.5", weight 32 oz. Rubber armored.
Price: **$1,089.30**

LEUPOLD 20x50 COMPACT 50mm objective, 20x. Field at 100 yards 11.5 ft.; eye relief 1"; length 9.4"; weight 20.5 oz.
Price: Armored model **$710.70**
Price: Packer Tripod **$89.30**

LEUPOLD 25x50 COMPACT 50mm objective, 25x. Field at 100 yds. 8.3 ft.; eye relief 1"; length overall 9.4"; weight 20.5 oz.
Price: Armored model **$758.90**
Price: Packer Tripod **$89.30**

LEUPOLD 30x60 COMPACT 60mm objective, 30x. Field at 100 yds. 6.4 ft.; eye relief 1"; length overall 12.9"; weight 26 oz.
Price: Armored model **$782.10**
Price: Packer Tripod **$89.30**

MIRADOR TTB SERIES Draw tube armored spotting scopes. Available with 75mm or 80mm objective. Zoom model (28x-62x, 80mm) is 11⅞" (closed), weighs 50 oz. Field at 1000 yds. 70-42 ft. Comes with lens covers.
Price: 28-62x80mm **$1,133.95**
Price: 32x80mm **$971.95**
Price: 26-58x75mm **$989.95**
Price: 30x75mm **$827.95**

MIRADOR SSD SPOTTING SCOPES 60mm objective, 15x, 20x, 22x, 25x, 40x, 60x, 20-60x; field at 1000 yds. 37 ft.; length 10¼"; weight 33 oz.
Price: 25x **$575.95**
Price: 22x Wide Angle **$593.95**
Price: 20-60x Zoom **$746.95**
Price: As above, with tripod, case **$944.95**

MIRADOR SIA SPOTTING SCOPES Similar to the SSD scopes except with 45° eyepiece. Length 12¼"; weight 39 oz.
Price: 25x **$809.95**
Price: 22x Wide Angle **$827.95**
Price: 20-60x Zoom **$980.95**

MIRADOR SSR SPOTTING SCOPES 50mm or 60mm objective. Similar to SSD except rubber armored in black or camouflage. Length 11⅛"; weight 31 oz.
Price: Black, 20x **$521.95**
Price: Black, 18x Wide Angle **$539.95**
Price: Black, 16-48x Zoom **$692.95**
Price: Black, 20x, 60mm, EER **$692.95**
Price: Black, 22x Wide Angle, 60mm **$701.95**
Price: Black, 20-60x Zoom **$854.95**

MIRADOR SSF FIELD SCOPES Fixed or variable power, choice of 50mm, 60mm, 75mm objective lens. Length 9¾"; weight 20 oz. (15-32x50).
Price: 20x50mm **$359.95**
Price: 25x60mm **$440.95**
Price: 30x75mm **$584.95**
Price: 15-32x50mm Zoom **$548.95**
Price: 18-40x60mm Zoom **$629.95**
Price: 22-47x75mm Zoom **$773.95**

MIRADOR SRA MULTI ANGLE SCOPES Similar to SSF Series except eyepiece head rotates for viewing from any angle.
Price: 20x50mm **$503.95**
Price: 25x60mm **$647.95**
Price: 30x75mm **$764.95**
Price: 15-32x50mm Zoom **$692.95**
Price: 18-40x60mm Zoom **$836.95**
Price: 22-47x75mm Zoom **$953.95**

MIRADOR SIB FIELD SCOPES Short-tube, 45° scopes with porro prism design. 50mm and 60mm objective. Length 10¼"; weight 18.5 oz. (15-32x50mm); field at 1000 yds. 129-81 ft.
Price: 20x50mm **$386.95**
Price: 25x60mm **$449.95**
Price: 15-32x50mm Zoom **$575.95**
Price: 18-40x60mm Zoom **$638.95**

NIKON FIELDSCOPES 60mm and 78mm lens. Field at 1000 yds. 105 ft. (60mm, 20x), 126 ft. (78mm, 25x). Length 12.8″ (straight 60mm), 12.6″ (straight 78mm); weight 34.5-47.5 oz. Eyepieces available separately.
Price: 60mm straight body **$610.00**
Price: 60mm angled body **$740.00**
Price: 60mm straight ED body **$1,090.00**
Price: 60mm angled ED body **$1,190.00**
Price: 78mm straight ED body **$1,860.00**
Price: 78mm angled ED body **$1,980.00**
Price: Eyepieces (15x to 60x) .... **$134.00** to **$290.00**
Price: 15-45x eyepiece (25-56x for 78mm) **$281.00**
NIKON SPOTTING SCOPE 60mm objective, 20x fixed power or 15-45x zoom. Field at 1000 yds. 145 ft. (20x). Gray rubber armored. Straight or angled eyepiece. Weighs 44.2 oz., length 12.1″ (20x).
Price: 20x60 fixed **$426.00**
Price: 15-45x zoom **$658.00**
PENTAX 30x60 HG 60mm objective lens, 30x. Field of view 86 ft. at 1000 yds. Length 12.1″; weight 35 oz. Waterproof, rubber armor, multi-coated lenses. Comes with lens cap, case, neck strap.
Price: **$450.00**
REDFIELD WATERPROOF 20-45x SPOTTER 60mm objective, 20-45x. Field at 1000 yds. 45-63 ft. Length 12.5″; weight 23 oz. Black rubber armor coat. With vinyl carrying case.
Price: **$557.95**
Price: As above, with adjustable tripod, aluminum carrying case with shoulder strap **$699.95**
REDFIELD REGAL IV Conventional straight through viewing. Regal IV has 60mm objective and interchangeable 25x and 20x-60x zoom eyepieces. Field at 1000 yds. 94 ft. (25x). With tripod and aluminum carrying case.
Price: Regal IV with black rubber Armorcoat **$925.95**
REDFIELD REGAL VI 60mm objective, 25x fixed and 20x-60x interchangeable eyepieces. Has 45° angled eyepiece, front-mounted focus ring, 180° tube rotation. Field at 1000 yds. 94 ft. (25x); length 12¼″; weight 40 oz. Comes with tripod, aluminum carrying case.
Price: Regal VI **$1,000.95**
SIMMONS 1205 COMPACT 50mm objective, 12-36x zoom. Textured black finish. Ocular focus and variable power magnification.
Price: With tripod **$239.95**
Price: Model 25109 (Mossy Oak camo finish) **$261.95**
Price: Model 24109 (Realtree rubber) **$249.95**
SIMMONS 1207 COMPACT 50mm objective, 25x fixed power. Ocular focus. Green rubber-armored finish.
Price: With tripod **$199.95**
Price: Model 1206 (black rubber-armored finish) **$199.95**
SIMMONS 1280 50mm objective, 15-45x zoom. Black matte finish. Ocular focus. Peep finder sight. Waterproof.
Price: With tripod **$299.99**
SIMMONS 1281 60mm objective, 20-60x zoom. Black matte finish. Ocular focus. Peep finder sight. Waterproof.
Price: With tripod **$349.99**
SIMMONS 24108 COMPACT 50mm objective, 25x fixed power. Ocular focus. Realtree rubber camo.
Price: With tripod **$229.95**
SWAROVSKI CT EXTENDIBLE SCOPES 75mm or 85mm objective, 20-60x zoom, or fixed 15x, 22x, 30x, 32x eyepieces. Field at 1000 yds. 135 ft. (15x), 99 ft. (32x); 99 ft. (20x), 5.2 ft. (60x) for zoom. Length 12.4″ (closed), 17.2″ (open) for the CT75; 9.7″/17.2″ for CT85. Weight 40.6 oz. (CT75), 49.4 oz. (CT85). Green rubber armored.
Price: CT75 body **$765.56**
Price: CT85 body **$1,100.00**
Price: 20-60x eyepiece **$327.78**
Price: 15x, 22x eyepiece .... **$211.11-$155.45**
Price: 30x eyepiece **$254.44**
SWAROVSKI AT-80/ST-80 SPOTTING SCOPES 80mm objective, 20-60x zoom, or fixed 15x, 22x, 30x, 32x eyepieces. Field at 1000 yds. 135 ft. (15x), 99 ft. (32x); 99 ft. (20x), 52.5 ft. (60x) for zoom. Length 16″ (AT-80), 15.6″ (ST-80); weight 51.8 oz. Available with HD (high density) glass.
Price: AT-80 (angled) body **$1,100.00**
Price: ST-80 (straight) body **$1,100.00**
Price: With HD glass **$1,543.33**
Price: 20-60x eyepiece **$327.78**
Price: 15x, 22x eyepiece .... **$211.11-$155.45**
Price: 30x eyepiece **$254.44**
SWIFT NIGHTHAWK M849U 80mm objective, 28-75x zoom, or fixed 25x, 31x, 50x, 75x eyepieces. Has rubber armored body, 1.8x optical finder, retractable lens hood, 45° eyepiece. Field at 1000 yds. 60 ft. (28x), 41 ft. (75x). Length 13.4 oz.,; weight 39 oz.
Price: Body only **$850.00**
Price: 28-75x eyepiece **$285.00**
Price: Fixed eyepieces .... **$90.00** to **$200.00**
Price: Model 849 (straight) body **$780.00**
SWIFT NIGHTHAWK M850U 65mm objective, 22-60x zoom, or fixed 20x, 25x, 40x, 60x eyepieces. Rubber armored with a 1.8x optical finder, retractable lens hood. Field at 1000 yds. 83 ft. (22x), 52 ft. (60x). Length 12.3″; weight 30 oz. Has 45° eyepiece.
Price: Body only **$630.00**
Price: 22-60x eyepiece **$285.00**
Price: Fixed eyepieces .... **$90.00** to **$200.00**
Price: Model 850 (straight) body **$560.00**
SWIFT LEOPARD M837 50mm objective, 25x. Length $9^{11}/_{16}$″ to 10½″. Weight with tripod 28 oz. Rubber armored. Comes with tripod.
Price: **$150.00**
SWIFT TELEMASTER M841 60mm objective. 15x to 60x variable power. Field at 1000 yds. 160 feet (15x) to 40 feet (60x). Weight 3.25 lbs.; length 18″ overall.
Price: **$399.50**
SWIFT M700R 10x-40x, 40mm objective. Field of 210 feet at 10x, 70 feet at 40x. Length 16.3″, weight 21.4 oz. Has 45° eyepiece.
Price: **$198.00**
SWIFT SEARCHER M839 60mm objective, 20x, 40x. Field at 1000 yds. 118 ft. (30x), 59 ft. (40x). Length 12.6″; weight 3 lbs. Rotating eyepiece head for straight or 45° viewing.
Price: **$460.00**
Price: 30x, 50x eyepieces, each **$65.00**
TASCO MS2530 MINI-SPOTTER 30mm objective, 25x. Field at 100 yds 11 ft., 6 in. Weighs 10.3 oz.; length 7¼″ overall. Comes with tripod, case.
Price: **$94.40**
TASCO WC26TZ SPOTTING SCOPE 60mm objective, 15-45x zoom. Field at 100 yds. 11.4 ft. (15x), 6.2 ft. (45x). Length 15″ overall; weight 28 oz. Comes with tripod.
Price: **$386.00**
Price: WC27TZ (45° model) **$386.00**
TASCO 5001 COMPACT ZOOM 50mm objective, 12-36x zoom. Field at 100 yds. 16 ft., 9 in. Includes photo adapter tube, tripod with panhead lever, case.
Price: **$288.00**
TASCO 37ZB SPOTTING SCOPE 50mm objective. 18-36x zoom. Field at 100 yds. 12 ft., 6 in. to 7 ft., 9 in. Black rubber armored.
Price: **$229.00**
Price: Model 37ZBC (brown camo rubber) **$229.00**
Price: Model 3700 (black, with tripod, case) **$271.00**
Price: Model 3701 (as above, brown camo) **$271.00**
TASCO CW50TZB, CW50TZBC ZOOM SPOTTING SCOPES 50mm objective lens, 12-36x zoom. Field at 100 yds. 16-9 ft. Available in black or brown camo rubber armor. With panhead lever tripod.
Price: CW50TZB (brown) **$314.00**
Price: CW50TZBC (camo) **$314.00**
TASCO CW50TR COMPACT SPOTTING SCOPE 50mm objective lens, 25x fixed power. Field at 100 yds. 11 ft. Comes with panhead lever tripod.
Price: **$226.00**
TASCO 21EB ZOOM 50mm objective lens, 15-45x zoom. Field at 100 yds. 11 ft. (15x). Weight 22 oz.; length 18.3″ overall. Comes with panhead lever tripod.
Price: **$119.00**
TASCO 22EB ZOOM 60mm objective lens, 20-60x zoom. Field at 100 yds. 7 ft., 2 in. (20x). Weight 28 oz.; length 21.5″ overall. Comes with micro-adjustable tripod.
Price: **$183.00**
TASCO 35TZB COMPACT ZOOM 50mm objective lens, 10-25x zoom. Field at 100 yds. 22 ft. (10x) Weight 23.3 oz.; length 11″ overall. Comes with panhead lever tripod.
Price: **$237.00**
TASCO MS2040 MINI SPOTTING SCOPE 40mm objective lens, 20x fixed power. Field at 100 yds. 7 ft., 8 in. Weight 12.4 oz.; length 8.5″ overall. Comes with tripod with bendable legs.
Price: **$113.75**
TASCO 9002T WORLD CLASS SPOTTING SCOPE 60mm objective lens, 15-60x zoom. Field at 100 yds. 14.6 ft. (15x). Fully multi-coated optics, includes camera adaptor, camera case, tripod with pan-head lever.
Price: **$628.00**
UNERTL "FORTY-FIVE" 54mm objective. 20x (single fixed power). Field at 100 yds. 10',10″; eye relief 1″; focusing range infinity to 33 ft. Weight about 32 oz.; overall length 15¾″. With lens covers.
Price: With multi-layer lens coating **$496.00**
Price: With mono-layer magnesium coating **$414.00**
UNERTL STRAIGHT PRISMATIC 63.5mm objective, 24x. Field at 100 yds., 7 ft. Relative brightness, 6.96. Eye relief ½″. Weight 40 oz.; length closed 19″. Push-pull and screw-focus eyepiece. 16x and 32x eyepieces **$100.00** each.
Price: **$369.00**
UNERTL 20x STRAIGHT PRISMATIC 54mm objective, 20x. Field at 100 yds. 8.5 ft. Relative brightness 6.1. Eye relief ½″. Weight 36 oz.; length closed 13½″. Complete with lens covers.
Price: **$343.00**
UNERTL TEAM SCOPE 100mm objective. 15x, 24x, 32x eyepieces. Field at 100 yds. 13 to 7.5 ft. Relative brightness, 39.06 to 9.79. Eye relief 2″ to 1½″. Weight 13 lbs.; length 29⅞″ overall. Metal tripod, yoke and wood carrying case furnished (total weight 80 lbs.).
Price: **$2,200.00**
WEAVER 20x50 50mm objective. Field of view 12.4 ft. at 100 yds. Eye relief .85″; weighs 21 oz.; overall length 10″. Waterproof, armored.
Price: **$385.00**
WEAVER 15-40x60 ZOOM 60mm objective. 15-40x zoom. Field at 100 yds. 119 ft. (15x), 66 ft. (60x). Overall length 12.5″, weighs 26 oz. Waterproof, armored.
Price: .... **NA**

PERIODICAL PUBLICATIONS

AAFTA News (M)
5911 Cherokee Ave., Tampa, FL 33604. Official newsletter of the American Airgun Field Target Assn.

Action Pursuit Games Magazine (M)
CFW Enterprises, Inc., 4201 W. Vanowen Pl., Burbank, CA 91505 818-845-2656. $3.95 single copy U.S., $4.50 Canada. Editor: Jessica Sparks, 818-845-2656. World's leading magazine of paintball sports.

Air Gunner Magazine
4 The Courtyard, Denmark St., Wokingham, Berkshire RG11 2AZ, England/011-44-734-771677. $U.S. $44 for 1 yr. Leading monthly airgun magazine in U.K.

Airgun Ads
Box 33, Hamilton, MT 59840/406-363-3805. $35 1 yr. (for first mailing; $20 for second mailing; $35 for Canada and foreign orders.) Monthly tabloid with extensive For Sale and Wanted airgun listings.

The Airgun Letter
Gapp, Inc., 4614 Woodland Rd., Ellicott City, MD 21042-6329/410-730-5496; airgnltr@clark.net; http://www.airgunletter.com. $18 U.S., $21 Canada, $24 Mexico and $30 other foreign orders, 1 yr. Monthly newsletter for airgun users and collectors.

Airgun World
4 The Courtyard, Denmark St., Wokingham, Berkshire RG40 2AZ, England/011-44-734-771677. Call for subscription rates. Oldest monthly airgun magazine in the U.K., now a sister publication to *Air Gunner.*

Alaska Magazine
4220 B St., Suite 210, Achorage, AK 99503. $24.00 yr. Hunting, Fishing and Life on the Last Frontier articles of Alaska and western Canada. Outdoors Editor, Ken Marsh.

American Firearms Industry
Nat'l. Assn. of Federally Licensed Firearms Dealers, 2455 E. Sunrise Blvd., Suite 916, Ft. Lauderdale, FL 33304. $35.00 yr. For firearms retailers, distributors and manufacturers.

American Gunsmith
Belvoir Publications, Inc., 75 Holly Hill Lane, Greenwich, CT 06836-2626/203-661-6111. $49.00 (12 issues). Technical journal of firearms repair and maintenance.

American Handgunner
591 Camino de la Reina, Suite 200, San Diego, CA 92108. $16.75 yr. Articles for handgun enthusiasts, competitors, police and hunters.

American Hunter (M)
National Rifle Assn., 11250 Waples Mill Rd., Fairfax, VA 22030 (Same address for both.) Publications Div. $35.00 yr. Wide scope of hunting articles.

American Rifleman (M)
National Rifle Assn., 11250 Waples Mill Rd., Fairfax, VA 22030 (Same address for both). Publications Div. $35.00 yr. Firearms articles of all kinds.

American Single Shot Rifle News* (M)
Membership Secy. Tim Mather, 1180 Easthill SE, N. Canton, Ohio. Annual dues $20 for 6 issues. Official journal of the American Single Shot Rifle Assn.

American Survival Guide
McMullen Angus Publishing, Inc., 774 S. Placentia Ave., Placentia, CA 92670-6846. 12 issues $19.95/714-572-2255; FAX: 714-572-1864.

American West
American West Management Corp., 7000 E. Tanque Verde Rd., Suite #30, Tucson, AZ 85715. $15.00 yr.

Arms Collecting (Q)
Museum Restoration Service, P.O. Box 70, Alexandria Bay, NY 13607-0070. $22.00 yr.; $62.00 3 yrs.; $112.00 5 yrs.

Australian Shooters Journal
Sporting Shooters' Assn. of Australia, Inc., P.O. Box 2066, Kent Town SA 5071, Australia. $45.00 yr. locally; $55.00 yr. overseas surface mail only. Hunting and shooting articles.

The Backwoodsman Magazine
P.O. Box 627, Westcliffe, CO 81252. $16.00 for 6 issues per yr.; $30.00 for 2 yrs.; sample copy $2.75. Subjects include muzzle-loading, woodslore, primitive survival, trapping, homesteading, blackpowder cartridge guns, 19th century how-to.

Black Powder Cartridge News (Q)
SPG, Inc., P.O. Box 761, Livingston, MT 59047. $17 yr. (4 issues). For the blackpowder cartridge enthusiast.

Black Powder Times
P.O. Box 234, Lake Stevens, WA 98258. $20.00 yr.; add $5 per year for Canada, $10 per year other foreign. Tabloid newspaper for blackpowder activities; test reports.

Blade Magazine*
700 East State St., Iola, WI 54990-0001. $19.95 for 12 issues. Foreign price (including Canada-Mexico) $50.00. A magazine for all enthusiasts of handmade, factory and antique knives.

Caliber
GFI-Verlag, Theodor-Heuss Ring 62, 50668 K"ln, Germany. For hunters, target shooters and reloaders.

The Caller (Q) (M)
National Wild Turkey Federation, P.O. Box 530, Edgefield, SC 29824. Tabloid newspaper for members; 4 issues per yr. (membership fee $25.00)

Cartridge Journal (M)
Robert Mellichamp, 907 Shirkmere, Houston, TX 77008/713-869-0558. Dues $12 for U.S. and Canadian members (includes the newsletter); 6 issues.

The Cast Bullet*(M)
Official journal of The Cast Bullet Assn. Director of Membership, 4103 Foxcraft Dr., Traverse City, MI 49684. Annual membership dues $14, includes 6 issues.

COLTELLI, che Passione (Q)
Casella postale N.519, (-20101 Milano, Italy/Fax:02-48402857. $15 1 yr., $27 2 yrs. Covers all types of knives—collecting, combat, historical. Italian text.

Combat Handguns*
Harris Publications, Inc., 1115 Broadway, New York, NY 10010. Single copy $3.25 U.S.A.; $3.75 Canada.

Deer & Deer Hunting Magazine
700 E. State St., Iola, WI 54990-0001. $16.96 yr. (8 issues)

The Derringer Peanut (M)
The National Association of Derringer Collectors, P.O. Box 20572, San Jose, CA 95160. A newsletter dedicated to developing the best derringer information. Write for details.

Deutsches Waffen Journal
Journal-Verlag Schwend GmbH, Postfach 100340, D-74503 Schwäbisch Hall, Germany/0791-404-500; FAX:0791-404-505 and 404-424. DM102 p. yr. (interior); DM125.30 (abroad), postage included. Antique and modern arms and equipment. German text.

Double Gun Journal
P.O. Box 550, East Jordan, MI 49727/800-447-1658. $35 for 4 issues.

Ducks Unlimited, Inc. (M)
1 Waterfowl Way, Memphis, TN 38120

The Engraver (M) (Q)
P.O. Box 4365, Estes Park, CO 80517. Mike Dubber, editor. The journal of firearms engraving.

The Field
King's Reach Tower, Stamford St., London SE1 9LS England. £36.40 U.K. 1 yr.; 49.90 (overseas, surface mail) yr.; £82.00 (overseas, air mail) yr. Hunting and shooting articles, and all country sports.

Field & Stream
Times Mirror Magazines, Two Park Ave., New York, NY 10016. $11.94 yr. Monthly shooting column. Articles on hunting and fishing.

FIRE
Euro-Editions, Boulevard Lambermont 140, B1030 Brussels, Belgium. Belg. Franc 2100 for 6 issues. Arms, shooting, ammunition. French text.

Fur-Fish-Game
A.R. Harding Pub. Co., 2878 E. Main St., Columbus, OH 43209. $15.95 yr. "Gun Rack" column by Don Zutz.

The Gottlieb-Tartaro Report
Second Amendment Foundation, James Madison Bldg., 12500 NE 10th Pl., Bellevue, WA 98005/206-454-7012;Fax:206-451-3959. $30 for 12 issues. An insiders guide for gun owners.

Gray's Sporting Journal
Gray's Sporting Journal, P.O. Box 1207, Augusta, GA 30903. $36.95 per yr. for 6 consecutive issues. Hunting and fishing journals. Expeditions and Guides Book (Annual Travel Guide).

Gun List†
700 E. State St., Iola, WI 54990. $29.95 yr. (26 issues); $54.95 2 yrs. (52 issues). Indexed market publication for firearms collectors and active shooters; guns, supplies and services.

Gun New Digest (Q)
Second Amendment Fdn., P.O. Box 488, Station C, Buffalo, NY 14209/716-885-6408;Fax:716-884-4471. $10 U.S.; $20 foreign.

The Gun Report
World Wide Gun Report, Inc., Box 38, Aledo, IL 61231-0038. $33.00 yr. For the antique and collectable gun dealer and collector.

Gunmaker (M) (Q)
ACGG, P.O. Box 812, Burlington, IA 52601-0812. The journal of custom gunmaking.

The Gunrunner
Div. of Kexco Publ. Co. Ltd., Box 565G, Lethbridge, Alb., Canada T1J 3Z4. $23.00 yr., sample $2.00. Monthly newspaper, listing everything from antiques to artillery.

Gun Show Calendar (Q)
700 E. State St., Iola, WI 54990. $14.95 yr. (4 issues). Gun shows listed; chronologically and by state.

Gun Tests
11 Commerce Blvd., Palm Coast, FL 32142. The consumer resource for the serious shooter. Write for information.

Gun Trade News
Bruce Publishing Ltd., Manor Farm The Green, Uffington, Oxon SN7 7RB, England/44-1367-820-882;Fax:44-1367-820-113. Britain's only "trade only" magazine exclusive to the gun trade.

Gun Week†
Second Amendment Foundation, P.O. Box 488, Station C, Buffalo, NY 14209. $35.00 yr. U.S. and possessions; $40.00 yr. other countries. Tabloid paper on guns, hunting, shooting and collecting (36 issues).

Gun World
Gallant/Charger Publications, Inc., 34249 Camino Capistrano, Capistrano Beach, CA 92624. $22.50 yr. For the hunting, reloading and shooting enthusiast.

Guns & Ammo
Petersen Publishing Co., 6420 Wilshire Blvd., Los Angeles, CA 90048. $21.94 yr. Guns, shooting, and technical articles.

Guns
Guns Magazine, P.O. Box 85201, San Diego, CA 92138. $19.95 yr.; $34.95 2 yrs.; $46.95 3 yrs. In-depth articles on a wide range of guns, shooting equipment and related accessories for gun collectors, hunters and shooters.

Guns and Gear
Creative Arts, Inc., 4901 Northwest 17th Way, Fort Lauderdale, FL 33309/305-772-2788; FAX:305-351-0484. Single copy $4.95. Covering all aspects of the shooting sports.

Guns Review
Ravenhill Publishing Co. Ltd., Box 35, Standard House, Bonhill St., London EC 2A 4DA, England. œ20.00 sterling (approx. U.S. $38 USA & Canada) yr. For collectors and shooters.

H.A.C.S. Newsletter (M)
Harry Moon, Pres., P.O. Box 50117, South Slope RPO, Burnaby BC, V5J 5G3, Canada/604-438-0950;Fax:604-277-3646. $25 p. yr. U.S. and Canada. Official newsletter of The Historical Arms Collectors of B.C. (Canada).

Handgunner*
Richard A.J. Munday, Seychelles house, Brightlingsen, Essex CO7 ONN, England/012063-305201. £ 18.00 (sterling).

Handgunning*
PJS Publications, News Plaza, P.O. Box 1790, Peoria, IL 61656. Cover price $3.95; subscriptions $19.98 for 6 issues. Premier journal for multi-sport handgunners: hunting, reloading, law enforcement, practical pistol and target shooting, and home defense.

Handgun Times
Creative Arts, Inc., 4901 NW 17th Way, Fort Lauderdale, FL 33309/305-772-2788; FAX: 305-351-0484. Single copy $4.95. Technical evaluations, detailed information and testing by handgun experts.

Handloader*
Wolfe Publishing Co., 6471 Airpark Dr., Prescott, AZ 86301/520-445-7810;Fax:520-778-5124. $22.00 yr. The journal of ammunition reloading.

Hunting Horizons
Wolfe Publishing Co., 6471 Airpark Dr., Prescott, AZ 86301. $6.95 Annual. Dedicated to the finest pursuit of the hunt.

INSIGHTS*
NRA, 11250 Waples Mill Rd., Fairfax, VA 22030. Editor, John E. Robbins. $15.00 yr., which includes NRA junior membership; $10.00 for adult subscriptions (12 issues). Plenty of details for the young hunter and target shooter; emphasizes gun safety, marksmanship training, hunting skills.

International Arms & Militaria Collector (Q)
Arms & Militaria Press, P.O. Box 80, Labrador, Qld. 4215, Australia. A$39.50 yr. (U.S. & Canada), 2 yrs. A$77.50; A$37.50 (others), 1 yr., 2 yrs. $73.50. Editor: Ian D. Skennerton.

International Shooting Sport*/UIT Journal
International Shooting Union (UIT), Bavariaring 21, D-80336 Munich, Germany. Europe: (Deutsche Mark) DM44.00 yr., 2 yrs. DM83.00; outside Europe: DM50.00 yr., 2 yrs. DM95.00 (air mail postage included.) For international sport shooting.

Internationales Waffen-Magazin
Habegger-Verlag Zürich, Postfach 9230, CH-8036 Zürich, Switzerland. SF 107.00 (approx. U.S. $87.00) surface mail for 10 issues. Modern and antique arms, self-defense. German text; English summary of contents.

IPPA News (M)
International Paintball Players Assn., P.O. Box 26669, San Diego, CA 92196-0669/619-695-8882. Call or write for subscription rates. Newsletter for members of the IPPA.

The Journal of the Arms & Armour Society (M)
A. Dove, P.O. Box 10232, London, SW19 2ZD England. œ15.00 surface mail; œ20.00 airmail sterling only yr. Articles for the historian and collector.

Journal of the Historical Breechloading Smallarms Assn.
Published annually. Imperial War Museum, Lambeth Road, London SE1 6HZ, England. $21.00 yr. Articles for the collector plus mailings of short articles on specific arms, reprints, newsletters, etc.

Knife World
Knife World Publications, P.O. Box 3395, Knoxville, TN 37927. $15.00 yr.; $25.00 2 yrs. Published monthly for knife enthusiasts and collectors. Articles on custom and factory knives; other knife-related interests, monthly column on knife identification, military knives.

Machine Gun News
Lane Publishing, P.O. Box 459, Dept. GD, Lake Hamilton, AR 71951/501-525-7514;Fax:501-525-7519. $34.95 yr. (12 issues); $5.00 sample copy. Informative articles on machine guns, tactical firearms, and suppressors; contains interviews, question & answer columns, legislative updates, ATF ruling, classified and display ads.

Man At Arms*
P.O. Box 460, Lincoln, RI 02865. $27.00 yr., $52.00 2 yrs. plus $8.00 for foreign subscribers. The N.R.A. magazine of arms collecting-investing, with excellent articles for the collector of antique arms and militaria.

The Mannlicher Collector (Q)(M)
Mannlicher Collectors Assn., Inc., P.O. Box 7144, Salem, OR 97303-0028. $20 yr. subscription included i. membership.

MAN/MAGNUM
S.A. Man (Pty) Ltd., P.O. Box 35204, Northway, Durban 4065, Republic of South Africa. SA Rand 125.00 for 12 issues. Africa's only publication on hunting, shooting, firearms, bushcraft, knives, etc.

The Marlin Collector (M)
R.W. Paterson, 407 Lincoln Bldg., 44 Main St., Champaign, IL 61820.

Muzzle Blasts (M)
National Muzzle Loading Rifle Assn., P.O. Box 67, Friendship, IN 47021. $30.00 yr. annual membership. For the blackpowder shooter.

Muzzleloader Magazine*
Scurlock Publishing Co., Inc., Dept. Gun, Route 5, Box 347-M, Texarkana, TX 75501. $18.00 U.S.; $22.50 U.S. for foreign subscribers a yr. The publication for blackpowder shooters.

National Defense (M)*
American Defense Preparedness Assn., Two Colonial Place, Suite 400, 2101 Wilson Blvd., Arlington, VA 22201-3061/703-522-1820; FAX: 703-522-1885. $35.00 yr. Articles on both military and civil defense field, including weapons, materials technology, management.

National Knife Magazine (M)
Natl. Knife Coll. Assn., 7201 Shallowford Rd., P.O. Box 21070, Chattanooga, TN 37424-0070. Membership $35 yr.; $65.00 International yr.

National Rifle Assn. Journal (British) (Q)
Natl. Rifle Assn. (BR.), Bisley Camp, Brookwood, Woking, Surrey, England. GU24, OPB. œ22.00 Sterling including postage.

National Wildlife*
Natl. Wildlife Fed., 1400 16th St. NW, Washington, DC 20036, $16.00 yr. (6 issues); *International Wildlife*, 6 issues, $16.00 yr. Both, $22.00 yr., includes all membership benefits. Write attn.: Membership Services Dept., for more information.

New Zealand GUNS*
Waitekauri Publishing, P.O. 45, Waikino 3060, New Zealand. $NZ90.00 (6 issues) yr. Covers the hunting and firearms scene in New Zealand.

New Zealand Wildlife (Q)
New Zealand Deerstalkers Assoc., Inc., P.O. Box 6514, Wellington, N.Z. $30.00 (N.Z.). Hunting, shooting and firearms/game research articles.

North American Hunter* (M)
P.O. Box 3401, Minnetonka, MN 55343. $18.00 yr. (7 issues). Articles on all types of North American hunting.

Outdoor Life
Times Mirror Magazines, Two Park Ave., New York, NY 10016. Special 1-yr. subscription, $11.97. Extensive coverage of hunting and shooting. Shooting column by Jim Carmichel.

La Passion des Courteaux (Q)
Phenix Editions, 25 rue Mademoiselle, 75015 Paris, France. French text.

Paintball Consumer Reports
14573-C Jefferson Davis Highway, Woodridge, VA 22191/703-491-6199. $19.95 1 yr. U.S., $27.95 foreign. Product testing for the paintball industry.

Paintball Games International Magazine
Aceville Publications, Castle House, 97 High St., Colchester, Essex, England CO1 1TH/011-44-206-564840. Write for subscription rates. Leading magazine in the U.K. covering competitive paintball activities.

Paintball Hotline†
American Paintball Media and Marketing, 15507 S. Normandie Ave. #487, Gardena, CA 90247/310-323-1021. $50 U.S. 1 yr. $75 Mexico and Canada, $125 other foreign orders. Weekly newsletter that tracks inside industry news.

Paintball News
PBN Publishing, P.O. Box 1608, 24 Henniker St., Hillsboro, NH 03244/603-464-6080. $35 U.S. 1 yr. Bi-weekly newspaper covering new product reviews and industry features.

Paintball Players Bible*
American Paintball Media and Marketing, 15507 S. Normandie Ave. #487, Gardena, Ca 90247/310-323-1021. $12.95 U.S. 1 yr., $19.95 foreign. Publications w. profiles of guns and accessories.

Paintball Sports (Q)
Paintball Publications, Inc., 540 Main St., Mount Kisco, NY 10549/941-241-7400. $24.75 U.S. 1 yr., $32.75 foreign. Covering the competitive paintball scene.

Performance Shooter
Belvoir Publications, Inc., 75 Holly Hill Lane, Greenwich, CT 06836-2626/203-661-6111. $45.00 yr. (12 issues). Techniques and technology for improved rifle and pistol accuracy.

Petersen's HUNTING Magazine
Petersen Publishing Co., 6420 Wilshire Blvd., Los Angeles, CA 90048. $19.94 yr.; Canada $29.34 yr.; foreign countries $29.94 yr. Hunting articles for all game; test reports.

P.I. Magazine
America's Private Investigation Journal, 755 Bronx Dr., Toledo, OH 43609. Chuck Klein, firearms editor with column about handguns.

Pirsch
BLV Verlagsgesellschaft mbH, Postfach 400320, 80703 Munich, Germany/089-12704-0;Fax:089-12705-354. German text.

Point Blank
Citizens Committee for the Right to Keep and Bear Arms (sent to contributors), Liberty Park, 12500 NE 10th Pl., Bellevue, WA 98005

POINTBLANK (M)
Natl. Firearms Assn., Box 4384 Stn. C, Calgary, AB T2T 5N2, Canada. Official publication of the NFA.

The Police Marksman*
6000 E. Shirley Lane, Montgomery, AL 36117. $17.95 yr. For law enforcement personnel.

Police Times (M)
3801 Biscayne Blvd., Miami, FL 33137/305-573-0070.

Popular Mechanics
Hearst Corp., 224 W. 57th St., New York, NY 10019. $15.94 yr. Firearms, camping, outdoor oriented articles.

Precision Shooting
Precision Shooting, Inc., 222 McKee St., Manchester, CT 06040. $29.00 yr. Journal of the International Benchrest Shooters, and target shooting in general. Also considerable coverage of varmint shooting, as well as big bore, small bore, schuetzen, lead bullet, wildcats and precision reloading.

Rifle*
Wolfe Publishing Co., 6471 Airpark Dr., Prescott, AZ 86301. $19.00 yr. The sporting firearms journal.

Rod & Rifle Magazine
Lithographic Serv. Ltd., P.O. Box 38-138, Wellington, New Zealand. $50.00 yr. (6 issues). Hunting, shooting and fishing articles.

Safari* (M)
Safari Magazine, 4800 W. Gates Pass Rd., Tucson, AZ 85745/602-620-1220. $55.00 (6 times). The journal of big game hunting, published by Safari Club International. Also publish *Safari Times*, a monthly newspaper, included in price of $55.00 national membership.

Second Amendment Reporter
Second Amendment Foundation, James Madison Bldg., 12500 NE 10th Pl., Bellevue, WA 98005. $15.00 yr. (non-contributors).

Shooter's News
23146 Lorain Rd., Box 349, North Olmsted, OH 44070/216-979-5258;Fax:216-979-5259. $29 U.S. 1 yr., $54 2 yrs.; $52 foreign surface. A journal dedicated to precision riflery.

Shooting Industry
Publisher's Dev. Corp., 591 Camino de la Reina, Suite 200, San Diego, CA 92108. $50.00 yr. To the trade $25.00.

Shooting Sports USA
National Rifle Assn. of America, 11250 Waples Mill Road, Fairfax, VA 22030. Annual subscriptions for NRA members are $5 for classified shooters and $10 for non-classified shooters. Non-NRA member subscriptions are $15. Covering events, techniques and personalities in competitive shooting.

The Shooting Times & Country Magazine (England)†
IPC Magazines Ltd., King's Reach Tower, Stamford St, 1 London SE1 9LS, England/0171-261-6180;Fax:0171-261-7179. œ65 (approx. $98.00) yr.; œ79 yr. overseas (52 issues). Game shooting, wild fowling, hunting, game fishing and firearms articles. Britain's best selling field sports magazine.

Shooting Times
PJS Publications, News Plaza, P.O. Box 1790, Peoria, IL 61656/309-682-6626. $21.98 yr. Guns, shooting, reloading; articles on every gun activity.

The Shotgun News‡
Snell Publishing Co., Box 669, Hastings, NE 68902/800-345-6923. $29.00 yr.; foreign subscription call for rates. Sample copy $4.00. Gun ads of all kinds.

SHOT Business
Flintlock Ridge Office Center, 11 Mile Hill Rd., Newtown, CT 06470-2359/203-426-1320; FAX: 203-426-1087. For the shooting, hunting and outdoor trade retailer.

Shotgun Sports
P.O. Box 6810, Auburn, CA 95604/916-889-2220; FAX:916-889-9106. $28.00 yr. Trapshooting how-to's, shotshell reloading, shotgun patterning, shotgun tests and evaluations, Sporting Clays action, waterfowl/upland hunting. Call 1-800-676-8920 for a free sample copy.

The Sixgunner (M)
Handgun Hunters International, P.O. Box 357, MAG, Bloomingdale, OH 43910

The Skeet Shooting Review
National Skeet Shooting Assn., 5931 Roft Rd., San Antonio, TX 78253. $20.00 yr. (Assn. membership of $30.00 includes mag.) Competition results, personality profiles of top Skeet shooters, how-to articles, technical, reloading information.

Soldier of Fortune
Subscription Dept., P.O. Box 348, Mt. Morris, IL 61054. $24.95 yr.; $34.95 Canada; $45.95 foreign.

Sporting Clays Magazine
5211 South Washington Ave., Titusville, FL 32780/407-268-5010; FAX: 407-267-7216. $29.95 yr. (12 issues).

Sporting Goods Business
Miller Freeman, Inc., One Penn Plaza, 10th Fl., New York, NY 10119-0004. Trade journal.

Sporting Goods Dealer
Two Park Ave., New York, NY 10016. $100.00 yr. Sporting goods trade journal.

Sporting Gun
Bretton Court, Bretton, Peterborough PE3 8DZ, England. œ27.00 (approx. U.S. $36.00), airmail œ35.50 yr. For the game and clay enthusiasts.

Sports Afield
The Hearst Corp., 250 W. 55th St., New York, NY 10019. $13.97 yr. Tom Gresham on firearms, ammunition; Grits Gresham on shooting and Thomas McIntyre on hunting.

The Squirrel Hunter
P.O. Box 368, Chireno, TX 75937. $14.00 yr. Articles about squirrel hunting.

TACARMI
Via E. De Amicis, 25; 20123 Milano, Italy. $100.00 yr. approx. Antique and modern guns. (Italian text.)

Trap & Field
1200 Waterway Blvd., Indianapolis, IN 46202. $25.00 yr. Official publ. Amateur Trapshooting Assn. Scores, averages, trapshooting articles.

Turkey Call* (M)
Natl. Wild Turkey Federation, Inc., P.O. Box 530, Edgefield, SC 29824. $25.00 with membership (6 issues per yr.)

Turkey & Turkey Hunting*
Krause Publications, 700 E. State St., Iola, WI 54990-0001. $12.95 (6 issue p. yr.). Magazine with leading-edge articles on all aspects of wild turkey behavior, biology and the successful ways to hunt better with that info. Learn the proper techniques to calling, the right equipment, and more.

The U.S. Handgunner* (M)
U.S. Revolver Assn., 40 Larchmont Ave., Taunton, MA 02780. $10.00 yr. General handgun and competition articles. Bi-monthly sent to members.

U.S. Airgun Magazine (Q)
2603 Rollingbrook, Benton, AR 72015/501-778-2615. Cover the sport from hunting, 10-meter, field target and collecting. Write for details.

The Varmint Hunter Magazine (Q)
The Varmint Hunters Assn., Box 759, Pierre, SD 57501/800-528-4868. $24.00 yr.

Waffenmarkt-Intern
GFI-Verlag, Theodor-Heuss Ring 62, 50668 K"ln, Germany. Only for gunsmiths, licensed firearms dealers and their suppliers in Germany, Austria and Switzerland.

Wild Sheep (M) (Q)
Foundation for North American Wild Sheep, 720 Allen Ave., Cody, WY 82414. Official journal of the foundation.

Wisconsin Outdoor Journal
Krause Publications, 700 E. State St., Iola, WI 54990-0001. $16.95 yr. (8 issues). For Wisconsin's avid hunters and fishermen, with features from all over that state with regional reports, legislative updates, etc.

Women & Guns
P.O. Box 488, Sta. C, Buffalo, NY 14209. $24.00 yr. U.S.; $72.00 foreign (12 issues). Only magazine edited by and for women gun owners.

World War II*
Cowles History Group, 741 Miller Dr. SE, Suite D-2, Leesburg, VA 22075-8920. Annual subscriptions $19.95 U.S.; $25.95 Canada; 43.95 foreign. The title says it—WWII; good articles, ads, etc.

*Published bi-monthly †Published weekly ‡Published three times per month. All others are published monthly.
M=Membership requirements; write for details. Q=Published Quarterly.

The ARMS LIBRARY

FOR COLLECTOR • HUNTER • SHOOTER • OUTDOORSMAN

IMPORTANT NOTICE TO BOOK BUYERS

Books listed here may be bought from Ray Riling Arms Books Co., 6844 Gorsten St., P.O. Box 18925, Philadelphia, PA 19119, phone 215/438-2456. Joe Riling is the researcher and compiler of "The Arms Library" and a seller of gun books for over 30 years.

The Riling stock includes books classic and modern, many hard-to-find items, and many not obtainable elsewhere. These pages list a portion of the current stock. They offer prompt, complete service, with delayed shipments occurring only on out-of-print or out-of-stock books.

NOTICE FOR ALL CUSTOMERS: Remittance in U.S. funds must accompany all orders. For U.S. add $2.00 per book for postage and insurance. Minimum order $10.00. For UPS add 50% to mailing costs.

All foreign countries add $5.00 per book. All foreign orders are shipped at the buyer's risk unless an additional $5 for insurance is included.

Payments in excess of order or for "Backorders" are credited or fully refunded at request. Books "As-Ordered" are not returnable except by permission and a handling charge on these of $2.00 per book is deducted from refund or credit. Only Pennsylvania customers must include current sales tax.

A full variety of arms books also available from Rutgers Book Center, 127 Raritan Ave., Highland Park, NJ 08904.

***New Book**

BALLISTICS and HANDLOADING

ABC's of Reloading, 5th Edition, by Dean A. Grennell, DBI Books, Inc., Northbrook, IL, 1993. 288 pp., illus. Paper covers. $19.95.

The definitive guide to every facet of cartridge and shotshell reloading.

Ammunition Making, by George E. Frost, National Rifle Association of America, Washington, D.C., 1990. 160 pp., illus. Paper covers. $17.95.

Reflects the perspective of "an insider" with half a century's experience in successful management of ammunition manufacturing operations.

***Barnes Reloading Manual #1,** Barnes Bullets, American Fork, UT, 1995. 350 pp., illus. $24.95.

Data for more than 65 cartridges from 243 to 50 BMG.

Basic Handloading, by George C. Nonte, Jr., Outdoor Life Books, New York, NY, 1982. 192 pp., illus. Paper covers. $6.95.

How to produce high-quality ammunition using the safest, most efficient methods.

Big Bore Rifles And Cartridges, Wolfe Publishing Co., Prescott, AZ, 1991. Paper covers. $26.00.

This book covers cartridges from 8mm to .600 Nitro with loading tables.

Black Powder Guide, 2nd Edition, by George C. Nonte, Jr., Stoeger Publishing Co., So. Hackensack, NJ, 1991. 288 pp., illus. Paper covers. $14.95.

How-to instructions for selection, repair and maintenance of muzzleloaders, making your own bullets, restoring and refinishing, shooting techniques.

***Blackpowder Loading Manual, 3rd Edition,** edited by Sam Fadala, DBI Books, Inc., Northbrook, IL, 1995. 368 pp., illus. Paper covers. $19.95.

Revised and expanded edition of this landmark blackpowder loading book. Covers hundreds of loads for most of the popular blackpowder rifles, handguns and shotguns.

The Bullet Swage Manual. MDSU/I, by Ted Smith, Corbin Manufacturing and Supply Co., White City, OR, 1988. 45 pp., illus. Paper covers. $10.00.

A book that fills the need for information on bullet swaging.

***Cartridges of the World, 8th Edition,** by Frank Barnes, edited by M. L. McPherson, DBI Books, Inc., Northbrook, IL, 1996. 480 pp., illus. Paper covers. $24.95.

Completely revised edition of the general purpose reference work for which collectors, police, scientists and laymen reach first for answers to cartridge identification questions. Available October, 1996.

***Complete Blackpowder Handbook, 3rd Edition,** by Sam Fadala, DBI Books, Inc., Northbrook, IL, 1996. 416 pp., illus. Paper covers. $21.95.

Expanded and refreshed edition of the definitive book on the subject of blackpowder. Available, September, 1996.

The Complete Handloader for Rifles, Handguns and Shotguns, by John Wootters, Stackpole Books, Harrisburg, PA, 1988. 214 pp., $29.95.

Loading-bench know-how.

***Designing and Forming Custom Cartridges,** by Ken Howell, Ken Howell, Stevensville, MT, 1995. 596 pp., illus. $59.95.

Covers cartridge dimensions and includes complete introductory material on cartridge manufacture and appendices on finding loading data and equipment.

Game Loads and Practical Ballistics for the American Hunter, by Bob Hagel, Wolfe Publishing Co., Prescott, AZ, 1992. 310 pp., illus. $27.90.

Hagel's knowledge gained as a hunter, guide and gun enthusiast is gathered in this informative text.

Gibbs' Cartridges and Front Ignition Loading Technique, by Roger Stowers, Wolfe Publishing Co., Prescott, AZ, 1991. 64 pp., illus. Paper covers. $14.95.

The story of this innovative gunsmith who designed his own wildcat cartridges known for their flat trajectories, high velocity and accuracy.

Handbook of Bullet Swaging No. 7, by David R. Corbin, Corbin Manufacturing and Supply Co., White City, OR, 1986. 199 pp., illus. Paper covers. $10.00.

This handbook explains the most precise method of making quality bullets.

Handbook for Shooters and Reloaders, by P.O. Ackley, Salt Lake City, UT, 1970, (Vol. I), 567 pp., illus. (Vol. II), a new printing with specific new material. 495 pp., illus. $17.95 each.

Handbook of Metallic Cartridge Reloading, by Edward Matunas, Winchester Press, Piscataway, NJ, 1981. 272 pp., illus. $19.95.

Up-to-date, comprehensive loading tables prepared by four major powder manufacturers.

Handgun Reloading, The Gun Digest Book of, by Dean A. Grennell and Wiley M. Clapp, DBI Books, Inc., Northbrook, IL, 1987. 256 pp., illus. Paper covers. $16.95.

Detailed discussions of all aspects of reloading for handguns, from basic to complex. New loading data.

***Handloader's Digest 1997, 16th Edition,** edited by Bob Bell, DBI Books, Inc., Northbrook, IL, 1996. 480pp., illus. Paper covers. $23.95.

Top writers in the field contribute helpful information on techniques and components. Greatly expanded and fully indexed catalog of all currently available tools, accessories and components for metallic, blackpowder cartridge, shotshell reloading and swaging.

Handloader's Guide, by Stanley W. Trzoniec, Stoeger Publishing Co., So. Hackensack, NJ, 1985. 256 pp., illus. Paper covers. $14.95.

The complete step-by-step fully illustrated guide to handloading ammunition.

Handloader's Manual of Cartridge Conversions, by John J. Donnelly, Stoeger Publishing Co., So. Hackensack, NJ, 1986. Unpaginated. $49.95.

From 14 Jones to 70-150 Winchester in English and American cartridges, and from 4.85 U.K. to 15.2x28R Gevelot in metric cartridges. Over 900 cartridges described in detail.

Handloading, by Bill Davis, Jr., NRA Books, Wash., D.C., 1980. 400 pp., illus. Paper covers. $15.95.

A complete update and expansion of the NRA Handloader's Guide.

Handloading for Hunters, by Don Zutz, Winchester Press, Piscataway, NJ, 1977. 288 pp., illus. $30.00.

Precise mixes and loads for different types of game and for various hunting situations with rifle and shotgun.

Hatcher's Notebook, by S. Julian Hatcher, Stackpole Books, Harrisburg, PA, 1992. 488 pp., illus. $29.95.

A reference work for shooters, gunsmiths, ballisticians, historians, hunters and collectors.

Hodgdon Data Manual No. 26, Hodgdon Powder Co., Shawnee Mission, KS, 1993. 797 pp. $22.95.

Includes Hercules, Winchester and Dupont powders; data on cartridge cases; loads; silhouette; shotshell; pyrodex and blackpowder; conversion factors; weight equivalents, etc.

The Home Guide to Cartridge Conversions, by Maj. George C. Nonte Jr., The Gun Room Press, Highland Park, NJ, 1976. 404 pp., illus. $24.95.

Revised and updated version of Nonte's definitive work on the alteration of cartridge cases for use in guns for which they were not intended.

Hornady Handbook of Cartridge Reloading, 4th Edition, Vol. I and II, Hornady Mfg. Co., Grand Island, NE, 1991. 1200 pp., illus. $28.50.

New edition of this famous reloading handbook. Latest loads, ballistic information, etc.

Hornady Handbook of Cartridge Reloading, Abridged Edition, Hornady Mfg. Co., Grand Island, NE, 1991. $19.95.

Ballistic data for 25 of the most popular cartridges.

Hornady Load Notes, Hornady Mfg. Co., Grand Island, NE, 1991. $4.95.

Complete load data and ballistics for a single caliber. Eight pistol 9mm-45ACP; 16 rifle, 222-45-70.

*__How-To's for the Black Powder Cartridge Rifle Shooter,__ by Paul A. Matthews, Wolfe Publishing Co., Prescott, AZ, 1995. 45 pp. Paper covers. $22.50.

Covers lube recipes, good bore cleaners and over-powder wads. Tips include compressing powder charges, combating wind resistance, improving ignition and much more.

The Illustrated Reference of Cartridge Dimensions, edited by Dave Scovill, Wolfe Publishing Co., Prescott, AZ, 1994. 343 pp., illus. Paper covers. $19.00

A comprehensive volume with over 300 cartridges. Standard and metric dimensions have been taken from SAAMI drawings and/or fired cartridges.

Loading the Black Powder Rifle Cartridge, by Paul A Matthews, Wolfe Publishing Co., Prescott, AZ, 1993. 121 pp., illus. Paper covers. $22.50.

Author Matthews brings the blackpowder cartridge shooter valuable information on the basics, including cartridge care, lubes and moulds, powder charges and developing and testing loads in his usual authoritative style.

*__Loading the Peacemaker—Colt's Model P,__ by Dave Scovill, Wolfe Publishing Co., Prescott, AZ, 1995. $24.95.

A comprehensive work about the most famous revolver ever made, including the most extensive load data ever published.

Lyman Cast Bullet Handbook, 3rd Edition, edited by C. Kenneth Ramage, Lyman Publications, Middlefield, CT, 1980. 416 pp., illus. Paper covers. $19.95.

Information on more than 5000 tested cast bullet loads and 19 pages of trajectory and wind drift tables for cast bullets.

Lyman Black Powder Handbook, ed. by C. Kenneth Ramage, Lyman Products for Shooters, Middlefield, CT, 1975. 239 pp., illus. Paper covers. $14.95.

Comprehensive load information for the modern blackpowder shooter.

*__Lyman Pistol & Revolver Handbook, 2nd Edition,__ edited by Thomas J. Griffin, Lyman Products Co., Middlefield, CT, 1996. 287 pp., illus. Paper covers. $18.95.

The most up-to-date loading data available including the hottest new calibers, like 40 S&W, 9x21, 9mm Makarov, 9x25 Dillon and 454 Casull.

Lyman Reloading Handbook No. 47, edited by Edward A. Matunas, Lyman Publications, Middlefield, CT, 1992. 480 pp., illus. Paper covers. $23.00.

"The world's most comprehensive reloading manual." Complete "How to Reload" information. Expanded data section with all the newest rifle and pistol calibers.

Lyman Shotshell Handbook, 4th Edition, edited by Edward A. Matunas, Lyman Products Co., Middlefield, CT, 1996. 330 pp., illus. Paper covers. $24.95.

Has 9000 loads, including slugs and buckshot, plus feature articles and a full color I.D. section.

Lyman's Guide to Big Game Cartridges & Rifles, by Edward Matunas, Lyman Publishing Corporation, Middlefield, CT, 1994. 287 pp., illus. Paper covers. $17.95.

A selection guide to cartridges and rifles for big game—antelope to elephant.

Making Loading Dies and Bullet Molds, by Harold Hoffman, H&P Publishing, San Angelo, TX, 1993. 230 pp., illus. Paper covers. $24.95.

A good book for learning tool and die making.

*__Metallic Cartridge Reloading, 3rd Edition,__ by M. L. McPherson, DBI Books, Inc., Northbrook, IL., 1996. 384 pp., illus. Paper covers. $21.95.

A true reloading manual with over 10,000 loads fro all popular metallic cartridges and a wealth of invaluable technical data provided by a recognized expert.

Modern Handloading, by Maj. Geo. C. Nonte, Winchester Press, Piscataway, NJ, 1972. 416 pp., illus. $15.00.

Covers all aspects of metallic and shotshell ammunition loading, plus more loads than any book in print.

Modern Practical Ballistics, by Art Pejsa, Pejsa Ballistics, Minneapolis, MN, 1990. 150 pp., illus. $24.95.

Covers all aspects of ballistics and new, simplified methods. Clear examples illustrate new, easy but very accurate formulas.

*__Mr. Single Shot's Cartridge Handbook,__ by Frank de Haas, Mark de Haas, Orange City, IA, 1996. 116 pp., illus. Paper covers. $21.50.

This book covers most of the cartridges, both commercial and wildcat, that the author has known and used.

*__Nick Harvey's Practical Reloading Manual,__ by Nick Harvey, Australian Print Group, Maryborough, Victoria, Australia, 1995. 235 pp., illus. Paper covers. $24.95.

Contains data for rifle and handgun including many popular wildcat and improved cartridges. Tools, powders, components and techniques for assembling optimum reloads with particular application to North America.

Nosler Reloading Manual No. 3, edited by Gail Root, Nosler Bullets, Inc., Bend, OR, 1989. 516 pp., illus. $21.95.

All-new book. New format including featured articles and cartridge introductions by well-known shooters, gun writers and editors.

The Paper Jacket, by Paul Matthews, Wolfe Publishing Co., Prescott, AZ, 1991. Paper covers. $13.50.

Up-to-date and accurate information about paper-patched bullets.

Precision Handloading, by John Withers, Stoeger Publishing Co., So. Hackensack, NJ, 1985. 224 pp., illus. Paper covers. $14.95.

An entirely new approach to handloading ammunition.

Propellant Profiles New and Expanded, 3rd Edition, Wolfe Publishing Co., Prescott, AZ, 1991. Paper covers. $16.95.

Reloader's Guide, 3rd Edition, by R.A. Steindler, Stoeger Publishing Co., So. Hackensack, NJ, 1984. 224 pp., illus. Paper covers. $11.95.

Complete, fully illustrated step-by-step guide to handloading ammunition.

Reloading for Shotgunners, 3rd Edition, by Edward A. Matunas, DBI Books, Inc., Northbrook, IL, 1993. 288 pp., illus. Paper covers. $17.95.

Expanded reloading tables with over 2,000 loads. Bushing charts for every major press and component maker. All new presentation on all aspects of shotshell reloading by one of the top experts in the field.

Sierra Handgun Manual, 3rd Edition, edited by Kenneth Ramage, Sierra Bullets, Santa Fe Springs, CA, 1990. 704 pp., illus. 3-ring binder. $19.95.

New listings for XP-100 and Contender pistols and TCU cartridges...part of a new single shot section. Covers the latest loads for 10mm Auto, 455 Super Mag, and Accurate powders.

Sierra Rifle Manual, 3rd Edition, edited by Kenneth Ramage, Sierra Bullets, Santa Fe Springs, CA, 1990. 856 pp., illus. 3-ring binder. $24.95.

Updated load information with new powder listings and a wealth of inside tips.

Sixgun Cartridges and Loads, by Elmer Keith, The Gun Room Press, Highland Park, NJ, 1986. 151 pp., illus. $24.95.

A manual covering the selection, uses and loading of the most suitable and popular revolver cartridges. Originally published in 1936. Reprint.

Speer Reloading Manual Number 12, edited by members of the Speer research staff, Omark Industries, Lewiston, ID, 1987. 621 pp., illus. $18.95.

Reloading manual for rifles and pistols.

Why Not Load Your Own?, by Col. T. Whelen, A. S. Barnes, New York, 1957, 4th ed., rev. 237 pp., illus. $20.00.

A basic reference on handloading, describing each step, materials and equipment. Includes loads for popular cartridges.

Wildcat Cartridges, Volume I, Wolfe Publishing Company, Prescott, AZ, 1992. 125 pp. Soft cover. $16.95.

From *Handloader* magazine, the more popular and famous wildcats are profiled.

Wildcat Cartridges, Volume II, compiled from *Handloader* and *Rifle* magazine articles written by featured authors, Wolfe Publishing Co., Prescott, AZ, 1992. 971 pp., illus. Paper covers. $34.95.

This volume details rifle and handtgun cartridges from the 14-221 to the 460 Van Horn. A comprehensive work containing loading tables and commentary.

Yours Truly, Harvey Donaldson, by Harvey Donaldson, Wolfe Publ. Co., Inc., Prescott, AZ, 1980. 288 pp., illus. $19.50.

Reprint of the famous columns by Harvey Donaldson which appeared in "Handloader" from May 1966 through December 1972.

COLLECTORS

The American Cartridge, by Charles R. Suydam, Borden Publishing Co., Alhambra, CA, 1986. 184 pp., illus. $18.00.

An illustrated study of the rimfire cartridge in the United States.

American Military Shoulder Arms: Volume 1, Colonial and Revolutionary War Arms, by George D. Moller, University Press of Colorado, Niwot, CO, 1993. 538 pp., illus. $75.00.

A superb in-depth study of the shoulder arms of the United States. This volume covers the pre-colonial period to the end of the American Revolution.

American Military Shoulder Arms: Volume 2, From the 1790's to the End of the Flintlock Period, by George D. Moller, University Press of Colorado, Niwot, CO, 1994. 496 pp., illus. $75.00.

Describes the rifles, muskets, carbines and other shoulder arms used by the armed forces of the United States from the 1790s to the end of the flintlock period in the 1840s.

Antique Guns, the Collector's Guide, 2nd Edition, edited by John Traister, Stoeger Publishing Co., S. Hackensack, NJ, 1994. 320 pp., illus. Paper covers. $19.95.

Covers a vast spectrum of pre-1900 firearms: those manufactured by U.S. gunmakers as well as Canadian, French, German, Belgian, Spanish and other foreign firms.

Arms & Accoutrements of the Mounted Police 1873-1973, by Roger F. Phillips and Donald J. Klancher, Museum Restoration Service, Ont., Canada, 1982. 224 pp., illus. $49.95.

A definitive history of the revolvers, rifles, machine guns, cannons, ammunition, swords, etc. used by the NWMP, the RNWMP and the RCMP during the first 100 years of the Force.

Arms Makers of Maryland, by Daniel D. Hartzler, George Shumway, York, PA, 1975. 200 pp., illus. $50.00.

A thorough study of the gunsmiths of Maryland who worked during the late 18th and early 19th centuries.

Artistry in Arms: The Guns of Smith & Wesson, by Roy G. Jinks, Smith & Wesson, Springfield, MA, 1991. 85 pp., illus. Paper covers. $19.95.

Catalog of the Smith & Wesson International Museum Tour 1991-1995 organized by the Connecticut Valley Historical Museum and Springfield Library and Museum Association.

Assault Weapons, 4th Edition, The Gun Digest Book of edited by Jack Lewis, DBI Books, Inc., Northbrook IL, 1996. 256 pp., illus. Paper covers. $19.95.

An in-depth look at the history and uses of these arms.

Astra Automatic Pistols, by Leonardo M. Antaris, FIRAC Publishing Co., Sterling, CO, 1989. 248 pp., illus. $45.00.

Charts, tables, serial ranges, etc. The definitive work on Astra pistols.

Basic Documents on U.S. Marital Arms, commentary by Col. B. R. Lewis, reissue by Ray Riling, Phila., PA, 1956 and 1960. *Rifle Musket Model 1855.* The first issue rifle of musket caliber, a muzzle loader equipped with the Maynard Primer, 32 pp. *Rifle Musket Model 1863.* The typical Union muzzle-loader of the Civil War, 26 pp. *Breech-Loading Rifle Musket Model 1866.* The first of our 50-caliber breechloading rifles, 12 pp. *Remington Navy Rifle Model 1870.* A commercial type breech-loader made at Springfield, 16 pp. *Lee Straight Pull Navy Rifle Model 1895.* A magazine cartridge arm of 6mm caliber. 23 pp. *Breech-Loading Arms* (five models) 27 pp. *Ward-Burton Rifle Musket 1871*-16 pp. Each $10.00.

Beretta Automatic Pistols, by J.B. Wood, Stackpole Books, Harrisburg, PA, 1985. 192 pp., illus. $24.95.

Only English-language book devoted to the Beretta line. Includes all important models.

Blacksmith Guide to Ruger Flat-top & Super Blackhawks, by H.W. Ross, Jr., Blacksmith Corp., Chino Valley, AZ, 1990. 96 pp., illus. Paper covers. $9.95.

A key source on the extensively collected Ruger Blackhawk revolvers.

*__Blue Book of Gun Values, 17th Edition,__ edited by E. P. Fjestad, Investment Rarities, Inc., Minneapolis, MN, 1996. 1301 pp., illus. Paper covers. $24.95.

Covers all new 1996 firearm prices. Gives technical data on both new and discontinued domestic and foreign commercial and military guns, modern commemoratives and major trademark antiques.

The Blunderbuss 1500-1900, by James D. Forman, Museum Restoration Service, Bloomfield, Ont., Canada, 1995. 40 pp., illus. Paper covers. $4.95.

The guns that had no peer as an anti-personal weapon throughout the flintlock era.

Boarders Away, Volume II: Firearms of the Age of Fighting Sail, by William Gilkerson, Andrew Mowbray, Inc. Publishers, Lincoln, RI, 1993. 331 pp., illus. $65.00.

Covers the pistols, muskets, combustibles and small cannon used aboard American and European fighting ships, 1626-1826.

The Book of the Springfield, by Edward C. Crossman and Roy F. Dunlap, Wolfe Publishing Co., Prescott, AZ, 1990. 567 pp., illus. $36.00.

A textbook covering the military, sporting and target rifles chambered for the caliber 30 Model 1906 cartridge; their metallic and telescopic sights and ammunition used in them.

Breech-Loading Carbines of the United States Civil War Period, by Brig. Gen. John Pitman, Armory Publications, Tacoma, WA, 1987. 94 pp., illus. $29.95.

The first in a series of previously unpublished manuscripts originated by the late Brigadier General John Putnam. Exploded drawings showing parts actual size follow each sectioned illustration.

The Breech-Loading Single-Shot Rifle, by Major Ned H. Roberts and Kenneth L. Waters, Wolfe Publishing Co., Prescott, AZ, 1995. 333 pp., illus. $28.50.

A comprehensive and complete history of the evolution of the Schutzen and single-shot rifle.

British Military Firearms 1650-1850, by Howard L. Blackmore, Stackpole Books, Mechanicsburg, PA, 1994. 224 pp., illus. $50.00.

The definitive work on British military firearms.

British Service Rifles and Carbines 1888-1900, by Alan M. Petrillo, Excaliber Publications, Latham, NY, 1994. 72 pp., illus, Paper covers. $11.95.

A complete review of the Lee-Metford and Lee-Enfield rifles and carbines.

British Small Arms Ammunition, 1864-1938, by Peter Labett, Armory Publications, Oceanside, CA, 1994. 352 pp., illus. $75.00.

The military side of the story illustrating the rifles, carbines, machine guns, revolvers and automatic pistols and their ammunition, experimental and adopted, from 577 Snider to modern times.

The British Soldier's Firearms from Smoothbore to Rifled Arms, 1850-1864, by Dr. C.H. Roads, R&R Books, Livonia, NY, 1994. 332 pp., illus. $49.00.

A reprint of the classic text covering the development of British military hand and shoulder firearms in the crucial years between 1850 and 1864.

British Sporting Rifle Cartridges, by Bill Fleming, Armory Publications, Oceanside, CA, 1994. 302 pp., illus. $60.00.

An expanded study of volume three of *The History & Development of Small Arms Ammunition.* Includes pertinent trade catalog pages, etc.

Browning Dates of Manufacture, compiled by George Madis, Art and Reference House, Brownsboro, TX, 1989. 48 pp. $5.00.

Gives the date codes and product codes for all models from 1824 to the present.

Browning Sporting Arms of Distinction 1903-1992, by Matt Eastman, Matt Eastman Publications, Fitzgerald, GA, 1995. 450 pp., illus. $49.95.

The most recognized publication on Browning sporting arms ever written; covers all models.

Bullard Arms, by G. Scott Jamieson, The Boston Mills Press, Ontario, Canada, 1989. 244 pp., illus. $35.00.

The story of a mechanical genius whose rifles and cartridges were the equal to any made in America in the 1880s.

Burning Powder, compiled by Major D.B. Wesson, Wolfe Publishing Company, Prescott, AZ, 1992. 110 pp. Soft cover. $10.95.

A rare booklet from 1932 for Smith & Wesson collectors.

The Burnside Breech Loading Carbines, by Edward A. Hull, Andrew Mowbray, Inc., Lincoln, RI, 1986. 95 pp., illus. $16.00.

No. 1 in the "Man at Arms Monograph Series." A model-by-model historical/technical examination of one of the most widely used cavalry weapons of the American Civil War based upon important and previously unpublished research.

California Gunsmiths 1846-1900, by Lawrence P. Sheldon, Far Far West Publ., Fair Oaks, CA, 1977. 289 pp., illus. $29.65.

A study of early California gunsmiths and the firearms they made.

Canadian Military Handguns 1855-1985, by Clive M. Law, Museum Restoration Service, Bloomfield, Ont. Canada, 1994. 130pp., illus. $40.00.

A long-awaited and important history for arms historians and pistol collectors.

***Cap Guns,** by James Dundas, Schiffer Publishing, Atglen, PA, 1996. 160 pp., illus. Paper covers. $29.95.

Over 600 full-color photos of cap guns and gun accessories with a current value guide.

Carbines of the Civil War, by John D. McAulay, Pioneer Press, Union City, TN, 1981. 123 pp., illus. Paper covers. $7.95.

A guide for the student and collector of the colorful arms used by the Federal cavalry.

Cartridges for Breechloading Rifles, by A. Mattenheimer, Armory Publications, Oceanside, CA, 1989. 90 pp. with two 15"x19" color lithos containing 163 drawings of cartridges and firearms mechanisms. $29.95.

Reprinting of this German work on cartridges. Text in German and English.

***Cartridges of the World, 8th Edition,** by Frank Barnes, edited by M. L. McPherson, DBI Books, Inc., Northbrook, IL, 1996. 480 pp., illus. Paper covers. $24.95.

Completely revised edition of the general purpose reference work for which collectors, police, scientists and laymen reach first for answers to cartridge identification questions. Available October, 1996.

Civil War Breech Loading Rifles, by John D. McAulay, Andrew Mowbray, Inc., Lincoln, RI, 1991. 144 pp., illus. Paper covers. $15.00.

All the major breech-loading rifles of the Civil War and most, if not all, of the obscure types are detailed, illustrated and set in their historical context.

Civil War Carbines Volume 2: The Early Years, by John D. McAulay, Andrew Mowbray, Inc., Lincoln, RI, 1991. 144 pp., illus. Paper covers. $15.00.

Covers the carbines made during the exciting years leading up to the outbreak of war and used by the North and South in the conflict.

Civil War Pistols, by John D. McAulay, Andrew Mowbray Inc., Lincoln, RI, 1992. 166 pp., illus. $38.50.

A survey of the handguns used during the American Civil War.

A Collector's Guide to United States Combat Shotguns, by Bruce N. Canfield, Andrew Mowbray Inc., Lincoln, RI, 1992. 184 pp., illus. Paper covers. $24.00

This book provides full coverage of combat shotguns, from the earliest examples right up to the Gulf War and beyond.

A Collector's Guide to Winchester in the Service, by Bruce N. Canfield, Andrew Mowbray, Inc., Lincoln, RI, 1991. 192 pp., illus. Paper covers. $22.00.

The firearms produced by Winchester for the national defense. From Hotchkiss to the M14, each firearm is examined and illustrated.

A Collector's Guide to the M1 Garand and the M1 Carbine, by Bruce N. Canfield, Andrew Mowbray, Inc., Publisher, Lincoln, RI, 1988. 144 pp., illus., paper covers. $22.00.

A comprehensive guide to the most important and ubiquitous American arms of WWII and Korea.

A Collector's Guide to the '03 Springfield, by Bruce N. Canfield, Andrew Mowbray Inc, Lincoln, RI, 1989. 160 pp., illus. Paper covers. $22.00.

A comprehensive guide follows the '03 through its unparalleled tenure of service. Covers all of the interesting variations, modifications and accessories of this highly collectible military rifle.

Collector's Illustrated Encyclopedia of the American Revolution, by George C. Neumann and Frank J. Kravic, Rebel Publishing Co., Inc., Texarkana, TX, 1989. 286 pp., illus. $29.95.

A showcase of more than 2,300 artifacts made, worn, and used by those who fought in the War for Independence.

Colonial Frontier Guns, by T.M. Hamilton, Pioneer Press, Union City, TN, 1988. 176 pp., illus. Paper covers. $13.95.

A complete study of early flint muskets of this country.

***The Colt Armory,** by Ellsworth Grant, Man-at-Arms Bookshelf, Lincoln, RI, 1996. 232 pp., illus. $35.00.

A history of Colt's Manufacturing Company.

Colt Heritage, by R.L. Wilson, Simon & Schuster, 1979. 358 pp., illus. $75.00.

The official history of Colt firearms 1836 to the present.

Colt Peacemaker British Model, by Keith Cochran, Cochran Publishing Co., Rapid City, SD, 1989. 160 pp., illus. $35.00.

Covers those revolvers Colt squeezed in while completing a large order of revolvers for the U.S. Cavalry in early 1874, to those magnificent cased target revolvers used in the pistol competitions at Bisley Commons in the 1890s.

Colt Peacemaker Encyclopedia, by Keith Cochran, Keith Cochran, Rapid City, SD, 1986. 434 pp., illus. $65.00.

A must book for the Peacemaker collector.

Colt Peacemaker Encyclopedia, Volume 2, by Keith Cochran, Cochran Publishing Co., SD, 1992. 416 pp., illus. $60.00.

Included in this volume are extensive notes on engraved, inscribed, historical and noted revolvers, as well as those revolvers used by outlaws, lawmen, movie and television stars.

Colt Percussion Accoutrements 1834-1873, by Robin Rapley, Robin Rapley, Newport Beach, CA, 1994. 432 pp., illus. Paper covers. $39.95.

The complete collector's guide to the identification of Colt percussion accoutrements; including Colt conversions and their values.

***Colt Pocket Pistols,** by Dr. John W. Brunner, Phillips Publications, Williamstown, NJ, 1996. 200 pp., illus. $50.00.

The definitive reference guide on the 25, 32 and 380 Colt automatic pistols.

Colt Revolvers and the Tower of London, by Joseph G. Rosa, Royal Armouries of the Tower of London, London, England, 1988. 72 pp., illus. Soft covers. $15.00.

Details the story of Colt in London through the early cartridge period.

Colt Revolvers and the U.S. Navy 1865-1889, by C. Kenneth Moore, Dorrance and Co., Bryn Mawr, PA, 1987. 140 pp., illus. $29.95.

The Navy's use of all Colt handguns and other revolvers during this era of change.

***Colt Rifles and Muskets from 1847-1870,** by Herbert Houze, Krause Publications, Iola, WI, 1996. 192 pp., illus. $34.95.

Discover previously unknown Colt models along with an extensive list of production figures for all models.

***Colt's SAA Post War Models,** by George Garton, The Gun Room Press, Highland Park, NJ, 1995. 166 pp., illus. $39.95.

Complete facts on the post-war Single Action Army revolvers. Information on calibers, production numbers and variations taken from factory records.

Colt Single Action Army Revolvers and the London Agency, by C. Kenneth Moore, Andrew Mowbray Publishers, Lincoln, RI, 1990. 144 pp., illus. $35.00.

Drawing on vast documentary sources, this work chronicles the relationship between the London Agency and the Hartford home office.

The Colt U.S. General Officers' Pistols, by Horace Greeley IV, Andrew Mowbray Inc., Lincoln, RI, 1990. 199 pp., illus. $38.00.

These unique weapons, issued as a badge of rank to General Officers in the U.S. Army from WWII onward, remain highly personal artifacts of the military leaders who carried them. Includes serial numbers and dates of issue.

Colt's Dates of Manufacture 1837-1978, by R.L. Wilson, published by Maurie Albert, Coburg, Australia; N.A. distributor I.D.S.A. Books, Hamilton, OH, 1983. 61 pp. $10.00.

An invaluable pocket guide to the dates of manufacture of Colt firearms up to 1978.

Colt's 100th Anniversary Firearms Manual 1836-1936: A Century of Achievement, Wolfe Publishing Co., Prescott, AZ, 1992. 100 pp., illus. Paper covers. $12.95.

Originally published by the Colt Patent Firearms Co., this booklet covers the history, manufacturing procedures and the guns of the first 100 years of the genius of Samuel Colt.

The Colt Whitneyville-Walker Pistol, by Lt. Col. Robert D. Whittington, Brownlee Books, Hooks, TX, 1984. 96 pp., illus. Limited edition. $20.00.

A study of the pistol and associated characters 1846-1851.

The Complete Guide to U.S. Infantry Weapons of World War Two, by Bruce Canfield, Andrew Mowbray, Publisher, Lincoln, RI, 1995. 303 pp., illus. $35.00.

A definitive work on the weapons used by the United States Armed Forces in WWII.

Compliments of Col. Ruger: A Study of Factory Engraved Single Action Revolvers, by John C. Dougan, Taylor Publishing Co., El Paso, TX, 1992. 238 pp., illus. $46.50.

Clearly detailed black and white photographs and a precise text present an accurate istory of the Sturm, Ruger & Co. single-action revolver engraving project.

Confederate Revolvers, by William A. Gary, Taylor Publishing Co., Dallas, TX, 1987. 174 pp., illus. $49.95.

Comprehensive work on the rarest of Confederate weapons.

Coykendall's 2nd Sporting Collectible Price Guide, by Ralf Coykendall, Jr., Lyons & Burford Publlishers, New York, NY, 1992. 223 pp., illus. Paper covers. $16.95.

The all-new second volume with new sections on knives and sporting magazines.

Cowboy Collectibles and Western Memorabilia, by Bob Bell and Edward Vebell, Schiffer Publishing, Atglen, PA, 1992. 160 pp., illus. Paper covers. $29.95.

The exciting era of the cowboy and the wild west collectibles including rifles, pistols, gun rigs, etc.

***Cowboy and Gunfighter Collectible,** by Bill Mackin, Mountain Press Publishing Co., Missoula, MT, 1995. 178 pp., illus. Paper covers. $25.00.

A photographic encyclopedia with price guide and makers' index.

The Deringer in America, Volume 1, The Percussion Period, by R.L. Wilson and L.D. Eberhart, Andrew Mowbray Inc., Lincoln, RI, 1985. 271 pp., illus. $48.00.

A long awaited book on the American percussion deringer.

The Deringer in America, Volume 2, The Cartridge Period, by L.D. Eberhart and R.L. Wilson, Andrew Mowbray Inc., Publishers, Lincoln, RI, 1993. 284 pp., illus. $65.00.

Comprehensive coverage of cartridge deringers organized alphabetically by maker. Includes all types of deringers known by the authors to have been offered to the American market.

Development of the Henry Cartridge and Self-Contained Cartridges for the Toggle-Link Winchesters, by R. Bruce McDowell, A.M.B., Metuchen, NJ, 1984. 69 pp., illus. Paper covers. $10.00.

From powder and ball to the self-contained metallic cartridge.

The Devil's Paintbrush: Sir Hiram Maxim's Gun, by Dolf Goldsmith, 2nd Edition, expanded and revised, Collector Grade Publications, Toronto, Canada, 1993. 384 pp., illus. $69.95

The classic work on the world's first true automatic machine gun.

Drums A'beating Trumpets Sounding, by William H. Guthman, The Connecticut Historical Society, Westport, CT, 1993. 232 pp., illus. $75.00.

Artistically carved powder horns in the provincial manner, 1746-1781.

***The Dutch Luger (Parabellum) A Complete History,** by Bas J. Martens and Guus de Vries, Ironside International Publishers, Inc., Alexandria, VA, 1995. 268 pp., illus. $49.95.

The history of the Luger in the Netherlands. An extensive description of the Dutch pistol and trials and the different models of the Luger in the Dutch service.

The Eagle on U.S. Firearms, by John W. Jordan, Pioneer Press, Union City, TN, 1992. 140 pp., illus. Paper covers. $14.95.

Stylized eagles have been stamped on government owned or manufactured firearms in the U.S. since the beginning of our country. This book lists and illustrates these various eagles in an informative and refreshing manner.

Early Indian Trade Guns: 1625-1775, by T.M. Hamilton, Museum of the Great Plains, Lawton, OK, 1968. 34 pp., illus. Paper covers. $12.95.

Detailed descriptions of subject arms, compiled from early records and from the study of remnants found in Indian country.

Encyclopedia of Ruger Rimfire Semi-Automatic Pistols: 1949-1992, by Chad Hiddleson, Krause Publications, Iola, WI, 1993. 250 pp., illus. $29.95.

Covers all physical aspects of Ruger 22-caliber pistols including important features such as boxes, grips, muzzlebrakes, instruction manuals, serial numbers, etc.

Encyclopedia of Ruger Semi-Automatic Rimfire Pistols 1949-1992, by Chad Hiddleson, Krause Publications, Iola, WI, 1994. 304 pp., illus. $29.95.

This book is a compilation of years of research, outstanding photographs and technical data on Ruger.

English Pistols: The Armories of H.M. Tower of London Collection, by Howard L. Blackmore, Arms and Armour Press, London, England, 1985. 64 pp., illus. Soft covers. $14.95.

All the pistols described and pictured are from this famed collection.

European Firearms in Swedish Castles, by Kaa Wennberg, Bohuslaningens Boktryckeri AB, Uddevalla, Sweden, 1986. 156 pp., illus. $50.00.

The famous collection of Count Keller, the Ettersburg Castle collection, and others. English text.

Fifteen Years in the Hawken Lode, by John D. Baird, The Gun Room Press, Highland Park, NJ, 1976. 120 pp., illus. $24.95.

A collection of thoughts and observations gained from many years of intensive study of the guns from the shop of the Hawken brothers.

'51 Colt Navies, by Nathan L. Swayze, The Gun Room Press, Highland Park, NJ, 1993. 243 pp., illus. $59.95.

The Model 1851 Colt Navy, its variations and markings.

Firearms and Tackle Memorabilia, by John Delph, Schiffer Publishing, Ltd., West Chester, PA, 1991. 124 pp., illus. $39.95.

A collector's guide to signs and posters, calendars, trade cards, boxes, envelopes, and other highly sought after memorabilia. With a value guide.

Flayderman's Guide to Antique American Firearms...and Their Values, 6th Edition, by Norm Flayderman, DBI Books, Inc., Northbrook, IL, 1994. 624 pp., illus. Paper covers. $29.95.

Updated edition of this bible of the antique gun field.

The .45-70 Springfield, by Joe Poyer and Craig Riesch, North Cape Publications, Tustin, CA, 1991. 112 pp., illus. Soft covers. $14.95.

A definitive work on the 45-70 Springfield. Organized by serial number and date of production to aid the collector in identifying models and rifle parts.

Frank and George Freund and the Sharps Rifle, by Gerald O. Kelver, Gerald O. Kelver, Brighton, CO, 1986. 60 pp., illus. Paper covers. $12.00.

Pioneer gunmakers of Wyoming Territory and Colorado.

French Military Weapons, 1717-1938, Major James E. Hicks, N. Flayderman & Co., Publishers, New Milford, CT, 1973. 281 pp., illus. $35.00.

Firearms, swords, bayonets, ammunition, artillery, ordnance equipment of the French army.

The French 1935 Pistols, by Eugene Medlin and Colin Doane, Eugene Medlin, El Paso, TX, 1995. 172 pp., illus. Paper covers. $25.95.

The development and identification of successive models, fakes and variants, holsters and accessories, and serial numbers by dates of production.

From the Kingdom of Lilliput: The Miniature Firearms of David Kucer, by K. Corey Keeble and **The Making of Miniatures,** by David Kucer, Museum Restoration Service, Ontario, Canada, 1994. 51 pp., illus, $25.00.

An overview of the subject of miniatures in general combined with an outline by the artist himself on the way he makes a miniature firearm.

Game Guns & Rifles: Percussion to Hammerless Ejector in Britain, by Richard Akehurst, Trafalgar Square, N. Pomfret, VT, 1993. 192 pp., illus. $34.95.

Long considered a classic this important reprint covers the period of British gunmaking between 1830-1900.

George Schreyer, Sr. and Jr., Gunmakers of Hanover, Pennsylvania, by George Shumway, George Shumway Publishers, York, PA, 1990. 160pp., illus. $50.00.

This monograph is a detailed photographic study of almost all known surviving long rifles and smoothbore guns made by highly regarded gunsmiths George Schreyer, Sr. and Jr.

The German Assault Rifle 1935-1945, by Peter R. Senich, Paladin Press, Boulder, CO, 1987. 328 pp., illus. $49.95.

A complete review of machine carbines, machine pistols and assault rifles employed by Hitler's Wehrmacht during WWII.

The German K98k Rifle, 1934-1945: The Backbone of the Wehrmacht, by Richard D. Law, Collector Grade Publications, Inc., Toronto, Canada, 1993. 336 pp., illus. $69.95.

The most comprehensive study ever published on the 14,000,000 bolt-action K98k rifles produced in Germany between 1934 and 1945.

German Machineguns, by Daniel D. Musgrave, Revised edition, Ironside International Publishers, Inc. Alexandria, VA, 1992. 586 pp., 650 illus. $49.95.

The most definitive book ever written on German machineguns. Covers the introduction and development of machineguns in Germany from 1899 to the rearmament period after WWII.

German Military Rifles and Machine Pistols, 1871-1945, by Hans Dieter Gotz, Schiffer Publishing Co., West Chester, PA, 1990. 245 pp., illus. $35.00.

This book portrays in words and pictures the development of the modern German weapons and their ammunition including the scarcely known experimental types.

German Pistols and Holsters 1934-1945, Vol. 2, by Robert Whittington, Brownlee Books, Hooks, TX, 1990. 312 pp., illus. $55.00.

This volume addresses pistols only: military (Heer, Luftwaffe, Kriegsmarine & Waffen-SS), captured, commercial, police, NSDAP and government.

German 7.9mm Military Ammunition, by Daniel W. Kent, Daniel W. Kent, Ann Arbor, MI, 1991. 244 pp., illus. $35.00.

The long-awaited revised edition of a classic among books devoted to ammunition.

German Pistols and Holsters, 1934-1945, Volume 4, by Lt. Col. Robert D. Whittington, 3rd, U.S.A.R., Brownlee Books, Hooks, TX, 1991. 208 pp. $30.00.

Pistols and holsters issued in 412 selected armed forces, army and Waffen-SS units including information on personnel, other weapons and transportation.

The Golden Age of Remington, by Robert W.D. Ball, Krause publications, Iola, WI, 1995. 208 pp., illus. $29.95.

For Remington collectors or firearms historians, this book provides a pictorial history of Remington through World War I. Includes value guide.

Great British Gunmakers: The Mantons 1782-1878, by D.H.L. Back, Historical Firearms, Norwich, England, 1994. 218 pp., illus. Limited edition of 500 copies. $175.00.

Contains detailed descriptions of all the firearms made by members of this famous family.

Great Irish Gunmakers: Messrs. Rigby 1760-1869, by D.H.L. Back, Historical Firearms, Norwich, England, 1993. 196 pp., illus. $150.00.

The history of this famous firm of Irish gunmakers illustrated with a wide selection of Rigby arms.

A Guide to the Maynard Breechloader, by George J. Layman, George J. Layman, Ayer, MA, 1993. 125 pp., illus. Paper covers. $17.95.

The first book dedicated entirely to the Maynard family of breech-loading firearms. Coverage of the arms is given from the 1850s through the 1880s.

Guide to Ruger Single Action Revolvers Production Dates, 1953-73, by John C. Dougan, Blacksmith Corp., Chino Valley, AZ, 1991. 22 pp., illus. Paper covers. $9.95.

A unique pocket-sized handbook providing production information for the popular Ruger single-action revolvers manufactured during the first 20 years.

Gun Collecting, by Geoffrey Boothroyd, Sportsman's Press, London, 1989. 208 pp., illus. $29.95.

The most comprehensive list of 19th century British gunmakers and gunsmiths ever published.

Gun Collector's Digest, 5th Edition, edited by Joseph J. Schroeder, DBI Books, Inc., Northbrook, IL, 1989. 224 pp., illus. Paper covers. $17.95.

The latest edition of this sought-after series.

Gunmakers of London 1350-1850, by Howard L. Blackmore, George Shumway Publisher, York, PA, 1986. 222 pp., illus. $35.00.

A listing of all the known workmen of gun making in the first 500 years, plus a history of the guilds, cutlers, armourers, founders, blacksmiths, etc. 260 gunmarks are illustrated.

Gunsmiths of Illinois, by Curtis L. Johnson, George Shumway Publishers, York, PA, 1995. 160 pp., illus. $50.00.

Genealogical information is provided for nearly one thousand gunsmiths. Contains hundreds of illustrations of rifles and other guns, of handmade origin, from Illinois.

The Gunsmiths of Manhattan, 1625-1900: A Checklist of Tradesmen, by Michael H. Lewis, Museum Restoration Service, Bloomfield, Ont., Canada, 1991. 40 pp., illus. Paper covers. $4.95.

This listing of more than 700 men in the arms trade in New York City prior to about the end of the 19th century will provide a guide for identification and further research.

***The Guns of Dagenham: Lanchester, Patchett, Sterling,** by Peter Laidler and David Howroyd, Collector Grade Publications, Inc., Cobourg, Ont., Canada, 1995. 310 pp., illus. $39.95.

An in-depth history of the small arms made by the Sterling Company of Dagenham, Essex, England, from 1940 until Sterling was purchased by British Aerospace in 1989 and closed.

Gun Tools, Their History and Identification by James B. Shaffer, Lee A. Rutledge and R. Stephen Dorsey, Collector's Library, Eugene, OR, 1992. 375 pp., illus. $32.00.

Written history of foreign and domestic gun tools from the flintlock period to WWII.

Gun Trader's Guide, 18th Edition, published by Stoeger Publishing Co., S. Hackensack, NJ, 1995. 575 pp., illus. Paper covers. $19.95.

Complete, fully illustrated guide to identification of modern firearms along with current market values.

Handbook of Military Rifle Marks 1870-1950, by Richard A. Hoffman and Noel P. Schott, Mapleleaf Militaria Publishing, St. Louis, MO, 1995. 42 pp., illus. Spiral bound. $15.00.

An illustrated guide to identifying military rifle and marks.

The Handgun, by Geoffrey Boothroyd, David and Charles, North Pomfret, VT, 1989. 566 pp., illus. $60.00.

Every chapter deals with an important period in handgun history from the 14th century to the present.

The Hawken Rifle: Its Place in History, by Charles E. Hanson, Jr., The Fur Press, Chadron, NE, 1979. 104 pp., illus. Paper covers. $15.00.

A definitive work on this famous rifle.

Hawken Rifles, The Mountain Man's Choice, by John D. Baird, The Gun Room Press, Highland Park, NJ, 1976. 95 pp., illus. $29.95.

Covers the rifles developed for the Western fur trade. Numerous specimens are described and shown in photographs.

High Standard: A Collector's Guide to the Hamden & Hartford Target Pistols, by Tom Dance, Andrew Mowbray, Inc., Lincoln, RI, 1991. 192 pp., illus. Paper covers. $24.00.

From Citation to Supermatic, all of the production models and specials made from 1951 to 1984 are covered according to model number or series.

Historic Pistols: The American Martial Flintlock 1760-1845, by Samuel E. Smith and Edwin W. Bitter, The Gun Room Press, Highland Park, NJ, 1986. 353 pp., illus. $45.00.

Covers over 70 makers and 163 models of American martial arms.

Historical Hartford Hardware, by William W. Dalrymple, Colt Collector Press, Rapid City, SD, 1976. 42 pp., illus. Paper covers. $10.00.

Historically associated Colt revolvers.

The History and Development of Small Arms Ammunition, Volume 1, by George A. Hoyem, Armory Publications, Oceanside, CA, 1991. 230 pp., illus. $60.00.

Military musket, rifle, carbine and primitive machine gun cartridges of the 18th and 19th centuries, together with the firearms that chambered them.

The History and Development of Small Arms Ammunition, Volume 2, by George A. Hoyem, Armory Publications, Oceanside, CA, 1991. 303 pp., illus. $60.00.

Covers the blackpowder military centerfire rifle, carbine, machine gun and volley gun ammunition used in 28 nations and dominions, together with the firearms that chambered them.

The History and Development of Small Arms Ammunition (British Sporting Rifle) Volume 3, by George A. Hoyem, Armory Publications, Oceanside, CA, 1991. 300 pp., illus. $60.00.

Concentrates on British sporting rifle cartridges that run from the 4-bore through the .600 Nitro to the .297/.230 Morris.

The History of Smith and Wesson, by Roy G. Jinks, Willowbrook Enterprises, Springfield, MA, 1988. 290 pp., illus. $27.95.

Revised 10th Anniversary edition of the definite book on S&W firearms.

The History of Winchester Firearms 1866-1992, sixth edition, updated, expanded, and revised by Thomas Henshaw, New Win Publishing, Clinton, NJ, 1993. 280 pp., illus. $24.95.

This classic is the standard reference for all collectors and others seeking the facts about any Winchester firearm, old or new.

History of Winchester Repeating Arms Company, by Herbert G. Houze, Krause Publications, Iola, WI, 1994. 800 pp., illus. $50.00.

The complete Winchester history from 1856-1981.

***Honour Bound: The Chauchat Machine Rifle,** by Gerard Demaison and Yves Buffetaut, Collector Grade Publications, Inc., Cobourg, Ont., Canada, 1995. $39.95.

The story of the CSRG (Chauchat) machine rifle, the most manufactured automatic weapon of World War One.

How to Buy and Sell Used Guns, by John Traister, Stoeger Publishing Co., So. Hackensack, NJ, 1984. 192 pp., illus. Paper covers. $10.95.

A new guide to buying and selling guns.

Identification Manual on the .303 British Service Cartridge, No. 1-Ball Ammunition, by B.A. Temple, I.D.S.A. Books, Piqua, OH, 1986. 84 pp., 57 illus. $12.50

Identification Manual on the .303 British Service Cartridge, No. 2-Blank Ammunition, by B.A. Temple, I.D.S.A. Books, Piqua, OH, 1986. 95 pp., 59 illus. $12.50

Identification Manual on the .303 British Service Cartridge, No. 3-Special Purpose Ammunition, by B.A. Temple, I.D.S.A. Books, Piqua, OH, 1987. 82 pp., 49 illus. $12.50

Identification Manual on the .303 British Service Cartridge, No. 4-Dummy Cartridges Henry 1869-c.1900, by B.A. Temple, I.D.S.A. Books, Piqua, OH, 1988. 84 pp., 70 illus. $12.50

Identification Manual on the .303 British Service Cartridge, No. 5-Dummy Cartridges (2), by B.A. Temple, I.D.S.A. Books, Piqua, OH, 1994. 78 pp. $12.50

Illustrations of United States Military Arms 1776-1903 and Their Inspector's Marks, compiled by Turner Kirkland, Pioneer Press, Union City, TN, 1988. 37 pp., illus. Paper covers. $4.95.

Reprinted from the 1949 Bannerman catalog. Valuable information for both the advanced and beginning collector.

Indian War Cartridge Pouches, Boxes and Carbine Boots, by R. Stephen Dorsey, Collector's Library, Eugene, OR, 1993. 156 pp., illus. Paper Covers. $25.00.

The key reference work to the cartridge pouches, boxes, carbine sockets and boots of the Indian War period 1865-1890.

An Introduction to the Civil War Small Arms, by Earl J. Coates and Dean S. Thomas, Thomas Publishing Co., Gettysburg, PA, 1990. 96 pp., illus. Paper covers. $10.00.

The small arms carried by the individual soldier during the Civil War.

Iver Johnson's Arms & Cycle Works Handguns, 1871-1964, by W.E. "Bill" Goforth, Blacksmith Corp., Chino Valley, AZ, 1991. 160 pp., illus. Paper covers. $14.95.

Covers all of the famous Iver Johnson handguns from the early solid-frame pistols and revolvers to optional accessories, special orders and patents.

Jaeger Rifles, by George Shumway, George Shumway Publisher, York, PA, 1994. 108 pp., illus. Paper covers. $25.00.

Thirty-six articles previously published in *Muzzle Blasts* are reproduced here. They deal with late-17th, and 18th century rifles from Vienna, Carlsbad, Bavaria, Saxony, Brandenburg, Suhl, North-Central Germany, and the Rhine Valley.

James Reid and His Catskill Knuckledusters, by Taylor Brown, Andrew Mowbray Publishers, Lincoln, RI, 1990. 288 pp., illus. $24.95.

A detailed history of James Reid, his factory in the picturesque Catskill Mountains, and the pistols which he manufactured there.

Jane's Infantry Weapons, 21st Edition, 1995-96, Jane's Information Group, Alexandria, VA, 1995. 750 pp., illus. $265.00.

Complete coverage on over 1,700 weapons and accessories from nearly 300 manufacturers in 69 countries. Completely revised and updated.

Japanese Handguns, by Frederick E. Leithe, Borden Publishing Co., Alhambra, CA, 1985. 160 pp., illus. $22.95.

An identification guide to all models and variations of Japanese handguns.

***Japanese Rifles of World War Two,** by Duncan O. McCollum, Excalibur Publications, Latham, NY, 1996. 64 pp., illus. Paper covers. $18.95.

A sweeping view of the rifles and carbines that made up Japan's arsenal during the conflict.

The Kentucky Rifle, by Captain John G.W. Dillin, George Shumway Publisher, York, PA, 1993. 221 pp., illus. $50.00.

This well-known book was the first attempt to tell the story of the American longrifle. This edition retains the original text and illustrations with supplemental footnotes provided by Dr. George Shumway.

Know Your Broomhandle Mausers, by R.J. Berger, Blacksmith Corp., Southport, CT, 1985. 96 pp., illus. Paper covers. $9.95.

An interesting story on the big Mauser pistol and its variations.

Krag Rifles, by William S. Brophy, The Gun Room Press, Highland Park, NJ, 1980. 200 pp., illus. $35.00.

The first comprehensive work detailing the evolution and various models, both military and civilian.

The Krieghoff Parabellum, by Randall Gibson, Midland, TX, 1988. 279 pp., illus. $40.00.

A comprehensive text pertaining to the Lugers manufactured by H. Krieghoff Waffenfabrik.

The Lee-Enfield Story, by Ian Skennerton, Ian Skennerton, Ashmore City, Australia, 1993. 503 pp., illus. $59.95.

The Lee-Metford, Lee-Enfield, S.M.L.E. and No. 4 series rifles and carbines from 1880 to the present.

Levine's Guide to Knives And Their Values, 3rd Edition, by Bernard Levine, DBI Books, Inc., Northbrook, IL, 1993. 480 pp., illus. Paper covers. $25.95

All the basic tools for identifying, valuing and collecting folding and fixed blade knives.

Longrifles of North Carolina, by John Bivens, George Shumway Publisher, York, PA, 1988. 256 pp., illus. $50.00.

Covers art and evolution of the rifle, immigration and trade movements. Committee of Safety gunsmiths, characteristics of the North Carolina rifle.

Longrifles of Pennsylvania, Volume 1, Jefferson, Clarion & Elk Counties, by Russel H. Harringer, George Shumway Publisher, York, PA, 1984. 200 pp., illus. $50.00.

First in series that will treat in great detail the longrifles and gunsmiths of Pennsylvania.

Lugers at Random, by Charles Kenyon, Jr., Handgun Press, Glenview, IL, 1990. 420 pp., illus. $49.95.

A new printing of this classic, comprehensive reference for all Luger collectors.

***The Luger Story,** by John Walter, Stackpole Books, Mechanicsburg, PA, 1995. 256 pp., illus. $39.95.

The standard history of the world's most famous handgun.

Marlin Firearms: A History of the Guns and the Company That Made Them, by Lt. Col. William S. Brophy, USAR, Ret., Stackpole Books, Harrisburg, PA, 1989. 672 pp., illus. $75.00.

The definitive book on the Marlin Firearms Co. and their products.

Massachusetts Military Shoulder Arms 1784-1877, by George D. Moller, Andrew Mowbray Publisher, Lincoln, RI, 1989. 250 pp., illus. $24.00.

A scholarly and heavily researched study of the military shoulder arms used by Massachusetts during the 90-year period following the Revolutionary War.

Matt Eastman's Guide to Browning Belgium Firearms 1903-1994, by Matt Eastman, Matt Eastman Publications, Fitzgerald, GA, 1995. 150 pp. Paper covers. $14.95.

Covers all Belgium models through 1994. Manufacturing production figures on the Auto-5 and Safari rifles.

Mauser Bolt Rifles, by Ludwig Olson, F. Brownell & Son, Inc., Montezuma, IA, 1976. 364 pp., illus. $47.50.

The most complete, detailed, authoritative and comprehensive work ever done on Mauser bolt rifles.

***Mauser Military Rifles of the World,** by Robert W. D. Ball, Krause Publications, Iola, WI, 1996. 240 pp., illus. $39.95.

The rifles produced by the Mauser Co. for their international market with complete production quantities, rarity and technical specifications.

Military Handguns of France 1858-1958, by Eugene Medlin and Jean Huon, Excalibur Publications, Latham, NY, 1994. 124 pp., illus. Paper covers. $24.95.

The first book written in English that provides students of arms with a thorough history of French military handguns.

Military Pistols of Japan, by Fred L. Honeycutt, Jr., Julin Books, Palm Beach Gardens, FL, 1991. 168 pp., illus. $34.00.

Covers every aspect of military pistol production in Japan through WWII.

Military Rifles of Japan, 4th Edition, by F.L. Honeycutt, Julin Books, Lake Park, FL, 1989. 208 pp., illus. $42.00.

A new revised and updated edition. Includes the early Murata-period markings, etc.

Military Small Arms of the 20th Century, 6th Edition, by Ian V. Hogg, DBI Books, Inc., Northbrook, IL, 1991. 352 pp., illus. Paper covers. $20.95.

Fully revised and updated edition of the standard reference in its field.

M1 Carbine, by Larry Ruth, Gunroom Press, Highland Park, NJ, 1987. 291 pp., illus. Paper $19.95.

The origin, development, manufacture and use of this famous carbine of World War II.

The M1 Garand: Post World War, by Scott A. Duff, Scott A. Duff, Export, PA, 1990. 139 pp., illus. Soft covers. $19.95.

A detailed account of the activities at Springfield Armory through this period. International Harvester, H&R, Korean War production and quantities delivered. Serial numbers.

The M1 Garand: World War 2, by Scott A. Duff, Scott A. Duff, Export, PA, 1993. 210 pp., illus. Paper covers. $39.95.

The most comprehensive study available to the collector and historian on the M1 Garand of World War II.

Modern Beretta Firearms, by Gene Gangarosa, Jr., Stoeger Publishing Co., S. Hackensack, NJ, 1994. 288 pp., illus. Paper covers. $16.95.

Traces all models of modern Beretta pistols, rifles, machine guns and combat shotguns.

Modern Guns Identification and Values, 10th Edition, by Steven and Russell Quertermous, Collector Books, Paducah, KY, 1994. 496 pp., illus. Paper covers. $12.95.

Over 2,500 models of rifles, handguns and shotguns from 1900 to the present are described and prices given for NRA excellent and very good.

***Modern Gun Values, The Gun Digest Book of,** 10th Edition, by the Editors of Gun Digest, DBI Books, Inc., Northbrook, IL., 1996. 560 pp. illus. Paper covers. $21.95.

Greatly updated and expanded edition describing and valuing over 7,000 firearms manufactured from 1900 to 1996. The standard for valuing modern firearms.

Modern Small Arms, by Ian Hogg, Book Sales, Edison, NJ, 1995. 160 pp., illus. $17.98.

Encyclopedia coverage of more than 150 of the most sought after small arms produced today—rifles, pistols, machine guns and shotguns are covered.

More Single Shot Rifles, by James C. Grant, The Gun Room Press, Highland Park, NJ, 1976. 324 pp., illus. $29.95.

Details the guns made by Frank Wesson, Milt Farrow, Holden, Borchardt, Stevens, Remington, Winchester, Ballard and Peabody-Martini.

Mortimer, the Gunmakers, 1753-1923, by H. Lee Munson, Andrew Mowbray Inc., Lincoln, RI, 1992. 320 pp., illus. $65.00.

Seen through a single, dominant, English gunmaking dynasty this fascinating study provides a window into the classical era of firearms artistry.

***Mossberg: More Gun for the Money,** by V. and C. Havlin, Investment Rarities, Inc., Minneapolis, MN, 1995. 304 pp., illus. Paper covers. $24.95.

The history of O. F. Mossberg and Sons, Inc.

The Muzzle-Loading Cap Lock Rifle, by Ned H. Roberts, reprinted by Wolfe Publishing Co., Prescott, AZ, 1991. 432 pp., illus. $30.00.

Originally published in 1940, this fascinating study of the muzzle-loading cap lock rifle covers rifles on the frontier to hunting rifles, including the famous Hawken.

The Navy Luger, by Joachim Gortz and John Walter, Handgun Press, Glenview, IL, 1988. 128 pp., illus. $24.95.

The 9mm Pistole 1904 and the Imperial German Navy. A concise illustrated history.

Pistols of the World, 3rd Edition, by Ian Hogg and John Weeks, DBI Books, Inc., Northbrook, IL, 1992. 320 pp., illus. Paper covers. $20.95.

A totally revised edtion of one of the leading studies of small arms.

The Number 5 Jungle Carbine, by Alan M. Petrillo, Excalibur Publications, Latham, NY, 1994. 32 pp., illus. Paper covers. $7.95.

A comprehensive treatment of the rifle that collectors have come to call the "Jungle Carbine"—the Lee-Enfield Number 5, Mark 1.

The '03 Era: When Smokeless Revolutionized U.S. Riflery, by Clark S. Campbell, Collector Grade Publications, Inc., Ontario, Canada, 1994. 334 pp., illus. $44.50.

A much-expanded version of Campbell's *The '03 Springfields*, representing forty years of in-depth research into "all things '03."

The P-08 Parabellum Luger Automatic Pistol, edited by J. David McFarland, Desert Publications, Cornville, AZ, 1982. 20 pp., illus. Paper covers. $10.00.

Covers every facet of the Luger, plus a listing of all known Luger models.

Packing Iron, by Richard C. Rattenbury, Zon International Publishing, Millwood, NY, 1993. 216 pp., illus. $45.00.

The best book yet produced on pistol holsters and rifle scabbards. Over 300 variations of holster and scabbards are illustrated in large, clear plates.

Patents for Inventions, Class 119 (Small Arms), 1855-1930. British Patent Office, Armory Publications, Oceanside, CA, 1993. 7 volume set. $350.00.

Contains 7980 abridged patent descriptions and their sectioned line drawings, plus a 37-page alphabetical index of the patentees.

Paterson Colt Pistol Variations, by R.L. Wilson and R. Phillips, Jackson Arms Co., Dallas, TX, 1979. 250 pp., illus. $35.00.

A book about the different models and barrel lengths in the Paterson Colt story.

Pennsylvania Longrifles of Note, by George Shumway, George Shumway, Publisher, York, PA, 1977. 63 pp., illus. Paper covers. $15.00.

Illustrates and describes rifles from a number of Pennsylvania rifle-making schools.

Pistols of the World, 3rd Edition, by Ian Hogg and John Weeks, DBI Books, Inc., Northbrook, IL, 1992. 320 pp., illus. Paper covers. $20.95.

A totally revised edition of one of the leading studies of small arms.

The Pitman Notes on U.S. Martial Small Arms and Ammunition, 1776-1933, Volume 2, Revolvers and Automatic Pistols, by Brig. Gen. John Pitman, Thomas Publications, Gettysburg, PA, 1990. 192 pp., illus. $29.95.

A most important primary source of information on United States military small arms and ammunition.

The Plains Rifle, by Charles Hanson, Gun Room Press, Highland Park, NJ, 1989. 169 pp., illus. $29.95.

All rifles that were made with the plainsman in mind, including pistols.

The Powder Flask Book, by Ray Riling, R&R Books, Livonia, NY, 1993. 514 pp., illus. $70.00.

The complete book on flasks of the 19th century. Exactly scaled pictures of 1,600 flasks are illustrated.

***Proud Promise: French Autoloading Rifles, 1898-1979,** by Jean Huon, Collector Grade Publications, Inc., Cobourg, Ont., Canada, 1995. 216 pp., illus. $39.95.

The author has finally set the record straight about the importance of French contributions to modern arms design.

***E. C. Prudhomme's Gun Engraving Review,** by E. C. Prudhomme, R&R Books, Livonia, NY, 1994. 164 pp., illus. $60.00.

As a source for engravers and collectors, this book is an indispensable guide to styles and techniques of the world's foremost engravers.

The Rare and Valuable Antique Arms, by James E. Serven, Pioneer Press, Union City, TN, 1976. 106 pp., illus. Paper covers. $4.95.

A guide to the collector in deciding which direction his collecting should go, investment value, historic interest, mechanical ingenuity, high art or personal preference.

Reloading Tools, Sights and Telescopes for Single Shot Rifles, by Gerald O. Kelver, Brighton, CO, 1982. 163 pp., illus. Paper covers. $15.00.

A listing of most of the famous makers of reloading tools, sights and telescopes with a brief description of the products they manufactured.

The Remington-Lee Rifle, by Eugene F. Myszkowski, Excalibur Publications, Latham, NY, 1995. 100 pp., illus. Paper covers. $22.50.

Features detailed descriptions, including serial number ranges, of each model from the first Lee Magazine Rifle produced for the U.S. Navy to the last Remington-Lee Small Bores shipped to the Cuban Rural Guard.

Revolvers of the British Services 1854-1954, by W.H.J. Chamberlain and A.W.F. Taylerson, Museum Restoration Service, Ottawa, Canada, 1989. 80 pp., illus. $27.50.

Covers the types issued among many of the United Kingdom's naval, land or air services.

Rhode Island Arms Makers & Gunsmiths, by William O. Archibald, Andrew Mowbray, Inc., Lincoln, RI, 1990. 108 pp., illus. $16.50.

A serious and informative study of an important area of American arms making.

Rifles of the World, by John Walter, DBI Books, Inc., Northbrook, IL, 1993. 320 pp., illus. Paper covers. $20.95.

Compiled as a companion volume to *Pistols of the World*, this brand new reference work covers all centerfire military and commercial rifles produced from the perfection of the metal-case cartridge in the 1870's to the present time.

The Rock Island '03, by C.S. Ferris, C.S. Ferris, Arvada, CO, 1993. 58 pp., illus. Paper covers. $12.50.

A monograph of interenst to the collector or historian concentrating on the U.S. M1903 rifle made by the less publicized of our two producing facilities.

Ruger, edited by Joseph Roberts, Jr., the National Rifle Association of America, Washington, D.C., 1991. 109 pp. illus. Paper covers. $14.95.

The story of Bill Ruger's indelible imprint in the history of sporting firearms.

Sam Colt's Own Record 1847, by John Parsons, Wolfe Publishing Co., Prescott, AZ, 1992. 167 pp., illus. $24.50.

Chronologically presented, the correspondence published here completes the account of the manufacture, in 1847, of the Walker Model Colt revolver.

Scottish Firearms, by Claude Blair and Robert Woosnam-Savage, Museum Restoration Service, Bloomfield, Ont., Canada, 1995. 52 pp., illus. Paper covers. $4.95.

This revision of the first book devoted entirely to Scottish firearms is supplemented by a register of surviving Scottish long guns.

***Scouts, Peacemakers and New Frontiers in .22 Caliber,** by Don Wilkerson, Cherokee Publications, Kansas City, MO, 1995. 224 pp., illus. $40.00.

Covers the 48 variations and numerous subvariants of the later rimfire Single Actions.

Sharps Firearms, by Frank Seller, Frank M. Seller, Denver, CO, 1982. 358 pp., illus. $50.00.

Traces the development of Sharps firearms with full range of guns made including all martial variations.

***Shooter's Bible, 1997, No. 87,** edited by William S. Jarrett, Stoeger Publishing Co., S. Hackensack, NJ, 1995. 576 pp., illus. Paper covers.

Contains specifications, photos and retail prices of handguns, rifles, shotguns and blackpowder arms currently manufactured by major U.S. and foreign gunmakers.

Simeon North: First Official Pistol Maker of the United States, by S. North and R. North, The Gun Room Press, Highland Park, NJ, 1972. 207 pp., illus. $15.95.

Reprint of the rare first edition.

The SKS Type 45 Carbines, by Duncan Long, Desert Publications, El Dorado, AZ, 1992. 110 pp., illus. Paper covers.

Covers the history and practical aspects of operating, maintaining and modifying this abundantly available rifle.

Small Arms: Pistols & Rifles, by Ian V. Hogg, Greenhill Books, London, England, 1994. 160 pp., illus. $19.95.

An in-depth description of small arms, focusing on pistols and rifles, with detailed information about all small arms used by the world's armed forces.

Smith & Wesson Handguns, by Roy McHenry and Walter Roper, Wolfe Publishing Co., Prescott, AZ, 1994. 233 pp., illus. $32.00.

The bible on Smith & Wesson handguns.

Southern Derringers of the Mississippi Valley, by Turner Kirkland, Pioneer Press, Tenn., 1971. 80 pp., illus., paper covers. $10.00.

A guide for the collector, and a much-needed study.

***Soviet Russian Postwar Military Pistols and Cartridges,** by Fred A. Datig, Handgun Press, Glenview, IL, 1988. 152 pp., illus. $29.95.

Thoroughly researched, this definitive sourcebook covers the development and adoption of the Makarov, Stechkin and the new PSM pistols. Also included in this source book is coverage on Russian clandestine weapons and pistol cartridges.

Soviet Russian Tokarev "TT" Pistols and Cartridges 1929-1953, by Fred Datig, Graphic Publishers, Santa Ana, CA, 1993. 168 pp., illus. $39.95.

Details of rare arms and their accessories are shown in hundreds of photos. It also contains a complete bibliography and index.

Soviet Small-Arms and ammunition, by David Bolotin, Handgun Press, Glenview, IL, 1996. 264 pp., illus. $49.95.

An authoritative and complete book on Soviet small arms.

Spencer Firearms, by Roy Marcot, R&R Books, Livonia, NY, 1995. 237 pp., illus. $60.00.

The definitive work on one of the most famous Civil War firearms.

Sporting Collectibles, by Jim and Vivian Karsnitz, Schiffer Publishing Ltd., West Chester, PA, 1992. 160 pp., illus. Paper covers. $29.95.

The fascinating world of hunting related collectibles presented in an informative text.

The Springfield 1903 Rifles, by Lt. Col. William S. Brophy, USAR, Ret., Stackpole Books Inc., Harrisburg, PA, 1985. 608 pp., illus. $49.95.

The illustrated, documented story of the design, development, and production of all the models, appendages, and accessories.

Springfield Shoulder Arms 1795-1865, by Claud E. Fuller, S. & S. Firearms, Glendale, NY, 1986. 76 pp., illus. Paper covers. $17.95.

Exact reprint of the scarce 1930 edition of one of the most definitive works on Springfield flintlock and percussion muskets ever published.

***Standard Catalog of Firearms, 6th Edition,** compiled by Ned Schwing and Herbert Houze, Krause Publications, Iola, WI, 1996. 1,116 pp., illus. Paper covers. $29.95.

1996 pricing guide in six grades with more than 2,300 photos and over 1,100 manufacturers.

***Standard Catalog of Smith and Wesson,** by Jim Supica and Richard Nahas, Krause Publications, Iola, WI, 1996. 256 pp., illus. $29.95.

Clearly details hundreds of products by the legendary manufacturer. How to identify, evaluate the condition and assess the value of 752 Smith & Wesson models and variations.

***Steel Canvas: The Art of American Arms,** by R. L. Wilson, Random House, NY, 1995, 384 pp., illus. $65.00.

Presented here for the first time is the breathtaking panorama of America's extraordinary engravers and embellishers of arms, from the 1700s to modern times.

Stevens Pistols & Pocket Rifles, by K.L. Cope, Museum Restoration Service, Alexandria Bay, NY, 1992. 114 pp., illus. $24.50.

This is the story of the guns and the man who designed them and the company which he founded to make them.

The Sumptuous Flaske, by Herbert G. Houze, Andrew Mowbray, Inc., Lincoln, RI, 1989. 158 pp., illus. Soft covers. $35.00.

Catalog of a recent show at the Buffalo Bill Historical Center bringing together some of the finest European and American powder flasks of the 16th to 19th centuries.

System Mauser—2nd Edition: An Illustrated History of the 1896 Self-Loading Pistol, by John W. Breathed, Jr. and Joseph J. Schrieder, Jr., Handgun Press, Glenview, IL, 1995. Illus. $49.95.

Newly revised and enlarged edition of the definitive work on this famous German handgun.

Textbook of Automatic Pistols, by R.K. Wilson, Wolfe Publishing Co., Prescott, AZ, 1990. 349 pp., illus. $54.00.

Reprint of the 1943 classic being a treatise on the history, development and functioning of modern military self-loading pistols.

***Thompson: The American Legend,** by Tracie L. Hill, Collector Grade Publications, Ontario, Canada, 1996. 584 pp., illus. $85.00.

The story of the first American submachine gun. All models are featured and discussed.

The Trapdoor Springfield, by M.D. Waite and B.D. Ernst, The Gun Room Press, Highland Park, NJ, 1983. 250 pp., illus. $39.95.

The first comprehensive book on the famous standard military rifle of the 1873-92 period.

United States Martial Flintlocks, by Robert M. Reilly, Andrew Mowbray, Inc., Lincoln, RI, 1986. 263 pp., illus. $39.50.

A comprehensive illustrated history of the flintlock in America from the Revolution to the demise of the system.

U.S. Breech-Loading Rifles and Carbines, Cal. 45, by Gen. John Pitman, Thomas Publications, Gettysburg, PA, 1992. 192 pp., illus. $29.95.

The third volume in the Pitman Notes on U.S. Martial Small Arms and Ammunition, 1776-1933. This book centers on the "Trapdoor Springfield" models.

U.S. Military Arms Dates of Manufacture from 1795, by George Madis, David Madis, Dallas, TX, 1989. 64 pp. Soft covers. $5.00.

Lists all U.S. military arms of collector interest alphabetically, covering about 250 models.

U.S. Military Small Arms 1816-1865, by Robert M. Reilly, The Gun Room Press, Highland Park, NJ, 1983. 270 pp., illus. $39.95.

Covers every known type of primary and secondary martial firearms used by Federal forces.

U.S. M1 Carbines: Wartime Production, by Craig Riesch, North Cape Publications, Tustin, CA, 1994. 72 pp., illus. Paper covers. $15.95.

Presents only verifiable and accurate information. Each part of the M1 Carbine is discussed fully in its own section; including markings and finishes.

U.S. Naval Handguns, 1808-1911, by Fredrick R. Winter, Andrew Mowbray Publishers, Lincoln, RI, 1990. 128 pp., illus. $26.00.

The story of U.S. Naval Handguns spans an entire century—included are sections on each of the important naval handguns within the period.

Variations of the Smooth Bore H&R Handy Gun, by Eric M. Larson, Eric M. Larson, Takoma Park, MD, 1993. 63 pp., illus. Paper covers. $10.00.

A pocket guide to the identification of the variations of the H&R Handy Gun.

Walther Models PP and PPK, 1929-1945, by James L. Rankin, assisted by Gary Green, James L. Rankin, Coral Gables, FL, 1974. 142 pp., illus. $35.00.

Complete coverage on the subject as to finish, proofmarks and Nazi Party inscriptions.

Walther P-38 Pistol, by Maj. George Nonte, Desert Publications, Cornville, AZ, 1982. 100 pp., illus. Paper covers. $11.95.

Complete volume on one of the most famous handguns to come out of WWII. All models covered.

Walther Volume II, Engraved, Presentation and Standard Models, by James L. Rankin, J.L. Rankin, Coral Gables, FL, 1977. 112 pp., illus. $35.00.

The new Walther book on embellished versions and standard models. Has 88 photographs, including many color plates.

Walther, Volume III, 1908-1980, by James L. Rankin, Coral Gables, FL, 1981. 226 pp., illus. $35.00.

Covers all models of Walther handguns from 1908 to date, includes holsters, grips and magazines.

***Weapons of the Highland Regiments 1740-1780,** by Anthony D. Darling, Museum Restoration Service, Bloomfield, Canada, 1996. 28 pp., illus. Paper covers. $5.95.

This study deals with the formation and arming of the famous Highland regiments.

Webley Revolvers, by Gordon Bruce and Christien Reinhart, Stocker-Schmid, Zurich, Switzerland, 1988. 256 pp., illus. $69.50.

A revised edition of Dowell's "Webley Story."

Weimar and Early Lugers, by Jan C. Still, Jan C. Still, Douglas, AK, 1994. 312 pp., illus.

Volume 5 of the series *The Pistol of Germany and Here Allies in Two World Wars.*

The Whitney Firearms, by Claud Fuller, Standard Publications, Huntington, WV, 1946, 334 pp., many plates and drawings, $50.00.

An authoritative history of all Whitney arms and their maker. Highly recommended. An exclusive with Ray Riling Arms Books Co.

Winchester: An American Legend, by R.L. Wilson, Random House, New York, NY, 1991. 403 pp., illus. $65.00.

The official history of Winchester firearms from 1849 to the present.

The Winchester Book, by George Madis, David Madis Gun Book Distributor, Dallas, TX, 1986. 650 pp., illus. $47.00.

A new, revised 25th anniversary edition of this classic book on Winchester firearms. Complete serial ranges have been added.

Winchester Dates of Manufacture 1849-1984, by George Madis, Art & Reference House, Brownsboro, TX, 1984. 59 pp. $5.95.

A most useful work, compiled from records of the Winchester factory.

Winchester Engraving, by R.L. Wilson, Beinfeld Books, Springs, CA, 1989. 500 pp., illus. $125.00.

A classic reference work, of value to all arms collectors.

The Winchester Handbook, by George Madis, Art & Reference House, Lancaster, TX, 1982. 287 pp., illus. $19.95.

The complete line of Winchester guns, with dates of manufacture, serial numbers, etc.

Winchester Lever Action Repeating Firearms, Vol. 1, The Models of 1866, 1873 and 1876, by Arthur Pirkie, North Cape Publications, Tustin, CA, 1995. 112 pp., illus. Paper covers. $19.95.

Complete, part-by-part description, including dimensions, finishes, markings and variations throughout the production run of these fine, collectible guns.

The Winchester Model 94: The First 100 Years, by Robert C. Renneberg, Krause Publications, Iola, WI, 1991. 208 pp., illus. $34.95.

Covers the design and evolution from the early years up to the many different editions that exist today.

Winchester Shotguns and Shotshells, by Ronald W. Stadt, Krause Publications, Iola, WI, 1995. 256 pp., illus. $34.95.

The definitive book on collectible Winchester shotguns and shotshells manufactured through 1961.

***The Winchester Single-Shot,** by John Cambell, Andrew Mowbray, Inc., Lincoln RI, 1995. 272 pp., illus. $55.00.

Covers every important aspect of this highly-collectible firearm.

Winchester Slide-Action Rifles, Volume 1: Model 1890 & 1906, by Ned Schwing, Krause Publications, Iola, WI, 1992. 352 pp., illus. $39.95.
First book length treatment of models 1890 & 1906 with over 50 charts and tables showing significant new information about caliber style and rarity.
Winchester Slide-Action Rifles, Volume 2: Model 61 & Model 62, by Ned Schwing, Krause Publications, Iola, WI, 1993. 256 pp., illus. $34.95.
A complete historic look into the Model 61 and the Model 62. These favorite slide-action guns receive a thorough presentation which takes you to the factory to explore receivers, barrels, markings, stocks, stampings and engraving in complete detail.
Winchester's 30-30, Model 94, by Sam Fadala, Stackpole Books, Inc., Harrisburg, PA, 1986. 223 pp., illus. $24.95.
The story of the rifle America loves.

A.G. Russell's Knife Trader's Guide, by A.G. Russell, Paul Wahl Corp., Bogata, NJ, 1991. 160 pp., illus. Paper covers. $10.00.
Recent sales prices of many popular collectible knives.
The American Blade Collectors Association Price Guide to Antique Knives, by J. Bruce Voyles, Krause Publications, Iola, WI, 1995. 480 pp., illus. Paper covers. $16.95.
In this complete guide to pocketknives there are 40,000 current values in six grades of condition for knives produced from 1800-1970.
The American Eagle Pommel Sword: The Early Years 1793-1830, by Andrew Mowbray, Publisher, Lincoln, RI, 1988. 224 pp., illus. $45.00.
Provides an historical outline, a collecting structure and a vast new source of information for this rapidly growing field.
American Indian Tomahawks, by Harold L. Peterson, The Gun Room Press, Highland Park, NJ, 1993. 142 pp., illus. $49.95.
The tomahawk of the American Indian, in all its forms, as a weapon and as a tool.
American Knives; The First History and Collector's Guide, by Harold L. Peterson, The Gun Room Press, Highland Park, NJ, 1980. 178 pp., illus. $24.95.
A reprint of this 1958 classic. Covers all types of American knives.
American Primitive Knives 1770-1870, by G.B. Minnes, Museum Restoration Service, Ottawa, Canada, 1983. 112 pp., illus. $24.95.
Origins of the knives, outstanding specimens, structural details, etc.
American Socket Bayonets and Scabbards, by Robert M. Reilly, Andrew Mowbray, Inc., Lincoln, RI, 1990. 209 pp., illus. $40.00.
A comprehensive illustrated history of socket bayonets, scabbards and frogs in America from the Colonial period through the Civil War period.
The American Sword, 1775-1945, by Harold L. Peterson, Ray Riling Arms Books, Co., Phila., PA, 1980. 286 pp. plus 60 pp. of illus. $45.00.
1977 reprint of a survey of swords worn by U.S. uniformed forces, plus the rare "American Silver Mounted Swords, (1700-1815)."
American Swords and Sword Makers, by Richard H. Bezdek, Paladin Press, Boulder, CO, 1994. 648 pp., illus. $79.95.
The long-awaited definitive reference volume to American swords, sword makers and sword dealers from Colonial times to the present.
The Ames Sword Company, 1829-1935, by John D. Hamilton, Andrew Mowbray Publisher, Linclon, RI, 1995. 255 pp., illus. $45.00.
An exhaustively researched and comprehensive history of America's foremost sword manufacturer and arms supplier during the Civil War.
The Arms and Armour of Arabia in the 18th-19th and 20th Centuries, by Robert Elgood, Scolar Press, Brookfield, VT, 1994. 190 pp., illus. $99.50.
An outstanding documentary on this aspect of Arab culture. Examines surviving weapons, identifies new centers of manufacture and questions the origin of "Damascus" swords.
Battle Blades: A Professional's Guide to Combat/Fighting Knives, by Greg Walker; Foreword by Al Mar, Paladin Press, Boulder, CO, 1993. 168 pp., illus. $30.00.
The author evaluates daggers, Bowies, switchblades and utility blades according to their design, performance, reliability and cost.
Bayonets from Janzen's Notebook, by Jerry L. Janzen, Cedar Ridge Publications, Broken Arrow, OK, 1994. 512 pp., illus. $34.50.
A very popular reference book covering bayonets of the World.
Bayonets of the Remington Cartridge Period, by Jerry L. Janzen, Cedar Ridge Publications, Broken Arrow, OK, 1994. 200 pp., illus. $39.95.
The story of the bayonets which accompanied the Remington Rolling Block and its many successors. Included are the rifles, the countries who used them, pictures of the bayonets in use and detailed descriptions of each bayonet.
The Book of the Sword, by Richard F. Burton, Dover Publications, New York, NY, 1987. 199 pp., illus. Paper covers. $12.95.
Traces the swords origin from its birth as a charged and sharpened stick through diverse stages of development.
Borders Away, Volume 1: With Steel, by William Gilkerson, Andrew Mowbray, Inc., Lincoln, RI, 1991. 184 pp., illus. $48.00.
A comprehensive study of naval armament under fighting sail. This first voume covers axes, pikes and fighting blades in use between 1626-1826.
The Bowie Knife, by Raymond Thorp, Phillips Publications, Wiliamstown, NJ, 1992. 167 pp., illus. $9.95.
After forty-five years, the classic work on the Bowie knife is once again available.
Bowie Knives, by Robert Abels, Sherwood International Corp., Northridge, CA, 1988. 30 pp., illus. Paper covers. $14.95.
Reprint of the classic work on Bowie knives.
British & Commonwealth Bayonets, by Ian D. Skennerton and Robert Richardson, I.D.S.A. Books, Piqua, OH, 1986. 404 pp., 1300 illus. $40.00.
Collecting the Edged Weapons of Imperial Germany, by Thomas M. Johnson and Thomas T. Wittmann, Johnson Reference Books, Fredricksburg, VA, 1989. 363 pp., illus. $39.50.
An in-depth study of the many ornate military, civilian, and government daggers and swords of the Imperial era.
Collector's Guide to Ames U.S. Contract Military Edged Weapons: 1832-1906, by Ron G. Hickox, Pioneer Press, Union City, IN, 1993. 70 pp., illus. Paper covers. $14.95.
While this book deals primarily with edged weapons made by the Ames Manufacturing Company, this guide refers to other manufactureres of United States swords.
Collector's Handbook of World War 2 German Daggers, by LtC. Thomas M. Johnson, Johnson Reference Books, Fredericksburg, VA, 2nd edition, 1991. 252 pp., illus. Paper covers. $25.00.
Concise pocket reference guide to Third Reich daggers and accoutrements in a convenient format. With value guide.
The Complete Bladesmith: Forging Your Way to Perfection, by Jim Hrisoulas, Paladin Press, Boulder, CO, 1987. 192 pp., illus. $25.00.
Novice as well as experienced bladesmith will benefit from this definitive guide to smithing world-class blades.
The Complete Book of Pocketknife Repair, by Ben Kelly, Jr., Krause Publications, Iola, WI, 1995. 130 pp., illus. Paper covers. $10.95.
Everything you need to know about repairing knives can be found in this step-by-step guide to knife repair.
Confederate Edged Weapons, by W.A. Albaugh, R&R Books, Lavonia, NY, 1994. 198 pp., illus. $30.00.
The master reference to edged weapons of the Confederate forces. Features precise line drawings and an extensive text.
The Craft of the Japanese Sword, by Leon and Hiroko Kapp, Yoshindo Yoshihara, Kodanska International, Tokyo, Japan, 1990. 167 pp., illus. $39.00.
The first book in English devoted to contemporary sword manufacturing in Japan.
Exploring the Dress Daggers of the German Army, by Thomas T. Wittmann, Johnson Reference Books, Fredericksburg, VA, 1995. 350 pp., illus. $59.95.
The first in-depth analysis of the dress daggers worn by the German Army.
German Clamshells and Other Bayonets, by G. Walker and R.J. Weinard, Johnson Reference Books, Fredericksburg, VA, 1994. 157 pp., illus. $22.95.
Includes unusual bayonets, many of which are shown for the first time. Current market values are listed.
German Military Fighting Knives 1914-1945, by Gordon A. Hughes, Johnson Reference Books, Fredericksburg, VA, 1994. 64 pp., illus. Paper covers. $24.50.
Documents the different types of German military fighting knives used during WWI and WWII. Makers' proofmarks are shown as well as details of blade inscriptions, etc.
The Handbook of British Bayonets, by Ian D. Skennerton, I.D.S.A. Books, Piqua, OH. 64 pp. $4.95
How to Make Folding Knives, by Ron Lake, Frank Centofante and Wayne Clay, Krause Publications, Iola, WI, 1995. 193 pp., illus. Paper covers. $13.95.
With step-by-step instructions, learn how to make your own folding knife from three top custom makers.
How to Make Knives, by Richard W. Barney and Robert W. Loveless, Krause Publications, Iola, WI, 1995. 182 pp., illus. Paper covers. $13.95.
Complete instructions from two premier knife makers on making high-quality, handmade knives.
***IBCA Price Guide to Commemorative Knives 1960-1990, by J. Bruce Voyles, Krause Publications, Iola, WI, 1996. 256 pp., illus. Paper covers. $16.95.**
Manufacturers, descriptions, quantities, prices and values for 1,200 limited edition commemorative knives.
Kentucky Knife Traders Manual No. 6, by R.B. Ritchie, Hindman, KY, 1980. 217 pp., illus. Paper covers. $10.00.
Guide for dealers, collectors and traders listing pocket knives and razor values.
Knife and Tomakawk Throwing: The Art of the Experts, by Harry K. McEvoy, Charles E. Tuttle, Rutland, VT, 1989. 150 pp., illus. Soft covers. $8.95.
The first book to employ side-by-side the fascinating art and science of knives and tomahawks.
Knifemaking, The Gun Digest Book of, by Jack Lewis and Roger Combs, DBI Books, Inc., Northbrook, IL, 1989. 256 pp., illus. Paper covers. $16.95.
All the ins and outs from the world of knifemaking in a brand new book.
Knife Throwing a Practical Guide, by Harry K. McEvoy, Charles E. Tuttle Co., Rutland, VT, 1973. 108 pp., illus. Paper covers. $8.95.
If you want to learn to throw a knife this is the "bible."
Knives, 4th Edition, The Gun Digest Book of, by Jack Lewis and Roger Combs, DBI Books, Inc., Northbook, IL, 1992. 256 pp., illus. Paper covers. $17.95.
Covers practically every aspect of the knife world.
***Knives '97, 17th Edition,** edited by Ken Warner, DBI Books, Inc., Northbrook, IL, 1996. 304 pp., illus. Paper covers. $19.95.
Visual presentation of current factory and custom designs in straight and folding patterns, in swords, miniatures and commercial cutlery. Available September, 1996.
Levine's Guide to Knives And Their Values, 3rd Edition, by Bernard Levine, DBI Books, Inc., Northbrook, IL, 1989. 512 pp., illus. Paper covers. $25.95.
All the basic tools for identifying, valuing and collecting folding and fixed blade knives.
The Master Bladesmith: Advanced Studies in Steel, by Jim Hrisoulas, Paladin Press, Boulder, CO, 1990. 296 pp., illus. $45.00.
The author reveals the forging secrets that for centuries have been protected by guilds.
Military Swords of Japan 1868-1945, by Richard Fuller and Ron Gregory, Arms and Armour Press, London, England, 1986. 127 pp., illus. Paper covers. $18.95.
A wide-ranging survey of the swords and dirks worn by the armed forces of Japan until the end of World War II.
Modern Combat Blades, by Duncan Long, Paladin Press, Boulder, CO, 1993. 128 pp., illus. $25.00.
Long discusses the pros and cons of bowies, bayonets, commando daggers, kukris, switchblades, butterfly knives, belt-buckle blades and many more.
On Damascus Steel, by Dr. Leo S. Figiel, Atlantis Arts Press, Atlantis, FL, 1991. 145 pp., illus. $65.00.
The historic, technical and artistic aspects of Oriental and mechanical Damascus. Persian and Indian sword blades, from 1600-1800, which have never been published, are illustrated.
The Pattern-Welded Blade: Artistry in Iron, by Jim Hrisoulas, Paladin Press, Boulder, CO, 1994. 120 pp., illus. $35.00.
Reveals the secrets of this craft—from the welding of the starting billet to the final assembly of the complete blade.
Randall Made Knives: The History of the Man and the Blades, by Robert L. Gaddis, Paladin Press, Boulder, CO, 1993. 304 pp., illus. $50.00.
The authorized history of Bo Randall and his blades, told in his own words and those of the people who knew him best.
Rice's Trowel Bayonet, reprinted by Ray Riling Arms Books, Co., Phila., PA, 1968. 8 pp., illus. Paper covers. $3.00.
A facsimile reprint of a rare circular originally published by the U.S. government in 1875 for the information of U.S. troops.
The Samurai Sword, by John M. Yumoto, Charles E. Tuttle Co., Rutland, VT, 1958. 191 pp., illus. $23.95.
A must for anyone interested in Japanese blades, and the first book on this subject written in English.
Scottish Swords from the Battlefield at Culloden, by Lord Archibald Campbell, The Mowbray Co., Providence, RI, 1973. 63 pp., illus. $15.00.
A modern reprint of an exceedingly rare 1894 privately printed edition.

Secrets of the Samurai, by Oscar Ratti and Adele Westbrook, Charles E. Tuttle Co., Rutland, VT, 1983. 483 pp., illus. $35.00.
A survey of the martial arts of feudal Japan.

Small Arms Identification Series, No. 6-British Service Sword & Lance Patterns, by Ian Skennerton, I.D.S.A. Books, Piqua, OH, 1994. 48 pp. $9.50.

Small Arms Series, No. 2. The British Spike Bayonet, by Ian Skennerton, I.D.S.A. Books, Piqua, OH, 1982. 32 pp., 30 illus. $9.00.

Sure Defence, The Bowie Knife Book, by Kenneth J. Burton, I.D.S.A. Books, Piqua, OH, 1988. 100 pp., 115 illus. $37.50.

Sword of the Samurai, by George R. Parulski, Jr., Paladin Press, Boulder, CO, 1985. 144 pp., illus. $34.95.
The classical art of Japanese swordsmanship.

Swords for the Highland Regiments 1757-1784, by Anthony D. Darling, Andrew Mowbray, Inc., Publisher, Lincoln, RI, 1988. 62 pp., illus. $18.00.
The basket-hilted swords used by private highland regiments in the 18th century British army.

Swords from Public Collections in the Commonwealth of Pennsylvania, edited by Bruce S. Bazelon, Andrew Mowbray Inc., Lincoln, RI, 1987. 127 pp., illus. Paper covers. $12.00.
Contains new information regarding swordmakers of the Philadelphia area.

The Scottish Dirk, by James D. Forman, Museum Restoration Service, Bloomfield, Ont., Canada, 1991. 60 pp., illus. Paper covers. $4.95.
More than 100 dirks are illustrated with a text that sets the dirk and Sgian Dubh in their socio-historic content following design changes through more than 300 years of evolution.

Swords and Blades of the American Revolution, by George C. Neumann, Rebel Publishing Co., Inc., Texarkana, TX, 1991. 288 pp., illus. $35.95.
The encyclopedia of bladed weapons—swords, bayonets, spontoons, halberds, pikes, knives, daggers, axes—used by both sides, on land and sea, in America's struggle for independence.

Tomahawks Illustrated, by Robert Kuck, Robert Kuck, New Knoxville, OH, 1977. 112 pp., illus. Paper covers. $15.00.
A pictorial record to provide a reference in selecting and evaluating tomahawks.

World of Dress Daggers, 1900-1945, Volume 1, by Robert Berger, Robert Berger, CT, 1995. 296 pp., illus. $34.95.
The photographs and illustrations, in conjunction with the author's descriptive outline for each model, help to clearly identify these collectible daggers.

GENERAL

Advanced Muzzleloader's Guide, by Toby Bridges, Stoeger Publishing Co., So. Hackensack, NJ, 1985. 256 pp., illus. Paper covers. $14.95.
The complete guide to muzzle-loading rifles, pistols and shotguns—flintlock and percussion.

Air Gun Digest, 3rd Edition, by J.I. Galan, DBI Books, Inc., Northbrook, IL, 1995. 258 pp., illus. Paper covers. $18.95
Everything from A to Z on air gun history, trends and technology.

American Gunsmiths, by Frank M. Sellers, The Gun Room Press, Highland Park, NJ, 1983. 349 pp. $39.95.
A comprehensive listing of the American gun maker, patentee, gunsmith and entrepreneur.

American and Imported Arms, Ammunition and Shooting Accessories, Catalog No. 18 of the Shooter's Bible, Stoeger, Inc., reprinted by Fayette Arsenal, Fayetteville, NC, 1988. 142 pp., illus. Paper covers. $10.95.
A facsimile reprint of the 1932 Stoeger's Shooter's Bible.

America's Great Gunmakers, by Wayne van Zwoll, Stoeger Publishing Co., So. Hackensack, NJ, 1992. 288 pp., illus. Paper covers. $16.95.
This book traces in great detail the evolution of guns and ammunition in America and the men who formed the companies that produced them.

Archer's Digest, 6th Edition, by Roger Combs, DBI Books, Inc., Northbrook, IL, 1995. 256 pp., illus. $18.95.
Authoritative information on all facets of the archer's sport.

Armed and Female, by Paxton Quigley, E.P. Dutton, New York, NY, 1989. 237 pp., illus. $16.95.
The first complete book on one of the hottest subjects in the media today, the arming of the American woman.

***Arms and Armour in Antiquity and the Middle Ages,** by Charles Boutell, Stackpole Books, Mechanicsburg, PA, 1996. 352 pp., illus. $22.95.
Detailed descriptions of arms and armor, the development of tactics and the outcome of specific battles.

***Arms & Armor in the Art Institute of Chicago,** by Walter J. Karcheski, Jr., Bulfinch Press, Boston, MA, 1995. 128 pp., illus. $35.00.
Now, for the first time, the Art Institute of Chicago's arms and armor collection is presented in the visual delight of 103 color illustrations.

Arms for the Nation: Springfield Longarms, edited by David C. Clark, Scott A. Duff, Export, PA, 1994. 73 pp., illus. Paper covers. $9.95.
A brief history of the Springfield Armory and the arms made there.

Arsenal of Freedom, The Springfield Armory, 1890-1948: A Year-by-Year Account Drawn from Official Records, compiled and edited by Lt. Col, William S. Brophy, USAR Ret., Andrew Mowbray, Inc., Lincoln, RI, 1991. 400 pp., illus. Soft covers. $29.95.
A "must buy" for all students of American military weapolns, equipment and accoutrements.

***Assault Weapons, 4th Edition, The Gun Digest Book of,** edited by Jack Lewis, DBI Books, Inc., Northbrook, IL. 256 pp., illus. Paper covers. $19.95.
An in-depth look at the history and uses of these arms.

A Bibliography of American Sporting Books, compiled by John C. Phillips, James Cummins, Bookseller, New York, NY, 1991. 650 pp. Edition limited to 250 numbered copies. $75.00.
A reprinting of the very scarce 1930 edition originally published by the Boone & Crockett Club.

Blackpowder Hobby Gunsmithing, by Sam Fadala and Dale Storey, DBI Books, Inc., Northbrook, IL., 1994. 256 pp., illus. Paper covers. $18.95.
A how-to-guide for gunsmithing blackpowder pistols, rifles and shotguns from two men at the top of their respective fields.

***Blackpowder Loading Manual, 3rd Edition,** edited by Sam Fadala, DBI Books, Inc., Northbrook, IL, 1995. 368 pp., illus. Paper covers. $19.95.
Revised and expanded edition of this landmark blackpowder loading book. Covers hundreds of loads for most of the popular blackpowder rifles, handguns and shotguns.

The Blackpowder Notebook, by Sam Fadala, Wolfe Publishing Co., Prescott, AZ, 1994. 212 pp., illus. $22.50.
For anyone interested in shooting muzzleloaders, this book will help improve scores and obtain accuracy and reliability.

***Bolt Action Rifles, 3rd Edition,** edited by Frank de Haas, DBI Books, Inc., Northbrook, IL, 1995. 576 pp., illus. Paper covers. $24.95.
A revised edition of the most definitive work on all major bolt-action rifle designs.

***The Book of the Crossbow,** by Sir Ralph Payne-Gallwey, Dover Publications, Mineola, NY, 1996. 416 pp., illus. Paper covers. $14.95.
Unabridged republication of the scarce 1907 London edition of the book on one of the most devastating hand weapons of the Middle Ages.

Bows and Arrows of the Native Americans, by Jim Hamm, Lyons & Burford Publishers, New York, NY, 1991. 156 pp., illus. $19.95.
A complete step-by-step guide to wooden bows, sinew-backed bows, composite bows, strings, arrows and quivers.

Bowhunter's Digest, 3rd Edition, by Chuck Adams, DBI Books, Inc., Northbrook, IL, 1990. 288 pp., illus. Soft covers. $17.95.
All-new edition covers all the necessary equipment and how to use it, plus the fine points on how to improve your skill.

British Small Arms of World War 2, by Ian D. Skennerton, I.D.S.A. Books, Piqua, OH, 1988. 110 pp., 37 illus. $25.00.

British Sniper, by Ian Skennerton, I.D.S.A. Books, Piqua, OH, 1983. 26 pp., over 375 illus. $40.00.

***Cartridges of the World, 8th Edition,** by Frank Barnes, edited by M. L. McPherson, DBI Books, Inc., Northbrook, IL, 1996. 480 pp., illus. Paper covers. $24.95.
Completely revised edition of the general purpose reference work for which collectors, police, scientists and laymen reach first for answers to cartridge identification questions. Available October, 1996.

***Combat Handgunnery, 4th Edition, The Gun Digest Book of,** by Chuck Taylor, DBI Books, Inc., Northbrook, IL, 1992. 256 pp., illus. Paper covers. $18.95.
This edition looks at real world combat handgunnery from three different perspectives—military, police and civilian. (Available October, 1996)

Competitive Shooting, by A.A. Yuryev, introduction by Gary L. Anderson, NRA Books, The National Rifle Assoc. of America, Wash., DC, 1985. 399 pp., illus. $29.95.
A unique encyclopedia of competitive rifle and pistol shooting.

***The Complete Blackpowder Handbook, 3rd Edition,** by Sam Fadala, DBI Books, Inc., Northbrook, IL, 1996. 416 pp., illus. Paper covers. $21.95.
Expanded and refreshed edition of the definitive book on the subject of blackpowder. (Available September, 1996.)

Complete Guide to Bowhunting Deer, by Chuck Adams, DBI Books, Inc., Northbrook, IL, 1984. 256 pp., illus. Paper covers. $16.95.
Plenty on equipment, bows, sights, quivers, arrows, clothes, lures and scents, stands and blinds, etc.

The Complete Guide to Game Care and Cookery, 3rd Edition, by Sam Fadala, DBI Books, Inc., Northbrook, IL, 1994. 320 pp., illus. Paper covers. $18.95.
Over 500 photos illustrating the care of wild game in the field and at home with a separate recipe section providing over 400 tested recipes.

Complete Guide to Guns & Shooting, by John Malloy, DBI Books, Inc., Northbrook, IL, 1995. 256 pp., illus. Paper covers. $18.95.
What every shooter and gun owner should know about firearms, ammunition, shooting techniques, safety, collecting and much more.

Cowboy Action Shooting, by Charly Gullett, Wolfe Publishing Co., Prescott, AZ, 1995. 400 pp., illus. Paper covers. $24.50.
The fast growing of the shooting sports is comprehensively covered in this text—the guns, loads, tactics and the fun and flavor of this Old West era competition.

Crossbows, edited by Roger Combs, DBI Books, Inc., Northbrook, IL, 1986. 192 pp., illus. Paper covers. $15.95.
Complete, up-to-date coverage of the hottest bow going—and the most controversial.

Death from Above: The German FG42 Paratrooper Rifle, by Thomas B. Dugelby and R. Blake Stevens, Collector Grade Publications, Toronto, Canada, 1990. 147 pp., illus. $39.95.
The first comprehensive study of all seven models of the FG42.

Encyclopedia of Modern Firearms, Vol. 1, compiled and publ. by Bob Brownell, Montezuma, IA, 1959. 1057 pp. plus index, illus. $60.00. Dist. By Bob Brownell, Montezuma, IA 50171.
Massive accumulation of basic information of nearly all modern arms pertaining to "parts and assembly." Replete with arms photographs, exploded drawings, manufacturers' lists of parts, etc.

Exploded Handgun Drawings, The Gun Digest Book of, edited by Harold A. Murtz, DBI Books, Inc., Northbrook, IL, 1992. 512 pp., illus. Paper covers. $20.95.
Exploded or isometric drawings for 494 of the most popular handguns.

Exploded Long Gun Drawings, The Gun Digest Book of, edited by Harold A. Murtz, DBI Books, Inc., Northbrook, IL, 512 pp., illus. Paper covers. $20.95.
Containing almost 500 rifle and shotgun exploded drawings.

Firearms Engraving as Decorative Art, by Dr. Fredric A. Harris, Barbara R. Harris, Seattle, WA, 1989. 172 pp., illus. $115.00.
The origin of American firearms engraving motifs in the decorative art of the Middle East. Illustrated with magnificent color photographs.

Firing Back, by Clayton E. Cramer, Krause Publications, Iola, WI, 1995. 208 pp., Paper covers. $9.95.
Proposes answers and arguments to counter the popular anti-gun sentiments.

Flayderman's Guide to Antique American Firearms...and Their Values, 6th Edition, by Norm Flayderman, DBI Books, Inc., Northbrook, IL, 1994. 624 pp., illus. Paper covers. $29.95.
Updated edition of this bible of the antique gun field.

***Frank Pachmayr: The Story of America's Master Gunsmith and his Guns,** by John Lachuk, Safari Press, Huntington Beach, CA, 1996. 254 pp., illus. First edition, limited, signed and slipcased. $85.00; Second printing trade edition. $50.00.
The colorful and historically significant biography of Frank A Pachmayr, America's own gunsmith emeritus.

The Frontier Rifleman, by H.B. LaCrosse Jr., Pioneer Press, Union City, TN, 1989. 183 pp., illus. Soft covers. $14.95.
The Frontier rifleman's clothing and equipment during the era of the American Revolution, 1760-1800.

Gatling: A Photographic Remembrance, by E. Frank Stephenson, Jr., Meherrin River Press, Murfreesboro, NC, 1994. 140 pp., illus. Paper covers. $25.00.
A new book on Richard Gatling and his famous gun; featuring 145 photographs, many rare and never before published.

The Gatling Gun: 19th Century Machine Gun to 21st Century Vulcan, by Joseph Berk, Paladin Press, Boulder, CO, 1991. 136 pp., illus. $29.95.
Here is the fascinating on-going story of a truly timeless weapon, from its beginnings during the Civil War to its current role as a state-of-the-art modern combat system.

Good Guns Again, by Stephen Bodio, Wilderness Adventures Press, Bozeman, MT, 1994. 183 pp., illus. $29.00.
A celebration of fine sporting arms.

Grand Old Lady of No Man's Land: The Vickers Machine Gun, by Dolf L. Goldsmith, Collector Grade Publications, Cobourg, Canada, 1994. 600 pp., illus. $79.95.

Goldsmith brings his years of experience as a U.S. Army armourer, machine gun collector and shooter to bear on the Vickers, in a book sure to become a classic in its field.

Great Shooters of the World, by Sam Fadala, Stoeger Publishing Co., So. Hackensack, NJ, 1991. 288 pp., illus. Paper covers. $18.95.

This book offers gun enthusiasts an overview of the men and women who have forged the history of firearms over the past 150 years.

Guerrilla Warfare Weapons, by Terry Gander, Sterling Publishing Co., Inc., 1990. 128 pp., illus. Paper covers. $9.95.

The latest and most sophisticated armaments of the modern underground fighter's armory.

***Gun Digest, 1997, 51st Edition,** edited by Ken Warner, DBI Books, Inc., Northbrook, IL, 1996. 544 pp., illus. Paper covers. $23.95.

All-new edition of the world's biggest selling gun book.

Gun Digest Treasury, 7th Edition, edited by Harold A. Murtz, DBI Books, Inc., Northbrook, IL, 1994. 320 pp., illus. Paper covers. $17.95.

A collection of some of the most interesting articles which have appeared in Gun Digest over its first 45 years.

***Gunfitting: The Quest for Perfection,** by Michael Yardley, Safari Press, Huntington Beach, CA, 1995. 128 pp., illus. $24.95.

The author, a very experienced shooting instructor, examines gun stocks and gunfitting in depth.

Gun Notes, by Elmer Keith, Safari Press, Huntington Beach, CA, 1995. 280 pp., illus. $30.00.

A collection of Elmer Keith's most interesting columns and feature stories that appeared in *Guns and Ammo* magazine from 1961 to the late 1970s.

Gunshot Injuries: How They Are Inflicted, Their Complications and Treatment, by Col. Louis A. La Garde, 2nd revised edition, Lancer Militaria, Mt. Ida, AR, 1991. 480 pp., illus. $34.95.

A classic work which was the standard textbook on the subject at the time of WWI.

***Guns Illustrated 1997, 29th Edition,** edited by Harold A. Murtz, DBI Books, Inc., Northbrook, IL, 1996. 336 pp., illus. Paper covers. $20.95.

Truly the journal of Gun Buffs, this all new edition consists of articles of interest to every shooter as well as a complete catalog of all U.S. and imported firearms with latest specs and prices. Available August, 1996.

Guns of the Wild West, by George Markham, Sterling Publishing Co., New York, NY, 1993. 160 pp., illus. Paper covers. $19.95.

Firearms of the American Frontier, 1849-1917.

Gun Talk, edited by Dave Moreton, Winchester Press, Piscataway, NJ, 1973. 256 pp., illus. $9.95.

A treasury of original writing by the top gun writers and editors in America. Practical advice about every aspect of the shooting sports.

The Gun That Made the Twenties Roar, by Wm. J. Helmer, rev. and enlarged by George C. Nonte, Jr., The Gun Room Press, Highland Park, NJ, 1977. Over 300 pp., illus. $24.95.

Historical account of John T. Thompson and his invention, the infamous "Tommy Gun."

The Gunfighter, Man or Myth? by Joseph G. Rosa, Oklahoma Press, Norman, OK, 1969. 229 pp., illus. (including weapons). Paper covers. $14.95.

A well-documented work on gunfights and gunfighters of the West and elsewhere. Great treat for all gunfighter buffs.

Gunproof Your Children/Handgun Primer, by Massad Ayoob, Police Bookshelf, Concord, NH, 1989. Paper covers. $4.95.

Two books in one. The first, keeping children safe from unauthorized guns in their hands; the second, a compact introduction to handgun safety.

Guns & Shooting: A Selected Bibliography, by Ray Riling, Ray Riling Arms Books Co., Phila., PA, 1982. 434 pp., illus. Limited, numbered edition. $75.

A limited edition of this superb bibliographical work, the only modern listing of books devoted to guns and shooting.

Guns, Loads, and Hunting Tips, by Bob Hagel, Wolfe Publishing Co., Prescott, AZ, 1986. 509 pp., illus. $19.95.

A large hardcover book packed with shooting, hunting and handloading wisdom.

Guns of the First World War, Rifle, Handguns and Ammunition from the Text Book of Small Arms, 1909, edited by John Walter, Presidio Press, Novato, CA, 1991. $30.00.

Details of the Austro-Hung. Mann., French Lebels, German Mausers, U.S. Springfields, etc.

Gunshot Wounds, by Vincent J.M. DiMaio, M.D., Elsevier Science Publishing Co., New York, NY, 1985. 331 pp., illus. $90.00.

Practical aspects of firearms, ballistics, and forensic techniques.

Gun Writers of Yesteryear, compiled by James Foral, Wolfe Publishing Co., Prescott, AZ, 1993. 449 pp. $35.00.

Here, from the pre-American rifleman days of 1898-1920, are collected some 80 articles by 34 writers from eight magazines.

Handgun Digest, 3rd Edition, edited by Chris Christian, DBI Books, Inc., Northbrook, IL, 1995. 256 pp., illus. Paper covers. $18.95.

Full coverage of all aspects of handguns and handgunning from a highly readable and knowledgeable author.

***Handguns '97,** edited by Ray Ordorica, DBI Books, Inc., Northbrook, IL, 1996. 352 pp., illus. Paper covers. $20.95.

Top handgun experts cover what's new in the world of handguns and handgunning. (Available August, 1996.)

***Handloader's Digest 1997, 16th Edition,** edited by Bob Bell, DBI Books, Inc., Northbrook, IL, 1996. 480pp., illus. Paper covers. $23.95.

Top writes in the field contribute helpful information on techniques and components. Greatly expanded and fully indexed catalog of all currently available tools, accessories and components for metallic, blackpowder cartridge, shothell reloading and swaging.

"Hell, I Was There!," by Elmer Keith, Petersen Publishing Co., Los Angeles, CA, 1979. 308 pp., illus. $24.95.

Adventures of a Montana cowboy who gained world fame as a big game hunter.

***HK Assault Rifle Systems,** by Duncan Long, Paladin Press, Boulder, CO, 1995. 110 pp., illus. Paper covers. $27.95.

The little known history behind this fascinating family of weapons tracing its beginnings from the ashes of World War Two to the present time.

Il Grande Libro Delle Incision (Modern Engravings Real Book), by Marco E. Nobili, Editrice Il Volo, Milano, Italy, 1992. 399 pp., illus. $95.00.

The best existing expressions of engravings on guns, knives and other items. Text in English and Italian.

Jim Dougherty's Guide to Bowhunting Deer, by Jim Dougherty, DBI Books, Inc., Northbrook, IL, 1992. 256 pp., illus. Paper covers. $17.95.

Dougherty sets down some important guidelines for bowhunting and bowhunting equipment.

***Kill or Get Killed,** by Col. Rex Applegate, Paladin Press, Boulder, CO, 1996. 400 pp., illus. $29.95.

The best and longest-selling book on close combat in history.

***Knives '97, 17th Edition,** edited by Ken Warner, DBI Books, Inc., Northbrook, IL, 1996. 304 pp., illus. Paper covers. $19.95.

Visual presentation of current factory and custom designs in straight and folding patterns, in swords, miniatures and commercial cutlery. (Available September, 1996.)

Lasers and Night Vision Devices, by Duncan Long, Desert Publications, El Dorado, AZ, 1993. 150 pp., illus. Paper covers. $29.95.

A comprehensive look at the evolution of devices that allow firearms to be operated in low light conditions and at night.

The Last Book: Confessions of a Gun Editor, by Jack O'Connor, Amwell Press, Clinton, NJ, 1984. 247 pp., illus. $30.00.

Jack's last book. Semi-autobiographical.

The Lewis Gun, by J. David Truby, Paladin Press, Boulder, CO, 1988. 206 pp., illus. $39.95.

The development and employment of this weapon throughout early decades of this century.

The Long-Range War: Sniping in Vietnam, by Peter R. Senich, Paladin Press, Boulder, CO, 1994. 280 pp., illus. $39.95.

The most complete report on Vietnam-era sniping ever documented.

Manual for H&R Reising Submachine Gun and Semi-Auto Rifle, edited by George P. Dillman, Desert Publications, El Dorado, AZ, 1994. 81 pp., illus. Paper covers. $12.95.

A reprint of the Harrington & Richardson 1943 factory manual and the rare military manual on the H&R submachine gun and semi-auto rifle.

The Manufacture of Gunflints, by Sydney B.J. Skertchly, facsimile reprint with new introduction by Seymour de Lotbiniere, Museum Restoration Service, Ontario, Canada, 1984. 90 pp., illus. $24.50.

Limited edition reprinting of the very scarce London edition of 1879.

Master Tips, by J. Winokur, Potshot Press, Pacific Palisades, CA, 1985. 96 pp., illus. Paper covers. $11.95.

Basics of practical shooting.

Military Rifle & Machine Gun Cartridges, by Jean Huon, Paladin Press, Boulder, CO, 1990. 392 pp., illus. $34.95.

Describes the primary types of military cartridges and their principal loadings, as well as their characteristics, origin and use.

Military Small Arms of the 20th Century, 6th Edition, by Ian V. Hogg, DBI Books, Inc., Northbrook, IL, 1991. 352 pp., illus. Paper covers. $20.95.

Fully revised and updated edition of the standard reference in its field.

***Modern Gun Values, 10th Edition, The Gun Digest Book of** by the editors of Gun Digest, DBI Books, Inc., Northbrook, IL, 1996. 560 pp., illus. paper covers. $21.95.

Greatly updated and expanded edition describing and valuing over 7,000 firearms manufactured between 1900 and 1995. The standard reference for valuing modern firearms.

Modern Law Enforcement Weapons & Tactics, 2nd Edition, by Tom Ferguson, DBI Books, Inc., Northbrook, IL, 1991. 256 pp., illus. Paper covers. $18.95.

An in-depth look at the weapons and equipment used by law enforcement agencies of today.

Modern Sporting Guns, by Christopher Austyn, Safari Press, Huntington Beach, CA, 1994. 128 pp., illus. $40.00.

A discussion of the "best" English guns; round action, over-and-under, boxlocks, hammer guns, bolt action and double rifles as well as accessories.

The More Complete Cannoneer, by M.C. Switlik, Museum & Collectors Specialties Co., Monroe, MI, 1990. 199 pp., illus. $19.95.

Compiled agreeably to the regulations for the U.S. War Department, 1861, and containing current observations on the use of antique cannon.

The MP-40 Machine Gun, Desert Publications, El Dorado, AZ, 1995. 32 pp., illus. Paper covers. $11.95.

A reprint of the hard-to-find operating and maintenance manual for one of the most famous machine guns of World War II.

***Naval Percussion Locks and Primers,** by Lt. J. A. Dahlgren, Museum Restoration Service, Bloomfield, Canada, 1996. 140 pp., illus. $35.00

First published as an Ordnance Memoranda in 1853, this is the finest existing study of percussion locks and primers origin and development.

L.D. Nimschke Firearms Engraver, by R.L. Wilson, R&R Books, Livonia, NY, 1992. 108 pp., illus. $100.00.

The personal work record of one of the 19th century America's foremost engravers. Augmented by a comprehensive text, photographs of deluxe-engraved firearms, and detailed indexes.

No Second Place Winner, by Wm. H. Jordan, publ. by the author, Shreveport, LA (Box 4072), 1962. 114 pp., illus. $15.95.

Guns and gear of the peace officer, ably discussed by a U.S. Border Patrolman for over 30 years, and a first-class shooter with handgun, rifle, etc.

***The One-Round War: U.S.M.C. Scout-Snipers in Vietnam,** by Peter Senich, Paladin Press, Boulder, CO, 1996. 384 pp., illus. $59.95.

Sniping in Vietnam focusing specifically on the Marine Corps program.

***OSS Weapons,** by Dr. John W. Brunner, Phillips Publications, Williamstown, NJ, 1996. 224 pp., illus. $44.95.

The most definitive book ever written on the weapons and equipment used by the supersecret warriors of the Office of Strategic Services.

Pin Shooting: A Complete Guide, by Mitchell A. Ota, Wolfe Publishing Co., Prescott, AZ, 1992. 145 pp., illus. Paper covers. $14.95.

Traces the sport from its humble origins to today's thoroughly enjoyable social event, including the mammoth eight-day Second Chance Pin Shoot in Michigan.

E.C. Prudhomme, Master Gun Engraver, A Retrospective Exhibition: 1946-1973, intro. by John T. Amber, The R. W. Norton Art Gallery, Shreveport, LA, 1973. 32 pp., illus. Paper covers. $9.95.

Examples of master gun engravings by Jack Prudhomme.

A Rifleman Went to War, by H. W. McBride, Lancer Militaria, Mt. Ida, AR, 1987. 398 pp., illus. $24.95.

The classic account of practical marksmanship on the battlefields of World War I.

Second to None, edited by John Culler and Chuck Wechsler, Live Oak Press, Inc., Camden, SC, 1988. 227 pp., illus. $39.95.

The most popular articles from *Sporting Classics* magazine on great sporting firearms.

Sharpshooting for Sport and War, by W.W. Greener, Wolfe Publishing Co., Prescott, AZ, 1995. 192 pp., illus. $30.00.

This classic reprint explores the *first* expanding bullet; service rifles; shooting positions; trajectories; recoil; external ballistics; and other valuable information.

Shooter's Bible, 1997, No. 88, edited by William S. Jarrett, Stoeger Publishing Co., So. Hackensack, NJ, 1996. 575 pp., illus. Paper covers. $21.95.

"The World's Standard Reference Book."

Shooting, by J.H. FitzGerald, Wolfe Publishing Co., Prescott, AZ, 1993. 421 pp., illus. $29.00.

A classic book and reference for anyone interested in pistol and revolver shooting.

***Sniper: The World of Combat Sniping,** by Adrian Gilbert, St Martin's Press, NY, 1995. 290 pp., illus. $24.95.

The skills, the weapons and the experiences.

***Sniper Training, FM 23-10,** Reprint of the U.S. Army field manual of August, 1994, Paladin Press, Boulder, CO, 1995. 352pp., illus. Paper covers. $25.00

The most up-to-date U.S. military sniping information and doctrine.

Sniping in France, by Major H. Hesketh-Prichard, Lancer Militaria, Mt. Ida, AR, 1993. 224 pp., illus. $24.95.

The author was a well-known British adventurer and big game hunter. He was called upon in the early days of "The Great War" to develop a program to offset an initial German advantage in sniping. How the British forces came to overcome this advantage.

The SPIW: Deadliest Weapon that Never Was, by R. Blake Stevens, and Edward C. Ezell, Collector Grade Publications, Inc., Toronto, Canada, 1985. 138 pp., illus. $29.95.
The complete saga of the fantastic flechette-firing Special Purpose Individual Weapon.

The Sporting Craftsmen: A Complete Guide to Contemporary Makers of Custom-Built Sporting Equipment, by Art Carter, Countrysport Press, Traverse City, MI, 1994. 240 pp., illus. $49.50.
Profiles leading makers of centerfire rifles; muzzleloading rifles; bamboo fly rods; fly reels; flies; waterfowl calls; decoys; handmade knives; and traditional longbows and recurves.

The Street Smart Gun Book, by John Farnam, Police Bookshelf, Concord, NH, 1986. 45 pp., illus. Paper covers. $11.95.
Weapon selection, defensive shooting techniques, and gunfight-winning tactics from one of the world's leading authorities.

Stress Fire, Vol. 1: Stress Fighting for Police, by Massad Ayoob, Police Bookshelf, Concord, NH, 1984. 149 pp., illus. Paper covers. $9.95.
Gunfighting for police, advanced tactics and techniques.

Survival Guns, by Mel Tappan, Desert Publications, El Dorado, AZ, 1993. 456 pp., illus. Paper covers. $21.95.
Discusses in a frank and forthright manner which handguns, rifles and shotguns to buy for personal defense and securing food, and the ones to avoid.

Thompson Guns 1921-1945, Anubis Press, Houston, TX, 1980. 215 pp., illus. Paper covers. $11.95.
Facsimile reprinting of five complete manuals on the Thompson submachine gun.

The Ultimate Sniper, by Major John L. Plaster, Paladin Press, Boulder, CO, 1994. 464 pp., illus. Paper covers. $39.95.
An advanced training manual for military and police snipers.

U.S. Marine Corp Rifle and Pistol Marksmanship, 1935, reprinting of a government publication, Lancer Militaria, Mt. Ida, AR, 1991. 99 pp., illus. Paper covers. $11.95.
The old corps method of precision shooting.

U.S. Marine Corps Scout/Sniper Training Manual, Lancer Militaria, Mt. Ida, AR, 1989. Soft covers. $14.95.
Reprint of the original sniper training manual used by the Marksmanship Training Unit of the Marine Corps Development and Education Command in Quantico, Virginia.

U.S. Marine Corps Scout-Sniper, World War II and Korea, by Peter R. Senich, Paladin Press, Boulder, CO, 1994. 236 pp., illus. $39.95.
The most thorough and accurate account ever printed on the training, equipment and combat experiences of the U.S. Marine Corps Scout-Snipers.

U.S. Marine Corps Sniping, Lancer Militaria, Mt. Ida, AR, 1989. Irregular pagination. Soft covers. $14.95.
A reprint of the official Marine Corps FMFM1-3B.

Unrepentant Sinner, by Charles Askins, Tejano Publications, San Antonio, TX, 1985. 322 pp., illus. Soft covers. $19.95.
The autobiography of Colonel Charles Askins.

Weapons of the Waffen-SS, by Bruce Quarrie, Sterling Publishing Co., Inc., 1991. 168 pp., illus. $24.95.
An in-depth look at the weapons that made Hitler's Waffen-SS the fearsome fighting machine it was.

Weatherby: The Man, The Gun, The Legend, by Grits and Tom Gresham, Cane River Publishing Co., Natchitoches, LA, 1992. 290 pp., illus. $24.95.
A fascinating look at the life of the man who changed the course of firearms development in America.

The Winchester Era, by David Madis, Art & Reference House, Brownsville, TX, 1984. 100 pp., illus. $14.95.
Story of the Winchester company, management, employees, etc.

With British Snipers to the Reich, by Capt. C. Shore, Lander Militaria, Mt. Ida, AR, 1988. 420 pp., illus. $24.95.
One of the greatest books ever written on the art of combat sniping.

You Can't Miss, by John Shaw and Michael Bane, John Shaw, Memphis, TN, 1983. 152 pp., illus. Paper covers. $12.95.
The secrets of a successful combat shooter; how to better defensive shooting skills.

GUNSMITHING

Advanced Rebarreling of the Sporting Rifle, by Willis H. Fowler, Jr., Willis H. Fowler, Jr., Anchorage, AK, 1994. 127 pp., illus. Paper covers. $32.50.
A manual outlining a superior method of fitting barrels and doing chamber work on the sporting rifle.

The Art of Engraving, by James B. Meek, F. Brownell & Son, Montezuma, IA, 1973. 196 pp., illus. $33.95.
A complete, authoritative, imaginative and detailed study in training for gun engraving. The first book of its kind—and a great one.

Artistry in Arms, The R. W. Norton Gallery, Shreveport, LA, 1970. 42 pp., illus. Paper covers. $9.95.
The art of gunsmithing and engraving.

Barrels & Actions, by Harold Hoffman, H&P Publishers, San Angelo, TX, 1990. 309 pp., illus. Sprial bound. $27.95.
A manual on barrel making.

Black Powder Hobby Gunsmithing, by Sam Fadala and Dale Storey, DBI Books, Inc., Northbrook, IL., 1994. 256 pp., illus. Paper covers. $18.95.
A how-to guide for gunsmithing blackpowder pistols, rifles and shotguns from two men at the top of their respective fields.

Checkering and Carving of Gun Stocks, by Monte Kennedy, Stackpole Books, Harrisburg, PA, 1962. 175 pp., illus. $34.95.
Revised, enlarged cloth-bound edition of a much sought-after, dependable work.

The Colt .45 Automatic Shop Manual, by Jerry Kuhnhausen, VSP Publishers, McCall, ID, 1987. 200 pp., illus. Paper covers. $22.95.
Covers repairing, accurizing, trigger/sear work, action tuning, springs, bushings, rebarreling, and custom .45 modification.

The Colt Double Action Revolvers: A Shop Manual, Volume 1, by Jerry Kuhnhausen, VSP Publishers, McCall, ID, 1988. 224 pp., illus. Paper covers. $24.95.
Covers D, E, and I frames.

The Colt Double Action Revolvers: A Shop Manual, Volume 2, by Jerry Kuhnhausen, VSP Publishers, McCall, ID, 1988. 156 pp., illus. Paper covers. $18.95.
Covers J, V, and AA models.

The Complete Metal Finishing Book, by Harold Hoffman, H&P Publishers, San Angelo, TX, 1992. 364 pp., illus. Paper covers. $29.95.
Instructions for the different metal finishing operations that the normal craftsman or shop will use. Primarily firearm related.

Custom Gunstock Carving, by Philip Eck, Stackpole Books, Mechanicsburg, PA, 1995. 232 pp., illus. $34.95.
Featuring a gallery of more than 100 full-size patterns for buttstocks, grips, accents and borders that carvers can use for their own projects.

Exploded Handgun Drawings, The Gun Digest Book of, edited by Harold A. Murtz, DBI Books, Inc., Northbrook, IL. 1992. 512 pp., illus. Paper covers. $20.95.
Exploded or isometric drawings for 494 of the most popular handguns.

Exploded Long Gun Drawings, The Gun Digest Book of, edited by Harold A. Murtz, DBI Books, Inc., Northbrook, IL. 512 pp., illus. Paper covers. $20.95.
Containing almost 500 rifle and shotgun exploded drawings. An invaluable aid to both professionals and hobbyists.

The Finishing of Gun Stocks, by Harold Hoffman, H&P Publishers, San Angelo, TX, 1994. 98 pp., illus. Paper covers. $17.95.
Covers different types of finishing methods and finishes.

Firearms Assembly/Disassembly, Part I: Automatic Pistols, Revised Edition, The Gun Digest Book of, by J.B. Wood, DBI Books, Inc., Northbrook, IL, 1990. 480 pp., illus. Paper covers. $19.95.
Covers 58 popular autoloading pistols plus nearly 200 variants of those models integrated into the text and completely cross-referenced in the index.

Firearms Assembly/Disassembly Part II: Revolvers, Revised Edition, The Gun Digest Book of, by J.B. Wood, DBI Books, Inc., Northbrook, IL, 1990. 480 pp., illus. Paper covers. $19.95.
Covers 49 popular revolvers plus 130 variants. The most comprehensive and professional presentation available to either hobbyist or gunsmith.

Firearms Assembly/Disassembly Part III: Rimfire Rifles, Revised Edition, The Gun Digest Book of, by J. B. Wood, DBI Books, Inc., Northbrook, IL., 1994. 480 pp., illus. Paper covers. $19.95.
Greatly expanded edition covering 65 popular rimfire rifles plus over 100 variants all completely cross-referenced in the index.

Firearms Assembly/Disassembly Part IV: Centerfire Rifles, Revised Edition, The Gun Digest Book of, by J.B. Wood, DBI Books, Inc., Northbrook, IL, 1991. 480 pp., illus. Paper covers. $19.95.
Covers 54 popular centerfire rifles plus 300 variants. The most comprehensive and professional presentation available to either hobbyist or gunsmith.

Firearms Assembly/Disassembly, Part V: Shotguns, Revised Edition, The Gun Digest Book of, by J.B. Wood, DBI Books, Inc., Northbrook, IL, 1992. 480 pp., illus. Paper covers. $19.95.
Covers 46 popular shotguns plus over 250 variants with step-by-step instructions on how to dismantle and reassemble each. The most comprehensive and professional presentation available to either hobbyist or gunsmith.

Firearms Assembly/Disassembly Part VI: Law Enforcement Weapons, The Gun Digest Book of, by J.B. Wood, DBI Books, Inc., Northbrook, IL, 1981. 288 pp., illus. Paper covers. $16.95.
Step-by-step instructions on how to completely dismantle and reassemble the most commonly used firearms found in law enforcement arsenals.

Firearms Assembly 3: The NRA Guide to Rifle and Shotguns, NRA Books, Wash., DC, 1980. 264 pp., illus. Paper covers. $13.95.
Text and illustrations explaining the takedown of 125 rifles and shotguns, domestic and foreign.

Firearms Assembly 4: The NRA Guide to Pistols and Revolvers, NRA Books, Wash., DC, 1980. 253 pp., illus. Paper covers. $13.95.
Text and illustrations explaining the takedown of 124 pistol and revolver models, domestic and foreign.

Firearms Bluing and Browning, By R.H. Angier, Stackpole Books, Harrisburg, PA. 151 pp., illus. $18.95.
A world master gunsmith reveals his secrets of building, repairing and renewing a gun, quite literally, lock, stock and barrel. A useful, concise text on chemical coloring methods for the gunsmith and mechanic.

Firearms Disassembly—With Exploded Views, by John A. Karns & John E. Traister, Stoeger Publishing Co., S. Hackensack, NJ, 1995. 320 pp., illus. Paper covers. $19.95.
Provides the do's and don'ts of firearms disassembly. Enables owners and gunsmiths to disassemble firearms in a professional manner.

Guns and Gunmaking Tools of Southern Appalachia, by John Rice Irwin, Schiffer Publishing Ltd., 1983. 118 pp., illus. Paper covers. $9.95.
The story of the Kentucky rifle.

Gunsmithing Tips and Projects, a collection of the best articles from the *Handloader* and *Rifle* magazines, by various authors, Wolfe Publishing Co., Prescott, AZ, 1992. 443 pp., illus. Paper covers. $25.00.
Includes such subjects as shop, stocks, actions, tuning, triggers, barrels, customizing, etc.

Gunsmith Kinks, by F.R. (Bob) Brownell, F. Brownell & Son, Montezuma, IA, 1st ed., 1969. 496 pp., well illus. $18.95.
A widely useful accumulation of shop kinks, short cuts, techniques and pertinent comments by practicing gunsmiths from all over the world.

Gunsmith Kinks 2, by Bob Brownell, F. Brownell & Son, Publishers, Montezuma, IA, 1983. 496 pp., illus. $18.95.
A collection of gunsmithing knowledge, shop kinks, new and old techniques, shortcuts and general know-how straight from those who do them best—the gunsmiths.

Gunsmith Kinks 3, edited by Frank Brownell, Brownells Inc., Montezuma, IA, 1993. 504 pp., illus. $19.95.
Tricks, knacks and "kinks" by professional gunsmiths and gun tinkerers. Hundreds of valuable ideas are given in this volume.

Gunsmithing, by Roy F. Dunlap, Stackpole Books, Harrisburg, PA, 1990. 742 pp., illus. $34.95.
A manual of firearm design, construction, alteration and remodeling. For amateur and professional gunsmiths and users of modern firearms.

Gunsmithing at Home, by John E. Traister, Stoeger Publishing Co., So. Hackensack, NJ, 1985. 256 pp., illus. Paper covers. $14.95.
Over 25 chapters of explicit information on every aspect of gunsmithing.

The Gunsmith's Manual, by J.P. Stelle and Wm. B. Harrison, The Gun Room Press, Highland Park, NJ, 1982. 376 pp., illus. $19.95.
For the gunsmith in all branches of the trade.

Home Gunsmithing the Colt Single Action Revolvers, by Loren W. Smith, Ray Riling Arms Books, Co., Phila., PA, 1995. 119 pp., illus. $24.95.
Affords the Colt Single Action owner detailed, pertinent information on the operating and servicing of this famous and historic handgun.

The Mauser M91 Through M98 Bolt Actions: A Shop Manual, by Jerry Kuhnhausen, VSP Books, McCall, ID, 1991. 224 pp., illus. Paper covers. $26.95.
An essential book if you work on or plan to work on a Mauser action.

*__Mr. Single Shot's Gunsmithing-Idea-Book,__ by Frank de Haas, Mark de Haas, Orange City, IA, 1996. 168 pp., illus. Paper covers. $21.50.
Offers easy to follow, step-by-step instructions for a wide variety of gunsmithing procedures all reinforced by plenty of photos.

The NRA Gunsmithing Guide—Updated, by Ken Raynor and Brad Fenton, National Rifle Association, Wash., DC, 1984. 336 pp., illus. Paper covers. $15.95.
Material includes chapters and articles on all facets of the gunsmithing art.

Pistolsmithing, The Gun Digest Book of, by Jack Mitchell, DBI Books, Inc., Northbrook, IL, 1980. 256 pp., illus. Paper covers. $16.95.
An expert's guide to the operation of each of the handgun actions with all the major functions of pistolsmithing explained.

Pistolsmithing, by George C. Nonte, Jr., Stackpole Books, Harrisburg, PA, 1974. 560 pp., illus. $29.95.
A single source reference to handgun maintenance, repair, and modification at home, unequaled in value.

*__Practical Gunsmithing,__ by the editors of American Gunsmith, DBI Books, Inc., Northbrook, IL, 1996. 256 pp., illus. Paper covers. $19.95.
A book intended primarily for home gunsmithing, but one that will be extremely helpful to professionals as well.

*__Professional Stockmaking,__ by D. Wesbrook, Wolfe Publishing Co., Prescott AZ, 1995. 308 pp., illus. $54.00.
A step-by-step how-to with complete photographic support for every detail of the art of working wood into riflestocks.

Recreating the American Longrifle, by William Buchele, et al., George Shumway, Publisher, York, PA, 1983. 175 pp., illus. $30.00.
Includes full-scale plans for building a Kentucky rifle.

The Remington M870 and M1100/M11-87 Shotguns: A Shop Manual, by Jerry Kuhnhausen, VSP Publishers, McCall, ID, 1992. 226 pp., illus. Paper covers. $26.95.
Covers everything about gunsmithing the most popular Remington shotguns from fitting a recoil pad to installing choke tubes, and everything in between.

Riflesmithing, The Gun Digest Book of, by Jack Mitchell, DBI Books, Inc., Northbrook, IL, 1982. 256 pp., illus. Paper covers. $16.95.
The art and science of rifle gunsmithing. Covers tools, techniques, designs, finishing wood and metal, custom alterations.

Ruger Double Action Revolvers, Vol. 1, Shop Manual, by Jerry Kuhnhausen, VSP Publishers, McCall, ID, 1989. 176 pp., illus. Soft covers. $18.95.
Covers the Ruger Six series of revolvers: Security-Six, Service-Six, and Speed-Six. Includes step-by-step function checks, disassembly, inspection, repairs, rebuilding, reassembly, and custom work.

The S&W Revolver: A Shop Manual, by Jerry Kuhnhausen, VSP Publishers, McCall, ID, 1987. 152 pp., illus. Paper covers. $24.95.
Covers accurizing, trigger jobs, action tuning, rebarreling, barrel setback, forcing cone angles, polishing and rebluing.

Shotgun Gunsmithing, The Gun Digest Book of, by Ralph Walker, DBI Books, Inc., Northbrook, IL, 1983. 256 pp., illus. Paper covers. $16.95.
The principles and practices of repairing, individualizing and accurizing modern shotguns by one of the world's premier shotgun gunsmiths.

The Story of Pope's Barrels, by Ray M. Smith, R&R Books, Livonia, NY, 1993. 203 pp., illus. $39.00.
A reissue of a 1960 book whose author knew Pope personally. It will be of special interest to Schuetzen rifle fans, since Pope's greatest days were at the height of the Schuetzen-era before WWI.

Survival Gunsmithing, by J.B. Wood, Desert Publications, Cornville, AZ, 1986. 92 pp., illus. Paper covers. $9.95.
A guide to repair and maintenance of the most popular rifles, shotguns and handguns.

The Trade Rifle Sketchbook, by Charles E. Hanson, The Fur Press, Chadron, NE, 1979. 48 pp., illus. Paper covers. $9.95.
Includes full-scale plans for 10 rifles made for Indian and mountain men; from 1790 to 1860, plus plans for building three pistols.

HANDGUNS

Advanced Master Handgunning, by Charles Stephens, Paladin Press, Boulder, CO., 1994. 72 pp., illus. Paper covers. $10.00.
Secrets and surefire techniques for winning handgun competitions.

*__The Ayoob Files: The Book,__ by Massad Ayoob, Police Bookshelf, Concord, NH, 1995. 223 pp., illus. Paper covers. $14.95.
The best of Massad Ayoob's acclaimed series in American Handgunner magazine.

Black Powder Hobby Gunsmithing, by Sam Fadala and Dale Storey, DBI Books, Inc., Northbrook, IL., 1994. 256 pp., illus. Paper covers. $18.95.
A how-to guide for gunsmithing blackpowder pistols, rifles and shotguns from two men at the top of their respective fields.

Blue Steel and Gun Leather, by John Bianchi, Beinfeld Publishing, Inc., No. Hollywood, CA, 1978. 200 pp., illus. $19.95.
A complete and comprehensive review of holster uses plus an examination of available products on today's market.

Browning Hi-Power Pistols, Desert Publications, Cornville, AZ, 1982. 20 pp., illus. Paper covers. $9.95.
Covers all facets of the various military and civilian models of the Browning Hi-Power pistol.

Colt Automatic Pistols, by Donald B. Bady, Borden Publ. Co., Alhambra, CA, 1974, 368 pp., illus. $25.00.
The rev. and enlarged ed. of a key work on a fascinating subject. Complete information on every automatic marked with Colt's name.

The Colt .45 Auto Pistol, compiled from U.S. War Dept. Technical Manuals, and reprinted by Desert Publications, Cornville, AZ, 1978. 80 pp., illus. Paper covers. $9.95.
Covers every facet of this famous pistol from mechanical training, manual of arms, disassembly, repair and replacement of parts.

*__Combat Handgunnery, 4th Edition,__ by Chuck Taylor, DBI Books, Inc., Northbrook, IL, 1996. 256 pp., illus. Paper covers. $18.95.
This all-new edition looks at real world combat handgunnery from three different perspectives—military, police and civilian. Available, October, 1996.

Combat Pistols, by Terry Gander, Sterling Publishing Co., Inc., 1991. Paper covers. $9.95.
The world's finest and deadliest pistols are shown close-up, with detailed specifications, muzzle velocity, rate of fire, ammunition, etc.

Combat Raceguns, by J.M. Ramos, Paladin Press, Boulder, CO, 1994. 168 pp., illus. Paper covers. $25.00.
Learn how to put together precision combat raceguns with the best compensators, frames, controls, sights and custom accessories.

*__Competitive Pistol Shooting,__ by Dr. Laslo Antal, A&C Black, London, England, 2nd edition, 1995. 176 pp., illus. Paper covers. $24.95.
Covers the basic principles followed in each case by a well illustrated and detailed discussion of the rules, technique, and training as well as the choice and maintenance of weapons.

The Complete Book of Combat Handgunning, by Chuck Taylor, Desert Publications, Cornville, AZ, 1982. 168 pp., illus. Paper covers. $16.95.
Covers virtually every aspect of combat handgunning.

The Custom Government Model Pistol, by Layne Simpson, Wolfe Publishing Co., Prescott, AZ, 1994. 639 pp., illus. Paper covers. $24.50.
The book about one of the world's greatest firearms and the things pistolsmiths do to make it even greater.

The CZ-75 Family: The Ultimate Combat Handgun, by J.M. Ramos, Paladin Press, Boulder, CO, 1990. 100 pp., illus. Soft covers. $16.00.
An in-depth discussion of the early-and-late model CZ-75s, as well as the many newest additions to the Czech pistol family.

Experiments of a Handgunner, by Walter Roper, Wolfe Publishing Co., Prescott, AZ, 1989. 202 pp., illus. $37.00.
A limited edition reprint. A listing of experiments with functioning parts of handguns, with targets, stocks, rests, handloading, etc.

Exploded Handgun Drawings, The Gun Digest Book of, edited by Harold A. Murtz, DBI Books, Inc., Northbrook, IL. 1992. 512 pp., illus. Paper covers. $20.95.
Exploded or isometric drawings for 494 of the most popular handguns.

The Farnam Method of Defensive Handgunning, by John S. Farnam, DTI, Inc., Seattle, WA, 1994. 191 pp., illus. Paper covers. $13.95.
A book intended to not only educate the new shooter, but also to serve as a guide and textbook for his and his instructor's training courses.

Fast and Fancy Revolver Shooting, by Ed. McGivern, Anniversary Edition, Winchester Press, Piscataway, NJ, 1984. 484 pp., illus. $18.95.
A fascinating volume, packed with handgun lore and solid information by the acknowledged dean of revolver shooters.

Firearms Assembly/Disassembly, Part I: Automatic Pistols, Revised Edition, The Gun Digest Book of, by J.B. Wood, DBI Books, Inc., Northbrook, IL, 1990. 480 pp., illus. Soft covers. $19.95.
Covers 58 popular autoloading pistols plus nearly 200 variants of those models integrated into the text and completely cross-referenced in the index.

Firearms Assembly/Disassembly Part II: Revolvers, Revised Edition, The Gun Digest Book of, by J.B. Wood, DBI Books, Inc., Northbrook, IL, 1990. 480 pp., illus. Soft covers. $19.95.
Covers 49 popular revolvers plus 130 variants. The most comprehensive and professional presentation available to either hobbyist or gunsmith.

.45 ACP Super Guns, by J.M. Ramos, Paladin Press, Boulder, CO, 1991. 144 pp., illus. Paper covers. $24.00.
Modified .45 automatic pistols for competition, hunting and personal defense.

The .45, The Gun Digest Book of, by Dean A. Grennell, DBI Books, Inc., Northbrook, IL, 1989. 256 pp., illus. Paper covers. $17.95.
Definitive work on one of America's favorite calibers.

Glock: The New Wave in Combat Handguns, by Peter Alan Kasler, Paladin Press, Boulder, CO, 1993. 304 pp., illus. $25.00.
Kasler debunks the myths that surround what is the most innovative handgun to be introduced in some time.

Great Combat Handguns, by Leroy Thompson and Rene Smeets, Sterling Publishing Co., New York, NY, 1993. 256 pp., illus. $29.95.
Revised and newly designed edition of the successful classic in handgun use and reference.

Hand Cannons: The World's Most Powerful Handguns, by Duncan Long, Paladin Press, Boulder, CO, 1995. 208 pp., illus. Paper covers. $20.00.
Long describes and evaluates each powerful gun according to their features.

Handgun Digest, 3rd Edition, edited by Chris Christian, DBI Books, Inc., Northbrook, IL, 1995. 256 pp., illus. Paper covers. $18.95.
Full coverage of all aspects of handguns and handgunning from a highly readable and knowledgeable author.

Handgun Reloading, The Gun Digest Book of, by Dean A. Grennell and Wiley M. Clapp, DBI Books, Inc., Northbrook, IL, 1987. 256 pp., illus. Paper covers. $16.95.
Detailed discussions of all aspects of reloading for handguns, from basic to complex. New loading data.

Handguns '97, 9th Edition, edited by Ray Ordorica, DBI Books, Inc., Northbrook, IL, 1995. 352 pp., illus. Paper covers. $20.95.
Top handgun experts cover what's new in the world of handguns and handgunning. Available August, 1996.

*__Hidden in Plain Sight,__ by Trey Bloodworth & Mike Raley, Professional Press, Chapel Hill, NC, 1995. Paper covers. $13.00.
A practical guide to concealed handgun carry.

High Standard Automatic Pistols 1932-1950, by Charles E. Petty, The Gunroom Press, Highland Park, NJ, 1989. 124 pp., illus. $19.95.
A definitive source of information for the collector of High Standard arms.

*__The Hi-standard Pistol Guide,__ by Burr Leyson, Duckett's Sporting Books, Tempe AZ, 1995. 128 pp., illus. Paper covers. $22.00.
Complete information on selection, care and repair, ammunition, parts, and accessories.

How to Become a Master Handgunner: The Mechanics of X-Count Shooting, by Charles Stephens, Paladin Press, Boulder, CO, 1993. 64 pp., illus. Paper covers. $10.00.
Offers a simple formula for success to the handgunner who strives to master the technique of shooting accurately.

Hunting for Handgunners, by Larry Kelly and J.D. Jones, DBI Books, Inc., Northbrook, IL, 1990. 256 pp., illus. Paper covers. $16.95.
Covers the entire spectrum of hunting with handguns in an amusing, easy-flowing manner that combines entertainment with solid information.

Illustrated Encyclopedia of Handguns, by A.B. Zhuk, Stackpole Books, Mechanicsburg, PA, 1994. 256 pp., illus. $49.95.
Identifies more than 2,000 military and commercial pistols and revolvers with details of more than 100 popular handgun cartridges.

Instinct Combat Shooting, by Chuck Klein, Chuck Klein, The Goose Creek, IN, 1989. 49 pp., illus. Paper covers. $12.00.
Defensive handgunning for police.

Know Your Czechoslovakian Pistols, by R.J. Berger, Blacksmith Corp., Chino Valley, AZ, 1989. 96 pp., illus. Soft covers. $9.95.
A comprehensive reference which presents the fascinating story of Czech pistols.

Know Your 45 Auto Pistols—Models 1911 & A1, by E.J. Hoffschmidt, Blacksmith Corp., Southport, CT, 1974. 58 pp., illus. Paper covers. $9.95.
A concise history of the gun with a wide variety of types and copies.

Know Your Walther P.38 Pistols, by E.J. Hoffschmidt, Blacksmith Corp., Southport, CT, 1974. 77 pp., illus. Paper covers. $9.95.
Covers the Walther models Armee, M.P., H.P., P.38—history and variations.

Know Your Walther PP & PPK Pistols, by E.J. Hoffschmidt, Blacksmith Corp., Southport, CT, 1975. 87 pp., illus. Paper covers. $9.95.
A concise history of the guns with a guide to the variety and types.

The Mauser Self-Loading Pistol, by Belford & Dunlap, Borden Publ. Co., Alhambra, CA. Over 200 pp., 300 illus., large format. $24.95.

The long-awaited book on the "Broom Handles," covering their inception in 1894 to the end of production. Complete and in detail: pocket pistols, Chinese and Spanish copies, etc.

Modern American Pistols and Revolvers, by A.C. Gould, Wolfe Publishing Co., Prescott, AZ, 1988. 222 pp., illus. $37.00.

A limited edition reprint. An account of the development of those arms as well as the manner of shooting them.

The Modern Technique of the Pistol, by Gregory Boyce Morrison, Gunsite Press, Paulden, AZ, 1991. 153 pp., illus. $45.00.

The theory of effective defensive use of modern handguns.

9mm Handguns, 2nd Edition, The Gun Digest Book of, edited by Steve Comus, DBI Books, Inc., Northbrook, IL, 1993. 256 pp., illus. Paper covers. $18.95.

Covers the 9mmP cartridge and the guns that have been made for it in greater depth than any other work available.

9mm Parabellum; The History & Developement of the World's 9mm Pistols & Ammunition, by Klaus-Peter Konig and Martin Hugo, Schiffer Publishing Ltd., Atglen, PA, 1993. 304 pp., illus. $39.95.

Detailed history of 9mm weapons from Belguim, Italy, Germany, Israel, France, USA, Czechoslovakia, Hungary, Poland, Brazil, Finland and Spain.

*__The Official 9mm Markarov Pistol Manual,__ translated into English by Major James Gebhardt, U.S. Army (Ret.), Desert Publications, El Dorado, AR, 1996. 84 pp., illus. Paper covers. $12.95.

The information found in this book will be of enormous benefit and interest to the owner or a prospective owner of one of these pistols.

The 100 Greatest Combat Pistols, by Timothy J. Mullin, Paladin Press, Boulder, CO, 1994. 409 pp., illus. Paper covers. $40.00.

Hands-on tests and evaluations of handguns from around the world.

P-38 Automatic Pistol, by Gene Gangarosa, Jr., Stoeger Publishing Co., S. Hackensack, NJ, 1993. 272 pp., illus. Paper covers. $16.95

This book traces the origins and development of the P-38, including the momentous political forces of the World War II era that caused its near demise and, later, its rebirth.

Pistol & Revolver Guide, 3rd Ed., by George C. Nonte, Stoeger Publ. Co., So. Hackensack, NJ, 1975. 224 pp., illus. Paper covers. $11.95.

The standard reference work on military and sporting handguns.

Pistol Guide, by George C. Nonte, Jr., Stoeger Publishing Co., So. Hackensack, NJ, 1991. 280 pp., illus. Paper covers. $13.95.

Covers handling and marksmanship, care and maintenance, pistol ammunition, how to buy a used gun, military pistols, air pistols and repairs.

Pistols of the World, 3rd Edition, by Ian Hogg and John Weeks, DBI Books, Inc., Northbrook, IL, 1992. 320 pp., illus. Paper covers. $20.95.

A totally revised edtion of one of the leading studies of small arms.

Pistolsmithing, The Gun Digest Book of, by Jack Mitchell, DBI Books, Inc., Northbrook, IL, 1980, 288 pp., illus. Paper covers. $16.95.

An expert's guide to the operation of each of the handgun actions with all the major functions of pistolsmithing explained.

Police Handgun Manual, by Bill Clede, Stackpole Books, Inc., Harrisburg, PA, 1985. 128 pp., illus. $18.95.

How to get street-smart survival habits.

Powerhouse Pistols—The Colt 1911 and Browning Hi-Power Source Book, by Duncan Long, Paladin Press, Boulder, CO, 1989. 152 pp., illus. Soft covers. $19.95.

The author discusses internal mechanisms, outward design, test-firing results, maintenance and accessories.

Practical Shooting: Beyond Fundamentals, by Brian Enos, Zediker Publishing, Clifton, CO, 1996. 201 pp., illus. $27.95.

This prize-winning master covers the advanced techniques of competitive shooting in all its facets.

Report of Board on Tests of Revolvers and Automatic Pistols, From the Annual Report of the Chief of Ordnance, 1907. Reprinted by J.C. Tillinghast, Marlow, NH, 1969. 34 pp., 7 plates, paper covers. $9.95.

A comparison of handguns, including Luger, Savage, Colt, Webley-Fosbery and other makes.

Revolver Guide, by George C. Nonte, Jr., Stoeger Publishing Co., So. Hackensack, NJ, 1991. 288 pp., illus. Paper covers. $10.95.

A detailed and practical encyclopedia of the revolver, the most common handgun to be found.

Ruger Automatic Pistols and Single Action Revolvers, by Hugo A. Lueders, edited by Don Findley, Blacksmith Corp., Chino Valley, AZ, 1993. 79 pp., illus. Paper covers. $14.95.

The definitive work on Ruger automatic pistols and single action revolvers.

The Ruger "P" Family of Handguns, by Duncan Long, Desert Publications, El Dorado, AZ, 1993. 128 pp., illus. Paper covers. $14.95.

A full-fledged documentary on a remarkable series of Sturm Ruger handguns.

The Ruger .22 Automatic Pistol, Standard/Mark I/Mark II Series, by Duncan Long, Paladin Press, Boulder, CO, 1989. 168 pp., illus. Paper covers. $12.00.

The definitive book about the pistol that has served more than 1 million owners so well.

The Semiautomatic Pistols in Police Service and Self Defense, by Massad Ayoob, Police Bookshelf, Concord, NH, 1990. 25 pp., illus. Soft covers. $9.95.

First quantitative, documented look at actual police experience with 9mm and 45 police service automatics.

The Sharpshooter—How to Stand and Shoot Handgun Metallic Silhouettes, by Charles Stephens, Yucca Tree Press, Las Cruces, NM, 1993. 86 pp., illus. Paper covers. $10.00.

A narration of some of the author's early experiences in silhouette shooting, plus how-to information.

Shoot a Handgun, by Dave Arnold, PVA Books, Canyon County, CA, 1983. 144 pp., illus. Paper covers. $12.95.

A complete manual of simplified handgun instruction.

Shoot to Win, by John Shaw, Blacksmith Corp., Southport, CT, 1985. 160 pp., illus. Paper covers. $15.50.

The lessons taught here are of interest and value to all handgun shooters.

Shooting, by J.H. FitzGerald, Wolfe Publishing Co., Prescott, AZ, 1993. 421 pp., illus. $29.00

Exhaustive coverage of handguns and their use for target shooting, defense, trick shooting, and in police work by an noted firearms expert.

Sig/Sauer Handguns, by Duncan Long, Desert Publications, El Dorado, AZ, 1995. 150 pp., illus. Paper covers. $16.95.

The history of Sig/Sauer handguns, including Sig, Sig-Hammerli and Sig/Sauer variants.

Sixgun Cartridges and Loads, by Elmer Keith, reprint edition by The Gun Room Press, Highland Park, NJ, 1984. 151 pp., illus. $24.95.

A manual covering the selection, use and loading of the most suitable and popular revolver cartridges.

Sixguns, by Elmer Keith, Wolfe Publishing Company, Prescott, AZ, 1992. 336 pp. Hardcover. $34.95.

The history, selection, repair, care, loading, and use of this historic frontiersman's friend—the one-hand firearm.

Smith & Wesson's Automatics, by Larry Combs, Desert Publications, El Dorado, AZ, 1994. 143 pp., illus. Paper covers. $27.95.

A must for every S&W auto owner or prospective owner.

Successful Pistol Shooting, by Frank and Paul Leatherdale, The Crowood Press, Ramsbury, England, 1988. 144 pp., illus. $34.95.

Easy-to-follow instructions to help you achieve better results and gain more enjoyment from both leisure and competitive shooting.

*__The Tactical Pistol,__ by Gabriel Suarez with a foreword by Jeff Cooper, Paladin Press, Boulder, CO, 1996. 216 pp., illus. Paper covers. $25.00.

Advanced gunfighting concepts and techniques.

The .380 Enfield No. 2 Revolver, by Mark Stamps and Ian Skennerton, I.D.S.A. Books, Piqua, OH, 1993. 124 pp., 80 illus. Paper covers. $19.95.

Webley & Scott Automatic Pistols, by Gordon Bruch, Stocker-Schmid Publishing Co., Dietikon, Switzerland, 1992. 256 pp., illus. $69.95.

The fundamental representation of the history and development of all Webley & Scott automatic pistols.

World's Deadliest Rimfire Battleguns, by J.M. Ramos, Paladin Press, Boulder, CO, 1990. 184 pp., illus. Paper covers. $14.00.

This heavily illustrated book shows international rimfire assault weapon innovations from World War II to the present.

HUNTING

NORTH AMERICA

Advanced Wild Turkey Hunting & World Records, by Dave Harbour, Winchester Press, Piscataway, NJ, 1983. 264 pp., illus. $19.95.

The definitive book, written by an authority who has studied turkeys and turkey calling for over 40 years.

*__After the Hunt With Lovett William,__ by Lovett Williams, Krause Publications, Iola, WI, 1996. 256 pp., illus. Paper covers. $15.95.

The author carefully instructs you on how to prepare your trophy turkey for a trip to the taxidermist. Plus help on planning a grand slam hunt.

Aggressive Whitetail Hunting, by Greg Miller, Krause Publications, Iola, WI, 1995. 208 pp., illus. Paper covers. $14.95.

Learn how to hunt trophy bucks in public forests, private farmlands and exclusive hunting grounds from one of America's foremost hunters.

*__Alaskan Adventures, Volume 1-The Early Years,__ by Russell Annabel, Safari Press, Huntington Beach, CA, 1996. 280 pp., illus. Limited, numbered, slipcased copies signed by David Annabel and Dell Annabel Lamey. $50.00.

A complete collection of previously unpublished magazine articles in book format.

All About Bears, by Duncan Gilchrist, Stoneydale Press Publishing Co., Stevensville, MT, 1989. 176 pp., illus. $19.95.

Covers all kinds of bears—black, grizzly, Alaskan brown, polar and leans on a lifetime of hunting and guiding experiences to explore proper hunting techniques.

All-American Deer Hunter's Guide, edited by Jim Zumbo and Robert Elman, Winchester Press, Piscataway, NJ, 1983. 320 pp., illus. $29.95.

The most comprehensive, thorough book yet published on American deer hunting.

All Season Hunting, by Bob Gilsvik, Winchester Press, Piscataway, NJ, 1976. 256 pp., illus. $14.95.

A guide to early-season, late-season and winter hunting in America.

American Duck Shooting, by George Bird Grinnell, Stackpole Books, Harrisburg, PA, 1991. 640 pp., illus. Paper covers. $17.95.

First published in 1901 at the height of the author's career. Describes 50 species of waterfowl, and discusses hunting methods common at the turn of the century.

Awesome Antlers of North America, by Odie Sudbeck, HTW Publications, Seneca, KS, 1993. 150 pp., illus. $35.00.

500 world-class bucks in color and black and white. This book starts up where the Boone & Crockett recordbook leaves off.

Bare November Days, by George Bird Evans et al, Countrysport Press, Traverse City, MI, 1992. 136 pp., illus. $39.50.

A new, original anthology, a tribute to ruffed grouse, king of upland birds.

The Bear Hunter's Century, by Paul Schullery, Stackpole Books, Harrisburg, PA, 1989. 240 pp., illus. $19.95.

Thrilling tales of the bygone days of wilderness hunting.

Bear in Their World, by Erwin Bauer, an Outdoor Life Book, New York, NY, 1985. 254 pp., illus. $32.95.

Covers all North American bears; including grizzlies, browns, blacks, and polars.

Becoming a Great Moose Hunter, by Richard Hackenburg, Frank Amato Publications, Portland, OR, 1994. 111 pp., illus. Paper covers. $10.95.

Explains habits and habitat of moose and how to hunt them with rifle or bow. Includes moose calling techniques.

The Best of Babcock, by Havilah Babcock, selected and with an introduction by Hugh Grey, The Gunnerman Press, Auburn Hills, MI, 1985. 262 pp., illus. $19.95.

A treasury of memorable pieces, 21of which have never before appeared in book form.

The Best of Field & Stream, edited by J.I. Merritt, with Margaret G. Nichols and the editor of *Field & Stream*, Lyons & Burford, New York, NY, 1995. 352 pp., illus. $25.00.

100 years of great writing from America's premier sporting magazine.

The Best of Jack O'Connor, by Jack O'Connor, The Amwell Press, Clinton, NJ, 1994. 192 pp., illus. $26.95.

Amwell Press presents 34 prime selections from the grand master of outdoor writers.

The Best of Nash Buckingham, by Nash Buckingham, selected, edited and annotated by George Bird Evans, Winchester Press, Piscataway, NJ, 1973. 320 pp., illus. $35.00.

Thirty pieces that represent the very cream of Nash's output on his whole range of outdoor interests—upland shooting, duck hunting, even fishing.

The Best of Sheep Hunting, by John Batten, Amwell Press, Clinton, NJ, 1992. 616 pp., illus. $47.50.

This "Memorial Edition" is a collection of 40 articles and appendices covering sheep hunting in the North American area of Canada, Alaska, the West and Midwest as well as Africa and Europe.

Big Game, Big Country, by Dr. Chauncey Guy Suits, Great Northwest Publishing and Distributing Co., Anchorage, AK, 1987. 224 pp., illus. $29.50.

Chronicles more than a decade of high-quality wilderness hunting by one of this country's more distinguished big game hunters.

Big Game Trails in the Far North, by Col. Philip Neuweiler, Great Northwest Publishing and Distributing Co., Inc., Anchorage, AK, 1990. 320 pp., illus. $35.00.

This book is the result of 50 years hunting big game in the Far North.

Birds on the Horizon, by Stuart Williams, Countrysport Press, Traverse City, MI, 1993. 288 pp., illus. $49.50.

Wingshooting adventures around the world.

Blacktail Trophy Tactics, by Boyd Iverson, Stoneydale Press, Stevensville, MI, 1992. 166 pp., illus. Paper covers. $14.95.

A comprehensive analysis of blacktail deer habits, describing a deer's and man's use of scents, still hunting, tree techniques, etc.

Bowhunter's Digest, 3rd Edition, by Chuck Adams, DBI Books, Inc., Northbrook, IL, 1990. 288 pp., illus. Soft covers. $17.95.

All-new edition covers all the necessary equipment and how to use it, plus the fine points on how to improve your skill.

Brown Feathers, by Steven J. Julak, Stackpole Books, Harrisburg, PA, 1988. 224 pp., illus. $16.95.

Waterfowling tales and upland dreams.

*__The Buffalo Harvest,__ by Frank Mayer as told to Charles Roth, Pioneer Press, Union City, TN, 1995. 96 pp., illus. Paper covers. $7.50.

The story of a hide hunter during his buffalo hunting days on the plains.

Bugling for Elk, by Dwight Schuh, Stoneydale Press Publishing Co., Stevensville, MT, 1983. 162 pp., illus. $18.95.

A complete guide to early season elk hunting.

Call of the Quail: A Tribute to the Gentleman Game Bird, by Michael McIntosh, et al., Countrysport Press, Traverse City, MI, 1990. 175 pp., illus. $39.50.

A new anthology on quail hunting.

Calling All Elk, by Jim Zumbo, Jim Zumbo, Cody, WY, 1989. 169 pp., illus. Paper covers. $14.95.

The only book on the subject of elk hunting that covers every aspect of elk vocalization.

Campfires and Game Trails: Hunting North American Big Game, by Craig Boddington, Winchester Press, Piscataway, NJ, 1985. 295 pp., illus. $23.95.

How to hunt North America's big game species.

Come October, by Gene Hill et al, Countrysport Press, Inc., Traverse City, MI, 1991. 176 pp., illus. $39.50.

A new and all-original anthology on the woodcock and woodcock hunting.

The Complete Guide to Bird Dog Training, by John R. Falk, Lyons & Burford, New York, NY, 1994. 288 pp., illus. $22.95.

The latest on live-game field training techniques using released quail and recall pens. A new chapter on the services available for entering field trials and other bird dog competitions.

The Complete Guide to Bowhunting Deer, by Chuck Adams, DBI Books, Inc., Northbrook, IL, 1984. 256 pp., illus. Paper covers. $16.95.

Plenty on equipment, bows, sights, quivers, arrows, clothes, lures and scents, stands and blinds, etc.

The Complete Guide to Game Care & Cookery, 3rd Edition, by Sam Fadala, DBI Books, Inc., Northbrook, IL, 1994. 320 pp., illus. Paper covers. $18.95.

Over 500 photos illustrating the care of wild game in the field and at home with a separate recipe section providing over 400 tested recipes.

The Complete Smoothbore Hunter, by Brook Elliot, Winchester Press, Piscataway, NJ, 1986. 240 pp., illus. $16.95.

Advice and information on guns and gunning for all varieties of game.

Confessions of an Outdoor Maladroit, by Joel M. Vance, Amwell Press, Clinton, NJ, 1983. $20.00.

Anthology of some of the wildest, irreverent, and zany hunting tales ever.

*__Corn-Fed Giants,__ by Tom Miranda and Bermie Barringer, Moving Mountain Publishing, Crystal Lake, IA, 1995. 190 pp., illus. Paper covers. $14.95.

A step-by-step guide to locating and harvesting whitetails in farmland.

Covey Rises and Other Pleasures, by David H. Henderson, Amwell Press, Clinton, NJ, 1983. 155 pp., illus. $17.50.

A collection of essays and stories concerned with field sports.

Coveys and Singles: The Handbook of Quail Hunting, by Robert Gooch, A.S. Barnes, San Diego, CA, 1981. 196 pp., illus. $11.95.

The story of the quail in North America.

Coyote Hunting, by Phil Simonski, Stoneydale Press, Stevensville, MT, 1994. 126 pp., illus. Paper covers. $12.95.

Probably the most thorough "How-to-do-it" book on coyote hunting ever written.

Deer & Deer Hunting, by Al Hofacker, Krause Publications, Iola, WI, 1993. 208 pp., illus. $34.95.

Coffee-table volume packed full of how-to-information that will guide hunts for years to come.

Deer and Deer Hunting: The Serious Hunter's Guide, by Dr. Robert Wegner, Stackpole Books, Harrisburg, PA, 1984. 384 pp., illus. Paper covers. $16.95.

In-depth information from the editor of "Deer & Deer Hunting" magazine. Major bibliography of English language books on deer and deer hunting from 1838-1984.

Deer and Deer Hunting Book 2, by Dr. Robert Wegner, Stackpole Books, Harrisburg, PA, 1987. 400 pp., illus. Paper covers. $16.95.

Strategies and tactics for the advanced hunter.

Deer and Deer Hunting, Book 3, by Dr. Robert Wegner, Stackpole Books, Harrisburg, PA, 1990. 368 pp., ilus. $29.95.

This comprehensive volume covers natural history, deer hunting lore, profiles of deer hunters, and discussion of important issues facing deer hunters today.

The Deer Book, edited by Lamar Underwood, Amwell Press, Clinton, NJ, 1982. 480 pp., illus. $25.00.

An anthology of the finest stories on North American deer ever assembled under one cover.

Deer Hunter's Guide to Guns, Ammunition, and Equipment, by Edward A. Matunas, an Outdoor Life Book, distributed by Stackpole Books, Harrisburg, PA, 1983. 352 pp., illus. $24.95.

Where to hunt for North American deer. An authoritative guide that will help every deer hunter get maximum enjoyment and satisfaction from his sport.

Deer Hunting, by R. Smith, Stackpole Books, Harrisburg, PA, 1978. 224 pp., illus. Paper covers. $14.95.

A professional guide leads the hunt for North America's most popular big game animal.

Deer Hunting Coast to Coast, by C. Boddington and R. Robb, Safari Press, Long Beach, CA, 1989. 248 pp., illus. $24.95.

Join the authors as they hunt whitetail deer in eastern woodlot, southern swamps, midwestern prairies, and western river bottom; mule deer in badland, deserts, and high alpine basins; blacktails in oak grasslands and coastal jungles.

Doves and Dove Shooting, by Byron W. Dalrymple, New Win Publishing, Inc., Hampton, NJ, 1992. 256 pp., illus. $17.95.

The author reveals in this classic book his penchant for observing, hunting, and photographing this elegantly fashioned bird.

Dove Hunting, by Charley Dickey, Galahad Books, NY, 1976. 112 pp., illus. $10.00.

This indispensable guide for hunters deals with equipment, techniques, types of dove shooting, hunting dogs, etc.

Dreaming the Lion, by Thomas McIntyre, Countrysport Press, Traverse City, MI, 1994. 309 pp., illus. $35.00.

Reflections on hunting, fishing and a search for the wild. Twenty-three stories by *Sports Afield* editor, Tom McIntyre.

Drummer in the Woods, by Burton L. Spiller, Stackpole Books, Harrisburg, PA, 1990. 240 pp., illus. Soft covers. $16.95.

Twenty-one wonderful stories on grouse shooting by "the Poet Laureate of Grouse."

Duck Decoys and How to Rig Them, by Ralf Coykendall, revised by Ralf Coykendall, Jr., Nick Lyons Books, New York, NY, 1990. 137 pp., illus. Paper covers. $14.95.

Sage and practical advice on the art of decoying ducks and geese.

The Duck Hunter's Handbook, by Bob Hinman, revised, expanded, updated edition, Winchester Press, Piscataway, NJ, 1985. 288 pp., illus. $15.95.

The duck hunting book that has it all.

Early American Waterfowling, 1700's-1930, by Stephen Miller, Winchester Press, Piscataway, NJ, 1986. 256 pp., illus. $27.95.

Two centuries of literature and art devoted to the nation's favorite hunting sport—waterfowling.

Eastern Upland Shooting, by Dr. Charles C. Norris, Countrysport Press, Traverse City, MI, 1990. 424 pp., illus. $29.50.

A new printing of this 1946 classic with a new, original Foreword by the author's friend and hunting companion, renowned author George Bird Evans.

The Education of Pretty Boy, by Havilah Babcock, The Gunnerman Press, Auburn Hills, MI, 1985. 160 pp., illus. $19.95.

Babcock's only novel, a heartwarming story of an orphan boy and a gun-shy setter.

Elk and Elk Hunting, by Hart Wixom, Stackpole Books, Harrisburg, PA, 1986. 288 pp., illus. $29.95.

Your practical guide to fundamentals and fine points of elk hunting.

Elk Hunting in the Northern Rockies, by Ed. Wolff, Stoneydale Press, Stevensville, MT, 1984. 162 pp., illus. $18.95.

Helpful information about hunting the premier elk country of the northern Rocky Mountain states—Wyoming, Montana and Idaho.

Elk Hunting with the Experts, by Bob Robb, Stoneydale Press, Stevensville, MT, 1992. 176 pp., illus. Paper covers. $15.95.

A complete guide to elk hunting in North America by America's top elk hunting expert.

Elk Rifles, Cartridges and Hunting Tactics, by Wayne van Zwoll, Larsen's Outdoor Publishing, Lakeland, FL, 1992. 414 pp., illus. $24.95.

The definitive work on which rifles and cartridges are proper for hunting elk plus the tactics for hunting them.

Encyclopedia of Deer, by G. Kenneth Whitehead, Safari Press, Huntington, CA, 1993. 704 pp., illus. $130.00.

This massive tome will be the reference work on deer for well into the next century.

Fair Chase, by Jim Rikhoff, Amwell Press, Clinton, NJ, 1984. 323 pp., illus. $25.00.

A collection of hunting experiences from the Arctic to Africa, Mongolia to Montana, taken from over 25 years of writing.

Firelight, by Burton L. Spiller, Gunnerman Press, Auburn Hills, MI, 1990. 196 pp., illus. $19.95.

Enjoyable tales of the outdoors and stalwart companions.

The Formidable Game, by John H. Batten, Amwell Press, Clinton, NJ. 1983. 264 pp., illus. $40.00.

Big game hunting in India, Africa and North America by a world famous hunter.

Fresh Looks at Deer Hunting, by Byron W. Dalrymple, New Win Publishing, Inc., Hampton, NJ, 1993. 288 pp., illus. $24.95.

Tips and techniques abound throughout the pages of this latest work by Mr. Dalrymple whose name is synonymous with hunting proficiency.

From the Peace to the Fraser, by Prentis N. Gray, Boone and Crockett Club, Missoula, MT, 1995. 400 pp., illus. $49.95.

Newly discovered North American hunting and exploration journals from 1900 to 1930.

Fur Trapping In North America, by Steven Geary, Winchester Press, Piscataway, NJ, 1985. 160 pp., illus. Paper covers. $19.95.

A comprehensive guide to techniques and equipment, together with fascinating facts about fur bearers.

A Gallery of Waterfowl and Upland Birds, by Gene Hill, with illustrations by David Maass, Petersen Prints, Los Angeles, CA, 1978. 132 pp., illus. $44.95.

Gene Hill at his best. Liberally illustrated with 51 full-color reproductions of David Maass' finest paintings.

Game Care and Cookery, 3rd Edition, by Sam Fadala, DBI Books, Inc., Northbrook, IL, 1994. 320 pp., illus. Paper covers. $18.95.

Over 500 photos illustrating the care of wild game in the field and at home with a separate recipe section providing over 400 tested recipes.

Game in the Desert Revisited, by Jack O'Connor, Amwell Press, Clinton, NJ, 1984. 306 pp., illus. $27.50.

Reprint of a Derrydale Press classic on hunting in the Southwest

Getting the Most Out of Modern Waterfowling, by John O. Cartier, St. Martin's Press, NY, 1974. 396 pp., illus. $22.50.

The most comprehensive, up-to-date book on waterfowling imaginable.

Getting a Stand, by Miles Gilbert, Pioneer Press, Union City, TN, 1993. 204 pp., illus. Paper covers. $10.95.

An anthology of 18 short personal experiences by buffalo hunters of the late 1800s, specifically from 1870-1882.

Gordon MacQuarrie Trilogy: Stories of the Old Duck Hunters, by Gordon MacQuarrie, Willow Creek Press, Minocqua, WI, 1994. $49.00.

A slip-cased three volume set of masterpieces by one of America's finest outdoor writers.

The Grand Passage: A Chronicle of North American Waterfowling, by Gene Hill, et al., Countrysport Press, Traverse City, MI, 1990. 175 pp., illus. $39.50.

A new original anthology by renowned sporting authors on our world of waterfowling.

The Grand Spring Hunt for America's Wild Turkey Gobbler, by Bart Jacob with Ben Conger, Winchester Press, Piscataway, NJ, 1985. 176 pp., illus. $15.95.

The turkey book for novice and expert alike.

*__Grouse and Woodcock, A Gunner's Guide,__ by Don Johnson, Krause Publications, Iola, WI, 1995. 256 pp., illus. Paper covers. $14.95.

Find out what you need in guns, ammo, equipment, dogs and terrain.

Grouse of North America, by Tom Huggler, NorthWord Press, Inc., Minocqua, WI, 1990. 160 pp., illus. $29.95.

A cross-continental hunting guide.

Grouse Hunter's Guide, by Dennis Walrod, Stackpole Books, Harrisburg, PA, 1985. 192 pp., illus. $16.95.

Solid facts, observations, and insights on how to hunt the ruffed grouse.

Gun Clubs & Decoys of Back Bay & Currituck Sound, by Archie Johnson and Bud Coppedge, CurBac Press, Virginia Beach, VA, 1991. 224 pp., illus. $40.00.

This book identifies and presents a photographic history of over 100 hunting clubs and lodges on Back Bay, VA and Currituck Sound, NC.

Gunning for Sea Ducks, by George Howard Gillelan, Tidewater Publishers, Centreville, MD, 1988. 144 pp., illus. $14.95.

A book that introduces you to a practically untouched arena of waterfowling.

Heartland Trophy Whitetails, by Odie Sudbeck, HTW Publications, Seneca, KS, 1992. 130 pp., illus. $35.00.
A completely revised and expanded edition which includes over 500 photos of Boone & Crockett class whitetail, major mulies and unusual racks.

Horns in the High Country, by Andy Russell, Alfred A. Knopf, NY, 1973. 259 pp., illus. Paper covers. $12.95.
A many-sided view of wild sheep and their natural world.

How to Hunt, by Dave Bowring, Winchester Press, Piscataway, NJ, 1982. 208 pp., illus. Paper covers. $10.95; cloth, $15.00.
A basic guide to hunting big game, small game, upland birds, and waterfowl.

The Hunters and the Hunted, by George Laycock, Outdoor Life Books, New York, NY, 1990. 280 pp., illus. $34.95.
The pursuit of game in America from Indian times to the present.

A Hunter's Fireside Book, by Gene Hill, Winchester Press, Piscataway, NJ, 1972. 192 pp., illus. $16.95.
An outdoor book that will appeal to every person who spends time in the field—or who wishes he could.

A Hunter's Road, by Jim Fergus, Henry Holt & Co., NY, 1992. 290 pp. $22.50
A journey with gun and dog across the American uplands.

Hunt High for Rocky Mountain Goats, Bighorn Sheep, Chamois & Tahr, by Duncan Gilchrist, Stoneydale Press, Stevensville, MT, 1992. 192 pp., illus. Paper covers. $19.95.
The source book for hunting mountain goats.

The Hunter's Shooting Guide, by Jack O'Connor, Outdoor Life Books, New York, NY, 1982. 176 pp., illus. Paper covers. $5.95.
A classic covering rifles, cartridges, shooting techniques for shotguns/rifles/handguns.

The Hunter's World, by Charles F. Waterman, Winchester Press, Piscataway, NJ, 1983. 250 pp., illus. $29.95.
A classic. One of the most beautiful hunting books that has ever been produced.

*__Hunting Adventure of Me and Joe__, by Walt Prothero, Safari Press, Huntington Beach, CA, 1995. 220 pp., illus. $22.50.
A collection of the author's best and favorite stories in the vein of the great adventure storytellers.

Hunting America's Game Animals and Birds, by Robert Elman and George Peper, Winchester Press, Piscataway, NJ, 1975. 368 pp., illus. $16.95.
A how-to, where-to, when-to guide—by 40 top experts—covering the continent's big, small, upland game and waterfowl.

Hunting Boar, Hogs & Javelinas, by Bob Gooch, Atlantic Publishing Co., Tabor City, NC, 1989. 204 pp., illus. Paper covers. $9.95.
Thorough in explaining where, when and how to hunt these elusive creatures, along with a state-by-state hunting guide and a list of recipes.

Hunting Ducks and Geese, by Steven Smith, Stackpole Books, Harrisburg, PA, 1984. 160 pp., illus. $17.95.
Hard facts, good bets, and serious advice from a duck hunter you can trust.

Hunting for Handgunners, by Larry Kelly and J.D. Jones, DBI Books, Inc., Northbrook, IL, 1990. 256 pp., illus. Soft covers. $16.95.
A definitive work on an increasingly popular sport.

Hunting in Many Lands, edited by Theodore Roosevelt and George Bird Grinnell, et al., Boone & Crockett Club, Dumphries, VA, 1990. 447 pp., illus. $40.00.
A limited edition reprinting of the original Boone & Crockett Club 1895 printing.

Hunting Mature Bucks, by Larry L. Weishuhn, Krause Publications, Iola, WI, 1995. 256 pp., illus. Paper covers. $14.95.
One of North America's top white-tailed deer authorities shares his expertise on hunting those big, smart and elusive bucks.

Hunting North America's Big Game, by Bob Hagel, Stackpole Books, Harrisburg, PA, 1987. 220 pp., illus. $34.95.
Complete coverage on how to approach, track, and shoot game in different terrains.

Hunting Open-Country Mule Deer, by Dwight Schuh, Sage Press, Nampa, ID, 1989. 180 pp., illus. $18.95.
A guide taking Western bucks with rifle and bow.

Hunting Predators for Hides and Profits, by Wilf E. Pyle, Stoeger Publishing Co., So. Hackensack, NJ, 1985. 224 pp., illus. Paper covers. $11.95.
The author takes the hunter through every step of the hunting/marketing process.

Hunting the American Wild Turkey, by Dave Harbour, Stackpole Books, Harrisburg, PA, 1975. 256 pp., illus. $14.95.
The techniques and tactics of hunting North America's largest, and most popular, woodland game bird.

Hunting Trips in North America, by F.C. Selous, Wolfe Publishing Co., Prescott, AZ, 1988. 395 pp., illus. $52.00.
A limited edition reprint. Coverage of caribou, moose and other big game hunting in virgin wilds.

Hunting Trophy Whitetails, by David Morris, Stoneydale Press, Stevensville, MT, 1993. 483 pp., illus. $29.95.
This is one of the best whitetail books published in the last two decades. The author is the former editor of *North American Whitetail* magazine.

Hunting Western Deer, by Jim and Wes Brown, Stoneydale Press, Stevensville, MT, 1994. 174 pp., illus. Paper covers. $14.95.
A pair of expert Oregon hunters provide insight into hunting mule deer and blacktail deer in the western states.

Hunting Wild Boar in California, by Bob Robb, new revised edition, Larsen's Outdoor Publications, Lakeland, FL, 1994. 160 pp., illus. Paper covers. $14.95.
The most complete guide to hunting California's most popular big game animal on public and private land.

Hunting Wild Turkeys in the West, by John Higley, Stoneydale Press, Stevensville, MT, 1992. 154 pp., illus. Paper covers. $12.95.
Covers the basics of calling, locating and hunting turkeys in the western states.

Hunting with the Twenty-two, by Charles Singer Landis, R&R Books, Livonia, NY, 1994. 429 pp., illus. $45.00.
A miscellany of articles touching on the hunting and shooting of small game.

I Don't Want to Shoot an Elephant, by Havilah Babcock, The Gunnerman Press, Auburn Hills, MI, 1985. 184 pp., illus. $19.95.
Eighteen delightful stories that will enthrall the upland gunner for many pleasurable hours.

In Search of the Wild Turkey, by Bob Gooch, Greatlakes Living Press, Ltd., Waukegan, IL, 1978. 182 pp., illus. $9.95.
A state-by-state guide to wild turkey hot spots, with tips on gear and methods for bagging your bird.

Indian Hunts and Indian Hunters of the Old West, by Dr. Frank C. Hibben, Safari Press, Long Beach, CA, 1989. 228 pp., illus. $24.95.
Tales of some of the most famous American Indian hunters of the Old West as told to the author by an old Navajo hunter.

Jack O'Connor's Gun Book, by Jack O'Connor, Wolfe Publishing Company, Prescott, AZ, 1992. 208 pp. Hardcover. $26.00.
Jack O'Connor imparts a cross-section of his knowledge on guns and hunting. Brings back some of his writings that have here-to-fore been lost.

Jaybirds Go to Hell on Friday, by Havilah Babcock, The Gunnerman Press, Auburn Hills, MI, 1985. 149 pp., illus. $19.95.
Sixteen jewels that reestablish the lost art of good old-fashioned yarn telling.

Jim Dougherty's Guide to Bowhunting Deer, by Jim Dougherty, DBI Books, Inc., Northbrook, IL, 1992. 256 pp., illus. Paper covers. $17.95.
Dougherty sets down some important guidelines for bowhunting and bowhunting equipment.

Last Casts and Stolen Hunts, edited by Jim Casada and Chuck Wechsler, Countrysport Press, Traverse City, MI, 1994. 270 pp., illus. $29.95.
The world's best hunting and fishing stories by writers such as Zane Grey, Jim Corbett, Jack O'Connor, Archibald Rutledge and others.

A Listening Walk...and Other Stories, by Gene Hill, Winchester Press, Piscataway, NJ, 1985. 208 pp., illus. $15.95.
Vintage Hill. Over 60 stories.

Longbows in the Far North, by E. Donnall Thomas, Jr. Stackpole Books, Mechanicsburg, PA, 1994. 200 pp., illus. $16.95.
An archer's adventures in Alaska and Siberia.

*__The Longwalkers: 25 Years of Tracking the Northern Cougar__, by Jerry A. Lewis, Wolfe Publishing Co., Prescott, AZ, 1996. 140 pp., illus. Paper covers. $24.95.
Trek the snow-covered mountain forests of Idaho, Montana, British Columbia, and Alberta with the author as he follows cougars/mountain lions on foot, guided by his keen hounds.

Making Game: An Essay on Woodcock, by Guy De La Valdene, Willow Creek Press, Oshkosh, WI, 1985. 202 pp., illus. $35.00.
The most delightful book on woodcock yet published.

Mammoth Monarchs of North America, by Odie Sudbeck, HTW Publications, Seneca, KA, 1995. 288 pp., illus. $35.00.
This book reveals eye-opening big buck secrets.

Matching the Gun to the Game, by Clair Rees, Winchester Press, Piscataway, NJ, 1982. 272 pp., illus. $17.95.
Covers selection and use of handguns, blackpowder firearms for hunting, matching rifle type to the hunter, calibers for multiple use, tailoring factory loads to the game.

Measuring and Scoring North American Big Game Trophies, by Wm. H. Nesbitt and Philip L. Wright, The Boone and Crockett Club, Alexandria, VA, 1986. 176 pp., illus. $15.00.
The Boone and Crockett Club official scoring system, with tips for trophy evaluation.

*__Meditation on Hunting__, by Jose Ortego y Gasset, Wilderness Adventures Press, Bozeman, MT, 1996. 140 pp., illus. In a slipcase. $60.00.
The classic work on the philosophy of hunting.

Mixed Bag, by Jim Rikhoff, National Rifle Association of America, Wash., DC, 1981. 284 pp., illus. Paper covers. $9.95.
Reminiscences of a master raconteur.

Modern Pheasant Hunting, by Steve Grooms, Stackpole Books, Harrisburg, PA, 1982. 224 pp., illus. Paper covers. $10.95.
New look at pheasants and hunters from an experienced hunter who respects this splendid gamebird.

Modern Waterfowl Guns and Gunning, by Don Zutz, Stoeger Publishing Co., So. Hackensack, NJ, 1985. 224 pp., illus. Paper covers. $11.95.
Up-to-date information on the fast-changing world of waterfowl guns and loads.

Montana—Land of Giant Rams, by Duncan Gilchrist, Stoneydale Press Publishing Co., Stevensville, MT, 1990. 208 pp., illus. $19.95.
Latest information on Montana bighorn sheep and why so many Montana bighorn rams are growing to trophy size.

Montana—Land of Giant Rams, Volume 2, by Duncan Gilchrist, Outdoor Expeditions and Books, Corvallis, MT, 1992. 208 pp., illus. $34.95.
The reader will find stories of how many of the top-scoring trophies were taken.

More and Better Pheasant Hunting, by Steve Smith, Winchester Press, Piscataway, NJ, 1986. 192 pp., illus. $15.95.
Complete, fully illustrated, expert coverage of the bird itself, the dogs, the hunt, the guns, and the best places to hunt.

More Grouse Feathers, by Burton L. Spiller, Crown Publ., NY, 1972. 238 pp., illus. $25.00.
Facsimile of the original Derrydale Press issue of 1938. Guns and dogs, the habits and shooting of grouse, woodcock, ducks, etc. Illus. by Lynn Bogue Hunt.

More Tracks: 78 Years of Mountains, People & Happinesss, by Howard Copenhaver, Stoney dale Press, Stevensville, MT, 1992. 150 pp., illus. $18.95.
A collection of stories by one of the back country's best storytellers about the people who shared with Howard his great adventure in the high places and wild Montana country.

Mostly Huntin', by Bill Jordan, Everett Publishing Co., Bossier City, LA, 1987. 254 pp., illus. $21.95.
Jordan's hunting adventures in North America, Africa, Australia, South America and Mexico.

Mostly Tailfeathers, by Gene Hill, Winchester Press, Piscataway, NJ, 1975. 192 pp., illus. $15.95.
An interesting, general book about bird hunting.

Movin' Along with Charley Dickey, by Charlie Dickey, Winchester Press, Piscataway, NJ, 1985. 224 pp., illus. $15.95.
More wisdom, wild tales, and wacky wit from the Sage of Tallahassee.

"Mr. Buck": The Autobiography of Nash Buckingham, by Nash Buckingham, Countrysport Press, Traverse City, MI, 1990. 288 pp., illus. $39.50.
A lifetime of shooting, hunting, dogs, guns, and Nash's reflections on the sporting life, along with previously unknown pictures and stories written especially for this book.

Murry Burnham's Hunting Secrets, by Murry Burnham with Russell Tinsley, Winchester Press, Piscataway, NJ, 1984. 244 pp., illus. $17.95.
One of the great hunters of our time gives the reasons for his success in the field.

My Health is Better in November, by Havilah Babcock, University of S. Carolina Press, Columbia, SC, 1985. 284 pp., illus. $19.95.
Adventures in the field set in the plantation country and backwater streams of SC.

North American Big Game Animals, by Byron W. Dalrymple and Erwin Bauer, Outdoor Life Books/Stackpole Books, Harrisburg, PA, 1985. 258 pp., illus. $29.95.
Complete illustrated natural histories. Habitat, movements, breeding, birth and development, signs, and hunting.

North American Elk: Ecology and Management, edited by Jack Ward Thomas and Dale E. Toweill, Stackpole Books, Harrisburg, PA, 1982. 576 pp., illus. $39.95.
The definitive, exhaustive, classic work on the North American elk.

The North American Waterfowler, by Paul S. Bernsen, Superior Publ. Co., Seattle, WA, 1972. 206 pp. Paper covers. $9.95.
The complete inside and outside story of duck and goose shooting. Big and colorful, illustrations by Les Kouba.

Of Bears and Man, by Mike Cramond, University of Oklahoma Press, Norman, OK, 1986. 433 pp., illus. $29.95.

The author's lifetime association with bears of North America. Interviews with survivors of bear attacks.

The Old Man and the Boy, by Robert Ruark, Henry Holt & Co., New York, NY, 303 pp., illus. $24.95.

A timeless classic, telling the story of a remarkable friendship between a young boy and his grandfather as the hunt and fish together.

The Old Man's Boy Grows Older, by Robert Ruark, Henry Holt & Co., Inc., New York, NY, 1993. 300 pp., illus. $24.95.

The heartwarming sequel to the best-selling *The Old Man and the Boy.* A warm and rewarding book.

The Old Pro Turkey Hunter, by Gene Nunnery, Gene Nunnery, Meridian, MS, 1980. 144 pp., illus. $12.95.

True facts and old tales of turkey hunters.

*__Once Upon a Time,__ by Nash Buckingham, Beaver Dam Press, Brentwood, TN, 1995. 170 pp., illus. $29.50.

The Only Good Bear is a Dead Bear, by Jeanette Hortick Prodgers, Falcon Press, Helena, MT, 1986. 204 pp. Paper covers. $12.50.

A collection of the West's best bear stories.

Outdoor Pastimes of an American Hunter, by Theodore Roosevelt, Stackpole Books, Mechanicsburg, PA, 1994. 480 pp., illus. Paper covers. $16.95.

Stories of hunting big game in the West and notes about animal pursued and observed.

Outdoor Yarns & Outright Lies, by Gene Hill and Steve Smith, Stackpole Books, Harrisburg, PA, 1984. 168 pp., illus. $18.95.

Fifty or so stories by two good sports.

The Outlaw Gunner, by Harry M. Walsh, Tidewater Publishers, Cambridge, MD, 1973. 178 pp., illus. $22.95.

A colorful story of market gunning in both its legal and illegal phases.

*__Pear Flat Philosophies,__ by Larry Weishuhn, Safari Press, Huntington Beach, CA, 1995. 234 pp., illus. $24.95.

The author describes his more lighthearted adventures and funny anecdotes while out hunting.

Pheasant Days, by Chris Dorsey, Voyageur Press, Stillwater, MN, 1992. 233 pp., illus. $24.95.

The definitive resource on ringnecks. Includes everything from basic hunting techniques to the life cycle of the bird.

Pheasant Hunter's Harvest, by Steve Grooms, Lyons & Burford Publishers, New York, NY, 1990. 180 pp. $18.95.

A celebration of pheasant, pheasant dogs and pheasant hunting. Practical advice from a passionate hunter.

Pheasants of the Mind, by Datus Proper, Wilderness Adventures Press, Bozeman, MT, 1994. 154 pp., illus. $25.00.

No single title sums up the life of the solitary pheasant hunter like this masterful work.

Pinnell and Talifson: Last of the Great Brown Bear Men, by Marvin H. Clark, Jr., Great Northwest Publishing and Distributing Co., Spokane, WA, 19880. 224 pp., Illus. $39.95

The story of these famous Alaskan guides and some of the record bears taken by both of them.

Quail Hunting in America, by Tom Huggler, Stackpole Books, Harrisburg, PA, 1987. 288 pp., illus. $19.95.

Tactics for finding and taking bobwhite, valleys, Gambel's Mountain, scaled-blue, and Mearn's quail by season and habitat.

Quest for Giant Bighorns, by Duncan Gilchrist, Outdoor Expeditions and Books, Corvallis, MT, 1994. 224 pp., illus. Paper covers. $19.95.

How some of the most successful sheep hunters hunt and how some of the best bighorns were taken.

Radical Elk Hunting Strategies, by Mike Lapinski, Stoneydale Press Publishing Co., Stevensville, MT, 1988. 161 pp., illus. $18.95.

Secrets of calling elk in close.

Records of North American Big Game 1932, by Prentis N. Grey, Boone and Crockett Club, Dumfries, VA, 1988. 178 pp., illus. $79.95.

A reprint of the book that started the Club's record keeping for native North American big game.

Records of North American Whitetailed Deer, by the editors of the Boone and Crockett Club, Dumfries, VA, 1987. 256 pp., illus. Flexible covers. $15.00.

Contains data on 1293 whitetail trophies over the all-time record book minimum, listed and ranked by state or province and divided into typical and non-typical categories.

Ridge Runners & Swamp Rats, by Charles F. Waterman, Amwell Press, Clinton, NJ, 1983. 347 pp., illus. $25.00.

Tales of hunting and fishing.

The Rifles, the Cartridges, and the Game, by Clay Harvey, Stackpole Books, Harrisburg, PA, 1991. 254 pp., illus. $32.95.

Engaging reading combines with exciting photos to present the hunt with an intense level of awareness and respect.

Ringneck! Pheasants & Pheasant Hunting, by Ted Janes, Crown Publ., NY, 1975. 120 pp., illus. $15.95.

A thorough study of one of our more popular game birds.

Ruffed Grouse, edited by Sally Atwater and Judith Schnell, Stackpole Books, Harrisburg, PA, 1989. 370 pp., illus. $59.95.

Everything you ever wanted to know about the ruffed grouse. More than 25 wildlife professionals provided in-depth information on every aspect of this popular game bird's life. Lavishly illustrated with over 300 full-color photos.

*__Secret Strategies from North America's Top Whitetail Hunters,__ compiled by Nick Sisley, Krause Publications, Iola, WI, 1995. 256 pp., illus. Paper covers. $14.95.

Bow and gun hunters share their success stories.

Shadows of the Tundra, by Tom Walker, Stackpole Books, Harrisburg, PA, 1990. 192 pp., illus. $19.95.

Alaskan tales of predator, prey, and man.

Sheep Hunting in Alaska—The Dall Sheep Hunter's Guide, by Tony Russ, Outdoor Expeditions and Books, Corvallis, MT, 1994. 160 pp., illus. Paper covers. $19.95.

A how-to guide for the Dall sheep hunter.

Sheep & Sheep Hunting, by Jack O'Connor, Safari Press, Huntington Beach, CA, 1992. 308 pp., illus. $35.00.

A new printing of the definitive book on wild sheep.

Shorebirds: The Birds, The Hunters, The Decoys, by John M. Levinson & Somers G. Headley, Tidewater Publishers, Centreville, MD, 1991. 160 pp., illus. $49.95.

A thorough study of shorebirds and the decoys used to hunt them. Photographs of more than 200 of the decoys created by prominent carvers are shown.

Shots at Big Game, by Craig Boddington, Stackpole Books, Harrisburg, PA, 1989. 198 pp., illus. $24.95.

How to shoot a rifle accurately under hunting conditions.

*__Southern Deer & Deer Hunting,__ by Larry Weishuhn and Bill Bynum, Krause Publications, Iola, WI, 1995. 256 pp., illus. Paper covers. $14.95.

Mount a trophy southern whitetail on your wall with this firsthand account of stalking big bucks below the Mason-Dixon line.

Sport and Travel; East and West, by Frederick Courteney Selous, Wolfe Publishing Co., Prescott, AZ, 1988. 311 pp., illus. $29.00.

A limited edition reprint. One of the few books Selous wrote covering North American hunting. His daring in Africa is equalled here as he treks after unknown trails and wild game.

*__Spring Gobbler Fever,__ by Michael Hanback, Krause Publications, Iola, WI, 1996. 256 pp., illus. Paper covers. $15.95.

Your complete guide to spring turkey hunting.

Spring Turkey Hunting, by John M. McDaniel, Stackpole Books, Harrisburg, PA, 1986. 224 pp., illus. $21.95.

The serious hunter's guide.

Squirrels and Squirrel Hunting, by Bob Gooch. Tidewater Publ., Cambridge, MD, 1973. 148 pp., illus. $14.95.

A complete book for the squirrel hunter, beginner or old hand. Details methods of hunting, squirrel habitat, management, proper clothing, care of the kill, cleaning and cooking.

*__Stand Hunting for Whitetails,__ by Richard P. Smith, Krause Publications, Iola, WI, 1996. 256 pp., illus. Paper covers. $14.95.

The author explains the tricks and strategies for successful stand hunting.

*__The Still Hunter,__ by Theodore S. Van Dyke, The Pine Creek Historian, Gateway Press, Inc., Baltimore, MD, 1995. 397 pp., illustrated by Carl Rungius.

Facsimile reprint of this classic, both which contains a great deal of valuable information not only on the secrets of still hunting, but on all aspects of deer and deer hunting.

Strayed Shots and Frayed Lines, edited by John E. Howard, Amwell Press, Clinton, NJ, 1982. 425 pp., illus. $25.00.

Anthology of some of the finest, funniest stories on hunting and fishing ever assembled.

Successful Goose Hunting, by Charles L. Cadieux, Stone Wall Press, Inc., Washington, DC, 1986. 223 pp., illus. $24.95.

Here is a complete book on modern goose hunting by a lifetime waterfowler and professional wildlifer.

Taking Big Bucks, by Ed Wolff, Stoneydale Press, Stevensville, MT, 1987. 169 pp., illus. $18.95.

Solving the whitetail riddle.

Taking Chances in the High Country, compiled and with an introduction by Jim Rikhoff, The Amwell Press, Clinton, NJ, 1995. 411 pp., illus. In a slipcase. $85.00.

An anthology by some thirty stories by different authors on hunting sheep in the high country.

Taking More Birds, by Dan Carlisle and Dolph Adams, Lyons & Burford Publishers, New York, NY, 1993. 160 pp., illus. $19.95.

A practical handbook for success at Sporting Clays and wing shooting.

Tales of Alaska's Big Bears, by Jim Rearden, Wolfe Publishing Co., Prescott, AZ, 1989. 125 pp., illus. Soft covers. $12.95.

A collection of bear yarns covering nearly three-quarters of a century.

Tales of Quails 'n Such, by Havilah Babcock, University of S. Carolina Press, Columbia, SC, 1985. 237 pp. $19.95.

A group of hunting stories, told in informal style, on field experiences in the South in quest of small game.

They Left Their Tracks, by Howard Coperhaver, Stoneydale Press Publishing Co., Stevensville, MT, 1990. 190 pp., illus. $18.95.

Recollections of 60 years as an outfitter in the Bob Marshall Wilderness.

Timberdoodle, by Frank Woolner, Nick Lyons Books, N. Y., NY, 1987. 168 pp., illus. $18.95.

The classic guide to woodcock and woodcock hunting.

Track of the Kodiak, by Marvin H. Clark, Great Northwest Publishing and Distributing Co., Anchorage, AK, 1984. 224 pp., illus. $39.95.

A full perspective on Kodiak Island bear hunting.

Trail and Campfire, edited by George Bird Grinnel and Theodore Roosevelt, The Boone and Crockett Club, Dumfries, VA, 1989. 357 pp., illus. $39.50.

Reprint of the Boone and Crockett Club's 3rd book published in 1897.

Trail of the Eagle, by Bud Conkle, as told to Jim Rearden, Great Northwest Publishing & Distributing Co., Anchorage, AK, 1991. 280 pp., illus. $29.50.

Hunting Alaska with master guide Bud Conkle.

Trap & Skeet Shooting, 3rd Edition, edited by Chris Christian, DBI Books, Inc., Northbrook, IL, 1994. 288 pp., illus. Paper covers. $17.95.

A detailed look at the contemporary world of trap, Skeet and Sporting Clays.

Trophy Mule Deer: Finding & Evaluating Your Trophy, by Lance Stapleton, Outdoor Experiences Unlimited, Salem, OR, 1993. 290 pp., illus. Paper covers. $24.95.

The most comprehensive reference book on mule deer.

The Turkey Hunter's Book, by John M. McDaniel, Amwell Press, Clinton, NJ, 1980. 147 pp., illus. Paper covers. $9.95.

One of the most original turkey hunting books to be published in many years.

Turkey Hunter's Digest, Revised Edition, by Dwain Bland, DBI Books, Inc., Northbrook, IL, 1994. 256 pp., illus. Paper covers. $17.95.

A no-nonsense approach to hunting all five sub-species of the North American wild turkey that make up the Royal Grand Slam.

Turkey Hunting with Gerry Blair, by Gerry Blair, Krause Publications, Iola, WI, 1993. 280 pp., illus. $19.95.

Novice and veteran turkey hunters alike will enjoy this complete examination of the varied wild turkey subspecies, their environments, equipment needed to pursue them and the tactics to outwit them.

The Upland Equation: A Modern Bird-Hunter's Code, by Charles Fergus, Lyons $ Burford Publishers, New York, NY, 1996. 86 pp. $20.00

A book that deserves space in every sportsman's library. Observations based on firsthand experience.

*__The Upland Gunner's Book,__ edited by George Bird Evans, The Amwell Press, Clinton, NJ, 1985. 263 pp., illus. In slipcase. $27.50.

An anthology of the finest stories ever written on the sport of upland game hunting.

Varmint and Small Game Rifles and Cartridges, by various authors, Wolfe Publishing Co., Prescott, AZ, 1993. 228 pp., illus. Paper covers. $26.00.

This is a collection of reprints of articles originally appearing in Wolfe's *Rifle* and *Handloader* magazines from 1966 through 1990.

Wegner's Bibliography on Dear and Deer Hunting, by Robert Wegner, St. Hubert's Press, Deforest, WI, 1993. 333 pp., 16 full-page illustrations. $45.00.

A comprehensive annotated compilation of books in English pertaining to deer and their hunting 1413-1991.

Western Hunting Guide, by Mike Lapinski, Stoneydale Press Publishing Co., Stevensville, MT, 1989. 168 pp., illus. $18.95.

A complete where-to-go and how-to-do-it guide to Western hunting.

Whispering Wings of Autumn, by Gene Hill and Steve Smith, Wilderness Adventures Press, Bozeman, MT, 1994. 150 pp., illus. $29.00.

Hill and Smith, masters of hunting literature, treat the reader to the best stories of grouse and woodcock hunting.

Whitetail: The Ultimate Challenge, by Charles J. Alsheimer, Krause Publications, Iola, WI, 1995. 228 pp., illus. Paper covers. $14.95.

Learn deer hunting's most intriguing secrets—fooling deer using decoys, scents and calls—from America's premier authority.

The Wild Turkey Book, edited and with special commentary by J. Wayne Fears, Amwell Press, Clinton, NJ, 1982. 303 pp., illus. $22.50.

An anthology of the finest stories on wild turkey ever assembled under one cover.

The Wilderness Hunter, by Theodore Roosevelt, Wolfe Publishing Co., Prescott, AZ, 1994. 200 pp., illus. $25.00.

Reprint of a classic by one of America's most famous big game hunters.

Wilderness Hunting and Wildcraft, by Townsend Whelen, Wolfe Publishing Co., Prescott, AZ, 1988. 338 pp., illus. $39.00.

A limited edition reprint. Plentiful information on sheep and mountain hunting with horses and on life histories of big game animals.

The Wildfowler's Quest, by George Reiger, Lyons & Burford, Publishers, New York, NY, 1989. 320 pp., illus. $24.95.

A richly evocative look into one man's passionate pursuit of ducks, geese, turkey, woodcock, and other wildfowl all over the world.

Wings for the Heart, by Jerry A. Lewis, West River Press, Corvallis, MT, 1991. 324 pp., illus. Paper covers. $14.95.

A delightful book on hunting Montan's upland birds and waterfowl.

The Woodchuck Hunter, by Paul C. Estey, R&R Books, Livonia, NY, 1994. 135 pp., illus. $25.00.

This book contains information on woodchuck equipment, the rifle, telescopic sights and includes interesting stories.

Woodcock, by John Alden Knight, Gunnerman Press, Auburn Hills, MI, 1989. 160 pp., illus. $21.95.

A new printing of one of the finest books ever written on the subject.

Woodcock Shooting, by Steve Smith, Stackpole Books, Inc., Harrisburg, PA, 1988. 142 pp., illus. $16.95.

A definitive book on woodcock hunting and the characteristics of a good woodcock dog.

***World Record Whitetail: The Hanson Buck Story,** by Milo Hanson with Ian McMurchy, Krause Publications, Iola, WI, 1995. 144 pp., illus. Paper covers. $9.95.

How do you top a deer hunting record that stood for 80 years? Milo Hanson shares in his firsthand account of bagging the largest whitetail ever scored in the history of B&C measurements.

AFRICA/ASIA/ELSEWHERE

African Adventures, by J.F. Burger, Safari Press, Huntington Beach, CA, 1993. 222 pp., illus. $35.00.

The reader shares adventures on the trail of the lion, the elephant and buffalo.

The African Adventures: A Return to the Silent Places, by Peter Hathaway Capstick, St. Martin's Press, New York, NY, 1992. 220 pp., illus. $22.95.

This book brings to life four turn-of-the-century adventurers and the savage frontier they braved. Frederick Selous, Constatine "Iodine" Ionides, Johnny Boyes and Jim Sutherland.

African Camp-fire Nights, by J.E. Burger, Safari Press, Huntington Beach, CA, 1993. 192 pp., illus. $32.50.

In this book the author writes of the men who made hunting their life's profession.

African Hunter, by Baron Bror von Blixen-Finecke, St. Martin's Press, New York, NY, 1986. 284 pp., illus. $14.95.

Reprint of the scarce 1938 edition. An African hunting classic.

***African Hunter,** by James Mellon, Safari Press, Huntington Beach, CA, 1996. 522 pp., illus. Clothbound. $110.00; Paper covers. $65.00.

Regarded as the most comprehensive title ever published on African hunting.

African Hunting and Adventure, by William Charles Baldwin, Books of Zimbabwe, Bulawayo, 1981. 451 pp., illus. $75.00.

Facsimile reprint of the scarce 1863 London edition. African hunting and adventure from Natal to the Zambezi.

African Jungle Memories, by J.F. Burger, Safari Press, Huntington Beach, CA, 1993. 192 pp., illus. $32.50.

A book of reminiscences in which the reader is taken on many exciting adventures on the trail of the buffalo, lion, elephant and leopard.

African Rifles & Cartridges, by John Taylor, The Gun Room Press, Highland Park, NJ, 1977. 431 pp., illus. $35.00.

Experiences and opinions of a professional ivory hunter in Africa describing his knowledge of numerous arms and cartridges for big game. A reprint.

The African Safari, by P. Jay Fetner, St. Martin's Press, Inc., N. Y., NY, 1987. 700 pp., illus. $70.00.

A lavish, superbly illustrated, definitive work that brings together the practical elements of planning a safari with a proper appreciation for the animals and their environment.

African Twilight, by Robert F. Jones, Wilderness Adventure Press, Bozeman, MT, 1994. 208 pp., illus. $36.00.

Details the hunt, danger and changing face of Africa over a span of three decades.

After Big Game in Central Africa, by Edouard Foa, St. Martin's Press, New York, NY, 1989. 400 pp., illus. $16.95.

Reprint of the scarce 1899 edition. This sportsman covered 7200 miles, mostly on foot—from Zambezi delta on the east coast to the mouth of the Congo on the west.

A Man Called Lion: The Life and Times of John Howar "Pondoro" Taylor, by P.H. Capstick, Safari Press, Huntington Beach, CA, 1994. 240 pp., illus. $24.95.

With the help of Brian Marsh, an old Taylor acquaintance, Peter Capstick has cumulated over ten years of research into the life of this mysterious man.

Argali: High-Mountain Hunting, by Ricardo Medem, Safari Press, Huntington Beach, CA, 1995. 304 pp., illus. Limited, signed edition. $150.00.

Medem describes hunting seven different countries in the pursuit of sheep and other mountain game.

Bell of Africa, compiled and edited by Townsend Whelen, Safari Press, Huntington Beach, CA, 1990. 236 pp., illus. $24.95.

The autobiography of W.D.M. Bell compiled and edited by his lifetime friend from Bell's own papers.

Big Game and Big Game Rifles, by John Taylor, Safari Press, Huntington Beach, CA, 1993. 215 pp., illus. $24.95.

A classic by the man who probably knew more about ammunition and rifles for African game than any other hunter.

Big Game Hunting and Collecting in East Africa 1903-1926, by Kalman Kittenberger, St. Martin's Press, New York, NY, 1989. 496 pp., illus. $16.95.

One of the most heart stopping, charming and funny accounts of adventure in the Kenya Colony ever penned.

Big Game Hunting Around the World, by Bert Klineburger and Vernon W. Hurst, Exposition Press, Jericho, NY, 1969. 376 pp., illus. $30.00.

The first book that takes you on a safari all over the world.

Big Game Hunting in Asia, Africa, and Elsewhere, by Jacques Vettier, Trophy Room Books, Agoura, CA, 1993. 400 pp., illus. Limited, numbered edition. $150.00.

The first English language edition of the book that set a new standard in big game hunting book literature.

Big Game Hunting in North-Eastern Rhodesia, by Owen Letcher, St. Martin's Press, New York, NY, 1986. 272 pp., illus. $15.95.

A classic reprint and one of the very few books to concentrate on this fascinating area, a region that today is still very much safari country.

Big Game Shooting in Cooch Behar, the Duars and Assam, by The Maharajah of Cooch Behar, Wolfe Publishing Co., Prescott, AZ, 1993. 461 pp., illus. $118.00.

A reprinting of the book that has become legendary. This is the Maharajah's personal diary of killing 365 tigers.

The Book of the Lion, by Sir Alfred E. Pease, St. Martin's Press, New York, NY, 1986. 305 pp., illus. $15.95.

Reprint of the finest book ever published on the subject. The author describes all aspects of lion history and lion hunting, drawing heavily on his own experiences in British East Africa.

Chui! A Guide to Hunting the African Leopard, by Lou Hallamore and Bruce Woods, Trophy Room Books, Agoura, CA, 1994. 239 pp., illus. $75.00.

Tales of exciting leopard encounters by one of today's most respected pros.

Death in a Lonely Land, by Peter Capstick, St. Martin's Press, New York, NY, 1990. 284 pp., illus. $19.95.

Twenty-three stories of hunting as only the master can tell them.

Death in the Dark Continent, by Peter Capstick, St. Martin's Press, New York, NY, 1983. 238 pp., illus. $15.95.

A book that brings to life the suspense, fear and exhilaration of stalking ferocious killers under primitive, savage conditions, with the ever present threat of death.

Death in the Long Grass, by Peter Hathaway Capstick, St. Martin's Press, New York, NY, 1977. 297 pp., illus. $17.95.

A big game hunter's adventures in the African bush.

Death in the Silent Places, by Peter Capstick, St. Martin's Press, New York, NY, 1981. 243 pp., illus. $15.95.

The author recalls the extraordinary careers of legendary hunters such as Corbett, Karamojo Bell, Stigand and others.

Duck Hunting in Australia, by Dick Eussen, Australia Outdoor Publishers Pty Ltd., Victoria, Australia, 1994. 106 pp., illus. Paper covers. $17.95.

Covers the many aspects of duck hunting from hides to hunting methods.

East Africa and its Big Game, by Captain Sir John C. Willowghby, Wolfe Publishing Co., Prescott, AZ, 1990. 312 pp., illus. $52.00.

A deluxe limited edition reprint of the very scarce 1889 edition of a narrative of a sporting trip from Zanzibar to the borders of the Masai.

East of the Sun and West of the Moon, by Theodore and Kermit Roosevelt, Wolfe Publishing Co., Prescott, AZ, 1988. 284 pp., illus. $25.00.

A limited edition reprint. A classic on Marco Polo sheep hunting. A life experience unique to hunters of big game.

Elephant, by Commander David Enderby Blunt, The Holland Press, London, England, 1985. 260 pp., illus. $35.00.

A study of this phenomenal beast by a world-leading authority.

Elephant Hunting in East Equatorial Africa, by A. Neumann, St. Martin's Press, New York, NY, 1994. 455 pp., illus. $26.95.

This is a reprint of one of the rarest elephant hunting titles ever.

Elephant Hunting in Portuguese East Africa, by Jose Pardal, Safari Press, Huntington Beach, CA, 1990. 256 pp., illus. $60.00.

This book chronicles the hunting-life story of a nearly vanished breed of man—those who single-handedly hunted elephants for prolonged periods of time.

Elephants of Africa, by Dr. Anthony Hall-Martin, New Holland Publishers, London, England, 1987. 120 pp., illus. $75.00.

A superbly illustrated overview of the African elephant with reproductions of paintings by the internationally acclaimed wildlife artist Paul Bosman.

Encounters with Lions, by Jan Hemsing, Trophy Room books, Agoura, CA, 1995. 302 pp., illus. $75.00.

Some stories fierce, fatal, frightening and even humorous of when man and lion meet.

Ends of the Earth, by Roy Chapman Andrews, Wolfe Publishing Co., Prescott, AZ, 1988. 230 pp., illus. $27.00.

A limited edition reprint. Includes adventures in China and hunting in Mongolia. Andrews was a distinguished hunter and scout.

First Wheel, by Bunny Allen, Amwell Press, Clinton, NJ, 1984. Limited, signed and numbered edition in the NSFL "African Hunting Heritage Series." 292 pp., illus. $100.00.

A white hunter's diary, 1927-47.

The Fomidable Game, by John Batten, The Amwell Press, Clinton, NJ, 1994. 336 pp., illus. $40.00.

Batten and his wife cover the globe in search of the world's dangerous game. Includes a section on the development of the big bore rifle for formidable game.

The Great Arc of the Wild Sheep, by J.L. Clark, Safari Press, Huntington Beach, CA, 1994. 247 pp., illus. $24.95.

Perhaps the most complete work done on all the species and subspecies of the wild sheep of the world.

Gun and Camera in Southern Africa, by H. Anderson Bryden, Wolfe Publishing Co., Prescott, AZ, 1989. 201 pp., illus. $37.00.

A limited edition reprint. The year was 1893 and author Bryden wandered for a year in Bechuanaland and the Kalahari Desert hunting the white rhino, lechwe, eland, and more.

Horned Death, by John F. Burger, Safari Press, Huntington Beach, CA, 1992. 343 pp., illus. $35.00.

The classic work on hunting the African buffalo.

Horn of the Hunter, by Robert Ruark, Safari Press, Long Beach, CA, 1987. 315 pp., illus. $35.00.

Ruark's most sought-after title on African hunting, here in reprint.

***Hunters of Man,** by Capt. J. Brandt, Safari Press, Huntington Beach, CA, 1995. 242 pp., illus. $18.95.

True stories of man-eaters, man killers and rogues in Southeast Asia.

***Hunting Adventures Worldwide,** by Jack Atcheson, Stoneydale Press Publishing Co., Stevensville, MT, 1996. 256 pp., illus. $29.95.

A variety of stories and photographs chronicling Atcheson's lifetime as a hunter in many parts of the world.

***Hunting in Ethiopia, An Anthology,** by Tony Sanchez-Arino, Safari Press, Huntington Beach, CA, 1996. 350 pp., illus. Limited, signed and numbered edition. $135.00.

The finest selection of hunting stories ever compiled on hunting in this great game country.

Hunting in Many Lands, by Theodore Roosevelt and George Bird Grinnel, The Boone and Crockett Club, Dumfries, VA, 1987. 447 pp., illus. $40.00.

Limited edition reprint of this 1895 classic work on hunting in Africa, India, Mongolia, etc.

Hunting in the Sudan, An Anthology, compiled by Tony Sanchez-Arino, Safari Press, Huntington Beach, CA, 1992. 350 pp., illus. Limited, signed and numbered edition in a slipcase. $125.00.
The finest selection of hunting stories ever compiled on hunting in this great game country.

Hunting in Tanzania, An Anthology, by Tony Sanchez-Arino, Safari Press, Huntington Beach, CA, 1991. 416 pp., illus. Limited, signed and numbered edition, in a slipcase. $125.00.
The finest selection of hunting stories ever compiled on that great East African game country, Tanzania.

Hunting in Zimbabwe, An Anthology, by Tony Sanchez-Arino, Safari Press, Huntington Beach, CA, 1992. 350 pp., illus. Limited, signed and numbered edition, in a slipcase. $125.00.
The finest selection of hunting stories ever compiled on hunting in this great game country.

Hunting the Elephant in Africa, by Captain C.H. Stigand, St. Martin's Press, New York, NY, 1986. 379 pp., illus. $14.95.
A reprint of the scarce 1913 edition; vintage Africana at its best.

Jaguar Hunting in the Mato Grosso and Bolivia, by T. Almedia, Safari Press, Long Beach, CA, 1989. 256 pp., illus. $35.00.
Not since Sacha Siemel has there been a book on jaguar hunting like this one.

The Jim Corbett Collection, by Jim Corbett. Safari Press, Huntington, CA, 1991. 1124 pp., illus., five volumes in slipcase. $105.00.
This slip-cased set of Jim Corbett's works includes: *Jungle Lore, The Man-Eating Leopard of Rudraprayag, My India, Man-Eaters of Kumaon, Tree Tops,* and *Temple Tiger*.

Jim Corbett's India, stories selected by R.E. Hawkins, Oxford University Press, New York, NY, 1993. 250 pp. $24.95.
Stories and extracts from Jim Corbett's writings on tiger hunting by his publisher and editor.

Karamojo Safari, by W.D.M. Ball, Safari Press, Huntington Beach, CA, 1990. 288 pp., illus. $24.95.
The story of Bell's caravan travels through Karamojo, his exciting elephant hunts, and his life among the uncivilized and uncorrupted natives.

*__Killers in Africa,__ by Alexander Lake, Alexander Books, Alexander, NC, 1996. 256 pp., illus. Paper covers. $12.95.
The truth about animals lying in wait and hunters lying in print. For lovers of big-game hunting and tales of the glory of African adventures past.

King of the Wa-Kikuyu, by John Boyes, St. Martin Press, New York, NY, 1993. 240 pp., illus. $19.95.
In the 19th and 20th centuries, Africa drew to it a large number of great hunters, explorers, adventurers and rogues. Many have become legendary, but John Boyes (1874-1951) was the most legendary of them all.

Lake Ngami, by Charles Anderson, New Holland Press, London, England, 1987. 576 pp., illus. $35.00.
Originally published in 1856. Describes two expeditions into what is now Botswana, depicting every detail of landscape and wildlife.

Last Horizons: Hunting, Fishing and Shooting on Five Continents, by Peter Capstick, St. Martin's Press, New York, NY, 1989. 288 pp., illus. $19.95.
The first in a two volume collection of hunting, fishing and shooting tales from the selected pages of The American Hunter, Guns & Ammo and Outdoor Life.

The Last Ivory Hunter: The Saga of Wally Johnson, by Peter Capstick, St. Martin's Press, New York, NY, 1988. 220 pp., illus. $18.95.
A grand tale of African adventure by the foremost hunting author of our time. Wally Johnson spent half a century in Mozambique hunting white gold—ivory.

*__Last of the Few: Forty-Two Years of African Hunting,__ by Tony Sanchez-Arino, Safari Press, Huntington Beach, CA, 1996. 250 pp., illus. $85.00.
The story of the author's career with all the highlights that come from pursuing the unusual and dangerous animals that are native to Africa.

Last of the Ivory Hunters, by John Taylor, Safari Press, Long Beach, CA, 1990. 354 pp., illus. $29.95.
Reprint of the classic book "Pondoro" by one of the most famous elephant hunters of all time.

*__The Lost Classics,__ by Robert Ruark, Safari Press, Huntington Beach, CA, 1996. 260 pp., illus. $35.00.
The magazine stories that Ruark wrote in the 1950s and 1960s finally in print in book form.

The Man-Eaters of Tsavo, by Lt. Col. J.H. Patterson, St. Martin's Press, New York, NY, 1986. 346 pp., illus. $14.95.
A reprint of the scarce original book on the man-eating lions of Tsavo.

Memories of an African Hunter, by Denis D. Lyell, St. Martin's Press, New York, NY, 1986. 288 pp., illus. $15.95.
A reprint of one of the truly great writers on African hunting. A gripping and highly readable account of Lyell's many years in the African bush.

*__Mundjamba: The Life Story of an African Hunter,__ by Hugo Seia, Trophy Room Books, Agoura, CA, 1996. 400 pp., illus. Limited, numbered and signed by the author. $125.00.
An autobiography of one of the most respected and appreciated professional African hunters.

The Nature of the Game, by Ben Hoskyns, Quiller Press, Ltd., London, England, 1994. 160 pp., illus. $37.50.
The first complete guide to British, European and North American game.

One Happy Hunter, by George Barrington, Safari Press, Huntington Beach, CA, 1994. 240 pp., illus. $40.00.
A candid, straightforward look at safari hunting.

Peter Capstick's Africa: A Return to the Long Grass, by Peter Hathaway Capstick, St. Martin's Press, N. Y., NY, 1987. 213 pp., illus. $29.95.
A first-person adventure in which the author returns to the long grass for his own dangerous and very personal excursion.

The Recollections of an Elephant Hunter 1864-1875, by William Finaughty, Books of Zimbabwe, Bulawayo, Zimbabwe, 1980. 244 pp., illus. $85.00.
Reprint of the scarce 1916 privately published edition. The early game hunting exploits of William Finaughty in Matabeleland and Nashonaland.

Robert Ruark's Africa, by Robert Ruark, Countrysport Press, Inc., Traverse City, MI, 1991. 256 pp., illus. $29.50.
A new release of previously uncollected stories of the wanderings through Africa of this giant in American sporting literature.

Safari: A Chronicle of Adventure, by Bartle Bull, Viking/Penguin, London, England, 1989. 383 pp., illus. $40.00.
The thrilling history of the African safari, highlighting some of Africa's best-known personalities.

Safari Rifles: Double, Magazine Rifles and Cartridges for African Hunting, by Craig Boddington, Safari Press, Huntington Beach, CA, 1990. 416 pp., illus. $37.50.
A wealth of knowledge on the safari rifle. Historical and present double-rifle makers, ballistics for the large bores, and much, much more.

Safari: The Last Adventure, by Peter Capstick, St. Martin's Press, New York, NY, 1984. 291 pp., illus. $15.95.
A modern comprehensive guide to the African Safari.

Sands of Silence, by Peter H. Capstick, Saint Martin's Press, New York, NY, 1991. 224 pp., illus. $35.00.
Join the author on safari in Nambia for his latest big-game hunting adventures.

Shoot Straight and Stay Alive: A Lifetime of Hunting Experiences, by Fred Bartlett, Trophy Room Books, Argoura, CA, 1994. 262 pp., illus. $85.00.
A book written by a man who has left his mark on the maps of Africa's great gamelands.

Skyline Pursuits, by John Batten, The Amwell Press, Clinton, NJ, 1994. 372 pp., illus. $40.00.
A chronicle of Batten's own hunting adventures in the high country on four continents since 1928, traces a sheep hunting career that has accounted for both North American and International Grand Slams.

Solo Safari, by T. Cacek, Safari Press, Huntington Beach, CA, 1995. 270 pp., illus. $40.00.
Here is the story of Terry Cacek who hunted elephant, buffalo, leopard and plains game in Zimbabwe and Botswana on his own.

South Pacific Trophy Hunter, by Murray Thomas, Safari Press, Long Beach, CA, 1988. 181 pp., illus. $37.50.
A record of a hunter's search for a trophy of each of the 15 major game species in the South Pacific region.

*__Spiral-Horn Dreams,__ by Terry Wieland, Trophy Room Books, Agoura, CA, 1996. 362 pp., illus. Limited, numbered and signed by the author. $85.00.
Everyone who goes to hunt in Africa is looking for something; this is for those who go to hunt the spiral-horned antelope—the bongo, myala, mountain nyala, greater and lesser kudu, etc.

Sport on the Pamirs and Turkestan Steppes, by Major C.S. Cumberland, Moncrieff & Smith, Victoria, Autralia, 1992. 278 pp., illus. $45.00.
The first in a series of facsimile reprints of great trophy hunting books by Moncrieff & Smith.

Tales of the Big Game Hunters, selected and introduced by Kenneth Kemp, The Sportsman's Press, London, 1986. 209 pp., illus. $15.00.
Writings by some of the best known hunters and explorers, among them: Frederick Courteney Selous, R.G. Gordon Cumming, Sir Samuel Baker, and elephant hunters Neumann and Sutherland.

Theodore Roosevelt Outdoorsman, by R.L. Wilson, Trophy Room Books, Agoura, CA, 1994. 326 pp., illus. $85.00.
This book presents Theodore Roosevelt as a rancher, Rough Rider, Governor, President, naturalist and international big game hunter.

Those Were the Days, by Rudolf Sand, Safari Press, Huntington Beach, CA, 1993. 300 pp., illus. $100.00.
Travel with Rudolf Sand to the pinnacles of the world in his pursuit of wild sheep and goats.

Through the Brazilian Wilderness, by Theodore Roosevelt, Stackpole Books, Mechanicsburg, PA, 1994. 448 pp., illus. Paper covers. $16.95.
Adventure and drama in the South American jungle.

Trophy Hunter in Africa, by Elgin Gates, Safari Press, Huntington Beach, CA, 1994. 315 pp., illus. $29.95.
This is the story of one man's adventure in Africa's wildlife paradise.

Trophy Hunter in Asia, by Elgin Gates, Charger Productions, Inc., Capistrano Beach, CA, 1982. 272 pp., illus. $19.95.
Facinating high adventure with Elgin T. Gates one of America's top trophy hunters.

Uganda Safaris, by Brian Herne, Winchester Press, Piscataway, NJ, 1979. 236 pp., illus. $12.95.
The chronicle of a professional hunter's adventures in Africa.

The Wanderings of an Elephant Hunter, by W.D.M. Bell, Safari Press, Huntington Beach, CA, 1990. 187 pp., illus. $24.95.
The greatest of elephant books by the greatest-of-all elephant hunter.

A White Hunters Life, by Angus MacLagan, an African Heritage Book, published by Amwell Press, Clinton, NJ, 1983. 283 pp., illus. Limited, signed, and numbered deluxe edition, in slipcase. $100.00.
True to life, a sometimes harsh yet intriguing story.

Wild Sports of Southern Africa, by William Cornwallis Harris, New Holland Press, London, England, 1987. 376 pp., illus. $35.00.
Originally published in 1863, describes the author's travels in Southern Africa.

*__With a Gun in Good Country,__ by Ian Manning, Trophy Room Books, Agoura, CA, 1996. Limited, numbered and signed by the author. $85.00.
A book written about that splendid period before the poaching onslaught which almost closed Zambia and continues to the granting of her independence. It then goes on to recount Manning's experiences in Botswana, Congo, and briefly in South Africa.

RIFLES

The Accurate Varmint Rifle, by Boyd Mace, Precision Shooting, Inc., Whitehall, NY, 1991. 184 pp., illus. $24.95.
A long overdue and long needed work on what factors go into the selection of components for and the susequent assembly of...the accurate varmint rifle.

The AK-47 Assault Rifle, Desert Publications, Cornville, AZ, 1981. 150 pp., illus. Paper covers. $10.00.
Complete and practical technical information on the only weapon in history to be produced in an estimated 30,000,000 units.

*__American Hunting Rifles: Their Application in the Field for Practical Shooting,__ by Craig Boddington, Safari Press, Huntington Beach, CA, 1996. 446 pp., illus. First edition, limited, signed and slipcased. $85.00. Second printing trade edition. $35.00.
Covers all the hunting rifles and calibers that are needed for North America's diverse game,

The AR-15/M16, A Practical Guide, by Duncan Long. Paladin Press, Boulder, CO, 1985. 168 pp., illus. Paper covers. $16.95.
The definitive book on the rifle that has been the inspiration for so many modern assault rifles.

*__Assault Weapons, 4th Edition,__ by Jack Lewis, DBI Books, Inc., Northbrook, IL, 1996. 256 pp., illus. Paper covers. $19.95.
An in-depth look at the history and uses of these arms.

Australian Military Rifles & Bayonets, 200 Years of, by Ian Skennerton, I.D.S.A. Books, Piqua, OH, 1988. 124 pp., 198 illus. Paper covers. $19.50.

Australian Service Machineguns, 100 Years of, by Ian Skennerton, I.D.S.A. Books, Piqua, OH, 1989. 122 pp., 150 illus. Paper covers. $19.50.

The Big-Bore Rifle, by Michael McIntosh, Countrysport Press, Traverse City, MI, 1990. 224 pp., illus. $39.95.
The book of fine magazine and double rifles 375 to 700 calibers.

The Big Game Rifle, by Jack O'Connor, Safari Press, Huntington Beach, CA, 1994. 370 pp., illus. $37.50.
An outstanding description of every detail of construction, purpose and use of the big game rifle.

Big Game Rifles and Cartridges, by Elmer Keith, reprint edition by The Gun Room Press, Highland Park, NJ, 1984. 161 pp., illus. $29.95.
Reprint of Elmer Keith's first book, a most original and accurate work on big game rifles and cartridges.

Black Powder Hobby Gunsmithing, by Sam Fadala and Dale Storey, DBI Books, Inc., Northbrook, IL, 1994. 256 pp., illus. Paper covers. $18.95.
A how-to-guide for gunsmithing blackpowder pistols, rifles and shotguns from two men at the top of their respective fields.

The Black Rifle, M16 Retrospective, R. Blake Stevens and Edward C. Ezell, Collector Grade Publications, Toronto, Canada, 1987. 400 pp., illus. $59.95
The complete story of the M16 rifle and its development.

Bolt Action Rifles, 3rd Edition, edited by Frank de Haas, DBI Books, Inc., Northbrook, IL, 1995. 576 pp., illus. Paper covers. $24.95.
A revised edition of the most definitive work on all major bolt-action rifle designs.

The Book of the Garand, by Maj.-Gen. J.S. Hatcher, The Gun Room Press, Highland Park, NJ, 1977. 292 pp., illus. $26.95.
A new printing of the standard reference work on the U.S. Army M1 rifle.

The Book of the Twenty-Two: The All American Caliber, by Sam Fadala, Stoeger Publishing Co., So. Hackensack, NJ, 1989. 288 pp., illus. Soft covers. $16.95.
The All American Caliber from BB caps up to the powerful 226 Barnes. It's about ammo history, plinking, target shooting, and the quest for the one-hole group.

British Military Martini, Treatise on the, Vol. 1, by B.A. Temple and Ian Skennerton, I.D.S.A. Books, Piqua, OH, 1983. 256 pp., 114 illus. $40.00.

British Military Martini, Treatise on the, Vol. 2, by B.A. Temple and Ian Skennerton, I.D.S.A. Books, Piqua, OH, 1989. 213 pp., 135 illus. $40.00.

British .22RF Training Rifles, by Dennis Lewis and Robert Washburn, Excaliber Publications, Latham, NY, 1993. 64 pp., illus. Paper covers. $10.95.
The story of Britain's training rifles from the early Aiming Tube models to the post-WWII trainers.

Combat Rifles of the 21st Century, by Duncan Long, Paladin Press, Boulder, CO, 1991. 115 pp., illus. Paper covers. $16.50.
An inside look at the U.S. Army's program to develop a super advanced combat rifle to replace the M16.

The Complete AR15/M16 Sourcebook, by Duncan Long, Paladin Press, Boulder, CO, 1993. 232 pp., illus. Paper covers. $35.00.
The latest development of the AR15/M16 and the many spin-offs now available, selective-fire conversion systems for the 1990s, the vast selection of new accessories.

Exploded Long Gun Drawings, The Gun Digest Book of, edited by Harold A. Murtz, DBI Books, Inc., Northbrook, IL, 512 pp., illus. Paper covers. $20.95.
Containing almost 500 rifle and shotgun exploded drawings. An invaluable aid to both professionals and hobbyists.

The FAL Rifle, by R. Blake Stevens and Jean van Rutten, Collector Grade Publications, Cobourg, Canada, 1993. 848 pp., illus. $129.95.
Originally published in three volumes, this classic edition covers North American, UK and Commonwealth and the metric FAL's.

The Fighting Rifle, by Chuck Taylor, Paladin Press, Boulder, CO, 1983. 184 pp., illus. Paper covers. $20.00.
The difference between assault and battle rifles and auto and light machine guns.

Firearms Assembly/Disassembly Part III: Rimfire Rifles, Revised Edition, The Gun Digest Book of, by J. B. Wood, DBI Books, Inc., Northbrook, IL., 1994. 480 pp., illus. Paper covers. $19.95.
Covers 65 popular rimfires plus over 100 variants, all cross-referenced in the index.

Firearms Assembly/Disassembly Part IV: Centerfire Rifles, Revised Edition, The Gun Digest Book of, , by J.B. Wood, DBI Books, Inc., Northbrook, IL, 1991. 480 pp., illus. Paper covers. $19.95.
Covers 54 popular centerfire rifles plus 300 variants. The most comprehensive and professional presentation available to either hobbyist or gunsmith.

F.N.-F.A.L. Auto Rifles, Desert Publications, Cornville, AZ, 1981. 130 pp., illus. Paper covers. $13.95.
A definitive study of one of the free world's finest combat rifles.

The Hammerless Double Rifle, by Alexander Gray, Wolfe Publishing Co., Prescott, AZ, 1994. 154 pp., illus. $39.50.
The history, design, construction and maintenance are explored for a better understanding of these firearms.

Hints and Advice on Rifle-Shooting, by Private R. McVittie with new introductory material by W.S. Curtis, W.S. Curtis Publishers, Ltd., Clwyd, England, 1993. 32 pp. Paper covers. $10.00.
A reprint of the original 1886 London edition.

The History and Development of the M16 Rifle and Its Cartridge, by David R. Hughes, Armory Publications, Oceanside, CA, 1990. 294 pp., illus. $49.95.
Study of small caliber rifle development culminating in the M16 with encyclopedic coverage of the .223/5.56mm cartridge.

***Hunting with the .22,** by C.S. Landis, R&R Books, Livonia, NY, 1995. 429 pp., illus. $45.00.
A reprinting of the classical work on .22 rifles.

Illustrated Handbook of Rifle Shooting, by A.L. Russell, Museum Restoration Service, Alexandria Bay, NY, 1992. 194 pp., illus. $24.50.
A new printing of the 1869 edition by one of the leading military marksman of the day.

Keith's Rifles for Large Game, by Elmer Keith, The Gun Room Press, Highland Park, NJ, 1986. 406 pp., illus. $39.95.
Covers all aspects of selecting, equipping, use and care of high power rifles for hunting big game, especially African.

Know Your M1 Garand, by E. J. Hoffschmidt, Blacksmith Corp., Southport, CT, 1975, 84 pp., illus. Paper covers. $9.95.
Facts about America's most famous infantry weapon. Covers test and experimental models, Japanese and Italian copies, National Match models.

Know Your Ruger 10/22 Carbine, by William E. Workman, Blacksmith Corp., Chino Valley, AZ, 1991. 96 pp., illus. Paper covers. $9.95.
The story and facts about the most popular 22 autoloader ever made.

The Lee Enfield No. 1 Rifles, by Alan M. Petrillo, Excaliber Publications, Latham, NY, 1992. 64 pp., illus. Paper covers. $10.95.
Highlights the SMLE rifles from the Mark 1-VI.

The Lee Enfield Number 4 Rifles, by Alan M. Petrillo, Excalibur Publications, Latham, NY, 1992. 64 pp., illus. Paper covers. $10.95.
A pocket-sized, bare-bones reference devoted entirely to the .303 World War II and Korean War vintage service rifle.

The Lee Enfield Story, by Ian Skennerton, I.D.S.A. Books, Piqua, OH, 1993. 504 pp., nearly 1,000 illus. $59.95.

The Lee Enfield Story, Deluxe Presentation Edition by Ian Skennerton, I.D.S.A. Books, Piqua, OH, 1993. 504 pp., nearly 1,000 illus. Leather cover. $150.00.

Legendary Sporting Rifles, by Sam Fadala, Stoeger Publishing Co., So. Hackensack, NJ, 1992. 288 pp., illus. Paper covers. $16.95.
Covers a vast span of time and technology beginning with the Kentucky Long-rifle.

***The Li'l M1 .30 Cal. Carbine,** by Duncan Long, Desert Publications, El Dorado, AZ, 1995. 203 pp., illus. Paper covers. $14.95.
Traces the history of this little giant from its original creation.

M14/M14A1 Rifles and Rifle Markmanship, Desert Publications, El Dorado, AZ, 1995. 236 pp., illus. Paper covers. $16.95.
Contains a detailed description of the M14 and M14A1 rifles and their general characteristics, procedures for disassembly and assembly, operating and functioning of the rifles, etc.

The M-14 Rifle, facsimile reprint of FM 23-8, Desert Publications, Cornville, AZ, 50 pp., illus. Paper $7.95.
Well illustrated and informative reprint covering the M-14 and M-14E2.

Military Bolt Action Rifles, 1841-1918, by Donald B. Webster, Museum Restoration Service, Alexander Bay, NY, 1993. 150 pp., illus. $34.50.
A photographic survey of the principal rifles and carbines of the European and Asiatic powers of the last half of the 19th century and the first years of the 20th century.

Military and Sporting Rifle Shooting, by Captain E.C. Crossman, Wolfe Publishing Co., Prescott, AZ, 1988. 449 pp., illus. $45.00.
A limited edition reprint. A complete and practical treatise covering the use of rifles.

The Mini-14, by Duncan Long, Paladin Press, Boulder, CO, 1987. 120 pp., illus. Paper covers. $12.00.
History of the Mini-14, the factory-produced models, specifications, accessories, suppliers, and much more.

***Mr. Single Shot's Book of Rifle Plans,** by Frank de Haas, Mark de Haas, Orange City, IA, 1996. 85 pp., illus. Paper covers. $22.50.
Contains complete and detailed drawings, plans and instructions on how to build four different and unique breech-loading single shot rifles of the author's own proven design.

M1 Carbine Owner's Manual, M1, M2 & M3 .30 Caliber Carbines, Firepower Publications, Cornville, AZ, 1984. 102 pp., illus. Paper covers. $10.95.
The complete book for the owner of an M1 Carbine.

***The M1 Garand Serial Numbers & Data Sheets,** by Scott A. Duff, Scott A. Duff, Export, PA, 1995. 101 pp. Paper covers. $9.95.
This pocket reference book includes serial number tables and data sheets on the Springfield Armory, Gas Trap Rifles, Gas Port Rifles, Winchester Repeating Arms, International Harvester and H&R Arms Co. and more.

***More Single Shot Rifles and Actions,** by Frank de Haas, Mark de Haas, Orange City, IA, 1996. 146 pp., illus. Paper covers. $22.50.
Covers 45 different single shot rifles. Includes the history plus photos, drawings and personal comments.

The Muzzle-Loading Rifle...Then and Now, by Walter M. Cline, National Muzzle Loading Rifle Association, Friendship, IN, 1991. 161 pp., illus. $32.00.
This extensive compilation of the muzzleloading rifle exhibits accumulative preserved data concerning the development of the "hallowed old arms of the Southern highlands."

The No. 4 (T) Sniper Rifle: An Armourer's Perspective, by Peter Laidler with Ian Skennerton, I.D.S.A. Books, Piqua, OH, 1993. 125 pp., 75 illus. Paper covers. $19.95.

Notes on Rifle-Shooting, by Henry William Heaton, reprinted with a new introduction by W.S. Curtis, W.S. Curtis Publishers, Ltd., Clwyd, England, 1993. 89 pp. $19.95.
A reprint of the 1864 London edition. Captain Heaton was one of the great rifle shots from the earliest days of the Volunteer Movement.

The Pennsylvania Rifle, by Samuel E. Dyke, Sutter House, Lititz, PA, 1975. 61 pp., illus. Paper covers. $5.00.
History and development, from the hunting rifle of the Germans who settled the area. Contains a full listing of all known Lancaster, PA, gunsmiths from 1729 through 1815.

Police Rifles, by Richard Fairburn, Paladin Press, Boulder, CO, 1994. 248 pp., illus. Paper covers. $30.00.
Selecting the right rifle for street patrol and special tactical situations.

***The Poor Man's Sniper Rifle,** by D. Boone, Paladin Press, Boulder, CO, 1995. 152 pp., illus. Paper covers. $14.95.
Here is a complete plan for converting readily available surplus military rifles to high-performance sniper weapons.

A Potpourri of Single Shot Rifles and Actions, by Frank de Haas, Mark de Haas, Ridgeway, MO, 1993. 153 pp., illus. Paper covers. $22.50.
The author's 6th book on non-bolt-action single shots. Covers more than 40 single-shot rifles in historical and technical detail.

The Remington 700, by John F. Lacy, Taylor Publishing Co., Dallas, TX, 1990. 208 pp., illus. $44.95.
Covers the different models, limited editions, chamberings, proofmarks, serial numbers, military models, and much more.

The Revolving Rifles, by Edsall James, Pioneer Press, Union City, TN, 1975. 23 pp., illus. Paper covers. $2.50.
Valuable information on revolving cylinder rifles, from the earliest matchlock forms to the latest models of Colt and Remington.

Rifle Guide, by Sam Fadala, Stoeger Publishing Co., S. Hackensack, NJ, 1993. 288 pp., illus. Paper covers. $16.95.
This comprehensive, fact-filled book beckons to both the seasoned rifleman as well as the novice shooter.

The Rifle: Its Development for Big-Game Hunting, by S.R. Truesdell, Safari Press, Huntington Beach, CA, 1992. 274 pp., illus. $35.00.
The full story of the development of the big-game rifle from 1834-1946.

Rifleman's Handbook: A Shooter's Guide to Rifles, Reloading & Results, by Rick Jamison, NRA Publications, Washington, DC, 1990. 303 pp., illus. $21.95.
Helpful tips on precision reloading, how to squeeze incredible accuracy out of an "everyday" rifle, etc.

***The Rifleman's Rifle,** by Roger Rule, Sherwoods, Beverly Hills, CA, 1996. 368 pp., illus. $79.95
The definitive book on the Model 70 Winchester with over 500 photographs many, in full color.

Riflesmithing, The Gun Digest Book of, by Jack Mitchell, DBI Books, Inc., Northbrook, IL, 1982. 256 pp., illus. Paper covers. $16.95.
Covers tools, techniques, designs, finishing wood and metal, custom alterations.

Rifles of the World, by John Walter, DBI Books, Inc., Northbrook, IL, 1993. 320 pp., illus. Paper covers. $20.95.
Compiled as a companion volume to *Pistols of the World*, this brand new reference work covers all centerfire military and commercial rifles produced from the perfection of the metal-case cartridge in the 1870's to the present time.

Ned H. Roberts and the Schuetzen Rifle, edited by Gerald O. Kelver, Brighton, CO, 1982. 99 pp., illus. $15.00.
A compilation of the writings of Major Ned H. Roberts which appeared in various gun magazines.

The Ruger 10/22, by William E. Workman, Krause Publications, Iola, WI, 1994. 304 pp., illus. Paper covers. $19.95.
Learn all about the most popular, best-selling and perhaps best-built 22 caliber semi-automatic rifles of all time.

Schuetzen Rifles, History and Loading, by Gerald O. Kelver, Gerald O. Kelver, Publisher, Brighton, CO, 1972. Illus. $15.00.
Reference work on these rifles, their bullets, loading, telescopic sights, accuracy, etc. A limited, numbered ed.

Semi-Auto Rifles: Data and Comment, edited by Robert W. Hunnicutt, The National Rifle Association, Washington, DC, 1988. 156 pp., illus. Paper covers. $15.95.
A book for those who find military-style self-loading rifles interesting for their history, intriguing for the engineering that goes into their design, and a pleasure to shoot.

Shooting the Blackpowder Cartridge Rifle, by Paul A. Matthews, Wolfe Publishing Co., Prescott, AZ, 1994. 129 pp., illus. Paper covers. $22.50.
A general discourse on shooting the blackpowder cartridge rifle and the procedure required to make a particular rifle perform.

Single-Shot Actions, Their Design and Construction, by Frank and Mark Delisse, de Haas Books, Orange City, IA 1991. 247 pp., illus. $45.00.
Covers the best single shot rifles of the past plus a potpourri of modern single shot rifle actions.

Single-Shot Rifle Finale, by James Grant, Wolfe Publishing Co., Prescott, AZ, 1992. 556 pp., illus. $36.00.
The master's 5th book on the subject and his best.

Single Shot Rifles and Actions, by Frank de Haas, Orange City, IA, 1990. 352 pp., illus. Soft covers. $27.00.
The definitive book on over 60 single shot rifles and actions.

Sixty Years of Rifles, by Paul A. Matthews, Wolfe Publishing Co., Prescott, AZ, 1991. 224 pp., illus. $19.50.
About rifles and the author's experience and love affair with shooting and hunting.

S.L.R.—Australia's F.N. F.A.L. by Ian Skennerton and David Balmer, I.D.S.A. Books, Piqua, OH, 1989. 124 pp., 100 illus. Paper covers. $19.50.

Small Arms Identification Series, No. 2—.303 Rifle, No. 4 Marks I, & I*, Marks 1/2, 1/3 & 2, by Ian Skennerton, I.D.S.A. Books, Piqua, OH, 1994. 48 pp. $9.50.

Small Arms Identification Series, No. 3—9mm Austen Mk I & 9mm Owen Mk I Sub-Machine Guns, by Ian Skennerton, I.D.S.A. Books, Piqua, OH, 1994. 48 pp. $9.50.

Small Arms Identification Series, No. 4—.303 Rifle, No. 5 Mk I, by Ian Skennerton, I.D.S.A. Books, Piqua, OH, 1994. 48 pp. $9.50.

Small Arms Identification Series, No. 5—.303-in. Bren Light Machine Gun, by Ian Skennerton, I.D.S.A. Books, Piqua, OH, 1994. 48 pp. $9.50.

Small Arms Series, No. 1 DeLisle's Commando Carbine, by Ian Skennerton, I.D.S.A. Books, Piqua, OH, 1981. 32 pp., 24 illus. $9.00.

Small Arms Identification Series, No. 1—.303 Rifle, No. 1 S.M.L.E. Marks III and III*, by Ian Skennerton, I.D.S.A. Books, Piqua, OH, 1981. 48 pp. $9.50.

The Springfield Rifle M1903, M1903A1, M1903A3, M1903A4, Desert Publications, Cornville, AZ, 1982. 100 pp., illus. Paper covers. $12.00.
Covers every aspect of disassembly and assembly, inspection, repair and maintenance.

*__Still More Single Shot Rifles,__ by James J. Grant, Pioneer Press, Union City, TN, 1995. 211 pp., illus. $27.50.
This is Volume Four in a series of Single-Shot Rifles by America's foremost authority. It gives more in-depth information on those single-shot rifles which were presented in the first three books.

The Sturm, Ruger 10/22 Rifle and .44 Magnum Carbine, by Duncan Long, Paladin Press, Boulder, CO, 1988. 108 pp., illus. Paper covers. $12.00.
An in-depth look at both weapons detailing the elegant simplicity of the Ruger design. Offers specifications, troubleshooting procedures and ammunition recommendations.

Successful Rifle Shooting, by David Parish, Trafalgar Square, N. Pomfret, VT, 1993. 250 pp., illus. $39.95.
For the beginner and advanced shooter as well. Each position and firing the shot are closely examined as is each stage of entry and participation in competition.

*__Target Rifle in Australia,__ by J.E. Corcoran, R&R, Livonia, NY, 1996. 160 pp., illus. $40.00.
A most interesting study of the evolution of these rifles from 1860 - 1900. British rifles from the percussion period through the early smokeless era are discussed.

To the Dreams of Youth: The .22 Caliber Single Shot Winchester Rifle, by Herbert Houze, Krause Publications, Iola, WI, 1993. 208 pp., illus. $34.95.
A thorougly researched history of the 22-caliber Winchester single shot rifle, including interesting photographs.

U.S. Marine Corps AR15/M16 A2 Manual, reprinted by Desert Publications, El Dorado, AZ, 1993. 262 pp., illus. Paper covers. $16.95.
A reprint of TM05538C-23&P/2, August, 1987. The A-2 manual for the Colt AR15/M16.

U.S. Rifle M14—From John Garand to the M21, by R. Blake Stevens, Collector Grade Publications, Inc., Toronto, Canada, revised second edition, 1991. 350 pp., illus. $49.50.
A classic, in-depth examination of the development, manufacture and fielding of the last wood-and-metal ("lock, stock, and barrel") battle rifle to be issued to U.S. troops.

War Baby!: The U.S. Caliber 30 Carbine, Volume I, by Larry Ruth, Collector Grade Publications, Toronto, Canada, 1992. 512 pp., illus. $69.95.
Volume 1 of the in-depth story of the phenomenally popular U.S. caliber 30 carbine. Concentrates on design and production of the military 30 carbine during World War II.

War Baby Comes Home: The U.S. Caliber 30 Carbine, Volume 2, by Larry Ruth, Collector Grade Pulications, Toronto, Canada, 1993. 386 pp., illus. $49.95.
The triumphant competion of Larry Ruth's two-volume in-depth series on the most popular U.S. military small arm in history.

The Winchester Model 94: The First 100 Years, by Robert C. Renneberg, Krause Publications, Iola, WI, 1991. 207 pp., illus. $34.95.
Covers the design and evolution from the early years up to today.

SHOTGUNS

Advanced Combat Shotgun: The Stress Fire Concept, by Massad Ayoob, Police Bookshelf, Concord, NH, 1993. 197 pp., illus. Paper covers. $9.95.
Advanced combat shotgun fighting for police.

The American Shotgun, by Charles Askins, Wolfe Publishing Co., Prescott, AZ, 1988. 321 pp., illus. $39.00.
A limited edition reprint. Askins covers shotguns and patterning extremely well.

The American Shotgun, by David F. Butler, edited by C. Kenneth Ramage, Lyman Publications, Middlefield, CT, 1973. 243 pp., illus. Paper covers. $14.95.
A comprehensive history of the American smoothbore's evolution from Colonial times to the present day.

American Shotgun Design and Performance, by L.R. Wallack, Winchester Press, Piscataway, NJ, 1977. 184 pp., illus. $16.95.
An expert lucidly recounts the history and development of American shotguns.

The American Single Barrel Trap Gun, by Frank F. Conley, Frank F. Conley, Carmel Valley, CA, 1989. 241 pp., illus. $39.95.
History, serial numbers, collecting and how they were made. Covers Baker, Fox, Ithaca, Levefer, Meriden, Parker, L.C. Smith, etc.

Best Guns, by Michael McIntosh, Countrysport, Inc., Traverse City, MI, 1989. 288 pp., illus. $39.50.
Devoted to the best shotguns ever made in the United States and the best presently being made in the world.

The Better Shot, by Ken Davies, Quiller Press, London, England, 1992. 136 pp., illus. $39.95.
Step-by-step shotgun technique with Holland and Holland.

Black Powder Hobby Gunsmithing, by Sam Fadala and Dale Storey, DBI Books, Inc., Northbrook, IL, 1994. 256 pp., illus. Paper covers. $18.95.
A how-to-guide for gunsmithing blackpowder pistols, rifles and shotguns from two men at the top of their respective fields.

The British Shotgun, Volume 1, 1850-1870, by I.M. Crudington and D.J. Baker, Barrie & Jenkins, London, England, 1979. 256 pp., illus. $59.95.
An attempt to trace, as accurately as is now possible, the evolution of the shotgun during its formative years in Great Britain.

The British Shotgun, Volume 2, 1871-1890, by I.M. Crudginton and D.J. Baker, Ashford Press, Southampton, England, 1989. 250 pp., illus. $59.95.
The second volume of a definitive work on the evolution and manufacture of the British shotgun.

*__Boothroyd on British Shotguns,__ by Geoffrey Boothroyd, Safari Press, Huntington Beach, CA,1995. 220 pp., illus. $35.00.
ains engraving, stock-making, Damascus barrels, light-game guns, pigeon guns, Birmingham guntrade, London and Birmingham proof houses, and includes the 1914 Webley & Scott catalog.

*__Boss & Co. Builders of Best Guns Only,__ by Donald Dallas, Safari Press, Huntington Beach, CA, 1996. 336 pp., illus. $75.00
om its founding by Thomas Boss (1790 - 1857) to the present day.

Clay Pigeon Shooting for Beginners and Enthusiasts, by John King, The Sportsman's Press, London, England, 1991. 94 pp., illus. $24.95.
John King has devised this splendid guide to clay pigeon shooting in the same direct style in which he teaches at his popular Barbury Shooting School near Swindon.

Clay Shooting, by Peter Croft, Ward Lock, London, England, 1990. 160 pp., illus, $29.95.
A complete guide to Skeet, trap and sporting shooting.

Clay Target Handbook by Jerry Meyer, Lyons & Buford, Publisher, New York, NY, 1993. 182 pp., illus. $22.95.
Contains in-depth, how-to-do-it information on trap, Skeet, sporting clays, international trap, international Skeet and clay target games played around the country.

Clay Target Shooting, by Paul Bentley, A&C Black, London, England, 1987. 144 pp., illus. $25.00.
Practical book on clay target shooting written by a very successful international competitor, providing valuable professional advice and instruction for shooters of all disciplines.

A Collector's Guide to United States Combat Shotguns, by Bruce N. Canfield, Andrew Mowbray Inc., Publishers, Lincoln, RI, 1993. 184 pp., illus. Paper covers. $24.00.
Full coverage of the combat shotgun, from the earliest examples to the Gulf War and beyond.

The Complete Clay Shot, by Mike Barnes, Trafalgar Square, N. Pomfret, VT, 1993. 192 pp., illus. $39.95.
The latest compendium on the clay sports by Mike Barnes, a well-known figure in shotgunning in the U.S. and England.

Cradock on Shotguns, by Chris Cradock, Banford Press, London, England, 1989. 200 pp., illus. $45.00.
A definitive work on the shotgun by a British expert on shotguns.

The Defensive Shotgun, by Louis Awerbuck, S.W.A.T. Publications, Cornville, AZ, 1989. 77 pp., illus. Soft covers. $12.95.
Cuts through the myths concerning the shotgun and its attendant ballistic effects.

The Double Shotgun, by Don Zutz, Winchester Press, Piscataway, NJ, 1985. 304 pp., illus. $20.95.
Revised, updated, expanded edition of the history and development of the world's classic sporting firearms.

Ed Scherer on Sporting Clays, by Ed Scherer, Ed Scherer, Elk Grove, WI, 1993. 200 pp., illus. Paper covers. $29.95.
Covers footwork, gun fit, master eye checks, recoil reduction, noise abatement, eye and ear protection, league shooting, shot sizes and chokes.

Exploded Long Gun Drawings, The Gun Digest Book of, edited by Harold A. Murtz, DBI Books, Inc., Northbrook, IL. 512 pp., illus. Paper covers. $20.95.
Containing almost 500 rifle and shotgun exploded drawings. An invaluable aid to both professionals and hobbyists.

Field, Cover and Trap Shooting, by Adam H. Bogardus, Wolfe Publishing Co., Prescott, AZ, 1988. 446 pp., illus. $45.00.
A limited edition reprint. Hints for skilled marksmen as well as young sportsmen. Includes haunts and habits of game birds and waterfowl.

Finding the Extra Target, by Coach John R. Linn & Stephen A. Blumenthal, Shotgun Sports, Inc., Auburn, CA, 1989. 126 pp., illus. Paper covers. $14.95.
The ultimate training guide for all the clay target sports.

Firearms Assembly/Disassembly, Part V: Shotguns, Revised Edition, The Gun Digest Book of, by J.B. Wood, DBI Books, Inc., Northbrook, IL, 1992. 480 pp., illus. Paper covers. $19.95.
Covers 46 popular shotguns plus over 250 variants. The most comprehensive and professional presentation available to either hobbyist or gunsmith.

A.H. Fox "The Finest Gun in the World", revised and enlarged edition, by Michael McIntosh, Countrysport, Inc., New Albany, OH, 1995. 408 pp., illus. $49.00.
The first detailed history of one of America's finest shotguns.

Fucili D'Autore (The Best Guns), by Marco E. Nobili, London Guns, Ltd., Santa Barbara, CA, 1992. 845 pp., illus. $125.00.
An exhaustive study on Italian luxury-grade shotguns and their makers, with information on European makers as well. Text in English and Italian.

The Golden Age of Shotgunning, by Bob Hinman, Wolfe Publishing Co., Inc., Prescott, AZ, 1982. $22.50.
A valuable history of the late 1800s detailing that fabulous period of development in shotguns, shotshells and shotgunning.

*__Grand Old Shotguns,__ by Don Zutz, Shotgun Sports Magazine, Auburn, CA, 1995. 136 pp., illus. Paper covers. $19.95
A study of the great smoothbores, their history and how and why they were discontinued. Find out the most sought-after and which were the best shooters.

Hartman on Skeet, By Barney Hartman, Stackpole Books, Harrisburg, PA, 1973. 143 pp., illus. $19.95.
A definitive book on Skeet shooting by a pro.

The Ithaca Gun Company From the Beginning, by Walter Claude Snyder, Cook & Uline Publishing Co., Spencerport, NY, 1991. 256 pp., illus. $59.95.
The entire family of Ithaca Gun Company products is described together with a photo gallery section containing many previously unpublished photographs of the gun makers.

L.C. Smith Shotguns, by Lt. Col. William S. Brophy, The Gun Room Press, Highland Park, NJ, 1979. 244 pp., illus. $35.00.
The first work on this very important American gun and manufacturing company.

The Little Trapshooting Book, by Frank Little, Shotgun Sports Magazine, Auburn, CA, 1994. 168 pp., illus. Paper covers. $19.95.
Packed with know-how from one of the greatest trapshooters of all time.

***Lock, Stock, and Barrel,** by C. Adams & R. Braden, Safari Press, Huntington Beach, CA, 1996. 254 pp., illus. $24.95.
The process of making a best grade English gun from a lump of steel and a walnut tree trunk to the ultimate product plus practical advise on consistent field shooting with a double gun.
A Manual of Clayshooting, by Chris Cradock, Hippocrene Books, Inc., New York, NY, 1983. 192 pp., illus. $39.95.
Covers everything from building a range to buying a shotgun, with lots of illus. & dia.
***The Model 12, 1912-1964,** by Dave Riffle, Dave Riffle, Ft. Meyers, FL, 1995. 274 pp., illus. $49.95.
The story of the greatest hammerless repeating shotgun ever built.
The Mysteries of Shotgun Patterns, by George G. Oberfell and Charles E. Thompson, Oklahoma State University Press, Stillwater, OK, 1982. 164 pp., illus. Paper covers. $25.00.
Shotgun ballistics for the hunter in non-technical language.
The Orvis Wing-Shooting Handbook, by Bruce Bowlen, Nick Lyons Books, New York, NY, 1985. 83 pp., illus. Paper covers. $10.95.
Proven techniques for better shotgunning.
Police Shotgun Manual, by Bill Clede, Stackpole Books, Harrisburg, PA, 1986. 128 pp., illus. $18.95.
Latest shotgun techniques for tough situations.
***Positive Shooting,** by Michael Yardley, Safari Press, Huntington Beach, CA, 1995. 160 pp., illus. $30.00.
This book will provide the shooter with a sound foundation from which to develop an effective, personal technique that can dramatically improve shooting performance.
Purdey's, the Guns and the Family, by Richard Beaumont, David and Charles, Pomfert, VT, 1984. 248 pp., illus. $39.95.
Records the history of the Purdey family from 1814 to today, how the guns were and are built and daily functioning of the factory.
Reloading for Shotgunners, 3rd Edition, by Edward A. Matunas, DBI Books, Inc., Northbrook, IL, 1993. 288 pp., illus. Paper covers. $17.95.
Expanded reloading tables with over 2,000 loads. Bushing charts for every major press and component maker. All new presentation on all aspects of shotshell reloading by one of the top experts in the field.
Robert Churchill's Game Shooting, edited by MacDonald Hastings, Countrysport Press, Traverse City, MI, 1990. 252 pp., illus. $29.50.
A new revised edition of the definitive book on the Churchill method of instinctive wingshooting for game and Sporting Clays.
75 Years with the Shotgun, by C.T. (Buck) Buckman, Valley, Publ., Fresno, CA, 1974. 141 pp., illus. $10.00.
An expert hunter and trapshooter shares experiences of a lifetime.
Scherer on Skeet 2, by Ed Scherer, Ed. Scherer, Waukesha, WI, 1993. 121 pp., illus. Paper covers. $19.95.
A "teaching" book, featuring the eight Skeet stations plus shootoff doubles.
Shooting at Clays, by Alan Jarrett, Stanley Paul, London, England, 1991. 176 pp., illus. $34.95.
This book unravels the complexities of clay pigeon shooting.
The Shooting Field with Holland & Holland, by Peter King, Quiller Press, London, England, new & enlarged edition, 1990. 184 pp., illus. $49.95.
The story of a company which has produced excellence in all aspects of gunmaking.
The Shotgun in Combat, by Tony Lesce, Desert Publications, Cornville, AZ, 1979. 148 pp., illus. Paper covers. $10.00.
A history of the shotgun and its use in combat.
Shotgun Digest, 4th Edition, edited by Jack Lewis, DBI Books, Inc., Northbrook, IL, 1993. 256 pp., illus. Paper covers. $17.95.
The all-new edition looking at what's happening with shotguns and shotgunning today.
Shotgun Gunsmithing, The Gun Digest Book of, by Ralph Walker, DBI Books, Inc., Northbrook, IL, 1983. 256 pp., illus. Paper covers. $16.95.
The principles and practices of repairing, individualizing and accurizing modern shotguns by one of the world's premier shotgun gunsmiths.
***The Shotgun: History and Development,** by Geoffrey Boothroyd, Safari Press, Huntington Beach, CA, 1995. 240 pp., illus. $35.00.
The first volume in a series that traces the development of the British shotgun from the 17th century onward.
Shotgun Stuff, by Don Zutz, Shotgun Sports, Inc., Auburn, CA, 1991. 172 pp., illus. Paper covers. $19.95.
This book gives shotgunners all the "stuff" they need to achieve better performance and get more enjoyment from their favorite smoothbore.
Shotgunner's Notebook: The Advice and Reflections of a Wingshooter, by Gene Hill, Countrysport Press, Traverse City, MI, 1990. 192 pp., illus. $24.50.
Covers the shooting, the guns and the miscellany of the sport.
Shotgunning: The Art and the Science, by Bob Brister, Winchester Press, Piscataway, NJ, 1976. 321 pp., illus. $18.95.
Hundreds of specific tips and truly novel techniques to improve the field and target shooting of every shotgunner.
Shotgunning Trends in Transition, by Don Zutz, Wolfe Publishing Co., Prescott, AZ, 1990. 314 pp., illus. $29.50.
This book updates American shotgunning from post WWII to present.
Shotguns and Cartridges for Game and Clays, by Gough Thomas, edited by Nigel Brown, A & C Black, Ltd., Cambs, England, 1989. 256 pp., illus. Soft covers. $24.95.
Gough Thomas' well-known and respected book for game and clay pigeon shooters in a thoroughly up-dated edition.
***Shotguns and Gunsmiths: The Vintage Years,** by Geoffrey Boothroyd, Safari Press, Huntington Beach, CA, 1995. 240 pp., illus. $35.00.
A fascinating insight into the lives and skilled work of gunsmiths who helped develop the British shotgun during the Victorian and Edwardian eras.
***Shotguns and Shooting,** by Michael McIntosh, Countrysport Press, New Albany, OH, 1995. 258 pp., illus. $30.00.
The art of guns and gunmaking, this book is a celebration no lover of fine doubles should miss.
Sidelocks & Boxlocks, by Geoffrey Boothroyd, Sand Lake Press, Amity, OR, 1991. 271 pp., illus. $35.00.
The story of the classic British shotgun.
Spanish Best: The Fine Shotguns of Spain, by Terry Wieland, Countrysport, Inc., Traverse City, MI, 1994. 264 pp., illus. $49.50.
A practical source of information for owners of Spanish shotguns and a guide for those considering buying a used shotgun.
The Sporting Clay Handbook, by Jerry Meyer, Lyons and Burford Publishers, New York, NY, 1990. 140 pp., illus. Soft covers. $15.95.
Introduction to the fastest growing, and most exciting, gun game in America.
Sporting Clays, The Gun Digest Book of, by Jack Lewis, DBI Books, Inc., Northbrook, IL, 1991. 224 pp., illus. Paper covers. $17.95.
A superb introduction to the fastest growing gun game in America.
Sporting Clays, by Michael Pearce, Stackpole Books, Harrisburg, PA, 1991. 192 pp., illus. $16.95.
Expert techniques for every kind of clays course.
The Story of the Sporting Gun, by Ranulf Rayner, Trafalgar Square, North Pomfret, VT, 1991. 96 pp., illustrated. $75.00.
This magnificent volume traces the story of game shooting from the early development of the shotgun to the present day.
Successful Clay Pigeon Shooting, compiled by T. Hoare, Trafalgar Square, N. Pomfret, VT, 1993. 176 pp., illus. $39.95.
This comprehensive guide has been written by ten leading personalities for all aspiring clay pigeon shooters.
Taking More Birds, by Dan Carlisle & Dolph Adams, Lyons & Burford, New York, NY, 1993. 120 pp., illus. $19.95.
A practical guide to greater success at sporting clays and wing shooting.
Trap & Skeet Shooting, 3rd Edition, edited by Chris Christain, DBI Books, Inc., Northbrook, IL, 1994. 288 pp., illus. Paper covers. $17.95.
A detailed look at the contemporary world of trap, Skeet and Sporting Clays.
Turkey Hunter's Digest, Revised Edition, by Dwain Bland, DBI Books, Inc., Northbrook, IL, 1994. 256 pp., illus. Paper covers. $17.95.
Presents no-nonsense approach to hunting all five sub-species of the North American wild turkey.
U.S. Shotguns, All Types, reprint of TM9-285, Desert Publications, Cornville, AZ, 1987. 257 pp., illus. Paper covers. $9.95.
Covers operation, assembly and disassembly of nine shotguns used by the U.S. armed forces.
U.S. Winchester Trench and Riot Guns and Other U.S. Military Combat Shotguns, by Joe Poyer, North Cape Publications, Tustin, CA, 1992. 124 pp., illus. Paper covers. $15.95.
A detailed history of the use of military shotguns, and the acquisition procedures used by the U.S. Army's Ordnance Department in both World Wars.
The Winchester Model Twelve, by George Madis, David Madis, Dallas, TX, 1984. 176 pp., illus. $19.95.
A definitive work on this famous American shotgun.
The Winchester Model 42, by Ned Schwing, Krause Pub., Iola, WI, 1990. 159 pp., illus. $39.95.
Behind-the-scenes story of the model 42's invention and its early development. Production totals and manufacturing dates; reference work.
Winchester's Finest, the Model 21, by Ned Schwing, Krause Publicatons, Inc., Iola, WI, 1990. 360 pp., illus. $49.95.
The classic beauty and the interesting history of the Model 21 Winchester shotgun.
The World's Fighting Shotguns, by Thomas F. Swearengen, T. B. N. Enterprises, Alexandria, VA, 1979. 500 pp., illus. $34.95.
The complete military and police reference work from the shotgun's inception to date, with up-to-date developments.

ARMS ASSOCIATIONS

UNITED STATES

ALABAMA

Alabama Gun Collectors Assn.
Secretary, P.O. Box 70965, Tuscaloosa, AL 35407

ALASKA

Alaska Gun Collectors Assn., Inc.
C.W. Floyd, Pres., 5240 Little Tree, Anchorage, AK 99507

ARIZONA

Arizona Arms Assn.
Don DeBusk, President, 4837 Bryce Ave., Glendale, AZ 85301

CALIFORNIA

California Cartridge Collectors Assn.
Rick Montgomery, 1729 Christina, Stockton, CA 95204
California Waterfowl Assn.
4630 Northgate Blvd., #150, Sacramento, CA 95834
Greater Calif. Arms & Collectors Assn.
Donald L. Bullock, 8291 Carburton St., Long Beach, CA 90808-3302
Los Angeles Gun Ctg. Collectors Assn.
F.H. Ruffra, 20810 Amie Ave., Apt. #9, Torrance, CA 90503
Stock Gun Players Assn.
6038 Appian Way, Long Beach, CA, 90803

COLORADO

Colorado Gun Collectors Assn.
L.E.(Bud) Greenwald, 2553 S. Quitman St., Denver, CO 80219/303-935-3850
Rocky Mountain Cartridge Collectors Assn.
John Roth, P.O. Box 757, Conifer, CO 80433

CONNECTICUT

Ye Connecticut Gun Guild, Inc.
Dick Fraser, P.O. Box 425, Windsor, CT 06095

FLORIDA

Unified Sportsmen of Florida
P.O. Box 6565, Tallahassee, FL 32314

GEORGIA

Georgia Arms Collectors Assn., Inc.
Michael Kindberg, President, P.O. Box 277, Alpharetta, GA 30239-0277

ILLINOIS

Illinois State Rifle Assn.
P.O. Box 637, Chatsworth, IL 60921
Mississippi Valley Gun & Cartridge Coll. Assn.
Bob Filbert, P.O. Box 61, Port Byron, IL 61275/309-523-2593
Sauk Trail Gun Collectors
Gordell M. Matson, P.O. Box 1113, Milan, IL 61264
Wabash Valley Gun Collectors Assn., Inc.
Roger L. Dorsett, 2601 Willow Rd., Urbana, IL 61801/217-384-7302

INDIANA

Indiana State Rifle & Pistol Assn.
Thos. Glancy, P.O. Box 552, Chesterton, IN 46304
Southern Indiana Gun Collectors Assn., Inc.
Sheila McClary, 309 W. Monroe St., Boonville, IN 47601/812-897-3742

IOWA

Beaver Creek Plainsmen Inc.
Steve Murphy, Secy., P.O. Box 298, Bondurant, IA 50035
Central States Gun Collectors Assn.
Avery Giles, 1104 S. 1st Ave., Marshtown, IA 50158

KANSAS

Kansas Cartridge Collectors Assn.
Bob Linder, Box 84, Plainville, KS 67663

KENTUCKY

Kentuckiana Arms Collectors Assn.
Charles Billips, President, Box 1776, Louisville, KY 40201
Kentucky Gun Collectors Assn., Inc.
Ruth Johnson, Box 64, Owensboro, KY 42302/502-729-4197

LOUISIANA

Washitaw River Renegades
Sandra Rushing, P.O. Box 256, Main St., Grayson, LA 71435

MARYLAND

Baltimore Antique Arms Assn.
Mr. Cillo, 1034 Main St., Darlington, MD 21304

MASSACHUSETTS

Bay Colony Weapons Collectors, Inc.
John Brandt, Box 111, Hingham, MA 02043
Massachusetts Arms Collectors
Bruce E. Skinner, P.O. Box 31, No. Carver, MA 02355/508-866-5259

MICHIGAN

Association for the Study and Research of .22 Caliber Rimfire Cartridges
George Kass, 4512 Nakoma Dr., Okemos, MI 48864

MINNESOTA

Sioux Empire Cartridge Collectors Assn.
Bob Cameron, 14597 Glendale Ave. SE, Prior Lake, MN 55372

MISSISSIPPI

Mississippi Gun Collectors Assn.
Jack E. Swinney, P.O. Box 16323, Hattiesburg, MS 39402

MISSOURI

Greater St. Louis Cartridge Collectors Assn.
Don MacChesney, 634 Scottsdale Rd., Kirkwood, MO 63122-1109
Mineral Belt Gun Collectors Assn.
D.F. Saunders, 1110 Cleveland Ave., Monett, MO 65708
Missouri Valley Arms Collectors Assn., Inc.
L.P Brammer II, Membership Secy., P.O. Box 33033, Kansas City, MO 64114

MONTANA

Montana Arms Collectors Assn.
Lewis E. Yearout, 308 Riverview Dr. East, Great Falls, MT 59404
Weapons Collectors Society of Montana
R.G. Schipf, Ex. Secy., 3100 Bancroft St., Missoula, MT 59801/406-728-2995

NEBRASKA

Nebraska Cartridge Collectors Club
Gary Muckel, P.O. Box 84442, Lincoln, NE 68501

NEW HAMPSHIRE

New Hampshire Arms Collectors, Inc.
James Stamatelos, Secy., P.O. Box 5, Cambridge, MA 02139

NEW JERSEY

Englishtown Benchrest Shooters Assn.
Michael Toth, 64 Cooke Ave., Carteret, NJ 07008
Jersey Shore Antique Arms Collectors
Joe Sisia, P.O. Box 100, Bayville, NJ 08721-0100
New Jersey Arms Collectors Club, Inc.
Angus Laidlaw, Vice President, 230 Valley Rd., Montclair, NJ 07042/201-746-0939

NEW YORK

Iroquois Arms Collectors Assn.
Bonnie Robinson, Show Secy., P.O. Box 142, Ransomville, NY 14131/716-791-4096
Mid-State Arms Coll. & Shooters Club
Jack Ackerman, 24 S. Mountain Terr., Binghamton, NY 13903

NORTH CAROLINA

North Carolina Gun Collectors Assn.
Jerry Ledford, 3231-7th St. Dr. NE, Hickory, NC 28601

OHIO

Ohio Gun Collectors Assn.
P.O. Box 9007, Maumee, OH 43537-9007/419-897-0861;Fax:419-897-0860
Shotshell Historical and Collectors Society
Madeline Bruemmer, 3886 Dawley Rd., Ravenna, OH 44266
The Stark Gun Collectors, Inc.
William I. Gann, 5666 Waynesburg Dr., Waynesburg, OH 44688

OKLAHOMA

Indian Territory Gun Collector's Assn.
P.O. Box 4491, Tulsa, OK 74159/918-745-9141

OREGON

Oregon Arms Collectors Assn., Inc.
Phil Bailey, P.O. Box 13000-A, Portland, OR 97213-0017/503-281-6864;off.:503-620-1024
Oregon Cartridge Collectors Assn.
Gale Stockton, 52 N.W. 2nd, Gresham, OR 97030

PENNSYLVANIA

Presque Isle Gun Collectors Assn.
James Welch, 156 E. 37 St., Erie, PA 16504

SOUTH CAROLINA

Belton Gun Club, Inc.
J.K. Phillips, 195 Phillips Dr., Belton, SC 29627
Gun Owners of South Carolina
Membership Div.: William Strozier, Secretary, P.O. Box 70, Johns Island, SC 29457-0070/803-762-3240;Fax:803-795-0711;e-mail:76053.222@compuserve.com

SOUTH DAKOTA

Dakota Territory Gun Coll. Assn., Inc.
Curt Carter, Castlewood, SD 57223

TENNESSEE

Smoky Mountain Gun Coll. Assn., Inc.
Hugh W. Yabro, President, P.O. Box 23225, Knoxville, TN 37933
Tennessee Gun Collectors Assn., Inc.
M.H. Parks, 3556 Pleasant Valley Rd., Nashville, TN 37204-3419

TEXAS

Houston Gun Collectors Assn., Inc.
P.O. Box 741429, Houston, TX 77274-1429
Texas Cartridge Collectors Assn., Inc.
Robert Mellichamp, Memb. Contact, 907 Shirkmere, Houston, TX 77008/713-869-0558
Texas Gun Collectors Assn.
Bob Eder, Pres., P.O. Box 12067, El Paso, TX 79913/915-584-8183
Texas State Rifle Assn.
4600 Greenville Ave., #292, Dallas, TX 75206/214-369-8772

WASHINGTON

Association of Cartridge Collectors on the Pacific Northwest
Robert Jardin, 14214 Meadowlark Drive KPN, Gig Harbor, WA 98329
Washington Arms Collectors, Inc.
Joyce Boss, P.O. Box 389, Renton, WA, 98057-0389/206-255-8410

WISCONSIN

Great Lakes Arms Collectors Assn., Inc.
Edward C. Warnke, 2913 Woodridge Lane, Waukesha, WI 53188
Wisconsin Gun Collectors Assn., Inc.
Lulita Zellmer, P.O. Box 181, Sussex, WI 53089

WYOMING

Wyoming Weapons Collectors
P.O. Box 284, Laramie, WY 82070/307-745-4652 or 745-9530

NATIONAL ORGANIZATIONS

Amateur Trapshooting Assn.
601 W. National Rd., Vandalia, OH 45377/513-898-4638;Fax:513-898-5472
American Airgun Field Target Assn.
5911 Cherokee Ave., Tampa, FL 33604
American Coon Hunters Assn.
Opal Johnston, P.O. Cadet, Route 1, Box 492, Old Mines, MO 63630
American Custom Gunmakers Guild
Jan Billeb, Exec. Director, P.O. Box 812, Burlington, IA 52601-0812/319-752-6114 (Phone or Fax)
American Defense Preparedness Assn.
Two Colonial Place, 2101 Wilson Blvd., Suite 400, Arlington, VA 22201-3061
American Paintball League
P.O. Box 3561, Johnson City, TN 37602/800-541-9169
American Pistolsmiths Guild
Alex B. Hamilton, Pres., 1449 Blue Crest Lane, San Antonio, TX 78232/210-494-3063
American Police Pistol & Rifle Assn.
3801 Biscayne Blvd., Miami, FL 33137
American Single Shot Rifle Assn.
Gary Staup, Secy., 709 Carolyn Dr., Delphos, OH 45833/419-692-3866
American Society of Arms Collectors
George E. Weatherly, P.O. Box 2567, Waxahachie, TX 75165
American Tactical Shooting Assn.(A.T.S.A.)
c/o Skip Gouchenour, 2600 N. Third St., Harrisburg, PA 17110/717-233-0402;Fax:717-233-5340

Association of Firearm and Tool Mark Examiners
Lannie G. Emanuel, Secy., Southwest Institute of Forecsic Sciences, P.O. Box 35728, Dallas, TX 75235; Membership Secy., Ann D. Jones, VA Div. of Forensic Science, P.O. Box 999, Richmont, VA 23208/804-786-4706;Fax:804-371-8328

Boone & Crockett Club
250 Station Dr., Missoula, MT 59801-2753

Browning Collectors Assn.
Secretary:Scherrie L. Brennac, 2749 Keith Dr., Villa Ridge, MO 63089/314-742-0571

The Cast Bullet Assn., Inc.
Ralland J. Fortier, Membership Director, 4103 Foxcraft Dr., Traverse City, MI 49684

Citizens Committee for the Right to Keep and Bear Arms
Natl. Hq., Liberty Park, 12500 NE Tenth Pl., Bellevue, WA 98005

Colt Collectors Assn.
25000 Highland Way, Los Gatos, CA 95030

Ducks Unlimited, Inc.
Natl. Headquarters, One Waterfowl Way, Memphis, TN 38120

Fifty Caliber Shooters Assn.
11469 Olive St. Rd., Suite 50, St. Louis, MO 63141/601-475-7545;Fax:601-475-0452

Firearms Coalition
Box 6537, Silver Spring, MD 20906/301-871-3006

Firearms Engravers Guild of America
Rex C. Pedersen, Secy., 511 N. Rath Ave., Lundington, MI 49431/616-845-7695(Phone and Fax)

Foundation for North American Wild Sheep
720 Allen Ave., Cody, WY 82414-3402

Freedom Arms Collectors Assn.
P.O. Box 160302, Miami, FL 33116-0302

Garand Collectors Assn.
P.O. Box 181, Richmond, KY 40475

Golden Eagle Collectors Assn.
Chris Showler, 11144 Slate Creek Rd., Grass Valley, CA 95945

Gun Owners of America
8001 Forbes Place, Suite 102, Springfield, VA 22151/703-321-8585

Handgun Hunters International
J.D. Jones, Director, P.O. Box 357 MAG, Bloomingdale, OH 43910

Harrington & Richardson Gun Coll. Assn.
George L. Cardet, 330 S.W. 27th Ave., Suite 603, Miami, FL 33135

High Standard Collectors' Assn.
John J. Stimson, Jr., Pres., 540 W. 92nd St., Indianapolis, IN 46260

Hopkins & Allen Arms & Memorabilia Society (HAAMS)
1309 Pamela Circle, Delphos, OH 45833

International Ammunition Association, Inc.
C.R. Punnett, Secy., 8 Hillock Lane, Chadds Ford, PA 19317/610-358-1258;Fax:610-358-1560

International Benchrest Shooters
Joan Borden, RR1, Box 250BB, Springville, PA 18844/717-965-2366

International Blackpowder Hunting Assn.
P.O. Box 1180, Glenrock, WY 82637/307-436-9817

IHMSA (Intl. Handgun Metallic Silhouette Assn.)
Frank Scotto, P.O. Box 5038, Meriden, CT 06451

International Handloaders Assn.
6471 Airpark Dr., Prescott, AZ 86301/520-445-7810;Fax:520-778-5124

International Paintball Field Operators Assn.
15507 S. Normandie Ave. #487, Gardena, CA 90247/310-323-1021

IPPA (International Paintball Players Assn.)
P.O. Box 26669, San Diego, CA 92196-0669/619-695-8882;Fax:619-695-6909

Jews for the Preservation of Firearms Ownership (JPFO) 501(c)(3)
2872 S. Wentworth Ave., Milwaukee, WI 53207/414-769-0760;Fax:414-483-8435

The Mannlicher Collectors Assn.
Rev. Don L. Henry, Secy., P.O. Box 7144, Salem, OR 97303-0028

Marlin Firearms Collectors Assn., Ltd.
Dick Paterson, Secy., 407 Lincoln Bldg., 44 Main St., Champaign, IL 61820

Miniature Arms Collectors/Makers Society, Ltd.
Ralph Koebbeman, Pres., 4910 Kilburn Ave., Rockford, IL 61101/815-964-2569

M1 Carbine Collectors Assn. (M1-CCA)
P.O. Box 4895, Stateline, NV 89449

National Association of Buckskinners (NAB)
Territorial Dispatch, 4701 Marion St., Suite 324, Livestock Exchange Bldg., Denver, CO 80216

The National Association of Derringer Collectors
P.O. Box 20572, San Jose, CA 95160

National Assn. of Federally Licensed Firearms Dealers
Andrew Molchan, 2455 E. Sunrise, Ft. Lauderdale, FL 33304

National Association to Keep and Bear Arms
P.O. Box 78336, Seattle, WA 98178

National Automatic Pistol Collectors Assn.
Tom Knox, P.O. Box 15738, Tower Grove Station, St. Louis, MO 63163

National Bench Rest Shooters Assn., Inc.
Pat Ferrell, 2835 Guilford Lane, Oklahoma City, OK 73120-4404/405-842-9585

National Firearms Assn.
P.O. Box 160038, Austin, TX 78716/403-439-1094; FAX: 403-439-4091

National Muzzle Loading Rifle Assn.
Box 67, Friendship, IN 47021

National Professional Paintball League (NPPL)
540 Main St., Mount Kisco, NY 10549/914-241-7400

National Reloading Manufacturers Assn.
One Centerpointe Dr., Suite 300, Lake Oswego, OR 97035

National Rifle Assn. of America
11250 Waples Mill Rd., Fairfax, VA 22030

National Shooting Sports Foundation, Inc.
Robert T. Delfay, President, Flintlock Ridge Office Center, 11 Mile @NORMAL:Hill Rd., Newtown, CT 06470-2359/203-426-1320; FAX: 203-426-1087

National Skeet Shooting Assn.
Mike Hampton, Exec. Director, 5931 Roft Road, San Antonio, TX 78253-9261

National Sporting Clays Association
5931 Roft Road, San Antonio, TX 78253-9261/800-877-5338

National Wild Turkey Federation, Inc.
P.O. Box 530, Edgefield, SC 29824

North American Hunting Club
P.O. Box 3401, Minnetonka, MN 55343

North American Paintball Referees Association (NAPRA)
584 Cestaric Dr., Milpitas, CA 95035

North-South Skirmish Assn., Inc.
Stevan F. Meserve, Exec. Secretary, 507 N. Brighton Court, Sterling, VA 20164-3919

Remington Society of America
Leon W. Wier Jr., President, 8268 Lone Feather Ln., Las Vegas, NV 89123

Rocky Mountain Elk Foundation
P.O. Box 8249, Missoula, MT 59807-8249/406-523-4500;Fax:406-523-4581

Ruger Collector's Assn., Inc.
P.O. Box 240, Greens Farms, CT 06436

Safari Club International
Philip DeLone, Executive Dir., 4800 W. Gates Pass Rd., Tucson, AZ 85745/602-620-1220

Sako Collectors Assn., Inc.
Jim Lutes, 202 N. Locust, Whitewater, KS 67154

Second Amendment Foundation
James Madison Building, 12500 NE 10th Pl., Bellevue, WA 98005

Single-Action Shooting Society
1938 North Batavia St., Suite C, Orange, CA 92665/714-998-0209;Fax:714-998-1992

Smith & Wesson Collectors Assn.
George Linne, 2711 Miami St., St. Louis, MO 63118

The Society of American Bayonet Collectors
P.O. Box 234, East Islip, NY 11730-0234

Southern California Schuetzen Society
Dean Lillard, 34657 Ave. E., Yucaipa, CA 92399

Sporting Arms & Ammunition Manufacturers Institute (SAAMI)
Flintlock Ridge Office Center, 11 Mile Hill Rd., Newtown, CT 06470-2359/203-426-1320; FAX: 203-426-1087

Sporting Clays of America (SCA)
Ellen McCormick, Director of Membership Services, 9 Mott Ave., Suite 103, Norwalk, CT 06850/203-831-8483; FAX: 203-831-8497

The Thompson/Center Assn.
Joe Wright, President, Box 792, Northboro, MA 01532/508-845-6960

U.S. Practical Shooting Assn./IPSC
Dave Thomas, P.O. Box 811, Sedro Woolley, WA 98284/360-855-2245

U.S. Revolver Assn.
Brian J. Barer, 40 Larchmont Ave., Taunton, MA 02780/508-824-4836

U.S. Shooting Team
U.S. Olympic Shooting Center, One Olympic Plaza, Colorado Springs, CO 80909/719-578-4670

The Varmint Hunters Assn., Inc.
Box 759, Pierre, SD 57501/Member Services 800-528-4868

Weatherby Collectors Assn., Inc.
P.O. Box 128, Moira, NY 12957

The Wildcatters
P.O. Box 170, Greenville, WI 54942

Winchester Arms Collectors Assn.
Richard Berg, Executive Secy., P.O. Box 6754, Great Falls, MT 59406

The Women's Shooting Sports Foundation (WSSF)
1505 Highway 6 South, Suite 101, Houston, TX 77077

ARGENTINA

Association Argentina de Colleccionistas de Armes y Municiones
Castilla de Correas No. 28, Succursal I B, 1401 Buenos Aires, Republica Argentina

AUSTRALIA

The Arms Collector's Guild of Queensland Inc.
Ian Skennerton, P.O. Box 433, Ashmore City 4214, Queensland, Australia

Australian Cartridge Collectors Assn., Inc.
Bob Bennett, 126 Landscape Dr., E. Doncaster 3109, Victoria, Austrlia

Sporting Shooters Assn. of Australia, Inc.
P.O. Box 2066, Kent Town, SA 5071, Australia

CANADA

ALBERTA

Canadian Historical Arms Society
P.O. Box 901, Edmonton, Alb., Canada T5J 2L8

National Firearms Assn.
Natl. Hq: P.O. Box 1779, Edmonton, Alb., Canada T5J 2P1

BRITISH COLUMBIA

The Historical Arms Collectors of B.C. (Canada)
Harry Moon, Pres., P.O. Box 50117, South Slope RPO, Burnaby, BC V5J 5G3, Canada/604-438-0950;Fax:604-277-3646

ONTARIO

Association of Canadian Cartridge Collectors
Monica Wright, RR 1, Millgrove, ON, LOR IVO, Canada

Tri-County Antique Arms Fair
P.O. Box 122, RR #1, North Lancaster, Ont., Canada KOC 1Z0

EUROPE

BELGIUM

European Catridge Researchers Assn.
Graham Irving, 21 Rue Schaltin, 4900 Spa, Belgium/32.87.77.43.40;Fax:32.87.77.27.51

CZECHOSLOVAKIA

Spolecnost Pro Studium Naboju (Czech Cartridge Research Assn.)
JUDr. Jaroslav Bubak, Pod Homolko 1439, 26601 Beroun 2, Czech Republic

DENMARK

Aquila Dansk Jagtpatron Historic Forening (Danish Historical Cartridge Collectors Club)
Steen Elgaard Moler, Ulriksdalsvej 7, 4840 Nr. Alslev, Denmark 10045-53846218;Fax:004553846209

ENGLAND

Arms and Armour Society
Hon. Secretary A. Dove, P.O. Box 10232, London, 5W19 22D, England

Dutch Paintball Federation
Aceville Publ., Castle House 97 High Street, Colchester, Essex C01 1TH, England/011-44-206-564840

European Paintball Sports Foundation
c/o Aceville Publ., Castle House 97 High St., Colchester, Essex, C01 1TH, England

Historical Breechloading Smallarms Assn.
D.J. Penn M.A., Secy., Imperial War Museum, Lambeth Rd., London SE 1 6HZ, England.
Journal and newsletter are $21 a yr., including airmail.

National Rifle Assn.
(Great Britain) Bisley Camp, Brookwood, Woking Surrey GU24 OPB, England/01483.797777

United Kingdom Cartridge Club
Ian Southgate, 20 Millfield, Elmley Castle, Nr. Pershore, Worcestershire, WR10 3HR, England

FRANCE

Syndicat National de l'Arquebuserie du Commerce de l'Arme Historique
B.P. No. 3, 78110 Le Vesinet, France

GERMANY

Bund Deutscher Sportschützen e.v. (BDS)
Borsigallee 10, 53125 Bonn 1, Germany

Deutscher Schützenbund
Lahnstrasse 120, 65195 Wiesbaden, Germany

SPAIN

Asociacion Espanola de Colleccionistas de Cartuchos
Secretary, APDO. Correos No. 682, 50080 Zaragoza, Spain

SWEDEN

Scandinavian Ammunition Research Assn.
Box 107, 77622 Hedemora, Sweden

NEW ZEALAND

New Zealand Cartridge Collectors Club
Terry Castle, 70 Tiraumea Dr., Pakuranga, Auckland, New Zealand

New Zealand Deerstalkers Assn.
Michael Watt, P.O. Box 6514, Wellington, New Zealand

SOUTH AFRICA

Historical Firearms Soc. of South Africa
P.O. Box 145, 7725 Newlands, Republic of South Africa

Republic of South Africa Cartridge Collectors Assn.
Arno Klee, 20 Eugene St., Malanshof Randburg, Gauteng 2194, Republic of South Africa

S.A.A.C.A. (South African Arms and Ammunition Assn.)
P.O. Box 4065, Northway, Kwazulu-Natal 4065, Republic of South Africa

SAGA (S.A. Gunowners' Assn.)
P.O. Box 4065, Northway, Kwazulu-Natal 4065, Republic of South Africa

DIRECTORY OF THE ARMS TRADE

The **Product Directory** contains 53 product categories. Note that in the Product Directory, a black bullet preceeding a manufacturer's name indicates the availability of a Warranty Service Center address, which can be found on page 445.

The **Manufacturers' Directory** alphabetically lists the manufacturers with their addresses, phone numbers, FAX numbers and Internet addresses, if available.

DIRECTORY OF THE ARMS TRADE INDEX

PRODUCT DIRECTORY

AMMUNITION, COMMERCIAL

ACTIV Industries, Inc.
American Ammunition
Arms Corporation of the Philippines
A-Square Co., Inc.
Bergman & Williams
Black Hills Ammunition, Inc.
Blammo Ammo
Brenneke KG, Wilhelm
Buffalo Bullet Co., Inc.
Bull-X, Inc.
BulletMakers Workshop, The
California Magnum
CBC
Cor-Bon Bullet & Ammo Co.
C.W. Cartridge Co.
Daisy Mfg. Co.
Delta Frangible Ammunition, LLC
Denver Bullets, Inc.
Diana
Dynamit Nobel-RWS, Inc.
Effebi SNC, Dr. Franco Beretta
Eley Ltd.
Elite Ammunition
Estate Cartridge, Inc.
Federal Cartridge Co.
Fiocchi of America, Inc.
Gamo
Garrett Cartridges, Inc.
Gibbs Rifle Co., Inc.
Goldcoast Reloaders, Inc.
Grand Falls Bullets, Inc.
Hansen & Co.
Hansen Cartridge Co.
Hart & Son, Inc., Robert W.
Hirtenberger Aktiengesellschaft
Hornady Mfg. Co.
ICI-America
IMI
Keng's Firearms Specialty, Inc.
Kent Cartridge Mfg. Co. Ltd.
Lapua Ltd.
M&D Munitions Ltd.
Mac-1 Distributors
Magnum Research, Inc.
MagSafe Ammo Co.
MAGTECH Recreational Products, Inc.
Maionchi-L.M.I.
Markell, Inc.
Men—Metallwerk Elisenhuette, GmbH
Moreton/Fordyce Enterprises
Mullins Ammo
Naval Ordnance Works
NECO
New England Ammunition Co.
Oklahoma Ammunition Co.
Old Western Scrounger, Inc.
Omark Industries
PMC/Eldorado Cartridge Corp.
Polywad, Inc.
Pony Express Reloaders
Precision Delta Corp.
Pro Load Ammunition, Inc.
Remington Arms Co., Inc.
Rocky Fork Enterprises
Rucker Dist. Inc.
RWS
Shooting Components Marketing
Slug Group, Inc.
Spence, George W.
Star Reloading Co., Inc.
Talon Mfg. Co., Inc.
TCCI
3-D Ammunition & Bullets
3-Ten Corp.
USAC
Valor Corp.
Victory USA
Vihtavuori Oy/Kaltron-Pettibone
Voere-KGH m.b.H.
Weatherby, Inc.
Widener's Reloading & Shooting Supply, Inc.
Winchester Div., Olin Corp.
Zero Ammunition Co., Inc.
Zonie Bullets

AMMUNITION, CUSTOM

Accuracy Unlimited (Littleton, CO)
AFSCO Ammunition
American Derringer Corp.
Arms Corporation of the Philippines
A-Square Co., Inc.
Ballistica Maximus North
Berger Bullets, Ltd.
Bergman & Williams
Black Hills Ammunition, Inc.
Blue Mountain Bullets
Bruno Shooters Supply
Brynin, Milton
Buck Stix—SOS Products Co.
BulletMakers Workshop, The
Carroll Bullets
CBC
CHAA, Ltd.
Christman Jr., David
Country Armourer, The
Cubic Shot Shell Co., Inc.
Custom Tackle and Ammo
C.W. Cartridge Co.
Dakota Arms, Inc.
Dead Eye's Sport Center
DKT, Inc.
Elite Ammunition
Elko Arms
Estate Cartridge, Inc.
Freedom Arms, Inc.
Gammog, Gregory B. Gally
GDL Enterprises
Glaser Safety Slug, Inc.
Grand Falls Bullets, Inc.
Granite Custom Bullets
Heidenstrom Bullets
Hirtenberger Aktiengesellschaft
Hoelscher, Virgil
Horizons Unlimited
Hornady Mfg. Co.
Jackalope Gun Shop
Jensen Bullets
Jensen's Custom Ammunition
Jensen's Firearms Academy
Jones, J.D.
Kaswer Custom, Inc.
Keeler, R.H.
Kent Cartridge Mfg. Co. Ltd.
KJM Fabritek, Inc.
Lapua Ltd.
Lindsley Arms Cartridge Co.
Lomont Precision Bullets
MagSafe Ammo Co.
MAST Technology
McMurdo, Lynn
Men-Metallwerk Elisenhuette, GmbH
Milstor Corp.
Moreton/Fordyce Enterprises
Mullins Ammo
Naval Ordnance Works
NECO
Old Western Scrounger, Inc.
Oklahoma Ammunition Company
Parts & Surplus
Personal Protection Systems
Precision Delta Corp.
Precision Munitions, Inc.
Precision Reloading, Inc.
Professional Hunter Supplies
Rolston, Inc., Fred W.
Sandia Die & Cartridge Co.
SOS Products Co.
Specialty Gunsmithing
Spence, George W.
Spencer's Custom Guns
SSK Industries
Star Custom Bullets
State Arms Gun Co.
Stewart's Gunsmithing
Swift Bullet Co.
Talon Mfg. Co., Inc.
TCCI
3-D Ammunition & Bullets
3-Ten Corp.
Vitt/Boos
Vulpes Ventures, Inc.
Warren Muzzleloading Co., Inc.
Weaver Arms Corp. Gun Shop
Wells Custom Gunsmith, R.A.
Westley Richards & Co.
Worthy Products, Inc.
Yukon Arms Classic Ammunition
Zonie Bullets

AMMUNITION, FOREIGN

AFSCO Ammunition
Armscorp USA, Inc.
A-Square Co., Inc.
Beretta S.p.A., Pietro
B-West Imports, Inc.
BulletMakers Workshop, The
CBC
Century International Arms, Inc.
Cubic Shot Shell Co., Inc.
Dead Eye's Sport Center
Diana
DKT, Inc.
Dynamit Nobel-RWS, Inc.
Fiocchi of America, Inc.
First, Inc., Jack
Fisher Enterprises, Inc.
Fisher, R. Kermit
FN Herstal
Forgett Jr., Valmore J.
Gamo
Gibbs Rifle Co., Inc.
Hansen & Co.
Hansen Cartridge Co.
Hirtenberger Aktiengesellschaft
Hornady Mfg. Co.
IMI
IMI Services USA, Inc.
Jackalope Gun Shop
JagerSport, Ltd.
K.B.I., Inc.
Keng's Firearms Specialty, Inc.
Lapua Ltd.
MagSafe Ammo Co.
Maionchi-L.M.I.
Mandall Shooting Supplies, Inc.
MAST Technology
Merkuria Ltd.
New England Arms Co.
Oklahoma Ammunition Co.
Old Western Scrounger, Inc.
Paragon Sales & Services, Inc.
Precision Delta Corp.
R.E.T. Enterprises
Rocky Fork Enterprises
RWS
Sentinel Arms
Stoeger Industries
Southern Ammunition Co., Inc.
Spence, George W.
Stratco, Inc.
SwaroSports, Inc.
Talon Mfg. Co., Inc.
T.F.C. S.p.A.
USA Sporting Inc.
Vihtavuori Oy/Kaltron-Pettibone
Yukon Arms Classic Ammunition

AMMUNITION COMPONENTS—BULLETS, POWDER, PRIMERS, CASES

Acadian Ballistic Specialties
Accuracy Unlimited (Littleton, CO)
Accurate Arms Co., Inc.
Action Bullets, Inc.
ACTIV Industries, Inc.
Alaska Bullet Works
Alliant Techsystems
Allred Bullet Co.
Alpha LaFranck Enterprises
Arco Powder
Armfield Custom Bullets
A-Square Co., Inc.
Atlantic Rose, Inc.
Ballard Built
Barnes Bullets, Inc.
Beartooth Bullets
Beeline Custom Bullets Limited
Bell Reloading, Inc.
Belt MTN Arms
Berger Bullets, Ltd.
Bergman & Williams
Berry's Bullets
Bertram Bullet Co.
Big Bore Bullets of Alaska
Big Bore Express Ltd.
Bitterroot Bullet Co.
Black Belt Bullets
Black Hills Shooters Supply
Black Powder Products
Brenneke KG, Wilhelm
Briese Bullet Co., Inc.
Brown Co., E. Arthur
Brownells, Inc.
BRP, Inc.
Bruno Shooters Supply
Buckeye Custom Bullets
Buckskin Bullet Co.
Buffalo Arms
Buffalo Rock Shooters Supply
Bullet, Inc.
Bull-X, Inc.
Butler Enterprises
Buzztail Brass
Calhoon Varmint Bullets, James
Canyon Cartridge Corp.
Carnahan Bullets
Cascade Bullet Co., Inc.
CCI
Champion's Choice, Inc.
Cheddite France, S.A.
CheVron Bullets
C.J. Ballistics, Inc.
Clark Custom Guns, Inc.
Classic Brass
Competitor Corp., Inc.
Cook Engineering Service
Cor-Bon Bullet & Ammo Co.
Crawford Co., Inc., R.M.
Creative Cartridge Co.
Cummings Bullets
Curtis Gun Shop
Custom Bullets by Hoffman
Cutsinger Bench Rest Bullets
D&J Bullet Co. & Custom Gun Shop, Inc.
Dakota Arms, Inc.
Diamondback Supply
DKT, Inc.
Dohring Bullets
Double A Ltd.
DuPont
Eichelberger Bullets, Wm.
Elkhorn Bullets
Epps, Ellwood
Federal Cartridge Co.
Finch Custom Bullets
Fiocchi of America, Inc.
First, Inc., Jack
Forkin, Ben
Fowler Bullets
Foy Custom Bullets
Freedom Arms, Inc.
Fusilier Bullets
G&C Bullet Co., Inc.
Gander Mountain, Inc.
Gehmann, Walter
GOEX, Inc.
Golden Bear Bullets
Gonic Bullet Works
Gotz Bullets
"Gramps" Antique Cartridges
Granite Custom Bullets

Grayback Wildcats
Green Bay Bullets
Grier's Hard Cast Bullets
Grizzly Bullets
Group Tight Bullets
Gun City
Hammets VLD Bullets
Hardin Specialty Dist.
Harris Enterprises
Harrison Bullets
Hart & Son, Inc., Robert W.
Haselbauer Products, Jerry
Hawk, Inc.
Hawk Laboratories, Inc.
Heidenstrom Bullets
Hercules, Inc.
Hirtenberger Aktiengesellschaft
Hobson Precision Mfg. Co.
Hodgdon Powder Co., Inc.
Hornady Mfg. Co.
HT Bullets
Huntington Die Specialties
IMI
IMI Services USA, Inc.
Imperial Magnum Corp.
IMR Powder Co.
J-4, Inc.
J&D Components
J&L Superior Bullets
Jensen Bullets
Jensen's Firearms Academy
Jester Bullets
JLK Bullets
Johnson's Lage Uniwad
JRP Custom Bullets
Ka Pu Kapili
Kasmarsik Bullets
Kaswer Custom, Inc.
Keith's Bullets
Ken's Kustom Kartridge
Keng's Firearms Specialty, Inc.
Kent Cartridge Mfg. Co. Ltd.
KJM Fabritek, Inc.
KLA Enterprises
Kodiak Custom Bullets
Lapua Ltd.
Lawrence Brand Shot
Legend Products Corp.
Liberty Shooting Supplies
Lightfield Ammunition Corp., The Slug Group
Lightning Performance Innovations, Inc.
Littleton, J.F.
M&D Munitions Ltd.
Magnus Bullets
Maine Custom Bullets
Maionchi-L.M.I.
Marchmon Bullets
MarMik Inc.
Marple & Associates, Dick
MAST Technology
Master Class Bullets
McMurdo, Lynn
MEC, Inc.
Meister Bullets
Men-Metallwerk Elisenhuette, GmbH
Merkuria Ltd.
Michael's Antiques
Miller Enterprises, Inc., R.P.
Mitchell Bullets, R.F.
MI-TE Bullets
MoLoc Bullets
Montana Precision Swaging
Mt. Baldy Bullet Co.
Mulhern, Rick
Murmur Corp.
Mushroom Express Bullet Co.
Nagel's Bullets
National Bullet Co.
Naval Ordnance Works
Necromancer Industries, Inc.
Norma
North American Shooting Systems
North Devon Firearms Services
Northern Precision Custom Swaged Bullets
Nosler, Inc.
Oklahoma Ammunition Co.
Old Wagon Bullets
Old Western Scrounger, Inc.
Omark Industries
Ordnance Works, The
Pacific Rifle Co.
Page Custom Bullets
Patrick Bullets
Pattern Control
Peerless Alloy, Inc.
Petro-Explo, Inc.
Phillippi Custom Bullets, Justin
Pinetree Bullets
Polywad, Inc.
Pomeroy, Robert
Powder Valley Services
Precision Components
Precision Components and Guns
Precision Delta Corp.
Precision Munitions, Inc.
Prescott Projectile Co.
Price Bullets, Patrick W.
Professional Hunter Supplies
Rainier Ballistics Corp.
Ranger Products
Red Cedar Precision Mfg.
Redwood Bullet Works
Reloading Specialties, Inc.
Remington Arms Co., Inc.
Radical Concepts
Rifle Works & Armory
R.I.S. Co., Inc.
R.M. Precision, Inc.
Robinson H.V. Bullets
Rolston, Inc., Fred W.
Rubright Bullets
Scharch Mfg., Inc.
Schmidtman Custom Ammunition
Schneider Bullets
Schroeder Bullets
Scot Powder
Seebeck Assoc., R.E.
Shappy Bullets
Shilen Rifles, Inc.
Shooting Components Marketing
Sierra Bullets
Silhouette, The
Specialty Gunsmithing
Speer Products
Spencer's Custom Guns
Stanley Bullets
Star Custom Bullets
Stark's Bullet Mfg.
Stewart's Gunsmithing
Talon Mfg. Co., Inc.
Taracorp Industr
ies
TCCI
TCSR
T.F.C. S.p.A.
Thompson Precision
3-D Ammunition & Bullets
TMI Products
Trico Plastics
Trophy Bonded Bullets, Inc.
True Flight Bullet Co.
USAC
Vann Custom Bullets
Vihtavuori Oy/Kaltron-Pettibone
Vincent's Shop
Vom Hoffe
Watson Trophy Match Bullets
Weatherby, Inc.
Western Nevada West Coast Bullets
White Shooting Systems, Inc.
Widener's Reloading & Shooting Supply
Williams Bullet Co., J.R.
Winchester Div., Olin Corp.
Windjammer Tournament Wads, Inc.
Winkle Bullets
Woodleigh
Worthy Products, Inc.
Wosenitz VHP, Inc.
Wyant Bullets
Wyoming Bonded Bullets
Wyoming Custom Bullets
Yukon Arms Classic Ammunition
Zero Ammunition Co., Inc.
Zonie Bullets

ANTIQUE ARMS DEALERS

Ackerman & Co.
Ad Hominem
Ahlman Guns
Antique American Firearms
Antique Arms Co.
Aplan Antiques & Art, James O.
Armoury, Inc., The
Bear Mountain Gun & Tool
Bob's Tactical Indoor Shooting Range & Gun Shop
Boggs, Wm.
British Antiques
Buckskin Machine Works
Buffalo Arms
Burgess & Son Gunsmiths, R.W.
Cabela's
Cannon's Guns
Cape Outfitters
Carlson, Douglas R.
Chadick's Ltd.
Chambers Flintlocks Ltd., Jim
Champlin Firearms, Inc.
Chuck's Gun Shop
Classic Guns, Inc.
Cole's Gun Works
D&D Gunsmiths, Ltd.
Delhi Gun House
Dixie Gun Works, Inc.
Dixon Muzzleloading Shop, Inc.
Duffy, Charles E.
Dyson & Son Ltd., Peter
Ed's Gun House
Enguix Import-Export
Fagan & Co., William
First, Inc., Jack
Fish, Marshall F.
Flayderman & Co., N.
Forgett Jr., Valmore J.
Frielich Police Equipment
Fulmer's Antique Firearms, Chet
Getz Barrel Co.
Glass, Herb
Goergen's Gun Shop, Inc.
Golden Age Arms Co.
Greenwald, Leon E. "Bud"
Gun Room, The
Gun Room Press, The
Gun Works, The
Guns Antique & Modern DBA/ Charles E. Duffy
Guncraft Sports, Inc.
Hallowell & Co.
Hansen & Co.
Hunkeler, A.
Johns, Bill
Kelley's
Ledbetter Airguns, Riley
LeFever Arms Co., Inc.
Lever Arms Service Ltd.
Liberty Antique Gunworks
Lock's Philadelphia Gun Exchange
Log Cabin Sport Shop
Martin's Gun Shop
Mathews & Son, Inc., George E.
Mendez, John A.
Montana Outfitters
Mountain Bear Rifle Works, Inc.
Museum of Historical Arms, Inc.
Muzzleloaders Etcetera, Inc.
Navy Arms Co.
N.C. Ordnance Co.
New England Arms Co.
Pioneer Guns
Pony Express Sport Shop, Inc.
Retting, Inc., Martin B.
S&S Firearms
Sarco, Inc.
Scott Fine Guns, Inc., Thad
Semmer, Charles
Shootin' Shack, Inc.
Steves House of Guns
Stott's Creek Armory, Inc.
Strawbridge, Victor W.
Track of the Wolf, Inc.
Vic's Gun Refinishing
Vintage Arms, Inc.
Wiest, M.C.
Winchester Sutler, Inc., The
Wood, Frank
Yearout, Lewis E.

APPRAISERS—GUNS, ETC.

Accuracy Gun Shop
Ahlman Guns
Antique Arms Co.
Armoury, Inc., The
Arundel Arms & Ammunition, Inc., A.
Blue Book Publications, Inc.
Bob's Tactical Indoor Shooting Range & Gun Shop
Bustani, Leo
Butterfield & Butterfield
Camilli, Lou
Cannon's Guns
Cape Outfitters
Chadick's Ltd.
Champlin Firearms, Inc.
Christie's East
Clark Custom Guns, Inc.
Clark Firearms Engraving
Classic Guns, Inc.
Clements' Custom Leathercraft, Chas
Cole's Gun Works
Colonial Repair
Corry, John
Costa, David
Custom Tackle and Ammo
D&D Gunsmiths, Ltd.
DGR Custom Rifles
Dixie Gun Works, Inc.
Dixon Muzzleloading Shop, Inc.
Duane's Gun Repair
Ed's Gun House
Epps, Ellwood
Eversull Co., Inc., K.
Fagan & Co., William
First, Inc., Jack
Fish, Marshall F.
Flayderman & Co., Inc., N.
Forgett, Valmore J., Jr.
Forty Five Ranch Enterprises
Frontier Arms Co., Inc.
Golden Age Arms Co.
Gonzalez Guns, Ramon B.
"Gramps" Antique Cartridges
Greenwald, Leon E. "Bud"
Griffin & Howe, Inc.
Groenewold, John
Gun City
Gun Room Press, The
Gun Shop, The
Gun Works, The
Guncraft Sports, Inc.
Hallowell & Co.
Hammans, Charles E.
HandiCrafts Unltd.
Hank's Gun Shop
Hansen & Co.
Hughes, Steven Dodd
Idaho Ammunition Service
Irwin, Campbell H.
Island Pond Gun Shop
Jaeger, Inc., Paul/Dunn's
Jensen's Custom Ammunition
Jonas Appraisers—Taxidermy Animals, Jack
Kelley's
Ledbetter Airguns, Riley
LeFever Arms Co., Inc.
Lever Arms Service Ltd.
Liberty Antique Gunworks
Lock's Philadelphia Gun Exchange
Mac's .45 Shop
Madis, George
Martin's Gun Shop
Montana Outfitters
Mowrey's Guns & Gunsmithing
Museum of Historical Arms, Inc.
Muzzleloaders Etcetera, Inc.
Navy Arms Co.
N.C. Ordnance Co.
New England Arms Co.
Nitex, Inc.
Orvis Co., The
Pasadena Gun Center
Pentheny de Pentheny
Perazzi USA, Inc.
Peterson Gun Shop, Inc., A.W.
Pettinger Books, Gerald
Pioneer Guns
Pony Express Sport Shop, Inc.
R.E.T. Enterprises
Retting, Inc., Martin B.
Richards, John
S&S Firearms
Safari Outfitters Ltd.
Scott Fine Guns, Inc., Thad
Shell Shack
Shootin' Shack, Inc.
Sipes Gun Shop
Sportsmen's Exchange & Western
Starnes Gunmaker, Ken
Steger, James R.
Stott's Creek Armory, Inc.
Stratco, Inc.
Strawbridge, Victor W.
Thurston Sports, Inc.
Vic's Gun Refinishing
Walker Arms Co., Inc.

Wayne Firearms for Collectors and Investors, James
Wells Custom Gunsmith, R.A.
Whildin & Sons Ltd., E.H.
Wiest, M.C.
Williams Shootin' Iron Service
Winchester Sutler, Inc., The
Wood, Frank
Yearout, Lewis E.

AUCTIONEERS—GUNS, ETC.

Butterfield & Butterfield
Christie's East
Kelley's
"Little John's" Antique Arms
Sotheby's

BOOKS (Publishers and Dealers)

American Handgunner Magazine
Armory Publications
Arms & Armour Press
Arms, Peripheral Data Systems
Arms Software
Ballistic Products, Inc.
Barnes Bullets, Inc.
Blackhawk West
Blacksmith Corp.
Blacktail Mountain Books
Blue Book Publications, Inc.
Brown Co., E. Arthur
Brownell's, Inc.
Buffalo Arms
Calibre Press, Inc.
Cape Outfitters
Colonial Repair
Colorado Sutlers Arsenal
Corbin, Inc.
Crit'R Call
Cumberland States Arsenal
DBI Books
Flores Publications, Inc., J.
Golden Age Arms Co.
Gun City
Gun Hunter Books
Gun List
Gun Parts Corp., The
Gun Room Press, The
Gun Works, The
Guncraft Books
Guncraft Sports, Inc.
Gunnerman Books
Guns, (Div. of D.C. Engineering, Inc.)
GUNS Magazine
H&P Publishing
Handgun Press
Harris Publications
Hawk, Inc.
Hawk Laboratories, Inc.
Heritage/VSP Gun Books
Hodgdon Powder Co., Inc.
Home Shop Machinist, The
Hornady Mfg. Co.
Hungry Horse Books
Info-Arm
Ironside International Publishers, Inc.
King & Co.
Krause Publications, Inc.
Lane Publishing
Lapua Ltd.
Lethal Force Institute
Lyman Products Corp.
Martin Bookseller, J.
McKee Publications
MI-TE Bullets
Mountain South
New Win Publishing, Inc.
NgraveR Co., The
OK Weber, Inc.
Old Western Scrounger, Inc.
Outdoorsman's Bookstore, The
Pejsa Ballistics
Petersen Publishing Co.
Pettinger Books, Gerald
Police Bookshelf
Precision Shooting, Inc.
Reloading Specialties, Inc.
R.G.-G., Inc.
Riling Arms Books Co., Ray
Rutgers Book Center
S&S Firearms
Safari Press, Inc.
Saunders Gun & Machine Shop
Shootin' Accessories, Ltd.
Sierra Bullets
S.P.G., Inc.
Stackpole Books
Stoeger Industries
Stoeger Publishing Co.
"Su-Press-On," Inc.
Thomas, Charles C.
Trafalgar Square
Trotman, Ken
Vega Tool Co.
VSP Publishers
WAMCO—New Mexico
Wiest, M.C.
Wilderness Sound Products Ltd.
Williams Gun Sight Co.
Wolfe Publishing Co.
Wolf's Western Traders

BULLET AND CASE LUBRICANTS

Bear Reloaders
Blackhawk West
Brass-Tech Industries
Break-Free, Inc.
Brown Co., E. Arthur
Buffalo Arms
Camp-Cap Products
CFVentures
Chem-Pak, Inc.
Cooper-Woodward
Elkhorn Bullets
E-Z-Way Systems
Forster Products
Green Bay Bullets
Guardsman Products
HEBB Resources
Hollywood Engineering
Hornady Mfg. Co.
Imperial
Le Clear Industries
Lithi Bee Bullet Lube
M&N Bullet Lube
MI-TE Bullets
NECO
Paco's
RCBS
Reardon Products
Rooster Laboratories
Shay's Gunsmithing
Small Custom Mould & Bullet Co.
S.P.G., Inc.
Tamarack Products, Inc.
Warren Muzzleloading Co., Inc.
Widener's Reloading & Shooting Supply, Inc.
Young Country Arms

BULLET SWAGE DIES AND TOOLS

Brynin, Milton
Bullet Swaging Supply, Inc.
Camdex, Inc.
Corbin, Inc.
Holland's
Hollywood Engineering
Necromancer Industries, Inc.
Niemi Engineering, W.B.
North Devon Firearms Services
Rorschach Precision Products
Sport Flite Manufacturing Co.

CARTRIDGES FOR COLLECTORS

Ad Hominem
Alpha 1 Drop Zone
Buck Stix—SOS Products Co.
Cameron's
Campbell, Dick
Cole's Gun Works
Colonial Repair
Country Armourer, The
Delhi Gun House
DGR Custom Rifles
Duane's Gun Repair
Eichelberger Bullets, Wm.
Enguix Import-Export
Epps, Ellwood
First, Inc., Jack
Forty Five Ranch Enterprises
Goergen's Gun Shop, Inc.
"Gramps" Antique Cartridges
Gun Parts Corp., The
Gun Room Press, The
Idaho Ammunition Service
MAST Technology
Michael's Antiques
Montana Outfitters
Mountain Bear Rifle Works, Inc.
Pasadena Gun Center
Pioneer Guns
Samco Global Arms, Inc.
San Francisco Gun Exchange
SOS Products Co.
Ward & Van Valkenburg
Yearout, Lewis E.

CASES, CABINETS, RACKS AND SAFES—GUN

Abel Safe & File, Inc.
Alco Carrying Cases
All Rite Products, Inc.
Allen Co., Bob
Allen Co., Inc.
Allen Sportswear, Bob
Alumna Sport by Dee Zee
American Display Co.
American Security Products Co.
Americase
Ansen Enterprises
Arizona Custom Case
Arkfeld Mfg. & Dist. Co., Inc.
Armes de Chasse
Art Jewel Enterprises Ltd.
Ashby Turkey Calls
Aspen Outdoors, Inc.
Bagmaster Mfg., Inc.
Barramundi Corp.
Berry's Mfg. Inc.
Big Sky Racks, Inc.
Big Spring Enterprises "Bore Stores"
Bill's Custom Cases
Bison Studios
Black Sheep Brand
Boyt
Brauer Bros. Mfg. Co.
Brell Mar Products
Browning Arms Co.
Brunsport, Inc.
Bucheimer, J.M.
Bushmaster Hunting & Fishing
Cannon Safe, Inc.
Cascade Fabrication
Chipmunk
Clark Custom Guns, Inc.
Cobalt Mfg., Inc.
D&L Industries
Dara-Nes, Inc.
Deepeeka Exports Pvt. Ltd.
D.J. Marketing
Doskocil Mfg. Co., Inc.
DTM International, Inc.
Elk River, Inc.
English Inc., A.G.
Enhanced Presentations, Inc.
Fort Knox Security Products
Frontier Safe Co.
Galati Internationl
Galazan
GALCO International Ltd.
Granite Custom Bullets
Gun Locker
Gun-Ho Sports Cases
Gusdorf Corp.
Hafner Creations, Inc.
Hall Plastics, Inc., John
Harrison-Hurtz Enterprises, Inc.
Hastings Barrels
Homak Mfg. Co., Inc.
Hoppe's Div.
Huey Gun Cases
Hugger Hooks Co.
Hunter Co., Inc.
Impact Case Co.
Johanssons Vapentillbehor, Bert
Johnston Bros.
Jumbo Sports Products
Kalispel Case Line
Kane Products, Inc.
KK Air International
Knock on Wood Antiques
Kolpin Mfg., Inc.
Lakewood Products, Inc.
Liberty Safe
Marsh, Mike
Maximum Security Corp.
McWelco Products
Morton Booth Co.
MPC
MTM Molded Products Co., Inc.
National Security Safe Co., Inc.
NCP Products, Inc.
Necessary Concepts, Inc.
Nesci Enterprises, Inc.
Outa-Site Gun Carriers
Outdoor Connection, Inc., The
Pachmayr Ltd.
Palmer Security Products
Penguin Industries, Inc.
Perazzi USA, Inc.
Pflumm Mfg. Co.
Poburka, Philip
Powell & Son (Gunmakers) Ltd., William
Protecto Plastics
Prototech Industries, Inc.
Quality Arms, Inc.
Savana Sports, Inc.
Schulz Industries
Southern Security
Sportsman's Communicators
Sun Welding Safe Co.
Surecase Co., The
Sweet Home, Inc.
Tinks & Ben Lee Hunting Products
Waller & Son, Inc., W.
WAMCO, Inc.
Wilson Case, Inc.
Woodstream
Zanotti Armor, Inc.
Ziegel Engineering

CHOKE DEVICES, RECOIL ABSORBERS AND RECOIL PADS

Accuright
Action Products, Inc.
Ahlman Guns
Allen Co., Bob
Allen Sportswear, Bob
Answer Products Co.
Arms Ingenuity Co.
Baer Custom, Inc., Les
Baker, Stan
Bansner's Gunsmithing Specialties
Bartlett Engineering
Black Sheep Brand
Briley Mfg., Inc.
B-Square Co., Inc.
Bull Mountain Rifle Co.
C&H Research
Cape Outfitters
Cation
Chuck's Gun Shop
Clark Custom Guns, Inc.
Clearview Products
Colonial Arms, Inc.
Connecticut Shotgun Mfg. Co.
Crane Sales Co., George S.
Danuser Machine Co.
Dayson Arms Ltd.
Dever Co., Jack
Dina Arms Corporation
D-Max, Inc.
Elsen, Inc., Pete
Fabian Bros. Sporting Goods, Inc.
Gentry Custom Gunmaker, David
Graybill's Gun Shop
Great 870 Co., The
Guns, (Div. of D.C. Engineering, Inc.)
Harper, William E.
Hastings Barrels
Holland's
I.N.C., Inc.
Intermountain Arms & Tackle, Inc.
Jaeger, Inc., Paul/Dunn's
Jenkins Recoil Pads, Inc.
J.P. Enterprises, Inc.
Kick Eez
London Guns Ltd.
Lyman Instant Targets, Inc.
Lyman Products Corp.
Mag-Na-Port International, Inc.
Marble Arms
Meadow Industries
Michaels of Oregon Co.
Morrow, Bud

Nelson/Weather-rite, Inc.
One Of A Kind
Pachmayr Ltd.
Palsa Outdoor Products
PAST Sporting Goods, Inc.
Powell & Son (Gunmakers) Ltd., William
Pro-Port Ltd.
Protektor Model
Que Industries
R.M. Precision, Inc.
Shotguns Unlimited
Spencer's Custom Guns
Stone Enterprises Ltd.
Trulock Tool
Uncle Mike's
Wise Guns, Dale

CHRONOGRAPHS AND PRESSURE TOOLS

Brown Co., E. Arthur
Canons Delcour
Chronotech
Competition Electronics, Inc.
Custom Chronograph, Inc.
D&H Precision Tooling
Hornady Mfg. Co.
Kent Cartridge Mfg. Co. Ltd.
Oehler Research, Inc.
P.A.C.T., Inc.
Shooting Chrony, Inc.
SKAN A.R.
Tepeco

CLEANING AND REFINISHING SUPPLIES

AC Dyna-tite Corp.
Acculube II, Inc.
Accupro Gun Care
ADCO International
American Gas & Chemical Co., Ltd.
Answer Products Co.
Armsport, Inc.
Atlantic Mills, Inc.
Atsko/Sno-Seal, Inc.
Barnes Bullets, Inc.
Belltown, Ltd.
Birchwood Casey
Blackhawk East
Blue and Gray Products, Inc.
Break-Free, Inc.
Bridgers Best
Brown Co., E. Arthur
Cape Outfitters
Chem-Pak, Inc.
Chopie Mfg., Inc.
Clenzoil Corp.
Colonial Arms, Inc.
CONKKO
Crane & Crane Ltd.
Creedmoor Sports, Inc.
Custom Products
D&H Prods. Co., Inc.
Dara-Nes, Inc.
Deepeeka Exports Pvt. Ltd.
Dewey Mfg. Co., Inc., J.
Du-Lite Corp.
Dutchman's Firearms, Inc., The
Dykstra, Doug
E&L Mfg., Inc.
Eezox, Inc.
Effebi SNC, Dr. Franco Beretta
Ekol Leather Care
Faith Associates, Inc.
Flitz International Ltd.
Fluoramics, Inc.
Forster Products
Frontier Products Co.
G96 Products Co., Inc.
G.B.C. Industries, Inc.
Goddard, Allen
Golden Age Arms Co.
Gozon Corp., U.S.A.
Guardsman Products
Half Moon Rifle Shop
Heatbath Corp.
Hoppe's Div.
Hornady Mfg. Co.
Hydrosorbent Products
Iosso Products
J-B Bore Cleaner
Johnston Bros.
Kellogg's Professional Products
Kent Cartridge Mfg. Co. Ltd.
Kesselring Gun Shop
Kleen-Bore, Inc.
Laurel Mountain Forge
LEM Gun Specialties, Inc.
Lewis Lead Remover, The
List Precision Engineering
LPS Laboratories, Inc.
Marble Arms
Micro Sight Co.
Minute Man High Tech Industries
Mountain View Sports, Inc.
MTM Molded Products Co., Inc.
Muscle Products Corp.
Nesci Enterprises, Inc.
Old World Oil Products
Omark Industries
Original Mink Oil, Inc.
Outers Laboratories, Div. of Blount
Ox-Yoke Originals, Inc.
P&M Sales and Service
Pachmayr Ltd.
Parker Gun Finishes
Pendleton Royal
Penguin Industries, Inc.
Precision Reloading, Inc.
Prolix® Lubricants
Pro-Shot Products, Inc.
R&S Industries Corp.
Radiator Specialty Co.
Rickard, Inc., Pete
RIG Products Co.
Rod Guide Co.
Rooster Laboratories
Rusteprufe Laboratories
Rusty Duck Premium Gun Care Products
Saunders Gun & Machine Shop
Shiloh Creek
Shooter's Choice
Shootin' Accessories, Ltd.
Silencio/Safety Direct
Sno-Seal, Inc.
Spencer's Custom Guns
Svon Corp.
Tag Distributors
TDP Industries, Inc.
Tetra Gun Lubricants
Texas Platers Supply Co.
T.F.C. S.p.A.
United States Products Co.
Van Gorden & Son, Inc., C.S.
Venco Industries, Inc.
Warren Muzzleloading Co., Inc.
WD-40 Co.
Wick, David E.
Williams Shootin' Iron Service
Willow Bend
Young Country Arms
Z-Coat Industrial Coatings, Inc.

COMPUTER SOFTWARE—BALLISTICS

Action Target, Inc.
AmBr Software Group Ltd.
Arms, Peripheral Data Systems
Arms Software
Ballistic Engineering & Software, Inc.
Ballistic Program Co., Inc., The
Barnes Bullets, Inc.
Beartooth Bullets
Bestload, Inc.
Blackwell, W.
Canons Delcour
Corbin, Inc.
Country Armourer, The
Data Tech Software Systems
Exe, Inc.
Ford, Jack
JBM Software
Jensen Bullets
J.I.T. Ltd.
JWH:Software
Kent Cartridge Mfg. Co. Ltd.
Load From A Disk
Maionchi-L.M.I.
Oehler Research, Inc.
P.A.C.T., Inc.
PC Bullet/ADC, Inc.
Pejsa Ballistics
RCBS
Sierra Bullets
Tioga Engineering Co., Inc.
Vancini, Carl

CUSTOM GUNSMITHS

A&W Repair
Acadian Ballistic Specialties
Accuracy Gun Shop
Accuracy Unlimited (Glendale, AZ)
Ace Custom 45's, Inc.
Ackerman & Co.
Ad Hominem
Adair Custom Shop, Bill
Ahlman Guns
Aldis Gunsmithing & Shooting Supply
Alpha Gunsmith Division
Alpine's Precision Gunsmithing & Indoor Shooting Range
Amrine's Gun Shop
Answer Products Co.
Antique Arms Co.
Armament Gunsmithing Co., Inc.
Arms Craft Gunsmithing
Arms Ingenuity Co.
Arnold Arms Co., Inc.
Arrieta, S.L.
Art's Gun & Sport Shop, Inc.
Arundel Arms & Ammunition, Inc., A.
AWC Systems Technology
Baelder, Harry
Baer Custom, Inc., Les
Bain & Davis, Inc.
Bansner's Gunsmithing Specialties
Barnes Bullets, Inc.
Barta's Gunsmithing
Baumannize Custom
Bear Arms
Bear Mountain Gun & Tool
Beaver Lodge
Behlert Precision, Inc.
Beitzinger, George
Belding's Custom Gun Shop
Bellm Contenders
Belt MTN Arms
Benchmark Guns
Bengtson Arms Co., L.
Biesen, Al
Biesen, Roger
Billeb, Stephen L.
Billings Gunsmiths, Inc.
BlackStar AccuMax Barrels
BlackStar Barrel Accurizing
Bond Custom Firearms
Borden's Accuracy
Borovnik KG, Ludwig
Brace, Larry D.
Briese Bullet Co., Inc.
Briganti & Co., A.
Briley Mfg., Inc.
Broad Creek Rifle Works
Brockman's Custom Gunsmithing
Broken Gun Ranch
Brown Precision, Inc.
Buckhorn Gun Works
Buckskin Machine Works
Budin, Dave
Bull Mountain Rifle Co.
Bullberry Barrel Works, Ltd.
Burkhart Gunsmithing, Don
C&J Enterprises, Inc.
Cache La Poudre Rifleworks
Camilli, Lou
Campbell, Dick
Cannon's Guns
Carolina Precision Rifles
Carter's Gun Shop
Caywood, Shane J.
Chambers Flintlocks Ltd., Jim
Champlin, R. MacDonald
Champlin Firearms, Inc.
Chicasaw Gun Works
Christman Jr., David
Chuck's Gun Shop
Clark Custom Guns, Inc.
Clark Firearms Engraving
Classic Arms Corp.
Classic Guns, Inc.
Cloward's Gun Shop
Cochran, Oliver
Coffin, Charles H.
Cogar's Gunsmithing
Cole's Gun Works
Coleman's Custom Repair
Colonial Repair
Colorado Gunsmithing Academy Lamar
Colt's Mfg. Co., Inc.
Competitive Pistol Shop, The
Conrad, C.A.
Corkys Gun Clinic
Costa, David
Cox, C. Ed
Craig Custom Ltd.
Creekside Gun Shop, Inc.
Cullity Restoration, Daniel
Cumberland Knife & Gun Works
Curtis Custom Shop
Custom Checkering Service
Custom Gun Products
Custom Gun Stocks
Custom Gunsmiths
Custom Shop, The
Cylinder & Slide, Inc.
D&D Gunsmiths, Ltd.
D&J Bullet Co. & Custom Gun Shop, Inc.
Dangler, Homer L.
Darlington Gun Works, Inc.
Davis, Don
Davis Service Center, Bill
Delorge, Ed
Dever Co., Jack
DGR Custom Rifles
DGS, Inc.
Dietz Gun Shop & Range, Inc.
Dilliott Gunsmithing, Inc.
Donnelly, C.P.
Dowtin Gunworks
Duane's Gun Repair
Duffy, Charles E.
Duncan's Gun Works, Inc.
Dyson & Son Ltd., Peter
Echols & Co., D'Arcy
Eckelman Gunsmithing
Eggleston, Jere D.
EGW Evolution Gun Works
Erhardt, Dennis
Eskridge Rifles, Steven Eskridge
Eversull Co., Inc., K.
Eyster Heritage Gunsmiths, Inc., Ken
Fanzoj GmbH
Ferris Firearms
First, Inc., Jack
Fish, Marshall F.
Fisher, Jerry A.
Fisher Custom Firearms
Flaig's
Fleming Firearms
Flynn's Custom Guns
Forkin, Ben
Forster, Kathy
Forster, Larry L.
Forthofer's Gunsmithing & Knifemaking
Francesca, Inc.
Francotte & Cie S.A., Auguste
Frank Custom Classic Arms, Ron
Frazier Brothers Enterprises
Frontier Arms Co., Inc.
Fullmer, Geo. M.
Gator Guns & Repair
Genecco Gun Works, K.
Gentry Custom Gunmaker, David
G.G. & G.
Gillmann, Edwin
Gilman-Mayfield, Inc.
Giron, Robert E.
Goens, Dale W.
Gonzalez Guns, Ramon B.
Goodling's Gunsmithing
Goodwin, Fred
Gordie's Gun Shop
Grace, Charles E.
Graybill's Gun Shop
Green, Roger M.
Greg Gunsmithing Repair
Griffin & Howe, Inc.
Groenewold, John
Gun Shop, The
Guns
Guns Antique & Modern DBA/ Charles E. Duffy
Gunsite Custom Shop
Gunsite Gunsmithy
Gunsite Training Center
Gunsmithing Ltd.
Hagn Rifles & Actions, Martin
Hallberg Gunsmith, Fritz
Hamilton, Alex B.
Hammans, Charles E.

Hammond Custom Guns Ltd., Guy
Hank's Gun Shop
Hanson's Gun Center, Dick
Hardison, Charles
Harold's Custom Gun Shop, Inc.
Harris Gunworks
Hart & Son, Inc., Robert W.
Hart Rifle Barrels, Inc.
Hartmann & Weiss GmbH
Hecht, Hubert J.
Heinie Specialty Products
Hendricks Gun Works
Hensler, Jerry
Hensley, Darwin
High Bridge Arms, Inc.
High Performance International
Highline Machine Co.
Hill, Loring F.
Hiptmayer, Armurier
Hiptmayer, Klaus
Hoag, James W.
Hobbie Gunsmithing, Duane A.
Hodgson, Richard
Hoehn Sales, Inc.
Hoelscher, Virgil
Hoenig & Rodman
Hofer Jagdwaffen, P.
Holland, Dick
Holland's
Hollis Gun Shop
Horst, Alan K.
Huebner, Corey O.
Hughes, Steven Dodd
Hunkeler, A.
Hyper-Single, Inc.
Imperial Magnum Corp.
Intermountain Arms & Tackle, Inc.
Irwin, Campbell H.
Island Pond Gun Shop
Ivanoff, Thomas G.
J&S Heat Treat
Jackalope Gun Shop
Jaeger, Inc., Paul/Dunn's
Jamison's Forge Works
Jarrett Rifles, Inc.
Jarvis, Inc.
Jensen's Custom Ammunition
Jim's Gun Shop
Jim's Precision
Johnston, James
Jones, J.D.
J.P. Enterprises, Inc.
Juenke, Vern
Jurras, L.E.
K-D, Inc.
KDF, Inc.
Ken's Gun Specialties
Ketchum, Jim
Kilham & Co.
Kimball, Gary
King's Gun Works
KLA Enterprises
Klein Custom Guns, Don
Kleinendorst, K.W.
Kneiper Custom Guns, Jim
Knippel, Richard
KOGOT
Kopp, Terry K.
Korzinek Riflesmith, J.
LaFrance Specialties
Lair, Sam
LaRocca Gun Works, Inc.
Lathrop's, Inc.
Laughridge, William R.
Lawson Co., Harry
Lebeau-Courally
LeFever Arms Co., Inc.
Liberty Antique Gunworks
Lind Custom Guns, Al
Linebaugh Custom Sixguns & Rifle Works
List Precision Engineering
Lock's Philadelphia Gun Exchange
Lomont Precision Bullets
London Guns Ltd.
Mac-1 Distributors
Mac's .45 Shop
Mag-Na-Port International, Inc.
Mahony, Philip Bruce
Makinson, Nicholas
Manley Shooting Supplies, Lowell
Martin's Gun Shop
Martz, John V.
Masker, Seely
Mathews & Son, Inc., George E.
Maxi-Mount
Mazur Restoration, Pete
McBros Rifle Co.
McCament, Jay
McCann's Machine & Gun Shop
McCann's Muzzle-Gun Works
McCluskey Precision Rifles
McFarland, Stan
McGowen Rifle Barrels
McKinney, R.P.
McMillan Rifle Barrels
MCS, Inc.
Mercer Custom Stocks, R.M.
Michael's Antiques
Mid-America Recreation, Inc.
Middlebrooks Custom Shop
Miller Co., David
Miller Arms, Inc.
Miller Custom
Mills Jr., Hugh B.
Mo's Competitor Supplies
Moeller, Steve
Monell Custom Guns
Moreton/Fordyce Enterprises
Morrison Custom Rifles, J.W.
Morrow, Bud
Mountain Bear Rifle Works, Inc.
Mowrey's Guns & Gunsmithing
Mullis Guncraft
Mustra's Custom Guns, Inc., Carl
NCP Products, Inc.
Nelson, Stephen
Nettestad Gun Works
New England Custom Gun Service
Newman Gunshop
Nicholson Custom
Nicklas, Ted
Nitex, Inc.
Norrell Arms, John
North American Shooting Systems
North Fork Custom Gunsmithing
Nu-Line Guns, Inc.
Oakland Custom Arms, Inc.
Old World Gunsmithing
Olson, Vic
Orvis Co., The
Ottmar, Maurice
Ozark Gun Works
P&S Gun Service
Pace Marketing, Inc.
Pagel Gun Works, Inc.
Parker Gun Finishes
Pasadena Gun Center
Paterson Gunsmithing
Pell, John T.
PEM's Mfg. Co.
Pence Precision Barrels
Penrod Precision
Pentheny de Pentheny
Perazone, Brian
Performance Specialists
Peterson Gun Shop, Inc., A.W.
Power Custom, Inc.
P.S.M.G. Gun Co.
Quality Firearms of Idaho, Inc.
Ray's Gunsmith Shop
Renfrew Guns & Supplies
Ridgetop Sporting Goods
Ries, Chuck
Rifles Inc.
Rigby & Co., John
RMS Custom Gunsmithing
Robar Co.'s, Inc., The
Roberts Products
Robinson, Don
Rocky Mountain Arms, Inc.
Rocky Mountain Rifle Works Ltd.
Rogers Gunsmithing, Bob
Romain's Custom Guns, Inc.
RPM
Rudnicky, Susan
Rupert's Gun Shop
Ryan, Chad L.
Sanders Custom Gun Service
Schiffman, Curt
Schiffman, Mike
Schiffman, Norman
Schuetzen Gun Co.
Schumakers Gun Shop, William
Schwartz Custom Guns, Wayne E.
Scott Fine Guns, Inc., Thad
Scott, Dwight
Scott, McDougall & Associates
Shaw, Inc., E.R.
Shay's Gunsmithing
Shell Shack
Shockley, Harold H.
Shooten' Haus, The
Shooter Shop, The
Shooters Supply
Shootin' Shack, Inc.
Shooting Specialties
Shotgun Shop, The
Shotguns Unlimited
Silver Ridge Gun Shop
Simmons Gun Repair, Inc.
Singletary, Kent
Sipes Gun Shop
Siskiyou Gun Works
Skeoch, Brian R.
Slezak, Jerome F.
Small Arms Mfg. Co.
Smith, Art
Smith, Sharmon
Snapp's Gunshop
Spencer Reblue Service
Spencer's Custom Guns
Spokhandguns, Inc.
Sportsmen's Exchange & Western Gun Traders, Inc.
Spradlin's
Springfield, Inc.
SSK Industries
Starnes Gunmaker, Ken
Steelman's Gun Shop
Steffens, Ron
Steger, James R.
Stiles Custom Guns
Storey, Dale A.
Stott's Creek Armory, Inc.
Strawbridge, Victor W.
Sullivan, David S.
Swampfire Shop, The
Swann, D.J.
Swenson's 45 Shop, A.D.
Swift River Gunworks, Inc.
Szweda, Robert
300 Gunsmith Service, Inc.
Talmage, William G.
Tank's Rifle Shop
Tarnhelm Supply Co., Inc.
Taylor & Robbins
Ten-Ring Precision, Inc.
Thompson, Randall
Thurston Sports, Inc.
Time Precision, Inc.
Titus, Daniel
Tom's Gun Repair
Tooley Custom Rifles
Trevallion Gunstocks
Upper Missouri Trading Co.
USA Sporting Inc.
Van Epps, Milton
Van Horn, Gil
Van Patten, J.W.
Vest, John
Vic's Gun Refinishing
Vintage Arms, Inc.
Volquartsen Custom Ltd.
Von Minden Gunsmithing Services
Walker Arms Co., Inc.
Wardell Precision Handguns Ltd.
Weaver Arms Corp. Gun Shop
Weber & Markin Custom Gunsmiths
Weems, Cecil
Weigand Combat Handguns, Inc.
Wells, Fred F.
Wells Custom Gunsmith, R.A.
Welsh, Bud
Werth, T.W.
Wessinger Custom Guns & Engraving
West, Robert G.
Western Design
Westley Richards & Co.
Westwind Rifles, Inc.
Wichita Arms, Inc.
Wiebe, Duane
Wild West Guns
Williams Gun Sight Co.
Williams Shootin' Iron Service
Williamson Precision Gunsmithing
Wilson's Gun Shop
Winter, Robert M.
Wise Guns, Dale
Wiseman and Co., Bill
Wood, Frank
Yankee Gunsmith
Zeeryp, Russ

CUSTOM METALSMITHS

Adair Custom Shop, Bill
Ahlman Guns
Aldis Gunsmithing & Shooting Supply
Allen, Richard L.
Amrine's Gun Shop
Answer Products Co.
Arnold Arms Co., Inc.
Arundel Arms & Ammunition, Inc., A.
Baer Custom, Inc., Les
Bansner's Gunsmithing Specialties
Baron Technology
Bear Mountain Gun & Tool
Behlert Precision, Inc.
Beitzinger, George
Benchmark Guns
Bengtson Arms Co., L.
Biesen, Al
Billingsley & Brownell
BlackStar AccuMax Barrels
BlackStar Barrel Accurizing
Brace, Larry D.
Broad Creek Rifle Works
Brockmans Custom Gunsmithing
Brown Precision, Inc.
Buckhorn Gun Works
Bull Mountain Rifle Co.
Campbell, Dick
Carter's Gun Shop
Champlin Firearms, Inc.
Checkmate Refinishing
Classic Guns, Inc.
Colonial Repair
Colorado Gunsmithing Academy Lamar
Craftguard
Crandall Tool & Machine Co.
Cullity Restoration, Daniel
Custom Gun Products
Custom Gunsmiths
D&D Gunsmiths, Ltd.
D&H Precision Tooling
Dietz Gun Shop & Range, Inc.
Duncan's Gunworks, Inc.
Erhardt, Dennis
Eyster Heritage Gunsmiths, Inc., Ken
First, Inc., Jack
Fisher, Jerry A.
Forster, Larry L.
Francesca, Inc.
Frank Custom Classic Arms, Ron
Fullmer, Geo. M.
Gentry Custom Gunmaker, David
Gordie's Gun Shop
Grace, Charles E.
Graybill's Gun Shop
Green, Roger M.
Griffin & Howe, Inc.
Gun Shop, The
Guns
Gunsmithing Ltd.
Hagn Rifles & Actions, Martin
Hallberg Gunsmith, Fritz
Hart & Son, Inc., Robert W.
Hecht, Hubert J.
Heilmann, Stephen
Heppler's Machining
Highline Machine Co.
Hiptmayer, Armurier
Hiptmayer, Klaus
Hoelscher, Virgil
Holland's
Hollis Gun Shop
Horst, Alan K.
Hyper-Single, Inc.
Intermountain Arms & Tackle
Ivanoff, Thomas G.
J&S Heat Treat
Jaeger, Inc., Paul/Dunn's
Jeffredo Gunsight
Johnston, James
Ken's Gun Specialties
Kilham & Co.
Klein Custom Guns, Don
Kleinendorst, K.W.
Kopp, Terry K.
Lampert, Ron
LaRocca Gun Works, Inc.
Lawson Co., Harry
Lind Custom Guns, Al
List Precision Engineering
Mac's .45 Shop
Mains Enterprises, Inc.
Makinson, Nicholas
Mazur Restoration, Pete
McCament, Jay
McFarland, Stan
Morrison Custom Rifles, J.W.
Mullis Guncraft
Nettestad Gun Works
Nicholson Custom

Nitex, Inc.
Noreen, Peter H.
North Fork Custom Gunsmithing
Nu-Line Guns, Inc.
Olson, Vic
Ozark Gun Works
P&S Gun Service
Pagel Gun Works, Inc.
Parker Gun Finishes
Pasadena Gun Center
Penrod Precision
Precision Metal Finishing
Precise Metalsmithing Enterprises
Precision Specialties
Rice, Keith
Rifles Inc.
Robar Co.'s, Inc., The
Rocky Mountain Arms, Inc.
Shirley Co. Gun & Riflemakers Ltd., J.A.
Simmons Gun Repair, Inc.
Sipes Gun Shop
Skeoch, Brian R.
Smith, Art
Snapp's Gunshop
Spencer's Custom Guns
Sportsmen's Exchange & Western Gun Traders, Inc.
Steffens, Ron
Stiles Custom Guns
Stott's Creek Armory, Inc.
Strawbridge, Victor W.
Talmage, William G.
Taylor & Robbins
Thompson, Randall
Tom's Gun Repair
Van Horn, Gil
Von Minden Gunsmithing Services
Waldron, Herman
Weber & Markin Custom Gunsmiths
Wells, Fred F.
Welsh, Bud
Werth, T.W.
Wessinger Custom Guns & Engraving
West, Robert G.
Westrom, John
White Rock Tool & Die
Wiebe, Duane
Williams Gun Sight Co.
Williamson Precision Gunsmithing
Winter, Robert M.
Wise Guns, Dale
Wood, Frank
Zufall, Joseph F.

DECOYS

A&M Waterfowl, Inc.
Baekgaard Ltd.
Boyds' Gunstock Industries, Inc.
Carry-Lite, Inc.
Deer Me Products Co.
Fair Game International
Farm Form Decoys, Inc.
Feather Flex Decoys
Flambeau Products Corp.
G&H Decoys, Inc.
Herter's Manufacturing, Inc.
Hiti-Schuch, Atelier Wilma
Klingler Woodcarving
Molin Industries
North Wind Decoy Co.
Penn's Woods Products, Inc.
Quack Decoy & Sporting Clays
Sports Innovations, Inc.
Tanglefree Industries
Waterfield Sports, Inc.
Woods Wise Products

ENGRAVERS, ENGRAVING TOOLS

Ackerman & Co.
Adair Custom Shop, Bill
Adams, John J. & Son Engravers
Adams Jr., John J.
Ahlman Guns
Alfano, Sam
Allard, Gary
Allen, Richard L.
Altamont Co.
American Pioneer Video
Anthony and George Ltd.
Baron Technology
Barraclough, John K.
Bates Engraving, Billy
Bell Originals, Inc., Sid
Bleile, C. Roger
Boessler, Erich
Bone Engraving, Ralph
Bratcher, Dan
Brooker, Dennis
Brownell Checkering Tools, W.E.
Burgess, Byron
Churchill, Winston
Clark Firearms Engraving
Collings, Ronald
Creek Side Metal & Woodcrafters
Cullity Restoration, Daniel
Cupp, Custom Engraver, Alana
Davidson, Jere
Delorge, Ed
Desquesnes, Gerald
Dixon Muzzleloading Shop, Inc.
Dolbare, Elizabeth
Drain, Mark
Dubber, Michael W.
Dyson & Son Ltd., Peter
Engraving Artistry
Evans Engraving, Robert
Fanzoj GmbH
Firearms Engraver's Guild of America
Flannery Engraving Co., Jeff W.
Floatstone Mfg. Co.
Forty Five Ranch Enterprises
Fountain Products
Francolini, Leonard
Frank Custom Classic Arms, Ron
Frank Knives
French, J.R.
Gene's Custom Guns
George, Tim
Glimm, Jerome C.
Golden Age Arms Co.
Gournet, Geoffroy
Grant, Howard V.
Griffin & Howe, Inc.
GRS Corp., Glendo
Gun Room, The
Guns
Gurney, F.R.
Gwinnell, Bryson J.
Hale/Engraver, Peter
Half Moon Rifle Shop
Hands Engraving, Barry Lee
Harris Gunworks
Harris Hand Engraving, Paul A.
Harwood, Jack O.
Hendricks, Frank E.
Hiptmayer, Armurier
Hiptmayer, Heidemarie
Hiptmayer, Klaus
Horst, Alan K.
Ingle, Ralph W.
Jaeger, Inc., Paul/Dunn's
Jantz Supply
Johns Master Engraver, Bill
Kamyk Engraving Co., Steve
Kane, Edward
Kehr, Roger
Kelly, Lance
Klingler Woodcarving
Koevenig's Engraving Service
Kudlas, John M.
Lebeau-Courally
LeFever Arms Co., Inc.
Leibowitz, Leonard
Lindsay, Steve
Lister, Weldon
Little Trees Ramble
Lutz Engraving, Ron
Mains Enterprises, Inc.
Master Engravers, Inc.
McCombs, Leo
McDonald, Dennis
McKenzie, Lynton
Mele, Frank
Mittermeier, Inc., Frank
Moschetti, Mitchell R.
Mountain States Engraving
Napoleon Bonaparte, Inc.
Nelson, Gary K.
New Orleans Jewelers Supply Co.
NgraveR Co., The
Oker's Engraving
Old Dominion Engravers
P&S Gun Service
Pedersen, C.R.
Pedersen, Rex C.
Pilgrim Pewter, Inc.
Pilkington, Scott
Piquette, Paul R.
Potts, Wayne E.
Rabeno, Martin
Reed, Dave
Reno, Wayne
Riggs, Jim
Roberts, J.J.
Rohner, Hans
Rohner, John
Rosser, Bob
Rundell's Gun Shop
Runge, Robert P.
Sampson, Roger
Schiffman, Mike
Sherwood, George
Sinclair, W.P.
Singletary, Kent
Skaggs, R.E.
Smith, Mark A.
Smith, Ron
Smokey Valley Rifles
Theis, Terry
Thiewes, George W.
Thirion Gun Engraving, Denise
Valade Engraving, Robert
Vest, John
Viramontez, Ray
Vorhes, David
Wagoner, Vernon G.
Wallace, Terry
Warenski, Julie
Warren, Kenneth W.
Weber & Markin Custom Gunsmiths
Welch, Sam
Wells, Rachel
Wessinger Custom Guns & Engraving
Willig Custom Engraving, Claus
Wood, Mel

GAME CALLS

Adventure Game Calls
Arkansas Mallard Duck Calls
Ashby Turkey Calls
Bostick Wildlife Calls, Inc.
Brell Mar Products
Carter's Wildlife Calls, Inc., Garth
Cedar Hill Game Calls, Inc.
Crawford Co., Inc., R.M.
Crit'R Call
Custom Calls
D&H Prods. Co., Inc.
D-Boone Ent., Inc.
Deepeeka Exports Pvt. Ltd.
Dr. O's Products Ltd.
Duck Call Specialists
Faulhaber Wildlocker
Faulk's Game Call Co., Inc.
Flow-Rite of Tennessee, Inc.
Gander Mountain, Inc.
Green Head Game Call Co.
Hally Caller
Haydel's Game Calls, Inc.
Herter's Manufacturing, Inc.
Hunter's Specialties, Inc.
Keowee Game Calls
Kingyon, Paul L.
Knight & Hale Game Calls
Lohman Mfg. Co., Inc.
Mallardtone Game Calls
Marsh, Johnny
Moss Double Tone, Inc.
Mountain Hollow Game Calls
Oakman Turkey Calls
Olt Co., Philip S.
Penn's Woods Products, Inc.
Primos, Inc.
Quaker Boy, Inc.
Rickard, Inc., Pete
Robbins Scent, Inc.
Rocky Mountain Wildlife Products
Salter Calls, Inc., Eddie
Savana Sports, Inc.
Sceery Game Calls
Scobey Duck & Goose Calls, Glynn
Scruggs' Game Calls, Stanley
Simmons Outdoor Corp.
Sports Innovations, Inc.
Stewart Game Calls, Inc., Johnny
Sure-Shot Game Calls, Inc.
Tanglefree Industries
Tink's & Ben Lee Hunting Products
Tink's Safariland Hunting Corp.
Wellington Outdoors
Wilderness Sound Products Ltd.
Woods Wise Products
Wyant's Outdoor Products, Inc.

GUN PARTS, U.S. AND FOREIGN

Accuracy Gun Shop
Ahlman Guns
Amherst Arms
Armscorp USA, Inc.
Aro-Tek, Ltd.
Badger Shooters Supply, Inc.
Bear Mountain Gun & Tool
Bob's Gun Shop
Briese Bullet Co., Inc.
British Antiques
Bushmaster Firearms
Bustani, Leo
Cape Outfitters
Caspian Arms Ltd.
Century International Arms, Inc.
Clark Custom Guns, Inc.
Cole's Gun Works
Colonial Repair
Cylinder & Slide, Inc.
Delta Arms Ltd.
DGR Custom Rifles
Dibble, Derek A.
Dilliott Gunsmithing, Inc.
Dixie Gun Works, Inc.
Duane's Gun Repair
Duffy, Charles E.
Dyson & Son Ltd., Peter
E&L Mfg., Inc.
Elliott Inc., G.W.
EMF Co., Inc.
Enguix Import-Export
Fabian Bros. Sporting Goods, Inc.
Fleming Firearms
Forrest, Inc., Tom
Forster Products
Galati International
Goodwin, Fred
Groenewold, John
Gun Parts Corp., The
Gun Shop, The
Guns Antique & Modern DBA/Charles E. Duffy
Gun-Tec
Hastings Barrels
High Performance International
Irwin, Campbell H.
I.S.S.
Jaeger, Inc., Paul/Dunn's
Johnson's Gunsmithing, Inc., Neal G.
K&T Co.
Kimber of America, Inc.
K.K. Arms Co.
Krico Jagd-und Sportwaffen GmbH
Laughridge, William R.
List Precision Engineering
Lodewick, Walter H.
Lothar Walther Precision Tool, Inc.
L.P.A. Snc
Mac's .45 Shop
Mandall Shooting Supplies, Inc.
Markell, Inc.
Martin's Gun Shop
Martz, John V.
Mathews & Son, Inc., George E.
McCann's Machine & Gun Shop
McCormick Corp., Chip
Merkuria Ltd.
Mid-America Recreation, Inc.
Morrow, Bud
Nu-Line Guns, Inc.
Pachmayr Ltd.
Parts & Surplus
Pennsylvania Gun Parts
Perazzi USA, Inc.
Performance Specialists
Peterson Gun Shop, Inc., A.W.
Pre-Winchester 92-90-62 Parts Co.
P.S.M.G. Gun Co.
Quality Firearms of Idaho, Inc.
Quality Parts Co.
Ranch Products
Randco UK
Retting, Inc., Martin B.
Ruvel & Co., Inc.
S&S Firearms
Sabatti S.R.L.
Sarco, Inc.
Scherer

Shockley, Harold H.
Silver Ridge Gun Shop
Sipes Gun Shop
Smires, C.L.
Smith & Wesson
Southern Ammunition Co., Inc.
Southern Armory, The
Sportsmen's Exchange & Western Gun Traders, Inc.
Springfield, Inc.
Springfield Sporters, Inc.
Starr Trading Co., Jedediah
"Su-Press-On," Inc.
Swampfire Shop, The
Tank's Rifle Shop
Tarnhelm Supply Co., Inc.
Twin Pine Armory
USA Sporting Inc.
Vintage Arms, Inc.
Vintage Industries, Inc.
Volquartsen Custom Ltd.
Walker Arms Co., Inc.
Weaver Arms Corp. Gun Shop
Westfield Engineering
Williams Mfg. of Oregon
Winchester Sutler, Inc., The
Wise Guns, Dale
Wolff Co., W.C.

GUNS, AIR

Air Arms
•Air Venture
Airrow
•Anschutz GmbH
Arms Corporation of the Philippines
Arms United Corp.
Baikal
•Beeman Precision Airguns
•Benjamin/Sheridan Co.
Brass Eagle, Inc.
Brocock Ltd.
•BSA Guns Ltd.
Compasseco, Ltd.
Component Concepts, Inc.
Crawford Co., Inc., R.M.
Creedmoor Sports, Inc.
•Crosman Airguns
Crosman Products of Canada Ltd.
•Daisy Mfg. Co.
Daystate Ltd.
•Diana
•Dynamit Nobel-RWS, Inc.
E.A.A. Corp.
•FAS
Frankonia Jagd
•FWB
•Gamo
Gamo USA, Inc.
•GFR Corp.
•Great Lakes Airguns
GZ Paintball Sports Products
Hebard Guns, Gil
•Interarms
Labanu, Inc.
List Precision Engineering
•Mac-1 Distributors
•Marksman Products
Maryland Paintball Supply
Merkuria Ltd.
•Pardini Armi Srl
Park Rifle Co., Ltd., The
Penguin Industries, Inc.
Powell & Son (Gunmakers) Ltd., William
•Precision Airgun Sales, Inc.
•Precision Sales Int'l, Inc.
Ravell Ltd.
Ripley Rifles
•RWS
Savana Sports, Inc.
S.G.S. Sporting Guns Srl
Shanghai Airguns, Ltd.
SKAN A.R.
Smart Parts
Sportsman Airguns, Inc.
•Steyr Mannlicher AG
Stone Enterprises Ltd.
•Swivel Machine Works, Inc.
Theoben Engineering
Tippman Pneumatics, Inc.
Trooper Walsh
UltraSport Arms, Inc.
Valor Corp.
Venom Arms Co.
Vortek Products
•Walther GmbH, Carl
•Webley and Scott Ltd.
•Weihrauch KG, Hermann
Whiscombe
World Class Airguns

GUNS, FOREIGN—IMPORTERS (Manufacturers)

Accuracy International (Anschutz GmbH)
AcuSport Corporation (Anschutz GmbH)
•Air Rifle Specialists (airguns)
•Air Venture (airguns)
Airguns-R-Us (Falcon Pneumatic Systems; air rifles and pistols)
•American Arms, Inc. (Fausti Cav. Stefano & Figlie snc; Franchi S.p.A.; Grulla Armes; Uberti, Aldo; Zabala Hermanos S.A.; blackpowder arms)
Amtec 2000, Inc. (Erma Werke GmbH)
Anics Firm, Inc. (Anics)
•Armes de Chasse (Armas Azor, J.A.; AYA; Francotte & Cie S.A., Auguste)
Arms United Corp. (Gamo)
•Armscorp USA, Inc.
Armsport, Inc. (airguns, blackpowder arms and shotguns)
•Autumn Sales, Inc. (Blaser Jagdwaffen GmbH)
Auto-Ordnance Corp. (Techno Arms)
•Beauchamp & Son, Inc. (Pedersoli, Davide & C.)
•Beeman Precision Airguns (Beeman Precision Airguns; FWB; Webley & Scott Ltd.; Weihrauch KG, Hermann)
•Bell's Legendary Country Wear (Miroku, B.C./Daly, Charles; Powell & Son, Ltd., William)
•Beretta U.S.A. Corp. (Beretta S.p.A., Pietro)
•Bohemia Arms Co. (BRNO)
British Sporting Arms
•Browning Arms Co. (Browning Arms Co.)
B-West Imports, Inc.
•Cabela's (Pedersoli, Davide & C.; blackpowder arms)
•Cape Outfitters (Armi Sport; Bertuzzi; Pedersoli, Davide & C.; San Marco; Societa Armi Bresciane Srl.; Westley Richards & Co.; blackpowder arms)
•Century International Arms, Inc. (Famas; FEG; Norinco)
Champion Shooters' Supply (Anschutz GmbH)
Champion's Choice (Anschutz GmbH; Lapua; Walther GmbH, Carl)
•Chapuis USA (Chapuis Armes)
Christopher Firearms Co., Inc., E.
•Cimarron Arms (Uberti, Aldo; blackpowder arms)
County Arms (I.T.S.)
•CVA (blackpowder arms)
•Daisy Mfg. Co. (Daisy Mfg. Co.; Gamo)
•Dixie Gun Works, Inc. (Pedersoli, Davide & C.; Uberti, Aldo; blackpowder arms)
•Dynamit Nobel-RWS, Inc. (Brenneke KG, Wilhelm; Diana; Gamo; Norma Precision AB; RWS)
•E.A.A. Corp. (Astra-Sport, S.A.; Benelli Armi S.p.A.; Sabatti S.r.l.; Tanfoglio S.r.l., Fratelli; Weihrauch KG, Hermann)
Eagle Imports, Inc. (Bersa S.A.)
•Ellett Bros. (Churchill)
•EMF Co., Inc. (Dakota; Hartford; Pedersoli, Davide & C.; San Marco; Uberti, Aldo; blackpowder arms)
Euroarms of America, Inc. (blackpowder arms)
Eversull Co., Inc., K.
•Fiocchi of America, Inc. (Fiocchi Munizioni S.p.A.)
First National Gun Bank Corp., The (Gamba S.p.A.-Societa Armi Bresciane Srl., Renato)
•Forgett Jr., Valmore J. (Navy Arms Co.; Uberti, Aldo)
•Galaxy Imports Ltd., Inc. (Laurona Armas Eibar, S.A.D.; Ugartechea S.A., Ignacio)
Gamba, USA (Societa Armi Bresciane Srl.)
Gamo USA, Inc. (Gamo)
Giacomo Sporting, Inc.
•Glock, Inc. (Glock GmbH)
•Great Lakes Airguns (air pistols)
Griffin & Howe (Arrieta, S.L.)
Groenewold, John (BSA Guns Ltd.; Paragon and Prometheus pellets; Webley & Scott Ltd.)
•GSI, Inc. (Mauser Werke Oberndorf; Merkel Freres; Steyr; Steyr-Mannlicher AG)
•G.U., Inc. (New SKB Arms Co.; SKB Arms Co.)
Gunsite Custom Shop (Accuracy International Precision Rifles)
Gunsite Training Center (Accuracy International Precision Rifles)
Gunsmithing, Inc. (Anschutz GmbH)
•Hammerli USA (Hammerli Ltd.)
Harris Gunworks (Peters Stahl GmbH)
•Heckler & Koch, Inc. (Benelli Armi S.p.A.; Heckler & Koch, GmbH)
•Hi-Grade Imports (Arrieta, S.L.)
Imperial Magnum Corp. (Imperial Magnum Corp.)
Import Sports Inc. (Llama Gabilondo Y Cia)
•Interarms (Helwan; Howa Machinery Ltd.; Interarms; Korth; Norinco; Rossi S.A., Amadeo Rua; Star Bonifacio Echeverria S.A.; Walther GmbH, Carl)
•JägerSport, Ltd. (Voere-KGH m.b.H.)
•Jansma, Jack J. (Arrieta, S.L.)
•J.O. Arms Inc. (KSN Industries, Ltd.)
•K.B.I., Inc. (Armscorp USA, Inc.; Baikal; FEG; K.B.I., Inc.; Sabatti S.R.L.)
•Keng's Firearms Specialty, Inc. (Lapua; Ultralux)
Kongsberg America L.L.C. (Kongsberg)
•Krieghoff International, Inc. (Krieghoff Gun Co., H.)
K-Sports Imports, Inc.
Labanu, Inc. (air rifles)
London Guns Ltd. (London Guns Ltd.)
Mac-1 Distributors (Venom Arms Co.)
•Magnum Research, Inc. (BRNO; CZ)
MAGTECH Recreational Products, Inc. (Magtech)
•Mandall Shooting Supplies, Inc. (Arizaga; Atamec-Bretton; Cabanas; Crucelegui, Hermanos; Erma Werke GmbH; Firearms Co. Ltd./Alpine; Hammerli Ltd.; Korth; Krico Jagd-und Sportwaffen GmbH; Morini; SIG; Tanner; Ugartechea S.A., Ignacio; Zanoletti, Pietro; blackpowder arms)
Marx, Harry (FERLIB)
•MEC-Gar U.S.A., Inc. (MEC-Gar s.r.l.)
•Mitchell Arms, Inc. (Mitchell Arms, Inc.)
•Moore & Co., Wm. Larkin (Bertuzzi; Garbi, Armas Urki; Piotti; Rizzini, Battista; Rizzini, F.LLI)
•Nationwide Sports Distributors, Inc. (Daewoo Precision Industries Ltd.)
•Navy Arms Co. (Navy Arms Co.; Pedersoli, Davide & C.; Pietta; Uberti, Aldo; blackpowder and cartridge arms)
•Nevada Cartridge Co. (Effebi SNC-Dr. Franco Beretta)
•New England Arms Co. (Arrieta, S.L.; Bertuzzi; Bosis; Cosmi Americo & Figlio s.n.c.; Dumoulin, Ernest; Lebeau-Courally; Rizzini, Battista; Rizzini, F.LLI)
New England Custom Gun Service (AYA; EAW)
•Nygord Precision Products (FAS; Morini; Pardini Armi Srl; Steyr; Steyr-Mannlicher AG; TOZ; Unique/M.A.P.F.)
OK Weber, Inc. (target rifles)
•Orvis Co., Inc., The (Arrieta, S.L.)
•Pachmayr Ltd.
•Para-Ordnance, Inc. (Para-Ordnance Mfg., Inc.)
•Paul Co., The (Norma Precision AB; Sauer)
Pelaire Products (Whiscombe)
•Perazzi USA, Inc. (Perazzi m.a.p. S.p.A.)
Powell Agency, William, The (William Powell & Son [Gunmakers] Ltd.)
P.S.M.G. Gun Co. (Astra Sport, S.A.; Interarms; Star Bonifacio Echeverria S.A.; Walther GmbH, Carl)
•Quality Arms, Inc. (Arrieta, S.L.)
Sarco, Inc.
Savage Arms, Inc. (Lakefield Arms Ltd.; Savage Arms, Inc.)
Schuetzen Pistol Works (Peters Stahl GmbH)
Sheridan USA, Inc., Austin
•Sigarms, Inc. (Hammerli Ltd.; Sauer; SIG-Sauer)
•Sile Distributors (Marocchi F.lli S.p.A.)
SKB Shotguns (SKB Arms Co.)
Sphinx USA Inc. (Sphinx Engineering SA)
Sportsman Airguns, Inc. (QB air rifles; Shanghai Airguns, Ltd.)
•Springfield, Inc. (Springfield, Inc.)
•Stoeger Industries (IGA; Sako Ltd.; Tikka; target pistols)
Stone Enterprises Ltd. (airguns)
•Swarovski Optik North America Ltd.
•Taurus Firearms, Inc. (Taurus International Firearms)
Taylor's & Co., Inc. (Armi San Marco; Armi Sport; I.A.B.; Pietta; Uberti, Aldo)
Tradewinds, Inc. (blackpowder arms)
Tristar Sporting Arms, Ltd. (Turkish made firearms)
Trooper Walsh (Venom Arms Co.)
Turkish Firearms Corp. (Turkish Firearms Corp.)
•Uberti USA, Inc. (Uberti, Aldo; blackpowder arms)
USA Sporting Inc. (Armas Kemen S.A.)
Vintage Arms, Inc.
•Weatherby, Inc. (Weatherby, Inc.)
Wingshooters Ltd. (Arrieta, S.L.)
World Class Airguns (Air Arms)

GUNS, FOREIGN—MANUFACTURERS (Importers)

Accuracy International Precision Rifles (Gunsite Custom Shop; Gunsite Training Center)
•Air Arms (World Class Airguns)
Anics (Anics Firm, Inc.)
•Anschutz GmbH (Accuracy International; AcuSport Corporation; Champion Shooters' Supply; Champion's Choice; Gunsmithing, Inc.)
•Arizaga (Mandall Shooting Supplies, Inc.)
Armas Azor, J.A. (Armes de Chasse)
Armas Kemen S.A. (USA Sporting Inc.)
Armi San Marco (Taylor's & Co., Inc.)
Armi Sport (Cape Outfitters; Taylor's & Co., Inc.)
Arms Corporation of the Philippines
Armscorp USA, Inc. (K.B.I., Inc.)
•Arrieta, S.L. (Griffin & Howe; Hi-Grade Imports; Jansma, Jack J.; New England Arms Co.; The Orvis Co., Inc.; Quality Arms, Inc.; Wingshooters Ltd.)
•Astra Sport, S.A. (E.A.A. Corp.; P.S.M.G. Gun Co.)
Atamec Bretton (Mandall Shooting Supplies, Inc.)
•ATIS Armi S.A.S.
•AYA (Armes de Chasse; New England Custom Gun Service)
•Baikal (K.B.I., Inc.)
•Beeman Precision Airguns (Beeman Precision Airguns)
•Benelli Armi S.p.A. (E.A.A. Corp.; Heckler & Koch, Inc.)
•Beretta S.p.A., Pietro (Beretta U.S.A. Corp.)
•Bernardelli S.p.A., Vincenzo
Bersa S.A. (Eagle Imports, Inc.)
•Bertuzzi (Cape Outfitters; Moore & Co., Wm. Larkin; New England Arms Co.)
•Blaser Jagdwaffen GmbH (Autumn Sales, Inc.)
Bondini Paolo (blackpowder arms)
Borovnik KG, Ludwig
Bosis (New England Arms Co.)
Brenneke KG, Wilhelm (Dynamit Nobel-RWS, Inc.)
•BRNO (Bohemia Arms Co.; Magnum Research, Inc.)
Brocock Ltd.
•Browning Arms Co. (Browning Arms Co.)
•BSA Guns Ltd. (Groenewold, John)

•See page 445 for Warranty Service Center Addresses

- •Cabanas (Mandall Shooting Supplies, Inc.)
- •CBC
- •Chapuis Armes (Chapuis USA)
- •Churchill (Ellett Bros.)
- •Cosmi Americo & Figlio s.n.c. (New England Arms Co.)
- •Crucelegui, Hermanos (Mandall Shooting Supplies, Inc.)
- •CVA (blackpowder arms)
- •CZ (Magnum Research, Inc.)
- •Daewoo Precision Industries Ltd. (Nationwide Sports Distributors, Inc.)
- •Dakota (EMF Co., Inc.)
- •Daisy Mfg. Co. (Daisy Mfg. Co.)
- •Diana (Dynamit Nobel-RWS, Inc.)
- Dumoulin, Ernest (New England Arms Co.)
- EAW (New England Custom Gun Service)
- Effebi SNC-Dr. Franco Beretta (Nevada Cartridge Co.)
- •Erma Werke GmbH (Amtec 2000, Inc.; Mandall Shooting Supplies, Inc.)
- •Fabarm S.p.A.
- F.A.I.R. Techni-Mec s.n.c.
- Falcon Pneumatic Systems (Airguns-R-Us)
- •Famas (Century International Arms, Inc.)
- •FAS (Nygord Precision Products)
- •Fausti Cav. Stefano & Figlie snc (American Arms, Inc.)
- •FEG (Century International Arms, Inc.; K.B.I., Inc.)
- FERLIB (Marx, Harry)
- Fiocchi Munizioni S.P.A. (Fiocchi of America, Inc.)
- •Firearms Co. Ltd./Alpine (Mandall Shooting Supplies, Inc.)
- FN Herstal
- •Franchi S.p.A (American Arms, Inc.)
- •Francotte & Cie S.A., Auguste (Armes de Chasse)
- •FWB (Beeman Precision Airguns)
- •Gamba S.p.A.-Societa Armi Bresciane Srl., Renato (First National Gun Bank Corp., The)
- •Gamo (Arms United Corp.; Daisy Mfg. Co.; Dynamit Nobel-RWS, Inc.; Gamo USA, Inc.)
- •Garbi, Armas Urki (Moore & Co., Wm. Larkin)
- Gaucher Armes S.A.
- •Glock GmbH (Glock, Inc.)
- •Grulla Armes (American Arms, Inc.)
- •Hammerli Ltd. (Hammerli USA; Mandall Shooting Supplies, Inc.; Sigarms, Inc.)
- Hartford (EMF Co., Inc.)
- Hartmann & Weiss GmbH
- •Heckler & Koch, GmbH (Heckler & Koch, Inc.)
- •Helwan (Interarms)
- •Heym GmbH & Co., Friedrich Wilh.
- Holland & Holland Ltd.
- •Howa Machinery Ltd. (Interarms)
- I.A.B. (Taylor's & Co., Inc.)
- •IGA (Stoeger Industries)
- •IMI
- Imperial Magnum Corp. (Imperial Magnum Corp.)
- •Interarms (Interarms; P.S.M.G. Gun Co.)
- I.T.S. (County Arms)
- •K.B.I., Inc. (K.B.I., Inc.)
- Kongsberg (Kongsberg America L.L.C.)
- •Korth (Interarms; Mandall Shooting Supplies, Inc.)
- •Krico Jagd-und Sportwaffen GmbH (Mandall Shooting Supplies, Inc.)
- •Krieghoff Gun Co., H. (Krieghoff International, Inc.)
- KSN Industries, Ltd. (J.O. Arms Inc.)
- •Lakefield Arms Ltd. (Savage Arms, Inc.)
- Lanber Armas S.A.
- Lapua (Champion's Choice; Keng's Firearms Specialty, Inc.)
- •Laurona Armas Eibar S.A.D. (Galaxy Imports Ltd., Inc.)
- •Lebeau-Courally (New England Arms Co.)
- •Llama Gabilondo Y Cia (Import Sports Inc.)
- London Guns Ltd. (London Guns Ltd.)
- Magtech (Magtech Recreational Products, Inc.)
- •Marocchi F.lli S.p.A. (Sile Distributors, Inc.)
- Mauser Werke Oberndorf (GSI, Inc.)
- •MEC-Gar s.r.l. (MEC-Gar U.S.A., Inc.)
- •Merkel Freres (GSI, Inc.)
- •Miroku, B.C./Daly, Charles (Bell's Legendary Country Wear)
- •Mitchell Arms, Inc. (Mitchell Arms, Inc.)
- •Morini (Mandall Shooting Supplies; Nygord Precision Products)
- •Navy Arms Co. (Forgett Jr., Valmore J.; Navy Arms Co.)
- New SKB Arms Co. (G.U., Inc.)
- Norica, Avnda Otaola
- •Norinco (Century International Arms, Inc.; Interarms)
- Norma Precision AB (Dynamit Nobel-RWS Inc.; The Paul Co., Inc.)
- •Para-Ordnance Mfg., Inc. (Para-Ordnance, Inc.)
- •Pardini Armi Srl. (Nygord Precision Products)
- •Pedersoli, Davide & C. (Beauchamp & Son, Inc.; Cabela's; Cape Outfitters; Dixie Gun Works, Inc.; EMF Co., Inc.; Navy Arms Co.)
- •Perazzi m.a.p. S.p.A. (Perazzi USA, Inc.)
- Perugini-Visini & Co. s.r.l.
- Peters Stahl GmbH (Harris Gunworks; Schuetzen Pistol Works)
- Pietta (Navy Arms Co.; Taylor's & Co., Inc.)
- •Piotti (Moore & Co., Wm. Larkin)
- •Powell & Son Ltd., William (Bell's Legendary Country Wear; Powell Agency, The, William)
- QB air rifles (Sportsman Airguns, Inc.)
- •Rigby & Co., John
- •Rizzini, Battista (Moore & Co., Wm. Larkin; New England Arms Co.)
- •Rizzini, F.LLI (Moore & Co., Wm. Larkin; New England Arms Co.)
- •Rossi S.A., Amadeo Rua (Interarms)
- •RWS (Dynamit Nobel-RWS, Inc.)
- Sabatti S.R.L. (E.A.A. Corp.; K.B.I., Inc.)
- •Sako Ltd. (Stoeger Industries)
- •San Marco (Cape Outfitters; EMF Co., Inc.)
- S.A.R.L. G. Granger
- •Sauer (Paul Co., The; Sigarms, Inc.)
- Savage Arms, Inc. (Savage Arms, Inc.)
- Shanghai Airguns, Ltd. (Sportsman Airguns, Inc.)
- •SIG (Mandall Shooting Supplies, Inc.)
- •SIG-Sauer (Sigarms, Inc.)
- •SKB Arms Co. (G.U., Inc.; SKB Shotguns)
- •Societa Armi Bresciane Srl. (Cape Outfitters; Gamba, USA)
- Sphinx Engineering SA (Sphinx USA Inc.)
- •Springfield, Inc. (Springfield, Inc.)
- •Star Bonifacio Echeverria S.A. (Interarms; P.S.M.G. Gun Co.)
- •Steyr (GSI, Inc.; Nygord Precision Products)
- •Steyr-Mannlicher AG (GSI, Inc.; Nygord Precision Products)
- •Tanfoglio S.r.l., Fratelli (E.A.A. Corp.)
- •Tanner (Mandall Shooting Supplies, Inc.)
- •Taurus International Firearms (Taurus Firearms, Inc.)
- Taurus S.A., Forjas
- Techni-Mec
- Techno Arms (Auto-Ordnance Corp.)
- T.F.C. S.p.A.
- •Tikka (Stoeger Industries)
- TOZ (Nygord Precision Products)
- Turkish Firearms Corp. (Turkish Firearms Corp.)
- •Uberti, Aldo (American Arms, Inc.; Cimarron Arms; Dixie Gun Works, Inc.; EMF Co., Inc.; Forgett Jr., Valmore J.; Navy Arms Co.; Taylor's & Co., Inc.; Uberti USA, Inc.)
- •Ugartechea S.A., Ignacio (Galaxy Imports Ltd., Inc.; Mandall Shooting Supplies, Inc.)
- Ultralux (Keng's Firearms Specialty, Inc.)
- •Unique/M.A.P.F. (Nygord Precision Products)
- Venom Arms Co. (Mac-1 Distributors; Trooper Walsh)
- •Voere-KGH m.b.H. (JägerSport, Ltd.)
- •Walther GmbH, Carl (Champion's Choice; Interarms; P.S.M.G. Gun Co.)
- •Weatherby, Inc. (Weatherby, Inc.)
- •Webley & Scott Ltd. (Beeman Precision Airguns; Groenewold, John)
- •Weihrauch KG, Hermann (Beeman Precision Airguns; E.A.A. Corp.)
- •Westley Richards & Co. (Cape Outfitters)
- Whiscombe (Pelaire Products)
- •Zabala, Hermanos S.A. (American Arms, Inc.)
- •Zanoletti, Pietro (Mandall Shooting Supplies, Inc.)
- Zoli, Antonio

GUNS, U.S.-MADE

- A.A. Arms, Inc.
- •Accu-Tek
- •Airrow
- •American Arms & Ordnance, Inc.
- •American Arms, Inc.
- •American Derringer Corp.
- •AMT
- Amtec 2000, Inc.
- •ArmaLite, Inc.
- •A-Square Co., Inc.
- •Auto-Ordnance Corp.
- •Baer Custom, Inc., Les
- •Barrett Firearms Mfg., Inc.
- Bar-Sto Precision Machine
- •Beretta U.S.A. Corp.
- •Braverman, R.J.
- •Brolin Arms
- •Brown Co., E. Arthur
- Brown Products, Inc., Ed
- •Browning Arms Co. (Parts & Service)
- Bullberry Barrel Works, Ltd.
- •Bushmaster Firearms
- •Calico Light Weapon Systems
- •Century Gun Dist., Inc.
- •Colt's Mfg. Co., Inc.
- •Competitor Corp., Inc.
- •Connecticut Valley Classics
- •Connecticut Shotgun Mfg. Co.
- •Coonan Arms
- •Cooper Arms
- •Cumberland Arms
- •CVA
- •Dakota Arms, Inc.
- Dangler, Homer L.
- •Davis Industries
- •Desert Industries, Inc.
- •Eagle Arms, Inc.
- •Emerging Technologies, Inc.
- •Essex Arms
- •Feather Industries, Inc.
- •Federal Engineering Corp.
- FN Herstal
- •Freedom Arms, Inc.
- •Gibbs Rifle Co., Inc.
- •Gilbert Equipment Co., Inc.
- •Gonic Arms, Inc.
- Gunsite Custom Shop
- Gunsite Gunsmithy
- •H&R 1871, Inc.
- Harrington & Richardson
- •Harris Gunworks
- •Hatfield Gun Co., Inc.
- •Hawken Shop, The
- Heritage Firearms
- Heritage Manufacturing, Inc.
- •High Standard Mfg. Co., Inc.
- •Hi-Point Firearms
- •HJS Arms, Inc.
- •H-S Precision, Inc.
- •Intratec
- •Jennings Firearms Inc.
- JS Worldwide DBA
- •Kahr Arms
- Kelbly, Inc.
- •Kel-Tec CNC Industries, Inc.
- •Kimber of America, Inc.
- •Kimel Industries
- K.K. Arms Co.
- •Knight's Mfg. Co.
- LaFrance Specialties
- •L.A.R. Mfg., Inc.
- •Laseraim, Inc.
- •Lorcin Engineering Co., Inc.
- •Magnum Research, Inc.
- •Marlin Firearms Co.
- •Maverick Arms, Inc.
- •McBros Rifle Co.
- McCann's Muzzle-Gun Works
- Miller Arms, Inc.
- •Mitchell Arms, Inc.
- •MKS Supply, Inc.
- •M.O.A. Corp.
- •Montana Armory, Inc.
- •Mossberg & Sons, Inc., O.F.
- NCP Products, Inc.
- •New Advantage Arms Corp.
- •New England Firearms
- Noreen, Peter H.
- •North American Arms, Inc.
- Nowlin Custom Mfg.
- Paragon Sales & Services, Inc.
- •Phoenix Arms
- •Precision Small Arms
- •Quality Parts Co.
- Recoilless Technologies, Inc.
- •Remington Arms Co., Inc.
- Rifle Works & Armory
- •Rocky Mountain Arms, Inc.
- Ruger
- •Seecamp Co., Inc., L.W.
- •Sharps Arms Co., Inc., C.
- •Shiloh Rifle Mfg.
- •Smith & Wesson
- •Sporting Arms Mfg., Inc.
- •Springfield, Inc.
- Stoeger Industries
- •Sturm, Ruger & Co., Inc.
- •Sundance Industries, Inc.
- •Survival Arms, Inc.
- •Swivel Machine Works, Inc.
- •Tar-Hunt Custom Rifles, Inc.
- •Taurus Firearms, Inc.
- •Texas Armory
- •Texas Longhorn Arms, Inc.
- •Thompson/Center Arms
- •Ultra Light Arms, Inc.
- •U.S. Repeating Arms Co.
- •Weatherby, Inc.
- •White Shooting Systems, Inc.
- •Wichita Arms, Inc.
- •Wildey, Inc.
- •Wilkinson Arms

GUNS AND GUN PARTS, REPLICA AND ANTIQUE

- Ahlman Guns
- Armi San Paolo
- Bear Mountain Gun & Tool
- Beauchamp & Son, Inc.
- Bob's Gun Shop
- British Antiques
- Buckskin Machine Works
- Buffalo Arms
- Burgess & Son Gunsmiths, R.W.
- Cache La Poudre Rifleworks
- Cape Outfitters
- Century International Arms, Inc.
- Chambers Flintlocks Ltd., Jim
- Cogar's Gunsmithing
- Cole's Gun Works
- Colonial Repair
- Curly Maple Stock Blanks
- Dangler, Homer L.
- Day & Sons, Inc., Leonard
- Delhi Gun House
- Delta Arms Ltd.
- Dilliott Gunsmithing, Inc.
- Dixie Gun Works, Inc.
- Dixon Muzzleloading Shop, Inc.
- Ed's Gun House
- Euroarms of America, Inc.
- Flintlocks, Etc.
- Forgett, Valmore J., Jr.
- Forster Products
- Galazan
- Golden Age Arms Co.
- Goodwin, Fred
- Groenewold, John
- Gun Parts Corp., The
- Gun-Tec
- Hastings Barrels
- Hunkeler, A.
- Liberty Antique Gunworks
- List Precision Engineering
- Lock's Philadelphia Gun Exchange
- Lucas, Edw. E.
- McKinney, R.P.
- Meier Works
- Mountain State Muzzleloading Supplies
- Munsch Gunsmithing, Tommy
- Museum of Historical Arms, Inc.
- Neumann GmbH
- Pasadena Gun Center
- Peacemaker Specialists

•See page 445 for Warranty Service Center Addresses

PEM's Mfg. Co.
P.M. Enterprises, Inc.
Pony Express Sport Shop, Inc.
Precise Metalsmithing Enterprises
Quality Firearms of Idaho, Inc.
Randco UK
Retting, Inc., Martin B.
S&S Firearms
Sarco, Inc.
Scattergun Technologies, Inc.
Schuetzen Gun Co.
Silver Ridge Gun Shop
Sipes Gun Shop
South Bend Replicas, Inc.
Southern Ammunition Co., Inc.
Stott's Creek Armory, Inc.
Taylor's & Co., Inc.
Tennessee Valley Mfg.
Tiger-Hunt
Track of the Wolf, Inc.
Uberti USA, Inc.
Vintage Industries, Inc.
Weisz Parts
Wescombe
Winchester Sutler, Inc., The

GUNS, SURPLUS—PARTS AND AMMUNITION

Ad Hominem
Armscorp USA, Inc.
Arundel Arms & Ammunition, Inc., A.
Aztec International Ltd.
Badger Shooters Supply, Inc.
Ballistica Maximus North
Bohemia Arms Co.
Bondini Paolo
Braun, M.
Century International Arms, Inc.
Chuck's Gun Shop
Cole's Gun Works
Combat Military Ordnance Ltd.
Delta Arms Ltd.
First, Inc., Jack
Flaig's
Fleming Firearms
Forgett, Valmore J., Jr.
Forrest, Inc., Tom
Fulton Armory
Galazan
Garcia National Gun Traders, Inc.
Goodwin, Fred
Gun Parts Corp., The
Hart & Son, Inc., Robert W.
Interarms
Lever Arms Service Ltd.
Lomont Precision Bullets
Moreton/Fordyce Enterprises
Mountain Bear Rifle Works, Inc.
Navy Arms Co.
Nevada Pistol Academy Inc.
Oil Rod and Gun Shop
Parts & Surplus
Pasadena Gun Center
Perazone, Brian
Quality Firearms of Idaho, Inc.
Ravell Ltd.
Retting, Inc., Martin B.
Samco Global Arms, Inc.
Sarco, Inc.
Shell Shack
Shootin' Shack, Inc.
Silver Ridge Gun Shop
Simmons Gun Repair, Inc.
Sipes Gun Shop
Southern Armory, The
Sportsmen's Exchange & Western Gun Traders, Inc.
Springfield Sporters, Inc.
Stratco, Inc.
Tarnhelm Supply Co., Inc.
T.F.C. S.p.A.
Thurston Sports, Inc.
Westfield Engineering

GUNSMITHS, CUSTOM (see Custom Gunsmiths)

GUNSMITHS, HANDGUN (see Pistolsmiths)

GUNSMITH SCHOOLS

Bull Mountain Rifle Co.
Colorado Gunsmithing Academy Lamar
Colorado School of Trades
Cylinder & Slide, Inc.
Lassen Community College, Gunsmithing Dept.
Laughridge, William R.
Mathews & Son, Inc., George E.
Modern Gun Repair School
Montgomery Community College
Murray State College
North American Correspondence Schools
Nowlin Custom Mfg.
NRI Gunsmith School
Pennsylvania Gunsmith School
Piedmont Community College
Pine Technical College
Professional Gunsmiths of America, Inc.
Southeastern Community College
Smith & Wesson
Spencer's Custom Guns
Trinidad State Junior College Gunsmithing Dept.
Weigand Combat Handguns, Inc.

GUNSMITH SUPPLIES, TOOLS, SERVICES

Actions by "T"
Aldis Gunsmithing & Shooting Supply
Auto-Ordnance Corp.
Baer Custom, Inc., Les
Bar-Sto Precision Machine
Bear Mountain Gun & Tool
Belltown, Ltd.
Belt MTN Arms
Bengtson Arms Co., L.
Biesen, Al
Biesen, Roger
Bill's Gun Repair
Blue Ridge Machinery & Tools, Inc.
Bowen Classic Arms Corp.
Break-Free, Inc.
Briley Mfg., Inc.
Brownells, Inc.
B-Square Co., Inc.
Bull Mountain Rifle Co.
Carbide Checkering Tools
Chapman Manufacturing Co.
Chem-Pak, Inc.
Choate Machine & Tool Co., Inc.
Chopie Mfg., Inc.
Chuck's Gun Shop
Clark Custom Guns, Inc.
Clenzoil Corp.
Colonial Arms, Inc.
Conetrol Scope Mounts
Craig Custom Ltd.
Cumberland Arms
Custom Checkering Service
Custom Gun Products
D&J Bullet Co. & Custom Gun Shop, Inc.
Dakota Arms, Inc.
Dan's Whetstone Co., Inc.
Dayton Traister
Dem-Bart Checkering Tools, Inc.
Dever Co., Jack
Dremel Mfg. Co.
Du-Lite Corp.
Dutchman's Firearms, Inc., The
Echols & Co., D'Arcy
EGW Evolution Gun Works
Faith Associates, Inc.
Fisher, Jerry A.
Forgreens Tool Mfg., Inc.
Forkin, Ben
Forster, Kathy
Forster Products
Frazier Brothers Enterprises
G.B.C. Industries, Inc.
Grace Metal Products, Inc.
Greider Precision
Gunline Tools
Gun-Tec
Half Moon Rifle Shop
Hastings Barrels
Henriksen Tool Co., Inc.
High Performance International
Hoelscher, Virgil
Holland's
Ivanoff, Thomas G.
J&R Engineering
J&S Heat Treat
Jantz Supply
JBM Software
JGS Precision Tool Mfg.
Kasenit Co., Inc.
KenPatable Ent., Inc.
Kimball, Gary
Kleinendorst, K.W.
Kmount
Korzinek Riflesmith, J.
Kwik Mount Corp.
LaBounty Precision Reboring
Lea Mfg. Co.
Lee Supplies, Mark
Lee's Red Ramps
List Precision Engineering
London Guns Ltd.
Mag-Na-Port International, Inc.
Mahovsky's Metalife
Marsh, Mike
MCS, Inc.
Menck, Thomas W.
Metalife Industries
Metaloy Inc.
Michael's Antiques
Millett Sights
MMC
Morrow, Bud
Mo's Competitor Supplies
N&J Sales
NCP Products, Inc.
Nowlin Custom Mfg.
Ole Frontier Gunsmith Shop
PanaVise Products, Inc.
Passive Bullet Traps, Inc.
PEM's Mfg. Co.
Perazone, Brian
Power Custom, Inc.
Practical Tools, Inc.
Precision Metal Finishing
Precision Specialties
Prolix® Lubricants
Reardon Products
Rice, Keith
Romain's Custom Guns, Inc.
Roto Carve
Royal Arms Gunstocks
Rusteprufe Laboratories
Savage Range Systems, Inc.
Scott, McDougall & Associates
Shirley Co. Gun & Riflemakers Ltd., J.A.
Shooter's Choice
Slug Group, Inc.
Smith Abrasives, Inc.
Starrett Co., L.S.
Sullivan, David S.
Talley, Dave
Texas Platers Supply
Time Precision, Inc.
Tom's Gun Repair
Tom's Gunshop
Trulock Tool
Turnbull Restoration, Doug
Van Gorden & Son, Inc., C.S.
Venco Industries, Inc.
Vintage Industries, Inc.
Washita Mountain Whetstone Co.
Weaver Arms Corp. Gun Shop
Weigand Combat Handguns, Inc.
Welsh, Bud
Westfield Engineering
Westrom, John
Westwind Rifles, Inc.
White Rock Tool & Die
Wilcox All-Pro Tools & Supply
Wild West Guns
Will-Burt Co.
Williams Gun Sight Co.
Williams Shootin' Iron Service
Willow Bend
Wilson's Gun Shop
Wise Guns, Dale

HANDGUN ACCESSORIES

A.A. Arms, Inc.
ADCO International
Adventurer's Outpost
Alpha Gunsmith Division
American Derringer Corp.
Armite Laboratories
Arms Corporation of the Philippines
Aro-Tek, Ltd.
Astra Sport, S.A.
Auto-Ordnance Corp.
Baer Custom, Inc., Les
Bar-Sto Precision Machine
Baumannize Custom
Behlert Precision, Inc.
Beretta S.p.A., Pietro
Bill's Custom Cases
Black Sheep Brand
Blue and Gray Products, Inc.
Bob's Gun Shop
Bond Custom Firearms
Bowen Classic Arms Corp.
Broken Gun Ranch
Brown Products, Inc., Ed
Brownells, Inc.
Bucheimer, J.M.
Bushmaster Firearms
Bushmaster Hunting & Fishing
Butler Creek Corp.
C3 Systems
Centaur Systems, Inc.
Central Specialties Ltd.
Clark Custom Guns, Inc.
Cobra Gunskin
Craig Custom Ltd.
D&L Industries
Dade Screw Machine Products
Delhi Gun House
Dewey Mfg. Co., Inc., J.
D.J. Marketing
Doskocil Mfg. Co., Inc
E&L Mfg., Inc.
E.A.A. Corp.
Eagle International, Inc.
EGW Evolution Gun Works
Faith Associates, Inc.
FAS
Feather Industries, Inc.
Feminine Protection, Inc.
Ferris Firearms
Fleming Firearms
Frielich Police Equipment
Galati International
GALCO International Ltd.
Glock, Inc.
Greider Precision
Gremmel Enterprises
Gun Parts Corp., The
Gun-Alert
Gun-Ho Sports Cases
Harvey, Frank
Haselbauer Products, Jerry
Hebard Guns, Gil
Heinie Specialty Products
Hill Speed Leather, Ernie
H.K.S. Products
Hoppe's Div.
Hunter Co., Inc.
Jarvis, Inc.
Jeffredo Gunsight
J.P. Enterprises, Inc.
Jumbo Sports Products
KeeCo Impressions
Keller Co., The
King's Gun Works
K.K. Arms Co.
Lakewood Products, Inc.
Lee's Red Ramps
Lem Sports, Inc.
Loch Leven Industries
Lohman Mfg. Co., Inc.
Mac's .45 Shop
Mag-Na-Port International, Inc.
Magnolia Sports, Inc.
Magnum Research, Inc.
Mahony, Philip Bruce
Mandall Shooting Supplies, Inc.
Markell Inc.
McCormick Corp., Chip
MEC-Gar S.R.L.
Merkuria Ltd.
Mid-America Guns and Ammo
Minute Man High Tech Industries
Mitchell Arms, Inc.
MTM Molded Products Co., Inc.
Mustra's Custom Guns, Inc., Carl
North American Specialties
No-Sho Mfg. Co.
Ox-Yoke Originals, Inc.
PAST Sporting Goods, Inc.
Penguin Industries, Inc.
Power Custom, Inc.
Practical Tools, Inc.
Protector Mfg. Co., Inc., The
Protektor Model

Quality Parts Co.
Ram-Line, Inc.
Ranch Products
Round Edge, Inc.
RPM
Slings 'N Things, Inc.
Southwind Sanctions
TacStar Industries, Inc.
TacTell, Inc.
T.F.C. S.p.A.
TMI Products
Trijicon, Inc.
Tyler Mfg.-Dist., Melvin
Valor Corp.
Vintage Industries, Inc.
Volquartsen Custom Ltd.
Weigand Combat Handguns, Inc.
Western Design
Wilson's Gun Shop

HANDGUN GRIPS

Ahrends, Kim
Ajax Custom Grips, Inc.
Altamont Co.
American Derringer Corp.
American Gripcraft
Arms Corporation of the Philippines
Art Jewel Enterprises Ltd.
Baer Custom, Inc., Les
Barami Corp.
Bear Hug Grips, Inc.
Bell Originals, Inc., Sid
Beretta S.p.A., Pietro
Bob's Gun Shop
Boone's Custom Ivory Grips, Inc.
Boyds' Gunstock Industries, Inc.
Brooks Tactical Systems
Brown Products, Inc., Ed
Clark Custom Guns, Inc.
Cobra Gunskin
Cole-Grip
Colonial Repair
Custom Firearms
Dayson Arms Ltd.
Desert Industries, Inc.
E.A.A. Corp.
Eagle Mfg. & Engineering
EMF Co., Inc.
Ferris Firearms
Fisher Custom Firearms
Fitz Pistol Grip Co.
Forrest, Inc., Tom
Harrison-Hurtz Enterprises, Inc.
Herrett's Stocks, Inc.
Hogue Grips
J.P. Enterprises, Inc.
KeeCo Impressions
Lett Custom Grips
Linebaugh Custom Sixguns & Rifle Works
Mac's .45 Shop
Mandall Shooting Supplies, Inc.
Masen Co., Inc., John
Michaels of Oregon Co.
Mid-America Guns and Ammo
Millett Sights
Monte Kristo Pistol Grip Co.
N.C. Ordnance Co.
Newell, Robert H.
North American Specialties
Pacific Rifle Co.
Pardini Armi Srl
Pilgrim Pewter, Inc.
Radical Concepts
Rosenberg & Sons, Jack A.
Roy's Custom Grips
Savana Sports, Inc.
Sile Distributors, Inc.
Smith & Wesson
Speedfeed, Inc.
Spegel, Craig
Taurus Firearms, Inc.
Triple-K Mfg. Co., Inc.
Tyler Mfg.-Dist., Melvin
Uncle Mike's
Vintage Industries, Inc.
Volquartsen Custom Ltd.
Wilson's Gun Shop

HEARING PROTECTORS

Brown Co., E. Arthur
Brown Products, Inc., Ed
Browning Arms Co.
Clark Co., Inc., David
Clark Custom Guns, Inc.
Cobra Gunskin
E-A-R, Inc.
Electronic Shooters Protection, Inc.
Faith Associates, Inc.
Flents Products Co., Inc.
Gentex Corp.
Hoppe's Div.
Kesselring Gun Shop
North American Specialties
North Specialty Products
Paterson Gunsmithing
Peltor, Inc.
Penguin Industries, Inc.
R.E.T. Enterprises
Rucker Dist. Inc.
Safesport Manufacturing Co.
Silencio/Safety Direct
Willson Safety Prods. Div.

HOLSTERS AND LEATHER GOODS

A&B Industries, Inc.
Action Products, Inc.
Aker Leather Products
Alessi Holsters, Inc.
American Sales & Kirkpatrick
Arratoonian, Andy
Bagmaster Mfg., Inc.
Baker's Leather Goods, Roy
Bandcor Industries
Bang-Bang Boutique
Barami Corp.
Bear Hug Grips, Inc.
Bianchi International, Inc.
Bill's Custom Cases
Black Sheep Brand
Blocker Holsters, Inc., Ted
Brauer Bros. Mfg. Co.
Brown, H.R.
Browning Arms Co.
Bucheimer, J.M.
Bull-X, Inc.
Bushwacker Backpack & Supply Co.
Carvajal Belts & Holsters
Cathey Enterprises, Inc.
Chace Leather Products
Churchill Glove Co., James
Cimarron Arms
Clark Custom Guns, Inc.
Clements' Custom Leathercraft, Chas
Cobra Gunskin
Cobra Sport
Colonial Repair
Counter Assault
Crawford Co., Inc., R.M.
Creedmoor Sports, Inc.
Davis Leather Co., G. Wm.
Delhi Gun House
DeSantis Holster & Leather Goods, Inc.
Desert Industries, Inc.
D-Max, Inc.
Easy Pull Outlaw Products
Ekol Leather Care
El Dorado Leather
El Paso Saddlery Co.
EMF Co., Inc.
Eutaw Co., Inc., The
F&A Inc.
Faust, Inc., T.G.
Ferdinand, Inc.
Flores Publications, Inc., J.
Fobus International Ltd.
Fury Cutlery
Gage Manufacturing
GALCO International Ltd.
Glock, Inc.
GML Products, Inc.
Gould & Goodrich
Gun Leather Limited
Gunfitters, The
Gusty Winds Corp.
Hafner Creations, Inc.
HandiCrafts Unltd.
Hebard Guns, Gil
Hellweg Ltd.
Henigson & Associates, Steve
High North Products, Inc.
Hill Speed Leather, Ernie
Holster Shop, The
Horseshoe Leather Products
Hoyt Holster Co., Inc.
Hume, Don
Hunter Co., Inc.
John's Custom Leather
Joy Enterprises
Jumbo Sports Products
Kane Products, Inc.
Keller Co., The
Kirkpatrick Leather Co.
Kolpin Mfg., Inc.
Korth
Kramer Handgun Leather, Inc.
L.A.R. Mfg., Inc.
Law Concealment Systems, Inc.
Lawrence Leather Co.
Leather Arsenal
Lone Star Gunleather
Magnolia Sports, Inc.
Markell, Inc.
Michaels of Oregon Co.
Minute Man High Tech Industries
Mixson Corp.
Nelson Combat Leather, Bruce
Noble Co., Jim
No-Sho Mfg. Co.
Null Holsters Ltd., K.L.
October Country
Ojala Holsters, Arvo
Oklahoma Leather Products, Inc.
Old West Reproductions, Inc.
Pathfinder Sports Leather
PWL Gunleather
Renegade
Ringler Custom Leather Co.
Rybka Custom Leather Equipment, Thad
Safariland Ltd., Inc.
Safety Speed Holster, Inc.
Savana Sports, Inc.
Schulz Industries
Second Chance Body Armor
Shoemaker & Sons, Inc., Tex
Silhouette Leathers
Smith Saddlery, Jesse W.
Southwind Sanctions
Sparks, Milt
Stalker, Inc.
Strong Holster Co.
Stuart, V. Pat
Tabler Marketing
Texas Longhorn Arms, Inc.
Top-Line USA Inc.
Torel, Inc.
Triple-K Mfg. Co., Inc.
Tyler Mfg.-Dist., Melvin
Uncle Mike's
Valor Corp.
Venus Industries
Viking Leathercraft, Inc.
Walt's Custom Leather
Whinnery, Walt
Wild Bill's Originals

HUNTING AND CAMP GEAR, CLOTHING, ETC.

A&M Waterfowl, Inc.
Ace Sportswear, Inc.
Action Products, Inc.
Adventure 16, Inc.
Allen Co., Bob
Allen Sportswear, Bob
Armor
Atlanta Cutlery Corp.
Baekgaard Ltd.
Bagmaster Mfg., Inc.
Barbour, Inc.
Bauer, Eddie
Bear Archery
Beaver Park Products, Inc
Better Concepts Co.
Big Beam Emergency Systems, Inc.
Boss Manufacturing Co.
Brown Manufacturing
Browning Arms Co.
Buck Stop Lure Co., Inc.
Bushmaster Hunting & Fishing
Bushnell Sports Optics Worldwide
Camp-Cap Products
Carhartt, Inc.
Catoctin Cutlery
Chippewa Shoe Co.
Churchill Glove Co., James
Clarkfield Enterprises, Inc.
Cobra Gunskin
Coghlan's Ltd.
Coleman Co., Inc.
Coulston Products, Inc.
Crawford Co., Inc., R.M.
Creedmoor Sports, Inc.
D&H Prods. Co., Inc.
Dakota Corp.
Danner Shoe Mfg. Co.
DeckSlider of Florida
Deer Me Products
Dr. O's Products Ltd.
Dunham Co.
Duofold, Inc.
Dynalite Products, Inc.
E-A-R, Inc.
Ekol Leather Care
Erickson's Mfg., Inc., C.W.
Eutaw Co., Inc., The
F&A Inc.
Flow-Rite of Tennessee, Inc.
Forrest Tool Co.
Fox River Mills, Inc.
Frankonia Jagd
G&H Decoys, Inc.
Game Winner, Inc.
Gander Mountain, Inc.
Gerber Legendary Blades
Glacier Glove
H&B Forge Co.
Hafner Creations, Inc.
Hawken Shop, The
Hinman Outfitters, Bob
Hodgman, Inc.
Houtz & Barwick
Hunter's Specialties, Inc.
K&M Industries, Inc.
Kamik Outdoor Footwear
Kolpin Mfg., Inc.
LaCrosse Footwear, Inc.
Langenberg Hat Co.
Lectro Science, Inc.
Liberty Trouser Co.
L.L. Bean
MAG Instrument, Inc.
Marathon Rubber Prods. Co., Inc.
Melton Shirt Co., Inc.
Molin Industries
Mountain Hollow Game Calls
Nelson/Weather-Rite, Inc.
North Specialty Products
Northlake Outdoor Footwear
Original Mink Oil, Inc.
Orvis Co., The
Palsa Outdoor Products
Partridge Sales Ltd., John
Pointing Dog Journal
Porta Blind, Inc.
Pro-Mark
Pyromid, Inc.
Randolph Engineering, Inc.
Ranger Mfg. Co., Inc.
Ranging, Inc.
Rattlers Brand
Red Ball
Refrigiwear, Inc.
Rocky, Shoes & Boots
Safesport Manufacturing Co.
Savana Sports, Inc.
Scansport, Inc.
Sceery Game Calls
Schaefer Shooting Sports
Servus Footwear Co.
Simmons Outdoor Corp.
Slings 'N Things, Inc.
Streamlight, Inc.
Swanndri New Zealand
10-X Products Group
Thompson, Norm
T.H.U. Enterprises, Inc.
Tink's Safariland Hunting Corp.
Torel, Inc.
TrailTimer Co.
Venus Industries
Wakina by Pic
Walker Co., B.B.
Walls Industries
Wilcox All-Pro Tools & Supply
Wilderness Sound Products Ltd.
Willson Safety Prods. Div.
Winchester Sutler, Inc., The
Wolverine Boots & Outdoor Footwear Division
Woolrich, Inc.
Wyoming Knife Corp.
Yellowstone Wilderness Supply

KNIVES AND KNIFEMAKER'S SUPPLIES FACTORY AND MAIL ORDER

Adventure 16, Inc.
Aitor-Cuchilleria Del Norte, S.A.
All Rite Products, Inc.
American Target Knives
Aristocrat Knives
Art Jewel Enterprises Ltd.
Atlanta Cutlery Corp.
B&D Trading Co., Inc.
Barteaux Machetes, Inc.
Bell Originals, Inc., Sid
Benchmark Knives
Beretta U.S.A. Corp.
Bill's Custom Cases
Blackjack Knives, Ltd.
Boker USA, Inc.
Bowen Knife Co. Inc.
Browning Arms Co.
Buck Knives, Inc.
Buster's Custom Knives
Camillus Cutlery Co.
Case & Sons Cutlery Co., W.R.
Catoctin Cutlery
Chicago Cutlery Co.
Christopher Firearms Co., Inc., E.
Clements' Custom Leathercraft, Chas
Coast Cutlery Co.
Cold Steel, Inc.
Coleman Co., Inc.
Colonial Knife Co., Inc.
Compass Industries, Inc.
Crawford Co., Inc., R.M.
Creative Craftsman, Inc., The
Crosman Blades
Cutco Cutlery
Cutlery Shoppe
Damascus-U.S.A.
Dan's Whetstone Co., Inc.
Degen Inc.
Delhi Gun House
DeSantis Holster & Leather Goods, Inc.
Diamontd Machining Technology, Inc.
EdgeCraft Corp.
EK Knife Co.
Empire Cutlery Corp.
Eze-Lap Diamond Prods.
Forrest Tool Co.
Forthofer's Gunsmithing & Knifemaking
Fortune Products, Inc.
Frank Knives
Frost Cutlery Co.
Fury Cutlery
Gerber Legendary Blades
Gibbs Rifle Co., Inc.
Golden Age Arms Co.
Gun Room, The
Gutmann Cutlery Inc.
H&B Forge Co.
HandiCrafts Unltd.
Harrington Cutlery, Inc., Russell
Harris Publications
Hawken Shop, The
Henckels Zwillingswerk, Inc., J.A.
High North Products, Inc.
Hoppe's Div.
Hubertus Schneidwarenfabrik
Hunter Co., Inc.
Hunting Classics
Ibberson (Sheffield) Ltd., George
Imperial Schrade Corp.
Iron Mountain Knife Co.
J.A. Blades, Inc.
Jantz Supply
Jenco Sales, Inc.
Johnson Wood Products
Joy Enterprises
KA-BAR Knives
Kasenit Co., Inc.
Kershaw Knives
Knife Importers, Inc.
Koval Knives
Lamson & Goodnow Mfg. Co.
Leatherman Tool Group, Inc.
Linder Solingen Knives
L.L. Bean
Mar Knives, Inc., Al
Matthews Cutlery
Molin Industries
Murphy Co., Inc., R.
Normark Corp.
North American Specialties
Outdoor Edge Cutlery Corp.
Penguin Industries, Inc.
Pilgrim Pewter, Inc.
Plaza Cutlery, Inc.
Precise International
Queen Cutlery Co.
R&C Knives & Such
Randall-Made Knives
Russell Knives, Inc., A.G.
Safesport Manufacturing Co.
Scansport, Inc.
Schiffman, Mike
Schrimsher's Custom Knifemaker's Supply, Bob
Sheffield Knifemakers Supply, Inc.
Smith Saddlery, Jesse W.
Soque River Knives
Spyderco, Inc.
Swiss Army Knives, Inc.
T.F.C. S.p.A.
Traditions, Inc.
Tru-Balance Knife Co.
United Cutlery Corp.
Utica Cutlery Co.
Venus Industries
Walt's Custom Leather
Washita Mountain Whetstone Co.
Weber Jr., Rudolf
Wenoka/Seastyle
Western Cutlery Co.
Whinnery, Walt
Wostenholm
Wyoming Knife Corp.

LABELS, BOXES, CARTRIDGE HOLDERS

American Sales & Kirkpatrick
Ballistic Products, Inc.
Berry's Mfg. Inc.
Brown Co., E. Arthur
Cabinet Mountain Outfitters Scents & Lures
Crane & Crane Ltd.
Del Rey Products
DeSantis Holster & Leather Goods, Inc.
Fitz Pistol Grip Co.
Flambeau Products Corp.
J&J Products Co.
Kolpin Mfg., Inc.
Lakewood Products, Inc.
Liberty Shooting Supplies
Loadmaster
Midway Arms, Inc.
MTM Molded Products Co., Inc.
Pendleton Royal

LOAD TESTING AND PRODUCT TESTING, (Chronographing, Ballistic Studies)

Ballistic Research
Bartlett, Don
Bestload, Inc.
Briese Bullet Co., Inc.
Briganti & Co., A.
Buck Stix—SOS Products Co.
CFVentures
Clerke Co., J.A.
D&H Precision Tooling
Dead Eye's Sport Center
Defense Training International, Inc.
DGR Custom Rifles
DKT, Inc.
Duane's Gun Repair
Gonzalez Guns, Ramon B.
Hank's Gun Shop
Hensler, Jerry
Hoelscher, Virgil
Jackalope Gun Shop
Jensen Bullets
Jurras, L.E.
Lomont Precision Bullets
Maionchi-L.M.I.
MAST Technology
Master Class Bullets
McCann's Machine & Gun Shop
McMurdo, Lynn
Moreton/Fordyce Enterprises
Multiplex International
Oil Rod and Gun Shop
Ransom International Corp.
RPM
Rupert's Gun Shop
SOS Products Co.
Spencer's Custom Guns
Vancini, Carl
Vulpes Ventures, Inc.
Wells Custom Gunsmith, R.A.
Whildin & Sons Ltd., E.H.
White Laboratory, Inc., H.P.
X-Spand Target Systems

MISCELLANEOUS

Actions, Rifle
Hall Manufacturing
Accurizing, Rifle
Richards, John
Stoney Baroque Shooters Supply
Adapters, Cartridge
Alex, Inc.
Adapters, Shotshell
PC Co.
Airgun Accessories
BSA Guns Ltd.
Airgun Repair
Airgun Repair Centre
Nationwide Airgun Repairs
Ray's Gunsmith Shop
Assault Rifle Accessories
Feather Industries, Inc.
Ram-Line, Inc.
Barrel Stress Relieving
Cryo-Accurizing
Bi-Pods
B.M.F. Activator, Inc.
Body Armor
A&B Industries, Inc.
Faust, Inc., T.G.
Second Chance Body Armor
Top-Line USA Inc.
Bore Illuminator
Flashette Co.
Bore Lights
N.C. Ordnance Co.
MDS, Inc.
Brass Catcher
Gage Manufacturing
M.A.M. Products, Inc.
Bullets, Rubber
CIDCO
Calendar, Gun Shows
Stott's Creek Printers
Cannons, Miniature Replicas
Furr Arms
R.G.-G., Inc.
Dehumidifiers
Buenger Enterprises
Hydrosorbent Products
Dryers
Peet Shoe Dryer, Inc.
E-Z Loader
Del Rey Products
Firearm Refinishers
Armoloy Co. of Ft. Worth
Firearm Restoration
Adair Custom Shop, Bill
Burgess & Son Gunsmiths, R.W.
Johns, Bill
Liberty Antique Gunworks
Mazur Restoration, Pete
Moeller, Steve
Nicholson Custom
FFL Record Keeping
Basics Information Systems, Inc.
PFRB Co.
R.E.T. Enterprises
Hunting Trips
J/B Adventures & Safaris, Inc.
Professional Hunter Specialties
Hypodermic Rifles/Pistols
Multipropulseurs
Industrial Dessicants
WAMCO—New Mexico
Insert Barrels
MCA Sports
Multi-Caliber Adapters
Lettering Restoration System
Pranger, Ed G.
Locks, Gun
Brown Manufacturing
Master Lock Co.
Magazines
Mag-Pack Corp.
Mats
Brigade Quartermasters
Military Equipment/Accessories
Alpha 1 Drop Zone
Amherst Arms
Photographers, Gun
Bilal, Mustafa
Hanusin, John
Macbean, Stan
Payne Photography, Robert
Semmer, Charles
Smith, Michael
Weyer International
White Pine Photographic Services
Pistol Barrel Maker
Bar-Sto Precision Machine
Power Tools, Rotary Flexible Shaft
Foredom Electric Co.
Saddle Rings, Studs
Silver Ridge Gun Shop
Safety Devices
P&M Sales and Service
Safeties
Harper, William E./ The Great 870 Co.
P.M. Enterprises, Inc.
Scents and Lures
Buck Stop Lure Co., Inc.
Cabinet Mountain Outfitters Scents & Lures
Dr. O's Products Ltd.
Flow-Rite of Tennessee, Inc.
Mountain Hollow Game Calls
Robbins Scent, Inc.
Tink's Safariland Hunting Corp.
Tinks & Ben Lee Hunting Products
Wellington Outdoors
Wildlife Research Center, Inc.
Scrimshaw
Boone's Custom Ivory Grips, Inc.
Dolbare, Elizabeth
Hoover, Harvey
Lovestrand, Erik
Reno, Wayne
Sherwood, George
Shooting Range Equipment
Caswell International Corp.
Passive Bullet Traps, Inc.
Savage Range Systems, Inc.
Shotgun Barrel Maker
Baker, Stan
Silencers
AWC Systems Technology
Ciener, Jonathan Arthur
DLO Mfg.
Fleming Firearms
S.C.R.C.
Sound Technology
Ward Machine
Slings and Swivels
DTM International, Inc.
High North Products, Inc.
Leather Arsenal
Pathfinder Sports Leather
Schulz Industries
Torel, Inc.
Treestands and Steps
A&J Products
Apache Products, Inc.
Brell Mar Products
Dr. O's Products Ltd.
Silent Hunter
Summit Specialties, Inc.
Trax America, Inc.
Treemaster
Warren & Sweat Mfg. Co.
Trophies
Blackinton & Co., Inc., V.H.
Ventilated Rib
Simmons Gun Repair, Inc.
Ventilation
ScanCo Environmental Systems
Video Tapes
American Pioneer Video
Calibre Press, Inc.
Eastman Products, R.T.
Foothills Video Productions, Inc.
New Historians Productions, The
Primos, Inc.
Rocky Mountain Wildlife Products
Trail Visions
Wilderness Sound Products Ltd.
Xythos-Miniature Revolver
Andres & Dworsky

MUZZLE-LOADING GUNS, BARRELS AND EQUIPMENT

Accuracy Unlimited (Littleton, CO)
Adkins, Luther
Allen Manufacturing
•Anderson Manufacturing Co., Inc.
Armi San Paolo
Bauska Barrels
•Beauchamp & Son, Inc.
Beaver Lodge
Bentley, John
Birdsong & Associates, W.E.
Blackhawk West
Blue and Gray Products, Inc.
Bridgers Best
Buckskin Machine Works
Burgess & Son Gunsmiths, R.W.
Butler Creek Corp.
Cache La Poudre Rifleworks
California Sights
•Cape Outfitters
Cash Manufacturing Co., Inc.
CenterMark
Chambers Flintlocks, Ltd., Jim
Chopie Mfg., Inc.
•Cimarron Arms
Cogar's Gunsmithing
Colonial Repair
•Colt Blackpowder Arms Co.
Cousin Bob's Mountain Products
•Cumberland Arms
•Cumberland Knife & Gun Works
Curly Maple Stock Blanks
•CVA
Dangler, Homer L.
Davis Co., R.E.
Day & Sons, Inc., Leonard
•Dayton Traister
deHaas Barrels
Delhi Gun House
Desert Industries, Inc.
Dewey Mfg. Co., Inc., J.
DGS, Inc.
Dyson & Son Ltd., Peter
•EMF Co., Inc.
•Euroarms of America, Inc.
Eutaw Co., Inc., The
Fautheree, Andy
Feken, Dennis
Fellowes, Ted
Fire'n Five
Flintlocks, Etc.
•Forster Products
Fort Hill Gunstocks
Frontier
Getz Barrel Co.
GOEX, Inc.
Golden Age Arms Co.
•Gonic Arms, Inc.
Green Mountain Rifle Barrel Co., Inc.
Hastings Barrels
•Hatfield Gun Co., Inc.
•Hawken Shop, The
Hege Jagd-u. Sporthandels, GmbH
Hoppe's Div.
•Hornady Mfg. Co.
House of Muskets, Inc., The
Hunkeler, A.
Jamison's Forge Works
Jones Co., Dale
K&M Industries, Inc.
Kennedy Firearms
Knight Rifles
Kwik-Site Co.
L&R Lock Co.
Legend Products Corp.
•Log Cabin Sport Shop
Lothar Walther Precision Tool, Inc.
•Lyman Products Corp.
McCann's Muzzle-Gun Works
Michaels of Oregon Co.
MMP
•Modern MuzzleLoading, Inc.
•Montana Armory, Inc.
Montana Precision Swaging
Mountain State Muzzleloading Supplies
•Mowrey Gun Works
MSC Industrial Supply Co.
Mt. Alto Outdoor Products
Mushroom Express Bullet Co.
Muzzleloaders Etcetera, Inc.
Navy Arms Co.
North Star West
October Country
Oklahoma Leather Products, Inc.
Olson, Myron
Orion Rifle Barrel Co.
Ox-Yoke Originals, Inc.
Pacific Rifle Co.
•Pedersoli, Davide & C.
Penguin Industries, Inc.
•Pioneer Arms Co.
Prairie River Arms
Radical Concepts
Rusty Duck Premium Gun Care Products
R.V.I.
S&B Industries
S&S Firearms
Selsi Co., Inc.
•Sharps Arms Co., Inc., C.
Shooter's Choice
•Sile Distributors
Single Shot, Inc.
Sklany, Steve
Slings 'N Things, Inc.
Smokey Valley Rifles
South Bend Replicas, Inc.
Southern Bloomer Mfg. Co.
Starr Trading Co., Jedediah
Stone Mountain Arms
Storey, Dale A.
Tennessee Valley Mfg.
Thompson Bullet Lube Co.
Thompson/Center Arms
•Thunder Mountain Arms
Tiger-Hunt
Track of the Wolf, Inc.
•Traditions, Inc.
Treso, Inc.
UFA, Inc.
•Uberti, Aldo
Uncle Mike's
•Upper Missouri Trading Co.
Venco Industries, Inc.
Walters, John
Warren Muzzleloading Co., Inc.
Wescombe
White Owl Enterprises
•White Shooting Systems, Inc.
Williams Gun Sight Co.
Woodworker's Supply
Young Country Arms

PISTOLSMITHS

Accuracy Gun Shop
Accuracy Unlimited (Glendale, AZ)
Ace Custom 45's, Inc.
Actions by "T"
Adair Custom Shop, Bill
Ahlman Guns
Aldis Gunsmithing & Shooting Supply
Alpha Precision, Inc.
Alpine's Precision Gunsmithing & Indoor Shooting Range
Armament Gunsmithing Co., Inc.
AWC Systems Technology
Baer Custom, Inc., Les
Bain & Davis, Inc.
Banks, Ed
Behlert Precision, Inc.
Bellm Contenders
Belt MTN Arms
Bengtson Arms Co., L.
BlackStar AccuMax Barrels
BlackStar Barrel Accurizing
Bowen Classic Arms Corp.
Campbell, Dick
Cannon's Guns
Caraville Manufacturing
Clark Custom Guns, Inc.
Colonial Repair
Colorado Gunsmithing Academy Lamar
Corkys Gun Clinic
Costa, David
Craig Custom Ltd.
Curtis Custom Shop
Custom Gunsmiths
D&L Sports
Davis Service Center, Bill
Ellicott Arms, Inc./Woods Pistolsmithing
Ferris Firearms
Fisher Custom Firearms
Forkin, Ben
Francesca, Inc.
Frank Custom Classic Arms, Ron
Frielich Police Equipment
Garthwaite, Jim
Giron, Robert E.
Gonzalez Guns, Ramon B.
Greider Precision
Gun Room Press, The
Guncraft Sports, Inc.
Guns
Gunsite Custom Shop
Gunsite Gunsmithy
Gunsite Training Center
Gunsmithing Ltd.
Hamilton, Alex B.
Hamilton, Keith
Hank's Gun Shop
Hanson's Gun Center, Dick
Hardison, Charles
Harris Gunworks
Hebard Guns, Gil
Heinie Specialty Products
High Bridge Arms, Inc.
Highline Machine Co.
Hoag, James W.
Intermountain Arms & Tackle, Inc.
Irwin, Campbell H.
Island Pond Gun Shop
Ivanoff, Thomas G.
J&S Heat Treat
Jarvis, Inc.
Jensen's Custom Ammunition
Johnston, James
Jones, J.D.
J.P. Enterprises, Inc.
Jungkind, Reeves C.
K-D, Inc.
Kaswer Custom, Inc.
Ken's Gun Specialties
Kilham & Co.
Kimball, Gary
Kopp, Terry K.
La Clinique du .45
LaFrance Specialties
LaRocca Gun Works, Inc.
Lathrop's, Inc.
Lawson, John G.
Leckie Professional Gunsmithing
Lee's Red Ramps
Linebaugh Custom Sixguns & Rifle Works
List Precision Engineering
Long, George F.
Mac's .45 Shop
Mahony, Philip Bruce
Marent, Rudolf
Martin's Gun Shop
Marvel, Alan
McCann's Machine & Gun Shop
McGowen Rifle Barrels
Middlebrooks Custom Shop
Miller Custom
Mitchell's Accuracy Shop
MJK Gunsmithing, Inc.
Mountain Bear Rifle Works, Inc.
Mullis Guncraft
Mustra's Custom Guns, Inc., Carl
Nastoff's 45 Shop, Inc., Steve
NCP Products, Inc.
North Fork Custom Gunsmithing
Novak's Inc.
Nowlin Custom Mfg.
Oglesby & Oglesby Gunmakers, Inc.
Paris, Frank J.
Pasadena Gun Center
Peacemaker Specialists
PEM's Mfg. Co.
Performance Specialists
Peterson Gun Shop, Inc., A.W.
Pierce Pistols
Plaxco, J. Michael
Precision Specialties
Randco UK
Ries, Chuck
Rim Pac Sports, Inc.
Robar Co.'s, Inc., The
Rogers Gunsmithing, Bob
Scott, McDougall & Associates
Seecamp Co., Inc., L.W.
Shooter Shop, The
Shooters Supply
Shootin' Shack, Inc.
Sight Shop, The
Singletary, Kent
Sipes Gun Shop
Springfield, Inc.
SSK Industries
Steger, James R.
Swampfire Shop, The
Swenson's 45 Shop, A.D.
300 Gunsmith Service, Inc.
Ten-Ring Precision, Inc.
Thompson, Randall
Thurston Sports, Inc.
Tom's Gun Repair
Vic's Gun Refinishing
Volquartsen Custom Ltd.
Walker Arms Co., Inc.
Walters Industries
Wardell Precision Handguns Ltd.
Weigand Combat Handguns, Inc.
Wessinger Custom Guns & Engraving
Whitestone Lumber Corp.
Wichita Arms, Inc.
Williams Gun Sight Co.
Williamson Precision Gunsmithing
Wilson's Gun Shop

REBORING AND RERIFLING

Flaig's
H&S Liner Service
Ivanoff, Thomas G.
Jackalope Gun Shop
K-D, Inc.
Kopp, Terry K.
LaBounty Precision Reboring
Matco, Inc.
Pence Precision Barrels
Redman's Rifling & Reboring
Rice, Keith
Ridgetop Sporting Goods
Shaw, Inc., E.R.
Siegrist Gun Shop
Simmons Gun Repair, Inc.
300 Gunsmith Service, Inc.
Tom's Gun Repair
Van Patten, J.W.
West, Robert G.
White Rock Tool & Die
Zufall, Joseph F.

RELOADING TOOLS AND ACCESSORIES

Action Bullets, Inc.
Advance Car Mover Co., Rowell Div.
American Products Co.
Ames Metal Products
•Ammo Load, Inc.
Anderson Manufacturing Co., Inc.
Arms Corporation of the Philippines
Atlantic Rose, Inc.
Bald Eagle Precision Machine Co.
Ballistic Products, Inc.
Ballisti-Cast, Inc.
Bear Reloaders
Belltown, Ltd.
Ben's Machines
Berger Bullets, Ltd.
Berry's Mfg. Inc.
Birchwood Casey
Blue Ridge Machinery & Tools, Inc.
Brass-Tech Industries
Break-Free, Inc.
Briganti & Co., A.
Brobst, Jim
•Brown Co., E. Arthur
BRP, Inc. High Performance Cast Bullets
Bruno Shooters Supply
Brynin, Milton
B-Square Co., Inc.
Buck Stix—SOS Products Co.
Buffalo Arms
Bull Mountain Rifle Co.
Bullet Swaging Supply, Inc.
Bullseye Bullets
C&D Special Products
•Camdex, Inc.
Canyon Cartridge Corp.
Carbide Die & Mfg. Co., Inc.
Case Sorting System
CFVentures
•C-H Tool & Die Corp.
Chem-Pak, Inc.
CheVron Case Master
Clark Custom Guns, Inc.
Claybuster Wads & Harvester Bullets
Clymer Manufacturing Co., Inc.
Coats, Mrs. Lester
Colorado Shooter's Supply
CONKKO
Cook Engineering Service

•See page 445 for Warranty Service Center Addresses

•Corbin, Inc.
Crouse's Country Cover
Custom Products, Neil A. Jones
Davis, Don
Davis Products, Mike
D.C.C. Enterprises
Denver Bullets, Inc.
•Denver Instrument Co.
Dever Co., Jack
Dewey Mfg. Co., Inc., J.
•Dillon Precision Prods., Inc.
Dropkick
Dutchman's Firearms, Inc., The
E&L Mfg., Inc.
Eagan, Donald V.
Eezox, Inc.
Engineered Accessories
Enguix Import-Export
Essex Metals
•4-D Custom Die Co.
F&A Inc.
Federal Cartridge Co.
Federated-Fry
Feken, Dennis
Ferguson, Bill
First, Inc., Jack
Fitz Pistol Grip Co.
Flambeau Products Corp.
Forgett Jr., Valmore J.
Forgreens Tool Mfg., Inc.
•Forster Products
•Fremont Tool Works
Fry Metals
Fusilier Bullets
G&C Bullet Co., Inc.
GAR
Goddard, Allen
GOEX, Inc.
Gozon Corp., U.S.A.
Graphics Direct
Graves Co.
Green, Arthur S.
Greenwood Precision
Grizzly Bullets
Hanned Line, The
Hanned Precision
Harrell's Precision
Harris Enterprises
Harrison Bullets
Haydon Shooters' Supply, Russ
Heidenstrom Bullets
Hensley & Gibbs
Hirtenberger Aktiengesellschaft
Hobson Precision Mfg. Co.
Hoch Custom Bullet Moulds
Hoehn Sales, Inc.
Hoelscher, Virgil
•Hollywood Engineering
Hondo Industries
•Hornady Mfg. Co.
Howell Machine
•Huntington Die Specialties
IMI Services USA, Inc.
Imperial Magnum Corp.
INTEC International, Inc.
Iosso Products
Javelina Lube Products
JGS Precision Tool Mfg.
JLK Bullets
Jonad Corp.
Jones Custom Products, Neil A.
Jones Moulds, Paul
•K&M Services
K&S Mfg. Inc.
Kapro Mfg. Co., Inc.
King & Co.
KLA Enterprises
Kleen-Bore, Inc.
Lane Bullets, Inc.
LBT
•Lee Precision, Inc.
Legend Products Corp.
Liberty Metals
Littleton, J.F.
Lomont Precision Bullets
Lortone, Inc.
Loweth, Richard
Luch Metal Merchants, Barbara
Lyman Instant Targets, Inc.
•Lyman Products Corp.
M&D Munitions Ltd.
MA Systems
•Magma Engineering Co.
MarMik Inc.
Marquart Precision Co., Inc.
MAST Technology
Master Class Bullets
Match Prep
McKillen & Heyer, Inc.
MCRW Associates Shooting Supplies
•MEC, Inc.
Midway Arms, Inc.
Miller Engineering
MI-TE Bullets
MKL Service Co.
MMP
Mt. Baldy Bullet Co.
MTM Molded Products Co., Inc.
Multi-Scale Charge Ltd.
Naval Ordnance Works
Necromancer Industries, Inc.
NEI Handtools, Inc.
Niemi Engineering, W.B.
North Devon Firearms Services
Old West Bullet Moulds
•Old Western Scrounger, Inc.
Omark Industries
Paco's
Pattern Control
Pedersoli, Davide & C.
Peerless Alloy, Inc.
Pend Oreille Sport Shop
Petro-Explo, Inc.
Pinetree Bullets
Plum City Ballistic Range
Policlips North America
Polywad, Inc.
Pomeroy, Robert
•Ponsness/Warren
Powder Valley Services
Prairie River Arms
Precision Castings & Equipment, Inc.
•Precision Reloading, Inc.
Prime Reloading
Prolix® Lubricants
Pro-Shot Products, Inc.
Protector Mfg. Co., Inc., The
Rapine Bullet Mould Mfg. Co.
Raytech
•RCBS
•Redding Reloading Equipment
R.E.I.
Reloading Specialties, Inc.
Rice, Keith
Riebe Co., W.J.
RIG Products
R.I.S. Co., Inc.
Roberts Products
Rochester Lead Works, Inc.
Rooster Laboratories
Rorschach Precision Products
Rosenthal, Brad and Sallie
SAECO
Sandia Die & Cartridge Co.
Saunders Gun & Machine Shop
Saville Iron Co.
•Scharch Mfg., Inc.
Scot Powder Co. of Ohio, Inc.
Scott, Dwight
Seebeck Assoc., R.E.
Sierra Specialty Prod. Co.
Silhouette, The
Silver Eagle Machining
Simmons, Jerry
Sinclair International, Inc.
Skip's Machine
S.L.A.P. Industries
Small Custom Mould & Bullet Co.
SOS Products Co.
Spence, George W.
Spencer's Custom Guns
Sport Flite Manufacturing Co.
Sportsman Supply Co.
•Stalwart Corp.
•Star Machine Works
Stillwell, Robert
Stoney Point Products, Inc.
Talon Mfg. Co., Inc.
Tamarack Products, Inc.
Taracorp Industries
TCCI
TCSR
TDP Industries, Inc.
Tetra Gun Lubricants
Thompson Bullet Lube Co.
Timber Heirloom Products
TMI Products
TR Metals Corp.
Trammco, Inc.
Trophy Bonded Bullets, Inc.
Tru-Square Metal Prods., Inc.
TTM
Tyler Scott, Inc.
Varner's Service
Vega Tool Co.
VibraShine, Inc.
Vibra-Tek Co.
Vihtavuori Oy
Vitt/Boos
Von Minden Gunsmithing Services
Walters, John
Webster Scale Mfg. Co.
Welsh, Bud
Werner, Carl
Westfield Engineering
White Rock Tool & Die
Whitetail Design & Engineering Ltd.
Widener's Reloading & Shooting Supply
•William's Gun Shop, Ben
Wilson, Inc., L.E.
Wise Guns, Dale
Wolf's Western Traders
Yesteryear Armory & Supply
Young Country Arms

RESTS—BENCH, PORTABLE—AND ACCESSORIES

Accuright
Adaptive Technology
Adventure 16, Inc.
Armor Metal Products
Aspen Outdoors, Inc.
Bald Eagle Precision Machine Co.
Bartlett Engineering
Browning Arms Co.
B-Square Co., Inc.
Bull Mountain Rifle Co.
Canons Delcour
Chem-Pak, Inc.
Clift Mfg., L.R.
Clift Welding Supply
Decker Shooting Products
Desert Mountain Mfg.
F&A Inc.
Greenwood Precision
Harris Engineering, Inc.
Hidalgo, Tony
Hoelscher, Virgil
Hoppe's Div.
J&J Sales
Kolpin Mfg., Inc.
Kramer Designs
Midway Arms, Inc.
Millett Sights
MJM Manufacturing
Outdoor Connection, Inc., The
PAST Sporting Goods, Inc.
Pease Accuracy, Bob
Penguin Industries, Inc.
Portus, Robert
Protektor Model
Ransom International Corp
Saville Iron Co.
Slug Group, Inc.
Stoney Point Products, Inc.
Thompson Target Technology
T.H.U. Enterprises, Inc.
Tonoloway Tack Drivers
Varner's Service
Wichita Arms, Inc.
Zanotti Armor, Inc.

RIFLE BARREL MAKERS (See also Muzzle-Loading Guns, Barrels and Equipment)

Airrow
Bain & Davis, Inc.
Bauska Barrels
BlackStar AccuMax Barrels
BlackStar Barrel Accurizing
Border Barrels Ltd.
Broad Creek Rifle Works
Brown Co., E. Arthur
Bullberry Barrel Works, Ltd.
Bustani, Leo
Canons Delcour
Carter's Gun Shop
Christensen Arms
Cincinnati Swaging
Citadel Mfg., Inc.
Clerke Co., J.A.
D&J Bullet Co. & Custom Gun Shop, Inc.
deHaas Barrels
Dilliott Gunsmithing, Inc.
Donnelly, C.P.
Douglas Barrels, Inc.
Gaillard Barrels
Getz Barrel Co.
Green Mountain Rifle Barrel Co., Inc.
Half Moon Rifle Shop
Harold's Custom Gun Shop, Inc.
Harris Gunworks
Hart Rifle Barrels, Inc.
Hastings Barrels
Hoelscher, Virgil
H-S Precision, Inc.
Jackalope Gun Shop
Jones, J.D.
K-D, Inc.
KOGOT
Kopp, Terry K.
Krieger Barrels, Inc.
LaBounty Precision Reboring
Lilja Precision Rifle Barrels
Lothar Walther Precision Tool, Inc.
Mac's .45 Shop
Matco, Inc.
McGowen Rifle Barrels
McMillan Rifle Barrels
Mid-America Recreation, Inc.
Nowlin Custom Mfg.
Obermeyer Rifled Barrels
Pac-Nor Barreling
Pell, John T.
Pence Precision Barrels
Rocky Mountain Rifle Works Ltd.
Rosenthal, Brad and Sallie
Sabatti S.R.L.
Schneider Rifle Barrels, Inc., Gary
Shaw, Inc., E.R.
Shilen Rifles, Inc.
Siskiyou Gun Works
Small Arms Mfg. Co.
Sonora Rifle Barrel Co.
Specialty Shooters Supply, Inc.
Springfield, Inc.
SSK Industries
Strutz Rifle Barrels, Inc., W.C.
Swivel Machine Works, Inc.
Volquartsen Custom Ltd.
Wells, Fred F.
Wilson Arms Co., The
Wiseman and Co., Bill

SCOPES, MOUNTS, ACCESSORIES, OPTICAL EQUIPMENT

Accuracy Innovations, Inc.
Ackerman, Bill
ADCO International
Adventurer's Outpost
•Aimpoint, Inc.
•Aimtech Mount Systems
•Air Venture
Alley Supply Co.
•Anderson Manufacturing Co., Inc.
Anschutz GmbH
Apel GmbH, Ernst
A.R.M.S., Inc.
•Armscorp USA, Inc.
Aro-Tek, Ltd.
Baer Custom, Inc., Les
•Barrett Firearms Mfg., Inc.
Bushnell Sports Optics Worldwide
Beaver Park Products, Inc.
•Bohemia Arms Co.
Boonie Packer Products
•Brown Co., E. Arthur
Brownells, Inc.
•Browning Arms Co.
Brunton U.S.A.
•B-Square Co., Inc.
Bull Mountain Rifle Co.
•Burris Co., Inc.
•Bushnell
Butler Creek Corp.
Celestron International
Center Lock Scope Rings
Champion's Choice, Inc.
Clark Custom Guns, Inc.
Clearview Mfg. Co., Inc.
Combat Military Ordnance Ltd.
Compass Industries, Inc.
Concept Development Corp.
Conetrol Scope Mounts
CRDC Laser Systems Group
Creedmoor Sports, Inc.

•See page 445 for Warranty Service Center Addresses

Custom Quality Products, Inc.
D&H Prods. Co., Inc.
D.C.C. Enterprises
Del-Sports, Inc.
DHB Products
Doctor Optic Technologies, Inc.
Eagle International, Inc.
Eagle Mfg. & Engineering
Edmund Scientific Co.
Ednar, Inc.
Eggleston, Jere D.
Emerging Technologies, Inc.
•Europtik Ltd.
Excalibur Enterprises
Farr Studio, Inc.
Feather Industries, Inc.
•Forster Products
From Jena
Fujinon, Inc.
Gentry Custom Gunmaker, David
G.G. & G.
Glaser Safety Slug, Inc.
Great Lakes Airguns
Guns, (Div. of D.C. Engineering, Inc.)
Hakko Co. Ltd.
•Hammerli USA
Harris Gunworks
Hermann Leather Co., H.J.
Hertel & Reuss
Holland's
H-S Precision, Inc.
Ironsighter Co.
•Jaeger, Inc., Paul/Dunn's
JagerSport, Ltd.
Jeffredo Gunsight
Jewell, Arnold W.
Jones, J.D.
•Kahles, A Swarovski Company
Kelbly, Inc.
•Keng's Firearms Specialty, Inc.
KenPatable Ent., Inc.
•Kesselring Gun Shop
Kimber of America, Inc.
Kmount
•Kowa Optimed, Inc.
Kris Mounts
KVH Industries, Inc.
Kwik Mount Corp.
Kwik-Site Co.
•L&S Technologies, Inc.
L.A.R. Mfg., Inc.
•Laser Devices, Inc.
•Laseraim
LaserMax
Lectro Science, Inc.
Lee Co., T.K.
•Leica USA, Inc.
•Leupold & Stevens, Inc.
List Precision Engineering
Lohman Mfg. Co., Inc.
London Guns Ltd.
Mac's .45 Shop
Masen Co., Inc., John
Maxi-Mount
McCann's Machine & Gun Shop
McMillan Optical Gunsight Co.
MDS
Michaels of Oregon Co.
Military Armament Corp.
Millett Sights
•Mirador Optical Corp.
Mitchell Arms, Inc.
MWG Co.
New Democracy, Inc.
New England Custom Gun Service
•Nikon, Inc.
North American Specialties
Oakshore Electronic Sights, Inc.
Olympic Optical Co.
Optical Services Co.
Orchard Park Enterprise
Outdoor Connection, Inc., The
Parsons Optical Mfg. Co.
PECAR Herbert Schwarz, GmbH
PEM's Mfg. Co.
•Pentax Corp.
Perazone, Brian
Precise Metalsmithing Enterprises
•Precision Sport Optics
Premier Reticles
•Ram-Line, Inc.
Ranch Products
Randolph Engineering, Inc.
•Ranging, Inc.
•Redfield, Inc.
Rice, Keith
Rocky Mountain High Sports Glasses
S&K Mfg. Co.
Saunders Gun & Machine Shop
•Schmidt & Bender, Inc.
Scope Control Inc.
ScopLevel
Seattle Binocular & Scope Repair Co.
Selsi Co., Inc.
•Shepherd Scope Ltd.
Sightron, Inc.
•Simmons Enterprises, Ernie
•Simmons Outdoor Corp.
Six Enterprises
SKAN A.R.
SKB Shotguns
Sportsmatch U.K. Ltd.
•Springfield, Inc.
SSK Industries
Steyr Mannlicher AG
Stoeger Industries
SwaroSports, Inc.
Swarovski Optik North America Ltd.
•Swift Instruments, Inc.
TacStar Industires, Inc.
Talley, Dave
Tank's Rifle Shop
•Tasco Sales, Inc.
Tele-Optics
•Thompson/Center Arms
•Trijicon, Inc.
Uncle Mike's
•Unertl Optical Co., Inc., John
United Binocular Co.
United States Optics Technologies, Inc.
Valor Corp.
Volquartsen Custom Ltd.
Warne Manufacturing Co.
Warren Muzzleloading Co., Inc.
WASP Shooting Systems
Weatherby, Inc.
Weaver Products
•Weaver Scope Repair Service
Weigand Combat Handguns, Inc.
Westfield Engineering
White Rock Tool & Die
Wideview Scope Mount Corp.
•Williams Gun Sight Co.
York M-1 Conversions
Zanotti Armor, Inc.
•Zeiss Optical, Carl

SHOOTING/TRAINING SCHOOLS

Accuracy Gun Shop
Alpine Precision Gunsmithing & Indoor Shooting Range
American Small Arms Academy
Auto Arms
Bob's Tactical Indoor Shooting Range & Gun Shop
Chapman Academy of Practical Shooting
Chelsea Gun Club of New York City, Inc.
Clark Custom Guns, Inc.
CQB Training
Daisy Mfg. Co.
Defense Training International, Inc.
Dowtin Gunworks
Executive Protection Institute
Firearm Training Center, The
Firearms Academy of Seattle
G.H. Enterprises Ltd.
Gonzalez Guns, Ramon B.
Gunsite Training Center
Hank's Gun Shop
I.S.S.
Jensen's Custom Ammunition
Jensen's Firearms Acadamy
J.P. Enterprises, Inc.
McMurdo, Lynn
Mendez, John A.
Middlebrooks Custom Shop
Modern Gun School
Nevada Pistol Academy Inc.
North American Shooting Systems
North Mountain Pines Training Center
Pacific Pistolcraft
Passive Bullet Traps, Inc.
Performance Specialists
Quigley's Personal Protection Strategies, Paxton
River Road Sporting Clays
Robar Co.'s, Inc., The
SAFE
Savage Range Systems, Inc.
Shooter's World
Shooting Gallery, The
Shotgun Shop, The
Smith & Wesson
Specialty Gunsmithing
Starlight Training Center, Inc.
300 Gunsmith Service, Inc.
Tactical Defense Institute
Western Missouri Shooters Alliance
Yankee Gunsmith
Yavapai Firearms Academy Ltd.

SIGHTS, METALLIC

Accura-Site
All's, The Jim J. Tembelis Co., Inc.
Alpec Team, Inc.
Andela Tool & Machine, Inc.
Anschutz GmbH
Armsport, Inc.
Aro-Tek, Ltd.
Baer Custom, Inc., Les
Bob's Gun Shop
Bo-Mar Tool & Mfg. Co.
Bond Custom Firearms
Bowen Classic Arms Corp.
Bradley Gunsight Co.
Brown Co., E. Arthur
Brown Products, Inc., Ed
Buffalo Arms
California Sights
Cape Outfitters
Champion's Choice, Inc.
C-More Systems
Colonial Repair
DHB Products
Engineered Accessories
Evans, Andrew
Evans Gunsmithing
Farr Studio, Inc.
Fautheree, Andy
GSI, Inc.
Gun Doctor, The
Gun South, Inc.
Guns, (Div. of D.C. Engineering, Inc.)
Heinie Specialty Products
Hesco-Meprolight
Innovative Weaponry, Inc.
Innovision Enterprises
Jaeger, Inc., Paul/Dunn's
Lee's Red Ramps
List Precision Engineering
Lofland, James W.
London Guns Ltd.
L.P.A. Snc
Lyman Instant Targets, Inc.
Lyman Products Corp.
Mac's .45 Shop
Marble Arms
Meier Works
Meprolight
Merit Corp.
Mid-America Recreation, Inc.
Millett Sights
Mitchell Arms, Inc.
MMC
Montana Vintage Arms
New England Custom Gun Service
North American Specialties
Novak's Inc.
Oakshore Electronic Sights, Inc.
OK Weber, Inc.
Pachmayr Ltd.
PEM's Mfg. Co.
P.M. Enterprises, Inc.
Quarton USA, Ltd. Co.
Robar Co.'s, Inc., The
RPM
Scattergun Technologies, Inc.
Shepherd Scope Ltd.
Slug Site Co.
Talley, Dave
T.F.C. S.p.A.
Trijicon, Inc.
WASP Shooting Systems
Wichita Arms, Inc.
Williams Gun Sight Co.

STOCKS (Commercial and Custom)

Accuracy Unlimited (Glendale, AZ)
Ackerman & Co.
Adair Custom Shop, Bill
Ahlman Guns
Amrine's Gun Shop
Anschutz GmbH
Arms Ingenuity Co.
Artistry In Wood
Bain & Davis, Inc.
Balickie, Joe
Bansner's Gunsmithing Specialties
Barnes Bullets, Inc.
Bartlett, Don
Beitzinger, George
Belding's Custom Gun Shop
Bell & Carlson, Inc.
Benchmark Guns
Biesen, Al
Biesen, Roger
Bob's Gun Shop
Boltin, John M.
Bowerly, Kent
Boyds' Gunstock Industries, Inc.
Burgess & Son Gunsmiths, R.W.
Brace, Larry D.
Briganti & Co., A.
Brockmans Custom Gunsmithing
Brown Co., E. Arthur
Brown Precision, Inc.
Brownell Checkering Tools, W.E.
Buckhorn Gun Works
Bull Mountain Rifle Co.
Bullberry Barrel Works, Ltd.
Burkhart Gunsmithing, Don
Burres, Jack
Butler Creek Corp.
Cali'co Hardwoods, Inc.
Camilli, Lou
Campbell, Dick
Caywood, Shane J.
Chambers Flintlocks Ltd., Jim
Champlin Firearms, Inc.
Chicasaw Gun Works
Christman Jr., David
Churchill, Winston
Clark Custom Guns, Inc.
Claro Walnut Gunstock Co.
Cloward's Gun Shop
Cochran, Oliver
Coffin, Charles H.
Coffin, Jim
Coleman's Custom Repair
Colonial Repair
Colorado Gunsmithing Academy Lamar
Conrad, C.A.
Cooper Arms
Costa, David
Crane Sales Co., George S.
Creedmoor Sports, Inc.
Curly Maple Stock Blanks
Custom Checkering Service
Custom Gun Products
Custom Gun Stocks
Custom Riflestocks, Inc.
D&D Gunsmiths, Ltd.
D&G Presicion Duplicators
D&J Bullet Co. & Custom Gun Shop, Inc.
Dahl's Custom Stocks
Dangler, Homer L.
D.D. Custom Stocks
Desert Industries, Inc.
de Treville & Co., Stan
Dever Co., Jack
Devereaux, R.H. "Dick"
DGS, Inc.
Dilliott Gunsmithing, Inc.
Dillon, Ed
Dowtin Gunworks
Dressel Jr., Paul G.
Duane Custom Stocks, Randy
Duncan's Gunworks, Inc.
Echols & Co., D'Arcy
Eggleston, Jere D.
Erhardt, Dennis
Eversull Co., Inc., K.
Fajen, Inc., Reinhart
Farmer-Dressel, Sharon
Fibron Products, Inc.
Fisher, Jerry A.
Flaig's
Folks, Donald E.
Forster, Kathy
Forster, Larry L.
Forty Five Ranch Enterprises
Frank Custom Classic Arms, Ron
Game Haven Gunstocks

•See page 445 for Warranty Service Center Addresses

Gene's Custom Guns
Gervais, Mike
Gilman-Mayfield, Inc.
Giron, Robert E.
Goens, Dale W.
Golden Age Arms Co.
Gordie's Gun Shop
Goudy Classic Stocks, Gary
Grace, Charles E.
Green, Roger M.
Greene Precision Duplicators
Greenwood Precision
Griffin & Howe, Inc.
Gun Shop, The
Guns
Guns, (Div. of D.C. Engineering, Inc.)
Gunsmithing Ltd.
Hallberg Gunsmith, Fritz
Halstead, Rick
Hanson's Gun Center, Dick
Harper's Custom Stocks
Harris Gunworks
Hart & Son, Inc., Robert W.
Hastings Barrels
Hecht, Hubert J.
Heilmann, Stephen
Hensley, Darwin
Heppler, Keith M.
Heydenberk, Warren R.
High Tech Specialties, Inc.
Hillmer Custom Gunstocks, Paul D.
Hiptmayer, Armurier
Hiptmayer, Klaus
Hoelscher, Virgil
Hoenig & Rodman
H-S Precision, Inc.
Huebner, Corey O.
Hughes, Steven Dodd
Intermountain Arms & Tackle, Inc.
Island Pond Gun Shop
Ivanoff, Thomas G.
Jackalope Gun Shop
Jaeger, Inc., Paul/Dunn's
Jamison's Forge Works
Jarrett Rifles, Inc.
Johnson Wood Products
J.P. Gunstocks, Inc.
KDF, Inc.
Keith's Custom Gunstocks
Ken's Rifle Blanks
Kilham & Co.
Klein Custom Guns, Don
Klingler Woodcarving
Knippel, Richard
Kokolus, Michael M.
Lawson Co., Harry
Lock's Philadelphia Gun Exchange
Lynn's Custom Gunstocks
Mac's .45 Shop
Marple & Associates, Dick
Masen Co., Inc., John
Mathews & Son, Inc., George E.
Mazur Restoraton, Pete
McCament, Jay
McCullough, Ken
McDonald, Dennis
McFarland, Stan
McGowen Rifle Barrels
McGuire, Bill
McKinney, R.P.
McMillan Fiberglass Stocks, Inc.
Mercer Custom Stocks, R.M.
Mid-America Recreation, Inc.
Miller Arms, Inc.
Morrison Custom Rifles, J.W.
Morrow, Bud
MPI Fiberglass Stocks
Nelson, Stephen
Nettestad Gun Works
New England Arms Co.
New England Custom Gun Service
Newman Gunshop
Nickels, Paul R.
Norman Custom Gunstocks, Jim
Oakland Custom Arms, Inc.
Oil Rod and Gun Shop
OK Weber, Inc.
Old World Gunsmithing
One Of A Kind
Or-Ün
Orvis Co., The
Ottmar, Maurice
Ozark Gun Works
P&S Gun Service
Pacific Research Laboratories, Inc.
Pagel Gun Works, Inc.
Paulsen Gunstocks
Pecatonica River Longrifle
PEM's Mfg. Co.
Pentheny de Pentheny
Perazone, Brian
Perazzi USA, Inc.
R&J Gun Shop
Ram-Line, Inc.
Reagent Chemical and Research, Inc.
Reiswig, Wallace E.
Richards Micro-Fit Stocks
Rimrock Rifle Stocks
RMS Custom Gunsmithing
Robar Co.'s, Inc., The
Robinson, Don
Robinson Firearms Mfg. Ltd.
Roto Carve
Royal Arms Gunstocks
Ryan, Chad L.
Sanders Custom Gun Service
Saville Iron Co.
Schiffman, Curt
Schiffman, Mike
Schuetzen Gun Co.
Schumakers Gun Shop, William
Schwartz Custom Guns, David W.
Schwartz Custom Guns, Wayne E.
Shell Shack
Sile Distributors, Inc.
Six Enterprises
Skeoch, Brian R.
Slug Group, Inc.
Smith, Art
Smith, Sharmon
Snider Stocks, Walter S.
Speedfeed, Inc.
Speiser, Fred D.
Stiles Custom Guns
Storey, Dale A.
Strawbridge, Victor W.
Swann, D.J.
Szweda, Robert
Talmage, William G.
Taylor & Robbins
Tecnolegno S.p.A.
T.F.C. S.p.A.
Tiger-Hunt
Tirelli
Tom's Gun Repair
Tom's Gunshop
Trevallion Gunstocks
Tucker, James C.
Turkish Firearms Corp.
Tuttle, Dale
Vest, John
Vic's Gun Refinishing
Vintage Industries, Inc.
Volquartsen Custom Ltd.
Von Minden Gunsmithing Services
Walnut Factory, The
Weatherby, Inc.
Weber & Markin Custom Gunsmiths
Weems, Cecil
Wells Custom Gunsmith, R.A.
Wells, Fred F.
Wenig Custom Gunstocks, Inc.
Werth, T.W.
Wessinger Custom Guns & Engraving
West, Robert G.
Western Gunstock Mfg. Co.
Williams Gun Sight Co.
Williamson Precision Gunsmithing
Windish, Jim
Winter, Robert M.
Wright's Hardwood Gunstock Blanks
Yee, Mike
Zeeryp, Russ

TARGETS, BULLET AND CLAYBIRD TRAPS

Action Target, Inc.
American Target
American Whitetail Target Systems
A-Tech Corp.
Barsotti, Bruce
Beomat of America Inc.
Birchwood Casey
Blue and Gray Products, Inc.
Bull-X, Inc.
Caswell International Corp.
Champion Target Co.
Champion's Choice, Inc.
Cunningham Co., Eaton
Dapkus Co., Inc., J.G.
Datumtech Corp.
Dayson Arms Ltd.
D.C.C. Enterprises
Detroit-Armor Corp.
Diamond Mfg. Co.
Erickson's Mfg., Inc., C.W.
Federal Champion Target Co.
Freeman Animal Targets
G.H. Enterprises Ltd.
Gun Parts Corp., The
Hiti-Schuch, Atelier Wilma
Hunterjohn
Innovision Enterprises
Jackalope Gun Shop
JWH: Software
Kennebec Journal
Kleen-Bore, Inc.
Littler Sales Co.
Lyman Instant Targets, Inc.
Lyman Products Corp.
M&D Munitions Ltd.
MSR Targets
National Target Co.
N.B.B., Inc.
North American Shooting Systems
Nu-Teck
Outers Laboratories, Div. of Blount
Ox-Yoke Originals, Inc.
Parker Reproductions
Passive Bullet Traps, Inc.
Pease Accuracy, Bob
PlumFire Press, Inc.
Quack Decoy & Sporting Clays
Red Star Target Co.
Remington Arms Co., Inc.
River Road Sporting Clays
Rockwood Corp., Speedwell Div.
Rocky Mountain Target Co.
Savage Range Systems, Inc.
Schaefer Shooting Sports
Seligman Shooting Products
Shooters Supply
Shoot-N-C Targets
Shotgun Shop, The
Thompson Target Technology
White Flyer Targets
World of Targets
X-Spand Target Systems
Z's Metal Targets & Frames
Zriny's Metal Targets

TAXIDERMY

African Import Co.
Jonas Appraisers—Taxidermy Animals, Jack
Kulis Freeze Dry Taxidermy
Parker, Mark D.
World Trek, Inc.

TRAP AND SKEET SHOOTER'S EQUIPMENT

Allen Co., Bob
Allen Sportswear, Bob
Bagmaster Mfg., Inc.
Baker, Stan
Ballistic Products, Inc.
Beomat of America Inc.
Clymer Manufacturing Co., Inc.
Colonial Arms, Inc.
Crane & Crane Ltd.
Dayson Arms Ltd.
Dewey Mfg. Co., Inc., J.
F&A Inc.
Fiocchi of America, Inc.
Gander Mountain, Inc.
G.H. Enterprises Ltd.
Great 870 Co., The
Harper, William E.
Hastings Barrels
Hillmer Custom Gunstocks, Paul D.
Hoppe's Div.
Hunter Co., Inc.
K&T Co.
Ljutic Industries, Inc.
Lynn's Custom Gunstocks
Maionchi-L.M.I.
Meadow Industries
Moneymaker Guncraft Corp.
MTM Molded Products Co., Inc.
Noble Co., Jim
Palsa Outdoor Products
Passive Bullet Traps, Inc.
PAST Sporting Goods, Inc.
Penguin Industries, Inc.
Perazzi USA, Inc.
Pro-Port Ltd.
Protektor Model
Quack Decoy & Sporting Clays
Remington Arms Co., Inc.
Rhodeside, Inc.
Savage Range Systems, Inc.
Shootin' Accessories, Ltd.
Shooting Specialties
Shotgun Shop, The
Titus, Daniel
Trius Products, Inc.
X-Spand Target Systems

TRIGGERS, RELATED EQUIPMENT

Actions by "T"
B&D Trading Co., Inc.
Baer Custom, Inc., Les
Behlert Precision, Inc.
Bob's Gun Shop
Bond Custom Firearms
Boyds' Gunstock Industries, Inc.
Bull Mountain Rifle Co.
Canjar Co., M.H.
Cape Outfitters
Clark Custom Guns, Inc.
Dayton Traister
Electronic Trigger Systems, Inc.
Eversull Co., Inc., K.
Galati International
Gentry Custom Gunmaker, David
Guns, (Div. of D.C. Engineering, Inc.)
Hastings Barrels
Hoelscher, Virgil
Holland's
Jaeger, Inc., Paul/Dunn's
Jewell, Arnold W.
J.P. Enterprises, Inc.
List Precision Engineering
Masen Co., Inc., John
Master Lock Co.
Miller Single Trigger Mfg. Co.
OK Weber, Inc.
Pease Accuracy, Bob
PEM's Mfg. Co.
Penrod Precision
Perazone, Brian
Perazzi USA, Inc.
S&B Industries
Shilen Rifles, Inc.
Timney Mfg., Inc.
Videki

MANUFACTURERS' DIRECTORY

A

A&B Industries, Inc. (See Top-Line USA, Inc.)
A&J Products, Inc., 5791 Hall Rd., Muskegon, MI 49442-1964
A&M Waterfowl, Inc., P.O. Box 102, Ripley, TN 38063/901-635-4003; FAX: 901-635-2320
A&W Repair, 2930 Schneider Dr., Arnold, MO 63010/314-287-3725
A.A. Arms, Inc., 4811 Persimmont Ct., Monroe, NC 28110/704-289-5356, 800-935-1119; FAX: 704-289-5859
AAL Optics, Inc., 2316 NE 8th Rd., Ocala, FL 33470/904-629-3211; FAX: 904-629-1433
Abel Safe & File, Inc., 124 West Locust St., Fairbury, IL 61739/800-346-9280, 815-692-2131; FAX: 815-692-3350
A.B.S. III, 9238 St. Morritz Dr., Fern Creek, KY 40291
AC Dyna-tite Corp., 155 Kelly St., P.O. Box 0984, Elk Grove Village, IL 60007/847-593-5566; FAX: 847-593-1304
Acadian Ballistic Specialties, P.O. Box 61, Covington, LA 70434
Acculube II, Inc., 4366 Shackleford Rd., Norcross, GA 30093-2912
Accupro Gun Care, 15512-109 Ave., Surrey, BC U3R 7E8, CANADA/604-583-7807
Accuracy Den, The, 25 Bitterbrush Rd., Reno, NV 89523/702-345-0225
Accuracy Gun Shop, 7818 Wilkerson Ct., San Diego, CA 92111/619-282-8500
Accuracy Innovations, Inc., P.O. Box 376, New Paris, PA 15554/814-839-4517; FAX: 814-839-2601
Accuracy International, 9115 Trooper Trail, P.O. Box 2019, Bozeman, MT 59715/406-587-7922; FAX: 406-585-9434
Accuracy International Precision Rifles (See U.S. importer—Gunsite Training Center)
Accuracy Unlimited, 7479 S. DePew St., Littleton, CO 80123
Accuracy Unlimited, 16036 N. 49 Ave., Glendale, AZ 85306/602-978-9089; FAX: 602-978-9089
Accura-Site (See All's, The Jim Tembellis Co., Inc.)
Accurate Arms Co., Inc., 5891 Hwy. 230 West, McEwen, TN 37101/615-729-4207, 800-416-3006; FAX 615-729-4211
Accuright, RR 2 Box 397, Sebeka, MN 56477/218-472-3383
Accu-Tek, 4525 Carter Ct., Chino, CA 91710/909-627-2404; FAX: 909-627-7817
Ace Custom 45's, Inc., 1880½ Upper Turtle Creek Rd., Kerrville, TX 78028/210-257-4290; FAX: 210-257-5724
Ace Sportswear, Inc., 700 Quality Rd., Fayetteville, NC 28306/919-323-1223; FAX: 919-323-5392
Ackerman & Co., 16 Cortez St., Westfield, MA 01085/413-568-8008
Ackerman, Bill (See Optical Services Co.)
Action Bullets, Inc., 1811 W. 13th Ave., Denver, CO 80204/303-595-9636; FAX: 303-595-4413
Action Products, Inc., 22 N. Mulberry St., Hagerstown, MD 21740/301-797-1414; FAX: 301-733-2073
Action Target, Inc., P.O. Box 636, Provo, UT 84603/801-377-8033; FAX: 801-377-8096
Actions by "T", Teddy Jacobson, 16315 Redwood Forest Ct., Sugar Land, TX 77478/713-277-4008
ACTIV Industries, Inc., 1000 Zigor Rd., P.O. Box 339, Kearneysville, WV 25430/304-725-0451; FAX: 304-725-2080
AcuSport Corporation, 1 Hunter Place, Bellefontaine, OH 43311-3001/513-593-7010; FAX: 513-592-5625
Ad Hominem, RR 3, Orillia, Ont. L3V 6H3, CANADA/705-689-5303
Adair Custom Shop, Bill, 2886 Westridge, Carrollton, TX 75006
Adams & Son Engravers, John J., 87 Acorn Rd., Dennis, MA 02638/508-385-7971
Adams Jr., John J., 87 Acorn Rd., Dennis, MA 02638/508-385-7971
Adaptive Technology, 939 Barnum Ave, Bridgeport, CT 06609/800-643-6735; FAX: 800-643-6735
ADCO International, 10 Cedar St., Unit 17, Woburn, MA 01801/617-935-1799; FAX: 617-935-1011
Adkins, Luther, 1292 E. McKay Rd., Shelbyville, IN 46176-9353/317-392-3795
Advance Car Mover Co., Rowell Div., P.O. Box 1, 240 N. Depot St., Juneau, WI 53039/414-386-4464; FAX: 414-386-4416
Adventure 16, Inc., 4620 Alvarado Canyon Rd., San Diego, CA 92120/619-283-6314
Adventure Game Calls, R.D. 1, Leonard Rd., Spencer, NY 14883/607-589-4611
Adventurer's Outpost, P.O. Box 70, Cottonwood, AZ 86326/800-762-7471; FAX: 602-634-8781
African Import Co., 20 Braunecker Rd., Plymouth, MA 02360/508-746-8552
AFSCO Ammunition, 731 W. Third St., P.O. Box L, Owen, WI 54460/715-229-2516
Ahlman Guns, Rt. 1, Box 20, Morristown, MN 55052/507-685-4243; FAX: 507-685-4247
Ahrends, Kim, Custom Firearms, Box 203, Clarion, IA 50525/515-532-3449; FAX: 515-532-3926
Aimpoint, Inc., 580 Herndon Parkway, Suite 500, Herndon, VA 22070/703-471-6828; FAX: 703-689-0575
Aimtech Mount Systems, P.O. Box 223, 101 Inwood Acres, Thomasville, GA 31799/912-226-4313; FAX: 912-227-0222
Air Arms, Hailsham Industrial Park, Diplocks Way, Hailsham, E. Sussex, BN27 3JF ENGLAND/011-0323-845853 (U.S. importers—Air Werks International; World Class Airguns)
Air Rifle Specialists, P.O. Box 138, 130 Holden Rd., Pine City, NY 14871-0138/607-734-7340; FAX: 607-733-3261
Air Venture, 9752 E. Flower St., Bellflower, CA 90706/310-867-6355
Airgun Repair Centre, 3227 Garden Meadows, Lawrenceburg, IN 47025/812-637-1463; FAX: 812-637-1463
Airguns-R-Us, 101 7th Ave., Columbia, TN 38401/615-381-4428; FAX: 615-381-1218
Airrow (See Swivel Machine Works, Inc.)
Aitor-Cuchilleria Del Norte, S.A., Izelaieta, 17, 48260 Ermua (Vizcaya), SPAIN/43-17-08-50; FAX: 43-17-00-01
Ajax Custom Grips, Inc., 9130 Viscount Row, Dallas, TX 75247/214-630-8893; FAX: 214-630-4942
Aker Leather Products, 2248 Main St., Suite 6, Chula Vista, CA 91911/619-423-5182; FAX: 619-423-1363
Alaska Bullet Works, P.O. Box 54, Douglas, AK 99824/907-789-3834
Alcas Cutlery Corp. (See Cutco Cutlery)
Alco Carrying Cases, 601 W. 26th St., New York, NY 10001/212-675-5820; FAX: 212-691-5935
Aldis Gunsmithing & Shooting Supply, 502 S. Montezuma St., Prescott, AZ 86303/602-445-6723; FAX: 602-445-6763
Alessi Holsters, Inc., 2465 Niagara Falls Blvd., Amherst, NY 14228-3527/716-691-5615
Alex, Inc., Box 3034, Bozeman, MT 59772/406-282-7396; FAX: 406-282-7396
Alfano, Sam, 36180 Henry Gaines Rd., Pearl River, LA 70452/504-863-3364; FAX: 504-863-7715
All's, The Jim J. Tembelis Co., Inc., 280 E. Fernau Ave., Oshkosh, WI 54901/414-426-1080; FAX: 414-426-1080
All American Lead Shot Corp., P.O. Box 224566, Dallas, TX 75062
All Rite Products, Inc., 5752 N. Silverstone Circle, Mountain Green, UT 84050/801-876-3330; 801-876-2216
Allard, Gary, Creek Side Metal & Woodcrafters, Fishers Hill, VA 22626/703-465-3903
Allen Co., Bob, 214 SW Jackson, P.O. Box 477, Des Moines, IA 50315/515-283-2191; 800-685-7020; FAX: 515-283-0779
Allen Co., Inc., 525 Burbank St., Broomfield, CO 80020/303-469-1857, 800-876-8600; FAX: 303-466-7437
Allen Mfg., 6449 Hodgson Rd., Circle Pines, MN 55014/612-429-8231
Allen, Richard L., 339 Grove Ave., Prescott, AZ 86301/602-778-1237
Allen Sportswear, Bob (See Allen Co., Bob)
Alley Supply Co., P.O. Box 848, Gardnerville, NV 89410/702-782-3800
Alliant Techsystems, Smokeless Powder Group, 200 Valley Rd., Suite 305, Mt. Arlington, NJ 07856/800-276-9337; FAX: 201-770-2528
Allred Bullet Co., 932 Evergreen Drive, Logan, UT 84321/801-752-6983
Alpec Team, Inc., 201 Ricken Backer Cir., Livermore, CA 94550/510-606-8245; FAX: 510-606-4279
Alpha 1 Drop Zone, 2121 N. Tyler, Wichita, KS 67212/316-729-0800
Alpha Gunsmith Division, 1629 Via Monserate, Fallbrook, CA 92028/619-723-9279, 619-728-2663
Alpha LaFranck Enterprises, P.O. Box 81072, Lincoln, NE 68501/402-466-3193
Alpha Precision, Inc., 2765-B Preston Rd. NE, Good Hope, GA 30641/770-267-6163
Alpine's Precision Gunsmithing & Indoor Shooting Range, 2401 Government Way, Coeur d'Alene, ID 83814/208-765-3559; FAX: 208-765-3559
Altamont Co., 901 N. Church St., P.O. Box 309, Thomasboro, IL 61878/217-643-3125, 800-626-5774; FAX: 217-643-7973
Alumna Sport by Dee Zee, 1572 NE 58th Ave., P.O. Box 3090, Des Moines, IA 50316/800-798-9899
AmBr Software Group Ltd., P.O. Box 301, Reistertown, MD 21136-0301/410-526-4106; FAX: 410-526-7212
American Ammunition, 3545 NW 71st St., Miami, FL 33147/305-835-7400; FAX: 305-694-0037
American Arms & Ordnance, Inc., P.O. Box 2691, 1303 S. College Ave., Bryan, TX 77805/409-822-4983
American Arms, Inc., 715 Armour Rd., N. Kansas City, MO 64116/816-474-3161; FAX: 816-474-1225
American Derringer Corp., 127 N. Lacy Dr., Waco, TX 76705/800-642-7817, 817-799-9111; FAX: 817-799-7935

American Display Co., 55 Cromwell St., Providence, RI 02907/401-331-2464; FAX: 401-421-1264
American Frontier Firearms Co., 40725 Brook Trails Way, Aguanga, CA 92536/909-763-0014; FAX: 909-763-0014
American Gas & Chemical Co., Ltd., 220 Pegasus Ave., Northvale, NJ 07647/201-767-7300
American Gripcraft, 3230 S. Dodge 2, Tucson, AZ 85713/602-790-1222
American Handgunner Magazine, 591 Camino de la Reina, Suite 200, San Diego, CA 92108/619-297-5350; FAX: 619-297-5353
American Pioneer Video, P.O. Box 50049, Bowling Green, KY 42102-2649/800-743-4675
American Products Co., 14729 Spring Valley Road, Morrison, IL 61270/815-772-3336; FAX: 815-772-7921
American Safe Arms, Inc., 1240 Riverview Dr., Garland, UT 84312/801-257-7472; FAX: 801-785-8156
American Sales & Kirkpatrick, P.O. Box 677, Laredo, TX 78042/210-723-6893; FAX: 210-725-0672
American Security Products Company, 11925 Pacific Ave., Fontana, CA 92337/909-685-9680, 800-421-6142; FAX: 909-685-9685
American Small Arms Academy, P.O. Box 12111, Prescott, AZ 86304/602-778-5623
American Target, 1328 S. Jason St., Denver, CO 80223/303-733-0433; FAX: 303-777-0311
American Target Knives, 1030 Brownwood NW, Grand Rapids, MI 49504/616-453-1998
American Whitetail Target Systems, P.O. Box 41, 106 S. Church St., Tennyson, IN 47637/812-567-4527
Americase, P.O. Box 271, 1610 E. Main, Waxahachie, TX 75165/800-880-3629; FAX: 214-937-8373
Ames Metal Products, 4324 S. Western Blvd., Chicago, IL 60609/312-523-3230; FAX: 312-523-3854
Amherst Arms, P.O. Box 1457, Englewood, FL 34295/941-475-2020; FAX: 941-473-1212
Ammo Load, Inc., 1560 E. Edinger, Suite G, Santa Ana, CA 92705/714-558-8858; FAX: 714-569-0319
Amrine's Gun Shop, 937 La Luna, Ojai, CA 93023/805-646-2376
Amsec, 11925 Pacific Ave., Fontana, CA 92337
AMT, 6226 Santos Diaz St., Irwindale, CA 91702/818-334-6629; FAX: 818-969-5247
Amtec 2000, Inc., 84 Industrial Rowe, Gardner, MA 01440/508-632-9608; FAX: 508-632-2300
Analog Devices, Box 9106, Norwood, MA 02062
Andela Tool & Machine, Inc., RD3, Box 246, Richfield Springs, NY 13439
Anderson Manufacturing Co., Inc., 22602 53rd Ave. SE, Bothell, WA 98021/206-481-1858; FAX: 206-481-7839
Andres & Dworsky, Bergstrasse 18, A-3822 Karlstein, Thaya, Austria, EUROPE, 0 28 44-285
Angelo & Little Custom Gun Stock Blanks, P.O. Box 240046, Dell, MT 59724-0046
Anics Firm, Inc., 3 Commerce Park Square, 23200 Chagrin Blvd., Suite 240, Beechwood, OH 44122/216-292-4363, 800-550-1582; FAX: 216-292-2588
Anschutz GmbH, Postfach 1128, D-89001 Ulm, Donau, GERMANY (U.S. importers—Accuracy International; AcuSport Corporation; Champion Shooters' Supply; Champion's Choice; Gunsmithing, Inc.)
Ansen Enterprises, Inc., 1506 W. 228th St., Torrance, CA 90501-5105/310-534-1837; FAX: 310-534-3162
Answer Products Co., 1519 Westbury Drive, Davison, MI 48423/810-653-2911
Anthony and George Ltd., Rt. 1, P.O. Box 45, Evington, VA 24550/804-821-8117
Antique American Firearms (See Carlson, Douglas R.)
Antique Arms Co., 1110 Cleveland Ave., Monett, MO 65708/417-235-6501
Apache Products, Inc., 4224 Old Sterington Rd., Monroe, LA 71203/318-325-1761; FAX: 318-325-4873
Apel GmbH, Ernst, Am Kirschberg 3, D-97218 Gerbrunn, GERMANY/0 (931) 707192
Aplan Antiques & Art, James O., HC 80, Box 793-25, Piedmont, SD 57769/605-347-5016
Arcadia Machine & Tool, Inc. (See AMT)
Arco Powder, HC-Rt. 1, P.O. Box 102, County Rd. 357, Mayo, FL 32066/904-294-3882; FAX: 904-294-1498
Aristocrat Knives, 1701 W. Wernsing Ave., Effingham, IL 62401/800-953-3436; FAX: 217-347-3083
Arizaga (See U.S. importer—Mandall Shooting Supplies, Inc.)
Arizona Custom Case, 1015 S. 23rd St., Phoenix, AZ 85034/602-273-0220
Arkansas Mallard Duck Calls, Rt. Box 182, England, AR 72046/501-842-3597
Arkfeld Mfg. & Dist. Co., Inc., 1230 Monroe Ave., Norfolk, NE 68702-0054/402-371-9430; 800-533-0676
ArmaLite, Inc., P.O. Box 299, Geneseo, IL 61254/309-944-6939; FAX: 309-944-6949
Armament Gunsmithing Co., Inc., 525 Rt. 22, Hillside, NJ 07205/908-686-0960
Armas Azor, J.A. (See U.S. importer—Armes de Chasse)
Armas Kemen S.A. (See U.S. importer—USA Sporting)
Armes de Chasse, P.O. Box 827, Chadds Ford, PA 19317/610-388-1146; FAX: 610-388-1147
Armfield Custom Bullets, 4775 Caroline Drive, San Diego, CA 92115/619-582-7188; FAX: 619-287-3238
Armi San Marco (See U.S. importer—Taylor's & Co., Inc.)
Armi San Paolo, via Europa 172-A, I-25062 Concesio, 030-2751725 (BS) ITALY
Armi Sport (See U.S. importers—Cape Outfitters; Taylor's & Co., Inc.)
Armite Laboratories, 1845 Randolph St., Los Angeles, CA 90001/213-587-7768; FAX: 213-587-5075
Armoloy Co. of Ft. Worth, 204 E. Daggett St., Fort Worth, TX 76104/817-332-5604; FAX: 817-335-6517
Armor (See Buck Stop Lure Co., Inc.)
Armor Metal Products, P.O. Box 4609, Helena, MT 59604/406-442-5560
Armory Publications, P.O. Box 4206, Oceanside, CA 92052-4206/619-757-3930; FAX: 619-722-4108
Armoury, Inc., The, Rt. 202, Box 2340, New Preston, CT 06777/203-868-0001
A.R.M.S., Inc., 230 W. Center St., West Bridgewater, MA 02379-1620/508-584-7816; FAX: 508-588-8045
Arms & Armour Press, Ltd., Wellington House, 125 Strand, London WC2R 0BB ENGLAND/0171-420-5555; FAX: 0171-240-7265
Arms Corporation of the Philippines, Bo. Parang Marikina, Metro Manila, PHILIPPINES/632-941-6243, 632-941-6244; FAX: 632-942-0682
Arms Craft Gunsmithing, 1106 Linda Dr., Arroyo Grande, CA 93420/805-481-2830
Arms Ingenuity Co., P.O. Box 1, 51 Canal St., Weatogue, CT 06089/203-658-5624
Arms, Peripheral Data Systems (See Arms Software)
Arms Software, P.O. Box 1526, Lake Oswego, OR 97035/800-366-5559, 503-697-0533; FAX: 503-697-3337
Arms United Corp., 1018 Cedar St., Niles, MI 49120/616-683-6837
Armscorp USA, Inc., 4424 John Ave., Baltimore, MD 21227/410-247-6200; FAX: 410-247-6205
Armsport, Inc., 3950 NW 49th St., Miami, FL 33142/305-635-7850; FAX: 305-633-2877
Arnold Arms Co., Inc., P.O. Box 1011, Arlington, WA 98223/800-371-1011, 360-435-1011; FAX: 360-435-7304
Aro-Tek, Ltd., 206 Frontage Rd. North, Suite C, Pacific, WA 98047/206-351-2984; FAX: 206-833-4483
Arratoonian, Andy (See Horseshoe Leather Products)
Arrieta, S.L., Morkaiko, 5, Elgoibar, E-20870, SPAIN/(43) 74 31 50; FAX: (43) 74 31 54 (U.S. importers—Griffin & Howe; Hi-Grade Imports; Jansma, Jack J.; New England Arms Co.; The Orvis Co., Inc.; Quality Arms, Inc.)
Art Jewel Enterprises Ltd., Eagle Business Ctr., 460 Randy Rd., Carol Stream, IL 60188/708-260-0400
Art's Gun & Sport Shop, Inc., 6008 Hwy. Y, Hillsboro, MO 63050
Artistry in Leather (See Stuart, V. Pat)
Artistry in Wood, 134 Zimmerman Rd., Kalispell, MT 59901/406-257-9003
Arundel Arms & Ammunition, Inc., A., 24 Defense St., Annapolis, MD 21401/301-224-8683
Ashby Turkey Calls, P.O. Box 1466, Ava, MO 65608-1466/417-967-3787
Aspen Outdoors, Inc., 1059 W. Market St., York, PA 17404/717-846-0255, 800-677-4780; FAX: 717-845-7447
A-Square Co., Inc., One Industrial Park, Bedford, KY 40006-9667/502-255-7456; FAX: 502-255-7657
Astra Sport, S.A., Apartado 3, 48300 Guernica, Espagne, SPAIN/34-4-6250100; FAX: 34-4-6255186 (U.S. importer—E.A.A. Corp.; P.S.M.G. Gun Co.)
A-Tech Corp., P.O. Box 1281, Cottage Grove, OR 97424
Atamec-Bretton, 19, rue Victor Grignard, F-42026 St.-Etienne (Cedex 1) FRANCE/77-93-54-69; FAX: 33-77-93-57-98 (U.S. importer—Mandall Shooting Supplies, Inc.)
ATIS Armi S.A.S., via Gussalli 24, Zona Industriale-Loc. Fornaci, 25020 Brescia, ITALY
Atlanta Cutlery Corp., 2143 Gees Mill Rd., Box 839 CIS, Conyers, GA 30207/800-883-0300; FAX: 404-388-0246
Atlantic Mills, Inc., 1325 Washington Ave., Asbury Park, NJ 07712/800-242-7374
Atlantic Research Marketing Systems (See A.R.M.S., Inc.)
Atlantic Rose, Inc., P.O. Box 1305, Union, NJ 07083
Atsko/Sno-Seal, Inc., 2530 Russell SE, Orangeburg, SC 29115/803-531-1820; FAX: 803-531-2139
Audette, Creighton, 19 Highland Circle, Springfield, VT 05156/802-885-2331
Austin's Calls, Bill, Box 284, Kaycee, WY 82639/307-738-2552
Auto Arms, 738 Clearview, San Antonio, TX 78228/512-434-5450
Autauga Arms, Inc., 817 S. Memorial Dr., Prattville, AL 36067-5734/800-262-9563; FAX: 334-361-2961
Automatic Equipment Sales, 627 E. Railroad Ave., Salesburg, MD 21801
Auto-Ordnance Corp., Williams Lane, West Hurley, NY 12491/914-679-4190; FAX: 914-679-2698
Autumn Sales, Inc. (Blaser), 1320 Lake St., Fort Worth, TX 76103/817-335-1634; FAX: 817-338-0119
AWC Systems Technology, P.O. Box 41938, Phoenix, AZ 85080-1938/602-780-1050
AYA (See U.S. importer—Armes de Chasse; New England Custom Gun Service)
A Zone Bullets, 2039 Walter Rd., Billings, MT 59105/800-252-3111; 406-248-1961
Aztec International Ltd., P.O. Box 1384, Clarkesville, GA 30523/706-754-7263

B

B&D Trading Co., Inc., 3935 Fair Hill Rd., Fair Oaks, CA 95628/800-334-3790, 916-967-9366; FAX: 916-967-4873
B&G Bullets (See Northside Gun Shop)

Badger Shooters Supply, Inc., P.O. Box 397, Owen, WI 54460/800-424-9069; FAX: 715-229-2332
Baekgaard Ltd., 1855 Janke Dr., Northbrook, IL 60062/708-498-3040; FAX: 708-493-3106
Baelder, Harry, Alte Goennebeker Strasse 5, 24635 Rickling, GERMANY/04328-722733; FAX: 04328-722732
Baer Custom, Inc., Les, 29601 34th Ave., Hillsdale, IL 61257/309-658-2716; FAX: 309-658-2610
Bagmaster Mfg., Inc., 2731 Sutton Ave., St. Louis, MO 63143/314-781-8002; FAX: 314-781-3363
Baikal (See U.S. importer—Air Werks International; K.B.I., Inc.)
Bain & Davis, Inc., 307 E. Valley Blvd., San Gabriel, CA 91776-3522/818-573-4241, 213-283-7449
Baker, Stan, 10,000 Lake City Way, Seattle, WA 98125/206-522-4575
Baker's Leather Goods, Roy, P.O. Box 893, Magnolia, AR 71753/501-234-0344
Balaance Co., 340-39 Ave. S.E. Box 505, Calgary, AB, T2G 1X6 CANADA
Bald Eagle Precision Machine Co., 101-K Allison St., Lock Haven, PA 17745/717-748-6772; FAX: 717-748-4443
Balickie, Joe, 408 Trelawney Lane, Apex, NC 27502/919-362-5185
Ballard Built, P.O. Box 1443, Kingsville, TX 78364/512-592-0853
Ballard Industries, 10271 Lockwood Dr., Suite B, Cupertino, CA 95014/408-996-0957; FAX: 408-257-6828
Ballistic Engineering & Software, Inc., 185 N. Park Blvd., Suite 330, Lake Orion, MI 48362/313-391-1074
Ballistic Products, Inc., 20015 75th Ave. North, Hamel, MN 55340-9456/612-494-9237; FAX: 612-494-9236
Ballistic Program Co., Inc., The, 2417 N. Patterson St., Thomasville, GA 31792/912-228-5739, 800-368-0835
Ballistic Research, 1108 W. May Ave., McHenry, IL 60050/815-385-0037
Ballistica Maximus North, 107 College Park Plaza, Johnstown, PA 15904/814-266-8380
Ballisti-Cast, Inc., Box 383, Parshall, ND 58770/701-862-3324; FAX: 701-862-3331
Bandcor Industries, Div. of Man-Sew Corp., 6108 Sherwin Dr., Port Richey, FL 34668/813-848-0432
Bang-Bang Boutique (See Holster Shop, The)
Banks, Ed, 2762 Hwy. 41 N., Ft. Valley, GA 31030/912-987-4665
Bansner's Gunsmithing Specialties, 261 East Main St. Box VH, Adamstown, PA 19501/800-368-2379; FAX: 717-484-0523
Barami Corp., 6689 Orchard Lake Rd. No. 148, West Bloomfield, MI 48322/810-738-0462; FAX: 810-855-4084
Barbour, Inc., 55 Meadowbrook Dr., Milford, NH 03055/603-673-1313; FAX: 603-673-6510
Barnes Bullets, Inc., P.O. Box 215, American Fork, UT 84003/801-756-4222, 800-574-9200; FAX: 801-756-2465; WEB: http://www.itsnet.com/home/bbullets
Baron Technology, 62 Spring Hill Rd., Trumbull, CT 06611/203-452-0515; FAX: 203-452-0663
Barraclough, John K., 55 Merit Park Dr., Gardena, CA 90247/310-324-2574
Barramundi Corp., P.O. Drawer 4259, Homosassa Springs, FL 32687/904-628-0200
Barrett Firearms Manufacturer, Inc., P.O. Box 1077, Murfreesboro, TN 37133/615-896-2938; FAX: 615-896-7313
Barska Optics Int'l., 1765 E. Colorado Blvd., Pasadena, CA 91106/818-568-0618; FAX: 818-568-9681
Barsotti, Bruce (See River Road Sporting Clays)
Bar-Sto Precision Machine, 73377 Sullivan Rd., P.O. Box 1838, Twentynine Palms, CA 92277/619-367-2747; FAX: 619-367-2407
Barta's Gunsmithing, 10231 US Hwy. 10, Cato, WI 54206/414-732-4472
Barteaux Machete, 1916 SE 50th Ave., Portland, OR 97215-3238/503-233-5880
Bartlett, Don, P.O. Box 55, Colbert, WA 99005/509-467-5009
Bartlett Engineering, 40 South 200 East, Smithfield, UT 84335-1645/801-563-5910; FAX: 801-563-8416
Basics Information Systems, Inc., 1141 Georgia Ave., Suite 515, Wheaton, MD 20902/301-949-1070; FAX: 301-949-5326
Bates Engraving, Billy, 2302 Winthrop Dr., Decatur, AL 35603/205-355-3690
Bauer, Eddie, 15010 NE 36th St., Redmond, WA 98052
Baumannize Custom, 4784 Sunrise Hwy., Bohemia, NY 11716/800-472-4387; FAX: 516-567-0001
Baumgartner Bullets, 3011 S. Alane St., W. Valley City, UT 84120
Bausch & Lomb Sports Optics Div. (See Bushnell Sports Optics Worldwide)
Bauska Barrels, 105 9th Ave. W., Kalispell, MT 59901/406-752-7706
Bear Archery, RR 4, 4600 Southwest 41st Blvd., Gainesville, FL 32601/904-376-2327
Bear Arms, 121 Rhodes St., Jackson, SC 29831/803-471-9859
Bear Hug Grips, Inc., 17230 County Rd. 338, Buena Vista, CO 81211/800-232-7710
Bear Mountain Gun & Tool, 120 N. Plymouth, New Plymouth, ID 83655/208-278-5221; FAX: 208-278-5221
Bear Reloaders, P.O. Box 1613, Akron, OH 44309-1613/216-920-1811
Beartooth Bullets, P.O. Box 491, Dept. HLD, Dover, ID 83825-0491/208-448-1865
Beauchamp & Son, Inc., 160 Rossiter Rd., P.O. Box 181, Richmond, MA 01254/413-698-3822; FAX: 413-698-3866
Beaver Lodge (See Fellowes, Ted)
Beaver Park Products, Inc., 840 J St., Penrose, CO 81240/719-372-6744
Beeline Custom Bullets Limited, P.O. Box 85, Yarmouth, Nova Scotia CANADA B5A 4B1/902-648-3494; FAX: 902-648-0253
Beeman Precision Airguns, 5454 Argosy Dr., Huntington Beach, CA 92649/714-890-4800; FAX: 714-890-4808
BEC, Inc., 1227 W. Valley Blvd., Suite 204, Alhambra, CA 91803-2438/818-281-5751; FAX: 818-293-7073
Behlert Precision, Inc., P.O. Box 288, 7067 Easton Rd., Pipersville, PA 18947/215-766-8681, 215-766-7301; FAX: 215-766-8681
Beitzinger, George, 116-20 Atlantic Ave., Richmond Hill, NY 11419/718-847-7661
Belding's Custom Gun Shop, 10691 Sayers Rd., Munith, MI 49259/517-596-2388
Bell & Carlson, Inc., Dodge City Industrial Park/101 Allen Rd., Dodge City, KS 67801/800-634-8586, 316-225-6688; FAX: 316-225-9095
Bell Originals, Inc., Sid, 7776 Shackham Rd., Tully, NY 13159-9333/607-842-6431
Bell Reloading, Inc., 1725 Harlin Lane Rd., Villa Rica, GA 30180
Bell's Gun & Sport Shop, 3309-19 Mannheim Rd, Franklin Park, IL 60131
Bell's Legendary Country Wear, 22 Circle Dr., Bellmore, NY 11710/516-679-1158
Bellm Contenders, P.O. Box 459, Cleveland, UT 84518/801-653-2530
Belltown, Ltd., 11 Camps Rd., Kent, CT 06757/860-354-5750
Belt MTN Arms, 107 10th Ave. SW, White Sulphur Springs, MT 59645/406-586-4495
Ben's Machines, 1151 S. Cedar Ridge, Duncanville, TX 75137/214-780-1807; FAX: 214-780-0316
Benchmark Guns, 12593 S. Ave. 5 East, Yuma, AZ 85365
Benchmark Knives (See Gerber Legendary Blades)
Benelli Armi, S.p.A., Via della Stazione, 61029 Urbino, ITALY/39-722-307-1; FAX: 39-722-327427 (U.S. importers—E.A.A. Corp.; Heckler & Koch, Inc.)
Bengtson Arms Co., L., 6345-B E. Akron St., Mesa, AZ 85205/602-981-6375
Benjamin/Sheridan Co., Crossman, Rts. 5 and 20, E. Bloomfield, NY 14443/716-657-6161; FAX: 716-657-5405
Bentley, John, 128-D Watson Dr., Turtle Creek, PA 15145
Beomat of America Inc., 300 Railway Ave., Campbell, CA 95008/408-379-4829
Beretta S.p.A., Pietro, Via Beretta, 18-25063 Gardone V.T. (BS) ITALY/XX39/30-8341.1; FAX: XX39/30-8341.421 (U.S. importer—Beretta U.S.A. Corp.)
Beretta U.S.A. Corp., 17601 Beretta Drive, Accokeek, MD 20607/301-283-2191; FAX: 301-283-0435
Berger Bullets, Ltd., 5342 W. Camelback Rd., Suite 200, Glendale, AZ 85301/602-842-4001; FAX: 602-934-9083
Bergman & Williams, 2450 Losee Rd., Suite F, Las Vegas, NV 89030/702-642-1901; FAX: 702-642-1540
Bernardelli S.p.A., Vincenzo, 125 Via Matteotti, P.O. Box 74, Gardone V.T., Brescia ITALY, 25063/39-30-8912851-2-3; FAX: 39-30-8910249
Berry's Bullets, Div. of Berry's Mfg., Inc., 401 N. 3050 E., St. George, UT 84770-9004
Berry's Mfg., Inc., 401 North 3050 East St., St. George, UT 84770/801-634-1682; FAX: 801-634-1683
Bersa S.A., Gonzales Castillo 312, 1704 Ramos Mejia, ARGENTINA/541-656-2377; FAX: 541-656-2093 (U.S. importer—Eagle Imports, Inc.)
Bertram Bullet Co., P.O. Box 313, Seymour, Victoria 3660, AUSTRALIA/61-57-922912; FAX: 61-57-991650
Bertuzzi (See U.S. importers—Cape Outfitters; Moore & Co., Wm. Larkin; New England Arms Co.)
Bestload, Inc., Carl Vancini, P.O. Box 4354, Stamford, CT 06907/203-978-0796; FAX: 203-978-0796
Better Concepts Co., 663 New Castle Rd., Butler, PA 16001/412-285-9000
Beverly, Mary, 3201 Horseshoe Trail, Tallahassee, FL 32312
Bianchi International, Inc., 100 Calle Cortez, Temecula, CA 92590/909-676-5621; FAX: 909-676-6777
Biesen, Al, 5021 Rosewood, Spokane, WA 99208/509-328-9340
Biesen, Roger, 5021 W. Rosewood, Spokane, WA 99208/509-328-9340
Big Beam Emergency Systems, Inc., 290 E. Prairie St., Crystal Lake, IL 60039
Big Bear Arms & Sporting Goods, Inc., 2714 Fairmount St., Dallas, TX 75201/214-871-7061, 800-400-BEAR; FAX: 214-754-0449
Big Bore Bullets of Alaska, P.O. Box 872785, Wasilla, AK 99687/907-373-2673; FAX: 907-373-2673
Big Sky Racks, Inc., P.O. Box 729, Bozeman, MT 59771-0729/406-586-9393; FAX: 406-585-7378
Big Spring Enterprises "Bore Stores", P.O. Box 1115, Big Spring Rd., Yellville, AR 72687/501-449-5297; FAX: 501-449-4446
Bilal, Mustafa, 908 NW 50th St., Seattle, WA 98107-3634/206-782-4164
Bill's Custom Cases, P.O. Box 2, Dunsmuir, CA 96025/916-235-0177; FAX: 916-235-4959
Bill's Gun Repair, 1007 Burlington St., Mendota, IL 61342/815-539-5786
Billeb, Stephen L., 1101 N. 7th St., Burlington, IA 52601/319-753-2110
Billings Gunsmiths, Inc., 1841 Grand Ave., Billings, MT 59102/406-652-3104
Billingsley & Brownell, P.O. Box 25, Dayton, WY 82836/307-655-9344
Birchwood Casey, 7900 Fuller Rd., Eden Prairie, MN 55344/800-328-6156, 612-937-7933; FAX: 612-937-7979
Birdsong & Assoc., W.E., 1435 Monterey Rd., Florence, MS 39073-9748/601-366-8270
Bismuth Cartridge Co., 3500 Maple Ave., Suite 1650, Dallas, TX 75219/800-759-3333, 214-521-5880; FAX: 214-521-9035
Bison Studios, 1409 South Commerce St., Las Vegas, NV 89102/702-388-2891; FAX: 702-383-9967
Bitterroot Bullet Co., Box 412, Lewiston, ID 83501-0412/208-743-5635
Black Belt Bullets, Big Bore Express Ltd., 7154 W. State St., Suite 200, Boise, ID 83703
Black Hills Ammunition, Inc., P.O. Box 3090, Rapid City, SD 57709-3090/605-348-5150; FAX: 605-348-9827

Black Hills Shooters Supply, P.O. Box 4220, Rapid City, SD 57709/800-289-2506
Black Sheep Brand, 3220 W. Gentry Parkway, Tyler, TX 75702/903-592-3853; FAX: 903-592-0527
Blackhawk East, Box 2274, Loves Park, IL 61131
Blackhawk West, Box 285, Hiawatha, KS 66434
Blackinton & Co., Inc., V.H., 221 John L. Dietsch, Attleboro Falls, MA 02763-0300/508-699-4436; FAX: 508-695-5349
Blackjack Knives, Ltd., 1307 W. Wabash, Effingham, IL 62401/217-347-7700; FAX: 217-347-7737
Black Powder Products, 67 Township Rd., P.O. Box 1411, Chesapeake, OH, 45619/614-867-8047
Blacksmith Corp., 830 N. Road No. 1 E., P.O. Box 1752, Chino Valley, AZ 86323/520-636-4456; FAX: 520-636-4457
BlackStar Accurizing, 11501 Brittmoore Park Drive, Houston, TX 77041/713-849-9999; FAX: 713-849-5445
BlackStar AccuMax Barrels (See BlackStar Accurizing)
BlackStar Barrel Accurizing (See BlackStar Accurizing)
Blacktail Mountain Books, 42 First Ave. W., Kalispell, MT 59901/406-257-5573
Blackwell, W. (See Load From a Disk)
Blair Engraving, J.R., P.O. Box 64, Glenrock, WY 82637/307-436-8115
Blammo Ammo, P.O. Box 1677, Seneca, SC 29679/803-882-1768
Blaser Jagdwaffen GmbH, D-88316 Isny Im Allgau, GERMANY (U.S. importer—Autumn Sales, Inc.)
Bleile, C. Roger, 5040 Ralph Ave., Cincinnati, OH 45238/513-251-0249
Blocker Holsters, Inc., Ted, Clackamas Business Park Bld. A, 14787 S.E. 82nd Dr./Clackamas, OR 97015
503-557-7757; FAX: 503-557-3771
Blount, Inc., Sporting Equipment Div., 2299 Snake River Ave., P.O. Box 856, Lewiston, ID 83501/800-627-3640, 208-746-2351; FAX: 208-799-3904
Blue and Gray Products, Inc. (See Ox-Yoke Originals, Inc.)
Blue Book Publications, Inc., One Appletree Square, Minneapolis, MN 55425/800-877-4867, 612-854-5229; FAX: 612-853-1486
Blue Mountain Bullets, HCR 77, P.O. Box 231, John Day, OR 97845/503-820-4594
Blue Ridge Machinery & Tools, Inc., P.O. Box 536-GD, Hurricane, WV 25526/800-872-6500; FAX: 304-562-5311
BMC Supply, Inc., 26051 - 179th Ave. S.E., Kent, WA 98042
B.M.F. Activator, Inc., 803 Mill Creek Run, Plantersville, TX 77363/409-894-2005, 800-527-2881
Bob's Gun Shop, P.O. Box 200, Royal, AR 71968/501-767-1970
Bob's Tactical Indoor Shooting Range & Gun Shop, 122 Lafayette Rd., Salisbury, MA 01952/508-465-5561
Boessler, Erich, Am Vogeltal 3, 97702 Munnerstadt, GERMANY/9733-9443
Boggs, Wm., 1816 Riverside Dr. C, Columbus, OH 43212/614-486-6965
Bohemia Arms Co., 17101 Los Modelos, Fountain Valley, CA 92708/619-442-7005; FAX: 619-442-7005
Boker USA, Inc., 14818 West 6th Ave., Suite 10A, Golden, CO 80401-5045/303-279-5997; FAX: 303-279-5919
Boltin, John M., P.O. Box 644, Estill, SC 29918/803-625-2185
Bo-Mar Tool & Mfg. Co., Rt. 12, Box 405, Longview, TX 75605/903-759-4784; FAX: 903-759-9141
Bonanza (See Forster Products)
Bond Custom Firearms, 8954 N. Lewis Ln., Bloomington, IN 47408/812-332-4519
Bondini Paolo, Via Sorrento, 345, San Carlo di Cesena, ITALY I-47020/0547 663 240; FAX: 0547 663 780
Bone Engraving, Ralph, 718 N. Atlanta, Owasso, OK 74055/918-272-9745
Boone Trading Co., Inc., P.O. Box BB, Brinnan, WA 98320
Boone's Custom Ivory Grips, Inc., 562 Coyote Rd., Brinnon, WA 98320/206-796-4330
Boonie Packer Products, P.O. Box 12204, Salem, OR 97309/800-477-3244, 503-581-3244; FAX: 503-581-3191
Borden's Accuracy, RD 1, Box 250BC, Springville, PA 18844/717-965-2505; FAX: 717-965-2328
Border Barrels Ltd., Riccarton Farm, Newcastleton SCOTLAND U.K. TD9 0SN
Borovnik KG, Ludwig, 9170 Ferlach, Bahnhofstrasse 7, AUSTRIA/042 27 24 42; FAX: 042 26 43 49
Bosis (See U.S. importer—New England Arms Co.)
Boss Manufacturing Co., 221 W. First St., Kewanee, IL 61443/309-852-2131, 800-447-4581; FAX: 309-852-0848
Bostick Wildlife Calls, Inc., P.O. Box 728, Estill, SC 29918/803-625-2210, 803-625-4512
Bowen Classic Arms Corp., P.O. Box 67, Louisville, TN 37777/615-984-3583
Bowen Knife Co., Inc., P.O. Box 590, Blackshear, GA 31516/912-449-4794
Bowerly, Kent, HCR Box 1903, Camp Sherman, OR 97730/541-595-6028
Bowlin, Gene, Rt. 1, Box 890, Snyder, TX 79549
Boyds' Gunstock Industries, Inc., 3rd & Main, P.O. Box 305, Geddes, SD 57342/605-337-2125; FAX: 605-337-3363
Boyt, 509 Hamilton, P.O. Drawer 668, Iowa Falls, IA 50126/515-648-4626; FAX: 515-648-2385
Brace, Larry D., 771 Blackfoot Ave., Eugene, OR 97404/503-688-1278
Bradley Gunsight Co., P.O. Box 340, Plymouth, VT 05056/860-589-0531; FAX: 860-582-6294
Brass and Bullet Alloys, P.O. Box 1238, Sierra Vista, AZ 85636/602-458-5321; FAX: 602-458-9125
Brass Eagle, Inc., 7050A Bramalea Rd., Unit 19, Mississauga, Ont. L4Z 1C7, CANADA/416-848-4844
Brass-Tech Industries, P.O. Box 521-v, Wharton, NJ 07885/201-366-8540
Bratcher, Dan, 311 Belle Air Pl., Carthage, MO 64836/417-358-1518
Brauer Bros. Mfg. Co., 2020 Delman Blvd., St. Louis, MO 63103/314-231-2864; FAX: 314-249-4952
Braun, M., 32, rue Notre-Dame, 2440 LUXEMBURG
Braverman Corp., R.J., 88 Parade Rd., Meridith, NH 03293/800-736-4867
Break-Free, Inc., P.O. Box 25020, Santa Ana, CA 92799/714-953-1900; FAX: 714-953-0402
Brell Mar Products, Inc., 113 Boyce Dr., Brookhaven, MS 39601/601-833-2050; FAX: 601-835-1817
Brenneke KG, Wilhelm, Ilmenauweg 2, 30851 Langenhagen, GERMANY/0511/97262-0; FAX: 0511/97262-62 (U.S. importer—Dynamit Nobel-RWS, Inc.)
Bretton (See Atamec-Bretton)
Bridgers Best, P.O. Box 1410, Berthoud, CO 80513
Briese Bullet Co., Inc., RR1, Box 108, Tappen, ND 58487/701-327-4578; FAX: 701-327-4579
Brigade Quartermasters, 1025 Cobb International Blvd., Dept. VH, Kennesaw, GA 30144-4300/404-428-1248, 800-241-3125; FAX: 404-426-7726
Briganti & Co., A., 475 Rt. 32, Highland Mills, NY 10930/914-928-9573
Briley Mfg., Inc., 1230 Lumpkin, Houston, TX 77043/800-331-5718, 713-932-6995; FAX: 713-932-1043
British Antiques, P.O. Box 7, Latham, NY 12110/518-783-0773
British Sporting Arms, RR1, Box 130, Millbrook, NY 12545/914-677-8303
BRNO (See U.S. importers—Bohemia Arms Co.; Magnum Research, Inc.)
Broad Creek Rifle Works, 120 Horsey Ave., Laurel, DE 19956/302-875-5446
Brobst, Jim, 299 Poplar St., Hamburg, PA 19526/215-562-2103
Brockman's Custom Gunsmithing, P.O. Box 357, Gooding, ID 83330/208-934-5050
Brocock Ltd., 43 River Street, Digbeth, Birmingham, B5 5SA ENGLAND/011-021-773-1200
Broken Gun Ranch, 10739 126 Rd., Spearville, KS 67876/316-385-2587; FAX: 316-385-2597
Brolin Arms, 2755 Thompson Creek Rd., Pomona, CA 91767/909-392-2352; FAX: 909-392-2354
Brooker, Dennis, Rt. 1, Box 12A, Derby, IA 50068/515-533-2103
Brooks Tactical Systems, 279-A Shorewood Ct., Fox Island, WA 98333/800-410-4747; FAX: 206-572-6797
Brown Co., E. Arthur, 3404 Pawnee Dr., Alexandria, MN 56308/612-762-8847
Brown, H.R. (See Silhouette Leathers)
Brown Manufacturing, P.O. Box 9219, Akron, OH 44305/800-837-GUNS
Brown Precision, Inc., 7786 Molinos Ave., Los Molinos, CA 96055/916-384-2506; FAX: 916-384-1638
Brown Products, Inc., Ed, Rt. 2, Box 492, Perry, MO 63462/573-565-3261; FAX: 573-565-2791
Brownell Checkering Tools, W.E., 9390 Twin Mountain Circle, San Diego, CA 92126/619-695-2479; FAX: 619-695-2479
Brownells, Inc., 200 S. Front St., Montezuma, IA 50171/515-623-5401; FAX: 515-623-3896
Browning Arms Co. (Gen. Offices), One Browning Place, Morgan, UT 84050/801-876-2711; FAX: 801-876-3331
Browning Arms Co. (Parts & Service), 3005 Arnold Tenbrook Rd., Arnold, MO 63010-9406/314-287-6800; FAX: 314-287-9751
BRP, Inc. High Performance Cast Bullets, 1210 Alexander Rd., Colorado Springs, CO 80909/719-633-0658
Bruno Shooters Supply, 111 N. Wyoming St., Hazleton, PA 18201/717-455-2281; FAX: 717-455-2211
Brunsport, Inc., 1131 Bayview Dr., Quincy, IL 62301/217-223-8844; FAX: 217-223-8847
Brunton U.S.A., 620 E. Monroe Ave., Riverton, WY 82501/307-856-6559; FAX: 307-856-1840
Brynin, Milton, P.O. Box 383, Yonkers, NY 10710/914-779-4333
BSA Guns Ltd., Armoury Rd. Small Heath, Birmingham, ENGLAND B11 2PX/011-021-772-8543; FAX: 011-021-773-0845
B-Square Company, Inc., P.O. Box 11281, 2708 St. Louis Ave., Ft. Worth, TX 76110/817-923-0964, 800-433-2909; FAX: 817-926-7012
Bucheimer, J.M., Jumbo Sports Products, 721 N. 20th St., St. Louis, MO 63103/314-241-1020
Buck Knives, Inc., 1900 Weld Blvd., P.O. Box 1267, El Cajon, CA 92020/619-449-1100, 800-326-2825; FAX: 619-562-5774, 800-729-2825
Buck Stix—SOS Products Co., Box 3, Neenah, WI 54956
Buck Stop Lure Co., Inc., 3600 Grow Rd. NW, P.O. Box 636, Stanton, MI 48888/517-762-5091; FAX: 517-762-5124
Buckeye Custom Bullets, 6490 Stewart Rd., Elida, OH 45807/419-641-4463
Buckhorn Gun Works, 8109 Woodland Dr., Black Hawk, SD 57718/605-787-6472
Buckskin Bullet Co., P.O. Box 1893, Cedar City, UT 84721/801-586-3286
Buckskin Machine Works, A. Hunkeler, 3235 S. 358th St., Auburn, WA 98001/206-927-5412
Budin, Dave, Main St., Margaretville, NY 12455/914-568-4103; FAX: 914-586-4105
Buenger Enterprises/Goldenrod Dehumidifier, 3600 S. Harbor Blvd., Oxnard, CA 93035/800-451-6797, 805-985-5828; FAX: 805-985-1534
Buffalo Arms, 123 S. Third, Suite 6, Sandpoint, ID 83864/208-263-6953; FAX: 208-265-2096

Buffalo Bullet Co., Inc., 12637 Los Nietos Rd., Unit A, Santa Fe Springs, CA 90670/310-944-0322; FAX: 310-944-5054
Buffalo Rock Shooters Supply, R.R. 1, Ottawa, IL 61350/815-433-2471
Bull Mountain Rifle Co., 6327 Golden West Terrace, Billings, MT 59106/406-656-0778
Bullberry Barrel Works, Ltd., 2430 W. Bullberry Ln. 67-5, Hurricane, UT 84737/801-635-9866
Bullet, Inc., 3745 Hiram Alworth Rd., Dallas, GA 30132
Bullet Swaging Supply, Inc., P.O. Box 1056, 303 McMillan Rd, West Monroe, LA 71291/318-387-7257; FAX: 318-387-7779
BulletMakers Workshop, The, RFD 1 Box 1755, Brooks, ME 04921
Bullseye Bullets, 1610 State Road 60, No. 12, Valrico, FL 33594/813-654-6563
Bull-X, Inc., 520 N. Main, Farmer City, IL 61842/309-928-2574, 800-248-3845 orders only; FAX: 309-928-2130
Burgess, Byron, P.O. Box 6853, Los Osos, CA 93412/805-528-1005
Burgess & Son Gunsmiths, R.W., P.O. Box 3364, Warner Robins, GA 31099/912-328-7487
Burkhart Gunsmithing, Don, P.O. Box 852, Rawlins, WY 82301/307-324-6007
Burnham Bros., P.O. Box 1148, Menard, TX 78659/915-396-4572; FAX: 915-396-4574
Burres, Jack, 10333 San Fernando Rd., Pacoima, CA 91331/818-899-8000
Burris Co., Inc., P.O. Box 1747, 331 E. 8th St., Greeley, CO 80631/970-356-1670; FAX: 970-356-8702
Bushmann Hunters & Safaris, P.O. Box 293088, Lewisville, TX 75029/214-317-0768
Bushmaster Firearms (See Quality Parts Co./Bushmaster Firearms)
Bushmaster Hunting & Fishing, 451 Alliance Ave., Toronto, Ont. M6N 2J1 CANADA/416-763-4040; FAX: 416-763-0623
Bushnell (See Bausch & Lomb)
Bushwacker Backpack & Supply Co. (See Counter Assault)
Bustani, Leo, P.O. Box 8125, W. Palm Beach, FL 33407/305-622-2710
Buster's Custom Knives, P.O. Box 214, Richfield, UT 84701/801-896-5319
Butler Creek Corporation, 290 Arden Dr., Belgrade, MT 59714/800-423-8327, 406-388-1356; FAX: 406-388-7204
Butler Enterprises, 834 Oberting Rd., Lawrenceburg, IN 47025/812-537-3584
Butterfield & Butterfield, 220 San Bruno Ave., San Francisco, CA 94103/415-861-7500
Buzztail Brass (See Grayback Wildcats)
B-West Imports, Inc., 2425 N. Huachuca Dr., Tucson, AZ 85745-1201/602-628-1990; FAX: 602-628-3602

C

C3 Systems, 678 Killingly St., Johnston, RI 02919
C&D Special Products (See Claybuster Wads & Harvester Bullets)
C&H Research, 115 Sunnyside Dr., Box 351, Lewis, KS 67552/316-324-5445
C&J Enterprises, Inc., 7101 Jurupa Ave., No. 12, Riverside, CA 92504/909-689-7758
Cabanas (See U.S. importer—Mandall Shooting Supplies, Inc.)
Cabela's, 812-13th Ave., Sidney, NE 69160/308-254-6644; FAX: 308-254-6669
Cabinet Mtn. Outfitters Scents & Lures, P.O. Box 766, Plains, MT 59859/406-826-3970
Cache La Poudre Rifleworks, 140 N. College, Ft. Collins, CO 80524/303-482-6913
Cadre Supply (See Parts & Surplus)
Calhoon Varmint Bullets, James, Shambo Rt., Box 304, Havre, MT 59501/406-395-4079
Calibre Press, Inc., 666 Dundee Rd., Suite 1607, Northbrook, IL 60062-2760/800-323-0037; FAX: 708-498-6869
Cali'co Hardwoods, Inc., 3580 Westwind Blvd., Santa Rosa, CA 95403/707-546-4045; FAX: 707-546-4027
Calico Light Weapon Systems, 405 E. 19th St., Bakersfield, CA 93305/805-323-1327; FAX: 805-323-7844
California Magnum, 20746 Dearborn St., Chatsworth, CA 91313/818-341-7302; FAX: 818-341-7304
California Sights (See Fautheree, Andy)
Camdex, Inc., 2330 Alger, Troy, MI 48083/810-528-2300; FAX: 810-528-0989
Cameron's, 16690 W. 11th Ave., Golden, CO 80401/303-279-7365; FAX: 303-628-5413
Camilli, Lou, 4700 Oahu Dr. NE, Albuquerque, NM 87111/505-293-5259
Camillus Cutlery Co., 54 Main St., Camillus, NY 13031/315-672-8111; FAX: 315-672-8832
Campbell, Dick, 20,000 Silver Ranch Rd., Conifer, CO 80433/303-697-0150
Camp-Cap Products, P.O. Box 173, Chesterfield, MO 63006/314-532-4340; FAX: 314-532-4340
Canjar Co., M.H., 500 E. 45th Ave., Denver, CO 80216/303-295-2638
Cannon's Guns, Box 1036, 320 Main St., Polson, MT 59860/406-887-2048
Cannon Safe, Inc., 9358 Stephens St., Pico Rivera, CA 90660/310-692-0636, 800-242-1055; FAX: 310-692-7252
Canons Delcour, Rue J.B. Cools, B-4040 Herstal, BELGIUM 32.(0)41.40.61.40; FAX: 32(0)412.40.22.88
Canyon Cartridge Corp., P.O. Box 152, Albertson, NY 11507/FAX: 516-294-8946
Cape Outfitters, 599 County Rd. 206, Cape Girardeau, MO 63701/314-335-4103; FAX: 314-335-1555
Caraville Manufacturing, P.O. Box 4545, Thousand Oaks, CA 91359/805-499-1234
Carbide Checkering Tools (See J&R Engineering)
Carbide Die & Mfg. Co., Inc., 15615 E. Arrow Hwy., Irwindale, CA 91706/818-337-2518
Carhartt, Inc., P.O. Box 600, 3 Parklane Blvd., Dearborn, MI 48121/800-358-3825, 313-271-8460; FAX: 313-271-3455
Carlson, Douglas R., Antique American Firearms, P.O. Box 71035, Dept. GD, Des Moines, IA 50325/515-224-6552
Carnahan Bullets, 17645 110th Ave. SE, Renton, WA 98055
Carolina Precision Rifles, 1200 Old Jackson Hwy., Jackson, SC 29831/803-827-2069
Carrell's Precision Firearms, 643 Clark Ave., Billings, MT 59101-1614/406-962-3593
Carroll Bullets (See Precision Reloading, Inc.)
Carry-Lite, Inc., 5203 W. Clinton Ave., Milwaukee, WI 53223/414-355-3520; FAX: 414-355-4775
Carter's Gun Shop, 225 G St., Penrose, CO 81240/719-372-6240
Carter's Wildlife Calls, Garth, Inc., P.O. Box 821, Cedar City, UT 84720/801-586-7639
Cartridge Transfer Group, Pete de Coux, 235 Oak St., Butler, PA 16001/412-282-3426
Carvajal Belts & Holsters, 422 Chestnut, San Antonio, TX 78202/210-222-1634
Cascade Arms, Inc., P.O. Box 268, Colton, Oregon 97017
Cascade Bullet Co., Inc., 2355 South 6th St., Klamath Falls, OR 97601/503-884-9316
Cascade Fabrication, 1090 Bailey Hill Rd. Unit A, Eugene, OR 97402/503-485-3433; FAX: 503-485-3543
Cascade Shooters, 2155 N.W. 12th St., Redwood, OR 97756
Case & Sons Cutlery Co., W.R., Owens Way, Bradford, PA 16701/814-368-4123, 800-523-6350; FAX: 814-768-5369
Case Sorting System, 12695 Cobblestone Creek Rd., Poway, CA 92064/619-486-9340
Cash Mfg. Co., Inc., P.O. Box 130, 201 S. Klein Dr., Waunakee, WI 53597-0130/608-849-5664; FAX: 608-849-5664
Caspian Arms Ltd., 14 North Main St., Hardwick, VT 05843/802-472-6454; FAX: 802-472-6709
Caswell International Corp., 1221 Marshall St. NE, Minneapolis, MN 55413-1055/612-379-2000; FAX: 612-379-2367
Catco-Ambush, Inc., P.O.Box 300, Corte Madera, CA 94926
Cathey Enterprises, Inc., P.O. Box 2202, Brownwood, TX 76804/915-643-2553; FAX: 915-643-3653
Cation, 2341 Alger St., Troy, MI 48083/810-689-0658; FAX: 810-689-7558
Catoctin Cutlery, P.O. Box 188, 17 S. Main St., Smithsburg, MD 21783/301-824-7416; FAX: 301-824-6138
Caywood, Shane J., P.O. Box 321, Minocqua, WI 54548/715-277-3866 evenings
CBC, Avenida Humberto de Campos, 3220, 09400-000 Ribeirao Pires-SP-BRAZIL/55-11-742-7500; FAX: 55-11-459-7385
C.C.G. Enterprises, 5217 E. Belknap St., Halton City, TX 76117/817-834-9554
CCI, Div. of Blount, Inc., Sporting Equipment Div., 2299 Snake River Ave.,, P.O. Box 856/Lewiston, ID 83501
800-627-3640, 208-746-2351; FAX: 208-746-2915
Cedar Hill Game Calls, Inc., Rt. 2 Box 236, Downsville, LA 71234/318-982-5632; FAX: 318-368-2245
Celestron International, P.O. Box 3578, 2835 Columbia St., Torrance, CA 90503/310-328-9560; FAX: 310-212-5835
Centaur Systems, Inc., 1602 Foothill Rd., Kalispell, MT 59901/406-755-8609; FAX: 406-755-8609
Center Lock Scope Rings, 9901 France Ct., Lakeville, MN 55044/612-461-2114
CenterMark, P.O. Box 4066, Parnassus Station, New Kensington, PA 15068/412-335-1319
Central Specialties Ltd., 1122 Silver Lake Road, Cary, IL 60013/708-639-3900; FAX: 708-639-3972
Century Gun Dist., Inc., 1467 Jason Rd., Greenfield, IN 46140/317-462-4524
Century International Arms, Inc., P.O. Box 714, St. Albans, VT 05478-0714/802-527-1252; FAX: 802-527-0470; WEB: http://www.generation.net/~century
CFVentures, 509 Harvey Dr., Bloomington, IN 47403-1715
C-H Tool & Die Corp. (See 4-D Custom Die Co.)
CHAA, Ltd., P.O. Box 565, Howell, MI 48844/800-677-8737; FAX: 313-894-6930
Chace Leather Products, 507 Alden St., Fall River, MA 02722/508-678-7556; FAX: 508-675-9666
Chadick's Ltd., P.O. Box 100, Terrell, TX 75160/214-563-7577
Chambers Flintlocks Ltd., Jim, Rt. 1, Box 513-A, Candler, NC 28715/704-667-8361
Champion Shooters' Supply, P.O. Box 303, New Albany, OH 43054/614-855-1603; FAX: 614-855-1209
Champion Target Co., 232 Industrial Parkway, Richmond, IN 47374/800-441-4971
Champion's Choice, Inc., 201 International Blvd., LaVergne, TN 37086/615-793-4066; FAX: 615-793-4070
Champlin, R. MacDonald, P.O. Box 132, Candia, NH 03034
Champlin Firearms, Inc., P.O. Box 3191, Woodring Airport, Enid, OK 73701/405-237-7388; FAX: 405-242-6922
Chapman Academy of Practical Shooting, 4350 Academy Rd., Hallsville, MO 65255/573-696-5544, 573-696-2266
Chapman Manufacturing Co., 471 New Haven Rd., P.O. Box 250, Durham, CT 06422/203-349-9228; FAX: 203-349-0084
Chapuis Armes, 21 La Gravoux, BP15, 42380 St. Bonnet-le-Chateau, FRANCE/(33)77.50.06.96 (U.S. importer—Chapuis USA)

Chapuis USA, 416 Business Park, Bedford, KY 40006
Checkmate Refinishing, 370 Champion Dr., Brooksville, FL 34601/904-799-5774
Cheddite France, S.A., 99, Route de Lyon, F-26500 Bourg-les-Valence, FRANCE/33-75-56-4545; FAX: 33-75-56-3587
Chelsea Gun Club of New York City, Inc., 237 Ovington Ave., Apt. D53, Brooklyn, NY 11209/718-836-9422, 718-833-2704
Chem-Pak, Inc., 11 Oates Ave., P.O. Box 1685, Winchester, VA 22604/800-336-9828, 703-667-1341; FAX: 703-722-3993
Cherry's Fine Guns, P.O. Box 5307, Greensboro, NC 27435-0307/919-854-4182
Chesapeake Importing & Distributing Co. (See CIDCO)
CheVron Bullets, RR1, Ottawa, IL 61350/815-433-2471
CheVron Case Master (See CheVron Bullets)
Chicago Cutlery Co., 1536 Beech St., Terre Haute, IN 47804/800-457-2665
Chicasaw Gun Works (See Cochran, Oliver)
Chipmunk (See Oregon Arms, Inc.)
Chippewa Shoe Co., P.O. Box 2521, Ft. Worth, TX 76113/817-332-4385
Choate Machine & Tool Co., Inc., P.O. Box 218, 116 Lovers Ln., Bald Knob, AR 72010/501-724-6193, 800-972-6390; FAX: 501-724-5873
Chopie Mfg., Inc., 700 Copeland Ave., LaCrosse, WI 54603/608-784-0926
Christensen Arms, 192 East 100 North, Fayette, UT 84630/801-528-7999; FAX: 801-528-7494
Christie's East, 219 E. 67th St., New York, NY 10021/212-606-0400
Christman Jr., David, 937 Lee Hedrick Rd., Colville, WA 99114/509-684-5686 days; 509-684-3314 evenings
Christopher Firearms Co., Inc., E., Route 128 & Ferry St., Miamitown, OH 45041/513-353-1321
Chronotech, 1655 Siamet Rd. Unit 6, Mississauga, Ont. L4W 1Z4 CANADA/905-625-5200; FAX: 905-625-5190
Chu Tani Ind., Inc., P.O. Box 2064, Cody, WY 82414-2064
Chuck's Gun Shop, P.O. Box 597, Waldo, FL 32694/904-468-2264
Churchill (See U.S. importer—Ellett Bros.)
Churchill, Winston, Twenty Mile Stream Rd., RFD P.O. Box 29B, Proctorsville, VT 05153/802-226-7772
Churchill Glove Co., James, P.O. Box 298, Centralia, WA 98531
CIDCO, 21480 Pacific Blvd., Sterling, VA 22170/703-444-5353
Ciener, Inc., Jonathan Arthur, 8700 Commerce St., Cape Canaveral, FL 32920/407-868-2200; FAX: 407-868-2201
Cimarron Arms, P.O. Box 906, Fredericksburg, TX 78624-0906/210-997-9090; FAX: 210-997-0802
Cincinnati Swaging, 2605 Marlington Ave., Cincinnati, OH 45208
Citadel Mfg. Inc., 5220 Gabbert Rd., Moorpark, CA 93021/805-529-7294; FAX: 805-529-7297
C.J. Ballistics, Inc., P.O. Box 132, Acme, WA 98220/206-595-5001
Clark Co., Inc., David, P.O. Box 15054, Worcester, MA 01615-0054/508-756-6216; FAX: 508-753-5827
Clark Custom Guns, Inc., 336 Shootout Lane, Princeton, LA 71067/318-949-9884; FAX: 318-949-9829
Clark Firearms Engraving, P.O. Box 80746, San Marino, CA 91118/818-287-1652
Clarkfield Enterprises, Inc., 1032 10th Ave., Clarkfield, MN 56223/612-669-7140
Claro Walnut Gunstock Co., 1235 Stanley Ave., Chico, CA 95928/916-342-5188
Classic Arms Corp., P.O. Box 106, Dunsmuir, CA 96025-0106/916-235-2000
Classic Brass, 14 Grove St., Plympton, MA 02367/FAX: 617-585-5673
Classic Guns, Inc., Frank S. Wood, 3230 Medlock Bridge Rd., Suite 110, Norcross, GA 30092/404-242-7944
Claybuster Wads & Harvester Bullets, 309 Sequoya Dr., Hopkinsville, KY 42240/800-922-6287, 800-284-1746, 502-885-8088; FAX: 502-885-1951
Clearview Mfg. Co., Inc., 413 S. Oakley St., Fordyce, AR 71742/501-352-8557; FAX: 501-352-8557
Clearview Products, 3021 N. Portland, Oklahoma City, OK 73107
Cleland's Gun Shop, Inc., 10306 Airport Hwy., Swanton, OH 43558/419-865-4713
Clements' Custom Leathercraft, Chas, 1741 Dallas St., Aurora, CO 80010-2018/303-364-0403
Clenzoil Corp., P.O. Box 80226, Sta. C, Canton, OH 44708-0226/330-833-9758; FAX: 330-833-4724
Clerke Co., J.A., P.O. Box 627, Pearblossom, CA 93553-0627/805-945-0713
Clift Mfg., L.R., 3821 Hammonton Rd., Marysville, CA 95901/916-755-3390; FAX: 916-755-3393
Clift Welding Supply & Cases, 1332-A Colusa Hwy., Yuba City, CA 95993/916-755-3390; FAX: 916-755-3393
Cloward's Gun Shop, 4023 Aurora Ave. N, Seattle, WA 98103/206-632-2072
Clymer Manufacturing Co., Inc., 1645 W. Hamlin Rd., Rochester Hills, MI 48309-1530/810-853-5555, 810-853-5627; FAX: 810-853-1530
C-More Systems, P.O. Box 1750, 7553 Gary Rd., Manassas, VA 22110/703-361-2663; FAX: 703-361-5881
Coast Cutlery Co., 609 SE Ankeny St., Portland, OR 97214/503-234-4545; FAX: 503-234-4422
Coats, Mrs. Lester, 300 Luman Rd., Space 125, Phoenix, OR 97535/503-535-1611
Cobalt Mfg., Inc., 1020 Shady Oak Dr., Denton, TX 76205/817-382-8986; FAX: 817-383-4281
Cobra Gunskin, 133-30 32nd Ave., Flushing, NY 11354/718-762-8181; FAX: 718-762-0890
Cobra Sport s.r.l., Via Caduti Nei Lager No. 1, 56020 San Romano, Montopoli v/Arno (Pi), ITALY/0039-571-450490; FAX: 0039-571-450492
Cochran, Oliver, Box 868, Shady Spring, WV 25918/304-763-3838
Coffin, Charles H., 3719 Scarlet Ave., Odessa, TX 79762/915-366-4729
Coffin, Jim, 250 Country Club Lane, Albany, OR 97321/541-928-4391
Cogar's Gunsmithing, P.O. Box 755, Houghton Lake, MI 48629/517-422-4591
Coghlan's Ltd., 121 Irene St., Winnipeg, Man., CANADA R3T 4C7/204-284-9550; FAX: 204-475-4127
Cold Steel, Inc., 2128-D Knoll Dr., Ventura, CA 93003/800-255-4716, 800-624-2363 (in CA); FAX: 805-642-9727
Cole's Gun Works, Old Bank Building, Rt. 4, Box 250, Moyock, NC 27958/919-435-2345
Cole-Grip, 16135 Cohasset St., Van Nuys, CA 91406/818-782-4424
Coleman Co., Inc., 250 N. St. Francis, Wichita, KS 67201
Coleman's Custom Repair, 4035 N. 20th Rd., Arlington, VA 22207/703-528-4486
Collings, Ronald, 1006 Cielta Linda, Vista, CA 92083
Colonial Arms, Inc., P.O. Box 636, Selma, AL 36702-0636/334-872-9455; FAX: 334-872-9540
Colonial Knife Co., Inc., P.O. Box 3327, Providence, RI 02909/401-421-1600; FAX: 401-421-2047
Colonial Repair, P.O. Box 372, Hyde Park, MA 02136-9998/617-469-4951
Colorado Gunsmithing Academy Lamar, 27533 Highway 287 South, Lamar, CO 81052/719-336-4099
Colorado School of Trades, 1575 Hoyt St., Lakewood, CO 80215/800-234-4594; FAX: 303-233-4723
Colorado Shooter's Supply, 1163 W. Paradise Way, Fruita, CO 81521/303-858-9191
Colorado Sutlers Arsenal (See Cumberland States Arsenal)
Colt Blackpowder Arms Co., 5 Centre Market Place, New York, NY 10013/212-925-2159; FAX: 212-966-4986
Colt's Mfg. Co., Inc., P.O. Box 1868, Hartford, CT 06144-1868/800-962-COLT, 203-236-6311; FAX: 203-244-1449
Combat Military Ordnance Ltd., 3900 Hopkins St., Savannah, GA 31405/912-238-1900; FAX: 912-236-7570
Companhia Brasileira de Cartuchos (See CBC)
Compass Industries, Inc., 104 East 25th St., New York, NY 10010/212-473-2614, 800-221-9904; FAX: 212-353-0826
Compasseco, Ltd., 151 Atkinson Hill Ave., Bardtown, KY 40004/502-349-0910
Competition Electronics, Inc., 3469 Precision Dr., Rockford, IL 61109/815-874-8001; FAX: 815-874-8181
Competitive Pistol Shop, The, 5233 Palmer Dr., Ft. Worth, TX 76117-2433/817-834-8479
Competitor Corp., Inc., Appleton Business Center, 30 Tricnit Road, Unit 16, New Ipswich, NH 03071-0508/603-878-3891; FAX: 603-878-3950
Component Concepts, Inc., 10240 SW Nimbus Ave., Suite L-8, Portland, OR 97223/503-684-9262; FAX: 503-620-4285
Concept Development Corp., 14715 N. 78th Way, Suite 300, Scottsdale, AZ 85260/800-472-4405; FAX: 602-948-7560
Condon, Inc., David, 109 E. Washington St., Middleburg, VA 22117/703-687-5642
Conetrol Scope Mounts, 10225 Hwy. 123 S., Seguin, TX 78155/210-379-3030, 800-CONETROL; FAX: 210-379-3030
CONKKO, P.O. Box 40, Broomall, PA 19008/215-356-0711
Connecticut Shotgun Mfg. Co., P.O. Box 1692, 35 Woodland St., New Britain, CT 06051-1692/203-225-6581; FAX: 203-832-8707
Connecticut Valley Arms Co. (See CVA)
Connecticut Valley Classics, P.O. Box 2068, 12 Taylor Lane, Westport, CT 06880/203-254-3202; FAX: 203-256-1180
Conrad, C.A., 3964 Ebert St., Winston-Salem, NC 27127/919-788-5469
Continental Kite & Key (See CONKKO)
Cook Engineering Service, 891 Highbury Rd., Vermont VICT 3133 AUSTRALIA
Coonan Arms (JS Worldwide DBA), 1745 Hwy. 36 E., Maplewood, MN 55109/612-777-3156; FAX: 612-777-3683
Cooper Arms, P.O. Box 114, Stevensville, MT 59870/406-777-5534; FAX: 406-777-5228
Cooper-Woodward, 3800 Pelican Rd., Helena, MT 59601/406-458-3800
Corbin, Inc., 600 Industrial Circle, P.O. Box 2659, White City, OR 97503/541-826-5211; FAX: 541-826-8669
Cor-Bon Bullet & Ammo Co., 1311 Industry Rd., Sturgis, SD 57785/800-626-7266; FAX: 800-923-2666
Corkys Gun Clinic, 4401 Hot Springs Dr., Greeley, CO 80634-9226/970-330-0516
Corry, John, 861 Princeton Ct., Neshanic Station, NJ 08853/908-369-8019
Cosmi Americo & Figlio s.n.c., Via Flaminia 307, Ancona, ITALY I-60020/071-888208; FAX: 39-071-887008 (U.S. importer—New England Arms Co.)
Costa, David, Island Pond Gun Shop, P.O. Box 428, Cross St., Island Pond, VT 05846/802-723-4546
Coulston Products, Inc., P.O. Box 30, 201 Ferry St., Suite 212, Easton, PA 18044-0030/215-253-0167, 800-445-9927; FAX: 215-252-1511
Counter Assault, Box 4721, Missoula, MT 59806/406-728-6241; FAX: 406-728-8800
Country Armourer, The, P.O. Box .308, Ashby, MA 01431-0308/508-827-6797; FAX: 508-827-4845
County Arms, 11020 Whitman Ln., Tamarac, FL 33321/305-720-2066; FAX: 305-722-6353
Cousin Bob's Mountain Products, 7119 Ohio River Blvd., Ben Avon, PA 15202/412-766-5114; FAX: 412-766-5114

Cox, C. Ed, RD 2, Box 192, Prosperity, PA 15329/412-228-4984
CP Bullets, 340-1 Constance Dr., Warminster, PA 18974
CQB Training, P.O. Box 1739, Manchester, MO 63011
Craftguard, 3624 Logan Ave., Waterloo, IA 50703/319-232-2959; FAX: 319-234-0804
Craig Custom Ltd., Research & Development, 629 E. 10th, Hutchinson, KS 67501/316-669-0601
Crandall Tool & Machine Co., 19163 21 Mile Rd., Tustin, MI 49688/616-829-4430
Crane & Crane Ltd., 105 N. Edison Way 6, Reno, NV 89502-2355/702-856-1516; FAX: 702-856-1616
Crane Sales Co., George S., P.O. Box 385, Van Nuys, CA 91408/818-505-8337
Crawford Co., Inc., R.M., P.O. Box 277, Everett, PA 15537/814-652-6536; FAX: 814-652-9526
CRDC Laser Systems Group, 3972 Barranca Parkway, Ste. J-484, Irvine, CA 92714/714-586-1295; FAX: 714-831-4823
Creative Cartridge Co., 56 Morgan Rd., Canton, CT 06019/203-693-2529
Creative Craftsman, Inc., The, 95 Highway 29 North, P.O. Box 331, Lawrenceville, GA 30246/404-963-2112; FAX: 404-513-9488
Creedmoor Sports, Inc., P.O. Box 1040, Oceanside, CA 92051/619-757-5529
Creek Side Metal & Woodcrafters (See Allard, Gary)
Creekside Gun Shop, Inc., Main St., Holcomb, NY 14469/716-657-6338; FAX: 716-657-7900
Crit'R Call, Box 999G, La Porte, CO 80535/970-484-2768; FAX: 970-484-0807
Crosman Airguns, Rts. 5 and 20, E. Bloomfield, NY 14443/716-657-6161; FAX: 716-657-5405
Crosman Blades (See Coleman Co., Inc.)
Crosman Products of Canada Ltd., 1173 N. Service Rd. West, Oakville, Ontario, L6M 2V9 CANADA/905-827-1822
Crouse's Country Cover, P.O. Box 160, Storrs, CT 06268/860-423-8736
CRR, Inc./Marble's Inc., 420 Industrial Park, P.O. Box 111, Gladstone, MI 49837/906-428-3710; FAX: 906-428-3711
Crucelegui Hermanos (See U.S. importer—Mandall Shooting Supplies, Inc.)
Cryo-Accurizing, 1160 South Monroe, Decatur, IL 62521/217-423-3070; FAX: 217-423-2756
Cubic Shot Shell Co., Inc., 98 Fatima Dr., Campbell, OH 44405/216-755-0349; FAX: 216-755-0349
Cullity Restoration, Daniel, 209 Old County Rd., East Sandwich, MA 02537/508-888-1147
Cumberland Arms, 514 Shafer Road, Manchester, TN 37355/800-797-8414
Cumberland Knife & Gun Works, 5661 Bragg Blvd., Fayetteville, NC 28303/919-867-0009
Cumberland Mountain Arms, P.O. Box 710, Winchester, TN 37398/615-967-8414; FAX: 615-967-9199
Cumberland States Arsenal, 1124 Palmyra Road, Clarksville, TN 37040
Cummings Bullets, 1417 Esperanza Way, Escondido, CA 92027
Cunningham Co., Eaton, 607 Superior St., Kansas City, MO 64106/816-842-2600
Cupp, Alana, Custom Engraver, P.O. Box 207, Annabella, UT 84711/801-896-4834
Curly Maple Stock Blanks (See Tiger-Hunt)
Curtis Custom Shop, RR1, Box 193A, Wallingford, KY 41093/703-659-4265
Curtis Gun Shop, Dept. ST, 119 W. College, Bozeman, MT 59715/406-587-4934
Custom Barreling & Stocks, 937 Lee Hedrick Rd., Colville, WA 99114/509-684-5686 (days), 509-684-3314 (evenings)
Custom Bullets by Hoffman, 2604 Peconic Ave., Seaford, NY 11783
Custom Calls, 607 N. 5th St., Burlington, IA 52601/319-752-4465
Custom Checkering Service, Kathy Forster, 2124 SE Yamhill St., Portland, OR 97214/503-236-5874
Custom Chronograph, Inc., 5305 Reese Hill Rd., Sumas, WA 98295/360-988-7801
Custom Firearms (See Ahrends, Kim)
Custom Gun Products, 5021 W. Rosewood, Spokane, WA 99208/509-328-9340
Custom Gun Stocks, Rt. 6, P.O. Box 177, McMinnville, TN 37110/615-668-3912
Custom Gunsmiths, 4303 Friar Lane, Colorado Springs, CO 80907/719-599-3366
Custom Hunting Ammo & Arms (See CHAA, Ltd.)
Custom Products (See Jones Custom Products, Neil A.)
Custom Quality Products, Inc., 345 W. Girard Ave., P.O. Box 71129, Madison Heights, MI 48071/810-585-1616; FAX: 810-585-0644
Custom Riflestocks, Inc., Michael M. Kokolus, 7005 Herber Rd., New Tripoli, PA 18066/610-298-3013
Custom Shop, The, 890 Cochrane Crescent, Peterborough, Ont. K9H 5N3 CANADA/705-742-6693
Custom Tackle and Ammo, P.O. Box 1886, Farmington, NM 87499/505-632-3539
Cutco Cutlery, P.O. Box 810, Olean, NY 14760/716-372-3111
Cutlery Shoppe, 5461 Kendall St., Boise, ID 83706-1248/800-231-1272
Cutsinger Bench Rest Bullets, RR 8, Box 161-A, Shelbyville, IN 46176/317-729-5360
CVA, 5988 Peachtree Corners East, Norcross, GA 30071/800-251-9412; FAX: 404-242-8546
C.W. Cartridge Co., 242 Highland Ave., Kearney, NJ 07032/201-998-1030
C.W. Cartridge Co., 71 Hackensack St., Wood Ridge, NJ 07075
Cylinder & Slide, Inc., William R. Laughridge, 245 E. 4th St., Fremont, NE 68025/402-721-4277; FAX: 402-721-0263
CZ (See U.S. importer—Magnum Research, Inc.)

D

D&D Gunsmiths, Ltd., 363 E. Elmwood, Troy, MI 48083/810-583-1512; FAX: 810-583-1524
D&G Precision Duplicators (See Greene Precision Duplicators)
D&H Precision Tooling, 7522 Barnard Mill Rd., Ringwood, IL 60072/815-653-4011
D&H Prods. Co., Inc., 465 Denny Rd., Valencia, PA 16059/412-898-2840, 800-776-0281; FAX: 412-898-2013
D&J Bullet Co. & Custom Gun Shop, Inc., 426 Ferry St., Russell, KY 41169/606-836-2663; FAX: 606-836-2663
D&L Industries (See D.J. Marketing)
D&L Sports, P.O. Box 651, Gillette, WY 82717/307-686-4008
D&R Distributing, 308 S.E. Valley St., Myrtle Creek, OR 97457/503-863-6850
Dade Screw Machine Products, 2319 NW 7th Ave., Miami, FL 33127/305-573-5050
Daewoo Precision Industries Ltd., 34-3 Yeoeuido-Dong, Yeongdeungoo-GU, 15th, Fl./Seoul, KOREA (U.S. importer—Nationwide Sports Distributors)
Dahl's Custom Stocks, N2863 Schofield Rd., Lake Geneva, WI 53147/414-248-2464
Daisy Mfg. Co., P.O. Box 220, Rogers, AR 72757/501-636-1200; FAX: 501-636-1601
Dakota (See U.S. importer—EMF Co., Inc.)
Dakota Arms, Inc., HC 55, Box 326, Sturgis, SD 57785/605-347-4686; FAX: 605-347-4459
Dakota Corp., 77 Wales St., P.O. Box 543, Rutland, VT 05701/802-775-6062, 800-451-4167; FAX: 802-773-3919
Daly, Charles (See B.C. Miroku/Charles Daly)
Damascus-U.S.A., 149 Deans Farm Rd., Tyner, NC 27980/919-221-2010; FAX: 919-221-2009
Dan's Whetstone Co., Inc., 130 Timbs Place, Hot Springs, AR 71913/501-767-1616; FAX: 501-767-9598
Dangler, Homer L., Box 254, Addison, MI 49220/517-547-6745
Danner Shoe Mfg. Co., 12722 NE Airport Way, Portland, OR 97230/503-251-1100, 800-345-0430; FAX: 503-251-1119
Danuser Machine Co., 550 E. Third St., P.O. Box 368, Fulton, MO 65251/573-642-2246; FAX: 573-642-2240
Dapkus Co., Inc., J.G., Commerce Circle, P.O. Box 293, Durham, CT 06422
Dara-Nes, Inc. (See Nesci Enterprises, Inc.)
Darlington Gun Works, Inc., P.O. Box 698, 516 S. 52 Bypass, Darlington, SC 29532/803-393-3931
Data Tech Software Systems, 19312 East Eldorado Drive, Aurora, CO 80013
Datumtech Corp., 2275 Wehrle Dr., Buffalo, NY 14221
Davidson, Jere, Rt. 1, Box 132, Rustburg, VA 24588/804-821-3637
Davis, Don, 1619 Heights, Katy, TX 77493/713-391-3090
Davis Co., R.E., 3450 Pleasantville NE, Pleasantville, OH 43148/614-654-9990
Davis Industries, 15150 Sierra Bonita Ln., Chino, CA 91710/909-597-4726; FAX: 909-393-9771
Davis Leather Co., G. Wm., 3990 Valley Blvd., Unit D, Walnut, CA 91789/909-598-5620
Davis Products, Mike, 643 Loop Dr., Moses Lake, WA 98837/509-765-6178, 509-766-7281 orders only
Davis Service Center, Bill, 7221 Florin Mall Dr., Sacramento, CA 95823/916-393-4867
Day & Sons, Inc., Leonard, P.O. Box 122, Flagg Hill Rd., Heath, MA 01346/413-337-8369
Dayson Arms Ltd., P.O. Box 532, Vincennes, IN 47591/812-882-8680; FAX: 812-882-8446
Daystate Ltd., Newcastle Street, Stone, Staffs, ST15 8JU ENGLAND/01785-812473; FAX: 01785-812105
Dayton Traister, 4778 N. Monkey Hill Rd., P.O. Box 593, Oak Harbor, WA 98277/206-679-4657; FAX:206-675-1114
DBASE Consultants (See Arms, Peripheral Data Systems)
DBI Books, Division of Krause Publications, 4092 Commercial Ave., Northbrook, IL 60062/847-272-6310; FAX: 847-272-2051; For consumer orders, see Krause Publications
D-Boone Ent., Inc., 5900 Colwyn Dr., Harrisburg, PA 17109
D.C.C. Enterprises, 259 Wynburn Ave., Athens, GA 30601
D.D. Custom Stocks, R.H. "Dick" Devereaux, 5240 Mule Deer Dr., Colorado Springs, CO 80919/719-548-8468
de Coux, Pete (See Cartridge Transfer Group)
de Treville & Co., Stan, 4129 Normal St., San Diego, CA 92103/619-298-3393
Dead Eye's Sport Center, RD 1, Box 147B, Shickshinny, PA 18655/717-256-7432
Decker Shooting Products, 1729 Laguna Ave., Schofield, WI 54476/715-359-5873
DeckSlider of Florida, 27641-2 Reahard Ct., Bonita Springs, FL 33923/800-782-1474
Deepeeka Exports Pvt. Ltd., D-78, Saket, Meerut-250-006, INDIA/011-91-121-512889, 011-91-121-545363; FAX: 011-91-121-542988, 011-91-121-511599
Deer Me Products Co., Box 34, 1208 Park St., Anoka, MN 55303/612-421-8971; FAX: 612-422-0526
Defense Training International, Inc., 749 S. Lemay, Ste. A3-337, Ft. Collins, CO 80524/303-482-2520; FAX: 303-482-0548
Degen Inc. (See Aristocrat Knives)

deHaas Barrels, RR 3, Box 77, Ridgeway, MO 64481/816-872-6308
Del Rey Products, P.O. Box 91561, Los Angeles, CA 90009/213-823-0494
Delhi Gun House, 1374 Kashmere Gate, Delhi, INDIA 110 006/(011)237375 239116; FAX: 91-11-2917344
Delorge, Ed, 2231 Hwy. 308, Thibodaux, LA 70301/504-447-1633
Del-Sports, Inc., Box 685, Main St., Margaretville, NY 12455/914-586-4103; FAX: 914-586-4105
Delta Arms Ltd., P.O. Box 1000, Delta, VT 84624-1000
Delta Co. Ammo Bunker, 1209 16th Place, Yuma, AZ 85364/602-783-4563
Delta Enterprises, 284 Hagemann Drive, Livermore, CA 94550
Delta Frangible Ammunition, LLC, 1111 Jefferson Davis Hwy., Suite 508, Arlington, VA 22202/703-416-4928; FAX: 703-416-4934
Dem-Bart Checkering Tools, Inc., 6807 Bickford Ave., Old Hwy. 2, Snohomish, WA 98290/360-568-7356; FAX: 360-568-1798
Denver Bullets, Inc., 1811 W. 13th Ave., Denver, CO 80204/303-893-3146; FAX: 303-893-9161
Denver Instrument Co., 6542 Fig St., Arvada, CO 80004/800-321-1135, 303-431-7255; FAX: 303-423-4831
DeSantis Holster & Leather Goods, Inc., P.O. Box 2039, 149 Denton Ave., New Hyde Park, NY 11040-0701/516-354-8000; FAX: 516-354-7501
Desert Industries, Inc., P.O. Box 93443, Las Vegas, NV 89193-3443/702-597-1066; FAX: 702-871-9452
Desert Mountain Mfg., P.O. Box 2767, Columbia Falls, MT 59912/800-477-0762, 406-892-7772; FAX: 406-892-7772
Desquesnes, Gerald (See Napoleon Bonaparte, Inc.)
Detroit-Armor Corp., 720 Industrial Dr. No. 112, Cary, IL 60013/708-639-7666; FAX: 708-639-7694
Dever Co., Jack, 8590 NW 90, Oklahoma City, OK 73132/405-721-6393
Devereaux, R.H. "Dick" (See D.D. Custom Stocks)
Dewey Mfg. Co., Inc., J., P.O. Box 2014, Southbury, CT 06488/203-264-3064; FAX: 203-262-6907
DGR Custom Rifles, RR1, Box 8A, Tappen, ND 58487/701-327-8135
DGS, Inc., Dale A. Storey, 1117 E. 12th, Casper, WY 82601/307-237-2414
DHB Products, P.O. Box 3092, Alexandria, VA 22302/703-836-2648
Diamond Machining Techonology (See DMT—Diamond Machining Technology)
Diamond Mfg. Co., P.O. Box 174, Wyoming, PA 18644/800-233-9601
Diamondback Supply, 2431 Juan Tabo, Suite 163, Albuquerque, NM 87112/505-237-0068
Diana (See U.S. importer—Dynamit Nobel-RWS, Inc.)
Dibble, Derek A., 555 John Downey Dr., New Britain, CT 06051/203-224-2630
Dietz Gun Shop & Range, Inc., 421 Range Rd., New Braunfels, TX 78132/210-885-4662
Dilliott Gunsmithing, Inc., 657 Scarlett Rd., Dandridge, TN 37725/615-397-9204
Dillon, Ed, 1035 War Eagle Dr. N., Colorado Springs, CO 80919/719-598-4929; FAX: 719-598-4929
Dillon Precision Products, Inc., 8009 East Dillon's Way, Scottsdale, AZ 85260/602-948-8009, 800-762-3845; FAX: 602-998-2786
Dina Arms Corporation, P.O. Box 46, Royersford, PA 19468/610-287-0266; FAX: 610-287-0266
Division Lead Co., 7742 W. 61st Pl., Summit, IL 60502
Dixie Gun Works, Inc., Hwy. 51 South, Union City, TN 38261/901-885-0561, order 800-238-6785; FAX: 901-885-0440
Dixon Muzzleloading Shop, Inc., RD 1, Box 175, Kempton, PA 19529/610-756-6271
D.J. Marketing, 10602 Horton Ave., Downey, CA 90241/310-806-0891; FAX: 310-806-6231
DKT, Inc., 14623 Vera Drive, Union, MI 49130-9744/616-641-7120; FAX: 616-641-2015
DLO Mfg., 10807 SE Foster Ave., Arcadia, FL 33821-7304
D-Max, Inc., RR1, Box 473, Bagley, MN 56621/218-785-2278
DMT—Diamond Machining Technology, Inc., 85 Hayes Memorial Dr., Marlborough, MA 01752-1892/508-481-5944; FAX: 508-485-3924
Doctor Optic Technologies, Inc., 4685 Boulder Highway, Suite A, Las Vegas, NV 89121/800-290-3634, 702-898-7161; FAX: 702-898-3737
Dogtown Varmint Supplies, 1048 Irvine Ave. No. 333, Newport Beach, CA 92660/714-642-3997
Dohring Bullets, 100 W. 8 Mile Rd., Ferndale, MI 48220
Dolbare, Elizabeth, P.O. Box 222, Sunburst, MT 59482-0222
Donnelly, C.P., 405 Kubli Rd., Grants Pass, OR 97527/541-846-6604
Doskocil Mfg. Co., Inc., P.O. Box 1246, 4209 Barnett, Arlington, TX 76017/817-467-5116; FAX: 817-472-9810
Double A Ltd., Dept. ST, Box 11306, Minneapolis, MN 55411
Douglas Barrels, Inc., 5504 Big Tyler Rd., Charleston, WV 25313-1398/304-776-1341; FAX: 304-776-8560
Dowtin Gunworks, Rt. 4, Box 930A, Flagstaff, AZ 86001/602-779-1898
Dr. O's Products Ltd., P.O. Box 111, Niverville, NY 12130/518-784-3333; FAX: 518-784-2800
Drain, Mark, SE 3211 Kamilche Point Rd., Shelton, WA 98584/206-426-5452
Dremel Mfg. Co., 4915-21st St., Racine, WI 53406
Dressel Jr., Paul G., 209 N. 92nd Ave., Yakima, WA 98908/509-966-9233; FAX: 509-966-3365
Dri-Slide, Inc., 411 N. Darling, Fremont, MI 49412/616-924-3950
Dropkick, 1460 Washington Blvd., Williamsport, PA 17701/717-326-6561; FAX: 717-326-4950
DTM International, Inc., 40 Joslyn Rd., P.O. Box 5, Lake Orion, MI 48362/313-693-6670
Duane Custom Stocks, Randy, 110 W. North Ave., Winchester, VA 22601/703-667-9461; FAX: 703-722-3993
Duane's Gun Repair (See DGR Custom Rifles)
Dubber, Michael W., P.O. Box 312, Evansville, IN 47702/812-424-9000; FAX: 812-424-6551
Duck Call Specialists, P.O. Box 124, Jerseyville, IL 62052/618-498-9855
Duffy (See Guns Antique & Modern DBA/Charles E. Duffy)
Du-Lite Corp., Charles E., 171 River Rd., Middletown, CT 06457/203-347-2505; FAX: 203-347-9404
Dumoulin, Ernest, Rue Florent Boclinville 8-10, 13-4041 Votten, BELGIUM/41 27 78 92 (U.S. importer—New England Arms Co.)
Duncan's Gun Works, Inc., 1619 Grand Ave., San Marcos, CA 92069/619-727-0515
Dunham Co., P.O. Box 813, Brattleboro, VT 05301/802-254-2316
Dunphy, Ted, W. 5100 Winch Rd., Rathdrum, ID 83858/208-687-1399; FAX: 208-687-1399
Duofold, Inc., RD 3 Rt. 309, Valley Square Mall, Tamaqua, PA 18252/717-386-2666; FAX: 717-386-3652
DuPont (See IMR Powder Co.)
Dutchman's Firearms, Inc., The, 4143 Taylor Blvd., Louisville, KY 40215/502-366-0555
Dybala Gun Shop, P.O. Box 1024, FM 3156, Bay City, TX 77414/409-245-0866
Dykstra, Doug, 411 N. Darling, Fremont, MI 49412/616-924-3950
Dynalite Products, Inc., 215 S. Washington St., Greenfield, OH 45123/513-981-2124
Dynamit Nobel-RWS, Inc., 81 Ruckman Rd., Closter, NJ 07624/201-767-7971; FAX: 201-767-1589
Dyson & Son Ltd., Peter, 29-31 Church St., Honley Huddersfield, W. Yorkshire HD7 2AH, ENGLAND/44-1484-661062; FAX: 44-1484-663709

E

E&L Mfg., Inc., 4177 Riddle by Pass Rd., Riddle, OR 97469/541-874-2137; FAX: 541-874-3107
E.A.A. Corp., P.O. Box 1299, Sharpes, FL 32959/407-639-4842, 800-536-4442; FAX: 407-639-7006
Eagan, Donald V., P.O. Box 196, Benton, PA 17814/717-925-6134
Eagle Arms (See ArmaLite, Inc.)
Eagle Grips, Eagle Business Center, 460 Randy Rd., Carol Stream, IL 60188/800-323-6144, 708-260-0400; FAX: 708-260-0486
Eagle Imports, Inc., 1750 Brielle Ave., Unit B1, Wanamassa, NJ 07712/908-493-0333; FAX: 908-493-0301
Eagle International, Inc., 5195 W. 58th Ave., Suite 300, Arvada, CO 80002/303-426-8100; FAX: 303-426-5475
Eagle Mfg. & Engineering, 2648 Keen Dr., San Diego, CA 92139/619-479-4402; FAX: 619-472-5585
E-A-R, Inc., Div. of Cabot Safety Corp., 5457 W. 79th St., Indianapolis, IN 46268/800-327-3431; FAX: 800-488-8007
Eastman Products, R.T., P.O. Box 1531, Jackson, WY 83001/307-733-3217, 800-624-4311
Easy Pull Outlaw Products, 316 1st St. East, Polson, MT 59860/406-883-6822
EAW (See U.S. importer—New England Custom Gun Service)
Echols & Co., D'Arcy, 164 W. 580 S., Providence, UT 84332/801-753-2367
Eckelman Gunsmithing, 3125 133rd St. SW, Fort Ripley, MN 56449/218-829-3176
Ed's Gun House, Rt. 1, Box 62, Minnesota City, MN 55959/507-689-2925
Edenpine, Inc. c/o Six Enterprises, Inc., 320 D Turtle Creek Ct., San Jose, CA 95125/408-999-0201; FAX: 408-999-0216
EdgeCraft Corp., P.O. Box 3000, Limestone and Southwood Rd., Avondale, PA 19311/215-268-0500, 800-342-3255; FAX: 215-268-3545
Edmisten Co., P.O. Box 1293, Boone, NC 28607
Edmund Scientific Co., 101 E. Gloucester Pike, Barrington, NJ 08033/609-543-6250
Ednar, Inc., 2-4-8 Kayabacho, Nihonbashi, Chuo-ku, Tokyo, JAPAN 103/81(Japan)-3-3667-1651; FAX: 81-3-3661-8113
Eezox, Inc., P.O. Box 772, Waterford, CT 06385-0772/860-447-8282, 800-462-3331; FAX: 860-447-3484
Effebi SNC-Dr. Franco Beretta, via Rossa, 4, 25062 Concesio, Italy/030-2751955; FAX: 030-2180414 (U.S. importer—Nevada Cartridge Co.
Eggleston, Jere D., 400 Saluda Ave., Columbia, SC 29205/803-799-3402
EGW Evolution Gun Works, 4050 B-8 Skyron Dr., Doylestown, PA 18901/215-348-9892; FAX: 215-348-1056
Eichelberger Bullets, Wm., 158 Crossfield Rd., King of Prussia, PA 19406
EK Knife Co., c/o Blackjack Knives, Ltd., 1307 Wabash Ave., Effingham, IL 62401
Ekol Leather Care, P.O. Box 2652, West Lafayette, IN 47906/317-463-2250; FAX: 317-463-7004
El Dorado Leather, P.O. Box 2603, Tucson, AZ 85702/520-586-4791; FAX: 520-586-4791
El Paso Saddlery Co., P.O. Box 27194, El Paso, TX 79926/915-544-2233; FAX: 915-544-2535
Eldorado Cartridge Corp. (See PMC/Eldorado Cartridge Corp.)
Electro Prismatic Collimators, Inc., 1441 Manatt St., Lincoln, NE 68521
Electronic Shooters Protection, Inc., 11997 West 85th Place, Arvada, CO 80005/303-456-8964; 800-797-7791
Electronic Trigger Systems, Inc., P.O. Box 13, 230 Main St. S., Hector, MN 55342/612-848-2760

Eley Ltd., P.O. Box 705, Witton, Birmingham, B6 7UT, ENGLAND/021-356-8899; FAX: 021-331-4173
Elite Ammunition, P.O. Box 3251, Oakbrook, IL 60522/708-366-9006
Elk River, Inc., 1225 Paonia St., Colorado Springs, CO 80915/719-574-4407
Elkhorn Bullets, P.O. Box 5293, Central Point, OR 97502/541-826-7440
Elko Arms, Dr. L. Kortz, 28 rue Ecole Moderne, B-7060 Soignies, BELGIUM/(32)67-33-29-34
Ellett Bros., 267 Columbia Ave., P.O. Box 128, Chapin, SC 29036/803-345-3751, 800-845-3711; FAX: 803-345-1820
Ellicott Arms, Inc./Woods Pistolsmithing, 3840 Dahlgren Ct., Ellicott City, MD 21042/410-465-7979
Elliott Inc., G.W., 514 Burnside Ave., East Hartford, CT 06108/203-289-5741; FAX: 203-289-3137
Elsen, Inc., Pete, 1529 S. 113th St., West Allis, WI 53214
Emerging Technologies, Inc. (See Laseraim Technologies, Inc.)
EMF Co., Inc., 1900 E. Warner Ave. Suite 1-D, Santa Ana, CA 92705/714-261-6611; FAX: 714-756-0133
Empire Cutlery Corp., 12 Kruger Ct., Clifton, NJ 07013/201-472-5155; FAX: 201-779-0759
Engineered Accessories, 1307 W. Wabash Ave., Effingham, IL 62401/217-347-7700; FAX: 217-347-7737
English, Inc., A.G., 708 S. 12th St., Broken Arrow, OK 74012/918-251-3399
Englishtown Sporting Goods Co., Inc., David J. Maxham, 38 Main St., Englishtown, NJ 07726/201-446-7717
Engraving Artistry, 36 Alto Rd., RFD 2, Burlington, CT 06013/203-673-6837
Enguix Import-Export, Alpujarras 58, Alzira, Valencia, SPAIN 46600/(96) 241 43 95; FAX: (96) (241 43 95) 240 21 53
Enhanced Presentations, Inc., 5929 Market St., Wilmington, NC 28405/910-799-1622; FAX: 910-799-5004
Enlow, Charles, 895 Box, Beaver, OK 73932/405-625-4487
Ensign-Bickford Co., The, 660 Hopmeadow St., Simsbury, CT 06070
EPC, 1441 Manatt St., Lincoln, NE 68521/402-476-3946
Epps, Ellwood (See "Gramps" Antique Cartridges)
Erhardt, Dennis, 3280 Green Meadow Dr., Helena, MT 59601/406-442-4533
Erickson's Mfg., C.W., Inc., 530 Garrison Ave. N.E., P.O. Box 522, Buffalo, MN 55313/612-682-3665; FAX: 612-682-4328
Erma Werke GmbH, Johan Ziegler St., 13/15/FeldiglSt., D-8060 Dachau, GERMANY (U.S. importers—Amtec 2000, Inc.; Mandall Shooting Supplies, Inc.)
Eskridge Rifles, Steven Eskridge, 218 N. Emerson, Mart, TX 76664/817-876-3544
Essex Arms, P.O. Box 345, Island Pond, VT 05846/802-723-4313
Essex Metals, 1000 Brighton St., Union, NJ 07083/800-282-8369
Estate Cartridge, Inc., 12161 FM 830, Willis, TX 77378/409-856-7277; FAX: 409-856-5486
Euber Bullets, No. Orwell Rd., Orwell, VT 05760/802-948-2621
Euroarms of America, Inc., P.O. Box 3277, Winchester, VA 22604/540-662-1863; FAX: 540-662-4464
European American Armory Corp. (See E.A.A. Corp.)
Europtik Ltd., P.O. Box 319, Dunmore, PA 18512/717-347-6049; FAX: 717-969-4330
Eutaw Co., Inc., The, P.O. Box 608, U.S. Hwy. 176 West, Holly Hill, SC 29059/803-496-3341
Evans, Andrew, 2325 NW Squire St., Albany, OR 97321/541-928-3190; FAX: 541-928-4128
Evans Engraving, Robert, 332 Vine St., Oregon City, OR 97045/503-656-5693
Evans Gunsmithing (See Evans, Andrew)
Eversull Co., Inc., K., 1 Tracemont, Boyce, LA 71409/318-793-8728; FAX: 318-793-5483
Excalibur Enterprises, P.O. Box 400, Fogelsville, PA 18051-0400/610-391-9105; FAX: 610-391-9223
Exe, Inc., 18830 Partridge Circle, Eden Prairie, MN 55346/612-944-7662
Executive Protection Institute, Rt. 2, Box 3645, Berryville, VA 22611/540-955-1128
Eyears, Roland C., 576 Binns Blvd., Columbus, OH 43204-2441
Eyster Heritage Gunsmiths, Inc., Ken, 6441 Bishop Rd., Centerburg, OH 43011/614-625-6131
Eze-Lap Diamond Prods., P.O. Box 2229, 15164 Weststate St., Westminster, CA 92683/714-847-1555; FAX: 714-897-0280
E-Z-Way Systems, P.O. Box 4310, Newark, OH 43058-4310/614-345-6645, 800-848-2072; FAX: 614-345-6600

F

F&A Inc., 50 Elm St., Richfield Springs, NY 13439/315-858-1470; FAX: 315-858-2969
Fabarm S.p.A., Via Averolda 31, 25039 Travagliato, Brescia, ITALY/030-6863629; FAX: 030-6863684 (U.S. importer—Ithaca Acquisition Corp.)
Fabian Bros. Sporting Goods, Inc., 1510 Morena Blvd., Suite "G", San Diego, CA 92110/619-275-0816; FAX: 619-276-8733
Fagan & Co., William, 22952 15 Mile Rd., Clinton Township, MI 48035/313-465-4637; FAX: 313-792-6996
Fair Game International, P.O. Box 77234-34053, Houston, TX 77234/713-941-6269
F.A.I.R. Tecni-Mec s.n.c. di Isidoro Rizzini & C., Via Gitti, 41 Zona Indu, triale/25060 Marcheno (Brescia), ITALY/030-861162-8610344; FAX: 030-8610179
Faith Associates, Inc., 1139 S. Greenville Hwy., Hendersonville, NC 28792/704-692-1916; FAX: 704-697-6827
Fajen, Inc., Reinhart, Route 1, P.O. Box 214-A, Lincoln, MO 65338/816-547-3030; FAX: 816-547-2215
Falcon Pneumatic Systems (See U.S. importer—Airguns-R-Us)
Famas (See U.S. importer—Century International Arms, Inc.)
Fanzoj GmbH, Griesgasse 1, 9170 Ferlach, AUSTRIA 9170/(43) 04227-2283; FAX: (43) 04227-2867
Far North Outfitters, Box 1252, Bethel, AK 99559
Farm Form Decoys, Inc., 1602 Biovu, P.O. Box 748, Galveston, TX 77553/409-744-0762, 409-765-6361; FAX: 409-765-8513
Farmer-Dressel, Sharon, 209 N. 92nd Ave., Yakima, WA 98908/509-966-9233; FAX: 509-966-3365
Farr Studio, Inc., 1231 Robinhood Rd., Greeneville, TN 37743/615-638-8825
Farrar Tool Co., Inc., 12150 Bloomfield Ave., Suite E, Santa Fe Springs, CA 90670/310-863-4367; FAX: 310-863-5123
FAS, Via E. Fermi, 8, 20019 Settimo Milanese, Milano, ITALY/02-3285846; FAX: 02-33500196 (U.S. importer—Nygord Precision Products)
Faulhaber Wildlocker, Dipl.-Ing. Norbert Wittasek, Seilergasse 2, A-1010 Wien, AUSTRIA/OM-43-1-5137001; FAX: OM-43-1-5137001
Faulk's Game Call Co., Inc., 616 18th St., Lake Charles, LA 70601/318-436-9726
Faust, Inc., T.G., 544 Minor St., Reading, PA 19602/610-375-8549; FAX: 610-375-4488
Fausti Cav. Stefano & Figlie snc, Via Martiri Dell Indipendenza, 70, Marcheno, ITALY 25060 (U.S. importer—American Arms, Inc.)
Fautheree, Andy, P.O. Box 4607, Pagosa Springs, CO 81157/303-731-5003
Feather Flex Decoys, 1655 Swan Lake Rd., Bossier City, LA 71111/318-746-8596; FAX: 318-742-4815
Feather Industries, Inc., 37600 Liberty Dr., Trinidad, CO 81082/719-846-2699; FAX: 719-846-2644
Federal Cartridge Co., 900 Ehlen Dr., Anoka, MN 55303/612-323-2300; FAX: 612-323-2506
Federal Champion Target Co., 232 Industrial Parkway, Richmond, IN 47374/800-441-4971; FAX: 317-966-7747
Federal Engineering Corp., 1090 Bryn Mawr, Bensenville, IL 60106/708-860-1938; FAX: 708-860-2085
Federated-Fry (See Fry Metals)
FEG, Budapest, Soroksariut 158, H-1095 HUNGARY (U.S. importers—Century International Arms, Inc.; K.B.I., Inc.)
Feinwerkbau Westinger & Altenburger GmbH (See FWB)
Feken, Dennis, Rt. 2 Box 124, Perry, OK 73077/405-336-5611
Fellowes, Ted, Beaver Lodge, 9245 16th Ave. SW, Seattle, WA 98106/206-763-1698
Feminine Protection, Inc., 10514 Shady Trail, Dallas, TX 75220/214-351-4500; FAX: 214-352-4686
Ferdinand, Inc., P.O. Box 5, 201 Main St., Harrison, ID 83833/208-689-3012, 800-522-6010 (U.S.A.), 800-258-5266 (Canada); FAX: 208-689-3142
Ferguson, Bill, P.O. Box 1238, Sierra Vista, AZ 85636/520-458-5321; FAX: 520-458-9125
FERLIB, Via Costa 46, 25063 Gardone V.T. (Brescia) ITALY/30-89-12-586; FAX: 30-89-12-586 (U.S. importers—Harry Marx)
Ferris Firearms, 30115 U.S. Hwy. 281 North, Suite 158, Bulverde, TX 78163/210-980-4811
Fibron Products, Inc., P.O. Box 430, Buffalo, NY 14209-0430/716-886-2378; FAX: 716-886-2394
Finch Custom Bullets, 40204 La Rochelle, Prairieville, LA 70769
Fiocchi Munizioni s.p.a. (See U.S. importer—Fiocchi of America, Inc.)
Fiocchi of America, Inc., 5030 Fremont Rd., Ozark, MO 65721/417-725-4118, 800-721-2666; FAX: 417-725-1039
Firearm Training Center, The, 9555 Blandville Rd., West Paducah, KY 42086/502-554-5886
Firearms Academy of Seattle, P.O. Box 2814, Kirkland, WA 98083/206-820-4853
Firearms Co. Ltd./Alpine (See U.S. importer—Mandall Shooting Supplies, Inc.)
Firearms Engraver's Guild of America, 332 Vine St., Oregon City, OR 97045/503-656-5693
Firearms Safety Products, Inc. (See FSPI)
Fire'n Five, P.O. Box 11 Granite Rt., Sumpter, OR 97877
First, Inc., Jack, 1201 Turbine Dr., Rapid City, SD 57701/605-343-9544; FAX: 605-343-9420
Fish, Marshall F., Rt. 22 N., P.O. Box 2439, Westport, NY 12993/518-962-4897
Fisher, Jerry A., 553 Crane Mt. Rd., Big Fork, MT 59911/406-837-2722
Fisher Custom Firearms, 2199 S. Kittredge Way, Aurora, CO 80013/303-755-3710
Fisher Enterprises, Inc., 1071 4th Ave. S., Suite 303, Edmonds, WA 98020-4143/206-771-5382
Fisher, R. Kermit (See Fisher Enterprises, Inc.)
Fitz Pistol Grip Co., P.O. Box 610, Douglas City, CA 96024/916-778-0240
Flaig's, 2200 Evergreen Rd., Millvale, PA 15209/412-821-1717
Flambeau Products Corp., 15981 Valplast Rd., Middlefield, OH 44062/216-632-1631; FAX: 216-632-1581
Flannery Engraving Co., Jeff W., 11034 Riddles Run Rd., Union, KY 41091/606-384-3127
Flashette Co., 4725 S. Kolin Ave., Chicago, IL 60632/312-927-1302; FAX: 312-927-3083
Flayderman & Co., N., Inc., P.O. Box 2446, Ft. Lauderdale, FL 33303/305-761-8855
Fleming Firearms, 7720 E 126th St. N, Collinsville, OK 74021-7016/918-665-3624

Flents Products Co., Inc., P.O. Box 2109, Norwalk, CT 06852/203-866-2581; FAX: 203-854-9322
Flintlocks, Etc. (See Beauchamp & Son, Inc.)
Flitz International Ltd., 821 Mohr Ave., Waterford, WI 53185/414-534-5898; FAX: 414-534-2991
Floatstone Mfg. Co., 106 Powder Mill Rd., P.O. Box 765, Canton, CT 06019/203-693-1977
Flores Publications, Inc., J., P.O. Box 830131, Miami, FL 33283/305-559-4652
Fluoramics, Inc., 18 Industrial Ave., Mahwah, NJ 07430/800-922-0075, 201-825-7035
Flow-Rite of Tennessee, Inc., 107 Allen St., P.O. Box 196, Bruceton, TN 38317/901-586-2271; FAX: 901-586-2300
Flynn's Custom Guns, P.O. Box 7461, Alexandria, LA 71306/318-455-7130
FN Herstal, Voie de Liege 33, Herstal 4040, BELGIUM/(32)41.40.82.83; FAX: (32)41.40.86.79
Fobus International Ltd., Kfar Hess, ISRAEL 40692/972-9-911716; FAX: 972-9-911716
Folks, Donald E., 205 W. Lincoln St., Pontiac, IL 61764/815-844-7901
Foothills Video Productions, Inc., P.O. Box 651, Spartanburg, SC 29304/803-573-7023, 800-782-5358
Ford, Jack, 1430 Elkwood, Missouri City, TX 77489/713-499-9984
Foredom Electric Co., Rt. 6, 16 Stony Hill Rd., Bethel, CT 06801/203-792-8622
Forgett Jr., Valmore J., 689 Bergen Blvd., Ridgefield, NJ 07657/201-945-2500; FAX: 201-945-6859
Forgreens Tool Mfg., Inc., P.O. Box 990, 723 Austin St., Robert Lee, TX 76945/915-453-2800
Forkin, Ben (See Belt MTN Arms)
Forrest, Inc., Tom, P.O. Box 326, Lakeside, CA 92040/619-561-5800; FAX: 619-561-0227
Forrest Tool Co., P.O. Box 768, 44380 Gordon Lane, Mendocino, CA 95460/707-937-2141; FAX: 717-937-1817
Forster, Kathy (See Custom Checkering Service)
Forster, Larry L., P.O. Box 212, 220 First St. NE, Gwinner, ND 58040-0212/701-678-2475
Forster Products, 82 E. Lanark Ave., Lanark, IL 61046/815-493-6360; FAX: 815-493-2371
Fort Hill Gunstocks, 12807 Fort Hill Rd., Hillsboro, OH 45133/513-466-2763
Fort Knox Security Products, 1051 N. Industrial Park Rd., Orem, UT 84057/801-224-7233, 800-821-5216; FAX: 801-226-5493
Fort Worth Firearms, 2006-B Martin Luther King Fwy., Ft. Worth, TX 76104/817-536-0718; FAX: 817-535-0290
Forthofer's Gunsmithing & Knifemaking, 5535 U.S. Hwy 93S, Whitefish, MT 59937-8411/406-862-2674
Fortune Products, Inc., HC04, Box 303, Marble Falls, TX 78654/210-693-6111; FAX: 210-693-6394
Forty Five Ranch Enterprises, Box 1080, Miami, OK 74355-1080/918-542-5875
Fouling Shot, The, 6465 Parfet St., Arvada, CO 80004
Fountain Products, 492 Prospect Ave., West Springfield, MA 01089/413-781-4651; FAX: 413-733-8217
4-D Custom Die Co., 711 N. Sandusky St., P.O. Box 889, Mt. Vernon, OH 43050-0889/614-397-7214; FAX: 614-397-6600
4W Ammunition, Rt. 1, P.O. Box 313, Tioga, TX 76271/817-437-2458; FAX: 817-437-2228
Fowler Bullets, 806 Dogwood Dr., Gastonia, NC 28054/704-867-3259
Fox River Mills, Inc., P.O. Box 298, 227 Poplar St., Osage, IA 50461/515-732-3798; FAX: 515-732-5128
Foy Custom Bullets, 104 Wells Ave., Daleville, AL 36322
Francesca, Inc., 3115 Old Ranch Rd., San Antonio, TX 78217/512-826-2584; FAX: 512-826-8211
Franchi S.p.A., Via del Serpente, 12, 25131 Brescia, ITALY/030-3581833; FAX: 030-3581554 (U.S. importer—American Arms, Inc.)
Francolini, Leonard, 106 Powder Mill Rd., P.O. Box 765, Canton, CT 06019/203-693-1977
Francotte & Cie S.A., Auguste, rue du Trois Juin 109, 4400 Herstal-Liege, BELGIUM/41-48.13.18; FAX: 32-41-48-11-70 (U.S. importer—Armes de Chasse)
Frank Custom Classic Arms, Ron, 7131 Richland Rd., Ft. Worth, TX 76118/817-284-9300; FAX: 817-284-9300
Frank Knives, Box 984, Whitefish, MT 59937/406-862-2681; FAX: 406-862-2681
Frankonia Jagd, Hofmann & Co., D-97064 Wurzburg, GERMANY/09302-200; FAX: 09302-20200
Frazier Brothers Enterprises, 1118 N. Main St., Franklin, IN 46131/317-736-4000; FAX: 317-736-4000
Freedom Arms, Inc., P.O. Box 1776, Freedom, WY 83120/307-883-2468, 800-833-4432 (orders only); FAX: 307-883-2005
Freeman Animal Targets, 5519 East County Road, 100 South, Plainsfield, IN 46168/317-487-9482; FAX: 317-487-9671
Fremont Tool Works, 1214 Prairie, Ford, KS 67842/316-369-2327
French, J.R., 1712 Creek Ridge Ct., Irving, TX 75060/214-254-2654
Frielich Police Equipment, 211 East 21st St., New York, NY 10010/212-254-3045
From Jena (See Europtik Ltd.)
Frontier, 2910 San Bernardo, Laredo, TX 78040/210-723-5409; FAX: 210-723-1774
Frontier Arms Co., Inc., 401 W. Rio Santa Cruz, Green Valley, AZ 85614-3932
Frontier Products Co., 164 E. Longview Ave., Columbus, OH 43202/614-262-9357
Frontier Safe Co., 3201 S. Clinton St., Fort Wayne, IN 46806/219-744-7233; FAX: 219-744-6678
Frost Cutlery Co., P.O. Box 22636, Chattanooga, TN 37422/615-894-6079; FAX: 615-894-9576
Fry Metals, 4100 6th Ave., Altoona, PA 16602/814-946-1611
FSPI, 5885 Glenridge Dr. Suite 220A, Atlanta, GA 30328/404-843-2881; FAX: 404-843-0271
Fujinon, Inc., 10 High Point Dr., Wayne, NJ 07470/201-633-5600; FAX: 201-633-5216
Fullmer, Geo. M., 2499 Mavis St., Oakland, CA 94601/510-533-4193
Fulmer's Antique Firearms, Chet, P.O. Box 792, Rt. 2 Buffalo Lake, Detroit Lakes, MN 56501/218-847-7712
Fulton Armory, 8725 Bollman Place No. 1, Savage, MD 20763/301-490-9485; FAX: 301-490-9547
Furr Arms, 91 N. 970 W., Orem, UT 84057/801-226-3877; FAX: 801-226-3877
Fury Cutlery, 801 Broad Ave., Ridgefield, NJ 07657/201-943-5920; FAX: 201-943-1579
Fusilier Bullets, 10010 N. 6000 W., Highland, UT 84003/801-756-6813
FWB, Neckarstrasse 43, 78727 Oberndorf a. N., GERMANY/07423-814-0; FAX: 07423-814-89 (U.S. importer—Beeman Precision Airguns)

G

G3 & Co., 18 Old Northville Rd., New Milford, CT 06776/203-354-7500
G96 Products Co., Inc., River St. Station, P.O. Box 1684, Paterson, NJ 07544/201-684-4050; FAX: 201-684-3848
G&C Bullet Co., Inc., 8835 Thornton Rd., Stockton, CA 95209/209-477-6479; FAX: 209-477-2813
G&H Decoys, Inc., P.O. Box 1208, Hwy. 75 North, Henryetta, OK 74437/918-652-3314; FAX: 918-652-3400
Gage Manufacturing, 663 W. 7th St., San Pedro, CA 90731
Gaillard Barrels, P.O. Box 21, Pathlow, Sask., S0K 3B0 CANADA/306-752-3769; FAX: 306-752-5969
Galati International, P.O. Box 326, Catawissa, MO 63015/314-257-4837; FAX: 314-257-2268
Galaxy Imports Ltd., Inc., P.O. Box 3361, Victoria, TX 77903/512-573-4867; FAX: 512-576-9622
Galazan, P.O. Box 1692, New Britain, CT 06051-1692/203-225-6581; FAX: 203-832-8707
GALCO International Ltd., 2019 W. Quail Ave., Phoenix, AZ 85027/602-258-8295, 800-874-2526; FAX: 602-582-6854
Gamba-Societa Armi Bresciane Srl., Renato, Via Artigiani, 93, 25063 Gardone Val Trompia (BS), ITALY/30-8911640; FAX: 30-8911648 (U.S. importer—The First National Gun Bank Corp.)
Gamba, USA, P.O. Box 60452, Colorado Springs, CO 80960/719-578-1145; FAX: 719-444-0731
Game Haven Gunstocks, 13750 Shire Rd., Wolverine, MI 49799/616-525-8257
Game Winner, Inc., 2625 Cumberland Parkway, Suite 220, Atlanta, GA 30339/770-434-9210; FAX: 770-434-9215
Gammog, Gregory B. Gally, 14608 Old Gunpowder Rd., Laurel, MD 20707-3131/301-725-3838
Gamo (See U.S. importers—Daisy Mfg. Co.; Dynamit Nobel-RWS, Inc.)
Gamo USA, Inc., 3721 S.W. 47th Ave., Suite 304, Ft. Lauderdale, FL 33314
Gander Mountain, Inc., P.O. Box 128, Hwy. "W", Wilmot, WI 53192/414-862-2331,Ext. 6425
GAR, 590 McBride Avenue, West Paterson, NJ 07424/201-754-1114; FAX: 201-742-2897
Garbi, Armas Urki, 12-14, 20.600 Eibar (Guipuzcoa) SPAIN/43-11 38 73 (U.S. importer—Moore & Co., Wm. Larkin)
Garcia National Gun Traders, Inc., 225 SW 22nd Ave., Miami, FL 33135/305-642-2355
Garrett Cartridges, Inc., P.O. Box 178, Chehalis, WA 98532/360-736-0702
Garthwaite, Jim, Rt. 2, Box 310, Watsontown, PA 17777/717-538-1566
Gator Guns & Repair, 6255 Spur Hwy., Kenai, AK 99611/907-283-7947
Gaucher Armes, S.A., 46, rue Desjoyaux, 42000 Saint-Etienne, FRANCE/77 33 38 92; FAX: 77 61 95 72
G.B.C. Industries, Inc., P.O. Box 1602, Spring, TX 77373/713-350-9690; FAX: 713-350-0601
G.C.C.T., 4455 Torrance Blvd., Ste. 453, Torrance, CA 90509-2806
GDL Enterprises, 409 Le Gardeur, Slidell, LA 70460/504-649-0693
Gehmann, Walter (See Huntington Die Specialties)
Genco, P.O. Box 5704, Asheville, NC 28803
Genecco Gun Works, K., 10512 Lower Sacramento Rd., Stockton, CA 95210/209-951-0706
General Lead, Inc., 1022 Grand Ave., Phoenix, AZ 85007
Gene's Custom Guns, P.O. Box 10534, White Bear Lake, MN 55110/612-429-5105
Gentex Corp., 5 Tinkham Ave., Derry, NH 03038/603-434-0311; FAX: 603-434-3002
Gentner Bullets, 109 Woodlawn Ave., Upper Darby, PA 19082/610-352-9396
Gentry Custom Gunmaker, David, 314 N. Hoffman, Belgrade, MT 59714/406-388-GUNS
George & Roy's, 2950 NW 29th, Portland, OR 97210/503-228-5424, 800-553-3022; FAX: 503-225-9409
George, Tim, Rt. 1, P.O. Box 45, Evington, VA 24550/804-821-8117
Gerber Legendary Blades, 14200 SW 72nd Ave., Portland, OR 97223/503-639-6161, 800-950-6161; FAX: 503-684-7008

Gervais, Mike, 3804 S. Cruise Dr., Salt Lake City, UT 84109/801-277-7729
Getz Barrel Co., P.O. Box 88, Beavertown, PA 17813/717-658-7263
GFR Corp., P.O. Box 1439, New London, NH 03257-1439
G.G. & G., 3602 E. 42nd Stravenue, Tucson, AZ 85713/520-748-7167; FAX: 520-748-7583
G.H. Enterprises Ltd., Bag 10, Okotoks, Alberta T0L 1T0 CANADA/403-938-6070
Giacomo Sporting USA, 6234 Stokes Lee Center Rd., Lee Center, NY 13363
Gibbs Rifle Co., Inc., Cannon Hill Industrial Park, Rt. 2, Box 214 Hoffman, Rd./Martinsburg, WV 25401
304-274-0458; FAX: 304-274-0078
Gilbert Equipment Co., Inc., 960 Downtowner Rd., Mobile, AL 36609/205-344-3322
Gillmann, Edwin, 33 Valley View Dr., Hanover, PA 17331/717-632-1662
Gilman-Mayfield, Inc., 3279 E. Shields, Fresno, CA 93703/209-221-9415; FAX: 209-221-9419
Gilmore Sports Concepts, 5949 S. Garnett, Tulsa, OK 74146/918-250-4867; FAX: 918-250-3845
Giron, Robert E., 1328 Pocono St., Pittsburgh, PA 15218/412-731-6041
Glacier Glove, 4890 Aircenter Circle, Suite 210, Reno, NV 89502/702-825-8225; FAX: 702-825-6544
Glaser Safety Slug, Inc., P.O. Box 8223, Foster City, CA 94404-8223/800-221-3489, 415-345-7677; FAX: 415-345-8217
Glass, Herb, P.O. Box 25, Bullville, NY 10915/914-361-3021
Glimm, Jerome C., 19 S. Maryland, Conrad, MT 59425/406-278-3574
Glock GmbH, P.O. Box 50, A-2232 Deutsch Wagram, AUSTRIA (U.S. importer—Glock, Inc.)
Glock, Inc., P.O. Box 369, Smyrna, GA 30081/770-432-1202; FAX: 770-433-8719
GML Products, Inc., 394 Laredo Dr., Birmingham, AL 35226/205-979-4867
Gner's Hard Cast Bullets, 1107 11th St., LaGrande, OR 97850/503-963-8796
Goddard, Allen, 716 Medford Ave., Hayward, CA 94541/510-276-6830
Goens, Dale W., P.O. Box 224, Cedar Crest, NM 87008/505-281-5419
Goergen's Gun Shop, Inc., Rt. 2, Box 182BB, Austin, MN 55912/507-433-9280
GOEX, Inc., 1002 Springbrook Ave., Moosic, PA 18507/717-457-6724; FAX: 717-457-1130
Goldcoast Reloaders, Inc., 2421 NE 4th Ave., Pompano Beach, FL 33064/305-783-4849
Golden Age Arms Co., 115 E. High St., Ashley, OH 43003/614-747-2488
Golden Bear Bullets, 3065 Fairfax Ave., San Jose, CA 95148/408-238-9515
Gonic Arms, Inc., 134 Flagg Rd., Gonic, NH 03839/603-332-8456, 603-332-8457
Gonic Bullet Works, P.O. Box 7365, Gonic, NH 03839
Gonzalez Guns, Ramon B., P.O. Box 370, Monticello, NY 12701/914-794-4515
Goodling's Gunsmithing, R.D. 1, Box 1097, Spring Grove, PA 17362/717-225-3350
Goodwin, Fred, Silver Ridge Gun Shop, Sherman Mills, ME 04776/207-365-4451
Gordie's Gun Shop, 1401 Fulton St., Streator, IL 61364/815-672-7202
Gotz Bullets, 7313 Rogers St., Rockford, IL 61111
Goudy Classic Stocks, Gary, 263 Hedge Rd., Menlo Park, CA 94025-1711/415-322-1338
Gould & Goodrich, P.O. Box 1479, Lillington, NC 27546/910-893-2071; FAX: 910-893-4742
Gournet, Geoffroy, 820 Paxinosa Ave., Easton, PA 18042/215-559-0710
Gozon Corp., U.S.A., P.O. Box 6278, Folson, CA 95763/916-983-2026; FAX: 916-983-9500
Grace, Charles E., 6943 85.5 Rd., Trinchera, CO 81081/719-846-9435
Grace Metal Products, Inc., P.O. Box 67, Elk Rapids, MI 49629/616-264-8133
"Gramps" Antique Cartridges, Box 341, Washago, Ont. L0K 2B0 CANADA/705-689-5348
Grand Falls Bullets, Inc., P.O. Box 720, 803 Arnold Wallen Way, Stockton, MO 65785/816-229-0112
Granite Custom Bullets, Box 190, Philipsburg, MT 59858/406-859-3245
Grant, Howard V., Hiawatha 15, Woodruff, WI 54568/715-356-7146
Graphics Direct, P.O. Box 372421, Reseda, CA 91337-2421/818-344-9002
Graves Co., 1800 Andrews Ave., Pompano Beach, FL 33069/800-327-9103; FAX: 305-960-0301
Grayback Wildcats, 5306 Bryant Ave., Klamath Falls, OR 97603/541-884-1072
Graybill's Gun Shop, 1035 Ironville Pike, Columbia, PA 17512/717-684-2739
Great 870 Co., The, P.O. Box 6309, El Monte, CA 91734
Great American Gun Co., 3420 Industrial Drive, Yuba City, CA 95993/916-671-4570
Great Lakes Airguns, 6175 S. Park Ave., Hamburg, NY 14075/716-648-6666; FAX: 716-648-5279
Green, Arthur S., 485 S. Robertson Blvd., Beverly Hills, CA 90211/310-274-1283
Green Bay Bullets, 1638 Hazelwood Dr., Sobieski, WI 54171/414-826-7760
Green Genie, Box 114, Cusseta, GA 31805
Green Head Game Call Co., RR 1, Box 33, Lacon, IL 61540/309-246-2155
Green Mountain Rifle Barrel Co., Inc., P.O. Box 2670, 153 West Main St., Conway, NH 03818/603-447-1095; FAX: 603-447-1099
Green, Roger M., P.O. Box 984, 435 E. Birch, Glenrock, WY 82637/307-436-9804
Greene Precision Duplicators, M.L. Greene Engineering Services, P.O. Box, 1150/Golden, CO 80402-1150/303-279-2383
Greenwald, Leon E. "Bud", 2553 S. Quitman St., Denver, CO 80219/303-935-3850
Greenwood Precision, P.O. Box 468, Nixa, MO 65714-0468/417-725-2330
Greg Gunsmithing Repair, 3732 26th Ave. North, Robbinsdale, MN 55422/612-529-8103
Greg's Superior Products, P.O. Box 46219, Seattle, WA 98146
Greider Precision, 431 Santa Marina Ct., Escondido, CA 92029/619-480-8892
Gremmel Enterprises, 2111 Carriage Drive, Eugene, OR 97408-7537/541-302-3000
Grier's Hard Cast Bullets, 1107 11th St., LaGrande, OR 97850/503-963-8796
Griffin & Howe, Inc., 33 Claremont Rd., Bernardsville, NJ 07924/908-766-2287; FAX: 908-766-1068
Griffin & Howe, Inc., 36 W. 44th St., Suite 1011, New York, NY 10036/212-921-0980
Grifon, Inc., 58 Guinam St., Waltham, MS 02154
Grizzly Bullets, 322 Green Mountain Rd., Trout Creek, MT 59874/406-847-2627
Groenewold, John, P.O. Box 830, Mundelein, IL 60060/708-566-2365
Group Tight Bullets, 482 Comerwood Court, San Francisco, CA 94080/415-583-1550
GRS Corp., Glendo, P.O. Box 1153, 900 Overlander St., Emporia, KS 66801/316-343-1084, 800-835-3519
Grulla Armes, Apartado 453, Avda Otaloa, 12, Eiber, SPAIN (U.S. importer—American Arms, Inc.)
GSI, Inc., 108 Morrow Ave., P.O. Box 129, Trussville, AL 35173/205-655-8299; FAX: 205-655-7078
GSS Scheller (See U.S. importer—American Bullets)
GTM, 15915B E. Main St., La Puente, CA 91744
Guardsman Products, 411 N. Darling, Fremont, MI 49412/616-924-3950
Gun Accessories (See Glaser Safety Slug, Inc.)
Gun-Alert, 1010 N. Maclay Ave., San Fernando, CA 91340/818-365-0864; FAX: 818-365-1308
Gun City, 212 W. Main Ave., Bismarck, ND 58501/701-223-2304
Gun Doctor, The, 435 East Maple, Roselle, IL 60172/708-894-0668
Gun Doctor, The, P.O. Box 39242, Downey, CA 90242/310-862-3158
Gun-Ho Sports Cases, 110 E. 10th St., St. Paul, MN 55101/612-224-9491
Gun Hunter Books, Div. of Gun Hunter Trading Co., 5075 Heisig St., Beaumont, TX 77705/409-835-3006
Gun Leather Limited, 116 Lipscomb, Ft. Worth, TX 76104/817-334-0225; 800-247-0609
Gun List (See Krause Publications, Inc.)
Gun Locker, Div. of Airmold, W.R. Grace & Co.-Conn., Becker Farms Ind. Park,, P.O. Box 610/Roanoke Rapids, NC 27870/800-344-5716; FAX: 919-536-2201
Gun Parts Corp., The, 226 Williams Lane, West Hurley, NY 12491/914-679-2417; FAX: 914-679-5849
Gun Room, The, 1121 Burlington, Muncie, IN 47302/317-282-9073; FAX: 317-282-5270
Gun Room Press, The, 127 Raritan Ave., Highland Park, NJ 08904/908-545-4344; FAX: 908-545-6686
Gun Shop, The, 5550 S. 900 East, Salt Lake City, UT 84117/801-263-3633
Gun Shop, The, 62778 Spring Creek Rd., Montrose, CO 81401
Gun South, Inc. (See GSI, Inc.)
Gun-Tec, P.O. Box 8125, W. Palm Beach, FL 33407
Gun Works, The, 247 S. 2nd, Springfield, OR 97477/541-741-4118; FAX: 541-988-1097
Guncraft Books (See Guncraft Sports, Inc.)
Guncraft Sports, Inc., 10737 Dutchtown Rd., Knoxville, TN 37932/423-966-4545; FAX: 423-966-4500
Gunfitters, The, P.O. 426, Cambridge, WI 53523-0426/608-764-8128
Gunline Tools, 2950 Saturn St., Suite O, Brea, CA 92621/714-993-5100; FAX: 714-572-4128
Gunnerman Books, P.O. Box 214292, Auburn Hills, MI 48321/810-879-2779
Guns, 81 E. Streetsboro St., Hudson, OH 44236/216-650-4563
Guns Antique & Modern DBA/Charles E. Duffy, Williams Lane, West Hurley, NY 12491/914-679-2997
Guns, Div. of D.C. Engineering, Inc., 8633 Southfield Fwy., Detroit, MI 48228/313-271-7111, 800-886-7623 (orders only); FAX: 313-271-7112
GUNS Magazine, 591 Camino de la Reina, Suite 200, San Diego, CA 92108/619-297-5350; FAX: 619-297-5353
Gunsight, The, 1712 North Placentia Ave., Fullerton, CA 92631
Gunsite Custom Shop, P.O. Box 451, Paulden, AZ 86334/520-636-4104; FAX: 520-636-1236
Gunsite Gunsmithy (See Gunsite Custom Shop)
Gunsite Training Center, P.O. Box 700, Paulden, AZ 86334/520-636-4565; FAX: 520-636-1236
Gunsmith in Elk River, The, 14021 Victoria Lane, Elk River, MN 55330/612-441-7761
Gunsmithing, Inc., 208 West Buchanan St., Colorado Springs, CO 80907/719-632-3795; FAX: 719-632-3493
Gunsmithing Ltd., 57 Unquowa Rd., Fairfield, CT 06430/203-254-0436; FAX: 203-254-1535
Gurney, F.R., Box 13, Sooke, BC V0S 1N0 CANADA/604-642-5282: FAX: 604-642-7859
Gusdorf Corp., 11440 Lackland Rd., St. Louis, MO 63146/314-567-5249
Gusty Winds Corp., 2950 Bear St., Suite 120, Costa Mesa, CA 92626/714-536-3587
Gutmann Cutlery Inc., 1100 W. 45th Ave., Denver, CO 80211/303-433-6506
Gwinnell, Bryson J., P.O. Box 248C, Maple Hill Rd., Rochester, VT 05767/802-767-3664
GZ Paintball Sports Products (See GFR Corp.)

H

H&B Forge Co., Rt. 2 Geisinger Rd., Shiloh, OH 44878/419-895-1856
H&P Publishing, 7174 Hoffman Rd., San Angelo, TX 76905/915-655-5953
H&R 1871, Inc., 60 Industrial Rowe, Gardner, MA 01440/508-632-9393; FAX: 508-632-2300
H&S Liner Service, 515 E. 8th, Odessa, TX 79761/915-332-1021
Hafner Creations, Inc., P.O. Box 1987, Lake City, FL 32055/904-755-6481; FAX: 904-755-6595
Hagn Rifles & Actions, Martin, P.O. Box 444, Cranbrook, B.C. VIC 4H9, CANADA/604-489-4861
Hakko Co. Ltd., Daini-Tsunemi Bldg., 1-13-12, Narimasu, Itabashiku Tokyo 175, JAPAN/03-5997-7870/2; FAX: 81-3-5997-7840
Hale/Engraver, Peter, 800 E. Canyon Rd., Spanish Fork, UT 84660/801-798-8215
Half Moon Rifle Shop, 490 Halfmoon Rd., Columbia Falls, MT 59912/406-892-4409
Hall Manufacturing, 1801 Yellow Leaf Rd., Clanton, AL 35045/205-755-4094
Hall Plastics, Inc., John, P.O. Box 1526, Alvin, TX 77512/713-489-8709
Hallberg Gunsmith, Fritz, 33 S. Main, Payette, ID 83661/208-642-7157; FAX: 208-642-9643
Hallowell & Co., 340 W. Putnam Ave., Greenwich, CT 06830/203-869-2190; FAX: 203-869-0692
Hally Caller, 443 Wells Rd., Doylestown, PA 18901/215-345-6354
Halstead, Rick, RR4, Box 272, Miami, OK 74354/918-540-0933
Hamilton, Alex B. (See Ten-Ring Precision, Inc.)
Hamilton, Keith, P.O. Box 871, Gridley, CA 95948/916-846-2316
Hammans, Charles E., P.O. Box 788, 2022 McCracken, Stuttgart, AR 72106/501-673-1388
Hammerli USA, 19296 Oak Grove Circle, Groveland, CA 95321/209-962-5311; FAX: 209-962-5931
Hammerli Ltd., Seonerstrasse 37, CH-5600 Lenzburg, SWITZERLAND/064-50 11 44; FAX: 064-51 38 27 (U.S. importer—Hammerli USA)
Hammets VLD Bullets, P.O. Box 479, Rayville, LA 71269/318-728-2019
Hammond Custom Guns Ltd., Guy, 619 S. Pandora, Gilbert, AZ 85234/602-892-3437
Hammonds Rifles, RD 4, Box 504, Red Lion, PA 17356/717-244-7879
Handgun Press, P.O. Box 406, Glenview, IL 60025/847-657-6500; FAX: 847-724-8831
HandiCrafts Unltd. (See Clements' Custom Leathercraft, Chas)
Hands Engraving, Barry Lee, 26192 E. Shore Route, Bigfork, MT 59911/406-837-0035
Hank's Gun Shop, Box 370, 50 West 100 South, Monroe, UT 84754/801-527-4456
Hanned Line, The, P.O. Box 2387, Cupertino, CA 95015-2387
Hanned Precision (See Hanned Line, The)
Hansen & Co. (See Hansen Cartridge Co.)
Hansen Cartridge Co., 244-246 Old Post Rd., Southport, CT 06490/203-259-6222, 203-259-7337; FAX: 203-254-3832
Hanson's Gun Center, Dick, 233 Everett Dr., Colorado Springs, CO 80911
Hanusin, John, 3306 Commercial, Northbrook, IL 60062/708-564-2706
Hardin Specialty Dist., P.O. Box 338, Radcliff, KY 40159-0338/502-351-6649
Hardison, Charles, P.O. Box 356, 200 W. Baseline Rd., Lafayette, CO 80026-0356/303-666-5171
Harold's Custom Gun Shop, Inc., Broughton Rifle Barrels, Rt. 1, Box 447, Big Spring, TX 79720/915-394-4430
Harper, William E. (See Great 870 Co., The)
Harper's Custom Stocks, 928 Lombrano St., San Antonio, TX 78207/512-732-5780
Harrell's Precision, 5756 Hickory Dr., Salem, VA 24133/703-380-2683
Harrington & Richardson (See H&R 1871, Inc.)
Harrington Cutlery, Inc., Russell, Subs. of Hyde Mfg. Co., 44 River St., Southbridge, MA 01550/617-765-0201
Harris Engineering, Inc., Rt. 1, Barlow, KY 42024/502-334-3633; FAX: 502-334-3000
Harris Enterprises, P.O. Box 105, Bly, OR 97622/503-353-2625
Harris Gunworks, 3840 N. 28th Ave., Phoenix, AZ 85017-4733/602-230-1414; FAX: 602-230-1422
Harris Hand Engraving, Paul A., 10630 Janet Lee, San Antonio, TX 78230/512-391-5121
Harris Publications, 1115 Broadway, New York, NY 10010/212-807-7100; FAX: 212-627-4678
Harrison Bullets, 6437 E. Hobart St., Mesa, AZ 85205
Harrison-Hurtz Enterprises, Inc., P.O. Box 268, RR1, Wymore, NE 68466/402-645-3378; FAX: 402-645-3606
Hart & Son, Inc., Robert W., 401 Montgomery St., Nescopeck, PA 18635/717-752-3655, 800-368-3656; FAX: 717-752-1088
Hart Rifle Barrels, Inc., P.O. Box 182, 1690 Apulia Rd., Lafayette, NY 13084/315-677-9841; FAX: 315-677-9610
Hartford (See U.S. importer— EMF Co., Inc.)
Hartmann & Weiss GmbH, Rahlstedter Bahnhofstr. 47, 22143 Hamburg, GERMANY/(40) 677 55 85; FAX: (40) 677 55 92
Harvey, Frank, 218 Nightfall, Terrace, NV 89015/702-558-6998
Harwood, Jack O., 1191 S. Pendlebury Lane, Blackfoot, ID 83221/208-785-5368
Haselbauer Products, Jerry, P.O. Box 27629, Tucson, AZ 85726/602-792-1075
Hastings Barrels, 320 Court St., Clay Center, KS 67432/913-632-3169; FAX: 913-632-6554
Hatfield Gun Co., Inc., 224 N. 4th St., St. Joseph, MO 64501/816-279-8688; FAX: 816-279-2716
Hawk, Inc., 849 Hawks Bridge Rd., Salem, NJ 08079/609-299-2700; FAX: 609-299-2800
Hawk Laboratories, Inc. (See Hawk, Inc.)
Hawken Shop, The (See Dayton Traister)
Haydel's Game Calls, Inc., 5018 Hazel Jones Rd., Bossier City, LA 71111/318-746-3586, 800-HAYDELS; FAX: 318-746-3711
Haydon Shooters' Supply, Russ, 15018 Goodrich Dr. NW, Gig Harbor, WA 98329/206-857-7557
Heatbath Corp., P.O. Box 2978, Springfield, MA 01101/413-543-3381
Hebard Guns, Gil, 125-129 Public Square, Knoxville, IL 61448
HEBB Resources, P.O. Box 999, Mead, WA 99021-09996/509-466-1292
Hecht, Hubert J., Waffen-Hecht, P.O. Box 2635, Fair Oaks, CA 95628/916-966-1020
Heckler & Koch GmbH, P.O. Box 1329, 78722 Oberndorf, Neckar, GERMANY/49-7423179-0; FAX: 49-7423179-2406 (U.S. importer—Heckler & Koch, Inc.)
Heckler & Koch, Inc., 21480 Pacific Blvd., Sterling, VA 20166-8903/703-450-1900; FAX: 703-450-8160
Hege Jagd-u. Sporthandels, GmbH, P.O. Box 101461, W-7770 Ueberlingen a. Bodensee, GERMANY
Heidenstrom Bullets, Urds GT 1 Heroya, 3900 Porsgrunn, NORWAY
Heilmann, Stephen, P.O. Box 657, Grass Valley, CA 95945/916-272-8758
Heinie Specialty Products, 301 Oak St., Quincy, IL 62301-2500/309-543-4535; FAX: 309-543-2521
Heintz, David, 800 N. Hwy. 17, Moffat, CO 81143/719-256-4194
Hellweg Ltd., 40356 Oak Park Way, Suite H, Oakhurst, CA 93644/209-683-3030; FAX: 209-683-3422
Helwan (See U.S. importer—Interarms)
Henckels Zwillingswerk, Inc., J.A., 9 Skyline Dr., Hawthorne, NY 10532/914-592-7370
Hendricks, Frank E., Master Engravers, Inc., HC03, Box 434, Dripping Springs, TX 78620/512-858-7828
Hendricks Gun Works, 1162 Gillionville Rd., Albany, GA 31707/912-439-2003
Henigson & Associates, Steve, 2049 Kerwood Ave., Los Angeles, CA 90025/213-305-8288
Henriksen Tool Co., Inc., 8515 Wagner Creek Rd., Talent, OR 97540/541-535-2309
Hensler, Jerry, 6614 Country Field, San Antonio, TX 78240/210-690-7491
Hensley & Gibbs, Box 10, Murphy, OR 97533/541-862-2341
Hensley, Darwin, P.O. Box 329, Brightwood, OR 97011/503-622-5411
Heppler, Keith M., Keith's Custom Gunstocks, 540 Banyan Circle, Walnut Creek, CA 94598/510-934-3509; FAX: 510-934-3143
Heppler's Machining, 2240 Calle Del Mundo, Santa Clara, CA 95054/408-748-9166; FAX: 408-988-7711
Hercules, Inc. (See Alliant Techsystems, Smokeless Powder Group)
Heritage Firearms (See Heritage Manufacturing, Inc.)
Heritage Manufacturing, Inc., 4600 NW 135th St., Opa Locka, FL 33054/305-685-5966; FAX: 305-687-6721
Heritage/VSP Gun Books, P.O. Box 887, McCall, ID 83638/208-634-4104; FAX: 208-634-3101
Hermann Leather Co., H.J., Rt. 1, P.O. Box 525, Skiatook, OK 74070/918-396-1226
Herrett's Stocks, Inc., P.O. Box 741, Twin Falls, ID 83303/208-733-1498
Hertel & Reuss, Werk für Optik und Feinmechanik GmbH, Quellhofstrabe, 67/34 127 Kassel, GERMANY
0561-83006; FAX: 0561-893308
Herter's Manufacturing, Inc., 111 E. Burnett St., P.O. Box 518, Beaver Dam, WI 53916/414-887-1765; FAX: 414-887-8444
Hesco-Meprolight, 2139 Greenville Rd., LaGrange, GA 30240/706-884-7967; FAX: 706-882-4683
Heydenberk, Warren R., 1059 W. Sawmill Rd., Quakertown, PA 18951/215-538-2682
Heym GmbH & Co. KG, Friedrich Wilh, Coburger Str.8, D-97702 Muennerstadt, GERMANY
Hi-Grade Imports, 8655 Monterey Rd., Gilroy, CA 95021/408-842-9301; FAX: 408-842-2374
Hi-Point Firearms, 5990 Philadelphia Dr., Dayton, OH 45415/513-275-4991; FAX: 513-522-8330
Hickman, Jaclyn, Box 1900, Glenrock, WY 82637
Hidalgo, Tony, 12701 SW 9th Pl., Davie, FL 33325/305-476-7645
High Bridge Arms, Inc., 3185 Mission St., San Francisco, CA 94110/415-282-8358
High North Products, Inc., P.O. Box 2, Antigo, WI 54409/715-627-2331
High Performance International, 5734 W. Florist Ave., Milwaukee, WI 53218/414-466-9040
High Standard Mfg. Co., Inc., 4601 S. Pinemont, 148-B, Houston, TX 77041/713-462-4200; FAX: 713-462-6437
High Tech Specialties, Inc., P.O. Box 387R, Adamstown, PA 19501/215-484-0405, 800-231-9385
Highline Machine Co., 654 Lela Place, Grand Junction, CO 81504/970-434-4971
Hill, Loring F., 304 Cedar Rd., Elkins Park, PA 19117

Hill Speed Leather, Ernie, 4507 N. 195th Ave., Litchfield Park, AZ 85340/602-853-9222; FAX: 602-853-9235
Hillmer Custom Gunstocks, Paul D., 7251 Hudson Heights, Hudson, IA 50643/319-988-3941
Hinman Outfitters, Bob, 1217 W. Glen, Peoria, IL 61614/309-691-8132
Hiptmayer, Armurier, RR 112 750, P.O. Box 136, Eastman, Quebec JOE 1P0, CANADA/514-297-2492
Hiptmayer, Heidemarie, RR 112 750, P.O. Box 136, Eastman, Quebec J0E 1PO, CANADA/514-297-2492
Hiptmayer, Klaus, RR 112 750, P.O. Box 136, Eastman, Quebec J0E 1P0, CANADA/514-297-2492
Hirtenberger Aktiengesellschaft, Leobersdorferstrasse 31, A-2552 Hirtenberg, AUSTRIA/43(0)2256 81184; FAX: 43(0)2256 81807
HiTek International, 484 El Camino Real, Redwood City, CA 94063/415-363-1404, 800-54-NIGHT; FAX: 415-363-1408
Hiti-Schuch, Atelier Wilma, A-8863 Predlitz, Pirming Y1 AUSTRIA/0353418278
HJS Arms, Inc., P.O. Box 3711, Brownsville, TX 78523-3711/800-453-2767, 210-542-2767
H.K.S. Products, 7841 Founion Dr., Florence, KY 41042/606-342-7841, 800-354-9814; FAX: 606-342-5865
Hoag, James W., 8523 Canoga Ave., Suite C, Canoga Park, CA 91304/818-998-1510
Hobbie Gunsmithing, Duane A., 2412 Pattie Ave., Wichita, KS 67216/316-264-8266
Hobson Precision Mfg. Co., Rt. 1, Box 220-C, Brent, AL 35034/205-926-4662
Hoch Custom Bullet Moulds (See Colorado Shooter's Supply)
Hodgdon Powder Co., Inc., P.O. Box 2932, 6231 Robinson, Shawnee Mission, KS 66202/913-362-9455; FAX: 913-362-1307; WEB: http://www.unicom.net/hpc
Hodgman, Inc., 1750 Orchard Rd., Montgomery, IL 60538/708-897-7555; FAX: 708-897-7558
Hodgson, Richard, 9081 Tahoe Lane, Boulder, CO 80301
Hoehn Sales, Inc., 75 Greensburg Ct., St. Charles, MO 63304/314-441-4231
Hoelscher, Virgil, 11047 Pope Ave., Lynwood, CA 90262/310-631-8545
Hoenig & Rodman, 6521 Morton Dr., Boise, ID 83704/208-375-1116
Hofer Jagdwaffen, P., Buchsenmachermeister, Kirchgasse 24, A-9170 Ferlach, AUSTRIA/04227-3683
Hoffman New Ideas, 821 Northmoor Rd., Lake Forest, IL 60045/312-234-4075
Hogue Grips, P.O. Box 1138, Paso Robles, CA 93447/800-438-4747, 805-239-1440; FAX: 805-239-2553
Holland & Holland Ltd., 33 Bruton St., London, ENGLAND 1W1/44-171-499-4411; FAX: 44-171-408-7962
Holland, Dick, 422 NE 6th St., Newport, OR 97365/503-265-7556
Holland's, Box 69, Powers, OR 97466/503-439-5155; FAX: 503-439-5155
Hollis Gun Shop, 917 Rex St., Carlsbad, NM 88220/505-885-3782
Hollywood Engineering, 10642 Arminta St., Sun Valley, CA 91352/818-842-8376
Holster Shop, The, 720 N. Flagler Dr., Ft. Lauderdale, FL 33304/305-463-7910; FAX: 305-761-1483
Homak Mfg. Co., Inc., 3800 W. 45th St., Chicago, IL 60632/312-523-3100, FAX: 312-523-9455
Home Shop Machinist, The, Village Press Publications, P.O. Box 1810, Traverse City, MI 49685/800-447-7367; FAX: 616-946-3289
Hondo Ind., 510 S. 52nd St.,I04, Tempe, AZ 85281
Hoover, Harvey, 5750 Pearl Dr., Paradise, CA 95969-4829
Hoppe's Div., Penguin Industries, Inc., Airport Industrial Mall, Coatesville, PA 19320/610-384-6000
Horizons Unlimited, P.O. Box 426, Warm Springs, GA 31830/706-655-3603; FAX: 706-655-3603
Hornady Mfg. Co., P.O. Box 1848, Grand Island, NE 68802/800-338-3220, 308-382-1390; FAX: 308-382-5761
Horseshoe Leather Products, Andy Arratoonian, The Cottage Sharow, Ripon HG4 5BP ENGLAND/44-1765-605858
Horst, Alan K., 3221 2nd Ave. N., Great Falls, MT 59401/406-454-1831
Horton Dist. Co., Inc., Lew, 15 Walkup Dr., Westboro, MA 01581/508-366-7400; FAX: 508-366-5332
House of Muskets, Inc., The, P.O. Box 4640, Pagosa Springs, CO 81157/303-731-2295
Houtz & Barwick, P.O. Box 435, W. Church St., Elizabeth City, NC 27909/800-775-0337, 919-335-4191; FAX: 919-335-1152
Howa Machinery, Ltd., Sukaguchi, Shinkawa-cho, Nishikasugai-gun, Aichi 452, JAPAN (U.S. importer—Interarms)
Howell Machine, 815$^1/_2$ D St., Lewiston, ID 83501/208-743-7418
Hoyt Holster Co., Inc., P.O. Box 69, Coupeville, WA 98239-0069/360-678-6640; FAX: 360-678-6549
H-S Precision, Inc., 1301 Turbine Dr., Rapid City, SD 57701/605-341-3006; FAX: 605-342-8964
HT Bullets, 244 Belleville Rd., New Bedford, MA 02745/508-999-3338
Hubertus Schneidwarenfabrik, P.O. Box 180 106, D-42626 Solingen, GERMANY/01149-212-59-19-94: FAX: 01149-212-59-19-92
Huebner, Corey O., P.O. Box 2074, Missoula, MT 59806-2074/406-721-7168
Huey Gun Cases, P.O. Box 22456, Kansas City, MO 64113/816-444-1637; FAX: 816-444-1637
Hugger Hooks Co., 3900 Easley Way, Golden, CO 80403/303-279-0600
Hughes, Steven Dodd, P.O. Box 545, Livingston, MT 59047/406-222-9377
Hume, Don, P.O. Box 351, Miami, OK 74355/918-542-6604; FAX: 918-542-4340
Hungry Horse Books, 4605 Hwy. 93 South, Whitefish, MT 59937/406-862-7997
Hunkeler, A. (See Buckskin Machine Works)
Hunter Co., Inc., 3300 W. 71st Ave., Westminster, CO 80030/303-427-4626; FAX: 303-428-3980
Hunter's Specialties, Inc., 6000 Huntington Ct. NE, Cedar Rapids, IA 52402-1268/319-395-0321; FAX: 319-395-0326
Hunterjohn, P.O. Box 477, St. Louis, MO 63166/314-531-7250
Hunting Classics Ltd., P.O. Box 2089, Gastonia, NC 28053/704-867-1307; FAX: 704-867-0491
Huntington Die Specialties, 601 Oro Dam Blvd., Oroville, CA 95965/916-534-1210; FAX: 916-534-1212
Hydrosorbent Products, P.O. Box 437, Ashley Falls, MA 01222/413-229-2967; FAX: 413-229-8743
Hyper-Single, Inc., 520 E. Beaver, Jenks, OK 74037/918-299-2391

I

I.A.B. (See U.S. importer—Taylor's & Co., Inc.)
IAI, 6226 Santos Diaz St., Irwindale, CA 91702/818-334-1200
IAR, Inc., 33171 Camino Capistrano, San Juan Capistrano, CA 92675/714-443-3642; FAX: 714-443-3647
Ibberson (Sheffield) Ltd., George, 25-31 Allen St., Sheffield, S3 7AW ENGLAND/0114-2766123; FAX: 0114-2738465
ICI-America, P.O. Box 751, Wilmington, DE 19897/302-575-3000
Idaho Ammunition Service, 2816 Mayfair Dr., Lewiston, ID 83501/208-743-0270; FAX: 208-743-4930
IGA (See U.S. importer—Stoeger Industries)
Illinois Lead Shop, 7742 W. 61st Place, Summit, IL 60501
IMI, P.O. Box 1044, Ramat Hasharon 47100, ISRAEL/972-3-5485222
IMI Services USA, Inc., 2 Wisconsin Circle, Suite 420, Chevy Chase, MD 20815/301-215-4800; FAX: 301-657-1446
Impact Case Co., P.O. Box 9912, Spokane, WA 99209-0912/800-262-3322, 509-467-3303; FAX: 509-326-5436
Imperial (See E-Z-Way Systems)
Imperial Magnum Corp., P.O. Box 249, Oroville, WA 98844/604-495-3131; FAX: 604-495-2816
Imperial Schrade Corp., 7 Schrade Ct., Box 7000, Ellenville, NY 12428/914-647-7601; FAX: 914-647-8701
Import Sports Inc., 1750 Brielle Ave., Unit B1, Wanamassa, NJ 07712/908-493-0302; FAX: 908-493-0301
IMR Powder Co., 1080 Military Turnpike, Suite 2, Plattsburgh, NY 12901/518-563-2253; FAX: 518-563-6916
I.N.C., Inc. (See Kick Eez)
Independent Machine & Gun Shop, 1416 N. Hayes, Pocatello, ID 83201
Info-Arm, P.O. Box 1262, Champlain, NY 12919
Ingle, Ralph W., 4 Missing Link, Rossville, GA 30741/404-866-5589
Innovative Weaponry, Inc., 337 Eubank NE, Albuquerque, NM 87123/800-334-3573, 505-296-4645; FAX: 505-271-2633
Innovision Enterprises, 728 Skinner Dr., Kalamazoo, MI 49001/616-382-1681; FAX: 616-382-1830
INTEC International, Inc., P.O. Box 5708, Scottsdale, AZ 85261/602-483-1708
Interarms, 10 Prince St., Alexandria, VA 22314/703-548-1400; FAX: 703-549-7826
Intercontinental Munitions Distributors, Ltd., P.O. Box 815, Beulah, ND 58523/701-948-2260; FAX: 701-948-2282
Intermountain Arms & Tackle, Inc., 1375 E. Fairview Ave., Meridian, ID 83642-1816/208-888-4911; FAX: 208-888-4381
International Shooters Service (See I.S.S.)
Intratec, 12405 SW 130th St., Miami, FL 33186/305-232-1821; FAX: 305-253-7207
Iosso Products, 1485 Lively Blvd., Elk Grove Village, IL 60007/708-437-8400; FAX: 708-437-8478
Iron Bench, 12619 Bailey Rd., Redding, CA 96003/916-241-4623
Iron Mountain Knife Co., P.O. Box 2146, Sparks, NV 89432-2146/702-356-3632; FAX: 702-356-3640
Ironside International Publishers, Inc., P.O. Box 55, 800 Slaters Lane, Alexandria, VA 22313/703-684-6111; FAX: 703-683-5486
Ironsighter Co., P.O. Box 85070, Westland, MI 48185/313-326-8731; FAX: 313-326-3378
Irwin, Campbell H., 140 Hartland Blvd., East Hartland, CT 06027/203-653-3901
Irwindale Arms, Inc. (See IAI)
Island Pond Gun Shop (See Costa, David)
Israel Military Industries Ltd. (See IMI)
I.S.S., P.O. Box 185234, Ft. Worth, TX 76181/817-595-2090
I.S.W., 106 E. Cairo Dr., Tempe, AZ 85282
I.T.S. (See U.S. importer—County Arms)
Ivanoff, Thomas G. (See Tom's Gun Repair)

J

J-4, Inc., 1700 Via Burton, Anaheim, CA 92806/714-254-8315; FAX: 714-956-4421
J&D Components, 75 East 350 North, Orem, UT 84057-4719/801-225-7007
J&J Products, Inc., 9240 Whitmore, El Monte, CA 91731/818-571-5228, 800-927-8361; FAX: 818-571-8704
J&J Sales, 1501 21st Ave. S., Great Falls, MT 59405/406-453-7549

J&L Superior Bullets (See Huntington Die Specialties)
J&R Engineering, P.O. Box 77, 200 Lyons Hill Rd., Athol, MA 01331/508-249-9241
J&R Enterprises, 4550 Scotts Valley Rd., Lakeport, CA 95453
J&S Heat Treat, 803 S. 16th St., Blue Springs, MO 64015/816-229-2149; FAX: 816-228-1135
J.A. Blades, Inc. (See Christopher Firearms Co., Inc., E.)
Jackalope Gun Shop, 1048 S. 5th St., Douglas, WY 82633/307-358-3441
Jaeger, Paul, Inc./Dunn's, P.O. Box 449, 1 Madison Ave., Grand Junction, TN 38039/901-764-6909; FAX: 901-764-6503
JagerSport, Ltd., One Wholesale Way, Cranston, RI 02920/800-962-4867, 401-944-9682; FAX: 401-946-2587
Jamison's Forge Works, 4527 Rd. 6.5 NE, Moses Lake, WA 98837/509-762-2659
Jansma, Jack J. (See Wingshooters, Ltd.)
Jantz Supply, P.O. Box 584-GD, Davis, OK 73030-0584/405-369-2316; FAX: 405-369-3082
Jarrett Rifles, Inc., 383 Brown Rd., Jackson, SC 29831/803-471-3616
Jarvis, Inc., 1123 Cherry Orchard Lane, Hamilton, MT 59840/406-961-4392
JAS, Inc., P.O. Box 0, Rosemount, MN 55068/612-890-7631
Javelina Lube Products, P.O. Box 337, San Bernardino, CA 92402/714-882-5847; FAX: 714-434-6937
J/B Adventures & Safaris, Inc., 2275 E. Arapahoe Rd. Ste. 109, Littleton, CO 80122-1521/303-771-0977
J-B Bore Cleaner, 299 Poplar St., Hamburg, PA 19526/610-562-2103
JBM, P.O. Box 3648, University Park, NM 88003
Jeffredo Gunsight, P.O. Box 669, San Marcos, CA 92079/619-728-2695
Jenco Sales, Inc., P.O. Box 1000, Manchaca, TX 78652/800-531-5301; FAX: 800-266-2373
Jenkins Recoil Pads, Inc., 5438 E. Frontage Ln., Olney, IL 62450/618-395-3416
Jennings Firearms, Inc., 17692 Cowan, Irvine, CA 92714/714-252-7621; FAX: 714-252-7626
Jensen Bullets, 86 North, 400 West, Blackfoot, ID 83221/208-785-5590
Jensen's Custom Ammunition, 5146 E. Pima, Tucson, AZ 85712/602-325-3346; FAX: 602-322-5704
Jensen's Firearms Academy, 1280 W. Prince, Tucson, AZ 85705/602-293-8516
Jester Bullets, Rt. 1 Box 27, Orienta, OK 73737
Jewell, Arnold W., 1490 Whitewater Rd., New Braunfels, TX 78132/210-620-0971
J-Gar Co., 183 Turnpike Rd., Dept. 3, Petersham, MA 01366-9604
JGS Precision Tool Mfg., 1141 S. Summer Rd., Coos Bay, OR 97420/503-267-4331; FAX:503-267-5996
Jim's Gun Shop (See Spradlin's)
Jim's Precision, Jim Ketchum, 1725 Moclips Dr., Petaluma, CA 94952/707-762-3014
J.I.T., Ltd., P.O. Box 230, Freedom, WY 83120/708-494-0937
JLK Bullets, 414 Turner Rd., Dover, AR 72837/501-331-4194
J.O. Arms Inc., 5709 Hartsdale, Houston, TX 77036/713-789-0745; FAX: 713-789-7513
Johanssons Vapentillbehor, Bert, S-430 20 Veddige, SWEDEN
John's Custom Leather, 523 S. Liberty St., Blairsville, PA 15717/412-459-6802
Johns Master Engraver, Bill, RR 4, Box 220, Fredericksburg, TX 78624-9545/210-997-6795
Johnson's Gunsmithing, Inc., Neal, 208 W. Buchanan St., Suite B, Colorado Springs, CO 80907/800-284-8671 (orders), 719-632-3795; FAX: 719-632-3493
Johnson Wood Products, RR 1, Strawberry Point, IA 52076/319-933-4930
Johnson's Lage Uniwad, P.O. Box 2302, Davenport, IA 52809/319-388-LAGE
Johnston Bros., 1889 Rt. 9, Unit 22, Toms River, NJ 08755/800-257-2595; FAX: 800-257-2534
Johnston, James (See North Fork Custom Gunsmithing)
Jonad Corp., 2091 Lakeland Ave., Lakewood, OH 44107/216-226-3161
Jonas Appraisals & Taxidermy, Jack, 1675 S. Birch, Suite 506, Denver, CO 80222/303-757-7347: FAX: 303-639-9655
Jones Co., Dale, 680 Hoffman Draw, Kila, MT 59920/406-755-4684
Jones Custom Products, Neil A., 17217 Brookhouser Road, Saegertown, PA 16433/814-763-2769; FAX: 814-763-4228
Jones Moulds, Paul, 4901 Telegraph Rd., Los Angeles, CA 90022/213-262-1510
Jones, J.D. (See SSK Industries)
Joy Enterprises (See Fury Cutlery)
J.P. Enterprises, Inc., P.O. Box 26324, Shoreview, MN 55126/612-486-9064; FAX: 612-482-0970
J.P. Gunstocks, Inc., 4508 San Miguel Ave., North Las Vegas, NV 89030/702-645-0718
JP Sales, Box 307, Anderson, TX 77830
JRP Custom Bullets, RR2-2233 Carlton Rd., Whitehall, NY 12887/802-438-5548 (p.m.), 518-282-0084 (a.m.)
JRW, 2425 Taffy Ct., Nampa, ID 83687
JS Worldwide DBA (See Coonan Arms)
Juenke, Vern, 25 Bitterbush Rd., Reno, NV 89523/702-345-0225
Jumbo Sports Products (See Bucheimer, J.M.)
Jungkind, Reeves C., 5001 Buckskin Pass, Austin, TX 78745-2841/512-442-1094
Jurras, L.E., P.O. Box 680, Washington, IN 47501/812-254-7698
JWH: Software, 6947 Haggerty Rd., Hillsboro, OH 45133/513-393-2402

K

K&M Industries, Inc., Box 66, 510 S. Main, Troy, ID 83871/208-835-2281; FAX: 208-835-5211
K&M Services, 5430 Salmon Run Rd., Dover, PA 17315/717-764-1461
K&P Gun Co., 1024 Central Ave., New Rockford, ND 58356/701-947-2248
K&S Mfg., 2611 Hwy. 40 East, Inglis, FL 34449/904-447-3571
K&T Co., Div. of T&S Industries, Inc., 1027 Skyview Dr., W. Carrollton, OH 45449/513-859-8414
KA-BAR Knives, 31100 Solon Rd., Solon, OH 44139/216-248-7000; 800-321-9316, ext. 329; FAX: 216-248-8651
Kahles, A Swarovski Company, 1 Wholesale Way, Cranston, RI 02920-5540/800-426-3089: FAX: 401-946-2587
Kahnke Gunworks, 206 West 11th St., Redwood Falls, MN 56283/507-637-2901
Kahr Arms, P.O. Box 220, 630 Route 303, Blauvelt, NY 10913/914-353-5996; FAX: 914-353-7833
Kalispel Case Line, P.O. Box 267, Cusick, WA 99119/509-445-1121
Kamik Outdoor Footwear, 554 Montee de Liesse, Montreal, Quebec, H4T 1P1 CANADA/514-341-3950; FAX: 514-341-1861
Kamyk Engraving Co., Steve, 9 Grandview Dr., Westfield, MA 01085-1810/413-568-0457
Kandel, P.O. Box 4529, Portland, OR 97208
Kane, Edward, P.O. Box 385, Ukiah, CA 95482/707-462-2937
Kane Products, Inc., 5572 Brecksville Rd., Cleveland, OH 44131/216-524-9962
Ka Pu Kapili, P.O. Box 745, Honokaa, HI 96727/808-776-1644; FAX: 808-776-1731
Kapro Mfg. Co., Inc. (See R.E.I.)
Kasenit Co., Inc., 13 Park Ave., Highland Mills, NY 10930/914-928-9595; FAX: 914-928-7292
Kasmarsik Bullets, 152 Crstler Rd., Chehalis, WA 98532
Kaswer Custom, Inc., 13 Surrey Drive, Brookfield, CT 06804/203-775-0564; FAX: 203-775-6872
K.B.I., Inc., P.O. Box 5440, Harrisburg, PA 17110-0440/717-540-8518; FAX: 717-540-8567
K-D, Inc., Box 459, 585 N. Hwy. 155, Cleveland, UT 84518/801-653-2530
KDF, Inc., 2485 Hwy. 46 N., Seguin, TX 78155/210-379-8141; FAX: 210-379-5420
KeeCo Impressions, Inc., 346 Wood Ave., North Brunswick, NJ 08902/800-468-0546
Keeler, R.H., 817 "N" St., Port Angeles, WA 98362/206-457-4702
Kehr, Roger, 2131 Agate Ct. SE, Lacy, WA 98503/360-456-0831
Keith's Bullets, 942 Twisted Oak, Algonquin, IL 60102/708-658-3520
Keith's Custom Gunstocks (See Heppler, Keith M.)
Kelbly, Inc., 7222 Dalton Fox Lake Rd., North Lawrence, OH 44666/216-683-4674; FAX: 216-683-7349
Keller Co., The, 4215 McEwen Rd., Dallas, TX 75244/214-770-8585
Kelley's, P.O. Box 125, Woburn, MA 01801/617-935-3389
Kellogg's Professional Products, 325 Pearl St., Sandusky, OH 44870/419-625-6551; FAX: 419-625-6167
Kelly, Lance, 1723 Willow Oak Dr., Edgewater, FL 32132/904-423-4933
Kel-Tec CNC Industries, Inc., P.O. Box 3427, Cocoa, FL 32924/407-631-0068; FAX: 407-631-1169
Ken's Gun Specialties, Rt. 1, Box 147, Lakeview, AR 72642/501-431-5606
Ken's Kustom Kartridges, 331 Jacobs Rd., Hubbard, OH 44425/216-534-4595
Ken's Rifle Blanks, Ken McCullough, Rt. 2, P.O. Box 85B, Weston, OR 97886/503-566-3879
Keng's Firearms Specialty, Inc., P.O. Box 44405, 875 Wharton Dr. SW, Atlanta, GA 30336/404-691-7611: FAX: 404-505-8445
Kennebec Journal, 274 Western Ave., Augusta, ME 04330/207-622-6288
Kennedy Firearms, 10 N. Market St., Muncy, PA 17756/717-546-6695
KenPatable Ent., Inc., P.O. Box 19422, Louisville, KY 40259/502-239-5447
Kent Cartridge Mfg. Co. Ltd., Unit 16, Branbridges Industrial Estate, East, Peckham/Tonbridge, Kent, TN12 5HF ENGLAND
622-872255; FAX: 622-872645
Keowee Game Calls, 608 Hwy. 25 North, Travelers Rest, SC 29690/803-834-7204
Kershaw Knives, 25300 SW Parkway Ave., Wilsonville, OR 97070/503-682-1966, 800-325-2891; FAX: 503-682-7168
Kesselring Gun Shop, 400 Hwy. 99 North, Burlington, WA 98233/206-724-3113; FAX: 206-724-7003
Ketchum, Jim (See Jim's Precision)
Kick Eez, P.O. Box 12767, Wichita, KS 67277/316-721-9570; FAX: 316-721-5260
Kilham & Co., Main St., P.O. Box 37, Lyme, NH 03768/603-795-4112
Kimball, Gary, 1526 N. Circle Dr., Colorado Springs, CO 80909/719-634-1274
Kimber of America, Inc., 9039 SE Jannsen Rd., Clackamas, OR 97015/503-656-1704, 800-880-2418; FAX: 503-656-5357
Kimel Industries (See A.A. Arms, Inc.)
King & Co., P.O. Box 1242, Bloomington, IL 61702/309-473-3964
King's Gun Works, 1837 W. Glenoaks Blvd., Glendale, CA 91201/818-956-6010; FAX: 818-548-8606
Kingyon, Paul L. (See Custom Calls)
Kirk Game Calls, Inc., Dennis, RD1, Box 184, Laurens, NY 13796/607-433-2710; FAX: 607-433-2711
Kirkpatrick Leather Co., 1910 San Bernardo, Laredo, TX 78040/210-723-6631; FAX: 210-725-0672
KJM Fabritek, Inc., P.O. Box 162, Marietta, GA 30061/404-426-8251
KK Air International (See Impact Case Co.)

K.K. Arms Co., Star Route Box 671, Kerrville, TX 78028/210-257-4718; FAX: 210-257-4891
KLA Enterprises, P.O. Box 2028, Eaton Park, FL 33840/941-682-2829; FAX: 941-682-2829
Kleen-Bore, Inc., 16 Industrial Pkwy., Easthampton, MA 01027/413-527-0300; FAX: 413-527-2522
Klein Custom Guns, Don, 433 Murray Park Dr., Ripon, WI 54971/414-748-2931
Kleinendorst, K.W., RR 1, Box 1500, Hop Bottom, PA 18824/717-289-4687
Klingler Woodcarving, P.O. Box 141, Thistle Hill, Cabot, VT 05647/802-426-3811
Kmount, P.O. Box 19422, Louisville, KY 40259/502-239-5447
Kneiper, James, P.O. Box 1516, Basalt, CO 81621-1516/303-963-9880
Knife Importers, Inc., P.O. Box 1000, Manchaca, TX 78652/512-282-6860
Knight & Hale Game Calls, Box 468 Industrial Park, Cadiz, KY 42211/502-924-1755; FAX: 502-924-1763
Knight Rifles (See Modern MuzzleLoading, Inc.)
Knight's Mfg. Co., 7750 9th St. SW, Vero Beach, FL 32968/407-562-5697; FAX: 407-569-2955
Knippel, Richard, 500 Gayle Ave, Apt. 213, Modesto, CA 95350-4241/209-869-1469
Knock on Wood Antiques, 355 Post Rd., Darien, CT 06820/203-655-9031
Knoell, Doug, 9737 McCardle Way, Santee, CA 92071
Kodiak Custom Bullets, 8261 Henry Circle, Anchorage, AK 99507/907-349-2282
Koevenig's Engraving Service, Box 55 Rabbit Gulch, Hill City, SD 57745
KOGOT, 410 College, Trinidad, CO 81082/719-846-9406
Kokolus, Michael M. (See Custom Riflestocks, Inc.)
Kolpin Mfg., Inc., P.O. Box 107, 205 Depot St., Fox Lake, WI 53933/414-928-3118; FAX: 414-928-3687
Kongsberg America L.L.C., P.O. Box 252, Fairfield, CT 06430/203-259-0938: FAX: 203-259-2566
Kopec Enterprises, John (See Peacemaker Specialists)
Kopp, Terry K., Route 1, Box 224F, Lexington, MO 64067/816-259-2636
Korth, Robert-Bosch-Str. 4, P.O. Box 1320, 23909 Ratzeburg, GERMANY/451-4991497; FAX: 451-4993230 (U.S. importer—Interarms; Mandall Shooting Supplies, Inc.)
Korzinek Riflesmith, J., RD 2, Box 73D, Canton, PA 17724/717-673-8512
Koval Knives, 5819 Zarley St., Suite A, New Albany, OH 43054/614-855-0777; FAX: 614-855-0945
Kowa Optimed, Inc., 20001 S. Vermont Ave., Torrance, CA 90502/310-327-1913; FAX: 310-327-4177
Kramer Designs, 36 Chokecherry Ln., Clancy, MT 59634/406-933-8658; FAX: 406-933-8658
Kramer Handgun Leather, P.O. Box 112154, Tacoma, WA 98411/206-564-6652; FAX: 206-564-1214
Krause Publications, Inc., 700 E. State St., Iola, WI 54990/715-445-2214; FAX: 715-445-4087; Consumer orders only 800-258-0929
Krico Jagd-und Sportwaffen GmbH, Nurnbergerstrasse 6, D-90602 Pyrbaum GERMANY/09180-2780; FAX: 09180-2661 (U.S. importer—Mandall Shooting Supplies, Inc.)
Krieger Barrels, Inc., N114 W18697 Clinton Dr., Germantown, WI 53022/414-255-9593; FAX: 414-255-9586
Krieghoff Gun Co., H., Boschstrasse 22, D-89079 Ulm, GERMANY/731-401820; FAX: 731-4018270 (U.S. importer—Krieghoff International, Inc.)
Krieghoff International, Inc., 7528 Easton Rd., Ottsville, PA 18942/610-847-5173; FAX: 610-847-8691
Kris Mounts, 108 Lehigh St., Johnstown, PA 15905/814-539-9751
KSN Industries, Ltd. (See U.S. importer—J.O. Arms Inc.)
K-Sports Imports, Inc., 2755 Thompson Creek Rd., Pomona, CA 91767/909-392-2345; FAX: 909-392-2354
Kudlas, John M., 622 14th St. SE, Rochester, MN 55904/507-288-5579
Kulis Freeze Dry Taxidermy, 725 Broadway Ave., Bedford, OH 44146/216-232-8352; FAX: 216-232-7305
KVH Industries, Inc., 110 Enterprise Center, Middletown, RI 02842/401-847-3327; FAX: 401-849-0045
Kwik Mount Corp., P.O. Box 19422, Louisville, KY 40259/502-239-5447
Kwik-Site Co., 5555 Treadwell, Wayne, MI 48184/313-326-1500; FAX: 313-326-4120

L

L&R Lock Co., 1137 Pocalla Rd., Sumter, SC 29150/803-775-6127
L&S Technologies, Inc. (See Aimtech Mount Systems)
La Clinique du .45, 1432 Rougemont, Chambly, Quebec, J3L 2L8 CANADA/514-658-1144
Labanu, Inc., 2201-F Fifth Ave., Ronkonkoma, NY 11779/516-467-6197; FAX: 516-981-4112
LaBounty Precision Reboring, P.O. Box 186, 7968 Silver Lk. Rd., Maple Falls, WA 98266/360-599-2047
LaCrosse Footwear, Inc., P.O. Box 1328, La Crosse, WI 54602/608-782-3020, 800-323-2668; FAX: 800-658-9444
Lady Clays, P.O. Box 457, Shawnee Mission, KS 66201/913-268-8006
LaFrance Specialties, P.O. Box 178211, San Diego, CA 92177-8211/619-293-3373
Lair, Sam, 520 E. Beaver, Jenks, OK 74037/918-299-2391
Lake Center, P.O. Box 38, St. Charles, MO 63302/314-946-7500
Lakefield Arms Ltd. (See Savage Arms, Inc.)
Lakewood Products, Inc., 275 June St., P.O. Box 230, Berlin, WI 54923/800-US-BUILT; FAX: 414-361-5058
Lampert, Ron, Rt. 1, Box 177, Guthrie, MN 56461/218-854-7345
Lamson & Goodnow Mfg. Co., 45 Conway St., Shelburne Falls, MA 03170/413-625-6331: FAX: 413-625-9816
Lanber Armas, S.A., Zubiaurre 5, Zaldibar, SPAIN 48250/34-4-6827702; FAX: 34-4-6827999
Lane Bullets, Inc., 1011 S. 10th St., Kansas City, KS 66105/913-621-6113, 800-444-7468
Lane Publishing, P.O. Box 459, Lake Hamilton, AR 71951/501-525-7514; FAX: 501-525-7519
Langenberg Hat Co., P.O. Box 1860, Washington, MO 63090/800-428-1860; FAX: 314-239-3151
Lanphert, Paul, P.O. Box 1985, Wenatchee, WA 98807
Lapua Ltd., P.O. Box 5, Lapua, FINLAND SF-62101/64-310111; FAX: 64-4388991 (U.S. importers—Champion's Choice; Keng's Firearms Specialty, Inc.
L.A.R. Mfg., Inc., 4133 W. Farm Rd., West Jordan, UT 84088/801-280-3505; FAX: 801-280-1972
LaRocca Gun Works, Inc., 51 Union Place, Worcester, MA 01608/508-754-2887; FAX: 508-754-2887
Laser Devices, Inc., 2 Harris Ct. A4, Monterey, CA 93940/408-373-0701, 800-235-2162; FAX: 408-373-0903
Laseraim, Inc. (See Emerging Technologies, Inc.)
Laseraim Arms, Inc., P.O. Box 3548, Little Rock, AR 72203/501-375-2227; FAX: 501-372-1445
Laseraim Technologies, Inc., P.O. Box 3548, Little Rock, AR 72203/501-375-2227; FAX: 501-372-1445
LaserMax, 3495 Winton Place, Bldg. B, Rochester, NY 14623/716-272-5420; FAX: 716-272-5427
Lassen Community College, Gunsmithing Dept., P.O. Box 3000, Hwy. 139, Susanville, CA 96130/916-251-8809 ext. 109 or 200; FAX: 916-257-8964
Lathrop's, Inc., 5146 E. Pima, Tucson, AZ 85712/520-881-0266, 800-875-4867; FAX: 520-322-5704
Laughridge, William R. (See Cylinder & Slide, Inc.)
Laurel Mountain Forge, P.O. Box 224C, Romeo, MI 48065/810-749-5742
Laurona Armas Eibar, S.A.L., Avenida de Otaola 25, P.O. Box 260, 20600 Eibar, SPAIN/34-43-700600; FAX: 34-43-700616 (U.S. importers—Galaxy Imports Ltd., Inc.)
Law Concealment Systems, Inc., P.O. Box 3952, Wilmington, NC 28406/919-791-6656, 800-373-0116 orders
Lawrence Brand Shot (See Precision Reloading, Inc.)
Lawrence Leather Co., P.O. Box 1479, Lillington, NC 27546/910-893-2071; FAX: 910-893-4742
Lawson Co., Harry, 3328 N. Richey Blvd., Tucson, AZ 85716/520-326-1117
Lawson, John G. (See Sight Shop, The)
LBT, HCR 62, Box 145, Moyie Springs, ID 83845/208-267-3588
Le Clear Industries (See E-Z-Way Systems)
Lea Mfg. Co., 237 E. Aurora St., Waterbury, CT 06720/203-753-5116
Lead Bullets Technology (See LBT)
Leather Arsenal, 27549 Middleton Rd., Middleton, ID 83644/208-585-6212
Leatherman Tool Group, Inc., 12106 NE Ainsworth Cir., P.O. Box 20595, Portland, OR 97294/503-253-7826; FAX: 503-253-7830
Lebeau-Courally, Rue St. Gilles, 386, 4000 Liege, BELGIUM/041-52-48-43; FAX: 32-041-52-20-08 (U.S. importer—New England Arms Co.)
Leckie Professional Gunsmithing, 546 Quarry Rd., Ottsville, PA 18942/215-847-8594
Lectro Science, Inc., 6410 W. Ridge Rd., Erie, PA 16506/814-833-6487; FAX: 814-833-0447
Ledbetter Airguns, Riley, 1804 E. Sprague St., Winston Salem, NC 27107-3521/919-784-0676
Lee Co., T.K., One Independence Plaza, Suite 520, Birmingham, AL 35209/205-913-5222
Lee Precision, Inc., 4275 Hwy. U, Hartford, WI 53027/414-673-3075
Lee Supplies, Mark, 9901 France Ct., Lakeville, MN 55044/612-461-2114
Lee's Red Ramps, 4 Kristine Ln., Silver City, NM 88061/505-538-8529
LeFever Arms Co., Inc., 6234 Stokes, Lee Center Rd., Lee Center, NY 13363/315-337-6722; FAX: 315-337-1543
Legend Products Corp., 1555 E. Flamingo Rd., Suite 404, Las Vegas, NV 89119/702-228-1808, 702-796-5778; FAX: 702-228-7484
Leibowitz, Leonard, 1205 Murrayhill Ave., Pittsburgh, PA 15217/412-361-5455
Leica USA, Inc., 156 Ludlow Ave., Northvale, NJ 07647/201-767-7500; FAX: 201-767-8666
L.E.M. Gun Specialties, Inc., The Lewis Lead Remover, P.O. Box 2855, Peachtree City, GA 30269-2024/770-487-0556
Lem Sports, Inc., P.O. Box 2107, Aurora, IL 60506/815-286-7421, 800-688-8801 (orders only)
Lenahan Family Enterprise, P.O. Box 46, Manitou Springs, CO 80829
Lethal Force Institute (See Police Bookshelf)
Lett Custom Grips, 672 Currier Rd., Hopkinton, NH 03229-2652
Leupold & Stevens, Inc., P.O. Box 688, Beaverton, OR 97075/503-646-9171; FAX: 503-526-1455
Lever Arms Service Ltd., 2131 Burrard St., Vancouver, B.C. V6J 3H7 CANADA/604-736-0004; FAX: 604-738-3503
Lewis Lead Remover, The (See LEM Gun Specialties, Inc.)
Liberty Antique Gunworks, 19 Key St., P.O. Box 183, Eastport, ME 04631/207-853-4116
Liberty Metals, 2233 East 16th St., Los Angeles, CA 90021/213-581-9171; FAX: 213-581-9351

Liberty Safe, 1060 N. Spring Creek Pl., Springville, UT 84663/800-247-5625; FAX: 801-489-6409
Liberty Shooting Supplies, P.O. Box 357, Hillsboro, OR 97123/503-640-5518
Liberty Trouser Co., 3500 6 Ave S., Birmingham, AL 35222-2406/205-251-9143
Lightfield Ammunition Corp., The Slug Group, P.O. Box 376, New Paris, PA 15554/814-839-4517; FAX: 814-839-2601
Lightning Performance Innovations, Inc., RD1 Box 555, Mohawk, NY 13407/315-866-8819, 800-242-5873; FAX: 315-866-8819
Lilja Precision Rifle Barrels, P.O. Box 372, Plains, MT 59859/406-826-3084; FAX: 406-826-3083
Lincoln, Dean, Box 1886, Farmington, NM 87401
Lind Custom Guns, Al, 7821 76th Ave. SW, Tacoma, WA 98498/206-584-6361
Linder Solingen Knives, 4401 Sentry Dr., Tucker, GA 30084/770-939-6915; FAX: 770-939-6738
Lindsay, Steve, RR 2 Cedar Hills, Kearney, NE 68847/308-236-7885
Lindsley Arms Cartridge Co., P.O. Box 757, 20 College Hill Rd., Henniker, NH 03242/603-428-3127
Linebaugh Custom Sixguns, Route 2, Box 100, Maryville, MO 64468/816-562-3031
List Precision Engineering, Unit 1, Ingley Works, 13 River Road, Barking, Essex 1G11 0HE ENGLAND/011-081-594-1686
Lister, Weldon, Route 1, P.O. Box 1517, Boerne, TX 78006/210-755-2210
Lithi Bee Bullet Lube, 1885 Dyson St., Muskegon, MI 49442/616-726-3400
"Little John's" Antique Arms, 1740 W. Laveta, Orange, CA 92668
Little Trees Ramble (See Scott Pilkington, Little Trees Ramble)
Littler Sales Co., 20815 W. Chicago, Detroit, MI 48228/313-273-6889; FAX: 313-273-1099
Littleton, J.F., 275 Pinedale Ave., Oroville, CA 95966/916-533-6084
Ljutic Industries, Inc., 732 N. 16th Ave., Suite 22, Yakima, WA 98902/509-248-0476; FAX: 509-576-8233
Llama Gabilondo Y Cia, Apartado 290, E-01080, Victoria, SPAIN (U.S. importer—Import Sports, Inc.)
L.L. Bean, 386 Main St., Freeport, ME 04032/207-865-3111
Load From A Disk, 9826 Sagedale, Houston, TX 77089/713-484-0935
Loadmaster, P.O. Box 1209, Warminster, Wilts. BA12 9XJ ENGLAND/01044 1985 218544; FAX: 01044 1985 214111
Loch Leven Industries, P.O. Box 2751, Santa Rosa, CA 95405/707-573-8735; FAX: 707-573-0369
Lock's Philadelphia Gun Exchange, 6700 Rowland Ave., Philadelphia, PA 19149/215-332-6225; FAX: 215-332-4800
Lodewick, Walter H., 2816 NE Halsey St., Portland, OR 97232/503-284-2554
Lofland, James W., 2275 Larkin Rd., Boothwyn, PA 19061/610-485-0391
Log Cabin Sport Shop, 8010 Lafayette Rd., Lodi, OH 44254/216-948-1082
Logan, Harry M., Box 745, Honokaa, HI 96727/808-776-1644
Lohman Game Call Company, 4500 Doniphan Dr., P.O. Box 220, Neosho, MO 64850/417-451-4438; FAX: 417-451-2576
Lomont Precision Bullets, RR 1, P.O. Box 34, Salmon, ID 83467/208-756-6819; FAX: 208-756-6824
London Guns Ltd., Box 3750, Santa Barbara, CA 93130/805-683-4141; FAX: 805-683-1712
Lone Star Gunleather, 1301 Brushy Bend Dr., Round Rock, TX 78681/512-255-1805
Long, George F., 1500 Rogue River Hwy., Ste. F, Grants Pass, OR 97527/541-476-7552
Lorcin Engineering Co., Inc., 10427 San Sevaine Way, Ste. A, Mira Loma, CA 91752/909-360-1406; FAX: 909-360-0623
Lortone, Inc., 2856 NW Market St., Seattle, WA 98107/206-789-3100
Lothar Walther Precision Tool, Inc., 2190 Coffee Rd., Lithonia, GA 30058/770-482-4253; Fax: 770-482-9344
Lovestrand, Erik, 206 Bent Oak Circle, Harvest, AL 35749-9334
Loweth, Richard, 29 Hedgegrow Lane, Kirby Muxloe, Leics. LE9 9BN ENGLAND
L.P.A. Snc, Via Alfieri 26, Gardone V.T., Brescia, ITALY 25063/30-891-14-81; FAX: 30-891-09-51
LPS Laboratories, Inc., 4647 Hugh Howell Rd., P.O. Box 3050, Tucker, GA 30084/404-934-7800
Lucas, Edward E., 32 Garfield Ave., East Brunswick, NJ 08816/201-251-5526
Lucas, Mike, 1631 Jessamine Rd., Lexington, SC 29073/803-356-0282
Luch Metal Merchants, Barbara, 48861 West Rd., Wixon, MI 48393/800-876-5337
Lutz Engraving, Ron, E. 1998 Smokey Valley Rd., Scandinavia, WI 54977/715-467-2674
Lyman Instant Targets, Inc. (See Lyman Products Corp.)
Lyman Products Corporation, 475 Smith Street, Middletown, CT 06457-1541/860-632-2020, 800-22-LYMAN; FAX: 860-632-1699
Lynn's Custom Gunstocks, RR 1, Brandon, IA 52210/319-474-2453

M

M&D Munitions Ltd., 127 Verdi St., Farmingdale, NY 11735/800-878-2788, 516-752-1038; FAX: 516-752-1905
M&M Engineering (See Hollywood Engineering)
M&N Bullet Lube, P.O. Box 495, 151 NE Jefferson St., Madras, OR 97741/503-255-3750
MA Systems, P.O. Box 1143, Chouteau, OK 74337/918-479-6378
Mac-1 Distributors, 13974 Van Ness Ave., Gardena, CA 90249/310-327-3582
Mac's .45 Shop, P.O. Box 2028, Seal Beach, CA 90740/310-438-5046
Macbean, Stan, 754 North 1200 West, Orem, UT 84057/801-224-6446
Madis, David, 2453 West Five Mile Pkwy., Dallas, TX 75233/214-330-7168
Madis, George, P.O. Box 545, Brownsboro, TX 75756
MAG Instrument, Inc., 1635 S. Sacramento Ave., Ontario, CA 91761/909-947-1006; FAX: 909-947-3116
Mag-Na-Port International, Inc., 41302 Executive Dr., Harrison Twp., MI 48045-1306/810-469-6727; FAX: 810-469-0425
Mag-Pack Corp., P.O. Box 846, Chesterland, OH 44026
Magma Engineering Co., P.O. Box 161, 20955 E. Ocotillo Rd., Queen Creek, AZ 85242/602-987-9008; FAX: 602-987-0148
Magnolia Sports, Inc., 211 W. Main, Magnolia, AR 71753/501-234-8410, 800-530-7816; FAX: 501-234-8117
Magnum Grips, Box 801G, Payson, AZ 85547
Magnum Power Products, Inc., P.O. Box 17768, Fountain Hills, AZ 85268
Magnum Research, Inc., 7110 University Ave. NE, Minneapolis, MN 55432/800-772-6168, 612-574-1868; FAX: 612-574-0109
Magnus Bullets, P.O. Box 239, Toney, AL 35773/205-828-5089; FAX: 205-828-7756
MagSafe Ammo Co., 2725 Friendly Grove Rd NE, Olympia, WA 98506/360-357-6383; FAX: 360-705-4715
MAGTECH Recreational Products, Inc., 5030 Paradise Rd., Suite A104, Las Vegas, NV 89119/702-736-2043; FAX: 702-736-2140
Mahony, Philip Bruce, 67 White Hollow Rd., Lime Rock, CT 06039-2418/203-435-9341
Mahovsky's Metalife, R.D. 1, Box 149a Eureka Road, Grand Valley, PA 16420/814-436-7747
Maine Custom Bullets, RFD 1, Box 1755, Brooks, ME 04921
Mains Enterprises, Inc., 3111 S. Valley View Blvd., Suite B120, Las Vegas, NV 89102-7790/702-876-6278; FAX: 702-876-1269
Maionchi-L.M.I., Via Di Coselli-Zona Industriale Di Guamo, Lucca, ITALY 55060/011 39-583 94291
Makinson, Nicholas, RR 3, Komoka, Ont. N0L 1R0 CANADA/519-471-5462
Malcolm Enterprises, 1023 E. Prien Lake Rd., Lake Charles, LA 70601
Mallardtone Game Calls, 2901 16th St., Moline, IL 61265/309-762-8089
M.A.M. Products, Inc., 153 B Cross Slope Court, Englishtown, NJ 07726/908-536-3604
Mandall Shooting Supplies, Inc., 3616 N. Scottsdale Rd., Scottsdale, AZ 85252/602-945-2553; FAX: 602-949-0734
Manley Shooting Supplies, Lowell, 3684 Pine St., Deckerville, MI 48427/313-376-3665
Manufacture D'Armes Des Pyrenees Francaises (See Unique/M.A.P.F.)
Mar Knives, Inc., Al, 5755 SW Jean Rd., Suite 101, Lake Oswego, OR 97035/503-635-9229; FAX: 503-223-0467
Marathon Rubber Prods. Co., Inc., 510 Sherman St., Wausau, WI 54401/715-845-6255
Marble Arms, P.O. Box 111, Gladstone, MI 49837/906-428-3710; FAX: 906-428-3711
Marchmon Bullets, 8191 Woodland Shore Dr., Brighton, MI 48116
Marent, Rudolf, 9711 Tiltree St., Houston, TX 77075/713-946-7028
Markell, Inc., 422 Larkfield Center 235, Santa Rosa, CA 95403/707-573-0792; FAX: 707-573-9867
Markesbery Muzzle Loaders, Inc., 7785 Foundation Dr., Ste. 6, Florence, KY 41042/800-875-0121; 606-342-2380
Marksman Products, 5482 Argosy Dr., Huntington Beach, CA 92649/714-898-7535, 800-822-8005; FAX: 714-891-0782
Marlin Firearms Co., 100 Kenna Dr., North Haven, CT 06473/203-239-5621; FAX: 203-234-7991
Marmik Inc., 2116 S. Woodland Ave., Michigan City, IN 46361-7508/219-872-7231
Marocchi F.lli SRL, Via Galileo Galilei 8, I-25068 Zanano di Sarezzo, ITALY (U.S. importers—Sile Distributors)
Marple & Associates, Dick, 21 Dartmouth St., Hooksett, NH 03106/603-627-1837; FAX: 603-627-1837
Marquart Precision Co., Inc., Rear 136 Grove Ave., Box 1740, Prescott, AZ 86302/602-445-5646
Marsh, Johnny, 1007 Drummond Dr., Nashville, TN 37211/615-833-3259
Marsh, Mike, Croft Cottage, Main St., Elton, Derbyshire DE4 2BY, ENGLAND/01629 650 669
Marshall Enterprises, 792 Canyon Rd., Redwood City, CA 94062
Martin Bookseller, J., P.O. Drawer AP, Beckley, WV 25802/304-255-4073; FAX: 304-255-4077
Martin's Gun Shop, 937 S. Sheridan Blvd., Lakewood, CO 80226/303-922-2184
Martz, John V., 8060 Lakeview Lane, Lincoln, CA 95648/916-645-2250
Marvel, Alan, 3922 Madonna Rd., Jarretsville, MD 21084/301-557-6545
Maryland Paintball Supply, 8507 Harford Rd., Parkville, MD 21234/410-882-5607
Masen Co., Inc., John, 1305 Jelmak, Grand Prairie, TX 75050/817-430-8732; FAX: 817-430-1715
Masker, Seely, 54 Woodshire S., Getzville, NY 14068/716-689-8894
MAST Technology, 4350 S. Arville, Suite 3, Las Vegas, NV 89103/702-362-5043; FAX: 702-362-9554
Master Class Bullets, 4209-D West 6th, Eugene, OR 97402/503-687-1263, 800-883-1263
Master Engravers, Inc. (See Hendricks, Frank E.)
Master Lock Co., 2600 N. 32nd St., Milwaukee, WI 53245/414-444-2800
Master Products, Inc. (See Gun-Alert/Master Products, Inc.)

Match Prep, P.O. Box 155, Tehachapi, CA 93581/805-822-5383
Matco, Inc., 1003-2nd St., N. Manchester, IN 46962/219-982-8282
Mathews & Son, Inc., George E., 10224 S. Paramount Blvd., Downey, CA 90241/310-862-6719; FAX: 310-862-6719
Matthews Cutlery, 4401 Sentry Dr., Tucker, GA 30084/770-939-6915
Mauser Werke Oberndorf Waffensysteme GmbH, Postfach 1349, 78722 Oberndorf/N. GERMANY (U.S. importer—GSI, Inc.)
Maverick Arms, Inc., 7 Grasso Ave., P.O. Box 497, North Haven, CT 06473/203-230-5300; FAX: 203-230-5420
Maxi-Mount, P.O. Box 291, Willoughby Hills, OH 44094-0291/216-944-9456; FAX: 216-944-9456
Maximum Security Corp., 32841 Calle Perfecto, San Juan Capistrano, CA 92675/714-493-3684; FAX: 714-496-7733
Mayville Engineering Co. (See MEC, Inc.)
Mazur Restoration, Pete, 13083 Drummer Way, Grass Valley, CA 95949/916-268-2412
MCA Sports, P.O. Box 8868, Palm Springs, CA 92263/619-770-2005
McBros Rifle Co., P.O. Box 86549, Phoenix, AZ 85080/602-780-2115; FAX: 602-581-3825
McCament, Jay, 1730-134th St. Ct. S., Tacoma, WA 98444/206-531-8832
McCann's Machine & Gun Shop, P.O. Box 641, Spanaway, WA 98387/206-537-6919; FAX: 206-537-6993
McCann's Muzzle-Gun Works, 14 Walton Dr., New Hope, PA 18938/215-862-2728
McCluskey Precision Rifles, 10502 14th Ave. NW, Seattle, WA 98177/206-781-2776
McCombs, Leo, 1862 White Cemetery Rd., Patriot, OH 45658/614-256-1714
McCormick Corp., Chip, 1825 Fortview Rd., Ste. 115, Austin, TX 78704/800-328-CHIP, 512-462-0004; FAX: 512-462-0009
McCullough, Ken (See Ken's Rifle Blanks)
McDonald, Dennis, 8359 Brady St., Peosta, IA 52068/319-556-7940
McFarland, Stan, 2221 Idella Ct., Grand Junction, CO 81505/303-243-4704
McGowen Rifle Barrels, 5961 Spruce Lane, St. Anne, IL 60964/815-937-9816; FAX: 815-937-4024
McGuire, Bill, 1600 N. Eastmont Ave., East Wenatchee, WA 98802/509-884-6021
McKee Publications, 121 Eatons Neck Rd., Northport, NY 11768/516-575-8850
McKenzie, Lynton, 6940 N. Alvernon Way, Tucson, AZ 85718/520-299-5090
McKillen & Heyer, Inc., 35535 Euclid Ave. Suite 11, Willoughby, OH 44094/216-942-2044
McKinney, R.P. (See Schuetzen Gun Co.)
McMillan Fiberglass Stocks, Inc., 21421 N. 14th Ave., Phoenix, AZ 85027/602-582-9635; FAX: 602-581-3825
McMillan Optical Gunsight Co., 28638 N. 42nd St., Cave Creek, AZ 85331/602-585-7868; FAX: 602-585-7872
McMillan Rifle Barrels, P.O. Box 3427, Bryan, TX 77805/409-690-3456; FAX: 409-690-0156
McMurdo, Lynn (See Specialty Gunsmithing)
MCRW Associates Shooting Supplies, R.R. 1 Box 1425, Sweet Valley, PA 18656/717-864-3967; FAX: 717-864-2669
MCS, Inc., 34 Delmar Dr., Brookfield, CT 06804/203-775-1013; FAX: 203-775-9462
McWelco Products, 6730 Santa Fe Ave., Hesperia, CA 92345/619-244-8876; FAX: 619-244-9398
MDS, P.O. Box 1441, Brandon, FL 33509-1441/813-653-1180; FAX: 813-684-5953
Meadow Industries, 24 Club Lane, Palmyra, VA 22963/804-589-7672; FAX: 804-589-7672
Measurement Group, Inc., Box 27777, Raleigh, NC 27611
MEC, Inc., 715 South St., Mayville, WI 53050/414-387-4500; FAX: 414-387-5802
MEC-Gar S.R.L., Via Madonnina 64, Gardone V.T., Brescia, ITALY 25063/39-30-8912687; FAX: 39-30-8910065 (U.S. importer—MEC-Gar U.S.A., Inc.)
MEC-Gar U.S.A., Inc., Box 112, 500B Monroe Turnpike, Monroe, CT 06468/203-635-8662; FAX: 203-635-8662
Meier Works, P.O. Box 423, Tijeras, NM 87059/505-281-3783
Meister Bullets (See Gander Mountain)
Mele, Frank, 201 S. Wellow Ave., Cookeville, TN 38501/615-526-4860
Melton Shirt Co., Inc., 56 Harvester Ave., Batavia, NY 14020/716-343-8750; FAX: 716-343-6887
Men-Metallwerk Elisenhuette, GmbH, P.O. Box 1263, D-56372 Nassau/Lahn, GERMANY/2604-7819
Menck, Thomas W., 5703 S. 77th St., Ralston, NE 68127-4201
Mendez, John A., P.O. Box 620984, Orlando, FL 32862/407-282-2178
Meprolight (See Hesco-Meprolight)
Mercer Custom Stocks, R.M., 216 S. Whitewater Ave., Jefferson, WI 53549/414-674-5130
Merit Corporation, Box 9044, Schenectady, NY 12309/518-346-1420
Merkel Freres, Strasse 7 October, 10, Suhl, GERMANY (U.S. importer—GSI, Inc.)
Merkuria Ltd., Argentinska 38, 17005 Praha 7, CZECH REPUBLIC/422-875117; FAX: 422-809152
Mesa Sportsmen's Assoc., L.L.C., 250 Main St., Box 854, Delta, CO 81416/970-874-4571
Metal Products Co. (See MPC)
Metalife Industries (See Mahovsky's Metalife)
Metaloy Inc., Rt. 5, Box 595, Berryville, AR 72616/501-545-3611
Michael's Antiques, Box 591, Waldoboro, ME 04572
Michaels of Oregon Co., P.O. Box 13010, Portland, OR 97213/503-255-6890; FAX: 503-255-0746
Micro Sight Co., 242 Harbor Blvd., Belmont, CA 94002/415-591-0769; FAX: 415-591-7531
Microfusion Alfa S.A., Paseo San Andres N8, P.O. Box 271, Eibar, SPAIN 20600/34-43-11-89-16; FAX: 34-43-11-40-38
Mid-America Guns and Ammo, 1205 W. Jefferson, Suite E, Effingham, IL 62401/800-820-5177
Mid-America Recreation, Inc., 1328 5th Ave., Moline, IL 61265/309-764-5089; FAX: 309-764-2722
Middlebrooks Custom Shop, 7366 Colonial Trail East, Surry, VA 23883/804-357-0881; FAX: 804-365-0442
Midway Arms, Inc., 5875 W. Van Horn Tavern Rd., Columbia, MO 65203/800-243-3220, 314-445-6363; FAX: 314-446-1018
Midwest Gun Sport, 1108 Herbert Dr., Zebulon, NC 27597/919-269-5570
Midwest Sport Distributors, Box 129, Fayette, MO 65248
Military Armament Corp., P.O. Box 120, Mt. Zion Rd., Lingleville, TX 76461/817-965-3253
Miller Arms, Inc., P.O. Box 260 Purl St., St. Onge, SD 57779/605-642-5160; FAX: 605-642-5160
Miller Co., David, 3131 E. Greenlee Rd., Tucson, AZ 85716/602-326-3117
Miller Custom, 210 E. Julia, Clinton, IL 61727/217-935-9362
Miller Enterprises, Inc., R.P., 1557 E. Main St., P.O. Box 234, Brownsburg, IN 46112/317-852-8187
Miller Single Trigger Mfg. Co., Rt. 209 Box 1275, Millersburg, PA 17061/717-692-3704
Millett Sights, 16131 Gothard St., Huntington Beach, CA 92647/714-842-5575, 800-645-5388; FAX: 714-843-5707
Mills Jr., Hugh B., 3615 Canterbury Rd., New Bern, NC 28560/919-637-4631
Milstor Corp., 80-975 E. Valley Pkwy. C-7, Indio, CA 92201/619-775-9998; FAX: 619-772-4990
Miniature Machine Co. (MMC), 2513 East Loop 820 North, Ft. Worth, TX 76118/817-595-0404; FAX: 817-595-3074
Minute Man High Tech Industries, 10611 Canyon Rd. E., Suite 151, Puyallup, WA 98373/800-233-2734
Mirador Optical Corp., P.O. Box 11614, Marina Del Rey, CA 90295-7614/310-821-5587; FAX: 310-305-0386
Miroku, B.C./Daly, Charles (See U.S. importer—Bell's Legendary Country Wear; U.S. distributor—Outdoor Sports Headquarters, Inc.)
Mitchell Arms, Inc., 3433-B. W. Harvard St., Santa Ana, CA 92704/714-957-5711; FAX: 714-957-5732
Mitchell Bullets, R.F., 430 Walnut St., Westernport, MD 21562
Mitchell's Accuracy Shop, 68 Greenridge Dr., Stafford, VA 22554/703-659-0165
MI-TE Bullets, R.R. 1 Box 230, Ellsworth, KS 67439/913-472-4575
Mittermeier, Inc., Frank, P.O. Box 2G, 3577 E. Tremont Ave., Bronx, NY 10465/718-828-3843
Mixson Corp., 7435 W. 19th Ct., Hialeah, FL 33014/305-821-5190, 800-327-0078; FAX: 305-558-9318
MJK Gunsmithing, Inc., 417 N. Huber Ct., E. Wenatchee, WA 98802/509-884-7683
MJM Mfg., 3283 Rocky Water Ln. Suite B, San Jose, CA 95148/408-270-4207
MKL Service Co., 610 S. Troy St., P.O. Box D, Royal Oak, MI 48068/810-548-5453
MKS Supply, Inc. (See Hi-Point Firearms)
MMP, Rt. 6, Box 384, Harrison, AR 72601/501-741-5019; FAX: 501-741-3104
M.O.A. Corp., 2451 Old Camden Pike, Eaton, OH 45320/513-456-3669
Modern Gun Repair School, P.O. Box 92577, Southlake, TX 76092/800-493-4114; FAX: 800-556-5112
Modern Gun School, 500 N. Kimball, Suite 105, Southlake, TX 76092/800-774-5112
Modern MuzzleLoading, Inc., 234 Airport Rd., P.O. Box 130, Centerville, IA 52544/515-856-2626; FAX: 515-856-2628
Moeller, Steve, 1213 4th St., Fulton, IL 61252/815-589-2300
Molin Industries, Tru-Nord Division, P.O. Box 365, 204 North 9th St., Brainerd, MN 56401/218-829-2870
MoLoc Bullets, P.O. Box 2810, Turlock, CA 95381-2810/209-632-1644
Monell Custom Guns, 228 Red Mills Rd., Pine Bush, NY 12566/914-744-3021
Moneymaker Guncraft Corp., 1420 Military Ave., Omaha, NE 68131/402-556-0226
Montana Armory, Inc., 100 Centennial Dr., Big Timber, MT 59011/406-932-4353
Montana Outfitters, Lewis E. Yearout, 308 Riverview Dr. E., Great Falls, MT 59404/406-761-0859
Montana Precision Swaging, P.O. Box 4746, Butte, MT 59702/406-782-7502
Montana Vintage Arms, 2354 Bear Canyon Rd., Bozeman, MT 59715
Monte Kristo Pistol Grip Co., P.O. Box 85, Whiskeytown, CA 96095/916-778-0240
Montgomery Community College, P.O. Box 787-GD, Troy, NC 27371/910-572-3691, 800-839-6222
Moore & Co., Wm. Larkin, 8727 E. Via de Commencio, Suite A, Scottsdale, AZ 85258/602-951-8913; FAX: 602-951-8913
Moreton/Fordyce Enterprises, P.O. Box 940, Saylorsburg, PA 18353/717-992-5742; FAX: 717-992-8775
Morini (See U.S. importers—Mandall Shooting Supplies, Inc.; Nygord Precision Products)
Morrison Custom Rifles, J.W., 4015 W. Sharon, Phoenix, AZ 85029/602-978-3754

Morrow, Bud, 11 Hillside Lane, Sheridan, WY 82801-9729/307-674-8360
Morton Booth Co., P.O. Box 123, Joplin, MO 64802/417-673-1962; FAX: 417-673-3642
Mo's Competitor Supplies (See MCS, Inc.)
Moschetti, Mitchell R., P.O. Box 27065, Denver, CO 80227
Moss Double Tone, Inc., P.O. Box 1112, 2101 S. Kentucky, Sedalia, MO 65301/816-827-0827
Mossberg & Sons, Inc., O.F, 7 Grasso Ave., North Haven, CT 06473/203-230-5300; FAX: 203-230-5420
Mountain Bear Rifle Works, Inc., 100 B Ruritan Rd., Sterling, VA 20164/703-430-0420; FAX: 703-430-7068
Mountain Hollow Game Calls, Box 121, Cascade, MD 21719/301-241-3282
Mountain South, P.O. Box 381, Barnwell, SC 29812/FAX: 803-259-3227
Mountain State Muzzleloading Supplies, Box 154-1, Rt. 2, Williamstown, WV 26187/304-375-7842; FAX: 304-375-3737
Mountain States Engraving, Kenneth W. Warren, P.O. Box 2842, Wenatchee, WA 98802/509-663-6123
Mountain View Sports, Inc., Box 188, Troy, NH 03465/603-357-9690; FAX: 603-357-9691
Mowrey Gun Works, P.O. Box 246, Waldron, IN 46182/317-525-6181; FAX: 317-525-9595
Mowrey's Guns & Gunsmithing, RR1, Box 82, Canajoharie, NY 13317/518-673-3483
MPC, P.O. Box 450, McMinnville, TN 37110-0450/615-473-5513; FAX: 615-473-5516
MPI Fiberglass Stocks, 5655 NW St. Helens Rd., Portland, OR 97210/503-226-1215; FAX: 503-226-2661
MSC Industrial Supply Co., 151 Sunnyside Blvd., Plainview, NY 11803-9915/516-349-0330
MSR Targets, P.O. Box 1042, West Covina, CA 91793/818-331-7840
Mt. Alto Outdoor Products, Rt. 735, Howardsville, VA 24562
Mt. Baldy Bullet Co., 12981 Old Hill City Rd., Keystone, SD 57751-6623/605-666-4725
MTM Molded Products Co., Inc., 3370 Obco Ct., Dayton, OH 45414/513-890-7461; FAX: 513-890-1747
Mulhern, Rick, Rt. 5, Box 152, Rayville, LA 71269/318-728-2688
Mullins Ammo, Rt. 2, Box 304K, Clintwood, VA 24228/703-926-6772
Mullis Guncraft, 3523 Lawyers Road E., Monroe, NC 28110/704-283-6683
Multi-Caliber Adapters (See MCA Sports)
Multipax, 8086 S. Yale, Suite 286, Tulsa, OK 74136/918-496-1999; FAX: 918-492-7465
Multiplex International, 26 S. Main St., Concord, NH 03301/FAX: 603-796-2223
Multipropulseurs, La Bertrandiere, 42580 L'Etrat, FRANCE/77 74 01 30; FAX: 77 93 19 34
Multi-Scale Charge Ltd., 3269 Niagara Falls Blvd., N. Tonawanda, NY 14120/905-566-1255; FAX: 905-276-6295
Mundy, Thomas A., 69 Robbins Road, Somerville, NJ 08876/201-722-2199
Munsch Gunsmithing, Tommy, Rt. 2, P.O. Box 248, Little Falls, MN 56345/612-632-6695
Murmur Corp., 2823 N. Westmoreland Ave., Dallas, TX 75222/214-630-5400
Murphy Co., Inc., R., 13 Groton-Harvard Rd., P.O. Box 376, Ayer, MA 01432/617-772-3481
Murray State College, 100 Faculty Dr., Tishomingo, OK 73460/405-371-2371 ext. 238, 800-342-0698
Muscle Products Corp., 112 Fennell Dr., Butler, PA 16001/800-227-7049, 412-283-0567; FAX: 412-283-8310
Museum of Historical Arms Inc., 2750 Coral Way, Suite 204, Miami, FL 33145/305-444-9199
Mushroom Express Bullet Co., 601 W. 6th St., Greenfield, IN 46140-1728/317-462-6332
Mustra's Custom Guns, Inc., Carl, 1002 Pennsylvania Ave., Palm Harbor, FL 34683/813-785-1403
Muzzleload Magnum Products (See MMP)
Muzzleloaders Etcetera, Inc., 9901 Lyndale Ave. S., Bloomington, MN 55420/612-884-1161
MWG Co., P.O. Box 971202, Miami, FL 33197/800-428-9394, 305-253-8393; FAX: 305-232-1247

N

N&J Sales, Lime Kiln Rd., Northford, CT 06472/203-484-0247
Nagel's Bullets, 9 Wilburn, Baytown, TX 77520
Napoleon Bonaparte, Inc., Gerald Desquesnes, 640 Harrison St., Santa Clara, CA 95050
Nastoff's 45 Shop, Inc., Steve, 12288 Mahoning Ave., P.O. Box 446, North Jackson, OH 44451/216-538-2977
National Bullet Co., 1585 E. 361 St., Eastlake, OH 44095/216-951-1854; FAX: 216-951-7761
National Security Safe Co., Inc., P.O. Box 39, 620 S. 380 E., American Fork, UT 84003/801-756-7706, 800-544-3829; FAX: 801-756-8043
National Target Co., 4690 Wyaconda Rd., Rockville, MD 20852/800-827-7060, 301-770-7060; FAX: 301-770-7892
Nationwide Airgun Repairs (See Airgun Repair Centre)
Nationwide Sports Distributors, Inc., 70 James Way, Southampton, PA 18966/215-322-2050, 800-355-3006; FAX: 702-358-2093
Naval Ordnance Works, Rt. 2, Box 919, Sheperdstown, WV 25443/304-876-0998
Navy Arms Co., 689 Bergen Blvd., Ridgefield, NJ 07657/201-945-2500; FAX: 201-945-6859
N.B.B., Inc., 24 Elliot Rd., Sterling, MA 01564/508-422-7538, 800-942-9444
N.C. Ordnance Co., P.O. Box 3254, Wilson, NC 27895/919-237-2440; FAX: 919-243-0927
NCP Products, Inc., 3500 12th St. N.W., Canton, OH 44708/330-456-5130: FAX: 330-456-5234
Necessary Concepts, Inc., P.O. Box 571, Deer Park, NY 11729/516-667-8509; 800-671-8881
NECO, 1316-67th St., Emeryville, CA 94608/510-450-0420; FAX: 510-450-0421
Necromancer Industries, Inc., 14 Communications Way, West Newton, PA 15089/412-872-8722
NEI Handtools, Inc., 51583 Columbia River Hwy., Scappoose, OR 97056/503-543-6776; FAX: 503-543-6799; E-MAIL: neiht@mcimail.com
Nelson Combat Leather, Bruce, P.O. Box 8691 CRB, Tucson, AZ 85738
Nelson, Gary K., 975 Terrace Dr., Oakdale, CA 95361/209-847-4590
Nelson, Stephen, 7365 NW Spring Creek Dr., Corvallis, OR 97330/541-745-5232
Nelson/Weather-Rite, Inc., 14760 Santa Fe Trail Dr., Lenexa, KS 66215/913-492-3200; FAX: 913-492-8749
Nesci Enterprises, Inc., P.O. Box 119, Summit St., East Hampton, CT 06424/860-267-2588; FAX: 860-267-2589
Nesika Bay Precision, 22239 Big Valley Rd., Poulsbo, WA 98370/206-697-3830
Nettestad Gun Works, RR 1, Box 160, Pelican Rapids, MN 56572/218-863-4301
Neumann GmbH, Am Galgenberg 6, 90575 Langenzenn, GERMANY/09101/8258; FAX: 09101/6356
Nevada Cartridge Co., 44 Montgomery St., Suite 500, San Francisco, CA 94104/415-925-9394; FAX: 415-925-9396
Nevada Pistol Academy Inc., 4610 Blue Diamond Rd., Las Vegas, NV 89139/702-897-1100
New Advantage Arms Corp., 2843 N. Alvernon Way, Tucson, AZ 85712/602-881-7444; FAX: 602-323-0949
New Democracy, Inc., 751 W. Lamar Blvd., Suite 102, Arlington, TX 76012-2010
New England Ammunition Co., 1771 Post Rd. East, Suite 223, Westport, CT 06880/203-254-8048
New England Arms Co., Box 278, Lawrence Lane, Kittery Point, ME 03905/207-439-0593; FAX: 207-439-6726
New England Custom Gun Service, 438 Willow Brook Rd., RR2, Box 122W, W. Lebanon, NH 03784/603-469-3450; FAX: 603-469-3471
New England Firearms, 60 Industrial Rowe, Gardner, MA 01440/508-632-9393; FAX: 508-632-2300
New Historians Productions, The, 131 Oak St., Royal Oak, MI 48067/313-544-7544
New Orleans Jewelers Supply Co., 206 Charters St., New Orleans, LA 70130/504-523-3839; FAX: 504-523-3836
New SKB Arms Co., C.P.O. Box 1401, Tokyo, JAPAN/81-3-3943-9550; FAX: 81-3-3943-0695
New Win Publishing, Inc., Box 5159, Clinton, NJ 08809/201-735-9701; FAX: 201-735-9703
Newark Electronics, 4801 N. Ravenswood Ave., Chicago, IL 60640
Newell, Robert H., 55 Coyote, Los Alamos, NM 87544/505-662-7135
Newman Gunshop, 119 Miller Rd., Agency, IA 52530/515-937-5775
NgraveR Co., The, 67 Wawecus Hill Rd., Bozrah, CT 06334/203-823-1533
Nic Max, Inc., 535 Midland Ave., Garfield, NJ 07026/201-546-7191; FAX: 201-546-7419
Nicholson Custom, Rt. 1, Box 176-3, Sedalia, MO 65301/816-826-8746
Nickels, Paul R., 4789 Summerhill Rd., Las Vegas, NV 89121/702-435-5318
Nicklas, Ted, 5504 Hegel Rd., Goodrich, MI 48438/810-797-4493
Niemi Engineering, W.B., Box 126 Center Road, Greensboro, VT 05841/802-533-7180 days, 802-533-7141 evenings
Nikon, Inc., 1300 Walt Whitman Rd., Melville, NY 11747/516-547-8623; FAX: 516-547-0309
Nitex, Inc., P.O. Box 1706, Uvalde, TX 78801/210-278-8843
Noble Co., Jim, 1305 Columbia St., Vancouver, WA 98660/206-695-1309
Noreen, Peter H., 5075 Buena Vista Dr., Belgrade, MT 59714/406-586-7383
Norica, Avnda Otaola, 16, Apartado 68, 20600 Eibar, SPAIN
Norin, Dave, Schrank's Smoke & Gun, 2010 Washington St., Waukegan, IL 60085/708-662-4034
Norinco, 7A, Yun Tan N Beijing, CHINA (U.S. importers—Century International Arms, Inc.; Interarms)
Norma Precision AB (See U.S. importers—Dynamit Nobel-RWS Inc.; Paul Co. Inc., The)
Norman Custom Gunstocks, Jim, 14281 Cane Rd., Valley Center, CA 92082/619-749-6252
Normark Corp., 10395 Yellow Circle Dr., Minnetonka, MN 55343-9101/612-933-7060; FAX: 612-933-0046
Norrell Arms, John, 2608 Grist Mill Rd., Little Rock, AR 72207/501-225-7864
North American Arms, Inc., 2150 South 950 East, Provo, UT 84606-6285/800-821-5783, 801-374-9990; FAX: 801-374-9998
North American Correspondence Schools, The Gun Pro School, Oak & Pawney St., Scranton, PA 18515/717-342-7701
North American Munitions, P.O. Box 815, Beulah, ND 58523/701-948-2260; FAX: 701-948-2282
North American Shooting Systems, P.O. Box 306, Osoyoos, B.C. V0H 1V0 CANADA/604-495-3131; FAX: 604-495-2816

North American Specialties, P.O. Box 189, Baker City, OR 97814/503-523-6954
North Devon Firearms Services, 3 North St., Braunton, EX33 1AJ ENGLAND/01271 813624; FAX: 01271 813624
North Fork Custom Gunsmithing, James Johnston, 428 Del Rio Rd., Roseburg, OR 97470/503-673-4467
North Mountain Pine Training Center (See Executive Protection Institute)
North Specialty Products, 2664-B Saturn St., Brea, CA 92621/714-524-1665
North Star West, P.O. Box 488, Glencoe, CA 95232/209-293-7010
North Wind Decoy Co., 1005 N. Tower Rd., Fergus Falls, MN 56537/218-736-4378; FAX: 218-736-7060
Northern Precision Custom Swaged Bullets, 329 S. James St., Carthage, NY 13619/315-493-1711
Northlake Outdoor Footwear, P.O. Box 10, Franklin, TN 37065-0010/615-794-1556; FAX: 615-790-8005
Northside Gun Shop, 2725 NW 109th, Oklahoma City, OK 73120/405-840-2353
No-Sho Mfg. Co., 10727 Glenfield Ct., Houston, TX 77096/713-723-5332
Nosler, Inc., P.O. Box 671, Bend, OR 97709/800-285-3701, 503-382-3921; FAX: 503-388-4667
Novak's, Inc., 1206½ 30th St., P.O. Box 4045, Parkersburg, WV 26101/304-485-9295; FAX: 304-428-6722
Nowlin Custom Mfg., Rt. 1, Box 308, Claremore, OK 74017/918-342-0689; FAX: 918-342-0624
NRI Gunsmith School, 4401 Connecticut Ave. NW, Washington, D.C. 20008
Nu-Line Guns, Inc., 1053 Caulks Hill Rd., Harvester, MO 63304/314-441-4500, 314-447-4501; FAX: 314-447-5018
Null Holsters Ltd., K.L., 161 School St. NW, Hill City Station, Resaca, GA 30735/706-625-5643; FAX: 706-625-9392
Numrich Arms Corp., 203 Broadway, W. Hurley, NY 12491
Nu-Teck, 30 Industrial Park Rd., Box 37, Centerbrook, CT 06409/203-767-3573; FAX: 203-767-9137
NW Sinker and Tackle, 380 Valley Dr., Myrtle Creek, OR 97457-9717
Nygord Precision Products, P.O. Box 12578, Prescott, AZ 86304/520-717-2315; FAX: 520-717-2198

O

Oakland Custom Arms, Inc., 4690 W. Walton Blvd., Waterford, MI 48329/810-674-8261
Oakman Turkey Calls, RD 1, Box 825, Harrisonville, PA 17228/717-485-4620
Oakshore Electronic Sights, Inc., P.O. Box 4470, Ocala, FL 32678-4470/904-629-7112; FAX: 904-629-1433
Obermeyer Rifled Barrels, 23122 60th St., Bristol, WI 53104/414-843-3537; FAX: 414-843-2129
October Country, P.O. Box 969, Dept. GD, Hayden, ID 83835/208-772-2068; FAX: 208-772-9230
Oehler Research, Inc., P.O. Box 9135, Austin, TX 78766/512-327-6900, 800-531-5125; FAX: 512-327-6903
Oglesby & Oglesby Gunmakers, Inc., RR 5, Springfield, IL 62707/217-487-7100
Oil Rod and Gun Shop, 69 Oak St., East Douglas, MA 01516/508-476-3687
Ojala Holsters, Arvo, P.O. Box 98, N. Hollywood, CA 91603/503-669-1404
Oker's Engraving, 365 Bell Rd., P.O. Box 126, Shawnee, CO 80475/303-838-6042
Oklahoma Ammunition Co., 4310 W. Rogers Blvd., Skiatook, OK 74070/918-396-3187; FAX: 918-396-4270
Oklahoma Leather Products, Inc., 500 26th NW, Miami, OK 74354/918-542-6651; FAX: 918-542-6653
OK Weber, Inc., P.O. Box 7485, Eugene, OR 97401/541-747-0458; FAX: 541-747-5927
Old Dominion Engravers, 100 Progress Drive, Lynchburg, VA 24502/804-237-4450
Old Wagon Bullets, 32 Old Wagon Rd., Wilton, CT 06897
Old West Bullet Moulds, P.O. Box 519, Flora Vista, NM 87415/505-334-6970
Old West Reproductions, Inc., 446 Florence S. Loop, Florence, MT 59833/406-273-2615
Old Western Scrounger, Inc., 12924 Hwy. A-l2, Montague, CA 96064/916-459-5445; FAX: 916-459-3944
Old World Gunsmithing, 2901 SE 122nd St., Portland, OR 97236/503-760-7681
Old World Oil Products, 3827 Queen Ave. N., Minneapolis, MN 55412/612-522-5037
Ole Frontier Gunsmith Shop, 2617 Hwy. 29 S., Cantonment, FL 32533/904-477-8074
Olsen Development Lab, 111 Lakeview Ave., Blackwood, NJ 08012
Olson, Myron, 989 W. Kemp, Watertown, SD 57201/605-886-9787
Olson, Vic, 5002 Countryside Dr., Imperial, MO 63052/314-296-8086
Olt Co., Philip S., P.O. Box 550, 12662 Fifth St., Pekin, IL 61554/309-348-3633; FAX: 309-348-3300
Olympic Optical Co., P.O. Box 752377, Memphis, TN 38175-2377/901-794-3890, 800-238-7120; FAX: 901-794-0676, 800-748-1669
Omark Industries, Div. of Blount, Inc., 2299 Snake River Ave., P.O. Box 856, Lewiston, ID 83501/800-627-3640, 208-746-2351
Omega Sales, P.O. Box 1066, Mt. Clemens, MI 48043/810-469-7323; FAX: 810-469-0425
One Of A Kind, 15610 Purple Sage, San Antonio, TX 78255/512-695-3364
Op-Tec, P.O. Box L632, Langhorn, PA 19047/215-757-5037
Optical Services Co., P.O. Box 1174, Santa Teresa, NM 88008-1174/505-589-3833
Orchard Park Enterprise, P.O. Box 563, Orchard Park, NY 14227/616-656-0356
Ordnance Works, The, 2969 Pidgeon Point Road, Eureka, CA 95501/707-443-3252
Oregon Arms, Inc., P.O. Box 20, Prospect OR 97536/503-560-4040; FAX: 503-560-4041
Original Mink Oil, Inc., 10652 NE Holman, Portland, OR 97220/503-255-2814, 800-547-5895; FAX: 503-255-2487
Orion Rifle Barrel Co., RR2, 137 Cobler Village, Kalispell, MT 59901/406-257-5649
Or-Un, Tahtakale Menekse Han 18, Istanbul, TURKEY 34460/90212-522-5912; FAX: 90212-522-7973
Orvis Co., The, Rt. 7, Manchester, VT 05254/802-362-3622 ext. 283; FAX: 802-362-3525
Ottmar, Maurice, Box 657, 113 E. Fir, Coulee City, WA 99115/509-632-5717
Outa-Site Gun Carriers, 219 Market St., Laredo, TX 78040/210-722-4678, 800-880-9715; FAX: 210-726-4858
Outdoor Connection, Inc., The, 201 Cotton Dr., P.O. Box 7751, Waco, TX 76714-7751/800-533-6076; 817-772-5575; FAX: 817-776-3553
Outdoor Edge Cutlery Corp., 2888 Bluff St., Suite 130, Boulder, CO 80301/303-652-8212; FAX: 303-652-8238
Outdoor Enthusiast, 3784 W. Woodland, Springfield, MO 65807/417-883-9841
Outdoor Sports Headquarters, Inc., 967 Watertower Ln., West Carrollton, OH 45449/513-865-5855; FAX: 513-865-5962
Outdoorsman's Bookstore, The, Llangorse, Brecon, Powys LD3 7UE, U.K./44-1874-658-660; FAX: 44-1874-658-650
Outers Laboratories, Div. of Blount, Inc., Sporting Equipment Div., Route 2,, P.O. Box 39/Onalaska, WI 54650
608-781-5800; FAX: 608-781-0368
Ox-Yoke Originals, Inc., 34 Main St., Milo, ME 04463/800-231-8313, 207-943-7351; FAX: 207-943-2416
Ozark Gun Works, 11830 Cemetery Rd., Rogers, AR 72756/501-631-6944; FAX: 501-631-6944

P

P&M Sales and Service, 5724 Gainsborough Pl., Oak Forest, IL 60452/708-687-7149
P&S Gun Service, 2138 Old Shepardsville Rd., Louisville, KY 40218/502-456-9346
Pac-Nor Barreling, 99299 Overlook Rd., P.O. Box 6188, Brookings, OR 97415/503-469-7330; FAX: 503-469-7331
Pace Marketing, Inc., P.O. Box 2039, Stuart, FL 34995/407-871-9682; FAX: 407-871-6552
Pachmayr, Ltd., 1875 S. Mountain Ave., Monrovia, CA 91016/818-357-7771, 800-423-9704; FAX: 818-358-7251
Pacific Pistolcraft, 1810 E. Columbia Ave., Tacoma, WA 98404/206-474-5465
Pacific Precision, 755 Antelope Rd., P.O. Box 2549, White City, OR 97503/503-826-5808; FAX: 503-826-5304
Pacific Research Laboratories, Inc., 10221 S.W. 188th St., Vashon Island, WA 98070/206-463-5551; FAX: 206-463-2526
Pacific Rifle Co., 1040-D Industrial Parkway, Newberg, OR 97132/503-538-7437
Pacific Tool Co., P.O. Box 2048, Ordnance Plant Rd., Grand Island, NE 68801
Paco's (See Small Custom Mould & Bullet Co.)
P.A.C.T., Inc., P.O. Box 531525, Grand Prairie, TX 75053/214-641-0049
Page Custom Bullets, P.O. Box 25, Port Moresby Papua, NEW GUINEA
Pagel Gun Works, Inc., 1407 4th St. NW, Grand Rapids, MN 55744/218-326-3003
Paintball Consumer Reports (International Paintball Pub. Inc.), 14573-C Je, ferson Davis Highway/Woodridge, VA 22191
703-491-6199
Paintball Games International Magazine (Aceville Publications), Castle House, 97 High St./Colchester, Essex, CO1 1TH ENGLAND
011-44-206-564840
Paintball Sports Magazine, 540 Main St., Mt. Kisco, NY 10549/914-241-7400
Palmer Manufacturing Co., Inc., C., P.O. Box 220, West Newton, PA 15089/412-872-8200; FAX: 412-872-8302
Palmer Security Products, 2930 N. Campbell Ave., Chicago, IL 60618/800-788-7725; FAX: 312-267-8080
Palsa Outdoor Products, P.O. Box 81336, Lincoln, NE 68501-1336/402-488-5288, 800-456-9281; FAX: 402-488-2321
PanaVise Products, Inc., 1485 Southern Way, Sparks, NV 89431/702-353-2900; FAX: 702-353-2929
Para-Ordnance Mfg., Inc., 980 Tapscott Rd., Scarborough, Ont. M1X 1E7, CANADA/416-297-7855; FAX: 416-297-1289 (U.S. importer—Para-Ordnance, Inc.)
Para-Ordnance, Inc., 1919 NE 45th St., Ft. Lauderdale, FL 33308
Paragon Sales & Services, Inc., P.O. Box 2022, Joliet, IL 60434/815-725-9212; FAX: 815-725-8974
Pardini Armi Srl, Via Italica 154, 55043 Lido Di Camaiore Lu, ITALY/584-90121; FAX: 584-90122 (U.S. importers—Nygord Precision Products)
Paris, Frank J., 17417 Pershing St., Livonia, MI 48152-3822
Park Rifle Co., Ltd., The, Unit 6a, Dartford Trade Park, Power Mill Lane, Dartford, Kent DA7 7NX/011-0322-222512 (U.S. importer—Air Werks International)
Parker Div. Reageant Chemical (See Parker Reproductions)
Parker Gun Finishes, 9337 Smokey Row Rd., Strawberry Plains, TN 37871/423-933-3286

Parker Reproductions, 124 River Rd., Middlesex, NJ 08846/908-469-0100; FAX: 908-469-9692
Parker, Mark D., 1240 Florida Ave. 7, Longmont, CO 80501/303-772-0214
Parsons Optical Mfg. Co., P.O. Box 192, Ross, OH 45061/513-867-0820; FAX: 513-867-8380
Parts & Surplus, P.O. Box 22074, Memphis, TN 38122/901-683-4007
Partridge Sales Ltd., John, Trent Meadows, Rugeley, Staffordshire, WS15 2HS ENGLAND/0889-584438
Pasadena Gun Center, 206 E. Shaw, Pasadena, TX 77506/713-472-0417; FAX: 713-472-1322
Passive Bullet Traps, Inc. (See Savage Range Systems, Inc.)
PAST Sporting Goods, Inc., P.O. Box 1035, Columbia, MO 65205/314-445-9200; FAX: 314-446-6606
Paterson Gunsmithing, 438 Main St., Paterson, NJ 07502/201-345-4100
Pathfinder Sports Leather, 2920 E. Chambers St., Phoenix, AZ 85040/602-276-0016
Patrick Bullets, P.O. Box 172, Warwick QSLD 4370 AUSTRALIA
Pattern Control, 114 N. Third St., P.O. Box 462105, Garland, TX 75046/214-494-3551; FAX: 214-272-8447
Paul Co., The, 27385 Pressonville Rd., Wellsville, KS 66092/913-883-4444; FAX: 913-883-2525
Paulsen Gunstocks, Rt. 71, Box 11, Chinook, MT 59523/406-357-3403
Payne Photography, Robert, P.O. Box 141471, Austin, TX 78714/512-272-4554
PC Bullet/ADC, Inc., 52700 NE First, Scappoose, OR 97056-3212/503-543-5088; FAX: 503-543-5990
PC Co., 5942 Secor Rd., Toledo, OH 43623/419-472-6222
Peacemaker Specialists, P.O. Box 157, Whitmore, CA 96096/916-472-3438
Pease Accuracy, Bob, P.O. Box 310787, New Braunfels, TX 78131/210-625-1342
Peasley, David, P.O. Box 604, 2067 S. Hiway 17, Alamosa, CO 81101
PECAR Herbert Schwarz, GmbH, Kreuzbergstrasse 6, 10965 Berlin, GERMANY/004930-785-7383; FAX: 004930-785-1934
Pecatonica River Longrifle, 5205 Noddingham Dr., Rockford, IL 61111/815-968-1995; FAX: 815-968-1996
Pedersen, C.R., 2717 S. Pere Marquette Hwy., Ludington, MI 49431/616-843-2061
Pedersen, Rex C., 2717 S. Pere Marquette Hwy., Ludington, MI 49431/616-843-2061
Pedersoli Davide & C., Via Artigiani 57, Gardone V.T., Brescia, ITALY 25063/030-8912402; FAX: 030-8911019 (U.S. importers—Beauchamp & Son, Inc.; Cabela's; Cape Outfitters; Dixie Gun Works; EMF Co., Inc.; Navy Arms Co.)
Peerless Alloy, Inc., 1445 Osage St., Denver, CO 80204-2439/303-825-6394, 800-253-1278
Peet Shoe Dryer, Inc., 130 S. 5th St., P.O. Box 618, St. Maries, ID 83861/208-245-2095, 800-222-PEET; FAX: 208-245-5441
Peifer Rifle Co., P.O. Box 192, Nokomis, IL 62075-0192/217-563-7050; FAX: 217-563-7060
Pejsa Ballistics, 2120 Kenwood Pkwy., Minneapolis, MN 55405/612-374-3337; FAX: 612-374-3337
Pelaire Products, 5346 Bonky Ct., W. Palm Beach, FL 33415/407-439-0691; FAX: 407-967-0052
Pell, John T. (See KOGOT)
Peltor, Inc., 41 Commercial Way, E. Providence, RI 02914/401-438-4800; FAX: 401-434-1708
PEM's Mfg. Co., 5063 Waterloo Rd., Atwater, OH 44201/216-947-3721
Pence Precision Barrels, 7567 E. 900 S., S. Whitley, IN 46787/219-839-4745
Pend Oreille Sport Shop, 3100 Hwy. 200 East, Sandpoint, ID 83864/208-263-2412
Pendleton Royal, c/o Swingler Buckland Ltd., 4/7 Highgate St., Birmingham, ENGLAND B12 0XS/44 121 440 3060, 44 121 446 5898; FAX: 44 121 446 4165
Pendleton Woolen Mills, P.O. Box 3030, 220 N.W. Broadway, Portland, OR 97208/503-226-4801
Penguin Industries, Inc., Airport Industrial Mall, Coatesville, PA 19320/610-384-6000; FAX: 610-857-5980
Penn Bullets, P.O. Box 756, Indianola, PA 15051
Penn's Woods Products, Inc., 19 W. Pittsburgh St., Delmont, PA 15626/412-468-8311; FAX: 412-468-8975
Pennsylvania Gun Parts, 1701 Mud Run Rd., York Springs, PA 17372/717-259-8010
Pennsylvania Gunsmith School, 812 Ohio River Blvd., Avalon, Pittsburgh, PA 15202/412-766-1812
Penrod Precision, 312 College Ave., P.O. Box 307, N. Manchester, IN 46962/219-982-8385
Pentax Corp., 35 Inverness Dr. E., Englewood, CO 80112/303-799-8000; FAX: 303-790-1131
Pentheny de Pentheny, 2352 Baggett Ct., Santa Rosa, CA 95401/707-573-1390; FAX: 707-573-1390
Perazone-Gunsmith, Brian, P.O. Box 275GD, Cold Spring Rd., Roxbury, NY 12474/607-326-4088; FAX: 607-326-3140
Perazzi m.a.p. S.P.A., Via Fontanelle 1/3, 1-25080 Botticino Mattina, ITALY (U.S. importer—Perazzi USA, Inc.)
Perazzi USA, Inc., 1207 S. Shamrock Ave., Monrovia, CA 91016/818-303-0068; FAX: 818-303-2081
Peregrine Sporting Arms, Inc., 14155 Brighton Rd., Brighton, CO 80601/303-654-0850
Performance Specialists, 308 Eanes School Rd., Austin, TX 78746/512-327-0119
Peripheral Data Systems (See Arms Software)
Personal Protection Systems, RD 5, Box 5027-A, Moscow, PA 18444/717-842-1766
Perugini Visini & Co. s.r.l., Via Camprelle, 126, 25080 Nuvolera (Bs.), ITALY
Peters Stahl GmbH, Stettiner Strasse 42, D-33106 Paderborn, GERMANY/05251-750025; FAX: 05251-75611 (U.S. importers—Harris Gunworks; Olympic Arms)
Petersen Publishing Co., 6420 Wilshire Blvd., Los Angeles, CA 90048/213-782-2000; FAX: 213-782-2867
Peterson Gun Shop, Inc., A.W., 4255 W. Old U.S. 441, Mt. Dora, FL 32757-3299/904-383-4258
Petro-Explo, Inc., 7650 U.S. Hwy. 287, Suite 100, Arlington, TX 76017/817-478-8888
Pettinger Books, Gerald, Rt. 2, Box 125, Russell, IA 50238/515-535-2239
Pflumm Mfg. Co., 10662 Widmer Rd., Lenexa, KS 66215/800-888-4867; FAX: 913-451-7857
PFRB Co., P.O. Box 1242, Bloomington, IL 61702/309-473-3964
Phil-Chem, Inc. (See George & Roy's)
Phillippi Custom Bullets, Justin, P.O. Box 773, Ligonier, PA 15658/412-238-9671
Phillips, Jerry, P.O. Box L632, Langhorne, PA 19047/215-757-5037
Phillips & Rodgers, 100 Hilbig, Suite C, Conroe, TX 77301/800-682-2247
Phoenix Arms, 1420 S. Archibald Ave., Ontario, CA 91761/909-947-4843; FAX: 909-947-6798
Photronic Systems Engineering Company, 6731 Via De La Reina, Bonsall, CA 92003/619-758-8000
Piedmont Community College, P.O. Box 1197, Roxboro, NC 27573/910-599-1181
Pierce Pistols, 2326 E. Hwy. 34, Newnan, GA 30263/404-253-8192
Pietta (See U.S. importers—Navy Arms Co.; Taylor's & Co., Inc.)
Pilgrim Pewter, Inc. (See Bell Originals Inc., Sid)
Pilkington, Scott, Little Trees Ramble, P.O. Box 97, Monteagle, TN 37356/615-924-3475; FAX: 615-924-3489
Pine Technical College, 1100 4th St., Pine City, MN 55063/800-521-7463; FAX: 612-629-6766
Pinetree Bullets, 133 Skeena St., Kitimat BC, CANADA V8C 1Z1/604-632-3768; FAX: 604-632-3768
Pioneer Arms Co., 355 Lawrence Rd., Broomall, PA 19008/215-356-5203
Pioneer Guns, 5228 Montgomery Rd., Norwood, OH 45212/513-631-4871
Pioneer Research, Inc., 216 Haddon Ave., Suite 102, Westmont, NJ 08108/800-257-7742; FAX: 609-858-8695
Piotti (See U.S. importer—Moore & Co., Wm. Larkin)
Piquette, Paul R., 80 Bradford Dr., Feeding Hills, MA 01030/413-781-8300, Ext. 682
Plaxco, J. Michael, Rt. 1, P.O. Box 203, Roland, AR 72135/501-868-9787
Plaza Cutlery, Inc., 3333 Bristol, 161, South Coast Plaza, Costa Mesa, CA 92626/714-549-3932
Plum City Ballistic Range, N2162 80th St., Plum City, WI 54761-8622/715-647-2539
PlumFire Press, Inc., 30-A Grove Ave., Patchogue, NY 11772-4112/800-695-7246; FAX:516-758-4071
PMC/Eldorado Cartridge Corp., P.O. Box 62508, 12801 U.S. Hwy. 95 S., Boulder City, NV 89005/702-294-0025; FAX: 702-294-0121
P.M. Enterprises, Inc., 146 Curtis Hill Rd., Chehalis, WA 98532/206-748-3743; FAX: 206-748-1802
Poburka, Philip (See Bison Studios)
Pohl, Henry A. (See Great American Gun Co.)
Pointing Dog Journal, Village Press Publications, P.O. Box 968, Dept. PGD, Traverse City, MI 49685/800-272-3246; FAX: 616-946-3289
Police Bookshelf, P.O. Box 122, Concord, NH 03301/603-224-6814; FAX: 603-226-3554
Policlips North America, 59 Douglas Crescent, Toronto, Ont. CANADA M4W 2E6/800-229-5089, 416-924-0383; FAX: 416-924-4375
Polywad, Inc., P.O. Box 7916, Macon, GA 31209/912-477-0669
Pomeroy, Robert, RR1, Box 50, E. Corinth, ME 04427/207-285-7721
Ponsness/Warren, P.O. Box 8, Rathdrum, ID 83858/208-687-2231; FAX: 208-687-2233
Pony Express Reloaders, 608 E. Co. Rd. D, Suite 3, St. Paul, MN 55117/612-483-9406; FAX: 612-483-9884
Pony Express Sport Shop, Inc., 16606 Schoenborn St., North Hills, CA 91343/818-895-1231
Porta Blind, Inc., 2700 Speedway, Wichita Falls, TX 76308/817-723-6620
Portus, Robert, 130 Ferry Rd., Grants Pass, OR 97526/503-476-4919
Potts, Wayne E., 912 Poplar St., Denver, CO 80220/303-355-5462
Powder Horn Antiques, P.O. Box 4196, Ft. Lauderdale, FL 33338/305-565-6060
Powder Horn, Inc., The, P.O. Box 114 Patty Drive, Cusseta, GA 31805/404-989-3257
Powder Valley Services, Rt. 1, Box 100, Dexter, KS 67038/316-876-5418
Powell & Son (Gunmakers) Ltd., William, 35-37 Carrs Lane, Birmingham B4 7SX ENGLAND/121-643-0689; FAX: 121-631-3504 (U.S. importer—Bell's Legendary Country Wear; The William Powell Agency)
Powell Agency, William, The, 22 Circle Dr., Bellmore, NY 11710/516-679-1158
Power Custom, Inc., RR 2, P.O. Box 756AB, Gravois Mills, MO 65037/314-372-5684

Practical Tools, Inc., Div. Behlert Precision, 7067 Easton Rd., P.O. Box 133, Pipersville, PA 18947/215-766-7301; FAX: 215-766-8681
Pragotrade, 307 Humberline Dr., Rexdale, Ontario, CANADA M9W 5V1/416-675-1322
Prairie River Arms, 1220 N. Sixth St., Princeton, IL 61356/815-875-1616, 800-445-1541; FAX: 815-875-1402
Pranger, Ed G., 1414 7th St., Anacortes, WA 98221/206-293-3488
Pre-Winchester 92-90-62 Parts Co., P.O. Box 8125, W. Palm Beach, FL 33407
Precise International, 15 Corporate Dr., Orangeburg, NY 10962/914-365-3500; FAX: 914-425-4700
Precise Metalsmithing Enterprises, 146 Curtis Hill Rd., Chehalis, WA 98532/206-748-3743; FAX: 206-748-8102
Precision, Jim, 1725 Moclip's Dr., Petaluma, CA 94952/707-762-3014
Precision Airgun Sales, Inc., 5139 Warrensville Center Rd., Maple Hts., OH 44137-1906/216-587-5005
Precision Cartridge, 176 Eastside Rd., Deer Lodge, MT 59722/800-397-3901, 406-846-3900
Precision Cast Bullets, 101 Mud Creek Lane, Ronan, MT 59864/406-676-5135
Precision Castings & Equipment, Inc., P.O. Box 326, Jasper, IN 47547-0135/812-634-9167
Precision Components, 3177 Sunrise Lake, Milford, PA 18337/717-686-4414
Precision Components and Guns, Rt. 55, P.O. Box 337, Pawling, NY 12564/914-855-3040
Precision Delta Corp., P.O. Box 128, Ruleville, MS 38771/601-756-2810; FAX: 601-756-2590
Precision Metal Finishing, John Westrom, P.O. Box 3186, Des Moines, IA 50316/515-288-8680; FAX: 515-244-3925
Precision Munitions, Inc., P.O. Box 326, Jasper, IN 47547
Precision Ordnance, 1316 E. North St., Jackson, MI 49202
Precision Reloading, Inc., P.O. Box 122, Stafford Springs, CT 06076/860-684-7979; FAX: 860-684-6788
Precision Sales International, Inc., P.O. Box 1776, Westfield, MA 01086/413-562-5055; FAX: 413-562-5056
Precision Shooting, Inc., 222 McKee St., Manchester, CT 06040/860-645-8776; FAX: 860-643-8215
Precision Small Arms, 9777 Wilshire Blvd., Suite 1005, Beverly Hills, CA 90212/310-859-4867; FAX: 310-859-2868
Precision Specialties, 131 Hendom Dr., Feeding Hills, MA 01030/413-786-3365; FAX: 413-786-3365
Precision Sport Optics, 15571 Producer Lane, Unit G, Huntington Beach, CA 92649/714-891-1309; FAX: 714-892-6920
Premier Reticles, 920 Breckinridge Lane, Winchester, VA 22601-6707/540-722-0601; FAX: 540-722-3522
Prescott Projectile Co., 1808 Meadowbrook Road, Prescott, AZ 86303
Price Bullets, Patrick W., 16520 Worthley Drive, San Lorenzo, CA 94580/510-278-1547
Preslik's Gunstocks, 4245 Keith Ln., Chico, CA 95926/916-891-8236
Prime Reloading, 30 Chiswick End, Meldreth, Royston SG8 6LZ UK/0763-260636
Primos, Inc., P.O. Box 12785, Jackson, MS 39236-2785/601-366-1288; FAX: 601-362-3274
Pro Load Ammunition, Inc., 5180 E. Seltice Way, Post Falls, ID 83854/208-773-9444; FAX: 208-773-9441
Pro-Mark, Div. of Wells Lamont, 6640 W. Touhy, Chicago, IL 60648/312-647-8200
Pro-Port Ltd., 41302 Executive Dr., Harrison Twp., MI 48045-1306/810-469-7323; FAX: 810-469-0425
Pro-Shot Products, Inc., P.O. Box 763, Taylorville, IL 62568/217-824-9133; FAX: 217-824-8861
Professional Firearms Record Book Co. (See PFRB Co.)
Professional Gunsmiths of America, Inc., Route 1, Box 224F, Lexington, MO 64067/816-259-2636
Professional Hunter Supplies (See Star Custom Bullets)
Prolix® Lubricants, P.O. Box 1348, Victorville, CA 92393/800-248-LUBE, 619-243-3129; FAX: 619-241-0148
Protecto Plastics, Div. of Penguin Ind., Airport Industrial Mall, Coatesville, PA 19320/215-384-6000
Protector Mfg. Co., Inc., The, 443 Ashwood Place, Boca Raton, FL 33431/407-394-6011
Protektor Model, 1-11 Bridge St., Galeton, PA 16922/814-435-2442
Prototech Industries, Inc., Rt. 1, Box 81, Delia, KS 66418/913-771-3571; FAX: 913-771-2531
ProWare,Inc., 15847 NE Hancock St., Portland, OR 97230/503-239-0159
P.S.M.G. Gun Co., 10 Park Ave., Arlington, MA 02174/617-646-8845; FAX: 617-646-2133
PWL Gunleather, P.O. Box 450432, Atlanta, GA 31145/404-822-1640; FAX: 404-822-1704
Pyromid, Inc., 3292 S. Highway 97, Redmond, OR 97756/503-548-1041; FAX: 503-923-1004

Q

QB air rifles (See U.S. importer—Sportsman Airguns, Inc.)
Quack Decoy & Sporting Clays, 4 Ann & Hope Way, P.O. Box 98, Cumberland, RI 02864/401-723-8202; FAX: 401-722-5910
Quaker Boy, Inc., 5455 Webster Rd., Orchard Parks, NY 14127/716-662-3979; FAX: 716-662-9426
Quality Arms, Inc., Box 19477, Dept. GD, Houston, TX 77224/713-870-8377; FAX: 713-870-8524
Quality Firearms of Idaho, Inc., 114 13th Ave. S., Nampa, ID 83651/208-466-1631
Quality Parts Co./Bushmaster Firearms, 999 Roosevelt Trail, Bldg. 3, Windham, ME 04062/800-998-7928, 207-892-2005; FAX: 207-892-8068
Quarton USA, Ltd. Co., 7042 Alamo Downs Pkwy., Suite 370, San Antonio, TX 78238-4518/800-520-8435, 210-520-8430; FAX: 210-520-8433
Quartz-Lok, 13137 N. 21st Lane, Phoenix, AZ 85029
Que Industries, Inc., P.O. Box 2471, Everett, WA 98203/800-769-6930, 206-347-9843; FAX: 206-514-3266
Queen Cutlery Co., P.O. Box 500, Franklinville, NY 14737/800-222-5233; FAX: 716-676-5535
Quigley's Personal Protection Strategies, Paxton, 9903 Santa Monica Blvd.,, 300/Beverly Hills, CA 90212
310-281-1762

R

R&C Knives & Such, P.O. Box 1047, Manteca, CA 95336/209-239-3722; FAX: 209-825-6947
R&J Gun Shop, 133 W. Main St., John Day, OR 97845/503-575-2130
R&S Industries Corp., 8255 Brentwood Industrial Dr., St. Louis, MO 63144/314-781-5400
Rabeno, Martin, 92 Spook Hole Rd., Ellenville, NY 12428/914-647-4567
Radiator Specialty Co., 1900 Wilkinson Blvd., P.O. Box 34689, Charlotte, NC 28234/800-438-6947; FAX: 800-421-9525
Radical Concepts, P.O. Box 1473, Lake Grove, OR 97035/503-538-7437
Rainier Ballistics Corp., 4500 15th St. East, Tacoma, WA 98424/800-638-8722, 206-922-7589; FAX: 206-922-7854
Ram-Line, Inc., 545 Thirty-One Rd., Grand Junction, CO 81504/303-434-4500; FAX: 303-434-4004
Ranch Products, P.O. Box 145, Malinta, OH 43535/313-277-3118; FAX: 313-565-8536
Randall-Made Knives, P.O. Box 1988, Orlando, FL 32802/407-855-8075
Randco UK, 286 Gipsy Rd., Welling, Kent DA16 1JJ, ENGLAND/44 81 303 4118
Randolph Engineering, Inc., 26 Thomas Patten Dr., Randolph, MA 02368/800-541-1405; FAX: 617-956-0337
Ranger Mfg. Co., Inc., 1536 Crescent Dr., P.O. Box 14069, Augusta, GA 30919-0069/706-738-2023; FAX: 404-738-3608
Ranger Products, 2623 Grand Blvd., Suite 209, Holiday, FL 34609/813-942-4652, 800-407-7007; FAX: 813-942-6221
Ranger Shooting Glasses, 26 Thomas Patten Dr., Randolph, MA 02368/800-541-1405; FAX: 617-986-0337
Ranging, Inc., Routes 5 & 20, East Bloomfield, NY 14443/716-657-6161; FAX: 716-657-5405
Ransom International Corp., P.O. Box 3845, 1040-A Sandretto Dr., Prescott, AZ 86302/520-778-7899; FAX: 520-778-7993; E-MAIL: ransom@primenet.com; WEB: http://www.primenet.com/˜ransom
Rapine Bullet Mould Mfg. Co., 9503 Landis Lane, East Greenville, PA 18041/215-679-5413; FAX: 215-679-9795
Rattlers Brand, P.O. Box 311, 115 E. Main St., Thomaston, GA 30286/706-647-7131, 800-825-7131; FAX: 706-647-6652
Ravell Ltd., 289 Diputacion St., 08009, Barcelona SPAIN/34(3) 4874486; FAX: 34(3) 4881394
Ray's Gunsmith Shop, 3199 Elm Ave., Grand Junction, CO 81504/970-434-6162; FAX: 970-434-6162
Raytech, Div. of Lyman Products Corp., 475 Smith Street, Middletown, CT 06457-1541/860-632-2020; FAX: 860-632-1699
RCBS, Div. of Blount, Inc., Sporting Equipment Div., 605 Oro Dam Blvd., Oroville, CA 95965/800-533-5000, 916-533-5191; FAX: 916-533-1647
Reagent Chemical & Research, Inc. (See Calico Hardwoods, Inc.)
Reardon Products, P.O. Box 126, Morrison, IL 61270/815-772-3155
Recoilless Technologies, Inc., 3432 W. Wilshire Dr., Suite 11, Phoenix, AZ 85009/602-278-8903; FAX: 602-272-5946
Red Ball, 100 Factory St., Nashua, NH 03060/603-881-4420
Red Cedar Precision Mfg., W. 485 Spruce Dr., Brodhead, WI 53520/608-897-8416
Red Diamond Dist. Co., 1304 Snowdon Dr., Knoxville, TN 37912
Red Star Target Co., P.O. Box 275, Babb, MT 59411-0275/800-679-2917; FAX: 800-679-2918
Redding Reloading Equipment, 1097 Starr Rd., Cortland, NY 13045/607-753-3331; FAX: 607-756-8445
Redfield, Inc., 5800 E. Jewell Ave., Denver, CO 80224-2303/303-757-6411; FAX: 303-756-2338
Redman's Rifling & Reboring, 189 Nichols Rd., Omak, WA 98841/509-826-5512
Redwood Bullet Works, 3559 Bay Rd., Redwood City, CA 94063/415-367-6741
Reed, Dave, Rt. 1, Box 374, Minnesota City, MN 55959/507-689-2944
Refrigiwear, Inc., 71 Inip Dr., Inwood, Long Island, NY 11696
R.E.I., P.O. Box 88, Tallevast, FL 34270/813-755-0085
Reiswig, Wallace E. (See Claro Walnut Gunstock Co.)
Reloaders Equipment Co., 4680 High St., Ecorse, MI 48229
Reloading Specialties, Inc., Box 1130, Pine Island, MN 55463/507-356-8500; FAX: 507-356-8800

Remington Arms Co., Inc., P.O. Box 700, 870 Remington Drive, Madison, NC 27025-0700/800-243-9700
Renegade, P.O. Box 31546, Phoenix, AZ 85046/602-482-6777; FAX: 602-482-1952
Renfrew Guns & Supplies, R.R. 4, Renfrew, Ontario K7V 3Z7 CANADA/613-432-7080
Reno, Wayne, 2808 Stagestop Rd., Jefferson, CO 80456/719-836-3452
R.E.T. Enterprises, 2608 S. Chestnut, Broken Arrow, OK 74012/918-251-GUNS; FAX: 918-251-0587
Retting, Inc., Martin B., 11029 Washington, Culver City, CA 90232/213-837-2412
R.G.-G., Inc., P.O. Box 1261, Conifer, CO 80433-1261/303-697-4154; FAX: 303-697-4154
Rhodeside, Inc., 1704 Commerce Dr., Piqua, OH 45356/513-773-5781
Rice, Keith (See White Rock Tool & Die)
Richards, John, Richards Classic Oil Finish, Rt. 2, Box 325, Bedford, KY 40006/502-255-7222
Richards Micro-Fit Stocks, 8331 N. San Fernando Ave., Sun Valley, CA 91352/818-767-6097; FAX: 818-767-7121
Rickard, Inc., Pete, RD 1, Box 292, Cobleskill, NY 12043/800-282-5663; FAX: 518-234-2454
Ridgetop Sporting Goods, P.O. Box 306, 42907 Hilligoss Ln. East, Eatonville, WA 98328/360-832-6422; FAX: 360-832-6422
Riebe Co., W.J., 3434 Tucker Rd., Boise, ID 83703
Ries, Chuck, 415 Ridgecrest Dr., Grants Pass, OR 97527/503-476-5623
Rifle Works & Armory, 707 N 12 St., Cody, WY 82414/307-587-4914
Rifles Inc., 873 W. 5400 N., Cedar City, UT 84720/801-586-5996; FAX: 801-586-5996
RIG Products, 87 Coney Island Dr., Sparks, NV 89431-6334/702-331-5666; FAX: 702-331-5669
Rigby & Co., John, 66 Great Suffolk St., London SE1 OBU, ENGLAND/0171-620-0690; FAX: 0171-928-9205
Riggs, Jim, 206 Azalea, Boerne, TX 78006/210-249-8567
Riling Arms Books Co., Ray, 6844 Gorsten St., P.O. Box 18925, Philadelphia, PA 19119/215-438-2456; FAX: 215-438-5395
Rim Pac Sports, Inc., 1034 N. Soldano Ave., Azusa, CA 91702-2135
Rimrock Rifle Stocks, P.O. Box 589, Vashon Island, WA 98070/206-463-5551; FAX: 206-463-2526
Ringler Custom Leather Co., 31 Shining Mtn. Rd., Powell, WY 82435/307-645-3255
Ripley Rifles, 42 Fletcher Street, Ripley, Derbyshire, DE5 3LP ENGLAND/011-0773-748353
R.I.S. Co., Inc., 718 Timberlake Circle, Richardson, TX 75080/214-235-0933
River Road Sporting Clays, Bruce Barsotti, P.O. Box 3016, Gonzales, CA 93926/408-675-2473
Rizzini, Battista, Via 2 Giugno, 7/7Bis-25060 Marcheno (Brescia), ITALY (U.S. importers—Wm. Larkin Moore & Co.; New England Arms Co.)
Rizzini, F.LLI (See U.S. importers—Moore & Co. Wm. Larkin; New England Arms Co.)
RLCM Enterprises, 110 Hill Crest Drive, Burleson, TX 76028
R.M. Precision, Inc., Attn. Greg F. Smith Marketing, P.O. Box 210, LaVerkin, UT 84745/801-635-4656; FAX: 801-635-4430
RMS Custom Gunsmithing, 4120 N. Bitterwell, Prescott Valley, AZ 86314/520-772-7626
Robar Co.'s, Inc., The, 21438 N. 7th Ave., Suite B, Phoenix, AZ 85027/602-581-2648; FAX: 602-582-0059
Robbins Scent, Inc., P.O. Box 779, Connellsville, PA 15425/412-628-2529; FAX: 412-628-9598
Roberts/Engraver, J.J., 7808 Lake Dr., Manassas, VA 22111/703-330-0448
Roberts Products, 25328 SE Iss. Beaver Lk. Rd., Issaquah, WA 98029/206-392-8172
Robinett, R.G., P.O. Box 72, Madrid, IA 50156/515-795-2906
Robinson, Don, Pennsylvania Hse., 36 Fairfax Crescent, Southowram, Halifax, W. Yorkshire HX3 9SQ, ENGLAND/0422-364458
Robinson Firearms Mfg. Ltd., 1699 Blondeaux Crescent, Kelowna, B.C. CANADA V1Y 4J8/604-868-9596
Robinson H.V. Bullets, 3145 Church St., Zachary, LA 70791/504-654-4029
Rochester Lead Works, 76 Anderson Ave., Rochester, NY 14607/716-442-8500; FAX: 716-442-4712
Rockwood Corp., Speedwell Division, 136 Lincoln Blvd., Middlesex, NJ 08846/908-560-7171, 800-243-8274; FAX: 980-560-7475
Rocky Fork Enterprises, P.O. Box 427, 878 Battle Rd., Nolensville, TN 37135/615-941-1307
Rocky Mountain Arms, Inc., 600 S. Sunset, Unit C, Longmont, CO 80501/303-768-8522; FAX: 303-678-8766
Rocky Mountain High Sports Glasses, 8121 N. Central Park Ave., Skokie, IL 60076/708-679-1012; FAX: 708-679-0184
Rocky Mountain Rifle Works Ltd., 1707 14th St., Boulder, CO 80302/303-443-9189
Rocky Mountain Target Co., 3 Aloe Way, Leesburg, FL 34788/904-365-9598
Rocky Mountain Wildlife Products, P.O. Box 999, La Porte, CO 80535/303-484-2768; FAX: 303-223-9389
Rocky Shoes & Boots, 294 Harper St., Nelsonville, OH 45764/800-848-9452, 614-753-1951; FAX: 614-753-4024
Rod Guide Co., Box 1149, Forsyth, MO 65653/800-952-2774
Rogers Gunsmithing, Bob, P.O. Box 305, 344 S. Walnut St., Franklin Grove, IL 61031/815-456-2685; FAX: 815-288-7142
Rohner, Hans, 1148 Twin Sisters Ranch Rd., Nederland, CO 80466-9600
Rohner, John, 710 Sunshine Canyon, Boulder, CO 80302/303-444-3841
Rolston, Inc., Fred W., 210 E. Cummins St., Tecumseh, MI 49286/517-423-6002, 800-314-9061 (orders only); FAX: 517-423-6002
Romain's Custom Guns, Inc., RD 1, Whetstone Rd., Brockport, PA 15823/814-265-1948
Rooster Laboratories, P.O. Box 412514, Kansas City, MO 64141/816-474-1622; FAX: 816-474-1307
Rorschach Precision Products, P.O. Box 151613, Irving, TX 75015/214-790-3487
Rosenberg & Sons, Jack A., 12229 Cox Ln., Dallas, TX 75234/214-241-6302
Rosenthal, Brad and Sallie, 19303 Ossenfort Ct., St. Louis, MO 63038/314-273-5159; FAX: 314-273-5149
Ross & Webb (See Ross, Don)
Ross, Don, 12813 West 83 Terrace, Lenexa, KS 66215/913-492-6982
Rosser, Bob, 1824 29th Ave., Suite 24, Birmingham, AL 35209/205-870-4422
Rossi S.A., Amadeo, Rua: Amadeo Rossi, 143, Sao Leopoldo, RS, BRAZIL 93030-220/051-592-5566 (U.S. importer—Interarms)
Roto Carve, 2754 Garden Ave., Janesville, IA 50647
Round Edge, Inc., P.O. Box 723, Lansdale, PA 19446/215-361-0859
Rowe Engineering, Inc. (See R.E.I.)
Royal Arms Gunstocks, 919 8th Ave. NW, Great Falls, MT 59404/406-453-1149
Roy's Custom Grips, Rt. 3, Box 174-E, Lynchburg, VA 24504/804-993-3470
RPM, 15481 N. Twin Lakes Dr., Tucson, AZ 85737/602-825-1233; FAX: 602-825-3333
Rubright Bullets, 1008 S. Quince Rd., Walnutport, PA 18088/215-767-1339
Rucker Dist. Inc., P.O. Box 479, Terrell, TX 75160/214-563-2094
Rudnicky, Susan, 9 Water St., Arcade, NY 14009/716-492-2450
Ruger (See Sturm, Ruger & Co., Inc.)
Rundell's Gun Shop, 6198 Frances Rd., Clio, MI 48420/313-687-0559
Runge, Robert P., 94 Grove St., Ilion, NY 13357/315-894-3036
Rupert's Gun Shop, 2202 Dick Rd., Suite B, Fenwick, MI 48834/517-248-3252,
Russ, 23 William St., Addison, NY 14801/607-359-3896
Russell Knives, Inc., A.G., 1705 Hwy. 71B North, Springdale, AR 72764/501-751-7341
Rusteprufe Laboratories, 1319 Jefferson Ave., Sparta, WI 54656/608-269-4144
Rusty Duck Premium Gun Care Products, 7785 Foundation Dr., Suite 6, Florence, KY 41042/606-342-5553; FAX: 606-342-5556
Rutgers Book Center, 127 Raritan Ave., Highland Park, NJ 08904/908-545-4344; FAX: 908-545-6686
Ruvel & Co., Inc., 4128-30 W. Belmont Ave., Chicago, IL 60641/312-286-9494; FAX: 312-286-9323
R.V.I. (See Fire'n Five)
RWS (See U.S. importer—Dynamit Nobel-RWS, Inc.)
Ryan, Chad L., RR 3, Box 72, Cresco, IA 52136/319-547-4384
Rybka Custom Leather Equipment, Thad, 134 Havilah Hill, Odenville, AL 35120

S

S&B Industries, 11238 McKinley Rd., Montrose, MI 48457/810-639-5491
S&K Manufacturing Co., P.O. Box 247, Pittsfield, PA 16340/814-563-7808; FAX: 814-563-7808
S&S Firearms, 74-11 Myrtle Ave., Glendale, NY 11385/718-497-1100; FAX: 718-497-1105
Sabatti S.R.L., via Alessandro Volta 90, 25063 Gardone V.T., Brescia, ITALY/030-8912207-831312; FAX: 030-8912059 (U.S. importer—E.A.A. Corp.; K.B.I., Inc.)
SAECO (See Redding Reloading Equipment)
Saf-T-Lok, 5713 Corporate Way, Suite 100, W. Palm Beach, FL 33407
Safari Outfitters Ltd., 71 Ethan Allan Hwy., Ridgefield, CT 06877/203-544-9505
Safari Press, Inc., 15621 Chemical Lane B, Huntington Beach, CA 92649/714-894-9080; FAX: 714-894-4949
Safariland Ltd., Inc., 3120 E. Mission Blvd., P.O. Box 51478, Ontario, CA 91761/909-923-7300; FAX: 909-923-7400
SAFE, P.O. Box 864, Post Falls, ID 83854/208-773-3624
Safesport Manufacturing Co., 1100 W. 45th Ave., Denver, CO 80211/303-433-6506, 800-433-6506; FAX: 303-433-4112
Safety Speed Holster, Inc., 910 S. Vail Ave., Montebello, CA 90640/213-723-4140; FAX: 213-726-6973
Sako Ltd., P.O. Box 149, SF-11101, Riihimaki, FINLAND (U.S. importer—Stoeger Industries)
Salter Calls, Inc., Eddie, Hwy. 31 South-Brewton Industrial Park, Brewton, AL 36426/205-867-2584; FAX: 206-867-9005
Samco Global Arms, Inc., 6995 NW 43rd St., Miami, FL 33166/305-593-9782
Sampson, Roger, 430 N. Grove, Mora, MN 55051/320-679-4868
San Francisco Gun Exchange, 124 Second St., San Francisco, CA 94105/415-982-6097
San Marco (See U.S. importers—Cape Outfitters; EMF Co., Inc.)
Sanders Custom Gun Service, 2358 Tyler Lane, Louisville, KY 40205/502-454-3338
Sanders Gun and Machine Shop, 145 Delhi Road, Manchester, IA 52057
Sandia Die & Cartridge Co., 37 Atancacio Rd. NE, Albuquerque, NM 87123/505-298-5729
Sarco, Inc., 323 Union St., Stirling, NJ 07980/908-647-3800
S.A.R.L. G. Granger, 66 cours Fauriel, 42100 Saint Etienne, FRANCE/04 77 25 14 73; FAX: 04 77 38 66 99

Sauer (See U.S. importer—Paul Co., The; Sigarms, Inc.)
Saunders Gun & Machine Shop, R.R. 2, Delhi Road, Manchester, IA 52057
Savage Arms, Inc., 100 Springdale Rd., Westfield, MA 01085/413-568-7001; FAX: 413-562-7764
Savage Arms, Inc., 248 Water St., P.O. Box 1240, Lakefield, Ont. K0L 2H0, CANADA/705-652-8000; FAX: 705-652-8431
Savage Range Systems, Inc., 100 Springdale RD., Westfield, MA 01085/413-568-7001; FAX: 413-562-1152
Savana Sports, Inc., 5763 Ferrier St., Montreal, Quebec, CANADA H4P 1N3/514-739-1753; FAX: 514-739-1755
Saville Iron Co. (See Greenwood Precision)
Savino, Barbara J., P.O. Box 1104, Hardwick, VT 05843-1104
Scanco Environmental Systems, 5000 Highlands Parkway, Suite 180, Atlanta, GA 30082/404-431-0025; FAX: 404-431-0028
Scansport, Inc., P.O. Box 700, Enfield, NH 03748/603-632-7654
Scattergun Technologies Inc., 620 8th Ave. S., Nashville, TN 37203/615-254-1441; FAX: 615-254-1449; WEB: http://www.scattergun.com
Sceery Game Calls, P.O. Box 6520, Sante Fe, NM 87502/505-471-9110; FAX: 505-471-3476
Schaefer Shooting Sports, 1923 Grand Ave., Baldwin, NY 11510/516-379-4900; FAX: 516-379-6701
Scharch Mfg., Inc., 10325 Co. Rd. 120, Unit C, Salida, CO 81201/719-539-7242, 800-836-4683; FAX: 719-539-3021
Scherer, Box 250, Ewing, VA 24240/615-733-2615; FAX: 615-733-2073
Schiffman, Curt, 3017 Kevin Cr., Idaho Falls, ID 83402/208-524-4684
Schiffman, Mike, 8233 S. Crystal Springs, McCammon, ID 83250/208-254-9114
Schiffman, Norman, 3017 Kevin Cr., Idaho Falls, ID 83402/208-524-4684
Schmidtke Group, 17050 W. Salentine Dr., New Berlin, WI 53151-7349
Schmidt & Bender, Inc., Brook Rd., P.O. Box 134, Meriden, NH 03770/603-469-3565, 800-468-3450; FAX: 603-469-3471
Schmidtman Custom Ammunition, 6 Gilbert Court, Cotati, CA 94931
Schneider Bullets, 3655 West 214th St., Fairview Park, OH 44126
Schneider Rifle Barrels, Inc., Gary, 12202 N. 62nd Pl., Scottsdale, AZ 85254/602-948-2525
School of Gunsmithing, The, 6065 Roswell Rd., Atlanta, GA 30328/800-223-4542
Schrimsher's Custom Knifemaker's Supply, Bob, P.O. Box 308, Emory, TX 75440/903-473-3330; FAX: 903-473-2235
Schroeder Bullets, 1421 Thermal Ave., San Diego, CA 92154/619-423-3523
Schuetzen Gun Co., P.O. Box 272113, Fort Collins, CO 80527/970-223-3678
Schuetzen Pistol Works, 620-626 Old Pacific Hwy. SE, Olympia, WA 98513/360-459-3471; FAX: 360-491-3447
Schulz Industries, 16247 Minnesota Ave., Paramount, CA 90723/213-439-5903
Schumakers Gun Shop, William, 512 Prouty Corner Lp. A, Colville, WA 99114/509-684-4848
Schwartz Custom Guns, David W., 2505 Waller St., Eau Claire, WI 54703/715-832-1735
Schwartz Custom Guns, Wayne E., 970 E. Britton Rd., Morrice, MI 48857/517-625-4079
Scobey Duck & Goose Calls, Glynn, Rt. 3, Box 37, Newbern, TN 38059/901-643-6241
Scope Control, Inc., 5775 Co. Rd. 23 SE, Alexandria, MN 56308/612-762-7295
ScopLevel, 151 Lindbergh Ave., Suite C, Livermore, CA 94550/510-449-5052; FAX: 510-373-0861
Scot Powder, Rt.1 Box 167, McEwen, TN 37101/800-416-3006; FAX: 615-729-4211
Scot Powder Co. of Ohio, Inc., Box GD96, Only, TN 37140/615-729-4207, 800-416-3006; FAX: 615-729-4217
Scott, Dwight, 23089 Englehardt St., Clair Shores, MI 48080/313-779-4735
Scott Fine Guns, Inc., Thad, P.O. Box 412, Indianola, MS 38751/601-887-5929
Scott, McDougall & Associates, 7950 Redwood Dr., Cotati, CA 94931/707-546-2264; FAX: 707-795-1911
S.C.R.C., P.O. Box 660, Katy, TX 77492-0660/FAX: 713-578-2124
Scruggs' Game Calls, Stanley, Rt. 1, Hwy. 661, Cullen, VA 23934/804-542-4241, 800-323-4828
Seattle Binocular & Scope Repair Co., P.O. Box 46094, Seattle, WA 98146/206-932-3733
Second Chance Body Armor, P.O. Box 578, Central Lake, MI 49622/616-544-5721; FAX: 616-544-9824
Security Awareness & Firearms Education (See SAFE)
Seebeck Assoc., R.E., P.O. Box 59752, Dallas, TX 75229
Seecamp Co., Inc., L.W., P.O. Box 255, New Haven, CT 06502/203-877-3429
Seligman Shooting Products, Box 133, Seligman, AZ 86337/602-422-3607
Selsi Co., Inc., P.O. Box 10, Midland Park, NJ 07432-0010/201-935-0388; FAX: 201-935-5851
Semmer, Charles, 7885 Cyd Dr., Denver, CO 80221/303-429-6947
Sentinel Arms, P.O. Box 57, Detroit, MI 48231/313-331-1951; FAX: 313-331-1456
Serva Arms Co., Inc., RD 1, Box 483A, Greene, NY 13778/607-656-4764
Service Armament, 689 Bergen Blvd., Ridgefield, NJ 07657
Servus Footwear Co., 1136 2nd St., Rock Island, IL 61204-3610/309-786-7741; FAX: 309-786-9808
S.G.S. Sporting Guns Srl., Via Della Resistenza, 37, 20090 Buccinasco (MI) ITALY/2-45702446; FAX: 2-45702464
Shanghai Airguns, Ltd. (See U.S. importer—Sportsman Airguns, Inc.)
Shappy Bullets, 76 Milldale Ave., Plantsville, CT 06479/203-621-3704
Sharps Arms Co., Inc., C. (See Montana Armory, Inc.)
Shaw, Inc., E.R. (See Small Arms Mfg. Co.)
Shay's Gunsmithing, 931 Marvin Ave., Lebanon, PA 17042
Sheffield Knifemakers Supply, Inc., P.O. Box 741107, Orange City, FL 32774-1107/904-775-6453; FAX: 904-774-5754
Shell Shack, 113 E. Main, Laurel, MT 59044/406-628-8986
Shepherd Scope Ltd., Box 189, Waterloo, NE 68069/402-779-2424; FAX: 402-779-4010
Sheridan USA, Inc., Austin, P.O. Box 577, 36 Haddam Quarter Rd., Durham, CT 06422/203-349-1772; FAX: 203-349-1771
Sherwood, George, 46 N. River Dr., Roseburg, OR 97470/541-672-3159
Shilen Rifles, Inc., P.O. Box 1300, 205 Metro Park Blvd., Ennis, TX 75119/214-875-5318; FAX: 214-875-5402
Shiloh Creek, Box 357, Cottleville, MO 63338/314-447-2900; FAX: 314-447-2900
Shiloh Rifle Mfg., 201 Centennial Dr., Big Timber, MT 59011/406-932-4454; FAX: 406-932-5627
Shirley Co. Gun & Riflemakers Ltd., J.A., P.O. Box 368, High Wycombe, Bucks. HP13 6YN, ENGLAND/0494-446883; FAX: 0494-463685
Shockley, Harold H., 204 E. Farmington Rd., Hanna City, IL 61536/309-565-4524
Shoemaker & Sons, Inc., Tex, 714 W. Cienega Ave., San Dimas, CA 91773/909-592-2071; FAX: 909-592-2378
The Shooten' Haus, 102 W. 13th, Kearney, NE 68847/308-236-7929
Shooter Shop, The, 221 N. Main, Butte, MT 59701/406-723-3842
Shooter's Choice, 16770 Hilltop Park Place, Chagrin Falls, OH 44023/216-543-8808; FAX: 216-543-8811
Shooter's Edge, Inc., P.O.Box 769, Trinidad, CO 81082
Shooter's World, 3828 N. 28th Ave., Phoenix, AZ 85017/602-266-0170
Shooters Supply, 1120 Tieton Dr., Yakima, WA 98902/509-452-1181
Shootin' Accessories, Ltd., P.O. Box 6810, Auburn, CA 95604/916-889-2220
Shootin' Shack, Inc., 1065 Silver Beach Rd., Riviera Beach, FL 33403/407-842-0990
Shooting Chrony Inc., 3269 Niagara Falls Blvd., N. Tonawanda, NY 14120/905-276-6292; FAX: 905-276-6295
Shooting Components Marketing, P.O. Box 1069, Englewood, CO 80150/303-987-2543; FAX: 303-989-3508
Shooting Gallery, The, 8070 Southern Blvd., Boardman, OH 44512/216-726-7788
Shooting Specialties (See Titus, Daniel)
Shooting Star, 1825 Fortview Rd., Ste. 115, Austin, TX 78747/512-462-0009
Shoot-N-C Targets (See Birchwood Casey)
Shotgun Shop, The, 14145 Proctor Ave., Suite 3, Industry, CA 91746/818-855-2737; FAX: 818-855-2735
Shotguns Unlimited, 2307 Fon Du Lac Rd., Richmond, VA 23229/804-752-7115
Siegrist Gun Shop, 8754 Turtle Road, Whittemore, MI 48770
Sierra Bullets, 1400 W. Henry St., Sedalia, MO 65301/816-827-6300; FAX: 816-827-6300; WEB: http://www.sierrabullets.com
Sierra Specialty Prod. Co., 1344 Oakhurst Ave., Los Altos, CA 94024/FAX: 415-965-1536
SIG, CH-8212 Neuhausen, SWITZERLAND (U.S. importer—Mandall Shooting Supplies, Inc.)
SIG-Sauer (See U.S. importer—Sigarms, Inc.)
Sigarms, Inc., Corporate Park, Industrial Drive, Exeter, NH 03833/603-772-2302; FAX: 603-772-9082
Sight Shop, The, John G. Lawson, 1802 E. Columbia Ave., Tacoma, WA 98404/206-474-5465
Sightron, Inc., Rt. 1, Box 293, Franklinton, NC 27525/919-494-5040; FAX: 919-494-2612
Signet Metal Corp., 551 Stewart Ave., Brooklyn, NY 11222/718-384-5400; FAX: 718-388-7488
Sile Distributors, Inc., 7 Centre Market Pl., New York, NY 10013/212-925-4111; FAX: 212-925-3149
Silencio/Safety Direct, 56 Coney Island Dr., Sparks, NV 89431/800-648-1812, 702-354-4451; FAX: 702-359-1074
Silent Hunter, 1100 Newton Ave., W. Collingswood, NJ 08107/609-854-3276
Silhouette Leathers, P.O. Box 1161, Gunnison, CO 81230/303-641-6639
Silhouette, The, P.O. Box 1509, Idaho Falls, ID 83403
Silver Eagle Machining, 18007 N. 69th Ave., Glendale, AZ 85308
Silver Ridge Gun Shop (See Goodwin, Fred)
Silver-Tip Corp., RR2, Box 184, Gloster, MS 39638-9520
Simmons, Jerry, 715 Middlebury St., Goshen, IN 46526/219-533-8546
Simmons Enterprises, Ernie, 709 East Elizabethtown Rd., Manheim, PA 17545/717-664-4040
Simmons Gun Repair, Inc., 700 S. Rogers Rd., Olathe, KS 66062/913-782-3131; FAX: 913-782-4189
Simmons Outdoor Corp., 2120 Kilarney Way, Tallahassee, FL 32308/904-878-5100; FAX: 904-878-0300
Sinclair International, Inc., 2330 Wayne Haven St., Fort Wayne, IN 46803/219-493-1858; FAX: 219-493-2530
Sinclair, W.P., Box 1209, Warminster, Wiltshire BA12 9XJ, ENGLAND/01044-1985-218544; FAX: 01044-1985-214111
Single Shot, Inc. (See Montana Armory, Inc.)
Singletary, Kent, 2915 W. Ross, Phoenix, AZ 85027/602-582-4900
Sipes Gun Shop, 7415 Asher Ave., Little Rock, AR 72204/501-565-8480
Siskiyou Gun Works (See Donnelly, C.P.)

Six Enterprises, 320-D Turtle Creek Ct., San Jose, CA 95125/408-999-0201; FAX: 408-999-0216
Skaggs, R.E., P.O. Box 555, Hamilton, IN 46742/219-488-3755
SKAN A.R., 4 St. Catherines Road, Long Melford, Suffolk, CO10 9JU ENGLAND/011-0787-312942
SKB Arms Co. (See New SKB Arms Co.)
SKB Shotguns, 4325 S. 120th St., P.O. Box 37669, Omaha, NE 68137/800-752-2767; FAX: 402-330-8029
Skeoch, Brian R., P.O. Box 279, Glenrock, WY 82637/307-436-9655; FAX: 307-436-9034
Skip's Machine, 364 29 Road, Grand Junction, CO 81501/303-245-5417
Sklany, Steve, 566 Birch Grove Dr., Kalispell, MT 59901/406-755-4257
SKR Industries, POB 1382, San Angelo, TX 76902/915-658-3133
S.L.A.P. Industries, P.O. Box 1121, Parklands 2121, SOUTH AFRICA/27-11-788-0030; FAX: 27-11-788-0030
Slezak, Jerome F., 1290 Marlowe, Lakewood (Cleveland), OH 44107/216-221-1668
Slings 'N Things, Inc., 8909 Bedford Circle, Suite 11, Omaha, NE 68134/402-571-6954; FAX: 402-571-7082
Slug Group, Inc., P.O. Box 376, New Paris, PA 15554/814-839-4517; FAX: 814-839-2601
Slug Site Co., Ozark Wilds, Rt. 2, Box 158, Versailles, MO 65084/314-378-6430
Small Arms Mfg. Co., 5312 Thoms Run Rd., Bridgeville, PA 15017/412-221-4343; FAX: 412-221-4303
Small Custom Mould & Bullet Co., Box 17211, Tucson, AZ 85731
Smart Parts, 1203 Spring St., Latrobe, PA 15650/412-539-2660; FAX: 412-539-2298
Smires, C.L., 28269 Old Schoolhouse Rd., Columbus, NJ 08022/609-298-3158
Smith & Wesson, 2100 Roosevelt Ave., Springfield, MA 01102/413-781-8300; FAX: 413-731-8980
Smith, Art, 230 Main St. S., Hector, MN 55342/612-848-2760; FAX: 612-848-2760
Smith, Mark A., P.O. Box 182, Sinclair, WY 82334/307-324-7929
Smith, Michael, 620 Nye Circle, Chattanooga, TN 37405/615-267-8341
Smith, Ron, 5869 Straley, Ft. Worth, TX 76114/817-732-6768
Smith, Sharmon, 4545 Speas Rd., Fruitland, ID 83619/208-452-6329
Smith Abrasives, Inc., 1700 Sleepy Valley Rd., P.O. Box 5095, Hot Springs, AR 71902-5095/501-321-2244; FAX: 501-321-9232
Smith Saddlery, Jesse W., 3601 E. Boone Ave., Spokane, WA 99202-4501/509-325-0622
Smokey Valley Rifles (See Lutz Engraving, Ron E.)
Snapp's Gunshop, 6911 E. Washington Rd., Clare, MI 48617/517-386-9226
Snider Stocks, Walter S., Rt. 2 P.O. Box 147, Denton, NC 27239
Sno-Seal (See Atsko/Sno-Seal)
Societa Armi Bresciane Srl. (See U.S. importer—Cape Outfitters; Gamba, USA)
Sonora Rifle Barrel Co., 14396 D. Tuolumne Rd., Sonora, CA 95370/209-532-4139
Soque River Knives, P.O. Box 880, Clarkesville, GA 30523/706-754-8500; FAX: 706-754-7263
SOS Products Co. (See Buck Stix—SOS Products Co.)
Sotheby's, 1334 York Ave. at 72nd St., New York, NY 10021/212-606-7260
Sound Technology, P.O. Box 1132, Kodiak, AK 99615/907-486-8448
South Bend Replicas, Inc., 61650 Oak Rd., South Bend, IN 46614/219-289-4500
Southeastern Community College, 1015 S. Gear Ave., West Burlington, IA 52655/319-752-2731
Southern Ammunition Co., Inc., 4232 Meadow St., Loris, SC 29569-3124/803-756-3262; FAX: 803-756-3583
Southern Armory, The, Rt. 2, Box 134, Woodlawn, VA 24381/703-238-1343; FAX: 703-238-1453
Southern Bloomer Mfg. Co., P.O. Box 1621, Bristol, TN 37620/615-878-6660; FAX: 615-878-8761
Southern Security, 1700 Oak Hills Dr., Kingston, TN 37763/423-376-6297; 800-251-9992
Southwind Sanctions, P.O. Box 445, Aledo, TX 76008/817-441-8917
Sparks, Milt, 605 E. 44th St. No. 2, Boise, ID 83714-4800
Spartan-Realtree Products, Inc., 1390 Box Circle, Columbus, GA 31907/706-569-9101; FAX: 706-569-0042
Specialty Gunsmithing, Lynn McMurdo, P.O. Box 404, Afton, WY 83110/307-886-5535
Specialty Shooters Supply, Inc., 3325 Griffin Rd., Suite 9mm, Fort Lauderdale, FL 33317
Speedfeed, Inc., 3820 Industrial Way, Suite N, Benicia, CA 94510/707-746-1221; FAX: 707-746-1888
Speer Products, Div. of Blount, Inc., Sporting Equipment Div., P.O. Box 856, Lewiston, ID 83501/208-746-2351; FAX: 208-746-2915
Spegel, Craig, P.O. Box 3108, Bay City, OR 97107/503-377-2697
Speiser, Fred D., 2229 Dearborn, Missoula, MT 59801/406-549-8133
Spence, George W., 115 Locust St., Steele, MO 63877/314-695-4926
Spencer Reblue Service, 1820 Tupelo Trail, Holt, MI 48842/517-694-7474
Spencer's Custom Guns, Rt. 1, Box 546, Scottsville, VA 24590/804-293-6836
Spezial Waffen (See U.S. importer—American Bullets)
S.P.G., Inc., P.O. Box 761-H, Livingston, MT 59047/406-222-8416; FAX: 406-222-8416
Sphinx Engineering SA, Ch. des Grandes-Vies 2, CH-2900 Porrentruy, SWITZERLAND/41 66 66 73 81; FAX: 41 66 66 30 90 (U.S. importer—Sphinx USA Inc.)
Sphinx USA Inc., 998 N. Colony, Meriden, CT 06450/203-238-1399; FAX: 203-238-1375
Spokhandguns, Inc., 1206 Fig St., Benton City, WA 99320/509-588-5255
Sport Flite Manufacturing Co., P.O. Box 1082, Bloomfield Hills, MI 48303/810-647-3747
Sporting Arms Mfg., Inc., 801 Hall Ave., Littlefield, TX 79339/806-385-5665; FAX: 806-385-3394
Sports Innovations, Inc., P.O. Box 5181, 8505 Jacksboro Hwy., Wichita Falls, TX 76307/817-723-6015
Sportsman Airguns, Inc., 17712 Carmenita Rd., Cerritos, CA 90703-8639/800-424-7486
Sportsman Safe Mfg. Co., 6309-6311 Paramount Blvd., Long Beach, CA 90805/800-266-7150, 310-984-5445
Sportsman Supply Co., 714 East Eastwood, P.O. Box 650, Marshall, MO 65340/816-886-9393
Sportsman's Communicators, 588 Radcliffe Ave., Pacific Palisades, CA 90272/800-538-3752
Sportsmatch U.K. Ltd., 16 Summer St., Leighton Buzzard, Bedfordshire, LU7 8HT ENGLAND/01525-381638; FAX: 01525-851236
Sportsmen's Exchange & Western Gun Traders, Inc., 560 S. "C" St., Oxnard, CA 93030/805-483-1917
Spradlin's, 113 Arthur St., Pueblo, CO 81004/719-543-9462; FAX: 719-543-9465
Springfield, Inc., 420 W. Main St., Geneseo, IL 61254/309-944-5631; FAX: 309-944-3676
Springfield Sporters, Inc., RD 1, Penn Run, PA 15765/412-254-2626; FAX: 412-254-9173
Spyderco, Inc., 4565 N. Hwy. 93, P.O. Box 800, Golden, CO 80403/303-279-8383, 800-525-7770; FAX: 303-278-2229
SSK Co., 220 N. Belvidere Ave., York, PA 17404/717-854-2897
SSK Industries, 721 Woodvue Lane, Wintersville, OH 43952/614-264-0176; FAX: 614-264-2257
Stackpole Books, 5067 Ritter Rd., Mechanicsburg, PA 17055-6921/717-234-5041; FAX: 717-234-1359
Stalker, Inc., P.O. Box 21, Fishermans Wharf Rd., Malakoff, TX 75148/903-489-1010
Stalwart Corporation, 76 Imperial, Unit A, Evanston, WY 82930/307-789-7687; FAX: 307-789-7688
Stanley Bullets, 2085 Heatheridge Ln., Reno, NV 89509
Star Bonifacio Echeverria S.A., Torrekva 3, Eibar, SPAIN 20600/43-107340; FAX: 43-101524 (U.S. importer—Interarms; P.S.M.G. Gun Co.)
Star Custom Bullets, P.O. Box 608, 468 Main St., Ferndale, CA 95536/707-786-9140; FAX: 707-786-9117
Starke Bullet Company, P.O. Box 400, Cooperstown, ND 58425/701-797-3431
Starkey Labs, 6700 Washington Ave. S., Eden Prairie, MN 55344
Starkey's Gun Shop, 9430 McCombs, El Paso, TX 79924/915-751-3030
Starline, 1300 W. Henry St., Sedalia, MO 65301/816-827-6640; FAX: 816-827-6650
Star Machine Works, 418 10th Ave., San Diego, CA 92101/619-232-3216
Star Reloading Co., Inc., 5520 Rock Hampton Ct., Indianapolis, IN 46268/317-872-5840
Stark's Bullet Mfg., 2580 Monroe St., Eugene, OR 97405
Starlight Training Center, Inc., Rt. 1, P.O. Box 88, Bronaugh, MO 64728/417-843-3555
Starnes Gunmaker, Ken, 32900 SW Laurelview Rd., Hillsboro, OR 97123/503-628-0705; FAX: 503-628-6005
Starr Trading Co., Jedediah, P.O. Box 2007, Farmington Hills, MI 48333/810-683-4343; FAX: 810-683-3282
Starrett Co., L.S., 121 Crescent St., Athol, MA 01331/617-249-3551
State Arms Gun Co., 815 S. Division St., Waunakee, WI 53597/608-849-5800
Steelman's Gun Shop, 10465 Beers Rd., Swartz Creek, MI 48473/810-735-4884
Steffens, Ron, 18396 Mariposa Creek Rd., Willits, CA 95490/707-485-0873
Stegall, James B., 26 Forest Rd., Wallkill, NY 12589
Steger, James R., 1131 Dorsey Pl., Plainfield, NJ 07062
Steves House of Guns, Rt. 1, Minnesota City, MN 55959/507-689-2573
Stewart Game Calls, Johnny, Inc., P.O. Box 7954, 5100 Fort Ave., Waco, TX 76714/817-772-3261; FAX: 817-772-3670
Stewart's Gunsmithing, P.O. Box 5854, Pietersburg North 0750, Transvaal, SOUTH AFRICA/01521-89401
Steyr Mannlicher AG, Mannlicherstrasse 1, P.O.B. 1000, A-4400 Steyr, AUSTRIA/0043-7252-896-0; FAX: 0043-7252-68621 (U.S. importer—GSI, Inc.; Nygord Precision Products)
Stiles Custom Guns, RD3, Box 1605, Homer City, PA 15748/412-479-9945, 412-479-8666
Stillwell, Robert, 421 Judith Ann Dr., Schertz, TX 78154
Stoeger Industries, 5 Mansard Ct., Wayne, NJ 07470/201-872-9500, 800-631-0722; FAX: 201-872-2230
Stoeger Publishing Co. (See Stoeger Industries)
Stone Enterprises Ltd., Rt. 609, P.O. Box 335, Wicomico Church, VA 22579/804-580-5114; FAX: 804-580-8421
Stone Mountain Arms, 5988 Peachtree Corners E., Norcross, GA 30071/800-251-9412
Stoney Baroque Shooters Supply, John Richards, Rt. 2, Box 325, Bedford, KY 40006/502-255-7222
Stoney Point Products, Inc., P.O. Box 234, 1815 North Spring Street, New Ulm, MN 56073-0234/507-354-3360; FAX: 507-354-7236

Storage Tech, 1254 Morris Ave., N. Huntingdon, PA 15642/800-437-9393
Storey, Dale A. (See DGS, Inc.)
Storm, Gary, P.O. Box 5211, Richardson, TX 75083/214-385-0862
Stott's Creek Armory, Inc., RR1, Box 70, Morgantown, IN 46160/317-878-5489
Stott's Creek Printers, RR1, Box 70, Morgantown, IN 46160/317-878-5489
Stratco, Inc., P.O. Box 2270, Kalispell, MT 59901/406-755-1221; FAX: 406-755-1226
Strawbridge, Victor W., 6 Pineview Dr., Dover, NH 03820/603-742-0013
Streamlight, Inc., 1030 W. Germantown Pike, Norristown, PA 19403/215-631-0600; FAX: 610-631-0712
Strong Holster Co., 39 Grove St., Gloucester, MA 01930/508-281-3300; FAX: 508-281-6321
Strutz Rifle Barrels, Inc., W.C., P.O. Box 611, Eagle River, WI 54521/715-479-4766
Stuart, V. Pat, Rt.1, Box 447-S, Greenville, VA 24440/804-556-3845
Sturm, Ruger & Co., Inc., Lacey Place, Southport, CT 06490/203-259-4537; FAX: 203-259-2167
"Su-Press-On," Inc., P.O. Box 09161, Detroit, MI 48209/313-842-4222 7:30-11p.m. Mon-Thurs.
Sullivan, David S. (See Westwind Rifles, Inc.)
Summit Specialties, Inc., P.O. Box 786, Decatur, AL 35602/205-353-0634; FAX: 205-353-9818
Sundance Industries, Inc., 25163 W. Avenue Stanford, Valencia, CA 91355/805-257-4807
Sun Welding Safe Co., 290 Easy St. No.3, Simi Valley, CA 93065/805-584-6678, 800-729-SAFE; FAX: 805-584-6169
Surecase Co., The, 233 Wilshire Blvd., Ste. 900, Santa Monica, CA 90401/800-92ARMLOC
Sure-Shot Game Calls, Inc., P.O. Box 816, 6835 Capitol, Groves, TX 77619/409-962-1636; FAX: 409-962-5465
Survival Arms, Inc., P.O. Box 965, Orange, CT 06477/203-924-6533; FAX: 203-924-2581
Svon Corp., 280 Eliot St., Ashland, MA 01721/508-881-8852
Swampfire Shop, The (See Peterson Gun Shop, Inc., A.W.)
Swann, D.J., 5 Orsova Close, Eltham North, Vic. 3095, AUSTRALIA/03-431-0323
Swanndri New Zealand, 152 Elm Ave., Burlingame, CA 94010/415-347-6158
SwaroSports, Inc. (See JagerSport, Ltd.)
Swarovski Optik North America Ltd., One Wholesale Way, Cranston, RI 02920/401-942-3380, 800-426-3089; FAX: 401-946-2587
Sweet Home, Inc., P.O. Box 900, Orrville, OH 44667-0900
Swenson's 45 Shop, A.D., P.O. Box 606, Fallbrook, CA 92028
Swift Bullet Co., P.O. Box 27, 201 Main St., Quinter, KS 67752/913-754-3959; FAX: 913-754-2359
Swift Instruments, Inc., 952 Dorchester Ave., Boston, MA 02125/617-436-2960, 800-446-1116; FAX: 617-436-3232
Swift River Gunworks, Inc., 450 State St., Belchertown, MA 01007/413-323-4052
Swiss Army Knives, Inc., 151 Long Hill Crossroads, 37 Canal St., Shelton, CT 06484/800-243-4032
Swivel Machine Works, Inc., 11 Monitor Hill Rd., Newtown, CT 06470/203-270-6343; FAX: 203-874-9212
Szweda, Robert (See RMS Custom Gunsmithing)

T

3-D Ammunition & Bullets, 112 W. Plum St., P.O. Box J, Doniphan, NE 68832/402-845-2285, 800-255-6712; FAX: 402-845-6546
3-Ten Corp., P.O. Box 269, Feeding Hills, MA 01030/413-789-2086; FAX: 413-789-1549
10-X Products Group, 2915 Lyndon B. Johnson Freeway, Suite 133, Dallas, TX 75234/214-243-4016, 800-433-2225; FAX: 214-243-4112
300 Gunsmith Service, Inc., at Cherry Creek State Park Shooting Center,, 12500 E. Belleview Ave./Englewood, CO 80111
303-690-3300
Tabler Marketing, 2554 Lincoln Blvd., Suite 555, Marina Del Rey, CA 90291/818-755-4565; FAX: 818-755-0972
TacStar Industries, Inc., 218 Justin Drive, P.O. Box 70, Cottonwood, AZ 86326/602-639-0072; FAX: 602-634-8781
TacTell, Inc., P.O. Box 5654, Maryville, TN 37802/615-982-7855; FAX: 615-558-8294
Tactical Defense Institute, 574 Miami Bluff Ct., Loveland, OH 45140/513-677-8229
Tag Distributors, 1331 Penna. Ave., Emmaus, PA 18049/610-966-3839
Talbot QD Mounts, 2210 E. Grand Blanc Rd., Grand Blanc, MI 48439-8113/810-695-2497
Talley, Dave, P.O. Box 821, Glenrock, WY 82637/307-436-8724, 307-436-9315
Talmage, William G., 10208 N. County Rd. 425 W., Brazil, IN 47834/812-442-0804
Talon Mfg. Co., Inc., 575 Bevans Industrial Ln., Paw Paw, WV 25434/304-947-7440; FAX: 304-947-7447
Tamarack Products, Inc., P.O. Box 625, Wauconda, IL 60084/708-526-9333; FAX: 708-526-9353
Tanfoglio S.r.l., Fratelli, via Valtrompia 39, 41, 25068 Gardone V.T., Brescia, ITALY/30-8910361; FAX: 30-8910183 (U.S. importer—E.A.A. Corp.)
Tanglefree Industries, 1261 Heavenly Dr., Martinez, CA 94553/800-982-4868; FAX: 510-825-3874
Tank's Rifle Shop, P.O. Box 474, Fremont, NE 68025/402-727-1317; FAX: 402-721-2573
Tanner (See U.S. importer—Mandall Shooting Supplies, Inc.)
Taracorp Industries, Inc., 1200 Sixteenth St., Granite City, IL 62040/618-451-4400
Tar-Hunt Custom Rifles, Inc., RR3, P.O. Box 572, Bloomsburg, PA 17815-9351/717-784-6368; FAX: 717-784-6368
Tarnhelm Supply Co., Inc., 431 High St., Boscawen, NH 03303/603-796-2551; FAX: 603-796-2918
Tasco Sales, Inc., 7600 NW 26th St., Miami, FL 33156/305-591-3670; FAX: 305-592-5895
Taurus Firearms, Inc., 16175 NW 49th Ave., Miami, FL 33014/305-624-1115; FAX: 305-623-7506
Taurus International Firearms (See U.S. importer—Taurus Firearms, Inc.)
Taurus S.A., Forjas, Avenida Do Forte 511, Porto Alegre, RS BRAZIL 91360/55-51-347-4050; FAX: 55-51-347-3065
Taylor & Robbins, P.O. Box 164, Rixford, PA 16745/814-966-3233
Taylor's & Co., Inc., 304 Lenoir Dr., Winchester, VA 22603/540-722-2017; FAX: 540-722-2018
TCCI, P.O. Box 302, Phoenix, AZ 85001/602-237-3823; FAX: 602-237-3858
TCSR, 3998 Hoffman Rd., White Bear Lake, MN 55110-4626/800-328-5323; FAX: 612-429-0526
TDP Industries, Inc., 606 Airport Blvd., Doylestown, PA 18901/215-345-8687; FAX: 215-345-6057
Techni-Mec (See F.A.I.R. Tecni-Mec s.n.c. di Isidoro Rizzini & C.)
Techno Arms (See U.S. importer—Auto-Ordnance Corp.)
Tecnolegno S.p.A., Via A. Locatelli, 6, 10, 24019 Zogno, ITALY/0345-91114; FAX: 0345-93254
Tele-Optics, 5514 W. Lawrence Ave., Chicago, IL 60630/312-283-7757; FAX: 312-283-7757
Ten-Ring Precision, Inc., Alex B. Hamilton, 1449 Blue Crest Lane, San Antonio, TX 78232/210-494-3063; FAX: 210-494-3066
Tennessee Valley Mfg., P.O. Box 1175, Corinth, MS 38834/601-286-5014
Tepeco, P.O. Box 342, Friendswood, TX 77546/713-482-2702
Testing Systems, Inc., 220 Pegasus Ave., Northvale, NJ 07647
Teton Arms, Inc., P.O. Box 411, Wilson, WY 83014/307-733-3395
Tetra Gun Lubricants, 1812 Margaret Ave., Annapolis, MD 21401/410-268-6451; FAX: 410-268-8377
Texas Armory, P.O. Box 154906, Waco, TX 76715/817-867-6972
Texas Longhorn Arms, Inc., 5959 W. Loop South, Suite 424, Bellaire, TX 77401/713-660-6323; FAX: 713-660-0493
Texas Platers Supply Co., 2453 W. Five Mile Parkway, Dallas, TX 75233/214-330-7168
T.F.C. S.p.A., Via G. Marconi 118, B, Villa Carcina, Brescia 25069, ITALY/030-881271; FAX: 030-881826
Theis, Terry, P.O. Box 535, Fredericksburg, TX 78624/210-997-6778
Theoben Engineering, Stephenson Road, St. Ives, Huntingdon, Cambs., PE17 4WJ ENGLAND/011-0480-461718
Thiewes, George W., 14329 W. Parada Dr., Sun City West, AZ 85375
Things Unlimited, 235 N. Kimbau, Casper, WY 82601/307-234-5277
Thirion Gun Engraving, Denise, P.O. Box 408, Graton, CA 95444/707-829-1876
Thomas, Charles C., 2600 S. First St., Springfield, IL 62794/217-789-8980; FAX: 217-789-9130
Thompson, Norm, 18905 NW Thurman St., Portland, OR 97209
Thompson, Randall (See Highline Machine Co.)
Thompson Bullet Lube Co., P.O. Box 472343, Garland, TX 75047-2343/214-271-8063; FAX: 214-840-6743
Thompson/Center Arms, P.O. Box 5002, Rochester, NH 03866/603-332-2394; FAX: 603-332-5133
Thompson Precision, 110 Mary St., P.O. Box 251, Warren, IL 61087/815-745-3625
Thompson Target Technology, 618 Roslyn Ave., SW, Canton, OH 44710/216-453-7707; FAX: 216-478-4723
Thompson Tool Mount (See TTM)
T.H.U. Enterprises, Inc., P.O. Box 418, Lederach, PA 19450/215-256-1665; FAX: 215-256-9718
Thunder Mountain Arms, P.O. Box 593, Oak Harbor, WA 98277/206-679-4657; FAX: 206-675-1114
Thunderbird Cartridge Co., Inc. (See TCCI)
Thurston Sports, Inc., RD 3 Donovan Rd., Auburn, NY 13021/315-253-0966
Tiger-Hunt, Box 379, Beaverdale, PA 15921/814-472-5161
Tikka (See U.S. importer—Stoeger Industries)
Timber Heirloom Products, 618 Roslyn Ave. SW, Canton, OH 44710/216-453-7707; FAX: 216-478-4723
Time Precision, Inc., 640 Federal Rd., Brookfield, CT 06804/203-775-8343
Timney Mfg., Inc., 3065 W. Fairmont Ave., Phoenix, AZ 85017/602-274-2999; FAX: 602-241-0361
Tink's Safariland Hunting Corp., P.O. Box 244, 1140 Monticello Rd., Madison, GA 30650/706-342-4915; FAX: 706-342-7568
Tinks & Ben Lee Hunting Products (See Wellington Outdoors)
Tioga Engineering Co., Inc., P.O. Box 913, 13 Cone St., Wellsboro, PA 16901/717-724-3533, 717-662-3347
Tippman Pneumatics, Inc., 3518 Adams Center Rd., Fort Wayne, IN 46806/219-749-6022; FAX: 219-749-6619
Tirelli, Snc Di Tirelli Primo E.C., Via Matteotti No. 359, Gardone V.T., Brescia, ITALY 25063/030-8912819; FAX: 030-832240

Titus, Daniel, Shooting Specialties, 119 Morlyn Ave., Bryn Mawr, PA 19010-3737/215-525-8829
TMI Products (See Haselbauer Products, Jerry)
TM Stockworks, 6355 Maplecrest Rd., Fort Wayne, IN 46835/219-485-5389
Tom's Gun Repair, Thomas G. Ivanoff, 76-6 Rt. Southfork Rd., Cody, WY 82414/307-587-6949
Tom's Gunshop, 3601 Central Ave., Hot Springs, AR 71913/501-624-3856
Tomboy, Inc., P.O. Box 846, Dallas, OR 97338/503-623-8405
Tombstone Smoke`n'Deals, 3218 East Bell Road, Phoenix, AZ 85032/602-905-7013; Fax: 602-443-1998
Tonoloway Tack Drives, HCR 81, Box 100, Needmore, PA 17238
Tooley Custom Rifles, 516 Creek Meadow Dr., Gastonia, NC 28054/704-864-7525
Top-Line USA, Inc., 7920-28 Hamilton Ave., Cincinnati, OH 45231/513-522-2992, 800-346-6699; FAX: 513-522-0916
Torel, Inc., 1708 N. South St., P.O. Box 592, Yoakum, TX 77995/512-293-2341; FAX: 512-293-3413
Totally Dependable Products (See TDP Industries, Inc.)
TOZ (See U.S. importer—Nygord Precision Products)
TR Metals Corp., 1 Pavilion Ave., Riverside, NJ 08075/609-461-9000; FAX: 609-764-6340
Track of the Wolf, Inc., P.O. Box 6, Osseo, MN 55369-0006/612-424-2500; FAX: 612-424-9860
Tradewinds, Inc., P.O. Box 1191, 2339-41 Tacoma Ave. S., Tacoma, WA 98401/206-272-4887
Traditions, Inc., P.O. Box 776, 1375 Boston Post Rd., Old Saybrook, CT 06475/860-388-4656; FAX: 860-388-4657
Trafalgar Square, P.O. Box 257, N. Pomfret, VT 05053/802-457-1911
Traft Gunshop, P.O. Box 1078, Buena Vista, CO 81211
TrailTimer Co., 1992-A Suburban Ave., P.O. Box 19722, St. Paul, MN 55119/612-738-0925
Trail Visions, 5800 N. Ames Terrace, Glendale, WI 53209/414-228-1328
Trammco, 839 Gold Run Rd., Boulder, CO 80302
Trappers Trading, P.O. Box 26946, Austin, TX 78755/800-788-9334
Trax America, Inc., P.O. Box 898, 1150 Eldridge, Forrest City, AR 72335/501-633-0410, 800-232-2327; FAX: 501-633-4788
Treadlok Gun Safe, Inc., 1764 Granby St. NE, Roanoke, VA 24012/800-729-8732, 703-982-6881; FAX: 703-982-1059
Treemaster, P.O. Box 247, Guntersville, AL 35976/205-878-3597
Treso, Inc., P.O. Box 4640, Pagosa Springs, CO 81157/303-731-2295
Trevallion Gunstocks, 9 Old Mountain Rd., Cape Neddick, ME 03902/207-361-1130
Trico Plastics, 590 S. Vincent Ave., Azusa, CA 91702
Trijicon, Inc., 49385 Shafer Ave., P.O. Box 930059, Wixom, MI 48393-0059/810-960-7700; FAX: 810-960-7725
Trilux Inc., P.O. Box 24608, Winston-Salem, NC 27114/910-659-9438; FAX: 910-768-7720
Trinidad State Junior College, Gunsmithing Dept., 600 Prospect St., Trinidad, CO 81082/719-846-5631; FAX: 719-846-5667
Triple-K Mfg. Co., Inc., 2222 Commercial St., San Diego, CA 92113/619-232-2066; FAX: 619-232-7675
Tristar Sporting Arms, Ltd., 1814-16 Linn St., P.O. Box 7496, N. Kansas City, MO 64116/816-421-1400; FAX: 816-421-4182
Trius Traps, Inc., P.O. Box 25, 221 S. Miami Ave., Cleves, OH 45002/513-941-5682; FAX: 513-941-7970
Trooper Walsh, 2393 N. Edgewood St., Arlington, VA 22207
Trophy Bonded Bullets, Inc., 900 S. Loop W., Suite 190, Houston, TX 77054/713-645-4499; FAX: 713-741-6393
Trotman, Ken, 135 Ditton Walk, Unit 11, Cambridge CB5 8PY, ENGLAND/01223-211030; FAX: 01223-212317
Tru-Balance Knife Co., P.O. Box 140555, Grand Rapids, MI 49514/616-453-3679
Tru-Square Metal Prods., Inc., 640 First St. SW, P.O. Box 585, Auburn, WA 98071/206-833-2310; FAX: 206-833-2349
True Flight Bullet Co., 5581 Roosevelt St., Whitehall, PA 18052/610-262-7630; FAX: 610-262-7806
Trulock Tool, Broad St., Whigham, GA 31797/912-762-4678
TTM, 1550 Solomon Rd., Santa Maria, CA 93455/805-934-1281
Tucker, James C., P.O. Box 15485, Sacramento, CA 95851/916-923-0571
Turkish Firearms Corp., 522 W. Maple St., Allentown, PA 18101/610-821-8660; FAX: 610-821-9049
Turnbull Restoration, Inc., Doug, 6426 County Rd. 30, P.O. Box 471, Bloomfield, NY 14469/716-657-6338; WEB: http://gunshop.com/dougt.htm
Tuttle, Dale, 4046 Russell Rd., Muskegon, MI 49445/616-766-2250
Twin Pine Armory, P.O. Box 58, Hwy. 6, Adna, WA 98522/360-748-4590; FAX: 360-748-1802
Tyler Mfg.-Dist., Melvin, 1326 W. Britton Rd., Oklahoma City, OK 73114/405-842-8044, 800-654-8415
Tyler Scott, Inc., 313 Rugby Ave., Terrace Park, OH 45174/513-831-7603; FAX: 513-831-7417

U

Uberti USA, Inc., P.O. Box 469, Lakeville, CT 06039/860-435-8068; FAX: 860-435-8146
Uberti, Aldo, Casella Postale 43, I-25063 Gardone V.T., ITALY (U.S. importers—American Arms, Inc.; Cimarron Arms; Dixie Gun Works; EMF Co., Inc.; Forgett Jr., Valmore J.; Navy Arms Co; Taylor's & Co., Inc.; Uberti USA, Inc.)
UFA, Inc., 6927 E. Grandview Dr., Scottsdale, AZ 85254/800-616-2776
Ugartechea S.A., Ignacio, Chonta 26, Eibar, SPAIN 20600/43-121257; FAX: 43-121669 (U.S. importer—Galaxy Imports Ltd., Inc.; Mandall Shooting Supplies, Inc.)
Ultimate Accuracy, 121 John Shelton Rd., Jacksonville, AR 72076/501-985-2530
Ultra Light Arms, Inc., P.O. Box 1270, 214 Price St., Granville, WV 26505/304-599-5687; FAX: 304-599-5687
Ultralux (See U.S. importer—Keng's Firearms Specialty, Inc.)
UltraSport Arms, Inc., 1955 Norwood Ct., Racine, WI 53403/414-554-3237; FAX: 414-554-9731
Uncle Bud's, HCR 81, Box 100, Needmore, PA 17238/717-294-6000; FAX: 717-294-6005
Uncle Mike's (See Michaels of Oregon Co.)
Unertl Optical Co., Inc., John, 308 Clay Ave., P.O. Box 818, Mars, PA 16046-0818/412-625-3810
Unique/M.A.P.F., 10, Les Allees, 64700 Hendaye, FRANCE 64700/33-59 20 71 93 (U.S. importer—Nygord Precision Products)
UniTec, 1250 Bedford SW, Canton, OH 44710/216-452-4017
United Binocular Co., 9043 S. Western Ave., Chicago, IL 60620
United Cutlery Corp., 1425 United Blvd., Sevierville, TN 37876/615-428-2532, 800-548-0835; FAX: 615-428-2267
United States Ammunition Co. (See USAC)
United States Optics Technologies, Inc., 5900 Dale St., Buena Park, CA 90621/714-994-4901; FAX: 714-994-4904
United States Products Co., 518 Melwood Ave., Pittsburgh, PA 15213/412-621-2130
Upper Missouri Trading Co., 304 Harold St., Crofton, NE 68730/402-388-4844
USAC, 4500-15th St. East, Tacoma, WA 98424/206-922-7589
U.S.A. Magazines, Inc., P.O. Box 39115, Downey, CA 90241/800-872-2577
USA Sporting Inc., 1330 N. Glassell, Unit M, Orange, CA 92667/714-538-3109, 800-538-3109; FAX: 714-538-1334
U.S. Patent Fire Arms, No. 25-55 Van Dyke Ave., Hartford, CT 06106/800-877-2832; FAX: 800-644-7265
U.S. Repeating Arms Co., Inc., 275 Winchester Ave., Morgan, UT 84050-9333/801-876-3440; FAX: 801-876-3737
Utica Cutlery Co., 820 Noyes St., Utica, NY 13503/315-733-4663; FAX: 315-733-6602
Uvalde Machine & Tool, P.O. Box 1604, Uvalde, TX 78802

V

Valade Engraving, Robert, 931 3rd Ave., Seaside, OR 97138/503-738-7672
Valmet (See Tikka/U.S. importer—Stoeger Industries)
Valor Corp., 5555 NW 36th Ave., Miami, FL 33142/305-633-0127; FAX: 305-634-4536
Van Epps, Milton, Rt. 69-A, Parish, NY 13131/315-625-7251
Van Gorden & Son, Inc., C.S., 1815 Main St., Bloomer, WI 54724/715-568-2612
Van Horn, Gil, P.O. Box 207, Llano, CA 93544
Van Patten, J.W., P.O. Box 145, Foster Hill, Milford, PA 18337/717-296-7069
Vancini, Carl (See Bestload, Inc.)
Vann Custom Bullets, 330 Grandview Ave., Novato, CA 94947
Varner's Service, 102 Shaffer Rd., Antwerp, OH 45813/419-258-8631
Vega Tool Co., c/o T.R. Ross, 4865 Tanglewood Ct., Boulder, CO 80301/303-530-0174
Venco Industries, Inc. (See Shooter's Choice)
Venom Arms Co., Unit 1, Gun Garrel Industrial Centre, Hayseech, Cradley, Heath/West Midlands B64 7JZ ENGLAND
011-021-501-3794 (U.S. importers—Mac-1 Distributors, Trooper Walsh)
Venus Industries, P.O. Box 246, Sialkot-1, PAKISTAN/FAX: 92 432 85579
Verney-Carron, B.P. 72, 54 Boulevard Thiers, 42002 St. Etienne Cedex 1, FRANCE/33-77791500; FAX: 33-77790702
Vest, John, P.O. Box 1552, Susanville, CA 96130/916-257-7228
VibraShine, Inc., P.O. Box 577, Taylorsville, MS 39168/601-785-9854; FAX: 601-785-9874
Vibra-Tek Co., 1844 Arroya Rd., Colorado Springs, CO 80906/719-634-8611; FAX: 719-634-6886
Vic's Gun Refinishing, 6 Pineview Dr., Dover, NH 03820-6422/603-742-0013
Victory USA, P.O. Box 1021, Pine Bush, NY 12566/914-744-2060; FAX: 914-744-5181
Vihtavuori Oy, FIN-41330 Vihtavuori, FINLAND/358-41-3779211; FAX: 358-41-3771643
Vihtavuori Oy/Kaltron-Pettibone, 1241 Ellis St., Bensenville, IL 60106/708-350-1116; FAX: 708-350-1606
Viking Leathercraft, Inc., 1579A Jayken Way, Chula Vista, CA 91911/800-262-6666; FAX: 619-429-8268
Viking Video Productions, P.O. Box 251, Roseburg, OR 97470
Vincent's Shop, 210 Antoinette, Fairbanks, AK 99701
Vintage Arms, Inc., 6003 Saddle Horse, Fairfax, VA 22030/703-968-0779; FAX: 703-968-0780
Vintage Industries, Inc., 781 Big Tree Dr., Longwood, FL 32750/407-831-8949; FAX: 407-831-5346
VIP Products, 488 East 17th St., Ste. A-101, Costa Mesa, CA 92627/714-722-5986

Viramontez, Ray, 601 Springfield Dr., Albany, GA 31707/912-432-9683
Visible Impact Targets, Rts. 5 & 20, E. Bloomfield, NY 14443/716-657-6161; FAX: 716-657-5405
Vitt/Boos, 2178 Nichols Ave., Stratford, CT 06497/203-375-6859
Voere-KGH m.b.H., P.O. Box 416, A-6333 Kufstein, Tirol, AUSTRIA/0043-5372-62547; FAX: 0043-5372-65752 (U.S. importers—JagerSport, Ltd.)
Volquartsen Custom Ltd., 24276 240th Street, P.O. Box 271, Carroll, IA 51401/712-792-4238; FAX: 712-792-2542; E-MAIL: vcl@netins.net
Vom Hofe (See Old Western Scrounger, Inc., The)
Von Minden Gunsmithing Services, 2403 SW 39 Terrace, Cape Coral, FL 33914/813-542-8946
Vorhes, David, 3042 Beecham St., Napa, CA 94558/707-226-9116
Vortek Products, Inc., P.O. Box 871181, Canton, MI 48187-6181/313-397-5656; FAX:313-397-5656
VSP Publishers (See Heritage/VSP Gun Books)
Vulpes Ventures, Inc., Fox Cartridge Division, P.O. Box 1363, Bolingbrook, IL 60440-7363/708-759-1229

W

Wagoner, Vernon G., 2325 E. Encanto, Mesa, AZ 85213/602-835-1307
Wakina by Pic, 24813 Alderbrook Dr., Santa Clarita, CA 91321/800-295-8194
Waldron, Herman, Box 475, 80 N. 17th St., Pomeroy, WA 99347/509-843-1404
Walker Arms Co., Inc., 499 County Rd. 820, Selma, AL 36701/334-872-6231
Walker Mfg., Inc., 8296 S. Channel, Harsen's Island, MI 48028
Walker Co., B.B., P.O. Box 1167, 414 E. Dixie Dr., Asheboro, NC 27203/910-625-1380; FAX: 910-625-8125
Wallace, Terry, 385 San Marino, Vallejo, CA 94589/707-642-7041
Waller & Son, Inc., W., 59 Stoney Brook Road, Grandtham, NH 03753/603-863-4177; WEB: http://shooter.com
Walls Industries, Inc., P.O. Box 98, 1905 N. Main, Cleburne, TX 76031/817-645-4366; FAX: 817-645-7946
Walnut Factory, The, 235 West Rd. No. 1, Portsmouth, NH 03801/603-436-2225; FAX: 603-433-7003
Walt's Custom Leather, Walt Whinnery, 1947 Meadow Creek Dr., Louisville, KY 40218/502-458-4361
Walters Industries, 6226 Park Lane, Dallas, TX 75225/214-691-6973
Walters, John, 500 N. Avery Dr., Moore, OK 73160/405-799-0376
Walther GmbH, Carl, B.P. 4325, D-89033 Ulm, GERMANY (U.S. importer—Champion's Choice; Interarms; P.S.M.G. Gun Co.)
WAMCO, Inc., Mingo Loop, P.O. Box 337, Oquossoc, ME 04964-0337/207-864-3344
WAMCO—New Mexico, P.O. Box 205, Peralta, NM 87042-0205/505-869-0826
Ward & Van Valkenburg, 114 32nd Ave. N., Fargo, ND 58102/701-232-2351
Ward Machine, 5620 Lexington Rd., Corpus Christi, TX 78412/512-992-1221
Wardell Precision Handguns Ltd., 48851 N. Fig Springs Rd., New River, AZ 85027-8513/602-465-7995
Warenski, Julie, 590 E. 500 N., Richfield, UT 84701/801-896-5319; FAX: 801-896-5319
Warne Manufacturing Co., 9039 SE Jannsen Rd., Clackamas, OR 97015/503-657-5590, 800-683-5590; FAX: 503-657-5695
Warren & Sweat Mfg. Co., P.O. Box 350440, Grand Island, FL 32784/904-669-3166; FAX: 904-669-7272
Warren Muzzleloading Co., Inc., Hwy. 21 North, P.O. Box 100, Ozone, AR 72854/501-292-3268
Warren, Kenneth W. (See Mountain States Engraving)
Washita Mountain Whetstone Co., P.O. Box 378, Lake Hamilton, AR 71951/501-525-3914
WASP Shooting Systems, Rt. 1, Box 147, Lakeview, AR 72642/501-431-5606
Waterfield Sports, Inc., 13611 Country Lane, Burnsville, MN 55337/612-435-8339
Watson Bros., 39 Redcross Way, London Bridge, London, United Kingdom, SE1 1HG/FAX: 44-171-403-3367
Watson Trophy Match Bullets, 2404 Wade Hampton Blvd., Greenville, SC 29615/803-244-7948
Watsontown Machine & Tool Co., 309 Dickson Ave., Watsontown, PA 17777/717-538-3533
Wayne Firearms for Collectors and Investors, James, 2608 N. Laurent, Victoria, TX 77901/512-578-1258; FAX: 512-578-3559
Wayne Specialty Services, 260 Waterford Drive, Florissant, MO 63033/413-831-7083
WD-40 Co., 1061 Cudahy Pl., San Diego, CA 92110/619-275-1400; FAX: 619-275-5823
Weatherby, Inc., 3100 El Camino Real, Atascadero, CA 93422/805-466-1767, 800-227-2016, 800-334-4423 (Calif.); FAX: 805-466-2527
Weaver Arms Corp. Gun Shop, RR 3, P.O. Box 266, Bloomfield, MO 63825-9528
Weaver Products, Div. of Blount, Inc., Sporting Equipment Div., P.O. Box 39, Onalaska, WI 54650/800-648-9624, 608-781-5800; FAX: 608-781-0368
Weaver Scope Repair Service, 1121 Larry Mahan Dr., Suite B, El Paso, TX 79925/915-593-1005
Webb, Bill, 6504 North Bellefontaine, Kansas City, MO 64119/816-453-7431
Weber & Markin Custom Gunsmiths, 4-1691 Powick Rd., Kelowna, B.C. CANADA V1X 4L1/604-762-7575; FAX: 604-861-3655
Weber Jr., Rudolf, P.O. Box 160106, D-5650 Solingen, GERMANY/0212-592136
Webley and Scott Ltd., Frankley Industrial Park, Tay Rd., Rubery, Rednal, Birmingham B45 0PA, ENGLAND/011-021-453-1864; FAX: 021-457-7846 (U.S. importer—Beeman Precision Airguns; Groenewold, John)
Webster Scale Mfg. Co., P.O. Box 188, Sebring, FL 33870/813-385-6362
Weems, Cecil, P.O. Box 657, Mineral Wells, TX 76067/817-325-1462
Weigand Combat Handguns, Inc., P.O. Box 239, Crestwood Industrial Park, Mountain Top, PA 18707/717-474-9804; FAX: 717-474-9987
Weihrauch KG, Hermann, Industriestrasse 11, 8744 Mellrichstadt, GERMANY/09776-497-498 (U.S. importers—Beeman Precision Airguns; E.A.A. Corp.)
Weisz Parts, P.O. Box 20038, Columbus, OH 43220-0038/614-45-70-500; FAX: 614-846-8585
Welch, Sam, CVSR 2110, Moab, UT 84532/801-259-8131
Wellington Outdoors, P.O. Box 244, 1140 Monticello Rd., Madison, GA 30650/706-342-4915; FAX: 706-342-7568
Wells Creek Knife & Gun Works, 32956 State Hwy. 38, Scottsburg, OR 97473/503-587-4202
Wells Custom Gunsmith, R.A., 3452 1st Ave., Racine, WI 53402/414-639-5223
Wells, Fred F., Wells Sport Store, 110 N. Summit St., Prescott, AZ 86301/520-445-3655
Wells, Rachel, 110 N. Summit St., Prescott, AZ 86301/520-445-3655
Welsh, Bud, 80 New Road, E. Amherst, NY 14051/716-688-6344
Wenig Custom Gunstocks, Inc., 103 N. Market St., P.O. Box 249, Lincoln, MO 65338/816-547-3334; FAX: 816-547-2881
Wenoka/Seastyle, P.O. Box 10969, Riviera Beach, FL 33419/407-845-6155; FAX: 407-842-4247
Werner, Carl, P.O. Box 492, Littleton, CO 80160
Werth, T.W., 1203 Woodlawn Rd., Lincoln, IL 62656/217-732-1300
Wescombe, P.O. Box 488, Glencoe, CA 95232/209-293-7010
Wessinger Custom Guns & Engraving, 268 Limestone Rd., Chapin, SC 29036/803-345-5677
West, Jack L., 1220 W. Fifth, P.O. Box 427, Arlington, OR 97812
West, Robert G., 3973 Pam St., Eugene, OR 97402/541-344-3700
Western Cutlery (See Camillus Cutlery Co.)
Western Design (See Alpha Gunsmith Division)
Western Gunstock Mfg. Co., 550 Valencia School Rd., Aptos, CA 95003/408-688-5884
Western Missouri Shooters Alliance, P.O. Box 11144, Kansas City, MO 64119/816-597-3950; FAX: 816-229-7350
Western Munitions (See North American Munitions)
Western Nevada West Coast Bullets, 2307 W. Washington St., Carson City, NV 89703/702-246-3941; FAX: 702-246-0836
Westfield Engineering, 6823 Watcher St., Commerce, CA 90040/FAX: 213-928-8270
Westley Richards & Co., 40 Grange Rd., Birmingham, ENGLAND B29 6AR/010-214722953 (U.S. importer—Cape Outfitters)
Westrom, John (See Precision Metal Finishing)
Westwind Rifles, Inc., David S. Sullivan, P.O. Box 261, 640 Briggs St., Erie, CO 80516/303-828-3823
Weyer International, 2740 Nebraska Ave., Toledo, OH 43607/419-534-2020; FAX: 419-534-2697
Whildin & Sons Ltd., E.H., RR2, Box 119, Tamaqua, PA 18252/717-668-6743; FAX: 717-668-6745
Whinnery, Walt (See Walt's Custom Leather)
Whiscombe (See U.S. importer—Pelaire Products)
White Flyer Targets, 124 River Road, Middlesex, NJ 08846/908-469-0100, 602-972-7528 (Export); FAX: 908-469-9692, 602-530-3360 (Export)
White Laboratory, Inc., H.P., 3114 Scarboro Rd., Street, MD 21154/410-838-6550; FAX: 410-838-2802
White Owl Enterprises, 2583 Flag Rd., Abilene, KS 67410/913-263-2613; FAX: 913-263-2613
White Pine Photographic Services, Hwy. 60, General Delivery, Wilno, Ontario K0J 2N0 CANADA/613-756-3452
White Rock Tool & Die, 6400 N. Brighton Ave., Kansas City, MO 64119/816-454-0478
White Shooting Systems, Inc., 25 E. Hwy. 40, Box 330-12, Roosevelt, UT 84066/801-722-3085, 800-213-1315; FAX: 801-722-3054
Whitehead, James D., 204 Cappucino Way, Sacramento, CA 95838
Whitestone Lumber Corp., 148-02 14th Ave., Whitestone, NY 11357/718-746-4400; FAX: 718-767-1748
Whitetail Design & Engineering Ltd., 9421 E. Mannsiding Rd., Clare, MI 48617/517-386-3932
Whits Shooting Stuff, Box 1340, Cody, WY 82414
Wichita Arms, Inc., 923 E. Gilbert, P.O. Box 11371, Wichita, KS 67211/316-265-0661; FAX: 316-265-0760
Wick, David E., 1504 Michigan Ave., Columbus, IN 47201/812-376-6960
Widener's Reloading & Shooting Supply, Inc., P.O. Box 3009 CRS, Johnson City, TN 37602/615-282-6786; FAX: 615-282-6651
Wideview Scope Mount Corp., 13535 S. Hwy. 16, Rapid City, SD 57701/605-341-3220; FAX: 605-341-9142
Wiebe, Duane, 33604 Palm Dr., Burlington, WI 53105-9260
Wiest, M.C., 10737 Dutchtown Rd., Knoxville, TN 37932/423-966-4545
Wilcox All-Pro Tools & Supply, 4880 147th St., Montezuma, IA 50171/515-623-3138; FAX: 515-623-3104
Wild Bill's Originals, P.O. Box 13037, Burton, WA 98013/206-463-5738

Wild West Guns, 7521 Old Seward Hwy, Unit A, Anchorage, AK 99518/907-344-4500; FAX: 907-344-4005
Wilderness Sound Products Ltd., 4015 Main St. A, Springfield, OR 97478/503-741-0263, 800-437-0006; FAX: 503-741-7648
Wildey, Inc., P.O. Box 475, Brookfield, CT 06804/203-355-9000; FAX: 203-354-7759
Wildlife Research Center, Inc., 4345 157th Ave. NW, Anoka, MN 55304/612-427-3350, 800-USE-LURE; FAX: 612-427-8354
Wilkinson Arms, 26884 Pearl Rd., Parma, ID 83660/208-722-6771; FAX: 208-722-5197
Will-Burt Co., 169 S. Main, Orrville, OH 44667
William's Gun Shop, Ben, 1151 S. Cedar Ridge, Duncanville, TX 75137/214-780-1807
Williams Bullet Co., J.R., 2008 Tucker Rd., Perry, GA 31069/912-987-0274
Williams Gun Sight Co., 7389 Lapeer Rd., Box 329, Davison, MI 48423/810-653-2131, 800-530-9028; FAX: 810-658-2140
Williams Mfg. of Oregon, 110 East B St., Drain, OR 97435/541-836-7461; FAX: 541-836-7245
Williams Shootin' Iron Service, The Lynx-Line, 8857 Bennett Hill Rd., Central Lake, MI 49622/616-544-6615
Williamson Precision Gunsmithing, 117 W. Pipeline, Hurst, TX 76053/817-285-0064
Willig Custom Engraving, Claus, D-97422 Schweinfurt, Siedlerweg 17, GERMANY/01149-9721-41446; FAX: 01149-9721-44413
Willow Bend, P.O. Box 203, Chelmsford, MA 01824/508-256-8508; FAX: 508-256-8508
Willson Safety Prods. Div., P.O. Box 622, Reading, PA 19603-0622/610-376-6161; FAX: 610-371-7725
Wilson Arms Co., The, 63 Leetes Island Rd., Branford, CT 06405/203-488-7297; FAX: 203-488-0135
Wilson Case, Inc., P.O. Box 1106, Hastings, NE 68902-1106/800-322-5493; FAX: 402-463-5276
Wilson, Inc., L.E., Box 324, 404 Pioneer Ave., Cashmere, WA 98815/509-782-1328
Wilson's Gun Shop, Box 578, Rt. 3, Berryville, AR 72616/501-545-3618; FAX: 501-545-3310
Winchester (See U.S. Repeating Arms Co., Inc.)
Winchester Div., Olin Corp., 427 N. Shamrock, E. Alton, IL 62024/618-258-3566; FAX: 618-258-3599
Winchester Press (See New Win Publishing, Inc.)
Winchester Sutler, Inc., The, 270 Shadow Brook Lane, Winchester, VA 22603/540-888-3595; FAX: 540-888-4632
Windish, Jim, 2510 Dawn Dr., Alexandria, VA 22306/703-765-1994
Windjammer Tournament Wads, Inc., 750 W. Hampden Ave. Suite 170, Englewood, CO 80110/303-781-6329
Wingshooters Ltd., 4320 Kalamazoo Ave., Grand Rapids, MI 49508/616-455-7810; FAX: 616-455-5212
Wingshooting Adventures, 4320 Kalamazoo Ave. SE, Grand Rapids, MI 49507/616-455-7810; FAX: 616-455-5212
Winkle Bullets, R.R. 1 Box 316, Heyworth, IL 61745
Winter, Robert M., P.O. Box 484, Menno, SD 57045/605-387-5322
Wise Guns, Dale, 333 W. Olmos Dr., San Antonio, TX 78212/210-828-3388
Wiseman and Co., Bill, P.O. Box 3427, Bryan, TX 77805/409-690-3456; FAX: 409-690-0156
Wolf's Western Traders, 40 E. Works, No. 3F, Sheridan, WY 82801/307-674-5352
Wolfe Publishing Co., 6471 Airpark Dr., Prescott, AZ 86301/602-445-7810, 800-899-7810; FAX: 602-778-5124
Wolff Co., W.C., P.O. Box 458, Newtown Square, PA 19073/610-359-9600, 800-545-0077
Wolverine Footwear Group, 9341 Courtland Dr. NE, Rockford, MI 49351/616-866-5500; FAX: 616-866-5658
Wood, Frank (See Classic Guns, Inc.)
Wood, Mel, P.O. Box 1255, Sierra Vista, AZ 85636/602-455-5541
Woodleigh (See Huntington Die Specialties)
Woods Wise Products, P.O. Box 681552, 2200 Bowman Rd., Franklin, TN 37068/800-735-8182; FAX: 615-726-2637
Woodstream, P.O. Box 327, Lititz, PA 17543/717-626-2125; FAX: 717-626-1912
Woodworker's Supply, 1108 North Glenn Rd., Casper, WY 82601/307-237-5354
Woolrich Inc., Mill St., Woolrich, PA 17701/800-995-1299; FAX: 717-769-6234/6259
World of Targets (See Birchwood Casey)
World Class Airguns, 2736 Morningstar Dr., Indianapolis, IN 46229/317-897-5548
World Trek, Inc., 7170 Turkey Creek Rd., Pueblo, CO 81007-1046/719-546-2121; FAX: 719-543-6886
Worthy Products, Inc., RR 1, P.O. Box 213, Martville, NY 13111/315-324-5298
Wosenitz VHP, Inc., Box 741, Dania, FL 33004/305-923-3748; FAX: 305-925-2217
Wostenholm (See Ibberson [Sheffield] Ltd., George)
Wright's Hardwood Gunstock Blanks, 8540 SE Kane Rd., Gresham, OR 97080/503-666-1705
Wyant Bullets, Gen. Del., Swan Lake, MT 59911
Wyant's Outdoor Products, Inc., P.O. Box B, Broadway, VA 22815
Wyoming Bonded Bullets, Box 91, Sheridan, WY 82801/307-674-8091
Wyoming Custom Bullets, 1626 21st St., Cody, WY 82414
Wyoming Knife Corp., 101 Commerce Dr., Ft. Collins, CO 80524/303-224-3454

X, Y

X-Spand Target Systems, 26-10th St. SE, Medicine Hat, AB T1A 1P7 CANADA/403-526-7997; FAX: 403-528-2362
Yankee Gunsmith, 2901 Deer Flat Dr., Copperas Cove, TX 76522/817-547-8433
Yavapai College, 1100 E. Sheldon St., Prescott, AZ 86301/602-776-2359; FAX: 602-776-2193
Yavapai Firearms Academy Ltd., P.O. Box 27290, Prescott Valley, AZ 86312/520-772-8262
Yearout, Lewis E. (See Montana Outfitters)
Yee, Mike, 29927 56 Pl. S., Auburn, WA 98001/206-839-3991
Yellowstone Wilderness Supply, P.O. Box 129, W. Yellowstone, MT 59758/406-646-7613
Yesteryear Armory & Supply, P.O. Box 408, Carthage, TN 37030
York M-1 Conversions, 803 Mill Creek Run, Plantersville, TX 77363/800-527-2881, 713-477-8442
Young, Paul A., RR 1 Box 694, Blowing Rock, NC 28605-9746
Young Country Arms, P.O. Box 3615, Simi Valley, CA 93093
Yukon Arms Classic Ammunition, 1916 Brooks, P.O. Box 223, Missoula, MT 59801/406-543-9614

Z

Z's Metal Targets & Frames, P.O. Box 78, South Newbury, NH 03255/603-938-2826
Zabala Hermanos S.A., P.O. Box 97, Eibar, SPAIN 20600/43-768085, 43-768076; FAX: 34-43-768201 (U.S. importer—American Arms, Inc.)
Zanoletti, Pietro, Via Monte Gugielpo, 4, I-25063 Gardone V.T., ITALY (U.S. importer—Mandall Shooting Supplies, Inc.)
Zanotti Armor, Inc., 123 W. Lone Tree Rd., Cedar Falls, IA 50613/319-232-9650
Z-Coat Industrial Coatings, Inc., 3375 U.S. Hwy. 98 S. No. A, Lakeland, FL 33803-8365/813-665-1734
ZDF Import/Export Inc., 2975 South 300 West, Salt Lake City, UT 84115/801-485-1012; FAX: 801-484-4363
Zeeryp, Russ, 1601 Foard Dr., Lynn Ross Manor, Morristown, TN 37814/615-586-2357
Zeiss Optical, Carl, 1015 Commerce St., Petersburg, VA 23803/804-861-0033, 800-388-2984; FAX: 804-733-4024
Zero Ammunition Co., Inc., 1601 22nd St. SE, P.O. Box 1188, Cullman, AL 35056-1188/800-545-9376; FAX: 205-739-4683
Ziegel Engineering, 2108 Lomina Ave., Long Beach, CA 90815/310-596-9481; FAX: 310-598-4734
Zim's Inc., 4370 S. 3rd West, Salt Lake City, UT 84107/801-268-2505
Zoli, Antonio, Via Zanardelli 39, Casier Postal 21, I-25063 Gardone V.T., ITALY
Zonie Bullets, 790 N. Lake Havasu Ave., Suite 26, Lake Havasu City, AZ 86403/520-680-6303; FAX: 520-680-6201
Zriny's Metal Targets (See Z's Metal Targets & Frames)
Zufall, Joseph F., P.O. Box 304, Golden, CO 80402-0304